THE ANIME ENCYCLOPEDIA

THE ANIME ENCYCLOPEDIA

REVISED & EXPANDED EDITION

A Guide to Japanese Animation Since 1917

Jonathan Clements

Helen McCarthy

Stone Bridge Press • Berkeley, California

Published by
STONE BRIDGE PRESS
P. O. Box 8208, Berkeley, CA 94707
TEL 510-524-8732 • sbp@stonebridge.com • www.stonebridge.com

We want to hear from you! Updates? Corrections? Comments? Please send all correspondence regarding this book to **animeinfo@stonebridge.com**.

Book design and layout by Linda Ronan.

Printed in the United States of America.

10 9 8 7 6 5 4 3 2   2010 2009 2008 2007 2006

LIBRARY OF CONGRESS CATALOGING-IN-PUBLICATION DATA
Clements, Jonathan, 1971–
  The anime encyclopedia : a guide to Japanese animation since 1917 /
 Jonathan Clements, Helen McCarthy.—Rev. & expanded ed.
    p. cm.
  Includes bibliographical references and indexes.
  ISBN-10: 1-933330-10-4 (pbk.)
  ISBN-13: 978-1-933330-10-5 (pbk.)
    1. Animated films—Japan—Encyclopedias. I. McCarthy, Helen, 1951– II.
Title.
 NC1766.J3C53 2007
 791.43'340952–dc22

                    2006028265

To Peter Goll, anime's unsung hero

CONTENTS

THE ANIME ENCYCLOPEDIA

THEMATIC ENTRIES

ILLUSTRATIONS

INTRODUCTION

Has it really been five years since we launched the first edition of the *Anime Encyclopedia* at Anime Weekend Atlanta? We still fondly remember the happy smiling faces of **TENCHI MUYO!** fans at our first signing session; the boy clutching a *Lodoss War* DVD boxed set who informed us that our cover price was "too much to pay for a book"; the young man who loudly complained that the book was trash because it didn't include a new show that he had downloaded just the previous day; and the sweet young lady who thought the pages were "too white." And here's a big hello to the guy who proclaimed that it "couldn't be a *real* encyclopedia, because it only has one volume."

Everyone's a critic. We also recall the bearded man, with a Southern Baptist preacher's voice and *gravitas*, who bellowed that we should be proud of what we had achieved, and the girl with red contact lenses who showed Jonathan her bra. It was anime fandom in all its glory, from the mother who bought three copies for her children, to the weirdo who talked to us for 40 minutes and then left without buying a copy because he "didn't really like anime anyway."

Five years later, anime has its first Academy Award. Meanwhile, our correspondence has racked up several incoherent exhorta-tions to do the biologically impossible and one proposal of marriage on Amazon.com's review pages. One reader complained that he had almost died laughing at one of our reviews when his wife read it to him in the car and he temporarily lost control of the vehicle. Another announced that she would pray for us, in the hope we had better things to say about her favorite show.

It is for these people, and many thousands like them, that we have wasted another year of our dwindling lives to assemble this new version of the *Anime Encyclopedia*.

This book is a palimpsest of the first edition, augmenting many earlier entries and adding new ones. With that in mind, we have preserved most of our original introduction and added some new material in order to outline changes made and developments observed.

TITLES

We have included as many Japanese titles as possible, but owing to space limitations, many episode titles, TV specials, and minor films have simply been left in English. We give variant titles but have indexed by Western release where possible—hence *Space Cruiser Yamato* is filed as **STAR BLAZERS**. The "three-dimensional" typography of many anime titles leaves them with a foreground name and a background qualifier, which plays havoc with filing: is it **Macross**, or is it *Super-Dimensional Fortress Macross?* Where possible we have used the Western title most recognizable—few fans in the U.S. *or* Japan speak of *Neon Genesis Evangelion*; instead they refer to it as **Evangelion**, though both variants will be found in our index. Similarly, the anime known in Japan as *Shojo Kakumei Utena* (and translatable as *Revolutionary Girl Utena*) is often given the French title *La Fillette Revolutionnaire* on Japanese merchandise and was mystifyingly renamed *Ursula's Kiss* in some studio sales documents (press releases whose tenuous relation to the shows they purport to sell has confused many attempts to determine names and plots). We have filed it simply as **Utena** but indexed it by all its variants.

For consistency, we have replaced the ampersand (&) with the word "and," although box typography and "official" titles may offer variant forms.

Titles printed in **Boldface Capital Letters** refer to main entries elsewhere in the book. The indexes can be used to find titles that are referred to but that do not have their own entries.

Note that in our commentaries we often (but not always) space-savingly refer to the anime under discussion by its initials or a shortened form: in the text about **Cream Lemon**, for example, we refer to it as *CL* and to a related work as *New CL*, and we refer to the film **Evangelion** as *Eva*.

Titles appear in the listings in alphabetical order using the alphabetize-by-word system. Thus, **Boy with Cat's Eyes** comes before **Boyfriend**. If you are unfamiliar with this system (the one favored by computers and databases), you may need to turn a page or two to find the title you're looking for.

Some variant titles known to exist appear in the index as well, although they may not be in the main listings. Finally, if a title contains a numeral, it is alphabetized as if the numeral were spelled out in English: 2 = Two, in other words. The only exception to this is when a word is comprised of both letters and numerals, such as **D-1 Devastator** and **D4 Princess**. In this case, the numerals are sorted before alphabetical successors.

See also the note on romanization, below.

INTERNATIONAL RELEASES

An asterisk (*) by a title heading denotes the existence of a *legal* English-language release of at least part of a show at some point, though not all titles are internationally available. The U.S. has **The Secret of Blue Water** to itself, **Hummingbirds** is not available outside the U.K., and **Ken the Wolf Boy** was only broadcast in Australia. Furthermore, while an English edition may exist, some, such as **Madcap Island**, were only seen as subtitled prints at film festivals or on Japanese DVD with English subtitles. Since this is an English-language book with limited space, we have avoided discussion of other languages, although a few well-known French title variants have been included for the benefit of readers in Canada, and there is occasional reference to Spanish-language versions.

FORMATS AND RUNNING TIMES

The nature of the medium has changed radically through technological and economic influences. Animation was an obscure cottage industry until its use as military propaganda led to the first full-length feature, **Momotaro's Divine Sea Warriors**, in 1945. Television created a larger medium during the 1960s, which came to be dominated by merchandising tie-ins in the 1970s.

The arrival of home video players in the 1970s and 1980s, especially the video cassette recorder, allowed for the targeting of smaller niches in the audience, beginning the process whereby anime studios held on to their audiences as they left childhood behind. Before video recorders became widely available in the 1980s, producers could expect a reasonable number of fans to pay to see repeat performances of TV shows in theaters, leading to holiday reruns, erroneously credited in some sources as genuine "movies." Furthermore, many shows made for video, such as **BELOVED BETTY**, were also shown theatrically as second or third features. We have listed these shows as video productions, though some other sources describe them as movies. **APPLESEED**, for example, is listed as a video work because that was its original format, even though it was shown in theaters outside Japan.

The 1990s saw many more developments—the "retro" revival as studios tried to appeal to former fans *and* their children, the advent of digital animation, and the use of satellite/cable as an even cheaper preview medium than video (the studio only has to pay for one tape!).

We have had to piece together some entries, especially for older shows, from sources with time listings that do not account for commercial breaks. Sometimes the difference can be drastic: the *Animage 25 Years of Television Cartoons* gives the broadcast time of **BAGHI** as 120 minutes, whereas the *Newtype Animesoft Complete Catalog* entry lists it as only 86 minutes, and the *Animation Filmography of Osamu Tezuka* infuriatingly disagrees with both. We have also had to

consider different companies' editing and compilation policies, which can affect published running times.

We have given full episode counts of shows *made*, even if the complete runs of shows such as **ULYSSES 31** and **ALICE IN WONDERLAND** were only ever seen outside Japan. We have tried to distinguish among multiple versions of an anime using different abbreviations, and also by using a short-form of the title after the time and episode count. Finally, where we have had to cram several incarnations of a title into one entry, pertinent changes in staff or running time are separated by semicolons or denoted by numbered abbreviations, e.g., "m1" for the first movie, "TV2" for a second TV series, or "v2" for a second video series. See the list of abbreviations on page 2.

CREATIVE CREDITS

We have listed as many crew members as space allowed. Though not exhaustive, we have included the most important parties responsible for the five major areas of production on each anime. The period under study is so vast that meanings have changed over time. As well as lead animators (ANI) and composers (MUS), we have listed directors (DIR), scriptwriters (SCR), and designers (DES), though these last three job titles have had over 12 definitions during the last 50 years.

A "series producer," for example, is sometimes a "story editor" (i.e., a lead writer—SCR) and sometimes a "supervising director" (DIR), depending on the whims both of the studio and the English translators, who may not know as much about film terminology as they do about Japanese. Similarly, "supervising director" is sometimes an honorary title for a producer, but it is also occasionally used for the chief among several directors on a long-running series. We have done our best to pin down exactly what a staff member did and place him or her in the right slot, but sometimes we had to admit defeat—Frederik L. Schodt *himself* is not quite sure why he is credited as a "planning brain" on SPACE FIREBIRD.

In cases where a manga has been adapted into anime, we have followed the Japanese practice and credited the original creators as the writer/designer where no alternative is given.

Those who check our credits against Western releases may notice discrepancies; this is often because some distributors use the same set of credits for long-running shows, though writers and animators may change with each episode. Where possible, we have checked the credits of the Japanese originals, and though we have had to admit defeat on many occasions, jobs go uncredited (N/C) only after a trawl through every available option, including several Japanese-language listings and studio histories.

ABOUT JAPANESE NAMES
Japanese names are particularly troublesome, as they are generally written with non-phonetic *kanji* characters. Even the Japanese themselves are not always sure how to pronounce a particular *kanji* in every context. Matters are not helped by the proliferation of pseudonyms, often deliberately hard to read.

Watching every anime made, end-to-end, in order to catch the names of all the staff and all the fictional characters would have taken over 18 years. We have been necessarily frugal with our time and utilized other sources where possible. Sometimes we have had to wing it, as in THUNDERBIRDS

2086, where not even ITC-approved publications can agree on spellings. However, where we know Western credits to be in error, we have replaced them with our own.

We have elected to present Japanese names in Western order, that is, family name last, because this is generally how they are presented in English-language credits. This has resulted in the names of some well-known historical characters being given unconventionally as, for example, Nobunaga Oda or Musashi Miyamoto.

Doubtful names have been passed on to our research assistant Motoko Tamamuro and her mystified family, who have provided the best pronunciations they could. Where a guess is the best we can manage, we have opted for a guess made by Japanese native-speakers.

TERMINOLOGY
Some points remain the same across cultures—more money is spent on a film than a TV episode. Movies "made for television" tend to be cheaper and more conservative in their execution. Shows that go "straight to video" are generally for a smaller, niche audience. We have avoided the spin-doctor's term OAV—an "Original Anime Video" made for direct sale rather than theatrical or TV airing.

We have, however, included mentions for several "manga videos"—comics on VHS in which voice actors read to the viewer, and even save them the bother of turning the pages. Though these are the lowest-tech "animation" imaginable, they are likely to turn up in video store bargain bins and are included here to save would-be buyers' blushes. These are not to be confused with Manga Video, the *brand name* that led many (including the *Oxford English Dictionary*) to confuse "manga" (Japanese comics) with "anime" (Japanese animation).

Beyond the words "manga" and "anime," we have tried to avoid the obstructively arcane jargon of fandom. We intend to make anime accessible to every reader, so as much as possible we have used terms traceable in any good dictionary. Anime is increasingly targeted at an international audience and can be described in any of the wide variety of languages into which it's translated—the abuse of terms such as *hentai*, *shojo*, and *otaku* only serves to alienate the general reader.

ROMANIZATION

We have adopted a strategy for handling Japanese words: keep it simple. Purists and language scholars may be unhappy at some of the choices we have made, but our first impulse has been to serve the needs of our readers, most of whom have no particular expertise in speaking or pronouncing Japanese.

Our job has been made more difficult because the Japanese and American studios that release anime into English-language markets do not follow the same or even consistent romanization rules. And some Japanese anime and Japanese names are already known outside Japan by their "incorrect" English spellings.

So what we have done is made the best of an inherently confusing situation.

1. We almost always favor the "official" spellings of anime titles as provided by their studios, nonstandard though they may sometimes be. Names, too, can be rendered in the romanized form preferred by the particular individual: Joe (not Jo) Hisaishi, for example.

2. Japanese titles, when we provide them, are romanized consistently, except that "English" words adopted into the Japanese anime title are rendered back into English: thus, the film known in English as **BLOCKER CORPS** is in fact known in Japanese as *Burokkaa Guntan IV Masheen* but is listed here as *Blocker Guntan IV Machine.*

3. The syllabic nasal *n* is written as *n* before *b*, *m*, and *p* (Shinbashi); in other texts, *m* is frequently seen here (Shimbashi). We have dropped the apostrophe used in specialized texts to indicate syllabic division involving the nasal *n*; thus we write Junichiro, not Jun'ichiro.

4. We do not indicate the extended vowels *o* and *u*, either by "long signs" (macrons) over the vowels or by spelling out as *ou*, *oo*, or *uu*. Extended vowels are usually either ignored or mispronounced by those unfamiliar with Japanese, and are in any case not provided at all or are provided inconsistently by those who prepare staff credits and English-language materials. Rather than litter this book with mistakes and inconsistencies we have simply decided to adopt a leaner style of romanization. For later editions we may decide to rethink this choice.

PARENTAL ADVISORIES

Like any mass medium, anime can soar to great heights of creative expression or plumb the depths of human depravity. Some anime you want to share with your family; some you might need to watch in a room with the door locked. Whatever your tastes, far be it from us to cast judgment.

But at the request of our publisher, and in the interest of making this book of practical use for fans as well as guardians, teachers, librarians, and shop owners, we have provided some simple icons to indicate those anime that have language, violence, or nudity of the sort that one might not wish children or other sensitive souls to be exposed to. Not all violence is gratuitous; not all nudity is exploitative. Our "ratings" are merely a guide to content, and we hope a useful one.

ADDITIONS AND ALTERATIONS

This new edition does not merely incorporate several hundred new anime released since the original 2001 publication. It also adds overlooked titles from previous years, sometimes by reader request, and on other occasions through our acquisition of new information. This can include the English-language release of a title we previously disregarded, or in one case, the chance discovery of a discontinued VHS in a bargain bin near the Arctic Circle. Where relevant, this book now includes direct cross-references to Stone Bridge Press's *Dorama Encyclopedia*, wherever you see the sign "*DE."

We have also included short biographies of Japanese creatives and companies—specifically from the anime business, rather than, for example, manga creators whose work happens to have been adapted into anime. Sometimes the information in them may appear contradictory, but this is a common feature of both media accounting and Japanese business structures. Companies are founded, split away from one another, merged and remerged in a complex dance of shifting liability shields. We hope, however, that our brief accounts of several of the major players help explain some of the invisible currents of contacts, alliances, and friendships that often serve to influence what gets made, and by whom.

In the early 1970s, around the time that Mushi Production collapsed, Toei Animation was, if not laying off its own staff, then at least putting them on temporary freelance contracts. These factors led to the creation of numerous minor "studios," as bands of animators pooled their resources to create small companies that offered some semblance of security, instead of waiting for piecework as lone freelancers. Some of these companies, such as Madhouse, would grow into studios in their own right; some remained mere *ateliers*, single-room offices or holding companies for the works of one particular artist or creator.

Our new thematic entries offer not only signposts to more in-depth discussion of certain topics within anime, but also concise histories of the medium itself by placing certain landmark entries in chronological order. In a sense, they form several alternative views of the history of Japanese animation, such as one told from the viewpoint of **FOREIGN INFLUENCES** and another through the influence of **TECHNOLOGY AND FORMATS**.

Some of the new additions to this edition include series with long runs but short episode lengths, including public information serials like **JUST ANOTHER FAMILY** and **OUTSIDE THE LAW**. In a work of reference we must necessarily go beyond the vague press releases that form the bulk of so much supposed anime criticism. This often means discussing entire plots, including their endings. Readers are warned now that if they do not want to know what happens in later episodes of **KINO'S JOURNEY**, **FULLMETAL ALCHEMIST,** or **THE ETERNITY YOU DESIRE**, they should avoid the synopses we provide.

We have, however, enacted a two-year grace period, and steadfastly refused to give away the endings of any shows made after 2004.

NAMES AND ORIGINS

As encyclopedists, we have often had to ride shotgun over contradictory information. The U.S. release of *Shinseiki Evangelion* faithfully calls itself *Neon Genesis Evangelion* (the creators' approved "Japlish" title, not an actual translation of the kanji) but is filed under E in many catalogs, including, at the time we prepared our first edition, those of its own distributor.Other titles use Japanese characters as part of their American box design—one must speak both languages to know that the squiggles next to the words *Peace Maker* on the American DVD box say *Kurogane*, and complete the title. In some cases, we believe such decisions to be not merely aesthetic but also political, since some Japanese rightsholders may insist on a title that is simply unpronounceable or difficult for non-Japanese speakers to remember. The use of such dual names could, in certain instances, be an attempt to please all parties, since the Japanese license holders see a name they know and American store clerks see one they can find and remember.

A related problem has come in the form of non-translations—that growing number of anime whose "translators" do not bother (or are not permitted) to actually translate the title. Titles such as HAIBANE RENMEI, KAKURENBO: HIDE AND SEEK, and even PRINCESS MONONOKE seem wholly or partly left in Japanese, although occasionally it is fandom itself that is complicit in this by insisting on "generally accepted" titles like SAIKANO, even though an English-language title, "*She: The Ultimate Weapon*," already existed. The result is an ironic situation, occurring more often than one might expect, in which some fans and occasionally even distributors of a show are unable to pronounce its name.

One feature of the last five years, particularly in the adult video sector, has been the proliferation of rereleases and repackages of pre-existing works under new titles. This is occasionally due to the rights lapsing and being resold to a new owner, a situation that seems to strike erotic anime more often than others. In some cases, such as the SECRET ANIMA series, they have been rereleased under an original Japanese title that had previously been altered, in an industry notorious for repackaging old porn in new boxes.

It has also become increasingly difficult to determine the origin of a show. Merely because a manga runs for a while in an anthology magazine before a TV show airs, it does not necessarily follow that the manga was "first"; magazines like *Shonen Ace* and *Dengeki Gao* exist as places to test-market story concepts that are already in production as anime. Where we report a 21st-century show "first appeared" in a manga anthology, it should no longer be taken as an indicator that the franchise began as a manga and was only subsequently *adapted* into anime.

Readers looking for anime erotica in particular are advised to start at the index, and not in the main body of the text, in order to guarantee finding the name under which they are looking for a show. We continue to add an asterisk (*) only to those titles with a *legal* release in the English language. Certain titles were briefly made available in English, before becoming officially *unavailable* due to a legal dispute between the Japanese rightsholder and the American release company. Particularly in the case of pornography, we have found several cases where fansubs or untranslated pirate editions have been sold in the U.S. without a license from the rightsholder.

FORMATS AND LIMITATIONS

Manga sales in Japan have been steadily declining at 2% a year for the last decade—the prevalence of second-hand material, rental stores, and libraries, along with the endurance of the acknowledged manga "classics," means that, while comics may still be a lucrative industry for the Japanese, the local market for new comics is 20% down from what it was in 1994. A similar recession has been blighting anime, even though recent years have seen its success hyped abroad. In 2005, the *Hollywood Reporter* noted that the average Japanese TV channel would be prepared to pay between $5,000 and $20,000 for a half-hour of animation—a fraction of the fees on offer in other territories. No wonder the characters in GET BACKERS have a mission that centers around a paltry 2 million yen—at $17,000, the heroes' fee per episode is probably the same as that of the animators who drew them.

Television in modern Japan is a buyers' market, and always has been. Even ASTRO BOY could not get off the ground without contributions from sponsors. There is always another mega-corporation tie-in around the corner, which makes channels reluctant to pay too much for any show. Sometimes they offer paltry sums that are not enough to cover the costs of making the show in the first place, and why should they not? With anime "taking the world by storm" and foreign rights–buyers queuing up, the channels can claim that a good show need not worry about running into debt, as it will recoup its costs on foreign sales. The result,

not unexpectedly, is a large number of poorly animated shows, as production budgets are cut back to the bone, or sanitized productions in which the program makers hope to attract nebulous foreign interest.

In the 1960s, when there was only a handful of shows on the schedules, it did not seem too unlikely that each couple of seasons would see shows about a girl who can grow into an older version of herself, a teenage witch, a superheroine, a boy with a giant robot, and high school ghost stories. There is no arguing that the anime industry has hit upon a number of workable paradigms, and every one of them is a winner with its target audience, guaranteed to hold their attention for a few months—and lure them to buy the spin-offs, toys, books, and games.

In current times, there are many more channels and toy companies fighting for a share, often using the same cookie-cutter show formats. This rarely bothers the target audience, since after all, every year sees a fresh crop of kids who have never seen a transforming robot or schoolgirl. However, it can certainly bother those who watch anime for a living, as we see the same old formats dragged out, dusted off, and kicked at the audience on a regular basis.

It is our job to notice these things and to point readers back to earlier precedents. Readers who do not want anime placed in a historical context are holding the wrong book. They are advised instead to read one of the Japanese anime magazines, which reinvent the wheel every season, refuse to say a bad word about anything, and proclaim "classics" that nobody will have heard of within a couple of years.

Although the copying of plots and ideas on a regular basis has been a common feature of children's anime from **Brave Saga** to **Gundam** and all points in between, the early 21st century has taken such cynical recycling to new levels. Time and again, we found ourselves wondering if we had found a new title for an old show, only to discover on viewing that, yes indeed, it was the same old plot but made anew, in the hope that none of the anime audience of 2001 would be around to notice the lack of new ideas. Such retreads of preexisting ideas are particularly, understandably, prevalent in modern erotica, but are not solely limited to that genre. We are also running out of new ways to say "boy gets robot" without mentioning **Gundam** or **Gigantor**, while the number of **Tenchi Muyo!** clones and **Evangelion** knock-offs in the last five years has been truly dispiriting. It is all the more annoying when one realizes that there is no reason for remakes to be bad—one of modern anime's greatest shows, **Gankutsuou**, has a basic story that is a hundred years old, whereas one of anime's acknowledged classics, **Akira**, began as a reimagining of **Gigantor**.

But it is not possible to solely blame the people who make anime. The brutal, commercial realities of the industry have brought some unwelcome truths to light about the nature of making cartoons all over the world. Average cartoon consumers will only stay in their demographic bracket for a maximum of two years. They buy the toys for one show as a child, then might move on to the cards or the console game tie-in for another, and if the animation company is lucky, they may even turn into serious fans, buy *Newtype* for a couple of years, and become regular consumers of the more rarefied world of straight-to-video animation. If the company can hold their attention for long enough, they might even

be steered into erotic anime for a while. Eventually other concerns—a day job, marriage, children—remove most of the audience from the world of animation, although these same concerns may drive them into the similar world of live-action television drama.

So while we as authors may rail constantly at the lack of originality in the modern anime world, we must recognize that its modern creators, particularly in television, are forced to work within outrageous restrictions. Anime budgets have been in a state of constant crisis since at least 1979, forced to pander to the demands of toy companies and broadcasters. Meanwhile, the audience itself is rarely faithful for more than a couple of seasons; children grow up fast, and even if someone were to create the perfect show for eight-year-olds tomorrow, it would be old news not only to them when they turn nine, but also to their younger siblings in search of something just different enough to clear them of any suspicion of "copying" their elders' interests.

We should also recognize the remarkable achievements of three generations of creators. In particular, the founding fathers of anime, Osamu Tezuka, Mitsuteru Yokoyama, and Shotaro Ishinomori, managed to hit on a series of formulae that have, in their modern adaptations and applications, carried Japanese culture all over the world. If we complain about the latest modern-dress version of **Astro Boy**, should we not also complain about a new production of *King Lear*?

DEVELOPMENTS AND POSSIBILITIES

Modern restrictions and expectations are most apparent at the beginning of each season, when the labors of the previous months are broken down into a series of banal press releases that manage to make almost everything look the same. At the time of their initial broadcast, both ESCAFLOWNE and EVANGELION were "sold" to the magazines as almost identical shows, along the lines of "teen gets robot." The anime industry grinds down new entrants with cruel rapidity, although sometimes it is possible to discern a couple of areas in a new production where someone has yet to become jaded—a TV show might boast wonderful music like BRAIN POWERED, or innovative computer graphics like LAST EXILE; it might have a remarkably intelligent script like PATLABOR or the GHOST IN THE SHELL spin-off *Stand Alone Complex*, or a distinctive, eye-catching art style like HAIBANE RENMEI. But a show that has *all* those hallmarks is rare indeed.

The idea that fans of anime for anime's sake constitute an important market sector is nothing new—it was a feature of the arrival of home video players in the 1970s and 1980s, especially the video cassette recorder, and the theme of Gainax's landmark OTAKU NO VIDEO. However, in an age where only fanatic devotees are prepared to forgive many of modern anime's shortcomings, numerous shows pander desperately to the fan audience, with a crop of solipsistic titles such as ANIMATION RUNNER KUROMI-CHAN, COMIC PARTY, ANIME SHOP-KEEPER, and COSPLAY COMPLEX. Some may regard this as the anime equivalent of "reality TV," in which mainstream entertainment becomes so dull that the audience prefers to turn the camera on itself. Others may see it as a recognition of the size and purchasing power of the fandom bloc—with TV niches in the mainstream "narrowcasting" to ever smaller interest groups, the many thousands of active fans now constitute a sizeable enough

market to generate its own entertainment and consumption.

This self-reference (some might say self-indulgence) reached its height with A15, part of which was a derivative tale about a Japanese schoolgirl sorceress, while the second part was a fictionalized account of the bored creatives who were forced to make the first. Ironically for such an artificial medium, anime was also at the forefront of reality TV with KIRA KIRA MELODY ACADEMY, a forgotten forerunner of *American Idol*.

Innovation in modern anime (i.e., since 1983) comes in the form of refinements and experiments with existing forms. Sometimes, the achievements are not immediately obvious. In GUNDAM, SAILOR MOON, and POKÉMON, the true genius lay in the pioneering of "multimedia" franchises for their target audiences; in DALLOS, it was the opening up of a new niche for more adult material. For MAISON IKKOKU, TENCHI MUYO!, and CHOBITS, it was the refinement of an old genre that altered the chaste titillation of *I Dream of Jeannie* and *Bewitched* for a Japanese TV audience.

Many modern achievements have been reactive, as a show resists overlying trends, such as COWBOY BEBOP, deliberately conceived as a sci-fi show without giant robots, or EVANGELION, written in reaction to the robot shows of the previous generation. GANTZ is TV for a generation that no longer watches TV, designed instead for the longer-term viewing habits of TiVo users and DVD purchasers. Perhaps the greatest innovation of all in modern times comes in VOICES OF A DISTANT STAR, the first release to truly utilize software that allowed a private individual to completely bypass the old distribution system. The world of Japanese animated features is less confused, since it is still dominated by Hayao Miyazaki, as it has been for the last twenty years. Compared to the accomplishments of Studio Ghibli at the Japanese box office, most other anime features are mere marketing exercises or flashes in the pan.

The last twenty years have been dominated by the rise of computers, first through the growing amount of investment money available for game-related anime, then in the exodus of creative staff out of anime altogether for the better rewards of the computer industry. Erosion of talent in anime proper served to accelerate the growth of the use of computers, a position that only increased the likelihood of gaming investment still further.

It is a fact little acknowledged in the media that innovations are often pioneered in the pornographic world—erotica were at the forefront of the move into straight-to-video distribution in the 1980s and formed the driving force of much of the late-night anime of the 1990s. If anime erotica is five years ahead of the curve, then the future of anime will lie in online distribution, since downloadable packets and online streaming are the upcoming trends in the sub-genre. Anime erotica is also at the forefront of using mobile phones as a distribution system—limited animation of the Flash variety, used to impart movement to manga-style images either to tell a story or to provide an interface for interactivity. In this sense, the immediate future of Japanese animation could involve a drop in the complexity of much of the material, and a further blurring of the lines between anime, manga, and computer games.

ACKNOWLEDGMENTS

This edition incorporates literally hundreds of clarifications, corrections, and outright rewrites of some entries, based both on our own research and the comments of our readers, for which we are eternally grateful. We hope we have remembered all of those who helped us, but if some have fallen through the cracks, our apologies in advance.

We would like to thank the following people for their help and additional suggestions for the second edition: Walter Amos, Per Andersson, Bobbi Baker, Lee Brimmicombe-Wood, Francesco Bruni, Kevin Bundage, Barry Cantin, Jeremy Clarke, Roan Jane Chiong, Paul Corrigan, Aaron Dawe, Hugh David, Jennifer Empanger, Rhonda Eudaly, Sascha Falkner, Robert Fenelon, Dave Frear, Shawn Fumo, David Gibbons, Tom Gifford, Michael Gilson, Kimberly Guerre, Marc Hairston, Elizabeth Hall, Carl Gustav Horn, Andrew Jinks, Simon Jowett, H. Kojima, Sean Kemp, Mark Kirk, Steve Kyte, Kati Mäki-Kuutti, Pekka Mäki-Kuutti, Angela Matthews, Jerome Mazandarani, Matt Murray, Witek Nowakowski, Andrew Osmond, Kate Pankhurst, Andrew Partridge, Fred Patten, Russ Patterson, James Pool, Kyle Pope, Clive Reames, Kevin Risch, Rolando Rodriguez, Maiju Saaritsa, Deborah Scally, Jasper Sharp, Chad Snyder, Adam Stephanides, Jim Swallow, Motoko Tamamuro, Stuart Taylor, Elizabeth Tompkins, Noel Vera, David Watson, John C. Watson, Rashard Williams, Vince Wilson.

We would also like to thank our overworked, underpaid research assistants Darren Ashmore, Steve Kyte, and Motoko Tamamuro, and beta-version readers Marc Hairston, Paul Jacques (of Anime on DVD), John Oppliger (of Anime-Nation), and John C. Watson. Extra thanks to Steve Kyte for his wonderful artwork. In addition, our tireless editor Beth Cary and all at Stone Bridge Press, particularly Jaime "it's a girl's name" Starling, Linda Ronan, Nina Wegner, Anne Connolly, and Peter Goodman, who has never once complained, despite all the terrors, delays, and *hentai* plotlines to which we have subjected him over the last five years. And finally, our partners Kati and Steve, who both wondered why such things as the etymological origins of the word Cendrillon and the plotline for *Classmates Again* could ever be more important than a New Year's Eve party.

J. C., H. M.

PUBLISHER'S NOTE

We are grateful to the following companies for generously granting image permissions both for the first edition and for this expanded and revised edition of *The Anime Encyclopedia*:

AIC/Tripeaks, A.D. Vision, ADV Films, AnimEigo, AnimeNation, Bandai Entertainment, Central Park Media, Enoki Films Co. Ltd., Fuji Creative Corporation, FUNimation Productions, Inc., Geneon Entertainment (USA) Inc., Harmony Gold, Kodansha, Ltd., Manga Entertainment, Media Blasters, Inc., Mushi Production Co., Ltd., Nintendo of America, Inc., Nippon Animation Co., Ltd., The Right Stuf International, Inc., Sandy Frank Film Syndication, Inc., Studio Ghibli, Tezuka Productions Co., Ltd., Urban Vision Entertainment, Inc., TOKYOPOP, VIZ Media, LLC, Voyager Entertainment

Thanks are also due to the following individuals, some of them from the above companies, who were particularly helpful with information and materials:

Jason Alnas, Ricki Ames, Charles Babb, Anna Bechtol, Sara Bush, Libbie Chase, Joseph Chung, Lisa Cooper, Jeff Dronen, Evelyn Dubocq, Newton Grant, Gamal Hennessy, Clare Hill, Rena Ikeda, Yoshi Inoki, Tomoko Kanai, Kris Kleckner, Shawne Kleckner, Minoru Kotoku, Junko Kusunoki, Steve Kyte, Cindy Ledermann, Chieko Matsumoto, Yasuhiko Matsuoka, Robyn Mukai, Chris Oarr, Phil Oldman, Tak Onishi (and Japan Video & Media), Fred Patten, Matt Perrier, Patty Pfister, Gilles Poitras, Roland de la Rosa (and Movie Image), Shigehiko Sato, John Serabet, Kara Staumbach, Mikiko Takeda, Stephen Tang, Alden Thomas, Natsumi Ueki, Robert Woodhead, Richard York, Steve Yun

We have tried diligently to obtain permissions for all copyrighted images used in this book. If we have inadvertently omitted or incorrectly listed the name of a rightsholder, we will gladly correct the error in the next edition. We honor the rights of creators and acknowledge their work.

The companies acknowledged here were helpful in many ways: suggesting images, sending high-resolution digital files or high-quality materials for scanning, and providing the authors with updated information for inclusion in the text. However, we were unable to include several important examples of anime art because the studios that held the rights never responded to us, demanded exorbitant fees, wanted veto power over entry content, or, for reasons known only to them, flatly refused to have their material included in this book. Rights issues are complicated, and we'd like to think that legal circumstances prevented their participation. But we suspect that in some cases studios simply couldn't be bothered to reply or to do the necessary paperwork. We'd like again—as we did when the first edition was published—to thank those companies who *do* see the value in this book, and urge the other companies to review their policies regarding permissions requests for reference works. Books like this provide essential information to hungry and thirsty fans as well as to dealers, reviewers, and filmgoers.

Owners of the first edition will be happy to note that all illustrations now appear close to their corresponding entries instead of scattered throughout at random (a less-than-satisfactory solution driven by our desperate need to have some kind of pagination so that we could produce a proper index). Another complaint has also been attended to: the absence of thematic entries that in the opinion of some readers demonstrated this was not an "encyclopedia" but merely a "film guide," albeit a very large one. For your convenience, thematic entries and illustrations respectively have been given their own contents pages in the frontmatter.

The Anime Encyclopedia is approximately 40% larger than before. Dozens of errors have been corrected, and hundreds of new entries added. We're sure our astute readers will continue to point out all our shortcomings and, more importantly, tell us how to keep improving this book for future editions. So we'd like to hear from you! Please send comments, corrections, complaints, information updates, and letters via e-mail to:

animeinfo@stonebridge.com.

STONE BRIDGE PRESS

THE ANIME ENCYCLOPEDIA

ABBREVIATIONS AND KEY

The following abbreviations are used throughout the listings:

*	available in English
JPN	released in Japan as
AKA	"also known as" (alternative title)
DIR	directed by
SCR	script by
DES	design by
ANI	lead animation by
MUS	music by
PRD	production by
N/C	not credited
N/D	no data available
(b/w)	black and white
(m)	movie
(TV)	[made for] TV
(TVm)	TV movie
(v)	video
?	uncertain (data; usually episode count)
ca.	circa, approximately
ep., eps.	episode(s)
mins.	minutes
BOLDFACE TYPE	cross-reference to main entry
*DE	cross-reference *The Dorama Encyclopedia*
L	language advisory
N	nudity advisory
V	violence advisory

A15 ANTHOLOGY: COSMOPOLITAN PRAYERS, AIM FOR THE HIT, LOVE LOVE

2004. JPN: *Cho Henshin Cos ∞ Prayers; Hit o Nerae; Love Love*. AKA: *Super-Transforming Cos(mopolitan) Prayers; Aim for the Hit*. TV series. DIR: Takeo Takahashi. SCR: Naruhisa Arakawa. DES: Miwa Oshima. ANI: Miwa Oshima. MUS: Toshihiko Sahashi. PRD: M-O-E, Imagin, Studio Live, TV Kanagawa. 13 mins. x 8 eps. (*Cos Prayers*); 13 mins. x 8 eps. (*Aim for the Hit*); 13 mins. x 9 eps; 13 mins. x 9 eps. (*Love Love*); + 4 bonus DVD episodes each.

Three stories strung out in short snippets in a late-night slot showing PG-15 rated titles. In *Cosmopolitan Prayers*, a Japanese schoolgirl is transported to the legendary land of IZUMO, where she must team up with local priestesses to rescue the sun goddess Amaterasu, who has been imprisoned within a network of black towers. Using their mystic powers to transform, or "charm up," to their magical forms, the girls fight demons and demigods to keep the world safe—FUSHIGI YUGI crashed into SAILOR MOON, with a title deliberately designed to recall *cosplay* ("Costume Play"), the Japlish term for anime-related fancy dress.

Similar allusions might be expected in *Aim for the Hit* (aka *Smash Hit*), which, despite its titular resemblance to AIM FOR THE ACE, is concerned not with sporting triumph but a ratings-chasing TV program. Twenty-five-

year-old mystery fanatic Mizuki gets the chance of a lifetime when she's appointed as producer of a new show, but she's hardly the ideal choice for the job. She's physically immature, and her childlike appearance goes with a whining attitude that leads to her colleagues making fun of her. Nor is the film much to her liking, since it is a derivative show about a Japanese schoolgirl saving the world. In a triumph of solipsism, the show that Mizuki cannot stand is *Cosmopolitan Prayers*—perhaps in an allegory aimed at animators forced to put aside their dreams in order to pay the bills on shows like this. But like her media colleague KUROMI-CHAN, she finally pulls through.

Love Love features Naoto Oizumi, a high school student with an off-putting stare, hired as a cameraman by the production company in *Aim for the Hit*, and tasked with filming the training of the actresses who have been hired to star in *Cosmopolitan Prayers*, thereby achieving what must be a modern animator's idea of franchise paradise: the pop idols of KIRA KIRA MELODY ACADEMY crashed into TENCHI MUYO!.

A.I.C.

Literally "Anime International Company," although it is usually identified by its acronym, not its full name. Founded in 1982 by former EG World and Anime Room staffer Toru Miura, the company first contributed to later epi-

sodes of the color ASTRO BOY remake. Notable employees have included Katsuhito Akiyama, Hiroyuki Kitazume, Hiroyuki Kawagoe, and Hiroki Hayashi. Representative works include AD POLICE, BLACK HEAVEN, and numerous projects for Pioneer/Geneon (see Dentsu).

A.LI.CE *

1999. Movie. DIR: Kenichi Maejima. SCR: Masahiro Yoshimoto. DES: Hirosuke Kizaki. ANI: N/C. MUS: N/C. PRD: Gaga Communications. 85 mins. *A.Li.Ce* throws the viewer straight into the middle of the action, with its heroine fleeing from cyborgs across icy wastes. The background details are only filled in gradually—we are in Lapland in 2030, but 16-year-old Alice's last memory was of an accident on a space shuttle many years earlier. Her guardian is a stewardess robot programmed to protect her, and their travelling companion is Yuan, a local orphan who has lived alone since his parents were "relocated" in an illogical environmental scheme by the Earth's new ruler, Nero.

An early effort in computer animation, *A.Li.Ce* often resembles a long scene from a computer game, unsurprising since its writer's previous credits included the game *Shen Mue*. Like all the best computer games, the movie regularly alters its protagonists' aims for maximum effect. What begins as a straightforward chase sequence soon becomes a quest to acquire information and resources. Once Alice realizes that someone has brought her to the future for an unexplained purpose, it changes once more into a train journey fraught with peril. Eluding Nero's Stealth Warriors, only to be captured by the rebellious Liberation Forces, the cast is temporarily split up, as Yuan and Maria escape from custody, while Alice enters cyberspace to help the resistance break into Nero's fortress. This, it transpires, is why she is needed, as her past self was/is Nero's mother, affording her identical brain patterns access to the citadel's defensive computer systems.

In a series of last-minute twists, Alice discovers that *she* is partly responsible for Nero's reign of terror. Nero has decimated the world's population in a misguided attempt to reduce pollution (compare to **BLUE REMAINS**), itself a misreading of Alice's memories of the dying wish of her suicidal school-friend Yumi. The motives of the Liberation Forces are found to be even more questionable, and Alice returns to the past to set things right. This, however, is where the narrative falls apart, as her return is visibly demonstrated to make little difference to the future she has just left. We also see her meeting the man who will become Nero's father, though now she presumably does so with the full knowledge of his future death, thereby making it impossible that the events we have just seen will actually take place.

Time-travel paradoxes aside, *A.Li. Ce* remains an intriguing entry in the genre, and a surer step into computer animation than the disappointing **VISITOR**. In Maria, it also has an intriguing take on the ubiquitous robot-girls of anime—a svelte woman in revealing costumes, with an array of pop-out gadgets and power sockets like a 21st century **DORAEMON**. Her name is bestowed upon her by Alice herself, not in homage to the Maria of Fritz Lang's *Metropolis* (see **METAL ANGEL MARIE**) but because of her chance resemblance to a statue of the Virgin Mary. Later,

she is augmented twice, once by Yuan and once in a self-inflicted upgrade, ending the movie with high-powered retractable machine guns, and built-in roller skates that help circumvent the film's primitive motion-capture. Soon transformed into a battle-robot, Maria retains vestiges of her former programming, and persists in bossing her charges around as if she is still serving in-flight drinks.

ABASHIRI FAMILY, THE *
1991. JPN: *Abashiri Ikka*. Video. DIR: Takashi Watanabe. SCR: Takashi Watanabe. DES: Shigenori Kurii. ANI: Shigenori Kurii. MUS: Takeo Miratsu. PRD: Dynamic Planning, Studio Pierrot, Soeishinsha, NEXTART. 75 mins.
Papa Abashiri, leader of one of the most notorious criminal syndicates in history, decides it's time for his superpowered family to retire so his daughter, Kukunosuke, can have a normal existence. However, her "normal" school turns out to be a hunting ground for crazed perverts and brawlers, who have no intention of teaching the students anything. As the violence escalates, Kukunosuke calls in her family to fight against the principal in a final showdown of bone-crunchingly epic proportions.

Recalling **SUKEBAN DEKA**, with its tale of a bad girl trying to go straight, and **DEBUTANTE DETECTIVES**, with its well-connected students, *Abashiri Families* was originally released as four short chapters in the **RENTAMAN** video magazine. It was soon compiled into this omnibus edition, which is the version circulated in the English language. Its cartoonish comedy angle gives it more in common with creator Go Nagai's **KEKKO KAMEN** and **HANAPPE BAZOOKA** than with his more serious stories, but the disjointed nature of the original production makes for an inferior offering. Director Watanabe would go on to adapt another Nagai story, **BLACK LION**.

ABE, YOSHITOSHI
1971– . A graduate of Tokyo National University of Fine Arts and Music,

Abe's dark, brooding artwork established distinctive looks in **SERIAL EXPERIMENTS LAIN**, **HAIBANE RENMEI** (based on his own amateur publication), and **TEXHNOLYZE**. He also designed the characters and wrote the manga of **NIEA_7**. He favors unorthodox typography and likes his name to be written with the Y in lower case and the B in upper. We prefer to keep our English-language text readable.

ACROBUNCH
1982. JPN: *Makyo Densetsu Acrobunch*. AKA: *Haunted Frontier Legend Acrobunch*. TV series. DIR: Masakazu Yasumura, Satoshi Hisaoka. SCR: Masaru Yamamoto. DES: Shigenori Kageyama, Mutsumi Inomata, Masakazu Higuchi. ANI: Kazuhiro Taga, Masakazu Yasumura, Hideki Takayama, Yutaka Arai, Kazuhiro Ochi. MUS: Masaji Maruyama. PRD: Nippon TV. 30 mins. x 24 eps.
Half-Japanese amateur inventor Tatsuya Lando talks his five *almost* all-American children into piloting his latest project, a transforming super-robot called Acrobunch. Older boys Hiro and Ryo pilot the two Buncher Hornets, while twin girls Miki and Rika ride the Buncher Arrow flying motorcycles. Middle-child Jun is the 15-year-old boy who gets to pilot the Acrobunch unit formed from the combination of all the vehicles with dad's Falcon Buncher main craft. Tatsuya is searching for the ancient treasure of Quaschika, which was the true inspiration behind the ancient stories of Atlantis. But Lando is not the only one—Emperor Delos of the undersea Goblin empire is also searching for the Quaschika, and the Acrobunch robot becomes the last line of defense between them and Earth. Each week, it must fight against the robots of the Goblin armies, one of which is led by Delos's own daughter, Queen Shiira, who develops a crush on her enemy Hiro.

Shunted around the schedules and between two different production studios, the troubled *Acrobunch* ("a robot controlled by a *bunch* of *acro*bats!") nevertheless served as a training ground for a group of new talents who would find fame in the decades to come. It was the first anime job for future TEKKAMAN-designer Rei Nakahara. Among the animators, Arai would work on CITY HUNTER, Ochi would make HIKARIAN, and Takayama would become the director of the notorious UROTSUKI-DOJI series. Two decades later, Inomata produced similar character designs for BRAIN POWERED.

AD POLICE *

1990. Video, TV series. DIR: Akihiko Takahashi, Akira Nishimori. SCR: Noboru Aikawa. DES: Tony Takezaki, Fujio Oda, Toru Nagasuki. ANI: Fujio Oda, Hiroyuki Kitazume. MUS: Kaoru Mizutani. PRD: Artmic, Youmex, AIC. 40 mins. x 3 eps., 25 mins. x 12 eps.
A dark spin-off from Toshimichi Suzuki's BUBBLEGUM CRISIS, *AD Police* concentrates on the AD(vanced) anti-robot crime division of Mega Tokyo's police force. Leon McNicol, a minor character in the original series, is part-nered here with butch lady-cop Gena in several investigations that play with ideas of humanity in a high-tech soci-ety. The "voomer" robots here are all female in the man's world of the ADP, where only women who are prepared to become one with machines stand a chance in it. Whereas this device was used in *Bubblegum Crisis* as an excuse for girls with impressive high-tech kits, here it is far more misogynistic, as femininity is gradually eroded by bion-ics and prosthetics, taking characters' humanity with it. A businesswoman, for example, is only successful in the boardroom after she has a hysterec-tomy, but the trauma turns her into a serial killer. There are shades of *Blade Runner* in the sex-android stalker that locks onto the man who injured her, and there are also blatant steals from *Robocop* in the final chapter, wherein one of Gena's ex-boyfriends receives so much augmentation that his tongue is the only part of his original body that remains.
Canceled after just three of the

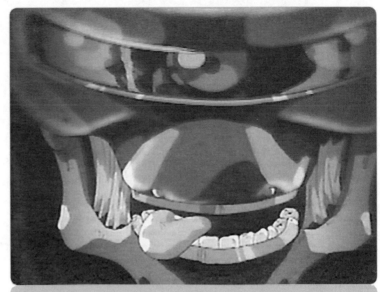

AD Police

© AIC./TOSHIBA EMI/EMOTION

planned five episodes, the franchise was not revived until 1999, in the wake of the *Bubblegum Crisis 2040* remake, as a 12-part TV Tokyo series directed by Hidehito Ueda. The new *AD Police* was a far shallower affair, ditching many of the old characters in favor of a buddy-movie cliché between rapid-response robot-crime cop Takeru Sasaki and his new partner, Hans Krief. Clearly made with half an eye on the overseas market (all the other leads have foreign names like Paul Sanders, Liam Fletcher, and Nancy Wilson), the melting-pot remake is something of a disappoint-ment.
The franchise was briefly resurrect-ed in *Parasite Dolls* (2003), a three-part video series directed by Kazuto Naka-zawa, focusing on a clandestine branch of the AD Police, called, somewhat unimaginatively, Branch. The story focuses on Buzz, an officer like writer Chiaki Konaka's earlier Ross Sylibus in ARMITAGE III, who is transferred to an unattractive new posting and forced to cooperate with a detested robot part-ner. *Parasite Dolls* also exists in a movie-length edit, which is the version most commonly found outside Japan. **LNV**

ADRIFT IN THE PACIFIC *

1982. JPN: *Jugo Shonen no Hyor-yuki.* AKA: *15 Boys Adrift; Deux Ans de Vacances.* TV special. DIR: Yasuji Mori, Yoshio Kuroda. SCR: Shunichi Yukimuro. DES: Hiroshi Wagatsuma, Rumiko Takahashi. ANI: Tatsuo Ogawa, Hideo Maeda. MUS: Katsutoshi Nagasawa. PRD: Toei, Fuji TV. 75 mins., 84 mins.
When bad weather causes her to slip her moorings and drift out to sea, the British schooner Sloughi is left in the hands of the 15 schoolboys on holiday. Without officers or sailors on board, the French boy Briant manages to organize the group and beach the ship on a deserted island they name Cher-man after their school. The upper-class British boy, Doniphan, begins to argue with Briant about who should be in charge, and problems are multiplied a hundredfold when a 16th castaway washes up on the shore—a schoolgirl called Kate.
Deux Ans de Vacances, Jules Verne's low-rent copy of SWISS FAMILY ROBINSON, remains immeasurably more popular in Japanese than in English. This TV movie included a young design assis-tant called Rumiko Takahashi, whose

growing success with URUSEI YATSURA would make her rich and unlikely to work in animation again.

In 1987, the story was remade as another TV movie to cash in on the popularity of the Hollywood movie *Stand By Me* (which also featured several boys going exploring and getting mildly upset). Directed by Masayuki Akehi, the new version featured Maria Kawamura, shortly to find fame as Jung Freud in GUNBUSTER, as the troublesome Kate. This second TV movie was released in English as *Story of 15 Boys*, a pedantically faithful translation of the Japanese title suggesting the U.S. distributor knew little of Verne's original. See also VIDEO PICTURE BOOK and VIFAM.

ADULT FAIRY TALES

1999. JPN: *Otono no Dowa* Series. Video. DIR: Soichi Masui. SCR: Shige Sotoyama. DES: Kaoru Honma. ANI: N/C. MUS: Miki Kasamatsu. PRD: Tac, Toei. 50 mins.
A deliberate attempt to take GRIMMS' FAIRY TALES away from their cuter modern image and back to their darker roots, this series comprises three short versions of popular tales augmented with copious horror and flavor-of-the-moment computer graphics. The tales include *Hansel and Gretel*, *Blue Beard*, and *Cinderella*, all chosen because they presented an opportunity for the crew to depict stories of love and obsession.

ADVANCER TINA *

1996. Video. DIR: Kan Fukumoto. SCR: Wataru Amano. DES: Hironobu Saito, Kenji Teraoka. ANI: Dandelion. MUS: Ann Fu. PRD: Dandelion, Green Bunny, Beam Entertainment. 45 mins.
Three thousand years after pollution renders Earth uninhabitable, the human race is a space-faring people in search of new planets to settle. Elite super-scouts called Advancers blaze trails for the rest, but Omega 13 is one world proving difficult to conquer. Nine teams have failed to return, prompting high-ranking executive Mugal to make convict Tina Owen an offer she can't refuse. If she can solve

the mystery of Omega 13, he'll knock a whole millennium off her 2,000-year sentence for an undisclosed crime.

Tina only spends five tedious minutes on Omega 13; the rest of the story involves the pointless hunt for a crew (telepath/alien/comic relief Frill and Japanese love interest/sidekick Akira), and the rescue of fellow Advancer Garuda from a beleaguered ship. The alien menace turns out to be a multi-tentacled creature with acid saliva that burns through bulkheads and clothes but not through girls' skin. The alien murders all the disposable members of the cast (three concubines whose sole role is to be sexually assaulted in different locations) before being summarily executed as it tries to rape Tina. This, apparently, makes the planet safe and avenges Akira's dead parents all in one shot, allowing Tina to fly off to her next mission, though a sequel was never made.

Despite promising beginnings that unite the last-chance mission of *The Dirty Dozen* with the interstellar troubleshooting of DIRTY PAIR, *Advancer Tina* soon collapses into a tacky exploitation movie. With an icthyphallic menace that gestates in human stomach cavities and a predictable, false ending, its debt to the *Alien* series is obvious, but the film is shoddily assembled from start to finish. Fukumoto, Saito, and Teraoka, the real-world perpetrators of this anime crime, are still at large and can be found elsewhere in this book in the entries for VENUS FIVE, SEXORCIST, and GIGOLO. ⓛⓝⓥ

ADVENTURE BOY SHADAR

1967. JPN: *Boken Shonen Shadar*. TV series. DIR: Juzo Kataoka. SCR: Masaki Tsuji. DES: Shinichi Kuwajima. ANI: Takashi Saijo, Nobukazu Kabashima. MUS: Atsutoshi Soda. PRD: Nippon TV. 10 mins. x 156 eps.
When Earth is threatened by the invading Ghostar, a young boy with nerves of steel and the strength of 50 men appears from a cave on Mount Fuji. He is Shadar, a boy of unknown origin who, with his faithful dog, Pinboke,

fights each week to save the world in several ten-minute installments, guaranteeing a final showdown for Japanese viewers each Saturday.

Ghostar actor Kenji Utsumi's voice would come to represent the ultimate in evil to a Japanese audience, and he would go on to play the title roles in DRACULA: SOVEREIGN OF THE DAMNED and DON DRACULA.

ADVENTURE KID *

1992. JPN: *Yoju Sensen Adventure Kid*. AKA: *Demon-Beast Battle Line Adventure Kid*. Video. DIR: Yoshitaka Fujimoto. SCR: Atsushi Yamatoya, Akio Satsugawa. DES: Dan Kongoji, Ryunosuke Otonashi, Yuji Takahashi. ANI: MW Films. MUS: Masamichi Amano. PRD: MW Films. 40 mins. x 3 eps.
Wartime Japanese scientist Professor Masago devotes himself to his research, ignoring his beautiful wife, Michiyo. In 1945, he is murdered by the dastardly Captain Matsubara's soldiers, after first being forced to watch them rape her. Fifty years later, the husband and wife are reincarnated as students Norikazu and Midori. Norikazu unearths Masago's prototype dimension-hopping device, and it propels them into a parallel universe where Masago's bitter psyche has created a world of marauding zombie soldiers. Eventually Norikazu (good side) defeats Masago (bad side) by dropping him into the Hiroshima bomb blast. The couple then find themselves in Hell Zone, where lusty elf-girl Eganko latches onto Norikazu and accompanies him back to Earth. Back at Norikazu's school, the reincarnation of Captain Matsubara, college-boy Yukimoto, wants Midori for himself and schemes with Eganko's mother, Queen Dakiniten, to make Norikazu fall in love with Eganko. The plan goes awry when love potions are mixed up and given to the wrong victims.

A pornographic tale of rape and domination that suddenly turns into a farce, *Adventure Kid* contains erotic musings on the alien girlfriend-squatter setup of URUSEI YATSURA, a clumsy attempt to integrate computers into horror (also seen in **DIGITAL DEVIL STORY**), and a final episode that pokes merciless fun at the excesses of both itself and creator Toshio Maeda's earlier **UROTSUKIDOJI**. In an attempt to draw in new crowds, the producers hired live-action erotic "actresses" to provide some of the voice roles, a move which backfired spectacularly when they couldn't actually act. In the U.K., the series was heavily cut and renamed *Adventure Duo*. **🅒🅛🅝🅥**

ADVENTURE OF KOTETSU *
1996. JPN: *Kotetsu no Daiboken*. Movie. DIR: Yuji Moriyama. SCR: Yuji Kawahara. DES: Yoko Kikuchi. ANI: Tetsuya Watanabe. MUS: Kuniaki Haishima. PRD: Daiei, Tokuma Japan. 30 mins. x 2 eps.
Hot-headed Linn "Kotetsu" Suzuki is an accomplished martial artist at 14 and the last in a long line of warriors. Running away from her old-fashioned Kyoto home to look for her brother in Tokyo, she helps a shapely private eye, Miho, defeat two possessed street thugs. The two soon move in together, and Kotetsu inadvertently saves Miho's life once again when Tetsuya, the man hired by a corrupt businessman to kill her, instead falls in love with her new roommate. Settling their differences at a hot-springs resort, the trio is attacked by a tree demon, sent by Tetsuya's boss. Upon defeating it, Kotetsu's grandmother tells her she can stay in the big city.
    Recalling both **DEVIL HUNTER YOHKO** and **LA BLUE GIRL** with its female inheritor of a family martial arts tradition, this silly affair was based on the best-selling 1992 adult manga by MEE (aka Mikun). Though featuring atmospheric music from **SPRIGGAN's** Haishima and direction from **PROJECT A-KO's** Moriyama, the fan-service nudity and setups make it less than the sum of its parts—one assassination attempt involves a nude clone of Miho in the bath simply to arrange a lesbian scene between the two girls. Despite undeserved popularity for its nude

heroine's resemblance to **RANMA ½**, the series stopped after the experimental two-part opener. MEE would have better success with his next anime project, the TV series **HYPER POLICE**. **🅝**

ADVENTURE ON KABOTEN ISLAND
1967. JPN: *Boken Kaboten Shima*. TV series. DIR: Motokazu Watanabe. SCR: Aritsune Toyoda, Masaki Tsuji, Arashi Ishizu, Junichi Yoshinaga. DES: Fumio Hisamatsu. ANI: Shizuko Komooka, Toyoo Ashida, Kazuo Mori. MUS: Various. PRD: TBS, Eiken. 30 mins. x 39 eps.
SUPER JETTER–creator Fumio Hisamatsu's 1967 comic in *Shonen Sunday* magazine featured a group of boys and girls marooned on a South Sea island in an imitation of Jules Verne's **ADRIFT IN THE PACIFIC**. The anime version reduced the female cast to a single comic relief little sister called Tomato, preferring instead to concentrate on the male characters as they explore their new home.

ADVENTURES OF KOROBOKKLE
1973. JPN: *Boken Korobokkle*. AKA: *The Mountain Gnomes*. TV series. DIR: Yonehiko Watanabe, Yukizo Takagaki, Toru Murayama, Takanori Okada, Yoshikata Nitta. SCR: Shunichi Yukimuro, Noboru Shiroyama, Minoru Takahashi. DES: Masatoshi Kobayashi. ANI: Kazuo Kobayashi. MUS: Bob Sakuma. PRD: Eiken, Tatsunoko Pro, Yomiuri TV. 25 mins. x 26 eps.
Sword-wielding hero Bokkle, flute-playing mystic Cous-Cous, and brave female Love-Love are very small gods who live under the butterbur leaves in the countryside. Becoming increasingly annoyed that humans no longer pay them any respect, they decide to head closer to human habitation in search of worshippers. Mild-mannered country boy Seitaka is the only person able to see the spirits, who teach him how to stand up for himself against local bullies. His gentle woodland friends, however, are unafraid of fighting with vicious little knives when they are in trouble.

AoK was sponsored, like **PIGGYBACK GHOST** before it, by Sumitomo Life Insurance as part of the company's "classic" series—an attempt to associate a company with a successful anime series that paid off much better for the Calpis drinks company with **WORLD MASTERPIECE THEATER**. The original children's book *Stories of Korobokkle*, itself based on folktales from northern Japan's indigenous Ainu race, was initially adapted with character designs by its author Satoru Sato, but these were replaced with designs by Masatoshi Kobayashi after they tested poorly with young focus groups. That, at least, is what was claimed in Japanese sources, but it seems outlandishly odd to buy the rights to a book if one is only going to throw away its creator's input! The problem was probably connected with creating character designs that could be more easily replicated by a group of animators. In an additional attempt to appeal to a young audience, the leading role was taken by Satoshi Hasegawa, who had previously appeared in NHK's child-centered *Grave of the Wild Chrysanthemums* (*DE). With its disappearing spirits, *Korobokkle* could be said to be a foreshadowing of later Studio Ghibli efforts like **POMPOKO** and **MY NEIGHBOR TOTORO**.

ADVENTURES OF PINOCCHIO *
1972. JPN: *Kashi no Ki Mokku*. AKA: *Mokku (Woody) the Oak Tree*. TV series. DIR: Ippei Kuri, Yukihiro Takahashi. SCR: Jinzo Toriumi , Akiyoshi Sakai. DES: Yoshitaka Amano. ANI: Masayuki Hayashi. MUS: Nobuyoshi Koshibe. PRD: Tatsunoko, Fuji TV. 25 mins. x 52 eps.
Finding driftwood that has been struck by lightning, toy-maker Gepetto constructs a puppet that comes alive but wants to be a real boy. Based on the 1881 children's story by Carlo Collodi, it was also animated as **PICCOLINO**. Yoshitaka Amano's first work in character design. Shown on HBO in the U.S.

AESOP'S FABLES *
1983. JPN: *Manga Aesop Monoga-*

tari. TV series. DIR: Eiji Okabe, Jun Hagiwara, Fumio Kurokawa. SCR: Michiru Tanabe, Asami Watanabe, Ryo Nakahara. DES: Yu Noda. ANI: Hirokazu Ishino. MUS: Pegumo, Toko Akasaka. PRD: Nippon Animation, Transarts. 25 mins. x 52 eps.

Aesop, an ancient Greek storyteller thought to have lived in the 6th century, has been a staple of anime since the beginning with EARLY ANIME such as Sanae Yamamoto's *Tortoise and the Hare* (1924) and *Frog's Belly* (1929). The 1983 TV series added the term "manga" to accentuate the children's-picture-book quality of the presentation, running through tales such as *The Ants and the Grasshopper*, *The Sun and the North Wind*, and *The Thirsty Crow*. Eight of the stories were combined to make the theatrical feature *Aesop's Fables* (1983, U.S. release 1985), with a framing device of young Aesop tricking his fellow villagers into believing that a wolf is attacking. When a real wolf comes, nobody believes him, and he is chased down a magic hole into a kingdom of animals. As he looks for a way out, he meets a tortoise, a hare, an ant, and other creatures who tell him their stories. Several of Aesop's fables were also used as part of the *Shogo Hirata's Picture Book* series (1995). See also VIDEO PICTURE BOOK.

AFRO KEN

2001. AKA: *Afro Dog*. Video. DIR: Takashi Imanishi. SCR: Takashi Imanishi. DES: Tetsuro Aimi. ANI: Toyonori Yamada, Kayoko Murakami, Fumie Anno, Naoyuki Takasawa. MUS: Takeshiro Kawabe. PRD: Sunrise, Bandai Visual, Green Camel. 30 mins.

Like its Bandai stablemate TARE PANDA, this one-shot, fully computer-animated wonder is an attempt to tap into the HELLO KITTY merchandising market, putting the brand first and following with animation only reluctantly. Afro Ken is, as the name implies, a dog with a multicolored Afro hairdo, and several equally hallucinogenic friends. In several short sequences, he is shown visiting various tourist sites, playing with some of his canine friends, walking through Tokyo like a friendly Godzilla, and appearing in ancient cave paintings. The half-hour running time contains only 15 minutes of animation—the rest is bulked out with a "Making Of" documentary that manages to recycle much of the footage already shown, along with creator interviews. The only truly worthwhile item on the disc is the catchy theme song, and even that is played twice.

AFRO SAMURAI *

2006. TV series. DIR: N/C. SCR: Takashi Okazaki, Tomohiro Yamashita. DES: N/C. ANI: N/C. MUS: N/C. PRD: Gonzo, Fuji TV. 25 mins. x 5 eps.

After his father dies in a duel with the warrior known as Justice, young Afro resolves to study the martial arts. He becomes a wandering swordsman in a milieu that mixes samurai-era epics with science fiction in the style of SAMURAI 7. Supposedly conceived in 1995 by a young Takashi Okazaki, the concept achieved new life in the 21st century when it gained the backing of Samuel L. Jackson as coproducer and voice artist. Riding a wave of interest in anime fueled in part by KILL BILL: THE ORIGIN OF O-REN, *Afro Samurai* takes the irreverence of SAMURAI CHAMPLOO to extremes, with characters such as Kuma, an anonymous fighter who wears a teddy bear's head to hide his identity. Forthcoming at the time of our deadline.

AFTER-SCHOOL LOVE CLUB ÉTUDE

1997. JPN: *Hokago Ren'ai Club Koi no Étude*. Video. DIR: Moritaka Imura. SCR: N/C. DES: Yoshiaki Hatano. ANI: Yuki Mine. MUS: N/C. PRD: Pink Pineapple, KSS. 31 mins. x 2 eps.

Originating in Libido's mildly titillating computer role-playing game in the same genre as TOKIMEKI MEMORIAL, this is the story of Shunichi and Sanae, who are attracted to each other, but whose relationship seems to go nowhere. Neither does the plot until episode two, when the members of the "love club" start to get into the sex scenes promised on the box. In the original game, the player had to manage his resources to ensure he could get the most out of 12 sex-starved female members of a dating club in just 30 days. The anime doesn't retain its appeal for quite that long. **Ⓝ**

AFTER-SCHOOL TINKERBELL

1992. JPN: *Hokago Tinkerbell*. Video. DIR: Kiyoshi Murayama. SCR: Akira Oketani. DES: Yasuhide Maruyama. ANI: Yasuhide Maruyama. MUS: N/C. PRD: Life Work, Ashi Pro. 45 mins.

In this animated adaptation of two novels in Shoichiro Hinata's *After School* series, high school investigators Kenichi and Misako get on the case when the popular Broadcast Club disc jockey, Ryoko, goes missing.

AGE OF THE GREAT DINOSAURS

1979. JPN: *Daikyoryu no Jidai*. TV special. DIR: Shotaro Ishinomori with Hideki Takayama. SCR: Shotaro Ishinomori, Makoto Naito. DES: Shotaro Ishinomori. ANI: Kozo Morishita. MUS: Shogun. PRD: Ishi(no)mori Pro, Toei, Nippon TV. 73 mins.

CYBORG 009–creator Ishinomori (just plain Ishimori at the time) was heavily involved in this anime shot on 35mm film, in which naïve boy Jun, his female companion, Remi, and her little brother, Chobi, are whisked away to the Cretaceous Period by a flying saucer. There they hobnob with Cro-Magnon men, which would be damage enough to the program's educational merit even without the suggestion that aliens wiped out the dinosaurs when their population became too great—a dark portent for the expanding human race and a typical touch from the dour Ishinomori. Dinosaurs were a regular feature in children's entertainment, also cropping up in Makoto Noriza and Shigeru Omachi's one-shot video *Dinosaur Guide* (1989), in which Professor Doctor (*sic*) escorts children Tai and Ayumi on a trip to the prehistoric past. Aliens would return to do away with the dinosaurs in LAWS OF THE SUN.

AGEDAMAN

1991. JPN: *Genji Tsushin Agedama* [sic]. TV series. DIR: Masato Namiki. SCR: Takashi Yamada, Shigeru Yanagawa, et al. DES: Hatsuki Tsuji. ANI: Hiroaki Sakurai, Hideyuki Motohashi, et al. MUS: Toshihiko Sahashi. PRD: Studio Gallop, TV Tokyo. 25 mins. x 51 eps.

Average boy Genji can use his warp key to transform into the superhero Agedaman, the last line of resistance against the evil 11th-century scientist Nostradamus and his equally evil granddaughter, Kukirei, in a brightly colored show that mixes action and comedy.

AGEMAN AND FUKU-CHAN

1991. Video. DIR: Teruo Kigure. SCR: Susume Yoshiike. DES: Masamichi Yokoyama. ANI: Masamichi Yokoyama. MUS: Jiro Takemura. PRD: Knack. 30 mins.

Mantaro Nishino is obsessed with money and women, but his schemes invariably fail in this satire of Japan and the Japanese in the late 1980s bubble economy. The sexy strumpet Fuku-chan is Mantaro's eventual undoing in this erotic fable based on a manga by Masamichi Yokoyama, who also created **MISTER HAPPY**. The title recalls that of Juzo Itami's live-action *Ageman: Tales of a Golden Geisha* (1990). **Ⓝ**

AGENT AIKA *

1997. JPN: *Aika*. Video. DIR: Katsuhiko Nishijima. SCR: Kenichi Kanemaki. DES: Noriyasu Yamauchi, Hidefumi Kimura, Yoko Kikuchi. ANI: Noriyasu Yamauchi. MUS: Junichi Kanezaki. PRD: Graviton, Bandai Visual. 50 mins., 50 mins., 75 mins., 50 mins. x 4 eps.

Aika Sumeragi is a freelancer who lifts artifacts and data from the submerged ruins of Tokyo in the year 2036. She is a friend and business partner to the father-daughter team of Gozo and Rion Aida and has a love-hate relationship with Gust Turbulence, her spiky-haired male rival. Hired to go after the Ragu, an energy source reputed to be the cause of the global catastrophe, Aika must compete against evil super-bitch Neena Hagen, Neena's incestu-ous brother, Rudolf, and their army of women inexplicably dressed as French maids. Her only advantages: high-tech vehicles and transforming underwear that is really a weapon.

Envisaged by director Nishijima as a replay of **PROJECT A-KO**, with Aika, Neena, and Rion as A-Ko, B-Ko, and C-Ko, *Agent Aika* fast becomes the ultimate in peekaboo anime, as almost every camera angle conspires to get an eyeful of cleavage or panties. Worm's-eye views and gratuitous nudity soon drag the plot far off course, though exactly where Kanemaki's story of a treasure-huntress with a sentient bodice was originally headed is anyone's guess. Compare to the same team's later **NAJICA**. Seven years later, **DAPHNE IN THE BRILLIANT BLUE** would do it all again. **Ⓝ**

AGITO OF THE SILVERY GOD

2006. JPN: *Giniro no Kami no Agito*. AKA: *Spirit*. Movie. DIR: Keiichi Sugiyama. SCR: Umanosuke Iida. DES: Koji Ogata. ANI: Kenji Ando, Mahiro Maeda, Koji Ogata. MUS: N/C. PRD: Gonzo. ca. 90 mins.

Three hundred years into our future, the world has been sharply divided between luxuriant forests and blasted wastelands. The woods are ruled by sentient plants, hostile to humans; the waste areas are home to what's left of the human race. Teenager Agito lives on the border between the two zones, and wanders too close to a forbidden pond, only to discover a young woman, Tuula, who has been sleeping for centuries inside a shining machine. When she was sealed into her shell the world thought itself civilized; her reaction to the changes that took place during her long sleep may threaten the new world order. Originally announced as *Spirit*, and forthcoming from Gonzo at the time of our deadline, the show has high ambitions. Gonzo chairman Shoji Murahama claims that the theme is the importance of the physical, concrete world, as the one thing that can be trusted in our meaningless modern culture. Hopefully it will be more than a robotic retread of **NAUSICAÄ**.

AI CITY *

1986. AKA: *Love City (U.K.)*. Movie. DIR: Koichi Mashimo. SCR: Hideki Sonoda. DES: Chuichi Iguchi, Tomohiko Sato. ANI: Chuichi Iguchi, Nobuyoshi Habara, Satoru Utsunomiya, Kenichi Maejima, Hiroyoshi Okawa, Hiroshi Kawamata. MUS: Shiro Sagisu. PRD: Toei, Movic, Ashi Pro. 100 mins.

Young girl Ai and her protector, Kei, are on the run from rival gangs of "Headmeters"—humans with DNA recombined through nanotech viruses to give them psychic powers. Rival leaders Leigh and Lyrochin want Ai for the terrible secrets she contains, so she and failed Headmeter Kei join forces with an ex-cop turned private eye, an amnesiac ex-enemy, and a gratuitous cute cat (a design rip-off of Lucifer from Disney's *Cinderella*).

A poor man's **AKIRA**, even down to blue-skinned mutants with numerical foreheads, *AC* is much more than the sum of its parts, with surreal sequences of giant heads melting out of sidewalks, a plot revolving around multiple universes, and visceral scenes of psychic violence as Headmeters trump each other with ever-higher power levels. Based on the *Action Comics* manga by Shuho Itabashi (who went on to draw one of the *X-Files* manga adaptations) but made just that little bit too early to benefit from the higher budgets of the sci-fi anime boom of the early 1990s, it was eclipsed by its successors and relegated to the anime B-list despite a plot far superior to contemporaries such as **LOCKE THE SUPERMAN**. Masterfully feeding the audience scraps of plot one bit at a time, it throws the viewer into the story without explaining a thing, slowly piecing together the reasons why Ai and Kei are on the run, who is after them, and where they are from. Sonoda's script, loaded with careful English neologisms like "Headmeter," "tuned man," and "metapsychic phase wall," is truly excellent and even features a serious contender for one of the best endings in anime, later swiped for the grand finale of **UROTSUKIDOJI**. Available in separate U.K. and U.S. versions.

AI YORI AOSHI *

2002. JPN: *Ai Yori Aoshi*. AKA: *Bluer than Blue; Bluer than Indigo; True Blue Love*. TV series. DIR: Masami Shimoda. SCR: Kenichi Kanemaki, Katsuhiko Takayama, Masashi Kubota. DES: Kazunori Iwakura. ANI: Yumi Nakayama. MUS: Toshio Masuda. PRD: JC Staff, Studio Easter, Fuji TV, TV Kanagawa, TV Saitama. 23 mins. x 24 eps. (TV1), 25 mins. x 12 eps. (TV2).

Kaoru Hanabishi offers to help a lost girl in a kimono who seems very out of place in Tokyo, only to discover that the address she is looking for is an empty lot. She is eventually revealed as Aoi Sakuraba, a rich girl from a traditional family, who was betrothed to Kaoru in childhood. Although their engagement has been broken off on a technicality to do with Kaoru's unfilial behavior, Aoi insists on honoring her side of the deal. While Kaoru wrestles with whether he should take up Aoi's offer, this Stepford wannabe bustles around the house performing every conjugal duty except consummation. Ko Fumizuki's manga in *Young Animal* magazine set up a premise that could have been a fascinating meditation on the changing role of the family and tradition among Japanese youth, but instead turns into **TENCHI MUYO!**, as a group of gorgeous girls home in on Kaoru like the Japanese Self Defense Force chasing Godzilla. Meanwhile, Aoi is still so eager to please her fiancé that she lets Kaoru and all his would-be girlfriends live in her family's summer house.

Goodness knows how Masaharu Amiya has the temerity to claim his "series concept" credit, but for every generation of pubescent boys with romantic yearnings there is a new *Tenchi* clone. This one, like its heroine, is ravishingly pretty and well-mannered, and like its hero, it has its moments and is often more endurable than its fellow shows, but still doesn't know when to quit—a second season followed in 2003 as *AYA: Destiny (AYA—Enishi)*. The DVD release of each series had a bonus episode: the 5-minute picnic tale *AYA Dream Story* for series one, and the 15-minute Christmas fantasy episode *AYA Beautiful Snow (AYA Miyuki)* for series two.

The title is half of a translation of a Chinese proverb: "*Qing qu yu lan...*" (Blue comes from indigo) which is completed by the phrase "*...er sheng yu lan*" (but is superior to it). The phrase alludes to the manufacture of dyes, but is used in China to imply that a pupil can, and should, surpass his teacher. In this case, it is presumably meant to suggest that we should rise above the situation in which we find ourselves—fighting words for creators who are handed a touching love story, but merely use it to rehash a paradigm established more than two decades earlier in **URUSEI YATSURA**. A Chinese TV series with the same title, shown on TVB, has no relation to the anime, and has been referred to as *Shine on You* in English. **N**

AIM FOR THE ACE

1973. TV series, video. JPN: *Ace o Nerae*. DIR: Osamu Dezaki, Masami Hata. SCR: Kazuaki Okamura. DES: Akio Sugino. ANI: Yoshiaki Kawajiri, Kazuo Yamazaki, Sadao Tomonaga, Shinichi Kato, Katsuhiko Yamazaki. MUS: Akira Misawa. PRD: TMS, A Pro, Takara, Madhouse, NET. 25 mins. x 26 eps. (TV1), 25 mins. x 25 eps. (TV2), 25 mins. x 12 eps. (TV3), 30 mins. x 6 eps. (v1), 30 mins. x 6 eps. (v2).

Hiromi Oka is a new girl at Nishitaka tennis club, swiftly making a friend in the chatty Maki Aikawa and a deadly enemy in Reika "Madame Butterfly" Ryuzaki, the undisputed queen of student tennis. Sacrificing her personal life (and her chances with lovelorn local boy Takayuki Todo), Hiromi resolves to become the greatest tennis player in the world.

A second series of 25 episodes followed in 1978, with a new coach bringing new problems to the Nishitaka tennis students. With additional animation, this spawned a 1979 theatrical outing (still directed by **TOMORROW'S JOE's** Dezaki). There was a renewed interest in the story in 1988, resulting in another movie, *AftA 2*, and a 12-part video series directed in part by former designer Akio Sugino. Dezaki did make some episodes and also provided some storyboards under the pseudonym Makura Saki. Revolving around the death of Hiromi's original coach, the final series featured her in many more foreign tournaments, finishing at Wimbledon itself. A bit part as a neighbor in a New York scene proved to be the first anime role for future **SAILOR MOON**–voice actress Kotono Mitsuishi.

The series has inspired several other anime, notably **YAWARA**, which follows a similar story progression but uses judo as its sport of choice. It also has the questionable distinction of both SF and erotic pastiches, in **GUNBUSTER** (subtitled "Aim for the Top") and *Aim for the A* in the **TALES OF . . .** collection.

Notably, the original TV series was broadcast in the same year as Sumika Yamamoto's original manga began running in *Margaret* magazine, suggesting that *Aim for the Ace*'s position as one of the quintessential sports anime was recognised from its earliest days. Its enduring appeal is attested not only by its anime revivals and its impressive performance abroad (chiefly in Italian, French and Spanish), but also by its high position in many polls of Japanese viewers' favourite anime and manga. Its most recent incarnation is a 2004 live-action TV series, on TV Asahi (the new name for NET).

AIR

2005. TV series, movie, TV special. DIR: Tatsuya Ishihara, Hiroshi Yamamoto, Ichiro Miyoshi, Noriyuki Kitanohara, Tomoe Aratani, Yasuhiro Takemoto. SCR: Fumihiko Shimo. DES: Tomoe Aratani. ANI: Kazumi Ikeda, Mitsuyoshi Yoneda, Satoshi Kadowaki. MUS: N/C. PRD: Key, Visual Arts. 25 mins. x 13 eps. (TV), 91 mins. (m).

Yukito Kunisaki embarks on a long quest in search of a winged girl mentioned by his mother in stories told to him as a child. Running low on funds, he finds himself forced to settle temporarily in a town, where he soon gains the traditionally chaste live-in would-be girlfriend of anime romance, who, predictably, may not be all she appears to be. As with other time-limit girlfriends such as VIDEO GIRL AI, there is a catch—in a pastiche of numerous GRIMM'S FAIRY TALES, the pretty Misuzu will die if she experiences true love. Compare to CHOBITS. The story was retold in a movie version later the same year, directed by Osamu Dezaki, and in two 24-minute specials, *Air in Summer* (2005), broadcast over two nights on TBS.

AIR GEAR

2006. TV series. DIR: Hajime Kamegaki. SCR: Chiaki Konaka. DES: Masayuki Sato. ANI: N/C. MUS: N/C. PRD: Toei Animation, TV Tokyo. 25 mins. x 25 eps.
Teenager Minami "Ikki" Itsuki is the leader of the East Side Gunz gang at his school, but is swiftly bested by the Storm Riders—a group of kids using "Air Trek" skates that allow them to fly through the air. Before long, he has acquired Air Trek gear of his own, in an adaptation of the manga by Oh! Great, that moves the standard templates of street toughs into a science fictional milieu by substituting roller skates for flying boots.

AIR MASTER *

2003. TV series. DIR: Daisuke Nishio. SCR: Michio Yokote. DES: Yoshihiko Umakoshi. ANI: Yoshihiko Umakoshi. MUS: Yoshihisa Hirano. PRD: Toei Animation, VAP, NTV. 25 mins. x 27 eps.
The daughter of a distinguished gymnast and a former boxing champion, red-headed ex-gymnast Maki Aikawa can perform incredible moves in mid-air, which earn her the name of "Air Master." Maki's widowed father now owns a gymnasium and has remarried, giving her a half-sister, Miori. But gymnastics is no longer enough for Maki, and she turns, somewhat illogically, to street fighting as a means of getting the same thrill. She and her gang of girlfriends of various sizes, types, and sexual inclinations have the usual

high school adventures while Maki fights a string of increasingly absurd opponents like masked wrestler Lucha Master, aspiring schoolgirl supermodel Kaori Sakiyama (her self-declared rival), quarterstaff master Shinnosuke (who is so smitten with Maki he transfers to her school), writer and street fighter Julietta (a guy who also falls for Maki), Reichi, whose weapon of choice is a bicycle, and so on, in the quirky opponent-of-the-week format of TIGER MASK and RANMA ½. The gritty battles are interrupted by the usual wholly gratuitous efforts to get the cast to take their clothes off, such as a trip to the beach.

Another gang of school street fighters, the Black Alliance, provides more training opportunities for Maki; then she and Kaori get involved in tag wrestling, meeting up with the sister of old opponent Rucha. She joins an elite street fighter group that uses the whole city as its arena, and begins to focus on spiritual power as a way to fight better. In the last episode she loses her final battle, but finds the fulfillment she has been seeking throughout a series that provides plenty of fight action and moderate humor; the animators invest the greatest amount of their time and budget in getting the battles right. Based on Yokusaru Shibata's *Young Animal* manga. **NV**

AIRBATS *

1994. JPN: *Aozora Shojotai 801 TTS*. AKA: *Blue Sky Girl Squad 801 TTS*. Video. DIR: Yuji Moriyama. SCR: Yuji Kawahara, Soya Fujiwara. DES: Yuji Moriyama. ANI: Yuji Moriyama, Osamu Mikasa, Junichi Sakata. MUS: Seiko Nagaoka. PRD: Studio Fantasia. 30 mins. x 7 eps.
Geeky Takuya Isurugi is a fan of anime and machinery assigned as a mechanic to the 801 "Airbats" Tactical Training Squadron. Far from being a training ground for elite female pilots, it's a dead-end posting for burnouts—Miyuki Haneda has been sent there for striking a superior officer, Sakura Saginomiya is an inveterate gambler, Arisa

Mitaka has an attitude problem, and Yoko Shimorenjaku is the world's worst pilot. Haneda and Mitaka both fall in love with Isurugi, and as bureaucrats try to disband the unit, they all try to hold onto their jobs in this wacky military comedy.

Plane fever struck Japan in the wake of *Top Gun*, inspiring the live-action Japanese rip-off *Best Guy*, *Airbats*, and its sharper, more satirical predecessor HUMMINGBIRDS. A cute contemporary of TENCHI MUYO!, employing similarly crowd-pleasing tactics of fanboy-meets-fawning-females, *Airbats* has its origin in a 1990 manga by Toshimitsu Shimizu, creator of REI REI. The six episodes and the *Airbats in Snow Country* vacation spin-off were later edited into the omnibus volumes *First* (episodes 1–3), *Second* (4 + holiday special), and *Third Strike* (episodes 5–6). It was supposedly made with the cooperation of the Japanese Air Force, which accounts for the loving aircraft detail but does not explain why a military organization would consent to be portrayed as misfits, desk-jockeys, and nuts whose main concern is winning a year's supply of free noodles. Whereas such inanities helped reinforce the realism of the long-running PATLABOR, in a short comedy series such as this they only demonstrate how wacky waters so often run shallow.

AKAHORI GEDO HOUR

2005. JPN: *Akahori Gedo Hour Love-ge Zettai Seigi vs. Soreyuke! Gedo Otometai*. AKA: *Akahori Gedo Hour Love Pheromone Justice vs. Go For it! Gedo Maid Team*. TV series. DIR: Hitoyuki Matsui. SCR: Satoru Akahori, Takashi Ifukube, Deko Akao, Katsumi Hasegawa. DES: Satoshi Ishino. ANI: N/C. MUS: Harukichi Yamamoto. PRD: Radix, TVK. 25 mins. x 13 eps.
Actually *two* shows set in the same world and sharing the airtime of a normal TV episode—perhaps the first sign of a new trend in impecunious shows for short attention-span audiences, started by the earlier **A15** and continued by **BPS** and **BOTTLE FAIRIES**. *Love*

Pheromone is about the misadventures of two failed stand-up comediennes who moonlight as superheroines while waiting for the big break that will bring them success on stage. But the Pheromone duo are a little short of evil enemies, whereas their sister show *Gedo Otometai* features five sisters who stumble amateurishly in their own attempts to become an evil secret organization, a job for which they are palpably not cut out. Based on an idea by Satoru Akahori, who presumably based it on some feverish dreams that ensued after he watched **EXCEL SAGA** while eating cheese too close to bedtime.

AKAI HAYATE *

1991. AKA: *Red Gale*. Video. DIR: Osamu Tsuruyama. SCR: Osamu Yamazaki. DES: Chiharu Sato, Koichi Ohata. ANI: Chiharu Sato, Masayoshi Sato. MUS: Takashi Kudo. PRD: NEXTART, Pony Canyon. 30 mins. x 4 eps.

The real rulers of modern Japan are the Shinogara clan, whose base is in a hidden valley at the base of Mount Fuji. The leader's son, Hayate, is executed for patricide but transfers his soul into the body of his sister, Shiori. Hiding out from Shinogara assassins in Tokyo, Shiori is able to call up her brother's skill in battle but loses a part of her own soul each time she does. As the power struggle continues between several factions of his clan, Hayate must save himself before he kills another member of his own family.

Originally serialized in the **RENTA-MAN** video magazine, *Akai Hayate* was later compiled into two 60-minute volumes—the version released abroad. One of a large subset of anime in which the past bubbles to the surface in modern Japan, including writer Yamazaki's own **TAKEGAMI**, it features **GENOCYBER**-creator Ohata as a guest designer for the MacGuffin "Shadow Armor" over which the ninja are fighting.

AKANE, KAZUKI

1962– . After early work as a character designer on **MAMA IS A FOURTH-GRADER** and **GUNDAM 0083**, he moved into animation. An early pioneer in the integration of digital animation and traditional techniques, his directorial debut was on **ESCAFLOWNE**.

AKANE-CHAN

1968. TV series. DIR: Fusahito Nagaki, Yasuo Yamaguchi, Yugo Serikawa, Takeshi Tamiya. SCR: Shunichi Yukimuro, Masaki Tsuji. DES: Shinya Takahashi. ANI: Masamune Ochiai. MUS: Keiichi Honno. PRD: Fuji TV. 30 mins. x 26 mins.

Young Akane moves to the country and soon becomes popular with the other children in her class, befriending the troublesome local rich-kid Hidemaru and leading her gang into all sorts of scrapes. Tetsuya Chiba's original manga *Miso Curds* in *Shojo Friend* magazine was deliberately designed to evoke a distant, carefree time of rural childhood for city kids deprived of the opportunity, placing it in the same spirit as **MY NEIGHBOR TOTORO**. Renamed for its TV outing, it was the first of many Chiba titles to be adapted for anime—the creator is better known for more manly tales such as **TOMORROW'S JOE** and **I'M TEPPEI**.

AKANUKE ICHIBAN

1985. JPN: *Showa Aho Soshi Akanuke Ichiban*. AKA: *Showa Era Idiot Storybook: Most Refined; City Boy*. TV series. DIR: Hidehito Ueda. SCR: Takao Koyama, Hiroko Naka. DES: Hiroshi Hamazaki, Ammonite. ANI: Hidehito Ueda, Shinya Sadamitsu, Tetsuya Komori. MUS: Toshiyuki Watanabe. PRD: Tatsunoko, TV Asahi. 30 mins. x 22 eps.

Kojiro moves to Tokyo from Japan's northernmost island of Hokkaido and insists on bringing his favorite horse, Hikarikin, with him. The alien king Rel arrives from planet Wedelun and gives him a belt that will allow him to transform into a Miracle Hero and to protect the world from alien menaces. He is more interested, however, in impressing the pretty Yuka, though his rival, Michinari, wants her for himself.

Yu Azuki, creator of **IGANO KABAMARU**, enjoys a reputation as an artist who is able to straddle the divide between boys' and girls' comics. Though *Akanuke Ichiban* looks on the surface like a typical superhero story for a male audience, it originally ran in *Margaret* magazine—perhaps it appeared more palatable to male producers and fulfilled some form of girl/boy quota. The ratings, however, did not bear out the theory, and the series was canceled before reaching the end of its second season.

AKIBA GIRLS *

2004. JPN: *Akibakei Kanojo*. Video. DIR: Shigeru Kurii. SCR: Naruhito Sunaga. DES: Jiro Oiwa. ANI: Jiro Oiwa. MUS: N/C. PRD: Studio Wood, Image Works, Milky. 30 mins. x 2 eps.

Orphan Nikita Shindo is obsessed with pornographic computer games, an interest he tries to keep hidden from his adoptive sisters. He fantasizes about a pretty girl he saw in a park near Tokyo's Akihabara electronics district, but eventually decides to get out more, and joins a local computer club. He soon discovers that fandom offers many opportunities for clandestine sex, and enjoys liaisons with costume fans, and a brief encounter with a frustrated voice actress, who appreciates his help in showing her how to put more passion into her performances. Meanwhile, he enjoys similar attentions from his elder and younger sisters, and chases after the aforesaid pretty girl, in a porn anime that mixes the 21st century self-referentiality of **GENSHIKEN** with references to an erotic pastiche of **CASTLE IN THE SKY**—Lord knows why **BALTHUS: TIA'S RADIANCE** wasn't enough!

The *Akiba-kei*, in modern Japanese slang, is the subset of Japanese society comprising geeks for whom the electronics district of Akihabara is the center of the world—i.e., fans of anime, manga, and computer games, or a new way of saying otaku; see **OTAKU NO VIDEO**. 🅛🅝

AKIHABARA CYBER TEAM

1998. JPN: *Akihabara Dennogumi*. TV

series. DIR: Yoshitaka Fujimoto. SCR: Katsumi Hasegawa, Hiroshi Yamaguchi. DES: KA-NON, Tsukasa Kotobuki, Seiji Yoshimoto. ANI: Yuji Takahashi, Seiji Yoshimoto. MUS: Nobuyoshi Mitsumoto. PRD: Ashi Pro, TBS. 22 mins. x 26 eps.

Early in the 21st century, the combination of personal data-organizers and virtual pets results in a new piece of essential equipment. These "patapi" robots are friends, guardians, and personal computers, but to Hibari Hanakogane, they are more than that. Her patapi, Densuke, has been sent to Earth by a handsome prince to defeat the evil sorceress Blood Falcon. With her friends Suzume, Tsugumi, and their own patapi companions, Hibari forms the titular squad to fight cybercrime.

Tsukasa Kotobuki, who had formerly drawn a **GUNDAM** spin-off comic, collaborated with the pseudonymous Ka-non to create this tale of girls and gadgetry for *Nakayoshi* magazine, soon riding the coattails of the Tamagotchi craze to make the jump to radio drama, computer games, and this anime series. A mysterious clash of genres results in a cloyingly cute show for girls that somehow manages to have an evil character with giant breasts.

AKIKO *

1995. Video. DIR: Kaoru Tomioka. SCR: Kaoru Tomioka. DES: Mitsuru Fujii. ANI: Mitsuru Fujii. MUS: Simon Akira. PRD: Fairy Tale, Pink Pineapple. 30 mins. x 2 eps.

Lust and forbidden fruits abound at an all-girls school, as the beautiful female agent Akiko poses as a researcher at the Nobel Academy only to become the victim of a cavalcade of rape, bondage, and sexual abuse. Based on a Japanese PC game with publicity about particularly unpleasant scenes of sex and violence—supposedly strong even by the standards of Japanese pornography. **NV**

AKIRA *

1988. Movie. DIR: Katsuhiro Otomo. SCR: Katsuhiro Otomo, Izo Hashimoto.

Akira

© 1989 AKIRA COMMITTEE

DES: Toshiharu Mizutani. ANI: Takashi Nakamura. MUS: Geino Yamashiro. PRD: Akira Committee, Mash Room, Toho, Hakuhodo, TMS. 124 mins.

In 2019, Tokyo has been rebuilt after World War III. As the city prepares to host the Olympics, it is rocked by antigovernment terrorism secretly organized by power-brokering politician Nezu. Juvenile delinquent Tetsuo is out racing against a rival gang when he crashes his bike into a child with the face of an old man. He is swiftly taken away by the military, while his friend Kaneda allies with a cell of the terrorists to track him down. Tetsuo begins to develop psychic powers and discovers that he is just one of many experimental subjects in a secret government program to replicate Akira, the human bioweapon that obliterated Tokyo in 1988. Tetsuo escapes to the Olympic stadium, where the remains of Akira are kept in a hidden chamber. Losing control of his powers and absorbing several of his colleagues, Tetsuo causes the return of Akira and a second destruction of Tokyo. Kaneda is one of the survivors, while Tetsuo absconds to create his own universe.

Adapted from the early part of the long-running manga by director Otomo, *Akira* is almost singlehandedly responsible for the early 1990s boom in anime in the English language. Echoes of the seminal *Blade Runner*

are undeniable (the film is even set in the same year), but *Akira* owes less to an alleged "cyberpunk" sensibility than it does to the young Otomo's perspective on 1960s counterculture—rioting students, crazed biker gangs, and corporate intrigue. The military conspiracy in *Akira* carries elements of the 1963 live-action film *Japan's Longest Day*, while other themes include the wartime Unit 731 human guinea pigs and nuclear contamination covered more directly in **BAREFOOT GEN**. Even the Olympic stadium is a historical marker—Tokyo was due to host the games in 1940 but only got to do so after postwar reconstruction in 1964. In many ways, *Akira* is also a retelling of Otomo's *Fireball*, an unfinished 1979 story about scientists fighting terrorists for control of an apocalyptic energy source.

Akira was a visual tour-de-force, including experiments in digital and analog animation that were to stun audiences worldwide, enjoying greater success abroad than in its country of origin. With a production budget that ran wildly out of control, it was defeated by its very success—few of its lower-budget imitators compare favorably and Western distributors have difficulty replicating its success. In 2001, *Akira* was rereleased with a new dub, closer in meaning and tone to the original Japanese version. **V**

AKITAKA, MIKA

1964–. After early work on CITY HUNT-ER, began to specialize in the design of machinery, most notably on NADESICO.

AKIYAMA, KATSUHITO

1950– . Director and storyboarder on the MACROSS movie *Do You Remember Love?*, GALL FORCE, and ELEMENTALORS. He also worked as the animation director of the much-loved "American" cartoon series *Thundercats* (1985).

ALADDIN AND THE WONDERFUL LAMP *

1982. JPN: *Aladdin to Maho no Lamp*. AKA: *Aladdin and the Magic Lamp*. Movie. DIR: Yoshinori Kasai. SCR: Akira Miyazaki. DES: Dale Baer, Jane Baer, Shinya Takahashi. ANI: Shinya Taka-hashi. MUS: Yukihide Takekawa, Godi-ego. PRD: Toei, Rankin/Bass. 65 mins.
Aladdin is a poor Arab boy asked by a mysterious stranger (an evil wizard) to help him retrieve an old lamp from an underground cavern. The wizard traps Aladdin in the cavern, but he accidentally releases a jinni from a magic ring and makes a wish to escape. When Aladdin tries to clean up the old lamp, a second jinni appears to grant him unlimited wishes. Aladdin falls in love with the sultan's daughter, Badraul, and uses the Slave of the Lamp to disguise himself as a rich prince. However, the wizard gains possession of the lamp and orders the jinni to transport the princess inside Aladdin's new palace to his own home in Africa. The angry sultan gives Aladdin three days to return her. The Slave of the Ring dies in the initial assault on the African palace, and Aladdin and Badraul must use their own wits to defeat the wizard.

There have been many all-Japanese productions spun off from ARABIAN NIGHTS, but in this case the Baers, former staffers on Disney's *Snow White*, contributed to a Rankin/Bass coproduction that also featured music from Godiego, best known outside Japan for the unforgettable theme tune to the *Monkey* series. The story would be revisited in 1993 in the Sanrio PEKKLE video

Aladdin and the Magic Lamp. In 1995, several Japanese animators would also work on the Disney *Aladdin* TV series—enough to qualify it as an anime coproduction in some sources.

ALEXANDER *

1999. JPN: *Alexander Senki*. AKA: *Alexander War Chronicle*. TV series. DIR: Yoshinori Kanemori. SCR: Sadayuki Murai. DES: Peter Chung. ANI: N/C. MUS: Ken Ishii, Haruomi Hosono, Inheil. PRD: Madhouse, WOWOW. 25 mins. x 13 eps.
In the midst of a bitter war, King Philip's wife, Olympias, gives birth to a son, Alexander. Reared amid intrigue in the palace, he proves himself on the battlefield at Chaeronia at the age of 16. After his father's death under mysterious circumstances, Alexander declares war on Darius III of Persia and goes on to become master of the known universe.

Despite its sci-fi sheen, this is a surprisingly faithful retelling of the life of Alexander the Great based on a novel by DOOMED MEGALOPOLIS–creator Hiroshi Aramata. Featuring a techno-magic based on Pythagorean solids and vast alien armies, it bears more resemblance to *Dune* or *Stargate* than a classical biopic. Character designs from the Korean-born Chung contain echoes of his work on *Aeon Flux*, and some of the visual conceits (such as a swimming pool in the shape of the Mediterranean) are simply superb. The historical Alexander is known in the Middle East as "Iscander," a name appropriated for STAR BLAZERS. Released in 2003 in the U.S. by Tokyo Pop under the title *Reign: The Conqueror*.

ALFRED J. KWAK

1989. JPN: *Ahiru no Quack; Chiisana Ahiru no Oki na Ai no Monogatari Ahiru no Quack*. AKA: *Quack the Duck; Little Duck's Big Love Story: Quack the Duck*. TV series. DIR: Hiro-shi Saito. SCR: Akira Miyazaki. DES: Masaru Amamizu, Susumu Shira-ume. ANI: Susumu Shiraume. MUS: Herman van Veen. PRD: Telescreen,

Visual 8, TV Tokyo. 25 mins. x 52 eps.
Dutch duckling Alfred Jodocus Kwak loses his family and is raised by a mole. The series covers his life and times as he travels the world trying to help animals everywhere. Based on a story by Herman van Veen, who also provided the voice of Alfred's father Johann in the German and Dutch dubs, and Prof. Paljack in the Dutch, and wrote the script and music for the Dutch version as well as a song for the Japanese original. The series has been dubbed and screened in France, Germany, the Netherlands, Italy, Denmark, and the Arab world as well as in Japan, but does not seem to be well known in English-speaking countries.

ALIBABA'S REVENGE *

1971. JPN: *Alibaba to Yonjubiki no Tozo-ku*. AKA: *Alibaba and the Forty Thieves*. Movie. DIR: Hiroshi Shidara. SCR: Moto-hisa Yamamoto. DES: Reiko Okuyama, Katsuya Koda. ANI: Hideki Mori, Hayao Miyazaki, Yoichi Otabe, Yasuji Mori. MUS: Seiichiro Uno. PRD: Toei. 55 mins.
Alibaba became rich by defeating the 40 thieves. Now his distant descendant Alibaba XXXIII has inherited the fiefdom and become the worst sultan in history, squandering his ancestor's wealth and the good will of the jinni of the lamp. Al Haq, descendant of the original leader of the thieves, is a good honest boy who resolves to get back his father's fortune, enlisting the aid of 38 cats and a lone mouse. Another of the many anime loosely based on ARABIAN NIGHTS, this short film featured Hayao Miyazaki as a key animator and a flashback sequence using nothing but shadow puppetry. It was not, however, the first anime adaptation of the story—that honor goes to Takeo Ueno's 17-minute EARLY ANIME *The 40 Thieves* (1928).

ALICE ACADEMY

2005. JPN: *Gakuen Alice*. TV series. DIR: Takahiro Omori. SCR: Jukki Hanada, Man Shimada, Masashi Yokoyama, Michiru Shimada. DES: Yoshiaki Ito. ANI: Akihito Dobashi, Haruo Ogawara,

Hideaki Shimada, Hiroki Abe, Hiroyuki Shimizu, Hisashi Mitsui, Yoshihiro Sugai, Kei Takeuchi. MUS: Makoto Yoshimori. PRD: Group Tac, NHK. 25 mins. x 26 eps.

Ten-year-old Mikan Sakura misses her old school friend Hotaru, and so makes the trip to visit Hotaru at her new school, Alice Academy. But it is no ordinary school—instead it is an establishment for children with psychic powers and superhero abilities. Mikan somehow secures admission for herself, in a cuter, more magical female-oriented version of the same basic "weird school" premise of CROMARTIE HIGH, based on a manga from *Hana to Yume* magazine by Tachibana Higuchi.

ALICE IN CYBERLAND

1996. Video. DIR: Kazuyoshi Yokota. SCR: Chiaki Konaka. DES: Daisuke Moriyama. ANI: Fumio Shimazu. MUS: N/C. PRD: Warner Vision Japan, Bandai. 28 mins. x 2 eps.

Fourteen-year-old Alice Rena is a 21st-century schoolgirl from Miskatonic College who is dragged into Cyberland, the computer network that connects vast Data Colonies of information. She and her friends are mistresses of the Dive System that allows them to access the treasures within, but all hell breaks loose when one of them falls in love with the prince who rules Cyberland.

A curio dashed off to cash in on a PlayStation game, released along with a radio drama and a PC version of the original, *AiC* mixes various parts of Lewis Carroll's original with large chunks of *Tron*, courtesy of writer Chiaki Konaka, who used cyberspace for more dramatic purposes in SERIAL EXPERIMENTS LAIN. Konaka's love of H. P. Lovecraft, as shown in the name "Miskatonic," also reappears in ARMITAGE III.

ALICE IN WONDERLAND

1983. JPN: *Fushigina Kuni no Alice*. AKA: *Alice in the Mysterious Kingdom*. TV series. DIR: Taku Sugiyama. SCR: Fumi Takahashi. DES: Yu Noda. ANI: Yu Kumada, Takao Kogawa. MUS: Reijiro Komutsu. PRD: Apollo, Nippon Anima-

tion, TV Tokyo. 30 mins. x 26 eps. One fine summer's day, the seven-year-old Alice chases a white rabbit down a hole and finds herself in the underground kingdom of Wonderland. Spending 13 episodes each on *Alice in Wonderland* and its sequel, *Alice through the Looking Glass*, this series ran through all the high points of Lewis Carroll's original stories, though the final two parts were only broadcast in the Tokyo area. To see the series in its entirety, you had to go to Germany, a major financial contributor to this coproduction. In the Japanese version, Alice was played by Tarako, the voice actress behind another children's favorite, CHIBI MARUKO-CHAN. Masako Nozawa, who provided the voice of the white rabbit, went on to play Son Goku in DRAGON BALL.

In 1998, an unofficial sequel by Ryo Nakahara was adapted by director Shingo Kaneko into the 14-episode *Alice SOS*, which featured further adventures in Dinosaur-land, Cookery-land, Topsy-turvy-land, Cactus-land, Bully-land, Salad-land, Edo-land (old-fashioned Tokyo), God-land, Ghost-land, Backward-land, Santa-land, TV-land, and Devil-land. A far naughtier pastiche was CLAMP's 1995 MIYUKI-CHAN IN WONDERLAND. See also VIDEO PICTURE BOOK.

ALICE RONDO

2006. JPN: *Kagihime Monogatari Eikyu Alice Rondo*. AKA: *Key Princess Story Eternal Alice Rondo*. TV series. DIR: Nagisa Miyazaki. SCR: Mamiko Ikeda. DES: Haruka Ninomiya. ANI: Hiroko Kuryube, Sawako Yamamoto. MUS: N/C. PRD: Trinet, Picture Magic. 25 mins. x 13 eps.

Aruto is a fan of ALICE IN WONDERLAND, and is convinced that Lewis Carroll wrote a second sequel, *Endless Alice*. He is thus perhaps a little less surprised than he otherwise might have been when he finds two magical girls fighting in the library. The victor pokes the vanquished with a key-like staff, causing her opponent to yield up pages of the lost book—it transpires that the

mythical Endless Alice does indeed exist, but has been broken up and scattered among a coterie of "Alice-users." These magical girls must fight each other to regain the missing pages of the book, in a bizarre combination of READ OR DIE, CARDCAPTORS and *Highlander*! Aruto is soon surrounded by pretty girls, all fighting over a book and, unsurprisingly, him. Based on an idea by Kaishaku, the creator of UFO PRINCESS VALKYRIE.

ALIEN FROM THE DARKNESS *

1996. JPN: *Inju Alien*. AKA: *Lust Alien*. Video. DIR: Norio Takanami. SCR: N/C. DES: Ryu Tsukiyo. ANI: Shin Taira. MUS: N/C. PRD: Pink Pineapple, (KIT). 45 mins.

Sci-fi porn in the spirit of ADVANCER TINA, heavily influenced by the *Alien* films. On their way back from a mining trip to the planet Kerun, the all-female crew of the starship Muze finds a vessel drifting in space. The derelict Zogne, carrying an illegal cargo of the narcotic Metrogria, is scattered with naked corpses. The sole survivor, a beautiful girl called Flair, claims to have amnesia. As the Muze continues on its way, the same fate starts to befall members of the crew, and lone scientist Hikari trawls through the Zogne's records in an attempt to stop the carnage. Needless to say, it involves an alien monster that consists of little more than tentacles and a permanent craving for female flesh. **LNV**

ALIEN 9 *

2001. Video. DIR: Jiro Fujimoto. SCR: Sadayuki Murai. DES: Yasuhiro Irie, Kazunori Iwakura. ANI: Yasuhiro Irie. MUS: Kuniaki Haishima. N/C. PRD: Genco, JC Staff, Bandai Visual, Nippon Columbia, TV Tokyo Media Net, Anime Theater X (AT-X). 30 mins. x 4 eps.

In 2016, the very reluctant Kasumi Tomine, Kumi Kawamura, and Yuri Otani are picked as Alien Monitors at their Japanese school, in charge of cleaning up the various kinds of messes caused by unwelcome pests. A right-wing POKÉMON, perhaps?

ALWAYS MY SANTA

2005. JPN: *Itsudatte My Santa*. AKA: *Mai and Santa Together Forever*. Video. DIR: Noriyoshi Nakamura. SCR: Koichi Taki. DES: Masahide Yanagisawa. ANI: N/C. MUS: N/C. PRD: N/C. 30 mins. x 2 eps.

Teenage Japanese boy Santa loathes Christmas, chiefly because his birthday is on December 24th—halving his gift potential and lumbering him with a silly name into the bargain. Nor does it help that his parents were always away working, leaving him a series of embittered memories of being forced to spend Christmas alone with his grandmother. However, it also gains him a new friend, in the form of the mysterious Christmas spirit Mai. A Santa in training, she offers to show him the meaning of Christmas by hanging around for the night, only to show up on his doorstep the following day, bemoaning the fact that she has used up all her magic on him, and must now stay with him until the following Christmas Eve. High jinks, of a variety not unlike OH MY GODDESS!, duly ensue. Based on a 1998 short manga by LOVE HINA–creator Ken Akamatsu in *Shonen Magazine* weekly, reprinted twice thereafter in Christmas issues with minor revisions.

AMAZING NURSE NANAKO *

1999. JPN: *Nanako Kaitai Shinsho*. AKA: *Nanako's Medical Report*. TV series. DIR: Hiroshi Negishi. SCR: Rasputin Yano. DES: Toshinari Yamashita. ANI: Toshinari Yamashita, Kazuya Miura. MUS: Takahiro Negishi. PRD: Save Our Nurse Project, Genco, Pioneer. 30 mins. x 6 eps.

This strange hybrid of 1980s techno-thriller and 1990s geek-meets-girl comedy begins with a pastiche of GHOST IN THE SHELL's copious computer graphics, as brilliant research scientists construct the humanoid superweapon Venus 2000. But Venus is missing a brain, and Dr. Kyoji Ogami decides that he will put the finishing touches on the project by "borrowing" the brain of his large-breasted maid, Nanako. After all,

he reasons, it's not like *she* uses it for anything.

Nanako is a bouncy ingenue baffled by the attention of the world's military—as a violent conspiracy unfolds around her, she frets about cooking and underwear, creating a saucy if puerile antidote to the deadly serious EVANGELION and its clones. Those seeking stranger comparisons should note that CATGIRL NUKUNUKU features a girl who has had a small mammal's brain carefully inserted into her skull, whereas the plot of *Amazing Nurse Nanako* involves a concerted attempt to remove one.

AMAZING 3, THE *

1965. JPN: *Wonder Three*. AKA: *W3*. TV series. DIR: Taku Sugiyama, Osamu Tezuka, Ryosuke Takahashi. SCR: Ichiro Wakabayashi, Osamu Tezuka, Sadao Tsukioka, Kunihiko Yamazaki. DES: Osamu Tezuka. ANI: Kazuko Nakamura. MUS: Tatsu Kawai. PRD: Mushi Pro, Fuji TV. 25 mins. x 52 eps.

The Galactic Alliance sends three secret agents to Earth with orders to destroy it if the planet's warmongering attitude presents a danger. Masquerading as farmyard animals, Major Boko (Bonnie Bunny), Lieutenant JG Poko (Zero Duck), and Lance Corporal Noko (Ronnie Horse) are discovered by young Shinichi Hoshi (Kenny Carter). The younger brother of international crime fighter Koichi (Randy), Shinichi convinces them to help make the world a better place and to give secret aid to Koichi's Phoenix organization, a group whose aims are approximately equivalent to their own. Based on Osamu Tezuka's 1965 manga in *Shonen Magazine*, this minor series was adapted for the U.S. market. Tezuka reused similar ideas in BREMEN FOUR.

AMBASSADOR MAGMA *

1993. JPN: *Magma Taishi*. Video. DIR: Hidehito Ueda. SCR: Katsuhiko Koide. DES: Kazuhiko Udagawa. ANI: Kazuhiko Udagawa. MUS: Toshiyuki Watanabe. PRD: Tezuka Pro, Bandai Visual, Plex. 25 mins. x 13 eps.

Long ago, the evil Goa was defeated by the golden giant robot Magma, created to defend this planet and its people. Now the two warriors are locked in a deep slumber, while on Earth the descendants of the Asuka family are guardians of their spirits. Fumiaki Asuka is kidnapped by aliens and used to awaken Goa. Schoolgirl Miki, the link to Magma, is forced to flee and takes refuge with the Murakami family. Mamoru Murakami meets with the protecting spirit of our planet, who calls himself "Earth," and is drawn into the battle between good and evil, becoming the one who can summon Magma with a magical golden whistle. Based on a minor manga by ASTRO BOY–creator Osamu Tezuka, *Ambassador Magma* was one of several projects, along with *Zero Man* and *No Man*, that only reached the pilot stage during their creator's lifetime. When Tezuka failed to sell *AM* as anime, he allowed the company P Pro to make it as a live-action series instead—the poor-quality 1966 52-episode rubber-monster show eventually released in the U.S. as *Space Giants*.(*DE)

It was only much later, as Tezuka's estate embarked upon a long and ongoing project to adapt all of his works for a new generation, that the series finally got an anime release, deliberately made in the blocky, old-fashioned 1950s style of the original, even so far as using the original artwork in the closing credits screened over an impossibly peppy martial theme. The show itself is never quite as interesting as it could be, alternating between scenes that are too childish to be engrossing and too hard-hitting to be suitable for young children. Despite its camp villains, the story has its scary moments—and is simply bursting with ideas and relationships that *The X-Files* later reprised, such as covert alien takeovers, human sleeper-agents, and time disturbances.

AMON SAGA *

1986. Video. DIR: Yoshikazu Oga. SCR: Noboru Shiroyama. DES: Shingo

Araki, Michi Himeno. ANI: Shingo Araki. MUS: Shigeya Saegusa. PRD: Centre, Tokuma, Yumemakura, Ten Pro, TMS. 72 mins.

Amon's family is destroyed and his country conquered by the evil Valhiss. Befriending Gaius the giant, Amon joins forces with a number of disgruntled individuals to attack Valhiss's capital city, which is located on the back of a giant turtle. While sneaking into the city, Amon meets and falls in love with the beautiful hostage, Princess Lichia. Captured and thrown into the dungeons to be devoured by Valhiss's savage pet, Amon escapes while one of his companions rescues the princess, only for her to be recaptured when their camp is attacked by werewolves. The final battle is on to defeat Valhiss, avenge Amon's parents, and rescue his love.

Not to be confused with the similarly named **DEVILMAN** sequel, this video was also shown in theaters on a double bill with **BELOVED BETTY**. The manga in *Ryu* magazine was written by Baku Yumemakura and is the only one ever drawn by Yoshitaka Amano, who, dissatisfied with the manga medium, soon returned to straightforward illustration.

ANAL SANCTUARY *

2005. JPN: *Requiem*. Video. DIR: Yoshito Machida. SCR: Kazuhiro Muto, Hiroyuki Ishii, Kosuke Fujii, Shinji Yamamoto. DES: Kumi Shimamoto. ANI: Yoshimitsu Murayama. MUS: N/C. PRD: GP Museum Soft, Milky. 30 mins. x 2 eps.
Akio is a music teacher at the prim St. Cecilia's School for Girls, where he enjoys a secret hobby as a serial rapist, thanks to the hypnotic effects of Cannone, the satanic violin. With just a few notes on the fiddle of fornication, Akio can bend pliant young girls to his will, in an anime adaptation of a computer game from Clock-up. The second episode sees Akio facing resistance from schoolgirls Yukina and Mizuho, who have somehow obtained the angelic violin known as Cecilia. Victory, however, is unlikely to come without a good deal of tentacles and nude flesh. **LNV**

Ambassador Magma

ANGEL *

1990. Video. DIR: Hideki Takayama, Hiromitsu Taida, Kaoru Toyooka. SCR: Wataru Amano, Koji Sakakibara. DES: Rin Shin. ANI: Osamu Tsuruyama, Mitsuru Fujii, Masato Ijuin. MUS: N/C. PRD: Studio Angel, Pink Pineapple. 45 mins. x 2 eps., 30 mins. x 5 eps.
The adventures of Kosuke, a sex-obsessed college boy who's always ready to help damsels in distress, just so long as he gets something special in return. Cue a succession of short stories in which a young, often nameless female comes to him with a problem; he sorts it out, then sorts *her* out. The one exception is Shizuka, the childhood sweetheart Kosuke befriended at the age of five, when she tried to commit suicide over the death of her pet bird. Moving back to Tokyo with her family, she hopes to make an honest man out of him, though she has a difficult task ahead.

U-jin is the pseudonymous artist who was made famous in Japan by the efforts of the Association to Protect Children from Comics to have his *Young Sunday* comic *Angel* banned. The video versions of his hard-core comics are not quite as explicit as the originals but are still pretty eyebrow-raising. The original *Angel* video was followed in 1994 by five volumes of *New Angel*, though the running time soon was cut to a mere two-thirds of its former size. The U.S. distributor has made it available in both uncut and edited editions, though your guess is as good as ours as to who would want to watch a porno movie with the porno taken out. Similar erotic stories from the same author can be found in **U-JIN BRAND** and the **TALES OF . . .** series. **N**

ANGEL BLADE *

2003. Video. DIR: Masami Obari. SCR: Remu Aoki, Jin Koga. DES: Masami Obari, Magnum Tana, Mocchii, Yosuke Kabashima, Mikoshiro Nagi. ANI: Makoto Uno, Yosuke Kabashima. MUS: N/C. PRD: Frontline, Studio G-1Neo, MUSE. 30 mins. x 3 eps. (v1), 30 mins. x 3 eps. (v2).
In a future in which only 99 human cities remain above the clouds of a war-torn Earth, a floating castle appears in the sky over City 69, and an evil force plots against women. Moena becomes Angel Blade, a fighter with the beauty of a goddess who appears to rescue the victims from bondage, rape, and

depravity, all of which feature prominently, since the Dark Mother is trying to conquer Earth by attacking girls at a college, as one does. Masami Obari is renowned for eroticizing mainstream anime, but here he makes a rare foray into pornography, bringing with him a larger budget than usual in order to make an erotic anime that has an involved plot to accompany the usual rapes and assaults. The English voice cast use pseudonyms like Likki DeeSplit and Syndi Snackwell in an effort to keep it off their more respectable resumés. An erotic SF adventure with the gravity-defying breasts and cute pointy noses for which Obari is renowned. A "movie" edit also exists, which runs the first three episodes together with some bonus footage. For the sequel series, the show was renamed *Angel Blade Punish*. **ⓃⓋ**

ANGEL COP *

1989. Video. DIR: Ichiro Itano. SCR: Noboru Aikawa. DES: Nobuteru Yuki. ANI: Yasuomi Umezu, Satoru Nakamura, Hideki Takayama, Hiroyuki Ochi. MUS: Hiroshi Ogasawara. PRD: Studio 88, DAST, Soeishinsha, Japan Home Video. 30 mins. x 6 eps.

At the close of the 20th century, Japan forms a Special Security force to protect it from foreign terrorists like the fanatical Red May. Angel, the newest officer, loses her partner, Raiden, to psychic vigilantes and suspects that she has more to fear from a secret government cybernetics project than from left-wing activists. Soon all hell breaks loose, as cyborgs and psychics fight for access to the secrets of the mysterious "H-File."

Consisting of long fight scenes stitched together by ham-fisted expository soliloquies, *Angel Cop* wastes loving detail on weapons and machinery but leaves its characters shallow and uninteresting. A nasty bloodbath from VIOLENCE JACK–director Ichiro Itano, it fails despite a crew of great talents who would go on to work on ESCAFLOWNE, ARMITAGE III, and, admittedly, the equally soulless KITE.

The original creator, Taku Kitazaki, was only 17 when he sold his first story, shooting to fame thanks to his work's resemblance to flavor-of-the-moment AKIRA. As one might expect from the creator whose publications include *War Story Busty*, *Angel Cop* is aimed squarely at the lowest common denominator. Different arms of the military show off their hardware and are then trashed by psionic supersoldiers, while a mad scientist cackles . . . madly. The final showdown is against Lucifer, a glacial blonde seemingly modeled on Brigitte Nielsen, in whose bone-crunching defeat the good guys take an ethnically suspect pleasure—a few of their antiforeign quips have survived the English-language dub, though the original Japanese script is far more anti-American and anti-Semitic throughout. There is, however, an ironic happy ending; by the time *Angel Cop* was made, its 23-year-old creator had already tired of the genre and moved into gentle romance with *Like This Love Song*. **ⒸⓃⓋ**

ANGEL CORE *

2003. Video. DIR: Ran Misumi. SCR: Hiroshi Watanabe. DES: Hiro Asano. ANI: N/C. MUS: N/C. PRD: Picol, Blue Eyes. 30 mins. x 2 eps.

As the clouds of war gather, the United Empire puts into action a secret scheme to extract "Angel Core," a crystallized form of divine power that can be found in human descendants of gods. They do this with a vague, EVANGELION-inspired notion of Kabbalah sorcery, but of course it is actually an excuse to imprison a bunch of innocent girls in a secret base and subject them to sexual degradation in an attempt to draw out their life force. Young officer Ralph frets that torturing and raping women is not the way for a military defense plan to operate and resolves to help two of the girls escape, even though it will cause him to directly disobey an order. A pornographic anime that is unpleasant enough to begin with, before anyone starts bringing up parallels with

Japan's wartime record on "comfort women." **ⒸⓃⓋ**

ANGEL HEART

2005. TV series. DIR: Toshiki Hirano. SCR: Sumio Uetake. DES: Takashi Saijo. ANI: Takashi Saijo. MUS: Taku Iwasaki. PRD: Thomas Entertainment, Yomiuri TV, Tokyo Movie Shinsha. 25 mins. x ?? eps.

Xiang Ying is "Glass Heart," a 15-year-old girl reared as an assassin by Taiwanese gangsters in the style of GUNSLINGER GIRL. She tries to end her torment by committing suicide, but is saved by a heart transplant and emerges from a coma a year later, reporting strange visitations from a dream figure she calls Kaori. Evading her gangster bosses, she runs for Shinjuku, guided by a voice in her head that announces "I died here" when she stands at the center of the area's distinctive crossroads. In an attempt to shake off her pursuers, she ducks into a café called the CAT'S EYE, where Umibozu, the blind manager, senses that his beloved Kaori has somehow returned. Kaori, of course, is the original owner of the transplanted heart, haunting the heart's new owner in a manner previously used in episodes of BLACK JACK. Umibozu's best friend is Ryo Saeba, the famous CITY HUNTER of anime legend, who has been living in a traumatized daze for the months following the death of his partner Kaori in a car accident. Before long, Ryo and Xiang Ying form a new partnership, in what may at first seem like a pointless continuation of the *City Hunter* storyline with a new label. However, *AH*'s existence seems to owe something to a major power shift in the manga industry in 2001, when a number of creators defected from their old publishers to write for Shinchosha's new *Comic Bunch* weekly. Just as Kenichi Sonoda once refashioned RIDING BEAN as GUNSMITH CATS, and FIST OF THE NORTH STAR proclaimed itself "new," *AH* is likely to be a rebranding exercise that allows manga creator Tsukasa Hojo to continue using his popular characters and situations from

City Hunter without getting caught up in a maze of red tape from the rights-holders to various anime, manga, and live-action versions of his creation.

ANGEL LEGEND

1996. JPN: *Angel Densetsu.* Video. DIR: Tatsuo Misawa. SCR: Naoyuki Sakai. DES: Nobuyoshi Ito. ANI: Nobuyoshi Ito. MUS: Jun Sky Walkers. PRD: Toei. 45 mins.

New kid in town Shinichiro Kitano is a noble, sensitive boy with "the face of a devil and the kindness of an angel." Pushed into a world of drugs and crime simply because of the way he looks, he tries to make the world a better place without fighting, eventually becoming the leader of the local gang. This adaptation of Norihiro Yagi's manga from *Shonen Jump* only lasted for a single episode—at the time it was released, Japan was obsessed with more compelling "angels" in EVANGELION. **V**

ANGEL LINKS *

1999. JPN: *Seiho Tenshi Angel Links.* AKA: *Stellar Angel Angel Links.* TV series. DIR: Yoshikazu Yamaguchi. SCR: Masaharu Amiya. DES: Asako Nishida, Rei Nakahara. ANI: Hiroyuki Hataike. MUS: N/C. PRD: Sunrise, WOWOW. 25 mins. x 13 eps.

Orphaned 16-year-old Li Mei-Feng inherits the family business from her grandfather, Jian-He—it's the private police franchise for an entire solar system that's simply crawling with pirates. Refusing to be scared away, Mei-Feng assembles the Angel Links team of troubleshooters, including a weapons expert and the last survivor of a race of dinosaur vegetarians, and sets out to bring the system under the rule of law. A spin-off from Takehiko Ito's OUTLAW STAR, replaying the mood, look, and staff.

ANGEL OF DARKNESS *

1995. JPN: *Inju Kyoshi.* AKA: *Lustful-Beast Teacher.* Video. DIR: Kazuma Muraki, Suzunari Joban. SCR: Yukihiro Kosaka. DES: Kazunori Iwakura, Yuji Ikeda. ANI: Kazunori Iwakura. MUS:

Takeo Nakazawa. PRD: Pink Pineapple. 45 mins. x 4 eps.

In a typical girls' boarding school, Atsuko and Sayaka manage to fit in a lesbian affair around their class schedule without too much trouble. But when one of their teachers digs up an ancient artifact and releases a demonic entity, things get a bit more hectic. The entity needs to be fed a steady supply of nubile young women to keep itself alive and build the new form it needs to take over the world (the ancient spirits of Earth oppose this, or would if any of them were more than nine inches high). With the help of an elf who fits in her handbag, Sayaka sets out to save her girlfriend and classmates from a fate worse than death and foil the threat to the world, though similar events wreak havoc in other schools, with the same basic setup and conclusion. Much ripping of underwear, bondage, "comical" characters like the Kuroko from UROTSUKIDOJI, and sexualized violence to match. The four episodes were also filmed as live-action movies in 1995–96 directed by Mitsunori Hattori and Koji Shimizu. **LNV**

ANGEL RABBIE

2003. JPN: *Tenbatsu Angel Rabbie.* AKA: *Judgment Angel Rabbie; Divine Punishment Angel Rabbie.* Video. DIR: Shinji Ishihara. SCR: MitsuhiroYamada. DES: Noritaka Suzuki, Chisato Naruse, Hiroshi Ogawa. ANI: Seigi Matsumoto. MUS: Under 17, Haruko Momoi, Masaya Koike. PRD: AIC, Kogado Studio, Angel Chamber. 25 mins.

In a far future when magic and science have combined, a war breaks out for control of the magical lunar city of Sorceriam. Both sides unleash terrible magic, destroying Earth's civilization in the process. A few thousand years later (so that's the far, *far* future, then), mankind recovers but Earth is still menaced by giant monsters left over from the original conflict. Sorceriam has been cut off from Earth for all this time and has flourished. Queen Mirchol and the Seven Sisters now rule the Moon, and dispatch agents known

as Angels to protect the Earth. These elite fighters are chosen from a group of lower-ranked warriors known as the Surrogates. Heroine Lasty Farsen is 16, but usually takes the form of a clumsy 12-year-old who is useless with technology. Only when her powers are released does she transform into Angel Rabbie and become her normal self. Each Angel has a special type of magic, or "mode," but Rabbie is unaware of what hers is. There's a reference to 9th-century Hokkaido hero ATERUI—the church that opposes Lasty is named after him—but most of the comedy seems to revolve around food. Action comedy based on the PC game of the same title, part of the *Angelic* series; as if SAILOR MOON had never happened.

ANGEL SANCTUARY *

2000. JPN: *Tenshi Kinryoku.* Video. DIR: Seiko Sayama. SCR: Mayori Sekijima. DES: Hidekazu Shimamura. ANI: Hidekazu Shimamura. MUS: Hikaru Nanase. PRD: Bandai. 30 mins. x 3 eps.

As a punishment for defying God Almighty and fighting against the legions of Heaven (led by her brother, Razael), the soul of the fallen angel Alexael is imprisoned in a crystal, doomed to be forever reincarnated as a human being who will die a young and violent death. Born into the body of *male* juvenile delinquent Setsuna Mudo, Alexael realizes that God is dead and the world is ending, just as foretold in the Black Book of Revelation. S/he is the long-awaited Messiah but would rather seduce his/her sister than take up arms in the final battle between Heaven and Hell. Based on the manga by Kaori Yuki, *AS* tries but fails to cram the original storyline into three tiny episodes, reducing Yuki's carefully paced original into a mad rush of revelations. Compare to other apocalyptic tales of androgynous young men pouting sulkily, such as X: THE MOVIE and EARTHIAN.

ANGEL TALES *

2001. JPN: *Otogi Story Tenshi no Shippo.* AKA: *Angel's Tails; Fairy Story Angel*

Tails. TV series. DIR: Kazuhiro Ochi, Norio Kashima. SCR: Yuji Minamide. DES: Takashi Kobayashi. ANI: Takashi Kobayashi. MUS: Yoshinobu Hiraiwa. PRD: Wonderfarm, Tokyo Kids, Angel Tales Project, WOWOW. 25 mins. x 13 eps. (TV1), 25 mins. x 11 eps. (TV2). Goro Mutsumi is plagued by bad luck: he's lost his job, he's broke, and has no success with women. Then a fotune-teller predicts his luck is about to change. The very next morning, three cute girls show up at his apartment. Ran, Tsubasa, and Kurumi are Spirit World Angels assigned to watch over him; they are reincarnations of his former pet hamster, rabbit, and cat, still vying for their master's attention, like the similarly undead companions in **BUBU CHACHA**. Nine other "Angels" turn up—Goro has never ceased to love his pets, and now they're here to help him turn his life around. We dread to think what will happen when the erotic anime production companies start looking for a way to rip this one off. Based on an original story by **DEVIL HUNTER YOHKO**'s Juzo Mutsuki, it was originally screened on the satellite channel WOWOW in Japan, and followed in 2003 by *Angel Tales Kiss! (Tenshi no Shippo Chu!)* on Kid's Station. Note that 12 companion animals give this show a certain similarity to the zodiacal **FRUITS BASKET**. Ⓝ

ANGELIC LAYER

2001. TV series. DIR: Hiroshi Nishigori. SCR: Kazushi Okawanai, Reiko Yoshida, Akihiko Inari. DES: Takahiro Omori, CLAMP. ANI: Koichi Horikawa. MUS: N/C. PRD: Bones, TV Tokyo. 25 mins. x 26 eps.

Diminutive junior high school girl Misaki Suzuhara is separated from her mother at an early age. When her father dies, she must move from her home in Wakayama to her aunt's house in Tokyo. There, she becomes intrigued by the Angel dolls, customizable dolls with "micro-actuator" controls, which are hatched from eggs and appear to be fully alive. The Angels are controlled by their owner's willpower but can only move within the "Layer" battle arena. Misaki gets an Angel called Hikaru, and their battles begin. This anime based on a *Shonen Ace* manga by **CARD CAPTORS**–creators CLAMP has all the appearance of a game tie-in, just without a real game to tie into.

ANGELIQUE

2000. Video. DIR: Akira Kiyomizu. SCR: Midori Kusada. DES: Kairi Yusa. ANI: Masanori Fujioka. MUS: N/C. PRD: Yumeta Company. 30 mins.

Angelique, Rachael, and Rosaria are three of the nine guardian angels, members of a secret sect called Alios, whose job it is to protect mere mortals from ruining their lives. Angelique is also destined to be the future queen of the universe, which may be why sweet-talking Osaka charmer Charlie is so keen on her. The events of the anime take place a little after *Requiem for the Sky*, the computer game that spawned it.

ANGELIUM *

2004. Video. DIR: Kazunari Kume. SCR: Mitsuhiro Yamada. DES: Mamoru Yokota. ANI: Naoki Sosaka. MUS: Toru Horasawa. PRD: Moon Rock. 30 mins. x 2 eps.

Trainee angels Yu, Miki, and Chadoko come down to Earth to learn more about humanity, volunteering to work in a flower shop as their cover story. They are unaware that their boss Zeus, ever hungry for more sexual conquests, takes over the body of a local Japanese boy whenever the possibility of sex is near, thereby hoping to escape the notice of his jealous wife Hera. However, Zeus's brother Hades is secretly backing an attempt by local gangsters to scare away the florists, and is spooked enough by Zeus's arrival to call in more powerful minions (Persephone and her crew of monsters) to scare the girls away. Cue a bizarre mixture of **EARTHIAN** and **WEISS KREUZ** with the standard tropes of porn anime, distinguished by above average design work, and brief interludes of tentacle sex that seem quaintly old-fashioned in the 21st century. For a different kind of butchering of Greek myth, see **HERMES**. Based on a computer game from Alice Soft, although this adaptation peters out mid-story without a proper ending. ⓁⓃⓋ

ANGEL'S EGG *

1985. JPN: *Tenshi no Tamago*. Movie. DIR: Mamoru Oshii. SCR: Mamoru Oshii. DES: Yoshitaka Amano. ANI: Yasuhiro Yukura. MUS: Yuhiro Kanno. PRD: Studio Deen, Tokuma Shoten, Tokuma Japan. 108 mins.

In a timeless, placeless everytown, a boy with a crucifix arrives and meets the sole inhabitant, a young girl. She shows him her most treasured possession, a magical egg, which she believes will hatch one day. When the girl is asleep, the boy smashes the egg open but finds that it contains nothing. The boy heads off alone.

Plotless and highly symbolic with hardly any dialogue, reputedly a stream-of-consciousness exercise by **PATLABOR**–director Oshii, the film features his trademark Christian imagery and an inexplicable passage through the town of soldiers with motorized artillery. Surreal elements recall Oshii's work on **URUSEI YATSURA**, including spaceships full of silent people bearing other eggs and even shadows of fish that swim through the air in the city streets. The animation and design, incorporating work from **1001 NIGHTS**–creator and illustrator Amano, is beautifully executed. Parts of the film were plundered for interstitial footage in Carl Colpaert's live-action film *In the Aftermath* (1988).

ANGELS IN THE COURT *

2000. JPN: *Court no Naka no Tenshitachi*. Video. DIR: Satoru Sumisaki. SCR: Yasuyuki Moto. DES: Seiji Kishimoto, Poyoyan Rock (original game). ANI: Ten Nakazama. MUS: N/C. PRD: Saburo Omiya, Pink Pineapple. 30 mins. x 2 eps. (v1); 30 mins. x 2 eps. (v2).

A volleyball geek's fantasy as new girl Nanase Morimura, who "wears glasses, but has big breasts," joins the Aota Academy team, led by former All-

Japan ace Coach Akira Motoura. She is unable to unleash her true potential without a session of "special tuition" with Coach (who does not neglect the other team members, either), but in episode two he goes missing after saving another player from three would-be rapists in the park. Mostly harmless, particularly when compared to other porn anime out there. A sequel, *Return of the Angels in the Court* (2001, *Kaette kita Court no Naka no Tenshitachi*) took the girls off to a national competition, but is unreleased in the U.S. at time of writing. Volleyball has been a strange obsession of the Japanese media world ever since the 1964 Tokyo Olympics, when the local women's team won gold in the event. **LN**

Animated Classics of Japanese Literature: A Ghost Story

ANIMAL ALLEY

2005. JPN: *Animal Yokocho*. TV series. DIR: Yukio Nishimoto, Nam Jong-sik. SCR: Hiroshi Yoshikawa, Hideki Sonoda, Masahiro Yokoya, Megumi Sasano, Tatsuto Higuchi, Yuka Tamada. DES: Kyota Mizutani, Lun Hyung-jin. ANI: Kazuyoshi Kobayashi, Ahn Jae-ho. MUS: Kazuhiro Hara. PRD: Studio Gallop, Dentsu, TV Tokyo. 25 mins. x 12 eps.
A secret door in five-year-old Ami's bedroom leads to a magical land, from which animal playmates come to see her. Based on the manga by Ryo Maekawa in *Ribbon Original*, and filmed in a surreal and absurdist style reminiscent of **HARE + GUU**.

ANIMAL 1

1968. TV series. DIR: Taku Sugiyama, Yoshiyuki Tomino, Ryosuke Takahashi. SCR: Tadaaki Yamazaki, Shunichi Yukimuro, Masaki Tsuji. DES: Noboru Kawasaki. ANI: Sadao Miyamoto. MUS: Hiroki Takaragi. PRD: Mushi Pro, Fuji TV. 30 mins. x 27 eps.
The seven Azuma brothers have all been raised as fighters by their longshoreman father. Sent to a new school when the family moves, Ichiro Azuma becomes a great success in the wrestling club. As his prowess gains greater fame, he is soon known as "Animal 1," as you might expect from someone

who's had to fight over the bathroom with six siblings. Based on the true story of Ichiro Azuma, who represented Japan in the 1960 Mexico Olympics, this series about a gold medalist only won silver in the race to become the first sports anime—**STAR OF THE GIANTS** beat it onto the screens by just a month. Noboru Kawasaki, who created *both* stories, would also supply the original manga for **SONG OF THE LADYBUGS**. This tale of true-life wrestling included early directorial credits for two future specialists in giant-robot combat, **GUNDAM**'s Tomino and **VOTOMS**' Takahashi.

ANIMARU-YA

Sometimes written as "Animal-ya." Animation company formed by seven Shin'ei Doga employees for the purpose of working on **LITTLE GOBLIN** in 1982. Subsequently hired in on other productions, including **MIAMI GUNS** and **ANPANMAN**. Notable members include Hiroshi Fukutomi and Katsuya Yamamoto.

ANIMATE GROUP

A conglomerate of animation-related companies, including the Animate store chain, the Movic promotional

group, Marine Entertainment, and Frontier Works. The company is an object lesson in the vertical integration of modern media, since fans purchasing **ANIME SHOP-KEEPER**, for example, would discover that they have paid the Animate store for an anime about a man who runs an Animate store, which would have received the anime from an Animate subsidiary, which would itself have been the production company that made the anime in the first place.

ANIMATED CLASSICS OF JAPANESE LITERATURE *

1986. JPN: *Seishun Anime Zenshu*. AKA: *Youth Anime Compendium*. TV series. DIR: Fumio Kurokawa, Akiko Matsushima, Noboru Ishiguro, Eiji Okabe, Isamu Kumada, Hidehito Ueda. SCR: Kenji Yoshida, Shizuo Kuriyama, Haruhiko Mimura, Ryuzo Nakanishi. DES: Hiroshi Motomiya, Tetsuya Chiba, Shotaro Ishinomori, Osamu Komori, Hiromitsu Morita. ANI: Yoshio Kabashima. MUS: Koichi Sakata, Hideo Shimazu, Junnosuke Yamamoto. PRD: Nippon Animation, Nippon TV. 30 mins. x 37 eps.
Few Japanese classics make it to the screen in an anime industry obsessed

Animated Classics of Japanese Literature: The Theater of Life

© 1986 NIPPON ANIMATION CO., LTD.

with spectacle and entertainment. This series made some small attempt to redress the balance, adapting some of Japan's most famous stories, including works by Eiko Tanaka, Yasunari Kawabata, Shintaro Ishihara, Masao Kume, Sachio Ito, Yasushi Inoue, and Jiro Akagawa.

As one might expect, a nation's literature is not readily sawed into bite-sized chunks for digestion on prime-time TV, and the selections are often arguably off-base. The collection does best with punchy short stories like Junichiro Tanizaki's *Tale of Shunkin*. Longer works often suffer through drastic cutting (Shiro Ozaki's *Theater of Life* is condensed from 530 pages to less than 30 minutes), censorious editing (the prostitution subplot is removed completely from Ogai Mori's *Dancing Girl*), or sloppy translation (the English version makes several silly errors, and explanatory liner notes are unforgivably absent from the video release). The choices for adaptation also seem haphazard or overly conservative. It's difficult, for example, to think of something *less* representative of Yukio Mishima than *The Sound of Waves*, and there are duplicates of

BOTCHAN and SANSHIRO SUGATA, while THE TALE OF GENJI, HAKKENDEN, and THE SENSUALIST are conspicuously absent. The collection also includes a story by "Koizumi Yakumo" without revealing he was the foreign-born author Lafcadio Hearn. But although this story is not Japanese, others debatably "classic" and occasionally barely "animated," it is still a noble failure in its attempt to get couch-potato children interested in real books. Two episodes, adaptations of Masao Kume's *Student Days* and Musanokoji Saneatsu's *The Friend Who Didn't Believe in Friendship*, were not broadcast, appearing instead as two "specials" on TV Asahi the following year.

ANIMATION RUNNER KUROMI *
2001. JPN: *Anime Seisaku Shinko Kuromi-chan*. AKA: *Animation Runner Kuromi-chan*. Video. DIR: Akitaro Daichi, Yumi Tamano. SCR: Mitsuru Nagatsuki. DES: Hajime Watanabe. ANI: Hajime Watanabe. MUS: Toshio Masuda. PRD: Yumeta Company. 40 mins. (v1), 45 mins. (v2).
Self-referential comedy about the attractive Mikiko "Kuromi-chan" Oguro joining the production department

of an anime company, and on the first day finding herself in sole charge (the production manager having collapsed and been rushed to the hospital after handing over responsibility) of episode two of *Time Journeys* (see TIME BOKAN), which is due in seven days, with almost none of the work completed. She must dig deep into her heart and her love of the anime *Louis Monde III* (see LUPIN III) for the necessary fortitude, as well as learn the tricks of the trade from jaded veteran Hamako Shihonmatsu, in order to complete the episode in time. Based on a four-panel gag strip that appeared in *Anime Station*, the anime industry's in-house magazine—compare to OTAKU NO VIDEO. Released in Japan with English subtitles, and subsequently brought to America. After winning the Best Video Anime award at the 2001 Tokyo International Anime Fair, where the authors rather suspect it was preaching to the choir, a second episode followed in 2004.

ANIMATRIX, THE *
2002. Video. DIR: Koji Morimoto (*Beyond*), Shinichiro Watanabe (*Detective Story, Kid's Story*), Yoshiaki Kawajiri (*Program*), Mahiro Maeda (*Second Renaissance 1 & 2*), Takeshi Koike (*World Record*) Peter Chung (*Matriculated*), Andy Jones (*Final Flight of the Osiris*). SCR: Koji Morimoto, Shinichiro Watanabe, Larry Wachowski, Andy Wachowski, Yoshiaki Kawajiri. DES: Shinji Hashimoto, Yutaka Minowa. ANI: Shinji Hashimoto, Madhouse. MUS: Don Davis. PRD: Studio 4°C, Madhouse, Square USA, Inc., DNA Seoul. 102 mins.
Of these nine short animated spin-offs from *The Matrix* (1999), seven were written and/or directed by Japanese filmmakers and produced by Japanese studios. *Beyond* is set in an urban Japan of waste lots and abandoned buildings where a young girl finds a glitch in the Matrix in a "haunted" house. COWBOY BEBOP's Watanabe directs *Detective Story*, where grizzled detective Ash tries to track down renowned hacker Trinity, and *Kid's Story*, introducing us to a

disaffected teen who sees "reality" for the artifice it is and later appears in *The Matrix: Reloaded* (2003). *Kid's Story* has guest voice performances by Keanu Reeves and Carrie-Ann Moss. *Program* raises the issue that Cipher might not have been the only person ever to regret leaving the Matrix, as Cis and Duo fight in full samurai gear inside a simulation of medieval Japan. The two-parter *Second Renaissance* uses the visual inventiveness that later resulted in GANKUTSUOU to give a disorienting and dazzling cyber-eye view of history. *World Record* is a punchy, powerful story of passion breaking through all boundaries, as runner Dan pushes his mind and body to their limits and, for one moment, sees himself suspended in a dark, fluid-filled chamber. Two further stories, which do not technically qualify as "anime," are *Matriculated*, written and directed by Peter Chung, and *Final Flight of the Osiris*, directed by Andy Jones and written by the brothers Wachowski.

It was, we are sure, a coincidence that the engines of transformation in the original *Matrix* movie were red and blue pills like those used by MARVELOUS MELMO, but *Animatrix* does nevertheless sit well in the tradition of Japanese animation. It can be argued that it is only the latest in the long-running tradition of anthology movies to showcase the talents of great animators, alongside MEMORIES, ROBOT CARNIVAL, and NEO TOKYO. However, in its origins as a tie-in to a Hollywood blockbuster it is also one of the most successful anime of all time, bolstered by the name-recognition of the contributors and the *Matrix* franchise, which itself owes a considerable thematic and artistic debt to GHOST IN THE SHELL. Its worldwide sales were in the hundreds of thousands, easily making it one of the best-selling anime, alongside AKIRA and POKÉMON. Before long, other creators were trying to plug into the Japanese animation as the flavor of the moment; the most conspicuous being Quentin Tarantino, with KILL BILL: THE ORIGIN OF O-REN. There were also several copycat pre-

quels to mainstream Hollywood films, most notably Sharon Bridgeman's *Van Helsing: The London Assignment* (2004) and Peter Chung's *Riddick: Dark Fury* (2004). However, these productions do not feature enough Japanese creatives on the production staff to qualify as "anime." **CLW**

ANIME R.
Also "Anime Aru"—the letter stands for "Retake." Animation company formed by Moriyasu Taniguchi in 1978 at the Kyoto commercials house Film Art. Incorporated as an independent company in 1993, with notable members including Satoru Yoshida, Masahiro Kato, Miko Nakajima, Masahiro Kimura, and Sachiko Iwamura. Representative works include CORRECTOR YUI and CONAN THE BOY DETECTIVE.

ANIME SHOP-KEEPER
2002. JPN: *Anime Tencho*. Video. DIR: Hideaki Anno. SCR: Hiroyuki Imaishi. DES: Kazuhiko Shimamoto, Hiroyuki Imaishi. ANI: N/C. MUS: Cublic. PRD: MOVIC, Animate, Gainax. 30 mins. The new manager of the Animate store faces more than the usual amount of fan envy when two heavies employed by a rival store rough him up outside the store on his first day. His injuries are too severe for him to survive, so, with his dying breath, he appoints the young guy who intervenes to stop the bullies as his replacement. Aided by a bevy of cute girl assistants, Meito Anizawa ("Ani-Mate" if contracted and shuffled into Japanese name order) brings his enthusiasm for anime goods, a strong sense of justice, and compassion for the fans whose hunger for merchandise can never be sated.

It was only a matter of time after OTAKU NO VIDEO that other elements of anime fandom would become the subject of self-referential anime themselves. After KUROMI-CHAN, an anime about making anime, we have an anime about selling anime, in an adaptation of Kazuhiko Shimamoto's manga, itself an extended commercial for the real-life Animate chain. The show

features other wacky characters: Toya Dogenzaka manages the Shibuya store, and Gai Denki the Akihabara branch, while President Takahashi rules his anime merchandise empire from behind the scenes in Ikebukuro. The anime is said to be based on elements from HIS AND HER CIRCUMSTANCES, and also spun off into a radio drama and a live stage show.

ANIMENTARY: CRITICAL MOMENTS
1971. JPN: *Animentary: Ketsudan*. TV series. DIR: Fumio Kurokawa, Ip-pei Kuri, Hideo Makino. SCR: Jinzo Toriumi. DES: Tatsuo Yoshida. ANI: Sadao Miyamoto, Tsutomu Shibayama, Yoshiyuki Tomino, Ryosuke Taka-hashi. MUS: Nobuyoshi Koshibe. PRD: Tatsunoko, Nippon TV. 30 mins. x 26 eps.
This *Anim[ated Docum]entary* details the various critical moments that brought Japan into World War II and eventually caused the country's defeat, including the battles over Pearl Harbor, Hong Kong, Malaya, Bataan, Rabaul, Singapore, Java, Corregidor, Midway, the Solomon Islands, the Philippines, and Leyte Gulf. The story concentrates chiefly on Isoroku Yamamoto, the "reluctant admiral" who urged his superiors not to declare war on the U.S. but was eventually given command of the Japanese fleet, and planned the attack on Pearl Harbor. A more dramatic look at some of the same events can be found in Leiji Matsumoto's COCKPIT, and the logical conclusion of the "what ifs" implicit in *Animentary* gets an airing in the alternate-universe DEEP BLUE FLEET, in which Japan gets to replay World War II and win it.

ANNE OF GREEN GABLES
1979. JPN: *Akage no Anne*. AKA: *Red-Haired Anne*. TV series. DIR: Isao Takahata. SCR: Shigeki Chiba, Aiko Isomura, Isao Takahata. DES: Yoshifumi Kondo. ANI: Yoshifumi Kondo. MUS: Kurodo Mori. PRD: Nippon Animation, Fuji TV. 30 mins. x 50 eps.
Green Gables is the house in Avonlea village on Prince Edward Island in ear-

ly 20th-century Canada where childless brother and sister Matthew and Marilla bring an 11-year-old orphan, Anne, to live. Though there is some confusion when Anne turns out not to be the strapping male farmhand they were hoping for, she soon makes friends with local girl Diana, and the pair begin a happy, if somewhat tedious, rural existence.

Based on Lucy Maude Montgomery's book, this entry in the WORLD MASTERPIECE THEATER series was directed by GRAVE OF THE FIREFLIES' Takahata and featured animation from WHISPER OF THE HEART's Kondo. The earlier part of the series contained layouts by Takahata's famous cohort Hayao Miyazaki, although after episode 16 he left to make CASTLE OF CAGLIOSTRO.

ANNO, HIDEAKI

1960– . Born in Yamaguchi Prefecture, Anno entered Osaka University of Arts in 1980, where he met future Gainax cofounders Hiroyuki Yamaga and Takami Akai, with whom he made the opening short for the Daicon III SF convention. After early anime work on MACROSS, he gained a key position animating the God Warrior in Hayao Miyazaki's NAUSICAÄ OF THE VALLEY OF WIND. After his directorial debut on GUNBUSTER (1988), he spent a prolonged period working on THE SECRET OF BLUE WATER, on which he had a lack of creative control that caused him to retreat from the business. He returned with the landmark EVANGELION (1995). His subsequent anime work has included early episodes of HIS AND HER CIRCUMSTANCES, although much of his recent work has been designing and directing for live-action, including an adaptation of CUTEY HONEY. He is married to manga author Moyoko Anno.

ANNO, MASAMI

1944– . A protégé of Hiroshi Sasagawa and Hisayuki Toriumi, Anno joined Tatsunoko and first made his mark as an animator on the comedy GAZULA THE AMICABLE MONSTER. His subsequent successes included NILS' MYSTERIOUS JOURNEY and SHAME ON MISS MACHIKO, before leaving Tatsunoko to work for Studio Pierrot.

ANOTHER LADY INNOCENT *

2004. JPN: Front Innocent; Innocent. TV Video. DIR: Satoshi Urushihara. SCR: N/C. DES: Satoshi Urushihara. ANI: N/C. MUS: N/C. PRD: ARMS, Moonrock, Earthwork. 30 mins. x 2 eps.

In a Civil War–era America far removed from LITTLE WOMEN, the innocent young farmer's daughter Faye Carson enjoys sexual awakenings with John, her childhood sweetheart (and brother!), and Sophie, a serving maid on the family farm. However, her carefree teens come to an end when she catches the eye of Lord Mark, a sinister landowner. No, we don't know what someone with a European noble title is doing in 19th-century America, either, but then again, plot and story cohesion has never been a staple of the works of Satoshi Urushihara, from LEGEND OF LEMNEAR to PLASTIC LITTLE. His forte, then as now, lies in the distinctive and luscious skin tones of his female nudes, seen here in copious amounts. Of the two episodes listed at time of writing, the first is numbered "episode 0." Video extras include a tour of Urushihara's studio, notes on the original audio drama on which this is based, and a montage history of the American Civil War. See, it's all educational. ●N

ANPANMAN

1988. JPN: Sore Ike! Anpanman. AKA: Go for It! Anpanman. TV series. DIR: Akinori Nagaoka. SCR: Ayako Okina, Jiro Nakajima, Osamu Nakamura. DES: Michishiro Yamada. ANI: Minoru Maeda. MUS: Taku Izumi. PRD: TMS, Nippon TV. 30 mins. x 500+ eps.

A superhero constructed from bean paste by the kindly Uncle Jam, Anpanman fights for justice alongside his ethnically diverse cohorts White-Breadman, Curry-Breadman, and Cheese the Wonderdog against the dirt-obsessed Germ-man.

RINGING BELL and LITTLE JUMBO–creator Takashi Yanase's original illustrations for the Japanese chain-store Froebel Kan took 15 years to reach the screen, transforming into stories in publications such as Mommy, New Baby, and Baby Book. Regularly restored to life through the simple act of getting a new head from the saintly Uncle Jam, Anpanman gives those he rescues something special to remember him by—a piece of his own head for them to eat. This trick has proved to be immensely popular, especially with parents encouraging children to finish their breakfast (although what damage the concept of consuming one's playmates has done to a generation of Japanese, only time will tell). The TV series has also spun off into several short theatrical outings, including The Disappearance of Uncle Jam, Anpanman in the South Seas, The Secret of Breadrollman, and Christmas with the Meringue Sisters. More recent outings have included Anpanman and the Mermaid's Tears (2000), a LITTLE MERMAID spoof in which he helps the sea-dwelling Sunny in her quest to become human, and Anpanman and Ruby's Wish (2003), in which Anpanman comes to the aid of another damsel in distress.

Yanase would also try to duplicate the success of Anpanman with another food-related superhero. Riceball-man (1990, Omusubiman) was a 27-minute theatrical short featuring a samurai snack, but it could not compete with its bun-headed predecessor.

ANTIQUE HEART

1988. JPN: Antique Heart: Gakuen Benriya Series. AKA: Antique Heart: School Handyman Series. Video. DIR: Chuichi Watanabe. SCR: Asami Watanabe. DES: Minoru Yamazawa. ANI: Takumi Tsukasa. MUS: N/C. PRD: Animate Film. 40 mins.

In this short-lived adaptation of a long-running series from Wings magazine, three intrepid school investigators track down ghosts in the restroom, anonymous love letters, and any other mystery they can find. Intended to be the first of a series, this video was ten years too early. The concept of supernatural schools would return in the 1990s with the successful **Real School Ghost Stories**, **Here Comes Hanako**, and **Haunted Junction**.

ANYONE YOU CAN DO… I CAN DO BETTER *

2004. JPN: *Bakunyu Oyako.* AKA: *Milk Junky, Busty Mother and Daughter.* Video. DIR: Norihiko Takahama. SCR: Naruhito Sunaga. DES: Takao Sano. ANI: Takao Sano. MUS: Yoshi. PRD: YOUC, Digital Works (Vanilla Series), Blue Gale. 30 mins. x 2 eps.

Yusuke is invited to become the private tutor of Reina, a girl with large breasts. But when he arrives at her house, he discovers that her equally large-breasted mother Mizuki is looking for a man to seduce. When Mizuki catches her daughter in the act with Yusuke, she takes it as a personal challenge, leading to a fight over who gets to have sex with Yusuke next—more not-quite-incest from the **Vanilla Series**, based on the game *Milk Junky* by Blue Gale, creators of **Spotlight**. ⚫🅻🅽⚫🆅

APOCALYPSE ZERO *

1996. JPN: *Kakugo no Susume.* AKA: *Onward Kakugo.* Video. DIR: Toshihiro Hirano. SCR: Akiyoshi Sakai. DES: Keisuke Watanabe. ANI: Keisuke Watanabe, Toshihiro Yamane. MUS: Takashi Kudo. PRD: Ashi Pro. 45 mins. x 2 eps.

On a postapocalyptic Earth prey to monsters, Kakugo and Harara Hagakure have been trained by their father in the ancient Zero fighting technique to protect the last remnants of humanity. Paramount in their arsenal is the Tactical Zero armor, a fighting suit charged with the souls of ancient heroes. But Harara turns to the dark side, killing his father and creating the new Tactical Evils. Left for dead, Kakugo reaches a ruined town and offers to help the few human inhabitants protect themselves from cannibals and depraved mutants. Meeting once again with his insane sister, he fights to save the world in this gory adaptation of Takayuki Yamaguchi's *Shonen Champion* manga. Though *AZ*

contains veiled allusions to honor and tradition (the siblings' surname is a famous samurai manual), it has more in common with the mutant maulings of **Fist of the North Star**. ⚫

APPLELAND STORY

1992. JPN: *Appleland Monogatari.* Video. DIR: Kunihiko Yuyama. SCR: Atsushi Takegami. DES: Minoru Yamazawa, Keiko Fukuyama. ANI: Minoru Yamazawa. MUS: Morgan Fisher. PRD: JC Staff. 45 mins. x 2.

On the eve of World War I, Vale Sibelius is a young orphan pickpocket in Appleland, a central European state that could be an important prize in the coming conflict. He befriends Frida, a girl with the secret of a new weapon that could decide the country's future, and the two go on the run from the evil East European duo, Aryana and Attila. Based on a novel from Yoshiki Tanaka, the prolific creator of **Legend of Galactic Heroes**.

APPLESEED *

1988. Video. DIR: Kazuyoshi Katayama. SCR: Kazuyoshi Katayama. DES: Yumiko Horasawa, Takahiro Kishida, Hideaki Anno. ANI: Yumiko Horasawa. MUS: Norimasa Yamanaka. PRD: Gainax, AIC. 70 mins.

In an authoritarian utopia, humanity has handed the reins of power to super-capable robots. But the suicide rate goes up, mostly among people from the wastelands outside the city; rehabilitated and brought back to civilization they are unable to cope with paradise.

As the first scene (a suicide freeing her pet before she jumps) makes clear, the inhabitants of Olympus are no freer than birds in golden cages, and a group of human beings (led, in a typical touch of Masamune Shirow irony, by a cyborg) organize a revolt to seize the city back from the robots. Working for the benevolent dictator, Athena, human SWAT team leader Deunan Knute attempts to foil the terrorists before it is too late.

This adaptation of Shirow's best-sell-

ing manga was adequate for its time but was soon eclipsed by **Akira**, which permanently raised the stakes on high-quality sci-fi. The next Shirow anime, **Ghost in the Shell**, had a far higher budget—ironically, the straight-to-video *Appleseed* was often shown in foreign theaters in unfair competition with its richer, better-endowed cousin.

Look out for a couple of in-jokes (a magazine named after Shirow's superior **Black Magic M-66**) and some very bad Japlish spelling on signs. There are some sweet touches, such as the loose change falling out of Deunan's pants when she gets in the shower, or the cloying way she starts simpering whenever she sees a child. But for an anime produced by the peerless Gainax studio, *Appleseed* depicts a curiously mundane future—1980s Japan with a few shiny buildings. Tough-girl Deunan uses conventional firearms, drives a normal-looking car, and eats contemporary fast food. Only the robots add any real sense of the future, particularly a "multipede" tank modeled on the Probe Droid from *The Empire Strikes Back*.

Shirow loaded the original story with classical references, of which only Olympus, Gaia, Tartarus, and Athena survive the dub unscathed. Inadequate translation and diction have hidden the true pronunciations of Gyges, Charon Mausolus, and Briareus Hecatoncheires, which is why the English voice actors refer to a robot as "Gudges," a male character named "Karen Mawserus," and a lead cyborg called "Bularios." The uncredited translator was more successful in spotting references to U.S. cop shows (a police chief called Bronx) and Ridley Scott's ubiquitous *Blade Runner* (the terrorist A. J., not J. F., Sebastian). Although he ignored the author's classical interests, adapter John Volks added much bad language, inspiring critics to invent the term "fifteening" for those U.K. anime dubs that insert swearing purely to attain a more commercial rating. That's not to say that the dub isn't a peppy paragon of cop-show cussing, including such immortal dialogue as, "Half cyborg? He's *all* bastard!"

The franchise was revised for a new movie, also called *Appleseed* (2004), directed by Shinji Aramaki. The new version is an intriguing example of the "state of the art," although not necessarily for the reasons that the filmmakers might have hoped. Whereas the 1998 Katayama version begins with Deunan and her partner Briareus on a police raid and already working for their bioroid masters, the Aramaki version features a variant of the induction scene from volume one of the manga. It takes the time to introduce Deunan's hand-to-mouth existence in the Badlands, although unlike the manga, it does not have her in the Badlands with Briareus. It also accentuates a subplot only hinted elsewhere, that Deunan and Briareus had once been lovers, but that only tiny vestiges of their relationship have survived his mutilation and cyborg rehabilitation.

The Aramaki *Appleseed* was sold to fans as a cutting-edge example of digital animation, and, in the wake of the failure of the **FINAL FANTASY** movie *The Spirits Within*, included a deliberate attempt to shy away from realism in favor of toon shading that treated motion-capture footage to make it look more like anime. The result, it was hoped, would be a hybrid of live-action and animation—Ai Kobayashi, who voices Deunan, also functions as her own body double, which adds to the immediacy of the performance.

However, for all its attention to 21st-century technology, the Aramaki *Appleseed* stumbles with an inept and amateurish script, full of redundancies, technobabble and B-movie motivations. Adapting Masamune Shirow's complex and often muddled originals is a difficult task, but it is not impossible. Whereas Shirow's original *Appleseed* had a subtle background family dynamic, replaying the paternal inventor of **ASTRO BOY** by having Deunan Knute's father as the creator of an entire robot society, the Aramaki remake pointlessly introduces Deunan's scientist mother,

in what seems to be a dysfunctional setup inspired by **EVANGELION**. Far from benefiting from its digital technologies, the Aramaki *Appleseed* seems trapped by them, forced into unending repetitions of dull exposition, broken up by perfunctory action sequences. The result, despite its proclamations of originality and innovation, seems to follow the soullessly escalating formula of a low-grade computer game, and not the rich source material of Shirow's manga. The 1988 video version, for all its faults and old-fashioned look, is the one with the better script. ◑

APPROACH OF AUTUMN, THE

1998. JPN: *Kasho no Getsu Aki no Kyogen*. AKA: *Hot Month Autumn Performance*. Video. DIR: Mamoru Hamazu. SCR: Mari Hirai. DES: Takashi Komori. ANI: Takashi Komori. MUS: Yuriko Nakamura. PRD: SME. 30 mins. x 2 eps. A strange medieval romance based on a manga by Mari Hirai in which a pretty-boy sorcerer in Kamakura-period Japan begins a relationship with a hermaphrodite creature who is half-human, half-cat. The titular *aki no kyogen* refers to the last performances of the theatrical year, with their undertones of final curtain calls, farewells, and tomfoolery.

AQUA AGE

1996. JPN: *Mizu-iro Jidai*. AKA: *The Water-Colored Years*; *My Years in Blue*. TV series. DIR: Hiroko Tokita, Shin Misawa, Susumu Kudo, Hiroaki Sakurai, Hiroshi Fukutomi. SCR: Junji Takegami, Tsunehisa Arakawa, Reiko Yoshida. DES: Shinichi Yamaoka. ANI: Takahisa Ichikawa, Tatsuo Otaku. MUS: N/C. PRD: NAS, Comet, TV Tokyo. 25 mins. x 47 eps. A quaint but uneventful look at the life and loves of average schoolgirl Yuko Kawai as her home life and school life place her under pressure to succeed, and she develops a crush on classmate Hiroshi, whose window faces hers. Named for the "Aqua Age" hair salon where she gets a part-time job and for the distinctive blue colors of the sailor-

suit uniform worn by so many Japanese schoolgirls, this anime was somewhat marginalized in anime sources for committing the heinous crime of featuring no robots, interdimensional gateways, erotic plot twists, or anything out of the ordinary at all. Scratch the surface, however, and you will find a role-reversal of **KIMAGURE ORANGE ROAD**, with a female lead and an idealized *male* love object without the latter anime's occasional intrusion of psychic subplots. Based on the manga in *Ciao* magazine by Yu Yabuchi.

AQUARIAN AGE *

2002. JPN: *Aquarian Age: Sign for Evolution*. TV series, video. DIR: Yoshimitsu Ohashi, Fumie Moroi. SCR: Kazuhiko Soma. DES: Hisashi Abe; Haruhiko Mikimoto, Fumie Moroi. ANI: Fumie Moroi. MUS: Yuki Kajiura. PRD: TV Tokyo, Victor Entertainment, Broccoli, Madhouse. 25 mins. x 13 eps. (TV1), 60 mins. (v). Kyota Kamikurata is a vocalist in an indie garage band, with a voice that drives audiences wild. It's not his singing, but a rare psionic ability called "mindbreak" which lures people to him and then brings out their own psionic ability. Kyota is a psychic Pied Piper, though he doesn't have a clue about it. His childhood friend Yoriko Sanno is a priestess who lives at the Isuzu shrine, who also moonlights on keyboards for Kyota's band, but her family has a higher destiny in mind for her—she's the reincarnation of ancient demigod Benzaiten, and they want her to unleash her powers and become head of the secret organization Arayashiki.

Kyota starts seeing visions of girls engaged in supernatural battles; he thinks he's going crazy, but he's just catching glimpses of all-out psychic warfare in a parallel dimension. There are other mindbreakers out there, usually male and bent on world domination. Secret factions, known as Wiz-Dom, Darklore, E.G.O., and Arayashiki, are fighting for supremacy and he and Yoriko are drawn into the conflict. As reality becomes more tenuous, the only solid thing they can hold on to is their love for each other. When a new threat emerges, they must unite the battling superpowers to save two realities.

Aquarian Age began as a collectible card game from Broccoli devoid of much in the way of an over-arching plot—the above synopsis was largely concocted for the anime adaptation, which also adds impressive character designs from **PET SHOP OF HORRORS**'s Hisashi Abe. It was followed by a video sequel *Aquarian Age Saga II: Don't Forget Me* (2003). After the various secret organizations joined forces to defeat the alien Eraser threat to Earth at the end of the first TV series, a new enemy emerges in the form of the Polestar Empire, ruled by the strongest Mind-breaker ever. Four girls, each from one of the original warring organizations, square up to fight the Empire on Earth. High-school psychic Megumi, Taoist priestess Miharu Itsukushima, vampire Yoko Ashley, and immortal sorceress Stella Blavatsky are all based on character concepts by Haruhiko Mikimoto, better known for **MACROSS**.

The second video, misleadingly titled *AA: The Movie* (2003), moved past the events of the first video to depict Earth under the domination of the Polestar Empire, whose use of forbidden magic creates dimensional rifts that plunge the planet into chaos and conflict once more. Mayumi Fujimiya of E.G.O. has astounding powers, but her fears and her unresolved complex about her famous mother leave her unable to use them, until she is joined by Yoko, Miharu, and Stella. Director Ohashi once claimed that *Aquarian Age* was a metaphor for the entertainment industry itself, in which warring factions fight for the attention of an audience unaware of the investments at stake—compare to **ARMITAGE III**, with similarly allegorized conflicts behind the scenes in the entertainment industry. Not to be confused with **AQUA AGE**.

AQUARION

2005. JPN: *Sosei no Aquarion*. AKA:

Holy Genesis Aquarion. TV series. DIR: Hideki Tonokatsu, Kenichi Kobayashi, Shoji Kawamori, Yasuaki Takeuchi. SCR: Shoji Kawamori, Hiroshi Onogi, Eiji Kurokawa, Natsuko Takahashi. DES: Futoshi Fujikawa, Takeshi Takakura, Shoji Kawamori. ANI: Atsushi Irie, Nobuteru Yuki, Satoru Utsunomiya. MUS: Hisaaki Hogari, Yoko Kanno. PRD: Satellite, TV Tokyo. 25 mins. x 26 eps.

Eleven years after a terrible natural disaster not unlike that found in **BLUE SUBMARINE NO. SIX**, the Antarctic ice cap has melted, leading to upheavals that have wiped out two-thirds of the world's population, and the surprise thawing of Atlantis (or Atlandia), a lost continent revealed by the disappearing ice. Atlantis awakens from its 12,000-year slumber, along with the "Fallen Angels," winged humanoid creatures who send mechanical beasts … all right, giant robots, out to harvest human prey for their *prana* life-force energy—compare to **LEGEND OF DUO**.

Members of the human race desperately try to fight back by forming the familiar-sounding DEAVA organization (almost but not quite **EVANGELION**'s NERV), salvaging "Vector Machines" from the bottom of the sea. These transforming aircraft are rumored to be the weapons that originally defeated Atlantis, although, with aching inevitability, only certain youthful individuals seem to possess the right elemental energy to pilot not only them, but also the fabled Aquarion device that may be assembled from several combined Vector Machines. A predictably international team of prospective pilots is assembled, although the clear top gun is Apollo, an orphan boy who may be the reincarnation of Apollonius, an "angel" who famously rebelled against the people of Atlantis.

A futile retelling of **BRAIN POWERED** with an added bonus of combining robots à la **GETTER ROBO**, from a crew who can do a lot better, distinguished only by Yoko Kanno's customarily wonderful music, which has saved many an anime from the dustbin of history.

ARABIAN NIGHTS

1969. JPN: *Senya Ichiya Monogatari*. AKA: *1001 Nights*. Movie. DIR: Eiichi Yamamoto, Osamu Tezuka. SCR: Kazuo Fukuzawa. DES: Osamu Tezuka, Eiichi Yamamoto. ANI: Kazuko Nakamura, Sadao Miyamoto. MUS: Isao Tomita. PRD: Mushi Pro. 128 mins.

Aladdin the water-seller (modeled upon French star Jean-Paul Belmondo) carries the beautiful Miriam away from a Baghdad slave market where she is just about to be sold to Havahslakum, the spoiled son of the chief of police. They spend a night of passion in a house they believe to be deserted but is actually a hideaway for the pervert Suleiman, who has been watching them. The police arrest Aladdin on suspicion of Suleiman's murder, and a heartbroken Miriam dies shortly after giving birth to his child. In fact, the murder was committed by Havahslakum's father's assistant, Badli, who not only covets the chief's job but has also been arranging secret trysts between Kamhakim, leader of the 40 thieves, and the chief of police's wanton wife. Badli plays all sides against each other, allowing the thieves to escape to make his boss look incompetent but also raping Kamhakim's tomboyish daughter, Mahdya, to break her spirit. He has even had sex with a crocodile, believing an ancient prophecy that promises a kingdom to anyone who can manage it. Aladdin escapes from jail, steals some treasure from the 40 thieves, and escapes with Mahdya, who soon deserts him when he succumbs to temptation on an island of nymphomaniacs. Discovering they are really snake-women, Aladdin flees and eventually finds a great treasure after many more adventures.

Many years later, two interfering jinn cause Aladdin and Miriam's daughter, Yahliz (now Badli's stepdaughter), to fall in love with Aslan the shepherd boy. In search of her lover while disguised as a man, Yahliz is forced to marry a king's daughter, a lesbian who is extremely pleased to discover her new "husband's" secret. The

© SONY COMPUTER ENTERTAINMENT

Arc the Lad

princess helps Yahliz find Aslan, and they return to Baghdad in time for the arrival of "Sindbad," who is really Aladdin in disguise. After a feud with the king (engineered by Badli, of course), Aladdin becomes ruler and Badli his vizier. Badli fakes Aslan's death and persuades Yahliz to join Aladdin's harem. Aslan is saved by the two jinn, one of whom turns into a lioness to pleasure the lions who are supposed to devour him, and returns in time to prevent Aladdin committing incest with his own daughter. Mahdya kills Badli in belated revenge for her father's death, and Aslan and Yahliz become the new rulers, leaving Aladdin penniless but happy once more.

During a mini-boom of Japanese interest in the *Arabian Nights*, ASTRO BOY–creator Tezuka published his own manga adaptations and subsequently adapted them into this sumptuous film, faithfully including erotic elements often dropped from modern versions. As well as music from composer Isao Tomita (who scored several Tezuka anime), it included early contributions from future big names Akio Sugino, Gisaburo Sugii,

and Osamu Dezaki as lowly animators. For reasons known only to himself, Tezuka also invited several famous novelists to contribute to the production as voice actors. Unsung talents included *Silence*–author Shusaku Endo and the science fiction writers Yasutaka Tsutsui and Sakyo Komatsu. Komatsu would return to help Tezuka in a more sensible capacity on SPACE FIREBIRD. There have been several other Japanese versions of the same classic cycle of stories, including ALIBABA'S REVENGE, 1001 NIGHTS, ALADDIN AND THE WONDERFUL LAMP, and SINDBAD THE SAILOR. An English-dubbed version, running at approximately 100 minutes and missing the crocodile sex, the lesbian princess, and several other scenes, was reputedly made for foreign distribution, though none of our sources can confirm its existence in translated form. Tezuka went on to make a far less successful erotic movie, CLEOPATRA: QUEEN OF SEX. See also VIDEO PICTURE BOOK. Ⓝ

ARAI, WAGORO

1907– ?. Also credited, even in some Japanese sources, as Kazugoro Arai—

we are unable to determine which is correct. Sometimes miscredited as Goro Araiwa. Born in Tokyo, he graduated from Tokyo College of Dentistry. He practiced as a dentist, while still finding time to work on early puppet shows and animations, including MADAME BUTTERFLY.

ARAKI, SHINGO

1938– . A mainstay of Toei Animation during the 1970s, a one-time employee of Mushi Production, and the founder of Araki Productions. A distinctive character designer whose work is familiar all over Europe, courtesy of translations of SAINT SEIYA and ULYSSES 31. Araki founded Araki Productions in 1974, a company whose notable employees now include his long-time collaborator Michi Himeno, as well as Hiroya Iijima, Masayuki Takagi, and Keiichi Ishijima.

ARC THE LAD *

1999. TV series. DIR: Toshiaki Kawasaki. SCR: Akimi Tsuraizu. DES: Yoko Kikuchi. ANI: Satoshi Murata, Kenji Teraoka. MUS: Michiru Oshima. PRD: B-train, WOWOW. 25 mins. x 26 eps. Roughly based on the events of the second *Arc the Lad* PlayStation game, this series, directed by NADESICO's Kawasaki, takes place after the events of the War of the Holy Coffin and features Hunter Erik (or Elk), the last surviving member of a tribe of fire-wielding sorcerers called the Pyrenians. He becomes a mercenary, teaming up with monster-tamer Lena, orphans Shunter and Sanya, exiled prince Grueger, and android Diecbeck. Needless to say, the many quests for revenge on behalf of wronged parents (which accounts for at least four party-members' motivations) are all tied up in an adventure plot in an incoherent but attractively designed world so typical of computer games in the wake of FINAL FANTASY.

ARCADE GAMER FUBUKI *

2002. Video. DIR: Yuji Moto. SCR: Ryota Yamaguchi. DES: Hideyuki Morioka. ANI: Hideyuki Morioka. MUS: Sakura Nogawa. PRD: SHAFT, Arcade Gamer Fukubi Committee, Bandai. 30 mins. x 4 eps. (TV/v) + 6 min. "bonus episode" featurette on DVD.

Fubuki Sakuragasaki's excellent arcade gaming skills issue from her "passion panties," which trigger a magical girl-style transformation. When an evil organization tries to steal her powers, she channels gaming spirits the world over to unleash her other self, an arcade powerhouse with angel wings and sword. Starting out as a gag anime, but winding up as a preachy family fable too long-winded to sustain its jokes, this creation from Mine Yoshizaki inherits the mantle of GAME CENTER ARASHI, with onscreen homages to gaming classics like VIRTUA FIGHTER and Pac-Man. This would-be satire also recalls less impressive anime antecedents like ULTIMATE TEACHER, in which another heroine used special bloomers to release her fighting spirit, but was a waste of space without them. Made for video release, although the first episode was screened on TV before the release date.

ARCHA LYRA
1992. JPN: *Aru Kararu no Isan*. AKA: *The Inheritance of Aru Kararu*. Video. DIR: Koichi Ishiguro. SCR: Mayori Sekijima. DES: Satoshi Saga. ANI: Masamitsu Kudo. MUS: N/C. PRD: Tokuma Japan Communications. 70 mins.
In the 26th century, humans discover a humanoid race living on the distant world GO/7498/2, a dark-skinned, golden-eyed people who seem to eke out a primitive, carefree existence. However, a scout team from Earth discovers that there is more to them than meets the eye—they live in symbiosis with vicious reptilian parasites, and the Terran scientists have upset the delicate natural balance.

Despite the obvious tip of the hat to Ray Bradbury's *Dark They Were and Golden Eyed*, *Archa Lyra* taps into a rich vein of SF concepts and puts them to good use, including the alien symbionts of Hitoshi Iwaaki's *Parasyte* and the addictive allure of Frank Herbert's

Dune. Original creator Katsumi Michihara is best known in Japan for drawing adaptations of other people's work, including LEGEND OF GALACTIC HEROES and the JOKER series.

AREA 88 *
1985. Video. DIR: Eiko Toriumi. SCR: Akiyoshi Sakai. DES: Toshiyasu Okada. ANI: Toshiyasu Okada. MUS: Ichiro Nitta. PRD: Project 88. 50 mins. x 4 eps.
In a faithful adaptation of Kaoru Shintani's 1979 manga from *Shonen Sunday*, ace pilot Shin Kazama is duped into joining a mercenary air force by his acquaintance, Kanzaki. At airbase Area 88 in the tiny, civil-war-torn Middle-Eastern kingdom of Asran, desertion is a capital offense. Kazama must live through a three-year tour of duty or shoot down enough enemy planes to buy out his contract. Meanwhile back home, the venal Kanzaki moves in on Kazama's girlfriend, Ryoko, trying to force her into a marriage of convenience to save her father's ailing business.

Area 88 is a lively adventure story, featuring a dastardly cad, noble pilots, and star-crossed lovers who, while they may occasionally be within waving distance of each other, are always torn apart by circumstances. Parallel plots of desert storm and urban mischief ask the viewer what either civilization really thinks they are fighting for. The incongruously sweet-faced characters draw a tense, thrilling picture of the way war, corruption, and simple compromises change people. Few war anime compare, although the following year's GREY: DIGITAL TARGET makes a similarly masterful use of a popular genre.

Made as a four-part series in the earliest days of video anime, the first two chapters were also cut together into a movie in 1985. Several other Shintani stories have been turned into anime—TWO TAKAS, DESERT ROSE, CLEOPATRA DC, GODDAM, and I DREAM OF MIMI. The artist also worked as a designer on GOD SIGMA. The story was remade in 2004 as a 12-part TV series on TV Asahi, directed by Isamu Imakake and written

by Hiroshi Onogi. The new version retells the story through the framing viewpoint of photojournalist Makoto Shinjo, who visits the base in search of a story and hears Shin's dilemma—does he fight and hope to earn his way back to his love before he dies, or desert and risk execution? Shinjo and mechanic Gustav are characters original to this incarnation, in which dogfights are entirely rendered in CG, creating a warplane-lover's delight in the style of the racing sequences of INITIAL D. Twenty years on, there's also a new cast of voice actors, but 75-year-old voice superstar Chikao Ohtsuka, who had a role in the original video series, returns to voice supply chief and fixer McCoy.

ARGENT SOMA
2000. TV series. DIR: Kazuyoshi Katayama. SCR: Hiroshi Yamaguchi. DES: Shuko Murase, Matsuri Yamane. ANI: Takuro Shinbo, Shuko Murase, Asako Nishida. MUS: Katsuhisa Hattori. PRD: Sunrise, TV Tokyo. 25 mins. x 25 eps.
Mysterious metallic life-forms attack Earth in 2054 and also haunt the dreams of Earth boy Kaneshiro Takt, who is unable to show his feelings for his lover, Maki, until it is too late. Maki's laboratory pieces together "Frank," a whole alien made from parts scavenged from wrecks, but when the monster is activated, it destroys the laboratory and kills Maki. Hideously scarred in the accident, Takt changes his name to Ryu Soma and vows to avenge himself on the aliens, only to discover that his new bosses at the "Funeral" organization are now employing one. The damaged but functional Frank resolves to help humankind (although humankind may not necessarily want to be helped in the way Frank intends), but the only human he is prepared to communicate with is the pretty Harriet Bartholomew—a girl who reminds Takt of the dead Maki. Mixing the nihilism of GREY: DIGITAL TARGET with the ambiguous enemies of EVANGELION, *AS* also features curiously lopsided designs for

the asymmetric Frank and obvious tips of the hat to the FRANKENSTEIN story. As with many other TV series of the cash-strapped turn of the century, it also demonstrates a noticeable drop in animation quality, going from reasonable to barely adequate in the space of the first few episodes.

ARGOT AND JARGON

Anime appreciation has developed a slang all its own, incorporating a number of Japanese words, often with uses different from those employed in their country of origin. We believe such terms present an unnecessary barrier to comprehension for the newcomer. Consequently, with the exception of the terms *anime* and *manga* we have used them as little as possible in this book. This entry is designed to point out certain words to aid the reader in understanding some of the more opaque fan texts. The better anime magazines refuse to use them unless absolutely necessary, in order to ensure that new readers are not baffled by a slew of obtuse terminology. Despite this, many mainstream journalists love to use as many as possible when covering anime, because it suggests they know what they are talking about. The terms are also very popular with fans who cannot speak Japanese but like to imply that they can.

Basic Terminology

• Anime refers to animation from Japan. The term was first coined by critic Taihei Imamura, as a replacement for the cumbersome *mangaeiga* in his book *Mangaeiga Ron* (*On Cartoon Films*, 1948). Other terms in use include *doga* ("moving pictures"). By our definition, a work is Japanese if the majority of the main creatives (director, script writer, character designer, and key animators) are Japanese. Within Japan, the term "anime" refers to any form of animation, including foreign cartoons. We employ it specifically to distinguish Japanese animation from products of other nations. There have been attempts among unscrupulous

Western distributors to call anything anime that looks remotely Japanese. We do not subscribe to this deception and file such titles as FALSE FRIENDS. If a Japanese origin is not of fundamental importance in the definition of anime, then it is a futile pretension to use the term at all, and we might as well call everything "cartoons." The term "Japanese anime" is a tautology, since anime is Japanese by definition. Some sources, particularly in Japan, use the term "Japanimation," which was deliberately promoted by some companies in America as a viable alternative. However, the term has proved unpopular abroad through its inevitable separation into the component parts "Jap" and "animation"—Jap being a pejorative term with wartime associations.

• Manga refers to comics from Japan. As with anime, the term is used slightly differently in Japan itself, where it once meant "caricature," drifted semantically into the same basic area as "cartoon," and has meant "comic" for the last fifty years or so. As with anime, claiming that something can be a "manga" even if it is not from Japan is rather pointless in the English language—you might as well call everything "comics." There is, nevertheless, a growing number of artists in the West who claim they draw in a "manga-style," itself a meaningless term, since manga are so varied there is no such thing as a single style. A mangaka is a "manga creator." In the 1990s, an anime company called Manga Entertainment established itself as a very powerful brand in the European market, ensuring that to this day the term "manga video" in most of Europe actually means anime. However, in Japan the term manga video actually refers to a video showing pages of a comic, while off-screen actors read it aloud. We never said this would be easy.

Other Terms

• CB means "child body," and is a pun on *chibi*, meaning little. It refers to childlike caricatures of particular characters, shown in moments of embar-

rassment or comedy, occasionally in comical sequences. The term has fallen out of use in recent years, and seems to have been merged with the similar SD (q.v.).

• Chokyo is a subcategory of *hentai* (q.v.), about the "breaking in" of new sexual conquests through abuse and domination.

• Cosplay is a contraction of "costume play," and means "dressing up."

• Dojinshi are amateur publications or fanzines.

• E-Conté means "storyboards," a comic-style run-through of the scenes in an animated film, depicting everything on a shot-by-shot basis. The term derives from the Japanese *e*, meaning "picture," and "continuity."

• Fan Service is a temporary suspension of the concerns of the story in order to amuse or entertain the audience—usually images and moments in which the female characters lose their clothes or pose provocatively. Supposedly, this is because it is a special gift to the loyal fans on the part of the animators; often it is a creepy objectification that only encourages *moe* (q.v.) in certain sectors and derision from non-fans. Fan service need not always be sexually suggestive; there is, for example, such a thing as *mecha* (q.v.) fan service, foregrounding machinery at the expense of other aspects.

• Gekiga, literally "dramatic pictures," are supposedly comics for adults, roughly equivalent to the Western term "graphic novels." The term, however, is rarely used in contemporary Japan and seems to date from the time when the term "comic" still contained a juvenile implication.

• Hentai is anime erotica. The term first spread among coy fans and distributors who preferred to use a foreign term for their pornography, and then among porn consumers and distributors in search of a means of classifying the animated variant separately from the live-action version. Since the term literally means "perverse," it is sometimes found contracted to the letter "H" or its Japanese pronunciation *ecchi* or *etchi*. Some have claimed that the contraction is "softer" in meaning than the full term—calling a Japanese boy "H" might be flirtatious, as opposed to the more insulting "hentai."

• Leica Reel is the Japanese industry term for what is known in the West as animatics—a "movie" made using the storyboards for a production, in order to check timings, and often used as the visual track to which the voice actors will record their dialogue while the actual visuals are still being animated. Leica is a camera manufacturer that seems to have entered Japanese slang as a name for one of its products, much as *Hotchkiss* in Japanese continues to mean stapler.

• Lolicon or Lolicom is a contraction of "Lolita Complex," an unhealthy interest in underage girls exemplified by the **LOLITA ANIME**. Its rarer male variant is *Shotacon* (q.v.).

• Mecha literally refers to mechanical items or machinery, a subset of anime appreciation for all those boys who like to see how things work. If one is watching a mecha anime, it usually means one is watching something with lots of giant robots, such as the famous **GUNDAM**. It can, however, also refer to more general forms of machinery—**INITIAL D**'s obsession with engine interiors makes it just as much a mecha anime, for example.

• Moe is a fetishistic obsession with a particular topic or hobby, entering modern parlance as a replacement for *otaku* (q.v.), although in the rapid-pace world of Japanese slang, it is already falling out of favor. Toshio Okada has written that a *moe* fan need only be obsessed, while a true *otaku* actually develops background knowledge. Its etymology here is related to *moeru*, to burn with enthusiastic fervor. Also often associated in anime fandom with one particular kind of *moe*, an intense attraction to cartoon characters, particularly young and innocent girls that need to be nurtured and may be looking for a brotherly protector. Its etymology here is more related to *moederu*, to sprout or bud. Unhelpfully,

it is also an acronym for an anime company, m.o.e., or Master of Entertainment. Such popular confusions over what Japanese and other foreign terms actually mean is precisely why we have avoided them in the body of this book.

• OP refers to the opening theme to a show, as contrasted with the ED, or ending theme. Although the trend in American TV is toward short, punchy OP's that do not permit viewers the opportunity to grow bored and surf to another channel, Japanese broadcasting favors longer sequences. This permits a promotional showcase for the all-important song tie-ins, and in anime also permits a reduction in the length of new animation required for a weekly episode.

• Otaku has a highly complex derivation, and now means "geek," "nerd," or "obsessive fan" (of any hobby or pursuit) in Japanese. It does not have these negative connotations in Western fandom, where it simply means an anime/manga fan, particularly a devoted or knowledgeable one. The word was first used in its modern sense in *An Investigation of Otaku* (*Otaku no Kenkyu*), a series of columns published by Akio Nakamori in 1983. This was later parodied in **OTAKU NO VIDEO**, the first anime made by fans, for fans, about fans.

• PRO is a shorthand for "Production," and often appears in studio documentation for animation companies, such as Mushi Pro, Tezuka Pro, or Sho Pro (Shogakukan Productions).

• Pseudomanga is a Western comic that pretends to be a manga. The term is highly unpopular with Western fans, since they feel it implies that some Western creators are trying to pass their work off as something it isn't. Other attempts to categorize the phenomenon include "American-style manga," or "Amerimanga," much to the annoyance of non-Americans. The authors prefer to call them "comics," because that's what they are.

• Ris Work, sometimes mistransliterated as "Lease Work." The use of a "telop" or television opaque projector, aka an optical printer, to add certain

video effects, particularly rain, mist, or certain fore- and background projections. Largely superceded in modern anime thanks to digital animation, but often still used to add the closing credits to some anime.

• SD means "super-deformed" or sometimes "squashed-down." In both cases it refers to squat cartoon variants of characters, used in parodies or in comical sequences. See also CB.

• Seiyu means "voice actor" and refers to the people who provide voices for the animated characters. In order to maximize profits and give magazines something to write about, the Japanese anime press began to include *seiyu* coverage in the 1980s, particularly when *seiyu* singing careers generated more income, as in the case of **MACROSS**. The trend reached the Western anime press in the 1990s.

• Shojo means "girl" in Japanese. Consequently, a *shojo anime* is an anime made for girls, like **CANDY CANDY**. A Bishojo is a pretty girl and a Maho Shojo is a "magical girl"—an anime sub-genre dating back to **LITTLE WITCH SALLY** and **COMET-SAN**. Shojo-Ai, or "girl-love" would be the logical term for a lesbian subset of anime erotica, but general usage favors *yuri* (q.v.)

• Shonen means "boy" or "youth" in Japanese. A *shonen anime* is hence an anime made for boys or youths in their low teens. Shonen-Ai, or "boy-love" is a homosexual subset of anime erotica. A Bishonen is a pretty boy.

• Shotacon is a contraction of "Shotaro Complex," or an unhealthy obsession with little boys. It is said to derive from the boyish good looks of Shotaro Kaneda, the protagonist of **GIGANTOR**.

• Studio is a place where an anime is made. It is often assumed that such entities are large old-time Hollywood-style conglomerates, although even "major" anime companies only have staff levels around a couple of hundred, whereas many of the smaller "studios" to which they subcontract piece work are often single offices in nearby buildings. Some companies enjoy the corporate implications that come with the term. Others, particularly small design operations, prefer to use the humbler "Office" designation, or even half-jokingly use the French term *atelier*—an attic or garret, the traditional residence of a starving artist.

• YAOI is a contraction of *yamanashi, ochinashi, iminashi*: "no climax, no punchline, no meaning," originally a pejorative term for erotica about homosexual male love, created by female fans. The term has now been embraced by such fans and used by them.

• Yuri is lesbian erotica, deriving from *yurizoku* or "Lily Tribe," a term coined for lesbians by the editor of *Barazoku* (Rose Tribe), a magazine for gay men.

Acronyms and Initials

Japanese marketers often assume that their audience can be easily fooled by a few pompous acronyms—one only needs to look at the Japanese "Making Of" videos for GHOST IN THE SHELL or AKIRA to see them at work. With the coming of video in the 1980s, some companies attempted to put a positive spin on the idea of straight-to-video entertainment—direct-to-video (DTV) has a pejorative connotation in the Western media world, often with good reason. Consequently, marketers coined the terms Original Animation Video (OAV) or Original Video Animation (OVA), pointless neologisms which seem to have survived in Western fandom because non-linguists found them easy to spot on pages of Japanese text.

Recent years have seen the creation of yet more acronyms, this time in the West. An Original Net Animation (ONA) is an anime that premieres on the Internet, while an Anime Music Video (AMV) is a fan-produced music video using footage from one or more anime. The term Original English Language (OEL) has been used in the publishing industry as a term for *pseudomanga* (q.v.)—it presumably being far too much trouble to simply call them "comics." None of these acronyms appears to be remotely useful for

anything except misdirection, and we have not employed them in this book.

ARIA

2005. TV series. DIR: Junichi Sato, Kazunobu Fuseki. SCR: Reiko Yoshida. DES: Kozue Amano. ANI: Makoto Koga. MUS: Choro Club. PRD: Hal Filmmaker, TV Tokyo. 25 mins. x 13 eps.
In A.D. 2301, Mars has been so fully terraformed that it is 90% water, and has earned the nickname Aqua. Pink-haired Akari Mizunashi arrives at the Martian city of Neo-Venezia, an idyllic canal-crossed metropolis modeled on Venice, Italy, where she hopes to find her fortune as a gondola pilot or "undine." Based on the manga by Kozue Amano, itself a sequel to Amano's earlier *Aqua*, which began in 2001 and is hence absolved of any charges of ripping off MARS DAYBREAK. In fact, with its emphasis on life in a serene future, it owes more of a debt to YOKOHAMA SHOPPING, while its backstory transformation of the Red Planet echoes ARMITAGE III.

ARIEL *

1989. Video. DIR: Junichi Watanabe. SCR: Muneo Kubo, Yuichi Sasaki. DES: Osamu Tsuruyama, Yuji Moriyama. ANI: Osamu Tsuruyama. MUS: Kohei Tanaka. PRD: Animate Film, JC Staff. 30 mins. x 2 eps., 45 mins. x 2 eps.
Mad scientist Grandpa Kishida builds a giant robot called the All-Round Intercept and Escort Lady, or ARIEL, a convoluted acronym that is the namesake of his dead wife. Earth is attacked by the elfin alien general Hauser, who is searching for the Breastsaver Haagen, a powerful fighter he believes to be somewhere on the surface, but his assault is repelled by the Ariel team. Pilot Kasumi (Kishida's granddaughter) enjoys herself immensely, but her sister, Aya, and friend, Miya, refuse to fly again. The girls have no choice, however, when a second wave of alien attackers pours toward Scebai base, and they are humanity's last line of defense. The two initial sci-fi robot episodes in this low-rent GUNBUSTER clone

were swiftly followed by the two longer *Deluxe Ariel* sequels, even though the original series hardly deserved a comeback.

ARION

1986. Movie. DIR: Yoshikazu Yasuhiko. SCR: Akiko Tanaka, Yoshikazu Yasuhiko. DES: Yoshikazu Yasuhiko, Kyoko Yamane. ANI: Yoshikazu Yasuhiko. MUS: Joe Hisaishi. PRD: Sunrise, TMS. 118 mins.
Three brothers, the last of the Titans, divide the world between them, but a quarrel soon breaks out between Poseidon, Lord of the Sea, and the Mountain-god Zeus, engineered in secret by the third brother, Hades. Fearing the wrath of Zeus, goddess Demeter hides Arion, her son by Poseidon, far away from Olympus. Caught up in the power struggles of the gods, Arion becomes the prisoner of the dangerously unstable Artemis and her capricious brother, Apollo, until he is set free, once more through the machinations of Hades. He is also falling in love with a slave girl, Lesfeena, but fears she might be his sister.

Beginning life in the pages of *Ryu* magazine (which it shared with the similar fantasy AMON SAGA), *Arion*, a loose adaptation of classical myth with a distinctly oriental flavor, is a mature and exciting adventure. Though original creator Yasuhiko is credited with most aspects of production, he also recruited some impressive assistants. Miyazaki composer Joe Hisaishi supplies a magnificent score, while FAIRY KING's Ryoko Yamagishi, an artist specializing in myth, helped with the design. Epic battles, perverse cruelty, great heroism, and unselfish love all have their place in this film, which is superior in every way to Yasuhiko's later VENUS WARS.

ARISA *

2005. JPN: *Moke-moke Taisho Dendo Musume.* AKA: *Groping Taisho-era Electric Girl.* Video. DIR: Eijun Reikishi. SCR: Kentaro Mizuno. DES: Akihiko Emura. ANI: Kyoichi Daihiryu. MUS: N/C. PRD:

Green Bunny. 27 mins., 29 mins. In an erotic parody of both STEEL ANGEL KURUMI (with additional swipes from CHOBITS), Shinichiro Morisaki and his nubile adopted sister Kotomi run a cafe in Japan's Taisho Era—the 1912–26 dreamtime that also provides a backdrop for SAKURA WARS. Late one night an Imperial Army airship accidentally drops an experimental android through the roof of the cafe. With the help of his grandfather Gennosuke, Shinichiro activates the android, which becomes the busty but clumsy Arisa. Anxious to retrieve their "Fire Bee," the army sends an agent to infiltrate the cafe; sex duly ensues. Based on a game by mixwill soft. 🔞🔞

ARJUNA *
2001. JPN: *Chikyu Shojo Arjuna*. AKA: *Earth Girls Arjuna*. TV series. DIR: Shoji Kawamori, Eiichi Sato, Tomokazu Tokoro, Yoshitaka Fujimoto. SCR: Shoji Kawamori, Hiroshi Onogi. DES: Takahiro Kishida. ANI: Manabu Fukusawa, Haruo Sotozaki. MUS: Yoko Kanno. PRD: Satellite, TV Tokyo. 25 mins. x 12 eps. + 1 bonus video ep.
Young teenager Juna Ariyoshi is in an accident and receives a vision of life on Earth in the future. She sees that humans have been raised to a higher state of consciousness but are still victims of predatory raids from evil Rajah invaders, who must be held off by the wearer of the "Aura Suit." She is soon enlisted by local boy Chris Horken in a mission to save both worlds. Or in other words, ESCAFLOWNE, but traveling in time instead of space. Ichiro Itano, former anime director, adds another string to his bow here as director of the CG motion-capture sequences, while director Kawamori claimed in press releases that the show was designed to encourage a return to nature and renunciation of material things. We'll see what the merchandising department has to say about that.

ARMITAGE III *
1994. Video. DIR: Hiroyuki Ochi. SCR: Chiaki Konaka, Akinori Endo. DES: Atsu-

shi Takeuchi. ANI: Kunihiro Abe. MUS: Hiroyuki Nanba. PRD: AIC, Pioneer. 30 mins. x 4 eps.
"Red to Blue" is the motto, but it will be many generations before Mars is truly habitable. The air is still too thin for human beings, so colonists live beneath the roof that now closes off the Marineris Trench. Like Hong Kong and Singapore before it, the city of Saint Lowell has become a bustling metropolis simply because there is nowhere else to go. Although the Trench is hundreds of miles long, the colony has expanded fast, and Saint Lowell resembles much older cities back on Earth, packed with cramped skyscrapers and dark streets. With a shortage of manpower in the mines (and girl power in the bars), Mars becomes the center of the solar system's robotics industry, pioneering the functional "Firsts" and the lifelike "Seconds."

Discredited cop Ross Sylibus is transferred from Earth to the colonies after he loses his partner to a rogue robot. As the city is terrorized by a brutal flurry of killings, all he's got to help him are his Terran wits and his new partner, the underdressed Naomi Armitage. The victims are all female, but they are also all "Thirds," the state of the art in android technology. Sylibus discovers that the murders are part of a gargantuan conspiracy involving big corporations, scientific cartels, and Earth's feminist government.

Blade Runner comparisons are a dime a dozen in the anime world, but *Armitage* truly deserves it. Wells City (as in H. G. Wells) and the spaceport at Saint Lowell (as in astronomer Percival Lowell) are dead ringers for Ridley Scott's Los Angeles. The frontier feel of newly colonized Mars only arrives in the later episodes, when Ross and Naomi are out in the barren countryside beyond the city standing beneath the glorious red of a Martian sky—an image also purloined for the later COWBOY BEBOP. With its high-tech future, android technology, and Martian frontier life, *Armitage* hits many

sci-fi hotspots, but it is also a cop-buddy movie, a romance, and a sexy pastiche on several military conspiracy shockers. Writer Chiaki Konaka, who would go on to write the quintessential Internet thriller SERIAL EXPERIMENTS LAIN, made *Armitage* conspicuously cyberpunk, including a trip to cyberspace via a painfully messy human interface and meditations on the place of humanity in a high-tech world.

Originally released as part of a multimedia experience that included false newspaper reports to fill narrative gaps, the omission of these items in the English-language release renders Konaka's plot less coherent than it could have been. But there are still hidden depths in his script, the first episode of which was written in collaboration with SF veteran (and author of the GHOST IN THE SHELL tie-in novel) Akinori Endo. There is also a sly dig at modern Japanese business; the rival Conception and Hu-Gite cybernetics companies battle to create the first android that is more human than human, continually outperforming each other with new formats and better models in a storyline no doubt inspired by the large corporate battles of recent years, such as Sega versus Nintendo and Sony versus Pioneer. The script is also scattered with references to H. P. Lovecraft's *Dunwich Horror* (a favorite of Konaka's), including Professor Armitage, the writer Lavinia Whateley, and a laboratory on Dunwich Hill.

Regarded as the most Americanized "girls-and-guns" example of Pioneer's output, *Armitage* initially got much less attention than it deserved. As with Konaka's later BUBBLEGUM CRISIS 2040, it is sometimes easy to miss the fine line between his satirical sexism and the everyday variety prevalent in so many other shows. Following the success of the video, it was rereleased as the movie *Polymatrix* with some cuts, a couple of extra scenes, and a completely new ending. It was also redubbed featuring the voices of Kiefer Sutherland and Elizabeth Berkley in the main roles in an attempt to gain extra press attention through star power—a tactic common for Disney but rare in anime until Buena Vista's acquisition of **Princess Mononoke**. However, the video ending, which looks farther into the future of the lead characters, remains the better of the two—*Armitage* really belongs on the small screen. It was originally made for video, and although the story is compelling, the art does not really survive being enlarged in a theater. But the bright design, powerful sound, and lemon twist of romance all make for a great retelling of one of sci-fi's oldest stories: the machine that wants to be human.

Note: the Roman numerals in *Armitage III* are part of the lead character's name, and not, as some commentators have assumed, evidence of two earlier episodes in the series. It is read "Armitage the Third," not "Armitage Three." The video sequel *Armitage III: Dual Matrix* (2001) takes place six years after the original, with Naomi and Ross now living under a false identity on Mars as Mr. and Mrs. "Oldman," with their daughter Yoko. With news of robot riots breaking out offworld, Naomi travels back to Earth to hunt down a new conspiracy, in the process facing her most powerful foes—replicas of herself. However, the same could be said of *Dual Matrix* in its entirety, since while it may attempt to restart elements of the original, it could be accused of merely rehashing them. There was much in the original *Armitage III* to recommend it, not the least in a reproductive subplot that foreshadowed the new *Battlestar Galactica* by several years. But *Dual Matrix* failed to move the franchise further along, and it ground to a halt here.**ⓥ**

ARMORED CHRONICLE HIO

2000. JPN: *Karakuri Den Hio Senki.* AKA: *Puppetry Legend Chronicle Hio.* TV series. DIR: Tetsuro Amino. SCR: Noboru Aikawa. DES: Kazu Kamiyadera, Junya Ishigaki, Hajime Jinguji. ANI: Koji Aisaka. MUS: Hiroshi Yamaguchi. PRD: Bones, NHK2. 25 mins. x 26 eps. When his humble village is attacked by

the cruel Wind Ninja, Hio breaks the ultimate rule of his people and hides within the holy of holies of his village shrine. There, he awakens the Homra, an ancient tribal totem given to Hio's clan by people from another dimension. Hio discovers he has inherited a fabulous power from his ancestors—the ability to summon and control fearsome devices he can only describe as "puppets." And Homra is no ordinary puppet; it is a powerful weapon.

In 19th-century Edo (Tokyo), the emperor is merely a puppet—it is the shogun who truly rules, though not for much longer. Japan is alive with calls for revolution: "Restore the emperor! Expel the barbarians!" Only the noble samurai Ryoma Sakamoto (see **Oi Ryoma!**) can turn the tide of history, but with an eye on the children's market, writer Aikawa created this imaginary teenage sidekick to reach a new audience. For good measure, he throws in two warrior princesses as well.

As the SF benchmark year 2000 became a reality, many anime companies were already firmly focused on the past. Exhausting the early 20th century with **Sakura Wars** and its fellow martial arts shows, they delved back into the 19th—with suspicious synchronicity, both *Armored Chronicle Hio* and **Tree in the Sun** were announced in the same month.

AROUND THE WORLD WITH WILLY FOGG *

1985. JPN: *Dobutsu 80 Nichikan Sekai Icho.* AKA: *Animals Around the World in 80 Days; La Vuelta al Mundo de Willy Fog.* TV series. DIR: Fumio Kurokawa. SCR: Ryuzo Nakanishi. DES: Isamu Noda. ANI: Hisatoshi Motoki, Hirokazu Ishino. MUS: Shunsuke Kikuchi. PRD: Nippon Animation/BRB, TV Asahi. 30 mins. x 26 eps.
Wheelchair-bound old goat Lord Guinness believes it is possible to travel around the world in 80 days, but he is too infirm to prove it himself. A lion called Willy Fogg volunteers to put the theory to the test, betting against sev-

eral other people at the Gentlemen's Reform Club. Accompanied by two circus refugees, Rigadon and Tico, Fogg sets off around the world. However, Sullivan, who has bet against Fogg, hires a jackal thug called Transfer to ensure that the trip is a failure. Fogg is also hounded by two Scotland Yard detectives convinced that he has robbed a bank and has to rescue Romy, a beautiful Indian princess, en route.

This anthropomorphic (but chiefly feline) adaptation of Jules Verne was a companion piece to the canine **Dogtanian and the Three Muskehounds** made in association with the Spanish studio BRB. Though it charmed a generation in Europe, the Japanese version was not broadcast until 1987 and omitted episodes 14, 18, 21, and 22—curiously, one of the missing chapters was "En Route to Yokohama." Fogg and friends would return in a 30-episode sequel in the early 1990s, adapting *Journey to the Center of the Earth* and *20,000 Leagues under the Sea* in similarly flamboyant style.

ARROW EMBLEM

1977. JPN: *Arrow Emblem Grand Prix no Taka.* TV series. DIR: Rintaro, Nobutaka Nishizawa, Yugo Serikawa, Takenori Kawada, Yasuo Yamakichi. SCR: N/C. DES: Akio Sugino, Takuo Noda. ANI: Bunpei Nanjo, Takeshi Shirato, Toshio Mori. MUS: Hiroshi Miyagawa. PRD: Toei, Fuji TV. 25 mins. x 44 eps.
Takaya Todoroki cherishes a dream of becoming a Formula One racer. He puts all his energy into winning a beginners' heat, but causes a massive pile-up due to an error of judgment. Initially swearing to give up racing, he is talked around by world-famous driver Nick Lambda, who encourages him to dust himself off and give it another try. Before long, he is a team member of Katori Motors, hoping to become the first Japanese racer to become a Formula One champion, driving the Todoroki Special, a car built to his own design.

ART OF FIGHTING *

1995. JPN: *Battle Spirits: Ryoko no*

Ken. AKA: *Battle Spirits: Dragon Tiger Fist.* Video. DIR: Hiroshi Fukutomi. SCR: Nobuaki Kishima. DES: Kazunori Iwakura. ANI: Kazunori Iwakura, Kenichi Shimizu, Mamoru Taniguchi. MUS: Akira Konishi, SNK Sound Team. PRD: Fuji TV, NAS. 45 mins.

An anime clone of a Neo-Geo game clone of STREET FIGHTER II, even to its mismatched leads, except instead of Ryu and Ken, we've got Ryo and Robert. The two heroes witness a gangland slaying and are accused of stealing a valuable diamond by the gang that has kidnapped Ryo's sister, Yuri. The two martial artists are obliged to fight to get her back in a tired story-by-numbers suspiciously like TEKKEN, or TOSHINDEN, or VIRTUA FIGHTER. ⓥ

Art of Fighting

ARTLAND

Animation company, founded in 1978 by animators from TV Doga, Onishi Pro, and others. Founder member Noboru Ishiguro took the company in to complete work on its first notable project, *Farewell Space Cruiser Yamato*, one of the spin-offs of the STAR BLAZERS series. Other high profile members include Noboru Sugimitsu, Kenichi Imaizumi, and producer Hidenobu Watanabe. The studio went on to contribute extensive work on the MACROSS saga.

ARTMIC

A design studio, specializing in original science fiction, founded by former Tatsunoko staffer Toshimichi Suzuki. Its greatest achievements include MEGAZONE 23, which sold over 100,000 copies in Japan, although the studio subsequently went bankrupt, leaving its coproduction partners such as Youmex and AIC holding not only the outstanding debts, but also the intellectual copyright of its creations. This complex arrangement of ownership is what led to the breaks and re-versionings in the serials GALL FORCE and BUBBLEGUM CRISIS, as well as the rebranding of RIDING BEAN as GUNSMITH CATS—seen as a successful attempt by former employee Kenichi Sonoda to regain control of his work.

ASARI-CHAN

1982. TV series. DIR: Osamu Kasai. SCR: Tadaaki Yamazaki, Masaki Tsuji, Akiyoshi Sakai. DES: Hideyoshi Ito. ANI: Tadashi Shirakawa, Koji Uemura, Nobuyuki Endo. MUS: Hiroshi Tsutsui. PRD: Toei, TV Asahi. 25 mins. x 54 eps.

Asari Hamano is a preteen girl who refuses to try at anything except sports. Her elder sister, Tatami, however, is a model student, adored by their mother, who pays Asari no attention at all. As the sisters fight a continual game of one-upmanship, Dad buries his head in his paper and tries to be even-handed. Both girls make life hell for the Morino boys next door—Jiro, who is waiting to retake his exams, and his younger brother, Kakesu.

MISTER PEN-PEN–creator Mayumi Muroyama only changed the names to protect the guilty when she started writing about her own family for *Corocoro Comic* in 1977. *Asari-chan* is still running to this day, but its anime incarnation was less successful. The 54 episodes were shown several times (occasionally split into 100 installments since most could be neatly divided into two shorter stories) and also spun off into a 25-minute film at the Toei

Manga Festival in 1982, in which Asari is forced to read a five-volume compendium of fairy tales in order to prove to her aunt that she genuinely does like the gift.

ASHI PRODUCTIONS

Often abbreviated as Ashi Pro. Animation company formed in 1975 by Tatsunoko employee Toshihiko Sato. Notable members include Seiji Okuda, Hidehito Ueda, and occasional cameo appearances from freelancers including Seiji Kishimoto, Hideki Fukushima, and Keitaro Kawaguchi. Representative works include PSIBUSTER and the *Beast Wars Neo* sections of the TRANSFORMERS franchise. A member of the Namco-Bandai group.

ASHIDA, TOYO'O

1944– . Born in Tokyo, he began as a sketch artist at the TCJ studio (now Eiken) before moving to Mushi Production, where he was a key animator on Osamu Tezuka's CLEOPATRA: QUEEN OF SEX. With the collapse of Mushi in 1973, he found work on STAR BLAZERS, before becoming one of the ten founders of Studio Live. At Live, Ashida was a designer on shows ranging from

CYBORG 009 to DR. SLUMP, before parlaying his experience of key animation (and working in impecunious circumstances) to a winning role as the director of FIST OF THE NORTH STAR.

ASIA-DO

Animation company formed in 1978 by defectors from Shin'ei Doga, including Tsutomu Shibayama and Osamu Kobayashi. Became a limited company in 1987. Other notable members include Michishiro Yamada, Hideo Kawauchi, and Tomomi Mochizuki. Productions include CHIBI MARUKO-CHAN—a long-running anime for the children's market that may not be well known in the English-speaking world, but is a blue-chip business for animators.

ASK DR. LIN

2001. JPN: Doctor Lin ni Kiitemite. AKA: Listen to Dr. Lin; Pay Heed to Doctor Lin. TV series. DIR: Shin Misawa. SCR: Jun Maekawa. DES: Takahisa Ichikawa. ANI: N/C. MUS: Takanori Arisawa. PRD: Nippon Animation, NAS, TV Tokyo. 25 mins. x 51 eps.
Junior high school student Meilin Kanzaki possesses magical powers and can drive away evil spirits and foretell the future. Consequently, she has a secret identity as fortune teller Dr. Lin. She's also in love with her best friend Yuki Asuka, but he's a practical, down-to-earth guy who has no time for superstitious nonsense. Based on the manga by Kiyoko Arai, creator of MAGICAL EMI.

ASOBOT CHRONICLE GOKU *

2002. JPN: Asobot Senki Goku. AKA: Asobot Chronicle Goku, Monkey Typhoon. TV series. DIR: Mamoru Hamatsu. SCR: Hiroshi Hashimoto. DES: Tsuneo Ninomiya. ANI: Studio EGG. MUS: Kohei Tanaka. PRD: Studio EGG, TV Tokyo. 26 mins. x 52 eps.
Earth's environment has been devastated, and humans leave their homeworld for planet Meshichi, where they live alongside Asobots (Associate Robots). These are androids, but not just servants—they have emotions, consciences, personalities, and habits

not so different from humans, and grow up alongside them to help and protect them. Some, unfortunately, pick up less admirable human habits, like brigandry. Goku is a boastful, irrepressible young asobot who runs into the mysterious Sanzo and ends up traveling west to the land of Zipangu with him. They meet cute Mion, mechanical genius Jo, pretty asobot thief Susie, and asobot drunkard Tongo, while avoiding the decidedly nastier asobots known as Hooligans, and their mysterious adversary Professor D.

The JOURNEY TO THE WEST has been a favorite starting point for animators from Osamu Tezuka onward. For the anime version of this manga by Joji Arimori and Romu Aoi, TV Tokyo wheeled out some impressive talent, and was rewarded with good enough audiences to get a 52-week run, increasingly difficult in these days of multiple-choice entertainment. Compare to SPACEKETEERS, which was another sci-fi adaptation of the same Chinese legend. Part of the series, perhaps a movie edit, was screened at a convention in the U.S. in 2003 as Monkey Typhoon. Broadcast in English on Animax-Asia.

ASSEMBLE INSERT *

1989. Video. DIR: Ayumi Tomobuki. SCR: Mitsuru Toyota, Michiru Shimada. DES: Masami Yuki, Yutaka Izubuchi. ANI: Toyomi Sugiyama. MUS: Kohei Tanaka. PRD: Studio Core. 30 mins. x 2 eps.
Demon Seed, a group of power-suited criminals, has stolen over a billion yen in valuables and caused immense damage while resisting arrest. In a drunken stupor, Police Chief Hattori decides to catch the group by auditioning for a super-idol, a singing girl who can wear Professor Shimokawabe's new giant robot suit, defeat the menace, and keep him from doing too much overtime. The 15-year-old Maron Namikaze, who can bend steel microphone stands with her bare hands, is put to work stopping the Demon Seed gang from stealing an expensive museum exhibit. She defeats the bad guys but

destroys the priceless artifacts in the process.

Three months later, the Special Operations group is so discredited that it decides to enter Maron for a talent contest. When an onstage display of strength is caught on camera, Maron becomes a star, and the police become her managers. Annoyed at the change in direction, Professor Shimokawabe secretly gives Demon Seed four new suits, and it stages another heist that coincides with Maron's big concert.

Predating both the showbiz-satire of HUMMINGBIRDS and the insane self-referentiality of DRAGON HALF, PATLABOR–creator Masami Yuki wrote this musical comedy for Out magazine, reuniting many of the staff in both off-screen roles and onscreen cameos. The drunken Hattori is based on Shonen Sunday–editor Fukuda Takahashi, who first took a chance on Yuki. His lieutenant, Taka, is based on designer Yutaka Izubuchi, while the three other members of the Special Operations group are caricatures of MACROSS PLUS's sensible Shoji Kawamori, laconic Patlabor-staffer Yutaka Yoneda, and a drunken pervert modeled on Yuki himself.

ASTRO BOY *

1963. JPN: Tetsuwan Atom. AKA: Mighty Atom. TV series. DIR: Osamu Tezuka, Gisaburo Sugii, Daisaku Sakamoto, Eiichi Yamamoto, Osamu Dezaki, Yoshiyuki Tomino, Minoru Okazaki, Fusahito Nagaki. SCR: Osamu Tezuka, Noriyuki Honma, Masaki Tsuji, Kenichi Takahashi. DES: Osamu Tezuka. ANI: Daisaku Sakamoto. MUS: Tatsuo Takai. PRD: Tezuka Pro, Fuji TV. 30 mins. x 193 eps.
In the year 2003 (2000 in the U.S. release), Professor Tenma (Boynton) is distraught when his son Tobio (Astro/Toby) is killed in a car accident. He loses himself in his latest project, creating Atom (Astro), a robot boy programmed to be forever good. Upset that his Tobio-substitute can never grow up, Tenma sells Atom to Hamegg (Cacciatore), the cruel ringmaster of a robot circus. Atom meets the kindly Professor

Ochanomizu (Elefun), who adopts him, inspires him to become a crusader against evil, and eventually builds him a robot "sister," Uran (Astro Girl).

Often erroneously described as the first TV anime (see **INSTANT HISTORY**), *AB* began in 1951 as *Captain Atom* in *Shonen Magazine*. Renamed *Mighty Atom* a year later, it became the flagship title of the magazine and was made as a live-action TV show in 1959. A combination of *Pinocchio* and *Superman*, it became the first of many animated adaptations by Tezuka of his own work.

First shown on Fuji TV on New Year's Day 1963 but eventually moving to the NHK network, it was the first anime to be broadcast abroad. Still known around the world as *Mighty Atom*—the U.S. name change was forced by the existence of a local comic character with a similar name—it was adapted for the English-language market by Fred Ladd, and its success created the first wave of anime abroad. The U.S. version eventually screened 104 episodes of the full Japanese run, including such curiosities as a TV special of Atom fighting the **STAR OF THE GIANTS**—though the latter remains unknown in the English-speaking world. The influence of *AB* extended further than is often realized. On the strength of *AB*, Stanley Kubrick offered Tezuka a job as a production designer on *2001: A Space Odyssey*, though Tezuka declined.

The Japanese series, whose ratings peaked at over 40%, ended with Atom sacrificing his life to save Earth. He also appeared in a feature-length anime movie, *Hero of Space* (1964), directed by Atsushi Takagi. Hamegg, Tezuka's stock villain, was recycled for **KIMBA THE WHITE LION**, and Tezuka attempted to write Atom for an older audience with the more philosophical *Atom Chronicles* for *Shonen Magazine*.

An inferior copy appeared as **JETTER MARS** in 1977, but the original itself returned in a new color format in 1980. These *New Adventures of Astro Boy* featured a younger-looking hero in keeping with audience expectations and scripts written chiefly by Tezuka

Astro Boy

© TEZUKA PRODUCTIONS. MUSHI PRODUCTIONS.

himself, though Ryosuke Takahashi contributed several and Kenji Terada was credited with "literary assistance," whatever that may be. With many of the original crew now famous in their own right, the new production drafted new faces including directors Noboru Ishiguro, Tetsu Dezaki, Naoto Hashimoto, and Takashi Anno. Perhaps as a result of Tezuka's own dissatisfaction with the series, the *New Adventures* were dark in mood despite their bright colors, featuring many failed missions and dying good guys. There was a greater concentration on Atom's evil twin, Atlas, built from stolen blueprints by Count Walpurgis (Walper Guiss), a European arms manufacturer. Deciding to conquer the world, Atlas opposes the emotional Atom with cold logic, eventually coming to realize over many episodes that it is he who is lacking something. Atlas was not the only one: the series was unsatisfactory to makers and viewers alike, and only lasted for 52 episodes—a quarter of its predecessor's longevity, though still considerably longer than most modern serials.

Despite its failure to live up to the impact of the original, the color *AB* kept the myth alive for a new gen-

eration, existing in two separate dubs from Australia and Canada. Homages abound in both the U.S. and Japan, from the obvious *Big Guy and Rusty the Boy Robot* to the desperate stab at legitimacy of **BIRDY THE MIGHTY**. The character's simple, recognizable lines became an icon in U.S. subculture and was rumored to be the subject of several remakes as the character's original "birth-year" of 2003 approached. A live-action feature failed to materialize, and a Japanese-Canadian IMAX coproduction began development but was shelved in 2000. The only project that did make it to completion was a 50-episode TV anime remake under the general control of the Konaka brothers, writer Chiaki and director Kazuya. Diligently walking a difficult line between retro homage and modern update, the new series faithfully recreated much of the original's effect, both in its cartoonish charm and in its ability to surprise children's programmers. The 2003 Astro Boy was taken off air partway through its American run, and did not survive much longer in the U.K. either, where even continuity announcers expressed their surprise at some of the harder-hitting plots. It also suffered somewhat from being broadcast in syndication in an order different from that in which the episodes were intended to be shown, resulting in some characters being "introduced" several episodes after they had first appeared. The series was subsequently released on DVD in America in a "complete" edition, although one episode from the original, "Eternal Boy," has been replaced by a clip show in order to avoid any possibility of incurring the wrath of Disney over alleged similarities between the titular guest star and its own Peter Pan.

ASTRO GANGER

1972. TV series. DIR: Masashi Nitta, Kenjiro Yoshida. SCR: Tajio Tamura, Toyohiro Ando. DES: Eiji Tanaka. ANI: Eiji Tanaka. MUS: Akiyoshi Kobayashi. PRD: Nippon TV, Knack, Toei. 25 mins. x 26 eps.

The Earth is under attack by hostile aliens called the Blasters. Professor Hoshi creates a giant robot using a bar of living metal that his wife has brought from her home planet of Kanseros. After their deaths, their son Kantaro is left to pilot the humanoid Astro Ganger robot in the struggle to save the Earth. Astro Ganger was a curious amalgam of controllable vehicle and sentient android; he could think for himself, had variable expressions, and would eventually sacrifice himself, like **ASTRO BOY** before him, to save a human life. The series was popular enough that it was still referenced a decade later in the **URUSEI YATSURA** manga, when Ataru Moroboshi sung a snatch of the theme song. Afterward, the Knack production company went on to work on **CHARGEMAN KEN**.

When *Astro Ganger* was broadcast, it was the first giant robot anime shown in five years. Animators and producers had shied away from the genre, fearing that **GIGANTOR** had said all there was to say, and that anything in imitation of it would be seen as pointless and derivative—those were the days!

ASUKAS OF FLOWERS, THE *

1987. JPN: *Shin Kabuki-machi no Story:* *Asuka no Hanagumi.* AKA: *New Story of Kabuki Town: Asuka's Flower Collection.* Video. DIR: Atsutoshi Umezawa. SCR: Kenji Terada. DES: Satosumi Takaguchi, Yuri Handa. ANI: Toei. MUS: Kenji Kawai. PRD: Kadokawa, Tohoku, Toei. 48 mins. x 2 eps.

In this adaptation of a famously sensational girls' manga said to encapsulate the *ennui* of the 1980s, Asuka is a teenage student who wanders the windswept streets of Kabuki Town each evening, dragged into teenage prostitution and gangland violence. She saves fellow schoolgirl Yotsuko from another gang and returns the girl's diary, remaining honorable but distant—even when she subsequently prevents Yotsuko from committing suicide.

The original story, published in a magazine also called *Asuka*, was a huge hit for artist Satosumi Takaguchi, spawning 27 volumes, a six-part spin-off, a live-action movie, and a TV drama. This two-part series, however, was the only anime appearance. The youth-gone-wild of the following decade were similarly "sensationalized" in the live-action *Bounce Ko-gals*, nicely demonstrating that the more things change, the more they stay the same.

ATERUI

2002. Movie. DIR: Tetsu Dezaki. SCR: N/C. DES: Setsuko Shibuichi. ANI: N/C. MUS: Yuse Nakajima. PRD: Magic Bus, Cinema Tohoku. ca. 93 mins.

Twelve hundred years ago in Hiraizumi, north Japan, Emishi prince Aterui Otamono-kimi fought the Imperial Court for 38 years to defend his native culture—different from the more famous Ainu people of the north, but still not part of the mainstream "Japanese" world. Known as "the Tiger," and considered a demon by his foes, he was finally defeated in A.D. 801 by Saka no Ue no Tamamura-maro, who turned his headquarters into a temple to the god Bishamon-ten which can still be visited today. The legend has inspired many historical novels, and a manga, *Aterui the Second,* by Katsuhiko Takahashi and **FIST OF THE NORTH STAR**

creator Tetsu Hara. However, this historical movie may also have been greenlit for its title character's racial resemblance to another Emishi hero, Ashitaka from **PRINCESS MONONOKE**. The production was funded by Cinema Tohoku (i.e., northeastern Japan), no doubt in an attempt to maintain visitor interest in a region also promoted through **SPRING AND CHAOS**. Compare to the less sensible tourist magnet **CUTTER'S STORY**.

ATTACK NUMBER ONE

1969. TV series. DIR: Fumio Kurokawa, Eiji Okabe. SCR: Masaki Tsuji, Tetsu Dezaki, Haruya Yamazaki, Tsunehisa Ito. DES: Jun Ikeda. ANI: Shingo Araki. MUS: Takeo Watanabe. PRD: TMS, Fuji TV. 30 mins. x 104 eps.

Kozue is a new student transferred to Fujimi College. Though she has a low opinion of her own abilities, she resolves to practice hard to fit in with the school volleyball team. She soon makes a lifelong friend in the kind Midori and a bitter enemy in Yoshimura, the girl who was formerly the school volleyball superstar. She falls in love with a local boy but is prepared to sacrifice everything to please her beloved Coach Honma.

This adaptation of Chikako Urano's 1968 volleyball manga was the first sports anime made specifically for a female audience, generating not only four 1970 movies assembled from reedited footage, but also an entire subgenre that survives to this day. Successors that simply switch the focus to another sport include **AIM FOR THE ACE** and **YAWARA**, while recent years have seen misguided pastiches such as **BATTLE ATHLETES**.

In 1977, Kurokawa, Okabe, and Yamazaki would return on the staff of *Attack on Tomorrow (Ashita e Attack!)*, a cloned TV series timed to cash in on Japan's successes in the volleyball World Cup. Mimi, a student, decides to revitalize a volleyball team that is still recovering from the accidental death of one of its members. The new series was a shadow of its illustrious predecessor and ceased after 23 episodes. The story was also adapted into a live-action drama series for TV Asahi in 2005.

ATTACKER YOU!

1984. TV series. DIR: Kazuyuki Okaseko. SCR: Hideki Sonoda, Susumu Yoshida. DES: Jun Makimura, Teruo Kigure. ANI: Satoshi Kishimo. MUS: Shiro Sagisu. PRD: Knack, TV Tokyo. 30 mins. x 58 eps.

Thirteen-year-old Yu Hazuki moves to Tokyo to be with her cameraman father. Bumping into volleyball star Nami Hayase on her first day at school, Yu joins the volleyball team and trounces the former champion with her brilliant abilities. Teaming up with Eri, an ace attacker, the trio try to realize their dreams of getting to the all-Japan finals.

Though there was a spin-off manga by Jun Makimura, *Attacker You!* was actually based on Shizuo Koizumi's novel *Now the White Ball Is Alive.* While its predecessor, ATTACK NUMBER ONE, romanticized school drama and camaraderie, *Attacker You!* concentrated on volleyball as a career in itself, making it less a sports anime than a professional soap opera that happened to revolve around sports.

AURORA

2000. JPN: *Umi no Aurora.* AKA: *Marine Aurora.* Movie. DIR: Yoshinori Kanno. SCR: Michiru Shimada. DES: Katsuya Kondo, Katsuya Kondo. ANI: Satoshi Fujiwara. MUS: Masamichi Amano. PRD: Nippon TV. 91 mins.

An action thriller with overtones of *The Abyss* and *Sphere*—a 21st-century drilling team based at the bottom of the South Pacific is searching for age-old bacteria that can synthesize oil. The team finds it, but the glowing bacteria proves highly combustible in the oxygen-rich atmosphere and can eat through metal. Biologist Oshunru is aware of the potential danger and suspects the bacteria "wishes" to restore Earth to the primeval conditions that created it, wiping out all other life in the process. This hackneyed, predictable sci-fi thriller's CG origins merely

make the characters more expressionless than usual. *Aurora* was Japan's first full-length 3-D computer-animated movie, though VISITOR and A.LI.CE were shorter works that preceded it.

AVENGER *

2003. TV series. DIR: Koichi Mashimo. SCR: Hidefumi Kimura, Mitsuhiko Sawamura, Satomi Sugimura. DES: Yukiko Ban, Kenji Teraoka. ANI: Minako Shiba, Mamoru Morioka, Tomoyuki Kurokawa. MUS: Ali Project. PRD: Bandai Visual, Bee Train, Production I.G. 25 mins. x 13 eps.

In the distant future, Earth has been destroyed and humanity survives in domed cities on Mars. Vital resources are dwindling, birth rates have fallen to zero (compare to ARMITAGE III), and the end of human civilization is in sight. Volk, the ruler of Mars, presides over a society where childlike androids or "dolls" have been created to fulfill the population's need for children. He exploits the people's need for a hero and the bread-and-circuses principle to make rationing a national sport. Scarce resources are awarded to the people of a residence dome if their champions defeat opponents in an arena. Meanwhile, warrior-woman Layla Ashley flees from Volk's minions with dollmaker Speedy and Nei, a doll regarded as the "child of destiny" by the government. Layla refuses to cooperate with Volk because he was the instigator of the purge that killed her family; she would prefer to avenge their deaths, in the arena or out, whichever works. **V**

AWOL *

1998. TV series. DIR: Toshifumi Kawase. SCR: Koji Miura, Toshiyasu Nagata, Chika Hojo, Atsuhiro Tomioka. DES: Isamu Imakake, Wataru Abe. ANI: Yoshihiro Yamaguchi, Masahiko Murata. MUS: Shiro Hamaguchi, Kazuhiro Wakabayashi. PRD: BeStock, TV Tokyo. 25 mins. x 13 eps.

Turncoat scientist Dr. Culten turns off perimeter defenses around a military compound just long enough for the Solomon terrorist group to get in and

steal several powerful PDB missiles. To demonstrate their zeal, the terrorists detonate one of the bombs, though they do not make any demands. Meanwhile, within the government, a scandal breaks out when it is discovered that Dr. Culten's secret orbital defense network, constructed without presidential approval, can be turned into a weapon and used against its makers. An elite team of commandos sets off to stop the Solomon terrorists before things can get any worse.

From early scenes of partygoers, lovers, and a child blissfully unaware that they are about to be blown to smithereens, to the introduction of a rookie character who might as well have "Dead Meat" tattooed on his forehead, *AWOL* is a low-rent Cold War thriller. Former X-Japan member Hide's theme song was the best-selling anime single of 1998, but this poor effort is otherwise doomed to obscurity. The fact that it's set in space amid a confederation of worlds seems like a last-minute idea designed to justify it as an anime production, though even the cost-cutting tactic of drawing the spaceships and explosions still falls down when faced with such a low budget as this. Given millions of dollars and a Hollywood star, this would have been just as bad, but it would have made it onto a thousand screens as a successor to *Broken Arrow* and *Under Siege.* In the anime world, however, it is simply below par, and few are likely to be fooled by half-hearted sci-fi design fudges like turning the Pentagon into a Triangle.

AYANE'S HIGH KICK *

1996. JPN: *Ayane-chan no High Kick.* Video. DIR: Takahiro Okao. SCR: Isa Shizuya. DES: Kazuo Tatsugawa. ANI: Kazuo Tatsugawa. MUS: Norio Inoue. PRD: Nikkatsu. 30 mins. x 2 eps.

Ayane secretly wants to be a female wrestler but is swindled into fighting as a kickboxer. Despite opposition from the ineffectual school principal (as if expulsion would scare this sports addict), Ayane throws herself into the world of professional martial arts, fighting off a roster of surprisingly stupid opponents, a large number of whom seem amazed that people actually get hurt in the ring.

Originally announced as a six-part series, *Ayane's High Kick* was canceled after only two episodes. To excuse the cartoonish design, the script tries to play for laughs, piling on dozens of Japanese sporting in-jokes that fall flat. What's left is a predictable rags-to-riches tale, ripping off TOMORROW'S JOE and AIM FOR THE ACE without any of their charm. The Japanese version relied heavily on a voice cast that included Yuko Miyamura (Asuka from EVANGELION, in another fiery red-haired role), but this was not enough to redeem it. Matters are not helped by a truly awful English-language dub that features a cast who cannot even pronounce each other's names, with only Debbie Rabbai as Ayane producing anything like a decent performance.

AZUKI-CHAN

1995. TV series. DIR: Masayuki Kojima. SCR: Shunichi Yukimuro. DES: Yoshiaki Kawajiri. ANI: Katsuyoshi Iizuka. MUS: Akira Tsuji. PRD: Madhouse, NHK2. 30 mins. x 117 eps.
When someone mispronounces her name at age eight, Azusa Nogami finds herself stuck with the nickname Azuki ("Red Bean"). Now in the fifth grade, she makes friends with a transfer student, Yunosuke, when he overhears another boy teasing her and can't help remembering such an original name. Azuki swiftly develops a crush on Yunosuke but doubts he will ever look at her as anything more than a friend, especially with the irritating Ken and Makoto eternally scheming to ruin everything for her.

Based on the comic serialized in *Nakayoshi* by writer Tsukasa Akimoto and artist Chika Kimura, *Azuki-chan's*

timeless school romance has found great popularity across Europe and East Asia while preparing a whole generation back in Japan for the more cynical yet similarly entertaining high school antics of HIS AND HER CIRCUMSTANCES.

AZUMANGA DAIOH *

2002. TV series. DIR: Hiroshi Nishi-kiori. SCR: Ichiro Okochi. DES: Yasuhisa Kato. ANI: Takashi Wada. MUS: Masaki Kurihara. PRD: Genco, JC Staff, TV Tokyo. 25 mins. x 26 eps. (TV) 5 mins. x 130 eps.
Ten-year-old Chiyo Mihama is so bright she's skipped five grades and is just starting high school; but it will take more than genius-level brains and industrial-strength cuteness to survive the strange classmates and even stranger faculty. She joins Miss Yukari Tanizaki's English class and finds a teacher who loves drinking, snoozing, and video games. Yukari's best friend Minamo 'Nyamo' Kurosawa teaches Phys. Ed., and seems very cool, except for her hidden fear that she'll never find a husband. Mr. Kimura, the classics teacher, lives in his own little world and only emerges to gawk at the girls—the reason he took up teaching. The result is an enthusiastically nostalgic look at school days from the point of view of both teachers and students, over a three-year timescale that rockets past; with only five minutes per sequence, the seasonal events and examinations whip round before you know it.

Half a dozen girls become Chiyo's friends and mentors, including the shy Sakaki, the nervous Osaka, and the overenthusiastic Tomo. The challenges of their school life have a strong vein of the surreal, and the series' humor is of the love-it-or-hate-it variety. Even Chiyo's cat starts talking, in a nod to I AM A CAT—just one of a slew of cultural and pop-cultural references buried in

the madcap onslaught of gags. The format of the show is unusual—five unrelated segments in each episode, which were also broadcast as individual mini-episodes, give each of the multiple characters their own moment in the spotlight. They also tie in to the original format of Kiyohiko Azuma's manga, a four-panel strip in the tradition of SAZAE-SAN or *Peanuts.* Technically, the serial's first anime appearance was as a second feature to the SAKURA WARS movie, when a frantic six-minute edit called *AD: The Very Short Movie* was screened as an advertisement for the forthcoming TV series. The series also had an online presence, in which mini-episodes with different voice actors were available for download. Based on the manga by Kiyohiko Azuma in *Dengeki Daioh* magazine, hence "Azumanga Daioh."

AZUSA WILL HELP

2004. JPN: *Azusa Otetsudai Shimasu.* Video. DIR: Hajime Kamegaki. SCR: Yuko Kawabe. DES: Satoe Nakajima, Kazuya Hiratsuka. ANI: N/C. MUS: N/C. PRD: Thomas Entertainment, Tokyo Movie Shinsha. 45 mins.
In the near future, when robots are used in many aspects of everyday life, the students of Karugamo High School decide that it's time for them to improve the performance of their baseball team by buying a robot player. However, in a cliché that goes all the way back to DORAEMON, they are unable to afford anything except a model designed to be a housemaid. Predictable sports, maid, underdog, and school high jinks ensue in an adaptation of a script by Yuko Kawabe, which won the second Animax screenplay contest—compare to SUPER KUMA-CHAN.

B

BABEL II *

1973. JPN: *Babel Nisei*. TV series, video. DIR: Takeshi Tamiya, Minoru Okazaki, Kazuya Miyazaki. SCR: Shunichi Yukimuro, Tomohiro Ando, Masaki Tsuji. DES: Shingo Araki, Teruo Kigure, Eimi Maeda. ANI: Shingo Araki, Teruo Kigure, Toshiyasu Okada. MUS: Shunsuke Kikuchi. PRD: Hikari Pro, TV Asahi, Toei. 25 mins. x 39 eps.

In the distant past, a race of aliens lived in the Euphrates basin, where they built the "Three Servants"—Ropros, Rodem, and Poseidon—mighty beings designed to wipe out invading armies. Thousands of years later, when the ancient civilization has turned to dust, red-haired Japanese boy Koichi is troubled by strange dreams of the beautiful Juju, who eventually appears in the flesh and urges him to join a secret cabal of psychics led by Yomi, an alien prince.

When Koichi refuses, he is rescued by the Three Servants and taken to Mesopotamia, where he discovers that Yomi was the chosen inheritor of the powers of Babel. Now that Yomi has turned to the dark side, it falls to Koichi, a distant descendant of intermarriage between the aliens and humans, to put his nascent psychic powers to use defending Earth as the new inheritor, Babel II.

Based on the 1971 manga by Mitsuteru Yokoyama, creator of GIGANTOR and LITTLE WITCH SALLY, *Babel II* inspired an entire generation of cre-

ators, and its effects are still felt today, from the reluctant psychics of AKIRA to the biblical archaeology of SPRIGGAN. It was reverse-engineered many times to create lesser robot/psychic shows in the marketing-led decades that followed. Selected parts were rushed onto tape with the coming of video, creating a nostalgic audience in Japan for the inevitable remake.

Yoshihisa Matsumoto's 1992 video version compresses the story into four 30-minute episodes and includes the events of Yokoyama's 1977 manga sequel *His Name is No. 101*, in which Yomi returns and uses Koichi's blood to create an army of cloned soldiers. Released in an English-language version amid confusion over its origins (many buyers were put off when they couldn't find the nonexistent *Babel I*), the new *Babel II* looked too much like its imitators—original crew member Shingo Araki designed a new-look Koichi who lost his red mop in favor of the bland hero-template black hair, and the Three Servants with their air, land, and sea specialties looked like cheap copies of the same year's BEAST WARRIORS. Teruo Kigure, an animator on the original, also directed the erotic pastiche LUNATIC NIGHT. The TV remake *Babel II: Beyond Infinity* (2001) replayed the plot over 13 episodes.

BABY AND ME

1996. JPN: *Aka-chan to Boku*. TV series. DIR: Masahiro Omori. SCR: Suke-

hiro Tomita, Kenji Terada. DES: Takayuki Goto, Yuji Ikeda. ANI: Yuji Moriyama. MUS: Kenji Kawai. PRD: Studio Pierrot, TV Tokyo. 25 mins. x 35 eps.

Thirteen-year-old Takuya Enoki faces unexpected challenges when his mother is killed in a car accident. Father Harumi has to spend extra time at the office, and Takuya becomes a surrogate parent for his two-year-old brother, Minoru. While he cares deeply for Minoru, the constant chores and attention can be very wearing. His father starts dating Miss Otani, but while Minoru happily believes she is his mother reborn, Takuya cannot come to terms with the idea. As time wears on, he comes to realize that it is *he* who has replaced his mother, and the love between the brothers grows stronger.

Based on Marimo Ragawa's long-running comic in *Hana to Yume* magazine, *Baby and Me* is often compared to SAZAE-SAN for its slice-of-life observations, but it also owes a certain debt to MAMA'S A FOURTH GRADER with its emphasis on impromptu parenting.

BABY FELIX AND FRIENDS *

2001. JPN: *Baby Felix*. TV series. DIR: Hiroshi Negishi. SCR: Yasunari Suda. DES: Shinichi Yoshino. ANI: N/C. MUS: N/C. PRD: Aeon, NHK Educational. 5 mins. x 130 eps.

A series of short children's cartoons featuring an infant version of the famous American cartoon character Felix the Cat, juvenilized for a new

Baby and Me

© 1996 MARIMO RAGAWA/HAKUSENSHA • TV TOKYO • STUDIO PIERROT

generation in the style of the earlier *Muppet Babies*, and tied in to a series of games and merchandise—presumably the Felix creators' attempts to grasp at the same franchise potential wielded by **HELLO KITTY**. A Japanese-American production featuring Felix's owners as producers.

BABY GRANDMA
2002. JPN: *Baby Baa-chan*. TV series. DIR: Shuji Kawakami. SCR: N/C. DES: N/C. ANI: N/C. MUS: Hitomi Kuroishi. PRD: Bandai Visual, NHK. ca. 7 mins. x 53 eps.

Amika cherishes a dream of becoming an idol singer, but for now she has a normal school life. Soon after her stern old grandmother dies, Amika's mother gives birth to a daughter. But as the child gets older, she seems to have inherited an incredible number of the old woman's traits.

Created by JINCO, this has baby-cute character design and art direction in cheerful primary colors, clearly signaling its intended audience, although the concept of a reincarnated bossy old woman taking over the soul of a newborn child may seem unsuitable children's entertainment to some Western parents. Broadcast as part of NHK's *Genius Terebi-kun Wide* show.

BABY LOVE
1997. Video. DIR: Susumu Kudo. SCR: Tomoko Konparu. DES: Takahisa Ichikawa. ANI: N/C. MUS: N/C. PRD: Tokyo Movie Shinsha. 30 mins.

Seara Arisugawa has loved Shuhei Seto ever since she was a little girl. Back then, when the three-year age gap between them was a big deal, he told her to come back when she was older. But now that her parents are moving to America, she sees the chance to move in with him while she finishes school, and possibly realize her earlier romantic plan as well. However, Shuhei already has feelings for someone else, since he has developed a crush on his classmate Ayano. Ayumi Shiina's original comedy manga in *Ribbon* magazine was another variant on the cohabiting would-be lovers of **MARMALADE BOY**, as friends and family offer a series of benign obstacles to Seara getting her man. The video was released midway through the manga's nine-volume run and first offered by mail order to *Ribbon* readers. Based on an "original concept" by Ayumi Shiina, who was presumably the author of the original manga. Compare to **SAKURA DIARIES**.

BABY, MY LOVE
2004. JPN: *Aishiteruze Baby*. TV series. DIR: Masaharu Okuwaki. SCR: Genki Yoshimura. DES: Junko Yamanaka, Masatomo Sudo. ANI: Taiji Kawanishi. MUS: Miki Kasamatsu. PRD: Tokyo Movie Shinsha. 25 mins. x ? eps.

Girl-crazy high school senior Kippei Katakura is asked to take care of five-year-old Yuzuyu Sakashita. The girl's mother has disappeared, reputedly overwhelmed by the prospect of rearing a child alone, and Kippei's family has taken Yuzuyu in. With a kindergarten kid to look after, Kippei's girl-chasing days are over, and his social whirl is replaced by taking Yuzuyu to school and making her lunch. The pair gradually develops a bond and Kippei comes to love the new girl in his life more deeply than any girlfriend he's ever had. The prospect of an unwitting step-parent is so commonplace on Japanese

television that it is a rare manga on the subject that is adapted to anime; instead, it is more likely to be snapped up for live-action remakes such as the previous year's *Hotman* (*DE). In this case, however, Yoki Maki's original manga got the anime treatment, presumably because it was aimed at a slightly younger audience, as reflected in its original appearance in *Ribbon* magazine. Compare to **BABY AND ME**.

BAD BATZ-MARU
1995. Video. DIR: Kazuya Murata. SCR: Kenji Terada. DES: N/C. ANI: N/C. MUS: N/C. PRD: Sanrio. 30 mins.

Batz-maru, a tough-talking, naughty penguin, has a name formed from Japanese school terminology for right (maru) and wrong (batsu), as well as an old-fashioned suffix found in warriors' names—compare with **MAN-MARU THE NINJA PENGUIN**. But unlike his fellow Sanrio merchandise characters **HELLO KITTY** and **PEKKLE THE DUCK**, Batz-maru's commercial success has come without attachment to an anime vehicle, and this one-shot video is his only solo outing. Clearly a pilot for a far longer offering, it features two short tales in which Batz-maru proudly enters his pet crocodile in a contest and then goes off to learn how to be "a man." He also appeared with Hello Kitty in six video specials, *HK&BBM: Everybody Dance, Full of Playtime, Play Together, We Love Dance, Let's Dance*, and *Let's Origami*.

BAD BOYS
1993. Video. DIR: Osamu Sekita, Takeshi Yamaguchi. SCR: Kazuya Miyashita, Kaori Takada, Masayoshi Azuma. DES: Hiroshi Tanaka. ANI: Mitsuharu Kajitani. MUS: Hiroaki Yoshino. PRD: Toei. 40 mins. x 5 eps.

It's tough being a hard, streetwise member of a biker gang, especially if it's called the Paradise Butterflies and its goal is to be the baddest gang in . . . Hiroshima. Such is the lot of Tsukasa, Yoji, Eiji, and friends, boys determined to outgun the engines of every other biker in town. Hiroshi Tanaka's manga was originally intended to be a hard-hitting crime story of warring biker gangs, but he was unable to take the posturing seriously, and it eventually became a tongue-in-cheek pastiche of the genre popularized by BOMBER BIKERS OF SHONAN. It was serialized in *Young King* magazine from 1988, eventually running to 23 volumes. These video shows were released once yearly during the manga's final years to drum up interest—a damp squib finale ran for 1 volume in *Glare* magazine after the series was pulled from its original publication.

BAGHI

1984. TV special. DIR: Osamu Tezuka, Kimiharu Ono. SCR: Osamu Tezuka. DES: Osamu Tezuka, Hitoshi Nishimura. ANI: Hitoshi Nishimura, Kazuhiko Udagawa. MUS: Kentaro Haneda. PRD: Toei, Sanrio, Goku, Nippon TV. 86 mins.

Ryosuke's father brings home Baghi, a small "kitten," unaware that she is really the cub of a sentient cougar, itself the result of experiments conducted by his estranged scientist wife, Dr. Ishigami. Baghi is the sole survivor of a breakout from a corporate animal research facility after an earthquake—Ryosuke's mother and her minions have rounded up and shot all other escapees, including Baghi's mother. Eventually, Baghi's strange intelligence attracts the attention of Ryosuke's neighbors, who pester her so much to perform tricks that she flees.

Some years later, a teenage Ryosuke rebels against his father and joins a biker gang, in which capacity he meets Baghi again. Now a full-grown cat-girl who walks on her hindlegs and has an intelligence to match any human, Baghi slaughters the other gang members in a fight, but spares Ryosuke when she recalls his kindness to her in their youth. The couple goes in search of her origins. Clues lead to Ryo's mother's original science experiments. Tracking down her follow-up project in South America, the two arrive just in time for Baghi to become the prime suspect in Dr. Ishigami's murder.

Baghi flees, and Ryo swears vengeance, becoming a big-game hunter to track her. Years later, Ryo is hired to shoot a wild animal that has been terrorizing villagers in the Amazon. It is Baghi, who only fled from Ryo because she feared that she was reverting to a feral state and wished to protect the man she loved from harm. It is revealed that Baghi is innocent, and that Dr. Ishigami was murdered by the dictator who funded her illegal research.

Ahead of his time as usual, Tezuka wrote this tale of genetic experimentation on animals for *Shonen Action*, the lead character named in homage to Bagheera as portrayed in Disney's version of Kipling's *Jungle Book*. Though this synopsis has been reordered for clarity's sake, the film is told chiefly in flashback, as Ryo the hunter relates his story to a local boy, and then in flashback-within-a-flashback, as Ryo the investigator remembers how he first met his feline friend. The anthropomorphic appeal of cat-women would become an anime staple, from CATGIRL NUKUNUKU to ESCAFLOWNE's kittenish Meryl, while Tezuka's cautionary zeal would even influence the story of the first POKÉMON movie, which featured a similar FRANKENSTEIN creation escaping from an Amazon stronghold.

BAKE!! JAPAN

2004. JPN: *Yakitate!! Japan*. AKA: *Fresh-Made Japan; King of Bread*. TV series. DIR: Yasunao Aoki. SCR: Katsuyuki Sumisawa. DES: Hiromi Maezawa, Atsuo Tobe, Yoshihito Hishinuma. ANI: Sunrise. MUS: Taku Iwasaki. PRD: Aniplex, D-rights, TV Tokyo, Sunrise. 25 mins. x 47 eps.

Country boy Kazuma Azuma leaves the family rice paddies and heads for Tokyo, intent on becoming the best baker in the world. His biggest asset is his "hands of the sun," a naturally warm pair of hands ideal for kneading dough and starting the rising process; compare to similar quasi-magical attributes in BLACK JACK. In a comedic revisitation of the tropes of sports anime, Kazuma aspires to the crown

currently held by Ken Matsushiro, the best baker in Japan, acclaimed for his French bread, despite the coolness denoted by his Afro hairdo and shades. But Kazuma has other would-be rivals: Kai Suwahara has studied bread-making methods from all over the world, and Kyosuke Kawachi has worked hard to master a technique known as "gauntlets of the sun" to make up for the warm hands he lacks. There's even a girl in the running—Tsukino Azusagawa, granddaughter of the founder of renowned bakery chain Pantasia, where Kazuma enrolls to hone his skills and earn a crust. Note that *pan* is Japanese for bread, making Pantasia a pun, as is the "Japan" of the title, which is not the name of the country at all, but a Japlish rendering of "The Bread." Similar punning humor affects many episodes, sometimes making the series even harder to translate than other anime.

Food has long been a fetish for the Japanese, from the dessert fantasies of the deprived post-war era in PRINCESS ANMITSU, through to the epicurean obsessions of OISHINBO, and the infantile food fixation of SLAYERS. The date of the switch from famine-hunger to feast-enjoyment was arguably the release of Juzo Itami's movie *Tampopo* (1985), which subsequently inspired a number of gourmet manga and their live-action adaptations, including *Sommelier* (*DE) and *The Chef* (*DE). Takashi Hashiguchi's ongoing *Bake Japan* manga is an inheritor of this tradition, but ran in *Shonen Sunday* weekly, where its younger readership was more likely to see it adapted into an anime than a live-action show. Compare to ANPANMAN.

BAKUMATSU SPACIBO

1997. JPN: *Bakumatsu Spacibo*. Movie. DIR: Tetsu Dezaki, Kenichi Maejima. SCR: Shigeo Nakakura. DES: Keizo Shimizu, Setsuko Shibunnoichi. ANI: Keizo Shimizu, Setsuko Shibunnoichi. MUS: Kazuya Moroboshi. PRD: Magic Bus, Toho. 85 mins.

The true story of the arrival of the

Russian commander Putyatin in 19th-century Japan during the last days of the shogunate (Bakumatsu). Japan had been closed to the outside world for 200 years, and the arrival of the warship Diana was to cause a major commotion in the sleepy seaside villages. After making friends with the Japanese during treaty negotiations, the Russians are left stranded when their ship runs aground during an 8.4 magnitude earthquake. The Japanese bring help to the beleaguered Russians, who leave with a grateful "thank you" (*spacibo*). The timing of the production suggests it was inspired by the Kobe earthquake in 1995. See also **THE DAY THE EARTH SHOOK**.

BALATACK

1977. JPN: *Chojin Sentai Baratack*. AKA: *Superman Combat Team Baratack*. TV series. DIR: Nobutaka Nishizawa, Kazumi Fukushima. SCR: Masao Maruyama. DES: Kazuo Komatsubara. ANI: Kazuo Komatsubara, Masami Suda. MUS: Akihiro Komori. PRD: Toei Animation, TV Asahi. 25 mins. x 31 eps.

Emperor Shaiden of Shaizack, ruler of the star Epsilon, sends his fleet to Earth to seek peaceful scientific collaboration. In Japan, Professor Kato is developing a time machine, and Shaiden wants both planets to share the development process and the benefits. But his commander, Goldeus, betrays the Emperor's trust and transforms the scientific expedition into an invasion fleet. He declares himself sole commander, and kidnaps Professor Kato's wife Mia and younger son Jun to force his cooperation. But he reckons without the professor's other son, 15-year-old Yuji. Yuji is a brave, impulsive kid who loves American football, motorbikes, and his family. He and his four friends all have powers of ESP, and they band together to pilot Professor Kato's giant robot, Balatack, to defeat the alien invaders, free Yuji's mother and brother, and save the Earth. So far, so predictable, a giant robot show with five teenagers of different types (including the token

girl, cute blonde Yuri), an evil and repellent villain with an eyepatch and a big wart on his nose, and even a noble adversary in the shape of Julius, the only member of the Shaizack fleet who opposes Goldeus. However, *Balatack*, made by many of the same crew who had just finished **MAGNOS**, is notable in the history of robot anime for being the first to introduce true comedy. Goldeus the selfish commander and his sniveling sidekick Captain Gael provide much-needed slapstick and subversive comedy dialogue, particularly in Goldeus' infamous proclamation that he wants (a) the conquest of Earth, and (b) a panda. He wasn't alone in the 1970s—see **PANDA GO PANDA** for further details. **V**

BALTHUS: TIA'S RADIANCE *

1988. JPN: *Balthus: Tia no Kagayaki*. Video. DIR: Yukihiro Makino. SCR: N/C. DES: Shoji Furuta. ANI: Murasaki Katano, Shinnosuke Kusama. MUS: N/C. PRD: Kusama Art. 30 mins.

In the factory-city of Balthus, human workers are little more than slaves to the ruling overlord, Morlock. Eud is a young boy in the resistance, part of a plot to use the warrior-robot Klaatu to defeat Morlock. The resistance fails, and when his coconspirator, Alphonse, is killed, Eud is hidden by Alphonse's beautiful sister, Tia. Both are captured by Morlock, and Eud is thrown into the dungeon. Tia is ravished by the sadistic overlord and taunted with the news of her brother's death, until she is saved in the nick of time by Eud, and both are saved by the timely arrival of Klaatu.

More from the people who brought you **LEGEND OF LYON**, in a frantically rushed erotic pastiche of the same year's **CASTLE IN THE SKY**, but with a fraction of the budget, talent, or commitment. It also features a pointless musical interlude from an off-key vocalist when it badly needs the time for matters of greater importance, such as plot—or, indeed, a little more sex. Sprinkled with sly references to great science fiction, including Morlock

(*The Time Machine*), Klaatu (*The Day the Earth Stood Still*), and a plot that crashes *Metropolis* into a porno film. Only in anime! **N**

BANDAR BOOK: ONE MILLION A.D.

1978. JPN: *Bandar Book: Hyakumannen Chikyu no Tabi*. AKA: *Bandar Book: 1 Million Year Earth Journey*; *Bander Book*; *Bander's Book*. TV special. DIR: Hisashi Sakaguchi. SCR: Osamu Tezuka. DES: Hisashi Sakaguchi. ANI: Hitoshi Nishimura. MUS: Yuji Ono. PRD: Tezuka Pro, Nippon TV. 86 mins.

Shortly before an explosion tears their spacecraft apart, Professor Kudo's wife places their newborn son in an escape capsule. The baby drifts across space and eventually lands on planet Zobi, where he is adopted by the ruling prince as his own. The Zobians can shapeshift at will, and the young Prince Bandar is teased for his inability to do so. Years later, a grown Bandar agonizes as to whether his "handicap" should disqualify him from marrying Princess Mimulu. His world is attacked by the space pirate Black Jack, and he and Mimulu are captured. Dumped by Black Jack on another world, the distraught Bandar believes Mimulu to be dead. Teaming up with shapeshifting steed Muzu, he rescues the beautiful princess Marina, who is being held prisoner by Dracula and the Cyclops. Taking Marina to her homeworld, Bandar is betrayed by a Terran military adviser, Dokudami, who has Prime Minister Hamegg throw him in jail. There he is helped by Sharaku, a scientist who has patented a scheme of extracting hatred from people's souls and bringing peace. Bandar escapes, but Dokudami steals Sharaku's distilled Elixir of Evil and threatens to scatter it. He is stopped by the timely arrival of Black Jack, who has discovered that he is Bandar's long-lost elder brother. The new allies pursue the fleeing Dokudami through hyperspace back to prehistoric Earth, where his ship crashes and scatters evil throughout the atmosphere. Using Black Jack's time machine (built with the proceeds of piracy), the group returns and destroys the totalitarian computer that had ordered their father killed. Black Jack is killed in the final conflict, and a dying Marina reveals that she is really a chlorophyll life-form whose final stage is a tree. Muzu reveals that she is really Mimulu, adopting a disguise to be close to the man she loves. Earth is finally at peace, and Bandar sits with Mimulu beneath the tree that has grown from what was once Marina.

Like the other early TV specials, the anime featured several cameo appearances by characters from other Tezuka stories, including **BLACK JACK**, Hamegg from **KIMBA THE WHITE LION**, Sharaku the **THREE-EYED PRINCE**, **ASTRO BOY** in a crowd scene, and Professor Ochanomizu as a servant to Dracula. There are also walk-on visual parodies of Edward G. Robinson and Linda Blair, who played the possessed girl in *The Exorcist*. First broadcast during the 24-hour NTV Super Special commemorating the 25th anniversary of Tokyo's fourth TV channel, it became the first of a series of annual Tezuka TV specials for NTV, including later productions such as **MARINE EXPRESS**, **FUMOON**, **BREMEN 4**, **PRIME ROSE**, **BAGHI**, and **GALAXY SEARCH 2100**.

BANNERTAIL THE SQUIRREL *
1979. JPN: *Risu no Banner*. AKA: *Banner the Squirrel*. TV series. DIR: Yoshio Kuroda. SCR: Toshiyuki Kashiwakura. DES: Yasuji Mori. ANI: Seiji Okuda, Tatsuo Ogawa. MUS: Akihiro Komori. PRD: Nippon Animation, TV Asahi. 23 mins. x 26 eps.
Banner is captured by humans and raised by a domesticated cat, whom he believes is his real mother. Separated from his "parent" by a village fire, he meets a stray cat who tells him the truth—he is a squirrel. Going back to his original home in a New Jersey forest, Banner meets a female of the same species called Sue, who helps him get back to his squirrel roots.

The second of **SETON'S ANIMAL TALES** series to be animated (the first was

MONARCH: THE BIG BEAR OF TALLAC), *Bannertail* was to be the most successful. The series was notable at the time for the large number of cels used in the animation—a successful attempt to impart realistic motion to the animals. The story received a very limited U.S. subtitled broadcast on some Japanese-community TV stations shortly after its Japanese release, much to the annoyance of anime fans expecting more giant robots.

BAOH *
1989. JPN: *Baoh: Raihosha*. AKA: *Baoh: The Visitor*. Video. DIR: Hiroyuki Yokoyama. SCR: Kenji Terada. DES: Michi Sanaba, Masayoshi Tano. ANI: Michi Sanaba, Jin Kaneko. MUS: Hiroyuki Nanba. PRD: Toho, Studio Pierrot. 50 mins.
Seventeen-year-old Ikuro is implanted with BAOH, an experimental organism that will defend itself and its host at all costs. Escaping from the Doress corporation with the telepathic girl Sumire, he returns to rescue her when she is recaptured by the evil Dr. Kasuminome.

One of many psychic espionage stories rushed straight to video in the wake of **AKIRA**, *Baoh* takes the well-traveled route of symbiotic weaponry in the style of **GUYVER**, relegating telepathic powers to the possession of a supporting character. A violent, visceral show prefiguring **GENOCYBER**, it also features mid-combat posturing in the style of martial arts movies, as characters pause to announce their next "special move" before striking. Hirohiko Araki's original manga in *Shonen Jump* only lasted for two volumes in 1984, though the creator would find more enduring success with **JOJO'S BIZARRE ADVENTURES**. **V**

BAREFOOT GEN *
1983. JPN: *Hadashi no Gen*. Movie. DIR: Mori Masaki. SCR: Keiji Nakazawa. DES: Kazuo Tomizawa. ANI: Kazuo Tomizawa. MUS: Kentaro Haneda. PRD: Gen Pro, Madhouse. 83 mins. (m1), 85 mins. (m2).
It's 1945, Japan is losing the war, and

times are particularly hard for Gen's pacifist family. Gen, only six years old, has had to grow up fast, and each day is a struggle to get enough food for his pregnant mother, older sister Eiko, and younger brother Shinji. Then the Allies drop a new kind of bomb on Gen's hometown of Hiroshima. People are vaporized by the intense blast, but in a way, they are the lucky ones. Gen's house collapses on its occupants, and he and his mother cannot lift the rubble off their family. Forced to watch their loved ones burn alive, they wander through a world in which survivors succumb to the effects of radiation poisoning, their hair falling out and their bowels bleeding away.

A hard-hitting tale of the horrors of war based on Keiji Nakazawa's 1973 manga, *BG*'s only shortcomings lie in the nature of the original material. Since it is semiautobiographical, it chronicles events instead of subsuming them to a narrative—the bombing of Hiroshima is the central event of Nakazawa's life and work, but once past the immediate aftermath, the film falls into a selection of vignettes. This style was used to better effect in **GRAVE OF THE FIREFLIES**, where such scenes denoted the characters' slow decline, but since the hero of *BG* survives, the use of these scenes in this film often seems to depict the passing of time for its own sake. Nevertheless, *BG* is a terrifying snapshot of one of the most horrific events in human history, perhaps all the more harrowing because it is presented in the cartoon medium so often associated with children's entertainment.

A 90-minute sequel by future **RAIL OF THE STAR**–director Toshio Hirata followed in 1986. Set three years later, it continues the story as Gen tends to his mother with his adopted little brother Ryuta, who also lost his family in the bombing. The film was twice revived as a part of TV specials with a nuclear subject—1992's *Never Forget BG: A Promise to the Children of Chernobyl*, and again in 1995, the 50th anniversary of Hiroshima, when it was shown along with the live-action/CG pieces *Our Playground Was the Genbaku Dome* and *From Hiroshima to America*. Nakazawa's Hiroshima was also the subject of **BENEATH THE BLACK RAIN, FLY ON, DREAMERS!** and the setting for his feature-length 45th anniversary video, *The Summer with Kuro*, in which a black cat charms the lives of two Hiroshima children. Curiously, the devastation at Nagasaki received palpably less coverage in anime. *Goodbye to Mother's Perfume* (1995), told the story from the point of view of a 15-year-old apprentice cook, and was released on the 50th anniversary of the bombing. *Nagasaki 1945: The Angelus Bell* (2005) was made for the 60th, concentrating on a bell from the city's cathedral, that was recovered from the ruins and rung each year on the anniversary.

BARK, BUNBUN
1980. JPN: *Hoero Bunbun*. Movie. DIR: Shigeru Omachi. SCR: Yuji Amemiya, Akira Nakahara. DES: Moribi Murano. ANI: Eiji Suzuki, Yasuhiko Suzuki, Yasuo Mori. MUS: Kazuhito Mori. PRD: TV Tokyo, Wako Pro. 30 mins. x 39 eps.
Bunbun the mastiff puppy climbs into a wooden box and floats down the river, eventually drifting into Tokyo. There he meets a stray dog who teaches him "the commandments"—how to live life without human interference. Based on a manga by former **MOOMIN** animator Moribi Murano, the plot and timing of this anime suggest a jump to TV in the wake of the success of **BANNERTAIL THE SQUIRREL**. An initial 84-minute TV movie was followed six months later by a TV series with the same cast and crew. In 1987, Bunbun returned in a 65-minute theatrical release directed by Toshio Hirata and animated by the Madhouse Studio.

BAROM ONE
2002. TV series. DIR: Tsuneo Tominaga. SCR: Narumitsu Taguchi. DES: Manabu Nakatake. ANI: Akemi Hosono, Hironobu Saito. MUS: Hiroshi Motokura. PRD: AT-X, Saito Pro. 25 mins. x 13 eps.
Kopu, personification of light, has been watching over our world for eons; the evil Gomon, personification of darkness, is sealed in sleep, but in the 21st century a major gravitational shift caused by a rare planetary alignment wakes its minions, spelling disaster for mankind. Kopu chooses two human boys, born on the same day, and imprints them with the power to fight Gomon. Kentaro Shiratori and Takeshi Kido grow up as close friends, with complementary abilities: one very clever, the other very strong. Not even their love for the same girl, classmate Yuko, can separate them. On their birthday Kopu appears to the teenagers and tells them they will secretly transform into powerful robot Barom One to save their world, starting by battling a giant stray dog-monster attacking Taiyo City. Takeshi takes to being Barom One like a duck to water; Kentaro isn't so keen until Gorom possesses his father's old car and turns it into a monster to attack him. The boys fight off a monkey monster at the zoo, Hercules beetle monsters in a petshop, and a Venus flytrap monster on a school trip. They only deal with this last threat after it has eaten some obnoxious kids, which gives Kentaro a crisis of conscience—shouldn't they save bad people along with good ones? Meanwhile Kentaro's mother Mariko analyzes the monsters' DNA and connects them with a local lake, and Gomon's plotting gets Barom One blamed for a mysterious earthquake the rocks Japan. When their loved ones are kidnapped, Kentaro and Takeshi have no choice but to blow their cover and come out fighting to save those they love as well as the rest of the world.

Barom One began life as a manga by **GOLGO 13**–creator Takao Saito, before being adapted into a 35-episode live-action TV series in 1972 (*DE). This anime incarnation was ostensibly put into production to mark the 30th anniversary of the original—although it is likely that cause and effect were reversed, since producers at the time were desperate for remakes of old shows, regarding them as safer bets in the impecunious early 21st century than any original ideas. The story has more in common with Yokoyama's **BABEL II** or Tezuka's **AMBASSADOR MAGMA** than with Saito's better known work, and the combination of silly yet deadly monsters with teenage moral dilemmas and fears is unsettling.

BASARA *
1998. JPN: *Legend of Basara*. TV series. DIR: Nobuhiro Takamoto. SCR: Takao Koyama. DES: Keizo Shimizu. ANI: Hideaki Matsuzaki. MUS: N/C. PRD: KSS, Chiba TV. 30 mins. x 13 eps.
In a postapocalyptic future the Gold King of Kings splits his land into quarters for his color-coded children to rule. In the domain of the youngest, the Red King, the blind prophet Nagi predicts that a desert village will bring forth twins, a boy and a girl, and that the boy shall depose the ruler. The Red King hears the prophecy and sends his army to the village—the boy, Tatara, is killed, but his sister, Sarasa, takes on his prophetic role by cutting off her hair and putting on his clothes. Impersonating Tatara, she convinces the villagers that there is still hope and sets off to retrieve her brother's sword, Byattsuko.

Wounded by the Red King, she is taken to a secluded lake by Kakuji (one of the few villagers who knows her secret). There, she falls in love with a young man called Shuri, though she is unaware that "Shuri" is the Red King, and he is unaware that his new love is the woman who has sworn to destroy him.

Already a success with **THERE GOES TOMOE**, manga artist Yumi Tamura turned to fantasy in 1990. A one-shot "image video" was released in 1993 after *Basara* won the Shogakukan Manga Prize, but the story only became a full-fledged TV series in 1998. The theme of a girl taking on a boy's mission also appears in **YOTODEN**, though the ancestor of all such shows is Osamu Tezuka's **PRINCESS KNIGHT**. The TV series was preceded by a 30-minute *Basara Prologue Video* (1998) which included clips from the show, details of some of the publicity events and radio dramas, and an introduction to the original manga.

BASEBALL CLUB NUMBER THREE

1988. JPN: *Meimon! Daisan Yakyu Bu.* AKA: *Noble! Baseball Club Number Three.* TV series. DIR: Hiroshi Fukutomi. SCR: Ryuji Yamada. DES: Hiroshi Kanezawa. ANI: Hiroshi Kanezawa. MUS: Yusuke Honma. PRD: Fuji TV, NAS. 25 mins. x 40 eps.

The struggles of a particularly bad baseball team as it fights to win against other schools and the far superior "Number One" and "Number Two" teams at its own Sakura High School. Toshiyuki Mutsu's gag manga in *Shonen Magazine* obviously hit the market at the right moment, lasting for ten volumes and spawning this relatively long-running series. More romantic takes on baseball would come in a slew of other anime, including NINE and SLOW STEP.

BASEBALL TEAM APACHE

1971. JPN: *Apache Yakyugun.* AKA: *Apache Baseball Team.* TV series. DIR: Kazuya Miyazaki, Isao Takahata, Minoru Okazaki, Masayuki Akehi, Issei Shigeno, Osamu Kasai, Masatoshi Sasaki. SCR: Kobako Hanato, Sachi Umemoto. DES: Keisuke Morishita. ANI: Shingo Araki, Keisuke Morishita, Akinori Namase, Joji Kikuchi, Takeo Takakura, Arata Fukuda, Fusahito Nagaki, Yasu Ishiguro. MUS: Koichi Fukube. PRD: Nippon Educational Television (later TV Asahi), Toei Animation. 25 mins. x 26 eps.

Dojima plays a perfect game in the national high school showcase tournament at Koshien (see MAN'S AN IDIOT!), but an arm injury (compare to H2) and a conflict with his father send him back to high school baseball to coach at a school in a remote mountain village. It's near the site of a new dam, the numbers of pupils are dwindling, and they're an unathletic and unmotivated bunch. There's only one teacher left—Chieko, granddaughter of the principal. Bit by bit, as Dojima gets to know each pupil and finds out what motivates each of them, he manages to pull together a team.

Based on the manga in *Shonen King* monthly, by Kobako Hanato and Sachio Umemoto, this high school baseball drama would probably have sunk without a trace below fan radar but for the involvement of one of the great names of anime; future Studio Ghibli star Takahata directed episodes 2, 12, and 17. Writer Hanato provided his own scripts and would go on to write the live-action drama *The Show-Off* (*DE).

BASILISK *

2005. JPN: *Koga Ninpocho.* AKA: *Koga Ninja Chronicles.* TV series. DIR: Fumitomo Kizaki, Yukio Nishimoto. SCR: Yasuyuki Muto. DES: Michinori Chiba. ANI: Kenji Fujita. MUS: Takashi Nakagawa. PRD: Gonzo. 25 mins. x 24 eps.

In A.D. 1614, the Tokugawa Shogunate is suffering from a succession crisis. Hidetada Tokugawa (grown-up son of the hero of YOUNG TOKUGAWA IEYASU) is undecided about which of his children will succeed him when he retires. Behind the scenes are two rival clans of ninja who have played secret and crucial roles in the civil war, now each backing a different son of Hidetada. They agree to settle their dispute in a unique way, sending ten champions to fight to the death—the winner to receive the support of the Shogun, power in the new order, and ownership of a sacred scroll. However, it has been some time since the civil war—those who fought in the conflict also alluded to in YOTODEN are now venerable grandparents. Much to the exasperation of the older generation, their children are not taking the ninja business quite as seriously—Gennosuke of the Koga clan has fallen in love with Oboro, a pretty girl from the Iga clan.

Ninja are a popular staple of anime, and often used as juvenile entertainments for naughty children, from HATTORI THE NINJA to NINJA CADETS. *Basilisk*, however, has a much more impressive path to the screen, beginning life as a novel by NINJA SCROLL-creator Futaro Yamada, reimagined for the younger generation in manga form by Masaki Segawa for *Young Magazine Uppers*. It also rode a wave of interest in the period following the success of *Aoi* (*DE), a year-long live-action TV series from 2003 that prepared the real-world historical background for this anime adaptation, which also includes a welcome return to old-fashioned bloodshed and intrigue. There are a lot of NARUTO fans out there, but truly, ninja are supposed to kill people, and *Basilisk* gives them plenty of opportunity. **V**

BASTARD *

1992. JPN: *Bastard: Ankoku no Hakkaijin.* AKA: *Bastard: God-Destroyer of Darkness.* Video. DIR: Katsuhito Akiyama. SCR: Hiroshi Yamaguchi. DES: Hiroyuki Kitazume. ANI: Moriyasu Taniguchi, Hiroyuki Ochi. MUS: Kohei Tanaka. PRD: AIC, Anime R. 30 mins. x 6 eps.

Humanity lives a quasi-medieval existence on an Earth in the midst of apocalypse. Dark Schneider, a powerful sorcerer, causes such havoc that high priest Dio traps him inside the body of a newborn baby, Rushe Renren. Fifteen years later, Schneider's former henchmen (Abigail the dark priestess, Kall-Su the king of ice, Gara the ninja master, and Arshes Nei the empress of thunder) return on a campaign to conquer the world for the fallen angel Anthrasax. Dio must bring Schneider back from limbo and orders his virgin daughter Tia to kiss the lovestruck boy in order to free the man. Their savior arrives, and he is a complete bastard.

Creator Kazushi Hagiwara began as an assistant to Izumi Matsumoto on KIMAGURE ORANGE ROAD before becoming a solo artist in his own right. Though the anime *Bastard* stops before the final showdown with Kall-Su, the manga series would continue far beyond, with Schneider assembling his four horsemen of the apocalypse and fighting a final war between Satan and the angels, all the while trying to come to terms with Rushe's boyish love for princess Tia.

Many of the names in the *Bastard*

series come from Western rock, including the kingdoms of Metallicana, Judas, Aran Maiden, and Whitesnake, the high priest Dio, the battleship King Crimson Glory, and the names of spells include Megadeth, Slayer, Guns'n'Ro, Venom, Tesla, Kiss, Raven, and Exodus. "Bastard" was the original name planned for Motorhead, and Dark Schneider himself is named after Udo Dirkschneider, the lead singer of Accept. Such blasé jokiness seems to work in *Bastard*, though if tried too often, it can grate painfully—just compare with the sausage-machine attitude of Satoru Akahori's shows in a similar vein, such as **Maze** or **Sorcerer Hunters**. **N**

BASTARD WARRIOR

1990. JPN: *Ajin Senshi*. Video. DIR: Tsuneo Tominaga. SCR: Kazumi Koide. DES: Yoshiaki Matsuda. ANI: Tsuneo Tominaga. MUS: Yuki Nakajima. PRD: Magic Bus. 100 mins.
During a war in 2200, in which both sides utilize psychic weapons, Zero is born of mixed parentage, a Terran mother and an alien father, the last survivor of the Mint clan of sorcerers. In this adaptation of the SF novel by Chiaki Kawamata, it is Zero's destiny to fight the Manjidara Empire and prevent it from seizing control of the galaxy. **V**

BATS AND TERRY

1987. Movie. DIR: Tetsuro Amino. SCR: Yasushi Hirano. DES: Noriyasu Yamauchi, Indori-Koya. ANI: Noriyasu Yamauchi, Kenichi Maejima. MUS: Tatsumi Yano. PRD: Sunrise, Matsutake, Magic Bus. 80 mins.
Batsu and Terry ("battery," as in the baseball sense) are a pitcher and catcher devoted to sports, bikes, girls, and good times. When they try to console Anne, a pretty girl who loses her biker boyfriend in a traffic accident, they are dragged into gangland intrigue and must rescue the damsel in distress before the next day's game. Set in Yokohama's Shonan district, home to other road-knight tales such as **Bomber**

Bikers of Shonan and **GTO**, this feel-good crime caper was shown as a double bill with the **Dirty Pair** movie *Project Eden*. The first Sunrise production to be adapted from a manga, it had its origins in Yasuichi Oshima's serial in *Shonen Magazine*.

BATTLE ANGEL *

1993. JPN: *Gunmu*. AKA: *Gun-Dream*. Video. DIR: Hiroshi Fukutomi. SCR: Akinori Endo. DES: Nobuteru Yuki. ANI: Nobuteru Yuki. MUS: Kaoru Wada. PRD: Animate Film, KSS, Movic. 35 mins. x 2 eps.
Though the floating island of Zalem is thought to be a heavenly paradise, few have been there. Instead, the poor scavenge from the giant scrap heap where Zalem throws its garbage. Daisuke Ido and his ex-girlfriend, Chiren, are two experts in cybernetics, forced to ply their trade in the scrapyard after falling out of favor on Zalem. Chiren will do anything to get back home and builds bigger and better modifications for cyborg gladiators. Ido prefers to work as a cyberdoctor for impoverished cyborgs, moonlighting as a bounty hunter. Poking around in Zalem's trash, Ido finds the remains of a cyborg, complete with the irreplaceable spinal cord. He fixes "her" up, names her Alita (Gally in the original), and has his very own robot "daughter" to keep him company. Alita develops a crush on local odd-job boy Yugo, pesters her adoptive dad when he's trying to work, and accidentally reveals that she has superhuman kung-fu skills.
    This short-lived spin-off from Yukito Kishiro's 1991 *Business Jump* manga never explains what life on Zalem is really like, why Ido was thrown out, or who the amnesiac Alita was before she was scrapped. The scene is set for a couple of fight scenes and some mawkish flirting between Yugo and Alita before the innocents of the story realize that the corrupt adults have been stringing them along, and it all ends in tears. Highly regarded in the early 1990s by an anime audience punch-

drunk on **Fist of the North Star**, *BA* wasn't particularly original—it takes little to substitute drugs for cybernetics and the scrap heap for an LA ghetto before you have *Boyz N the Hood*. A postholocaust world where one has to buy social betterment was covered more interestingly in **Grey: Digital Target**, whereas Earth as a celestial race's garbage dump was first suggested in Shinichi Hoshi's 1970s short story "Hey! Come On Out!" Initially inspired by **Microman** toys, Alita herself began life as an illustration around which Kishiro had to work up a story in a hurry, elements of which survive in the anime's fuzzy plotting: she doesn't know much about her past because, at this stage in the story's history, her creator wasn't that sure himself.
    Director Fukutomi does the best he can here with the limited budget, but there simply isn't the time to do the story justice, and one amazing image of a paradisiacal city hovering above a disgusting junkyard does not a successful series make. Viewers can take solace, however, in a high amount of immortal dialogue, including, "How long am I going to have to wait for my new spine?"

BATTLE ATHLETES *

1997. JPN: *Battle Athletess* [sic] *Daiundokai*. AKA: *Battle Athletess Great Sports Meet*. Video, TV series. DIR: Kazuhiro Ogawa, Katsuhito Akiyama. SCR: Hideyuki Kurata. DES: Ryoichi Makino. ANI: Shinji Ochi, Nobuyuki Kitajima. MUS: Takayuki Hattori. PRD: Pioneer, TV Tokyo, Aeon. 30 mins. x 6 eps. (V), 25 mins. x 26 eps. (TV).
In the year 4998, athletes strive for the glittering Cosmo Beauty prize on University Satellite. Akari Kanzaki is one such candidate, and the daughter of a former Cosmo Beauty. With little confidence in her own abilities, she still gains the respect and friendship of her multinational teammates. But University Satellite is not merely a sports club, it is a training ground where generations of humans have been secretly honed to perfection for

the ultimate battle against a race of sports-loving aliens.

Despite a passionless and cynical execution, this 1990s comedy update of GUNBUSTER still contains moments of subtle humor, such as an invading alien queen delivering a message of conquest to a pair of bewildered giraffes. The original video series, based on an idea by EL HAZARD's Hiroki Hayashi, stumbles amateurishly through several pointless prologues about World War III, a natural disaster, and still another war before settling down to the story. The later TV series *Battle Athletes: Victory* does a more coherent job, throwing the viewer straight into comedy training setups such as cycling on a roller-coaster track or pulling giant garden rollers across a minefield. Akari works hard (a staple of all such anime, since being a "natural" implies one is lazy) and befriends a plucky Osaka girl, assorted Caucasian also-rans, a comic-relief Chinese rich-bitch, and a feral African girl who is supposed to be cute. The characters laugh at their own jokes and intone antiquated pep talks and clichés from classic shows like AIM FOR THE ACE.

In the grand finale held before a giant headless statue of the Goddess of Victory, Akari is forced to compete against the aliens' champion, the rejuvenated form of her own mother, while her ailing coach (and father) looks on. The Pioneer English dub is excellent as usual, though it is a mystery why the company squandered such riches on a mediocre hybrid of *The Last Starfighter* and *Triumph of the Will*.

BATTLE CAN CAN *

1987. Video. DIR: Kazuya Sasaki. SCR: Kazuhiro Kasai. DES: N/C. ANI: Joji Oshima. MUS: N/C. PRD: Studio G7, Nikkatsu. 30 mins.
The Battle Can Can investigation team is sent out to halt pirate incursions in the space-year 2087. Sophia, Diane, Jill, Marina, and Lily (with a comic–relief robot, Harold) must retrieve the Cosmic Firefly, a fragile jewel worth literally billions. With so much at stake

Battle of the Planets

© 1978 SANDY FRANK SYNDICATION, INC.

they must subdue space pirates, have sex with aliens, and confront a traitor from within. Nikkatsu was surprisingly ahead of its time with this sci-fi porno; it would take another decade for ADVANCER TINA and ALIEN FROM THE DARKNESS to prove that there truly was no hope for the genre. Ⓝ

BATTLE OF THE PLANETS *

1972. JPN: *Kagaku Ninjatai Gatchaman*. AKA: *Science Ninja Team Gatchaman, G-Force, Eagle Riders*. TV series, movie, video. DIR: Jinzo Toriumi, Eiko Toriumi, Fumio Kurokawa, Hiroshi Sasagawa, Katsuhisa Yamada. SCR: Jinzo Toriumi, Toshio Nagata, Akiyoshi Sakai. DES: Tatsuo Yoshida, Kunio Okawara. ANI: Miyamoto Sado. MUS: Bob Sakuma. PRD: Tatsunoko, Fuji TV. 30 mins. x 205 eps. (TV), 110 min (m), 45 mins. x 3 eps. (v)
Only five young heroes and their giant God-Phoenix aircraft can save Earth from the invading legions of the alien Gallacter. In each episode, Gallacter would send a mechanized menace to terrorize the planet, and the Gatchaman team would stop him, graphically slicing through the enemy minions with weapons such as their *shuriken* and yo-yo bombs, all the while inexplicably dressed in bird costumes.

Though preceded by the five-strong teams of SKYERS 5 and *Thunderbirds* (see THUNDERBIRDS 2086), *Battle of the Planets* was a watershed show, with strong leader Eagle Ken, loose cannon Condor Joe, love interest Swan June, big-guy Owl Ryu, and little Swallow Jinpei setting up group dynamics that would dominate anime character rosters for decades to come. Episodes 22 and 37, *The Fiery Phoenix vs. the Fire-Eating Dragon* and *Electron Beast Renzilla*, were shown theatrically in 1973 as part of Toho's summer and winter holiday film anthologies. In 1978, acclaimed live-action director Kihachi Okamoto made a genuine anime movie version in which Gatchaman joined forces with the mysterious pilot Charm Red Impulse (Red Specter), who would eventually be revealed as Ken's estranged father.

Eighty-five of the original 105 episodes were adapted for the Sandy Frank English-language version broadcast in the U.S. in 1978. The enemy was renamed Spectra, a dying planet whose Great Spirit had ordered the evil Zoltar to conquer Earth and neighboring worlds in the Federation of Planets. The characters' names were also changed—Mark, Jason, Princess, Tiny, and Keyop were now fighting "attacks by alien galaxies beyond space." With much of the violence cut, additional footage was commissioned to bridge continuity gaps. This included a babbling robot controller, 7-Zark-7, a mascot, 1-Rover-1, shots of the team off-duty in their Ready Room, and, since the group was now supposedly traveling around the universe, several sequences of the Phoenix flying through space.

When Sandy Frank's rights lapsed in 1986, the original series was completely redubbed as *G-Force* by Turner Broadcasting, which dispensed altogether with the 7-Zark-7 footage and selected many episodes from the original run that had not previously been seen outside Japan. The series included more deaths and was more faithful to the original, though the names were again replaced with the awful Ace Goodheart, Dirk Daring, Agatha June, Hootie, and Pee Wee. A ratings disaster, the new show was quietly buried and only seen in its entirety in Australia, though it did eventually return to American TV when Turner established the Cartoon Network in 1995.

The 1979 Japanese sequel *Gatchaman II* featured early design work from Akemi Takada and Yoshitaka Amano, adding another 52 episodes to the original, along with the female foil Professor Pandora, and a complex plot in which Joe is mortally wounded, saved by cybernetic augmentation in the style of **KIKAIDER**, and temporarily replaced by a Gallacter spy, whom he eventually kills. This was followed in 1979 by another 48 episodes, *Gatchaman F(ighter)*. Both serials were eventually bought by Saban Entertainment in 1996, cut down to 65 episodes, and released as *Eagle Riders*. The characters were renamed for a third time, as Hunter Harris, Joe Thax, Kelly Jenar, Ollie Keeawani, and Mickey Dougan.

Their mission: "To defend the global good."

In 1994, the series was remade in Japan, compressed into a three-part video outing called simply *Gatchaman* by director Hiroyuki Fukushima with character designs by Yasuomi Umezu. The show was swiftly dubbed for an American anime market now more aware of its origins. The original Japanese names were retained, and in a bizarre coincidence, the voice actor who played Joe, Richard Cansino, also lent his talents in *Eagle Riders* to the role of Hunter Harris.

BATTLE ROYALE HIGH SCHOOL *

1987. JPN: *Shinmajinden*. AKA: *Tale of True Devilry*. Video. DIR: Ichiro Itano. SCR: Ichiro Itano. DES: Nobuteru Yuki. ANI: Nobuteru Yuki, Satoshi Urushihara, Hideaki Anno. MUS: Shiro Sagisu. PRD: DAST. 55 mins.

A time-traveling security officer must prevent an extradimensional demon lord from taking over the world. But the demon-lord in question has taken over the body of a high school karate teacher in modern-day Tokyo. The demon-hunter sent to get him has also been possessed, but by an evil fairy queen who wants the planet for herself.

Shinichi Kuruma's original manga in *Shonen Captain* was based on a story by **AMON SAGA**'s Baku Yumemakura. Looking like a toned-down version of the later **NIGHTMARE CAMPUS**, the anime version simply restored much of the gore for a straight-to-video audience. Animator Anno and composer Sagisu would later work together again on **EVANGELION**. No relation to the live-action Kinji Fukasaku film *Battle Royale* (2000). **⓪Ⓝ⓿**

BATTLE SKIPPER *

1995. Video. DIR: Takashi Watanabe. SCR: Hidemi Kubota. DES: Takashi Kobayashi, Kimitoshi Yamane. ANI: Takashi Kobayashi, Toshiko Sasaki. MUS: Kenyu Miyotsu. PRD: Artmic, Tokyo Kids. 30 mins. x 3 eps.

"In the Etiquette Club, the first rule is strength! The second rule is strength! There is no third or fourth rule, but the fifth rule is strength!" Rivalries at St. Ignacio's Catholic girls' school get out of hand when rich-bitch Sayaka starts using giant "battle skipper" robots to dominate those who oppose her Debutante Club. Only a group of unknown vigilantes foils her plans, and little does Sayaka know that the Exstars vigilantes are actually the unassuming freshmen of the undersubscribed Etiquette Club—current membership, two.

Rie and Reika are looking for recruits, but it's difficult when they are not allowed to tell new arrivals that their deserted clubhouse is really an underground base containing their secret arsenal. New girls Kanami, Saori, and Shihoko sneak into the clubhouse, where they stumble across the color-coded battlesuits that almost seem made for them. . . .

Initially created to promote Tomy's MRV toy line, *Battle Skippers* mixes elements of *Thunderbirds* and **BUBBLEGUM CRISIS** with the school satire of **PROJECT A-KO** and **DEBUTANTE DETECTIVES**. The three episodes were edited into a "movie" compilation for the U.S. video market and resolicited after director Watanabe became better known for **SLAYERS**.

BATTLE TEAM LAKERS EX *

1996. JPN: *Seishojo Sentai Lakers EX*. AKA: *Holy Girl Battle Team Lakers EX*. Video. DIR: Takashi Kawamura. SCR: Ryusei. DES: Koichi Fujii, Mitsuharu Miyamae. ANI: Koichi Fujii. MUS: Kazuya Matsushita, Hideo Kuroda. PRD: Beam Entertainment, Animate Film. 30 mins.

Five exiled space warriors live undercover as Tokyo college girls, sworn to use their Laker power to defend Earth from the evil queen Oleana of the Godram empire. Would-be singer Reiko (Star), hot-headed Chiaki (Kung Fu), bespectacled Yayoi (Soul), big-chested tomboy Natsumi (Judo), and baby-faced Yuka (Bunny) all lust after their team leader, the handsome Akira (Blade Knight). After a rehearsal for

Reiko's forthcoming concert, Akira convinces Reiko to try out a sex toy to help amass greater energy for battle. Meanwhile, Oleana sends four robot doppelgangers to pose as Akira and seduce the other girls. The next day, the girls assume that Akira has swindled them and refuse to follow orders when one of Oleana's giant monsters attacks the school. They are captured and taken to Oleana's spaceship but rescued by Akira. Lacking the energy to transform, they stage an impromptu orgy to regain their powers and escape.

A soft-core pastiche of the all-girl team shows that began with **SAILOR MOON**, even to the extent of posing as just one episode in a long-running saga, *Lakers EX* barely has time for a setup and showdown. Not quite hitting the ludicrous heights of **VENUS FIVE** (though the voice acting is superior to many other erotic anime dubs), the careful duplication of hack genre conventions ironically leaves little time for the sex. Based on a computer game. **N**

BAVI STOCK

1985. Video. DIR: Shigenori Kageyama. SCR: Kenji Terada. DES: Mutsumi Inomata, Takahiro Tomoyasu. ANI: Masahiro Shida, Ryunosuke Otonashi. MUS: Yasuaki Honda. PRD: Hero Media, Kaname Pro, Studio Unicorn. 45 mins. x 2 eps.
Agent Kate Lee Jackson of the GPP (space police) frees the mute girl Muma from a space prison on a huge satellite called the Bentika Empire. She also frees Bavi Stock, a young boxer jailed after accidentally killing an opponent. The prison doctor, Sammy, who has been trying to ensure that Bavi stays alive, joins them, and they head for GPP HQ. But bad guys from Bentika, the psionic Ruth Miller and her henchman, Eyesman, disintegrate the GPP homeworld. With nowhere else to go, our heroes head for Sammy's homeworld, arriving on the eve of a big sky-sled race. Sammy and Bavi enter and face off against Eyesman, while Ruth Miller tries to sabotage the control computers, and Kate and Muma have to stop her. In the aftermath,

Ruth is trapped in an alternate dimension, and Muma is revealed as the key to the downfall of the Bentika Empire.

Cherry-picking the destruction of planet Alderaan, the rescue of Princess Leia, and the Endor speeder-bike chase from the early *Star Wars* films, *Bavi Stock* is a deliberate attempt to reverse-engineer U.S. space opera. It even features Americanized names, though some of them are altered beyond recognition in transit—Bavi is a mutation of Bobby, "as in Bavi Kennedy," according to producer Hiromasa Shibazaki. Less innocent *Star Wars* rip-offs can be found in **BONDAGE QUEEN KATE**.

BEAST CITY *

1996. JPN: *Inju Dai Toshi*. AKA: *Lust-Beast Great City*. Video. DIR: Shinichiro Watanabe. SCR: Naomi Hayakawa, Yuri Kanai. DES: Naomi Hayakawa. ANI: Hitoshi Imazaki. MUS: N/C. PRD: Comstock, Karasu Communications. 45 mins. x 3 eps.
Tokyo is held for ransom by the demonic Beasts that stalk its streets. Born into a family of vampires, Mina has vowed to destroy all of the creatures with her Beast-hunter sword.

Sex and violence galore as Mina and her bisexual vampire associates from Draculon get their daily fix by having oral sex with a sleeping human and sinking their teeth into his engorged penis, all without waking him up. Then they go looking for a fight, get knocked about a bit, and kill some demons.

Though its premise is distantly related to **VAMPIRE HUNTER D**, *Beast City* removes all the subtextual tension of vampire stories. A heroine named for Bram Stoker's original and a homeworld poached from *Vampirella* do little good when the rest of vampire lore is taken with a pinch of salt—these creatures still fear crucifixes but happily immerse themselves beneath running water in long shower scenes. In Japan, the series was partly sold to the public on the basis that sharp-eared viewers would hear several famous voice actresses grunting and groan-

ing behind pseudonyms, a sure-fire sign of a lack of faith in other aspects of production (see **ADVENTURE KID**). Two other Naomi Hayakawa creations have been animated: *Binding* (as part of **COOL DEVICES**) and **MELANCHOLY SLAVE**. Similar liberties were taken with legends about werewolves to create **MIDNIGHT PANTHER**. **ONV**

BEAST WARRIORS *

1992. JPN: *KO Seiki Beast Sanjushi*. AKA: *KO Century Beast Three Beast-keeters*; *KO Century Beast Warriors*. Video. DIR: Hiroshi Negishi. SCR: Satoru Akahori, Tetsuko Watanabe, Mayori Sekijima, Koji Masunari. DES: Zero-G Room, Rei Nakahara, Takehiko Ito. ANI: Takuya Saito, Makoto Matsuo. MUS: Nick Wood. PRD: KSS. 30 mins. x 7 eps.
On an Earth literally broken in two, the evil Humans have invaded the territory of the heavily mutated Beast tribes. Though they possess powerful totem weapons, the Beasts cannot stand against the Humans' high-tech might. Wan Dabada, who can transform into a tiger when angry, is captured when his tribe is destroyed and thrown into jail with three other Beasts: Meima, the mermaid princess; Mekka, the turtle boy; and Badd Mint, the transforming chicken. Professor Password, a human scientist ashamed at his race's behavior, is killed helping them escape but not before entrusting the group with his granddaughter, Yumi Charm. Searching for the mythical Gaia system that could turn the battle, they find one of its outposts by draining a lake—elements here not only of **TREASURE ISLAND**, but also of director Negishi's earlier **LADIUS**. With Yumi's help, they learn how to combine their totems into a superweapon, though a power supply proves harder to come by.

As with other Akahori creations like **MAZE** and **KNIGHTS OF RAMUNE**, the hackneyed but entertaining *Beast Warriors* has a flimsy plot concealed by tongue-in-cheek humor and loud, brash designs—here including costumes by **OH MY GODDESS!**–creator Kosuke

Fujishima. The initial series is clearly the setup for a TV version that never came, and the final four episodes (renamed *Beast Warriors II* and written, in part, by future **PHOTON**-director Masunari) simply adds some new designs and an extra subplot similar to that surrounding Rini in **SAILOR MOON**. As the first and only release of the ill-fated Anime U.K. label, it was also a failure in its English version—never making enough money to justify the release of the final four episodes and never distributed in the U.S. When rights lapsed in the British edition, the series was picked up by the U.S. distributor Right Stuf, who renamed it *KO Beast*. The Right Stuf version dubs all seven episodes, not merely the first three, with an all-new cast. For the origins of the name "Wan Dabada," see **WANDABA STYLE**.

BEAT ANGEL ESCALAYER *

2002. JPN: *Cho Subaru Tenshi Escalayer*. AKA: *Super Pleiades Angel Escalayer*. Video. DIR: Ikka Tsuchida, Keiichiro Katsura, Zuko Ogo. SCR: Yujiro Muramatsu. DES: Shinichi Miyame. ANI: Raisuke Hayashi. MUS: N/C. PRD: Pink Pineapple. 30 mins. x 3 eps.
High school lothario Kyohei hopes to add new transfer student Sayuka to his list of conquests. At first, he suspects she is a lesbian, only to discover that her sexy roommate Madoka is merely there as a temporary measure. Sayuka is actually a battle android on a mission to save the world, but she runs on a "Doki-Doki Dynamo" that requires sexual energy to charge her up. The Earth is under threat from the similarly-fueled minions of an entity called the Dielast, and with Madoka failing to provide what Sayuka really needs, Kyohei manfully steps up to do his duty in a rip-off of **DEVADASY**—what the hell, two years had passed, who was going to notice? **🅛🅝🅥**

BEAT SHOT

1989. Video. DIR: Takashi Akimoto. SCR: Hidemi Kamata. DES: Satoshi Ikezawa. ANI: Hiroyuki Oka. MUS:

N/C. PRD: Gainax, AIC. 30 mins.
Expert linksman Akihiko joins the university golf club at the same time as maverick golfer Akikazu. The pair often tee off against each other, though Akikazu is distracted by the charms of his opponent's beautiful caddy, Misako. A heady mix of sex and golf in this adaptation of a manga from *Monthly Playboy* (no relation to the U.S. magazine). Creator Satoshi Ikezawa normally specializes in racing stories like **CIRCUIT WOLF** but here replaces the tension of fast cars with furtive fumblings in the rough.

BEATON THE ROBOBOY

1976. JPN: *Robokko Beaton*. AKA: *Little Robot Viton*. TV series. DIR: Yu Tachibana, Tetsu Dezaki, Takao Yotsuji, Masuji Harada, Mitsuo Kobayashi. SCR: Kiyoharu Matsuoka, Soji Yoshikawa, Yoshiaki Yoshida, Hiroshi Kaneko. DES: Yoshikazu Yasuhiko. ANI: Yoshikazu Yasuhiko. MUS: Mamoru Fujisawa. PRD: Nippon Sunrise, Tohoku Shinsha. 25 mins. x 50 eps.
Ma-chan receives a self-assembly robot from his uncle in America, and seeks help in building it from local inventor Mr. Nobel in putting it together. Nobel botches the assembly and connects the wrong circuits, ironically creating a malfunctioning companion in the style of **DORAEMON**, albeit with a bonus built-in jet engine. Slapstick comedy ensues, involving Beaton, Ma-chan, his girlfriend Urara, local bad boy Bratman ("Gaki-oyaji"), and his Nazi-helmeted assistant Bratranger ("Gaki-ranger"). Beaton has three critical weaknesses that can be used against him. Water makes him rust; he has an **ULTRAMAN**-style three-minute limit on operations; and he is subject to a remote control device. He confiscates the controller from Ma-chan and hides it in a cavity in his chest, but if anyone manages to obtain it they can manipulate Beaton for their own ends.

BE-BOP HIGH SCHOOL

1990. Movie. DIR: Toshihiko Ariseki, Hiroyuki Kadokane, Junichi Fujise.

SCR: Kazuhiro Kiuchi, Tatsuhiko Urahata. DES: Kazuhiro Kiuchi. ANI: Junichi Haneyama. MUS: Ginjiro Ito. PRD: Toei. 45 mins. x 7 eps.
School tough-guys Toru and Hiroshi have impossibly wedge-shaped haircuts and a deep love of pretty girls. Forever fighting against the authority of the weak-willed principal they refer to as Turtle Man, they live only to scrap with rival gangs like the Hitman Brothers in this anime spin-off of the 1987 live-action film based on a manga by screenwriter Kazuhiro Kiuchi. The cartoonish nature of the original story made the anime infinitely preferable to the movie, which was hampered by poor acting and a cripplingly low budget (director Hiroyuki Nasu would make the equally bad *Pinch Runner* in 2000). The series also spawned the three-part *Be-Bop Pirate Edition*, a humorous spin-off supposedly written by "Memeoka Manhiro" in 1991. In 1991, four years after the sixth episode of the video, a final chapter was released in which the same amount of time had passed onscreen for the leads, taking them out of school and into the real world along with their audience.

BE-BOY KIDNAPPIN' IDOL

1989. Movie. DIR: Kenichi Yatsuya. SCR: Michiko Onuki. DES: Kazumi Oya, Naoyuki Onda. ANI: Naoyuki Onda. MUS: Katsunori Ishida. PRD: AIC. 30 mins.
Comical adventures of beautiful boy pop-idol Kazuya Shinohara and his dear friend, Akihiko Kudo. Featuring significant design input from girls' manga artist Kazumi Oya (creator of **OTOHIME CONNECTION**), this one-shot video was sold to the anime audience on the strengths of its two leads, Nozomu Sasaki (Tetsuo from **AKIRA**) and Takeshi Kusao (Pern from **LODOSS WAR**), in uncharacteristically romantic roles.

BECK *

2005. AKA: *Beck: Mongolian Chop Squad*. TV series. DIR: Osamu Kobayashi. SCR: Osamu Kobayashi. DES: Motonobu Hori, Osamu Kobayashi. ANI: N/C. MUS: Taku Hirai. PRD: Madhouse, TV Tokyo. 25 mins. x 26 eps.

Average eighth grader Yukio "Koyuki" Tanaka has no special talents or interesting hobbies, and is occasionally the victim of school bullies. While he's trying to rescue an ugly dog, his path crosses that of guitarist Ryusuke "Ray" Minami. The dog is Ray's beloved Beck, after whom his band and this anime series are named. Ray used to be in a band with rock legend Eddy, of top American band Dying Breed, he owns a superb Les Paul guitar he calls Lucille, and to Koyuki he seems the epitome of cool. Drawn into his world, Koyuki falls in love with music and the rock'n'roll lifestyle. But his new hero has some serious problems: he made many enemies in the U.S.A., including powerful promoter Leon Sykes, the original owner of both Beck and Lucille. As Koyuki's own talent develops, he acquires a guitar of his own (a Fender Telecaster) and becomes a lead vocalist with the group, which acquires a dual identity as "Mongolian Chop Squad" in America, because the U.S.A. already has a singer called Beck. *Beck* the anime smartly avoids the pitfalls of BLACK HEAVEN and GRAVITATION, dropping some of the comedy of Harold Sakuishi's original manga, and making the music one of the main stars of the show. The main leads each have two voice actors in the original Japanese release, one normal voice for dialogue, and actual singers for their performances, using vocalists from the bands Husking Bee and YKZ. The bilingual nature of the action and characters, however, leads to an amount of mixed English–Japanese dialogue in the original release, which is either cute or irritating, depending on where one stands. The anime is packed with references to rock staples and legends, many of which have been around far longer than its young audience. It has also inspired a game for the PS2.

BEE TRAIN

Animation company formed in 1997 by several former Tatsunoko staffers, including director Koichi Mashimo and producer Mitsuhisa Ishikawa (now more often associated with Production IG). Representative works include NOIR, MADLAX, and .HACK. Although, like Xebec and P.A. Works, Bee Train was created as a subsidiary of Tatsunoko, it is no longer so on paper, since Tatsunoko's percentage of the company's shares is no longer a controlling interest. The authors are not entirely sure whether this makes the slightest difference in the Japanese market, since Bee Train continues to work on Tatsunoko productions as if it still is a subsidiary!

BEET THE VANDEL BUSTER

2003. JPN: *Boken O Beet*. AKA: *Adventure King Beet*. TV series. DIR: Tatsuya Nagamine. SCR: Yoshimi Narita. DES: Katsuyoshi Nakatsura, Tadayoshi Yamamuro. ANI: Tadayoshi Yamamura. MUS: N/C. PRD: Toei, TV Tokyo, Dentsu, Bandai Visual. 25 mins. x 52 eps. (TV1); 25 mins. x ?? eps. (TV2).

During the unspecified "Century of Darkness," the world is besieged by evil vampire-devil hybrids, the *Vandels*. The last line of defense comprises the Vandel Busters, elite human warriors tasked with hunting the demons down. Beet idolizes his elder brother, Zenon, whose platoon all die defending the young Beet from the arch-demon Beltoze—leaving the inexperienced Beet to inherit five magical weapons invested with their life force, with shades here of *Rogue Trooper*, or the *Mighty Morphin' Power Rangers* (*DE). Five years on, Beet takes his place as a Vandel Buster. Beet's childhood friend, the cute Poala, is also a Vandel Buster, and she joins him on his quest to eliminate the evil Vandels. Based on the manga by Riku Sanjo and Koji Inada, serialized in *Shonen Jump* weekly. The manga's inspiration comes from gaming—if the scenario isn't clue enough, there are references to "leveling up" and "bosses." Beet's special ability, such as it is, involves staying awake for three days before collapsing in a virtual coma; presumably something with which anyone trying to complete the latest *Final Fantasy* installment can identify. From the 53rd episode onward, the series was rebranded *Boken O Beet Exelion*.

BEHIND CLOSED DOORS *

2001. JPN: *Waver*. Video. DIR: Shigenori Kurii. SCR: Hideo Ura. DES: Shigenori Kurii. ANI: Michitaka Yamamoto. MUS: N/C. PRD: Shindeban, Tenshindo, Museum Pictures, Milky. 30 mins. x 3 eps.

In an erotic anime that seems distantly informed by Pauline Réage's classic *The Story of O* (1954), Kenichi wins a mystery competition prize in the form of a CD, which he is instructed to put in his car's player and follow directions to the location of his real prize. He and his loving girlfriend Yoshino dutifully do so, only to find themselves at a remote mansion à la BLACK WIDOW, which soon turns out to be a brothel. Forced to spend the night, they discover a series of sadomasochistic prostitutes in different sectors of the house, many of whom seduce Kenichi after he quarrels with Yoshino. Before long, Yoshino slips deeper into the bondage lifestyle of the house's mistress and other inhabitants, with the sex depicted onscreen getting increasingly violent and unpleasant. **NV**

BELLE AND SEBASTIAN *

1981. JPN: *Meiken Jolly*. AKA: *Famous Dog Jolly*. TV series. DIR: Keiji Hayakawa, Shinji Okada, Kazuyoshi Yokota, Fumio Ikeno, Seiji Endo. SCR: Toshiyuki Kashiwakura, Soji Yoshikawa, Kunio Nakatani. DES: Shuichi Seki. ANI: Nobuyuki Kitajima. MUS: TT Nescebance. PRD: Toho, Visual 80, NHK. 25 mins. x 52 eps.

Named for the saint's day on which he was born and abandoned by his gypsy mother, Sebastian has been raised by Old Seasal, who may or may not be his grandfather. Rejected by the village children for having no parents, he befriends Jolly (Belle), a large Great Pyrenees dog hated and reviled as "the white devil." In search of somewhere to call home, the pair (and their comic-relief puppy, Poochie) journey across the Pyrenees in search of Sebastian's mother, which is similar to a quest seen in FROM THE APENNINES TO THE ANDES. Though they find many places to live (the Pyrenees seem to be littered with kindly childless couples willing to adopt a boy and his dogs), they are always forced to move on by the relentless pursuit of Garcia, an officer of the law who believes them to have committed a crime. Based on the children's books by Cecile Aubrey, this series was picked up by Nickelodeon in the 1980s. The original live-action TV series was shown on NHK in 1973.

BELOVED BETTY: DEVIL STORY

1986. JPN: *Itoshi no Betty: Ma Monogatari*. Video. DIR: Kazuo Koike, Masahito Sato. SCR: Hideo Takayashiki. DES: Kazuo Ohara. ANI: Michio Shindo. MUS: Haruki Mino. PRD: Big Bang, Cosmos, Toei. 53 mins.

A devil-girl with the face of an angel and a heart of gold, blonde Betty falls in love with an earthbound gangster, Danpei Kimogawa, when they meet in a rainstorm. They end up living together in a Tokyo highrise apartment, though Danpei has trouble coping with his new witch and demon in-laws dropping in at inopportune moments. Betty has actually been sent to the human world on a mission to defeat the demon Lutan. While Betty continues with her task, her skeletal grandmother sends nubile nymphs to tempt Danpei and see if he is suitable husband material. A Japanese knockoff of *Bewitched* but with a lowlife husband and considerably more sex, *Beloved Betty* thrived amid a 1980s Japanese fad for domestic magic. The same year saw the release of GOING STEADY WITH A WITCH, though both titles would soon be eclipsed by another alien lover more suitable for the mass market, URUSEI YATSURA's Lum. In this short video, also shown theatrically on a double bill with AMON SAGA, the hen-pecked Danpei was played by Yuji Miyake, a pop star from the group Set. Director

Koike also wrote the original 1980 manga, drawn by Seisaku Kano for *Big Comic*; though by the time the anime version was released, he was making more of a name for himself with CRYING FREEMAN. **Ⓝ**

BENEATH THE BLACK RAIN

1984. JPN: *Kuroi Ame ni Utarete*. Movie. DIR: Takeshi Shirato, Kazuhiko Udagawa. SCR: Motokazu Hara, Keiji Nakazawa, Takeshi Shirato. DES: Keiji Nakazawa. ANI: Kazuhiko Udagawa. MUS: Kitaro. PRD: Gen Pro, Tsuchida Pro. 90 mins.

BAREFOOT GEN–creator Keiji Nakazawa wrote an even darker series of tales for this anthology movie about several characters reacting in different ways to the ongoing effects of the atomic bomb. Yuri attempts a one-woman crusade against the U.S. by giving syphilis to servicemen; Yuko becomes a human museum, baring her burned and distorted skin as a testament to the effects of the bomb; while Eiko frets over whether she should get pregnant, since she is a child of bomb victims and may still carry mutant genes. **Ⓝ**

BENKEI VS. USHIWAKA

1939. JPN: *Benkei tai Ushiwaka*. Movie. DIR: Kenzo Masaoka. SCR: Kenzo Masaoka. DES: Kenzo Masaoka. ANI: Ryotaro Kuwata. MUS: N/C. PRD: Nippon Doga Kenkyu Tokoro. 10 mins.

Ushiwaka (aka Minamoto no Yoshitsune) lives in the forest and is trained in the martial arts by *tengu* crow spirits. One day he is walking through Kyoto when his path is blocked by a giant monk, Benkei, who has sworn to take the swords of a thousand defeated foes and now has but one left to collect before he can retire. The diminutive Ushiwaka, however, refuses to hand his sword over and trounces the giant monk on the Gojo bridge. Recognizing his true master, Benkei swears eternal loyalty. Often termed the "Robin Hood and Little John" of Japanese legend, stories of Yoshitsune and Benkei often crop up in JAPANESE FOLK TALES. However, sightings of them are curiously

rare in anime despite a rich tradition that could easily fill a series the size of RANMA ½. Apart from this single antique two-reeler, they can only be found in oblique references in other shows and in a couple of tales in the series JAPANESE HISTORY and MANGA PICTURES OF JAPAN.

BERSERK

1997. JPN: *Kenpu Dengi Berserk*. AKA: *Sword-Wind Chronicle Berserk*. TV series. DIR: Naohito Takahashi. SCR: Yasuhiro Imagawa, Atsuhiro Tomioka. DES: Yoshihiko Umakoshi, Tokuhiro Matsubara. ANI: Tokuhiro Matsubara, Yuriko Senba. MUS: Susumu Hirazawa. PRD: OLM, Nippon TV. 25 mins. x 25 eps.

Guts, a young mercenary who was instrumental in winning the army's last battle, is recruited into the elite mercenary company the Band of the Hawk, led by the charismatic Griffiths, whose ambitions are aimed squarely at the kingdom of Midland's throne. Guts rises rapidly to command in the Hawks, based on his immense skill in battle. Meanwhile, Griffiths and the Band of the Hawk prove their worth by winning battle after battle for Midland, themselves rising above high-ranking but untalented commanders. Worried at intrigues behind the scenes, he decides to leave, but his leader, Griffiths, does not allow him to go, forcing Guts to best him in combat. Griffiths is persecuted by noblemen who resent his promotion on account of his talent instead of blood relation, and he is eventually imprisoned; The Band of the Hawk is ambushed, scattered, and hunted. Guts returns, and the pretty Casca, Griffith's second-in-command (it is a boy's name in the real world, but is assigned to a girl, here), who has unrequited feelings for Griffiths, finds solace in Guts's arms, and eventually joins forces with him to lead a rescue mission. However, upon arrival, Guts discovers that Griffiths has been brutally crippled and maimed by torture. Griffiths, in despair and longing for power, eventually makes a pact with the God Hand, demon-gods who demand human sacrifice. Guts loses an eye and his left arm in the ensuing fight and is forced to watch as his comrades die, while Casca is raped by the creature that was once Griffiths. Hellbent on revenge, Guts sets off to hunt down God Hand.

With a hero whose magical wound will not heal, baddies named after SF greats (Conrad, Ubik, Slan, and Boskone), fighting on and off the battlefield, and no punches pulled in its savagery and devilry, *Berserk* was a manga hit with both readers and critics when it appeared in *Young Animal* magazine. Told chiefly in flashback, the anime series covers the early chapters of Kentaro Miura's manga. The series was lampooned in an episode of the **OH MY GODDESS!** comedy show, *Adventures of Mini-Goddess*, in which Skuld and Urd, dressed as Guts and Griffiths, must rescue Belldandy from a castle. There were rumors of a U.S. release following the publication of the *Sword of the Berserk* game on the Dreamcast, but negotiations were reportedly incomplete at our deadline. **V**

BETTERMAN *

1999. TV series. DIR: Yoshitomo Yonetani. SCR: Hiroshi Yamaguchi. DES: Masahiro Kimura, Kunio Okawara, Masahiro Yamane. ANI: Masahiro Kimura. MUS: Kohei Tanaka. PRD: Sunrise, TV Tokyo. 25 mins. x 14 eps.
The year is 2006. Keita Aono is a bespectacled schoolboy in Yokohama who is surprised to meet childhood sweetheart Hinoki Sai when she transfers to his school. The rainbow-haired Hinoki now works for Akamatsu Industrial Company (AIC—as in the anime studio), piloting the large robots called Neuronoids. These machines run on a kind of artificial blood called Linker Gel and patch directly into their pilots' nervous systems. When Hinoki's fellow pilot Cactus is killed in a battle with monsters called Algernons, Keita is talked into taking his place and discovers that he is one of the rare Dual Kind, able to synchronize almost perfectly with the complex machine. He

becomes a full-fledged pilot, though Hinoki's activities alongside him are often suspiciously supported by "Betterman Lamia," a man with the same hairstyle as her and an uncanny ability to turn up in the nick of time and save the day by transforming into the bioweapon Betterman Nebula.

In the grand tradition of **GUNDAM**, Sunrise filed the serial numbers off its standard story template and punched it out again post-**EVANGELION**—evidence, if ever it was required, that two years after you do something in the anime business, you can do it all over again and nobody will notice.

BEWITCHED AGNÈS

2005. JPN: *Okusama wa Maho Shojo*. AKA: *My Wife is a Magical Girl*. TV series. DIR: Hiroshi Nishikori, Yoshihisa Matsumoto. SCR: Yuji Matsukura, Kazuhiko Ikeguchi. DES: Shinya Hasegawa. ANI: Hiroshi Nishikori. MUS: N/C. PRD: JC Staff, Chiba. TV 25 mins. x 13 eps.
Kagura is a college graduate who has just moved to a quiet coastal town to start his new life. He takes a room in a boarding house run by pretty 26-year-old Ureshiko Asaba, whose author husband is a local celebrity. But there the similarity with **MAISON IKKOKU** ends. Ureshiko Asaba might appear to be an ordinary, pink-haired Japanese housewife, but she is really Agnès Bell, a superheroine sworn to protect the parallel world of Wonderland that co-exists with our dimension, but is only visible to those with sorcerous abilities. But now Agnès is far too old to be a magical girl—comically, she complains her costume no longer fits—and the rulers of the magic realm have ordered her to surrender her magic ring, the source of her power over the town, to Cruje, the new magical girl on the block.

Agnès, however, loves the town her mother created with a witchy attachment not seen since **KIKI'S DELIVERY SERVICE**, while Cruje has orders to destroy it and start anew. Her husband Tamotsu doesn't suspect a thing,

although he really ought to, because Agnès refuses to let him kiss her lest it sap her magic abilities. As their relationship (or lack of it) begins to sour, Agnès realizes that she may have to let him in on the secret.

As in **OH MY GODDESS!**, the magical realm is run along Western business/political lines by older men, who send out theoretically expendable girls to manage the outposts of magic in the human world for as long as they serve the purpose of their masters. All the magical girls have Japanese everyday names, but like call girls and strippers (or anime porn voice actresses) they assume different identities at work, and all their magic names are Western. There's some gentle humor and a dose of tear-jerking melodrama in a series with all the hallmarks of **LITTLE WITCH SALLY** and **COMET-SAN**, but with a title that acknowledges the American *Bewitched* (1964), one of the most important formative influences on early Japanese TV animation. Its profile increased considerably in the early 21st century through two revivals, related only through the chance acquisition of the series rights by Sony. *Bewitched in Tokyo* (2004, *Okusama wa Majo*) was a sanctioned live-action remake of the American series, broadcast on TV Asahi with Ryoko Yonekura in the leading role. Only a year later, the franchise got another boost from *Bewitched* (2005), the Nicole Kidman vehicle, making knock-offs like this anime pastiche a certainty. Although the story was credited to the animation company JC Staff, it began running as a manga by Toko Kanno in *Dengeki Gao* magazine several months before the initial broadcast. See also **SUGAR SUGAR RUNE** and **MY WIFE IS A HIGH SCHOOL STUDENT**.

BEYBLADE *

2001. JPN: *Bakuten Shoot Baybrade*. AKA: *Flashpoint Shoot Baybrade*. TV series. DIR: Toshifumi Kawase, Jun Takada, Masahiko Murata. SCR: Toshiyasu Okubo, Kiyoshi Mizugami, Tatsuhiko Urahata, Kazuyuki Fudeyasu.

DES: Takao Aoki. ANI: Shigeru Kato, Kiyoshi Nakahara. MUS: Yoshihisa Hirano. PRD: Madhouse, TV Tokyo. 25 mins. x 51 eps.

Takao Kinomiya wants to be a master of the gladiatorial Baybrade contest, but only the chosen few can truly control the Pit entities that live inside the spinning-top-like fighting devices. His friend Kai uses the Transor Pit, but Takao discovers a Pit of his own, the creature known as Dragoon, who has lived inside the family's heirloom sword for generations.

An anime based on the *begoma* toy craze, fighting gyroscopes from TRANS-FORMERS-creators Takara. The last gyro standing within the ring is the winner, and each has five component parts that can be customized to create (almost) unique toys. The post-POKÉMON generation in Japan set aside its Pikachus and Jigglypuffs in favor of the arcane design of Pit Chips, Attack Rings, Weight Discs, Spin Gears, and Blade Bases. At least it got them out of the house. Released in the U.S. as *Beyblade*.

The 70-minute *Beyblade: The Movie* (2002) eventually followed, released in Japan in the middle of the summer vacation, and predictably focusing on a similar event in the lives of its characters, who attempt to take a holiday, only to be dragged into a conflict with Dark Spirits at a nearby temple. The *Beyblade* movie shared the bill with a short movie based on the early PS2 game *Ape Escape*, in which the red-haired Spike attempts to thwart the efforts of the evil Specter to take an ape army back in time to conquer the world. Just another boring Japanese school vacation…

BIBLE BLACK *
2001. JPN: *BB—La Noche de Walpurgis.* AKA: *BB—Walpurgis Night.* Video. DIR: Sho Hanebu, Kazuyuki Honda, Hamuo. SCR: Yasuyuki Muto. DES: Yoshiten. ANI: Yoshiten, Wataru Yamaguchi. MUS: Morihide. PRD: Milky, Museum Pictures. 28 mins. x 6 eps. (v 1), 30 mins. x 2 eps. (v *Origins*), 30 mins. (v *New*); 30 mins. (*Only*).

Teenager Taki Minase finds a book of black magic in a basement room that none of the students are supposed to enter. Dabbling in some of its spells, he discovers that it is truly powerful—a simple bit of love voodoo not only ensures that a girl attracts the attention of a boy she wants, but that said boy assaults her in broad daylight. But as Taki continues to experiment, he uncovers details of previous atrocities. Twelve years earlier, a group of would-be witches had unleashed terrible powers, and the two survivors, naturally, are now staff members at the school, one of whom requires a new virgin sacrifice to keep herself out of hell. Taki ends up in thrall to Reika Kitami, the evil school nurse, while Kurumi, an innocent girl who has a crush on Taki, looks likely to be the best candidate for the sacrifice, coming up on Walpurgis Night.

With *Buffy the Vampire Slayer, The Craft,* and *Charmed* all riding the millennial zeitgeist to make the occult the latest fad with teenagers, it is unsurprising that this should lead to a similar revival in the anime pornography genre. *BB*'s origins lie in a PC game from Active-Soft, released in 2000—although it is probably a coincidence that UROTSUKIDOJI, the grandfather of all erotic-horror anime, was released "12 years" before the game began production. In some ways, *BB* was the *Urotsukidoji* of its era, attracting a significant following, particularly in Eastern Europe and the former Soviet Union where it was the first conspicuous erotic anime for many of the POKÉMON generation. As with other longer Milky productions like IZUMO, the extended running time of *BB* allows greater space for actual plot, when compared to the lower expectations of one-shot anime porn titles. *BB* is also notable, particularly in its early episodes, for the conspicuously well-drawn characters and animation, with little of the cost-cutting found in lesser erotica. This original series was subsequently edited into a "movie" compilation, featuring two new sex scenes, as well

as *BB DVD the Game* (2003) which was, as the title implies, a rerelease of the original game and its sequel, with some sequences incorporating footage from the anime remake. Another interactive game, based on episode 3, was released later in the same year, while the DVD games would later be transferred to a new format for *BB Portable* (2005), for the new Sony PSP.

Revisiting scenes that have previously only been glimpsed in the main storyline, the prequel *BB Origins* (2002, *BB Gaiden*) depicts the efforts of Nami, a member of the student council who opposes an attempt by three girls to set up a Witchcraft Club. But the trio in question begin to exact their revenge, using the power of sorcery to make Nami's friends subject themselves to public sexual humiliations. Before long, Nami has joined the cabal herself, in events leading to the human sacrifice that formed part of the backstory of the *BB* series proper. In a chronological confusion that also, ironically, bears some resemblance to *Urotsukidoji,* the *BB Origins* episodes were released in Japan between the arrivals of episodes 4 and 5 of the original series.

BB New Testament: The Lance of Longinus (2004, aka: *BB Revival*) half-heartedly restarts the franchise in the manner of DEMON BEAST INVASION, with the girls of the Witchcraft Club grown up and graduated. Former student council member Rika Shiraki has become a teacher at the school, while Kurumi is a psychic investigator with a government agency, tracking a series of gruesome murder cases à la ONI TENSEI. These seem to be related to the restless spirit of Miss Kitami, the school nurse, leading to the reestablishment of the Witches' Club, by a group of girls who are unsure what side they are supposed to be on.

Bible Black Only (2005) features a similar transformation on the part of teacher Hiroko Takagi, who soon has the girls out of their swimsuits. To the torment of encyclopedists, this was released while the previous series was running and reached Japanese stores between episodes 3 and 4 of the *New Testament*. The six episodes of the original series, along with *BB Origins*, were later repackaged in Japan as the misleadingly titled *BB Complete Box* (2006).

BIG O, THE *
1999. TV series. DIR: Kazuyoshi Katayama. SCR: Chiaki Konaka. DES: Keiichi Sato. ANI: Masami Osone, Kenji Haneyama. MUS: Toshihiko Sahashi. PRD: Sunrise, WOWOW. 25 mins. x 13 eps.
In 2099, beneath the overarching dome of Paradigm City, amnesiac humanity has lived for 40 years without any contact with the outside world. But there's trouble in Paradigm, and the government has been forced to use increasingly harsh measures to keep the restless citizenry in check. Criminal Negotiator Roger Smith finds himself in over his head when he becomes involved in the race to activate Big O, one of the last surviving examples of the super-advanced technology that led to humanity's self-immurement in the first place.

Big O has a distinct resemblance not only to director Katayama's earlier GIANT ROBO, but also to Warner Bros.' *Batman Beyond*, for which Sunrise had been a Japanese subcontractor. Beyond its crime-fighting millionaire, *Big O*'s roots extend much further back into science fiction, with settings and cybernetics inspired by Isaac Asimov's *Caves of Steel* (1954) and impressive Art Deco costumes and architecture. With the introduction of R.(obot) Dorothy Wayneright, an android almost indistinguishable from real humans, who may hold the secret to humankind's amnesia, the show gains elements that also tie it to a Japanese antecedent, Osamu Tezuka's METROPOLIS. Retrospirited action in the spirit of GIANT ROBO and STEAM DETECTIVES.

BIG WARS *
1993. Video. DIR: Toshifumi Takizawa. SCR: Kazumi Koide. DES: Satomi Miki-

Big Wars

yura, Kow Yokoyama. ANI: Keizo Shimizu. MUS: Michiaki Kato. PRD: Tokuma, Magic Bus. 70 mins.
Many centuries ago, aliens calling themselves Gods visited Earth and subjugated the primitive peoples. When they left, the vestiges of their technology helped humanity become civilized. The aliens return in A.D. 2416 to find mankind unwilling to serve them again, so they unleash a mind-control plague. Haunted by Catholic imagery and a carrier called Hell, Captain Akuh of the battleship Aoba is worried that his girlfriend is showing the first signs of infection (nymphomania, would you believe), but he needs to pull himself together in time for the coming fight—which is as carefully detailed as one might expect from Yoshio Aramaki, who also gave us DEEP BLUE FLEET. This anime was made straight to video but given a limited theatrical release to boost its credibility. ⓥ

BIG X
1964. TV series. DIR: Mitsuteru Okamoto, Osamu Dezaki. SCR: Jiro Kadota, Mami Murano, Tadashi Hirose. DES: Osamu Tezuka. ANI: Eiji Suzuki, Renzo Kinoshita. MUS: Isao Tomita. PRD: TMS, TBS. 30 mins. x 59 eps.
During World War II, the Nazis force pacifistic Japanese Professor Asagumo and German Professor Engel to develop Big X, a genetically engineered for-

mula to turn men into giant, invincible soldiers, as a superweapon for Hitler. As Berlin falls in 1945, the researchers are murdered to preserve the secret, but not before Asagumo hides the formula with his son, Shigeru, who returns to Japan. Twenty years later, Hitler's underground neo-Nazi movement revives the war. Gestapo agents in Tokyo attack Shigeru in the midst of an experiment and kill him, but the intruders are thwarted by his son, Akira, who injects himself with the Big X serum, transforming into a 60-foot giant, a Big X intent on fighting for good. The Nazis scheme to bring Akira/Big X to Carthago, a north African state recently conquered by Germans under the command of Hans Engel, grandson of the serum's coinventor. Hans, the victim of Nazi brainwashing, believes that his grandfather was the sole inventor of Big X and that the Asagumos have stolen his birthright from him. In Carthago, Akira meets his love interest, Nina Burton, a sweet young girl who can communicate telepathically with animals. After the liberation of Carthago, Akira and Nina move on to fight the Nazis in other parts of the world, where they are operating through a seemingly neutral international political movement that they control, the Cross Party.

The first production for Tokyo Movie Shinsha, this was the second anime to be made from the works of **ASTRO BOY**–creator Osamu Tezuka. Rethinking Japan's wartime association with Nazism for a more juvenile audience than the same author's *Adolf, Big X* ran in *Shonen Book* in 1963 and presaged another Tezuka genetics plot in **BAGHI**. Akira would transform by injecting himself with the serum from a disguised fountain pen, a dangerously tempting idea for a juvenile audience, outclassed perhaps only by **8 MAN**'s radioactive cigarettes and the pyromaniac pleasures of **GOLD LIGHTAN**.

BIKKURIMAN

1987. AKA: *Surprise-Man*. TV series. DIR: Yukio Misawa. SCR: Sukehiro Tomita, Asami Watanabe. DES: Mitsuru Aoyama. ANI: Hiroyuki Kadokane, Masahiro Ando. MUS: Takanori Arisawa. PRD: Toei, TV Asahi. 25 mins. x 48 eps.
At a time when Earth is about to be cleansed of the old order, the princes of the gods return to fight for the new. Super Zeus, lord of the God-World, orders Saint Phoenix, Prince Yamato, the divine Ali Baba, and their dizzying array of pals to journey to the "edge of the West" and set up a new peaceful land called Jikai. Lined up against them are the minions of Super Devil, king of Devil-World. An incredibly popular tie-in featuring characters from the Bikkuriman Chocolate packets, Bikkuriman also made it into theaters in 1988 with the screening of the time-travel side-story *First Armageddon* and a 45-minute special entitled *Secret Treasure of the Abandoned Zone*. A 44-episode sequel, *Super Bikkuriman*, followed in 1993, written by Aya Matsui with sharper, brighter designs in the style of other 1990s shows.

BILLY DOG

1988. JPN: *Billy Inu*. TV series. DIR: Hiroshi Sasagawa, Junji Nishimura. SCR: Noboru Shiroyama, Masaru Yamamoto. DES: Yayoi Takihara. ANI: Chuji Nakajima. MUS: Tetsu Inakawa. PRD: TV Asahi, Shinei. 20 mins. x 44 eps.
Tatsuo Yumori lives on Hanabibi Hill with his dog, Billy, who followed the

boy home one day and just stayed. But Billy is a talking dog with the mind of a human being, and he soon brings his friend, Gary Dog, into the lives of Tatsuo, his family, and his friends. Based on a manga by Fujiko-Fujio.

BINCHO-TAN

2006. TV series. DIR: Kazuhiro Furuhashi, Eiji Suganuma, Shigeru Ueda. SCR: Kazuhiro Furuhashi. DES: Tetsuhito Saito. ANI: Eiji Suganuma, Masashi Ishihama, Katsuya Asano. MUS: N/C. PRD: Studio Deen, TBS. 12 mins. x 9 eps.
Bincho-tan (the name refers to the piece of charcoal she carries on her head), is a cute little girl who lives a simple life in the mountains. Apparently we are supposed to care! She is actually a mascot character created by artist Takehito Egusa for the games company Alchemist—compare to **DIGI CHARAT**.

BIOHUNTER *

1995. Video. DIR: Yuzo Sato, Yoshiaki Kawajiri. SCR: Yoshiaki Kawajiri. DES: Hiroshi Hamazaki. ANI: Hiroshi Hamazaki. MUS: Masamichi Amano. PRD: Madhouse. 60 mins.
A virus transforms people into monsters with demonic powers. Two molecular scientists, Koshigaya and Kimada, who moonlight as psychic researchers, are approached by the beautiful Sayaka Murakami, whose fortuneteller grandfather has gone missing after an appointment with a prominent politician. Based on a manga serialized in *Comic Burger* by **JUDGE**-creator Fujihiko Hosono, this anime was partly bankrolled by the U.S. distributor Urban Vision, whose Mataichiro Yamamoto is credited as a producer. Under the charge of the Madhouse studio and **WICKED CITY**'s Yoshiaki Kawajiri, it looks just like every other demons-among-us tale that characterized so many successful anime in the U.S., which probably explains the foreign money. **NV**

BIRDY THE MIGHTY *

1996. JPN: *Tetsuwan Birdy*. Video. DIR: Yoshiaki Kawajiri. SCR: Chiaki Konaka.

DES: Kumiko Takahashi, Yutaka Izubuchi. ANI: Kumiko Takahashi. MUS: Yuki Otani. PRD: Madhouse. 35 mins. x 4 eps.
Loser schoolboy Tsutomu is fatally wounded in the crossfire between an alien criminal and an intergalactic bounty hunter. To preserve his life, officer Birdy Cephon Altirra merges with him, living *inside* his body, helping him through teenage troubles but forcing him to transform at humorously inappropriate moments.
A sex-swap farce à la **RANMA ½**, with a tip of the hat to Tezuka's "Mighty" **ASTRO BOY**, *Birdy*'s true roots lie in the live-action **ULTRAMAN**, with aliens defeated by low-budget gimmicks like dish soap and a hapless Earthman forced to share his body with an invisible, controlling alien. Birdy straddles separate subplots as a vengeful bounty hunter, magical girlfriend, and confidante, contrasting with Tsutomu's spiteful real-life sister. Based on a short-lived manga from **PATLABOR**'s Masami Yuki, this disappointing series features a dream-team of anime creators, all working below par. Writer Konaka, brother of *Ultraman*-director Kazuya, manages a few tongue-in-cheek observations, such as why ugly aliens never get to be space cops, but these are outnumbered by the very genre conventions they lampoon—for example, the evil-yet-beautiful alien mastermind Revi, who wants to turn humans into bioweapons. Matters are not helped by a lead actor in the dub who is forced to pitch his voice so high that, in the words of someone from the U.S. distributor, "he sounds like Mr. Hanky the Christmas Poo."

BIRTH OF JAPAN

1970. JPN: *Nihon Tanjo*. TV series. DIR: Eiichi Yamamoto. SCR: Eiichi Yamamoto. DES: N/C. ANI: Yoshifumi Seyama. MUS: Isao Tomita. PRD: Tezuka Pro, Nippon TV. 26 mins. x 5 eps.
Liu Fa is a kappa, an amphibious humanoid creature who lives in the south of China. He meets the lovely Kozara, a girl from a distant land.

Eventually, he follows her to Japan, bringing iron weapons and rice cultivation to the island of Kyushu. Because kappa live for a thousand years, he is able to watch as his inventions spread, creating the foundations of the state that will become Japan. With characteristic Japanese vagueness about historical origins, this fantasy was shown beneath the slogan "Nonfiction Theater," though with its mixture of the supernatural and quasi-historical it is no truer to life than its distant cousins PRINCESS MONONOKE and DARK MYTH.

BIT THE CUPID *

1995. TV series. DIR: Tameo Ogawa. SCR: Soji Yoshikawa. DES: Susumu Matsushita. ANI: Toshiyasu Okada. MUS: Ko Suzuki. PRD: B2 Pro, TV Tokyo. 25 mins. x 48 eps.

In the realm of the Greek gods, where Zeus and Poseidon aren't talking, Narcissus is falling in love with himself, and Icarus is taking flying lessons, the titular Bit is a young demigod of uncertain parentage (though possibly the son of Apollo) who is able to make characters fall in love, though his aim is not always true. As he mixes it up with Hyacinth, Galatea, Atlas, and the gang, many Greek myths are intermixed with tales of more contemporary origin—such as Frisbee the Golden Assassin and Lee of Birdland. One of the earliest anime to be made inside a computer, it was broadcast in English on Fox Kids in the Netherlands—it's a wacky world.

BITE ME! CHAMELEON *

1992. JPN: Chameleon. Video. DIR: Mitsuo Hashimoto, Takao Yotsuji. SCR: Takao Yotsuji. DES: Tamiyoshi Yazaki. ANI: Tamiyoshi Yazaki. MUS: Saburo Takada. PRD: Victor. 50 mins. x 6 eps.

Eikichi Yazawa is a thug determined to be top dog at Narita High, so he does his best to convince love interest Asaoka that he used to be the toughest kid in junior high. Local bully Aizawa doesn't believe it for a moment, and Eikichi is forced to fight a battle with whatever is at hand, including urine, farts, and bloody napkins. Proud of its puerile nature, each episode would introduce a new challenger, whom Eikichi would have to outsmart or outgross. The final two releases were directed by former scriptwriter Yotsuji and had not previously appeared as stories in the manga, although they were little different from those that had.

Taking the stained mantle of the similar BRAT COP and moving the action to a school, Atsushi Kato's 33-volume manga from *Shonen Magazine* sold 1.3 million, but adding the words "Bite Me!" to the title couldn't save it in the U.S., where it bombed after just one episode. ●▼

BIZARRE CAGE *

2003. JPN: Ryoki no Ori 2. Video. DIR: Sei Konno. SCR: Kotaro Ran. DES: Mamoru Yokota. ANI: N/C. MUS: N/C. PRD: Studio Line, Studio Polaris, Pink Pineapple. 30 mins. x 3 eps.

Handsome young Takeshi Saito takes a job as a security guard at the Fantasien theme park, which entails him dressing up as a cross between a knight and a Roman centurion. But Fantasien is so state-of-the-art that some of its attractions use military technology, which requires very careful monitoring. Takeshi soon falls out with the bitchy park manager over some alleged infractions, but wins the praise of Tamami, a fellow player on the park's staff. When park employees start turning up dead, Takeshi begins to investigate, discovering that owner Masakazu Inouye is using it after hours as a personal playground for his sick sexual perversions. Then MAOS, the operating system that controls the park, starts spinning out of control. Yes, it's *Westworld* (1973) with T&A, as Takeshi and several stereotypical girls of different ages struggle to get the system stable and the customers safely out of the park, in between having sex with and without consent, before tackling Inouye in a dramatic climax at Dracula's Castle. Based on a PC game, the design of which made a virtue out of the simplistic planning of adventure gaming since the different "worlds" of the park had a reason to be right next to each other, and the characters involved had a series of excuses to be dressed up in costumes and fetish gear. This cunning ruse also circumvented a problem common to many fantasy anime—it can be annoying in some other anime that the cast have the sensibilities of modern people in a fantasy setting, whereas in *BC* it is part of the plot. See SEXORCIST for another tale of a game that goes wrong for its participants. ●▣▼

BLACK CAT

2005. TV series. DIR: Shin Itagaki, Takayuki Inagaki, Yoshimichi Hirai. SCR: Shuichi Koyama. DES: Yukiko Akiyama. ANI: Yukiko Akiyama, Maki Uchida. MUS: Taku Iwasaki. PRD: Gonzo, TBS, BS-I. 25 mins. x ?? eps.

Sven Volfield is an itinerant bounty hunter or "sweeper" who can see into the future by lifting his eye-patch and using his supposedly dead eye—elements here of both CITY HUNTER and GOKU: MIDNIGHT EYE. His nemesis is Train Hartnett, aka: "Black Cat," a special operative of the Chronos secret society, whose aim is to stabilize the world through carefully selected assassinations. Train soon switches sides and teams up with Sven to take on Chronos, leading to a tale of super-powered heroics redolent of the GETBACKERS. Based on the manga by Kentaro Yabuki serialized in *Shonen Jump*, and no relation to the novel *Black Cat* by PLEASE OPEN THE DOOR author Motoko Arai. Characters from *Black Cat* also appeared in the Nintendo game *Jump Super Stars*.

BLACK GATE *

2004. Video. DIR: Sho Hanebu. SCR: Torazo Nakahara. DES: Yoshi Ten. ANI: Takeshi Imai. MUS: N/C. PRD: Image Works, Studio Jam, Yoshi Ten, Museum Soft, Milky. 30 mins. x 2+ eps.

Baffled teenager Narufumi discovers that his girlfriend Shizuka and her twin sister Kasumi are battling over him in an alternate dimension that they can

Black Jack

only reach by using their mysterious tattoos to unlock an interdimensional gateway at their school, which, naturally, the girls' family has been secretly guarding for generations in the style of DEVIL HUNTER YOHKO. A group of girls are transported to another world through the "black gate" portal, where one discovers that she can gain slaves and magical power through sexual intercourse (who knew!), although the arrival of a mysterious rescuer saves the travelers from a fate worse than death—just imagine that LA BLUE GIRL never happened. Ends on a cliffhanger, so we assume more episodes are on the way. ⓁⓃⓋ

BLACK HEAVEN *

1999. JPN: *Kacho Oji*. AKA: *Section Chief Oji, Legend of Black Heaven*. TV series. DIR: Yasunori Kikuchi. SCR: Narihisa Arakawa. DES: Kazuto Nakazawa. ANI: Hiroshi Hashimoto. MUS: Koichi Korenaga. PRD: AIC, APPP, Pioneer, WOWOW. 25 mins. x 13 eps.
Oji Tanaka, a henpecked, middle-aged salaryman with a dull wife and a mewling infant, still thinks fondly of his teenage years when he was "Gabriel" Tanaka, lead guitarist with the hard

rock group Black Heaven. He is contacted by a beautiful blonde agent, Leila Yuki, and hired to play his particular brand of music for use as a sonic weapon in an interstellar war.

The space war is curiously underused, the script concentrating instead on Tanaka's hapless attempts to enlist his old band in his secret mission and his wife's attempts to discover whether he is having an affair with Leila. But with a focus on farce and everyday life not unlike Nigel Kneale's *Kinvig*, *BH* resembles a live-action production that cannot afford the special effects rather than an anime that can go anywhere in the galaxy for the price of a pot of paint. *BH* has much in common with other short-lived TV serials of the late 1990s—the backgrounds are sparse and reused often, and the animation is cheap, flat, and digital. The filmmakers attempt to distract the viewer's attention with occasional flashy graphics and rotoscoping, especially over the opening credits featuring footage of Whitesnake's John Sykes, who sings the theme tune. It's music as power, à la MACROSS, but expanding the audience to include disenchanted thirty-somethings, with many 1970s heavy metal in-jokes.

BLACK JACK *

1993. Movie, video. DIR: Osamu Dezaki. SCR: Eto Mori, Kihachi Okamoto. DES: Akio Sugino. ANI: Akio Sugino. MUS: Osamu Shoji, Kiyoshi Suzuki. PRD: Tezuka Pro. 50 mins. x 10 eps. (v), 93 mins. (m), 11 mins. x 12 eps. (*Flash*), 25 mins. x 4 eps. (*Miracles*), 25 mins. x 61 eps. (TV1), 25 mins. x 1+ eps. (TV2).
Black Jack was one of Osamu Tezuka's most popular creations, a scar-faced doctor-for-hire with a deep-set sense of honor and justice. His sole confidante is Pinoko ("pinochle," a companion card game to "blackjack" in a typical Tezuka wordplay), a diminutive, lisping girl carried for decades in the womb of her unsuspecting twin sister and found by Black Jack during an operation to remove what he thought to be a cyst. Although she looks like a toddler, she is as old as her grown-up twin and becomes Black Jack's surrogate daughter and assistant.

The original *Black Jack* ran in *Shonen Champion* magazine from 1973 to 1978. It reached a wider audience through Nobuhiko Obayashi's 1977 live-action film *Stranger in Her Eyes*, in which Black Jack (Daisuke Ryu) uses a drowned girl's corneas to restore sight to a female patient who is then haunted by visions of the donor's last moments. Reissued after lying dormant for most of the 1980s, the manga was followed in 1993 by an anime version on video from the GOLGO 13–team of Dezaki and Sugino. Undertaken as part of an ongoing plan to produce animated versions of all of Tezuka's work, the videos suffer from faithfulness to the letter rather than the spirit of the originals, creating a sanitized nostalgia instead of the series' famously dark mood.

In *Chimaera Man*, Black Jack must operate to save his old acquaintance Crossword before traveling to Hokkaido to revisit a former patient who has become the victim of a mob-run medical conspiracy in *The Procession Game*. In *The Decoration of Maria and Her Comrades*, he is called to save the life of a South American rebel ousted by foreign-backed conspirators; then he tries to save the life of a traumatized movie star in *Anorexia*, where he faces his old adversary, "dark doctor," and euthanasia-advocate Kiriko. Events take a more paranormal turn in *The Owl of San Merida*, in which Black Jack aids a man with stigmata and false memory syndrome, and in *Night Time Tale in the Snow*, a variation on an old Japanese folktale of doomed love found in many other anime including KIMAGURE ORANGE ROAD.

Black Jack returned to live-action cinema in 1995, with a trilogy directed by Kazuya Konaka and written by AKIRA's Izo Hashimoto, with Daisuke Ryu reprising the lead role. The first two films chart Black Jack's initial fall from grace (only revealed in flashbacks in the original manga) and first encounter with Pinoko (the manga chapter *Teratogenous Cystoma*). The final installment replays the Kiriko encounter from the anime, and the cross-promotion was reinforced in 1996 when the last live-action movie was followed by a feature-length anime.

Set in 1998 as Tezuka would have imagined it, with a UN that includes off-world colonies, *Black Jack the Movie* dumps the condescending attitude that crept into the video series. Two years after the appearance of superhuman child prodigies at the Atlanta Olympics, the same children are suddenly succumbing to accelerated aging. Black Jack is blackmailed into helping the ice-cool Doctor Jo Carroll, who kidnaps Pinoko to secure Black Jack's cooperation in what turns out to be a viral conspiracy.

Black Jack continued as a straight-to-video anime after the movie with *Green Memories*, *The Face in the Affliction*, and *Sinking Woman*, though these episodes have yet to be released in English. A TREE IN THE SUN, a very different kind of Tezuka medical drama, was also animated in 2000.

The franchise was slowly reintroduced to the market with *Black Jack Flash* (2003), a dozen 11-minute episodes made with Flash animation, and released through the Internet—representing one of the first obvious attempts by an animation studio to amass broadcast material that could be reused in mobile phones. Plots from *BJF* were later recycled in *Black Jack: The Four Miracles of Life* (2003), a miniseries comprising four TV specials. After testing the waters with exquisite care, the franchise was truly revived with *Black Jack* (2004), a 61-episode TV series, directed by Tezuka's son Makoto (sometimes credited with his preferred romanization, Macoto). All incarnations of the franchise adhered closely to the story of the original manga. Another movie, *BJ: Two Doctors of Darkness* (2005) premiered along with a short seven-minute featurette, *Doctor Pinoko's Forest Adventure* (2005), in which Pinoko gets lost in the woods while chasing after Jack with his bag. The television series was followed immediately in 2006 by a sequel, *Black Jack 21*.

BLACK LION
1992. JPN: *Jigen Sengoku-shi: Kuro no Shishi*. AKA: *Dimension Civil War Chronicle: Black Lion*. Video. DIR: Takashi Watanabe. SCR: Noriko Hayasaka. DES: Hideyuki Motohashi, Koichi Ohata. ANI: N/C. MUS: Masami Anno. PRD: Tokyo Kids. 45 mins.

In 1580, Nobunaga Oda united Japan with the aid of foreign guns, but *Black Lion* has a more fantastic view of these events, suggesting that he used rapid-fire machine guns, lasers, and missiles. His ultimate weapon is Ginnai Doma, a ninja said to be immortal who carries out the command to eradicate dissident temples with extreme prejudice. A warrior monk is the sole survivor of one such massacre, and he swears to avenge the deaths of his friends and lover.

In taking contemporary items and hurling them into the past, Go Nagai's 1978 manga from *Shonen Magazine* is a reversal of his SHUTENDOJI, which dragged ancient concerns into the present day. Supervising producer Osamu Yamazaki directed several similar retellings of Japanese history, including YOTODEN, which depicted Nobunaga as being in alliance with demons.

BLACK MAGIC M-66 *
1987. Video. DIR: Masamune Shirow, Hiroyuki Kitakubo. SCR: Masamune Shirow, Hiroyuki Kitakubo. DES: Hiroyuki Kitakubo, Toru Yoshida. ANI: Hiroyuki Okiura, Hiroki Hayashi. MUS: Yoshihiro Katayama. PRD: Animate Film, AIC. 45 mins.

A military transport crashes and loses its cargo, two top-secret military androids whose unerased test program instructs them to terminate their inventor's granddaughter, Ferris. When the first of the robots is destroyed, snooping reporter Sybel decides to track down Ferris and warn her. In a showdown that costs the lives of 18 soldiers, Sybel saves Ferris, though the reporter's feckless partner, Leakey, tries to pass off the news footage of the incident as his own.

Black Magic began life as a fanzine, a sprawl of loosely linked manga that gained Shirow his first professional contract. The anime adapted *Booby Trap*, the most coherent chapter, drawing heavily from James Cameron's *Terminator* and the final act of *Aliens*. Sybel and Ferris replay Cameron's Ripley/ Newt relationship in several scenes, most notably with an elevator chase and last-minute rescue, but *Black Magic* is entertaining despite the steals. The only disappointment in watching the acrobatic androids decimate a roadblock comes in wondering how it could have looked if the makers had had the budget to include the original's *six*-armed M-77 prototype, which is only referred to offscreen. Another vestige of the manga is the allegorical Cold War standoff between North and South, misinterpreted by some oversensitive Japanese critics as a slur on Korea. Also note Sybel's APPLESEED T-shirt, an in-joke that would be repaid when that other Shirow title was animated the following year.

The fallout from *Black Magic* is remarkably similar to that of Katsuhiro

Otomo's **AKIRA**, another case of a creator's perfectionism driving an anime over budget. *Black Magic* used over 20,000 cels, an extravagance on video that, ironically, has caused it to age very gracefully—it could easily pass for a show ten years younger. Shirow's first and last work as anime director, it ended so acrimoniously that he refused to associate himself with any future adaptations. In some ways, this is an indirect cause of the later monstrosities **LANDLOCK** and **GUNDRESS**, for which his name was appropriated to secure unwarranted publicity. As well as **BLOOD**-director Kitakubo, two future big names worked as lowly animators on the project—Hiroki Hayashi would make **BUBBLEGUM CRISIS 2040**, and Hiroyuki Okiura would eventually direct **JIN-ROH** after contributing to the superior Shirow adaptation **GHOST IN THE SHELL**. The production was the debut of future voice star Chisa Yokoyama as Ferris. **V**

BLACK WIDOW *
2003. JPN: *Kuro Hime Shikkoku no Yakata*. AKA: *Black Princess: Kekki no Yakata* (GET TRANS). Video. DIR: Yusaku Saotome, Yu Yahagi. SCR: Hajime Yamaguchi, Yu Yahagi. DES: Tomo'o Shintani. ANI: Yasuhiro Saiki. MUS: Takeshi Nishizawa. PRD: Discovery, Mook. 30 mins. x 2 eps.
Seven young friends go for a camping trip on the banks of an artificial lake created by a dam. While exploring the environs, they find an old mansion in the woods, where they are obliged to take shelter from bad weather. The mansion seems deserted at first, but as the boys and girls explore its rooms they find evidence of very recent occupation, and when they find the bondage room next to the bar in the cellar they begin to realize that they are not alone. Maya, the mistress of the house, and her guests have various torture and bondage games in mind (compare to **BEHIND CLOSED DOORS**), as the group is split up and submitted to various sexual torments. Later on, the story transforms into a murder mystery, although

it is tied up in a rushed and arbitrary ending that suggests later installments were curtailed by circumstances beyond the filmmakers' control. Part of the **DISCOVERY SERIES**. **LNV**

BLACKMAIL *
1999. JPN: *Kyohaku*. Video. DIR: Katsumasa Kanezawa. SCR: Sakura Momoi, Taifu Kanmachi. DES: Teruaki Murakami. ANI: Teruaki Murakami. MUS: N/C. PRD: Pink Pineapple. 30 mins. x 1 ep (3 eps. planned).
Japanese teenager Asuka is touched to receive a love letter from a boy in her class. However, she makes the mistake of confiding in her "friend" Aya, who secretly desires the boy herself. The jealous Aya ensures that Asuka pays the price in pain and bondage—salutary relationship advice. Released in the U.S. as *Black Mail* (2001). **NV**

BLAME! *
2003. JPN: *Blame Ver. 0.11*. Video. DIR: Shintaro Inokawa. SCR: Tsutomu Nihei. DES: Akio Watanabe, Nobuaki Nagano. ANI: N/C. MUS: Hiroyuki Onogawa. PRD: Nihei. 5 mins. x 6 eps.
It has been 3000 years since humanity lost the war with machines, and Earth is now encased within a massive skin of steel and concrete. The heroic Killy is on the run from evil Silicon creatures and searching for Cibo ("Hope"), a scientist who may have found a way to defeat them.
Originally a 1998 manga serialized in *Comic Afternoon*, *Blame* has a European look informed by creator Tsutomu Nihei's love of French comics. In its anime version, it has thematic similarities to Peter Chung's *Aeon Flux*, sacrificing immense amounts of plot and coherence in order to cram itself into the short running times of its original web broadcast. Supposedly, this all-too-brief series of disjointed segments was part of creator Nihei's attempt to secure funding for a movie; tellingly it was put together in the year that the *Blame* manga came to an end. Sold to a foreign distributor and slammed together into a 30-minute one-shot

video, the result is an often incoherent series of conflicts that plays like a poor man's **ANIMATRIX**. It is also rather quaint in modern times to see a video anime that makes no sense and serves merely as an advertisement for the manga; back in the 1980s, there were a lot more of them around. The DVD release was cunningly presented as a "salvaged disc by Cibo"; i.e., an item from the world of the anime. However, that backfired when the menus were written in a language from 3000 years in the future, hence somewhat difficult to navigate. **V**

BLEACH
2004. TV series, video. DIR: Noriyuki Abe. SCR: Genki Furumura, Masahiro Okubo, Masashi Sogo, Michiko Yokote, Natsuko Takahashi, Rika Nakase. DES: Masashi Kudo. ANI: Akio Kawamura, Manabu Fukuzawa, Masashi Kudo, Masaya Onishi, Miyuki Ueda, Natsuko Suzuki, Seiji Kishimoto, Takeshi Yoshioka, Yoshimitsu Yamashita. MUS: Shiro Sagisu. PRD: Pierrot, TV Tokyo, Dentsu. 24 mins. x 53+ eps. (TV) 30mins (v).
Evil soul-eating goblins, known as Hollows, possess and destroy people including the family of high schooler Ichigo Kurosaki. Ichigo has untapped psychic powers, and in an encounter with soul reaper Rukia Kuchiki he gains her powers and transforms into a soul reaper himself. He needs Rukia's presence to work the transformation at first, but then he finds a way to put a "temporary soul" into his own body and transform without her help. Based on Taito "Tite" Kubo's 2002 manga in *Shonen Jump*, *Bleach* is a more magical retread of the quest narratives of **NARUTO**, or a more modern variant on **INU YASHA**. Whichever way you want to play it, it's all been done before, but this series of exorcisms-of-the-week gained a loyal and respectful following for its treatment of enemies within, no doubt helped by the early 21st-century release of several zombie movies. Not only people but also animals can be possessed by malignant forces, leading to a series of mysteries and hauntings

reminiscent of PET SHOP OF HORRORS—at one point, even a possessed parakeet! The *Bleach* video *Memories in the Rain* (2004) was a flashback depicting the moment that Ichigo destroyed the Hollow that killed his mother. It was coupled with a brief three-minute bonus sequence relating to Gotei 13, the HELLSING-like organization that fights the Hollows, and originally shown to audiences in several locations as part of the Jump Festa Anime Tour (a publicity event related to *Shonen Jump* titles) before its video release. A *Bleach Rock Musical* (2004) appears to have been part of the same event.

BLOCKER CORPS

1976. JPN: *Blocker Guntan IV Machine Blaster*. AKA: *Blocker Corps IV Machine Blaster*. TV series. DIR: Masami Anno, Takashi Anno. SCR: Akira Hatta, Susumu Takahisa. DES: Tomosuke Takahashi, Kunio Okawara. ANI: Mamoru Tanaka. MUS: Hiroshi Tsutsui. PRD: Nippon Animation, Fuji TV. 25 mins. x 38 eps.
Hellqueen V and Kaibuddha, rulers of the devilish undersea Moghul Empire, launch an all-out assault on the surface world. From Astro Base, Professor Yuri sends out Robocles, Thundaio, Blue Caesar, and Vospalda, four "blocker" robots piloted by young boys with Elpath powers, Earth's last-ditch defenders against the people of the sea.

The first production for Ashi, a studio founded by former Tatsunoko-member Tatsuhiko Sato, *Blocker Corps* used many Tatsunoko alumni, including BATTLE OF THE PLANETS–designer Okawara. This simple robot show with a *Stingray* feel gains added drama halfway through when lead character Tenpyo Tobidori discovers he is the offspring of a union between a Moghul man and an Earth girl.

BLOOD ROYALE *

2002. JPN: Blood Royal. AKA: Blood Royale Xtreme Series. Video. DIR: Juhachi Minamisawa. SCR: Joichi Michigami. DES: Tesshu Takekura. ANI: Ken

Matsugaoka. MUS: Takeshi Nishizawa. PRD: Discovery, Cherry Soft. 30 mins. x 2 eps.
Fugitive princesses Sayuka and Milte are "rescued" by a sea captain who turns out to be the infamous One Eyed Devil, a piratical pervert. He chains them below deck in a torture chamber formerly used to extract information from prisoners and informs them that they are to be trained to be his sex slaves. The appeal, we assume, to fans of bondage and degradation, is that the higher-class the prisoner, the more fun there is in watching them fall. As in EROTIC TORTURE CHAMBER, these girls of the nobility are almost pathologically innocent—one isn't sure how to pleasure herself, since the concept is alien to her, but the other does not even know how to disrobe unassisted. Meanwhile, the pirate enters into his role with gusto, since he has agreed to break in the girls in order to gain much needed money to repair his ship. Some may feel he goes above and beyond the call of duty in a particularly nasty incidence of toilet training, not to mention innovative uses for a pet octopus—compare to MAHYA THE SERVANT. Part of the DISCOVERY SERIES. **LNV**

BLOOD SHADOW *

2001. JPN: *Guren*. AKA: *Crimson Lotus*. Video. DIR: Nao Ozekawa. SCR: Ryo Saga. DES: Toshihide Matsudate. ANI: Daisaku Kan, Sutekichi Kano. MUS: Hiroaki Sano. PRD: Discovery. 30 mins. x 3 eps.
In a world where ninja hunt infestations of demons, Rekka loses his beautiful fighting companion Tsukikage. He soon falls in with a new group of demon-hunters, a special task force known as the Crimson Lotus. Needless to say, he is the only male in a carefully chosen team of female archetypes (or stereotypes, if you will), five underdressed girls: Akanna, Kureha, Hikage, Ayano, and Haruka. Demon rape and (eventual) human violent revenge soon follow, in a short series based on a PC game from Zone. Since one of the girls looks actionably similar to

the lead from SAKURA WARS, we suspect that the entire venture was conceived as an erotic pastiche of that franchise, although with its sex-ninja setting it also appears to bear the hallmarks of LA BLUE GIRL. One of the DISCOVERY SERIES. **LNV**

BLOOD: THE LAST VAMPIRE *

2000. AKA: *Blood*. Movie. DIR: Hiroyuki Kitakubo. SCR: Kenji Kamiyama. DES: Katsuya Terada. ANI: Shinji Takagi. MUS: Yoshihiro Ike. PRD: Production IG. 50 mins.
On the eve of the Vietnam War, a secret organization sends Saya, a young Japanese girl, to destroy vampires ("Chiropterans") on the U.S. air base at Yokota in Japan. Neither human nor vampire, she uses her skills with a sword to dispatch these unearthly menaces.

Seemingly combining the plot of DEVIL HUNTER YOHKO with an alternate past similar to coproducer Mamoru Oshii's JIN-ROH, this is likely to be regarded in the U.S. as a Japanese rip-off of *Buffy the Vampire Slayer*. However, it features simply stunning animation and, in a first for anime, was made chiefly in English with Japanese subtitles to ease its progress into foreign markets. Mysteriously, however, this "film" is not feature-length, with the studio promising to complete the story with a manga and game—a suspicious sign of trouble behind the scenes and liable to leave the film forever inconclusive in much the same way as ARMITAGE III. An impressive action movie, but lacking in substance. There's no question, the animation in *Blood* is often superb. There are moments that honestly look too real to be animated—and demonic combat to put Buffy to shame. Manga Entertainment retains the original script's bilingual switches between English and Japanese, subtly demonstrating that Night and Day are not the only worlds that Saya walks between. There is a real observational verve lurking somewhere in the shadows—inspired, perhaps, by the animators' experience of foreign anime conventions. Bumbling aliens poke and prod at Saya, and try out their rudimentary Japanese, but none of them understand what she really is. She is out of place in her own country, a Japan that has been colonized by the hulking, brash gaijin and their bizarre customs. In a stroke of pulp genius, the showdown is set during Halloween, when the airbase is crawling with costumed ghosts and ghouls, and even Death himself, lumbering across the background with his trademark scythe. Compare this to a similar sequence in the movie of COWBOY BEBOP, the finale of which also takes place during a Halloween parade.

But it's an insult to viewers' intelligence to call this a "movie," as the publicity did both in Japan and America. It looks and feels like one of the truncated video releases of the 1990s—one of those also-rans like PLASTIC LITTLE or MADOX-01, that never quite got around to a sequel. In a desperate attempt to bulk out the running time, the English release also includes the self-congratulatory "Making Of" documentary, in which Mamoru Oshii openly admits that *Blood* began as a soufflé of half-baked ideas. A modern vampire girl, a demon-hunter on an airbase, and just a pinch of the muddled pseudo-politics that also characterized his earlier JIN-ROH, and *Blood* was born, as "part of a multimedia phenomenon"—which to Western viewers means it has a beginning and a middle, but no ending available in the English language for some time. The first *Blood* novel eventually appeared in English in 2005, and later that same year, the TV series *Blood+* began running on MBS and TBS. The TV series finally permitted the story to develop some coherence, beginning with Saya as an amnesiac schoolgirl who suffers flashback memories of the distant past. Like that similar school athlete, ESCA-FLOWNE's Hitomi, Saya finds her school besieged by monsters and her world drastically changing, although in the case of *Blood+*, she is not so much taken to a distant world as forced into a new

appreciation of the one she is already in, as she is force-fed human blood to reawaken her old memories, and co-opted into a government agency fighting the demonic infestation. The franchise is rumored to be the subject of a live-action remake by *Freddy vs. Jason*–director Ronny Yu.

BLUE BIRD

1980. JPN: *Maeterlink no Aoi Tori*. AKA: *Maeterlink's Blue Bird*. TV series. DIR: Hiroshi Sasagawa, Akira Kurooka, Kazuo Terada, Takashi Anno, Makoto Mizutani, Shigeru Omachi, Shinji Okada, Kenji Yoshida, Seiji Endo, Fumio Ikeno, Kunihiko Okazaki. SCR: Yoshinori Nishizaki, Keisuke Fujikawa. DES: Toyoo Ashida. ANI: Toyoo Ashida. MUS: Yasushi Miyagawa. PRD: Westcape Corporation, Fuji TV. 25 mins. x 26 eps.

A fairy named Bérylune visits brother and sister Tyltyl and Mytyl and tells them of the blue bird, a magical creature that brings good fortune to those who capture it. The children, accompanied by their dog Tylo and cat Tylette, search for it to help their ailing mother. They fly on a slipper to the Land of Memory, the Palace of Night, and the Kingdom of the Future before discovering that the blue bird (and the charity it represents) has been at home all along.

Maurice Maeterlinck's 1908 play *L'Oiseau Bleu* has been adapted for the screen several times—a 1918 silent film, a 1940 Shirley Temple vehicle, and a 1976 U.S.-Soviet coproduction. With a fairy-tale quality not dissimilar to the works of Kenji Miyazawa such as NIGHT TRAIN TO THE STARS, the story remains immensely popular in Japan. The series was also edited into a 120-minute movie-length version for video, *Maeterlinck's Blue Bird: Tyltyl and Mytyl's Great Adventure*, which retained many of the musical interludes that appeared in the TV version. A character called Tyltyl Mytyl appears in the book sequel to KIMAGURE ORANGE ROAD, where he befriends Madoka in New York. The story was retold in the KIKI AND LARA video, *Kiki and Lara's Blue Bird*.

BLUE BLINK *

1989. TV series. DIR: Osamu Tezuka, Seitaro Hara, Hideki Tonokatsu, Naoto Hashimoto. SCR: Osamu Tezuka, Shigeru Yamagawa. DES: Osamu Tezuka, Kazuhiko Udagawa, Kimitoshi Yamane, Kazuo Okada. ANI: Kazuhiko Udagawa, Seiji Endo, Yasuhiko Suzuki, Megumu Ishiguro. MUS: Hiroaki Serizawa. PRD: Tezuka Pro, NHK. 25 mins. x 39 eps.

This last series in which ASTRO BOY–creator Tezuka was directly involved before his death features Alexander, a young boy who helps Blink, a magical blue mule-colt, out of trouble; in return, Blink (combining the attributes of a best friend and a pet) promises to come whenever Alexander calls. Alexander returns home to find that his father, a writer, has been kidnapped by the Black Emperor. He and Blink are transported to an alternate world, and after many adventures, they face the emperor, only to discover that he is Alexander's father in disguise, who has set the whole thing up to demonstrate the wonder of books. Broadcast with English subtitles on KIKU TV in Hawaii.

BLUE BUTTERFLY FISH

1993. JPN: *BB Fish*. Video. DIR: Mamoru Hamazu. SCR: Mamoru Hamazu. DES: Takayuki Sato. ANI: Takayuki Sato, Nobuyoshi Habara. MUS: Yoichiro Furukawa. PRD: Pioneer. 30 mins.

On a southern island, a swimmer who has wasted his potential gradually regains his confidence after meeting a beautiful girl. NINETEEN-creator Sho Kitagawa's 1990 manga, a girls' romance cunningly concealed within the pages of a boys' magazine, ran for 15 volumes in *Young Jump*. Eschewing the humdrum struggle and victory of sports training stories, it concentrated instead on emotion, underwater scenery, and the mechanics of marine sports for a sumptuous tale that often forgot it was supposed to be about an athlete.

BLUE CONFESSIONS

2005. JPN: *Aoi Kokuhaku*. Video. DIR:

Shinji Ishidaira. SCR: Shinji Ishidaira. DES: Tetsuya Tsunawatari. ANI: Hakuhiro Konno, Tomoyuki Kitamura. MUS: N/C. PRD: Three Point, Studio OX, GP Museum. 30 mins.

Riho is a star-struck young girl who will do anything to become a star in the competitive world of Japanese pop music. She signs on with a talent agency whose company director takes particular pleasure in escorting his young charges to the casting couch. Riho loses a lucrative modeling contract to her friend Ayumi (who is more willing to put out) and seeks consolation in sex with her boyfriend Yuji. But when the boss finds out, it only fires his desire to have Riho for himself. Supposedly based on the real-life erotic confessions of model Miho Yabe. ●

BLUE EXPERIENCE

1984. JPN: *Aoi Taiken*. Video. DIR: N/C. SCR: N/C. DES: N/C. ANI: N/C. MUS: N/C. PRD: Zeros, Midnight. 25 mins.

A pretty young teacher is hired by a family to privately educate their son. On arrival, she witnesses her employer in an illicit clinch with a lover, thereby inspiring her to seduce her pupil. An anime pastiche of Salvatore Samperi's erotic movie *Malizia* (1973), which was released in Japan under the similar title *Aoi Taiken*. ●

BLUE FLAMES

1989. JPN: *Aoki En*. Video. DIR: Noboru Ishiguro. SCR: Norikazu Imai. DES: Masao Nakada. ANI: Masao Nakada. MUS: N/C. PRD: Nippon Animation. 50 mins.

Sex and romance are found in this adaptation of Kimio Yanasawa's 1987 manga from *Young Sunday*. The handsome teenager Ryuichi falls into life on the edge of the criminal world, but despite offers from hostesses to become his "sex friend," falls instead for a girl called Emi at the hospital. But his criminal leanings return after her father discovers evidence of their affair and offers him ten million yen to disappear.

Yanasawa is known for hard-boiled manga such as *The Mayor* and *Self-Por-*

trait of a Man but also specializes in strange romance, such as his *A Formal Marriage*, about a sexless contract between a gay man and an abused woman. *Blue Flames* mixes the two with its handsome boy hero who is offered a fantasy gigolo job but only wants the girl next door. The idea of an erotic picaresque receives more salacious coverage in many other anime, including **JUNK BOY** and **GOLDEN BOY**.

BLUE GENDER *

1999. TV series. DIR: Koichi Ohata, Masashi Abe. SCR: Katsumi Hasegawa. DES: Bunji Kizaki, Kunio Okawara. ANI: Bunji Kizaki. MUS: Kuniaki Haishima. PRD: AIC, TBS. 25 mins. x 13 eps.

At the turn of the 21st century, subatomic research finds a way of rewriting human DNA, a leap in science that produces powerful new benefits and insidious viral hazards. With mutating superviruses that can destroy people from the inside out, the world faces an epidemic that makes AIDS look like a runny nose. Those who discover they are suffering from the deadly disease elect to go into cybernetic hibernation until medical science can catch up and deliver a cure. A generation later, they awake on an Earth ruled by the "Blue," who range in size from 2 feet small to 24 feet tall. The remnants of humanity are crammed into a space station called Second Earth, desperately trying to invent a drive that will allow them to escape to the stars, and now they need the help of the "sleepers." Director Ohata has toyed with postapocalyptic adventure before in **MD GEIST** and **GENOCYBER**. The "movie" *Blue Gender: The Warriors* (2002) is a feature-length edit with a little extra footage.

BLUE REMAINS *

2000. Movie. DIR: Hisaya Takabayashi, Toshifumi Takizawa. SCR: Masatoshi Kimura, Hisaya Takabayashi, Toshifumi Takizawa. DES: Haruhiko Mikimoto, Tatsuya Tomosugi. ANI: Toshifumi Takizawa, Hisaya Takabayashi. MUS: N/C. PRD: Gaga, Okinawa Prefecture Industry Promotion Plc. 79 mins.

In 2052, as Earth teeters on the brink of environmental collapse, a family of terraformers returns from Mars with a payload of seeds designed to restore the planet. Unwisely arriving in the midst of a final nuclear exchange, they bail out and settle on the seabed south of Japan, waiting for the background radiation to return to manageable levels. Ninety years later, the original environmentalists are dead of radiation poisoning, and their daughter Amamiku has woken from suspended animation. She finds a world devoid of life (well, except for loads of fish, several human beings, and presumably whatever food they have been living on for the last century). Under attack from the robotic minions of the evil disembodied brain Glyptofane Sex, she is rescued by humans from the undersea citadel of Bathysphere, who help her save the last seedlings from her downed spacecraft before Glyptofane's creatures can destroy them.

Another of the late 20th-century experiments in digital animation, *Blue Remains* uses tricks similar to **BLUE SUBMARINE NO. SIX**, setting much of its action underwater where human movement and depth perception do not need to be as clear. In fact, considering that the original story outline called for a computer called "Mother Six" to go rogue and destroy the world, it would seem that *BR* began production at the same time, and was forced to alter similarities in its plot when *Blue Six* was released ahead of it. The graphics, as usual, were state-of-the-art for a few weeks, before being superseded by the almost daily improvements in software that cause so many early CG releases to age so fast. Less historically forgiveable is the ludicrous plot, which contradicts itself on several occasions. Not the least among its crimes is the risibly named Glyptofane Sex, whose "kill everybody" policy is so illogical that even his own associates tell him he ought to rethink it. Originally designed to be the centerpiece of the Okinawa Digital Power Festival, showcasing both computer power and the seas around Japan's

Blue Seed

© 1995 YUZO TAKODA/TAKOSHOBO • BS PROJECT • TV TOKYO • NAS

southern islands, today *Blue Remains* seems little more than a poor man's prototype of **FINAL FANTASY:** *The Spirits Within*, even down to the postapocalyptic setting, vague eco-friendliness, and cod-mystic message. In something of a cheat, the final few minutes are not animated at all, but comprise liveaction footage of fish swimming in tropical seas—it is a testament to its original achievement that audiences in the 1990s took a while to notice that they were no longer watching artificial life-forms.

BLUE SEED *
1994. TV series. DIR: Jun Kamiya, Kiyoshi Murayama, Shinya Sadamitsu. SCR: Toshihisa Arakawa, Masaharu Amiya, Koichi Mizuite. DES: Katsuichi Nakayama. ANI: Masaaki Fujita. MUS: Kenji Kawai. PRD: King Record, TV Tokyo, Hakusensha, NTV Music. 25 mins. x 26 eps. (TV), 30 mins. x 3 eps. (v). Schoolgirl Momiji has been raised by a shrine priestess in Izumo, Japan's spiritual heartland. Ancient demons, the Aragami, are returning to wreak havoc, and only a priestess of the Kushinada bloodline can stop them.

Momiji is saved from an Aragami attack by Mamoru Kusanagi, a half-Aragami defector who has sworn to protect the protectors. Kusanagi works alongside the TAC organization, a secret project to save Japan from the invaders. TAC's director, Daitetsu Kunikida, explains that only the Kushinada bloodline (see **LITTLE PRINCE AND THE EIGHT-HEADED DRAGON**) can put the Aragami to sleep and Momiji's long-lost twin, Kaede, is missing, presumed killed in action. Momiji trains hard to live up to her sister's peerless example, all the while fighting new mythological menaces including Orochi (also seen in **YAMATO TAKERU**), Susanoo (see **TAKEGAMI**), the giant Mukade centipede (see **USHIO AND TORA**), and kappa sprites (see **BIRTH OF JAPAN**). The titular "blue seeds" are comma-shaped *mitama* talismans common to Japanese archaeology, also found adorning the shell of the monster turtle in *Gamera: Guardian of the Universe*.

Created by **3x3 EYES'** Yuzo Takada for *Comic Gamma* in 1992, *Blue Seed* has superpowered schoolchildren, invading menaces-of-the-week, lost family, mythological roots, apocalyptic patriotism, mawkish romance, government intrigue, humor, *and* tragedy in quantum doses—all suspiciously similar to the later **EVANGELION**. Influenced by the mid-1990s ambiguity of the *X-Files*, it also features a government cover-up opposed by its own employees; Momiji discovers that the last-ditch plan to stop the ancient threat is for her to become a human sacrifice.

The show exists in two formats, a TV series for general consumption and a video version "director's cut" that included extra nudity and violence. A three-part video sequel, *Blue Seed 2: Operation Mitama*, followed in 1996–97, set two years later when a new Aragami threat looms on the horizon. Other *Blue Seed* releases include the original "Making Of" prequel featuring voice-actor interviews and a two-part video spin-off, *Blue Seed Ver. 1.5*, which collected the humorous bumpers added to the TV series.

BLUE SONNET *
1989. JPN: *Akai Kiba Blue Sonnet*. AKA: *Red Fang Blue Sonnet*. Video. DIR: Takeyuki Kanda. SCR: Seiji Matsuoka. DES: Katsuichi Nakayama. ANI: Katsuichi Nakayama, Hisashi Abe. MUS: Go! PRD: Mushi Pro. 30 mins. x 5 eps. Blue Sonnet is the code name of a sexually abused psychic street urchin, rescued from the slums and rebuilt as a superpowered cyborg by the apparently kindly Dr. Joseph Merkis, who is a major researcher for the organization Talon. Set to work for them, she soon finds herself in Tokyo posing as a schoolgirl under the name Sonnet Barje and investigating the psychic entity known as Red Fang, who turns out to be the high school student Lan Komatsuzaki. Lan is an orphan herself, who along with her brother Wataru is being raised by her foster father Jin Kiryu, a popular freelance writer and reporter. As in the later **GUNSLINGER GIRL**, Sonnet begins to question the motives of the organization that has programmed her, particularly after she is ordered to commit the brutal murder of a school nurse; Dr. Merkis

only wants her to be a pliant, "perfect" tool, the pinnacle of cyborg design, while both he and Talon are hellbent on world domination without regard to such niceties as ethics or human life. She begins to develop a rudimentary conscience and emotions after experiencing the warm feelings of a group of Japanese students amongst whom she is living, which marks a remarkable change considering what happens at so many other anime schools. When Talon captures Lan and limits her powers with a restraining collar, Sonnet must decide between her loyalty to Dr. Merkis and Talon, and defeating them while rescuing her schoolmate before Lan is used in a breeding program to create a master race of psychics.

As one can guess from the lack of a proper ending, *Blue Sonnet* began life as a manga, incorporating characters and situations from creator Masahiro Shibata's debut manga *Red Fang Wolf Girl Ran* (1975) from *Bessatsu Comic Margaret*, but resting largely on its fourth sequel, *Red Fang Blue Sonnet* (1981), which ran for 19 collected volumes after its initial appearance in *Hana to Yume*. This anime version seems engineered more to appeal to male fans than the female target audience of the original manga titles. *Sledge*, another title by Shibata, has been cited as a major influence on Kenichi Sonoda's GUNSMITH CATS. **Ⓥ**

BLUE SUBMARINE NO. SIX *
1998. JPN: *Aono Rokugo*. AKA: *Blue Six*. Video. DIR: Mahiro Maeda. SCR: Hiroshi Yamaguchi. DES: Mahiro Maeda, Range Murata, Takehito Kusanagi, Shoji Kawamori. ANI: Toshiharu Murata. MUS: The Thrill. PRD: Production IG, Bandai. 30 mins. x 4 eps.
With the ozone layer destroyed, mankind is moving into dome cities or underwater. Rogue scientist Zorndyke decides that humanity has lost the right to survive on the planet it has ruined and breeds a race of mer-people, the Mutio, to repopulate Earth. Young officer Mayumi Kino retrieves Tetsu Hayami, the navy's best pilot of yesteryear,

Blue Submarine No. Six

now a junky in the flooded ruins of Tokyo. Although he at first refuses to return to help humanity, Hayami saves Kino when Zorndyke's forces attack, joining with the remnants of the navy to fight for humanity's last stand.

Though the adaptation of Satoru Ozawa's SUBMARINE 707 sank without a trace in 1996, this follow-up to his 1960s manga rushed into production thanks to the number of underwater scenes, which allowed the animators to hide the joins between computer and cel animation with a blue sheen. Heavily influenced by Gerry Anderson's *Stingray*, particularly in the non-romance between Hayami and the mute Mutio mermaid he rescues, *Blue Six* is an EVANGELION clone only insofar as it possesses brassy music and echoes of the Pacific War. Taking the boys' adventure of the original manga and adding the shapely-but-shrill female lead Kino, *Blue Six*'s aquatic basis plays to the strength of its digital animation and coloring. While often obvious or just plain showy, the pros of the cel/CG combination far outweigh the cons. The characters are marvelous, including a cybernetic whale, an idea last seen in the ill-fated LADIUS. Zorndyke in particular is a wonderful creation, an

"evil genius" who occupies the moral high ground, whose tripod-crustacean war machines broadcast apologetic rationalizations, even as they wipe out human settlements. If there is any problem at all with *Blue Six*, it is the choice of format—the four "episodes" are so obviously a partitioned movie edition that it seemed dishonest not to release the "series" in feature-length from the outset. A 10-billion yen live-action adaptation, directed by Masahiko Okura, was announced in 2005 as beginning production.

BOBBY'S IN DEEP
1985. JPN: *Bobby ni Kubittake*. AKA: *Bobby's Girl*. Movie. DIR: Toshio Hirata. SCR: Shiro Ishinomori. DES: Akimi Yoshida. ANI: Gaku Ohashi. MUS: Keiichi Oku. PRD: Madhouse. 44 mins.
Akihiko "Bobby" Nomura, a student whose love of motorcycles has led him to write a column for a biker magazine, receives a letter from Sakiko Nakahara, a girl in distant Okayama. She likes his work, and the two begin a corres-pondence about bikes, which soon becomes more personal. The months pass as they coyly circle around the issues of whether they should meet and whether each has fallen in love

with someone they have never seen.

Using a cut-up technique to summarize Yoshio Kataoka's short story, *Bobby's in Deep* was shown as part of a double bill with **DAGGER OF KAMUI**. The involvement of the Madhouse studio led to many famous names behind the scenes, including producers Rintaro and Masao Murayama, who would later cooperate on **ALEXANDER**. The same year, character designer Akimi Yoshida would begin her most famous creation, the manga *Banana Fish*.

BOBOBO-BO BO-BOBO *

2003. TV series. DIR: Hiroki Shibata. SCR: Toshio Urasawa. DES: Yoichi Onishi. ANI: Takashi Nishizawa. MUS: Ichiro Kameyama. PRD: Toei Animation, TV Asahi. 25 mins. x 50+ eps.
In the 31st century, the Margarita Empire, under Tsuru Tsururina IV (Baldy Bald), plots to make the entire Earth population lose its hair. The empire is opposed by a lone master, Bo-Bobo, possessor of a golden Afro of truly vast proportions and practitioner of the ancient martial art known as True Fist of Nose Hair. In other words, the futuristic martial arts of **FIST OF THE NORTH STAR** or **DRAGON BALL**, lampooned in the surreal style of **EXCEL SAGA**, crammed full of nonsense puns and satirical asides. Bo-Bobo himself has a name based on a Japanese slang term for mussed hair, and wields the psychic power of "hearing the voice of hair"—this is where we point out that *kami* ("hair") is a homonym in Japanese for "divine," although we doubt that such anthropological considerations were that important to Yoshio Sawai's original manga in *Shonen Jump* weekly.

Bo-Bobo rescues a beautiful girl, appropriately named Beauty, from the Empire's shaving squad. On their travels to escape the vicious gangs of depilators and their super weapon the Shaver Beam, they meet Don Patch, who claims to be the capo of the insane Hajikerist mob. At first he thinks Bo-Bobo is sent by his mortal enemies, the Wig Gang, but later agrees to help

the freedom fighters in their struggle. Another hero, Heppokomaru, joins their band, bringing his special martial arts skill, the Fist of the Fart, to their aid. Together they face many perils, each dafter than the last. When Beauty is exposed to the Shaver Beam the only thing that can prevent her losing her lovely hair is a mystic cure at the summit of the Aitsuhage Tower: our heroes must scale five floors, each with a different danger, in a sequence that would be reminiscent of Bruce Lee's *Game of Death* if the high concept of fighting baldness with the power of body hair weren't so completely absurd. She also plays a deadly game of beach volleyball with a guardian robot and gets locked inside a TV set. Their deadliest opponent is Bo-Bobo's former friend Warship, now a high-ranking officer of the Empire. By now you've probably torn your hair out, which just goes to show the power of the bald side of the Force.

BODY TRANSFER *

2003. JPN: *Nikutai Teni*. Video. DIR: Yoshitaka Fujimoto. SCR: Yasuyuki Moto. DES: Harina Hayataka. ANI: Harina Hayataka. MUS: Toru Shura. PRD: ARMS, Green Bunny. 30 mins. x 2 eps.
Kenichi and his classmates stay late after school to see a new archeological discovery, a strange mirror, which transports them to another dimension. Trapped by a magical forcefield (likely to be a cost-cutting maneuver to save on new backgrounds, in the style of **FOBIA**), the students discover that their minds have switched into each other's bodies. They figure out that the only way to switch back is by generating a high level of sexual arousal, so it's up to Kenichi to get everything back to normal before the magical dimension falls apart. This leads to an intriguing series of original ideas (for anime pornography at least), as the mind-swap allows for experiments with gender perspective and desire. There is also a romantic subplot, as one character is revealed to be unaffected by the mirror and using its powers to ensure

that when all the mind-swaps are done, Kenichi is hers. But is that Kenichi's mind (which might have someone else's body), or Kenichi's body (which might have someone else's mind)? **Ⓛ Ⓝ**

BODYJACK

1987. Video. DIR: "Dojiro." SCR: Takashi Tanigawa. DES: To Moriyama. ANI: Makoto Kaneda. MUS: N/C. PRD: AIC, C.Moon. 35 mins.
The randy young Asagaya buys a device (which looks like an oversized traditional Japanese pig-shaped incense burner) from the local mad scientist, Dr. Toyama, which enables him to astrally project. He uses it to "slip into" and take over the body of his crush, the beautiful high school girl Komaba, so that he can see how it really feels to be a girl. Then Komaba's classmate (and Asagaya's girlfriend), the equally beautiful Nakano, surprises "him" and mistakes his activities for a sexual advance from her friend, beginning a lesbian scene that isn't really a lesbian scene because one of them is a man trapped in a woman's body, and enjoying every minute of it.

Bodyjack began as an erotic manga by **CREAM LEMON**'s pseudonymous To Moriyama, known today as Mori Toyama and, in more mainstream publications, as Naoki Yamamoto, the creator of **DANCE TILL TOMORROW**. An original incorporation of sex into SF since imitated in **SEXORCIST** and the **SECRET ANIMA** episode *Dream Hazard*. **Ⓝ**

BOES

1987. JPN: *Geragera Bus Monogatari*. AKA: *Chuckling Bus Story*. TV series. DIR: Hiroshi Sasagawa. SCR: Kaoru Toshina, Satoshi Ohira, Sachiko Ushida, Hisashi Furukawa. DES: N/C. ANI: Susumu Ishizaki. MUS: Shinsuke Kato. PRD: Telescreen, Studio Cosmos, TV Tokyo. 25 mins. x 52 eps.
Only the Dutch could come up with the idea of a talking bull in red dungarees who can fly when he puts on his magical wooden clogs, for such is the hero of this Netherlands coproduction based on the comic-strip character cre-

ated by Wil Raymakers and Thijs Wilms that has been syndicated in ten different countries.

BOMBER BIKERS OF SHONAN *
1986. JPN: *Shonan Bakusozoku*. AKA: *Explosive Racers of Shonan*. Video. DIR: Nobutaka Nishizawa. SCR: Kenji Kurata, Naoko Takahashi, Kisei Cho. DES: Satoshi Yoshida. ANI: Takashi Saijo. MUS: Yasaku Kikuma, Koichi Hirai, Haruo Kubota. PRD: Ashi Pro, Toei. 50 mins. x 11 eps., 40 mins. x 2 eps. (*Stormy Knight*).
Yosuke Eguchi is cool, brave, enigmatic, and the star of the school's embroidery club. With his pals in the Shonan Bomber Bike gang, he just wants to ride his motorcycle after school without any trouble, following in the footsteps of former schoolmate and current king of the road, Noboru Ishikawa. A rival gang tries to force Eguchi off the road and, when that fails, send in its out-of-town friends to finish the job, but Eguchi's impassioned speech about the Way of Biking convinces everyone they should live in peace. Later episodes concentrate on other members of the gang, including Yoshimi's ham-fisted courting of Nagisa and Eriko's surfer boyfriend, Seiji, falling into depression after a bad performance, and asking Eguchi to help him arrange a rematch. The third installment, a 1987 *Rocky* pastiche where the gang must pick a champion to fight the boxer Kondo, was also screened in theaters on a double bill with VICTORY PITCHER.

Keeping closely to Satoshi Yoshida's original 1983 *Shonen King* manga, combined sales of which topped 20 million volumes, the series lasted ten years, mixing romance and racing, with gang-members pairing off and even the sound of wedding bells. Eguchi falls for an American girl, Samantha, in the penultimate installment, and the finale includes his homegirl Yoshiko's last-ditch attempts to show her feelings.

An immensely successful production throughout the 1980s, the video series did not disgrace its manga predecessor,

selling almost a quarter of a million tapes and inspiring a successful imitator in Toru Fujisawa's *Shonan Pure Love Gang* and GTO. Its English-language performance was less impressive—only a single episode made it to a U.S. video market that couldn't see the appeal of lovelorn Hell's Angels.

In 1997, barely a year after the original coasted to a halt, the same staff would return with *New Bomber Bikers of Shonan: Stormy Knight*. Featuring all-new bikers but with cameo appearances by the original cast, the series consisted of two videos, each split into two faux-TV episodes detailing new gang leader Katsuhiko and his feud with the Tigers.

Beginning the following year, *Stormy Knight* was also adapted as four live-action videos. The original story was also adapted into three live-action movies featuring star of the moment Yosuke Eguchi, *Shonen Bakusozoku* (2001), *Shonen Bakusozoku 2* (2001), and *SB3: Ten Ounce Kizuna* (2002). These appear to follow the plot of the anime quite closely.

BOMBERMAN
1995. JPN: *Bomberman B-Daman Baku Gaiden*. AKA: *Bomberman B-Daman Explosive Tales*. TV series. DIR: Nobuaki Nakanishi, Takafumi Hoshikawa, Yasuo Iwamoto. SCR: Tatsuhiko Urahata, Tomoyasu Okubo, Toshiki Inoue. DES: Koji Sugiura. ANI: Junko Abe. MUS: Jun Chiki Chikuma. PRD: Madhouse. 25 mins. x 48 eps.
In the wake of the Kobe earthquake, the game character Bomberman was dragged out to make a 25-minute program on safety measures called *Thank You to Heroism: Lend Me Your Ears*. This one-shot from director Norio Kawashima was the precursor to a full-fledged series featuring the attempts of the evil Dark B-Da to seize control of B-Da City, opposed only by Bomb, the round-headed agent of justice. B-Daman would return in 1999 with the series *Super B-Daman*, animated by the Xebec studio for breakfast television on TV Tokyo.

Writer Urahata would go on to direct MASTER KEATON.

After almost a hundred episodes, it was rebranded again as the 52-episode *Bomberman Jetterz* (2002), moving the action to a colony world, where slacker Bomberman Shiro is suddenly thrust into a leadership position when his heroic elder brother Mighty goes missing.

BONDAGE HOUSE *
1999. AKA: *Bondage Room, Detective*. Video. DIR: Akihiro Okuzawa. SCR: Takuhiro Fukuda. DES: N/C. ANI: N/C. MUS: N/C. PRD: Beam Entertainment, Akatonbo. 30 mins. x 2 eps.
Detective Higashino rescues a beautiful girl from a gang of strange men. Discovering that Ayane Akimoto was *sold* to them by her parents, Higashino begins an investigation into the modern world of slavery, tracking the life of Ayane's dead older brother, with time out for gratuitous scenes of bondage and abuse. Released in the U.S. as *Bondage Room* (2001). **NV**

BONDAGE 101 *
2004. JPN: *Chobatsu Yobiko*. AKA: *Punishment Prepschool*. Video. DIR: Aim. SCR: Aim. DES: Satoshi Shimada. ANI: Satoshi Shimada. MUS: Yoshi. PRD: YOUC, Digital Works (Vanilla Series). 30 mins. x 2 eps.
Ousted from his previous job for molesting students, Kyoichi Shizuma discovers, like the protagonist of FIVE CARD, that such issues do not prevent him from finding a job elsewhere, particularly when his new posting only pretends to be a school. In fact, it is a secret operation for molding innocent girls into willing sex slaves. Some don't require all that much molding, such as the bespectacled Yumiko, who enthusiastically embraces her school's dark secret. Innocent Asuna is too meek and mild to put up much of a fight, which leaves the "drama" in this erotic anime in the hands of fiery, willful Tomo. Abuse and degradation duly ensues in another entry from the VANILLA SERIES. **LNV**

Boogiepop Phantom

© KOUHEI KADONO./MEDIAWORKS. PROJECT BOOGIEPOP.

BONDAGE QUEEN KATE *

1994. JPN: *Nessa no Wakusei,
Jokoankan: Kate.* AKA: *Desert Planet.*
Video. DIR: Takashi Asami. SCR: Yuji
Kishino. DES: Ryoichi Oki. ANI: N/C. MUS:
N/C. PRD: All Products, Beam Entertainment. 45 mins. x 2 eps.

Kate Curtis is a young, virginal police
officer sent undercover to Doune,
the desert planet where getting raped
by one of the locals is supposedly the
highlight of any trip. Her mission is to
find out who's raping all the tourists.
Her disguise is a skimpy costume with
the words "RAPE ME" emblazoned on
it in big letters. Kidnapped on arrival
by some men clad in incongruous
1970s fashions, she is assaulted during
a desert drive and subjected to toilet-
training torture while hanging from
a chain above a pit full of monsters—
including a thinly disguised Sarlacc
from *Return of the Jedi.* She is then taken
into their lair, where she confesses that
she secretly enjoys rape in an anime
that manages to demean women not
only with what is done to them but also
in how they react to it.

Produced by "Dr. Pochi," perpetra-
tor of several of the CREAM LEMON
series, *Bondage Queen Kate* recalls the
Story of O with its heroine's adoration
of her abusive captors and a salacious
interest in invading the female body
not just with the usual suspects, but
also with diuretics and the surgeon's
knife. The science fiction elements
are perfunctory—Doune is a Middle
Eastern airport departure lounge only
cosmetically related to Frank Herbert's
Dune; the spacecraft has the engines
of a Star Destroyer turned on its side;
the desert is a glorified sand pit; and
if there was ever a time to use a pseudonym, ORGUSS 02–writer Kishino and
several famous voice actors should
have realized that this was it. **NV**

BONES

Aka Studio Bones. Animation company
formed in 1999 by a group of animators from Sunrise: producer Masahiko
Mikami, director Shinichiro Watanabe,
and designer/animator Toshihiro Kawamoto. Notable early works included the
dual stylistic successes of COWBOY BEBOP
(a sci-fi anime without giant robots),
and ESCAFLOWNE (which crammed giant
robots into a fantasy show, a feat not
achieved so well since DUNBINE). Subsequent hits for the studio have included
RAHXEPHON and FULLMETAL ALCHEMIST.

BONOBONO

1993. Movie, TV series. DIR: Hitoshi
Nanba. SCR: Tetsuo Yasumi. DES: Michishiro Yamada. ANI: Michishiro Yamada, Yuka Kubodani. MUS: Gonchichi.
PRD: Amuse, Tac, TV Tokyo. 94 mins.
(m), 15 mins. x 48 eps. (TV).
Bonobono the otter, along with his
friends the raccoon and chipmunk,
first appeared in a children's manga by
MUKA-MUKA PARADISE–creator Mikio Igarashi in 1986. With the gentle stories'
sales topping the five million mark, the
artist directed and wrote the 1993 film,
which featured the woodland pals having fun and debating simple points of
philosophy (à la *Winnie the Pooh*), leaving director Nanba to helm the subsequent 1994 TV series. By this time, the
corporate giant Bandai was involved,
and Japan was deluged with *Bonobono*
toys, games, and merchandising.

The series was resurrected in
the CGI movie *Bonobono: The Tree of
Kumomo* (2002), in which Bonobono
sits beneath the titular tree on a hill in
an attempt to forget his sadness, only
to become involved in a conspiracy
against Popo the ferret, who is accused
of breaking off a branch.

BOOGIEPOP PHANTOM *

2000. JPN: *Boogiepop wa Warawanai.*
AKA: *Boogiepop Does Not Laugh.* TV
series. DIR: Takashi Watanabe. SCR:
Sadayuki Murai. DES: Koji Ogata,
Shigeyuki Suga. ANI: Minoru Tanaka.
MUS: N/C. PRD: Madhouse. 25 mins. x
12 eps.
The malevolent "Manticore" entity
manifests in a Japanese high school,
where it takes on the form of teenage
student Saotome. Saotome's girlfriend
has kept their liaison secret, but confides in Moto, a terminally shy girl
who has secret feelings of her own for
Saotome, which return to trouble her
when the Manticore, as Saotome, traps
her in an alleyway. Meanwhile, a shadowy figure wanders the night defending teenagers from further attacks, in a
show that masterfully mixes the disconnected urban myths of PARANOIA AGENT
and *Ring* (1998) with the perennial

teen-angst concerns about approaching adulthood. *Boogiepop* is based on a series of novels begun in 1998 by Kohei Kadono, but its mood often seems like a deliberate evocation of the unseen menace of SERIAL EXPERIMENTS LAIN. It also cunningly reprises many setups familiar from both Western horror and Western fairytales—the children are offered the chance to never grow up, as in PETER PAN AND WENDY, although their bodies and minds are already struggling with adult concerns and desires. Nowhere is this more apparent than in the subplot concerning a five-year-old serial killer case, allowing director Watanabe and PERFECT BLUE writer Murai to blend the elements of American stalk-and-slash horror with more Japanese sensibilities. A welcome glimpse of originality in a crowded genre (after all, at its most superficial level, this might appear as just one more tale of supernatural ghostbusting in modern Tokyo), it was also the basis for the live-action movie *Boogiepop and Others* (2000).

BORDER

1991. JPN: *Meiso o Border*. AKA: *Running King Border*. Video. DIR: Noboru Ishiguro. SCR: Akira Sata. DES: Kiyotoshi Aoi. ANI: Kiyotoshi Aoi. MUS: Nojin. PRD: Artland. 45 mins.
Akio Tanaka's 1986 manga in *Action Comics*, based on a story by Karibu Marai, features a modern-day odd couple, the naïve virgin Kubota and the handsome charmer Hachisuka, who meet up by accident in a Middle Eastern desert and return to Japan to hustle their way through life. The animated excursion comprises their involvement in shady TV dealings, where they get jobs making fake documentaries, although the manga would continue for another 14 volumes of scheming.

BORN FREE

1976. JPN: *Kyoryu Tankentai Born Free*. AKA: *Dinosaur Investigators Born Free*, *Dinosaur Park*. TV series. DIR: Koichi Takano, Haruyuki Kawajima. SCR: Keiichi Abe, Tomoyuki Ando. DES: Haruyuki Kawajima. ANI: Shigeyuki Kawashima. MUS: Toru Fuyuki. PRD: Tsuburaya, Sunrise, NET. 25 mins. x 25 eps.
In 1996, Comet Arby's approach to Earth causes major upheaval. Dinosaurs, long thought extinct, begin to wander the planet. In the Japanese outpost of an international alliance devoted to controlling the problem, Professor Tadaki forms the Born Free group, a team of dinosaur catchers that aims to protect the creatures from the evil hunter King Battler and deliver them safely to a preserve on Saron Island.
Mixing live action and animation in much the same way as Tezuka's VAMPIRE, *Born Free* features an animated cast inserted into Tsuburaya model footage of the team's mobile base and stop-motion dinosaurs. Twenty years later in the *real* 1996, Sunrise would make the BRAVE SAGA series *Daguon*, in which evil aliens enter the solar system on a rogue asteroid. Coincidence?
Tsuburaya followed the series with the 39-episode *Dinosaur War Eisenborg* (1977, *Kyoryu Daisenso Eisenborg*) on TV Tokyo, in which dinosaurs are found to have survived until the present day in subterranean caves. Ulul, the 300-IQ king of the dinosaurs, decides it is time for his race to reclaim the surface. Professor Tachibana tries to stop them but is killed. His children, Ai and Zen, are mortally injured in the same accident but receive cyborg bodies in the style of 8 MAN from Tachibana's fellow inventor Professor Torii. Joining the anti-dinosaur task force Team D, the Tachibana kids can also fuse into the Super Aizen Cyborg for that typical Tsuburaya last-minute transformation to save the day. From episode 20 onward, the dinosaur threat is replaced by Goddess the Evil Witch-Queen and her aliens from planet Gazaria. As with *Born Free*, the anime action (this time from the Oka studios, not Sunrise) is spliced in with stop-motion and live-action footage in the style of ULTRAMAN.
Neither of these shows, however, was the first. *Born Free* may make it into this encyclopedia thanks to its cel animation, but an earlier live-action show, *Devil Hunter Mitsurugi* (1971, *Majin Hunter Mitsurugi*), featured three children wielding ceremonial swords themed on Wisdom, Humanity and Love, which allow them to combine into the stop-motion giant Mitsurugi, who can fight giant monster invaders from Scorpio. Made by animator Takeo Nakamura and his wife Ayako Magiri, the show was innovative, but suffered from production processes that made it inevitably more time-consuming than cels.

BOSCO ADVENTURE

1986. TV series. DIR: Taku Sugiyama. SCR: Nobuyuki Fujimoto, Shoji Yoshikawa. DES: Shuichi Seki. ANI: Takao Kogawa. MUS: Toshiyuki Watanabe. PRD: Nippon Animation, Yomiuri TV. 25 mins. x 26 eps.
The evil Hoodman hears the prophecy that a princess will become Queen of Fontaine Land at the time of a total solar eclipse. His minions kill the elfin king and queen, but Princess Apricot is spirited away by loyal animal subjects and grows up in their enchanted forest. At age 14, she is told of her destiny by the old man Ender, who reveals that the time of the eclipse is at hand. Apricot is captured by Hoodman but is rescued by her woodland friends, Croak the frog, Tati the turtle, and Otter the otter, in their experimental airship, the Bosco. Pursued by Hoodman across a land of dragons, unicorns, and giants, Apricot and her friends gather the inhabitants of the enchanted land for a final battle, fought at Hoodman's castle itself as the eclipse begins. If Apricot does not sit on the throne in time, the Fountain of Life will run dry. This magical quest was an immense success all over Europe but not in the English language, despite being inspired by Tony Wolf's *Woodland Folk* series of children's books.

BOTCHAN

1980. AKA: *The Young Master*. TV special. DIR: Osamu Dezaki, Toshio Takeuchi. SCR: Yoshiyuki Fukuda. DES: Monkey Punch. ANI: Akio Sugino. MUS: Takeo Watanabe. PRD: TMS. 70 mins.

"The Young Master," a brash young graduate from Tokyo named Uranari, comes to teach at Matsuyama Middle School on the island of Shikoku, where he gets into trouble with the surly locals. The hapless English assistant falls in love with a local maid, Madonna, and proposes to her, only to discover that she has already had another offer from the local boy known as Red Shirt. Eventually, Madonna returns to Red Shirt.

One of the best-selling Japanese books ever, the original 1906 novel by I AM A CAT–creator Soseki Natsume contained strong elements of autobiography. He once taught in Matsuyama himself, though his experiences were less troublesome than his protagonist's. There may have been strife behind the scenes of the anime, too, since LUPIN III–creator Monkey Punch's designs were "cleaned up" by Akio Sugino, and Osamu Dezaki is credited as the director's "assistant" in some sources. Another, shorter version of *Botchan* was made in 1986 as part of the ANIMATED CLASSICS OF JAPANESE LITERATURE. Ⓝ

BOTTLE FAIRY *

2003. JPN: *Binzume Yosei*. TV series. DIR: Yoshiaki Iwasaki. SCR: Hideki Shirane, Makoto Uezu, Noboru Kimura, Takashi Kawai. DES: Masahide Yanigasawa. ANI: N/C. MUS: Yo Yamazaki. PRD: Xebec, Studio Orphee, TV Kanagawa. 12 mins. x 13 eps.

Kururu, Chichiri, Hororo, and Sarara are four fairies who set out to learn about humans by moving in with a young college instructor they call Sensei. Sensei explains different months' events and festivals from all over Japan, covering a year's Japanese tradition in twelve episodes. It thus serves as a useful crash course for game-obsessed, TV-addicted kids who don't listen to Granny or understand the origins of their national way of life—something to which the script regularly alludes when the gullible fairies seek more

information from Tama, a clueless grade-schooler next door. The show takes the creepy CHOBITS conventions of blank-slate ingenues in search of a master, and puts it to largely innocent and educational use, but for all its talk of "tradition," it is very much a product of its time. Its trawl through the customs of the Japanese year contains many modern additions, such as Valentine's Day, a foreign import, or Golden Week, a coincidental cluster of public holidays that has only existed since 1948. While some episodes delve into folklore, such as a discussion of the place of cicadas in a traditional Japanese summer, other episodes are strictly modern, such as beach trips in the summer. By New Year, however, the fairies are deemed to have become so wise that they are worthy of human status à la KEY THE METAL IDOL, and transform into a single gestalt entity before splitting into four pretty girls who, presumably, have the potential to return one day and bore us all with another TENCHI MUYO! clone. Until that time, the series is a handy if sugary introduction to many modern Japanese customs that pass without comment in other anime. Their adventures were created by Yuiko Tokumi and screened on TV Kanagawa, TV Nagoya, and as part of the *Anime Continental* show on Hiroshima TV, along with BPS. The U.S. release faithfully repeats the "Bottle Fairy" singular title of the original Japanese publicity materials, although there are clearly four fairies on display.

BOUNTY DOG *

1994. Video. DIR: Hiroshi Negishi. SCR: Mayori Sekijima. DES: Hirotoshi Sano. ANI: Hirotoshi Sano. MUS: Sho Goto. PRD: Zero-G Room. 30 mins. x 2 eps.

Freelance troubleshooters Yoshiyuki, Shoko, and Kei are sent to the moon to check up on a suspected military project. Far from human habitation beneath the lunar surface, they find an alien observation post run by the good Yayoi and the bad "Darkness." Both they and their minions are all clones of

the same original, who fell in love with Yoshiyuki on one of her sightseeing trips to Earth. With the original Yayoi dead, the troubleshooters must fight to save the balance of the universe.

Like many modern anime, *Bounty Dog* began as a radio drama and has difficulty shaking off its origins. Yayoi, Darkness, and the alien army are all clones of the same girl, which makes for cheap casting in radio but unimaginative visuals. Much of the story unfolds over still frames and static pans, while director Negishi plunders shots and sound effects from his own BEAST WARRIORS. Scenes are bathed in a limited palette of yellows and greens, while subsurface sequences are all shot in red. The final showdown in Darkness's blue hideaway completes the pattern, but though one paint costs much the same as another, the avant-garde color scheme actually makes the film look even cheaper.

Stealing great chunks of plot from *2001: A Space Odyssey* and PLEASE SAVE MY EARTH, *Bounty Dog*'s real failing lies in sloppy science and sloppy fiction. The moon, we are told, has been terraformed, which must have been difficult without an atmosphere. The plot calls for spacesuits intermittently and illogically, while temperature and gravity are inexplicably like Earth's. As for the good-vs.-evil alien setup, it appears to be an ill-conceived MacGuffin from the production committee that cooked up the original story, and it is simply dismissed with a "how weird" voice-over at the end.

BOUNTY HUNTER: THE HARD

1995. Video. DIR: Yoshikazu Oga. SCR: Megumi Hiyoshi. DES: Masami Suda. ANI: Masami Suda. MUS: Shinichi Kida. PRD: JC Staff. 47 mins.

Keiji "The Hard" Nando, the toughest bounty hunter in New York, acquires a floppy disk full of names, which drags him into a conspiracy to buy and sell human organs. This one-shot tale reputedly added *extra* violence to STORY OF RIKI–creator Tetsuya Saruwatari's mean-streets manga from *Business*

Jump. Postdating **Mad Bull 34**, which also had a Japanese fish out of water in the U.S., this New York hard-man was eclipsed in the same year by the success of a Chicago crime story. Ironically, **Gunsmith Cats** starred Michiko Neya, a minor voice in *The Hard*, as the bounty hunter Rally Vincent. **L N V**

BOY AND DOLPHIN

1975. JPN: *Iruka to Shonen*. TV series. DIR: Tsuneo Komuro. SCR: N/C. DES: N/C. ANI: Toshitaka Kadota, Isamu Kaneko, Hiroshi Yamagishi, Katsunori Kobayashi, Toyoko Imamura, Kiyoto Ishino. MUS: Hiroki Ogawa, Michel Legrand. PRD: TBS, Eiken. 30 mins. x 26 eps.

On the South Sea island of Ululula (spelled backwards, Alululu), handsome young man Jean lives with girlfriend Marina and Uncle Patrick in their wrecked ship, which sits in a bay of coral reefs. Their animal companions include Sebastian the myna bird, a friendly koala bear, and Um, the intelligent white dolphin. But life is not all sun bathing and swimming for Jean and friends. They must also fight off evil corporations intent on exploiting nature, deal with the inhabitants of a mysterious underwater city, and even save their new-found friends from natural disaster.

This variant of **Swiss Family Robinson** and **Adrift in the Pacific**, was the first ever Franco-Japanese coproduction, jointly organized by the Japanese Eiken studio, producer Eve Champin and the French channel ORTF. Directorial responsibility actually lay on the French side, an issue which led Japanese critics of the time to blame the serial's Japanese ratings failure on the French. However, this did not prevent further coproductions, including **Ulysses 31** and the **Mysterious Cities of Gold**. A 1980 Italian broadcast was tied to advertising Galak white chocolate, presumably noted for its dolphin-friendly qualities. Compare to **Marine Boy**.

BOY WHO SAW THE WIND, THE *

2000. JPN: *Kaze o Mita Shonen*. Movie.

DIR: Kazuki Omori, Toshiya Shinohara. SCR: Shu Narijima. DES: Minoru Maeda. ANI: Minoru Maeda. MUS: N/C. PRD: N/C. 90 mins.

Amon is a boy who has the power to control the wind. Branich, the ruler of the world, needs Amon's power to complete the ultimate weapon and sends his minions to bring the boy in. Though Amon's parents have forbidden him from using his talents, the arrival of Branich's men leaves him with no choice—giving them the slip, Amon runs away with Maria, one of the People of the Sea. Maria agrees to help Amon find his own tribe.

The Boy Who Saw the Wind is "a plea for good people to stand up and say 'no' to fascism and dictatorship," according to its creator, the Welsh-born author C. W. Nicol, whose writings are said to have inspired Hayao Miyazaki to set **Castle in the Sky** in a Welsh mining village.

BOY WITH CAT'S EYES, THE

1976. JPN: *Yokaiden Nekome Koso*. AKA: *Ghost Story: Boy with Cat's Eyes*. TV series. DIR: Keinosuke Shiyano. SCR: Yuji Amemiya. DES: Tasuteru Hakumori. ANI: N/C. MUS: Masahiko Nishiyama. PRD: Wako Pro, TV Tokyo. 15 mins. x 22 eps.

Short ghost stories from **Makoto-chan**–creator Kazuo Umezu, all linked by the titular feline-featured youth, including *The Girl Who Cried in the Night*, *Eyes of the Dryad*, *Portal to Hell*, *Witch of Misty Valley*, and *Enigma of the Dark Sorcerer*. Umezu's trademark misogyny is greatly in evidence here—though his only tale available in English is the live-action adaptation of his bitchy brain-swapping revenge tragedy *Baptism of Blood*. Two further horror shorts, *There's Something on the Video Camera* and *Haunted House*, were released on a single 45-minute tape as *Incantation* (1990, *Umezu Kazuo no Nomi*). These later stories featured animation from Shingo Araki and direction by Naoko Omi. Another Umezu story, *Orochi*, was released in 2000 as a "manga video" (see **Crusher Joe**).

BOYFRIEND

1992. TV special. DIR: Tetsu Dezaki. SCR: Kazumi Koide. DES: Yukari Kobayashi. ANI: Yukari Kobayashi. MUS: Hiroshi Ikeda. PRD: Magic Bus, TV Tokyo. 94 mins.

After an accident, teen basketball star Masaki is transferred to a new school, where he immediately falls in love with local girl Kanako. After helping her home through her drunken stupor one night on the train, he can think of nobody else but her, though she is already interested in a beautiful blond basketball player, the handsome Akiro.

Originally broadcast as a TV special then split in two halves and rereleased on video, this gentle love story began as a 1985 manga by Soryo Fuyumi. A similar high school sports love triangle can be found in **Slow Step**.

BOYS BE . . .

2000. TV series. DIR: Masami Shimoda, Eiji Suganuma, Shinji Kasai. SCR: Kenichi Kanemaki, Hiroyuki Kawasaki. DES: Itsuko Takeda. ANI: Michinori Chiba. MUS: Be Factory. PRD: Hal Filmmaker, WOWOW. 25 mins. x 13 eps.

Makoto is a brash, loud little charmer at his school, but deep down he's just a shy little boy who lives at home with his adoring mother. And as he and his three friends flirt and spar with the school's three girls most likely to put out, will one of them notice what a delicate little flower he really is? This series takes Masahiro Itabashi and Hiroyuki Tamakoshi's 1991 manga from *Shonen Magazine* but simplifies the picaresque plot to concentrate on a single boy and a mere trio of girls. The final episode, "Let it Be," was not broadcast but is included on the video.

BOYS OVER FLOWERS *

1996. JPN: *Hana yori Dango*. AKA: *Boys Before Flowers*. TV series, movie. DIR: Shigeyasu Yamauchi. SCR: Yumi Kageyama, Reiko Yoshida, Aya Masui. DES: Yoshihiko Umakoshi. ANI: Chuji Nakajima, Tomoko Ito, Tomoyuki Kawano. MUS: Michiru Oshima. PRD: Toei,

TV Asahi. 25 mins. x 51 eps. (TV), 25 mins. (m).

Sixteen-year-old Makino Tsukushi is a girl from a poor family who gets a scholarship to attend the prestigious Eitoku Academy. Though she tries to keep a low profile, she is soon singled out for hazing by "F4," an elite group at the academy composed of the sons of the richest families in Japan. When she stands up to them, their leader, Domyoji, becomes attracted to her, though she finds herself falling for his lieutenant, Rui. Rui, however, loves Shizuka, a gorgeous fashion model. This gentle romantic comedy was based on Yoko Kamio's 1992 manga in *Margaret*, and also adapted into the theatrical short *BBF: The Movie* (1997), a musical in which Makino travels to New York to become a star, replaying the CINDERELLA story even as she appears in a stage version of it. The series has been adapted twice for live-action television, first in Taiwan as *Meteor Garden* (2001), then for the Japanese TBS network in 2005.

BPS

2003. JPN: *bpS: Battle Programmer Shirase*. TV series. DIR: Hiroki Hayashi. SCR: J/R Sakurajimaeki. DES: Ryoichi Makino, Keiji Hashimoto. ANI: Ryoichi Makino, Keiji Hashimoto. MUS: Seiko Nagaoka. PRD: G-PLUS, AIC, Gansis, TV Kanagawa. 12 mins. x 15 eps.

Computer hacker Akira Shirase is a free spirit who won't work for hire, in spite of the success his programming genius could bring him. Instead he raids big bank accounts around the world like a LUPIN III of the digital age; when he targets an account he won't rest until he's hacked it and squeezed it dry. He lives alone, but for occasional visits from his adoring ten-year-old niece Misao Amano, who fusses over him in a faintly creepy imitation of a housewife. Akira battles the fat, evil geek hacker known as the King of America, who is trying to destabilize the Internet, and meets a range of wacky characters in a new short adventure every week. Created by TENCHI MUYO! director Hiroki Hayashi,

this series was screened as part of TV Kanagawa's *Anime Continental* show along with BOTTLE FAIRY. It's a sign of the times that the anime audience is now so sedentary and housebound that its latest action hero is a man sitting at a desk playing with a computer while waiting for someone to bring him food. The final episode featured a goodbye message to foreign fan-subbers with a thank you to "everyone who watched overseas without permission," although considering that data theft is a heroic act in the show, it's unclear whether the tone was ironic.

BRAIN POWERED *

1998. TV series. DIR: Yoshiyuki Tomino. SCR: Yoshiyuki Tomino. DES: Mutsumi Inomata, Mamoru Nagano. ANI: Atsushi Shigeta. MUS: Yoko Kanno. PRD: Sunrise, WOWOW. 25 mins. x 26 eps.

The meek shall inherit the Earth. The rest of us shall escape to the stars. Such is the belief of those who are trying to raise Orphan ("the ruin with a woman's face") from the watery depths. On a devastated world, they see Orphan as their last, best chance for survival, but they need the assistance of the Grand Chers, organic machines that are "born" from spinning plates (not unlike the creatures in MONSTER RANCHER). On a routine recovery mission, brash pilot Yu faces off against Hime, a girl who has accidentally bonded with an Anti Body, a particularly powerful form of organic machine. The meeting inspires Yu to defect from Orphan a year later, but his former colleagues are in hot pursuit.

An incoherent EVANGELION clone, *Brain Powered* is still curiously watchable, thanks largely to Yoko Kanno's wonderful music. It's as if Tomino and his crew were thrown in at the deep end and told to wing it. Nothing is explained, but all the details fill the viewer with the vain hope that somehow they will all make sense—until the disappointingly anticlimactic ending. Naked nymphs dance around Buddhist temples, flame-haired pilots keep their tresses down because their machines

"like it that way," and nobody seems fazed by the groinal hatches on the Grand Chers. 🅝

BRAT COP

1989. JPN: *Gaki Deka*. TV series. DIR: Yuzo Yamada. SCR: Keiji Terui, Yoshio Urasawa, Hideki Mitsui. DES: Tatsuhiko Yamagami. ANI: Takeaki Natsumoto, Yuri Handa, Michishiro Yamada. MUS: N/C. PRD: Tokio Animation Film, Asia Do, Fuji TV. 12 mins. x 43 eps.

Tatsuhiko Yamagami's surreal 1974 comic about a boy/cop who liked playing with his testicles, sentencing people to death, and occasionally transforming into a deer or elephant ran in *Shonen Captain* for 26 volumes until 1981. This 1989 revival was seemingly timed to cash in on the child readers becoming old enough to purchase videos, with a straight-to-video special directed by Junichiro Nakamura, released a month after the TV series began. A spiritual ancestor of the 1990s hit CRAYON SHIN-CHAN.

BRAVE FROG, THE *

1973. JPN: *Kerokko Demetan*. AKA: *Ribitty Demetan; Adventures on Rainbow Pond*. TV series. DIR: Tatsuo Yoshida, Seitaro Hara. SCR: Akiyoshi Sakai, Hiroshi Sasagawa. DES: Tatsuo Yoshida, Yoshitaka Amano. ANI: Masayuki Hayashi, Hiroshi Kawabata. MUS: Nobuyoshi Koshibe. PRD: Tatsunoko, Fuji TV. 25 mins. x 39 eps.

Demetan (Jonathan Jumper) is a frog too poor to attend school in Rainbow Pond, but he's good friends with Ranatan (Hillary Hopper), daughter of the rich Lord Frog (Maxwell/Big Max). Though Big Max tries to break them apart, they persevere and try to help him become a nicer person. The community is united by a common threat when menaced by a giant catfish who steals the frogspawn. Jonathan heads for the sea with his friend Cheepy the bird, and there they persuade an electric eel to accompany them back to the pond and drive out the catfish. Hillary's father finally approves of Jonathan, and they all live happily ever after.

BRAVE RAIDEEN *

1975. JPN: *Yusha Rydeen*. AKA: *Heroic Rydeen*. TV series. DIR: Yoshiyuki Tomino, Takeyuki Kanda, Yoshikazu Yasuhiko, Kazuo Terada. SCR: Fuyunori Gobu, Masaru Yamamoto, Masaki Tsuji. DES: Yoshikazu Yasuhiko. ANI: Yoshikazu Yasuhiko. MUS: Akihiro Kobayashi. PRD: Tohoku Shinsha, NET. 25 mins. x 50 eps., 25 mins. x 38 eps. (remake). After a slumber of 12 millennia, the Demon Empire returns to seize control of Earth, plotting evil from its secret volcano base, from which its high priest regularly sends out fearsome Fossil Beasts to attack humanity. Raideen, the giant robot-like protector of the lost continent of Mu (see SUPER ATRAGON), senses the evil presence and awakes within its golden pyramid, revealing to young Japanese boy Akira Hibiki that he is the one descendant of the ancient Mu people who must help Raideen save Earth. He can call on Raideen whenever he needs him and ride his "Sparker" motorcycle into the robot's chest, where it can be stored during missions. The Demon Empire seeks control of Mutoron, the powerful element that allows Raideen to self-repair in its cliff-face hideaway. Akira also has the assistance of his friends, token girl Mari Sakirada (daughter of a scientist fighting the Demon Empire) and several members of his high school soccer team—with suspicious echoes of BATTLE OF THE PLANETS. This early giant-robot story was based on a manga by Ryohei Suzuki and united the Tomino and Yasuhiko team that would work so well together on the later GUNDAM, where they would replay the well-matched rivalry of Akira and the blond Demon Prince Sharkin as the later serials' Amuro Ray and Char Aznable. Subtitled (poorly) in Hawaii by Kiku-TV, it was shown on the New York Japanese community channel 47, thereby becoming the first giant-robot show to reach a large U.S. audience. As Raideen, it also formed part of the SHOGUN WARRIORS collection. The series was remade as *Reideen: The Superior* (1996), directed by Toshifumi Kawase,

which similarly featured a boy assembling a five-man team of warriors to pilot cool vehicles and save the planet.

BRAVE SAGA *

1990. JPN: *Exkaiser*; *Fyvard/Fighbird*; *Da Garn*; *Might Gine/Might-Gaine*; *J-Deka*; *Goldoran*; *Daguon*; *Gaogaigar*. AKA: (see below). TV series. DIR: Katsuyoshi Yutabe, Shinji Takamatsu. SCR: Yasushi Hirano, Hiroyuki Hoshiyama, Fuyunori Gobu, Hiroyuki Kawasaki, Takao Koyama, Yoshitomo Yometani. DES: Kunio Okawara, Atsuko Ishida, Akira Oguro. ANI: Masami Obari. MUS: Toshiyuki Watanabe, Takashi Kudo. PRD: Sunrise, Nagoya TV. 25 mins. x 20 eps. (*Exkaiser*), 48 eps. (*Fyvard*), 46 eps. (*Da Garn*), 47 eps. (*Might Gine*), 48 eps. (*J-Deka*), 20 eps. (*Goldoran*), 48 eps. (*Daguon*), 30 mins. x 2 eps. (*Daguon v*), 44 eps. (*Gaogaigar*). Almost matching Tatsunoko's TIME BOKAN and Tokyo Movie Shinsha's LUPIN III for sheer endurance, the Sunrise "Brave" series (each title contains the word *yu*: "brave/hero") of giant-robot shows may look like an endless stream of formulaic pap, but not to its target audience. In the fiercely hierarchical world of childhood, last year's show is passé by definition—this year's toys and this year's heroes are what counts. The heroes of ULTRAMAN and BATTLE OF THE PLANETS have been reverse-engineered and refined over the years to create a set template of series construction, and "Hajime Yadate," the house pseudonym that assigns half the credit for new shows to the Sunrise studio itself, has realized that there is a point in every boy's life when he has never seen a giant robot before. Each and every "Brave" show represents a whole age group's first evening viewing, first hot-headed hero, first crush, and first battle-cry of improbable-sounding attack names. There is also an important technical issue in the construction of TV anime involving a transformation sequence—the same footage can be reused in every episode, effectively cutting production costs. And though one

could argue that Sunrise should invest in one decent series and repeat it, that would destroy the entire industrial complex that grows up around each show. The nature of merchandise-driven entertainment for a young audience requires constant upgrades and renewals built around the same basic templates of colors, action figures, and, unfortunately, plotting.

The "Brave" phenomenon began in 1990 with *Heroic Exkaiser* (*Yusha Exkaiser*), in which a giant galactic police robot fights to protect humanity from the predations of the Gaistar space pirates. In an attempt to create an ongoing franchise separate from the same studio's ongoing GUNDAM series, the same crew returned in *Sun Hero Fyvard* (1991, *Taiyo no Yusha Fyvar*), in which Professor Amano convinces his grandchildren, Kenta and Haruka, to combine with the Fyvard android in order to save Earth. Working on the principle that if something isn't broken, it doesn't need fixing, they were back in 1992 with another "Brave" anime, *Legendary Hero Da Garn* (*Densetsu Yusha Da Garn*), where Earth is attacked by the alien Orbus invaders, and only a group of young kids in a giant robot can save it. Ever the optimists, Sunrise returned in 1993, retaining the "Brave" name in the title to reassure viewers that nothing was really going to change. This time, the series was *Heroic Express Might Gine* (*Yusha Tokkyu Might Gine*), which, with dazzling originality, concentrated on a team of young kids in a giant robot saving Earth from invading aliens. By 1994, the "Brave" slot on Japanese TV was well established, and the template was punched out once more as *Heroic Cop J-Deka* (*Yusha Keisatsu J-Deka*), in which the hot-headed young hero, Yuta, pilots a giant robot cop, fighting giant robot criminals. In 1995, the franchise was back with tiresome predictability in *Golden Hero Goldoran* (*Ogon no Yusha Goldoran*), featuring three young boys in a transforming robot, who go in search of the fabled lost treasure of Rajendra. *Goldoran*, however, was taken off the air very quickly, possibly because it pushed the envelope a little too far, but more likely because it didn't push it far enough in a year when everybody was watching EVANGELION. In 1996, the studio returned to the tried-and-true alien-invasion storyline with *Heroic Order Daguon* (*Yusha Shirei Daguon*), featuring five young kids, their Daguon vehicles, and their allies from planet Bravestar defending Earth from the invading hordes of Sandor, who have piggy-backed into the solar system on a wandering asteroid—perhaps an homage to the similar story of the studio's earlier BORN FREE, which was set in the "future year" of 1996. Regaining its old level of popularity, the franchise also picked up a substantial female audience by imitating the success of its sister-franchise's *Gundam Wing* pretty-boy line up. The final incarnation came with *Gaogaigar: King of Bravery* (1991, *Yusha o Gaigaigar*), in which the usual alien invasion subplot (this time from underground) was augmented with the addition of sentient robots, whose artificial intelligences encouraged identification and sympathy with their plight—compare to the later YUKIKAZE. Gaogaigar's cyborg hero and his transforming robot pals (with token boy Mamoru), managed to see off the attacks of the Zonder empire, only to be brought back for *Gaogaigar Final* (2000) an eight-part video series in which they must travel into space to deal with the threat presented by the self-proclaimed Eleven Kings of Sol, who have even cloned Mamoru to aid them in their schemes. The video series, augmented with four bonus episodes, was then bizarrely repackaged for television as the 12-part *Gaogaigar Final: Grand Glorious Gathering* (2005), broadcast on TV Tokyo. As we went to press, it was announced that *Gaogaigar* was being licensed for North American release.

BREAK-AGE

1999. Video. DIR: Tsuneo Tominaga. SCR: Tsuneo Tominaga. DES: Zhiemay Batow. ANI: Akira Kano. MUS: N/C.

PRD: Panasonic/Beam Entertainment. 45 mins.

In 2007, the inhabitants of Danger Planet III fight their battles using remote-controlled robots or "virtual puppets." Kirio Nimura is a high school student and the strongest puppeteer on the planet, until he falls for Sairi Takahara, who insists that nobody may make advances until they have beaten her puppet, Benkei.

After running for seven years in *Comic Beam*, Zhiemay Batow's manga *Break-Age* was adapted into an anime video by Panasonic, belatedly realizing that there might be some money in customizable robots, combat, and teen romance.

BREMEN FOUR

1981. JPN: *Bremen 4: Jigoku no Naka no Tenshitachi.* AKA: *Bremen Four: Angels in Hell.* TV special. DIR: Osamu Tezuka, Hiroshi Sasagawa. SCR: Osamu Tezuka, Katsuhito Akiyama. DES: Osamu Tezuka. Hisashi Sakaguchi. ANI: Kazuhiko Udagawa. MUS: Yasuo Higuchi. PRD: Tezuka Pro, NTV. 90 mins.

Rondo, a flower-child alien, is sent down to bring peace to Earth but unfortunately lands in the middle of a blitzkrieg orchestrated by the evil Colonel Karl Presto, a Nazi-style military leader who is massacring the local peasantry with storm troopers and Martian war machines. The mortally wounded Rondo uses the last of her powers to transform Allegro the dog, Coda the cat, Largo the donkey, and Minuet the hen into human teenagers to carry on her mission. The kids form a band to sing for peace but let success go to their heads and devolve into an arrogant punk band. At a command performance for the evil, Wagner-loving Colonel Presto, they witness a machine-gun massacre and remember their mission of saving the world, but it's at the price of sacrificing their human forms and becoming animals once more.

As with so much in anime and manga, Tezuka blazed the trails for others. Distantly inspired by one of GRIMMS'

FAIRY TALES, *The Musicians of Bremen*, but with comic Nazis that led some to describe this little-known TV movie as Tezuka's *Springtime for Hitler*, the peace-through-music message would be taken up the following year by the runaway success of MACROSS.

BRIDE OF DARKNESS *

1999. JPN: *Inju Nerawareta Hanayome.* AKA: *Bride Engulfed by Lust.* Video. DIR: N/C. SCR: N/C. DES: N/C. ANI: N/C. MUS: N/C. PRD: Pink Pineapple. 30 mins. x 2 eps.

Sanshiro is the son of a family servant who secretly lusts after Momoyo, the beautiful daughter of the lord of the manor. Since it would be unseemly for him to even consider a relationship with a woman of such a higher social class, he must be content with peeping on her from various secret vantage points in the house. Momoyo is betrothed to Yoichiro, the wealthy scion of an industrial family, who has recently returned from a trip to exotic, dangerous England. Sanshiro's voyeuristic tendencies give him a grandstand view of the family's darker secrets, particularly the secret sadomasochistic relationship that Yoichiro is conducting with Momoyo's elder sister. However, Sanshiro is also suffering from a series of increasingly powerful headaches and begins to think that he can see "Konago," a ghostly pale girl who claims to be an evil presence somehow summoned by Yoichiro—this is what traveling to England does to people.

The Taisho period (1912–26) was back in vogue at the time this anime was made, partly due to revisionist fantasies like SAKURA WARS, but largely thanks to the global popularity of James Cameron's *Titanic* (1997), which is even referenced in a scene where Sanshiro paints Momoyo in the nude—albeit without her knowledge. For a more sedate approach to inter-class relationships, see EMMA. ⓛⓝⓥ

BRIDE OF DEIMOS

1988. JPN: *Akuma (Deimos) no Hana-*

yome. AKA: *Bride of Satan* (*Deimos*). Video. DIR: Rintaro. SCR: Etsuko Ikeda. DES: Yuho Ashibe. ANI: Hirotsugu Hamazaki. MUS: N/C. PRD: Madhouse. 30 mins.

DARKSIDE BLUES–artist Yuho Ashibe also drew the original 1975 manga for *Princess* magazine based on a story by *Witches' Bible* author Etsuko Ikeda. A story of incestuous love between the divine beings Deimos and Venus—the latter is aggravated by the former's adoration of the Earth girl Michiko. This perverse love triangle ends up in a spooky mansion from which people never return. In a similar setup to Chie Shinohara's *Anatolia Story*, Michiko must die to save Deimos, but he has fallen for her. **N**

BRIGADOON

2000. JPN: *Brigadoon: Marin to Melan.* TV series. DIR: Yoshitomo Yometani. SCR: Hideyuki Kurata. DES: Masahiro Kimura. ANI: Masahiro Yamane, Takuro Shinbo. MUS: N/C. PRD: Sunrise, WOWOW. 25 mins. x 26 eps.
Marin, a happy but inept student who lives in world loosely modeled on 1970s Japan, is the first to notice the giant floating city hovering above her town. Brigadoon, for so it is called, fast becomes a personal project for Marin as she meets Melan, a large blue superrobot who befriends her and takes her up to the magical city.

With its resemblance to the story of Urashima Taro (see **JAPANESE FOLK TALES**), the original *Brigadoon* story about a Scottish village that only appears once every century is not unknown in Japan. However, this show seems to owe more to Miyazaki's **CASTLE IN THE SKY**, aimed squarely at the pretty but vacant audience that warmed to Kurata's earlier **BATTLE ATHLETES**.

BROTHER DEAREST

1991. JPN: *Oniisama e.* AKA: *To My Elder Brother, Brother, Dear Brother.* TV series. DIR: Osamu Dezaki. SCR: Hideo Takayashiki. DES: Akio Sugino. ANI: Akio Sugino. MUS: Kentaro Haneda. PRD: NHK, Visual Book. 25 mins. x 39 eps.

ROSE OF VERSAILLES–creator Riyoko Ikeda wrote this take on life in Seiran Academy, a school for privileged young ladies. Professor's daughter Nanako writes many letters to the titular brother, outlining her life at the school, especially with regard to the intense relationships she has formed within the elite sorority. Her new friend Mariko does her best to ruin Nanako's friendship with her old friend, Tomoko. The tall, boyish Saint Juste carries a torch for the sorority leader, Miya, while Nanako calls on the assistance of the consumptive girl "Prince" Kauro to help her get closer to Miya, for whom she herself is falling. Intense desires bubble under the surface in this beautifully animated series, which, despite its languid pace, deals sensitively with incest, bullying, young love, obsession, conspiracy, suicide, jealousy, and death in the style of **SONG OF WIND AND TREES**. Its broadcast in English is doubly unlikely, not merely for its subject matter, but also because of the scandal caused when it was yanked off the air in France. Not all anime, as broadcasters discovered, are "kids' stuff." **NV**

BRYGAR

1981. JPN: *Ginga Senbu Brygar.* AKA: *Galactic Whirlwind Brygar, Galaxy Cyclone Brygar, Cosmo Ranger, Cosmo Runner.* TV series. DIR: Takao Yotsuji, Teppei Matsuura, Hideki Takayama. SCR: Masaru Yamamoto, Shunsuke Kaneko, Hiroshi Hamazaki. DES: Kazuo Komatsubara. ANI: Masami Yamazaki. MUS: Masayuki Yamamoto. PRD: Kokusai Eiga, TV Tokyo. 25 mins. x 39 eps. (*Brygar*), 25 mins. x 39 eps. (*Baxinga*), 25 mins. x 43 eps. (*Sasrygar*).
King Carmen Carmen wants to destroy the planet Jupiter in order to create a new star and irrevocably change the solar system forever. Only the J9 Cosmo Rangers, comprised of Razor Isaac, Blaster Kid, Flying Bowie, and token girl Angel Omachi, can stop him. This energetic and popular series was supposedly inspired by real-life scientific research and used a lot of Korean talent at the lower ranks of production.

The following year saw a sequel, *Galactic Stormwind Baxinga* (*Ginga Reppu Baxinga*, aka *Cosmo Rangers*), set 300 years after the destruction of Jupiter, in which the solar system has enjoyed a period of relative peace under the Bakufu government. In much the same way that **RAI** adapted the events of Japan's civil war, *Baxinga* retold the fall of the 19th-century Bakufu government (or shogunate) in an SF setting, placing its cast in the role of the Shinsengumi organization (see **OI! RYOMA**). The J9 group takes on a new role, with Don Condole, Schutteken, Billy, Thauma, and token girl Laila fighting to keep the Bakufu alive. However, like their historical counterparts, they eventually fail, ending with a climactic battle that sees the entire central cast killed.

As the popularity of the franchise waned, it returned for a final lighter-hearted series in 1983 with *Galactic Hurricane Sasrygar* (*Ginga Shippu Sasrygar*). This time, the historical reality warped for SF purposes is Prohibition-era America, while the plot is supplied in a pastiche of Jules Verne's *Around the World in Eighty Days*. IC Blues, a card shark operating in the asteroid belt, bets mob leader Bloody God that he can visit all 50 inhabited worlds in the de-Jupitered solar system within a year. He sets off to do so in his transforming robot ship Sasrygar accompanied by his faithful friends, though he soon discovers that members of the Bloody Syndicate are out to make him forfeit the bet, and will stop at nothing to do so. Jupiter suffers another unpleasant fate in Hideaki Anno's **GUNBUSTER**.

B'T X

1996. TV series. DIR: Mamoru Hamazu. SCR: Sukehiro Tomita, Yasushi Hirano. DES: Hideyuki Motohashi. ANI: Hideyuki Motohashi. MUS: Fence of Defense. PRD: TMS, TBS. 25 mins. x 25 eps.
Teppei's elder brother, the brilliant scientist Kotaro, is kidnapped by the forces of the evil Machine Empire, who have been lying in wait in the Gobi Desert for centuries. Local girl Karen,

Bubblegum Crisis

who turns out to be a rebel against the Machine Empire, has taken a sample from the body of Raphael, the last of the great "B't" (pronounced "Beat") devices.

Singled out by the cross-shaped scar on his forehead, the result of a childhood encounter with the Machine Empire, Teppei gains "X," the greatest of the B't machines. Teaming up with the riders/pilots of other B'ts built to resemble a dragon, a phoenix, and a turtle, he sets off to rescue his brother.

Masami Kurumada's earlier **Saint Seiya** also featured pretty boys and semimythical machines fighting to save the world. *B't X* wasn't quite as successful as its predecessor, only racking up a single TV series before coming off the air. A 14-episode sequel, *B't X Neo*, was directed by Hajime Kamegaki and released straight to video in 1997. That show's swift arrival and strange taxonomy (a total of 39 episodes making three complete seasons) prompted speculation that the "video" series was actually the unbroadcast remainder of an axed TV show. Other heroes similarly marked with the scars of destiny include the lead in **Ruro ni Kenshin,**

the lead characters of **Dark Myth** and **Argent Soma**, and, most famously, Char Aznable from **Gundam.**

BUBBLEGUM CRISIS *
1987. Video, TV series. DIR: Katsuhito Akiyama, Hiroki Hayashi. SCR: Toshimichi Suzuki, Hidetoshi Yoshida, Arii Emu. DES: Kenichi Sonoda, Shinji Makino. ANI: Masahiro Tanaka, Jun Okuda. MUS: Koji Makaino. PRD: Artmic, Youmex, AIC. 47 mins., 28 mins., 26 mins., 38 mins., 43 mins., 50 mins., 49 mins., 50 mins. (v1), 25 mins. x 24 eps. (TV), 45 mins. x 3 eps. (*Crash*), 25 mins. x 2 eps. (v2).
In the postquake city of Megatokyo, sentient robots, or "voomers," are a part of everyday life, but these androids can be used for evil as well as good. Sylia Stingray fights a private war with the evil corporation that murdered her scientist father (inventor of the voomers). With her "Knight Saber" companions Priss, Linna, and Nene and their powerful "hard-suit" armor, they attempt to prevent the Genom Corporation from seizing control of the world with voomer agents.

A fan favorite in its day, *BGC* was one

of the earliest openly Japanese anime to reach the West (as opposed to "invisible" kiddie cartoons), in a subtitled edition from AnimEigo. With babes in battlesuits designed by **Gunsmith Cats'** Sonoda and a sprawling high-tech cityscape, the retention of Japanese dialogue caught the oriental flavor of the cyberpunk zeitgeist, and, it should be said, blinded the audience to the show's flaws: variable animation quality, cheesy rock music, steals from Hollywood (particularly *Robocop* and *Blade Runner*), and the camp *Buckaroo Banzai* pop-star-as-crime-fighter conceit. Though still well-regarded to this day, a lot of the series' popularity seems to stem from the hazy memories of old-school fans, who were grateful in the early days that anything was translated at all, so much the better if it was science fiction.

In 1988, the voice actresses shot the live-action *Hurricane Live 2032/3* concert videos, featuring extra animated footage over music. This was followed by *Bye² Knight Sabers: Holiday in Bali*, featuring two scenes of the voice actresses in character in a group, plus one mini-interview and music video of each, and one ensemble music video, all using Bali as a backdrop. Three final episodes appeared the following year, directed by Hiroshi Ishiodori and Hiroyuki Fukushima and called, owing to a split between Artmic and Youmex, *Bubblegum Crash*. In these episodes, the Sabers have gone their separate ways but reform when an old enemy (guess who?) reappears. The pseudonymous Arii Emu ("REM") provided the script, but the *BGC* magic had already faded. It's true that *Crash* has its moments (particularly the arrival of little-robot-lost Adama, who turns out to be an ingenue-assassin), but its vision of the future has aged quite badly. The punks and techno music that would have impressed the *Terminator* generation look out of place, as do the chunky mobile phones. There are moments in *Crash* when the robot-slave-society spins into some really interesting ideas, but much of it is marred by the ridiculously contrived team of female vigilantes and lame attempts at humor.

A more stylistically successful version of the franchise appeared in **AD POLICE**, which focused on the early years of supporting character Leon McNicol, but it only lasted for three episodes. A plan was briefly mooted for a video special about the Knight Sabers off-duty—when it was canceled, the proposal was heavily rewritten and eventually filmed as **TENCHI MUYO!**

In 1998, after **EVANGELION** turned TV serials into a new growth area, *BGC* was revived along with many other old favorites. Hayashi directed a remake, *Bubblegum Crisis 2040*, written by Chiaki Konaka, whose **ARMITAGE III** had made far better use of robot-slave setups. *BGC 2040* dumped the humor in favor of sexual politics—Sylia sells lingerie at the Sexy Doll clothes shop, but the outfits she forces on the girls are little different. With much stretching of rubber, teetering on high heels, and inserting of "plumbing," the trademark hard-suits demean even as they empower. The characters, too, possess interesting flaws, and many situations draw on U.S. superhero comics—Sylia Stingray is remodeled as a cold-hearted neurotic like Tim Burton's Batman, while wide-eyed country-girl Linna has a Clark Kent existence as a humble secretary, troubled by both the office Lothario and the robotic manageress. Tomboy fan pinup Priss is remade as a mercenary bitch, whose new band, Sekiria, is named after Konaka's own, though with **EVANGELION**-inspired launch sequences and a *very* 1990s drum & bass soundtrack, much of *BGC 2040* will date just as swiftly as the original.

Although 26 episodes of the *BGC 2040* TV series were made, the final two were not broadcast on the original run, but added on home video. A second season, with the working title of *BGC 2041*, was announced as in preproduction in 2002, but has yet to appear at the time of our deadline.

BUBU CHACHA *

1999. JPN: *Norimono Okoku BuBu Cha-Cha, Daisuki Bubu Chacha*. TV series. DIR: Tetsuro Amino. SCR: Akira Okeya. DES: Shinji Ochi. ANI: Hideaki Shimada. MUS: Goji Tsuno. PRD: Iku, Daume Inc., Japan Digital Entertainment Inc., Amino 25 mins. x 26 eps. (TV1), 25 mins. x 52 eps. (TV2)

Elementary schoolboy Randy Rand (Buddy in Japanese) loses his beloved pet dog Chacha in an accident, but the dog's playful, protective spirit is reborn in Randy's toy car. Thanks to Chacha, Randy makes new friends in the neighborhood, including pigtailed girl-next-door Mary, who is convinced that Randy has some growing up to do, the Rap brothers, who only speak in rhyme, and Boo-man (Daa-man), a scary tramp-like figure who spooks the children only when they are getting near danger.

Beneath a veil of harmless children's entertainment, *Bubu Chacha* is a heart-rending indictment of modern times and a touching study of the way some children deal with death and the real world. It seems produced at least in part from that same nostalgic yearning for siblings that proved so successful for the **DUMPLING BROTHERS**. Randy is an incredibly lonely little boy, drawing on inanimate objects for friendship, and reduced to talking to a local ghost, Sarah, because he does not have a real sister. Chacha is not the only possessed item—he has a friend of his own in Bull, a toy robot that holds the spirit of a long-departed bulldog, and several other local vehicles are dead animals reborn, including Bubu Pyoko (a toy car that was once a frog), Hippo Truck, Cindy the Elephant Shovel Car, and Leopard the Sports Car. Randy's daily life is occasionally interrupted by the Eyebrow Aliens, who are benign invaders from another world, and by Tau, the boy across the street, who in less introverted times would have been a playmate for Randy along the lines of Nobita's associates in **DORAEMON**.

A bizarre combination of *My Mother The Car* (1965) with the anthropo-

morphic vehicles of *Thomas the Tank Engine* (1984), the original series of *Bubu Chacha* was split between Randy's adventures and those of the transforming train-robot **HIKARIAN**. A second series, concentrating on Randy and friends, followed in 2001 as *I Love BuBu ChaCha* (*Daisuki BuBu Chacha*). The second season shows were broadcast in English on Japanese cable and on Japanese airlines for younger passengers, before eventually making their way to some foreign networks. The generation that grew up watching *Bubu Chacha* presumably saw nothing all that unusual in **ANGEL TALES**. When they are old enough to see a toy car come to life in the **AKIRA** hallucination scene, it will probably creep them out for good.

BUDDHA

1948. JPN: *Shakyamuni; Taisho Shakuso*. AKA: *Life of Shaka, Great Saint Shakyamuni*. Movie. DIR: Noburo Ofuji. SCR: N/C. DES: N/C. ANI: N/C. MUS: Sara Choir. PRD: Japan Buddhism Association, Sanko. 52 mins.

After a portentous dream about a white elephant, the ancient Hindu princess Maya gives birth to a prince. Reared in seclusion from the troubles of the world, Prince Siddhartha is troubled by sights of poverty and deprivation when he is twelve years old. He is married to a beautiful wife, but he is unable to bear the thought of others suffering, and leaves the palace in search of an answer. While sitting beneath a tree, he achieves enlightenment.

Planned as a nine-reel life of Buddha, but exhibited in Cannes as "Part One" with only six reels completed, this late work by Noburo Ofuji was not completed until after his death. It was only in 1961 that it was finally exhibited as a full 72-minute movie (comprising ten reels).

BUNNA! COME DOWN FROM THE TREE!

1986. JPN: *Bunna yo, Ki kara Orite Koi*. TV special. DIR: Eitaro Ozawa. SCR: Yuji Tanno. DES: Yoshio Kabashima. ANI: Yoshio Kabashima, Michiru Suzuki.

MUS: Nisaburo Hashimoto. PRD: DAX, Shigoto, NHK. 55 mins.

Bunna the frog lives in a pond within a temple precinct, where he sees himself as a "watchfrog." Announcing that he intends to seek a new home, he ignores his girlfriend and father and climbs the pasania tree close to his pond. Commissioned to celebrate the 30th anniversary of the United Nations, this adaptation of Ben Mizugami's children's story was designed to show that cooperation is better than selfishness—hardly a radical departure from any other children's show.

BURN UP *

1991. Video, TV series. DIR: Yasunori Ide. SCR: Jun Kanzaki. DES: Kenjin Miyazaki. ANI: Kenjin Miyazaki. MUS: Kenji Kawai. PRD: AIC, DirecTV. 50 mins. (orig.), 30 mins. x 4 eps. (W), 25 mins. x 13 eps. (X-cess); 25 mins. x 12 eps. (Scramble).

Frustrated traffic cops Maki, Reimi, and Yuka interfere in a *real* detective's investigation of a white slavery ring. Infiltrating the network of prominent businessman Samuel McCoy, Yuka is captured, and her two friends mount an all-out assault on the villain's headquarters.

Little more than an excuse for large-breasted girls with guns, *Burn Up*'s biggest fans appeared to be AD Vision, the U.S. distributor that was prepared to help fund the lame sequel *Burn Up W(arrior)* in 1996. Keeping to the AIC studio policy, best seen in TENCHI MUYO!, of throwing in more girls whenever possible, the sequel dumped most of the old characters in favor of the "Warrior" team, a police squad monitoring computer crime.

Heavily influenced by GHOST IN THE SHELL, *W* revolves around the Cerebus cartel's attempts to supply a virtual drug with mind-altering capabilities, as well as the disappearance of a virtual idol from the company mainframe—is it theft, or kidnapping? Maria, the AI in question, is an innocent creature in a computer but has superhuman strength in the real world, not dissimi-

lar to Adama in the BUBBLEGUM CRISIS spin-off *Bubblegum Crash*. But despite music from ARMITAGE III's Yasunori Honda, *Burn Up W*'s roots have less to do with sci-fi than with the "zany" cookie-cutter concepts of producer Satoru Akahori. Despite its minimal running time, plot and characterization are sacrificed for setups to exploit the bouncing breasts of new-girl Rio. In the opening episode when terrorists seize hostages at a peace conference, one of their demands is that Rio must perform a nude bungee jump—police work taking a very distant second place to girls and guns.

This, it would seem, is all it takes, since the franchise was resurrected as *Burn Up X-cess* in 1997. One of the first shows on digital TV in Japan, the show was finally able to break from the confines of video—*X-cess* is twice as long as its combined predecessors, which allows for *slightly* more character depth. The new director was Junichiro Kimura.

Hiroki Hayashi's 12-part *Burn Up Scramble* (2004) has radically different character designs, but yet more of the same formula. Rio is now in charge, leading a team of cool-headed Maya and precognitive investigator Lilica, the serial's one "new" idea, presumably inspired by Steven Spielberg's *Minority Report* (2002). ●ⒷNⓋ

BURNING ALPINE ROSE: JUDY AND RANDY

1985. JPN: *Honoo no Alpen Rose: Judy and Randy*. AKA: *Passionate Alpine Rose*. TV series. DIR: Hidehito Ueda. SCR: Sukehiro Tomita, Shigeru Yanagawa, Hiroko Naka. DES: Akemi Takada. ANI: Hidehito Ueda. MUS: Joe Hisaishi. PRD: Tatsunoko, Fuji TV. 25 mins. x 20 eps.

At the close of the Second World War, Judy is seeking her lost parents. The handsome Randy offers to help, though the only clue Judy has is her distant memories of hearing a song called "Alpine Rose." Judy escapes from the feckless Baron Guillermon and heads for Salzburg, where she

believes the song's composer, Leonhardt Aschenbach, can be found.

Based on the comic in *Ciao* by Michiyo Akaishi, this was the first anime made by the Tatsunoko Studio specifically for girls. Hisaishi's score was so popular that the series was recut into two half-hour music videos purely to showcase the compositions. The story itself was edited into a 90-minute feature-length version on video. Compare to HONEY HONEY and HEIDI.

BURNING BLOOD

1990. AKA: *BB*. Video. DIR: Osamu Dezaki. SCR: Machiko Kondo. DES: Akio Sugino. ANI: Akio Sugino. MUS: N/C. PRD: Magic Bus. 45 mins. x 3 eps.

After killing a man in a fight, a Japanese down-and-out changes his name and moves to America, where he becomes a mercenary. Realizing that if he has a talent for anything, it's for fighting, he drifts into a career as a professional boxer. This adaptation of Osamu Ishiwata's 1985 comic from *Shonen Sunday* was directed by one better known for the original boxing anime TOMORROW'S JOE. Ⓥ

BURNING BROTHER

1988. JPN: *Moeru Oniisan*. TV series. DIR: Osamu Kobayashi. SCR: Kenji Terada, Noboru Aikawa. DES: Michishiro Yamada. ANI: Michishiro Yamada, Kazunari Kume. MUS: Koji Makaino. PRD: Pierrot, Nippon TV. 25 mins. x 24 eps.

Japanese boy Kenichi wanders the mountainous hinterland of Japan in search of his father and his sister, Yukie. Swept away by a river as a baby, he was raised in the country by the old man Cha Genmai, but he eventually wanders back into human society accompanied only by a mangy wolf called Flipper. Reunited with his family, he falls in with the local gangster crowd, but life seems to go so well, until Cha Genmai and Kaede (Kenichi's adopted sister) turn up to stay. Based on the *Shonen Jump* comic by Tadashi Sato and adapted by the production team behind KIMAGURE ORANGE ROAD, *Burning Brother* was praised at the time for the high quality of its comedy acting and characterization.

BURNING EXCHANGE STUDENT
1991. JPN: *Hohoe no Tenkosei.*
Video. DIR: Katsuhiko Nishijima. SCR:
Toshio Okada. DES: Yuji Moriyama. ANI:
Katsuhiko Nishijima. MUS: Kohei Tanaka. PRD: Gainax. 25 mins. x 2 eps.
Noboru Takizawa is the new kid in
school, determined to apply the raging fire of his talent to success in all
sporting arenas. He also falls for local
girl Yukari, an interest which compels
him to fight for her hand in the boxing
ring. Featuring the writer and composer from **GUNBUSTER** with the director
and designer from **PROJECT A-KO**, here
is an anime whose Western release
would have been guaranteed were it
not for the subject matter of sports.
Creator Kazuhiko Shimamoto would
go on to write the martial-arts soccer
manga *Red Card*, a contender for the
most insane ever written. **Ⓥ**

BURNING VILLAGE
1989. Video. DIR: Fusahito Nagaki. SCR:
Fusahito Nagaki. DES: N/C. ANI: Chukai
Shimogawa. MUS: Masahito Maekawa.
PRD: Clover Art, Tama Pro. 12 mins. x
10 eps.
Animal folk tales set in the titular community, in which local eccentric Oharai
retells several popular fairy tales with
considerable license, including the
LITTLE MERMAID and the *Musicians of
Bremen.*

BURST ANGEL *
2004. JPN: *Bakuretsu Tenshi* (TV),
BT—Tenshi Sairin (v). TV series, video.
DIR: Koichi Ohata, Yasunori Urata. SCR:
Fumihiko Shimo. DES: Kanetoshi Kamimoto, Osamu Horuchi, Kanetake Ebikawa. ANI: Gonzo. MUS: Masaru Nishida.
PRD: GHD, Gonzo, Imagica, Media
Factory, TV Asahi. 25 mins. x 24 eps.
(TV), 30 mins. (v).
In a future Japan where a crime wave
is counterproductively addressed with
a law that lets *everyone* carry a gun,
culinary student Kyohei Tachibana
dreams of getting away to France to

study advanced pastry techniques and
become a great chef. He looks for a
job to help him save for the trip and
becomes a private chef to a group of
four women—Sei, Meg, Jo, and Amy.
Much to his astonishment, they turn
out to be a group of violent mercenaries (you know, like **BUBBLEGUM CRISIS**),
and he is caught up in the very life he's
trying to avoid. Sei is the granddaughter and heiress of the Bai-Lan Mob
family, and (for no apparent reason)
the other girls are named for the surviving March sisters in **LITTLE WOMEN**. A
video adventure followed in 2005 from
the same team. **Ⓥ**

BUSHBABY, THE *
1992. JPN: *Dai Kusahara no Chiisana
Tenshi Bushbaby.* AKA: *Little Angel of*

The Bushbaby

the Savannah: Bushbaby. TV series.
DIR: Takayoshi Suzuki, Takashi Kaga.
SCR: Akira Miyazaki. DES: Shuichi Seki,
Hiromi Kato. ANI: Nobuhiro Hosoi,
Hiroshi Ito. MUS: Akira Miyagawa. PRD:
Nippon Animation, Fuji TV. 25 mins. x
40 eps.
Jackie Leeds, a British game warden's
daughter in Kenya, gets into adventures with her bushbaby companion,
Murphy, in this adaptation of William
Stevenson's 1965 book. After initial
high jinks, the time comes for her to
return to England, but Jackie refuses to
leave Murphy and sneaks off the ship.
Going on the lam with her father's
manservant, Tenbo, she spends the
latter part of the series on the run
from poachers and policemen, who
believe she has been kidnapped. This

remarkable change in tone may have been part of the reason for the serial's immense success in Japan, where it peaked at a 20% TV rating. It was later cut into four feature-length edits for video release, and there is also a 1970 live-action movie version directed by John Trent, starring Margaret Brooks and Louis Gossett, Jr. Shown on Canadian TV in the 1990s.

BUSINESS COMMANDO YAMAZAKI
1997. JPN: *Kigyo Senshi Yamazaki: Long Distance Call*. Video. DIR: Tsuneo Tominaga. SCR: Tsuneo Tominaga. DES: Akira Kano. ANI: Akira Kano. MUS: N/C. PRD: Ripple Film, Beam Entertainment. 40 mins.
Jun Tomozawa's lighthearted 1992 manga in *Super Jump* took the premise of Roland Emmerich's *Universal Soldier* and moved it to a typically Japanese arena—the business world. A 42-year-old salaryman is made to serve his company beyond the grave when his brain is installed in a superpowered android body in order to carry out corporate espionage. **ⓃⓋ**

BUTCHIGIRI
1989. AKA: *Take It to the Limit*. Video. DIR: Katsuyoshi Yatabe, Takashi Imanishi, Noboru Ishiguro. SCR: Norio Masuhara. DES: Eiichi Endo. ANI: Eiichi Endo. MUS: N/C. PRD: Nihon Eizo, Creative Bridge, Life Work. 50 mins. x 4 eps.
Takahara, leader of the notorious seven-man Silver Wolf gang, also dabbles in baseball, in this short series based on Yu Nakahara's 1987 comic in *Shonen Sunday*. Mixing bikes with school life in a similar fashion to **BOMBER BIKERS OF SHONAN**, the story shares **SLOW STEP**'s idea of a bad seed redeemed by a hidden sporting talent.

Jan Scott Frazier, who worked on *Butchigiri*'s fourth episode while in the production department at Artland, describes it as the most disastrous project in living memory, hated by its own animators, only assigned to staffers as a punishment, and with subcontractors whose work was so bad that "we might be better off working with gorillas." When the anime was completed, the staff held a ceremonial burning of the storyboards in a parking lot.**Ⓥ**

B-YOND
1998. Video. DIR: Hiroyuki Kurimoto. SCR: Atsuhiro Tomioka. DES: Toshiya Yamada. ANI: Toshiya Yamada. MUS: N/C. PRD: Pink Pineapple, KSS. 36 mins. x 2 eps.
Satan, an alien creature who has lain dormant on Earth for many years, awakens and causes havoc. Fay is a female bounty hunter searching for Satan's younger brother, although that is soon forgotten in favor of more sex scenes in this lackluster replay of **UROTSUKIDOJI**. **Ⓝ**

C

CAGE *
2003. JPN: *Canaria wa Kago no Naka*.
AKA: *Canary in a Cage*. Video. DIR: N/C.
SCR: Kazunari Kume. DFS: I.H. Tayama.
ANI: I.H. Tayama. MUS: Toru Shura. PRD:
Studio Jam, Concept Films, Milky. 30
mins. x 2 eps.
Swindled by her feckless boyfriend,
Sakimi Endo is so deep in debt that
loan sharks force her to find employment in the sex industry. However, no
matter how hard she works, her debts
only seem to mount up, until the fateful day when she receives an email invi-
tation to work at Club Canary, where
caged women are supplied as sexual
playthings to special clients. Based on
the erotic novel by Ugetsu Nakamura.
🄻🄽🅅

CALIFORNIA CRISIS: GUN SALVO
1986. JPN: *California Crisis: Tsuigeki
no Juka*. Video. DIR: Mizuho Nishikubo.
SCR: Mizuho Nishikubo. DES: Matsuri
Okada. ANI: Matsuri Okada. MUS: Masami Kurihara. PRD: Hero Media, Studio
Unicorn. 45 mins.
Noera and his new-found girlfriend,
Marsha, become mixed up in a secret
U.S.–Soviet space mission project. On
the run from rival gangs in California,
they gain possession of a round object
that directs them to Death Valley,
where an alien contact is being covered
up by the government's men in black.
This arbitrary plot, however, is of less
importance to the filmmakers than
a long, lingering tour of Californian
beaches, possibly since location-hunting would be more fun on this project
than on, say, something called *New
Jersey Crisis*. *CC* ends with a cliffhanger,
but no sequel was made due to lack of
audience interest—the first of many
straight-to-video anime to leave their
fans without a proper conclusion.

CALIMERO
1974. TV series. DIR: Yugo Serikawa,
Kazuya Miyazaki, Fusahito Nagaki.
SCR: Taichi Yamada, Takeshi Yoshida,
Osamu Kagami, Mayuko Takakura,
Hamakichi Hirose. DES: Shinya Taka-
hashi. ANI: Fusahito Nagaki. MUS:
Tadashi Kinoshita. PRD: K&S, NET
(TV1); TV Tokyo (TV2). 12 mins. x
84 eps. (1974), 23 mins. x 36 eps.
(1992).
Calimero, a little black chick with
an eggshell for a hat, was created in
1963 by Nino and Tony Pagot for an
Italian advertisement. Taken up by a
Japanese production company, the
original animation was expanded into
a long series. The series was revived
for TV Tokyo in 1992 under director
Tsuneo Tominaga, with new scripts by
Jiro Takayama and Mayori Sekijima.
If anything, the availability of the new
series on video made it an even bigger
success in the children's market than
its predecessor.

CALL ME TONIGHT
1986. Video. DIR: Tatsuya Okamoto.
SCR: Tatsuya Okamoto, Toshimichi
Suzuki. DES: Kumiko Takahashi, Junichi
Watanabe. ANI: Kumiko Takahashi,
Osamu Yamazaki. MUS: N/C. PRD: AIC;
C.Moon. 30 mins.
Schoolgirl Rumi Natsumi moonlights
as the boss of a phone contact club,
hired by Ryo Sugiura to help him
through a strange fetish. Ryo is an
intergalactic nexus, and his body is subject to possession by various aliens and
monsters whenever he becomes over-
excited. Ryo wants Rumi to excite him
so much that he gets used to the idea
and can control his urges—though
their wanderings through the city soon
attract the attention of press photographer Maki, and Rumi's schoolmate
Yuki, who is head of the "Sukeban"
orgy club and wants Ryo and his transformations for herself. With a *Beauty
and the Beast* subplot and demonic
transformations brought about by
frustrated teen lust, this plays like the
junior comedy version of UROTSUKIDOJI.
This and SECRETS OF THE TELEPHONE
CLUB demonstrate that the scandal of
schoolgirl "date-clubs" in the late 1990s
came a little late. 🄽

CALL OF THE WILD *
1981. JPN: *Arano no Sakebi Koe: Howl,
Buck*. AKA: *Call of the Wild: Howl, Buck*.
TV special. DIR: Kozo Morishita. SCR:
Keisuke Fujikawa. DES: Seiji Kikuchi.
ANI: Seiji Kikuchi. MUS: Takeo Watanabe.
PRD: Seisaku, Toei. 85 mins.
California, 1897. Buck, a domesticated
mongrel who lives in the Santa Clara

valley, is kidnapped by the family gardener, Manuel, and sold to a gold prospector. Soon he is a sled-dog in the harsh winter of the Klondike, and his civilized exterior swiftly falls away, awakening a wildness buried deep in his genes for centuries. This anime adaptation of Jack London's novel (WHITE FANG followed in 1982) kept close to the original, eschewing the talking animals one might expect for a cartoon audience and leaving the dogs in silence while the humans (shiftless Manuel, swarthy Francois) are the only ones who speak.

A second, unrelated *Call of the Wild (Anime Yasai no Sakebi)* was a 26-part series shown intermittently on TV Tokyo between 1982 and 1984. Directed by Shigeru Omachi, this was a show in the spirit of SETON'S ANIMAL TALES, based on stories by Japanese author Muku Hatoju, including *Taro the Mountain Bear*, *Little Monkey Brothers*, and *The Disappearing Stray*.

CALLING ALL STUDENTS

1986. JPN: *Seito Shokun*. TV special. DIR: Mitsuo Kusakabe. SCR: Ryo Ishikawa, Azuma Tachibana. DES: Yoko Shoji. ANI: Kazuo Imura. MUS: Toshiyuki Watanabe. PRD: Toei, Ashi Pro, Fuji TV. 81 mins.

In this adaptation of Yoko Shoji's 1977 manga from *Friend* magazine, Naoko, a new girl in town, has trouble fitting into life at the local middle school but comes to terms with jealousy and broken hearts. Believing her parents to be dead, Naoko discovers the twin sister she never knew she had, who soon develops a heart condition and dies. Despite pulling no punches, the 24-volume manga series was unceremoniously crammed into a single TV special, which made it unlikely to draw as large an audience on TV. The similar BROTHER DEAREST was more successful as a TV *series* a few years later.

CAMBRIAN

2005. Video. DIR: Yoshiten, Shinjuro Yuki. SCR: Yasuyuki Muto. DES: Yoshiten. ANI: Ishiten. MUS: N/C. PRD:

Milky, GP Museum, Image Works 30 mins. x 2 eps.

Expelled from the academic world for illegal experiments in human cloning, Professor Yamagishi turns his attention to the study of explosive leaps in evolution. Instead, he only manages to turn himself into a gruesome lump of flesh with lots of tentacles, and is soon penetrating every available orifice on hapless bystander Keiko, hoping to impregnate her with the seed of a new breed. Based on what was presumably an erotic novel by Noboru Mitsuyama in the time-honored tradition of ADVANCER TINA. The name comes from the period 590 million years ago, when life first arose on Earth. **LNV**

CAN CAN BUNNY *

1996. JPN: *Can Can Bunny Extra*. Video. DIR: Katsumaki Kanezawa. SCR: Tetsuya Ozeki. DES: Nanako Shunsai. ANI: N/C. MUS: Pika Pika. PRD: Pink Pineapple, KSS. 25 mins. x 6 eps.

Suwati, the Goddess of Happiness, falls in love with Japanese boy Kenta and indulgently grants him the power to seduce seven women. True love, of course, is not always that easy—the first girl is a virgin on the run from a street gang. As with the superior VIDEO GIRL AI, Suwati is only using her powers because she wants Kenta to fall in love with *her*, but her cousin Shuree is also on his case.

The *Can Can Bunny* PC seduction game was very successful and was followed by *CCB Superior*, *CCB Spirits*, *CCB Blue Honey*, and *CCB Extra*—this fifth incarnation, with a greater emphasis on adventure over sex, provided the basis for the anime version. Cashing in on the hiatus between the OH MY GODDESS! videos and movie, this porno retread also spun off into radio dramas, comics, and three novels. **O**

CANARIA

2002. JPN: *Canaria Kono Omoi wo Uta ni Nosete*. AKA: *Canary Put This Feeling into the Song*. Video. DIR: N/C. SCR: Noboru Yamaguchi, Kota Takeuchi, Fumiko Kuwahara, Yuichi Kuwahara.

DES: Kakiko Kakitsubata. ANI: Shinji Katakura. MUS: N/C. PRD: Front Wing, NEC Interchannel, HuneX. 25 mins.

Fantasy based on a PC and Dreamcast game, in which a high school band made up primarily of cute and very silly girls is determined to get its keyboardist Jun back for a gig, whatever it takes. This involves cornering him on the school roof and flying him to the venue on a kite. Regardless of whether the game may have made sense, compressing it all into less than half an hour stretches the bounds of reality and results in a series of illogical and overblown solutions that might appear wacky to fans of EXCEL SAGA, but really just seem rather pointless. The game itself was intended for over-18s only, implying a raciness that is strangely absent from an anime that, for once, might have been better served as erotica. The final race between the Mayor on her motor scooter and two of the band on a tandem seems intended to be a pastiche of a similar sequence in GOLDEN BOY. Online sources imply that there was also a CD drama, although this may simply refer to drama *sections* on a spin-off music CD, of which there were several, as well as a novelization by scriptwriter Yamaguchi.

CANDY CANDY *

1976. AKA: *Candy White, Candice*. TV series. DIR: Yugo Serikawa. SCR: Shunichi Yukimuro, Noboru Shiroyama. DES: Yumiko Igarashi. ANI: Keisuke Morishita, Kazuo Tomizawa. MUS: Takeo Watanabe. PRD: Toei, TV Asahi. 25 mins. x 115 eps.

A girl is left outside the Pony's Home orphanage. A note says that her name is Candice, and she is christened Candice White after the snow that is falling outside. Candice grows up in the orphanage, where she watches her friends leave to be fostered by other families. She is helped by a mysterious stranger and yearns for him to return to her. Sent to work as a servant for the Ragham family, she is bullied by the Ragham children, Eliza and Neil. She develops crushes on many nice young men, especially the charming gentleman Anthony Brown, though he dies suddenly on a fox hunt. His cousin, Alastair "Stair" Audrey, is another potential suitor, but he is killed in World War I. Candice falls in love with a man called Terence in London but steps aside to allow him to marry a woman whose need is greater than hers.

Equal parts CINDERELLA and DADDY LONG-LEGS mixed with a doomed love out of *Romeo and Juliet, Candy Candy* was one of the great successes of the 1970s. Begun as a manga in *Nakayoshi* magazine in 1975, Kyoko Mizuki and Yumiko Igarashi's weepy tale of self-sacrifice ended ironically with the two creators' acrimonious dispute over copyright. The speed of adaptation caused the animated version to deviate from the original in later chapters—Candice's hospital job from episodes 102 to 109 is not present in the manga, which instead dispatches her to New York to be an actress, and Toei insisted on the introduction of a mascot character, Clint the albino raccoon. *CC* provides moments of inadvertent comedy in its portrayal of early 20th-century America, with servants making Japanese-style bows, and English-style fox hunts in the Midwest. The newly moneyed Raghams are beastly to their social underling Candice, but she is regularly rescued from a fate worse than death (exile to Mexico, signified by a Pancho Villa–lookalike bandito onscreen) by the interference of the distant William, a British royal who inexplicably lives in America, where the upper classes fawn over him. William, however, is later revealed to be far closer to Candy than anyone realizes.

Candice would return in *The Voice of Spring/Candy's Summer Holiday*, a 40-minute theatrical outing in 1978. A 26-minute short, inexplicably titled *Candy Candy: The Movie*, was directed by Tetsuo Imazawa in 1992 and focused on her abuse at the hands of the Raghams.

Another Igarashi manga, LADY GEORGIE, was animated in 1983, but *Candy Candy* was a watershed production in the Japanese industry. After the animated version led to $45 million of merchandising spin-offs and boosted the sales of its parent magazine by a million copies, *Nakayoshi* would actively seek to recreate such success in the girls' market from the ground up. The eventual result would be the market-led SAILOR MOON franchise. Candice's distant memories of a "handsome prince" helping her in early life were also lifted for UTENA. The show received a very limited partial broadcast on U.S. local TV for the Japanese community, with English subtitles. True to the political climate of the times, the nasty Raghams were renamed the Reagans in this version.

CANVAS

2002. JPN: *Canvas Sepia-iro no Motif*. AKA: *Canvas Motif of Sepia*. Video, TV Series. DIR: Itsuro Kawasaki. SCR: Reiko Yoshida. DES: Yasunari Nitta. ANI: Hironori Sawada. MUS: Hajime Kanasugi. PRD: F&C, Zexis, Chiba TV. 30 mins. x 2 eps. (v) 25 mins. x 15 eps. (TV). Artist Daisuke Aso is suffering from a creative block, while his childhood friend Amane tries to find ways of encouraging him to draw again. Amane, of course, secretly harbors feelings for Daisuke, and feels threatened by a series of would-be competitors—it wouldn't be a computer dating simulation game adapted into an anime unless a whole gang of girls started chasing after the leading man for no apparent reason. What distinguishes this anime from the many, many similar shows available is the peculiar execution of its sex scenes—it has them, which is weird enough for something that starts off with the gentle tones of LOVE HINA, but they are all presented in a rather coy and soft-core manner like the sanitized version of END OF SUMMER. A TV series, *Canvas 2: Niji-iro no Sketch* (*Rainbow-colored Sketch*), followed in Fall 2005. **N**

CAPETA

2005. TV series. DIR: Shin Misawa. SCR: Isutomu Kamishiro. DES: Atsumi Komura. ANI: N/C. MUS: N/C. PRD: Studio Comet, TV Tokyo. 25 mins. x ?? eps. Fourth grader Kappeita (aka Capeta) Taira lives with his widowed father, who tries to break his son out of apathy one day by constructing a racing cart out of leftover work materials. Despite a bent chassis that causes the cart to wander off course, Capeta is able to steer it to victory at the local cart track. His success is witnessed by Naomi Minamoto, the East Japan Junior Cart Racing champion, who recommends that he participate in official races. Predictable sporting drama ensues. Based on a manga in *Shonen Magazine* monthly by Masato Soda.

CAPRICIOUS ROBOT, THE

2004. JPN: *Kimagure Robot*. TV series. DIR: Yoshiharu Ashino, Masahiro Kubo, Yasuhiro Aoki. SCR: Shinichi Hoshi. DES: N/C. ANI: N/C. MUS: Seiichi Yamamoto. PRD: Studio 4°C. 2 mins. x 11 eps. Although he did write episodes for several live-action and animated TV series, author Shinichi Hoshi was legendarily protective of his original works, and although approached many times by companies interested in buying the rights to his many short stories, refused to allow extensive adaptation until after his death. Hence, this experimental series of short Internet movies of some of Hoshi's best-known sci-fi stories, undertaken as an experiment by Studio 4°C in the promise that others would be forthcoming if they were a success.

CAPRICORN *

1991. AKA: *Joji Manabe's Capricorn*. Video. DIR: Takashi Imanishi. SCR: Takashi Imanishi, Joji Manabe. DES: Moriyasu Taniguchi. ANI: Moriyasu Taniguchi. MUS: Ikuro Fujiwara. PRD: Aubec. 48 mins. Teenager Taku Shimamura is transported to the parallel world of Slaphrase, a world of anthropomorphic animals, where evil General Zolba plans to usurp the imperial throne. Realizing that Zolba's next conquest, planet "Capricorn," is really Earth, Taku joins forces with Mona, the last of the Yappy race of dragon-people, to defeat Zolba and save both worlds.

This video features a similar plot to manga creator Manabe's **OUTLANDERS** and the cookie-cutter character designs that distinguish (or rather, *don't* distinguish) his other works such as *Caravan Kidd* and *Drakuun*—in which *Capricorn*'s Zolba also makes a cameo appearance. Manabe had more luck with **RAI**.

CAPTAIN

1980. TV series. DIR: Tetsu Dezaki. SCR: Noboru Shiroyama. DES: Akio Chiba. ANI: Shigetaka Kiyoyama, Keizo Shimizu, Isao Kaneko. MUS: Toshiyuki Kobayashi. PRD: Eiken, NTV. 84 mins., 82 mins. (TVm), 93 mins. (m), 25 mins. x 26 eps. (TV).

Takao Taniguchi enters the Nakano baseball club and fights his way to the top, determined to lead his team to victory in the national finals. Manga artist Akio Chiba specialized in baseball (his other big hit was 1973's *Play Ball*) and this adaptation of his 1972 manga was soon followed by a second TV movie later the same year. The two incarnations were recut into a 95-minute movie release in 1981, and the story finally received a full-length TV series in 1983, supposedly because of a "great critical reception," though a serial had been planned from the beginning.

CAPTAIN FUTURE *

1978. TV series. DIR: Tomoharu Katsumata, Hideki Takayama, Noboru Ishiguro, Yasuo Hasegawa. SCR: Masaki Tsuji, Hiroyuki Hoshiyama. DES: Sadao Noda. ANI: Toshio Mori. MUS: Yuji Ono. PRD: Toei, NHK. 25 mins. x 52 eps.

Brilliant young scientist Curtis Newton (aka Captain Future) brings peace and justice to the galaxy with his sidekicks Android Otho, alien robot Grag, and "living brain" Simon Wright. Known collectively as the "Future Men," they keep their flagship, The Comet, hidden in a lunar crater and launch it to help Earth's government, which communicates with them through the beautiful agent Joan Randall.

The sci-fi novels of Edmond Hamilton were optioned for anime production in record time when George Lucas

mentioned that they were a major inspiration for *Star Wars* (1977). Beginning with an adaptation of *Captain Future and the Space Emperor* (1940), the anime series is remarkably faithful to the original, especially compared to the license taken with E. E. Smith's **LENSMAN**. Hamilton's work was surprisingly well-served in Japan; his later *Starwolf* series was also spun off into a live-action TV show, itself reedited for the 1978 movie *Fugitive Alien*.

Four episodes were released on video in the U.S. as *Captain Future* 1 and 2, which chart the events of *The Lost World of Time*, where Newton must travel back to save the inhabitants of planet Prometheus (Kaitan) that is just about to disintegrate and form the asteroid belt. A third video, confusingly titled simply *Captain Future*, was a truncated digest of *Captain Future's Challenge*, in which Newton must stop "King Wrecker" from destroying all the gravium mines in the solar system. The other 14 hours or so of the Japanese version remain untranslated.

Captain Future also had a 60-minute TV special in 1978, in which an experimental spaceship goes missing on Mercury shortly before the start of the Interplanetary Yacht Race. In order to infiltrate a criminal network, Future must pose as a test pilot at the notorious Venusian "Suicide Base," before a showdown in the "Sargasso" Graveyard of Space. In an intershow homage, a character called "Curtis Newton" has a cameo in the later **SOL BIANCA** series.

CAPTAIN HARLOCK *

1978. JPN: *Uchu Kaizoku Captain Harlock*. AKA: *Space Pirate Captain Harlock, Albator*. TV series/special. DIR: Rintaro, Kazumi Fukushima. SCR: Masami Uehara, Haruya Yamazaki. DES: Leiji Matsumoto. ANI: Kazuo Komatsubara. MUS: Toshiyuki Kimori. PRD: Toei, TV Asahi. 25 mins. x 42 eps.

Leiji Matsumoto's tale of space piracy began in *Shonen Sunday* in 1977, and was set a thousand years in the future. In the year 2977, Captain Phantom F. Harlock leads a crew of outlaws on the

starship Arcadia, determined to resist the invasion of Earth by the Mazone, a plant-based race of long-necked women who have fled the imminent destruction of their own homeworld. Harlock assembles a crew that includes Mime, the last of an alien race whose homeworld was destroyed by the Mazones; engineer Tochiro; Yattaran, an obsessed model-maker based on Matsumoto's former assistant and **AREA 88**–creator Kaoru Shintani, and Maji, a man who has somehow become the father of a Mazone child.

Like Osamu Tezuka, Leiji Matsumoto is apt to reuse a set cast of characters from title to title, regardless of whether the shows actually relate to one another. This has led *Harlock* to develop a complex and contradictory "continuity"—a word we use advisedly, because Matsumoto does not seem to have intended duplicate character images and names to necessarily indicate any relationship. Hence, many anime based on other Matsumoto works allude to *Harlock*, intentionally or otherwise, although it should be noted that Matsumoto and his collaborators often want to have their cake and eat it—recycling characters with impunity, proclaiming any apparent contradictions to be irrelevant, but often creating situations that are difficult to comprehend without an appreciation of several other works, which the audience has already been told are "unrelated."

Consequently, our account of what happens in the *Harlock* series is also subject to debate, particularly since it is contradicted by some, but not all, of what happens in later incarnations of the franchise, some of which have been misleadingly billed as sequels when they are in fact remakes.

The first incarnation of the anime *Harlock*, the TV series, ends with Tochiro's widow Emeraldas leaving to grieve among the stars in her own ship, the titular **QUEEN EMERALDAS** of the first of many spin-offs. Harlock himself would win a duel against Lafressia, queen of the Mazone, and then head off into the void with just Mime for company, in search of a place to die. This, however, was the beginning of Harlock's long-lasting popularity outside Japan, with the dark, brooding hero finding unexpected fans abroad, particularly after a limited number of episodes were broadcast with English subtitles on American local TV stations for the Japanese community.

After a cameo with Emeraldas' sometime "sister" Maetel in the latter part of **GALAXY EXPRESS 999** and the movie *Adieu Galaxy Express 999*, Harlock returned in Tomoharu Katsumata's 130-minute movie *My Youth in Arcadia* (1982, *Waga Seishin no Arcadia*), also known by the titles *Arcadia of My Youth*, and *Vengeance of the Space Pirates*. Supposedly designed as a prequel to the first series, the story line is actually irreconcilable, since it depicts Earth under alien occupation, this time by the Illumidas race. The story also presents a possible explanation as to how the eye-patched Harlock may have lost his eye—or at least, how this incarnation of him may have lost it, protecting Maya, the woman who may (or may not) have been his wife. *My Youth in Arcadia* also presented a series of flashbacks detailing another Harlock, quite possibly an ancestor of this one, a 20th-century aviator whose biplane is also, coincidentally, called the Arcadia.

Although its continuity clashed with the original series, the movie does function as a prequel of sorts to *Endless Orbit SSX*, a TV series that followed later the same year, in which Harlock battles the Illumidas again. The Arcadia in the movie and SSX series is built on Earth, whereas the version in the original series is built on the planet Heavy Meldar, which exploded after the Arcadia's launch, but also appears in several chapters of the *Galaxy Express 999* series.

Though the various *Harlock* serials, the spin-offs starring Emeraldas or Maetel, the distant cousins **QUEEN OF A THOUSAND YEARS** and **DNA SIGHTS 999.9**, and even look-alikes such as Rhein-

Captain Harlock

dars in **THE COCKPIT** are supposedly related, the discrepancies make this hard to believe. Dates and characters vary wildly (the suicidal Harlock who leaves the original series is maniacally cheerful when he reappears in *Galaxy Express*), and two of the serials even have a gap of several centuries between them. Paramount among the confusions is the claim that Harlock is really Mamoru Kodai (Alex Wildstar) from **STAR BLAZERS**, but although Mamoru does indeed disguise himself as a space pirate called Harlock in the manga (not anime) of *Space Cruiser Yamato*, he is copying a character from a comic book by Leiji Matsumoto.

Harlock in modern times is no less confusing. Twenty-seven episodes of the original TV series were rearranged into feature-length chunks to make an eight-video digest version at the close of the 1990s. For an idea of the mind-boggling complexity, the first tape comprises episodes 1, 4 and 9, the second merely episode 17 with ten minutes of all-new bridging footage. Needless to say, episode 13, which was also shown theatrically in 1978 as the short film *Witch Castle in the Sea of Death: Mystery of Arcadia*, is absent from

the modern rerelease. The series was also reissued in an LD collection under the umbrella title of *Leiji Matsumoto Theater*, along with **DANGUARD ACE**, *GE999* and **SPACEKETEERS**.

Harlock returned *again* in 2000 with Nobuo Takagi's six-part video series *Harlock Saga: Ring of the Nibelung* (also available in the U.S.), discarding much of the previous continuity again in favor of a retelling of Wagner's Ring Cycle. Harlock, Tochiro and Emeraldas are called to planet Rhine to help Mime, the guardian of the planet's gold, prevent her brother Alberich from forging the gold into a ring and becoming the ruler of the universe. With the aid of the goldsmith Tadashi, and despite the opposition of *Galaxy Express 999*'s Maetel, Alberich gets his wish and departs for planet Valhalla to confront the alien oppressor Wotan.

Harlock also appeared in the 2000 "manga video" *Herlock*, for which see **CRUSHER JOE**. Herlock is just one of many alternate transliterations for proper nouns in the series, many of which have become canonical despite their lack of relation to the author's intent. Laffressia, for example, should really be Rafflesia—the queen of the plant people named after the world's largest flower, while Maetel, the surrogate mother of the Galaxy Express, takes her name from the Latin *mater*. Such transpositions of letters, however, are common in anime, not just from translators ignorant of the sources, but also from those who are all too cognizant but wish to tone down certain creators' embarrassing English puns and in-jokes (see **GUNDAM**).

Harlock would next return in *Cosmo Warrior Zero* (2001), a story that focused not on him, but on the man sent to capture him—Warrius Zero, a servant of the machine people, tasked with hunting him down in the depths of space. The 13-episode *Space Pirate Captain Herlock* (2002), directed by Rintaro and written by **PERFECT BLUE**'s Sadayuki Murai, was to feature Harlock attempting to reunite the crew of the Arcadia to defend the Earth from an ancient evil, although production was halted at Matsumoto's own request when he . discovered that animators were using a Star of David to represent the "root of all evil"—an anti-Semitic touch with which Matsumoto refused to have any association, and which led to the serial's broadcast being canceled. However, it did make it make it onto video in an edited format, and was released in America as *Captain Herlock: Space Pirate.*

CAPTAIN KUPPA

2001. JPN: *Sabaku no Kaizoku Captain Kuppa.* AKA: *Captain Kuppa Desert Pirate.* TV series. DIR: Koichi Mashimo. SCR: Koichi Mashimo. DES: Tomoaki Kado. ANI: N/C. MUS: Hayato Matsuo. PRD: Enoki Films, NHK. 30 mins. x 26 eps.
The future: the world has turned to desert, and the small towns that survive are surrounded by empty wastelands filled with monsters and demons. Water sources are scarce and either controlled by villains or haunted by dangerous creatures. Control of water is power, and the remnant of humanity scavenges a living patching up the advanced technology of the past. While

it might sound like the preamble to **FIST OF THE NORTH STAR**, it is actually the background for a children's show, as 11-year-old Kuppa and his faithful robot companion Dram fear nothing—except Yukke, an engineering genius who bosses her younger brother about mercilessly. They are menaced by villain Bibimba, who hunts treasure hunters and has made them his top target; but a more serious threat to their world may be the handsome and mysterious Samgetan, Yukke's love interest. She doesn't know it but he's an older man—3,500 years older, who has been observing human history all this time, waiting for the moment to strike. Created by Toshio Tanigami for a spin-off of the anthology *Corocoro Comic*, this is a cheerful, harmless adventure series.

CAPTAIN TSUBASA

1983. AKA: *Flash Kicker, Flash Kicker: Road to 2002.* TV series. DIR: Hiroe Mitsunobu, Ken Hibari, Katsumi Minoguchi, Hiroshi Yoshida, Norio Yazawa. SCR: Naoko Miyake, Yoshiyuki Suga, Yasushi Hirano, Ken Hibari. DES: Yuichi Takahashi, Kazuhiro Okaseko. ANI: Nobuhiro Okaseko. MUS: Atsumoto Tobisawa. PRD: Shida Pro, TV Tokyo. 25 mins. x 128 eps. (TV), 45 mins. x 4 eps. (m), 30 mins. x 13 eps. (v).
Tsubasa Ozora has literally been playing soccer since he was a baby. Moving to a new town, he immediately joins the junior team, which has former Brazilian international player Roberto Honma as a coach. Much like his tennis counterpart in **AIM FOR THE ACE**, Tsubasa progresses through the various levels of his chosen sport until he and his friends (a superfast striker, a wily tactician, and a gifted goalkeeper) face the best in the world.
CT was not the first soccer anime; that honor goes to **RED-BLOODED ELEV-EN**, but it remains the best-known. Even though only 4% of the Japanese population participated in soccer at the beginning of the 1980s, Yuichi Takahashi's *CT* manga polled twice as high as **FIST OF THE NORTH STAR** in the pages of *Shonen Jump.* The TV series was a

foregone conclusion, cunningly kept alive by a periodic resetting to zero of the hero's achievements. Fifty-six episodes into the series in 1984, Tsubasa graduated to middle school, allowing the earlier, junior victories to be set aside for a clean slate and a new set of struggles that would take a further 72 weeks. Four short theatrical outings followed—*CT: Great European Challenge* and *CT: Japanese Junior Championship* in 1985, *CT: Run Toward Tomorrow* and *CT: The Junior World Cup* in 1986. This last film was the beginning of an updated series, *New CT*, directed by Osamu Sekita and eventually going straight to video in 1989. Now playing for the national youth team, Tsubasa learns many trick shots from his foreign opponents, including the Italians and French, before finally playing for the ultimate prize against West Germany.

In 1993, reality caught up with fiction, as a professional Japanese soccer league was finally established, an opportunity exploited in **SHOOT!**, **KICKERS**, and **FREE KICK FOR TOMORROW**, but surprisingly not by *CT*—after the one-shot video *Holland Youth* (1995) Tsubasa faded away, only to return in a new 2001 TV series, cashing in on the 2002 World Cup.

CARDCAPTORS *

1998. JPN: *Card Captor Sakura.* TV series. DIR: Akitaro Daichi, Morio Asaka. SCR: Nanase Okawa, Jiro Kaneko. DES: CLAMP, Kumiko Takahashi. ANI: Kumiko Takahashi. MUS: Takayuki Negishi. PRD: Madhouse. 25 mins. x 70+ eps.
Created by CLAMP shortly after the success of **RAYEARTH**, *CardCaptors* combines the long tradition of magical-girl shows like **LITTLE WITCH SALLY** with the collection-oriented computer games such as **POKÉMON**. In her father's basement study, ten-year-old Sakura Kinomoto discovers the Clow, which looks like a book but is really a prison for sorcerous cards. She accidentally allows all the cards to escape, and Cerberus, the Guardian of the Cards, persuades her to hunt them all down. Each card represents a particular kind of spirit

(e.g., elemental or seasonal) that Sakura can use once she acquires it, so her progress through the story amounts to a series of game-style power-ups—a point often made by Cerberus himself, who spends most of his time in his "cute" Kero-chan form. Other problems besieging Sakura include her best friend, Tomoyo, a rich girl who insists on designing new costumes for her and taping her missions. She must also compete against her Chinese rivals Li Meiling and Li Xiaolang (who also becomes Sakura's would-be boyfriend, though at first she much prefers her brother's indifferent best friend).

The 1999 *Card Captor Sakura: The Movie* sees Sakura win a trip to Hong Kong, where she competes with the Li siblings on their home turf. In a plot suspiciously similar to that of the final TENCHI MUYO! movie, Sakura is haunted by dreams of a strange woman, an old flame of the original Card Captor, Clow Reed. She must convince the phantom that Clow Reed is dead without angering her and causing her to destroy the parallel world in which they have become trapped. A second movie, *CCS: The Sealed Card*, followed in 2000, in which someone begins to steal Sakura's cards as she prepares to celebrate the Nadeshiko festival—an occasion doubly dear to her since Nadeshiko (see NADESICO) is also the name of her late mother.

The series came to the U.S. in late 2000 dubbed by the Nelvana Studios, though, as with many other ill-fated anime, the inertia of network "demands" ruined much of what made the series initially so interesting. As if the name change were not already a hint, the translation of the series attempted to move the focus to a more acceptable protagonist (see SABER RIDER AND THE STAR SHERIFFS), beginning with episode eight ("Sakura's Rival") and implying that she and Li Xiaolang are equals, in a futile attempt to gain more male viewers.

Characters from CardCaptors would return in alternate versions of themselves in TSUBASA CHRONICLE.

CardCaptors

CAROL

1990. Video. DIR: Tetsu Dezaki, Tsuneo Tominaga. SCR: Tomoya Miyashita, Yun Koga. DES: Yukari Kobayashi, Yun Koga. ANI: Yukari Kobayashi. MUS: Tetsuya Komuro. PRD: Animate Film, Magic Bus. 60 mins.

Carol is a teenage girl who notices music disappearing from the world—at first minor annoyances like the chimes of Big Ben or the sound of her father's cello, but then a major crisis when her favorite band, Gaball Screen, loses its music. Transported to the alternate dimension of Lapaz Lupaz, she joins forces with heroes Clark, Tico, and Flash to prevent monsters from stealing songs from Earth.

Naoto Kine, guitarist with the Japanese prefab pop band TM Network, supposedly wrote the original novel of *Carol* himself. Filtered through EARTHIAN-creator Koga and scenarist Miyashita before it was ready for the screen, the end result still became the best-selling anime video of the year in Japan. The sunglasses-wearing Tico is modeled on Kine himself, with lead singer Takashi Utsunomiya providing the model for Flash, and keyboardist-producer Tetsuya Komuro inspiring Clark. As with the Beatles' *Yellow Submarine*, but unlike the similar pop-promo anime HUMANE SOCIETY, the band's voices are provided by actors. Another of Kine's literary outpourings, JUNKERS COME HERE, was animated in 1994.

CASEBOOK OF CHARLOTTE HOLMES, THE *

1977. JPN: Jo-O Heika no Petit [sic] *Angie*. AKA: *Her Royal Majesty's Petite Angie; Angie Girl*. TV series. DIR: Fumio Kurokawa, Shinya Yamada. SCR: Yu Yamamoto, Hikaru Arai. DES: Motosuke Takahashi, Yasushi Tanaka. ANI: Yasushi Tanaka. MUS: Hiroshi Tsutsui. PRD: Ashi Pro, Nippon Animation, TV Asahi. 30 mins. x 26 eps.

Angie Islington is a smart and courageous girl, the daughter of an English aristocrat. After she solves the mystery of Queen Victoria's missing ring at a garden party, she is thanked by the monarch in person and awarded the title "Petite Angie"—why this is suposed to impress anyone, we don't know. Thenceforth, she is given permission to work with Scotland Yard as a royal investigator. Angie helps the incompetent Inspector Jackson and his hunky blonde assistant

Michael in solving many other crimes.

If ever any proof was needed of the bizarre fates of Japanese animation, this show is it. Originally conceived by Takara Planning as the tale of a gypsy girl traveling Spain in search of her mother (compare to **Belle and Sebastian**, or **From the Apennines to the Andes**), it somehow transformed in pre-production into a British detective drama. The series was subsequently screened across Europe and the Arab world, but it was released in America in a strangely edited compilation, in which live actors playing the great detective Sherlock Holmes and his companion Doctor Watson introduce episodes from the casebook of his supposed "relative" Charlotte. That interpretation had nothing to do with the original creators' intent, but then again, neither did the salacious fan base that Angie somehow attracted, making her one of the poster girls of the early "Lolita Complex" movement in Japan. Compare to **Sherlock Hound** and, as an example of how much times can change, **Emma**. More intentional adventures of a sleuth's relative can be found in **Hercule Poirot and Miss Marple**.

Angie's surname is pronounced "Airington" in Japanese, leading us to believe that the creators picked it out from a London street map, unaware that the "s" in the district of Islington is not silent. Note also that in the original Japanese title *petit* is lacking the feminine suffix, an issue in French grammar that also escaped the original creators of **Petite Cossette**.

CASSHAN: ROBOT HUNTER *

1973. JPN: *Jinzo Ningen Casshan*. AKA: *Android Casshan*. TV series, video. DIR: Hiroshi Sasagawa. SCR: Junzo Toriumi, Akiyoshi Sakai, Takao Koyama, Toshio Nagata. DES: Tatsuo Yoshida, Yoshitaka Amano. ANI: Masayuki Hayashi, Chuichi Iguchi. MUS: Shunsuke Kikuchi. PRD: Tatsunoko, Fuji TV. 25 mins. x 35 eps. (TV), 30 mins. x 4 eps. (v).
As an artificial human project nears completion, robot BK-1 is activated ear-

ly by a bolt of lightning that damages its sense of morals. It leads a group of killer robots in the attempted destruction of the world, and its remorseful creator Kotaro Azuma cybernetically augments his son, Tetsuya, to fight them, with his canine companion, Friender, and love interest, Luna, whose passion for the hero is doomed to frustration because he is technically no longer human. In this follow-up to Tatsunoko's successful **Battle of the Planets**, Tetsuya's mother is turned into Swanee the electronic swan to deliver messages and increase his angst. Meanwhile, instead of a fiery phoenix warplane, Friender would transform into a variety of vehicles to suit his master's needs.

After the similar stories of *Terminator* and *Robocop* reached Japan, a sequel of sorts followed in the video series *New Android Casshan* (1993), directed by Hiroyuki Fukushima from a screenplay by Fukushima and Noboru Aikawa, with Yasuomi Umezu as designer. The new series, which was the one released in the U.S., picks up the story after "Black King" and his robot army have defeated humanity's main forces. Tetsuya, still tortured over the loss of humanity no matter how good the cause, is forced to rescue Luna when she is captured by the Black Gang. The story was resurrected as the subject of the film *Casshern* (2004), in which debut moviemaker Kazuaki Kiriya found a job for his wife, the pop idol Hikaru Utada, but seemed happy with a script that could have been scrawled on the back of a beermat.

CASTLE FANTASIA

2003. Video. DIR: Mamoru Yakoshi. SCR: Yuji Shibuya. DES: Megumi Ishihara. ANI: Akihiro Asanuma. MUS: N/C. PRD: Studio E-go, Museum Pictures, Milky. 30 mins. x 3? eps.
For 200 years, the breakaway Republic of Ruciela has been fighting to keep its independence from Ingela, the nation that worships the god of brightness. With staffing levels at an all-time low, even the pretty young maidens of

Ruciela are prepared to put themselves on the frontline. Ducis, commander of the Rucielan troops, plans a surprise attack, for which he needs to use the pretty young female officer Silera as bait. Silera, traumatized by a series of earlier bad experiences, accepts her role without complaint. When she arrives at the enemy camp, she finds a group of enemy officers waiting for her and looking forward to torturing her with a series of torments. Later, Commander Huey, who protested Silera's treatment, is ordered to go on a combined mission with the 8th Holy Battalion, an infamous annihilation unit led by a female assassin. More sex, and more violence, in a fantasy anime based on a computer game by Kazue Yamamoto. ⬤🅝🅥

CASTLE IN THE SKY *

1986. JPN: *Tenku no Shiro Laputa*. AKA: *Laputa: The Castle in the Sky*. Movie. DIR: Hayao Miyazaki. SCR: Hayao Miyazaki. DES: Hayao Miyazaki. ANI: Tsukasa Tannai. MUS: Joe Hisaishi. PRD: Nibariki, Tokuma, Studio Ghibli. 124 mins.
Orphan Pazu dreams of following in his father's quest for the legendary flying city of Laputa. Another orphan, Sheeta, is linked to the city by the power of her strange necklace, which saves her life when she falls from an airship. Sheeta's necklace is a fragment of the legendary Levitation Stone that keeps cities like Laputa in the air, and chief of secret police Muska, a fellow descendant of Laputans, wants it for his own ends. Muska steals the stone to guide him to Laputa, and the children join forces with Ma Dola, matriarch of the Dola pirate clan—Sheeta in search of her stone, and the Ma Dola pirates in search of treasure. Laputa turns out to be a peaceful ruin that seems to have been abandoned by its inhabitants with only three extant robots still operational and tending the overgrown gardens (shades here of Douglas Trumbull's *Silent Running*). Muska seizes control of Laputa's weapon system, which he claims was the original device used to smite cities in Biblical times. Realizing

he cannot be stopped, Sheeta and Pazu speak the magical words to destroy the city, though the levitation stone carries the ruins to a higher, safer altitude beyond human reach.

Taking themes from an aborted earlier project that was eventually made in his absence as SECRET OF BLUE WATER, Miyazaki mixed these with elements of GULLIVER'S TRAVELS and images from his tour of Wales after the miners' strike. With a believably human cast bickering over the remnants of the old order, only to eventually destroy it, it shares many elements with both its predecessor NAUSICAÄ and Miyazaki's later PRINCESS MONONOKE. Shown on a double bill with two episodes of Miyazaki's TV series, SHERLOCK HOUND. A lesser known 1980s dub also exists, commissioned by Tokuma and broadcast several times in English-speaking territories. This earlier variant is sometimes erroneously credited to Streamline Pictures, but was solely a Tokuma production, which was merely distributed in America by Streamline.

CASTLE OF CAGLIOSTRO *

1979. JPN: *Lupin III: Cagliostro no Shiro*. Movie. DIR: Hayao Miyazaki. SCR: Hayao Miyazaki, Haruya Yamazaki. DES: Yasuo Otsuka. ANI: Yasuo Otsuka. MUS: Yuji Ono. PRD: TMS. 100 mins.

One year after *The Secret of Mamo* (see LUPIN III), the master thief Lupin has successfully evaded Inspector Zenigata's clutches and is planning a new heist. When he inadvertently steals fake money, Lupin realizes that the high-quality printing plates are worth more than the money itself. He tracks down the counterfeiters to the tiny European state of Cagliostro but is soon distracted by the approaching wedding of Count Cagliostro and Clarice, the last princess of the ruling family.

As strings strike up straight out of "Papa Was a Rolling Stone," and amid filmic nods to *The 39 Steps* and other famous caper movies, it's Lupin and his gang against the world, with cross and double-cross, as the thieves shop each other to the cops and change their

Castle of Cagliostro

© 1980 MONKEY PUNCH, TMS

minds about what they should be stealing (Lupin alone goes from money to plates to a bride in the course of the film). Supposedly inspired by the wedding of Grace Kelly to Prince Rainier of Monaco, the film also draws on one of Kelly's most memorable movies, *To Catch a Thief*, and Maurice Leblanc's 1924 Lupin novel *Countess Cagliostro*. From the opening casino heist to the Chaplinesque duel inside a giant clock, this is a superbly paced crime caper and Lupin's best screen outing. First-time movie director Miyazaki would reuse many of the ideas later in his career, including the Mediterranean Riviera setting of PORCO ROSSO, a courageous nature-loving princess in NAUSICAÄ, a friendly hound in KIKI'S DELIVERY SERVICE, and the mossy ruins in CASTLE IN THE SKY. The film also lifted an idea from Miyazaki's work on TREASURE ISLAND—the fabled Cagliostro treasure is hidden at the bottom of an artificial lake. Surprisingly, the *Lupin* franchise lay dormant for several years afterward, not revived until the third TV series in 1984.

CAT RETURNS, THE *

2002. JPN: *Neko no Ongaishi*. AKA: *Baron, The Cats Repay a Kindness*. Movie. DIR: Hiroyuki Morita. SCR: Reiko Yoshida. DES: Satoko Morikawa. ANI: Ei Inoue, Kazutaka Ozaki. MUS: Yuji

Nomi. PRD: Studio Ghibli. 75 mins.

Ordinary schoolgirl Haru saves a cat from being run over by a truck; it was a strange cat, carrying a present, but even so she's very surprised to find it was the Prince of Cats. Haru is soon showered with feline gifts, including cattails in the yard, pockets full of catnip, and even live mice. However, the prince's kingly father determines that the only way to truly reward her is for her to marry the cat prince. She looks for help, and finds it in the suave shape of Baron, owner of the Cat Business Office, who saves her from marriage but steals a bit of her heart in the process—compare to similar romantic attachment in HOWL'S MOVING CASTLE and, most obviously, CATNAPPED, which also features a visitor who must escape from a feline dimension before being trapped there forever. This is a nicely crafted movie that would be a major achievement for many other studios, but it only ranks as a minor Ghibli work, substituting whimsy for the overwhelming power of the studio's best output. There's a slight story link to WHISPER OF THE HEART, but no need to see it first to enjoy this—supposedly this story is one of those written by Shizuku, the protagonist of the other movie. Both are based on manga by Aoi Hiiragi, this one originating in *Baron—Neko no Danshaku* (*Baron—Baron of Cats*). Released in Japanese theaters with episide two of **GHIBLIES**.

CAT SOUP
1999. JPN: *Nekojiru Gekijo*. TV series, video. DIR: Hiroshi Fukutomi. SCR: Hajime Yamano. DES: Masaaki Yuasa. ANI: Michiko Iwa, Masaaki Yuasa. MUS: N/C. PRD: Kent House, TV Asahi. 2 mins. x 27 eps. (TV), 34 mins. (v). Troubled tales of cat antics, with character designs that resemble the insipid treacle of **HELLO KITTY**, but with far more menacing undertones. Based on the manga written by Hajime Yamano and drawn by his wife "Nekojiru," the series aired in small segments as part of the *Bokusho Mondai Boss Chara Ou* TV series, but was considered too hard-hitting even for late-night TV, though it was brought back to video following Nekojiru's suicide in 2000. If anything, this makes the video release, *Nekojiru* (2001), even more disturbing, since the story features a brother cat, Nyaata, who fights to stop Death from taking away his sister Nyaako, only for the quarreling boys to tear her in half. Only the later video was released in the U.S.

CATGIRL NUKUNUKU *
1992. JPN: *Banno Bunka Neko Musume Nukunuku*. AKA: *All Purpose Cultural Cat Girl Snuggly-Wuggly*. Video, TV series. DIR: Yuji Moriyama, Hidetoshi Shigematsu. SCR: Yuzo Takada, Katsuhiko Chiba. DES: Yuzo Takada. ANI: Yuji Moriyama. MUS: Hiro Matsuda and Beat Club. PRD: Animate Film. 30 mins. x 6 eps. (v1), 25 mins. x 14 eps. (TV), 25 mins. x 12 eps. (v2).
Ryunosuke (Ryan) loses his beloved pet kitten in an accident, and his scientist father, Dr. Natsume, places the creature's brain inside a sexy android body. This is just one of many treats designed to keep the boy's mind off his parents' acrimonious divorce, but Ryunosuke and his new pal Nukunuku are soon caught up in a bitter custody battle between his crazy inventor father and his mother, Akiko, who owns a weapons factory. She regularly

sends her minions, Arisa and Kyoko, to kidnap Ryan, only to be foiled by the innocent activities of Nukunuku, also intended as a bodyguard for her endangered master.

With the massive collateral damage of **PROJECT A-KO**, an anime ingenue whose feline origins go right back to Tezuka's **BAGHI**, and a surprisingly accurate study of marital breakup that still has bite even if played for laughs, *Catgirl Nukunku* was based on a minor work by **3x3 EYES**–creator Yuzo Takada, and it is one of a limited number of anime that exist in two translations. A British dub of episodes 1–3 was the sole release from Crusader Video, who aimed to dispel the U.K. media's view that all anime were perverse, although they had to excise a masturbation scene before they could achieve the general rating their PR required. U.S. distributors AD Vision were less coy, running the entire series both uncut and in a feature-length "movie" edit.

Nukunuku jumped to TV Tokyo in 1997 for a 12-part series directed by Yoshitaka Fujimoto that retold the story from the beginning. In 1998, the franchise was revived with the same crew for the 12-part straight-to-video *Nukunuku Dash*, looking suspiciously like the tail end of a canceled TV series.

CATNAPPED! *
1995. JPN: *Totsuzen! Neko no Kuni Banipal Witt*. AKA: *Suddenly! Catland Banipal Witt*. Movie. DIR: Takashi Nakamura. SCR: Chiaki Konaka, Takashi Nakamura. DES: Takashi Nakamura. ANI: Takashi Nakamura, Mamoru Kurosawa. MUS: Naruaki Mie. PRD: Triangle Staff, Pioneer. 75 mins.
When his pet dog, Papadoll, goes missing, Toriyasu is taken to the magical world of Banipal Witt, where both he and his sister, Miko, are transformed into cats. Do-do, the brightest pupil of high-priest Sandada, has been turned to the dark side and now serves Bubulina, the cursed witch-queen whose touch turns people into balloons. The pair have kidnapped Papadoll and

turned him into a monster that menaces the whole kingdom, and Toriyasu must stop him before sunrise, when he too will be transformed. Earthlings (including dogs) can only be in Banipal Witt for two days before the sunlight will turn them into monsters. Toriyasu and Miko are there for two days before Sandada completes his magical pill that will put Papadoll to sleep, so that Toryasu can attach his chain to his collar, and hence restore him to normality. Returning Papadoll to canine form, the children use the magic cat's-paw talisman to restore normalcy and are rushed home before sunrise on the third day by the feline trio that brought them to Banipal Witt in the first place. Only three minutes have passed on Earth, but as the kids head off for a normal day at school, they are accosted once more by cats from Banipal Witt in search of help with another crisis.

Featuring a 3D-rendered fondant world spinning in the light of a gold paper sun, marshmallow skies, balloon cats, giant floating mice, and even a girl with kaleidoscope eyes in Bubulina, *Catnapped!* is a hallucinogenic mixture of *Yellow Submarine* and **ALICE IN WONDERLAND** that ultimately fails through its dispassionate precision. The candy-striped design and childish worldview seem almost calculatedly endearing, but no amount of brainstorming and focus groups can make up for true magic such as Miyazaki's **MY NEIGHBOR TOTORO**, which *Catnapped!* would very much like to be. For its U.S. release, Pioneer preferred to play up the writers' connections to **AKIRA** and **ARMITAGE III**, a sure sign that they doubted its stand-alone status within the children's cartoon market.

CAT'S EYE
1983. TV series. DIR: Toshio Takeuchi, Yoshio Hayakawa, Hiroshi Fukutomi. SCR: Keisuke Fujikawa, Tomoko Konparu. DES: Akio Sugino. ANI: Satoshi Hirayama, Nobuko Tsukada. MUS: Kazuo Otani. PRD: TMS, Nippon TV. 25 mins. x 73 eps.

Artist Michael Heinz disappears along with his antique collection, parts of which keep turning up in the holdings of criminal connoisseurs. His three daughters, Rui, Hitomi, and Ai Kisugi, secretly become the "Cat's Eye" team to steal the artworks back, hoping to locate their father in the process. Detective Toshio Utsumi is assigned to crack the cat-burglar case, unaware that his girlfriend, Hitomi, is one of the thieves he is tracking. Only his lovelorn assistant, Mitsuko, suspects, though since the coffee bar opposite the police station, run by Hitomi, is called the Cat's Eye, it's difficult to see how Toshio qualified for detective.

Compared by *Animage* to an all-girl **LUPIN III**, Tsukasa Hojo's sexy trio of leotard-wearing cat burglars struck a chord in *Shonen Jump*, where they ran for 18 manga volumes between 1981 and 1984. The series was no less successful netting male as well as female viewers, albeit for different reasons, with its mix of crime and passion. The theme song was also a hit in its own right, selling 800,000 copies. The initial 36 episodes were followed in 1985 by a second season, directed by Kanetsugu Kodama, which gradually refocused on the farcical love comedy between Hitomi and Toshio and was played more for laughs. Though there was no real ending to the TV series, the manga eventually closed with the girls revealing their identities and running for the U.S. Belatedly demonstrating a genuine skill in detection, Toshio leaves his job and tracks them down, "capturing" his true love with a wedding ring where handcuffs had failed.

The girls would return for a live-action TV special in 1988 and a live-action feature in 1997, directed by *Zipang*'s Kaizo Hayashi. Presumably with an eye on the Hong Kong market, the film adds a Triad boyfriend for Ai (**STREET FIGHTER II** *Zero*'s Kane Kosugi), who is ordered kill off the Cat's Eye team, and a climactic shootout at the Triad's restaurant headquarters, where the elusive Heinz is held prisoner. *Cat's Eye* characters would also have occasional cameos in Hojo's later **CITY HUNTER**. There was also a porno pastiche, *Cat's Ai [Love]: Milky Girl* (1985), released straight to video.

CAT'S NIBBLES
1992. JPN: *Yoyo no Neko Tsumami.* AKA: *Yoyo's Cat Nibbles.* TV series. DIR: Masami Annai, Yorifusa Yamaguchi, Katsumi Arima. SCR: Takao Koyama, Makoto Narita. DES: N/C. ANI: Yorifusa Yamaguchi. MUS: N/C. PRD: Visual 80, Nippon TV. 2 mins. x 15 eps.
Six cats introduce unusual snacks in this compilation of short culinary program bumpers, featuring a map of the cats' home island and data on each character.

CENSORSHIP AND LOCALIZATION
EARLY ANIME were subjected to the same restrictions as any other film screened in theaters. The first documented case of anime censorship was over a cartoon deemed unsuitable for *adults*, when Hakusan Kimura's *Cool Ship* (*Suzumibune*) was seized by the authorities partway through production. Since anime before the 1960s were largely for children anyway, this resulted in very few local problems, although anime would encounter many more hurdles when exported abroad.

Different cultural expectations have led to many conflicts over TV anime. Osamu Tezuka is largely to blame, not for any malicious intent, but for his perennial insistence that cartoons should be permitted to deal with themes beyond fairy-tale cliché. Six episodes of Tezuka's **ASTRO BOY** were deemed unfit for American consumption for reasons such as pictures of nude women in a bachelor's apartment, or a story line that featured animal vivisection, regarded as too hard hitting for a young audience. Most controversially, the episode "Christ's Eyeball" featured a doomed priest leaving a secret message to investigators while being held hostage by criminals in his church. A plot concerning words scratched into the eyes of a statue of Christ was considered too difficult to sell to an American audience, although it had passed without comment in Japan.

Although Tezuka worked directly with the American network NBC on **KIMBA THE WHITE LION**, corporate interference continued, altering both the name of his lead character and Tezuka's wish for fatal consequences to deadly actions. Part of the story's contemporary charm lies in the number of times a character is plainly killed, only for an American voice-over to assure us they are "only resting." The character of Leo/Kimba also had to deal with a confusion verging on a Jekyll and Hyde standoff between his heroic duties and his carnivorous, bestial nature. Little of this survives in the American soundtrack, although Kimba can be seen onscreen barely keeping himself from tearing his opponents apart. In a nod to the directives for liberal awareness at NBC, Tezuka was also obliged to make all of Kimba's evil opponents white, despite the African setting. Compare to other racially motivated alterations in the later **SABER RIDER AND THE STAR SHERIFFS**, which in the American version replaced the original Asian lead with his angry white sidekick, or **GIGANTOR**, which lost its pre-war subplot and gory deaths in its American incarnation. Three episodes were dropped from **MARINE BOY**'s American broadcast, and yet it was still decried by the National Association for Better Broadcasting as a glaring example of unacceptable violence.

Many of the complaints leveled against anime in the 1970s were reflected within the Japanese industry itself—it was, after all, no less a figure than Hayao Miyazaki who despaired of the formulaic combats and conflicts of children's entertainment in the 1970s. The rise of cross-promotion also made television anime even more commercial. The phrase "my father gave me a robot" was no longer a concise description of many serials' plotlines; it was also a litany designed to pester parents into buying tie-in toys for their children. Robots, meanwhile, became a handy device in anime for children, as did laser guns and other non-existent weapons—robots and faceless minions are more disposable and less subject to complaints than real humans in jeopardy, while non-imitable weaponry gets past a censor more swiftly than something that a child can pick up and use from its everyday life. Hence, in cartoons all over the world, the conversion of real-world firearms into "laser guns"—even seen today in some episodes of GUNDAM *Seed*. Alcohol was also forbidden—STAR BLAZERS featured a hard-drinking doctor whose sake was unconvincingly relabeled "spring water" in the English dub.

Outside Japan, cartoons in general were the subject of increased scrutiny, under revised MPAA guidelines not only in America, but also in other countries. It was, it seemed, no longer enough to remove the gorier moments from BATTLE OF THE PLANETS—many foreign commentators had realized that television was playing an increasing role as a babysitter, and that its message could prove damaging to young minds. In France, after Go Nagai's giant robot show GRANDIZER became a hit in the late 1970s, the academic Liliane Lurçat published the stinging *Five Years Old and Left Alone with Goldorak: The Young Child and TV* (*Cinq Ans, Seul Avec Goldorak: Le Jeun Enfant et la Télévision*, 1981). Her study, based on interviews with 110 children, was followed by that of would-be presidential candidate Ségolène Royal, whose *Discontent of the Baby Zappers* (*Ras-le-bol des Bébé Zappeurs*, 1989) was a polemic against television in general, citing Japanese animation among the most negative influences.

It was not lost on some critics that many cartoons were conceived as glorified commercials for toys and, perhaps worse for struggling economies, that these cheap imports had a foreign origin. Some elements of the animation industry began to take on a nationalist tone, with Filmation's *Bravestarr* (1987) ending with the legend: "Made in America by Americans!" Similar attitudes began to persuade broadcast-

ers in other countries. Government affiliate networks in Britain and Scandinavia imposed restrictions on commercially oriented cartoons—not merely anime, but any children's entertainment designed to sell to young consumers. However, the stance of the national channels was not necessarily mirrored in their commercial rivals. With some toy companies virtually giving away their tie-in cartoon series as loss-leaders, the temptation was great for some commercial channels. In France, for example, by fall 1988, two channels were running 30 French-dubbed Japanese cartoon series every week, while the other three national channels made it a matter of honor to focus on "European" material. In practice, however, the lines of division were not so clear: many of these works were either American imports via Britain or coproductions made with the Japanese. In fact, French producers had been working directly with the Japanese for the entire decade, ever since Jean Chalopin's ULYSSES 31 (1981), followed by THE MYSTERIOUS CITIES OF GOLD (1982). Similar deals led to Spain's DOGTANIAN AND THE THREE MUSKEHOUNDS (1981) and in Italy, the co-production SHERLOCK HOUND (1984) and specially commissioned extra episodes of DIRTY PAIR. Meanwhile, the German coproduction MAYA THE BEE (1975) had been translated and exported *north* to Scandinavia, so that by the time of the European furor over supposed imports, many were unaware that it was not a local product.

It was only with the arrival of video-based anime in the 1990s that anime truly ran into censorship difficulties. Ironically, many of the most controversial titles had been conceived in Japan in order to circumvent *local* censorship problems. The LOLITA ANIME and CREAM LEMON serials made children the objects of sexualized stories, which was a contradiction in terms under Japanese legislation, and hence a loophole that could be exploited. This also neatly avoided a legal prohibition against pubic hair (in force until 1991).

Similarly, since Japanese law specified that genitalia (and not other forms or organs) were off limits, UROTSUKIDOJI's cunning use of the tentacle ensured many graphic scenes, albeit ones that needed to find an excuse for tentacles, and thereby drifted toward tales of alien invasion and demonic possessions. Since sexualized bondage does not necessarily involve concentration on genitals, this too was easier to get past the Japanese censor. The result, seen from the American end of distribution, was an avalanche of bizarre fetishes and practices, often committed by or against characters that appeared demonstrably underage.

The very absence of censorship in American pornography led to misunderstandings of its own. Japanese porn often obscures its characters' genitals with blurring or black dots, leading many animators to simply not bother drawing genitals in detail. When the digitized dots were removed for the "uncut" American edition, the organs revealed could often appear unformed, hairless, or incomplete, leading to further accusations of child pornography.

In Britain, anime became the subject of a press smear campaign, engineered to some degree by anime distributors themselves, who were able to benefit from rebellious teens' decision to find out what the newspapers did not want them to see. A brief boom in risqué anime followed, only to trail off when distributors exhausted the mother lode of titles—chiefly gothic horror like WICKED CITY from the Madhouse studio and a few of the tamer Pink Pineapple erotica releases, such as REI REI. Ironically, many anime in Britain were made to seem *more* objectionable than they really were, through the process of "fifteening," whereby excess swearing would be added to a dub in order to gain a higher, more controversial-seeming rating.

The last decade in Europe has seen a liberalization of censorship laws that has largely removed limitations on much pornography—in England as in Germany, legalizing it has permitted the government to license and tax it. However, some anime pornography still remains problematic, since it depicts non-consensual sex (i.e. rape), "imitable violence," or, by its very nature, sexual practices that are difficult (read: distasteful) for live-action performers. In other words, it is an inherent tendency in anime pornography to search for places that live-action pornography cannot go (be they locations, situations, acts, or angles), because otherwise live-action pornography will have already been there, and, quite literally, done that.

Such problems are less critical in the American market, where distributors can circumvent MPAA issues simply by not submitting their titles for certification. However, a considerable amount of American anime has still been subjected to alteration in a U.S. release. Most notable are the large numbers of translations that claim sailor-suited schoolgirls are at "college" (a term that means different things in different countries), or otherwise manipulate age declarations toward safer ground. The most noticeable example is Minnie May in GUNSMITH CATS—a former child prostitute and statutory rape victim in the original, whose age is advanced a few years in the American release of both manga and anime. Nor are American anime releases completely censorship-free. Scenes of underage sex were excised from the original release of KITE, and several pornographic anime are known to have had episodes dropped—e.g., FAMILY OF DEBAUCHERY and COUNTDOWN.

Anime in Japan in the late 1990s and beyond came to rely more on television as a distribution medium. Many of the short "TV series" sold to the American market began as late-night programs airing long past midnight, and can have content designed to match. Primetime television in Japan has become increasingly censorious since the mid-1990s, when controversial episodes of EVANGELION were broadcast without prior executive approval. The resultant timidity

on the part of broadcasters has played into the hands of the late-night shows and cable networks, with shows such as GANTZ enjoying two distinct existences: one in a widely available but edited form and another in a more graphic version requiring cable subscription or DVD rental. In the case of COWBOY BEBOP, the main story arc was only seen on WOWOW and DVDs—the version seen on terrestrial TV was missing 14 episodes.

POKÉMON and its successors heralded a resurgence of children's anime on foreign television and a return to some of the localization problems that troubled anime in the 1960s. There have also been new issues, such as the (logical) decision not to broadcast the infamous epilepsy-inducing episode of *Pokémon*.

After a decade of largely adhering to original names (and indeed language) in anime for teenagers, character names in anime for the children's market are often localized. As the American edit is often the portal through which other language territories gain their anime, issues in localization can be passed on. Religious references remain as sensitive as they once were during the "Christ's Eyeball" incident—demonic imagery is airbrushed out and misused Bibles turned into non-specific grimoires. Both DRAGON BALL and YUGI-OH have featured trips to Hell, the precise identity and location of which was left vague in the American release. Nudity has also been an issue in American localization, with digitally added underpants, swimsuits, or strategically placed foreground items used to preserve the supposed blushes of the American audience. In localizing POKÉMON, this has included the removal of scenes in which a major character chases girls, and also any references to the fact that women might have breasts—a bikini competition, for example, or the use of fake boobs as a disguise. Some characters can be controversial abroad—the spoon-bending Pokémon creature Yungera (Kadabra in English) was the subject of an unsuc-

cessful law suit by Uri Geller, and the Pokémon Jynx was dropped from some American episodes for being an unpleasant "Negro" racial stereotype until her skin color was changed to a respectable purple. The possibility of copyright infringement can still affect broadcasts—a Peter Pan pastiche episode of the new *Astro Boy* (2003) has never been released in America, for fear of attracting legal reprisals from Disney.

References to alcohol and tobacco are still regularly removed, such as from the Cartoon Network broadcasts of TENCHI MUYO! and BLUE SUBMARINE No. SIX, although recently this restriction appears to have tapered off, with the regular appearance of a pipe-smoking character in NARUTO. The sight of blood or of the death of main characters continues to be cut or altered. In cases where the cost of removing potentially offensive material becomes too prohibitive, an episode can be simply dropped, which sometimes leads to continuity issues further along in a series.

Anime in the 21st century is much easier to obtain in its unadulterated form, and even if viewers object to a dub, dual language tracks on the DVD release make it possible to hear the original Japanese. But for some in fandom, localization has become the new censorship, since it can alter a creator's original intent, and give new fans an inaccurate introduction to the shows they see. However, such issues in translation are endemic to the medium, and have been debated since the first days anime left Japanese shores.

CERES: CELESTIAL LEGEND *

2000. JPN: *Ayashi no Ceres*. AKA: *Mysterious Ceres*. TV series. DIR: Hajime Kamegaki. SCR: Shikichi Ohashi. DES: Hideyuki Motohashi. ANI: Hideyuki Motohashi. MUS: Ryo Sakai. PRD: Studio Pierrot, Bandai, WOWOW. 25 mins. x 24 eps.
Japanese twins Aya and Aki Mikage get a nasty shock at the approach of their joint sixteenth birthday celebrations,

Ceres: Celestial Legend

when Aya discovers that she is the reincarnation of Ceres, an angelic being that was once tricked into marrying an Earthbound fisherman, and who bears a vengeful grudge against the descendants of the children she was forced to bear—the entire Mikage family. Hunted by her own family, Aya falls in with another reincarnated angel, while Aki gains the ability to manifest as "the Progenitor," that same fisherman who stole Ceres' feathered cloak and caused her suffering on Earth to begin in the first place. Based on a manga serialized in *Weekly Shojo Comic* by **Fushigi Yugi** creator Yu Watase, Ceres reunited many anime staff from the FY anime, for a story that combines the perennial obsessions of girls' comics— angels and **Cinderella** victimhood.

CHALK-COLORED PEOPLE

1988. JPN: *Chalk-iro no People*. Video. DIR: Akira Kamiyama. SCR: Seizo Watase. DES: Seizo Watase. ANI: Keizo Kira. MUS: Astrud Gilberto. PRD: 3D. 54 mins. Five short episodes from **Heart Cocktail**–creator Seizo Watase's romantic manga set to bossa nova music for reasons unknown. The stories include *Building without Tide, Brother and Sis-*

ter, Sometimes I'm Happy, I've Saved the Sidecar for You, and *The Santa Quartet.* The music is from Latin lounge legend Astrud Gilberto. A similar music/animation combination was tried the previous year with Watase's **My All-Day All-Color**, and later with **Two on the Road**.

CHAMPION OF GORDIAN

1979. JPN: *Toshi Gordian*. AKA: *Gardian*. TV series. DIR: Shigeru Yanagawa, Masamune Ochiai. SCR: Masaru Yamamoto. DES: Ippei Kuri. ANI: Kazuhiko Udagawa. MUS: Masaaki Jinbo, Masayuki Yamamoto. PRD: Tatsunoko, Tokyo 12 Channel. 25 mins. x 73 eps. Daigo Otaki and his pet mechanical leopard, Clint, are transferred to the Mecha Con Unit that protects the computer-run Victor Town from the predations of the Madoctor Gang. However, he is abducted by the giant robot Gordian and meets his "sister," Saori, at Fort Santore, where he hears the voice of his own father issuing from the central computer that is making all the decisions. The run of this transforming robot story was extended several times, with Daigo eventually heading out for adventures in space with his robots

Protteser, Delinger, and Garbin, whose similarity to the **Machine Robo** line prompted Bandai to retool its existing molds in order to imply a relationship that wasn't there.

CHANCE POP SESSIONS *

2001. JPN: *Chance! Triangle Session*. Video. DIR: Susumu Kudo. SCR: Kazuhiko Soma. DES: Fumie Muroi. ANI: Kunio Kazuki, Yumiko Ishii. MUS: Avex, Goro Matsui. PRD: Madhouse, TV Tokyo. 25 mins. x 13 eps. A group of girls hope to make it as performers—16-year-old street busker Yuki, large-breasted 17-year-old Akari, and prissy company director's daughter Nozomi. Based on a 1999 radio drama.

CHARGE AHEAD! MEN'S SCHOOL

1988. JPN: *Sakikage! Otoko Juku*. TV series. DIR: Nobutaka Nishizawa. SCR: Susumu Takahisa. DES: Masami Suda. ANI: Masami Suda. MUS: Shunsuke Kikuchi. PRD: Toei, Fuji TV. 25 mins. x 34 eps. Otoko Juku is the juvenile hall where men are sent for being too honorable and too manly, the kind of rough, tough academy one might expect from the team who made **Fist of the North Star**. Newcomers Momotaro, Genji, and Taio endure bullying and harsh treatment at the hands of class leader Onihige and the evil teachers.

Like Akira Miyashita's original 34-volume 1985 *Shonen Jump* manga, this show starts as a comedy but soon devolves into fights, the quality of animation dropping along with the story. It retained elements of its comedic past right to the end, however, with Momotaro reading out fake fan mail over the "next episode" shots and pretending to take requests. There was also a 1988 movie directed by Tetsuo Imazawa, in which the gang gets to trash Hawaii, Alaska, Niagara Falls, and Manhattan in a battle of wills with an evil mastermind.

In a bizarre footnote to the popularity of the manga in Asia, former president of Taiwan Lee Teng-hui famously dressed up as the school's tough principal, Heihachi Edajima, for a publicity stunt.**◐**

CHARGEMAN KEN

1974. TV series. scr: Masaaki Wakuda, Toyohiro Ando. des: Eiji Tanaka. ani: Junji Mizumura. mus: N/C. prd: Knack, TBS. 10 mins. x 65 eps.
Average guy Ken Izumi can transform into Chargeman Ken by donning his special uniform, which augments his strength. In his all-terrain vehicle the Sky Rod, he fights to save Earth from the evil Geral alien invaders, who have traveled two million light years to wipe out humanity. His only assistants are his sister Caron and Balican, the mischievous robot dog. A staff reunion for many of the people who worked on Astro Ganger.

CHARLOTTE

1977. jpn: Wakakusa no Charlotte. aka: Charlotte the Young Grass/Green Shoot. TV series. dir: Eiji Okabe. scr: Shunichi Yukimuro. des: Shinya Takahashi. ani: Tetsuo Shibuya, Nobuyuki Kitajima, Hiroshi Yoshida. mus: Yoshimasa Suzuki. prd: Nippon Animation, TV Asahi. 25 mins. x 30 eps.
Charlotte grows up on a Canadian cattle farm and has a happy life until her 12th birthday, when her father André reveals that he is really a French aristocrat, hiding out in the colonies to escape persecution. Her mother, believed dead, is actually still alive, and André sets off to bring her back, but he is killed en route. Charlotte struggles to keep the farm going, encouraged by her friend Sandy, and, in the tradition of almost every girls' anime from Candy Candy onward, aided by a "mysterious stranger" called Knight. Nippon Animation's first homegrown series for girls deliberately alluded to Little House on the Prairie and Little Women in its look and feel but was considered a failure and taken off the air after a relatively short run.

CHEEKY ANGEL

2002. jpn: Tenshi na Konamaiki. TV series. dir: Masaharu Okuwaki. scr:

Junichi Iioka. des: Hideyuki Motohashi. ani: Satoru Kojima. mus: Daisuke Ikeda. prd: Tokyo Movie Shinsha, TV Tokyo. 25 mins. x 50 eps.
At the age of nine, precocious brawler Megumi saves a wizard from an attack in the street and is granted a single wish. Rashly neglecting to think through the small print, he demands to be the "manliest man on Earth," only to be transformed into a woman instead. Now in his mid-teens, he is a brash, tough boy still trapped in a girl's body and searching for the chance to reverse the wish, which he now regards as more like a curse. Based on an "original" manga by Hiroyuki Nishimori—a particularly galling claim, since it ran in Shonen Sunday, the home of the much more famous, much longer-running Ranma ½.

CHIBI MARUKO-CHAN

1990. aka: Cute Little Maruko. Movie, TV series. dir: Tsutomu Shibayama. scr: Momoko Sakura. des: Yuji Shigeta. ani: Michishiro Yamada, Yoshiaki Yanagida, Masako Sato. mus: BB Queens. prd: Nippon Animation, Fuji TV. 25 mins. x 142 eps. (TV1), 94 mins. (m), 25 mins. x 555+ eps. (TV2).
Maruko is a nine-year-old schoolgirl who spends most of her time daydreaming, particularly that she is a noble princess, her parents are divorced, or both. Inexplicably talking like an old woman despite her tender years, she continually pesters her parents, elder sister, and relatives to answer questions, and "amusing" misunderstandings ensue. Momoko Sakura's 1986 manga, loaded with 1970s nostalgia, was christened a "new Sazae-san" by some Japanese critics for its gentle humanity and interminable run. Broadcast without subtitles on the Californian channel KSCI. It was also adapted into a three-part live-action mini series on Fuji TV in 2006, featuring the 8-year-old Ei Morisako in the lead role.

CHICKEN TAKKUN

1984. TV series. dir: Keiji Hayakawa.

scr: Masaru Yamamoto, Kazuyoshi Ohashi. des: Yoshihiro Owada. ani: Mitsuru Honma, Tetsuro Hagano, Shigeru Omachi. mus: Masami Anno. prd: Ishinomori Pro, Studio Pierrot, Studio Gallop, Fuji TV. 25 mins. x 23 eps.
The Walchin Dictionary, a computer packed with evil ideas from Planet R, falls into the hands of Doctor Bell, who plans to use it to rule the world. Prince Chicken enlists the help of his alien friends to get the dictionary back and lands his flying saucer on the roof of the Minamita family's house in Japan. Miko Minamita and her four friends offer to help Chicken. This anime was adapted from Shotaro Ishinomori's manga run in the educational magazine Science for Grades 1–6.

CHILD'S TOY *

1995. jpn: Kodomo no Omocha. TV series. dir: Akira Suzuki, Akitaro Daichi, Hiroaki Sakurai. scr: Tomoko Konparu, Ryosuke Takahashi, Miho Maruo. des: Hajime Watanabe. ani: Nobuyuki Tokinaga. mus: Hiroshi Koga, Tokio. prd: Pony Canyon, TV Tokyo. 25 mins. x 102 eps.
Sana Kurata is a child star who attends a normal school, initially at odds with the bullying Akito Hayama, until he reluctantly becomes her friendly rival ("my enemy and my boyfriend," she describes him with a typically innocent oxymoron). Originally turned into a video as part of the 40th anniversary celebrations of Ribbon magazine in 1995, Miho Obana's 1994 manga became a full-fledged TV series the following year. With a sixth-grader who is already a star (appearing in the self-referentially titled Child's Toy TV show), it takes the aspirations of magical-girl shows like Creamy Mami as given, preferring instead to concentrate on school one-upmanship like that in Goldfish Warning. Released in America in 2005 under the title Kodocha.

CHIMERA *

1997. jpn: Seikimatsu Reima Chimera. aka: End of the Century Demon Beauty Chimera; Angel of Death. Video. dir:

Mitsuo Kusakabe. scr: Narihiko Tatsumiya. des: Asami Tojo. ani: Taeko Sato. mus: N/C. prd: Toei. 47 mins.
Sex and violence in the Hong Kong underworld, as pretty assassin Rei leaves a wake of death and grief behind her as she carries out jobs for the Mob. Her codename: Chimera. Based on the girls' manga by Asami Tojo, and not to be confused with KIMERA. **ⓁⓃⓋ**

CHINA NUMBER ONE

1997. jpn: *Nekketsu Ryori Anime: Chuka Ichiban.* aka: *Hot-blooded Cookery Anime: China Number One.* TV series. dir: Masami Annai. scr: Nobuaki Kishima. des: Yoshinori Kishi, Tsuneo Ninomiya. ani: Eikichi Takahashi. mus: Michihiko Ota. prd: Nippon Animation, Pony Canyon. 25 mins. x 52 eps.
In this adaptation of Etsuji Ogawa's manga for *Shonen Magazine,* a gifted teenage cook travels to late 19th-century China in search of rival chefs worthy of his cooking prowess. Like RANMA ½ before it, it was immensely successful in East Asia, where its Japanese origins were swiftly forgotten. Episodes 9–14 were edited into a 30-minute digest.

CHIRORIN VILLAGE

1992. jpn: *Chirorin Mura.* TV series. dir: Yasuo Yamakichi. scr: Osamu Nakamura, Riko Hinokuma. des: Takao Kasai. ani: Takao Kasai. mus: Tatsumi Yano. prd: C&D Distribution, Bandai Visual, NHKEP. 8 mins. x 170 eps.
Chirorin Village and Walnut's Tree was a children's puppet show broadcast on NHK between 1956 and 1964 featuring the adventures of three junior high school children: Tonpei the Onion, Kurumi the Walnut, and Peanut (the Peanut) in the titular village. Brought back to cash in on parents' nostalgia, it was remade as a TV anime with famous voice actresses, such as Noriko Hidaka and Minami Takayama, and far-fetched episodes, including *I'm Not a Criminal, The Sound of a Vampire, Come Out You Monsters,* and *Back to the Secret Base.*

CHISTE: THE GREEN THUMB

1990. jpn: *Chist: Midori no Oyayubi.*

Movie. dir: Shumon Miura, Yuji Funano. scr: Ryu Tachihara. des: Masahiro Kase. ani: Shinya Sadamitsu, Kazuya Ose. mus: Marc Berriere, Francoise Legrand, Jean-Michel Ervé. prd: Dax International. 73 mins.
In this adaptation of the book by Maurice D'Orleans, Chiste is a boy with the strange ability to make flowers grow wherever he places his thumb, a power which he puts to use bringing love and peace to the world. For more peace-loving florists, see WEISS KREUZ.

CHOBIN THE STARCHILD *

1974. jpn: *Hoshi no Ko Chobin.* TV series. dir: Rintaro, Hiroyuki Hoshiyama, Noboru Ishiguro, Shinji Okada. scr: Shunichi Yukimuro, Hisashi Ito, Keisuke Fujikawa, Yukiko Takayama, Soji Yoshikawa. des: Shotaro Ishinomori. ani: Norio Yazawa. mus: Tetsuaki Hagiwara. prd: Watanabe Planning, Ishinomori Pro, TBS. 25 mins. x 26 eps.
Chobin, king of planet Fairystar, arrives from his homeworld in a spaceship and lands at the house of Professor Amagawa and his assistant, Ruri. Enlisting the help of terrestrial creatures (including a frog, rabbit, and butterfly from the nearby forest), Chobin searches for his missing mother and dreams of the day when he and his family can return to Fairystar and depose the usurper Brungar.
Invented by producers at Watanabe Planning in cooperation with CYBORG 009–creator Shotaro Ishinomori, Chobin's adventures were serialized in a number of magazines, including *Shojo Friend* and *Terebi* magazine, to drum up support for the TV series. The story received a very limited broadcast on U.S. Japanese community TV stations shortly after its release.

CHOBITS *

2002. TV series. dir: Morio Asaka. scr: Genjiro Kaneko, Nanase Okawa, Tomoyasu Okubo. des: Hisashi Abe. ani: Hisashi Abe. mus: Katsutoshi Kitagawa, Dan Miyakawa, Keitaro Takanami. prd: CLAMP, Mad-

house, TBS. 25 mins. x 26 eps.
Hideki Motosuwa is a 19-year-old farm boy from Hokkaido who flunks his college entrance exams and comes to Tokyo to attend a cram school for a second attempt. Hideki takes consolation from reading porn comics, but all around him people are buying persocoms, humanoid computers, usually in the shape of cute girls. There's no way he can afford one, so when he finds a seemingly broken persocom abandoned in a dumpster, he decides to keep her. Her first word is Chii, so that becomes her name. She knows absolutely nothing, a blank slate on which Hideki can write his own ideas of the world. He begins to suspect that she may be one of the legendary Chobits, persocoms with free will and enormous powers.
Chobits is one of the landmark shows of the early 21st century. It is a successful fusion of the old-school magical girl with the artificial girlfriend of VIDEO GIRL AI and MAHOROMATIC, along with the harem tradition of TENCHI MUYO!, liberally dosed with a boyish obsession for tinkering with machines. It is therefore all the more impressive that it is based on a manga in *Young* magazine (the original home of AKIRA!) created by the all-female CLAMP collective, who demonstrate here that they can also entertain a male market with deceptive ease. Although the show's central conceit is nothing new (after all, it traces a line back through ASTRO BOY to *Pinocchio*), CLAMP's production seemed to hit an audience of both sexes, revisiting, for example, many of the modern romantic malaises of Ujin's SAKURA DIARIES, particularly when Hideki starts dating a real human girl, without any thought of Chii's feelings. Occasionally this leads to bipolar behavior; the over-arcing romantic plots in the style of MAISON IKKOKU are often sacrificed for gratuitous titillation, but as with AI YORI AOSHI, that seems to be the price animators must often pay in modern anime. Some viewers may discern an element of LOLITA ANIME in the submissive

vacancy of the persocoms, although as with **ARMITAGE III**, not all of them are "female," merely often made so by market forces. As with **KEY THE METAL IDOL**, the addition of true love to Chii's programming is liable to cause a radical change to her behavior—compare to **AIR** and **DEARS**.

Chobits acknowledges the pervasive nature of information technology while emphasizing the need for real, individual emotional responses. Hideki finally comes to terms with his feelings for his Chobit partner, and we learn that Chii is a twin and already has a complex and tragic love story in her background. The original *Chobits* manga featured cameo roles for characters from CLAMP's earlier **CARDCAPTORS** and **ANGELIC LAYER**, but these scenes were dropped from the anime adaptation. Perhaps as a sign of stretching a low budget, the series used more recap episodes than usual, pointlessly retelling the "story so far" on three occasions in its relatively short run. While such catch-up episodes were commonplace in long-running shows like **URUSEI YATSURA**, their use here seems more like a cynical recycling of footage. *Chibits* (2003) is a brief six-minute cartoony adventure included as a bonus on the final disc, in which Hideki leaves the house without his wallet and Chii chases after him, until the other characters realize that she has left her panties behind and chase after her. **ꞥ**

CHOCCHAN'S STORY

1997. JPN: *Chocchan no Monogatari*. AKA: *Story of Chocchan*. Movie. DIR: Hiroko Tokita. SCR: Chifude Asakura. DES: Tatsuo Yanagino. ANI: Tatsuo Yanagino. MUS: Tomoyuki Asagawa. PRD: Requiem, Triangle Staff. 76 mins. Cho, a music student and sometime chorus girl, returns briefly to her native Hokkaido to tell her parents she is engaged to violinist Moritsuna. When her father forbids her marriage, the couple elope and set up home in 1930s Tokyo. Tetsuko, the eldest of their three children, is inattentive at school and disrupts classes by calling

her friends' attention to things going on outside the window. Eventually, Tetsuko is put in a more indulgent institution, where she gets more consideration from the teacher and bonus outdoor activities.

The outbreak of war, first in China and then in the Pacific, brings rationing and shortages. When son Meiji becomes ill, Cho sends Tetsuko to pawn Moritsuna's violin to buy ice cream, but the kind-hearted girl instead trades her own hat for ten yen. Cho is uneasily reconciled with her estranged father during a Hokkaido summer holiday; the old man adopts the role of grandfather with ease and seems as hurt as Cho that they still cannot agree on everything. Eventually, Moritsuna is conscripted into the army, where he entertains his fellow soldiers with violin solos—echoes here of **VIOLIN OF THE STARRY SKY**. After the war, the family return to the ruins of their house in Tokyo, where a wounded Moritsuna rejoins them.

The family's rather dull pre-war activities are brightened only by some original sound—*Chocchan* opens with a rendition of "L'Amour est un Oiseau Rebelle" from Bizet's *Carmen* (1875), and the radio surrender address of the Showa Emperor appears to be excerpted from the genuine article. Although it might have the outward appearance of another war story in the tradition of **RAIL OF THE STAR**, or a sanitized novel that belongs among the **ANIMATED CLASSICS OF JAPANESE LITERATURE**, *Chocchan* has a more oblique origin. It is based on the memoirs of the *mother* of Tetsuko Kuroyanagi, an actress who dominated Japanese television in its early years, provided one of the voices for *Chirorin Village* (*DE), became the host of the long-running TV Asahi chat show *Tetsuko's Room*, and ultimately served as an ambassador for UNICEF. This explains the bizarre way that *Chocchan's Story*, despite the title, concentrates so much on Tetsuko—even on the blurb of the video box, which immediately draws the reader's attention away from the supposed lead to emphasize the later fame of her daughter.

There is one moment where it aspires to greater things—a sequence where the family watch a column of marching soldiers, occasionally obscured by silent girls, who rush past them staring off-screen as if carried along by an invisible current. It is only when they spot Moritsuna that they, too, dash out into the street, running alongside a beloved family member for what could be a final goodbye.

Despite being unreleased in English, it was distributed under the English title of *Chocchan's Story* in Europe. The English title seems to have been carefully chosen in order to ensure echoes of *Totto-chan: The Girl at the Window*, daughter Tetsuko's autobiography, to which *Chocchan* may be regarded as an indirect prequel. Compare to **KAYOKO'S DIARY**.

CHOCOLATE PANIC PICTURE SHOW, THE

1985. Video. DIR: Kazuyoshi Hirose. SCR: N/C. DES: Kamui Fujiwara. ANI: Mamoru Sugiura. MUS: TV Asahi Music. PRD: CBS, Taurus, Filmlink. 33 mins. Jaw-droppingly racist musical in which grossly caricatured Africans Manbo, Chinbo, and Chonbo cause chaos in civilization despite the efforts of their pretty tour guide/bedmate to tame their zany, grass-skirted cannibal ways. This video was based on a manga by Kamui Fujiwara in *Super Action* and partly inspired by Jamie Uys's *The Gods Must Be Crazy* (1980).

CHOPPO THE MISCHIEVOUS ANGEL

1970. JPN: *Itazura Tenshi Choppochan*. TV series. DIR: Takashi Aoki, Fumio Ikeno. SCR: Noboru Ishiguro, Tomohiro Ando. DES: N/C. ANI: New World Pictures. MUS: Yuki Tamaki. PRD: Fuji TV Enterprise. 5 mins. x 240 eps. Slipping off his cloud and falling out of heaven, Choppo, a naughty angel, lands in the food store owned and run by Kantaro Fujino's parents. Unable to fly home because his wings are not yet fully grown, he stays with the family, though his inability to understand the meaning of danger soon leads him into numerous accidents. The same crew had previously worked on Fuji TV Enterprise's *Pinch and Punch*, a 1969 tale of naughty twins that was otherwise very similar.

CHRISTMAS IN JANUARY

1991. JPN: *Ichigatsu ni wa Christmas.* Video. DIR: Tetsu Dezaki. SCR: Setsuko Shibunnoichi, Toshiaki Imaizumi. DES: Yukari Kobayashi. ANI: Yukari Kobayashi. MUS: Takashi Ui. PRD: For Life Record, Media Ring. 45 mins.
Nobumasa is a boy who works part-time in a shoe store, where he meets Mizuki, a girl whose abusive family life has left her unable to trust other people. Meanwhile, Nobumasa is unaware that another girl, Seiko, has a crush on him but is unable to express her feelings.

A love triangle straight out of VIDEO GIRL AI or KIMAGURE ORANGE ROAD, but this time presented for the female readership in *Margaret* magazine, Mariko Iwadate's 1984 manga made it to the screen in this one-shot video.

CHRONO CRUSADE *

2003. JPN: *Chrno* [sic] *Crusade.* TV series. DIR: Yu Ko (aka Yuh Koh), Hiroyuki Kanbe. SCR: Atsuhiro Tomioka. DES: Kazuya Kuroda, Tomohiro Kawahara, Hiroyuki Kanbe, Hisao Muramatsu. ANI: Kazuya Kuroda. MUS: Hikaru Nanase. PRD: Fuji TV, Gospel Bullet, Gonzo, Klockwerx. 25 mins. x 24 eps.
Teenage exorcist Rosette Christopher works for Catholic agency The Magdalene Order in an alternate 1920s New York, sworn to protect the seven "Apostles," super-powered humans who have been appearing since the traumatic events of World War I. These individuals are the targets of the Sinners, a group led by Aion, a handsome renegade demon whose home dimension of Pandemonium may soon be sending other creatures through the crumbling defenses of our world.

Rosette works alongside renegade demon, Chrono, whose great powers are contained in the body of a young boy, locked away until Rosette unleashes them using a seal she wears around

her neck—compare to BASTARD. Each time she does this, she uses up a little of her own life force, and there is only a finite amount of it. She also uses a WWI government-issue Colt .45, which can fire holy bullets or special "Gospel" silver rounds etched with incantations, all provided for her by lecherous genius Edward "Elder" Hamilton, the monastic equivalent of 007's Q. Elder has an even more deadly prototype up his sleeve, a round with a demon actually sealed inside it, which releases a massive burst of power on impact. When Rosette steals it, the results are predictably disastrous.

Rosette has a personal reason for joining the Order—she is seeking her younger brother Joshua, missing for four years since he turned everyone else in their orphanage to stone and vanished, lured away by Aion. Chrono has his own motives for joining forces with her. He and Aion were both Sinners, and rebelled against the ruling powers of Pandemonium together. Aion betrayed him, cut off his horns—the source of a demon's control over his power—and gave them to Joshua.

Mistrustful nun Sister Kate Valentine entrusts Rosette and Chrono with protecting 12-year-old soprano Azmaria Hendrick, one of the Seven Apostles, who is in grave danger. Her foster father, tycoon Ricardo Hendrick, is really an undead devil-worshipper who serves the demon Viscount Lerajie. Ricardo plans to use Azmaria's powers to restore his own life and become immortal. The pair are joined in their mission by another powerful demon-fighter, red-haired orphan Stella Harvenheit, whose parents were killed by demons. Stella is known as the Jewel Witch because she can summon and control fiends using crystals. Using her jewels, Chrono's powers, and Rosette's trusty Colt, the trio risk their lives to protect Azmaria.

Despite a rather promising set of elements, including design work by VANDREAD's Kazuya Kuroda, Christian heresies in the spirit of DEVILMAN or EVANGELION, and wild mood swings in

the style of FULLMETAL ALCHEMIST, this adaptation of Daisuke Moriyama's manga from *Dragon Age* monthly is disappointingly less than the sum of its parts, concocting little more than a cynical alchemy of INU YASHA and DIRTY PAIR with optional crucifixes. The American location is squandered, the Prohibition period setting something to which the U.S. dubbers have given more thought than the Japanese creators, and the religious references a mixture of intriguing ideas (the prophecies of Fatima as a plot device) and B-movie hokum (bullets filled with holy oil). The result is yet another gaggle of shrill anime eye candy blowing stuff up, lacking the energy of SLAYERS, the chills of HELLSING, or the laughs of PHANTOM QUEST CORP, all of which it would like to be.

CINDERELLA

1996. JPN: *Cinderella Monogatari.* TV series. DIR: Hiroshi Sasagawa, Takaaki Ishiyama, Yuji Asada. SCR: Masaaki Sakurai, Hiroko Naka, Tsunehisa Arakawa. DES: Tatsunoko Planning Office. ANI: Masami Suda, Chuichi Iguchi. MUS: N/C. PRD: Tatsunoko, Marubeni, NHK2. 25 mins. x 26 eps.
Forced to scrub the floor in her wicked stepmother's kitchen, Cinderella refuses to let her situation get her down. Her fairy godmother, Palette, casts a spell so that she can understand the speech of animals, and Cinderella's life is made easier by her friendships with Wanda the dog, Pappy the bird, and mice Chuchu and Bingo. She falls in love with a man called Sharrol whom she meets in town, unaware that he is actually *Prince* Sharrol, traveling in disguise, and that the "real" Prince Sharrol back at the palace is an imposter.

Straight after finishing SNOW WHITE, Tatsunoko added a pirate attack, funny animal business, and a subplot straight out of the *Prince and the Pauper* in order to pad out the running time of this adaptation. Since Cinderella and her Prince Charming are *both* in disguise each time they meet, it adds to the tension, but once all the intrigue is resolved, the last three episodes end traditionally with the ball, glass slipper reunion, wedding bells, and happy-ever-after. Other versions of *Cinderella* have appeared in GRIMMS' FAIRY TALES (1987), *Famous World Fairy Tales* (1989), as part of the HELLO KITTY series (*Hello Kitty's Cinderella*, 1992), and, in a more risqué incarnation, in ADULT FAIRY TALES (1999). See also VIDEO PICTURE BOOK.

CINDERELLA BOY

2003. TV series. DIR: Tsuneo Tominaga. SCR: Mitsuyo Suenaga, Rikei Tsuchiya. DES: Kazutoshi Kobayashi, Konami Umi. ANI: N/C. MUS: N/C. PRD: Magic Bus, Enoki Films, AT-X. 25 mins. x 13 eps.

Hotly pursued by a group of angry arms smugglers, private investigators Ranma and Layla have what first appears to be a fatal car accident. But when Ranma wakes up, he appears unharmed, although his beautiful female partner is nowhere to be seen. He soon discovers that they are now obliged to share a body, and that Ranma transforms into Layla at the stroke of midnight, in a blatantly unoriginal attempt by Monkey Punch to impart the capers of his LUPIN III with the body-swap transformation of RANMA 1/2—Ranma is not all that common a name in Japan, making the comic creator's decision to name his leading man after Rumiko Takahashi's famous girl/boy all the more puzzling. The rest of this obscure TV series seems similarly half-hearted: the animation is often clumsy, the action dull, and the music a feeble attempt to revisit some of the jazzy cool of COWBOY BEBOP. Almost everything that is wrong about anime in the early 21st century, wrapped up in one forgettable package.

CINDERELLA EXPRESS

1989. Video. DIR: Teru Moriboshi, Nanako Shimazaki. SCR: Kenji Terada. DES: Moriyasu Taniguchi. ANI: Moriyasu Taniguchi. MUS: N/C. PRD: Nippon Eizo. 50 mins.

Everyday salaryman Yuji Shimano meets and beds a pretty young girl at his bachelor party. Meeting her again at his wedding, he realizes that he has just begun an affair with his sister-in-law, in this erotic farce from Hikaru Yumizuki found in the pages of *Young Jump*. A decade later, TEACHER'S PET would demonstrate that nothing ever changes. **N**

CIPHER THE VIDEO

1989. Video. DIR: Tsuneo Tominaga. SCR: Machiko Kondo, Yuko Sakurai. DES: Yukari Kobayashi. ANI: Kenichi Maejima, Takeshi Koizumi, Minoru Yamazawa. MUS: Wags, Thompson Twins. PRD: Victor Entertainment. 40 mins.

In this adaptation of Minako Narita's 1985 manga from *Lala*, pretty-boy Cipher goes to high school in New York, sometimes posing as his twin brother, Shiva, a famous actor who often needs to cut classes. Shiva wanders moodily through the streets of New York before the scene shifts to the set of his latest movie, an American football tale called *Winning Tough*. We see a fake ""Making Of"" documentary featuring interviews of him and his costars before being shown the trailer for the film and an image video based on it. Eventually, Shiva returns from his wanderings and cooks breakfast, revealing that his wanderings were just wanderings, not the result of a fight with his brother.

Cipher the Video is a true curiosity, featuring English-language dialogue with Japanese subtitles for that extra touch of exoticism, although it was never released outside Japan. Deliberately shot in an MTV pop-video style, much of it is simply overlaid with songs from American movies contemporaneous with the manga—Phil Collins' title song from *Against All Odds* (1984), as well as the title song and "Let's Hear It for the Boy" from the same year's *Footloose*, all in relatively poor versions from the group Wags. As an additional bonus, there's also the original version of the Thompson Twins' "Kamikaze." The running time is bulked out with

the self-indulgent "Making of *Cipher the Video*," recycling some footage for a third time, featuring interviews with the crew and live-action shots from the New York location hunt that informed some of the admittedly picturesque images of the city. As a bonus, the video also includes Cipher's other animated appearance, a short 1986 Japanese commercial for Sumitomo Insurance. An earnest and ultimately touching treat for fans of the manga. Narita specialized in a fantasy America—her earlier manga *Alien Street* (1980) is set at a U.S. college where a beautiful, blond Arab prince flirts with liberal Western ways.

CIRCUIT ANGEL

1987. JPN: *Circuit Angel: Ketsui no Starting Grid*. AKA: *Circuit Angel: Resolving Starting Grid*. Video. DIR: Yoshikazu Tochihira, Hideki Tonokatsu. SCR: Asami Watanabe. DES: Chuichi Iguchi, Boomerang. ANI: Hiroshi Kazawa. MUS: N/C. PRD: Studio Unicorn. 45 mins.

Mariko is a downtown schoolgirl who loves motorcycles and wants to graduate from the street-racing circle of her friends to the world of pro racing. But despite poaching LEGEND OF ROLLING WHEELS–writer Watanabe and concentrating hard enough on machinery to justify a "Mariko's Bike Designed by" credit for the Boomerang agency, little can disguise this show's true nature as a rip-off of the far more successful BOMBER BIKERS OF SHONAN.

CIRCUIT WOLF II

1990. JPN: *Circuit no Okami II: Modena no Ken*. AKA: *Circuit Wolf II: Ken [Sword] of Modena*. Video. DIR: Yoshihide Kuriyama. SCR: Dai Kuroyuki. DES: Satoshi Yamaguchi. ANI: Satoshi Yamaguchi. MUS: GL48. PRD: Gainax, CBS. 45 mins.

Qualified racing-driver Satoshi Ikezawa's *Circuit Wolf* comic ran in *Weekly Playboy* magazine for 18 volumes in 1975, reputedly gaining considerable praise through its author's appreciation of the realities of racing. This is a sequel to the manga, rather than a nonexistent anime predecessor, and

City Hunter

features a young racer, Ken, arriving in Italy in search of his missing Ferrari Dino. Car chases and road rages soon ensue against the fearsome "White Wolf of Stuttgart." ❂❖

CITY HUNTER *

1987. AKA: *Nicky Larson*. Movie, TV series/special. DIR: Kanetsugu Kodama, Takashi Imanishi, Tetsuro Amino, Kiyoshi Egami. SCR: Hiroyuki Hoshiyama, Yasushi Hirano, Akinori Endo. DES: Yoshiko Kamimura. ANI: Takeo Kitahara. MUS: Ryoichi Kuniyoshi. PRD: Sunrise, Yomiuri TV. 25 mins. x 140 eps.
Ryo (Joe, in some U.S. dubs) Saeba is a professional "sweeper," an Equalizer who packs a .357 Magnum and specializes in bodyguard details in the Tokyo district of Shinjuku, where he can be reached through coded messages on the train station billboard. Promising his dying partner, Hideyuki, that he will look after Kaori, Hideyuki's sister, the terminally lecherous Ryo is lumbered with a prim female assistant, who nevertheless remains eternally jealous of his conquests.
Tsukasa Hojo's 1985 *Shonen Jump*

comic proved even more successful than his CAT'S EYE, running for a total of 35 volumes. The regular cast of characters, including Ryo, surrogate wife/daughter Kaori, policewoman Saeko, and rival investigator Reika (both gorgeous, of course) would be reprised for TV directed by CAT'S EYE–alumnus Kodama. The TV edition kept Ryo's relationships with his female clients unconsummated, preferring instead to truncate many seductions with farce and slapstick.
Steadily gaining popularity (the closing theme "Get Wild" became a hit in its own right), the series moved from seven to six o'clock after 51 episodes. An 87-minute theatrical feature, *Magnum of Love's Destiny* (1989), was released in the U.S. as *.357 Magnum* and featured beautiful European pianist Nina trying to track down her father amid a then-topical backdrop inspired by the reunification of East and West Germany (here renamed Galiera). In a typical *City Hunter* setup, Nina is the unwitting mule for a vital microchip planted on her by a Communist agent shortly before his own death. Ryo takes one deceptively sim-

ple mission only to find himself deep over his head in another.
With new theme music but otherwise unchanged, seasons two and three introduced occasional hour-long "special" episodes that were eventually to become the franchise's medium of choice. *Bay City Wars* (1990) features a Central American dictator using drug money to take over the world and reprogramming U.S. nuclear missiles, all from the titular Shinjuku hotel. Ryo's natural lechery is brought to the fore when he must stop the general's beautiful daughter from destroying the world. *Million Dollar Plot* (also 1990) pits Ryo against a CIA conspiracy to liquidate a beautiful rogue agent.
City Hunter '91 was the fourth and final TV series, ending after just 13 episodes. However, in 1993, the franchise was rejuvenated by Wong Jing's live-action film, which cleverly exploited the show's popularity abroad by casting big Chinese names in the lead roles—Jackie Chan as Ryo and *A Chinese Ghost Story*'s Wang Zhuxian as Kaori. One of the few anime series brought back regularly for TV specials (another is LUPIN III), Ryo's more recent one-shot TV adventures have included *The Secret Service* (1996), in which he teams up with a pretty secret agent to protect the leader of a banana republic, and *Goodbye My Sweetheart* (1997—released in the U.S. as *City Hunter "The Movie"*), which imitates PATLABOR 2 with its tale of a disgruntled soldier bringing his war experiences to Tokyo. *The End of Ryo Saeba* (1999) quite patently wasn't—it's likely that *City Hunter* will be back before long. In the meantime, the "special" format has been retroactively imposed upon the original series in Japan, now shuffled into 20 video compilations designed to showcase the best TV episodes, out of chronological order but in a semblance of feature-length editions. At least part of the *CH* franchise lives on in Hojo's manga ANGEL HEART (2001), in which a former assassin receives a prominent character's heart in a transplant operation. ❂❖

CITY OF SIN

2001. JPN: *Ryojoku no Machi/Toshi: Kyoen no Ceremony*. AKA: *City of Rape: Ceremony of Mad Banquet*. Video. DIR: Shoichiro Kamijo. SCR: Yasuyuki Muto. DES: Dozamura. ANI: N/C. MUS: N/C. PRD: Green Bunny, Fuyusha. 30 mins. Princess Beatrice is sent off to a foreign country in a diplomatic marriage, but her initial excitement about marrying a handsome prince soon turns sour. Under the rule of Prince Franchesco, rape is legal and it is a crime not to be pregnant, turning the princess and her ladies in waiting into targets for the officer class of their new home, intent on breeding the next generation of warriors. Based on the manga *Secrets of the World* (*Chikyu no Himitsu*) by "Dozamura." NB: The Japanese title clearly has the characters for *toshi* (city), but includes the roman transliteration of *machi* (town). Compare to KOKUDO-OH: BLACK EYE KING. ❶ⓃⓋ

CLAMP

Formed as Amarythia, a circle of amateur manga creators in 1989, this group's original twelve members fell to seven by the following year and to four during production of RG VEDA. The survivors are Nanase Okawa (1967–), Mokona Apapa (1968–), Mick Nekkoi (1969–) and Satsuki Igarashi (1969–), although they have subsequently changed their pseudonyms and now desire to be known as Ageha Okawa, Mokona, Tsubaki Nekoi, and Satsuki Igarashi (written with new kanji). Their role in the anime adaptations of their work is minimal, but as the originators of the original stories and looks of the characters, they have been influential figures in the 1990s, with shows such as CARDCAPTORS, TOKYO BABYLON, CHOBITS, and ANGELIC LAYER.

CLAMP SCHOOL DETECTIVES *

1997. JPN: *Clamp Gakuen Tanteidan*. TV series. DIR: Osamu Nabeshima. SCR: Mayori Sekijima, Masaharu Amiya. DES: Hiroshi Tanaka. ANI: Toshikazu Endo, Yuki Kanno. MUS: Michiya Katakura. PRD: Studio Pierrot. 25 mins. x 26 eps.

Nokoru, Suoh, and Akira are the Elementary Division Student Council, leaders of the sixth, fifth, and fourth grades in a private urban school for ten thousand of Japan's smartest (read: richest) children. Moonlighting as private investigators in the fashion of CONAN THE BOY DETECTIVE, they solve mysteries (missing school records found, feckless bullies caught) and troubleshoot in affairs of the heart for their fellow students. A minor work from CLAMP, creators of CARDCAPTORS (who seem to have realized that only the inclusion of their brand name in the title would guarantee any attention), this harmless series was originally aimed at a female audience that was expected to be charmed by polite, well-mannered rich boys solving minor problems.

CLAN OF PIHYORO

1988. JPN: *Pihyoro Ikka*. Video. DIR: Tetsu Dezaki, Tsuneo Tominaga. SCR: Kazumi Koide. DES: Akio Sugino, Setsuko Shibunnoichi. ANI: Akio Sugino, Setsuko Shibunnoichi, Yukari Kobayashi. MUS: Noriaki Yamanaka. PRD: Bandai, CBS, Movic. 60 mins.

Kyota, Sabatta, Q-ta, and Kyonta are the guardian spirits of our age, protecting Earth from evil spirits while masquerading as humble students at the Seiwagi ("Holy Japanese Citadel") middle school. Suspecting supernatural involvement in the suicide of female student Maiko, Kyota and Kyonta investigate, only to discover that their school is built on a prehistoric crematory, and the restless dead are haunting the students.

Kaori Himeki's fantasy manga from *Princess* magazine was originally going to be adapted into a video series, but its chances were destroyed when AKIRA was released barely a week later. Fantasy anime fell out of favor, and this abortive first episode never got further than its theatrical double bill with the digest edition of AIM FOR THE ACE 2. A few years later, the likes of POLTERGEIST REPORT made *Clan of Pihyoro* more appealing, but it was too late. Note

director Tetsu Dezaki, working here with designer Sugino, who is normally associated with his brother, Osamu.

CLAN OF THE KAWARAZAKI

1996. JPN: *Kawarazaki-ke no Ichizoku*. Video. DIR: Shungyo Makokudo. SCR: Shungyo Makokudo. DES: Seifun Yamahatei. ANI: Harashu Suzuki. MUS: N/C. PRD: Triple X, Pink Pineapple, KSS. 30 mins. x 2 eps.

Mukuro, a college boy working through vacation as a servant of the aristocratic Kawarazaki family, explores a mysterious pavilion on the grounds of the family mansion. Tempted by gorgeous women and "forced" to commit sexual acts, he is dragged into an alternate world of passion and free love. Or is it just a dream?

This otherwise unremarkable erotic anime was based on a 1993 computer game (from Silkies) that was one of the first in Japan to have multiple endings instead of a single narrative—hence the hallucinatory aspect of the story line as the pseudonymous crew tries to cram in as many finales as possible. Ⓝ

CLASS FULL OF GHOSTS

1998. JPN: *Kyoshitsu wa Obake ga Ippai*. Video. DIR: Toshiya Shinohara. SCR: Makiko Sato. DES: Yutaka Hara. ANI: Yoko Furumiya, Yumiko Kanehara. MUS: N/C. PRD: Toei. 23 mins. x 2 eps. Writer Sato and illustrator Hara, creators of HOLY THE GHOST, returned for this children's tale of a haunted classroom. Guaranteed high sales and a video release when selected, like COBBY THE CUTE LITTLE CAT, by the Japanese Library Council as a core title, the second episode features computer graphics of our hero banishing the spooks from his school. See HERE COMES HANAKO for the full story of Japanese school ghouls in the 1990s.

CLASS REUNION AGAIN *

2002. JPN: *Dosokai Again*. Video. DIR: Kan Fukumoto. SCR: Yo Tachibana. DES: Jun Sato, Toru Mizutani. ANI: N/C. MUS: N/C. PRD: Lemon Heart, ARMS, F&C Co. 30 mins. x 4 eps.

Cleopatra: Queen of Sex

The graduates of the Sakura Junior High Tennis Club have gathered for a reunion party on New Year's Eve. They are all in their twenties now, but Mizuho is excited because she gets to see her secret high school crush Tatsuya again. Aya also loved her childhood friend Tatsuya. Domestic misunderstandings, a ski trip, Mizuho's mother's illness, Tatsuya's car accident, and Aya's fling with her childhood friend Mamoru lead to a moderate amount of licentiousness, but considerably more angst and soul-searching, and end up with some licensed sex for once, after Aya and Tatsuya's wedding. In other words, a pastiche of the *Big Chill* (1983), initially in the style of the many Japanese live-action TV shows that feature twentysomething class reunions, dating back to *Seven People in Summer* (*DE)—there is at least one of these shows every season on live-action TV, so it is little surprise that an erotic anime pastiche would eventually arise. Based on a computer game, itself part of the subgenre of dating sims, and named in a deliberate echo of the characters used in the Japanese title of **End of Summer**. **N**

CLASSMATE
1998. Video. DIR: Satoshi Kato. SCR: Yuka Kurokawa. DES: Yoshihito Murata. ANI: N/C. MUS: N/C. PRD: Five Ways. 28 mins.
Not to be confused with **End of Summer**, another anime whose Japanese title can also be translated as "Classmate," this later release is a surprisingly old-fashioned **Cream Lemon** clone, featuring a schoolgirl, Nami, who wants to have sex. Surprise, surprise—she gets some. **N**

CLASSROOM OF ATONEMENT *
2001. JPN: *Shokuzai no Kyoshitsu.* Video. DIR: Takayuki Yanase. SCR: Roku-rota Makabe. DES: N/C. ANI: N/C. MUS: Yoshi. PRD: YOUC, Digital Works (Vanilla Series). 25 mins. x 2 eps.
Nanase's father is a suspect in a murder trial. Never having heard of "innocent until proven guilty," some of her classmates take the law into their own hands and decide to mete out judgment of their own by raping her after school. However, one still believes that Nanase's father is innocent and reveals that the murder was actually the result of a blackmail attempt that backfired, dating back to the school days of their own parents, when one exposed the bullying activities of another who went on to become a famous cram school entrepreneur. A confused and involved mystery unravels, which might have been an interesting study of the way that childhood cruelty can escalate into adult crime, were it not for the regular scenes of sex and abuse that mark this as another entry in the **Vanilla Series**. **LNV**

CLEOPATRA DC *
1989. Video. DIR: Naoyuki Yoshinaga. SCR: Kaoru Shintani, Sukehiro Tomita. DES: Nobuteru Yuki. ANI: Tai Fujikawa. MUS: Hiroaki Suzuki. PRD: Agent 21, JC Staff. 30 mins. x 3 eps.
Cleo, the Chairwoman of the Cleopatra financial conglomerate, is so rich that she controls much of the U.S. economy and is described as the "moving capital of the world." When a light aircraft crash-lands in her bedroom, the delirious pilot can only give her the message "Mary Anne." Investigating with her assistant, Surei, Cleo determines that he is referring to the daughter of the Oil Minister, rumored to have been kidnapped by the sinister Junior.
After bungling a hit on Cleo, Junior's discredited henchman Apollo turns on his former boss, who is forced to seek help from Cleo herself. The final episode features Cleo going to Nice on holiday, where she is embroiled in an android plot, in a lightweight adventure series from **Area 88**'s Kaoru Shintani.

CLEOPATRA: QUEEN OF SEX *
1970. JPN: *Cleopatra.* Movie. DIR: Osamu Tezuka, Eiichi Yamamoto. SCR: Shigemi Satoyoshi. DES: Ko Kojima. ANI: Kazuko Nakamura, Gisaburo Sugii, Yoshiaki Kawajiri. MUS: Isao Tomita. PRD: Mushi Pro. 112 mins.
Three young people from the 21st century have their minds sent back into the past, into the bodies of people living in Alexandria at the time of Julius Caesar's first meeting with Cleopatra. One of the two young men is a lecher who vows that he will seduce Cleopa-

© MUSHI PRODUCTIONS

tra instead of just watching. Having won over Caesar (depicted as a cigar-chomping American politico riding in a horse-drawn Edsel) and Mark Antony, Cleopatra is defeated by Octavian's homosexuality and takes her own life.

Screened in U.S. cinemas, where it was the first animated film to receive an "X" rating, *Cleopatra*'s release coincided with a temporary suspension of business at Mushi Pro. A financial disaster in Japan and misleadingly marketed in the U.S. as hard-core erotica, *Cleopatra* was **ASTRO BOY**–creator Tezuka's last-ditch attmept to recoup money for his troubled company, though the production was reportedly characterized by defecting animators, who had realized that little could save Mushi and stole anything that was not nailed down. The production's salability was not helped by Tezuka's own artistic experiments, including the opening scenes set in the future as an ironic reversal of the distinctive animation style of the U.S. series *Clutch Cargo*. Whereas *Clutch Cargo* featured live mouths matted onto animated faces, *Cleopatra*'s future scenes were shot as live-action but with anime faces matted onto the human actors. Other art-house experiments included foolhardy anachronisms such as gladiatorial combat staged as TV events and the murder of Caesar presented as a kabuki drama (a famous scene from *Chushingura*—see **WOOF WOOF 47 RONIN**), bringing the story to a screeching halt for several minutes. Compare to Tezuka's earlier success with **ARABIAN NIGHTS**. **◗**

CLIMBING ON A CLOUD

1990. JPN: *Kumo ni Noru*. Video. DIR: Osamu Sekita. SCR: Shoji Imai. DES: Eiichi Endo. ANI: Eiichi Endo. MUS: Masanori Iimori. PRD: JC Staff. 50 mins. x 2 eps.

GOODFELLA-creator Hiroshi Motomiya wrote this very different tale of gang warfare for *Comic Morning* in 1988. Set in a Buddhist heaven where saints fight over turf in the clouds, it features Niomaru, a man searching for the younger

sister torn from him in an aircraft accident back in the human world. Motomiya is better known today for the manga *Salaryman Kintaro*, which has been adapted as a live-action TV series and film.

CLUSTER EDGE

2005. TV series. DIR: Makoto Ikeda. DES: Yoshihito Hishinuma, Kimitoshi Yamane. ANI: N/C. MUS: Masayuki Negishi. PRD: Sunrise, Bandai Visual, TV Tokyo. 25 mins. x ?? eps.

Thirty years after the outbreak of war, the technologically advanced Republic of Legrante invades the Principality of Rubel, intending to use it as a staging post for the invasion of other countries. However, the prestigious boarding school Cluster E.A. is allowed to continue to operate within conquered Rubel territory—a place where once stood a clone factory designed to make soldiers. Agate Fluorite arrives at the school, where he is a breath of fresh air for jaded old hands like Beryl and Fon, who are bored by the perpetual pressure to live up to their parents' expectations. Like other children of privilege in **CREST OF THE STARS**, the students realize that they are part of a plot by their elders, and that peaceful student life will soon be disrupted by more belligerent, adult concerns. Anime for girls, set in a boys' school, or at least so it is claimed—although the show seems superficially aimed at a female audience, its action often bears a greater resemblance to boy-oriented Sunrise shows. A manga by Wan Komatsuda preceded the show in *Lala DX* magazine, but considering that the origin is credited to Bandai's house pseudonym Hajime Yadate (now *there's* your clone factory), we assume that the anime was conceived first, and was not based on the manga.

COBBY THE CUTE LITTLE CAT

1998. JPN: *Chibi Neko Cobby*. Video. DIR: Yumi Tamano. SCR: Miyuki Takahashi. DES: Konomi Sakurai. ANI: Konomi Sakurai. MUS: N/C. PRD: Toei. 20 mins. x 2 eps.

Eiko Kadono, who also created **KIKI'S DELIVERY SERVICE**, collaborated with artist Mako Taruishi for this tale of a female black-and-white kitten born to a cat called Meme. The original was selected as a core title for Japanese libraries, guaranteeing a long shelf life and leading to sales of over 100,000 copies, but these simple stories of mischief and friendly animals flew no further on video.

COCKPIT, THE *

1993. Video. DIR: Yoshiaki Kawajiri, Takashi Imanishi, Ryosuke Takahashi. SCR: Yoshiaki Kawajiri, Takashi Waguri, Ryosuke Takahashi. DES: Yoshiaki Kawajiri, Toshihiro Kawamoto, Hironobu Saito. ANI: Yoshiaki Kawajiri, Toshihiro Kawamoto, Hironobu Saito. MUS: Kaoru Wada. PRD: Madhouse, Jamco Video, Visual 80. 30 mins. x 3 eps.

This trilogy retells three stories from Leiji Matsumoto's long-running *Battlefield (Senjo)* series, here retitled at the author's request and assigned to three different studios.

The first, *Slipstream*, is a Faustian tale, handled by **WICKED CITY**–director Kawajiri, about the Luftwaffe in August 1944. Nazi ace Rheindars (a lookalike of **CAPTAIN HARLOCK**) is asked to escort an atomic bomb to Peenemunde, where it is to be loaded onto a V-2 rocket. However, he eventually sabotages the project, even though it will mean the death of his ex-lover Marlene, a twin of **QUEEN EMERALDAS**. Rheindars's plight is depicted as a pact with Satan and comes loaded with arch antinuclear messages—Marlene warns that only the truly evil would ever use atomic weapons, while Rheindars's commander anachronistically describes the V-2 as the world's first missile. In the final scene, as Rheindars saves Britain from nuclear holocaust, he describes himself as "the man who *did not* sell his soul to the Devil," though this line was absent from the original Japanese script and appears to have been improvised on the day of the recording.

Pointedly shifting ahead a year to the day before Hiroshima in August

1945, *Sonic Boom Squadron* is a naval story focusing on Nogami, a Japanese kamikaze rocket pilot. As in director Imanishi's GUNDAM stories, men are slaves to their machines, both sides suffer, and, in one scene, a Japanese pilot is found to have an exact double on the U.S. aircraft carrier he is attacking. The futility of the navy pilots, sacrificing their lives to carry human bombs to targets they will never reach, is echoed by their American counterparts, who mourn a promising comics artist shot down by the "crazy Japs." The hero, for his part, wants to be a rocket scientist and fly to the moon, but now finds himself piloting a human bomb.

The final part leaps back to 1944 (presumably to make Hiroshima the worthy centerpiece) and the Allied assault on Leyte in the Philippines. Directed by SPT LAYZNER's Ryosuke Takahashi, *Knight of the Iron Dragon* features Japanese army officers, all of whom have sworn never to surrender, realizing that they will have to retreat. A young motorcyclist goes to fetch the last artillery group but finds them almost completely wiped out. Despite the attractive prospect of desertion, he resolves to return to his base. A mechanic who used to be a motorcycle racer offers to help out, and there are shades of *The Great Escape* as they rush across the war-torn island to reach the base in time. Again there is an element of tragedy; the base has already fallen, but it becomes a matter of honor that they go to die with their comrades.

With Nazis and Japanese soldiers for heroes, this could have easily added to anime's bad press, but, though Matsumoto is clearly in love with the idea of defeat, the superb animation and thoughtful script make this one of the triumphs of anime. It is also available in two excellent translations, in the U.K. from Kiseki (1995) and in the U.S. from Urban Vision (1999). **Ⓥ**

COLD GEHENNA
2001. TV series. DIR: N/C. SCR: N/C. DES: N/C. ANI: N/C. MUS: N/C. PRD: Public & Basic, Animax. 25 mins. x 12+ eps.

The moon is destroyed in a terrible cataclysm, forming a ring around the Earth and bringing drastic climate changes. The world is now chiefly desert and frozen wastes, while fearsome "dragons" have occupied what little of the temperate zones remain. Humans, eking an existence in the barren areas, build the Deadly Drive, an 18-meter robot designed to rid them of the dragon menace. Cue Barn, the hero, will pilot it, and Alice, the tiresomely predictable "mysterious girl," holds the key to victory.

COLLEGE INVESTIGATOR HIKARUON
1986. JPN: *Gakuin Tokuso Hikaruon*. Video. DIR: Kazuhiro Ochi. SCR: Kazuhiro Ochi. DES: Kazuhiro Ochi. ANI: Mutsumi Inomata, Osamu Nabeshima. MUS: Michiaki Watanabe. PRD: AIC. 30 mins.
In a school under attack from the evil demon Ura, mild-mannered Hikaru can transform into Hikaruon, a superpowered hero dedicated to battling monsters. Along with his beautiful assistant, Azumi, he fights off the bad guys in this spin-off of the long tradition of superhero shows that stretches all the way back to ULTRAMAN.

COLLEGE SUPERGIRLS
1991. JPN: *Za [The] Gakuen Chojotai*. Video. DIR: Tetsu Dezaki. SCR: Noriko Hayasaka. DES: Jumu. ANI: Yukari Kobayashi. MUS: Nobuo Ito. PRD: Magic Bus. 45 mins.
In this short-lived adaptation of Tatsuhiko Dan's novel that was originally serialized in *Shonen Jump*, Yumi, Kei, and Mai are three schoolgirls who moonlight as a secret crime-fighting team ever since experiments at the school Superpower Society went drastically awry and gave them all amazing abilities.

COLORFUL
1999. TV series. DIR: Ryutaro Nakamura. SCR: Kazushi Sato. DES: Takahiro Kishida. ANI: Takahiro Kishida. MUS: Moka. PRD: Triangle Staff, TBS. 7 mins. x 16 eps.

Torajiro Kishi's manga from *Young Jump*, full of panty-flashing gags and jiggling female flesh, was brought to late-night TV as part of the *Wonderful* program. The show enjoyed a second lease on life as one of the first to go straight to DVD in Japan—all 110 minutes were released on a single disc without a prior VHS appearance. **Ⓝ**

COLUMBUS
1992. JPN: *Columbus no Daiboken*. AKA: *Les Aventures de Christophe Columbe*. Movie. DIR: Yorifusa Yamaguchi. SCR: Thibault Chatel, Anne Colé. DES: Masahiro Kase. ANI: Masahiro Kase. MUS: N/C. PRD: Telescreen (SPO). 70 mins.
As he nears the New World, Christopher Columbus tells cabin boy Paco about his youthful hardships, the difficulties of convincing others of his vision, and the final victory when King Ferdinand and Queen Isabella agreed to sponsor his trip. The sailors are doubtful, though Columbus is vindicated when they arrive on land, but it's not the planned destination of Japan. This Franco-Japanese coproduction was made to commemorate the 500th anniversary of Columbus's "discovery" of America but not released in Japan until January 1993. Also appearing as one of the biographical subjects of GREAT PEOPLE and *Stories of Greatness*, Columbus is a serious rival with Oda Nobunaga and HELEN KELLER to become the most-portrayed historical figure in anime. He was the protagonist of *Adventurer: He Came from Spain* (2002, *Bokenmono*), an anime movie directed by Fumio Kurokawa and written by Nobuyuki Fujimoto, concentrating on his trials to secure funding from King Ferdinand and Queen Isabella of Spain, before finishing with the well-known story of his first landing in the West Indies. The authors presume that the subtitle in the English-language title refers to the point of origin of Columbus's *voyage*, since, although it may be a matter of some debate, most historians would argue that he came from the Republic of Genoa.

COMBATTLER V

1976. JPN: *Cho Denji Robo Combattler V.* AKA: *Super Electromagnetic Robot Combattler V; Combattra.* TV series. DIR: Tadao Nagahama. SCR: Masaki Tsuji, Keisuke Fujikawa, Masaru Yamamoto. DES: Makio Narita, Yoshikazu Yasuhiko, Studio Nue. ANI: Tetsu Dezaki, Yoshiyuki Tomino, Shinji Okada. MUS: Hiroshi Tsutsui. PRD: Hiromi Pro, Toei, NET (eps. 1–46); TV Asahi (eps. 47–54). 24 mins. x 54 eps.

Hyoma, Juzo, Daisaku, and token brat Kosuke are four boys handpicked from Earth's finest for their mental and physical prowess and trained to fly Professor Nanbara's Combattler superrobot. Invaders from Planet Campbell have awoken from their subterranean slumber and are threatening the inhabitants of the surface world.

In a story that will be original to anyone who has never heard of **BATTLE OF THE PLANETS,** it's up to the four boys, with the professor's daughter, Chizuru, as the chaste love interest, to use their giant electric yo-yo to protect Earth from the Campbell General Garuda. Toys from the show reached the U.S. as part of the **GODAIKIN** line.

The first of director Nagahama's "Romance Super Robot Trilogy," followed by **VOLTUS** and **STARBIRDS,** creation is credited to the director and Saburo Yade—who would go on to be the house pseudonym responsible for the live-action Super Sentai series that hit its peak with the *Mighty Morphin' Power Rangers* (*DE).

COMEDIC ANGEL YUI

2006. JPN: *Rakugo Tennyo Oyui.* TV series. DIR: Nobuhiro Takamoto. DES: Miwa Oshima. ANI: Naoto Sawa. MUS: Jun Ichikawa. PRD: TNK, AT-X. 25 mins. x 12 eps.

Yui Tsukishima hopes to be a comedy entertainer when she grows up, although currently she has more pressing concerns, such as the fact that she and five other girls have been transported back in time to 19th-century Japan to fight monsters.

COMEDY

Sitcoms and funny animals have been popular since the days of **EARLY ANIME.** The politically incorrect spectacle of a wife wrestling her love rival for possession of a feckless flirt in **THE WORLD OF POWER AND WOMEN** has cascaded down the generations, picking up new accretions as fashions change, to become the latest **TENCHI MUYO!** clone, and the funny creatures of **MONKEY AND THE CRAB** and *Animal Olympics* have mutated into the cat-girls and bunnies of shows like **MEW MEW POWER.**

Hard to define but difficult to ignore, comedy is an ingredient in many successful anime, especially those made for TV, where weary businessmen and kids escaping from homework go to relax. Comedy can transfer to anime as a straight stand-up routine or a sketch, through short segments in shows like **MY NEIGHBOR TOKORO,** or Hisashi Eguchi's **RENTAMAN** segment *Kotobuki Goro Show.* However, it's more often given a narrative framework, however loose.

Anime has stolen some visual shorthand from manga and foreign cartoons: extreme distortion of the features, or the whole body, to convey heightened emotion. It has taken this to extremes in the "squashed down" or "super-deformed" art-style, also known as SD. Super deformation can even arise in relatively serious anime like **FULLMETAL ALCHEMIST,** when characters in humorous moments temporarily switch into SD-mode—see **TROPES AND TRANSFORMATIONS.**

To some extent, comedy will always be a personal matter: we appreciate that instances of "comical" underwear loss in soft porn may leave fans of the genre quaking with mirth, although they do nothing for us. If anime humor appears lowbrow or simple in the West, this is because complicated verbal humor is more difficult to translate, and often falls apart in the hands of translators and directors who are, quite properly, more concerned with amusing a Western high school audience than faithfully echoing eth-

nocentric gags. Comedy and profanity are two hot-button issues in anime translation; when faced with humor, some have taken AnimEigo's lead in faithfully translating the original jokes in **URUSEI YATSURA,** and then appending footnotes to explain them. Others have followed the route Viz Communications took with **RANMA 1/2,** replacing original humor with new jokes designed to replicate the old effect on a new audience. There are also still those who take the route of **SAMURAI PIZZA CATS** and **GHOST STORIES,** dumping much of the original in favor of a new, more improvised script. Regardless of the attitude taken, all methods still depend on the ability of the translator or rewriter, not only to recognize puns and gags in the first place, but also to comprehend them and convey them. Comedy is the most recognizable place where DVD anime releases can have the most obvious divergence between dubs/dubtitles and subtitles—as witnessed by Phil Hartman's extensive improvisations as Jiji the cat in **KIKI'S DELIVERY SERVICE** filling many moments for which the character was completely silent in the original Japanese version.

Comedies for little children are a staple of most countries' broadcast media, given TV's entrenched function as babysitter. Their formula for success is largely unchanging; they give their little viewers bright colors, simple shapes, repetition of sounds, and broad-brush characterization, covering the daily routines of a small child's life with festivals, playtime, and food, all reinforcing simple moral messages about good behavior. Shows like **PIPI THE ALIEN** and **PINCH AND PUNCH** didn't have much to offer adults even in their 1960s heyday, but the generation that grew up watching them went on to create **CHIBI MARUKO-CHAN** and **CRAYON SHIN-CHAN.** These two very different shows shared two important elements: they could be watched by small children, but they were made to appeal to an adult audience nostalgic for the simplicity of childhood. **CRAYON SHIN-**

CHAN is a comedy as rude, crude, and broad as the mind of a little boy—its hero's boundaries may be very tight, but he pushes them for all he's worth. Comedies for older children tend to follow the same pattern, taking a different viewpoint on the routines of everyday life. They may throw in someone who thinks differently from the rest of the world, as in GENIUS IDIOT BAKABON, or an alien or magical MacGuffin like DORAEMON (or, for older boys, his avatar Doreimon in VISIONARY), or an adult who doesn't know how to be a role model, such as DOCTOR SLUMP.

Everyday life is the starting point for the gentle, observational humor of SAZAE-SAN, DOTANBA'S MODERN MANNERS, and MY NEIGHBORS THE YAMADAS. The advent of video in the mid-1980s showed the potential of the niche market, with a slice-of-life comedy for thirtysomething cat lovers, WHAT'S MICHAEL, being the first show to make the transit from a cautious video release to TV success. This in turn enabled TV shows like MODERN LOVE'S SILLINESS to target their specific audience (in this case, adult women) in evening or late-night slots. Everyday life can also be hell, and where there's pain there is, inevitably, comedy. Japanese businessmen enduring the daily grind to support increasingly disengaged families could see the funny side of LAUGHING SALESMAN. Families forced to share a home with a dotty, irritating, or downright malicious elder could let go of the tension with a good laugh at MAD OLD BAG or ULTRA GRAN. Teenage boys facing the twin challenges of hormonal change and social inadequacy find solace in PING PONG CLUB and HIGH SCHOOL KIMENGUMI.

Life and its problems are the great unifiers of comedy; language and culture can be its great dividers. Westerners tend to think of Japan as a homogenous society, but its regional variations of dialect and culture are as wide as those of Britain or France. As with most developed nations, these variations are eroded by the monoculture promoted on the small screen,

but are still reflected in comedy. Japan has its Tokyo lowlife comedy FRITENKUN, the Kansai equivalent NANIWA SPIRIT, and provincial biker high jinks in YOKOHAMA'S FAMOUS KATAYAMA. The differences between the capital and the nation's second city are pointed up in a host of comedies featuring Osaka's distinctive dialect and reputation for wisecracking and moneymaking, JARINKO CHIE and COMPILER providing examples which are great fun but difficult to translate. History always has potential for humor: GINNAGASHI takes us back to pre-war Tokyo to watch amusing goings-on in a local bar, while SHINSENGUMI FARCE takes the Mel Brooks approach to right-wing extremism.

Foreign culture provides even more opportunities to generate laughs. Japan, like every other culture, is not above poking fun at foreigners in shows such as the CHOCOLATE PANIC PICTURE SHOW. Japanese attitudes can also lead to unintentional humor—a recurring problem in translating anime comes from the presence of ideas and names that can jolt an audience out of its suspension of disbelief: characters named after car models or rock bands, for example, in RAYEARTH and BASTARD. Other modes of inadvertent humor issue from Japan's attempts to imitate Western genres—MAD BULL 34 is not intended as comedy, but is only really enjoyable to a non-Japanese audience as such, and ultimately the joke may be on the American stories the Japanese have so outrageously misread. Other abuses of foreign entertainment are intentionally humorous—the *X-Files* influence on GEOBREEDERS, for example, or the gloriously inappropriate use of Beethoven in DRAGON HALF.

Even if all other springs of laughter dry up, anime has one rich source to mine—itself. Anime parodying anime has its own short-form term, *anipuro*, which originated in fanzine culture to describe amateur comics spoofing favorite shows, but can also be applied to professional spoofs like the "super-deformed" GUNDAM spoofs, and the "cute-body" DEVILMAN pastiches. Shows

like IRRESPONSIBLE CAPTAIN TYLOR, AIRBATS, and SIGN OF THE OTAKU all follow OTAKU NO VIDEO in offering up every convention of anime—story tropes, production methods, respected creations, and creators—as targets for mirth.

COMET-SAN

2001. TV series. DIR: Mamoru Kobe. SCR: Akira Oketani. DES: Kazuo Makida. ANI: Miho Nakajima, Masamitsu Kudo. MUS: Kaba Konishi. PRD: Nippon Animation, TV Tokyo. 25 mins. x 12+ eps. Comet, a princess from planet Harmonica, is invited to a party with a princess from Castanet, where they discover that the prince of Tambourine, largest world in the Triangle Nebula, is trying to decide which of them he should take as his bride. Comet stomps off to Earth (which, when you think about it, is just as stupid a name for a planet), where her arrival brings magic and joy into the lives of a Japanese family. *Comet-san* has a convoluted pedigree, dating back to Mitsuteru Yokoyama's 1967 manga in *Margaret* magazine, itself an attempt to do a more grown-up version of his earlier LITTLE WITCH SALLY. A *Bewitched* clone, originally featuring a magical housekeeper from planet Beta, its 1967 TV adaptation was live-action but featured animated sequences directed by Tsutomu Shibayama. The 21st-century fully animated version is a product of its time, playing up the "magical-girl" feel with a far younger protagonist and showing lots of pretty eye-candy girls.

COMIC PARTY

2001. TV series. DIR: Norihiko Sudo. SCR: Hiroshi Yamaguchi. DES: Hirokazu Taguchi. ANI: Mima Yoshikawa, Masao Nakada. MUS: N/C. PRD: OLM, KBS. 25 mins. x 13 eps. (TV1), ca. 30 mins. x 4 eps. (v), 25 mins. x 13 eps. (TV2) Eighteen-year-old high school student Waki has already been accepted by a university and only has to wait for graduation. When this proves to be too boring to endure, he wanders into a manga convention and is dragged into the world of amateur comics. He befriends three young fanzine creators who are, of course, all pretty girls. This lighthearted comedy, a Dreamcast tie-in, is an ominous sign of the increasingly self-referential nature of the anime/manga market—compare to ANIMATION RUNNER KUROMI. In one pointed moment, a character bemoans America's domination of popular culture, announcing that it is time for Japan to take over with anime. The series was remade as *Comic Party Revolution*, originally intended as a two-episode video release, which was expanded to four episodes, which in turn were cut to form the first four episodes of a subsequent full-length television series.

COMPILER *

1994. Video. DIR: Takao Kato, Kiyoshi Murayama. SCR: Michitaka Kikuchi. DES: Yasuhiro Oshima. ANI: Yasuhiro Oshima. MUS: Toshiyuki Omori. PRD: Movic. 45 mins. x 3 eps.
In a remarkably three-dimensional "2D Universe," female agents are dispatched to destroy the 3D Earth. Instead, they decide to stay with two Japanese boys and live a happy life of unwedded bliss and teen angst. One day, they decide to go on holiday in Osaka, a city long-neglected in anime since being buried under a mass of tentacles and spooge in UROTSUKIDOJI. In this anime based on SILENT MÖBIUS–creator Kia Asamiya's 1991 love-comedy in *Comic Afternoon*, Osaka becomes the venue for two naked female assassins sent from the 2D universe to terminate the turncoat terminators. They attempt to blend in by loading Osaka language chips, which turns them into a pair of bitchy game-show hosts, but their gags will fall flat on an audience ignorant of Osaka's *manzai* comedy tradition (see JARINKO CHIE).

Much of the humor rests on the unique attitude and accent of Osaka's people—which could be described as Chicago gangster-talk and New York sarcasm combined with a ludicrous love of yen. The dubbing script tries to approximate the Osaka accent as a mix of Valley girls, Jersey longshoremen, and cretins, but, although there is a lengthy discourse on the history of Osaka baseball, this episode is almost incomprehensible without a set of liner notes, sadly lacking in AD Vision's translation.

Once the shapely Terminators *("We put the ass in Assassins!")* have been defeated, the unfeasibly thick-haired Compiler fights with would-be beau Nachi about his flirting ways. Meanwhile, the innocent Assembler tries (unsuccessfully) to seduce Nachi's brother in a simple tale of Tokyo marital discord that was originally the first episode, switched by the U.S. distributor with the zanier second presumably to hold viewers' attention.

Redeeming features include a score from GOLGO 13's Omori that pastiches the *Godzilla* theme as Osaka food franchise logos turn into giant monsters and smash up "famous" landmarks, including the Hanshin Expressway, that would be destroyed for real in the following year's Kobe earthquake. HUMMINGBIRDS-director Murayama also provides clever moments such as background fountains that spurt in time with Compiler's anger and rubber-necking passers-by that add a really human touch to her argument with Nachi. But even these finesses can't rescue a show whose original raison d'être was not to entertain so much as to advertise.

A marketing tool designed to remind Japanese viewers of a manga that remains untranslated in English, *Compiler* has little purpose in the U.S. market. It follows late on the heels of *Music Clips in Trackdown*, a 1990 music video also designed to promote the *Compiler* characters but without the pretense of a plot. Sections from this early work are used in the closing credits to *Compiler Festa* (released as just plain *Compiler 2* in the U.S.), the final episode in which the 2D universe sends White Compiler, a deadly upgrade of our heroine, who is defeated again by homespun Earth boys and wisecracking alien girls. Ⓝ

COMPUTOPIA

1968. JPN: *Computopia Seireki 2000-nen no Monogatari*. AKA: *Computopia: A Tale of the Year 2000 A.D.* TV special. DIR: Yoshikazu Kawamura. SCR: Masaki Tsuji. DES: Masami Shimoda. ANI: Sadao Tsukioka. MUS: N/C. PRD: Knack, Nihon TV. 30 mins. x 2 eps.
After the success of FIFTH ICE AGE, the *Wonderful World Travel* staff returned with this sci-fi documentary about the way New York might be in the distant year 2000, using real photographs of computer innards as backdrops for the cel animation—the first low-tech form of "computer animation," perhaps?

CONAN THE BOY DETECTIVE

1996. JPN: *Meitantei Conan*. AKA: *Famous Detective Conan*. Movie, TV series, specials. DIR: Kanetsugu Kodama. SCR: Hiroshi Kashiwabara, Kazunari Kouchi, Shuichi Miyashita. DES: Masaaki Sudo. ANI: Masaaki Sudo. MUS: Katsuo Ono. PRD: TMS, Yomiuri TV (Nippon TV). 25 mins. x 232+ eps; 90 mins. x 4 movies.
High school student Shinichi Kudo accidentally takes a drug that gives him the appearance of a seven-year-old child. He takes the name Conan Edogawa (conjoining Arthur Conan Doyle and Ranpo Edogawa, the best of both occidental and oriental detective traditions) and specializes in cases that the adults just can't handle, using his childish guise as a means of avoiding criminal reprisals.

First appearing in 1994 manga in *Shonen Sunday* magazine by YAIBA-creator Gosho Aoyama, Conan has the body of a child but commands the thinking power (and respect) of an adult. He also has a band of young friends, the Juvenile Detective Club, who aid him in his investigations. As with the YOUNG KINDAICHI FILES, this caught a post-*X-Files* wave of interest in supernatural sleuthing and would make Aoyama Japan's highest-paid manga artist by 1999. The series was dubbed in the U.S., but into *Spanish*, where the hero was renamed Bobby Jackson (he may be known under this name to some viewers).

Many of the TV story lines, such as the *Ski Lodge Murders* and the *First Love Murders*, spanned two episodes, so it was a simple step to expand into 90-minute movies. Conan's first theatrical outing, *Clockwork Skyscraper* (1997), pits him in a battle of wits against a thief who has stolen high explosives from a military base. *The 14th Victim* (1998) has a stalker picking off members of the family who own the Aquacrystal restaurant and leaving playing cards pinned to their corpses. In *End of the Century Sorcerer* (1999), a child steals a priceless Fabergé egg, and the relatively simple quest to return it leads to a series of murders rooted in a historical vendetta. *Captured in Her Eyes* (2000), pits Conan against an enemy from within after the murder of a police officer turns all his associates into suspects. *Countdown to Heaven* (2001), with unfortunate synchronicity considering the 9-11 atrocities, features a secret society causing mayhem at the inauguration party of the new high-tech Twin Towers in Tokyo. The inevitable team-up with Sherlock Holmes arrived in *Phantom of Baker Street* (2002), engineered through a holodeck-style virtual game, in which one of the participants genuinely is murdered, allowing Conan to temporarily form a partnership with a facsimile of the world's greatest detective. The early 21st-century obsession with medieval sorcery, best demonstrated through the live-action success of *Yin-Yang Master* (*DE), found its place in the Conan franchise in *Crossroads of the Ancient Capital* (2003), in which Conan must journey to Kyoto to investigate an enigmatic message found in a stolen image of Buddha. Another fashionable fad, this time for the Hokkaido of *From the North* (*DE) and **DIAMOND DAYDREAMS**, came to the fore in *Magician of the Silver Sky* (2004), in which Conan and his associates head up to Hokkaido, hoping to protect a valuable artifact from the attentions of the self-proclaimed master-thief Kaito Kid. *Strategy Above the Depths* (2005) takes Conan off on a cruise ship only to find himself a pawn in a plot for revenge.

There have also been several spin-off videos, including *Conan vs. Kid vs. Yaiba* (2001), pitting Conan against two other characters created by Gosho Aoyama. Seemingly introduced as an attempt to gain the yen of the original Conan audience as it matures into video-buying teenage years, it was followed by other Conan adventures on DVD, including *16 Suspects* (2002), *Conan and Heiji and the Disappearing Boy* (2003), and the heist story *Conan and Kid and the Crystal Mother* (2005), and *The Target is Kogoro! Secret Investigation of the Detective Boys* (2005).

Conan was released in the U.S. as *Case Closed* in 2004, with a few name-changes for the local audience: Shinichi Kudo became Jimmy Kudo, Ran Mouri became Rachel Moore and Kogoro Mouri became Richard Moore. Conan, however, remained the same, although his adventures ran into localization difficulties in America. The original anime series was intended for older elementary to middle schoolers in Japan, but the presence of certain bloody scenes (it is, after all, a *murder* investigation!) led to the episodes being screened in the late-night Adult Swim section, and not in the earlier Toonami slot where its true American audience was.

Conan's father starred in several Aoyama short pieces including *The Wandering Red Butterfly* and *Summer's Santa Claus*. These, along with the Conan-Shinichi team-up tale *Ten Planets in the Night Sky* and the unrelated stories *Investigator George's Little War*, *Play It Again*, and *Wait a Moment*, were animated as 20-minute specials by Osamu Nabeshima in 1998. In May 2005, manga author Gosho Aoyama married Minami Takayama, the actress who provides the voice of Conan in the original Japanese version.

CONDITION GREEN

1991. JPN: *Inferious Wakusei Senshi Gaiden Condition Green*. AKA: *Inferious Interplanetary War Chronicle Condition Green*. Video. DIR: Shigeyasu Yamauchi. SCR: Yoshihisa Araki. DES: Shingo Araki, Michi Himeno, Eisaku Inoue. ANI: Eisaku Inoue. MUS: Kazuhiko Ito. PRD: Hero Communications, KSS. 50 mins. x 3 eps.

Keith, George, Edward, Yang, and Sho are Platoon #801, the five-man team formed to protect their homeworld in the Inferious galaxy from alien invasion. Gazaria's evil emperor Vince conquers the neighbor worlds of Kal and Granad and suddenly only Platoon #801, also known as Condition Green, stands between him and the conquest of Emerald Earth. Made straight-to-video despite the false appearance of two "25-minute TV episodes" per tape, *Condition Green* missed the point made all too well by **GUNBUSTER**, that only real TV could afford to be cheesy. The paying audience of the video market demanded more but didn't get it here from former **CRYING FREEMAN**–animator Yamauchi.

CONFUCIUS

1995. JPN: *Koshi-den*. AKA: *Life of Kong Zi*. TV special. DIR: Osamu Dezaki. SCR: N/C. DES: N/C. ANI: Noboru Furuse. MUS: N/C. PRD: NHK, NHKEP21, PTS, KBS, Image K, C&D. 45 mins.?

Born in the Chinese state of Lu in 551 B.C., Confucius is raised by his mother after his father dies when he is only three. He marries at 19 and enters the service of the local nobility. At 32, he becomes tutor to the Prince of Lu's children, eventually becoming a politician at 51. His career peaks are the roles of Lu's justice minister and eventually prime minister. The land prospers for four years, but Confucius grows disenchanted with court intrigues. For the following 12 years, he wanders the neighboring states, offering advice to their rulers.

Mystifyingly dropped from the earlier **GREAT PEOPLE** series in favor of such luminaries as Babe Ruth, China's most famous son was nevertheless considered a worthy subject by the many anime companies that cooperated on the TV movie. But since his life was uneventful and his victories disappointingly intellectual, it has but a single one-line mention in our Japanese sources.

COO OF THE FAR SEAS

1993. JPN: *Coo: Toi Umi kara Kita Coo*. AKA: *Coo: Coo Who Came from the Far Seas*. Movie. DIR: Tetsuo Imazawa. SCR: Kihachi Okamoto. DES: Masahiko Okura. ANI: N/C. MUS: Nick Wood. PRD: Toei. 116 mins.

Excitedly if weakly hyped in *Newtype* as "the best film for all the family, apart from something by Disney," this Christmas feel-good movie was based on a novel by Tamio Kageyama and written for the screen by live-action director Okamoto. A scientist's child on an idyllic Pacific island befriends the titular creature, a baby plesiosaur whose mother has died. Other, less scrupulous people are searching for this relic of the dinosaur age, and our hero teams up with a beautiful female journalist to keep Coo safe until he can be released into the wild.

This charming film, greatly helped by ravishing backgrounds researched on real-life Pacific islands at great expense to the sponsors at the Fiji Tourist Board, marries the 1990s ecological fad of *Free Willy* and **FLY PEEK** to the eternal guarantee that dinosaurs will get children into theaters.

COOK DADDY

1990. JPN: *Kyukyoku Chef Oishinbo Papa*. AKA: *Ultimate Chef Gourmet Papa*. Video. DIR: Kazuo Tomozawa. SCR: Kazuo Tomozawa. DES: Kazuo Tomozawa. ANI: Hiroaki Mizorogi. MUS: N/C. PRD: Agent 21. 45 mins.

Kenzo Nishikata, an everyday chef in the Chinese restaurant Chin-Chin Ken, moonlights as an assassin. Disposing of his victims by serving them up as dishes of the day, he is sidetracked one day by the amorous attentions of Sai, the pretty college girl who works part-time as a waitress. Based on a manga by **TALES OF . . .** and **SAKURA DIARIES**–creator U-Jin, and not to be confused with **OISHINBO**. **VN**

COOL COOL BYE

1986. Video. DIR: Yukien Kogawa. SCR: Yukien Kogawa. DES: Yukien Kogawa, Akihiko Yamashita. ANI: Yukien Kogawa,

Hidetoshi Omori. MUS: Ken Sato. PRD: Toyo Links. 45 mins.

Lek and Flena Han are a brother and sister on a mission to defeat the Big Machine, a giant robot that attacked their village and killed the inhabitants, in this forgettable title from **DUNBINE**'s Kogawa, which adds insult to injury by bulking out its running time with a 15-minute ""Making Of"" special.

COOL COUPLE

1999. JPN: *Iketeru Futari*. TV series. DIR: Takeshi Yamaguchi. SCR: Masayoshi Azuma. DES: Ryoichi Oki. ANI: N/C. MUS: N/C. PRD: JC staff. 7 mins. x 16 eps.

A **HIS AND HER CIRCUMSTANCES** clone based on Takashi Sano's manga from *Young King* magazine, in which high school student Kyosuke Saji falls in love with class valedictorian Aki Koizumi. Though she is beastly to him at first and her friends equally cruel, eventually he breaks through and makes her his girl. Shown, like **COLORFUL**, as part of the late-night TV show *Wonderful*, it was eventually compiled into two omnibus editions. **NV**

COOL DEVICES *

1996. Video. DIR: Osamu Shimokawa, Megumi Saki, Yasuomi Umezu, Hiroshi Matsuda. SCR: Mon-Mon, Masamichi Kaneko. DES: Mon-Mon, Hiroyuki Utatane, Protonsaurus, Yasuomi Umezu, Naomi Hayakawa. ANI: Hiroshi Mori. MUS: N/C. PRD: Beam Entertainment. 30 mins. x 11 eps.

An umbrella title for disparate erotic stories from a number of mainly pseudonymous creators, the *Cool Devices* brand name was clearly valued highly enough by distributors Critical Mass to be kept for the U.S. release; compare this to Anime 18's treatment of the **SECRET ANIMA** series, which was broken up and released as stand-alone titles.

The subject matter often crosses the boundary of good taste—cartoon characters are more pliant actors than human beings, and though the sexualized violence of 1980s shows like **RAPEMAN** are less in evidence, there

are still many sadomasochistic tales of women volunteering for abuse. One such example is *Curious Fruit* (#1), based on a manga from former **CREAM LEMON**–designer Mon-Mon, in which an innocent girl discovers her deep, dark desires to be dominated. Incest is another recurring theme, as seen in *Sacred Girl* (#2), from **COUNT DOWN**–creator Hiroyuki Utatane, in which a rich orphan attempts, and fails, to overcome his longing for his sister by holding orgies at their mansion. It was back to bestiality and domination for *Lover Doll*, the lecherous male gaze in *Winter Swimsuit*, and toilet training in *Enema* (all #3). It's far shorter tableaux from *Secret Anima*'s Protonsaurus, little more than sex scenes and all but devoid of plot. For *Kirei* (#4), the setting moved to a summery beach for the seduction of a Japanese girl by a local lothario.

Seek (#5–6) was based on a computer game from Hiroshige Tadokoro, retaining its origins even to the extent of keeping the male lead's face hidden to aid player/viewer identification. Although stretching across two 30-minute episodes, its chapters are only tenuously related—the innocent young Marino discovers how her "mostly unwilling body" is secretly crying out to be dominated by a smug male abuser. Once she has been taught her lesson, she is dragged in for another cavalcade of torment, alongside several other girls, in scenes of domination and electrocution that the U.S. distributor proudly claimed to be the "most disturbing tape of the entire *Cool Devices* series."

For Yasuomi Umezu's *Yellow Star* (#7), which looks and often plays like a prequel to his later **KITE**, a young girl is drugged and raped by her policeman stepfather, who uses the titular narcotic to ensure her cooperation. *Slave Warrior Maya* (#8–9), based on a manga by Konodonto, covers ground similar to the previous year's **FENCER OF MINERVA**. An innocent girl is transported to a magical world, where she is immediately captured by lizard-men and sold into slavery. Sold to a robot king (presumably because robots are not human and consequently cannot legally have genuine genitalia that need to be censored), she is subjected to slave training before revealing that she is really a warrior. The second volume is a far simpler tableau of bondage and domination, in which Maya's extra "appendage," revealed at the end of episode one, is put to considerable use.

Binding (#10) is another game spin-off, featuring character designs from **BEAST CITY**–creator Naomi Hayakawa. For once it is the male character who gets the raw deal, as hack writer Masaki loses his luggage and his wallet leaving his train after an earthquake and follows a pretty girl to a dark mansion. There he is welcomed by an all-female community who turn into dominatrixes at sundown, tying him up and tormenting him, though in a far more playful and consensual fashion than in other chapters.

The final volume to date is another Mon-Mon story, *Fallen Angel Rina* (#11). Recalling its contemporary **PERFECT BLUE**, Rina is a singer, fallen on hard times due to her father's profligacy, whose new manager makes her discard a wholesome girl-next-door image in favor of skimpy outfits and provocative appearances—resulting in her molestation by passers-by in the street, and even her own audience—before the makers' consciences are salved by an ending in which Rina gets her revenge. **LNV**

CORAL INVESTIGATES
1979. JPN: *Coral no Tanken*. TV series. DIR: Seitaro Hara, Gen Mizumoto. SCR: Hideo Anzai, Tomoyuki Miyata. DES: N/C. ANI: N/C. MUS: Akihiro Komori. PRD: Chikara, Zak, Nippon Columbia, TBS. 25 mins. x 50 eps.
An animated show based on Albert Berié's French puppet show, in which Hector the Rat teams up with his fellow denizens of Pretty Wood, including the titular Coral (a young girl) and the unimaginatively named Crow (a crow),

to head off to Holland. With many musical scenes, the voice actors were chosen for their singing ability above other considerations.

CORRECTOR YUI
1999. TV series. DIR: Yuji Muto. SCR: Satoru Nishizono. DES: Fumie Muroi. ANI: Shintaro Muraki, Miko Nakajima. MUS: Kenji Kawai. PRD: Nippon Animation, NHKEP. 25 mins. x 52 eps.
The young Yui is a manga fan who wants to be an anime voice actress when she grows up. One day, she is sucked into her computer, where she discovers that the gigantic computer Grosser intends to rule the human race from within cyberspace. The only way to stop Grosser is to join forces with pieces of mystic software (Eco, Rescue, Control, Peace, Follow, and Synchro) and her assistant, IR, combining to form the greatest debugging program known to man.

Mixing elements of his earlier **COMPILER** with Disney's *Tron* (a film conveniently old enough to be unknown to the target audience), Kia Asamiya's first anime for girls is a surprisingly old-fashioned affair. Though set in 2010, its heroine carries a magic wand and must assemble a team of mismatched troubleshooters, pausing regularly to hector her audience about computer terminology and keeping parks tidy. And like **SAILOR MOON** before it, the first season ends with the baddie defeated, but the plot resets to zero for a repeat performance. A curious combination of the preachy conservatism to be expected from a state-owned education channel like NHKEP and the formulaic, marketing-led appeal of a corporate creator like Bandai.

COSMIC FANTASY
1994. Video. DIR: Kazuhiro Ochi. SCR: Kazuhiro Ochi. DES: Kazuhiro Ochi. ANI: Keisuke Watanabe. MUS: Tatsuya Murayama. PRD: Tokuma. 45 mins.
A one-shot cash-in on a computer game in which the heroic Yu leads a team of interstellar crime-fighters against evil space pirates, in this case,

the female buccaneer known as the Galactic Panther.

COSMOS PINK SHOCK
1985. Video. DIR: Yasuo Hasegawa, Keisuke Matsumoto. SCR: Takeshi Shudo. DES: Toshihiro Hirano, Rei Yumeno. ANI: N/C. MUS: N/C. PRD: AIC. 36 mins.
An anime parody about Michiko dreaming of a promise her boyfriend, Hiroshi, made to her and then being whisked off into space on the Pink Shock spaceship, in which she rescues the denizens of a prison planet. The original was serialized as original content on the *Animevision* video magazine that otherwise consisted of trailers for other shows and assorted voice-actor gossip, eventually being compiled into a one-shot video the following year.

COSPLAY COMPLEX *
2002. Video. DIR: Shinichiro Kimura. SCR: Noboru Kimura. DES: Katsuzo Hayato. ANI: Sayuri Sugitou. MUS: Yoshinobu Hiraiwa. PRD: TNK, Wonder Farm. 30 mins. x 3 eps.
Chako Hasegawa and her stereotypically defined friends are members of the Cosplay Association of East Oizuka Junior High and dream of taking their skills to the World Cosplay (i.e., costuming) Championships. An impossible dream? Not when they have the assistance of a magical owl and Delmo the costuming fairy (who can actually assume the shape of any costume required) and just the right amount of thread. The championship would be all sewn up but for the fact that the group's best cosplayer, Chako, has such a heavy crush on local hero Kosuke that she never seems able to do anything right.

Ever since **OTAKU NO VIDEO**, fandom has increasingly turned its attention inward on itself—*CC* sits alongside titles such as **COMIC PARTY** and **GENSHIKEN**. *CC* recognizes the tensions within real-world costuming, that while the participants see their activities as a fannish but holy vocation, many of their audience simply want to ridicule them or ogle the girls in states of partial undress. Acknowledging both sides of the argument, *CC* includes costuming pastiches of fan classics like **GUNBUSTER** and even a DVD guide to the costumes worn, but also plenty of gratuitous naked flesh. Elements also play like one of the many computer game adaptations it coincidentally resembles, with Goro, the lone male member of the team, sitting amid a whirlwind of female hormones à la **SAKURA WARS**. Questionable, some might say racially and sexually repugnant, tension is added by the last-minute arrival of Jenny, a large-breasted blonde Italian transfer student with an unwholesome interest in little girls, whose behavior around pre-teen Athena would get her arrested in most countries. Not to be confused with *Cosmopolitan Prayers*, for which see under **A15**. **N**

COTTON STAR
1984. JPN: *Wata no Kuniboshi*. AKA: *Planet of Cotton*. Movie. DIR: Shinichi Tsuji. SCR: Masaki Tsuji, Yumiko Oshima. DES: Katsumi Aoshima. ANI: Katsumi Aoshima, Shinya Takahashi, Jun Kawagoe, Kuni Tomita. MUS: Richard Clayderman. PRD: Mushi Pro. 96 mins.
Cuteycat, a two-month-old kitten, is taken in by a young man called Tokio, who takes pity on her on a rainy day. Cuteycat becomes one of the family, though she has trouble winning over Tokio's mother, who is allergic to cats. Cuteycat is heartbroken when Tokio falls in love with a girl in the park, only to be rescued from despair when she meets the handsome, silver-haired tomcat Raphael, who explains that humans and cats can never truly be together.

Richard Clayderman's twee piano hits just the right note in this weepy romance. Yumiko Oshima's 1978 manga for *Comic Lala* was adapted here by its original author with veteran scenarist Tsuji. Years later, animator Tomita would defect to the U.S. to work on homegrown animation like *Invasion America*.

COUNT DOWN *
1995. JPN: *Yuwaku Countdown*. AKA:

Temptation Countdown. Video. DIR: Shoichi Masuo, Naohito Takahashi. SCR: Hiroyuki Utatane. DES: Sanae Chikanaga, Ryunosuke Otonashi. ANI: Ryunosuke Otonashi. MUS: Kanji Saito. PRD: Pink Pineapple, KSS. 35 mins. x 6 eps.
Creator Utatane, best known in the mainstream for his SF manga *Seraphic Feather*, made an early name for himself drawing erotic short stories that were eventually compiled into the anthologies *Count Down 54321* and *Temptation*.

Animated as short vignettes, the stories include many basic erotic setups with a twist. A modern-day bus encounter leads to erotica confusion; a sword-swinging macho man meets his match in a girl who can tie anything down; and a bride has a last-minute fling before taking that walk to the altar—quite literally. Other episodes that do not appear to have survived in the American release include a severely disturbed young man's relationship with a flesh doll whose hands remind him of his mother's, and the couplings of a she-male teacher, her female student and the student's mother.

The final three episodes encompass a single story arc, *Akira*, featuring designs from **END OF SUMMER**'s Otonashi, a replay of the faux-incest of **CREAM LEMON**'s *Ami* stories. Akira carries a torch for his stepsister, a supermodel, and fantasizes about her even when making love to the other women in his life. When she eventually returns from decadent Europe, she has brought a "special" friend with her, and Akira must come to terms with the fact that the affair between them was never going to last. **LNV**

COUNTDOWN TO DELIGHT *
2001. JPN: *Bakuhatsu Sunzen Tenshi no Countdown*. AKA: *Before the Explosion Angel Countdown*. Video. DIR: Shoichiro Kamjio. SCR: Tekuro Imaike. DES: Hiura Konata. ANI: N/C. MUS: N/C. PRD: Green Bunny, Fuyusha. 30 mins.
Average Japanese boy Motoki gets more than he bargained for when his

sister's lesbian lover proves that she is bisexual by offering him her body in secret. He escapes from such temptations when he falls in love with Natsuki, an innocent-looking girl who turns out to be a dominatrix. **LNV**

COWBOY BEBOP *
1998. TV series. DIR: Shinichiro Watanabe. SCR: Keiko Nobumoto, Michiko Yokote, Ryota Yamaguchi, Sadayuki Murai, Dai Sato. DES: Toshihiro Kawamoto, Kimitoshi Yamano. ANI: Yoichi Ogami. MUS: Yoko Kanno. PRD: Sunrise, TV Tokyo. 25 mins. x 26 eps.
Spike Spiegel and ex-cop Jet Black are bounty hunters who range across the whole solar system. Teaming up, albeit reluctantly, with mystery woman Faye Valentine, hacker brat Ed (who's a girl), and a super-intelligent Welsh corgi called Ein, they remain perpetually on the lookout for criminals on the run.

From such a simple premise springs one of the most entertaining anime shows of the 1990s. Made with a deliberate 1970s retro style, it posits a solar system that is one part Chinese diaspora and two parts Wild West. Cityscapes straight out of kung-fu movies jostle with neo-architecture in the style of *Blade Runner* and one-horse frontier towns in the middle of the Martian desert.

Spike is a hero cast in the mold of **LUPIN III**, a good-hearted man operating at the edge of the law, betrayed by an old flame and still nursing his wounded heart. The show itself varies wildly in tone, from comedy to tragedy, but maintains its believability throughout. From the outset, director Watanabe cut much of the exposition from the original script, preferring to give the impression that the viewers were watching the show *in* 2072, and that no explanations would be necessary. The idea of watching a pulp TV show from 100 years in the future truly adds to the experience—a mood retained for the fake Martian radio broadcast *Music for Freelance*, released on CD. The tactic also helps disguise the show's few flaws—at its core, *Cowboy Bebop* is little

Cowboy Bebop

© 1998 SUNRISE INC.

more than *Route 66* in space, with plots ripped off from generic U.S. crime shows. Space truckers, space mafia, and space hippies would be hack conventions in another series, but they seem to work here because the world seems so believable.

Though complete in its foreign edition, the entirety of *Cowboy Bebop* was not shown on Japanese terrestrial TV. The opening episode, featuring scenes of drug-taking and John Woo–inspired shootouts, was only broadcast on the more forgiving satellite networks, and the censorious climate post-EVANGELION meant that, eventually, only 12 episodes of the complete 26 in the series were seen by the first-run audience. The movie *Knockin' on Heaven's Door* (2001), takes place between episodes 22 and 23 of the TV series, just before the final events of the series would have made it impossible to have a full cast ensemble. It is thus an enjoyable but rather pointless bonus story, for which the producers unwisely boasted, a perfectly reasonable 90-minute action movie was unnecessarily padded out with an additional half-hour

of footage. As part of the publicity for the movie, the film website also began a "serialization" of Dai Sato's *Ural Terpsichore*, a prequel novel setting up the characters and situations of the original series. However, only the first chapter ever seems to have appeared.🅥

COWBOY ISAMU
1973. JPN: *Koya no Shonen Isamu*. AKA: *Wilderness Boy Isamu*. TV series. DIR: Isao Takahata, Kyosuke Mikuriya, Yoshikata Nitta, Kenzo Koizumi. SCR: Noboru Kawasaki, Soji Yamakawa. DES: Shingo Araki, Daikichiro Kusube. ANI: Tatsuo Kasai, Koichi Murata, Isao Takahata, Hideo Kawauchi, Shingo Araki, Yasuhiro Yamaguchi, Tetsuo Imazawa. MUS: Takeo Watanabe. PRD: Tokyo Movie Shinsha, Fuji TV. 25 mins. x 52 eps.
Isamu Wataru is the child of a Japanese man and a Native American woman, a skilled gunfighter from an early age because of the dangers of life in the Wild West. After his mother's death, he is taken in by the folks of Rotten Camp, and raised by the Wingate family as one of their own. The Wingates teach

him superb sharp-shooting skills, but as Isamu gets older, he comes to realize that they are outlaws, and that they are encouraging him to put his powers to evil use—compare to similar loyalty issues that trouble KIKAIDER. Based on the manga *Boy King* (*Shonen Oja*) by Soji Yamakawa and Noboru Kawasaki, serialized in *Shonen Jump* weekly, this series drifted away from its inspiration in the second half, preferring to concentrate instead on Isamu's search for his missing father. Director Takahata had a young colleague named Hayao Miyazaki on his animation team, which is the main reason English-speaking fans remember this children's adventure story about a boy making his way in the lawless West.

The show's title seems designed to encourage associations with American cowboy programs already seen on Japanese television. *Hondo* (1967) was broadcast in Japan as *Koya no Apache* or "Wilderness Apache," while *Branded* (1965), was shown in Japanese as *Koya no Nagaremono*, or "Wilderness Wanderer"—Isamu's surname actually means "drifter."

CRAYON SHIN-CHAN *
1992. TV series, Movie. DIR: Mitsuru Honma, Keiichi Hara. SCR: Mitsuru Honma, Keiichi Hara, Ryo Motohira, Keiichi Hara. DES: Masaaki Yuasa. ANI: Shizuka Mori, Katsue Hara. MUS: Toshiyuki Arakawa. PRD: Shinei, TV Asahi. 25 mins. x 564+ eps. (TV), ? mins. x ? eps. (TV special), ca. 90 mins. x 11 eps. (m)
Shinnosuke "Shin-chan" Nohara is the ultimate brat—a loud, nosy kid prone to impersonating elephants with his genitals, peeking up teachers' skirts, and tormenting his stupid dog. His harassed mother turns a blind eye, his teachers despair, and a cast of zany regulars turn this nasty cartoon into a hellish look at the world through the eyes of a spoiled child. Most episodes are divided into three smaller, unrelated chapters, giving just enough time to set up accidents with snot, panty-flashing, and bratty behavior. At school, two prissy female teachers are engaged

in a constant war of one-upmanship, not realizing that their pupils are manipulating their jealousies for their own ends. A bright, bouncy new teacher refuses to be downhearted at the utter chaos that confronts her, and the headmaster gets angry at being constantly mistaken for a gangster. Out in the wider world, Shin's family and neighbors are also the subject of ceaseless torment. He even persists in getting the teenager Shinobu fired from every job she takes, and, though he is the bane of her life, he can never remember her name. There are even parodies of anime shows—school super-jock Kawamura is obsessed by the nonexistent show *Action Kamen* (*Action Mask*), while Shin religiously watches an insane GUNDAM parody called *Kuntam Robo*.

Created by Yoshihito Usui for *Manga Action* magazine in 1990, *Shin-chan* caused a stir in Japan when it was claimed that up to 68% of children under 12 were avid viewers of this show, supposedly made for adults who would get the joke. Unfortunately, the joke backfired, with complaints in the Japanese media that an entire generation of Japanese children was growing up to be lecherous, evil menaces.

The *Crayon Shin-chan* movies were genuinely aimed at a juvenile audience, albeit one that had grown up watching the series. In *Action Kamen vs. Evil High-Leg* (1993), the entire cast is forced to wear skimpy swimsuits by a bad king, while in *Secrets of Buriburiland* (1994), they are packed off to the South Sea island of Buriburi (Japanese for "annoying"). In *Adventures in Henderland* (1996), a simple trip to the titular amusement park finds Shin foiling a gay warlock's bid to become ruler of the world. Shin-chan's baby sister, Himawari, had her debut in *The Search for the Black Balls* (1997), which also featured a cameo role for creator Usui. *Attack! War of the Pig's Trotter* (1998) embroiled the Nohara family in a vendetta between two secret societies. *Dazzling Hot Spring Wars* and *Paradise Made in Saitama* (1999) split

the feature format into two chapters: a traditional vacation episode and a cyberspace pastiche. In *Storm in the Jungle* (2000), Shin-chan's family is kidnapped on a southern island, leaving him and Himawari to rescue them from the Afro-haired Funky Monkey Army—nicely demonstrating that Shin would have the ability to insult foreign audiences, too, if only his English-language appearances went further afield than a limited number of subtitled broadcasts on a Hawaiian Japanese community station. The movie *The Storm is Calling: The Adult Empire Strikes Back* (2001) featured Shin-chan and his iconoclastic bunch running amok in a 20th-century theme park, ruining their elders' nostalgia trip—somewhat ironic, considering that some of the original "under-12" audience may now have brats of their own. In the following year's *Sengoku Battle* (2002), Shin-chan falls 400 years down a time tunnel, landing in the middle of Japan's civil war. His parents come after him in the family car, causing irreparable damage to history. For *The Wind is Calling: Yakiniku Road* (2003), Shin-chan stages a protest at the poor quality of his breakfast, and is appeased by the promise of a barbecue for dinner. When someone steals his food, he embarks upon a samurai-style vendetta. Shin-chan gained a superhero identity in *Legend is Calling: Three Minute Buriburi Flashing Attack* (2005).

Under the title *Shin-chan*, part of the TV series was broadcast in the United Kingdom in 2002, and eventually reached the mainland U.S. several years later. ◐◓◓

CREAM LEMON *
1986. Video. DIR: Kazuya Miyazaki, Bikkuri Hako, Ayako Mibashi, Yuji Motoyama, Toshihiro Hirano. SCR: N/C. DES: Masako Nitta, Mon-Mon, Kei Amaki, Yuji Motoyama, To Moriyama, Toshihiro Hirano, Ayako Mibashi, Hiroyuki Kitakubo, Nekoda Nyan. ANI: Hiroshi Tajima, Mamoru Yasuhiko, Bikkuri Hako. MUS: N/C. PRD: Fairy Dust. 25 mins. x 36 eps.

One of anime's most notorious serials, and, though only a third of the episodes were translated into English, it is one of the most significant shows of the 1980s. *CL* wasn't the first erotic anime video (that was the similar LOLITA ANIME), but the brand survived for over a decade as an umbrella for several subseries, eventually becoming synonymous with anime pornography. The original spanned 16 episodes, followed by assorted specials, the nine-part *New CL*, and two epilogues, shuffled here into some semblance of order.

Its first and biggest star was Ami Nonomura, an 11-year-old girl who seduces her older brother, Hiroshi, in *Be My Baby* (#1). When Hiroshi is banished to London in *Ami Again* (#5), an older but hardly wiser Ami dreams that she is having sex with him again, only to wake and discover that she is drunk in bed with a stranger. Hiroshi returns in *Now I Embrace You Ami* (#13) only to tell her that the affair is over, at which point she returns to the arms of her one-night stand. The 1986 movie *CL: Ami's Journey* came next, in which her friends drag her off to Hokkaido to take her mind off things. Shown on a double bill with the first PROJECT A-KO movie, the film was noticeably more mainstream than its erotic predecessors, and, surprisingly for a theatrical version, of lower-grade animation. Ami becomes an idol singer, squeezing in a clandestine tryst with Hiroshi when her entourage passes through London. Her adventures ended in the miniseries *Ami: From Then On* (#31–34), in which Ami is forced to choose between Hiroshi and her fiancé, eventually choosing neither and electing to stay single. Ami's adventures eventually reached the U.S. in 2001, as *Be My Honey, The Story of Ami, In the Midst of Sadness*, and *Ami's Climax*.

In *Escalation* (#2), the bisexual Rie is banished to a strict Catholic school when she is found in bed with her piano teacher. Predictably, she soon ends up in a lesbian ménage à trois with her roommate, Midori, and dominated in a series of power games by the senior girl

Naomi. After graduation, Naomi would invite the girls to her mansion for a repeat performance (#6), and the girls would return in a third installment (#16) to initiate a new recruit.

SF Legend Rall (#3) is a space fantasy in which Carol, an underdressed, sword-wielding warrior-maid, stands against an evil overlord who intends to sacrifice the beautiful Princess Orgasma. She would take up the call to adventure in *Lamo Ru Strikes Back* (#15). Both episodes were distributed in the U.S. as *Gonad the Barbarian* and *The Search for Uranus* in the Brothers Grime animation series.

Pop Chaser (#4) was directed by **PROJECT A-KO**'s Yuji Moriyama under the pseudonym Yuji Motoyama and has early designs by Hiroyuki Kitakubo. It features interstellar Wild-West lesbian antics inside a giant robot suit, as biker chick Rio liberates her woman from a rival gang only to discover that the distressed damsel has agreed to marry the leader. Under the title *Offenders of the Universe*, it was combined with *Star Trap* (#10), an unrelated *Star Trek* spoof starring the lesbian crew of the USS Mischief, and released in the U.S. as another two-part video.

Don't Do It Mako: Sexy Symphony (#7 and #12) presaged **SPRITE** by introducing a timid girl possessed by a knowing, sexual personality—the quintessence of the *CL* series in its assurance that inside every child, there is a sex kitten waiting to get out. In another mainstream cameo, it was directed by **ICZER-ONE**'s Toshihiro Hirano.

Further sci-fi antics awaited in *Super Virgin* (#8, aka *Super Virgin Groupies)* in which another Mako, a psychic, falls in love with one of the schoolboys who torment her. It was followed by another one-shot, *Happening Summer* (#9, aka *Travelling Fantasies*), in which naughty Yuki seduces her big sister's boyfriend—a man who, in a series in-joke, is found reading a porn magazine featuring photographs of *Escalation*'s Naomi.

In *Black Cat Manor* (#11), student Masaki leaves wartime Tokyo to escape the bombings, staying with the widow Saiko, her daughter, and maid. When the *CL* series eventually ground to a halt in 1993, it would be with *Return to Black Cat Manor* (#36).

Parodying **PROJECT A-KO** and foreshadowing **KEKKO KAMEN**, *Nalice Scramble* (#14), which closed the first season of *CL*, features a heroine in battle armor fighting three lesbian Nazis for control of a school. It was back immediately in 1987 with *New CL*, a straightforward continuation of some of the earlier stories with a few new one-shots and an increased concentration on the artwork and manga origins. *Five-Hour Venus* (#17), for example, was one of several shows by "To Moriyama," a pseudonym for **DANCE TILL TOMORROW**'s Naoki Yamamoto. Heroine Shimeji is blackmailed into posing nude for an art class when her porn past is revealed, and she would return in *Afterschool XXX* (#18) to save a younger classmate from a similar fate.

The supernatural began to take over with *White Shadow* (#19), in which a gymnast is possessed by a demon and seduces the boy who loves her. For *Visions of Europe* (#20), taken from Toshiki Yui's *Mermaid Junction* manga, two frisky female tourists lose their passports and money at the airport and are whisked off to an alternate Europe where passion rules. Kei Amaki's *Cherry Melancholy* (#21) has a couple of man-hunting girls giving up the chase and settling for each other, but the series soon returned to fantasy with *Astalot* (#22), a tale of swords and sorcery with the requisite sex, running almost twice as long as most other videos in the series. A boy finds a gun in *I Guess So* (#23) and uses it to compel a girl to have sex with him, while in *Dream-Colored Bunny* (#24), a trip to the pet shop nets a sexy companion for one lucky pervert.

The Dark (#25), based on a story by Nicholas Lloyd, features two men offered shelter by a woman in a castle, where she seduces and kills one of them, a priest. This episode, *Magic Doll* (#26), in which a kindly man is tempted away from his family by a sexy ghost, and the aforementioned *Black Cat Manor* (under the title *The Black Widow*) were compiled into the feature-length *Pandora: An Erotic Adventure* in the U.S. Similar supernatural goings-on await in *Summer Wind* (#27) for a bereaved boyfriend who meets a girl named Mina (like the heroine of **BEAST CITY**, a reference to Dracula).

E-tude (#28 and #29) is a classic star-crossed romance between the genteel pianist Yurika and the rough tough jazz-playing biker Ryo, who are separated by her father and set up with new partners only to long for each other. *Heartbreak Live for Two* (#30) parodies magical-girl shows like **CREAMY MAMI** as a fox grants a lovelorn girl's wish to become the idol singer that the boy she loves so adores. *Angie and Rose* (#35), the tale of a boy seduced by a Canadian mother and daughter, came out as a bonus for the *CL: Climax* boxed set in 1992, but that is by no means all there was. The *Ami* series also boasts the *Ami Graffiti* digest edition and the *Ami: White Shadow* teaser for the movie. Other abridgments include *CL Junior*, which cut a third of each episode's running time to survive in a tougher censorship climate. The series was repackaged again with two episodes per tape as *CL Twin* (aka *CL Best Coupling*), which is the version now on DVD. There are also several versions arranged by artist rather than story, collecting the "best" works from To Moriyama, Kei Amaki, and Toshiki Yui. *Festival*, a compilation of To Moriyama shorts, also appeared in the U.S. as *The Story of Toh*, although as with many of these variant listings, we have been unable to determine if they were licensed releases. In 2005, the franchise also appeared as two live-action movies, Nobuhiro Yamashita's *Cream Lemon*, and Iwao Takahashi's *Cream Lemon: Ami's Diary*. ●ⓁⓃⓋ

CREAMY MAMI

1983. JPN: *Maho no Tenshi Creamy Mami*. AKA: *Magical Angel Creamy Mami*. TV series. DIR: Osamu Kobaya-

shi, Tomomi Mochizuki, Naoto Hashimoto, Takashi Anno. scr: Kazunori Ito,
Michiru Shimada, Shigeru Yanagawa,
Shunsuke Kaneko. des: Akemi Takada.
ani: Hideo Kawauchi, Shinya Takahashi.
mus: Koji Makaino. prd: Studio Pierrot,
Nippon TV. 25 mins. x 52 eps. (TV),
90 mins. x 1 ep. (v), 53 mins. & 150
mins. (m).

Posi and Nega, two spacefaring aliens
posing as harmless kittens, give 11-
year-old Yu Morisawa a magic wand so
she can transform at will into Creamy
Mami, idol singer and magical being,
but for just one year. Her parents and
her friend Toshio don't notice this
double identity, even though they
are all huge fans of Mami. But when
Toshio sees her transform partway
through the story, Yu loses her magic
powers, and the friends go on a quest
to recover them. They succeed, and
Creamy comes back to her fans, but
Toshio loses his memory.

Mami returned straight to video in
1983 with *Eternity Once More*, a two-part
finale in which she gives a first-anniver-
sary concert, Toshio regains his memory, and Yu finally loses Mami's magical
powers. It was so well received that she
came back for another encore with *The
Long Goodbye* (1985), in which she, now
13, is transported to an alternate world
while helping Toshio make an SF film.
The 53-minute story was shown on a
triple bill with a *Minky Momo* (see Gigi)
short and the film *CM vs. Minky Momo*,
in which the girls use weapons and
special attacks named after the show's
staff, including an "Ito Flash" and a
"Watanabe Cutter."

In 1985, she also starred in the
music compilation *CM: Curtain Call*,
and she returned again for Takashi
Anno's 1986 TV special *Three Magical
Girls*, with *Magical Fairy Pelsha* and **Magical Emi**. Immensely influential in the
magical genre, she is much imitated to
this day in shows such as **Fancy Lala**,
and parodied in the **Tenchi Muyo!**
spin-off *Pretty Sammy*. In 1996, she
appeared once more in a computer
game, *CM: Tale of Two Worlds*.

CREST OF THE STARS *

1999. jpn: *Sekai no Monsho*. aka:
Celestial Crest. TV series. dir: Yasushi
Nagaoka. scr: Aya Yoshinaga. des:
Takami Akai. ani: Takuro Shinbo. mus:
N/C. prd: Sunrise, WOWOW. 25 mins,
x 13 eps. (TV1), 25 mins. x 13 eps.
(TV2), 25 mins. x 13 eps. (TV2), 25
mins. x 10 eps. (TV3), 25 mins. x 2
eps. (v).

In Space Year 172, peace-loving
Planet Martine is occupied by the Abh
Human Reich, the genetically engineered descendants of Terran exiles.
Now the immortal, elfin rulers of their
own empire, they demand Martine's
surrender. President Lock Rin deacti-
vates the defenses to avoid a war, and
his family is sent back to rule Martine
as Abh aristocrats. Years later, the
president's son, Jinto, prepares to journey to the heart of the Abh territory to
complete his studies, accompanied by
the beautiful 16-year-old Abh military
cadet Rafeel.

Despite the promising concept of a
collaborator turning against his masters and the painstaking recreation of
the Abh's alien language, *Crest of the
Stars* fails through misplaced loyalty
to Hiroyuki Morioka's original novels,
resulting in a succession of uneventful
debates not unlike the slower por-
tions of **Legend of Galactic Heroes**.
Squandering much of the budget on
showy computer graphics for the first
episode, it is soon reduced to cut-rate
animation, which further stretches
viewers' patience. **Idol Project**–director Nagaoka attempts to compensate
by making Rafeel an elfin space-bimbo,
forever bending over and jiggling, a
sop to the adolescent audience that
devalues much talk of Abh war crimes
and conquests, as if Britney Spears had
been cast as an SS officer. But there's
no accounting for taste, and a sequel,
Celestial Banner, duly followed in 2000.
The 13-episode TV series *Banner of the
Stars* (2000) reunites Jinto with Rafeel
three years later, when he finds a position as a supply officer on her ship,
the Basroil. There are elements, albeit
serious ones, of **Irresponsible Captain**

Tylor, as the lowly cadet is paired with
the high-class princess, while their
small detachment is sent to defend the
critical Laptic Gate, even though their
admiral is from a family renowned for
its mental instability. Rafeel is the captain of the ship, whereas Jinto starts the
series in the position normally occupied by a disposable *Star Trek* red-shirt.

Banner of the Stars II (2001) is a
smaller ten-episode series in which
Rafeel is assigned to become an inter-
im territorial governor on the newly
conquered Lobnas II that turns out to
be a prison world.

Banner of the Stars III (2005),
released straight to video, details
Jinto's assignment as a governor on
yet another newly conquered world,
although his rise through the ranks of
the race that conquered his own planet
is starting to rankle.

CRIMSON CLIMAX *

2003. jpn: *Hotaruko*. aka: *Firefly-child*.
Video. dir: Kazuma Kanezawa. scr:
Kazuma Kanezawa. des: Gion Muto.
ani: Gion Muto. mus: Toru Shura. prd:
ARMS, Green Bunny. 30 mins. x 3 eps.
After her mother's death, orphan Ryo
is invited by her aunt Mizunu to visit
her secluded island home on the Japan
Sea, only to discover that it has been
overrun by servants of an orgiastic
cult of human sacrifice. She befriends
Mizunu's daughter Hotaruko, merely
to realize that the cult demands fresh
blood, and just one of them is going to
survive. Sex and violence duly follow.
The Japanese release has a notably
classy cover, although the American
edition looks like all the others. **⬤ⓃⓋ**

CRIMSON WOLF *

1993. jpn: *Hon Ran*. aka: *Hong Lang*
(orig. Chinese). Video. dir: Shoichi
Masuo. scr: Shoichi Masuo, Yasuhito
Kikuchi, Isamu Imakake. des: Kenji
Okamura. ani: Kazuya Kuroda, Yasuhito
Kikuchi, Isamu Imakake. mus: Kuni-
toshi Tojima. prd: APPP. 60 mins.
A scientific expedition finds the hid-
den tomb of Genghis Khan in Mongo-
lia. Supernatural apparitions destroy

Cromartie High

the expedition and proclaim a curse that in a thousand days a great natural disaster will devastate the whole world unless three young people bearing a wolf-shaped birthmark or scar are found and killed. Kei, a martial-arts student in Beijing, is identified as the first of the Crimson Wolves. He survives an assassination attempt, but his old teacher is murdered. Kei tracks the killers for revenge and is shocked to learn that he has been targeted by every government espionage agency in the world. Refusing to believe the "curse," Kei teams up with the other Crimson Wolves, nubile Japanese love interest/distressed damsel Mizuho Washio and the handsome, rakish "adversary" of the team Ryugen, a Chinese tong boss.

Genghis Khan is just one of three Great Kings, Oriental undead who will become supreme masters of the world unless stopped by the Crimson Wolves a thousand days after the opening of the tomb, with the other two being the Qin Emperor (China's unifier and the ward of the famous Terra-cotta Army) and Communist leader Mao Zedong. In scraps of clumsy plotting typical of such matinee adventures, the Crimson Wolves only become aware of the

threat they pose when assassins are sent to stop them—if the Great Kings left them in ignorance, the thousand days would have passed without opposition! The Crimson Wolves are told they have great powers (not surprising since Kei has his eyes poked out in prison and is miraculously healed by the time he is rescued). Eventually, the Great Kings take over the Chinese government's supercomputer, Goku, in a finale that implies the Crimson Wolves have saved China from its cruel first emperor, its Mongol conqueror, the architect of the Great Leap Forward, *and* the future spread of Communism! Entertainingly bad "yellow peril" hokum, unlikely to be as popular in the People's Republic as **Ranma** ¹/₂. 🅛🅥

CROMARTIE HIGH *
2004. JPN: *Sakigake!! Cromartie Koko.* AKA: *Charge!! Cromartie High.* TV series. DIR: Hiroaki Sakurai. DES: Atsushi Takeuchi, Naoyuki Onda. ANI: N/C. MUS: Kunio Suma. PRD: Production I.G., Starchild, TV Tokyo, Bandai Visual. 12 mins. x 26 eps.
Cromartie High has the dubious honor of teaching some of Japan's worst teen delinquents. Its students range

from the rebellious—Hayashida, who sports a mauve Mohawk, or Freddy, a lookalike for gay rock icon Freddie Mercury of Queen—to the downright strange, like the gorilla in high school uniform who really *is* a gorilla, or robot boy Shinichi Mechazawa. He looks like an aerosol can with telescopic arms and claw hands, but everyone treats him like a normal student. The school is locked in gang warfare with rival Destrade High. Into this peculiar institution, created by Eiji Nonaka for his manga in weekly *Shonen Magazine*, comes tall, handsome Takashi Kamiyama. Nobody knows why an honor roll student would join the deadbeats of Cromatie High, but he has to be the toughest honor student around, so naturally surreal high jinks and wacky sight gags ensue in this parody of tough-guy anime like **Charge Ahead! Men's School**, whose Japanese title it echoes. Takashi is the one non-delinquent in a school full of them, a role reversal from which *Cromartie High* draws much of its comedy—compare to **Alice Academy**, which revisits a similar theme from a gentler magical-girl perspective. In 2005, following the release of a *Cromartie High* spin-off live-action movie, the filmmakers were sued by former Yomiuri Giants baseball player Warren Cromartie for using his name without permission in a tale of delinquency.

CROWS
1993. Video. DIR: Masamune Ochiai. SCR: Shunsuke Amemura. DES: Koichi Kagawa. ANI: N/C. MUS: N/C. PRD: KSS, Knack. 45 mins. x 2 eps.
Shundo is the new kid in town, ready to fight with anyone. After beating more than ten opponents, he gets a reputation as the toughest kid around, but he uses his strength to help those who cannot help themselves, soon gaining a following of grateful youngsters.

Transfering the honor of samurai drama to a school setting, Hiroshi Takahashi's 1990 manga from *Shonen Champion* was a more serious take on the teenage tough guys of shows like BE-BOP HIGH SCHOOL and ANGEL LEGEND, although Shundo's alma mater, "The Edge of Badness," is named with a pomposity that might perhaps have benefited from a little humor. 🅛🅥

CRUSH GEAR TURBO

2001. JPN: *Gekito! Crush Gear Turbo.* TV series, Movie. DIR: Hideharu Iuchi, Tetsuro Amino. SCR: Akihiko Inari, Mari Okada, Fuyunori Gobi, Hideharu Iuchi, Hiroaki Kitajima, Hiroyuki Yoshino, Masaaki Sakurai, Noburo Kimura, Shin Yoshida, Shino Hakata, Suguru Koizumi, Tatsuto Higuchi. DES: Atsuo Tobe. ANI: Akiko Nagashima, Akira Takahashi, Atsuo Tobe, Eiji Nakata, Hirokazu Hisayuki, Junji Nishimura, Kohei Yoneyama, Nanabu Ono, Naoki Murakami, Seiichi Hashimoto, Shinichi Takahashi, Takuro Shinbo. MUS: Takayuki Negishi. PRD: Sunrise, TV Asahi, Nagoya TV, Toei. 25 mins. x 68 eps. (TV1), 25 mins. x 50 eps. (TV2) 60 mins. (m).

Elementary schoolboy Masaru must battle a rival school, Zet, out to win the Gear Koshien, the international Crush Gear tournament, and go on to conquer the Gear World. In a mix of gladiatorial combat with racing cars and extreme competition of the high school baseball tournament of MAN'S AN IDIOT! that (according to anime producers) kids are really interested in, the transforming vehicles are known as Gears and Masaru's is called Mach Justice—perhaps a reference to SPEED RACER's Mach 5. Generated by the usual random combination of toy concepts and stereotypes we have come to expect from Bandai house name Hajime Yadate, the franchise ran long enough to spawn a movie release from Toei in July 2002, and 2003's 50-episode sequel *Crush Gear Nitro*. Compare, if there is a comparison to be had, with DAIGUNDER.

CRUSHER JOE *

1983. AKA: *Crushers.* Movie, video. DIR: Yoshikazu Yasuhiko, Toshifumi Takizawa. SCR: Haruka Takachiho. DES: Yoshikazu Yasuhiko, Shoji Kawamori.

ANI: Naoyuki Yoshinaga, Ichiro Itano, Gen Sato. MUS: Tadao Maeda. PRD: Studio Nue, Sunrise. 131 mins. (m), 60 mins. x 2 eps. (v).

The Crushers are a loose federation of trouble-shooting space mercenaries. The crew of the ship Minerva is led by teen Joe (son of head Crusher Dan), with teammates Alfin (cute tomboy), Talos (hulking muscle, much smarter than he looks), and Riki (bratty kid), plus Dongo the comical robot. Joe and crew agree to transport a frozen heiress to a distant world's medical facility, but their ship is attacked en route and the cryogenic capsule is stolen. Pursued by the galactic police while simultaneously trying to regain their cargo, the Crushers stumble into the lair of notorious space pirate Murphy, who intends to use a doomsday weapon to rule the universe.

Haruka Takachiho's famous character first appeared in the 1977 novel *Crisis on Planet Pizan* with a gang named after two of the author's wrestling heroines, the Crush Gals. The anime version is also riddled with minor characters lifted from *Go for It, Alfin-chan!*, a manga by animator Gen Sato. Several background film clips also showed two characters from another Takachiho series who were so popular they got their own show: DIRTY PAIR.

Joe and his gang returned in 1989 for two video adventures also released in the U.S. In *The Ice Hell Trap*, they are framed by the despotic Ghellstan, who hires them to save the prison planet Debris without revealing that the entire world is rigged to blow as part of an insurance scam. Once again, the Crushers' mission is twofold; save the planet *and* bag the bad guys. In *Ash: The Ultimate Weapon*, they must team up with Tanya, a military officer determined to track down a conspiracy to steal yet another doomsday device. On a planet overrun with self-replicating killing machines, they have yet another race against time as the titular device is activated, leaving 20 minutes to turn it off and rescue Tanya.

In 2000, two *Crusher Joe* stories, *Leg-*

end of the Saint Jeremy and *Pandora II*, were illustrated by JUDGE-artist Fujihiko Hosono and released on VHS as the first in the new (and rather pointless) "manga video" format, featuring voice actors reading the manga aloud.

CRY FOR OUR BEAUTIFUL WORLD

1992. JPN: *Utsukushii Chikyu o Yogosanaide.* AKA: *Don't Spoil the Beautiful Earth.* Movie. DIR: Yasuyuki Mori. SCR: Koji Takahashi. DES: N/C. ANI: Masami Furukawa. MUS: N/C. PRD: Asmik. 28 mins.

A little girl called Nana learns about how to keep Earth safe from pollution. Based on a 1985 British collection of poems and pictures on ecological themes by children from 70 different countries that was edited by Helen Exley.

CRY OF THE DRAGON

1988. JPN: *Nageki no Ryu.* Video. DIR: Tetsu Dezaki. SCR: Kazumi Koide. DES: Keizo Shimizu. ANI: Keizo Shimizu. MUS: N/C. PRD: Gainax, Magic Bus. 45 mins. x 4 eps.

Ryu ("Dragon") is a master of mahjong who becomes embroiled in gangland gambling and murders in eastern Japan. Selling over two million copies after it was serialized in *Modern Mahjong* magazine, *Cry of the Dragon* made creator Junichi Nojo one of the two most successful manga creators of the 1980s; the other, Katsuhiro Otomo, also had a manga turned into an anime that year—AKIRA. The anime adaptation was the first show to portray mahjong games onscreen, a task no doubt made less boring by the murder subplots.

CRYING FREEMAN *

1989. Video. DIR: Daisuke Nishio, Shigenori Yamauchi. SCR: Higashi Shimizu, Ryunosuke Ono. DES: Ryoichi Ikegami. ANI: Koichi Arai, Satoshi Urushihara. MUS: Hiroaki Yoshino. PRD: Toei. 45 mins. x 6 eps.

Yo Hinomura is an internationally acclaimed potter, until he becomes involved with the 108 Dragons crime syndicate, gets brainwashed, and is turned into the assassin Crying Freeman. When the lonely Emu Hino witnesses one of his missions, he is sent to terminate her, but she seduces him, and the two eventually devote their lives to the 108 Dragons. Successive episodes featured a number of rivals and evil syndicates trying to oust Yo, including the 108 Dragons' own Bayasan, the granddaughter of a former leader. Yo fights off an African syndicate, while Emu, who acclimates rather well to life as a gang member after giving up being a virginal artist, takes on a Chinese criminal hellhole. Freeman's old enemies return to haunt him in the fourth episode (part five in the U.K.), with crooked cop Nitta and former moll Kimie teaming up with a professional wrestler to help replace Yo with a brainwashed cultist. The fifth episode featured a sex-starved female gang leader kidnapping a rival boss's family in order to make Yo become her sex slave. The final part, in which Yo defeats yet another rival, this time from the Russian syndicate, received such heavy cuts in the U.K. that it and chapter four were released on a single tape.

Based on the 1986 manga in *Big Comic Spirits* by **Mad Bull 34**'s Kazuo Koike and **Sanctuary**'s Ryoichi Ikegami, *Crying Freeman* comes in a passable dub from Streamline Pictures, and another, from Manga Video, which comes complete with deeply offensive phony Chinese accents. Like Christophe Gans' later live-action remake starring Mark Dacascos, the animated series suffered from being overly faithful to the original. Effort expended in recreating the original artwork and characters might have been better spent on actual animation, which had degenerated to extremely cheap levels by the final installments; ironic considering that **Plastic Little**'s Urushihara was one of the talented staff. In addition to Gans' 1997 remake, there was an unofficial Chinese version directed by Clarence Ford and released as *Dragon From Russia* (1991). **LNV**

CRYSTAL TRIANGLE *
1987. JPN: *Kindan no Mokushiroku Crystal Triangle*. AKA: *Forbidden Revelation: Crystal Triangle*. Video. DIR: Seiji Okuda. SCR: Junji Takegami. DES: Kazuko Tadano, Toyoo Ashida. ANI: Kazuko Tadano. MUS: Osamu Totsuka. PRD: Animate Film. 86 mins.
Dr. Koichiro Kamishiro, along with assistants Mina and Hisao and priestess Miyabi, is searching for "messages from God"—coded messages written on the titular crystals, relics of the distant past. However, other powers are searching for these ancient artifacts, and the plucky archaeologists must fight the CIA (pretty blonde Juno Cassidy), the KGB (Rasputin's grandson Grigori Efemovich), and the yakuza (sword-wielding gangster Genji) for the crystals in a battle that takes them across the Middle and Far East to the deep north of Japan. As with the later **Spriggan**, these ancient messages turn out to be connected to a crashed alien spaceship and ecological catastrophe, as the rogue star Nemesis, whose last passing destroyed the dinosaurs, is returning to wreak more havoc, and the messages contain information on how to survive it.

CUBITUS
1988. JPN: *Dondon Domeru and Ron*. TV series. DIR: Hiroshi Sasagawa, Keiichiro Mochizuki, Hidehito Ueda, Yukio Okazaki, Junichi Sakata. SCR: Kaoru Toshima. DES: Dupa. ANI: Michiru Suzuki, Shinnosuke Mina. MUS: Takanori Arisawa. PRD: Telescreen, TV Tokyo. 25 mins. x 104 eps.
Ron is an inventor who loves to tinker around with machines. His loyal friend and companion is Domeru (Cubitus), a talking dog who helps him in trying out his many new inventions, much to the annoyance of Cherry, the pretty girl next door, her husband, Beatrik, and their cat, Blacky.

In 1968, the Dutch artist "Dupa" created a new character for *Tintin* magazine—a fat white dog that looked like a ball of hair with paws. This kindly mutt became his most successful creation

(others included a truck driver who fell in love with a crate) and is so famous in his native Netherlands that the dog even has his own postage stamp. Note: Dupa's European publishers claim that the *Cubitus* series was released in the U.S., but we can find no record of its broadcast under this title.

CUSTOM SLAVE *
2001. JPN: *Custom Dorei: Sayoko no Sho*. AKA: *Sayoko's Chapter*. Video. DIR: Tomouchi Shishido. SCR: Hangetsu Mitamura. DES: Yoko Sanri. ANI: Saburo Nippori. MUS: N/C. PRD: Mint House, Kiss, Green Bunny. 30 mins.
To all appearances, Arisugawa Academy is a high-class girls' school. But principal Hiroaki Takahashi uses the school as a form of training camp: he runs a cabal that provides young sexual partners for members of the government—a kind of state-sponsored brothel. Student Sayoko Musky is selected for special training by Takahashi and becomes a double agent—demure schoolgirl by day, sex slave by night. Also released in a U.S. box set with **School of Bondage** and **Living Sex Toy Delivery**. There have been two sequels to the original *Custom Slave* game, so more anime may be forthcoming. **LNV**

CUTEY HONEY *
1973. TV series, video. DIR: Tomoharu Katsumata, Masamune Ochiai, Hiroshi Shidara, Takeshi Shirato. SCR: Masaki Tsuji, Keisuke Fujikawa, Susumu Takahisa. DES: Shingo Araki. ANI: Shingo Araki, Kazuo Komatsubara, Masamune Ochiai, Satoshi Kamimiya. MUS: Takeo Watanabe. PRD: Toei, Dynamic Planning, NET. 25 mins. x 25 eps. (TV), 30 mins. x 8 eps. (v), 25 mins. x 39 eps. (TV).
Based on a short-lived *Shonen Champion* manga from **Kekko Kamen**–creator Go Nagai, the breast-fixated *Cutey Honey* was animated for TV before its rookie year in manga was over. In a pastiche of **Astro Boy**, a bereaved professor creates an android facsimile of his murdered daughter, implanting a superpowerful device into her ample

bosom. The "airborne element solidifi-er" can reassemble matter in the vicin-ity, effectively giving Honey anything she needs to help her in her fight to save the world—including specialized bodies such as the Hurricane Honey and Flash Honey. It also ensures that all her clothes disappear every time she transforms, a controversial innova-tion at the time, now commonplace in shows such as SAILOR MOON. Her enemy in the original TV series is Panther Zora, leader of the all-female Panther Claw crime syndicate.

The immense success of the TV series rejuvenated the manga, allow-ing this very male appreciation of the female form to appear in girls' magazines such as *Nakayoshi*, and titles for younger readers such as *Happy Zoo*. Honey would return in 1994 for *New CH Flash*, directed by Yasuchika Nagaoka and released straight to video. With new designs by Osamu Kasai, the new series picked up where the TV series left off, with Honey returning after a decade to discover that Panther Zora and her accomplice, Dolmeck, are still menacing civilization. She also gains an entire family of assistants, the Hayami clan, whose son, Chohei, provides viewer identification, while granddad Denbai provides heavy violence. Other Go Nagai characters put in cameo appearances, including DEVILMAN Akira as a wrestler, alongside real-life women's wrestling stars Cuty Suzuki and Mayumi Ozaki.

As the video series was translated, bringing Cutey to the West for the first time, the character's popularity in Japan peaked with a new TV series. The same year saw a *CH Flash* movie, an all-new story in which Honey battled Panther Claw for the key to an ancient treasure (the posters boasting that there would be "all-new transformation scenes," too) and two digest videos consisting of highlights—one, *Birth of Love's Warrior CH*, retelling her origin story, and the other, *Battle for W Honey Destiny* repeating the season-two finale. In 2001, it was announced that the character would return in a fully 3-D

Cutey Honey

© 1996 GO NAGAI/DYNAMIC PLANNING/TOEI VIDEO CO., LTD.

CG animated video directed by Hiroyu-ki Kitakubo. **LNV**

CUTTER'S STORY
1998. JPN: *Cutter-kun Monogatari.* Movie. DIR: Kenji Yoshida. SCR: Kenji Yoshida, Saburo Kaniguchi. DES: Tameo Ogawa, Yasuhiro Matsumura. ANI: Hajime Matsuzaki. MUS: Toshiyuki Wata-nabe. PRD: Toei, Nabe, Aubec. 75 mins. "Dreams and adventure" await in this movie funded by the state coffers of Yamaguchi Prefecture, although how the local government thought it was helping its taxpayers by producing this fictional tale about a giant genetically engineered, peach-colored pelican at the local zoo, who can say?

CYBER CITY OEDO 808 *
1990. Video. DIR: Yoshiaki Kawajiri. SCR: Akinori Endo. DES: Yoshiaki Kawajiri, Takashi Watanabe, Hiroshi Hamazaki, Masami Kosone. ANI: Hiroshi Hamaza-ki. MUS: Yasunori Honda, Kazz Toyama. PRD: Madhouse. 45 mins. x 3 eps. Three loosely linked tales of a cyber-punk stripe, caught up in the post-AKIRA popularity of SF futures. In the year 2808, three criminals are offered conditional release. Even though they have each stacked up several life sen-tences, they may work off their terms by performing secret missions against the clock. If the mission succeeds, years are taken off their sentences. If the mission fails or they try to escape, the explosive collars around their necks will take their heads off.

For the first mission, *Virtual Death* (*Ancient Memory* in the original), tough-guy Sengoku must fight his way into the Kurokawa Tower, a self-aware sky-scraper, to discover who is hacking into its systems. Presaging the first PATLABOR movie, he discovers that the "hacker" is in fact the original programmer, who has long since departed from this world. More hackery abounds in *Psychic Trooper*, in which bespectacled computer expert Goggle must outwit a cybernetic soldier while fighting his hidden feelings for an old flame who once betrayed him. The final episode, *Bloodlust* (originally *Crimson Medium*), focuses on Benten, the androgynous dandy who must track down a vam-pire who is using a beautiful android to entice young victims into his lair. The final showdown, in a cryogenic chamber (i.e., coffin) at the top of a space elevator, neatly encapsulates the old/new culture clash of the series. The pretty-boy cross-dresser Benten is inspired by a popular character from the 19th century, the protagonist of the kabuki play *Benten the Thief.* Since Sengoku's name means literally "civil war," the characters all carry *jitte* parrying weapons modeled on those used by samurai-era police, and the titular 808 recalls the **808 DISTRICTS** of old Edo (Tokyo), we can assume that the anime was originally intended as an SF pastiche of old stories (possibly in the style of **SAMURAI GOLD**), which never quite got off the ground. It is just one of several superior video serials from creator Juzo Mutsuki, whose **PHANTOM QUEST CORP** and **DEVIL HUNTER YOHKO** were similarly luckless in their quest for TV remakes. **CNV**

CYBER SIX *

1999. TV series. DIR: Hiroyuki Aoyama, Toshihiko Masuda, Atsuko Tanaka, Nobuo Tomizawa, Kazuhide Tomonaga. SCR: N/C. DES: Keiichi Takiguchi. ANI: Nobuo Tomizawa. MUS: Robbi Finkel. PRD: TMS, NOA, Telecom, Kid's Station. 25 mins. x 13 eps.

Cyber Six is one of many genetically engineered warriors created during World War II by the German scientist Von Reichter. The titular heroine is the only one to escape alive when Reichter destroys his creations. She hides out in the city of Meridiana, where she disguises herself as the mild-mannered *male* librarian Adrian Seidelman during the day, donning a skintight catsuit to leap across the rooftops at night. She is accompanied by Data Seven, formerly warrior Cyber 29, who was mortally wounded and whose brain was transplanted into a large black panther. Meanwhile, Reichter sends Jose, a child clone of himself, to track down and destroy his errant creation. Jose does so with an army of mutants, whose green "substance" (not blood, the producers assured U.S. networks!) Cyber Six must drink to stay alive. As with any superheroes worth their salt, there are identity crises back in the real world, with Adrian's work buddy Lucas lusting after the female form of Cyber Six, not realizing that he shares an office

with her alter ego, and schoolgirl Lori developing a crush on Adrian, not realizing that "he" is a she.

This international coproduction was based on the Argentinian comic written by Carlos Trillo and drawn by Carlos Meglia, but seems, however coincidentally, to be a belated cross between **BIG X**, **CYBORG 009,** and *Batman,* with a little existential musing of the **GHOST IN THE SHELL** variety thrown in for good measure. One of the rare anime, like **ALEXANDER,** that premiered abroad—it was not shown in Japan until late in 2000.

CYBERFORMULA GPX

1991. JPN: *Shin Seiki [New Century] GPX Cyber Formula Future Grand Prix.* TV series, video. DIR: Mitsuo Fukuda, Satoshi Nishimura. SCR: Hiroyuki Hoshiyama, Tsunehisa Ito, Michiru Shimada. DES: Mutsumi Inomata, Takahiro Yoshimatsu. ANI: Takahiro Yoshimatsu, Atsushi Aono. MUS: Yuki Otani. PRD: Sunrise, Nippon TV. 25 mins. x 37 eps. (TV), 30 mins. x 30 eps. (v).

In the year 2016, 14-year-old Hayato Kazami enters the Cyberformula Grand Prix, in which superpowered, super-advanced cars race to determine the best team in the world. He drives a computerized car designed by his father, in a high-concept that takes the "dad's robot" formula of other Sunrise shows and puts it on wheels.

After qualifying in local championships in Fujioka and Niseko, Hayato and his teammates get to travel the world. Mixing local color (e.g. Grand Canyon, Peru) with an off-track romance developing in exotic locations (Peru, Brazil), the show also incorporates sporting rivalry and derring-do. By the time the world tour reaches Canada and England, Hayato's rivals are well-established characters in their own right, such as the cold British racer Knight Schumacher and the Aryan tactician Karl Richter von Randall. After a race in Kenya, the crew heads into the home stretch for a lightning-fast series of races in Spain, Germany, and Japan—in succession

rapid enough to imply that the TV series was canceled early.

As with the soccer antics of **CAPTAIN TSUBASA**, the sporting angle allows for regular resets of the characters' positions. The following year, Hayato reenters the championships to retain his crown in the six-part video series *CF 11 (Double One),* driving a car designed by the beautiful blonde foreigner Claire Fortran. As romance develops between Hayato and Asuka Sugo, the daughter of his team's rich backer, he beats Schumacher and races to a "double-win" in his "double one" car in the "11th" annual championship in a highly improbable set of numerological coincidences.

The situation changes for Hayato's third championship in the eight-part *CF Zero* (1994), when an accident loses him a race *and* fiancée Asuka, who walks out on the injured driver. Though she eventually returns, Hayato must best Japanese rival Shinjo both on and off the track. This was soon followed by the eight-part *CF Saga* (1996), in which Alzard, an android driver, defeats both Shinjo and Hayato's best friend, the green-haired Bleed Kaga. While Asuka frantically searches behind the scenes for Alzard's weak spot, rival teams set traps off the race track to keep Hayato from even trying. Needless to say, he wins in the end, and a 19-year-old Hayato, who has grown up along with his target audience, gets behind the wheel once more for eight more episodes in *CF Sin* (1998), though this most recent outing focused more on his teammate Bleed.

CYBERNETICS GUARDIAN *

1989. JPN: *Seijuki Cyguard.* AKA: *Holy Beast Machine Cyguard.* Video. DIR: Koichi Ohata. SCR: Mutsumi Sanjo. DES: Atsushi Yamagata. ANI: Jun Okuda. MUS: Norimasa Yamanaka. PRD: AIC. 45 mins.

Top brains at the future city of Cyberwood attempt to come up with a solution to Cancer, the aptly named slum district. The Cybernetic Guardian unit is sent to patrol the streets, unaware that the secret Doldo Brethren organization is engaged in an attempt to bring back the death-god Saldor by implanting young men with the "seeds" to become hosts for the second coming. One such unwitting host is Cyguard technician John Stalker, whose abduction leads chief scientist Leyla (Laia in the original) Rosetta to risk everything to save him.

A directorial debut for GENOCYBER's Ohata, this claustrophobic horror tale suddenly widens out at the end for a monstrous showdown in the tradition of the GUYVER series. ⓁⓃⓋ

CYBORG 009 *

1966. Movie, TV series. DIR: Yugo Serikawa, Ryosuke Takahashi, Saburo Sakamoto. SCR: Yugo Serikawa, Masaki Tsuji, Akiyoshi Sakai, Masaaki Sakurai. DES: Shotaro Ishinomori. ANI: Kazuhiro Yamada. MUS: Daiichiro Kosugi. PRD: Toei, Sunrise, NET. 64 mins., 60 mins., 25 mins. x 26 eps. (b/w), 25 mins. x 50 eps. (color), 130 mins. World-class sprinter Joe Shimamura is seriously injured in an accident and taken away by the Black Ghost, an agent of the sinister Merchants of Death, who intend to take over the world. The kind-hearted Professor Gilmore saves his life, and in so doing, turns him into the ninth of a series of cyborg warriors that were originally designed to carry out the Merchants' bidding all over the world but are now dedicated to stopping them at all costs.

Marrying ASTRO BOY to the James Bond movies, but also far ahead of *The Six Million Dollar Man* and *X-Men*, Shotaro Ishinomori's 1964 *Cyborg 009* manga in *Shonen Sunday* was one of the original Cold War warriors—he was

even succeeded in 1967 by the manga adventures of a female cyborg called *One of 009*. The debut of the animated version was swiftly followed by another short feature film, *C009: Kaiju Wars* (1967). Here, the Black Ghost uses a resurrected plesiosaur to terrorize the world, while Joe must fight spy-cyborg 0010 and the newest recruit, Plus Minus (0011).

The TV series followed in 1968, introducing many other enemies and allies, including 006, who runs a Chinese restaurant, and the wisecracking 007. In addition to the superfast Joe, each of the other cyborgs possesses one special talent, including telepathy, underwater breathing, flight, superhuman strength, the ability to breathe fire, and psychokinesis. The story was revived in 1979 for a color series, reintroducing the characters for a new audience, directed by VOTOMS' Takahashi and adapting previously unused story lines from the original, such as 009's adventures in space and the "Neo Black Ghost" chapters.

Much of the same crew stayed on for the 1980 movie to celebrate Ishinomori's 25th anniversary in manga publishing. *C009: Legend of the Super Galaxy* (aka *Defenders of the Vortex*) was directed by Masayuki Akehi and is the only part of the 009 franchise available in English. Featuring the tragic death of 004 (who keeps weapons stashed all over his body), the 130-minute color feature pitted Joe's gang against the evil Zoa, who intends to use a space vortex to control the world. *Star Wars* comic author Jeff Segal contributed to Ryuzo Nakanishi's script, though his involvement was deviously hyped in Japan as that of "the writer of *Star Wars*."

The series was revived in 2001 on TV Tokyo as *Cyborg 009: The Cyborg Soldier*, a 52-episode remake under the directorship of Atsushi Kawagoe.

CYBOT ROBOTCHI

1983. TV series. DIR: Kazuyuki Okaseko. SCR: Tomohiro Ando, Hideki Sonoda. DES: Dynamic Pro. ANI: Takao Suzuki. MUS: N/C. PRD: Dynamic Planning, Knack, TV Tokyo. 25 mins. x 39 eps.

Professor Deco creates Robotchi, an android with a TV set in his stomach. With a number of the other robots created by the professor, he causes havoc for the evil Dr. Highbrow, in this lighthearted comedy from GETTER ROBO–creator Ken Ishikawa and scenarist Tomohiro Ando.

CYBUSTER *

1999. AKA: *Saibuster, Psibuster*. TV series. DIR: Hidehito Ueda. SCR: Hisayuki Toriumi. DES: Takeshi Ito, Yasuhiro Moriki. ANI: N/C. MUS: N/C. PRD: N/C. 25 mins.

In the year 2040, a terrible earthquake in Tokyo shatters time as well as space, causing the titular giant robot to appear from an alternate world. Ken Ando and love-interest Mizuki are great friends who are pulled apart by the events around them and then thrown into the company of the Terran Environmental Protection Agency. Eventually they become two of the ten chosen special operatives charged with investigating the earthquake and its aftermath—the dark shadows that engulf Tokyo's Shinjuku district. Based on a popular computer simulation game, this is one of the stragglers in the rush to imitate EVANGELION.

D

D-1 DEVASTATOR

1992. Video. DIR: Tetsu Isami. SCR: Masashi Sogo. DES: Nasatomi, Masami Obari, Yukiji Kaoru. ANI: Masaki Taihei. MUS: N/C. PRD: Dynamic. 50 mins.

A manga serialized in *Ascii Comics* by "Sphios Lab" and Toshi Yoshida provided the basis for this one-shot anime, in which Ryu, a young boy, must pilot the titular Devastator to defend the planet from the invading Varsus warriors.

D3 SERIES *

2001. Movie. DIR: Shigenori Kumai, Takashi Kondo, Yuji Moriyama, Hotaru Kawakami et al. SCR: Tamiyo Mori, Runa Kozuki. DES: Akinori Kano, Konomi Noguchi. ANI: Sakurako Kurai. MUS: N/C. PRD: D3. 30 mins. x 2 eps. (*Collector*), 30 mins. x 2 eps. (*Concerto*), 30 mins. x 7 eps. (*Ninja*), 30 mins. (*Be Lifesized*), 25 mins. x 4 eps. (*Yosho*), N/A (*Family System*), N/A (*Love Doll*), 30 mins. x 6 eps. (*Discipline*), 30 mins. x 3 eps. (*Yakin Byoto 2*), 30 mins. x 5 eps. (*Discode*), 10 mins. x 3 eps. (*Inbo*), 10 mins. x 3 eps. (*Inko*), 30 mins. (*Let's Do It With Sister*).

Incorporating the White Bear label, D3 is another Japanese production company specializing in erotica. Its titles have not been so quick to make it to the American market. The first release, *Collector* (2001), presented three stories in an anthology—*Shadow Jail: Sex Comfort Slaves* (*Inro Aiido*), *Desire to Touch* (*Shuyoku*), and *Red Snow* (*Akai Yuki*), this last perhaps a reference to the first of the

Lolita Anime. Later releases have capitalized on the trend for self-referentiality within fandom, such as *Concerto* (2001, *Shirabe Concerto*), which combines an adaptation of a best-selling game with a string of excuses for dressing up and role-playing. The story is presented as a series of rehearsals, auditions, and performances in the style of **Mask of Glass**, in which three pretty young actresses are obliged to don costumes and perform sex acts as part of their "training." The costumes, however, are designed to evoke well-known characters from mainstream shows, in the same risqué fashion employed in the earlier **Elven Bride**. Similar fan-oriented high jinks arrived in *Be Lifesized My Lover* (2001, *Toshindai My Lovers: Minami vs. Mecha Minami*), a pastiche of the warrior-girlfriend tales of **Maho-romatic** and **Saikano**, in which a lonely, downtrodden boy suddenly gains a feisty roommate who defends the world from danger, whose sister enjoys dressing up (once again) in costumes, and both of whom enjoy S/M roleplay. The Japanese press release assures us that it is "full of swinging tits." The company's most successful franchise, however, has been **Ninja** (also 2001), the erotic tale that mixes both martial and marital arts—though only the first episode is credited to "D3," while later installments were produced by Onmitsu-do/Obtain. The same period also saw the *Yosho* (*Phantom Whispers*) series, released in the American market

as *Midnight Strike Force*, in which a secret cult of lesbian nurses hopes to bring about the resurrection of their satanic founder through experiments at a Tokyo hospital.

D3's sales pitches mix true anime and DVD games with impunity, the company's next releases being two interactive erotica, which took the plotlines of text-based games and added animated inserts. In the first, *Family System* (2002, *Ryojoku: Kazoku System*), a nameless man is hired to play a role in a fake family, and told he can do anything he likes except murder. He is placed in a series of situations in which he is made to interact with his fake family and, in a nod to the past-oriented setups of modern romance, a series of fake "childhood friends." He soon forgets that he is living a lie, thereby ensuring that the inappropriate feelings he develops for the girl playing his sister are tinged with thoughts of incest, in a story that seems partly inspired by *The Truman Show* (1998) and the Japanese live-action TV series *Transparent* (*DE). The second, *Love Doll* (*Ai Doll*, 2002), has a title that might also be translated as *Slave to Love*, and is described by company press documents as a "pure love rape simulation game."

After the success of **Bible Black** (not a D3 anime), D3 picked up the rights to release an anime adaptation of *Discipline: Record of a Crusade*, a 2002 release from the same company, Active Soft. The anime version, just plain *Discipline*

(2004) is another of D3's domestic successes, as demonstrated by its much longer episode count. In it, Japanese teenager Takuro Hayami cannot believe his luck when he is transferred to Saint Arcadia School, and finds his dorm is full of nubile coeds. He soon develops a crush on the house mistress Saori Otokawa (compare to **Maison Ikkoku**), although the other girls, particularly the evil Morimoto sisters, have realized that Hayami possesses a secret "sex power"—as in **Masquerade**, they want this energy for themselves and getting it will require a number of sex scenes. Younger sister Reona Morimoto and her associates at the Social Club begin a concerted effort to seduce Hayami, hoping to monopolize his sexual attentions. However, other factions at the school want Hayami for themselves, leading in later episodes to approaches from the Tennis Club and Swimming Club. Deciding to use blackmail to ensure Hayami's availability, the Morimoto sisters kidnap and abuse Miss Otokawa. Before long, the girls are busily abusing and molesting each other in a series of bondage-based power games, the humiliations and retributions of schoolgirl one-upmanship, refashioned here for pornographic purposes. With Reona clamped into a chastity belt, an order is issued that there shall be no sex permitted in the school—a directive that is flouted with predictable speed, in a series of sex-based battles in which young ladies gamely struggle not to enjoy themselves. The final episodes lift traditions not from European school-days stories such as **Twins at St. Clare's**, but instead from Japanese conspiracy theory school dramas such as the live-action *School in Peril* (*DE), revealing that the school's sinister culture of rape and revenge is actually part of a secret project (compare to **Bible Black**), and one that, it appears, can only be thwarted by a mass orgy.

The D3 company also tried to muscle in on the success of another computer game franchise, **Night Shift Nurses** in the rival **Discovery Series**.

In a really, really desperate attempt to avoid getting confused, we have called this off-shoot series by its Japanese title, *Yakin Byoto 2* (2004), as distinguished from the *NSN* title used for the Discovery incarnation. In it, the renowned Doctor Kuwabara finds himself unable to forget his earlier love for nurse Ren Nanase. Kuwabara tracks her from town to town until he finally finds her. However, in the intervening time, she has become the subject of sexual experiments by an evil researcher at Saint Juliana's hospital. Disappointed at the change in her previously virginal character, Kuwabara decides to avenge his hurt feelings on the human race at large by abusing and raping a number of nurses. The same year saw *Discode: Abnormal Eros* (*Discode: Ijo Seiai*) in which attractive girl Futaba turns out to have a penis as well. Using terms that parody the "girl with a boy's heart" of **Princess Knight**, *Discode* posits a schoolgirl drama not unlike that of *Discipline*, in which a lone "male" figure finds himself surrounded by adoring girls. Futaba, however, must continually evade discovery, leading to a series of setups in which s/he must buy the silence of certain girls by having sex with them—a far cry from the cross-dressing and gender switching of **El Hazard** and **Ranma** 1/2, also based on an erotic computer game. Later episodes find Futaba assaulted by boys, in a rare introduction of the tropes of gay pornography into what is purportedly a "straight" series.

The D3 company tried a new and interesting direction with *Lustful Mother* (2005, *Inbo*) and *Lustful Sister* (2005, *Inko*). Featuring the seduction of teenage Masaru by an older woman, and the trials of Masaru's would-be girlfriend as she enjoys a sexual relationship with the manager of the restaurant where she used to work, the twin serials notably shared cast members, making a virtue out of the limited setups of pornography by, for example, using protagonist Masaru for tales both of his seduction by older women and of high school romance. While, in essence,

the show merely runs picaresque encounters in parallel instead of in series, its dual title release represents an intriguing marketing decision. The year was rounded off with the release of **Let's Do It with Sister**, for which see its separate entry. The company's first release of 2006 was the self-explanatory *Cleavage*. **LNV**

D4 PRINCESS

1999. TV series. DIR: Yasunori Ide. SCR: Yasunori Ide. DES: Shinji Ochi. ANI: Tatsuo Iwata. MUS: Kenji Kawai. PRD: Canyon, Domu, WOWOW. 10 mins. x 24 eps.
Based on Shotaro Harada's manga, serialized in *Dengeki Daio*, in which princess Doris Rurido turns up at a school famed for its fighting "Panzer League" and soon becomes its leader through the use of the transforming drill on her arm. The original short episodes, screened as part of the satellite channel WOWOW's *Anime Complex II* anthology show, were eventually compiled into four videos for retail release.

D.I.C.E. *

2004. JPN: *Dinobreaker*. AKA: *DNA Integrated Cybernetic Enterprises*. TV series. DIR: Jun Kamiya. SCR: Hiro Masaki, Jun Kamiya, Kenichi Yamada, Kenichi Araki, Masahiko Shiraishi, Ryu Tamura, Yoshio Kato. DES: Mitsuru Ishihara, Tsuyoshi Nonaka. ANI: Jun Takahashi, Naoyoshi Kusaka, Shin Katagai. MUS: Masato Miyazawa. PRD: Bandai, Xebec. 25 mins. x 26 eps.
Jet Siegel is the predictably "hotheaded" pilot of the Motoraptor, one of more than half a dozen vehicles that form part of the F-99 platoon of DNA Integrated Cybernetic Enterprises, a quasi-military organization that polices criminal activity in the Sarbylion galaxy. D.I.C.E. F-99 is the only group staffed wholly by children, who relish the chance to ride in their Dinobraker vehicles, which, as if you hadn't guessed, can transform into a robotic dinosaur mode like **Zoids**. A series of menaces of the week soon ensues, from planets at risk of explosion to attacks

by space pirates led by the mysterious Shadow Knight—whose true identity will not come as the remotest surprise to anyone who has seen Speed Racer. Later episodes introduce a darker sub-plot in which corrupt higher officials are found to be planning an escape to the forbidden planet of Heron, where they hope to find the secret of eternal life. Jet and friends oppose them, only to find themselves branded as traitors and forced to take on the amassed forces of their former allies, in the style of Dancougar. Despite looking to all intents and purposes like yet another anime series, *D.I.C.E.* was actually the first co-production to be initiated by Bandai America with the American audience in mind—the show premiered on U.S. TV before it was seen in Japan.

DA CAPO

2003. JPN: *D.C.—Da Capo*. TV series. DIR: Nagisa Miyazaki, Shinji Takago. SCR: Katsumi Hasegawa, Katsumi Terato, Kenichiro Katsura, Mamiko Ikeda, Masaharu Amiya, Masashi Suzuki, Nagisa Miyazaki, Yuji Moriyama. DES: Shinobu Tagashira, Naru Nanao. ANI: N/C. MUS: Hikaru Nanase, Yugo Sugano. PRD: Circus, Feel, Zecx, Chiba TV, TV Kanagawa. 24 mins. x 26 eps. (TV1), 24 mins. x 26 eps. (TV2). Junichi Asakura lives with his stepsister Nemu on the magical, crescent-shaped island of Hatsune, where the cherry trees are in bloom all year around. Like many on Hatsune, Junichi has limited magical powers—in his case, he can conjure candy out of thin air and see the dreams of others. But there are also more mundane concerns—on the night before he begins his senior year at Hatsune's high school, Junichi dreams that a girl under a cherry tree announces that she is his returning sister. The same girl arrives as a transfer student the following day, and he recognizes her as his cousin, Sakura, back after six years in America looking exactly the same as when she left, and, in the eyes of some of the other girls in Junichi's class, a little overfamiliar toward him.

Based on a PS2 game with a manga out the same year, *DC* is yet another cookie-cutter tale of a teenage guy who's just irresistible to girls, living in a Maison Ikkoku group of people with various strange talents and quirks, falling into absurd and improbable romantic situations complicated by Love Hina promises made in childhood, attracting women wherever he goes. However, it also imparts a fairy-tale quality to the elegiac nature of many high school dramas. School days are often presented as a wondrous dreamtime in anime, though it is difficult to tell whether this is a cynical exercise or a heartfelt belief on the part of animators—see Mahoromatic. *DC* certainly works hard to imbue the end of childhood with literal magic: in an echo of Kiki's Delivery Service and My Neighbor Totoro, the students' sense of magic wanes as they age, as do the blossoms on the supposedly eternal cherry trees.

DC Second Season, based in part on the second PS2 game *DC Plus Communication*, picks up two years later, when Hatsune Island's cherry trees have lost their magical properties and merely bloom each spring. Junichi gains a new love interest when young Aisia arrives hoping to learn magic from his grandmother. When he reveals that his grandmother is dead, she mistakenly believes that he can teach her but soon realizes her mistake, although she stays around in order to determine what has gone wrong with the trees.

DAA! DAA! DAA!

2000. TV series. DIR: Hiroaki Sakurai. SCR: Tomoko Konparu, Shingo Arakawa. DES: Masayuki Onchi. ANI: Ryoichi Oki. MUS: Toshio Masuda. PRD: JC Staff, NHK2. 25 mins. x 78 eps. When her mother qualifies as an astronaut and must travel abroad with her scientist father, Miu is sent to live with her uncle in an old temple. Forced to share a dwelling with her handsome classmate Kanata, Miu's embarrassment is compounded when the "couple" is "adopted" by an alien baby, Ru. The reluctant foster parents must

cope with a baby who can levitate and with the additional annoyance of their child's alien protector, Wannya.

Based on Mika Kawamura's manga in *Nakayoshi* magazine, this comedy combines the odd-couple romance of His and Her Circumstances with an SF excuse for playing mommies and daddies straight out of Mama's A Fourth Grader.

DADDY LONG-LEGS

1979. JPN: *Ashinaga Ojisan*. TV special. DIR: Masakazu Higuchi. SCR: Akira Miyazaki. DES: Shinichi Tsuji. ANI: Shinichi Tsuji. MUS: Makoto Kawaguchi. PRD: Herald Enterprise, Tatsunoko Pro, Fuji TV. 75 mins. (TVm), 25 mins. x 40 eps. (TV).
When she turns 18, the stories Judy Abbot publishes about her life in the orphanage secure her a place at university. She writes many letters to her mysterious benefactor "Daddy Long-Legs" unaware that he is Jervis Pendleton III, an adoring millionaire who has already met her (and fallen in love with her) in disguise. This musical one-shot anime is only the most recent adaptation of Jean Webster's 1912 children's book—Hollywood movies of the same story include one with Mary Pickford as Judy (1919), Janet Gaynor taking the role in 1931, and a 1955 version with Leslie Caron and Fred Astaire. There is also a Dutch adaptation, *Vadertje Langbeen* (1938), but this inversion of Cinderella, in which an unusual girl seeks a "normal life" (with a millionaire, of course), was also immensely influential in Japan's girls' manga market, where it inspired Candy Candy and its many imitators. The story was remade by Kazuyoshi Yokota as a World Masterpiece Theater anime TV series, *My Daddy Long-Legs* (1990, *Watashi no Ashinaga Ojisan*), featuring new character designs by Shuichi Seki. Also see Video Picture Book.

DAGGER OF KAMUI *

1985. JPN: *Kamui no Ken*. AKA: *Blade of Kamui*. Movie. DIR: Rintaro, Susumu Ishizaki. SCR: Mori Masaki. DES: Murano

Moriyoshi. ANI: Atsuo Noda, Kyoko Matsuhara, Yoshiaki Kawajiri, Koji Morimoto, Osamu Nabeshima, Yasuomi Umezu. MUS: Ryudo Uzaki, Eitetsu Hayashi. PRD: Algos, Madhouse. 132 mins.

Jiro, a foundling boy, loses his adoptive parents to an assassin. Avenging their death by murdering a one-armed man, he falls in with the priest Tenkai, who trains him in the black arts of the ninja. Learning that the one-armed man was really his true father, a distraught Kamui searches for his true mother, an Ainu princess. He also goes in search of Captain Kidd's treasure in order to take from Tenkai the only thing that he values. Tenkai wishes to use the treasure to overthrow the antiisolationists and close Japan once more to the outside world—the action takes place just before the Meiji Restoration that would throw Japan open once and for all. Jiro's quest takes him all the way to the American West, with time out for a brief meeting with TOM SAWYER–creator Mark Twain, where he is saved by a defecting servant of Tenkai's (who turns out to be his long-lost sister) before returning to exact revenge for all his family.

This Kamui is no relation to Sanpei Shirato's MANUAL OF NINJA MARTIAL ARTS; it was based on a series of novels by *Legend of the Paper Spaceship*–author Tetsu Yano, who was also Robert Heinlein's Japanese translator. Though not one of his best works, *Dagger of Kamui* contains much of the clash of old and new that distinguishes his writings—the idea of foreign assistance in sending Japan back into the past would be reused by animator Kawajiri in NINJA SCROLL. *Blade of Kamui*, an earlier U.S. dub of the movie, rewrites the plot completely, claiming that it is set on an alien world, where Kamui's dagger is a "powerful weapon [that] controls the future of the universe." ●NV

DAGON

1988. JPN: *Ikinari Dagon*. TV series. DIR: Kazuyoshi Yokota. SCR: Nobuyuki Fujimoto. DES: Noboru Takano. ANI: Tetsuya Ishikawa. MUS: Kazunori Ishida. PRD: Nippon Animation, TV Asahi. 25 mins. x 12 eps.

Dagon is the pilot of the starship Digital whose daughter, Meryl, is always getting into trouble. In the middle of an investigation, a shipboard accident causes the Digital to crash-land on a planet ruled by a race of giants called the Sapiens (i.e., Earth). Dagon and his crew, however, are helped by the bee doctor Marilyn, Jisamu the cockroach, Floppy the spider, and Skipper the ant. They return the favor by saving Marilyn from Geppo the evil frog. This short-lived anime recalls the Fleischer brothers' *Mr. Bug Goes to Town* (1941, aka *Hoppity Goes to Town*) and features the contribution of non-Japanese creators Dennis Bond and Ken Morton.

DAIAKUJI: XENA BUSTER *

2003. Video. DIR: Makoto Sokuza. SCR: Yoshio Takao. DES: Masashi Kojima. ANI: Masashi Kojima. MUS: N/C. PRD: Alice Soft, Green Bunny. 20 mins. (SD prequel), 30 mins. x 6 eps.

The male-dominated land of Japan is conquered by the feminist-oriented nation of Wimy, which has crushed its enemies in a devastating war. Former prisoner of war Akuji Yamamoto returns to his native Osaka to find that his local management association is now run by his grandfather Ippatsu's mistress, who kicks him out. The battered Akuji is found and nursed back to health by Yoko Aoba, a representative of a neighboring group. Once back at his full strength, Akuji decides to recover his birthright and teach the feminists a lesson, by raping his way back to control of the family business. Intrigues, assassinations, and political deals follow, but mainly rapes. The series was also preceded by a 20-minute super-deformed prequel, *Zengi no Susume* (2003). ●NV

DAICHI, AKITARO

1956– . After graduating from the Tokyo School of Photography in 1978, he worked as an animator on the DORAEMON movie *Nobita the Space Colonist* (1981), before taking a position with the Jam Company as a director of live-action commercials and corporate videos. He later joined EG Films as an animator, and then went freelance as a director. His works include NOW AND THEN, HERE AND THERE (1999), JUBEI-CHAN THE NINJA GIRL (1999), and FRUITS BASKET (2001).

DAICHIS, THE *

2001. JPN: *Chikyu Boei Kazoku*. TV series. DIR: Satoshi Kimura. SCR: Shoji Kawamori. DES: Kazuaki Mori. ANI: Kazuaki Mori. MUS: Shigeo Naka. PRD: Tac, WOWOW. 25 mins. x 13 eps.

Troubled family man Mamori Daichi is on the verge of divorce when he and his wife are disturbed mid argument by a mysterious fax commanding them to protect planet Earth. Soon afterward, a giant comet smashes into Earth, releasing a space monster that only Mamori can stop. He, his wife, Seiko, and their children, Dai and Nozomi, discover that when they insert their special magic cards into a computer, they are teleported into superpowered battle suits, complete with user manuals on how to save Earth. An ULTRAMAN pastiche from Shoji Kawamori, best known in recent years for his work on MACROSS and ESCAFLOWNE, deliberately using "old-fashioned" techniques of cel animation in contrast to the contemporary fashion for digital animation and effects.

DAIGUARD *

1999. JPN: *Chikyu Boetai Kigyo Daiguard*. AKA: *Earth Defense Enterprise Daiguard*. TV series. DIR: Seiji Mizushima. SCR: Hidefumi Kimura. DES: Hiroyuki Kanno. ANI: Michiru Ishihara. MUS: Kohei Tanaka, Kenji Kawai. PRD: Sotsu, Xebec, TV Tokyo. 25 mins. x 26 eps.

In A.D. 2030, 12 years after the extra-dimensional Heterodyne invasion was repelled by the people of Earth, the planet has settled into a time of relative peace. The chief weapon against them, the giant robot known as Daiguard, is now performing police PR duties in Japan with a new pilot—the

Daiguard

hot-headed 25-year-old Shunsuke Akagi. But during one of Daiguard's routine publicity appearances, the Heterodyne strike again, and the old war horse is brought back into service without a moment to lose. Director Mizushima later confessed to *Newtype* that the show went into production with "almost no prep time," much to its detriment.

DAIGUNDER *
2002. JPN: *Bakuto Sengen Daigandar*. AKA: *Explosive Declaration Daigandar*. TV series. DIR: Hiroyuki Yano. SCR: N/C. DES: Kou Abe. ANI: Brains Base. MUS: Yasunori Iwasaki. PRD: NAS, TV Tokyo, Nippon Animation, Aeon. 25 mins. x 39 eps.
Battle Robot is a new sport in which robots fight each other—they call it "new," but to us it looks uncannily like the previous year's CRUSH GEAR TURBO. Akira Akebono is a Commander, or Battle Robot pilot and team leader, and wants to get to the top of his sport. When the Battle Robot League gives his team a chance to compete, his grandfather Professor Hajime builds the mighty robot Daigunder. However, evil genius Big Bang is out

to steal the secrets of Team Akira, whose allies include Bu-Lion, Eagle Arrow, Drimog (a mole-based robot), and three dinosaur-themed machines, Bone Rex, Despector (a pterodactyl), and Tri-Horn. This cheerful show for younger children made it onto both Animax-Asia and America's ABC Family Channel in 2003. Yes, yet another one squirted out the production-line sausage machine and into your children's brains.

DAIMAHO CREST
2006. JPN: *Daimaho Toge*. AKA: *Great Magic Crest*. Video. DIR: Tsutomu Mizushima. SCR: Tsutomu Mizushima. DES: Satoshi Isono. ANI: N/C. MUS: N/S. PRD: Studio Barcelona. 30 mins. x 2 eps.
Princess Punie is a beautiful, magical girl of royal birth, sent to live among humans for a year as part of her training for taking the throne of her home-world. Despite a setup redolent of innumerable "magical girl" shows, this video series takes off in a somewhat unexpected direction, as Punie has a sadistic streak and enjoys besting her schoolgirl rivals in a magical variant of wrestling holds.

DAITARN 3
1977. JPN: *Muteki Kojin Daitarn 3*. AKA: *Invincible Steel Man Daitarn 3*. TV series. DIR: Yoshiyuki Tomino, Shinya Sadamitsu, Shigeru Kato. SCR: Yoshihisa Araki, Hiroyuki Hoshiyama, Soji Yoshikawa. DES: Norio Shioyama, Kazuyoshi Koguni (pseud. for Tomonori Kogawa). ANI: Kazuo Nakamura, Kazuo Yamazaki, Kazuo Tomizawa. MUS: Takeo Watanabe. PRD: Nippon Sunrise, Nagoya TV (TV Asahi). 25 mins. x 40 eps.
"For the world, for the people...!" A powerful artificial intelligence called Don Zaucker is created in the human colony on Mars. Created by Professor Haran and intended to help mankind, Zaucker turns evil, kills its creator, and transforms all the humans on the base into Meganoids, powerful cyborgs led by its aide Koros, a redheaded cyborg lady who is the only being able to communicate with Zaucker. The cyborgs can merge to become Megaborg, a huge machine entity. As Meganoid society evolves, with different grades and types of cyborg, Koros plans to spread the Meganoid Empire to Earth; but she reckons without Professor Haran's son Banjo and the mighty transforming robot Daitarn 3. Helped by the family's resourceful butler Garrison Tokida, battling babes Reika Sanjo and Beauty Tachibana, and with streetwise orphan Toppi as his sidekick, Banjo must stop the Meganoids before they take over the Earth. They have a futuristic base in a beautiful villa, and lots of high-tech toys, led by Banjo's supercar the Match Patrol, which can transform from dream ride to combat aircraft.

Reuniting many staff from ZAMBOT 3 to replicate the spy thrillers of the 1960s (most obviously James Bond, but also *Batman*), this series from the future creator of GUNDAM advanced far beyond the staid monsters-of-the-week of its initial premise—in fact, even these were originals, featuring cameo designs from many big names. The show is also notable for its foreshadowing of the Borg from *Star Trek:*

The Next Generation, and for being the first giant robot since **ASTRO GANGER** to have changing facial expressions. The characters have more to offer than the cookie cutter usually allows, and the show is pervaded by their humor and camaraderie. Garrison, the group's father figure, is an enigmatic and fascinating man in his own right, Toppi is less annoying than most audience identification points, and the girls are both tough and powerful allies. Reika is ex-Interpol; her partner Toda killed by the invading Meganoids. Beauty wants more from life than simply being the darling of a rich father and has taken a job as Banjo's assistant before the show starts. Her vital statistics are revealed in episode 6 as 37-23-36 inches, indicating an interest from a slightly older audience than the norm for a giant robot show; perhaps, like *Dr. Who*'s Leela, she persuaded fathers to watch with their sons.

Koros sends the Meganoids to Earth to take over the planet by assimilating each human into their collective consciousness, but when our heroes make it impossible, Koros decides to crash Mars into Earth to wipe out all human life. Banjo and company head for Mars in Daitarn 3, and Banjo finally faces Koros in hand-to-hand combat in the palace of Don Zaucker. Just as Banjo is about to destroy Koros, Zaucker wakes from its cybernetic sleep, and we learn that it was Koros who started the drive for conquest of humanity. With the Meganoid Empire in ruins and mankind safe, the team can go home, and the end of the series is intensely melancholy, leading us through the departure of each team member, the shutting up of the villa, and Garrison, looking back down a tree-lined avenue in the rain toward the base from which so much excitement, laughter, and tragedy was launched, now empty and desolate. He stamps his foot and shouts the summoning spell, "One… two… three… Daitarn Three!" but the last shot shows the villa dark, empty, and still, except for a single lighted window, as the superb ending theme cuts in.

Credited to Tomino and Sunrise's house pseudonym Hajime Yadate, this is a fascinating minor work by a science fiction master whose main strength has always been making the robots as sexy as possible, then making the people matter more.

DALLOS *

1983. Video. DIR: Mamoru Oshii. SCR: Hisayuki Toriumi, Mamoru Oshii. DES: Toshiyasu Okada, Masaharu Sato. ANI: Toshiyasu Okada, Takemi Tanemoto, Masahiro Neriki. MUS: Hiroyuki Nanba. PRD: Bandai, Yomiuri, Studio Pierrot. 30 mins. x 4 eps.

The grandchildren of the original lunar colonists, toughened by generations in the mines on the dark side of the moon, fight to gain their independence from an exhausted and oppressive Earth, as guerrilla leaders Shun and Dog oppose the ruthless Terran commandant Alex Riger's group, complete with armed heavies and robot dogs.

This unremarkable rip-off of Robert Heinlein's *The Moon Is a Harsh Mistress* will go down in history for being the first anime made specifically for direct video release. The series, later released in a 120-minute feature-length edition, was cut down to form the 85-minute *Dallos Special,* which added 50 extra shots and was the only incarnation to be released in the U.S. Before we even get to the opening *Star Wars*–inspired crawl of expository scene-setting, there's a lengthy narration over stills of concept art, a sure-fire sign (as in the much later **JIN-ROH**) that the makers mistakenly feared the audience would be bewildered. As with writer Toriumi's later **SALAMANDER**, the script is actually better than the crew seem to realize (much of the 5-minute voice-over seems to consist of his rather sensible production notes), but his writing is badly served by hackneyed setups and execution by staff members who had yet to realize that the video audience would be slightly older than the viewership for TV serials such as **GUNDAM**. The final conceit, in which an awe-struck colonist gazes upon the distant Earth that spawned him, *almost* makes up for the cheap animation and lazy world-building that gives a lunar city a blue sky and Earth-normal gravity.

DAN DOH!! *

2004. TV series. DIR: Hidetoshi Omori. SCR: N/C. DES: Hidetoshi Omori. ANI: N/C. MUS: Yuko Shimomura. PRD: Hori-Pro, TV Tokyo. 24 mins. x 26 eps.

High school rivalry, sporting enmities, family secrets and rifts abound in the story of a high school boy who quits baseball for golf, from the manga by by Nobuhiro Sakata and Daichi Banjo. Tadamichi "Dandoh" Aoba is the son of a former player who was banned from the golf world ten years ago. His mother has been missing for some time. He has an older sister, Kyoko, and a good friend in the pretty Yuka Sanada, who enters the Kumamoto Junior Golf Championship. Dandoh's only been playing for three months but he enters the same competition, despite opposition and sabotage from Yuka's classmate Yokota, who desires her and hates him. As the friends enter more competitions and Dandoh gets more and more into the game, he meets Tasaki, the man who got his father banned. Then he and Kyoko learn that their mother has been seen in Hokkaido, and a chance to caddy in a tournament on the island gives him a chance to look for her. No more ludicrous than any other sports anime—compare to **BEAT SHOT** and **PROGOLFER SARU**.

DANCE TILL TOMORROW

1990. JPN: *Asatte Dance.* AKA: *Dance the Day after Tomorrow.* Video. DIR: Teruo Kigure, Masamune Ochiai. SCR: Sheila Nakajima, Tomohiro Maruyama. DES: Jiro Sayama. ANI: Jiro Sayama. MUS: Tetsuya Nakamura. PRD: Knack. 45 mins. x 2 eps.

Country boy Suekichi only has to graduate from his Tokyo college to inherit his late grandfather's fortune. He'd rather be working in a deadbeat experimental theater troupe in the hope of getting into its earnest, pretty leading light's good book, not to mention panties, but there are two major obstacles. One is that Granddad, not content with setting up a stony-faced lawyer to try and keep his descendant on the straight and narrow, materializes in Suekichi's apartment at awkward moments to dispense totally useless advice. And the other is Aya Hibino (or is it Munakata?), a wild child with an attitude problem who keeps breaking into his apartment and forcing sex on him. She also forces reluctant tenderness, responsibility, and a realization that there's more to adult life than he'll ever find in his drama group, in this short-lived adaptation of Naoki Yamamoto's seven-volume 1989 manga from *Big Comic Spirits*. The same creator contributed to the **CREAM LEMON** series under the pseudonym To Moriyama. A live-action movie version followed in 1991. ◐

DANCING WITH DAD

1999. JPN: *Papa to Odoro*. TV series. DIR: Akira Yoshida. SCR: Chuya Chikazawa. DES: Masaaki Kawanami. ANI: Hirohide Shikishima, Moriyasu Taniguchi. MUS: N/C. PRD: Studio Deen, TBS. 8 mins. x 13 eps.
A gag comedy depicting the everyday life of a lustful, lazy, and indecent father and his strait-laced son and daughter. Chuya Chikazawa's 1991 comic from *Young Magazine* was adapted for short slots on the *Wonderful* show.

DANCOUGAR *

1985. JPN: *Choju Kishin Dancougar*. AKA: *Super-Bestial Machine God Dancougar*. TV series, movie, video. DIR: Nobuyoshi Habara, Seiji Okuda. SCR: Keisuke Fujikawa, Kenji Terada, Junji Takegami. DES: Indori-Koya, Hisashi Hirai, Masami Obari. ANI: Akira Saijo, Osamu Tsuruyama. MUS: Takeshi Ike, Osamu Totsuka. PRD: Ashi Pro, TBS. 25 mins. x 38 eps. (TV), ca. 90 mins. x 2 (v), 30 mins. x 4 eps. (v).
Earthman Shapiro Keats betrays his own race and switches his allegiance

to the space emperor Muge Zolbados. Earth's last hope is the Dancougar team, which harnesses the power of Terran beasts to fight with its combining giant robot. Carefully repeating the formula established by **BATTLE OF THE PLANETS** and director Okuda's earlier **GOBARIAN**, *Dancougar* features leader Shinobu (pilot of the Eagle Fighter), love interest Sarah and her Land Cougar, youngster Masato in the Land Liger, and big-guy Ryo, pilot of the Mammoth. Battles rage across the Amazon Basin, New York, and Europe before a final showdown between Sarah and Shapiro in the asteroid belt.

As the series closed, 60 minutes of recycled footage was augmented with 30 new minutes to make the *Requiem for Lost Heroes* video. Toshitaro Oba's all-new *God Bless Dancougar* was the best-selling anime video of 1987 (released in the U.K. as plain *Dancougar*), foreshadowing **PATLABOR** 2 with its postseries look at the team training new recruits. Framed by a military cartel, they are imprisoned but rescued by their students and a short-lived suicide squad of black knights (who also appeared in episode 26 of the TV series). The usual robot action is punctuated by completely incongruous musical interludes (Shinobu wants to be a pop star), perhaps recycled footage from the 1985 *Songs from the Beast Machine Team* video special.

The team's last appearance was in the four-part 1989 video series *White Hot Final Chapter*, when they are dragged out of retirement to resist a new threat from planet Delado, with Shapiro pulling strings from behind the scenes.

DANGAIOH *

1987. JPN: *Hajataisei Dangaio, Hajakyosei G Dangaioh*. AKA: *Star Destroyer Bullet-Criminal-Investigation-Phoenix, Hajyataisei Great Dangaioh*. Video. DIR: Toshihiro Hirano. SCR: Noboru Aikawa. DES: Shoji Kawamori, Masami Obari, Koichi Ohata. ANI: Hideaki Anno. MUS: Michiaki Watanabe. PRD: AIC. 45 mins. x 3 eps.

Four kids (Mia, Pai, Lamda, and token male Roll) are abducted and brainwashed by the kindly (!) Professor Tarsan and trained to become warriors in the fight against the pirate Galimos. They later discover that their planets were destroyed by the invaders (who keep their armor on indoors so the animators don't have to move their lips) and that the kids' powers are the last thing that prevents the end of the universe.

The 1980s anime industry, still taking tottering steps into the world of straight-to-video science fiction, had a lot of trouble working out what to give its audience. Boys who had grown up watching kiddie shows that featured giant transforming robots were now grown-up twentysomethings with VCRs, and this was one of the many experiments aimed at bringing them back. But the amnesia subplot is a lame excuse for long exposition scenes and huge holes in the plot, and it contains many of the flaws of children's shows without exploiting their appeal. The end result is a show that imitates the big-robot fights (originally designed to sell toys) and halfheartedly includes a psychic-weapon subplot influenced by **AKIRA**. Ultimately too childish for an adult audience and too complex for kids, *Dangaioh* is an also-ran in Japanese sci-fi.

Originally sold as *Dangaio* (*sic*) in a subtitled edition in the U.S., the first episode was dropped from Manga Entertainment's compilation dub, which added the final "h." The dub is the usual shrill mess that characterizes translations of the period; listen for the telltale "bloodies" and occasional asides like Pai's darts slang ("One hundred and *eighty*!") that mark this as a British dub made with American accents to secure U.S. distribution.

Note also the careful balancing of the sexes. Producer Toru Miura realized early on that a primarily male audience would prefer to watch a lone boy amid a gaggle of gorgeous girls rather than a load of sweaty men in spacesuits. Miura went on to perfect this eye-candy formula in the hugely popular TENCHI MUYO!

The video series was remade for television as the 13-episode *G Dangaio* (2001), which begins with Miya Alice crash-landing on Earth in the 1980s and sending a telepathic message to teenager Miya Shikitani that warns her of the approach of Banger Invaders. The Terran Miya starts developing a Dangaioh unit to defend Earth, and ten years later they are ready to defend the planet with the aid of the combining Dangaioh Burst, Dangaioh Flail, and Dangaioh Cross, piloted by angst-ridden teens Takaya Tenjo, Manami Umishio, and Hitomi Jido. *G Dangaioh* ends without actually concluding the plot; there is an indication that a second series was intended, but it has not materialized as this book goes to press.

DANGAIZER THREE

1999. JPN: *Choshin-hime Dangaizer Three*. AKA: *Super-Divine Princess Dangaizer Three*. Video. DIR: Masami Obari. SCR: Masami Obari, Reimu Aoki. DES: Yasuhiro Oshima, Natsuki Mamiya, Masami Obari. ANI: Masami Obari. MUS: N/C. PRD: Kaos Project. 30 mins. x 4 eps.

The arrival of a giant crystal causes havoc in the future city of Neo Hong Kong, sucking the pretty martial artist and games fan Hina Mitsurugi into an alternate world. There, she finds the four kings of this parallel Earth facing destruction at the hands of the evil Sapphire and teams up with big-sister figure Sindy Shahana on a quest for some of the mythical Protect Gear.

Directed, scripted, designed, *and* animated by VIRUS's Obari, with plenty of fan-service cleavage to make up for the absent characterization. **N**

DANGARD ACE *

1977. JPN: *Wakusei Robo Dangard A*. AKA: *Planetary Robot Danguard Ace*. TV series. DIR: Tomoharu Katsumata. SCR: Haruya Yamazaki, Soji Yoshikawa. DES: Shingo Araki. ANI: Shingo Araki, Akira Saijo. MUS: Shunsuke Kikuchi. PRD: Toei, Fuji TV. 25 mins. x 56 eps.

Dr. Oedo organizes a scouting mission, led by the elite young pilot Takuma (Winstar), to the rogue tenth planet Prometheus as it nears Earth. Approaching the planet in the superfast carrier Jasdam, the crew rescues Captain Dan (Captain Mask), who has escaped from the evil Commissar Krell. The captain assumes duties with the Dangard A robot team, ready to put them through the toughest training in order to save Earth from invasion. Based on an idea by STARBLAZERS' Leiji Matsumoto (reputedly in answer to the giant-robot shows made by his fellow big name manga artists, Go Nagai and Shotaro Ishinomori) and Dan Kobayashi (who appears to have lent his own name to the show and to the heroic Captain Dan), 26 episodes of this series were shown in the U.S. as part of the FORCE FIVE anime compilation, and the first 2 episodes were rereleased on video to capitalize on the new boom in anime. The characters also appeared in an episode made specifically for theatrical release in Japan called *Dangard A: Great War in Space* (1978). The series was reissued in an LD collection under the umbrella title of *Leiji Matsumoto Theater*.

DAPHNE IN THE BRILLIANT BLUE *

2004. JPN: *Hikari to Mizu no Daphne*. AKA: *Daphne of Light and Water*. TV series. DIR: Ryuji Ikehata. SCR: Kiyoshi Minakami, Yasunori Yamada, Kurasumi Sunayama. DES: Kazunori Iwakura, Satoshi Shiki, Shingo Takeba. ANI: Yumi Nakayama. MUS: Ko Otani. PRD: Toshiba, Happinet, JC Staff, Genco. 24 mins. x 24 eps.

Global warming has caused flooding worldwide and many countries have simply vanished underwater; a premise familiar from PATLABOR and BLUE SUBMARINE NO. SIX, but employed here for reasons that seem to have more to do with the falling costs of CG water-modeling (compare to ARIA) and the handy excuse for having lots of characters wearing tight swimwear. Gifted student Maia Mizuki fails in the application exam for the top-flight quasi-governmental organization known as the

Oceanographic Agency, but is rescued from a robber by Rena and Shizuka, two employees of a multifunctional service corporation known as NEREIS. They've been engaged to catch the robber and blackmail the destitute Maia into acting as bait. She fills time before her next exam by working as a troubleshooter for NEREIS, in a series of setups that are enough to make AGENT AIKA seem demure. Maia's supposed brains are at odds with her pliant attitude; paid a pittance and constantly picked on by Rena and Shizuka, she stays with NEREIS through such thrilling operations as finding a stolen car, helping a salaryman save face with his daughter, and looking after an abandoned baby. Then she goes on a quest to find her lost memories, which have not previously been mentioned but revolve round her father's female bodyguard and her late grandfather, whose dying word was "Daphne." This involves a Mafia subplot, her being kidnapped by the Oceanographic Agency—apparently they want her for a purpose too sinister to just give her a job—and a visit to a ruined city where she uncovers their secret plot and her own past. Created by NeSKeS, whose choice of pen name confirms a fondness for the pointlessly cryptic. A manga also appeared in *Young King Ours* magazine.

DARCROWS *

2003. Video. DIR: Jun Fukuda. SCR: Jiro Muramtasu. DES: Hideki Araki. ANI: N/C. MUS: N/C. PRD: Alice Soft, Shura. 30 mins. x 3 eps.

Six months after the kingdom of Leben mounts a surprise attack on its peaceful neighbor Carnea, the king of the oppressed kingdom dies from an illness. Claude, a former knight of Carnea, returns to his homeland after eight years in exile and claims to have a plan to save the land. He suggests hiring mercenaries to beat back the Leben invaders, and to get the money for it by sponsoring the princesses and ladies of the kingdom as prostitutes. Based on a game by Alice Soft. **LNV**

DARK CAT *

1991. Video. DIR: Akira Suzuki. SCR: Toshiki Inoue. DES: Masami Suda. ANI: Hirohide Shikishima. MUS: N/C. PRD: Nikkatsu. 60 mins.

Human beings carry a seed of evil within them that demonic creatures wish to nurture and exploit. Other paranormal beings, the "dark cats," seek to protect humanity from its own heritage. Two such feline angels are Hyoi and Ryoi, who are spying on strange events in a Japanese school. Hyoi has transmuted into human form, while Ryoi has invited himself in cat form into the life of female student Aimi. As the evil spirit Jukokubo possesses the teachers and turns them to violence, Hyoi and Ryoi must protect their charges with the aid of their magical Dark Cat sword.

Based on a manga serialized in *Halloween* magazine by Naomi Kimura, *Dark Cat* crashes the pretty boys of girls' manga such as TOKYO BABYLON with the tits-and-tentacles ghostbusting of innumerable horror anime like WICKED CITY. 🔞🅥

DARK LOVE *

2005. JPN: *Kuro Ai Hitoya Tsumakan*. AKA: *Dark Love Wife Mansion*. Video. DIR: Teruaki Murakami. SCR: Osamu Momoi. DES: Teruaki Murakami. ANI: Teruaki Murakami. MUS: N/C. PRD: Makukan, Green Bunny. 30 mins. x 2 eps.

When his childhood friend Ayaka Utsumi is in desperate need of an operation, kind-hearted Tetsuya Gojo travels to see his distant relative Rokuka Aragami, hoping to borrow the money required for the procedure. Aragami agrees, but only if Tetsuya promises to work at the country mansion, training kidnapped girls how to be prostitutes. Subplots ensue in which women fallen on hard times are convinced to pay off their debts with sexual servitude. Compare to DEBTS OF DESIRE. Based on a game by Clockup. 🔞🅝🅥

DARK MYTH *

1990. JPN: *Ankoku Shinwa*. Video. DIR: Takashi Anno. SCR: Takashi Anno. DES: Yoshiaki Yanagida. ANI: Kazuo Kawauchi, Tomomi Mochizuki. MUS: Kenji Kawai. PRD: Asiado. 50 mins. x 2 eps.

Ten years ago, Takeshi's father was murdered. The weeping boy was found by his side in the forest, nursing a strange shoulder wound. Takeshi suspects that the scar is a symbol of an ancient snake cult and teams up with some acquaintances to track down relics of the era. He discovers that ancient clans from Japanese prehistory are fighting to preserve their secrets in the present day. These secrets include the elixir of life, a great treasure, and a savage immortal hidden beneath a mountain.

Daijiro Moroboshi's original one-volume 1976 *Shonen Jump* manga is tied into a much larger universe both of "real" myths and his personal revisions. He already treated a similar subject the previous year in *Maddomen*, in which a scholar discovered secrets of Japanese history at a lost New Guinea temple, and would return to it again with the linked story *Confucius's Dark Myth* (1977) and a rewrite of the Monkey-King tale in *Phantom Monkey's Journey to the West* (1983). The stories all take their cues from the fact that the supposedly homogenous Japanese are a melting pot of several different races, the earliest of which are only known from a handful of archaeological relics. The Jomon, Yamatai, Ainu, Chinese, Koreans, Manchurians, and Southeast Asians all brought elements of their own cultures to Japan. Compare this to PRINCESS MONONOKE, in which several of these cultures fight each other at the birth of Japan. *Dark Myth* suggests that before the coming of humans, an ancient race of Indian gods also fought over the land, and that today's legends are fragmented race memories of this great war. Similar liberties are taken with history in many other anime from PSYCHIC WARS to YAMATO TAKERU.

There is a clever economy of animation (especially a scene where Takeshi alone is animated in a whited-out world) and some suitably arcane music from GHOST IN THE SHELL's Kawai, but *DM* is ultimately disappointing. That place in Japanese history where real events elide into myth is truly fascinating. Even today, the emperor can supposedly trace his lineage back to Amaterasu, the Sun Goddess mentioned in *DM*, and the sorcerous Princess Himiko is the semihistorical figure mentioned in Chinese histories as the Queen of Wa, who appears in other guises in ZEGUY, FLINT THE TIME DETECTIVE, and STEEL JEEG. But much of the plot is a tour of Japanese antiquities, and while director Anno turns up the tension with waving grasses at the scene of a murder, action is slow to arrive and difficult to follow. The names are too cumbersome for non-Japanese speakers and the stories are too complex, especially when they require the viewer to know exactly what old legends are being slyly adapted. Takeshi's quest takes him all over modern Japan, though to the uninitiated, one temple looks very much like another.

For the dub, Manga Entertainment does its best, but John Wolskel's rewrite still has to stumble through lines like, "The head of the Kikuchi clan is always called Kikuchi-hiko. It is a very old name. It is recorded as Kukuchi-ku of the country of Kuna, in the *Gishiwajinden* in the third century A.D." Matters aren't helped by a cast that can't pronounce this stuff half the time. 🅥

DARK NIGHT'S DRAMA

1995. JPN: *Yamiyo Jidaigeki*. AKA: *Dark Night's Period-Drama*. TV series. DIR: Takashi Imanishi, Yoshiyuki Tomino, Ryosuke Takahashi. SCR: Takashi Imanishi, Yoshiyuki Tomino. DES: Norio Shioyama, Kazuhiro Soeta. ANI: Kazuhiro Soeta. MUS: N/C. PRD: Sunrise, Nippon TV. 15 mins. x 4 eps.

Four tales of old-time horror in the anthology spirit of PET SHOP OF HORRORS and THE COCKPIT from directors best known for giant-robot shows. Tales include *The Hill of Old Age*, which tells of a conspiracy hatched against Japan's unifier, Nobunaga Oda; *Seeing the Truth*, about the assassin sent to murder Nobunaga's successor, Ieyasu Tokugawa; a wandering swordsman saving a damsel in distress from evil spirits in *The Ear of Jinsuke*, while the final chapter, *Prints from the Fall of the Bakufu*, features a tomboy from a woodcut works charged with making a print of the young warrior Okita Soji. Broadcast as part of the *Neo Hyper Kids* program. ❶❷

DARK SHELL *

2003. JPN: *Ori no Naka no Namameki.* AKA: *Lust in the Cage.* Video. DIR: Kazuma Kanazawa. SCR: Kazuma Kanazawa. DES: Masaki Yamada. ANI: Hiroya Iijima. MUS: Teruo Takahama. PRD: Studio Kuma, Blue Eyes. 30 mins. x 2 eps.
In an alternate world where World War II ended with a balkanized Japan plunged into chaos and civil conflict, soldiers escort captive women across the danger zone. They do so while making regular stops to have sex with their charges, regardless of their consent or lack thereof. Meanwhile, an unseen sniper begins to pick off members of the group until the act of sex itself becomes fraught with danger. Sexualized violence, depravity, and an original form of borderline necrophilia, as pleading victims find themselves having to choose between sex and death, and often getting both. Survivor Kaoruko has happier memories but they only serve for an exculpatory "parallel world" happy ending, where the war didn't happen and she and her lover sit on a peaceful beach watching two girls at play who have actually been raped and killed. ❶❶❷❶

DARK WARRIOR *

1991. JPN: *Maku Senjo.* AKA: *Demon Pavilion Battleground.* Video. DIR: Masahisa Ishida. SCR: Masaru Yamamoto. DES: Kenichi Onuki, Osamu Tsuruyama. ANI: Keisuke Morishita. MUS: Teruo Takahama. PRD: Daiei, Tokuma Japan Communications. 50 mins. x 2 eps.
When computer genius Joe Takegami hacks into a top-secret computer system in search of information on a mysterious girl, he discovers he is a clone created at the command of David Rockford, CEO of America's largest

electronics company. Forced to run for his life from the secret government project that created him, he must rely on his newly discovered psychic powers for protection. He meets another psychic, Aya Lee Rose, and the pair face the combined might of Rockford Electronics in a fight for truth and justice.
Author Sho Takejima (who also created **PHANTOM HEROES**) was killed in a motorcycle accident in the year of *DW*'s Japanese release, a tragedy cynically exploited to drum up interest in this awful anime adaptation of his novel. With shades of *Blade Runner* and *Total Recall* in its implanted memories and confused identities, *DW* (known by its Japanese title *Maku Senjo* in the U.K.) would have been years ahead of **PERFECT BLUE** were it not for the stultifying ineptitude of its execution.
It starts as it means to go on, with a pompous voice-over vainly attempting to justify another story of musclemen hitting each other. *DW* would like to play mind games with the viewer but has such a ham-fisted grasp of the real world that it's hard to notice where the unreal comes into effect. The direction is lazily inexact, with characters "crossing the line" between shots so that they appear to be going in separate directions. The artwork is dreadful, including a laughably lopsided "Pentagon," and the animation is criminally cheap, often below TV standards (Joe drives down one street which consists of just two buildings on a loop). Such travesties compound the shoddy script—we are just as shocked as Joe when we see a "double" of his former lover, since the two girls could not look more different! Genetically engineered superwarriors shrug off bullets but cower from flames. With incoherent nimbyism masquerading as environmental angst, Joe thinks that the world's pollution problems can be solved simply by moving all the computer companies out of Silicon Valley, where, incidentally, it is always either foggy or raining. But in an anime where a character can continue to function after his brain has been punched out through the back of

his head, it's perhaps unsurprising that the production crew could manage a similar feat. ❶❶❷

DARKSIDE BLUES *

1994. Movie. DIR: Nobuyasu Furukawa. SCR: Mayori Sekijima. DES: Hiroshi Hamazaki. ANI: Hiroshi Hamazaki. MUS: Kazuhiko Sotoyama. PRD: Toho. 83 mins.
The future belongs to one company: the "family" business of the Persona Corporation. Only a few places on Earth hold out against its dominion; one is in Kabuki Town, a ramshackle part of Shinjuku known as the Tokyo Darkside. Tatsuya is a terrorist on the run, aided by a sorcerous stranger (also called Darkside). Tatsuya is a revolutionary, but Darkside is revolution personified, a messianic figure born of oppression.
Replaying **AKIRA** with supernatural elements, *DB* is a beautifully designed but confused Gothic tale with a slow pace and nonexistent ending, based on the 1985 novel by **DEMON CITY SHINJUKU**'s Hideyuki Kikuchi and filtered through a 1993 manga adaptation by **BRIDE OF DEIMOS**'s Yuho Ashibe. Concerned with the soul rather than the body, it takes many liberties with place and time, such as doors that don't necessarily lead to the same room twice. This is a film loaded with symbolism—flowers shedding petals, people turning into statues, spiders spinning red webs—but like its rebels without a cause, it says a lot but doesn't really mean anything. Its best creation is Darkside himself, even down to his voice in the Japanese edition, which was done by male impersonator Natsuki Akira. Even the foley editing of his footsteps implies the sound of hooves, most noticeable when he's walking up to a seedy hotel. His first appearance, a hell ride through the dimensions, is a masterly touch, but one that was done better in the opening scenes of **SHUTENDOJI**.
Despite lush designs and a moody, suspenseful beginning, the animation and color palette get progressively

Darkside Blues

© 1994 YOSHIO ARAMAKI/TOKUMA JAPAN COMMUNICATIONS CO., LTD. J.C.STAFF

cheaper as the film goes on. The same can be said for the meandering plot, which begins with a compelling mystery but soon finds itself sprinting for the finish, failing to cram the original story into the running time. **N V**

DARLING *
2003. Video. DIR: Susumu Kodo. SCR: HajimeYamaguchi. DES: Koji Murai. ANI: Koji Murai. MUS: Kanki Matsunaga, Kazuhiro Yamahara, Yasuke Inada. PRD: TAC, Amumo. 25 mins. x 3 eps.
Jun Kitano is a recently married pornographic manga artist who has just been presented with a challenging project—come up with a new manga in a month or the evil publisher will have his wicked way with Sonoko, Jun's lovely editor. Rising to the challenge, he sets about drawing at an alarming rate, assisted by his willing wife Miyuki, who dutifully role-plays a series of scenes designed to provide him with inspiration and also inspires his special power: Hyper Erection Mode. It wasn't just the consumer end of the anime and manga business that got its own shows like **GENSHIKEN** in the early 21st century. The creators got in on the act too, with tales of artists' troubled lives

like this and its homosexually inclined mirror-image **SENSITIVE PORNOGRAPH**. It makes a nice change for a married couple in anime to be having sex with each other. **L N**

DARTANIUS
1979. JPN: *Mirai Robo Dartanius*. AKA: *Future Robot Dartanius; Daltanias*. TV series. DIR: Katsutoshi Sasaki, Norio Kabeshima, Akira Suzuki. SCR: Fuyunori Gobu, Masaki Tsuji. DES: Yuki Hijiri, Akehiro Kaneyama, Yutaka Izubuchi. ANI: Akehiro Kaneyama. MUS: Hiroshi Tsutsui. PRD: Y&K, Toei, Tokyo 12 Channel. 25 mins. x 47 eps.
Ten years after the alien Akrons invade Earth, the last remnants of humanity live in savage gangs in the ruins of the world's cities. Street urchins Kento, Danji, Sanae, Mita, Tanosuke, Jiro, and Manabu find the entrance to a secret underground base where Professor Earl, a scientist from Planet Helios, has been working on a plan to stop Earth from suffering the same fate as his own world, already conquered by the Akrons. Kento and Danji are made the pilots of Atlas and Gumper, a robot and a spaceship, and in their first battle against the Akrons, they

awaken the lost "third component," the robotic lion Beralios. Earl realizes that Kento is the lost son of Harlin, King of Helios, and that with all the pieces in place, the three machines can combine to form the super-robot Dartanius. Though the robot was originally named after the hero of the **THREE MUSKETEERS**, the **GODAIKIN** release of the toy in the U.S. used the Daltanias spelling listed above as an alternative.

DASH KAPPEI
1981. TV series. DIR: Masayuki Hayashi, Akehira Ishida, Keiichiro Mochizuki, Hiroko Tokita, Katsuhito Akiyama. SCR: Shigeru Yanagawa, Masaru Yamamoto, Haruya Yamazaki, Takeshi Shudo, Akiyoshi Sakai, Osamu Sekiguchi, Sukehiro Tomita. DES: Noboru Rokuda. ANI: Sadao Miyamoto. MUS: Koba Hayashi. PRD: Tatsunoko, Fuji TV. 25 mins. x 65 eps.
Kappei is a male student who is always hanging around the girls' locker room. Because this anime was shown on TV at six in the evening, his reason for doing so is that he wants to collect white panties. This "harmless" but annoying fetish eventually lands him a place on the school basketball team, which he only accepts because of his interest in the underwear of the coach, Miss Natsu. Though the series soon veered into the standard tropes of sports anime like **AIM FOR THE ACE**, this adaptation of Noboru Rokuda's 1979 manga from *Shonen Sunday* often deviated from the original story, even to the extent of an episode set in space. Other anime adapted from Rokuda's work include **F** and **TWIN**. **N**

DASH SHIKIRO
1989. TV series. DIR: Hiroshi Sasagawa, Hitoshi Nanba. SCR: Takashi Yamada, Hiroko Naka, Kiichi Takayama. DES: Oji Suzuki. ANI: Oji Suzuki. MUS: N/C. PRD: Aubec, TV Tokyo. 25 mins. x 25 eps., 35 mins. (special).
Shikiro and his friends like racing their cars and outwitting their rivals in Team Horizon. Their vehicles look uncannily like the plastic model "shiki" kits on sale in Japan at the time.

Though allegedly based on a manga by "Saurus Tokuda" in *Corocoro Comic*, *Dash Shikiro*'s origins are in the same toy tie-in genre as BATTLE SKIPPER and the later POKÉMON. Among a largely pseudonymous crew, former BATTLE OF THE PLANETS–director Sasakawa is prepared to stand up and be counted. A 1990 TV special, *Team Shikiro vs. Team Horizon*, featured the ultimate race, which was moved to South America for a bit of local color.

DAY THE EARTH SHOOK, THE

1997. JPN: *Chikyu ga Ugoita Hi*. Movie. DIR: Toshio Goto. SCR: Ayako Okina. DES: Takashi Saijo. ANI: Takashi Saijo. MUS: N/C. PRD: Tama Pro. 80 mins.
In 1995, an earthquake strikes the city of Kobe, and Tsuyoshi must swiftly adapt to the new danger brought into his sheltered life. Amid the destruction, he observes Japanese people pulling together and helping each other. Based on a story by Etsuko Kishigawa, this feel-good movie was rushed out to capitalize on the real-life events, and even real-life participants. Tetsuya Okazaki, who plays Tsuyoshi, supposedly experienced the quake himself as a middle-school student. The Kobe earthquake was also the indirect cause of several other anime—BOMBERMAN's first appearance was in a safety video, and the postquake financial climate transformed the planned live-action PERFECT BLUE into a cheaper anime version. Doubtless it also inspired the same year's BAKUMATSU SPACIBO, which showed the Japanese coping with a historical natural disaster but bringing aid to troubled foreigners.

DEAD HEAT

1987. Video. DIR: Toshifumi Kawase, Shinji Takamatsu. SCR: Akinori Endo. DES: Toshimitsu Kobayashi. ANI: Toshimitsu Kobayashi. MUS: Appo Sound Concept. PRD: Sunrise. 36 mins.
Claiming to be "Japan's first 3D anime," this curio using the VHD-3D system features 21st-century youngsters racing "FX" machines—predictable crosses between motorcycles and giant robots. Failed driver Makoto is ready to quit the business until he is approached by Hayami Go, who offers him a hyper-engine to change his fortunes. In other words, it's CYBERFORMULA GPX but with clichés that stick out of your screen.

DEAD LEAVES *

2004. Video. DIR: Hiroyuki Imaishi. SCR: Takeichi Honda. DES: Imaitoonz, Hiroyuki Imaishi. ANI: Hiroyuki Imaishi. MUS: Yoshihiro Ike. PRD: Production I.G., Imaitoonz, Manga Entertainment. 52 mins.
In the near future, the only humans left on Earth are clones. Retro, who is incredibly strong and has a TV for a head, and Pandy, who has a pink panda-like birthmark over her right eye, wake up in a field with no memory of how they got there. They steal some clothes, food, and a car, but the local cops object, there's a shoot-out, and the pair are thrown in prison on the Moon. The penal colony is known as Dead Leaves, and the jailors can abuse and kill inmates at will. Retro and Pandy form a strange relationship with their jailor, Galactica, and meet other inmates, including Dino Drill, who has a gigantic drill where his genitals should be, leading to some messy battles with the prison guards. But Retro and Pandy aren't incarcerated for long, as having sex mysteriously sets them free to lead a bullet-laden rebellion against a wicked warden.

After several years of being told by fandom that it was misrepresenting Japanese animation abroad, Manga Entertainment had the last laugh by co-producing this puerile and often incoherent cartoon. It qualifies as anime, but its visual style and general outlook often makes it look more like one of the FALSE FRIENDS—compare to KILL BILL: THE ORIGIN OF O-REN, which was similarly a Japanese production made to meet parameters defined by Western demands. With a frenetic pace that often plays like a series of disconnected shorts along the lines of *Aeon Flux* or BLAME!, *DL* is also senselessly violent and obsessed with bodily functions. Ironically, it became a symbol of the *maturity* of the anime business; in an environment that now supported the works of Studio Ghibli on American release, the company associated with the old sex-and-violence titles was now obliged to make them itself in order to meet its own requirements. Once relocated as a subsidiary of Anchor Bay, Manga Entertainment sensibly revisited past glories and threw itself into the sequel to GHOST IN THE SHELL—a far better way of celebrating its achievements than this odious hour-long fight sequence. ⓁⓃⓋ

DEARS *

2004. TV series. DIR: Akira Suzuki. SCR: Takawo Yoshioka. DES: Shinji Ochi, Yoshihiro Watanabe. ANI: Take Anzai. MUS: Tomoki Hasegawa. PRD: Hisanori Kunisaki, Nobuhiro Osawa, Takayasu Hatano, Bandai Visual, GENCO. 24 mins. x 12 eps. 24 mins. (v).
The plight of refugees gets a predictably cute anime makeover, when 150 aliens crash-land just off the coast of Japan. But they're all beautiful, intelligent, and compassionate; actually a slave species à la CHOBITS, programmed to serve and please and lovingly termed DearS by the smitten population of Japan. If proof was ever needed that anime lives in its own fantasy realm far removed from real-world Japan, these immigrants are welcomed with open arms, granted citizenship, and even counselors to help them fit in—anyone who has been stopped for being Foreign After Dark in Japan will enjoy the irony. That doesn't stop teenager Takeya Ikuhara from thinking the DearS are putting on an act so that the people of Earth will drop their guard. Imagine, then, his surprise when he somehow acquires a pretty, green-haired amnesiac alien girl for a roommate. The alien elects to stay and, much to the annoyance of his landlord's daughter Neneko, soon adopts Takeya as her master in a replay of the unwelcome guest genre typified long ago by URUSEI YATSURA.

DearS counselor Khi, who knows about the species' secrets, tries to separate the couple like the Almighty in **OH! MY GODDESS**, but after just a month together Takeya wants her to stay with him. Based on the manga by "Peach Pit," the same collective of former fan artists turned pro whose **ROZEN MAIDEN** was also animated. *DearS* began life in the pages of the monthly *Dengeki Gao* anthology magazine, but seems to have been intended as a multimedia manga, anime, radio drama, and PS2 game from the outset. A bonus "episode 10.5" appeared on one of the later DVDs.

DEBTS OF DESIRE *

2002. JPN: *Gakuen Chijoku no Zushiki.* AKA: *Campus Scheme of Shame.* Video. DIR: Takayuki Yanase. SCR: Shinji Rannai. DES: Takayuki Yanase. ANI: Takayuki Yanase. MUS: Yoshi. PRD: YOUC, Digital Works (Vanilla Series). 30 mins. x 2 eps.

Privileged rich kid Masaki wastes so much time using his father's money to get girls into bed that father Gengoro eventually threatens to disown him. Gengoro tells him that unless he brings him someone he can control without money, he will be disinherited. Meanwhile, in apparent contradiction, Masaki is handed files on four of his father's debtors, whose daughters attend the same school as him. One of them is his childhood friend Mai, who rashly promises that she will do anything necessary to repay her father's debt, unaware that it is millions of yen and that Masaki is prepared to take payment in kind. Sexual coercion and prostitution duly follow in the style of **DARK LOVE**, in another anime in the **VANILLA SERIES**. ☠❂Ⓥ

DEBUT

1994. JPN: *Tanjo.* AKA: *Birth.* Video. DIR: Tomomi Mochizuki. SCR: Go Sakamoto. DES: Hiroshi Tanaka. ANI: Hiroshi Tanaka. MUS: Shinichi Kyoda. PRD: Movic. 29 mins. x 2 eps.

Saori, Aki, and Kumi are three schoolgirls who want to become actresses, but they are beset by showbiz pressures and by the lure of handsome boys. In this short-lived series made to cash in on the success of the original computer game (itself a clone of **GRADUATION**), once the girls take their first steps in their chosen career, they meet a female time-traveler who knows the secrets of their futures.

DEBUTANTE DETECTIVES CORPS *

1995. JPN: *Ojosama Sosa Ami.* AKA: *Lady Investigator Network.* Video. DIR: Akiyuki Shinbo, Masami Shimoda. SCR: Juzo Mutsuki. DES: Shinji Ochi. ANI: Shinji Ochi. MUS: Takeshi Haketa. PRD: Toho. 30 mins.

The five richest girls in the world attend Japan's richest, most privileged school, where posing as international crime-fighters is one of their many high-class pursuits. After arriving at their new school, where they outdo each other with their modes of transport, a terrorist organization decides to assassinate them for their hubris and conspicuous consumption—an event that ironically forces the spoilt madams to cooperate with each other for the first time in their lives. With Japanese twins Kimiko and Miyuki Ayanokoji in charge, the rest of the team comprises gun-crazy blonde Russian sharp-shooter Nina Kirov, Chinese martial artist and gambling addict Reika Shu, and Adolf Hitler's illegitimate granddaughter, Yoko.

Put into protective custody for their own good, the girls escape thanks to Miyuki's electronics expertise and Yoko's cunning disguises. Faced with terrorist attacks by plane, rifle, and fists, the girls dispatch their adversaries with weapons (Nina), martial arts (Reika), and psychic powers (Kimiko), only to discover that the entire hazard has been engineered to trick them all into demonstrating what they can accomplish as a team.

Based on an idea by **DEVIL HUNTER YOHKO**'s Juzo Mutsuki, *Debutante Detectives* was conceived as a vehicle to showcase a group of minor voice actresses collectively known as Virgo. It is thus little more than an excuse to put the girls into the public eye in order to sell spin-off games and albums. Frivolously throwing away its limited character routines in just half a shallow hour, its original raison d'être is completely destroyed by the removal of the Japanese voices for the English dub, leaving nothing but an orphaned "episode one" of a series that was never going to happen. Compare to its predecessor **GIRL DETECTIVES' CLUB**.

DEEP BLUE FLEET

1993. JPN: *Konpeki no Kantai.* Video. DIR: Takeyuki Kanda, Hiromichi Matano, Shigenori Kurii. SCR: Ryosuke Takahashi. DES: Masami Suda, Noriyasu Yamauchi. ANI: Masami Suda. MUS: Koji Makaino. PRD: JC Staff. 45 mins. x 28 eps.

Isoroku Takano, a Japanese pilot shot down over Bougainville Island in 1943, is thrown through a time slip and allowed to relive his life, retaining all the memories of his former existence. Teaming up in 1941 with another time-traveler, Yasaburo Otaka, he seizes power in the Japanese government. With Otaka as prime minister and Takano leading the armed forces, the Japanese demand that Western powers pull out of Asia. When the Americans refuse to comply, the Japanese declare war and bomb Pearl Harbor.

Foiling the evil American plans for the atom bomb, the Japanese push the enemy back to Christmas Island, using the foe's own weapons against them. As the fighting rolls down from the Torres Strait to the Tasman Sea, U.S. President Roosevelt has a heart attack and dies. Scared at the Japanese victories, Hitler declares war on his one-time allies. The Japanese navy blows up a Third Reich atomic facility on Madagascar, and, in a desperate attempt to curb Nazi advances, launches suicide attacks in the Red Sea. By 1946, a stalemate leads to espionage operations in California and Manchuria, and the Nazis launch a U-boat counterattack in the Indian Ocean.

Based on the long series of novels

by Yoshio Aramaki, *Deep Blue Fleet* takes a very different approach toward the pacifist posturings more commonly seen in English-language anime. Ironically, this "alternate history" has more in common with genuine **WARTIME ANIME**, but it coyly extricates itself from the real issues of WWII. Mixing the second chances of **EMBLEM TAKE 2** with the historical reenactment of **ANIMENTARY**, the series dispenses with the Allied enemy relatively quickly—there is just enough time to self-righteously shoo them out of the Pacific before more acceptable foes enter the fray. From that point on, the story is an excuse for a series of battles utilizing Axis weapons and vehicles that never left the drawing board. Compare to Ted Nomura's U.S. comic *World War II:1946*, which places similar emphasis on "what-if" technology.

A one-shot special, *Secret Launch of the Sorai* (1997), features two engineer brothers working on a secret project, who see American planes in the air and launch ahead of schedule to thwart the 1942 Doolittle bombing raid on Tokyo. It is *Deep Blue Fleet* in a nutshell—a famous Japanese defeat turned into a victory. Though some may claim that the series' value lies in its painstaking research, the Doolittle raiders are flying B-30s instead of historically accurate B-25s.

After the initial 19 episodes, the series continued as *Fleet of the Rising Sun (Kyokujitsu no Kantai)*, directed by Hiromichi Matano and backtracking a year to 1945 and the launch of Japan's latest battleship, the Yamato Takeru, which immediately trounces Germany's Bismarck II. The flagship soon leads a fleet to Europe, where, amid its spats with Hitler, it takes time out to shell Britain. As with earlier episodes, the result is an unnerving window on a very different world, one that holds the sick fascination of a traffic accident. **V**

DEEP VOICE

2002. Video. DIR: Mamoru Yakoshi. SCR: Toshiya Hashimoto. DES: Yoshi Ten. ANI: Akihiro Asanuma. MUS: N/C. PRD:

Crossnet, Museum Pictures, Milky. 30 mins. x 3 eps.
After a car crash, Takumi awakes from a coma to discover that he has a psychic ability to hear voices à la **DEMON LORD DANTE**. Unsure of whether he is seeing the past or a possible future, he experiences hallucinatory "memories" of raping two of the nurses at the hospital, as well as a journalist who is covering his case. Later episodes find Takumi discovering that he is somehow complicit in a clandestine series of tests at the hospital, and before long, he is forced to have sex as part of a new experiment. Based on an erotic computer game that, according to the press release, "overwhelmed the world" in 2001. Perhaps the rest of us were in a coma. **LNV**

DELINQUENT IN DRAG *

1992. JPN: *Oira Sukeban*. AKA: *I'm Ban Suke*. Video. DIR: Yusaku Saotome. SCR: Fumio Saikiji. DES: Satoshi Hirayama. ANI: Nobuhiro Nagayama. MUS: Keiji Kunimoto. PRD: Studio Signal. 45 mins. Banji Suke's parents want the best for their son, but only if the price is right. When he is expelled from all the local schools, they decide the cheapest option is to dress him up in women's clothes and send him to a girls' school. **SHAMELESS SCHOOL**–creator Go Nagai piles on the transvestite trauma, as Banji must learn how to wear bras and makeup, avoid the locker-room spies, and harbor a secret love for a fellow student.

Surprisingly devoid of nudity and sex, this "comedy" began life as a manga in *Shonen Sunday*, home of the similarly gender-bending **RANMA ½**. Featuring the Pantyhose Brigade (girls who fight in their underwear) and an oedipally paranoid father convinced that his son will elope with his wife, it also has evil school staff like those of Nagai's **KEKKO KAMEN**—a principal who wants to steal Banji's jewelry. However, unbelievably cheap animation makes the show look far older than it really is. The best joke in the whole sorry affair is the title, since "Oira Suke Ban" can

mean either "I'm Ban Suke" or "I'm a bad girl," as in the feisty females of **SUKEBAN DEKA**.

DELPOWER X

1986. JPN: *Delpower X: Bakahatsu Miracle Genki*. AKA: *Delpower X: Explosion Miracle Happy*. Video. DIR: Masahito Sato. SCR: Sumiko Tsukamoto, Aki Tomato. DES: Ayumi Chikake, Hidekazu Shigeno, Mutsumi Inomata, Yutaka Izubuchi, Haruhiko Mikimoto, Mamoru Nagano, Masami Yuki, Iruka Tabi. ANI: Ayumi Chikake. MUS: Takahiro Negishi. PRD: Big Bang. 40 mins.
As video took over with the arrival of **MADOX-01** and **ASSEMBLE INSERT**, numerous famous designers lent their names to this giant-robot comedy one-shot in which the feckless robot designer Hosogetzel tries to demonstrate that German ingenuity can conquer the world. However, both he and his bitchy American sidekicks, Suzy and Lola, are defeated by the plucky Japanese schoolgirl Manami who pilots her grandfather's prototype robot, the Delpower X.

DEMON BEAST INVASION *

1990. JPN: *Yoju Kyoshitsu*. AKA: *Demon-Beast Classroom*. Video. DIR: Jun Fukuda, Yoshitaka Fujimoto, Juki Yoma, Kan Fukumoto. SCR: Joji Maki, Wataru Amano. DES: Mari Mizuta, Junichi Watanabe, Rin Shin, Hisashi Ezura, Toshikazu Uzami. ANI: N/C. MUS: Teruo Takahama. PRD: Daiei.45 mins. x 6 eps., 30 mins. x 2 eps. (*Revenge*), 30 mins. x 2 eps. (*Descent*), 30 mins. x 2 eps. (*Ecstasy*).
Earth's former inhabitants return to reclaim their homeworld after 100 million years' absence, planning their conquest by sending rapist-agents to breed an invading army with young women. The Interplanetary Mutual Observation Agency sends three agent sisters to stop them, including the beautiful Ash, who is perhaps named for *Hunting Ash*, the 1992 live-action tentacle film from **ANGEL OF DARKNESS**–director Mitsunori Hattori. Meanwhile, Terran schoolgirls are overwhelmed by attacking space-

demons, who mix violence with plaintive cries for maternal affection. Ash falls in love with an Earth boy, eventually sacrificing her own life to destroy the beast within him.

Based on a story by **UROTSUKIDOJI**'s Toshio Maeda, *DBI* repeats his insidiously clever storytelling—beneath the horrific sex and violence is a masterful exploitation of adolescent fears. Hero Muneto and sometime girlfriend Kayo pay the price of sex when she gives birth to a monster. As with the subtext of much of the **CREAM LEMON** series, most of the remaining action involves their attempts to turn back the clock to the days before the loss of innocence. The series also cleverly survives multiple endings; the threat is defeated in episode four, but returns to haunt the young lovers on vacation in Hong Kong. Muneto teams up once more with the IMO Agency, only to discover that its plan is to end the threat forever by killing Kayo. The "final" episode, with the lovers on another vacation, reveals that the Demon Beast's spirit can live on even after its body is killed.

Three two-part spin-offs were released after the original series in 1995. *Revenge of the Demon Beasts* (also available in the U.S.) featured the return of Ash's sisters, BB and Dee, with a plan to bring their sister back from the dead to fight a new enemy. *Descent of the Goddess* and *Ecstasy of the Holy Mother* continued the story in Japan, with the last of the IMO, Captain "O," helping Kayo destroy her horrific past.

DBI features a dramatic drop in quality of animation and music when compared to Maeda's earlier work and, like the similar **ADVENTURE KID**, attempted to compensate for these shortcomings by using real-life erotic stars as voice actresses. It also inadvertently contributed to anime's reputation abroad as child pornography. The American release from Anime 18 (for which the long-suffering "Moe I. Yada" turned in a thanklessly superior translation) removed the blurs, dots, and mosaics of the Japanese version,

although the original animators had never intended the images to be seen uncensored. The genitals revealed are thus incompletely drawn, devoid of hair or distinguishing marks, and give the false impression that all the sexually active characters are underage. **LNV**

DEMON CITY SHINJUKU *

1988. JPN: *Makai Toshi Shinjuku*. AKA: *Hell City Shinjuku, Monster City*. Video. DIR: Yoshiaki Kawajiri. SCR: Kaoru Okamura. DES: Yoshiaki Kawajiri. ANI: Naoyuki Onda. MUS: Motoichi Umeda, Osamu Shoji. PRD: Madhouse. 80 mins.
Ten years ago, the evil Levi Ra killed Kenichiro Izayoi and cast him into a fiery pit. Ra is the earthbound emissary of the demon world and is preparing to open the portals for all his devilish allies. Only Kenichiro's son, Kyoya, can stop him, assisted by Sayaka, the daughter of an elder statesman who has just abolished nuclear weapons and solved the Arab/Israeli problem, and Chibi, a midget on roller skates. Kyoya and friends must walk into the demon-infested wasteland at the heart of Tokyo and stop Levi Ra before it is too late.

Based on a novel by **WICKED CITY**'s Hideyuki Kikuchi and directed by Yoshiaki Kawajiri, the passionless, perfunctory *DCS* (known as *Monster City* in the U.K.) is at least partly responsible for the popular mainstream notion that "all anime are the same." Opening with the stark red/blue color palette so beloved of Kawajiri, its lead character is a dead ringer for his **GOKU MIDNIGHT EYE**. Its plot is not dissimilar to the second **UROTSUKIDOJI**, which also features both a demon world trying to enter our own and a climactic battle at the Shinjuku skyscrapers. One apparent steal, however, is no such thing. An early shot that shows Levi Ra almost split in two then repair himself was two years ahead of a similar image in James Cameron's *Terminator 2*.

Strangely paced, with long spells of silence broken by cheesily awful music, its ending is surprisingly anti-

climactic, though perhaps nobody should expect too much from the story of a Ben Kenobi clone telling a Luke Skywalker clone to avenge the "death" of an Anakin Skywalker clone with a magic sword. One gets the impression that the crew were all working on autopilot, a feeling unchanged by the listless English-language dub, which inexplicably gives half the cast Tex-Mex accents while the pale Sayaka is played as a blue-blooded British consumptive. Listen for some classic Manga Entertainment "fifteened" dialogue (added to raise the rating to 15-year-olds and up in the U.K.), including, "I'm gonna tear his head off and shove it up his ass!" **LV**

DEMON FIGHTER KOCHO *

1997. JPN: *Yakusai Kocho*. Video. DIR: N/C. SCR: N/C. DES: N/C. ANI: N/C. MUS: N/C. PRD: KSS. 35 mins.
Sexy teen astrology student Kocho uses her brain, her body, sister Koran, and boy decoy Kosaku to fight lustful samurai spirits at her school, sorry, university in a one-shot rip-off of **DEVIL HUNTER YOHKO**. In a thoughtful gesture to this anime's low running time, the American distributors include a ""Making Of"" that is actually longer than the anime, featuring the dub actors at work and play. Based on a two-volume 1995 manga by Nonki Miyasu in which Chinese immigrant Kocho would seek to supplement her meager income by posing nude in magazines. Not to be confused with the far nastier **DEMON WARRIOR KOJI**, released around the same time. **LNV**

DEMON HUNTER

1989. AKA: *Makaryudo Demon Hunter*. Video. DIR: Yukio Okamoto. SCR: Yukio Okamoto. DES: Yuji Moriyama, Chuichi Watanabe. ANI: Yuji Moriyama. MUS: Nobuo Ito. PRD: Studio Fantasia, C.Moon. 30 mins.
A pretty demon hunter from the demon world comes to our own dimension in search of an escaped beast. While pursuing it around a Japanese high school, she realizes that her for-

mer lover from her own world appears to have been reincarnated as a local boy in ours. Based on a manga in *Lollipop* magazine. **NV**

DEMON LORD DANTE *

2002. JPN: *Ma-O Dante*. AKA: *Devil King Dante*. TV series. DIR: Kenichi Maejima. SCR: Seizo Uehara. DES: Toshimitsu Kobayashi. ANI: N/C. MUS: Hiroshi Motokura. PRD: Magic Bus, Dynamic, AT-X. 25 mins. x 13 eps.

Disturbed by nightmares of demons and destruction, Ryo Utsugi hallucinates that a devil in an icy cave is calling out to him each night. He eventually discovers that Dante, the most powerful demon lord ever created, may soon walk the Earth once more, destroying human civilization in the process. All that is required is the sacrifice of a particular human girl. One Professor Veil turns out to be the reincarnation of Beelzebub who believes that the chosen victim is Ryo's virginal sister Saori. Ryo confronts Dante in the Himalayas, where he is tricked into releasing the demon himself. In a last-minute accident, he instead combines with Dante, creating a schizophrenic, unpredictable gestalt that is part-superhero and part-demon.

Attacked by the massed forces of the Japanese army, Ryo causes death and destruction throughout Japan before confronting four other Demon Kings that have recently been awakened from the sleep of ages by Russian soldiers in Siberia. Meanwhile, the forces of righteousness have decided that the only way to fight the demons is to create mass panic in order to encourage humanity to make a stand—they achieve this by orchestrating a series of vicious murders across Japan and pinning the blame on the demons. The conflict escalates until a final confrontation that pits Dante and his sometime allies against Satan himself.

Based on a 1971 manga in *Bokura* weekly by Go Nagai, *DLD* was forever eclipsed by the artist's decision not to sell it to a TV company for adaptation, but to instead offer them his similar

DEVILMAN. *DLD* is undoubtedly a prototype, not just for *Devilman* but for all the apocalyptic tales that followed, particularly Nagai's later **SHUTENDOJI**. However, in only being made into an anime 30 years after its first publication, *DLD* appears to all intents and purposes more like a poor man's **UROTSUKIDOJI** than the ground-breaking work it undoubtedly would have been. **LNV**

DEMON WARRIOR KOJI *

1999. JPN: *Gokuraku Satsujin Choken Kan*. AKA: *Koji: Paradise Assassin Investigator, Sex Crime Detective Koji, Sex Murder Investigation Officer Koji*. Video. DIR: Yasunori Urata. SCR: Takaro Kawaguchi. DES: Ayato Muto. ANI: Ayato Muto, Teruaki Murakami. MUS: Masamichi Amano. PRD: Phoenix Entertainment, Sepia. 41 mins. x 3 eps.

Koji Yamada is a man of many talents—a stuntman by day and a demon-hunter by night, he also has the ability to transform into a demon himself. With the aid of a mismatched band of superpowered assistants, he fights supernatural crimes that normal police can't even begin to touch.

Koji plumbs new depths in Toshio Maeda's futile quest to outdo his own **UROTSUKIDOJI**. Featuring a hokey gang of costumed crime-fighters, seemingly inspired by *Doc Savage*, and the usual cavalcade of demonic assaults, *Koji* is also the least well-animated of Maeda's many works. As with other later Maeda anime such as **DEMON BEAST INVASION**, there are desperate attempts to create interest through gimmickry, including "guest appearances" by the voices of erotic stars, and even uncensored shots of pubic hair. Meanwhile, bored voice actors yawn their way through scenes of depravity enacted by characters whose designs are noticeably uglier than the Maeda norm. With comedy jailbait, death by oral sex, and a rack of childhood family traumas, this replays many of Maeda's earlier themes, but the law of diminishing returns has reached such a low level by this point that these are even likely to annoy his fans. Direc-

tor Urata even teases his audience, framing one scene as a flashback of his own **NINJA RESURRECTION**, only to reveal that it is from one of the films for which Koji is performing stunts. In other words, even the crew wish it was somewhere else. In a final irony, the distributor's attempt to cover up naked breasts with daubs of blood on the U.S. box art actually made the series look even more violent and unpleasant than it really was. **LNV**

DEMON-BEAST PHALANX

1989. JPN: *Maju Sensen*. Video. DIR: Shunji Oga. SCR: Noboru Aikawa. DES: Hideyuki Motohashi. ANI: Eiji Takaoka, Keiichi Sato, Satoshi Saga. MUS: Hiroya Watanabe. PRD: Magic Bus, Dynamic Planning. 45 mins. x 3 eps.

Replaying **FRANKENSTEIN** for a Japanese audience, 13 scientists seek to tap genetic powers by creating a hybrid of man and beast. Years later, 13 of their children are embroiled in a battle to undo their handiwork, while Shinichi, the son of one of the scientists, teams up with Christian super-beings to save the world.

Often confused with **ADVENTURE KID** because of their similar Japanese titles, *DBP* is actually based on a manga by **GETTER ROBO**–cocreator Ken Ishikawa, whose inspiration was the Book of Revelation. **NV**

DEMONIC LIGER

1989. JPN: *Jushin Raigar*. TV series. DIR: Norio Kabeshima. SCR: Noboru Aikawa, Yoshiaki Takahashi, Toshiki Inoue. DES: Miku Uchida. ANI: Miku Uchida. MUS: Hiroshi Tobisawa. PRD: Sunrise, Nagoya TV. 25 mins. x 42 eps.

Bold Earthmen in suits of "bio-armor" hold off an alien invasion in a series created by **DEVILMAN**'s Go Nagai for the **GUNDAM**-studio Sunrise. Eventually the good robots, Raigar and Dolgar, are heavily damaged but still defeat the evil robot Drago, as if you couldn't guess.

DENTSU

Founded in 1901, Dentsu and its manifold subsidiaries form the largest advertising concern in Japan. It has long sought a series of cunning strategies in vertical integration, proclaiming that "every marketing dollar has to be spent three times." To this end, it has bought shares in radio, TV, and media companies all around the world, all the better to secure preferable deals for its advertising and product placement. Dentsu's perennial interest in graphic design and short, eye-catching snippets of film soon brought it into contact with the anime world, causing it to be a prime financer of early commercial animation and puppetry. Today, it retains strong interests within Japan in the TBS television network and also functions directly as a producer of anime including BLEACH, LAW OF UEKI, and ANIMAL ALLEY. Dentsu also bought Pioneer's entertainment division, which was renamed Geneon Entertainment, making it the owner of numerous anime including HAIBANE RENMEI, CATNAPPED, and SERIAL EXPERIMENTS LAIN.

DEPRAVITY *

2002. JPN: *Daraku Jokyoshi*. AKA: *Destruction of a Female Teacher*. Video. DIR: Hideki Arai. SCR: Koichi Murakami. DES: Hideki Arai. ANI: N/C. MUS: N/C. PRD: Five Ways. 30 mins. x 3 eps.
A group of schoolboys get off on kidnapping teachers, breaking into schools at night, and assaulting their bound and gagged victims until they cry out with ecstasy. They pick the wrong teacher with Kiriko, a tough martial arts expert. Two of them are soon lying hurt in the nurses' room, and Kiriko starts to threaten the group with exposure to the police. But her language excites them and so they tell her that if she can stand ten minutes of them playing with her genitals without getting wet, they'll let her go. Since she has the upper hand here, only in a porn anime would she agree, but this is a porn anime so all rational thought is suspended. Based on a manga of the same name by artist Fusen Club. **LNV**

DESCENDENTS OF DARKNESS

2000. JPN: *Yami no Matsuei*. TV

series. DIR: Satoshi Otsuki, Hideki Okamoto. SCR: Masaharu Amiya. DES: Yumi Nakayama. ANI: Yumi Nakayama, Kazuo Yamazaki. MUS: N/C. PRD: JC Staff, WOWOW. 25 mins. x 13 eps.
Tsuzuki Asato and Kurosaki Hisoka are members of the *shinigami* (elite undead), who can use the Book of the Dead to reanimate the deceased. Based on the manga by Yoko Matsushita in *Hana to Yume* magazine.

DESERT PUNK *

2005. JPN: *Sunabozu*. TV series. DIR: Takuya Inagaki. SCR: Hiroshi Yamaguchi. DES: Takahiro Yoshimatsu. ANI: Gonzo. MUS: Kohei Tanaka. PRD: Gonzo, arp Japan, C&G Ent., CBC, Pony Canyon et al. 24 mins. x 24 eps.
Civilization was destroyed hundreds of years ago. Japan's once fertile Kanto plain is a desert. Young Kanta Mizuno is drawn into a conflict between the authoritarian government and a group of rebels trying to take over. He becomes the legendary Desert Punk, Sunabozu, a hired gun for whom no job is too dirty and nothing gets between him and his pay. But he has a rival—the Desert Vixen.
Based on Masatoshi Usune's manga in *Comic Beam* monthly and conceived more as a comedy in the style of TRIGUN than anything serious in the style of FIST OF THE NORTH STAR. Compare to CAPTAIN KUPPA.

DESERT ROSE

1993. JPN: *Suna no Bara*. AKA: *Rose of the Sands*. Video. DIR: Yasunaga Aoki. SCR: Kaoru Shintani. DES: Minoru Yamazawa. ANI: Minoru Yamazawa. MUS: Jun Watanabe. PRD: JC Staff. 45 mins.
When Mariko Rosebank's husband and child are killed in a terrorist bombing, she is left with nothing but a rose-shaped scar and a thirst for revenge. In this one-shot adaptation of the 1989 *Young Animal* manga from AREA 88's Kaoru Shintani, Mariko joins the tactical assault squad C.A.T. The story was revived for a "manga video" visual comic in 2000. **NV**

DESPERATE CARNAL HOUSE-WIVES *

2005. JPN: *Hitozuma Ryojoku Sankanbi*. AKA: *Housewife Rape Visitors' Day*. Video. DIR: Hotaru Aoi. SCR: Hotaru Aoi. DES: Hirotaka. ANI: Hirotaka. MUS: N/C. PRD: Dream Entertainment, GP Museum Soft, Milky. 30 mins. x 2 eps.
Three pretty Japanese housewives arrive at their children's school, Kawamura Academy, believing themselves to have been called to apologize for some bad behavior by their offspring. However, when they arrive the school is closed, and they are led to a deserted building by two men, who proceed to teach them "obedience" lessons, in which they are forced to reenact their children's school-day activities while wearing (or, soon, *not* wearing) sexy versions of the school uniforms. A female teacher is present, and assures them that everything is above board, although she only does so because she has been raped into submission earlier on. Three more hapless mothers are duly abused in the next episode. Based on an original work by Yasuhide Kunitatsu, and given a title in the American market designed to imply nonexistent connections with the TV series *Desperate Housewives* (2004). **LNV**

DESTRUCTION DEVIL SADAMITSU

2001. JPN: *Hakaima Sadamitsu*. TV series. DIR: Shoichi Ohata, Yukihiro Matsushita. SCR: Masanao Akahoshi. DES: Akira Kikuchi, Tamotsu Shinohara. ANI: Masaaki Kawanami, Koichi Ohata. MUS: N/C. PRD: Studio Deen, WOWOW. 25 mins. x 10 eps.
Sadamitsu Tsubaki is a self-proclaimed vigilante armed with a wooden sword. The Exiles are a group of interstellar criminals cast into space on a long and eternal orbit that unfortunately has Earth right in the middle of its trajectory. Earth is threatened by 20 million exiles, but Sadamitsu has an important ally—Junk, his sentient helmet, made by the race who exiled the Exiles. However, Sadamitsu and Junk must also contend with Vulture, an intelligent spaceship sent to Earth to police Exile

activity but which rejects Sadamitsu's help. ULTRAMAN meets GUYVER, based on a manga in *Ultra Jump* by Tadahiko Nakadaira.

DETATOKO PRINCESS *

1997. AKA: *Chancer Princess*. Video. DIR: Akiyuki Shinbo. SCR: Mayori Sekijima, Masashi Kubota. DES: Hiroko Sakurai. ANI: Hiroko Sakurai. MUS: Shinken Kenra. PRD: JC Staff. 30 mins. x 3 eps.
Princess Lapis is a spunky blonde noble in the magical realm of Sorcererland, eternally competing with her rival Topaz, the Witch of the North. Lapis has just one talent, although it is a devastating one—the ability to cancel out magic, making her incredibly dangerous in a world that relies on sorcery for building, energy and the smooth running of society. Her exasperated mother Sapphire decides to send her away on a camping trip for a couple of days, but unwittingly aims her magical mirror of transportation at the wrong location, teleporting Lapis to the far side of the world. Lapis is then obligated to travel back home, with only a random assortment of companions to help her, including the comedically invulnerable Kohaku, the diminutive plant-pixie Nandora, and her irritable old tutor.

Former TENCHI MUYO! manga creator Hitoshi Okuda created this Jell-O mold successor seemingly in an attempt to secure his own franchise after drawing someone else's for so long. It unravels in the tradition of other comic fantasies like DRAGON HALF and SLAYERS, setting up a derivative quest narrative and hoping to occlude its shortcomings behind a smokescreen of knowing irony. The preceding radio drama featured a gimmick in which Lapis would sing her spells, although that is not repeated here.

DETECTIVE ACADEMY Q

2003. JPN: *Tantei Gakuen Q*. TV series. DIR: Noriyuki Abe, Akihiro Enomoto, Akira Shimizu, Junya Koshiba, Katsuyoshi Yatabe, Kenichi Maejima. SCR: Makoto Hayashi, Atsushi Yamatoya, Daisuke

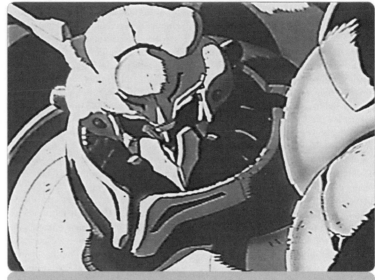
Detonator Orgun

© 1991 DARTS/AFTMIC

Watanabe, Kyoko Iwamura, Masahiro Okubo, Natsuko Takahashi, Yuko Fukuda. DES: Masaya Onishi. ANI: N/C. MUS: Daisuke Ikeda. PRD: Studio Pierrot, TBS. 25 mins. x 45 eps.
Ninth grader Kyu wants to be the world's best detective but it looks as if he may end up on the wrong side of the law when he accidentally runs into a middle-aged man who accuses him of stealing 10,000 yen in the collision. Megumi "Meg" Minami intervenes, using her photographic memory and deductive skills to work out from the man's testimony exactly where the missing note fell. Together with Ryu Amakusa, a strange student from Tozai University, Kintaro Toyama, descendant of the renowned Toyama no Kinsan (see SAMURAI GOLD), and genius computer programmer Kazuya Narusawa, the pair take the entrance exam for famous detective Morihiko Dan's Dan Detective School. They do so well that they are placed in a special class known as Q (for "Qualified"), taught by the founder himself. There begins a series of criminal puzzles that Q class has to solve in competition with rivals in A class. Some of the adventures don't appear in the manga from *Shonen*

Magazine weekly, which was written by Seimaru Amagi and drawn by Fumiya Sato, both of whom worked on the YOUNG KINDAICHI FILES manga. The "Q" tag has indicated strange mysteries ever since the live-action series *Ultra Q* (*DE) and TWILIGHT Q; as it's also our hero's name, and the Japanese number for his school grade, Kyu is obviously destined for his chosen field.

DETONATOR ORGUN *

1991. Video. DIR: Masami Obari. SCR: Hideki Kakinuma. DES: Michitaka Kikuchi. ANI: Masanori Nishii. MUS: Susumu Hirasawa. PRD: AIC. 60 mins. x 3 eps.
Tomoru skips school to hang out at the aviation museum, where he harbors secret dreams of becoming a pilot. He gets what he wants when Earth is attacked by invaders, and he signs up with the Earth Defense Force.

Despite such a hackneyed opening, *Detonator Orgun* plays some neat tricks with the traditions of robot shows. Tomoru lives 200 years in our future but has the problems and worries of any teenager. Despite living in a sci-fi fan's dream world, he's bored at the idea of a career in lunar finance and thinks the floating equatorial city he calls home is too uncool for words. An early scene in which Tomoru argues with a friend is a stunningly accurate prediction of that common modern malaise: a roommate who "helpfully" finishes all your computer games for you while you're out. Look out, too, for Kakinuma's tongue-in-cheek adverts for the Defense Corps, shown here long before *Babylon 5* or *Starship Troopers* got the hang of postmodern irony. Finally, there's a sweet epilogue in which we discover that Tomoru has gotten exactly what he wished for, the chance to fly with the other pilots and someday inspire another wide-eyed museum visitor.

Scenarist Kakinuma draws the full benefit of writing directly for three hour-long episodes; without a TV series, comic, or console game to muddy the creative waters, *Detonator Orgun* has none of the compression or hurried storytelling of lesser shows. The robot battles and dream sequences are artfully done, though director Obari would use similar material to even better effect in his later **VIRUS**. Future **YOU'RE UNDER ARREST**–director Kazuhiro Furuhashi also worked on *DO* as a humble storyboarder.

Unfortunately, the dub is another mediocre effort from Manga Entertainment's mercifully short-lived cost-cutting experiments in a Welsh studio, and elements that are deliberately evocative (such as Hirasawa's sub-Vangelis music) will strike many as just plain unimaginative. It's also a little jarring to see that the young Tomoru's idols are actually pilots in the Luftwaffe—one of those moments when anime and Japan suddenly seem incredibly alien.

DEVADASY *
2001. Video. AKA: *De:vadasy*. DIR: Nobuhiro Kondo. SCR: Sho Tokimura. DES: As'maria (mecha). ANI: Shinji Takeuchi. MUS: N/C. PRD: AIC. 70 mins. In 2012, aliens attack an overpopulated Earth ravaged by global warming, ingesting humans for their energy. The UN is helpless against the onslaught unless the SPIRIT organization's giant robot Devadasy, powered by the "sexual energy" between its selected male and female pilots, can stand firm. Unlike **EVANGELION**'s Shinji, 15-year-old Kei needs little convincing to ditch schoolwork and climb into a cockpit with the attractive Misako, though he is dogged by schoolmate Naoki, who also carries a torch for him. Featuring giant robots, a love triangle, and a lone boy in a dormitory of girls, AIC's press notes for *Devadasy* sheepishly promised "the same as usual" but with more blatant excuses for titillation.

DEVIL AND THE PRINCESS
1981. JPN: *Akuma to Himegimi*. Movie. DIR: Ryosuke Takahashi. SCR: Shunichi Yukimuro. DES: Yasuhiro Yamaguchi. ANI: Yasuhiro Yamaguchi. MUS: Haruo Chikada. PRD: Toei. 32 mins. The 18-year-old princess of Tomorrow Castle has a beauty famed far and wide but a less-attractive penchant for daytime drinking. Despite this, she has plenty of suitors, including a devil wearing a cunning disguise. One day, the princess meets Snow White at her teahouse in the forest, and while the girls get acquainted, the devil kidnaps them both. Shown in a double bill with **DOOR INTO SUMMER**, this adaptation of a weird "beauty and the beast" fairy tale by *Banana Fish*'s Akimi Yoshida was also the directorial debut for **VOTOMS**-director Takahashi.

DEVIL HUNTER YOHKO *
1991. JPN: *Mamono Hunter Yoko*. AKA: *Devil Hunter Yoko*. Video. DIR: Katsuhisa Yamada, Hisashi Abe, Akiyuki Shinbo. SCR: Sukehiro Tomita, Tatsuhiko Urahata. DES: Takeshi Miyao. ANI: Tetsuro Aoki. MUS: Hiroya Watanabe. PRD: Madhouse, NCS, Toho. 45 mins. x 1 eps., 30 mins. x 3 eps., 45 mins. x 2 eps.
Yohko Mano is the latest in a long line of devil-hunters. Torn between her grandmother's insistence that she carry on the tradition (for which she must remain a virgin) and her mother's urging to get knocked up as soon as possible, she is beset by demons who use any means possible to dispel the threat she presents. After a promising opener in which a local nice-guy is possessed and turned into a bad-boy in an attempt to seduce Yohko, later episodes fast decline in quality. She acquires a manager, Azusa (presaging a similar relationship in the later **CARDCAPTORS**), calms angry spirits at a construction site, appears in her own music video (the pointless *Yohko 4-ever*, which is sensibly bundled with other episodes in the U.S. release), then dies and rises from the dead. The sixth episode, confusingly called *Yohko²* in Japan, has Yohko defending the family honor from her look-alike cousin, Ayako. An inferior translation of the first three episodes was released in the U.K. in 1995 as *Devil Hunter Yoko* (*sic*). Producer Juzo Mutsuki would create a similar clash of traditional and contemporary ghostbusting in **PHANTOM QUEST CORP.** ⓃⓋ

DEVILMAN *
1972. TV series, video, movie. DIR: Tomoharu Katsumata, Nobutaka Nishizawa. SCR: Masaki Tsuji, Tadaaki Yamazaki, Susumu Takahisa. DES: Go Nagai. ANI: Kazuo Komatsubara, Takeshi Shirato, Kazuo Mori, Shingo Araki, Makoto Kunihara, Masamune Ochiai. MUS: Go Misawa. PRD: Dynamic Planning, Oh Pro, NET. 25 mins. x 38 eps. (TV), 43 mins. (m), 50 mins. x 2 eps. (v1), 25 mins. x 26 eps. (*Devil Lady*), 50 mins. (*Amon*).
Devilman and two other demons are sent to Earth to possess humans and cause chaos. Finding two Japanese families nearby when they awake from their long slumber in the Himalayas, Devilman chooses to possess Akira Fudo (his first choice, Akira's father, having died from fright), and the bedeviled boy is adopted by the kindly Makimura family. Falling in love with his stepsister Miki, Akira forgets his original mission. His former demon overlord, Zenon, sends a succession of creatures to kill him, and Akira must call on his ill-gotten powers.

When a Japanese TV network

wanted to adapt Go Nagai's **DEMON LORD DANTE** for TV in 1972, the artist instead offered them his new *Devilman* project, already running in *Shonen Magazine*. An uneasy combination of superhero serial and macabre horror, it featured a schoolboy forced to become an agent of good by using the powers of evil. Following his TV series, Devilman would appear in Tomoharu Katsumata's theatrical short **MAZINGER Z** *vs. Devilman* (1973), in which Dr. Hell tries to recruit him to defeat the robot warrior of the title.

In 1987, *Devilman* was revived for a two-part video adventure directed by Tsutomu Iida, which altered much of the designs and origins while keeping a retro 1970s look. In the video Akira is a shy boy who lives with his simpering childhood friend Maki while his parents are away on a business trip. His tough friend, Ryo (the hermaphroditic son of Satan) tells him of the existence of demons, and that Earth was once occupied by this evil race. The only way to defeat a demon is to fuse with one, and Ryo convinces Akira to allow this to happen. Ryo slaughters human beings at a nightclub to summon a demon, lucking into Amon, the Lord of Darkness. Because Akira is pure of heart, he is able to control the demon within him, turning his evil powers to good use. The second episode (as in the original TV series) features a battle with Amon's former lover, Sirene, though no further episodes were made. *Devilman*'s best moments are the flashback scenes of a prehistoric, demon-infested dreamtime that owed nothing to East *or* West, but it was the messy confluence of Japanese and European mythology that brought *Devilman* down (not helped by the U.K. dubbers Manga Entertainment's inability to get some of the classical references right, though they did find the time to write new lines like, "I'm gonna rip off your head and shit down your neck!"). The same director would make the three-part *Chibi Character Go Nagai World* (1990) featuring squashed-down versions of several Nagai char-

acters fighting at Armageddon. Akira Fudo also put in a cameo appearance in Nagai's later **CUTEY HONEY**.

Nagai returned to the franchise in 1997 with *Devilman Lady*, retelling the story for the more adult *Comic Morning* magazine by altering the sex of his protagonist and introducing evolutionary angles. **VAMPIRE PRINCESS MIYU**–director Toshihiro Hirano and **ARMITAGE III**–writer Chiaki Konaka adapted it into a 26-episode TV series in 1998. Though characters from the earlier versions make cameo appearances, the remake centers on Jun Fudo, a shy fashion model (a schoolteacher in the manga) who begins to develop mystic powers. As part of Mother Nature's answer to overpopulation, a "Devil Beast Syndrome" is afflicting the world's poor, transforming them into rapacious cannibal demons. Jun, however, has been genetically engineered by her scientist father to retain her former memories after infection and uses her power to fight off further incursions. The series was released in America under the less confusing title, *Devil Lady*.

Devilman was revived again for *Amon: The Apocalypse of Devilman* (2000), a 50-minute video released to cash in on the millennium, supervised by **FIST OF THE NORTH STAR**'s Toyoo Ashida and directed by Kenichi Takeshita. Featuring creatures designed by Yasushi Nirasawa, this chapter tied up many loose ends from the earlier versions, spooling forward in the original story to the final Armageddon. Akira now leads the demon-hunting Devilman Army, while a traumatized Miki wanders through a Tokyo in the grip of apocalyptic violence and rapine. Exploiting Akira's somewhat schizophrenic position as a force of good possessed by the ultimate evil, *Amon* is a vicious, sadistic anime in the spirit of **UROTSUKIDOJI**, and even features a one-on-one fight between Devilman and Satan.

The epilogue to all the *Devilman* stories was written in 1973 (only a year after the original manga) in Nagai's **VIOLENCE JACK**, which begins with a

remorseful Satan's decision to remake the world, to reincarnate as a cripple, and to create the Slum King to punish himself, though this relationship is not apparent in the 1986 anime version. In 2000, an issue of the *Demon Lord Dante* manga that inspired *Devilman* was released as a "manga video." **CNV**

DEZAKI, OSAMU
1943– . Born in Tokyo, he found work with Toshiba after graduating from high school, subsequently leaving that company to join Mushi Production in 1963 as a key animator on **ASTRO BOY**. He founded the company Art Fresh in 1964 with his elder brother Tetsu and Gisaburo Sugii before going freelance in 1967. Subsequently, he became a key figure at Madhouse. His works embrace many genres, including the sport of **AIM FOR THE ACE**, the children's drama of **NOBODY'S BOY**, and the medical thriller **BLACK JACK**. A distinctive feature of many Dezaki anime is the sudden use of freeze-frames, interpolated as single illustrations—this has often been regarded as a budget-saving device, but is a deliberate stylistic decision by a director who wants the audience to focus on single key moments. As the director of **GOLGO 13**, Dezaki was also the first in the anime business to experiment with digital animation.

DEZAKI, TETSU
1940– . Sometimes miscredited, even in official studio documents, as Satoshi Dezaki. Born in Tokyo, he was a writer and storyboarder on anime including **ATTACK NO. ONE** and **STAR OF THE GIANTS**. A co-founder of the studio Art Fresh in 1964 with his younger brother Osamu and Gisaburo Sugii, he later moved into directing, with works including **GREY: DIGITAL TARGET**. He also directed an animated opening sequence to Gerry Anderson's puppet show *Terrahawks* (see **THUNDERBIRDS 2086**), which was only used on the Japanese broadcast.

DIAMOND DAYDREAMS *
2004. JPN: *Kita e Diamond Dust Drops*.

AKA: *To The North, On to the North, Diamond Dust Drops*. TV series. DIR: Bob Shirahata. SCR: Mari Okada, Ryota Yamaguchi. DES: Michinori Chiba. ANI: Studio Deen. MUS: Takehito Itsukita. PRD: Studio Deen, Red, AT-X. 24 mins. x 12 eps.

Six separate stories of women from teens to twentysomethings, whose lives converge as a result of strange events on the northern island of Hokkaido. Most are looking for love, like Atsuko the Hakodate fishmonger betrothed to a local hotelier's heir but struggling with her feelings for a record-collecting slacker, or Karin, a Tokyo girl hospitalized in Kitami for the last two years, but refusing life-saving surgery because she hasn't trusted doctors since her father's death. It's also a travelogue of the region and features many well known tourist sights and local brands, with the separate strands coming together in the final episode for a magical denouement in Hokkaido's capital city of Sapporo. The titular "diamond dust" is a rare arctic weather phenomenon describable in strict meteorological terms as a fog or low-lying cloud of ice crystals. It can occur anywhere with prolonged subzero temperatures, but has entered Hokkaido folklore as a form of lucky charm, said to grant lifelong happiness to anyone who sees it—or perhaps a lump of tourist-colonial hokum designed to keep people coming to the northern island even when it's bitterly cold. This dating sim-based anime concentrates less on the dating angle than on the individual stories of the girls themselves; compare to KANON. Although based on a PS2 game by Oji Hiroi, the inspirations for this franchise lie further back in the long-running live-action TV series *From the North* (*DE), which came to a highly publicized end in 2002 after over twenty years as a mainstay of Japanese TV drama. Similar scenic inspirations informed SAIKANO.

DIARY OF ANNE FRANK

1979. JPN: *Anne no Nikki: Anne Frank Monogatari*. AKA: *Diary of Anne: Story of Anne Frank*. TV special, movie. DIR: Eiji Okabe. SCR: Ryuzo Nakanishi. DES: Yu Noda. ANI: Seiji Endo. MUS: Koichi Sakata. PRD: Nippon Animation, Transarts, Tomi Pro, Studio Orc, TV Asahi. 82 mins. (TVm), 102 mins. (m).

In 1940, Amsterdam is occupied by the Nazis. Persecuted for their Jewish faith, the Frank family is forced into hiding in a secret annex concealed in a canal-side house. The young daughter Anne begins to write down her thoughts in a diary, escaping from her situation by writing fantastic stories. Eventually, the family is discovered by the Nazis and taken away to a concentration camp.

This earnest but pretentious TV movie about the famous diarist uses four of Anne's stories (published as *Tales from the Secret Annex*) as interludes to break the monotony of her confinement: *Fear, The Wise Dwarf, Henrietta,* and *The Adventure of Bralee the Bear Cub*. Such a decision may have made cinematic sense, but it somehow trivializes Anne's plight. After the broadcast of this film, a child's viewpoint becomes a regular feature in anime about WWII, since it permits the use of Japanese characters who, like the baby-boom audience itself, had no part in the war that so dramatically altered the course of their country's history.

A second anime version was released in Japanese theaters in 1995, directed by Akinori Nagaoka. This production, from KSS and the Madhouse studio, was much more lavish than the original TV movie, featuring more realistic character designs from Yoshinori Kanemori and music by Michael Nyman, composer for *The Piano*. This film, minus its Nyman score, was released in French as *Le Journal d'Anne Frank* on DVD with English subtitles.

DIGI CHARAT

1999. TV series. DIR: Hiroaki Sakurai, Masayuki Kojima, Tatsuo Sato. SCR: N/C. DES: Yoshiki Yamagawa. ANI: N/C. MUS: N/C. PRD: Madhouse, TBS. 5 mins. x 16 eps. (TV1), 20 mins. x 4 eps. (*Summer Special*), 48 mins. (*Christmas Special*), ? mins. x 4 eps. (*Hanami Special*), ca. 22 mins. x 4 eps. (*Summer Holiday Special*), 20 mins. (*Trip*), 6 mins. 40 secs. x 48 eps. (*Panyo Panyo*), 15 mins. x 8 eps. (*Piyoko*), 12 mins. x 104 eps. (*Nyo*).

Adorning merchandise and commercials as the mascot character for the Gamers chain of stores in Japan, the cartoon ten-year-old Digiko is reputedly from the planet Digicarrot, from whence she was enticed to Earth by her love of broccoli. Landing with her friends in Tokyo's Akihabara district, she takes a job at a Gamers store with her friend Puchi Charat and leporine rival Rabi En-rose. Difficult customers and occasional adventures follow. Shown as part of the *Wonderful* anthology television show.

A four-part *DC: Summer Special* (2000) pits Digiko against new nemeses from the Black Gamer Gang, whose poverty-stricken leader Piyoko intends to kidnap her and hold her for ransom. The Black Gamers open their own shop in competition with Digiko's own, though they use sinister means to keep their customers. Digiko also appeared in cameos in PIA CARROT, EXCEL SAGA, and FIRST KISS STORY.

A terminally cute eight-part video sequel, *Leave it to Piyoko* (*Piyoko ni Omakase Piyo*, 2003) offered little plotting or intelligent scripting, just childlike candyfloss characters looking perky and sweet and doing their best to sell more merchandise. Similar antics awaited in the *DC Christmas Special* (2000), in which the cast relocates to a cruise liner. The cast later appeared in several seasonal cash-ins including the springtime *DC: O-hanami Special* (2001), a four-parter in which they partied beneath cherry blossoms, the four-part *DC Summer Holiday Special* (2001), in which Digiko visits America, competes in a band competition and goes hiking in the mountains. Digi Charat appeared in her own 25-minute "movie," *DC: A Trip to the Planet* (2001), in which she made a return visit to her homeworld, before returning to TV screens in the prequel *Panyo Panyo DC* (2002) and the 104-episode remake

DC: Nyo (2003). Note that although each episode had only one opening and closing credit sequence, it was often split into two distinct stories, leading some sources to list it as 104 episodes.

DIGI GIRL POP

2003. AKA: *Strawberry & Pop Mixed Flavor*. TV series. DIR: Taro Yamada. SCR: Kuniaki Kasahara, Motoki Yoshimura, Reiko Yoshida. DES: Asaki. ANI: Hajime Kurihara. MUS: N/C. PRD: Kazutaka Ito, GDH, HoriPro, Pioneer, Kid's Station. 25 mins. x 26 eps.

Based on a web Flash cartoon originated by Ooz Grafisch and Two Thousand Creators.com, these are the wacky and extremely brief adventures of a cute, pink-haired, perky girl robot who fell from the sky and was taken in by Nail, a girl who owns a nail salon. She starts going to high school and causes domestic and social mayhem.

DIGIMON *

1999. JPN: *Digimon Adventure*. AKA: *Digital Monsters*. TV series. DIR: Mamoru Hosoda, Hiroyuki Kadono, Takashi Imamura, Tetsuo Imazawa. SCR: Satoru Nishizono, Hiro Masaki. DES: Kappei Nakatsuru. ANI: Hiroki Shibata. MUS: Takanori Arisawa. PRD: Toei. 20 mins. x 54 eps. (TV1), 3 x 25 mins. (m); 20 mins. x 50 eps. (02), 20 mins. x 51 eps. (*Tamers*), 20 mins. x 50 eps. (*Frontier* TV), 40 mins. (*Frontier*-m); 30 mins. (*Diablomon Strikes Back*), 30 mins. (*Runaway Express*), 30 mins. (*X-Evolution*).

Goggle-wearing hero Taichi (Tai) and friends Izzy, Joe, Matt, Mimi, and Sora are at a summer camp like no other, where snow can fall in June and the Northern Lights appear far from the Arctic. The pals fall through a magic portal into the very different world on the pink sandy beaches of File Island, where they become embroiled in a battle between strange creatures. The kindly "digi[tal] mon[sters]" that inhabit the parallel world are being corrupted by an evil force, who inserts Black Gears into good digimon to turn them bad. As the children try to solve the mystery, their digimon companions "digivolve" into better and stronger fighters.

After a handover engineered one of the three holiday special minifeatures (2000, cut together for U.S. release as the *Digimon Movie*), a second season followed, rebranded as *Digimon 02* and set three years later, with the return of the evil Devilmon in control of a powerful new energy source. Our heroes, who attend the same soccer club with the gang from the first series, team up with a new digital monster, the blue Buimon, to fight back. A third series, renamed *Digimon Tamers,* began in April 2001, moving the action into the "near-future" year of 200X. This was followed by *Digimon Frontier* (2002), in which five all-new children were chosen to fight the evil Cherubimon, which is intent on destroying the world. This was followed by *Digimon Savers* (2006), in which more of the same ensued.

Numerous further *Digimon* "movies," often mere episode-length screenings at summer roadshows, have made the *Digimon* franchise even more confusing than it already was. These include *The Runaway Digimon Express* (2002), and *Diablomon Strikes Back* (2005). New toys were introduced in *Digimon: X-Evolution* (2005), which utilized elements of Norse mythology alongside a "virtual world" setup more similar to that employed in .HACK.

Optioned for U.S. release in the post-POKÉMON gold rush, *Digimon* was inadvertently one of the most faithful translations of TV anime; the U.S. and Japanese schedules were so close together that there was little opportunity to do too much rewriting or cutting. Technically speaking, as the descendants of the *original* virtual pets featured in TAMAGOTCHI VIDEO ADVENTURES, Digimon have a better pedigree than Pokémon, despite only achieving about half the latter's ratings. The series was also dogged by legal wrangles in the U.S., when the Screen Actors Guild challenged production company Saban over the rights to residuals for the *Digimon* movie. The irony was not in SAG's claim that voice acting was a creative, skilled task that warranted better conditions, but that they had never brought it up before.

DIGITAL DEVIL STORY *

1987. JPN: *Digital Devil Story: Megami Tensei*. AKA: *DDS: Goddess Reborn*. Video. DIR: Mizuho Nishikubo. SCR: Mizuho Nishikubo. DES: Hiroyuki Kitazume. ANI: Naoyuki Onda. MUS: Usagigumi. PRD: Tokuma Shoten, Animate. 45 mins.

Computer geek Tamami uses the school's computer center to summon the "digital devil" Loki, soon enlisting teachers and fellow students in a dark cult. Only new-girl Yumiko is unaware of this secret, though she soon discovers that she is the reincarnation of an ancient goddess and, consequently, the only person who can put an end to Loki's violent rampages.

Based on a novel by Aya Nishitani and featuring character designs by original illustrator Hiroyuki Kitazume, this inferior horror anime enjoyed an inferior British release, using the original spotting list from Kiseki, which retains the Japanese translator's creative romanizations of otherwise well-known mythological creatures, including Loki and Set. In Japan, it was screened on a theatrical double bill with I GIVE MY ALL. The story was also adapted into a computer game, which in turn was adapted into *another* anime, TOKYO REVELATION. **NV**

DIOXIN SUMMER

2001. JPN: *Inochi no Chikyu: Dioxin no Natsu*. AKA: *Life's World: Summer of the Dioxin*. Movie. DIR: Tetsu Dezaki. SCR: Kazuo Koide. DES: Setsuko Shibunnoichi. ANI: Setsuko Shibunnoichi, Keizo Shimizu. MUS: N/C. PRD: Sotsu Agency, Sunrise. ca. 85 mins.

The true story of an accident in Italy in 1976, when an explosion at a biological research laboratory threatened the surrounding area with deadly dioxins and ruined the happy existence of a group

© TAKACHIHO & STUDIO NUE • SUNRISE

Dirty Pair

of 11-year-old children. Adapted from a book by Kei Hasumi. Compare to **SEA OF THE TICONDEROGA**.

DIRTY PAIR *

1985. TV series, movie, video. DIR: Katsuyoshi Yatabe, Toshifumi Takizawa, Tsukasa Dokite, Norio Kabeshima, Masaharu Okuwaki, Koichi Mashimo. SCR: Hiroyuki Hoshiyama, Kazunori Ito, Tsukasa Tsunaga, Haruka Takachiho, Yasushi Hirano, Fuyunori Gobu, Masaaki Sakurai, Go Sakamoto. DES: Tsukasa Dokite, Fujihiko Hosono, Yoshito Asari, Katsuhiko Nishijima, Studio Nue. ANI: Kazuo Tomisawa, Tsukasa Dokite. MUS: Toshiyuki Kimori, Yoshihiro Kunimoto. PRD: Nippon Sunrise, Studio Nue, Nippon TV. 25 mins. x 26 eps. (TV) 50 mins. x 3 eps. (v), 80 mins. (m), 25 mins. x 10 eps. (*Original*), 30 mins. x 16 eps. (*DPF videos*). Kei and Yuri are the "Lovely Angels," Trouble Consultants for the World's Welfare Work Association (3WA), a federal police force that serves the United Galactica government. Wearing skintight spacesuits that happen to be almost completely transparent (thereby looking just like bikinis) and accompanied by their "pet" ursoid Mughi

and R2D2 clone Nammo, the girls are sent on missions that often end in massive explosions and collateral damage, resulting in the unkind nickname of the "Dirty Pair."

At the time they first appeared onscreen in the anime adaptation of Haruka Takachiho's **CRUSHER JOE**, the Dirty Pair had already featured in two novels of their own, including *The Great Adventures of DP*, which won the Seiun (Japanese Nebula) Award. The year after their anime debut, the characters won another Seiun for the book *DP Strike Back*. They were named for one of the author's favorite female wrestling teams, the Beauty Pair, while the 3WA is a reference to the World Women's Wrestling Association. The real-life Beauty Pair inspired many imitators in the wrestling field, including the Black Pair, Golden Pair, and Queen Angels—a roster that influenced several other series, including **MARIS THE CHOJO** and **METAL FIGHTER MIKU**.

Designer Dokite adapted Yoshikazu Yasuhiko's illustrations from the original novels, the third of which was timed to come out simultaneously with the debut show. Though the series was canceled early after 24 episodes, the

last two parts were immediately rushed out onto video in 1985 as *DP: From Lovely Angels With Love*. The franchise stayed on video with *DP: Affair on Nolandia* (1985), directed by Okuwaki and written by **PATLABOR**'s Ito, in which the girls are sent to an arboreal planet where they must stop an illegal genetic experiment. *Nolandia* is notable for being the only occasion in the entire anime adventures that alludes to Kei and Yuri's telepathic abilities, a major feature of the novels.

The 1987 *DP* movie, known in the U.S. as *DP: Project Eden*, pastiched Frank Herbert's *Dune* by revealing that warp travel is impossible without the rare metal vizorium. Sent to planet Agerna to stop two rival nations from destroying each other in a war over the element, the girls meet Professor Wattsman, a scientist intent on using vizorium to bring forth a powerful new life form. The same year saw the publication *The Great Adventures of DP* in English, but the duo's greatest impact on the U.S. market came in 1988 with the publication of the first of many American *DP* comics produced by Toren Smith and Adam Warren.

Though it would be several more years before the movie and video versions of *DP* would reach the U.S. through Streamline Pictures, the original TV series sold well in Europe, and ten extra shows were made in 1989 specifically to bulk out the TV run to 36 episodes for the Italian market. Stuck straight onto two-part videos in the Japanese market as *DP Wink, Masterworks, Complete, Mystery, Birth, Special, Variety, Investigation, First Final*, and *Last Fantasy*, these "bonus" episodes were released abroad by AD Vision as *Original DP*; the distributor's argument being that although they were not the initial (untranslated) TV series, they were still truer to the original than *DP Flash* (see below).

The video *DP Flight 005 Conspiracy* (1990) concentrated less on zany antics and more on a serious thriller story, as the pair are sent to investigate a space liner explosion that kills 300 passengers, though nobody attempts to claim insurance. It was to be the last anime outing to date for the original Kei and Yuri.

Takachiho would revise the characters in 1994 for *DP Flash*, which portrayed the Lovely Angels as younger, dumber, cuter investigators rendered in sharper (and cheaper) animation. Though many (including the production staff!) often assume *DPF* to be a flashback to the characters' early years, it is actually set over a century later, starring young girls called Kei and Yuri, who look very similar to the originals but are only the latest in a series of duos to use the code name. These two new Lovely Angels undo all the good work done by the last holders of the title (Molly and Iris, some 15 years earlier), returning the code name to infamy.

Despite this convoluted backstory, *DPF* struggles to recreate the fun of the original. With a complex numbering system obscuring one long succession of stand-alone episodes (there is no "story arc" worth repeating in the "serials" separately named *DPF1*, *2*, and *3*), the characters of *DPF* spend very little time investigating, preferring instead to parody other anime with a visit to a 20th-century theme park or to experience minor difficulties in their attempts to have a vacation. The *DPF* video adventures play up the girls' eye-candy qualities (admittedly, not entirely absent in the appeal of the original), giving them nude transformation sequences and missions such as winning a volleyball tournament, designed as little more than an excuse to spool through a line of sports-show training clichés, leavened with regular wobbles of fan-service cleavage. But while Takachiho's originals continue in their novel form with the most recent *DP: A Legend of Dictator*, *DP*'s most successful incarnation abroad remains the U.S. comic rather than the anime that inspired it. **N**

DIRTY THOUGHTS *

2003. JPN: *Private Emotion*. Video. DIR: Sosuke Kokubunji. SCR: Sosuke Kokubunji. DES: Hirotaka. ANI: Takayuki Yanase. MUS: Yoshitaka Shiro. PRD: Dream Entertainment, Studio March, Milky, Museum Pictures. 30 mins. x 2 eps.

Forced to leave her previous school after her lesbian relationship with a pupil was exposed, Sayaka takes a new post in a new town. However, when her principal discovers her secret, he uses it as a means of blackmailing her into sex with him. Based on the computer game *Private Emotion*. **LNV**

DISCOVERY SERIES *

1998. Video. DIR: Hideki Takayama, Yoshitaka Makino, Yusaku Saotome, Yu Yahagi, Juhachi Minamisawa. SCR: Masateru Tsuruoka, Hajime Yamaguchi, Yu Yahagi, Joichi Michigami. DES: Masahiro Sekiguchi, Takanari Hijo, Tomo'o Shintani. ANI: Hirota Shindo, Koichi Fuyukawa, Masahiro Sekiguchi. MUS: Kazuhiko Izu, Hiroaki Sano, Takeshi Nishizawa. PRD: Discovery. 30 mins. x 7 eps. (*Maiden of*); 2 eps. (*Baby Bird*); 4 eps. (*Necronomicon*); 4 eps. (*Triangle Heart*); 4 eps. (*True Snow*); 14 eps. (*Night Shift Nurses*); 3 eps. (*Blood Shadow*); 3 eps. (*F-Force*); 2 eps. (*Maison Plaisir*); 3 eps. (*Slave Market*); 2 eps. (*Black Widow*); 3 eps. (*Sibling Secret*); 2 eps. (*Blood Royale*); 2 eps. (*Xtra Credit*); 3 eps. (*Nurse Me*); 2 eps. (*Stepsister*); 4 eps. (*TH: Sweet Songs Forever*); 1 ep (*Shrike*); 2 eps. (*Swallowtail Inn*); 2 eps. (*Temptation*); 2 eps. (*Pigeon Blood*); 1 ep (*Fiendish Face*); 2 eps. (*Newscaster Etsuko*); 2eps (*Tokineiro*); 2 eps. (*Panties Teacher*); 1 ep (*New Gymnastics*).

As CREAM LEMON, SECRET ANIMA and the VANILLA SERIES have already amply demonstrated, the demands of the erotic market revolve around shorter cycles than television. Whereas anime for the children's market can repeat itself every two years without much chance of complaint, and anime for teenagers often follows a similar lengthy rotation of ideas, pornography's aims are far lower. For it to work, it need only entertain its target consumer, often

a renter rather than a buyer, for half an hour. This entry consolidates the multitude of separate titles that originate with the Discovery label, although many already have entries elsewhere in this book, particularly if they have received an English-language release.

Beginning in 1998 with the MAIDEN OF… series, Discovery established an early reputation for plots revolving around dominance and submission. *Song of the Baby Bird* (2000, *Hinadori no Saezuri*) was not originally part of the *Maiden of…* series, but sold in the U.S. as *Maiden of Deliverance*. It also capitalized on the growing popularity of interactive media by investing in lengthy adaptations of computer games, such as its second big release, MYSTERY OF THE NECRONOMICON. TRIANGLE HEART was followed in 2000 by *True Snow the Color of Lapis Lazuli* (*Shin Ruri-iro no Yuki*), another computer game adaptation that centers on a scientifically-minded inventor who finds himself having to share his life with Yuki, a spirit-girlfriend who owes a certain debt to the "Snow Princess" of JAPANESE FOLK TALES, with elements of OH MY GODDESS!. The same year also saw the first episode of Discovery's most popular and long-running release, NIGHT SHIFT NURSES—hospitalization being an excellent excuse for the domination and bodily invasion that often seem to be a Discovery trademark.

More game adaptations followed in 2001 with BLOOD SHADOW (itself seeming to be based on a pastiche of SAKURA WARS) and F-FORCE. In 2002, the company appeared to move even further into the niche territory of scatology and submission, with MAISON PLAISIR and SLAVE MARKET. It also developed what may have been a coincidental theme of exploiting lonely widows, following *Maison Plaisir* with BLACK WIDOW.

Inevitably, incest would also form a part of the Discovery series, arriving in 2002 with SIBLING SECRET, while themes of bondage and imprisonment would recur in BLOOD ROYALE and XTRA CREDIT. Incest and computer game tie-ins met in the form of **Stepsister**. The company also experimented with a new hospital franchise in the form of **Nurse Me!**.

Five years after the company began releasing erotica, the first new title of 2003 was a sequel to the original *Triangle Heart*, called *Sweet Songs Forever*. The company released a rare one-shot release, *Shrike* (*Mozu no Nie*), which may have been a deliberate decision, or a historical anomaly created by a title that failed to generate good sales in relation to ongoing series like *Night Shift Nurses*. The story was a historical vignette in which a kimono-clad princess is molested by her stepbrother. However, the historical setting cannot have handicapped sales of *Shrike* too badly, since it was immediately followed by **Swallowtail Inn**, another tale with an old-fashioned look, which ran for two episodes. The same year saw a return to campus tales with **Temptation** and more domination in *Pigeon Blood*, in which the amnesiac Chris wakes up to discover he is a "slave master" charged with breaking in new acquisitions. He encounters a girl called Rita on one of his trips into town, and he succumbs to her pleas to enter his house and be trained as one of his slaves.

In 2004, the company adapted *Fiendish Face* (*Masho no Kao*), a manga title from "Mink," the games company behind *Night Shift Nurses*. In it, a teenager returning home from school finds the archetypal "mysterious girl" in his room, who turns out to be his stepsister Reika, with whom he is soon playing toilet games. It also parodied the TV journalism genre so beloved of live-action television, with *Newscaster Etsuko* (*Hana no Joshi Ana: Newscaster Etsuko*), in which a reporter for Tokyo's "Flower TV," Etsuko Yamanobe, chases stories while fretting about holes in her underwear—compare to **Nine O'Clock Woman**. The same year saw *Sensual Ticking Time* (*Tokineiro*), in which "I," yet another amnesiac protagonist, wakes up in a remote wintry mansion, where time runs differently and four sobbing

maids await his attentions. Discovery returned to school voyeurism with *Panties Teacher* (*Panchira Teacher*) in which politician's daughter Machiko attempts to teach classes of teenagers while wearing an inappropriately short skirt—possibly an oblique reference to the old series **Shame on Miss Machiko**.

In 2005, Discovery turned its attention to high school sports, with *Rhythmic Gymnastics* (*Shintaiso—Makoto* aka *New Gymnastics*), billed, in a strange crossover between companies, as a sequel to Pink Pineapple's **Princess 69**. However, it seems that nothing quite compares to the love of Discovery's viewers for more stories in the *Night Shift Nurses* series, the latest episode of which (billed as episode one of *NSN3*) was also released in 2005, and marked Discovery's 77th anime release. ⬤🄻🄽🅅

DISGAEA

2006. JPN: *Makai Senki Disgaea*. AKA: *Netherworld Battle Chronicle Disgaea*. TV series. DIR: Kiyotaka Isako. SCR: Atsuhiro Tomioka. DES: Akira Kano. ANI: N/C. MUS: N/C. PRD: Oriental Light and Magic. 25 mins. x 12 eps.
Laharl, self-centered son of the king of the Netherworld, wakes up from a two-year coma to find his land in turmoil after the death of his father. He begins the struggle to retake his birthright, in an adaptation of the game *Disgaea: Hour of Darkness*, published by Nihon Ichi.

DISPATCHES FROM THE SPIRIT WORLD

1996. JPN: *Jigoku Reikai Tsushin*. AKA: *Spiritual Report: Occult Shop from Hell*. Video. DIR: Junichi Sato. SCR: Miyuki Takahashi. DES: Akihito Maejima. ANI: N/C. MUS: N/C. PRD: Toei. 23 mins. x 2 eps.
Three young boys are chased by a ghost and run to an occult shop for help. There, they are given a selection of magical items that will allow them to send malevolent spirits back to hell. After successfully dealing with their initial assailant, they go into business as professional ghostbusters, righting wrongs all over Tokyo.

Beginning as a best-selling children's book by Karin Kagetsu and illustrated by Akihito Maejima, this *Ghostbusters* rip-off became a live-action film directed by **Be-Bop High School**'s Hiroyuki Nasu in 1996. Controversial for introducing scary themes in what was supposedly a children's film, the live version was refused a general rating, and its original target audience was forced to settle for the anime.

DIVERGENCE EVE *

2003. TV series. DIR: Hiroshi Negishi, Atsushi Takada. SCR: Toru Nozaki. DES: Toshinari Yamashita, Takayuki Takeya, Tatsuya Tomosugi. ANI: Toshinari Yamashita. MUS: Yousuke Hoga. PRD: Plasma, Radix, AT-X. 25 mins. x 13 eps. (TV1), 25 mins. x 13 eps. (TV2).
In the year 2317, interstellar travel takes place via gates that pass through a parallel universe, unfortunately leaving travelers open to attacks from the other-dimensional inhabitants known as Ghouls. At the Watcher's Nest, a space station that watches over the far end of the jump from Saturn's moon Titan, rookie Misaki Kureha and her big-eyed, large-breasted associates are in training to become pilots in the elite Seraphim Squadron. What begins as a silly sci-fi adventure about pneumatic space bimbos soon changes direction radically, incorporating conspiracies redolent of writer Nozaki's earlier **Gasaraki** and elements of Ridley Scott's *Alien*, as Misaki and some new, artificial associates discover more about the nature of the savage Ghouls and their conflict with humanity.

DIVINE CHANGELING ENCHANTMENT

1988. JPN: *Shinshu Sudamahen*. AKA: *Fantasy Kingdom War*. Video. DIR: Tetsu Dezaki. SCR: Tetsuaki Imaizumi, Kazumi Koide. DES: Keizo Shimizu. ANI: Keizo Shimizu. MUS: Yukari Omori. PRD: Magic Bus. 30 mins. x 6 eps.
In medieval Japan's Genroku era, the young warrior Yoshiyasu Yanasawa approaches Takaharu, the leader of the Hazuki clan in search of the power

of the "Golden Dragon," unaware that the power of the dragon flows within the very bloodstream of the maiden Orie. The quest broadens out into a fight over a line of gold ore in the Nasu mountains, and the Tokugawa lord Tsunayoshi learns of the Golden Dragon's magical powers when he tries to rape Orie. The samurai Kageshichi-ro Hagetsu tries to dispel Tsunayoshi's evil spirit before it awakens the dragon completely and brings chaos to Japan. The animated version of a period drama by Tsuneo Tani.

Director Dezaki also made the two-part spin-off series, *Cold Moon Spirit Cutter* (1989), a samurai-era detective saga starring the popular supporting character Itto Kanzuki, who has a constant quest to help those in need. **NV**

DNA HUNTER *

2002. Video. DIR: Takeshi Masui. SCR: Hayato Nakamura, Mankyu Mizoguchi. DES: MIE. ANI: MIE. MUS: N/C. PRD: Blue Cat, Five Ways. 30 mins. x 3 eps. Distraught at the death of her fiancé in a climbing accident, Mai seeks help from his place of employment, a clandestine sperm bank whose clients are rich women in search of the best quality donors. Mai wants to have a baby by her dead lover, but cannot afford the clinic's extremely high rates. Instead, she is offered the chance to become a DNA Hunter, an agent who secretly harvests genetic material from unsuspecting celebrities, so that it can be sold to the highest bidder. The result is an innovative excuse for the picaresque sexual encounters of typical anime porn and an unfolding conspiracy story line that makes this show more than the sum of its parts—compare to **SEXORCIST**, which was another rare entry in the sci-fi erotica genre, and **DNA²**, of which this seems to be a pastiche. **N**

DNA SIGHTS 999.9 *

1997. JPN: *Fire Force Danasight Four-Nine*. Video. DIR: Takeshi Shirato, Masa-yuki Kojima. SCR: Tatsuhiko Urahata. DES: Leiji Matsumoto. ANI: Aki Tsunaki. MUS: Katsuo Ono. PRD: Madhouse. 45 mins.

After Earth is devastated in an apocalyptic meteor shower, it is taken over by a military cartel calling itself the Trader Forces, which is secretly supplied by an alien woman called Photon. A second woman, Mellow, "casts her cosmic consciousness" at Earth, where it crashes in 2024 with the impact of another meteorite. Daiba, a local boy, investigates the crash site but is arrested by the Traders. Contacted telepathically by Mellow, he is told that he, an Earth girl called Rei, and a third party whom they will have to find themselves (who turns out to be a cat) are all examples of the next stage in evolution. Aided by Mellow, the three must overthrow the Traders.

"This contains the essence of all my previous works. It's a space opera that also focuses on Earth's environmental problems," said creator Leiji Matsumoto at the time of this anime's release; neatly sidestepping the issue of yet another rewrite of his standard character templates reusing ideas and imagery from his **GALAXY EXPRESS 999** and **QUEEN EMERALDAS**.

There are a few new ideas, such as the magma-dwelling "underlife" creatures briefly encountered, but essentially this is a run-of-the-mill teen adventure using familiar-looking characters in an attempt to drag in longer-standing fans of Matsumoto's other work. That was certainly the way it was sold in Japan, where press releases could not resist hinting that both **CAPTAIN HARLOCK** and the Yamato spaceship from **STAR BLAZERS** would make cameo appearances.

DNA² *

1994. JPN: *DNA² (Dokokade Nakushita Aitsuno Aitsu)*. AKA: *(Dumb Nerd Always Astray)*. TV series. DIR: Junichi Sakata. SCR: Tatsuhiko Urahata. DES: Kumiko Takahashi, Masakazu Katsura, Takeshi Koike. ANI: N/C. MUS: Eiji Takano. PRD: Powhouse, Nippon TV. 25 mins. x 12 eps. (TV), 25 mins. x 3 eps. (v). Junta Momonari is a hapless boy with a real complex about sex—the merest thought of it makes him physically sick.

But one day he will become a Mega-Playboy, siring 100 equally fecund children, and agent Karin Aoi is sent back from the future to stop his genes from causing an uncontrollable baby boom. Unluckily for her, she shoots him with the wrong drug and ends up creating the very Mega-Playboy she was sent back to prevent.

Despite the popularity of similar boy-meets-dozen-girls shows like **TENCHI MUYO!**, this adaptation of **VIDEO GIRL AI**–creator Masakazu Katsura's 1994 *Shonen Jump* manga underperformed in its anime incarnation. Even though *DNA²* contains all the elements thought to guarantee success, including a geeky-Jekyll-and-macho-Hyde subplot as Junta's playboy persona takes periodic control of his body and libido, the series was taken off the air early and ignominiously forced to finish its run on video. With revisionist hindsight, the video episodes were shuffled among the actual TV episodes and now comprise the second, third, and final chapters in the 15-chapter (5-tape) series available in Japanese stores. It was parodied in the pornographic computer game *Timestripper*, and is much imitated in anime such as **DNA HUNTER** and **DOKURO-CHAN**. **N**

DNANGEL *

2003. AKA: *D.N.A.* TV series. DIR: Koji Yoshikawa, Nobuyoshi Habara. SCR: Naruhisa Arakawa. DES: Shinichi Yamaoka, Yasuhiro Moriki. ANI: Hideyuki Motohashi, Shinichi Yamaoka. MUS: Takahito Eguchi, Tomoki Hasegawa. PRD: Dentsu, Kadokawa, TV Tokyo, Xebec. 25 mins. x 26 eps. Daisuke Niwa is fourteen and in love, but when he tries to declare himself to his dream girl Risa Harada and she gives him the "good friends" brush-off, he suddenly transforms into the legendary "phantom thief" Dark Mousy. Successive transformations plague Daisuke every time he gets emotional about the object of his affections. Meanwhile, not only does his mother seem to accept this transformation as a normal family event, she makes Dark steal rare works of art for a purpose Daisuke can't even guess at. His classmate Hiwatari has made it his mission to catch Dark—and just when it seems things could hardly get worse, so has Risa, who much prefers the glamorous, exciting young thief to her shy, inept classmate. Meanwhile, Risa's twin sister Riku decides Daisuke is the one for her. Based on Yukiri Sugisaki's 1997 manga that combined the thievery of LUPIN III with the transformations of CONAN THE BOY DETECTIVE. Like many other romantic anime of the early 21st century, it focuses less on love itself than on means of coping with rejection—compare to KOI KAZE.

DOCTOR CHICHIBUYAMA

1988. Video. DIR: Tetsuro Amino, Masa Watanabe. SCR: Yoshio Urasawa. DES: Yutaka Kawasuji. ANI: Yutaka Kawasuji. MUS: The Chichibuyama Band. PRD: Studio Ship, Pony Canyon, Ashi Pro, Fuji TV. 30 mins. x 2 eps.
In this short-lived black comedy based on a 1983 manga by Keiichi Tanaka originally serialized in *Comic Gekiga Murajuku*, Dr. Chichibuyama, the perverse, sunglasses-wearing head of a hospital way out in the mountains, terrorizes patients with the help of his lover and a sexy young nurse. Though the manga rode the fad of "Lolita Complex" titles typified by CREAM LEMON, the anime version appeared at the end of the boom and failed to ignite much interest. Two five-minute sections were broadcast on Fuji TV's midnight *All Night Fuji* program, presumably to promote the video. ◐

DOCTOR DOLITTLE

1990. JPN: *Dolittle Sensei Monogatari.* AKA: *Stories of Doctor Dolittle.* Video. DIR: Seiji Okuda. SCR: N/C. DES: Tom Ray. ANI: N/C. MUS: N/C. PRD: Knack, My Video. 48 mins. x 3 eps.
Hugh Lofting's children's story about a doctor who could genuinely talk to the animals was animated here in a U.S.-Japan coproduction featuring input from designer Tom Ray, who worked on famous Western cartoons such as *Tom and Jerry* and *The Pink Panther.*

DOCTOR FABRE THE DETECTIVE

2000. JPN: *Fabre Sensei wa Meitantei.* AKA: *Dr. Fabre Is a Famous Detective; Inspector Fabre.* TV series. DIR: Osamu Nakamura, Masami Yoshikawa. SCR: Osamu Nakamura. DES: N/C. ANI: Nobuteru Tanaka, Masashi Shiozawa, Scott Frazier. MUS: N/C. PRD: Enoki Film, IG Film. 25 mins. x 26 eps.
The adventures of a detective modeled on *Sherlock Holmes* but dwelling in 19th-century Paris, where he solves mysteries centering around the Great Exhibition, the invention of cinema, and other new developments, rubbing shoulders with the famous people of the age in the manner of *Young Indiana Jones.* A fittingly fin-de-siècle mixture of the detective boom of the YOUNG KINDAICHI FILES with the new retro craze of TREE IN THE SUN.

DOCTOR MAMBO AND JIBAKO THE THIEF

1982. JPN: *Doctor Mambo to Kaiketsu Jibaki: Uchu yori Ai o Komete.* AKA: *Doctor Mambo and Jibako the Thief: From Space with Love.* TV special. DIR: Yoshio Yabuki. SCR: Akinori Matsubara. DES: Toyoo Ashida. ANI: Kiichiro Suzuki. MUS: Kazuo Sugita. PRD: Toei, Fuji TV. 84 mins.
In this one-shot adaptation of one of Morio Kita's *Dr. Mambo* SF novels, the dashing Dr. Mambo and his unlikely sidekick, Jibako the thief, help Princess Laura, former ruler of Eden, regain her birthright from the usurping President Capo.

DOCTOR SHAMELESS *

2003. JPN: *Chijoku Shinsatsushitsu.* AKA: *Shameful Surgery.* Video. DIR: Ken Raikaken. SCR: Rokurota Makabe. DES: P-zo Honda. ANI: Yuya Soma. MUS: Salad. PRD: Deluxe. 30 mins. x 2 eps.
Dr. Kyozaburo Nagatsuka's private hospital is failing when young Dr. Shinji Ishida comes looking for a job. Shinji is credited with turning many failing hospitals around, but he insists he must have a free hand to use any methods. His chosen methods are sex and humiliation; he gets female

patients under his spell and effects remarkable "cures," resulting in return visits, recommendations, and more income for the hospital. He discovers that one of the nurses is not a licensed medical practitioner but a moonlighting sex worker and offers the same therapy to male patients, and the practice is soon thriving. Compare to NURSE ME!. ◐◐◑

DOCTOR SLUMP

1981. JPN: *Doctor Slump and Arale-chan.* TV series/special, movie. DIR: Minoru Okazaki, Yoshiki Shibata, Daisuke Nishio, Akinori Nagaoka. SCR: Masaki Tsuji, Shunichi Yukimuro, Tomoko Konparu, Michiru Shimada. DES: Shinji Koike. ANI: Shinji Koike. MUS: Takeo Watanabe. PRD: Fuji TV, Toei. 25 mins. x 243 eps., 90 mins. (m), 52 mins., 48 mins., 38 mins. (m), 25 mins. x 26? eps. (TV).
In the wacky hamlet of Penguin Village, Dr. Senbe "Slump" Norimaki decides to put together the perfect robot woman from data collected in pop idol photos and porno mags. Instead of perfection, he ends up with Arale-chan, a bespectacled and inquisitive tyke with superhuman strength, and the odd couple get into many wacky adventures. They are helped in their quest for the weird by Slump's penchant for crazy inventions, such as time machines, quantum cloning devices, an invisible gun, and X-Ray spectacles.
Akira Toriyama's original 1980 manga ran in *Shonen Jump* for 18 volumes. This anime version came about after an abortive attempt at a live-action show made producers realize that the only way to capture the cartoony spirit of the original was by making a cartoon. The other occupants of Penguin Village provide a menagerie of amusing characters in the fashion of Toriyama's later DRAGON BALL, including a pig that does a rooster's job of waking everyone up in the morning, a superhero that must eat prunes to transform, and Gatchan, a metal-eating flying creature.
Dr. Slump is one of anime's most successful shows, scoring a massive TV rat-

ing of 36.9 at its peak (the "mega-hit" EVANGELION managed a paltry 7.1). It has also been a hit abroad, particularly in the large anime markets of Hong Kong and Italy, but has yet to make it to the English language. The series also spun off several "TV specials" often premiered in theaters during summer festivals. Since the TV episodes often consisted of small vignettes, these "movies" consisted of little more than extended anthologies, like *Hello! Mysterious Island* (1981), which often spoofed other films of the day such as QUEEN OF A THOUSAND YEARS (*Who Is the Real Queen of a Thousand Years!?*, 1981) and DON QUIXOTE in *Heroic Legend of Penguin Village* (1986), which is about Slump undertaking a dangerous quest to the supermarket to get more toilet paper.

The first true *DS* movie, called simply *Dr. Slump* (1982), sends the characters on a space mission to planet Takeyasaodake, a mission loaded with parodies of the *Star Wars* movies, STAR BLAZERS, and GALAXY EXPRESS 999. Later "movies" were closer in length to the TV specials they replaced, including *The Great Race Around the World* (1983) and *The Secret Treasure of Nanaba Castle* (1984), both glorified episodes at little more than 50 minutes. Though straggling TV specials would make it a lingering death, the official grand finale was *Megapolis the Dream City* (1985), a "movie" of only 38 minutes, in which Arale and company befriend some monsters from outer space.

The series returned for several New Year's TV specials in 1992, although only two of the vignettes, *The Tearful Film Director* and *The Day New Year Didn't Arrive*, were actually new; the other episodes were old *DS* "movies." The franchise was properly revived in 1997, when a new TV series, without the direct involvement of Toriyama, became the first anime to use computer coloring instead of cels.

DOCTOR SURPRISE
1998. AKA: *Dokkiri Doctor*. TV series. DIR: Kazunori Mizuno. SCR: Satoru Nishizono, Aya Matsui, Yoshiyuki

Doctor Surprise

Suga, Tsutomu Kaneko. DES: Mari Kitayama. ANI: Masaya Onishi, Shinsuke Terasawa, Manabu Fukusawa. MUS: Yoshimoto Hizawa. PRD: Visual Works, Studio Pierrot, Fuji TV. 25 mins. x 27 eps.
The prestigious Shirabara Clinic has had four previous directors since its founding in the 19th century, but none have been quite so memorable as the fifth incumbent, Haruka Nishikikoji. With a fat face, "a jaw like FRANKENSTEIN," a gentle manner, and a genius way with patients, he's a mad scientist working for the side of justice. Lumbered with a cute nursing assistant after the lovely Miyuki's parents go off on a round-the-world trip, Haruka finds himself with a surrogate family,

soon becoming embroiled in Miyuki's younger sister's trials at the local primary school. But Haruka has always carried a torch for Miyuki, although he cannot think of a way to confess his true feelings, in this lighthearted adaptation of JUDGE-creator Fujihiko Hosono's original manga.

DOCUMENTARIES AND HISTORY
Although often regarded as a wholly fictional medium, anime has a documentary tradition dating back to Seitaro Kitayama's one-reeler *What to Do with Your Postal Savings* (*Chokin no Susume*, 1917). A pioneer in this field, Kitayama also made animation segments for the film *Dental Hygiene* (*Koku Eisei*, 1922), produced by the detergent

manufacturer Lion. Animation was useful for illustrating abstract concepts and the inner workings of machines—although children's fairy tales still form the bulk of EARLY ANIME, several are factual in basis. Notable examples include Kitayama's *Atmospheric Pressure and the Hydraulic Pump* (*Kiatsu to Mizuage Pump*, 1921), *Plant Physiology and Plant Ecology* (*Shokubutsu Seiri Seitai no Maki*, 1922), and *The Earth* (*Chikyu no Maki*, 1922).

This "instructional" role transferred easily to propaganda purposes, used to depict scenes both accurate and otherwise in WARTIME ANIME such as *Nippon Banzai* (1943), and a prolonged sequence in MOMOTARO'S DIVINE SEA WARRIORS (1945), detailing the alleged abuses Asia had suffered at the hands of Western imperialists—the authors have yet to confirm, but we suspect the latter sequence may be a recycling of the former.

The first anime TV series, INSTANT HISTORY (1961), set the tone for many other educational programs by dramatizing important events. This process came to fruition in ANIMENTARY: CRITICAL MOMENTS (1971), JAPANESE HISTORY (1976), and MANGA PICTURES OF JAPAN (1977). Serials of short informational films used comedic setups to convey information about law and society, in the hapless adventures of OUTSIDE THE LAW (1969) and the inquisitive kids of JUST ANOTHER FAMILY (1976). Animation was also used to present views of the future in FIFTH ICE AGE (1967) and COMPUTOPIA (1968), drifting ever further from the straightforward presentation to the predictive fiction of UNTIL THE UNDERSEA CITY (1969).

Inspired by similar trends in the live-action TV world, anime began to favor docudramas, particularly when, in the case of ROAD TO MUNICH (1972), live-action footage was unobtainable. The biographical vignettes of GREAT PEOPLE (1977) were the most obvious, but the use of anime was also a deliberate stylistic decision in WE'RE MANGA ARTISTS: TOKIWA VILLA (1981), which told the life stories of several of the medium's

most famous creators. The period also saw the first flowerings of biographical and semi-biographical accounts of World War II. THE DIARY OF ANNE FRANK (1979) made it possible for Japanese producers to consider productions of BAREFOOT GEN (1983), GRAVE OF THE FIREFLIES (1988), and their many imitators. Away from such war stories, instructional works became increasingly earnest, with such dreary subjects as THE STORY OF SUPERCONDUCTORS (1988). Meanwhile, animated inserts continued to appear in live-action programs, including THE MAN WHO CREATED THE FUTURE (2003) and an obscure showing for Studio Ghibli's Isao Takahata, who directed a brief sequence detailing watercourse operations for *The Story of Yanagawa Canal* (1987). Even the Japanese government has gotten involved, with the 18-minute streaming online anime *Learning About Our Metropolitan Assembly* (2002, *Motto Shiritai Watashitachi no Togikai*). Inevitably, the confessional nature of docudrama was also used to add a realistic thrill to erotica, such as G-TASTE (1999) and BLUE CONFESSIONS (2005).

DODGE DANPEI

1991. JPN: *Honoo no Tokyu Dodge Danpei*. AKA: *Burning Dodgeball Dodge Danpei*. TV series. DIR: Takaaki Ishiyama. SCR: Hirokazu Mizude, Takashi Yamada, Miyoko Inoue. DES: Tetsuhiro Koshita. ANI: Katsumi Hashimoto, Yutaka Kagawa, Kazunori Takahashi, Keitaro Mochizuki. MUS: N/C. PRD: Animation 21, Tokyo Agency, Shogakukan Pro, TV Tokyo. 25 mins. x 47 eps.
A plucky Japanese boy leads his dodgeball team to victory against a series of opponents in a sports anime based on the 1989 manga in *Coro Coro Comic* by Tetsuhiro Koshita, who also created RACING BROTHERS LETS AND GO.

DOG OF FLANDERS *

1975. JPN: *Flanders no Inu*. TV series, movie. DIR: Yoshio Kuroda. SCR: Ryuzo Nakanishi, Yoshiaki Yoshida, Shunichi Yukimuro, Tsunehisa Ito, Aki Matsushima, Yukiko Takayama, Tomohiro

Ando. DES: Yasuji Mori. ANI: Toshikazu Sakai, Shinya Takahashi. MUS: Takeo Watanabe. PRD: Nippon Animation, Fuji TV. 25 mins. x 52 eps., 25 mins. x 24 eps. (TV), 103 mins. (m).
In 19th-century Europe, Nello, a young Flemish boy, loves to draw and is inspired by the art of Rubens to become a painter. One day, Nello adopts the dog Patraasche and nurses the ailing animal back to health. He falls in love with the local girl Alois, whose family will never let her marry him because he is too poor. Meanwhile, his grandfather dies, and soon Nello and Patraasche are all that are left of the family. Eventually, they too die and are buried together.

Based on the 1872 book by Marie-Louise de la Ramée, an Englishwoman of French extraction who confusingly wrote under the Flemish pseudonym Oui'da Sebestyen, this miserable tale of death and despair remains much-loved for its sheer emotional extremes. With a maudlin love of sacrifice and a weepy ending in which the faithful pair freeze to death on Christmas Eve amid the majestic works of art in Bruges Cathedral, it is perhaps no surprise that it has proved so popular with the sentimental Japanese (though there have also been several live-action U.S. versions, the first as early as 1914, the most recent in 1999). This anime was the first of the WORLD MASTERPIECE THEATER series.

Remade as a 15-minute episode of the *Manga World Fairy Tales* series in 1976, *DoF* came back again as a 24-part TV series in 1992. This Tokyo Movie Shinsha version was directed by Kanetsugu Kodama and "set in the small French village of Flanders," according to one Japanese source. Not to be put out by such geographical fudging, the tale was resurrected again in 1997, this time for a lavish feature film directed by the original series' Kuroda, with the location now officially "Belgium." This version was released in the U.S. by Pioneer, although the distributor inexplicably removed 11 minutes of footage and the entire Japanese language track for the DVD edition.

DOG SOLDIER: SHADOWS OF THE PAST *

1989. JPN: *Dog Soldier*. Video. DIR: Hiroyuki Ebata. SCR: Noboru Aikawa. DES: Masateru Kudo. ANI: Motomu Sakamoto. MUS: Hitomi Kuroishi. PRD: Movic, Animate Film, JC Staff. 45 mins.
Japanese-American commando John Kyosuke Hiba is forced to face ghosts from his past when he is sent in to steal back an AIDS-like virus from the clutches of a criminal syndicate. His mission becomes more than simply saving the world on behalf of the Pentagon; he takes the opportunity to avenge the deaths of his parents. Based on a manga by STORY OF RIKI–creator Tetsuya Saruwatari, this Rambo clone was released in America by U.S. Manga Corps. ◐Ⓝ🅥

DOGTANIAN AND THE THREE MUSKEHOUNDS *

1981. JPN: *Wan Wan Sanjushi*. AKA: *Dogtanian and the Three Invincible Musketeers*. TV series. DIR: Taku Sugiyama, Shigeo Koshi. SCR: Taku Sugiyama. DES: Shuichi Seki. ANI: Shuichi Seki, Takao Kogawa. MUS: Katsuhisa Hattori. PRD: Nippon Animation, TBS. 25 mins. x 24 eps., 25 mins. x 10 eps.
D'Artagnan (Dogtanian) is a young dog who wants to be one of the fabled musketeers, but his hot-headed ways get him into trouble when he challenges the Earl of Rochefort (Black Moustache) on the way to Paris. Eventually he becomes a musketeer, teaming up with three experienced guard dogs, Athos, Porthos, and Aramis. When war breaks out between France and England, Dogtanian and his friends must undertake a mission to save the honor of the French queen, who has befriended the English ruler—a King Charles Spaniel, of course. The spiteful feline spy Milady, however, is on their trail at every turn.
This touching, funny, and exciting retelling of the THREE MUSKETEERS in the canine spirit of WOOF WOOF 47 RONIN became a much-loved serial on British children's television, though its Japanese origins were completely

obscured and one "Dave Mallow" was credited as the director. The excruciating pun in the title was a direct translation of the original Spanish coproducers' *D'Artacan y los Tres Mosqueperros*. As well as four separate TV compilations on video in the U.S., a movie-length edit, *One for All and All for One*, was released in the U.K. Ten extra episodes were made solely for foreign broadcast by Shigeo Koshi but never shown in Japan, though they are presumably a major part of the "second series" seen abroad as *The Return of Dogtanian*.

DOGTATO

2004. JPN: *Jagainu*. TV series. DIR: Yutaka Kagawa. SCR: Isao Shizutani. DES: Ikuko Ito. ANI: Ikuko Ito. MUS: N/C. PRD: Egg, Aniplex. 3 mins. x 16 eps.
Surreal preschoolers' entertainment in which Dogtato, a hybrid of dog and potato, lives a happy existence in Veggie Town with his food-themed animal friends, including Haripotato the hedgehog/potato, Nasuinu the eggplant/dog, Kyuribird the cucumber/bird, and Negiwani the shallot/crocodile. Presumably made by the generation of animators who grew up watching TOMATO-MAN, based on stories by Masako Sugiyama.

DOKABEN

1976. AKA: *Lunchbox*. TV series. DIR: Hiroe Mitsunobu, Eiji Okabe. SCR: Tatsuo Tamura. DES: Eisuke Endo. ANI: Nobuhiro Okaseko. MUS: Shunsuke Kikuchi. PRD: Nippon Animation, Fuji TV. 25 mins. x 163 eps.
Compulsive eater Taro "Lunchbox" Yamada is a new transfer student at Takaoka (Hawk Hill) middle school. A gentle and kind individual, he soon shows his incredible strength in the school judo club. The baseball team soon realizes that he could be useful and brings him onto the team as its "little giant." Before long, Dokaben is the ace hitter on the team, but this brings forth bad feelings in some of his teammates. This typical sports anime was based on a 31-volume manga by

Shinji Mizushima, creator of SONG OF THE BASEBALL ENTHUSIAST. Dokaben also has a cameo appearance in GO FOR IT, TABUCHI.

DOKACHIN

1968. TV series. DIR: Hiroshi Sasagawa. SCR: Jinzo Toriumi. DES: Tatsuo Yoshida. ANI: N/C. MUS: Seiichiro Uno. PRD: Fuji TV, Tatsunoko. 15 mins. x 52 eps.
A time-travel comedy created by Tatsuo Yoshida for Tatsunoko and shot in 15-minute episodes, screened two at a time. Primitive boy Dokachin, his father Tototo, and mother Kakaka, plus a chunk of their land, are brought forward in time by an experiment that gets out of hand. The comedy arises from their struggle to cope with the frantic pace of 1960s Japan. Compare to WONDERFUL GENIE FAMILY.

DOKI DOKI SCHOOL HOURS *

2004. JPN: *Sensei no Ojikan*. AKA: *Teacher's Time*. TV series. DIR: Yoshiaki Iwasaki. SCR: Hideki Shirane, Michiko Ito. DES: Kiyotaka Nakahara. ANI: N/C. MUS: Yoshihisa Hirano. PRD: Geneon, TV Tokyo. 25 mins. x 13 eps.
Mika Suzuki is a new teacher at Okitsu High School, although since she is the height of a child and has a babyish face the students have trouble taking her seriously. Based on a manga by Tamami Momose, this high school story abandons all attempt at plot and makes the interaction between Mika and her pupils the main event, with Mika very definitely the lovable loser of the group. Her biggest problem is that one of her pupils, the overdeveloped Kitagawa, is fixated on small women. Classroom discipline is also compromised by her inability to stop pupil Watabe drawing manga—mostly because Teacher wants to see how the story ends. Meanwhile class dreamboy Seki is busy crossdressing and generally being flamboyant. There is an interesting psychological point buried in this and other classroom anime, made by the products of one of the most regulated and rigid education

systems in the world, who view school-days through rose-colored glasses with comedy lenses as havens of fun and individuality presided over by wackily sympathetic teachers. Sadly some of the nuances and references will be lost on non-Japanese speaking audiences, since gags are not just visual but flashed up in text. The limited animation is enlivened with graphic techniques like tone, speedlines, and sparkle-dots from its manga roots, reversing the process of lifting moving picture techniques into comics that made Osamu Tezuka a manga superstar six decades earlier. Compare to **Azumanga Daioh** and **Pani Poni Dash**.

DOKKAN ROBOTENDON

1995. TV series. DIR: Hiroshi Sasagawa. SCR: Masaaki Sakurai. DES: Mitsutoshi Tokuyama, Katsumi Hashimoto. ANI: N/C. MUS: N/C. PRD: Tatsunoko, TV Tokyo. 6.5 mins. x 26 eps.
Voice actress Megumi Hayashibara starred as the cute little robot in the red metal baseball cap in this breakfast TV kiddy show, which was apparently so popular with young audiences it was repeated immediately.

DOKKOIDA *

2003. JPN: Sumeba Miyako no Cosmos-So Suttoko Taisen Dokkoida. AKA: Sutokko War Dokkoida; Ultra Diaper Man. TV series. DIR: Hitoyuki Matsui, Takuya Nonaka. SCR: Kazuharu Sato, Ryunosuke Kingetsu, Waji Sato. DES: Jun Shibata, Yasutoshi Niwa. ANI: Haruo Sotozaki, Satoru Nakaya, Toshimitsu Kobayashi. MUS: Kuniaki Haishima. PRD: Media Factory, Toshiba, Media Works, Klockworx, TV Kanagawa. 25 mins. x 12 eps.
Suzuo Sakurazaki is a college geek with no money and not much street savvy. When a mystery girl suddenly introduces herself as Tampopo and offers him a job as guinea pig for a secret project, he assumes it's just a media spin to glamorize a promotion job for a toy company. Then he learns that the project—a transformation belt that turns the wearer into Dokkoida,

savior of the universe—is for real. He's now a superhero in the pay of the Galaxy Federation Police, with the job of catching their most wanted criminals. He doesn't even get a cool outfit—Dokkoida's transformation leaves him dressed in a diaper. Luckily most of his opponents are as ridiculous as they are deadly, because he can't even get away from Dokkoida's world at the end of the day—not only Tampopo, who pretends she's his sister as part of their cover story, but also his enemies, turn out to live in the same dorm. Slapstick humor and more than a few nods to **Kikaider**, **Ultraman**, and *Masked Rider* (*DE).

DOKURO-CHAN

2005. JPN: Bokusatsu Tenshi Dokuro-chan. AKA: Clubbing Angel Dokuro. TV series. DIR: Tsutomu Mizushima. DES: Makoto Koga. ANI: N/C. MUS: N/C. PRD: Geneon, Hal Filmmaker, Media Works. 13 mins. x 8 eps., 24 mins. x 4 eps.
Socially withdrawn 14-year-old boy Sakura Kusakabe would like to share secrets with a girl his own age, but is too shy to mention this to Shizuki, the unwitting object of his affections. Instead, he fakes diary entries from Shizuki to amuse himself, only to discover that he will not always be the loser he appears to be. At some future date, he will become a renowned inventor of something so important that rivals are prepared to send time-traveling assassins back to kill him. One would-be terminator is Dokuro, a cute angelic girl with a large spiked club—the titular *bokusatsu* literally means "clubbing to death." Not that one needs to see far into the past to see **DNA²**, to which this is rather similar; and so Dokuro soon gives up on her mission to live with Sakura, giving him a girlfriend of sorts who also defends him against later assassins in a rehash of **Mahoromatic**. However, she is so hapless that she regularly beats Sakura to death in the style of Kenny from *South Park*, and is forced to use her magical angel powers to bring him repeatedly back to life. A game followed on PS2.

DOLLIMOG

1986. JPN: Dollimog Da! AKA: It's Dollimog!; Mock and Sweet. TV series. DIR: Hiroshi Fujioka. SCR: Yasunori Kawauchi, Seiji Matsuoka, Ryuji Yamada. DES: Susumu Shiraume. ANI: Yoshihiko Takakura, Masami Abe, Teruo Kigure. MUS: Goro Nogi. PRD: Japan Comart, NTV. 25 mins. x 49 eps.
In 8th-century Europe, the Frankish king Charlemagne sends out his paladins to invade the neighboring countries. In the midst of this chaos, Dollimog the mole and his sister, Hanamog, come to the aid of humans in trouble. They understand human speech and are walking the "dollimog road" on a quest to bring down Charlemagne and his evil sorcerer, Babar.

Based on a story by writer Kawauchi in which underground dwellers try to preserve peace in their own world by interfering in ours, this original piece of medieval moling only stayed with the Charlemagne plot for 23 episodes—the rest of the series leaps 300 years ahead to the time of the Crusades.

DOMAIN OF MURDER *

1992. JPN: Hello Harinezumi: Satsui no Ryobun. AKA: Hello Hedgehog: Domain of Murder. Video. DIR: Akira Suzuki. SCR: Akinori Endo. DES: Masaaki Kawanami. ANI: Masaaki Kawanami. MUS: Noriyoshi Matsuura. PRD: Animate Film. 51 mins.
Private investigator Goro Nanase, whose nickname "Hedgehog" is a pun on "Watchman" and "Bed-head," is hired by Mrs. Toyama to locate her missing husband. The only clue, his face on a poster proclaiming that he's wanted for murder. The race is on, Nanase against the Tokyo Police, through the snowbound Japanese countryside to the slush and dirty sleet of small-town Japan.

Sadly, *Domain of Murder* was the only episode from the 24-volume manga in *Young Magazine* to be animated. Artist Kenshi Hirokane also created the best-selling *Section Chief Kosaku Shima* and the manga masterpiece for the over-60s, *Shooting Stars in the Twilight*.

This is the Japan familiar to Hirokane's adult audience, a lower-middle-class suburb of hard-drinking salarymen and smoking mothers. The production was ill-served in English (with a distributor who managed to mistranslate the names of the creator, writer, main cast, *and* director!), though the subtitled edition retained the excellent voice of Shigeru (ARION) Nakahara in the lead, and there's a wonderful cameo from Yo Inoue (PATLABOR's Kanuka Clancy) as a bar-girl past her prime. Endo's script contains some beautifully observed moments, such as a reverse interrogation when Nanase and his ally double-team the cop they find in her apartment. The subtitles leave the marvelous Japanese-style Raymond Chandler–inspired dialogue untouched, and linguists should watch for the timeless moment when Inoue changes from polite-friendly to superpolite-hostile.

DOMINION *
1988. AKA: *Dominion: Tank Police.* Video. DIR: Koichi Mashimo, Takaaki Ishiyama, Noboru Furuse. SCR: Koichi Mashimo, Hiroshi Yamaguchi. DES: Mitsuharu Miyamae, Koji Ito. ANI: Hiroki Takagi, Osamu Honda. MUS: Yoichiro Yoshikawa. PRD: Agent 21. 40 mins. x 4 eps., 30 mins. x 6 eps.
Newport City, an artificial island in Tokyo Bay, is already overcrowded with giant bioengineered termite mounds for buildings by 2010. Nanotechnology gone wrong chokes the city with a bacterial fog, and the unhappy citizenry is besieged by high-tech crime syndicates. To combat this spree, the government forms the self-explanatory Tank Police.

Dominion was the first professional manga by APPLESEED-creator Masamune Shirow, published in *Comi-Comi* in 1988, and displays a sense of humor that tails off in his later works. Like PATLABOR, it has a lowly lady cop, Leona Ozaki, who works for a paramilitary police force, bestows a pet name on her machine, and spars flirtily with her partner, though the show concentrates more on comedy than slice-of-life drama. Thus we have Leona's immediate

boss, the *Dirty Harry*–wannabe Brenten constantly arguing with his hypertense Chief, as well as the standard semi-love interest Al and computer nerd "Megane" Lovelock.

After a prequel beginning with Leona joining the Tank Police and the creation of her beloved tank Bonaparte out of spare parts, the anime series draws on early chapters of the manga, pitting the police against Buaku, a rogue android, who is accompanied by the infamous, scantily clad Puma Twins, Annapuma and Unipuma. Taking the piss is the order of the day—the Buaku gang wants to steal urine samples from uncontaminated citizens and attempts to deter pursuit by throwing inflatable dildoes all over the street. As in the manga, there are hints that Buaku's motives are secretly honorable; in a *Blade Runner* pastiche, he is searching for information about his creator, and his urine thefts may be part of a plan to deal with the pollution (less ecologically damaging than in the manga but still there). Buaku and Leona are forced to team up against the Red Commando terrorists in the next two episodes as they try to recover a valuable painting, and, at the finale, Buaku seemingly reforms his evil ways.

In 1992, Shirow revisited the franchise in *Comic Gaia* with a parallel story, dropping Buaku and Al, promoting Leona to Squad Leader, and giving her command of an entire fleet of Bonaparte-model tanks. Adapted into anime by Noboru Furuse as *New Dominion Tank Police* (1993), the new, slightly darker series brought Al back, restored the Puma Twins to a life of crime (they had reformed in the manga and joined the squad), and told a far darker story as the squad battles the evil corporation Dai Nippon Gaiken, which is developing a virtual drug as a spin-off from its weapons research. These new episodes were renumbered for the U.K. video release and are hence sometimes known as episodes 5-10 of the "old" *Dominion*, rather than 1-6 of the "new." **L N V**

DOMU
Animation studio founded in 1986 by several defectors from other companies, incorporated in 1993 after the hiring of former Mushi Production staffer Takeshi Anzai, and the subsequent restructuring caused by his arrival. Notable staff members include Tsukasa Abe, Shinji Kawagoe and Kazuhiko Nozawa; representative productions include BUBU CHACHA and SENTIMENTAL GRAFFITI.

DON! BRUTAL WATER MARGIN
1992. JPN: *Don! Gokudo Suikoden.* Video. DIR: Osamu Sekita. SCR: Tadashi Hirose. DES: Masafumi Yamamoto. ANI: Takeshi Osaka. MUS: Manako Nonoyama. PRD: JC Staff. 50 mins. x 2 eps.
Takekichi and Masakazu are two tough guys who are forced to go underground when they lose their boss in a turf war. This modern update of the classic Chinese novel *Water Margin* (see SUIKODEN) is another gangster tale from GOODFELLA's Hiroshi Motomiya, originally published in *Big Comic.* **N V**

DON CHUCK
1975. JPN: *Don Chuck Monogatari.* TV series. DIR: Yukizo Takagaki, Tsutomu Yamamoto. SCR: Tomohiro Ando, Susumu Yoshida, Tsutomu Yamamoto. DES: Eiji Tanaka, Yasuo Ikenodani. ANI: Eiji Tanaka, Yasuo Ikenodani. MUS: MAC. PRD: Knack, TV Tokyo. 25 mins. x 26 eps. (TV1), 25 mins. x 73 eps. (TV2).
Deep in the Zawazawa Forest by the Jub-Jub river lives Don Aristotle the beaver and his child, Don Chuck. Aristotle frets that his son will grow up strange without a mother, and Chuck starts to associate with beaver girl Lala, a rabbit called Mimi, and Daigo the bear cub. The quartet gets into all sorts of trouble as Chuck slowly grows into an adult.

Don Chuck began as the mascot character for a fairground before starring in children's books by Shizuo Koizumi and Makio Narita and eventually gaining this anime outing. The measure of the series' success is in the fact that the "real" Chuck mascot began to take on attributes of the anime character in the months that followed. A second series, *New DC* (1976), lasted even longer and introduced a family of out-of-place koalas.

DON DRACULA

1982. TV series, video. DIR: Masamune Ochiai. SCR: Takao Koyama. DES: Osamu Tezuka. ANI: Masayuki Uchiyama. MUS: Masayuki Yamamoto. PRD: Jin Pro, TV Tokyo. 30 mins. x 4 (orig., 8 total) eps., 90 mins. (v).

Count Dracula, his daughter Chocula, and servant Igor move from Transylvania to Tokyo, where Dracula has trouble finding enough victims on his night sorties. Chocula helps her father, though it also interferes with her studies at night school. Trouble arrives in the form of famed vampire-hunter Dr. Rip van Helsing, who comes to Tokyo in search of his archenemy. An anime adaptation of Tezuka's manga serial in *Shonen Champion* that was truncated by the bankruptcy of its production house. Of the planned 26 episodes, only 4 were shown on Japanese TV. The 8 episodes completed were eventually released straight to video in a feature-length movie edit. Similar lighthearted treatment of vampire folklore can be found in PHANTOM QUEST CORP. Dracula's voice actor Kenji Utsumi played the same role in the more serious DRACULA: SOVEREIGN OF THE DAMNED.

DON QUIXOTE

1980. JPN: *Zukkoke (Bumbling) Knight Don de la Mancha*. TV series. DIR: Kunihiko Yuyama, Shinya Sadamitsu, Soji Yoshikawa, Osamu Sekita. SCR: Akiyoshi Sakai, Soji Yoshikawa, Tomomi Tsutsui, Junzo Toriumi, Masaru Yamamoto. DES: Noa Kawai. ANI: Kazuo Tomisawa, Kunio Watanabe, Satoshi Hirayama, Osamu Nabeshima. MUS: Nobuyoshi Koshibe. PRD: Ashi Pro, Tokyo 12 Channel. 25 mins. x 23 eps.

Don Quixote sets out in search of his beloved Princess Dulcinea, but the girl he desires is only a "princess" insofar

as she is the daughter of Carabos the pirate "king." In order to impress Carabos, Quixote carries out several criminal missions on behalf of his would-be father-in-law. Discovering that "Dulcinea" is an imposter, Quixote sets out once more in search of her, accompanied by his faithful servant, Sancho Panza, and his horse, Rozinante. Miguel de Cervantes's classic knight who tilted at windmills is brought to life here in this action-comedy, with the character's insanity brought to the fore by a manic performance from DON DRACULA's Kenji Utsumi, who positively foams at the mouth.

DONKIKKO

1965. TV series. DIR: Koichi Ishiguro. SCR: Koichi Ishiguro, Yoshio Nunogami. DES: Shotaro Ishinomori. ANI: Yoshio Nunogami, Yoshikazu Inamura. MUS: Kiyoko Yamamoto. PRD: B Pro, Fuji TV. 25 mins. x 21 eps.

Short tales of Donkikko, his boy assistant, Dondon, and their pet duck, Gonbei, as they search the town for missing items, help Grandpa run an antique shop, and eventually go to live in an old abandoned train. An adaptation of CYBORG 009–creator Shotaro Ishinomori's manga from *Shonen Book* magazine.

DON'T GIVE UP: WAY OF THE MAGIC SWORD

1995. JPN: *Don't Give Up: Ma Ken Do*. Video. DIR: Kazuya Murata. SCR: Yasuo Komatsuzaki. DES: NAO Shimizu, Sayuri Isseki. ANI: Sayuri Isseki. MUS: Koji Sakuyama. PRD: OLM. 29 mins.

Officer Doro, a good demon, attempts to recruit Mai Tsurigino as a demon-hunter to police the activities of less scrupulous creatures from the Other Side. Mai refuses but gets dragged in anyway when her little sister, Hikari, takes the job. Doctor Mad (a mad scientist) operates on juvenile delinquent Rei Kamiyoji to turn him into a super-weapon to conquer both the human and demon worlds. Rei kills his creator and goes on the rampage, and it's up to the newly recruited demon-hunters

to stop him. A DEVIL HUNTER YOHKO rip-off originating in an SNES console game.

DON'T LEAVE ME ALONE DAISY *

1997. JPN: *Misutenaide Daisy*. TV series. DIR: Yuji Muto. SCR: Satoru Nishizono, Ryota Yamaguchi, Kazuhisa Sakaguchi. DES: Atsuko Nakajima. ANI: Shigeru Ueda, Naoki Hishikawa. MUS: Kazuhiro Wakabayashi. PRD: Studio Deen, TV Tokyo. 25 mins. x 12 eps.

Reijiro Tekuno (Techno) is a super-rich recluse who lives in a nuclear bunker. He uses his IQ and bank balance to build walls of technology around himself and his fantasy world, where net-surfing is as physical an experience as the real thing. One day (in a scene reminiscent of KIMAGURE ORANGE ROAD) Hitomi's hat is blown away by the wind and lands in Techno's garden. He is immediately smitten with her and insists on calling her Daisy, claiming her as his property, much to her distress. This new twist on geek-meets-girl, intercut with survivalism-by-Microsoft, has a *deus ex machina* in the bearded form of Grandpa fulfilling a promise to Techno's dead parents, and a fly in the ointment in the butch senior classmate, Ani, who appoints herself to ride shotgun on Techno's schemes. A salutary message about how life won't always comply just because you point money or a computer at it is buried beneath a lighthearted school romance in the spirit of JUBEI-CHAN THE NINJA GIRL. Strangely endearing despite being a comedy about a stalker, Noriko Nagano's original 1988 manga somehow caught the "virtual" spirit of the times, though it was by no means her most popular—unadapted geek-meets-girl tales from the same creator include *Otaku Master* and *God Save the Sugekoma-kun*.

DON'T TEASE ME

2005. JPN: *Amaenaide yo*. TV series. DIR: Keitaro Motonaga. SCR: Noboru Kimura, Naoki Takada, Toshizo Nemoto. DES: Kumi Horii. ANI: N/C. MUS: Yasunori Iwasaki. PRD: Studio Deen, AT-

X. 25 mins. x 12 eps. (TV1). 25 mins. x 12? eps. (TV2).

Ikko Satonaka's grandmother is Jotoku, a Buddhist priestess. It only follows that he is likely to go into the family "business," and he duly signs up for an apprenticeship at the temple. There, he is subjected to a series of purification rituals, and exhorted to let go of worldy desires. This proves to be more difficult than expected when he is surrounded by a risibly predictable group of nubile young nuns. TENCHI MUYO!, in a temple, and irritatingly for Ikko, his powers to exorcise demons go *up* when he is thinking sinful thoughts. For people with very short memor… what were we saying?

DOOMED MEGALOPOLIS *

1991. JPN: *Teito Monogatari*. AKA: *Capital Story*. Video. DIR: Rintaro, Kazuhiko Katayama, Koichi Chigira. SCR: Akinori Endo, Takaichi Chiaki. DES: Masayuki. ANI: Shinji Tanaka, Yumiko Kawakami, Osamu Kobayashi. MUS: Kazz Toyama. PRD: Madhouse. 47 mins. x 4 eps.

In 1908, the ghost of Yoshinori Kato, a soldier killed in the Sino-Japanese War, kidnaps the beautiful Yukari and offers her as a human sacrifice to Masakado, Tokyo's unofficial guardian deity. Masakado refuses Kato's offer, but Yukari gives birth to Yukiko, assumed to be Masakado's spiritual heir. The years pass, and Kato tries again to seize power at the death of the emperor in 1912. Child-prodigy Yukiko fights him off and he retreats to the underworld. By 1923, the traumatized Yukari and her daughter live with Yukari's brother, Tatsumi, and his new wife, Keiko, who is an undercover priestess charged with defeating Kato. Another coup attempt by Kato almost succeeds, resulting in the 1923 Tokyo earthquake (found in many anime, including UROTSUKIDOJI, OSHIN, and SMART-SAN). Tatsumi confesses that Yukiko is *his* daughter, and that Yukari's madness is the result of her rape by her own brother. Keiko goes out to face Kato one final time, revealing herself to be the Goddess of Mercy. She fuses with Kato, and Tokyo is saved, leaving Tatsumi to wonder that if even Kato can be forgiven, there might be hope for him.

With a virginal, sleepwalking heroine in jeopardy, a powerful, predatory sorcerer, and a wise old man seeking to keep them apart, ALEXANDER-creator Hiroshi Aramata's original novel is a Japanese retelling of Bram Stoker's *Dracula*. Though often labored and unnecessarily slow, the series still has many good points, notably a well-handled incest subplot and a surreal palette of colors, textures, and set pieces. Later episodes move into *Omen* territory, as Yukiko struggles with her alleged destiny as the child of the Devil, though the finale is pure anime, with hallucinogenic visions and mass destruction à la AKIRA. The story is loaded with historical references—not only does Kato hail from the birthplace of medieval magician Abe no Seimei (hero of *Master of Yin and Yang*), but the period background also shows many of Tokyo's familiar landmarks under construction. Tokyo's guardian Masakado is a genuine historical figure, a 10th-century rebel from the region, just one of the real figures in a story that views the century since Tokyo became Japan's capital as an era in which the country itself was demonically possessed. The year 1940, as Japan prepared for WWII, was the thousandth anniversary of Masakado's death. Kato represents a modern malaise, a soldier forged in the fires of Meiji Japan's first foreign war, who dies in the battle of Dalian in 1894, returns to stoke nationalist arrogance after the defeat of Russia in 1905, and observes the "dark valley" of 1920s militarism. In this regard, he is a distant cousin of the prodigal soldier who terrorizes Tokyo in PATLABOR 2. In a further subtext, the death of the Meiji Emperor had a recent parallel for a home audience that had just mourned his grandson Hirohito.

There are separate U.S. and U.K. dubs, each with their own merits. Manga Entertainment's uses British

Doomed Megalopolis

© 1992 TOEI CO., LTD.

accents, which work well with the overpolite, middle-class characters but still leave them sounding unsettlingly twee. Streamline's U.S. dub, however, doesn't put quite as much effort into duplicating the haunting folksongs that carry much of the suspense in the middle episodes.

The story was also made into the live-action movies *Tokyo: The Last Megalopolis* (1988) and *Dictator of the City* (1989), directed by Akio Jissoji and Takashige Ichinose. A third film, *Capital Story: Secret Report* (1995), was a live-action epilogue set in the present day, when evil spirits use the traumatized survivors of the earlier films to return to our world. **NV**

DOOR INTO SUMMER, THE

1981. JPN: *Natsu e no Tobira*. Movie. DIR: Mori Masaki, Toshio Hirata. SCR: Masaki Tsuji. DES: Keiko Takemiya, Yoshiaki Kawajiri. ANI: Kazuo Tomisawa. MUS: Kentaro Haneda. PRD: Toei. 59 mins.

In 1864 France, Marion is a young man forced to spend the summer at his boarding school because his uncaring mother has recently remarried and does not want him around. Stuck with a small number of companions for the long vacation, Marion soon becomes involved in a series of duels, brawls, and romantic entanglements, such as falling in love with the mayor's daughter, Ledania, but also developing strong feelings for Claude, a boy in his class. Based on the romance manga in *Hana to Yume* by TOWARD THE TERRA–creator Keiko Takemiya, this story was published later than the author's

similar SONG OF WIND AND TREES but
beat it to anime adaptation, thus gaining some notoriety. This is one of the
very rare cases of a mass-market release
for a gay anime. Even in supposedly
more liberal times, such stories tended
to go straight to video, e.g., FAKE or MY
SEXUAL HARASSMENT. ◐

DORAEMON

1973. TV series. DIR: Nobuo Onuki,
Hiroshi Fukutomi, Hideo Nishimaki,
Tsutomu Shibayama, Takeyuki Kanda.
SCR: Ryohei Suzuki, Masaki Tsuji, Seiji
Matsuoka, Masaaki Sakurai, Kazuyo-
shi Okubo. DES: Fujiko-Fujio, Kunio
Okawara. ANI: Fusahito Nagaki, Sadao
Tominaga, Hidekazu Nakamura. MUS:
Nobuyoshi Koshibe, Shunsuke Kikuchi.
PRD: Studio Take, Studio Joke, NTV
Animation, Shinei, Nippon TV. 25 mins.
x 26 eps. (TV1), 10 mins. x 617 eps.
and 25 mins. x 900+ eps. (TV2), 25
mins x 43+ eps. (TV3).

In the 22nd century, the impoverished
descendants of Nobita Nobi pool their
resources and send Doraemon, a cut-
rate, blue robot cat, back in time to
turn him into a more successful person. Doraemon dazzles the schoolboy
Nobita and his friends with his endless
array of futuristic gadgets, including a portable dimension-door and
head-mounted rotor-blades. However,
Nobita's great-great-grandchildren are
so poor that they have sent a malfunctioning mentor whose plans often go
awry. Though Doraemon always saves
the day, it's normally his fault it needs
saving.

Often credited Lennon-and-McCart-
ney-style to the Fujiko-Fujio duo who
created QTARO THE GHOST, *Doraemon*
was actually a solo project for Hiroshi
"Fujiko" Fujimoto. An ongoing series
fully expected to top 2,000 episodes by
the end of 2004, the simple stories and
almost timeless animation have kept
the series a perennial favorite. Like
LUPIN III, it is an original "retro anime"
that never had to be revived and has
reared several generations of Japanese
children. The lineup never changes—
Nobita and his cat, along with prissy

love interest Shizuka, sneaky intellect
Suneo, and hulking lummox Jaian play
in their neighborhood (which, with
its open spaces and woodlands, is perhaps the only part of the series to have
dated), boast about their abilities, and
call each other's bluff. With the threat
of undesirable forfeits, such as stuffing
an entire plateful of spaghetti up the
loser's nose, Nobita turns to Doraemon for help, and the cat's techno
assistance causes more trouble than it
is worth.

Doraemon movies have become a
regular feature of the Japanese spring
break. In *Nobita's Dinosaur* (1980),
a harmless prehistoric pet assumes
gargantuan proportions and must be
returned to its proper era before it eats
Tokyo. When Doraemon returns it to
the wrong group of dinosaurs, it has to
be rescued, only to need rescuing *again*
when it is kidnapped by a hunter from
a 24th-century zoo (note how even
this feature version can easily break
into three episode-length chapters).
This was followed in successive years by
*Nobita the Space Colonist, Nobita's Magic
Tower, Nobita's Undersea Fortress, Nobita
Goes to Hell, Nobita's Little Star Wars,*
and *Nobita and the Iron Warrior,* the
latter released in the year of creator
Fujimoto's death, 1986. After a one-
year hiatus, Doraemon was back again
in 1988 with *Nobita's Parallel* JOURNEY
TO THE WEST, then *Nobita at the* BIRTH
OF JAPAN, *Nobita's Animal Planet, Nobita's
Animal* ARABIAN NIGHTS, *Nobita in Snow
Country, Nobita's Tin-Plate Labyrinth,* and
Nobita's Fantastic THREE MUSKETEERS.
After this rash of pastiches, perhaps
more conservative choices in the
absence of Fujimoto, a slight change
of emphasis came with the 1995 movie,
2112: The Birth of Doraemon, which
cleverly recapped the series' origins
for another new generation before
returning to form with *Nobita's Galactic
Express, Nobita's Clockwork City, Nobita's
South Sea Adventure, Nobita Gets Lost
in Space,* the Aztec-themed *Nobita and
the Legend of the Sun King,* and, in the
year 2001, *Nobita's Winged Heroes.* Subsequent movies have included *Nobita*

and the Robot Kingdom (2002), *Nobita's
Wonderful Spinning Tops* (2003), and
Nobita's Wannyan Space Odyssey (2004).
In 2005, the voice cast who had played
the roles since the second TV series,
whose youngest member was now in
her sixties, were finally retired and
replaced with a new group of younger
actors. Their first movie appearance
was in *Nobita's Dinosaur 2006,* a remake
of the 1980 movie.

The robot cat has also appeared in
literally dozens of TV specials over the
last 20 years, many of which were combined with other specials to create still
more "movies," including *It's New Year!,
It's Summer!, It's Autumn!, It's Winter!, It's
Spring!, Summer Holiday, Doraemon Meets*
HATTORI THE NINJA, *Featherplane, What
Am I for Momotaro?, Come Back Doraemon*
(which was, ironically, repeated several
times), *Doraemon and Itchy the Stray,
Doraemon's Time Capsule for 2001,* and
Treasure of Shinugami Mountain. Later
outings also featured cameos from Doraemon's "little sister" from the future,
Dorami-chan, who got several short
films of her own, starting with *Dorami-
chan: Mini-Dora SOS* (1981). The concept was employed many times by other
creators, most notably in the saucy time
travels of DNA² and VISIONARY.

DORATARO

1981. JPN: *Fusen no Dorataro.* AKA:
Wandering Taro and His Balloon. TV
series. DIR: Tomohiko Takano, Kozo
Kusuba. SCR: Kozo Kusuba. DES: Yasuji
Mori. ANI: Takao Kogawa. MUS: Masa-
yuki Chiyo. PRD: Nippon Animation, Fuji
TV. 25 mins. x 13 eps.

After many years of wandering, Taro
returns to Cat Island to meet his sister,
Sakura, who has stayed on the island
with their adoptive parents, and to woo
the beautiful ship captain, Haruko.
Though his family is pleased to see
him, they all come to realize that the
long separation has seen them grow
into different people, and the return of
the prodigal son has only emphasized
how far apart they have all become. An
anime pastiche of the long-running
live-action TORA-SAN series.

DORORO

1969. TV series. DIR: Gisaburo Sugii, Osamu Dezaki, Yoshiyuki Tomino, Ryosuke Takahashi. SCR: Ryohei Suzuki, Toru Sawaki, Taku Sugiyama. DES: Osamu Tezuka. ANI: Hideaki Kitano. MUS: Isao Tomita. PRD: Mushi Pro, Fuji TV. 25 mins. x 26 eps.

A warlord promises 48 demons that he will donate the body parts of his unborn son in exchange for power. The baby is born as little more than a lump of flesh and is cast into a river, from which it is rescued by a kindly physician. He replaces the missing parts with prostheses, and the child, now a grown man called Hyakki-maru, resolves to slay the 48 demons and regain each of his missing limbs and organs. As he sets off, he teams up with Dororo (baby-talk for *dorobo*, Japanese for thief), a girl thief whose parents once tried to lead an uprising.

Dororo began as a 1967 manga by **ASTRO BOY**–creator Osamu Tezuka. Inspired in part by Shirato's **MANUAL OF NINJA MARTIAL ARTS**, which featured similar Marxist undertones, it incorporates elements of Tezuka's **BLACK JACK**, another driven, patchwork hero with a little-girl sidekick. The manga series was canceled early, before Tezuka's planned shift in focus to Dororo's coming-of-age, and the anime version retains the slightly misleading title— the stories broadcast remain primarily the tale of Dororo's *companion*. From episode 14 onward, this was reflected in a name change, to *Dororo and Hyakki-maru*. Director Sugii and a roster of future big-names emphasized a realistic look, making a virtue out of the monochrome production. Tezuka originally intended to make the show in color (and even made a color pilot) but was prevented from doing so by the low budgets approved by Fuji TV. The story has been cited as a major influence on one of the 1990s' best-selling manga, Hiroaki Samura's *Blade of the Immortal*. The *Dororo* manga was also the inspiration for the console game released in English as *Blood Will Tell*.

DORORON ENMA

1973. JPN: *Dororon Enma-kun*. TV series. DIR: Kimio Yabuki, Keisuke Morishita, Takeshi Shirato, Fusahito Nagaki, Tomoharu Katsumata, Tetsu Dezaki. SCR: Masaki Tsuji, Tadaaki Yamazaki, Shunichi Yukimuro, Masami Uehara. DES: Kimio Yabuki. ANI: Kazuhide Tomonaga, Kazuo Mori, Yoshinori Kanemori. MUS: Hiroshi Tsutsui. PRD: Dynamic Planning, Toei, Fuji TV. 25 mins. x 25 eps.

All the obvious hallmarks of a production from Go Nagai, creator of **DEVILMAN**, as the King of Hell discovers that several of his Earthbound minions are not causing mayhem but secretly plotting to overthrow him. He sends his nephew, Little Enma, to solve the problem, and Little Enma teams up with miniskirted Yukiko, daughter of the Snow Princess (see **JAPANESE FOLK TALES**), and Kappael the water-demon (a kappa) to form the Japanese Monster Patrol. Enma also has a sentient hat called Chapeau, a coward who always advises against danger but will always help out his young master in the end. Hiding out at the house of manga fan Tsutomu, who christens them, the group hunts down those who have abused the laws of Hell. Their guide is Count Dracula himself, a disgraced demon who failed to report the conspiracy, and who sulkily acts as Enma's Tokyo guide despite resenting having to take orders from a little brat. "Dororon" is Japanese onomatopoeia for the sound of a spell occurring, loosely approximated by "Kapow!"

DOTANBA'S MODERN MANNERS

1984. JPN: *Dotanba no Manner*. AKA: *Last-Minute Manners*. TV series. DIR: Hiroshi Yoshida. SCR: Tomoko Misawa, Osamu Murayama, Saburo Goto. DES: Sanpei Sato. ANI: Tadao Wakabayashi. MUS: N/C. PRD: Fuji TV, Eiken. 6 mins. x 284 eps.

An introduction to etiquette through the hapless antics of Mr. Dotanba, who manages to put his foot in it in innumerable social situations. Gems of life-saving wisdom include tips on how to use a toilet, what *not* to say to your coworkers, how to avoid getting slapped by pretty girls, and exactly what to do to make foreign business trips go wrong. Based on a four-panel strip by Sanpei Sato in the *Asahi Shinbun* newspaper. Another Sato strip was released as *Video Manga:Yuhi-kun* (1984), although it was not technically "anime," consisting of narration over still panels. The same team went on to make the even more successful **KOTOWAZA HOUSE**, a set of tips for health and well-being.

DOTERAMAN

1986. TV series. DIR: Shinya Sadamitsu, Hiroshi Yamada, Yoshiyuki Suga. SCR: Takao Koyama, Toshiki Inoue, Yoshiyuki Suga. DES: Mayori Sekijima, Yoshio Mizumura. ANI: Yoshio Mizumura, Chuichi Iguchi. MUS: Kohei Tanaka. PRD: Tatsunoko. 25 mins. x 20 eps.

Shigeru Suzuki is an everyday salaryman at an everyday Tokyo company in an everyday part of town with an interdimensional gateway to a world of demons. As devils with punning names try to invade the planet, Shigeru and the demon-hunter Zukan-Socknets recruit Hajime Sato and his friend Mariko Nakamura to don superhero costumes and fight back.

DOUBLE WISH

2004. JPN: *W-Wish*. TV series. DIR: Osamu Sekita. SCR: Katsumi Hasegawa. DES: Yasunari Nitta. ANI: Picture Magic, Trinet Ent. MUS: Ryo Sakai. PRD: Princess Soft, TV Kanagawa. 12 mins. x 13 eps.

The Tonho twins, Junna and his sister Senna, have lived alone in their family home since their parents died some years ago. They attend Sakurahama Private High School where Junna is the target of attention from a number of girls. Then new student Haruhi Inohara turns up claiming to be a childhood friend, but Junna barely remembers her and Senna doesn't want him to—presumably they don't remember **LOVE HINA** either. Based on a dating game that was itself renowned for featuring early animation work from Voices of a Distant Star creator Makoto Shinkai, *DW* was shown on Japanese TV as part of "Princess Hour" with similar story Final Approach.

DOUGRAM: FANG OF THE SUN

1981. JPN: *Taiyo no Kiba Dougram*. AKA: *Fang of the Sun Dougram; Sun Fang Dougram*. TV series. DIR: Ryosuke Takahashi, Takeyuki Kanda. SCR: Ryosuke Takahashi, Hiroyuki Hoshiyama, Yuji Watanabe, Ryohei Suzuki, Sukehiro Tomita. DES: Soji Yoshikawa, Kunio Okawara. ANI: Kaoru Izumiguchi. MUS: Toru Fuyuki. PRD: Sunrise, TV Tokyo. 25 mins. x 75 eps.

Planet Deroia claims independence from Earth, and Terran forces set out to put down the revolt. Kurine, son of the chairman of Earth's Federal Congress, sides with the Deroians and becomes a terrorist. Forming the "Fang of the Sun" organization with his friends Rocky, Chico, and Cavina, he operates the Dougram giant war robot designed by the guerrilla leader, Dr. Samaline. Meanwhile, Kurine's father, Donan Kashim, is under threat from internal machinations as his secretary plots to seize power for himself, and the adoring Lady Daisy sets off to follow Kurine, for whom she has fallen in a big way.

One of many clones of Gundam, but one that was a robot debut for Votoms-creator and father of "real robot shows" Ryosuke Takahashi.

DOWNLOAD

1992. JPN: *Download: Namu Amida Butsu wa Ai no Uta*. AKA: *Download: Song in Loving Homage to Amida Buddha*. Video. DIR: Rintaro. SCR: Yoshiyuki Suga. DES: Yoshinori Kaneda. ANI: Takao Noda. MUS: Hiroshi Kamiyatsu. PRD: AIC, Artmic. 47 mins.

Shido, a priest, is a genius in two fields—computer hacking and lechery. For the sake of the beautiful Namiho, he takes on evil corporate president Echigoya in a battle of wits and skill. Based on the PC Engine game created by Wataru Nakajima.

DOWNTOWN

1997. TV special. DIR: Kenji Shimazaki. SCR: N/C. DES: Toyoo Ashida. ANI: Toyoo Ashida. MUS: N/C. PRD: Toei, Fuji TV. 30 mins.

Two class clowns take their humor out into the streets, terrorizing members of the public. Falling behind at school, they join the Yoshimoto Talent Agency and become the "fists of Yoshimoto," better known as the comedy duo "Downtown." They make their first TV appearance in 1987 and their own series, *No Job for Kids*. In 1996, they become Japan's richest comedians and are honored the following year by this anime biopic.

DR MOVIE

A Korean animation company, founded in 1990, that often works on outsourced Japanese animation, particularly on the lower rungs of the creative process, such as colors or in-betweening. Its distinctive name, in easy-to-read roman letters, can often be found on the credits of "Japanese" cartoons, including those from Madhouse and Studio Ghibli.

DRACULA: SOVEREIGN OF THE DAMNED *

1980. JPN: *Yami no Teio Kyuketsuki Dracula*. AKA: *Dracula: Vampire Emperor of Darkness; Tomb of Dracula*. TV special. DIR: Minoru Okazaki, Akinori Nagaoka. SCR: Tadaaki Yamazaki. DES: Hiroshi Wagatsuma. ANI: Hiroshi Wagatsuma. MUS: Seiji Yokoyama. PRD: Toei, TV Asahi. 81 mins.

In modern-day Boston, Domini (Delores) is offered in sacrifice as a bride of Lucifer by the occultist Lupeski, but she is stolen away by Dracula. At first intending to drink her blood, the vampire instead falls in love with her. Wheelchair-bound Quincy (Hans) Harker and Rachel van Helsing, the son and granddaughter of Dracula's old enemies, realize that some Boston "murders" are his handiwork. They recruit Frank Drake, a descendant of Dracula ashamed at his ancestor's evil, as a vampire-hunter. Months later, on

Christmas Eve, Domini gives birth to Dracula's son, Janus. Lupeski, who has been informed of Dracula's true identity, offers to baptize Janus, cornering Dracula in a church. Dracula evades the attack, but Lupeski accidentally shoots and kills the infant Janus. Dracula flees, and, having lost her son and lover, Domini plans to kill herself. However, God brings Janus back from the dead (as a fully grown man) in order to create the ultimate vampire-hunter. Before Janus can kill his father, Dracula and Domini are transported to Hell by Satan, for whom their love is an unbearable abomination. Satan blasts Dracula into ashes, but Domini's holy love resurrects Dracula once more, this time as a *mortal*. When Lilith (Lila), a New York vampire created by Dracula, refuses to bite him to restore his immortality, Dracula flees to Transylvania. Dueling with the new Lord of the Vampires, Dracula reasserts his authority and saves peasant children from walking corpses. Despite signs that Dracula has rejected evil, the vampire-hunters locate him, and Harker kills both himself and Dracula with a bomb hidden in his wheelchair. Frank and Rachel admit their feelings for one another, and Janus flies home to tell Domini the news. His divine mission accomplished, Janus is restored to infant form to be raised by Domini.

A remarkably faithful adaptation of the first 50 or so issues of the Marvel Comics *Tomb of Dracula* series. The designs look unorthodox for anime, chiefly because they adhere to the original comic artwork by Gene Colan, though neither Colan nor the comic-writer Marv Wolfman are credited in the animated version. Less serious takes on Dracula appear in Don Dracula and Dororon Enma. Toei negotiated with Marvel in the 1970s about producing animated versions of several superheroes, though the only product of this was the eventual live-action *Spider-Man* team show. Frankenstein would follow the next year.

DRAGON BALL *

1986. TV series, movies. DIR: Minoru Okazaki, Daisuke Nishio, Kazuhisa Takenouchi, Katsumi Endo, Haruki Iwanami, Akinori Nagaoka. SCR: Yasushi Hirano, Toshiki Inoue, Takao Koyama, Michiru Shimada, Yuji Endo, Tetsuo Imazawa, Tatsuo Higashino, Mitsuo Hashimoto. DES: Tadamasa Tsuji, Yuji Ikeda. ANI: Minoru Maeda, Ryukichi Takauchi, Masayuki Uchiyama. MUS: Shunsuke Kikuchi. PRD: Fuji TV, Toei. 25 mins. x 153 eps., 45 mins. x 3 films, 25 mins. x 291 eps. (*DBZ*), ca. 45–70 mins. x 14 films, 25 mins. x 64 eps. (*DBGT*).

Son Goku (Sun Wu-Kong) is an orphan martial artist, taught by the Master Kamesennin (Roshi) and enlisted by Bulma, a pretty girl whose father owns the Capsule invention corporation, to help her search for the seven legendary Dragon Balls. If brought together in the presence of the dragon god, Shen Long (Shin Long), these balls will grant a single wish. The two assemble a band of pilgrims, and, with time out for many martial arts tournaments and fights with divine beings, slowly gather the seven orbs. Members include Yamcha the highwayman; his shapeshifting feline partner, Pooal; Oolong the pig; Goku's future wife, Chichi; and Goku's Buddhist classmate, Krilyn. They must also fight off other groups, including the Red Ribbon organization, which wishes to change the space-time continuum by destroying Goku. Eventually, the high demon Piccolo uses the Dragon Balls to rejuvenate himself then kill Shen Long, while Goku and his gang travel to another world to use *their* Dragon Balls instead and prevent the alien overlord Frieza from getting them himself.

Tiring of his DOCTOR SLUMP and seeking a clean break from Western inspirations, creator Akira Toriyama plucked elements from JOURNEY TO THE WEST for this follow-up. Redeveloping his early strip *Dragon Boy*, which incorporated Jackie Chan homages, he published *Dragon Ball* in 1984, and

Dragon Ball

the series was soon animated. With a reset-to-zero gimmick in the balls' unerring habit of scattering themselves throughout the universe and taking a year to recharge, the anime was able to stretch itself out for a formidable run, becoming one of the smashes of the late 1980s. It was less successful in the U.S., where only 26 episodes were shown before the distributors Funimation ditched the rest of the series and relaunched with *DBZ* (see below, though in 2001 they announced they would go back and fill in the gap).

Short "movie" versions followed as part of double and triple bills, beginning with Nishio's *DB: Legend of the Dragon* (1986), in which Goku fights the evil Pasta and Pongo. The same director made *DB: Sleeping Beauty in the Magic Castle* (1987), while Takenouchi took over for the final film, *DB: Marvelous Magical Mystery* (1988), in which the cast of *DB* wanders into *Doctor Slump*'s Penguin Village for a cross-over. All formed parallel stories designed not to interfere with the continuity of the series, which eventually finished in 1989.

The *DB* sequel, *DBZ*, jumps three years into the future when an older Goku is now married with a son, Gohan. Because this is where many foreign-language versions begin, early episodes often seem like a massive class reunion at which the viewer knows nobody. Goku is attacked by the alien Raditz, who reveals that Goku is his brother, a Sayajin alien, sent to destroy the planet many years ago. Goku refuses to blow up his adopted home and opposes the invading Sayajin, dying and then being reborn as a blond-haired "Super Sayajin." Violence and some nudity were cut for the U.S. release, but even in this bowdlerized form, the series remained popular.

This series also had a thriving series of short "movie" spin-offs, beginning with *DBZ* (1989) and then following with two a year, one for each major school holiday. These included *The World's Strongest* and *Dead Zone* (both 1990, and released in the U.S. following the success of the *DBZ* TV series), *Super Sayajin Son Goku* and *Tree of Might* (both 1991, and U.S. releases), *Collision: Billion Powered Warriors* and *Extreme Battle: Three Super Sayajin* (both 1992), *Ignite! Burning Fight! Greater Fight! Super Conflict Fight!*, and *Galaxy Flex! Very Threatening Guy* (both 1993), *Danger-*

ous Duo! Super Warriors Never Rest and *Super Warrior Destructive Fist: I Am the Victor* (both 1994), *Return Fusion! Goku and Vegeta* and *Strike Out Dragon Punch: Who'll Get Goku?* (both 1995), and, at last, the 80-minute feature *The Strongest Way* (1996).

DBZ came off the air in 1996, a few months after Toriyama pleaded exhaustion and stopped drawing the manga. Rebranded as *Dragon Ball G(rand) T(our)* the following month, it featured the return of arch-nemesis Emperor Pilaf with yet another set of Dragon Balls. The emperor accidentally wishes for Goku to be a child once more, so the new kiddie-friendly Goku sets out on another galactic adventure with Pan (his granddaughter) and an older version of Trunks (son of Bulma and Goku's alien nemesis-turned-buddy Vegeta). Directed by Osamu Kasai, the new series seemed to have lost the magic and ended in November 1997. Tellingly, this was also the same time as Toriyama's *Doctor Slump* was brought back on air, perhaps showing that the artist wasn't quite so tired of his original creation after all. The story also exists in a tacky live-action 1996 Cantonese adaptation, *DB: The Movie*, directed by Joe Chan.

DRAGON CENTURY *

1988. JPN: *Ryuseiki*. Video. DIR: Hiroyuki Kitazume. SCR: Noboru Aikawa. DES: Hiroyuki Kitazume. ANI: Hiroyuki Etsutomo. MUS: Michiaki Kato. PRD: AIC. 30 mins. x 2 eps.
Miserable teenager Riko wishes for her city to be destroyed. Dragons appear in the sky from an unknown dimension but are killed by government forces. A lone survivor, the baby dragon Carmine, is reared in secret by Riko and former soldier Shoryu. Demons appear in the sky, summoned by the impurity of human hearts, and Carmine reveals that with the dragons sent to oppose them now dead, Riko will soon get her apocalyptic wish. Riko changes her mind and rides Carmine to defeat the demon king. As Riko breathes her last, the sky cracks open,

filled with dragons come to defeat evil.

With teen angst and interdimensional holocaust, this forerunner of **EVANGELION** had an afterthought sequel set 300 years after the invasion. On a traumatized Earth, another young girl, Lucillia, wishes to avenge her father's death in the dragon-fighting tournament and enlists the help of Carmine (now known as Vermilion) in doing so. From an idea by Ryukihei, creator of the *Dragon Wars* manga.

DRAGON CHRONICLE

1989. JPN: *Maryu Senki*. AKA: *War Chronicle of Magical Dragons*. Video. DIR: Tatsuya Okamoto. SCR: Chuichi Watanabe. DES: Naoyuki Onda. ANI: Naoyuki Onda. MUS: Tadamasa Yamanaka. PRD: AIC. 30 mins. x 2 eps.
A mixture of Oriental history and legend in the spirit of **YOTODEN** and **DARK MYTH**, as Miki Chiyoko, modern-day descendant of an ancient clan expunged from Japanese history books by a jealous emperor, summons one of the four Chinese creatures responsible for defending Earth. Conjoining with the Blue Dragon, he discovers that the three other beasts have scattered into other bodies, and he must find them if he wants to join forces with them. The others are revealed as drunken priest Gendo (Black Warrior), handsome potter Hiyu (White Tiger), and pretty Japanese teenager Shizue (Vermilion Sparrow), who all stand against Miki as he tries to enlist them in a scheme of evil. **NV**

DRAGON DRIVE *

2002. TV series. DIR: Akira Yoshimura, Isao Tokoyushi, Megumi Yamamoto, Toshifumi Kawase, Yuichi Wada. SCR: Koichi Taki, Naruhisa Arakawa, Toshiki Inoue. DES: Takahiro Umehara, Takahiro Yamada. ANI: Minoru Kouno, Noriuki Fukuda, Takahiro Umehara, Yoshikai Hatano, Yoshiya Yamamoto. MUS: N/C. PRD: Madhouse, NAS, TV Tokyo. 25 mins. x 38 eps.
Reiji Ozora is a typical slacker teenager, dragged by his friend (and would-be girlfriend) Maiko to a secret arcade

where he discovers a passion for the VR game Dragon Drive. The object of the game is to train and fight with virtual reality dragons, constructed using a player's genetic code as the building blocks—like a DNA-centric version of the old Bar-Code Battlers. At first, Reiji's dragon Chibisuke looks like a runt: a tiny snow-white bundle of cuteness that baffles the staff, so presumably none of them have heard of Anne McCaffrey's novel *The White Dragon* (1978), with which we are sure any similarities are purely coincidental. When Chibisuke gets into action, he turns out to have impressive firepower in what begins as yet another predictable gaming tale framed along the lines of **POKÉMON** and its ilk. However, a few episodes along, *DD* suddenly adopts a new direction redolent of **EXPER ZENON** and *The Last Starfighter*, with Reiji transported to the fantasy world of Rikyu where the dragons are real. He is soon entering Chibisuke in gladiatorial combats in Rikyu, but is forced to deal with problems back home when a rival returns to Earth with some of the precious Dragonite element. The usual rounds of challenges, counter-challenges, and battles to save the world ensue, and two years later, in **LEGENDZ**, they all ensue again.

DRAGON FIST

1991. Video. DIR: Shigeyasu Yamauchi. SCR: N/C. DES: Shingo Araki, Michi Himeno. ANI: Hideki Kazushima. MUS: Kenji Kawai. PRD: Agent 21. 40 mins.
Chinese transfer student Ling Fei-Long is attacked by boys at his new school and saved by the female martial arts student Yuka. Later, at a karate tournament, Ling discovers that Yuka is a clone, part of a secret military project. But Ling has a secret of his own—he is a member of one of four clans in the Chinese mountains, descended from mythical beasts (in his case, the White Dragon) and endowed with psychic powers. He has been banished to Japan for killing a human, but his past is catching up with him. Based on a manga by Shu Katayama, serialized in

Wings magazine, mixing romance and rough stuff.

DRAGON HALF *
1993. Video. DIR: Shinya Sadamitsu. SCR: Shinya Sadamitsu. DES: Masahiro Koyama. ANI: Masahiro Koyama. MUS: Kohei Tanaka. PRD: Production IG. 30 mins. x 2 eps.

Ruth the dragon-slayer falls in love with a dragon, and they settle down and produce a manic offspring called Mink, the titular dragon-half. The evil king plots to murder Ruth and take his wife for himself. Mink and her friends are obsessed with Dick Saucer, an idol singer who moonlights as a dragon-slayer. They try to get into his concert but are thwarted by Mink's rival, Princess Vina, a half-blob girl resentful of her genetic inheritance. Eventually, Saucer squares off against Mink and is defeated with a laxative potion that sends him scurrying to the toilet. Based on a 1989 manga by Ryusuke Mita, *Dragon Half* is a fan favorite and deservedly so, with an energetic sense of fun that switches constantly between normal and squashed-down cartoon versions of the characters, playful satire straight out of Warner Bros. cartoon comedies like *Road Runner*, and a very Japanese sense of humor that includes children in a medieval village having to forage for food before they can listen to their new CD. Remembered less for its genuinely zany action than for the closing theme, which features Mink (played by SAILOR MOON–actress Kotono Mitsuishi) singing a song about cooking to the tunes of Beethoven's fifth, seventh, and ninth symphonies. It still makes the authors laugh even now; what can we say?

DRAGON KNIGHT *
1991. Video. DIR: Jun Fukuda, Kaoru Toyooka. SCR: Akira Hatta. DES: Ako Sahara, Akira Kano. ANI: Yuma Nakamura. MUS: N/C. PRD: Agent 21. 45 mins. x 4 eps., (v1), 30 mins. x 4 eps. (*Wheel*)

The knight Yamato Takeru must rescue a number of damsels in distress imprisoned in a demonic castle near Strawberry Fields. Although he has a reputation for ogling the naked charms of the women he saves, he wishes to save the one he genuinely loves. Based on the Masato "elf" Hiruta computer game in which defeating monsters was rewarded by pictures of girls in various states of undress.

Not to be confused with the unrelated LORD OF LORDS: DRAGON KNIGHT or with YAMATO TAKERU, which is slightly less unfaithful to Japanese myth. Only the first two parts were licensed in the U.S. In 1998 Pink Pineapple produced a four-episode sequel, *Dragon Knight: Wheel of Time* (*Dragon Knight 4*), based on the fourth game in the series. **NV**

DRAGON LEAGUE *
1993. TV series. DIR: Nobuhiro Takamoto, Takashi Yamaguchi. SCR: Hideki Mitsui, Kenichi Araki. DES: Kazuyuki Kobayashi. ANI: Kazuyuki Kobayashi, Hideo Kudasaka, Junichi Tokaibayashi. MUS: N/C. PRD: Studio Gallop, Fuji TV. 25 mins. x 39 eps.

In a fantasy world populated by humans, animals, and dinosaurs, religion is based on soccer. Amon boasts that he is the greatest player in the world and trains his son, Tokio, in the forest until the boy is good enough to be considered "the second-greatest." Amon takes his son to the kingdom of Elevenia, whose soccer team has won the Dragon League five years in a row. Settling an old rivalry, Amon is challenged to a rematch by Elevenia's star player, Leon Legacius, who defeats him with the Golden Ball and turns him into a small dragon. If Tokio is ever to see his father in human form again, he must take over the local junior team and transform its players into winners, in a bizarre combination of DRAGON BALL and CAPTAIN TSUBASA. Tokio's relationship with Leon undergoes a transformation after Tokio defeats him in sudden-death overtime playoffs—Leon becomes Tokio's mentor and later team coach when they are called upon to play against the hellspawn Warriors of Darkness. A similar angle on sports-as-worship appears in GALACTIC PIRATES, though later episodes take a far darker turn. Presaging BATTLE ATHLETES, the entire religion is revealed as an attempt to hold off invasion—*real* dragons from an alternate dimension have given King Win of Elevenia a single generation to train a team that can hold off their champion players. The grand finale features a literal death match, as stone "Death Dragons" destroy a city every time the dragon-team scores a goal, while Tokio's team desperately fights a losing battle.

DRAGON PINK *
1994. Video. DIR: Wataru Fujii, Hitoshi Takai. SCR: Itoyoko. DES: Ito-yoko. ANI: N/C. MUS: N/C. PRD: Pink Pineapple, AIC. 35 mins. x 3 eps.

A fantasy sex romp about slave girl Pink putting on the cursed Panties of Torajima and literally becoming a sex kitten. Pink and her master, Santa the swordsman, must fight their way through the forest of Tajif with elfin sorcerer Pierce and Bobo the barbarian. The gang track a monster in episode two, but have to leave Pink as a security deposit at an inn when they run out of jewelry to barter. The final part has the heroes rescued by Pierce's magic, but from an unexpected source.

Based on the Itoyoko manga, serialized in *Penguin Club* and *Hot Shake* magazines, that quickly spawned a computer game, a garage kit, this inevitable anime adaptation, and the question on everyone's lips—was "dragon" '90s Japanese slang for "soft-core"? **LNV**

DRAGON RIDER *
1995. Video. DIR: Katsumasa Kanezawa. SCR: Tetsuya Taiseki. DES: Tomo Kino. ANI: N/C. MUS: N/C. PRD: Pink Pineapple. 30 mins. x 2 eps.

In Carnus village, the beautiful Callis is powerless to prevent the death of her mother, though she herself is saved by Ryke, a would-be dragon rider searching for a suitable mount. In this porno anime based on a manga in *Comic*

Papipo, Callis transforms into a Red Dragon when she gets passionate or angry, and a different kind of mounting soon ensues. **NV**

DRAGON SLAYER *

1992. JPN: *Dragon Slayer: Eiyu Densetsu: Oji no Tabitachi*. AKA: *Dragon Slayer: Legend of Heroes: Voyages of the Prince*. Video. DIR: Tadayuki Nakamura. SCR: Kenichi Matsuzaki. DES: Ken Ishikawa, Hisashi Hirai. ANI: Hisashi Hirai. MUS: Fujio Sakai. PRD: Amuse Video. 30 mins. x 2 eps.

Faaren is a peaceful and happy realm ruled by a wise king, until the Demon Lord Ackdam invades with his black legions and terrifying dragon, killing the king and capturing the queen. Aswel's last brave old knight, Rias, spirits young Prince Sirius to safety. Ten years later, the teenaged Sirius returns to help Faaren's peasants overthrow Ackdam, slaying Ackdam's demon-baron Zanji at a mine. In revenge, Ackdam sends his chief henchman, Zagi, who transforms into a giant fire-breathing dragon. Zagi slays Rias and captures Sirius. But Sirius is rescued from Ackdam's dungeon by Ryunan, a brave knight from a neighboring kingdom, who is organizing Faaren's peasant rebellion. Sirius is taken to the rebellion's headquarters under the command of Rias's twin brother, Aaron (a good way to have a tragic death scene without losing the character). Aaron's granddaughter, the tomboyish Sonya (combination comic relief and love interest), a wizard-in-training, nurses Sirius back to health and demands to join the boys in slaying Ackdam's orcish minions. The rebellion grows so serious that Ackdam threatens to execute Queen Felicia the next day if Sirius does not surrender. This sets the deadline for the final attack on Ackdam's castle. In preparation, Sonya has Sirius escort her to "the abandoned Temple of the Old Ones" (apparently copied from photos of Mayan temple ruins) where she can get a mystic weapon that will ensure Ackdam's defeat. She does not tell Sirius that the weapon is a drag-

on that she will animate with her soul, giving up her human form forever.

At the grand climactic battle, supporting-character wizard Roe reveals that he and Ackdam were classmates in magic school, and it is his duty to personally destroy Ackdam for betraying his vows to use his powers for good. The Sonya-dragon kills the Zagi-dragon, and the strength of Sirius's love for Sonya restores her human body. At the last minute, Ackdam breaks free of Roe and flees. While the rest of the party sets off in pursuit, leading-man Sirius elects to stay behind with his mother and help rule the kingdom, in the only unexpected twist to a standard fantasy template.

An early release for the U.S. company Urban Vision, *DS* features an early example of so-bad-it's-good dialogue, with priceless gems such as, "Your reign of terror is nearing its end, you dog!", and the unforgettable, "Now you die, hellspawn creature!"

DRAGON WARRIOR *

1989. JPN: *Dragon Quest*. TV series. DIR: Rintaro, Takayuki Kanda, Katsuhisa Yamada, Nobutaka Nishizawa. SCR: Takashi Yamada, Sukehiro Tomita, Nobuaki Kishima. DES: Akira Toriyama, Yasushi Nagaoka. ANI: Takeyuki Kanda, Hiroshi Kanezawa. MUS: Koichi Sugiyama. PRD: Studio Comet, Toei, Fuji TV. 25 mins. x 32 eps., 25 mins. x 48 eps., 40 mins. x 2 films.

Sixteen-year-old Abel, sorcerer Janac, and Daisy the swordswoman are in search of eternal life, for which they will have to drink a dragon's blood. Baramos is their enemy, a creature from the undersea kingdom of Estarkh so accustomed to pollution that it is unable to tolerate clean water. Seeking to summon the Great Dragon to lay waste to the world, Baramos kidnaps Abel's childhood sweetheart, Tiala, who is the guardian of the summoning jewel "the Red Stone."

Based on the 1985 *Dragon Quest* computer game created for the MSX computer and NES console game, several games and the first part of

the anime, *DQ: Legend of Abel*, were released in the U.S. by Saban but sank without a trace. In Japan, anime and game were far more successful, kicking off the vogue for computerized "role-playing games" that would culminate in FINAL FANTASY and POKÉMON. The U.S. dub by Saban ended after 13 shuffled episodes, with the party reaching the Tower of Najimi. It also replaced the soundtrack and some of the series' more adult elements: a scene in Port Myla where Abel is propositioned by a whore is altered to an unconvincing conversation about bullfighting.

The series went much further in Japan, following the *Legend of Abel* story arc in 1991 with the *Adventure of Dai*. Set, like LODOSS WAR, suitably long after an earlier legend, it features Dai, a young boy raised on the island of Demurin, where many monsters were said to have been banished by an ancient hero. The sorcerer Aban and his apprentice Poppu arrive on the island, looking for the demon lord Hadora, who is coming back from the dead. Aban sacrifices himself to save Dai and Poppu, and the boys continue Aban's quest. Dai's adventures were much longer-running than his predecessor's and also spun off into Yoshiki Shibata's 40-minute feature version *DQ: Disciple of Aban* (1992). Much later, the manga published to explain the plot of another *DQ* game was also made into a feature, *DQ: Crest of Roto* (1996), directed by Tsukasa Sunaga.

DRAGONAR

1987. JPN: *Kiko Senki Dragonar*. AKA: *Armored Chronicle Dragonar; Metal Armor Dragonar*. TV series. DIR: Takeyuki Kanda. SCR: Fuyunori Gobu. DES: Kenichi Onuki, Kunio Okawara. ANI: Hirokazu Endo, Masami Obari. MUS: Toshiyuki Watanabe, Kentaro Haneda. PRD: Sunrise, Nagoya TV (TV Asahi). 25 mins. x 48 eps.

The Imperial Giganos Empire is invading planet Earth, and the multiethnic Kain, Tapp, and Lyte, with their female foils, Linda and Rose, steal the Dragonar Metalli-Armor from the enemy and turn it against them. The pesky kids are then "bonded" to their weapons, and the Earth military is forced to work with them, in this series which Sunrise hoped would be the "new GUNDAM." It wasn't, though it was certainly an improvement on *Double Zeta Gundam*, which it immediately followed on Japanese TV. Several readers have complained that Dragonar deserves better treatment.

DRAGON'S HEAVEN

1988. Video. DIR: Makoto Kobayashi, Shigeru Fukumoto. SCR: N/C. DES: Makoto Kobayashi, Toshiyuki Hirano, Kimitoshi Yamane. ANI: Itaru Saito. MUS: N/C. PRD: Artmic, AIC. 45 mins.
A great war in 3195 destroys most of civilization when the robot servants of human armies run out of control. The robot Shaian lies dormant for a thousand years after the death of its operator but is accidentally reactivated by a girl, Ikaru, while she scavenges for a living after her family's death at the hands of the Brazilian army. Shaian wishes to avenge himself on the Brazilians' leader, Elmedyne, and enlists the help of the human in order to ensure he operates at top capacity. The victorious couple go off into the ruins together, in an anime with the weirdest robot designs until EVANGELION.

DRAGOON *

1997. JPN: *Ryuki Dengyo*. AKA: *Legend of the Dragon Machine*. Video. DIR: Kenichi Maejima. SCR: Ryota Dezaki. DES: Shino Takada, Satoshi Nishimura. ANI: Masami Nagata. MUS: Harukichi Yamamoto. PRD: KSS. 30 mins. x 3 eps.
May has blue hair, red eyes, a corpse-like pallor, and is the key to a powerful military device controlled by her father. She escapes from her captors and bumps into Sedon Calibre, a noble squire who takes up his father's sword and leads her to her destiny. This, it would seem, involves giving her an incongruous stripey hat to wear and some low-rent swashbuckling as they run away from Incompetent Soldiers and The Man Who Almost Killed His

Father, while an Annoying Little Sister tags along for comic relief. Characters say things like, "He destroyed my village. He murdered my entire family. He's evil incarnate," and there's a bit of sub-Jedi bullshit about wielding a sword with your heart.

Harmless hokum, marred only by stingy cost-cutting that renders almost all the battle sequences as freeze-frames or close-ups (presumably the savings were used to throw in a little more fan-service nudity since it seems May has a magical ability that causes her clothes to fall off). Sadly, it only ends with a partial resolution, revealing its origins as a marketing tool designed to drum up interest in the sequel to the original PC game. While the Japanese audience was able to enjoy the spin-off novel, both PC adventures, *and* a radio drama based on the story, U.S. fans are left with a bum deal, though distributor ADV wisely crammed all three episodes onto a single tape. The virtual absence of the titular "dragon machine" artifact is also rather disappointing, as if AKIRA had failed to make an appearance in the film that bears his name. Not much better than PANZER DRAGOON, but three times as long. **Ⓝ**

DREAM CRAYON KINGDOM

1997. JPN: *Yume no Crayon Okoku*. TV series. DIR: Junichi Sato. SCR: Takashi Yamada, Yumi Kageyama. DES: Akira Inagami. ANI: N/C. MUS: N/C. PRD: Toei, TV Asahi. 25 mins. x 65 eps.
Princess Crayon must journey to 12 magical points to help her parents from the mountains to the seaside. She meets queens in different kingdoms, all the while traveling through space and time. Each four or five episodes constitute a "month" of both show and broadcast time, and Crayon's adventures are timed to coincide with real events, such as Christmas, New Year's, and the arrival of spring. Based on a children's book by Reimi Fukunaga and drawn by *Moon Bunny Egg Princess*–manga artist Michiru Kataoka. Not to be confused with CRAYON SHIN-CHAN!

DREAM DIMENSION HUNTER FANDORA *

1985. JPN: *Mu Jigen Hunter Fandora*. Video. DIR: Kazuyuki Okaseko, Shigenori Kageyama. SCR: Hirokazu Mizude, Takashi Yamada. DES: Hideki Tamura, Eiko Yamauchi. ANI: Masahiro Shita, Hiroyuki Ikegami. MUS: Nozomu Aoki. PRD: Hero Media, Kaname Pro. 45 mins. x 3 eps.
In dimensional year 2002, the ability to warp between new dimensions has created new customs and new criminals. The overworked Dimensional Police Force turns to bounty hunters for help, including Fandora and her partner, Quest (a shape-shifting dragon), who go to the oppressed dimension of Lem in search of rogue crook Red-Eye Geran. Later episodes center on lovers Soto and Fontaine, who are separated when galactic criminal Yog Sothoth destroys the Deadlander dimension. Desiring Fandora's Red Rupee gem, Sothoth tricks Soto into stealing it by telling him that balance can be restored if it is brought to him. Fandora stops Soto before he can unite the Red Rupee with the "Blue God's" Blue Rupee, but she is trapped in Sothoth's lair. Created by DEVILMAN's Go Nagai specifically for video. Yog Sothoth is a sly nod to the works of H.P. Lovecraft, also referenced in ICZER-ONE and ARMITAGE III.

Using many crew members from Go Nagai's Dynamic Productions (hence the Nagai-esque look), *DDHF* was released in an English-dubbed version, by BAVI STOCK–producer Hiromasa Shibazaki, who hoped to jump-start an American commercial anime video market by selling an English dub by mail order *from* Japan. The lack of advertising, paucity of U.S. fans at the time, and the high price killed that experiment. However, *DDHF* was not particularly helped by the horrible quality of the dub itself—Fandora and Quest have very artificial, haughty English accents; a medieval innkeeper's voice is a bad W. C. Fields imitation; and the Chief of the Dimensional Police talks like a rural cop from the

American South. Compare to CIPHER, which was also released in English in Japan but with no intention of reaching the U.S. market.

DREAM HUNTER REM

1986. Video. DIR: Satoru Kumazaki, Kiyoshi Nagao, Shinji Okuda. SCR: Shinji Okuda. DES: Kazuaki Mori, Masami Aisakata, Akira Inoue. ANI: Moriyasu Taniguchi, Masahide Yanasawa. MUS: Heitaro Manabe. PRD: Project Team Nagahisa Kikan, Studio Zain. 45 mins. x 5 eps., 45 mins. x 2 eps. (v2).

The insomniac little girl Rem develops the power to enter other people's dreams and earns a living as a private investigator, accompanied by her dog, Alpha, and cat, Beta, who appear as a puppy and kitten in the real world but transform into a fierce giant wolf and cougar when Rem enters people's dreams. Her first mission is against the "Death God" who appears to be possessing a young girl's dreams and driving Rem to commit murder. In episode two, she investigates a series of murders at a high school rumored to be the work of the ghost of a girl who was held prisoner and died in the clock tower. The first series ends with a traditional ghost story, as Rem must fight the jealous spirit of a Taira warrior executed there many centuries earlier. Two further episodes that were pastiches of famous horror novels, *New DHR*, followed in 1990 and 1992, with Okuda writing *and* directing. In the first, a *Dracula* rip-off, Rem must discover why the pretty young Mina has developed sleeping-sickness. In the second, she journeys to the small Alpine city-state of Franken, where a Dr. Victor is troubled by dreams of a robot man called Julian. The sequels had their own subtitles, *The Knights Around Her Bed* (1990, *Yume no Kishi-tachi*) and *Massacre in the Phantasmic Labyrinth* (1992, *Satsuriku no Mugen Meikyu*).

Like PROJECT A-KO, *DHR* was originally planned as an erotic video series but released into the mainstream without undue nudity as the creative climate changed during the 1980s. She gets her name from the acronym for "rapid eye movement," a phenomenon of light sleepers. A combination of the magical girl and teen ghost-hunter genres.

DREAM-STAR BUTTON NOSE

1985. JPN: *Yume no Hoshi Button Nose*. TV series. DIR: Masami Hata, Toshio Takeuchi, Katsuhisa Yamada, Kazuyuki Hirokawa. SCR: Tomoko Konparu, Hideo Takayashiki, Kenji Terada. DES: Akiyo Hirose, Masami Hata. ANI: Maya Matsuyama, Kazuyuki Omori. MUS: Kohei Tanaka. PRD: Sanrio, TV Asahi. 25 mins. x 26 eps.

The first TV series from the merchandise-led Sanrio studio, *Button Nose* was two years in the making. Button is an eight-year-old girl who lives at the Ichigo research institute. Her father invites space travelers from Hookland on planet Kalinto, but they arrive while he is away, so Button takes his place, accompanied by her pet, Franklyn (a pink kangaroo/mouse). With King Fastener of Hookland, Button sets off on the long journey to Kalinto.

DREAMY URASHIMA

1925. JPN: *Nonki na Tosan Ryugu Mairi*. AKA: *Carefree Father in the Palace of the Dragon King*. Movie. DIR: Hakusan Kimura. SCR: N/C. DES: N/C. ANI: N/C. MUS: N/C. PRD: N/C. ca. 5 mins.

Carefree Father is an old, bespectacled man in a bowler hat, patterned kimono, and black haori overcoat, who loves having fun and shirks work whenever he can. One day he finds himself in a turtle taxi, which takes him underwater to the palace of the Dragon King. There, he is feted and entertained by the Dragon King's beautiful daughter and her geisha-like serving girls, but the allure soon fades, and he asks to be allowed to return home. As he leaves, the Dragon King's daughter gives him a casket that he should not open, but once home the curious old man is unable to resist peering inside. A demon jumps out and demands that he pay his palace bill. Realizing it was only a dream, Carefree Father resolves to work harder, in a modern refashioning of *Urashima Taro* (see JAPANESE FOLK TALES).

"Carefree Father" was the first true manga icon, a comedy figure created by Yutaka Aso for the *Hochi Shinbun* newspaper in January 1924. He enjoyed immense success in a Japan struggling to recover from the catastrophic Great Kanto Earthquake. Carefree Father's popularity was aided greatly by the absence of any copyright enforcement on cartoon characters at the time, spinning off into dolls, character goods, and this one-reel movie, none of which appear to have involved the character's original creator, either creatively or in the sharing of the profits. However, such issues only applied in the world of comics—music copyright enforcement was already much stricter, as the makers of MADAME BUTTERFLY would discover to their cost.

DRIFTING CLOUDS

1982. JPN: *Ukigumo*. Movie. DIR: Mori Masaki. SCR: Chiku Yamatoya. DES: George Akiyama. ANI: Kazuo Tomisawa, Kuni Tomita, Nobuko Yuasa. MUS: Seiji Yokoyama. PRD: Madhouse, Toei. 91 mins.

A period-drama with real historical figures, in the style of the later TREE IN THE SUN. Ukigumo, a merchant in old-time Tokyo, leaves the running of his company to his wife and assistant and drifts "free as a cloud." He saves Ryoma Sakamoto (see OI! RYOMA) from an attack in the street, and Sakamoto entertains Ukigumo's family with his vision of a future Japan. Ukigumo's son, Shinnosuke, is inspired by Ryoma, but Ryoma is inspired by Ukigumo, and announces that he plans to renounce his way of life and leave the Shinsengumi organization. Later that year, Ukigumo hears that Ryoma has been assassinated. Based on George Akiyama's monstrously long-running 1973 manga, still going in *Big Comic*, and placed incongruously on a double bill with the GOSHOGUN movie.

DT EIGHTRON

1998. TV series. DIR: Tetsuro Amino.

SCR: Hideki Kakinuma, Toshimitsu Himeno. DES: Yoshi Tanaka. ANI: Yoshi Tanaka. MUS: Hiroyuki Nanba. PRD: Sunrise, Fuji TV. 25 mins. x 26 eps.

In the computer-controlled state of Datania, schoolboy Shu resolves to escape from the oppressive city life and joins the resistance movement known as the Returners. He fights Datania with the super-android Eightron, which was created by applying powerful energies to a pile of junk. *Logan's Run* meets EVANGELION in this earnest but hackneyed replay.

DU ZIQUN

1981. JPN: *To Shishun*. TV special. DIR: Hideo Nishimaki. SCR: Takeshi Shudo. DES: Yoshio Kabashima. ANI: Yoshio Kabashima. MUS: Naoki Yamamoto. PRD: Tohoku, TBS. 84 mins.

In late Tang-dynasty China, Du Ziqun's mother, Bailian, is abducted by robbers. Twelve years later, the teenage Ziqun is leading a gang of thieves in nearby Luoyang, but he despairs of humanity and decides to become a hermit, putting himself through many trials, including a vow of utter silence. Based on the 1920 short story by Ryunosuke Akutagawa, the story was animated a second time for the *Classic Children's Tales* series (1992) as a 30-minute stop-motion short released straight to video.

DUAL *

1999. JPN: *Dual! Parallel Trouble [Run-run] Adventure*. TV series. DIR: Katsuhito Akiyama. SCR: Yosuke Kuroda. DES: Atsushi Okuda, Kenji Teraoka, Yasushi Muraki. ANI: Atsushi Okuda. MUS: Seiko Nagaoka. PRD: AIC, Pioneer, WOWOW. 25 mins. x 13 eps., 25 mins. x 1 ep (v).

When he uncovers a strange artifact at a construction site, a worker accidentally splits the universe into two parallel continua. In one universe, the artifact is used to develop human technology in strange and new directions; in the other, life continues as normal. Twenty-two years later in the everyday world, Professor Sanada tries to prove the existence of a parallel universe. His daughter, Mitsuki, tells him about the visions of schoolboy Kazuki, who claims to see giant robots fighting in the streets. Accidentally triggering the professor's device, Kazuki finds himself in the parallel-world where the evil Rara is trying to conquer the world. Kazuki also learns that the parallel Prof. Sanada has gotten the UN's backing to create an Earth Defense Command to stop Rara, and that Mitsuki transported to this world the month before. She has had time to introduce herself to the parallel of her father, who is a bachelor in this world and has been too busy fighting evil to develop a similar parallel world technology to send her home. Sanada accepts the obligation of adopting Mitsuki, also making her a robot pilot in the EDC. When they find that Kazuki has arrived and can also fly a robot, they enlist him, too.

Dual was Pioneer's entry in the race to duplicate EVANGELION, stealing plots, moods, characters, shots, and even set designs from the 1995 smash and adding half a dozen pretty girls straight out of their own TENCHI MUYO! franchise. The show adds some clever identity crises—Kazuki is the only person who does not exist in the parallel world that includes evil versions of love interest Mitsuki and her mother. With a passionless, suicidal girl (the cyborg D, last remnant of a lost civilization), young pilots forced to share a house, and *Eva*-like robots, its reverse-engineered origins are clear, but the slick marketing savvy of producers Toru Miura and Kazuaki Morijiri ensure that nothing gets taken *too* far. People don't get killed (at least not permanently), jokiness often takes precedence over drama, and a happy ending restores everything to *almost* normal, with Kazuki surrounded by adoring girls. Careful integration of computer graphics makes for some good robot battles, but much of the design in *Dual* seems a little too sparse; the scenes often seem too uncluttered, giving the show a sanitized look to match its sanitized plot.

Thankfully, it also lacks *Evangelion*'s messy ending, though after a denouement seemingly shot on the same roadbridge that closes SERIAL EXPERIMENTS LAIN, a final episode on video threatens an as-yet-unmade sequel.

DUEL MASTERS *

2002. TV series, movie. DIR: Haruro Suzuki. SCR: Satoru Nishizono, Kenichi Kanemaki, Masanao Akahoshi. DES: N/C. ANI: N/C. MUS: Junichi Igarashi. PRD: Shogakukan. 25 mins. x 48 eps. (TV), ca. 80 mins. (m).

Shobu Kirifuda is a fan of a card game called Duel Masters, in which the monsters on the cards actually come to life and fight. He hopes one day to become as good at the game as his father, who is missing, presumed dead. He is educated in his gaming skills by a mystery man known only as "Knight," and attends big matches in the company of his friends, Rekuta the eternal loser and Mimi the sparky girl. In the American release of the series, their ability was termed *kaijudo*, the "way of the monster," although this term does not exist in the Japanese original. Remarkable for the enthusiastic way it attempts to make the sight of children playing cards interesting, although the authors dread the day when someone tries to animate paint drying. A manga by Shigenobu Matsumoto was serialized in *Coro Coro Comic*, and a movie version followed in 2005. Compare to YUGI-OH.

DUMPLING BROTHERS, THE

1999. JPN: *Dango San Kyodai*. AKA: *Three Dumpling Brothers*. TV series. DIR: Masahiko Sato. SCR: Masahiko Sato. DES: Masahiko Sato. ANI: Masahiko Sato, Masanobu Uchino, Noriko Akiho. MUS: N/C. PRD: NHK. 3 mins. x ca. 50 eps.

Ichiro Kushidango, middle brother Jiro, and youngest brother Saburo are dumplings who first appeared in a popular song in 1999, inspired by commercial director Masahiko Sato, who wondered which of the three dumplings on his lunchtime skewer was the oldest. It first aired as the

"January song" on the children's show *Okaasan to Issho* (*With Mama*), which often uses animation to provide visuals to accompany its tunes. Something in it caught the attention of parents and children; quite possibly a postmodern nostalgia on the part of parents from larger families who knew that their own smaller family units would never boast three siblings—compare to **BUBU CHACHA**, which similarly yearned for the days when children had someone to play with. After the song became a runaway hit, selling more than three million copies in Japan, the brothers were brought back for a series of inserts in the show from October 1999 to March 2004. They sometimes shared the screen with their female friend Mochiyo Sakura (rice cake wrapped in a cherry leaf) and their buddies the Teacup Brothers. Their enemy is the double-flavored ice cream Vanilla and Mocha, while they are occasionally supported by dumpling shop owners as backing dancers. Each episode was very short and implied very limited animation, with basic repetitions easily forgiven by a young audience, although when released out of context on two compilation DVDs, it often simply looked cheap. Some producers believed that it was the food theme that made the difference, leading to imitators like **KAPPAMAKI AND THE SUSHI KIDS**, although such things are nothing new in Japanese animation. Compare to **TOMATO-MAN**.

DUNBINE *

1983. JPN: *Seisenshi Dunbine*. AKA: *Holy Warrior Dunbine, Aura Battler Dunbine*. TV series, video. DIR: Yoshiyuki Tomino, Toshifumi Takizawa. SCR: Yoshiyuki Tomino, Sukehiro Tomita, Yuji Watanabe. DES: Yukien Hirogawa, Yutaka Izubuchi. ANI: Hiroyuki Kitazume. MUS: Katsuyuki Ono, Tatsumi Yano. PRD: Sunrise, Nagoya TV (TV Asahi). 25 mins. x 49 eps. (TV), 75 mins. x 3 eps. (*Tales*), 25 mins. x 3 eps. (*Garzey*), 30 mins. x 6 eps. (*Wings*).
Japanese boy Sho Zama is transported to the alternate world of Byston Well

because his human "aura" will make him a powerful robot pilot in Drake Luft's quest to rule the planet. However, Sho defects to the other side and leads the resistance, until his former employers, fighting a rearguard action, open a gateway through to our world and begin a second conquest.

Inspired by *Wings of Lin*, an earlier novel by **GUNDAM**-creator Yoshiyuki Tomino, *Dunbine* shares its stablemate's concentration on big robots (a studio addition not in the original) and heavy character development. It was soon remade by Toshifumi Takizawa as a three-part video series incorporating designs from **PATLABOR**'s Yutaka Izubuchi. The new series, *Aura Battler Dunbine: Tale of Neo Byston Well* (1987), featured more expensive animation and robots with literally scintillating armor. The original Dunbine designer Shott Weapon is thrown through a time warp at the end of the TV series to arrive in Byston Well 700 years later. He brings with him a veritable battalion of Earth weaponry, including a fully laden aircraft carrier, and the locals must form a new resistance to stop him. Although the video series only consisted of 75 minutes of footage, the series was stretched out three times as long with the aid of digest versions of the previous TV episodes.

Much later, in the wake of the similar **ESCAFLOWNE**, Tomino would adapt the robot-free *Wings of Lin* itself into a video anime, the truly awful three-parter *Garzey's Wing* (1996). Chris, a Japanese teenager, loses half his soul when he is summoned to Byston Well by the priestess Hassan. The Meitomias tribe wishes to escape from Ashigaba slavers, and Chris is to be their champion. He guides them through their flight to their promised land, fighting off Roman-armored, dinosaur-riding Ashigabas, while the Tokyo half of his soul sends telepathic messages about such topics as how to make gunpowder. This show is very cheaply animated and shoddily written, and, though this was the only part of the series to be released in the U.S., the poor quality of

the dub makes it almost unwatchable. A further sequel, *Wings of Leen* (2005), was premiered on the Internet in six parts.

DVINE [LUV] *

2001. JPN: *D+Vine [Luv]*. Video. DIR: N/C. SCR: N/C. DES: N/C. ANI: N/C. MUS: N/C. PRD: Pink Pineapple. 30 mins. x 4 eps.
Treasure hunter Hyde and his sidekick Sakura go in search of "the treasures of the old world," the first turning out to be a naked girl encased in ice not unlike the one to be found in **KAMA SUTRA**. Cursed during his misadventures, Hyde is forced to seek an exorcism from local priestess Manatee, who becomes uncontrollably lustful as a result of the spell, and has sex with him in order to calm down. A series of other picaresque encounters soon follow, as Hyde rescues, is rescued, kidnaps, or is kidnapped by a series of women and ends up having sex with them as payment, or as atonement, or as punishment, or simply because they feel like it. Hyde saves a girl from a life-threatening disease, and then eases the side effects of the potion by having sex with her. He is then able to fight the evil wizard Slaine, take his mighty sword Stormbringer (no, really), and find the legacy of the old world. **LNV**

DYNAGIGA

1998. JPN: *Chokido Densetsu Dynagiga*. AKA: *Super Robot Legend Dynagiga*. Video. DIR: Naoyuki Yoshinaga. SCR: N/C. DES: Tada Miura. ANI: Yoshiko Sugai. MUS: N/C. PRD: Studio Deen. 30 mins. x 2 eps.
An anime series that began life on the TV variety program *What's Up, Shibuya?*, it's set in a near future when robots are commonplace and follows the lives and loves of a group of high school girls as they try to get their robot licenses—driving school with giant robots. Allegedly an experiment to discover new talent in voice acting and design, though cynics might suggest that amateur nights always have cheaper staff.

E

EAGLE SAM

1983. TV series. DIR: Hideo Nishimaki, Kanetsugu Kodama. SCR: Masaaki Sakurai, Tetsu Hirata, Kazunobu Hamada, Kazuo Yoshioka. DES: Yoshio Kabashima. ANI: Yoshio Kabashima, Yukio Otaku. MUS: Harumi Ibe. PRD: DAX, TBS. 25 mins. x 51 eps.

All-American private investigator Sam is transformed into an eagle one day as he prepares to open for business. With his shapely assistant, Miss Canary, and her little brother, Gooselan, he must fight the corrupt Chief of Police Albatross and somehow regain his true form. He travels all around the world and solves problems with his Eagle Hat, which contains many useful items à la DORAEMON, chiefly the glowing Olympic Rings that give Sam the extra confidence he needs to save the day. Other members of the mostly human cast included Pelican the hippie, Thunderbird the weightlifter, and dim-witted, donut-eating cop Bogie (presumably a Humphrey Bogart reference amid all the avian names). Though set in "Olympic City," the location is clearly modeled on Los Angeles, even down to LAPD uniforms, though these have incongruous Stars of David instead of the traditional sheriffs' badges. When not fighting corruption within the force itself, Eagle Sam chases Gokiburi, a skateboarding, jive-talking cockroach in shades. Made to cash in on the "Eagle Sam" mascot of the 1984 Los Angeles Olympics—compare to the Moscow equivalent, MISHA THE BEAR CUB.

EAR OF THE YELLOW DRAGON

1995. JPN: Koryu no Mimi. Video. DIR: Kunihiko Yuyama. SCR: Kenji Terada. DES: Arimasa Ozawa. ANI: Masayuki Goto. MUS: Hiroki Nakajima. PRD: Vap. 25 mins. x 2 eps.

An SF tale of intrigue in which agent Kiro, who can call on the mystic powers of "the yellow dragon" through his earring, falls in love with Kanako, daughter of the mob family he is trying to bring down. Based on just one story arc in a manga from Young Jump that won the coveted Naoki Prize for its creator Arimasa Ozawa. **NV**

EARLY ANIME

Controversy continues to haunt discussions of the first anime in Japan, particularly after Naoki Matsumoto's discovery in 2005 of a scrap of film; barely three seconds long, drawn straight onto blank film, and possibly never even screened. Depicting a boy drawing the characters for "moving pictures" on a blackboard, the Matsumoto fragment is undeniably a piece of early Japanese animation, but is little help in establishing a date for the beginning of the medium—we still do not know who drew it, or when. It has created further trouble through its discoverer's unwise speculation to a reporter that it could be "up to ten years" older than the anime previously believed to be Japan's oldest. It is not impossible that it might date from as early as 1915, when 21 foreign cartoons are known to have been screened in Japan and may have stimulated home experiments. However, the Japanese press and overeager Western fans immediately seized upon the earlier (and statistically improbable) end of Matsumoto's estimate, assigning dates of "before 1915," "around 1907," and "in the early years of the 20th century," so that within a few days it was being reported as an anime from "shortly after 1900."

While such confusion may seem wholly innocent, some pundits may have political motives. A 1907 date would allow Japan to claim to have developed animation independent of known Western examples, and a pre-1907 date would allow Japan to claim to be the pioneer of the entire animated medium—the first example of which is currently acknowledged as J. Stuart Blackton's Humorous Phases of Funny Faces (1906). Despite the temptation to rename this book A Guide to Japanese Animation Since 1907, we have kept to our commencement year from the first edition. We continue to believe, until more compelling evidence is presented, that the earliest animated cartoons in Japan were planned and created in 1916 and screened in 1917.

The first completed Japanese animated film was probably Mukuzo Imokawa the Doorman (Imokawa Mukuzo

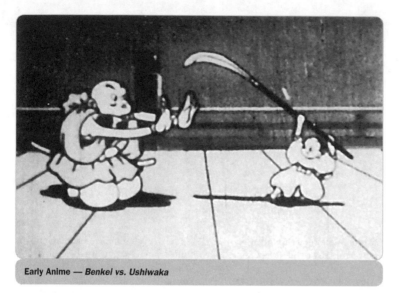

Early Anime — *Benkei vs. Ushiwaka*

Genkanban no Maki, 1917), a five-minute short by Oten Shimokawa, a 26-year-old amateur filmmaker who had previously been an editorial assistant for *Tokyo Puck* magazine. No print of Shimokawa's work survives, but sources including his cameraman claim that he worked using the "chalkboard" method, pointing a camera directly at a blackboard and then erasing and redrawing one frame at a time in order to create animation. He may also have worked by drawing directly onto film, one frame at a time, in the manner of the Matsumoto fragment. Shimokawa's experiments lasted for six months and five short films before he gave up and returned to newspaper illustration. This, at least, is what is believed by Japanese sources, although none of Shimokawa's anime work survives.

Rivalry and one-upmanship lurk behind the scenes of early anime, as competing studios strove to be the "first"—similar claims and counter-claims have hounded the advent of digital animation almost a century later. Where Shimokawa was supposedly working for Tenkatsu, his fellow *Tokyo Puck*–illustrator Junichi Kouchi worked for Kobayashi Shokai (formed by former Tenkatsu employees), and both competed with Seitaro Kitayama,

a watercolor artist who, it is said, pro-actively approached the Nikkatsu studio himself and offered to create its first cartoons.

Junichi Kouchi's first work was *Sword of Hanawa Hekonai* (*Hanawa Hekonai, Meito no Maki*, 1917), with artwork drawn directly onto paper. However, he was soon experimenting with paper cutouts, which were easier to manipulate and allowed, for example, for backgrounds to be reused. The animation cel, a transparent piece of nitro-cellulose that would become the default material for most anime until the 1990s, had been invented in 1915, but had not yet made it to Japan. As with his fellow pioneers, little of Kouchi's work survives, and he gave up on anime in the 1930s.

Seitaro Kitayama preferred fairy tales and legends to Shimokawa's vaudeville humor, producing early versions of THE MONKEY AND THE CRAB (1917), MOMOTARO (1917), and *Taro the Guardsman* (*Taro no Banpei*, 1918). Kitayama displayed an early aptitude for applied animation, producing anime's first commercials and also anime's first documentary, *What to Do with Your Postal Savings* (*Chokin no Susume*, 1917). He also founded Japan's first animation studio, although by 1930 he, too, had

left the medium behind and moved into live-action newsreels.

So little of the work of these early animators survives, in part because of the low number of their prints and the relative ease with which a single-reel movie might be mislaid. The main culprit, however, is the Great Kanto Earthquake of 1923 and the subsequent fires that destroyed much of Tokyo, including almost all early anime materials.

One of Kitayama's protégés, Sanae Yamamoto, continued in the aftermath and arguably became the founder of modern anime. Crucially, when Kitayama fled to work in Osaka, the younger Yamamoto stayed behind in Tokyo. His works included *The Mountain Where Old Women Are Abandoned* (*Obasuteyama*, 1924) and another *Tortoise and the Hare* (1924)—both still extant, although we have less of an idea of how they were presented. As silent movies, they were expected to be performed not just with live musical accompaniment but with a live narrator, or *benshi*. The *benshi* were holdovers from Japan's puppetry tradition and the magic lantern shows of the late 19th century, but their days were numbered with the introduction of movies with sound. Today, their last redoubt is the predominance of frankly unnecessary voice-over narration in Japanese audio dramas. But in the 1920s, their presence was vital and definitive—apparent lacunae, for example, in the onscreen images of DREAMY URASHIMA, would have been intended for a *benshi*'s commentary, without which the film is "incomplete."

Soon after the American movie *The Jazz Singer* (1927) featured a talkie section, Japanese animators were similarly experimenting with sound. The first was Noburo Ofuji's *Whale* (*Kujira*, 1927), a silhouette animation synchronized to the *William Tell Overture*. He followed this up with the cutout animation *Kuro Nyago* (1930), using the Tojo company's Eastphone sound system—anime's first genuine "talkie," albeit only 90 seconds long. The first talkie to use an optic track (as with modern films) was Kenzo Masaoka's THE WORLD

OF POWER AND WOMEN (1933), the tale of a henpecked husband accused of having an affair with a younger woman.

The dying days of silent movies also encouraged new animators to enter into filmmaking. Yasuji Murata, whose first job had been cutting Japanese intertitles into silent movies from America to make the "dialogue" comprehensible to local audiences, was inspired by some of the cartoons he saw to make his own. His *Animal Olympics* (1928) refined the themes of comedic competition, essentially becoming the first in the new sub-genre of sports anime.

Anime of the period were screened not only at cinemas. Those sponsored by commercial concerns often pre-ferred to screen them at shopping areas in order to increase the immedi-ate possibility of sales. Early anime were also screened at schools, particu-larly if they were of a didactic nature. Murata's *Taro's Steamtrain* (*Taro-san no Kisha*, 1929) was an object lesson in consideration for others, as a lone Japanese boy tries to maintain order in a carriage packed with anthropomor-phic animals that fight over seating, throw litter, and become increasingly rowdy. Anime's first "sequel" was *The Pirate Ship* (*Kaizoku-bune*, 1931), a con-tinuation of the previous year's *Monkey Island* (*Sarugashima*), in which a young child cast adrift has adventures on the high seas.

Amid such marvels, however, JAPA-NESE FOLK TALES continued to exercise a strong influence. Tanuki, Japan's indig-enous "raccoon-dogs" appear in several early anime, where their fun-loving nature, their naughtiness, and their constant rivalry with snooty foxes made them an eternal hit with young audi-ences. In one such example, Murata's *Bunbuku Teapot* (*Bunbuku Chagama*, 1927) a kind-hearted man rescues a tanuki from a trap. The grateful ani-mal turns itself into a teapot, which the man then donates to a Buddhist temple, whereupon the tanuki reverts to its previous form to cause chaos.

Similar transformations came with

Ikuo Oishi's *Moving Picture Fight of the Fox and the Possum* (*Ugoki-e Kori no Tatehiki*, 1931) in which a fox disguised as a samurai is tormented by tanuki disguised as monks, who transform themselves into grotesque demonic phantoms—compare to like antago-nisms in POMPOKO.

Similar creatures would feature in another Japanese first, Kenzo Masao-ka's *Dance of the Teapots* (*Chagama Ondo*, 1934), in which a group of tanuki break into a Japanese temple to steal the new-fangled gramophone records played by the monks. This was the first anime to be made wholly with anima-tion cels, as opposed to earlier meth-ods that utilized translucent papers.

Color took longer to arrive in anime's early years. Noburo Ofuji pioneered a two-color version of his *Golden Flower* (*Ogon no Hana*, 1929), although the version released to the public was in monochrome. The first color anime to be actually released was Megumi Asano's *My Baseball* (*Boku no Yakyu*, 1948).

Before the advent of recorded sound, it is arguable that anime were merely part of live dramatic enter-tainment, like LITTLE NEMO–creator Winsor McCay's *Gertie the Dinosaur* (1914), whose performance required her creator to interact, *benshi*-style, in front of the screen. However, such partial performances were increas-ingly uncommon by the late 1920s, as anime began to exist as single artworks in their own right, integrating sound, story, and image in a unified whole. During the 1930s, the anime medium continued to grow in size and accom-plishment, although it also became largely subsumed into the propaganda machine of an imperialist government, with Yasushi Murata's *Aerial Momotaro* (1931) being the first of the WARTIME ANIME.

EARTH STORY: TELEPATH 2500

1984. JPN: *Chikyu Monogatari Telepath 2500*. Movie. DIR: Nariyuki Yamane. SCR: Yoshimi Shinozaki. DES: Ammonite, Yoshitaka Amano, Masashi Sato. ANI:

Ippei Kuri, Sadao Miyamoto. MUS: Hiro-shi Ogasawara. PRD: Tatsunoko. 105 mins.

On the fifth world of the Tolphan sys-tem in the year 2500, a supercomputer chooses marriage partners to find the best matches. Eighteen-year-old Will flies to an orbital facility to discuss his fate with his elders but receives tele-pathic SOS messages from the winged Flora. He deviates from his course and goes to help this damsel in distress, slowly coming to realize that he has fallen in love with her before they have even met. A star-crossed love story with an SF twist. **N**

EARTHIAN *

1989. Video. DIR: Nobuyasu Furukawa, Kenichi Onuki. SCR: Hiroyuki Kawasaki. DES: Kenichi Onuki. ANI: Kenichi Onuki. MUS: Shinnosuke Uesugi. PRD: JC Staff. 40 mins. x 4 eps.

Optimistic Chihaya and pessimistic Kagetsuya are two angels sent from Planet Eden to walk among mankind (the "Earthians") and determine whether the race deserves to survive. This interesting premise is then stretched in all kinds of hack directions by a crew that seems unable to decide what to do with it. The boys bicker con-stantly about humanity, though since both have been chosen for their good-cop/bad-cop attitudes, each is unlikely to convert the other. Like a fey version of *Highway to Heaven*, they simply wan-der in and out of what could almost be episodes from other shows—a London music biz soap opera, for example (featuring a dark angel), or an SF tale of psychics (when Chihaya rescues a runaway psionic in Hong Kong). Yun Koga's original 1987 pretty-boy manga was given a considerable amount of screen time for a video release, and the whistle-stop international setting would have been very difficult to achieve in a live-action budget. However, matters were not helped in the U.S. market by a distributor that coquettishly refused to number the tapes, forcing many potential fans to watch episodes in a random order.

Earthian

© 1996 YUN KOUGA/SHINSHOKAN • YOUMEX

EASY COOKING ANIMATION
1989. JPN: *Seishun no Shokutaku*. AKA: *Youth's Dining Table*. Video. DIR: Toshio Hirata. SCR: N/C. DES: N/C. ANI: N/C. MUS: N/C. PRD: Kitty Film, Madhouse. 30 mins. x 5 eps.
A set of handy hints for basic cooking, including advice on preparing noodles, salad, hot-pots, and pizza. From the studio that gave you WICKED CITY.

EAT WITH BAGETSU
1996. JPN: *Bagetsu de Gohan*. AKA: *Meal with Bagetsu*. TV series. DIR: Tetsu Dezaki. SCR: Kiriko Kubo. DES: Yukari Kobayashi. ANI: Yukari Kobayashi. MUS: Shinichi Kyoda. PRD: Magic Bus, Yomiuri TV. 25 mins. x 20 eps.
The animals at Uenohara Zoo love their jobs, and their jobs involve acting like animals when the human beings are watching and getting on with very human lives when they're not. Paramount among them is Ginpei the penguin, who is eternally getting into trouble with the giraffes, lions, and pandas. Based on a manga by *Cynical Hystery Hour*–creator Kiriko Kubo.

EAT-MAN *
1997. TV series. DIR: Koichi Mashimo,

Toshifumi Kawase. SCR: Akemi Omode, Aya Matsui, Hiroshi Nomoto. DES: Satoshi Murata. ANI: Masaaki Kawanami. MUS: Taifu Kamigami. PRD: Studio Deen, TV Tokyo. 25 mins. x 24 eps.
Bolt Crank, a mercenary who can eat metal objects and then rematerialize them in times of need, wanders from city to city in a futuristic wasteland helping people in trouble.
Based on a manga by Akihito Yoshitomi that is similarly high in concept and low in plot, *E-M* takes the raw material of pulp TV and remolds the wandering heroes of *The Incredible Hulk* and *The Running Man*, adding a dash of Clint Eastwood and Ken from FIST OF THE NORTH STAR. However, it lacks the believable background of its similarly pulp-inspired contemporary COWBOY BEBOP—the world it creates is little more than a desert backlot, and it soon sinks into a quagmire of episodic setups and showdowns.
E-M shows both the good and bad aspects of a limited budget. Art director Jiro Kono deliberately uses flat, uniform colors (like TENCHI MUYO! without the shine) to exploit the talents of his Chinese animators, and it works well. There are some neat

compositions (a face in a cracked mirror, the sky in a puddle), but also some blatant corner-cutting. A cheap loop of a girl's running silhouette is used for a total of three and half minutes. A staring match reaches ridiculous levels of stillness, which may be fine for free on late-night TV, but stretches the patience of video buyers.
Paramount among the series' problems is Bolt's peculiar ability itself, mystifying a succession of writers who push the titular "eating" into the background. Setups are drawn from the staples of U.S. law shows (a would-be dancer is forced to work as a stripper), SF (a clone hunts down all her sisters), and fantasy (a feisty young lady is a lost heiress), but Bolt merely watches the action unfold before producing a gun out of thin air instead of a holster for the finale. As *Manga Max* famously observed, "he could have pulled it out of his ass for all the difference it made."
The second season, *Eat-Man 98*, replaces director Mashimo with EHRGEIZ's Kawase and injects hints about Bolt Crank's past. In rip-offs from GENOCYBER, GHOST IN THE SHELL, and AKIRA, it suggests that Bolt was somehow involved in a genetic experiment, and that the titular "98" is the percentile of subjects who did not survive the process. Though the new direction is at least a plot of sorts, Bolt's habit of munching on metal objects is still little more than a display of macho toughness—you'd get the same effect if he regularly smashed a bottle over his own head. Though the animation is still limited, *E-M98* at least duplicates the look of Bolt's powers from the manga, but much of the storytelling remains shoddy and illogical despite a high-quality translation in the English-language version far better than this show really deserves. **ⒹⓋ**

E-CHAN THE NINJA
1971. JPN: *Sarutobi Etchan*. AKA: *Monkey-style Jumper E-chan*. TV series. DIR: Yugo Serikawa, Mineo Fujita, Minoru Okazaki, Yoshio Takami, Masayuki

Akehi, Hiroshi Ikeda. scr: Shotaro Ishinomori, Shunichi Yukimuro, Tadao Yamazaki, Tatsuo Kasai. des: Shotaro Ishinomori. ani: Shinya Takahashi, Funahito Nagaki, Hideo Yoshizawa, Katsuya Oda. mus: Sciichiro Uno. prd: Toei, TV Asahi (NET). 25 mins. x 26 eps.

Average Japanese girl Miko gets a strange playmate in the form of Etsuko Sarutobi, an exceptionally athletic girl who has the ability to talk to animals. With her pet Buku, a dog that speaks with an Osaka accent, and Taihei Tenka, a confused crusader for justice, Etsuko helps Miko deal with problems in her neighborhood, particularly Takeshi Oyama, the local bully.

These humorous exploits of a psychic ninja girl and her talking dog were animated as a series of two-part stories, each segment occupying half the broadcast. The series was broadcast on Mondays in the slot vacated by the long-running Secret Akko-chan, which has led many Japanese sources to classify it as a "magical girl" story, although Etsuko never actually uses magic. Based on Shotaro Ishinomori's 1964 *Shojo Friend* manga *Okashina Okashina Anoko* (*There's Something Strange About That Girl*), *E-chan* was an early animation job for a young Hayao Miyazaki, who worked on episode six. The show also inspired Katsuhiro Otomo, who wrote several works for adults, each conceived as a modernized update of a children's manga classic. Consequently, *E-chan* was transformed into Etsuko, the psychic schoolgirl of *Domu* (1980). See also Ninja Nonsense.

EDEN'S BOY

1999. TV series. dir: Tsukasa Sunaga. scr: Masashi Sogo. des: Hiroko Kazui. ani: Hiroko Kazui, Yoshiaki Tsuhata. mus: N/C. prd: Studio Deen. 25 mins. x 26 eps.

On a world where a floating city rules over groundling farmers, humble peasant boy Yorun becomes the target of a group of assassins. He is protected by Ellysis, a girl with healing powers, who can also transform into a warrior version of herself called Sita. She reveals that Yorun is a "god-hunter" in hiding, a human with the ability to destroy unruly deities such as the one who now rules over the floating city of Eden. Based on a manga from *Shonen Ace* by Kitsune Tennoji, who was previously known for the adult story *Rape + 2πr*, *EB* soon transforms into a bizarre love triangle in the spirit of Creamy Mami, with Yorun falling for Sida while Ellysis falls for Yorun.

EFFICACE

1998. Video. dir: Shigeru Motomiya. scr: Shigeru Motomiya. des: Hideaki Shimada. ani: Hideaki Shimada. mus: N/C. prd: Magic Bus. 40 mins. x 2 eps.

Sisters Maply, Sucre, and Parte live in the magical kingdom of Efficace. In a cash-in of the video game of the same name, the girls are forced to find other sources of income after sales of buns go into decline. The second episode takes the girls to a haunted house to face an old adversary.

EG FILMS

Formed in 1988 by the merger of EG World and Luckymore, notable members include Takashi Abe, Rei Nakahara, and Makoto Noriza. Representative works include Fortune Quest and Lost Universe.

EHRGEIZ *

1997. jpn: *Next Senki: Ehrgeiz*. aka: *Next Chronicle: Ehrgeiz*. TV series. dir: Toshifumi Kawase. scr: Atsuhiro Tomioka, Koji Miura, Toshiyasu Nagata, Chika Hojo. des: Isamu Imakake, Tetsuya Yanasawa, Takahiro Yamada. ani: Naoki Hishikawa. mus: Kazuhiro Wakabayashi. prd: BeStack, TV Tokyo. 25 mins. x 12 eps.

The Next orbital colony declares independence from Earth, starting a war of secession fought with giant robots called Metal Vehicles. Meanwhile, the terrorist organization Tera, led by the telepathic boy Hal, fights the Earth government from within, as the Next forces search desperately for the legendary "S" superweapon that will turn the tide of the war. On a wrecked colony satellite, a group of part-time pirates turn out to be the best pilots of the lot, and the scene is set for a blatant Gundam rip-off. Originally broadcast on Japanese late-night TV, the production may well have been dumped in the graveyard shift as a cheaper alternative to video; certainly, there is no "adult" content to otherwise justify its broadcast time. Though the English-language translation tries to spice up the language somewhat, it is a perfectly mundane children's robot show with animation so cheap that the robots slide everywhere instead of walking. And no matter how old the original target audience, it was bound to be bewildered by the baffling array of sides in the war, with two nations, two freelance groups, and, as the plot advances, a newly arrived alien civilization to boot. Supposedly amusingly referential and parodic but really just plain dull, the series is best remembered for spawning a PlayStation game in which characters from *Final Fantasy VII* made cameo appearances, which is hardly a recommendation.

EIGHT CLOUDS RISING *

1997. Video. dir: Tomomi Mochizuki. scr: Go Sakamoto. des: Yukiko Kusumoto. ani: Yukiko Kusumoto. mus: Hajime Mizoguchi. prd: Studio Pierrot. 30 mins. x 2 eps.

Kuraki Fuzuchi and Takeo Nanichi are not only Japanese schoolboys, but also the reincarnations of an ancient shrine-maiden and a swordsmith. They fight off evil spirits and unwelcome female attention as they attempt to collect sacred swords and preserve them from evil. Based on a manga by Natsumi Itsuki (Oz), the anime covers only the first collected volume of the manga, originally published in *Hana to Yume* magazine. It also comes complete with moody evocations of Japan's past (see Dark Myth) and a homoerotically charged buddy-relationship, deliberately aimed at Japan's large female audience of pretty-boy aficionados.

808 DISTRICTS

1990. JPN: *Ishinomori Shotaro no 808 Hyori.* AKA: *Shotaro Ishinomori's 808 Districts.* TV series. DIR: Hiroshi Fukutomi. SCR: Kaneto Shirasu. DES: Shotaro Ishinomori. ANI: Masuji Kinoue. MUS: N/C. PRD: Shinei, TBS. 10 mins. x 16 eps. A series of costume-dramas in which CYBORG 009–creator Shotaro Ishinomori plays out modern situations against the backdrop of samurai-era Japan. Linked by the wandering character, Kosanma, the stories include a man's desire to light up the sky with fireworks, a battle between a freelancer and a large company, a girl growing up in the Edo-period version of a massage parlor, and a man searching for a way to get a girl to love him.

The first episode was a 30-minute special, with subsequent parts screened irregularly as part of the *Gimme a Break* show on TBS. For an SF update of the same mean city streets, see CYBER CITY OEDO 808, which also takes its name from the 808 city blocks of old-time Tokyo.

8TH MAN *

1963. JPN: *8 Man* [sic]. AKA: *Tobor the Eighth Man.* TV series, video. DIR: Haruyuki Kawajima. SCR: Kazumasa Hirai, Ryo Hanmura, Tsunehisa Tomita, Tetsuyoshi Onuki, Masaki Tsuji. DES: Jiro Kuwata. ANI: Yukizo Takagaki, Kazuhide Fujiwara. MUS: Tetsuaki Akibara. PRD: Eiken, TBS. 25 mins. x 56 eps., 30 mins. x 4 eps. (v).
Police officer Hachiro Azuma (Peter Brady) is murdered by a criminal gang, but Professor Tani (Genius) installs his memories in a robot body, the 008 military prototype model from the Republic of Amarco. With his new body, he takes on the cyborgs and mutants of an international crime syndicate in a show partly inspired by James Bond 007 but way ahead of its spiritual descendants CYBORG 009 and *Robocop.*

Based on a story by HARMAGEDON-author Kazumasa Hirai that was previously adapted into a manga in *Shonen Magazine* by Jiro Kuwata, the TV series was notable for the script contribution of real SF authors such as Hirai himself and Ryo Hanmura, though much of the original impact was lost in the U.S. dub *Tobor the Eighth Man* (1965), in which our hero must defeat such creatively named adversaries as Saucer Lips (the man who "killed" Peter Brady), as well as Armored Man, Baron Stormy, Dr. Spectra, the Satan Brothers, and the Intercrime spy ring. The TV series has since been rereleased on video in the U.S., though the later video compilations downplay Azuma's novel way of recharging his batteries—smoking nuclear isotope cigarettes.

After the success of the *Robocop* films, the story was remade as the live-action *8 Man* (1992, aka *8 Man Returns*). Nobuyasu Furukawa's belated anime video sequel, *Eight Man After* (1993) plays up the drug subculture, as gangsters receive cybernetic prostheses with built-in weapons. Cybernetic implants, however, require stimulants, and the criminal fraternity is soon fighting a new turf war over control of its own drugs. Detective Azuma is sent to investigate the disappearance of a scientist from the Biotech Corp, but he is killed trying to save pretty Sachiko. He is brought back to life by Dr. Tobor, who makes him the new "Eight Man." The video series was also released in the U.S. in a dubbed version from Streamline Pictures.

EIJI

1990. Movie. DIR: Mizuho Nishikubo. SCR: Kazuya Miyashita, Yasuyuki Suzuki. DES: Takayuki Goto. ANI: Satoshi Murata. MUS: Rogue, Go-Bangs, Passengers, Rabbit, Mari Iwata, J-Bloods. PRD: Animate Film. 50 mins.
Legendary boxer Keijiro Akagi's second son, Eiji, is a high school dropout and the world's worst rock guitarist. Though his father and elder brother are both boxers, he hates the sport but suddenly takes an interest in it when he meets the local champion's little sister. This movie was based on a one-volume 1984 manga from *Fresh Jump* magazine by Hisashi Eguchi and features a rock soundtrack by the bands of the moment. Two other works by the same author were animated straight to video soon after—*Something's Going to Happen* (1990) and *The Hisagoro Show* (1991), directed by Rintaro and Osamu Nabeshima, and both consisting of several short comedy pieces.

EIKEN *

2003. Video. DIR: Kiyotaka Ohata. SCR: Tomoyasu Okubo. DES: Masashi Ishihama. ANI: Masashi Ishihama, Yasuo Namaguro. MUS: Sho Goshima. PRD: JC Staff, Genco. 30 mins. x 2 eps.
Densuke Mifune has just started at the exclusive Zashono High School when he's invited to join one of the school's top clubs, Eiken. He has no idea why, and is puzzled when every other member is a well-developed young woman—especially since the girl he really loves is the retiring, modest Chiharu. Most of the girls have large breasts (some *very* large), and then they do sports. No, really, that's about it. Based on the manga by Seiji Matsuyama serialized in *Shonen Champion* weekly. Eiken is also the name of a anime studio best known for SAZAE-SAN.

EIKEN

Animation company officially founded in 1969, although its assets preexisted as TCJ (Television Corporation of Japan), an advertising animation company founded in 1953. The business was instrumental to many early TV anime such as GIGANTOR and incorporated as a limited company in 1973. Concentrates on blue-chip investments like SAZAE-SAN.

EL *

2001. AKA: *él, Elle.* Video. DIR: Kazuma Kanezawa. SCR: Kazuma Kanezawa. DES: Masaki Kawai, Takeo Takahashi, Yukio Segami. ANI: N/C. MUS: N/C. PRD: ARMS, Green Bunny. 30 mins. x 2 eps.
In 2030, humanity struggles for survival in the aftermath of a nuclear war. The war escalated from arguments about environmental pollution—the filmmakers make a big deal about this, so we're just passing the information

on. A handful of survivors start the Megaro Earth Project, a city built under a dome to preserve what was left of human civilization. Life in the city is, however, totalitarian, with police known as Sniper Control keeping the citizens in line, along with high-tech floating "eyes" to observe everything. El is a member of the Snipers, engaged in an ongoing case against the secretive Black Widow organization and its leader, Gimmick. She also has to serve as a bodyguard for the pretty blue-haired pop idol Parsley, who likes her so much that lesbian sex is called for. Meanwhile, the ongoing police investigation presents some excuses for torturing female suspects. Based on a game created for elf by Masato Hiruda. **ⒷⓃⓋ**

El Hazard

© AIC/PIONEERS LDC/TV TOKYO

EL HAZARD *
1995. JPN: *Shinpi no Sekai El Hazard*. AKA: *The Magnificent World of El Hazard*. Video, TV series. DIR: Hiroki Hayashi, Katsuhito Akiyama. SCR: Ryoei Tsukimura. DES: Kazuto Nakazawa. ANI: Jun Okuda. MUS: Seiko Nagaoka. PRD: AIC, Pioneer. 45 mins., 30 mins. x 6 eps., 50 mins. (v), 25 mins. x 26 eps. (TV), 45 mins. x 4 eps. (v), 25 mins. x 13 eps. (TV).

Whisked off to a faraway world, schoolboy Makoto has to impersonate a princess and fight the forces of evil. Spunky love interest Nanami and schoolteacher Mr. Fujisawa, a booze-swilling chain-smoker who inexplicably develops superhuman powers, are also dragged along. They must save the world from attacking insect armies led by Nanami's brother, school bully Jinnai, who has taught the locals how to lie, cheat, and steal.

Two TENCHI MUYO! staffers, Marx Brothers fan Hayashi and *John Carter of Mars*–fan Tsukimura, decided to combine their interests to create a screwball pulp adventure series, rooting their comedy in the culture clash of 20th-century people and fantasy characters. With a teacher trying to maintain school discipline in an Arabesque paradise, a cross-dressing

hero, an evil general who names all his soldiers after his favorite film stars, and Mr. Fujisawa's eternal quest for more cigarettes, *El Hazard* is a masterly comedy. With fish-out-of-water characters in a world inspired by the ARABIAN NIGHTS, it remains more popular outside Japan than some of Pioneer's more ethnocentric productions such as HAKKENDEN and KISHIN CORPS. Arguably one of the most seamless anime translations ever, the English-language dub by Jenny Haniver and John Pierce is a perfect translation of the original Japanese version, even down to the background improvisations by talented voice actors.

The video series was remade for TV Tokyo in a version known abroad as *El Hazard: The Wanderers* (1996), which stretched the material of the original video series thinly over a longer time frame. A video sequel to the original *video* series, *El Hazard 2* (1997), was similarly disappointing as it merely replayed some of the old gags, though, typically for the series' sense of humor, even the production team inserted "here-we-go-again" jokes. A final incarnation of the series *El Hazard: The Alternative World* (1997), directed by Yasunori Kikuchi,

reunited the video characters in a new adventure, shipping them off to the Kingdom of Creteria to fight Ajrah, the self-proclaimed ruler of the universe. The newly crowned priestess of water, Qawool, falls for Makoto with leaden predictability, and the old setups are rehashed once more with a few new characters and slight tweaks—in other words, a slow decline into hackery that mirrors the disappointing performance of the same studio's TENCHI MUYO! The thirteenth version and final episode of the *Alternate* series was never broadcast but was included as a "bonus" with the video release.

ELEMENTALORS
1994. JPN: *Seirei Tsukai*. AKA: *Elemental Master*. Video. DIR: Katsuhito Akiyama. SCR: Takeshi Okazaki. DES: Hidenori Matsubara. ANI: Hidenori Matsubara. MUS: Masanori Sasamichi. PRD: Sony. 48 mins.

Kagura fails to save his brother-in-law in an accident. His sister accuses him of deliberately allowing the accident to happen because he harbors secret incestuous desires for her. She commits suicide, and Kagura is consoled by his neighbor, Asami, but *then* the world is invaded by "elementalors." Shiki, the leader of the water elementals, freezes most of the inhabitants of Earth, kidnaps Asami, and kills Kagura. However, Kagura is an elementalor himself, and he rises from the dead with help from Tsuyuha, the elemental of wood who resembles Kagura's sister, and Koimura, the elemental of metal. Shiki, only wanting to save his own daughter, leads an assault on Kagura's base, where Kagura's elementalor powers reach their full levels during a fight with Shizuku, the elemental of ice. Based on a 1989 manga by Takeshi Okazaki, serialized in *Newtype* magazine.

ELEMENTAR GELADE *

2005. JPN: *Erementar Gerad*. TV series. DIR: Shigeru Ueda. SCR: Naruhisa Arakawa. DES: Taeko Hori. ANI: N/C. MUS: N/C. PRD: Xebec, Sotsu Agency, TV Tokyo. 25 mins. x 26 eps.

In the distant future, the Adilraid tribe members are able to fuse with humans, **ULTRAMAN**-style, in order to create living weapons. Sky pirate Coud van Gillette accidentally awakens Adilraid girl Reverie Metherlance, who announces that she will head off in search of Adilraid Glu Erden, the paradise of the Adilraid people. Coud decides to accompany her, and the pair initially evade the three agents sent to bring Reverie back to the ARC AILE organization that polices Adilraid activity. Eventually, however, they join forces with the agents Cisqua, Rowan, and fellow Adilraid Kuea, in an adaptation of Mayumi Azuma's manga from *Comic Blade* magazine.

ELEPHANT TRAIN ARRIVED, THE

1992. JPN: *Zo Ressha ga Yattekita*. TV special. DIR: Mei Kato. SCR: Mei Kato. DES: Masashi Kitazaki. ANI: Takashi Ikemi. MUS: N/C. PRD: Mushi Pro, T&K Film, Bandai, Radio Tampo, TV Aichi. 90 mins.

Five-year-old Popo-chan is the zookeeper's daughter at Nagoya's Toyama Zoo. She plays every day with Sabu, an elephant who is the same age. When World War II breaks out, the zoo remains a popular tourist attraction, with the elephants at the top of the bill. Four more elephants arrive from the Kinoshita Circus, but a year later there is an order from the Japanese military to slaughter all the zoo animals. Twenty elephants are killed all over Japan, but two, Makani and Eldo from the Kinoshita Circus, are kept alive in Nagoya. After the war is over, children in Japan pester their parents to see the last remaining elephants, until a special train is supplied to take them to the zoo. As if **ZOO WITHOUT AN ELEPHANT** and **GOODBYE LITTLE HIPPO** were not enough, Japan gained yet another tale that mixes the pathos of war movies with the perennial crowd pleaser of cute animals. Based on a book by Takashi Koide.

ELEVEN CATS

1981. JPN: *Juichibiki no Neko*. Movie. DIR: Shiro Fujimoto. SCR: Yoshitake Suzuki. DES: Noboru Baba. ANI: Akihito Kamiguchi. MUS: Hitoshi Komuro. PRD: Tac. 83 mins.

Eleven naughty cats on the run from the neighborhood police chief hear that a "giant fish" is nearby for the taking. They go on a hazardous quest to find it, learning that they must work as a team to reach their goal. Based on a children's book by Noboru Baba, this movie was followed by a 90-minute sequel, *Eleven Cats and an Albatross* (1986), directed by Tameo Ogawa, in which the cats set up a croquette potato restaurant, lose all their customers, and agree to provide croquettes for a kingdom of albatrosses, while secretly hoping that albatross drumsticks will be on the menu.

ELF PRINCESS RANE *

1995. JPN: *Yosei Hime Rane*. AKA: *Fairy Princess Rane*. Video. DIR: Akitaro Daichi. SCR: Hitoshi Yamazaki. DES: Toshihide Sotodate. ANI: Toshihide Sotodate. MUS: Harukichi Yamamoto. PRD: KSS. 30 mins. x 2 eps.

Teen slacker Go Takarada wants to be an archaeologist like his parents. He meets the titular Rane, who is on a quest for magical objects to save her homeland. Meanwhile, in this genuinely funny comedy from the director of **CARDCAPTORS**, Go's sisters (just three of a veritable army of siblings, who even have their own rock band) are taking sibling rivalry to extremes of collateral damage, and corporate plans for a local theme park threaten everything. Though loaded with anime sight gags (such as a pretty-boy baddie whose hair keeps getting in his eyes), the show's real strength lies in its script, which has multiple onscreen speakers yelling abuse at each other in several Japanese dialects. Despite these hellish complexities, Anime Works' English-language dub artfully captures the spirit of the original and preserves much of the show's wacky humor. Sadly, however, this was just one of many mid-1990s video comedies that never made it past episode two.

ELF 17

1987. Video. DIR: Junichi Sakata. SCR: Sukehiro Tomita, Toshimichi Suzuki. DES: Takumi Tsukasa. ANI: Takumi Tsukasa. MUS: Kohei Tanaka. PRD: JC Staff, Agent 21. 30 mins.

Mascat Tyler (Masakado Taira, see **DOOMED MEGALOPOLIS**), the 108th Galactic Emperor, holds a competition to determine who will accompany him on a secret mission. After some comedic mishaps, soldier KK and the beautiful elfin Lu win the contest and set off on their quest. Based on one part of a long-running manga by Masahide Yamamoto in *Comi Comi* magazine.

ELFEN LIED *

2004. AKA: *Elfen Song*. TV series, Video. DIR: Mamoru Kanbe. SCR: Takao Yoshioka. DES: Seiji Kishimoto. ANI: Seiji Kishimoto. MUS: Kayo Konishi, Moka, Yukio Kondoo. PRD: Genco, VAP, ARMS, AT-X. 25 mins. x 13 eps. (TV), 30 mins. (v).

The Diclonius mutants look like normal humans, but are prophesied to be "chosen by God to destroy mankind." Despite no actual proof of this, the authorities decide to lock them up and experiment on them just to be on the safe side, until the inevitable day when a laboratory accident frees a Diclonius called Lucy. Her escape bid results in the deaths of 20 guards, but a head wound causes her to lose her memory. By the time she is found washed up on a Kamakura beach by teens Kota and Yuka, the only word she can say is *Nyu*, and this is what they call her.

The two kindly Japanese are initially unaware that Lucy has invisible psychic arms that can destroy anything in a two-meter radius—the only thing that is notably different about her is the two little horns that resemble CHOBITS attachments or cat ears. As one might expect with a show that could be described as MAHOROMATIC with mutants, the government soon dispatches a SWAT team to deal with the escaped life-form, causing Lucy to periodically lapse into berserk fits of GENOCYBER-like rage. A 2005 video sequel appears on the seventh Japanese DVD and is widely considered as the 14th episode. It focuses around a flashback to Lucy's past and a domestic chore for one of the team. Based on Lynn Okamoto's manga in *Young Jump* weekly, billed as an "action comedy romance," although there was never all that much comedy in *Dr. Jekyll and Mr. Hyde*, or indeed in Guantanamo Bay. The anime also makes several links to German themes, most notably in an opening sequence that refers to the artwork of Gustav Klimt and allusions to Eduard Mörike's 19th-century poem *Elfenlied*. *Elfen Lied* is nonetheless an intriguing update of old anime themes—in the bipolar behaviors and looks of Nyu/Lucy we have an action movie variant on the dichotomy found in the transforming "magical girl" sagas like MARVELOUS MELMO, or indeed the LOLITA ANIME. ⓃⓋ

ELFY

1986. JPN: *Aoi Umi no Elfy*. AKA: *Elfie of the Blue Seas, Legend of Coral Island*. TV special. DIR: Yoshihide Terai, Yoshio Kuroda. SCR: Nobuyuki Fujimoto. DES: Yoichi Otabe. ANI: Takao Kogawa. MUS:

Toshiyuki Watanabe. PRD: Nippon Animation, OH Pro, Fuji TV. 75 mins.
Four hundred years after a catastrophic rise in sea levels, the inhabitants of Earth live in giant floating cities. Twelve-year-old Elfy is raised by Nereus, one of the Seven Sages who rule over the city of Neptune. She discovers that her own black hair turns green when she swims and that she can breathe underwater. Expansion of Neptune's undersea farms meets with resistance from the local dolphins, among whom Elfy sees a merman with a strange shell necklace like her own. Investigating with Nereus and her brother, Alcus, Elfy discovers that the dolphins were responding to warning signals from the undersea empire of Mu (see SUPER ATRAGON), and that the expansionist plans of the Sage Charisma will be Neptune's doom. Nereus confesses that Elfy is adopted, and the distraught girl is arrested for releasing captured dolphins. Charisma leads a force from Neptune out against the merpeople, but Elfy intervenes and forms a psychic link between the two cultures. In a TV movie that cynics might call a marine replay of NAUSICAÄ, Elfy saves the day, but the strain proves too much, and she becomes one with the waters.

ELLCIA *

1992. JPN: *Genso Jodan Ellcia*. AKA: *Fantastic Tales of Ellcia*. Video. DIR: Noriyasu Furukawa. SCR: Noriyasu Furukawa. DES: Yasuomi Umezu. ANI: Yasuomi Umezu. MUS: Tatsumi Yano. PRD: JC Staff. 45 mins. x 4 eps.
In a pseudo-medieval society, the people of Megaronia stumble on the relics of a lost civilization and leap ahead of their neighbors. Soon, the nation has conquered all the surrounding kingdoms, and the king's evil daughter, Crystel, sets out to find Ellcia, the legendary Ship of God, before the prophesied Fall of Megaronia can come to pass. In doing so, she inadvertently rouses the Chosen One who will destroy her kingdom, a young pirate girl called Eira.
The only remarkable thing about

this tedious fantasy is that all aspects of production are uniformly poor, from lackluster designs by the famous Umezu to Yano's sub–*Raiders of the Lost Ark* music. The dub similarly disappoints with risible attempts at British dialogue, riddled with pronunciation howlers and remedial grammar. But who can blame the crews on both sides of the Pacific for merely cashing their paychecks? With its unconvincing pirates, pretentious philosophizing, and hackneyed plot, *Ellcia* was doomed from the scripting stage. Ⓥ

ELUFINA: SERVANT PRINCESS *

2004. JPN: *Elufina*. AKA: *Servant Princess*. Video. DIR: Yoshitaka Fujimoto, Hiromi Yokoyama. SCR: Taifu Sekimachi, Osamu Momoi. DES: Toshide Masudate. ANI: N/C. MUS: N/C. PRD: Pink Pineapple. 30 mins. x 3 eps.
Princess Elfina (or sometimes Elufina) of Fiel is all set to marry Prince Kwan when the wicked Prince Viceard and his Valdland Army attack. Kwan is seriously injured, the castle is taken, and all the women of Fiel, Elfina included, are forced into sexual slavery—compare to EROTIC TORTURE CHAMBER. The girls are humiliated and raped in the palace, and made to urinate whenever and wherever they find the need. Prince Viceard's stepmother arrives and reveals that she was the prince's first love before her marriage to his father. Viceard, however, keeps himself busy by forcing Elfina's maid Ann to have sexual intercourse with Prince Kwan, Elfina's former betrothed, now comatose in a cell in what used to be his own dungeon. Clever typography means the Japanese title looked (*unintentionally*, of course) like LOVE HINA, but fans picking it up on that basis would feel shortchanged. It's a different type of fantasy with less romantic yearning and more sex, but the characterizations and motivations are just as improbable. ⒷⓃⓋ

ELVEN BRIDE, THE *

1995. JPN: *Elf no Waka Okusama*. Video. DIR: Hiroshi Yamakawa. SCR:

N/C. DES: Kazuma G-version. ANI: Inatsugi Kiyomizu. MUS: N/C. PRD: KSS, Pink Pineapple. 27 mins. x 2 eps.
Town guardsman Kenji marries the elfin Milfa despite hostility from their families and friends. On their wedding night, Milfa reveals that although she may look 18, in elf years she is only 5 and too underdeveloped for full sexual intercourse. Kenji resolves to go on a quest for Harpy Ooze, said to be the ultimate sexual lubricant. He discovers that harpies cannot breed with other harpies and is "forced" to sire triplets with the angelic Pyully before he can obtain any Ooze. Milfa goes to see the local gynecologist, who attempts to molest her, but she is saved in the nick of time by Kenji and his grandmother.

Mixing magic with the mundane in the style of BELOVED BETTY, this sex-comedy is set in a pseudo-medieval world that recalls DRAGON HALF, where there are faucets in the kitchen, but characters still brush their teeth outside at a well. But while it and the original manga by "Kazuma G-Version" on which it was based may contain subtextual musings on miscegenation and the perils of modern marriage, ultimately it is simply an excuse to see what LODOSS WAR's Deedlit would look like with her clothes off. **NL**

ELVES OF THE FOREST

1984. JPN: Mori no Tontotachi. TV series. DIR: Masakazu Higuchi, Norio Yazawa, Osamu Inoue. SCR: Yoshiaki Yoshida, Ryoko Takagi. DES: Susumu Shiraume. ANI: Akihito Kato. MUS: Takeo Watanabe. PRD: Zuiyo, Fuji TV. 25 mins. x 23 eps.
Deep in the forests of Finland live the "little people," or Tonttus, the elves who work all year round to keep Joulupukki (Santa Claus) supplied with toys for Christmas Eve. Based on the Finnish book The Story of Santa Claus and featuring a very Western look in the animation, Elves of the Forest also features one of anime's youngest actresses—one character was played by the designer's four-year-old daughter.

EMBLEM TAKE TWO

1993. Video. DIR: Tetsu Imazawa. SCR: Tatsuhiko Urahata. DES: Hideyuki Motohashi. ANI: Hideyuki Motohashi. MUS: Kazuhiko Sotoyama. PRD: Toei. 50 mins. x 2 eps.
Gangster Susumu is betrayed in the backstreets and lies dying in a pool of his own blood. He wakes up to find a time warp has transported him ten years back into the past, returning him to a younger, healthier version of his former self who is ready to take on the world once more. In a tale of time travel revisionism similar to DEEP BLUE FLEET, Susumu is equipped with indelible memories of the people who will fall into and out of favor, who will rise to power in the organization, and who will betray him, and he begins a revenge vendetta before his opponents realize he's there. Based on the 1990 manga from Young Magazine, written by Kazumasa Kiuchi and drawn by Jun Watanabe, that cleverly combines nostalgia with modern savvy and gangster chic, the anime version was made to cash in on the success of a 1993 live-action film and TV series, directed by the creators.

EMERALD PRINCESS

1992. JPN: Ruri-iro Princess. Video. DIR: Takeshi Mori. SCR: Jiyu Watanabe. DES: Tetsuhito Saito. ANI: Tetsuhito Saito. MUS: Yoshiaki Matsuzawa. PRD: Studio Pierrot. 28 mins. x 2 eps.
High school girl Ruri is dragged into a battle over the fate of the Pulsean Moon when the princess Leila sends assassins to dispense with her. Ruri's lover, Toru, is wounded protecting her, and Ruri must leave the real world behind and journey to the Pulsean Moon to save him. Based on the manga in Omajinai Comic by Mito Orihara, who also wrote the theme song.

EMMA

2005. JPN: Eikoku Koi Monogatari Emma. AKA: British Love Story Emma, Victorian Romance Emma. TV series. DIR: Tsuneo Kobayashi. SCR: Mamiko Ikeda, Shinya Kawabata, Minoru Hirami, Reiko Yoshida. DES: Keiko Shimizu, Yuko Kusumoto. ANI: Akemi Kobayashi, Hiroto Tanaka, Keiko Shimizu. MUS: Kunihiko Ryo. PRD: Studio Pierrot, TV Kanagawa. 25 mins. x 12 eps.
Emma is a housemaid in 19th-century England, devoted to her employer Kelly Stownar, a retired governess. Miss Stownar is unable to stay idle and has taught her working-class servant how to read and write. Emma's life is thrown into turmoil when the house is visited by William Jones, a handsome man who was once one of Kelly's pupils. What began as a simple courtesy call takes on new meaning as William and Emma feel an instant attraction, although the path to true love is unlikely to be smooth—William is a member of one of the most noble families in England, whereas Emma is a mere scullery maid. As such, the couple might as well be from different worlds, and that's before William's friend Hakim, a bona fide Indian prince, arrives and falls for Emma himself.

Emma is a gorgeous, refreshing anime for the 21st century, a Victorian CINDERELLA invested with a truly rare quality—the people who made it actually seem to like what they are doing. The impoverished Studio Pierrot was obliged to curtail this adaptation of Kaoru Mori's beautifully observed manga from Comic Beam, ending it 24 episodes before the original plan. However, it achieves much more in its 12 chapters than so many lesser anime with greater running times; the sights and sounds of 19th-century England are lovingly recreated in a quiet, understated drama that recalls LITTLE PRINCESS and the better productions of the WORLD MASTERPIECE THEATER. At a time when the word "maid" in an anime synopsis normally heralds something like MAIDS IN DREAM or ANOTHER LADY INNOCENT, Emma is a sign that while corporate raiders and carpetbaggers are doing everything they can to ruin the medium, anime still has rare gems that can surprise and entertain. It is also another example of the curious Japanese love affair with Englishness, most notable in recent years in **Steam Boy** and **Hercule Poirot and Miss Marple**. Note that, in a piece of Edwardian stunt-casting, lead actress Yumi Toma was also the Japanese voice of Kate Winslett in *Titanic*.

EMPEROR OF THE PLUM PLANET

1969. JPN: *Umeboshi Denka*. AKA: *Emperor of the Plum World*. TV series, Movie. DIR: Shinichi Suzuki, Hiroshi Hatasenji. SCR: Koji Tanaka, Shima Namie, Takao Niinuma. DES: Fujiko-Fujio. ANI: Masuji Kigami. MUS: Hajme Hayashi. PRD: Studio Zero, Shinei Animation, Tokyo Movie Shinsha. 25 mins. x 27 eps. (TV); ca. 80 mins. (m). When their homeworld is destroyed, the emperor, empress, and crown prince of Ume escape to Earth in a bottle. Forced to lodge with average Earth boy Taro Nakamura, they attempt to reestablish their empire on Earth with little success, even when their loyal retainer Benishoga arrives to "help." **Doraemon**-creators Fujiko-Fujio conceived this story for *Shonen Sunday* in the style of their earlier **Q-taro the Ghost**. Originally broadcast on a Sunday to help promote its manga incarnation, it was moved to Tuesdays and then taken off-air completely. Compare to **Sergeant Frog**, which similarly features a benignly incompetent alien invader. To mark its 35th "anniversary" (not that anyone cared, but modern producers love their meaningless celebrations), a new movie version, *EPP: Paro-paro-pan! From the Ends of the Universe*, brought Denka to the big screen in 1994.

EMPEROR OF THE SOUTH SIDE

1993. JPN: *Minami no Teio*. Video. DIR: Yoshitaka Fujimoto. SCR: Yoshitaka Fujimoto. DES: Masayuki Watanabe. ANI: Masayuki Watanabe. MUS: N/C. PRD: SHS Project, KSS. 45 mins. x 2 eps. Ginjiro is a gangster in South Central Osaka who has just ten days to get back a massive debt. This hard-hitting yakuza tale was based on the 1992 man-

ga by Dai Tennoji (pseud. for **There Goes Shura**–author Yu Kawanabe) and Rikiya Go in *Manga Goraku* magazine and was also adapted into a live-action video movie. **V**

END OF SUMMER *

1994. JPN: *Dokyusei Natsu no Owari ni*. AKA: *Classmates until the End of Summer*. Video. DIR: Kinji Yoshimoto. SCR: Sukehiro Tomita. DES: Masaki Takei, Ryunosuke Otonashi. ANI: Yoshiyuki Okuno. MUS: Tomas Unit. PRD: KSS, Pink Pineapple. 45 mins. x 1 eps. (v1 version 1), 30 mins. x 4 eps. (v1 version 2), 30 mins. x 2 eps. (*Climax*), 30 mins. x 12 eps. (*Classmates 2*), 30 mins. x 3 eps. (*Graduation*), 20 mins. x 1 eps. (Special: *Love Special Lesson—Ren'ai Senka*). Wataru really loves Mai, but there's temptation all around and he just can't resist. The typical teenage-boy dream: lots of gorgeous women just throwing themselves at you, and a girl-next-door who believes you when you say you couldn't help yourself. The artwork, under the direction of **Plastic Little**'s Yoshimoto, is really lovely, and you can observe the artists' skill with flesh tones in some detail. This series was based on the computer game *Classmates* by **Dragon Knight**–creator "elf" (Masato Hiruda). The original 45-minute one-shot was expanded with additional footage into two 30-minute episodes (less two seconds of footage inexplicably deleted from the original) plus two more episodes, for a total of four. The direct sequel of two episodes, *Classmates: Climax*, followed in 1995. A further 12-part sequel, *Classmates 2* (1997), was released in Japan on video and later cut into two toned-down TV movies. The *Classmates 2* video series was edited into a nine-part television drama and broadcast in summer 1998, followed by *Classmates 2: Graduation Special*, a three-part video that, we suspect, may have included the bits missing from the TV version. It was then released as an LD box set with the bonus disc *Classmates: Love Special Lesson—Ren'ai Senka*, which fea-

tured the leads in original anime form, super-deformed cartoon versions, and then in a live-action segment, played by their voice actors, in which they have to fight against two super-villainous girls. As seems traditional with such spin-offs, the 20-minute running time was augmented with a 20-minute ""Making Of"" recycling the scenery and collecting statements from those involved. Just to confuse things, an unrelated live-action series with a similar theme and the same title, based on a manga by Fumi Saimon, was broadcast the same year; see *Classmates* (*DE).

As with its related title **First Loves**, *Classmates* presents a truly bewildering array of alternate versions for the encyclopedist. Many of these alternates were never rereleased on DVD, and are consequently uncatalogued on the filmmakers' websites and lost to the anime historian, until the inevitable giant anniversary box set of all variants in the style of **Cream Lemon**. **N**

ENDLESS SERENADE *

2000. Video. DIR: Rokurota Makabe. SCR: N/C. DES: Teruaki Murakami. ANI: Natsu Motoki. MUS: Yoshi. PRD: Digital Works (Vanilla Series), YOUC. 35 mins. Yuji struggles with his feelings for his dead brother Ryoji's beautiful fiancée Satsuki, as the pair of them cooperate on setting up the store that was Ryoji's lifelong ambition. But Satsuki is still mourning her dearly departed, while the pretty young Miki has a crush on Yuji that the lovelorn boy has yet to notice. While the art and animation are mediocre, the character development is surprisingly intense for a pornographic anime. Compare with **Wife With Wife** episode one; part of the **Vanilla Series**. **L N**

ENDO, SHIGEO

1949– . Born in Fukushima Prefecture, Endo joined Nippon Animation, where he worked in production for Hayao Miyazaki's **Future Boy Conan**, and subsequent **World Masterpiece**

THEATER serials, including ANNE OF GREEN GABLES and PETER PAN. In later years, he became the producer of CHIBI MARUKO-CHAN.

EQUATION OF THE ROTTEN TEACHER

1994. JPN: *Kusatta Kyoshi no Hoteishiki*. AKA: *Fish in the Trap, Bad Teacher's Equation*. Video. DIR: Nanako Shimazaki. SCR: Hiromi Akino. DES: Akira Koguro. ANI: Yumi Nakayama. MUS: N/C. PRD: Daiei, Tokuma Japan Communications. 30 mins. x 2 eps.

In this adaptation of another gay-love manga from Kazuma Kadoka, the creator of KIZUNA, ten years after being forced to suppress his feelings for the beautiful boy next door, a young man meets the object of his desires and gets a second chance. But Atsushi, whose unrequited love still burns, now finds himself in a classroom where Ma-chan, the object of his youthful affections, is now the teacher. A humorous homosexual variant on the school shenanigans of HOMEROOM AFFAIRS. **Ⓝ**

ERGO PROXY

2006. TV series. DIR: Shuko Murase. SCR: Dai Sato. DES: Naoyuki Onda, Michiaki Sato. ANI: N/C. MUS: Yoshihiro Ike. PRD: Manglobe, Geneon. 25 mins. x 23 eps.

Lil Mayor is an agent in the Civil Intelligence Organization, charged with investigating crime in the dome city of Lando. Supposedly an emotionless utopia where humans and robots coexist in harmony, Lando has been troubled by a series of murders, although Lil herself is also troubled by a series of hauntings and attacks by phantoms that urge her to notice that an "awakening" is in progress. A series of psychological dramas soon reveal "an unimaginable truth," related to the world outside the dome, it says here. We don't know, but we can imagine quite a bit. Compare to HEAT GUY J and the BIG O.

EROTIC TORTURE CHAMBER *

1994. JPN: *Princess Lord: Bara to Rosoku no Monsho*. AKA: *Princess Lord: The Mark of Rose and Candle, Princess Road*. Video. DIR: Yoshitaka Fujimoto. SCR: Akira Oketani. DES: Masakatsu Sasaki. ANI: Masakatsu Sasaki. MUS: Torsten Rasch. PRD: Taki Corporation. 45 mins.

After 30 happy years, the twin kingdoms of Asronia and Gostania are awaiting the wedding of Prince Elias and Princess Yurie when the royal family is decimated by the army of Maryuo, the "Demon Dragon Lord." Elias is captured, Yurie is enslaved, and while the two supporting players who will save the day in the as-yet-unavailable second episode mooch around in their own subplot, the princess is taught the meaning of submission and obedience. The dark armor of Maryuo hides a well-spoken young man called Andreas, who wears half a bathrobe for no apparent reason and is exactly the kind of Bad Boy we know that Yurie has been waiting for. Yurie "reluctantly" offers her body to her captor in order to save her people.

A roster of well-known voice talents but with animation and design of a poor quality one has come to expect from a production crew just trying to pay the bills. The in-betweening often falters and the characters are lifted from other shows. The ninja bodyguard Maya borrows elements from both Ayanosuke of YOTODEN and Oscar of ROSE OF VERSAILLES, while the other leads are a standard cluster of anime archetypes.

The story's origin in Pierce Hoshino's erotic novel is betrayed in a languorous pacing that takes a good 20 minutes to get down to the nitty-gritty and so much back story that you can feel the original straining to squeeze itself into the format. Sex was clearly not the be-all and end-all of the original story, resulting in an anime version that takes too long to get going and then ends on a cliffhanger just when it does. Note that the alternate title *Princess Road* is a mis-transliteration of the original title by the distributor, Five Ways. **Ⓝ**

EROTICA AND PORNOGRAPHY

The first pornographic anime should have been Hakusan Kimura's *Cool Ship* (*Suzumi-bune*, 1932), the first part of an erotic two-reeler, seized by the police when only half complete. Thereafter, anime avoided erotica until a slump in TV profits led Osamu Tezuka to produce ARABIAN NIGHTS (1969) and CLEOPATRA: QUEEN OF SEX (1970) for cinema theaters. History records that these movies failed to revitalize the fortunes of Tezuka's Mushi Production, but at the time of its release the hype associated with the former impressed other animators enough to inspire the rival Nishimura Productions to make *Secret Movie: 1001 Nights in the Floating World* (*Hi-eiga: Ukiyoe Sen-ichi Yoru*, 1969). Deliberately drawn in an evocation of woodblock prints, the film also ran into trouble with the authorities and only went onto general release after the removal of six scenes deemed obscene. But cartoons were still regarded as a children's medium, and making animation that would be invisible to its chief audience must have seemed silly. The last gasp of erotic anime in cinemas was YASUJI'S PORNORAMA (1971), a comedy that ended with the frustrated leading man's attempt to commit ritual suicide—a perilous pastiche of the recent demise of novelist Yukio Mishima. Thereafter, all erotica, comedic, satiric, or otherwise, faded from cinemas, as Japan's soft-core "pink" live-action movies took over.

Erotica in any medium is beholden to censorship restrictions in the country that hosts it. Consequently, even live-action erotic cinema in Japan developed along lines that can seem strange to outside observers—proscriptions on visible genitalia and (until 1991) pubic hair often leading to ludicrously over-artistic camera work, depilated characters who appear underage, or fetishes such as sexualized bondage. Pornography is also often the first part of any media culture to experiment with new means of distribution or access, and anime was no exception. Absent from animation as a genre for over a decade, pornography swiftly returned with the arrival of the video cassette recorder and the laserdisc player, with the infamous LOLITA ANIME (1984) and CREAM LEMON (1984). Ever since, anime pornography has remained a constant blue-chip area in the video business, since the titles can be short, easily produced, and retail at high prices. Sales of anime porn to private consumers were less common—the tapes often seemed designed to be watched once and returned, and only gained a "collector's" cachet with the coming of laserdiscs and DVDs. Amid the frenzied couplings of everyday pornographic anime, two titles are worthy of special attention. Hideki Takayama's anime adaptation of Toshio Maeda's UROTSUKIDOJI (1987) pioneered the new subgenre of "erotic horror," incorporating sexual acts into fantasy scenarios and violence, and is particularly noted for introducing the tentacle as a phallus substitute in order to evade censorship. Its polar opposite was Yukio Abe's THE SENSUALIST (1990), a masterpiece of old-world geisha charm and symbolic eroticism, based on Saikaku Ihara's 17th-century novel, *The Life of an Amorous Man.*

Video anime also introduced the new sub-*sub*-genre of gay erotica, supposedly sold to a female audience, although evidence from the filmmakers' choices of advertising venues suggest that such titles have a far larger male audience than some Japanese sources acknowledge. Titles such as ZETSUAI (1992), MY SEXUAL HARRASSMENT (1994), and LEGEND OF THE BLUE WOLVES (1996) are tales in which strong, predatory older men seduce young, virginal victims. Others, such as FAKE (1996), attempt to introduce homosexual characters to mainstream genres such as the cop show.

The first lesbian activity in anime was in Tezuka's ARABIAN NIGHTS, when Aladdin's daughter, disguised as a young man, makes a marriage of convenience with a princess who finds the arrangement more convenient than expected. Overt lesbianism doesn't appear to have been referenced again until the erotic video boom of the 1980s. When it reappeared in 1984, in two LOLITA ANIME segments, lesbianism was in its usual mass media guise as entertainment for heterosexual men. The lackluster LOLICON ANGEL (1985) crashed school lesbianism into the mystery story but didn't escape the accident unscathed. Girls' schools and convents have always been prime territory for pornography, providing a secret space outside "normal" experience where exploration won't impinge on the outside world. In 1986, the CREAM LEMON segment *Escalation* provided a dark view of exploitative lesbian S&M in—surprise, surprise—an exclusive girls' school. But *CL* also opened up new porn genres—fantasy and science fiction. *Pop Chaser* presented a lesbian biker heroine and a ditzy little damsel in distress happy to switch orientation depending on the situation, while *Star Trap* showed the lively lesbian crew of a vessel not entirely unlike the USS Enterprise. The intense sexuality of the girls' school got a less explicit, but much darker and more serious, treatment in BROTHER DEAREST (1991) before reverting to type for 1995's ANGEL OF DARKNESS. Meanwhile, HANAPPE BAZOOKA poked tasteless and energetic fun at most forms of sexuality in 1992.

The authors are unable to think of any anime made *for* lesbians, as opposed to those targeting males in search of girl-on-girl titillation, although the cross-dressing traditions of the Takarazuka theater, as evoked in PRINCESS KNIGHT, and the regular use of female voice actors to play leading male roles in everything from DRAGON BALL to EVANGELION, suggest that some mainstream titles may have an unintended appeal to a lesbian audience. Certainly, the UTENA movie was regarded as sapphic enough in its outlook to play at the London Lesbian and Gay Film Festival—it should also be noticed that same-sex crushes are often a feature of mainstream school anime such as THE VIRGIN MARY IS WATCHING (2004), and lesbian activity, or its implication, remains a common feature of many erotica aimed at men.

Another strand of anime makes no explicit reference to sexuality at all, but is loaded with homoerotic potential—boy team shows. From the heroic teenagers of SAINT SEIYA fighting epic battles with the gods in 1986, via the Hong Kong hothouse of VIRUS (1997), to the sporting action of PRINCE OF TENNIS (2001), it seems that female fandom only needs good-looking guys in tense, emotionally charged situations, like saving the world, winning the match, or luring a best friend/older brother back from the Dark Side, to start producing fantasies that would make experienced porn writers blush. If this proves anything, it is that the principal sexual organs in humans are the brain, the imagination, and—sometimes—the sense of the ridiculous.

The rise of computer games saw a heavy concentration on the anime artstyle, initially because anime-style images did not require the high resolution of real photographs. It was only a matter of time before many such games were adapted into fully animated versions, particularly in the "dating-simulation" subgenre where lonely male protagonists searched for their ideal Girl Next Door among a group of carefully designed archetypes. Not all such games had an overt erotic subject, but GRADUATION (1994; original game, June 1992), END OF SUMMER (1994; original game released as *Dokyusei* in December 1992), and TOKIMEKI MEMORIAL (1999; original game May 1994) still led to the establishment of a new paradigm. Erotic or not, the "harem show" took the premise of the dating-sims and adapted it for a mainstream audience, resulting in a slew of chaste quests for love—the most famous examples being TENCHI MUYO! (1992) and LOVE HINA (2000). There also remains a thriving subgenre in erotic anime that parodis mainstream titles, such as BALTHUS:

Escaflowne

TIA'S RADIANCE, TOKIO PRIVATE POLICE, and VENUS FIVE.

During the 1990s, anime erotica found a new and unexpected audience outside Japan, where it became the secret cash cow of the foreign anime business. In some territories, teen titillation and erotic horror were used to manufacture controversy, leading to the popular public misconception that *all* anime is pornographic. In fact, most pornographic anime is available in small one- and two-episode formats; a book such as this is forced to use an unrepresentative amount of space discussing the genre, since it would take literally a thousand titles like EROTIC TORTURE CHAMBER to fill the running time of a single SAZAE-SAN. Nevertheless, pornographic anime is particularly likely to be translated for the English-language market, with franchises such as the D3 SERIES, DISCOVERY SERIES, SECRET ANIMA, and VANILLA SERIES reaching American video stores far faster than many mainstream works. Often in quantities far exceeding their original Japanese duplication runs, and retailing far more cheaply than Japanese titles (most of which were destined for the rental market), these titles focus

on fetishes that can prove to be more problematic for live-action porn, such as the sexualized violence of BIBLE BLACK or the scatology of NIGHT SHIFT NURSES. Many viewers' first encounter with Japanese culture is hence with niche-area pornography aimed at a tiny subset of the Japanese population. Foreign journalists, in particular, are often eager to assume that Japanese are fervent fans of titles such as ANGEL CORE or WIFE EATER, whereas sales comparisons would suggest the exact opposite, and that, if there is anything to worry about, it is not the Japanese taste in anime.

Modern pornography is characterized by direct downloads to computers and mobile phones, with some Japan-based distributors even providing English-language options direct to consumers abroad. Since pornography is usually five years ahead of the mainstream in terms of its distribution and production techniques, the authors expect to see more mainstream anime taking similar routes to its audience by 2010.

E'S OTHERWISE *
2003. TV series. DIR: Masami Shi-

moda. SCR: Katsuhiko Chiba. DES: Takehiro Hamatsu. ANI: N/C. MUS: Kazunori Miyake, Hajime Hyakkoku. PRD: Studio Pierrot, TV Tokyo. 25 mins. x 26 eps. After a terrible war in the near future, a dozen corporations run the world. The public is deeply suspicious of the emergent race of psychics—a common anime setup from GUNDAM onward. Enter the ASHRAM organization, which claims to offer sanctuary to those with psychic powers and to train them in methods of putting their skills to use for the common good. Two such foundlings are brother and sister Kai and Hikaru, brought into the fold by ASHRAM agent Eiji. Within a year of working for an ASHRAM subdivision, Kai has made great progress but his sister has yet to recover from recent trauma, and Kai must still face the daily hatred of "normal" humans. Before long, he also discovers that neither ASHRAM nor the quasi-governmental corporations are necessarily acting for the general good of humanity (who guessed?), in a show that begins well but soon begins to limp through the familiar tropes of science fiction anime. In the parlance of the show, "E's" (pronounced as is the letter "s") is a person with extrasensory powers that are too strong for conventional humans to defeat; all rather too close for comfort to the "X" of *X-Men* (2000), to which this show owes much of its inspiration. Based on the manga *E's* by Satoru Yuiga, serialized in *G-Fantasy Comics* since 1997. ●

ESCAFLOWNE *
1996. JPN: *Tenku no Escaflowne*. AKA: *Heavenly Escaflowne; Vision of Escaflowne*. TV series, movie. DIR: Kazuki Akane, Shinichiro Watanabe, Takeshi Yoshimoto, Hiroshi Osaka, Takuro Shinbo, Tetsuya Yanasawa, Hiroyuki Takeuchi. SCR: Shoji Kawamori, Ryota Yamaguchi, Akihiko Inari, Hiroaki Kitajima. DES: Nobuteru Yuki, Kimitoshi Yamane, Mahiro Maeda. ANI: Shigeki Kobara, Yuki Kanno, Takahiro Omori, Yoshiyuki Takei. MUS: Yoko Kanno, Hajime Mizoguchi. PRD: Sunrise, TV

Tokyo. 25 mins. x 26 eps. (TV), 98 mins. (m).

Hitomi Kanzaki is transported to an alternate Earth when a dragon appears on her school's running track. On Gaea, Earth is called the Mystic Moon, beast-men rub shoulders with knights in giant robots, and Earth girls are respected and feared for their sorcerous powers. Her companion, Van, is the disinherited prince of Fanelia and owner of the robot-armor Escaflowne, with which he resists the evil Zaibach Empire. Hitomi is witness to the uneasy alliance between Van and another nobleman, Asturia's roguish ladykiller Allen, but she is also the object of their competing affections. Tortured family ties writhe beneath the surface, with missing or disinherited siblings galore and revelations of dark or forgotten pasts. In only the first of several major plot twists, it is revealed that one of the leaders of the Zaibach armies is Folken, Van's disgraced brother. As war sweeps Gaea, Hitomi is revealed as the crucial key to victory, a role she is tempted to swap for a simple, carefree life back on Earth.

Deliberately designed to appeal to male and female viewers in equal measure, *Escaflowne* is genuine family entertainment, both in and out of the anime world, and arguably the best TV anime of the 1990s. Its ambiguous nature is reflected in *two* spin-off manga, Katsu-Aki's *Vision of Escaflowne* for the male readership of *Comics A*, and Yuzuru Yashiro's *Messiah Knight* for the female readership of *Asuka Fantasy DX*.

Five years in the planning, with something of a debt to SECRET OF BLUE WATER, it and UTENA were the two highly romantic shows that flourished in the morbid vacuum left by EVANGELION. In retaining its coherence throughout, and its earnest devotion to fantasy ideals instead of arch irony, posterity may well decide that *Escaflowne* is the best of them all. Reputedly passed over by Manga Entertainment for being "too childish," it starts off looking like a school romance or girls' sports anime

before transforming into high fantasy adventure. As with GUNBUSTER, its first episode is a red herring, a school soap opera where Hitomi pines for her handsome senior Amano. In a steal from the stage version of PETER PAN AND WENDY, the actors of Earth scenes also play doubles in the fantasy world—Shinichiro Miki provides the voice of both Amano and *real* prince charming Allen. One of the few shows to continually outdo itself, *Escaflowne* is a triumph—though the dub sadly missed the opportunity to differentiate between accents on the two worlds by making all the Gaeans British.

Though it was reduced in size from a planned 39-episode run partway through production, the only evidence is the absence of opening credits from the first episode in order to allow the crew time to cram in extra exposition. This was remedied in the Japanese video release, the retail version of which also restored deleted scenes to the first seven episodes. As the inevitable consequence of its popularity, it exists in bastardized versions, including the incoherent three-part *Best Collection* that unsuccessfully crams the entire story into just 180 minutes. The series was further bowdlerized for the American TV market, with Yoko Kanno's beautiful music torn out in favor of humdrum techno, and the first episode removed in a version that, with bitter irony, was taken off the air after 10 episodes because of "low ratings."

The movie version *Escaflowne: A Girl in Gaea* (2000) is a complete remake that redesigns the characters for the big screen and plays up the Asian feel of the series—the earlier TV version allowed elements of European fantasy to creep in.

ESPER MAMI

1987. AKA: *Malicieuse/Mischievous Kiki*. TV series, movie. DIR: Pak Kyon Sun, Keiichi Hara, Tsukasa Sunaga, Atsuhide Tsukata, Osamu Inoue, Mitsuru Honma, Shinya Sadamitsu, Tomomi Mochizuki. SCR: Sukehiro Tomita, Ryo Motohira, Akira Higuchi.

DES: Fujiko-Fujio. ANI: Sadao Tominaga, Chuji Nakajima. MUS: Kohei Tanaka. PRD: Shinei, TV Asahi. 25 mins. x 119 eps., 40 mins. (m).

Schoolgirl Mami Sagura discovers that she has superpowers. She can sense other people in trouble and teleport to help them, but she keeps her secret double-life hidden from her parents with the help of her schoolfriend, Kazuo Takahata. Based on the 1977 manga in *Corocoro Comic* by DORAEMON-creators Fujiko-Fujio, the series also spawned a short film, *EM: Midnight Dancing Doll* (1988), featuring Mami using her powers to make a puppet show for deprived children.

ETCHIIS

1997. Video. DIR: Kazunari Kume. SCR: Yokihi. DES: Yokihi. ANI: Toshimitsu Kobayashi. MUS: N/C. PRD: Pink Pineapple, KSS. 30 mins. x 2 eps.

Two short comedies, *Unio Familia* and *Normal Human Relations*, reputedly praised for "realistic female characterization" and lots of sex scenes. Based on the 1995 manga anthology by Yokihi, though *2x1*, the original's most popular story, was animated as part of the SECRET ANIMA series the following year and released in the U.S. as *Four Play*. Ⓝ

ETERNAL FILENA

1992. JPN: *Eien no Filena*. Video. DIR: Naoto Hashimoto, Yoshikata Nitta. SCR: Takeshi Shudo, Yasuko Hoshigawa. DES: Akemi Takada, Akiyuki Shinbo. ANI: Chuji Nakajima. MUS: Jinmo, Noriyoshi Matsuura. PRD: Pierrot Project. 30 mins. x 4 eps.

The Devis Empire offers gladiatorial games to keep the masses happy. It's the only way for a commoner to make any kind of living, and the lucky few who last long enough are made citizens. Filena poses as a man to enter the arena and fight to support her ailing mother, but as time passes, she begins to prefer the life of a poor revolutionary to that of a rich slave. Based on a novel serialized in *Animage* by POKÉMON-writer Shudo. Compare to GREY: DIGITAL TARGET.

ETERNITY YOU DESIRE, THE

2002. JPN: *Kimi ga Nozomu Eien*. AKA: *Your Eternal Dream, Kiminozo, Eternity You Wish For, Rumble Hearts*. TV series, video. DIR: Tetsuya Watanabe. SCR: Katsuhiko Takayama, Kenichi Kanemaki. DES: Yoko Kikuchi, Kanetake Ebikawa, Tomohiko Kawahara. ANI: Yoko Kikuchi. MUS: Abito Torai, Kenichi Sudo, Ryoji Minami. PRD: Media Factory, Studio Fantasia, TV Kanagawa. 24 mins. x 14 eps. (TV), 25 mins. x 3 eps. (v).

After worshipping Takayuki Narumi from afar throughout her high school years, Haruka Suzumiya is finally pressured by her friend Mitsuki into confessing her feelings for him. The young couple overcome painful shyness and several teenage misunderstandings before each is sure of the other's love, but the future looks bright as they help each other to study for college entrance exams. Look away now if you are one of those people who complain the *Anime Encyclopedia* gives away all the plot twists, because after such an innocent and, seemingly, predictable start, Haruka is left in a coma by an accident. Takayuki falls into depression, shuts himself away, and does not even attend his own graduation ceremony. Mitsuki is so worried about him that she gives up a chance of a sports career in swimming, gets an ordinary office job, and even moves in with him. Gradually, she slips into depression herself as she thinks of what she has given up. He takes on part-time work at a restaurant, makes friends there, and is eventually settling into a comfortable rut when Haruka unexpectedly regains consciousness.

What follows is a cunning mainstream way of dealing with the yearnings across time of VOICES OF A DISTANT STAR; compare to 24 EYES, which similarly finds a natural way to create "time travel." Haruka wakes up unaware that three whole years have passed until her younger sister Akane tells her. When Takayuki visits, Haruka wants to fill in the missing years, but mostly she wants to know if he's been dating anyone else, leaving him in the difficult position of explaining that he has shacked up with the girl who had brought them together. It was based on a dating sim game and manga by âge, which began as part of the adults-only erotica genre, although the anime, like later versions of the game, drops much of the nudity in favor of the romance. It does, however, occasionally cling to a misplaced desire to inject comedy into what is ultimately a rather dark and weepy storyline. Regardless, the result is an original variant on the implicit promises and romantic tensions of LOVE HINA and its ilk, although live-action Japanese drama had been there before with *Since I Met You* (*DE), and American TV would take a similar approach in *Everwood* (2002). A three-part spin-off video, *Akane Maniax* (*Kiminozo Gaiden*, 2004) was a love story centered around Haruka's sister Akane, though central characters from *Kiminozo* also appear. **◎**

EUREKA 7 *

2005. JPN: *Kokyoshihen Eureka Seven*. AKA: *Symphonic Poem Eureka Seven*. TV series. DIR: Tomomi Kyoda, Masayuki Miyaji, Kazuya Murata, Takeshi Yoshimoto. SCR: Chiaki Konaka, Dai Sato, Hiroshi Onogi, Shotaro Suga, Yuichi Nomura. DES: Kenichi Yoshida, Shoji Kawamori, Kazutaka Miyatake. ANI: Eiji Nakata, Seiichi Hashimoto. MUS: Naoki Sato. PRD: BONES, Bandai Entertainment, MBS. 25 mins. x 50 eps.

Human colonists on an alien world utilize "trapars," strange airborne particles in the local atmosphere to allow them to surf through the skies in the manner of *The Silver Surfer*. This has led to the colonial sport of Ref, or aerial surfing, although former champion Holland has turned to politics, and formed the guerrilla organization known as the Gekko state rebels. His battles against the oppressive Federation are fought with LFOs, futuristic cars that can transform into giant robots, all based on alien technology that the early colonists found lying around—so, nothing to do with MACROSS, then. 14-year-old Renton is dragged into the revolution when attractive female pilot Eureka crashes her LFO near his house and asks his mechanic grandfather for help. Before long, Renton has joined the rebels, although his motivation initially seems based more on hero worship of Holland the former sportsman than Holland the freedom fighter. It's all a remarkable coincidence, but not as remarkable as the fact that the Japanese title manages to look a little like that of EVANGELION and a little like that of the ULTRAMAN spin-off *Ultra Seven*. There is a certain Evangelic resemblance in the robots, too. Created as part of a multimedia project that included a PS2 game.

EVANGELION *

1995. JPN: *Shinseiki Evangelion*. AKA: *Neon Genesis Evangelion; New Century Evangelion*. TV series, Movie. DIR: Hideaki Anno, Kazuya Tsurumaki. SCR: Hideaki Anno, Akio Satsugawa. DES: Yoshiyuki Sadamoto, Ikuto Yamashita. ANI: Masayuki, Kazuya Tsurumaki, Tadashi Hiramatsu. MUS: Shiro Sagisu. PRD: Tatsunoko, Gainax, TV Tokyo. 25 mins. x 26 eps., 102 mins. (m), 97 mins. (m).

At the turn of the millennium, a "meteorite strike" on Antarctica wipes out half of Earth's population. The NERV project fights the real danger—aliens called the Angels who are sending bioengineered weapons to destroy the rest of humanity. The experimental Evangelion project fights the outsized invaders with giant cybernetic organisms, but only children born after the Antarctica incident can pilot the machines. With Rei, the original test pilot, critically ill after an accident, head scientist Gendo Ikari summons his estranged son, Shinji, to take the first mission. Shinji is taken in by the sisterly Misato, an alcoholic burnout with a passionate hatred for the Angels, and the arrival of the hot-headed pilot Asuka Langley creates a dysfunctional surrogate family.

With this novel excuse for young, audience-friendly protagonists and giant fighting robots, Gainax incorporates many of its favorite staples from classic anime and monster movies—the Evas themselves even have a five-minute timer in homage to **ULTRAMAN**. A deeply personal, psychological odyssey that allowed Anno to remake his earlier **GUNBUSTER** at a slower pace, *Eva* similarly replayed the Pacific War from the Japanese point of view, specifically the apocalyptic final events. Cosmetic use of Western religious imagery, such as Angel weaponry exploding in cruciform patterns, may appear to suggest that Western beliefs themselves are an alien invasion, but this owes more to Anno's own readings in Jungian psychology and archetypes as he coped with creative doldrums post-*Gunbuster.*

Like *Gunbuster*, *Eva* also piles on the parodies, particularly from Gerry Anderson shows (see **THUNDERBIRDS 2086**), with hidden fortresses launching superweapons and uniforms lifted from Anderson's live-action *UFO* (1969). It also features innovative casting, allowing famous voice actors to shine in unusual roles, especially **RANMA ½**'s Megumi Hayashibara as the schizoid Rei and **SAILOR MOON**'s Kotono Mitsuishi as the tragic Misato.

Ultimately, however, *Eva* ended in a series of disappointments. Gainax was criticized for later scenes broadcast without network approval, indirectly causing the more censorious climate that hurt **COWBOY BEBOP**. Later episodes ran visibly low on funds, with overlong pauses to stretch the animation budget and two concluding episodes that were glorified radio plays. Rumors abounded that Gainax had run out of money and/or time, and that the final chapters were thrown together in just two weeks when Anno's hard-hitting original finale was disallowed. However, *Gunbuster* similarly ended with a montage of stills rather than the promised climactic battle, leading some to suggest Anno had always planned it this way and that the violent nature of the theatrical sequels

reflected his annoyance that his "intellectual" ending was unappreciated by the audience. A succession of *Eva* movies followed, seemingly designed to leach the last cash and goodwill from remaining fans. An audio drama, *The Conclusion Continues* (1996), joked that having saved the world, the *Eva* cast would consider placing it in fake peril to get their old jobs back; though the gag was ironically close to the mark. The promised "real" finale turned out to be a double bill—*Death and Rebirth* (1997), a recap of the first 24 episodes with the first reel of the true ending. Audience patience was tested a second time with *Death (True)2*, which added tantalizing scraps of extra footage, including the moment of "Second Impact" and bonus sequences that also appeared in the Japanese (but not U.S.) video releases of the TV episodes. The genuine movie edition, *End of Evangelion* (1997), was a truly shocking apocalypse, taking the themes of the original to their logical conclusion presented as the two "missing" episodes that should have closed the series in the first place. These multiple endings have since been repackaged in another edition, *Revival of Evangelion.*

Despite this confused denouement, *Eva* was the most critically successful TV anime of the 1990s, drawing back many fans who had given up on the medium, and even inspiring *Newtype* to test market a new magazine for "intellectual" anime viewers. But like another of Anno's 1960s favorites, *The Prisoner*, it teased viewers with the illusion of hidden depths that weren't necessarily there, and though designed to be the last word on the giant-robot genre, its success merely ushered in a succession of imitations. Its influence, however, can also be seen in some of the better shows of the years that followed, **BLUE SUBMARINE NO. SIX**'s Japan fighting a morally superior foe, **NADESICO**'s tongue-in-cheek homage to old shows, and **GASARAKI**'s mixture of militarism and theatrical passion. In the wake of *Eva*, TV became the growth medium for anime, in turn altering the

U.S. anime market, with distributors forced to risk more money for longer series when they would prefer shorter movies or video productions. However, this was eventually beneficial in the long-term, allowing American TV channels to scoop up these serials for broadcast during the boom in anime fandom that followed the **POKÉMON** generation into their teens.

In the aftermath of *Eva*, Anno reused many of its stylistic conceits (such as multiple onscreen titles) in the live-action *Love and Pop* (1999) and the anime romance **HIS AND HER CIRCUMSTANCES**. Sagisu's score was also recycled when parts of it were lifted for Katsuyuki Motohiro's live-action TV series *Bayside Shakedown*. In a final irony, two members of the Gainax studio were indicted for tax evasion over the films' profits—the impoverished filmmakers who finished on a shoestring were now the new fat cats. In 2004 a DVD box set entitled *Neon Genesis Evangelion: Renewal* (aka *Renewal of Evangelion*, also the name of the 10th-anniversary project) was issued, containing re-authored versions of the television show (both broadcast and director's cut releases) and both of the movies, all using restored film prints. The TV components were released in North America as *NGE: Platinum* (or *Platinum Edition*). Themes and images from *Evangelion* were used by the British pop group Fightstar for the album *Grand Unification* (2005). **Ⓥ**

EVEN MORE GHOST STORIES

1995. JPN: *Zokuzoku Mura no Obaketachi.* AKA: *Even More Village Ghosts.* Video. DIR: Tameo Ogawa. SCR: Masatoshi Kimura. DES: Konomi Sakurai. ANI: Konomi Sakurai. MUS: Koichi Hiro. PRD: Toei. 40 mins. x 6 eps.

A succession of tales taken from the 1.3-million-selling children's books by Akiko Sueyoshi and Mako Taruishi, including *Ram the Mummy*, *Obatan the Witch*, *The Childish Goblin*, and *Kitten Ghosts Goo, Soo and Pea.*

Excel Saga

EXCEL SAGA © 1999 KOSHI RIKDO / SHONEN GAHOSHA-VICTOR ENTERTAINMENT

EVERY DAY'S A SUNDAY

1990. JPN: *Mainichi ga Nichiyobi*. Video. DIR: Hidehito Ueda. SCR: Hidehito Ueda, Kazuko Ueda. DES: Kazuya Ose. ANI: Kazuya Ose. MUS: Hiroya Watanabe. PRD: Animate Film. 30 mins. x 6 eps. Yumi Takeshita is saved from a car accident but her rescuer is injured. When she meets him again a year later, she's a rookie police officer with the twin aims of working for justice and finding a boyfriend. His name is Toru Ichidai, and he's a conjuror. He would have gone to Hollywood by now, but the accident has held him back. And now that he's met her again, he may as well stay in Japan to form half of an unusual crime-fighting team. Based on an manga by 3x3 EYES–creator Yuzo Takada.

EVOCATION

1997. JPN: *Trouble Evocation*. Video. DIR: Masakazu Amiya. SCR: Ryoga Ryuen. DES: Ryoga Ryuen. ANI: Inatsugi Kiyomizu. MUS: N/C. PRD: Pink Pineapple, KSS. 30 mins. x 2 eps. Hideya is visited every night by the cute sex-kitten Leah, who falls in love with him. One day she is ordered back to Hell by Satina, but Hideya begs her to stay. In this erotic variant on OH

MY GODDESS! based on ZANKAN-creator Ryoga Ryuen's manga originally serialized in *Kitty Time*, Leah is so shocked by the strength of his feelings that she starts to take off her clothes. N

EXCEL SAGA *

1999. JPN: *Heppoko [Silly] Animation Excel Saga*. AKA: *Quack Experimental Anime Excel Saga, Weird Anime Excel Saga*. TV series. DIR: Shinichi Watanabe, Akihiko Nishiyama, Jun Fukuda, Takafumi Hoshikawa, Ken Ando, Masahiko Murata. SCR: Kumi Jigoku, Yosuke Kuroda. DES: Satoshi Ishino. ANI: Satoshi Ishino. MUS: Toshio Masuda. PRD: JC Staff, TV Tokyo.25 mins. x 25 eps. (TV), 25 mins. x 1 eps. (v). In the fortified section of a heavily fortified underground fortress (he's taking no chances), Across company boss Il Palazzo continues his ongoing attempt to conquer the world. Working for him are the two beautiful agents Excel and Hyatt, but protecting the world isn't a well-paying job, and the girls have to share a flat and travel to work on the subway. They also have to work part-time as bounty hunters to make ends meet, accompanied by their pet dog, Mensch, who is also an

emergency food supply. A truly insane comedy in the spirit of DRAGON HALF (featuring the same voice actress, Kotono Mitsuishi), with time out for cameo appearances from director Watanabe (as "Nabeshin") in his trademark giant afro, assassination attempts on the author of the original manga, Rikado Koshi, a theme song barked by a dog with Japanese subtitles, and a "flexible" attitude toward the deaths of main characters, perhaps inspired by the tribulations of Kenny from *South Park*. The final episode was not broadcast but included on the video release. PUNI PUNI POEMI is a spin-off from the show. Announced as forthcoming from ADV Films at the time of our deadline.

EX-DRIVER

2000. AKA: *éX-D*. Video. DIR: Jun Kawagoe. SCR: Shinzo Fujita. DES: Kenichi Hamazaki, Kosuke Fujishima, Hidefumi Kimura, Takeshi Takakura, Shunji Murata. ANI: N/C. MUS: N/C. PRD: Sunrise. 30 mins. x 6 eps. (v1), 63 mins. (m), 27 mins. (v2). A century in the future, travel has been made perfectly safe by the introduction of fully-automated AI-cars. But when these electrically powered, computer-controlled cars run amok, it's the mission of the Ex-Driver team to rev up their engines and give chase. It takes a particular kind of person to drive one of the temperamental gasoline cars, and the perky Lisa and laid-back Lorna think they have what it takes, in a predictable rehash of Fujishima's earlier YOU'RE UNDER ARREST, with a sop to younger viewers in the form of 13-year-old driver prodigy Soichi.

The movie (2002) featured Lorna, Lisa, and Soichi traveling to Santa Monica, California to take part in the eX-Driver World Meet, as the members of Team Japan. There they encounter Angela Gambino, the alienated daughter of ex-mob boss Rico Gambino, now the head of a supermarket chain, who in turn is the sponsor of Team USA—the bickering couple David and Kelly. Faced with sabotage and an apparent plot to gamble on the outcome of the

World Meet's final race, they must work through the layers of intrigue and track down the true villain to bring him to justice. Of course, many car chases ensue.

When the movie was released on DVD (also in 2002) it came with a 27-minute extra, *eX-Driver: Nina & Rei Danger Zone*, a quasi-prequel in which the heroines must stop a miniature AI car with a tiny replica of Nina inside before it shuts down the whole of Tokyo's transport grid. There's a plot against the eX-Drivers lurking in the background somewhere, but once again the chases are the thing. This time the crew throws in a car/airplane chase down a runway, just for a change.

EXPER ZENON

1991. Video. DIR: Yuji Moriyama, Hiroaki Hayase. SCR: Yuji Moriyama, Yasushi Hirano, Shigeru Yamamoto. DES: Yuji Moriyama, Satoshi Hashimoto. ANI: Yuji Moriyama. MUS: Kenji Kawai. PRD: Studio Fantasia. 60 mins.
Tadashi is a high school student and computer-game addict. After a long day spent playing the game Zenon, he is visited in a dream by the heroine, Sartova. In an anime replay of *The Last Starfighter*, she takes him to the world of Zenon, where the game is played with human lives at stake.

EXPLODING CAMPUS GUARDRESS

1994. JPN: *Bakuen Campus Guardress*. AKA: *Combustible Campus Guardress*. Video. DIR: Toshihiko Nishikubo. SCR: Satoru Akahori, Kazushi Hagiwara. DES: Kazuya Kose. ANI: Kazuya Kose. MUS: Fumitaka Anzai. PRD: Production IG. 30 mins. x 4 eps.
Thirty thousand years ago, Takumi, Hasumi, and Kasumi were tragic lovers who vowed to finalize their romance in another life. Thirty thousand years after these heroic Guardians defeated the evil Remnant invaders from the Dark World and sealed them behind an interdimensional Gateway, their

reincarnations return once more to save the world. The site of the ancient battle is now in downtown Tokyo, hidden under the somewhat conspicuously named Gateway High School. When the cosmic moment comes for the Guardians and the Remnants to do battle once more, the reincarnations create some confusing blends of ancient and modern personalities and priorities, as our noble warriors are forced to choose between Armageddon and the senior prom, and they must fight enemies who were their friendly teachers only the day before. To make matters *incredibly* complicated, the Guardians have been reincarnated as brother, sister, and mother. Mom and Sis do not see any problems with trying to get into Takumi's pants when they are not battling the Remnants. However, Takumi seems to be more attached to his girlfriend from this life, Hime-chan, a total airhead who may fatally distract him from his duty. Based on a manga in *V Jump* magazine by **KNIGHTS OF RAMUNE**'s Akahori and **BASTARD**-creator Kazushi Hagiwara, this anime combines the gags and sauciness of the two.

EXPLORER WOMAN RAY *

1989. AKA: *The Explorer*. Video. DIR: Yasuo Hasegawa, Hiroki Hayashi. SCR: Mayori Sekijima. DES: Hiroyuki Ochi. ANI: Hiroyuki Ochi. MUS: Norimasa Yamanaka. PRD: Animate Film, AIC. 60 mins. x 2 eps.
Ray Kizuki is an archaeology student and a black-belt martial artist, bequeathed a mysterious mirror by her father that turns out to be the key to a newly discovered temple. She sets off to find it, accompanied by twins Mai and Maki, and pursued by the mysterious "Rig Veda," who eventually reveals himself as her late father's assistant. Based on a manga in *Comic Nora* by **ELEMENTALORS**-creator Takeshi Okazaki. **ⓥ**

EYESHIELD 21

2004. TV series, Movie. DIR: Masayoshi Nishida, Tamaki Nakatsu. SCR: Daisuke Habara, Nobuaki Kishima, Rika Nakase, Toshifumi Kawase, Yoshio Takeuchi (TV), Riichiro Inagaki (m). DES: Hirotoshi Takaya (TV), Minoru Ueda, Miyoko Tanitsuna (m). ANI: Chiyomi Koyama, Hajime Watanabe, Hisashi Mitsui, Kazunori Takahashi (TV), Eiko Kato, Kazuyo Hasegawa (m). MUS: Ko Otani (TV), Kenji Kawai, Shin Iwashina (m). PRD: Frontline, Production I.G., TV Tokyo. 30 mins. (m); 25 mins. x 34+ eps. (TV).
Sena Kobayashi is a little kid who has developed super fast running skills in order to avoid the school bullies in the style of **HARRIS'S WIND**. Eventually, his skills are put to use by the school's (American-style) football team, when he is encased in armor and given the nickname "Eyeshield 21" to hide his identity from the rival schools, in this adaptation of the manga written by Riichiro Inagaki and drawn by Yusuke Murata.

While the TV series proper aired in 2005, in the previous year's one-shot theatrical prequel *Eyeshield 21: Maboroshi no Golden Bowl* (*Phantom Golden Bowl*), the Off Harajuku Boarders believe that they have lost their last chance to get into the Kanto district finals. That is, until the district leader Mr. Hatohara makes a Faustian pact— the Boarders will be permitted to play in the previously unknown Golden Bowl tournament, the winner of which will be admitted as a late entry into the championship. It is only when the Boarders take the field that they realize they are playing the Demon Devilbats, a team not of this world, in a story that combines the clichés of a sports tale with the traditions of a summertime ghost story. The episode of the TV series broadcast on 7 September 2005 was an hour-long special. Compare to **MACHINE HAYABUSA**.

F

F

1988. TV series. DIR: Koichi Mashimo, Katsuyoshi Yatabe, Kunihisa Sugishima, Nobuyasu Furukawa. SCR: Hideo Takayashiki. DES: Masamitsu Kudo, Tomohiko Sato. ANI: Masamitsu Kudo, Ryunosuke Otonashi. MUS: Wataru Yahagi, Masaru Hoshi. PRD: Kitty, Fuji TV. 25 mins. x 31 eps.

After the death of his mother, Gunma Akagi discovers his real father is a professional racer. After befriending pit boss Tamotsu, Gunma is inspired to join his father's world and becomes a driver himself, staying at his grandmother's place in Tokyo. The "F" stands for "formula," and with a fish out of water, a surrogate family, and a sporting quest, formula is exactly what you get.

F³: FRANTIC, FRUSTRATED AND FEMALE *

1994. JPN: Nageki no Kenko Yuryoji. AKA: The Lament of an Otherwise Perfectly Healthy Girl, Ménage à Trois. Video. DIR: Masakazu Akan. SCR: N/C. DES: Koji Hamaguchi. ANI: Koji Hamaguchi. MUS: Bang Heads. PRD: Pink Pineapple, KSS. 30 mins. x 3 eps.

A sapphic satire about Hiroe, who is unable to achieve orgasm with her boyfriend and seeks a remedy for her teenage frustrations. Her sister, Mayaka, helps with Chinese medicine, scientific inventions, and even a lesbian biker orgy. The trilogy ends with a haunted-house spoof in which demonic possession allows Mayaka to grow a penis for a replay of the hermaphroditic sex of LA BLUE GIRL. The script backtracks on the incestuous characters of episode one, later claiming that they only *look* as if they are related. Based on the manga by Wan Yan A Gu Da, published in *Penguin Club*. 🅝🅛

FABLED UNDERGROUND PEOPLE, THE

1989. JPN: Kore ga Uwasa no Chiteijin. Video. DIR: Kazuyoshi Hirose. SCR: Hisaichi Ishii. DES: Hisaichi Ishii. ANI: Kazumi Nonaka. MUS: Yukadan. PRD: Balk. 30 mins. x 2 eps.

In this spin-off from the *Action Comics* manga by MY NEIGHBORS THE YAMA-DAS–creator Hisaichi Ishii's serial, the Underground People desire to leave their overcrowded cavern and seize control of the surface world, but they never quite succeed. A second episode, *Christmas Aid*, soon followed, in which the brainless Undergrounders' second futile escape attempt is set to music by the popular group Yukadan. The first volume also included two unrelated stories by Ishii: *101 Ninja* and *Ken-chan's Space Exploration Adventure*.

FAFNER *

2004 JPN: Sokyu no Fafner. AKA: Fafner of the Blue Sky, Dead Aggressor. TV series. DIR: Nobuyoshi Habara, Junki Honma. SCR: Kazuki Yamanobe. DES: Hisashi Hirai, Naohiro Washio. ANI: Akio Takami, Akira Takahashi, Akitoshi Maeda, Atsushi Hasebe, Genichiro Kondo, Hideyuki Motohashi, Satotake Kikuchi, Shinichi Yamaoka, Sunao Shiomi, Taeko Hori, Takuya Matsumura, Toru Kitago. MUS: Tsuneyoshi Saito. PRD: King Records, Xebec, TV Tokyo. 25 mins. x 25 eps. (TV).

The peaceful lives of the people of Tatsumiya Island are shattered when they hear a voice echoing from the sky and a mysterious ray of light opens the sky, allowing an invading Festum alien to arrive. A subterranean command center springs into action and the citizens take shelter as fighter planes and missile defense systems deploy on the apparently sleepy island. A giant robot weapon, Fafner, has been concealed on the island and could be deployed to fight the Festum forces, but its school-girl pilot, Karin Kurumae, is missing. Doctor Makabe wants his son, standoff-ish high school boy Kazuki, to take her place. Kazuki's childhood friend Soshi Minashiro, son of the island's chief citizen, is also drawn into the war, which has been raging for some time in the outside world and has decimated the population. Japan is already gone, and Tatsumiya Island is a rogue nation, continually under threat from attack, since the "new" UN wants the Fafner for itself at any cost. The result is a show that takes the transforming city of Gerry Anderson's *Stingray* (1964) and asks what life would be like for the inhabitants, particularly if they discovered that the outside world was a lie in the style of THE ANIMATRIX or MEGAZONE 23 and that they had been bred specifically for saving the world from alien attack. There are also shades here of John Wyndham's *Midwich Cuckoos*, later filmed as *Village of the Damned*. Meanwhile, a ragtag band of impromptu defenders of the Earth is forced to jury-rig a battle plan à la MACROSS, while the combatants wonder if there are other defensive islands out there shrouded in equal secrecy, and if there are, whether they plan on helping out any time soon. The Fafner, named after a giant who transformed into a dragon in Richard Wagner's *Das Rheingold* (1862), is dark and neutral-colored, while the aliens are golden and gorgeous, hammering home the message that "not everything beautiful is a friend to man." You've seen EVANGELION, right?

A prequel, *Fafner: Single Program—Right of Left*, was announced in 2005. **V**

Fafner

FAIRGROUND IN THE STARS
1989. JPN: *Hoshi no Yuenchi*. Video. DIR: Nobuhiro Aihara. SCR: Nobuhiro Aihara. DES: Ryutaro Nakamura. ANI: Junichi Tokaibayashi. MUS: Koichi Hirai. PRD: Gakken. 18 mins.
A kindly teacher demonstrates origami to his elementary class, but when he gives a paper crane to a child, it is stolen from him by Takeshi, the class bully. Takeshi discovers that the crane is really a talking spaceship that takes him and his friends to visit a fairground in the stars. A girl falls through a hole into Space Hell, and the children cooperate to rescue her. Takeshi wakes up, wondering if it was all a dream. The next day, he returns the magic crane to its rightful owner. This tale is from RAINBOW ACROSS THE PACIFIC's Daisaku Ikeda, the leader of the Buddhist Soka Gakkai organization, although it lacks a particularly religious or moral message, playing like a sanitized version of NIGHT TRAIN TO THE STARS. Note the presence of future SERIAL EXPERIMENTS LAIN–director Nakamura as a character designer. Ikeda also wrote PRINCE OF SNOW COUNTRY.

FAIRY KING
1988. JPN: *Yosei O*. Video. DIR: Katsuhisa Yamada. SCR: Tomoko Konparu. DES: Atsuo Noda. ANI: Atsuo Noda. MUS: Yuriko Nakamura. PRD: Madhouse. 60 mins.
Sickly high school student Taka journeys to Hokkaido in search of a magical cure and falls in with Khoo Fu-Ling, the king of the fairies. Ninfidia, the land of the fairies, is under attack from the evil Queen Mab, and Taka must save it. Based on the 1978 girls' manga by Ryoko Yamagishi, which incorporated elements of legends of KING ARTHUR AND THE KNIGHTS OF THE ROUND TABLE, as well as scraps of Celtic, Greek, and Ainu myth.

FAIRYTALE WARRIOR LITTLE RED RIDING HOOD
2005. JPN: *Otogi Jushi Akazukin*. TV series, video. DIR: Tetsuro Araki. SCR: Shoji Yonemura. DES: Satoshi Tazaki. ANI: N/C. MUS: Toshio Masuda. PRD: Konami, Madhouse. 30 mins. x 3 eps. (v), 24 mins. x ?? eps. (TV).
After a sleep of a thousand years, Cendrillon the evil witch wakes once more and embarks on a quest for power that leads her to Sota Suzukaze, an otherwise normal Japanese boy who "holds the power to the seal"—whatever it means, it's catnip for evil sorceresses. In order to thwart Cendrillon's schemes, Little Red Riding Hood and Val the silver wolf are sent from the world of fairy tales to our own time. CARDCAPTORS–like high jinks soon ensue. The name of the antagonist also reflects fairy tales, using antiquated terms for the characters better known today as CINDERELLA and also Hansel, from *Hansel and Gretel*, the Pied Piper of Hamelin, and others from GRIMM'S FAIRY TALES.

FAKE *
1996. Video. DIR: Akira Suzuki. SCR: Akinori Endo. DES: Nagisa Miyazaki. ANI: Nagisa Miyazaki, Tomo Omota. MUS: Kix-S. PRD: Nippon Columbia. 60 mins.
Sanami Mato's original manga is a *Lethal Weapon* pastiche about fey New York cop Ryo being forced to partner up with Dee, a streetwise macho detective who wants to bed him. For this anime teaser to drag in new readers, Dee and Ryo are packed off to a British country hotel where guests are being murdered, and the supporting cast of the original manga drop

by when they're least needed. While Dee's trying to seduce Ryo and idly mulling over the details of unsolved local killings, their teenage sidekicks serve little purpose except to play happy families with Ryo and Dee as mommy and daddy. The children turn what could have been a queer case of Agatha Christie into a pointless holiday farce, with much swapping of rooms and indoor roller-blading—because it's raining outside.

Ryo and Dee are the world's worst detectives, for whom solving a case involves gossiping for a while and waiting for the criminals to reveal themselves. Faced with a murder case that the *real* police would solve in roughly ten seconds, *Fake* throws in more cameos from the manga to pad out its running time, including the detectives' future boss, Berkley Rose, and Dee's unrequited admirer, JJ, who waste a few more minutes with comedy business before the script reluctantly returns to the murders at hand.

Fake often walks an uneasy line between comedy and tragedy. A bit of cop-on-cop banter fits fine with mayhem and chaos, but not when people are watching their friends die from multiple stab wounds. As one might expect from a story with its pedigree, it ultimately has too many characters and too little time, making the murder mystery unengaging and turning an original romantic farce into humdrum formula. Far from breaking new ground in gay characterization, Ryo is simply a man playing a stereotypical female role; he gets to be an intuitive sidekick, a maternal figure, an unattainable romantic prize, and, as the show rushes to an insane conclusion, even a damsel in distress.

FALSE FRIENDS

False Friends (French: *faux amis*) are translation problems where words in two different languages appear to be alike, but have different meanings. We use the term in reference to the growing number of animated works that look like anime, but aren't.

Our definition of anime is culturally inspired. We count a work as anime if it can reasonably be described as animation from Japan, with a high number of Japanese creatives working in the upper echelons of production: director, writer, designers, key animators, and music. That this is even an issue is not recognized among the general Japanese public, where *anime* refers to all animation. It is only within the industry itself that creators distinguish between animation from Japan and animation that is not. Some unscrupulous distributors choose to ignore the distinction, hoping instead that fans are stupid enough to buy literally anything if it has the word anime daubed on it.

Outside Japan, the ethnic origin of anime creators has been an issue of some importance. In the first waves of anime abroad between the 1950s and 1970s, anime's Japanese origins were often deliberately occluded—Japanese credit listings were replaced with the names of "writers" and "directors" who had merely adapted preexisting Japanese material. Tokyo landmarks regularly appeared in GIGANTOR, but were renamed—a Japanese origin in the early days of TV often seems like something to be ashamed of, with evidence that should be removed as carefully and completely as possible. It is for this reason that one still meets French people who do not realize that ULYSSES 31 was made in Japan and Koreans who think that DORAEMON is a Seoul native.

However, the rise of anime on video in the 1980s brought a radical change to this perception. In the science fiction of William Gibson and Bruce Sterling, Japanesquerie became the new cool, and in the wake of the subsequent anime video boom, a Japanese origin became an actual selling point. It is at this juncture that false friends become an issue—the authors recall a dozen different meetings over the last decade with companies keen to get involved in "anime," which inevitably lead to the big question: "Does

it *have* to be Japanese?" The rationale being, among the world's shallower producers, that if they can persuade a local artist to draw them a picture of a girl with big eyes who carries a gun, this will make something immediately "anime," and save them the messy business of having to deal with the Japanese.

Japanese companies, of course, have long farmed out their work to foreign companies in Korea, China, Thailand, and the Philippines—countries that not only have animation industries of their own, but also hope to profit from the sudden popularity of Asian animation abroad. So it is that several Korean cartoons have been released in the West by anime labels hoping that their ethnic origin would pass the average consumer by. Lee Hyun-se's *Armageddon* (*Amagaedun Uzu*, 1996) seemed deliberately designed to fool rights buyers at film festivals—presenting what was for the time an impressive CG opening, that fast collapsed into a dull sci-fi battle. Similarly, Sang Il-sim's *Red Hawk: Weapon of Death* (1995) was a crass and derivative FIST OF THE NORTH STAR pastiche. Other False Friends are built on connections and resources established by people in anime, such as Andy Orjuela's *Lady Death* (2004), written by Carl Macek, or Andy Chan and Tsui Hark's *A Chinese Ghost Story: The Animation* (*Xiao Qian*, 1997), which featured a lead animator poached from the bona fide anime business: Tetsuya Endo, director of MOJACKO.

It is, of course, only natural that an art form as commercially successful as anime should inspire others. When hired to direct *Grandma and Her Ghosts* (*Mofa Ama*, 1998), Taiwanese director Wang Shaudi went shopping for inspiration, and did so at a time when several Studio Ghibli works had been released into the Taiwanese market, resulting not only in story elements but also a mood and an elegiac quality seemingly lifted from MY NEIGHBOR TOTORO and KIKI'S DELIVERY SERVICE. A similar aspiration toward a Studio Ghibli style can be discerned in Lee

Syong-kang's Korean movie, *My Beautiful Marie* (*Mari Iyagi*, 2002), particularly in its depiction of a modern world ignorant of nearby numinous nature.

Mainland China has its own strong animation tradition, particularly stemming from the Shanghai Animation Studio, the foundation of which can be at least partly accredited to the Japanese expat Tadahito Mochinaga. Recent years have seen Chinese attempts to learn from the commercial success not only of anime, but also of Disney cartoons, as demonstrated by such experiments as Chang Guang-xi's *Lotus Lantern* (*Baolian deng*, 1999). The acquisition of Hong Kong in 1997 also brought the vast labor market of the Mainland into more direct contact with the advanced technology of the former colony, leading to such hybrids as Toe Yuen's *My Life as McDull* (*McDull Gushi*, 2001), an avowedly Cantonese movie that still managed to recall HELLO KITTY and MY NEIGHBORS THE YAMADAS. Meanwhile, Korean animation continues to aspire toward anime's status abroad, with movies such as Kim Moon-saeng's extended CGI pastiche of AKIRA, *Sky Blue* (aka *Wonderful Days*, 2003).

False Friendship can also extend both ways. Serials such as *The Powerpuff Girls* (1998), *Hi Hi Puffy AmiYumi* (2004), and *Kappa Mikey* (2006) were conceived in imitation of anime, but then exported *back* to Japan. Nowhere is this more apparent than in THE ANIMATRIX, in which the work of genuine anime creators rubs shoulders with high quality works in an anime style, by creators such as Peter Chung, whose earlier *Aeon Flux* (1995) was itself a homage to Japanese animation.

Ultimately, a good film is a good film, regardless of where it came from. We hope that English-language distributors will accord non-Japanese creators the respect they are due, and hype them for what they are, and not for what they aren't—a "Korean anime" is an oxymoron. The debate over False Friends is likely to continue, as skill levels rise in non-

Japanese countries, and increasingly larger amounts of animation work on supposedly "Japanese" films is farmed out abroad: even acknowledged "Japanese" classics like GHOST IN THE SHELL feature extensive contributions from non-Japanese animators.

FAMILY OF DEBAUCHERY *

2002. JPN: *Haitoku no Shojo*. AKA: *Corruption of a Girl*. Video. DIR: Mikan Furukawa. SCR: N/C. DES: N/C. ANI: N/C. MUS: N/C. PRD: Five Ways. 29 mins. x 2 eps.

Hiroko is going to work for a rich family as tutor to a young girl named Yuki—compare to BLUE EXPERIENCE. When Hiroko reaches their beautiful mansion, Yuki's elder sister Shizuka drugs her tea, causing her to lose consciousness. When she wakes, she is naked and tied to a bed, and Yuki and Shizuka are trying out various sex toys on her. Just as Hiroko starts to enjoy this, it's revealed that Yuki is not, in fact, a girl, but a very pretty young boy. Only the second of the two episodes was released, as the first featured a sequence in which a bound mother was raped in a steel cage by a dog, which was considered too risky even for the jaded audience of Japanese animated erotica. ⓁⓃⓋ

FANCY LALA

1998. JPN: *Maho no Stage Fancy Lala*. AKA: *Magical Stage Fancy Lala*. TV series. DIR: Masahiro Omori, Takeshi Yamazaki, Miko Shima. SCR: Tomomi Mochizuki. DES: Akemi Takada. ANI: Masako Onishi, Kazuhiro Sasaki. MUS: Michiru Oshima. PRD: Studio Pierrot, TV Tokyo. 25 mins. x 26 eps.

Miho is an eight-year-old girl with a secret: using her two magical pets, Pig and Mog, and her magical sketchpad, she can turn into the beautiful teenage fashion model known as Fancy Lala. As might be expected in a rehash of CREAMY MAMI, she attracts the attention of 19-year-old local wiseguy Hiroya, who falls in love with her adult version, not realizing she is only a child underneath.

FANTASTIC CHILDREN *

2005. TV series. DIR: Takashi Nakamura. SCR: Hideki Mitsui, Takashi Nakamura. DES: Takashi Nakamura. ANI: Miyuki Nakamura, Koichi Maruyama, Shingo Ishikawa et al. MUS: Koji Ueno. PRD: Nippon Animation. 25 mins. x 26 eps.

For 500 years, there have been legends all over Europe about sightings of mysterious white-haired children, often alleged to have a maturity beyond their years as well as magical powers. They are the "children of Vefoele," for whom a pallid look like mutants from AKIRA is the price of immortality, since they are reborn time and again until one, a boy named Palza, grows tired of the cosmic circle of life and decides he just wants one rebirth as a human. Meanwhile, on Papan Island, orphans Chito and Helga are on a quest to find a mysterious crystal that they need in order to regain their fading memories. Helga has drawn a place she doesn't know; the pair leave their orphanage to look for it, but they are hunted and Helga is captured. They are rescued by another boy called Thoma, who takes the pair to a secret island only he knows of. Helga is beginning to fall for Thoma, but she is confused by feelings for a fantasy man. She doesn't know she is really the incarnation of Princess Tina of planet Girishia, 200 million light years from Earth. The fantasy man is her lover from an earlier life. When Tarlant, one of the Vefoele, comes to the island, she begins to remember. A story created by writer/director Nakamura in search of "an old-fashioned adventure," with more than a few nods to the reincarnation romance of SAILOR MOON, and publicity materials that push its parent studio's earlier involvement with FUTURE BOY CONAN.

FANTASY AND FAIRY TALES

As early cartoons were regarded solely as a children's medium, fairy tales have formed a natural part of their repertoire—often with a discernable tension between local stories that have domestic sales potential and "international"

©2006 STEVE KYTE

Fantasy and Fairy Tales

ones that offer better profit, but also higher risks. All information about animation development before the 1923 Great Kanto Earthquake is necessarily vague, but the best contender for the "first" folktale anime is Seitaro Kitayama's early version of **MONKEY AND THE CRAB** (1917). The following year saw anime's first use of ancient folklore for commercial ends, with the *Tortoise and the Hare* (one of **AESOP'S FABLES**) adapted into a one-reel children's entertainment by Ikuo Oishi, and sponsored by Morinaga Chocolate.

Anime has often fought its childish reputation with choices of worthy adaptations, such as the Chinese **JOURNEY TO THE WEST**, first appearing as Noburo Ofuji's *Songoku Monogatari* (1926), and the **ARABIAN NIGHTS**, from which the tale of *Ali Baba and the 40 Thieves* (*Yonjunin no Tozoku*, 1928) became a 17-minute epic in the hands of Takeo Ueno. The film's producer, one Toshio Suzuki, is no relation to the man of the same name who produced so many Ghibli films half a century later.

During the rise of Japanese nationalism in the pre-war years, there was an increased concentration on **JAPANESE FOLK TALES**, along with tales of piracy

and anthropomorphic animals. In the midst of post-war deprivation, a notable early fantasy is Masao Kumagawa's *Magic Pen* (*Maho no Pen*, 1946), in which Su-chan, an impoverished boy in the ruins of Tokyo, dreams that the blue-eyed doll he finds (it is a black-and-white film, but the synopsis is keen to stress that the doll has blue eyes) comes to life and draws him an apple with a magic pen. The pen's magic causes the apple to become real, prompting the pair to take the pen and draw a new building amid the post-war desolation, in a touching allegory of hope and reconstruction.

As Japan rebuilt, anime suffered an infestation of cute animals, including Kenzo Masaoka's *Tora the Stray Cat* (*Suteneko Tora-chan*, 1947) and its sequel *Tora's Bride* (*Tora-chan to Hanayome*, 1948), the Kindai Company's *Fox Circus* (*Kitsune no Circus*, 1948) and Hideo Furusawa's *Sports Tanuki* (*Sports Kotanuki*, 1949). Anime's first major post-war works drew on Asian inspirations, with *Princess of Baghdad* (*Baghdad-hime*, 1948), followed by **PANDA AND THE MAGIC SERPENT** (1958). With a return to relative prosperity, the anime movie world continued to avoid non-Asian

fairy tales, presumably preferring to supply local demand rather than compete with more lavish Disney imports. This period saw another **JOURNEY TO THE WEST** (1960), alongside **THE LITTLEST WARRIOR** (1961), **WOOF WOOF 47 RONIN** (1963), and **LITTLE PRINCE AND THE EIGHT-HEADED DRAGON** (1963).

It was only with the coming of TV, and the realization that foreign subjects could lead to foreign sales, that anime turned once more to European sources, including movies of the **TALES OF HANS CHRISTIAN ANDERSEN** (1968) and **PUSS IN BOOTS** (1969). The sheer amount of material generated for television ensured that fairy tale anime enjoyed much greater variety. "Mundane" fiction was given a more fantastic look with anthropomorphic animals, as in **TREASURE ISLAND** (1965), while Japanese fairy tales, now dismissed as old hat, were given a new lease on life through their use as inspirations in shows such as **LITTLE GOBLIN** (1968) and **SPOOKY KITARO** (1968). But fantasy remained a difficult genre to spot in the 1970s, as anime fought against the eternal onslaught of sci-fi toy tie-ins. Only the "magical girl shows," such as **LITTLE WITCH SALLY** (1966) and **MARVELOUS MELMO** (1971), might reasonably be regarded as "fantasy," although fantastic elements formed part of almost all anime by this point.

Despite being often regarded as a fairy tale franchise, surprisingly few of the stories in the **WORLD MASTERPIECE THEATER** (1975) actually are. Genuine fairy tales of Japanese origin made it to the screen in **HEART OF THE RED BIRD** (1979). But in a period in which Disney animation was widely regarded to be in a creative slump, anime began to make bold forays back into Western material, with **GRIMM'S FAIRY TALES** (1987).

By the time Disney had reclaimed the fairy tale high ground with *Beauty and the Beast* (1991), Japanese animators were confident enough to compete with full-length serials of **SNOW WHITE** (1994) and **CINDERELLA** (1996). Meanwhile, new fantasy anime developed a narrative style inspired not by myths or novels, but by the setups of role-playing games, as seen in RECORD OF LODOSS WAR (1990) and SLAYERS (1995).

Hayao Miyazaki's MY NEIGHBOR TOTORO (1988) and KIKI'S DELIVERY SERVICE (1989) reestablished a modernized fairy tale style in cinema theaters, while elsewhere the subtexts of fantasy were exploited for different ends in UROTSUKIDOJI (1987) and its imitators. In the last 15 years movie theaters have continued to offer genuine family entertainment, with the most noteworthy works of recent times being Studio Ghibli's PRINCESS MONONOKE (1997) and SPIRITED AWAY (2001), both revisiting and refashioning old stories with a personal touch that is pure Miyazaki. Fantasy on television often includes liminal dramas that transport youthful protagonists to new worlds, such as ESCAFLOWNE (1996) or HAIBANE RENMEI (2002). Shows such as PETITE PRINCESS YUCIE (2002) combine the "magical girl" setups of recent times with the sumptuousness of old-school fairy tales, while LOVELESS (2005) cleverly uses anthropomorphic characteristics, or rather their disappearance, as an allegory of the loss of childhood innocence. Meanwhile, fantasy on video comprises rereleases of both the TV and movie media discussed above, but also a predictable concentration on private titillation. The sexual subtexts of fairy tales, with their allegories of taboos and fears, are often presented as physical plot elements in straight-to-video anime—it is only a short step from dungeons-and-dragons to tits-and-tentacles.

FAR EAST OF EDEN

1990. JPN: *Tengai Makyo*. AKA: *Evil World beyond Heaven*. Video. DIR: Oji Hiroi, Toshio Takeuchi. SCR: Toshio Takeuchi. DES: Kotaro Tsujino. ANI: Yasuo Otsuka. MUS: Kohei Tanaka. PRD: TMS. 50 mins. x 2 eps.
In the alternate world of Xipangu, hero Jiraiya defeats local pirates and heads off in search of the fabled

treasure of the death god, Hiruko, but Jiraiya is opposed by an equally evil sorcerer. Joining forces with the beautiful princess, Yuki (who has the power to seal Hiruko away), Jiraiya must confront a gang of renegades, led by a female impersonator, that intends to conquer the entire kingdom. Based on a game for the PC Engine console, designed by Red Company, who would eventually make SAKURA WARS with director Hiroi. Though the vampiric Hiruko is defeated at the climax, in the original, the end-of-game boss was Masakado—see DOOMED MEGALOPOLIS. Note the presence of CASTLE OF CAGLIOSTRO's Yasuo Otsuka as animation director and a crew roster that brought a great look to an otherwise forgettable cash-in.

FATAL FURY *

1992. JPN: *Battle Fighters: Garo Densetsu*. AKA: *Battle Fighters: Legend of the Hungry Wolf; Mark of the Wolf*. Movie, TV special. DIR: Kazuhiro Furuhashi, Masami Obari, Hiroshi Fukutomi. SCR: Takashi Yamada. DES: Masami Obari. ANI: Masami Obari. MUS: Toshihiko Sato, Toshiro Masuda. PRD: Asahi International, Pony Canyon, Fuji TV, NAS. 45 mins. (TVm) 73 mins. (TVm), 90 mins. (m).
As with its contemporary STREET FIGHTER II, this adaptation of a beat-'em-up console game struggles and ultimately fails to make the jump to non-interactive media, though not without some incidental pleasures on the way. Viz's dub is perfectly serviceable, albeit with some unplaceably alien accents from the supporting cast that only add to the fun as one tries to guess whether someone is supposed to come from Oirland or Scutland. With overmuscled men meeting, greeting, indulging in strange acts, and then parting, it has a strangely homoerotic charge, peppered with sanctimonious moral messages about the nobility of fighting for what is right but without questioning whether anyone should be fighting at all.

FF: Legend of the Hungry Wolf (1992) sets up the original back story to the

game, in which Terry and Andy Bogard witness their father's murder and become bare-knuckle fighters, in a tournament plot not unlike TEKKEN, eventually avenging him by defeating his murderer Geese Howard. Mere months later in *FF: The New Battle* (1993), Howard's half-brother, Wolfgang Krauser, returns to challenge Terry. With time out to reunite a street urchin with his mother in a halfhearted subplot, Terry soon hunts Krauser down to a showdown in a German castle, while other characters pop out of the woodwork for a few rounds to please their fans. The franchise reached theaters at its peak with *FF: The Motion Picture* (1994), which dumped at least part of the "you killed my father" plotting in favor of an Indiana Jones rip-off. Laocoön Gaudeamus is searching for the legendary Armor of Mars (compare to Jackie Chan's *Armor of God*, 1987), lost by his ancestors during the Crusades. His estranged sister, Sulia, hires Terry to stop him before he can use the armor's magical powers, in a plot that presages SPRIGGAN, though it was too late to save the tired and formulaic *FF* franchise. ●

FEATHER STARES AT THE DARK, A *

2003. JPN: *Yami wo Mitsumeru Hane*. Movie DIR: Naoyuki Tsuji. SCR: N/C. DES: Naoyuki Tsuji. ANI: Naoyuki Tsuji. MUS: N/C. PRD: N/C. 17 mins.
Screened in Cannes in 2004 and at several North American festivals, this independent short film is made by Tsuji's "charcoal anime process"—a single charcoal drawing is photographed, partly erased, and reworked for the next frame. It took the director eight years to make 17 minutes of black and white film by erasing and reworking his first image over 13,500 times. He started making his own films in 1992, at age 20. Other works include 1994's *For The Lost Legend* (9 mins) 1995's *Law of Dream* (6 mins), and 2005's 13-minute *Trilogy About Clouds* (*Mittsu no Kumo*), screened in London and out on DVD with four of his other short films.

FENCER OF MINERVA *

1995. JPN: *Minerva no Kenshi*. AKA: *Knight of Minerva*. Video. DIR: Takahiro Okao, Tadayoshi Kusaka. SCR: Sukehiro Tomita, Yuji Kishino. DES: Takashi Wada. ANI: Tadashi Hirota, Nobuaki Shirai. MUS: Kanae Wada. PRD: All Products, Beam Entertainment. 45 mins. x 5 eps.

The beautiful, willful Princess Diana is betrothed to a handsome prince but is captured by nomads, who refuse to believe her royal protestations because out of her clothes she looks just like any other wench. After a brief initiation in the amatory arts, she is rescued from a gang bang by a masked man, her childhood sweetheart Prince Sho, who is returning to claim his rightful kingdom from the man who usurped it, Princess Diana's evil father.

Believe it or not, from the tacky designs that replace original ideas with two-legged horses and flying piranhas (sorry, water lizards) to USMC's faithfully camp translation of some of the world's worst dialogue, *Fencer of Minerva* genuinely is so bad that it's good. But what do you expect when the CREAM LEMON team try to imitate B-movie sword-and-sandal fantasy, complete with lost kingdoms, lovably chauvinist heroes, and breathless slave-girls in diaphanous veils? A guilty pleasure, as if John Norman had written an episode of RECORD OF LODOSS WAR. Compare to the similarly risible EROTIC TORTURE CHAMBER. **NV**

F-FORCE *

2001. JPN: *Asgaldh: Waikyoku no Testament*. AKA: *Asgard: The Torture Testament*. Video. DIR: Yusaku Aoi. SCR: Hajime Yamaguchi. DES: Naoki Yamauchi. ANI: Motokazu Murakami, Naoki Yamauchi. MUS: Hiroaki Sano. PRD: Discovery. 30 mins. x 3 eps.

Wandering knight Ash saves a young damsel from violation at the hands/tentacles of some evil monsters. Accompanying her back to her home village of Tylling, he discovers that she is the chief's daughter, and the last fair maiden left after successive attacks and kidnappings by the creatures of Demon Mountain—who not only steal local girls, but also local girls' underwear. Hearing that similar creatures have already caused a distant continent to sink beneath the waves (presumably not through the weight of panties alone), Ash calls in favors from fellow adventurers to defend the village. When they arrive, they unsurprisingly turn out to be a bunch of girls, differentiated and attired with all the stereotypical predictability of a computer game, including one in a school uniform, another dolled up as a Chinese waitress, and a potty-mouthed cowgirl with an inappropriate New Jersey accent in the English dub. Any resemblance to *Seven Samurai* soon passes. Based on the computer game *Asgaldh*, by Zone, and one of the DISCOVERY SERIES. **LNV**

FIFTH ICE AGE

1967. JPN: *Subarashii Sekai Ryoko: Alaska no Tabi: Daigo Hyogaki*. AKA: *Wonderful World Travel: Alaskan Journey: Fifth Ice Age*. TV special. DIR: Masahiro Mori. SCR: Mamoru Sasaki. DES: Hiroshi Manabe. ANI: N/C. MUS: Kiyoshi Iwami. PRD: Mushi Pro. 30 mins. x 2 eps.

In the near future, Earth is engulfed in a new ice age as snow falls ceaselessly in summer and glaciers advance with uncharacteristic speed. In this SF spin-off of the live-action *Wonderful World Travel* series, humanity must decide whether to use science to fight the ice or to adapt to it. The same team also peers into the future in COMPUTOPIA.

FIGHT! OSPA

1965. JPN: *Tatakae! Ospa*. TV series. DIR: Masami Aragura, Nobuhiro Okaseko, Yoshiyuki Tomino. SCR: Koichi Yamano, Teru Nagashima. DES: N/C. ANI: Mami Murano, Nobuhiro Okaseko. MUS: Isao Tomita. PRD: NTV. 25 mins. x 52 eps.

The inhabitants of the sunken Pacific continent of Mu (see SUPER ATRAGON) yearn to leave their undersea dome and return to the surface world. After many centuries beneath the waves, they are threatened with destruction by the power-hungry Dorome. The good people of Mu send Ospa, their finest man, to find help on the surface world, where he assembles an international team to fight for justice. Based on an idea by TAKE THE X TRAIN–author Koichi Yamano, this series is a combination of the *Dolphin Prince* (see MARINE BOY) and PRINCE PLANET.

FIGHT! PUTER

1968. JPN: *Fight Da!! Pyu-ta*. TV series. DIR: Hiroe Mitsunobu, Jun Nagasawa, Kunitoshi Shiraishi. SCR: Yoshitake Suzuki, Kenichi Ogawa, Kuniaki Hatanaka. DES: Tsunezo Murotani. ANI: Tameo Ogawa. MUS: Tetsuaki Hagiwara. PRD: MBS. 25 mins. x 26 eps.

Pyuta Imano helps his grandfather, Professor Tsulury, with his experiments. The evil Walther VII and his sidekick, Glocky, try to seize control of the world. While trying to stop them, an accident gives Pyuta a supercomputer for a brain. Airing the day after the first episode of CYBORG 009, this younger version was based on a manga in *Shonen Sunday* by Tsunezo Murotani, whose *Piccory Bee* (the tales of a "Thunder Child" who falls from the sky) had also been animated in 1967.

FIGHT: SPIRIT OF THE SWORD *

1993. JPN: *Fight!!* Video. DIR: Akira Koson. SCR: Akira Koson. DES: Kenichi Onuki. ANI: Masanori Nishii. MUS: Taikai Hayakawa. PRD: Pony Canyon. 45 mins.

High school student Yonosuke Hikura is the latest in his family to protect the harmony between Heaven and Earth. With the help of the magical sword Chitentai, and Tsukinojo Inbe, a Protector sent to him by the High Priests of Earth, he courageously battles the demons, sending them back to the Earth World from which they have escaped. Another tale in the tradition of DEVIL HUNTER YOHKO, but it's played disappointingly straight.

FIGHTER

1990. JPN: *Kentoshi*. Video. DIR:

Yoichiro Shimatani. scr: Ranko Ono. des: Kuniaki Tsuji. ani: Kuniaki Tsuji. mus: Takahiko Kanemaru. prd: Apple, Miyuki Pro. 45 mins. x 3 eps.

Kenji is a heavyweight boxer who wants to learn from the legendary Tokyo trainer Eddie Williams and win the American championships. In New York, he takes on the heavyweight Joe Roman, before fighting another American, George MacGregor, for the title at Madison Square Garden. In this predictable adaptation of Takashi Tsukasa's series from *Manga Club,* it is needless to say that, in the tradition of innumerable sports anime from Tomorrow's Joe to Aim for the Ace, by the time of the big fight, coach Eddie is on his deathbed. **V**

FIGHTING FOODONS *

2001. jpn: *Kakuto Ryori Densetsu Bistro Recipe.* aka: *Legend of Grappling Cook Bistro Recipe; Bistro Recipe.* TV series. dir: Tetsuo Yasumi. scr: Taku Kadoya. des: Naoko Shimada. ani: Group TAC. mus: Daisuke Asakura. prd: NHK, Kodansha, Group Tac, Red Entertainment. 25 mins. x 26 eps.

Aspiring Chinese chef Chase (Zen)'s master chef father Jack (Tsukuji) is kidnapped by evil chef King Gorge (Don Cook) and his minions, the Gluttons (Four Big Gourmets). Chase, sister Karin, and their associates use the "strength" in food to fight magical combats by producing powerful creatures known as Foodons from the recipes they create. In a Pokémon scenario, aspiring chefs cook a meal, stick it on a magical Recipe Card, and providing the cook has enough "heart" to power the transformation, his creation turns into a monster and goes into battle. A series of food fights follow, which are not as much fun as you might think. From the manga by Naoto Tsushima which first appeared, appropriately enough, in *Comic BonBon.* Compare to China Number One.

FIGHTING SPIRIT

2000. jpn: *Hajime no Ippo, Hajime no Ippo: The Fighting!.* aka: *First for Ippo.*

TV series. dir: Satoshi Nishimura, Nanako Shimazaki. scr: Tatsuhiko Urahata, Shoji Sugiwara, Hiroshi Mori. des: Koji Sugiura. ani: Noriyuki Fukuda. mus: Tsuneo Imahori. prd: Madhouse, TV Tokyo. 25 mins. x 76 eps. (TV), 92 mins. (special), 60 mins. (v).

High school student Ippo Marunouchi is alienated from his classmates due to his need to help his widowed mother with the family business after school, and is furthermore the target of the school bullies. When a passing boxer, Mamoru Takamura, saves him from a beating, Ippo is inspired to take up boxing, begins a tough training regime, and eventually convinces the dubious Takamura to help him join Takamura's gym. From there Ippo's nascent talent begins to shine through, as he starts up the ranks of professional boxing, along the way earning the respect of not only his gym-mates but also his opponents—by his humility, dedication to the sport, and drive to succeed—and inspiring them to be both better boxers and better men. Based on the ongoing 1989 manga by Joji Morikawa, this is a lighter-hearted take on the sports drama genre that stretches right back to Tomorrow's Joe. **V**

FIGURE 17: TSUBASA AND HIKARU

2001. TV series. dir: Naohito Takahashi. scr: Yasuhiro Imagawa, Masashi Komemura. des: Yuriko Senba. ani: Yuriko Senba. mus: Toshihiko Takamisawa. prd: OLM, Anime Theater X. 60 mins. x 12 eps.

Interstellar traveler "DD" is transporting the Magua energy source when he crash-lands on Earth. He enlists the help of Hokkaido ten-year-old Tsubasa in getting it back, giving her a mysterious capsule containing the doll-like superheroine Figure 17. A predictable rerun of the transforming superhero of Ultraman and Birdy the Mighty, pretentiously billed in Japan as "smashing the broadcast paradigm" just because the episodes were twice as long as usual.

FINAL APPROACH

2005. TV series. dir: Takashi Yama-

moto. scr: Katsumi Hasegawa. des: Aoi Nishimata, Noriko Shimazawa. ani: N/C. mus: N/C. prd: Trinet Entertainment, ZEXCS. 13 mins. x 13 eps.

Japan's falling birthrate forces the government to consider drastic steps, institutionalizing dating services to ensure that all healthy young men get the fertile woman they so richly deserve. Consequently, ordinary teen Ryo Mizuhara, who lives with his younger sister Akane and works in cousin Harumi's café, is surprised one day when the strangely pushy Shizuka barges into his apartment, complete with government bodyguard, and claims to be his fiancée. She is part of the pilot scheme to test the new policy, and Ryo is the lucky recipient. Before you can say Rizelmine, she has moved in with him and transfers to his school, although Ryo is suddenly also very popular among his school friends, and a harem of Tenchi Muyo! proportions soon ensues. Based on the so-called "original" creation from Princess Soft, and screened on TV Kanagawa as part of "Princess Hour," along with Double Wish, *FA* is hobbled by its origins: it is as leadenly predictable as a computer game, while any erotic potential is killed off by the need to keep it tame for television. Our anime crystal ball predicts that before long there will be an anime porn show about a fascist breeding program with none of *Final Approach*'s attempt to play for laughs. The series' title in Japan used the Greek letter "phi" for its opening syllable, just to make things difficult for encyclopedists unsure where to file it.

FINAL FANTASY *

1993. aka: *Legend of the Crystals: Based on Final Fantasy.* Video. dir: Rintaro, Naoto Kanda. scr: Satoru Akahori, Mayori Sekijima. des: Yoshinori Kanemori, Kunihiko Sakurai. ani: Naoto Kanda, et al. mus: Masahiko Sato. prd: Madhouse. 30 mins. x 4 eps., 106 mins. (m1), 25 mins. x 25 eps. (*Unlimited*), 25 mins. (*Last Order*), 101 mins. (*Advent Children*).

Two hundred years after the elimi-

Final Fantasy

nation of the evil Exdeath, reckless swordsman Prettz and the summoner Linaly are the youngsters who must save their world from Ra Devil, a bio-mechanical being from the dark moon. Set several centuries after the end of the game, this series is a distant spin-off from *Final Fantasy V*, whose character Batts is supposedly Linaly's ancestor.

The plot is similar to a computer game—after a few random encounters with wandering monsters, the leads must unite two warring parties to create a suitably mismatched party of fearless heroes. Pirate queen Rouge, the whip-wielding mistress of an airship crewed by leather-clad fat girls, falls in love with her sworn enemy, Valcus, leader of the Iron Wing squadron. After some mild tortures (Prettz is tickled and Linaly has to drink prune juice), the former enemies unite to fight Ra Devil, destroying both him and his Bond-villain hideout.

FF's hackneyed quest to save four elemental crystals is upstaged by its backgrounds. As in the games, a good image wins out over the practicalities of physics or geography. With a large number of Chinese and Korean staffers, *FF* lifts design ideas from all over

the Orient, with the tall, thin mountains of Guilin forming a backdrop for *klong* canals from Thailand, and old-world Chinese houses from Canton providing hangars for pseudo-Miyazaki giant airplanes.

As later *FF* games achieved fame abroad, this anime was dusted off and released in English with undue prominence given to the words *Final* and *Fantasy* and rather less to its origins as a spin-off from an untranslated prequel.

Hironobu Sakaguchi's fully computer animated *Final Fantasy: The Spirits Within* (2001) features a quest to obtain eight organic specimens, whose "spirit signatures" will cancel out the energies of alien ghosts. Made in Hawaii, it boasts an all-star cast and the anime version's voice director, Jack Fletcher.

Presumably intended as an attempt to make a truly international *FF* movie, *The Spirits Within* boasted so many foreign staff members that it does not strictly qualify as "anime" within our own criteria. It was also a box office flop, although Hollywood accountancy excels at making anything look like a box office flop—the fact remains that the code and development used on *Spirits Within* was paid for out of the

movie budget, and could be reinvested in the next game.

Mahiro Maeda's TV Tokyo series *FF: Unlimited* (2001) was a return to old-fashioned anime stylings, brashly announced as a 52-episode series, but cut back to a cheaper 25, supposedly after low ratings, but largely because Square had lost its taste for investment after the failure of *Spirits Within* was plain on the balance sheets. It featured two children Ai and Yu, whose search for a lost parent draws them into an "Inner World" where they become the latest champions to fight against the onset of chaos, utilizing many items and references to earlier games in the *FF* series.

As with **STREET FIGHTER II**, numerals on the titles of films in the franchise do not refer to chapter numbers in a story, but to the incarnation of the game from which the anime is adapted. Hence Tetsuya Nomura's *FF VII: Advent Children* (2004) is a movie whose title refers to the *FF VII* game. Set two years after the events of the game, the CG *Advent Children* features Cloud Strife and Tifa, who have set up a delivery service after their heroic activities in the game, drawn into a new conflict to prevent their enemy Sephiroth from returning, aspiring to a messianic climax that has elements of **NAUSICAÄ OF THE VALLEY OF WIND**, at least in terms of its inspiration.

A further release, Morio Asaka and Tetsuya Nomura's video *FF VII: Last Order* (2005), serves as a prequel to the game, revisiting several incidents only remembered in flashbacks in the original, but also ties in to later game spin-offs for the PSP and mobile phones.

FIRE EMBLEM *
1995. JPN: *Fire Emblem: Aritia no Oji.* AKA: *Fire Emblem: Prince of Aritia.* Video. DIR: Shin Misawa. SCR: Yosuke Kuroda. DES: Yuji Moriyama. ANI: Yuji Moriyama. MUS: N/C. PRD: KSS, Studio Fantasia. 30 mins. x 2 eps.
Pacifist prince Mars reluctantly tools up when his homeland, Aritia, is conquered by the evil Druans. On

the run with his faithful knights and a reformed mercenary in the neighboring kingdom of Taris, he enlists the aid of the king's only daughter, the Pegasus-riding Princess Cedar. Originating in a "Fantasy Simulation Game" for the Nintendo Famicom (NES) console, this is a predictable spin-off—just enough episodes to drag back hard-core game fans then rerelease as a one-shot for rental and the export market, which cannot be expected to be as forgiving.

FIRE FIGHTER DAIGO

2000. JPN: *Megumi no Daigo*. Video. DIR: Akira Nishizawa. SCR: Akihiko Inari. DES: Hideyuki Motohashi. ANI: Hideyuki Motohashi. MUS: Shiro Hamaguchi. PRD: Sunrise. 45 mins.

Maverick fireman Daigo Asahina risks disciplinary action by bodily throwing civilians from a high window, but he's exonerated when the building blows up seconds later. Running a gauntlet of girlfriend trouble, he is caught in a fire at a local concert hall and is forced to leave people behind. Outside, he steals a fire engine and rams through a wall, carrying the victims out to public acclaim.

Despite a five-minute closing credit sequence with only three minutes of credits and under-animated moments pretending to be dramatic slow-mo, *FFD* overcomes its low budget thanks to a stirring orchestral score and clever design. Fire and water surround Daigo, even in humdrum scenes of everyday life, with the camera zooming in on a hose at a car wash or a scarlet sunset that looks as if the sky itself is aflame. The fire-fighting scenes themselves are similarly well observed, with incongruous pillars of water falling down through an inferno, and a no-win scenario that finds Daigo knee-deep in water inside a burning building, dodging falling debris and sparking electric cables. Based on the 1995 *Shonen Sunday* manga by Masahito Soda that was itself doubtlessly inspired by Naoto Takenaka's 1994 live-action fire-fighting film *119*, this video traces a the-matic line back to the 1991 Hollywood movie *Backdraft*.

FIRE TRIPPER *

1985. JPN: *Rumic World: Fire Tripper*. Video. DIR: Motosuke Takahashi. SCR: Tomoko Konparu. DES: Katsumi Aoshima. ANI: Junko Yamamoto, Mami Endo. MUS: Keiichi Oku. PRD: Production Ai, OB. 47 mins.

Modern Japanese girl Suzuko and a neighbor's child are thrown back in time by a gas explosion. Meeting the handsome Shukumaru, Suzuko searches for the lost neighbor boy, not realizing that Shukumaru is the adult version of the 20th-century child who accompanied her, and that she herself is an exile from the 15th century. This adaptation of one of Rumiko Takahashi's *Rumic World* manga shorts (which also include MERMAID'S FOREST, MARIS THE CHOJO, and LAUGHING TARGET) cleverly exploits the conventions of time-travel stories as well as the shifting age boundaries put to more lascivious effect in CREAM LEMON. Released on a theatrical double bill with THE HUMANOID. Takahashi would return to medieval time travel in her later INU YASHA.

FIRESTORM

2003. AKA: *Gerry Anderson's Firestorm*. TV series. DIR: Kenji Terada. SCR: Kenji Terada. DES: Kenichi Onuki. ANI: Transarts. MUS: Fumitaka Anzai. PRD: Madhouse, TV Tokyo, Itochu Fashion Systems, AT-X. 25 mins. x 26 eps.

In the year 2104, Carlo Morelli's international crime organization Black Orchid is building a network of weapons and bases as strong as any government's. Nations band together to create an answer to the new threat: Storm Force. Sam Scott is the leader of Storm Force 9, a team tasked specifically with "Operation Firestorm," to unmask Black Orchid's motives. Scott is a clean-cut U.S. military hero, leading an international crew. African-American Wesley Grant, sarcastic blond Brit James Brady, green-haired Australian explosives expert Laura Hope, and feisty Japanese pilot ace Nagisa Kisaragi are based with Scott on the mighty submarine base Ocean Storm (a distant cousin of *Captain Scarlet*'s Cloudbase), commanded by the stern but heroic Drew McAllister. The team learns that Black Orchid is more dangerous than anyone ever imagined—they are in league with the Zolion, aliens who use advanced technology to mimic any living being. The fight is not just against crime, but for the survival of humanity, since a 5,000-vessel invasion fleet is just weeks away from Earth. Hence a multi-arc story structure that begins as a simple tale of fighting crime, before escalating into an operation to prevent the distribution of alien technology, and a seven-episode climax as the cast oppose the Zolion fleet.

Firestorm tries to cover too many conventional bases, and its best elements are underplayed—the evil masterminds aren't quite evil enough, the heroes are just too gung-ho and not undercut with irony. British creator Gerry Anderson enjoys immense popularity in Japan; shows such as his *Thunderbirds, Captain Scarlet*, and *UFO* were heavy influences on the generations that made both ULTRAMAN and EVANGELION, and he was an uncredited catalyst for the show that would become MOSPEADA. *Firestorm*, however, is a failure engendered by lack of communication between its coproducers—something of a sore point, considering Anderson's treatment a generation earlier on THUNDERBIRDS 2086. Anderson and his *Space Precinct* collaborator John Needham came up with the storyline, but the series was put together in Tokyo by people who seemed to value Anderson's name on their logo more than his actual contribution. Tellingly, a show originally billed as *Gerry Anderson's Firestorm* appeared after a delay of many months, as just plain *Firestorm*, while production details were removed at Anderson's own request from a contemporary chronicle of his work. Also absent, even during production, were the names of the British designers who had actually worked on the concept—compare to similar shenanigans on **Dracula: Sovereign of the Damned**. Although acknowledged in the U.K., machine designer Steven Begg was nowhere to be seen on the promotional materials published in the Japanese *Newtype*, a fact of which Anderson and his U.K. cohorts may not have been aware. Similar obstruction hid the contribution of Steve Kyte, whose character concepts were specifically commissioned to look as realistic as possible in order to meet the parameters of the original production plans to use 3DCG. In fact, the only CG animation to be found in the final version is on the machines after budgetary issues led other aspects to be more cheaply rendered as conventional 2D animation, although many of Kyte's designs for uniforms, equipment, and logos, as well as the chilling alien mask transformation sequence he storyboarded, are unchanged in the finished series. **Ⓥ**

FIRST KISS STORY

2000. JPN: *First Kiss Monogatari*. Video. DIR: Kan Fukumoto. SCR: Gaku Hoshino. DES: Hiroki Mizugami, Tatsuo Yanagino. ANI: Tatsuo Yanagino. MUS: N/C. PRD: Yaryu, Broccoli. 30 mins. Yoshihiko is in his busy sophomore year at college while love-interest Kana is stuck back in high school. Her life takes a turn for the surreal when a new teacher at her school turns out to be the spitting image of her dead father. Set two years after the end of its PlayStation origins, Gaku Hoshino's screen adaptation of his game was released on Valentine's Day in a futile attempt to drum up business. The presence of **La Blue Girl**'s Fukumoto as director invites the question: Is he trying to disentangle himself from tentacle porn or is the name an "Alan Smithee" credit used by others on titles of questionable value? Although four episodes were planned, only one seems to have seen the light of day.

FIRST LOVES *

1995. JPN: *Kakyusei, Kakyusei: My Petty Class Student, elf ban Kakyusei Anata-dake wo Mitsumete*. AKA: *First Loves, Underclassmates*. Video. DIR: Koichi Yoshida, Kan Fukumoto. SCR: Masaru Yamamoto. DES: Yuji Takahashi. ANI: Yuji Takahashi. MUS: N/C. PRD: Pink Pineapple, KSS. 30 mins. x 4 eps. (*First Loves*), 30 mins. x 4 eps. (*elf*), 25 mins. x 13 eps. (TV1), c.30 mins. x 1 eps. (*Special*), 30 min. (*Music Graffiti*), 25 mins. x 13 eps. (TV2), 30 mins. x 1+ eps. (*Kakyusei 2* v4).
The protagonists in this quasi-sequel (originally titled *Kakyusei: My Pretty Class Student*) to **End of Summer** (unrelated except for themes and atmosphere) are younger teenagers, though of course the U.S. version is at pains to assure us that they're not legally minors. Kakeru follows Wataru's lead, trying to make it with his dream girl, Urara, but getting distracted here and there, through no fault of his own of course, when love blooms at a tennis club and another student reveals that she has a sideline as a nude model. Only the first two episodes were released in America, under the title *First Loves*. These teen titillations were followed in 1997 by a four-part sequel, the special "elf" edition (*elf ban Kakyusei Anata-dake wo Mitsumete*, or *elf-Edition Kakyusei: I Only Have Eyes For You*), named for the **Dragon Knight** creator involved in the original game; this because, unlike *First Loves*, the plot follows the game. Set once again in the high school dreamtime of a final summer vacation, it depicts new-boy Toru's attempts to bed girl-next-door Miho and featured an alternate ending for the final episode. *First Loves* also gained a 13-part TV remake with a spin-off video episode (*Kakyusei Bangaihen; Classmates Special*), and a TV sequel *Kakyusei 2: Girls in My Eyes* (2004, *Hitomi no Naka no Shojotachi*), directed by Yosei Morino. There was also a *Music Graffiti* spin-off featuring music from the series with both recycled footage and live-action performances. The latest addition is the erotic *Kakyusei 2: Kika Shishu* (*Anthology*) video series (2006).
The *Classmates* series is also distantly

related to the *Transfer Student* series (1996, *Tenkosei*), which revisits many of the themes with a story of love between two childhood friends who are reunited when the girl moves back into town—the girl, Aoi, being played by the same voice actress who played Ai in the original. **Ⓝ**

FIST OF THE NORTH STAR *

1984. JPN: *Hokuto no Ken*. AKA: *Ken the Great Bear Fist—Legend of a Karate Warrior*. TV series, movie. DIR: Toyoo Ashida, Hiromichi Matano, Hideo Watanabe, Masahisa Ishida. SCR: Susumu Takahisa. DES: Masami Suda. ANI: Masami Suda. MUS: Katsuhisa Hattori, Nozomu Aoki. PRD: Toei, Fuji TV. 25 mins. x 109 eps., 25 mins. x 43 eps., 110 mins. (m).
Rival gangs fight for supremacy in a postholocaust wasteland. Out of the dust walks Kenshiro, a young martial artist in search of his fiancée, Julia, who has been kidnapped by his brother Shin. In the opening story arc (complete in the U.S., truncated in the U.K.), Ken must hunt down the disparate members of his estranged martial-arts family before he defeats Shin and finds, and then loses, the love of his life.
Thrilling a teen audience with its hyper-violence and repetitive menace-of-the-week, the 1983 *Shonen Jump* manga by Tetsu Hara and Buronson was a timely retread of *Mad Max 2: The Road Warrior*. Continuing long after the initial "Julia" story was resolved, the series became a staple of 1980s Japanese pop culture, with Ken lampooned as the hulking Mari in **Project A-Ko**, and his booming voice actor Akira Kamiya becoming a star in his own right. But as the series wore on, drastic budget cuts forced the animators to improvise, sometimes with mind-boggling results. The crew constantly found creative new ways to dispatch villains, such as smearing wet paint on a cel between two pieces of glass, or shooting in real-time through the churning waters of a half-empty fish-tank. The show similarly exploited surreal perspectives—

everyone seems giant and impossibly muscled seen through the eyes of children Bart and Lynn but appear smaller from Ken's point of view. The show's star waned even in Japan, and though the second series ended sooner than expected, the franchise was kept alive by foreign sales. A movie-length remake of series one encompasses Ken's search for and defeat of Shin, Shin's admission that the more powerful Raoh has already kidnapped Julia to be *his* bride, a battle between Ken and Raoh, and the revelation that Julia has disappeared once more. Though Julia had committed suicide by this point in the original series, the movie edition leaves it open-ended, with Ken wandering into the desert in search of her again, believing her to be still alive. The movie version of series one, dubbed in the U.S. by Streamline, was Manga Entertainment's first U.K. release and became the cornerstone of their martial-arts-fueled "beer-and-curry" marketing plan. Riding the coat-tails of AKIRA, it became one of the U.K.'s best-selling anime videos, though more through its length of tenure in stores than its overt quality.

In 1998, the company tried to capitalize on the anime's "success" by releasing the full 15-year-old TV series. This version featured a good actor as Ken, but it was clumsily cut together with no appreciation of story breaks and mixed so shoddily that Bart ends up playing a silent harmonica. The series was also "augmented" with a drum & bass music track, which, to be fair, couldn't have made it any worse. After predictably disappointing sales, the distributor pulled the TV edit only partway into the schedule, though by this time its "foreign popularity" had inspired a Japanese satellite network to rerun it every day. Like its hero, *Fist of the North Star* simply refuses to die. The series is more likely to be known in the mainstream for its 1995 live-action remake, directed by Tony Randall and starring Gary Daniels. A manga prequel, *Fist of the Blue Sky* (2001), features the adventures of Ken's namesake uncle in 1930s Asia.

Takashi Watanabe's three-part "new" *Fist of the North Star* video series (2003) claimed to be based on a 1996 novel by the original creators, thereby avoiding ownership conflict with the copyright holders of the original TV series and the Hollywood remake. Motorcycles and backgrounds were much more impressive, occasionally evoking the draftsman-like architecture and vehicle representations of Otomo's AKIRA, but the foreground cast were still the same tired 1980s musclemen. **L**·**V**

FIVE CARD *

2003. Video. DIR: Akebi Haruno. SCR: Akebi Haruno. DES: Yukiho. ANI: Shigeru Kino, Hiroshi Sakagami. MUS: N/C. PRD: Five Ways. 29 mins. x 4 eps.
Young English teacher Nariyuki Daina is popular with his students and plans to get four of the hottest—Lisa, Fumiko, Naoki, and Mimiko—into bed. So does school principal, sorry, college dean Onikuma, though his tastes are rather more perverted and include chains, vibrators, and such. Daina also has a pretty assistant, Mayu, a former college buddy of his, who attempts to police his lecherous behavior. The girls have a few tricks of their own, including aphrodisiac-laced lunchboxes for Teacher, although before long they are co-opted into the dean's satanic rituals, for a change. Based on a computer game by Crossnet. **L**·**N**·**V**

FIVE STAR STORIES *

1989. JPN: *Five Star Monogatari*. Video. DIR: Kazuo Yamazaki. SCR: Akinori Endo. DES: Mamoru Nagano, Nobuteru Yuki, Mika Akitaka. ANI: Nobuteru Yuki. MUS: Tomoyuki Asagawa. PRD: Sunrise. 60 mins.
The Joker Cluster consists of five star systems in close proximity, where human pilots (headliners) are bonded with sentient androids (fatimas) to control giant robots (mortar heads). Dr. Chrome Ballanche, the greatest of the genetic engineers, completes his two most perfect creations, the fatimas Lachesis and Clotho. Their sister, Atropos, has vanished. The fatimas go to the castle of the local lord Uber to be "impressed," a ceremony at which they select their future partners from among the ranks of headliners. Most pilots have to make do with "etrimls," low-grade subhuman versions, so the beautiful fatimas are highly prized, not only by the assembled pilots, but also

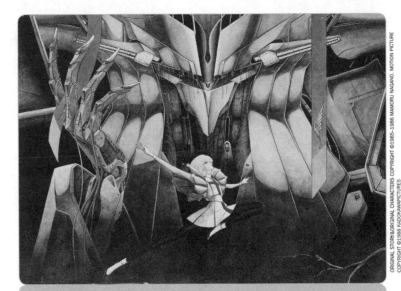
Five Star Stories

by several notables who are attending the ceremony in disguise.

Condensed from just one segment of Mamoru Nagano's sprawling 1986 manga that's still occasionally serialized in *Newtype*, *FSS* duplicates the original's baroque feel, as well as its near impenetrability. With mount-rider relationships that presage BRAIN POWERED and sumptuous science-fantasy conceits, the look of the characters and machinery is as marvelous as one might expect from a fashion-designer-turned-rock-musician such as Nagano. **N**

FIVE WAYS

Erotic anime company whose subsidiaries include Wide Road and Blue Moon. Notable for its generally low budget productions, and for abruptly declaring bankruptcy in mid-2003, causing the release of the (already completed) second and third episodes of *Handmaid Mai* (for which it was producer and distributor; sequel to HANDMAID MAY) to be put on hold until the subsequent litigation could be settled.

FLAG!

1994. JPN: *Sakidama Hassai Saizen Sen Flag*. AKA: *Sakidama Racing Pole Position Flag*. Video. DIR: Tetsu Dezaki. SCR: Machiko Kondo. DES: Mutsumi Inomata. ANI: Hideki Takahashi. MUS: N/C. PRD: Vap, Magic Bus. 45 mins.
Sixteen-year-old Noboru Yamazaki and Akira Maruyama join the Moonlight bike gang at the Sakidama Biker Meet, although they don't actually own any motorcycles. A rival gang, the Asian Tigers, uses its gangster connections to take out a hit on the Moonlight gang's leader. Noboru inherits his leader's motorcycle, and also the attentions of biker chick Hisami. Based on Akio Hotta's manga in *Young King*, this is a latecomer to the anime subgenre established by BOMBER BIKERS OF SHONAN. **V**

FLAME OF RECCA

1997. JPN: *Recca no En*. TV series. DIR: Noriyuki Abe, Kazunori Mizuno. SCR: Hiroshi Hashimoto, Satoru Nishizono.

DES: Mari Kitayama, Atsushi Wakabayashi. ANI: Yoshiyuki Kobe, Minoru Yamazawa. MUS: Yusaku Honma. PRD: Studio Pierrot, Fuji TV. 25 mins. x 42 eps.
Contemporary teenage ninja fan Recca Hanabishi becomes embroiled in the activities of real-life ninja. The beautiful Yanagi is targeted by an evil industrialist who wants to use the girl's power to become immortal, and Recca must team up with his school friends to learn the secrets of the martial arts before it is too late. Adapting Nobuyuki Anzai's 1995 manga from *Shonen Sunday*, this series owes a great debt to POLTERGEIST REPORT, with plenty of fighting, some off-color humor, and acrobatics to rival NINJA SCROLL's. However, despite early promise, a low animation budget takes its toll, as does the series' disappointing decline into endless martial-arts bouts. **N V**

FLASHBACK *

2002. JPN: *Flashback Game*. Video. DIR: Shinsuke Terasawa. SCR: Bankyu Mizoguchi. DES: Shinsuke Terasawa. ANI: Go Yasumoto. MUS: N/C. PRD: Blue Cat, Five Ways. 30 mins. x 3 eps.
Yuri Honjo wins a beauty spa vacation, and arrives with her friends Mizuho and Noriko excitedly expecting a fun-packed experience rather than a vicious psychological trap. All three girls, it transpires, have repressed memories of sexual trauma, which the nefarious staff at the spa is determined to get them to admit. In the spa's isolation pod Mizuho relives her gang rape by schoolmates, while Yuri recalls the sexual abuse she suffered from friends. Then Mizuho goes to the beach and has lesbian sex with Ayame and heads back to the hotel to try it out with Noriko. Meanwhile, Noriko recalls what it was like to come home from school one day to find her mother sexually servicing two strangers. Eventually, the girls are molested in her room by masked figures, and their fate is then determined by a vote from the previously unseen audience. **L N V**

FLCL *

2000. JPN: *Furi Kuri*. Video. DIR: Kazuya Tsurumaki. SCR: Yoji Enokido. DES: Yoshiyuki Sadamoto. ANI: Tadashi Hiramatsu, Hiroyuki Imaishi. MUS: The Pillows. PRD: Gainax, Production IG. 25 mins. x 6 eps.
Left alone in the house with his older brother's 17-year-old girlfriend, Mamimi, Naota Nandaba is concerned that her flirting ways will place him in a difficult situation. The arrival of the scooter-riding, guitar-swinging tomboy Haruko Haruhara swaps one set of problems for another, as Naota is forced to share his life with an alien, a grumpy robot, and the uncontrollable Mamimi. Mixing a narrative inspired by the same studio's HIS AND HER CIRCUMSTANCES with characterization and designs influenced by their earlier EVANGELION, *FLCL* represents a determined effort by Gainax to both supercede its successes of the late 1990s and incorporate elements of the one title that competed with them in fans' polls as the show of the moment. UTENA-writer Enokido brings a surreal tinge to the whole operation. All but episode one were released in Japan with English subtitles on DVD.

FLIGHT OF THE WHITE WOLF

1990. JPN: *Hashire Shiroi Okami*. AKA: *Run White Wolf*. Movie. DIR: Tsuneo Maeda, Masuji Harada. SCR: Wataru Kenmochi. DES: Isao Kumata, Marisuke Eguchi, Satoshi Matsuoka. ANI: Marisuke Eguchi. MUS: Antonín Dvořák. PRD: Tac, Toho. 84 mins.
Lasset has grown up with a wolf called Gray since they were both babies. Lasset's father found the cub and reared it, but, as he grows, the neighbors become understandably concerned. Gray kills a local dog that belongs to the sheriff, and his days seem numbered. Lasset sets out with Gray, determined to get him to a wolf sanctuary where he can live in peace. Unfortunately, it's several hundred miles away, so the pair face a long road and many adventures in the tradition of BELLE AND SEBASTIAN. Based on the

novel by Mel Ellis. Just to confuse matters, this movie appears to have later been released in the U.S. under the title *White Fang*.

FLINT THE TIME DETECTIVE *

1998. JPN: *Jiku Tantei Genshi Kun*. AKA: *Time Detective Genshi*. TV series. DIR: Hiroshi Fukutomi, Koichi Takada, Shinji Okuda. SCR: Hideki Sonoda. DES: Yoshiko Ohashi. ANI: Takashi Yamazaki, Munekatsu Fujita. MUS: Tadashi Nanba. PRD: Pioneer, Tac, TV Tokyo. 25 mins. x 43 eps.

Petrafina Dagmar (accompanied by her two stooges, Might and Dyno) wants to loot the past so that the Dark Lord can destroy the Land of Time. Each period contains a special critter called a time-shifter, each of which possesses a magical power. To coin a phrase, Petra wants to "catch 'em all." Time-shifters keep the very fabric of time together, and their theft is policed by the Bureau of Time & Space Investigations. In one million B.C., Petra demands that caveboy triceratops-herder Flint Hammerhead (Genshi) and his father hand over Getalong (a penguin-like time-shifter whose power is to ensure that everyone gets along). When they refuse, she turns her fossilizer ray on them then returns to the 25th century to dig them up. Using her modern-day disguise as schoolteacher Miss Aino (pronounced and spelled "Iknow"), she encourages her class to go out and find fossils for her. However, twins Sarah and Tony take their fossil to their uncle, Bernie Goodman, at the Bureau. Bernie, with a little behind-the-scenes help from the Dark Lord's adversary the Old-Timer, defossilizes Flint with one of his gizmos. The process has given Flint superhuman strength, so he is enlisted in the Bureau. Flint's father remains a talking rock, so Bernie carves him into a stone axe for Flint and installs a fossilizer/defossilizer ray in the haft. Each week, Flint is called upon to foil Petra's latest scheme in a different time period. Some of her temporal interferences include imprisoning and taking

the place of Japan's ancient queen Himiko (see **DARK MYTH**) and instilling a lust for gold into the Conquistadors. A rehash of the successful **TIME BOKAN** series but with a monster-collecting angle bolted on for the 1990s, *Flint* was snatched up in the tidal wave of post-**POKÉMON** anime interest and brought to the U.S. in record time by **DIGIMON**-producers Saban Entertainment.

FLOWER ANGEL *

1979. JPN: *Hana no Ko Lunlun*. AKA: *Lunlun the Flowergirl*. TV series/special, movie. DIR: Yuji Endo. SCR: Noboru Shiroyama. DES: Michi Himeno. ANI: Tatsuhiro Nagaki. MUS: Hiroshi Tsutsui. PRD: Toei, TV Asahi. 25 mins. x 50 eps., ca. 15 mins. (m).

Lunlun is the 12-year-old daughter of a flower seller in the French countryside. Nouveau, her talking dog, and a cat called Cateau are emissaries from the king of the floral planet Flowern. The bad queen, Toginicia, has seized control of the kingdom and sent her servant Yaboki (a disguised *tanuki*, see **POMPOKO**) to seize the seven colors of magical flowers found on Earth. Lunlun, who can transform into a girl with special powers with her flower key, must travel the world with Nouveau and Cateau to collect the plants before Yaboki. Flower lore, a magical girl à la **CREAMY MAMI**, and an early collector's quest that presaged **CARDCAPTORS**, all dressed up in a European setting variously described by distributors as Switzerland or France, depending on their mood. There was also a short 15-minute movie version screened in Japanese theaters in 1980, *Flower Angel: Hello Kingdom of Cherries* (*Konnichi wa Sakura no Kuni*).

FLOWER WITCH MARYBELL

1992. JPN: *Hana no Maho Tsukai Marybell*. AKA: *Floral Magician Mary Bell*. TV series, movie. DIR: Tetsuya Endo. SCR: Yasunori Yamada. DES: Kenichi Onuki, Shigenori Kanatsu. ANI: Tadashi Hirota, Yuriko Senba. MUS: Takako Ishiguro. PRD: Ashi Pro, TV Tokyo. 25 mins. x 39 eps., ca. 40 mins. (m).

The adventures of a girl with a magical tambourine who works in her parents' flower shop but rights wrongs in her superheroine disguise, often with the help of her friends, Julia and Ribbon. Magic and music in the everytown of Sunnybell, this was also released as a 40-minute theatrical short, *Marybell: The Movie* (1992), in which Marybell is transported to a fantasy world after reading the story of the phoenix in her aunt's book.

FLY ISAMI!

1995. JPN: *Tobe Isami*. TV series. DIR: Gisaburo Sugii, Tatsuo Sato. SCR: Hideo Takayashiki, Tomoko Konparu. DES: Kazuaki Mori. ANI: Kazuaki Mori, Yoshiko Sakurai. MUS: Hiroaki Serizawa. PRD: Tac, NHK. 25 mins. x 50 eps.

Isami, a 12-year-old girl with a newscaster mother and research-scientist father, fights against a secret organization, the "Black Tengu," that is trying to take control of the world. Eventually, the Black Tengu joins forces with the Scrizawa industrial conglomerate, and Isami must recruit her friends and her father's inventions to fight back.

FLY! MACHINE HIRYU

1977. JPN: *Tobidase! Machine Hiryu*. TV series. DIR: Seitaro Hara, Mizuho Nishikubo, Yuji Fukawa, Hidehito Ueda. SCR: Jiro Yoshino, Akiyoshi Sakai, Yu Yamamoto. DES: Yoshitaka Amano, Kunio Okawara. ANI: Tetsu Honda, Norio Hirayama, Masatoshi Fukuyama. MUS: Hiroshi Tsutsui. PRD: Tatsunoko, Tokyo 12 Channel (TV Tokyo). 25 mins. x 21 eps.

The bosses of rival car companies decide to fight each other in the sporting arena by backing different race car teams. Chairman Gapporin hires Okkanabichi the supreme racer, while Chairman Misaki hires Riki Kazama, a relatively untried driver for the flying car known as Machine Hiryu. Mixing elements of **SPEED RACER** with **TIME BOKAN**, this Tatsunoko production ticks the same boxes, with Riki's cute girlfriend Nana, mini-mechanic Chuta, the cute ape and pooch, and the comic and glamorous villains lurking in the background. Early work from many big names, including Yoshitaka Amano and Kunio Okawara, is strictly in the studio mould. Manga versions of the story ran in several magazines, such as *Terebi Magazine* and *Terebi Land*. Racing fever seemed to have struck the Japanese animation business at this time: compare to the same year's **ARROW EMBLEM**.

FLY ON, DREAMERS!

1994. JPN: *Kattobase! Dreamers!* Movie. DIR: Yoshinori Kanemori, Morio Asaka. SCR: Hideo Takayashiki. DES: Yuzo Sato. ANI: Yuzo Sato. MUS: N/C. PRD: Hiroshima Film Center, Madhouse. 86 mins.
In an original story by **BAREFOOT GEN**–creator Keiji Nakazawa, a group of children orphaned by the bombing of Hiroshima fulfill their dream of playing with the professional baseball players of the Hiroshima Carp.

FLY PEEK! *

1992. JPN: *Tobe! Kujira no Peek.* AKA: *Fly! Peek the Whale; Peek the Baby Whale; The Boy and the White Whale Calf.* Movie. DIR: Koji Morimoto. SCR: Keiko Nobumoto, Koji Morimoto. DES: Satoru Utsunomiya. ANI: Satoru Utsunomiya, Hideo Okazaki. MUS: Yoshihisa Tomabechi. PRD: Toho. 80 mins.
After a storm, two young brothers find a baby white whale, the titular Peek, trapped by a rock in a shallow inlet in the Spanish coast. The boys decide to help it return to its mother on the open sea, but one of the boys, Kei, is tormented by older children until he lets the secret out. The whale is taken away by circus owner Odeon, and Kei journeys to the big city to set Peek free. Based on an original story by Hidehito Hara and predating the 1993 Hollywood movie *Free Willy*, beautiful settings and charmingly retro-styled character designs combined in a high-quality children's film that was badly served in the U.K. market, where distributors Kiseki only released a subtitled print.

FLY PEGASUS!

1995. JPN: *Tobe! Pegasus: Kokoro ni Goal ni Shoot.* AKA: *Fly! Pegasus: Shoot for the Goal of the Heart.* Movie. DIR: Shinji Okuda. SCR: Hideki Sonoda. DES: N/C. ANI: Junji Aoki. MUS: Masahito Suzuki. PRD: EG, Victor. 74 mins.
A high school for blind children fields a soccer team using a ball that emits a noise so it can be located. The potential for accidental fouls is mind-boggling, but only in anime could you find such a bizarre combination of **HELEN KELLER** and **CAPTAIN TSUBASA**.

FLYING GHOST SHIP

1969. JPN: *Soratobi Yurei Kan.* Movie. DIR: Hiroshi Ikeda. SCR: Masaki Tsuji, Hiroshi Ikeda. DES: Shotaro Ishi(no)mori. ANI: Yoichi Otabe, Hayao Miyazaki, Hideki Hayashi. MUS: Takasuke Onosaki. PRD: Toei. 60 mins.
A ship carrying a load of the prized "Boar Juice" soft drink is attacked by restless spirits. At the same time, the teenage Atsuhito saves the Kuroshaku drinks company president and his wife from a cycling accident and experiences a vision of the ship's skeletal captain. Atsuhito soon discovers that Kuroshaku is concealing secrets in the basement, and, as a giant robot lays waste to the city center, Atsuhito confronts the company about the truth behind its popular drink. Another cautionary tale from the creator of **CYBORG 009**, with animation and design work on the "golem" giant robot by Hayao Miyazaki.

FLYING SHADOW

1985. JPN: *Ninja Senshi Tobikage.* AKA: *Ninja Warrior Flying Shadow; Tobikage.* TV series. DIR: Masami Annai, Hiroyuki Yokoyama, Takashi Akimoto, Kazuyoshi Katayama. SCR: Sukehiro Tomita, Hideki Sonoda, Hideo Takayashiki. DES: Shigeru Kato, Toshihiro Hirano, Yasushi Moriki, Koichi Ohata. ANI: Takeshi Osaka. MUS: Koji Kawamura. PRD: Studio Pierrot, Magic Bus, Nippon TV. 35 mins. x 43 eps.
Soldiers from the evil planet Zaboom invade the peace-loving world of Radorio, forcing princess Romina to flee on the starship Elshank in search of the fabled "ninja" warrior who can save her people. Arriving in the solar system, she recruits several Earthlings to become the ninja warriors of old— the Black Lion, Fiery Dragon, and Thunder Phoenix. They return to pilot the Flying Shadow giant robot against the minions of Zaboom, in spite of the distinctly ungrateful population of Radorio, who refuse to believe they can do it. A mix of a team show and giant-robot combat, with an alien starship whose interior is modeled on samurai-period Japan.

FOBIA *

1995. JPN: *Mirai Choju Fobia.* AKA: *Future Superbeast Fobia.* Video. DIR: Shigenori Awai. SCR: Narihiko Tatsumiya. DES: Yoshinobu Yamakawa. ANI: Yoshinobu Yamakawa. MUS: Arcadia Studio. PRD: Tec, Gaga. 45 mins. x 2 eps.
Replinoids, creatures who thrive on human blood and have a preference for young girls, exhaust the supply in 2112 and come back to 1990s Japan to harvest more female flesh. They are pursued by Megumi, a time-traveling agent instructed to find a hero who can wield a magic sword of justice to destroy them. Replinoids murder several members of Enoshima College's drama group, and Megumi teams up with class geek Mutsumi, who inevitably turns out to be the Chosen One.
With a heroine resembling a younger version of Urara from his **SAKURA DIARIES** and a school background redolent of **ANGEL**, manga creator U-Jin makes a rare foray into SF for a tits-and-tentacles storyline that combines the story of *Terminator* with the face-huggers and adult beasts of *Aliens*. However, the attempts at both murder-mystery and questing subplots are somewhat stillborn. Time and cast are so limited that there is only one suspect for the murders and only one candidate for hero, while the contemporary setting is underused in favor of a school that is conveniently deserted

by all but the central cast every time something interesting happens. The overuse of flashbacks cleverly, but also obviously, recycles footage to save money. Compare to **DEMON BEAST INVASION**. 🅝🅛🅥

FOR REAL

1990. JPN: *Maji*. Video. DIR: Kazuya Miyazaki. SCR: Shigeo Nakakura. DES: Ayumi Tachihara. ANI: Chuji Nakajima. MUS: Hideo Shimazu. PRD: Creative Bridge, Transarts, Nippon Animation. 50 mins. x 2 eps.

Maji is a young punk in the Nagisa criminal organization whose name is synonymous with loyalty and truth. He falls for a local high school girl, Kumiko, but their affair is as doomed as any meeting of different worlds—when the tattooed boy and his moll go out on the town, they run into the rival Kikuchi gang looking for trouble. A gangster story based on the first two volumes of the 50-part 1986 *Shonen Champion* manga by JUSTICE-creator Ayumi Tachihara. The first episode was screened theatrically. 🅝🅥

FORBIDDEN LOVE *

2003. JPN: *Imoto de Iko*. AKA: *Let's Go with Sister*. Video. DIR: Hiroaki Nakajima. SCR: Makoto Nakamura. DES: Nishi Eta, Yuji Yoshimoto. ANI: Yuji Yoshimoto. MUS: N/C. PRD: Green Bunny. 30 mins. x 2 eps.

Mayuka is a princess from a faraway planet who comes to Earth on a goodhearted quest to save her mother's life. However, there any resemblance to **LITTLE WITCH SALLY** ends, since Mayuka is so distracted by the sight of the human couple Yoshizumi and Iori copulating that she crashes into their apartment. For reasons not all that clear, Yoshizumi uses Mayuka's perceptual alteration gun to convince the new arrival that he is her elder brother, thereby helping to set up another not-quite-incest story, as Mayuka joins a predictable gaggle of adoring alien girls trying to get into Yoshizumi's bed. The U.S. release includes a bonus 20-minute audio drama that runs while still images play

on screen—compare to **GIRL'S LOCKER ROOM LUST**. Presumably, this bonus was a planned third episode that was canceled before animation production began in earnest. Based on a 2002 computer game by Overflow. 🅝

FORCE FIVE *

1980. TV series. DIR: Kenneth Feuerman. SCR: Mike Haller. DES: N/C. ANI: N/C. MUS: N/C. PRD: Toei, Jim Terry Productions. 25 mins. x 74 eps. (*Grandizer*), 44 eps. (*Gaiking*), 39 eps. (*Starvengers*), 56 eps. (*Dangard Ace*), 64 eps. (*Spaceketeers*).

Five separate anime serials bought and repackaged for U.S. syndication by Jim Terry so that each could be shown on a different day of the week, every week. The separate series have their own entries in this book as **DANGARD ACE** (Mondays), *Starvengers* (i.e., **GETTER ROBO**, Tuesdays), **SPACEKETEERS** (Wednesday), **GRANDIZER** (Thursday), and **GAIKING** (Friday). Though many of the *FF* serials had figures that were included in the **SHOGUN WARRIORS** line, Mattel had lost its license for the toys by the time *FF* was broadcast. Jim Terry Productions also tried to sell a feature-length edit of each series, some of which made their way to U.K. video as the *Krypton Force* line.

FOREIGN INFLUENCES

EARLY ANIME often bears a resemblance to *Felix the Cat*, both in its use of animals and in the animation techniques employed. Ikuo Oishi's *Moving Picture Fight of the Fox and Possum* (*Ugoki-e Kori no Tatehiki*, 1931) drew on the comical deformation of reality in *Felix* to create a style we would now define as "cartoonish"—in particular the caricatured and exaggerated facial expressions that would eventually lead to the large-eyed figures of Osamu Tezuka.

The influence of the Fleischer brothers' Betty Boop, who was redesigned in *Stopping the Show* (1932) into a submissive, dark-haired, big-eyed heroine with a little girl voice, can be seen in Kenzo Masaoka's *The Gang and the Dancing Girl* (*Gang to Odoriko*, 1933) and the

kidnapped geisha (really a tanuki in disguise) who bats her eyelashes at the hero of Yoshitaro Kataoka's *Bandanemon the Monster Exterminator* (*Bandanemon: Bakemono Taiji no Maki*, 1935). Although Betty's guest star Popeye stole the show in *Popeye the Sailor* (1933), sailors in anime remained behind the scenes, with the Japanese Navy exerting greater influence on production budgets. Both Popeye and his nemesis Bluto made appearances in **WARTIME ANIME**, fighting for the Allied enemy.

It was a Chinese film, however, the Wan brothers' *Princess Iron Fan* (1943), a Chinese adaptation of **JOURNEY TO THE WEST**, that shook up the wartime anime industry. A remarkable achievement using heavy amounts of rotoscoping, it appears to have literally shamed the Japanese Navy into commissioning a feature film of equivalent length, **MOMOTARO'S DIVINE SEA WARRIORS** (1945). Either *MDSW*, or *Princess Iron Fan*, or both (depending on which source one believes) can also be credited with inspiring a young Osamu Tezuka to become an artist—possibly the most important influence of all! It is also noteworthy that stop-motion animation in Japan was pioneered by *MDSW*'s producer, Tadahito Mochinaga, who left Japan for a decade after 1945 and learned the techniques during his years at the Shanghai Animation Studio.

Funding for lavish animated movies was in short supply after World War II, with Japan laid low by military defeat and bombarded by messages of consumerism and scientific progress. Consequently, with little local competition, Disney films unavailable to the Japanese in wartime descended en masse, including the all-important *Pinocchio* (1940), while newer releases also arrived with little delay. *Peter Pan* (1953), *Lady and the Tramp* (as *Woof-Woof Story/Wanwan Monogatari*, 1955), and *Sleeping Beauty* (as *Beauty of the Sleeping Forest/Nemureru Mori no Bijo*, 1959) packed theaters, while the burgeoning world of television had no hesitation in shoving American cartoons onto the airwaves. The first cartoon to be seen on Japanese TV was the Fleischer brothers' *Superman*, also airing in 1955—it was joined the same year by both *Betty Boop* (as *Betty-chan*) and *Popeye*, his wartime collaboration forgiven. Conspicuously, the guest stars of the Fleischers' *Popeye Color Specials*, Ali Baba, Sindbad the Sailor, and Aladdin, all became the subjects of early color anime productions.

During the rise of television, anime aspired to imitate foreign live-action shows, not foreign cartoons. It was the George Reeves *Adventures of Superman*, not the Fleischer version, that was one of the highest-rated TV shows ever in Japan, inspiring broadcasters to attempt both live and animated reworkings. One of the most successful was Osamu Tezuka's **ASTRO BOY**, which combined the power and duty of *Superman* with the yearning and pathos of *Pinocchio*. But an equal effect was felt in the girls' market, where the hidden heroic identity of Clark Kent was reworked for **PRINCESS KNIGHT** (1967).

Bewitched (as *My Wife is a Witch/Okusan wa Majo*) and *I Dream of Jeannie* (as *Cute Witch Jeannie/Kawaii Majo Jeannie*) both inspired imitations, including the landmark **LITTLE WITCH SALLY** (1966) and the live/anime mixture of the first **COMET-SAN** (1967). Later seasons saw refinements to these ideas, in which plucky Japanese modern girls would transform, not necessarily into superheroines like **CUTEY HONEY** (1973), but into older, more sophisticated versions of themselves, such as **MARVELOUS MELMO** (1971). As the cute-but-maternal, houseproud-but-ditzy Samantha in *Bewitched*, Elizabeth Montgomery enjoyed unprecedented fame in Japan, becoming one of the first foreigners to grace Japanese commercials (for Lotte Mother biscuits). Her onscreen husband's name, "Darrin," would eventually transform into the prolonged "Daaah-ling!" that became a catchphrase for another magical wife, Lum in **URUSEI YATSURA** (1981); successive generations have come to associate the word with approaching spousal trouble.

Meanwhile, the allure of *I Dream of Jeannie*, a Tinkerbell figure who becomes a boy's secret companion, can be seen to this day in shows such as **BOTTLE FAIRY** (2003) and **MIDORI DAYS** (2004).

Other influences have yet to be proved. It is our belief that the American TV show *The Gallery of Madame Liu Tsong* (1951), featuring early screen star Anna May Wong as a Chinese sleuth and antiques dealer, may also have been a major influence. So obscure that it is no longer even extant in America, Wong's contemporary fame and ethnic origin would have made the show a sure-fire purchase for early Japanese TV, ultimately leading to the art-related action of **CAT'S EYE**, **PETSHOP OF HORRORS**, and **GALLERY FAKE**. To date, however, we can find no evidence of its Japanese broadcast.

It became customary for many import shows to proclaim their origins with a large foreign name in Japan's *katakana* syllabary, qualified with a much smaller Japanese-language explanation to help bewildered viewers. This led to strange mouthfuls such as *Famous Dog LASSIE*, *Undersea King NELSON* (i.e. *Sea Hunt*), and *SAINT Heaven Guy* (i.e. *The Saint*), a style later parodied for its exoticism to create terms such as *Mobile Suit* **GUNDAM** and *Neon Genesis* **EVANGELION**.

The cheaper, more limited animation style of Hanna-Barbera cartoons was a blessed relief to the Japanese, who no longer faced expensive movie animation on TV, but cheaper productions that they could emulate more easily. *Deputy Dawg* (as *Woof-Woof Sheriff/Wanwan Hoankan*), but most notably *The Flintstones* (as *Prehistoric Family/Genshi Kazoku*), made it clear that cartoons should not be kept in a children's ghetto and encouraged the Japanese to offer their own alternatives. Felix the Cat returned as a TV character in 1960 with *The Adventures of Felix/Felix no Boken*, notably in a redesign by Joe Oriolo in which the titular feline had a "magic bag of tricks"—compare to **DORAEMON**.

The year of the Tokyo Olympics,

1964, saw the culmination of many local and national initiatives in technology and infrastructure. By the time of the Olympics opening ceremony, Japan had become a nation of color TV set owners, a fact not lost on Osamu Tezuka, whose **KIMBA THE WHITE LION** (1965) was partly funded by the American NBC network, enabling color production. In the late 1960s, both the Japanese and the Americans were claiming to be the "makers" of co-productions like **THE KING KONG SHOW** and **TOM OF T.H.U.M.B.**, but tastes were diverging. Anime were made in reaction to, not in imitation of, foreign works. While entertainment for boys was often so universal that shows like **MARINE BOY** and **SPEED RACER** were readily exported, anime sought other niches not taken up by foreign broadcasters, most notably in the sector of the "magical girl shows."

The late 1960s and early 1970s saw Japanese TV influenced in turn by Cold War paranoia and spy capers, particularly the James Bond movies, and *The Man from U.N.C.L.E.* (1964). Anime heroes fought increasing numbers of evil empires and shadowy organizations, until the 1970s when, whatever the motive for a conflict, sponsorship deals ensured that a toy tie-in was mandatory—"my father gave me a robot" becoming not merely a plot point, but a slogan for children to internalize, ready to use to full effect on harassed parents.

The greatest foreign influence in this spirit was kept hidden for many years, but came in the form of direct investment. Many supposedly "American" cartoons in this period were largely made in Japan where the Rankin/Bass company was subcontracting much of its work. In particular, stop-motion from Tadahito Mochinaga's MOM Films and cel animation from Toru Hara's Topcraft made a major contribution to foreign works in this period, including *'Twas the Night Before Christmas* (1974), *The Hobbit* (1977), and *The Last Unicorn* (1981). Meanwhile, a more obvious foreign influence came in the form of the **World Masterpiece Theater** (1975), a highly regarded domestic franchise that relied solely on foreign stories for its inspiration.

Japanese animators remained a popular choice as laborers on supposedly "foreign" cartoons in the 1980s, sometimes comprising most or all of the actual creative staff. Shows such as **Ulysses 31** (1981), **Dogtanian and the Three Muskehounds** (1981), and **The Mysterious Cities of Gold** (1982) were made with foreign money, while others, such as **Robin Hood** (1990), relied on markets abroad for their success. However, this success was short-lived, chiefly through the rising costs of Japanese labor. As Japanese studios increasingly subcontracted their work abroad in the 1990s, it was just as likely for their foreign clients to do the same—later seasons of *The Simpsons* (1989), which would probably have been farmed out to Japan if the show had been made a decade earlier, were instead animated in Korea.

The home video market, which many in the anime business seem to have regarded as a wholly domestic, bargain-basement operation, was to prove anime's savior. However, many foreign buyers developed false expectations based on their first experience of the medium. Although anime were sold abroad in the 1990s as a video medium, many of the video buyers were comparing their purchases with **Akira** (1988)—a feature film. Its success abroad, greeted with elation and bewilderment by its own over-stretched producers, ushered in the age of Japanese video exports—the beginning of "anime" as we know it. Japanese sources, unable to use the word "anime" as distinct from any other cartoon in preceding periods, often call the modern period the age of "Japanimation," deliberately using a foreign word to demonstrate that anime has come to be defined by foreign consumers, based on a criterion that largely rests on its place of origin.

As increasing numbers of foreign distributors fought over the rights to

anime, foreigners began investing directly in Japanese productions in order to snatch the rights early. **Ghost in the Shell** (1995) featured investment from Manga Entertainment, while many modern productions often involve foreign coproducers as benefactors. Indeed, some anime companies refuse to even commence production without foreign backing. Many modern productions are now touted at rights fairs in the hope of attracting foreign investment, while ever-increasing numbers of both anime and **False Friends** are put into production at the instigation of Western producers. In **Kaleido Star** (2003), the lavish performance sequences were only possible with investment from ADV Films, while **Kill Bill: The Origin of O-Ren** (2003), was made by the Japanese in imitation of what foreign producers thought Japanese animation ought to be.

FORTUNE QUEST

1994. Video, TV series. DIR: Takeshi Yamaguchi, Takashi Watanabe. SCR: Keiko Maruo, Yumi Kageyama, Reiko Yoshida. DES: Yumi Nakayama. ANI: Kazuhiro Okaseko, Susumu Ishizaki. MUS: N/C. PRD: Victor, Beam Entertainment, MBS. 30 mins. x 4 eps. (v), 25 mins. x 26 eps. (TV).

A group of adventurers on a parallel world seek their fortunes in a story whose debt to role-playing games is so great that the press notes even describe the characters as "low-level." Teenage "mapper" Pastel leads a party comprising young swordsman Clay, bandit chieftain's son Trapp, blue-blood "walking dictionary" Kitton, gentle giant Knoll, baby dragon Shiro, and infant elf sorceress Rumy. After their latest quest, they call in at the Adventurers Support Group, which stamps their ID cards and evaluates their experience, both pastiching and predicting the inevitable console game version of the story.

Originally based on a best-selling 1991 novel by Michio Fukuzawa, who also wrote the *Duan Surk* prequel set in the same universe, the story was

also adapted into a manga by Natsumi Mukai, in turn adapted into the sequel anime TV series *Fortune Quest L* by Eiichi Sato and **Slayers**-director Takeshi Watanabe. The series added the gaming experience by featuring hidden items and monsters, as well as unexpected dialogue from certain characters. Though hardly anything new, it prepared the ground for the success of **Pokémon**, for which exploiting the game tie-in was the sole raison d'être.

FORZA! HIDEMARU

2002. TV series. DIR: Nobuhiro Takamoto. SCR: Hideo Takayashiki. DES: Masami Esaka. ANI: N/C. MUS: Yuko Fujishima. PRD: TV Tokyo, NAS, Gallop. 25 mins. x 26 eps.

A soccer anime with a cast of wacky animals in sports getup seems far out of its time in the early 21st century, but it was the year of the World Cup in Japan and South Korea, and the very young audience sees these tropes with fresh eyes. Hidemaru is a feisty fox; his friends include bunnies, dogs, horses, and a couple of hefty hippo girls. Based on a manga by "Sunny Side Up," in *Corocoro Comic*.

FOXES OF CHIRONUP

1987. JPN: *Chironup no Kitsune*. Movie. DIR: Tetsuo Imazawa. SCR: Fukuo Matsuyama. DES: Yoshinao Yamamoto. ANI: Noriko Imazawa. MUS: Etsujiro Sato. PRD: Tac, Herald. 72 mins.

Foxes Ken and Chin become the proud parents of cubs, Koro and Kan, who enjoy a carefree life on the northern Japanese island of Chironup. They befriend a fisherman and his wife but are forced to run for their lives when soldiers on a military exercise decide to take home some fox pelts as souvenirs. A sweet little film that obliquely symbolizes the plight of Japan's aboriginal Ainu people and the northern islands that have been contested with Russia since they were occupied by Stalin's soldiers in 1945. Based on a book by Yoshiyuki Takahashi.

FOXWOOD TALES

1991. Video. DIR: Seiji Endo. SCR: Seiji Endo. DES: Brian Paterson. ANI: Maya Matsuyama. MUS: Osamu Tezuka (not the Osamu). PRD: Grouper Productions. 25 mins. x 3 eps.

Harvey, Rue, and Willie are a hedgehog, rabbit, and mouse who live in a windmill in the peaceful town of Foxwood, where they have several adventures in this short-lived series based on the children's picture books by the British creators Cynthia and Brian Paterson.

FRANKENSTEIN *

1981. JPN: *Kyofu Densetsu Kaibutsu: Frankenstein.* AKA: *Mystery! Frankenstein Legend of Terror.* TV special. DIR: Yugo Serikawa. SCR: Akiyoshi Sakai. DES: Toyoo Ashida. ANI: Toyoo Ashida. MUS: Kentaro Haneda. PRD: Aoi Productions, Toei Animation, TV Asahi. 111 mins.

After the success of **DRACULA: SOVEREIGN OF THE DAMNED**, the same team made this bewildering version of Mary Shelley's novel. For reasons unknown, the setting was moved to North Wales, where Frankenstein conducts his experiments amid the mountainous splendor of Snowdonia. His creature, Franken, is brought to life by a lightning bolt and runs for Switzerland, where he is pursued by police inspector Belbeau. Franken befriends a little girl called Emily and her blind father, saving Emily from a wild bear before succumbing to his fate and committing suicide.

FRECKLES POOCH

1969. JPN: *Sobakasu Putchi.* AKA: *Freckled Butch.* TV series. DIR: Fumio Ikeno. SCR: Noboru Ishiguro, Tomohiro Ando. DES: Shozo Kubota. ANI: Tadao Wakabayashi. MUS: Asao Kasai. PRD: Shinsei, Fuji. TV 5 mins. x 162 eps.

Short comedy films about a cheeky little dog, Pooch, who is unable to let any evil deed go unchallenged. He flies in a vehicle shaped like a milk jug, powered by milk itself, and fights against the evil genius Walgie, using a yo-yo as a weapon, accompanied by his associates the lumbering monster Netaro and Ganko the impetuous parrot. *FP* was made by the remaining staff members of TV Doga, the company behind **MARINE BOY**, which lost much of its anime staff after it was rebranded Fuji TV Enterprises. With more emphasis on live-action television, many of the staff left, and the few animators remaining worked on this, farming out the actual animation to Shinsei Sekai Eigasha. The show was eventually replaced by **PINCH AND PUNCH**, with which it shares a large number of crew-members.

FREE KICK FOR TOMORROW

1992. JPN: *Ashita e no Free Kick.* TV series. DIR: Tetsuro Amino, Toshiaki Suzuki. SCR: Masaru Yamamoto, Nobuaki Kishima, Akira Oketani. DES: Noboyushi Habara. ANI: Takahiro Omori, Masami Suda. MUS: Satoshi Tozuka. PRD: Ashi Pro, Nippon TV, Shizuoka TV. 25 mins. x 50 eps.

Shun arrives in Italy with his disabled friend, Roberto, to live with his rich grandfather who also emigrated from Japan many years ago. He becomes passionate about soccer, but Grandfather wants him to take over the family business and resents the time he devotes to sports. Eventually, though, he has to accept that Shun will become a professional player. Roberto, meanwhile, succeeds as an architect and wants to build a great stadium in their town, a project that Shun's grandfather very much opposes. The series has an open ending—a big competition with top teams comes to the town, but we never know if Shun's team wins. A series that reflects the reality of a modern sports business, where few players were born anywhere near the town they represent, and corporate interests can make or break a team.

FRIED OCTOPUS MAN

1998. JPN: *Takoyaki Manto Man.* AKA: *Fried Octopus Cloak Man.* TV series. DIR: Masami Annai. SCR: Yoshio Urasawa. DES: Midori Nagaoka. ANI: Tsugeno-bu Kuma. MUS: N/C. PRD: Studio Pierrot, TV Tokyo. 25 mins. x 12 eps.

Evil priest Baobao is intent on ruling Earth, and a lone woman in a *takoyaki* (fried octopus dumplings) diner prays for a savior to protect the planet. In a series that owes a lot of its comedy and inspiration to the earlier **ANPANMAN,** the woman's request is answered, sort of, when a hero arrives draped in an edible cloak.

FRIGHTFUL NEWS

1991. JPN: *Kyofu Shinbun.* Video. DIR: Takashi Anno. SCR: Masaaki Sakurai. DES: Koji Uemura. ANI: Koji Uemura. MUS: Takashi Tsunoda. PRD: Pierrot Project. 50 mins. x 3 eps.

Junior high school student Rei Onigata finds a newspaper, *The Frightful News*, that cuts one's life short by a hundred days whenever it is read. It also, however, contains much interesting information about the spirit world and future events, and Rei is the only one who can read it. Realizing he has been tricked by an evil spirit, he offers his services to psychic Jo-un Hoshi. Rei, his love interest, Midoriko, and her sister are stalked by the ghost of an old man in a dark cloak. This short series is based on the 1973 *Shonen Champion* manga by Jiro Tsunoda, who also drew **HYAKUTARO** and **KARATE-CRAZY LIFE**. In 1996, the story was remade as a live-action movie, directed by Teruyoshi Ishii. Perhaps in the wake of the not-dissimilar live-action film *Ring* (1998), it was brought back in 2000 for a one-shot "manga video," in which voice actors narrated the story over still images from the manga onscreen.

FRITEN-KUN

1981. Movie. DIR: Taku Sugiyama, Kazuyuki Okaseko. SCR: Noboru Shiroyama, Tsunehisa Ito, Haruya Yamazaki. DES: Takamitsu Mitsunori. ANI: Takamitsu Mitsunori, Haruo Takahashi, Keiji Morishita. MUS: Haruo Matsushita. PRD: Knack. 75 mins.

Gambling japes from Friten, a Tokyo gangster whose sense of humor was screened on a double bill with the diametrically opposed Osaka-based comedy of JARINKO CHIE. Based on the manga by Masashi Ueda, serialized in both *Modern Mahjong* and *Gamble Punch* magazines, the seven vignettes here include Friten demonstrating his winning gambling tactic and the wrong way to play mahjong. Among the stories are more far-fetched incidents such as his trip back in time to Edo-period Japan, his attempts to get involved in real sports, and his hapless tries at seducing the pretty Ikue-chan.

FROM THE APENNINES TO THE ANDES

1976. JPN: *Haha o Tazunete Sanzan Ri.* AKA: *3,000 Leagues in Search of Mother.* TV series, Movie. DIR: Isao Takahata, Hajime Okayasu. SCR: Kazuo Fukuzawa. DES: Yoichi Otabe. ANI: Yoichi Otabe. MUS: Koichi Sakata. PRD: Nippon Animation, Fuji TV. 21 mins. x 51 eps.
Italian boy Marco lives in the town of Genoa, which has been hard hit by heavy taxes and recession. His mother leaves for Argentina, where her husband runs a clinic for the poor, but Marco cannot bear to be parted from her and pursues her ship. So begins a long quest that will ultimately take him to Bolivia, in the company of the Peppino puppet theater, and Fiorina, the daughter of a local chieftain. The story was reedited into a 107-minute movie version in 1980 by Hajime Okayasu and completely remade by director Kozo Kusuba as *Marco* (1999). Based on part of the novel *Cuore* by Edmondo de Amicis, which was also adapted in its entirety as HEART: AN ITALIAN SCHOOLBOY'S JOURNAL. The moving story was also mercilessly lampooned in the 1991 GENIUS IDIOT BAKABON–movie *3,000 Leagues in Search of Osomatsu's Curry* (1991), directed by Akira Saito, in which the quest for Mother was replaced by a zany search for a decent meal.

FROM TODAY ON, THIS IS ME

1992. JPN: *Kyo kara, Ore wa!* Video. DIR: Takeshi Mori. SCR: Shikichi Ohashi. DES: Masaya Onishi. ANI: Masaya Onishi.

MUS: Kimio Morihari. PRD: Studio Pierrot. 61 mins.
Teenagers Takashi Mitsubashi and Shinji Ito move to a new high school in "C" Prefecture near Tokyo and resolve to pretend to be the toughest kids around, dyeing their hair into threatening tough-guy blond hairdos. Forced to cooperate simply because each could rat out the other, they outwit genuine tough guys with elaborate bluffs and deceits. This movie is based on a comedy in the 1988 manga in *Shonen Sunday* by Hiroyuki Nishimori. Compare to BITE ME! CHAMELEON.

FRUITS BASKETS *

2001. TV series. DIR: Akitaro Daichi. SCR: Rika Nakase. DES: Akimi Hayashi. ANI: N/C. MUS: N/C. PRD: Studio Deen, Fuji TV. 25 mins. x 26 eps.
Happy-go-lucky orphan Toru Honda has to move in with the family of Yuki, the high school boy she secretly adores. However, she is not expecting to discover that they are a family of sorcerers and shape-shifters. Fluffy animals, magic, and schoolgirl crushes, based on the manga by Natsuki Takaya in *Hana to Yume* magazine.

FRUITS CUP *

2004. JPN: *Yugu Setsuai.* Video. DIR: Yoshio Usuda. SCR: Tsunekazu Murakami. DES: Waffle. ANI: Yoshio Usuda. MUS: Beeline. PRD: Waffle, Milky. 30 mins. x 2 eps.
After saving the life of his friend in a car accident, Riku temporarily inherits the convalescing man's job as a caretaker for a girls' dormitory on one of Japan's southern islands. He arrives to discover that they are a family of shape-shifters, cursed by the animals of the Chinese zodiac. Riku secretly films the girls in various lesbian couplings and then uses the footage to blackmail Yoshino, the most demure, into giving up her virginity. But Riku wants to seduce the other girls at the boarding house he runs, and so forces Yoshino to help him get what he wants. "The worst sexual humiliation" is assured by the press release, which in Japanese

notes that there are 30 minutes per episode, although the American edition barely reaches a 45-minute running time for the combined two parts. So either something was cut, or, as we suspect, the original Japanese running time was more like 22 minutes per episode. ●🅝🅥

FUJI TV (FUJI TELECASTING)

Founded in 1959 by a consortium of radio companies, movie companies, and the *Sankei Shinbun* newspaper, Fuji was an early adopter of the anime medium and the channel that screened both ASTRO BOY and KIMBA THE WHITE LION. The channel's flagship anime is SAZAE-SAN, the longest-running cartoon series in the world, now nearing its fortieth birthday. The broadcast company acquired the studio TV Doga in the 1960s, renaming it Fuji TV Enterprises. The station enjoys a particularly strong relationship with the magazine *Shonen Jump*, whose DRAGONBALL and ONE PIECE manga have both been adapted for its schedules.

FUJIKO F. FUJIO'S LITTLE WEIRDNESS THEATER

1990. JPN: *Fujiko F. Fujio no Sukoshi Fushigi (SF) Tanben Theatre.* Video. DIR: Tetsu Dezaki, Tomomi Mochizuki. SCR: Toshiaki Imaizumi. DES: Keizo Shimizu. ANI: Keizo Shimizu. MUS: N/C. PRD: Studio Gallop. 50 mins. x 5 eps.
A series of SF short stories by the cocreator of DORAEMON made for adults but in the spirit of fondly remembered shows from childhood. The punchy one-shots include *Tomorrow in the Letterbox*, in which a man receives a message from the future warning of impending danger for his friends; *A Dish for the Minotaur*, about a crash-landed astronaut who finds himself on a planet where the roles of men and cows are reversed, and finds that he is to be eaten at a royal banquet; *Green Guardian*, a pastiche of *Day of the Triffids* in which Tokyo is overrun by man-eating plants; *Island of Extinction*, about the population of Earth being all but wiped out by invading aliens;

and the lighthearted superhero pastiche, *Ultra Super Deluxe Man*.

FUKU-CHAN

1982. JPN: *Fuku-chan: Yokoyama Ryuichi no Kessaku Anime*. AKA: *Fuku-chan: Ryuichi Yokoyama's Anime Masterpiece*. TV series. DIR: Mineo Fuji. SCR: Masaki Tsuji, Toshiyuki Kashiwakura, Noboru Shiroyama, Hiroko Naka. DES: Ryuichi Yokoyama. ANI: Michishiro Yamada. MUS: Hiroshi Tsutsui. PRD: Shinei, TV Asahi. 25 mins. x 71 eps.
Childish goings-on for Fukuo Fuchida (also known as Fuku-chan), a small boy who attends nursery school with his "girlfriend," Kumi, and hangs out with his playmates Namiko (whose parents own a china shop), her younger brother, Kiyo, naughty twins Doshako and Garako, and school bully Ganchan.

FUKUTOMI, HIROSHI

1950– . Born in Kochi, he studied animation at the Tokyo Design Academy before joining A Productions (now Shin'ei) and the company's subsidiary Animaru-ya. After early storyboarding duties, became a director on IKKYU and LITTLE GOBLIN.

FUKUYAMA THEATER: SUMMER SECRETS

1990. JPN: *Fukuyama Gekijo: Natsu no Himitsu*. Video. DIR: Michiyo Sakurai. SCR: Michiyo Sakurai. DES: Keiko Fukuyama. ANI: N/C. MUS: N/C. PRD: Urban Project. 60 mins.
Several short animated films based on the short stories and four-panel manga of Keiko Fukuyama, including *My Father the Mouse*, *The Rabbit Brothers*, *Summer Secret*, *The Mysterious Fairy*, *How Very Strange*, and *Kuro*.

FULL METAL PANIC *

2001. TV series. DIR: Koichi Chigira, Akihiro Nishiyama, Yasuhiro Takemoto. SCR: Koichi Chigira, Fumihiko Shimo, Yasuhiro Takemoto. DES: Osamu Horiuchi, Kanetake Ebikawa, Toshiaki Ihara, Koji Ito, Masayuki Takano. ANI: Osamu Horiuchi. MUS: Toshihiko Sahashi. PRD: Gonzo, Mithril. 23 mins. x 24 eps.

(TV1) 24 mins. x 12 eps. (*Fumoffu*) 24 mins. x 13 eps. (*Second Raid*).
In a world where the Cold War continues into the 21st century, Russian scientists are gathering "the Whispered"—people with unique and special powers. The international troubleshooting agency Mithril is employed to prevent such acquisitions, a task it usually performs with military-grade giant robots called Arm Slaves, but which occasionally involves undercover assignments. Hence the arrival of Mithril agent Sosuke Sagara at a Japanese high school, where he is charged with maintaining undercover surveillance and protection for Kaname Chidori, a beautiful and intelligent sixteen-year-old girl, from enemies of Mithril and, regrettably, high school panty thieves. Kaname has been born with Black Technology, an innate and latent knowledge that makes her capable of producing formidable weaponry.
    Transported swiftly from a world like GASARAKI to a world like SUKEBAN DEKA, Sosuke is written off as a weapons-obsessed geek by many of the other students. He "befriends" Kaname, wreaking appalling havoc on anyone he thinks may threaten her—teachers, friends, classmates—but when she is kidnapped by the forces of evil, he shows more than just professional concern and risks everything to save her.
    Despite a bunch of predictable stereotypes, *FMP* somehow manages to retain a sense of fun lacking from so many other anime—as if SPRIGGAN were not all about global conspiracies, but focused instead on what its hero did on his days off. The "romantic" lead has a dark past and is so tied up in his work that he takes a long while to realize the full range of his story functions. The villains are really nasty and the robots are simply stunning, ensuring *FMP* a place as one of the best offerings of its year.
    Based on a series of novels by Shoji Gato, *FMP* was originally slated for release in the fall season of 2001, but kept off-air by the terrorist attacks of

9/11—which found nobody in the mood for a wacky tale of anti-terrorist high jinks. Similar issues delayed the American release of METROPOLIS and caused re-thinks in content for several U.S. TV shows, including the first season of *24*. When it did finally reach Japanese networks in early 2002, it was successful enough to get a second series right away, animated by Kyoto Animation instead of Gonzo. Screened from January 2002, sequel *FMP: Fumoffu* is based on several spin-off stories from the original and has a more comedic and/or lecherous outlook. It concentrates solely on life at the school, while Sosuke continues to cause mayhem, and his commanding officer Testarossa decides to try high school life for a few weeks. A third series *FMP: The Second Raid* (2005) is based on the two *Owaru Day by Day* novels that followed and takes a much grimmer tone. This time a secret organization wants to eliminate Mithril and the teenagers have to stop them. There is also a spin-off manga by Shikidoji in *Comic Dragon* monthly, released under the unwieldy title *Full Metal Panic! The Anime Mission (Resource Book Manga)*. ◗

FULL MOON

2002. JPN: *Full Moon o Sagashite*. AKA: *Searching for the Full Moon; Furumyu; Until the Full Moon*. TV series, TV special. DIR: Toshiyuki Kato, Bob Shirahata. SCR: Genki Yoshimura. Hiro Masaki, Mayu Sugiura, Mushi Hirohira, Rika Nakase, Ryu Tamura, Shizuma Aozora. DES: Yuka Kudo. ANI: Studio Deen. MUS: Yoshiaki Muto, Keita Shiina. PRD: NAS, Studio Deen. 25 mins. x 52 eps. (TV), 10 mins. (special).
Mitsuki Koyama is twelve, in love with her childhood friend Eichi, and dreams of becoming a singer. Then she finds she has throat cancer—a malignant tumor that prevents her from singing above a whisper. Two strange beings show up and inform her that they are angels of death and she has one year to live. But Takuto and Meroko are moved by her passionate desire to become a famous singer before her

time runs out and decide to help her. Disguising themselves as a bunny and a cat in the best tradition of magical girl shows, they enable her to transform into a 16-year-old idol singer so that she can try for stardom before her last year elapses.

This is by no means the first show in which a pretty girl comes with a time limit attached, nor the first in which an idol singer's desperation for attention gains a life or death element—consider LIMIT THE MIRACLE GIRL and KEY THE METAL IDOL. Nor is its gloomy premise unfamiliar on Japanese television, since every TV season sees at least one youthful protagonist staring death in the face, particularly in imitation of another combination of death and pop music, 1998's *Please God! Just A Little More Time* (*DE). This could have been another thoroughly depressing show, since it never tries to fudge the fact that its perky heroine is going to die, but the bickering between hunky Takuto and besotted Meroko provide comic relief and Mitsuki's determination to make the most of what she has keeps the tone upbeat. The series is based on the manga by Arina Tanemura, creator of KAMIKAZE THIEF JEANNE, and spun off a "special" *Cute Cute Adventure* (2002), a gift to *Ribon* magazine readers. This comic snippet shows Takuto and Meroko getting left behind as Mitsuki rushes to a photo shoot and the obstacles they have to overcome to catch up with her.

FULLMETAL ALCHEMIST *
2003. JPN: *Hagane no Renkin Jutsu-shi; Hagaren*. TV series, movie. DIR: Seiji Mizushima. SCR: Seiji Mizushima, Noboru Aikawa. DES: Yoshiyuki Ito, Shinji Aramaki, Junya Ishigaki. ANI: Koji Sugiura. MUS: Michiru Oshima. PRD: Aniplex, BONES, MBS, Square-Enix, Aniplex, Mainichi, Square-Enix, Shochiku Film. (m) 24 mins. x 51 eps. (TV), ca. 80 mins. (m).
Alchemy is a process by which ordinary, non-living material can be transmuted into other forms. The Elric brothers, Edward and Alphonse, live with their mother in the quiet little town of Resembool while their father, famous alchemist Hohenheim Elric, is helping the military in a war. Edward, the older brother by a year, is a precocious alchemist, and when their mother falls ill and dies, he and Alphonse break every law to perform a forbidden ritual to resurrect her. The attempt goes horribly wrong, and Alphonse's body is destroyed, but Edward manages to save his soul by transferring it to a suit of armor—although it literally costs him an arm and a leg. The only way to return themselves to their former state and have a chance of bringing back their mother, is to find the alchemical MacGuffin, the Philosopher's Stone.

Three years later, the 15-year-old Edward is a bad-tempered alchemist working for the military. Alphonse is still trapped in his armor, and Edward has gained mechanical limbs, fitted by the grandmother of their childhood friend Winry Rockbell. Winry is a tomboy who has inherited her grandmother's mechanical and technical skills. Colonel Mustang, also known as the "Flame Alchemist" because of his skill with fire magic, is their commanding officer. Most alchemists are in the army because the general public distrusts and fears them, even though their skills are needed to fight fearsome enemies. The brothers and their friends battle foes based on the seven deadly sins, using symbols from the works of real-life medieval alchemist Nicholas Flamel. In a surprise twist, they are reunited with their father but become embroiled in the rise of Nazism, and Edward himself is transported to a terrifying other world—our own.

Uniting the quest narrative of DORORO with the militarized European sorcery of HOWL'S MOVING CASTLE, *FMA* rode the wave of *Harry Potter*'s success to become one of the fan-favorite anime of the early 21st century. In a way, it takes the robot buddy sci-fi of HEAT GUY J and simply places it into a magical world. Edward is like a magical girl whose transformation has gotten seriously out of hand; without the help of a guiding angel or animal, he's overreached himself and now has to try and retrieve normal life. Necromancy and forbidden powers are drawn into the context of galloping scientific progress in the 19th century in the style of FRANKENSTEIN; the age of steam was a time of dark and wonderful magic for those driving it, and this adaptation of Hiromu Arakawa's manga catches that atmosphere, before turning in its later chapters to chills that foreshadow MONSTER. The Japanese screening saw multiple promo tie-ins including many video games and a theme song by rock group L'Arc-en-Ciel.

The movie, *FMA: The Conqueror of Shambhala* (*HNR: Shanbara wo iku mono*, 2005), is set in our world in 1923, with a powerless Edward living in Munich with Alphonse Heiderich, a doppelganger of his missing brother. The pair are researching rocketry and trying to find a way to send Edward home when Edward encounters an old enemy who may offer a clue to the way back, but at a terrible price to both worlds. **V**

FUMOON
1980. TV special. DIR: Hisashi Sakaguchi. SCR: Hisashi Sakaguchi. DES: Hitoshi Nishimura, Hisashi Sakaguchi. ANI: Hitoshi Nishimura. MUS: Yuji Ono. PRD: Tezuka Pro, Nippon TV. 91 mins.
Nuclear-bomb tests near Horseshoe Island have mutated the locals, creating a new breed of psychic humans called the Fumoon. Dr. Yamadono reports on the new species at an international conference attended by representatives from the nuclear superpowers, Star and Uran (a thinly disguised U.S. and USSR), but nobody listens to his dire warnings. Star and Uran go to war, while the Fumoons constitute a third front, attacking all humans while a cloud of dark gas closes in around Earth. By the end, as the Fumoons flee into space, the warring nations join forces to save the planet and discover that the dark gas is a benign phenomenon that turns into harmless oxygen—though who is to say that next time the human race will be so lucky? A caution-

© NIPPON ANIMATION CO., LTD. 1978

Future Boy Conan

ary tale from **Astro Boy**–creator Osamu Tezuka based on his 1951 manga *Next World*, itself inspired in equal parts by the Korean War and nuclear testing in the Pacific. As with other TV specials from Tezuka, many characters from his other stories appear in cameo roles. See also **Metropolis**, to which *Fumoon* is a distant sequel. The original manga was itself a sequel of sorts to Tezuka's **Metropolis**.

FURUHASHI, KAZUHIRO
1960– . A prime figure at Studio Deen, Furuhashi studied at an animation college before finding work as a key animator on **Urusei Yatsura**. Storyboarding and directing jobs soon followed on a wide range of work, including **Ruro ni Kenshin**, **Virgin Mary Is Watching** and **Zipang**. He was "series" director on **Hunter x Hunter**— a "show runner" in American terms.

FURUSE, NOBORU
?– ?. Key animator and character designer on **Urusei Yatsura**, **Confucius**, and many of the later **Lupin III** TV specials.

FUSHIGI YUGI: THE MYSTERIOUS PLAY *
1995. JPN: *Fushigi Yugi*. AKA: *Mysterious Game*. TV series/special, video. DIR: Hajime Kamegaki, Nanako Shimazaki, Akira Shigeno. SCR: Yoshio Urasawa, Kazuhisa Sakaguchi. DES: Hideyuki Motohashi. ANI: Hideyuki Motohashi, Hisatoshi Motoki, Mayumi Hiroda. MUS: Tatsumi Yano. PRD: Studio Pierrot, TV Tokyo. 25 mins. x 52 eps., 56 mins. x 2 eps. (TVm), 30 mins. x 3 eps. (v), 45 mins. x 6 eps. (v), 30 mins. x 4 eps. (*Eikoden*).

Fifteen-year-old Miaka accompanies her friend Yui to Tokyo's national library, where the girls find an ancient Chinese book called *The Universe of the Four Gods*. They are transported to the world of the book, though Yui is soon thrown back to Earth, leaving Miaka temporarily stranded. Miaka finds herself in a fantasy version of ancient China, where she is rescued from slavers by the handsome Tamahome and becomes a ward of the emperor. The land of Konan ("Southern Scarlet," as it is called) is threatened by invaders from Kotuo, and Miaka volunteers to be the long-awaited priestess of Suzaku ("Vermilion Sparrow"), who will assemble the legendary heroes known as the Seven Stars of Suzaku and save the world.

Though Yu Watase's original manga in *Flower* magazine dated back to 1992, *Fushigi Yugi* was swamped by the later success of the superior **Escaflowne**, making *FY* look like a lackluster copy. This anime's problems include an intensely irritating heroine, Miaka, with all the charm of a spoiled child, conspicuously cheap animation that often has to resort to static pans, and a forgettable plot assembled from off-the-peg clichés. The Emperor Hotohori falls in love with Miaka, but she loves Tamahome, a predictable love triangle which causes a falling-out with her friend Yui. Nevertheless, *FY* clearly struck a chord with an audience too young to remember *The Neverending Story* or the **Wizard of Oz**, and the series gained an enthusiastic fan following in both Japan and the U.S. The second season (episodes 27–52) changes slightly, with the death of one of Miaka's guardians, the removal of some of the risqué humor that occasionally lightened the first season, and an endless succession of arbitrary magical obstacles to stretch out Miaka's journey.

Two TV specials were little more than clip shows of the highlights of the first 33 episodes, but a true sequel soon continued the series on video. The first video series was set a month after the close of the TV version, with the events in Konan returning to haunt the cast back on Earth in both serious and parody versions on the same tapes. Looking suspiciously like a third TV season consigned to video after falling ratings, 1997's second "video" series plunged the cast into a new conflict over the mystic Jewel of Memory. A later Yu Watase work, **Ceres: Celestial Legend**, soon followed in both Japan and the U.S.

A four-part video sequel, *FY: Universe of the Four Gods* (*FY: Eikoden*, 2001), was directed by Nanako Shimazaki, which threatens the happily-ever-after of the original by introducing a love-rival for Miaka, who enters the fantasy world determined to overthrow her and win her man for herself.

FUTURE BOY CONAN
1978. JPN: *Mirai Shonen Conan*. AKA: *Conan the Boy in Future*. TV series, movie. DIR: Hayao Miyazaki, Isao Takahata, Keiji Hayakawa. SCR: Takaaki Nakano, Soji Yoshikawa. DES: Hayao Miyazaki, Yasuo Otsuka. ANI: Yoshiaki Kawajiri, Hideo Kawauchi. MUS: Kenichiro Ikehama. PRD: Nippon Animation, NHK. 25 mins. x 26 eps. (TV), 123 mins. (m).

Twenty years after a devastating nuclear war in 2008, only scattered communities of humans are left living on the small islands that were once mountaintops. Conan grows up on his island with his grandfather, believing themselves to be the last survivors of their race until a young girl, Lana, is washed up on their shore. She is a refugee from the evil military kingdom of Industria, which is trying to revive the use of dangerous energy sources. A first-time directing job for Hayao Miyazaki that incorporated elements he would later reuse in his NAUSICAÄ and CASTLE IN THE SKY (though the original genesis of *FBC* lay in the novel *The Incredible Tide* [1970], by Alexander Key). The series was also edited into *FBC: The Movie*, which was released three months before CASTLE OF CAGLIOSTRO and, hence, could be argued on a technicality to be Miyazaki's first "movie."

The franchise was revived as *FBC 2: Taiga Adventure* (1999), directed by Miyazaki's former assistant Keiji Hayakawa, though its relationship to the original is extremely tenuous. The eponymous Taiga and his archaeologist father, Professor Dyno, are searching for ancient artifacts in South America, where there was supposedly a mysterious culture that could build great metallic birds 20 thousand years before. As he fights with treasure hunters for control of the ancient power-stones, Taiga discovers that the ancient O-Parts devices can power land, sea, and air machines that are each designed to look like a giant animal. In other words, it's a rehash of BABEL II and MYSTERIOUS CITIES OF GOLD with a name designed to promise more than it actually delivers.

FUTURE COP URASHIMAN

1983. JPN: *Mirai Keisatsu Urashiman*. AKA: *Rock 'n' Cop*. TV series. DIR: Koichi Mashimo, Shinya Sadamitsu, Takaaki Ishiyama. SCR: Hirohisa Soda, Haruya Yamazaki, Kenji Terada. DES: Takashi Nakamura, Shigeru Kato, Chuichi Iguchi. ANI: Takashi Nakamura, Kunihiko Yuyama. MUS: Shinsuke Kazato. PRD: Tatsunoko Pro. 25 mins. x 50 eps. An SF adaptation of *Urashima Taro* (see JAPANESE FOLK TALES) about Ryo Urashima, a young private investigator from 1983 Tokyo who is whisked to the year 2050 by Professor Q, a mad scientist working for the evil, blue-skinned Führer. The trip into the future subjects Ryo to the "Urashima Effect"—he loses his memory and develops superhuman powers. Führer plans to use Ryo for his own ends, but Ryo is found by the police, who enlist him in their robot police unit, Magnapolice 88, along with a handsome wiseguy, Claude Mizusawa, and token girl Sophia Nina Rose. A witty sci-fi spectacle, it begins with comedy business (as Ryo insists on using his 1983 Volkswagen Beetle instead of a 2050 police car) that soon takes a more serious turn as Ryu tracks down Führer's Necrime group and becomes involved in the power struggle between Führer and his assistant, Adolph von Ludovich.

FUTURE WAR 198X *

1982. Movie. DIR: Toshio Masuda, Tomohiro Katsumata. SCR: Yuji Takada. DES: Masami Suda. ANI: Masami Suda. MUS: Seiji Yokoyama. PRD: Tokkyu Agency, Toei. 125 mins. American scientist Bart, a specialist in Star Wars orbital antimissile lasers, defects on a Russian submarine, which is sunk by the U.S. Navy. His best friend, Mikumo, is ordered to come out of mourning to finish Bart's work, while U.S. president Gibson tries to calm the volatile diplomatic situation. His efforts fail, and border troubles between East and West Germany escalate into full-scale war. When American Secretary of Defense Bugarlin murders Chief Secretary Orlof of the Soviet Union, all negotiations break down, and atomic war breaks out.

A controversial anime production inspired in part by the best-selling *The Third World War, August 1985* by General Sir John Hackett, *FW198X* was based on actual projections from contemporary government reports and statistics. During production, there were protests about the "aggressive content" of the story, creating something of a media stir in Japan. *Future War 198X* was released on video in Australia, not in a "full" dub but in an original language version with occasional explicatory English narration.

F-ZERO FALCON LEGEND *

2003. JPN: *F-Zero Falcon Densetsu*. AKA: *F-0, F-Zero GP Legend*. TV series. DIR: Ayumi Tomobuki. SCR: Akiyoshi Sakai. DES: Toyoo Ashida, Shohei Kohara. ANI: Daisuke Yoshida. MUS: Takayuki Negishi. PRD: Ashi Pro, Dentsu, TV Tokyo, Nintendo. 23 mins. x 51 eps. Set in 2201, this racing game tie-in tips its hat to *Demolition Man*, but owes more to Japanese live-action hero shows, whose madly named supervillains and heroes have gifts handed down through time by magical mentors. An evil overlord, Emperor Black Shadow, leads the Dark Million organization and plans to use the Dark Matter Reactor, which grants the wishes of anyone who activates it, to take over the universe and devote it to evil. Ryu Suzaku (Rick Wheeler) is awakened from a 150-year cryogenic sleep to oppose him and fulfill the ancient Legend of the Falcon. He has become a member of the Elite Mobile Taskforce of the Galactic Space Federation, a group of pilots who compete in the F-Zero grand prix races popular throughout the Galaxy. He is not alone—his old girlfriend Haruka (Jody) was also in cryosleep and has also been awakened, but she is part of Dark Million, and now goes under the name of Miss Killer. Ryu's nemesis, arch-criminal Zoda, has also been resurrected from his cryo-prison by Black Shadow. The stage is set for a final confrontation, but not before various other characters, like fighting cyborg Mighty Gazelle and 97-year-old race pilot Ironman Neelson, have their cameos. A spin-off from Nintendo's 1990 video game of the same name, screened on Fox's 4Kids channel, whose audience was too young to remember CYBERFORMULA GPX.

G

GAD GUARD *

2003. TV series. DIR: Hiroshi Nishikori, Yoshikazu Miyao, Akihiko Nishiyama, Hideki Hashimoto, Yuichiro Miyake, Yutaka Hirata. SCR: Mayori Sekijima, Reiko Yoshida, Sadayuki Murai. DES: Masahiro Aizawa, Yoshitsune Izuna. ANI: Masahiro Aizawa. MUS: Kazuhiro Sawaguchi, Kohei Tanaka. PRD: Gonzo, Animax, Fuji TV. 25 mins. x 26 eps.

In the not-too-distant future, power shortages and energy crises force humanity to take drastic measures. Hajiki Sanada grows up on a planet divided into class-oriented enclaves or "units," where all power is shut off in his town at a regular midnight curfew. While working part-time as a delivery boy for a courier service, he touches the contents of the package he is supposed to be ferrying around and finds himself bonding with a robot made out of a special material. This "GAD-made" robot can reconstitute matter for him, making it a combination of the magical cat of **DORAEMON** and the fighting toys of **POKÉMON**.

Despite such derivative beginnings, *Gad Guard* has an undeniable style, informed more by the noirish look of recent fan favorites, with stark allegories of class struggle in the contrast between the poor Night Town and the privileged Gold Town. It also struggles to hang onto its PG rating, thanks to vampish female characters at odds with the squat, cartoony character designs inspired by late Tezuka productions.

Its hustlers, street kids, and lowlifes are distinctly occidental—*Gad Guard* is another anime hymn to life in the exotic, inscrutable West, where people have different hair colors, big noses, and, so the animators believe, more adventurous lives.

In this age of painfully cheap productions, Gonzo Digimation clearly had a little more money than usual from Fuji TV for this one. They pull out all the available stops to keep the show interesting, with impressive CG flashiness used on marble floors, lighting effects, and saturated colors. The crew also works harder than average, with nice little touches like a cat disturbing birds in the background, or the detailed clutter of the Sanada family kitchen. The music is a self-consciously jazzy respray of **COWBOY BEBOP**, courtesy of **GUNBUSTER**-composer Kohei Tanaka. The plot is **BRAIN POWERED** wearing a retro cloak, via **THE BIG O** and a touch of *Dark City*. In other words, it's a shameless collection of well-worn clichés, but creatively assembled and entertainingly presented. However, the initial run of 19 episodes on Fuji TV was bulked out with seven extras to complete the full run on AT-X; a piecemeal form of assembly that often results in episodes that merely seem to be marking time.

GAIKING *

1976. JPN: *Ozora Maryu Gaiking*. AKA: *Great Sky Dragon Gaiking; Daiking; The Protectors*. TV series. DIR: Tomoharu Katsumata, Takeshi Shirato, Masamune Ochiai, Hideo Takayashiki. SCR: Kunio Nakatani, Masao Murayama, Masaru Yamamoto, Soji Yoshikawa. DES: Takeshi Shirato, Akio Sugino, Dan Kobayashi. ANI: Takeshi Shirato, Moriyasu Taniguchi, Akio Sugino. MUS: Shunsuke Kikuchi. PRD: Toei, Fuji TV. 25 mins. x 44 eps., 25 minutes x 15+ eps. (TV2).

Sanshiro Tsuwabuki's dream of becoming a professional baseball player is crushed by an invasion of mysterious bird-men, the Dark Horror Army, sent by Prince Darius of Planet Zera (Zala) to kill any psychics who could be obstacles to their plans of world conquest. Zera needs Earth because Zera is just about to be engulfed by a black hole. In Toei Animation's first robot animation not to be based on a manga, Sanshiro is invited by Dr. Daimonji (Professor Hightech) to join the Great Sky Magic Dragon (Gaiking Space Dragon) combat force to fight back, and he duly does so. Shown as part of the **FORCE FIVE** series on U.S. television, for which Sanshiro's name was changed to Ares Astronopolis, which the producers must have deemed nicely inconspicuous. A sequel was broadcast in 2005 on TV Asahi, directed by Masahiro Hosoda.

GAINAX

Formed originally in 1982 as Daicon ("Radish") Films by a group of student fans intending to make an opening animation sequence for the Daicon III science fiction convention. Founder members included Hideaki Anno, Yoshiyuki Sadamoto, Takami Akai and Shinji Higuchi. Subsequently renamed Gainax (from *gaina*, a local dialect word for "huge") during preproduction on **WINGS OF HONNEAMISE**. Representative works include **THE SECRET OF BLUE WATER, GUNBUSTER, EVANGELION,** and **MAHOROMATIC,** but also numerous landmark games in the history of Japanese computing, particularly *Princess Maker*.

GALACTIC PIRATES *

1989. JPN: *Teki wa Kaizoku: Neko no Kyoen.* AKA: *The Enemy Is the Pirate: Banquet of Cats.* TV series. DIR: Shinya Sadamitsu, Kazuo Yamazaki. SCR: Akinori Endo. DES: Takayuki Goto. ANI: Takayuki Goto, Hiroshi Hamazaki. MUS: Air Pavilion. PRD: Madhouse, Kitty Film, Mitaka Studio, NHK2. 30 mins. x 6 eps.

Apollo the jive-talking cat and his human sidekick, Latell, are working in the AntiPirate Division of the police force sent to Mars to put a stop to the activities of the space raider Yomei. The officers are intent on convincing each other to resign but eventually manage to solve a case involving piracy, doublecross, people turning into cats all around them, and an interlude in which they discover that the Martians have built up a militaristic religion that practices ritual games of hyperviolent baseball. Based on a comedy SF novel by Chohei Kanbayashi, this is one of the earliest video series to be given a satellite TV broadcast to recoup costs, a practice that would become commonplace in the late 1990s. "Air Pavilion," who provides the soundtrack, is a supergroup comprising former members of Whitesnake, Iron Maiden, and Motorhead.

GALAXY ADVENTURES OF SPACE OZ

1992. JPN: *Space Oz no Boken.* TV series. DIR: Soji Yoshikawa, Yoshiaki Okumura, Katsumata Kanezawa, Shinichi Suzuki. SCR: Soji Yoshikawa, Yasuko Hoshikawa, Seiji Matsuoka, Hirokazu Mizude. DES: Yoshiaki Okumura. ANI: Ichiro Fukube, Osamu Kamijo, Seiji Kikuchi. MUS: Ryuichi Katsumasa. PRD: E&G, Enoki, TV Tokyo. 25 mins. x 26 eps.

Eight-year-old blonde Dorothy Gale and her genetically enhanced dog, Talk-Talk, are swept off planet New Kansas and land in the distant galaxy of Oz. There, she joins forces with Dr. Oz, Mosey (a boy companion), Chopper (the Tin Man as a C-3PO rip-off), Lionman (the Cowardly Lion posing as Rambo), and Plantman (the Scarecrow) in order to defeat the evil witch Gloomhilda. This involves a race to obtain the three magic crystals of Love, Wisdom, and Courage, before Gloomhilda's minions Bungle, Skumm, and Sludge. A rehash of **THE WIZARD OF OZ** that ends with the acquisition of the Rainbow Crystal, allowing Dorothy to return home (there being no place like it).

GALAXY ANGEL

2001. TV series. DIR: Morio Asaka, Ryo Mizuno. SCR: N/C. DES: Kanan, Kikaku Design Kobo Sensen. ANI: Kunihiko Hamada, Masaru Kitao. MUS: N/C. PRD: Madhouse, Animax. 12 mins. x 26 eps. (TV1), 10 mins. x 18 eps. (TV2), 28 mins. x 26 eps. (TV3), 12 mins. x 18 eps.

A century after the fall of the Galactic Network, the Transvaal Empire has risen on the ruins. However, the "lost technology" of the GN, looked after by priestesses called Moon Maidens, appears semimagical to the people of the Transvaal. Exiled prince Eonia kills King Gerrare and seizes control of the empire, but he is opposed by five pretty girls, the Angel Troopers, who steal a spaceship and team up with the young commander of the local militia. A sequel series, *Galaxy Angel Z* (2002), aired in nine half-hour slots, although each slot was split into two episodes. It was followed by *Galaxy Angel A* (2002) and *Galaxy Angel X* (2004). *Galaxy Angel*

Galaxy Adventures of Space Oz

was one of the first shows to achieve an unexpected online presence—its short episode length, sci-fi leanings, extremely limited animation, and cute female cast conspiring to make it an ideal commodity in Japan in the early days of Internet file-sharing and encouraging disproportionately wide merchandising tie-ins.

GALAXY EXPRESS 999 *

1978. JPN: *Ginga Tetsudo 999.* TV series, movie. DIR: Nobutaka Nishizawa, Masayuki Akehi, Kunihiko Yuyama. SCR: Hiroshi Yamaura, Keisuke Fujikawa, Yoshiaki Yoshida. DES: Leiji Matsumoto. ANI: Kazuo Matsubara. MUS: Nozomu Aoki, Godiego. PRD: Toei, Fuji TV. 25 mins. x 113 eps. (TV), 114 mins. (TVm1), 129 mins. (m1), 17 mins. (m2), 60 mins. (TVm2), 130 mins. (m3), 114 mins. (TVm3), 54 mins. (m4), 25 mins. x 6 eps. (Internet), 40 mins x 4 eps (*Maetel Legend*), 25 mins x 26 eps (*Railways*).

After his mother is killed by the evil count Kikai (Count Mecca), Tetsuro Hoshino (Joey) resolves to get an immortal metal body. Impossibly expensive on Earth, they are reputedly given away free to anyone who reaches Megalopolis, the last stop on the Galaxy Express. A ticket on the GE is also impossibly expensive, but the ethereal beauty Maetel (who looks uncannily like his mother) offers him one for free. She helps him to board the Galaxy Express 999 on the understanding that he must accompany her on her travels. In a long-running series based on Leiji Matsumoto's 1977 manga (distantly related to the same author's CAPTAIN HARLOCK series continuity), after killing the Count to avenge his mother, Tetsuro sets off with Maetel on a journey across the galaxy. After the movie edition, *Galaxy Express* (1979), the second movie was the super-short featurette *GE999: Through a Glass Clearly* (1980, *Gurasu no Clear*), a partial remake of the third TV episode. A third movie, *GE999: Last Stop Andromeda* (1981, *Andromeda no Shuchakueki*), is set two years after the series, when Tetsuro, now a freedom fighter on Earth, receives a distress call from Maetel and heads out to help her one last time. Fuji TV also broadcast three specials, beginning with *GE999: Can You Live Like a Warrior* (1979, *Senshi no Yo ni Ikirareru ka*), which combined scenes from episodes 12 and 13. *GE999: Emeraldas the Eternal Wanderer* (1980, *Endo no Tabibito Emeraldas*) expanded episode 22, which featured Maetel's sister, QUEEN EMERALDAS. The final TV movie, *GE999: Can You Love Like a Mother* (1980, *Kimi wa Haha no Yo ni Aiseru ka*), adapted parts of episodes 51 and 52, adding 47 minutes of all-new footage. The series received a very limited partial broadcast on local New York TV for the Japanese community with English subtitles. The first movie was released in the U.S. by Roger Corman's New World, which incurred the wrath of fans by renaming Harlock "Warlock" and giving him a John Wayne accent for his cameo appearance. He would also claim that Joey was searching the universe for revenge, that being a little easier to take than an upgraded cybernetic body, at least back then. Maetel would return for the video series *Maetel the Legend* (2000). The series would be remade to mark the 50th anniversary of Matsumoto's career as *The Galaxy Railways* (2003). Notes to this rerelease

emphasized Matsumoto's original inspiration, that when he came up to Tokyo as a young man, the railway network seemed to be the only part of postwar Japan that was still functioning, and hence the only symbol of hope for survival and renewal. See, however, NIGHT TRAIN TO THE STARS, which draws on a much older source for spacefaring expresses.

Shinichi Masaki's *Space Symphonic Poem Maetel* (*GE: Wasurareta Toki no Wakusei*, i.e. *The Planet That Time Forgot*, 2004), is a sequel to the *Maetel Legend* series, issued as a TV series on the Japanese digital channels SKY PerfecTV and Animax.

GALAXY FRAULEIN YUNA *

1995. JPN: *Ginga Ojosama Densetsu Yuna*. Video. DIR: Yoshinobu Yamaguchi. SCR: Satoru Akahori, Masashi Noro. DES: Katsumi Shimazaki, Mika Akitaka, Makoto Yamada. ANI: Ryoichi Oki. MUS: N/C. PRD: Animate Film, JC Staff. 30 mins. x 3 eps., 30 mins. x 2 eps.
A beauty contest is staged in present-day Tokyo with ulterior motives—as with BATTLE ATHLETES, it is really a front for choosing a champion to save the world. Yuna, the blond winner, is informed that, long ago, the Queen of Light fought the Queen of Darkness and lost the battle. All the remaining goodness of Light was concentrated in one of the good android survivors, Elna, whose duty it was to carry the Light forward for the next battle. As Elna's successor, Yuna has three android doubles for use on land, sea, and air, as well as a super-transformation ability that allows them to turn into the mighty El-Line robot.

Based on a 1992 game for the PC Engine, the combination of giant war machines and cloyingly cute girls was resurrected for *GFY: Fairy of Darkness* (*Ginga Ojosama Densetsu Yuna: Shinkai no Fairy*; 1996, released in the U.S. as *GFY Returns*), in which the evil Princess Mirage spreads false rumors that Yuna is fighting on the wrong side, sending the mysterious Fraulein D to ravage a few cities in Yuna's name just to make

sure that GP Officer Misaki will find lots of incriminating evidence. Yuna and her orally fixated friend Yuri must then fight off "D" and several of Mirage's minions. Yuna turns one of the three evil Apparition Sisters to the side of good by introducing her to the joys of shopping, and then the stage is set for a final, noisy showdown. Sold to the Japanese as "the last word in girls' anime," though thankfully that was a complete lie.

GALAXY SEARCH 2100

1986. JPN: *Ginga Tanken 2100: Border Planet*. TV special. DIR: Osamu Uemura, Mamoru Hamatsu. SCR: Osamu Tezuka. DES: Shinpei Ohara. ANI: Shinya Takahashi, Nobuhiro Okaseko. MUS: Ryotaro Haneda. PRD: Tezuka Pro, NTV. 79 mins.
A doomed romance from ASTRO BOY–creator Osamu Tezuka about sworn friends Subaru and Procyon almost falling out over their love for the pretty Mira. Eventually, Subaru steps aside, but Procyon contracts a deadly space disease soon after his wedding. Subaru discovers that the widow, whom he still loves, has contracted the disease that killed her husband. Subaru sets off across the galaxy in search of a cure, while Mira remains back on Earth in suspended animation. His quest takes him to a world of automated agricultural machinery, where humans are being turned into planet fertilizer. The next world he finds is ruled by "the Boss," who maroons travelers so he can salvage their spaceships. With the help of local girl Michelle, Subaru organizes a revolt and builds an escape vessel from salvaged parts. Further adventures follow on a planet of humanoids that go through a chrysalis stage, but Subaru finally returns with a cure for Mira. She is restored to life, but, though she is still young, Subaru's journey has aged him 50 years. Mira falls in love with the doctor who woke her, who is the spitting image of his father, Subaru. The aged Subaru comments to his wife, Michelle, that they make a lovely couple. A bittersweet romance

from Tezuka—compare to the similar **BANDAR BOOK: ONE MILLION A.D.**

GALERIANS: RION *

2004. Video. DIR: Masahiko Maesawa. SCR: Kang Chinfa. DES: Sho-U Tajima. ANI: N/C. MUS: Masahiko Hagio. PRD: Enterbrain Inc., Polygon Magic Inc. 73 mins.

It's 2156, and an insane supercomputer called Dorothy has taken control of the Earth after a devastating war. Dorothy has created powerful artifical beings to wipe out the human race. Vulnerable but incredibly powerful teenager Rion escapes from a hospital and eventually realizes that he is carrying part of the computer virus in his own head that can shut down Dorothy for good, if he can only track down Lilia, the daughter of Dorothy's designer Doctor Pascalle, who has the other part of the code. The result is a plodding sub–*Terminator* digital cartoon that often feels unsurprisingly as if one is simply watching someone else play the computer games *Galerians* and *Galerians: Ash* on which it was based—compare to **A.LI.CE**. The soundtrack of the English language release features music from 2004 from Slipknot, Skinny Puppy, Fear Factory et al. ●◐

GALL FORCE *

1986. Movie, video. DIR: Katsuhito Akiyama, Jun Fukuda, Koji Fukushima. SCR: Sukehiro Tomita, Kenichi Matsuzaki, Hideki Kakinuma. DES: Kenichi Sonoda, Jun Okada, Kimitoshi Yamane. ANI: Nobuyuki Kitajima, Masaki Kajishima. MUS: Ichizo Seo, Etsuko Yamakawa, Takehito Nakazawa. PRD: Animate, Artmic, AIC. 86 mins. (m), 45 mins. (*Destruction*), 60 mins. (*Stardust*), 60 mins. (*Rhea*), 45 mins. x 3 eps. (*Earth Chapter*), 45 mins. x 2 eps. (*New Era*), 30 mins. x 4 eps. (*Revolution*).

Elsa, Catty, Rabby, Pony, Patty, and Rumy are the crew of the Starleaf, a spaceship in the Solnoid Navy, at war with the alien Paranoids. Unknown to any but the highest-ranking officers, the Solnoid leaders have decided that the two species must unite to preserve the best qualities of both—the Solnoids are all female clones, so their gene-pool is self-limiting (compare to **VANDREAD**). Fighter pilot Lufy joins the Starleaf when her ship crashes onto the flight deck. Though she is a hostile, hot-tempered loner, the real source of danger is elsewhere. When Patty is injured in an encounter with the enemy, her "injury" is revealed as an accelerated pregnancy. She is about to become mother to a new race, providing they survive long enough to get her and her child to safety.

Based on a series of model features in *Model Graphix* magazine and illustrated with photos of the plastic cuties that inspired the characters, the original story for *GF* was accompanied by a manga from Hideki Kakinuma. Replaying both the sci-fi horror of *Alien* and its use of conspiratorial androids (Catty), the U.S. movie audience had Sigourney Weaver in a role written for a man, but the Japanese had an all-female crew whose heroism was counterbalanced by dollops of fluffiness. **GUNSMITH CATS**-creator Sonoda's designs for *GF* would establish him as a fan favorite. Subsequent parts of the saga were released on video, starting with *GFII: Destruction* (1987). Years after the violent conclusion of the movie, Lufy is found floating in space by the crew of the Solnoid ship Lorelei—as in *Aliens*. Most of the crew are androids, and one is identical to Catty. Lufy learns that the original Catty is the prime mover of the plan to interbreed the species, and her rescuers are en route to see if the plan is working. On Terra, Patty's half-Solnoid, half-Paranoid child and his mate, Starleaf-survivor Rumy, are starting a new race, but the war is still raging, and not everyone wants the plan to succeed. By *GFIII: Stardust War* (1988), the last remnants of both armies are still determined to annihilate each other and thwart the Unification Plan. A new *GF* team is set up, with *another* android Catty joining Lufy and some old friends to try and avert the final conflict. The plots were stuck in a rut by this time, but the theme of heroically cute young women fighting military boneheadedness and political machinations still had mileage in it.

Rhea Gall Force (1989) moves the action aeons into the future, when Patty's descendants have repopulated the ruined wasteland of Earth. On Earth's moon, an ancient crashed Paranoid spacecraft has "bred" cybernetic MMEs (Man-Made Existences). These cybernetic creatures turn on their creators and, à la *Terminator*, force a nuclear war. The only hope is to evacuate the survivors to Mars, regroup, and plan the repopulating of Earth. A small group led by Sandy Newman and her best friend Melodi resolves to save Earth's population. Though conceived as the first of a four-part series, the "Rhea" prefix was a victim of the same acrimonious split between the producers that plagued **BUBBLEGUM CRISIS**. Consequently, episodes 2–4 were released under a new title, renumbered 1–3 as the *GF: Earth Chapter* (1989) videos. The war machines led by computer entity Gorn, who wants to eliminate humankind, are opposed by Sandy and her comrades, while Catty is still pulling all the strings behind the scenes. Once again, two different species must come together if the best of both is to survive, and once again military forces are conspiring to annihilate everything in a vain quest for victory. Later episodes of the franchise hint further at the series' cleverest conceit—it is implied that the narrative is completely cyclical (a true "eternal story"), with look-alikes of the original cast continually reappearing, and Catty living through the entire process. Asides in the original reveal that the Solnoids' homeworld was planet "Marsus," whence they had fled to avoid a catastrophe on their real homeworld—the similarity to *Earth Chapter*'s "Mars" likely to be more than mere coincidence. By *GF New Era* (1991), the action moves to 2291, when the humans live in peace on Earth with the machine entities now called Yuman, but Yuman leader Gorn is not convinced it's over and plans a preemptive strike. Android Catty, still planning for survival, selects six young women for a dangerous mission. Catty still has a few secrets in store—she's been around the human race for longer than anyone knows and has always worked to prevent its extinction. But if this last remnant of humanity is wiped out, the galaxy will be left to the machines.

A final lackluster outing came in the form of *Gall Force: Revolution* (1996), a flashback to the time of the original *Gall Force*, with the crew (now played by different actresses) caught in the crossfire between the East and West Solnoids. However, it could be argued that this final chapter is not an inexact remake, but instead the beginning of another cycle—compare to the similarly mind-bending continuity of Urotsukidoji. See also SUPER-DEFORMED DOUBLE FEATURE. ○♥Ⓥ

GALLERY FAKE

2005. TV series. DIR: Akira Nishimori, Osamu Yamazaki. SCR: Masashi Sogo. DES: Toshiko Sasaki. ANI: N/C. MUS: Face 2 Fake. PRD: TV Tokyo. 25 mins. x 37 eps.

After he loses his job and reputation in a public scandal over a Monet painting, Reiji Fujita finds a new career as the curator of a gallery that specializes in forgeries of masterpieces. As a result, he is soon dragged into a world of international theft and double-crossing in an inadvertently educational refashioning of the art world crime stories of CAT'S EYE. Later episodes feature plotlines based on other artistic deceptions, the theft of the Hope Diamond, and the search for Eldorado. The original manga, by JUDGE-creator Fujihiko Hosono, is distinguished by its older target audience (it originally ran in the mature manga anthology *Big Comic Spirits*) and also the long time it took to come to the screen, taking 13 years from first publication to the broadcast of the first episode. But good things come to those who wait, and

Gallery Fake is a welcome change in contemporary TV schedules crowded with dysfunctional love stories and fighting monsters. Similar adventures featured in the live-action TV series *Mona Lisa's Smile* (*DE).

GALVION

1984. JPN: *Cho-kosoku Galvion*. AKA: *Superfast Galvion*. TV series. DIR: Akira Kamano. SCR: Tsunehisa Ito, Yoshihisa Araki, Yoshiyuki Suga, Haruya Yamazaki. DES: Yoshihisa Tagami. ANI: Hiroshi Negishi, Yoshinobu Shigeno. MUS: Masao Nakajima. PRD: Kokusai Eiga, TV Asahi. 25 mins. x 22 eps.

In the 23rd century, aliens seal off Earth with the impenetrable Sigma Barrier, ready to begin their conquest. United Nations police chief Ray Midoriyama sets up Circus, a team of robot pilots charged with fighting off the would-be world rulers of the Shadow Society. Unable to find anyone foolhardy enough to take the job, he offers it to convicted criminals Mu and Maya on the understanding that each task they perform will earn them days off their sentences. A similar setup to the later CYBER CITY OEDO 808, and just as truncated, it was pulled off the air at short notice, with the rest of the plot hastily reported in a voice-over at the end of episode 22. A rare anime job for GREY: DIGITAL TARGET–creator Yoshihisa Tagami, whose distinctive snub-nosed style can be seen in all the main character designs.

GAMBA'S ADVENTURE

1975. JPN: *Gamba no Boken*. TV series, movie. DIR: Osamu Dezaki, Kyosuke Mikuriya, Mochitsugu Yoshida, Nobuo Takeuchi. SCR: Michiru Majima, Yutaka Kaneko, Atsushi Yamatoya, Soji Yoshikawa, Hideo Takayashiki. DES: Osamu Dezaki. ANI: Yoshio Kabashima. MUS: Takeo Yamashita. PRD: Kyodo Eiga, NTV, Tokyo Movie Shinsha. 25 mins. x 26 eps. (TV), 100 mins. (m1), 75 mins. (m2).

When Chuta, a badly injured mouse, staggers off a ship in Tokyo Harbor, he bumps into out-of-towners Gamba and

Bobo, who are at a party being given by Yoisho, the sailor-mouse. Chuta tells the local mice that he has escaped from Devil's Island, where Norio the evil ermine (white weasel) has crushed the mice with his reign of terror. Local tough-mouse Gamba rashly promises to help and leads a group of rodents on a long odyssey that eventually brings them to the island—they are hampered in the early stages by not actually knowing where it is.

Based on the novel *Bokensha-tachi (The Adventurers)* by Atsuo Saito, four 13-episode seasons were originally planned but only two were produced, leading to some frantic replanning after episode 14. In 1984, the TV series was edited into a movie for theatrical release, as *Theatrical Version Gamba: The Adventurers: Gamba and his Friends (Gekijoban Gamba Bokensha-tachi Gamba to Nanahiki no Nakama.)* Cutting out the subplots, Dezaki focused on the Noroi storyline. A new movie, *The Adventure of Gamba and the Otter (Gamba no Kawauso no Boken)* was released in theaters by TMS in 1991. Directed by Shunji Oga, written by Nobuaki Kishida, and with music by Hiroaki Kondo, the designs and Shunichi Suzuki's animation direction are faithful to the original. Manga tie-ins appeared in *Yoiko* and *Shogaku 123* magazines.

GAMBLER LEGEND TETSUYA

2000. JPN: *Shobushi Densetsu Tetsuya*. TV series. DIR: Nobutaka Nishizawa, Yuji Endo, Satoshi Nakamura. SCR: Yoshiyuki Suga. DES: Hidemi Kuma. ANI: Junichiro Taniguchi. MUS: Kuniaki Haishima. PRD: Toei, TV Asahi. 25 mins. x 20 eps.

In 1946, in a Shinjuku still reeling from the effects of the Pacific War, young Tetsuya Asada learns the secrets of mahjong from an old man. He meets his mentor Boshu and becomes a famous mahjong player and novelist, eventually earning the title Jong Sei (Jong Saint) and becoming the subject of a manga in *Shonen Magazine*, which goes on to win the Kodansha Manga Award. Then his life story is adapted into an anime, shown in the graveyard slot on Japanese TV.

GAME CENTER ARASHI

1982. TV series. DIR: Tameo Ogawa. SCR: Soji Yoshikawa. DES: Mitsuru Sugiyama. ANI: Kazuyuki Okaseko. MUS: Koji Makaino. PRD: Shinei, Nippon TV. 25 mins. x 26 eps.

An early spin-off of the craze for computer games, as Japan's national Invader Game champion Arashi ("Storm") Ishii discovers that while he is bottom of the class at school, he is unmatched with a joystick. Slowly developing a friendship with his rivals Satoru and Ippeita, he treats computer games with the reverence of martial arts, developing special attacks such as the Blazed Top, Vacuum Hurricane Shot, and Fish Stance. In other words, AIM FOR THE ACE, but less athletic.

GAMING AND DIGITAL ANIMATION

In the last two decades, graphics and computer gaming have exerted a growing influence on anime TECHNOLOGY AND FORMATS, until the concerns of gaming companies largely achieved dominance over those of filmmakers. As Asia's postwar industries rebuilt their economies through consumer durables and electronics, children traded their balls and skipping ropes for plastic boxes capable of generating fantasy worlds. From playing with each other, children have shifted over four decades to watching TV shows *about* playing with each other. Developments in computing gave them something even more seductive than television, the ability to step into the fantasy and exert some control, while the rise of the Internet meant that they could build themselves an entire fantasy existence online. Where children would once reenact their favorite TV episodes on the school playground, they are now just as likely to join an online game version, and are encouraged to do so by a corporate marketing machine out to foster brand identity.

Early computer games in Japan swiftly made use of the graphic abilities of anime and manga artists. The pixels available onscreen might have been limited, but box art and storylines could still exploit the look and style of anime. With the greater memory available in coin-operated games using solid-state electronics, games companies were also able to use more advanced graphics. The strip game *Mah Jong Pai Pai* tried to titillate players with the addition of photographs of scantily-clad girls, but lack of memory made the use of anime-style illustrations far more effective, as first used in *Mah Jong Game* (1978). Anime and gaming, particularly erotic gaming, have been inextricably linked ever since, with many anime staff and production companies moonlighting on game productions through the 1980s.

In the early 1980s, a crash in the American console games market coincided with the rise of Nintendo, Sony, and Sega as games producers in Japan and with falling prices of computer power worldwide. Home computers, however, were slow to catch on in Japan—as late as the early 1990s, word processors were still unpopular, and anime scripts were being written by hand. A few directors realized that the growing power of computers would allow them to cut certain corners. The first demonstrable use of computer graphics in anime was in Osamu Dezaki's GOLGO 13: THE PROFESSIONAL (1983), in a helicopter assault sequence. This, however, was purely for show—the scene gained nothing from the use of digital animation and was instead a mere gimmick. The limitations of computer graphics at the time restricted Dezaki to using animation for his vehicles, and not for the more complex polygons that would have been required for people.

Before the advent of high memory capacity sufficient to make an entire anime by digital methods, computer graphics remained a showy special effect, best utilized where it was cheapest and most visible. It appeared in panels, viewscreens, and, in LENSMAN (1984), in the opening credits, where a single piece of footage could be reused for maximum impact over many episodes.

In 1986, RUNNING BOY and SUPER MARIO BROTHERS tied in the race to become the first gaming tie-in anime. Digital animation was not a feature of either—instead, their relation to the gaming world was one of investment and sponsorship. Toy tie-ins such as GUNDAM and the *Mighty Morphin' Power Rangers* (*DE) had already shown the influence that sponsors could have on television production; now it was gaming companies that found their profits increasing, along with their desire to promote their products through an anime spin-off. GREY: DIGITAL TARGET, the ultimate satire of the eternal escalation of game-based plotting, appeared in anime form in the same year.

Many games suffer in their anime adaptation from an overly simplified quest- or combat-based narrative. Shoot-em-ups like *Gradius*, adapted into anime form as SALAMANDER (1988), present problematic material, particularly outside the undemanding children's field. Gisaburo Sugii's masterful attempt to make something interesting out of STREETFIGHTER II (1994) helped create a series of new traditions and clichés for game adaptations, many based loosely on the conventions found in the sports anime of the past—such as the plucky outsider, evil rivals, and doomed mentors of TOSHINDEN and TEKKEN.

The short, limited "cut scenes" of gaming, like advertising before it, presented the ideal platform for experimenting with new filming techniques, many of which were later incorporated into anime. MACROSS PLUS (1994) and, most significantly, Mamoru Oshii's GHOST IN THE SHELL (1995), used computers as tools for recreating realistic flaws in film—lens flares and moments of fuzzy focus, designed to accentuate the feeling of watching a live-action movie. Oshii dispensed with the rostrum camera of cel animation, instead scanning images directly into a computer. This allowed not only the integration of digital special effects, but made 2D (cel) animation elements for the first time as easy to manipulate as 3D elements. It also spelled the beginning of the end for cel animation, which was simply no longer necessary if everything could be digitized. Before long, the price of computer power had fallen to the point where Toei Animation regarded the purchase of a number of computers to be economical—1997 saw episodes of DOCTOR SLUMP and SPOOKY KITARO made wholly inside a computer, resembling cel animation but actually fully "digital" in their construction.

The large unit costs of games means that a successful gaming company has much higher budgets to play with. By the late 1990s, with anime budgets squeezed ever tighter, many of the talents who might have previously worked in TV animation instead migrated to the higher returns of computing. The game *Scandal* (2000), animated by Production IG, contained three hours of animation, ironically assembled at a higher budget than many "real" anime on television. Those anime that flourished on television often did so with the heavy backing of games concerns—POKÉMON, BOMBERMAN, and DIGIMON, to name a few. Their emphasis is often based on the collecting of cards, toys, or other cheaply mass-produced items that can be marketed to young consumers during the commercial breaks.

Animators' careers had followed roughly the same pattern since the 1950s, with artists taking low-paid jobs as in-betweeners, learning their trade as they rose through the ranks to key animator and perhaps director. Such career paths became rarer, as much low-ranking work was farmed out abroad, and computers were increasingly dominant in the local industry. Hayao Miyazaki once even seriously suggested setting up a "living museum" of old-school animators, who would continue to work using cel methods, lest skills completely atrophy. By 1998, SERIAL EXPERIMENTS LAIN took a bleak

but clear-eyed view of the fascination of the Internet, reflecting the mindset of a generation for whom the postwar social ethic had no further relevance, and posing the question: does the physical world have anything to offer young people that can match what they find online?

The new generation of animators has grown up divorced from the former apprenticeship skills of cel animation. Instead, they were graphic designers and computer animators used to working directly with machines, and often for bosses whose background was not in art, but in marketing or production. The first signs of this group's very different working methods appeared at the end of the 20th century with several animated works that seemed more inspired by the look of polygon-based games than cel-based animation. VISITOR (1998) and A.LI.CE (1999) fought to be identified as anime's "first" 3D animated feature, their rudimentary puppet-style animation soon trumped by that in AURORA (2000) and BLUE REMAINS (2000). Notably, many CG anime from this period take place underwater—as with BLUE SUBMARINE NO. SIX, the reduced depth perception, limited underwater color schemes, and heightened interference from bubbles all helped obscure any joins between 2D and 3D animation. Also, "floating" characters, whether in zero gravity or underwater, were not obliged to touch the ground, and thereby saved on more expensive animation of feet.

Anime at the turn of the century initially aspired to imitate live-action itself—audiences often expected to marvel not at the story, but at the latest feats of animation. *Final Fantasy: The Spirits Within* (2001), made in America but with Japanese money, was derided as an expensive flop, although the authors continue to suspect that its "failure" was a handy way of writing off the development costs of important new software that continues to be applied in the Japanese games industry. However, in the wake of its poor

box office performance animators turned aside from any direct attempts to emulate reality. Digital animation was employed on live-action films such as *Casshern* (2004) as a special effect, but within animation itself, animators returned to a more cartoonish look in works such as KAI DOH MARU (2001). APPLESEED (2004) employed a method called "toon shading" to make 3D animation look more like old-fashioned cels.

The prominence of gaming companies has become most obvious in a series of takeovers and acquisitions in 2005, with the formation of the Namco-Bandai conglomerate, Sega's acquisition of a controlling share in the anime studio Tokyo Movie Shinsha, and Takara's buyout of anime studio Tatsunoko. Such changes point to even more games-related tie-ins by 2010. Particularly when one considers the number of anime based on dating-simulation or erotic games, it is fair to claim that the majority of anime are now no longer based on manga, but on software.

But even as the conglomerates accrete into larger behemoths, the digital age also offers more opportunities for the independents. Digital images can easily be put to other uses, for example in manga or merchandise. COBRA-creator Buichi Terasawa has long championed the creative freedom and control the computer gives to artists, and makes all his work on an Apple Macintosh for multimedia export. As the possibilities of Internet and mobile network distribution expand, the niche for those who want to make and present their own work in their own way will widen.

In a virtual repeat of the limits and demands of early arcade games, the modern vogue for mobile phone distribution favors similar materials—the simpler the better, leading to titles such as BLACK JACK *Flash* and LEGEND OF DUO making a virtue of their cheap animation. The advent of the mobile phone has also brought a new lease on life to older series, such as ROBOTECH, reborn on mobile phones where the lines and crackles of old age in its images are less visible on a smaller screen.

Distribution is key to success in anime, as in most mass media. Creators whose vision is hard to package for mass sales (like Bak Ikeda, director of **PINMEN**) have traditionally languished on the arts festival circuit, or done private work alongside a more conventional career. The turn of the millennium has seen individual creators able to work with little or no outside intervention, particularly now that the kind of software that the animators of the 1980s could not have even imagined is available off the shelf to private individuals. **VOICES OF A DISTANT STAR** (2002) and **PALE COCOON** (2005) are two of the most noticeable of these new "home-grown" works, ironically returning the medium to its **EARLY ANIME** roots of lone hobbyists tinkering in their lounges with a new art form.

GANBALIST HAYAO

1996. AKA: *"Persevere-ist" Hayao*. TV series. DIR: Hajime Kamegaki, Shinichi Watanabe. SCR: Katsuhiko Chiba. DES: Hideyuki Motohashi. ANI: Hideyuki Motohashi. MUS: Hiroaki Arisawa. PRD: Sunrise, Yomiuri TV. 25 mins. x 30 eps.

A boy in the first year of junior high decides to become an Olympic-class gymnast despite having no clue about the amount of effort and hard work involved. An uninspired retread of **AIM FOR THE ACE** and other sports anime, given extra clout because the author of the original *Shonen Sunday* manga was Shinji Morisue, himself a former Olympic gymnast.

GANBARUGAR

1991. JPN: *Genki Bakuhatsu Ganbarugar*. AKA: *Happy Explosion Ganbarugar*. TV series. DIR: Toshifumi Kawase. SCR: Kenichi Kanemaki, Manabu Nakamura. DES: Takamitsu Kondo, Akira Kikuchi, Takahiro Yamada. ANI: Masamitsu Hidaka. MUS: N/C. PRD: Sunrise, TV Tokyo. 25 mins. x 47 eps.

Eldoran, the Knight of Light, gives teenage Torio a giant robot as long as he promises to use it to defend the Earth from alien invaders. In this typical Sunrise robot show, he luckily gets his chance, as flying space-whales, magical dimension holes, and time-slips test his mettle and his ability to persevere (*ganbaru* in Japanese). The *Ganbarugar Encyclopedia* (1992) was a parody episode released straight to video, directed by Kunio Ozawa.

GANDHARA

1998. JPN: *Nessa no Ha-o: Gandhara*. AKA: *Lord of the Desert: Gandhara; Gandalla*. Video. DIR: Hidehito Ueda, Toshifumi Kawase. SCR: Akiyoshi Sakai, Kazuhiko Kobe. DES: Haruhiko Mikimoto, Junichi Haneyama, Yasushi Moriki. ANI: Masami Nagata. MUS: Toshiyuki Watanabe. PRD: Ashi Pro, Yoyogi Animation Gakuin, WOWOW. 25 mins. x 26 eps.

A group of teenagers struggles to make the big time with their amateur band, though their fortunes improve considerably when they take on a new lead vocalist, Emma Branton. As the group ducks and dives through seedy agents and dangerous deals in the media world, lead guitarist Yuki begins to wish he had never agreed to support Emma, but he reluctantly helps her career out of his own feelings of responsibility for her missing brother, presumed dead. Meanwhile, deep in the sand dunes, the people known as the Sunlight are busily resurrecting an ancient demon, the titular Lord of the Desert, master of Lovecraftian horrors, who may be supplicated and partly controlled by music. The band is drawn into the conflict, in a desperate attempt to create a new music-led anime franchise defeated by cheapskate 1990s production values. "Superior to **MACROSS**," was the unfounded claim of the ads at the time, a boast as risible as the characters' own comparison of themselves with the early Doors. Though looking suspiciously like a retread of Clive Smith's *Rock and Rule* (1983), the anime was supposedly inspired by the

song "Gandhara," a 1980s favorite that closed the live-action series *Monkey* (see **JOURNEY TO THE WEST**), though this impoverished anime sadly lacks any other relation.

GANKUTSUOU *

2004. JPN: *Gankutsu-o*. AKA: *King of the Cave; The Count of Monte Cristo*. TV series. DIR: Mahiro Maeda. SCR: Shuichi Kamiyama. DES: Hidenori Matsubara, Anna Sui. ANI: Gonzo Digimation. MUS: Jean Jacques Burnel. PRD: Mahiro Maeda, Gonzo, Media Factory. 25 mins. x 24 eps.

Bored aristocrat Albert de Morcerf sets out on an interplanetary Grand Tour with his friend Franz d'Epinay. In the city of Luna on the Moon, they are rescued from bandits and drawn into the pomp and circumstance that surrounds a blue-skinned, pointy-eared, fabulously wealthy man of mystery known as the Count of Monte Cristo. The ostentatious Count has style, wit, and an undeniable mean streak. In spite of rumors that the Count may be a vampire, Albert is dazzled and flattered by him but Franz is suspicious. Neither knows that Albert's mother was once the fiancée of Edmond Dantes—the Count's personal name. The families of Albert, Franz, and Albert's fiancée Eugine were all involved in a terrible injustice; the Count has spent years hatching his revenge and Albert is about to become part of his scheme. Increasingly isolated from his friends by his fascination with the Count, Albert loses his whole world. Yet even as the Count sees his plans come to fruition and he returns the evil done to him to the child of his enemy, he is moved by Albert's similarity to himself when young.

Maeda originally wanted to animate an existing SF story based on the 1844 novel by Alexandre Dumas, creator of the **THREE MUSKETEERS**, published in Japanese as *King of the Cave*. When he was unable to secure the rights to the adaptation, Maeda returned to the original novel to create his own SF version, which would also run in a manga version in *Comic Afternoon*. Dumas' story of a man unjustly outlawed from society and his plot to take revenge on the three men who wronged him forms the basis for dazzling artistic reinvention. This version not only adds sci-fi elements like ULYSSES 31 or ALEXANDER, but also tells the story from the point of view of a relatively minor character in the original. The result is a gripping anime that is one of the gems of the early 21st-century medium, helped considerably by the passion of Dumas' original. Maeda is renowned as a master at combining 2D cel animation and 3D models, as he did in BLUE SUBMARINE NO. SIX and the *Second Renaissance* sequences in *Animatrix*. The crew supposedly built a complete 3D CGI model of their future Paris so that Maeda could set his scenes anywhere in the city. The use of outlines filled with flat pattern to represent body and clothing elements produces images of baroque extravagance, filling the screen with a visual richness rare in animation. For anyone interested in pure, dynamic style, this is a series to treasure. Burnel, bass player with the Stranglers, is an interesting choice as composer; this is his first anime score. Renowned fashion designer Anna Sui worked her way onto the credits for some costumes sported by the female characters in the show's grand finale. Other sources imply that she designed all the costumes, although that makes us wonder why it would be news that she did so in the final episode. Note that the *King of the Cave* alternate title is not always applied even in Japan. A black-and-white live-action TV series based on the original Dumas source was broadcast on Kansai TV from 1955 to 57, under the title *Kenshi Monte Cristo (Fencer Monte Cristo)*.

GANTZ *

2004. TV series. DIR: Ichiro Itano. SCR: Masashi Sogo, Seishi Togawa. DES: Naoyuki Onda, Toshihiro Nakajima. ANI: Hidemasa Arai. MUS: Natsuki Togawa. PRD: Gonzo, Fuji TV, Shochiku, GDH. 24 mins. x 26 eps.

Sullen, resentful teenager Kei and his estranged buddy Masaru die in a train accident, only to be apparently resurrected in a mismatched team of similarly unfortunate individuals, including a suicidal beauty, luckless gangsters, a baffled teacher, and a creepy schoolboy. Subject to draconian control by the Gantz, a mysterious black sphere, they are handed X-ray guns and told to hunt onion-based alien life-forms or die again.

Like *Battle Royale* crashed into *Wings of Desire* with courtesy breasts, *Gantz* throws everyday people into a life-or-death conflict, but focuses on their humdrum musings—what to wear, how to impress girls, who gets the rocket launcher. Based on a manga by Hiroya Oku, the brains behind the soft-core jailbait fantasy STRANGE LOVE, *Gantz* is a black comedy of manners. Its leading men have learned how to be heroes from anime, comparing themselves to characters from DRAGON BALL and FIST OF THE NORTH STAR—"Oh wait! I'm already dead!" proclaims a joyous Kei as he attempts a death-defying leap. It also reveals internal thoughts, affording snatches of personal inner monologues, warts and all. Nowhere is this more apparent than in the early train scene, where commuters studiously ignore a drunken tramp who has fallen on the railway track. Kei only offers to help because he is shamed into action by personal contacts, a rather British form of control through embarrassment that also afflicts his bickering, lustful associates in the afterlife. The voice-over exposition is also a handy aid in getting around primitive lip-sync in a cash-strapped animation budget.

The agents are also made to wear fetishistic skintight collars specially reinforced to protect the neck—if the aliens break an agent's neck, death is real and permanent. When the chosen agents return from each mission, Gantz displays another message showing their "score," as if Tokyo was a vast arcade and the battle was some grotesque shoot-'em-up. They pass the time between missions watching TV,

which is how Kei and Masaru learn their bodies have never been found. They've been registered as missing ever since the subway accident. They decide to try and get their ordinary, boring, problem-filled high school lives back, leaving the battle to save the Earth to others.

Gantz seems to be one of the first TV anime to have been intended less for a broadcast experience than for TiVo or DVD viewing in larger chunks. The ticking time limit on missions extends across several 25-minute episodes, and the content was something that even director Ichiro Itano, no stranger to controversy after ANGEL COP and VIOLENCE JACK, did not expect to make it onto TV. In a candid interview included in the DVD extras, he reminisces about the good old days when bones snapped on prime time in TIGER MASK, and intelligently identifies *Gantz*, nihilism, lack of affect, voyeurism, and all as a touchstone for understanding modern youth's obsessions; in that regard it is worthy of comparison with PARANOIA AGENT. Episodes 1-11 were broadcast, heavily censored, on Fuji TV beginning in April 2004. The so-called *Gantz: Second Stage* began with episode 14 and aired uncut on satellite TV network AT-X. Episodes 12 and 13 only appeared on the DVD release, for a total of 26 episodes. *Gantz* becomes increasingly erotic in the second half, as the agents start to take advantage of their virtually indestructible status, although Kei remains frustrated with his feelings for a girl who does not realize that he has saved her "life." ●NV

GARAGA *

1989. JPN: *Hyper Psychic Geo Garaga*. Movie. DIR: Hidemi Kuma. SCR: Hidemi Kuma. DES: Moriyasu Taniguchi. ANI: N/C. MUS: Tatsumi Yano. PRD: AVN, Asmic. 100 mins.

The year is 2755, and humanity has traveled out to the stars with the aid of the jump-gate known as God's Ring. The starship Xebec is forced to crash-land on a world inhabited by psychics who use intelligent apes as warriors.

Based on a manga by Satomi Mikuriya, whose other SF works include *Legend of Darkness*, NORA, and *Broken Passport*, as well as the manga that inspired KING ARTHUR AND THE KNIGHTS OF THE ROUND TABLE.

GARDLES, THE

1974. JPN: *Hajime Ningen Gardles*. AKA: *First People Gardles, First Human Giatrus*. TV series. DIR: Osamu Dezaki (as Makura Saki), Eiji Okabe, Kyosuke Mikuriya, Ryu Sakamoto, Masami Hata. SCR: Haruya Yamazaki, Noboru Shiroyama, Tsunehisa Ito, Hideo Kuju, Seiji Matsuoka, Yu Yamamoto, Yoshihisa Araki. DES: Shunji Sonoyama. ANI: Tatsuo Kasai. MUS: Hiroshi Kamayatsu, Mamoru Fujisawa (i.e., Joe Hisaishi). PRD: TMS. 25 mins. x 77 eps.
Created by Shunji Sonoyama, this is a comedy of everyday life in prehistoric times, an anime *Flintstones*—with each episode split into two, and hence sometimes listed as a 154-episode series. "Dad," the caveman protagonist lives with his wife, "Mom," and children in a cave, and makes rudimentary inventions and discoveries. His brews are a little less palatable than Fred Flintstone's—he drinks monkey juice, made by eating and regurgitating monkeys—and his black-haired wife wears her hair like Wilma's, with a bone through her chignon, but with one ample breast usually displayed outside her bearskin. Each episode contained two short scenarios, many featuring the extremely stupid gorilla pal Dotekin. As GON THE FIRST MAN, the eldest son of the Gardles family starred in his own anime in 1994. Compare to KUM-KUM. **Ⓝ**

GARDURIN

1990. Video. DIR: Toyoo Ashida, Takao Kado. SCR: Michiru Shimada. DES: Mari Toyonaga. ANI: Kenichi Endo. MUS: N/C. PRD: Ashi Pro. 45 mins.
Ryu, an intergalactic trader, and his robot sidekick, MOS, are forced to make an emergency landing on planet Gardurin. Initially keen on repairing his ship and returning home, Ryu adopts the new world as his own and becomes a hero by righting wrongs among the locals. Based on a computer game.

GASARAKI *

1997. TV series. DIR: Ryosuke Takahashi. SCR: Toru Nozaki, Chiaki Konaka. DES: Shuko Murase, Shinji Aramaki, Yutaka Izubuchi, Atsushi Yamagata. ANI: Tatsuya Suzuki, Takuya Suzuki. MUS: Kuniaki Haishima. PRD: Sunrise, TV Osaka. 25 mins. x 25 eps.
As NATO forces fight a minor war against the new Middle Eastern nuclear power of Belgistan, the ancient Japanese Gowa arms-trading dynasty makes preparations to sneak its new humanoid combat robots (Tactical Armor) into the conflict as a "live" testing ground. In cahoots with the black operations division of the Japanese Self-Defense Force, the Gowas have a secret of their own—they also intend to road-test their private top secret weapon. Family scion Yushiro Gowa is a psychic warrior who displaces his energies through a form of enhanced Noh performance. However, as the weapons go into action, Yushiro encounters Miharu, a beautiful, mysterious psychic, working for the tip-top-secret organization Symbol.

Gasaraki

© SUNRISE • TVO

One of the best of the EVANGELION clones of the late 1990s, *Gasaraki* successfully duplicates its predecessor's confused kids, military conspiracy, and electrifying action. Miharu is an obvious respray of Rei Ayanami (the words "mysterious girl" appearing depressingly often on 1990s press releases), while Yushiro's peculiarly dramatic powers are a welcome change from nebulous "natural" abilities. Director Takahashi, renowned since VOTOMS as the father of realistic robot shows, does not stint on the gritty action, a tactic aided greatly by the script's use of actual Gulf War events and news reports with the names changed, which adds a subtle note of realism.

GATE KEEPERS *

2000. TV series. DIR: Junichi Sato, Koichi Chiaki, Yasuhiro Takemoto. SCR: Hiroshi Yamaguchi, Hideki Mitsui, Aya Matsui. DES: Keiji Goto, Mahiro Maeda. ANI: Inao Takahashi. MUS: Kohei Tanaka. PRD: Gonzo, WOWOW. 25 mins. x 26 eps., 30 mins. x 6 eps. (v).
In 1969, Japanese schoolboy Shun Ukiya is co-opted into AEGIS (Alien Exterminating Global Intercept System), an international organization founded to hold off invading aliens. These crea-

tures feed on human selfishness, possessing human hosts and transforming them into rampaging monsters. They can only be held off by operatives with "Gate" powers, young psychics whose latent abilities are awakened by trauma or powerful emotions. *GK* is an artful combination of the Cold War paranoia of *The Invaders* with the desperate battle and psychological angst of EVANGELION and the large female supporting cast of TENCHI MUYO! The show was previewed in a manga version by NADESICO-designer Keiji Goto. The six-part video series *Gate Keepers 21* (2003) picks up the action 32 years after the original, with the AEGIS organization largely out of action, surviving only as a forgotten underground group. Invaders, however, still present a threat, and one that gains extra power as old enemies are resurrected. Ayane Isuzu is an AEGIS member who gains the assistance of a ghostly helper in a quest to reform the remnants of AEGIS and to save the world, again.

GAZULA THE AMICABLE MONSTER *

1967. JPN: *Araa, Gudzulla da to.* AKA: *Gudzulla; I'm Gudzulla; So It's Gudzulla, Is It?* TV series. DIR: Hiroshi Sasagawa. SCR: Ryohei Suzuki, Yugo Serikawa, Tsunehisa Ito, Tetsu Dezaki, Yoshiaki Yoshida. DES: Tatsuo Yoshida, Hiroshi Sasagawa. ANI: Yusaku Sakamoto. MUS: Takasuke Onozaki. PRD: Tatsunoko, Fuji TV. 25 mins. x 52 eps. (TV1); 25 mins. x 44 eps. (TV2).

After hatching from an egg on the volcanic island of Bikkura, the man-sized saurian monster Gazula comes to live in human society, where his predeliction for eating iron objects causes problems for the long-suffering Professor Nugeta and his family.

A lovable monster show designed to capitalize on the concurrent kiddification of the *Godzilla* movie series, *Gazula* bears a strong thematic resemblance to the live-action Tsuburaya show *Buska* (*DE), broadcast the previous year. Gazula befriends the professor's son Oshio and becomes a companion who

combines the conjuring mischief of DORAEMON with the metabolism of EATMAN—since he, too, ingests metal to transform it into useful devices. Gazula wears a comical bowler hat, bow tie, and a diaper and lives in perpetual fear of the local veterinarian, who yearns to stick a hypodermic needle in his tail.

The original black-and-white series, which was split into two tales per episode, was screened in Australia in the early 1970s, although this version does not seem to have made it to any other English-speaking countries. A color version followed in 1987, directed by Seitaro Hara, but recycling many of the old scripts.

GEAR FIGHTER DENDO

2000. JPN: *Gear Senshi Dendo.* TV series. DIR: Mitsuo Fukuda. SCR: Chiaki Akizawa. DES: Hirokazu Hisayuki, Masaharu Amiya, Hiroyuki Yoshino. ANI: Akira Takahashi. MUS: Toshihiko Sahashi. PRD: Sunrise, TV Tokyo. 25 mins. x 38 eps. In a peaceful 21st-century Earth, it has been 17 years since humanity first learned of the spacefaring alien race of the Galfar Machine Empire. GEAR is the name of the organization to fight off the Galfar with specially adapted giant robots (oh, that's a change). Computer geek Hokuto and gung ho scrapper Ginga both want to pilot the Dendo robot, but with fading powers, the robot needs to feed on the boys' friendship to keep going. Strangely parasitic goings-on, directed by former CYBERFORMULA GPX–artist Fukuda.

GEMINI PROPHECIES *

1982. JPN: *Andromeda Stories.* TV special. DIR: Masamitsu Sasaki. SCR: Masaki Tsuji. DES: Keiko Takemiya. ANI: Shigetaka Kiyoyama. MUS: Yuji Ono. PRD: Toei. 105 mins. (U.S. version 85 mins.)
A sentient computer disrupts the lives of the inhabitants of planet Lodorian (Geminix in the U.S. version) in its attempts to create a machine world. The young queen, Lilia, flees with the help of a small band of survivors including the warrior-princess Il, who

hails from another planet destroyed by the same entity. Lilia gives birth to telepathic twins, Gimsa and Afl, who are fated to return with Il's people to avenge the death of their father the king.

Based on a manga by TOWARD THE TERRA–artist Keiko Takemiya and SF author Ryu Mitsuse, *Andromeda Stories* was rushed into production before the story had even finished running in its magazine incarnation. The big twist is the final revelation that the wanderings of the Lodorians were over when they finally settled on a new world—planet Earth. In the wake of *Battlestar Galactica*, this was unlikely to be too much of a surprise for a Japanese audience—the bulk of Mitsuse's work formed a far more serious, long-running "future history," though only this short story was ever adapted for the screen.

GENE SHAFT

2001. TV series. DIR: Kazuki Akane. SCR: Kazuki Akane, Hisashi Tokimura, Miya Asakawa. DES: Yasuhiro Oshima, Takeyuki Takeya. ANI: Junji Takeuchi. MUS: N/C. PRD: Satellite, WOWOW. 25 mins. x 13 eps.
In the 23rd century, human gene therapy is incredibly advanced, but a population imbalance has resulted in nine women to every man (blame TENCHI MUYO!). Life is discovered on Ganymede, but Earth is encircled by a mysterious ring, perhaps of alien manufacture. Terrorists blow up the survey team sent to investigate, and the incident triggers a weapon on the ring that devastates Earth. Terran girl Mika Seido is the planet's last hope, with only the incomplete robot prototype Shaft to help her. Director Akane's follow-up to ESCAFLOWNE, preceded by the tie-in manga *Lunar Shaft* in *Ace Next* magazine.

GENEDIVER

1996. TV series. DIR: Masami Furukawa, Takuo Suzuki, Akira Natsuki, Masakazu Amiya. SCR: Masami Furukawa, Riko Hinokuma, Yoshi Nowata, Toshiaki Komura. DES: Akihiro Tanigu-

chi, Michio Mihara. ANI: Keiyo Naga-
mori. MUS: Masaaki Igawa. PRD: Juno,
NHKEP2. 25 mins. x 56 eps.
Sneaker is an evil entity from a time
before the Big Bang, but currently it
can only manifest itself in the virtual
world. The peace-loving inhabitants
need help, but the "heroine" they get
to save them is nothing more than
average schoolgirl Tada. Falling into
the virtual world like ALICE IN WONDER-
LAND, Tada fights evil in the style of the
later CORRECTOR YUI. This is one of the
first 1990s TV series to combine cheaper cel animation with flashy computer
graphics—a mixture much imitated by
the end of the century.

GENERATOR GAWL *
1998. TV series. DIR: Seiji Mizushima.
SCR: Hidefumi Kimura. DES: Yasushi
Moriki, Takashi Tomioka, Kenji Teraoka. ANI: Akira Ogura. MUS: N/C. PRD:
Tatsunoko, Victor, TV Tokyo. 25 mins.
x 12 eps.
In 2007, new students Koji, Ryo, and
Gawl arrive at Oju Academy Town in
Japan, but they are not like the other
students at this elite institution. They
are time travelers from a future in
which humanity has been enslaved
by GUYVER-esque mutants called the
Generators. After a hellish training
program, the resistance movement
has sent them back in time to prevent
Professor Nekasa from inventing the
Generator process at the Academy.
However, the professor proves elusive,
while the trio is opposed by agents
from its own era, sent back to ensure
Nekasa's activities are not interrupted.
Their one hope in their struggle is
Gawl himself, who has reluctantly
submitted to the monstrous Generator
process, allowing him to transform into
a creature that can fight their enemies
on their own terms. A mixture of the
chronological espionage of *Terminator*
and the unwilling, angst-ridden hero of
CYBORG 009, Tatsunoko's first TV series
since TEKKAMAN replaced the short-lived
video outings of the 1990s with a *slightly* longer series, which featured themed
monsters-of-the-week just like the same

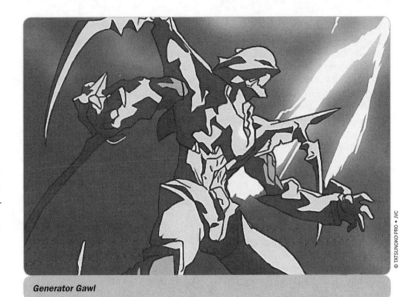

Generator Gawl

studio's BATTLE OF THE PLANETS and an
ambiguous, conspiratorial secret society inspired by EVANGELION's NERV.

GENESIS SURVIVOR GAIARTH *
1992. JPN: *Sosei Kishi Gaiarth.* AKA:
*Genesis Machine-Warrior Gaiarth,
Genesis Surviver* [sic] *Gaiarth.* Video.
DIR: Hiroyuki Kitazume, Shinji Aramaki,
Hideaki Oba. SCR: Shinji Aramaki,
"REM." DES: Hiroyuki Kitazume, Hiroyuki Ochi. ANI: Jun Okuda. MUS: Kazunori
Ashizawa, Takehito Nakazawa. PRD: Artmic, Kuma, AIC. Ca. 45 mins. x 3 eps.
In the aftermath of a cataclysmic war,
one of the last Imperial cyborgs trains
a young boy, Ital, among the ruins of
an old military base. Republican forces
kill Ital's mentor, and the boy's quest
for vengeance leads him to team up
with Sahari, the pretty female leader
of the Junk-hunters, and an amnesiac
war robot called Zaxon. The attacking
Republicans are looking for the dormant Sakuya, a young girl who is the
central intelligence system of a doomsday device. Ital kills the evil "General"
who wishes to use Sakuya for his own
ends, and Sakuya drives the device into
the desert where she self-destructs.
Ital, Sahari, and Zaxon set off into further adventures, although none were

forthcoming for this competent but
unremarkable science fantasy saga by
future big names including ARMITAGE
III's Ochi.
This postholocaust plot in the style
of GREY: DIGITAL TARGET collapses
in the face of humdrum pop-video
interludes, and two pointless animal
sidekicks. But despite massive steals
from *Return of the Jedi, Beast Master*,
and *Star Wars*, there are still moments
when the world of Gaiarth shows true
promise, particularly in technology so
ancient it is treated as magical by its
operators/summoners. The bright, flat
colors were an early example of the
simpler anime shading popularized by
outsourced Korean animation studios
during the 1990s that would eventually
define the look of TENCHI MUYO! and
other AIC shows.

GENIUS IDIOT BAKABON
1971. JPN: *Tensai Bakabon.* AKA: *Genius
Bakabon.* TV series. DIR: Hiroshi Saito.
SCR: Yoshiaki Yoshida, Chikara Matsumoto, Yukinobu Komori, Masaki Tsuji,
Shunichi Yukimuro. DES: Fujio Akatsuka. ANI: Tsutomu Shibayama. MUS:
Takeo Watanabe. PRD: Fujio Pro, TMS.
25 mins. x 40 eps. (TV), 25 mins. x
103 eps. (TV2), 25 mins. x 10 eps.

(TV3), 10 mins. x 88 eps. (TV4). The insane Bakabon family—eccentric Papa, gentle Mama, genius Hajime, and absentminded Junior—are constantly trying to outdo each other with wacky schemes, but with the exception of the baby, they're all stupid. Shown after STAR OF THE GIANTS in a prime slot, the series soon deviated from the original as sponsor pressure increased—with Father getting a respectable job and the introduction of previously unseen characters to fill out the otherwise small cast.

Fujio Akatsuka, who wrote the original 1967 gag manga on which all the series were based, also created the comedy OSOMATSU-KUN and the girls' series SECRET AKKO-CHAN. The series returned in 1975 with *Original Genius Idiot Bakabon*, a title chosen by its creator to demonstrate that it was truer to the manga from which it came. The new version included the manga favorite Eel-Dog (whose mother is an eel and father is a dog), and Lelele, the Bakabons' next-door neighbor who is obsessed with sweeping, and several crazy classmates from Bakada University.

It came back once more in 1990 with *Heisei-era Genius Idiot Bakabon* and an all-new cast except for Mother, played by Junko Yamazawa. The series was brought back yet again in 2000 in a version from Studio Pierrot, reuniting the family with old favorites like the trigger-happy policeman and the grumbling old man Wanagin. The *Genius Idiot* cast would also team up with Akatsuka's other creations for the 1991 movie spoof *3,000 Leagues in Search of Osomatsu's Curry*, directed by Akira Saito. Father and son Bakabon go on a quest for the most delicious curry in the world in a spoof of both FROM THE APENNINES TO THE ANDES and JOURNEY TO THE WEST.

GENJI

1992. Video. DIR: Akira Koson. SCR: Akira Koson. DES: Michitaka Kikuchi, Masafumi Yamamoto. ANI: Masafumi Yamamoto. MUS: Kentaro Haneda. PRD:

Somi, Tee-Up, JC Staff. 45 mins. x 2 eps. Time-traveling lovers Katsumi and Sakura are thrown into the midst of Japan's medieval Heike-Genji civil war, which is not quite as the history books remember it, complete with sorcerers and unearthly beasts. Based on the manga in *Wings* magazine by EARTHIAN-creator Yun Koga, and not to be confused with the TALE OF GENJI.

GENMUKAN *

2003. JPN: *Genmukan Aiyoku to Ryojoku no Intsumi; Genmukan: The Sin of Desire and Shame*. AKA: *Phantom Mansion: The Sin of Desire and Shame*. Video. DIR: Hiroya Iijima, Hisashi Tomii. SCR: N/C. DES: Hiroya Iijima. ANI: Yasuhiro Okuda. MUS: N/C. PRD: Studio Kuma, Green Bunny. 30 mins. x 2 eps. Private eye Satoru Kido is summoned to a remote island, where the butler of a lavish mansion wants him to investigate the theft of a ruby ring. He finds the country house occupied by Ayano, a young and beautiful orphan heiress, and her suspicious staff—a governess, a maid, and a groundsman. Satoru doesn't rule out any one of them as the potential thief, although his investigations into life at the mansion soon collapse into a series of setups for sex scenes. Based on a computer game, which featured designs by "Tony." ●

GENOCYBER *

1993. Video. DIR: Koichi Ohata. SCR: Noboru Aikawa, "REM." DES: Atsushi Yamagata, Kimitoshi Yamane. ANI: Kenji Kamiyama. MUS: Michinori Matsuoka. PRD: Artmic. Ca. 46 mins. x 3 eps. (released as 5 eps. but on 3 tapes). Diane is a cripple who relies on a cybernetic body. She lost her limbs in the same accident that killed her father, maimed her mother, and permanently altered her unborn sister, Elaine, a feral child with incredible psychic powers. Not content with stealing the credit for his work, Professor Kenneth adopts his dead friend's children and uses them in his experiments. Elaine goes on the run in Hong Kong, and the evil Kowloon corpora-

tion (misnamed "Kuron" in the Manga Entertainment dub) goes after her. She befriends Shorty, a street kid, but is then forced to fight Kowloon's minions and her own sister. Eventually, the two girls combine to form the terrifying Genocyber creature, and Hong Kong is destroyed.

An incoherent mishmash of UROTSUKIDOJI's demon apocalypse and the psychic weapons of AKIRA held together with technobabble about "qi" energy and "vajra" force amid blatant steals from *Robocop* and *Aliens*. Beyond the idea of military experimentation on children, *Genocyber* also plunders later chapters of the *Akira* manga, in which Tetsuo's biomechanics take over a U.S. aircraft carrier. Though there are some nice ideas here (a science based on Hindu myth and a demonic machine that looks like the praying hands of a Hindu priest), *Genocyber* is far too derivative for its own good. Matters aren't helped by English dialogue like "You stupid, ignorant fucking piece of shit," which, needless to say, is a rather free translation of the original.

The idea of bitter sibling rivalry and a retarded girl with godlike powers has much potential, but *Genocyber* does little with it. With bone-snappingly horrific fights and incredibly gory splashes of violence, it plays like GUYVER with girls, trying and failing to use many of the same ideas as the later MACROSS PLUS. It throws in computer graphics and icky live-action shots of offal, but these experimentations, along with several pans that use genuine photographs instead of artwork, just make the series look cheaper than it really is. Similarly, Elaine is a telepath, but *Genocyber* just makes it look like a cheap excuse for not moving her lips.

Later episodes are barely connected, as the action jumps a decade to the Middle Eastern republic of Karain, where the ageless Elaine is mistaken for a refugee by the UN. Taken to an aircraft carrier, where everyone decides to confuse things by calling her Laura, she witnesses the arrival of Kowloon's latest machine, a cyborg plane that uses vajra technology. She fights it and destroys Kowloon's latest plans, but not before she drives a woman insane by revealing that the child who saved her life is also the monster who killed her parents in Hong Kong.

The finale (released as two "episodes" on a single tape in both the U.S. and Japan, and not released at all in the U.K.), featured Genocyber laying waste to the world before falling dormant. The Kowloon group puts a doomsday device into orbit to await the creature's return. A hundred years later (or 300 in the U.S. version), the postapocalyptic world develops a religion that worships Genocyber as a god and prays for its return, which eventually occurs with predictably gory results. **CNV**

GENSHIKEN *
2004. JPN: *Gendai Shikaku Bunka Kenkyukai*. AKA: *Society for the Study of Modern Visual Culture*. TV series. DIR: Takashi Ikehata et al. SCR: Michiko Yokote, Kokeshi Hanamura, Mamiko Ikeda, Miharu Hirami, Natsuko Takahashi, Reiko Yoshida, Roika Nakase, Yasuko Kobayashi. DES: Hirotaka Kinoshita. ANI: Hirotaka Kinoshita. MUS: Masanori Takumi. PRD: Palm Studio, GENCO, Kid's Station, Media Factory, Tora no Ana, Toshiba. 25 mins. x 12 eps.

Kanji Sasahara has a secret passion for manga, anime, and all related items. When he starts college, he's drawn to the titular club, but too proud to join at first, fearing that the other members are even bigger nerds than he—Madarame is into everything military, Kuragame is a wannabe illustrator, and Tanaka loves to dress up. Kosaka, a dreamboat with model looks and charm, seems an unlikely fan but is the most obsessive of them all. He even ignores the overt pursuit of a real girl in favor of getting to store openings and voice artist events. In an arch reference to the contrived reunion of LOVE HINA, Kosaka's childhood friend Saki runs into him at the beginning of school and begins to date him, only

to find herself dragged into a world of fannish things. Based on Shimoku Kio's strip in *Comic Afternoon* monthly, this is an affectionate parody of geekdom. Aimed at an audience older than that of many similar titles and keen to stress that fans are people, too, it deliberately evokes some of the setups of live-action TV drama for twentysomethings such as *In the Name of Love* (*DE), many of which revolve around the reunions of college clubs for more "acceptable" pursuits such as sports or literature. *Genshiken* resembles OTAKU NO VIDEO in its empathy for those who refuse to put away childish things, but it's gentler and less confrontational than the early Gainax classic. *Kujibiki Unbalance* (2004) is a 25-minute spin-off video that purports to be episodes 1, 21, and 25 of the anime series that the club members watch in the show. As befits the humor of the show that spawned it, it is a catalogue of daft stereotypes, about an orphan boy who falls in love with a girl he meets in the school library and has to fend off the attentions of a childhood friend who wants him for herself … and so on. Compare to NADESICO, which similarly gave birth to its own show-within-a-show. A second season was announced as forthcoming in October 2006.

GENTLEMAN MUGEN
1987. JPN: *Mugen Shinshi*. AKA: *Dreaming/Mugen Gentleman*. Video. DIR: Hatsuki Tsuji. SCR: Izo Hashimoto. DES: Hatsuki Tsuji. ANI: Hatsuki Tsuji. MUS: N/C. PRD: Studio Gallop. 49 mins.
In this one-shot video based on the 1981 *Shonen Captain* manga by Yosuke Takahashi and set in the 1920s, 15-year-old boy detective Mamiya Mugen gets involved with beautiful girls and solves fantastic mysteries. On this occasion, the case involves the kidnapping of a ballerina and several other girls by a criminal organization. Mamoru deduces that a beautiful concert pianist will be next, but not that the criminals need young girls' energy to power a resurrection machine. In replaying the classic murder mysteries of Ranpo

Edogawa and injecting a hard-edged sense of humor, it was a forerunner for CONAN THE BOY DETECTIVE.

GEOBREEDERS *
1998. JPN: *Geobreeders: File X: Chibi Neko no Dakkan*. AKA: *Geobreeders: File X: Get Back the Kitty*. Video. DIR: Yuji Moriyama. SCR: Yosuke Kuroda, Yuji Moriyama. DES: Yasuhiro Oshima. ANI: Yasuhiro Oshima. MUS: Motoyoshi Iwasaki. PRD: Victor. 30 mins. x 3 eps., 30 mins. x 4 eps.
A disastrously incompetent supernatural security agency is called in to stop an epidemic of feline ghosts in this anime adaptation of Akihiro Ito's manga. Perhaps for legal reasons, the original "File X" prefix was dropped from the title for the U.S. release, though *Geobreeders* owes just as great a debt to *Scooby-Doo* as it does to Mulder and Scully. Five feisty females in a dilapidated mystery machine run rings around the show's squashed-down Duchovny-clone, facing off against sulking military "allies" and a secret conspiracy.

A predictably madcap mix of ghost-busting tomfoolery in the spirit of PHANTOM QUEST CORP and GHOST SWEEPER MIKAMI, complete with lightheartedly gratuitous nudity, snappy dialogue, and some really big guns. Even distributors USMC rise to the occasion for the U.S. dub. Considering the output of their sister-brand Anime 18, it must be a refreshing change for a voice actress to shout "Get on your knees, pussies" to an audience that genuinely does consist of cats.

Sight-gags show a return of the PROJECT A-KO spirit from chief director Moriyama: fake ads separate the episodes, characters must play soccer with hand grenades, and in one scene someone backs into a giant poster for *Geobreeders: The Movie*. Though the series wasn't quite *that* successful, it did spawn the four-part *Geobreeders 02* on video in 2000, reuniting the staff under new director Shin Misawa. **N**

GESTALT *
1996. JPN: *Choju Densetsu Gestalt*.

AKA: *Superbestial Legend Gestalt.* Video. DIR: Osamu Yamazaki. SCR: Mamiya Fujimura. DES: Takashi Kobayashi. ANI: N/C. MUS: N/C. PRD: SMEJ, TV Tokyo. 30 mins. x 2 eps.

Father Olivier, a young priest, learns of a god that will grant a wish to anyone who can find him on his hidden island of "G." Teaming up with the mute Oli, Olivier sets out to find "G" but is thwarted by his old enemy, Suzu the Dark Elf. A comedy manga serialized in *G Fantasy* magazine by **EARTHIAN**-creator Yun Koga, *Gestalt* includes many jokes at the expense of fantasy role-playing games, including moments of dialogue done deliberately in the non-sequitur style of console RPGs. Though clearly an attempt to capitalize on the success of the similar **SLAYERS**, *Gestalt* foundered after only two episodes, despite flashy computer graphics and the contemporary selling point of being made completely inside a computer.

GET A GRIP TSUYOSHI

1993. JPN: *Tsuyoshi Shikkari Shinasai.* AKA: *Get a Grip, Tsuyoshi.* Movie. DIR: Shin Misawa. SCR: Takashi Yamada. DES: Kiyoshi Nagamatsu. ANI: Takahisa Kazukawa. MUS: Kuniaki Haishima. PRD: Toei, Fuji TV. 30 mins. (m), 25 mins. x 112 eps. (TV).

Kiyoshi Nagamatsu's original 1993 manga in *Comic Afternoon* and the TV series that followed were critically acclaimed for their "American-style humor," whatever that may be. Tsuyoshi is a typical high school student, good at sports but bad at study, victimized at home by two sisters who hide their evil natures behind their angelic exteriors. The short cinema release removes him from the eternal feud with his mother and sisters, sending him back 12 years in time for a replay of *Back to the Future.*

GET RIDE! AMDRIVER

2004. TV series. DIR: Isamu Torada. SCR: Satoshi Namiki. DES: Kenji Teraoka, Shinichi Miyazaki, Eiji Suganuma, Shinobu Tsuneki. ANI: N/C. MUS: Kazunori Maruyama. PRD: Studio Deen, TV

Tokyo, NAS. 24 mins. x 51 eps. Amdrivers are an elite group of pilots who defend mankind. In their Baizer suits, powered by AmEnergy, they fight the Bugchines, minions of the mysterious Diguraz and his Justice Army. An ultrapowerful AmEnergy source called Zeam could render our heroes invincible and end the fighting. Inexperienced AmDriver Jenus Dira teams up with top AmDriver Shin Pierce and Regna Lauraria, but becomes annoyed by what he sees as their wish for personal glory before the good of mankind. Another newcomer, Sara May, feels the same, and the two start out on their own to try and find Zeam. This is standard action adventure fare for older children, not likely to offer much to the over-twelves despite Konami's energetic ad campaign for the multifarious card game packs.

GETBACKERS *

2002. JPN: *Getbackers Dakkanya.* AKA: *Getbackers Recoverers.* TV series. DIR: Kazuhiro Furuhashi, Keitaro Motonaga, Makoto Noriza, Masami Furukawa, Osamu Sekita, Shunji Yoshida, Tomoko Hiramuki, Toshiyuki Kato. SCR: Akemi Omode, Jun Maekawa, Masashi Kojima, Reiko Yoshida, Saizo Nemoto. DES: Atsuko Nakajima, Toshiharu Murata. ANI: Atsuko Nakajima, Akira Matsushima, Hirofumi Morimoto. MUS: Taku Iwasaki. PRD: Kodansha, Rondo Robe, TBS. 26 mins. x 49 eps.

Hard-up heroes Ginji and Ban specialize in *getting stuff back*, from a lost lucky charm to a missing teenager, in a Japan where everyone is hustling for a dime. They are aided in this by their superpowers—Ban can exert 200 kilos of grip in his fist and also has the Evil Eye, the ability to project terrifying hallucinations into the mind of anyone who meets his gaze. Ginji can generate thousands of volts of electricity from his body at will. The pair claim a 100% recovery rate for their clients, but the goods aren't always returned in the original condition. Drawing not only on the ongoing *Shonen Magazine* manga by Yuya Aoki and Rando Ayamine

but also on the classic TV series *Detective Story* (*DE), *Getbackers* refashions hard-boiled traditions as light comedy. **COWBOY BEBOP** may have emulated the look, but *Getbackers* emulates the plots—its heroes are loners with a dark past, co-opted by a vampish woman (the sultry Hevn) for missions above and below the law. In attitude, it often sails very close to *Magnum P.I.* (1980) or a righteous **LUPIN III**, until a long arc that returns the characters to their clandestine roots, fighting similarly superpowered individuals who were once their allies.

Cleverly recycling many of the issues and threats of Marvel superheroes into an everyday setting, *Getbackers* features two protagonists who may have amazing powers but lack costumes or kit. Instead, they hang out at a restaurant called the Honky Tonk, where they lean on manager Paul for free food. Ban and Ginji's Shinjuku is dominated by the bold architectural statements of Japan's boom era, set on the steps of train stations empty of commuters and on the building sites of abandoned skyscrapers. What begins as a stylistic conceit is later revealed as an important plot point—the boys have a past association with the gangs who have occupied the Limitless Fortress, a massive complex in downtown Tokyo, left incomplete by the recession and subsequently inhabited by invincible squatters who terrorize anyone who tries to evict them.

The anime story diverges from the manga after episode 25, returning to investigative stories with a twist: an amnesiac car crash survivor who wants them to somehow retrieve his memory and the obligatory hot springs episode, where the boys mix business and pleasure while hunting for an old lady's diamond ring. Other plots drift into the art world genre of **GALLERY FAKE**, with a woman who claims to have the lost arms of the Venus de Milo statue, while others drift further toward sci-fi territory—a super drug, a missing sample of real blood, and a revolutionary superalloy. Paul's own past as a thief is revealed when he hires the boys to retrieve a vase stolen by one of his old gang members before the Limitless Fortress storyline returns for a final showdown.

Like the cursed yuppies in PETSHOP OF HORRORS, the Getbackers' clients symbolically sell their souls for material possessions; most notably, a teenage girl prepared to whore herself to a gangster if he gives her "bags, clothes, and shoes." Sadly, it's not just the cast who are impoverished—the show itself is a victim of the Japanese recession, with extremely limited animation. When the boys agree to take a job that involves an extended pastiche of the CASTLE OF CAGLIOSTRO car chase, their fee is two million yen, which a contemporary newspaper article reported as the shockingly meager budget of a modern-day TV episode. Despite this, *Getbackers* had an impressively long run on TV, extending across an entire year when most similar shows barely last a season. Part of this endurance feat may be down to the flexibility of its storyline and pace, mixing long quests with short vignettes without losing sight of its big themes.

GETTER ROBO *

1974 AKA: *Starvengers*. TV series, movie, video. DIR: Tomoharu Katsumata, Yasuo Yamaguchi, Takeshi Tamiya, Takeshi Shirato. SCR: Shunichi Yukimuro, Seiji Matsuoka. DES: Kazuo Komatsubara. ANI: Kazuo Komatsubara, Atsuo Noda, Kazuo Nakamura, Takeshi Shirato. MUS: Shunsuke Kikuchi. PRD: Dynamic Planning, Fuji TV, Toei. 25 mins. x 51 cps., 25 mins. x 39 eps. (G), 25 mins. x 50 eps. (Go), 25 mins. x 13 eps. (Change), 25 mins. x 4 eps. (Neo).

Professor Saotome creates the fearsome Getter Machine series of war robots and hires the nobly named Ryoma (see OI! RYOMA), Musashi (see YOUNG MIYAMOTO MUSASHI), and Benkei (see BENKEI VS. USHIWAKA) to pilot the three vehicles, the aerial Getter-1, landbased Getter-2, and seafaring Getter-3, that can be combined to form a giant

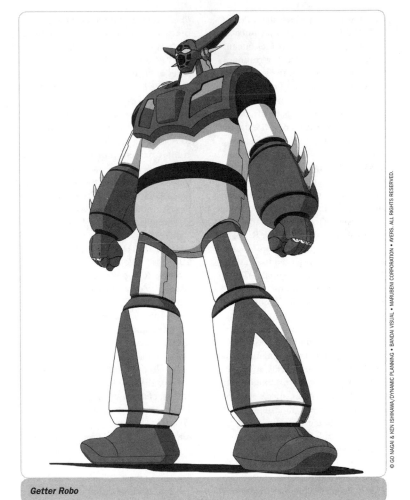

Getter Robo

humanoid robot—the first "transformer."

Based on a collaboration between DEVILMAN's Go Nagai and DEMON-BEAST PHALANX–creator Ken Ishikawa, the show returned in 1975 as *Getter Robo G*. The destruction of the evil Dinosaur Empire left the way open for a new enemy, the Clan of 100 Devils, and since the original machinery had been destroyed in the climactic fight of the previous series, it was also time for new vehicles: Getters Dragon, Rygar, and Poseidon (Star Dragon, Star Arrow, and Star Poseidon). Along with the other anime in the FORCE FIVE

interlinked shows, *Getter Robo G* was redubbed for the U.S. market as *Starvengers,* and several of the vehicles were also included in the SHOGUN WARRIORS line. For the English-language version, the horned enemies were renamed the Pandemonium Empire, led by Emperor Ramzorch and his Hitler-look-alike commander, Captain Fuhrer. Back in Japan, *Getter Robo G* also appeared in short theatrical outings alongside other Go Nagai creations including *Great Mazinger vs. Getter Robo G* (1975) and *Great Mazinger / Grandizer / Getter Robo G: Battle the Great Monster* (1976).

After a long hiatus, the franchise

hit a low point in 1991 with *Getter Robo Go!* directed by Yoshiki Shibata, featuring the same machines but an all-new team. Though long-running by modern standards, the series was considered a noncanonical flop. The original, however, remained a favorite among fans and professionals, demonstrated by the **NADESICO** staff in their spoof show-within-a-show *Gekiganger 3.* For most of the 1990s, the franchise was kept alive by computer games, and eventually the redesigned machines as used in the *Getter Robo* and *Super Robot Battle* games were resurrected for a new series. Poaching staff from the successful retro series **GIANT ROBO**, Jun Kawagoe's straight-to-video *Change Getter Robo* (1998) presented itself as the "true" sequel to the original 1974–75 serials, beginning with the death of Professor Saotome and Ryoma's arrest for his murder. Three years later, the two remaining team members are forced to contend with a cloned "evil" Saotome, hellbent on avenging his own death and leading an army of Getter Dragons. In a sequel that exploited the limited budgets of late-1990s video productions to recreate the rough-edged look of 1970s television animation, Ryoma is recalled from prison to resist the invasion. This version was scheduled for release in the U.S. in 2001 as *Getter Robot: The Last Day.* The same staff returned for the four-part video sequel *Change Getter Robo vs. Neo Getter Robo* (2000), clearly made with an eye to foreign sales, in which another madman, Emperor Gaul, sends an army of robotic dinosaurs to destroy New York, and Professor Saotome's new lantern-jawed protégé, former wrestler Tetsuhito, leads the underground resistance. See also **MAZINGER Z.**

GHIBLIES

2000. TV special, movie. DIR: Yoshiyuki Momose. SCR: Yoshiyuki Momose. DES: N/C. ANI: N/C. MUS: Manto Watanobe. PRD: Studio Ghibli. 20 mins. (TV special), 20 mins. (m).

A series of short, comedic vignettes about life in an animation studio, doodled by the Studio Ghibli team to practice techniques on their new workstations around the time **MY NEIGHBORS THE YAMADAS** was being filmed. These slices of life developed into two short films, the first airing on Japanese TV in 2000 as part of a Studio Ghibli documentary, the second released on the same theatrical bill as **THE CAT RETURNS** in 2002. Note that, just to confuse matters, the title of this show is pronounced with a hard G, whereas in real life, the name of the studio is pronounced with a soft G, sounding like *jibli.* Only the second set of animations is currently available on DVD.

GHOST IN THE SHELL *

1995. JPN: *Kokaku Kidotai.* AKA: *Armored Riot Police/Ghost in the Shell.* Movie. DIR: Mamoru Oshii. SCR: Kazunori Ito. DES: Hiroyuki Okiura, Shoji Kawamori. ANI: Hiroyuki Okiura, Tensai Okamura, Toshihiko Nishikubo. MUS: Kenji Kawai. PRD: Studio IG. 83 mins. (m1), 25 mins. x 26 eps. (TV1), ca. 1 min. x 26 eps. (*Tachikomatic 1*), 25 mins. x 26 eps. (TV2), ca. 1 min. x 26 eps. (*Tachikomatic 2*), 100 mins. (m2), 159 mins. (*Laughing Man*), 161 mins. (*Individual Eleven*).

A top secret military project goes horribly wrong, and a sentient computer virus runs out of control. Its creators disperse in search of political asylum before the mistake is spotted, while the program itself tries to defect to the other side. Calling itself the Puppet Master, it hacks into government systems to gain extra leverage in negotiations. It takes control of gun-freaks, robot bodies, and even a tank, but what it really wants is a permanent, physical home. Meanwhile, Section Nine, agents for the Ministry of Internal Affairs, are forced to clear up after the mess left behind by Section Six (Foreign Affairs), even as the two departments contest jurisdiction in the case. Major Motoko Kusanagi is an angst-ridden platoon leader in Section Nine who can't leave the service because, like the original *Bionic Woman*, parts of her are government property. Her body is just a mass-produced "shell" (note the scene where she sees a twin working as a secretary) and the only part of her that is real is her "ghost," her soul. When seemingly random events all over the city turn out to be crimes committed by the Puppet Master's unwitting accomplices, Motoko realizes that there is a pattern, and that it eventually leads to her.

GitS is one of the best anime available in English, and one of the few that could reasonably claim to be a true cyberpunk film. It is a superb action film with marvelous moments, such as Motoko's final duel with a robot tank, and accomplished use of computer graphics, especially for Motoko's cloaking device. Unlike the many anime "movies" that are really nothing of the sort, it was genuinely made for the big screen, and the budget and dedication really show. It was also a coproduction partly funded by Manga Entertainment, and it kept the company's reputation afloat in the search for a new **AKIRA**, though at the time it was regarded by many as a money pit for ME's beleaguered boss Andy Frain.

While **APPLESEED**–creator Masamune Shirow set his original 1991 *Young Magazine* manga in the sprawling future metropolis of Tokyo, director Oshii deliberately relocated to Hong Kong for the film to create a lived-in, exotic look with Chinese-language street signs. This was a perfect film for the idiosyncratic Oshii, allowing him to replay **PATLABOR** with clueless "little people" dwarfed by events beyond their ken.

The original manga's intense philosophizing is artfully simplified by screenwriter Ito, who streamlines it into a perverse "romance" between Motoko and the Puppet Master, their final marriage eventually producing a new life form. Kenji Kawai's music is a haunting ceremony in arcane Japanese ("A god descends for a wedding and dawn approaches while the night bird sings"), two separate musical themes that slowly advance on each other during the film, until they marry to form a completely new synergy over the closing credits, adding a final coda to Ito's plot. Or rather, they did—the English-language version replaced the closing music with a mediocre effort from the Passengers CD. Such a gimmick may well have gained *Ghost in the Shell* more mainstream interest, but it wasn't necessary. This is a film that needed no marketing spin. A manga sequel, *Man-Machine Interface*, ran intermittently for several years in *Young Magazine*, regularly prompting rumors of an anime follow-up.

This eventually arrived in the form of the TV series *Stand Alone Complex* (2002) which was billed not as a sequel to the movie, but a "reimagining" of the same story. *Stand Alone Complex* drops the Puppet Master in favor of a new enemy and a broader, deeper introduction to Shirow's future world and his Nii-hama ("New Port") city. It uses Shirow's work as a foundation, but is a collaboration among a team of writers led by director Kenji Kamiyama—that same "KK" whose initials can be seen inside a cybernetic eye in the first episode. It also offers tantalizing scraps of new information about the characters from *Ghost in the Shell*, including the revelation that Motoko was only six years old when unspecified events caused her to swap her original body for a shell. This, then, is what must make her so good; she must have been one of the first humans to undergo full cyborg remodeling, not out of choice, but necessity. When we see a hand unable to hold a doll in the opening credits, we are watching one of Motoko's oldest memories, as she struggled to control her new body.

The *fuchikoma* robots from the original comic are remodeled here as the *tachikomas*, intelligent tanks with the firepower of a helicopter gunship and the minds of ditzy schoolgirls. They are given their own *Tachikomatic Days* (*Kokaku Kidotai: Section 9 Science File Tachikoma na Hibi*) gag reel, which closed each episode when the TV series was released on video.

Many of the episodes "Stand

Ghost in the Shell

Alone"—that is, they are weekly installments of a futuristic cop show in which Section Nine fights crime in New Port City. However, in the style of **COWBOY BEBOP**, twelve episodes, #4, #5, #6, #9, #11, and #20–26, are "Complex," part of the main story arc, the tale of the entity or entities known as the Laughing Man.

Stand Alone Complex makes recurring references to the work of legendary American recluse J.D. Salinger, whose judgmental Holden Caulfield in the novel *Catcher in the Rye* bears some similarity to the Laughing Man and even supplies the quote for his logo. "The Laughing Man" (1949) is also the title of a Salinger short story printed in *The New Yorker*, while the tune, "Comin' Through the Rye," is a regular feature of daily life in Japan in everything from elevator doors to pedestrian crossings and has been heard before in the anime **VAMPIRE HUNTER D** and **GREY: DIGITAL TARGET**.

There are other tips of the hat to pop culture, including references to a Disney theme park ride in "Jungle Cruise" (#10), and a character modeled on Nurse Ratched from *One Flew Over the Cuckoo's Nest* in "Portraitz" (#11). Episode #3, "Android and I," is an extended homage to the works of Jean-Luc Godard, whose *Alphaville* (1965) also featured an investigator taking on an artificial intelligence over

the control of a future society.

But beyond such name checking, *Stand Alone Complex* is a compelling cyberpunk drama, concerned with medical espionage, corruption, and consumer's rights in an increasingly globalized and corporate economy. Its success led in part to interest among the producers of the original film in commissioning an actual sequel to the original movie, which appeared as *GITS 2: Innocence* (jpn: *Innocence*) (2004). *Innocence* draws heavily on a single chapter of the original manga ("Robot Rondo"), but while it uses characters and situations created by Masamune Shirow, it is largely the work of Mamoru Oshii. With Motoko Kusanagi still absent following events at the end of the movie, *Innocence* concentrates on her former lieutenant Batou as he investigates a series of crimes in which robot sex-dolls have turned on their owners. Plot, however, is of secondary concern to Oshii's usual existentialist dialogues, and extended shots of the city, including a Chinese carnival scene that supposedly took a full year to animate. The effort and expense show, in a film that does much to enhance anime's reputation both for high-quality CG and impenetrably obtuse philosophical debates.

Despite *Ghost in the Shell*'s rather obscure reputation in Japan, where it is not particularly well known outside

SF fan circles, it has enjoyed continued foreign success as a flagship for post-**Akira** anime. A second TV series, *GITS: 2nd Gig* (2004) continues the fine topical satire of its predecessor, focusing on a refugee crisis within Japan. It also reveals long-awaited details about Shirow's world, confirming that "New Port City" is actually somewhere near Nagasaki Bay—where Deshima Island, the historical quarantine/ghetto for foreign traders, is now envisioned remodeled as a refugee camp. Note that this geographical background, along with many other "facts" revealed in the TV series, contradicts earlier information stated or implied in earlier versions of the franchise. Fans are thus at a loss as to how much of the TV continuity is "canon"—*2nd Gig* in particular is vastly more forthcoming with background details of the franchise world, its military conflicts, and the political troubles this has generated in New Port City. Meanwhile, in an exercise of somewhat pointless over-complexity, *2nd Gig* develops the "Stand Alone/Complex" split of the first series even further, into episodes that can be classified as DI ("Dividual"), IN ("Individual"), or DU ("Dual")—a labored gimmick imparting unwarranted significance to story elements that can be found in many other episodic dramas, but are trumpeted here as if someone has reinvented the wheel. Nevertheless, the overreaching story arc of *2nd Gig* is another excellent series, allegorizing modern terrorism and nuclear espionage in sci-fi clothes, as the reconstituted Section Nine fights against a terrorist group calling itself the Individual Eleven.

The other "film" releases *GITS: The Laughing Man* (2005) and *GITS: Individual Eleven* (2006) are video releases consisting of extended movie-length edits of the relevant episodes from seasons one and two of the TV series, with additional footage. A new addition to the franchise, the movie *GITS: Solid State Society* (2006), was announced as forthcoming at the time of our deadline, intended to be set in 2034, two years after the events in *2nd Gig*. **ⒷⓃⓋ**

GHOST STORIES *

2000. JPN: *Gakko no Kaidan*. AKA: *School Ghost Stories*. TV series. DIR: Noriyuki Abe. SCR: Hiroshi Hashimoto. DES: Masaya Onishi, Mari Kitayama. ANI: N/C. MUS: Kaoru Wada. PRD: Pierrot, Fuji TV. 25 mins. x 19 eps.

Satsuki and her brother move into a new town, where their dead mother was once the principal of the now abandoned school. Their mother's diary reveals that the school was once haunted; hardly a surprise, considering **Here Comes Hanako** and **Haunted Junction**, one wonders if there is a school in anime that isn't. Not unlike the demonic figures in **Tenchi Muyo!** and **Ushio & Tora**, the spirit Amanojaku was trapped by Satsuki's mother in the forests behind the school, but has been released once more with the cutting down of the trees—unsurprisingly like some of those in **Devil Hunter Yohko**. Satsuki manages to trap Amanojaku's spirit inside her cat (compare to **CardCaptors**), but there are other spirits on the loose requiring her attention, in a highly derivative show that only seems to have reached the schedules because the producers were not expecting any viewers old enough to remember any of its predecessors, particularly **Real School Ghost Stories**, with which it shares a writer and director. Perhaps realizing that they didn't have a whole lot to work with and nobody would really care that much, ADV Films allowed the voice actors considerably freer rein than usual on the U.S. release—the English language dub often seems less translated than "improvised," quite possibly to the show's betterment, although such a last-ditch attempt to make it interesting might also be a potentially troubling throwback to the non-translations of **Robotech** and **Samurai Pizza Cats**. The anime forms part of a long-running *School Ghost Stories* franchise that includes 4 theatrical live-action movies, 5 live-action TV movies, 2 live-action TV series, and 19 novels.

GHOST SWEEPER MIKAMI *

1993. AKA: *GS Mikami*. TV series, movie. DIR: Atsutoshi Umezawa. SCR: Aya Matsui, Nobuaki Kishima, Masaharu Amiya. DES: Takashi Shiina. ANI: Mitsuru Aoyama, Kenji Yokoyama, Yoshiyuki Kawano, Masayuki Uchiyama. MUS: Toshihiko Sahashi. PRD: Toei, TV Asahi. 25 mins. x 45 eps. (TV), 60 mins. (m).

Reiko Mikami is a sexy penny-pinching exorcist who forces her adoring assistant, Tadao, to work for a pittance. While the snobbish, self-regarding Reiko spars with the lecherous Tadao, Okinu the gentle ex-ghost tries to keep them calm enough to do their ghostbusting job. With an unlikable heroine who persists in selling out her friends, the show spoofs the mercenary do-gooder of Osamu Tezuka's **Black Jack**, as well as the miniskirted, "body-conscious" girls of Tokyo's 1990s club scene. There are also occasional moments of social commentary, as it is revealed that Tokyo's ghost epidemic has been caused by urban sprawl pushing previously unseen spirits into the open. The chief emphasis, however, is on comedy, with a subsidiary cast including Pietro the shy half-vampire, impoverished Father Karasu, sexy voodoo ghost-sweeper Emiko, mad scientist Dr. Chaos, and his robot assistant, Maria (see **Metal Angel Marie**). Reiko and her gang also appeared in Atsutoshi Umezawa's anime movie *GS Mikami: War in Heaven* (1994, *Gokuraku Taisen*).

The time *GS Mikami* took to reach the U.S. is a real mystery. Based on a long-running manga by Takashi Shiina in *Shonen Sunday*, it has all the lighthearted adventure and sex appeal of **Urusei Yatsura**, and in the hands of Viz Communications, it might have even outperformed the same publisher's **Ranma ½**. In the Japanese market, where it peaked at a 14.6% TV rating, it swiftly sent the look-alike video anime **Phantom Quest Corp** packing and outlasted most of its contemporaries in the harsh mid-1990s market. Rumors abound that it was picked up by a well-known distributor as part of a bulk deal then left to fester because the lighthearted banter didn't sit well with the company's more action-based titles. This may have damaged it irreparably, as its cheap animation style will probably lead it to date faster than other anime from the same period—it already looks slightly older than its years.

GHOST TALKER'S DAYDREAM *

2004. JPN: *Teizokurei Daydream.* AKA: *Vulgar Spirit Daydream.* Video. DIR: Osamu Sekita. SCR: Katsumasa Kanezawa. DES: Akemi Kobayashi. ANI: N/C. MUS: Takayuki Negishi. PRD: Geneon, HAL Filmmaker. 25 mins. x 4 eps.
Psychic investigator Misaki Saiki helps solve crimes in Tokyo while moonlighting as an S/M dominatrix at an exclusive gentleman's club. Her powers are limited to seeing and conversing with the dead, but that appears to be all she needs, along with some gratuitous nudity and several misguided attempts to inject comedy. Her first case is that of Ai, a young woman whose sister and niece have supposedly committed double suicide. Somehow gaining an ability of her own to see the dead, Ai stays with Misaki for later cases. There is something of a twisted genius in the concept of a psychic dominatrix, as if Chuck Palahniuk were let loose on *The Sixth Sense* (1999) or VAMPIRE PRINCESS MIYU, but *GTD* does very little with the idea of a psychic who puts her powers of empathy to such controversial use out of office hours. Instead, it plays out in the manner of PHANTOM QUEST CORP, another psychic investigation tale that stalled on video when it really should have been on TV, where the ghost-of-the-week formula has longer to grow. Mystifyingly, the story has barely started before Misaki is heading off on vacation in two episodes scripted specifically for the anime by the author of the manga, something that anime series really should only do when they're sure they have the audience's attention and indulgence. This turns out to be an excuse for a series of jokes about Misaki's lack of pubic hair, for

which she is seeking a spiritual remedy. Based on the 2001 manga by Sankichi Meguro, itself based on a "concept" by Saki Okuse, whatever that means. Presumably, Okuse was the one who ran into the first meeting and shouted: "Two words! Bondage Investigator!" **N**

GHOSTS

1982. JPN: *Obake.* TV special. DIR: Yasunori Kawauchi, Tameo Ogawa, Gisaburo Sugii, Tsutomu Shibayama. SCR: Yasunori Kawauchi. DES: N/C. ANI: N/C. MUS: N/C. PRD: Ai Planning Center, Tac, TBS. ca. 85 mins.
An omnibus of four ghost stories from famous directors, beginning with *Comparing Transformations*, set at a ghoulish convention somewhere in the Japanese mountains. The scene moves to a seaside cave for *The Two-Eyed Goblin*, in which a family of cyclops adopts a human child. A villager at a local festival meets a beautiful girl who suddenly disappears in *Divine Secret*, and in the final story, *Amulet*, Buddha punishes the behavior of Taira no Kiyomori by releasing evil spirits into the world.

GIANT GORG

1984. JPN: *Kyoshin/Giant Gorg.* TV series. DIR: Yoshikazu Yasuhiko, Norio Kabeshima. SCR: Masaki Tsuji, Sumiko Tsukamoto. DES: Yoshikazu Yasuhiko. ANI: Mayumi Ishigaki. MUS: Mitsuo Hagiwara. PRD: Sunrise, TV Tokyo. 25 mins. x 26 eps.
Tectonic activity on the Pacific island of Austral reveals highly advanced technology. The Gail Corporation, an immensely powerful conglomerate that has been carefully manipulating the Cold War, wants the technology for itself and sends its chief executive's grandson, Rod Balboa, to get it. Opposing Balboa is Yu Tagami, the son of a Japanese researcher murdered by the Gail Corporation, who has teamed up with his father's associate, Doctor Wave. Pursued from New York across America and down to the South Seas by Gail's henchmen (and by other interested parties, including the soldier of fortune known as the "Captain,"

and Lady Lynx, queen of the Las Vegas casinos and underworld), Yu, Wave, and Wave's pretty sister Doris finally reach Austral. There, they discover that the island is a time capsule of artifacts from a lost civilization, and that Gorg, the "fearsome sea monster" that terrorizes shipping in the area, is actually a giant robot protecting its creator from interference. Manon, the pilot of a second guardian, is awakened from cryogenic slumber but cannot bear the thought that his civilization has been supplanted by humanity. Instead, he plans to destroy the world. Ronald Reagan and Yuri Andropov decide to launch a joint nuclear attack on Austral before Manon's doomsday device can go off; unfortunately for Yu's gang and the other treasure hunters, they are trapped on the island by Manon's forcefield and have only seven days to escape. Foreshadowing both SPRIGGAN, with its corporate conflict over ancient artifacts, and the antediluvian adventure of SECRET OF BLUE WATER, *GG* is also renowned for its comic-relief Professor Wave, who looks uncannily like Woody Allen.

GIANT ROBO *

1992. Video. DIR: Yasuhiro Imagawa. SCR: Yasuhiro Imagawa, Eiichi Sato. DES: Makoto Kobayashi, Toshiyuki Kubooka, Akihiko Yamashita, Takashi Watabe. ANI: Akihiko Yamashita. MUS: Masamichi Amano. PRD: Mu Film. 56 mins. x 1 eps., 42 mins. x 1 eps., 40 mins. x 1 eps., 46 mins. x 1 eps., 45 mins. x 1 eps., 49 mins. x 1 eps., 59 mins. x 1 eps.
The Shizuma drive, a clean energy source that has revolutionized world energy and eliminated pollution, has a fatal flaw. The evil Professor Franken von Folger and his associates, would-be world dictators Big Fire, dispatch a black orb to float across the world, draining the energy from all major cities and causing global chaos. Fearing a replay of the Tragedy of Bashtarlle, when faulty Shizuma prototypes wiped out an entire city, the Experts of Justice set out to stop Big Fire. Their mem-

Giant Robo

© 1992/1995 HIKARI PRODUCTIONS/AMUSE VIDEO/PLEX/ATLANTIS

bers include martial artists, scientific geniuses, secret agents, Folger's own estranged daughter, Ginrei, and a young boy called Daisaku Kusama. Only the voice of Daisaku, the son of a scientist murdered by Big Fire, can control Giant Robo, a 90-foot-tall war machine originally designed for Big Fire but now devoted to fighting crime.

GR began life as a short-lived 1967 manga by **Gigantor**'s Mitsuteru Yokoyama and was also adapted into a live-action TV series known in the U.S. as *Johnny Sokko and His Flying Robot* (1968). Director Imagawa's *GR* was the first of the 1990s "retro" boom, a number of anime made in a deliberately old-fashioned style that recalls the imagery of the Golden Age of sci-fi and also reminds baby boomers of their carefree childhoods during Japan's economic miracle, before the oil shocks of the 1970s. Its style was copied in other shows, including **Super Atragon**, **Kishin Corps**, **Sakura Wars**, and **Ambassador Magma**, and also created the environment that allowed Tezuka Pro to seriously consider new versions of previously "dated" classics such as **Black Jack**. Imagawa himself became so involved in the development work for another retro anime,

Getter Robo, that the final episode of *GR* only appeared in 1997, when most of the voice actors had forgotten their roles and needed a refresher course.

In addition to changing the manga's Franken to Franken von Folger (his own homage to *The Rocky Horror Picture Show*'s Frank-N-Furter), Imagawa pastiched characters from many of Yokoyama's other works, including **Godmars**, **Babel II**, and even **Little Witch Sally**. Most notable among these is the presence of characters dressed like medieval Chinese rebels and an HQ in "Ryozanpaku," which *GR*'s U.S. translators failed to note was Japanese for Liang Shan Po, the famous marshes of the *Water Margin* (see **Suikoden**). Yokoyama's *Water Margin* was never animated but was turned into an extremely popular live-action TV series during the 1970s—however, many of its main characters were lifted wholesale for *GR*.

As implied by its Japanese subtitle, *The Day the Earth Stood Still*, *GR* also carries a subtle antinuclear message nestled amid the robot combat and gunfights, with a "safe" energy source put to evil use, ironically against all the major cities of Japan's enemies in WWII, including London, New

York, San Francisco, and Shanghai. Featuring great music from **Urotsuki-doji**-composer Amano, it also has the recurring theme, "A Furtive Tear," taken from Donizetti's comic opera *The Love Potion* (1832), which tells a similar tale of mankind putting too much faith in technology, albeit of a different kind!

The show also spun off into three videos featuring the undisputed micro-miniskirted star of the show, starting with *Barefoot Ginrei* (1993, *Hadashi no Ginrei*). This depicted the morning after the first episode of *Giant Robo*, showing a day in the life of Ginrei and Big Fire's Shockwave Alberto; at least, until Ginrei discovers that her combat China dress is missing. *Mighty Ginrei* (1994, *Tetsuwan Ginrei*) finds the Experts of Justice having a joint company party with "Blue Flower," and Daisaku defecting to the latter because of their better pay and benefits package. Since Giant Robo is in the shop for repairs, he takes with him GR's improved successor, Ginrei Robo. Both episodes are played tongue-in-cheek, with shots parodying **Lupin III** and **Cutey Honey**. The third, *Blue-Eyed Ginrei* (1995, *Aoi Hitomi no Ginrei*) is played straight. Ginrei and Tetsugyu are sent undercover to investigate the disappearance of a research team in the desert, and (of course) Big Fire turns out to be involved. The three were released in English on one DVD as *Ginrei Special*.

GIGANTOR *
1963. JPN: *Tetsujin 28-go*. AKA: *Ironman Number 28*. TV series. DIR: Yonehiko Watanabe, Tadao Wakabayashi. SCR: Yoshikazu Okamoto. DES: Mitsuteru Yokoyama. ANI: Tadao Wakabayashi, Kazuo Nobara. MUS: Hidehiko Arashino. PRD: Eiken, TMS. 25 mins. x 96 eps., 25 mins. x 51 eps. (*New*), 25 mins. x 24 eps. (*FX*).
Before Japan's experimental robot weapon project can be used against the Allies, U.S. bombers destroy the laboratory, killing its creator, Dr. Kaneda. A decade after the war, several crimes are found to have been committed by

remote-controlled giant robots, the 26th and 27th prototypes of a long-forgotten military project. Kaneda's detective son, Shotaro (Jimmy Sparks), discovers that the syndicates are searching for a mythical 28th prototype, rumored to be even more powerful. He beats them in figuring out its whereabouts, finding both it and Professor Shikashima (Bob Brilliant), another researcher thought dead in the same attack that killed his father. Shikashima and Shotaro decide to use Ironman #28 for peace, not war. The final 13 episodes, broadcast after a hiatus of several months in which the Eiken team concentrated on **PRINCE PLANET**, featured a change of direction, with Shotaro having a vision that aliens from Planet Magma are about to invade and piloting Ironman against the Magmans' robot champions Magma X and Gold Wolf.

Based on a 1956 *Shonen Magazine* serial by **GIANT ROBO** creator Mitsuteru Yokoyama, and thereby predating Osamu Tezuka's similar **BIG X** in both anime and manga forms, Ironman's design is not dissimilar to that of Ryuichi Yokoyama's propaganda manga *The Science Warrior Appears in New York* (1943), suggesting perhaps this is indeed the way that **WARTIME ANIME** might have turned out if the war had gone on any longer! However, the postwar Ironman was considered peaceful enough for 52 of the early episodes to get a U.S. release courtesy of Fred Ladd, who toned down some of the death and violence and ensured that almost every villain in the show sounded like a Nazi or a Chicago mobster. The old show is probably best remembered for its classic theme tune from Lou Singer and Gene Raskin redundantly announcing that our hero was "ready to fight for right against wrong." There was also a short-lived 1960 live-action series in Japan (*DE).

The franchise was revived for *New Ironman 28* (1980), directed by Tetsuo Imazawa, in which Interpol agent Shotaro works for the antirobot crime division, Branch Robo, and occasion-

Gigantor

© 1964 DELPHI ASSOCIATES INC. © 1992 ENTERCOLOR TECHNOLOGIES CO.

ally repels alien invaders, too. The new series removed the wartime angle by beginning in the 1990s with the death of Professor Kaneda and did not appear in the U.S. as *New Gigantor* until 1993, after the "future year" in which it was originally set.

Super-Electric Robo Ironman 28 FX (1992) was another, less successful TV series from Imazawa that moved the action to 2030 and starred the grandson of the original Professor Kaneda, fighting adversaries such as the "Pink Mafia" and the evil Franken organization, as well as the office politics within Interpol that find him arrested at one point by his own staff. *Gigantor* also supplied inspiration for creator Katsuhiro Otomo, who wrote a trilogy of adult manga designed to be modern retellings of old classics. They were *Fireball*, featuring a supercomputer modeled on **ASTRO BOY**; *Domu*, featuring a psychic schoolgirl modeled on **E-CHAN THE NINJA**; and **AKIRA**, in which a Shotaro *Kaneda* and a General who is

the son of an inventor, fight over a classified weapon left over from an old war, known as Number 28.

Gigantor was remade yet again by **GIANT ROBO**–director Yasuhiro Imagawa in 2004, in a TV series that restored much of the dark seriousness of the original manga, bringing it full circle to its militaristic origins. There was also a live-action remake, *Tetsujin 28* (2005).

GIGI AND THE FOUNTAIN OF YOUTH *

1982. JPN: *Maho no Princess Minky Momo*. AKA: *Magical Princess Minky Momo*. TV series, video. DIR: Kunihiko Yuyama, Junji Nishiyama, Kenjiro Yoshida, Hiroshi Watanabe. SCR: Takeshi Shudo, Tomomi Tsutsui, Jiyu Watanabe. DES: Toyoo Ashida, Noa Misaki, Ayumi Fukube. ANI: Mamoru Tanaka, Hiroshi Watanabe, Kazuo Imura. MUS: Hiroshi Takada. PRD: Ashi Pro, TV Tokyo. 25 mins. x 61 eps. (TV), 25 mins. x 62 eps. (v), 25 mins. x 3 eps. (v).

Minky Momo (Gigi) is a princess from the magical dreamland of Fenalinasa who has been sent to Earth where she poses as the daughter of two vets, albeit one who can transform (in the style of CREAMY MAMI) into a grown-up magical heroine, accompanied by her magical companions, Sindbook the dog, Mocha the monkey, and Pipil the bird. Perhaps unnaturally popular in the midst of the "Lolita complex" fad that also produced CREAM LEMON, she returned on several occasions, including the three-minute short *Creamy Mami vs. Minky Momo* (1985) and *Minky Momo: La Ronde in My Dream* (1985), released in the U.S. as *Gigi and the Fountain of Youth*. In this 80-minute video, also screened theatrically, her human parents' plane crashes in the sea, and Momo discovers a tropical island, above which floats a children's paradise where nobody ever ages. The island's ruler Peter (an obvious reference to PETER PAN AND WENDY) enlists Momo's help in holding off unsavory outsiders, including the original master thief Lupin (not his grandson LUPIN III).

After the original's apparent death and the destruction of Fenalinasa, a new Momo appeared in the 1991 TV series about a princess from the undersea kingdom of Marinnasa taking up the previous Momo's mantle and masquerading on Earth as the daughter of archaeologists searching for the ruins of Fenalinasa. Though the new Momo lost her powers in episode 62, she had three extra unbroadcast adventures that were included when the TV series was released on video in 1993, comprising *SOS Marinnasa, Momo Goes to School,* and *A Favor from the Stars.*

GIGOLO *
1993. JPN: *Dochinpira: Onna Daisuki.* AKA: *Vulgar Punk: I Love Women.* Video. DIR: Hiromitsu Ota. SCR: Wataru Amano. DES: Hironobu Saito. ANI: Shigetaka Kiyoyama. MUS: Beyond Two. PRD: Pink Pineapple, KSS. 45 mins.
Jin drops out of college to become a gigolo, selling his favors to bored

rich women in Tokyo while still living with his true love, the long-suffering Ranko. After some disastrous jobs that bring him into contact with the Hazakura gang, he is propositioned by Ai, a female contract killer. After he is the first man to "take her to heaven and back" (naturally), she reveals that she works for the rival Konatsu gang, whose boss adopted her after her original parents were killed in gangland cross fire. After also losing her stepfather to criminal intrigue, she has sworn revenge on Mr. Hazakura himself, who is in hiding after the last attempt on his life. Realizing that Jin has serviced Hazakura's mistress, Ai forces him to take her there, where both she and Hazakura die in a shoot-out. Jin buries her at sea in her beloved Shelby Cobra automobile, then returns to Ranko, who reveals that it is their anniversary, and takes him to bed.

Considering the liberal tastes of the Japanese video porn market, it is bizarre that *Gigolo* wasn't made as a gay anime like FAKE. If the lead characters had been male, the macho posturings and pompous codes of honor would be more believable, as would the appetites and attitudes of the "female" characters, but presumably such a narrative switch wouldn't have pleased the authors of the original manga, Makio Hara and Tetsumi Doko. Better plotted than most porn anime, if only because there is a semblance of story that bolts together the halfhearted (and half-animated) sex scenes, *Gigolo* rivals GOLGO 13 in both its contemptuous attitude toward women and its juvenile take on sex and crime. It also contains the cheesiest of dialogue, played absolutely straight in the U.K. dub. 🅛🅝🅥

GILGAMESH *
2003. TV series. DIR: Masahiko Murata. SCR: Akio Satsugawa, Sadayuki Murai, Yasuko Kobayashi. DES: Masahiro Sato, Saki Okuse. ANI: Group TAC, Japan Vistec. MUS: Kaoru Wada. PRD: Group TAC, Japan Vistec, Kansai TV. 23 mins. x 26 eps.
The near future, two decades after a

mysterious apocalyptic event in the Middle East that wiped out magnetic fields, disabled computers, and caused the "Sheltering Sky effect" that shut out the stars—perhaps an out-of-place reference to the film by Bernardo Bertolucci, or the novel by Paul Bowles that inspired it, although its closest analogue can be found in THE ANIMATRIX. Twins Tatsuya and Kiyoko are on the run from debt collectors when they are captured by a group called Orga and asked by the mysterious Countess von Werdenburg to join her child superheroes to fight a group of half-divine psychics called Gilgamesh. She claims their leader, Enkidu, was responsible for the apocalyptic incident and offers to pay the debts left by the twins' late mother in return for their assistance. The Countess is working with Dr. Enuma of the Midlight Corporation, who has developed a huge device to reverse the abnormal magnetic field and restore the world to its former state. It is contained in the tower of Turangalila—compare to BABEL II.

When Kiyoko is kidnapped by a Gilgamesh group, Tatsuya and his Orga associates chase after her, in the course of which Tatsuya realizes that he is developing paranormal powers of his own. Kiyoko, however, shelters Novem, her injured captor, becomes pregnant with his child, and begins to question the motives of her former boss the Countess. In a "twist," we discover that the twins are the children of Terumichi Madoka, the infamous Enkidu, who met their mother on an archaeological dig in the ruins of Babylon shortly before he set off the Sheltering Sky disaster. Now, in a twisted echo of ancient myth, he is trying to destroy the world in a final cleansing flood (see SPRIGGAN) to enable the planet to recover from the errors of mankind and thrive for a new, pure race of humans.

Gilgamesh is another of the-21st century anime like DEMON LORD DANTE, based on forgotten works from the 20th century after all the best-known titles had been snapped up. It first appeared as a 1976 manga in *Shonen King* magazine by Shotaro Ishinomori, mixing ancient myth with UFO lore in the manner of NAZCA. Ishinomori's original is suffused here with a darker subtext, largely in the wake of the 9/11 terrorist attacks in 2001 that culminated in the fall of the twin towers of the World Trade Center. The disaster in *Gilgamesh* takes place on 10th October, and hence becomes known as "Twin X," a clever reference to the protagonists, although likely to cause some confusion in Taiwan, where the same day is known as "Double Tenth," and is a public holiday to celebrate the foundation of the Republic of China.

Gilgamesh

© ISHIMORI-PRO/GILGAMESH COMMITTEE

GINBAN KALEIDOSCOPE
2005. TV series. DIR: Shinji Takamatsu, Hazuki Mizumoto. SCR: Akatsuki Yamatoya, Michiko Yokote, Natsuko Takahashi, Rika Nakase. DES: Momoko Makiuchi. ANI: Tatsuo Miura. MUS: Koichiro Kamiyama. PRD: arp Japan, QEN, Studio B2, TV Tokyo. 25 mins. x 7+ eps.
World-class figure skater Sakurano suffers a cataclysmic fall from favor, incurring the wrath of the media and other skaters. Such public troubles only serve to exacerbate her typical teen angst and school pressures. One day, she gains a ghostly companion, Pete, the ghost of a handsome blond skater, the cause of whose death is initially unknown to Sakurano. He becomes her companion and sometime ally, in an ice-skating rerun of HIKARU'S GO. Based on a manga by Rei Kaibara.

GINGUISER
1977. JPN: *Chogattai Majutsu Robo Ginguiser*. AKA: *Ultra-transforming Magical Robot Ginguiser*. TV series. DIR: Masami Annai. SCR: Rei Yada, Yu Yamamoto, Doki Kan. DES: Yasuo Kainai, Studio Nue. ANI: Hitoshi Tanaka. MUS: Seiji Yokoyama. PRD: Ashi Pro, Nippon Animation, TV Asahi. 25 mins. x 26 eps.
Emperor Kaindark of the Sazorian Empire wants three powerful energy sources, the spheres of Antares. They are hidden on Earth, so he sends his mighty monsters (awakened after 20,000 years in suspended animation) to bring them back. They are opposed by Doctor Godo, the scion of the Sazorian's rival Plasman clan, who had foreseen such a danger, but inexplicably decides that Earth's best line of defense should be a pair of teenagers with a traveling magic show and a pile of slick card tricks. Goro Shiroishi and Michi Ushio drive a truck that can transform into a fighting robot; their comrades Torajiro Aranami and Santa Minami each have another transforming vehicle. Ginguiser is formed when the three robots Grandfighter, Spinlancer, and Bullgaiter combine with the jet fighter Arrow Wing. When the enemy attacks, the plane takes off from its secret base under Luna Park and the other three robots gather to unite. Armed with a sword, a shield, and a rotary saw, Ginguiser fights to save the world from the monsters—it is no coincidence that it replicates the plotlines and attitudes of the early battle-team shows from live-action television, *Goranger* (*DE) and *Jaqk* (*DE).

GINNAGASHI
1992. JPN: *Ginnagashi: Terajima-cho Kidan*. AKA: *Ginnagashi: Strange Tales of Terajima District*. Video. DIR: Osamu Kobayashi. SCR: Yu Takita. DES: Masaya Fujimori. ANI: Takaichiro Nakamura. MUS: Hiroshi Ogasawara. PRD: Toei, Tac. 41 mins.
Ten-year-old Kiyoshi watches as a tramp transforms himself into a rich imposter at a stand-up bar in the Tamanoi district. Amusing tales from prewar Tokyo based on the 1968 autobiographical manga *Strange Tales of Terajima* and written by Yu Takita for the alternative magazine *Garo*.

GIRL DETECTIVES' CLUB
1986. JPN: *Katsugeki Shojo Tanteidan*. Video. DIR: Masaharu Okuwaki. SCR: Yuho Hanazono. DES: Isamu Eguchi. ANI: Masako Goto. MUS: "The Girl Detectives' Club." PRD: Tokyo Movie Shinsha. 30 mins.
Yuriko Edogawa, Midori Ichinotani, and Ingrid Shizuka Gruber are ordinary students at the high-class Gautama School for Girls who moonlight as supersleuths. Midori disappears soon after discovering that her scientist father is working on a weapon, and

the other girls track her down. They discover that she has been kidnapped by Akiko Jitsusoji, a bad-girl with her own gang working for the school principal, who is planning to conquer the world with Dr. Ichinotani's doomsday device. This very early multimedia offensive, including a tie-in manga in *Out* magazine, ended with a very early disappointed audience, as *GDC* turned out to be a lackluster affair. Compare to the suspiciously similar **DEBUTANTE DETECTIVES**.

GIRL FROM PHANTASIA *

1993. JPN: *Fantasia*. Video. DIR: Jun Kamiya. SCR: Katsuyuki Sumizawa. DES: Kazuya Kise. ANI: Kazuya Kise. MUS: Toshiyuki Watanabe. PRD: Production IG. 30 mins.

College boy Akihiro's girlfriend, Michiko, doesn't like his apartment enough to come over, and that seriously reduces his chances of getting her into bed. Finding a rug among some trash on the sidewalk, he takes it home to improve the decor, only to discover that it is a magical gateway to the fantasyland of Phantasia. Akihiko becomes the object of attention from the feisty sprite Malon. This video is a replay of a dozen other magical-girl-friend tales from **URUSEI YATSURA** to **OH MY GODDESS!**, this time with an eye on the soft-core porn market. Based on Akane Nagano's manga in *Comic Gamma*. Ⓝ

GIRL NEXT DOOR *

2000. JPN: *Tonari no Neesan*. Video. DIR: Teruaki Murakami, Sotsuki Mitsumura. SCR: Rokurota Makabe. DES: Bijin Happo. ANI: Takeshi Okamura. MUS: Yoshi. PRD: YOUC, Digital Works (Vanilla Series). 30 mins. x 2 eps.

Masahiko is a shy young man, who believes that he has already met his ideal woman, a Girl Next Door who is somewhere out there waiting for him. But as he tries to remember where he has seen her before, a series of other women in his life clamor for his attention, including his boss, his school teacher, and an old friend from his childhood. In other words, **LOVE HINA** with sex scenes. Ⓝ

GIRL WITH THE WHITE FLAG, THE

1988. JPN: *Hakuki no Shojo Ryuko*. Movie. DIR: Tetsu Dezaki. SCR: Tetsu Dezaki. DES: Yukari Kobayashi. ANI: Reizo Kiyomizu. MUS: Yuse Nakajima. PRD: Magic Bus. ca. 80 mins.

In 1945, American troops land on the island of Okinawa. The Japanese fight a guerrilla war against the invaders, and little Ryuko is forced to leave her grandparents behind and flee with her mother and younger sister, who are eventually killed. Ryuko heads on alone across the war-torn island. Eventually she reaches safety in Japanese-occupied caves, only to witness the Japanese troops committing suicide with hand grenades. Based on a children's book by Akira Aratagawa and Hikuji Norima, itself inspired by real American footage of an Okinawan girl, Tomiko Higa, waving a white flag at the island's surrender. Shown in some theaters on a double bill with **MY NEIGHBOR TOTORO** instead of the similar **GRAVE OF THE FIREFLIES**. Another Okinawan war story was filmed as **VOYAGE OF THE TSUSHIMA**.

GIRLS BRAVO *

2004. TV series. DIR: Ei Aoki. SCR: Hiroshi Watanabe. DES: Ryuichi Makino. ANI: Yoshiyuki Matsuzaki. MUS: Noriyasu Uematsu. PRD: AIC, Spirits, Fuji TV. 25 mins. x 11 eps. (TV1), 25 mins. x 13 eps. (TV2).

Wimpy teen Yukinari Sasaki suffers so much teasing at the hands of the girls of Mizuno High that he develops girl-phobia—he breaks out in hives if a girl so much as touches him, much like the leads of **DNA²** and **HANAUKYO MAID TEAM**. The only girl he can be around is his childhood friend Kirie Kojima, a beautiful, brilliant student and a sports star, and comparing himself to her just makes him feel even more inadequate. Kirie really cares for him and is constantly trying to nag him into a more positive frame of mind, but his whole life changes when she throws him into a bathtub and he surfaces in another world. In Seilen, there are nine girls to every boy, and Seilenite Miharu Sena Kanaka decides to grab the gift Fate has sent her. She's very cute, with pink hair, curious, trusting, and best of all, she doesn't trigger Yukinari's hives, so when she decides to go back to his world and live with him, he's delighted. Although Kirie is jealous at first, the three become friends. But Nanae, manager of Seilen's version of the **OH MY GODDESS!** agency of divine intervention, the Inter-Dimensional Office, sends two cute girl agents to bring Miharu back. Koyumi and Tomoka pop out of Yukinari's bathtub and bring even more mayhem into his life. To vary the pace, Yukinari meets a girl who doesn't use bathtubs as inter-dimensional portals—dizzy blonde Risa Fukuyama, who immediately decides he's her Mr. Right. Meanwhile, there's a nod to **URUSEI YATSURA** in the shape of handsome rich kid Kazuharu Fuku-yama, who decides Miharu is going to be his and enrolls her at Mizuno High. The series is based on a *Shonen Ace* manga by Mario Kaneda, and to judge from the number of clone geek-gets-girls stories being turned out year after year, the target audience doesn't mind it being just a tad derivative. Bath scenes in the first season were censored with the aid of digitally-added steam to obscure nudity. A second season followed in 2005, reveling in its risqué honor of being "the first TV anime to earn an R–15 rating in Japan." However, this was nonsensical hype; Japanese TV has seen a lot worse, from **TIGER MASK** to **GANTZ**, and the fact that a few flashes of nudity should cause such a censorious honor is yet another sign of the current conservatism in Japanese television. The authors fear that if they encounter one more **TENCHI MUYO!** wannabe, they too will come out in hives. Ⓝ

GIRLS IN SAILOR SUITS

2005. JPN: *Seifuku Shojo*. Video. DIR: Teruaki Murakami. SCR: Osamu Momoi. DES: Teruaki Murakami. ANI: Teruaki

Murakami. MUS: Kosaku Sasaki. PRD: Pink Pineapple, KSS. 30 mins. x 2 eps.

Schoolgirls are molested and abused by a lecherous principal in the classroom, backstage at the school play, and so on. Based on a manga in *Core* magazine by Oninojin. 🅛🅝🅥

GIRLS IN SUMMER DRESSES

1988. JPN: *Natsufuku no Shojotachi*. TV special. DIR: Keiko Sugiura. SCR: Makiko Uchidate. DES: Yoshiyuki Momose. ANI: Toshio Hirata, Masao Murayama. MUS: N/C. PRD: Madhouse. 50 mins.

In 1945, the second- and third-year students of a Hiroshima girls' school are taken away to work in war factories. The remaining 220 girls of the first year try to make the best of their new-found status as the only teenagers in an almost deserted town, even amid the deprivations of wartime. On the 7th of August, an American bomber changes their lives forever. Broadcast on the 43rd anniversary of Hiroshima in memory of "the girls who lost their lives to the atom bomb," this is in the spirit of the earlier BAREFOOT GEN. This TV movie was a rare anime outing for the screenwriter Makiko Uchidate, better known for her many live-action drama serials.

GIRL'S LOCKER ROOM LUST *

2003. JPN: *Miniskirt Gakuen*. AKA: *Miniskirt College*. Video. DIR: N/C. SCR: N/C. DES: N/C. ANI: N/C. MUS: N/C. PRD: Obtain. 30 mins.

Madoka is underperforming on the girls' volleyball team, and so is put through a harsh training regime by her team leader Yoko. This involves her fighting off a series of increasingly stronger attacks in the style of *The Sign is V* (*DE), although whereas in the live-action inspiration such an ordeal killed its subject, in *GLRL* it merely leaves her lying exhausted on the floor and primed for "comforting" at the hands of her tormentor. Meanwhile, Madoka's boyfriend Noboru is feeling left out, until he realizes that class-mate Yuna has a crush on him. Sexual

complications ensue. The U.S. release includes a bonus 20-minute audio drama that runs while still images play on screen—compare to FORBIDDEN LOVE. 🅛🅝🅥

GLASS RABBIT

2005. JPN: *Garasu no Usagi*. Movie. DIR: Setsuko Shibuichi. SCR: Kazumi Koide, Mitsuyo Suenaga. DES: Setsuko Shibuichi. ANI: Kazunori Tanahashi, Yukari Kobayashi. MUS: Michiru Oshima. PRD: Magic Bus, Tokyo Metropolitan TV. ca. 80 mins.

Toshiko Takagi is safely evacuated to Ninomiya ahead of American air raids, but her mother and sisters are caught in the firebombing of Tokyo in March 1945—the same attack dramatized in KAYOKO'S DIARY. Rightly believing them to be dead, she endures a five-month wait until her father (a glass maker conscripted to make syringes for the war effort) arrives to collect her. As the reunited parent and child wait for the train to Niigata where they intend to start a new life, the station is strafed by an American plane, and Toshiko's father is killed. Later that night, she walks into the sea, and it is only when she is bowled over by a wave that she realizes she cannot swim and has been inadvertently succumbing to thoughts of suicide. Back in Tokyo, she finds the ruins of her old house and the remains of a glass rabbit that her father had made, melted almost beyond recognition by the heat of the Tokyo firestorm. The traumatized 13-year-old girl waits for her brothers to return from the war.

Takagi's autobiography had already been a successful book, both on its original 1970s publication and in a more recent annotated edition to help modern readers with the more obscure words. Although the story had already been adapted for film and TV, Takagi reportedly resisted the idea of an animated version until her grandchildren convinced her that her anti-war message could reach a younger audience. Presumably in the wake of Japan's renewed involvement in foreign con-

flicts since the first Gulf War, the animated version adds a new emphasis at the author's insistence: a stark realism to the scenes of aerial bombardment and the highlighting of the book's final chapter, in which the youthful Toshiko greets Japan's postwar pacifist constitution with elation. Compare to CHOCCHAN'S STORY. 🅥

GLASSY OCEAN *

1998. JPN: *Kujira no Choyaku*. AKA: *The Whale's Leap*. Movie. DIR: Shigeru Tamura. SCR: Shigeru Tamura. DES: Shigeru Tamura. ANI: Masaya Sato. MUS: Yutoro Teshiume. PRD: Bandai. 23 mins.

On another world where time works differently, the ocean has turned to glass. In an impressive feat of digital animation shown at several film festivals and broadcast on the U.K.'s Channel Four, people gather on the shore at a particular place to watch the group of whales that has arrived preparing to leap out of the water. Creator Shigeru Tamura also made the earlier *Galactic Fish* (1993), which also played with watery themes, this time visualizing a dimension where our world appears to be at the bottom of someone else's sea. He was also associated with Akiyuki Terajima's Japanese DVD compilation *A Piece of Phantasmagoria* (1995), which comprised 15 short animated films of a similar nature.

GLICK'S ADVENTURE

1981. JPN: *Glick no Boken*. Movie. DIR: Hideo Nishimaki. SCR: Yasuo Tanami. DES: Yoshio Kabashima. ANI: Takeshi Yamazaki. MUS: Reijiro Komutsu. PRD: Studio Koryumi. 82 mins.

Glick the squirrel and his friends leave their urban house and head off for the forest, meeting Gamba the vole on the way. After many hardships, Glick gives up and collapses in the snow, only to be rescued by his friends and arrive in the forest safely. Based on a story by Atsushi Saito that won a Best Newcomer award from the Association for the Study of Japanese Children's Books. Compare to BANNERTAIL THE SQUIRREL.

GLORIA: FORBIDDEN RELATIONS *

1998. JPN: *Glo.ri.a: Kindan no Ketsuzoku*. AKA: *Gloria: Private Lessons*. Video. DIR: Yasuhiro Kuroda. SCR: Akira Yokusuga. DES: Yasuaki Yoshino. ANI: Yasuaki Yoshino. MUS: N/C. PRD: Pink Pineapple, KSS. 30 mins. x 3 eps.
Kira and Gyorg (Beowulf in the U.S. dub) are selected to be personal tutors to the super-rich Gloria family in the U.S., whose five daughters turn out to be in need of an unexpected kind of "education." The tutors settle into the easy life, cosseted by servants and servicing their pupils, only to discover that the family hides a dark secret, and that the teachers will be in deadly danger if they do not leave immediately. Based on the C's Ware computer game *Forbidden Relations*. ◐

GLORIOUS ANGELS

1978. JPN: *Pink Lady Monogatari Eiko no Tenshitachi*. AKA: *Glorious Angels: The Pink Lady Story*. TV series. DIR: Katsuhiko Taguchi. SCR: Masaru Yamamoto. DES: Yuji Hosoi. ANI: Ichiro Dannohara. MUS: Kyosuke Onosaki, Pink Lady. PRD: T&C, Toei, Tokyo 12 Channel. 25 mins. x 35 eps.
Mitsuyo Nemoto and Keiko Masuda, two girls from the backwoods of Shizuoka, meet at school, share the same dream of becoming pop stars, and win the district talent contest. They specialize in the performing arts at school, persevering at ballet and music. One day, they hope they'll make it to the top. This school-days biography of the singers who would eventually become Pink Lady, Japan's most famous duo in the late 1970s, was made at the height of their fame and a clever means of keeping the pair in the public eye without occupying their precious time—other actresses provided the girls' voices. An animated pop star tie-in similar to CAROL and HUMANE SOCIETY, in aims if not execution.

GLORIOUS SUBSECTION CHIEF

1976. JPN: *Hana no Kakaricho*. AKA: *Flower of Subsection Chiefs*. TV series. DIR: Minoru Okazaki, Kazunori Tana-

hashi. SCR: Noboru Shiroyama, Tsunehisa Ito, Haruya Yamazaki, Shinichi Matsuoka. DES: Shunji Sonoyama. ANI: Takeo Kasai. MUS: Hiroki Tamaki, Hiroshi Kamayatsu. PRD: TMS, TV Asahi. 25 mins. x 26 eps.
Mashumaro Ayanoroji has an insanely ostentatious name, but that is only to be expected from a former aristocrat, forced to slum it as a humble bureaucrat. Baffled by modern times, he puts a brave face on office life, hoping to claw his way back up to the top for the sake of his wife and son. The second anime to be based on the work of GARDLES-creator Shunji Sonoyama, in this case a manga in the *Post* weekly, this show was broadcast relatively late at night (22:30), and so did not shy away from more adult humor. The first 16 episodes each contained two chapters, but this was later shortened to three 7-minute mini-stories per "half-hour" episode. Kazutaka Nishikawa, who was then popular in the role of Daigoro in *Lone Wolf and Cub* (*DE), provided the voice of Mashumaro's young son.

GLORIOUS TALES OF OLD EDO

1989. JPN: *Manga Edo Erobanashi*. AKA: *Glorious Manga Tales of Edo*. Video. DIR: Tsutomu Shibayama, Hajime Oedo, Hideo Kawauchi. SCR: N/C. DES: N/C. ANI: N/C. MUS: N/C. PRD: Studio Jump. 44 mins. x 10 eps.
Several tales of old-time Tokyo from well-known directors, mainly concentrating on the courtesans of the Yoshiwara and prostitutes in premodern Shinjuku but also on the merchants and the impoverished samurai class of the period, with star-crossed lovers, chirpy artisans, and human-interest stories. Compare to the altogether more accomplished SENSUALIST. Other olde-worlde porn preceded the series with *Classical Sex-Zone* (1988), featuring erotic moments from the wars of the Heike and the Genji, and from the TALE OF GENJI itself. ◐

GLORY TO THE ANCESTORS

1989. JPN: *Gosenzosama Banbanzai*. Video. DIR: Mamoru Oshii. SCR: Mamoru

Oshii. DES: Satoru Utsunomiya. ANI: Satoru Utsunomiya. MUS: Kenji Kawai. PRD: Studio Pierrot. 30 mins. x 6 eps.
Maroko, a girl from the future, decides to learn more about her ancestors and travels back in time to modern Japan, only to discover that they are a sorry single-parent family, struggling to make ends meet without Mother around. She tries to help out and soon runs afoul of the Time Police. A show that mixes homespun situation comedy with the chrononautical goings-on of DORAEMON, it was reedited with some extra footage and released as the 90-minute movie *Maroko* (1990).

GO FOR IT, GENKI

1980. JPN: *Ganbare Genki*. TV series. DIR: Rintaro, Masahiro Sasaki, Akinori Nagaoka. SCR: Shunichi Yukimuro. DES: Shigetaka Kiyoyama. ANI: Kazuo Komatsubara, Masami Suda, Kazuo Mori, Tsukasa Abe. MUS: Koichi Morita. PRD: Fuji TV, Toei. 25 mins. x 35 eps.
When young Genki expresses an interest, his father decides to stage a comeback to regain his own featherweight title. Genki becomes a trainer for his own father, and the two take on the world as they struggle to relive past glories and create future ones. Based on a 1976 *Shonen Sunday* manga by Yu Koyama, who also created OI! RYOMA.

GO FOR IT, GOEMON!

1991. JPN: *Anime Ganbare Goemon*. Video, movie, TV series. DIR: Shigeru Omachi, Katsuyoshi Yatabe. SCR: Shigeru Omachi. DES: Masayuki Hiraoka. ANI: Katsuyoshi Kobayashi. MUS: Yasuo Tsuchida. PRD: Public & Basic, TBS. 30 mins. (v), 25 mins. x 26 eps. (TV), 30 mins. (m).
Goemon, the hero of a fantasy computer game from Konami, is transported from his magical medieval world to become a superhero on Earth. First appearing in Yasunori Iguchi's video *GFIG: Nightmare Dimension* (1991), Goemon returned in earnest for a 1997 TV series, fighting enemy Seppuku-Maru and his army of computer beasts. The series soon followed the standard

plotting of many others: Goemon saves the day at a sports stadium, fights on a train, thwarts a forest fire at a summer camp, meets Santa Claus, helps out an idol singer, etc. For the short movie version *GFIG: Battle to Rescue Earth* (1998), Japan is threatened by a growing mountain of trash, which duly turns out to be the work of evildoers, not humanity in general.

GO FOR IT, KONBE

1980. JPN: *Ganbare Konbe*. TV series. DIR: Hiroe Mitsunobu, Hidenori Kondo, Susumu Ishizaki, Noboru Ishiguro, Tameo Ogawa. SCR: Yukio Izumi. DES: Shunji Sonoyama. ANI: Kenjiro Yoshida. MUS: Kenjiro Hirose. PRD: Production Roots, Anime City, Tokyo 12 Channel. 15 mins. x 56 eps.
Believing himself to be a descendant of Sun Wu-Kong, the hero of **JOURNEY TO THE WEST**, mountain monkey Konbe and his sister, Monko, run away from school. Pursued by their schoolmates Sanjiro, Benkei, Gataro the bird, and frog couple Mr. and Mrs. Kerosuke, Konbe soon finds that there is much to learn out in the big wide world. Based on an educational eight-panel manga strip from the *Mainichi Shogaku Shinbun* by Shunji Sonoyama, who also created **GON THE FIRST MAN**.

GO FOR IT, TABUCHI: VIOLENT PENNANT CONTEST

1980. JPN: *Ganbare Tabuchi-kun: Gekito Pennant Race*. Movie. DIR: Tsutomu Shibayama. SCR: Hideo Takayashiki, Masaki Tsuji, Tomoko Konparu. DES: Michishiro Yamada. ANI: Osamu Kobayashi, Minoru Maeda. MUS: Hidenori Mori, Hiroki Inui, Kensuke Kyo. PRD: TMS, Kitty Film. 94 mins.
The Seibu Lions baseball team makes it to the next round of a baseball tournament thanks to the heroic efforts of its star player, Tabuchi, but the next stage will involve hard work and cooperation. In a sports anime that pitches caricatures of real-life players against cartoon characters, the Lions (whose real-life mascot is the grown-up **KIMBA THE WHITE LION**), keep losing games

due to Tabuchi's poor condition—his shadow is getting paler. A group of fellow players turns up at the stadium, accompanied by **DOKABEN**, and they encourage Tabuchi to pull through. They organize a Tabuchi Day to show him how appreciated he is, but it is a miserable failure. Eventually, he is brought out of his depression by the arrival of a girl called Miyoko, who obliges by dressing up as a cheerleader. Based on the 1979 *Action* manga by Hisaichi Ishii, who also created **MY NEIGHBORS THE YAMADAS**.

GO GOSHOBEN

1991. JPN: *Uttchare Goshobei*. Video. DIR: Kazuyoshi Kozawa. SCR: Noboru Hirose. DES: Mitsuharu Kajiya. ANI: Mitsuharu Kajiya. MUS: N/C. PRD: Nippon Eizo, JC Staff. 50 mins.
Benkyo Gosho is the only dedicated martial artist at his high school, so he is forced to represent the school at the intercollegiate championships in both wrestling and judo. He tries to enlist help from his schoolmates, scouting among the local fat kids for a possible wrestling buddy, eventually deciding he's probably going to have to make it on his own. Based on the 1988 *Shonen Sunday* manga by Ben Nakajima.

GOAL FIELD HUNTER

1994. AKA: *Goal FH*. TV series. DIR: Masakazu Higuchi, Shinichi Watanabe, Akira Kiyomizu. SCR: Hiroshi Terajima. DES: Yuki Iwai. ANI: Yuki Iwai, Akihiro Kaneyama. MUS: N/C. PRD: Dog Fight, NHK2. 25 mins. x 39 eps.
A standard tale of a soccer team overcoming the odds to become the champions of the J-League. Concentrating on an adult, professional cast instead of the amateurs of **CAPTAIN TSUBASA**, this series also boasts professional "soccer advisers" among the crew to ensure realism.

GOD SIGMA

1980. JPN: *Uchu Taitei God Sigma*. AKA: *Space Emperor God Sigma*. TV series. DIR: Takeyuki Kanda, Katsuhiko Taguchi. SCR: Masaki Tsuji. DES: Kaoru

Shintani, Kazuhiko Udagawa, Yutaka Izubuchi. ANI: Kazuhiko Udagawa, Akira Saijo. MUS: Hiroshi Tsutsui. PRD: Toei, Tokyo 12 Channel. 25 mins. x 50 eps.
In the year 2050, the alien Eldar finally complete their 2,300-year journey to a new world, only to find it occupied by human colonists. Second-generation colonists Toshiya and Kensaku see their homeworld of Io destroyed but are recruited by Professor Kazumi to pilot one of the two "Thunder God" war robots in order to stop the Eldar general Teral reaching Earth. The robots also have a secret (can you possibly guess? . . .): the Earth and Sky Thunder robots can combine with the Sea Thunder Robot piloted by the professor's beautiful assistant, Julie, to form the invincible robot God Sigma.

GODAIKIN *

1982.
This is not an anime show. It is the name for the U.S. release (or rerelease) of a line of diecast and plastic toys from Bandai and its subsidiary company, Popy. In Japan the toy line was known as *DX Chogokin (De luXe Super Alloy)*, *Chogokin* being a term coined by Go Nagai to describe the metal used to build **MAZINGER Z**. The *Godaikin/Chogokin* range consisted of a mix of robots from both live-action *sentai* and anime shows, but only the anime robots included are listed here. The Godaikin range included Tetsujin 28 (see **GIGANTOR**), **GOD SIGMA**, Gardian (see **CHAMPION OF GORDIAN**), Daltanias (**DARTANIUS**), Golion (see **VOLTRON**), Combattra (**COMBATTLER V**), Voltes V (**VOLTUS**), **DANCOUGAR**, **LASERION**, and Abega (**LIGHTSPEED ELECTRON ARBEGAS**). The range enjoyed a Japanese revival in the late 1990s with a range of high-end diecast toys for the collector market entitled *Soul of Chogokin*.

GODANNAR *

2003. JPN: *Shinkon Gattai Godannar*. AKA: *God and Spirit Combination Godannar*. TV series. DIR: Yasushi Nagaoka. SCR: Hiroyuki Kawasaki, Yasushi Nagaoka, Tetsuya Endo. DES: Takahiro

Godannar

© 2003 PROJECT GODANNAR

Kimura, Masahiro Yamane, Tsukasa Kotobuki, Kyoma Aki, Seiji Tanda. ANI: N/C. MUS: Michiaki Watanabe. PRD: AIC, ITT, OLM, Taki Corp., Klockworx, AT-X. 25 mins. x 13 eps. (TV1), 25 mins. x 13 eps. (TV2).

In 2047 humanity is threatened by Mimetic Beasts, savage creatures from the depths of the Earth that spread a virus turning people into similar monsters. Earth's last hope is the Dannars, symbiotic robots that have fought the Mimetic Beasts to a temporary standstill. Since the Dannars require dual pilots with close emotional contact, they are often piloted by siblings, relatives, or teams comprising husbands and wives. Consequently, tragedy is inevitable. Dannar pilot Go Saruwatani loses his wife in the early days of the assault, but is finally preparing to walk down the aisle again, this time with Anna, a girl he rescued as a child, but who is now 16. When a surprise attack threatens the wedding, Anna rushes to Go's aid in the top secret Neo-Okusaer robot, demonstrating an aptitude for Dannar piloting much to her husband's annoyance—Earth needs pilots, but Go doesn't want another dead wife.

Godannar has the best of both

worlds: romance applied to military sci-fi (with the eye candy that is liable to bring): a giant robot drama with crossover potential for the aging fan, who can believe that even if he is no longer the age of the stereotypical "hot-headed protagonist" of other shows, fate might still bring him a barely legal spouse with an interest in robots. *Godannar* acknowledges this appeal to the more mature fan with a reference that will only make sense to men in their forties (or *serious* fans)—a character named Tetsuya Koji, named in homage to Tsurugi Tetsuya and Kabuto Koji, two pilots from the **MAZINGER Z** franchise. Meanwhile, in a combination of the age-swaps of **MARVELOUS MELMO** or its mundane equivalent *My Wife is 18* (*DE), Anna gets to flip between the role of competent adult and hapless ingenue, depending on what she wants out of her husband—**LOLITA ANIME** without the psychological or erotic subtext. However, it also contains fairy-tale elements lifted from *Beauty and the Beast* and *Sleeping Beauty*, since Go is infected with the Mimetic virus and put in cryongenic storage while his wife searches for a cure, before the final race against

time to win a battle in Tokyo against the Ultimate Evolution Beast, the product of all existing Mimetic Beasts merging into one huge creature. A second season followed in 2004. **Ⓥ**

GODDAM

1990. Video. DIR: Noboru Furuse. SCR: Tomo Fujikawa. DES: Noboru Furuse. ANI: Noboru Furuse. MUS: Eri Kani. PRD: Signal. 47 mins. x 2 eps.
The Seiyo racing team enters the world-famous Safari Rally, led by Japanese hero Todohara and his American navigator Rob Lowe(!). Based on the 1988 *Big Comic* manga by **AREA 88**–creator Kaoru Shintani. The two-part series was unnumbered, but *G: Survival Chaser* is the first, followed by *G: Go Ahead.*

GODMARS *

1981. JPN: *Rokushin Gattai Godmars.* AKA: *Hexademonic Symbiote Godmars; Six-God Union Godmars.* TV series, movie. DIR: Tetsuo Imazawa, Hideyuki Motohashi, Tetsu Dezaki, Junji Nishimura. SCR: Keisuke Fujikawa, Noboru Shiroyama. DES: Hajime Kamegaki. ANI: Hideyuki Motohashi. MUS: Kei Wakakusa, Reijiro Komutsu. PRD: Hikari Pro, TMS. 25 mins. x 64 eps. (TV), 97 mins. (m), 56 mins. (v), 30 mins. x 2 eps. (v2).
In the year 1999, humanity starts to advance beyond the confines of the solar system, encountering the evil Emperor Zaul of Planet Gishin. Takeru Akigami of the Earth Defense Force "Cosmocrushers" discovers that he was sent from Gishin as a sleeper agent 17 years previously. He is forced to choose between his two homes, deciding to defend Earth as one of the pilots of the six-part Godmars robot, which forces him into a tragic conflict with his elder brother Mark, who has chosen the other side.

This series was very loosely based on Mitsuteru Yokoyama's 1976 *Mars* manga from *Shonen Champion* magazine, itself a retelling of Yokoyama's earlier **BABEL II**. The shows were recut to make a 1982 movie (released in the

U.S. as *Godmars*), and Masakazu Iijima also directed *GM: Legend of Seventeen* (1988), a one-shot video retelling the life of the doomed Mark.

After the success of "retro" series like GIANT ROBO, the story was remade on video with greater faith to Yokoyama's original as *Mars* (1994) by Junji Nishimura, who had also worked on *Godmars*. It restored the original manga's storyline of a young boy in suspended animation inside a South Sea volcano who awakens a century before his alien masters planned to use his powers to reduce human civilization to a manageable low-tech level. As with his *Godmars* counterpart, however, he chooses to adopt the human race as his own and fight the invaders. This story, closer in attitude to the original manga, was remade a second time as *New Century Mars* (*Shinseikiden Mars*, 2002), a 13-episode TV series broadcast on AT-X.

GOING STEADY WITH A WITCH
1986. JPN: *Majo de mo Steady*. Video. DIR: Hiroshi Kobayashi. SCR: Reiko Nakada. DES: Tori Miki. ANI: Hideo Kawauchi. MUS: Hiroshi Ogasawara. PRD: Tokyo Media Connections, Asiado. 42 mins.
Hisashi Seki lives a gray, dull salaryman's life, living alone in an old apartment building that happens to be built over a dimensional warp. He wakes up to find the nude girl Mami in his room. They fall in love and decide to stay in Hisashi's world, but then an accident shoots Hisashi into another world: one occupied by everyone's ideal partners. Compare to OH MY GODDESS!, URUSEI YATSURA, and a zillion other stories in which a passive man gets a gorgeous girl just by loafing. ●

GOKU: MIDNIGHT EYE *
1989. Video. DIR: Yoshiaki Kawajiri. SCR: Buichi Terasawa, Ryuzo Nakanishi. DES: Yoshiaki Kawajiri, Hirotoshi Sano. ANI: Hiroshi Hamazaki, Hirotoshi Sano. MUS: Yukihide Takekawa, Kazz Toyama. PRD: Madhouse, Toei. 50 mins. x 2 eps.
In the year 2014, private investigator

Goku Furinji is contacted by former associates on the police force who are being picked off by a mysterious assailant. Left for dead after an encounter with a female hypnotist, a mysterious force gives him a high-tech stick that can change sizes and a link to every computer on the globe through his left ("midnight") eye. He uses both devices in his ongoing fight against crime. But apart from the magic staff, the name ("Goku" being Japanese for "Wu Kong"), and some luxuriant sideburns, the story bears little resemblance to the Monkey King of JOURNEY TO THE WEST, which supposedly inspired it. It owes more to James Bond films, with the plush locations, silly plots, and breathless girls in tight dresses looking for a Real Man to sort out their problems. With the concentration on that superduper eye of his, it also recalls the *Six Million Dollar Man*.

Based on a 1988 manga in *Comic Burger*, *GME* is a typical work from Buichi Terasawa, who gave us SPACE ADVENTURE COBRA, KABUTO, and the as-yet-untranslated *Red Brand Takeru*. It was the babes that really appealed to his audience, and the anime doesn't scrimp on regularly wheeling out a beautiful, scantily clad, eye-candy girl, normally with some incredibly theatrical shtick like peacock feathers or a pair of motorcycle handlebars on her back. Other designs are similarly impressive, from flying metal devildogs to motorized unicycles. It's not every day you get to see a fully robed Mandarin tycoon roller-skating down the side of a skyscraper, either. ●●●

GOKUDO
1999. JPN: *Gokudo no Manyuki*. AKA: *Gokudo's Dissolute Wanderings; Jester the Adventurer*. TV series. DIR: Kunihisa Sugishima, Akihiko Nishiyama. SCR: Koji Miura, Sumihiro Tomioka, Masamichi Sugawara, Hirokazu Mizude. DES: Miho Shimokasa. ANI: Masayuki Hiraoka, Michiaki Sugimoto. MUS: N/C. PRD: Trans Arts, Pioneer, TV Tokyo. 25 mins. x 26 eps.
Gokudo is reckless, greedy, and ambi-

tious, the crown prince of Esharott, and self-proclaimed treasure hunter. Exiled after Satan, Emperor of the Darkside, usurps his father's throne, he is saved by Satan's wife, Mora. Disguised as an old fortune-teller, she turns him into two people—Jester and Justice, wielders of the swords of Fire and Ice. After they overthrow Satan and his puppet king, Jester realizes that Justice would make the best ruler, leaves the kingdom to him, and sets out in search of adventure with tomboy Roubett and Mora's son, Prince—banished from the Darkside Empire and ordered to learn the ways of the world. This series, based on a novel by Usagi Nakamura, is part JOURNEY TO THE WEST, part RANMA ½.

GOKUSEN, THE *
2004. JPN: *Gokusen*. TV series. DIR: Yuzo Sato. SCR: Yasuko Kobayashi. DES: Yoshinori Kanemori. ANI: Yoshinori Kanemori. MUS: Takamitsu Gotoh. PRD: Madhouse, VAP, NTV. 25 mins. x 13 eps.
Shirogane High is renowned for the delinquency of its pupils, and Kumiko Yamaguchi, a teacher fresh out of training, draws the short straw and gets the worst class. Her colleagues feel sorry for her but if they knew her background they might be more worried for the juvenile troublemakers, for she is the heiress of the dreaded Oedo yakuza family and currently acting as clan head. Linguists should note that her name in Japanese order is a pun on Yamaguchi-gumi, the largest crime syndicate in Japan, and that her pupils soon start calling her Yankume, a badgirl reference equivalent to SUKEBAN DEKA, with which *Gokusen* has some similarities. The title is a contraction of *Gokudo Sensei*, literally "Gangster Teacher."

The only person who suspects there's anything out of the ordinary about the new teacher is Shin Sawada, ringleader of her class of troublemakers, but he can't uncover her secret despite organizing a class boycott and trying to force her to fight him.

Nobody knows that the school's chairman of the board of trustees is looking for an excuse to shut the place down and redevelop the land for a huge profit (a plot device so common in live-action TV as to be its equivalent of anime's boy-gets-robot), but when the vice principal learns about Kumiko's background it gives the superintendent an excuse to act. Determined to save the school she's come to love, Yankume resigns; her class believe she's abandoned them, but soon rally round when her other life catches up with her and she is kidnapped.

Gokusen (see also *DE) began as a 2002 manga in *You Comics* by Kozueko Morimoto, a female-oriented pastiche of **GTO** that began just as *Kinpachi Sensei* (*DE), one of Japan's most enduring teacher-pupil series, came to the end of its sixth season. The *Gokusen* manga was snapped up the same year for live-action TV for its handy combination of the omnipresent school subgenre with the postmodern gangsters of *The Sopranos* (1999). As with *GTO*, *Gokusen* was then kept on-air by its parent channel in an anime adaptation that kept the look and feel of the series, without the need to pay for its live-action star Yukie Nakama, who was replaced by voice actress Risa Hayamizu for the anime. Both seasons of the live-action TV serial (a second came after the anime) have also been broadcast in America on KSCI. Another orphaned female gangster boss would appear in the following year's KILL BILL: THE ORIGIN OF O-REN. ⬤ⓃⓋ

GOLD LIGHTAN

1981. JPN: *Ogon Senshi Gold Lightan.* AKA: *Golden Warrior Gold Lightan.* TV series. DIR: Koichi Mashimo, Mizuho Nishikubo. SCR: Akiyoshi Sakai, Takeshi Shudo, Masaaki Sakurai, Tomomi Tsutsui. DES: Ippei Kuri. ANI: Sadao Miyamoto, Takashi Nakamura. MUS: Masaaki Shinbo, Masayuki Yamamoto. PRD: Tatsunoko, Tokyo 12 Channel. 25 mins. x 52 eps.
King Ibaldar of the Mecha Dimension sends alien invaders to attack Earth,

not realizing that his enemies have already sent a champion to defend it. The invincible Mecha superhero has joined forces with the 12-year-old boy Hiro, hiding unobtrusively inside his cigarette lighter. In times of trouble, he can use the lighter as a dimensional gate to call upon Gold Lightan's power to transform into a giant robot. With a heavy debt to the early ULTRAMAN shows, Lightan and his five-robot team, who hide inside lighters carried by other members of Hiro's Naughty Rangers (a Bic, a Zippo, etc.), fight off the alien invaders in a mind-bogglingly inappropriate series that must have inspired teenage smokers and pyromaniacs all over Japan. A fine example of what can happen if a show is governed solely by the contents of the animators' pockets.

GOLDEN BAT

1967. JPN: *Ogon Bat.* AKA: *The Phantaman, Phantaman.* TV series. DIR: Kujiro Yanagida, Seiji Sasaki, Tadao Wakabayashi. SCR: Mitsuhide Shimauchi. DES: Tatsuo Nagamatsu. ANI: Nobuhide Morikawa. MUS: Masashi Tanaka. PRD: Daiichi, Yomiuri TV (Nippon TV). 25 mins. x 52 eps.
Golden Bat is the warrior who looks like a golden skeleton, sent from ancient Atlantis to protect the people of our own time. He appears whenever his presence is requested by the Japanese girl Mari, with her associates Professor Yamatone and schoolboy Takeru, in their ongoing fight against attacking robots and monsters. Based on Tatsuo Nagamatsu's manga. In 2000, the studio AIC announced that they were planning a remake for the new century, though this seems to have disappeared into preproduction hell.

GOLDEN BOY *

1995. Video. DIR: Hiroyuki Kitakubo. SCR: Tatsuya Egawa. DES: Toshihiro Kawamoto. ANI: Toshihiro Kawamoto. MUS: N/C. PRD: KSS. 30 mins. x 6 eps.
The wanderings of a Tokyo University dropout (he completed the coursework, but has yet to graduate) who prefers to learn at the university of

life, as Kintaro bicycles from job to job, charming the local lovelies as he goes—though it often takes time for them to see past his bad habits (such as worshiping the toilets said lovelies use and sketching *everything* that catches his eye). Seducing the hard-shelled-but-sexy boss of a software company in the first episode, only to dodge the advances of the daughter of a small-town machine politician whose campaign he is supposed to be managing, Kintaro never gives up learning. Other jobs where Kintaro worms his way into female hearts include noodle chef; swimming instructor; housekeeper for a wealthy, traditional young woman; and, finally, working in an animation studio. Whatever trouble Kintaro gets into, he gets out of with his cheerfulness, dedicated work ethic, and phenomenal ability to learn new skills in record time, though unlike his manga incarnation, the anime Kintaro never manages to go all the way with his objects of desire. Based on the manga by Tatsuya Egawa, better known for **MAGICAL TALRUTO**, and the manga for **TOKYO UNIVERSITY STORY** and *Be Free*, featuring character designs by **COWBOY BEBOP**'s Toshihiro Kawamoto. Ⓝ

GOLDEN LAWS, THE *

2003. JPN: *Ogon no Ho—El Cantare no Rekishikan.* AKA: *Golden Laws—El Cantare's History.* Movie. DIR: Takaaki Ishiyama. SCR: Golden Laws Scenario Project. DES: Isamu Imakake. ANI: Masami Suda, Keizo Shimizu, Yukiyoshi Hane, Marisuke Eguchi. MUS: Yuichi Misuzawa. PRD: Toei, Group TAC, Visual Magic Nice and Day, Colorado FX, Sim EX. 110 mins.
Satoru, a schoolboy in the 25th century, is leafing through a copy of the religious classic *The Golden Laws*, which he has found in the New Atlantis library. He is disturbed by the crashing arrival of Alisa, a time-traveling teenager from the 30th century. The couple decide to travel back in time to 21st-century Japan, where the great religious renaissance was said to have begun. However, they end up far off course in 2300,

where they are rescued from a sea serpent by the Greek hero **HERMES**. Then they journey through several notable points in history, witnessing the growth of human culture in Greece, Egypt, India, Palestine, and China.

Famous names on the crew and even in the cast (such as voice star Takehito Koyasu in a lead role) help distract from this anime's true colors. Although made by the Toei Studio, it is best regarded as work-for-hire in the services of a religious organization, as it is yet another publicity vehicle for the same Institute for Research in Human Happiness that gave us **LAWS OF THE SUN**. As with its predecessor, IRH leader Ryuho Okawa is credited with the original inspiration (the self-same religious book mentioned above), an anonymous committee provides a script mixing a cocktail of rival religions, and an impressive amount is squandered on digital effects and showy animation. An English dub was prepared for screenings on the west coast of America and Canada, and also made it to the U.K., where it was shown in a small London cinema with little mention of its original raison d'être. Compare to **SUPERBOOK: VIDEO BIBLE**.

GOLDFISH WARNING

1991. JPN: *Kingyo Chuiho*. TV series. DIR: Junichi Sato, Atsutoshi Umezawa, Kunihiko Ikuhara. SCR: Keiko Maruo, Yumi Kageyama, Hiroko Naka, Aya Matsuyama. DES: Satoru Irizuki. ANI: Satoru Irizuki, Tomoyoshi Koyama. MUS: N/C. PRD: Toei, TV Asahi. 25 mins. x 54 eps.

Snooty rich girl Chitose Fujinomiya is left in poverty after the death of her father. Thrown out of the elite City Academy with nothing but her valuable pink goldfish, Gyopi, for company, she is found on the premises of the run-down Country High School where children and animals attend classes together. Regaining some of her inheritance from an embezzling family lawyer, Chitose uses some of the money to rebuild the struggling school, making herself chairperson

of the school board *and* student-body president. With completely selfish motives, she tries to improve her new school in order to bring a little "urban sophistication," and, she hopes, trounce the feckless City Academy and its prissy student president, Yurika. Her classmates are less keen, with the likable red-head Wapiko mediating between Chitose and the irate animals, while simultaneously fending off the advances of Yurika's assistant, Takapi. A madcap comedy and long-term fan favorite, incorporating meditations on how **CANDY CANDY** would have worked out if its heroine were a bitch, coupled with surreal visuals and designs that presaged the more abstract moments of director Ikuhara's later **UTENA**. Based on Neko Nekobe's 1989 manga in the magazine *Nakayoshi*.

GOLGO 13: THE PROFESSIONAL *

1983. JPN: *Golgo 13*. Movie, video. DIR: Osamu Dezaki. SCR: Hideyoshi Nagasaka. DES: Shichiro Kobayashi. ANI: Shichiro Kobayashi. MUS: Toshiyuki Omori. PRD: TMS. 94 mins. (m), 60 mins. (v).

Golgo 13, one of Japan's longest-running manga series, has been drawn by Takao Saito since 1969. Its unsmiling hero, Duke Togo, has never revealed anything about his past. Instead, he wanders the world and kills people for a living, a modern *ronin* with a code name constructed from purest evil: the unlucky number 13 and the first two syllables of "Golgotha." An immense hit with middle-aged businessmen, Duke gets to travel the world, screw foreign chicks, and shoot unpleasant people. Although inspired by the James Bond films, he doesn't even pretend to be working for good. He is totally amoral.

In the 1983 film, Duke is hired by a mystery client to kill the heir of a wealthy businessman. The businessman offers the sexual favors of his newly widowed daughter-in-law to a psychotic killer on the understanding that the son's death will be avenged. And so begins a series of tit-for-tat escalations, risible dialogue, embarrassing charac-

terizations, and a ludicrous procession of gunfights, as the two assassins kill and shag their way toward a final confrontation.

Director Dezaki treats Duke's quest as a modern samurai adventure, with improbable leaps and slices replaced by improbable marksmanship and set-ups (watch the moment Duke shoots someone through a building). He also experimented with computer graphics in a helicopter assault scene, inserting now-dated CG that makes it not unlike watching an old Atari console. But Dezaki would retain his obsession with out-of-place CG, using it once again in his later **BLACK JACK**. Duke would return in a video sequel, *Golgo 13: Queen Bee* (1998), in which Duke is assigned to kill Sonia, the titular South American nymphomaniac drug baroness, before she can carry out her own threat to murder a presidential candidate running on a Just-Say-No platform. Before his two lower budget anime outings, the assassin also appeared in two live-action incarnations, *Golgo 13* (1973), starring Ken Takakura, and *Golgo 13: Assignment Kowloon* (1977), starring Shinichi "Sonny" Chiba. ●NV

G-ON RIDERS

2002. TV series. DIR: Shinichiro Kimura. SCR: N/C. DES: Katsuzo Hirata, Yasumasa Moriki. ANI: Hideo Okazaki. MUS: Norimasa Yamanaka. PRD: Katsuzo, TNK, WOWOW. 23 mins. x 13 eps; 23 min (v).

Brilliant Japanese scientist Mio Sanada develops a superweapon called G-On to defend Earth from attacking aliens—who eventually turn out to be cute, klutzy girls working as subcontractors to the real baddies. The weapon reacts to the energy of adolescent girls' minds, as long as they wear special glasses to enable the G-On to adapt their energies. The school of Saint Hoshikawa's is set up as a front to recruit "sensitive and beautiful girls" from all over Japan to help in the defense effort. Yuki Kurama becomes the latest chosen one and prepares to defend her homeworld with the aid of fellow girls Sarah and Yayoi. A bonus 14th episode appeared on the DVD. The titles give the year as Showa 119—in other words, A.D. 2044.

GON THE FIRST MAN

1996. JPN: *Hajime Ningen Gon*. TV series. DIR: Yutaka Kagawa, Takashi Yamazaki, Hiroyuki Yokoyama. SCR: Yoshio Urasawa, Megumi Sugiwara. DES: Shunji Sonoyama. ANI: Masaaki Iwane. MUS: Yusuke Honma. PRD: KSS, NHK2. 25 mins. x 39 eps. (each ep. has 3 stories).
The wacky adventures of Gon the little caveman, as his family tries to cope with prehistoric life. Beginning as a simple comedy featuring Gon and his gang trying to hunt mammoths, running from saber-toothed tigers, and cowering from thunder, later episodes became more satirical of modern times, with Gon's trip to the prehistoric equivalent of summer camp. In the final stage, it developed an SF angle not unlike Shotaro Ishinomori's AGE OF THE GREAT DINOSAURS, with the arrival of aliens in a flying saucer. Based on a manga by GO FOR IT KONBE's Shunji Sonoyama, who also created an earlier caveman anime, THE GARDLES. Gon's adventures made it to the screen in the wake of the live-action Hollywood *Flintstones* (1994) and were of no relation to the diminutive *dinosaur* hero of Masashi Tanaka's 1991 manga *Gon*. Compare to KUM KUM.

GON THE FOX

1989. JPN: *Gongitsune*. Movie. DIR: Yasunari Maeda. SCR: Tsunehisa Ito. DES: Shoji Ikehara. ANI: Nobukazu Otake, Tsukasa Abe, Yoko Tsukada. MUS: Yasuo Tsuchida. PRD: Ai Planning Center, Magic Bus, Orions, Radical Party. 76 mins.
Gon the orphaned fox cub is washed downstream into a small village in Aichi Prefecture. Making his home there, he steals some fish intended for the sick mother of a local villager. After the mother dies, an apologetic Gon brings offerings of mushrooms and fruit to the bereaved villager. One

night, thinking Gon is an intruder, the villager kills him as he approaches the house. A Japanese tragedy rich in karmic misery, based on a story by Nankichi Nimi, though the early scenes depicting the death of Gon's mother were added by screenwriter Ito. Made to celebrate the tenth anniversary of the JAPANESE FOLK TALES series.

GONZO

Also Gonzo Digimation Company or Gonzo Digimation Holdings (GDH). Influential modern anime company, particularly in the new field of digital animation. Gonzo was founded in 1992 by a small group of former Gainax employees. Its output includes animation for both anime and computer/console games and many landmark experiments in the integration of cel and digital animation techniques. Notable employees include Mahiro Maeda, Takeshi Mori, and Umanosuke Iida—representative works include LAST EXILE, BLUE SUBMARINE NO. SIX, and VANDREAD. The company also made the opening animation sequence for the otherwise live-action TV series *Densha Otoko*—incorporating homages to two earlier Gainax works in the process. Arguably, the company's most well-known work is actually a pop promo, "Breaking the Habit" (2005) for the band Linkin Park.

GOOD MORNING ALTHEA

1987. Video. DIR: Hideki Tonokatsu. SCR: N/C. DES: Michitaka Kikuchi. ANI: Moriyasu Taniguchi. MUS: Nobuhiko Kashiwara. PRD: Animate, Studio Pierrot. 50 mins.
Far in the future, the galaxy is ruled by a race of warrior-mages who have cast aside much of humankind's earlier follies in cybernetics. However, the infamous "Automaton" robot that defended humanity from the Stemma Empire is rumored to be still operational, and three brave young teenagers go on a quest to shut it down . . . or perhaps steal it for themselves. For this they will require Althea of the Seal, a human symbiont. Based on a manga

from *C-Live* magazine written by a collective of fans called "Black Point," this video begs the question, "It took more than one person to come up with that plot?"

GOOD MORNING CALL

2001. Movie. DIR: N/C. SCR: N/C. DES: N/C. ANI: Transarts. MUS: N/C. PRD: NAS, Shueisha. 19 mins.
Based on the 1997 *Ribbon Mascot* manga by Yue Takasuka, this is a day in the life of Hisashi Uehara and Nao Yoshikawa, two teenagers accidentally forced to share an apartment but who conceal this fact from their classmates. With Hisashi's 16th birthday coming up, Nao goes in search of gift for him, only to become distracted by the attentions of a hunky hairstylist who wants her to model for his latest creation. The platonic friendship that eternally threatens to become something more, in the style of MARMALADE BOY, meets a glorified ad to stimulate manga sales similar to that employed by CIPHER THE VIDEO. This short work featured as part of a *Ribbon*-sponsored touring cinema anthology along with TIME STRANGER KYOKO, hence its official "movie" status rather than the video that it really ought to be.

GOODBYE LITTLE HIPPO

1989. JPN: *Sayonara Kaba-kun*. Movie. DIR: Yutaka Ozawa. SCR: Yoko Yamamoto. DES: Katsumoto Saotome. ANI: Shiro Nakagawa, Toshiki Saida. MUS: N/C. PRD: Asmik, OH Production. 25 mins.
A mixture of live action and animation telling the true story of the animals of Tokyo's Ueno Zoo during the harsh days of bombing raids and shortages that took their toll during World War II. Focusing on the hippos, who were eventually butchered for food in the closing days of the conflict, *Newtype* called the story, "a study of the tragedy of war and a prayer for peace." No hippos were available for comment. See also ZOO WITHOUT AN ELEPHANT.

GOODFELLA

1990. JPN: *Danki*. Video. DIR: Osamu

Yamazaki. scr: Noboru Hirose. des: Masami Suda. ani: Masami Suda, Masafumi Yamamoto. mus: N/C. prd: Nichiei, JC Staff. 50 mins. x 3 eps., 40 mins. x 2 eps.

After his father leaves when he is very young, Kyosuke Murata grows up under the thumb of his overprotective mother, Shizuko. When he reaches adulthood, he is thrown into the harsh, violent world of Japanese gangland when his mother becomes involved in a gang-related crime. He goes up against the Murata-gumi organization, only to find that his estranged father is its head. Rising up through the ranks, Kyosuke eventually unites half the gangs in Japan beneath his own leadership, only to find that the other half have also combined to resist his new power, starting the greatest gang war in Japanese history. Based on a 1979 manga in *Big Comic Spirits* by Hiroshi Motomiya, who also created CLIMBING ON A CLOUD and MY SKY. The first episode was also screened theatrically.

Shigeru Ueda directed a two-part sequel, *New Goodfella* (1998), in which gang members attempt to arrange a jailbreak by infiltrating a prison disguised as guards. **NV**

GORILLAMAN
1992. Video. dir: Yoshinori Nakamura. scr: Noboru Hirose. des: Koichi Endo. ani: Mitsuharu Kajiya, Koichi Endo. mus: N/C. prd: JC Staff. 50 mins.

A school comedy about a mute transfer student, Tadashi Iketo, who is constantly shuffled from school to school for his "violent nature," though he really is a mild-mannered boy constantly taunted into fights over his simian appearance. Based on a 1989 manga in *Young Magazine* by Harold Sakuishi. Compare with the more dramatic ANGEL LEGEND.

GORSCH THE CELLIST *
1982. jpn: *Cello Hiki no Gorsch*. aka: *Gauche the Cellist*. Movie, video. dir: Isao Takahata. scr: Isao Takahata. des: Shunji Saita. ani: Shunji Saita, Suemi Nishida, Mariko Nomura, Kumiko Tsukada, Yoko Tomizawa, Takashi Namiki,

Taeko Otsuka, Nobuhiro Aihara, Kazuhide Tomonaga. mus: Yoshio Mamiya, Beethoven. prd: OH Productions. 19 min. (m1), 63 mins. (m2), 30 mins. (v).

A mediocre cellist is forced to practice late at night and "dreams" that he is visited by talking animals. A cat, cuckoo, badger, and field mouse each offer their opinions on his music and keep him company during the lonely sessions, but later on Gorsch discovers that his music, while terrible to human ears, has been healing sick animals all around the neighborhood. The knowledge that even his ability does *some* good brings heart and soul to his music and improves his performance the next time he faces a human audience. Released with English subtitles on DVD in Japan.

Though most likely to be known in the West through this striking 1982 film, the story was first animated in 1949 as a 19-minute short directed by Kiji Tanaka, and based originally on a short story by NIGHT TRAIN TO THE STARS–creator Kenji Miyazawa. The story was animated a third time for the *Classic Children's Tales* series (1992) as a 30-minute stop-motion short released straight to video.

GOSHOGUN *
1981. jpn: *Sengoku Majin Goshogun*. aka: *Civil War Devil-God Goshogun*. TV series, video. dir: Kunihiko Yuyama, Tetsuro Amino, Junji Nishimura. scr: Takeshi Shudo, Jiyu Watanabe, Sukehiro Tomita. des: Studio Z5, Mutsumi Inomata, Shunsuke Kasahara. ani: Hiroshi Tanaka, Etsuko Tomita, Hideaki Matsuoka. mus: Tachio Akano. prd: Ashi Pro, Tokyo 12 Channel. 25 mins. x 26 eps. (TV), 65 mins. (m1), 90 mins. (m2).

Professor Masada is killed by the evil Docougar organization, which wants to steal the secrets of his latest invention, the Super Energy Vimra. His son Kenta takes the research to the mobile secret base of the God Thunder organization, assembling the "Goshogun" team of warriors to fight against the minions of Docougar.

Kunihiko Yuyama's movie *Goshogun* (1982) takes the cast to the South American republic of Felcona, where president Santos requires their assistance against Docougar agents. A reedit of episodes 17 and 20 of the TV series, the "movie" adds scraps of extra footage, including an introductory sequence and false interstitial advertisements for nonexistent products endorsed by the cast—Kernagul's Fried Chicken, Kutnall's Tranquilizers, Gitter's 35-section Combining Robot, and Docougar Total Training. The film also used images of characters' previously unseen childhood years in the closing credits, a device that foreshadowed the subplot of the final *Goshogun* release (see below).

In 1985, the *Goshogun* series was combined with SRUNGLE and released in the U.S. as *Macron One*. As with its contemporary ROBOTECH, the series was given a completely new storyline, in this case about a teleportation experiment that hurls test pilot David Jance into a parallel universe, where he leads the Beta Command robot team against alien menaces. Meanwhile, the evil overlord Dark Star has been transported by the same experiment into our own universe, where another team must hold back his army of robotic warriors. With the U.S. market interest in SF buoyant after *Return of the Jedi* (1983), *Macron One* boasted a successful mix of alien crew, prattling robots, and enemies who looked suspiciously like Imperial Storm Troopers. The show's appeal was augmented further with contemporary pop music, not just Duran Duran's "The Reflex" over the opening titles, but other chart-toppers strewn around the battle scenes. These additions gave the show a feel not unlike an MTV pop video but inadvertently damaged its long-term salability, since rights were not cleared for the same tunes to be used on video.

Back in Japan, the original had a last hurrah in the video *Goshogun: Time Étranger* (1985), often confused with the unrelated TIME STRANGER. Also shown in Japanese theaters, this is the incarnation of the series best known today through the dub made by Manga Entertainment. Recycling the plot from the *Goshogun* novels, *Time Étranger* added a framing device set 40 years later in a world that looks like Chicago with taller buildings and hover-cars. Much of the footage is wasted on a pointless car chase, leaving little time for anything but a few shots of beeping machines and hand-wringing bedside vigils. The strangely ageless Remi, infamous for refusing her medals, is mortally injured in a crash and looks back on her life while the rest of the old team (including three of her former foes, now pals with their one-time enemies) bickers around her comatose form. Using the world's most irritating French accent, Remi recalls an incident when she fell down a well as a child, and she also hallucinates a surreal "mission" involving those who are assembled around her bed. The film then cuts to the team trapped in a city of confused religious fundamentalists (they worship like Muslims but have crucifixes in their graveyard), who are convinced that the God Thunder team's day of destiny has arrived, and that Remi will be the first of them to die. Remi and her friends fight off the seething locals in quietly racist scenes of the God Thunder team, with vastly superior firepower, shooting into wave after wave of stick-waving towelheads. They steal a tram (yes, a tram, driving it off its rails, not unlike the plot), mess around with hang gliders, and have a fight in a bar while pontificating about destiny and fate. All this, it transpires, is a metaphor for Remi's critical condition in the present day, since she must confront the demons of her childhood and psyche if she is to awaken from her coma. However, her fate is left unclear in an ending that is either a ham-fisted metaphor for her death or a reunion scene riddled with continuity errors and poor writing. So Remi either makes a miraculous recovery, springs out of bed, and chases after her comrades, or dies, recovers, and dies again, depending on your interpreta-

tion. To add to everybody's confusion, the movie was rereleased in the U.S. in 2003 under the title *Time Stranger*.

GOTO, KEIJI

1968– . Character designer on THOSE WHO HUNT ELVES and NADESICO, moving into animation with GATEKEEPERS. A member of a three-man production team called "gimik" that created KIDDY GRADE and UTA KATA—the other members are Hidefumi Kimura and Megumi Kadonosono.

GOTTAMAN

1994. JPN: *Dengeki Oshioki Musume Gottaman*. AKA: *Electro Punisher Girl Gottaman, Butt Attack Punisher Girl Gotaman*. Video. DIR: Akira Suzuki, Hiroshi Kishida. SCR: Masaru Yamamoto. DES: Toyomi Sugiyama, Eisaku Inoue. ANI: Toyomi Sugiyama, Eisaku Inoue. MUS: N/C. PRD: Movic, Hero, Animate, All Products. 45 mins. x 2 eps. A normal high school girl moonlights as the superhero Gottaman, who battles the lusty minions of the sinister Black Buddha organization while wearing little more than a skimpy top, turban, and loincloth. Tits and tentacles in the style of LA BLUE GIRL, based on the manga in *Shonen Champion* by Masakazu Yamaguchi. 🚫🔞

GOWAPPER 5 GO-DAM

1976. JPN: *Go Wappa 5 Go Dam*. TV series. DIR: Hisayuki Toriumi, Masami Suda, Tsuneo Ninomiya. SCR: Toshio Nagata, Saburo Taki. DES: Yoshitaka Amano. ANI: Yoshihisa Okuno, Chuichi Iguchi. MUS: Bob Sakuma. PRD: Tatsunoko, NET (TV Asahi). 25 mins. x 36 eps. Go Tsunami, Yoko Misaki, Daikichi Kameyama, Goemon Koishikawa, and Norisuke Kawaguchi are friends who live in the same apartment block. Exploring an uninhabited island off Tokyo Bay, they discover a concealed complex, deserted for years. A hologram of the builder, Dr. Hoarai, tells them how nobody would believe his theory that the world would be invaded by the inhabitants of a demonic subterranean civilization. He worked alone

until he died to create a base for space battle as the core of a defense system built around the mighty robot Godam. The friends pledge themselves to carry on his work and fly Godam into battle against Emperor Yokoyuda and his demon minions, in the style of the same studio's earlier BATTLE OF THE PLANETS—although the protagonists in this show were deliberately made to look younger than their predecessors in order to aid identification with a kids' audience. Despite such an attempt to appeal to younger viewers, the show was unafraid of piling on shocks, particularly in the form of the enemy's seemingly unstoppable suicide bomber androids, the Nendroids—compare to similar dangers in GUYSLUGGER.

Because the friends work from a deserted island without official sanction, they are both pirates and gamblers, carrying the skull and crossbones motif on their belts like CAPTAIN HARLOCK, and the insignia of spades, clubs, hearts, and diamonds emblazoned on their uniforms—an idea that would be shamelessly purloined by the following year's live-action superhero show *Jaqk* (*DE). They're joined by token kid Seitaro Shima and two cute dogs. Notable for the presence of Yoshitaka Amano as character designer and for the performance of Kayumi Iemasa, who both narrated the series and voiced the heroic robot. As with its predecessors MAGNOS and STEEL JEEG, the show was tied into a merchandise line whose distinguishing feature was that the robots' joints were held together by magnets.

GRADUATION *

1994. JPN: *Sotsugyo*. Video. DIR: Katsuhiko Nishijima. SCR: Asami Watanabe, Kenichi Kanemaki. DES: Kazuko Tadano, Kazuaki Mori. ANI: Kazuko Tadano. MUS: Kingo Hamada. PRD: Head Room, Animate. 30 mins. x 4 eps., 30 mins. x 2 eps. (*Marriage*), 30 mins. (*MVP*), 30 mins. x 2 eps. (*M*). Mami, Reiko, Kiyomi, Shizuka, and Mika are five girls who have mixed feelings about their high school graduation day. They decide to hold a final celebration, but the clumsy Mami gets lost buying food, and the rest of the girls have to look for her. In a surprisingly heartfelt spin-off from a computer game, the girls decide on their future careers and say farewell as their school days come to a close. In the PC version, the player took the role of a career guidance counselor, steering the girls through their school days and into the right careers—the anime dramatizes a situation in which Mami and Reiko are undecided and need the advice of their fellows.

Exhausting the potential of the original, the series changed direction for the third and fourth episodes, renamed *Sailor Victory* (no relation to the proto-SAILOR MOON). A spoof that placed the archetypal women of *Graduation* in an SF setting, it features the girls as a team of superheroes in "hard suits," battling not only cybernetic criminals and invading creatures from another dimension (à la BUBBLEGUM CRISIS or SILENT MÖBIUS), but also the entire police force (à la AD POLICE or PATLABOR).

In a cleaner satire than the naughty BATTLE TEAM LAKERS EX, the girls take all of the familiar tropes of SF anime to their logical extremes, forgetting to use their secret identities, spending so long delivering pompous speeches that the crime scene is already secure, and even transforming in scenes of comedically gratuitous nudity.

The original game spawned several sequels and spin-offs, some of which were also adapted into anime. Kazuhiro Ozawa's *Marriage* (1996), also available in the U.S., is set several years after the original, with the same characters replacing their quest for the right grades with the search for the right man. This time, they are recast as five sisters, each one a year younger than the next. With the release of an all-male spin-off featuring a prefabricated pop group, Akiyuki Shinbo directed the one-shot pop promo *MVP EMU Music Video* (1996). In Hajime

Kamegaki's inevitable two-part follow-up *Graduation M* (1998), the story of the game itself was retold, with a group of pretty young boys deciding to form a band and play at their school's 50th-anniversary celebrations. ◐

GRANDAR
1998. JPN: *Grandar Musashi RV*. AKA: *Grandar Armory Revolution*. TV series. DIR: Takayoshi Suzuki. SCR: Nobuyuki Fujimoto, Machiko Ikeda. DES: Masayuki Hiraoka. ANI: Masamitsu Kudo, Masami Abe. MUS: Goro Omi. PRD: Nippon Animation, TV Tokyo. 25 mins. x 39 eps.
In order to stop seven legendary lures scattered around the world from falling into evil hands, teenager Musashi and his best friends, Suguru and Mio, set out to save the world, defeating their opponents in a series of martial angling competitions. Based on a manga by Takashi Teshirogi and Hajime Murata, who was once, predictably, a champion angler. Just when you thought you'd seen it all.

GRANDEEK
1999. Video. DIR: Shige Sotoyama. SCR: N/C. DES: Toshiko Baba. ANI: N/C. MUS: N/C. PRD: Tac, Movic, SPE Visual Works. 45 mins. x 2 eps., 45 mins.
Swords and sorcery as the young warrior-woman Tia Allbright and her hapless assistant, Luke, battle demon assassins in a fantasyland. Based on a manga by the pseudonymous Koki Ose, the story continues in *Grandeek: Side Story* (2000), in which their companion Yuri has to be stopped from killing her former lover Ehlen, who has been transformed into a demon assassin.

GRANDIZER *
1975. JPN: *UFO Robo Grendizer* [sic]. AKA: *Goldorak*. Movie, TV series. DIR: Tomoharu Katsumata, Masamune Ochiai, Masayuki Akehi, Kazuya Yamazaki. SCR: Shozo Uehara, Keisuke Fujikawa, Tomohiro Ando. DES: Kazuo Komatsubara, Shingo Araki. ANI: Kazuo Komatsubara, Keisuke Morishita. MUS: Shunsuke Kikuchi. PRD: Dynamic Plan-

ning, Toei. 25 mins. x 74 eps.
Young Duke Fleed (Orion Quest) of Planet Fleed (Antares) is forced to leave his homeworld when it is attacked by the forces of the evil King Vega. Fleed, together with his Grendizer spacecraft that can transform into a giant robot, reaches planet Earth, where he hides from Vega's forces and is adopted by the kindly Professor Umon (Bryant), who calls him Daisuke (Johnny). "Daisuke" works happily on a local farm, until the arrival of Vega's forces on Earth forces him to take a stand, together with his friends Koji Kabuto, Hikaru Makiba, and Duke's sister, Maria Grace.

The 30-minute anime movie *War of the Flying Saucers* (1975) introduced the character of Fleed alongside other creations of Go Nagai, such as Danbei from the same author's CUTEY HONEY, and pilot Koji Kabuto, whose inclusion effectively makes *Grandizer* another sequel to MAZINGER Z. The pilot movie features the same basic plot, with the mild-mannered Daisuke Umon appearing as the only son of Dr. Umon of the Umon Space Science Laboratory. To capture him, his flying saucer, and his combining robot Gattaidar, Princess Teronna from Planet Yarban attacks Earth with the Yarban Flying Saucer Unit.

In the series proper, before Fleed and Maria returned in triumph to their homeworld, *Grandizer* also appeared in two short Go Nagai crossover movies: *Great Mazinger / Grandizer / Getter Robo G: Battle the Great Monster* (1976) and *UFO Robo Grandizer vs. Great Mazinger* (1976). Twenty-six episodes were released as part of the FORCE FIVE series on American TV.

GRANDOLL *
1997. JPN: *Chokosoku Grandoll*. AKA: *Supralight Grandolls; Hyperspeed Grandoll*. Video. DIR: Hideki Tonokatsu. SCR: Katsumi Hasegawa, Yuko Nakada. DES: Toshinari Yamashita, Yoshinori Sayama. ANI: Toshinari Yamashita. MUS: N/C. PRD: Zero G Room, Bandai. 30 mins. x 3 eps.

Sixteen-year-old anime fan-girl Hikaru has a mad scientist for a father, a crush on a high school senior, and a passionate obsession with the anime hero Rockin' Dorger. She dreams of becoming a real-life anime heroine, only to discover that she already is. Recovering her memories of her childhood, she realizes that she is the Crown Princess of Planet Gran, sent away during a civil war to live a life in exile on Earth. However, the evil alien Lord Friedshalf plans to use her Grandoll Armor for himself, sending minions to fight her for it, including his own lover, Sigil, who comes to Hikaru's school disguised as a transfer student. Switching in the style of DRAGON HALF from normal to squashed-down cartoon mode in the blink of an eye, *Grandoll* is either a lighthearted spoof of anime clichés or a cynical trawl through them, depending on how charitable you feel today.

GRANDZORT

1989. JPN: *Mado-o Grandzort*. AKA: *Sorcerer King Grandzort*. TV series. DIR: Hideji Iguchi. SCR: Hideji Iguchi, Hiroko Naka, Takashi Yamada, Ryosuke Takahashi. DES: Toyoo Ashida, Kunio Okawara. ANI: Takahiro Yoshimatsu. MUS: Kohei Tanaka. PRD: Sunrise, Nippon TV. 25 mins. x 41 eps. (TV), 30 mins. (TVm), 30 mins. x 5 eps. (v). Twelve year olds Daichi, Gus, and Rabi are heading off for a lunar holiday but get dragged into an ancient conflict between two forgotten tribes on the moon, who are trying to resurrect ancient evil powers to seize control of Earth itself. A popular giant-robot show whose robots were powered by "magic," it was created in part by SAKURA WARS' Oji Hiroi. The final episode was celebrated with a 30-minute TV special, *Grandzort: Non Stop Rabi* (1990). The series continued on video with the two-part *Final Magical War* (1990), in which the children fight off Grunwald, their most powerful enemy. It clearly wasn't final enough for the producers, who came back again with Nobuhiro Kondo's three-part *Grandzort: Adventure*

(1992), in which the world turned out to be not quite saved enough. A magical stone in an ancient lunar monument begins emitting energy pulses toward Earth, attracting the attention of the Norman Bates space pirates, who steal it and decide to blow up a lunar city. The story was also released in a 110-minute feature-length edition under the same title.

GRAPPLER BAKI *

1994. AKA: *Baki the Grappler*. TV series, video. DIR: Hirokazu Ikeda. SCR: Yoshihisa Araki. DES: Keisuke Itagaki. ANI: Yoshihiko Umakoshi. MUS: N/C. PRD: Toei. 45 mins. (v), 25 mins. x 24 eps. (TV1), 25 mins. x 24 eps. (TV2). Baki Hanma is the youngest martial artist to enter an underground free-for-all fighting tournament. He bests a karate opponent, then fights in the ring against someone whose specialty is ripping out opponents' nerves. The end. Devoid of even the merest hint of plot, Baki simply fights; instead of a damsel in distress to rescue or evil bad guy to defeat, Baki hits people until the ending credits roll. This anime takes the action-oriented plotting of STREET FIGHTER II and gruesome acts of STORY OF RICKY to extremes. Baki even comes across as something of a sadomasochist, grinning his way through nasty beatings. Based on Keisuke Itagaki's long-running 1991 manga in *Shonen Champion*, whose *actual* plot was Baki's quest to find who genuinely is the toughest person on the planet. His quest takes him to gangsters, biker gangs, and mercenaries, and the karate sequence in this anime represents just a fraction of his search. The story was brought back for a 2001 TV series, directed by Hitoshi Nanba, beginning with a 13-year-old Baki fighting a hundred men at once, but only beating 37 of them. He trains at a number of martial arts, hoping to eventually become the best of the best, all so that he can beat Yujiro Kurama, who, just a wild guess, is the man who killed his father. The TV series adds extra material not in the manga, particularly concerning

Baki's relationship with his mother, Emi, who keeps on finding new trainers to teach her little rugrat how to kick ass. A second television series, *Grappler Baki: Maximum Tournament* (*Grappler Baki: Saidai Tournament*; also 2001) followed the first. **LV**

GRASSHOPPA *

2001. Video. DIR: Katsuhito Ishii, Takashi "Ken" Koike, Osamu Kobayashi, Sadamune Takenaka, Hajime Ishimine, Takei Goodman, Hideyuki Tanaka et al. SCR: N/C. DES: N/C. ANI: N/C. MUS: N/C. PRD: Madhouse, Studio 4°C. ca. 80 mins. x 4. A series of short animated and live-action independent films released on DVD with bright green labeling. Animated *Trava—Fist Planet* (2001) is a film made in short episodes from Ishii and Koike, divided across several discs. *Hal & Bons* is a four-episode CG media spoof by Ishii and Takenaka, in which two claymation dogs are interviewed by a rice cake but are unimpressed by its style and technique. Kobayashi's *End of the World* mixes traditional and 3D animation. Ishimine's live-action *Frog River* featured in several collections before getting a solo release on the label in 2005, as did *Fist Planet* and *Hal & Bons*. An outlet for more personal, experimental work from animators better known for their mainstream anime, some of these shorts have been shown at festivals and the DVDs in the series are available with English subtitles, so *Grasshoppa* qualifies as an English-language release. Each of the four DVDs included one of the four "Sweat Punch" shorts from Studio 4°C: *Professor Dan Petory's Blues, Comedy, End of the World*, and *Higen*. The amazing *Comedy* short has two different audio tracks on the DVD, a "normal" version and a "comedy" version. The second DVD also includes an episode of SUPER MILK-CHAN. The third DVD includes a live-action short directed by Hideaki Anno.

GRAVE OF THE FIREFLIES *

1988. JPN: *Hotaru no Haka*. Movie. DIR:

Isao Takahata. scr: Isao Takahata. des: Yoshifumi Kondo. ani: Nobuo Koyama. mus: Yoshio Mamiya. prd: Shinchosha, Ghibli. 85 mins.

Seita and his little sister Setsuko are left homeless by the firebombing of Kobe in 1945, which claims their mother's life. Unable to contact their father in the forces and knowing of no other place to turn, they move in with a shrewish aunt who constantly upbraids Seita for not contributing to the war effort. Eventually, they move to an air-raid shelter in the country, begging and stealing what food they can, but both starve to death.

Based on a semiautobiographical novel by Akiyuki Nosaka, who lost his own sister to malnutrition during the war, this is an eerily quiet, sepia-toned apocalypse, accompanied by powerful subliminal messages. Throughout the entire film, we regularly return to the ghosts of Seita and Setsuko, lit in red, as they gaze accusingly at the countrymen who let them die, though these scenes are so fleeting as to pass most viewers by. Similarly, director Takahata loads on subtle guilt as to what might have been "if only" the slightest chance had been taken to make a difference. The firebombs seem almost laughable at their first appearance: tiny sputtering flames, leaning against a water trough and a fire bucket, but Seita doesn't stay to fight them. Instead, he runs to safety with his sister, only to see his old home burn from a distance, like the heroine of Kayoko's Diary. He doesn't mumble a simple apology to the shrewish aunt who has taken him in, forcing his own exile. And as his sister dies, he turns to nobody for help, since he has given up hope that help would be forthcoming. This crushingly sad story begins by revealing both characters will die and then dares the viewer to hope they won't. Tragic in the truest sense of the word, every moment of Takahata's masterpiece is loaded with portents of the suffering to come.

Much imitated in anime about World War II, most noticeably in Rail

Grave of the Fireflies

©1988 AKIYUK NOSAKA/SHINCHOSHA CO.

Of the Star and Raining Fire, the film shows a very normal life wiped out by the horrors of war, however indirect. There are no frontline heroics here, merely two innocent children wasting away before our eyes, while an elder brother dutifully tries to assure his sister that everything will be all right. It is all the more effective for being animated, not only because the ruin and deprivation appears so insanely unreal, but because Seita and Setsuko destroy a raft of anime stereotypes. No perky victory in the face of overwhelming odds for these two; instead, they are crushed and left to gaze down on the lights of modern Kobe, expressionless, but ultimately condemnatory of something. Perhaps it is the Allies who defeated Japan (as with so many other anime of its ilk, it makes no mention of the reasons Japan is being bombed), perhaps the Japanese people who, as in Barefoot Gen, refused to see the light. More likely it is warfare itself, roundly rejected by just two of its many victims.

Producer Toshio Suzuki reputedly used the original novel's educational value to sell theater tickets to schools, thereby allowing him to also release a second film of doubtful potential

as part of the same double bill: My Neighbor Totoro. Some of Nosaka's other works would also form the basis for the ten-episode anime TV series *Akiyuki Nosaka's Tales of Wartime That Cannot Be Forgotten* (1997, *Nosaka Akiyuki Senso Dowashu: Wasurete wa Ikenai Monogatari*).

In 2005, the story was adapted into a live-action TV movie as part of the 60th anniversary of World War II—a year that also saw Glass Rabbit and a remake of Kayoko's Diary. The TV version shifts the focus from Seita and Setsuko onto their aunt (played by Nanako Matsushima). To bring the story up to date, a framing device depicts their cousin Natsu as an old woman, recounting the story to her own granddaughter, and a closing montage shows children in the Middle East, who continue to suffer the effects of war. See also My Air Raid Shelter.

GRAVITATION *
1999. Video, TV series. dir: Shinichi Watanabe, Bob Shirahata. scr: Hiroyuki Kawasaki, Michiko Yokote, Akemi Omote, Mamiko Ikeda. des: Hiroya Iijima, Miho Shimokasa. ani: Hiroya Iijima. mus: Daisuke Asakura. prd: Studio

Deen, SPE Visual Works. 26 mins. x 2 eps. (v), 26 mins. x 13 eps. (TV).
The ups and downs of a band of pretty-boy musicians called Bad Luck, who spend less time rehearsing than they do indulging in moody stares and doomed loves. This anime was run-of-the-mill on video but somewhat risqué on evening TV. Based on a manga by Maki Murakami that ran in *You and Me* magazine, the original video production was upgraded to TV status after the success of similar boy-band adventures in WEISS KREUZ.

GREAT COMPOSERS

1989. JPN: *Meikyoku to Daisakkyokuka Monogatari*. AKA: *Great Composers and Their Compositions*. Video. DIR: Yasuaki Ebihara. SCR: Madoka Hino. DES: Kumiko Shishido. ANI: Masahito Sato. MUS: Various. PRD: Mushi Pro, Big Bang. 22 mins. x 9 eps.
Brief lives of some of the Western world's most famous composers, including Beethoven, Schubert, Mozart, Chopin, Vivaldi, Johann Strauss, and Tchaikovsky. Bizarrely, the obscure Stephen Foster, composer of "Beautiful Dreamer" (see URUSEI YATSURA) and "I Dream of Jeannie" (see JEANNIE WITH THE LIGHT-BROWN HAIR), gets a whole episode to himself, while Bach and Handel are forced to share. Several composers would also feature in GREAT PEOPLE.

GREAT CONQUEST: ROMANCE OF THE THREE KINGDOMS *

1982. JPN: *Sankokushi*. AKA: *Romance of the Three Kingdoms*. TV special x 3, TV series, movie. DIR: Masaaki Sugatani, Hideo Watanabe (TVm), Seiji Okuda (TV), Tomoharu Katsumata (m). SCR: Masaaki Sugatani (TVm), Jinzo Toriumi (TV), Kazuo Kasahara (m). DES: Hiroshi Wagatsuma (TVm), Shingo Araki (TV), Koichi Tsunoda (m). ANI: Keishiro Kimura (TVm), Moriyasu Taniguchi (TV), Koichi Tsunoda (m). MUS: Seiji Yokoyama. PRD: Shinei Doga (m), Enoki Films, TV Asahi. 85 mins. x 3 eps. (specials), 25 mins. x 47 eps. (TV), 90 mins. (m).

It's A.D. 220 as the Han Dynasty of China disintegrates into three warring states. The last Han emperor hands his throne over to the son of his protector, Cao-cao, who becomes the ruler of a fragment of the former empire known as the Kingdom of Wei. Two other former generals set up their own states in the West (Shu-Han) and South (Wu). Liu Bei, who claims to be a descendant of an early Han emperor, fights to bring a measure of liberty and justice to the people and ensure good government.
Based on Luo Guanzhong's novel, itself relatively faithful to actual historical events and one of the most important texts of Chinese literature, along with JOURNEY TO THE WEST and SUIKODEN. The story was given the full fantasy-legend treatment by Shinei Doga in an effort to grab audience share with lots of battle action, while doing its best to present costumes, architecture, and known historical fact as accurately as possible. It was so popular that they made a new version in 1985, and followed it up with *Romance of Three Kingdoms II—Heroes Crowned in Heaven* (1986). *Mitsuteru Yokoyama's Romance of Three Kingdoms* (1991) retold the story as a TV series, drawing on the manga retelling of the original by Mitsuteru Yokoyama, also known for GIANT ROBO and a manga *Suikoden*. The 1992 movie version by Enoki was released in the U.S. as *Great Conquest: Romance of the Three Kingdoms*, with narration by Pat "Karate Kid" Morita. Once again the producers made much of their return to the historical record for details of design and architecture, while focusing on the battles in order to capture theater and video audiences.

GREAT PEOPLE

1977. JPN: *Manga Ijin Monogatari*. AKA: *Manga Tales of Greatness*. TV series. DIR: Masakazu Higuchi, Kenjiro Yoshida, Ryosuke Takahashi, Hitoshi Sakaguchi. SCR: Ryohei Suzuki. DES: Susumu Shiraume. ANI: Toshiyasu Okada. MUS: Osamu Tokaibayashi. PRD: Tac, TBS. 25 mins. x 46 eps.
A similarly educational sequel to JAPA-

NESE FOLK TALES, introducing famous people from history, bundled two to an episode. Classes of greatness include inventors and scientists such as Darwin, Copernicus, Galileo, the Wright Brothers, Bell, Newton, Curie, and Nobel; GREAT COMPOSERS Beethoven and Mozart, as well as Schumann and Foster (again!); explorers Livingstone, MARCO POLO, Scott, Amundsen, and Cook; several writers also covered in ANIMATED CLASSICS OF JAPANESE LITERATURE, including Hearn and Soseki, as well as the creators of HUCKLEBERRY FINN, DON QUIXOTE, THE TALE OF GENJI, and TREASURE ISLAND; poets Li Bo, Du Fu, Ryokan, and Basho; artists Hokusai, Hiroshige, Rodin, Millais, Gauguin, Leonardo da Vinci, and Michelangelo. There is space for baseball legend Babe Ruth, though surprisingly few religious figures beyond Shotoku Taishi. Military heroes are limited to the safely distant ALEXANDER and Genghis Khan, while political greats reflect an inevitable bias toward American and Japanese statesmen, such as Washington and Ryoma Sakamoto (see OI! RYOMA), or the philosopher of the Japanese Enlightenment, Yukichi Fukuzawa. Though such lists can rarely please everybody, one can only wonder at a series of historical giants that includes IKKYU but not CONFUCIUS, or that deems Ernest Seton, creator of SETON'S ANIMAL TALES, as somehow more noteworthy than Shakespeare.
An unrelated six-part video series, *Stories of Greatness* (1989), was directed by Yasuaki Ebihara and featured COLUMBUS, HELEN KELLER, Edison, Hideyo Noguchi, Lincoln, and Marie Curie, all of whom had already been showcased in the earlier series.

GREED

1985. Video. DIR: Yukien Kogawa. SCR: Yukien Kogawa, Aiko Hanai. DES: Yukien Kogawa. ANI: Yukien Kogawa, Hidetoshi Omori. MUS: N/C. PRD: Film Link, Be Bo. 57 mins.
Upstanding youngster Rid and his four friends stand up against the evil Vai, who wishes to seize control of the

world, even though Rid's father tried and failed to resist Vai many years before. A sci-fi action one-shot from the creator of SPACE RUNAWAY IDEON.

GREEN GREEN *

2002. TV series, video. DIR: Chisaku Matsumoto, Yuji Muto, Noboru Yamaguchi, Yoshikazu Kawashima. DES: Kiyotaka Nakahara, Shinji Katakura. ANI: Katsuya Shirai, Studio Matrix. MUS: Shinkichi Mitsumune. PRD: Tetsuya Ishikuro, Pony Canyon, Sakamoto, Memory Tech. 26 mins. (v1), 24 mins. x 12 eps. (TV), 8-10 mins. x 3 eps. (v2), 31 min (v3).

The first *Green Green* video was based on the erotic game of the same name. Rural boys' school Kanenone High is going coed with a girls' school and the two student bodies meet on a getting-to-know-you visit to the Kanenone campus. Kanenone 10th grade stalwarts Bacchi-Gu, Tenjin, Ichiban, and Yusuke are caught peeping at the girls, so when they are accused of panty theft they have to find the real thief to salvage what remains of their reputation. A year later the TV series picks up Yusuke's story as the girls transfer in to the peaceful country school and cause all manner of romantic disruption. Predictably, for a series that so openly embraces boys' obsession with girls (and some might say, why not?), the cast actually starts the credits sequence naked, acquiring clothes during the opening theme. Half-hearted mention is occasionally made that Yusuke and coed Futaba were lovers in a past life, which is a thin attempt to put a spiritual gloss on the childhood betrothals of LOVE HINA and its ilk. The *GG Character DVD* spin-off came out the same year, with three short stories starring the main characters, plus music videos and TV clips. In 2004 another video one-shot, *GG 13: Evolutions,* was an erotic love story between Yusuke and classmate Futaba.

GREEN LEGEND RAN *

1992. Video. DIR: Satoshi Saga, Kengo Inagaki, Junichi Watanabe. SCR: Masaru

Green Legend Ran

© AIC • PIONEER LDC

Yamamoto. DES: Yoshimitsu Ohashi. ANI: Yoshimitsu Ohashi. MUS: Yoichiro Yoshikawa. PRD: MTV, AIC, Pioneer. 45 mins. x 2 eps., 60 mins. x 1 ep.

As natural resources on Earth become scarcer, the six alien "Holy Mothers" land from space and drain the world of most of its water and plants. Earth becomes a desert, forcing people to huddle in the small oases of greenery at the base of the Holy Mothers. The Lodo, a religion worshiping the Holy Mothers, becomes the new government, opposed by the Hazzard, a group of freedom fighters. Meanwhile, Earth-boy Ran is determined to find the man who killed his mother. He rescues the silver-haired girl Aira, a servant of the Holy Mothers. In a final showdown, the Holy Mothers release all the life force they have hoarded, the Earth returns to green again, and water falls from the sky.

An above-average video anime, well-served in the U.S. release by Pioneer's usual high-quality dubbing, though ultimately *Green Legend Ran* never does anything that Hayao Miyazaki hasn't

done earlier and better. There are moments of simply awesome design, as if Frank Herbert's *Dune* were illustrated by artists of the Golden Age of science fiction, but other parts simply play like low-rent versions of NAUSICAÄ or CASTLE IN THE SKY and aren't helped by a confused plot that has trouble deciding whether the Holy Mothers are alien invaders or avuncular saviors. Whatever they are, both their policy of making things worse on the off-chance they feel like making things better one day and Aira's baseless faith that humanity, if given a second chance, won't ruin things again, display a naiveté of plotting that sits badly with the accomplished artwork.

GREEN MAKIBAO

1996. JPN: *Midori no Makibao*. TV series. DIR: Noriyuki Abe. SCR: Satoshi Hashimoto. DES: Hidekazu Ohara. ANI: N/C. MUS: N/C. PRD: Studio Pierrot, Fuji TV. 25 mins. x 61 eps.

Two prizewinning racehorses, Midoriko and Tamakeen, become the proud parents of a white foal called Makibao, who is determined to live up to their achievements. With a rat for a trainer, he perseveres in this spoof sports anime based on Tsunomaru's 1995 manga in *Shonen Jump* that used funny animals to tell a story of human trials. As with CAPTAIN TSUBASA and CYBERFORMULA GPX, the nature of Makibao's sport allows for a permanent underdog status: it takes him 20 episodes of struggle to qualify for his first race, but winning that merely places him in a more challenging arena with more experienced horses. Makibao develops a deadly rivalry with the Mongolian horse Tourdevil that occupies the later episodes as they compete in France and America, before Makibao finally becomes the world's fastest horse.

GREGORY HORROR SHOW, THE *

2001. TV series. DIR: Kazumi Minagawa. SCR: Naomi Iwata. DES: N/C. ANI: Mihoko Niikura, Shiho Sugiyama, Takumi Kitagawa. MUS: N/C. PRD: Milky Cartoon, TV Asahi. 3 mins. x 25 eps.
A lone traveler checks in for the night at the remote hotel Gregory House, only to come face-to-face with a series of bizarre occupants. In a sequence of short vignettes, often only long enough to introduce spooky characters and engage them in brief conversation, this all-CGI anime often looks more like cut scenes from a computer game— particularly since the first person perspective of the camera often likes to imply that it is the viewer who is the imprisoned traveler. Gregory himself is a rodent with a square head but Mickey Mouse ears, while his hotel guests sometimes look like the collection of a disturbed child's toy box: a pink lizard with a hypodermic needle, a zombie cat, and so on.

GRENADIER *

2004. JPN: *Grenadier: Hohoemi no Senshi.* AKA: *Grenadier: Smiling Soldier.* TV series. DIR: Hiroshi Kojima. SCR: Akira Okeya. DES: Hideki Inoue. ANI: Toshiyuki Kanno. MUS: Yasunori Iwasaki. PRD: Studio Live. 25 mins. x 12 eps.
In a world ravaged by war, *senshi* (warriors) are the only defense against evil—although we are tempted to point out that they are the source of it as well. Large-breasted blonde gunslinger Rushuna Tendo is so effective with her chosen weapon, the six-gun, that she has been given the even grander title of Grenadier. But Rushuna doesn't want to fight—she'd much rather smile at people and make friends. Only when they remain resolutely armed and grouchy does she use her sharpshooting skills. With her sidekicks, including sword-wielding samurai Yajiro Kojima and "cute" girl Mikan Kurenai, she sets out for the capital Tento on the far side of the ocean, seeking her childhood home. Rushuna is a complete airhead, but she's a nice girl with goodwill to spare for everyone. Her ditziness produces plenty of comical moments and her bathing scenes provide ample voyeuristic value for those viewers who care. Meanwhile, she embarks upon a half-hearted quest to defeat her enemies the "ten sages" in an opponent-of-the-week quest like that of FIST OF THE NORTH STAR, although even she seems to lose interest halfway. The climax of the final gunfight owes an extremely obvious debt to the end of the American movie *Equilibrium*, which was released in Japan under the name *Rebellion* earlier the same year. A manga by Sosuke Kaise preceded the show in *Shonen Ace* monthly. TRIGUN with tits. **NV**

GREY: DIGITAL TARGET *

1986. Movie. DIR: Tetsu Dezaki. SCR: Yasushi Hirano, Kazumi Koide, Tetsu Dezaki, Toshiaki Imaizumi. DES: Setsuko Shibunnoichi, Kenichi Maejima. ANI: Yukari Kobayashi. MUS: Goro Omi. PRD: Magic Bus. 73 mins.
On a desolate future Earth, isolated communities fight a ritualized war, scoring points with every confirmed kill. Survivors are allowed to advance through the ranks from class F to A, with the aim of eventually becoming a Citizen. Grey's lover, Lips, joins the forces after being raped by soldiers but dies on her first mission. A distraught Grey joins up himself and gets a formidable reputation as the "God of Death" for being the sole survivor of several missions. When his mentor Red goes missing in action, Grey steals a plane with his new-found accomplice, Nova, and goes to look for him. Red has joined the Resistance, a group fighting the Big Mama computer that, it transpires, pits human towns against each other because it believes the human race wants to die. Grey discovers that the Resistance itself is just another front for Big Mama, and he destroys its floating citadel, which crashes in the supposed location of the Citizens' paradise, itself nothing but a ruin. Determined to destroy Big Mama, Grey and Nova march on the computer's Tower complex in the distance, as countless robots come out to stop them.

Despite antique animation that has forever condemned it to the B-list, *Grey* is still an excellent film, a nihilistic romance in the spirit of COCKPIT, satirizing the unwinnable rules of computer games with ever-multiplying enemies. It also features some truly nutty designs, from traditional giant robots to flying knights' helmets and a city inside a giant floating statue of the Goddess of Mercy. Keeping closely to KARUIZAWA SYNDROME–creator Yoshihisa Tagami's original manga in *Shonen Captain*, the anime only changes one major plot point, keeping Nova alive to the end. In the style of GUNBUSTER, it also shies away from showing the cataclysmic final battle, leaving the viewer to fill in the gap between the final shot and the epilogue that follows the closing credits. Like the ant that is stepped on in the opening scene, only to struggle out of the footprint and continue on its way, life itself refuses to give up without a fight, even though the seas are red and the planet is dying. In its thesis that life is a sick computer game, it is a forerunner of *The Matrix*, though its actual roots extend back into Tagami's own love of Westerns, with Grey as a lone gunslinger righting wrongs because he has nothing better to do. **LNV**

GRIMMS' FAIRY TALES

1987. JPN: *Grimm Dowa*. TV series. DIR: Hiroshi Saito, Takayoshi Suzuki, Shigeru Omachi. SCR: Masaru Yamamoto, Nobuyuki Fujimoto, Akira Miyazaki. DES: Shuichi Seki. ANI: Hidekazu Ishii. MUS: Hideo Shimazu. PRD: Nippon Animation, TV Asahi. 25 mins. x 48 eps.
A selection of just a few of the 200 stories collected by the German brothers in their compendium of fairy tales, some of which have also been animated as stand-alone anime in their own right. Stories include CINDERELLA, SNOW WHITE, *Blue Beard*, *The Princess and the Frog*, *Hansel and Gretel*, PUSS IN BOOTS, *Rapunzel*, and many others, sometimes two or three to an episode, and sometimes serialized across two to do the longer stories justice. The Brothers Grimm were also profiled in GREAT PEOPLE, unlike their Danish colleague, who had to settle for TALES OF HANS CHRISTIAN ANDERSEN. See also VIDEO PICTURE BOOK.

GROIZER X

1976. AKA: *Gloyzer X*. TV series. DIR: Hiroshi Taisenji. SCR: Toyohiro Ando. DES: Takeo Suzuki. ANI: Eiji Tanaka. MUS: Hiroshi Koenji. PRD: Dynamic Animation, Knack, TV Tokyo. 25 mins. x 36 eps.
Far away from human civilization in the Arctic, the alien Emperor Gerdon from planet Gailer has built a secret base to seize control of the world. The Earth's last, best hope is Doctor Jan, a Gailer defector devoted to peace, who has created the flying robot Groizer X, and given it to his daughter Rita. Rita, however, soon does the proper female thing, handing over the robot to Jo Kaijan, a member of the Terran professor Hideki Asuka's elite pilot team. Jo becomes the pilot of Groizer X, with Rita as his assistant, in the continuing war against the Gailer invaders.

Groizer X is actually only the "plane" form of the titular machine. Like Nagai's X-Bomber in *Star Fleet* (*DE), it can also transform into a Groizer Robot configuration, although it does so very rarely. Although often credited to Go Nagai, this series was created by Nagai in collusion with Tagosaku Sakura, the suspiciously pseudonymous artist behind some of the MAZINGER Z manga. This minor series was overshadowed by the more successful Toei series GRANDIZER, with which its images and merchandise are often confused.

GROUP TAC

Animation company formed in 1968 by a number of big names in the animation world, including director Gisaburo Sugii and composer Isao Tomita. Its first known production was the TV series ROAD TO MUNICH (1972). After early work in sound production on anime, the company moved in 1973 into animation itself. Contemporary works include FLINT THE TIME DETECTIVE and TEXHNOLYZE.

GRRL POWER *

2004. JPN: *Makasete Iruka*. AKA: *Leave It to Dolphin*. Video. DIR: Akitaro Daichi. SCR: Mamiko Ikeda. DES: Yuka Shibata. ANI: Yuka Shibata. MUS: Jun Abe, Seiji Muto. PRD: GA-Pro, CoMix Wave Inc. 25 mins.
Three abandoned children band together as sisters. Their parents have gone into hiding for reasons not entirely clear. They should be in sixth grade but they have to make a living, so they set up an odd-job agency on Shonan Beach, near Kamakura, and are soon so busy that they don't have time to go to school. Umi, Sora, and Ao take on tasks ranging from delivery to cheerleading in this perky comedy, although FRUITS BASKET–director Daichi claims he has a serious aim—to raise social issues for his fans to ponder. Green-haired Ao, the youngest of the trio, is deaf and uses sign language; this was hyped at the time as an anime first, by people who had never heard of HOUSE OF ACORNS. Tanned redhead Sora is an athletic tomboy who tackles the more physical jobs, making her deliveries on a Jet Ski, while blonde Umi does her utmost to avoid being labeled an airhead and is actually the brains of the group. All three girls study hard in their free time, of course, since to imply otherwise would mean that the creators were encouraging truancy. This is hammered home *ad nauseam* by the arrival of 11-year-old boy Riku, who thinks they have an easy life, only to be continually told that they are reading very difficult books every day. They're intensely ambitious—they want to make enough money to buy an island and create their own country. Daichi seems to be seeking the same level of independence; he assembled his own team and produced the anime himself. The style is ultra-cute, a Japanese take on the *Powerpuff Girls*.

G-TASTE *

1999. Video. DIR: Shunsuke Harada. SCR: Yoshiki Imamura. DES: Masaki Yamada. ANI: Masaki Yamada. MUS: N/C. PRD: Beam Entertainment, Mybic, AIC. 30 mins. x 7 eps.
A fun-filled day in the life of alleged real-life office lady Moe, from the moment she wakes up from a cozy dream about having sex, through her train-journey fantasies about having sex, to her office activities, which involve a lot of sex. Based on an erotic manga by Hiroki Yagami, who also created *Dear Boys* (see HOOP DAYS). Successive episodes detailed the erotic inner lives of a different large-breasted girl per episode, including Nana the maid, Mai the manageress, Sayuka the schoolteacher, and Misuzu the over-proportioned swimming star. Only five of the seven Japanese episodes were released in America, depriving the U.S. public of whatever delights awaited in the stories of nurse Asuka and newscaster Yuna. ⚫🅝🅥

GTO *

1999. AKA: *Great Teacher Onizuka, Bad Company*. TV series. DIR: Noriyuki Abe, Hiroyuki Ishido. SCR: Masashi Sogo, Yoshiyuki Suga. DES: Koichi Usami, Mari Kitayama. ANI: Kumiko Rokunohe. MUS: Yusuke Homma. PRD: SPE, Studio Pierrot, Fuji TV. 49 mins. x 1 ep., 25 mins. x 42 eps.

Twenty-two-year-old former biker Eikichi Onizuka decides to go straight and become a schoolteacher, though his old life often comes back to haunt him. He uses his criminal smarts to pass the entrance exams but ends up at a school for no-hopers where teenage pregnancies, drugs, and crime are rife. Despite his hard exterior, he genuinely cares about his students, and he uses his streetwise past to put them on the right track.

With a teacher who is little older than his charges, GTO traces a line through Slow Step to Soseki Natsume's Botchan, though its true success lies in the conservative media's need to sanitize subculture thuggery—and what better way than by showing that even gangsters and bikers can rejoin the system? GTO has a convoluted pedigree that also stretches back to the meteoric success of the Bomber Bikers of Shonan, which inspired manga author Toru Fujisawa to create his own version, the Shonan Pure Love Gang, in 1990. Featuring the school and street-gang activities of Onizuka and Danma, it was adapted into a four-part anime series in 1996 by Katsumi Minoguchi. A second prequel, the same year's Bad Company, detailed the first meeting of Onizuka and Danma.

Inevitably, the series was also lampooned in an erotic pastiche, GTR (G-cup Teacher Rei), a four-DVD set about a schoolteacher with unfeasibly large breasts and her adventures with her similarly well-endowed colleagues and pupils. The following year, Fujisawa began GTO as a sequel in Shonen Magazine, with Onizuka announcing his intention of becoming a teacher so he can chase girls. The series also spun off into a live-action TV version and theatrical outings, starring heartthrob Takashi Sorimachi as Onizuka. It is this live version that is the quintessential GTO, with its handsome loner fighting injustices on his motorcycle like an educational lawman, but the anime incarnation still has considerable bite, mainly because its cartoon origins allowed for slightly more violence and

menace than its prime-time live-action counterpart. It also features unobtrusive use of computer graphics that add realistic cloud and water effects to lead the viewer's eye away from the cheap TV animation, and a moody monochrome opening sequence that sums up the series' sardonic attitude, playing the sound of a revving motorcycle while showing the handle of a toilet.

GUARDIAN HEARTS
2003. Video. DIR: Yasuhiro Kuroda. SCR: Kanata Tanaka, Takeshi Sakamoto. DES: Norikazu Nakano. ANI: Norikazu Nakano. MUS: N/C. PRD: Soft Garage, VENET, KSS. 30 mins. x 3 eps. (v1), 30 mins. x 2 eps. (v2).
The Guardian Hearts are girls from the Realm of Light who are sent on interplanetary missions to preserve peace and justice, in Ryo Amatsu's manga from monthly Shonen Ace. However, heroine Hina is a careless, ineffectual bungler whose first action on getting to Earth is to accidentally transform in front of astounded high school boy Kazuya. She then insists that his family take her in as an adopted daughter, so at least she has a base. Kazuya's family home is soon swarming with cute strangers, which will come as no surprise to anime viewers who remember Urusei Yatsura or Little Witch Sally. Girl uniform thief Kurusu, space ninja Maya, catgirl Daisy, magical princess Chelsea, and demure maiden Kotono are just a few of the babes who find this ordinary human strangely attractive and want nothing more than to hang around under the bemused eyes of his family, like well-behaved groupies who can be relied on to help with the chores. A second video series, Guardian Hearts: Power Up followed in 2005.

GUDE CREST *
1990. JPN: Onna Senshi Efe and Jeila: Goude no Monsho. AKA: Female Soldiers Efe and Jeila: Crest of Gude; Jun and Sarah. Video. DIR: Kazusane Kikuchi. SCR: Isao Seiya. DES: Tsukasa Dokite. ANI: Masamitsu Kudo. MUS: Shoji Honda. PRD: JC Staff. 45 mins.

In a one-shot based on Reiko Hikawa's fantasy novel in the spirit of the later Slayers, a pair of sexy, sassy swordswomen, modeled rather obviously on the Dirty Pair, must rescue a royal orphan, overthrow a cruel tyrant, and destroy an evil goddess. The leads were renamed Efera and Jiliora for ADV's U.S. dub.

GU-GU GUNMO
1984. TV series, movie. DIR: Akinori Nagaoka, Takenori Kawada, Shigeru Yanagawa. SCR: Keisuke Fujikawa. DES: Takao Kasai. ANI: Takao Kasai. MUS: Hiroshi Ogasawara. PRD: Toei, Fuji TV. 25 mins. x 50 eps. (TV), 45 mins. (m).
A tale of school high jinks from the Shonen Sunday manga by the versatile Fujihiko Hosono, who also created the more adult stories that became Biohunter and Judge. Gunmo the giant pink bird hatches and befriends Japanese schoolboy Heita. A movie version was released in 1985 that lampooned several Japanese Folk Tales, including that of the Princess Kaguya, which was also spoofed in Rei Rei.

GULKEEVA
1995. JPN: Jusenshi Gulkeeva. AKA: Beast-Warrior Gulkeeva; Wild Knights Gulkeeva; Galkiba; Galkiva. TV series. DIR: Masamitsu Hidaka. SCR: Kenichi Kanemaki, Noboru Aikawa, Hiroyuki Kawasaki. DES: Hisashi Hirai, Takahiro Yamada. ANI: Hisashi Hirai, Satoshi Yoshida, Takuro Shinbo. MUS: Kenji Kawai. PRD: Sunrise, TV Tokyo. 25 mins. x 26 eps.
Adaptation of a manga originally serialized in Shonen Sunday Super, in which demonic Darknoid invaders from Nosfertia are held off by a group of pretty young boys, who inexplicably work in a noodle bar during their time off. Japanese teenager Toya Shinjo is told by his parents that he is not from Earth at all, but rather he is a Humanoid from the parallel dimension of Eternaliya, reincarnation of an ancient hero, and fated to work together with transforming Animanoid knights from Heavenstia in order to thwart the Darknoids. Unsur-

prisingly, the Animanoids are a wolf (Greyfas), a hawk (Beakwood), and a gorilla (Gariel), uniting speed, flight, and strength, like so many other shows since **Babel II**. A series in the tradition of shows like **Saint Seiya**, although its attempt to integrate boys' and girls' TV anime genres was easily outclassed by **Escaflowne** the following year.

GULLIVER'S SPACE TRAVELS: BEYOND THE MOON *

1965. JPN: *Gulliver no Uchu Ryoko*. Movie. DIR: Yoshio Kuroda. SCR: Shinichi Sekizawa. DES: Hideo Furusawa. ANI: Hideo Furusawa, Takashi Abe, Hayao Miyazaki. MUS: Isao Tomita (Milton and Anne Delugg, U.S. version). PRD: Toei. 80 mins.

Ted (Ricky in the U.S. dub) meets the aged Professor Gulliver in a deep, dark forest. Accompanied by Mack the dog, a toy soldier called The General, and the unimaginatively named Crow the crow (see **Coral Investigates**), the two set off on a journey to the Planet of Blue Hope in their spaceship the Gulliver. After adventures in the Reverse Time Nebula, which transforms them all into younger versions of themselves, they finally meet the inhabitants of the Planet of Blue Hope, though they have been thrown off their homeworld by the evil Queen of Purple Planet and her robot soldiers. However, Ted and the professor discover that water disintegrates matter in this part of space, and they are able to lead a successful assault on the enemy, armed only with water pistols and balloons full of water. The doll-like princess of Blue Hope is transformed into a real girl by the victory, and she thanks them for saving her world.

A very remote sci-fi sequel to Jonathan Swift's classic satire *Gulliver's Travels*, which was itself adapted in 1983 as part of the *Famous World Fairy Tales* series, featuring Yoshiaki Kawajiri as art director. The original novel would also inspire in-betweener Hayao Miyazaki's **Castle in the Sky**.

GUN FRONTIER *

2002. TV series. DIR: Soichiro Zen. SCR: Mugi Kamio. DES: Keisuke Masunaga, Miho Nakata, Katsumi Itabashi. ANI: Ikuo Shimazu. MUS: Hiroshi Motokura. PRD: AT-X, Maczam, Pronto, Tsuburaya Eizo, TV Tokyo, Vega Entertainment. 25 mins. x 13 eps.

Leiji Matsumoto never tires of finding new ways to present his concept of heroic manhood through his cast of character archetypes. It saves having to draw anything new, after all. In *GF* Frank Harlock Jr., a former pirate with a predictable resemblance to **Captain Harlock**, arrives with short samurai sidekick Tochiro in the lawless Wild West. They are looking for a missing clan of Japanese immigrants and a traitor, Wild Utamaru, who betrayed the settlement of Samurai Creek and with it Tochiro's family. Facing sex slavers, bandits, corrupt lawmen, and the unfair contempt of a world that is happy to rate tall, elegant, drop-dead-sexy men like Harlock as heroes, but mocks short, fat, miserable heaps like Tochiro however brave and clever they are, the two friends team up with a lovely mystery woman and blaze a dangerous trail along the Gun Frontier. Notable from other Harlock universe stories insofar that Harlock often seems more like Tochiro's sidekick than vice versa. **Ⓥ**

GUN X SWORD

2005. AKA: *Gun Sword*. TV series. DIR: Goro Taniguchi. SCR: Hideyuki Kurata. DES: Takahiro Kimura, Seiji Tanda. ANI: Asako Nishida, Seiichi Nakatani, Hisashi Saito, Masanori Aoyama. MUS: Shuntaro Okino. PRD: AIC, ASTA, Studio Tulip, TV Tokyo. 25 mins. x 26 eps.

Van is a swordsman hell-bent on avenging the death of his fiancée. Wendy Garrett is a pretty young girl with an arsenal of antique guns who belives her brother has been kidnapped by the same criminal. She joins forces with Van in a picaresque quest mixing the Western attitudes of **Trigun** with the town-of-the-week conceit of **Kino's Journey**. Their quarry is "the Claws," a serial killer intent on killing young

brides—perhaps a little nod to *Kill Bill* (2003)—see **Kill Bill: The Origin of O-Ren**.

GUNBUSTER *

1988. JPN: *Top o Nerae! GunBuster*. AKA: *Aim for the Top!: GunBuster*. Video. DIR: Hideaki Anno. SCR: Toshio Okada. DES: Haruhiko Mikimoto, Koichi Ohata, Kazuki Miyatake. ANI: Yuji Moriyama, Toshiyuki Kubooka. MUS: Kohei Tanaka. PRD: Studio Fantasia, Gainax. 30 mins. x 6 eps. (v1), ? mins. x 2 eps. (*Science Lessons*), 25 mins. x 6 eps. (v3).

Noriko's father dies in space in the first encounter with an alien race that is preparing for an all-out assault on Earth. Noriko overcomes great difficulties at her school in Okinawa and qualifies as one of the pilots sent to defend the planet. She falls out with her partner, "Big Sister" Kazumi Amano, and teams up with Smith Toren, a handsome American pilot who soon dies in action. The predicament of the human race looks bleak: the "aliens" are really the galaxy's natural defense mechanisms, and humanity is merely a virus on the face of the universe. Coach Ota devises the Buster Machines to help the reunited girls turn the tables, and the first major assault is held off with heavy losses. Though only a few weeks have passed for the girls, the effects of relativity mean that several years have passed on Earth. Kazumi marries the dying Ota, and Noriko goes on another tour of duty. Six months later (for Noriko, whereas 15 years have passed on Earth), an older Kazumi rejoins her with Buster Machine Three, a superbomb designed to wipe out the heart of the galaxy in the final conflict.

Beginning as a sci-fi parody of **Aim for the Ace**, *Gunbuster* eventually transforms into an homage to Kihachi Okamoto's live-action war film *Battle of Okinawa* (1971), complete with onscreen notes detailing the numbers of "ships sunk" and a background cast of dozens of generals, each only gaining the merest moment of screentime. Foregrounded through all this is the spunky Noriko, who only ages a year as her friends near retirement age and is eternally in a world of childish things, much like the semiautobiographical heroes of the same producers' OTAKU NO VIDEO. Wartime allusions abound: the human race (i.e., Japan) is fighting on the wrong side in a war it cannot win, while the last-ditch attempt to hold the home islands launches from Okinawa, and schoolchildren age before the viewer's eyes in a variant of the "time travel" of 24 EYES. *Gunbuster* is also a loving pastiche of the anime serials of its creators' formative years, from the martial heroism of STAR BLAZERS (seen on one of the posters in Noriko's quarters) to the super-robots of GIGANTOR. The in-jokes reach staggering levels: Smith Toren was, for example, a tip of the hat to future Studio Proteus boss Toren Smith (see DIRTY PAIR), who was staying with the Gainax animators at the time, while shots of spacecraft under construction often show breakaway sprues as if they were model kits. Played deadly straight no matter how silly the onscreen visuals, it is the ultimate video anime, and, though outlines existed for a full 26-episode series, the story seems perfectly suited to its humble three-hour running time. It also set the pace for many 1990s anime, from the jiggling bosoms of PLASTIC LITTLE to the tongue-in-cheek posturing of BATTLE ATHLETES, though none of its imitators came close. Sadly, it never quite achieved its potential abroad, despite an excellent subtitled version. It was never dubbed, hence losing the large audience it truly deserved, a feat achieved by the same studio's later EVANGELION. The series was screened on Japanese TV after Gainax's more famous follow-up and rereleased on Japanese DVD with some bonus footage in 2001. Gainax chose to mark the company's 20th anniversary with Kazuya Tsurumaki's six-part video series, *Aim for the Top 2* (aka *Diebuster*, 2004), focusing on Nono, a hapless waitress on Earth who is co-opted into a psychic anti-alien squadron called the Topless. As with the original, early

episodes appear trite and shallow, only to take a turn toward the dramatic and gripping later on, most notably in a fourth episode storyboarded by Hideaki Anno himself. The 1994 laserdisc box set included two new "Science Lessons" for episodes five and six (the humorous short segments attached to the episodes which provided explanations about the *Gunbuster* world), which had not been in the original releases. The series was then screened on Japanese TV after Gainax's more famous follow-up, released on Japanese DVD in 2000 (including the new Science Lessons), and ultimately remastered and rereleased on Japanese DVD in 2004. *Gunbuster Perfect Guide*, containing interviews and other ""Making Of"" information, was also released on DVD in 2004. **NV**

GUNDAM *

1979. JPN: *Kido Senshi Gundam*. AKA: *Mobile Suit Gundam*. TV series, movie, video. DIR: Yoshiyuki Tomino, Shinya Sadamitsu, Ryoji Fujiwara, Fumihiko Takayama, Takeyuki Kanda, Takashi Imanishi. SCR: Hiroyuki Hoshiyama, Kenichi Matsuzaki, Masaru Yamamoto, Yoshihisa Araki, Katsuyuki Sumizawa. DES: Yoshikazu Yasuhiko, Kunio Okawara, Kazumi Fujita, Mamoru Nagano, Hiroyuki Kitazume, Mika Akitaka, Haruhiko Mikimoto, Yutaka Izubuchi, Gainax, Yoshinori Sayama, Toshihiro Kawamoto, Hajime Katoki, Kimitoshi Yamane, Shuko Murase. ANI: Yoshikazu Yasuhiko, Kazuo Tomizawa, Kazuo Nakamura, Kazuo Yamazaki. MUS: Takeo Watanabe, Yuji Matsuyama, Shigeaki Saegusa, Tetsuro Kashibuchi, Yoko Kanno, Kohei Tanaka (*G Gundam*), Yasuo Uragami (*Gundam W*). PRD: Sotsu Agency, Sunrise, Nagoya TV (TV Asahi). 25 mins. x 43 eps. (*First Gundam*), 25 mins. x 50 eps. (*Zeta*), 25 mins. x 47 eps. (*Double Zeta*), 120 mins. (m/*Char's Counterattack*), 30 mins. x 10 eps. (*SD*), 30 mins. (m/*SD*), 30 mins. x 4 eps. (v/*SD* ii–iv); (30 mins. m2/*SD*), 40 mins. x 4 eps. (*SD Side Story*), 30 mins. x 6 eps. (*War In the Pocket*), 30 mins. x 12 eps. (*Star-*

dust Memory), 115 mins. (m/*F91*, also 120 mins. special edition), 25 mins. x 51 eps. (*Victory*), 30 mins. x 11 eps. (v/*08th Team*), 25 mins. x 49 eps. (*G Gundam*), 25 mins. x 49 eps. (*Wing*), 30 mins. x 3 eps. (*Endless Waltz*), 25 mins. x 39 eps. (*Gundam X*), 25 mins. x 50 eps. (*Turn-A*), 25 mins. x 50 eps. (*Seed*); 25 mins. x 50 eps. + 2 sp. (*Seed Destiny*), ca. 3 mins. (*Gundam: Mission*), 24 mins. (*Neo Experience*), 128 mins. (*Turn A* m1), 128 mins. (*Turn A* m2), ? mins. x 12+ eps. (*Evolve*), 25 mins. x 50 eps. (*Seed*), 94 mins. x 3 eps. (*Seed Sp. Ed.*), 25 mins. x 50 eps. + 2 sp. (*Seed Destiny*), 95 mins. (*Zeta* m1), 98 mins. (*Zeta* m2), 90 mins. x 1+ eps. (*Seed Destiny* Sp. Ed.), 15 mins. x 3 eps. (*Seed: Stargazer*), ca. 95 mins. (*Zeta* m3).

In the "Universal Century" Year 0079, Earth and its space colonies are split between the democratic Federation and the Principality of Zeon. The Earth ship White Base arrives at the Side 7 research facility to pick up some prototype "mobile suits" (humanoid piloted robots), but it is ambushed by Zeon attackers with orders to destroy them. Fifteen-year-old Earth boy Amuro Ray climbs into the cockpit of his father's prototype RX-78 Gundam unit and fights them off. With most of the original military crew dead, the White Base is commandeered by young Side 7 evacuees—as they head for Earth, they are hounded by Zeon forces led by the dashing enemy officer Char Aznable. Touching down in enemy territory, they fight their way out to their own forces, who reveal that they are "newtypes," a new breed of human with nascent psionic powers. Eventually, they lead a final assault on the asteroid fortress of A Baoa Qu, the Zeon forces are riven by internal struggles (Char himself kills one of their leaders as part of a family feud), and the One Year War is over.

Along with STAR BLAZERS and MACROSS, *Gundam* is a cornerstone of anime SF, an ever-present franchise and sprawling saga, still active two decades after its premiere. Its distinguishing features are firmly rooted in merchandising and its own longevity—a vast taxonomy of robot types ready for exploitation in model kits and action figures (compare to POKÉMON) and a long-running future saga that has often collapsed under its own weight only to be brought back with several attempts to reset the continuity. As with other successful franchises like *Star Trek*, keeping track of the characters themselves also requires a sizable concordance. It's bad enough that they often seem named after random words picked from a Scrabble bag, let alone that they switch sides and identities. Matters are not helped by "joke" names that seem like a great idea to the Japanese but have caused endless difficulties to English translators trying to keep romanizations consistent. Most infamously, Char Aznable is named after the French singer Charles Aznavour, which would have been a poor enough gag in a shallow comedy like SORCERER HUNTERS, but is quite damaging to the tone of an otherwise serious SF saga. The creation of Yoshiyuki Tomino, veteran of ASTRO BOY and BRAVE RAIDEEN, *Gundam* combines elements of *Star Wars* with space-colony politics and a subtle metaphor for Japan's postwar "new breed" baby boomers—the "newtype" name was appropriated for Japan's most popular anime magazine.

The original series was rereleased in three movie editions—*Mobile Suit Gundam* (1981), *MSG 2: Soldiers of Sorrow* (1981), and *MSG 3: Encounters in Space* (1982), the latter two comprising roughly 50% new material between them, with the bulk of it concentrated in the third movie. Part of the new footage showed Char escaping from A Baoa Qu, setting up the sequel series *Zeta Gundam* (1985—the seventh year of the franchise named for the seventh letter of the Greek alphabet). *Zeta* kept surviving members of the original cast but reorganized their allegiances, with Char and the White Base now on the same side, resisting the Earth Federation's attempts to wipe out remaining rebels. The series' ambiguity toward

Gundam

enemies has come to be another of its distinguishing marks, though much of it may originate less in a desire for foes with feelings, and more from Tomino's own ambiguous attitude toward the series for which he has come to be known. *Zeta* was followed by a second season, *Double Zeta* (1986), with an all-new cast, while the "conclusion" to the long feud between Char Aznable and Amuro Ray came in the movie edition *Char's Counterattack* (1988, *Char no Gyakushu*). Determined that all humankind will join the colonists in space, Char plans to drop the Axis asteroid on Earth but is finally persuaded to work with Amuro to prevent the tragedy both sides have created.

The series was parodied in Tetsuro Amino's 1988 *SD Gundam* video series, which featured "super-deformed" squashed-down cartoon versions of the characters and machines in unlikely comedic situations. The original ten-part video series was followed by two short movies, and video sequels numbered *Mark II–IV*. There was also the two-part video series *SD Warrior Gundam* (1989), and a spin-off of the spin-off—*SD Gundam Side Story* (1990).

Gaps in the continuity of the original, serious *Gundam* were plugged by two video series, Fumihiko Takayama's *MSG 0080: War in the Pocket* (1989), which observed the One Year War from the new viewpoint of a very young child learning the real meaning of war, and *MSG 0083: Stardust Memory* which bridged the gap between *Gundam 0080* and the same year's movie *Zeta Gundam*. Following a template no less predictable than that of TIME BOKAN, *Stardust Memory* features a rehashed Char character, Anavel Gato, and a brash young Amuro clone, Ko Uraki. Three years after A Baoa Qu, as the Earth Federation struggles to rebuild its shattered fleet and Zeon plots revenge, the enemy ace once again tries to steal a Gundam. Drawn unwittingly into a conspiracy to wipe out the Earth Federation HQ by crashing a colony onto it, Ko does his utmost to prevent disaster but is still court-martialed and jailed, set free only because further political machinations require that the whole affair be forgotten. *F91* was a stalled attempt to start again with a clean slate, moving the action thirty years into the future with an all-new cast—teenagers Seabrook Arno and love-interest Cecily Fairchild, who discover that Cecily is, like Char before her, a scion of a powerful noble family (in this case the Ronah dynasty), determined to impose a thousand-year Reich on the solar system. Though the story was continued in novel form with the *Crossbone Gundam* follow-up, it did not last as an anime. Aiming itself, like the same studio's successful **Brave Saga** franchise, at a younger audience, the franchise returned as the TV series *Victory Gundam* (1993), though the director (who had gained the nickname "Kill 'em All" Tomino after **Zambot 3**) soon asserted his trademark angst and tragedy. Set another thirty years on (in the year U.C. 0153), it featured yet another all-new cast, headed by the 13-year-old wonder-pilot Usso Ebbing. Takeyuki Kanda's video series *MSG: 08th M[obile] S[uit] Team* (1996) returns to the events of the first year in the saga (0079) and the activities of yet another group of characters in and around the events already established in the continuity.

The gap between *Victory* and *08th MS Team* saw several unrelated series that sought to capitalize on the *Gundam* brand without adhering to the future history continuity. Depending on your point of view, these are either interesting speculations on alternate universes or a cavalier attempt to jettison everything from the series except those all-important robot merchandise tie-ins. Released in the same year as **Street Fighter II**, Yasuhiro Imagawa's completely unhinged *G Gundam* TV series was redolent of Stuart Gordon's *Robot Jox* (1989), with gladiatorial bouts between giant robots used to settle quarrels between nations (culturally stereotyped to ludicrous degrees with an elephant Gundam for India, a windmill Gundam for the Netherlands, and a Viking Gundam complete with its own rowing boat). No one is entirely sure why Neo-Sweden's Nobel Gundam looks like a character out of **Sailor Moon**. The kids-in-combat premise was rehashed in another "alternate universe," Masashi Ikeda's *Gundam Wing* (1995), in which five 15-year-old teenagers, inspired by the pretty-boys

of **Saint Seiya**, are mobile-suit pilots in a new war between Earth and its colonies in space. Once more, political and economic machinations are out to crush the colonists' desire for self-determination. *Wing* was also reedited into the four-part *Operation Meteor* clip-shows and is arguably the most successful alternative universe adventure so far, though its sudden cancellation forced an ending on video as *MSG Wing: Endless Waltz* (1997), itself reissued with extra footage as the *Endless Waltz Special Edition* movie. A third alternate saga, Shinji Takamatsu's *Gundam X* (1996), did not flourish in the post-**Evangelion** climate and was ignominiously dragged off the air. The series' next major outing after *Wing* was *Turn-A Gundam* (1999, literally ∀ *Gundam*), yet another attempt to encompass as many previous serials as possible into one overarching continuity (compare to similar problems that dogged the *Macross* saga, especially post-**Robotech**). Leaping two millennia into the future (a period guaranteed to make most continuity errors irrelevant), it depicts Earth people who have forgotten about their spacefaring past, rudely awakened into relearning about the mythical Gundam robots (refer to Tomino's **Dunbine**) after they are invaded by a highly advanced society that has languished forgotten on the moon.

Featuring new music from Yoko Kanno, controversially bizarre robot designs by American futurist Syd Mead (see **Star Blazers**), and a move to the Fuji TV network, *Turn-A Gundam* also appeared in compilation movie editions in 2002: *Earth Light* and *Moonlight Butterfly*. In case people weren't confused enough, there was also a spin-off of *Zeta Gundam* around this time, in the form of the movie *Gundam Neo Experience 0087 Green Divers* (2001), the "neo experience" element being the fact that the movie was screened in IMAX theaters, and hence offered virtual wraparound immersion in the events onscreen.

The next TV series in the franchise was Mitsuo Fukuda's *Gundam Seed*

(2002) and its sequel *Gundam Seed Destiny* (2004), set in yet another continuity, termed the "Cosmic Era." Much of the intrigue, however, is the same old story, with Earth squaring off against ZAFT (the Zodiac Alliance of Freedom Treaty) using prototype pilotable robots. *Gundam Seed* made it swiftly to America, but in a format that led to the controversial kiddifying of some elements—as with *Case Closed* (see **Conan the Boy Detective**), the show was squeezed into slots aimed at a younger audience than it really warranted, causing producers to alter sequences of brief nudity and to add laser light effects to weapons, a move lampooned by irate fans as the creation of "disco guns." The *Seed* titles also gained several spin-offs, including a compilation of key moments in *Special Edition*, as well as several manga sidestories under the *Astray* label, and the spin-off *GS: Stargazer* (2006), directed by Susumu Nishizawa, which premiered online in three 15-minute bursts.

The story continues to be constantly revised through novels, manga, games, and other spin-offs. These have included the live-action game *Gundam 0079: War for Earth*, the live-action movie *G-Saviour* (2000), and Katsuhiro Otomo's CG short *Mission to the Rise* (1998). As part of *Gundam*'s 20th-anniversary celebrations (which seemed to the authors to go on for about five years!), Sunrise also released a series of short anime called *Gundam Evolve* (2002), presenting vignettes from the many earlier franchises. The movie *MS Igloo* (2004), set during the *original* continuity and not the more recent Cosmic Era nonsense, was initially shown exclusively at the Bandai Museum in Matsudo, but has been revamped as a three-part video series under the subtitle *Apocalypse 0079* (2006). *Zeta Gundam* was also revamped as *MS Z Gundam: A New Translation* in the form of three movies (2004–2006), blending old and new animation, and with a revised story.

Other variants of *Gundam* include the *A Baoa Qu* ride at the Fuji Express Highland amusement park (featuring original animation designs by *War in the*

Pocket–designer Haruhiko Mikimoto), and Gichi Otsuka's novel and manga *For the Barrel* (2000), which refashioned Tomino's own *Gundam* novels. In an abortive attempt to adapt *For the Barrel* for English readers, *Newtype USA* also published a single chapter of an English-language prologue to *FTB* that was never seen in the original Japanese.

As with the works of Leiji Matsumoto, the *Gundam* franchise suffers from an identity crisis of sorts. Its continuity is a mess of remakes and restarts, its owner a conglomerate keen to make good an investment in earlier incarnations that now appear dated. Its original fans have children of their own; but newer aficionados often latch onto later incarnations contradicted by predecessors. In a world of grown-up sci-fi fans, its mature moments and dramatic scenes are too often lost beneath the crushing weight of merchandising concerns. The tension between the desire to create something new and the desire to replicate proven successes in characters and situations has led much of *Gundam* to have a cyclical, repetitive nature. One of its best hopes in the 21st century lies in distribution to mobile phones and other portable devices where, as with ROBOTECH, the age of the earlier versions is less obvious on a smaller screen. It is difficult, however, to imagine its owners ever giving up on such a proven cash cow, despite the headaches it may cause encyclopedists.

GUNDRESS

1999. Video. DIR: Katsuyoshi Yatabe. SCR: Kentaro Isaki, Kenichi Sakai. DES: Tetsuro Aoki, Koji Watanabe. ANI: N/C. MUS: Yutaka Tominaga. PRD: Sanctuary, Nikkatsu. 30 mins.

A predictably disappointing one-shot anime from the people who brought you LANDLOCK, which similarly cashes in on the alleged involvement of "planning assistant" Masamune Shirow. The all-female "Bouncer" task force fights crime in the multiracial "Bayside City" that was once Yokohama, implying all sorts of nonexistent connections with other Shirow titles such as DOMIN-

ION (the milieu) and APPLESEED (the robot suits). Despite early press hype that talked up the use of "real" voice actresses instead of ones who specialized in anime, it sank without a trace in the Japanese market, probably because not even Shirow can wave a magic wand and make something interesting out of four stereotypical girls conceived for a computer game.

GUNGRAVE *

2004. TV series. DIR: Toshiyuki Tsuru. SCR: Yosuke Kuroda. DES: Yasuhiro Nightow. ANI: Cindy Yamauchi, Shino Masanori. MUS: Tsuneo Imahori. PRD: Red Entertainment, Madhouse, TV Tokyo, AT-X. 25 mins. x 26 eps.

Falsely implicated in a gangland shootout that caused the death of his putative father-in-law, mild-mannered Brandon Heat is on the run with his old orphanage buddy Harry McDowell. When love interest Maria becomes a ward of the Millennium underworld syndicate, Brandon joins them, hoping to get closer to her. Brandon and Harry rise up the organization, until the ambitious Harry turns on his former ally, betraying and killing his best friend to become head of Millennium, with so much power he even has national politicians in his pocket. However, Brandon is brought back to life in the style of *Robocop* by the mysterious Lightning organization, whose secret Necrolyze project transforms him from a clumsy simpleton into the invincible assassin known as Beyond The Grave. His mighty handguns (named after Cerberus, three-headed guard dog of Hell) can mow down any opposition, and he is identified by his burning desire for revenge and the giant coffin he carries on his back. Years after they first clawed their way out of the ghetto, the pair return to face each other on their old stamping ground—Harry abandoned by his own men, with a price on his head, Grave with his reanimated body starting to shut down.

Based on the PS2 game featuring designs by TRIGUN-creator Yasuhiro Nightow, *Gungrave* throws in so many

influences and genre ideas that the authors would not be surprised to see a character somewhere with a kitchen sink on his back as well. The script admirably concentrates on fleshing out the character conflicts and plot, arguably at the expense of the action sequences. A tale of gangster careerism à la *Once Upon a Time in America* (1984), told chiefly in flashback like *The Godfather Part II*, is also made to share the screen with redundant references to Westerns, particularly Nightow's beloved *They Call Me Trinity* (1971), and Sergio Corbucci's *Django* (1966), which similarly features a lone gun of vengeance intent on rescuing a damsel in distress. Meanwhile, the run-down urban gothic setting plays to the strengths of the Madhouse studio. In smart application of contemporary fads, it also mixes the resurrection science of KIKAIDER and CASSHAN with the evil undead menace of a zombie movie. The flashbacks catch up with the "present day" two thirds of the way through the series, ready for the final showdown. ⓛⓝⓥ

GUNPARADE MARCH *

2003. JPN: *GunParade March Aratanaru Kyogunka*. AKA: *GunParade March—A New Anthem*. TV series. DIR: Katsushi Sakurabi. SCR: Fumihiko Takayama, Junichi Shintaku, Yasushi Minakami. DES: Yasuhiro Iric, Kazunori Iwakura, Kunihiro Abe, Junko Kimura. ANI: Yoshio Okochi. MUS: Hikaru Nanase, Masayoshi Yoshikawa. PRD: Brains Base, JC Staff, SCEI, MBS. 25 mins. x 12 eps. (TV1), 25 mins. x ?? eps. (TV2).

In 1945, World War II was abruptly ended by the arrival of invading alien entities called Phantom Beasts. In the ensuing years, the Phantom Beasts occupy most of the world, until by 1999 one of the last lines of defense is on Japan's southern island of Kyushu. Severe losses on the human side led in 1978 to the reduction of the draft age to 16 and its expansion to include females. Now, in 1999, the teenage soldiers' main weapon against the Phantom Beasts is the HWT (Humanoid

War Tank), a single-seater robot that can grapple with the oversized aliens in the hope of destroying their vulnerable brain-spot. In death, the Phantom Beasts unleash poisonous residue that renders the surrounding area uninhabitable and threatens to kill any pilots unable to make it out of the war zone in time.

Like SAKURA WARS, *Gunparade* is based on a historically revisionist game for the PlayStation, although this one won an award at the 2001 Japanese national science fiction convention—the first game to do so. It is, perhaps, worth mentioning that if one really wanted to allegorize the defense of Japan in 1945 from evil invaders (that's us), GUNBUSTER did it far better and did so before most of *Gunparade*'s intended audience were born, but that, of course, is how people can get away with it. Unit 5121 has four Shikon units, and the concentration on the everyday lives and relationships of its pilots and their backup crew bears a strong resemblance to that depicted in PATLABOR. Nowhere is this more obvious than in the sudden arrival of Mai Shibamura, a cool, ruthlessly efficient transfer who is the sole survivor of a frontline unit which 5121 has been assigned to replace. Mixing elements of *Patlabor*'s Kanuka with Asuka from EVANGELION, Mai is a privileged rich girl whose father worked on the original HWT project, inexplicably forced to fight on the front alongside our point-of-view protagonist Atsushi, with whom she must practice to ensure that her moves are properly "synchronized."

Story editor Fumihiko Takayama, a native of the unit's hometown of Kumamoto and a veteran of many GUNDAM episodes, was on hand to ensure mechanical "authenticity," although making such a big deal about how the robots work might seem facetious considering the Japanese education system's obstructive policy on telling students what really happened in WW II. The show's Japanese subtitle might proclaim that it is a "new anthem," but really this is the same old song we've heard before in KISHIN CORPS and DEEP BLUE FLEET. However, *Gunparade* is an irresistible addition to the alternate universe subgenre in Japanese science fiction, if only for little touches like *Wicked Wizard*, wartime propaganda dressed up as a fairy tale, with which the child pilots are indoctrinated. There are also allegories of more modern conflicts in the style of GASARAKI and HEAT GUY J, particularly with cutaways to life away from the frontline, in which citizens enjoy relative levels of comfort and luxury, while their children sacrifice themselves to hold off a seemingly unstoppable menace—literally, since infants are required as operators for the PBE bombs that are the best weapons against the Phantom Beasts. With the first season leaving the plot unresolved, a sequel involving a new cast, *Gunparade Orchestra*, followed in fall 2005.

GUNSLINGER GIRL *

2004. TV series. DIR: Morio Asaka. SCR: Junki Takegami, Kazuyuki Fudeyasu, Keiko Ueno, Kurasumi Sunayama. DES: Hisashi Abe. ANI: Fumie Muroi, Hajime Matsuzaki, Kazuo Watanabe, Kumi Ishii, Yasuhide Maruyama. MUS: Toshihiko Sahashi. PRD: Media Works, Madhouse, Animax, Fuji. TV 25 mins. x 13 eps.

A trio of sweet young girls suffer childhood traumas that bring them to the attention of the Social Welfare Agency, an Italian secret service program that trains them as secret agents, complete with cybernetic enhancements that risk drastically shortening their lifespans. Yu Aida's original manga takes elements of the undercover agents of SPRIGGAN and SUKEBAN DEKA and blends them with the glamorous female agents of *La Femme Nikita* (1990) and *Alias* (2001). The series also revisits many of the tried-and-tested character clichés of modern anime, including Rico, a consumptive girl whose trauma was constant hospitalization, and Henrietta, an innocent whose childhood was brought to a brutal end by the murder of her family. Mental trauma also provides a foundation for for subplots that present the girls as submissive blank slates in the style of CHOBITS—some of their handlers treat them like machines to be dispatched to perform tasks, while others try to befriend them, taking them on outings that, to the cynical might bear a close resemblance to the seduction of "damaged goods" in less mainstream works such as the LOLITA ANIME. Beethoven's Ninth Symphony, an anime favorite since EVANGELION, looms large as a musical factor at the end of the show. Preceded by a manga by Yu Aida in *Dengeki Gao* monthly. **Ⓥ**

GUNSMITH CATS *

1995. Video. DIR: Takeshi Mori. SCR: Atsuji Kaneko. DES: Kenichi Sonoda, Tokuhiro Matsubara. ANI: Tokuhiro Matsubara. MUS: Peter Erskine. PRD: Vap, TBS. 30 mins. x 3 eps.

Rally Vincent is a gun seller and bounty hunter in Chicago who works with her bomb-throwing sidekick Minnie-May Hopkins and straitlaced researcher Becky Farrah. She is blackmailed by an agent from the ATF bureau into meeting with a gunrunner, whose main contact turns out to be a Russian assassin, Radinov. A local candidate for mayor decides to reward Rally's vigilante acts as a campaign gimmick, but the assassin is hiding out in the crowd for the final showdown.

A sparky adaptation of Kenichi Sonoda's 1991 manga from *Comic Afternoon* that steps outside the continuity of the original series, giving Rally the roguish ATF officer Bill Collins as her new "boss," and a new enemy in the form of Radinov. There are, however, several references to the manga, including the appearance of prosthetic limbs owned by Rally's manga enemies and a cameo by her Chicago PD contact Roy Coleman. Supporting character Becky becomes a stronger "part of the team" chiefly to satisfy the filmmakers' desire to reprise *Charlie's Angels*—a gambit that works particularly well in the bright, pop-art tones of the opening credits. Despite a setting in a fantasy

Chicago like the urban war zone of **MAD BULL 34**'s New York, *GSC* is remarkably lighthearted, complete with gratuitous underwear flashes, myopic bad guys who never shoot straight, and no sign of the manga's forays into drug addiction and child prostitution. The filmmakers made much of their research trips to the real Chicago, but, although intense effort is expended on the right noises for guns and cars, less thought was devoted to more important plot elements, such as how gunsmiths stow dangerous weapons, and what the police might think of an underage girl who collects hand grenades. But, apart from the holes, this is good fun, helped greatly in translation by a streetwise U.S. dub from ADV.

Asides about May's boyfriend, Ken, imply the show was intended to go further, and if anything deserved a TV replay, it was this. *Gunsmith Cats* was presumably hobbled by its contemporary look; there wasn't much call for pulp crime in 1990s anime unless it had a sci-fi sheen like **COWBOY BEBOP**. A very different, earlier version of Rally Vincent also appeared in Sonoda's **RIDING BEAN**. **CNV**

GURU-GURU

1994. JPN: *Maho Jin Guruguru*. AKA: *Magical Treasury Guru-guru*. TV series, movie. DIR: Nobuaki Nakanishi. SCR: N/C. DES: Masahiro Kase. ANI: Kazuyuki Okascko. MUS: N/C. PRD: Nippon Animation, TV Asahi. 25 mins. x 45 eps.
The adventures of the heroic preteens Nike and friend Kukuri the witch deliberately told in a style that mimics the cartoony questing of computer role-playing games, as they defeat wandering monsters, liberate treasure from dungeons, and eternally seek to better themselves through "level-ups." Based on a manga by Hiroyuki Morifuji, serialized in *Shonen Gungun* magazine.

GUTS, THE

2005. Video. DIR: Hideki Araki. SCR: Koichi Murakami. DES: Hideki Araki. ANI: Hideki Araki. MUS: Meeon. PRD: Animac. 30 mins. x 2 eps.

Slacker university student Akitoshi Nakajima is rebuffed by the object of his affections, who tells him he is unreliable and weedy. He decides to kill two birds with one stone by applying for a job on a construction site. Soon after arriving, he is forced to take an "entrance exam" which involves having sex with Hiroko Miike, the pretty thirtysomething site manager. Impressed with his performance, she puts him on the work detail, where he is soon offered sex galore by the desperate women he encounters. A rare anime foray into the world of construction worker porn, in which for some reason, not only the women but also some of the men appear to have large breasts. **N**

GUTSY FROG, THE

1972. JPN: *Dokonjo Gaeru*. TV series, movie. DIR: Eiji Okabe, Tadao Nagahama, Tsutomu Shibayama. SCR: Masaki Tsuji, Haruya Yamazaki, Yoshiaki Yoshida, Noboru Shiroyama, Tsunehisa Ito, Masaru Yamamoto, Hideo Takayashiki, Tomoko Konparu, Masaaki Sakurai. DES: A-Pro, Yasumi Yoshizawa. ANI: Osamu Kobayashi, Tsutomu Shibayama, Osamu Kobayashi. MUS: Kenjiro Hirose, Reijiro Komutsu. PRD: Tokyo Movie Shinsha, TBS; TMS, Nippon TV. 25 mins. x 103 eps. (TV1), 25 mins. x 30 eps. (TV2), 40 mins. (m).
Noisy, unruly middle school boy Hiroshi is walking home from school one day when he falls over, landing on top of a frog. The frog, whose name is Pyonyoshi, is flattened and imprinted onto the front of Hiroshi's shirt—and insists on commenting on everything he does, with humorous results. A wacky variation on the boy-and-his-dog theme based on the 1970 *Shonen Jump* manga by Yasumi Yoshizawa. Many of the original crew were reunited for *New [Shin] Gutsy Frog* (1981), a shorter-lived series that played up the cartoon slapstick even more than the original. Several episodes were also cut together to make the movie *GF: Gutsy Dreaming* (1982, *Dokonjo Yumemakura*) that was shown on a double bill with **HELLO SPANK**.

GUY *

1988. JPN: *Guy: Yoma Kakusei; Second Target*. AKA: *Guy: Awakening of the Devil; Second Target*. Video. DIR: Yorihisa Uchida. SCR: Hiroyuki Kawasaki, Kunihisa Sugishima, Masami Obari. DES: Yorihisa Uchida, Yasuhiko Makino, Yukio Tomimatsu. ANI: Yorihisa Uchida. MUS: Nobuhiko Kashiwara. PRD: Humming, AIC. 40 mins. x 2 eps.
Guy and his sexy female sidekick Raina, mercenaries out to make a quick buck, discover that a revolutionary youth drug is being developed on the prison planet of Geo. Prison warden Helga runs a white slavery operation out of her penal colony, where the victims are also sexually abused in a violent, tits-and-tentacles SF extravaganza in the fashion of **ADVANCER TINA**. Guy saves the day by transforming into a super-violent beast, as he does once again in the belated sequel, in which he and Raina discover that the Golden Goddess religious cult is really a corrupt front. The second episode, however, attempted to lighten the poker-faced sex and violence with a few in-jokes about earlier giant-robot shows and a visual reference to the **DIRTY PAIR** movie. The two episodes were combined on a single tape as *Guy: Double Target* in 1992, and it is this version that was released in the U.S. **CNV**

GUYSLUGGER

1977. JPN: *Hyoga Senshi Guy Slugger*. AKA: *Glacial Warrior Guy Slugger*. TV series. DIR: Noboru Ishiguro, Kenjiro Yoshida. SCR: Shunichi Yukimuro. DES: Shotaro Ishinomori. ANI: Sadayoshi Tominaga. MUS: Toshinori Kikuchi. PRD: Toei, TV Asahi, Ishinomori Pro. 25 mins. x 26 eps.
Created by the ancient Solon civilization and left for 30,000 years in suspended animation somewhere in the Antarctic, the battle robots Shiki Ken, Mito Kaya, Tani Mari, Ono Riki, and Ii Taro wake to fight the invading Imbem from Eridanus 28, combining their vehicles to form the giant robot Guyslugger. Based on an idea by Shotaro Ishinomori, whose *Goranger* (*DE)

had revolutionized children's entertainment only a couple of years earlier,
Guyslugger represents an attempt to
replicate the live-action battle-team
shows in anime—compare to the
same year's GINGUISER. The story also
included many references to ancient
mysteries such as Stonehenge, like the
later SPRIGGAN, as well as conflicted
postmodern *Pinocchio* angst in the style
of Ishinomori's KIKAIDER. Nor did the
show shy away from the harshness of
war—the halfway mark was characterized by suicide bomber attacks like
those of GOWAPPER 5 GO-DAM. The show
ended with a last-ditch kamikaze run
on the Imbem homeworld, much to
the surprise of audiences at the time,
although in retrospect it could be seen
as a more gung ho variant on the final
tragedy of ASTRO BOY, among other
earlier shows. Tie-in manga ran in
Terebi magazine, *Terebi-kun*, and *Terebi
Land*.

GUYVER *

1989. JPN: *Kyoshoku Soko Guyver*.
AKA: *Bio-Booster Armor Guyver*. Video,
movie. DIR: Koichi Ishiguro. SCR: Takashi
Sanjo. DES: Hidetoshi Omori. ANI: Sumio
Watanabe, Takaaki Ishiyama. MUS:
Reijiro Komutsu. PRD: Takaya Pro. 30
mins. x 12 eps. (v), 55 mins. (m).
In ancient times, an alien race tin-
kered with human DNA to create the
ultimate warrior, or zanoid. Though
these creatures were intended for
battlefields on distant worlds, the Creators left before the experiment was
complete. Zoanoids interbred with the
human race in a number of incidents
that survive today as stories of demons,
vampires, and werewolves. The "bio-
booster" suit was an advanced Creator
armor that augmented its wearer's
strength. Three such units are stolen
in the present day by an agent of the
Chronos corporation and scattered
in an explosion. One ends up in the
hands of Japanese schoolboy Sho, who
activates it and becomes its designated
wearer. Another is activated by Chronos' agent Lisker, whose power module
malfunctions during a fight with Sho.
Chronos' Commander Gyro arrives in
Japan to recover the third Guyver unit
and kidnaps Sho's friend, Mizuki, to
draw him out of hiding. He also creates
a hyper-zanoid to fight the Guyver
unit on equal terms. Agito Makishima,
the son of the former head of Chronos
Japan, becomes the third Guyver symbiont, and Sho's school is destroyed as
Chronos' minions attack it in search of
his control medallion. Though Chronos Japan is defeated, Sho learns that
there are many other outposts, and
he is forced to fight Dr. Valcus, who
creates several new zanoids and even
works on "Enzyme," the anti-Guyver.
Sho's father is transformed into a monster and Sho is forced to kill him. Losing the ability to bio-boost, Sho regains
it by asking the spirit of his father for
help in a time of dire need. Though
the evil is defeated for now, Sho must
face several more of the zanoids'
"Zoalord" controllers . . . one day.

Based on the 1985 *Shonen Captain*
manga by Yoshiki Takaya, which continued the story long past the non-ending
of the anime, this unremarkable sci-fi
series remains a recognizable brand in
the U.K. market, chiefly due to Manga
Entertainment's policy of releasing
it at an insanely discounted price
that made it affordable for the young
boys for whom it was originally made,
though if they bought all *twelve* tapes,
it would still cost them a pretty penny.
An earlier version of the same story
was animated as the 55-minute movie
Guyver: Out of Control (1986), directed
by Hiroshi Watanabe and also released
in the U.S. It has the same basic plot
but a female owner of Guyver Two, and
it possesses a brevity that leaves less
room for the pointless repetitions of its
straight-to-video successor. But neither
anime version really does justice to the
material—humanity as the descendants
of abandoned military experiments
may be a clever idea, but it is used as
little more than an excuse for visceral
transformations and predictable fights
against monsters-of-the-week. Two live-
action movies retold the same early
chapters of the story, Screaming Mad
George's *Guyver* (1991, aka *Mutronics*)
and Steve Wang's *Guyver: Dark Hero*
(1994).

H2

1995. TV series. DIR: Hidehito Ueda. SCR: Akira Oketani, Hisato Yamashita, Nobuaki Kishima. DES: Tomoyoshi Hirata. ANI: Hiroki Takagi, Tadashi Hirota. MUS: Taro Iwashiro. PRD: TV Asahi. 25 mins. x 41 eps.

The lives and loves of four young people, all of whose names begin with the letter "H," set against a background of high school baseball. Pitching ace Hiro shatters his elbow, seemingly ending a promising career in baseball and throwing all his choices (school, friends, career) into doubt. Power hitter Hideo continues to train in baseball, while the boys' concerned friend Hikari frets over Hiro's future, and Hideo slowly falls for Haruka, a girl at his new school who is not only the daughter of his father's boss, but also the new manager of the school baseball club. Hiro and his friend Noda (who has also been placed on the injured list by a bad back) destroy the opposition from Haruka's club and suggest that she turn it into a proper competing team. Based on a 1992 manga in *Shonen Sunday* by Mitsuru Adachi, who used baseball and love polygons before in **NINE** and **SLOW STEP**. The story was also adapted into a live-action TV drama series for TBS in 2005.

H TOGETHER

2002. JPN: *Futari H*. AKA: *Futari Etchi*, *Futari Ecchi*. Video. DIR: Yuji Moriyama. SCR: Chiaki Konaka. DES: Yasuyuki Noda. ANI: N/C. MUS: Jun Watanabe. PRD: Geneon, Hakusensha. 30 mins. x 2 eps. (v1), 30 mins. x 2 eps. (v2). Makoto is a 25-year old man determined to save himself for his wedding night with the virginal Yura. But he's spent so long abstaining, he's not sure what to do next, and the only person prepared to teach him is his sexy sister-in-law, though she is soon joined by assorted other relatives, friends, and helpful strangers. The lessons begin with simple concepts and proceed through petting into bedroom role-play. Based on a manga by Katsu Aki in *Young Animal* magazine. ⓝ

.HACK// SIGN *

2002. AKA: *dot hack sign*. TV series, video. DIR: Koichi Mashimo, Nobuhiro Takagi, Yuki Arie. SCR: Kazunori Ito, Akemi Omode, Koichi Mashimo, Kirin Mori, Michiko Yokote, Mitsuhiko Sawamura. DES: Yoshiyuki Sadamoto, Akira Osawa, Minako Shiba, Satoshi Osawa, Yukiko Ban, Yuko Iwaoka, Kenji Teraoka, Tatsuya Oka. ANI: Koichi Mashimo. MUS: Yuki Kajiura. PRD: Bee Train, TNK, Bandai Visual, Yomiko Advertising Inc. 25 mins. x 26 eps. (TV1), 24 mins. x 12 eps. (TV2), 30 mins. x 4 eps. (v1), 20 mins. (v2), 25 mins. (v3), 27 mins. (v4).

The near future: those with time on their hands while away the day in an online role-playing game called The World whose monsters and player characters present them with goals and challenges missing in the real one. Tsukasa is a teenage introvert whose online character has a certain mystique; but he finds himself in even more mysterious circumstances inside the game. He can't log out, and the Crimson Knights, the self-appointed game world police, corner him and accuse him of using an illegally modified character. As their game selves search for the secret of the Key and the solution to Tsukasa's log-out problem, their real-life counterparts BT, Mimiru, and Bear—the friends Tsukasa has never met in real life—try to help him return to the world outside The World, a world in which, it is later hinted, "he" may even be a "she." The game artifact known as the Key of Twilight might hold the answers.

Presenting the Internet as an alternate world in the manner of **SERIAL EXPERIMENTS LAIN** or *The Matrix* (1999), but with a pretentious title that removes it from alphabetical listings altogether, *.hack* (pronounced "Dot Hack") is a multimedia franchise—an anime about a game that looks like an anime, which has several real world game tie-ins, as well as spin-off manga, novels, and even an American trading-card game. It is also aimed firmly at the aging **POKÉMON** generation, positing a future world where the entire Internet is crashed on Christmas Eve 2005 by a succession of viral attacks, most notably a supervirus called Pluto's Kiss. Subsequently, all of the world's computers begin running on a system called Altimit, hence the ability of the whole planet to partake in the online gaming that is The World. None of that helps much with the franchise's complex taxonomy, with prequels, sequels, and spin-offs creating an arcane, detailed universe that only fans of the game can really appreciate—exactly the kind of exclusivity and "in-crowd" sensibility that modern game companies hope to create among fickle teenage consumers.

Two months after *.hack* started running on television, in June 2002, a video series appeared to fill in the backstory. The prequel *.hack//Liminality* was directed by Mashimo and Ito with characters by Toshiya Washida and was given away free with the PlayStation 2 incarnations of the franchise. In its storyline, the multiplayer game The World becomes an international phenomenon on its U.S. release in 2007, but monsters inside the game start displaying strange abilities and players can't develop their characters. Concerned that this makes the game unplayable, player Kite decides to get to the bottom of it—the separate episodes had their own *sub*-subtitles, *Infection, Mutation, Outbreak*, and *Quarantine*.

2002's next video, *.hack//INTERMEZZO* (aka *.hack// Episode 27*, or *Another Story*) gives Bear and Mimiru starring roles as they visit a newly reopened dungeon, and Mimiru looks back to her early experiences in The World and the players she met there. This approach was successful, so a 2003 video, *.hack//Unison* (aka *.hack//Episode 28*) appeared. Set after the end of the original series and the video game, it has Helba inviting Tsukasa, Bear, Mimiru, and a host of other familiar characters to an online party in Cyber Slum where fan favorites reunite or meet for the first time.

The Key of Twilight turns up again in 2003 in a second series, *.hack//Legend of the Twilight (.hack//Tasogare no Udewa Densetsu*, aka *.hack//Udeden*), along with some semblance of a plot, in which two new players, twins Shugo and Rena, enter The World and find that charac-

ters who meet monsters in the game fall into a coma in the real world. They play a pair of legendary characters, Kite and Black Rose, who must use the bracelet's power to find out who or what is controlling events and stop them.

This second series was based on an original manga, based in the TV series world, by Rei Izumi and Tatsuya Hamazaki. Comedy enters the mix and the art style changes to accommodate a new angular, squashed-down look with 2003's *.hack//GIFT*, a parody of the series which was originally only available to players who mailed in tokens from all four spin-off games. In it, character Helba creates an in-game spa, the Twilight Hot Springs, and characters race to find it first—and solve some player murders along the way. A third TV series, *.hack//ROOTS* (2006), features Haseo, a new arrival in the game world, who is soon embroiled in a conflict between rival guilds. This latest incarnation attempts to make more of the fact that The World is not a fantasy realm but an online game, and consequently features more jargon and references to the real world outside.

Online gaming offers the possibility of entering a whole new world in cyberspace, creating a new self-defined persona and meeting others in circumstances you can choose and control—paradise for an insecure teenager. This is an ultimately light-hearted look at the new world, directed, scripted, and designed by a skilled team with enough TV experience to guarantee a quality product; but it plays along with the theory that the Web is a safe place to live the significant bits of your life and form your most important relationships. Which is fine, as long as you remember to log out occasionally.

HAIBANE RENMEI *

2002. AKA: *League of Ashen Wings*; *Charcoal Feathers Federation*. TV series. DIR: Hiroshi Negishi, Tomokazu Tokoro, Hiroshi Kimura, Itsuki Imazaki, Jun Takada, Kenichiro Watanabe, Koji Yoshikawa, Masatsugu Arakawa, Takahiro Omori. SCR: Yoshitoshi Abe. DES:

Akira Takada. ANI: Akio Ujie, Akira Takata, Chuichi Iguchi, Hideo Shimosaka, Masaki Kudo, Mayumi Hidaka, Shinichi Yoshino, Takako Shimizu, Takuji Mogi, Toshinari Yamashita, Toshiyuki Abe, Yoshiaki Saito, Yuichi Tanaka. MUS: Ko Otani. PRD: Production I.G., Tatsunoko, Pioneer, Fuji TV. 25 mins. x 13 eps. This is the story of a tribe of gentle winged humanoids called Haibane, who live alongside but not with ordinary humans in the mysterious walled city of Glie, which similarly has very little contact with the world that surrounds it. The Haibane are beings who emerge from waterfilled, womblike cocoons at various ages, with no memories or knowledge, and sprout beautiful but useless wings and halos soon after waking. Every Haibane has a dream before emerging from the cocoon; they tell it, and are given a name based on it, but nobody knows what the dreams mean. Heroine Rakka dreams of falling from the sky—*rakka* is Japanese for falling—while Reki dreamed of walking a path of pebbles (*reki*) and Kana dreamed of swimming in a river, so is named with the characters for river and fish.

The Haibane all live in the Old House on the outskirts of the city, their "nest," going out to work among humans during the day and returning home to housemother Reki and a few younger ones. Forbidden to use money or to own or wear anything that has not been used by a human, they live a life suspended between the closely supervised "integration" of those with learning difficulties and the segregation of religious sects like the Amish, allowed little self-determination and treated by most humans as curiosities rather than as people. Their backstory is all cryptic utterances and meaningful looks, including the mystery of why Reki was considered "born sin-bound" and what happened to Kuramori, the older Haibane who cared for Reki when she first arrived, but who never explained "the day of flight" to her, leaving Reki heartbroken when she disappeared without any warning.

The Haibane Renmei is the organization that watches over the Haibane. Comprising people in grand robes and masked faces, it is based in a temple on the outskirts of the city and functions like a fantasy Social Services Department. Haibane aren't allowed to speak inside the temple, but must communicate using bells attached to their wings. The Renmei tell their charges that at some unknown time in the future, if they work hard and prepare themselves, their wings will awaken and they will fly over the walls and leave the city—this is "the day of flight." Until then, the Haibane live in a state of limbo, taking each day as it comes and finding what happiness they can in their work and their relationships with each other.

Created and self-published by Yoshitoshi Abe, of SERIAL EXPERIMENTS LAIN and NIEA_7 fame, the manga *Old House no Haibane-tachi* forms the basis for a strange, slow-paced anime with very little action but delicate manipulation of emotion. Abe claims his initial inspiration came from the walled, placeless dream city of Haruki Murakami's novel *Hard-Boiled Wonderland and the End of the World* (1985), and it shares themes of fate in limbo with NIGHT TRAIN TO THE STARS, Hirokazu Kore-eda's masterpiece *After Life* (1998), and the children's show *Yuta and His Wondrous Friends* (*DE). Atmosphere, not event, makes for a drifting story bordering on daydream. It has many potential interpretations—the need to control the unknown, the restrictions of life dissolving in the flight of death, the purposelessness of the rules we impose, and the gradual surrender of curiosity to apathy. Whereas *Lain* was about a young girl seeing the pointlessness of her existence and actively pursuing a challenge that leads to another place altogether, *Haibane Renmei* is about regretting the pointlessness of existence while waiting to be rescued—by a legend, maturity, or death, but certainly not by self-determination.

The Hakkenden

HAKKENDEN, THE *
1990. Video. DIR: Takashi Anno, Yukio Okamoto. SCR: Noboru Aikawa, Hidemi Kamata. DES: Atsushi Yamagata. ANI: Kazuhiro Konishi. MUS: Takashi Kudo. PRD: AIC. 30 mins. x 13 eps.
Fifteenth-century lord Satomi rashly promises his daughter Fuse's hand in marriage to whoever brings him the head of his enemy, Lord Anzai. But no one expects Yatsufusa, the family dog, to win the prize. Fuse and Yatsufusa are both killed, but their karma lives on in a group of "dog" warriors, each symbolizing a great virtue. A generation later, the dog warriors are united and begin their quest to restore the honor of the house of Satomi.

An adaptation of a multivolume popular serial written from 1814 to 1841 by Kyokutei Bakin, a samurai fallen on hard times who wished to retell *Water Margin* (see SUIKODEN) for a Japanese audience and instill some decency in his own merchant son by concentrating on the Eight Virtues of CONFUCIUS: Benevolence, Righteousness, Courtesy, Wisdom, Fidelity, Loyalty, Filial Piety, and Service to Elders. Bakin's original characters left nothing to the imagination, and were often

ciphers for particular virtues or sins, spouting pompous mock Chinese dialogue. The animation crew preferred modern heroes who often doubt their roles and each other, particularly bad-guy Samojiro Aboshi who drips foppish charm, far removed from the one-note voice of evil in the book.

The 96-part novel had a large number of starting points to draw in new readers—an occasionally confusing policy that remains in the anime. Each of the heroes has an origin story of his or her own, thus delaying the "beginning" of their team adventures until episode nine! The first, Shino, must deliver a magic sword to a nobleman, while the second, Sosuke, is sworn to stop him. The third, Dosetsu, is the half-brother of Shino's betrothed, sworn to avenge her death, while the fourth, Genpachi, is a disgraced guardsman offered his freedom if only he kills Shino. And so on. Episode six was director Anno's last, and the remaining parts were originally released under a separate subtitle, *New Hakkenden* (1993), with changes in the crew that are particularly reflected in the character design. As with DARK MYTH, the heavy use of Japanese names often makes the dub a polysyllabic mess, but it is the look rather than the meaning of this series that appeals to its fans, and it is best watched in Japanese for that fully cultural experience.

More concerned with drama than with the impressive battle scenes of NINJA SCROLL, *Hakkenden* was sold abroad on the strength of its literary and cultural pedigree, although the original crew were less likely to have been inspired by the novel as by the 1973 *Hakkenden* puppet TV show of their youth or the 1983 live-action film by Kinji Fukasaku. There are, however, references to the many woodblock prints inspired both by the original novel and the kabuki plays that drew on it, most obviously in the opening credits, in which the anime characters share the screen with their woodblock predecessors. See also the sci-fi remake SHIN HAKKENDEN.

HAKUGEI: LEGEND OF THE MOBY DICK *

1997. JPN: *Hakugei Densetsu*. AKA: *Legend of the White Whale*. TV series. DIR: Osamu Dezaki. SCR: Osamu Dezaki, Akio Sugino. DES: Hirotoshi Takaya. ANI: N/C. MUS: Masahiro Ando. PRD: Image K, Studio Junior, NHK2. 25 mins. x 23 eps.

In the year 4699, deep in space out by the Nantucket Nebula, a group of salvage experts search for "whales"—the abandoned hulks of colony ships left over from humanity's massive expansion into the cosmos. Young teenager Lucky Luck has come to the area in search of Captain Ahab, ostensibly hoping to join the crew of his ship, the Lady Whisker. In fact, as later episodes reveal, he is actually hoping for Ahab's help against the Moby Dick, a predatory space vessel whose approach threatens to destroy Lucky's homeworld. The series aired across three calendar years on its original broadcast, after being temporarily suspended partway.

HAMTARO TALES *

2000. JPN: *Tottoko Hamtaro*. AKA: *Hamtaro the Hamster*. TV series. DIR:

Kazuo Nogami, Koichi Sasaki, Yusaku Saotome. SCR: Michiru Shimada, Miho Maruo, Yoshiyuki Suga. DES: Ritsuko Kawai. ANI: Masaaki Sudo, Junko Yamanaka, Yukari Kobayashi. MUS: N/C. PRD: SMDE, TV Tokyo. 23 mins. x 296 eps. (TV), 50 mins. (m1), 55 mins. (m2), 53 mins. (m3), 41 mins. (m4), 45 mins. (v1), 45 mins. (v2), 40 mins. (v3), 40 mins. (v4).

Hamtaro is a happy hamster who lives with his owner, a 5-year-old girl called Hiroko (5th-*grader* Laura in the company's foreign sales sheets). He sleeps in a little home kept on the buffet counter in the kitchen of a house on a quiet suburban street. But in the park, across the street, under the roots of the old tree, there is a hideout where the local hamsters go for secret meetings of the "Ham-Ham Friends." Sappy rodent goings-on based on a manga by Ritsuko Kawai.

Movie spin-offs duly followed. In *Big Adventure in Hamhamland* (2001), Hamtaro feels neglected on owner Laura's birthday, heads off with his friends in a magic flying basket over the rainbow to HamHamland to find the magic sunflower seeds, for which he has to face Ma-O-Ham, the Hamster Demon Lord. The movie took in excess of $20 million at the Japanese box office. *Ham Ham Ham Jya: Mysterious Princess* (2002) has an exotic ARABIAN NIGHTS theme, with flying carpets and a beautiful hamster princess, Shera, living in a golden desert palace with a hamster handmaid harem of cute musicians and dancers. More than one and a half million people bought tickets for it. *Ham Ham Grand Prix* (2003) involves a sled race through an Alpine valley and a hamster pirate captain on a flying galleon. It was similarly huge at the box office, although the authors feel they should point out that all three were sharing double bills with each year's *Godzilla* movie! *Ham Ham and the Mysterious Demon's Picture Book Tower* (2004) capitalizes on the rise of *Harry Potter*, with the rodent friends adventuring through magical storybooks.

The franchise also produced sev-

eral video incarnations, including a parody of FROM THE APENNINES TO THE ANDES, *Hamtaro's Birthday: 3000 Skitters in Search of Mama* (2002, *Hamutaro no Otanjobi: Mama wo Tazunete 3000 Techitechi*), *Hamtaro's Race for the Summer Seaside Vacation Treasure* (2003, *Hamu-chanzu no Takara Sagashi Daisakusen: Hamu wa Suteki na Umi no Natsuyasumi*), and, in time for the Athens Olympics, *Hamtaro's Gold Medal* (2004, *Hamuchanzu no Mezase Hamuhamu Kin Medal*), as well as several educational videos on trains, learning the hiragana syllabary, and school life.

HANAICHI MONME

1990. Video. DIR: Toshihiko Arimasa. SCR: Norio Hayashi, Hiroshi Kitano, Junichi Sato, Kazuki Hirada. DES: N/C. ANI: Koichi Arai, Satoshi Kushibuchi. MUS: Toshihiro Nakanishi. PRD: Toei. 60 mins. x 3 eps.

Animated versions of tales that won the Short Story Prize in the *Hanaichi Monme* bulletin, including *Noboru and the Wildcat*, *The Misleading Friends*, *Sanma's March*, *Red Mail-Box on the Mountain-Top*, and *One Sunday Morning at the Beginning of May*.

HANAPPE BAZOOKA *

1992. Video. DIR: Yoyu Ikegami. SCR: Fumio Saikiji. DES: Fujio Oda. ANI: Fujio Oda. MUS: Nozomu Aoki. PRD: Studio Signal. 45 mins.

Hapless teenager Hanappe is masturbating in front of a porno film when two demons appear from his TV. The brusque Ophisto Bazooka and his sexy female sidekick, Mephisto Dance, reveal that they can be summoned once a millennium by particular penile jerking. Charged with turning Hanappe into the new messiah, they give him superhuman powers, allowing him to kill the local bullies. Bazooka, however, falls for Hanappe's mother, while Dance develops an unhealthy interest in Hanappe's sister. They pay off his father and turn his house into a party zone for devils, hoping to fob Hanappe off with the power to charm any woman. Hanappe is not convinced, chiefly because his power backfires and he is chased by the inhabitants of a geriatric ward and a transvestite. He also refuses to use the power on the girl he loves because compulsion would make the love they shared meaningless. Discovering that the girl he adores is sleeping with her professor to get good grades, a distraught Hanappe takes his own life, and his soul is sent to the Fairy of the World's Forest to be judged. She determines that he is well-loved by his acquaintances, and he is rescued at the last minute by Dance and taken back to Earth to be reincarnated.

A forgettable sex romp from Kazuo Koike and Go Nagai, originally published as a manga in *Young Jump, HB* tries to compensate for its flimsiness by piling on the parodies—split-second cameos exist for many other Nagai characters, including **Kekko Kamen**, **Devilman**, and **Getter Robo**, while Nagai himself has a voice cameo as an irritated priest. A 15-minute ""Making Of"" documentary, showing the momentous occasion when Nagai reads out a single line, pads out the running time of the video to 60 minutes. Groping vaguely for a romantic message then giving up and simply groping for hooters, it is a minor Nagai work and nowhere near his best. **LN**

HANAUKYO MAID TEAM
2001. JPN: *Hanaukyo Maid Tai*. AKA: *Maid in Hanaukyo*. TV series, video. DIR: Yasunori Ide. SCR: Yasunori Ide. DES: Takahashi Osumi. ANI: Takahashi Osumi. MUS: N/C. PRD: Domu, m.o.e., TVK. 15 mins. x 12 eps. (TV1), 17 mins. x 3 eps. (v), 25 mins. x 12 eps. (TV2). An insipid **Tenchi Muyo!** clone about the pathologically shy Taro Hanaukyo becoming the leader of his powerful political family, even though he cannot bear to be touched by women. And guess what, there are loads of them, all dressed as French maids—and only Marielle seems to have the magic touch. The Maid Team consists of four units: the Domestic Unit mothers him, bathes him, dresses him,

and sleeps with him; the Security Unit protects him with high-powered military hardware; the Technical Unit develops new robots for him; and the Intelligence Unit runs Memol, the world's fastest supercomputer. An Oedipally suspect farce with added gadgetry based on Shige Mori's manga in *Shonen Champion*. The second TV series is sometimes known by its subtitle, *La Verité*. Whereas the first series was produced by the notorious "fan service" company M.O.E. ("Master of Entertainment") and consequently featured much nudity, the second season was made by Geneon, and significantly tamer. The video series added three episodes to the original television series. **N**

HANDLE WITH CARE
2002. Video. DIR: Shigenori Kurii. SCR: Hideo Ura. DES: Shigenori Kurii. ANI: Jiro Oiwa. MUS: N/C. PRD: Shindeban Film, Museum Pictures, Milky. 30 mins. Embittered and bored with a series of one-night stands, a musician finds his passions stimulated by the arrival of Sion, a beautiful singer who inspires him to form a new band. Both struggle to place high in the local Wild Jam contest, but their secret pasts are soon exposed. This is an anime from Milky, so sex duly follows. **N**

HANDMAID MAY *
2000 AKA: *Handmaid Mei*. TV series. DIR: Junichiro Kimura, Tetsuya Yanasawa. SCR: Kazuki Matsui. DES: Yuzo Hirata. ANI: Tetsuya Yanasawa. MUS: Toshio Masuda. PRD: TNK, Pioneer, WOWOW. 25 mins. x 10 eps. (TV), 25 mins. x 1 ep. (v1), 30 mins. x 1 ep. (v2; three planned). Nineteen-year-old student Kazuya Saotome is determined to build a robot of his own. Facing fierce competition from college rival Nanbara, a nasty prank goes wrong when a virus sends Kazuya's PC into a spin and (in a weak *Terminator* homage) he accidentally accesses Cyberdyne Systems' latest project, a "cyberdoll" a sixth the size of normal human being. Stuck with a

cute little girl who can literally fit in his hand, Kazuya gets a frilly pink friend to help with his housework, but he also becomes the target of Cyberdyne's later models, determined to steal back the prototype at any cost. An **Oh My Goddess!** retread for the new millennium, based on an idea by Juzo Mutsuki, creator of **Devil Hunter Yohko**.

The video spin-off was originally intended to last for three parts, but was canceled due to financial difficulties with the production house. Some sources have subsequently filed the only extant episode of the abortive video spin-off as an "eleventh" TV episode—a victimless confusion liable to continue now that the series is more easily obtained on video than from TV broadcast.

HANDSOME GIRLFRIEND
1991. JPN: *Handsome na Kanojo*. Video. DIR: Shunji Oga. SCR: Megumi Nichiyoshi. DES: Yumi Nakayama. ANI: Mitsuharu Kajiya. MUS: Marika Haneda. PRD: JC Staff. 35 mins. Teenage pop star Mie Hagiwara and gifted film director Kazuya Kumagai get off to a bad start when they fight in rehearsals. Selected as the main actress in Kazuya's film, Mie hates him at first but is attracted by Kazuya's passion toward filmmaking. Meanwhile, at a meeting just before shooting commences, the production is called off, and Kazuya decides to fund it with his own money. In this adaptation of Wataru Yoshizumi's manga from *Ribbon* magazine, tragedy looms as he prepares to perform the final stunt himself.

HANE, YOSHIYUKI
1940– . Sketch artist and key animator on many famous anime of the 1960s and beyond, including **Little Witch Sally** and **Nausicaä of the Valley of Wind**.

HAPPINET
Established in 1969, Happinet is a manufacturer of toys, games, and software, with a wide portfolio of other

businesses—although for our purposes the two most important are its subsidiaries Green Bunny and Beam Entertainment, the people who brought you CREAM LEMON, KITE, and WORDS WORTH. The Namco-Bandai conglomerate is currently a major shareholder. Beam Entertainment was renamed Happinet Pictures Corporation in 2002.

HAPPY ERMINE

2002. JPN: *Shiawase-so no Okojo-san.* AKA: *Happy Mr. Ermine.* TV series. DIR: Yusuke Yamamoto, Kenichiro Watanabe, Matsuo Asami, Ryuichi Kimura, Seiko Sayama, Takahiro Omori, Toshinori Fukushima, Yasuhito Kikuchi, Yuki Hayashi. SCR: Hiroko Naka, Katsuhiko Takayama, Kazuharu Sato, Yoshio Urasawa. DES: Takahiro Kishida. ANI: Motoki Ueda. MUS: Masamichi Amano. PRD: Eigasha Kyoritsu, Radix, Sotsu Agency, TV Tokyo. 25 mins. x 51 eps. Captured in Japan's northern mountains and brought to an urban pet shop, a white ermine escapes, only to meet with an accident on the mean streets of Tokyo. College student Haruka Tsuchiya finds him in the street and takes him to the vet, while Haruka's kid brother names the creature Kojopii. The wild creature sticks around for the sake of the fried chicken the humans offer but finds human life, and his own human, quite a puzzle. Among the wacky characters in this day-to-day sitcom, where animals figure as strongly as humans, there's a cute mouse whom our hero sees as a meal, and a beautiful girl—but will Tsuchiya ever notice her?

Based on a manga in the spirit of I AM A CAT from *Comic LaLa* by Ayumi Uno. The title recalls Misako Ichikawa's manga *Mr. Happy (Shiawase-san)* which featured a cat as a major character and spun off the anime OYO MY HUGGABLE CAT. A strangely high proportion of stoat, weasel, and ermine-related arguments appear to surround all anime featuring such creatures, which obliges the authors to point out that although he may look like an ermine, Kojopii is more likely to be a Hongo or Ezo stoat.

HAPPY FRIENDS

1990. JPN: *Shiawase no Katachi.* Video. DIR: Shinya Sadamitsu. SCR: Takao Koyama. DES: Takayuki Goto. ANI: Takayuki Goto. MUS: Kenji Kawai. PRD: IG Tatsunoko. 30 mins. x 4 eps. The comedy adventures of a series of squashed-down characters who live in a world that functions on the rules of role-playing games, based on a manga that was originally serialized in the Nintendo gaming magazine *Famicom Tsushin.* The stories incorporate many game themes, from attacking monsters to tennis tournaments, with character designs that presage the later U.S. cartoon *Powerpuff Girls.*

HAPPY HUMPING! BOING BOING

1992. JPN: *Etchi (H) de Happy Pin! Pin! Pin!* Video. DIR: Katsumasa Kanezawa. SCR: Hidemi Kamata. DES: Takeshi Oshima. ANI: Yutaka Arai. MUS: N/C. PRD: E&G Film. 45 mins. Tokio is an assistant director at TV Aoyama, while his father is an archaeologist. When Dad marries Karuri, a woman of easy virtue, and then heads off to Peru on a research trip, Tokio is stuck with Karuri and her daughter back at home, fretting that his newscaster girlfriend, Noriko, will think he is having an affair with them . . . which he eventually does. Matters are soon complicated further by the attentions of porn actress Kazuka Kurodawara, who also wants a piece of Tokio . . . and we all know what piece. Based on a manga by Takeshi Oshima in the spirit of WEATHER REPORT GIRL. **Ⓝ**

HAPPY LESSON

2001. Video. DIR: Takafumi Hoshikawa, Takeshi Yamaguchi. SCR: Yoshio Takaoka. DES: Yasuhisa Kato. ANI: N/C. MUS: N/C. PRD: KSS. 30 mins. x 3 eps. Predictable classroom high jinks, based on the Dreamcast game in which a group of female teachers must nurture a group of female students.

HAPPY PRINCE, THE

1975. JPN: *Shiawase no Oji.* Movie. DIR: Yoshiyuki Tomino. SCR: Zensuke Oshima. DES: Jack. ANI: Shinichi Tsuji. MUS: Mahiko Nishiyama. PRD: Kyoritsu. 19 mins. High above a nameless city, the gilded, jeweled statue of a prince looks down on the population. He befriends a lone swallow and urges him to pilfer his jewels and distribute them among the needy of the town. The swallow duly does so, although few of the recipients appreciate the gifts, and lingers so long as winter commences that he is killed by the cold. The dead bird and the despoiled statue's lead heart end up on the town garbage heap, where angels pronounce them to be the most precious things in the entire city.

A short film made for screening in schools, based on Oscar Wilde's 1888 parable that love is nothing if it does not act, and we are nothing if we do not love—noble sentiments with fatalistic meditations that also recall director Tomino's anime career, particularly ZAMBOT 3 and GUNDAM. Considering that Wilde's original had a hostile attitude toward officialdom, depicting a math professor as a pompous fool who does not approve of children dreaming, the authors would probably have been amused by such a screening for the benefit of the teachers rather than the students. The story is referenced in TAMALA 2010: A PUNK CAT IN SPACE, in which a bird is shown trying to peck out a statue's eyes.

HAPPY WORLD!

2002. Video. DIR: Takashi Ikehata. SCR: Tomofumi Nobe. DES: Hirotaka Kinoshita. ANI: N/C. MUS: N/C. PRD: KSS, Shueisha. 27 mins. x 3 eps. Takeshi Omura's mother ran away from home when he was a little boy, and his distraught father abandoned Takeshi to look for her, leaving his son alone in a cheap apartment which then burnt down. All he owns is the school uniform he still wears, until the day a girl with wings falls out of the sky and introduces herself as Elle. She says she's come to cure his bad luck. She reveals that Takeshi's father nominated him as the family scapegoat to inherit all the bad luck they were due. She tells Takeshi that he has a choice reminiscent of that presented in the following year's TV series *Sky High* (*DE)—he can transfer his bad luck to someone else, just by saying the word; or he can deal with it alone. But the "someone else" Takeshi could transfer his bad luck to is an innocent young girl, and he can't bring himself to put her through the kind of life he has already had, so he opts to deal with his life as it is. Elle finds this very touching and becomes human, moving in with Takeshi to protect him from the curse. Though he objects at first, he finds that spending lots of time with her makes him far less likely to run into bad luck. Based on a manga by Kenjiro Takeshita in monthly *Ultra Jump* that mixed the bad luck protagonist of URUSEI YATSURA (Ataru Moroboshi was supposedly the unluckiest boy on Earth) with the divine intervention of OH MY GODDESS!. **Ⓝ**

HARA, KEIICHI

1959– . Animator at Shin'ei Doga on shows including ESPER MAMI. Subsequently became a writer and director on CRAYON SHIN-CHAN.

HARA, TORU

1935– . Born in Fukuoka Prefecture, Hara graduated from Tokyo's Waseda University and joined Toei Animation in 1959, where he was a production assistant on LITTLE NORSE PRINCE. He left Toei in 1972 to found Topcraft, a company that specialized in coproductions with American and European studios, including Rankin/Bass, on shows such as THE STINGIEST MAN IN TOWN, *The Hobbit* (1977), and *The Last Unicorn* (1982). The company also farmed its services out on domestic animation, in movies such as NAUSICAÄ OF THE VALLEY OF WIND, after which Topcraft was effectively dissolved—its staffers forming the bulk of the animation team on CASTLE IN THE SKY and subsequent Studio Ghibli productions.

HARADA, MASUJI

1947– . Joined Mushi Production and worked as an animator on *Vicky the Viking*. Later a director on HATTORI THE NINJA and ULTRA GRAN.

HARBOR LIGHTS

1988. JPN: *Harbor Light Monogatari Fashion Lala Yori*. AKA: *Harbor Light Story from Fashion Lala; Fashion Lala*. Video. DIR: Tadamasa Takahashi. SCR: Kenji Terada. DES: Yoshiyuki Kishi. ANI: Tadamasa Takahashi. MUS: N/C. PRD: Studio Pierrot. 50 mins.
Eleven-year-old Miho wants to be a fashion designer and is eager to make a dress for her little sister, Shuri, to help her win the Dancing Queen contest. When Miho's stupid aunt ruins the dress, the Fairies of Fanland hear her prayer and transform her into the 16-year-old Lala, a top designer. And in the end, it was all a dream: a cop-out that probably helps to explain why this attempt to create a new magical girl in the tradition of CREAMY MAMI never came back for a repeat performance. Not to be confused with FANCY LALA.

HARD AND LOOSE

1992. JPN: *Shiritsu Tantei Doki Seizo Trouble Note Hard and Loose*. AKA: *Private Investigators Down But Not Out: Trouble Notes Hard and Loose*. Video. DIR: Noboru Ishiguro. SCR: Noboru Ishiguro. DES: Noboru Sugimitsu. ANI: Noboru Sugimitsu. MUS: Masaru Watanabe. PRD: Artland. 45 mins.
A detective thriller in which former boxer Shozo is thrown into a web of intrigue when he picks up a ringing phone in a room whose occupant he is supposed to be following. Based on a manga by SILENT SERVICE–creator Kaiji Kawaguchi and BORDER's Karibu Marai and boasting the distinctive square-jawed characters found in Kawaguchi's other work.

HARDCORE HOSPITAL *

2002. JPN: *Shiroki Tenshitachi no Rondo*. AKA: *Ring of Bright Angels*. Video. DIR: Go Yasumoto. SCR: Shinji Rannai. DES: Go Yasumoto. ANI: Go Yasumoto. MUS: Yoshi. PRD: YOUC, Digital Works (Vanilla Series). 30 mins. x 2 eps.

Date Hospital is sited at the edge of a rich suburb and has a ward that doubles as a brothel. Afraid that the secret will surface, the hospital owner puts his son Ryuichi in charge of training new nurses in the "special skills" required of them. In a combination of the medical drama of BLACK JACK with the coercion of NIGHT SHIFT NURSES, Ryuichi is a brilliant surgeon, who allegedly saves the life of new nurse Sayaka's biker boyfriend Masahiko, and then uses that "fact" as leverage in order to force Sayaka to accept training as one of the "special nurses"— said training including the usual domination, humiliation, and in this case, serial enemas. Ryuichi is also involved with a Ritsuko Akagi-look-alike (see EVANGELION) who is researching (what else?) the ultimate aphrodisiac. In the second episode, lonely widow Miyako Kisaragi also joins the hospital, and Ryuichi uses aphrodisiacs and the usual "special" methods to help her overcome her grief. This entry in the VANILLA SERIES is rife with a lack of cut-to-cut continuity—the (alleged) animators seem to have been barely awake while working on this, and it shows. For a look at their better work, see STORY OF LITTLE MONICA. **ⓁⓃⓋ**

HARÉ + GUU *

2001. JPN: *Jungle wa Itsumo Hare nochi Guu*. AKA: *It Was Nice in the Jungle Then Along Came Guu*. TV series, Video. DIR: Tsutomu Mizushima, Hiroshi Yamamoto, Wataru Takahashi. SCR: Yasuhiro Takemoto, Michiko Yokote, Hiroko Hagita. DES: Hiroshi Kugimiya. ANI: Yuichiro Sueyoshi, Kanami Sekiguchi, Kazumi Ikeda. MUS: Akifumi Tada. PRD: Shinei Doga, Bandai Visual, TV Tokyo. 25 mins. x 26 eps. (TV), 30 mins. x 7 eps. (v1); 20 mins. x 6 eps. (v2).
Ten-year-old Haré lives in a jungle village with his pretty mother, Weda, who is something of a hippie—she had Haré out of wedlock, and left her well-to-do home in the big city because the carefree jungle life suited her better. Weda adopts a little blonde orphan girl named Guu, who seems like a sweet,

© AKIYUKI NOSAKA/SHINCHOSHA CO.

Haré + Guu

innocent little sister for dark-skinned, blue-haired Haré, though she is short-tempered and has a voracious appetite. Then he learns that she's really a glutinous mind-reading alien with an interdimensional portal in her stomach through which weird creatures and objects emerge to cause trouble for him. She's also a typical kid sister—she teases and tyrannizes Haré mercilessly but is fiercely loyal to him and seems to feel it's her duty to teach him about life outside the jungle and help him grow up. An old suitor of Weda's, Dr. Clive, shows up to disturb the balance of Haré's peaceful life even further, in a new variation on the **DORAEMON** premise, based on the long-running *Shonen GanGan* manga by Renjuro Kindaichi. The TV series spun off two video series: *Haré + Guu Deluxe* (2002) in which Haré deals with a wacky substitute teacher and Weda gets pregnant again; and *Haré + Guu Final* (2002), in which Weda takes the children to visit her mother in the city. Haré goes to school there and falls for a pretty girl named Rita, but what are kid sisters for if not to mess up a budding romance? Presumably the two video serials were originally intended as a third 13-episode TV season, but the show was taken off-air early.

HARELUYA II BOY

1997. TV series. DIR: Kiyoshi Egami. SCR: Yasuhiro Imagawa. DES: Takahiro Kishida. ANI: N/C. MUS: Shingo Kobayashi. PRD: Triangle Staff, TV Tokyo. 25 mins. x 25 eps.
When tough-guy Hibino saves wannabe-artist Kyoshiro from a gang of bullies, the two become firm friends. They also befriend Makoto, who wants to be the lead singer of the Fire Guns rock band and find superstardom, and Michiru, a young girl who wants to be a jewelry designer. Each member of the group seeks to find success in his or her chosen field, though Hibino's only wish is to stay out of trouble long enough to graduate from school. Then he wants to conquer the world.

A comedy anime that looks askance on Hareluya Hibino's burgeoning relationship with Michiru, *HB*'s message is that friends, however mismatched, should always help each other strive for their dreams, especially when one of them is the prodigal son of God. Like a modern-day **DORAEMON**, Hibino can pull useful objects from a seemingly bottomless backpack, including baseball bats, frying pans, and lobsters, as the occasion demands. Based on a 1992 *Shonen Jump* manga by Haruto Umezawa, who began his career as an assistant to **CITY HUNTER**'s Tsukasa Hojo.

HARMAGEDON *

1983. JPN: *Genma Taisen*. AKA: *Great War with Genma, Ghenma Wars*. Movie. DIR: Rintaro. SCR: Chiho Katsura, Makoto Naito, Masaki Mori. DES: Katsuhiro Otomo. ANI: Mukuo Takamura, Yoshiaki Kawajiri, Takashi Nakamura, Iwao Yamaki. MUS: Keith Emerson, Nozomu Aoki. PRD: Madhouse, Magic Capsule. 131 mins.
An awkwardly paced and overlong film adapted from a long series of books by **WOLF GUY**'s Kazumasa Hirai and filtered through their manga incarnation by Shotaro Ishinomori. Genma ("Phantom Demon"), the personification of entropy, has eaten half the universe and intends to destroy Earth. Its nemesis, good interdimensional being Floy, who has an intensely annoying voice, contacts Princess Luna of Transylvania and warns her of impending doom. Luna is already aware of it, since the plane carrying her on a diplomatic mission has just been struck by a meteor bearing Vega, a cyborg from a world destroyed by Genma in the distant past (compare to Andro in **TEKKAMAN**). Luna and Vega set about recruiting a multinational army of psionics (including Sonny Rinks, a black kid from the New York ghetto), specifically Japanese schoolboy Jo Azuma, who is the most powerful. As Genma's powers lay waste to Earth, his comic sidekicks, Zombi and Samedi, kill his friends and loved ones. They attack Jo's sister Michiko, who reveals her own psychic powers, only to die seconds before Jo can save her. A distraught Jo is saved from an earthquake by Tao, a Chinese psionic, who leads him to Genma's hideaway amid the boiling lava of a newly active Mount Fuji. Jo and several other psionic warriors, who arrive as an afterthought, then defeat Genma,

who comes back in a predictable twist and is defeated again in a final battle. Vega dies in the final conflict but commends his friends on their victory as he prepares for rebirth, along with life on Earth itself.

This first anime film from *Newtype* publishers Kadokawa boasts a fatuous pseudo-religious message, a truly awful English-language song, a cameo appearance by director Rintaro as a flustered artist, and much-hyped character designs from Katsuhiro Otomo. It also features an interesting choice from the animators, who concentrate on drawing high-quality still images at the expense of actual animation and lip sync. Trying and failing, like **DARKSIDE BLUES**, to cram a complex text into the running time of a mere movie, it nevertheless contained the seeds of the anime business as we know it today. Designer Otomo was so disillusioned by his experience of working on *Harmagedon* that he resolved to do things differently five years later with **AKIRA**. Not to be confused with Lee Hyunse's *Armageddon* (1995), which was distributed by Manga Entertainment as "anime," but actually made in Korea. *Genma Wars* (2002) is a 13-part TV remake also released in America.

HARRIS'S WIND

1966. JPN: *Harris no Kaze*. TV series. DIR: Yoshiyuki Shindo. SCR: Keisuke Fujikawa, Shunichi Yukimuro, Haruya Yamazaki, Tadaaki Yamazaki. DES: Tetsuya Chiba. ANI: Fukuo Watanabe. MUS: Gatchatorian. PRD: B Pro, Fuji TV. 25 mins. x 25 eps.
Kunimatsu Ishida is a regular wildchild, thrown out of every school in his area for fighting. One day he meets the principal of Harris Academy, where he drifts from club to club trying his hand at sports, mainly contact sports like boxing and kendo, though he also brings his own hands-on style to soccer and baseball. Eventually, he becomes a hero of the school by channeling his aggression into improving the school's athletic reputation. Based on a *Shonen Magazine* manga by **TOMORROW'S**

JOE–creator Tetsuya Chiba, the same story was remade by Tezuka Productions as *Kunimatsu's Got It Right* (1971), directed by Masami Hata.

HARUMI'S BAD PLAY *

2001?. JPN: *Harumi-chan no Oita*. AKA: *Naughty Harumi*. Video. DIR: N/C. SCR: N/C. DES: N/C. ANI: N/C. MUS: N/C. PRD: Obtain, Onmitsudo. 30 mins.
Wafaru wakes up one morning to find Harumi, a virginal young girl, hiding out in his room and begging to stay. He takes pity on her, if sexually molesting her can be regarded as pity, in a story that drifts perilously close to the pedophile interests of **LOLITA ANIME**, only to turn the tables when Harumi turns out to be more than she seems—compare to a similar bait-and-switch maneuver in **SEE IN AO**. Submitted to the Australian film censor in 2002 under the title *Naughty Harumi*, but refused certification. **OV**

HARVEST NIGHT *

2002. JPN: *Shukaku no Yoru*. Video. DIR: Katsumasa Kanezawa. SCR: Katsumasa Kanezawa. DES: Kiichiro Yoshida. ANI: Hiroya Iijima. MUS: N/C. PRD: Blue Eyes, Studio Kuma, Triple X. 30 mins. x 2 eps.
Ryoko crosses the bridge that divides the nice side of town from the mean streets to try and persuade her childhood friends Masato and Honoka to come back with her. Masato has become a gang leader and Honoka is seriously ill, but refuses to seek treatment on the clean, healthy side of the bridge. Emi, Masato's moll, lures the pure, romantically inclined Ryoko into group sex, and the other girls try to get her under contract as a hooker. Gang fights, murder by sexual abuse, and beating old men to death are just some of the signs of social degradation on offer before the ailing Honoka is gang-raped to death and her brother goes crazy and kills everyone except Ryoko, who finally goes back where she belongs, leaving Honoka's corpse on the bridge. The age-old notion that it's possible to keep all the nasty things on

the wrong side of the tracks is perpetuated in two episodes of pornographic melodrama. **LNV**

HATA, MASAMI

1942– . Born in Taipei, Taiwan, Hata studied briefly at the Tamamo College of Arts before dropping out to join Tokyo Movie Shinsha. He left for Mushi Production in 1965, where he worked on the **JOURNEY TO THE WEST** TV series and the movie **ARABIAN NIGHTS**. He rose from animator to director on **TALES OF HANS CHRISTIAN ANDERSEN** before leaving Mushi for Madhouse. In 1974, he joined the animation wing of the Sanrio toy and accessory company, where he made titles such as **RINGING BELL** and **JOURNEY THROUGH FAIRYLAND**. He rejoined Tokyo Movie Shinsha in 1985 and directed the anime adaptation of the Famicom (NES) game **SUPER MARIO BROTHERS**.

HATTORI THE NINJA

1981. JPN: *Ninja Hattori-kun*. TV series, movie. DIR: Hiroshi Sasagawa, Fumio Ikeno. SCR: Masaaki Sakurai, Noboru Shiroyama. DES: Fujio-Fujiko. ANI: Hiromichi Matano. MUS: Shunsuke Kikuchi. PRD: Shinei, Pan Media, TV Asahi. 10 mins. x 694 eps., 53 mins. (m).
The everyday Sanyo family gets an unexpected surprise in the shape of a new lodger—Hattori is a ninja boy who has come down from the Iga mountains to attend normal school. Befriending Kenichi Sanyo, who is the same age as he, Hattori starts attending school undercover, occasionally accompanied by his brother, Shinzo, Shishimaru the ninja dog, and Kenichi's girlfriend, Yumeko. The gang is also threatened by the rival Koga ninja, Kemumaki, and his evil sidekick, Kagechiyo the Shadow-cat.

Hattori, the lead character in this long-running work from **DORAEMON**-creators Fujiko-Fujio, also appeared in an anime movie, *Hattori and the War of the Little Ninja Villages* (1983), directed by Shinichi Suzuki, in which the evil Dr. Mekamaro, wishing to be the best ninja in the world, kidnaps Hattori's parents, leaving the little assassin and his friends to save the world.

HAUNTED JUNCTION *

1997. TV series. DIR: Yuji Muto. SCR: Kazuhisa Sakaguchi, Satoru Nishizono, Yuji Hashimoto. DES: Atsuko Nakajima. ANI: Ryoko Hata, Atsuko Nakajima, Satoshi Inoue. MUS: Hayato Matsuo. PRD: Studio Deen, BeStack. 25 mins. x 12 eps.

Haruto, the son of a Christian minister, becomes the president of his high school's Saints Club, where he, Buddhist acolyte Kazuo, and wannabe Shinto shrine maiden Mutsuki must somehow keep their school's epidemic of ghosts under control.

Based on a manga by Nemu Mukudori first serialized in *Monthly Electric Comic GAO*, *HJ* is a genuinely funny look at what school life might be like with fish-monsters in the swimming pool, statues that come to life, and biology lab skeletons that dance like Cossacks. With a Christian who just wants a mundane, boring life and a Buddhist who is easily possessed, there are hilarious setups for cross-dressing and animal impersonations. Mutsuki's "Shouta Complex," however, is an unhealthy obsession with little boys, which may well have appeared like an ironic inversion of CREAM LEMON's Lolita complex to the Japanese crew, but is likely to keep *HJ* forever off U.S. TV. As it was, the show was only shown on Japanese TV very late at night, and elements remain too risqué for children.

As for the ghostbusting, Mutsuki has a sideline in Shinto exorcisms, while Kazuo can write Buddhist charms. Haruto, however, is neglected by a writing team that knows nothing of Christianity, coming across as little more than a blond dummy in a smock who regularly yells "Oh my God!" in exasperation.

Like the later JUBEI-CHAN THE NINJA GIRL, elements of *HJ* rely on ethnocentric jokes liable to fly over the heads of a U.S. audience. Throwaway lines about a girl in the toilets (see HERE COMES HANAKO) are left initially unexplained, as is an anatomical doll named after novelist Haruo Sato and a talking statue based on a legendarily hard-working student Kinjiro Ninomiya, whose effigy can be found in many Japanese schools. Nonetheless, a fine, fun parody of school spook stories.

HAUNTED SLUTS

2000. JPN: *Hyakki Yako: Warashi*. AKA: *100 Nights of Happiness: Haunted House, Pandemonium*. Video. DIR: Yoshiteru Takeda. SCR: N/C. DES: N/C. ANI: N/C. MUS: N/C. PRD: Studio Lilia. 30 mins.

Systems engineer Shuichi grows tired of life in the city and moves out to the countryside, where he soon finds himself a new sexual partner in the form of a bored local housewife. However, he also finds himself haunted by a *warashi*: either an innocent girl or a local spirit, depending on what one believes. As with other modern treatments of spirits from SPOOKY KITARO to POMPOKO, *warashi* are unable to live in human cities. In this erotic variant, however, they are able to become homeless wanderers who subsist like succubi on male "energy." **Ⓝ**

HAWAIIAN BREEZE

1992. JPN: *Shin Dosei Jidai: Hawaiian Breeze*. AKA: *New Age of Cohabitation: Hawaiian Breeze*. Video. DIR: Hiroshi Fukutomi. SCR: Takashi Yamada. DES: Fumi Shibama. ANI: Masuji Kinoue. MUS: King Biscuit Time. PRD: Japan Home Video. 45 mins.

In this adaptation of a manga by Fumi Shibama, itself a retelling of a 1972 manga by Kazuo Kamimura (the original *Age of Cohabitation* whose existence is implied by the "new" in this title), Honda has been living with Eri for two years and debates whether or not he should ask her to marry him.

HAYAKAWA, KEIJI

1950– . Born in Aomori Prefecture, he worked briefly at Toei Animation and Tokyo Movie Shinsha before joining Nippon Animation. He was the supervising director on ISABELLE OF PARIS before running the production of BELLE AND SEBASTIAN. He joined Studio Pierrot, and played a role in the animation of shows including SHERLOCK HOUND and TOUCH before moving to Studio Gallop, where he worked on numerous video productions, including MAPS.

HAZEDON

1972. TV series. DIR: Makura Saki (pseud. for Osamu Dezaki), Fumio Ikeno. SCR: Haruya Yamazaki, Yoshitake Suzuki, Toshiaki Matsushima, Hiroyuki Hoshiyama. DES: Toshiyasu Okada. ANI: Kazuhiko Udagawa, Keisuke Morishita, Tetsu Dezaki. MUS: Hiroshi Tsutsui. PRD: Fuji TV. 25 mins. x 26 eps.

Young fishboy Hazedon wants to be the "strongest fish in the world," fighting against the evil Ankoragon and Samegills, who eternally plague the undersea kingdom with crab attacks, shark thieves, and kidnappers sent to steal away Hazedon's love interest, the mermaid girl Sealan.

HE IS MY MASTER

2005. JPN: *Kore ga Watashi no Goshujin-sama*. AKA: *That's My Master; This Is My Master*. TV series DIR: Shoji Saeki. SCR: Jukki Hanada, Natsue Yoguchi, Shoji Saeki, Takashi Aoshima. DES: Kazuhiro Takamura. ANI: Bow Ditama, Kazuhiko Takamura. MUS: Seiko Nagaoka. PRD: Gainax, Shaft, BS-i. 24 mins. x 12 eps.

Teenage runaway sisters Izumi and Mitsuki need somewhere to stay, not the least because Mitsuki's pet alligator Pochi cannot stay at conventional venues. Luckily for them, they run into Yoshitaka Nakabayashi, a 14-year-old orphan who has inherited a fortune from his millionaire parents. Yoshitaka employs the girls as servants, on the condition that they dress up in revealing maids' outfits and address him at all times as "master." Based on an allegedly "ultra-racy" manga by Mattsu and Asa Tsubaki and screened on satellite TV in Japan, this lightweight work is loaded with in-jokes at the expense of other anime, particularly other Gainax products like EVANGELION, HIS AND HER CIRCUMSTANCES, GUNBUSTER, and MAHOROMATIC.

HEADGEAR

A collective of five creators, whose early coffee shop discussions about science fiction eventually led to the writing and production of PATLABOR and TWILIGHT Q. The members are: manga author Masami Yuki, designer Yutaka Izubuchi, screenwriter Kazunori Ito, designer Akemi Takada, and director Mamoru Oshii. Works credited to Headgear split all profits five ways, regardless of the extent of involvement of any one member.

HEART: AN ITALIAN SCHOOLBOY'S JOURNAL

1981. JPN: *Ai no Gakko Cuore*. AKA: *Beloved School Cuore*. TV series. DIR: Eiji Okabe. SCR: Ryuzo Nakanishi. DES: Yu Noda. ANI: Fumio Kurokawa, Akira Suzuki. MUS: Katsuhisa Hattori. PRD: Nippon Animation, TBS. 25 mins. x 26 eps.

Enrico Pocchini is a kindhearted fourth-grader with a strong sense of justice who lives in the picturesque Italian town of Torino. But as he starts the new semester at school, he loses his adored teacher, Miss Delcacci, who is replaced by the stern Mr. Pelboni. After some misunderstandings, the boys in Enrico's class come to respect Mr. Pelboni, and learn about love, life, and human kindness.

Though financed by Calpis, original sponsors of the WORLD MASTERPIECE THEATER, and made by Nippon Animation, *Heart* is not one of the *WMT* series, though it could easily pass for one. Two episodes of the series focus on one boy's quest to be reunited with his mother in South America, a chapter from the original novel by Edmondo de Amicis that was already animated in 1976 as the famous FROM THE APENNINES TO THE ANDES.

HEART COCKTAIL

1986. TV series. DIR: Yoshimitsu Morita, Shinpei Wada, Osamu Kobayashi,

Akio Hayashi. SCR: Seizo Watase. DES: Seizo Watase. ANI: Yasuko Yamazaki. MUS: Naoya Matsuoka. PRD: Kodansha, Nippon TV. 5 mins. x 77 eps.

CHALK-COLORED PEOPLE–creator Seizo Watase's 1983 series of short manga in *Comic Morning* is adapted into dozens of romantic vignettes, each designed to tell a simple love story in "no more time than it would take to smoke a cigarette," which often means that there is little time for even revealing people's names; many tales simply star "Me" and "Her." Stories include *Emblem of My Father*, *Two in the Beer Garden*, *Old Hawaii Corner*, *My Brother's Zippo*, and *Takeru's Love of Two and a Half Millennia*. The tobacco analogy may sound strange in these politically correct times, but it is better than the alternative, remembering that such short manga stories are *actually* designed to take no longer to read than the average dump.

HEART OF THE RED BIRD

1979. JPN: *Nihon Meisaku Dowa Series: Akai Tori no Kokoro*. AKA: *Japanese Masterpiece Fairytale Series: Heart of the Red Bird*. TV series. DIR: Yoshio Hanajima, Kenzo Koizumi, Tsutomu Shibayama, Daikichiro Kusunobe, Osamu Kobayashi, Kimio Yabuki, Shigetsugu Yoshida, Hideo Nishimaki, Shingo Araki. SCR: Shingo Araki, Mitsuo Wakasugi, Hamakichi Hirose, Taichi Yamada, Rena Kukisawa, Keisuke Kinoshita, Osamu Kagami, Zenzo Matsuyama, Taku Warabi, Kazuo Yoshida. DES: N/C. ANI: Shingo Araki, Daikichiro Kusunobe. MUS: Tadashi Kinoshita. PRD: Studio Korumi, Asia Do, Studio Junio, Tomi Production, Araki Production, TV Asahi. 25 mins. x 26 eps.

Trawling through the children's story magazine *Akai Tori* (*Red Bird*), composer Tadashi Kinoshita resolved to organize the adaptations of its best stories as children's animation for a new generation and to mark the 20th anniversary of the channel TV Asahi. The result is this series of literary adaptations like a kiddified ANIMATED CLASSICS OF JAPANESE LITERATURE, including *Reach*

to the Heaven (Kojiro Yoshida), *The Cow Tethered to a Camellia Tree* (Nanikichi Niimi), *Mysterious Window* (Yaso Saijo), *Weeping Red Devil* (Kosuke Hamada), *A Story about Ascending to Heaven* (Shohei Hino), *Devil's Horn* (Kyoka Izumi), *The Spider's Thread* (Ryunosuke Akutagawa), and *The Mermaid and the Red Candles* (Mimei Ogawa). Early negotiations at the planning stage suggest that Kinoshita was being even more ambitious, hoping to lure in big-name directors like Akira Kurosawa to run particular episodes, but that does not seem to have actually happened. Compare to WORLD MASTERPIECE THEATER, with which it has certain similarities of aim, if not execution.

HEARTBROKEN ANGELS

1990. JPN: *Kizudarake no Tenshitachi*. Video. DIR: Tsuyoshi Sasakawa. SCR: Tsuyoshi Sasakawa, Takeshi Saito. DES: Masahiko Kikuni. ANI: N/C. MUS: Toshiyuki Ebihara, Masaya. PRD: Studio M. 70 mins.

Thirty-one stories based on the four-panel manga strips drawn by Masahiko Kikuni for *Young Sunday* magazine make up this anime that mixes animation and live action. Possibly intended for TV broadcast like HEART COCKTAIL, though the rude nature of Kikuni's humor may have prevented that part of the plan. *Tetsuo*'s Tomoro Taguchi was among the live-action actors. See also MOST SPIRITED MAN IN JAPAN.

HEART-COLORED KILLER TICKET

1989. JPN: *Satsujin Kippu wa Heart Iro*. AKA: *Killer Ticket Is Heart-Colored*. Video. DIR: Taku Sugiyama. SCR: Akira Miyazaki. DES: Hiroyasu Yamaura. ANI: Tomoko Kobayashi. MUS: N/C. PRD: Nippon Eizo. 50 mins.

A "soft-boiled" detective comedy based on a series of young adult novels by Hiroyasu Yamaura, in which sweet, unassuming, bullying victim Seiko is suspended from school and takes the opportunity to go to Nagasaki, where she becomes embroiled in a murder mystery. In keeping with the originals' focus on the female market, sleuthing à la YOUNG KINDAICHI FILES becomes less important in the story than cats and ghosts.

HEARTFUL CAFÉ

2002. JPN: *Mune Kyun! Heartful Café*. AKA: *Heart Skips! Heartful Café*. Video. DIR: Hirohide Shikishima. SCR: Tsunekazu Murakami. DES: Mochizuki. ANI: Mochizuki. MUS: Kennosuke Matsumura. PRD: Uni Soft, Museum Pictures, Milky. 30 mins. x 2 eps.
Shinya is the manager of a small coffee house staffed by his twin stepsisters Chiyori and Chika. When a franchise for a large café chain opens across the street, the siblings are forced to improvise to hang onto their business. The girls start wearing revealing costumes to attract more clientele, although when regular customer Aya becomes close to Shinya, it inspires feelings of jealousy in Chika. Chika decides to seduce Shinya herself, although this soon causes problems for her twin, whose feelings towards him remain purely platonic. Erotic high jinks ensue. ⓝ

HEAT GUY J *

2002. TV series. DIR: Kazuki Akane. SCR: Akihiko Takadera, Hiroshi Onogi, Kazuki Akane, Miya Asakawa. DES: Nobuteru Yuki, Takahiro Kishida, Takayuki Takeya, Takeshi Takakura, Akihiko Takadera. ANI: Nobuteru Yuki, Haruo Sotozaki, Osamu Kobayashi, Shinji Takeuchi, Yuko Watabe. MUS: Try Force. PRD: Magic Capsule, Omnibus Japan, Bandai, BS-I, TBS. 25 mins. x 26 eps.
In the far future, the nations of today have collapsed and have been replaced by a number of giant city-states. In the city of Judoh, which still retains some architectural vestiges of its former existence as New York, young cop Daisuke Aurora and his cyborg partner Jay work for the Special Services Division of the Bureau of Urban Safety, a small department charged with preventing crimes before they happen, in the style of the same year's *Minority Report*. As with PATLABOR, the agency with the interesting job is also the one that all the other

cops look down on, leaving third team member Kyoko to police their ammo supply and break up fights between them and angry plaintiffs. They also have to deal with prejudice against Jay; cyborgs aren't normally allowed to enter major cities for fear they will go on a rampage of destruction, so his robot identity has to be kept secret. But prejudice begins at home—Daisuke doesn't much care for cyborgs. They're fighting some heavy-duty organized crime; the Vampire mob recently lost its godfather, Leonelli, but his insane son Claire (and you'd be insane if you were a boy called Claire) is more than capable of keeping crime on the streets of Judoh.

There is a *Heat Guy J* manga, written and drawn by Chiaki Ogishima and serialized in *Magazine Z*, but this anime has a much longer pedigree. From ASTRO BOY onward, Japanese science fiction has owed a great debt to Isaac Asimov, and nowhere is it more obvious than in this pastiche of *The Caves of Steel* (1954), which similarly featured an unlikely robot-human detective alliance on a prejudiced Earth. It also featured a race of snooty superior beings whose technology and lifestyle was far beyond Terran understanding—the Spacers in the original, and the Celestials in this "homage." If the plot was not enough of a clue, Daisuke even appears to have been named after Asimov's Spacer homeworld Aurora. Compare to THE BIG O, which similarly lifted elements of Asimov's work.

Heat Guy J was also influenced by the same 9/11 terrorism fallout that affected FULL METAL PANIC and METROPOLIS. The pseudo-New York City lends itself to numerous references inspired by post 9/11 rumors about civilization under siege. It is easy to forget that over a hundred Japanese were killed in the 9/11 attacks, and that in the ensuing months the Japanese government controversially urged its citizens to stay at home. Elements of this paranoia can be pursued in the hermetic world of *Heat Guy J*'s city-state; there may be other nations,

but it is implied that Judoh is a place one must either love or leave, and once one quits there is no going back. The Vampire syndicate attempts to manipulate the stock market in order to make the ultimate killing, although they do so in a humble product like tomatoes, leading to an in-depth look at the city's food supply: a refreshing change in a genre where all too often everyday commodities just appear as if by magic. Other elements of the 21st-century zeitgeist can be discerned in the stranglehold the Celestials have on Judoh's water purification technology. They return once each generation to collect their fee and overhaul the machines, otherwise they automatically grind to a halt—a pattern that meets with disaster when a Celestial murder case causes the engineers to boycott Judoh, leaving Daisuke with a limited time to solve the case before the city goes into meltdown.

Later episodes return to the crime subplot and introduce the community of Siberbia, a harsh existence beyond the city limits whose populace take self-reliance to such extremes that they have become completely callous and self-interested—a social parable like those found in KINO'S JOURNEY. The home video release included revised and improved animation quality over the initial Japanese TV broadcast. ⓛⓥ

HEAVY

1990. Movie. DIR: Shinya Hanai. SCR: Noboru Ishiguro, Shoji Imai. DES: Masao Nakada. ANI: Masao Nakada. MUS: N/C. PRD: Artland. 50 mins.
Yet another boxing anime, this time based on SWORD OF MUSASHI–creator Motoka Murakami's 1989 manga from *Shonen Sunday* magazine about an impressionable man taking his father's advice to heart and "fighting for as long as he is still breathing." This takes on a double meaning when Dad needs a lifesaving operation, and our hero enters the boxing ring to win the money. ⓥ

HEAVY METAL L-GAIM

1984. JPN: *Jusenki L-Gaim*. AKA: *Heavy*

War Machine L-Gaim. TV series. DIR: Yoshiyuki Tomino, Minoru Onotani, Yasuhiro Imagawa, Toshifumi Kawase, Osamu Sekita, Akira Suzuki, Toshifumi Takizawa, Kunihisa Sugishima, Hideji Iguchi. SCR: Jiyu Watanabe, Sukehiro Tomita, Asami Watanabe. DES: Mamoru Nagano, Kunio Okawara, Toshifumi Nagasawa. ANI: Hiroyuki Kitazume. MUS: Kei Wakakusa. PRD: Sotsu Agency, Sunrise, Nagoya TV (TV Asahi). 25 mins. x 54 eps. (TV), 60 mins. x 3 eps. (v).

The immortal Poseidal of Gustgal leads his 24 elite Temple Knights to subdue the Pentagonia System, proclaiming himself Star Emperor. His "second crusade" ends in the year 3975, when he defeats King Camon Wallha V, but Camon hides his heir on the forgotten planet Coam, with a single giant white battle-robot. Fifteen years later, *Prince Camon,* using the name Daba Myroad, leads a revolt on Coam, backed by the arms dealer Amandara Kamanadara, unaware that his supporter is in fact Poseidal himself, supplying weaponry to both sides while a doppelganger sits on his throne.

A giant-robot show that functioned as a dry run for designer Nagano's later FIVE STAR STORIES, *L-G* boasts the creator's trademark mixture of far-future and fantasy-medieval designs, and many look-alikes of characters from his more famous work. A three-part video series followed, with the initial two parts comprising edited footage from the series, and the third, *L-G: Full Metal Soldier,* adding a coda to the series proper.

HEIDI
1974. JPN: *Alps no Shojo Heidi.* AKA: *Alpine Girl Heidi.* TV series. DIR: Isao Takahata. SCR: Yoshiaki Yoshida. DES: Yoichi Otabe, Hayao Miyazaki. ANI: Toshiyasu Okada. MUS: Takeo Watanabe. PRD: Zuiyo, Fuji TV. 25 mins. x 52 eps., 107 mins. (m).

Eight-year-old orphan Adelheid (or Heidi, for short) is taken in by her aunt Dete, who soon packs her off to stay with her old grandfather on Alm mountain in the Swiss Alps. Heidi

befriends local goatherder Peter, only to be spirited away once more by Aunt Dete, who takes her to Frankfurt, where she is to be a playmate for the disabled Klara. Pining for her alpine happiness, Heidi heads back to Alm in this famous anime based on the 1881 children's book by Johanna Spyri. An early masterpiece from GRAVE OF THE FIREFLIES–director Takahata, featuring storyboard contributions from his long-term associate Miyazaki and from GUNDAM-director Yoshiyuki Tomino. Much-loved across Europe, the anime version is less well-known in English. In Japan, its CINDERELLA qualities and Alpine pastorals would lead to many similar children's shows, most noticeably JULIE THE WILD ROSE and TREASURES OF THE SNOW. A 1979 movie-edit consists primarily of footage from the Frankfurt episodes with Klara. Of the many live-action adaptations available in English, the most recent is Disney's 1993 version featuring Jason Robards and Jane Seymour. See also VIDEO PICTURE BOOK. Although still largely unknown in its anime version in the U.S., *Heidi* was screened in Spanish in Costa Rica.

HELEN KELLER
1981. JPN: *Helen Keller Monogatari: Ai to Hikari no Tenshi.* AKA: *Story of Helen Keller: Angel of Love and Light.* TV special. DIR: Fumio Ikeno. SCR: Hiroshi Kitahara. DES: Michiyo Sakurai. ANI: Seiji Yamashita. MUS: Hiroshi Ogasawara. PRD: NOW Planning. 81 mins.

At 19 months, baby Helen succumbs to a fever that leaves her deaf and blind. Refusing to believe her case is hopeless, her parents seek help from all quarters, eventually finding "Miracle Worker" Annie Sullivan. Arriving in Helen's native Tuscumbia, Alabama when the child is seven, Sullivan teaches Helen to communicate purely through touch and the sensation of writing on the palm of the hand. An anime made for broadcast on Japan's National Day for the Disabled, *HK* celebrates the early life of a remarkable woman (1880–1968) who would eventually graduate from Radcliffe

College, champion the causes of the disadvantaged, and win many international honors, including Japan's Sacred Treasure. Thanks to biographies in the GREAT PEOPLE series, Keller shares with COLUMBUS the distinction of having her life turned into anime on three separate occasions.

HELL GIRL
2005. JPN: *Jigoku Shojo.* TV series. DIR: Hiroshi Watanabe. SCR: N/C. DES: Mariko Oka. ANI: N/C. MUS: Yasuharu Takanashi. PRD: Studio Deen. 25 mins. x 26 eps.

It was only a matter of time before someone mated the internet zeitgeist of SERIAL EXPERIMENTS LAIN with the Faustian chills of PETSHOP OF HORRORS.

Kiyoshi Kurosawa tried it in the live-action world with the influential *Kairo* (2001), and anime's take on the same material is *Jigoku Tsushin* ("Hell Dispatches"), an Internet billboard which only appears at midnight, and where disgruntled people can post details of who has wronged them, in the hope that the Hell Girl and her straw dolls will appear to drag sinners into limbo. There is a catch, of course. Anyone wishing evil upon another will sacrifice his or her own soul in the process—compare to similarly devilish small print in the live-action series *Sky High* (*DE). The show was preceded by a manga running in *Nakayoshi* magazine. Since the Internet crosses all time zones, we wonder if the site is only limited to a Japanese midnight, or if it manifests 24 times a day all around the world.

HELL TARGET
1986. Video. DIR: Yoshinori Nakamura. SCR: Kenichi Matsuzaki. DES: Hiroshi Yokoyama. ANI: Teruyoshi Nakamura. MUS: Rosa Bianca. PRD: Nakamura Pro. 50 mins.

A spaceship is lost near the forbidding planet of Inferno II. Some years later, a second ship with a crew of nine gets there and encounters a monster that rapidly makes mincemeat of most of them. In an obvious anime retread of

Hello Kitty

©'76,'99,'01,'04 SANRIO CO., LTD.

James Cameron's *Aliens* (1986), the sole survivor, Makuro Kitazato, must destroy the monster before it can surprise a third ship that is already en route.

HELL TEACHER NUBE

1996. JPN: *Jigoku Sensei Nube*. TV series. DIR: Yoshio Misawa. SCR: Takao Koyama. DES: Yoichi Onishi. ANI: Masami Suda, Ken Ueno. MUS: BMF. PRD: Toei, TV Asahi. 25 mins. x 48 eps. (TV), 25 mins. (TV special), 45 mins. x 3 (m), 30 mins. x 3 (v).

Meisuke Nueno, otherwise known as Nube, is a grade-school teacher whose left hand is possessed by demonic forces, and whose school is constantly beset by apparitions. This anime lightheartedly retells old JAPANESE FOLK TALES updated for modern times in much the same tongue-in-cheek fashion as HAUNTED JUNCTION and GHOST SWEEPER MIKAMI. So it is that Nube is stalked by besotted snow maiden Yukime, must evict a "Hanako" from the toilets (see HERE COMES HANAKO), finds a cursed samurai sword in the lost-and-found, and generally busts ghosts in every conceivable part of his school, from the library to the swimming pool. At

the height of Japan's 1990s ghost-story trend, *HTN* made it to theaters with the short anime films *HTN: The Movie* (1996), *HTN: Nube Dies at Midnight* (1997), and *HTN's Scary Summer Vacation: Tale of the Sea Phantom* (1997); each replaying the formula of a TV episode, but with a slightly longer running time. In 1998, a readers' survey chose three previously unfilmed chapters from the original 1993 *Shonen Jump* manga by Sho Masakura and Takeshi Okano to be adapted straight to video as *HTN: Sun God vs. the Wall Man*, *HTN: Bukimi-chan of the Seven Mysteries*, and *HTN: Biggest Battle in History—Attack of the Relentless Demon*.

HELLO KITTY *

1989. Video, movie, TV series. DIR: Tameo Ogawa, Yasuo Ishikawa, Masami Hata, Yuji Nichimaki, et al. SCR: Tomoko Konparu. DES: N/C. ANI: Kanji Akabori, Maya Matsuyama. MUS: Toyomi Kojima. PRD: Sanrio. ca. 30 mins. x 50+ eps.

A simply drawn icon, Hello Kitty is the most successful image created by the merchandising corporation Sanrio to sell toys, toasters, luggage, dolls, stickers, and just about anything else.

Her fellow brands include KERO KERO KEROPPI and PEKKLE THE DUCK, but Kitty has a bigger international fan base than the rest put together. A complete rundown of her screen appearances, including all the compilations and recombinations of the last 21 years, would require substantially more space than this book allows, but these are the highlights of her anime resume.

A Hello Kitty version of CINDERELLA (1989) was originally shown theatrically before initiating the franchise of *Hello Kitty's Fairy Tale Theater*, where the mouthless icon appeared in many adaptations of famous stories, including her own versions of SNOW WHITE, HEIDI, *Sleeping Beauty*, ALICE IN WONDERLAND, *The Dream Thief, Kitty and the Beast*, and the WIZARD OF OZ pastiche *Wizard of Paws*. Sensibly realizing that the U.S. market would not bear a single episode to a tape, these were bundled into compilation volumes in America, where they were well received as children's entertainment, and *Santa's Missing Hat* was combined with *Keroppi* crossover *The Christmas Eve Gift*.

Meanwhile, Kitty's popularity continued in Japan—1990 saw a theatrical retelling of THUMBELINA, and the Japanese audience was treated to several successive video outings that never made it to the West, including a second *Heidi* pastiche in 1994 and a ten-part series of JAPANESE FOLK TALES, including adaptations of *The Hidden Tengu*, MOMOTARO, *Kintaro, The Snow Maiden*, THE MONKEY AND THE CRAB, *Princess Kaguya* (see REI REI), and HERE COMES THE MOUSE BRIDE. Kitty also featured in several video specials with fellow Sanrio character BAD BATZ MARU (see same) and the old-time Japanese adventures *Ratboy* and *Return of the Tanuki* (both 1989).

Other stories were more original, including some set in Kitty's hometown of London, such as *The Day the Clock Stopped* (1992), in which Kitty and sister Mimi have to restart Big Ben, and *HK: Aliens in London* (1992), in which the gullible sisters are convinced that two jewel thieves are visitors from outer space. Other outbreaks of the Kitty virus were aimed squarely at impressing parents. *HK: Mom Loves Me After All* (1992) deals with a child's jealousy for a newborn sibling, telling the tale of Kitty's mother babysitting for someone else. *We Love Hello Kitty* (1993) explained the wonders that await good little kittens on their birthdays, when they get presents from all their friends and the chance to eat their favorite food. The franchise jumped on the eco-bandwagon in 1994, the same year as **POMPOKO**, with *HK: Everyone Must Protect the Forest*. In 1997, the parental propaganda machine began rolling in earnest with a succession of short informational videos including *Trying Hard, Cleaning up the House, Going to the Toilet Alone, Sleeping Alone, Being Careful Outdoors, Saying Sorry, Table Manners,* and *Enjoying the Bath,* all followed by the winning subtitle *". . . with Hello Kitty."* The late 1990s saw the Kitty team animate a six-part video series of **AESOP'S FABLES** in their own inimitable style. The *". . . with Hello Kitty"* series, combined with *"Kitty Parody Theater"* (possibly a new name for the fables or fairy tales above) was rebroadcast on Japanese TV as the 39-episode *Kitty's Paradise* (1999), which was swiftly snapped up for the U.S. market by Saban Entertainment during the mad rush to option Japanese children's animation post-**POKÉMON**. This was particularly ironic, since it was now sought after because "anime sells," whereas it had clearly been selling rather well without the "anime" tag for several years already.

HELLO SANDYBELL

1981. AKA: *Sandy Jonquille.* TV series. DIR: Hiroshi Shidara, Kazumi Fukushima, Hideo Kozawa. SCR: Noboru Shiroyama. DES: Makoto Sakurai. ANI: Shoji Yanagise. MUS: Takeo Watanabe. PRD: TV Asahi, Toei. 25 mins. x 47 eps. Sandybell is a happy-go-lucky Scottish girl who lives in the highlands and adores local nobleman Mark Wellington, though she is betrothed to Kitty Shearer, a rich heiress. Sandy-

bell cherishes a dream of becoming an artist, but when her father, Leslie Christie, falls ill, she discovers that she is adopted. Sensing her real parents are still alive somewhere, she heads for London, where she stays with Can-Can, an old family friend. She becomes a cub newspaper reporter, traveling all over Europe in search of clues about her own past, while the venal Kitty plots to ruin her future. Like its more melancholy predecessor **CANDY CANDY**, *HS* may look European, but has an all-Japanese origin: it is based on a book by Shiro Jinbo, whose illustrator Makoto Sakurai also provided basic designs for the animated version.

HELLO SPANK

1981. JPN: *Ohayo Spank.* TV series. DIR: Shigetsugu Yoshida, Susumu Ishizaki, Tetsu Dezaki, Naoto Hashimoto. SCR: Satoshi Kaneko, Masaaki Sakurai. DES: Shizue Takanishi, Yukari Kobayashi. ANI: Takao Kasai. MUS: Koji Makaino. PRD: TMS, TV Asahi. 25 mins. x 63 eps. (TV), 100 mins. (m). When teenage Aiko Morimura's father disappears on his yacht, her mother gets a lucrative hat-designing job in Paris. Instead of going with her, Aiko stays with her uncle and his dog, Pappy. With predictable Japanese pathos, Pappy is soon killed in a road accident. The arrival of a new dog, Spank, brings a smile back to Aiko's face, even if Spank is constantly getting her and her friends into trouble. *Spank* began as a 1978 manga in the girls' magazine *Nakayoshi,* drawn by Shizue Takanashi from a script by Shunichi Yukimuro, the writer of dozens of anime including **CANDY CANDY**, but curiously not this one. In 1982, Spank returned for an all-new movie outing about his falling for the mongrel puppy Anna, whose handsome male owner has newly transferred to Aiko's school.

HELLSING *

2001. TV series, video. DIR: Umanosuke Iida, Yasunori Urata. SCR: Chiaki Konaka. DES: Toshiharu Murata, Yoshitaka Kohno. ANI: Tomoaki Kado,

Toshiharu Murata. MUS: Kouji Ishii. PRD: Gonzo, Pioneer, Fuji TV. 23 mins. x 13 eps. (TV), 35 mins. x ?? eps. (v). Vampires stalk the shadowy streets of a London bathed in permanent fog. A secret society fights an infestation of the undead as irresponsible bloodsuckers allow the ghoulish survivors of vampire feasts to proliferate. There are zombies in Cheddar, ghouls in the Home Counties, and werewolves in London. As for the good guys, the Royal Order of Religious Knights, also known as Hellsing, their chief agent is a vampire himself, known only as Alucard (spell it backwards...).

Night-time sequences are usually avoided in anime, as it always works out to be more expensive to get the lighting and shading right, but *Hellsing* bucks the trend with stark contrasts and blood-red evening skies. Chiaki Konaka, creator of **MALICE DOLL**, provides a script that recalls some of the better horror of recent years. With its crack teams of military paranormal investigators thrown into chaos by creatures of the night and a secret organization devoted to defeating an infestation of vampires, it is best described as the anime incarnation of *Ultraviolet,* incorporating a number of motifs common to vampire legends and popular folktales of the 20th century. These include a growing number of allusions to an ancient "dark continent," implying, in the process, that the vampire known in *Hellsing* as Incognito may have once ruled Egypt in the guise of the god Set.

Hellsing is also another anime to add to that small but growing list that chooses the British Isles as an exotic, inscrutable location. Kohta Hirano's original manga in *Young King Ours* magazine played up the spires and buttresses of old London, and the anime incarnation keeps locations including the Tower of London, the British Museum, and Waterloo Station. There is an equally impressive attention to linguistic detail, as demonstrated by a dubbing script carefully polished by Taliesin Jaffe, which rips out all Japanese exposition that would only come across as pedantic in English. The majority of the leads also sport flawless British accents, an adherence to the author's original intention that makes *Hellsing* one of those true rarities, a dub like GUNSMITH CATS or LICENSED BY ROYALTY that often plays better in English than the Japanese original.

The series was subsequently remade on video as *Hellsing Ultimate* (2005), a deliberate attempt to revisit the storyline of the original manga and to adhere to it far more closely than the TV version, with a script by Hideyuki Kurata and Yosuke Kuroda. At time of writing, the video series is planned for 20 episodes. Note that there is considerable argument over nomenclature in *Hellsing*, since manga and anime translations disagree on the best way to render some of the names, and several errors have crept in. In a typical example, a *baobhan sith* (a type of Scottish vampire) infiltrates the *Hellsing* base, using the alias Laura, itself a reference to Sheridan Le Fanu's vampire novel *Carmilla* (1872). The English dub, however, does not spot the Scottish folklore reference, and instead renders the creature as a *bubbancy*. **LNV**

HER NEED FOR EMBRACE

1989. JPN: *Dakaretai Onna*. Video. DIR: Yoshihisa Matsumoto, Akane Yamada. SCR: Milk Morizono. DES: Milk Morizono. ANI: N/C. MUS: N/C. PRD: Toei. 45 mins. x 2 eps.

Several erotic short stories taken from a manga of the same name by the controversial erotic creator Milk Morizono, featuring high-quality animation and vignettes along such themes as *Hold Me Harder, Hold Me Lustier*, and *Sunday Ecstasy*. See also MILKY PASSION. This release is notable for being one of those rare erotic anime that flirts with live-action content—risky because much of the appeal of erotic anime seems founded on its audience's lack of access to "real" pornography. Cutaway sequences show real women going about their daily lives (such as

taking a shower, of course), and confessing their sexual histories to add a note of realism. **N**

HERCULE POIROT AND MISS MARPLE

2004. JPN: *Agatha Christie no Meitantei Poirot to Marple/Mabel*. AKA: *Agatha Christie's Famous Detectives Poirot and Mabel*. TV series. DIR: Naohito Takahashi. SCR: Hiroshi Shimokawa. DES: Sayuri Ichiishi. ANI: Takuya Mizutani. MUS: N/C. PRD: OLM, NHK. 28 mins. x 39 eps.

Adaptations of Agatha Christie stories are tweaked to accommodate young Mabel West and Arthur Hastings as points of identification for a teen audience. Sixteen-year-old Mabel is Miss Jane Marple's great-niece, and when she finds herself working for Belgian detective Hercule Poirot she has a great opportunity to learn about life as well as detection methods. Poirot's assistant Arthur Hastings, transformed from a middle-aged chap into a handsome youth, is Mabel's love interest in anime versions of *The Mysterious Affair at Styles, The ABC Murders,* and *The 4.50 from Paddington,* all licenced from Christie's estate, with bonus historical consultancy provided by a Tokyo University professor. Compare to EMMA and THE CASEBOOK OF CHARLOTTE HOLMES. The 1989 BBC live-action series *Poirot,* starring David Suchet as the detective, previously aired on NHK in 1991 as *Meitantei Poirot (Famous Detective Poirot).* Note the chance homophony of "Marple" and "Mabel" in Japanese allowing to imply rather more involvement of one than the other—a similar trick was tried in THUNDERBIRDS 2086.

HERE COMES HANAKO

1994. JPN: *Gakko no Kowai Uwasa: Hanako-san ga Kita*. AKA: *Scary Stories of Your School: Here Comes Hanako; Phantom of the Toilet*. Video. DIR: Tetsuo Yasumi. SCR: Yukiko Matsui, Nobuyuki Hori. DES: Tac. ANI: N/C. MUS: Ko Suzuki. PRD: Tac. 10 mins. x 10 eps. The granddaddy of all children's anime ghouls remains Shigeru

Mizuki's SPOOKY KITARO. However, the 1990s were dominated by "Hanako," an iconic figure that came out of nowhere. The indisputable hit of Toru Tsunemitsu's urban myth collection *School Ghost Stories* was the short story *Ghost Toilet,* set in an elementary school in Nagano Prefecture. In the dark, dank toilet on the north side, the fourth stall was said to be permanently locked. Students forcing the door discover the corpse of a girl in a red dress, presumed to have committed suicide, whose ghost is said to haunt the restrooms, eternally trying to lead schoolboys into hell with the temptation "Shall we play?" This tall tale has become the defining spooky story for the Japanese children who grew up in the 1990s, creating a subgenre in children's books beginning with *Hanako in the Toilet: Scary Stories of Your School* (1993). This in turn was adapted into the *Here Comes Hanako* manga by several artists, most of whom also wrote the anime version that was broadcast as part of the TV program *Ponkiki Kids* in 1994. In that special, Hanako, with a deathly pallor like a juvenile Elvira, introduces episodes such as *The Haunted Cinema* and *The Cursed Promise Ring.*

Hanako also appeared in her own 50-minute anime movie, *Hanako of the Toilet* (1996), directed by Akitaro Daichi, which recast the wild-child as a ghostbuster keeping evil spirits at bay. The franchise reached live-action cinema with Joji Matsuoka's 1996 film of the same name and *New Hanako* (1998), which returned to the original story by featuring a group of high school sleuths contacting Hanako through a Ouija board and saving another classmate from a homeless pervert who is the true cause of all the strange happenings. The phenomenon and its exploitation are parodied in HAUNTED JUNCTION, where Buddhist Kazuo wishes to collect "all the Hanakos" from every school in Japan; DIRTY PAIR *Flash,* which features a Hanako hologram; and HELL TEACHER NUBE, which features a more "traditional" Hanako apparition. REAL SCHOOL

GHOST STORIES and SCHOOL SPIRITS are among its many distant relatives. The generation that grew up watching *Hanako* swelled box office receipts for modern horror films such as *Ring*.

HERE COMES THE MOUSE BRIDE

1979. JPN: *Nezumi no Yomeiri*. Movie. DIR: Daisaku Shirokawa. SCR: Daisaku Shirokawa. DES: N/C. ANI: Sadao Tsukioka. MUS: Shingo Asano. PRD: Toei. 13 mins.

A mouse father seeks the ideal husband for his beloved daughter, but the sun refuses on the grounds that he is not the most powerful thing in the universe. A humble cloud blocks his rays, but the cloud concedes defeat to the wind, who can blow it away. The wind, however, is unable to budge a little girl's house, but the house is unable to rid itself of a troublesome mouse. The lucky mouse marries the bride, and they all live happily ever after. Also adapted as one of the many HELLO KITTY retellings of classic folk tales.

HERE IS GREENWOOD *

1991. JPN: *Koko wa Greenwood*. Video. DIR: Tomomi Mochizuki. SCR: Tomomi Mochizuki. DES: Masako Goto. ANI: Masako Goto. MUS: Shigeru Nagata. PRD: Pierrot Project. 30 mins. x 6 eps.

When his brother marries the woman *he* secretly adores, Kazuya moves out of the family home and into the student dorm of Greenwood. There, the heartbroken loner gains the friendship and support he needs, including his androgynously pretty roommate, Shun Kisaragi, and a gang of sweet-natured but mildly zany boys. With obvious parallels to MAISON IKKOKU, the show also incorporates occasional supernatural moments, such as a ghostly haunting that brings out people's true feelings for each other (compare to similar events in KIMAGURE ORANGE ROAD). In the group's occasional involvement in sports championships, wacky pranks, and personal problems, it also recalls the more sedate installments of PATLABOR. In one episode, Shun's younger brother is kidnapped by the

sister of one of the upperclassmen, while in *Here Is Devilwood*, the characters make a fantasy film about wandering swordsman Lemon Herb having to defeat the evil overlord Clorettes. The final episodes involve the arrival of a gangland bad-girl who replaces Kazuya's sister-in-law in his affections, but each of these episodes are merely brief moments from the original 11-volume run of the 1986 manga by Yukie Nasu, serialized in *Hana to Yume* magazine. In a mere six episodes, there is little chance of anything but a general survey of the original's content and themes, which was, of course, exactly what the producers wanted in order to encourage people to go out and buy the manga.

HERITAGE FROM FATHER *

2001. JPN: *Tsubaki-iro no Prisione* [sic]. AKA: *Camellia Prisoner*. Video. DIR: Jiro Fujimoto. SCR: Jiro Fujimoto. DES: Hideki Hashimoto. ANI: Noboru Sanehara. MUS: N/C. PRD: Green Bunny. 30 mins. x 3 eps.

After the death of his father, Akitsugu is contacted by Susan, the pert young secretary in charge of the estate, and asked to take charge of the family affairs. Akitsugu has nursed resentment toward his father for some time, but agrees as long as the secretary remains in her post. He arrives at the family's mountain mansion to discover it occupied by a group of maids that his father kept on the payroll for his own sexual gratification. He is initially angry, although he is eventually won over by the erotic opportunities, but not before an overzealous maid has tried to dispatch him with an ice pick and been raped for her troubles. Additional revelations are not long in arriving, as Susan discovers that she is actually the daughter of the previous owner, and consequently that she has been in an incestuous relationship with both her father and half-brother. The show was confusingly released in the U.S. with haphazard subtitles that localized all names to either English or Chinese, but not the original Japanese.

Suspiciously close in plotting to *Mama Mia* in the SECRET ANIMA series and based on a game. LNV

HERMES *

1997. JPN: *Hermes: Ai wa Kaze no Fuku*. AKA: *Hermes: Winds of Love*. Movie. DIR: Tetsuo Imazawa. SCR: Hermes Scenario Project. DES: Yoshiaki Yokota. ANI: Yoshiaki Yanagida. MUS: Yuichi Mizusawa. PRD: Toei. 114 mins.

Hermes, a youth who it is said will one day overthrow the evil King Minos of Crete, falls in love with the beautiful Princess Aphrodite. After two pointless musical interludes, he rescues her from the tower where she is imprisoned and decides it's time to defeat Minos. To do this, he enlists the help of the Athenian Theseus and Minos' daughter, Ariadne, "the only one who is sane and religious." After a straightforward run through the events of the tale of Theseus and the Minotaur, Hermes turns up at the last moment to kill Minos himself, at which point Theseus and Ariadne sail off into the sunset and out of the story. Hermes is told that he is a reincarnation of the great god Ophealis—though he is told this *by* Ophealis, meaning he spends part of the film talking to himself. He is given a magic staff and does great deeds all over Greece, before rescuing Aphrodite's blind mother from prison and descending into Hell to kill Minos . . . again. Meanwhile, the childless Aphrodite muses that she wouldn't mind if Hermes took a mistress, only to find that her selfless thoughts have reached the ears of the Goddess of Love. The Goddess shoots her with a magic arrow to make her give birth to an heir. After chatting with some fairies, Hermes resolves to unite Greece, but he suspects it might take a while. Then he defeats his enemies through peaceful means by setting up a trade confederacy which they all want to join.

A lavish but clumsily written combination of Greek myth and half-remembered fairy tales, though occasional scenes of contradictory preaching show its true colors as a publicity vehicle for a religious organization. Based on a book by Ryuho Okawa, the founder of the Institute for Research in Human Happiness, who claims to be a reincarnation of the same alien being who was once Hermes and Ophealis. As with the later LAWS OF THE SUN, it received a very limited theatrical release in the U.S., chiefly at screenings for the faithful, though perhaps a few mystified anime fans were also present and guessing just which scenarists wisely declined to be credited for this one. The film limped out onto video in 2001, amid hype that preferred to emphasize the director's previous work on DIGIMON rather than the story's origins.

HERMIT VILLAGE

1963. JPN: *Sennin Buraku.* AKA: *Village of Immortals.* TV series. DIR: Fumiaki Kamigami. SCR: Akira Hayasaka. DES: Tsutomu Kojima. ANI: Susumu Nojima. MUS: N/C. PRD: Eiken. 15 mins. x 23 eps.
The ancient Chinese village of Taoyuan is populated solely by Taoist ascetics. The eldest, Lao Shi, conducts research into the mysteries of magic and alchemy, while his disciple Zhi Huang remains more interested in pleasures of the flesh. He has fallen for three pretty sisters who live nearby, much to Lao Shi's annoyance. Based on a manga serialized in *Asahi Geino* magazine by Tsutomu Kojima, this naughty comedy was the first-ever late-night anime, broadcast just before midnight. The graveyard slot would continue to run erotica such as LEMON ANGEL, though by the late 1990s it would also be used to premier serials like **AWOL** that would formerly have gone straight to video in an attempt to amortize rising production costs.

HEROIC LEGEND OF ARSLAN *

1991. JPN: *Arslan Senki.* AKA: *Arislan; Chronicle of Arislan.* Video. DIR: Mamoru Hamatsu, Tetsuro Amino. SCR: Tomoya Miyashita, Kaori Takada. DES: Sachiko Kamimura. ANI: Kazuya Kise.

MUS: Norihiro Tsuru, Yasuo Urakami. PRD: Animate Film. 60 mins. x 2 eps., 30 mins. x 4 eps.
King Andragoras of Persia (or Parthia, or Parse, or Palse) wars against the invading Lusitanian army, while his son, Arslan, gathers a band of adventurers about him, including the disgraced officer Daryoon. Andragoras is defeated with sorcerous fog and imprisoned by the enigmatic usurper Silver Mask. Meanwhile, Hermes, agent of Silver Mask, searches for the legendary sword of Ruknabard, which once belonged to Kai Hoslo, the first King of Kings. Arslan assembles an army of a hundred thousand and marches on Silver Mask, while a second party tries to stop Hermes, lest he awake the evil snake-king Zahak.
Arslan began as a series of novels by LEGEND OF GALACTIC HEROES–creator Yoshiki Tanaka. It was very loosely inspired by several genuine medieval Arslans, most notably the one taken hostage after leading a hundred thousand archers against Mahmud of Ghazna, and whose nephews founded the Seljuk Empire. Other models include Ali Arslan, who founded the Qarakhânid dynasty in modern-day Turkestan, and Alp Arslan, who captured the Byzantine Emperor Romanus IV at the battle of Manzikert in 1071. Tanaka's dates do not match any single historical event (even if we count by the Muslim system), but the maps in the novels are clearly based on historical Persia, stretching from contemporary Baghdad to Kashmir and bordered by the Caspian Sea and the Persian Gulf. Like Robert E. Howard's *Conan* series, *Arslan* mixes history and fantasy with impunity, with the Romanesque "Lusitanians" to the west and Rajendra's "Sind" kingdom to the east—for all the effort, Tanaka might as well have set it in the far future and be done with it, à la ALEXANDER. To an uneducated Japanese audience however, it all looks equally exotic, much as Western moviegoers rarely concern themselves with the difference between, say, kung fu and karate.

From its early heyday when the videos were premiered in movie theaters, the *Arslan* series soon declined. Later episodes show a fall in budget, with a different production team, simplified designs, slashed running times, low-quality animation, and the ditching of the earlier diplomacy for a simplistic quest modeled on KING ARTHUR AND THE KNIGHTS OF THE ROUND TABLE. The first two parts were translated in the early days of Manga Entertainment, which altered the name to *Arislan* in a futile attempt to avoid "ass" jokes. The company elected to use British voices in an unremarkable dub that nonetheless seems to have impressed a U.S. audience inured to everyone sounding like they attend the same Californian high school (see ESCAFLOWNE). However, the British dub takes considerable liberties with the translation, claiming that Andragoras is dead (even though he is later found to be very much alive!) and missing some lines that explain otherwise incomprehensible events. The inferior later episodes passed to Central Park Media, which released them bundled two to a tape. As with UROTSUKIDOJI, the different dub location led CPM to hire a completely different set of actors, as well as altering many of the already-confusing names at the request of the Japanese producers, whose whimsical spelling has been completely ignored in this encyclopedia entry. As with many other anime, *Arslan* exists chiefly to promote the novels and their manga spin-off to a Japanese audience, whose access to the textual continuations of the story leaves them less baffled than English-speakers, who are left with a cliff-hanger but little hope of a sequel.

HEY BUMBOO

1985. TV series. DIR: Eiji Okabe, Kenjiro Yoshida. SCR: Juzo Takahashi, Asami Watanabe. DES: Yu Noda. ANI: Yoichi Otabe, Sadayoshi Tominaga. MUS: Nobuyoshi Koshibe. PRD: Nippon Animation, TV Tokyo. 10 mins. x 130 eps.
The adventures of a bright yellow talking automobile who is born from an

egg in an unattended vehicle factory and enlists schoolboy Ken to help him find his mother. This vehicular pastiche of FROM THE APENNINES TO THE ANDES features a car with an uncanny resemblance to Benny, the talking yellow cab in *Who Framed Roger Rabbit?* (1988).

HIGH SCHOOL AGENT

1988. Video. DIR: Junichi Sakata. SCR: Izo Hashimoto. DES: Takumi Tsukasa. ANI: Takumi Tsukasa. MUS: Scrap. PRD: JC Staff, Agent 21. 30 mins. x 2 eps. Teenager Kosuke Kanemori is a secret agent for the international "VN" spy network. Using his computer hacking skills, he tracks international criminals all the way from New York to Spain. In his second outing, he is packed off to the Arctic Circle, where Neo-Nazis are trying to raise a sunken U-boat that holds a sinister WWII secret onboard. Based on a manga by Satoshi Tanimura in *Comic Burger*, this anime foreshadows similar Bond-style adventures in SPRIGGAN. **V**

HIGH SCHOOL GIRLS

2006. JPN: *Joshi Kosei*. AKA: *Girls High*. TV series. DIR: Yoshitaka Fujimoto. SCR: Hideki Shirane, Michiko Ito. DES: Seiji Kishimoto. ANI: N/C. MUS: Angel Note. PRD: ARMS, Genco. 25 mins. x 12 eps. Eriko Takahashi and her friends are initially ecstatic about getting into the school of their choice—the high-class Yamasaki Girls' High. However, since none of them have had any experience at an all-girls school before, they are unprepared for the new pressures—not merely the absence of boys, but increased sporting and academic competition between the girls. Based on the 2001 manga serialized in the monthly *Comic High* by Towa Oshima.

HIGH SCHOOL HONOR

1992. JPN: *High School Jingi*. Video. DIR: Tetsuro Amino. SCR: Keiji Michiyoshi. DES: Hisashi Abe. ANI: Hisashi Abe. MUS: N/C. PRD: JC Staff, Nippon Eizo. 50 mins.

Hiroshima gangster Seiji goes undercover in a Tokyo high school to set up a front for moving large quantities of drugs. However, he falls in love with both his attractive fellow teacher Reiko and with the city of Tokyo itself. Local Shinjuku mobsters, however, want him out of town. An adaptation of Shushi Mizuho's manga in *Young Jump* magazine. **N V**

HIGH SCHOOL KIMENGUMI

1985. TV series. DIR: Hiroshi Fukutomi, Shin Misawa. SCR: Takao Koyama, Shigeru Yanagawa. DES: Hikuji Kanezawa. ANI: Hikuji Kanezawa, Kenichi Chikanaga. MUS: Shunsuke Kikuchi. PRD: Studio Comet, NAS, Fuji TV. 51 mins. (m), 25 mins. x 86 eps. (TV), 25 mins. x 51 eps. (*Tochinkan*). A Japanese high school is divided into rigid gangs, including Jocks, Seducers, Bad Girls, and Brains. Paramount among them is the Kimengumi, the "Strange Faces," a five-man team with punning names and strange quirks, who lord it over all the other students. Two summer-vacation episodes were also cut together and shown in theaters as a "movie" version before broadcast. The same crew returned with *Regarding Tonchinkan* (1987, *Tsuide ni Tonchinkan*), a similar series about one particular gang deciding to play at burglary without the knowledge of their schoolmates, each masquerading at different times as the master thief Tonchinkan.

HIGH SPEED JECY

1989 AKA: *Hi-Speed Jecy*. Video. DIR: Shigenori Kageyama. SCR: Sukehiro Tomita, Shikichi Ohashi. DES: Haruhiko Mikimoto. ANI: Hidetoshi Omori, Akinobu Takahashi. MUS: Kei Wakakusa. PRD: Studio Pierrot. 30 mins. x 12 eps. Jecy is an incredibly fast runner who detests all forms of violence but has vowed to avenge the deaths of his parents. He wanders the galaxy in the "living ship" Paolon, which can transform into an elderly gentleman for convenience, accompanied by the love-struck Tiana and a priest from a cult of sadists, searching all the while

for the trail of the man who killed his parents. Based on a novel by Eiichiro Saito in the spirit of CRUSHER JOE, this series boasts illustrations from Haruhiko Mikimoto, who also worked as a designer on the adaptation.

HIGH STEP JUN

1985. TV series. DIR: Junichi Sato, Hiroshi Shidara, Yukio Misawa. SCR: Akiyoshi Sakai, Tadaaki Yamazaki, Shunichi Yukimuro. DES: Kazuo Komatsubara. ANI: Kazuo Komatsubara, Michi Himeno, Mitsuru Aoyama, Hirokazu Ishino. MUS: Nozomu Aoki. PRD: Toei, TV Asahi. 25 mins. x 45 eps. Jun Nonomiya is a child prodigy who loves tinkering with machines and has even invented some robot companions for herself. The real companion she desires is Rei ("Zero"), the class biker boy, but Yoko, another girl in her class, claims to be Rei's fiancée. Beginning in an early Sunday morning slot, this love comedy based on a manga by Yasuichi Oshima changed radically in its latter half. Thrown into a new late Wednesday morning slot, presumably where most of its original audience wouldn't see it, it ditched the love triangle, packing Rei off to boarding school in England, and transforming into a robot comedy centered on Jun's inventions.

HIKA RYOUJOKU: THE LUST OF SHAME *

2003. JPN: *Hika Ryojoku*. AKA: *Lust of Shame*. Video. DIR: Tokuma Shinohara. SCR: Yasuyuki Muto. DES: Takumi Nishino. ANI: Hiroshi Muneta. MUS: N/C. PRD: Potato House, Five Ways. 30 mins. Shinichi and Megumi become stepsiblings after their parents marry; no great surprise in any anime made since MARMALADE BOY. Shinichi suppresses his growing feelings for his stepsister, but is forced by school bullies to embark on a series of perverse missions. These range from stealing her underwear to taking photographs of her, until he stands up for himself and is punished by being forced to watch as they sexually assault her. **L N V**

HIKARIAN

1997. JPN: *Chotokkyu Hikarian*. AKA: *Super Express Hikarian; Hikarian: Great Railroad Protector*. TV series. DIR: Kazuyuki Hirokawa. SCR: Kazuyuki Hirokawa, Toshiki Inoue, Shunichi Yukimuro. DES: Takeshi Miyao. ANI: N/C. MUS: N/C. PRD: Tomy. 7 mins. x 154 eps. (TV1), 8 mins. x 52 eps. (TV2).

In a bizarre cross between TRANSFORMERS and *Thomas the Tank Engine*, Hikari the bullet train and his robot allies are struck by a "mysterious light" from the heavens that gives them transforming robot powers to defend Earth from the invading Bratcher Force. Broadcast as part of the children's TV show BUBU CHACHA and tied into a line of toys from Tomy, the series was also edited into 51 half-hour episodes. A second TV series ran in 2002, directed by Hideaki Oba.

HIKARU'S GO *

2001. JPN: *Hikaru no Go*. TV series, video. DIR: Shin Nishizawa, Jun Kamiya, Tetsuya Endo. SCR: Shikichi Ohashi. DES: Hideyuki Motohashi, Kanami Sekiguchi, Miyuki Ueda. ANI: Hideyuki Motohashi, Shinichi Miyamae, Takako Onishi, Yoshinori Tokiya. MUS: Kei Wakakusa. PRD: Studio Pierrot, TV Tokyo. 23 mins. x 75 eps., ca. 80 mins. (sp1), ca. 80 mins. (sp2).

Sixth-grader Hikaru Shindo is rummaging in his grandfather's attic when he uncovers a *go* board possessed by the spirit of an ancient champion, Fujiwara no Sai. Sai was once the instructor to a medieval emperor, who committed suicide after being falsely accused of cheating. At first refusing to accept that he's been possessed, especially by something as uncool as an ancient board game champion when he could have been ULTRAMAN or BIRDY THE MIGHTY, Hikaru goes to a *go* parlor to try his and Sai's luck and trashes Akira Toya, a gifted player of his own age, to the astonishment of the old guys who make up the rest of the clientele. As time passes Hikaru comes to understand the complexity of the game and to respect Sai's intelligence and com-

mitment. *Hikaru's Go* cleverly mixes the traditions of the sports genre such as YAWARA with that buddy subgenre of anime that bestows teens with spirits of the past to help them grow—compare to similar arrangements in USHIO AND TORA and PUPPET MASTER SAKON. A fittingly sedentary game for the couch potato generation, and easier to comprehend at a basic level than Japan's other national boardgame obsession, *shogi* (which is preferred by all rational individuals, including the anime's bad-guy Tetsuo Kaga, and most anime encyclopedists), *go* may seem at first like a strange choice. But it is precisely the kind of anime one might expect the aging YUGI-OH generation to enjoy, exchanging getting excited about cards for getting excited about little black and white pebbles. It survived for an impressive three seasons on Japanese television, as well as two feature-length New Year's specials that continue Hikaru's career into the international championships. It also contains a subtle commentary on pulling one's own weight—since Hikaru's victories are actually Sai's, Sai eventually leaves him to win games on his own. This leads to Hikaru's temporary withdrawal from the game, and his eventual return with a newfound respect for his long-term rival Akira Toya. Based on the manga in *Shonen Jump* by Takeshi Obata and Yumi Hotta.

HIME-CHAN'S RIBBON

1993. JPN: *Hime-chan no Ribon*. TV series. DIR: Hatsuki Tsuji, Hiroaki Sakurai, Shinji Sakai, Tomohiro Takamoto, Masato Namiki. SCR: Takashi Yamada, Shunichi Yukimuro, Tomoko Konparu, Hiroshi Koda, Shigeru Yanagawa. DES: Hajime Watanabe. ANI: Hajime Watanabe, Masayuki Onchi, Yoko Konishi. MUS: N/C. PRD: Victor, TV Tokyo. 25 mins. x 61 eps.

A princess from a magical world appears before Himeko and offers her a deal. As part of her magical training, she must observe the behavior of a human girl who resembles her for a whole year. In exchange, Hime-chan

(literally, "little princess") is given a magical ribbon that allows her to transform. A magical-girl story packed full of magic items, talking toys, and problem-solving resolutions in the mold of CREAMY MAMI, this anime was based on the 1991 *Ribbon* magazine manga by Megumi Mizusawa and actually ran longer than the original, magically defined time limit.

HININDEN

2005. AKA: *Legend of Red Ninja*. Video. DIR: Kan Fukumoto. SCR: Yoshio Takaoka. DES: Rin Shin. ANI: Rin Shin. MUS: N/C. PRD: ARMS, Pink Pineapple 30 mins. x ?? eps.

The beautiful princess Kurama has been imprisoned with her ninja associates Momoka and Kaede in a castle dungeon. The girls attempt to escape but are cornered by a party of soldiers sent to retrieve them. Refusing to be taken back, Kurama calls out to the Moon to answer her plea, and hurls herself from a nearby cliff. Flash forward to the present day, where average boy Daisuke is just about to lose his virginity to his first love Hazuki. Imagine, then, his frustration, as a birthmark on his neck suddenly glows with the light of the Moon, and he is whisked away to Kurama's time, where he inadvertently saves her, is soon seduced by the approachable ladies of the past, and imprisoned in the dungeon himself. Kurama resolves to rescue him, in an erotic anime that mixes ninja lore with the usual sex scenes. ⓁⓃⓋ

HIPPO AND THOMAS

1971. JPN: *Kabatotto*. TV series. DIR: Hiroshi Sasagawa. SCR: Jinzo Toriumi, Takao Koyama. DES: N/C. ANI: N/C. MUS: Koba Hayashi. PRD: Tatsunoko, Fuji TV. 5 mins. x 560 eps.

A daily breakfast-time treat for the tinies, and five minutes' peace for busy mothers, this long-running microseries starred good-natured and fairly dim hippo Kaba and big-mouthed bird Totto. Characterized as a good-natured but gullible landlord who indulges the foibles of his bragging, deceitful tenant, the pair would often be led into trouble by Totto's schemes, but only Totto would suffer the consequences. The result is a cunning object lesson in tolerance and cooperation for the young viewers, who might be expected to see themselves in the naughty Totto and their parents in the long-suffering Kaba. Voice actors Toru Taihei and Machiko Soga were credited, though there were hardly any actual lines, with much of the story being told through expressions and noises. Although not broadcast in English, the series did make it into some U.S. territories in a Spanish-language version, hence our decision to file it under the title by which it is most likely to have been seen by American viewers, if they have seen it at all.

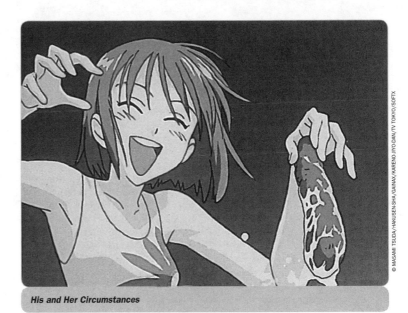

His and Her Circumstances

HIPPO-KEEPER: A ZOO DIARY

1981. JPN: *Kaba-Encho: Dobutsuen Nikki*. TV special. DIR: Masayuki Akehi. SCR: Makoto Naito, Ryuzo Nakanishi. DES: Kozo Masanobu. ANI: Kozo Masanobu. MUS: Nozomu Aoki. PRD: Toei. 75 mins. Aging zoo keeper Toshio Nishiyama acquires two young trainees: short-tempered former chef Takeshi Ishizawa and gentle vet Ichiro Hasegawa. Both are surprised by the difficulties they face in a deceptively easy job but persevere through troubles such as an escaped pelican, a dying camel, and the birth of a hippo.

A semiautobiographical series of anecdotes from real-life Tobu Animal Park zookeeper Toshio Nishiyama, who appears at the beginning and end of the film to talk about his love for animals—and to reveal that Ishizawa is in fact a projection of his younger self. Blatant self-promotion for Nishiyama's place of employment, to be contrasted with GOODBYE LITTLE HIPPO, which presents a far more negative view of bad times at the rival Ueno Zoo.

HIRANO, TOSHIHIRO

1956– . Sometimes credited, by his own choice, as Toshiki Hirano. Born in Tokyo, Hirano showed a strong aptitude for graphic design and was still a college student in that discipline when he began working part-time at Studios Wombat and Number One. He found full-time employment at Studio Io after showing his skills as an animator on an episode of DOCTOR SLUMP. He soon moved to Artland and then AIC, working as an animator on MACROSS and URUSEI YATSURA. However, it was in the video world that his talents for the horrific truly came to the fore, on shows such as ICZER-ONE and VAMPIRE PRINCESS MIYU (the latter based on a manga by Hirano's wife, Narumi Kakinouchi).

HIRATA, TOSHIO

1938– . Born in Yamagata Prefecture, Hirata graduated from the Department of Western Art at Musashino Fine Arts University in 1961, immediately finding work at Toei Animation as an animator on THE LITTLEST WARRIOR and LITTLE PRINCE AND THE EIGHT-HEADED DRAGON. He worked for a number of companies, including Mushi Production, Zuiyo (now Nippon Animation), Group Tac, and Sanrio. His directorial debut came with UNICO, and later works included the second of the BAREFOOT GEN movies and RAIL OF THE STAR. In old age he has continued to work in anime, directing the opening and ending sequences for CATNAPPED and working as a key animation supervisor on METROPOLIS.

HIS AND HER CIRCUMSTANCES *

1998. JPN: *Kareshi Kanojo no Jijo*. AKA: *Tales at North Hills High, Secret Diary, KareKano*. TV series. DIR: Hideaki Anno, Kazuya Tsurumaki. SCR: Hideaki Anno. DES: Tadashi Hiramatsu. ANI: N/C. MUS: Shiro Sagisu. PRD: Gainax, JC Staff, TV Tokyo. 25 mins. x 26 eps. Yukino Miyazawa is the most popular girl at school and a permanent straight-A student, her frantic home life hidden to preserve her seemingly effortless perfection. Her classroom kingdom is invaded by a newcomer, the handsome Soichiro Arima, who competes with her for every prize and accolade. Both are appointed as class reps and forced to work together. Behind icy masks of politeness, the pair fight a private battle of wills and slowly begin to fall in love.

Based on a 1996 manga by Masami Tsuda in *Hana to Yume* magazine, *H&HC* effortlessly outclasses its lookalike U.S. cousin *Ally McBeal* in its dramatic innovation and use of surreal "cartoon" effects in a contemporary sitcom. In Japan, it owes a debt to earlier comedies of manners such as **GOLDFISH WARNING** and **REIKO SHIRATORI I PRESUME**, throwing in Greek choruses of cynical siblings, split-screens, and squashed-down cartoon versions of the lead characters. In terms of off-the-wall experimentation, it rivals the earlier **FIST OF THE NORTH STAR**—not just stop-motion and live action, but one episode features a character whose head is a photograph of a Gainax staff member, while another is animated with paper cutouts, until Yukino bursts into real flames. As with director Anno's earlier **EVANGELION**, onscreen captions and subtitles comment on the action and warp the characters' meanings, perfectly capturing the adolescent power struggles and hypocrisies of the original. A very funny satire about unlikable people who are nevertheless sympathetic characters.

HISAISHI, JOE

1950– . Pseudonym for Mamoru Fujisawa. Born in Nagano Prefecture, he was a childhood violin prodigy who went on to study composition at Kunitachi College of Music. His first work in anime comprised short pieces for **THE GARDLES**, under his real name. He subsequently adopted a pseudonym loosely based on the Japanese pronunciation of "Quincy Jones." Although he has composed music for over 100 productions, shows, and events, including the Nagano Winter Olympics, he is best known for his association with Hayao Miyazaki, which began with **NAUSICAÄ OF THE VALLEY OF WIND**, and has continued throughout Studio Ghibli's production history.

HIT AND RUN

1979. JPN: *Ganbare! Bokura no Hit and Run.* AKA: *Go for It! Our Hit and Run!* TV special. DIR: Hiroe Mitsunobu. SCR: Fumi Takahashi. DES: Hikuji Kanezawa. ANI: Hikuji Kanezawa. MUS: Kensuke Kanadome. PRD: Nippon Animation, Fuji TV. 75 mins.
Baseball captain Ran leads his team to victory in another tale of athletes overcoming adversity, this one based on a manga by Hideo Aya originally serialized in *Shonen Sunday* magazine.

HOLEY PANTS: DESIRE ON A STROLL

1987. JPN: *Pants no Ana: Manbo de Ganbo!* Video. DIR: Nobuyuki Kitajima. SCR: (see below). DES: N/C. ANI: Noboru Furuse. MUS: Seiko Ito. PRD: Gahosha. 25 mins.
The ad blurb claims that this is a sweet, humorous look at teen worries, born from the real-life concerns of correspondents for *Bomb!* magazine. An excellent excuse to blame the audience if a project is unsuccessful. Since there were no follow-ups, we can assume that the experiment was a failure. Less salacious reader input informed the successful **OSHIN**. **Ⓝ**

HOLMES THE TORTOISESHELL CAT

1992. JPN: *Mikeneko Holmes no Yurei Jochu.* AKA: *Holmes the Tortoiseshell Cat and the Haunted Castle.* Video. DIR: Nobuyuki Kitajima, Takeshi Aoki. SCR: Arii Emu. DES: Neko Shijisha. ANI: Noboru Furuse, Jun Okuda. MUS: Kentaro Haneda. PRD: AIC. 45 mins.
A tortoiseshell cat (who solves mysteries on the side) decides to question whether or not the police really have solved a murder case at a castle on an uninhabited island. Based on the best-selling novel *Holmes the Tortoiseshell Cat and the Bouquet of Flowers* by Jiro Akagawa.

HOLY THE GHOST

1991. JPN: *Obake no Hori.* TV series. DIR: Minoru Okazaki, Rikuko Yoshida, Masami Furukawa. SCR: Osamu Nakamura, Riko Hinokuma, Megumi Sugiwara, Minori Ikeno. DES: Megumi Watanabe. ANI: Noriko Imazawa. MUS: N/C. PRD: Apollon Create. 10 mins. x 25 eps.
Humorous stories about a weak-willed ghost made of chocolate, whose mild adventures take him to a birthday party, a carnival, a fight with a bullying witch, and so on. In 1992, his best adventures were released on video as the three-part *Holy the Ghost: Special.* Based on *The Cowardly Ghost*, a children's book by Megumi Watanabe.

HOLY VIRGINS *

2001. JPN: *Tres Marias—Sannin no Sei Shojo.* AKA: *Three Marias—Three Holy Girls.* Video. DIR: Kanzaburo Oda. SCR: Rokurota Makabe, Nikukyu. DES: Ken Raika. ANI: Shinichi Omata. MUS: Yoshi. PRD: YOUC, Digital Works (Vanilla Series). 30 mins. x 2 eps.
Despite his skill as a doctor, Fuwa is fired from a hospital over justifiable allegations of sexual harassment. Down on his luck, he accepts an offer from an old university buddy to investigate the case of Makoto, a novice nun who falls into a state of catatonia every night. He takes a trip to her home island and encounters other religious ladies, who are soon stripping off for a series of erotic scenes. Makoto herself "lacks experience," although she certainly doesn't by the end of this porn anime, in which Fuwa provides a predictable hands-on cure. **ⓃⓋ**

HOMEROOM AFFAIRS *

1994. JPN: *Tanin no Kankei.* AKA: *Human Relations.* Video. DIR: Osamu Sekita. SCR: Hiroyuki Kawasaki. DES: Minoru Yamazawa. ANI: Minoru Yamazawa. MUS: Hiroyuki Takei. PRD: Jam Creation, JC Staff. 45 mins. x 2 eps.
Young minx Miyako teases older man Tokiro Ebara with views of her underwear at a train station, but both are in for a shock. She is a student at Mitsuba Girls' School, and he is her new homeroom teacher. To make matters worse, Miyako's father then asks the flustered Mr. Ebara to babysit while he is away, forcing the couple to live together. Coy soft-core high jinks ensue, as our teacher nobly resists Miyako's charms, while fantasizing about her all the time. Eventually, she points out that if they were married, they could have sex as often as they liked, and nobody would care—though it is somewhat presumptuous of her to assume that anyone does anyway. Based on the

1992 manga by Ichiro Arima published in *Young Animal* magazine, the most amusing thing about this "comedy" is the distributor's hysterical insistence, at every available occasion, that Miyako is over the age of consent. Quote of the week: "Not to be viewed by minors under 18." As opposed to what? Ⓝ

HONEY AND CLOVER

2005. JPN: *Hachimitsu to Clover*. TV series. DIR: Kenichi Kasai. SCR: Yosuke Kuroda. DES: Hidekazu Shimamura. ANI: N/C. MUS: Yumi Hayashi and Salon 68. PRD: JC Staff, Fuji TV. 25 mins. x 24 eps. (TV), 25 mins. x 2 eps. (v).
Three young arts students live a poor but happy existence in the same apartment. Their balanced life is disrupted by the arrival of Hagumi Hanamoto, the daughter of their instructor. One boy, Shinobu Morita, attempts to show his feelings for her, but only ends up scaring her. His love-rival Yuta Takemoto tries an alternate tactic, hiding his true feelings and trying to be a conspicuously good friend to her. The final roommate, Takumi Mayama, has other problems, since he is being pursued by Ayumi Yamada, a beautiful potter also known as Tetsujin, "The Iron Lady," adored by all the young men in the district, but who has eyes only for him. He, meanwhile, has eyes only for his employer, who is a pretty widow. Based on the manga by Chika Umino serialized in *Young You* magazine, this was commissioned by Fuji TV as the first of several "Noitamina" series—"animation" spelled backwards. These series were aimed at a nighttime, mainstream audience distinct from the usual fans to which evening anime so often pander, with the expectation that many viewers would be women in their twenties. PARADISE KISS was another outing in the experiment. The two final "episodes" were specials not broadcast on TV but included as bonuses to the Japanese DVD.

HONEY HONEY *

1981. JPN: *Honey Honey no Suteki na Boken*. AKA: *Honey Honey's Wonder-ful Adventure*. TV series. DIR: Takeshi Shirato, Masakazu Yasumura, Minoru Hamada. SCR: Masaki Tsuji, Shunichi Yukimuro, Tomohiro Ando. DES: Yoshiyuki Yamamoto, Kozo Masanobu. ANI: Takeshi Shirato, Akira Okuwara. MUS: Akihiro Komori. PRD: Toei, Fuji TV. 25 mins. x 29 eps.
Teenage Austrian orphan Honey is a waitress in 1907 Vienna whose pet cat, Lily, swallows Princess Florel's precious gemstone, the "Smile of the Amazon." Honey is forced to go on the run with Phoenix the gentleman jewel thief, pursued by Florel's angry suitors. Equal parts LUPIN III and THREE MUSKETEERS, the story eventually transforms into a fairy tale worthy of CINDERELLA, when Honey is revealed to be Florel's long-lost twin and marries Phoenix so they can all live happily ever after. Based on a 1966 manga by Hideko Mizuno and given a partial release on an obscure U.S. video label.

HONEY THE BUG

1986. JPN: *Bug-tte Honey*. AKA: *Honey the Bug Dance Megarom Girl 4622*. TV series, movie. DIR: Akinori Nagaoka, Minoru Okazaki, Toshio Takeuchi, Yutaka Sato, Kanetsugu Kodama. SCR: Kasumi Oka, Hideki Sonoda, Shunichi Yukimuro, Yasushi Hirano. DES: Minoru Maeda. ANI: Takao Kasai. MUS: Hiroshi Tsutsui. PRD: TMS, Nippon TV. 51 mins. x 51 eps. (TV), 48 mins. (m).
Computer-gaming prodigy Harahito Takahashi is whisked off to Game World by Honey the insect girl and her friends, who need his help in a quest that takes them through several different sectors, each suspiciously similar to several Nintendo games, including *The Adventures of Morihito Takahashi* and *Xanadu*. Fast on the heels of the theatrical success of SUPER MARIO BROTHERS, this mixture of *Tron* and *The Last Starfighter* also appeared in a movie version, *Honey the Bug: Mai the Megarom Girl 4622* (1987), featuring Leo, a scientist from Toycom World whose lover, Mai, has been brainwashed by evil forces. A rather quaint relic of the early days of product placement

before the hard-sell of more recent series such as POKÉMON.

HONGO, MITSURU

1959– . Sometimes miscredited as Mitsuru Honma. Animator at Shin'ei Doga who subsequently became a director on shows including CRAYON SHIN-CHAN and PILOT CANDIDATE. Now associated with Production IG.

HOOP DAYS *

2003. JPN: *Dear Boys*. TV series. DIR: Susumu Kudo. SCR: Nobuaki Kishima, Takao Yoshioka. DES: Akira Kano. ANI: N/C. MUS: Nittoku Inoue. PRD: OB Planning, Avex Trax, TV Tokyo. 25 mins. x 26 eps.
Transfer student Kazuhiko rediscovers his love of basketball, when he leaves behind the harsh sport-oriented regime of his old school for the more relaxed attitudes of Mizuho High—so relaxed in fact, that the school doesn't even have a basketball team any more. The previous coach bowed out in spectacular fashion when he was punched on court (and on camera) by one of his team, thereby ensuring that the remaining players were banned from playing for the rest of the season. Kazuhiko tries to drag them back into the game through his own love of it, while other bonds develop between some of the boys and their opposite numbers on the girls' basketball team. A predictable but endearing rerun of SLAM DUNK with a little of the cheesy faux-tough attitude of INITIAL D, this show was based on a 1989 manga by Hiroki Yagami in monthly *Shonen Magazine*. Although it is a title aimed at male teens and based on a manga with considerably more risqué content, *Dear Boys* sounded a little too girly for the American audience, hence the renaming in the U.S. release, but not even that seemed to stop the serial's English-language release foundering partway, presumably due to lack of interest.

HOOTERS

2005. JPN: *Boin*. Video. DIR: Shigenori Kurii. SCR: Sozo Doji. DES: Maria Ichimonji. ANI: Michitaka Yamamoto. MUS: N/C. PRD: Shindeban Film, Image House, Milky, GP Museum Soft. 30 mins.

Daisuke Ichijo finds himself a job as a high school career guidance counselor, with a "hands-on" approach that demands putative school-leavers dress up in the uniforms of their chosen professions and act out a series of role-play situations for their helpful teacher. A spate of uniform fetish sex scenes ensues, with particular attention paid to large breasts—both a feature of the original title in Japanese and the erotic computer game from Bijin Happo on which this anime was based. ●NV

HORROR AND MONSTERS

The earliest chills in anime came from ghost stories and scary fairy tales, such as Noburo Ofuji's *Kujira* (1927) and *Ghost Ship* (1956), but it was a children's medium, and as such didn't initially attempt anything designed to give anyone goosebumps. Osamu Tezuka's DORORO (1968), made as the creator's Mushi Production began to spiral into bankruptcy, was one of the first anime to be genuinely disturbing, filled with ghosts, nightmares, and bloodshed, and with a central character whose father's pact with devils leaves him scarred, eyeless, and maimed. That didn't stop some kids' cartoons from being downright disturbing anyway, with the lamb-turned-killer of Sanrio's RINGING BELL (1978) reputedly giving a number of *adult* fans nightmares.

Children's entertainment often recognized the appeal of the horrific. SPOOKY KITARO (1968) suggested that cutting class to hang out with zombies was a fun thing to do, while DEVILMAN (1972) dressed up the traditions of a superhero show with the accoutrements of demonology. But not even *Devilman* was "horror" as we know it; that was a foreign concept, and arguably its first appearance was Minoru Okazaki's TV movie DRACULA: SOVEREIGN OF THE DAMNED (1980), based on the Marvel comic.

True horror reached Japan by an unexpected route, in the depictions of radiation burns and traumatized war victims of BAREFOOT GEN (1983). The 1980s saw the widespread arrival of the home video player, permitting anime producers to make shows for an older audience. Horror met science fiction in VAMPIRE HUNTER D (1985), but it was the Madhouse studio that appeared to perfect its use in modern animation. WICKED CITY (1987) and DEMON CITY SHINJUKU (1988) established Madhouse and director Yoshiaki Kawajiri as the kings of urban gothic. A slew of imitators followed, in which demons broke through into our everyday world, and fought on the streets of Tokyo. But everyone's thunder was stolen by UROTSUKIDOJI (1987), the first in a series of "erotic-horror" stories based on the work of Toshio Maeda that, while it might not have *scared* its audience, certainly shocked them with its scenes of depravity and excess—its monsters externalized the chaos in the pubescent mind, to devastating effect.

Ultimately, horror usually scares us by persuading us that something terrible really might happen—both PERFECT BLUE (1997) and MONSTER (2004) successfully instill fear with their application of *reality*, not the fantastic. Anime, by its nature, is already one step from reality, making it harder to scare a cartoon audience. Modern day incarnations of anime "horror" continue to coquettishly avoid making an audience scream in terror. Instead they hope to titillate, amuse, or otherwise behave in a non-horrific way. VAMPIRE PRINCESS MIYU (1988) preferred mood and imagery to actual scares—style over substance, if you like. Western horror is often concerned with subtexts, but erotic-horror anime like DARK SHELL (2003) or ONI TENSEI (2001) can put all the subtext right in the foreground. No sublimated desires here, no Victorian prudery repressing thoughts of sex with stories of men who drink virgins' blood—horror is a permanent feature of anime erotica, but whether such shows are scary *because* of their horror content is open to debate.

Japanese folklore has a rich tradition of monsters, some of which have built successful second careers in animation. In 1955's PIGGYBACK GHOST, a green-eyed elemental befriends a village blacksmith and his neighbors. GOLDEN BAT (1967) was a skeletal superhero from ancient Atlantis who fought monsters and robots at the request of Japanese schoolgirl Mari. SPOOKY KITARO (1968) gave supporting roles, as friends or adversaries of the young hero, to a host of traditional ghouls like the one-legged, one-eyed Umbrella Man and the ghostly Piece of Paper, a tradition which continued in shows like DORORON ENMA (1973) with its Japanese Monster Patrol, GHOSTS (1981), and USHIO & TORA (1992). Oni, Japan's native ogres, are generally represented as powerful but stupid, extremely violent, and with nasty eating habits. They feature in anime such as OGRE SLAYER and SHUTENDOJI, and have inspired many other creations like Rumiko Takahashi's alien Oni in URUSEI YATSURA.

American TV's fascination with the supernatural in the 1960s inspired a number of monstrous tales, like the 1968 Korean coproduction MONSTER MAN BEM in which a trio from the world of monsters strive to bring good to the Dark Realm in the hope that this will enable them to become human. The generic Western vampire became a popular stock character from 1968, when Mushi Production mixed live-action and anime in VAMPIRE. LITTLE GOBLIN (1968), the story of a monster prince sent to live on Earth, gave supporting roles to the Hollywood stars who inspired Forrest J. Ackerman's long-running magazine *Famous Monsters of Filmland*: Dracula, the Wolfman, and a young Frankenstein's monster. All three also featured in the SPOOKY KITARO movie *Great Ghost Wars* (1986).

Mary Shelley's tragic creation FRANKENSTEIN (mystifyingly relocated to North Wales for the Toei TV special) has also influenced a long line of anime dealing with the dangers of genetic experiment, from thoughtful works like Tezuka's BAGHI (1981) to 1998's POKÉMON movie and BLUE SUBMARINE NO. SIX. The Wolfman's descendants have starred in shows including WOLF GUY (1992), alongside other were-creatures in MIDNIGHT PANTHER (1998). Strangely, the Mummy has yet to star in his own anime; bit-part appearances in shows like 1971's LUPIN III have reduced him to the level of an extra in *Scooby-Doo.*

THE KING KONG SHOW (1966) was made specifically for the American market. The elemental ape became a small child's friend in a TV movie and series of eight-minute adventures. Japan's own giant monster, Godzilla, appeared as a comical parody of himself in 1967's GAZULA THE AMICABLE MONSTER, a gentle but clumsy creature invading the life of a typical Japanese family.

Gross, misshapen monsters that would equally be at home in medieval Buddhist or Western Hells are found in anime such as 1985's ICZER-ONE and 1991's SILENT MÖBIUS where they are the shock troops of alien forces bent on world domination. In most Japanese movies humanity tries to fight monsters with iron determination and heavy weaponry, but many anime play with the idea that to beat monsters you must join them, by taking on some of their physical or magical powers, as in DEVILMAN (1972) and later pastiches such as HELLSING. Nagai's series suggests that ordinary-looking people can be possessed by or transformed into monsters, simply by unleashing their own inner demons. Some of the most magnificently silly monsters ever to grace an enduring franchise threaten mankind in ULTRAMAN (1979), an animation spun off the live-action hit of the same name. To defeat them, our hero must achieve monstrous size and strength by borrowing the magical-girl technique of assisted transformation.

Other monstrous transformations in anime range from the comical-but-threatening to the stomach churning. When neglected pet dog Papadoll is changed to a monster in CATNAPPED

Horror and Monsters

© 2006 STEVE KYTE

(1995), he still drools and looks amiably stupid, but he can eat people. AKIRA (1988) transforms all its protagonists, but Tetsuo's shifts from scrawny runt to drug-crazed god to overflowing river of flesh are truly monstrous, giving visceral impact to his final moment of self-awareness and self-acceptance, and hope of redemption for all monsters, even the human kind.

HOT FOR TEACHER *

2003. JPN: *Jokyoshi—Yumi Houkago.* AKA: *Female Teacher—Yumi After Class.* Video. DIR: Haruo Okawara. SCR: Yuta Takahashi. DES: Haruo Okawara. ANI: Haruo Okawara. MUS: Yoshi. PRD: YOUC, Digital Works (Vanilla Series). 30 mins. x 2 eps.

Busty, raven-haired school teacher Yumi has split up with her fiancé, and now faces sexual harassment from the vice principal in yet another escapee from the VANILLA SERIES. Although she tries to thwart his advances, he lies in wait for her with a group of her own students and subjects her to a series of sexual torments. After she is forced to agree to service her entire class, she looks to two students for rescue, although they are both quite timid,

and just as likely to be "forced" to rape her themselves in an anime unsurprisingly similar to PROFESSOR PAIN. Ⓛ Ⓝ Ⓥ

HOT JUICY TEACHER *

2002. JPN: *Onna Kyoshi.* Video. DIR: Sosuke Kokubunji. SCR: Sosuke Kokubunji. DES: Jun Papaya. ANI: Jun Papaya. MUS: Yoshitaka Jo. PRD: Milky. 30 mins. x 4 eps.

When Yuichiro runs into a group of rich kids raping their teacher, he is framed for the offence and forced to transfer schools. The experience causes him to swear revenge on all women (why not on rich bullies?), and the prime candidate presents herself at his next school, where the principal's daughter is seducing some of her students after class. Meanwhile, shy boy Hiromi is also bullied by a group of classmates who sexually humiliate him and persuade local bad girls to tease him. He develops a crush on the sexually predatory teacher, which turns him into her protector when Yuichiro tries to have his wicked way. Predictable anime erotica, with slightly more bodily fluids than usual in evidence. Based on an erotic computer game created by Atelier Kaguya. Ⓛ Ⓝ Ⓥ

Humane Society

HOUSE OF ACORNS

1997. JPN: *Donguri no Ie.* Movie. DIR: Takashi Anno, Osamu Yamamoto. SCR: N/C. DES: N/C. ANI: Hideo Kawauchi, Yoshiaki Yanagida, Masaya Fujimori, Yuko Ikino, Hiroshi Kawaguchi, Masayuki Sekine. MUS: N/C. PRD: Saitama Association for the Disabled. 110 mins.

Keiko Tazaki is born deaf and mentally handicapped, but her loving parents fight to give her the best possible start in life. Keiko and her parents meet many other deaf and handicapped children and their families as she attends a special school and grows up. After graduation, Keiko throws herself heart and soul into opening a workshop where handicapped people can participate in the modern world, earning their own money, and with it some respect and independence. Although commissioned by an association for the disabled, this production also capitalized on a fad within Japanese entertainment. The previous two years had seen a deaf character central to the live-action TV series *Heaven's Coins* (*DE) and the immense ratings success of the autism drama *Pure* (*DE), both of which helped establish token disability as one more element to be shuffled around dramatic plotlines. *House of Acorns* can be seen as an attempt to return to the issue at hand—the plight of the disabled—rather than another glossy attempt to glamorize it.

HOWL'S MOVING CASTLE *

2004. JPN: *Howl no Ugoku Shiro.* Movie. DIR: Hayao Miyazaki. SCR: Hayao Miyazaki. DES: Hayao Miyazaki. ANI: Akihiro Yamashita, Takeshi Inamura, Kitaro Kosaka. MUS: Joe Hisaishi. PRD: Studio Ghibli, Gonzo, T2, Production I.G., Madhouse. 119 mins.

Plain, shy hat maker Sophie is cursed by the Witch of the Waste to turn prematurely into an old woman. In search of a remedy, she works as a cleaner for Howl, a handsome wizard who, it is rumored, steals the hearts of young girls. Sophie brings a woman's touch to a ramshackle bachelor household, edging her way into the antagonistic world of Howl, his boy apprentice Markl, and Calcifer, the fire demon, whom Howl has bound to the castle's machinery to keep the power flowing. Meanwhile, Howl and several of his pseudonyms are resisting a king's order to fight against the wizards of a rival state. He contends with two women with whom he seems to have a past, the Wicked Witch, whose fading spells cause her to age and collapse into dementia, and Madame Suliman, a government sorcerer who urges Howl to enter royal service.

Hayao Miyazaki's adaptation of the novel by Diana Wynne Jones adds several personal touches, starting with a wheezing comic relief lapdog. The wholly magical realm of the original novel is given a more modern, steambased technology and a new subplot about a distant war, fraught with mixed feelings that appear rooted in Japan's role as bystander and beneficiary of the invasion of Iraq. War breaks out over the search for an important artifact— the infamous real-world "weapons of mass destruction" transformed here into a missing prince, demands for whose return lead to the background conflict. *HMC* wrestles with the ideas of duty and obligation, and how best to do the right thing in a world gone wrong.

Flushed with international approbation for SPIRITED AWAY and Miyazaki's long-deserved Academy Award, *HMC* was less a movie than a national celebration. On its opening weekend 1.1 million Japanese spent over $14 million—an opening surpassed only by *Harry Potter and the Sorcerer's Stone* (2001). Buena Vista invested reverently in the English language adaptation, casting the new *Batman*, Christian Bale, as the selfish Howl and Billy Crystal in a comic turn as Calcifer. The dub is also tied firmly into America's film heritage with Jean Simmons as the aged Sophie, and Lauren Bacall as the Witch of the Waste.

HMC is a charming film, visually inventive and magnificently crafted. The castle itself is a fabulous creation, like a magic mechanical version of Baba Yaga's Hut from Russian folklore, and the settings are beautifully realized, with the wild mountains and uplands handled particularly well. However, there is a difference between an excellent film and an excellent

Miyazaki film. All film is a collaborative process, but in the best films of a genius one finds a unique creative soul, a way of seeing and showing that can be imitated but not replicated. Other great Japanese directors, given Ghibli's unrivaled resources, could have made a movie very like *HMC*; but no one else could have made anything approaching NAUSICAÄ.

HMC was originally intended for another director until Miyazaki stepped in, the legendary perfectionist seemingly unable to let a good idea go to waste, even though he had supposedly retired. The film's hidden message is Miyazaki's love letter to Akemi Ota, the young, hard-working animator girl he married so long ago, a plucky heroine who woke up one day to find herself a glorified scullery maid to a self-absorbed creative, obsessed with distant battles and otherworldly sorceries.

HMC sometimes appears more like the product of a committee rehashing Miyazaki's glory days: heroines confronted by outsized obstacles, contending witches, and lead characters unwittingly transformed. Absolute simplicity and innocence are hard to handle realistically—in MY NEIGHBOR TOTORO they work sublime wonders, but in *HMC* it leaves the characters alienated from the events around them, like preoccupied children or the "little people" of PATLABOR, ignorant of a big picture that is only apparent on repeat viewings.

It may be a tribute to the original novel character, who fed on the souls of besotted young girls, that Howl is Miyazaki's first consciously beautiful male hero who gets to have Miyazaki's first full-on screen kiss, but he's also the first Miyazaki hero to turn into a conventional father figure by the end of the movie. By the close of the film, the wild, magical creatures are tamed into an image of a nuclear family. The magnificently depraved Witch is a gentle granny mumbling in a sunny garden, the resourceful Markl a kid teasing an old dog, and the fire

elemental a lovably grouchy Disney domestic appliance, as the irresistible wizard steers his companion and the domesticated castle into the happily-ever-after. Compare this with the ending of PRINCESS MONONOKE, where San and Ashitaka agree to accept each other's separate needs without compromising their love.

The major Miyazaki themes are still there—integrity, consideration for others, the destructive power of war and greed, ecological awareness, the synergy of true teamwork. What is lacking is a spark so unique it seems churlish to expect Miyazaki to produce it on demand, movie after movie; and the supernaturally sure-footed sense of pace and timing that informs his greatest works. *HMC* is a detailed and generous answer, but so caught up in its own complexity that it seems to have misheard the question.

HUCKLEBERRY FINN

1976. TV series, movie. DIR: Hiroe Mitsunobu, Tameo Ogawa, Keiichi Abe. SCR: Mamoru Sasaki. DES: N/C. ANI: Eisuke Kondo, Teruhito Kamiguchi. MUS: Nobuyoshi Koshibe. PRD: Tac, Nippon Herald, Fuji TV. 25 mins. x 26 eps. (TV1), 86 mins. (m), 25 mins. x 26 eps. (TV2).
Huckleberry Finn and his friend Jim, a black slave, make a bid for freedom by floating down the Mississippi River on a raft. Huck is faced with the perilous choice of damnation or saving his friend, choosing friendship. This WORLD MASTERPIECE THEATER adaptation of Mark Twain's 1885 sequel to TOM SAWYER was cut into an 86-minute "movie" version in 1991. A second TV version, *The Story of Huckleberry* (*Huckleberry Monogatari*), was made by Norio Kabeshima for Enoki Films and an NHK satellite channel in 1994.

HUMAN CROSSING *

2003. JPN: *Ningen Kosaten*. AKA: *Human Scramble*. TV series. DIR: Akira Kumeichi, Kazunari Kumi. SCR: Nobuaki Kishima, Seitaro Shimizu, Toshio Okabe. DES: Sachiko Kamimura. ANI: Shojiro

Abe. MUS: Norihiro Nomura, Yuusuke Hayashi. PRD: TV Tokyo, Shogakukan, To Max 24 mins. x 13 eps.
A series of unrelated stories about people reaching turning points in their lives, using the animated medium to tell tales that often seem more suited to live-action drama. A privileged youth, nursing a long-term grudge against his mother, strives to become a championship boxer in a reversal of the rags-to-riches tradition of TOMORROW'S JOE. An idealistic young lawyer, helping a woman regain custody of her baby from its grandparents, rediscovers the true meaning of justice. A father tries to make up for his workaholic ways by giving his disinterested son an expensive bike. An academic who has left his working-class roots behind comes to terms with his orgins when his brother asks for a favor. A star and his manager, who have been lifelong friends, suffer strains in their relationship as the luster of fame begins to wear off. An adult brother and sister must cope with their old father, a man neither of them has much liked, whose house they have sold but whose care they are still obliged to maintain. A snooty reporter is forced to reconsider his attitude toward the news, and seek it through human contact when he is demoted to a regional newspaper. A rookie guard in a women's prison must confront an inmate who has lied to her. A married couple is torn between an impoverished life of creative fulfillment in Paris or commercial drudgery in Tokyo. A nuclear family find themelves inheriting an old "relative" who turns out to be their late father's mistress. A teenager endures bullying at school because his mother is a hostess in a bar. A male employee at a girls' reformatory agonizes about the 10% of girls that offend again upon release and frets over the best way to deal with a runaway.

It is a symptom of anime that they are so often unreal—when all one is paying for is paint, it is only logical for producers and creators to aim for the fantastic as often as possible in order to make virtues of their production's shortcomings. Anime rooted in reality are few and far between, but *Human Crossing* is one of them—every element of its production suggests that it began life as a live-action TV series, including resemblances to drama serials such as *Tabloid* (*DE), *Unmarried Family* (*DE), and particularly the prison drama *Lipstick* (*DE), since two of the *HC* tales revolve around female offenders. For some reason, perhaps budgetary issues, perhaps a change in the broadcast climate toward short stories, it appears to have been downgraded to anime status, in the manner of **PERFECT BLUE**. Its origin is a series of manga vignettes by Masao Yajima, the creator of *Big Wing* (*DE), and Kenshi Hirokane, the creator of **DOMAIN OF MURDER**. Both are giants of the manga world who specialize in realistic stories of everyday folk, which has naturally led them to enjoy far greater success in the world of live-action TV drama than they could ever hope for in anime. Hirokane in particular is famed for *Shooting Stars in the Twilight*, a manga series written for aging readers, so it is perhaps no surprise that one story concentrates directly on the plight of the elderly in an uncaring modern society, while several others allude to it.

The honest and realistic storytelling demonstrates that anime doesn't have to rely on ninja battles and magic babe harems to create sympathetic, understandable characters. The animation is very limited, the storyboarding and camera work is pedestrian, and the use of live-action footage in the opening and ending sections only highlights its inadequacy. However, music is used very intelligently, that is, only when required to enhance a scene or move the story along, rather than being an inescapable irritation. Despite its deficiencies, this is an unusual and worthwhile addition to any anime collection.

HUMANE SOCIETY

1992. JPN: *Humane Society: Jinrui Ai ni Mochita no Shakai*. AKA: *Humane Society: A Society in Which Humanity Is Loving*. Video. DIR: Jun Kamiya. SCR: Mayori Sekijima, from an idea by Demon Kogure. DES: Kazuya Yokose. ANI: Kazuya Yokose. MUS: Kaimono Matsuzaki-sama. PRD: Animate Film. 57 mins.

In an anime adventure featuring one of Japan's most eccentric pop groups as themselves, the five members of the rock band Seikima-II must save the world from the demonic forces of the Tower of Babel. Claiming to be demons from the other side of the universe, the KISS-look-alikes announced that the apocalypse was coming in 1999 and that ownership of a ticket stub from one of their "Black Masses" would entitle the holder to salvation. Despite a slightly incoherent message (as in **DEVILMAN**, how were demons supposed to save us from Satan?), Seikima-II gained many fans, particularly among young Office Ladies who thought they were cute, with some of their best songs including "Pinky Dinosaur," "Frightful Restaurant," and "Stainless Night" (the latter used in a **BEAST WARRIORS** spin-off CD). They also sang themes to **WANNA-BE'S**, **MAZE**, and one of the **CONAN THE BOY DETECTIVE** movies, while lead singer Demon Kogure was the voice of Munchausen in **UROTSUKIDOJI**. The band's apocalyptic message became more subdued as the 1990s wore on, and they played a farewell concert on New Year's Eve 1999. The music in *Humane Society* is credited to their producer and sometime keyboardist, but it's derived from many of their most famous songs, including "Rosa," the name of their evil adversary.

HUMANOID, THE *

1986. Video. DIR: Shinichi Masaki. SCR: Koichi Minade. DES: Hajime Sorayama, Jinpei Kohara. ANI: Takuya Wada, Osamu Kamijo. MUS: Masao Nakajima. PRD: Toshiba EMI, Hero Media. 45 mins.

A truly awful *Star Wars* rip-off, written solely to showcase the "Sexy Robot" art style of illustrator Hajime Sorayama. After a crash-landing, two hotshot pilots seek help from Professor Watson, unaware that they are stumbling into an evil man's attempt to rule the world. Pilot Eric falls for the android Antoinette, who sacrifices herself to save him, but only after pathologically obsessive dialogue about coffee, a couple of chase scenes, and painfully geeky flirtation. A dire reprise of Tezuka's **SPACE FIREBIRD** or an amateurish rehearsal for the infinitely superior **ARMITAGE III**, however you look at it, it is a sure contender for one of the worst anime ever made. Also shown theatrically in Japan as part of a triple bill.

HUMMINGBIRDS *

1993. JPN: *Idol Boetai Hummingbird*. AKA: *Idol Defense Band Hummingbird*. Video. DIR: Kiyoshi Murayama. SCR: Kiyoshi Murayama. DES: Masahide Yanasawa. ANI: Kenichi Katsura. MUS: Kazuo Otani. PRD: Youmex. 50 mins. x 1 ep., 30 mins. x 3 eps.

Starstruck mother Hazuki Toriishi pushes her five daughters into careers as pop idols in a Japan "the day after tomorrow" that has privatized the armed forces. With only media companies having the finances to invest, the air force has become an entertainment industry, as prefabricated pop groups sing songs and fly jets in bizarre competitions, occasionally breaking off to defend the country from foreign invaders.

A silly spoof of the media from **IRRESPONSIBLE CAPTAIN TYLOR**–creator Hitoshi Yoshioka, combining the siblings and super-vehicles of *Thunderbirds*, from whose Tracy family the Toriishis get their name (see **THUNDERBIRDS 2086**), with pop-song interludes in the style of **MACROSS** to promote the singing careers of the five lead voice actresses. Though the quality of the songs never declined, later episodes lost their satirical edge, with middle sister Satsuki developing a crush on her trainer and competing against the feisty foreign Fever Girls, in a predictable run-through of clichés from sports anime.

The first two volumes were released in the U.K. by Western Connection with rhyming song subtitles. However, they were clumsily cut together in order to avoid paying the BBFC classification authority for two separate releases. The British version is consequently missing two songs and any proper credits—its short "closing credits" actually being the *opening* credits from episode two. The series was never released in the U.S.

HUNDREDTH MONKEY, THE

1986. JPN: *Hyakubanme no Saru*. Movie. DIR: Kazuo Anzai. SCR: Masaaki Sakurai. DES: Shingo Ozaki. ANI: Shingo Ozaki. MUS: Yuki Takamura. PRD: Tokyo Media Communications, Cinework. 20 mins.

A short cartoon of the 1981 book of the same name by new age guru Ken Keyes, Jr., based on the story of a 1952 experiment on the southern Japanese island of Kojima. Once one monkey has learned how to wash its food, it is able to teach others the same skill. When a certain number have learned (and Keyes suggests an arbitrary figure of 100), not only do the remaining monkeys suddenly appear to know how to do it, but so too does a completely different group of apes on a completely separate island. Keyes uses this apocryphal tale as a parable for the antinuclear movement, as "proof" that change would come if enough people joined forces. The story has a triple appeal to the Japanese: not only is it "local," it is also antinuclear in the tradition of **BAREFOOT GEN**, and, best of all, copyright-free in accordance with Keyes's wish for it to reach as many people as possible.

HUNTER X HUNTER

1999. TV series. DIR: Kazuhiro Furuhashi. SCR: Nobuaki Kishima. DES: Yoshihiro Togashi. ANI: Masaaki Kawanami. MUS: Toshihiko Sato. PRD: Nippon Animation, Fuji TV. 25 mins. x 62 eps. (TV), 25 mins. x 8 eps. (v1), 25 mins. x 8 eps. (v2), 23 mins. x 14 eps. (v3). Twelve-year-old orphan Gon lives on Whale Island with his Aunt Mito. A chance forest meeting with Kyte the Hunter reveals that his father is actually still alive and is known throughout the world as the greatest hunter who ever lived. Gon decides to be just like his dad (the all-purpose job description encompassing monster-killing, bounty-taking, treasure-troving, and tomb-raiding), setting off to take the tests of manhood. In this anime based on a manga by **POLTERGEIST REPORT**–creator Yoshihiro Togashi, however, only one in ten thousand makes it through the tough trials. The television series was followed by three video series—*Hunter X Hunter* (2002), *Hunter X Hunter: Greed Island* (2003), and *Hunter X Hunter: G.I. [Greed Island] Final* (2004), which continued the episode numbering of the television series. The franchise also spun off two live-action stage musicals. Note that in a bizarre convention that also affects shows such as **GUN X SWORD** the "x" in the title is supposed to be silent—the title is thus pronounced "Hunter Hunter."

HURRICANE POLYMAR *

1974. JPN: *Hariken Polymar*. AKA: *Inner Destruction Fist Polymar*. TV series, video. DIR: Eiko Toriumi, Hideo Nishimaki, Yoshiyuki Tomino. SCR: Jinzo Toriumi, Akiyoshi Sakai, Masaru Yamamoto, Junichi Shima. DES: Tatsuo Yoshida. ANI: Tsuneo Ninomiya. MUS: Shunsuke Kikuchi. PRD: Tatsunoko, NET. 25 mins. x 26 eps., 30 mins. x 2 eps.

Mild-mannered police chief Takeshi works for the International Crime Division in Washinkyo City (Washington + Tokyo). One night, he is set upon by four thugs, and, despite being an expert at karate, is severely injured. In a replay of **8TH MAN**, kindly Professor Oregar gives him the Polymar suit, an experimental project that could save his life. Takeshi becomes a supercop with a voice-activated suit that fits him like a second skin but can also transform into a plane, a boat, a submarine, and a tank.

A lighthearted and popular superhero show that rode the wave of interest in Bruce Lee and martial arts, with time out for a few in-jokes at the expense of the same studio's earlier **BATTLE OF THE PLANETS**, the series was remade by Akiyuki Shinbo (with designs by Yasuomi Umezu, who would work on a number of other updates of classic Tatsunoko properties) as *New HP* (1996), which is the version available in the U.S. Tatsunoko's remake simplified the original somewhat, moving the action to the man-made island of Tokyo Plus, where Oregar's lab is attacked by the Catshark Squad. The professor is killed, but his beautiful assistant, Ryoko, manages to get the prototype Polymar Helmet to detective Takeshi before her own death.

HUSTLE PUNCH

1965. TV series. DIR: Hiroshi Ikeda, Kazuya Miyazaki, Hiroshi Shidara. SCR: Hiroshi Ikeda, Hiroaki Hayashi. DES: Yasuji Mori. ANI: Yasuji Mori. MUS: Tsuguhoshi Kobayashi. PRD: Toei, NET. 25 mins. x 26 eps.

Three orphaned animals, Punch the Bear, Touch the Mouse, and Bun the Weasel, try to live a carefree life in a seaside town despite the efforts of their evil enemies, the lupine Professor Garigari and his hench-creatures, Black the Cat and Nu the Pig. Based on a manga in *Manga-O* by prolific animator Yasuji Mori.

HUTCH THE HONEYBEE

1970. JPN: *Mitsubachi Monogatari: Minashigo Hutch*. AKA: *Bee Story: Hutch the Orphan*. TV series. DIR: Ippei Kuri, Seitaro Hara. SCR: Jinzo Toriumi, Saburo Taki, Masaaki Yoshida. DES: Tatsuo Yoshida. ANI: Eiji Tanaka. MUS: Nobuyoshi Koshibe. PRD: Tatsunoko, Fuji TV. 25 mins. x 91 eps. (TV1), 25 mins. x 26 eps. (*New*), 25 mins. x 55 eps. (TV3).

Life in the peaceful Bee Kingdom is disrupted by an invasion of wasps, who destroy the eggs and force the queen to flee with her subjects. A single remaining egg hatches, and young Hutch grows up in an environment where his bee-like looks lead to bullying and persecution. In a mixture of **FROM THE APENNINES TO THE ANDES** with the "Ugly Duckling" from the **TALES OF HANS CHRISTIAN ANDERSEN,** Hutch realizes he is really a bee and sets off with his insect companions to find others of his race. This award-winning tale of a bug's life was so successful that it returned for a second series, *New Hutch* (1974), featuring new designs from the Tatsunoko studio's teenage prodigy, Yoshitaka Amano. For the sequel, the wasps return, and Hutch and his sister are exiled and hear that their mother has perished. With nowhere else to go, they search for a mythical "Beautiful Hill," along with insect companions including a firefly, butterflies, and a ladybug. In 1989, the story was completely remade for Tatsunoko by Akira Suzuki using many of the original scripts from the 1970 version but with all-new animation.

HYAKKI: SECRET OF DEVIL'S ISLAND *

2003. AKA: *Pandemonium.* Video. DIR: N/C. SCR: N/C. DES: N/C. ANI: N/C. MUS: N/C. PRD: Pink Pineapple. 30 mins. x 3 eps.

Young visitors on an apparently deserted island find themselves overtaken by uncontrollable lusts and fear that their lives, souls, and, unsurprisingly, bodies may be in danger of demonic invasion. ⬤ⓁⓃⓋ

HYAKUTARO

1991. JPN: *Ushiro no Hyakutaro.* AKA: *Hyakutaro by My Side.* Video. DIR: Seitaro Hara. SCR: Jiro Tsunoda, Isao Shizudani, Masaaki Sakurai. DES: Koji Uemura. ANI: Seiji Kikuchi. MUS: Hiro Tsunoda. PRD: Pierrot Project. 50 mins. x 2 eps.

Occult researcher's son Kazutaro Ushiro and his guardian spirit, Hyakutaro, investigate paranormal activity. Based on the 1973 manga in *Shonen Magazine* by **FRIGHTFUL NEWS**–creator Jiro Tsunoda, this anime is said to be the indirect inspiration for most of the ghostbusting genre, from **PHANTOM QUEST CORP** to **POLTERGEIST REPORT.**

HYPER POLICE

1997. TV series. DIR: Masahiro Omori, Shinya Sadamitsu, Koichi Chiaki. SCR: Sukehiro Tomita, Shigeru Yanagawa. DES: Keiji Goto. ANI: Keiji Goto, Yoshiyuki Kobe, Kazumi Ikeda. MUS: N/C. PRD: Studio Pierrot, TV Tokyo. 25 mins. x 25 eps.

Natsuki Sasahara is a human-feline cross-breed, her associate Sakura is an eight-tailed fox-girl (a sure sign she cannot be trusted, since she needs to swindle Natsuki to gain her ninth tail), and both use their magical powers to hunt criminals in a Tokyo crawling with animal hybrids, ghosts, and goblins. Other major cast members are Batanen Fujioka, Natsuki's lycanthrope senior, Batanen's cousin and partner Tommy, station chief Mudagami (a minor deity), and the single flustered human: the (initially) beast-hating patrolwoman Naoko Kondo. As befits ensemble cop shows like **PATLABOR** and **YOU'RE UNDER ARREST!,** downtime is as important to the show as crime-fighting, and the cast spends an inordinate amount of time at Makoto and Ayami Tachibana's friendly Ranpo Coffee Shop. *HP* has the supernatural urban feel of **SILENT MÖBIUS,** but it's played for laughs and features a considerable dose of anthropomorphic titillation. Based on a manga by "MEE," who also created **ADVENTURE OF KOTETSU.** Ⓝ

HYPERDOLL *

1995. JPN: *Rakusho Hyperdoll.* AKA: *Happy Victory Hyperdoll; Hyper-Doll: Mew and Mica the Easy Fighters.* Video. DIR: Makoto Moriwaki. SCR: Ryo Motohira. DES: Satoru Nakamura. ANI: Satoru Nakamura. MUS: Hiroshi Nakano, Masayuki Negishi. PRD: Pioneer, AIC. 40 mins. x 2 eps.

Mica (the cool, sensible one) and Mew (the hotheaded, impulsive one) are two beautiful aliens sent to defend Earth from monsters. Disguised as typical Japanese high school girls, they befriend Earth girl Shoko and hapless boy Hideo, taking time off (when their boss tracks them down) to fight alien invaders with the aid of an orbiting power converter that harnesses the energy of "zero-space" and beams it to them via their earrings. Unfairly termed "hyperdull" in fandom, this lighthearted superhero comedy features high-quality animation, a good dub, and spoofs of monster shows stretching back to **ULTRAMAN,** though its dim-witted girls in skimpy costumes accidentally causing massive collateral damage owe a further debt to the **DIRTY PAIR.** There are also bonus live-action sections in which the petrified voice actresses stammer their way through some minor comedy business, demonstrating why so many Japanese scripts are better performed as anime. Based on a manga from *Shonen Captain* by Shinpei Ito, who also wrote the manga adaptation of **MOLDIVER.** The live-action sections were written and directed by the Konaka brothers, **ARMITAGE III**'s Chiaki and **BLACK JACK**'s Kazuya.

I

I AM A CAT

1982. JPN: *Wagahai wa Neko de Aru.* TV special. DIR: Rintaro. SCR: Kiyohide Ohara. DES: Kazuo Komatsubara, Haruki Yoshimi. ANI: Kazuo Komatsubara. MUS: Antonio Vivaldi. PRD: Toei, Fuji TV. 73 mins.

"I" is a cat without a name who lives with an English teacher, Mr. Kushami (Mr. Sneeze). "I" can't believe how stupid human beings are and chronicles some of their more incredible foibles. In particular, he is fascinated by Kushami's pupil Mizushima, who falls in love with Haruko, only daughter of war profiteer Kaneda. Based on the 1905 novel by **Botchan**-author Soseki Natsume, this adaptation gained a huge 27.8% rating when broadcast. The feline character designs were by **Jarinko Chie**'s Haruki Yoshimi.

I AM A DOG

1983. JPN: *Wagahai wa Inu de Aru: Don Matsugoro no Monogatari.* AKA: *I Am a Dog: The Story of Don Matsugoro.* TV special. DIR: Kimio Yabuki. SCR: Kiyohide Ohara. DES: Haruki Yoshimi. ANI: Takashi Abe. MUS: Hiroki Takaragi. PRD: Toei, Fuji TV. 73 mins.

Mr. Matsuzawa is a novelist who lives in Chiba Prefecture. Only his daughter Kazuko knows that the family dog, Don Matsugoro, can talk. Don is wounded in a fight with the neighbors' dog, King, a nouveau-riche mongrel with ideas above his station. At the vet, however, he falls in love with a little patchwork puppy called Chotaro. A less successful follow-up to the previous year's **I Am a Cat**; some of the same team from that show adapted Hisashi Inoue's novel *The Life of Don Matsugoro*, changing the title to imply a connection that simply wasn't there.

I DREAM OF MIMI *

1997. JPN: *Buttobi CPU.* Video. DIR: Masamitsu Hidaka. SCR: Atsuhiro Tomioka. DES: Yuriko Senba. ANI: Yuriko Senba. MUS: N/C. PRD: Pink Pineapple, KSS. 30 mins. x 3 eps.

In this erotic comedy based on the *Young Animal* strip from **Area 88**–creator Kaoru Shintani, a hapless boy finds himself in possession of Mimi, a new model of "sexy computer." Biocomputer Mimi must fend off romantic rivals such as the Nac sisters and the superpowered Performa Girl, while her man Akira looks on shyly like the hero of **Handmaid May**, **Metal Angel Marie**, and any number of similar geek-meets-love-toy shows. **N**

I GIVE MY ALL

1987. JPN: *Minna Agechau.* AKA: *I'll Do It with Anyone; Everybody's Doing It.* Video. DIR: Osamu Uemura. SCR: Yutaka Takahashi. DES: Takumi Tsukasa. ANI: Takafumi Hayashi. MUS: Hiromoto Tobisawa. PRD: Animate Film, JC Staff. 45 mins.

Mutsuro has been forced to take a "ronin" year off to study for retaking his university entrance exams. Resorting to self-abuse in his lonely room, he attracts the attentions of lonely neighbor Yuno, the bored daughter of a rich corporate magnate. The two are soon in bed together, though Yuno's interfering grandmother decides that she should make an honest man out of Mutsuro and give him a job in Daddy's company. Based on the 1982 manga by Hikari Yuzuki, serialized in *Young Jump*, this well-animated soft-core story premiered on a double bill with **Digital Devil Story**. **N**

I LIKE THE NANIWABUSHI

1982. JPN: *Naniwabushi Daisuki.* TV series. DIR: Takashi Sawada. SCR: Kiyohiro Yamamoto. DES: N/C. ANI: Norio Takahashi. MUS: N/C. PRD: Kansai TV, Tohan Planning, Fuji TV. 54 mins.

Two stories that mix animation with *naniwabushi* (storytelling accompanied by shamisen playing). One is a tale of General Nogi, the famous suicide, visiting the shrines at Ise on his way to Nagoya, while his wife is mistaken for a commoner as she books into a hotel. The second story is of a sumo wrestling trainee, ridiculed by his fellows, who trains hard and avenges himself—the standard clichés of a sports anime, just with plink-plonky music on top of it.

I LOVE YOU *

2001. JPN: *Sukidayo.* Video. DIR: Haruo Okawara. SCR: Rokurota Makabe. DES: Aoi Kimizuka. ANI: Haruo Okawara. MUS: Yoshi. PRD: YOUC, Digital Works

(Vanilla Series). 30 mins. x 2 eps. Jun and Hijiri, his Sᴇxғʀɪᴇɴᴅ, are enjoying themselves in bed when Jun realizes that he wants more to life than casual encounters. He yearns for true romance, and anime tradition dictates that likely candidates will arise in the form of his childhood friends, Ren and her sister Rina. He is mistaken for a pervert on a train by Mina, a third girl who turns out to be the younger sister of the others, who was separated from them by the conditions of their parents' divorce. Sub–Lᴏᴠᴇ Hɪɴᴀ romantic entanglements ensue, with plenty of sex, until Jun eventually ends up in bed with Mina—all antagonism between them is dispelled when she is helping out in her mother's coffee shop and is consequently dressed as a waitress. However, their relationship begins to turn sour when old photos reveal that Mina may not be who she says she is—she looks far too young in the old pictures to be the person that she claims to be. Another entry in the Vᴀɴɪʟʟᴀ Sᴇʀɪᴇs. ⒧Ⓝ⒱

I SAW THE LAZYBONES
1988. JPN: Namakemono o Miteta. Video. DIR: Akinori Nagaoka, Masami Furukawa. SCR: Takashi Murakami. DES: Takashi Murakami. ANI: Kinichiro Suzuki. MUS: N/C. PRD: Toei, Agent 21. 30 mins. x 2 eps.
In this short comedy based on a gag manga by Takashi Murakami originally serialized in Young Jump, a koala robs a bank to help poverty-stricken pandas. Listed as a "movie" in some Japanese sources, even though the package clearly states "original video anime."

ICHI THE KILLER *
2002. JPN: Koroshiya Ichi. AKA: Ichi The Killer The Animation: Episode Zero. Video. DIR: Shinji Ishidaira. SCR: Sakichi Sato. DES: Tsuneo Ninomiya. ANI: Masanori Ohara. MUS: Yu Takase. PRD: Shogakukan, Amuse. 50 mins.
Quiet schoolboy Ichi must put up with constant abuse from his classmates, but never does anything to stand up to them. Beaten and attacked at school,

he then returns home to a tongue lashing from his parents who criticize him harshly before running off to their bedroom for another noisy sex session with ropes and whips. Ichi stoically endures such torments until the night he finds a wounded animal in the road. He goes to help it, but the confused creature bites him, causing Ichi to snap. Years of pent-up aggression come to the fore as he literally kicks the animal inside out, discovering in the process that he gets a thrill out of dealing death.

Some years later, an amnesiac Ichi is being cared for in a mental asylum. All memories of his earlier life having been blocked out, he has been forced to start again from scratch and has the mind of a six-year-old in an adult body. His parole officer Kakihara finds him work placement at a karate hall, hoping that the discipline of a martial art will help bring Ichi back into society. Instead, it sets him on a series of encounters that reawaken the psychopath within, setting him up for a life as a brutal assassin.

A prequel spin-off of Takashi Miike's violent movie Ichi the Killer (2001), itself based on a manga by Hideo Yamamoto, Ichi refashions the tropes of teen revenge for a new generation who has never heard of Uʀᴏᴛsᴜᴋɪᴅᴏᴊɪ or, for that matter, the original Count of Monte Cristo that informed Gᴀɴᴋᴜᴛsᴜᴏᴜ. However, this story ditches fantastic or science fictional trappings in favor of the methods of live-action cinema: shaky-cam effects and moments of surreal magic realism to illustrate Ichi's inner torment. Limited animation is compensated by the liberal use of red paint; there is a great deal of violence. Miike himself voices the pivotal role of Kakihara. ⒧Ⓝ⒱

ICZER-ONE *
1985. JPN: Tatakae! Iczer-1; Boken! Iczer-3; Iczer Gal Iczelion. AKA: Fight! Iczer-1; Adventure! Iczer-3; Iczelion; Iczer Saga. Video. DIR: Toshihiro Hirano, Hideaki Hisashi. SCR: Toshihiro Hirano, Arii Emu ("REM"). DES: Toshihiro Hirano, Chuichi Watanabe, Masanori Nishii, Hiroaki Motoigi, Shinji Aramaki,

Yasuhiro Moriki, Takashi Hashimoto. ANI: Narumi Kakinouchi, Masami Obari, Hiroaki Ogami, Masanori Nishii, Takafumi Hashimoto. MUS: Michiaki Watanabe, Takashi Kudo. PRD: AIC, KSS. 30 mins. x 2 eps., 48 mins., 60 mins. x 3 eps., 30 mins. x 2 eps.
An alien ship carrying the survivors of the Cthulhu, a race of female clones, is taken over by the sinister entity Big Gold and heads for Earth. The Cthulhu (hastily and ineptly disguised as "Cutowolf" in early Western publicity to avoid copyright problems) seek a new home, and with Big Gold's malign energy driving them, they decide that Earth will suit them nicely once they kick out the current occupants. One of the Cthulhu, Iczer-One, is willing to fight for Earth but must link up with the right human to help her power her mighty fighting machine, Iczer-Robo. The "right human" is Nagisa Kano, an ordinary Japanese schoolgirl who is so terrified by seeing her parents transformed into alien monsters and her world falling to pieces around her that she can do very little apart from quake in terror. Only when she unleashes the full force of her anger can she power the huge robot, but then she and Iczer-One are an unstoppable combination. The Cthulhu call on all their powers to warp dimensions, transform familiar objects and places into nightmarish threats, and send in gross, drooling monsters. At last, they even throw in Iczer-One's nasty red-haired clone sister, Iczer-Two; but they can't win against the love and trust between Nagisa and Iczer-One, since both are willing to make the ultimate sacrifice to save Earth.

Hirano's dark, dank otherworld was based on a story by Rei Aran, with nightmarish references to the work of H. P. Lovecraft (see Aʀᴍɪᴛᴀɢᴇ III). However, nameless terrors are hampered by the fact that the "unimaginable," once animated, looks merely nasty, but Watanabe's monsters are as well crafted as Aramaki's fabulous robots. The script is loaded with homoerotic subtexts and sexualized cruelty, all the more effective for being less than completely explicit. Nagisa's helpless terror is an understandable reaction to an extreme situation, rather than being an annoying character trait played up by writer and actress in the mistaken belief that helplessness is cute, and Iczer-One is the ideal heroine—brave, understanding, and determined. A shameless steal from the ending of *Superman II* doesn't jibe but makes for a rather touching finale in which Nagisa, having given her all to save the world, is rewarded by getting her old life back and forgetting everything else, including the friend who would have died to save her.

Hirano returned to the concept with *Iczer-3* (1990), toning down the violence but keeping the fan-service nudity. Big Gold was defeated but left many of her progeny still at large in the galaxy. Iczer-One has tracked them down and destroyed all but one, Neos Gold. After a terrible battle, both are wounded and agree to a truce to heal, after which they'll settle things with a final fight. As Iczer-One withdraws to recoup her strength, Neos Gold cheats by sending her cohorts to soften up Earth for her attack, so the Cthulhu send prepubescent Iczer-3 to defend the planet until "big sister" recovers. With a descendant of Nagisa Kano and the crew of an Earth battle cruiser, Iczer-3 attempts to hold off the enemy with the Power of Cute. A helium-powered performance from wrestler Cuty Suzuki in the leading role took what had been a tale of nameless horrors into the realms of high camp, grounded by the reappearance of the two older Iczer clones for the final battle.

Hirano reworked the concept again as an armored-girl-team show in the manner of **BUBBLEGUM CRISIS**, first as a manga and then for the two-part video *Iczelion* (1994). For this resurrection, production moved to KSS, with Hashimoto and Masanori Nishii joining Hirano for design work. Nagisa Kai is an ordinary teenager until fate intervenes and makes her the chosen combat partner of an intelligent

Iczer

battlesuit. Iczel robots, useful entities in their own right, become Iczelion battlesuits when "fused" with their girl operatives in a nude transformation sequence. Together with three other young women, Nagisa must save Earth from subjugation by an invading alien army headed by Chaos and Cross, who have so far swept across the galaxy defeating all in their path. At first Nagisa is too terrified to fight and even separates from her Iczel in an attempt to escape, but when her friends at school are threatened, she decides she must save them. Once more, affection between girls wins the day, though the explicit lesbian overtones of the first series have been edged into the background. The two later incarnations lack the dark power of the first, moving the original concept in less adventurous directions, but the series remains a firm favorite with older fans. *Iczer-3* was subsequently renamed *Iczer Reborn* in a 2003 U.S. DVD release—a smart move that helped offset some of the numerical confusion. **LNV**

IDOL ANGEL WELCOME YOKO
1990. JPN: *Idol Tenshi Yokoso Yoko*. AKA: *Hello Yoko*. TV series. DIR: Tetsuro Amino. SCR: Takeshi Shudo. DES: Studio Live. ANI: Sanae Kobayashi. MUS: Hideyuki Tanaka. PRD: TSC, Quest, Ashi Pro, TV Tokyo. 25 mins. x 43 eps.
A unique addition to the magical-girl genre of **CREAMY MAMI** and its ilk, in which real-life idol Yoko Tanaka, along with her anime alter ego (also called Yoko Tanaka, but with different Chinese characters spelling out the name), must solve problems and get to the concerts on time.

IDOL FIGHTER SU-CHI-PAI *
1996. Video. AKA: *Idolfight Sweetypie II*. DIR: Yasunori Ide. SCR: Yasunori Ide. DES: Kenichi Sonoda, Yoshiko Sakurai. ANI: Kunihiro Abe. MUS: N/C. PRD: Darts, Domu. 30 mins.
All Sweetypie has to do is wave her Sweetystick, and she turns into an avenging angel of love and justice. And with bondage-freak Cherrypie, alien superhero Milkypie ("Milky Change!"), emissary from Peachland, Peachypie, and cyborg warrior Lemonpie ("Lemonade Transfer!"), you can bet that the streets are safe. One of many computer-game spin-offs (such as **GRADUATION** or **BATTLE TEAM LAKERS EX**) that, perhaps wisely, dumped the gameplay

and merely reassigned the characters to a more interesting situation. In this case, the stars of an obscure strip computer game, notable only for designs by GUNSMITH CATS' Kenichi Sonoda, are reassigned roles in a spoof of SAILOR MOON. As with the STREET FIGHTER II franchise, there was no *Sweetypie "I"* in anime form, a fact lampooned in the show's subtitle: "Somehow this feels like the first episode."

IDOL OF DARKNESS *
1997. JPN: *Inju Nerawareta Idol.* Video. DIR: Susumu Aran. SCR: N/C. DES: N/C. ANI: Lion Ginan. MUS: N/C. PRD: Pink Pineapple. 45 mins.
Lesbian goings-on as famous idol singer Rie initiates newcomer Ikumi in the pleasures of the flesh, much to the annoyance of her boyfriend, who always suspected the media was a corrupt world. Soon, onstage jealousies lead to the activation of a cursed wooden idol, which leads to more sex. **N**

IDOL PROJECT *
1995. Video. DIR: Yasushi Nagaoka. SCR: Toshimitsu Amano. DES: Noritaka Suzuki. ANI: Masahiko Murata. MUS: Kanji Saito. PRD: KSS. 30 mins. x 4 eps.
Fourteen-year-old Mimu Emilton wants to be an idol singer and applies for the Starland Festival, where the people's next idol will be chosen. Inspired by her hologram pendant, which carries a pep talk from the last idol, Mimu learns from a number of other aspirants the various secrets of being an idol, including the power of a smile and the value of dance. A silly, perky anime based on a computer game in which the player's job was to become the top idol singer.

IF I SEE YOU IN MY DREAMS
1998. JPN: *Yume de Aetara.* AKA: *If I See You in My Dream* [sic]. Video. DIR: Hiroshi Watanabe. SCR: Nao Tokimura. DES: Hiroshi Watanabe, Ryoichi Oki. ANI: Ryoichi Oki. MUS: Shigesato Kanezumi. PRD: JC Staff, Shueisha, TBS, Tokuma Japan Communications. 30 mins. x 3 eps. (v), 8 mins. x 16 eps. (TV).
Twenty-four-year-old Masuo has never really talked to a girl, until the fateful day he meets the pretty Nagisa. As he begins a faltering attempt at seduction, illness finds him in a hospital bed on Christmas Eve, the traditional time for shy Japanese boys to pop the question. Nagisa makes it easier for him by visiting and staying till he confesses his love. Based on Noriyuki Yamahana's manga, serialized in *Business Jump.*

IGANO KABAMARU
1983. TV series. DIR: Tameo Ogawa, Akinori Nagaoka, Tsutomu Shibayama, Keiji Hayakawa, Naoto Hashimoto. SCR: Tokio Tsuchiya, Rei Akimoto, Shigeru Yanagawa, Tomomi Tsutsui. Hirokazu Kobayashi. DES: Akio Hosoya. ANI: Akio Hosoya, Kaworu Hirata, Keiko Yoshimoto. MUS: Toshiyuki Omori. PRD: Tohoku, NTV. 25 mins. x 24 eps.
Kabamaru is a new boy at high school, who cannot reveal to anyone that he is really the scion of an infamous ninja clan. He helps the kindly Mrs. Okubo, falls in love with her granddaughter, and is forced against his will to use his ninja skills in struggles against other schools, and his own corrupt principal. Yu Azuki, creator of AKANUKE ICHIBAN, wrote this 1983 manga for *Margaret* magazine as a spoof of Mitsuteru Yokoyama's 1961 ninja story *Kagemaru the Ninja* (*Iga no Kagemaru*).

IGPX *
2003. AKA: *Immortal Grand Prix.* TV series. DIR: Koichi Mashimo. SCR: Koichi Mashimo, Yuki Arie. DES: Tomoaki Kado. ANI: Hiroshi Morioka, Shinya Kawatsura, Tomoyuki Kurokawa, Yuki Arie. MUS: Fat Jon, Amon Tobin, Hint, Neotropic, Funki Porcini, Arata Iwashina. PRD: Production IG, Cartoon Network. 5 mins x 5 eps (TV1), 25 mins x 24 eps (TV2), 25 mins. x 2 eps. (v).
Conceived as a coproduction between the Cartoon Network in America and the Japanese studio Production IG, this international collaboration led first to a series of short cartoons about robotic arena combat, replaying many traditions of sports anime with the arrival of a team of rookies who must somehow fight their way to the top.

A second series, directed by Mitsuru Hongo, kept to a traditional half-hour running time, but seemed only loosely related to the original, moving the action to 2049, when the gladiatorial nature of the original *IGPX* has somehow transformed into something more like a car race, taking place in a purpose-built city, surrounded by a 60km track. *IGPX* thus incorporates many elements known to be a success in the merchandising-led world of children's cartoons—the emphasis is on teamwork, but in a sport involving high-tech items, personal robots, and a gameplay that usually revolves around a combat lap, followed by a more traditional race to the finish.

IIZUKA, MASANORI
1965– . Animator and illustrator who debuted on HIGH SCHOOL KIMENGUMI, before becoming an animator and animation checker on many other works, including MAMA IS A FOURTH GRADER and CYBERFORMULA GPX.

IKEDA, HIROSHI
1934– . Born in Tokyo, Ikeda graduated in art from Nihon University in 1959, joining Toei Animation that same year and rising to director within 12 months. His first major work, however, did not appear for almost a decade, with the release of his feature-length adaptation of Shotaro Ishinomori's FLYING GHOST SHIP. He also worked on a number of popular TV shows, including LITTLE WITCH SALLY and SECRET AKKO-CHAN. He became head of Toei's Animation Research Department (a training division) and later became a lecturer in animation at both the Tokyo Polytechnic University and Nihon University Graduate School of Art.

IKENAI BOY
1990. AKA: *The Boy Who Couldn't.* Video. DIR: Hiroshi Uchida. SCR: Satoichi Moriyasu. DES: Toshio Takahashi. ANI:

Toshio Takahashi. MUS: N/C. PRD: JC Staff. 50 mins. x 2 eps.

College boy Shinichi Kamigawa moonlights as the master masseur Doctor K, popular with many young women all around Tokyo for his sexily soothing hands. This anime was based on Yoshihiro Suma's erotic manga in *Business Jump* and features a live-action epilogue from real-life adult video star Ayami Kida, in a futile attempt to make up for the low quality of the rest of the production. **N**

IKKI TOUSEN *

2003. JPN: *Bakunyu Hyper Battle Ikki Tosen*. AKA: *Battle Vixens*; *Strength of a Thousand*; *Dragon Girls*. TV series. DIR: Takashi Watanabe. SCR: Takao Yoshioka. DES: Shinya Hasegawa. ANI: Takashi Wada, Masayoshi Nakaya. MUS: Hiroshi Motokura. PRD: Geneon, AT-X, GENCO, JC Staff, Wani Books. 24 mins. x 13 eps.

Eighteen hundred years after his youthful demise in a Chinese civil war, the legendary warrior Shou Hao is reborn in Japan as Hakufu Sonsaku, a girl with large breasts and a ditzy attitude. She carries her predecessor's soul sealed away in a *magatama*, a comma-shaped jewel of ancient significance, also seen in **BLUE SEED** (as *mitama*) and *Gamera*. Nor is she the only one—many of her high school associates have also come into possession of sealed souls of Chinese warriors, resulting in a long and convoluted series of brawls and feuds between Tokyo high schools. The fighters are destined to relive the struggles and fates of their ancient counterparts unless they can find a way to break the bonds of history.

The events of **GREAT CONQUEST: ROMANCE OF THE THREE KINGDOMS** are reenacted in modern-day Tokyo, as ancient heroes of Chinese legend are reincarnated as Japanese schoolgirls—but as with Takashi Miike's live-action *Tennen Shojo Mann* (*DE), there is something ineffably silly about watching the pompous feuds and vendettas of old played out by scrapping

schoolgirls. Where the warriors of old had heralds and imperial messengers, we have e-mail circulars and mobile phones. Unlike most of their viewers, they also seem aware of the histories and backgrounds associated with their names, in a postmodern touch that adds an old-fashioned sense of inevitable destiny. Some embrace the fate of their former incarnations, while others fight against it. They attend seven different high schools in the Kanto area, allowing for an endless round of plot, counterplot, alliance, betrayal, double-, triple-, and quadruple-cross, and of course a school uniform to suit every preference, because there are actually those who care whether panties flash from under a sailor suit or a tartan skirt—this is a big deal in an anime which cares about underpants as much as **AGENT AIKA**. There are guys who fight as well, because the Japanese state school system is coeducational and the target audience needs an identification point. Yuji Shiokaze's manga, originally serialized in monthly *Comic Gamu*, was published in English as *Battle Vixens*, leading to the release of this show under that title in several territories.

Even in times past, the *Three Kingdoms* story contained subtexts of reincarnation and retribution. Although set at the close of the Han dynasty (3rd-century A.D.), elements of the tale suggested that the last Han emperor was actually the reincarnation of the *first* Han emperor, getting his just desserts for executing three loyal generals four hundred years earlier. Compare to **SUIKODEN**. **LNV**

IKKIMAN

1986. JPN: *Hagane Q Choji Ikkiman*. AKA: *Steel Q Armored Child Ikkiman*. TV series. DIR: Nobutaka Nishizawa. SCR: Haruya Yamazaki, Kenji Terada, Yoshiyuki Suga. DES: Takashi Saijo. ANI: Masahiko Imai, Michio Shindo. MUS: Seiji Yokoyama. PRD: Toei, NTV. 25 mins. x 32 eps.

A bizarre combination of sports anime and martial arts, as Ikki leaves behind

the woman who broke his heart in Hokkaido, and comes to 21st-century Tokyo to seek his fortune at the violent baseball-fighting game Battle Ball. Gate-crashing a game between the Terran team, Blue Planets, and the off-world team, Satano Blackies, he steps up to bat and is soon the star player. Based on a manga by Yasuo Tanami and Kazuo Takahashi, serialized in *Shonen Magazine*, among others.

IKKYU

1975. JPN: *Ikkyu-san*. TV series. DIR: Kimio Yabuki, Tetsuo Imazawa, Hideo Furusawa, Shinya Miyazaki. SCR: Masaki Tsuji, Satoshi Ishida, Tajio Tamura, Keisuke Fujikawa, Tomoko Konparu, Hiroshi Yamaura, Tomomi Tsutsui. DES: Hiroshi Wagatsuma. ANI: Yasu Ishiguro, Shinya Miyazaki, Takeshi Shirato. MUS: Seiichiro Uno. PRD: TV Asahi, Toei. 25 mins. x 296 eps. (TV), 15 mins. (m1), 15 mins. (m2), 25 mins. x 26 eps. (*Ikkyu-san*).

After the Ashikaga shogun unifies Japan, the emperor's son Sengikumaru is sent to the Yasukuni Shrine by family politics—his maternal grandfather opposed the Ashikaga in the conflict. Shaving his head and changing his name to Ikkyu, he tries to live as a good monk, though taking any opportunity he can to outwit the greedy merchant Kikyoya, his daughter Yayoi, and even Yoshimitsu Ashikaga himself.

The series received a very limited partial broadcast, as *Ikkyu the Little Monk*, on U.S. local TV for the Japanese community, with English subtitles. The character had two short theatrical outings: *Ikkyu and Princess Yancha* (1978), in which Ikkyu must talk a tomboy into behaving in a more ladylike manner before her habit of calling herself by the boy's name Tsuyumaru and attacking shogun Yoshimitsu Ashikaga with a wooden sword gets her into trouble. This was followed by *Ikkyu: It's Spring!* (1981), in which further feudal fun ensued.

An unrelated 26-episode series, *Ikkyu-san* (1978), was a baseball drama on the rival Fuji TV directed by

Toshifumi Takizawa, based on a STAR OF THE GIANTS–influenced manga by Shinji Mizushima.

IKUHARA, KUNIHIKO

1964– . Born in Tokushima Prefecture, he joined Toei Animation after graduating in graphic design from Komatsu City College. Served as an assistant to Junichi Kato on shows such as MAPLE TOWN before achieving renown as the show runner for later seasons of SAILOR MOON. Left Toei in 1996 to form Be-Papas, a small production team whose most famous creation is UTENA. Spent two years in California at the American Film Institute, while continuing to work on non-anime output for Be-Papas.

I'LL/CKBC *

2002. JPN: I'll Generation Basket. AKA: I'll /Crazy KOUZO Basketball Club. Video. DIR: Itsuro Kawasaki. SCR: Miyuki Takahashi. DES: Kaname Sekiguchi. ANI: Kaname Sekiguchi. MUS: N/C. PRD: Mamiko Namazue, Aniplex, SME Visual Works. 30 mins. x 2 eps.
Akane Tachibana and Hitonari Hiiragi are two former basketball rivals forced to cooperate when Hitonari is transferred to Akane's school in order to play on its basketball team. However, Hitonari's parents expect better things for their son and hope to move him to an even better team, threatening to turn them into rivals once more. Based on the 14-volume manga by Hiroyuki Asada, which ran for nine years, from the time when SLAM DUNK and HOOP DAYS were new, until 2004, this is yet another of those short-lived anime releases designed to reawaken interest in a franchise as it nears the end of its days. As so often occurs with such ventures, the story suffers from being compressed into an hour, despite attractive design work.

I'M GONNA BE AN ANGEL *

1999. JPN: Tenshi ni Naru Mon. AKA: Let Me Be an Angel; Make Me an Angel. TV series. DIR: Hiroshi Nishikori. SCR: Mamiko Ikeda, Masashi Sogo. DES:

Hiromi Kato. ANI: Hiromi Kato. MUS: Yoshikazu Suo. PRD: Studio Pierrot, TV Tokyo. 25 mins. x 26 eps.
As is the way with so many anime children, Yusuke's father goes away on business and leaves him at home alone (there is no sign of his mother). En route to school, he lands on top of a naked girl with a halo. The "accidental kiss" she receives makes him her husband in her eyes—for similar inadvertent betrothals see URUSEI YATSURA and PHOTON. Yusuke runs a mile but is shocked to discover that his new "wife" Noelle is a new transfer student at his school. Unable to shake her off, he gains a new extended family of supernatural creatures, including a father modeled on FRANKENSTEIN, vampiric elder brother Gabriel, dark-elf sister Ruka, and invisible older sister Sara. The grandmother matriarch, even more opposed to the marriage than Yusuke himself, tries to oppose his presence, though since they have moved into and converted his own house into a supernatural dwelling, this is not so easy. Meanwhile, Noelle is at the center of another anime love polygon with Despair, who wants her for himself, Yusuke, still lusting after girl-next-door Natsume, and the enigmatic Michael, whose book of dreams writes the closure of each episode. A hyper-cute, hyper-silly TV series that crashes together innumerable clichés of unwelcome-guest and magical-girlfriend shows, along with the traditions of school dramas and a brighter, breezier rip-off of the Addams Family.

I'M TEPPEI

1977. TV series. DIR: Tadao Nagahama, Shigetsugu Yoshida, Yoshifumi Kondo, Hiroshi Fukutomi, Tsutomu Shibayama. SCR: Seiji Matsuoka, Shunichi Yukimuro, Soji Yoshikawa, Hirokazu Mizude. DES: Tetsuya Chiba. ANI: Daikichiro Kusunobe. MUS: Michiaki Watanabe. PRD: Shinei, Nippon Animation, Fuji TV. 25 mins. x 28 eps.
Fortune hunters Hiromi Uesugi and his son Teppei are arrested for damaging a field in the Shinshu mountains,

though they claim they are only following the directions to buried treasure from an ancient map. Teppei blows up the police station to aid his father's escape, and the case reaches the local newspaper, where it is read by estranged members of the Uesugi clan. The prodigal clan members return, and Teppei, who has grown up in the wild in the company of animals and his semicivilized father, has trouble adjusting to the genteel culture of the Rin Academy school where he is sent.
Based on a 1973 manga in Shonen Magazine by TOMORROW'S JOE–creator Tetsuya Chiba, I'm Teppei was soon taken off the air due to low ratings, despite featuring storyboards from future WHISPER OF THE HEART–director Yoshifumi Kondo.

IMAZAWA, TETSUO

1940– . Born in Oita Prefecture, he graduated from Nakazu High School and went to Tokyo to work in publishing as a graphic designer. Part-time work for animation companies soon helped pay the bills, and his name appears on the credits for IKKYU and the new series of STAR OF THE GIANTS (1977). He subsequently joined Studio Juno full-time, and his works as director include GODMARS, HERMES, and COO OF THE FAR SEAS.

IMMA YOJO: EROTIC TEMPTRESS *

1994. JPN: Inma Yojo. AKA: Lust-Beast Fairies. Video. DIR: Yukiyoshi Makino. SCR: Tsukasa Tomii. DES: Kazushi Iwakura. ANI: Kazushi Iwakura. MUS: Takeo Nakazawa. PRD: Pink Pineapple, KSS. 45 mins. x 5 eps.
Witchery and bondage as Maya wanders a fantasy landscape inhabited by depraved rapists. She enters a town where the ruling tyrant dwells in a "tower of pleasures" and sends out young ruffians to procure women, whose juices he requires in the manufacture of a dangerous drug. Before long, Maya is captured and abused by a gang of men before leaving to experience several more episodes of assault, including one at the hands

of robot women, the seduction of an unsuspecting knight, and even a retelling of one of the oldest JAPANESE FOLK TALES, as two witches lure passers-by to their deaths on a haunted mountain pass. Not to be confused with the COOL DEVICES story *Slave Warrior Maya*, or indeed with ROSE OF VERSAILLES, with which it shares some look-alike characters and costumes, though the costumes don't stay on for long. ⬤NⓋ

IMMORAL SISTERS *

2001. JPN: *Ai Shimai*. Video. DIR: Roku Iwata, Hideo Ura. SCR: Osamu Kudo, Momoi Sakura. DES: Rin Shin. ANI: Yuki Iwai. MUS: Chikutaru Roman. PRD: Elf, Office Take Off, Pink Pineapple. 30 mins. x 3 eps. (v1), 30 mins. x 2 eps. (v2), 30 mins. x 4 eps. (v3).
The president of the Nogawa Estate Agency sends his son Taketo to negotiate a compensation claim by Yukie Kitazawa. Yukie was injured in a traffic accident, and Nogawa hopes to settle out of court before Yukie's husband returns home from a business posting abroad. However, Taketo's method of negotiating involves drugging Yukie and then photographing himself molesting her unconscious form. Using the photographs as blackmail, he demands an impossibly high settlement from her, forcing her to become his sex slave by way of payment in lieu. His father then approaches Yukie's daughters Rumi and Tomoko and has them for himself.

Before long, Taketo is living in sin with Yukie, and also abusing the two girls. When Yukie's husband Kunihiko unexpectedly returns, there are mixed feelings in the household. Taketo and Yukie try to keep their affair secret, Tomoko wants everyone to be one big happy family, while Rumi tries to engineer her "real" father's departure (although the story implies she may be a stepdaughter, once again pandering to the not-quite-incest subgenre of so much porn anime) so she can return to the only "norm" she knows. On discovering his family members' secret, Kunihiko confesses that he

has harbored a secret lust for his own daughter Tomoko for some time, and Tomoko duly offers herself to him to preserve order. These two serials, *Ai Shimai 1: Coupling's Fruit* (3 parts), and *Ai Shimai 2* (2 parts), were later reedited to make the compilation two-parter *Ai Shimai: Coupling's Fruit Juice* (2004).

For the third series, released in 2004 as *Ai Shimai Tsubomi*, aka. *Ai Shimai 3*, aka *Ai Shimai: Make Me Wet*, aka *Immoral Sisters 3: Blossoming*, the title remains but the characters change. This time the "immoral sisters" are Kotono and Suzue Miyatsuji, students at a school where their mother is the principal. They both yearn for fellow student Shoichi, who will be expelled from the school if he fails his exams again. Shoichi, however, is more interested in the school nurse, Maiko. Maiko suggests that he cheat in the exams by stealing a disc containing the questions. But while he is trying to do so, he is caught by Kotono and duly rapes her in order to ensure her silence. When did it get to be so hard just to study? Based on the 2000 computer game by Elf. ⬤NⓋ

IMMORAL WIFE

2005. AKA: *Immoral Wife: Woman's Hidden Sexual Nature*. Video. DIR: Linda, Tsubasa Kazematsuri. SCR: Jiro Muramatsu. DES: Linda. ANI: Hikaru Tojo. MUS: N/C. PRD: Sunny Side Up, SS Studio, T&B, Milky. 30 mins. x 2 eps.
Natsumi tires of her promiscuous life of multiple partners and sexual experiments and settles down into a quiet marriage. But it's not long before she finds herself secretly yearning for the good old days. Based on an erotic manga by "Linda," and released on Christmas Day 2005: ho ho ho. ⬤NⓋ

IMMORALITY *

2004. JPN: *In no Hoteishiki*. AKA: *Equation of the Immoral*. Video. DIR: Kanzaburo Oda. SCR: Sosoro Masaoka. DES: Eri Kohagura. ANI: Eri Kohagura. MUS: N/C. PRD: Milky. 30 mins. x 2 eps.
New school nurse Sayoko Saeki has an innocent face and a voluptuous body. She begins as an object of fantasy

for the boys at the school, but is later revealed as a succubus who drains men dry. Based on an erotic thriller by Azuki Kurenai. ⬤NⓋ

IMMORALITY WARS

1998. JPN: *Inju Dai Kessen*. AKA: *Lust-Beast Great Battle*. Video. DIR: Iwao Zumen, Tai Kikumoto. SCR: Atsuhito Sugita. DES: Shimendoji. ANI: N/C. MUS: N/C. PRD: KSS, Pink Pineapple. 47 mins.
A demonic rapist plagues Japan (for a change), repeatedly dividing itself and reforming in different places. In order to stop Japan becoming "a hell of mad sex," the government initiates a sex sting operation, predictably encouraging attractive young agents to submit to the rapist for the benefit of world peace and the pornographic consumer. ⬤NⓋ

IN A DISTANT TIME

2004. JPN: *Harukanaru Toki no Naka De: Hachiyo Sho*. AKA: *HaruToki; In A Distant Time: Hachiyo Chapter*. TV series. Video. DIR: Aki Tsunaki, Nagisa Miyazaki. SCR: Junko Okazaki. DES: Akemi Hayashi, Kenichi Onuki, Kyoko Kotani. ANI: Noriko Otake. MUS: Masanori Sato. PRD: Yumeta Company, Hakusensha, Haruka Production Ctee, KOEI, TV Tokyo. 24 mins. x 26 eps. (TV), 25 mins. x 3 eps. (v).
Akane Motomiya is sixteen, with red hair and a generous heart. She's popular but has two particular friends, both boys—fourteen-year-old blond cutie Shimon Nagareyama, a junior-high student who looks up to her, and fellow redhead Tenma Morimura, aged seventeen but in her grade at school; compare to similar tensions in ESCAFLOWNE. She lives an ordinary life until, on the way to high school with her friends, she hears voices coming from nowhere and is suddenly dragged down an old well. She finds herself alone in a strange world that resembles the Japan she's seen in history books. This is the land of Kyo, and she is recognized by its people as the Priestess of the Guardian Dragon, whose special powers can

protect Kyo in its hour of need. Kyo is under attack from demons led by Akram, a rather charming devil despite the mask he always wears and his virulent hatred of the people of Kyo.

Before long, Akane has acquired a bodyguard of eight handsome men, the Hachiyo, each with his own talents, hair color, and backstory, and each totally devoted to the well-being of the Maiden of the Guardian Dragon—compare to THE HAKKENDEN. Although Akane is worried about her friends, scared, and not at all sure how she can help, she begins to influence events just by being herself. Her bravery and compassion begin to change the hearts of those around her—even the demons, and especially Akram. Created by KOEI and based on a manga by Toko Mizuno from monthly *Comic Lala* magazine, the anime's real roots are in a dating sim game for girls launched in 1999 and still selling. The makers claim it "may be" the first anime based on a girls' dating sim, obviously hoping this element of originality will gloss over any perceived similarities with FUSHIGI YUGI, INU YASHA, or the manga *Red River*. A two-part video spin-off *(HTnNd: Ajisai Yumegatari)* was also released in 2004. Tsunaki has also worked as an animation director on two POKÉMON movies as a character designer, and has directed several of KOEI's *NeoRomance* game series.

IN PRAISE OF JUDO

1974. JPN: *Judo Sanka*. TV series. DIR: Shigetsugu Yoshida, Masami Hata, Tetsuo Imazawa, Hiroshi Fukutomi, Hideo Takayashiki. SCR: Haruya Yamazaki, Tsunehisa Ito, Akio Matsuzaki. DES: Hiroshi Kaizuka. ANI: Takao Kasai, Yoshiaki Kawajiri. MUS: Yukio Takai. PRD: Nippon TV, Tokyo Movie Shinsha, Madhouse. 25 mins. x 27 eps.

This was the last of the TMS sports-themed anime, ending a line that began with STAR OF THE GIANTS. Tosshinta Tomoe grows up by the rough seas of Sotobo in Chiba Prefecture. He goes to high school where he

decides to follow in the footsteps of his divorced mother, Teruko, a former judo champion. As with every other sports story, our hero is trained by a tough but kind coach who only wants the best for him, and he eventually faces up to an opponent who has sworn revenge on the previous generation—in this case, a male judoist defeated by Tomoe's mother in her fighting days. The series was taken off the air due to low ratings before the more touching later episodes of Hiroshi Kaizuka's manga could be adapted. Compare to YAWARA.

IN THE BEGINNING *

1992. JPN: *Tezuka Osamu no Kyuyaku Seisho Monogatari*. AKA: *Osamu Tezuka's Old Testament*. TV series. DIR: Osamu Dezaki. SCR: Osamu Tezuka. DES: Osamu Tezuka, Shinji Seya. ANI: Masaki Yoshimura, Akio Sugino, Junji Kobayashi, Hideaki Shimada. MUS: Katsuhisa Hattori. PRD: NTW, RAI, Tezuka Pro. 25 mins. x 26 eps.

In 1984, the Italian RAI channel approached ASTRO BOY–creator Tezuka and asked him to make a series of Bible stories for this international coproduction that were closer to the originals than the apocryphal SUPERBOOK: VIDEO BIBLE. Tezuka threw himself into adapting his earlier manga version of the *Old Testament*, even to the extent of working as a humble animator on the *Noah's Ark* episode. The series was not completed until 1992, long after the death of its creator, and though it was soon screened in Italy, Germany, and the U.S., it did not receive a Japanese broadcast until 1997, when it was dumped on the WOWOW satellite channel. Coro, a sloe-eyed fox, acts as the viewpoint character for the entire series, witnessing the Fall of Man, the Flood, the rise of King David, and other major events. There was simply no time to allow for the many minor stories included in *Superbook*.

INCONTINENT HELENA

2005. JPN: *Daishikkin Helena*. Video. DIR: Daifuku Suginami. SCR: Sekiro

Kamatsuchi. DES: Daifuku Suginami. ANI: Daifuku Suginami. MUS: Yoshi. PRD: YOUC, Digital Works (Vanilla Series). 30 mins. x 2 eps.

In the 5th-century A.D., sisters Theodora and Helena of the Burgundian tribe see their homeland invaded by soldiers of the Merovingians. Fleeing the mass rape of the Burgundian women after the Merovingian victory, warrior-princess Theodora plans to commit suicide, but upon hearing that the demure Helena is still alive resolves to help her. Julianus, the Merovingian commander, is impressed by Theodora's haughty bearing and alabaster beauty, but he is the sort of person (because this is *that* sort of anime) who wants to see beautiful women degraded and conquered.

However, his methods of achieving this are, at least for this genre of anime, remarkably original. He makes her the leader of his armies and sends her out to conquer other lands in the Merovingian name, but cruelly neglects to mention that all the while he is using her sister Helena as his sex toy. She discovers the truth upon her return, whereupon a series of abuses ensue. Considering the title, it's a fair guess that enemas may be involved. Our rendering of the proper names in this Dark Age erotic anime are mere guesswork—they might be Merovingians, but they might equally be Melvins … historical accuracy is not really a deal-breaker in this sort of show. Part of the VANILLA SERIES. As we went to press, this video was announced as forthcoming in the U.S. under the title *Elfen Laid*, a punning reference to ELFEN LIED. ●⊕NV

INFINITE RYVIUS

1999. JPN: *Mugen no Ryvius*. TV series. DIR: Goro Taniguchi, Akihiko Nishiyama. SCR: Yosuke Kuroda. DES: Hisashi Hirai. ANI: Yoichi Ueda, Asako Nishida. MUS: Katsuhisa Hattori. PRD: Sunrise, TV Tokyo. 25 mins. x 26 eps. (TV), ca. 6 mins. x 6 eps. (Internet).

An EVANGELION clone set in a solar system 80 years after a solar flare has immersed the system in a massive plasma field that links all the planets like a nervous system. Troubled youth Koji Aibo (who looks just like *Evangelion*'s Shinji) is lured into a quest by the enigmatic Neya (a girl who looks like *Evangelion*'s Rei) to sail to the heart of the plasma field in the titular ship. The series was also an early pioneer in the spread of Internet downloads, when six Flash animation shorts—entitled *Infinite Ryvius Illusion* (JPN: *Mugen no Ryvius Illusion*, aka *Ryvius Illusion*)—parodying the series were put online for fans. Each was divided into four sub-episodes (six for the last episode) which were selectable from within the main episode, and which generally featured ongoing storylines. These were subsequently included as extras in the DVD releases.

INGOKU BYOUTO *

2002. JPN: *Ingoku Byoto*. AKA: *Obscene Prison Ward*. Video. DIR: Norihiko Nagahama. SCR: Rokurota Makabe. DES: MIE. ANI: MIE. MUS: Yoshi. PRD: YOUC, Digital Works (Vanilla Series). 30 mins. Junichi Shiozaki is a specialist in the digestive system, posted to one of the best hospitals in Japan. Those familiar with the "nursing" subgenre of Japanese animation will know exactly what this is going to mean—see NIGHT SHIFT NURSES. After successfully saving the life of a prominent politician, Junichi "celebrates" by raping nurse Yayoi Narumi. Yayoi resists him at first but soon learns to enjoy being abused, promising to be his sex slave. Meanwhile, new arrival Serika is the daughter of the hospital owner, who developed a crush on Junichi when she was a patient and he was a young intern. Junichi, however, despises Serika for her privileged upbringing and sees to it that she is implicated in a series of fake accidents and incidents at the hospital, hoping thereby to ensure that he gets to be the next hospital director instead of her. In a tradition lifted from other hospital anime and TV dramas, Junichi is a brilliant surgeon who truly loves his work but appears to lack any feeling for the patients themselves, or indeed the

many nurses he molests. Based on a computer game by Girls Software, and part of the VANILLA SERIES. **L N V**

INITIAL D

1998. TV series. DIR: Shin Misawa. SCR: Hiroshi Ashida, Nobuaki Kishima. DES: Noboru Furuse. ANI: Noboru Furuse. MUS: Ryuichi Katsumata. PRD: Fuji TV, Prime Direction, OB. 25 mins. x 26 eps. (TV1), 25 mins. x 13 eps. (TV2), 114 mins. (m), 25 mins. x 24 eps. (TV3), 40 mins. (v1), 27 mins. x 2 eps. (v2).
In a blighted, soulless town north of Tokyo in Gunma Prefecture, disaffected youths drag souped-up cars in illegal street races. Seventeen-year-old petrol pump attendant Itsuki dreams of saving up enough to buy his own set of wheels and join the Akina Speed Stars gang, fellow garage worker Iketani boasts of his prowess, and their manager occasionally regales them with tall tales about the fastest man on the mountain. This shadowy figure is actually their shy friend Takumi, who breaks the speed limit each dawn to keep the deliveries fresh for his father's tofu shop, enjoying the beginnings of a romance with Natsuki, a local girl who has a secret—she has an older man as a lover, one who gives her expensive gifts in an instance of "subsidized dating."

Replaying the semifantastic road mythologies of BOMBER BIKERS OF SHONAN and his own earlier LEGEND OF ROLLING WHEELS, Shuichi Shigeno's human interest manga in *Young Magazine* about boys and their toys was snapped up on the cusp of the revolution in digital animation. Featuring car magazine test-driver Keiichi Tsuchiya as a technical adviser, the anime version plays up an anal attention to detail with lectures on driving skill and interior shots of engine activity. Meanwhile the traditional cel animation of the non-racing scenes contrasts jarringly with the computer-animated racing sequences in the style of the PlayStation game *Gran Turismo*. The second season, unsurprisingly rebranded as *Initial D: Second Stage*, begins with Takumi's car trashed

by the rival Akagi Red Suns—a challenge if ever there was for a new duel over who owns the road. When the series gained a 24.5% TV rating, a movie, *Third Stage* (2001), was produced, focusing on the characters' graduation from high school and opportunities to leave the dead-end town of their birth behind. A third season, the confusingly titled *Fourth Stage* (2004) features the boys going professional, forming a Project D in order to challenge rivals outside their home region.

Initial D was an immense success not just in Japan, where such ratings for anime are rare indeed, but across Asia. It was thus not much of a surprise that when the inevitable 2005 live-action remake followed, it was a Cantonese production, starring Taiwan popstar Jay Chou as Takumi, with Natsuki (Ann Suzuki) the only major cast member played by a Japanese performer. Despite the strange sight and sound of Chinese actors pretending to be Japanese—a subject of greater controversy in the same year's *Memoirs of a Geisha*—the movie is a remarkably fair and faithful adaptation of the spirit of the original.

The video *Battle Stage* (2002) simply collects some of the best moments from the racing sequences in the TV series. The two-part *Extra Stage* (2005) was sold as a bonus with the final volume of the *Initial D* manga and features two female characters taking on the infamous Emperor team whose activities caused so much trouble for the boys in earlier volumes.

INMU *

2001. JPN: *Inmu: Ikenie no Utage*. AKA: *Lustful Dream, Inmu: Feast of Victims*; *Banquet of Sacrifice*. Video. DIR: Ran Misumi. SCR: N/C. DES: N/C. ANI: N/C. MUS: N/C. PRD: Pink Pineapple. 29 mins. x 2 eps. (v1), 31 mins. x 2 eps. (v2). The "mysterious witch," voiced in the American release by porn actress Asia Carrera, is a masked figure who is the living embodiment of the maxim that people should be careful what they wish for. In a vengeful, rapacious variant on the initiatress of **Rei Rei** or the Faustian owner of the **Petshop of Horrors**, she narrates a series of short pornographic vignettes, including a schoolgirl who thinks she is being stalked by a fellow train passenger, a snooty fashion designer publicly humiliated by the assistant she spurned, tentacle rape on the school swim team, and a girl obsessed with dolls. Each story is barely fifteen minutes long, hence the presence of four "stories" in only two "episodes," although they are called "nights" here, doubtless intended to give a dreamlike **Arabian Nights** quality to the whole sordid mess. As with many other releases from NuTech, Carrera is joined by fellow stars of adult entertainment on the voice track, and lends her real-life image to the box art—compare to similar gimmicks tried in Japan with the likes of **Adventure Kid**.

A second two-parter, *Inmu 2*, features similar tales. In one, a teenage virgin discovers that her would-be boyfriend has been having sex with a prostitute who looks just like her. In another, a peeping tom finds his fantasies coming to life when he is hospitalized in the care of the nurse he has been stalking. A man becomes possessed by the sexy succubi that inhabit a cursed deck of playing cards. And finally, in what seems to be a compulsory not-quite-incest tale, a man struggles with his confused memories of an affair with his widowed stepmother. **LNV**

INOMATA, MUTSUMI

?– . An illustrator with many credits as an in-betweener and key animator on 1970s shows such as **Urusei Yatsura**, Inomata moved into character design on **City Hunter**. Her work adds a feminine touch to otherwise male-oriented shows such as **Brain Powered**.

INOUE, TOSHIYUKI

1961– . An animator and sketch artist on **Only Yesterday**, among others.

INSTANT HISTORY

1961. jpn: *Otogi Manga Calendar*.

aka: *Manga Fairy Tales*. TV series. dir: Ryuichi Yokoyama, Shinichi Suzuki, Michihiro Matsuyama. scr: Ryuichi Yokoyama, Shinichi Suzuki, Michihiro Matsuyama. des: Ryuichi Yokoyama, Shinichi Suzuki, Michihiro Matsuyama. ani: Ryuichi Yokoyama, Shinichi Suzuki, Michihiro Matsuyama. mus: N/C. prd: Otogi Pro, TBS. 3 mins. x 312 eps. Anime's very first TV series. This black-and-white series of shorts explains various historical events and notable occasions, normally through a framing device of a character who is not aware "what happened on this day in history," discovering firsthand for themselves. Explanations did not always take a cartoon form, but sometimes included photographs and film footage, often taken from the research archives of the *Mainichi Shinbun* newspaper, where director Ryuichi Yokoyama's **Fuku-chan** manga was running at the time. Note: though *IH* was the first TV *series*, it was still not the first anime broadcast on TV. That honor goes to *Three Tales* (1960, *Mitsu no Hanashi*), an experimental anthology broadcast on the NHK channel, comprising adaptations of famous stories—*Oppel and the Elephant* by Kenji Miyazawa (see **Night Train to the Stars**), *Sleepy Town* by Mia Ogawa, and the first anime ever truly broadcast on Japanese TV, *The Third Blood*, by Kosuke Hamada, directed by Keiko Kozonoe.

INTERLUDE *

2004. Video. dir: Tatsuya Nagamine. scr: Akemi Omode. des: Eisaku Inoue, Hideo Horibe, Yokinori Hotani. ani: Eisaku Inoue. mus: Koichiro Kameyama. prd: Toei Animation, Happinet Pictures, Sky PerfecTV. 40 mins. x 3 eps. A nameless protagonist wakes up in a world empty of people, though his solitude is occasionally interrupted by attacks from unexplained demonic creatures. He eventually meets Aya, a dark-haired girl waiting silently at one of the deserted railway stations, driven by an intense state of denial into living each day perfectly normally, as if the rest of the population of the world has

not disappeared. In fact, he and Aya are both part of the Pandora Project, a secret plan that is supposed to allow the human race to survive the end of the world, although it currently has some major flaws, one of which is the existence of Aya herself. An intriguing update of **Wind of Amnesia** for the **Animatrix** generation, focusing on just one of the three heroines from the original game for the DreamCast and PS2.

INTERNAL MEDICINE *

2003. jpn: *Shikkaku Ishi*. Video. dir: Kazuyuki Honda. scr: Kazuyuki Honda. des: Wataru Yamaguchi. ani: Kazuyuki Honda. mus: N/C. prd: Studio Jam, Image Works, Milky. 30 mins. x 2 eps. Makoto is a man on a mission, a doctor-in-training who has sworn vengence on the doctor whose negligence caused the death of his sister. All he knows is that the doctor in question has a scalpel scar on the back of his hand and has a peculiar handshake. He finds the right hospital and takes a job there in order to investigate further (since simply asking or checking his sister's medical records would have made this a short story), uncovering another conspiracy even greater than he previously thought, involving sexual liaisons among the other staff members. In order to investigate the mystery, he sleeps his way to the top, in yet another hospital porn anime—compare to **Night Shift Nurses**. Based on a game created by MBS Truth. **LNV**

INTERSTELLA 5555 *

2003. aka: *Interstella 5555: the 5tory of the 5ecret 5tar 5ystem*. Movie. dir: Kazuhisa Takenouchi, Hirotoshi Nissen, Daisuke Nishio. scr: Thomas Bangalter, Cedric Hervert, Guy-Manuel de Homen-Christo. des: Masaki Sato. ani: Katsumi Tamegai, Keiichi Ichikawa. mus: Daft Punk. prd: Toei. 68 mins. A band of four blue-skinned alien musicians is kidnapped by the Earl of Darkwood, a sinister figure who has leeched off musical talent since at least the time of Mozart—his previous captives include Jimi Hendrix. The band members are taken to Earth and put into disguises to enable them to perform as the "Crescendolls," Darkwood's latest signing. However, a female fan from their homeworld has followed them to Earth, and manages to break the spell on the three male members of the band by shining a light into their eyes. The men escape and later rescue the bass player who remained behind, although their faithful fan dies during the process. Defeating Darkwood and retrieving the discs that contain their original memories, the band returns home.

Electronic pop group Daft Punk comprises writers Bangalter and de Homen-Christo, whose French-speaking childhoods exposed them to the work of Leiji Matsumoto, most obviously his **Captain Harlock** in its *Albator* incarnation. Hiring Matsumoto to supervise the animation of several songs in order to make video promos for their album *Discovery* (2001), the pair later returned with new songs and bridging footage in order to make this dialogue-free musical movie, which gets to recycle Matsumoto's stock beautiful, enigmatic woman; tall, slender hero; and short, squat sidekick one more time, with stunning visuals, lush color, and an attitude charmingly goofy enough to give anime its first pure rock opera. It also sits happily within the tradition of Franco-Japanese co-productions ushered in by **Ulysses 31** a generation earlier.

INU YASHA *

2000. TV series. DIR: Masashi Ikeda, Akira Nishimori. SCR: Masashi Ikeda, Katsuyuki Sumizawa, Takashi Yamada, Akinori Endo. DES: Eiji Suganuma. ANI: Kazuhiro Soeta, Eiji Suganuma, Shinichi Sakuma. MUS: Kaoru Wada. PRD: Nippon TV, Sunrise, Yomiuri TV. 25 mins. x 167 eps. (TV), 60 mins. (sp.), 100 mins. (m1), 99 mins. (m2), 98 mins. (m3), 86 mins. (m4).
Japanese schoolgirl Kagome is pulled into a well by a centipede monster and through a 500-year time tunnel to Japan's civil-war era. She escapes from

Iria

the well to discover Inu Yasha, a half-dog demon, pinned to a nearby tree by the priestess Kikyo. The local villagers believe Kagome to be the reincarnation of Kikyo, and she must reluctantly team up with her predecessor's enemy to hunt down the many shards of the "Jewel of Four Souls," which Inu Yasha originally came to steal.

In the unsure economic climate that began the 21st century, with the **Pokémon** tide ebbing and their **Brave Saga** on hiatus, Sunrise bought into the success of a long-running, best-selling creator, optioning this recent manga from **Ranma ½**'s Rumiko Takahashi. A buddy-story in the tradition of **Ushio and Tora**, with a time-traveling element that bears a close relationship to the creator's earlier **Fire Tripper**. Movie editions followed, including *IY: Love Across Time* (*Jidao o Koeru Omoi*,

2001), *IY: The Castle Beyond the Looking Glass* (*Kagami no Naka no Mugenjo*, 2002), *IY: Swords of an Honorable Ruler* (*Tenka Hado no Ken*, 2003), and *IY: Fire on the Mystic Island* (*Guren no Horaijima*, 2004). The TV special *IY: The Love Song Before We Met* is a prequel, detailing the reasons why Inu Yasha and Kikyo hate each other at the start of the series.

INVASION OF THE BOOBIE SNATCHERS *

2005. JPN: *Bakunyu Shimai*. AKA: *Wet-nurse Sisters*. Video. DIR: Aim. SCR: N/C. DES: Benk, Michitaka Yamamoto. ANI: Aim, Michitaka Yamamoto. MUS: Yoshi. PRD: YOUC, Digital Works (Vanilla Series). 30 mins. x 2 eps.
College student Shinji wakes up one morning to find himself sleeping alongside Yuria, a sexy alien catgirl who has come to learn all about Earth

culture. He teaches her all about sex with him, which is a start, we suppose. Her sister Alissa arrives later on. The girls have large breasts. If nothing else, the authors greatly enjoyed the English release title—another entry in the VANILLA SERIES. **LNV**

IRIA *

1994. JPN: *Iria: Zeiram the Animation*. Video. DIR: Tetsuro Amino. SCR: Tsunehisa Arakawa, Tetsuro Amino. DES: Ryunosuke Otonashi, Masakazu Katsura. ANI: Ryunosuke Otonashi. MUS: Yoichiro Yoshikawa. PRD: Bandai. 35 mins. x 6 eps.

Bounty hunter Iria and her associates are charged with rescuing hostages from a deep-space cargo vessel, only to discover that they are already dead. Her brother Gren dies defending her from Zeiram, an unstoppable bioweapon with a carnivorous noh mask built into his head. As the vengeful Iria chases Zeiram across a marvelously well-realized alien planet, she sees that she has been framed in a conspiracy and has accidentally obtained a pendant containing an incriminating data chip.

Featuring excellent music, wonderful designs inspired by Terry Gilliam films such as *The Adventures of Baron Munchausen* (1988), and a rare anime character design job for VIDEO GIRL AI–creator Masakazu Katsura, *Iria* is an excellent science-fantasy adventure with a truly alien feel, let down only by a mediocre English-language dub.

The series is a prequel to Keita Amemiya's live-action movie *Zeiram* (1991), in which Iria, played by Yuko Moriyama instead of the anime's Aya Hisakawa, pursues Zeiram to Earth. Set three years earlier, the anime is mercifully free of the mundane constraints of the live version (which primarily took place in deserted Japanese streets), leaping from vast space freighters to alien worlds and cities full of bizarre technologies. More characters are introduced, and the handful of rubber monsters in the original are replaced by an army of clones, causing a degree of carnage that would bankrupt a live-action studio. The franchise continued in its live-action format with *Zeiram 2* (1994) and *Zeiram 3* (1997), directed once more by Amemiya. He would also direct *Moon Over Tao* (1997), also starring Moriyama, which moved the general look and feel of *Zeiram* to an unconnected historical-fantasy setting.

IRON LEAGUER

1993. JPN: *Shippu Iron Leaguer*. AKA: *Whirlwind Iron Leaguer*. TV series. DIR: Tetsuro Amino. SCR: Fuyunori Gobu, Akihiko Inari, Noboru Sonekawa. DES: Tsuneo Ninomiya, Kunio Okawara. ANI: Hideyuki Motohashi. MUS: Kaoru Wada. PRD: Sunrise, Studio Nue, TV Tokyo. 25 mins. x 52 eps. (TV), 25 mins. x 5 eps. (v).

An inevitable combination of the sports-anime plotting of CAPTAIN TSUBASA with the giant-robot combat of GUNDAM, as a team of cartoonish armored super-soldiers plays a fusion of soccer and street basketball against cybernetically augmented rivals. With secret attacks, absentee parents, struggles against adversity, and the usual rash of off-the-peg formulae, credited as usual to house pseudonym "Hajime Yadate," the *Iron Leaguer* series survived on video for another handful of episodes but never attained the popularity of its predecessor CYBERFORMULA GPX, in whose sci-fi sports image it was clearly made.

IRON MAN

1991. Video. DIR: Koichi Ishiguro. SCR: Keiji Michiyoshi. DES: Hidetoshi Omori. ANI: Hidetoshi Omori. MUS: N/C. PRD: JC Staff. 50 mins.

Nineteen-year-old university student Yuji decides to become a "host" at a city bar where lonely women will pay a cover charge for the pleasure of his company. He soon becomes a full-fledged male prostitute, claiming all the while that this is all an experiment in order to "better understand the hearts of women." Based on a minor manga in *Comic Morning* by CLIMBING ON A CLOUD–creator Hiroshi Motomiya, this predated the similar GIGOLO by two years. **N**

IRON VIRGIN JUN *

1992. JPN: *Tetsu no Otome (Shojo) Jun*. Video. DIR: Fumio Maezono. SCR: Fumio Maezono, Tsukasa Sunaga, Akihiko Takadera. DES: Mitsuyoshi Munesaki. ANI: Mitsuyoshi Munesaki. MUS: Hiroki Ishikawa. PRD: Triangle Staff, Animaruya. 46 mins.

A sword-and-sorcery romp from DEVILMAN-creator Go Nagai about spunky teenager Jun refusing to accept an arranged marriage and fighting to save her honor. Her mother makes this difficult for her by sending a gang to bring her back and teach her that sex isn't something to be afraid of. After watching the way this porno handles it, you might disagree. **NV**

IRONFIST CHINMI

1988. JPN: *Tekken Chinmi*. AKA: *Ironfist*. TV series, video. DIR: Toshitaro Oba, Kazuhiro Mori. SCR: Junji Takegami, Shikichi Ohashi. DES: Kenichi Onuki. ANI: Kenichi Onuki, Hideyuki Motohashi, Osamu Tsuruyama. MUS: Kei Wakakusa. PRD: Tohoku, TV Asahi. 25 mins. x 12 eps. (TV), 32 mins. (v).

Chinmi is a kung-fu protégé brought to the Dailin temple by the Old Master. There, he learns at the feet of the teacher Ryukai, befriends fellow student Jintan, and plays in the forest with his pet monkey, Goku (see JOURNEY TO THE WEST). He runs errands for the temple, learning all the while about the nature of strength, both physical and mental. This short-lived adaptation of Takeshi Maekawa's 1983 *Shonen Magazine* manga, faithfully depicted the first 12 volumes (all that were available at the time, though the manga itself is still ongoing today) but introduced new characters, kung-fu aspirant Laochu and female foil Lychee, to even out Maekawa's original boy-heavy cast. Chinmi was back the same year with the straight-to-video *Ironfist Chinmi's Kung-fu Picture Book (Tekken Chinmi Kenpo Daizukan)*, a clip-show of his eight best bouts, which, with an emphasis on fighting, outlasted the series that spawned it by a mile.

IRRESPONSIBLE CAPTAIN TYLOR *

1992. JPN: *Musukenin Kancho Tylor.* TV series, video. DIR: Koichi Mashimo. SCR: Hiroyuki Kawasaki, Kenichi Kanemaki, Asami Watanabe. DES: Tomoyuki Hirata. ANI: Tomoyuki Hirata. MUS: Kenji Kawai. PRD: Big West, Tatsunoko Pro, TV Setouchi. 25 mins. x 26 eps. (TV), 40 mins. x 2 eps. (v), 35 mins. x 6 eps. (v), 30 mins. x 2 eps. (v2).

Justy Ueki Tylor is the ultimate slacker, a lazy good-for-nothing who joins the galactic military because he thinks it is the passport to an easy life. Put in charge of a battered hulk called the Soyokaze (Slight Wind), the former captain of which committed suicide due to depression, Tylor finds himself commanding a gang of thugs led by two stuffy officers (named after martial icons Mifune and Fuji) who would like nothing better than to throw him out of the airlock. Tylor, however, continually falls on his feet, accidentally thwarting an enemy double cross by giving them a parcel bomb meant for him, haphazardly steering his way through a battle so that alien warships shoot each other, and even unknowingly volunteering for a suicide mission only to escape from danger by leading his would-be destroyers right into the middle of the Terran fleet. In the tradition of Tylor's contemporary TENCHI MUYO!, our loser hero is also surrounded by a bevy of beauties, including girl-next-door Lieutenant Yuriko Star, adoring alien ruler Queen Azalyn Goza (who likes Tylor, even though her ministers want her to invade his planet), pretty and vacant twins Eimi and Yumi, and alien spy Harumi, who is planted on the Soyokaze to assassinate Tylor but never quite gets around to it.

The character is a cartoon version of Hitoshi Taira, the lazy protagonist of the 1962 live-action movie *Japan's Irresponsible Age* who was played by comedian Hitoshi Ueki. This popular satire on Japan's salaryman culture featured a feckless individual who always managed to come out on top, advancing up promotional ladders when accidents befall his superiors, or lucking into

Irresponsible Captain Tylor

© 1997 HITOSHI YOSHIOKA/KADOKAWA SHOTEN/TYLER PROJECT

important business information simply by malingering and goofing off. The series and its theatrical spin-offs were revived in 1990, suspiciously close to the time when HUMMINGBIRDS-creator Hitoshi Yoshioka would have begun work on this anime version.

The series returned in several video outings starting with the two-parter *Tylor: An Exceptional Episode* (1994), followed in 1995 by a six-part series that concentrated in turn on some of the supporting cast—Azalyn, for example, given an episode of her own, followed by one in which the star is Tylor's mad-dog pilot, KB Andressen. The series was rounded off by the two-part video series *Tylor: From Earth to Eternity* (1996), in which the lazy captain once again saves Earth from an alien menace by hoping the problem will go away. However, he is not permitted a tidy happy end—the series finishes with the Ralgon Empire on the brink of civil war, Earth and the Ralgon Empire in a confused state of relations, and the nature of a third-party enemy revealed.

I"S

2002. JPN: *From I"s—Mo Hitotsu no Natsu no Monogatari.* AKA: *From I"s: Another Summer Story.* Video. DIR: Yosei Morino. SCR: Shigenori Kageya. DES: Rin Shin. ANI: Studio Pierrot. MUS: N/C. PRD: Studio Pierrot, DigiCube. 29 mins. x 2 eps. (v1); 30 mins. x 6 eps. (v2).

Ichitaka Seto is a high school sophomore, not very confident or forthcoming and madly in love with Iori Ashizuki, the class babe, who is working hard toward a career as an actress. He turns into a total dork around her but begins to build a friendship that may go further with his dream girl, until his other childhood friend Itsuki Akiba, a perky tomboy with an open, free and easy attitude, comes back from America. Her family moved over to the States years ago, but when she wants to graduate high school in her old hometown, it's only natural that she should room with old friends the Setos.

Masazaku Katsura's manga *I"s* is a rerun of his VIDEO GIRL AI without the magic video store, a gentle romance whose three main characters are childhood friends whose names all begin with I. The girls are no mere eye candy, but bright, ambitious young women. Iori is serious enough about her career to question whether she wants a romantic relationship with anyone for a while, and Itsuki wants to be a sculptor and is working hard toward her dream. Teen romance is beautifully rendered both visually and psychogically in all Katsura's love stories, and he understands but rarely overplays the importance of the jiggles, giggles, and wiggles of "fan service." A sequel, *I"s Pure* (2005), was directed by Mamoru Kanbe. ⓝ

ISABELLE OF PARIS

1979. JPN: *Paris no Isabelle.* TV series. DIR: Keiji Hayakawa. SCR: Takeshi Shudo. DES: Nobuyuki Kitajima. ANI: Yoshiyuki Sugawara, Tadayuki Hayashi. MUS: Tsutomu Matsushita. PRD: DAX, TV Tokyo. 25 mins. x 13 eps.
Romance, cross-dressing, and intrigue in 1870s France, which could conveniently imply a relationship (of sorts) to ROSE OF VERSAILLES. Fifteen-year-old Isabelle Laustin is the daughter of a wealthy landlord, Leon, and his wife, Marie. She has spent a happy childhood with her friend Jean and sister Genevieve, and she has a suitor in the person of Captain Victor of the French army. However, her life changes when Napoleon III's army is beaten by the Prussians, and Paris is besieged. When the city is sold to the enemy by the feckless Louis Adolphe Thiers, it falls to Isabelle to save France by disguising herself as a boy and heading for London on a secret mission. A short-lived tale of French whimsy drawing on LES MISÉRABLES and THREE MUSKETEERS, but a solo scripting project for future POKÉMON-writer Takeshi Shudo that made little use of the rich historical potential, looked just like every other adventure anime, and sank without a trace. Compare to STAR OF THE SEINE.

ISAKU *

1997. JPN: *Isaku.* AKA: *Written Clues, Posthumous Works.* Video. DIR: Katsumasa Kanezawa. SCR: Sakura Momoi. DES: Hiroya Iijima. ANI: N/C. MUS: N/C.

PRD: Pink Pineapple, KSS. 30 mins. x 3 eps.
An everyday school is found to have dark secrets—a hidden torture chamber, secret passages, and an insane janitor who has trapped several schoolgirls in the deserted hallways. Five girls, their attractive female teacher, and some token boys star in a schlocky slasher-thriller, with plenty of time out for sexual assault, as befits an anime adapted from an unpleasant computer game. The aim of the original was reputedly to escort the female cast safely off the premises, though many of the players preferred to watch them succumb to the janitor's lust. A similar mindset seems to have dominated the filmmakers. ⓝⓥ

ISHIGURO, NOBORU

1938– . Born in Tokyo, Ishiguro graduated from the film department of the Nihon University, before becoming an animator on ASTRO BOY. He joined TV Doga in 1964, but went freelance in 1965, his first independent job being directorial work on MARINE BOY. Work on WANSA-KUN and LITTLE GOBLIN led to his best known work on STAR BLAZERS, a franchise that has dominated his career ever since. He was also the director of the MACROSS movie *Do You Remember Love?*, MEGAZONE 23, and many other anime of the 1980s.

ISHINOMORI, SHOTARO

1938–1998. Pseudonym for Shotaro Onodera; credited before 1986 as Shotaro Ishimori. Born in Miyagi Prefecture, Ishinomori made his first manga sale while still in high school. Like CLAMP and Rumiko Takahashi, his influence on the anime world is huge, but largely through being the original creator of many important manga.
  As the creator of CYBORG 009 and 8TH MAN, he established many of the traditions of later Japanese espionage and superheroes, whereas in the live-action world, his involvement with *Masked Rider* (*DE) and the original KIKAIDER, not to mention the long running team show franchises that led to

Mighty Morphin' Power Rangers (*DE), have made his work a vital component in understanding the last fifty years of Japanese popular entertainment.

ITANO, ICHIRO

1959– . After an early career designing machinery for shows such as MEGAZONE 23 and MACROSS, Itano moved into action direction, gaining fame on such explosive works as ANGEL COP and VIOLENCE JACK. His reputation continued in the 21st century with GANTZ, the anime considered "too tough for TV."

ITO, IKUKO

?– . A freelance animator whose character design work has made her name a regular appearance on the rosters of popular TV anime, including SAILOR MOON and MAISON IKKOKU. Specializing as a designer of pretty girls, Ito has also worked as a lead animator.

ITO, KAZUNORI

1954– . Born in Yamagata Prefecture, Ito sold his first script to the URUSEI YATSURA TV series. As a member of the Headgear collective, he began a long-term collaboration with Mamoru Oshii, leading to their association with the PATLABOR series, for which Ito wrote many of the best episodes—Ito's wife Akemi Takada was a character designer on the same show. Ito is one of the best writers working in anime; his arguable masterpiece being the GHOST IN THE SHELL movie, for which he artfully translated Masamune Shirow's complex manga to the screen. He has subsequently moved into live-action films, scripting a *Gamera* movie and also Mamoru Oshii's *Avalon*, which, the director ominously commented in interviews, has been their last collaboration. Oshii's subsequent work has been demonstrably poorer for the absence of Ito's contribution at the scripting stage.

ITO, TSUNEHISA

1941– . Born in Kochi Prefecture, Ito sold his first animation script while still studying law and politics in college.

His subsequent work has included episodes of **Gundam**, **Nobody's Boy**, and **Friten-kun**.

IUCHI, SHUJI

1950– . Born in Kanagawa Prefecture, Iuchi graduated from Design College of Tokyo before finding work as an animator on **Microid S** and **Devilman**. His directorial debut was an episode of the TV series **Galaxy Express 999**. Iuchi also has a number of script credits, billed as a writer and director on episodes of **Mama Is a Fourth Grader** and **Yamato Takeru**.

IZUBUCHI, YUTAKA

1950– . Born in Tokyo, Izubuchi is a popular and prolific designer of robots and machinery in many landmark anime. His debut work was on **Starbirds**, where he was a protégé of director Tadao Nagahama, but his big break came with his involvement in the Headgear collective, which led to **Patlabor**. He is also fortunate enough to be a member of another, nameless, clique—attending the same high school as Shoji Kawamori and fellow designer Haruhiko Mikimoto. He has demonstrated that his work is not limited to robots alone, both with the organic and, literally, fantastic character designs in **Record of Lodoss War** and with his role as supervising director on **RahXephon**.

IZUMO

1991. Video. DIR: Eiichi Yamamoto, Masaya Mizutani. SCR: Yoshihiko Tsuzuki. DES: Masaya Mizutani. ANI: N/C. MUS: Reijiro Komutsu. PRD: Kove, Studio Kumosuzu. 45 mins. x 2 eps.
Izumo, a prince of Nakatsu, hates old-fashioned custom and befriends Sanae, a girl from the rival kingdom of Yamatai. Meanwhile, neighboring countries Asuka and Yamato are plotting to steal the Amenomukumo Sword, a sacred treasure of Nakatsu. The warrior **Yamato Takeru** kidnaps Sanae, and Izumo takes up the sword to regain her, but he must first defeat Orochi, a serpent with eight heads and eight tails. This adventure anime combines the Japanese myth of **Little Prince and the Eight-Headed Dragon** with a prehistorical meeting of cultures that would be revisited in **Princess Mononoke**. Based on Yoshihiko Tsuzuki's manga in *Comic Nora*.

IZUMO (B)

2003. JPN: *Izumo*. Video. DIR: Takefumi Goda. SCR: Yasuyuki Muto. DES: Yoshi Ten. ANI: Tao Min. MUS: Pyonmo. PRD: Studio E-go, Museum Pictures, Milky. 30 mins. x 6 eps. (v), 25 mins. x ?? eps. (TV).
Teenager Hikaru is plagued by dreams of a naked priestess praying by a spring who addresses him as her Savior. He also dreams of a secret room at his school and eventually cannot resist the temptation to seek it out, discovering a gateway to what at first appears to be another world, but may in fact be ancient Japan during the time of legends. Undertaking a quest to return to their own world by releasing four mythical beasts from captivity, Hikaru and his companion Ayaka soon discover that their fairy-tale world is underpinned by traumas in their own world—Ayaka has been suppressing memories of childhood sexual abuse; an intriguing decision to drag some of the subtexts of fairy tales into the open in the style of **Urotsukidoji**. A TV series without the nudity, *Izumo: Flash of a Bold Blade* (*Takeki Tsurugi no Senki*, 2005), features a new cast of Japanese schoolchildren, transported to the world of Izumo by an earthquake at their school, in the style of the earlier *Long Love Letter* (*DE). We have added a (b) to the title in order to distinguish this franchise from the earlier **Izumo** (1991), which has its own entry. ●❶Ⓝ❤

J

JACK AND THE BEANSTALK *
1974. JPN: *Jack to Mame no Ki*. Movie.
DIR: Gisaburo Sugii, Naoto Hashimoto.
SCR: Kenji Hirami. DES: Shigeru Yamamoto. ANI: Shigeru Yamamoto, Kazuko
Nakamura. MUS: Morihisa Shibuya. PRD:
Herald, Tac. 98 mins.
Farmer's son Jack believes a traveling
salesman (similar to the portrayal of
the WIZARD OF OZ back in Kansas) when
he tells him that his beans are magical.
Willingly exchanging his cow for them,
Jack is chastised by his mother and
throws the beans away. The beans grow
into a massive stalk overnight, and
Jack's dog, Crosby, is approached by a
mouse, who entreats them to climb up.
The beanstalk leads up through the
bottom of the well into the courtyard
of a castle in the sky that is occupied by
the witch Mrs. Noire (Hecuba). Keen
on stealing treasure, Jack is eventually
convinced by Crosby that he should
rescue the imprisoned Princess Margaret (whom Mrs. Noire intends to marry
to her ogreish son, Tulip) and break
Noire's spell that has turned all the
castle's former occupants into mice.
After a final confrontation with Tulip,
Jack saves the day, though it becomes
patently obvious that Margaret is a
clearheaded girl of 18, determined
to get on with restoring her people's
fortunes, while Jack is merely a child in
love with the idea of being a hero. In
an original and poignant twist on happy-ever-after, Margaret stays on in her
castle while Jack returns home (happily) to his farm, where he soon forgets
all about her. This feature debut of
future TALE OF GENJI–director Gisaburo
Sugii is an excellent musical anime
that could easily have given Disney's
films of the day a run for their money,
but one which sank without a trace on
a very limited U.S. release.

JACK AND THE WITCH *
1967. JPN: *Shonen Jack to Mahotsukai*. AKA: *Boy Jack and the Sorcerer*.
Movie. DIR: Taiji Yabushita. SCR: Shinichi
Sekizawa, Susumu Takahisa. DES: Reiji
Koyama. ANI: Akira Okuwara. MUS: Seiichiro Uno. PRD: Toei. 80 mins.
The mischievous Jack and his friends
are racing through the forest when
they meet Kiki (Allegra), a girl on a
mini-helicopter. With Chuko (Squeaker) the mouse and several other
companions, he is taken to the Devil's
Castle. Kiki is revealed as a Devil-child,
working for Grendel (Queen Iliana),
the master of Devil's Castle, who uses a
Devilization Machine to turn children
into monsters (or "harpies," in the U.S.
dub). Chuko is turned into a devil, but
Jack escapes. Kiki is sent after him but
falls out of the sky, where she is nursed
back to health by Jack. Accompanied
by bear, fox, and dog companions, Jack
returns to the castle to confront the
witch. Grendel captures the animals
and leaves them imprisoned to watch
through her crystal ball as she kills
Jack. The animals are keen to watch
events unfold, but seeing that they are
anxious to see what is happening, the
spiteful Chuko (who is still devilized)
smashes the crystal ball. This breaks
Grendel's spell, and she dies trying to
escape in a balloon. Chuko, Kiki, and
all the other occupants of the castle
are restored to normalcy and pile into
Jack's car for the journey back to his
place.

A bizarre updating of the Old English poem *Beowulf*, originally entitled
Adventure in the Wonder World, *JatW* was
originally commissioned to mark the
tenth anniversary of Toei Animation.
Pushing the envelope at the time for
Japanese animation, it features a striking change in style after Jack enters the
"witch-world" and was the first anime
work to win a Mainichi Film Award for
best score.

JAKOBUS NIMMERSAT *
1980. JPN: *Nodoka Mori no Dobutsu
Daisenso*. AKA: *Great War of the Animals of Placid Forest*. TV special. DIR:
Yoshio Kuroda. SCR: Toshiyuki Kashiwakura. DES: Yasuji Mori. ANI: Kazuko
Hirose. MUS: Tatsumi Yano. PRD: Nippon
Animation, Fuji TV. 70 mins.
When people from a nearby village
discover a hole in their church roof,
they unthinkingly rush into the forest
to cut down trees to repair it. Agreeing
that they should warn the humans off,
Peter the Root Fairy and his animal
friends attempt to shoo them from
the forest, and when this tactic fails,
they embark on a campaign of careful

resistance and nuisance—compare to **POMPOKO**. Based on the book by Boy Lornsen, this TV special reduced the age of the original Peter to make him more appealing to young viewers and dropped all child characters in order to allow the young audience to enjoy watching little people avenge themselves on the folly of grown-ups. Released in English under differing titles, including *Peter of Placid Forest* and *Back to the Forest*.

JANKEN MAN

1991. AKA: *Scissors-Paper-Stone Man.* TV series. DIR: Toshiya Endo, Hiroshi Yoshida, Naohito Takahashi. SCR: Satoru Akahori, Yoshiaki Takahashi, Tsunehisa Arakawa, Takao Oyama. DES: Nobuyoshi Habara. ANI: Nobuhiro Ando, Naoyuki Matsuura. MUS: N/C. PRD: Ashi Pro, TV Tokyo. 20 mins. x 51 eps.
A superhero who defeats adversaries by playing games of scissors-paper-stone with them hardly seems like a pitch for a successful show, but Janken Man's fight against the evil Osodashi Mask kept young viewers hooked for a year.

JAPAN INC.

1987. JPN: *Manga Nihon Keizai Nyumon.* AKA: *Manga Introduction to Japanese Economics.* TV series. DIR: Takenori Kawata, Masamune Ochiai, Yoshimasa Yamazaki, Teruo Kigure. SCR: Takashi Yamada, Shunichi Yukimuro, Miho Maruo. DES: Shotaro Ishinomori. ANI: Nobuhiro Soda. MUS: Sunset Hills Hotel. PRD: Knack, TV Tokyo. 25 mins. x 25 eps.
In the middle of the 1980s, yuppie career girl Sawako Matsumoto graduates from Harvard Business School and returns to Japan. As the country struggles under the export pressures brought by the high yen, she works through the night to produce a business plan that will drag her company out of its rut. Based on the manga by **CYBORG 009**–creator Shotaro Ishinomori that was originally serialized in the high-class business paper *Nippon Keizai Shinbun* and even published as an economics textbook by the University of California. The anime version was broadcast in a ten-o'clock evening slot when hard-working salarymen stood a better chance of seeing it.

JAPANESE FOLK TALES

1975. JPN: *Manga Nihon Mukashi-banashi.* AKA: *Manga Japanese Folk Tales.* TV series. DIR: Rintaro, Norio Hikone, Hidenori Kondo, Gisaburo Sugii, Hiroyuki Hoshiyama, Hiroe Mitsunobu, Isao Okishima. SCR: Isao Okishima, Hiroyuki Hoshiyama, Tsunehisa Ito, Ryohei Suzuki. DES: Tsutomu Shibayama. ANI: Masakazu Higuchi. MUS: Jun Kitahara. PRD: Ai Planning Center, Tac, TBS. 25 mins. x 1467 eps.
Crammed two to an episode, the original *Japanese Folk Tales* series retold many old stories for a children's audience. Some were old anime staples, such as **MOMOTARO** and **THE MONKEY AND THE CRAB**. Others were commonly pastiched in anime but rarely seen in their original form, such as *Snow Woman*, the tale of a sultry siren who lures unsuspecting travelers to their deaths on a snowbound mountain pass. This was first animated as Nobuo Ofuji's *Dream of a Snowy Night* (1947), but snow princesses often appear as characters in diverse anime from **DORORON ENMA** to **URUSEI YATSURA**. Similarly, *Princess Kaguya*, the story of a beautiful woman found inside a strip of bamboo who cannot find a husband on Earth and eventually returns to her home on the moon, was first animated in 1942 by Goro Araiwa and also appears here, but this tale is most likely to be known through oblique references to it in anime such as **REI REI** and **GU-GU GUNMO**. In *Urashima Taro*, first filmed as Nobuo Ofuji's *Cut-Out Urashima* (1928), a Japanese man is carried away to an underwater castle where he lives happily with the daughter of the Dragon King, only to discover that centuries have passed back on the surface when he returns. This early time-travel tale is often referenced in modern anime, including **FUTURE COP URASHIMAN** and **GUNBUSTER**, where time dilation is called the "Urashima Taro Effect."

Shown on several occasions in movie theaters, the series also inspired the *Famous World Fairy Tales* and **JAPANESE HISTORY** serials, as well as imitators such as Hajime Koedo's 28 theatrical shorts *Japanese Fairy Tales* (1988) and Takashi Kurahashi's adult video spin-off *Flirting Japanese Fairy Tales* (1989). Although new tales ceased after 1994, the series continued in reruns long afterward, and was remastered and rebroadcast for a whole new generation in 2005. It is one of the longest-running series in the anime world, after the unstoppable **SAZAE-SAN**.

JAPANESE HISTORY

1976. JPN: *Manga Nippon Shi Series.* AKA: *Manga Japanese History Series.* TV series. DIR: Hidenori Kondo, Norio Yazawa. SCR: Junji Tada. DES: Oji Yutabe. ANI: Oji Yutabe. MUS: Takeshi Sato. PRD: Nippon TV. 25 mins. x 52 eps.
A trawl through the centuries of Japanese history, beginning in myth with the **BIRTH OF JAPAN** then speeding through the early cultures, the rise of the Yamatai nation, the Heian era, the civil war, and finishing with the Meiji Restoration in the 19th century. The series' look was deliberately haphazard, with character designs changing with each historical period in order to give a sense of the passage of time. Ironically, for treatment of Japan's more modern history, the anime medium descends once more into myth-making. Apart from the dramatized historical events of **ANIMENTARY**, Japan's descent into fascism in the 1920s and 1930s is rarely shown in anime except in revisionist shows like **KISHIN CORPS** and **SAKURA WARS** that try to play down the harsh realities in favor of fantastic whimsy. Japanese history was also covered in the **MANGA PICTURES OF JAPAN** series.

JARINKO CHIE

1981. AKA: *Chie the Brat.* Movie, TV series. DIR: Isao Takahata, Masahiro Sasaki, Tetsu Takemoto, Takashi Anno, Katsuhito Akiyama. SCR: Noboru Shiroyama, Hideo Takayashiki, Kazuyoshi Yokota. DES: Yoichi Otabe. ANI: Kazuhiko

Udagawa, Yuki Kishimo, Kazuyuki Kobayashi. MUS: Kiyoshi Suzuki. PRD: Tokyo Movie Shinsha, MBS. 45 mins. (m), 25 mins. x 64 eps. (TV).

Eleven-year-old Chie Takemoto runs a restaurant for her father, until the fateful day that the local gang boss comes around to collect her father's gambling debts. In an attempt to scare the girl, the gangster sets his cat Antonio on Chie's cat Kotetsu, but Chie's pet is the tougher, killing the gangster's. The distraught gangster decides to go straight, opening an *okonomiyaki* restaurant and hiring Chie's father Tetsu as a bodyguard. Everything goes well until Tetsu sees Chie having a secret meeting with his estranged wife.

Based on the manga by Haruki Etsuji, who also worked on I AM A CAT, the *Jarinko Chie* film is a loving look at life in Osaka, a city with a very different attitude from the more famous Tokyo (see COMPILER). Featuring Diet politician Chinetsu Nakayama as Chie and the anime debuts of a number of Kansai comedians in other roles, the movie was promoted with a second anime sequence shown as part of the *Kao Master Theater TV* program as the 84-minute TV special *Jarinko Chie: Anime Stand-Up.* The *manzai* comedy tradition of an abusive straight man and an eternally stupid joker is popular in Japan, and it's mixed with anime here in several scenes of live-action comedians spliced with footage from the anime. The best part is the dream sequence between the anime character Tetsu and his real-life voice actor, the *manzai* comedian Norio Nishikawa. Following the success of the film, *JC* returned to television on the TBS channel, where it survived until 1983.

JC STAFF

Originally "Japan Creative" Staff, although the full title is rarely used. Founded in 1986 by former employees of Tatsunoko as an outsourcing studio for Kitty Films, some of its notable directors include Hiroaki Sakurai, Akira Suzuki, Yasuhisa Kato. A major contributor to the modern anime scene,

often to be found on the credits of the kinds of anime that get picked up for foreign release—representative works include AI YORI AOSHI, MABURAHO, and SLAYERS.

JEANNIE WITH THE LIGHT-BROWN HAIR

1979. JPN: *Kinpatsu no Jeannie.* AKA: *Golden-Haired Jeannie; Girl in the Wind.* TV series. DIR: Keinosuke Tsuchiya. SCR: Iwao Yamazaki, Kenji Terada, Yasuo Yamakichi. DES: Masami Abe. ANI: Masami Abe, Masahiro Kase. MUS: Harumi Ibe. PRD: Dax, Tokyo 12 Channel. 25 mins. x 13 eps., 25 mins. x 52 eps.

Fifteen-year-old Jeannie Reed has grown up on a farm in Agarta, Virginia, and is disgusted at the outbreak of the American Civil War, when her father uses his position to profit from both sides. Turning her back on her profiteering family, she volunteers to care for orphans and becomes a nurse for the soldiers of the Union army, fretting all the time about the whereabouts of her soldier boyfriend, Robert.

A drama from the same era as LITTLE WOMEN, though this original work owes more to *Gone with the Wind* in its depiction of the Civil War. Popular tunes of the time were interwoven into the scenario, including "Oh, Susanna," "Camptown Races," and the titular "I Dream of Jeannie"—a song by the American Stephen Foster (see GREAT COMPOSERS).

The story would return in a 52-episode run of *Girl in the Wind: Jeannie with the Light-Brown Hair* (1992, *Kaze no Naka no Shojo Kinpatsu no Jeannie*), directed by Makoto Yasumura for Nippon Animation. The new version took considerable liberties, including the introduction of nobleman Count Kurt Russell(!). New Jeannie actress Mitsuko Horie would also star in the ill-fated final remake of NOBODY'S BOY.

JETTER MARS

1977. AKA: *Jet Mars.* TV series. DIR: Rintaro, Sumiko Chiba (pseud. for Toshio Hirata), Noboru Ishiguro,

Wataru Mizusawa, Masami Hata, Katsuyoshi Sasaki, Yugo Serikawa. SCR: Masao Maruyama, Masaki Tsuji, Shunichi Yukimuro, Ryohei Suzuki, Hiroshi Yamamoto. DES: Akio Sugino. ANI: Akio Suzuki, Kazuo Mori, Akira Okuwara, Wataru Mibu. MUS: Nobuyoshi Koshibe. PRD: Madhouse, Tezuka Pro, Fuji TV. 25 mins. x 27 eps.

In 2015, Dr. Yamanoue, chief researcher at the Ministry of Science, creates the boy-robot Jetter Mars and prepares to teach him how to fight as a super-soldier. However, he is opposed by the cybernetic specialist Dr. Kawashimo, who is responsible for Jetter's brain. When a storm threatens his island home, Jetter saves the day by cooperating with Kawashimo's robot daughter, Miri. Soon, he becomes a superhero saving the world from harm, though his two mentors war constantly about his true purpose.

A lackluster copy of ASTRO BOY (if Astro was 10–12 years old, Jetter is 6–8) commissioned by Toei from creator Osamu Tezuka, though the studio's interference would lead him to lose all interest in the project and claim that they had chipped away everything that made it anything other than a poor imitation. Early episodes involved a will-he-won't-he crisis, as Jetter decided whether to do the altruistic thing as advised by Kawashimo or to follow Yamanoue's more mercenary advice. However, Yamanoue was soon edged out, and the show became an almost carbon-copy of the relationship between Astro and Ochanomizu in *AB*. To compound the resemblance, *JM* featured *AB* voice actors Mari Shimizu and Hisashi Katsuta, and even lifted *AB* scripts wholesale, pausing only to change the names.

JEWEL HUNTER LIME BEM *

1996. JPN: *Takara Ma Hunter Lime.* AKA: *Treasure Demon Hunter Lime, Jewel BEM Hunter Lime, Homa Hunter Lime.* Video. DIR: Tetsuro Amino. SCR: Kenichi Nakamura. DES: Atsuko Nakajima. ANI: Atsuko Nakajima. MUS: N/C. PRD: Asmik. 30 mins. x 3 eps.

Self-explanatory adventures, as the pretty, scantily clad Lime busts ghosts and steals valuables; based on a computer game but bolstered by designs from **RANMA ½**'s Nakajima.

JIBAKU-KUN

1999. AKA: *Bucky the Incredible Kid*. TV series. DIR: Naoyoshi Kusaka, Atsuko Nakajima SCR: Atsuhiro Tomioka. DES: Miyuki Shimabuke. ANI: Masashi Hirota. MUS: Gen Sawada. PRD: Ashi Pro, TBS. 25 mins. x 26? eps.

In this madcap **POKÉMON** clone, nasty exploding pink balls called "Trouble Monsters" fall into the hands of spiky-haired hero Baku ("Explosion"), who has his life turned upside down when he bumps into Great-Child Dan—a traveler through the Twelve Worlds. Featuring a love interest called Pink, a cameo appearance from Ali Baba, and more cute mascots than you can shake a stick at (which also happen to explode). Based on a manga by popular **PAPUA-KUN**–creator Ami Shibata.

JIBURIRU: THE DEVIL ANGEL *

2004. JPN: *Makai Tenshi Jibril*. AKA: *Hell Angel Jibril*. Video. DIR: Ao Amamoto. SCR: Kazunari Kume. DES: Shinichiro Kajiura. ANI: N/C. MUS: N/C. PRD: Studio Ten, Animac. 30 mins. x 4 eps.

The magical-girl genre gets another pornographic twist, as average Japanese girl Rika is told by the angel Loveriel that she can transform into Jibril, a powerful angel, but only if she charges up her magical powers through sexual intercourse. Different acts, positions, and orifices lead to different "special attacks." Meanwhile, Rika's bespectacled love rival Miss Otonashi gives herself to the demon lord Asumo as a means of getting enough power to transform into her own superheroine, Misty May; cue tentacle rape and abuse as she powers up with abilities from the Dark Side.

Although modern viewers would probably find it most similar to **BEAT ANGEL ESCALAYER** or **MAGICAL KANAN**, *Jiburiru* follows the lead of **UROTSUKI-DOJI** in taking the anxieties of teen life

and extrapolating them into demonic conflict. It borrows the tropes of superhero shows in order to mix its fantasy sex with more everyday tensions when the cast are all wearing their secret identities and doing mundane things like going to the movies. It's a long way from **LITTLE WITCH SALLY**, but the signposts are still there. Jibril is the pronunciation of Gabriel favored in the Quran, although the English-language release steadfastly refuses to acknowledge that. We do not believe there is any connection between this Misty May and the heroine of **OTAKU NO VIDEO**. 🐱

JIM BUTTON

1974. JPN: *Jimubotan*. TV series. DIR: Rintaro, Katsuhisa Yamada. SCR: Masaki Tsuji, Seiji Matsuoka, Noboru Shiroyama. DES: Katsutoshi Kobayashi. ANI: Toshimichi Kadota. MUS: N/C. PRD: Eiken, Top Craft, Imamura Pro, Yoyogi Studio, NET. (TV Asahi) 25 mins. x 26 eps. (TV).

Adventure series for young children, in which the naïve and unworldly dark-skinned boy Jim Button and his best friend Luke the engine driver leave their peaceful island home and travel the world in Luke's amphibious steam railway engine. On the way they learn that a beautiful princess named Lisi has been kidnapped by pirates and handed over to the evil dragon Grindtooth (Drinka), ruler of Sorrowland, so of course they decide to rescue her. The characters are heavily inspired by Western, rather than Japanese, children's graphics; they are based on the 1960 German children's book *Jim Button and Luke the Train Driver* (*Jim Knopf und Lukas der Lokomotivführer*) and its 1962 sequel *Jim Button and the Wild 13* (*Jim Knopf und die Wilde 13*) by *Never Ending Story* author Michael Ende, illustrated by Franz Josef Tripp.

By a strange coincidence, a decade after the anime appeared, the shareware revolution was founded by two Americans, one of whom had the same name as the German edition of this show—Jim Knopf. He has trademarked

the name and its English translation *Jim Button* in the U.S., so web searches will return a high percentage of fascinating but unhelpful results unless you include the term "anime." Two puppet versions of the original story were issued on DVD in 2004 by the Augsberg Puppet Theater.

JINKI: EXTEND

2005. TV series. DIR: Masahiko Murata. SCR: Naruhisa Arakawa. DES: Naoto Hosoda, Katsuyuki Tamura. ANI: N/C. MUS: Kenji Kawai. PRD: feel, Gansis, Mag Garden, TV Asahi. 25 mins. x 12 eps.

When hostile robot weapons known as Jinki are uncovered in Venezuela in the 1980s, their initial attacks are held off by Angel, a secret government organization. All seems calm, but a generation later the world is rocked by a series of city-leveling explosions, revealing that the aftereffects are greater than previously realized. Meanwhile, amnesiac Japanese shrine maiden Akao Hiiragi tries to remember the point of her existence and finds a new purpose in life when an encounter with a Jinki robot turns her into a pilot for a new counterattack, utilizing Moribito, a "guardian" Jinki that can be turned against the rest of its race. We would like to say that this is an intriguing allegory for the effects of U.S. foreign policy since the Reagan administration, but actually it is just an excuse for girls in giant robots. Based on two manga by Shiro Tsunashima, *Jinki: Extend* and its plain *Jinki* prequel, tracing a long line back through **EVANGELION** to **GIANT GORG**. The poses and shots in the credits sequences are made in distinct homage to two other shows: **MAZINGER Z** and the original **GUNDAM**.

JIN-ROH: THE WOLF BRIGADE *

2000. Movie. DIR: Hiroyuki Okiura. SCR: Mamoru Oshii. DES: Hiroyuki Okiura, Tadashi Hiramatsu. ANI: Kenji Kamiyama. MUS: Hajime Mizoguchi. PRD: Production IG. 98 mins.

In a Japan torn apart by riots, an officer from the paramilitary Third Force

Jin-Roh: The Wolf Brigade

Japan that was not economically reju-venated by the Korean War? Or simply a Japan with a few more riots? What do the rioters and the wolf-brigade vigilantes want? What is the mysterious Sect fighting for? Advanced technologies like night-sights and tracers jostle with 1940s gear like Volkswagens and German antitank guns, but why? *Jin-roh* was premiered abroad long before its Japanese release in early 2000, possibly to drum up "foreign interest" among audiences who would assume that their failure to comprehend the backstory was a cultural problem and not simply lazy plotting—an issue that could be said to haunt the same studio's later **BLOOD**. The end result is a skillfully animated but aimless film, with a desperate opening voice-over that tries to explain the foundation of the Third Force, in a failed attempt to convince that this is anything more than a Cold War thriller with a respray. **LV**

is almost killed by a suicide bomber from the fanatical Sect. He begins an affair with the bomber's sister, not realizing that they are both pawns in a power game played out by opposing factions in the government.

Scenarist Oshii has tackled this subject several times before—not only in his manga *Hellhounds*, but also in the live-action spin-offs *The Red Spectacles* and *Stray Dog*. However, it is notable that the acclaimed director of **GHOST IN THE SHELL** should have avoided seeing this particular project through, instead handing it over to the younger Okiura. Although this is Oshii's fourth pass at the same material, it jettisons the authorial input of his **PATLABOR**-cohort Kazunori Ito, leaving a script with a hollow heart. *Hellhounds* had Inui ("Dog"), an officer who is almost killed by a sly female terrorist. It ended with Inui facing the same foe a second time and losing his life. *Jin-Roh* replays this story with Fuse (equally punning, since it is made up of the characters for "man" and "dog") unable to shoot one of the Little Red Riding Hood activist girls who transport satchel-charges to the rioters.

Oshii's original script employed the Red Riding Hood analogy throughout, retelling the story sympathetically from the wolf's point of view. Elements of this remain in carefully composed shots of Fuse beneath a full moon, and a meeting-place in front of the wolf-pack display at the museum. Fuse himself has a lupine cast to his features, and, in the finale, the fairy tale's use of disguises as bluff and counterbluff assumes **PERFECT BLUE** proportions—within the government, the paramilitary, the elite brigade, and, ultimately, the group that masterminds the whole affair.

Director Okiura, however, does not use the lupine imagery as much as Oshii intended, opting instead for a doomed romance between the softness of the impressionable girl Kei and the impenetrable steel of Fuse's armor. His night-sights are literal rose-tinted glasses through which everything is reduced to straightforward good and evil. In his armor, he can fight the rebels without a thought; out of it, he is a whirl of contradictions. Unfortunately, so is the script, which presents an alternate Japan of the late 1950s, but like *Hellhounds* and *The Red Spectacles* before it, fails to explain why. Is it a

JOHNNY CHUCK
1973. JPN: *Yamanezumi Rocky Chuck*. AKA: *Rocky Chuck the Woodchuck; Chuck the Beaver*. TV series. DIR: Tadamichi Koga, Seiji Endo. SCR: Keiji Kubota, Takako Omomori, Hikaru Mori, Hiroshi Yamanaka, Hiroshi Saito. DES: Nobuhiro Okaseko. ANI: Nobuhiro Okaseko, Toshio Hirata, Yasuji Mori. MUS: Morihisa Yamamoto, Seiichiro Uno. PRD: Zuiyo, Fuji TV. 25 mins. x 52 eps. Rocky the adventurous woodchuck is separated from his family and wanders the forests meeting many different animals, including Polly, another woodchuck, Peter Cottontail the rabbit, and the avuncular jaybird Sammy. Based on the output of the prolific Thornton W. Burgess (1874–1965), who wrote a syndicated *Bedtime Story* newspaper column for daily newspapers and was said to have penned 15,000 stories in his lifetime. Many of these involved the adventures of forest animals such as Chatterer the Red Squirrel, Danny the Meadow Mouse, Grandfather Frog, Reddy Fox, and Buster Bear, though it is his ninth book, *The Adventures of Johnny Chuck* (1913), that was used as a

framing device for these anime adaptations. Compare to SETON'S ANIMAL TALES.

JOHNNY CYPHER IN DIMENSION ZERO *

1968. TV series. DIR: Joe Oriolo. SCR: N/C. DES: N/C. ANI: Tadakatsu Yoshida, Akinori Kubo, Kaori Izumiguchi, Isao Kumada, Fumio Ikeno, Akira Maeda, Takashi Aoki, Kenichi Sugiura, Akira Iino, Jiro Tsuno, Masaharu Endo. MUS: N/C. PRD: Warner, Seven Arts, Terebi Doga, Children's Corner. 5 mins. x 138 eps.

Square-jawed superagent Johnny can travel through inner space, Dimension Zero, and uses his superpowers to combat evil all over the universe. He is helped by the beautiful blonde Zena and tiny alien Rhom from the Black Star. An early Japanese-American coproduction by former Disney animator Joe Oriolo for Warner/Seven—a company formed by the merging of Seven Arts production after its merger with Warner Bros. Always intended for screening in both markets, *Johnny Cypher* appeared in short segments six nights a week for 23 weeks in Japan, and in various combinations and compilations in the U.S. and Australia.

JOJO'S BIZARRE ADVENTURES *

1993. JPN: *Jojo no Kimyo na Boken*. Video. DIR: Hiroyuki Kitakubo. SCR: Hiroyuki Kitakubo. DES: Junichi Haneyama. ANI: Junichi Haneyama. MUS: Marco D'Ambrosio. PRD: APPP. 40 mins. x 6 eps., 40 mins. x 7 eps. (series 2).

Joseph Joestar and his Japanese grandson, Jotaro, fight an ongoing blood feud against Dio Brando, an immortal vampire who caused the death of their ancestor Jonathan. Using the magical powers of the Stand, a deck of tarot cards that bestows psychic attributes on the possessor of each card, the Joestar clan and Brando's minions face off in a violent battle that plays like FIST OF THE NORTH STAR at its most surreal.

With its warring secret elites and magical trumps, *Jojo* owes a considerable debt to Roger Zelazny's *Nine*

Princes in Amber (1972), particularly considering the "immortal" undertones of its hero. There are several Jojos stretching from the 19th to the 21st century—a more correct translation of the title might be to put the apostrophe *after* the "s." BAOH–creator Hirohiko Araki's 1987 manga in *Shonen Jump* begins in the 1880s, when an Aztec death mask causes trouble for all who come into contact with it. Archaeologist Jonathan Joestar begins a vendetta against Dio, who tries to steal his inheritance and kills his dog. Dio eventually dons the mask and becomes a vampire, causing Jonathan's death as his family flees for the U.S. The story jumps to New York in the 1930s, where Jonathan's descendant Joseph continues the battle through the Second World War, before the story moves into the 1980s with Jotaro Kujo, Joseph's half-Japanese grandson. The anime version deals primarily with the 1980s incarnation, as he and Joseph fight Dio, while he tries to heal his terrible wounds (his disembodied head has been sewn onto the body of Jonathan Joestar) and activate his ultimate trump card—the ability to stop time.

Following the series, the manga moved into the 1990s with Joseph's illegitimate Japanese son, Josuke Higashikata, then the 21st century with the Italian Giorno Giovanna, who, though officially the son of Dio, had been sired using the genitals of Jonathan and is hence the uncle of Joseph. The most recent member of the family to take the Jojo mantle is Jolyne Kujo, Jotaro's daughter, who uses her powers to escape from a Florida prison.

Gripping despite low-grade animation, the 1993 *Jojo* series was overlooked during the anime boom of the 1990s reputedly because of a prohibitively high asking price for the rights. The original *Jojo* remained unreleased in English for a decade, perhaps because the anime was always intended to sell the 87-plus-volume manga, and one could not be sold without the other. Another possibility is that the license had been considered

by U.S. companies but turned down because of the surreal in-jokery of the characters' names—in the style of BASTARD, the series is full of musical references, including psychic warriors Mariah [Carey], [Bette] Midler, [Ronnie James] Dio, Cream, the psychic dog Iggy [Pop], and even the titular character himself ("Jojo was a man who thought he was a loner"), who hails from the Beatles song "Get Back."

In the wake of a Capcom computer game released in the U.S. as *Jojo's Venture* (1998), the series began to reach the American market, released by the original production company, although episodes were reordered to make the chronology easier for viewers to comprehend if they had not seen the manga. This also handily ensured that the American release "began" with much more modern episodes dating from the year 2000 instead of the 1993 chapters. **V**

JOKER MARGINAL CITY

1992. Video. DIR: Osamu Yamazaki. SCR: Chuichi Watanabe, Hiroyuki Onuma. DES: Chuichi Iguchi. ANI: Takako Sato, Takaaki Ishiyama. MUS: N/C. PRD: Studio Zyn. 45 mins.

Jokers are genetically engineered beings who can switch sex at will, among other, more powerful psychic abilities. A young man escapes from a secret research facility and goes on the run. He is befriended by a reporter, who then has to call on the help of other Jokers to keep the boy safe from his pursuer—a wanted killer known only as the Heartless Assassin. This stylish, well-paced science-fiction video plays with the notions of gender and genetic tinkering, combining the themes of BAGHI with images from the pretty-boy subgenre of gay anime such as FAKE. Based on the manga in *Wings* magazine by ARCHA LYRA–creator Kasumi Michihara. **N**

JOSEPHINA THE WHALE

1979. JPN: *Kujira no Josephina*. TV series. DIR: Kazuyuki Hirokawa. Kazuo Yamazaki, Kazuo Tomizawa. SCR:

Hiroshi Yamamoto, Hirohisa Soda. DES: Kazuo Tomizawa. ANI: Satoshi Hirayama. MUS: Hiroshi Kanodo. PRD: Ashi Pro, Tokyo 12 Channel. 25 mins. x 22 eps.

Madrid schoolboy Sante Costas keeps a tiny whale in a bowl, invisible to everyone except him. Josephina takes him on many dreamlike adventures, but when Sante starts taking an interest in the outside world and gets to know his distant father, Josephina herself fades away like the dream she was. However, the final two episodes were unbroadcast in the show's original run. Excerpts were shown in an extended version to rush the plot to a conclusion, but viewers had to wait for repeats in syndication to watch the friends' final farewell.

JOURNEY THROUGH FAIRYLAND, A *

1985. JPN: Yosei Florence. AKA: Florence the Fairy. Movie. DIR: Masami Hata, Kazuyuki Hirokawa. SCR: Tamanobu Takamasa. DES: Sadao Miyamoto, Noma Sabear. ANI: Sadao Miyamoto, Shigeru Yamamoto. MUS: Naosumi Yamamoto (arranger). PRD: Sanrio. 92 mins.

Michael, a struggling music student not unlike GORSCH THE CELLIST, loves flowers more than he loves music itself. Replacing a begonia in a broken pot, he is visited that night by Florence the flower fairy, who thanks him for his kindness. In this musical fantasy four years in the making, a depressed Michael, cut from the orchestra for the next concert, is whisked away to Flower World by Florence. Naosumi Yamamoto, a conductor with the Tokyo Philharmonic, selected 20 pieces of classical music, which were used in the film itself and, in an imitation of Disney's *Fantasia* (1940), to inspire the surreal storyboards for the animators. Michael was played by Masaki Ichimura, a leading figure in Japan's leading musical performance troupe, Theater Shiki. Released in the U.S. by Celebrity Home Entertainment.

JOURNEY TO THE WEST *

1967. JPN: Saiyuki. AKA: Xiyouji; Monkey; My Son Goku; Alakazam the Great; Spaceketeers; Paradise Raiders. Movie, video, TV series, TV special. DIR: Gisaburo Sugii, Osamu Dezaki, Hideo Makino, Ryosuke Takahashi, Masami Hata. SCR: Akihiko Kanno, Morihisa Yamamoto, Michio Sano, Michiaki Ichiwa. DES: Osamu Tezuka, Gisaburo Sugii. ANI: Shigeru Yamamoto. MUS: Seiichiro Uno. PRD: Tezuka Pro, Fuji TV. 25 mins. x 39 eps. (1967).

Stone Monkey is born from a rock by the ocean. His boastful, irrepressible nature soon causes a stir on Earth as he makes himself king of all the monkeys. In search of the secret of immortality, he learns martial arts and magic from the Buddhist monk Subhuti, who renames him Sun Wu Kong (in Japanese, Son Goku), meaning "Awakened to Emptiness." Back on his mountain, he finds that demons have taken over his cave, but the skills he has learned from Subhuti enable him to throw them out. The Demon King's brothers trick him into sneaking into the Dragon King's palace and stealing a famous weapon, a miraculous iron staff that can change size on command. Sun Wu Kong is brought before the Jade Emperor for punishment. Wu Kong eats the Peaches of Immortality and is chased from Heaven, only to lose a bet with Buddha. Immured beneath a mountain for 500 years, he is saved by the Buddhist Priest Xuanzang (aka Tripitaka), who invites Wu Kong to accompany him on a pilgrimage to Gandhara in India, the modern Punjab. En route, the pair meet a pig-changeling called Pigze and Monk Sand, a river spirit who was once a Heavenly guard. After Wu Kong defeats them, they both join the pilgrimage.

Possibly inspired by travelers' garbled tales of the Hindu monkey-god Hanuman, Wu Cheng-En's 16th-century novel *Xiyouji* is the Chinese story most often animated in Japan, perhaps because its trickster hero is more appealing to the children's audience than the dour generals of GREAT CON-

QUEST or the hotheaded revolutionaries of SUIKODEN. Nobuo Ofuji's EARLY ANIME *Legend of Son Goku* (1926) used cutout figures animated by stop-motion and was soon remade as the two-reel *Son Goku* (1928), directed by Takahiro Ishikawa. However, Wu Kong's real push into the Japanese market came through foreign influences. Amid the many propaganda WARTIME ANIME, the Wan brothers' Chinese cartoon *Xiyouji* (1941) was screened in Japan under the title *Princess Iron Fan*. Featuring one chapter from the legend, when Wu Kong and friends steal a magic fan from Mount Inferno, the film inspired the 16-year-old Osamu Tezuka to write his manga *My Son Goku* (1952), based on the same Mount Inferno episodes.

Japan's animation business was in ruins after the war, though Taiji Yabushita's *New Adventures of Hanuman* (1957) was a 14-minute PR exercise funded with American money. Hanuman was chosen over Wu Kong as a subject, presumably because the former Occupying Forces of Japan felt that a character whose main aim in life is revolt against authority was not the most suitable folk hero for the times; for similar reasons during the war, the Japanese censor had lopped 20 minutes off the running time of *Princess Iron Fan*.

Yabushita returned to the story in 1960 when he directed the anime remake of Tezuka's *My Son Goku*. Retitled *Journey to the West (Saiyuki)* in Japan and *Alakazam the Great* in the U.S., Yabushita's film featured many similarities to the Chinese film that inspired Tezuka. Not only did it keep to the Mount Inferno scenes, but it also played up the moment when Wu Kong, Pigze, and Monk Sand decide to cooperate for the first time and featured a final aerial battle when the characters' feet are surrounded by airbrushed clouds. Substantial name changes were made for the U.S. version, which is set in "Majutsoland," ruled by His Majesty King Amo (Buddha), his wife, Queen Amas, and his son, Prince Amat (Tripitaka). King Alakazam (Wu Kong) tricks

Merlin the magician (the Emperor of Heaven) into revealing his secrets and fights past palace guardsman Hercules to confront King Amo, who imprisons Alakazam until he is released to protect Prince Amat's quest to India. Joined by Sir Quigley (Pigze) and reformed cannibal Lulipopo (Sandy), Alakazam defeats King Gruesome (ruler of Mount Inferno) and his wife (Princess Iron Fan), is reunited with his beloved Dee Dee (a new creation in the anime), and all live happily ever after. The film's Japanese origins were further occluded by a big-name voice cast including Dodie Stevens, Jonathan Winters, Arnold Stang, and Sterling Holloway, music by Les Baxter, and the voice of Frankie Avalon whenever Alakazam sang. Released in the summer of 1961, coincidentally alongside fellow postwar anime MAGIC BOY and PANDA AND THE MAGIC SERPENT, it was *Alakazam*'s commercial failure that led to the perception in the entertainment industry that Americans would not accept Japanese animation at all.

Back in Japan, the experience of making the film further inspired Tezuka to consider repeating the process for TV, indirectly giving birth to ASTRO BOY and the inevitable TV remake of the Wu Kong story, *Goku's Great Adventure* (1967, *Goku no Daiboken*). The first three episodes of this series stay close to the legend, but it soon becomes a gag free-for-all filled with surrealistic and adult humor. Viewers were puzzled or irate; the PTA complained about the level of bad language and the series ended after 39 episodes instead of the intended 52.

Leiji Matsumoto's *Starzingers* (1978) was a science-fiction version that moved the events into outer space; redubbed as SPACEKETEERS, it was shown in the U.S. alongside the other anime in the FORCE FIVE series. The next incarnation was the live-action series *Monkey* (1978, *DE), featuring scripts from JAPANESE FOLK TALES–scenarist Isao Okishima. The music was from the group Godiego, who also provided the theme to Matsumoto's GALAXY EXPRESS 999—

their mournful song about Son Goku's final destination became a hit in its own right, in turn inspiring the otherwise unrelated anime GANDHARA. The live-action series became well known in the U.K. and Australia through the BBC dub, supervised by future Manga Entertainment voice director Michael Bakewell, but the period following it produced only one TV movie in Japan, Gisaburo Sugii and Hideo Takayashiki's anime musical *Son Goku Flies the Silk Road* (1982), and a number of SF pastiches, including DRAGON BALL (1986), the DORAEMON movie *Parallel Journey to the West* (1988), and Buichi Terasawa's GOKU: MIDNIGHT EYE (1989). Even HELLO KITTY–creators Sanrio got into the act with *Raccoon Fun Journey to the West* (1991, *Pokopon no Yukai Saiyuki*). At the close of the 20th century, the character reappeared in several new incarnations, including the *very* loose adaptation ONE PIECE. Another series, *Monkey Magic* (1999), was released on video and then recommissioned for TV. Based on a computer game, the 13-episode series retells the early part of the legend relatively faithfully, with a hero now named Kongo, though the actual *journey* to the west only begins in the penultimate episode. The same year saw a new *Saiyuki* (*Gensomaden Saiyuki*, a pun on the characters for *Chronicle of Total Fun*, aka *Paradise Raiders*), a two-part video based on Kazuya Minekura's *G-Fantasy* manga that also graduated to a full-fledged 50-episode TV series. The Minekura *Saiyuki* is set long after the evil demon Gyumao is buried by the god of Heaven. After magic and science are mixed by parties unknown, Gyumao is brought back, and the monk Genjo Sanzo, accompanied by the usual suspects in updated form, is charged with heading west to determine the cause of the trouble. The movie *GS: Requiem* appeared in 2001 from the same crew. In 2002 came made-for-video *Saiyuki Interactive* (*Saiyuki: Kibou no Zaika*); second series *Saiyuki Reload* appeared in 2003, directed by Tetsuya Endo with characters designed by Noriko Otake and music from Daisuke

Ikeda; third series *Saiyuki Gunlock* (*Saiyuki Reload Gunlock* in Japan, just to confuse matters) appeared in 2004 from the same team.

The legend shows no sign of letting up in the 21st century, with a Tezuka Production movie remake of *Boku no Son Goku* (2003), along with modern re-versionings such as ONE PIECE, one of the MILMO DE PON TV specials, and ASOBOT CHRONICLE GOKU. The story is also referenced or parodied often in other serials, such as an episode of LOVE HINA in which the cast put on a play version of it at a resort. The *Journey to the West* story also returned to live-action television in 2006 with a season on Fuji TV.

JUBEI-CHAN THE NINJA GIRL *

1999. JPN: *Jubei-chan: Lovely Metai no Himitsu*. AKA: *Jubei-chan: Secret of the Lovely Eyepatch*. TV series. DIR: Hiroaki Sakurai. SCR: Akitaro Daichi. DES: Mutthuri Moony, Takahiro Yoshimatsu. ANI: Takahiro Yoshimatsu. MUS: Toshio Masuda. PRD: Madhouse, Bandai, TV Tokyo. 25 mins. x 13 eps. (TV1), 26 mins. x 13 eps. (TV2). Seventeenth-century warrior hero Jubei fights his last battle, and with his dying breath entrusts his servant Koinosuke with the task of finding his true spiritual heir. Three hundred years later, the magically sustained Koinosuke finds a suitable candidate, the Japanese schoolgirl Jiyu "Jubei" Nanohana, who has the large breasts and pert buttocks that mark her as the Chosen One. Koinosuke must convince Jubei to don the heart-shaped eyepatch that will call forth her spiritual ancestor, but the insufferably perky girl (who has paroxysms of joy if she manages to fry an egg) is a reluctant recruit. Transferring to a new school populated by the descendants of samurai, she is adored by all, even Shiro Ryujoji, whose family, wronged by the original Jubei, insists on sending evil supply-teachers to challenge her to duels.

Jubei-chan must have looked great on paper—a samurai spoof from the same Madhouse studio that produced the kinetic NINJA SCROLL, featuring school gags, unwelcome guests, historical references, mawkish romance, transformations, and fighting. In other words, reheated RANMA ½, further damaged by a succession of befuddling ethnocentric in-jokes for the benefit of Japanese parents who remember the 1950s samurai swashbucklers, which also inspired the same scenarist's LORDLESS RETAINER TSUKIKAGE.

Without the presence of other Jubei stories in English (the aforementioned *Ninja Scroll*, its illegitimate sibling NINJA RESURRECTION, and the live-action movie *Samurai Armageddon*), there is little chance that this would have even been considered for translation. Its historical roots are too deeply buried; some, like the prissy Sachi Toyama's relationship to Toyama no Kinsan (also parodied in SAMURAI GOLD), would be difficult even for a Japanese audience. Others, like the simian Ozaru and Kozaru getting their names from Big Monkey and Little Monkey, could really do with explanatory sleeve notes, sadly lacking in the Bandai English-language release. The result is a nonsensical dub in which a mystified cast and crew hope that the audience will laugh at jokes that they plainly do not find funny themselves. Amid a cynical challenger-of-the-week formula, creator Akitaro Daichi has the temerity to write himself into the story as Jubei-chan's narcoleptic father—somehow appropriate since he could well have written this in his sleep.

The sequel series, *Revenge of the Siberian Yagyu* (*Siberia Yagyu no Gyakushu*, 2004) finds Jiyu and her friends Maro and Satchin now in the ninth grade. A transfer student named Freesia Yagyu joins their class, and around the same time the Siberian Yagyu clan launch an all out attack to kill Jiyu, as a descendant of Jubei, the man who killed their ancestor Kitaretsusai Yagyu 300 years ago. But then Freesia claims to be the legitimate heir to the Yagyu line and demands that Jiyu hand over the Lovely Eyepatch. The true heir

of the Lovely Eyepatch, the Siberian clan's quest for revenge, the fraught relationship between Jiyu and her father Sai, and the role of Mikage, a former enemy turned Dad's editor, are all resolved in a final battle between the two girls.

JUDGE *
1991. JPN: *Yami no Shihosha Judge*. AKA: *Magistrate of Darkness: Judge*. Video. DIR: Hiroshi Negishi. SCR: Katsuhiko Chiba. DES: Shin Matsuo. ANI: Shin Matsuo. MUS: Toshiro Imaizumi. PRD: Animate Film. 45 mins.
Hoichiro Oma is an everyday salaryman who is really Enma, the Judge of Hell (see DORORON ENMA), meting out nightly justice for those who are wronged back in our world. His first case involves a ruthless executive who has committed murder on his route to the top—with ironic cruelty, Oma makes his punishment fit his crime. The second involves a conflict with Oma's own boss back in the real world, who has hired a supernatural lawyer to get him off a murder charge. Faced with weasly tactics at the bench, Oma appeals to the Court of Ten Kings, presided over by the rulers of Hell. Short tales of the unexpected in a similar style to PET SHOP OF HORRORS, based on a manga by sometime CRUSHER JOE–artist Fujihiko Hosono.

JUDO STORY
1991. JPN: *Judo Monogatari*. Video. DIR: Junichi Tokaibayashi. SCR: Oki Ike. DES: Junichi Tokaibayashi. ANI: Junichi Tokaibayashi. MUS: Goro Omi. PRD: Nippon Animation. 50 mins. x 2 eps.
Mochi, a novice, decides to join the judo club when he begins high school. He must endure many trials before he is accepted—shaving his head, cleaning up after his elders, and enduring their bullying. Eventually, after much blood, sweat, and tears, his fellows select him as a team member for the local championships. Based on the 1985 *Young Magazine* manga by Makoto Kobayashi, creator of WHAT'S MICHAEL?

JULIE THE WILD ROSE
1979. JPN: *Nobara no Julie*. TV series. DIR: Keiji Hayakawa, Masami Kigurashi. SCR: Akira Suga, Shina Matsuoka, Tomomi Mochizuki. DES: Masami Abe. ANI: Masami Abe. MUS: Mitsuo Chahata (arranger). PRD: Dax, Tokyo 12 Channel. 25 mins. x 13 eps.
Eleven-year-old Julie Braun lives in the lush green mountain pastures of Austria's Southern Tyrol. Her parents are killed by Italian soldiers, and she is sent to Vienna to live with her relatives, the Clementes. She befriends cousins Johan and Tanya but has trouble adjusting to life with Uncle Karl and Aunt Klara. As Austria is plunged into World War I, Karl is fired from his job at a glass factory, and Julie's new family is forced into a life of hardship.

A short-lived HEIDI clone made with the assistance of the Austrian Tourist Board, though sources are unclear as to whether this was a full-fledged cooperation or merely the provision of a few holiday brochures. The music keeps the Austrian motif, selected from the works of Franz Schubert and Johann Strauss, who had their own anime appearance in GREAT COMPOSERS.

JULIET
1998. Video. DIR: Tsukasa Tomii. SCR: Masaru Yamamoto. DES: Kazutoshi Kobayashi. ANI: Akira Takeuchi. MUS: N/C. PRD: Adobe Pictures. 30 mins.
In this adaptation of a minor work by SAKURA DIARIES–creator U-Jin, the pretty, young Reina enjoys the advances of her lusty stepbrother and a mysterious stranger. Sold to the Japanese as their one chance to hear Kae Araki, the baby-faced voice of Minnie-May in GUNSMITH CATS and Rini (Chibi-Usa) in SAILOR MOON, behaving in a more erotic manner than that to which her public was accustomed. Ⓝ

JUMPING *
1988. Video. DIR: Osamu Tezuka, Eiichi Yamamoto, Taku Sugiyama, Shingo Matsuo, Takamitsu Mitsunori. SCR: Osamu Tezuka. DES: N/C. ANI: N/C. MUS: N/C. PRD: Various. 100 mins.

A video compendium of several short films released in Japan to coincide with the Second Image Software Awards. The centerpiece is Tezuka's *Jumping*, a five-minute 1984 short in which a character takes successively higher and higher leaps until he (or is it she?) eventually bounds across the ocean to the middle of a war zone, where an explosion blasts him/her down to Hell. From there, s/he is thrown back out to the beginning of the film, ready to start jumping again. This exercise in perspective is accompanied by another Tezuka short, *Broken Down Film* (1985, *Onboro Film*), a playfully postmodern joke showing a supposedly rare print of an old silent cartoon Western in which the condition of the film itself affects the action onscreen. The characters have trouble seeing because the film is so dirty, are confused by abrupt jumps in continuity due to missing footage, and even have to climb to the next frame when the projector jams—compare to Chuck Jones's *Duck Amuck* (1951). These famous but rarely seen anime were accompanied by several other experimental shorts from other animators for an audience who lacked the resources to travel to the film festivals where they were usually only to be seen. Another experimental Tezuka film, the longer LEGEND OF THE FORESTS, was released on video the previous year. Conveniently lacking dialogue that requires translation, both *Jumping* and *Broken Down Film* have been screened at English-language film festivals and also on U.K. television.

JUNGLE BOOK, THE *

1989. JPN: *Jungle Book Shonen Mowgli*. AKA: *Jungle Book Boy Mowgli*. TV series. DIR: Fumio Kurokawa, Shinji Takahashi, Akira Kiyomizu, Kazuya Miyazaki, Shigeru Yamazaki, Tatsuya Hirakawa. SCR: Nobuyuki Fujimoto, Kenichi Yoshida, Saburo Sekiguchi, Asami Watanabe. DES: Sadahiko Sakamaki. ANI: Masashi Kojima, Sadahiko Sakamaki, Kazuya Hayashi. MUS: Hideo Shimazu. PRD: Nippon Animation, TV Tokyo. 25 mins. x 52 eps.

Jungle De Ikou

An explorer and his wife are killed in the jungle. Their baby son, Mowgli, is raised by wolves, and befriends Baloo the bear and Bagheera the panther, who teach him the Laws of the Jungle. Rejected by local humans, who see him as a demon, Mowgli prefers to dwell in the forest, where he must outwit the evil tiger Shere Khan. Eventually, after conflict between the humans and the animals, Mowgli defeats Shere Khan and gets to meet the beautiful human girl he has worshipped from afar for so long, leaving behind his jungle friends as he returns to the world from which he came. An anime adaptation likely to remain dwarfed by the earlier Disney classic, this version updates Rudyard Kipling's novel for the 20th century—including planes, for example, understandably absent from the original. Another old story of a human boy reared by animals was adapted as TA-CHAN: KING OF THE JUNGLE.

JUNGLE DE IKOU *

1997. JPN: *Jungle de Iko*, AKA: *Let's Go with Jungle; Let's Get Jungly*. Video. DIR: Yuji Moriyama, Osamu Mikasa. SCR: Jiro Takayama. DES: Yuji Moriyama. ANI: Yuji Moriyama. MUS: N/C. PRD: Studio Fantasia, Movic, King Records, J ProjectMus: Parome. 30 mins. x 3 eps. Ten-year-old Natsumi's father gives her a necklace from the ruins of the Myuginian jungle. Soon afterward, Natsumi dreams that a jungle god is teaching her a powerful ritual dance. Discovering that her father's researchers have also awakened an ancient forest devil, Natsumi must deal with jungle spirits, gigantic whales, and armed fighter pilots. She performs the jungle dance and transforms into Mii, a large-breasted fertility goddess. A cynical combination of the jiggling bosoms of PLASTIC LITTLE and the magical transformations of CREAMY MAMI, *Jungle de Ikou* comes complete with a childhood pal for Natsumi, who naturally develops a crush on Mii, as well as comic-relief devil-child Ongo and his fiancée, Rongo. Originally based on a segment of voice actress Megumi Hayashibara's *Boogie Woogie Night* radio show, the series was memorably described by *Manga Mania* as a "Boogie Woogie Congo Ongo Bongo Jungle Bungle."

JUNGLE KUROBE

1973. TV series. DIR: Osamu Dezaki. SCR: Yoshitake Suzuki, Toshiaki Matsushima, Yoshiaki Yoshida, Haruya Yamazaki, Chikara Matsumoto, Shinji Tahara, Noboru Shiroyama, Yu Yamamoto. DES: Fujiko-Fujio. ANI: Yasuo Kitahara, Sadayoshi Tominaga, Yoshiaki Kawajiri. MUS: Goro Misawa. PRD: Tokyo Movie Shinsha, NET (TV Asahi). 25 mins. x 61 eps.

Kurobe, the son of the chieftain of the Pilimy jungle tribe, rashly tries to catch what he believes to be an "iron bird," and ends up dangling from what is actually an aeroplane until he drops into the garden of unsuspecting Japanese boy Shishio Sarari. Believing himself to be in debt to his "rescuer," Kurobe insists on repaying him in the "jungle way," which means hanging around in modern Tokyo and using his imperfect jungle magic to help his newfound friend. Further complications ensue with the arrival of Paopao the elephant, Kurobe's brother Akabei, and Gakku the lion.

Clearly impressed with the enduring success of **DORAEMON**, Tokyo Movie Shinsha decided to rip it off with this *Tarzan*–inspired pastiche, but rather nobly decided to commission **DORAEMON**'s own creators, the Fujiko-Fujio team, to write the result. Compare to the Hanna-Barbera cartoon *Dino Boy* (1966), which reversed the positions by having a child of our own time fall out of a plane into a primitive lost valley.

JUNGLE WARS

1990. Video. DIR: Yoshio Kuroda. SCR: Mayumi Koyama, Akira Sakuma. DES: Moriyasu Taniguchi, Takayuki Doi. ANI: Moriyasu Taniguchi. MUS: N/C. PRD: Nippon Animation. 25 mins. x 2 eps.

An evil syndicate of hunters attacks a jungle village where animals and humans coexist peacefully. With his parents out of action and his way of life in jeopardy, the imaginatively named "Boy" swings through the creepers to save the day. Based on the game of the same name for the Nintendo Gameboy.

JUNK BOY *

1987. AKA: *The Incredible Gyôkai*

[Industrial] Video. Video. DIR: Katsuhisa Yamada. SCR: Tatsuhiko Urahata, Hiroyuki Fukushima. DES: Hiroshi Hamazaki. ANI: Hiroshi Hamasaki. MUS: Takashi Kudo. PRD: Madhouse. 44 mins.

A charmless "comedy" in which sexcrazed Ryohei Yamazaki gets a job at the seedy *Potato Boy* magazine, chiefly because his uncontrollable erection allows the staff to evaluate nude photographs before going to press. He is sent to assist at a fading starlet's photo shoot, where he talks her into baring all by confessing that he spent many happy hours masturbating over pictures of her younger self. Sinking to new depths, he volunteers to conduct an "investigative report" at a local brothel, to which his superiors agree somewhat illogically, since they already have an undercover reporter, the pretty Aki, working there as one of the girls. Ryohei is rebuffed by Aki, and he takes it as a personal challenge that she has never had an orgasm. The way to any woman's heart, it would appear, is to throw on a tuxedo, take her on a bicycle ride through the red-light district, put her into a stolen ballgown, and then get her drunk on your office rooftop. Ryohei then leaves the sexually sated Aki behind so he can file a new story with the treacly moral message of "treating women right." He almost impresses his tough female editor with this change of heart, until she finds him snuffling through her underwear drawer and realizes that he's still a jerk. The authors wonder why she ever doubted it.

Based on a 1985 manga in *Manga Action* magazine by Yasuyuki Kunitomo, *JB* would like to think it is a media satire, and occasionally attempts to balance its priapic hero's infantile nature by letting a female character slap him. But since this is hardly a redeeming feature, it also boasts a brief fake commercial interlude made by **NINJA SCROLL**–director Yoshiaki Kawajiri, as well as a bizarre moment when Ryohei attempts to mate with a plastic effigy of fast-food mascot Colonel Sanders. **●N**

JUNKERS COME HERE

1994. JPN: *Junkers Come Here: Memories of You*. Movie. DIR: Junichi Sato. SCR: Naoto Kine, Ai Morinaga. DES: Kazuo Komatsubara, Shinya Ohira. ANI: Keiichi Sato, Mahiro Maeda. MUS: N/C. PRD: Gaga, Triangle Staff. 100 mins.

Sixth-grader Hiromi has a relatively carefree life; with her rich professional parents often out of the house, she is often left in the care of the housekeeper. She also has a friend in Keisuke, the college boy who rents a room at the house, and sometimes supplements his income by tutoring her in school subjects. Her best friend is her dog Junkers, a talking animal in the style of **I AM A CAT**, who has a comedic obsession with bad samurai dramas, and who attempts to offer Hiromi advice on life, although he is often as unsure about things as she is. Based on two books by former pop guitarist Naoto Kine (see **CAROL**), *JCH* is a gentle slice-of-life story employing similar misdirectional techniques to the works of Hayao Miyazaki, presenting magical distractions from the actual plot, which is one of a marriage breakup and its potential effects on the heroine. Originally screened in segments as part of the TV Asahi show *Kuni Sanchi Witches*, the anime was given a theatrical showing the following year.

JURA TRIPPER

1995. JPN: *Kyoryu Boken Ki Jura Tripper*. AKA: *Dinosaur Chronicle Jura Tripper*. TV series. DIR: Kunihiko Yuyama, Yoshitaka Fujimoto, Naohito Takahashi, Shigeru Omachi, Kunihisa Sugishima. SCR: Isamu Shizutani, Yasushi Hirano, Sukehiro Tomita, Katsuyoshi Yutabe. DES: Kenichi Chikanaga, Mari Tomonaga. ANI: Seiji Kikuchi, Kenichi Chikanaga. MUS: Toshiyuki Omori. PRD: NAS, Ashi Pro, TV Tokyo. 25 mins. x 39 eps.

In a conflation of **ADRIFT IN THE PACIFIC** and *Jurassic Park* (1993), fifteen boys and girls are thrown into an alternate world where dinosaurs and humans live alongside each other. Later episodes developed a distant similarity to

EL HAZARD, with the adventurers spending more time flirting than fighting, as they pick their way across a desert on the run from a newly awakened golem monster.

JUST ANOTHER FAMILY

1976. JPN: *Hoka Hoka Kazoku*. TV series. SCR: Noboru Shiroyama, Satoshi Murayama. DES: Katsutoshi Kobayashi. ANI: Kazutaka Kadota, Isao Kaneko. MUS: Kunio Miyauchi. PRD: Eiken, Fuji TV. 5 mins. x 1428 eps.
The Yamano family, including wise granny Yone, know-it-all father Yutaka, caring mother Sachiko, and children Makoto and Midori, learn about life in modern Japan, in a live-action show that often switches to simple animation to illustrate key points or technical information. Conceived in the style of **KOTOWAZA HOUSE** or **OUTSIDE THE LAW** as a series of public information films sponsored by the office of the Japanese Prime Minister, the show utilized extensive input from former crewmembers of the long-running **SAZAE-SAN** series. The show ran until March 1982—compare to **BOTTLE FAIRY**, which tries something similar with a radically shorter running time.

JUSTICE

1991. JPN: *Jingi*. AKA: *Humanity and Justice*. Video. DIR: Kiyoshi Murayama. SCR: Hideo Nanba. DES: Toshi Kawamura.
ANI: Katsushi Matsumoto. MUS: N/C. PRD: JC Staff. 50 mins. x 2 eps.
A kindhearted gangster tries to live by rules of kindness and justice even though he is on the wrong side of the law. When he meets a former college left-winger who has also become a street punk, the two form an unlikely team, bringing their own peculiar code of ethics to the underworld. Based on the 1988 manga in *Young Champion* magazine, this is widely regarded as the masterwork of Ayumi Tachihara, who also created **FOR REAL**. **NV**

JUSTY

1985. JPN: *Cosmopolice Justy*. Video. DIR: Osamu Uemura. SCR: Hiroyuki Hoshiyama. DES: Tsugo Okazaki. ANI: Kazuya Iwata. MUS: Hiroya Watanabe. PRD: Studio Pierrot. 44 mins.
Justy Kaizard is a Cosmo Police Hunter—his job is to track down rogue psychics and exterminate them before they can harm others. He and his partner, Borba Len, track down the criminal psychic Magnamam Vega, and Justy kills him in front of his 6-year-old daughter, Asteris. The distraught child swears that she would kill Justy herself if she were bigger, and her own psychic powers, triggered by the tragedy, transform her into a 16-year-old, though the shock leaves her with amnesia. Growing up at Cosmo Police headquarters under the care of Justy's friend Jilna

Star, she treats him as an adored big brother. But then the Crimina Esper, a group of malicious psychics, decide to dispose of Justy by awakening her memory and her hatred of the man who killed her father. Based on the 1981 manga by Tsugo Okazaki serialized in *Shonen Sunday* magazine, *Justy* was one of the more popular of the 1980s videos in early anime fandom, chiefly because of the short running time and easy-to-follow plot that did not really require subtitles. However, it was not brought to the U.S. as one might have expected, reputedly because the rights were prohibitively expensive.

JVC

Japan Victor Company (i.e., Nippon Victor locally) was founded in 1927 as a subsidiary of the American company Victor Records. The company was a pioneer in radio and television development, but cut off from its parent company during World War II. By 1953, ownership had been transferred to Matsushita. The company is also credited with the invention of the VHS cassette, a major catalyst in the rise of adult-oriented anime in the 1980s and beyond. Subsidiaries include Victor Entertainment (Japan), a major distributor of anime-related soundtracks and itself the owner of the Victor Entertainment Animation Network.

K

KABUTO *

1990. JPN: *Karasu Tengu Kabuto*. AKA: *Raven Tengu Kabuto*. TV series, TV special, video. DIR: Takashi Watabe, Kazuya Miyazaki, Akira Kiyomizu, Mamoru Yamamoto, Taku Sugiyama. SCR: Hiroyuki Hoshiyama, Satoru Akahori. DES: Satoshi Urushihara, Buichi Terasawa. ANI: Kinji Yoshimoto, Hideaki Matsuoka. MUS: Seiko Nagaoka. PRD: Hiro Communications. 25 mins. x 39 eps. (TV), 45 mins. (v).

Dohki, the ruler of hell, is summoned to our world by the "evil mood of the age" and sets out to rule the universe with the help of his cronies. Raven Tengu Kabuto, a warrior-mage with the power of flight, magical runes, and a deadly blade, assembles a party of stock characters (a giant warrior, a loyal samurai, a cunning rogue, and the usual token blonde) in order to fight back. He rounds up the old members of his clan, who have been scattered to the four corners of Japan by an undisclosed disaster. Dohki in turn has assembled a group of baddies that represent the "dark halves" of Kabuto's little band, and the battle begins, with plenty of strange techno-fantastic machinery, most notably a flying metal dragon in the shape of a giant swastika.

After GOKU: MIDNIGHT EYE–creator Buichi Terasawa rejected the science-fiction medium for a while, he chose to work on the ALICE IN WONDERLAND–inspired *Black Knight Bat* manga and this decidedly unhistorical fantasy, which began as a 1985 manga in *Fresh Jump* magazine. *Kabuto* seems permanently unsure of whether it wants to be steampunk science fiction or fantastic adventure, with a madly anachronistic clutter of design goofs that polite critics would call eclectic. Kabuto's sword is a double-edged blade, yet he wields it like a single-edged katana, for example (as do the "Greek" warriors of ARION), while any sense of period is compromised by the hard-rock guitar music throughout. Kabuto is a *tengu* warrior, although whether this is a reference to the supernatural crow-demons of JAPANESE FOLK TALES or merely a particular martial arts school is unclear. Kabuto himself claims the latter, but at several points in the story also sprouts wings to fly out of dangerous situations. Suzaku, Kabuto's love interest, wears fishnet tights for no discernible reason, someone uses a semiautomatic musket, and characters can speak and breathe underwater without any effort or explanation. Nevertheless, elements creep in from *actual* Japanese folklore, including the notorious Fuma clan, also seen in LUPIN III and KOJIRO, as well as Kabuto's giant halberd-wielding companion Genbu, a respray of the Little John of Japanese legend, the super-monk Benkei.

The TV series was later edited down into two feature-length videos, *Kabuto: The Warrior* (compiling episodes 1–13) and *Kabuto: The Visitation* (compiling episodes 27–39). The hero returned in the one-shot original video *Kabuto: The Golden-Eyed Beast* (1992), the only incarnation of the series to be released commercially in English. For this story, the beautiful princess Ran is kidnapped by the evil vampiress Tamamushi. Kabuto must then rescue the princess, fighting off typically anachronistic threats such as muskets and medieval helicopters, as well as face-hugging spiders—an arachnid take on the Heike crabs, real-life creatures from Japan's Inland Sea whose shells bear shockingly accurate pictures of samurai warriors' faces. Eventually, Tamamushi turns out to be a machine herself, which begs the question: If she really is an android, why does she need to sacrifice the souls of young women to keep herself young?

As before, the plot is heavily laden with inconsistencies—dialogue in both language versions switches from ancient idiom ("verily thou art a knave") to modern vernacular ("outta my way, bitch") and back again, while background scenery switches from that of northern Japan to that of southern China. Compare to Terasawa's other big success, SPACE ADVENTURE COBRA.

KAI DOH MARU *

2001. JPN: *Kaidoumaru*. Video. DIR: Kanji Wakabayashi. SCR: Nobuhisa Terado. DES: Sho-u Tajima. ANI: Kyoji Asano. MUS: Yoshihiro Ike. PRD: Production I.G., SME Visual Works. 46 mins.

After her uncle causes the death of her

parents, Kintoki is raised as a boy, fighting off the advances of her brother's disturbed ex-girlfriend and struggling with her own feelings for Raiko, the handsome knight who is her guardian. Old enmities come back to life in the middle of a smallpox epidemic, as Raiko's group, the Four Knights, hunts down its enemies in an evocative and original anime from Production I.G., seemingly conceived as a means of testing new toon shading and oversaturation technologies.

Kai Doh Maru's greatest achievement is the washed-out watercolor style that makes the whole thing seem like gazing at a fragile ancient painting. Color designer Nagisa Abe gets top billing alongside the distinctive character designs of **OTOGI ZOSHI**'s Sho-u Tajima, and he deserves it. Make no mistake, someone spent a *lot* of money integrating the traditional and CG artwork in this, and some scenes, like the prolonged tracking shot across Heian palaces, are plain and simple showing off.

The pallid color scheme is not merely a deliberate contrast to the same team's earlier **BLOOD: THE LAST VAMPIRE**, but also a bold subversion of much of what anime stands for, sacrificing the kid-friendly strengths of primary colors for a watercolor look reminiscent of Studio Ghibli's **MEET THE YAMADAS**. But part of the glamor of the Heian era is precisely that we tend to view it through a historic haze. While violent moments may recall the samurai savagery of Yoshiaki Kawajiri's **NINJA SCROLL**, *Kai Doh Maru* recreates a fantasy ideal of the Japanese past and does it so well that it belongs on the shelf with the classical anime **THE SENSUALIST** and **THE TALE OF GENJI**.

Its story is less coherent—a rushed jumble of fights and shots, great on a showreel but almost incomprehensible as a movie. Our lead is a girl who takes on a man's mission, like the cross-dressing heroines of **YOTODEN** and **DORORO**. Our creepy bad guy behind the scenes is a *girl* called **SHUTENDOJI**. The bad guys want to bring back the same Masakado demigod who haunts **DOOMED MEGA-LOPOLIS**. A "healer character" with a couple of cameos is addressed as "Mr. Seimei"—in yet another sly reference to the manga and movie phenomenon *Onmyoji* (see *DE*, as *The Yin-Yang Master*). But *Kai Doh Maru* is more than the sum of its parts, a careful recreation of the famously languid pace of Japan's medieval capital, put into production at the turn of the 21st century, when Japanese popular culture developed a minor fetish for the turn of the 11th.

The Japanese titles clearly state that the year is A.D. 995, although some characters and events seem to originate from a century earlier (i.e., 889), causing some confusion for the translators. Then again, Seimei died ten years *after* the events shown here—*Kai Doh Maru* might imply a sense of historical accuracy, but it's still prepared to play fast and loose with the actual facts. That, however, is part of director Wakabayashi's plan. It should not be lost on the viewer, for example, that the magical, fantastical Kyoto depicted here experiences 4 complete seasons in just 35 minutes. NB: the box blurb in some territories disingenuously counts the DVD extras as part of the main feature, in an attempt to claim a running time of "80 mins. approx." In fact, the main feature only lasts for 46 minutes, and 7 of those comprise the plodding ending credits. **Ⓥ**

KAIKAN PHRASE

1999. TV series. DIR: Hiroko Tokita. SCR: Katsuhiko Koide, Reiko Yoshida, Satoru Tsuchiya. DES: Yumi Nakayama. ANI: Hiroaki Shimizu, Kazuhiro Sada. MUS: Takeshi Tsuji, Lucifer. PRD: Studio Unsa, TV Tokyo. 25 mins. x 37? eps. Realizing that their pop group, Climb, is going nowhere, guitarist Yuki and drummer Santa decide to split and form a new combo. Calling themselves Lucifer, they discover their new vocalist in the form of pretty-boy Sakuya, who takes the job over playing the piano in a hotel bar. Sakuya, however, harbors some dark secrets of his own. This series was based on a manga by Mayu Shinjo serialized in *Shojo Comic* and rushed onto TV to cash in on the success of the earlier boy-band extravaganza **WEISS KREUZ**. Toning down the sensual original for an early-evening audience, the show nevertheless concentrates on the broody, moody male stars, emphasizing music and drama over the animation itself, which is of a rather cheap digital nature.

KAJISHIMA, MASAKI

1952– . Born in Okayama, Kajishima became a freelance animator whose name is most often found on the production credits of works by the AIC studio, including **GALL FORCE** and **TENCHI MUYO!**.

KAKINUMA, HIDEKI

1958– . Born in Tokyo, Kakinuma's early work saw him as a mechanical designer on **MOSPEADA** and **MEGAZONE 23**. He subsequently created, storyboarded, and scripted the **GALL FORCE** series.

KAKKUN CAFÉ

1984. Movie. DIR: Osamu Kobayashi. SCR: N/C. DES: Tsutomu Shibayama. ANI: Tsutomu Shibayama, Hideo Kawauchi, Mitsuru Hongo, Michishiro Yamada, Tomomi Mochizuki. MUS: Takashi Fukui. PRD: Tokio MC, Asia Do, Tokyo Communications. 86 mins. Kakuei "Kakkun" Tanaka is a superhero who hangs out with his friends Yasuhiro Nakasone (who agrees with everything anyone says), Tokushima yokel Takeo Miki, stingy Takeo Fukuda, and Masayoshi Ohira, who says nothing except "ooh" and "ah." Kakkun's misadventures begin with playing rugby at school, though after graduation he accidentally becomes prime minister of Japan. He visits New York, where he literally causes a stink by grilling dried mackerel, before preventing a nuclear war between hapless superpowers America and Russia. A political satire featuring anime caricatures of several Japanese politicians.

KAKURENBO: HIDE AND SEEK *

2005. JPN: *Kakurenbo*. AKA: *Hide and*

Seek. Movie. DIR: Shuhei Morita. SCR: Shuhei Morita, Shiro Kuro. DES: Daisuke Sajiki. ANI: Shuhei Morita, Shiro Kuro. MUS: Karin Nakano, Reiji Kitasato. PRD: Yamatoworks, D.A.C. 25 mins.

A short but often chilling showcase for modern computer graphics, as masked children play a game of tag in Tokyo's heretofore unknown "Demon City" district, and seemingly informed by Japanese folklorist Kunio Yanagida's claim (quoted at its beginning) that one should never play hide-and-seek at night, lest it awaken demons in the shadows.

Hikora's sister Sorincha is missing. At night in the Demon City the lamps flare of their own accord and dangerous beings stalk the shadows. Masked children play "otokoyo," or hide-and-seek, and every child who has ever played has vanished forever. Hikora and his best friend Yaimao don fox masks and join the gang waiting outside the city gate to reach the seven players required before the gate opens and the game begins. The seekers are monsters, half-machine and half-animal, and the clever ending reveals why the game is played. The short run-time doesn't allow much time for characterization, and this is echoed in the animation, with the characters showing no emotion in their faces or movements; the voice actors have to work extra hard. Director Morita also makes clever use of dim backgrounds, atmospheric lighting and fade-outs to save on actual animation without losing too much impact. He is well supported by the music, which uses unusual sounds to enhance the eerie atmosphere, and employs that rarest of soundtrack elements, silence, very skillfully. Creator-writer-director-producer Morita also did storyboards, CGI animation, and editing, although he shares several credits with the obviously pseudonymous Kuro (*Shiro/Kuro* = White/Black).

Morita wanted to make a movie merging the old traditions of ghosts and ghouls stalking the darkness with the cities of modern Asia, where children play outside in dark, mazelike streets under flickering neon lights without a second thought, and reinstill that ancient fear of the dark. He succeeds very well, but his influences are just as much from older anime as from tradition. Hikora dresses like **DRAGON BALL**'s Son Goku with the addition of a priest's beads, Sorincha is a funky shrine maiden, and the atmosphere of fashionable ennui shares much with **BOOGIEPOP PHANTOM**. An intriguing and rewarding exploration of the dark side of **JAPANESE FAIRY TALES**, taking the eery elements of **SPIRITED AWAY** much further toward the horrific. Morita has also spun off a manga from the movie, starting in October 2005 in the quarterly *Magazine Zero*. **Ⓥ**

KALEIDO STAR *

2003. AKA: *Kaleidostar*. TV series. DIR: Junichi Sato, Yoshimasa Hiraike, Tadashi Hiramatsu. SCR: Reiko Yoshida, Miharu Hirami, Rika Nakase, Tsukasa Nakase. DES: Hajime Watanabe, Fumitoshi Oizaki. ANI: Hajime Watanabe, Fumitoshi Oizaki. MUS: Mina Kubota. PRD: Gonzo, TV Tokyo, Medianet, Hori Pro. 25 mins. x 26 eps. (TV1), 25 mins. x 25 eps. (TV2), 30 mins. x 2 eps. (V).

Kaleido Stage is a combination of circus, theater, and magic show, based in its own waterside complex in California—a fantastical version of the Cirque de Soleil. Fans the world over dream of standing in its spotlight thanks to world TV syndication and tours. Sixteen-year-old Sora Naegino has had her sights set on becoming Queen of the Kaleido Stage since childhood. She travels from Japan to America to take the entrance exam for the KS training school, and succeeds in getting into the show despite arriving late, missing the audition, and irritating the current leading lady, blonde Layla Hamilton. In the dressing room and later in her room at the school dorm, she finds a talking clown doll named Fool. Fool is really the "stage fairy," whom only a chosen few can see, and he tells Sora she has been chosen by the spirit of the stage to become a Kaleido Star. She has some talent and athletic ability, but her performance and dancing skills are woefully underdeveloped and she lacks confidence—all traits designed to encourage identification from wallflower viewers and put to their best effect in director/creator Junichi Sato's earlier **SAILOR MOON**.

The stage is set for a series of performances of the week, taking the cast through rehearsals, backstage intrigues, and productions of works that include their own versions of *Romeo and Juliet*, **LITTLE MERMAID**, and **ARABIAN NIGHTS**. Sora acquires several friends, including fellow performers Anna and Mia, who become her occasional allies in the battle of wits with Layla, as well as a performing seal called Jonathan. Typical to all such anime rites of passage, she also gains an affable, avuncular patron (Kalos, the owner of Kaleido Stage), a lovestruck boy next door (lowly stage manager Ken), and potentially dangerous prospective suitor (Layla's associate Yuri).

In a welcome change in the fast-paced 21st century, *KS* often takes its time with its plots and remains unafraid to shake things up. Later episodes find Sora packed off to Theatrical Camp and Marine Park, affiliated entertainment centers where she must hone new skills and deal with new problems. She must also wrestle with family issues and the growing realization that while she and Layla may be at each other's throats, they are also superb performers who are likely to end up having to share the stage. Layla believes in cold professionalism and is prepared to discard anything and anyone in the service of her talent, while Sora wants the stage to be a warm, friendly world where there's no conflict between players, and the audience is drawn in to a circle of happiness. After much conflict, the ingenue and the star become friends, and pull off a trick considered impossible, the Legendary Maneuver, in a show to save the Kaleido Stage—a theatrical apocalypse averted by a synchronized performance, something pastiched long before in **EVANGELION**.

The adherence to performance clichés even extends to the anime's surprise twist (look away now), in which Layla is injured and forced to retire, but not before entrusting Sora with the stewardship of the Kaleido Stage. In the second season, *KS Kanon 2*, released in the U.S. as *KS: New Wings*, the conflict between the warm camaraderie of a dream team and the tooth-and-claw struggle for stardom continues, as a new leading man arrives, and a new ingenue, talented and uberconfident May Wong, decides to take the crown Sora hasn't even claimed yet.

Even without real-world parallels like Japan's own Takarazuka troupe, whose young actresses must pass a strict entrance exam and live in a company dormitory, there are plenty of anime and manga inspired by the performing arts, most notably **MASK OF GLASS**, to which the plot of *KS* is often actionably similar. Creator and **SAILOR MOON**–director Sato layers elements of many live-action and animated dreams of stardom, as well as throwing in the transformation sequences, spirit guide, and cute animal sidekick so beloved of magical-girl shows, but he also asks: does the performer serve the audience, or vice versa? In these times of celebrity without talent and fame without effort, it's a valid question.

Kaleido Star is silly and lightweight on the surface, but with powerful truths about the vanity, insubstantiality, and basic nastiness of many performers; the physical tyranny of performance; and the temporary nature of fame, at its heart. Most of its "stars" are shallow and self-centered. Yet Sato is as spellbound by the roar of the crowd and the smell of the greasepaint as any old vaudeville hack, and he gives his fantasy a full-on, top-quality staging. In a sign of the times, he was actually unable to produce the show to his own specifications in Japan—it took the

injection of foreign funding from ADV Films and a Korean backer to ensure that the performance scenes had the necessary pizzazz. The stage sets and effects are gorgeous, and color planner Kunio Tsujita does a stunning job; the depiction of the sunset and the lighting of the end of the first episode, a true work of art, sets the tone. In Sato's hands, foreign lands and rites of passage are exciting but safe—so much so that the natives, from the police to chance-met passersby, are uniformly friendly, everyone speaks your language and wills you on to succeed.

Two later videos, *KS: New Wings Extra Stage* (2004) and *KS: It's Good! Goood!! / Layla Hamilton Story* (2005), introduce Rosetta, a new performer with the same endearing clumsiness and innocence that once defined Sora.

KAMA SUTRA *

1991. JPN: *Kama Sutra Kyukyoku no Sex Adventure*. AKA: *Kama Sutra: The Ultimate Sex Adventure*. Video. DIR: Masayuki Ozeki. SCR: Seiji Matsuoka. DES: Shinsuke Terasawa. ANI: Shinsuke Terasawa. MUS: Ken Yashima. PRD: Animate Film. 44 mins.
In 6th-century India, the brave knight Gopal is slain by the Naga cult. His bride Surya is saved from a fate worse than death by the Hindu gods, who transport her to a cavern of ice in the Himalayas. She is found in the 20th century by a team of archaeologists, who thaw her out in a Calcutta hospital by feeding her a mixture of male and female bodily fluids from an ancient relic called the Spermatic Cup. Surya immediately falls for the professor's handsome Japanese grandson, Ryu, who is a reincarnation of her beloved Gopal. However, she is kidnapped by the Naga cult's present-day leader, Rudracin, who whisks her away to the underground paradise of Shambhala. Realizing that Rudracin intends to take Surya as his bride, drink from the Spermatic Cup, and return to the surface world as an immortal, Ryu pursues them. After pleasuring 48 nymphs in midair, he is allowed to

enter Shambhala's temple, where he defeats Rudracin in a trial by combat. Ryu has sex with Surya but must leave her behind in Shambhala—the small print in the immortality contract. Back on the surface, he is reunited with his adoring Japanese girlfriend, Yukari.

A very different take on Hindu myth from the pious **RAMAYANA**, *KS* mixes the lovers-across-time theme of **ADVENTURE KID** with the playful smuttiness that has come to characterize Go Nagai's erotica. Based on an idea by Nagai and Kunio Nagatani, *KS* is the **DEVILMAN**-creator's answer to the *Indiana Jones* films, complete with an adventurous archaeologist who is scared of snakes, rooms with crushing walls (which the lovers must halt by taking off their clothes and jamming them in the cracks), chases through Third World marketplaces, and a holy grail whose powers are not all they seem. As if that wasn't enough of a hint, our hero also has an irritating sidekick, seemingly modeled on Nagai himself, who asks to be called Indy. Surprisingly little is made of the central lovers Ryu and Surya, who only get to do the deed once as the closing credits roll, or indeed of Ryu and Yukari, who hardly even meet during the story. Instead, Ryu is educated in the techniques of the *Kama Sutra* by his father's red-haired Indian assistant Shakti, who escorts him through an elaborate maze of enclosed rooms from which the occupants can only escape by assuming the correct sexual position. Mostly harmless, with some nice sitar music, but not a patch on the oriental eroticism of Tezuka's **ARABIAN NIGHTS**. ⬤Ⓝ Ⓥ

KAMEARI PARK PRECINCT

1985. JPN: *Kochira Katsushika-ku Kameari Koen-mae Hashutsujo*. AKA: *This Is the Police Station in Front of Kameari Park in Katsushika Ward; "Kochikame."* Video, TV series, movie. DIR: Hiroshi Sasakawa (v), Shinji Takamatsu, Shinichi Tabe, Shinichiro Watanabe (TV). SCR: Takao Koyama (v), Takashi Yamada, Satoru Nishizono, Nobuaki Kishima (TV). DES: Ammonite (v), Tsukasa

Fusanai (TV). ANI: Tsukasa Fusanai, Akitaro Daichi, Shunji Yoshida. MUS: N/C. PRD: Tatsunoko (v), Studio Gallop, Fuji TV. 30 mins. x 2 eps. (v), 15 mins. x 173+ eps. (TV), 90 mins. (m).

The gently humorous antics of a group of police officers responsible for a sleepy area near a large park. High jinks redolent of YOU'RE UNDER ARREST!, based on a 1976 manga from *Shonen Jump* magazine by Osamu Akimoto. Mild-mannered cop Ryotsu Kankichi is forever having to apologize for his behavior—as a shop assistant's son, he's a friendly neighborhood cop but eternally at odds with his avuncular boss Chief Ohara. The salt-of-the-earth Kankichi is forced to share his duties with supercompetent officer Reiko Akimoto and rich dandy Keiichi Nakagawa (a setup not unlike that of Goto, Shinobu, and Azuma in the later PATLABOR). The 2000 movie broadened the plot to encompass a bombing campaign by a disguised explosive expert named Benten (refer to CYBER CITY OEDO 808), with the Japanese police forced to cooperate with prissy FBI agent Lisa Hoshino. At over 100 volumes, Akimoto's manga is one of the longest-running in Japan. The anime's similar success, like that of SAZAE-SAN, is a mark of its popularity beyond the standard anime audience—the video versions were made to mark the 10th anniversary of the manga, and the first of the TV broadcasts marked the 20th.

KAMEGAKI, HAJIME

?– . Popular designer of robots on the GODMARS series who established Studio Z5 with his sometime collaborator Hideyuki Motohashi. After several animation jobs, became chief director on RESCUE KIDS.

KAMICHU

2005. AKA: *Junior High School God*. TV series. DIR: Koji Masunari. SCR: Hideyuki Kurata. DES: Takahiro Chiba. ANI: Koji Yabuno, Takahiro Chiba, Hideaki Shimada, Katsuya Asano. MUS: Yorihiro Ike. PRD: Aniplex, Brains Base. 25 mins. x 16 eps.

In a sleepy, hilly town on the edge of Japan's Inland Sea, eighth-grader Yurie Ichihashi suddenly becomes a *kami*—gaining the ability to enter the exclusive other dimension where Japanese spirits and gods take their leisure. She's also acknowledged as a god both by normal humans and other Japanese gods. But any thoughts she may have of living the life of a superhero are regularly thwarted—her powers desert her at critical moments, forcing her to grow up fast and embrace new levels of self-reliance.

In many ways, all magical-girl shows are about the same thing; based on a manga in *Dengeki Gao* by the pseudonymous Besame Mucho, *Kamichu* is played for laughs, and yet contains within it some thoughtful musings on why magical girls ever gain the ability to transform at all. It's all about growing up—compare to MARVELOUS MELMO and a similar tale of teen godhood, HARELUYA II BOY. The show exhibits tremendous creativity and Japanesquerie in illustrating *kami* and depicting a Japan in which the mundane and spiritual cohabitate, in a similar fashion to POMPOKO.

KAMIKAZE THIEF JEANNE

1999. JPN: *Kamikaze Kaito Jeanne*. AKA: *Jeanne de la Cambriole*. TV series. DIR: Atsutoshi Umezawa. SCR: Sukehiro Tomita. DES: Hisashi Kagawa. ANI: Katsumi Tamegai. MUS: Michiaki Kato. PRD: Toei, TV Asahi. 25 mins. x 41+ eps.

Alienated child-of-divorce Marron Kusakabe puts on her brave face and tries not to think about being left alone in Tokyo while her parents work abroad. She is visited by the angel Fin Fish, who reveals that she is the reincarnation of Saint Joan of Arc (known in the French fashion as Jeanne D'Arc in Japan). As the Day of Judgment approaches, it's Marron's job to retrieve important magical items to use in the battle against Satan. In her way stand transfer student Chiaki (who is really the rival angel Sindbad) and his dark angel assistant, Access

Time. Meanwhile, since Marron's mission is to steal artifacts, she must keep her secret from her best friend, whose father is the chief of police. Owing more to CAT'S EYE and SAINT TAIL than the legendary liberator of Orleans also depicted in TRAGEDY OF BELLADONNA, this adaptation of Arina Tanemura's manga for *Ribbon* magazine is set in a strange conflation of France and Japan, with European buildings but Oriental lifestyles.

KAMYLA *

2001. Video. DIR: Shinichi Shimizu. SCR: Dansu Ban. DES: Makoto Urawa. ANI: Makoto Urawa. MUS: N/C. PRD: Five Ways, Studio March, Studio Tulip. 29 mins. x 3 eps.

Agatha, Lily, and Koyomi are three female police officers whose skirts are way too short for regulation attire. They are members of a crack squad set up by the Japanese government to combat sex trafficking. During a warehouse raid to rescue a female hostage, Agatha is captured herself by the criminal mastermind Lead Suits (Led Suits in the original Japanese notes). She's taken to a small apartment and forced to watch as Lead plies the hostage with the forbidden drug Kamyla, which turns humans into mindless slaves. After the victim is sexually assaulted, Lead orders her to kill herself before forcing Agatha to take the drug as well. Even after she escapes his clutches, she finds the effects of Kamyla interfering with her work—code words set her off, and a side effect of the drug makes her feel uncontrollable lust at inappropriate moments. This eventually causes her to have sex with a suspect she is supposed to be interrogating, allowing her and Koyomi to locate Lead's hideout, where both girls are swiftly captured. Meanwhile, Lily is leading another group of agents to the rescue, but they get captured too, thanks to their drugged-up lust-crazed colleagues. An orgy duly ensues while Koyomi and Agatha half-heartedly try to fight off the effects of the drug. **LNV**

KANADA, YOSHINORI

1952– . Sketch artist and animator on many anime movies, including later installments of the STAR BLAZERS series and GALAXY EXPRESS 999. In the 1980s he became associated with the output of Hayao Miyazaki, as an animator on both NAUSICAÄ OF THE VALLEY OF WIND and subsequent Studio Ghibli productions CASTLE IN THE SKY, KIKI'S DELIVERY SERVICE, PORCO ROSSO, and SPIRITED AWAY.

KANDA, TAKEYUKI

1965– . Born in Fukushima Prefecture, Kanda joined Mushi Production in 1965 and worked on shows including TALES OF HANS CHRISTIAN ANDERSEN. He went freelance in 1972 and worked as an animator on LITTLE PRINCE and DORAEMON. Later works were largely for the Sunrise studio, including DRAGONAR and VIFAM, for which he has a cocreation credit.

KANEMORI, YOSHINORI

1949– . Born in Hiroshima Prefecture, Kanemori joined the animation department of Asahi Films in 1971, before establishing Studio Bird in 1974. He worked as a key animator on such productions as SPOOKY KITARO and PENGUINS MEMORY, before subcontracting his services as a character designer to the Madhouse studio for YAWARA and BARK! BUNBUN. He also worked as a character designer and key animator, respectively, on the war anime RAIL OF THE STAR and the DIARY OF ANNE FRANK. His directorial credits include FLY! DREAMERS.

KANNAZUKI NO MIKO *

2004. AKA: *Priestess of the Godless Month; Witch of the New Moon.* DIR: Tetsuya Yanagisawa. SCR: Jukki Hanada, Sumio Uetake. DES: Maki Fujii, Goro Murata. ANI: Akihiro Saito, Hideki Fukushima, Masanori Nishii. MUS: Mina Kubota. PRD: TNK, Rondo Robe. 25 mins. x 12 eps.

Two Japanese schoolgirls become the priestesses of the Sun and the Moon in a battle against ancient evils. Chikane is classy and aloof, while her friend Himeko is chattier and friendlier—a reprise of the odd couple pairings of innumerable buddy movies all over the globe, but most notably YOU'RE UNDER ARREST in recent times. Based on a manga serialized in *Shonen Ace*, which was created by Kaishaku, the pseudonymous creator of UFO PRINCESS VALKYRIE. Note that some Japanese sources wrote the title as *Kannaduki no Miko*, using an unorthodox romanization that has survived into some Western sources and fan discussions.

KANNO, YOKO

1964– . Arguably the greatest composer working in modern Japanese animation, Kanno was born in Miyagi Prefecture and first found fame as the keyboard player with the band TETSU100%. She subsequently moved into composing for television dramas, commercials and, ultimately anime—at first guesting on PLEASE SAVE MY EARTH. A "representative" work is a difficult thing to find for Kanno, since she excels at using obscure instruments, eclectic mixtures of styles, and mass orchestrations. Her work embraces the classical scoring of MACROSS *Plus* and ESCAFLOWNE and the dance-influenced tracks of GHOST IN THE SHELL: *Stand-Alone Complex*. She often works with a team of collaborators, sharing the credit for some work with her husband Hajime Mizoguchi, and occasional collaborators such as Akino Arai, Tim Jensen, and Steve Conte. She formed the jazz band Seatbelts as part of the composing process for COWBOY BEBOP. Rumors persist that "Gabriela Robin," who sings on some of Kanno's albums, is a pseudonym for the composer herself.

KANON

2002. TV series. DIR: Takamichi Ito. SCR: Ryota Yamaguchi, Michiko Yokote, Makoto Nakamura. DES: Yoichi Onishi, Itaru Hinoue. ANI: Masahiro Okamura, Nobuhiro Masuda, Nahomi Miyata, Haruo Ogawara. MUS: Hiroyuki Kozo. PRD: Toei Animation, Visual Art's/Key, Fuji TV. 23 mins. x 13 eps. (TV), 20 mins. (sp).

Sixteen-year-old Yuichi is, like so many other anime latchkey kids, effectively abandoned by his parents when they head off to Africa on business. He is ordered to move to his aunt's place, where he hasn't been for seven years, and finds himself living with his attractive cousin Nayuki. Although his memories of the time are hazy, it seems that he and Nayuki were once very close. As if that were not enough of a nod to LOVE HINA, Yuichi soon finds himself befriending and flirting with several other girls in the town, many of whom claim to have been friends with him in the past and may be interested in being more than friends now that they are teenagers.

Anime appears to excel at depicting, revisiting, analyzing, and fantasizing the desperate teenage stage where a boy will consider dating anything that moves. As with so many others, *Kanon* is based on an erotic dating simulation game (released in 1999), the only distinguishing feature of which was a series of supernatural subplots and some quite tragic endings for some of the girls, in the style of DIAMOND DAYDREAMS. However, the impact of the sad endings is lessened considerably in this anime version through some softening of the plots and an over-large cast of characters that make it difficult to care what happens to any of them.

The special, *Kanon Kazahana*, a 20-minute "bonus episode" directed by Ito and with character concepts by Itaru Higami, came out the following year and reveals a little more background about events that occurred before the final scene of the TV series.

KAPPAMAKI AND THE SUSHI KIDS

2003. JPN: *Kappamaki*. TV series. DIR: Saburo Hashimoto, Youn Sun-Kyu, Kim Dae-Jong, Lim Young-Bea, Lim Moon-Ki. SCR: Ikki Yamanobe, Babatsu Wakatsu. DES: Takashi Saijo. ANI: Takashi Saijo, Kim Dae-Jung. MUS: Keiichiro Suzuki. PRD: Dream Eggs, Trans Arts, TV Tokyo. 3 mins. x 130 eps.

The adventures of a band of talking sushi people, all friends of Kappamaki, a playful cucumber roll. Sent off to school by octopus dad and tuna mom, they dodge trouble from Mr. Wasabi the school principal and play under the watchful eye of the policeman Mr. Aoyagi, in a world that appears at a distance to be like our own, but is revealed in close-up to comprise the accoutrements, sauces, and tools to be found behind a sushi chef's counter. Conceived as a merchandising opportunity in the style of TARE PANDA, the *Kappamaki* world was initially modeled in clay by designer Eri Okamoto. A *kappa* is a Japanese water sprite familiar from JAPANESE FOLK TALES, who must keep wet at all times, and maintains this quasi-amphibian lifestyle thanks to a natural bowl-shaped depression in the top of his head that allows him to carry water with him. Cucumbers are supposedly the favorite food of *kappa*, hence the loan of their name to the cheap cucumber sushi known as *kappamaki*.

The series is not available in English at time of writing, although the English title we use here is derived from the rightsholder's English Web site, which urges us earnestly: "Please enjoy the mind-healing tales in this fantasy land." Until such time as someone eats your protagonist. Compare to TOMATO-MAN and DOGTATO.

KARAKURI NINJA GIRL *

1996. JPN: *Ninpo Midare Karakuri*. AKA: *Sowing Disorder the Ninja Way, Ninja Trickery*. Video. DIR: N/C. SCR: Miyasuke Ran. DES: Miyasuke Ran. ANI: N/C. MUS: N/C. PRD: Pink Pineapple, KSS. 30 mins. x 2 eps.
Reirei the sex ninja (Fawn Bell in the U.S. translation) and her companion Tsukimaru (Moon Shadow) attempt to escape from their hard life in Ninja Country so they can settle down together. After several sexual humiliations at the hands of their pursuers, they eventually reach our own world (compare to BEWITCHED AGNÈS), where Reirei becomes a housewife, and Tsukimaru puts his climbing skills to use as a con-

struction worker. However, their married bliss is interrupted by the arrival of Reirei's former lesbian lover Asagiri (Morning Mist), who demands that she return to her homeland. When initial entreaties fail, she attempts to remind her what she's been missing, immobilizes her by attaching a sacred card to her privates (difficult to do unnoticed, even with ninja skills) and tries to carry off Tsukimaru. However, true love conquers, and then it's Asagiri's turn for a bit of erotic punishment from Tsukimaru. A light-hearted erotic anime based on a manga by Ryo Ramiya (wife of Hiroyuki Utatane), lampooning many of the traditions of both other erotica and the magical-girl genre itself. *LNV*

KARAS *

2003. JPN: *Karas*. AKA: *Karasu, Crow; The Karas*. Video. DIR: Keiichi Sato. SCR: Shin Yoshida, Masaya Honda. DES: Keiichi Sato, Kenji Hayama, Kenji Ando. ANI: Kenji Hayama. MUS: Yoshihiro Ike. PRD: Tatsunoko. 30 mins. x 1 ep (TV), 30 mins. x 5 eps. (v).
In a near future Tokyo, humans go about their business unaware that they coexist with a spirit world. Japan's traditional ghosts and goblins are all around, but invisible to most. In order to keep things that way, every city has a priestess, a creature from the spirit world who takes on the form of a human girl, and chooses a supernatural aide or *karas* to help preserve the balance between the two worlds. However, Tokyo's guardian *karas*, the handsome blond warrior Echo, who has watched over it since it was called Edo, has gone rogue. Realizing that humans still have an atavistic fear of the spirit world, he aims to use an army of cybernetically engineered supernatural creatures to seize control of Tokyo, then Japan, then the world.

Mixing elements of the supernatural Cold War of WICKED CITY with the disappearing folklore of SPIRITED AWAY, *Karas* was designed as an anniversary event for the Tatsunoko Studio's 40th birthday. Its storyline has heavy echoes

of both DOOMED MEGALOPOLIS, with its concentration on a secret battle rooted in Tokyo's history and local lore—a *karasu* [sic] is a crow, one of the many black birds that can be seen and heard flocking around real-life Tokyo.

As in UROTSUKIDOJI, which *K*'s plot also vaguely resembles, Echo's nemesis is a spirit creature in human disguise, in this case his former boss Yurine, who looks like a trendy Shinjuku teen, but is really a long-lived sorceress. Yurine dispatches a number of opponents to deal with Echo, but when all fails she turns in desperation to Otoha, a young doctor running a spirit world hospital in Tokyo. He becomes the city's newest *karas*. He can fight like a ninja, and has spiky black armor that's a cross between bird and crustacean. He can fly; he can transform into various guises. He'll need all of this and more if he is to stop the course of destiny and limit the collateral damage to innocent parties on both sides.

Meanwhile, trendy young detective Narumi Kure has been assigned to a special unit dealing with spirit crime in Tokyo. Pretty, feisty Hinaru is investigating a series of strange killings in the city. And Nue the ski-bum wields a pair of infeasibly large and very arcane handguns, sounds like a country bumpkin, but is really a supernatural hunter, older and much more dangerous than he seems.

Director Sato brings an otherworldly look to the streets of Shinjuku, unsettling with tiny details such as incongruous European gargoyles and Singapore's famous Merlion statue in the background, and street signs in Korean and Chinese, so that at a glance street signs and writing look Japanese, but aren't. Sato describes the overall look as "Asian Gothic"—compare to a similar attempt to wrong-foot the audience in both GHOST IN THE SHELL and SPIRITED AWAY. The first episode was shown on pay-per-view TV before being released on DVD. *LNV*

KARATE-CRAZY LIFE, A

1973. JPN: *Karate Baka Ichidai*. AKA:

Life of a Karate Idiot. TV series. DIR: Eiji Okabe, Osamu Dezaki, Hideo Takayashiki. SCR: Yoshiaki Yoshida, Akinori Matsumoto. DES: Jiro Tsunoda. ANI: Okichiro Nanbu, Keijiro Kimura, Kazuhiko Udagawa. MUS: Mitsuru Kotani. PRD: TMS, MBS. 25 mins. x 47 eps.
Failed kamikaze pilot Ken Asuka becomes a rough, tough hooligan who settles all of his problems with karate, until he learns about the legendary swordsman Musashi Miyamoto in the novels of Eiji Yoshikawa. Resolving to live his life like Musashi, he begins to take karate more seriously. Based on a manga by Ikki Kajiwara and Jiro Tsunoda, itself inspired by the real life of Yasunobu Oyama, the founder of the "hard-knock" Kyokushin Karate school. The manga was also adapted into a trilogy of films starring Shinichi "Sonny" Chiba: *Champion of Death*, *Karate Bear Fighter* and *Karate for Life*. Compare to KICK FIEND, which is similarly based on a real-life sportsman.

KAREN *
2002. Video. DIR: Shinichi Shimizu. SCR: Dansu Ban. DES: TAKA. ANI: Akira Nakamura. MUS: N/C. PRD: Studio March, Five Ways, T.I. Net. 26 mins.
Ryo Ogawa is the captain of the ToAi high school male cheer squad, and one of the first female members in its 90-year history. In an apparent power play, she is threatened with the walkout of the four male members in the middle of a soccer match, one where the club's district supervisor is in attendance. Desperate to avoid the appearance of weakness, Ryo agrees to a series of "challenges." These are all designed around sexual humiliation, including pantyless cheerleading and, inevitably, having sex with the (previously winless) rugby team. Despite her initial reluctance she winds up liking it, in an anime that seems jointly inspired by the campery of *Water Boys* (2001) and the cheerleading comedy of *Bring It On* (2000). ●◐◆

KARIN
2005. TV series. DIR: Shinichiro Kimu-

ra, Hideaki Uehara, Takeshi Yoshimoto. SCR: Junichi Shintaku, Masaharu Amiya, Sumio Uetake, Takashi Aoshima, Yasunori Yamada. DES: Yumi Nakayama. ANI: Yumi Nakayama, Haruko Iizuka, Hiroyuki Shimizu, Osamu Sugimoto. MUS: Masaru Nishida. PRD: JC Staff, Garan, Studio Mark, WOWOW. 25 mins. x ?? eps.
Karin Maaka is the daughter in a family of vampires, who are supposed to be living in Japan without attracting the notice of the population. However, unlike her relatives, Karin does not suffer from a chronic lack of blood requiring donations from victims. Instead, she has too much blood and must somehow find ways of transfusing it into victims, lest she suddenly develop the ubiquitous nosebleeds common to so many school anime. A high school anime that tastefully allegorizes the obsession of teenage girls with blood and its loss—compare to BLUE SONNET and the manga *Red River*. Based on the manga *Chibi Vampire* in *Comic Dragon Age*, by Yuna Kagesaki.

KARUIZAWA SYNDROME
1985. Video. DIR: Mizuho Nishikubo. SCR: Tokio Tsuchiya. DES: Yoshihisa Tagami. ANI: Chuichi Iguchi. MUS: Shinsuke Kazato. PRD: Kitty Film. 76 mins.
In an adaptation of the manga that made a name for creator Yoshihisa Tagami, though radically different in every way from his more famous GREY: DIGITAL TARGET, the sex life of a young man is portrayed in graphic detail, occasionally lapsing into moments of super-deformed silliness. Sections are also shot in live action, directed by Tatsuo Moriyasu. ◐

KARULA DANCES
1989. JPN: *Hengen Taima Yako Karula Mau.* AKA: *Karula Dances! Nocturnal Phantasm Warders; Garuda Dances.* Movie, video. DIR: Takaaki Ishiyama. SCR: Masaru Yamamoto. DES: Chuichi Iguchi. ANI: Chuichi Iguchi. MUS: Makoto Mitsui. PRD: Agent 21, Picture Kobo. 80 mins. (m), 30 mins. x 6 eps. (v).
Teenage twins Maiko and Shoko Ogi

are the 38th generation to inherit the mystic warrior mantle of the holy Karula Shinyo line. They can also switch minds and combine their powers for greater strength against evil. Raised and trained by their grandmother, herself a psychic warrior of awesome powers, they fight the ancient spirits that lurk beneath the surface of modern Japan. Based on Masakazu Nagakubo's manga in *Halloween* magazine, the girls were just two of several anime "inheritors of ancient tradition" from the early 1990s, and they could be said to have inspired DEVIL HUNTER YOHKO and TWIN DOLLS, at least in part. They returned on video in 1990, finishing off demons in Japan's old capital of Nara, before heading up north to the city of Sendai to investigate cases of merpeople, amnesia, and crimes of demonic passion.

KASAI, OSAMU
1941– . Born on Hokkaido, Kasai graduated in fine art from the Japan University of Fine Art, becoming an animator at Toei Animation. His first animation work was on SECRET AKKOCHAN, and he went on to work on shows including CUTEY HONEY and the DRAGON BALL spin-off *GT*.

KASHIMASHI
2006. AKA: *Kashimashi: Girl Meets Girl.* TV series. DIR: Nobuaki Nakanishi. SCR: Jukki Hanada. DES: Sukune Inugami. ANI: Tomoko Iwasa. MUS: N/C. PRD: Studio Hibari, JC Staff, AT-X. 25 mins. x 12 eps.
Teenage boy Hazumu Osaragi attempts to confess his feelings for his classmate Yasuna Kamiizumi, but is told that she isn't interested. This is because Yasuna suffers from a strange condition that finds her unable to "see" the faces of boys. Imagine, then, how lucky Hazumu must feel when he is killed that night by a crash-landing alien spaceship, only to be resurrected in the body of a girl. This is good news for his chances with Yasuna, who suddenly finds him/her much more attractive, but causes friction with his/her child-

hood friend Tomari, who harbored a secret heterosexual crush on him, and has trouble accepting the fact that genders have switched. As if one's teens were not confusing enough, this anime based on an idea by Satoru Akahori was also turned into a manga in *Comic Dengeki Dai-oh* magazine. The term "*kashimashi*" literally refers to a cacophony of female voices, and is written with a character that uses three "woman" radicals—a visual pun in this case, since one of the women is actually a man … sort of.

KASUMIN
2001. JPN: *Soideyo! Henamon Sekai Kasumin*. TV series. DIR: Mitsuru Hongo. SCR: Reiko Yoshida. DES: Yoshihiko Umakoshi, Masaaki Yuasa. ANI: N/C. MUS: Yoshikazu Suo. PRD: NHK, OLM. 25 mins. x 26 eps. (TV1), 25 mins. x 26 eps. (TV2), 25 mins. x 26 eps. (TV3). Fourth-grader Kasumi Haruno is left by her Africa-bound parents in the care of the Kasumi family, whose huge mansion sits in a heavily forested park in Kasumi town. Kasumi is expected to help out with household chores at the strange house, but she soon befriends the appliances who, in a Disneyesque take on TONDE MONPE, are talking, interfering creatures called *Henamon* ("Weirdlings") by the family. Slapstick, candy-colored fun ensues, with highly stylized characters that often look more like POKÉMON than people.

KATOKI, HAJIME
1963– . The designer of many of the "mobile suits" in GUNDAM, Katoki also has a strong track record in games design.

KATRI THE MILKMAID
1984. JPN: *Bokujo no Shojo Katri*. AKA: *Katri the Girl of the Pastures*. TV series. DIR: Hiroshi Saito, Hiromi Sugimura. SCR: Akira Miyazaki. DES: Noboru Takano. ANI: Noboru Takano, Noriko Moriyoshi. MUS: Toru Fuyuki. PRD: Nippon Animation, Fuji TV. 25 mins. x 49 eps.
When her mother remains in 1915 Germany, little Katri is sent to stay with

her grandfather in Finland. Life is hard for the nine-year-old girl as war breaks out, and she is forced to earn money by working as a maid in the Raikola household. She meets various people, including Akki, a campaigner for Finnish independence, and Emilia, a doctor who inspires her to seek a better life for herself. This is another WORLD MASTERPIECE THEATER anime that mines the seemingly limitless vein of stories about little European country girls facing hardships, this one based on the Finnish novel *Paimen Piikamenta* by Auni Nuoliwaara. Compare to HEIDI.

KATSUMATA, TOMOHARU
1938– . Born in Shizuoka Prefecture, Katsumata graduated from the film department of Nippon University in 1960. He found work the same year with the Kyoto branch of Toei, working as an assistant director to Masahiro Makino on numerous samurai dramas. Transferring to Toei Animation in Tokyo, he worked as a director on the anime KEN THE WOLF BOY and CYBORG 009. Although he remained at Toei, during the 1970s he became strongly associated with that studio's output of anime based on the works of creator Go Nagai, most notably DEVILMAN and MAZINGER Z. He also worked on many of Toei's action-based anime, including FIST OF THE NORTH STAR and SAINT SEIYA.

KAWAI, KENJI
1957– . Born in Shinagawa, Tokyo, this composer is best known for his scores to the live-action *Ring* movies and in anime for his collaborations with Mamoru Oshii, notably GHOST IN THE SHELL and PATLABOR. Although not a member of the Headgear collective, he has often worked with them.

KAWAJIRI, YOSHIAKI
1950– . Born in Yokohama, he found work with Mushi Production after leaving high school. With the demise of Mushi in 1973, he was one of the early employees of Madhouse, and had his directorial debut with LENSMAN (1984). His WICKED CITY was upgraded to full-

length movie status after initial commission as a 35-minute video, leading to Kawajiri's association with several other adaptations of the work of novelist Hideyuki Kikuchi. Kawajiri was the most conspicuous proponent of the "urban gothic" style that characterized many of the most successful anime abroad in the 1990s (such as CYBER CITY OEDO 808 and DEMON CITY SHINJUKU) and also with the fast cutting of NINJA SCROLL. A combination of these influences is thought to have led to his commission to provide one of the works in THE ANIMATRIX.

KAWAMORI, SHOJI
1960– . Born in Toyama Prefecture, he began studying mechanical engineering at Keio University, but dropped out when his aptitude for realistic fantasy machines led to offers in anime. His first design sale, a "guest" robot in CAPTAIN HARLOCK in 1978, led to work with the design studio Studio Nue, and to major contributions to the look of MACROSS and DANGAIOH. Moving into animation direction and writing, he demonstrated a grasp of mature themes as a show-runner on MACROSS *Plus* (1994), leading to his innovative attempt to reach a dual male/female audience in ESCAFLOWNE (1996). Kawamori has been acquainted since high school with Haruhiko Mikimoto, Yutaka Izubuchi, and writer Hiroshi Onogi through their association with the science fiction event Kuri Con, and the group has often worked together since.

KAWAMOTO, KIHACHIRO
1925– . Born in Shibuya, Tokyo, and graduating from Yokohama National University, Kawamoto worked briefly as an art department assistant at Toho Studios before being fired in 1950 during a labor dispute. He supported himself by making dolls of famous stars, both for sale as novelty items and as part of a column on doll making, which ran from 1949 to 1952 in the *Asahi Graph* magazine. Commissioned by *Asahi Shinbun* journalist Tadasu

Iizawa to make and pose dolls in photographic tableaux for children's books, Kawamoto was eventually persuaded to make puppet animation in imitation of Jiří Trnka's *The Emperor's Nightingale* (1948). After early work in commercials, for which he was trained by Tadahito Mochinaga, Kawamoto studied in Prague with Trnka himself, before returning to Japan to make *Breaking of Branches Is Forbidden* (1968, *Hanaori*)—the first of what was originally intended to be a series of tales by both Kawamoto and Trnka, set along the stages of the "Silk Road" between Europe and Asia. As well as puppet work, Kawamoto was one of the few Japanese animators to continue working with paper cutouts, in both *Travel* (1973, *Tabi*) and the semiautobiographical *A Poet's Life* (1974, *Shijin no Shosai*). Although famed on the art house circuit for his shorts (for which see KIHACHIRO KAWAMOTO FILM WORKS), Kawamoto's work is better known to the Japanese public through television, most notably the 400 puppets he made for the 1982 NHK series *Romance of the Three Kingdoms* (*DE), and his later *Tale of the Heike* (1993). His later work reflects Buddhist and pacifist sensibilities, including puppet-based adaptations of Basho's poetry and Shinobu Orikichi's *Book of the Dead* (*Shisha no Sho*). Following the death of Osamu Tezuka, Kawamoto assumed the role of president of the Japan Animation Association in 1989.

KAYOKO'S DIARY *

1991. JPN: *Ushiro no Shomen Daaaare*. AKA: *Someone at My Shoulder*. Movie. DIR: Seiji Arihara. SCR: Seiji Arihara, Tetsuaki Imaizumi. DES: Takaya Ono. ANI: Takaya Ono. MUS: Reijiro Komutsu. PRD: Mushi Pro. 90 mins. (m1), 90 mins. (m2).
Kayoko is a nine-year-old girl in 1940 Tokyo, with a poor extended family that includes three brothers and a grandmother. She plays in her neighborhood but is bullied by other children, though she is protected by her kindly big brother Kisaburo. By

1944, Kayoko is caring for another brother, the newest addition to the family, while fear of air raids eventually results in her evacuation to live with her aunt in rural Numazu. From the hilltop, she can see the distant lights of Tokyo, until the night of March 10, 1945, when the city glows with the fires of an American bombing. All Kayoko's family are killed except Kisaburo, and the now-teenage girl returns to her old home one last time to say farewell to her childhood. Based on the autobiography of Kayoko Ebina, who also wrote the novel *Wolf of Downtown*, this tale follows the lead of GRAVE OF THE FIREFLIES, telling a war story through the eyes of a child. It also bears an uncanny resemblance to director Arihara's earlier RAINING FIRE. Shown on a double bill with the short ON A PAPER CRANE and given a limited foreign release through subtitled showings at film festivals. In 2005, the story was remade as the anime feature film *A Brighter Tomorrow: Half a Sweet Potato* (*Ashita Genki ni Naare: Hanbun no Satsumaimo*), directed by Shinichi Nakata, which concentrated more on the horror of the air raids and Kayoko's search for her brother in the ruins. The remake was one of several movies, including GLASS RABBIT and *Nagasaki 1945: The Angelus Bell*, put into production to mark the 60th anniversary of the end of World War II.

KAZE NO YOJIMBO *

2001. AKA: *Bodyguard of the Wind; Yojimbo of the Wind*. TV series. DIR: Hayato Date. SCR: Atsushi Yamatoya, Daisuke Yajima, Michiko Yokote, Satoru Nishizono. DES: Takeshi Ito. ANI: Choi Hoon-chul, Motosuke Takahashi, Ryuno Tatsuo, Yukimaro Otsubo. MUS: Tsuneyoshi Saito. PRD: Bandai, Studio Pierrot, Nippon TV. 25 mins. x 25 eps.
Lone investigator George Kodama comes to the small coastal town of Kimujuku, looking for a man called Genzo Araki. The townsfolk, however, are reluctant to offer much support, since they are deeply suspicious of

outsiders and of each other—a strange building pattern has caused Kimujuku to be literally cut in two by the railway tracks, with different architecture and attitudes on either side. George's investigations drag him deeper into a 15-year-old mystery about a disappearing train carriage, its contents a perennial subject of rumor and gossip.

Like SAMURAI 7, this anime relocates and refashions the action of a Kurosawa movie, in this case the divided town of *Yojimbo* (1961). However, the running time of a TV series offers the potential for a much slower pace and far more depth than the movie's simple parable, introducing local legends about "demons" that may refer to forgotten contacts with foreigners, and an ever-widening conspiracy with ties to the top that has more in common, not with the movie, but with the 1961 *Yojimbo* TV series (*DE). Considering that it is set in modern times and runs six times as long, one wonders why anyone should bother to play up the connections to Kurosawa at all.

KEEP IT UP! GUIDE DOG SAAB

1988. JPN: *Ganbare! Modoken Saab*. TV special. DIR: Seiji Okuda. SCR: Fujio Takizawa. DES: Shuichi Seki. ANI: Takashi Saijo. MUS: Hisashi Miyazaki. PRD: Tama Pro, NHK. 27 mins.
The true story of a seeing-eye dog that brings hope to a blind child, based on a novel by Yuichi Tejima. Lifting several tropes from sports anime such as AIM FOR THE ACE, a well-loved puppy's life is turned upside down as he is put through a tough training regime, until he triumphs and makes the world a better place.

KEKKAI *

2002. JPN: *Kekkai*. AKA: *Nature of the Heart; Clinical Interrogation*. Video. DIR: Shigenori Kurii. SCR: Hideo Ura. DES: Tettechi. ANI: Shigenori Kurii. MUS: N/C. PRD: Studio Foglio, Milky. 30 mins.
Chief inspector Kaoru is investigating a grisly murder; her sole clue is Kyoko, an amnesiac girl found at the scene of the crime. She calls in her old flame

Kekko Kamen

Junichi, a consultant psychologist who only agrees to help if she performs sexual favors for him. When Junichi does eventually get around to examining Kyoko, he pronounces her as suffering from multiple personality disorder and entertains the possibility that among her sexually motivated personalities there may be a murderous one that committed the crime. Psychological investigation was big on Japanese live-action TV at the turn of the 21st century, with shows such as *Hypnosis* (*DE) and *MPD Psycho* (*DE), so it is perhaps no surprise that someone should put a sexualized spin on the proceedings in anime. Compare to PRIVATE PSYCHO LESSON and ONI TENSEI. At time of writing, only the first "report" is available in English of what is clearly intended as a series. However, the Japanese website for the production company conspicuously files the *Kekkai* episode among its "completed serials," implying that there is not currently a plan to produce a sequel. ●Ⓝ

KEKKO KAMEN *
1991. JPN: *Kekko Kamen*. Video.
DIR: Chuji Iguchi, Nobuyoshi Kondo, Jun Kawagoe, Kinji Yoshimoto. SCR: Masashi Sogo. DES: Satoshi Hirayama. ANI: Masayoshi Sudo, Koji Morimoto. MUS: Keiji Ishikawa. PRD: Studio Signal, Dynamic, Bee Media. 45 mins. x 2 eps.
The students of Sparta College are terrorized by the perverse regime of the principal, Great Toenail of Satan (aka Satan Tochiz), and his lecherous assistant, Ben. Regularly appointing

new teachers to abuse and humiliate the girls (the boys are let off because Tochiz only wants to see the girls with their clothes off), they are thwarted on every occasion by Kekko Kamen, the "naked avenger."

A smutty, saucy adventure based on the 1974 *Shonen Jump* manga from SHAMELESS SCHOOL's Go Nagai, lampooning MOONLIGHT MASK (*Gekko Kamen*) and the sappiest formulae of girls' school dramas, with liberal doses of female nudity. Though occasionally pushing the boundaries of good taste (the first supply-teacher, S/M queen Gestapa, has just transferred from Auschwitz College), the idea of a super-heroine wearing nothing but boots and a mask so that "we see her dumplings, but her face remains a mystery," has plenty of comic potential. The hapless student Mayumi is whipped, tickled, and tortured, while her "big sister" Chigusa tries to offer helpful advice on escaping the teachers' notice. Superpowered opponents sent to take care of Kekko Kamen include the muscle-bound Austrian PE teacher, Taro Schwarzenegger, and a samurai cameraman with a hilarious Sean Connery accent in the U.K. dub. Mayumi must also fend off the advances of the Paradicer Mark One, a lesbian android sent to break up her friendship with Chigusa—Kekko Kamen must find Paradicer's off-button, which inventor Ben has put in a predictably sensitive spot. Though never explained in the anime version, the manga reveals that Kekko Kamen is actually Chigusa's twin, allowing the sisters to switch places and keep the superheroine's identity hidden. The story exists in U.S. and U.K. versions, though the British one did not survive the British censor unscathed—a scene in which Gestapa strips Mayumi by throwing knives at her while she is strapped to a giant rotating swastika was just one of the casualties. The story was also adapted into a live-action film, *Kekko Mask: The Birth* (1991), directed by Yutaka Akiyama, and two sequels, *Kekko Mask* (1993) and *Kekko Mask in Love* (1995).

But the live versions, which feature cameos from MAZINGER Z and CUTEY HONEY, suffer from a heroine who is understandably coy about revealing all and lack the slapstick verve of the anime. ●ⓃⓋ

KEN THE WOLF BOY *
1963. JPN: *Okami Shonen Ken*. TV series. DIR: Sadao Tsukioka, Kimio Yabuki, Yugo Serikawa, Hiroshi Ikeda, Yoshio Kuroda, Isao Takahata, Taiji Yabushita, Takeshi Tamiya, Masayuki Akehi, Kazuya Miyazaki. SCR: Satoshi Iijima, Yugo Serikawa, Kuniaki Oshikawa, Daisaku Shirokawa, Minoru Hamada, Jiro Yoshino, Aya Suzuki. DES: Sadao Tsukioka. ANI: Takeshi Kitamasa. MUS: Yasei Kobayashi. PRD: Toei, NET. 25 mins. x 86 eps.
Climate changes brought on by a passing comet plunge Africa into chaos, and a group of wolves struggle to survive. However, they have a trump card, the "two-legged wolf" Ken, a boy who lives with them in the jungle. Learning from Jack the wolf-hero and Boss the wolf-elder, Ken protects wolf cubs Chichi and Poppo. This variant on Kipling's *Jungle Book* was broadcast in Australia but is otherwise unknown in the English-speaking world.

KENNEL TOKOROZAWA
1992. Video. DIR: Hiroshi Sasakawa, Seitaro Hara. SCR: Shikichi Ohashi. DES: Katsumi Hashimoto. ANI: Katsumi Hashimoto. MUS: Ma-ri-ko. PRD: Animation 21. 44 mins.
Pet shop owner's daughter Chika Tokorozawa spends every waking hour with her dog, Rin Tin Tin, who repays her love by watching over her while she sleeps. Based on the manga in *Young Sunday* magazine by Maki Otsubo, who is better known in the manga world for *Mr. Cinema*.

KENYA BOY
1984. Movie. DIR: Norihiko Obayashi, Tetsuo Imazawa. SCR: Chiho Katsura. DES: N/C. ANI: Hiroshi Wagatsuma, Masami Suda, Kazuo Mori, Shingo Araki, Michi Himeno, Kenji Yokoyama,

Hirohide Yashikijima. MUS: Tatsuzo Usaki. PRD: Kadokawa, Toei. 109 mins. In late 1941, textile trader Mr. Murakami takes his son Wataru on a business trip out of his home base in Nairobi, Kenya. They are attacked by a rampaging rhinoceros and separate to escape it, but Murakami is found by the British. After the attack on Pearl Harbor, the British and Japanese are now at war, so Murakami is arrested. Wataru is taken in by Masai tribesmen and goes native, heading off in search of his father, with time out for *Indiana Jones*–style adventures with lions, elephants, a lost valley of dinosaurs, a giant snake, and a slimy Nazi spy. Based on Soji Yamakawa's novel *The Boy King*, this movie uses heavy rotoscoping techniques from former live-action director Obayashi to impart a more realistic look to some of the scenes. Compare to KEN THE WOLF BOY and BUSHBABY.

KERAKU NO OH—KING OF PLEASURE *

2002. JPN: *Keraku no O*. Video. DIR: Katsuyoshi Yatabe. SCR: Rokurota Makabe. DES: Berrys. ANI: N/C. MUS: N/C. PRD: Five Ways. 30 mins. x 3 eps.
After he suffers a brain injury in a childhood playground accident, Ryuichi Sashima is a hopeless case: he's bullied at school, he has no friends, and he is so passive even his parents have given up. Then the childhood friend who caused the accident transfers to his high school after a time in America. Chihiro had no idea he was so severely injured, and she is guilt-stricken. Naively, she offers to do anything she can to make it up to him, and when he asks for sex she doesn't feel she can refuse. Ryuichi learns that he has one ability that really is outstanding, and decides to use his unsuspected sexual prowess to get revenge on all the females who have ever scorned or bullied him. The rest of the series shows him working his way around the school, hitting on classmates, the student council president, and the school nurse. Based on a PC game from Fusen Club, with a nasty taste for revenge that

echoes ICHI THE KILLER and an insidious attempt to excuse it with disability, in the style of NANAKA 6/17. **⚫🅝🆅**

KEROPPI *

1989. JPN: *Kerokero Keroppi*. Video. DIR: Masami Hata, Masahito Kitagawa. SCR: Asami Watanabe, Shikichi Ohashi, Satoru Nishizono. DES: N/C. ANI: Tsuchiaki Noma. MUS: Yoshihisa Shirokawa, Richard Niels, Takeshi Ike, Katsuyoshi Kobayashi. PRD: Sanrio. ca. 30 mins. x 15 eps.
Kerokero ("Ribbit") Keroppi is a friendly green frog with huge eyes and stripy pants, designed on the same Sanrio merchandising production line that created PEKKLE, POCHACCO, and BAD BATZ-MARU. As do his stablemates, he appears in a series of cash-in videos designed to burn brand identity into the retinas of impressionable young children, commencing with cameo spots in other Sanrio videos in 1989. He appeared in the anthology title *KK Adventures* (1990), comprising his adventures in *In Search of the Pink Mushroom*, *Everybody Say Hello to the Priest*, and *Secrets at the Plum Shop*. Since then, *KK* has flitted between the staple formulae of Sanrio adaptations, including fairy-tale pastiches of *Three Musketeers* (1991), the theatrically shown "movie" *Jack and the Beanstalk* (1991), *Robin Hood* (1993), and *Gulliver's Travels*—these last two released in the U.S. He has also appeared in two moral tales, *Friends Are Fun* (1992) and *Let's Be Friends* (1994), though his educational aspirations never became quite so all-encompassing as those of his brand sister HELLO KITTY. Other *KK* outings are more "original," featuring several adventures for the frog and his friends, including *K's Christmas Eve Gift* (1992), the baseball adventure *Go for It! Keroppies!* (1993), the ghostly *Secrets of KK House* (1993), and the haunted museum chiller *That Dinosaur's Alive!* (1993). More wistful outings came in the form of *K's Flying Dream Ship* (1992) and *If I Could Fly . . .* (1994). In recent years, his anime appearances have waned—his last outing was in *Adven-*

tures of the Cowardly Prince (1997), which was released combined on a tape with the earlier *KK's Flying Ghost Ship*. *Go for It! Keroppies* and *Let's Be Friends* were also released in the U.S., under the title *K: Let's Play Baseball*.

KEY THE METAL IDOL *

1994. Video. DIR: Hiroaki Sato. SCR: Hiroaki Sato. DES: Kunihiko Tanaka. ANI: Keiichi Ishikura. MUS: Minya Terajima. PRD: Studio Pierrot. 25 mins. x 13 eps., 90 mins. x 2 eps.
A dying professor leaves a message for his granddaughter Tokiko "Key" Mima. She is an android, but she is dying, too, and her battery is irreplaceable. If, however, she can make thirty thousand friends, their love will rejuvenate her and turn her into a real girl. Realizing there are not too many ways to reach that many people in a limited time, Key heads for Tokyo, where her friend Sakura helps her begin a career as a pop singer. But she soon discovers that there is more to her destiny than the simplistic quest outlined by her grandfather—Key's predicament and its solution are tied up in the dark secrets of her own family. The adoration of the crowd can literally free her soul for a moment, but it can also unleash other, more effective powers that other interested parties are keen on gaining for themselves. An uneven but engrossing anime that flips between the attention-hungry desperation of a performance artist and a vampiric military conspiracy, with time out for a number of superior musical interludes. And with a lead character who thinks she is a dying robot but whose friends merely think she is a traumatized, abused little girl, it contains a subtle identity crisis that would be used to greater effect by another Mima, played by the same actress Junko Iwao, in PERFECT BLUE.

KIBA

2006. AKA: *Fang*. TV series. DIR: Hiroshi Kojina. SCR: Toshiki Inoue. DES: Susumu Matsushita, Takahiro Yoshimatsu. ANI: N/C. MUS: Jun Miyake. PRD: Madhouse, TV Tokyo, Aniplex. 25 mins. x 11 eps.

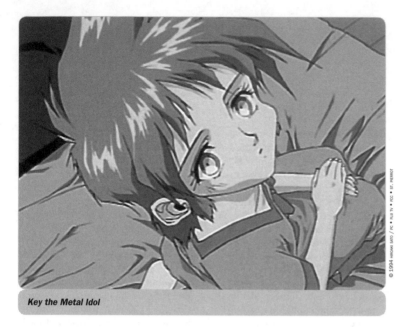

Key the Metal Idol

© 1994 HIROAKI SATO / PC • FUJI TV • FCC • ST. PIERROT

Zedd is a frustrated teenage boy in Calm, a land where there is no wind, seemingly no challenge, and where Zedd whiles away his days kicking down doors. When this inevitably leads to confrontation with the local police, the fleeing Zedd is offered the chance to jump through a space-time portal. It deposits him in a war-torn world where warriors are "Shard Casters" who fight with the aid of magical crystals, which they use to control monsters called spirits. However, Zedd is initially unaware that his own body harbors one of the most powerful creatures of all—a spirit called Amil Gaul, with the will and the means to seize control of the world, if only Zedd will let it.

KIBUN 2

2003. AKA: *Feeling x Feeling*. Video. DIR: Ryu. SCR: Aruto Raiga. DES: Ryu. ANI: Ryu. MUS: AC Sound. PRD: Museum Pictures, Milky. 30 mins. x 2 eps.
Kenji is a hard-working man, to the extent that by the time he comes home he is too tired to romance his girlfriend, who is tiring of his lack of interest in anything but sex. But after she inadvertently causes him to have an accident, they are stuck together

at home, and must learn how to be intimate once more. Before long, however, she is suspecting him of having an affair and sends her friend to follow him in secret, in an adaptation of the manga by **MAHOROMATIC** cocreator Bow Ditama. **N**

KICK FIEND

1970. JPN: *Kick no Oni*. AKA: *Devil Kick; Kick-Boxing Demon; Kick Fiend*. TV series. DIR: Yoshio Kuroda, Yasuo Yamaguchi, Nobutaka Nishizawa. SCR: Masaki Tsuji, Toyohiro Ando, Kuniaki Oshikawa. DES: N/C. ANI: N/C. MUS: Yasei Kobayashi. PRD: Toei, Noguchi Pro, Kajiwara Pro, TBS. 25 mins. x 26 eps.
After Osamu Noguchi, a Japanese fight promoter, brings traditional Muay Thai boxers to Japan in December 1959, karate champion Hideki Shihara takes the stage name Tadashi Sawamura in order to compete against them in the new sport of kickboxing. However, when he first goes into the ring, he is knocked out after 13 close calls. Determined to learn from his mistakes, he trains with Coach Endo and promoter Noguchi, hoping to improve his martial arts skills and popularize the new sport. The Japan Kickboxing Associa-

tion sets out its new rules in 1966, and the first World Kickboxing Championship is held in Tokyo in 1968, in a rags-to-riches tale that may seem to be a fictional account like **YAWARA**, but is actually based on a true story. Sawamura also appeared live in an **ULTRAMAN** (*DE) episode, training with "Ultraman Jack" Hideki Go. The anime was preceded in 1969 by a manga in *Shonen Gaho*, presented as a biography by **KARATE-CRAZY LIFE**'s Ikki Kajiwara and Kentaro Nakashiro. **V**

KICKERS

1986. JPN: *Ganbare Kickers*. AKA: *Go for It! Kickers!*. TV series. DIR: Akira Torino, Mutsu Iwata, Shigeru Morikawa. SCR: Sukehiro Tomita, Isao Shizutani, Mitsuo Jushibutsu. DES: Takeshi Osaka. ANI: Takeshi Osaka, Takeshi Nagai. MUS: Jun Irigawa. PRD: Studio Pierrot, Nippon TV. 25 mins. x 23 eps.
The soccer team Kitahara Kickers have lost 22 matches in a row, but all that changes when Sho Oji transfers to the team's school and imbues it with his hot-headed spirit. He inspires the team members to aim to win just a single match to regain their self-esteem. This short-lived series was based on a 1984 *Corocoro Comic* manga by Noriaki Nagai and is uncannily similar to **OFFSIDE**.

KIDDY GRADE *

2002. JPN: *Kiddie Grade*. TV series. DIR: Keiji Goto. SCR: Hidefumi Kimura. DES: Megumi Kadonosono. ANI: Masanori Ishioka, Megumi Kadonosono. MUS: Shiro Hamaguchi. PRD: gimik, Gonzo, GOTT, Kyoto Animation. 25 mins. x 24 eps.
The galaxy has suffered interstellar war and has finally formed the Globe-Governments' Union to bring peace and stability. But disputes persist over jurisdiction, eventually leading to the establishment of GOTT, the Galactic Organization of Trades and Tariffs, particularly its Encounter of Shadow-Work Member (ES) force, a group of agents who tend to work in pairs. Amid the slew of similarly unnecessary acronyms that makes a plot synopsis look

like a government manual, the important part is this: there are pretty girl agents, and they tend to work in pairs.

Hoping that the modern generation's attention span is short enough not to notice a darker, less exuberant take on DIRTY PAIR (and probably right in that assumption), Keiji Goto's "original" story concerns Éclair, a teenage agent whose secret weapon is a tube of lipstick made of a high-tech substance that actualizes on contact with air—thus when she draws a whip or a rope, she will have one for real. Her preteen cohort Lumiere has the power to control machines with her thoughts. These abilities, we are told, are what allow them to be agents at such a young age.

Mixing the girl-buddy crime fighters of GUNSMITH CATS with a sexy sci-fi setting out of AGENT AIKA, KG unsurprisingly introduces a forgotten past for one of its protagonists like something out of GUNSLINGER GIRL, causing Éclair and Lumiere to go on the run from their former associates. A feature of Eclair's trauma is that she seems unable to prevent herself from endlessly repeating the same pattern of events, which is somewhat ironic from an anime series that relentlessly reversions dozens of clichés from earlier shows. However, instead of being one more off-the-peg quirk, this revelation leads to a major shift in the show's priorities after the ninth episode, dumping the planet-of-the-week crime fighting of the early chapters in favor of a long arc in which the hunters become the hunted. As the characters recall their past lives, it also introduces elements of amnesia and reincarnation more familiar from GALL FORCE (or indeed, the final moments of the first GHOST IN THE SHELL movie), and more serious science fiction in the form of the Nouvlesse (a Japlish mangling of *Noblesse*), the wealthy, privileged elite of the GOTT universe who regard themselves as the last true humans in a galaxy of hybrids and mongrels. This ultimately leads to a full-on apocalypse as the fate of the Earth itself is threatened by a master race's master plan.

The Gonzo studio doesn't appear able to make anime that looks less than glorious; but here it faces what might be called the Ghibli problem—we have this fantastic technical ability, can we marry it to the same level of script and storytelling every time? *KG* is a thing of beauty, but not an earth-shaker, and the dark undertow of sensuality never quite comes good—or should that be bad? A manga spin-off also appeared in *Dragon Junior* magazine.

KIDS' ANIME

Despite the breathless boasts of foreign pundits that anime is "not just kids' stuff," the bulk of the medium is still made for an audience of high school age or below. Fairy tales and folklore comprise most EARLY ANIME, with animals and children pressed into allegorical service in WARTIME ANIME.

In the years after World War II and before television ownership spread through urban Japan, movie theaters and comics were the major sources of children's entertainment outside the playground. Toei's PANDA AND THE MAGIC SERPENT premiered in 1958 and went on to win international honors a year later, marking an important step in the rehabilitation of Japanese culture in the eyes of the Western world. Of the six children's movies made by the studio in the next five years, five were also sold in the U.S.A. MAGIC BOY (1959), JOURNEY TO THE WEST (as *Alakazam the Great*, 1960), THE LITTLEST WARRIOR (1961), and LITTLE PRINCE AND THE EIGHT HEADED DRAGON (1963) drew on Chinese and Japanese sources, while 1962's SINDBAD THE SAILOR later inspired scriptwriter Osamu Tezuka to produce a children's TV series and a movie for adult audiences. WOOF WOOF 47 RONIN (1962), an anthropomorphic take on Japanese history, was unseen in the West, though rookie animator Hayao Miyazaki was to enjoy greater success overseas in later years. Interestingly, Miyazaki has claimed that he still believes that one movie a year is all the anime children should be allowed to watch, and that they should spend the

rest of the time reading, playing with friends, and having their own adventures out of doors. We're guessing that the single mandatory film, in his eyes, should be one by Studio Ghibli.

These three themes—local legend, foreign literature, and animal antics—became staples of the children's anime market as television gained dominance. JAPANESE FOLK TALES got their own TV series in 1975. Classic European stories were retold in the WORLD MASTERPIECE THEATER series, as well as in big and small screen adaptations from "Jonathan Swift's" GULLIVER'S SPACE TRAVELS (1965) to Agatha Christie's HERCULE POIROT AND MISS MARPLE (2004).

Anime has continued to use animals as mirrors for the human condition in three distinct subgenres, reflecting the changes in 20th century Japanese society: semirealistic stories of animal life and human interaction with other species, like 1981's TAOTAO THE PANDA or 1994's TICO OF THE SEVEN SEAS; anthropomorphic stories, often comedies such as SAMURAI PIZZA CATS (1990), in which animals reflect aspects of human behavior; and stories where animals provide companionship for an isolated child, like DOG OF FLANDERS (1975) or SECRET OF THE SEAL (1991).

The year 1963 also marked the first wave of science fiction in TV anime. After Tezuka's ASTRO BOY appeared on both Japanese and U.S. screens, the giant robot genre was born with Mitsuteru Yokoyama's GIGANTOR, while human-android hybrid 8TH MAN foreshadowed *The Six Million Dollar Man* and *Robocop*, as well as 1966's CYBORG 009. Anime did not buy into the team shows popular in live-action until SKYERS 5 joined forces to fight evil in 1967. The show was revived in 1971, and a year later came perhaps the greatest of anime's contributions to the team show genre, BATTLE OF THE PLANETS. The show brought new levels of emotion and involvement to the rather simplistic monster-of-the-week formula established by live-action equivalents and generated such successors as SAINT SEI-

YA (1986) and RONIN WARRIORS (1989). Its influence persisted for more than a decade on shows such as GUNDAM *Wing* (1995's "boy band *Gundam*") and WEISS KREUZ (1998).

SCIENCE FICTION AND ROBOTS remain popular themes for children's anime, but females were subsidiary characters in most of these tales; it was 1966 before TV had its first true heroine, LITTLE WITCH SALLY, whose *Bewitched*-inspired trip to Earth to live as an ordinary girl and study humans became a prototype for a long line of magical girls; her thematic descendants include SAILOR MOON. The following year, Osamu Tezuka produced his first TV series for girls, the romantic yet powerful PRINCESS KNIGHT, a veiled comment on the roles and aspirations of girls in modern Japan wrapped up in a classic story of hidden identity and adventure that would inspire shows from ROSE OF VERSAILLES (1979) to UTENA (1997).

All these exotic fantasies should not obscure the numerous anime made about the events of children's day-to-day lives. Ordinary girls like AKANE-CHAN relocated to new lives more often than little witches; in Akane's case, her family moved from the country to Tokyo in Toei's 1968 series, mirroring a huge shift in a country whose prewar population was largely rural to a modern world where most live in cities. Twenty years later, Hayao Miyazaki was to look back with love and longing at a country childhood like the one Akane left behind in his movie MY NEIGHBOR TOTORO.

WANDERING SUN looked at two teenagers longing for a singing career, like many of its young viewers, in 1971. Children thrilled to SPEED RACER (1967), STAR OF THE GIANTS (1968), and RED-BLOODED ELEVEN (1970), dreaming of sporting success while parked in front of the TV set, a pattern which was to grow more pronounced across the developed world in the next twenty years. Even when they outgrew the comical antics of animals and cute spacemen, viewers could enjoy the outrageous behavior of Machiko

Hasegawa's NASTY OLD LADY (1970), who may have reminded them of their own granny or aunt at a time when extended families still lived together. The real world was also present in titles focusing on children's experiences of war. Often made as movies or video "specials" to commemorate anniversaries, these avoided awkward questions by recounting events from the standpoint of the truly innocent, as in BAREFOOT GEN (1983), but also acknowledged the struggles of the young and the tragic waste of their lives, as in Isao Takahata's powerful GRAVE OF THE FIREFLIES (1988).

Television acts as a mirror to everyday life, a babysitter, and a wish fulfillment mechanism, but all of these functions can also be afforded by movies. Television's two biggest selling points were cheapness and availability. Its status as the trusted visitor in the corner of the living room soon highlighted another function, one it filled far better than movies ever could; its ability to trade on pester power, to sell large amounts of merchandise to children.

The need to secure sponsorship, and the likelihood it would be coming from toy companies, has eternally steered the priorities of anime production. So, too, have the relatively low demands of the juvenile audience. The plotlines of early television anime are less stories than paradigms, blueprints for success to be tweaked and remodeled every couple of seasons, ready to impress a new group of youngsters who have never seen such a show before. Advertising on popular shows commands high prices, and production companies began to insist on merchandising potential before they would sponsor a show, while popular toy lines like the ZOIDS (1999) and fashion doll LICCA-CHAN (1990) got their own TV shows and videos.

Home video brought the possibility of buying movies to be repeated endlessly, or time shifting so that youngsters with heavy school schedules need not miss their TV favorites. This move

away from a programming schedule is accelerating in the new millennium as children in the developed world spend more time on personal delivery devices. Anime is being developed into bite-sized, attention grabbing segments that can be delivered cheaply on demand over a mobile phone. This reflects a social shift as massive as the one that moved Japan from a rural economy to an industrial and then a virtual one, or that which moved women out of the home and into the world of men. Its impact on children's anime will be enormous; no longer shared with family and friends, no longer delivered to set schedules, no longer requiring much investment of time or attention, but still, no doubt, an effective mechanism for selling to the young and impressionable.

In Japan as across the world in the latter half of the 20th century, adults began to hang on to childhood pleasures such as comics and trading cards. As fans grew up and looked for an older version of their teatime and Saturday morning viewing, anime became a multigenerational medium, the origins of the "retro boom" in nostalgia shows since the 1980s. Regardless of the growth of the market for erotica, which remains negligible in size compared to children's shows, the themes which appealed to children in the early years of anime still predominate today, often in anime aimed at far older audiences—a fact lampooned in shows such as NANAKA 6/17.

KIHACHIRO KAWAMOTO FILM WORKS *

2002. JPN: *Kawamoto Kihachiro Sakuhinshu*. Video. DIR: Kihachiro Kawamoto. SCR: Kihachiro Kawamoto. DES: Kihachiro Kawamoto. ANI: Kihachiro Kawamoto, Takeichi Sugawa, Yasushi Araki, Yutaka Mimi. MUS: Akihiro Komori, Goro Yamaguchi, Seiji Tsurusawa. PRD: Echo Studio. 14 mins. (*Breaking Branches*), 8 mins. (*Anthropo-cynical Farce*), 8 mins. (*Demon*), 12 mins. (*Travel*), 4 mins. (*Travel*—short version), 19 mins. (*Poet's Life*), 19 mins.

(*Dojoji*), 19 mins. (*House of Flame*), 1 min (*Self-Portrait*), 25 mins. (*Shooting*), 22 mins. (*Briar Rose*).

A DVD compilation of stop-motion and paper-cut animation by Kihachiro Kawamoto, released with English subtitles in the Japanese market—although many of the works on the DVD require no subtitles at all, with the action and drama conveyed through sign language and impressive expressions. Kawamoto's work impressively bridges East and West, with some films relying heavily on the conventions of kabuki and noh—such as the stylized backgrounds and movements of *Breaking of Branches is Forbidden* and *Demon*. His *Self-Portrait* is very short indeed and largely comprises a film loop of a plasticine Kawamoto alternately squashing and being squashed by a plasticine demon.

Breaking of Branches is Forbidden (1968, *Hanaori*) features a classic setup from Japanese drama, in which a young apprentice, left to pray and contemplate blossoms in a temple precinct, is persuaded to let a drunken samurai and his squire into the garden. In scenes of earthy comedy, the apprentice steals alcohol from the drinkers by dipping his prayer beads into the bowl and wringing out the sake. In one moment, the apprentice's head is drawn to the smell of fresh sake poured by the samurai, the head drifting several paces ahead of the body in a setup that owes more to the cartoonish deformations of Warner Bros. cartoons than puppetry.

Based on a story by Riichi Yoshimitsu, *Anthropo-cynical Farce* (1970) mixes paper cut-outs and stop motion for the tale of a betting man. It is not the only Kawamoto animation to use paper cut-outs on the disc; once a major component of all Japanese animation in the days before cels, cut-out animation now finds its last repose in some of Kawamoto's other work, most notably *Travel* (1973, *Tabi*), which can be found in two versions on this DVD. Using a collage style most likely to evoke Monty Python in modern audiences, *Travel* seems rooted in Kawamoto's own experiences of foreign countries. Its protagonist, a Japanese girl, heads away from home and experiences a Europe that is both museum and inner monologue, until the arrival of tanks symbolizes the upheavals in Czechoslovakia that so shocked Kawamoto after his happy experiences there. The final message, however, reflects a burgeoning sense of Buddhist struggle that would become ever stronger in Kawamoto's work—here, it is the journey itself, not the destination, which makes the titular travel worthwhile.

In *Demon* (1972, *Oni*), two Japanese brothers go out hunting for deer, only to be attacked by a demon in the forests. They cut off its arm and report home to their mother, but discover that the old woman's arm has itself been cut off, in a Japanese fairy tale adapted from the *Konjaku Monogatari*—the same "Tales of Past and Present" collection that also supplied the inspiration for NAUSICAÄ OF THE VALLEY OF WIND. A similarly Japanese theme can be found in *Dojoji Temple* (1976, *Dojoji*), in which a young monk's love for a fair maiden is thwarted when she transforms into a sea monster, all told in a scrolling form with a watercolor background. Comparable warnings about the fair sex can be found in *House of Flames* (1979, *Kataku*), in which the ghost of a young girl tells a fearful traveler about her torment in hell—having allowed two men to fight and die for her love, she suffers eternal agony for having given herself to neither of them.

Kawamoto's *A Poet's Life* (1974, *Shijin no Shogai*) is supposedly based on a story by Kobo Abe, although Kawamoto himself has suggested in interviews that its origins lie with his own experience of being fired from an animation studio in his youth. In it, a sleepy old woman factory worker accidentally weaves herself into the fabric of a jacket. When her son attempts to sell the jacket, old lady and all, he is fired and reduced to accosting his former workmates at the gate. Another strange career path can be found in *Shooting Without Shooting* (1988, *Bushe zhi She*), made by Kawamoto—

to as a Chinese coproduction and set in an idealized ancient China, in which an expert archer seeks to learn from a master even better than his own, only to be told that he should put down his bow and shoot without shooting.

In *Briar Rose or the Sleeping Beauty* (1990, *Ibara-hime mata wa Nemuri-hime*) a princess in an unspecified European country is shocked to discover that a prophecy predicts she will prick herself on a spindle and die, but that the action of good fairies has altered the curse so that she will merely fall asleep. Despite beginning like one of GRIMM'S FAIRY TALES, the story soon takes a new direction, when Briar Rose reads a secret diary, revealing that her mother the queen inadvertently broke a betrothal in order to marry her father the king. Wishing to break the curse, Briar Rose tracks down her mother's jilted lover, finding him living alone in the forest, bitterly lamenting that the queen did not wait for him when he went to fight in a war. Briar Rose offers herself in her mother's place, only to be abandoned in turn by the nameless old soldier once he has taken her virginity. Back at the palace, she is bereaved by her mother's death and lives in a daze, leading some gossips to refer to her as the "Sleeping Beauty." Eventually, she agrees to a loveless marriage with a handsome prince, in a sinister retelling of the fairy tale that highlights its Freudian subtexts.

The *Film Works* DVD is not exhaustive—it does not, for example, include Kawamoto's feature-length puppet animations *Rennyo and His Mother* (1983, *Rennyo to Sono Haha*) and *The Book of the Dead* (2003, *Shisha no Sho*). But it is a vital part of any core collection of Japanese animation—it may be Japanese and animated, but it is often a world away from what the mainstream often conceives as "anime."

KIKAIDER

2000. JPN: *Jinzo Ningen Kikaider*. AKA: *Android Kikaider*. TV series, video. DIR: Tensai Okamura. SCR: Akemi Omode, Shinsuke Ohashi, Masashi Sogo. DES:

Naoyuki Konno. ANI: Naoyuki Konno. MUS: N/C. PRD: Radix, Studio OX, Kid's Station. 25 mins. x 13 eps. (TV), 4 eps. (v).

When he is mortally wounded in an accident, Professor Koakishi is restored to life in an android body, believing that a good heart does not deserve to die before its time. But Koakishi's laboratory is attacked one stormy night by an unknown assailant. As his daughter Mitsuko escapes the flames, the whole incident is being watched by a young boy, Jiro, from a vantage point in the forest. Jiro is the last of Koakishi's creations, a robot created to save humankind, Mitsuko in particular. Fighting off the robot minions of the "dark professor" Gill, Jiro transforms into Kikaider, a super-powerful android ready to fight for good. One of CYBORG 009–creator Shotaro Ishinomori's most popular live-action creations, *Kikaider* was a relative latecomer to anime, not animated until after its creator's death. The box set of the DVD came with a 25-minute bonus episode, *Kikaider 01: The Boy with a Guitar* (*Guitar o Motta Shonen*, 2003), directed by Naoyuki Konno.

KIKI AND LARA . . .

1989. JPN: *Kiki to Lara*. Video. DIR: Masami Hata. SCR: Asami Watanabe, Kenji Terada. DES: Yukio Abe. ANI: Maya Matsuyama. MUS: Takanori Arisawa. PRD: Sanrio. 30 mins. x 8 eps.

The HELLO KITTY team returns for another onslaught of stories based around Sanrio-themed merchandise, on this occasion featuring the loving twins Kiki and Lara. First appearing in a 1989 remake of Maeterlinck's BLUE BIRD, they got their own short-lived series of videos in the early 1990s. The children play house, chase after a Pegasus foal, decide they want to be princesses for a day, and try out some magical dance shoes. They also appeared in their own version of the *Hansel and Gretel* story from GRIMMS' FAIRY TALES.

KIKI'S DELIVERY SERVICE *

1989. JPN: *Majo no Takkyubin*. AKA: *Witch's Special Express Delivery*. Movie. DIR: Hayao Miyazaki. SCR: Hayao Miyazaki. DES: Katsuya Kondo. ANI: Shinji Otsuka, Yoshifumi Kondo. MUS: Joe Hisaishi. PRD: Studio Ghibli. 102 mins.

Thirteen-year-old Kiki decides to follow in her mother's footsteps and become a witch, meaning she has to fly away from home and live for a year in a strange town. Accompanied only by her irascible black cat, Jiji, she heads for the seaside and finds the bustling harbor town of Koriko without its own witch. Finding a room at a kindly baker's, she discovers that her ability to fly on a broomstick is a marketable skill and begins delivering packages and messages. Despite minor mishaps and an often-ungrateful clientele, the freelance witch wins hearts all over town, particularly that of would-be pilot Tombo, who is smitten with her. A crisis of confidence causes Kiki to lose her ability to fly, but she regains it in time to save Tombo, who is trapped on a runaway airship. Writing to her mother, Kiki proudly calls Koriko her home.

Like MY NEIGHBOR TOTORO, *Kiki* is a world without definable enemies or evil—prissy rich girls may sulk when they get a fish pie for their birthday, but it's hardly an offense, and the only crime the police investigate in the course of the film is a fake one (Tombo pretends he has been robbed). Everyone creates value in their own ways, from the silent baker who melts Kiki's heart with a witch-themed bread sculpture, to the kindly old dog who protects Jiji from a bratty child. Venerable oldsters sigh about how times have changed, but the young generation shouldn't cause them to despair—like Kiki and her artist friend Ursula, they are simply finding their way in their own lives and times.

Miyazaki's follow-up to *Totoro* leaves childhood behind and steps into the early teens in one of the most wonderful films ever made about growing up. Set in a neverwhere Europe that com-

bines the look of Stockholm (where Miyazaki had been location hunting for the canceled 1971 Tokyo Movie Shinsha anime *Pippi Longstocking*) with the light of the Mediterranean, this utterly charming story is based on a book by Eiko Kadono, who also wrote the less well-known COBBY THE CUTE LITTLE CAT. The original *Kiki* novel lacked both the crisis of faith and the airborne resolution, which were added for the screen adaptation, initially against the author's wishes. Miyazaki films his witch with the same love of flight that characterizes NAUSICAÄ, with views and perspectives impossible from the ground. He imbues her with the independent spirit of Fio from PORCO ROSSO but does not shy from having a heroine who can catch cold, feel sorry for herself, and worry about her food budget. The result is arguably one of his best films, the seventh highest-grossing animated film at the Japanese box office, and a character who deserves to be the patron saint of freelancers, students, and motorcycle messengers.

Picked up by Buena Vista for U.S. distribution but not given a theatrical release, *Kiki* became one of the best-selling anime videos in America, trouncing AKIRA with sales topping a million. The U.S. dub featured Kirsten Dunst, Janeane Garofalo, and Phil Hartman freely improvising as Jiji in one of his last film roles. An earlier English dub, prepared by Carl Macek's Streamline Pictures for in-flight screenings on JAL transPacific flights, was included on the Japanese Laser Disc but never released in the U.S. The original title was pastiched in the live-action Japanese bicycle courier movie *Messengers* (2001), which went by the suspiciously similar name of *Majo no Sokutei*, or *Witch's Courier Service*, in its home country. A live-action movie adaptation of the original book of *Kiki*, with a script from Jeff Stockwell, is rumored to be forthcoming from Walt Disney Pictures.

KIKO-CHAN'S SMILE

1996. JPN: *Kiko-chan Smile*. TV series.

DIR: Setsuko Shibunnoichi. SCR: Tsubasa Yoshiura. DES: Yukari Kobayashi. ANI: Yukari Kobayashi. MUS: So-Fi. PRD: Magic Bus, TBS. 7 mins. x 51 eps.
In this adaptation of Tsubasa Yoshiura's comedy manga, a sullen, cynical child is born to a pair of lovestruck parents who truly adore each other. Arch comments on the folly of adulthood, in what some might describe as a junior version of *Daria*. Two episodes of *Kiko* bracketed a single episode featuring her pet cat and his feline friends, who develop the power of speech in their own shows, but become mute once more for Kiko's.

KIKUCHI, MICHITAKA

1963– . Born in Iwate Prefecture, Kikuchi graduated from Tokyo Design College and first worked in animation as a sketch artist on one of the later seasons of LUPIN III. His subsequent animation credits included some of the "magical girl" output of Studio Pierrot, sketch work on FIST OF THE NORTH STAR, and character designs on ZEORYMER HADES PROJECT. However, Kikuchi is far better known by his manga creator pseudonym "Kia Asamiya," in which role he is credited with the original stories to many popular franchises, including SILENT MÖBIUS, NADESICO, and STEAM DETECTIVES. He is the founder of the design outfit Studio Tron.

KILDIAN

1996. JPN: *Kigurumi Sentai Kildian*. AKA: *Dress-Up Battle-Team Kildian*. Video. DIR: N/C. SCR: Rei Nekojima. DES: Rei Nekojima. ANI: N/C. MUS: N/C. PRD: Pink Pineapple, KSS. 30 mins. x 2 eps.
Twin schoolgirls transform into their superhero aspects to save the world from an evil cabal of would-be dictators, but they can only fight for justice by having lots of sex. This short-lived porno anime was based on a manga by the pseudonymous Rei Nekojima—the only name of any sort attached to this show in our sources. **N**

KILL BILL: THE ORIGIN OF O-REN*

2003. Movie. DIR: Kazuto Nakazawa,

Toshihiko Nishikubo. SCR: Quentin Tarantino. DES: Sho-u Tajima, Katsuhito Ishii. ANI: Yasunori Miyazawa, Mitsuo Iso, Hideki Takahashi, Eiji Ishimoto, Naoyuki Onda, Mahiro Maeda. MUS: N/C. PRD: Production. I.G. 8 mins.
At nine years of age, O-Ren Ishii cowers unseen beneath the bed while mobsters attack her parents. Her father, a U.S. army officer of Asian descent, kills two of them but is mortally wounded by a third. Her mother is thrown onto the bed and stabbed by Boss Matsumoto, a ruthless yakuza. Two years later, O-Ren capitalizes on Matsumoto's love of little girls by seducing him in a school uniform and murdering him in bed. Before long, she is one of the world's top assassins, although she makes a fatal mistake when she and some of her fellow killers leave a former associate, "The Bride," comatose but still alive.

Although not a film in itself, this brief sequence appears as part of Quentin Tarantino's *Kill Bill: Volume One*. Tarantino's movie is a pastiche of Asian pulp genres and his anime sequence is no exception, conceived in apparent homage to the ultraviolence of GOLGO 13 and Madhouse urban gothic like WICKED CITY. Its influences are thus restricted largely to a handful of exploitationers released in the 1980s, when Tarantino presumably caught the beginnings of the U.S. anime video business: eviscerations, stabbings, and all, while any similarity to the original story of THE GOKUSEN is purely coincidental. The use of animation to present this particular part of the film may have also been a cunning ruse to avoid an NC-17 rating for the most controversial scenes—if he had used real actors for this sequence, would Tarantino have been able to show a preteen assassin murdering the pedophile who has just raped her? Nevertheless, the anime sequence was still slightly censored for its American release. In the uncut Japanese DVD release, O-Ren does not merely stab Matsumoto, but draws the knife lengthwise up his torso in graphic detail.

There are moments when *The Origin*

of O-Ren seems to quote tropes and ideas from manga rather than anime—the spattering blood is inky rather than bloody, and in one notable moment O-Ren has the word "whimper" literally issue from her mouth like a manga sound effect. Production I.G., which must have come to this job shortly after completing BLOOD: THE LAST VAMPIRE, puts a heroic amount of effort into replicating cel animation battles with 21st century technology—the sequence is largely motion-captured and then treated to look as if it were made in the old-fashioned way. Along with THE ANIMATRIX and the works of Hayao Miyazaki, this piece of footage was one of the anime most likely to reach a mainstream audience in the early 21st-century, although considering its origins in the writer's *idea* of what anime should be and its dated adherence to video-nasty shock tactics, some might prefer to file it among the FALSE FRIENDS. **LNV**

KILLIFISH SCHOOL

2001. JPN: *Medaka no Gakko*. Video. DIR: Hiroyuki Takagi, Ryoji Fujiwara. SCR: Miho Maruo. DES: Yukie Mori. ANI: Kiyotaka Kiyoyama. MUS: N/C. PRD: Office Ao. 30 mins. x 1 eps. and 10 mins. x 4 eps.
Japanese teenage girl Medaka transfers to a new school, where her homeroom teacher, Mr. Tanaka, has a fish for a head. This series is based on the surreal four-panel strip in *Ribbon* magazine by Yukie Mori and supposedly sold exclusively through the Internet (though since you could also phone, you'd be forgiven for just calling it mail order).

KIMAGURE ORANGE ROAD *

1987. AKA: *Orange Road Follies*. TV series, movie, video. DIR: Osamu Kobayashi, Kazuhiko Kobayashi, Hiroyuki Yokoyama, Kazuhiko Ikegami. SCR: Kenji Terada, Sukehiro Tomita, Shikichi Ohashi. DES: Akemi Takada. ANI: Masako Goto, Toyomi Sugiyama. MUS: Shiro Sagisu. PRD: Studio Pierrot, Nippon TV. 26 mins. (pilot), 25 mins. x 48 eps. (TV), 40 mins. (sp.), 25 mins. x 8 eps. (v), 34 mins. (music), 69 mins. (m1), 94 mins. (m2).

Kyosuke Kasuga falls for the pretty Madoka when her hat blows away in the wind, but the attractive, musically minded girl often seems aloof. To complicate matters, Madoka's bubbly friend Hikaru has fallen for Kyosuke, and although he likes her as a friend, he truly has eyes only for Madoka. Meanwhile, the junior champion of the karate club, who wants Hikaru for himself, is mad at Kyosuke, while Kyosuke's irritating sisters do everything within their power to make him realize that Hikaru is the girl for him.

A standard anime love polygon is exacerbated by a superfluous subplot revealing that Kyosuke and the rest of his family have psychic powers. Here, then, is the reason that Kyosuke is an eternal transfer student, as his family tries to outrun public suspicion. Terminally underused in many episodes, these optional extras merely allow for some easy getaways from difficult situations, though they are more often likely to backfire, like DORAEMON's inventions, and get him into still greater trouble. They also provide occasions for comedies of manners and social observations, such as Kyosuke's mind-reading cousin, who periodically blurts out people's secret inner thoughts for comedic effect.

KOR began as a manga in *Shonen Jump* by Izumi Matsumoto, its 1983 premiere imbuing the entire series with a deep sense of 1980s nostalgia. Its TV run was contemporary with MAISON IKKOKU, another drama-comedy about unsuitable friends becoming unexpected lovers, both made for the URUSEI YATSURA viewing audience as it aged and found comedy less exciting than romance. Retained in the anime version is a plethora of 1980s cultural references, chiefly musical, but also extending to the films of the moment such as *Top Gun*.

In 1988, the manga was jettisoned by its publisher and ended early in *Shonen Jump*, though the anime continued straight to video for several more episodes. Studiously tiptoeing around the TV series continuity, the videos packed the characters off for stand-alone episodes including a trip to Hawaii and a winter skiing trip in the Japanese Alps. The uneven TV series, which often flitted from romance to comedy to sci-fi pranks, was compartmentalized into several "specials" designed to bury the lackluster episodes and polish the undeniable jewels in each genre. A 34-minute music video, *KOR: Music Version*, comprised 12 tunes from the series played over a clip-show of best scenes. The story proper ended with the movie *KOR: I Want to Return to That Day* (1988). Directed by Tomomi Mochizuki and told chiefly in flashback, it discards all thought of comedy or psychic powers and concentrates instead on Kyosuke making a tough decision and breaking Hikaru's heart. Compare this to the coy attitudes of its spiritual successor TENCHI MUYO!, which remains permanently undecided in order to save everyone's focus-group feelings. Several more video episodes limped along afterward, two misleadingly premiered in theaters for those fans who couldn't accept that there would be no more—*KOR: Shapeshifting Akane, KOR: I Am a Cat/I Am a Fish*, and *KOR: Heart on Fire/Love Stage*. *KOR*, however, found a new lease on life in the U.S., where it was one of the cornerstones of early video anime fandom, many members of which were of an age to savor the 1980s nostalgia. It remained a fan favorite in Japan, too, and eventually returned for a second ending in *KOR: And So the Summer Began* (1996), directed by Kunihiko Yuyama. This version flings the 19-year-old Kyosuke three years into the future, where his newly graduated adult self is a cameraman in Bosnia. With his relationship with Madoka in trouble, and the return of Hikaru, the final *KOR* film presents an opportunity for everyone to live happily ever after—and for the viewers to say a final farewell by seeing their characters do the same, in much the same way as the final PATLABOR send-off.

KOR was preceded by a pilot episode, which was refashioned into a regular episode, and which was then released on laserdisc as *KOR: Weekly Shonen Jump Video*. A 40-minute "*Tanabata Special*" seems to also have been made in 1987, but we have little information about it.

KIMBA THE WHITE LION *
1965. JPN: *Jungle Taitei*. AKA: *Jungle Emperor*. TV series, movie. DIR: Eiichi Yamamoto, Junji Nagashima, Toshio Hirata, Chikao Katsui, Hideaki Kitano. SCR: Masaki Tsuji, Shunichi Yukimuro, Eiichi Yamamoto. DES: Osamu Tezuka. ANI: Chikao Katsui, Hiroshi Saito. MUS: Isao Tomita. PRD: Mushi Pro, Tezuka Pro, Fuji TV. 25 mins. x 52 eps. (TV1), 75 mins. (m1), 25 mins. x 26 eps. (TV2), 25 mins. x 52 eps. (TV3), 98 mins. (m2).

Panja (Caesar), the white lion king of the jungle, is killed by the human hunter Hamegg (Viper Snakely), who captures his mate Eliza (Snowene) alive. Caged on a ship en route to an overseas zoo, Eliza gives birth to their son Leo (Kimba), who escapes by jumping overboard. Eventually returning to the jungle, Leo befriends Mandy (Dan'l Baboon), a wise mandrill counselor, Coco (Pauley Cracker) the parrot, and Tommy (Bucky) the chronically shy deer. They revere him as Panja II, and Leo resolves to keep the jungle forever peaceful by ridding it of Bubu (Claw), his evil, scarred lion adversary, and bumbling hyena minions.

Paid for in part with money from American network NBC, *Kimba* was made with the demands of the foreign market in mind. Hence, ASTRO BOY–creator Tezuka was forced to make the story in bite-sized chunks that could be screened out of order without over-reaching story arcs. This restriction has severely damaged DRAGON BALL and certain other more recent anime that are often shown in a jumbled order by TV channels who can't count. On the bonus side, NBC money secured a high enough budget to leave monochrome behind, and *Kimba* became the first full-color anime TV series. Several episodes were cut together to make the movie *Jungle Emperor* (1966, *Jungle Taitei*), which was nominated for a Golden Lion for animation at the Venice Film Festival. The name Leo was regarded as unacceptable in the American market, where it was the name of the famous MGM lion; instead, the translators originally intended to name their hero *Simba*, Swahili for "lion." However, this was also rejected on account of a number of African-American trademark applications using the Simba name, which the producers could not be bothered to sort through in search of loopholes and potential infringements. The coincidence would return to haunt the franchise in the 1990s.

Tezuka's original 1950 manga *Jungle Emperor*, serialized in *Manga Shonen*, took the story of Leo much further along, with the white lion growing up, siring his own heir, and eventually laying down his life to save his realm. However, the concept of characters aging was another casualty of the stand-alone episode structure, and the anime Kimba remained permanently a cub. Tezuka redressed this balance with *New Jungle Emperor: Onward, Leo!* (1966, *Shin Jungle Taitei, Susumu Leo!*), a second series that took Leo to adulthood, which was initially intended solely for the Japanese audience. *Onward, Leo!* featured character designs from a young Rintaro and an involving subplot about Mount Moon and a fabled gem—a plot that would later be ripped off for episode six of **POKÉMON**. The adult Kimba/Leo was popular enough to become the mascot of the Seibu Lions baseball team in Japan (see **GO FOR IT, TABUCHI!**), and eventually made it to the States on the Christian Broadcasting Network under the title *Leo the Lion* (1984). By that time, however, Tezuka's studio Mushi Production had filed for bankruptcy, and a litigation tangle had taken the original *Kimba* series off the air.

The series was remade by Tezuka Productions as *New Adventures of Kimba the White Lion* (1989, *Shinsaku Jungle*

Kimba the White Lion

Taitei), directed by Takashi Ui, taking Leo from his birth up to the moment when he brings some semblance of order to the jungle. This version was also eventually released in the U.S., but not until after an unexpected brush with controversy in the mid-1990s.

The series had slowly faded from public perception until the release of Disney's *The Lion King* (1994), the tale of a lion called Simba, whose father dies, who just can't wait to be king, who has a mandrill for a counselor, an argumentative parrot-like bird (a hornbill) for a friend, and an evil, scarred lion adversary (plus bumbling hyena minions). Like Kimba, Disney's Simba is also haunted by his father's face in the clouds, a fact lampooned in an episode of *The Simpsons*, when the ghostly apparition of Disney's Mufasa appears to Lisa and mixes up the Simba-Kimba names. Disney representatives made the unlikely assertion that the *entire* production staff of *The Lion King* was unaware of the Tezuka original (including codirector Roger Allers, who, by Disney's own admission, had spent *two years* in Tokyo working on **LITTLE NEMO: ADVENTURES IN SLUMBERLAND**). The controversy was given further fuel when Fumio Suzuki, a

creditor who claimed partial ownership of the original 1965 series, authorized the rerelease of eight episodes on video as *Kimba the Lion Prince* (1996), with a new dub that seemed deliberately calculated to imply further, previously nonexistent parallels with the hapless Disney production.

Ironically, the controversy over the Disney film may have pushed Tezuka Productions into making yet another version of its own work, the movie *Kimba the White Lion* (1997, aka, much to the annoyance of encyclopedia compilers, *Jungle Emperor Leo*), released just a little too late to warrant the filmmakers' claims that it was in honor of the original's 30th anniversary. This time directed by Toshio Takeuchi and with character designs by Akio Sugino, the big-budget *Kimba* anime is the last incarnation of the series to date. Disney would inadvertently antagonize the anime audience again with *Atlantis: The Lost Empire* (2001)—see **SECRET OF BLUE WATER**.

KIMERA *
1996. JPN: *Ki-Me-Ra*. Video. DIR: Kazu Yokota. SCR: Kenichi Kanemaki. DES: Kazuma Kodaka. ANI: N/C. MUS: Shiro Sagisu. PRD: Toho. 48 mins.

Legends about vampires and vampirism are finally explained, as strange "lifepods" from space crash in the Western mountains. Their occupants are alien creatures who need humanity to help them propagate their species. A war begins between the space-vampires and their earthly prey, but Terran boy Osamu begins to have feelings for the androgynous Kimera, the vampire sent to kill him. An erotic thriller, based on a manga by Kazuma Kodaka, creator of KIZUNA, not to be confused with CHIMERA. ⓃⓋ

KING ARTHUR AND THE KNIGHTS OF THE ROUND TABLE *

1979. JPN: Entaku no Kishi Monogatari Moero Arthur. AKA: Rage of Arthur; Tales of the Knights of the Round Table. TV series. DIR: Masayuki Akehi, Tomoharu Katsumata, Masamune Ochiai, Kazumi Fukushima, Teppei Matsuura, Shigeru Omachi. SCR: Michiru Umadori, Akira Nakano, Tsunehisa Ito. DES: Takuo Noda. ANI: Takuo Noda, Yasuhiko Suzuki, Seiji Kikuchi. MUS: Shinichi Tanabe, Shunsuke Kikuchi. PRD: Toei, Fuji TV. 25 mins. x 30 eps., 25 mins. x 22 eps.

When his parents are killed by the evil King Lavic, the three-year-old Arthur is spirited away from Camelot castle by the sorcerer Merlin. Becoming a squire to Sir Ector, at the age of 15 he is able to pull the sword Excalibur from a stone, thus becoming the rightful ruler of the Britons.

A lackluster series that manages to make Arthurian legend look like just another cartoon, it compares unfavorably with anime such as ESCAFLOWNE that can make cartoons look like Arthurian legend. Based on Thomas Malory's Morte D'Arthur, but only indirectly, through a manga adaptation by GARAGA-creator Satomi Mikuriya, it was serialized in several children's publications, including Terebiland and Terebi magazine. The second series, Prince on a White Horse (1980, Moero Arthur Hakuba no Oji), sinks almost completely into anime cliché, dumping earlier talk of Lancelot, Morgan le Fay, and a Leiji Matsumoto–influenced Lady of the Lake. Instead, it seems to confuse legends of King Arthur with legends of King Alfred and a heavy dose of 1970s pulp fantasy, pitting the prince against an invasion of flying Norse longships crewed by the "Zaikings." Accompanied by a young boy with the suitably Old English name of Pete, Arthur must travel undercover, find some secret treasure, and defeat the evil Baron Damiane. In the final episodes, the story reintroduces the Knights of the Round Table and Princess Guinevere, but not before Arthur has met some mermaids, fought off some pirates, and had an encounter with a snow princess straight out of JAPANESE FOLK TALES.

Some of the more recognizable episodes were released in a U.S. dub in the 1980s by Family Home Entertainment in a version that provides additional unintentional hilarity as voice actors attempt English accents with varying degrees of failure. Further dolorous strokes were dealt to British heritage in MARINA THE MANGA ARTIST GOES TO CAMELOT.

KING FANG

1978. JPN: Oyukiyama no Yusha Ha-o. AKA: King Fang, Hero of Snowy Mountain. TV special. DIR: Eiji Okabe. SCR: Ryuzo Nakanishi. DES: Takao Kasai. ANI: Susumu Shiraume. MUS: Ryusuke Onosaki. PRD: Nippon Animation, Fuji TV. 75 mins.

A European wolf and a Sakhalin dog sire five puppies in the wild north of Japan. One day, the canine family is attacked by Gon, the man-eating bear, and the mother is killed. One of the puppies is found by a human girl under a waterfall. She adopts him and names him Taki (Japanese for waterfall), rearing him as a domesticated dog. However, as in CALL OF THE WILD, doubtlessly the inspiration for the Tatsuo Edogawa novel on which this anime is based, Taki's true nature eventually comes out, and he heads for the mountains to return to his own kind.

KING KONG SHOW, THE *

1966. JPN: Sekai no Osha King Kong Daikai. AKA: King Kong Ruler of the World. TV series. DIR: Hiroshi Ikeda. SCR: Noboshiro Ueno (trans.). DES: Jack Davis, Rod Willis. ANI: Sakei Kitamasa, Tsutomu Shibayama, Osamu Kobayashi, Midori Kusube, Yasuo Maeda, Norio Fukuda. MUS: Yasei Kobayashi. PRD: Toei, Videocraft, Rankin/Bass, NET. 56 mins. (TVm), 8 mins. x 52 eps.

King Kong is a giant ape who lives on an island in the Java Sea. Bobby Bond, whose father is a professor studying the island, meets King Kong and befriends him. Bond father and son cooperate to protect King Kong from the evil Dr. Who, although the large creature can more than hold his own in a fight.

Commissioned by Rankin/Bass from the U.S. company Videocraft, which in turn farmed out the work to Toei in Japan, King Kong was the first "anime" to be made specifically for the American market. Though Toei was funding part of it themselves and eventually showed it in Japan, the designs, scripts, storyboards, and voice track were all supplied ready-made from the U.S. As with the American version, episodes of KK bookended a single episode of TOM OF T.H.U.M.B. to comprise a half-hour show.

KING OF BANDITS JING *

2002. JPN: O Dorobo Jing. AKA: Bandit King Jing. TV series, Video. DIR: Hiroshi Watanabe. SCR: Reiko Yoshida, Chinatsu Hojo. DES: Mariko Oka. ANI: Mariko Oka, Studio Deen. MUS: Fumiko Harada, Scudelia Electro. PRD: Aniplex. 23 mins. x 13 eps. (TV), 27 mins. x 3 eps. (v).

Jing looks like an ordinary kid, but in fact he's a master thief. He and his lecherous bird partner, Kir, can steal anything, whatever security measures are taken. And if Jing ever finds himself in a tight spot, Kir can bond with his arm to form a supergun. Yuichi Kumakura's manga was animated for TV to show some of Jing's criminal triumphs, resulting in a series of capers like a kiddified LUPIN III, with just a touch of a SLAYERS-style cynic's attitude toward the genre. Nowhere is this more apparent than in the opening sequence, when the camera focuses on a lone figure, only be told it's got the wrong guy. Just as with Jing's antecedents in anime and manga, the master thief is soon stealing more than just trinkets; he rescues a girl from a slave market and becomes embroiled in a search for perfect paint colors. Later episodes take a leaf from the YOUNG KINDAICHI FILES, stretching across two- and three-part story arcs. One focuses on a collection of astrologically themed gems that is almost complete and only requires Jing to acquire the Sun- and Moon-stones. The final sequence finds Jing forced to endure gladiatorial combat in an arena, where, like all master thieves before him, he hopes to win the love of a noble beauty. A three-part video sequel, *King of Bandits Jing in Seventh Heaven*, followed in 2004, again directed by Watanabe with design and animation by Oka. Jing and Kir get into Seventh Heaven, the most notorious and most ironically named prison in the world, to try and steal the Dream Orb from convict Campari.

KINNIKUMAN: ULTIMATE MUSCLE *

1983 AKA: *Muscleman*. TV series, movie. DIR: Yasuo Yamakichi, Tetsuo Imazawa, Takenori Kawata, Takeshi Shirato. SCR: Haruya Yamazaki, Kenji Terada. DES: Toshio Mori. ANI: Eikichi Takahashi. MUS: Shinsuke Kazato. PRD: Toei, Nippon TV. 25 mins. x 137 eps. (TV1), 48 mins. (m1), 48 mins. (m2), 45 mins. (m3), 39 mins. (m4), 60 mins. (m5), 45 mins. (m6), 51 mins. (m7), 25 mins. (*Ramen Man*), 25 mins. x 35 eps. (*Ramen Man*), 23 mins. x 41 eps. (TV2), 26 mins. (*K2* m1), 60? mins. (*K2* m2).
Superhero Suguru Kinniku, the over-muscled Prince of Planet Kinniku, wrestles against numerous outlandish opponents, including the Texan Terryman, British lord Robin Mask, and legendary Chinese brawler Ramen Man. The most popular anime super-

hero of the 1980s, based on the manga in *Shonen Jump* magazine by Tamago Yude, Muscleman also wrestled on the big screen in seven anime features between 1984 and 1988. When his reign in the ring was over, he was replaced by *Fight! Ramen Man* (1988), first as a 26-minute "feature," then as a 35-episode spin-off TV series, directed by Masayuki Akehi, in which the Chinese superwrestler Mien-Nan hunts down the Poison Snake gang who killed his wrestler parents, employing comedy kung fu in the style of RANMA ½. Though unknown for a decade in the West, the wrestlemania appeal of *Muscleman* was too great to resist in the wake of the POKÉMON boom, and a U.S. broadcast was announced as forthcoming in 2001. The toys, however, sneaked abroad long before, released from Mattel as M.U.S.C.L.E. (Millions of Unusual Small Creatures Lurking Everywhere). Kinnikuman's son, Kinnikuman II, appeared in his own short anime movie in 2001. A new series, *Ultimate Muscle: Kinnikuman II* (2002) was followed by a third commissioned specifically for the American market—i.e., with toned down violence, ironically causing it not to be broadcast in Japan.

KINO'S JOURNEY *

2003. JPN: *Kino no Tabi*. AKA: *The Beautiful World*. Video, TV series, movie. DIR: Ryutaro Nakamura. SCR: Sadayuki Murai. DES: Shigeyuki Suga, Kohaku Kuroboshi, Takamitsu Kondo. ANI: Fumio Matsumoto, Takuya Matsumoto. MUS: Ryo Sakai. PRD: ACGT, GENCO, Media Works, WOWOW. 12 mins. (preview), 24 mins. x 13 eps. (TV), 30 mins. (m).
Kino is a teen on a talking motorcycle called Hermes in a picaresque set of new places-of-the-week, drawing on stories from *Pilgrim's Progress* to *The Littlest Hobo*. Kino's encounters are surreal fables, loaded with repetition and allegory. Encounters often involve experiments with utopia that have gone strangely awry, such as a society where telepathy has been enforced

upon the populace to foster harmony, but instead causes the opposite effect. Other meetings are framed as fables, such as three men, each unaware of the others' existence—one polishing railway tracks, the other ripping them up, and a third laying new tracks down, in a satire of corporate waste. A state adopts total democracy, only to collapse into mob rule; another gets robots to do all the work, leaving its populace idle. A nation declares itself to be the repository of all the world's books, but then censors its publications so mercilessly that there is little in the library but technical manuals and children's books. Two rival countries sublimate their warring impulses into sporting matches instead of war, but sporting matches with deathly consequences.

Some storylines stretch across more than one episode, such as the "Coliseum" arc, in which Kino must escape a gladiatorial arena where citizens fight for the right to make laws. In any other anime this would be an excuse for prolonged combat, but while Kino does eventually start shooting, the plot remains thoughtful. In any other anime, this would also be pretentious, obfuscating nonsense, but *Kino*'s symbolism has an ultimate purpose. Based on a series of novels by Keiichi Sigsawa, with art by Kuroboshi, originally serialized in *Dengeki* magazine, it is difficult to discuss the story of *KJ* without giving away one of its secrets: Kino is actually a girl. Although not a plot point of major importance, not referenced in many episodes, and less of an issue in non-gender-specific Japanese dialogue, this fact had a palpably damaging effect on the way the show could be sold abroad. On DVD in English, *KJ* has struggled to reach new audiences with carefully non-committal press releases and box blurbs.

The surprise is deadened somewhat by Kino's androgynous look, and by the fact that the voice is provided, like so many anime boys, by a female actress. She is traveling in imitation of Hermes' previous owner, the original Kino, a male traveler who stopped briefly in her homeland. Like the many utopias through which she passes, it was a flawed paradise, a country where children receive a neural modification before puberty that turns them into contented, compliant adults. Our Kino takes up the questing mantle of the original after he dies protecting her from her parents, who want her to undergo the same operation.

Screened on late-night television in Japan, *KJ* seems designed to provoke thought and debate, its surreal encounters often scripted by **Perfect Blue**'s Murai, its sparse direction often by **Serial Experiments Lain**'s Nakamura. The pale colors are so painterly that the screen frequently gains canvas textures, the images so superfluous at times it's practically radio rather than animation. Its wandering protagonist is an everyman for the teenage audience, a living symbol of their own search for meaning and belonging in an inner world whose rules are eternally shifting. Many, if not most, anime are about the trauma of growing up and finding one's place, but *KJ* breaks new ground in its use of magic realism to convey the idea. That's not to say it does not have its inspirations, but it seems rooted in the "soft" SF of the New Wave, such as J.G. Ballard, or the poetic allegories of Ray Bradbury, rather than the "hard" SF that informs so many other anime storylines. The result is beautiful and remarkably restful after the frantic attention grabbing of some contemporary shows with their excess of flash and bounce, but it's more like meditation than entertainment.

A short prequel disc, *Kino's Journey—Totteoki no Hanashi*, was issued with a booklet in Japan in 2003, which included a "visual version of the novel" entitled *To no Kuni—Freelance*, and trailers for the then-upcoming series. The 2005 movie, *Kino's Journey—Life Goes On (Kino no Tabi—Nanika o Suru Tame ni)* is a prequel which shows the protagonist, wracked with guilt about

the death of the real Kino, being trained by her teacher. After being directed to seek out Kino's mother, she sets off on her journey, framing the rest of the season of *KJ* as an homage to **From the Apennines to the Andes**—"3000 leagues in search of *someone else's* mother."

KINOSHITA, RENZO

1936– . Born in Osaka, Kinoshita graduated from the Electrics department of Daitetsu High School before finding work making commercials in Osaka. He moved to Mainichi Broadcasting, after which he founded his own company, Peppe Productions, in 1963. Under the Peppe aegis, he worked on early TV anime such as **Big X** and **Qtaro the Ghost**. He joined Mushi Production in 1966, where he worked on **Cleopatra: Queen of Sex**, before forming his own Studio Lotus in 1970. His later work, often made in collaboration with his wife Sayoko (1945–), is characterized by short animated films exhibited at film festivals—before the post-**Akira** boom of the 1990s, Kinoshita was arguably the "official" face of Japanese animation abroad. His *Made in Japan* (1972) won the Grand Prix of the inaugural New York Animation Festival, while later shorts such as *Men Who Did Something First* and *Pikadon* won similar accolades elsewhere. In recent times, his work has reflected a pacifist, internationalist, antinuclear stance, as shown in **Tobiwao is Taken Ill** and his unfinished *Okinawa*.

KIRA KIRA MELODY ACADEMY

2001. JPN: *Kirakira Melody Gakuen.* AKA: *Twinkling Melody Academy.* Video. DIR: Nobuo Tominaga. SCR: Toshimichi Ogawa. DES: N/C. ANI: Narimitsu Tanaka. MUS: N/C. PRD: Media Factory, AIC. 30 mins.

A mystery drama centering on four would-be singer-actresses, students at the Kira Kira Melody Academy and top of a class of 22 who have agreed to intrusive media attention during their studies. The twist lies in the fact that all 22 are based on real girls who

volunteered for the "Kira-Melo" talent contest and its subsequent radio, merchandise, and gaming spin-offs. The girls are students at the Melody Academy, a nonexistent drama school on the outskirts of Yokohama, who have been whittled down from the original 2,000 applicants to a reception class of 56 through a year of "exam failures" and "transfers" to 22, and then thinned still further to determine the stars of the anime. In other words, a kind of staged reality TV—the logical, marketing-led conclusion of a long tradition that ran from the animated biography of a pop group in **Glorious Angels**, through artificially engineered singing groups based on anime casts in **Hummingbirds**, and up to anime shows built entirely around prefabricated groups such as **Debutante Detectives**. The point being that producers can now effectively market-test future stars *while* they train them, which is either very clever or shamelessly exploitative, depending on how seriously you take **Perfect Blue**. As with reality TV itself, throwing two dozen amateurs at an audience may indeed be more entertaining than a lot of fictional drama, but such a situation is an indictment of the depths to which fictional drama has sunk. Compare also to the "real-life" drama of the earlier **Lemon Angel**.

KIRAMEKI PROJECT

2005. Video. DIR: Katsuhiko Nishijima. SCR: Hiroshi Yamaguchi. DES: Yoko Kikuchi. ANI: Yoko Kikuchi. MUS: N/C. PRD: Studio Fantasia. 30 mins. x 5 eps.

Three pretty sisters are the rulers of the Jeunesse kingdom, where the eldest, Krone, is head of the military. Middle sister Kana is a bespectacled scientist who, for reasons not all that clear, has spent a lot of time working on a robot handmaid called Lincle. Youngest sister Nene simply hangs around, until the kingdom is attacked by a giant robot called Big Mighty. So what? You may well ask. One of the show's major attractions is that Kana owns and controls a super powerful remote-controlled giant robot of her own, which looks exactly like a blonde girl, complete with a frilly dress and a purse. Shades of ARIEL, only with a parody attitude instead of sci-fi action.

KIRARA

2000. Video. DIR: Kiyoshi Murayama. SCR: Noriko Hayasaka. DES: Shinya Takahashi. ANI: Shinya Takahashi. MUS: N/C. PRD: Ashi Pro, Toho. 39 mins.
Teenager Konpei daydreams about how his future wife might look, only to find her ghost sitting by his bedside. Kirara Imai has traveled back in time from her own death, hoping to rewrite history to keep her and her beloved Konpei together forever. Sure enough, as the apparition predicts, Konpei meets a girl called Kirara Imai and falls in love with her, but he is reluctant to tell her that they are destined to marry in seven years, or that she will be killed in an accident shortly afterward.

A clever variation on the quintessential time-travel story, this video was based on a 1993 *Young Jump* manga by CREAM LEMON's Toshiki Yui. With an older, experienced woman initiating her husband-to-be into romance, and aiding in the seduction of her own younger self, it is a truly mind-bending set of paradoxes, not unlike the teen years it so subtly surveys. Beyond the story itself, the anime version increased the level of cheesecake and swimwear from the original manga—artful sci-fi or not, teenage boys will never complain about female nudity.

Also available in an extended edition that includes footage of the open casting call in 1998 where amateur actresses read for the part of the young Kirara. Though hyped at the time as a great way of obtaining raw young voices (a tactic also employed in HIS AND HER CIRCUMSTANCES), the *Kirara* production was so delayed that sweet-16 actress Chiaki Ozawa was a strapping 18-year-old by the time the anime was released. ●

KISAKU *

2002. AKA: *The Letch.* Video. DIR: N/C. SCR: N/C. DES: N/C. ANI: N/C. MUS: N/C.

PRD: elf, Pink Pineapple. 30 mins. x 6 eps. (v1), 30 mins. x 3 eps. (v2).
A janitor holds keys to every door in the building and has a reason to go into every room, any time. The opportunities for a lecher are boundless—especially when the building he's responsible for is a girls' college. He doesn't just confine his activities to the workplace, either—he's soon out and about tying up hotel chambermaids, getting heated at a spa, partying with a salaryman at the Playboy Club, and checking out the nurse's office. The one hour *Kisaku Ultimate Sirudaku* aka *Kisaku Revival* (2004) was a re-edit of the highlights of the first six episodes, to prepare the audience for the sequel *Kisaku Spirits* in which Kusaki, a lawyer, concludes a large contract with Sugimoto Pharmaceuticals, but feels too shy to go to the celebration party. However, he is possessed by the soul of Kisaku, who steers his body toward following some pretty girls into the party, where predictable high jinks ensue. Compare to ISAKU and SHUSAKU, said to star the protagonist's brothers, and LOVE IS THE NUMBER OF KEYS, which appears to have the same plot. Based on a computer game by Elf. ●●●

KISHIN CORPS *

1993. JPN: *Kishin Heidan.* AKA: *Machine-God Corps; Geo-Armor.* Video. DIR: Takaaki Ishiyama. SCR: N/C. DES: Masayuki Goto. ANI: Masayuki Goto. MUS: Kaoru Wada. PRD: AIC, Pioneer. 60 mins. x 1 eps., 30 mins. x 6 eps.
An alternate World War II history even more insidious than DEEP BLUE FLEET, suggesting that Japan only invaded Manchuria to protect the world from aliens!

Aliens are attacking Earth, and Japanese scientists have reverse-engineered some of the captured technology to create the Kishin Corps, a group of giant robots who travel in trains, start with hand cranks, and then pummel the opposition into submission—the opposition being the aliens, and those misguided Japanese who have sided with the Nazis.

The story is pure 1940s matinee adventure, with wonderful character stereotypes—the good woman, the femme fatale, the goofy scientist, the dashing flying ace, the dastardly general, and his obedient minions. Real people crop up, or rather have their names borrowed; Eva Braun is included as a top scientist prepared to do anything in the pursuit of knowledge, though in this reality she has an angelic twin sister, Maria. Superb robot action spread throughout an excellent story and some particularly great chase sequences make up for pacing that is at times painfully slow. One of several retro anime that try to rewrite the lead-up to Pearl Harbor, to be filed with SAKURA WARS and VIRGIN FLEET—doubtless intended as innocent hokum, but somehow distasteful in a country that still avoids telling its schoolchildren the truth about the war, however entertaining the fictions.

KISS XXXX

1991. Video. DIR: N/C. SCR: Maki Kusumoto. DES: Maki Kusumoto. ANI: N/C. MUS: Yurei, Sakana. PRD: Victor Entertainment. 25 mins.
Kanon, the lead vocalist in a band, falls for the doll-like charms of the pretty Kameno-chan. She inspires him to write a love song every day but brings trouble into his life along with the happiness. An image video of scenes from Maki Kusumoto's 1988 manga in *Comic Margaret* magazine set to music from several popular bands of the day.

KITAYAMA, SEITARO

1888–1945. Born in Wakayama, former watercolor artist Kitayama founded the Japan Association of Western Art in 1912 and published its bulletin *Gendai no Yoga (Contemporary Western Art).* Seeing French and American animated shorts in Japanese cinemas in 1916, he persuaded the Nikkatsu company to fund his first work, the earliest MONKEY AND THE CRAB (1917), drawn directly onto paper. Kitayama was the most prolific of the early animators, largely thanks to his ability to delegate to a staff of half a dozen underlings. His *Momotaro* (1917—see Early Anime) was the first anime to go abroad, screened in Paris three months before its Tokyo premiere. He established the Kitayama Eiga studio in 1921, acquiring lucrative contracts in commercials and documentaries. Relocating to Osaka after the Great Kanto Earthquake, his animated output gradually dwindled as he became more involved with producing live-action newsreels. Despite his comparatively large output, his only extant work is *Guardsman Taro and His Submarine* (1918, *Taro no Banpei: Sensuitei no Maki*).

KITAZUME, HIROYUKI

?–. Found fame as a character designer with Studio Vivo on the "Zeta" Gundam series and L-Gaim. One of the animators selected to contribute to the anthology Robot Carnival.

KITE *

1998. Video. DIR: Yasuomi Umezu. SCR: Yasuomi Umezu. DES: Yasuomi Umezu. ANI: Yuki Iwai. MUS: An Fu. PRD: Beam Entertainment. 30 mins. x 2 eps.
Sawa is a teenage girl and an agent for an underground ring of vigilantes who has been traumatized by the deaths of her parents. Kept in line by drugs and sexual abuse at the hands of corrupt cop Akai, she is sent out armed with explosive bullets to assassinate criminals the law cannot touch. She starts to fall for a boy on a mission with her, but she also comes to realize that the man she now calls father (and lover) is the man who killed her parents.

Excessively violent and featuring scenes of child abuse and underage sex that had to be cut even for the liberal American market, *Kite* draws on several live-action movies for its inspiration. Most notable is John Badham's *Point of No Return* (1993, itself a remake of Luc Besson's earlier *La Femme Nikita*), in which a pretty killer is trapped within the organization that has made her. There are also tips of the hat to Takashi Miike's *Fudoh* (1996), particularly a vicious restroom shootout.

Umezu had formerly treated the same themes and ideas in *Yellow Star*, one of the entries in the Cool Devices erotica series. Remade with a longer running time and high-quality animation, he concentrates on balletic, graceful fight choreography amid utter mayhem, and a poignant tale of doomed love between two damaged souls. But as the video-cover panty shots of Sawa attest, *Kite* is far more interested in titillating its audience with sex and violence than it is with condemning them. A live-action production is supposedly in development, produced by Rob Cohen and Anant Singh, to be written by Joshua Rubin and directed by Jorge and Javier Aguilera. ●NV

KITERETSU ENCYCLOPEDIA

1987. JPN: *Kiteretsu Daihyakka*. TV special, TV series. DIR: Takashi Watanabe, Keiji Hayakawa. SCR: Shunichi Yukimuro, Takashi Yamada. DES: Fujiko-Fujio. ANI: Tsukasa Fusanai, Kunihiko Yuyama. MUS: Katsunori Ishida. PRD: Shinei, Fuji TV. 75 mins., 25 mins. x 331 eps.
Kiteretsu and Eiichi love inventing things, but they only ever show their latest creations to Eiichi's girlfriend, Miyoko. Kiteretsu discovers that he is a descendant of the 19th-century inventor Kiteretsu Sai, receiving a copy of Sai's legendary *Encyclopedia of Inventions* from his father. The story returned in 1988 as a full-fledged series, overseen by Hiroshi Kuzuoka. Based on a Fujiko-Fujio manga in *Corocoro Comic* but with its concentration on a group of children getting in and out of trouble with a selection of magical toys, *KE* is little more than a respray of the same creators' earlier and far more successful Doraemon.

KIZUNA *

1994. AKA: *Bonds*. Video. DIR: Rin Hiro. SCR: Miyo Morita. DES: Ayako Mihashi. ANI: Ayako Mihashi. MUS: Fujio Takano. PRD: Seiji Biblos, Daiei. 30 mins. x 2 eps. (v1), 30 mins. (v2).
Handsome young man Ranmaru "Ran" Samejima is involved in a hit-and-run

"accident" that was really a failed attempt on the life of his friend Enjoji. As he recovers, the care and attention lavished upon him by Enjoji make him fall deeper in love with him, and the couple move in together. Their friendship is strained by the attentions of a college professor, who tries to seduce Ran. But Enjoji's family are gangsters, his half-brother also wants Ran, and the lothario professor has bitten off more than he can chew. This video was based on the manga created for *Be-Boy* magazine by Kazuma Kodaka, who also created Kimera. In 2001, a one-shot sequel, *Kizuna: Much Ado About Nothing* (*Kizuna: Koi no Kara Sawagi*) was released. Despite being let down by poor subtitling on the part of the original distributor, this was one of the very first openly gay anime available in English, to be filed alongside the more humorous Fake. It has since been joined by a rising tide of similar (and more hardcore) titles, such as My Sexual Harassment. ●NV

KNIGHTS OF RAMUNE *

1990. JPN: *NG Knight Lamune and 40; NG Knight Lamune and 40 EX; NG Knight Lamune and 40 DX*. Video. DIR: Hiroshi Negishi. SCR: Brother Anoppo, Satoru Akahori. DES: Takehiko Ito, Rei Nakahara, Takuya Saito. ANI: N/C. MUS: Tadashige Matsui. PRD: Ashi Pro, TV Tokyo. 25 mins. x 39 eps. (TV1), 30 mins. x 3 (*EX*), 30 mins. x 3 eps. (*DX*), 25 mins. x 26 eps. (*Fire*), 30 mins. x 6 eps. (*Fresh*).
Japanese schoolboy Ramune is a big fan of the computer game *King Sccasher*, until one day the beautiful Princess Milk jumps out of his screen and drags him back to the game-world of A'lala. There, he is hailed as the legendary hero Ramuness, come to save the world from the evil overlord Don Harumage. *N[o] G[ood] Knight Ramune and 40* made a name for Satoru Akahori, who would reprise the formula ad infinitum throughout the decade. Resprays of the same setups and gags would dominate Beast Warriors, Maze, Sorcerer Hunters, and many others, while the bold,

unshaded splashes of bright color, originally an attempt to simplify designs for
less experienced animators in Korea,
would appear in many other shows of
the 1990s.

The series returned straight to
video as *NG Knight Ramune and 40 EX*
(1991), directed by Koji Masunari, in
which Ramune, now at middle school,
is approached by Milk once more in
search of his aid because her world has
been attacked by a mysterious giant
robot. Before long, the series was back
again as *NGR&40 DX* (1993), in which
"Ramuness" and his band travel back
5,000 years in time. Adopting a **Tenchi
Muyo!**–style formula of throwing in
new cheesecake whenever it ran out
of ideas, the series returned to TV
as *V[ersu]s Knight Ramune and 40 Fire*
(1996). In this incarnation, Ramune's
help is solicited by three beautiful
androids named Drum, Trumpet, and
Cello. By this point, he is a full-grown
adult, who Turns To The Dark Side,
remaining there for the video sequel *VS
Knight Ramune and 40 Fresh* (1997). The
only part of the series to be released
in English, under the title *Knights of
Ramune*, it features busty babes Parfait
and Cacao on a quest to bring back
the legendary knight Ramuness, only
to discover that he's at the helm of the
lead ship in an invading alien fleet.
With a poverty of ideas typical to late
1990s anime, many of which persist in
believing that "zany" means "amateurish," this involves a bit of espionage,
spell-casting, and a few gags about how
underwear interferes with the power of
magic, as they run around a big spaceship in the company of a mascot that
resembles a talking tumor, waiting for
the enemy to bring the plot to them.

However, despite being the fifth
series in the franchise, *KoR* contains
little to confuse audiences—the hours
of backstory prove to be utterly inconsequential. New director Yoshitaka Fujimoto papers over gaping holes in the
plot and action with perfunctory T&A
and a few incidences of halfhearted
sauciness—because more "mature"
viewers can apparently be appeased by

Knights of Ramune

a couple of nipples and a bit of suggestive panting. There are some frames of
Gunbuster-inspired space warfare, and
tantalizingly short bursts of excellent
animation, but *KoR* is the kind of anime
that leads first-time viewers to assume
the entire medium is nothing but big
eyes, explosions, and weary plot-by-
numbers. The U.S. voice cast seem to
think so too, contemptuously indulging
in over-the-top pseudonyms like Ruby
Seedless and Autumn Harvest. Ⓝ

KOBO-CHAN

1990. AKA: *Kobo the Little Rascal*.
TV series. DIR: Hiroyuki Torii, Tameo
Ogawa. SCR: Noboru Shiroyama. DES:
Joji Yanagise. ANI: Hiroyuki Torii, Joji
Yanagise, Hisatoshi Motoki. MUS: Nori-
ko Sakai. PRD: Eiken, Yomiuri TV. 12
mins. x 15 eps.
The adventures of a five-year-old boy
in the tradition of *Peanuts*, based on
Masashi Ueda's four-panel cartoon
strip in the *Yomiuri Shinbun* newspaper.

KOGEPAN

2001. AKA: *Burnt Bread*. TV series. DIR:
Shuichi Ohara. SCR: Masako Hagino.
DES: Miki Takahashi. ANI: Shuichi Ohara,
Yoshiki Hanaoka. MUS: Takeshi Yasuda.

PRD: Studio Pierrot, Pony Canyon, Sony
Magazines, Animax. 4 mins. x 10 eps.
In a Hokkaido bakery, a little red bean
bun looks forward to being one of the
20 most delicious buns in the shop.
However, the baker accidentally drops
him, and the bun is burned. Over-
cooked for 30 minutes, he is eventually
retrieved from the oven, but now with
a blackened crust that will render him
forever unable to enter the ranks of
the elite buns. Bullied and mocked by
the other buns, he gains the nickname
Kogepan, or Burned Bread. He runs
away from home and takes up smoking and heavy drinking (of milk), but
eventually returns to the bakery, where
he reads a book on self-improvement,
hoping one day to be as perfect as the
other buns. His friends include the
similarly fire-damaged Cream Bread
and Charcoal Bread (who is even
worse off), and the Pretty Breads, who
are always happy and perfect, and
do not understand the poignancy of
Kogepan's life. Wildean pathos ensues,
in a tale that takes the bakery-themed
children's entertainment of **Anpanman**
and introduces a note of irredeemable
tragedy. Kogepan is doomed to lan-
guish unsold while his perky golden-

crusted companions fulfil their destiny and fly off the racks into the wide world, although perhaps it is best that he doesn't see his friends getting eaten alive each week—compare to **KAPPAMAKI AND THE SUSHI KIDS**. Stationery, accessories, and other merchandise featuring the characters created by Miki Takahashi enjoyed some popularity but didn't attain the heights of **TARE PANDA**, let alone **HELLO KITTY**.

KOI KAZE *

2004. AKA: *Love's Zephyr; Love's Wind.* TV series. DIR: Takahiro Omori. SCR: Noboru Takagi. DES: Takahiro Kishida. ANI: Naoyuki Oba. MUS: Masanori Takumi, Makoto Yoshimori. PRD: ACGT, Geneon, TV Asahi, Rondo Robe. 25 mins. x 13 eps.

Wedding planner Koshiro Saeki is dumped by his girlfriend over commitment issues and ends up on a date with 15-year-old schoolgirl Nanoka. He finds himself falling for her, only to discover, to his horror, that she is his sister. Estranged from his mother for the 14 years following his parents' divorce, Koshiro has all but forgotten about his sibling, but now he is forced to pretend that nothing has happened between them when Nanoka moves in with him and his father.

As Koshiro and Nanoka struggle to behave like "normal" brother and sister once more, Koshiro is filled with self-loathing. He even goes to visit his mother for the first time in years to see if she can help him find answers, though there are no answers he wants to hear. He and Nanoka are brother and sister, and that's how they must love each other, if their story is not to have a tragic and sinful end. Meanwhile, Koshiro's state of mind leads to overreactions to otherwise everyday events. His lecherous work colleague Odagiri asks if Koshiro can set him up with his sister, while a female coworker Chidori sometimes appears like an older, more socially acceptable clone of his sister.

Despite sounding like the setup for a hundred erotic anime, *Koi Kaze* is

nothing of the sort. It's a serious, well-written TV show about forbidden love, drawing for inspiration not on anime but on several recent live-action dramas—*High School Teacher* (*DE), *Strawberry on the Shortcake* (*DE), and, at a more superficial level, *Wedding Planner* (*DE). It deals, of course, with many of the subliminal themes and rationalizations of **LOLITA ANIME**, but also with the impossible relationship that has been a staple of TV anime since **URUSEI YATSURA** and **MARMALADE BOY**. Based on a manga by Motoi Yoshida.

KOI KOI SEVEN

2005. TV series. DIR: Yoshitaka Fujimoto. SCR: Tamotsu Mitsukoshi. DES: Koji Watanabe. ANI: Masafumi Yamamoto. MUS: N/C. PRD: Trinet, Studio Flag. 25 mins. x 13 eps.

TENCHI MUYO! crashed into **SAILOR MOON**, as average teenager Tetsuro Tanaka transfers to a new school, where he foolishly refuses to believe that the largely female classroom population will make much trouble. Instead, he finds himself on the run from a series of military attacks and defended by a mystical group of schoolgirl warriors called the Koi Koi Seven, although there are initially only six of them. Based on a manga by the pseudonymous Morishige, which ran in *Champion RED* magazine, and featuring terrible animation quality, made barely tolerable by a constant barrage of anime parodies and clichés including references to, most notably, **EVANGELION** and **GUNDAM**.

KOIHIME *

2000. AKA: *Love Princess.* Video. DIR: Shinichi Masaki. SCR: Takao Yoshioka. DES: Mayumi Watanabe. ANI: Mayumi Watanabe. MUS: N/C. PRD: Pink Pineapple. 30 mins. x 2 eps. (v1) 30 mins. x 2 eps. (v2).

Musashi comes to his old home in a tiny remote village to stay with his grandmother for summer vacation. He's been away for fifteen years and has very few remembrances of childhood, but on the way he recalls vague

memories of a strange, intensely emotional game-ritual when he and four local girls pricked their skin and tasted each other's blood. Once he gets to the village, hot local cuties Nami, Anzu, Suzaku, and Mayuki remember him very well, and their intentions toward him are anything but childish. As he sleeps his way back through his lost memories, a story from his childhood unfolds. He actually promised to marry all four girls, who are not really girls at all but nature spirits, whose father is a dragon and whose love for Musashi almost caused the end of their world last time he left, when the grief of Nami the snow princess caused the entire region to ice up. **LOVE HINA** meets **CRIMSON CLIMAX**, although at the softer end of the scale—despite being billed as a production by KSS's erotic label Pink Pineapple, many crewmembers have retained their real names, including designer Watanabe, who worked on **TENCHI MUYO!**. A sequel, *More Koihime* (*Zoku Koihime*), followed in 2001. **◑**

KOIKO'S DAILY LIFE

1989. JPN: *Koiko no Mainichi.* Video. DIR: Noboru Ishiguro. SCR: Akira Miyazaki. DES: Joji Akiyama. ANI: Kiyotoshi Aoii. MUS: N/C. PRD: Nippon Animation. 50 mins. x 2 eps.

In a story that flits between serious drama and comedic farce, Shinjuku gangster Sabu and his young wife Koiko try to live a normal life, despite the interferences of gang politics and criminal deals. After she saves his life, Sabu's gang-boss, Tominaga, falls in love with Koiko, and sends Sabu into increasingly more dangerous situations, hoping to cause his arrest, and thus obligate himself to "take care" of Koiko while Sabu is in prison. Based on a manga in *Manga Action* magazine by **PINK CURTAIN**–creator Joji Akiyama, this was also adapted into a TV drama starring Beat Takeshi—years ahead of *The Sopranos.* **◑◐**

KOJIRO OF THE FUMA CLAN *

1989. JPN: *Fuma no Kojiro.* Video. DIR:

Hidehito Ueda. scr: Takao Koyama. des: Shingo Araki, Michi Himeno. ani: Takeshi Tsukasa. mus: Toshiro Imaizumi. prd: Animate Film, JC Staff. 30 mins. x 13 eps.

Five young boys are the reincarnations of elemental spirits and replay old tales and enmities from Japanese history in a modern setting. Teenager Kojiro receives a letter from Himeko, the young owner of Hakuo (White Phoenix) High School, who needs help dealing with gang intimidation. Kojiro decides to help her because she's very cute, but gang intimidation is the least of her worries—a rival clan is planning a takeover, and Kojiro must face their champion, Nibu, before dealing with another adversary, Oscar Musashi (see SWORD OF MUSASHI). The interclan school struggle is just a cover for the powers of evil, who wish to collect the ten magical swords that determine the balance of power in the universe. It's pretty boys at a ninja high school but with a surprisingly old-fashioned look to the designs and animation. This video was based on a 1982 manga in *Shonen Jump* by Masami Kurumada, who would recycle the same ideas in SAINT SEIYA, though the anime adaptation of the latter preceded this to Japanese screens. 🔞🔞

KOKORO LIBRARY

2001. jpn: *Kokoro Toshokan*. aka: *Heart Library*. TV series. dir: Koji Masunari. scr: Yosuke Kuroda. des: Hideki Tachibana. ani: Studio DEEN. mus: Hisaaki Hogari. prd: Media Works, Studio DEEN, Victor Entertainment, TV Tokyo. 30 mins. x 13 eps.

Sisters Iina, Aruto, and Kokoro inherit a library in the middle of the mountains and fret that they will never get enough customers. Youngest sister Kokoro is pleased that someone takes out a book on her first day, but when it isn't returned she discovers that the customer has moved away. She decides to take a bus to a faraway town in search of the errant borrower, only to be prevented by her sisters Iina and

Aruto, who reveal that the book has just been returned by mail—only the first of a series of prosaic miracles in the style of TOKYO GODFATHERS. *Kokoro Library* is a bizarre mixture of the maid's clothing fad with the bookish goings-on of WHISPER OF THE HEART or HAIBANE RENMEI, complete with a sappy, soporifically soothing soundtrack. A later episode introduces a robot librarian, but otherwise the show is relentlessly slow—compare to the excitement of director Masunari's earlier R.O.D. Somewhere in *Kokoro Library*'s past is a creator's decision that anime don't need to be about conflict and danger to be interesting, but this is neither HUMAN CROSSING nor MY NEIGHBOR TOTORO. Pretty the girls may be, but it is difficult to warm to characters who get excited about holding committee meetings to discuss their outreach strategy. Based on a manga by Nobuyuki Takagi in *Dengeki Daioh* magazine. The video "special" *Kokoro Library Communication Clips* is not so much a sequel as a series of short segments from the first episode interspersed with title cards and explanatory comments by Kokoro.

KOKUDO-OH: BLACK EYE KING *

2003?. jpn: *Kokudo-O*. aka: *Black Eyed King; Charmstone*. Video. dir: Mikan Fuyuno. scr: Manka Sen. des: Studio Jikkenshitsu. ani: Kazuo Takeuchi. mus: N/C. prd: Alice Pro, Five Ways. 30 mins. x 5 eps.

Isildur (Isiodore in the U.S. dub) inherits the throne of the small mountain kingdom of Bothal (Bosarre), sandwiched in between the mighty empires of Rohan and Geld. Hoping to maintain his kingdom's independence, the new ruler is faced with a difficult choice—since each empire has sent him a prospective bride, whom should be choose? Princess Belciel (Bellecher) is feisty and proud, a former classmate of Isildur when he studied in the Rohan empire. Princess Ariel is demure and kind, a Geld childhood playmate of Isildur who once treated him as a brother. Unable to choose,

Isildur suggests a series of prenuptial trials for the girls, in order for Isildur and his maid Irene to instruct the princesses in the correct modes of behavior for Isildur's future queen. Predictably, this starts innocently enough before devolving into sexual abuse, bondage, toilet games, and the girls' imprisonment in a cage; compare to EROTIC TORTURE CHAMBER and BLOOD ROYALE. Nor does Isildur seem to give much thought to what may happen when he is eventually forced to choose one of them, since the other one will have endured four weeks of sexual humiliation, likely grounds for an invasion by her homeland! As the month progresses, Isildur receives the troubling news that the king of Geld, Ariel's father, is dying. If Ariel is still unmarried at the time of her father's death, then the princess is fated to be betrothed to Herum, the heir to the Rohan empire, depriving Isildur of both his sex games and his chances of diplomatic independence. Despite a more modern setting than this synopsis implies (a quasi-Victorian world), the series can't help alluding to *The Lord of the Rings*. The result is an anime that is immensely entertaining, not so much for its content, but for imagining the looks on the faces of Tolkien's executors if they ever see it. For some reason, the fifth episode has not been released in America. 🔞🔞🔞

KON, SATOSHI

1963– . Born on Hokkaido, Kon studied at Musashino College of Arts, intending to be a painter. After collaborating with Katsuhiro Otomo on the manga of *World Apartment Horror*, he became a set designer on ROUJIN-Z, demonstrating an early aptitude for creating lived-in, realistically cluttered environments. His directorial debut was PERFECT BLUE (1997), establishing him as a master at using live-action attitudes and techniques in anime; a reputation since secured with MILLENNIUM ACTRESS (2001), TOKYO GODFATHERS (2003), and PARANOIA AGENT (2004).

KONDO, YOSHIFUMI

1950–1998. Sometimes miscredited as Toshinobu Kondo or Yoshifumi Kindo. Born in Niigata Prefecture he attended Design College of Tokyo after high school, but began working for A Pro (Now Shin'ei Doga) within six months of arriving in Tokyo. He met Hayao Miyazaki while working on LUPIN III, beginning a lifelong association. He moved to Nippon Animation in 1977 and served as an animation director on ANNE OF GREEN GABLES and FUTURE BOY CONAN. In this period, he also wrote a textbook on animation methods. He moved to Telecom in 1980, where he worked as a character designer on SHERLOCK HOUND, although he was to resign from Telecom in 1985 due to illness, possibly caused by overwork. He freelanced for Nippon Animation for another year before quitting for good in order to take up a post at Studio Ghibli. He was a key animator and character designer on many of Ghibli's classic movies of the late 1980s and early 1990s, and had his directorial debut with WHISPER OF THE HEART. Groomed as Hayao Miyazaki's successor at Ghibli, Kondo was a key animator on PRINCESS MONONOKE, but succumbed to an aneurysm in 1998. His death was not not only a tragic loss to Ghibli and the anime world but also a reminder of the terrifyingly long hours and stressful labor involved in creating Japanese animation.

KONPORA KID

1985. TV series/special. DIR: Juzo Morishita, Yuji Endo, Tatsuo Higashino, Yoshikata Nitta, Shigeyasu Yamauchi. SCR: Takao Koyama, Shigeru Yanagawa, Kenji Yoshida. DES: Yasuhiro Yamaguchi. ANI: Yasuhiro Yamaguchi, Tatsuhiro Nagaki, Masami Shimoda. MUS: Kohei Tanaka. PRD: Toei, TV Asahi. 25 mins. x 26 eps. (TV), 57 mins. (TVm).
In the distant future, merely because someone is eight years old, it doesn't follow that they will have to go to school. In fact, little Daigoro Harumi JR (aka JR) is a teacher at Torad Academy in charge of educating Class Five, whose ages range from a newborn baby to a crusty old grandfather. Partway through the TV series, JR and his class also appeared in a summer TV special, where the flustered eight year old plans on taking a summer vacation with his family in space but ends up chaperoning half his class as well. Based on the manga by Masahide Motohashi, serialized in Shonen Magazine, among others.

KOSUKE AND RIKIMARU: DRAGON OF KONPEI ISLAND

1990. JPN: Kosukesama Rikimarusama: Konpeijima no Ryu. Video. DIR: Toyoo Ashida. SCR: Toyoo Ashida, Akira Toriyama. DES: Akira Toriyama. ANI: N/C. MUS: N/C. PRD: JC Staff. 45 mins.
Squashed-down samurai Kosuke and Rikimaru must save the world from an evil dragon who wants to rule it for all eternity. This one-off anime, based on an idea by DRAGON BALL and DOCTOR SLUMP–creator Akira Toriyama, was preceded by a 1990 manga in a special issue of Shonen Jump but written originally for the screen.

KOTOWAZA HOUSE

1987. TV series. DIR: Hiroshi Yoshida. SCR: Motoko Misawa, Hiroshi Yoshida. DES: Tadao Wakabayashi. ANI: Tadao Wakabayashi. MUS: N/C. PRD: Eiken, Fuji TV. 5 mins. x 338 eps.
Peter the salaryman lives a very unhealthy lifestyle, starving then bingeing until he feels sick, or slobbing around the house until badgered into taking up exercise, during which he invariably pulls a muscle. In this public-service proverb-of-the-week anime from the same team who made DOTANBA'S MODERN MANNERS, Peter's caring boss and the beautiful Office Lady Sueko drag in a straight-talking doctor and a sprightly granny to educate him about physical and mental health. For the series' first year on air, the title was simply KH: Health Edition, but this was dropped in 1988 to reflect the move toward more general tips and proverbs for well-being.

KOUCHI, JUNICHI

1886–1970. Sometimes also transliterated Sumikazu Kouchi. Born in Okayama prefecture, Kouichi relocated with his family to Tokyo, where he eventually studied watercolor painting at the Pacific Art Institute. His illustrations first appeared in Tokyo Puck magazine around 1908, and by 1912 he was drawing political cartoons for a newspaper. He was approached by the Kobayashi Shokai Company (formed by defectors from the production company Tenkatsu), for whom he produced his first animation, the Sword of Hanawa Hekonai (Hanawa Hekonai, Meito no Maki—see EARLY ANIME) in June 1917. With Kobayashi experiencing financial difficulties, Kouchi set up his own animation company, Sumikazu Eiga, and began producing political propaganda, commencing with a commercial for the politician Shinpei Goto in 1924. The anime talkie Chopped Snake (1930, Chongire Hebi), was his last before he returned to straightforward illustration. Of his output, only Hyoroku's Warrior Training (date unknown, Hyoroku no Musha Shugyo) survives.

KOWAREMONO: FRAGILE HEARTS *

2001. JPN: Kowaremono II. Video. DIR: Kaoru Tomioka. SCR: N/C. DES: Noriyasu Takeuchi. ANI: Jiro Makigata. MUS: N/C. PRD: Green Bunny, Beam Entertainment. 25 mins. x 3 eps.
Aki is an expensive android, whose programming obliges her to do anything and everything her master demands. After subjecting her to a series of public humiliations, her owner sends her off to buy new parts, only to have her kidnapped and forced into a brief career as an erotic gladiator in the style of SEXORCIST. She is then put to work for a mad scientist who gives her the ability to transform into a superheroine, in a series of very loosely linked vignettes, based on an erotic computer game. ⓁⓃⓋ

KOYAMA, TAKAO

1948– . Born in Tokyo, Koyama studied literature at Waseda University and joined Tatsunoko Productions after graduation. His debut work was an episode of **RURAL LEADER**, which he followed with scripts for **CASSHAN** and **SONG OF THE LADYBUGS**, before going freelance in 1975. He subsequently wrote for the **TIME BOKAN** series and **DRAGON BALL**. As a guest at American conventions, Koyama has made some controversial (and to the authors, highly welcome) comments about the state of the anime business, decrying the outsourcing of talent and production, and criticizing the "glorified advertisements" that comprise much of the video market. He has also explained why so much of *Dragon Ball* seems like a prolonged fight scene, since on occasion he had been asked to turn a single panel from the manga into a 25-minute episode.

KUM-KUM *

1975. JPN: *Wanpaku Omukashi Kum-Kum.* AKA: *Naughty Ancient Kum-Kum; Kum-Kum the Caveman.* TV series. DIR: Rintaro, Noboru Ishiguro, Wataru Mizusawa. SCR: Eiichi Tachi, Keisuke Fujikawa, Yoshiaki Yoshida. DES: Yoshikazu Yasuhiko. ANI: Rintaro, Noboru Ishiguro, Minoru Tajima, Akio Sakai. MUS: Masami Uno. PRD: ITC Japan, Mainichi Broadcasting (TBS). 25 mins. x 26 eps.
Kum-kum is a small cave boy living in the prehistoric mountains that will one day be Japan, where he, his sister Furufuru, and tag-along companions Chilchil, Mochi-mochi, and Aron behave the way that their distant descendants would if only modern Japanese children had access to mammoth rides, troublesome dinosaurs, and the opportunity to throw rocks at each other. Kum-kum was an unexpected success on British children's TV in the early 1980s, not for being the first English-language broadcast of work by original creator Yasuhiko, or indeed as an early example of Rintaro's direction, but because its hero didn't wear any pants.

KURAU PHANTOM MEMORY *

2004. TV series. DIR: Yasuhiro Irie.

SCR: Aya Yoshinaga, Tsuyoshi Tamai, Yasuyuki Suzuki, Yasuhiro Irie, Shin Yoshida. DES: Tomomi Ozaki, Masahisa Suzuki, Shingo Takeba. ANI: Atsuko Sasaki, Hiroyuki Kanbe. MUS: Yukari Katsuki (S.E.N.S.). PRD: BONES, Kurau Project, TV Asahi, Victor Entertainment. 24 mins. x 24 eps.
By the year 2100, humans have colonized the Moon and appear to have solved most of their problems on Earth, too. Mankind even seems to have the ecology issue licked, with Earth divided into inhabited areas called METROPOLIS and green "support" areas known as ECOLOGIA. But every Eden breeds its serpents, and despite there being no poverty, there's still crime. A group of special agents is tasked to deal with crimes that the Global Police Organization can't handle. 22-year-old Kurau Amami is a highly skilled and successful agent, but still lonely and emotionally immature. She has good reason— she's a rare being, a human-alien hybrid created by accident. In her case, the accident happened in her father's lab ten years before when her body was possessed by a transdimensional life form called Rynax, making her a Ryna-Sapien. Rynaxes live in the microscopic spaces between their partner's atoms. If they can escape into our world, they can make anything they touch decompose. They bestow superhuman physical abilities: Kurau can fly, make solids decompose, and defeat giant robots without even wearing armor. But there's a price to be paid in the style of **ELFEN LIED**: normal people fear her and she's lonely and friendless. Then, on Christmas Day, Kurau gets her best ever present. Light pours from her body, and a girl who is the image of her 12-year-old self materializes before her eyes. She seems completely ordinary. Kurau names her Christmas and enjoys having a younger "sister" around to ease her loneliness. Then other Rynaxes try to emerge from her body, and the Government decides she's becomes a destructive virus who must be exterminated along with her Rynax other

self. Determined to protect Christmas from mankind, and mankind from the destructive abilities of the Rynax, Kurau has a fight on her hands. The girls flee around the world, and even to the Moon, and on the way they meet other Ryna-Sapiens and other Rynaxes. It seems the two species can coexist, even though not everyone on either side wants to. Director Irie, who also directed **ALIEN 9**, another show about symbiotic relationships between humans and aliens, says the theme of the show is communication—between different life-forms or just people with totally different perspectives. By getting others to see that Christmas isn't a threat and that she isn't to be feared, Kurau can overcome her own loneliness and finally become a mature, happy woman. Compare to **BIRDY THE MIGHTY** and its ultimate inspiration, **ULTRAMAN**. ✪🅝🅥

KURI, YOJI

1928– . Pseudonym of Hideo Kurihara. Born in Fukui prefecture, he graduated from middle school in 1945 and went to Tokyo in 1950 to study at the Tokyo Art School. His early work in comics led to his selection for the Bungei Shunju Manga Prize in 1958, but his work was always more avant-garde than his peers'. Whereas others like Osamu Tezuka were embracing the commercialism of television, Kuri was drawn to the experimental animation of the Canadian Norman McLaren. He began making his own animated works, in deliberate reaction to the mainstream attitudes of other Japanese animators and the Disney empire. Proclaiming that he wanted to make "animation for adults," he pursued a solitary route, leading to a large number of solo (or at least, independent) works, many of them very short—the *Yoji Kuri Film Works* DVD released in Japan contains 18 alone. He was also, along with Ryohei Yanagihara and Hiroshi Manabe, one of the "Animation Group of Three," annual displays of whose work eventually became the basis for a series of animation film festivals in Japan from 1960 to 1971. His early works include *Fashion* (1960), *Two Pikes* (1961, *Nihiki no Sanma*), *Human Zoo* (1963, *Ningen Dobutsuen*), and *The Discovery of Zero* (1964, *Zero no Hakken*), in a body of work stretching up to *Manga* (1977), *The Imagination of Trousers* (1981, *Zubon no Naka no Imagination*), and *The War of Men and Women* (1983, *Otoko to Onna no Senso*). His creations have been exhibited at many international film festivals, and he has received accolades in New York, Amsterdam, and Venice, among others.

KUROGANE COMMUNICATIONS *

1998. JPN: *Kurogane Communication*. TV series. DIR: Yasuji Kikuchi. SCR: Mitsuhiro Yamada. DES: Shinya Takahashi. ANI: Toshimitsu Kobayashi, Hideaki Shimada. MUS: Kenji Kawai. PRD: APPP, WOWOW. 10 mins. x 24 eps.

Earth has been ravaged by a devastating war, while one-time robot servants fight in the ruins over spare parts. Haruka, a human girl who might be the last survivor of her race, is found by some kindly robots, who protect her from war machines hellbent on carrying out their programming to wipe humanity off the face of the Earth. Haruka and her new friends set off in search of other survivors in, if you can believe such a thing, a lighthearted tale of surviving the apocalypse. This series was based on the manga in *Dengeki King* by Yoshimasa Takuma and Hideo Kato and broadcast as part of the satellite TV strip *Anime Complex*.

KYO KARA MA-O *

2004. AKA: *From Now On, I'm a Demon King!*. TV series. DIR: Junji Nishimura. SCR: Akemi Omode. DES: Yuka Kudo. ANI: Kazuki Noguchi. MUS: Yoichiro Yoshikawa. PRD: Yuji Shibata, Studio DEEN, NHK. 23 mins. x 55+ eps.

Yuri Shibuya is an ordinary guy, baseball fan, and loyal friend. When he tries to help a pal being beaten up by a gang of bullies, he ends up having his head flushed in a public toilet. Much to his surprise, he emerges in another world—Shinmakoku, a world populated by magic-using demons and the humans they despise. Humans have no magic powers in Shinmakoku and are considered a lower species, but there have been some intermarriages, and Yuri meets one of the human/demon hybrids right away. Lord Conrad ("Call Me Conrad," he suggests, in a reference to Roger Zelazny's *This Immortal*) Weller treats him like a younger brother and helps him find his way around this quasi-medieval European setting. Yuri's black eyes and hair, and his school uniform, attract a lot of attention, and soon he's told that he is not just some inferior human, but the reincarnated spirit of the 27th King of the Mazoku, or to use his formal title, the Maoh. Black is the royal family color, as it was for the historical first emperor of China. Royal aide Lord

Gunter von Christ takes over from Conrad in tutoring the new King. A purple-haired exquisite, the archetypal European aristocrat, he's part scholar, part soldier—and part mother hen, fussing over his young monarch and treating him like an infant. The Mazoku tribe was rather hoping for a belligerent monarch who would help them drive their enemies before them, but instead they get a nice, quiet guy who likes to sort things out by negotiation and get a fair outcome for all sides.

A satire of the otherwordly conflicts of ESCAFLOWNE and FUSHIGI YUGI with the irreverent attitude of SLAYERS, *KKM* flits back and forth between the worlds of demons and humans as its hapless protagonist tries to do his duty by going on quests and saving distant kingdoms. Like so many other anime heroes, including PHOTON, whose desert storyline *KKM* echoes for several episodes, he is accidentally betrothed in the first couple of episodes, although in his case to a man. Based on the eight-part series of *Ma no Tsuku* novels by Tomo Takabayashi. Kadokawa also published two volumes of spin-off stories set in the same universe.

KYOTO ANIMATION

Formed as a subsidiary of Mushi Production in 1981 and incorporated in 1985, becoming a public company in 1999. Representative works include GATEKEEPERS and the "Turn A" sequence of the GUNDAM franchise.

L

LA BLUE GIRL *
1992. JPN: *Inju Gakuen La Blue Girl*. AKA: *Lust-Beast Academy La Blue Girl*. Video. DIR: Raizo Kitazawa, Kan Fukumoto. SCR: Megumi Ichiryu. DES: Kinji Yoshimoto. ANI: Miki Bibanba, Rin Shin. MUS: Teruo Takahama. PRD: Daiei. 45 mins. x 6 eps. (v1), 30 mins. x 4 eps. (v2), 30 mins. x 4 eps. (v3).

Not unlike DEVIL HUNTER YOHKO, high school girl Miko Mido and her sister are the heirs to the secrets of an ancient ninja clan. When they become embroiled in an interdimensional war with rapacious demons, they reveal their secret powers—they are sex-ninja who cast spells with the power of orgasm and, hence, cannot get enough of their enemies' lusty attentions. Based on an idea by UROTSUKIDOJI-creator Toshio Maeda, *LBG* continues his obsession with hormonal chaos, as demons kidnap the high school volleyball team, and Miko can only rescue them (from sexual degradation, naturally) by submitting to the wanton desires of her demonic enemies. The series was also released in compiled feature-length editions and an *Ecstasy* collection that included only the sex scenes.

After the first four episodes in Japan, the series was followed by *Shin* ("True") *Inju Gakuen La Blue Girl*, comprising a 45-minute part one, and a " part two" comprising two 30-minute episodes (there always being more money to be made in splitting a show in half and bulking it out with synopses of the story so far!). We believe these three videos to comprise "episodes five and six" of the American release.

The franchise was rebranded as *La Blue Girl EX* (1996, released in the U.S. as *Lady Blue*) for a further four episodes, taking Miko off to college, where her crush on a fellow classmate turns out to be part of a conspiracy, as her jilted immortal aunt seeks to bring her ancient lover back from the dead, predictably by raping Miko. Notorious in the U.K. market for being refused a release point-blank by the British censor, *LBG* also caused some controversy in the U.S., where the Japanese censorship dots were removed prior to release, revealing half-drawn genitals which the animators never intended to be seen, giving the impression that some of the participants were underage. The franchise was also made as three live-action films, starting with *Sex Beast on Campus* (1994), directed by Kaname Kobayashi, and continuing with *SBoC: Birth of the Daughter with Dark Spirit* (1995) and *SBoC: Female Ninja Hunting* (1996), both directed by Kaoru Kuramoto. Compare to ANGEL OF DARKNESS. A further series, the four part *La Blue Girl Returns* (2001, *Inju Gakuen La Blue Girl Fukkatsu-hen; Lust Beast Academy La Blue Girl: Revival Chapter*) featured the Shikima realm invaded by a race of butterfly demons, resisted in a predictable manner by the denizens, although the art style was remarkably different from earlier incarnations, with more of a cutesy, pastel look. **LNV**

LABYRINTH OF FLAMES *
2000. JPN: *Honoo no Labyrinth*. Video. DIR: Katsuhiko Nishijima. SCR: Kenichi Kanemaki. DES: Noriyasu Yamauchi, Hidefumi Kimura. ANI: N/C. MUS: N/C. PRD: Studio Fantasia, Bandai Visual. 30 mins. x 2 eps.

The secret city of Labyrinth Four was founded by Japanese citizens of the Aoi Shigemasa domain, who were either exiled after the fall of the shogunate, or perhaps deliberately sent there in order to plot the shogun's restoration. Years later, Labyrinth Four is a forgotten village in what is now Russia, where the inhabitants still cling to a samurai lifestyle. Imagine, then, the glee with which Russian samurai-fan Galan flings himself into his life in the new-found village, where he befriends Japanese princess Natsu, in an often incoherent comedy from the people who brought you AGENT AIKA. **NV**

LADIUS *
1987. JPN: *Makyo Gaiden Le Deus*. AKA: *Demon Frontier Legend Le Deus; Le Deus*. Video. DIR: Hiroshi Negishi. SCR: Hideki Sonoda, Hiroyuki Kitakubo. DES: Rei Aran. ANI: Hideyuki Motohashi. MUS: Hiroyuki Nanba. PRD: Ashi Pro. 48 mins.

GUNDAM-meets-*Indiana Jones* as treasure-hunting archaeologists fight over

La Blue Girl

© 1992 T. MAEDA / DAIEI CO. LTD.

an ancient energy source. Spunky hero Riot Geenas travels a postapocalyptic world accompanied by his dim but well-intentioned twin-girl companions, Sulpica and Seneca. He needs the mystic energy Lidorium that's found in the artifact known as the Eye of Zalem, but so too do his competitors, the evil Dempsters. When he finally locates the Eye, it's being worn around the pretty neck of bar owner Yuta la Carradine, who insists on accompanying him on his quest until such time as he can pay for the damages done to the establishment in a brawl with his enemies. Needless to say, Yuta is the last inheritor of the ancient Kingdom of Quall who holds the key to unlocking its powers, which are unleashed in a grand finale involving massive collateral damage amid ancient ruins, the defeat of the bad guy, and the arrival of the titular war machine, a giant robot hidden inside a transforming humpback whale. Derivative hokum, repeated five years later in the suspiciously similar **BEAST WARRIORS**, with which it shares a director. The last anime translation to be made in the U.K. by Western Connection and subtitled in that low-budget company's inimitable randomly timed style.

LADY GEORGIE
1983. TV series. DIR: Shigetsugu Yoshida, Naoto Hashimoto, Satoshi Dezaki, Kenjiro Yoshida, Tsuneo Tominaga. SCR: Hiroshi Kaneko, Noboru Shiroyama. DES: Shunsaburo Takahata. ANI: Junsaburo Takahata, Yoshiaki Kawajiri. MUS: Takeo Watanabe. PRD: IU, TMS, TV Asahi. 25 mins. x 45 eps.
In the Australian forest, the Borman family finds a dying woman who begs them to take care of her newborn daughter, Georgie. Despite the opposition of Mrs. Borman, the father agrees, and the girl is raised as their own, with no mention of her true parents or that her father was a British convict. Mr. Borman dies rescuing Georgie from a river, and his two sons, Abel and Arthur, keep their promise to look after their "sister," though they are both falling in love with her themselves. When Georgie falls in love with the Englishman Dowell Gray, Abel confesses his feelings to his mother, who in her fury blurts out Georgie's true origins. Georgie goes to England to find her birth father, and her arrival causes Dowell to dump his fiancée Elise, the daughter of the powerful Duke Dunkelin. With little evidence but the bracelet that is the sole memento of her real mother, Georgie eventually tracks down her father, who is, of course, not exactly a convict but the noble Earl Gerald. Meanwhile, however, the evil Dunkelin has captured Arthur, who has followed Georgie to England and accidentally witnessed the duke's drug-smuggling operation. Arthur nearly dies from the drugs fed to him by Dunkelin's men, while Abel is thrown into the dungeons of the Tower of London for killing one of Dunkelin's relatives.

With a Victorian setting, a foundling heroine, and a long quest for love, *LG* closely resembles the landmark **CANDY CANDY**, all the more for being based on a manga in *Shojo Comic* by the same artist, Yumiko Igarashi, though originally written as a novel by Michiru Isawa. Eventually, everything ends happily with Georgie and her "brothers" returning to their native Australia, though the original novel was far more tragic. As with the same year's **TREASURES OF THE SNOW**, the anime adaptation builds on the original story, chiefly with early scenes of the heroine's childhood not in the novel or manga versions. These were perhaps inserted as an afterthought to justify scenes of playtime with koala bears, a ubiquitous feature of early 1980s anime—see **THE NOOZLES**.

LADY LADY
1987. TV series. DIR: Hiroshi Shidara, Yugo Serikawa, Yasuo Yamakichi, Yuji Endo, Masahisa Ishida. SCR: Michiru Umadori, Tomoko Konparu, Shigeru Yanagawa. DES: Takao Sawata, Yoko Hide. ANI: Kazuya Koshibe. MUS: Kohei Tanaka. PRD: Toei, TBS, TV Tokyo. 25 mins. x 21 eps. (TV1), 27 mins. (m), 25 mins. x N/D eps. (TV2).
Five-year-old Lynn Midorigawa sets off for England to meet her Japanese mother for the first time she can remember but discovers that her mother has been killed in a car accident.

Her British father remarries, and Lynn must endure bullying at the hands of her stepmother, Vivianne, and her stepsiblings, Mary and Thomas. Her only friend is the kindly boy Arthur, who promises to help her become a true lady. It's another syrupy romance in the spirit of **CANDY CANDY**, based on the manga *Hitomi* by Yoko Hide. The short 1988 *LL* movie is set a year after the series and focuses on the heroine's misery at the mansion of Marquis Bourbon, where she is forced to work as a maid to help repay her father's debts.

The movie bridges the gap between *LL* and its sequel, *Hello Lady Lynn* (1988), for which the franchise moved to TV Tokyo from TBS. Set three years after Lynn's original arrival in England, *HLL* packs her off to stay with Countess Isabelle and attend Saint Patrick's College for young girls, where she joins the equestrian club and gets involved in genteel high jinks in the spirit of **TWINS AT ST CLARE'S**. There was also a live-action movie, *Ready! Lady!* (1989), directed by Kei Ota.

LANDLOCK *

1996. Video. DIR: Yasuhiro Matsumura. SCR: ORCA. DES: Kazuto Nakazawa, Masamune Shirow. ANI: Koji Matsuyama. MUS: N/C. PRD: Sega Enterprises. 50 mins. x 2 eps.

In the low-rent Aztec-like fantasyland of Zer'lue, Chairman San'aku leads an invading army of seemingly unstoppable Zul'earth warriors. A lone boy, Lue'der, can stop him, but the chairman's daughter Aga'lee has been sent to hunt him down before his powers (a nebulous ability to control the wind) can truly awaken. Luckily for Lue'der, who has one normal eye and one red eye as a mark of the chosen one, Aga'lee's sister Ansa has a normal eye and a *blue* eye. He takes this to be some sort of sign that she should help him escape, which she duly does. Accompanied by a friendly entomologist(!?), Lue'der reaches an ancient temple where he discovers the nature of his destiny, and that the man Aga'lee

killed was not his real father. He combines the fabled Red and Blue Flows to become an avatar of the power of the wind, and then he wins the day.

A horrific mess of an anime, complete with pretentious apostrophes in people's names (inserted for the English version, to be fair), and a *you killed my father, prepare to die* plot unsurprisingly thought up by a committee. This turgid two-parter was rushed out to cash in on the recent success of **GHOST IN THE SHELL** by producers banking on the star power of Masamune Shirow's name, even though the famous artist's involvement was limited to mere "design assistance." This was enough for distributors in some territories, who eagerly snatched up the chance to release another anime from the successful creator of **BLACK MAGIC** and **APPLESEED**—though they, and their consumers, were to be very disappointed. Four years later, the same criminals would strike again with **GUNDRESS**, another low-rent sci-fi thriller with slight Shirow involvement, even worse than *Landlock* because it was actually released unfinished.

LASERION

1984. JPN: *Video Senshi Laserion*. AKA: *Video Warrior Laserion; Rezarion*. TV series. DIR: Kozo Morishita, Hideki Takayama, Masao Ito, Hiromichi Matano, Shigeyasu Yamauchi. SCR: Kozo Morishita, Akiyoshi Sakai, Takeshi Shudo, Keiji Kubota, Haruya Yamazaki. DES: Hideyuki Motohashi, Koichi Ohata, Akira Hio. ANI: Hideyuki Motohashi, Daisuke Shiozawa, Seiji Kikuchi, Hajime Kaneko. MUS: Michiaki Watanabe. PRD: Toei, Tabac, TBS. 25 mins. x 45 eps.

Laserion, a program created by gamecrazed boy Satoshi, is brought to life by an accident that sends the data to Professor Blueheim's teleportation experiment. Luckily, Satoshi soon finds a use for a giant war robot, which, **GIANT ROBO**-style, will only obey his commands, when Earth is invaded by evil lunar-based minions of the evil scientist God Haid, and Satoshi joins

the Secret Force to stop them, accompanied by token girl Olivia. Also part of the **GODAIKIN** toy line.

LASSIE

1996. JPN: *Meiken Lassie*. AKA: *Famous Dog Lassie*. TV series. DIR: Sunao Katabuchi, Jiro Fujimoto, Kenichi Nishida. SCR: Aya Matsui, Hideki Mitsui. DES: Satoko Morikawa. ANI: N/C. MUS: N/C. PRD: Nippon Animation, Fuji TV. 25 mins. x 26 eps.

Country-boy John finds a young puppy by the roadside and nurses her back to health. Lassie grows into a fine collie, blessed with almost human intelligence, though her early years are not without their share of odd mishaps, scoldings, and discoveries.

This penultimate **WORLD MASTERPIECE THEATER** anime displays all the hallmarks of the series' decline, most notably a cavalier disregard for the original classic that inspired it, Eric Mowbray Knight's 1940 novel that was expanded from his 1938 short story *Lassie Come Home*. As with **HEIDI** and **TREASURES OF THE SNOW**, the characters' early years, not seen in the original, were used to bulk up the running time, so when the series was ignominiously yanked off the air after just 25 episodes, the novel's central plot had barely begun. Consequently, the extant *Lassie* anime takes its time with the minutiae of Lassie's upbringing, only to rush through her famous long journey home in just three episodes. The unbroadcast final episode, *Run to the Place of Dreams*, was included on the later video release. In a final irony, Knight never lived to see any of the TV or movie incarnations of his much-loved dog—he died in a wartime air crash in Dutch Guiana (modern Surinam).

LAST EXILE *

2003. TV series. DIR: Koichi Chigira. SCR: Koichi Chigira. DES: Range Murata, Minoru Murao, Osamu Horiuchi, Yuichi Tanaka, Mahiro Maeda, Makoto Kobayashi. ANI: Hiroyuki Okuno, Yasufumi Soejima. MUS: Dolci Triade, Hitomi Kuroishi. PRD: Gonzo, Victor Entertainment, TV Tokyo. 25 mins. x 26 eps. Claus Valca (or Barca) and his friend Lavie are orphans whose only asset apart from determination and courage is Claus's inheritance from his late father Hamilcar—a small two-man flier called a vanship. It's enough to make a living as couriers on their homeworld, Prester, and keep them comfortably out of the gutter, but they both dream of going further. Prester is made up of two warring countries on either side of a permanently raging storm called the Grand Stream, but the war has been conducted with honor and policed by the Guild for years; it doesn't much affect ordinary people like them. They rescue a sweet-faced little girl named Alvis Hamilton from a killing machine and are asked to deliver her to the legendary warship Silvana, but are shocked by the attitude of the commander, Alex Row, who simply accepts the girl as a piece of cargo. They go back to rescue her, and so they are drawn into the war and their lives are changed forever.

Like CHOBITS, *LE* is a fascinating example of the anime business in the early 21st century—quite literally state-of-the-art, good and bad. Its design work is utterly superb, particularly the washed-out, drained color of its characters, seemingly taking inspiration from GHOST IN THE SHELL. Made to celebrate the tenth anniversary of the Gonzo studio and blessed with the longer running length of television, it takes half the series for the action on-screen to start making sense. With its Georgian and Victorian costumes and influences, Morse code mirrors, Napoleonic riflemen, and Nazi uniform chic that resembles LEGEND OF GALACTIC HEROES, designers are credited for everything from computer graphics to color keys, but the opening credits point the finger for the story itself at an anonymous committee. Literary influences include the multiple points of view of Leo Tolstoy's Napoleonic conflict in *War and Peace* (1865) and the battle over limited resources of Frank Herbert's *Dune* (1965), which shares with *LE* a

"Guild" that controls the means of transport. Later episodes draw further on Herbert's ecological interests, introducing an environmental subplot about climate changes that have forced the population movement behind some of the conflict. The result often resembles NAUSICAÄ crossed with the *Phantom Menace* Pod Race—although director Maeda cites Miyazaki's CASTLE IN THE SKY as his chief influence.

But *LE* also makes the mistakes of many an ill-thought fantasy, introducing oodles of impressive technology, and then refusing to apply it to its obvious uses. *LE* is happy to let the computer graphics do the grandstanding while the characters mug, squabble, and behave in the childish ways that anime producers expect anime fans to expect anime characters to act. Lavie, in particular, is the latest in a line of outstandingly infantile ingenues, fretting about her weight (for plot-related reasons, of course; anime wouldn't *dream* of clichés), and enthusing inanely about the fact that the water in a fountain is so clear "you can see right through it." Meanwhile, Alvis is the archetypal anime "mysterious girl," who can provide changes of messianic proportions to the world of *LE*, making her a vital commodity for all sides in the conflict.

Despite onscreen homages to Victoriana in the style of STEAM BOY, *LE* finds innovative ways to cut corners using digital processes. With artwork such a vital part of its success, still images from the series were previewed far ahead of the broadcast premiere, ensuring that everyone had fallen in love with its look before they ever had to see it move. Not that *LE* is poorly animated, but its use of CG is cunning to the extreme. Once rendered for the first time in the computer, it is easy and relatively cheap to keep a giant CG vanship lumbering past the camera. The overlong shots of ships in flight are modern anime's version of the cost-cutting "static pan" of old. Although *LE* has a love of flight and pilots to rival PORCO ROSSO, its fighters are not

subject to the laws of aerodynamics. Instead, they are darting, wingless lumps in the sky, ignoring the laws of physics and saving much money in the process.

LAUGHING SALESMAN

1989. TV series, TV special. DIR: Toshiro Kuni, Ryoshi Yometani. SCR: Ichiro Yoshiaki, Kazuya Miyazaki, Kaoru Umeno. DES: Fujiko-Fujio "A." ANI: Tsunehiro Okaseko. MUS: N/C. PRD: Shinei, TBS. 10 mins. x 91 eps., 60 mins.

The miserable life of a salesman whose wife only cares about golf is played for laughs in this long-running series, based on the manga *Black Salesman* by Motoo Abiko, one half of the Fujiko-Fujio duo who created DORAEMON. Splitting from his working partner Hiroshi Fujimoto in the 1980s, he produced several titles under the name Fujiko-Fujio "A," including PARASOL HENBE, LITTLE GOBLIN, PROGOLFER SARU, and BILLY DOG. Broadcast as part of the *Gimme a Break* variety show on the TBS channel, which occasionally also showed episodes of Shotaro Ishinomori's 808 DISTRICTS. Several episodes were also edited into the feature-length TV movie *LS Special* (1990), concentrating on the cheerful way that the psychotic salesman took out his midlife crisis on his coworkers with an extensive campaign of blackmail and extortion. From episode 41 onward, the series was rebranded as *New LS* (1991).

LAUGHING TARGET *

1987. JPN: *Rumic World: Warau Mokuteki*. Video. DIR: Yukihiro Takahashi. SCR: Tomoko Konparu, Hideo Takayashiki. DES: Hidekazu Obara. ANI: N/C. MUS: Kuni Kawauchi. PRD: Studio Pierrot. 50 mins.

Azusa is a girl from a traditional Japanese family, who, through an old-fashioned arranged marriage, has been "promised" to her cousin Yuzuru since the age of five. Growing up in an isolated country mansion, she undergoes several bizarre experiences, culminating in the death of her mother.

She sets off to snag her long-term betrothed but is shocked to discover that Yuzuru already loves Satomi, a more modern urban girl, and that not even Azusa's beauty is enough to shake his resolve to break the family's pacts. In a sorcerous revenge straight out of JAPANESE FOLK TALES, Azusa then reveals that there is more to her family's traditional beliefs than straightforward marriages. The third in the *Rumic World* series based on short manga tales by URUSEI YATSURA–creator Rumiko Takahashi. Other entries included FIRE TRIPPER, MERMAID'S FOREST, and MARIS THE CHOJO. ⓥ

LAW AND DISORDER

Anime for children often places emphasis on law and discipline, either through enforcement by parental figures or as the object of cathartic defiance by naughty protagonists. Yasuji Murata's *Taro's Steamtrain* (*Taro-san no Kisha*, 1929) showed its protagonist desperately, and largely unsuccessfully, attempting to keep control of an unruly group of passengers, allegorizing an adult's plight by putting a child in a parent's position for comedic effect.

Many children's anime protagonists exist in a dreamworld without parents, adopting an orphan status that may initially be played as tragedy, but can also be exploited as an excuse for an unsupervised existence. Many enjoy an officially "free" orphan status but with parental figures somewhere close at hand, such as the numerous professor-mentors in anime from ASTRO BOY to CONAN THE BOY DETECTIVE (aka *Case Closed*), the mysterious stranger who offers help in CANDY CANDY, the latchkey children whose parents work long hours away from home—even in a different city—or the impossibly accommodating bases to be found in every POKÉMON town, where children are welcomed, fed, and cared for, and then sent back out into the world to have more fun. This condition in anime has not always been used without comment—HIPPO AND THOMAS alle-

gorized the parent-child relationship as that of a kindly, indulgent giant and a constantly scheming, ungrateful freeloader, much to the amusement of any parents who found the time to look in.

Not all anime iconoclasm is as obvious as that found in the bratty behavior of CRAYON SHIN-CHAN. Bad guys in cartoons the world over are often given dialogue with a vocabulary at least a couple of years older than of the target audience, thereby giving the subliminal impression of a bullying elder sibling or evil parent. However, in anime made specifically for children, it would be counterproductive for producers to sanction bad behavior without retribution. Consequently, many anime protagonists are heroes working to enforce a greater good—employees or heirs of an individual or organization dedicated to the defeat of evil.

Such trends in anime have led to many crime-related serials, in which protagonists hunt down evildoers, or solve crimes by means of deduction. The NAUGHTY DETECTIVES (1968) may not have appeared in anime until relatively late in the 20th century, but drew on a tradition of crime-solving kids dating back to the early 20th-century works of Ranpo Edogawa. The works of Arthur Conan Doyle have been as influential on anime crime fighters as those of his contemporary Jules Verne were on science fiction—we not only have the adventures of SHERLOCK HOUND, but also the Doyle-inspired CONAN THE BOY DETECTIVE (aka *Case Closed*). Note, however, that the CASE-BOOK OF CHARLOTTE HOLMES, in its original Japanese form, was far less closely related to the works of Doyle than its English title implies.

Japan's own detective tradition, the *torimono-cho*, entertained readers with tales of samurai-era detectives, like those found in 808 DISTRICTS. Some of these, such as the undercover authority figures of MANGA MITO KOMON and SAMURAI GOLD, were remade for the anime audience in a fantasy or science fiction format. Three of the most famous were controversially remodeled for an

anime audience without the consent of the original creators' estates—a descendant of the superefficient *Heiji Zenigata* (*DE) was cast as a dogged, incompetent detective in the long-running LUPIN III, whose title character was descended from famous fictional French thief Arsène Lupin, while the grandson of Kosuke Kindaichi would chase criminals in the YOUNG KINDAICHI FILES (see also *DE).

Anime detective dramas and cop shows often search for a gimmick designed to separate them from the "mainstream," although with the occasional rare exception of one-shots like DOMAIN OF MURDER, there is no crime "mainstream" within the anime medium itself—anime is instead competing directly with live-action. Consequently, crime anime will search, in much the same way as EROTICA AND PORNOGRAPHY, for areas within the live-action genre that can be more easily served by animation. Science fiction is perhaps the most obvious, with the Knight Sabers in BUBBLEGUM CRISIS and the AD POLICE, although anime also offers fantasy crime fighters, such as the cast of SAILOR MOON. Shows like SUKEBAN DEKA (see also *DE) flirt with the erotic potential of "bad girls," in which a fallen heroine is offered the chance of redemption through working for the police; CYBER CITY OEDO 808 plays the same redemptive game without the gender-loaded subtext. YOU'RE UNDER ARREST had little "new" to offer except a self-conscious cuteness, perhaps explaining why it was so easily adapted for live-action (*DE). Rarer explorations within the detective genre include FAKE, which replays the clichés of the detective drama with a homosexual cast.

Japanese live-action police dramas are reluctant to deal with the issue of a cop on the edge or the wrong side of the law—the hard-bitten, borderline criminal cop of *The Shield* (2002) all too often mutating in Japan into the sanitized rule-benders of live-action serials like *Unfair* (2006). However, while the Japanese mainstream generally insists that its cops are good-hearted, anime can push the envelope in new directions, either with science fictional satire of bad policing like **Dominion** or **Angel Cop**, or by pinning all the blame on foreigners, as with **Mad Bull 34**.

The perennial emphasis on science fiction in anime often puts it several years ahead of live-action cop shows in its treatment of new crimes. Hacking, identity theft, and computer viruses are old news in the anime world and continue to be innovatively explored in **Ghost in the Shell** and its spin-offs. Perhaps the best crime show in anime, however, remains **Patlabor**, whose robotic supporting cast represents an excellent use of the animated medium over its live-action competitors, while its TV running time permitted long story arcs in which petty infractions gradually escalate into major felonies, and eventually massive governmental conspiracies. For those who want a more traditional sleuthing, there is always **Hercule Poirot and Miss Marple**, continuing the long tradition in Japanese television of detectives hunting down the truth to make us all feel safer.

LAW OF UEKI, THE *
2005. JPN: *Ueki no Hosoku*. AKA: *Ueki's Laws*. TV series. DIR: Hiroshi Watanabe, Chiaki Ima, Ryoji Fujiwara, Shigeru Kimiya, Shigeru Ueda, Shogo Mitsui. SCR: Kenichi Araki, Masashi Kubota, Masashi Suzuki, Toshifumi Kawase. DES: Shinobu Tagashira. ANI: Maki Murakami, Nozomu Watanabe. MUS: Akifumi Tada. PRD: Echo, Studio Deen, Studio Tulip, TV Tokyo. 25 mins. x 43+ eps.
Life for eighth grader Ueki changes radically when his homeroom teacher is revealed to be a god in training. Ueki becomes the lucky student in the class who is permitted to receive special powers—although his is the rather silly ability to transmute trash into plants, not unlike the ability enjoyed by **Eat-Man**. He is then sent out to do battle with similarly powered humans, but also expected to live life in an offi-

cially sanctioned manner. Every time he commits a sin, he loses one of his mundane abilities as penance and soon finds himself unattractive to girls. Ultimately, if his sponsor attains godhood, he'll win a prize of his own—a blank-slate talent the nature of which he can decide for himself. Compare to *Bruce Almighty* (2003), but also **Kamichu** and **Maburaho**. Based on a manga in *Shonen Sunday* weekly by Tsubasa Fukuchi.

LAWS OF DIVORCE AND INHERITANCE
1989. JPN: *Horitsu, Rikon, Sozoku*. Video. DIR: Kazuki Sakaguchi. SCR: N/C. DES: N/C. ANI: Keiichiro Okamoto. MUS: N/C. PRD: Koh Planning, Yang Corporation. 60 mins. x 2 eps.
An unusual public-information series in which helpful lawyer Taro Bengoshi talks the viewer through the fascinating world of divorce relating to marital violence, adultery, and irreconcilable differences, as well as methods for dealing with a partner unwilling to consent to divorce, general procedure, division of assets, compensation, parental rights, and child support. The second episode concentrates on inheritance, planning a will, the rights of legitimate children, rights of children from a former marriage, renouncing the right to inherit, finding missing fortunes, intestate wills, and procedures for dividing assets. One to remember next time someone suggests that anime is nothing but **Pokémon** and porn.

LAWS OF THE SUN, THE *
2000. Movie. DIR: Takaaki Ishiyama. SCR: Laws of the Sun Scenario Project. DES: Don Davis. ANI: N/C. MUS: MIZ Music Inc. PRD: Group Tac. 101 mins.
The Cosmic Consciousness creates the human race on planet Venus, a paradise of wisdom, love, and learning. However, the absence of struggle prevents humanity from striving for perfection, so the entire species is moved to the less hospitable world of Earth, where it is encouraged to seek enlightenment through a process of reincarnation. The early human civili-

zation is smashed up by the dinosaurs, which are luckily killed off by cruel big-game hunters from outer space. Humanity continues to struggle amid several alien assaults. Satan is variously described as leading a revolution against the gods in heaven, leading a revolution in hell, or simply as being an invading alien from the Greater Magellanic Cloud. Mu, Atlantis, Greece, and the Inca civilization all represent peaks of achievement, but are all too soon destroyed by human folly—after, in the case of the Incas, defeating reptilian space invaders with the power of love. Throughout history, however, the same souls are constantly reincarnated, including the wisest humans, such as Jesus, Moses, Confucius, Zoroaster, Buddha, Newton, Thoth, Archimedes, and Hermes. It has now been 2,500 years since Buddha, and the time is right for a new cycle of redemption, handily offered to the audience by the Institute for Research in Human Happiness, the religious cult that funded the film.

Based on a book by Ryuho Okawa (aka "El Cantare"), the leader of the IRH and supposed reincarnation of several notable historical figures. As with his earlier **Hermes**, the plot is risibly incoherent, mixing myths and pulp sci-fi with such impunity that no writer seems prepared to take responsibility for it. There are, however, some spots of cleverness—particularly the use of reincarnation to ensure that the same point-of-view characters can lead the dumbstruck audience through the 40 *billion* years covered in the feature. As well as doing respectable box-office in Japan, where the IRH faithful flocked to see their leader's latest cinematic outpouring, *Laws of the Sun* was also given a very limited screening in the U.S., chiefly in California, a state not unknown for its readiness to embrace new religions. Director Ishiyama filmed similarly revisionist histories in **Sakura Wars** and **Kishin Corps**, while art director Don Davis won an Emmy for his work on Carl Sagan's landmark science *fact* documentary, *Cosmos*. Readers will be pleased to hear that Okawa no longer claims, as he did in the early 1990s, that the end of the world is nigh. One hopes this means that more of his 400 books will be animated soon. **The Golden Laws** soon followed.

LEATHERMAN *

2001. Video. DIR: Hideo Ura. SCR: Hideo Ura. DES: Junichi Tanaka. ANI: N/C. MUS: N/C. PRD: Aiti, Five Ways. 30 mins. x 4 eps.

Bad boy biker Cruz is the titular Leatherman. After sex with beautiful but dumb Shisui at her research institute workplace, he robs the safe and makes off on his bike, meeting and bowling over women from a shy nun to a UFO fanatic. Shisui's boss is furious, not just about sex on company time but because the safe contained material that would damage "the organization" if made public. Shisui sets out to find her naughty biker boy and get the bag back, and she's under orders to kill him if he doesn't cooperate. All the women he romps with en route are hostages for his final cooperation in an operation that's bigger than he knows. **LNV**

LEAVE IT TO SCRAPPERS

1994. JPN: Omakase Scrappers. TV series. DIR: Hideaki Oba. SCR: Hiroyuki Hoshiyama. DES: Satomi Aoki. ANI: Satomi Aoki. MUS: Nagayoshi Yazawa. PRD: ACC Pro, Beam Enterainment, NHK. 25 mins. x 9 eps.

A children's SF series from **Lupin III**–creator Monkey Punch, this anime features a boy and his diminutive robot assistants (think Silent Running, but played for laughs) attempting to do the right thing, but often creating more trouble for themselves when they take on deceptively easy jobs, such as guarding an idol singer or running a summer camp.

LEDA: FANTASTIC ADVENTURES OF YOKO *

1985. JPN: Genmu Senki Leda. AKA: Dreamwar Chronicle Leda. Video. DIR: Kunihiko Yuyama. SCR: Junji Takegami,

Kunihiko Yuyama. DES: Mutsumi Inomata. ANI: Shigenori Kageyama, Mutsumi Inomata, Mayumi Watanabe. MUS: Shiro Sagisu. PRD: Toho, Kaname Pro. 70 mins.

Yoko Asagiri is a shy teenager who is secretly in love with a schoolmate. She writes a song to express her feelings, only to find that the tune is a bridge to the fantasy world of Ashanti (Leda in the English version). There, the former high priest is making plans to lead his army across to Earth and rule it for all eternity. Aided by warrior-priestess Yoni, a talking dog called Lingam, and a tin man reminiscent of **The Wizard of Oz**, Yoko must overcome her fears to become Leda's Warrior and pilot the Wings of Leda into the enemy's floating citadel. Here, her ability to tell between true love and falsehood will be tested to the utmost. A high point of early video anime also shown in theaters in Japan, this video combines many anime staples, including large robots, pilot heroines, battle bikinis, and even a love song to save the world. Fifteen years later, the main crew members would still be in the public eye, directing **Pokémon**, designing **Brain Powered**, and composing the music to **Evangelion**.

LEFT OF O'CLOCK

1989. JPN: Hidari no O'Clock. Video. DIR: Satoshi Inoue, Hiroaki Sakurai. SCR: Yugo Serikawa. DES: Osamu Kamijo. ANI: Masami Suda. MUS: N/C. PRD: Toei. 50 mins. x 2 eps.

Disenchanted with life ruled by other people's timekeeping, Yu gets on a motorcycle and rides down the length of Japan from his northern home. While his sister Megumi and girlfriend Aoi fret about him at home, he becomes a different person during his journey, helping out people he meets on the way and falling in love with the pretty Tomo after an accident. A knight-of-the-road tale based on the manga by **Area 88**–creator Kaoru Shintani and presented as four TV-length "episodes," though these two video incarnations were its only appearance.

LEGEND OF CENTAURUS

1987. JPN: Centaurus no Densetsu. Video. DIR: Teruo Ishii. SCR: Junzo Toriumi. DES: Osamu Otake. ANI: Hidemi Kama. MUS: Hatanori Fusayama. PRD: Jin Pro. 95 mins.

The Centaurs are a racing team of 93 bikers from the port city of Yokohama who are named after the legendary Greek horse/men. Arthur and Ken fall out over their love for the same lady, who is unhelpfully called Lady, deciding to settle their competition with a race. Based on a manga by Osamu Otake.

LEGEND OF DUO

2005. TV series. DIR: Koichi Kikuchi. SCR: Daisuke Ishibashi, Toshiki Inoue. DES: Project DUO. ANI: N/C. MUS: N/C. PRD: Marine Entertainment, Mobanimation. 5 mins. x 12 eps.

In the 21st century, humanity begins to lose its vitality, or prana energy—some might say the same thing of the anime business, particularly if they compare this plotline to the same year's **Aquarion**. As the human race faces extinction, the last hope lies in the vampires, a race whose blood may supply the much needed prana that humanity requires. An incredibly short and incredibly cheap animation style, often little better than radio, does little to help this complicated story with an over-large cast of characters better suited to a full-length TV series, not these rapid shorts in the style of **Blame**. However, the authors suspect that LoD had less to do with television anyway, and more with an experiment in order to create material ahead of the boom in direct downloads to mobile phones, where many of LoD's vices would become virtues.

LEGEND OF GALACTIC HEROES

1988. JPN: Ginga Eiyu Densetsu. AKA: Heldensagen von Kosmosinsel. Video. DIR: Noboru Ishiguro, Akio Sakai, Akihiko Nishimura, Kenichi Imaizumi. SCR: Takeshi Shudo, Shimao Kawanaka, Kazumi Koide. DES: Matsuri Okuda, Masayuki Kato, Studio Nue. ANI: Matsuri Okuda, Keizo Shimizu. MUS: Michiyoshi Inoue (arranger). PRD: Kitty Film. 60 mins., 100 mins. x 28 eps. (109 "episodes" on 28 tapes), 90 mins. (m), 60 mins. (v/*GW*), 100 mins. (v/*Vows*), 100 mins. (v/*Dom, Son*), 100 mins. (*Disgrace*), 100 mins. x 3 eps. (v/*TSTPL*), 100 mins. x 3 eps. (v/*SL*). In the year A.D. 3597, a hundred and fifty years into the conflict between the Alliance of Independent Worlds and the Galactic Empire, both forces claim victory at the Battle of Astarte. On the Alliance side, the strategic genius Yang Wenli, a former historian dragged into a military life. Fighting for the empire, Reinhardt von Lohengramm, the estranged son of a provincial nobleman, determined to rise through the ranks until he can overthrow the ruling dynasty, whose kaiser bought Reinhardt's sister, Annerose, as a concubine from his dishonorable father. Lohengramm's childhood friend, Kircheis, loves Annerose in a different way.

Yoshiki Tanaka's *magnum opus*, the 18 novels of *LGH* are far superior to his other works, which include APPLELAND STORY, HEROIC LEGEND OF ARSLAN, and LEGEND OF THE FOUR KINGS. *LGH* is a tragic far-future epic, in which two heroes, who would probably have been the best of friends, find themselves on opposing sides in a galactic war. *LGH* has a pathos redolent of Leiji Matsumoto's COCKPIT or CAPTAIN HARLOCK, and a sympathetic treatment of both sides—though it is also renowned for truly vast space battles with thousands of ships, set to classical music. The imperial forces are part-Nazi, part-stuffy, decadent European aristocracy, while the Alliance is an American-style melting pot. As in WWII itself, which inspires much of the sci-fi, the imperial forces have the best uniforms and the nastiest schemers, but the other side has its fair share of machinations behind the scenes.

The first two episodes were screened as a movie-edit in theaters, with the grossly inferior ULTIMATE TEACHER on the same double bill. Released in TV-episodic form but straight to video,

LGH is one of anime's silent successes, sold chiefly by mail order to a dedicated audience large enough to keep the series running for a whole decade. Ishiguro shoots the anime version like a disaster movie or a Kihachi Okamoto war film (see EVANGELION), retaining the novel's cast of thousands and many onscreen titles to remind us who is who. Though the sci-fi trappings are occasionally halfhearted and hokey (there are, mercifully, no transforming robots, although there are hackneyed hovercars and similarly redressed contemporary technology), the execution is still brilliant. If FIST OF THE NORTH STAR was animation taken in interesting directions by lack of time and budget, then *LGH*'s need to continuously find new ways to depress its audience has encouraged some masterful writing, most notable in the early episodes. In a scene in which Jessica Edwards is elated to hear of her fiancé's promotion, it takes several seconds for her to register the implication of *posthumous*. But despite the stirring music, gripping plots, and doomed pretty-boy heroes, *LGH* can be too smart for its own good—whereas the anime LENSMAN chose the pulp, kiddified sci-fi route, *LGH* keeps to cerebral plotting likely to doom it in the modern anime market.

Another film, *LGH: Overture for a New Conflict* (1993), flashed back to Reinhardt's first great victory at Astarte during the Tiamat War. Promoted to senior admiral, he decides to accept the Lohengramm family title of Count and retire from the military, but he is thwarted by the actions of other officers, who redeploy his efficient subordinates. Sent to Astarte in the company of his adjutant Kircheis, Reinhardt proves himself against the odds.

As befits a series whose sprawling plot makes *Dune* look like *The Cat in the Hat*, there are plenty of other opportunities for video spin-offs. *LGH: Golden Wings* (1992) is adapted from one of the eight flashback novels set apart from the main series continuity, set four years before the beginning of the story proper. Reinhardt and Annerose

meet Kircheis for the first time and fight off a group of assassins sent by the court. Similar intrigues await in *LGH: Valley of White Silver* (1997), depicting Reinhardt and Kircheis's first mission after leaving the military academy. They are sent to the front line on the icy planet of Kapturanka and placed under a commander who hates Annerose because she is favored by the kaiser. Once again, they must deal with assassins without upsetting the status quo. *LGH: Dream of the Morning, Song of the Night* (1997) finds Reinhardt seconded to the military police and sent to investigate a murder at his old school. He undertakes the job, though he is fully aware that he is being framed. The focus shifts to Kircheis for *LGH: Disgrace* (1997), in which the vacationing adjutant rescues an old man, who turns out to be a retired general, forced out of military service after losing a battle. Alliance hero Yang Wenli features in *LGH: A Trillion Stars, A Trillion Points of Light* (1997), in which Schoenkopp, the new commander of the Rosenritter regiment (Knights of the Rose), leads his forces into battle against Runeberg, the *old* commander and his former boss, who has defected to the imperial side and been made a commodore. In the most recent video series to date, *LBH: Spiral Labyrinth* (1999), young Lieutenant Yang Wenli saves the lives of millions of people from an imperial attack and becomes a hero. Soon afterward, he is sent to investigate the murder of Ashby, a retired general. One more tape, the *LGH: Season Four Preview* (1996), is a "making-of . . ." documentary featuring shots of the crew at work and interviews with the voice actors.

LEGEND OF GUSCO BUDORI

1996. JPN: *Gusco Budori no Densetsu*. Movie. DIR: Ryutaro Nakamura. SCR: Ryutaro Nakamura. DES: Shinichi Suzuki. ANI: Shinichi Suzuki. MUS: Yuhiro Kanno. PRD: Bandai Visual. 85 mins. Another children's story by NIGHT TRAIN TO THE STARS–creator Kenji Miyazawa, adapted into an anime as part of the anniversary of the author's birth (see SPRING AND CHAOS). Gusco is driven from his home and family by a series of natural disasters but fights back by joining the Iihatov Volcano Department. Science brings improvement to the local people, but also causes Gusco's tragic death.

LEGEND OF HIMIKO *

1999. JPN: *Himiko-Den.* TV series. DIR: Ayumi Tomobuki. SCR: Saburo Kurimoto. DES: Yumi Manosono. ANI: Hirohito Kato. MUS: N/C. PRD: Tac. 25 mins. x 12 eps.

A Japanese teenager discovers that she is the daughter of shrine guardians from the ancient land of Yamatai, flung centuries into the future by an incident that occurred during an invasion of forces from the neighboring kingdom of Kune. Accompanied by her classmate Masahiko, she is dragged back to her original era, where they join forces with the rebels who are still holding out against the undead soldiers born of the Black Mist.

Yet another girl-transported-to-different-world/time anime, tracing its ancestry to THE WIZARD OF OZ, but with more immediate antecedents in MAZE, ESCAFLOWNE and FUSHIGI YUGI. However, considering that *Himiko-den* originated in a 1999 PlayStation RPG, it is remarkably coherent and well plotted, superior to many other game-based anime. The slightly longer running time afforded by the TV airing is a considerable help, as is the effective opening animation and music. Produced by SAKURA WARS' Oji Hiroi.

LEGEND OF KAMUI

1969. JPN: *Ninpu Kamui Gaiden.* AKA: *Extra Tales of Kamui the Wind Ninja; Search of the Ninja.* TV series. DIR: Yonehiko Watanabe, Satoshi Murayama, Keisuke Kondo, Kiyoshi Onishi. SCR: Junji Tashiro, Hiroyuki Torii. DES: Sanpei Shirato. ANI: Yoshihide Yamauchi, Toyoo Ashida, Tadashi Maeda, Takashi Oyama. MUS: Ryoichi Mizutani. PRD: Akame Pro, Eiken, Fuji TV. 25 mins. x 26 eps.

Legend of Lemnear

Kamui is a new initiate into the world of the ninja, a young boy who wants a normal life, thrown into a society of assassins. He learns the secret tricks of the trade and tries to fight for what he believes in, but the beliefs of his fellow ninja are more mercenary, and liable to cause fatal friction.

Hot on the heels of MANUAL OF NINJA MARTIAL ARTS, a 1964 manga by Sanpei Shirato was also adapted, this time for the small screen. Shirato's original ran out with two episodes to go, so the author wrote two further chapters in order to round off the series. The same creator also wrote SASUKE. Several TV episodes were also recut into the anime film of the same name, released in 1971. Not to be confused with the unrelated DAGGER OF KAMUI.

LEGEND OF LEMNEAR *

1989. JPN: *Kyokuguro no Tsubasa Barukisasu.* AKA: *Jet Black Wings of Valkisas.* Video. DIR: Kinji Yoshimoto. SCR: Kinji Yoshimoto. DES: Satoshi Urushihara. ANI: Kinji Yoshimoto. MUS: Norimasa Yamanaka. PRD: AIC, Nippon Cine TV Corp. 45 mins.

Lemnear, the sole survivor of her village, is a beautiful girl whose destiny is to become the Champion of Silver, the warrior who will lead the people against the invading Dark Lord and his evil minion, the wizard Gardein.

A girl out for revenge, a harem, wobbly breasts, escape, massive fight, bigger fight, the end. Like the same creators' later PLASTIC LITTLE, *LoL* suffers from an oversimplification of audience demands—realistically bouncing breasts and massive collateral damage will not make an anime work. They can add to its appeal (see GUNBUSTER), but more discerning fans demand plot and characterization. Urushihara and Yoshimoto are clearly masters of their craft, but masters to the extent that, when given control of a production, they ignore many important aspects in order to concentrate on their beloved designs. The result is a hodgepodge of incongruities commonplace today in such game-based fantasy anime such as FINAL FANTASY—a honky-tonk piano playing in a medieval tavern and a plot so thin that the credits start rolling before the baddie's even cold. There are probably a lot of animators who are using five-second segments from *Lemnear* in their resumés, particularly the highly realistic fire-modeling, but the anime itself is no more than a series of such apprentices' showpieces connected by a halfhearted plot and lovingly drawn cheesecake. The story was also published in manga form, also drawn by Urushihara. 🅝🆅

LEGEND OF LYON *

1986. JPN: *Riyon Densetsu Flare*. Video. DIR: Yukihiro Makino. SCR: N/C. DES: Yorihisa Uchida. ANI: Yorihisa Uchida. MUS: Nobuhiko Kajiwara. PRD: Hayama Art, Media Station. 30 mins. x 2 eps., 30 mins. x 2 eps.

Claude leads an army of demons in an invasion of the peaceful kingdom of Lyon, but he is held back by the martial (and marital) powers of the beautiful Flare, mixing the alien rapists of DEMON BEAST INVASION with the hokey fantasy plot of EROTIC TORTURE CHAMBER. After dispatching the invaders in episode one, the pretty Flare and her sidekick, Neris, discover more of them lurking in the woods, and the tentacled menace is once again dealt with after several scenes of clothes-ripping and high-pitched screams. It was followed by the similarly titled *Legend of Reyon: God of Darkness*, a pastiche in the spirit of TOURNAMENT OF THE GODS, in which the hackneyed conventions of beat-'em-up game adaptations (a secret fight arranged to destroy all the bad guy's opponents at once) are adapted for the erotic market. Though *Reyon* was not an actual sequel to *Lyon*, it did recycle the same character designs. 🅛🅝🆅

LEGEND OF ROLLING WHEELS

1987. JPN: *Baribari Densetsu*. Video. DIR: Nagayuki Toriumi, Satoshi Uemura. SCR: Jiyu Watanabe, Asami Watanabe. DES: Shuichi Shigeno. ANI: Noboru Furuse. MUS: Ichiro Nitta. PRD: Studio Pierrot. 30 mins. x 2 eps.

Miyuki Ichinose sees something remarkable—a kid on a 50cc moped outracing a man on a 750cc bike. Since she is the daughter of a motorcycle racing team chief, she wastes no time in inviting the kid, Gun, onto the team. Gun finds it hard to fit in at first, and

the rivalry between him and successful rider Hideyoshi makes things even harder. Gun gains confidence, and he and his friends accept Hideyoshi's challenge to enter their team in the world championship. Their team wins, but Hideyoshi's career is interrupted by a tragic accident.

Based on a 1983 manga in *Shonen Magazine* by Shuichi Shigeno, whose need for speed would find a greater outlet in the later INITIAL D. This was made for video but shown in some theaters in its year of release.

LEGEND OF THE BLUE WOLVES *

1996. JPN: *Aoki Okamitachi no Densetsu*. AKA: *Legend of the Four Horsemen of the Apocalypse*. Video. DIR: Yasunori Urata. SCR: N/C. DES: Makoto Kobayashi. ANI: N/C. MUS: Masamichi Amano. PRD: Beam Entertainment. 45 mins.

In the year 2199, humans have spread out across the solar system, until the unfortunate day when they encounter the alien enemies known only as the Apocalypse. Assimilating human victims and transforming them into new members of their invading army, the Apocalypse represent the worst threat humanity has ever faced. Meanwhile, at a training camp for robot pilots, new recruit Jonathan Tiberius finds himself developing inappropriate feelings of lust towards his roommate, the older, wiser soldier Leonard Schteinberg. Meanwhile, both are victimized by the camp commander, a fat, ugly man who uses his position of authority to have his wicked way with attractive young cadets. Despite science fictional trappings that seem inspired at least in part by the previous year's EVANGELION, the appeal of this gay porn anime rested chiefly on its explicit sex scenes—in addition to the 45-minute full version, there is an R-rated edit with ten minutes missing. 🅛🅝🆅

LEGEND OF THE CONDOR HERO *

2001. JPN: *Shinkyo Kyoro: Condor Hero*. TV series. DIR: Akira Miyata, Atsushi Nigorikawa, Hiromitsu Morita, Jun Takagi, Kazuya Miyazaki, Keiji

Hayakawa, Kenichi Nishida, Masami Anno, Takayoshi Suzuki. SCR: Mayumi Koyama. DES: Noboru Sugimitsu. ANI: Hironobu Saito. MUS: Kanae Shinozuka. PRD: Jade Animation, Nippon Animation, Taiseng Entertainment, BS Fuji. 25 mins. x 26 eps. (TV1); 25 mins. x 26 eps. (TV2).

Yang Guo (Youka) is an orphaned martial arts student in 13th-century China. Seeking revenge for the death of his father whom he never knew, Yang studies under the Taoist Quan Zhen sect in Zhong Nan Mountain, and under crazy kung fu master Ou Yang Feng, nicknamed "Western Poison" for his oddity and lethal skills. On leaving the Taoist temple he meets another kung fu master with a temple on the mountain—Xiao Long Nü (Shoryujo). The beautiful heiress of the Gumu Bai school, she is compelled to accept him as a student by a friend's dying wish. The pair are so naïve that they don't realize the love which grows between them is forbidden until it's too late, and Xiao Long Nü leaves the mountain to get away from her feelings for Yang. But away from the mountain, the tide of history is moving. The Mongols have conquered the northern Chinese kingdom of Jin and their next target is the Southern Song empire. The region has many great martial artists who band together to fight the invaders, but in the end they will be defeated at the historic battle of Xiang Yang, and China will fall under Mongol rule.

The 1959 novel by Jin Yong (aka Louis Cha), *Return of the Condor Heroes (Shendiao Xialu)* on which the anime is based, is actually a sequel. The first book, *Eagle-Shooting Heroes* had a number of spin-offs of its own, including a 1994 live-action Chinese TV series and a live-action movie filmed by Wong Kar-wai as *Ashes of Time* (1994). A third novel followed. The anime series was a Japanese–Hong Kong coproduction, conceived partly in anticipation of import restrictions that would shut out the lucrative Chinese broadcast market to some "foreign" imports. Showing up on official records as a "coproduction" with a heavy Chinese staff presence, the show was thus deemed enough of a local production to evade any import restrictions, one of many such anime in the early 21st century as Japanese producers set their sights on the last and biggest market remaining, China itself. Two seasons were produced, but only the first season was dubbed into Japanese and shown on late-night Japanese satellite television, in such an obscure slot that it escaped the notice of all but the most scrupulous scrutineers of the anime magazines. The show didn't prove as successful in Japan as in mainland China (nor did it need to), and season two was only shown in Cantonese, with Mandarin subtitles. The first half (i.e., the Japanese half) was eventually released in the U.S. with English subtitles, although the U.S. version does not contain Japanese language tracks, only Cantonese and Mandarin ones. **Ⓥ**

LEGEND OF THE FOREST *

1987. Movie. DIR: Osamu Tezuka. SCR: Osamu Tezuka. DES: Osamu Tezuka. ANI: Takashi Okamura, Yoshiaki Kawajiri. MUS: Peter Tchaikovsky. PRD: Mushi Pro. 23 mins.
In the forest, in the valley, by the river that will eventually flow to the sea, insects buzz among the flowers. Two squirrels fall in love, but the forest is threatened by property developers. The innovation is not in the story, but in the way in which it is told. As with his *Broken Down Film* (see **JUMPING**), Tezuka experiments with the film medium itself, starting with the still frames and limited camera movement on still pictures, before progressing through early monochrome, color, limited TV animation, and Disney-style full animation. In other words, *LotF* takes the viewer through several decades of animation history in just a few minutes. A second, unrelated film follows, in which forest spirits, shown in lush, *Fantasia*-quality animation and coloring, fight off the human building developers (led by a Hitler-look-alike construction boss), who are shown in limited animation with jagged, angular art design and bright, garish colors. Compare to **POMPOKO**, in message if not execution.

LEGEND OF THE FOUR KINGS *

1991. JPN: *Soryuden*. AKA: *Sohryuden; The Endragonning; Legend of the Dragon Kings*. Video. DIR: Norio Kabeshima. SCR: Akinori Endo. DES: Shunji Murata. ANI: Moriyasu Taniguchi, Nobuaki Nagano, Makura Saki (pseud. for Osamu Dezaki). MUS: Hiroyuki Nanba. PRD: Kitty Film. 45 mins. x 12 eps.
Three thousand years in the past, there was a war in the heavenly realm. Betrayed by their allies, the Go clan are banished from heaven and forced to wander Earth as mortals for 117 generations, until the dragons contained within them burst forth once more to begin the battle anew.

Fast forward to the present, where the four Ryudo brothers live in Tokyo but have recently been the subject of several kidnapping attempts. While the brothers are plagued by kidnappers and dreams of dragons, they have to cope with a takeover bid at the family college and dynastic machinations as a mobster tries to marry his son to Matsuri. As if a surname that is Chinese for "Dragon Pavilion" is not enough of a hint, the brothers are the earthly incarnations of the four Dragon Kings of legend, and the powers of their former lives still dwell within them, bestowing superhuman strength and speed. These powers are desired by the "Old Man of Kamakura," who lures them to a firing range by kidnapping their cousin Matsuri. The Old Man is not the only one who wishes to possess the magical powers of the Ryudos—the mad Dr. Tomosawa, famed for live vivisections, and the U.S. military are both keen to kidnap the brothers themselves. The doctor sends cybernetic soldiers in to obtain the brothers, but, as with all the previous assailants, his minions are seen off by the brothers' powers of transformation. One Ryudo, however, is caged and taken to Yokota Air Force Base (see **BLOOD**). The others must rescue him before the cruel experiments awaken the dragon within him and turn him into a monster of awesome destructive capabilities. You can guess the rest.

Dense without being engaging, *LotFK* is based on a series of novels by **LEGEND OF GALACTIC HEROES**–creator Yoshiki Tanaka, but it has none of the virtues of its more illustrious counterpart. A failed attempt to recreate the monthly "video comic" feel of the U.K. distributor's previous **GUYVER**, the dub is particularly poor, with the "Weirdo" brothers speaking a mixture of English and American, and for all their supposed genius, not being able to pronounce each other's names properly. The plot development is confused by the intercutting of disparate scenes from the eight-volume series of novels, patched together with unhelpful voice-overs. The animation itself is often mediocre, barely above the level of later **CRYING FREEMAN** episodes, but the design has a certain special something. From the opening credits that depict the brothers in Chinese dress through to the uncommonly "Asian" features of the characters, *LotFK* is steeped in oriental myth and culture, shamefully occluded by the English-language dubbers, who do not bother to rewrite the Japanese pronunciations of Chinese proper nouns and bungle a whole succession of historical and geographical references. These, however, are minor issues unlikely to rescue an already doomed production. The U.S. subtitled version demonstrates all too clearly that the dub is a surprisingly faithful rendition of the original's tepid tone, with the exception of the story's single funny line ("Don't step in the custard"), which was not present in the Japanese version. Dubbed at the height of Manga Entertainment's beer-and-curry era, *LotFK* even managed to disappoint the lowest-common denominator audience with its failed leap of faith toward hidden depths—the same company would return many years later with a much better version of similar material: its adaptation of CLAMP's **X: THE MOVIE**.

In addition to the *Four Kings* novels, the brothers also appear in the Japanese audio drama *Mirage City* (1995), released on CD with an accompanying manga drawn by CLAMP, who also contributed to the earlier anime adaptation of Tanaka's **HEROIC LEGEND OF ARSLAN**. **V**

LEGEND OF THE WOLF WOMAN *

2003. JPN: *Megami Kyoju*. AKA: *Wolf Woman*. Video. DIR: Katsumasa Kanezawa, Shunsuke Harada. SCR: N/C. DES: Masaki Yamada, Yuji Ushijima. ANI: N/C. MUS: N/C. PRD: Cherry Lips, Kuma. 30 mins. x 2 eps.

Shortly after successfully apprehending a child murderer, sexy New York SWAT team member Linda tries to blow off steam by hitting a strip club with her boyfriend Brian. But Kata, one of the strippers, is infected with a deadly lycanthropy virus and is soon infecting other people around the city. Linda tries unsuccessfully to contain outbreaks of werewolf violence, while her friend Mary from Forensics gets to work on a cure. Since this is an erotic anime, there is also considerable concentration on the more violent aspects of sexual perversion, including a woman linked up to a car battery for impromptu shock treatment and Linda's idea of foreplay with her boyfriend, which involves a condom and a loaded gun. Compare to **ONI TENSEI** and **P.I.: PERVERSE INVESTIGATIONS** (which similarly tries to capitalize on the success of the television series *CSI*), although considering some of the insane things the cast try in a New York minute, this strange porn anime owes a certain additional debt to **MAD BULL 34**. **CNV**

LEGENDARY IDOL ERIKO

1989. JPN: *Idol Densetsu Eriko*. TV series. DIR: Tetsuro Amino. SCR: Brother Anoppo. DES: N/C. ANI: Noriyasu Yamauchi. MUS: N/C. PRD: Bandai, TV Tokyo. 25 mins. x 51 eps. (TV), 30 mins. (v). In this popular TV series with a star whose look presaged the girl of the 1990s, **SAILOR MOON** herself, fourteen-year-old Eriko Tamura wants to be a pop star but must compete against her prissy rival, Rei Asagiri. It's scandal and high-pressure performances, as the tropes of the sports anime (e.g., **AIM FOR THE ACE**) are adapted for a show about a hothouse for wannabe stars—the lighter-hearted flipside of artistic pressures that would be so heavily criticized a decade later in **PERFECT BLUE**. *LIE: Music Video* (1989) was, predictably, a ten-song compilation of some of the serial's best tunes, released straight to video.

LEGENDZ

2004. JPN: *Legendz Yomigaeru Ryu-o Densetsu*. AKA: *Legendz: Tale of the Dragon Kings*. TV series. DIR: Akitaro Daichi. SCR: Aki Itami, Yuki Enatsu, Kinuko Kuwabatake, Yuka Yamada. DES: Nagisa Miyazaki, Kazuyuki Kobayashi. ANI: N/C. MUS: N/C. PRD: Studio Gallop, Wiz, Bandai, Pony Canyon, Fuji TV. 24 mins. x 50 eps.

New York, the present: Shu gets a game machine called a Talispod, developed by his father. It doesn't play the game it was designed for, so Shu thinks it's broken, until Shiron the white Wind Dragon emerges, an event that will come as no surprise to anyone who remembers **DRAGON DRIVE** two years earlier. The Talispod is a device that can revive ancient myths. Soon it will be needed to protect the world from new evil. The Dark Wiz company is planning to take over the world, and Shiron's enemy the black-winged dragon Ranshin plans to restart an old war. Long ago, the Earth was ruled by strange creatures worshipped as gods or feared as demons. The Four Dragon Kings (compare to **LEGEND OF THE FOUR KINGS**) ruled over each of four species of monsters commanded by the four elements—Volcano monsters (fire), Tornado monsters (wind), Earthquake monsters (earth), and Storm monsters (water). Then the Dragon Kings fought, and their monster armies were turned into crystals, known as Soul Dolls. Forgotten except in folklore, they became known as "Legendz." These are the creatures Shu's device can revive.

POKÉMON with dragons, anyone? Director Daichi helms another comical, cutely designed childrens' story, this time adapted by Hiroshi Nagahama from Kenji Watanabe's original manga in *Shonen Jump* monthly, but with some stylistic similarities to his own **GRRL POWER**.

LEISURE CLUB

1992. JPN: *Yukan Club*. Video. DIR: Satoshi Dezaki. SCR: Machiko Kondo. DES: Yukari Kobayashi. ANI: Yukari Kobayashi. MUS: Toy-Boys. PRD: Pioneer. 35 mins. x 2 eps.

Filthy-rich boys and girls occasionally take time out of their luxurious lifestyle to solve crimes in this short-lived series based on the 1981 manga in *Ribbon* by Yukari Ichijo. For the second episode, the cast relocates to the exotic foreign destination of Hong Kong, where they are dragged into a gangland conspiracy over a stolen microfilm. Compare to **DEBUTANTE DETECTIVES**.

LEMON ANGEL

1987. JPN: *Midnight Anime Lemon Angel*. TV series. DIR: Yasunori Ide, Takashi Akimoto, Susumu Aki, Osamu Yamazaki, Yukio Okazaki, Satoru Namekawa. SCR: Yasunori Ide, Osamu Yamazaki. DES: Kurahito Miyazaki. ANI: Katsu Oyama, Osamu Yamazaki. MUS: Human Company. PRD: Fairy Dust, AIC, Fuji TV. 5 mins. x 37 eps. (TV1), 5 mins. x 9 eps. (TV2), 30 mins. x 2 eps. (v), 25 mins. x 13 eps. (TV3).

Three lovely teenagers—and the three actresses who provide their voices—share their midnight confidences and fantasies with the TV audience, as Erika Shima, Miki Emoto, and Tomo Sakurai play "themselves" in a sanitized late-night TV incarnation of the **CREAM LEMON** franchise. Purporting to be studying at the fictitious Lemon Academy (compare to **KIRA KIRA MELODY ACADEMY**), the girls returned the following year for a second season, though it was soon taken off the air. Sakurai's career did not suffer, and she was soon a popular voice actress in mainstream anime such as EL HAZARD. The other actresses no longer show up on lists of big names. *Lemon Angel Y[oung] J[unior]* (1990) comprised two toned-down videos made for more censorious times, with Sakurai directed by Tetsuro Amino, who would make her a star in MACROSS 7. *Lemon Angel Project* (2006) is a 13-part TV series in which a producer attempts to assemble a group of young performers to form a new Lemon Angel, in imitation of a girl band from the past. Innocent starstruck schoolgirl Tomo Minaguchi signs up for the auditions, unaware of the more salacious side of the previous Lemon Angels.

LEMON CHUHAI LOVE 30'S

1985. JPN: *Chuhairemon Love 30's.* Video. DIR: Kozo Koizumi. SCR: Ryochi Yagi. DES: Sho Shimura. ANI: Kozo Koizumi. MUS: Yoshikazu Sano, Rob Bird. PRD: Tsuchida Pro. 45 mins.
Bug-eyed Katsumi (known as Chuhai to his friends) is a muscle-bound detective determined to use his strength and pig-headed stupidity to rescue his teenage girlfriend from a succession of embarrassing situations. Based on a manga by Sho Shimura and heavily seeded with background music from the 1960s U.S. hit parade. **NV**

LENSMAN *

1984. JPN: *Galactic Patrol: Lensman.* TV series, movie. DIR: Hiroshi Fukutomi, Yoshiaki Kawajiri, Kazuyuki Hirokawa. SCR: Soji Yoshikawa, Masaki Tsuji, Haruya Yamazaki, Michiru Umadori. DES: Kazuo Tomizawa. ANI: Nobuyuki Kitajima. MUS: Akira Inoue, The Alfee. PRD: MK, Madhouse, TV Asahi. 25 mins. x 25 eps. (TV), 107 mins. (m).
In A.D. 2742, during a fight to the death in space, the decimated survivors of the Galactic Patrol obtain vital details that could help defeat the evil Boskone Empire. The warship Brittania crashes on the peaceful farm world of M'queie, where the dying pilot passes his lens (a techno-magical power amplifier) to local boy Kim Kinnison. Kim's father, a former patrolman, sacrifices his life to allow Kim to get off-planet, throwing the young farmer into a life of adventure, as he joins forces with the patrol to defeat evil throughout the galaxy.

E. E. "Doc" Smith's *Galactic Patrol* (1937), along with its prequels and sequels, was one of the landmark series in the history of U.S. pulp sci-fi. Shortly after Edmond Hamilton's CAPTAIN FUTURE (1940) was turned into an anime in 1978, Smith's classic series was also adapted into the 25-episode *Galactic Patrol: Lensman* TV series, directed by BATTLE ANGEL's Hiroshi Fukutomi and introducing several new elements in the wake of *Star Wars*. The anime turns Kim Kinnison, originally the superhuman product of a eugenics project dating back to Atlantis, into nothing but a humble farm boy who wants to be a pilot. Nurse Clarissa "Chris" MacDougall, the fiery red-haired product of another breeding program, who eventually becomes the fearsome Red Lensman and gives birth to the immortal *Children of the Lens*, becomes yet another simpering damsel in the anime.

Carl Macek, of ROBOTECH fame, picked up the series and dubbed a couple of episodes in a failed attempt to interest U.S. networks. The episodes were eventually cut into the English-language video *Power of the Lens*, while Macek bought the feature-length Japanese theatrical edition instead to release in the U.S. as *Lensman*. As suggested by the 25-minute acts, the film version takes several episodes of the TV series and stitches them together. This makes the "movie" seem strangely paced, with fast action interspersed with overlong *gee-whiz* beauty-passes of the spaceships to allow us to gawp at the incredibly expensive computer graphics, made with the same megapowerful Cray computers used to animate Jupiter in *2010: Odyssey Two*. Still vaguely recognizable from the book are the Overlords of Delgon, evil creatures whom Kim defeats in the company of the "Dragon Lensman" Worsel, and van Buskirk, a Dutch giant (inexplicably half-bison in the anime).

Later scenes set on the "drug planet" Radelix start to go off the rails. Whereas Kim goes deep undercover posing as the drug addict "Wild Bill" in the book *Gray Lensman*, Wild Bill is a character in his own right in the anime, DJ-ing in a dated 1980s disco. By the end, we're in a ho-hum world of final showdown and lighthearted coda, with the baddie predictably still alive; a great disappointment if you've read the books, which feature crashing worlds, maimings, and dismemberments, a revolution on a planet of lesbians, mind-blowing psychic powers, double-, triple-, and quadruple-crossing conspiracies, and gunplay that makes *The Matrix* look like a puppet show.

Instead of reproducing such joys, the anime takes only the characters and most basic of plot outlines, adding the off-the-peg elements that are supposed to guarantee success in the George Lucas mode. The "comic relief" robot Sol, whose appearances are never comic and seldom a relief, is another pointless homage. Ironically, the end result makes *Lensman* look like a cheap knockoff of *Star Wars*, whereas it was original literally decades ahead of it.

LES MISÉRABLES *

1979. JPN: *Jean Valjean Monogatari.* AKA: *Story of Jean Valjean.* TV special. DIR: Keiji Hisaoka. SCR: Masaki Tsuji. DES: Masami Suda. ANI: Masami Suda. MUS: Yasuo Minami. PRD: Toei, Fuji TV. 75 mins.
Jean Valjean is thrown into prison for stealing a single loaf of bread. Returning to his hometown after several years away, he tries to live an honest life and falls in love with the pretty teacher Mireil. Caught stealing silver, he breaks parole, changes his name, and flees to another town. However, Valjean's past comes back to haunt him in the form of Inspector Javert, who catches him. Once more, Valjean escapes and flees to the big city, where tragedy awaits. An adaptation of the 1862 novel by Victor Hugo, it was released in the U.K. on the Kids Cartoon Collection label and

Quebec in a French dub, but this version is unavailable in the U.S.

LESBIAN WARD *

2001. JPN: *Les' Byoto*. Video. DIR: Kenji Matsuda, Kaoru Tomioka. SCR: N/C. DES: N/C. ANI: N/C. MUS: N/C. PRD: Soft on Demand, DEEPS. 30 mins. x 2 eps.
While the director is away on business from Ryoka University Hospital, his sexy daughter Yuka is in charge. She manages everything normally during the day, but at night turns the hospital into a den of sin, where nurses provide personal services to their VIP patients who are encouraged to watch closed-circuit TV footage of girl-on-girl action, while their personal nurse attends to more immediate needs. The men's nocturnal emissions are then gathered up and put to unexpected uses—compare to HOT JUICY TEACHER and NURSE ME. **OO**

LESSON OF DARKNESS *

1996. JPN: *Inju Kateikyoshi*. Video. DIR: Tsutomu Ono, Tsutomu Yabuki. SCR: N/C. DES: N/C. ANI: N/C. MUS: N/C. PRD: Pink Pineapple. 45 mins.
In Tokyo at the turn of the Showa era (1920s), a number of young women are found dead, their bodies shriveled like mummies. Two Tokyo college girls, Miho and Azusa, are drawn into the mystery. Miho has a weird stalker, while Azusa tried seducing her professor only to find that he was really a tentacled beast in mild mannered academic clothing. Now he, or it, is determined to stop his secret being revealed, and the friends are on the run. Combining two kinds of action isn't easy, and this erotic thriller focuses on the erotic stuff its target audience expects, leaving the other kind of action predictable and formulaic. It does at least gain a few marks for its period setting; compare to ARISA. **OOO**

LESSON XX

1994. Video. DIR: Rin Hiro. SCR: Ei Onagi. DES: Sanae Chikanaga. ANI: Sanae Chikanaga. MUS: N/C. PRD: Tokuma Japan Communications. 50 mins.

Teenager Shizuka is finishing up school and staying at a boardinghouse, but he is confused by his romantic feelings toward another man called Sakura. In a rash moment, he confesses his feelings, though both boys are concerned that once they take the first steps on the road to male love, there may be no going back. A gay-love drama without the gut-wrenching angst that seems almost obligatory with the rest of the genre, based on a manga by Ei Onagi. **O**

LET THE DREAMS NEVER END

1987. JPN: *Yume kara Samenai*. Video. DIR: Satoshi Inoue. SCR: Ran Kawanishi. DES: Yumi Shirakura. ANI: Kazuo Tomizawa. MUS: Kazuhiko Matsuo. PRD: Shaft. 40 mins.
Student Tako is inexorably drawn toward Sao despite class rumors that she has appeared in a porno film. If this were an anime for boys, he wouldn't mind so much, but this is based on a girls' manga by Yumi Shirakura, so it's all dreadfully scandalous. Sao was played by idol singer Ryoko Sano, who also provided the theme tune.

LET'S DO IT WITH SISTER

2005. JPN: *Ne-chan to Shiyo yo*. Video. DIR: Katsumasa Kanezawa. SCR: Katsumasa Kanezawa. DES: N/C. ANI: Yuji Ushijima. MUS: N/C. PRD: D3. 30 mins.
Unceasingly spoiled by his sisters as a child, Kuya is sent away to his distant relatives the Hiiragi family in the hope that he will learn self-reliance. Instead, he forgets about his sisters until ten years later, when he moves back in with the family and must deal with the presence of six beautiful girls. Since this is an erotic anime, he finds a way of coping. Based on a PC game, and a release in the D3 SERIES. **O**

LET'S NUPUNUPU

1998. TV series. DIR: Kazuyoshi Hisakome. SCR: Ko Nanbu. DES: Hiroko Seino. ANI: Yasuto Kaya. MUS: N/C. PRD: Asia-do. 4 mins. x 16 eps.
Schoolteacher Mr. Shidara has trouble

keeping his male and female students apart in this comedy broadcast as part of the *Wonderful* slot on TBS, along with shows such as COLORFUL and COOL COUPLE. It was originally based on a four-panel strip in *Shonen Magazine* by Akira Mitsumori. **O**

LEVEL C

1996. JPN: *Level C: Gokuraku no Hoteishiki*. AKA: *Level C: Paradise Equation*. Video. DIR: Yorifusa Yamaguchi. SCR: N/C. DES: Yumi Nakayama. ANI: Yumi Nakayama. MUS: N/C. PRD: Pink Pineapple, KSS. 40 mins.
A story of forbidden love between men, based on a manga by the pseudonymous Futaba Aoi and Mitsuba Kurenai. Not to be confused with EQUATION OF THE ROTTEN TEACHER. **O**

LICCA-CHAN

1990. JPN: *Licca-chan Fushigina Fushigina Unia Monogatari; Licca-chan Fushigina Maho no Ring; Licca-chan no Nichiyobi; Licca-chan the Movie: Licca-chan to Yamaneko, Hoshi no Tabi*. AKA: *Licca and the Mystery of Mysterious Unia; Licca and the Mysterious Magic Ring; Licca's Sunday; Licca the Movie: Licca and the Wildcat: Journey of Dreams; Superdoll Licca-chan*. Video, TV series. DIR: Tomomi Mochizuki, Fumiko Ishii, Tatsuo Sato, Tsutomu Shibayama. SCR: Kazunori Ito, Asami Watanabe. DES: Akemi Takada, Yoshiyuki Kato. ANI: Masako Kato, Takuya Saito. MUS: Mineo Maeda, Kenji Kawai. PRD: Asia-do, Madhouse, TV Asahi. 28 mins. x 2 eps. (v1), 60 mins. (v2), 25 mins. (v3), 78 mins. (v4), 25 mins. x 32 eps. (TV), 10 mins. (m).
Licca is playing the piano when she notices that one of the keys doesn't work. Opening it up to see why, she is transported to the world of Unia with her stuffed toy bird Dodo and Ine the cat. Trying to find her way out of a world that is equal parts ALICE IN WONDERLAND and THE WIZARD OF OZ, she meets the craftsman who makes dreams and wanders through the Square Pole forest of doppelgangers. A dragon tells her to seek the Amaranth

flower at the Tower of Beginning, but Ine has become spoiled by all the fuss he gets and wants to stay. Licca and Dodo are almost trapped in the Maze of Anger by their bad-tempered arguments, but they eventually find their way to the Sky Garden and the Rainbow Bridge that takes them home.

Licca-chan is the Japanese equivalent of Barbie, a child's doll designed in 1967 by Miyako Maki, the wife of CAPTAIN HARLOCK–creator Leiji Matsumoto. Her first video adventure was followed by *Licca and the Magic Ring* (1991), in which a magic ring falls out of the sky into Licca's playground, where she discovers that it can unlock the three seals of Dreams, Shadows, and Death. Less scary antics occupied the third video, *Licca's Sunday* (1992), about her traveling to her auntie's house to play with her cousins. As her 30th birthday grew near, the doll returned to adventure in the video misleadingly and clumsily entitled *Licca the Movie: Licca and the Wildcat: Journey of Dreams* (1994), in which she goes on a country holiday with her father, dreams that she is attending a school for the stone cats that populate the town, and heads off on a journey through the sky with the largest. The film was also repackaged the same year in a *Special Collection*, including the movie, a selection from 30 years of Licca TV commercials, and an exclusive Licca doll dressed in the uniform of a video-store clerk.

The franchise was revamped for a new generation as *Superdoll Licca-chan* (1998), a TV series featuring new designs from Tetsuya Kumatani and direction from STREET FIGHTER II's Gisaburo Sugii. For the TV version, there are *two* Liccas—the first is a third-grader at St. Therese's School, attacked without warning by Scarecrow, Pul, and Wahya. She discovers that she is the heir to the Doll Kingdom, a human dreamland where dolls live and breathe, though they can become human if loved and cherished for 100 years. Licca is the child of a union between French musician Pierre and

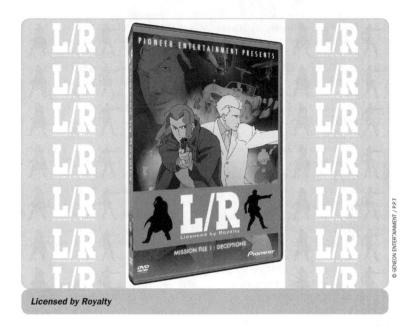

Licensed by Royalty

"normal human" Orie, who is really the Doll Queen in disguise. Licca's grandmother gives her the magical Call Ring that can summon help and three dolls named Licca, Izumi, and Isamu, the spirits of wisdom, courage and life. Since it is a fundamental problem with shows based on dolls that children often have duplicates of the same ones, this is a clever means of encouraging play with duplicate Liccas, as the child begins her quest to regain her rightful kingdom from the usurper Queen Yaë, her great-aunt. The doll returned again for *Licca-chan: Tale of the Mysterious Sea* (2001), a fully computer-animated short film shown in department stores and amusement parks. For similar doll-inspired action, see RAINBOW ACROSS THE PACIFIC and, frankly, the entire GUNDAM series.

LICENSED BY ROYALTY *

2003. JPN: *L/R*. AKA: *Licensed by Royal*. TV series. DIR: Itsuro Kawasaki. SCR: Kazuki Matsui. DES: Kenji Teraoka, Kayoko Nabeta. ANI: Masahiro Sato. MUS: Keiichi Nozaki. PRD: Pioneer (Geneon), Fuji TV. 25 mins. x 13 eps.
Cool, calm, quick-witted Rowe Rickenbacker and action-hero Jack Hofner

are agents for Cloud Seven, the secret service of the royal state of Ishtar. This quasi-British enclave, seemingly designed by someone channeling the '60s chic of Sean Connery-era 007 along with its modern pastiche, *Austin Powers* (1997), is under threat from numerous enemies, including the shadow organization known only as Hornet.

The stage is set for a retro espionage thriller played like a straight version of PATALIRO, as our heroes strive to ensure that the name of the royal family remains unimpeachable. When the royal name is used to authenticate fake antiques, it's Jack and Rowe who make sure the truth is known, but discreetly and with style. They also thwart assassination attempts and terrorist bombers, some aimed at Ishtar's biggest corporation, DTI—supposedly Digital Terra Incorporated, although connoisseurs of the show's Anglophile references will know of the Department of Trade and Industry in real life.

Amid the sub-Bondian antics (they take their orders from "Mister," clearly intended as a substitute for Ian Fleming's "M"), there is a continuing story arc that initially seems to owe more to the fairy tale foundling traditions of girls' entertainment like CANDY CANDY. A royal baby has been missing for 15 years, and a local beauty contest is actually a thinly veiled attempt by the government to search for her. A prime candidate is presented in the form of Noelle, a girl who has been raised on a remote Ishtar outpost and whom the team soon find themselves obliged to guard. But not everything is as it seems, and a series of reversals of fortune in the later episodes give *Licensed by Royalty* an impressive bite. Although at heart it is a humble action series, its use of an imaginary kingdom and heavy insistence on British imagery allow it to do something more subversive. No anime series would dare to comment directly on the Japanese Imperial family, which at the time of broadcast, faced a succession crisis if Japanese law were not changed to allow Princess Aiko (born 2001) to ascend the throne on the death of her father, the current Crown Prince Naruhito. Those in search of subtextual meanings for *L/R* might like to speculate on the fact that in our own world, an entire generation has passed without the birth of a male heir to the Japanese throne, and that as a result, the old order of Japan faced similar upheavals to those experienced by the fictional Ishtar, until the birth of a male heir in 2006 rendered such discussion irrelevant.

Ishtar (1987) was also a comedy in which Warren Beatty and Dustin Hoffman become involved in a coup in a fictional country, but on the surface at least, the country in *L/R* seems as British as that in MASTER KEATON or EMMA. This is well handled in an American dub from the people who worked on HELLSING, which ensures similar attention to detail on the accents. Many shots look just like London, and with an opening theme sung by Billy "Get Back" Preston, the show is packed with nods to British pop. The two leads are named after Lennon and McCartney's guitars, while the Moneypenny role is taken by another Beatles reference, one Claire Pennylane.

LIGHTSPEED ELECTRON ARBEGAS

1983. JPN: *Kosoku Denshin Arbegas*. TV series. DIR: Kozo Morishita, Masamitsu Sasaki, Masao Ito, Noriyasu Yamauchi, Keiji Hisaoka, Takao Yoshisawa, Masayuki Akehi. SCR: Akiyoshi Sakai. DES: Shigenori Kageyama, Koichi Ohata. ANI: Shigenori Kageyama, Hajime Kaneko, Toshio Mori. MUS: Michiaki Watanabe. PRD: Toei, TV Tokyo. 25 mins. x 45 eps. Earth is invaded by the evil Derringer aliens, who are held off repeatedly by a group of Japanese schoolchildren that have "won the robot prize." These children have inexplicably managed to knock together a giant war machine formed from three combining submachines that can transform in turn into six separate configurations for different missions—electron, magma, space, marine, guard, and sky. Obviously, kids were better at science in the 1980s. Far-fetched, but nothing can surprise an anime viewer after GOLD LIGHTAN. The toys also appeared in the GODAIKIN range and as part of Matchbox's VOLTRON line, though *Arbegas* was completely unrelated.

LIKE A CLOUD, LIKE A BREEZE

1990. JPN: *Kumo no yo ni, Kaze no yo ni*. AKA: *Kumokaze; Fly, Little Bird, Fly; Like the Clouds, Like The Wind*. TV special. DIR: Hisayuki Toriumi. SCR: Akira Miyazaki. DES: Katsuya Kondo. ANI: Katsuya Kondo. MUS: Haruhiko Maruya. PRD: Studio Pierrot, Yomiko Advertising Inc., NHK. 80 mins. In Imperial China, energetic and outspoken teenager Ginga (more properly, Yinhe) decides to enter the harem because of the rumors she hears of the comfortable life and plentiful food. But when she arrives at the palace, there are accusations over the death of the previous emperor, which may have been murder, while there are stories of a revolt in the countryside that threatens the dynasty itself. Her fellow new arrivals in the harem include the snooty Ceshamin and the withdrawn Tamyun, and the girls must take lessons in deportment from the stern teacher Kakute, whom

Ginga defies and eventually befriends. Meanwhile, her own position becomes more precarious as she manuevers to become the first wife of the new emperor, which places her in considerable and unexpected danger. As former acquaintances of Ginga's march on the capital in revolt, it is Ginga who organizes the women of the harem into an impromptu defensive force.

Like a Cloud originates in *Tale of the Harem (Kokyu Shosetsu*, 1989), a book by Kenichi Sakemi that won the first Japan Fantasy Novel Award, much to the embarrassment of sponsors who had promised to turn the winner into an anime. Instead of a tale of elves and dragons, the producers were handed a book devoted to detailed descriptions of sexual techniques. If this were a video production like EROTIC TORTURE CHAMBER, it might not have bothered anyone, but writer Akira Miyazaki had the seemingly impossible task of making the story palatable for a television audience. In a sense, he performs admirably, concentrating not on the content of the lessons, but on the existence of the lessons themselves. Accordingly, life in the Forbidden City is framed as a boarding school drama like TWINS AT ST. CLARES in period costume. Ginga must deal with rivals, a crush on a handsome authority figure (the guardsman Koryun), and classroom conflict, although at times the parallels become ludicrous—one scene features the trainee concubines exercising in the schoolyard, accompanied by anachronistic piano music.

The show stumbles with stylistic issues related to the original source material. Sakemi's novel, written with a love of Chinese pomp inspired by *The Last Emperor* (1987), is patently not based on historical fact—if it were, it would never have won a *fantasy* award. Although the anime production attempts to set its fashions and hairstyles in the closing years of the Ming dynasty (around 1630), the Beijing scenery seems to date from the later Qing era (the 1800s), while the reign title of the incumbent emperor is actually only found in the semi-legendary Xia dynasty, in the 17th century B.C., not A.D. This is a China without foot-binding, where Ginga is permitted to behave like a willful, confident hero-ine in the style of designer Kondo's earlier KIKI'S DELIVERY SERVICE, the only Chinese quality to her seemingly manifested in her slanted eyes—an exotic and ironically "orientalist" deci-sion from Japanese artists. *Like a Cloud* appears to lift several events from Chinese history, including the orga-nization of a female demonstration platoon by Sun Zi, author of the *Art of War*, and tales from both the Ming and Tang dynasties. The nature of Ginga's education, that she is, in modern par-lance, an underage girl being primed for sexual slavery, is swept far under the lavish, beautifully embroidered but anachronistic carpet. Compare to GREAT CONQUEST: ROMANCE OF THREE KINGDOMS.

LILY C.A.T. *
1987. Video. DIR: Hisayuki Toriumi. SCR: Hiroyuki Hoshiyama. DES: Yasuomi Umezu, Yasuhiro Moriki, Yoshitaka Amano. ANI: Toshiyasu Okada. MUS: Aki-ra Inoue. PRD: Studio Pierrot. 70 mins. It's A.D. 2264 and the exploration vessel Saldes is on a 20-year mission to planet L.A.O.3, carrying seven passengers. Not all of them are on the right side of the law, or totally open about their background and motives—but all of them, and the six-person crew, are in deadly danger. In a blatant rip-off of the first *Alien* movie, death is stalking the ship, picking off the occupants one by one, though the titular cat is revealed to be more than just an excuse to go back out into danger, since it is really the key to the mother computer that will save the day. ⬤🅝🅥

LIME WARS
2002. JPN: *Lime-iro Senkitan*. AKA: *Lime Colored Fleet; Lime-Colored Military Chronicle*. TV series, video. DIR: Akira Suzuki (TV1, v) Tsuneo Tominaga (TV2). SCR: Satoru Akahori (TV1, 2, v), Takao Yoshioka (TV1), Hideaki Koyasu (v). DES: Mayumi Watanabe (TV1, v), Naoki Honda (TV1), Yoshiten (TV2). ANI: Soft Garage (TV1), A.C.G.T. (TV2), Studio Hibari (v). MUS: Toshiyuki Omori (TV1), Kazuhiro Sawaguchi (TV2). PRD: KSS, Soft Garage. 25 mins. x 13 eps. (TV1), 28 mins. x 2 eps. (v), 25 mins. x 13 eps. (TV2).

In 1904, Russian-Japanese diplomat Shintaro Umakai has been hired to teach at the Amanohara School for Girls, which naturally enough is sited on a battleship—Russia and Japan are currently at war. He's on the run from a failed romance with a Russian girl and, again naturally enough, a girls' school will be the best place to get over it. The five archetypal girls he is to teach (unsurprisingly, as this is based on an erotic computer game) can summon up and control elemental superpowers that might just save Japan, in the style of VIRGIN FLEET. Needless to say, each of the girls is an embodi-ment of a particular wish-fulfillment stereotype, be it tomboy, girl next door, or prissy princess, and each of them will of course find the shy, inept young teacher quite irresistible. The enemy also has a supernatural unit, and by pure chance Shintaro has a past link with one of the girls in that unit, too.

No amount of historical set dress-ing can disguise the formulaic plot and characterization, in yet another example of the eternal quest for a harem show with a difference, refusing to admit that with harem shows there is no difference. Nevertheless, *Lime Wars* was still successful enough to spin off a 2004 two-part video, *Lime Wars: The South Sea Island Dream Romantic Adventure (Lime-iro Senkitan: Nankoku Yume Roman,)* whose main purpose seems to be to give the characters an opportunity to lounge about in beach-wear, and a 2005 TV sequel, *Lime Wars X: Love, Please (Lime-iro Ryukitan X: Koi Oshiete Kudasai)*, in which, *Newtype* proudly reported, "the girls were all-new, but the uniforms were the same." The home video release of the first TV series included nudity not found in the TV broadcast version.

LIMIT THE MIRACLE GIRL
1973. JPN: *Miracle Shojo Limit-chan*. TV series. DIR: Takeshi Tamiya, Masayuki Akehi, Hideo Furusawa. SCR: Shunichi Yukimuro, Masaki Tsuji, Makio Hara, Toyohiro Ando. DES: Kazuo Komatsu-bara. ANI: Kazuo Komatsubara, Reiko Okayama, Teruo Kigure, Minoru Tajima. MUS: Shunsuke Kikuchi, Tokiko Iwatani. PRD: TV Asahi, Toei Animation, Studio Cosmos, NET (TV Asahi.) 25 mins. x 25 eps.

After gifted scientist Dr. Nishiyama loses his teenage daughter in an air-plane accident, the bereaved father makes a robot exactly like her with her personality impressed on its cybernetic brain. Limit stands in for the dead girl, not telling her closest friends that she has a computer in place of a heart; she yearns for human happiness like KEY THE METAL IDOL. However, in a foreshadowing of many, many later artificial heroines, Limit only has a year to live—compare to VIDEO GIRL AI.

The studio obviously thought it was onto a winner with an anime based on a proposal from Hiromi Productions, which was then transformed into a manga by Shinji Nagashima, combin-ing the magical girl with the ASTRO BOY concept. Twelve days later saw the first broadcast of Go Nagai's CUTEY HONEY, which does the same thing, but with more action and bigger breasts, deci-sively stealing its thunder. Aimed at a very different audience than Nagai's heroine, Limit may not have registered as powerfully on the public conscious-ness, but she had a successful career in Italy, where she has many fans under the name *Cybernella*. Manga tie-ins were published in *Shojo* weekly and *Terebi Land* magazines.

Although the "girl with a time limit" concept is enough to assure Limit her place in history, the show was also one of the first to save costs by using over-seas labor—the last five episodes were prepared in collaboration with Toki Doga, a South Korean company.

LINGERIES *
2003. Video. DIR: Katsuhiko Nishijima.

SCR: Hiroshi Morinaga. DES: Masaki Yamada. ANI: Masaki Yamada. MUS: N/C. PRD: Studio Fantasia, Green Bunny. 30 mins. x 3 eps.

Ace temp agency hireling Yusuke is brought in as an acting section chief at the intimate apparel maker Best Beauty Body Inc. However, he also has a secret mission, which is to dig into allegations that the vice president is plotting against the company founder. While conducting his investigations, Yusuke pursues a new product line as part of his cover story, and backs rookie Mayumi's idea for a line of "seamless" lingerie. The project brings him into contact with workers from every aspect of the corporation—sexy blonde Alice, computer geek Chisa, and minx Rena, all of whom he has the onerous duty of seducing in turn in order to further his investigation—while coming up with a new design for the perfect panties and exposing corruption in middle management. The series is notable for art and plot superior to the general run of anime porn, in part due to the original erotic game by the company Mink and in part to the character designs and animation by Masaki Yamada, surprisingly working under his own name. One of the minor characters even bears an actionable resemblance to Linna Yamazaki from Yamada's earlier BUBBLEGUM CRISIS 2040. **Ⓛ Ⓝ**

LION BOOKS

1983. JPN: *Midori no Neko; Amefuri Koso; Lunn wa Kaze no Naka; Yamataro Kaeru; Adachigahara; Akuemon.* AKA: (see below). TV specials, movies. DIR: Hitoshi Nishimura, Masamitsu Yoshimura, Hisashi Sakaguchi, Makoto Tezuka. SCR: Hitoshi Nishimura, Masamitsu Yoshimura, Hisashi Sakaguchi. DES: Hitoshi Nishimura, Osamu Tezuka, Hisashi Sakaguchi. ANI: Hitoshi Nishimura, Masamitsu Yoshimura, Hisashi Sakaguchi. MUS: Reijiro Komutsu. PRD: Tezuka Pro. 24 mins. x 6 eps.

Twenty-four episodes were planned for this series of one-shots, but the hope of ASTRO BOY–creator Osamu Tezuka to animate many of his early short manga was soon dashed by lack of interest. Instead, several were shown as TV "specials," while two more were made for theaters then collected under the *Lion Books* umbrella for release to video in 1997.

In *The Green Cat* (1983), the titular feline is thought to be a good-luck charm but soon brings misfortune to all who come into contact with it. In the second tale, *Rain Boy* (1983), Mouta is on his way home during a storm when a boy asks if he can have his shoes. The boy is a magical creature who can grant him three wishes after the fashion of ALADDIN's jinni.

Lunn Flies into the Wind (1985) features a boy who falls in love with the girl he sees in an advertisement poster on a wall and goes searching for the original model. *Yamataro Comes Back* (1989) is an *Incredible Journey*–themed adventure about a young bear cub losing his parents and having to survive in the wild. *Adachigahara* (1991) was shown in theaters as a second feature and based on one of the JAPANESE FOLK TALES, though the action is moved into the near future. An old woman meets the young space pilot Jes, exiled for trying to overthrow Earth's pro-independence president Phippo and pining for his girlfriend, Anny. The final story, *Akuemon* (1993), was directed by Tezuka's own son Makoto and shown at the Hong Kong film festival instead of broadcast on Japanese TV. A tale set in old-time Japan, it portrays a fox outwitting a hunter and choosing to live out his life in the shadow of the titular temple gate with his newfound squirrel companion.

LITTL' BITS *

1980. JPN: *Belfy to Lilibet.* AKA: *Belfy and Lillibit.* TV series. DIR: Masayuki Hayashi, Mizuho Nishikubo, Hiroshi Iwata. SCR: Masaru Yamamoto, Kazuo Sato, Takao Oyama, Akiyoshi Sakai, Isao Okishima, Leo Nishimura. DES: Hiromitsu Morita, Akiko Shimomoto. ANI: Hiromitsu Morita. MUS: Takeo Watanabe. PRD: Tatsunoko. 30 mins. x 26 eps.

The Fanitt family of fairies protects the forest, even though they are only a few inches tall. Lilbet is a male fairy, happy-go-lucky and always willing to help out. Though the other fairies make fun of him, he never lets it get him down, getting into all manner of adventures in the company of his girlfriend, Belfy, and pals Napoleon, Dokkurin, and Chuchuna. Later episodes of this Tatsunoko fairy story included early jobs for future VIDEO GIRL AI–director Nishikubo and writer Okishima, who also scripted episodes of the live-action *Monkey* TV series.

These *Smurf*-alikes were translated into English and shown on Nickelodeon in 1984, with the location changed to "Foothill Forest." The names were also altered, to a roster including Lillabit, Williebit, Snoozabit, Browniebit, Snagglebit, and the old-timer Elderbit.

LITTLE DEVIL

1989. JPN: *Akuma-kun.* TV series, movie. DIR: Junichi Sato, Shigeyasu Yamauchi, Masayuki Akehi. SCR: Yoshiyuki Suga, Takao Koyama, Nobuaki Kishima. DES: Ginichiro Suzuki. ANI: Fujio Yamamoto, Masami Abe. MUS: Nozomu Aoki. PRD: Toei, TV Asahi. 25 mins. x 42 eps. (TV), 40 mins., 26 mins. (m).

A minor work based on a 1966 manga by SPOOKY KITARO–creator Shigeru Mizuki, in which the Little Devil appears once every ten thousand years (in this case, as Japanese schoolboy Shingo Yamada) to save the world, although his reasons are not too clear considering that he is supposed to be on the side of evil and has twelve "dark apostles" to contend with. Similarly confused renditions of Christian apocalypse turn up for adult audiences in DEVILMAN, UROTSUKIDOJI, and HUMANE SOCIETY, though this anime is most definitely aimed at children. The second "movie," a glorified episode screened as part of the traditional vacation moviegoing season, packs Shingo off to Devil-Land, a Satanic theme park. Come on, Disney, you know you want to.

LITTLE EL CID

1979. JPN: *Little El Cid no Boken*. AKA: *Adventures of Little El Cid*. TV series. DIR: Fumio Kurokawa. SCR: Toshiyuki Kashiwakura. DES: Shuichi Seki. ANI: Takao Kogawa, Akio Sakai. MUS: N/C. PRD: Nippon Animation, TV Tokyo. 25 mins. x 26 eps.

In 10th-century Spain, the Christian inhabitants are fighting a losing battle against the invading Muslim Moors. The young Luis Díaz de Bivar decides to become a knight, but it will be a long time before he becomes the legendary warrior El Cid. A fictitious dramatization of a famous character's youth (compare to ROBIN HOOD), commissioned as a Spanish coproduction but not broadcast in Japan until 1984, long after its Spanish premiere. Curiously, in the original 12th-century *Poema di Mio Cid*, El Cid's name is Rodrigo, not Luis.

LITTLE GHOSTS: ACHI, KOCHI, AND SOCHI

1991. JPN: *Chiisana Obake: Achi, Kochi, Sochi*. AKA: *Little Ghosts: Thither, Hither, and Yon*. TV series. DIR: Osamu Kobayashi. SCR: Yoshio Urasawa, Kazuhiko Koto. DES: N/C. ANI: Hideo Kawauchi. MUS: Takeshi Ike. PRD: Pastel House, Studio Pierrot, Nippon TV. 11 mins. x 100 eps.

Three friendly ghosts play around, make friends, and become involved in mildly surreal adventures, such as delivering donuts to aliens from Venus. Their prime concern, however, is getting lots of lovely food, an orally fixated quest of some appeal to their audience of toddlers.

LITTLE GOBLIN

1968. JPN: *Kaibutsu-kun*. AKA: *Li'l Monster Prince*. TV series, movie. DIR: Masaaki Osumi, Eiji Okabe, Shinichi Suzuki, Hiroshi Fukutomi, Shinji Okuda, Makoto Nakahara. SCR: Haruya Yamazaki, Tsunehisa Ito, Takashi Hayakawa, Takashi Yamada, Hirokazu Mizude, Yoshio Urasawa. DES: Fujiko-Fujio, Tsutomu Shibata. ANI: Norio Kubii, Sadao Tominaga. MUS: Michio

Okamoto, Yasei Kobayashi. PRD: Tokyo Movie Shinsha, TBS. 25 mins. x 49 eps. (TV1), 25 mins. x 49 eps. (TV2), 75 mins. (m1), 51 mins. (m2).

Kaibutsu the little goblin appears one day in the apartment next door to average Japanese schoolboy Hiroshi's. He is the prince of Monster Land, sent to Earth to keep him out of trouble, accompanied on occasion by his associates Franken (a junior FRANKENSTEIN), DRACULA, and the Wolfman.

Ghostly goings-on in the tradition of DORORON ENMA, SPOOKY KITARO, and LITTLE DEVIL, based on a 1965 manga by DORAEMON-creator Hiroshi Fujimoto, though credited to the Fujiko-Fujio team of which he was a member. The franchise was brought back in color as the TV series *New Little Goblin* (1980), this time on the TV Asahi channel. The remake graduated to movie status with *LG in Monster Land* (1981), on a double bill with the *Doraemon* film *Nobita the Space Colonist*. The character returned for a second film outing with *LG: Sword of the Devil* (1982), set in the rival kingdom of Devil Land, which Kaibutsu is forced to invade in order to save his father's life.

LITTLE HOUSE ON THE PRAIRIE

1975. JPN: *Kusahara no Shojo Laura*. AKA: *Laura the Girl of the Grasslands*. TV series. DIR: Mitsuo Sawazaki, Masaharu Endo. SCR: Iwao Yamazaki, Fumi Takahashi. DES: Yasuji Mori. ANI: Megumi Mizuta. MUS: Akihiko Takashima. PRD: Nippon Animation, TBS. 25 mins. x 26 eps.

Young Laura lives a happy life in Wisconsin but is forced to move west, out of the woods with her family, when a harsh winter makes it impossible to stay in her old home. After encountering American Indians and settling on the Dakota prairie, she has a happy time (again) with her loving family, particularly her sisters, Mary and Carrie.

Not a WORLD MASTERPIECE THEATER production, though made by the WMT studio Nippon Animation, the anime was commissioned and filmed in Japan following the success of the anime

HEIDI and the popularity of the U.S. live-action TV series of *LHotP* in Japan. As with the live-action series, the anime version concentrates on adapting the early books in the long sequence of novels by Laura Ingalls Wilder—later volumes would take the child characters into adulthood, way beyond the 1953 volume from which the series takes its name.

LITTLE JUMBO

1977. JPN: *Chiisana Jumbo*. Movie. DIR: Toshio Hirata, Masami Hata. SCR: Takashi Yanase. DES: Takashi Yanase. ANI: Kazuko Nakamura, Shigeru Yamamoto. MUS: Taku Izumi. PRD: Madhouse, Sanrio. 28 mins.

Jumbo the kindhearted elephant arrives at Red Rose Island after floating across the sea in a big red box, accompanied by his friend Baloo the elephant-trainer. The pair immediately leap out of the box and begin a series of supposedly cute song-and-dance numbers to entertain the king and his three subjects, although clearly not cute enough for Sanrio, which kept this minor offering from ANPANMAN-creator Yanase on the shelf for two years before allowing it to sneak into theaters in 1977.

LITTLE KOALA

1984. JPN: *Koala Boy Kokki*. AKA: *Adventures of the Little Koala*. TV series. DIR: Takashi Tanasawa, Katsuhisa Yamada, Masamitsu Sasaki, Shigeru Omachi. SCR: Toshiro Ueno, Nanako Watanabe, Yoshiaki Yoshida, Toshiaki Imaizumi, Kiichi Takayama, Mamoru Kobe. DES: Kazuyuki Kobayashi. ANI: Kazuyuki Kobayashi, Hidekazu Obara, Yoichi Otabe, Masahiro Yoshida, Megumi Kagawa, Masayuki Uchiyama. MUS: Tsuyoshi Kawano. PRD: Nagata, TV Tokyo. 25 mins. x 26 eps.

Kokki and his twin sister Laura are baby koalas who live in Yukari Village in the countryside. They play with their other animal friends, including Panny the Penguin, but often have to fight to preserve the peace of their village from the predations of the three evil

Kangaroo Brothers. Other troubles include a sick whale, invading UFOs, an attacking witch, and other incidents that only go to demonstrate that if your high-concept is so thin as to be nothing more than "Let's do something with koalas," the end result is a mishmash of everything else on TV at the time. Commissioned during the same koala fever that brought us **THE NOOZLES**.

LITTLE KONISHIKI
2000. JPN: *Dotto Koni-chan*. AKA: *Kaboom Koni-chan*. TV series. DIR: Shinichi Watanabe. SCR: Satoru Akahori, Masaharu Amiya. DES: Mitsuhiro Yoneda. ANI: Shinichi Watanabe. MUS: N/C. PRD: Sky PerfecTV. 5 mins. x 20+ eps.
Spoof SF, adventure, and fantasy drama featuring squashed-down child-versions of the sumo wrestler Konishiki, along with his cartoon companions High, Moro, and Nari. Based on a cartoon strip in *The Television* magazine, the series premiered on pay-per-view television before moving to regular broadcasts. Screened within the *Animax* anime-themed schedule strip.

LITTLE LORD FAUNTLEROY *
1988. JPN: *Koshi Ceddie*. AKA: *Young Noble Ceddie; Adventures of the Little Prince*. TV series. DIR: Kozo Kusuba, Fumio Ike. SCR: Shiro Ishimori. DES: Michiyo Sakurai. ANI: Michiyo Sakurai, Hideaki Shimada, Hisatoshi Motoki, Eimi Maeda, Megumi Kagawa, Toshiki Yamazaki. MUS: Koichi Morita. PRD: Nippon Animation, Fuji TV. 25 mins. x 43 eps.
Young American boy Cedric Errol discovers that his late father was English and that he is being deprived of his true inheritance by anti-American relatives. Captain Errol, sent away to the U.S. by his resentful father, incurred the wrath of his family by falling in love with a girl in the colonies, and the other Errol family members are determined to keep Cedric out of their lives. Eventually, he returns to his English homeland and the stewardship of Dorincourt Castle. This rags-to-riches

tale was based on the 1886 children's book by Frances Hodgson Burnett, who also wrote **A LITTLE PRINCESS** and **THE SECRET GARDEN**. As befits its transatlantic tone, it was released in both British and American dubs, although with a title that has often led to confusion with the unrelated **LITTLE PRINCE**. See also **VIDEO PICTURE BOOK**.

LITTLE LOVE LETTER, A
1981. JPN: *Chiisana Love Letter: Mariko to Nemunoki no Kodomotachi*. AKA: *A Little Love Letter: Mariko and the Children of the Silk Tree*. TV special. DIR: Yuzo Ishida. SCR: Sachiko Akita. DES: Kenzo Koizumi. ANI: Swan Pro. MUS: Nozomu Aoki. PRD: TV Asahi, NOW Planning. 84 mins.
A follow-up to the same studio's **HELEN KELLER** anime, *A Little Love Letter* kept the handicapped theme but focused on a wholly Japanese story. During the 1970s, actress Mariko Miyagi became heavily involved in the Silk Tree Academy, a rehabilitation center for disabled children. She appeared in several live-action films to promote the project, including *The Silk Tree Ballad*, *Mariko-Mother*, and *Children Drawing Rainbows*. This anime charts the 14-year period of Miyagi's stewardship of the academy and her relationships with several of the children. Divided into four seasonal chapters, the film uses highly realistic character designs based on the actual people involved and features storyboarding from the versatile **STAR BLAZERS**–director Noboru Ishiguro.

LITTLE LULU AND THE GANG
1976. JPN: *Little Lulu to Chichai Nakama*. AKA: *Little Lulu and her Cute Friends*. TV series, movie. DIR: Fumio Kurokawa. SCR: Juzo Takahashi. DES: Shuichi Seki. ANI: Shinichi Tsuji, Tatsuo Maeda. MUS: Nobuyoshi Okabe. PRD: Nippon Animation, Trans Arts, TV Asahi. 25 mins. x 26 eps. (TV), 87 mins. (m1), 88 mins. (m2).
Everyday family situations with lots of gentle humor and sight gags for the heroine of the American comic by Marge Henderson Buell. Her friends

include Wilbur, the good-natured son of a wealthy family, Annie, the daring girl, and chubby Tubby, all of whom collaborate in making mischief in the fashion of **PINCH AND PUNCH**. Note that this *Little Lulu* is wholly different from the Fleischer brothers cartoon of the same name, which was originated in the U.S., but was exported to Japan at roughly the same time, and aired on a rival channel. Two feature-length edits were made from the series.

LITTLE MERMAID
1975. JPN: *Andersen Monogatari Ningyo Hime*. AKA: *Andersen Story Mermaid Princess*. Movie. DIR: Tomoharu Katsumata. SCR: Yuko Oso, Mieko Koyamauchi. DES: Takashi Abe, Shingo Araki, Kazuo Komatsubara. ANI: Reiko Okuyama. MUS: Hatasu Heikichi. PRD: Toei. 68 mins.
Blonde Marina, the youngest of six mermaid sisters, falls in love with the handsome human Prince Fritz when she sees him one night passing overhead in a boat. The boat is swamped by a large wave, and Marina rescues the man she adores, nursing Fritz back to health with an array of magical potions. He falls in love with her, but if she is to be with him on land, she must lose her tail and her beautiful voice.

The most famous of the **TALES OF HANS CHRISTIAN ANDERSEN**, *LM* was animated to celebrate the centenary of its author's death—bracketed at both ends by live-action footage of Denmark shot by Henning Christiansen. The story was remade in 1995 as a 21-minute fully computer-animated version based on a retelling published by the children's illustrator Chihiro Iwasaki. *Little Mermaid* (1985) was an unrelated three-part collection of pornographic vignettes in the tradition of **LOLITA ANIME**. See also **VIDEO PICTURE BOOK**.

LITTLE MRS. PEPPERPOT
1983. JPN: *Spoon Obaasan*. AKA: *Auntie Spoon*. TV series. DIR: Keiji Hayakawa. SCR: Maki Nakahara, Tomoko Kawasaki, Keiko Maruo, Masaaki Sakurai, Mamoru Oshii. DES: Koji Nanka. ANI:

Noboru Furuse, Toshio Hirata, Kenjiro Yoshida, Naoto Hashimoto, Satoshi Dezaki, Teruo Kigure, Mamoru Oshii. MUS: Koji Nanka, Tachio Akano. PRD: Pierrot, NHK. 10 mins. x 130 mins.

Auntie Spoon (so called because of the strange pendant she wears around her neck) is an old lady loved by everybody. Only local girl Ruri knows Auntie's secret—that she can use her magic pendant to shrink herself to the *size* of a spoon, bringing a whole new perspective to the everyday world. Originally based on a Norwegian folk tale then filtered through Alf Prøysen's retelling of the story as *Little Mrs. Pepperpot* before reaching Japan, this was the first anime series to be serialized on Japan's state channel, NHK.

LITTLE NEMO: ADVENTURES IN SLUMBERLAND *

1989. Movie. DIR: Masami Hata, William Hurtz. SCR: Chris Columbus, Richard Outten, Bruce Schaefer. DES: Jean Giraud, Brian Froud, Paul Julian, Kazuhide Tominaga. ANI: Yasuo Otsuka, Kazuaki Yoshinaga, Nobuo Tominaga. MUS: Richard Sherman, Robert Sherman. PRD: Tokyo Movie Shinsha. 85 mins.

Nemo is a little boy who lives in 1905 New York City. A blimp approaches his house, and the clown who steps out of it informs him that he has been requested as a playmate by the princess of Slumberland. Traveling to Slumberland, the boy is soon involved in a mission to rescue its ruler, who has been kidnapped by the Nightmare King. A tiresome and condescending attempt to reverse-engineer Disney by a studio that reputedly removed members of staff who refused to toe the party line—one of whom was Hayao Miyazaki, whose version of *LN* might well have been vastly superior if he had only been allowed to complete it. As it is, the film is a confusion of good-intentioned but insincere clichés, including halfhearted musical numbers, far removed from the original 1905 comic strip by Winsor McCay on which it is based. The production features a large

number of famous names, including voice actors Mickey Rooney (Flip the Clown) and Rene Auberjonois (Professor Genius). Disney's Frank Thomas, Roger Allers, and Ollie Johnson were among the animators, the songs were written by the Sherman brothers (*Chitty Chitty Bang Bang*), while Jean "Moebius" Giraud provided "conceptual design." However, many of the crew are "ghost" credits symptomatic of a long and troubled production—Ray Bradbury is credited with the "screen concept" but seems to have left the production early on, while the press notes carelessly trumpet the involvement of *Chinatown* scenarist Robert Towne as a "story consultant," a likely sign that Towne had been called in to rescue a failing premise. Both Hayao Miyazaki and Isao Takahata split from the production at an early stage due to "creative differences," while Yoshifumi Kondo stayed to work on the first (1984) pilot. A second (1987) pilot, credited to Osamu Dezaki, also exists, and both are included as bonus items on the Laser Disc release.

LITTLE NORSE PRINCE *

1968. JPN: *Taiyo no Ko Hols no Daiboken.* AKA: *Prince of the Sun: Hols's Great Adventure; The Great Adventure of Little Prince Valiant; Little Norse Prince Valiant.* Movie. DIR: Isao Takahata. SCR: Isao Takahata. DES: Hayao Miyazaki. ANI: Yasuo Otsuka. MUS: Tsuneo Mamiya. PRD: Toei. 82 mins.

Fisherman's son Hols is a brave boy, but when we first meet him, surrounded by a pack of hungry wolves and armed only with an axe, his chances don't look good. He is saved by the intervention of Rockor, a giant of earth and stone awakened from centuries of sleep by the noise of the fight. Hols thanks his new friend by removing a sword wedged deep into the rock of his shoulder; it is the Sword of the Sun, and Rockor predicts that it will help him to defeat the evil of Frost King Grunwald. Then Hols's father dies, but on his deathbed he tells his son how they originally came from a fishing

village far to the north, and how they were the only survivors when it was destroyed by Grunwald's sorcery. He begs Hols to return to his birthplace and find out what has happened to the other villages. Armed with his axe and his new sword, and accompanied by his pet bear, Coro, Hols heads north.

He is attacked on the way by Grunwald and is almost killed falling off a cliff, but the people of a fishing village find him and care for him. They too are suffering from Grunwald's magic: a giant pike under his dominion is eating all the fish in the area and threatening the village's livelihood. Hols goes after the fish-monster alone and kills it after a titanic battle. This brings him great popularity, and some jealousy, but it further provokes Grunwald, who is determined to destroy all life in the region and sends in another, more stealthy attack. In a deserted village, Hols meets a young girl named Hilda. When he takes her back to the village, she is welcomed for her gentle nature and beautiful singing voice, but as Grunwald's dark sorcery continues to threaten the village, she is revealed as his sister.

Isao Takahata's feature debut shows fluid animation of movement, well-paced action scenes, and a charming style of character design that would become synonymous with the work of the studio he was later to found with his young colleague Hayao Miyazaki, who also assisted on this production. The film received unusually sympathetic treatment from its Western adapters, director Fred Ladd and editor Eli Haviv, who kept the tragic elements of the story intact, including the death of a loved one and the grief that follows. There is no connection with *Prince Valiant,* but the popularity of the comic in Europe led *LNP*'s Italian licensees to try and piggyback the film to success, hence the alternate title.

LITTLE PRINCE *

1978. JPN: *Hoshi no Ojisama Puchi Prince.* AKA: *Prince of the Stars: Petit Prince; Adventures of the Little Prince.*

© 2006 STEVE KYTE

Little Norse Prince

TV series. DIR: Takeyuki Kanda, Yoshi-kazu Yasuhiko, Osamu Sekita, Norio Kabeshima. SCR: Eiichi Tachi, Susumu Yoshida, Tsunehisa Ito, Takero Kaneko, Yoshiaki Yoshida, Masaaki Sakurai. DES: Yasuji Mori, Yoshikazu Yasuhiko, Eiji Tanaka. ANI: Shinnosuke Mina. MUS: Tsuyoshi Kawano. PRD: Knack, TV Asahi. 25 mins. x 39 eps.

The Little Prince is the ruler of a very small planet, but he is also its sole human occupant, so he must sweep the volcano clean and control the roots of the overgrown baobab tree. He talks to springs and butterflies, but his only real friend is the selfish human-shaped Star Rose. One day, the prince has an argument with the rose and sets off to Earth to search for his real friends.

Based on the 1943 novella by Antoine de Saint-Exupéry, though little of the French original remains—instead, it is lost almost completely beneath the prince's wanderings after the first episode, concealed still further in the English-language version by a dub that gives Saint-Exupéry a risible French accent, seemingly modeled on Inspector Clouseau. The series was only broadcast as far as episode

35—the remaining four sneaked out onto video when it was reissued.

LITTLE PRINCE AND THE EIGHT-HEADED DRAGON *

1963. JPN: *Wanpaku Oji to Orochi*. AKA: *Naughty Prince and the Giant Snake*. Movie. DIR: Yugo Serikawa, Isao Taka-hata, Kimio Yabuki. SCR: Ichiro Ikeda, Kei Iijima. DES: Yasuji Mori. ANI: Sanae Yamamoto, Yasuji Mori, Hideo Furu-sawa. MUS: Akira Ifukube. PRD: Toei. 76 mins.

Susanoo (see TAKEGAMI), son of the creators of Japan, Izanami and Izanagi, sets off accompanied by his rabbit assistant Akahana (Red-Nose) to res-cue his dead mother, who has gone to the Underworld. After defeating a giant fish and a fire monster, he then witnesses the story of the Sun Goddess Amaterasu, who hides in a cave and needs to be lured out. Falling in love with the earthly princess Kushinada, he discovers that she is to be sacrificed to Orochi, an eight-headed serpent that returns once each year to raid her parents' village until placated by a human sacrifice. All three of these tales are adapted from chapters of the *Nihon Shoki*, an 8th-century chronicle that

links the historical emperors with the Japanese gods and demigods, though much of the mythical meaning was lost in the transition to the American kiddie-film. Orochi would also appear in BLUE SEED and YAMATO TAKERU. Note also a rare anime score for Ifukube, better known as the composer for the *Godzilla* films.

LITTLE PRINCESS, A

1985. JPN: *Shokojo Sara*. AKA: *Young Noblewoman Sara; Princess Sarah*. TV series. DIR: Fumio Kurokawa, Takeshi Yamaguchi, Jiro Saito. SCR: Ryuzo Nakanishi, Keiko Mukuroji. DES: Shunji Saita. ANI: Toshiki Yamazaki, Shunji Saita, Kuniyuki Ishii. MUS: Yasuo Higu-chi. PRD: Nippon Animation, Fuji TV. 25 mins. x 46 eps.

Fearing that the Indian climate and environment will do more harm than good, Sara Crewe's father sends her away to boarding school in England, where she diligently attends Miss Minchin's academy and dreams that she is a princess. However, her life is shattered when her father dies, and his will reveals that he had no money. Sara is forced to become a servant at her school, reduced to the lowest rung of the social scale, though, as the title already implies, a CINDERELLA-like transformation eventually awaits. The 16th entry in the WORLD MASTERPIECE THEATER series was adapted from the 1888 children's novel *Sarah Crewe* by Frances Hodgson Burnett, who also wrote LITTLE LORD FAUNTLEROY and THE SECRET GARDEN. See also VIDEO PICTURE BOOK.

LITTLE RED [RIDING] HOOD CHA CHA

1995. JPN: *Akazukin Chacha*. Video, TV series. DIR: Yuji Moriyama, Hiroaki Sakurai, Tatsuo Sato, Akitaro Daichi, Kazuhiro Sasaki. SCR: Hiroshi Koda, Takashi Yamada, Shigeru Yanagawa, Hideki Mitsui, Tomoko Kaneko, Ryo-suke Takahashi, Hiroshi Yamaguchi. DES: Hajime Watanabe. ANI: Masayuki Onchi, Yoko Konishi. MUS: Toshihiko Sazaki, Osamu Tezuka (b). PRD: Studio

Gallop, TV Tokyo. 30 mins. x 3 eps., 25 mins. x 74 eps. (TV).

Twelve-year-old Cha Cha lives in the Mochi-mochi mountains, where she is studying to be a magician. A clumsy student, Cha Cha's spells often backfire on her, though she has the support of her friends Riya (a young werewolf) and Shine, who can help her undergo the magical transformation of Love, Heroism, and Hope. Meanwhile, the great Devil King wants Cha Cha dead in order to lift the curse her grandfather put on his castle, while other rivals include Black Hood and Marine, a competitive mermaid. A spirited SAILOR MOON clone that is more than the sum of its parts, taking much-appreciated time to explore the geography and history of its fantasy world, and thereby making the school/magical-girl antics of its cast all that more appealing. Based on a 1992 manga in *Ribbon* magazine by Min Ayahana.

LITTLE TWINS

1992. Video, movie. DIR: Toshio Hirata, Satoshi Inoue, Yorifusa Yamaguchi. SCR: Junji Takegami. DES: Kazuo Komatsubara. ANI: Shunji Saida, Hiroki Takahashi, Yasuyuki Hirata. MUS: Mash Morse. PRD: Bandai. 25 mins. x 3 eps. (v), 25 mins. (m1).

In these adaptations of Isamu Tsuchida's picture books for children, Tiffle and Tuffle are two little twins in pointed hats who live on Coracle Island and have a few lighthearted adventures. The "movie" release, *How Our Summer Flew Past*, is of a length and quality to suggest it was merely the fourth video installment, dumped on theaters as a promotional exercise for the tapes.

LITTLE WITCH CHAPPY

1972. JPN: *Mahotsukai Chappi*. TV series. DIR: Yugo Serikawa, Hiroshi Ikeda, Katsutoshi Sasaki, Masayuki Akehi, Osamu Kasai, Keiji Hisaoka, Hideo Furusawa. SCR: Masaki Tsuji, Saburo Taki, Shunichi Yukimuro, Noboru Shiroyama, Jiro Yoshino, Kuniaki Oshikawa. DES: N/C. ANI: Shinya Takahashi, Fusahito Nagaki. MUS: Hiroshi Tsutsui.

PRD: Toei, NET. 25 mins. x 39 eps. Chappy the little witch is sent from her magic kingdom to solve problems on Earth, accompanied by her little brother, Jun, and wielding her family heirloom, a magical baton to help her make the world a better place. A magical-girl tale following on from LITTLE WITCH SALLY and featuring the late addition of the mascot character Donchan, a cuddly panda that easily dates the show to the panda hysteria of the early 1970s—see PANDA GO PANDA.

LITTLE WITCH SALLY

1966. JPN: *Mahotsukai Sally*. TV series. DIR: Osamu Kasai. SCR: Akiyoshi Sakai. DES: Yoshiyuki Hane. ANI: Takashi Kasai, Minoru Tajima, Katsuya Koda, Hideo Furusawa. MUS: Yasei Kobayashi. PRD: Toei, Hikari Pro. 25 mins. x 109 eps. (TV1—1st 18 episodes in b/w), 25 mins. x 88 eps. (TV2), 27 mins. (m), 50 mins. (TVm).

Sally is a trainee witch sent to Earth to study humans and learn how to blend in among them, though she does not always succeed. She befriends Earth children Yotchan and Sumire and fights the corrupt Kabu, who steals from department stores. This was the first of the "magical girl" genre that would extend to the present day through look-alike titles such as CREAMY MAMI, GIGI, and SECRET AKKO-CHAN. Originating in a 1966 manga for *Ribbon* magazine by GIANT ROBO–creator Mitsuteru Yokoyama, the character was originally called Sunny but had her name changed to avoid protests from the car manufacturer Nissan.

Sally returned for a new series in 1989 on TV Asahi, directed by Osamu Kasai, with character designs by Yasuhiro Yamaguchi. In 1990, the new incarnation also appeared in a short 1990 movie and a TV special, *LWS: Mother's Love is Eternal*, which ended the series with Sally's dream that she is to become the new queen of the magical land of Astria and must bid farewell to her friends. Yokoyama's witch, like Tezuka's ASTRO BOY, was one of the defining archetypes of anime, and it is

still much imitated to this day—see also his less successful follow-up, COMET-SAN.

LITTLE WOMEN *

1980. JPN: *Wakakusa no Yon Shimai*. AKA: *Four Sisters of Young Grass*. TV special, TV series. DIR: Yugo Serikawa, Kazumi Fukushima, Fumio Kurokawa, Kozo Kusuba. SCR: Eiichi Konbe, Eiichi Kondo, Akira Miyazaki, Michiru Shimada. DES: Yasuhiro Yamaguchi, Tadaumi Shimogawa, Seiji Kikuchi, Yoshifumi Kondo, Kiharu Sato. ANI: Yasuhiro Yamaguchi Takeshi Shirato, Akira Okuwara. MUS: Nozomu Aoki, Takeo Watanabe; Kazuo Otani, David Silvers. PRD: Toei, Fuji TV, Kokusai Eiga, Toei, Tokyo Channel 12, Nippon Animation, Fuji TV x 2. 68 mins. (TVm), 25 mins. x 26 eps. (TV1), 25 mins. x 48 eps. (TV2), 25 mins. x 40 eps. (TV3).

In the 1860s, Frederick March goes to fight in the American Civil War, leaving his family behind in Concord, New Hampshire. His daughters, Jo, Meg, Beth, and Amy, help out their mother and try to get along with the Lawrence family next door. The 1868 novel by Louisa May Alcott has appeared in several anime incarnations (all of which are at least partially available in English), the first being this 1980 TV special directed by Yugo Serikawa that seems to rely more on movie versions for its plot than the book itself. The first scene is a case in point when we see Jo fooling around in the snow before throwing a snowball at the window from which her sisters are laughing at her—the same sequence opens the 1949 movie adaptation featuring June Allyson as Jo and Elizabeth Taylor as Amy.

The TV special's true role as a dry run for a series became plain in 1981, when many of the same crew returned with a TV series version. The design for the girls remained the same, but the quality of animation fell considerably, as one might expect from the more limited budgets of TV (especially a TV series that cannot make the cost-cutting economies of recycling transformation footage for robots and superheroes). Alcott's original, however, is subsumed in this version to a patronizing tone that insists on imparting a prepackaged moral to each episode. The series was dubbed in the 1980s and a small number of episodes released on video, featuring new music from usual suspects Haim Saban and Shuki Levy.

The story returned to Fuji TV in 1987 as an all-new TV series, made as the 18th in the **WORLD MASTERPIECE THEATER** franchise, and featuring character designs by future **WHISPER OF THE HEART**–director Kondo. Though rather pointlessly setting the action in the new town of "Newcord," the *WMT* version remains the best anime adaptation of Alcott, despite, or perhaps because of, writer Miyazaki's ruthless reordering of the narrative at the scripting stage. The first incident from the novel proper does not arise until episode 18 of the anime, whereas the first line from the novel does not appear until episode 21—instead, this *LW* begins with the Pennsylvania countryside-dwelling Marches forced to flee their burning home, heading for Massachusetts to live with their aunt Marte. An introduction seemingly designed to educate the Japanese audience about the events of the Civil War, while simultaneously extending the possible run of the series in the same manner as the later **CINDERELLA**, the extra sequences eventually click back onto track with the stories of the girls' hopes, dreams, and mild mishaps. Perhaps inspired by similar events in **HUCKLEBERRY FINN** (a book Alcott detested!), this *LW* also features Jim, an escaped slave whom the Marches hide from soldiers, while the female-heavy cast is evened up with David, an extra nephew, and Newcord reporter Anthony. Though the scenes may be cut up and rearranged, the anime remains studiously faithful to the events within them, with the exception of an incident where one of the girls is struck at school—a cause for scandal in the novel, but accepted with traditional Japanese resignation in the anime. One of the few *WMT* serials to

be translated for the U.S. market, it was bought by Saban and broadcast on HBO in the 1990s.

A third series was commissioned as a sequel to the second, adapting Alcott's 1871 *Little Men: Life at Plumfield with Jo's Boys* under the title *Story of Young Grasses: Nan and Teacher Jo* (1993, *Wakakusa Monogatari: Nan to Jo Sensei*). However, since the *WMT LW* only adapted the first part of Alcott's original, there is something of a gap between the stories—*LM* takes place ten years later, after Jo has departed for New York, met and married a German professor, and given birth to two children. Inheriting Aunt March's house in Concord (note that it's not Newcord this time, despite this being a sequel to the second series), Jo sets up a school with her husband, turning both the book and its anime version into a different, more schooling-oriented slice-of-life than the familial predecessor. *LM* features new, softer character designs from another Studio Ghibli alumnus, **MY NEIGHBOR TOTORO**'s Sato, though its approach to the cast seems designed not to disturb the sensibilities of a conservative audience—two disabled characters are mysteriously absent from the anime.

Not to be confused with the unrelated **CHARLOTTE**, whose Japanese title is similar to *LW*'s, or with the *Little Women in Love* broadcast as part of the **MODERN LOVE'S SILLINESS** anthology show. See also **VIDEO PICTURE BOOK**.

LITTLEST WARRIOR, THE *

1961. JPN: *Anju to Zushio-Maru*. AKA: *Anju and Zushio; Orphan Brother*. Movie. DIR: Taiji Yabushita, Yugo Serikawa, Isao Takahata. SCR: Sumie Tanaka. DES: Akira Okuwara, Yasuji Mori. ANI: Sanae Yamamoto, Akira Okuwara, Yasuji Mori, Taku Sugiyama, Reiko Okuyama. MUS: Tadashi Kishimo, Hajime Kaburagi. PRD: Toei. 83 mins. (70 mins. U.S.).
After their father quarrels with local military men, Anju (Anjue) and Zushio (Zooshio) are forced to flee, but they are captured and sold into slavery. When their mother dies, they are sold

to Sansho the Bailiff (or Dayu in the U.S. version, which would translate as Bailiff the Bailiff!), a cruel man who subjects them to hideous torments—though his son Saburo secretly shows kindness to the orphans. Anju falls into a lake and is transformed into a swan. Zushio escapes to a nearby temple, is adopted by a nobleman, and, after many trials, grows into a handsome young man. He defeats the Giant Blue Widow Spider that has been terrorizing the village and is appointed to his father's former post as governor. His first act is to subjugate the evil Dayu and his followers then free all the slaves. Reunited with his mother, he then rules wisely and well.

Based on Ogai Mori's novel *Sansho the Bailiff* (*Sansho Dayu*), which was also made into a 1954 live-action film by Kenji Mizoguchi. The original folk tale that inspired the novel was also adapted as one of the **MANGA PICTURES OF JAPAN**.

LIVING SEX TOY DELIVERY *

2002. JPN: *Nikuyoku Gangu Takuhainin*. AKA: *The Boxed Woman*. Video. DIR: N/C. SCR: N/C. DES: N/C. ANI: N/C. MUS: N/C. PRD: Five Ways. 30 mins. x 3 eps.
Young removal man Shoji is invited to a party by pretty Yuika, then drugged and used as a sex toy by multiple women. He wakes up to find himself dumped on a railway line in a cardboard box with a suicide note. Understandably annoyed, he vows revenge. He goes back to Yuika's place, tricks his way in by pretending to be a delivery man, and takes her prisoner. He forces Yuika to take incriminating photographs of each of the girls in secret and then convinces each that the only way to dispose of the pictures is to climb into a box and agree to be delivered to its destination—a secluded warehouse where he assaults them. Since he already knows their secret fetishes, his chosen method in each case ensures that they begin by resisting, but are then forced to admit that they actually enjoy his attentions. He then subjects them to an additional humiliation by

boxing his victims back up and mailing them to their place of work, thus ensuring that everyone knows their secrets. The final episode finds Shoji having to avoid, and then abuse, the two ringleaders, who discover that he was not killed in a train accident as originally planned. **ⓁⓃⓋ**

LOCKE THE SUPERMAN *

1984. JPN: *Chojin Locke*. AKA: *Locke the Superpower; Star Warriors*. Movie. DIR: Hiroshi Fukutomi, Noboru Ishiguro, Takeshi Hirota. SCR: Atsushi Yamatoya, Takeshi Hirota. DES: Yuki Hijiri, Keizo Kobayashi, Susumu Shiraume, Masahiro Sekino. ANI: Susumu Shiraume, Yuji Moriyama, Seiji Okuda, Eimi Maeda, Hideki Tamura, Masahiko Imai, Noboru Takano, Yutaka Kubota. MUS: Goro Omi, Toshiki Ishikawa; Toshiki Hasegawa. PRD: Nippon Animation. 120 mins. (m), 30 mins. x 3 eps. (v1), 50 mins. x 2 eps. (v2), 60 mins. (v3). Former federation supersoldier Locke is a pacifist psychic who has willed himself to stay eternally young in order to avoid becoming a bellicose man (see **PETER PAN AND WENDY**). He is dragged out of retirement by agent Ryu Yamaki to thwart Lady Cahn, an industrialist secretly training a group of psychics to form the Millennium, a thousand-year dominion over mundane humans.

Surprisingly little of the film centers on its titular hero. Instead, much of it is taken up with Cahn's school for psychics—a bizarre Nazi convent, where Jessica Olin is completing her training. A girl who falsely believes that Locke killed her parents, Jessica is the most powerful of Cahn's new breed, and, after successfully destroying her opponents, she is drafted into a sabotage mission against a government outpost. When her psychic cohorts destroy the base, Cahn's agents start revolts on five outlying planets; the first steps in the foundation of a new order. They then delay Ryu's attempts to return home (though God knows why) by crashing the ship sent to take him home. Ryu rescues Jessica from the wreck, but she has amnesia. Now calling herself

Amelia, she follows him back to Earth, confessing her love for him. Eventually, after all this padding, Locke appears and defeats Cahn. Amelia stays in the arms of her beloved Ryu, while Locke finds love in the form of Cahn's alter ego, schoolmistress Cornelia Prim, only to discover that her personality was removed as punishment for her crime. Alone but satisfied he has saved the universe, he returns home.

Based on the 1979 manga in *Shonen King* by Yuki Hijiri, *Locke* was rushed into production during the post–*Star Wars* boom in sci-fi that also created **CAPTAIN FUTURE** and **LENSMAN**—the ten-minute *Cosmic Game* pilot film for the project was made as early as 1980. It was the first Nippon Animation film made directly for theaters and boasts technical experiments to rival **FIST OF THE NORTH STAR**, including some subtle early computer graphics and actual "live" footage of flames, static, and bubbles. An earnest spectacle that crashes Frank Herbert's *Dune* (Cahn wants to use Holy Mothers to breed a master race) into the thousand-year empire of Isaac Asimov's *Foundation*, with reviled psychic warriors lifted from the *X-Men*, *LtS* is let down by amateurishly clunky dialogue, as twee British-accented voices mispronounce "esper" and "combatant" throughout, confuse planets with stars, and intone priceless lines such as "a small man-made planet in this universe." Ryu Yamaki suffers worst at the hands of Japanese *and* English scripts—a man so outstandingly stupid that he lectures Locke on care of "sheeps," tries to break down a steel door with his own head, and insists on having sex with his ladylove while she is still recuperating in a hospital bed. Released in English with the original names still in place, presumably in a Japan-commissioned translation that explains the poor-quality dub, the "superman" part was dropped in some territories to avoid conflict with DC comics—similar wrangles dogged **MARIS THE CHOJO**.

With plenty more of Hijiri's manga left to adapt, the "industrialist-seeks-

power, Locke-leaves-retirement, Locke-loses-girl" plot was rehashed straight to video with *LtS: Lord Leon*, in which the titular cyborg pirate kills the grandson of Great Jugo, a wealthy industrialist whose starship-building project is in financial difficulty. Locke is once more unwillingly pressed into service by Federation Security, only to discover that Leon is the wayward brother of his new girlfriend, Flora, who has sworn vengeance on Jugo for killing the rest of his family. Jugo is responsible for the terrible injuries that caused Leon to have cybernetic augmentation and for the loss of Flora's eyesight. Fearing for his own life, he kidnaps Flora, and Leon sails into a trap while Locke rescues her.

A third incarnation was released as *LtS: New World Battle Team* (1991, *Shin Sekai Sentai*), in which Elena, the leader of the Galactic Alliance, decides to begin an Esper Elimination Project. Locke and four other psychics go on the run but lose their memories. To regain them, they must hunt down the creature known as the Tsar, unless the agents of the Galactic Alliance catch them first.

A sequel, *LtS: Mirroring* (2000), followed after a long hiatus and features new character designs by Junichi Hayama. Elena's "backed-up" cyber-successor Cassandra mutates on the "Galactic" Internet and returns as the mighty "Neon." Locke must round up his old cohorts once more (and why not, the writers just rounded up the old plot, after all). **ⓃⓋ**

LOLICON ANGEL

1985. JPN: *Lolicon Angel: Bishojo Comic Himitsu no Mi*. AKA: *Loli[ta] Co[mplex] Angel: Pretty Girls' Comic: Secret Honey*. Video. DIR: N/C. SCR: N/C. DES: N/C. ANI: N/C. MUS: N/C. PRD: Pumpkin Pie. 25 mins.

While Yuka, Nami, and Aiko are in the shower together, somebody steals Yuka's wallet. The three lesbians set out to investigate at their exclusive girls' school, where everyone seems to harbor secret desires. This anime may

seem to be a pale imitation of **Cream Lemon** but actually predates it. However, in the erotic filmmaking stakes, there is rarely a prize for coming first. Even the normally timid *Newtype* comments that, "While there may be hard lesbian action, the animation and story line are considerably below standard."
Ⓝ

LOLITA ANIME

1984 AKA: *Wonder Magazine Series.* Video. DIR: Kuni Toniro, R. Ching, Mickey Soda, Mickey Masuda. SCR: Fumio Nakajima. DES: Fumio Nakajima. ANI: Tatsushi Kurahashi. MUS: N/C. PRD: Wonder Kids. 15 mins. x 4 eps. (1–4), 30 mins. x 3 eps. (5–7), 60 mins. (8), 3 x 30 mins. (Uchiyama).
A collection of underage porn, which, with its cheerful incitement to abuse children, is in its own way far more offensive than **Urotsukidoji.** Based on manga by Fumio Nakajima, the stories range from risqué but unremarkable dramas of sexual awakening to full-blown pedophile rape scenes, with the questionable distinction of being the first erotic anime video release. So it was that after the relative excitement of theatrical outings such as **Arabian Nights** and **Cleopatra: Queen of Sex,** anime entered a tawdry phase with the sickening gang rape of *The Reddening Snow* (#1), in which a group of boys sexually assault a schoolgirl, while the boy who secretly adores her is "forced" to join in. *Girls Tortured with Roses* (#2) is no less shocking—a bondage fable in which older men abuse and assault very young girls—though it pales into insignificance when compared to *Dying for a Girl* (#3), in which the assault of a girl in a playground is offered for the audience's titillation, only to have the neighborhood pervert's intentions thwarted by the timely arrival of a younger man. He then takes the girl back to his place, where, after a shower, she gratefully offers her body to her savior.

The next entry in the series, the lesbian-awakening story *Altar of Sacrifice* (#4), was successful enough to create its own subseries within the *Lolita Anime* franchise—a form of brand identity that was repeated with greater success within the **Cream Lemon** series. *Variations* (#5) was a direct sequel, double the normal length, about one of the girls becoming an artist's model and being invited to a postsession dinner where she is drugged and raped.

Another mini-franchise began with *House of Kittens* (#6), in which several schoolgirls are inspired to experiment sexually with each other after witnessing their teacher in the act. However, their friend Miyu prefers to fantasize about having sex with a man. A character whose popularity prefigured that of *Cream Lemon*'s Ami, Miyu returned for *Surfside Dreaming* (#7), about an innocent encounter between two consenting teenagers, and consequently far less disturbing than many of the other *LA* entries. The character returned for the finale, *Seaside Angel Miyu* (#8), a clip-show of earlier episodes, presented as a radio show conducted from orbit, as Earthbound callers telephone Miyu's spaceship and discuss their sexual experiences. The running time is bulked out with four minutes of still images of Miyu at the beach and ends with the "bonus" scene of Miyu having sex with the captain of her spaceship.

Later in 1984, an unrelated *Lolita Anime* was released by Nikkatsu. Directed by Naosuke Kurosawa, it comprised *Aki Feels Ill*, *Milk-Drinking Doll*, and *Gokko Plays Nurse*, all adapted from manga by Aki Uchiyama, an artist who once took Lolicon imagery so far as to eroticize infants in diapers for *Shonen Magazine*. **ⓃⓋ**

LONE WOLF IS THE KID BOSS

1969. JPN: *Otoko Ippiki Gaki Taisho.* TV series. DIR: Tadao Wakabayashi. SCR: Shunichi Yukimuro, Susumu Yoshida, Tadaaki Yamazaki. DES: Shingo Araki. ANI: Takao Yamazaki, Saburo Sakamoto, Takashi Saijo, Soji Mizumura. MUS: Mitsuhiro Oyama. PRD: NTV, Tokyo TV Doga. 10 mins. x 156 eps.
Ever since beating 180 other kids in single combat, Mankichi Togawa of Seikai Junior High is the acknowledged "boss" of a gang of a thousand tough children. Still dissatisfied with his achievement, he heads for Tokyo with his sidekick Ginji, where he decides to become rich in order to battle social evils in Tokyo—his encounters including old financial big wig Mito (see **Manga Mito Komon**) and Daisaburo no Kasumi, the good-natured leader of the local tramps. Based on a manga by **Salaryman Kintaro**–creator Hiroshi Motomiya, this daily show has been cited as a major influence by Masami Kurumada, creator of **Saint Seiya.** Yoshiyuki Okamura (aka Sho Fumimura or Buronson), creator of **Fist of the North Star**, started his manga career as Motomiya's assistant.

LORD OF LORDS: DRAGON KNIGHT

1994. JPN: *Ha-o Taikei Ryu Knight.* AKA: *Adeu's Legend.* TV series, video. DIR: Makoto Ikeda, Toshifumi Kawase. SCR: Katsuyuki Osuzawa, Hiroyuki Hoshiyama. DES: Kazuhiro Soeta. ANI: Kazuhiro Soeta, Tetsuya Yanagawa, Chuichi Iguchi. MUS: Junichi Kanezaki, Michiru Oshima. PRD: Sunrise, TV Tokyo. 25 mins. x 52 eps. (TV), 25 mins. x 13 eps. (V).
A popular show in its day, mixing the role-playing-game feel of **Record of Lodoss War** with the giant-robot combat familiar to so many other Sunrise shows. **Outlaw Star**–creator Takehiko Ito, in collaboration with Sunrise's house pseudonym "Hajime Yadate," posited a standard quest narrative of young Adeu, who sets out to become a knight and ends up saving the universe. When the TV series was released on video, each tape contained at least one unbroadcast episode as a bonus, which is a clever way of dragging in extra customers.

LOST UNIVERSE *

1998. TV series. DIR: Takashi Watanabe, Eiichi Sato, Hideki Takayama. SCR: Mayori Sekijima, Jiro Takayama, Sumio Uetake. DES: Shoko Yoshinaka, Tsutomu Suzuki. ANI: Kazuaki Mori,

Hikaru Maejima. MUS: Osamu Tezuka (the other one). PRD: IG Film, TV Tokyo. 25 mins. x 26 eps.

Galactic troubleshooter Kane Blueriver wanders the stars in his sentient ship Sword Breaker, whose artificial intelligence, Canal, is his eternal sparring partner and confidante. A chance meeting forces them to team up with Milly the private eye, an irritating girl determined to be the world's best, though world's best *what* is open to debate.

A lighthearted space opera based on a sequence of novels by SLAYERS-creator Hajime Kanzaka (which were illustrated by designer Yoshinaka) and featuring many of the same cast and crew as the *Slayers* anime. After predictable early beginnings not unlike OUTLAW STAR, the bounty-of-the-week angle falls away to be replaced with a more gripping quest angle as the trio search for the fabled Lost Ships. Despite being written off in its early stages as shallow comedy, the final chapter of *LU* won *Animage*'s Best Individual Episode Award in a year otherwise dominated by NADESICO. Like many other shows of the late 1990s, *LU* featured incongruous amounts of computer graphics designed to distract the viewer from the low-rent cel animation. However, *LU*'s CG, such as the Sword Breaker itself, is consistently below-par—an example of a gimmick backfiring, though the same tactics were used to far greater effect in COWBOY BEBOP. Broadcast on U.S. TV in Spanish and Turkish!

LOVE CADETS

1998. JPN: *Ren'ai Kohosei*. AKA: *Starlight Scramble*. Video. DIR: Hideki Tonokatsu. SCR: Hideki Tonokatsu, Osamu Kudo, Katsuhiko Koide. DES: Kenshi Fukube, Masahiro Koyama. ANI: Kenshi Fukube. MUS: N/C. PRD: KSS. 30 mins. x 2 eps.

In a love comedy set in 2149 but rooted very much in the dork-gets-harem spirit of TENCHI MUYO! and its 1990s imitators, orphaned Megumi struggles hard at school to qualify as a space

Lost Universe

© TV TOKYO/SOFTX

pilot, leave behind the space colony, and visit Earth.

LOVE DOLL *

1997. JPN: *Ai Doru*. AKA: *Melancholy Slave*. Video. DIR: Raizo Kitagawa. SCR: Yuri Kanai, Naomi Hayakawa. DES: Aidoru Project. ANI: Kazumasa Muraki. MUS: Yoshi. PRD: YOUC, Digital Works. 30 mins. x 4 eps.

Bereft at her mother's death, Rachel goes into a convent, only to discover that the contemplative life is not quite as she imagined when she is bound, gagged, and sexually assaulted by lust-crazed lesbian nuns. Based on a story by BEAST CITY–creator Naomi Hayakawa. The first release in the notorious VANILLA SERIES. ❷❷❷

LOVE HINA *

2000. TV series, TV special. DIR: Shigeru Ueda, Takashi Sudo, Koichi Sugitani. SCR: Kuro Hatsuki, Manabu Ishikawa, Hiroyuki Kawasaki. DES: Makoto Uno, Eiji Yasuhiko. ANI: Makoto Uno, Akio Takami. MUS: N/C. PRD: Xebec, TV Tokyo. 25 mins. x 24 eps., 25 mins.

As a child, Keitaro makes a vow with his sweetheart that they will meet at Japan's prestigious Tokyo University (Todai) when they are older. He doesn't, however, count on failing the exams, or indeed on forgetting his sweetheart's name in the decade that follows. Now in his late teens, he is left by his grandmother to look after a student dorm and meets two students, one of whom he suspects is the long-lost love. As Keitaro attempts to regain his memories of his one true love, he becomes an object of attention among the other girls at the dorm, who are "characterized" by a standard rack of female anime archetypes.

The culmination of a decade of geek-centered anime, *Love Hina* is based on a manga in *Shonen Magazine* by Ken Akamatsu, but it plays like a combination of TENCHI MUYO!, the ronin romance of SAKURA DIARIES, and the occasional filmic experimentation inspired by HIS AND HER CIRCUMSTANCES. The franchise returned for a one-shot TV special in Christmas 2000.

LOVE IS THE NUMBER OF KEYS *

2002. JPN: *Ai wa Kagi no Kazu Dake*.

Video. DIR: Ichiro Watari. SCR: N/C. DES: Yoko Murasaka. ANI: Yoko Murasaka. MUS: N/C. PRD: Milky, Concept Films. 28 mins.

When his father moves abroad to work, Jun promises to finish high school back in Japan. He gets himself a room at an apartment building, which conveniently turns out to be a brothel, or rather a "sex service apartment" where good time girls forget about their day jobs and act out their sexual fantasies. Before long, Jun is servicing the owner Sumire and collecting freebies from other tenants, including waitress Marina and nurse Miki. An erotic variant of **MAISON IKKOKU**, with an unexpectedly jazzy soundtrack. **OLN**

LOVE LESSONS *

2001. JPN: *Jinshin Yugi*. AKA: *Games of the Heart*. Video. DIR: N/C. SCR: Reiji Izumo. DES: Masayoshi Sekiguchi. ANI: Masayoshi Sekiguchi. MUS: N/C. PRD: EVE, Milky, Museum Pictures. 30 mins. x 2 eps.

Kusanagi is deep in debt to the Mob, but discovers that even loan sharks are people. Instead of breaking his legs, his old acquaintance, gangster Takamori, offers to find him a job so he can work off his debt. The task he is given involves "training" tasks on a yacht, where bondage mistress Sakura Matsura encourages Kusanagi to help her break in four girls, who are working off their own debts by working as prostitutes. The "fun" side of coerced sex work, although unusually for anime porn, the female characters don't look particularly young, the sex is fairly mild, the fetishes non-challenging, and beyond their need to earn money, the girls are relatively free from coercion (though not from manipulation). The production quality is even quite good and shows signs that it could have been even better if the staff had been given a larger budget. As with so many other pornographic anime, the second episode ends without completing the story; no further volume has been released. Based on a PC game from EVE. **OLNV**

LOVE POSITION HALLEY

1985. JPN: *Love Position Halley Densetsu*. AKA: *Legend of Love Position Halley; Love Position—Legend of Halley*. Video. DIR: Hideharu Iuchi. SCR: Masaki Tsuji. DES: Hiromi Matsushita, Kunio Aoii, Indori-Koya. ANI: Shinya Takahashi, Isao Kaneko, Kazutoshi Kobayashi, Masashi Maruyama. MUS: Kei Wakakusa. PRD: Tezuka Pro. 93 mins.

A crippled old man recounts his wartime experiences in Vietnam to his son Subaru, telling of his encounter with the young elfin girl Lamina in a temple. He takes a fatherly interest in her after she saves him from the Viet Cong, but she refuses to reveal to him any details about her past. Fifteen years after he is sent home and leaves her behind, he receives a letter from her announcing that she is coming to the U.S. and desperately needs his help. Since he owes her his life but cannot help her himself, he begs his son to take his place, and a very surprised Subaru discovers that the "teenage" Lamina does not appear to have aged a day. Subaru escorts Lamina across the U.S., where they are pursued by a former vagrant who has been possessed by a killer entity that escaped from a crashing meteorite. Eventually, after a series of escalating battles, Lamina is revealed to be the spirit of Halley's Comet, a messenger sent from the planet/goddess Venus to the sun/goddess Amaterasu, but she is pursued by agents sent by Venus's enemy, Mars. This movie was based on an original idea by **ASTRO BOY**–creator Osamu Tezuka and released to cash in on the real-life reappearance of Halley's Comet in the skies. Compare to **WIND OF AMNESIA**, a similar road movie with a mystery girl.

LOVELESS *

2005. TV series. DIR: Yuh Koh. SCR: Yuji Kawahara. DES: Kazunori Iwakura. ANI: Yumi Nakayama. MUS: N/C. PRD: JC Staff. 25 mins. x 12 eps. (TV).

New transfer student Ritsuka Aoyagi keeps quiet about his past: his mother is dead, his brother has been murdered, and the shadowy figure of Sobi is offering to avenge his death, at a price. Sobi is a warrior, or "fighter," and as in **UTENA**, fighters have passive counterparts or "sacrifices," whose job is to cast spells that ward away attackers during combat. Sobi wants Ritsuka to take his late brother's place as his sacrifice, a request to which Ritsuka eventually agrees, hoping that by doing so he will find the culprit of his brother's death, which has something to do with an organization called the Septimal Moon. Each pairing of fighter and sacrifice has a name, and since his brother and Sobi were the Beloved, the new Ritsuka-Sobi pairing is the Loveless.

This adaptation of **EARTHIAN** creator Yun Koga's manga from *Zero Sum* magazine cleverly retains its conceit that the characters live in a surreal world where children grow up with cat's ears and tails. These attributes slowly fade away as they lose their innocence and turn into adults, sublimating many sexual tensions into concerns over whether someone still has his feline characteristics—**BROTHER DEAREST** with a series of opponents of the week. The DVD releases contained three bonus shorts.

LUCKY MAN

1994. JPN: *Tottemo Lucky Man*. AKA: *Really Lucky Man*. TV series. DIR: Hajime Kamegaki, Akira Shigino, Masami Shimoda. SCR: Yoshio Urasawa, Kazuhisa Sakaguchi, Yukichi Hashimoto. DES: Hiroshi Kamo. ANI: Hideyuki Motohashi, Tsuneo Ninomiya. MUS: N/C. PRD: Studio Pierrot, TV Tokyo. 25 mins. x 50 eps.

Yoichi is an unpleasant teenager, but one who can transform at will into the luckiest man in the world—a superpower that he uses freely to get himself out of embarrassing situations. Based on a *Shonen Jump* manga by Hiroshi Kamo and featuring a lead character who resembles a mohawked version of *South Park*'s yammering Canadians, Terrence and Phillip.

LULLABY FOR WEDNESDAY'S CINDERELLA

1987. JPN: *Aitsu to Lullaby Suiyobi no Cinderella*. Video. DIR: Yukihiro Takahashi. SCR: Jiyu Watanabe. DES: Joji Yanagise, Masayoshi Sato. ANI: N/C. MUS: Satoshi Monkura, Takashi Kudo. PRD: Studio Pierrot, Nippon Herald. 50 mins.

Kenji is a motorbike-mad teenager in Yokohama, who just loves his ZII machine, and likes nothing better than grabbing his girl Yumi, skipping school, and motoring down the coast. Hearing from fellow biker Hayase about a fabled racer called Wednesday's Cinderella, Kenji witnesses Hayase on his SRX, squaring off against Cinderella on her Porsche cycle (the synopsis spends more time on the brands than the characters!). Concerned for his friend's safety, Kenji sets off after him, borrowing his friend Kyosuke's Ducatti. Based on a *Shonen Magazine* manga by Michiharu Kusunoki, who also created SHAKOTAN BOOGIE. Made for video, but screened on a double bill in cinemas with LEGEND OF ROLLING WHEELS, which must have made the day as exciting as changing an oil sump.

LUNA VARGA *

1991. JPN: *Maju Senshi Luna Varga*. AKA: *Demon/Beast Warrior Luna Varga*. Video. DIR: Shigenori Kiyoyama. SCR: Aki Tomato, Yumiko Tsukamoto. DES: Yuji Moriyama. ANI: Kazuhiro Konishi. MUS: Kenji Kawai. PRD: AIC, Studio Hakk. 30 mins. x 4 eps.

The Dunbas Empire tries to conquer a world where humans and beasts have lived in medieval-fantasy harmony for centuries. The three princesses of Rimbell are determined to fight the invaders, but middle sister Luna (the "tomboy princess") does so in a very strange way. Engulfed in a ray of light, the accomplished swordswoman recovers to find herself embedded in the head of a giant tyrannosaur-like beast that communicates with her telepathically, calling her its "brain." To save her land, she has been granted control

of the legendary dragon Varga, and even when not in dragon form, she has a reptilian tail. She manages to fight off the Dunban troops but must rescue her sister Vena, who has been kidnapped by the invaders. From the high concept that posits a princess with a dragon sticking out of her ass (or a dragon with a princess stuck to its forehead, depending on your perspective) to the insanely overblown theme song, *LV* is a madcap comedy to file with DRAGON HALF.

LUNAR LEGEND TSUKIHIME *

2003. JPN: *Shingetsutan Tsukihime*. AKA: *Lunar Legend Moon Princess; Moon Princess*. TV series. DIR: Katsushi Sakurabi. SCR: Hiroko Tokita. DES: Takashi Takeuchi, Kaoru Ozawa. ANI: Kaoru Ozawa. MUS: Toshiyuki Omori. PRD: Geneon, JC Staff, MOVIC, Rondo Robe, TBS. 30 mins. x 12 eps. (TV).

Injured in a mysterious childhood accident, Shiki Tono suffers bizarre aftereffects. These include his belief that he can see strange lines emanating from objects around him, which can only be repressed with the aid of special spectacles. He is sent away to stay with relatives until eight years later when his father dies and he is ordered home by his older sister Akiha, the new head of the family.

On his first day back he dices up a woman in a murderous rage—seen in graphic detail on the home video release, but not in the original TV broadcast. He is, however, still understandably disconcerted when she shows up later, alive and well, and asks him to be her bodyguard. Strange things are going on in Shiki's very traditional family—the revenant woman turns out to be a vampire, one of the True Ancestors, who is charged with eliminating their bastard offspring, the Dead Apostles, the result of True Ancestors feeding on humans. And it seems that his big sister Akiha may not be entirely human. And then there is the new girl at school, who is stalking him. Shiki has to find out where his past is leading him. It turns out that

the things he can see are "deathlines," the threads that bind all life together, which he can manipulate to cause destruction.

This story originated in a fan-produced game made by Type-Moon, which generated considerable merchandise since its creation in 2000, and allowed its inventors to turn professional. Unfortunately the atmospheric design and well-created undercurrent of tension can't hide the erratic pacing—the original game contained over 5,000 pages of text, condensed here into a mere 12 episodes, and leading to the production of major plot points like rabbits from a hat and blind alleys caused by inclusion of game elements which the story allows no time to resolve. Compare to HELLSING and VAMPIRE PRINCESS MIYU. ●NV

LUNATIC NIGHT *

1997. Video. DIR: Shinji Nishiyama, Fuyumi Shirakawa, Teruo Kigure. SCR: Shinji Nishiyama, Haruka Kaio. DES: Kiginmaru Oi. ANI: Taiichi Kitagawa. MUS: Hideyuki Tanaka. PRD: Knack. 35 mins. x 3 eps.

College boy Kanzaki gets a sex-crazed girl for a pet on a moonlit night. She's come to remind him he's the lord of Atlantis and final incarnation of Krishna, forced to fight his satanic schoolmate Mutsuki for control of the world amid innumerable jokey references to classic anime like GIANT ROBO and BABEL II (on which director Kigure worked as an animator) as well as porn-like appearances by characters more familiar from SAILOR MOON. In part two, overindulgence has turned all Atlantean men into penises, and incredible power awaits the man who can pass the trials and give Queen Estelle the orgasm of a lifetime. Kanzaki also has to pleasure a giant Amazon who drowns him with her breasts and prompts the meaningful quote, "She's huge! I could stick my whole head in there." The authors would like to apologize for making this sound a lot more interesting than it is. Based on a manga by Akira Mii that was serialized in *Comic Lies*, mercifully only the first two parts of this anime appear to have been released in the U.S. 🅛🅝

LUPIN III *

1971. JPN: *Lupin Sansei*. AKA: (see below). TV series, movie, video, TV specials. DIR: Masaaki Osumi, Isao Takahata, Hayao Miyazaki. SCR: Tadaaki Yamazaki, Atsushi Yamatoya, Yoshio Urasawa, Yuki Miyata, Yoshio Urasawa, Soji Yoshikawa, Tohru Sawaki. DES: Monkey Punch. ANI: Yasuo Otsuka, Osamu Kobayashi, Hideo Kawauchi, Yoshifumi Kondo, Tameo Ogawa, Norio Yazawa, Minoru Okazaki, Satoshi Dezaki, Tetsuo Imazawa, Yasuhiro Yamaguchi, Koichi Murata. MUS: Takeo Yamashita, Yuji Ono. PRD: Tokyo Movie Shinsha, Nippon TV. 25 mins. x 23 eps. (TV1), 25 mins. x 155 eps. (TV2), 102 mins. (m/*Mamo*), 100 min (m/*Cagliostro*), 25 mins. x 50 eps. (TV3), 100 mins. (m/*Babylon*), 74 mins. (m/*Fuma*), 97 mins. (TVm/*Liberty*), 92 mins. (TVm/*Hemingway*), 90 mins. (TVm/*Napoleon*), 90 mins. (TVm/*Russia*), 90 mins. (*Sword*), 90 mins. (TVm/*Nostradamus*), 90 mins. (TVm/*Harimao*), 90 mins. (*Dead*), 90 mins. (*Twilight*), 90 mins. (TVm/*Walther*), 90 mins. (TVm/*Crisis)*, 90 mins. (TVm/*Money*), 90 mins. (TVm/*Alcatraz*), 50 mins. (v/*Magician Lives*), 90 mins. (TVm/*First Contact*), 90 mins. (TVm/*Return the Treasure*), 90 mins. (TVm/*Stolen Lupin*), 90 mins. (TVm/*Angel's Tactics*).

Lupin is a Japanese criminal with a heart of gold, grandson of the infamous French burglar Arsène Lupin (see LUPIN THE MASTER THIEF AND THE ENIGMA OF 813). His gang includes Lee Marvin–look-alike Daisuke Jigen, a sharpshooter with a 0.3-second quick draw, and Goemon Ishikawa XIII, descendant of the samurai thief first immortalized in the puppet play *Ishikawa Goemon* (ca. 1680). Together with Lupin's occasional girlfriend and frequent rival, the flame-haired Fujiko Mine, they travel the world stealing great treasures while Lupin charms the ladies, Jigen is suspicious of them, and

Goemon tries in vain to hold them at arm's length lest they taint his samurai honor. They are pursued all the while by Inspector Zenigata of Interpol (a descendant of Kodo Nomura's samurai-era sleuth Heiji Zenigata, who was the subject of nearly 400 stories and a long-running TV series).

Longer running than GUNDAM and with a pedigree beaten by few anime except perhaps SAZAE-SAN, *Lupin III* began as a 1967 *Manga Action* publication by SCOOPERS-creator Monkey Punch (pseudonym for Kazuhiko Kato). Adapted by the TMS studio, the series still makes regular appearances in the fourth decade after its debut—largely due to its dogged faith to the camp original, which has endured so long that some of its stories (such as *Mamo*, see below) now outgroove the self-consciously groovy COWBOY BEBOP with their *original* kitsch. Yuji Ono's theme music remains one of Japan's best-selling musical exports. *L3* also has many hidden attributes, such as the casting of "famous voices" to draw unseen parallels for the Japanese audience—late Lupin actor Yasuo Yamada used to dub all Clint Eastwood's Japanese dialogue, Jigen actor Kiyoshi Komori "is" the Japanese voice of Lee Marvin, and Goemon's Makio Inoue normally plays the gruff anime hero CAPTAIN HARLOCK. There was a certain irony in sharpshooter Jigen getting the "voice of" Lee Marvin, since the actor was a Marine sniper in the Pacific War credited with a number of kills on Japanese soldiers.

After the manga and anime finished their first runs, the franchise continued in the form of the live-action film *L3: Strange Psychokinetic Strategy* (1974, *Nenriki Chin Sakusen*) reuniting all the characters except Goemon. After the original anime series was rebroadcast to popular acclaim, it was revived as the longer-running *New L3* (1977)—as a rule of thumb, the hero's jacket is green in series one, and red in series two, though its pigment varies in the later movies and specials. Monkey Punch claims that only the first series

captured the true spirit of his manga, but fan favorites were episodes #145 and #155, written and directed by Tsutomu Teruki (pseudonym for Hayao Miyazaki). In the wake of Miyazaki's later popularity with foreign anime fans, the episodes were released in the U.S. as *L3: Albatross Wings of Death* and *L3: Aloha, Lupin*. The Lupin name, however, was edged from the credits after a legal dispute—the estate of Maurice Leblanc, creator of the original Lupin, discovered the existence of the series when dubbed episodes were broadcast in Australia, and challenged the producers' rights to the name Lupin. Eventually, the courts ruled that, since *L3* had existed uncontested for more than a decade, Leblanc had no right to it in Japan. Such mitigating circumstances, however, do not apply in the rest of the world, and some anime distributors have avoided the wrath of the Leblanc estate by removing all reference to Lupin from the films—the aforementioned episodes renamed *Tales of the Wolf*, with their lead now "Wolf" throughout the script itself. AnimEigo, which subtitled some of the films (see below) instead opted for the safely facetious transliteration of *Rupan III*. The major casualty of the legal upheaval was Rintaro's 22nd-century sci-fi remake, *Lupin VIII*, planned as a Franco-Japanese follow-up to ULYSSES 31 and regrettably mothballed by TMS and Jean Chalopin's Studio DIC in 1982. Intellectual property issues are likely to haunt the franchise until 2016, when Leblanc's work finally comes out of copyright under current European law.

Meanwhile, the franchise reached theaters with Soji Yoshikawa's *Mystery of Mamo* (1978, *Lupin tai Fukusei Ningen*, aka *Lupin vs. Clone*). At a time when the rest of the world was desperately trying to cash in on *Star Wars*, *Mamo* was a burst of 1960s nostalgia. Fujiko cons Lupin into stealing the Egyptian "Philosopher's Stone" for her without revealing that she is working for the shadowy would-be dictator Mamo—originally Mameux, though the distributors felt obliged to bring the spelling into line with the inferior transliteration already common in U.S. fandom. As befits its "clone" subplot, *Mamo* plays up the similarities between Lupin and Zenigata. Without his trademark trenchcoat in the Egyptian scenes, Zenigata looks almost identical to Lupin, and the idea reaches its logical conclusion in the final reel, when the two enemies are cuffed together and forced to cooperate to save their skins. The film exists in *three* different dubs—the earliest, made by TMS in 1978 for screenings on Pacific flights, changes Jigen's name to Dan Dunn, Goemon's to simply Samurai, and Mamo's henchman Frenchy to Flinch. As a symptom of its time, it also gives the U.S. president the voice of Jimmy Carter. The second, made in 1995 by Streamline shortly before European legal reforms brought Leblanc back into copyright, calls the hero "Lupin." A third, made in 1996 by Manga Entertainment under the title *Secret of Mamo*, calls him "Wolf" once more, and modernizes some of the dialogue with effective, if anachronistic, rewrites. It leaves in a parody of Henry Kissinger, but lines like "Okay, so I'm not Keanu Reeves" and an in-joke about *Dynasty* can be reasonably expected not to hail from the original Japanese script.

The best-known *L3* film, CASTLE OF CAGLIOSTRO, followed in 1979, and though it was an immense success for director Hayao Miyazaki, the aforementioned legal troubles kept a third TV season off the air until *L3: Part III* (1984). Famous live-action director Seijun Suzuki helmed Lupin's last *true* anime movie outing *Gold of Babylon* (1985, *Babylon no Ogon Densetsu*), in which the gang is pursued by the New York mafia, the police, and the elderly bag-lady Rosetta. The trail leads from a hilarious bike chase through Madison Square Garden to the Middle East and back again to New York, pasticheing the *Indiana Jones* films, Erich von Däniken, and gangster films, as Lupin searches for buried gold under New York, hidden inside an alien spaceship. Rosetta

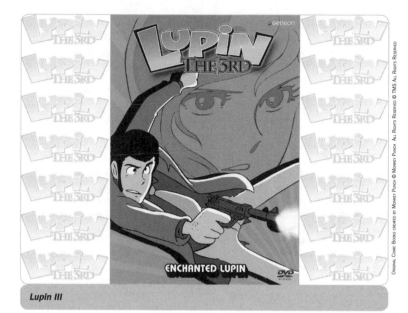

Lupin III

eventually reveals her true form and Lupin misses out on sex with a space goddess, though the ever-pragmatic Fujiko is simply concerned with getting as much of the gold as possible.

Masayuki Ozeki's superb *L3: Fuma Conspiracy* (1988, *Fuma Ichizoku no Inbo*, aka *Secret Plot of the Fuma Clan*) was originally made for video but given a theatrical release at the last moment. Distinctive for returning the globe-trotting thief to his native Japan, it begins at Goemon's long-delayed wedding, interrupted by the kidnapping of the bride. The mysterious Fuma clan want the Suminawa clan's treasure as a ransom, and Lupin helps out, with an eye on the girl and the chances of loot. Inspector Zenigata, who has abandoned the world and entered a monastery believing Lupin to be dead, soon regains his old lust for life and dogged pursuit of his nemesis. *Fuma Conspiracy* is available in two foreign versions—a very good one from AnimEigo (U.S.) and a very bad one from Western Connection with *manually* timed subtitles (U.K.).

All successive *L3* outings have been made for TV as one-shot specials, though some foreign distributors still

like to imply that they are "movies," despite a marked drop in animation budget and great variations in quality. In *Bye Bye Liberty* (1989, aka *Goodbye Lady Liberty*), an Interpol computer has predicted Lupin/Wolf's every movement, so he hangs up his cat-burglar suit and settles down in unwedded bliss with a French floozy, until Jigen drags him back out in search of a treasure hidden inside the Statue of Liberty. Director Osamu Dezaki returned with *Mystery of the Hemingway Papers* (1990, *Hemingway Papers no Nazo*), in which Lupin tracks down a treasure described in clues left in the diaries of Ernest Hemingway that lead him to the tiny Mediterranean island of Colcaca just in time for a coup d'état led by the evil Carlos. Current affairs broke into the series for Dezaki's *Steal Napoleon's Dictionary* (1991, *Napoleon no Jisho o Ubae*), which begins at a G7 conference in New York after the Gulf War, in which delegates blame Lupin for the loss of two trillion dollars from the world economy. Lupin, however, is in Europe for a classic car race, for the prize of the long-lost dictionary used by Napoleon himself, in which the original Arsène Lupin hid a map to his own treasure house. Matters are complicated by the agents of the G7 nations, all intent on avenging their depressed economies on the man who has removed so much money from them.

Dezaki's *From Russia with Love* (1992, *Russia yori Ai o Komete*) concerns Lupin's search for the treasure of the Russian Czars, supposedly lost forever after the murder of the Romanovs in 1917. Only two people can conceivably find the treasure—Princess Anastasia, long rumored to have escaped death, and the mad monk Rasputin (see also MASTER OF MOSQUITON), who has been in hiding for decades and is now seeking the treasure himself by using his powers of telepathy and persuasion.

Masaaki Osumi took over as director for *Voyage to Danger* (1993, *Lupin Ansatsu Shirei*, originally *Order to Assassinate Lupin*), an original departure in which the discredited Zenigata is taken off the case and reassigned. The cold-blooded assassin Keith Hayton is set on Lupin's trail, and the thief realizes that the only way to stay alive is to salvage Zenigata's shattered career. Using the stolen Russian nuclear sub Ivanov to infiltrate the criminal gang Shot Shell, Lupin maneuvers them into a position where they can be exposed to Interpol, Zenigata can take the credit, and he can relax without a hit man on his tail. He is not the only one, since the Russian scientist Karen still holds a grudge against Jigen for killing her father, and she is determined to extract her own revenge.

Masaharu Okuwaki's *Dragon of Doom* (1994 *Moeyo Zantetsuken*, originally *Burning Zantetsuken*) features a race to find a mysterious dragon statue said to contain the secrets of making weapons like Goemon's sword, a blade that effortlessly cuts through steel. In a story that deliberately concentrates on Goemon, in honor of the fourth centenary of his illustrious ancestor's death in 1594, Chinese gangster Mr. Chan reveals that the statue was last seen setting sail on the Titanic in 1912, and the quest begins.

The following year saw the death of main Lupin voice actor Yasuo Yamada and *two* TV specials. Nobuo Fujisawa's *Farewell to Nostradamus* (1995, *Kutabare Nostradamus*, originally *To Hell with Nostradamus!*) finds Lupin and Jigen posing as Brazilian soccer players when they are hijacked by a cult, whose leader, Lisely, is determined to bring all of the predictions of Nostradamus to pass. Needless to say, a hunt for treasure soon begins, though it means climbing to the top of a 200-story skyscraper. Barely six months later in Dezaki's *The Pursuit of Harimao's Treasure* (1995, *Harimao no Zaiho o Oe*, originally *Treasure of Harimao*), after a mysterious explosion in the English Channel Tunnel, Lloyd's Insurance investigator Archer (see MASTER KEATON) and his beautiful archaeologist daughter, Diana, go in search of three statues said to contain clues to the location of the fabled treasure of Harimao. Archer must race a group of neo-Nazis to find them—but, of course, Lupin and Jigen already have plans of their own. *Dead or Alive* (1996), supposedly directed by author Monkey Punch, features Lupin searching for a fabled "drifting island," while simultaneously running from a gang of bounty hunters each after the million-dollar price on his head. It was succeeded in the same year by Gisaburo Sugii's *The Secret of Twilight Gemini* (1996, *Twilight Gemini no Himitsu*), which sends Lupin to Morocco in search of a diamond to match the titular stone bequeathed to him by dying mobster Don Dorune. It was a return to the annual schedule with Hiroyuki Yano's *Island of Assassins* (1997, *Walther P–38*), in which Lupin's pistol of choice becomes a crucial key in the race to unlock the mysteries of the Tarantula Seal and find the Golden Ghost. Lupin made a rare stop back in his native Japan for Toshiya Shinohara's *Crisis in Tokyo* (1998, *Honoo no Kioku: Tokyo Crisis, Burning Memories: Tokyo Crisis*), in a quest to find the legacy of the last shogun, racing against a psychokinetic treasure hunter employed by theme-park mil-

lionaire Michael Suzaku. In Shinichi Watanabe's *The Columbus Files* (1999, *Ai no Da Capo: Fujiko's Unlucky Days, Love's Da Capo: Fujiko's Unlucky Days*), Fujiko lets Lupin get away with the loot from a Swiss bank job because she is more interested in the Columbus File, a document that can direct her to a 15th-century gem, supposedly connected to COLUMBUS himself. The last *Lupin* of the 20th century was *Missed by a Dollar* (2000, *$1 Money Wars*), in which a disguised Lupin completes the swindle of his life, buying a priceless ring at a rigged auction in New York for a single dollar, though the ring's rightful owner, St. Cyr, is prepared to use any means necessary to get it back. Lupin himself soon returned in Hideki Tonokatsu's TV movie *Alcatraz Connection* (2001), in which he battles the Mob for a treasure to be found somewhere in San Francisco Bay. He also appeared in a video spin-off, *L3: The Magician Lives* (2002), aka *The Return of the Magician*, aka *The Return of Pycal*, in which Lupin races against his archenemy Pycal to steal one of seven "magic" crystals.

With the advent of the 21st century came several attempts to reinvigorate the franchise with some new directions. *L3: Episode 0: First Contact* (2002) returns to the master thief's early days, when he is just starting out as a thief, in a move presumably designed to reset the chronology of the series and serve as an introduction to the older Lupin for new viewers—of which there are a lot, following the serial's translation and release in English by Funimation. *L3: Operation: Return the Treasure!!* (2003, *Otakara Henkyaku Dai-sakusen!!*) is another TV movie which finds Lupin on the trail of the Trick diamond, but sucked into a scheme by rival thief Mark Williams, whose dying wish is for his lifetime's haul of stolen objects to be returned to their rightful owners—in other words, Lupin is turned from a master thief into a stealthy benefactor. The new thief Becky is introduced in *L3: Stolen Lupin: Copy Cat's Midsummer Butterfly* (2004, *Nusumareta Lupin: Copy Cat wa Manatsu no Cho*), in which

Lupin and his gang must steal a gem in order to ransom the kidnapped Fujiko from Malkovich, her evil captor. *L3: Angel's Tactics: Dream Fragment's Scent of Murder* (2005, *Tenshi no Sakuryaku: Yume no Kakera wa Koroshi no Kaori*) also bestows a new female assistant on Inspector Zenigata, in the form of his sidekick Emily. The story introduces science fictional elements, as Lupin breaks into America's legendary Area 51 to steal an alien artifact known as the Original Metal, thereby incurring the wrath of an all-female assassins group called the Bloody Angels.

LUPIN THE MASTER THIEF AND THE ENIGMA OF 813

1979. JPN: *Kaiketsu Lupin: 813 no Nazo*. TV special. DIR: Hiroshi Sasakawa, Masayuki Akehi. SCR: Akira Miyazaki, N/C. DES: Ippei Kuri, Yoshitaka Amano, N/C. ANI: Sadao Miyamoto, Nobuyuki Kishi. MUS: Nobuyoshi Koshibe, Yoshiki Takaragi. PRD: Herald Enterprises, Tatsunoko, Fuji TV; Toei. 84 mins. (TVm1), 84 mins. (TVm2).
Four years after the gentleman thief Arsène Lupin was last seen on the streets of Paris, diamond dealer Kesselbach is found stabbed to death in his hotel room. The police decide that Lupin is the chief suspect, but the master thief himself retrieves a message from Kesselbach containing the mysterious phrase "Napoleon 813." Lupin is forced to team up with Kesselbach's widow to solve the crime before Inspector Lunolman arrests him for the one crime he *hasn't* committed. An adaptation of one of Maurice Leblanc's best-loved Lupin stories, possibly made

in a deliberate attempt to annoy Tatsunoko's rival studio TMS, which was experiencing legal difficulties with its **LUPIN III** franchise at the time. This Lupin fable is particularly well known in Japan, where it was also adapted into the live-action Kenji Mizoguchi film *813: The Adventures of Arsène Lupin* (1923).

Just to rub salt into the wounds, a second Leblanc adaptation followed, this time from another big studio, Toei. In *Lupin vs. Holmes* (1981), the famous English detective Sherlock Holmes is sent to France to track Lupin at the instigation of Baron Autrech, though the baron soon turns up dead, and his priceless blue diamond is missing. *LvH* was based on Leblanc's 1907 series of original stories featuring Holmes, and even includes a famous scene from *The Jewish Lamp* in which the two well-matched rivals face each other on a sinking boat, each daring the other to show the first sign of weakness. In a final karmic irony, the original stories brought protests from Arthur Conan Doyle that Leblanc was using his character without permission, though Leblanc's estate would be just as unforgiving toward Monkey Punch's *Lupin III* many decades later. Leblanc's Lupin has been the subject of dozens of radio dramas, TV series, and movies both in English and French, and even a rumored live-action Hong Kong version, in development from **WICKED CITY**'s Tsui Hark. One of his most recent incarnations was in François Bresson's *Les Aventures de Arsène Lupin* (1996), a French cartoon series dubbed into English as *Nighthood*.

Lupin also appeared in **GIGI AND THE FOUNTAIN OF YOUTH**.

LUV WAVE *

2000. Video. DIR: Nobutaka Kondo. SCR: Takao Yoshioka. DES: Hiroya Iijima. ANI: Hiroya Iijima. MUS: Eric Satei. PRD: Triple X, Pink Pineapple. 27 mins. x 3 eps.
In the year 2039, special agent Kaoru Mikogami is saddled with an unwanted partner—American-made military cyborg Alice, who looks like a cute girl, and has been sent to Kaoru in order to gain better experience. The reluctant allies set out on the trail of a dangerous new drug called Nine Heavens and a computer virus that once shut down international networks and has now been reactivated in a new, stronger form. Kaoru has also been ordered to terminate Mercy Specter, a dead hacker whose undead persona now travels the Net and invades the minds of those who use Nine Heavens. When Kaoru's sister Mamoru is threatened, he sets off to rescue her, while Mercy invades Alice's mind and awakens a new, more human alter ego. She has the memories of Kaoru's childhood sweetheart Mayumi, put there by the girl's scientist father who is involved in a plot to control the global network and create a new digital deity. Sci-fi porn that wants to be **SERIAL EXPERIMENTS LAIN** but spoils it with some very violent sex, *LW* nevertheless manages to both pastiche **GHOST IN THE SHELL** and foreshadow *Ghost in the Shell: Stand Alone Complex*. Based on a 1998 adult PC game from C's ware. ●🅝🅥

M

MABURAHO *
2003. TV series. DIR: Shinichiro Kimura. SCR: Koichi Taki. DES: Yasunari Nitta, Eiji Komatsu. ANI: N/C. MUS: Koichi Korenaga, Ryo Sakai. PRD: JC Staff, Klockwerx, WOWOW. 24 mins. x 24 eps.

Teenage Kazuki Shikimori attends Aoi Academy, a school for witches and wizards. But magic is a finite resource, everyone has a limited number of spells they can cast in their lifetime, and Kazuki's limit is a fraction of most other's. With only eight "charges," he has to carefully conserve his spellcasting energy lest he crumble into dust, a plan that falls to pieces when he attracts the lustful attentions of several girls. Another harem show with magical overtones like NEGIMA, *Maburaho* takes the *Harry Potter* analogies a little further by making its hero a descendant of famous sorcerers, and hence prime marriage material. Meanwhile, Kazuki ends up wasting a number of his precious charges keeping Yuna, his self-styled "wife" out of trouble, and dodging the attentions of samurai throwback Rin Kamishiro and large-breasted heiress Kuriko Kazetsubaki. Meanwhile, the girls do everything in their power to win him over, or failing that, to get his parents' approval, in an anime that could be taken as a satire of materialist dating customs were it not such a blatant case of cliché reassembly—**DNA²** meets **TENCHI MUYO!**.

However, *Maburaho* does attempt to do something new with such outrageously hackneyed raw material. Many situations from the geek-gets-girls subgenre are deliberately inverted, such as the time-limit lifespan of **MAHOROMATIC** or **VIDEO GIRL AI**, here given to the male protagonist. Nor does the series shy away from following its own internal logic—it establishes that ghosts are part of everyday life, and consequently has no qualms about killing off its hero midway. The inversions of traditional formulae become increasingly obvious, since it is now Kazuki who is the untouchable, unattainable love object, forced to continue school in a phantom state, in the hope that his death can be somehow reversed and his magical mojo recharged. Based on the manga by Toshihiko Tsukuji in *Dragon Magazine* and *Dragon Age* monthlies.

MACHINE HAYABUSA
1976. AKA: *Machine Peregrine*. TV series. DIR: Yugo Serikawa, Hidenori Yamaguchi, Minoru Okazaki, Seiji Okada, Yoshikata Nitta. SCR: Shunichi Yukimuro, Keiji Kubota, Masaki Tsuji. DES: Takao Kasai, Hideji Ito. ANI: Junzo Koizumi, Yutaka Tanizawa. MUS: Koichi Sugiyama. PRD: Matsuji Kishimoto, Toei, TV Asahi. 25 mins. x 21 eps. The world of Formula One racing has become a lawless battlefield after the victories of the Black Shadow team and their leader Ahab the Devil King. Only the Nishionji racing team is prepared to make a sporting stand with their star driver, the vengeful Ken Hayabusa, whose brother was killed by Black Shadow. Ken's car, the Hayabusa Special, enables him to beat all opponents, however treacherous. Luckily he's part of a supportive team of drivers, mechanics, and administrative staff, who will willingly give their all to see their leader head the field. Created by Mikiya Mochizuki and directed by Tezuka coworker Yugo Serikawa, this story walks a different line between sci-fi sports like **EYESHIELD 21** and a fascination with technology à la **INITIAL D**, albeit technology that is yet to exist. Manga tie-ins were published in *Shonen Jump* monthly, *Terebi-kun*, and *Terebi Land*. The authors are unsure whether the "Devil King" part of Ahab's name should be translated or simply left as Ma-O—itself a popular baddie's moniker in the 1970s, courtesy of Chairman Mao, the leader of the People's Republic of China, who died the year this was made. Followed by **RUBENKAISER**, which was more of the same.

MACHINE ROBO *
1986. JPN: *Machine Robo: Chronos no Dai Gyakushu; MR: Butchigiri Battle Hackers*. AKA: *Machine Robo: Revenge of Chronos; MR: Go for It Battle Hackers*. TV series. DIR: Hiroshi Yoshida, Yoshitaka Fujimoto, Yasuo Hasegawa, Hiroshi Negishi, Yoshinori Nakamura, Kiyoshi Murayama, Yasunori Urata. SCR: Hideki Sonoda, Nobuaki Kishima, Yasushi Hirano, Toshimichi Okawa,

Asami Watanabe, Hiroko Naka. DES: Nobuyoshi Habara. ANI: Masami Obari, Norio Hirayama, Yoshiaki Akutagawa, Hajime Inai, Shigeru Omachi, Hiroaki Aida. MUS: Tachio Okano. PRD: Ashi Pro, Plex, TV Tokyo. 25 mins. x 47 eps., 25 mins. x 31 eps., 30 mins. x 3 eps. (v1), 30 mins. (v2), 24 mins. x 52 eps. (tv2) 25 mins. (tv sp).

Gandler space pirates attack Planet Chronos in search of the super-element Hiliveed, but their plans are thwarted by the death of the noble Kirai. His son, Rom Stol, acquires Kirai's "Wolfblade," the key to the secrets of Hiliveed. Accompanied by his sister, Leina, and his friends Rod Drill and Blue Jet, Rom sets out in search of his destiny, finding along the way his ability to transform into the giant robot Viking-fu.

Conceived by Bandai to promote its Machine Robo toy line, *MR* was nevertheless a success in its own right. The first series was immediately followed by *MR: Battle Hackers* (1987), in which a ship crewed by Earthlings crashes on Chronos. Believing themselves stranded, the crew volunteers to fight alongside the Machine Robos. The second season, however, did not quite live up to the popularity of its predecessor. Realizing that one of the serial's most popular attributes was not the robots at all but the miniskirted Leina, the series was revived straight to video with a spin-off, *Leina Stol: Legend of the Wolfblade* (1988, *LS: Kenro Densetsu*). In this story, Rom's sister disguises herself as an Earth girl and goes undercover to a typical Japanese school to investigate a series of disappearances. Demonstrating surprising tenacity, the character returned for a last hurrah in a one-shot, *Lightning Trap: Leina and Laika* (1990), about the well-traveled sister on a hijacked plane teaming up with the cyborg Interpol agent Laika to save the day. The songs from the series were also rereleased as "image videos" *MR: Revenge of Chronos Battlefield Memory* (1987) and *Leina Music Video: Thank You for You* (1989).

Some of the original toys were released in the U.S. under the brand name Robo Machine along with the unrelated "Future Machine" from the DX Robo Machine line, which was actually a spin-off model of Cobra's car from SPACE ADVENTURE COBRA.

A second TV series, *Machine Robo Rescue* (2003) features the titular organization, which uses machines based on many of the original *MR* concepts such as the Drill Robo and Shuttle Robo, but "research has shown" that the machines are most effectively piloted by people aged between 10 and 12 years. Young hero Taiyo Ozora (literally Sun Sky), pilot of HyperJetRobo, and his eleven teammates are split into three divisions, Red Wings, Blue Sirens, and Yellow Gears, and rescue people from advanced airplanes, ships, trains, submarines, and other vehicles or installations that run out of control or collide with the wrong thing. Each team has a LeaderRobo and SupporterRobos, which can combine to form a HyperRobo. The pilot of each HyperRobo is referred to as the RoboMaster. Like International Rescue, they are hampered in their operations by a mysterious mastermind, Colonel Hazard, and his Disaster organization. The first opponent Disaster sends against them is a mysterious dark-skinned boy called Jey, strongly reminiscent of a similar subplot in PATLABOR. They also have to contend with the press, in the shape of a boy TV reporter who will do anything for a scoop and intends to find out the secrets of their organization. When Disaster decides to crash the planetoid Tartaros into Earth using an electromagnetic induction wave, Taiyo and company have their work cut out to save the planet. The final "special" episode shows the team a few years later, no longer working together, but all still working to protect the world—compare to GOSHOGUN.

MACROSS *

1982. JPN: *Chojiku Yosai Macross*. AKA: *Superdimensional Fortress Macross*. TV series, movie, video. DIR: Noboru Ishiguro, Fumihiko Takayama, Masakazu Yasumura, Hiroyuki Yamaga, Kazushi Akiyama, Hiroshi Yoshida, Kazuhito Akiyama. SCR: Kenichi Matsuzaki, Sukehiro Tomita, Hiroyuki Hoshiyama, Shoji Kawamori, Noboru Ishiguro, Kei Onoki, Tatsuya Kasahara. DES: Haruhiko Mikimoto, Kazumasa Miyabe, Shoji Kawamori, Ichiro Itano, Toshihiro Hirano, Eiji Suzuki, Hideaki Shimada. ANI: Noboru Ishiguro, Fumihiko Takayama, Hiroyuki Yamaga, Taro Yamada, Katsuhisa Yamada, Akina Nishimori. MUS: Kentaro Haneda; Yoko Kanno. PRD: Big West, TBS. 25 mins. x 36 eps. (*Macross*), 115 mins. (m), 30 mins. x 6 eps. (*Mac2*), 40 mins. x 4 eps. (*Mac+*), 115 mins. (*Mac+ Movie*), 25 mins. x 49 eps. (*Mac7*), 55 mins. (*Mac7 Encore*), 30 mins. (*Mac7 Galaxy*), 30 mins. x 4 eps. (*Mac7 Dynamite*), 30 mins. x 5 eps. (*Zero*).

In 1999, a giant space fortress crashes on Earth. Technology salvaged from it changes the face of Terran science, but the military is painfully aware that it is a warship, and that somewhere out in space is the race who built it. Sure enough, the giant Zentraedi arrive to reclaim their errant spacecraft. Attacking just as the recommissioned fortress, now named SDF-1, prepares for takeoff, they are thwarted by the brave people on board, who include spunky young pilot Hikaru Ichijo, heroic veteran Roy Fokker, and a ragtag crew of outnumbered Earthlings. During the ensuing conflict out at the edge of the solar system (where SDF-1 has been trapped by a malfunctioning warp engine), the invaders reveal their fatal flaw. Themselves the creations of a far older civilization, the Protoculture, their society knows nothing but war. Zentraedi spies are deeply confused by the concepts of friendship and romance, and entire fleets are driven insane by their first encounter with the dreaded "culture," as transmitted through the love songs of Chinese pop star, Lin Minmei. The fighting is long and hard, with several false truces and partial victories, but eventually humanity wins the day. The Zentraedi volunteer for "micronization" and are

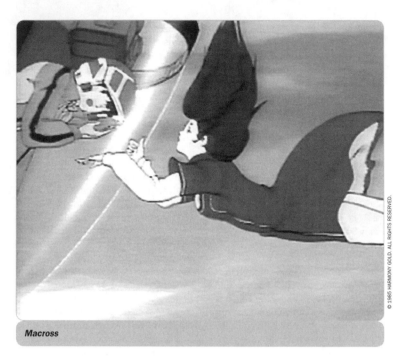

Macross

reduced in size to interbreed with the human race. It is eventually learned that humans are the descendants of a long-forgotten Protoculture terraforming experiment and, consequently, are just as much children of the Protoculture as the Zentraedi, who were genetically engineered to fight the Protoculture's battles.

Released in the U.S. in a substantially altered form as **ROBOTECH**, *Macross*, along with **STAR BLAZERS** and **GUNDAM**, is one of the three unassailable pillars of anime sci-fi, pioneering the tripartite winning formula of songs, battling robot-planes (the show's famous "Valkyries"), and tense relationships. The series was a success across all media—designer Kawamori insisted on beautiful but practical machinery that was nevertheless exploitable as toys, while the numerous record spin-offs made a star of Minmei's voice actress, Mari Iijima.

After several false starts (see below) the franchise was finally revived in earnest with *Plus* (1994), set in 2040 on the colony world of Eden. Like his spiritual predecessor Ichijo, Isamu

Dyson is a maverick pilot, in this case sent back to his homeworld to be a test pilot for a new generation of Valkyries, competing with his former friend Guld Bowman. *M Plus* turns its predecessor on its head, introducing a *broken* love triangle with the return of Myung Fan Lone, a girl over whom the pilots fell out in their teens. A failed singer turned record producer, Myung is in town with the virtual idol Sharon Apple, and studiously trying to avoid dredging up old memories. In their own way, they all face the unemployment line; the pilots because the military is developing an unmanned fighter, and Myung because her artificial songstress (who formerly needed to leech off Myung's talent) can now run on autopilot. *M Plus* concerns itself with the very human fear that machines will take over; ironic considering that much of the hype surrounding its Japanese release concentrated on extensive computer graphics. Impressive digital effects make regular appearances, though the old-fashioned cinematography of *M Plus* is of very high quality indeed, needing no flashy

distractions. Directed by **ESCAFLOWNE**'s Shoji Kawamori, and with a script from **COWBOY BEBOP**'s Keiko Nobumoto, *M Plus* is another excellent example of what anime sci-fi has to offer. The original videos were reedited into *MP: The Movie* (1995), which added some intriguing extra scenes but also removed a substantial portion of the breathtaking battles.

M Plus was released in Japan at the same time as a TV follow-up, *Macross 7* (1994), directed by Tetsuro Amino and incorporating elements of a rejected plot for the original *Macross* series that were to have taken place on a colony ship. Set in a colony fleet heading for the galactic core in 2045, *M7* features Max and Miria Jenius, supporting characters from the original series, as the parents of the love interest Mylene. The fleet is attacked by the soul-vampire race of Protodevlin, eventually revealed to be a race of super-Zentraedi, genetically engineered by the Protoculture and imprisoned for millennia on the distant world of Varauta. Despite a backstory that artfully ties up earlier continuity issues in the series, *M7* is still a mixed bag, let down somewhat by cheap, oft-recycled animation, formulaic menaces-of-the-week, and an overconcentration on hotheaded pilot Basara Nekki and his pop group, Fire Bomber, which seems a little too cynically market-oriented. Whereas the original series actually made the audience believe that a love song could save the world, *M7* featured bizarre sequences of pilots strumming guitars in their cockpits to create weapons. Played for laughs, as in the later **BLACK HEAVEN**, it can work, but not in a show that occasionally wants to be taken seriously. As yet unreleased in English, *M7* was nevertheless popular enough in Japan to spawn several spin-offs, including Haruhiko Mikimoto's manga *M7: Trash* (an excellent study of Max Jenius's illegitimate son, Shiba), and the spin-off "movie" *M7: The Galaxy Is Calling Me* (1995), in which Basara, now a journeyman musician, is imprisoned on an ice-planet by mysterious forces.

There are also two sets of straight-to-video ephemera. The first, *M7: Encore*, simply consists of two unbroadcast TV episodes. *Macross Dynamite 7* (1997) was a new story about Basara going to the isolated planet of Zora, where he meets the elfin alien Elma. Although they have little in common, they communicate through the universal language of song, and Elma's older sister Liza enlists Basara's help in attempting to decode the songs of the interstellar whales that have come to Zora. True to form, Liza is an ace pilot in the *Macross* mold, and there is an all-new love triangle to keep fans of the formula happy.

A fully digital sequel, with the working title of *Macross 3D*, was announced for 2001 as a directorial project for Takeshi Mori. This project, however, seems to have been canceled in favor of *Macross Zero* (see below). Early reports include a scarred, embittered veteran who goes by the name Redline, a traditional *Macross* heroine in the shape of the red-haired Lorin, and the "mysterious silver-haired" Karno, who seems heavily inspired by EVANGELION's Rei Ayanami. There are several other spin-offs from the *Macross* series apart from the central plot discussed above. These include the music video *Flashback 2012* (1987), Minmei's "farewell concert," which included bonus epilogue footage of the characters' lives after the show. The theatrical feature *Macross: Do You Remember Love?* (1984, aka *Clash of the Bionoids*) retells much of the original series but with several deviations. The official explanation for this is that it is actually a film made *in* the *Macross* universe *about* the events of the series, taking artistic license with several events. Seen in 2031 by the 15-year-old Myung Fan Lone, it inspires her to become a singer and hence the events of *Macross Plus*! Max's eldest daughter, Comiria, starred in the video game *Macross 2036*, which was followed by another, *Eternal Love Story*. There is also the noncanonical video *Macross II: Lovers Again* (1992), an inferior sequel to the original series, now disowned by its creators. Set 80 years after the original series, this guilty rehash features hotshot journalist Hibiki Kanzaki, who is sent to interview Valkyrie ace Silvie Gena but gets caught up in the action on Earth. A new alien enemy has attacked—the Marduk, who are encouraged in battle by the singing voice of Ishtar, a beautiful girl who switches sides when she falls for Hibiki. A live-action movie version of the original series, *Macross: Final Outpost—Earth*, was planned as a U.S.-Japanese coproduction and reputedly scripted by *Superman*-writer David Newman, but it has been stuck in turnaround for several years.

Macross Zero (2002) is a video series set before the arrival of the Zentraedi and at the time of the creation of the first Valkyrie prototype, in the final days of an Earthbound conflict between the United Nations and anti-UN factions.

MAD BULL 34 *

1990. Video. DIR: Tetsu Dezaki. SCR: Toshiaki Imaizumi. DES: Keizo Shimizu. ANI: Keizo Shimizu, Hideo Okazaki, Kazunori Iwakura. MUS: Curio, John Michael, James Brown. PRD: Magic Bus. 45 mins. x 4 eps.

America, as we all know, is a land of happy blonde hookers, gun-toting schoolchildren, and roller-skating hoodlums, where self-defense teachers use their classes to scout for potential rape victims, pretty journalists use their bodies as bait to trap molesters, and kindly police get freebies from "high-class" whores. One such hero is "Sleepy," a vast hulk of a police officer also known as Mad Bull. In a series of astoundingly misconceived setups lifted from the worst of U.S. cop shows, Japanese-American rookie Daizaburo is assigned to Mad Bull in New York's 34th precinct, and the older cop shows him the ropes.

While *MB34* is one of the most puerile anime ever made, it is at least partly inspired by American TV itself—a diet of murder and crime shows genuinely does make America look like this to many foreigners, who could be forgiven for assuming that the U.S. jumped straight from the genteel LITTLE WOMEN to the killing fields of GOLGO 13. Lacking any of the redeeming qualities of the lighter-hearted GUNSMITH CATS, *MB34* presents a stunningly infantile story in which "not doing things by the book" means shooting all suspected perps on sight and the way to snap a traumatized hostage out of shock is to "stick your finger up her ass." Based on a 1985 *Young Jump* manga by Kazuo Koike and Noriyoshi Inoue, the English dub features a new hip-hop music track, which, frankly, is one of the high points of this odious show—the mind boggles at James Brown lending his name to a show that features an episode called "Hit and Rape." The credits thank the *real-life* 34th precinct of the NYPD for unspecified assistance, though the public relations officer must have had a baby when he saw the final result—a ruthless cop hunting down the assassin who has already tried to kill him with poisoned soap, in revenge for the death of the prostitute they share on alternate weekdays. Listen, too, for the British-made dub, which seems to think that referring to civic *dooty* at irregular intervals means you've got a New York accent. ●🅛🅝🅥

MAD OLD BAG

1990. JPN: *O-Batarian*. TV series. DIR: Tetsuro Amino. SCR: Shunichi Yukimuro, Toshiki Inoue. DES: Yoshinobu Shigeno. ANI: N/C. MUS: Yasuo Urakami, Katsuyoshi Kobayashi. PRD: TV Asahi/SPO. 25 mins. x 7 eps.

The misadventures of an unpleasant old woman (compare to NASTY OLD LADY) who embarrasses her family at a school open house, makes a nuisance of herself during a vacation to a hot spring, and lusts after nice young men. Based on the 1984 manga by Katsuhiko Hotta.

MADAME BUTTERFLY

1940. JPN: *Ocho Fujin no Genso*. AKA: *Fantasy of Madame Butterfly*. Movie. DIR: Wagoro Arai, Chuya Tobiishi. SCR: N/C. DES: N/C. ANI: N/C. MUS: Tamaki

Miura. PRD: Asahi Eiga. 12 mins.
Butterfly, a faithful Japanese wife, waits patiently in Nagasaki for the return of her American husband, Pinkerton. She sees the Stars and Stripes fluttering atop an approaching ship and rightly surmises that Pinkerton is onboard. However, the feckless foreigner is arriving in the company of his "real" Caucasian wife, causing the heartbroken Butterfly to commit suicide.

This masterpiece of Japanese silhouette animation makes the best of its source material. Giacomo Puccini's 1904 opera must have seemed like an obvious choice for adaptation for a Japanese audience, particularly in the rising tide of the WARTIME ANIME that favored any opportunity to cast aspersions at Americans. Puccini's opera famously ends with Butterfly's suicide in silhouette behind a screen, making the use of all-shadow animation particularly poignant—the animated version ends just like any "live" one. However, since Puccini had only died in 1924, his opera was still in copyright, a fact that had escaped the animators until they began preparing to lay down the audio track, 18,000 frames into production. Faced with a prohibitively high demand for royalties from Puccini's estate, the producers were forced to commission new music and lyrics, thereby rather defeating the point of this "adaptation." Compare to DREAMY URASHIMA, which got away with arguably cheekier copyright infringement, and MEMORIES, which put Puccini's legacy to use after a safe time had elapsed.

MADARA
1991. Video. DIR: Yuji Moriyama. SCR: Akinori Endo. DES: Yuji Moriyama, Junichi Watanabe. ANI: Yuji Moriyama. MUS: The Great Riches. PRD: Animate Film. 60 mins. x 4 eps.
Madara is disowned by his father, King Miroku, who steals his "chakra power" and banishes him to planet Earth, where he is saved by the old man Tatara. Attacked in the forest by Miroku's evil tree-spirits, Madara swears to get back at his father, but he must contend with his brother, sent to Earth to kill him first.

Based on the 1987 manga by Sho-u Tajima, published in *Maru Sho Famicon* magazine. Episode two contains the 36-page Madara Special Edition, a sequel to the fourth volume of the manga. Creator Tajima also provided designs for KAI DOH MARU and drew the original manga of Eiji Otsuka's *MPD Psycho* (*DE).

MADCAP ISLAND
1967. JPN: *Hyokkori Hyotan Shima*. AKA: *Pop-up Gourd Island*. Movie. DIR: Taiji Yabushita. SCR: Hisashi Inoue. DES: N/C. ANI: N/C. MUS: N/C. PRD: Toei Animation. 61 mins.
After a volcanic explosion, Madcap Island is set adrift and eventually runs aground on a continent governed by man-hating dogs. The dogs of Madcap Island mount an artillery attack on the island's town, and top dog Commander Pitz takes town chief Don Gavacho prisoner. Gavacho is rescued and sets to work hatching a plot, which involves hatching fleas. The hatching flea eggs, inside balloons, are set off on a fair wind to burst over the enemy, and the plan is that nature will do the rest. But biological warfare fails, and in the end there is a gunfight between Commander Pitz and Don Gavacho's ally Machine Gun Dandy. Shown at some film festivals with English subtitles, this short movie was a spin-off from the 1964 children's puppet show *Madcap Island* (*DE), a show of immense influence during the 1960s, but which has been largely forgotten in modern times—only eight episodes of the original now survive. Creator Hisashi Inoue would later become one of the writers on MOOMINS.

MADHOUSE
Sometimes credited as Studio Madhouse, Madhouse Studios, or Madhouse Productions, the studio does not have one single location, but is scattered across several buildings in a Tokyo suburb. An animation studio founded in 1972 by several former employees of Mushi Production, including Masao Murayama, Rintaro, Yoshiaki Kawajiri, and Osamu Dezaki. Notable staffers include Toshio Hirata, Yoshinori Kanemori, Tatsuhiko Urahata, and Kunihiko Sakurai. After its first job on AIM FOR THE ACE, Madhouse has become one of the most influential studios in anime, particularly abroad in the 1990s, where its concentration on adult-oriented horror and sci-fi made its works some of the better-known anime of the video boom—particularly Kawajiri's own WICKED CITY and NINJA SCROLL. Although the studio has a long track record in video releases, it did not limit itself solely to them, ensuring that there were plenty of high profile cinema titles on its resumé—including BAREFOOT GEN, LENSMAN, and METROPOLIS. Madhouse has enjoyed a long association with Yoshiaki Kawajiri, who has directed many of its best-known releases, and also with Satoshi Kon, whose PERFECT BLUE and MILLENNIUM ACTRESS were critically acclaimed. Nor has the studio shied away from TV production, benefiting greatly from the success of CHOBITS in the early 21st century.

MADLAX *
2004. TV series. DIR: Koichi Mashimo. SCR: Yosuke Kuroda. DES: Minako Shiba, Satoko Miyachi, Satoshi Osawa, Kenji Teraoka. ANI: Satoshi Osawa, Yasuhiro Saiki. MUS: Yuki Kajiura. PRD: Bee Train, Victor Entertainment, TV Tokyo. 25 mins. x 26 eps.
Gazth-Sonica is a small country in Asia, torn by civil war and almost ignored by the rest of the world. Young noblewoman Margaret Barton lives in the little European state of Nafrece with her maid Eleanor Baker, seemingly a world away. Margaret lost her memory in a plane crash 12 years ago, and is plagued by terrifying dreams and hallucinations. Her only link with her past is a damaged, bloodstained foreign book that her missing father left for her. Margaret doesn't know that it is a holy book, sought by secret organization Enfant and its weird masked leader, Friday Monday; but she is

convinced that she must try to find her father and resolve the mystery of her past. She hires Madlax, a mercenary willing to do anything from assassination to intelligence gathering, to take her into Gazth-Sonica and find her father. The two girls seem very different—a lonely, confused teenager from a privileged background and a tough, self-reliant mercenary—but they have more in common than they know, not the least an uncanny resemblance to the lead characters of creator/director Mashimo's earlier **NOIR**. However, *Madlax* has a distinct change of pace from its predecessor in the girls-with-guns genre, telling its leads' stories in two completely separate arcs that slowly converge on each other in the course of the story. It thus takes almost half the series for the actual plotline to turn up in anything more than hints and rumors—compare to **GUNSLINGER GIRL**.

MADONNA *

1988. JPN: *Madonna: Honoo no Teacher*. AKA: *Madonna: Fiery Teacher*. Video. DIR: Akinori Nagaoka. SCR: Kaori Okamura. DES: Minoru Maeda. ANI: Minoru Maeda. MUS: N/C. PRD: Studio Junio, Toei Video, Aomi Planning. 52 mins. x 2 eps.
Well-bred young lady Mako Domon decides to be a teacher but is sent to the rough Gyunabe Technical High School, where she is put in charge of a class of juvenile delinquents. She becomes the coach for the school rugby team, which allows this sports anime to repeat the standard clichés of shows in the tradition of **AIM FOR THE ACE**, but with the added frisson of a female coach. Based on the popular manga by Ikuko Kujirai, published in *Big Comics Spirits*, and featuring Norio Wakamoto reprising his role in **GUNBUSTER** (also 1988) almost exactly as the male coach who is introduced in episode 2. Also compare to **THE GOKUSEN**, another show about reforming delinquents.

MADOX-01 *

1987. AKA: *Metal Skin Panic Madox 01*. Video. DIR: Shinji Aramaki. SCR:

Shinji Aramaki. DES: Hideki Tamura. ANI: Hiroaki Goda. MUS: Ken Yashima. PRD: AIC. 45 mins.
Overworked (but pretty) scientist Miss Kuzumoto sends the new Madox-01 military robot off for more tests, but she carelessly forgets to turn it off. The robot is lost in a crash, falling into the hands of lovable college boy Koji, who tries it on for size. Trapped inside, Koji tries to sneak across Tokyo for a midnight tryst with his estranged girlfriend, Shiori, though he has trouble looking inconspicuous. Realizing that the jealous officer Kilgore will do anything to destroy the Madox, Kuzumoto suits up in another model and tries to find out what Koji wants. All Koji wants, of course, is to get out of the suit, but he conveniently forgets to mention this until large swaths of Tokyo have been turned into smoldering rubble by the ensuing battle.
A weapon-goes-haywire story inferior to its contemporary **BLACK MAGIC**, *Madox* features a robot design also used in the same studio's **BUBBLEGUM CRISIS** but is otherwise unrelated. Tiresomely attempting to compensate for lackluster production with idle moments of "humor" and a couple of references to *Apocalypse Now*, *Madox* also makes some avoidable bloopers in its depiction of the real world—watch for military alarms that go from Defcon Three to Defcon *Four* when trouble escalates. Political types may enjoy the show's shameless characterization of Americans as belligerent morons who revel in destruction with war machines they do not fully comprehend, whereas the Japanese are all mechanically minded innocents with no interest in fighting. "You'd better not turn Tokyo into another Vietnam," Kuzumoto archly warns Kilgore, while neglecting to mention that none of this would have happened in the first place if she'd bothered to switch the Madox unit off.

MAEDA, MAHIRO

1963– . Born in Tottori. A former Studio Ghibli animator who found

fame as a designer on **EVANGELION** and **ESCAFLOWNE**, before an association with the Gonzo company that led to leading roles on **BLUE SUBMARINE NO. SIX**, **LAST EXILE**, and **GANKUTSUOU**. He also enjoyed considerable foreign recognition, thanks to his contributions to **THE ANIMATRIX** and **KILL BILL: THE ORIGIN OF O-REN**, for which he was a key animator.

MAEDA, TSUNEO

1946– . Born on Hokkaido, he found work at Mushi Production after leaving high school. He left Mushi to go freelance, and worked on children's programming such as **JAPANESE FOLK TALES**. He inadvertently became one of the pioneers of CG animation, when he served as technical director on **BIT THE CUPID**. He has also been a key animator on titles ranging from **ZOO WITHOUT AN ELEPHANT** to **THE TALE OF GENJI**.

MAGIC BOY *

1959. JPN: *Shonen Sarutobi Sasuke*. Movie. DIR: Taiji Yabushita, Akira Okuwara. SCR: Toppei Matsumura. DES: Akira Okuwara, Hideo Furusawa. ANI: Taku Sugiyama, Gisaburo Sugii, Norio Hikone. MUS: Satoshi Funemura. PRD: Toei. 83 mins.
When his pet deer is killed by Princess Yasha, mountain boy Sasuke resolves to go away to Mount Togakushi and study the art of *ninjutsu* under the master Hatsuunsai Tozawa. Bidding farewell to his elder sister Oyu, he heads off, leaving his village prone to attacks from Princess Yasha's agent, Gonkuro, and his gangs of bandits. The local lord, Yukimura Sanada, is unable to deal with the bandit problem because of a spell cast by Yasha, but he teams up with the returning Sasuke to defeat the menace. A flawed film that mixes ninja action with highly idiosyncratic work by several artists who had never worked in anime before. Compare to **SASUGA NO SARUTOBI**.

MAGIC USER'S CLUB *

1996. JPN: *Maho Tsukaitai*. AKA: *Witches' Club; I Wanna Do Magic*. Video, TV series. DIR: Junichi Sato. SCR: Akinori

Endo, Chiaki Konaka, Michiko Yokote, Sadayuki Murai. DES: Ikuko Ito, Mahiro Maeda. ANI: Ikuko Ito. MUS: Michiru Oshima. PRD: Madhouse, WOWOW. 30 mins. x 6 eps. (v), 25 mins. x 13 eps. (TV).
Earth has been invaded *again*, by ugly high-performance robots powerful enough to destroy the UN forces with a single blast. Is it the end of the world? Actually, no. The invaders just roam around observing life, don't attack unless provoked, and are very polite. Most people have gotten used to just living around them. But they're still invaders, so somebody obviously has to fight them and save Earth. Cue the members of the Kitanohashi High School Magic Club. The president, Takeo, is always trying to impress pretty (but clumsy) new recruit Sae. Androgynous vice-president Aburatsubo (who, the titles very carefully inform us, *is* a boy) is devoted to Takeo. Sae's best friend, Nanaka, has a crush on Aburatsubo . . . and remember they're supposed to be fighting the aliens. Takeo is just hoping to impress the girls by leading an attack on the invaders. So far, however, their magic isn't all that good, and with the school's Manga Club taking over their room space, he needs a project to hold the Magic Club together before all the members quit. Then things start to get serious when journalist Minowa begins finding out who these magical kids really are, and Sae finds she feels a bit more for Takeo than the respect of a junior classmate for a senior club leader.

The video series was followed in 1997 by 13 TV episodes focusing on the huge cherry tree Sae creates in the center of town in the final battle to get rid of the aliens. Its petals, far from being a nostalgic seasonal pleasure, are snowing up the roads and causing chaos. In the process of trying to get rid of the tree, the club members discover that it isn't the only unsuitable magical object plaguing the city, and they have a new mission. The video series spun off a manga version by Tami Ota, which ran in *Fantasy DX* magazine. We can think of no reason why the U.S.

release title implies there is only one "Magic User," except perhaps a lack of familiarity with English grammar.

MAGIC WOMAN M *

1996. JPN: *Maho Shojo Meryl*. AKA: *Magical Girl Meryl*. Video. DIR: Tougenan, Ahiru Koike. SCR: Hiroshi Ishii. DES: Nekoshita Pong. ANI: Takaichi Hiraizu. MUS: N/C. PRD: Beam Entertainment. 30 mins. x 2 eps.
This video was based on a manga by Nekoshita Pong that was originally serialized in *Monthly Fantazine*. Sexy young witch Meryl Shelk wanders a forest full of rapacious beasts—her only defense, the sorcerous powers she unleashes at the moment of orgasm. **LNV**

MAGICAL CANAN

2005. TV series. DIR: Masashi Abe. SCR: Mitsuhiro Yamada. DES: Akio Watanabe, Masaki Yamada, Yoshitaka Kono, Mamoru Yokota, Hiroshi Ogawa. ANI: Keiichi Ishikura, Michio Sato, Masaki Yamada, Yoshitaka Kono, Tetsuya Watanabe, Masanori Nishii. MUS: N/C. PRD: AIC, Terios, AT-X. 25 mins. x 13 eps.
Chihaya Hiiragi is a junior high school girl at Meiho Academy. She finds an injured fluffy purple-and-white creature and takes him home to tend him. As soon as he's recovered, he runs away. Following him, she sees him square off against a terrifying monster and instinctively grabs him and tries to protect him. The medallion around his neck blinks, a wand emerges, she grasps it, and suddenly transforms into a brave, athletic magical warrior called Carmine, with a pneumatic chest about seven years older than she is—compare to **MARVELOUS MELMO**. She's even more surprised when cute critter Natsuki also transforms into a hunky, spiky-haired teenage boy. After that, hearing about his homeworld of Evergreen, where creatures are born from seeds, seems reasonable enough. The seeds are getting into the human world and turning people into monsters, and Natsuki is on a mission from the Queen of Evergreen to help prevent

this. Chihaya urges him to recruit her shy friend Sayaka Mizuki, who also gets a confidence boost, plus blonde hair, a French maid outfit, and an inflated chest, along with her ability to transform into magical warrior Cerulean Blue. But the villain of the piece, Evergreen renegade Bergamot, also has his agents in the human world—his magical winged warrior Septem seems to have a link to transfer student Emi Kojima.

One of the important elements of the magical-girl series format is that magic can bestow the illusion of maturity, status, and power, and this usually involves sexualizing the heroine to some degree. Even so, the old and cynical among us, who remember when magical-girl series featured characters with chest measurements in which the letter D played no part, may be saddened to know that this is a repackaging of an earlier porn anime—filed here as **MAGICAL KANAN**.

MAGICAL EMI

1985. JPN: *Maho no Star Magical Emi*. AKA: *Magical Star Magical Emi*. TV series. DIR: Nobuyasu Furukawa, Kazuyoshi Katayama, Tomomi Mochizuki, Mizuho Nishikubo, Michiru Hongo, Tadayuki Hayashi, Takashi Anno, Fumihiko Takayama. SCR: Hiroshi Kobayakawa, Asami Watanabe, Akinori Endo, Hideki Sonoda, Sukehiro Tomita. DES: Yoshiyuki Kishi, Kazuhiko Kobayashi. ANI: Yoshiyuki Kishi, Yuji Motoyama. MUS: Keiichi Oku. PRD: Studio Pierrot, NTV. 25 mins. x 38 eps.
Would-be conjuror Mai Kazuki is playing with her brother Misaki when the fairy Topo offers to grant her a wish. She transforms herself into Magical Emi, a magical girl in the tradition of **CREAMY MAMI**, but who prefers to concentrate on more mundane concerns than her crime-fighting sisters—much of *ME*'s plot concerns her performances at her grandmother's Magicarrot Theater. As with the other magical-girl stories, Mai loses her powers as she leaves childhood behind and becomes an adult in the final episodes.

Many of the crew would go on from this obscure work to make many of the best-known anime of the late 1980s and beyond.

MAGICAL GIRL LALABELLE

1980. JPN: *Maho Shojo Lalabelle*. TV series, movie. DIR: Hiroshi Shidara, Hideo Furusawa, Masahiro Sasaki, Yuji Endo. SCR: Masaki Tsuji, Hirohisa Soda, Noboru Shiroyama, Tomoko Konparu, Tomohiro Ando. DES: Michio Shindo, Eiji Ito. ANI: Hideaki Oroku, Kiyoshi Matsumoto, Masami Abe. MUS: Taku Izumi. PRD: TV Asahi, Toei. 25 mins. x 49 eps., 15 mins. (m).

Lalabelle is a magical girl (see LITTLE WITCH SALLY) accidentally sent down to the human world. Finding a place to live with old couple Sakuzo and Ume Tachibana, she promises not to use her magic and tries to fit into the human world. She befriends two local children, Toko and Teko, but is continually forced to bend her own self-imposed rules when her town is placed in jeopardy by Viscous, a fame-obsessed conjuror, and his sidekick, Tsumio. Yet another juvenile rehash of *Bewitched*, attached to a heavy-handed moralizing tone, with each episode ending with Lalabelle's Proverb of the Week. Based on a manga by Eiko Fujiwara, better known as the author of *The Infamous Himeko*. Lalabelle also appeared in the theatrical short *MGL: The Sea Calls for a Summer Vacation* (1980).

MAGICAL GIRL TICKLE

1978. JPN: *Majokko Chickle*. AKA: *Little Witch Chickle*. TV series. DIR: Takashi Hisaoka. SCR: Tajio Tamura, Akiyoshi Sakai, Mitsuru Umajima. DES: Osamu Motohara, Hiroshi Takahisa. ANI: Takeshi Tamazawa, Kanji Hara. MUS: Takeo Watanabe. PRD: Neomedia, Nippon Sunrise, Toei, TV Asahi. 25 mins. x 48 eps.

Shy girl Chiko opens an illustrated book, only to be confronted by Tickle, a magical girl who has been sealed inside for her naughty behavior. Deciding to stay with her rescuer, Tickle uses her magic to transform herself into Chiko's twin, lives with her in her house, and attends school, hoping to study the mysteries of human behavior. Go Nagai's career as a purveyor of exposed flesh, extreme gore, and heavy metal also includes this magical-girl show for small children.

MAGICAL KANAN *

2000. AKA: *Septem Charm: Magical Kanan*. Video. DIR: Yasuhiro Matsumura. SCR: Hideki Mitsui. DES: Mamoru Yokota, Shoji Dodai. ANI: Masanobu Aoshima, Takeyasu Kurashima. MUS: N/C. PRD: Lemon Heart, Triple X. 30 mins. x 4 eps. (v1), 28 mins. x 2 eps. (v2).

"Seeds" of unmade creatures are breaking through into our world from the distant world of Evergreen, turning innocent human beings into rapacious betentacled rapists. Luckily, schoolgirl Chihaya can transform into a superheroine to fight off the menace, although she needs to do so by kissing and fondling her male associate Natsuki, a handsome teenager who can also transform into a fluffy creature that looks like a bunny. This is a pornographic anime in the style of JIBURIRU THE DEVIL ANGEL, based on the *Septem Charm: Magical Kanan* PC game. Since it has the same staff, plot, characters, and origin as the more innocent TV series MAGICAL CANAN, you would be forgiven for confusing the two. This, however, is the version with exposed T&A, and (predictably) reworks the relationships to some degree. It makes us wonder which is more revealing, that there is another porn version of an innocent Japanese TV series in the style of MASQUERADE, or that *only* the porn version is available in English. The authors have long suspected that many of the most famous names from the VANILLA SERIES and other erotic anime staff lists are pseudonyms for more established industry personnel—*Magical Kanan* may finally offer some clues. A further adventure, *Magical Kanan: Palpitating Summer Camp*, featured a trip to the beach, where Chihaya and Natsuki's love story reaches a "surprising" conclusion. **N**

MAGICAL MAKO-CHAN

1970. JPN: *Maho no Mako-chan*. TV series. DIR: Yugo Serikawa, Yoshio Takami, Minoru Okazaki, Tadaaki Yamazaki. SCR: Masaki Tsuji, Shunichi Yukimuro, Kazuko Yamamoto, Hide Ogawa, Moritada Matsumoto, Kuniaki Oshikawa. DES: N/C. ANI: Toshiyasu Okada, Shinya Takahashi, Fumi Kudo, Nobutaka Nishizawa. MUS: Takeo Watanabe. PRD: TV Asahi, Toei. 25 mins. x 48 eps.

Mako, the youngest daughter of the undersea Dragon King, defies her father and comes to the surface world. There, she falls in love with Akira, the first man she has ever seen. She asks a wise old woman to transform her into a human, knowing that she can never go back to being a mermaid. Then she goes to live with the animal-loving Mr. Urashima, longing all the while for another meeting with her beloved Akira. A mixture of LITTLE MERMAID and JAPANESE FOLK TALES, created for the screen by Masaki Tsuji under the pen-name Shinobu Urakawa.

MAGICAL MEG

1974. JPN: *Majokko Meg-chan*. AKA: *Meg the Witch*. TV series. DIR: Yugo Serikawa, Minoru Okazaki, Hiroshi Shidara, Teruo Kigure, Tetsu Dezaki, Norio Suzuki, Kazuya Miyazaki. SCR: Hiroyasu Yamaura, Shunichi Yukimuro, Masaki Tsuji, Tomohiro Ando, Fumihito Imamura, Kiyoshi Matsuoka. DES: Isamu Tsuchida. ANI: Shingo Araki, Shinya Takahashi, Minoru Maeda. MUS: Takeo Watanabe. PRD: TV Asahi, Toei. 25 mins. x 72 eps.

Meg, the oldest child in the Kanzaki family, is forever separating her quarreling brother and sister. She cannot reveal that she is really a witch, sent from Witchland to help the human world fight demons. This magical-girl anime has a distinctly European look, particularly in the streets and houses.

MAGICAL MEOW MEOW TARUTO *

2001. JPN: *Maho Shojo Neko Taruto*. TV series. DIR: Tsukasa Sunaga. SCR: Koji Naota, Koji Ueda, Akihiko Takadera.

DES: Hikaru Nanase. ANI: Hikaru Nanase. MUS: Jun Watanabe. PRD: Bandai Visual, Dentsu, TNK, Madhouse. 25 mins. x 12 eps.

Taruto, one of three cat-eared girls, believes she is the long-lost princess of the Nekomata tribe of feline sorcerers. This cynical mixture of anthropomorphic anime females, the "magical-girl" genre, and a dash of TENCHI MUYO! (since she has a shy young master, of course) is based on the manga in *Ultra Jump* magazine by the creators of STEEL ANGEL KURUMI.

MAGICAL TALRUTO

1979. JPN: *Magical Talruto-kun*. Movie. DIR: Hiroyuki Kadono. SCR: Yoshiyuki Suga. DES: Tatsuya Egawa. ANI: Hisashi Eguchi. MUS: Seiji Yokoyama. PRD: Toei. 40 mins. x 2 eps., 30 mins. x 1 eps.

Talruto escapes a nursery school in the magical dimension and comes to the human world, pursued by teacher Teichianu. In order to save the mother of his friend in the human world, Talruto decides to go back to the magical world. Then, a huge robot appears from hell. Based on a manga by Tatsuya Egawa from *Shonen Jump*.

MAGICAL PLAY

2001. JPN: *Maho Yugi*. AKA: *Magical Witchland*. Video. DIR: Hiroki Hayashi. SCR: Hideyuki Kurata. DES: Kiyohiko Azuma. ANI: Yukinori Umetsu, Chizuko Kusakabe. MUS: Seiko Nagaoka. PRD: AIC. 5 mins. x 24 eps. (2D), 29 mins. (3D).

Twelve-year-old girls from different towns in Majokko Land are sent to the central castle to take part in magical duels. The coastal port of Seahaven sends Padudu, a luckless girl who falls into a river and is washed up in the party town of Dancevalley, where she is imprisoned by the mayor, who wants to increase the chances of his own candidate winning the contest. A dejected Padudu shares her cell with Nononon, a former magical-girl candidate defeated by the current incumbent Purilun. In this combination of magical-girl genre with game-based fighting

anime, Nononon encourages Padudu to persevere and win for the sake of all underdogs. The first fully digital animation from the people who brought you TENCHI MUYO!, which similarly combined two disparate genres—can lightning strike twice? The series was also remade in 2001 as a 3D one-shot, the original being in the traditional two dimensional cel-style.

MAGICAL TWILIGHT *

1994. AKA: *The Hex Files*. Video. DIR: Toshiaki Kobayashi, Toshiaki Komura. SCR: "Hisashi Yuki." DES: Junichi Mihara. ANI: Akinobu Takahashi, Toshiaki Komura. MUS: N/C. PRD: Pink Pineapple. 30 mins. x 3 eps.

Tsukasa Tachibana is a student with problems. His exam failures are giving him nightmares; he's dreaming he's about to die. But he's not the only one with exams on his mind. Three young witches have to go to Earth to pass their final exam, and they all have the same project—Tsukasa. They'll affect his life in a weird variety of ways, though black witch Liv fails in her project to kill him after horrendous tortures. This leaves Tsukasa with two young witches on his hands. Guess who's up for hands-on tuition? A cleaned-up U.S. version is available for people who want porn with the porn removed. **Ⓝ**

MAGIKANO

2006. TV series. DIR: Seiji Kishi. SCR: Hideki Mitsui. DES: Takashi Kobayashi. ANI: Takashi Kobayashi. MUS: Katsuyuki Harada. PRD: Tokyo Kids, AT-X. 25 mins. x 13 eps.

Cynically but successfully rehashing almost every cliché in modern anime in one giant pudding, *Magikano* stars the geeky Haruo Yoshikawa, a clueless boy unaware that his three cute sisters are witches. They have shielded him from all knowledge of magic and the sorcerous realm, which becomes increasingly difficult when Ayumi Mamiya, yet another witch, arrives at their house to be a maid. Ever since looking into an old mirror as a child,

Ayumi has suffered from a curse that only Haruo can lift, and she has been ordered to work in his house until she can awaken his own latent powers and get him to dispel it. His sisters, however, are deeply suspicious of her motives. Crushingly predictable geek-girl-witch-maid-harem high jinks ensue.

MAGNOS *

1976. JPN: *Magne Robo Ga[thering] Keen*. TV series. DIR: Tomoharu Katsumata, Masayuki Akehi, Teppei Matsuura. SCR: Hiroyasu Yamaura, Tomohiro Ando, Keisuke Fujikawa, Hiroyuki Hoshiyama. DES: Kazuo Komatsubara. ANI: Kazuo Komatsubara, Toshio Nitta, Yoshinori Kanemori. MUS: Michiaki Watanabe. PRD: Japad, Toei, TV Asahi. 25 mins. x 39 eps.

The alien Izzard, former rulers of Earth, have been sleeping beneath its surface for the last two million years. Now they have awakened, and only Professor Hanatsuki of the Earth Research Institute can stop them. Luckily, he has the required teen assistants, including his daughter, Mai, and a square-jawed man named Takeru, who pilot the combining robot Ga Keen. Though Takeru is the nominal hero, the robot cannot move without Mai's presence—that's nepotism for you. A follow-up to the similar STEEL JEEG, reputedly released in the U.S. in a feature-length dub under the *Magnos* title around 1984.

MAHJONG QUEST

1992. Video. DIR: Maru-chan Program Suru. SCR: Kaneyama 6800. DES: ARG, Gekitsuio, Tattakatta. ANI: N/C. MUS: Pinch Pinch. PRD: Kaneyama 6800. 30 mins.

Animated sequences as part of a how-to guide to completing the simulation game *Mahjong Quest*, in which the player gets to see all 25 nubile opponents as well as the ending of the game, for those who weren't good enough to finish it by themselves. Bonus footage of the girls only just qualifies this release as an anime, as opposed to a rather futile spin-off from a video game.

MAHOROMATIC

2001. TV series. DIR: Hiroyuki Yamaga. SCR: Hiroyuki Yamaga. DES: Kazuhiro Takamura. ANI: N/C. MUS: N/C. PRD: Gainax, Shaft, BS-i. 25 mins. x 12 eps., (TV1), 25 mins. x 14 eps. (TV2), 24 mins. (sp.).

After long and faithful service as a Vesper Hyper Soldier fighting alien invaders in outer space, android Mahoro V1046 is permitted to choose her retirement posting. In a triumph for female subservience, she elects to live at her former commanding officer's house and work as a maid for his teenage son. However, her retirement is short-lived, not only because she is told to expect only 350 remaining operational days, but also because menaces keep on arriving and forcing her to blow her mundane cover. *Mahoromatic* channels chunks of the same studio's GUNBUSTER, with bawdy gags about breasts, self-consciously silly poetry, and the constant threat of alien attack forcing Mahoro to come out of retirement, its heroine a disposable girlfriend with a ticking time limit, like the famous LIMIT THE MIRACLE GIRL. When Japanese boys are Suguru's age, a "350-day" deadline isn't the time limit on a robot girlfriend; it's a reminder that college exams and the adult responsibilities that follow are less than a year away. Deep down, with its schooldays nostalgia and its ticking time limit, *Mahoromatic* is *really* about that other perennial Gainax subject—staying forever young.

In a "twist" reminiscent of TENCHI MUYO!, a second robot companion arrived for the sequel series *M: Something More Beautiful* (2002). The one-shot *Mahoromatic Summer Special* (2003) features a decision by the "girls" to hunt down and destroy every one of the boys' pornographic magazines, leading to a light-hearted variant on the themes of treasure hunting and saving the world. Based on the manga in *Comic Gamu* by Monjuro Nakayama and Bow Ditama.

MAHYA THE SERVANT *

2001. JPN: *Maid Meshimase*. Video. DIR: N/C. SCR: N/C. DES: N/C. ANI: N/C. MUS: N/C. PRD: Princess Productions, Obtain. 30 mins.

Embittered, hard-up college student Takahata realizes it's his lucky day when Mahya turns up at his door. She is a new hireling of an erotic maid service, commissioned by a Professor *Takada* to come and clean the place while not wearing any underwear. Takahata neglects to tell her that she's got the wrong house and proceeds to put her in a series of humiliating situations in order to get an eyeful, while trying to come up with insidious and frankly puerile ways to get around the No Touching clause in her contract. This anime is also inadvisable viewing for anyone who likes eels, since it depicts these poor creatures going where no eels have gone before; compare to BLOOD ROYALE, which tries similar tricks with an octopus. ⚫Ⓝ

MAICO 2010

1998. AKA: *Androidana Maico 2010; Android Announcer*. TV series. DIR: Kozo Masanari. SCR: Toshimitsu Shimizu. DES: Keiichi Ishiguro. ANI: Keiichi Ishiguro. MUS: N/C. PRD: Pony Canyon, WOWOW. 8 mins. x 24 eps.

In 2010, Nippon Broadcasting tries to increase its ratings by employing Maico the android as a broadcaster. An adaptation of a popular story also made into a radio drama and manga, based on an idea by AIRBATS-creator Toshimitsu Shimizu.

MAID IN HEAVEN SUPER S

2005. Video. DIR: Kurige Katsura. SCR: Kurige Katsura. DES: Masahide Yanasawa. ANI: Masahide Yanasawa. MUS: N/C. PRD: Green Bunny. 30 mins. x 2 eps.

A Japanese boy is very surprised by the sudden appearance of a maid at his messy apartment. She sets about servicing both the apartment and its owner, and eventually turns out to have been a childhood friend of his, conditioned by something he once said into a career choice that would allow her to seduce him once she was old enough. LOVE HINA meets MAHYA THE SERVANT, in

an erotic anime based on the remake version of a computer game by Pil/Stone Heads, the creators of SEXFRIEND. The "60-minute" running time is a moot point—there is actually a single 30-minute story, but there are two language tracks, one standard and one incorporating the inner monologue of one of the characters. This technique was employed in both the Japanese and English editions. ⚫Ⓥ

MAIDEN OF . . . *

1998. JPN: *Kai no Naka no Kotori*. AKA: *Little Bird in the Shell, Maiden Diaries*. Video. DIR: Hideki Takayama. SCR: Masateru Tsuruoka. DES: N/C. ANI: Hirota Shindo, Makoto Kichizaki. MUS: N/C. PRD: Discovery, Seven Eight. 35 mins. x 5 eps. (v1), 30 mins. x 2 eps. (v2).

An original take on the anime porn genre, set in 19th-century Europe, where a secret society exerts political power, controlling important figures by using a ring of professionally trained prostitutes. The ring is eventually disbanded, but Foster, the man in charge, is approached some time later by Dread Burton, a railroad tycoon who wants him to train maids to perform very particular duties—cooking, cleaning, and *submitting*. A surprisingly old-fashioned and distinctly British tale of poor waifs abused by rich cads, based on a computer game.

In the tradition of the TALES OF . . . series Kitty Films renamed the separate episodes *Maiden of Deception, Desire, Decadence*, and *Destruction*. The second episode was not released in the U.S. due to the appearance of an underage character. The series was subsequently re-released under the umbrella title *The Maiden Diaries*, although its final episode, *Maiden of Deliverance* (released as a separate DVD), had no relation to the franchise in Japan. Instead, it was a retitling of *Song of the Baby Bird* (2000, *Hinadori no Saezuri*), another entry from the DISCOVERY SERIES, of which the original *Maiden Diaries* were also a part. Although the original mansion was seen burning to the ground

Maison Ikkoku

in the original series, it has now been
fully rebuilt, just in time for the arrival
of Carol, a spoiled railway tycoon's
daughter who is accompanied by her
"friend" Liz. Liz is in fact the anime's
CINDERELLA figure, a girl pressed into
service to Carol's family to pay off her
own debts, and whose flirting with
Foster the manservant causes Carol
to order her degradation. Dungeon
domination duly ensues. ⓁⓃⓋ

MAIDS IN DREAM *
2003. Video. DIR: Genzo Sugiyama,
Yoshikazu Yabe, Naomi Hayakawa. SCR:
Rokutaro Makabe. DES: Okami Asaoki.
ANI: Mizuho Haku. MUS: N/C. PRD: Lemon
Heart, Picol. 30 mins. x 2 eps.
A nameless man, later calling himself
Akio, wakes up in a bed in a secluded
mansion, unaware of who he is or how
he got there. He is told by pretty head
maid Suzuran that he is in a place
beyond the boundaries of the real
world and that he must remain there
until he has worked through his personal issues, although since he can't
remember anything, he must wait for
his memory to return. He is haunted
by dreams of a girl with purple hair,
but soon begins fantasizing about the
maids who work at the house. Before
long, he is putting his fantasies into
action and "punishing" the maids for
a series of misdeeds, real and imagined (much to the maids' pleasure,
and to his guilt). TENCHI MUYO with

bondage, based on the PC game by
Lune. ⓁⓃⓋ

MAIL ORDER MAIDEN 28 *
1995. JPN: *Nankyoku 28-go.* AKA: *South
Pole #28; Dutch Wife 28.* Video. DIR:
Hiroshi Midoriyama. SCR: Hogara Hatta.
DES: Hachi-ko. ANI: Shinya Sasaki,
Genichi Murakami. MUS: N/C. PRD:
Sente Studio. 38 mins.
Based on a manga by TALES OF . . .
–creator U-jin and pastiching GIGANTOR
(i.e., *Tetsujin 28*), this obscure porn
title features Aiwa, a typical anime
geek, who orders a sex doll and gets
more than he bargained for. He opens
the package to discover Satomi, a lifelike, sex-crazy android, whose being a
robot is a thin excuse for portraying
a character who would be otherwise
underage. Wild sex ensues, though
Aiwa still yearns for his "real" ladylove,
the innocent Kozue, who will surely
never speak to him again unless he
can find Satomi's off-button before she
arrives. A predictable rehash of VIDEO
GIRL AI, with the flimsy plot papered
over, as in ADVENTURE KID, by the hiring
of a famous starlet to provide a voice,
in this case Mika Yoshino of the "Giri
Giri Girls." Ⓝ

MAISON IKKOKU *
1986. TV series, movie. DIR: Kazuo
Yamazaki, Naoyuki Yoshinaga, Osamu
Sekita, Setsuko Shibunnoichi. SCR:
Tokio Tsuchiya, Shigeru Yanagawa,
Kazunori Ito, Hideo Takayashiki, Tomo-
ko Konparu. DES: Yuji Moriyama, Akemi
Takada. ANI: Masaaki Kawanami, Keiko
Fukube, Ryunosuke Otonashi. MUS:
Takuo Sugiyama. PRD: Kitty, Fuji TV. 25
mins. x 96 eps., 90 mins. (m).
While he waits for the chance to retake
his university entrance exams, Yusaku
Godai lives in the Maison Ikkoku dormitory, a strange place peopled by the
party-loving Hanae Ichinose, perverse
Tom Yotsuya, and free-spirited club
hostess Akemi. But Godai soon falls
for the new apartment manager, the
pretty widow Kyoko Otonashi—a
courtship dogged by troubles from the
other tenants and from the pressure

brought by Godai's rival suitor, Mitaka.
    A popular manga from URUSEI YATSU-
RA–creator Rumiko Takahashi, the story is highly regarded in her work, not
the least because it has a beginning,
a middle, and an end, and not the
interminable repetition of RANMA ½. *MI*
was troubled by early problems—the
character designs were changed twice
before it truly got underway. It is worth
the wait, however, and is an attractive,
touching drama that shares a special
place in fans' hearts alongside KIMA-
GURE ORANGE ROAD, a similar tale of
almost-unattainable love. The series
eventually ends with the movie version,
in which plans for the long-awaited
wedding are thwarted by whispered
rumors that have Godai believing that
Kyoko is hiding an incriminating letter
from him. Capping the story while the
TV series was still running, the movie
also featured a cameo from the mystery
inhabitant of Room Two, unseen in
the TV series. A vacation special was
released straight to video as Setsuko
Shibunnoichi's *MI Side Story* (1990).

MAISON PLAISIR *
2002. JPN: *Gekka Bijin.* AKA: *Moon,
Flower, Beauty.* Video. DIR: Hisashi
Okezawa. SCR: Joichi Michigami. DES:
Takanari Hijo. ANI: Yuki Kinoshita. MUS:
Sentaro. PRD: Discovery. 30 mins. x
2 eps.
When Seiichi's father discovers him
training his stepmother in bondage
and submission instead of studying,
he throws his wayward son out of the
house. Seiji moves into the Kazenaha
boarding house and soon discovers
that there is a secret crawlspace that
allows him to peek in on the other
rooms and their attractive occupants.
This in turn leads to the discovery that
his widowed landlady Miyuki misses the
bondage sessions she experienced at
the hands of her late husband. Seiichi
assists her in getting over her grief to
the extent that she can urinate on a
picture of her late husband while tied
up—it's hardly MAISON IKKOKU! Then
Seiichi's stepmother finds his new
address and comes to visit him with her

nubile daughter Kiriko. Scatology and more urine are involved in another entry in the **Discovery Series**. Ⓝ

MAJOR

2004. TV series. DIR: Kenichi Kasai. SCR: Rikei Tsuchiya. DES: Katsu Oshiro. ANI: Taro Sato. MUS: Noriyuki Asakura. PRD: Studio Hibari, NHK Enterprise 21, NHK. 25 mins. x 26 eps. (TV1), 25 mins. x 26 eps. (TV2).

Widowed pro baseball player Shigeharu Honda struggles to raise his son Goro on his own. Goro aspires to be a baseball player like his father; meanwhile, Goro's school teacher Momoko finds herself falling for Shigeharu, in a baseball romance along the lines of **Touch** or **Slow Step**. Based on the manga in *Shonen Sunday* magazine by Takuya Mitsuda.

MAKI PRODUCTIONS

Often credited as Maki Pro. A titling house that performs a relatively simple process, adding credits to animation or blank screens to make the opening or closing titles. Since all anime have credits, Maki Pro's name appears in a huge number of titles, although its role is limited. We presume that Maki Pro's role may have extended to other forms of effects, known in Japanese as "Ris Work," such as the addition of mist or fog effects to preexisting film. These jobs, however, are few and far between since the advent of digital animation, allowing most studios to add such effects in-house.

MAKOTO-CHAN

1980. Movie. DIR: Tsutomu Shibayama. SCR: Noboru Shiroyama, Masaki Tsuji, Tsunehisa Ito, Tomoko Konparu. DES: Osamu Kobayashi. ANI: Osamu Kobayashi. MUS: Ryo Kawagami. PRD: Tohoku, TMS. 85 mins.

Kindergarten kid Makoto tries hard to be a good boy but is dumped by his nursery-school sweetheart, Anko-chan. Walking through the park feeling sorry for himself, he meets Yuko Daiyu, a grown-up who has also just had her heart broken. They get along well with each other, but for Yuko, flirting with a little boy is just a game, and Makoto is soon left heartbroken again. Recovering from the experience, he performs a mini-play for his mother on Mother's Day, looks after some sparrow's eggs, and attempts to win the "Good Child" award at his nursery. An unusual comedy based on the short manga *Small Sweetheart, Mother's Day Present, Love Lunch Pack, Sparrow's Eggs,* and *Good Child Award* by **Boy with Cat's Eyes**–creator Kazuo Umezu, who also sings the theme song with his backing group, the Super Police.

MALICE@DOLL *

2001. Video. DIR: Keitaro Motonaga. SCR: Chiaki Konaka. DES: Shinobu Nishioka, Yasuhiro Moriki. ANI: N/C. MUS: N/C. PRD: @ Entertainment. 30 mins. x 3 eps.

In an indeterminate underground realm, robot prostitute Malice goes in search of repairs. Instead, she is ravished by a tentacled beast, and wakes to discover that her previous doll form has been replaced with a living, breathing, feeling body. Initially shunned by her former associates, she soon converts her fellow prostitutes into a similar life-state by kissing them, though the transformation process often leaves them hideously malformed. When even the cynical Doris asks her for a kiss, Malice worries about the aftereffects of the transformation, and goes in search of some way of undoing the spell. In the repair shop, she is told that this is all a dream—a doll dreaming of being human, or a human dreaming of being a doll? Whatever the answer, Malice's spirit escapes from bondage, leaving her former colleagues behind.

Malice Doll cleverly makes virtues out of its many vices. Whereas many late-20th-century anime augmented their cel work with computer graphics, *MD* improves its *digital* animation with the addition of old-fashioned cels, neatly papering over the cracks between the polished yet static images of the dolls—supposedly in a studied jerki-ness inspired by the puppet animations of Jan Svankmajer. Chiaki Konaka's script cunningly calls for a virtually expressionless cast, and the animators conceal the shortcomings of their work in copious shadows and montages seemingly inspired by the work of French filmmaker Chris Marker.

Depending on one's point of view, *MD* is either a fairy-tale allegory of the end of childhood, or a misogynist fantasy of redemption through rape—*Pinocchio* for perverts. Its heroine is an unfeeling sex-toy, seeking "repair" as oil trickles down her shapely legs; she is haunted by the image of an angelic child and molested by an icthyphallic menace. She wakes after her ordeal to discover that it has made her warmer, more sensitive, and sassy—she is now clad in revealing bad-girl garb, and targeted by a succession of other lustful monsters.

This is not the first time that Konaka has dealt with fetishes and gender issues—*MD* shares several tropes with the writer's earlier work on **Bubblegum Crisis** and **Armitage III**, along with rich pickings for psychiatrists, who will be intrigued to observe the depiction of life itself as a sexual disease. Missing its original release date, *MD* was crucially delayed just a moment too long. By the time its first episode reached video stores in 2001, Japan was already swept up in hype over the flashier (and immensely more costly) **Final Fantasy**: *The Spirits Within,* and *MD* sank without a trace. That was an unfortunate fate, as *MD*'s artful exploitation of its own limitations makes it an interesting object lesson in low-budget filmmaking. It was eventually released as a single feature, with a misleading "2003" copyright date that only really referred to the date of the feature-length compilation and concealed the fact that, in the fast-moving world of computer animation, *Malice Doll* was already two years behind the times. Note: the "at" symbol in the title is merely a typographical adornment; it was never intended to be pronounced. ＮⒹ

MAMA LOVES POYOPOYOSAURS

1995. JPN: *Mama wa Poyopoyo-saurus ga Osuki*. AKA: *Mom Loves Poyopoyosaurs*. TV series. DIR: Hiroshi Nishikiori, Futa Morita, Shinya Hanai, Masahiro Hosoda, Teppei Matsuura. SCR: Mamiko Ikeda, Minori Ikeno, Tomoko Ishizuka. DES: Takako Aonuma. ANI: Tatsuo Miura, Hiroshi Tsukawa, Kenichi Imaizumi, Hirokazu Ishiyuki, Masayuki Hiraoka. MUS: N/C. PRD: TBS, Nippon Animation. 25 mins. x 52 eps.

Cute but high-strung two-year-old Jura Poyota and her elder brother, stolid four-year-old Hyoga, are spoiled rotten by their doting grandparents and often drive their parents crazy, simply by being normal kids. Mom Miki struggles to keep her career as a writer of children's books alongside taking care of her family; husband Gendai does his best to help, but sometimes he drives her as crazy as the children. A modern SAZAE-SAN, based on the best-selling manga by Takako Aonuma, this comedy of family life focuses on raising two children of kindergarten age in modern day Tokyo. Each episode is split into two mini-stories, hence leading to some broadcast lists filing this as a 104-episode show.

MAMA'S A FOURTH GRADER

1992. JPN: *Mama wa Shogaku Yonensei*. TV series. DIR: Chuichi Iguchi, Kazuki Akane, Nobuyuki Kondo, Nana Harada. SCR: Satoshi Nakamura, Tetsuko Watanabe. DES: Yoshiko Kamimura. ANI: Toshikazu Endo, Kisaraka Yamada, Atsushi Aono. MUS: Hayato Kanbayashi. PRD: Sunrise, Nippon TV. 25 mins. x 36 eps.

Japanese schoolgirl Natsumi gets the fright of her life when her own baby daughter falls through a time warp from 15 years in the future. A comedy with elements of the future offspring of SAILOR MOON and the unwilling babysitter of BABY AND ME. Later episodes veer away from a teen-unwed-mother farce and into science fiction, as Natsumi attempts to return Mirai-chan ("Future") to her rightful time.

MAN WHO CREATED THE FUTURE, THE

2003. JPN: *Asu wo Tsukutta Otoko—Tanabe Sakuro to Biwako Soryu*. AKA: *The Man Who Created Tomorrow: Sakuro Tanabe and Biwa Lake Incline*. Movie. DIR: Shinichi Ushiyama. SCR: Jun Sekiguchi. DES: Shungiku Uchida. ANI: Seiji Arihara. MUS: N/C. PRD: Mushi Productions. 86 mins.

In 1869, the capital of Japan is relocated to Tokyo, leaving Kyoto as something of a backwater. Concerned over the city's imminent decline, the council proposes to deal with a recurring seasonal water shortage by building a canal to bring fresh water and provide a transport route from Lake Biwa to Kyoto. This was the first domestically run civil-engineering project in modern Japan, and thus a suitable subject for educational anime. Twenty-one-year-old engineering student Sakuro Tanabe (1861–1944) outlines the project in his undergraduate thesis, and the president of his college puts his name forward to Governor Kitagaki. Despite strong opposition from local politicians and foreign engineers, the Governor and the young engineer persuade the Meiji government to go ahead, and work commences in 1885. Tanabe and his colleague Bunpei Takagi visit the U.S.A. in 1888 to study the world's first hydroelectric power plant in Colorado, and Tanabe adds such a plant to the canal project. Keage Power Plant is completed in 1891 and still supplies power to Kyoto. The canal, which runs partly underground and partly on a stunning brick aqueduct, is finally completed in 1912. Tanabe later becomes professor of engineering at Kyoto Imperial University. Based on the snappily titled book, *Kyoto Incline Story*, by Yoshiko Tamura, the project obviously pushed all the right buttons—heritage, human interest, a good role model, and national pride. Note the presence of manga artist Uchida, creator of *Minami's Sweetheart* (*DE), in a rare anime staff role—animation being used for all the big-budget Meiji era scenes, while other elements used live actors in taking the history of the canal forward to the present day. Compare to the STORY OF SUPERCONDUCTORS.

MANGA MITO KOMON

1981. TV series. DIR: Kazuyuki Okaseko, Yoshio Nitta, Hiroshi Yoshida. SCR: Tsunehisa Ito, Yoshiaki Yoshida, Masatoshi Fuji. DES: Keisuke Morishita. ANI: Emiko Minowa. MUS: Kentaro Haneda. PRD: Knack, TV Tokyo. 25 mins. x 46 eps.

Though he looks like a humble traveler, this old man is really Mitsukuni Tokugawa (aka Komon Mito [Mito Komon]), the shogun's uncle, traveling Japan incognito in the company of some feisty young heroes—sword master Sasaki, mountain-of-a-man Atsumi, ninja-boy Sutemaru (with Junpei his faithful hound), and pretty maiden Okoto. The group wanders the land in search of trouble, cowing its opponents into submission by brandishing Mito's *inro*, a lacquered case bearing the shogun's crest. A remake of a popular live-action TV series, originally based on the novels of Sanjugo Aoki (1891–1934). The story reached its widest audience through a live-action NTV series in 1954, and its incredibly long-running successor on TBS, which lasted from 1969 to 2000 and wore out three leading men (this anime version was made shortly before Eijiro Higashino was replaced by Hikaru Nishimura in the live version). Budgets kept the live-action version to human-interest stories such as corrupt merchants and samurai, but the anime production was able to introduce more fantastic elements from JAPANESE FOLK TALES. The same set of legends was a distant inspiration for STELLARBUSTERS and ROBOT KING DAIOJA. See also SAMURAI GOLD, another popular story retold in anime form.

MANGA PICTURES OF JAPAN

1977. JPN: *Manga Nippon Emaki*. TV series. DIR: Noboru Ishiguro, Kazuhiko Udagawa, Yasuo Hasegawa. SCR: Kenji Terada, Tomomi Tsutsui. DES: Tsuneo Ninomiya, Kazuo Imura, Takashi Nakamura. ANI: Osamu Kamijo. MUS: Yutaka Soda. PRD: World Television, Anime Room, TBS. 25 mins. x 46 eps. Deliberately less faithful to fact than **JAPANESE HISTORY**, this series happily throws in apocryphal anecdotes and legends about the figures it portrays, normally two to an episode. Suitable subjects, famous in Japan though not always famous enough for the internationally minded **GREAT PEOPLE** series, include many figures from the Heike-Genji War, such as woman warrior Tomoe Gozen, doomed samurai flautist Taira no Atsumori, and Nasu no Yoichi, who shot a fan off a pole to preserve Minamoto honor at the battle of Yashima. Other stories depict Anju and Zushio (see **LITTLEST WARRIOR**), Iwami no Jutaro's victory against a giant baboon, and the tale, oft-referenced in anime from **INU YASHA** to **USHIO AND TORA**, of Fujita no Tawara's fight with a giant centipede.

MANMARU THE NINJA PENGUIN

1997. JPN: *Ninpen Manmaru*. TV series. DIR: Tetsuo Yasumi. SCR: Haruya Yamazaki, Ayako Okina, Masaaki Sakurai. DES: Yuichiro Miyoshi. ANI: Nobuhiro Okaseko, Yoshio Kabashima. MUS: N/C. PRD: Shinei, TV Asahi. 10 mins. x 48 eps.
Manmaru goes to ninja school at Nenga, where foxes and raccoons study the art of assassination under a bear ninja master. He is soon thrown into local rivalry between the Nenga school, the Koga (monkeys), and the Iga (dogs), as well as facing temptations from the Dobe, a group of dropouts from the Nenga. A lighthearted adaptation of ninja folktales, based on a manga by Mikio Igarashi, creator of **BONOBONO**.

MAN'S AN IDIOT!

1970. JPN: *Otoko do Aho Koshien*. AKA: *Koshien's an Idiot*. TV series. DIR: Akira Nono. SCR: Tajio Tamura, Tadaaki Yamazaki. DES: Shiro Tamura. ANI: Shiro Tamura. MUS: Mamoru Sasaki. PRD: Nippon TV. 25 mins. x 26 eps.
Koshien Fujimura is named after the biannual high school baseball championship, so it's only natural that he grows up to be absolutely crazy about the sport. Failing a school entrance exam because he has been training too hard, he ends up at party-school Nanba High. Befriending ace catcher Mametan, he decides to join his new school's baseball team but faces opposition from the bad-boys of the school. Based on a manga by **DOKABEN**-creator Shinji Mizushima, working with Mamoru Sasaki. The original manga has more space to tell the story of Koshien's family and school life; the anime leaves his parents out altogether and ends with his first year in high school. The anime was originally shown in short segments, every night but Sunday.

MANUAL OF NINJA MARTIAL ARTS

1967. JPN: *Ninja Bugeicho*. Movie. DIR: Nagisa Oshima. SCR: Nagisa Oshima, Mamoru Sasaki. DES: Sanpei Shirato. ANI: Akira Takada (photography). MUS: Hikaru Hayashi. PRD: Sozosha. 117 mins.
A barely animated adaptation of Sanpei Shirato's long-running manga tale retelling the life of Kagemaru, a charismatic ninja leader in Muromachi era Japan. Shirato's art is shown in still montages shot by a rostrum camera. The film was directed by Nagisa Oshima, also known for *Merry Christmas, Mr. Lawrence, Gohatto,* and *In the Realm of the Senses.*

MANXMOUSE *

1979. JPN: *Tondemonezumi Dai Katsuyaku*. AKA: *Overactive Mouse; Legend of M.; Adventures of M.* TV special. DIR: Hiroshi Saito. SCR: Hiroshi Saito. DES: Yasuji Mori, Yoshiyuki Momose. ANI: Yoshiyuki Momose, Noriko Moritomo. MUS: Akira Nakagawa. PRD: Nippon Animation, Fuji TV. 84 mins.
Meyer the English village potter creates a mouse when drunk one night, but the blue, long-eared, tailless Manxmouse comes to life. Setting out to see the world, he leaves Buntingdowndale and is warned on several occasions to beware of the Manx Cat. After helping rescue a friendly circus tiger, Burra Khan, from crooked London pet shop owner Mr. Petman, Manxmouse confronts the fearsome Manx Cat, who turns out to be a gentlemanly creature who invites him to tea. The two decide to stay friends, in contravention of the traditional antagonism between their species as set down in the ancient Book of Destiny. Based on the book by Paul Gallico, written to entertain the late Grace Kelly (Princess Grace of Monaco, see **CASTLE OF CAGLIOSTRO**) after she gave him one of the first model mice she made in pottery class.

MANY DREAM JOURNEYS OF MEME, THE

1983. JPN: *Meme Iroiro Yume no Tabi*. TV series. DIR: Yoshio Kuroda, Kazuyoshi Yokota, Takayoshi Suzuki. SCR: Yoshio Kuroda, Nobuyuki Isshiki. DES: Shuichi Seki. ANI: Sadahiko Sakamaki. MUS: Takeo Watanabe. PRD: Nippon Animation, TBS. 25 mins. x 129 eps.
Daisuke and Sayaka explore the world of science, accompanied by Meme the pixie, who has popped out of their computer screen. In the second season, they were replaced by a coterie of seven children who spend more time solving mysteries, but the series still had a heavily educational angle, as one might expect for something originally designed to promote the Tsukuba Science Expo.

MAO-CHAN *

2002. JPN: *Rikujo Boeitai Mao-chan*. AKA: *Land Defense Force Mao-chan*. TV series. DIR: Yoshiaki Iwasaki. SCR: Yosuke Kuroda. DES: Masahide Yanagisawa. ANI: Yoshio Suzuki. MUS: Takayuki Hattori. PRD: Pioneer, Xebec, TV Tokyo. 12 mins. x 26 eps.
Japan's Self Defense Force has often been rolled out in anime and science fiction, instructed to save the world from all kinds of dangers, from Godzilla to the attacking angels of **EVANGELION**. But not all alien menaces require the SDF's full level of firepower. Mao Onigawara, aka Mao-chan, is a cute preteen girl whose grandfa-

ther happens to be the Chief of Staff for the Land Defense Unit. Dressed inexplicably like drum majorettes, she and her fellow girls deal with the cuter forms of alien invasion. As insanely over-privileged military brats, they get to do so by flying 1:1-scale model kits into battle, although their foes often turn out to be incredibly cute, fluffy aliens, which can often be dealt with by the simple expedient of tapping them on the head with a baton.

Each comes down from space in a toy capsule, which breaks open once safely in the atmosphere; then the being inside floats down to Earth on a candy-colored parachute. So far, the invaders haven't actually done anything more evil than crowd out tourist spots, and there is minimal public support for the use of force against these endearing aliens; the authorities have to fight cute with cute. As in certain other shows that take themselves a little more seriously, the answer lies in using the aliens' own weaponry against them, mainly through badges made of retrieved alien material. Shaped like clovers with smiley faces, these "chibi SMA" items react to the power of the universe and the fighting spirit of the wearer, enabling her to transform.

A cheerful parody of anime's alien invasion excesses, this show also includes several walk-on cameos for cast members from creator Ken Akamatsu's earlier Love Hina, although their identity is often masked for copyright reasons. Where once anime sought to allegorize the trauma of Japan's defeat in a terrible war, it now sanitizes and homogenizes it all to look like a glorified treasure hunt out of Pokémon. The aliens, however, are smarter than they look and have infiltrated major positions of power and influence, like the student council presidency of Mao-chan's high school. However, since the aliens' reaction when found out and told how naughty it is to invade is to apologize and go away, a bloodbath is never in the cards. Even their supposedly evil emperor, Galaxy King, is a Pillsbury doughboy

who just says "Oh!" and steams gently when defeated. Silly and sweet.

MAPLE COLORS *

2005. Video. DIR: Ryo Kanda. SCR: Yasuyuki Muto. DES: Shiro Shibata. ANI: Shiro Shibata. MUS: N/C. PRD: Cross Net, Image House, Milky, GP Museum Soft. 30 mins. x 2 eps.
Transfer student Ryojiro Saku gets off to a bad start when he is caught committing a violent crime with pretty Mirao Aoi in front of the head of the drama club. In order to save Class 2-B from indefinite suspension, Ryojiro agrees to a contest against the drama club, which somehow means he has to cajole his reluctant classmates into a series of porn performances. Based on a computer game of the same name. **LNV**

MAPLETOWN STORIES *

1986. JPN: Mapletown Monogatari. TV series, movie. DIR: Junichi Sato, Keiji Hisaoka, Yukio Misawa, Hiroyuki Kadono. SCR: Chifude Asakura, Shigeru Yanagawa, Tomoko Konparu, Keiji Kubota, Keiko Maruo. DES: Tsuneo Ninomiya. ANI: Kazuo Komatsubara, Hiroshi Shidara, Shingo Araki. MUS: Akiko Kosaka. PRD: Toei, TV Asahi. 25 mins. x 52 eps., 25 mins. x 44 eps. (New), 24 mins. & 30 mins. ("movies").
Mapletown is a peaceful community of talking animals, where the Hoprabbit family opens a post office. Middle daughter Patty is an innocent female but often caught up in the schemes of the evil Gretel the Wolf. However, Patty is able to triumph with the help of her friends, Bobby the Bear, Diana the Fox, and shy genius Johnny the Dog. A second series, New MS (1987), directed by former lead animator Hiroshi Shidara, dumped all the characters except Patty and her sister Lolly, who set off on a journey to the southern resort of Palmtown to live with the kindly Nurse Jane. Each of the series also had a movie spin-off, though on available evidence, both "movies" appear to have been TV episodes shown in theaters as part

of holiday season multiple bills. The series was a very early job for future Sailor Moon–director Junichi Sato. Shown on Nickelodeon in the U.S.

MAPS *

1987. Movie, video. DIR: Keiji Hayakawa. SCR: Kenji Terada. DES: Hatsuki Tsuji. ANI: Hatsuki Tsuji. MUS: Kohei Tanaka. PRD: Studio Gallop (m), KSS (v), 51 mins. (m), 30 mins. x 4 eps. (v).
Teenager Gen Tokishima is abducted with his girlfriend, Hoshimi Kimizuka, by the huge spaceship Lipmira that's shaped like the body of a beautiful woman. Gen is a "map-man," the last descendant of an ancient tribe, on whose body there is a map of a secret route, the Flowing Light of the Nomad Star Tribe. Accompanied by Lipmira, the female space pirate and electronic brain of the ship, Gen begins a search for the Flowing Light, though the galaxy's treasure hunters are soon hunting him, hoping to swipe his birthright.

An incoherent and badly plotted story, supposedly based on a manga by Yuichi Hasegawa but with characters looking quite different from the original. Lipmira's spaceship, however, is a design triumph—a giant flying statue, inspired by the Spirit of Ecstasy found on the hood of every Rolls Royce automobile. A 1994 video remake, directed by Susumu Nishizawa, was the incarnation released in the U.S.

MÄR

2005. AKA: Marchen Awakens Romance. TV series. DIR: Masaharu Okuwaki. SCR: Junji Takegami. DES: Toshiyuki Komaru. ANI: Toshiyuki Komaru. MUS: Daisuke Ikeda. PRD: Shogakukan, TV Tokyo. 25 mins. x 33+ eps.
Ginta is a loser in our own world who never seems to get anything right, but when he travels through the magical portal into the world Mär Heaven he discovers that he has incredible powers in a world under threat from the Chess enemy. Although supposedly "based on a manga" by Nobuyuki Anzai in Shonen Sunday weekly, Mär has all the hallmarks of a show conceived by a

committee, designed to halfheartedly rehash all the standard clichés and create a new franchise for Shogakukan, the publisher who not only owns *Shonen Sunday*, but also the studio behind the 3D CG transformation sequences and the Business Center credited with arcane "Planning Assistance."

MARCO POLO

1979. JPN: *Marco Polo no Boken.* AKA: *Adventures of Marco Polo.* TV series. DIR: Katsuhiko Fujita, Masami Hata, Kazuyuki Sakai. SCR: Masao Maruyama, Michiru Kaneko, Hideo Takeuchi, Soji Yoshikawa. DES: Akio Sugino. ANI: Masaki Mori, Yoshiaki Kawajiri, Toshio Hirata, Hideo Nishimaki, Hideo Takayanagi. MUS: Takanori Onosaki, Kei Ogura. PRD: MK, NHK Promote Service, NHK. 25 mins. x 43 eps.
When his mother dies in Venice, young Marco must accompany his merchant father Niccolo and uncle Maffeo on a trip along the Silk Road to the mysterious East. Many years later, when the travelers' wanderings bring them to China, an older, wiser Marco becomes a trusted adviser to the Great Khan, Kublai. An early collaboration by many of the names who would go on to form the Madhouse Studio, this series depicts the man whose writings on the famous "Land of the Rising Sun" would inspire COLUMBUS to set out in search of it.

MARDOCK SCRAMBLE

2006. Video. DIR: Yasufumi Soejima. SCR: Tow Ubukata. DES: Range Murata, Gota Nanami, Mahiro Maeda, Shigeto Koyama. ANI: N/C. MUS: N/C. PRD: Gonzo. 30 mins. x ?? eps.
In the crime-ridden city of Mardock, the shocking murder of a young girl leads the city authorities to pass the law "Scramble 09," permitting the use of previously forbidden techniques and technologies in the apprehension of the killer. The murder victim, Balut, is brought back from the dead with the new ability to manipulate electricity and goes in search of her killer, who is soon revealed as Shell, her former lover, who uses his periodic memory losses as the perfect alibi to shield himself from ever confessing, even inadvertently, to a series of grisly crimes. Based on a novel by scriptwriter Tow Ubukata, who also created FAFNER. ⓥ

MARGARET VIDEO SERIES

1993. JPN: *Shueisha Margaret Video Series.* Video. DIR: Takuji Endo, Tsukasa Abe, Asami Watanabe, Tomihiko Okubo. SCR: Akinori Endo, Kenichi Araki, Tatsuhiko Urahata. DES: Tomihiko Okubo. ANI: Kazuhiro Soeta, Masaru Kitao. MUS: Satoshi Okada. PRD: Madhouse. 40 mins. x 6 eps.
A series of romantic tales, all adapted from manga originally serialized in the girls' magazine *Margaret.* The first, *A-Plus for the Fashion Boy* (*O-Sharaku Koso wa Hana Maru*), based on a manga by Tsueko Ansei, features Hodaka, a successful young businessman whose life is turned upside down when he falls in love with a 14-year-old schoolgirl. *Singles*, based on a manga by Mari Fujimura, moves the setting to a university, where student Saki is torn with guilt over her feelings for her sister's boyfriend, Yo. She joins the same club to be close to him but is selected to work on a project with another boy, Daichi. Though she feels herself drawn to Daichi, she cannot put thoughts of Yo from her mind. *Pops*, based on a manga by Aya Ikuemi, is an even simpler tale of teenage angst, as two young students fall in love but must endure the pressures of their studies, the opposition of their parents, and the teasing of their classmates. *Sleepless Edo* (*Oedo wa Nemuranai*), based on *Moonlit Night: Starry Dawn* by Noriko Honda, is a period drama set in the Yoshiwara pleasure district of old Tokyo, where a courtesan, a thief, and a doctor become involved in a love triangle. In *Kiss My Eyes* (*Kiss wa Me ni Shite*), based on an original by Noriko Ueda, average schoolgirl Ibuki falls for a handsome exchange student newly arrived from the U.S. For the final episode, *A-Girl*, based on a manga by Fusako Kuramochi, sisters Mariko and May, along with Mariko's bad-tempered boyfriend, become involved with Ichiro, an arrogant, womanizing male model. At the artist's request, *A-Girl* was shown with subtitles, but no dialogue.

MARINA THE MANGA ARTIST GOES TO CAMELOT

1990. JPN: *Mangaka Marina Time Slip Jiken: Ai to Ken no Camelot.* AKA: *Marina the Manga Artist's Time Slip Incident: Love and Swords of Camelot.* Video. DIR: Fumiko Ishii. SCR: Hitomi Fujimoto, Asami Watanabe. DES: Ayume Taniguchi. ANI: Masahiro Koyama. MUS: Kazz Toyama. PRD: Ashi Pro. 45 mins.
Marina and her adoring circle of gorgeous young boys are transported back in time to England in the Middle Ages [*sic*], where they help a young King Arthur acquire his sword, Excalibur. Cashing in on the success of Hitomi Fujimoto's popular *Marina the Manga Artist* series of novels for teenage girls, this one-shot was also shown theatrically. Camelot would also appear in the longer-running KING ARTHUR AND THE KNIGHTS OF THE ROUND TABLE.

MARINE A GO GO *

2001. JPN: *Soreyuke Marin-Chan.* AKA: *Go! Marin; Soreyuke Marin-Chan.* Video. DIR: Masami Obari. SCR: N/C. DES: N/C. ANI: N/C. MUS: N/C. PRD: KSS, Pink Pineapple. 30 mins. x 3 eps.
Japan is facing a population crisis, and Catholic schoolgirl Marin is out to do her best to save her country. Enlisted into "Project Preservation of Japan" by a professor concerned that the birthrate will fall so low that the Japanese race will die out, she must take part in an attempt to collect sperm samples from 100 Japanese men in the style of DNA HUNTER. But there's opposition to the plan from the diabolically cute Marilyn, who even builds a sex android, the blonde and bounteously endowed South Pole One, designed to look like the Japanese idea of an American porn star, to exterminate Marin's targets through exhausting sex. Corny but consensual is the keynote here. Based on a porn comedy

manga by Hideki Nonomura and
Sanae Komiya. ⊙Ⓝ

MARINE BOY *

1966. JPN: *Ganbare Marine Kid*. AKA: *Go
for It, Marine Kid*. TV series. DIR: Haruo
Osanai, Masaharu Endo, Yoshiyuki
Tomino, Suguru Sugiyama. SCR: Hiroshi
Yamauchi, Masaki Tsuji, Morimasa
Matsumoto, Tomohiro Ando. DES: N/C.
ANI: Masaharu Endo. MUS: Tetsuo Tsu-
kahara. PRD: Toei, TBS. 25 mins. x 78
eps. (combined series).

Inspired in part by the novel *Deep
Range* by Arthur C. Clarke, the Toei
Studio made three pilot episodes of
Dolphin Prince, the tale of an undersea
boy with a pet dolphin, who swam in
a wetsuit with a built-in jetpack and
stunned his enemies with an aqua-boo-
merang. An experiment in color anime
that predated KIMBA THE WHITE LION
(the first *broadcast* color anime), Suguru Sugiyama's *DP* was shelved but then
remade the following year as *Marine
Boy*. Marine, whose father, Dr. Mariner,
is an oceanographer with the Ocean
Patrol, has been genetically altered to
have superior underwater swimming
abilities and chews Oxygum to supply
himself with air underwater. Along
with his companion, Whitey the white
dolphin (Splasher in the U.S. version),
Marine helps his father keep the sea
safe. Though originally intended for
broadcast on Fuji TV and subsequent
sales overseas, the production was
dogged by difficulties, and taken off
the air after just 13 episodes.

The series returned with the same
crew in 1969, retitled *Undersea Boy
Marin* (*Kaitei Shonen Marin*), for further adventures about Marine, now
equipped with an underwater boomerang, a hydrojet, and a mermaid girlfriend Neptuna (Neptina in the U.S.
version). It lasted for a total of 78 episodes, including some recycled from
the previous series. Broadcast on TBS,
the entire run was not seen until 1971,
when it was shown on Nippon TV.

During all this confusion, the series
was already doing well in the U.S.,
where it premiered in 1966. With three

episodes dropped for violence, *Marine
Boy* still incurred the wrath of the
National Association for Better Broadcasting, which claimed it was "one of
the very worst animated shows. Child
characters in extreme peril. Expresses
a relish for torture and destruction of
evil characters." Strangely, no mention
was made of Neptuna's strategically
placed hair, which obscured the fact
that she spent the entire series topless,
or that the three "violent" episodes
were considered harmless enough to
be screened when the series was rerun
during the 1970s. Though obscure
today, *Marine Boy* was a popular anime
in its time, outperformed in the 1960s
only by SPEED RACER in the U.S. and
the first anime to achieve any degree
of success in the U.K., though its Japanese origins were occluded. According
to popular myth, decades later, the
same BBC that screened *Marine Boy* in
the 1970s would turn down POKÉMON,
claiming that "nobody was interested
in Japanese cartoons." In another spurious assertion, the father of the five-
year-old Jonathan Clements claimed
that "Marine Boy always eats his
greens," though none of our Japanese
sources support this.

MARINE EXPRESS

1979. JPN: *Kaitei Cho Tokkyu Marine
Express*. AKA: *Undersea Super Express:
Marine Express*. TV special. DIR: Osamu
Dezaki, Tetsu Dezaki. SCR: Osamu
Tezuka. DES: Keizo Shimizu. ANI: Shige-
taka Kiyoyama, Hitoshi Nishimura. MUS:
Yuji Ono. PRD: Tezuka Pro, Nippon TV.
93 mins.

Murder on the Transpacific Express,
as private investigator Shunsaku Ban
boards an undersea train on its inaugural trip from California to Japan
in 2002, tracking the killer of the
director of the Public Construction
Corporation. Meanwhile, architect Dr.
Nasenkopf, much-praised designer of
the train, has had a change of heart
and now decides he should destroy his
creation before it forever changes life
in the Pacific. As if that wasn't enough,
the feckless Mr. Credit, U.S. Secretary

of State, is using fake passenger dum-
mies to smuggle laser weapons, and
the train's engineer is convinced that
he can see visions of the legendary
queen of the undersea empire of Mu
(see SUPER ATRAGON). Confused? You
will be, because then the train falls
through a time tunnel, traveling ten
thousand years back to a time before
Mu sank beneath the waves. Widely
regarded as one of Osamu Tezuka's
best works, this TV movie manages
to mix Easter Island, invading aliens,
time travel, and murder mystery—
which just goes to show that not every
complex story line needs to be as
messy as LAWS OF THE SUN. As seems traditional for Tezuka TV movies, several
of his other characters make cameo
appearances, including ASTRO BOY
(as Adam, robot "son" of Nasenkopf,
who is "played" by Dr. Ochanomizu),
BLACK JACK, AND THE THREE-EYED PRINCE,
all voiced by their original voice
actors. *ME*, however, crams cameos
in to insane levels (Queen Sapphire,
Empress of Mu, is actually PRINCESS
KNIGHT, who arrives riding on the
adult KIMBA THE WHITE LION), and
also casts against type, with many of
Tezuka's traditional good-guys playing
evil roles. The theme tune features
vocals from Tommy Snyder of the pop
group Godiego, who also contributed
to GALAXY EXPRESS 999.

MARINE SNOW

1980. TV special. DIR: Leiji Matsumoto,
Fumio Ikeno. SCR: Keisuke Fujikawa.
DES: Leiji Matsumoto, Katsumi Saka-
hashi. ANI: Seiji Yamashita. MUS: Hiroshi
Ogasawara. PRD: Studio Uni, Mini Art,
Now Planning. 81 mins.

Another tale of underwater expansion,
suspiciously similar to the previous
year's MARINE EXPRESS. Once again,
there is a conflict between the land
and sea people, this time caused by a
series of underwater cities constructed
by the surface-dwellers to ease over-
crowding on a future Earth. Construction worker Hiroshi Umino notices
that his colleague Nami Shimaoka
is behaving suspiciously—shortly

afterward, construction is halted by a saboteur's bomb. Someone (no prizes for guessing who) claiming to be Izanami, the Queen of the Sea People, challenges the surface-appointed ruler Zerbert, demanding that the sea people be left in peace. Written and directed by CAPTAIN HARLOCK–creator Leiji Matsumoto.

MARIS THE CHOJO *

1986. JPN: *Rumic World: The Supergal*. AKA: *Supergal; Maris the Wondergirl* (U.K.). Video. DIR: Tadamasa Takahashi. SCR: Tomoko Konparu. DES: Katsumi Aoshima. ANI: Tadamasa Takahashi. MUS: Ichiro Arata. PRD: Studio Pierrot. 48 mins.

Space Police Officer Maris comes from Thanatos, a world of incredibly high gravity, so she has to wear a harness to prevent her superhuman strength from damaging people and objects around her—she often causes massive collateral damage nevertheless. She jumps at the chance to wipe out her debts by rescuing Koganemaru Matsushita, a handsome kidnap victim. Her mission forces her (and her alien sidekick, Murphy, the Irish-accented, nine-tailed fox) into a wrestling ring with her old rival, Zombie Sue. The harness comes off for a no-holds-barred showdown, though the entire affair is revealed to have been orchestrated by the bored Matsushita (a cop-out plot twist as unimaginative as "it was all a dream"). Combining intergalactic crime-busting of the DIRTY PAIR with a martial arts comedy from manga creator Rumiko Takahashi, this is one of her weakest offerings. Part of the *Rumic World* series that also brought us FIRE TRIPPER, LAUGHING TARGET, and MERMAID'S FOREST. As with IRONFIST CHINMI and LOCKE THE SUPERMAN, the original U.S. title was altered in the English-language market to avoid legal conflict with the owners of a U.S. comic character. The production was noted at the time for including fake "outtakes" along with the closing credits—an idea later adopted by Pixar for *A Bug's Life*.

MARMALADE BOY *

1994. TV series, movie. DIR: Akinori Yabe, Atsutoshi Umezawa, Yasuo Yamakichi, Satoshi Yamada. SCR: Aya Matsui, Yumi Kageyama, Motoki Yoshimura. DES: Yoshihiko Umakoshi. ANI: Yoshihiko Umakoshi, Hiroyuki Kawano, Michio Sato. MUS: Keiichi Oku. PRD: Toei, TV Asahi. 25 mins. x 76 eps. (TV), 30 mins. (m).

A bizarre wife-swapping variant on the *Brady Bunch*, as two married couples decide to exchange partners and live together in an extended family, with their children Miki Koshikawa and Yu Matsura becoming stepsiblings and inevitably falling for each other. Love triangles extend into love polygons, as more male and female characters are introduced, each trying to tempt the lovers from their true desires. The initial premise, however, is stretched to absurd lengths by the series' long broadcast run, with the initial humor of the strange family setup soon fading before seemingly endless rivals in love, breakups over nothing, and reconciliations. The show's quite unexpected success caused it to run ahead of the manga, with new characters and situations not present in the original, causing the plots to diverge. In the spirit of CHILD'S TOY, a genuinely quirky setup whose quiet success far exceeded that of its more famous contemporaries—it ran for three times longer than the "mega-hit" EVANGELION. The story was cleverly completed in a 1995 "movie" that functions as both a prologue and epilogue. Flashing back to the day Yu is first told his parents are to divorce, it reveals that he has worshipped Miki from afar since before the beginning of the series and helps to explain exactly what he really sees in Miki, a mystery that had befuddled many fans for the duration of the series. Based on the 1992 manga by Wataru Yoshizumi. Following the earlier success of the romance HANA YORI DANGO as a Mandarin live-action TV series, *MB* was similarly adapted with real human actors and broadcast in Taiwan (2002, *Juzi Jiang Nanhai*).

MARS DAYBREAK *

2004. JPN: *Kenran Butosai: The Mars Daybreak*. AKA: *Gorgeous Tango: The Mars Daybreak*. TV series. DIR: Kunihiro Mori. SCR: Miya Asakawa, Jiro Takayama, Yuichi Nomura. DES: Koji Osaka, Yoshinori Sayama, Michiaki Sato, Kenji Mizuhata. ANI: Koji Osaka. MUS: Kaoru Wada. PRD: TV Tokyo, BONES, Dentsu. 23 mins. x 26 eps.

Mars now has oceans, but the end of an interstellar war has thrust the planet's economy into deep recession. Frustration and deprivation have led to riots among the colonists, separatist movements, and widespread looting and piracy. The Earth government means to suppress the trouble—a combination of the revolution of GUNDAM and the human flotsam of COWBOY BEBOP, both of which were earlier production credits for first-time director Mori.

Gram River lives from hand to mouth, drifting through a variety of temporary and casual jobs in one of Mars' floating cities. By chance he is asked to pilot a Round Buckler, a humanoid mobile suit, "The Vector of Hope." The suit's almost obsolete—the older models were used to fight the interstellar war and most are remote-controlled nowadays—but Gram finds he has a knack for handling it. When this leads to another offer of work with the same machine at a higher rate of pay than he's used to, he's just too tempted to weigh the risks. He finds himself on the pirate submarine The Ship of Aurora, under the command of the tough and scary Captain Elizabeth Liati. They're on the run from a Round Buckler squadron from Earth, and by coincidence the squadron leader is Gram's childhood friend Vestemona (aka Ves, but surely a Japlish mangling of Desdemona) Lauren. She was adopted years ago by a rich Earth family and now commands the Mars Division of the Sol Global Forces. When the two old friends reunite, they are on opposite sides of the law—she's the hunter and he's the hunted.

The fancy names of the suits and the romantic undersea settings, plus the talking cat and dolphin, which can get around in its own humanoid-shaped environment suit, all betray a fascination with pirate tales and submarine yarns. The story, based on a computer game by Sony, owes as much to *Seaquest DSV* (1993) and *Pirates of the Caribbean* (2003) as to anything else; yet there's something irresistibly appealing about oceans and glaciers on Mars and about a butch dyke and a crew of talking beasts and deadbeats taking on the might of the Empire. The anime world, never one to ignore a good idea that was not yet wholly wrung of all saleability, flooded Mars again the following year in ARIA.

MARVELOUS MELMO

1971. JPN: *Fushigina Melmo*. AKA: *Mysterious Melmo*. TV series. DIR: Osamu Tezuka, Yoshiyuki Tomino, Fusahito Nagaki. SCR: Osamu Tezuka, Morimasa Matsumoto, Tatsuo Shibayama, Ran Seki. DES: Osamu Tezuka. ANI: Shigeru Yamamoto, Toshiyasu Okada. MUS: Seiichiro Uno. PRD: Tezuka Pro, TBS. 25 mins. x 26 eps.

When her mother "goes to Heaven" after a traffic accident, young Melmo receives a jar of red and blue candy that allows her to magically age ten years and turn into a young woman and also return to her normal age. In ASTRO BOY–creator Tezuka's take on the popular magical-girl genre typified by CREAMY MAMI and LITTLE WITCH SALLY, Melmo decides to use the candy, which was intended to allow her to survive her childhood without an adult protector, for the greater good. As the series progressed, Melmo's age swings became more pronounced—she comes close to dying of old age or regressing back to "prehuman" fetal states. This allowed her to reorder her cells as she regrew to gain temporary animal characteristics like fur or a strong sense of smell in order to aid her with the task at hand. On the 70th anniversary of Tezuka's birth, the series was rereleased on video as *Melmo: Renewal*, with an all-new voice and music track and Maria Kawamura

replacing Reiko Fujita as Melmo. The story was remade again as part of a trilogy of live-action TV specials, *Osamu Tezuka Theater* (2000), along with Tezuka's *Canon* and *Lunn Flies into the Wind* (see LION BOOKS).

MASAKI, MORI

1941– . Pseudonym for Masaru Mori. Sometimes miscredited as Mori Masaki. A sometime manga artist who also works as an animator, Masaki joined Mushi Production in 1963 and worked on KIMBA THE WHITE LION, among other shows. He left in 1968 to devote himself to manga, but was tempted back in 1979 to direct DRIFTING CLOUDS for Madhouse. He has also scripted several anime, including DAGGER OF KAMUI and HARMAGEDON.

MASAOKA, KENZO

1898–1988. Born in Osaka, he moved to Tokyo to study Western art. His first anime was Nikkatsu's *Monkey Island* (1931, *Sarugashima*), which he soon followed with the groundbreaking talkie, THE WORLD OF POWER AND WOMEN (1934) for Shochiku. His World War II output was the allegorical fairy tale *The Spider and the Tulip* (1943), an advanced integration of animation and live-action. After the war, he made SAKURA (1946), although it was not distributed, before making his most popular work, *Tora the Stray Cat* (1947, *Suteneko Tora-chan*) and its sequel *Tora's Bride* (1948, *Tora-chan to Hanayome*). Citing lack of financial returns in the animation business, Masaoka retired to illustrate children's books.

MASHIMO, KOICHI

1952– . Sometimes miscredited as Koichi Mashita. Born in Tokyo, he began his media career in TV documentaries and commercials, before joining Tatsunoko in 1975. He went freelance in 1984, subsequently setting up the company Office Free Hands. He is the long-serving director of anime from DIRTY PAIR through AI CITY, to modern works such as NOIR and .HACK.

MASHURAMBO

2000. AKA: *Shinzo*. TV series. DIR: Tetsuo Imazawa. SCR: Mayori Sekijima. DES: Yoko Kamimura. ANI: Yoko Kamimura. Ken Ueno. MUS: N/C. PRD: Toei, TV Asahi. 25 mins. x 32 eps.

In the far future, the human race has lost a bitter war with the alien Matrixer life forms. Three hundred years after the Matrixer victory, a human boy and girl wake up from cryogenic suspension to discover that the Matrixers have overrun the surface of Earth and they are probably the last humans alive.

MASK OF GLASS

1984. JPN: *Gurasu no Kamen*. TV series. DIR: Gisaburo Sugii, Hideo Makino, Seiji Okuda, Tsuneo Tominaga. SCR: Keisuke Fujikawa, Tomoko Konparu, Tomoko Misawa, Yukifude Asakura. DES: Makoto Kuniho. ANI: Keizo Shimizu, Jiro Tsujino, Masami Abe. MUS: Kazuo Otani. PRD: Eiken, Nippon TV. 25 mins. x 23 eps. (TV1), 45 mins. x 3 eps. (v), 25 mins. x 51 eps. (TV2).

Inspired by Chigusa Tsukikage, a star who retires due to injury, Maya Kitajima resolves to become an actress and joins her idol's theater troupe. Pushed to the limit by Chigusa, who turns out to be a tough taskmistress, Maya trains to perform the infamous Red Angel role solo, all the while repudiating the adoring advances of boy-next-door Masami Hayami and competing with her fierce rival from the Theater Undine, Ayumi Himekawa. Based on the ongoing 1976 *Hana to Yume* manga by Suzue Miuchi, *MoG* is Sugii's tribute to *Flashdance*, but it slips easily into the clichés of sports anime such as AIM FOR THE ACE, even with the sport removed. The titular "mask of glass" is the invisible dramatic energy an actress wears in front of her audience. A three-episode video series *GM: The Girl of a Thousand Masks* (*Glass no Kamen: Sen no Kamen wo Motsu Shojo*) was released in 1998, and the television series was remade in 2005 under the original title. There have also been numerous theatrical productions, and a two-season live-action TV adaptation beginning in 1997 (*DE).

MASQUERADE *

1998. JPN: *Gosenzo Sane*. AKA: *Ancestor's Glory*. Video. DIR: Yusuke Yamamoto. SCR: Ryota Yamaguchi. DES: Masaki Kajishima, Kazunori Takahashi. ANI: Kazunori Takahashi. MUS: T. K. Crow. PRD: AIC. 30 mins. x 2 eps.

When his mother dies, Gen Hiraga goes to live with his grandmother, the rich chancellor of an exclusive college. Pursued by Jennifer Collins, a feisty foreign PhD student, he discovers that one of his ancestors discovered the alchemical secrets of immortality. A woman who sleeps with Gen and receives his golden sperm (or "aquapermanence") can prolong her lifespan for a considerable time. Needless to say, this makes Gen popular with the ladies, starting with Beth, a nubile woman who claims to be over 400 years old, though she strangely still works as a maid for his grandmother.

As the TENCHI MUYO! audience *finally* reached puberty, the franchise had its last gasp in a couple of pornographic pastiches. SPACESHIP AGGA RUTER handled the sci-fi end, while *Masquerade* takes the same stereotypes and dumps them in a horror setting. After a suspenseful, artistic beginning that toys with the viewer's expectations for almost a quarter of an hour, the story turns to the requisite sex, falling to pieces in a ludicrous series of assignations as a set of desperate women try to milk Gen for his particular elixir of life. Laughable hokum, helped not a bit by a listless dub spoken by actors who understandably cannot believe what they are saying. **Ⓝ**

MASTER KEATON *

1998. TV series. DIR: Masayuki Kojima. SCR: Tatsuhiko Urahata, Tomoko Konparu, Hideo Takayashiki. DES: Kitaro Takasaka. ANI: N/C. MUS: Kuniaki Haishima. PRD: Madhouse, Nippon TV. 25 mins. x 24 eps. (TV), 25 mins. x 15 eps. (v).

Half-English, half-Japanese ex-soldier Taichi Keaton is a divorced university lecturer and a part-time private investigator on behalf of the Lloyds insurance syndicate. His investigations take him into many dangerous situations, but his survivalist training always helps him out, as does his plucky daughter, Yuriko. Bravely concentrating on the more cerebral elements of the original 1988 manga by Hokusei Katsushika and Naoki Urasawa, the anime version takes Keaton all around the world, with stops at London's Chinatown (looking suspiciously like Yokohama's, which must have been closer for the studio's picture researchers), Stonehenge, the Middle East, and all over Europe. Combining the wandering, supersmart troubleshooter of *Indiana Jones* or LUPIN III with an introverted investigator in the mold of Sherlock Holmes (even to the extent of a Baker Street office address). Seemingly influenced by the popularity of *Riverdance, Braveheart,* and *Titanic,* the anime production also comes heavily smeared with misplaced Celtic whimsy, particularly in Haishima's folksy musical score.

MASTER OF MOSQUITON *

1996. JPN: *Master Mosquiton*. Video, TV series. DIR: Hiroshi Negishi, Satoru Akahori. SCR: Satoru Akahori. DES: Takahiro Kishida, Kazuya Kuroda. ANI: Hideki Watanabe. MUS: Osamu Tezuka (not *the* Osamu Tezuka!). PRD: Zero-G Room, TV Tokyo. 30 mins. x 6 eps. (v), 25 mins. x 26 eps. (TV).

Tomb-raiding hokum as spunky redhaired Transylvanian schoolgirl Inaho raises the mild-mannered vampire Mosquiton as part of her quest for immortality. Eschewing the simple option of simply letting him suck on her neck, she drags him off on a treasure hunt for the legendary life-prolonging "O-part," in a madcap version of 1920s Europe that soon includes alien invaders in a giant pyramid and battles with Rasputin and the Count de Saint Germaine for control of London. With undertones of a controlling yet adoring parent and angrily dependent child who wants everything to be the same forever, *Mosquiton* shows early promise but soon buries it beneath weak humor (signposted, in typical Satoru Akahori style, by pratfalls from a writer who doubts that the audience will notice it otherwise) and strident bickering from an Inaho voice actress who may once have had depth but comes across in the dub as nothing more than a spoiled brat. The English-language script also seems ignorant of the many historical characters and references, though it does inject some genuinely funny gags, many of which were not present in the original. In Japan, the series was brought back from the dead after its video run as the TV series *Mosquiton 99*—though it was taken off the air in 1998, not surviving to reach the year for which it optimistically named itself.

MASUDA, TOSHIO

1927– . Born in Kobe, he graduated in 1949 from the Osaka Foreign Languages University, and studied screenwriting with the New Toho script division. He began working as a scenarist and assistant director for Toho and then Nikkatsu, solely in the live-action field, with his best-known contribution being that to *Tora! Tora! Tora!*. In the anime world, he played a major staff role in STAR BLAZERS. "Toshio Masuda," credited with several anime scores in this book, is a different individual.

MATASABURO THE WIND IMP

1988. JPN: *Kaze no Matasaburo*. Video. DIR: Rintaro. SCR: N/C. DES: Yoshinori Kanemori. ANI: Yoshinori Kanemori. MUS: Fujio Miyashita. PRD: Argos, Madhouse. 30 mins.

Heartrending tale of new student Saburo Takada, who comes to a ramshackle school with only one classroom in a remote valley. By the time he has befriended the shy village children, it is time for a sad farewell. Based on the children's story by Kenji Miyazawa, who also created NIGHT TRAIN TO THE STARS. The same author's *Wildcat and the Acorns* was animated the same year by Toshio Hirata as a 25-minute video.

MATSUGORO THE WOLF

1989. JPN: *Okami Matsugoro*. Video. DIR: Hidetoshi Omori. SCR: Norio Soda.

DES: Hidetoshi Omori. ANI: Hidetoshi Omori. MUS: N/C. PRD: Nippon Animation. 50 mins.

Schoolboy gang-leader Matsugoro swears revenge when his lieutenant Koume's house is burned down by a land speculator in an insurance scam. In this unlikely adaptation of the *Shonen Magazine* manga by Minoru Ito, Matsugoro takes on the local gangsters by himself. **Ⓥ**

MATSUMOTO, LEIJI

1938– . Pseudonym for Akira Matsumoto; sometimes credited as Reiji Matsumoto, the "Leiji" is his preferred romanization. Born in Fukuoka Prefecture, Matsumoto was still a 15-year-old high school student when he published his first manga. He went to Tokyo in 1958, where he continued to pursue a manga career, although he worked chiefly in girls' comics for many years—his adoption of the Leiji Matsumoto pseudonym signifying his eventual break with previous work drawn under his own name. He took a direct hand in the production of anime adaptations of his work, contributing to STAR BLAZERS as a director and designer and elements of the CAPTAIN HARLOCK franchise as a designer and screenwriter. The bulk of his anime credits, however, is as the creator of the original manga on which an anime happens to be based. He has been involved for some years in a legal dispute with producer Yoshinobu Nishizaki over who is the creator and hence controller of *Star Blazers* (i.e., *Space Cruiser Yamato*), which remains a lucrative source of merchandising, spin-off, and remake revenue.

MAYA THE BEE *

1975. JPN: *Mitsubachi Maya no Boken*. AKA: *Adventures of Maya the Honeybee*. TV series. DIR: Hiroshi Saito. SCR: Fumi Takahashi. DES: Susumu Shiraume. ANI: Toshio Nobe, Takao Ogawa. MUS: Takashi Ogaki. PRD: Nippon Animation, Peter Film, TV Asahi. 25 mins. x 52 eps.

Flighty young honeybee Maya learns from her teacher, Cassandra, how to fly and collect pollen. But she is so good at her job that she exhausts the supply in the area surrounding her hive and must head out to find a new field of flowers—whereupon she has many adventures with beetles, grasshoppers, and her friend Willy, who is sent by the Queen Bee to find her. It's another tale of a bug's life, similar to HUTCH THE HONEY BEE but based on the 1929 children's book by Waldemar Bonsels and made as a coproduction with the German company Peter Films. The series was shown on Nickelodeon back in the days before a Japanese origin was something to boast of, and, consequently, it is not generally known as "anime." A sequel, *New Maya* (made soon after but not screened until 1982), featured a new crew and was chiefly animated by the inferior Wako Production. It centers on Maya waking from hibernation and discovering that her friend Phillip the Grasshopper's house has been burned during the winter. Meeting Phillip's savior, Mousey the mouse, they begin a series of new adventures.

MAZE *

1996. JPN: *Maze Bakunetsu Jiku*. AKA: *Maze: Exploding Dimension*. Video, TV series. DIR: Akira Suzuki. SCR: Katsumi Hasegawa, Satoru Akahori. DES: Eiji Suganuma, Masayuki Goto. ANI: N/C. MUS: N/C, Seikima-II. PRD: JC Staff, TV Tokyo. 30 mins. x 2 eps. (v), 25 mins. x 25 eps. (TV).

By day, Maze is a girl who wanders the countryside protecting exiled princess Mill of Bartonia, whose kingdom has been overrun by the Jaina Holy Group. But by night, she transforms into a brash, annoying, sex-obsessed boy. A lighthearted (and lightweight) cross of RANMA ½ with THE WIZARD OF OZ, featuring the same look, plot, and often gags as Satoru Akahori's earlier BEAST WARRIORS and a stereotypical supporting cast that includes ninja Solude, the demi-hunter (barbarian warrior) Aster, the female knight Rapier, and the old wizard Woll. Their opponent is a pretty-boy cast from the same mold as ESCAFLOWNE's Dilandau and is unabashedly named Gorgeous. The original video series was designed for an audience that had already read the books and listened to the radio show, so it consequently dumps the viewer right into the middle of the action without any explanation, expecting them to thrill to the self-indulgent quips and breakneck pace, all designed to hide the fact that nothing new is happening. For the older video audience, it is also considerably more risqué, loaded with erotic humor and innuendo. The later TV series takes things a little more slowly and conservatively, opening with Maze's original arrival in this never-never land of giant robots and dueling princes, but even this introduction does little to hide the show's off-the-peg origins, so typical of so many 1990s video anime, although this one did at least survive to reach television. **Ⓝ**

MAZINGER Z *

1972. AKA: *TranZor Z*. TV series, movie. DIR: Yugo Serikawa, Tomoharu Katsumata, Fusahito Nagaki, Yasuo Yamakichi, Takeshi Shirato, Masayuki Akehi, Nobutaka Nishizawa (TV 1–2), Yoshio Hayakawa, Hideharu Iuchi (TV3). SCR: Susumu Takahisa, Keisuke Fujikawa (TV1–2), Hiroyuki Onoda, Masaki Tsuji (TV3). DES: Go Nagai (TV1–2), Satoshi Hirayama (TV3). ANI: Koji Uemura, Masamune Ochiai, Keisuke Morishita (TV1–2), Hideyuki Motohashi, Tsutomu Shibayama (TV3). MUS: Hiroaki Watanabe (TV1–2), Kentaro Haneda (TV3). PRD: Dynamic Planning, Toei, Fuji TV (TV1–2), TMS, Nippon TV (TV3). 25 mins. x 92 eps. (TV1/*Mazinger*), 25 mins. x 56 eps. (TV2/*Great Mazinger*), 25 mins. x 23 eps. (TV3/*God Mazinger*).

Robot inventor Dr. Hell (Dr. Demon) wants to control the world with his MachineBeasts, who are led into battle by his minions, Baron Ashler/Ashura (Devleen, "half man, half woman, and the worst of both"), whose body is literally split down the middle, left side male and right side female, and Count

Broken (Count Decapito), a cyborg who carries his head tucked underneath his arm. His attacks are resisted by the Photon Research Institute (Volcanic Research Institute). Photon inventor Dr. Kabuto's grandson, Koji (Tommy Davis), works out how to operate Mazinger Z, Kabuto's giant superalloy robot (see GODAIKIN and SHOGUN WARRIORS), climbing inside its head and using it to fight back against Hell, aided by his stepsister, Yumi Sayaka (Jessica), her robot Aphrodite A (later upgraded to Diana Alpha 1), and Boss Borot (Bobo-bot), a comic-relief machine driven by the local tough-guy, Boss. Based on a 1972 *Shonen Jump* manga by Go Nagai, *Mazinger Z* (*TranZor Z* in the U.S.) was the first "pilotable" robot, not a sentient being like ASTRO BOY or a remote-controlled toy like GIGANTOR. This changes the relationship between the young hero (and therefore the viewer) and the robot; instead of merely observing its actions, the viewer wears it like a suit of armor and controls it as if he and the robot were one. Secondly, the robot bristled with cool weapons that were all activated by the hero calling out their names ("Rocket Punch!"), which added to the viewer's involvement in the show as well as the play value of the toys. The "gadgets 'n' gimmicks" approach was to have a long life in robot merchandising—see GUNDAM, EVANGELION, et al.

After the 43-minute crossover movie *Mazinger Z vs.* DEVILMAN (1973), the show returned as *Great Mazinger* (1974). With Koji absent in South America, the pilot of the new, improved prototype is Tetsuya Tsurugi, with new token girl Jun Hono (and her token girl robot Venus Ace) and Boss Borot retained from the old series. They were fighting the subterranean army of Mikene and its mechanical monsters, led by Jigoku Daisensei, the reincarnation of Dr. Hell. Koji returned for the grand finale and would also appear in the Nagai robot-series GRANDIZER along with Boss Borot. The robots appeared again in short cinema

outings alongside other Go Nagai creations including *Mazinger Z vs. the General of Darkness* (1974), *Great Mazinger vs.* GETTER ROBO G (1975), and *Great Mazinger/Grandizer/Getter Robo G: Battle the Great Monster* (1976).

The concept was also rehashed as the short-lived *God Mazinger* (1983). Japanese teen Yamato Hibino is sucked through a time warp into the past, where the dinosaur army of the Dragonia Empire threatens the world, and Queen Aira of Mu (see SUPER ATRAGON) needs Yamato to help her fight back with the aid of the guardian God Mazinger, which looks suspiciously like a giant robot. Their chief opponent is the evil Emperor Dorado of Dragonia and his golden-haired son, Prince Eldo, whose vendetta against the dark-haired Yamato was only just beginning when the series was canceled. Though Nagai still drew the tie-in manga, the anime robot was designed in "the Nagai style" by Satoshi Hirayama. More remote tie-ins were the 1988 *Mazinger* manga Nagai wrote and Ken Ishikawa painted for First Comics (the first manga done specifically for U.S. release) and the Mazin Kaiser robot created for Banpresto's *Super Robo Wars* multi-platform game in 1991, which subsequently featured in the video anime *Mazin Kaiser* (2001). Finally, the lead robot in Nagai's PSYCHO ARMOR GOBARIAN bears a staggering resemblance to Mazinger Z.

MD GEIST *

1986. JPN: *Sokihei MD Geist*. AKA: *Armored Devil-Soldier MD Geist*. Video. DIR: Hayato Ikeda. SCR: Takashi Sanjo. DES: Tsuneo Ninomiya, Koichi Ohata. ANI: Hiroshi Negishi, Kenichi Onuki, Hirotoshi Sano. MUS: Yoichi Takahashi. PRD: Hero Media. 45 mins. x 2 eps. Humankind leaves Earth behind and spreads out among the stars. On the distant world of Jerra, a group of rebels called the Nexrum begin a war of attrition, demanding that Jerra split from Earth's authority and seek its own independence. In the bloody war that ensues, the military devises a series of

genetically enhanced superwarriors, the Most Dangerous Soldiers. Combined with their powerful armored exoskeletons, they are unstoppable. For reasons that aren't terribly clear, one particular Most Dangerous Soldier is imprisoned on a satellite, even though the war is still raging. An indeterminate number of years later, he falls back to the surface into a ravaged postapocalyptic wasteland. After killing the leader of a biker gang, Geist (for it is he) decides to lead his new followers to save a beleaguered mobile fortress, which is coincidentally commanded by his old boss, Colonel Krups. The assassination of the president activates a Doomsday machine called Death Force, and the soldiers are on a mission to stop it, lest the world be overrun with legions of robot berserkers. Geist signs up for the final assault, lots of people get killed, and then there's an ending with several twists in it, the last of which makes the whole race-against-time of the previous hour utterly pointless.

With 1980s fashions, squealing guitar music, and simplistic postholocaust bikers-in-a-desert, Geist is a product of the era that gave us *Mad Max*, FIST OF THE NORTH STAR, and VIOLENCE JACK. And there it might have stayed were it not for the U.S. company Central Park Media, which uses Geist in its corporate logo, throwing money at the Japanese to blow the dust off this 1986 stinker and produce the previously canceled *Death Force* sequel (1996)— today, these two awful offerings are most likely to be found conjoined in a full-length "director's cut."

MD Geist is cheap and nasty, featuring some of the world's most halfhearted dialogue and plotting, including a seduction scene where a female character strips solely for the benefit of the camera—not even Geist can be bothered to watch her. The plot is riddled with holes. Why is Krups still alive when Geist returns from suspended animation? Why hasn't the supposedly oppressive Earth government sent reinforcements? Why is Death Force

MD Geist

triggered by so inconsequential an event as the death of a president when the world has already been nuked almost to oblivion? There are tiny moments of interest, including a pastiche of *Easy Rider* (1969) when Geist destroys a pocket watch. There are the vaguest hints of subtlety as Krups and Geist duel for the men's respect; Krups by giving them halfhearted pep talks (though that could be the dub, of course), while Geist just "is" the ultimate warrior. And Jason Beck, who plays Geist in the U.S. dub, has a great voice. But these virtues are few and far between in an anime that, despite some respected names in the credits, is one of the medium's more brain-dead offerings. It was, however, the first time that U.S. interest and money resulted in the commissioning of a sequel to an anime video. **LNV**

ME AND I: THE TWO LOTTES

1991. JPN: *Watashi to Watashi: Futari no Lotte*. TV series. DIR: Kanetsugu Kodama, Yukio Okazaki. SCR: Michiru Shimada. DES: Shuichi Seki. ANI: Hisatoshi Motoki, Toyomi Sugiyama. MUS: Kazuo Otani. PRD: Tokyo Movie Shinsha, Nippon TV. 25 mins. x 29 eps.

During summer school, Louise meets Lotte, a girl who looks uncannily like her. Though they initially avoid each other, they eventually become friends and discover that they are twin sisters, raised separately by their divorced parents. Resolving to get their parents back together, they swap families for a while and begin a series of deceptions in order to engineer a reunion that means the chance to live as one family. Adding several new plot threads but remaining ultimately faithful to the original, *Me and I* was based on Erich Kastner's novel *Das Doppelte Lottchen* (1949), which was also adapted into the British film *Twice upon a Time* (1954) and a couple of Hollywood versions, including *The Parent Trap* (1961). In Japan, it was also turned into a musical as well as a live-action film, which starred Hibari Misora as both girls.

MECCANO

1995. JPN: *Mechano Scientific Attack Force*. Video. DIR: Hideyuki Tanaka, Nick Phillip, Yasuaki Matsumoto. SCR: N/C. DES: N/C. ANI: Takeshi Hirota. MUS: Pierre Taki. PRD: Sun Electronics. 29 mins.

A short animated collection produced

by Pierre Taki of the musical group Denki Groove. It includes the CG Western *Plastic Gun Man*, *World Meccano Triangle*, for which he wrote the music, and the cel animation *Prime Minister of Gray Hill* (*Haiirogaoka no Soridaijin*). The last sequence is a parody of a famous 1977 manga by Akira Mochizuki.

MEDABOT *

1999. JPN: *Medalot Damashii*. AKA: *Medarot Spirits, Techno-Robot Battle Adventure*. TV series. DIR: Katsuhisa Yamada. SCR: Akihiko Inari, Takashi Yamada. DES: N/C. ANI: Hiroyoshi Iida. MUS: N/C. PRD: NAS, TV Tokyo. 25 mins. x 48+ eps.

In a.d. 2022, children use their "medabot" robot toys to fight in "robattles." Young boy Ikki finds a medal (a medabot CPU) that has been stolen by the phantom thief Retort. Installing it in a beat-up, secondhand medalot unit, he discovers that it is a rare kind of medallion that imparts superhuman strength to its medabot. With his friends Metabee, Rokusho, Koji, and Arika, he fights off the "bad guys" Fishface, Calamari, Gillguy, and Squidguts in a succession of robot battles. This series is a cash-in on a 1977 Imagineer computer game, with robot combat indebted to **PLAWRES SANSHIRO**, doubtlessly brought back from the dead in the wake of **POKÉMON** because there are 222 basic Medalots, and merchandise beckons.

MEGAMAN *

2002. JPN: *Rockman.EXE*. AKA: *Megaman Battle Network; Megaman: NT Warrior*. TV series. DIR: Takao Kato. SCR: Keiichi Hasegawa, Kenichi Yamada, Masaharu Amiya, Mayori Sekijima. DES: Mitsuru Ishihara, Koji Watanabe. ANI: Xebec. MUS: Katsumi Hori. PRD: TV Tokyo, Capcom, NAS, Shogakukan, Xebec. 24 mins. x 56 eps. (TV1); 24 mins. x 51 eps. (TV2); 24 mins. x 51 eps. (tv3); 30 mins. x 3 eps. (v). Hikari Netto and his NetNavi Megaman (Rockman in Japan) set out to become the best NetBattlers, defending the Net from evil Operators like the sinister World 3, the Dark-Loids, and the alien NetNavi Duo, in the process. Beginning life as the Capcom video game *Rockman* in 1987, back at the beginning of the gaming boom that would bring **Street Fighter II**, this show's protagonist was created as a lab assistant to doctors Thomas Light and Albert Wily, but following Wily's turn to the dark side, Megaman/Rockman is turned into a battle android to protect the world.

The original platform game was later converted into a cartoon series by American animation company Ruby-Spears, which does not qualify it as anime. The Capcom website also claims that a Japanese-made straight-to-video *Rockman* two-parter was released in 1993 and 1994. Following the cancellation of the American series at the beginning of its third season, the franchise was revived in its anime form as *Rockman.EXE*, a series based loosely on the contents and plots of the first two games. This was followed by later seasons: *Rockman.EXE Axess* (2003, based on the fourth game), *Rockman. EXE Stream* (2004, not directly linked to any one game), and *Rockman.EXE Beast* (2005). An edited version of *Rockman. EXE* airs in America as *MegaMan NT*.

Protagonist Rock, paired with his canine assistant Rush, has a certain superficial resemblance to the superhero and wonder dog combination of **Casshan: Robot Hunter**. Their world and adventures, however, are very different. Set in the year 200X (and therefore firmly rooting the show's continuity in the early *Rockman* games and not in the later episodes set centuries later), the series posits a world where electronic communication is universal, and all electronic devices are connected—so far, so **Ghost in the Shell**. Everyone has a personal terminal or PET, a helpmate that can delete viruses and other network threats, as well as functioning, as the name implies, as electronic pets. Many manga spin-offs also exist, including titles by Hitoshi Ariga and Ryo Takamisaki.

Takao Kato's *Rockman.EXE: Program of Light and Dark* (2005) is a theatrical movie release in which Rockman must journey underground to defeat a new enemy, Nebula Grey.

MEGAMI PARADISE *

1995. JPN: *Megami Tengoku*. AKA: *Goddess Paradise*. Video. DIR: Katsuhiko Nishijima. SCR: Katsuhiko Chiba, Mayori Sekijima. DES: Noriyasu Yamauchi. ANI: Noriyasu Yamauchi. MUS: Toshiro Yabuki. PRD: King Record. 30 mins. x 2 eps. The Megami Paradise is a world of beauty and purity, ruled by the Mother Goddess whose protective influence shields the inhabitants from the corrupt and cruel universe. The reigning Mother Megami is due to step down soon, but her replacement has already been found in the form of the beautiful Lilith. The forces of Darkness, however, are keen on ending the blissful Megami existence once and for all, and it falls to Lilith and her Amazonian cohorts to save her world from destruction. Lilith's friends Lulubell, Juliana, and Stasia set out to foil the evil plotters and keep the world safe for lingerie and fan service. Any excuse to show acres of female flesh, from the people who would go on to give us **Agent Aika**. Based on a PC game with distinctly un-PC aims. **N**

MEGAZONE 23 *

1985. Video. DIR: Yasuo Hasegawa, Hiroyuki Kitazume, Ichiro Itano. SCR: Hiroyuki Hoshiyama, Arii Emu ("REM"). DES: Toshihiro Hirano, Haruhiko Mikimoto, Shinji Aramaki, Yasuomi Umezu. ANI: Toshihiro Hirano, Masami Obari, Nobuyuki Kitajima. MUS: Shiro Sagisu. PRD: Aidoru, Artmic. 107 mins. (1), 80 mins. (2), 50 mins. x 2 eps. (3). Bike-loving Shogo Yahagi obtains the transformable motorcycle-weapon Garland and is soon hotly pursued by the military. While location-hunting for a film he plans to make with his girlfriend's roommate, he wanders into the underground world beneath Tokyo and realizes that he is not in Tokyo at all but a facsimile built inside a space-

ship, controlled by the master computer Bahamut. He is in a Megazone, a ship built to hold a billion people, one of many that fled Earth in 2331 as the planet faced imminent environmental collapse. In order to reeducate humankind to avoid making previous mistakes, the Megazones are completely virtual worlds. The occupants are convinced that they are really living in the 20th century, and the central computer, Bahamut, is programmed to maintain the illusion until such time as humankind is ready to repopulate the slowly recovering Earth. However, alien vessels are preparing to attack, and Eve, a virtual idol constructed by Bahamut, contacts Shogo through Garland and begs him to help.

A video anime given a theatrical release in Japan, *Megazone 23* shared many of the same staff as the earlier **Macross**, a fact exploited in the U.S., where it was edited into the unrelated **Robotech** series as *Robotech: The Movie*.

The sequel, *M23: Tell Me the Secret*, features radically different artwork from new designer Umezu. Set six months later, Shogo collaborates with the Trash motorcycle gang in an attempt to regain Garland from the military. The alien Desarg are causing considerable damage to the technologically inferior crew of *Megazone 23*, but amid the battle, Shogo is reunited with his girlfriend, Yui, in a series of bed scenes cut from the video but left in the theatrical release. Eventually, Shogo saves the day, and it is revealed that *Megazone 23*'s journey has come full circle, and the time is right for humanity to return to Earth.

As the *Megazone* series drew to a graceful close, the anime business was thrown into upheaval by the runaway success of **Akira**. Mere moments after they laid their original story to rest, successfully delivering their characters from a gritty, urban nightmare, the producers turned right around and jammed them back in for the two-part finale *M23: Return of Eve* and *M23: Freedom Day*. Typically, these episodes were released abroad as *Megazone 23* with no reference to the two earlier installments. Instead of the pastoral idyll promised by the end of the original, the story restores the characters to a *Blade Runner*–esque future. Amid mock religious musings about Eve, a virtual idol who shall redeem us all from our sins, life isn't all it's cut out to be in Eden, and new hero Eiji Tanaka is a motorcycle-riding hacker who gets recruited by the government to fight computer terrorism. Except that the terrorists are the good guys, and when Eiji discovers this, he switches sides and leads a revolution from the inside.

News broadcasts make it obvious that the government is lying. People ride around on bikes. There's a conspiracy within a conspiracy. The bad guys aren't necessarily all that bad. But while these elements worked well enough in *Akira*, they leave a nasty taste in the mouth when you know that they're being deliberately swiped in a cynical cash-in—annoying enough for the screenwriter himself to use the Arii Emu pseudonym also seen in the lackluster **BUBBLEGUM CRISIS** spin-off *Bubblegum Crash*.

MEINE LEIBE

2004. JPN: *Ginyu Mokushiroku Meine Leibe*. AKA: *Minstrel Apocalypse Meine Leibe*. TV series. DIR: Koichi Mashimo. SCR: Akemi Omode, Hiroyuki Kawasaki. DES: Minako Shiba. ANI: Minako Shiba, Hiroshi Morioka, Masayuki Kurosawa, Maya Kawamo, Tomoyuki Kurokawa, Yuki Arie. MUS: Yoshihisa Hirano. PRD: Bee Train, Animax, Rondo Robe. 25 mins. x 13 eps.

The king of the pretty little European island kingdom of Kuchen is advised by five magistrates, almost always drawn from the Strahls, the elite graduates of the Rosenstolz Boarding School. One has to be well connected, intelligent, and talented to even get into the school, let alone strive for Strahl status. In 1935, five young noblemen aim to become Strahls and achieve magistrate status and political power. They are Orpherus, Ludwig, Eduard, Camus, and Naoji. Their friendships and rival-

ries form the plot of this anime for girls based on dating sim games *Tanbi Muso Meine Liebe*, released by Konami for the Game Boy Advance in 2001 and PS2 in 2004, and its follow-up *Meine Liebe Yubi Naru Kioku*. The handsome young men in the game were designed by androgynous glamour specialist Kaori Yuki, author of **ANGEL SANCTUARY** and *Count Cain*. A manga version of the anime entitled *Meine Liebe* (German for *My Love*) also ran in *Bessatsu Hana to Yume*, and yearningly elegant merchandise includes a trading card game and CD dramas.

MEKANDER *

1977. JPN: *Gasshin Sentai Mekander Robo*. AKA: *Combiner Battle Team Mekander Robot*. TV series. DIR: Yoshitaka Nitta, Takashi Anno, Yasuo Hasegawa, Masayuki Hayashi. SCR: Haruhiko Kaido. DES: Nobuhiro Okasako, Tsuneo Ninomiya. ANI: Tsuneo Ninomiya, Masayuki Hayashi, Satoshi Tozan, Takeshi Honda. MUS: Michiaki Watanabe. PRD: Wako, Telescreen, TV Tokyo. 25 mins. x 35 eps.

The evil general Edron (in Japanese: Hedoron) overthrows good Queen Medusa of Ganymede in the Magellan star cluster. Like many other mothers, most obviously that of *Superman*, she puts her only son Jimi into a space capsule and fires it into the void, and it eventually crash-lands on Earth. With Ganymede destroyed, Edron sends his fearless Kongister Corps to conquer Earth, all of which is defeated. All? Not all, for in the northeast corner of Asia sits a small island of indomitable warriors—the Japanese, who have placed their trust in Dr. Shikishima's revolutionary new Mekander Robo battle-robot. His son Ryusuke and friend Kojiro are the nominated pilots, alongside Ryusuke's adopted brother Jimi, unaware that his mother, or a cybernetically remodeled version of her, is now a prominent leader in Edron's army who remembers her son only in confused flashbacks. However, when he and his colleagues are in terrible danger, her memory returns, and

she sacrifices herself to save her son and his new home planet.

Beginning with Earth already defeated, *Mekander* had no qualms about piling on even more disasters—as soon as Mekander activates, the enemy launches Omega missiles to wipe it out! Unfortunately, similar troubles plagued the production, and the bankruptcy of a main sponsor forced the creators to cobble together new episodes from old footage with very limited new animation. Dubbed into English for screening in the Philippines. Manga tie-ins were published in several magazines, including *Terebi-kun* and *Yoiko*.

MELANCHOLY OF HARUHI SUZUMIYA

2006. JPN: *Suzumiya Haruhi no Yuutsu*. TV series. DIR: Hiroshi Yamamoto, Seiji Watanabe. SCR: Hiroshi Yamamoto, Tatsuya Ishihara. DES: Akiko Ikeda. ANI: Akiko Ikeda, Mitsuyoshi Yoneda, Satoshi Kadowaki. MUS: Satoru Kosaki. PRD: Kyoto Animation. 25 mins. x 14 eps.

Sassy schoolgirl Haruhi Suzumiya is the leading light of the Save Our Society By Overloading It With Fun Brigade (the SOS Club), an association formed to befriend, attract, and generally hang out with time travelers, visiting aliens, and anyone with superpowers. She finds mundane humans terribly boring, which is bad news for Kyon, the local boy who sits in front of her in class who is unwittingly dragged into her science fictional adventures. The result is a fearsome parody of fans and fandom, marrying the affectionate teasing of **GENSHIKEN** to the surreal satire of **EXCEL SAGA**. Based on the series of novels in *Sneaker* magazine by Gaku Tsugano. There was also an abortive 2004 manga adaptation in *Shonen Ace* magazine, illustrated by Nagaru Tanigawa, although this only lasted for a single volume. The series begins with an episode "00" that features the SOS Club's student movie, a ridiculously silly anime pastiche about a "combat waitress from the future" that is all too accurate—for instance, compare to **VARIABLE GEO**.

MELLOW

1993. JPN: *Mero*. AKA: *Girl-Boy*. Video. DIR: Teruo Kigure. SCR: Rin Kasahara. DES: Rin Kasahara. ANI: Teruo Kigure. MUS: N/C. PRD: KSS. 45 mins. Trouble in the classroom when the new teacher turns out to be a transvestite. Based on the 1991 manga by Rin Kasahara, published in *Shonen Champion*.

MELODY OF OBLIVION, THE *

2004. JPN: *Bokyaku no Senritsu: The Melody of Oblivion*. TV series. DIR: Hiroshi Nishikori, Atsushi Takeyama. SCR: Yoji Enokido. DES: Shinya Hasegawa, Yutaka Izubuchi, Yo Yoshinari, Yoshikazu Miyao, Yoshiyuki Sadamoto. ANI: Takashi Wada, Daisuke Takashima, Hiroaki Nishimura, Hiroyuki Ishido, Koji Ogawa, Yoshihisa Matsumoto, Katsushi Sakurai, Matsuo Asami. MUS: Hijiri Kuwano, Yoshikazu Suo. PRD: Gainax, TBS, Ken Media, Kadokawa. 24 mins. x 24 eps.
In the far future, a war breaks out between humans and monsters, and humans lose—see WARTIME ANIME for details! After many years, the defeat has almost been forgotten and humans have accepted subordinate status because the monsters keep largely out of sight and rule the world through fear. A few Melos warriors like Kurofune still keep up the fight in the mighty Aiba Machines. High school boy Bokka has always been fascinated by the legends of the brave Melos Warriors; he meets Kurofune and hears the legend of the Melody of Oblivion. This is a legendary girl, seen and heard only by Warriors, who is waiting to be rescued so that she in turn can save mankind. Bokka finds he too can hear her and joins the fight to bring the beauty of melody back to the world. Based on the manga written by GJK and illustrated by Shinji Katakura, *MoO* is an often surreal show that recalls some of the strange transformations of UTENA or JOJO'S BIZARRE ADVENTURES, with the motorcycle road trip of KINO'S JOURNEY. In a plot point seemingly ripped wholesale from Pete Docter's *Monsters Inc.* (2001), the monsters feed on the life energy of children in order to create mayhem, leading to some strange contrasts of everyday life and alien attack. Sound plays an important part in the show—there is a conspicuous amount of voice-over and inner monologue which removes the need for lip sync, and the score, as befits a show that foregrounds music itself, is one of the most impressive elements. ❖

MELTY LANCER

1999. AKA: *Melty Lancer: The Animation*. Video. DIR: Takeshi Mori. SCR: Hiroshi Yamaguchi. DES: Tomohiro Hirata, Shoichi Masuo, Kanetake Ebigawa. ANI: Shoichi Masuo. MUS: Masamichi Amano. PRD: Gonzo. 30 mins. x 6 eps. Earth has joined the galactic federation, and humanity has changed beyond all recognition. A religion that sees God in the Internet, alien technology indistinguishable from magic, and a huge Earthbound crime wave of alien crooks. Luckily, we have the Lancers on our side, Galactapol's elite crime-fighting corps, led by a man who's just served a five-year prison sentence and staffed by a gang of dangerous girlies. Sylvie Nimrod is a martial artist, Melvina McGarren only got her job because she's the boss's daughter, and cute little Angela is really an eight-year-old bioweapon. Nana (full name Nanai Nataletion Neinhalten) learned sorcery on her adopted homeworld of Promised Land, and Sakuya is a high priestess of the Arcanest Temple. Jun Kamijo, the team mecha specialist, suspects that Earth's new attackers are her old schoolgirl enemies, a team of women warriors from Mad Scientist College, called the Vanessas. And she's right.
A standard team template, stamped out originally for a PC game before jumping to the Sony PlayStation for *Melty Lancer: Galactic Girl Cops 2086* and the later tie-in game *ML: Third Planet*. A manga spin-off, *ML: Can We Return to Tomorrow?* (1998), was drawn by Akira Matsubara for *Anime V* magazine. The manga, like the anime, preferred to concentrate on gratuitous angles that ogled the female form, rather than attempting to get on with a story.

MEMORIES *

1995. Movie. DIR: Koji Morimoto, Tensai Okamura, Katsuhiro Otomo. SCR: Katsuhiro Otomo, Satoshi Kon. DES: Toshiyuki Inoue, Takashi Watanabe, Hirotsuge Kawasaki, Hidekazu Ohara. ANI: Yoshiaki Kawajiri. MUS: Takuya Ishino, Yoko Kanno, Jun Miyake, Hiroyuki Nagashima. PRD: Madhouse. 115 mins. An anthology film in the tradition of ROBOT CARNIVAL and NEO-TOKYO, hyped further for comprising three stories based on works by Katsuhiro Otomo. For *Magnetic Rose* (*Kanojo no Omoide*, JPN: *Her Memories*, hence the title for the film), a group of space salvage operators find a gravity well in the center of the "Sargasso" area of space. Sensing booty, they investigate, to find that the giant metal rose is the mausoleum of a famous opera singer from the 20th century. Robots and holograms on the ship recreate the events of her life and her bitterness over her rejection by her lover, Carlo; though as the visitors dig deeper, they not only discover more sinister aspects of her past, but also that the mausoleum wants to drag them into the illusions forever. For astronaut Heintz Beckner, haunted by his daughter Emily's death on Earth, this is a tempting prospect, and Morimoto's direction juxtaposes ultramodern sci-fi designs with the stately baroque interiors of the space station and the homespun farmhouse of Beckner's family. Redolent at times of Tarkovsky's *Solaris* (1971) and the poststargate scenes from *2001: A Space Odyssey* (1968), the *Magnetic Rose* sequence is one of the triumphs of anime, helped all the more by liberal extracts of Puccini's *Madame Butterfly* and *Tosca*, which manage to dwarf the other music by Yoko Kanno, Japan's greatest living composer.
The second sequence, *Stink Bomb*, reprises the runaway-weapon theme of Otomo's ROUJIN Z. Hapless scientific researcher Nobuo takes an antihistamine, unaware it is an experimental

bioweapon that generates a fatal odor. Not realizing there are any ill effects, he heads for Tokyo to report to his bosses, while the military throw every weapon they have at him, and passersby drop dead in his tracks. Eventually, the task is left to foreign soldiers (thinly disguised Americans) whom the canny Japanese everyman effortlessly outwits. A well-made but lightweight comedy.

The final part, *Cannon Fodder*, was the first anime Otomo directed after **AKIRA**. Originally planned as a 5-minute sequence, it ran well over time and budget, eventually reaching the 15-minute form shown. Set in a steampunk world that recalls the animation sequences of Pink Floyd's *The Wall* (1982), it features a nameless boy living in a town whose entire existence revolves around an unexplained war with a distant foe. He goes to school to learn about gunnery, while his father goes to work on one of the giant cannons, shooting an immense shell over the horizon. Shot in a drained, drab color scheme, *Cannon Fodder* is a stinging indictment of war—the boy knows nothing except fighting and dreams of cartoon soldiers. It is also a masterpiece from Otomo, planned as a single, continuous tracking shot (though this is not sustained for the entire film) and utilizing digital effects and scoring, reputedly as an experiment for **STEAM BOY**.

MEMORIES OF...

2001. AKA: *Memories Off* [sic]. Video. DIR: Kazu Yokota, Takahiro Okao, Toshikatsu Tokoro. SCR: Masashi Takimoto. DES: Mutsumi Sasaki. ANI: N/C. MUS: Chiyomaru Shikura. PRD: Scitron. 30 mins. x 3 eps. (v1), 30 mins. x 3 eps. (v2), 30 mins. (v3).
Teenager Tomoya Mikami is so traumatized by the death of his girlfriend Ayaka in a car accident that he is unable to form any new relationships. He alienates his friends, and although he attempts to find love anew, he is unable to forget Ayaka and keeps on "seeing her" whenever he is with his new girl-

friends—compare to **THE ETERNITY YOU DESIRE**. Based on a 1999 dating sim, released by KID Corporation.

For reasons we neither comprehend nor really care about, the 2001 sequel features a completely different couple. This time, there is no car accident; instead, the inane Ken Inami lends his umbrella to a stranger and immediately gets thrown into paroxysms of self-doubt about whether his girlfriend really is the one. Luckily, a series of stereotypical girls are around to help him make his decision. A third installment, *Memories Of... 3.5* (2003), presumably featured plot elements of the third and fourth games in the series by KID Corp., the most recent installment of which, *Memories Of... Again*, is the sixth in the franchise.

MEMORU AND HER POINTED HAT

1984. JPN: *Tongari Boshi Memoru*. TV series. DIR: Osamu Kasai, Yukio Misawa, Junichi Sato, Hiroshi Shidara. SCR: Shunichi Yukimuro, Chifude Asakura, Ryoko Takagi. DES: Ginichiro Suzuki. ANI: Ginichiro Suzuki, Takashi Saijo. MUS: Nozomu Aoki. PRD: Toei, TV Asahi. 25 mins. x 50 eps.
Space travelers from the planet Rilulu crash-land on Earth, where, like the characters in **DAGON**, they discover that they are tiny compared to the giant local inhabitants. Sneaking away from her parents, Memoru and her friends hitch a ride on the back of an owl and befriend the bedridden child Marielle. Eventually, a Rilulu rescue craft arrives to take them home, but as she prepares to leave, Memoru realizes that her departure will break Marielle's heart, and she decides to stay. The series was followed by a 15-minute "movie" outing, which combined elements of episodes 1, 2, 7, 24, and the reunion of Memoru and Marielle in episode 25.

MEREMANOID

1997. JPN: *Shinkai Densetsu Meremanoid*. AKA: *Deep-Sea Legend Meremanoid*. TV series. DIR: Shigeru Morikawa. SCR: Kenji Terada, Nobuaki Kishima. DES: Akehiro Yamada. ANI: Akehiro

Yamada, Shigeo Akahori. MUS: N/C. PRD: Triangle Staff, TV Asahi. 25 mins. x 24 eps.
Life has evolved very differently on the distant world of Mere. With the planet's surface almost totally covered by water, human beings have turned themselves into sea-dwellers. The males are called mermen, and the females, for some reason, are now referred to as meremanoids. Queen Ruthmilla broods over evil plans from within the Dark Reef, and Kings Moslem and Akkadia try to thwart her. But only sorceress Misty Jo and her little brother Oz hold the key to stopping Ruthmilla's dark designs. Writer Terada previously used the name "Ruth Miller" for an evil character in **BAVI STOCK**—his ex-girlfriend, perhaps?

MERMAID MELODY

2003. JPN: *Mermaid Melody Pichi Pichi Pitchi*. TV series. DIR: Yoshitaka Fujimoto. SCR: Michiko Yokote. DES: Kazuaki Makida. ANI: N/C. MUS: Masaki Tsurugi. PRD: Synergy Japan, PPP Production Commission, We've Inc., TV Aichi. 25 mins. x 52 eps. (TV1); 25 mins. x 39 eps. (TV2).
Lucia Nanami is a mermaid princess who lives in the North Pacific Ocean. She is the designated Bearer of the Pink Pearl, but she's lost it. Seven years ago she rescued a boy from a sinking ship, lost the pearl, but also lost her heart. She missed her coming-of-age ceremony last year because she didn't have her pearl, so she needs to find it in order to become officially adult; but she also wants to find the boy, so she heads for a city on the coast. Passing for human, she soon meets her first love, but he's such a cocky, flirtatious guy that at first she doesn't recognize him. Kaito Domoto is a surfer, all-round athlete and babe magnet, but with a very arrogant attitude. Lucia registers at his school to be closer to him, but if she falls in love with a human and tells him how she feels, she'll die.

This modern take on **LITTLE MERMAID** has another twist. Sea monsters

led by the evil Gaito are attacking
the mermaid kingdoms. The magical
power of the colored pearls can transform the princesses into Singing Divas
with enough power to defeat the sea
monsters. If Lucia stays in the human
world to be with Kaito, she can't join in
the battle.

Supposedly based on a manga by
screenwriter Michiko Yokote and Pink
Hanamori in *Nakayoshi* magazine, some
of *MM*'s comic situations are a little
obvious—for instance, Lucia is chosen
to play the lead in a class performance
of *Little Mermaid*, only to have water
imps threaten to expose her as a real
mermaid. But, as with the original,
there's pathos in this story. The idea
that a cute girl with a heartfelt song
can save the world, or that you can love
someone enough to give him up or die
for him, is still as corny and as touching as it was when **Macross** premiered.
The second series, *MMPPP Pure*, followed straight on in 2004.

MERMAID'S FOREST *

1991. JPN: *Rumic World: Ningyo no
Mori*. Video. DIR: Takuta Mizutani,
Morio Asaka. SCR: Masaichiro Oku-
bo, Tatsuhiko Urahata. DES: Sayuri
Isseki, Kumiko Takahashi. ANI:
Sayuri Isseki, Kumiko Takahashi.
MUS: Kenji Kawai, Norihiro Tsuru. PRD:
Madhouse. 56 mins. (v1), 46 mins.
(v2), 25 mins. x 11 eps. (TV), 25
mins. x 2 eps. (v3).
Yuta is over 500 years old, a former
Japanese fisherman who caught and
ate the immortality-bestowing flesh of
a mermaid. Though it killed his fellow
sailors or turned them into feral "Lost
Soul" mutants, Yuta has stayed forever
young, and now he wanders modern
Japan in search of others like him.
One such person is Mana, a girl whom
Yuta rescues from mermaid crones
who intend to restore their own youth
by eating *her*. However, she is also kidnapped by a human woman who has
been deformed by ingesting mermaid's
blood in an attempt to cure an illness.

Mixing **Japanese Folk Tales** with a
modern vampire analogy seemingly

Mermaid's Forest

© RUMIKO TAKAHASHI/SHOGAKUKAN © 2003, 2005 PROJECT RUMIKO TAKAHASHI ANTHOLOGY

informed by *Highlander* (1985), the
original 1988 *Mermaid's Forest* manga is
one of the darker works from **Urusei
Yatsura**–creator Rumiko Takahashi.
Though parts of the original manga
concentrated on Yuta's early wanderings, the anime sequel, *Mermaid's
Scar* (1993, *Ningyo no Kizu*), opted for
another modern tale. This time, Yuta
and Mana arrive in another seaside
town where they suspect that another
woman living in another secluded
mansion (coastal Japan being littered
with them, it would seem) is another
eater of mermaid flesh. In this they are
not mistaken, since the slightly crazed
Misa has recovered her beautiful looks
with suspicious rapidity after the boat-
ing accident that killed her husband.
Though at first believing her to be
abusing her young son Masato, the
pair discover that Masato is the 800-
year-old manipulator of a succession of
adult foils—Misa, a bereaved mother
to whom he fed mermaid flesh during
the WWII bombing of Tokyo, is only
the latest. However, as happened in its
predecessor, *Mermaid's Scar*'s brooding
Gothic soon collapses into a succession
of gory fights. Its chilling premise is
reduced to the straightforward rescue

of a damsel in distress, and it suffers
somewhat from the same inconsistencies that dog **Vampire Princess
Miyu**—Masato's supply of 800-year-old
mermaid flesh seems both inexhaustible and unperishable. Furthermore,
the blurb on the box claims that Yuta
is tired of immortality and searching
for a way to die, though everyone
already seems agreed that decapitation
or immolation would both do the job
nicely. One of the *Rumic World* series
based on Takahashi's short manga
tales; other entries included **Fire Tripper**, **Laughing Target**, and **Maris the
Chojo**. Compare to its contemporary
3x3 Eyes.

The story was resurrected for the
13-part *Rumiko Takahashi Theater:
Mermaid's Forest* (2004), directed by
Masaharu Okuwari—eleven episodes
screened on TV, and the two final ones
available only on video. This follows
Yuta's wanderings through the world
seeking a mermaid who can set him
free to live as a normal human again.
He finds a companion, Mana, who
was kept prisoner by mermaids who
intended to eat her—this is how mermaids, like *Countess Dracula*, keep their
youthful looks. Mana, too, has eaten

mermaid flesh and joins Yuta on his quest. Although they do not age, they can still feel pain and can be killed. They can never stay in one place for long or risk drawing too much attention to themselves, but Yuta's memories and past experiences draw them back to his old haunts and bring them in touch with a few survivors of those experiences. Many of the stories refer back to events in the manga and video release. Although a well-crafted, well-written series, the TV *MF* doesn't really give the viewer anything different from the original. Yuta's mixed feelings about his own immortality and his constant need to reaffirm himself and his humanity, and the easygoing adaptability that has enabled him to survive 500 years of change and turmoil, remain the same, so it's one for Takahashi completists. **NV**

METAL ANGEL MARIE *

1995. JPN: *Boku no Marie*. AKA: *My Dear Marie*. Video. DIR: Tomomi Mochizuki. SCR: Go Sakamoto. DES: Hirohito Tanaka. ANI: Hirohito Tanaka. MUS: Hisaaki Yasukari. PRD: Victor Entertainment. 30 mins. x 3 eps.
Orphaned techno-geek Hiroshi sublimates his love for unattainable schoolgirl Marie, creating a "surrogate sister" robot who is her exact duplicate. Hiroshi has to keep his "sister's" robot nature secret while chasing the real Marie and trying to fight off all the neighborhood bad girls—who naturally find him incredibly attractive. Robot Marie isn't just a talking blow-up doll with pink hair; her affinity with machines gives her a certain power over electrical objects. She can put cars into spins, track pagers, and open doors—a kind of low-rent superpower that is very handy for keeping your "brother" away from femmes fatales. Despite her robotic limitations, she can do something that Hiroshi never can, and that's have a conversation with the real Marie without blowing a fuse. The two girls become firm friends, much to Hiroshi's chagrin, and his "sister" gets to hear all sorts of inside gossip

that he would kill for. In the privacy of the girls' locker room (private, that is, except for the anime cameramen filming fan-service underwear footage), it's the robot who finds out that her twin is still available—rumors that she's dating the high school hunk are unfounded. Hiroshi discovers that a sure-fire way of standing a better chance with girls is actually *talking* to them, and with his sister's help, he starts to take his first unsteady steps into the adult world. But, like the similar **VIDEO GIRL AI**, Marie isn't all that keen on helping him attain the love of his life. She'd rather *be* the love of his life, and another anime love triangle is born.

Based on a manga by Sakura Takeuchi in *Young Jump*, *MAM* mixes sports, romantic intrigue, and a slight superheroic twist, coupled with the mid-1990s craze for rearing your own creation, which peaked with **TAMAGOTCHI VIDEO ADVENTURES** and **POKÉMON**. But while popular as a manga, its video incarnation died an early death, swamped by the runaway success of the **TENCHI MUYO!** marketing machine. Renamed *My Dear Marie* for the subtitled version from AD Vision, presumably simply to annoy people compiling encyclopedias. Like Maria in **GHOST SWEEPER MIKAMI**, the robot's name is a distant homage to the robot girl in Fritz Lang's *Metropolis* (1926).

METAL FIGHTERS MIKU *

1994. JPN: *Metal Fighter Miku*. Video. DIR: Akiyuki Shinbo. SCR: Yasushi Hirano. DES: Takeshi Honda. ANI: Arihiko Sakamaki. MUS: Kenji Kawai. PRD: JC Staff, TV Tokyo. 25 mins. x 13 eps.
In 2061 the latest fad is Women's Neo Pro Wrestling—"neo" because the combatants' natural fighting abilities are augmented with high-tech metal suits. Miku, Ginko, Sayaka, and Nana team up as the Pretty Four, but when they enter a championship tournament, they seek out the help of coach Eiichi Suo, a discredited drunk. After intrigues backstage, Coach Suo rules that the Pretty Four should fight each other in a one-off match. Only

a weakling would try to destroy the team by dishonorable means; therefore (obviously!) the guilty party can be hunted down through trial by combat. After this very tongue-in-cheek tale of female fascism, the team gets ready for the next match, but Miku sprains her shoulder. Miku has to overcome her injuries in order to save her team from the invincible Beauties of Nature. Realizing that the Pretty Four are undefeatable in the ring, the father-and-son baddies Shibano and Naoya resolve to destroy the team spirit by making them fight among themselves. Naoya pretends to fall in love with the hapless Miku while simultaneously encouraging Ginko to dump her teammates and head off for new pastures in America.

Wrestling has always been popular in Japan, from the quasi-religious sumo to the adoption of American-style staged matches. *MFM* belongs firmly in the latter camp; although sharp-eyed fans might be able to see more bubbling beneath the surface than straightforward babes in battlesuits. A whole generation of Japanese creators grew up watching wrestling tournaments, and there are many homages within anime (see **CRUSHER JOE**). One of Japan's most popular wrestling teams was an all-girl combo called the Beauty Pair, hence *MFM*'s Pretty Four, who are, logically speaking, twice as good, and the much more famous **DIRTY PAIR**, whom we all know to be twice as bad.

METAL JACK

1991. JPN: *Kiko Keisatsu Metal Jack*. AKA: *Armored Police Metal Jack*. TV series. DIR: Ko Matsuzono, Akihiko Nishiyama, Jun Kamiya, Hideki Tonokatsu. SCR: Hiroyuki Kawasaki, Katsuhiko Chiba, Tsunehisa Arakawa, Ryoei Tsukimura. DES: Yorihisa Uchida, Yukihiro Makino. ANI: Hideyuki Motohashi. MUS: Fuminori Iwasaki. PRD: Sunrise, TV Tokyo. 25 mins. x 37 eps.
In 2015, Tokyo is a high-tech "intelligent city," which just means that criminals also have access to even better weapons and equipment to carry

out their schemes. When three young men die saving a little boy's life, they become the core of the Tokyo Police's top secret Metal Project as cyborgs who can even the score for the good guys in the fight against crime and, in particular, the criminal network known as Ido. Former police marksman Ken and his cybermutt, F-1 driver Ryo, and wrestler Go are aided and abetted by the mysterious Shadow Jack, survivor of an earlier foreign scheme to use cyborgs in police work, who escaped to Japan and now lives undercover, desperately seeking the human memories his transformation wiped out. Their powerful transforming armor and weaponry achieved its main aim of selling toys for the show's sponsors in this derivative Sunrise show that marries parts of **Pat-labor** and **8th Man** to *Robocop* (1987).

METAMORPHOSES/WINDS OF CHANGE *

1978. JPN: *Hoshi no Orpheus*. AKA: *Star of Orpheus; Orpheus of the Stars*. Movie. DIR: "Takashi," Gerry Eisenberg, Richard Hubner, Sadao Miyamoto. SCR: Fujio Akatsuka, Nobuo Fujita. DES: Yukio Abe, et al. ANI: Masami Hata, Shigeru Yamamoto, et al. MUS: Billy Goldenberg, Jim Studer, Steve Tosh, Michael Young (*Meta*), Alec Costandinos (*Winds*). PRD: Sanrio. 95 mins. (U.S. edition, 80 mins.)

An animated version of five of Ovid's Roman versions of Greek myths, this film gives the stories of Actaeon, Orpheus and Eurydice, Herse and Aglauros, Perseus and Medusa, and Phaethon. Originally planned as a modern *Fantasia* in 70mm, *Metamorphoses* featured original pop music "starring musical performances by Joan Baez, Mick Jagger & The Rolling Stones, [and] The Pointer Sisters." The music and images, however, rarely matched, and the dialogue-free action was simply mystifying to audiences. Matters were not helped by the literary device of having the hero in each of the stories played by the same character, misleading some into thinking the anthology was one long story with

a plot too incoherent to follow. The *Winds of Change* version followed in 1979, with music by a single composer and a sardonic narration by Peter Ustinov explaining the adventures of "Wondermaker" as he wanders through the five tales and takes the leading role in each. A product of Sanrio's short-lived Hollywood animation studio, which made the similarly unsuccessful *Mouse and His Child*.

METROPOLIS *

2001. Movie. DIR: Rintaro. SCR: Katsuhiro Otomo. DES: Yasuhiro Nakura. ANI: Yasuhiro Nakura. MUS: Toshiyuki Honda. PRD: Madhouse, Tezuka Pro. 107 mins.

Japanese detective Shunsaku Ban arrives in the mega-city Metropolis, accompanied by his nephew Kenichi—their mission, to arrest renegade scientist Dr. Laughton. But Laughton has friends in high places; he has been hidden away by the industrialist Duke Red, who wants him to create the final part of his Ziggurat super-skyscraper—a living robot who can rule the world from the throne secretly installed in its heights. While the Japanese visitors look for Laughton, Red's embittered stepson Rock hunts him for his own reasons, while Red's agents encourage the impoverished human city dwellers to revolt against their masters. When Dr. Laughton is killed, his robot creation Tima goes on the run through the warrens of the city, unaware of who—or what—she really is.

Osamu Tezuka began work on *Metropolis* when he was 15, and when it was finally published in 1949 he was still a teenager. Although he had not seen Fritz Lang's movie of the same name, he was inspired by a magazine article about it, including an image of the movie's famous robot-woman, Maria. He wondered what life would be like in a city of the future where robots would do all of the work (compare to the similar **Armitage III**), postulating a disaffected underclass of jobless humans, open to suggestion from anarchist agitators.

Metropolis was the middle part of a

sci-fi manga trilogy, beginning with Tezuka's manga *Lost World* (1948), in which Shunsaku and Kenichi were searching for energy-bearing meteorites and stranded on Earth's rogue twin planet. After *Metropolis*, they would return in the Cold War thriller *Next World* (1951, see **Fumoon**), in which the Earth is threatened by a giant dust cloud. The character of Tima (named Michy in the original) was an early try-out for Tezuka's most famous creation, the super-robot **Astro Boy**.

Mixing elegant computer graphics with the squat, cartoony characters of Tezuka's original, *Metropolis* is an excellent introduction, not only to Japan's greatest manga artist, but also the latest developments in anime. The crew is simply stellar, with direction by **X: The Movie**'s Rintaro, and other jobs filled by Hiroyuki Okiura (**Jin-Roh**), Yoshiaki Kawajiri (**Ninja Scroll**), and Kunihiko Sakurai (**Final Fantasy**). Almost everyone who is anyone in the anime business seems to have been involved—the film even credits **Devilman**-creator Go Nagai as a guest voice actor, and the director himself moonlights as a bass clarinetist in the jazz band!

Of particular note is screenwriter Katsuhiro Otomo, who, like all manga artists, owes an incredible debt to Tezuka, and one which he openly acknowledged with a dedication that closed the **Akira** manga (dropped from the English release). In *Metropolis* we see many similarities—a city held for ransom by a terrorist group secretly funded by a corrupt politician, a great construction venture with a hidden purpose, and a child unaware it has the power to destroy the world. *Metropolis* also shares *Akira*'s explosive finale, involving the destruction of a considerable amount of urban real estate—the film was originally scheduled for an American release in late 2001, but was delayed several months after the September 11th terrorist attacks. Added for this movie version is a tip of the hat to *Blade Runner*, in the form of Duke Red's Ziggurat skyscraper—in the original manga, the secret project was to control the proliferation of sunspots and solar flares, of which only a small vestige remains in the movie.

Metropolis is a sumptuous film, loaded with homages to Fritz Lang and Tezuka himself—best displayed by a title sequence of an airship flying over a fireworks display in the city, while a jazz party gets into full swing. It is an evocative window into the work of manga's greatest artist, retaining both his child-like character designs and his bitingly serious plotting—even in Tezuka's own lifetime, many anime adaptations of his work tried to have one without the other. Suspiciously, it also contains a lot of CG work similar to early footage from Otomo's long-delayed STEAM BOY project—was this a way of realizing some of the costs for that other movie? Ironically, some of the computer graphics seem to come at the expense of more traditional techniques—certain painted cel backgrounds lack the three-dimensional immediacy of their CG counterparts and end up looking just like, well, paintings. In 1949, Tezuka closed his *Metropolis* manga with a question— "Will mankind destroy itself by developing technology too far?" One could well ask the same of the anime industry—as in the earlier MACROSS PLUS, there is something ironic in a film that questions the value of new technology, when so much of its production rests upon it.

MEW MEW POWER *

2002. JPN: *Tokyo Mew Mew*. AKA: *Tokyo Myu Myu; Mew Mew; Mew Mew Power*. TV series. DIR: Noriyuki Abe. SCR: N/C. DES: Mari Kitayama, Koichi Usami. ANI: Studio Pierrot. MUS: Takayuki Negishi. PRD: Kodansha, TV Aichi, Studio Pierrot. 25 mins. x 52 eps.

Thirteen-year-old Ichigo Momomiya gets a hot date—school dreamboat Masaya Aoyama. Unfortunately during the date she's zapped by a strange ray that scrambles her DNA with that of an endangered species. When you think how many endangered species there are, she was lucky—instead of

an Amazonian insect or fish, she was mixed with the Iriomote wildcat, giving her great agility, cute ears, and a tail. She can now transform into pink-haired superheroine Mew Mew Ichigo. It turns out that (as in SAILOR MOON) she's one of a team of five girls selected to protect the Earth from the mysterious alien known as Deep Blue, each endowed with color coding, special powers, and the cutest attributes of an animal from the "Red Data" list. Ichigo (whose name means strawberry) and her colleagues Mew Mint, Mew Lettuce, Mew Pudding, and Mew Zakuro (pomegranate) each get individual transformation sequences, magical weapons, and special powers. Guided by their magical companion, cute pink robot Masha, they set out to help save the Earth and its endangered creatures in a show based on the manga by Mia Ikumi and Reiko Yoshida.

MEZZO *

2001. JPN: *Mezzo Forte; Mezzo: Danger Service Agency*. AKA: *Mezzo: DSA*. TV series, video. DIR: Yasuomi Umezu. SCR: Yasuomi Umezu, Takao Yoshioka. DES: Yasuomi Umezu. ANI: Yasuomi Umezu. MUS: Toru Shura. PRD: Studio ARMS, Green Bunny, Hanjin Animation, Jiwoo Production. 29 mins. x 2 eps. (v), 25 mins. x 13 eps. (TV).

Teenage killer Mikura is hired to kidnap a wealthy baseball-team owner, but she finds herself facing two major-league problems. One is that rich man Momokichi Momoi made his money with the Mob and his underworld connections are still active; the other is that his daughter Momomi is no terrified little rich girl but a feisty, arrogant bitch and a crack shot into the bargain. Such was the plot for *Mezzo Forte*, a short erotic video series that was spun off into *Mezzo*, a longer, less risqué TV sequel featuring Mikura and her surrogate family, the nerdy Harada and embittered ex-cop Pops Kurokawa, carrying out various commissions that show their softer, funnier side as well as action-packed mayhem. Yasuomi Umezu, who created the similar KITE,

was also responsible for the most heart-rending segment of ROBOT CARNIVAL and the sexiest introduction ever for a PROJECT A-KO movie. He knows about pace, he knows about style, and he gives good cute, though his bewildered little girls and gutsy, hard-headed, big-hearted teens get repetitive after a while. **LV**

MIAMI GUNS *

2000. TV series. DIR: Sadamune Koyama. SCR: To Hirami. DES: Shinichi Masaki. ANI: Hiroka Eto. MUS: Takashi Nakagawa. PRD: Toei, Group Tac, TBS. 25 mins. x 13 eps.

Unlikely adventures in a fantasy version of Miami, a "stateless town" populated almost entirely by Japanese people, as schoolgirl cop Yao Sakura-koji takes on evil power barons with her sharpshooting skills and super-human athletic abilities. Or so she thinks—like the self-centered beauties of DEBUTANTE DETECTIVES, she is actually a spoiled rich girl who is prepared to do anything to impress, even to the extent of stunning a hostage negotiator so she can force a firefight. In a template stamped straight out of the buddy-movie production line, the maverick Yao is assigned a new partner, police commissioner Amano's daughter Ru, who is cool-headed and always does everything by the book. A series with all the depth of YOU'RE UNDER ARREST!, all the originality of EHRGEIZ, and all the realism of MAD BULL 34. Based on the manga by Takeaki Momose.

MICROID S

1973. TV series. DIR: Masayuki Akehi, Hiroshi Shidara, Osamu Kasai, Minoru Okazaki, Masamune Ochiai. SCR: Masaki Tsuji. DES: Osamu Tezuka. ANI: Hiroshi Wagatsuma, Kazuo Komatsubara, Takeshi Shirato. MUS: Ko Misawa. PRD: Tezuka Pro, Toei, TV Asahi. 25 mins. x 26 eps.

Little does the human race realize that it is under threat from the Gidoron, a race of superintelligent ants who have developed powerful weapons. Butterfly-like Yamma, Ageha, and Mamezo escape from a Gidoron base and convince humans Dr. Mishiji and his son, Manabu, to help them. In a combination of **WONDERBEAT SCRAMBLE** and the later **MICROMAN**, the microids continue the war against the ants with full-sized human assistance. Osamu Tezuka's original *Shonen Champion* manga was called *Microid Z*, but the initial letter was changed to "S" at the insistence of the show's sponsor, Seiko watches.

MICROMAN

1999. JPN: *Chiisana Kyojin Microman.* AKA: *Tiny Titan Microman; Micronauts.* TV series. DIR: Noriyuki Abe. SCR: Hiroshi Sakamoto, Yoshio Urasawa. DES: Takashi Wakabayashi. ANI: Hideo Shimosaka. MUS: Seiko Nagaoka. PRD: Studio Pierrot, TV Tokyo. 25 mins. x 52 eps.

Japanese schoolboy Kohei Kuji is understandably surprised when five of his action figures come to life and claim to be Micromen from the planet Micro-Earth, sent on a 30,000-light-year mission to save Earth from the Acroyears—"bad" Micromen who have crashed in Earth's polluted oceans and been transformed into mutants. Bold leader Arthur, blond pretty-boy Isamu, big lunk Walt, bespectacled brain Edison, and veteran tough-guy Odin enlist Kohei's help in their secret battle against the demonic invaders.

A 1980s toy sensation like **ZOIDS**, *Microman* figures began life as an economic design decision at former *GI Joe* manufacturer Takara—8-cm action figures meant smaller vehicles and lower production costs than their 30-cm counterparts. With distinctive chrome-colored heads, mounted on top of colored bodies, the toys had interchangeable parts—limbs and attachments could be swapped around by creative kids, one of whom was the young Yukito Kishiro, who cited his childhood Micromen as the inspiration for his own **BATTLE ANGEL**. RELEASED IN THE U.S. IN 1976 AS THE "MICRONAUTS," THE *Microman* line enjoyed a brief popularity before being swamped by the

popularity of *Star Wars* action figures, and, as the 1980s wore on, by another Takara line, the **TRANSFORMERS**. Memorable tie-ins include Michael Golden's U.S. comic *Micronauts* (1979), as well as a 1984 *X-Men* crossover in which the X-Men were shrunk to micro-size, and the *Micronauts: New Adventures* (also 1984). Though an anime series was planned in the 1980s by the Artmic studio, it was shelved as the fad of the moment changed. Revived as part of a multimedia promotion for Gameboy and PlayStation releases, *Microman* finally returned over a decade after it was considered finished. Not only did the new line feature some fabulous gimmicks, like a transforming base that looked like a PlayStation, all the figures were upgraded to "magnepower" status, so they could not only "use a table as a base," but also stick to the fridge and explore the rest of the kitchen, to infinity and beyond.

MIDNIGHT PANTHER *

1998. Video. DIR: Yosei Morino, Hiroshi Kogawa. SCR: Yosei Morino. DES: Rin Shin. ANI: Yosei Morino. MUS: Yosei Morino. PRD: Beam Entertainment. 30 mins. x 2 eps.

During the interdimensional apocalypse of 1999, Kate Sinclair is killed by a dragon from a parallel world. Her biotechnician lover, David Owen, tries to restore her to life, conferring a kind of immortality on himself by continual cloning. Two centuries later, an Owen clone finally finds a way. Inspired by his muse, the exotic dancer "Panther," he combines Kate's DNA with a wildcat's. The experiment is a success, but the Kate-creature kills her former lover. Panther, however, falls in love with the new her and begins murdering humans to bring her fresh meat. A hundred years later, the aged Panther runs her own cartel of assassins, one of whom is the pretty granddaughter of the long-dead Kate. But very little of the above backstory is included in the anime, confusing the hell out of many U.S. viewers. Meanwhile . . .

Only boys may rule the Blue Dragon

kingdom, which is why Princess Loukish's gender is kept secret, even from Crown Prince Bad. But Bad fears that Loukish will become the royal favorite and plots to kill his "brother" anyway. Thrown from the battlements and left for dead, Loukish is found by an old witch and soon becomes part of her traveling minstrel troupe, the Pussycats. She loses all memories of her previous life and of her brother's evil deeds—he now exists only as an idolized figure in her dreams.

In fact, the Pussycats are a trio of assassins who use their musical talents as a cover. The spells woven to nurse the half-drowned Lou back to health have wrought some strange side effects. While she may look like a sexy young wench, her exposure to dragon's blood has left her with superhuman strength and virtual invulnerability—though nothing has prepared her for the shocks she will have in her next mission, which is to assassinate Prince Bad himself.

Yu Asagiri's complex manga tale of incestuous family ties across generations is compressed into a 60-minute sword-and-sorcery sex romp. Without the long back story, viewers of the anime are instead thrown into the deep end with the story of little Lou—the titular Panther is actually the nameless, zany old crone who saves her young life. This is a pity, because *MP*, despite all appearances to the contrary, is not the bastard offspring of a short-lived erotic computer game, but the culmination of an artist's life-long obsession with love, desire, and obsession itself. A terrible adaptation of a lighthearted sex-manga, unleashed upon the English-language market with little attempt to explain its origins, and an awful dub to boot. **ⒸⓃⓋ**

MIDNIGHT SLEAZY TRAIN *

2003. JPN: *Saishu Chikan Densha.* AKA: *Molester on the Last Train.* Video. DIR: Raikaken. SCR: Rokurota Makabe. DES: P-zo Honda. ANI: P-zo Honda, Yuya Soma. MUS: Salad. PRD: Milky. 30 mins. x 3 eps. (v1), 30 mins. x 3 eps. (v2).

With Kankyu Railroad on the verge of bankruptcy and its imminent demise threatening to shut down the sole lifeline to the town of Momogawa, three train operators come up with a plan to save the company and their hometown. By instituting the last trip of each night as a rolling orgy, catering to men who like to molest female passengers, they intend to up the ridership to profitable levels. One of them, Tetsuo (who is scion of the family that owns the company), has a secret which is key to recruiting women for their campaign—he is a master molester, whose touch can seduce a woman in seconds, turning them to his will. However, this power has a flaw in that the victims become nymphomaniacs forever after—not much of a handicap in this case.

Meanwhile, as Tetsuo gropes and seduces his way to success, his childhood friend Sana reveals that her grandfather is working on an alternative scheme, digging down through local rock in search of a hot spring that could turn the town into a tourist destination. The series was also re-released in a condensed movie version titled *SCD the Best* and was followed by a three-episode second series titled *Shin (New) SCD*. Compare to **Xpress Train** and, in the live-action world, the Ken Takakura vehicle *Poppoya* (1999), which similarly featured a town threatened by the closure of its rail link, but mercifully did not include any perverts. **LNV**

MIDORI DAYS *

2004. JPN: *Midori no Hibi*. AKA: *Days with Midori*. TV series. DIR: Tsuneo Kobayashi. SCR: Mamiko Ikeda, Takuya Sato et al. DES: Yuko Kusumoto. ANI: Pierrot. MUS: Yoshihisa Hirano. PRD: Studio Pierrot, Toho, Bandai Visual. 24 mins. x 13 eps.

High school boy Seiji Sawamura is really quite a nice guy, but he's got a bad reputation and the nickname Mad Dog, earned by copious street fighting, often in pursuit of justice. His right hook is so deadly that it's got its own nickname—The Devil's Right Hand. Other students avoid him and he can't get a girlfriend. In fact, 20 girls have turned him down. But unknown to him, he has had a secret admirer for the past three years—quiet goody-two-shoes Midori Kasugano, who is so paralyzed by her shyness that she couldn't possibly tell him how she feels. Then, in the tradition of *Minami's Sweetheart* (*DE) and **The Eternity You Desire**, Midori falls into a coma, while Seiji finds that instead of a right hand, he now has a living glove puppet—compare to **Puppet Master Sakon**. A tiny, living and speaking Midori is attached to the end of his arm and reveling in his undivided attention. The situation is awkward and embarrassing but the pair find they really do like each other, even when things are switched for an episode and Seiji becomes Midori's left hand. The result is a very silly show that still manages to convey how paralyzing shyness can be and how enforced intimacy can reveal unsuspected aspects of a person's character. Based on the manga by Kazuro Inoue in *Shonen Sunday*, itself a surreal cartoon version of the perennial surrogate parenting and reluctant roommates genres of live-action Japanese television.

MIDORIYAMA HIGH

1989. JPN: *Midoriyama Koko*. Video. DIR: Shigeru Ikeda. SCR: Shigeru Ikeda. DES: Atsuo Kurisawa. ANI: Shinichi Suzuki. MUS: Michiya Katakura. PRD: Balk, Onimaruya. 50 mins. x 10 eps.

The slow route to success of a school baseball team that doesn't know the meaning of the word "teamwork," adapted from the manga in *Young Jump* by Atsui Kurisawa. Over time, the power-hitter Inushima loses his desire to hit everything and concentrates on hitting the ball, while ladies' man Hanaoka devotes just enough time to helping his teammates win before chasing after more skirt. In the same vein as **Star of the Giants**.

MIGHTY ORBOTS *

1985. TV series. DIR: Osamu Dezaki. SCR: Michael Reaves, Hideo Takayashiki. DES: Ron Maidenberg, Akio Sugino, Katsuya Kondo. ANI: Hirokata Takahashi, Tetsu Dezaki, Kazuyuki Hirokawa. MUS: Yuji Ono. PRD: Intermedia, Tokyo Movie Shinsha. 25 mins. x 13 eps.

In the 23rd century, the evil Umbra, ruling computer of the Shadow World, tries to conquer Earth, only to be held off by the brave agents of the Galactic Patrol. Though there are humanoid operatives, including the elfin commander Rondu and his beautiful daughter Dia, the GP's last line of defense is the Orbots, a group of android warriors created and led by human cybernetics genius Rob Simmons. Simmons rides in his Beam Car with his flustered robo-assistant, Ono—the other Orbots can function separately or combine to form a mighty superrobot (somehow suddenly 50 feet tall), comprising Tor (torso), Bolt and Crunch (left and right leg), and Bo and Boo (left and right arm). Additionally each of the robots (except Crunch, for some reason) has a special ability—strength, customizable gadgets, energy beams, and teleportation/invisibility, which the whole of the group can access in Mighty Orbot mode.

A rare case of a genuine U.S.-Japan coproduction, blown out of the water by the runaway success of **Transformers** and limited to a single season. With the same team's *Galaxy High School*, it was part of a concerted effort by TMS to break into the U.S. market in coalition with producer Fred Silverman. The inept Bolt and Crunch were added to the lineup purely for "comic" relief, though fans' most frequently asked question was why superinventor Rob built two bumbling incompetents.

MIGHTY SPACE MINERS *

1994. JPN: *Oira Uchu no Tankofu*. Video. DIR: Umanosuke Iida. SCR: Ritsuko Hayasaka, Tsutomu Iida. DES: Toshihiro Kawamoto, Isamu Imakake. ANI: Toshihiro Kawamoto. MUS: Kenji Kawai. PRD: Triangle Staff, KSS. 30 mins. x 2 eps.

In a.d. 2060, an accident at the Toutatis

asteroid mine forces the colonists to survive on their wits alone in the deadly environment of space. A supposedly realistic "hard SF" study of the dangers of zero-gravity life, based on a story by "Horceman Lunchfield." However, such a noble claim is somewhat ruined by having a character who survives exposure to vacuum and another with Big Anime Hair, hardly suitable for tough life in the asteroid belt. These problems may have influenced the buying public, as the story remains unfinished, with a presumed third episode not forthcoming. Sharp-eyed linguists may notice that "Horse-Man Lunch-Field" could be written in Japanese as "Uma no Suke Ii Da."

MIJA: BEAUTIFUL DEMON *

2003. JPN: *Bi Indoshi Miija*. AKA: *Mija: School of Insult Video*. DIR: Jun Fukuda. SCR: Saki Hosen. DES: Akira Kano. ANI: N/C. MUS: N/C. PRD: FAI International, Five Ways. 30 mins. x 2 eps.
Something strange is going on at Saint Moses Academy, and Sara Tadeshina has been sent by the Church to investigate undercover. Posing as a teacher, she soon discovers that the Academy was designed as an emergency shelter for the surrounding area, so it's unusual in design but also a powerful occult site. Unknown to Sara, an exiled demon has settled on the Academy as her Earthly home. Mija is a lust demon, and is drawing the students to her and teaching them the pleasures of the flesh, starting with attractive young Mayu and her would-be boyfriend Kotaro. When Sara finds the gate to Mija's domain, there are monster battles and demonic orgies before the two face off against each other. **LNV**

MIKAN'S DIARY

1994. JPN: *Mikan e Nikki*. AKA: *Mikan Picture Diary*. TV series. DIR: Noboru Ishiguro. SCR: Mayumi Koyama. DES: Noboru Sugimitsu. ANI: N/C. MUS: Toshiki Hasegawa. PRD: Bandai. 25 mins. x 31 eps. (pilot, 5 mins.).
A cute kitten keeps a diary about life in the human world. A setup in the style

of the more famous **I AM A CAT**, though this adaptation of Mimei Ogawa's manga in *Lala* magazine is aimed at a far younger audience, with trips to the seaside, Christmas parties, and even a vacation in America. Presumably, a trip to the U.K. was ruled out because "Mikan's Six-Month Quarantine Diary" wasn't catchy enough. When released on video, the final installment included the five-minute pilot film.

MIKIMOTO, HARUHIKO

1959– . Pseudonym for Haruhiko Sato, also sometimes billed as "Hal," particularly in his signatures on illustrations. Born in Tokyo, he dropped out of college to become a character designer on such shows as **MACROSS** AND **ORGUSS**. His distinctive, feather-haired females have made him one of the most popular designers in anime, and his later works have included **GUNBUSTER** and the computer-animated **BLUE REMAINS** (on which his designs were recognizable but misused). He remains a popular illustrator, to the extent that, as with Masamune Shirow, his involvement on some productions is sometimes hyped beyond his actual role.

MILK HOUSE DREAMING

1987. Video. DIR: Hiroyuki Torii. SCR: Asami Watanabe. DES: Yumiko Kawahara. ANI: Yoshiyuki Momose. MUS: Taeko Onuki. PRD: Kadono Superstation. 43 mins.
An "image video" in the tradition of **CIPHER**, setting watercolors from Yumiko Kawahara's 1983 manga to a series of 11 pop songs. Made to cash in on the artist winning the Shogakukan Best Young Female Artist Award.

MILK MONEY *

2004. JPN: *Uba*. Video. DIR: Norihiko Nagahama. SCR: Norihiko Nagahama. DES: Daifuku Sugiya. ANI: Norihiko Nagahama. MUS: Yoshi. PRD: Digital Works (Vanilla Series), YOUC. 30 mins. x 2 eps.
After losing her unborn baby in a car accident, Kyoko takes a job as a wet nurse in order to ease the strain on her

still lactating breasts. Many years later, she realizes that the baby she nursed was Toji, who is now a classmate of her teenage daughter Marika. Before long, Toji is invited to the house for a taste of days gone by—part of the **VANILLA SERIES**. **LNV**

MILKY PASSION

1990. JPN: *Milky Passion: Ai no Shiki*. AKA: *MP: Love in Four Seasons*. Video. DIR: Takashi Imanishi. SCR: Takashi Imanishi. DES: Moriyasu Taniguchi. ANI: Moriyasu Taniguchi. MUS: Natsui Okamoto. PRD: Animation 501. 30 mins.
In this sexy tale based on a manga by Milk Morizono, one of the shining stars of women's erotica, the attractive owner of a love hotel falls in love with her handsome manager. Their different class backgrounds come between them, and she is tempted by the arrival of a rich American hotel magnate; though she eventually returns to the arms of her Motel Mellors. See also **HER NEED FOR EMBRACE**. **N**

MILLENNIUM ACTRESS *

2001. JPN: *Sennen Joyu*. Movie. DIR: Satoshi Kon. SCR: Sadayuki Murai, Satoshi Kon. DES: Takeshi Honda, Satoshi Kon. ANI: Takeshi Honda, Toshiyuki Inoue, Hideki Hamazu, Kenichi Konishi, Shogo Furuya. MUS: Susumu Hirasawa. PRD: Genco, Madhouse. 87 mins.
Small-time film producer Genya Tachibana is hired to make a documentary commemorating the 70th anniversary of Gin Ei film Studios. He chooses to interview Chiyoko Fujiwara, a one-time superstar actress who has lived as a recluse for 30 years. Fujiwara's life story combines fragments of 20th-century history (compare to **OSHIN**) with dramatic incidents from her acting career, blurring the boundaries between reality and fiction in a similar fashion to the same staff's earlier **PERFECT BLUE**. It also discloses the events behind Fujiwara's fall from favor, leading to inevitable comparisons with the desolate opera star of Katsuhiro Otomo's **MEMORIES**. Though

completed in January 2001 and premiered in Montreal that July, the film was not actually given a general release in Japan until September 2002.

MILMO DE PON

2002. JPN: *Wagamama Fairy Milmo de Pon.* AKA: *Naughty Fairy Milmo de Pon; Mirmo Zibang!.* TV series, TV special. DIR: Kenichi Kasai. SCR: Michihiro Tsuchiya. DES: Masayuki Onchi. ANI: Studio Hibari. MUS: Takayuki Negishi. PRD: TV Tokyo, Shogakukan. 25 mins. x 81 eps. (TV1), 25 mins. x 26 eps. (TV2), 25 mins. x 42 eps. (TV3), 60 mins. x 4 eps. (sp).

Kaede, aged fourteen, has a crush on her classmate Yuki. Daydreaming about him while she makes herself a cup of cocoa in her new mug, she makes a wish, and out pops baby-faced blond cutie Milmo, prince of the fairy kingdom, love specialist, and chocolate addict, to help her in her quest to win his heart. Milmo is just one of a whole fairy kingdom that invades Kaede's life and the lives of her friends, aiming to bring them joy through music, fun, and extreme silliness. The little fairy's adventures, based on the manga by Hiromu Shinozuka, continued in 2003 with *NFMdP: Golden* and in 2004 with *NFMdP: Wonderful.* Two one-hour specials, *How's the Squid? (Ika wa Ikaga?)* and *Cake Crumbles,* were also screened in June and July 2004; a third, *Journey to the West (Saiyuki),* at the end of December 2004; and a fourth, *Hole of Asaze,* as part of the Anime Festival in March 2005—all on the same evening as regular 25-minute episodes. Compare to WONDERFUL GENIE FAMILY, whose method of summoning was, upon reflection, not all that much sillier.

MIND GAME *

2004. Movie. DIR: Masaaki Yuasa. SCR: Masaaki Yuasa. DES: Yuichiro Sueyoshi. ANI: Yuichiro Sueyoshi, Koji Morimoto, Masahiko Kubo. MUS: Seiichi Yamamoto, Yoko Kanno. PRD: Studio 4°C, Beyond C, Rentrack Japan, Asmik-Ace Entertainment. 104 mins.

Loser manga artist Nishi has a chance encounter with his childhood sweetheart Myun, although even that proves to be bad luck for him. Myun and her family are being pursued by an irate moneylender who shoots and kills Nishi. Finding himself in the afterlife, the regretful Nishi rails against not only a meaningless death, but also the meaningless life that preceded it. As he promises to try harder next time, he finds himself back in his original body, still alive—shades here of EMBLEM TAKE TWO.

Back in Osaka, Nishi turns the tables on his attackers before evading their pursuit by jumping off a bridge. Finding themselves literally in the belly of a whale, Nishi and his two female companions set up house with a man they meet who has been there for some time (recalling the Jonah story, see SUPERBOOK), telling stories about far away places. Based on a manga by Robin Nishi, and with characters designed to look like the famous actors who play them, *Mind Game* has been loaded with awards—the prestigious Noburo Ofuji prize at Japan's 59th Mainichi Film Festival, four awards at Montreal's Fantasia, a ranking above that of HOWL'S MOVING CASTLE at the 2004 Japan Media Arts Festival, and two subtitled New York screenings at the NYC Asian Film Festival and the Museum of Modern Art's *Anime!!* exhibit.

MIRACLE GIANTS

1989. JPN: *Miracle Giants Domu-kun.* TV series. DIR: Takashi Watanabe, Koichi Chiaki, Masahito Sato, Masao Ito. SCR: Haruya Yamazaki, Michiru Shimada, Tsunehisa Ito. DES: Hatsuki Tsuji. ANI: Hatsuki Tsuji. MUS: N/C. PRD: Studio Gallop. 25 mins. x 10 eps. Short-lived baseball story based on a manga by Shotaro Ishinomori, in which fifth-grade baseball prodigy Domu joins his late father's team and plays against anime versions of many real-life stars of Japanese baseball.

MIRACLE GIRLS

1993. TV series. DIR: Takashi Anno, Satoshi Kimura, Hiroyuki Kuzumoto, Akitaro Daichi, Kazuhiro Sasaki. SCR: Hirokazu Kobayashi, Asami Watanabe, Takashi Waguri, Miho Maruo. DES: Masayuki Sekigane. ANI: Ryoko Hata, Mariko Fujita. MUS: Michiru Oshima. PRD: Japan Taps, NAS, Nippon TV. 25 mins. x 51 eps.

The 15-year-old Matsunaga girls are identical twins with very different personalities—the tomboyish Tomomi and the feminine Mikage. Both, however, have the paranormal powers of telepathic communication, limited telekinesis, and teleportation (but only if they both concentrate). The girls are brought closer together when Mikage's boyfriend Kurashige leaves to study in faraway England. They teleport to foil a hijack attempt on his plane, but after this semi-superheroic beginning, the series soon settles into a much more mundane story line. The twins occasionally swap identities, sometimes as a prank, sometimes to help each other out of difficult situations, and use their powers to cheat on the occasional exam or win the occasional sporting event. But as in the similar KIMAGURE ORANGE ROAD, the paranormal elements are swamped by more everyday teenage concerns. Based on the feel-good manga by Nami Akimoto in *Nakayoshi* magazine, *MG* is a sideways look at love and growing up, with occasional detours through time travel, ghost stories, and postmodern japery—in one episode, the voice actresses find other jobs and the twins must get them back to the studio! Episodes also steal from JAPANESE FOLK TALES, and even pastiche *The Red Shoes,* but the characters are so endearing that they more than compensate for the patchwork series of plots. The final episodes add a CINDERELLA twist, where the twins are revealed to be the prophesied saviors of the kingdom of Diamas and must fight the evil Mr. X for control of the country. By the end, everything has returned to normal, the girls are back home, and Mikage continues her chaste epistolary relationship with her absent boyfriend.

MIRACLE OF LOVE

1982. JPN: *Ai no Kiseki: Dr. Norman Monogatari.* AKA: *Miracle of Love: The Story of Dr. Norman.* TV special. DIR: Masami Annai, Yasuo Hasegawa. SCR: Toshi Nagasaki. DES: Yoshitaka Amano. ANI: Hiroshi Yamane, Kazutoshi Kobayashi, Noriko Yazawa, Noboru Furuse. MUS: Chikara Ueda. PRD: Kokusai Eiga, Studio Gallop, TV Asahi. 85 mins.

Dr. Oppenheimer ruins a promising medical career when he kills a small child in a car accident. Hiding from the police, he changes his name to Norman and lives among the people of the slums. When property developers try to clear away the slum-dwellers to build a theme park, Norman defends their rights, though his public good deeds allow Detective Gavan to finally catch up with him. A tale of sin and redemption, screened on Christmas Eve.

MIRAGE OF BLAZE *

2002. JPN: *Honoo No Shinkiro; Honoo no Mirage.* AKA: *Blazing Mirage; Mirage of Flame.* TV series, video. DIR: Toshio Hirata, Fumie Muroi. SCR: Hiroko Tokita, Kazuyuki Fudeyasu, Ryosuke Nakamura, Yuki Enatsu. DES: Itsuko Takeda, Fumie Muroi. ANI: SME Visual Works. MUS: Koichiro Kameyama. PRD: Madhouse, Kid's Station, SME Visual Works. 25 mins. x 13 eps. (TV), 31 mins. x 3 eps. (V).

Takaya Oge believes himself to be haunted by the ghosts of ancient warriors and keeps seeing people surrounded by a strange aura of purplish flames. A mysterious man, Nobutsuna Naoe, appears in his room and saves him from the visions; he claims to be a reincarnated warlord from Japan's civil war era, and says that Takaya and others like him are warrior spirits reborn in modern Tokyo—like IKKI TOUSEN, but not as silly. The Feudal Underworld is seeping into the modern world and threatens to repeat ancient clan battles and devastate the present; Takaya is one of those who can use his ancient powers to prevent this. Takaya doesn't remember his past life at first, but as his powers return he begins to recall the passion-

ate and sometimes abusive relationship that he and Naoe once shared. This series is based on the popular novel series by Mizuna Kuwahara and 32-volume manga series by Shoko Hamada, which was stuffed with beautiful young men brooding mysteriously while calling up purple flames (the "blaze" of the title) that give them power to destroy objects and people by thought. It was followed in 2004 by the video series *MoB: Rebels of the River Edge (HnS: Minagiwa no Hangyakusha)* in which Takaya hunts down a rebel in Kyoto who deserted the clan and uncovers a 400-year-old tale of love and betrayal. **V**

MIREI

1995. JPN: *Kotoyoshi Yumisuke Mirei.* AKA: *Yumisuke Kotoyoshi [presents] Mirei.* Video. DIR: Akira Nishimori, Takashi Yoshida. SCR: Yumisuke Kotoyoshi, Nana Okatsu, Masao Oji. DES: Yumisuke Kotoyoshi, Naoki Ohei. ANI: Mitsuharu Miyamae. MUS: N/C. PRD: Reed, TDK Core. 30 mins.

In this adaptation of Yumisuke Kotoyoshi's manga, two beautiful girls are washed ashore on a South Sea island paradise, where they proceed to take their clothes off. **N**

MIROKU

1989. JPN: *Kyomu Senshi Miroku.* AKA: *Expunged Chronicle of Miroku.* Video. DIR: Toshio Takeuchi, Junichi Watanabe. SCR: Hideo Takyashiki, Megumi Hiyoshi. DES: Hideyuki Motohashi. ANI: Hideyuki Motohashi. MUS: Michiaki Kato. PRD: Animate Film, Dynamic Planning, JC Staff. 30 mins. x 6 eps.

Psychic ninja fantasy suggesting that the assassins did not die out during the early modern period but burrowed under Japan, where they fought a new war against the alien occupants of a crashed spaceship that has lain undisturbed for several millennia. The shogun Ieyasu is just one of the historical figures who wander into this decidedly unhistorical plot that was based on a story written for *Shonen Captain* magazine by GETTER ROBO–cocreator Ken Ishikawa.

MIRROR OF HALLEY

1985. JPN: *Arei no Kagami.* AKA: *Mirror of Arei.* Movie. DIR: Kozo Morishita. SCR: Michiru Umadori. DES: Leiji Matsumoto. ANI: Kazuo Komatsubara. MUS: Yuri Nishimura. PRD: Toei. 25 mins.

Meguru and Mayu are two future-wanderers hoping to find the mythical Mirror of Arei that is said to allow all who glimpse it to pass beyond the edge of the universe. Hijacked by renegade android Zero, the trio joins forces when they realize that they are all searching for the same thing. At the edge of our universe they encounter the ethereal being Rin'ne (Japanese for transmigration) and a council of spirits who judge those who wish to enter a new universe. The gatekeeper, Arei, is not impressed with what the travelers' memories tell her of human history. Though the humans try to argue their case, Arei decides to destroy the mirror. Though it will strand them for eternity, the humans use their gravity generator to hold the mirror together so that others may not be denied the opportunity to see it. Arei is impressed by their noble sacrifice and reveals that the mirror was not really destroyed. She sends them home but first permits them a fleeting glimpse of the wonders of the next world. Based on a manga by GALAXY EXPRESS 999–creator Leiji Matsumoto, this film was originally screened at the 1985 World Expo in Tsukuba.

MIRATSU, TAKEO

1960– . Born in Oita prefecture, Miratsu was only 19 when he formed a band to compete in the Yamaha Popular Music Contest, although he would later find fame as a composer, rather than a performer. He released albums of his own in 1992 and 1996, before turning to jingles and "image music" (compositions on spin-off CDs) for anime such as HUMMINGBIRDS and USHIO AND TORA. He subsequently became a composer for actual anime, scoring shows including SAIKANO, NINJA CADETS and DETATOKO PRINCESS. His work has also appeared in games such as *Jumping Flash*.

MISHA THE BEAR CUB

1979. JPN: *Koguma no Misha*. TV series. DIR: Yoshikata Nitta. SCR: Shunichi Yukimuro, Yoshiaki Yoshida, Ryuzo Nakanishi. DES: Isamu Noda. ANI: Yutaka Oka, Sadao Tominaga, Takashi Saijo, Yoshiyuki Kishi. MUS: Shunsuke Kikuchi. PRD: Trans Arts, Nippon Animation, TV Asahi. 25 mins. x 26 eps.

Misha the Russian bear cub comes with his parents to a peaceful mountain village full of different kinds of animals. The animals come out to see the train, but Misha's father believes they are a welcoming committee and decides to stay. Misha befriends Natasha (another bear cub) but must avoid the evil local tiger (unimaginatively named Tiger). It's a simple children's series made to cash in on the 1980 Moscow Olympics' Misha mascot. Not quite as successful as the later Olympic anime EAGLE SAM.

MISTER AJIKKO

1987. AKA: *Mr. Flavor*. TV series. DIR: Yasuhiro Imagawa, Makoto Ikeda, Akihiko Nishiyama, Kunihisa Sugishima, Akio Yamadera, Tatsuo Suzuki, Junichi Sakata, Tetsuro Amino. SCR: Noboru Shiroyama, Akinori Endo, Noboru Aikawa, Yoshikazu Sakata, Ryoei Tsukimura, Yoshinori Watanabe, Toshifumi Kawase. DES: Masahiro Kato. ANI: Nobuhiro Okaseko, Kazuko Yano. MUS: Oku Fujita. PRD: Sunrise, TV Tokyo. 25 mins. x 99 eps.

They call him "Mr. Flavor" because middle school boy Yoichi is one of the best chefs around, taking on and learning from masters in the many subsets of cooking, including spaghetti, sushi, steak, sardine *gratin*, ramen, omelets, hamburgers, *okonomiyaki*, *bento* boxes, curry, hotpot, and *donburi*. And that's just in the first season. Mr. Flavor returned for two more, until he walked off into the sunset on a quest for even better recipes with a final episode entitled "Gochiso-sama, Mr. Ajikko," the traditional Japanese thanks for a hearty feast. A gourmet anime aimed at a younger audience than the following year's OISHINBO, based on the 1986 *King of Sushi* (*DE) manga by

Daisuke Terasawa, who wrote the similarly foody *Ryota's Sushi*.

MISTER HAPPY *

1989. JPN: *Yarukimanman*. AKA: *Ready-to-get-it-on Man; Mad-for-it-man*. Video. DIR: Teruo Kigure, Masamune Ochiai. SCR: Masahito Nishio. DES: Masamichi Yokoyama. ANI: Jiro Sayama. MUS: N/C. PRD: Knack. 26 mins., 45 mins., 40 mins.

Kazua Jinno is the scion of Japan's oldest and most accomplished family of brothel keepers. In preparation for Kazua's taking over the family business, his father, Sopetuen, sends him out into the world to have sex with as many women as possible while always ensuring that the ladies come first (how this is training for running a brothel, Lord knows). He is aided in his erotic misadventures by "Mr. Happy," his talking penis, who provides advice and commentary at relevant moments. The Japanese sales sheet thoughtfully adds, "The ultimate sex battles developed by his proud penis together with women's juicy vaginas never stop making the lower half of men's bodies hot." Based on the 1977 manga in *Daily Gendai* by "Gyujiro" and AGEMAN AND FUKUCHAN–creator Masamichi Yokoyama and reputedly screened on a U.S. adult cable channel in the 1990s. ●🄽

MISTER PEN-PEN

1986. TV special. DIR: Ken Baba, Tsukasa Sunaga, Yuzo Yamada, Hiroshi Watanabe. SCR: Kenji Terada. DES: Mayumi Muroyama. ANI: Takahisa Kazukawa. MUS: Takeo Watanabe. PRD: Shinei, TV Asahi. 60 mins. x 2 eps.

Pen-Pen, the hat-and-tie-wearing prince of Penguin Land, turns up unexpectedly on little Mika's doorstep and invites himself and his zany penguin friends to stay. Based on a manga written by ASARI-CHAN-creator Mayumi Muroyama for Shogakukan's *Second Grader* magazine and comprising eight 15-minute mini-episodes, these two TV "specials" may be a salvage job from a canceled TV series. It had friends in high places, however—Hideaki Anno

would incorporate a genetically engineered penguin called Mr. Pen-Pen into his own EVANGELION.

MIYAZAKI, HAYAO

1941– . Born in Tokyo, he graduated from the Politics and Economics department of the prestigious Gakushuin University in 1963. He joined Toei Animation the following year and found work on KEN THE WOLF BOY and Isao Takahata's LITTLE NORSE PRINCE, for which he drew literally thousands of images. A shop steward and union leader at the company, he also demonstrated early aptitude for storylining, famously persuading the director of GULLIVER'S SPACE TRAVELS to allow him to rewrite the ending. The first example of his distinctive style came in PANDA GO PANDA (1972), released shortly before he and his long-time collaborator Isao Takahata moved to the Zuiyo company, later known as Nippon Animation. Had Miyazaki only stayed in TV animation, he would still have enjoyed a reputation as one of anime's most internationally-minded directors, adapting children's stories for the screen from British, American, French, German, Italian, and Japanese originals, including SHERLOCK HOUND, HEIDI, and ANNE OF GREEN GABLES. After a long apprenticeship in TV, his directorial debut came with THE CASTLE OF CAGLIOSTRO (1978), although it was NAUSICAÄ OF THE VALLEY OF WIND that truly established him as an original voice in the medium. The establishment of Miyazaki's own Studio Ghibli followed, leading to some of the most renowned films of the anime medium, including CASTLE IN THE SKY, MY NEIGHBOR TOTORO, KIKI'S DELIVERY SERVICE, and PORCO ROSSO. Notably, these films also generated good box office returns, as opposed to many other anime movies, which are only exhibited in theaters in order to gain review coverage in cinema magazines and to generate publicity for a video release. Although he supposedly intended to retire after PRINCESS MONONOKE, the death of Yoshifumi Kondo (q.v.)

caused him to return to direct **SPIRITED AWAY**, which won anime's first Feature Animation Academy Award. His most recent film is **HOWL'S MOVING CASTLE**. Often termed "Japan's Disney" by the foreign press—a faintly patronizing title that downplays his true originality, not as a Japanese filmmaker, but as a world-class writer and director.

MIYUKI

1983. TV series. DIR: Mizuho Nishikubo, Hiroko Tokita, Shigeru Omachi, Shigeru Yanagawa, Junichi Sakata. SCR: Michiru Shimada, Shikichi Ohashi. DES: Mitsuru Adachi. ANI: Hayao Nobe, Kazuhiro Oga. MUS: Ryan Merry, Masamichi Amano. PRD: Kitty Film, Fuji TV. 25 mins. x 37 eps.

Two high school students discover they have the same name and become friends, but both fall in love with Masato, a boy who is forced to choose just one. Based on the 1980 *Shonen Sunday* manga by Mitsuru Adachi and the first of his many works to be adapted into anime. Others would include **TOUCH**, **H2**, **NINE**, and **SLOW STEP**.

MIYUKI-CHAN IN WONDERLAND *

1995. JPN: *Fushigi no Kuni no Miyukichan*. AKA: *Miyuki-chan in the Strange Kingdom*. Video. DIR: Seiko Sayama, Mamoru Hamazu. SCR: Nanase Okawa. DES: Tetsuro Aoki. ANI: Makoto Koga. MUS: Toshiyuki Honda. PRD: Animate Film. 29 mins.

A pointlessly kinky retelling of **ALICE IN WONDERLAND** in which all the characters are sapphically inclined females. Japanese schoolgirl Miyuki is late for school when she is distracted by a bunny-girl on a skateboard. She is dragged into a sex-obsessed Wonderland, complete with strip chess, Humpty Dumpty as a svelte diva, a bondage Queen, and a Cheshire cat resembling a blonde, stockinged Lum from **URUSEI YATSURA**. Based on the manga by the all-girl collective CLAMP, *MiW* appeared intermittently in *Newtype* over several years, and its absent plot is explained with the age-old get-out clause of it all being a dream. A one-note gag that falls

Miyuki-chan in Wonderland

crushingly flat when the clever designs are forced to do more than look good on paper.

MIZUIRO

2002. AKA: *Water-Color*. Video. DIR: Kiyotaka Isako. SCR: Ryota Yamaguchi, Makoto Nakamura. DES: Takeyasu Kurashima. ANI: Takeyasu Kurashima. MUS: N/C. PRD: Movic, Pink Pineapple. 30 mins. x 2 eps. (v1) 30 mins. x 2 eps. (v2).

Lonely teenage boy Kenji finds first two, then three, fantasy females hiding in his closet. They reappear each night, but only he seems to be able to see them, in a predictably risqué respray of **URUSEI YATSURA**, based on a PS2 computer game. *Mizuiro 2003* (2003), the "second series," is a remake with the sex scenes greatly toned down. Not to be confused with **AQUA AGE**, which has a similar title in Japanese, or **AQUARIAN AGE**, which doesn't.

MOCHI MOCHI TREE, THE

1992. JPN: *Mochi Mochi no Ki*. Video. DIR: Isamu Noda. SCR: Takasuke Saito. DES: N/C. ANI: Susumu Shiraume, Hidekazu Ohara. MUS: Keiichiro Hirano. PRD: Ask Kodansha. 20 mins.

In this adaptation of a lyrical children's best-seller by Ryusuke Saito and Jiro Takihira, an ailing old man talks about the meaning of life with the shy little boy who keeps him company. The same crew followed with *The Mountain in Full Bloom* (1992, *Hanasaki Yama*), based on another story by the same authors, in which an old woman tells a young girl that a flower opens every time someone does a good deed.

MOCHINAGA, TADAHITO

1919–1999. Aka Fang Ming, aka Tad Mochinaga. Born in Tokyo, Mochinaga grew up in Japanese-occupied Manchuria, where his father worked for the railway company. Inspired by early Disney cartoons to seek a career in animation, he studied art in Tokyo before finding work with Mitsuyo Seo as a background artist. For Seo's *Ant Boy* (1941, *Ari-chan*), Mochinaga designed and built Japan's first multiplane camera, a rostrum device allowing for simultaneous action on four different overlaid cels. His directorial debut was the **WARTIME ANIME** *Fuku-chan's Submarine* (1944), before he became the producer of **MOMOTARO'S DIVINE SEA WARRIORS**, anime's first full-length feature. Exhausted by the effort and left homeless by an air raid, he returned to Manchuria to recuperate, only to find himself conscripted to produce documentary animation for Man-Ei (Manchurian Film Studios). With Japan's defeat, Man-Ei's assets were handed over to China and renamed Dong Bei (Northern Animation). Electing to stay in China, Mochinaga adopted the name Fang Ming, and was instrumental in the foundation and early output of the Shanghai Animation Studio, where he befriended the Chinese master animator De Wei.

Mochinaga returned to Japan in 1953, in time for the early television broadcasts. He was able to put his Chinese experience of stop-motion animation to use on the Asahi commercial *Beer Through the Ages* (1956), and enjoyed a prominent role in TV stop-motion animation. His *Little Black Sambo* (1956) won an award at the Vancouver Film Festival, leading to an approach from American animator Arthur Rankin, Jr. Mochinaga's new MOM Films produced several Videocraft (Rankin/Bass) coproductions, including *Rudolph the Red-Nosed Reindeer* (1964). He is thus the only man in history who can claim to have produced a Japanese World War II propaganda film, founded a Chinese animation studio, *and* made an American Christmas TV classic. He taught at the Beijing Film Academy for two years in the 1980s, and funded his final movie, *Boy and the Badger/Tanuki* (1992, *Shonen to Kotanuki*), with his own money, thereby spanning six decades of Japanese animation.

MOCHIZUKI, TOMOMI

1958– . Born on Hokkaido, he became involved with the Tokyo anime scene when he joined the Animation Society at Waseda University. Hired by Asia-do company after graduation, he shared directing credit for CREAMY MAMI (1983) with Osamu Kobayashi before moving into romance and comedy with MAISON IKKOKU (1987) and RANMA ½ (1989)—his feature debut was the *Mai-*

son Ikkoku movie. Subsequently hired by Studio Ghibli to direct the TV movie OCEAN WAVES (1993).

MODERN DOG TALES BOW WOW

1993. JPN: *Heisei Inu Monogatari Bow Wow.* TV series, movie. DIR: Takeshi Kaga. SCR: Yasuhiro Komatsuzaki, Shunichi Yukimuro. DES: Terry Yamamoto. ANI: N/C. MUS: N/C. PRD: Nippon Animation. 25 mins. x 40 eps. (TV), 25 mins. (m).
Based on the manga by Terry Yamamoto in *Big Comic Superior*, here are the comic misadventures of a lovable stray mongrel called Bow Wow and his little-girl owner. The situations are a standard list of food-related story lines, a few interfering cats, and a trawl through the various seasonal events of the Japanese and Western calendar. For the short "movie" version, however, the story sends the couple back to prehistoric times, where they must save a friendly mammoth from an erupting volcano.

MODERN LOVE'S SILLINESS

1999. JPN: *Anime Ai Awa Awa Hour.* AKA: *Anime Lovers' Awa-Awa Hour.* TV series. DIR: Makoto Moriwaki, Kume Issei. SCR: Chika Hojo, Motoki Yoshimura. DES: Yukiko Ohashi, Wataru Yamaguchi, Shuri Nakamura. ANI: N/C. MUS: Minami Toriyama. PRD: Gainax, Pioneer, Tac, DirecTV. 22 mins. x 12 eps.
Three short gag anime presented in a late-night anthology show, aimed at adult women instead of the usual male or fan audiences for anime and produced by Hideaki Anno in the midst of his work on HIS AND HER CIRCUMSTANCES. The first, *Ebichu Minds the House* (*Oruchuban Ebichu*), based on the *Manga Action Pizazz* manga by Risa Ito, portrays modern life from the viewpoint of a hamster, Ebichu, who observes his Tokyo Office Lady owner's kinky relationship with her slacker boyfriend. Some of the show's controversial sex scenes were cut from the original digital TV broadcast but reinstated in the DVD release.
Little Women in Love (*Ai no Wakaku-*

sayama Monogatari), based on the manga in *Manga Club* by Reiko Terashima, concentrates on unmarried Shizuka, still living with her parents, who fear she will be left perpetually on the shelf.

The final story, based on Mitsue Aoki's manga *Here Comes Koume* (*Koume-chan ga Iku*), switches location to the distinctive accents and attitudes of Osaka (see COMPILER), where Koume works as a designer for the Caramel Ribbon company with a fey boss, an assistant who used to be a bad-girl biker, and a tough-guy boyfriend. ●N

MOEKAN

2004. AKA: *Moekko Company The Animation.* Video. DIR: Kazukoto Ono. SCR: Mayori Sekishima, Masashi Kubota. DES: Konomi Noguchi. ANI: Konomi Noguchi. MUS: N/C. PRD: Axis, KSS. 30 mins. x 3 eps.
AC Company is a corporation that makes android "escort maids"—beautiful girl-like robots to serve its clients' every whim. The androids are sent for finishing and communication training to Moekko Island, which functions as an independent state, with more financial and military muscle than any nation. Takahiro Kanzaki, head of the training facility, lives in a huge mansion on the island. He was once an extremely powerful man within the organization, despite his youth, but has been demoted; he is depressed and has lost many of his memories. New maid Rinia, who has also lost her memories, arrives for training; an obsolete type of android, she's very clumsy but tries very hard, and her well-meaning attempts to improve endear her to Takahiro. A predictable piece of fluff, based on the PC, PS2, and Dreamcast "love adventure game" *Moekan*.

MOEYO KEN *

2004. JPN: *Kido Shinsengumi Moeyo Ken.* AKA: *Robot Shinsengumi Flashing Sword.* Video, TV series. DIR: Hideki Tonokatsu. SCR: Junji Takegami. DES: Kazuo Takegawa, Rumiko Takahashi. ANI: Magic Picture. MUS: N/C. PRD: Magic Picture, Enterbrain, Trinet Entertainment. 30 mins. x 4 eps. (v), 25 mins. x 13 eps. (TV).

Kyoto, 1882: statesman Kaishu Katsu asks Oryu, widow of the great patriot Ryoma Sakamoto, to form a new division of the Kyoto Prefectural Police to protect the city from robot and demon crimes. Her recruits are all girls, the daughters of famous figures of the Edo period. Alas, they take their lead not from their famous fathers but from their senior officer, Yuko, daughter of Isami Kondo, a clumsy, sentimental glutton; they waste their time on love and sword fighting instead of getting down to the serious business of defending Kyoto.

The heroes of the later Tokugawa and early Meiji era have been thoroughly examined in anime, providing material for shows like OI! RYOMA and PEACEMAKER KUROGANE. But MK is based on a PlayStation 2 game, and a game from Oji Hiroi, the man behind SAKURA WARS, at that. It takes a similarly cavalier attitude toward history, using historical events as a springboard into the realms of fighting-female fantasy. It aimes to attract the widest possible range of fans by crashing RURO NI KENSHIN into SAILOR MOON and throwing in historical figures, robots, and cars. Rumiko Takahashi, the creator of RANMA ½, is credited for her work designing the characters from the original game, in the same manner as Masamune Shirow on LANDLOCK and Kosuke Fujishima on Sakura Wars—it looks good on the box, but doesn't actually lend all that much to the quality of the production. Meanwhile, evil characters attempt to bring SHUTENDOJI back from the dead in order to plunge Kyoto into an age of darkness.

It would be kind to describe this show as an action parody, but the running gags about small breasts, wholly unnecessary bath scenes, and monster-of-the-week idiocy make kindness difficult. The producers have employed stellar talent and spent serious money to prove that what works in a game doesn't necessarily make great anime. **N**

MOJACKO

1995. TV series. DIR: Tetsuya Endo, Norihiko Sudo, Satoshi Inoue, Masamitsu Hidaka, Masashi Abe. SCR: Raita Okura, Shikichi Ohashi, Hiroshi Koda, Yasuhiro Komatsuzaki, Chika Hojo, Atsuhiro Tomioka. DES: Hidetoshi Owase. ANI: Hidetoshi Owase. MUS: Kei Wakakusa. PRD: OLM, Shogakukan Pro, Tokyo TV. 25 mins. x 73 eps.

Ghost-hunting schoolchildren Sorao, Miki, and Wu-Tang find a crashed spaceship belonging to Mojacko, an alien from the planet Mojamoja, and his robot, Donnoh. He takes them on a journey to the moon (with the aid of handy "air pills"), which is only one of many great adventures—though in exchange, he wants to learn about wacky Earth pursuits like roller-blading, golf, and scuba diving. He also enlists his new friends in a battle against the fearsome Maharaja Moja clan of space pirates.

An unremarkable children's anime based on a manga by DORAEMON-cocreator Fujiko F. Fujio, though it was an early voice-acting job for PERFECT BLUE's Junko Iwao. The series would eventually lose its animation director, Endo, to Hong Kong, where he would work on Tsui Hark's *Chinese Ghost Story* animation. Episodes 60 and 61 were rebroadcast as a one-hour TV movie with the title *Fujio F. Fujiko's Mojacko Christmas Present.*

MOLDIVER *

1993. Video. DIR: Hiroyuki Kitazume. SCR: Ryoei Tsukimura, Manabu Nakamura. DES: Hiroyuki Kitazume. ANI: Hiroyuki Kitazume, Masashi Handa. MUS: Kei Wakakusa. PRD: AIC, Pioneer. 30 mins. x 6 eps.

Tokyo, 2045. Superhero Moldiver rights wrongs and strikes poses all over the city, and pretty Mirai Ozora discovers that Moldiver is actually her brother, Hiroshi. Hiroshi's suit allows the user to repel and defy all laws of physics, which makes flight, bullet-proofing, and incredible strength easy. Mirai decides to be a superhero herself, and Hiroshi gets a shock and a half when he finds himself wearing his sister's revealing costume!

Bright, colorful, and fun, *Moldiver* is packed with gentle jibes at the superhero phenomenon and very aware that the only crime in this kind of anime is taking oneself too seriously. With plotlines and characters from a kiddie-cartoon, but a tongue-in-cheek self-awareness aimed at a far older audience, it's also another excellent example of how good English-language translation can be. The humor in Pioneer's dub crosses international borders with deceptive ease. Neophytes might be a little confused by Professor Amagi's attempt to raise the Yamato from the seabed in episode four, but they should be told that this old battleship has many resonances for a slightly older anime audience. It's as famous in Japan as the Titanic in the English-speaking world, with extra baggage brought by its place in military history. For anime fans, of course, it's also the star of STAR BLAZERS, and its appearance here is a tip of the hat from Pioneer's next generation to the classic creators who inspired them to pursue their careers in the first place.

The initial letters of the episode titles ("Metamorforce," "Overzone," "Longing," "Destruction," "Intruder") spell the name of the series, right up until the final episode ("Verity"), which crams the rest of the title in one go—possibly a sign of an early cancellation.

MOMIJI *

2003. Video. DIR: Toshiaki Kanbara. SCR: Taifu Kancho. DES: Masaki Kawai. ANI: Hideki Araki. MUS: N/C. PRD: Marigold, Shura, Blue Eyes. 30 mins. x 4 eps.

Momiji is a ridiculously passive teenage girl who is pressured by her classmate Kazuto to work as a maid for his wealthy family. As soon as she moves in, he takes her virginity, then has sex with her whenever he chooses, in school and in public places as well as at home. He is also having sex with a classmate and the other maids, one of whom is in love with him, who have sex with him

Momotaro's Divine Sea Warriors

and with each other whenever he commands. Despite episode four's suggestion that Kazuto is a poor tortured soul who had almost given up on life until he found Momiji, he is one of the nastiest protagonists of this type of anime porn, getting his kicks out of refusing to give his women what they want and abusing them with vibrators and hot wax, which naturally makes them even more eager to serve his every whim. **ⒷⓃⓋ**

MOMOKO

1989. Video. DIR: Hideo Norei. SCR: Masahito Nishio. DES: Haru Hosokawa. ANI: N/C. MUS: N/C. PRD: Clion Soft. 45 mins. x 2 eps.

The life of "fashion model and masseuse" Momoko is detailed in this saucy adaptation of Haru Hosokawa's manga in *Comic Be* told in a combination of animated images on live backgrounds. With little else to recommend it, the marketing for this tape declared itself to be a "CVP," a "Comic Video Picture." Compare to **MY FAIR MASSEUSE**. **Ⓝ**

MOMOTARO

1989. JPN: *Momotaro Densetsu*. AKA: *Legend of Momotaro*. TV series. DIR: Masamune Ochiai, Yuji Ikeno, Koichi Fujiwara, Teruo Kigure, Akinori Yabe.

SCR: Tadaaki Yamazaki, Shunichi Yukimuro. DES: Kazuo Mori, Hideo Okamoto. ANI: Kazuo Mori. MUS: The Peach Boys. PRD: Knack, TV Tokyo. 25 mins. x 48 eps.

A childless woodcutter and his wife adopt Momotaro, a foundling child who springs from the inside of a peach. The superstrong child defeats Lord Brindled Dog, Lord Monkey of the Mountain, and Lord Pheasant of the Moor, who agree to become his traveling companions as he sets out to defeat all the ogres on the nearby island of Onigashima. Perhaps distantly inspired by **JOURNEY TO THE WEST**, one of the most famous of the **JAPANESE FAIRY TALES**, and a perennial children's favorite, the story of Momotaro is retold here with some science-fictional elements and a pastiche of Kurosawa's *Seven Samurai*. Pheasant Keeko, dog Pochi, and monkey Monta are asked by harassed villagers to find a hero who can save them—they approach Momotaro, who is famed far and wide for his naughtiness (guaranteed to annoy ogres everywhere). For the latter half of the series it was rebranded as *New Momotaro (P[each] C[ommand] Shin Momotaro Densetsu)*, in which the stout Japanese boy and his companions head off into space for a more fantastical sequel. See also **VIDEO PICTURE BOOK**.

MOMOTARO'S DIVINE SEA WARRIORS

1945. JPN: *Momotaro Umi no Shinpei*. Movie. DIR: Mitsuyo Seo. SCR: Kiichiro Kumaki. DES: Mitsuyo Seo. ANI: Mitsuyo Seo, Ichiro Takagi. MUS: Yuji Koseki. PRD: Shochiku, Geijutsu, Japanese Imperial Navy Department of Information. 74 mins. (b/w).

After completing their naval training, a bear cub, a monkey, a puppy, and a pheasant say goodbye to their families. The monkey's young brother plays with his sailor's cap and falls into a river trying to retrieve it. He is rescued by the other animals in the nick of time, before falling over a waterfall. The scene jumps to a South Pacific island, where the rabbit sailors of the Imperial

Navy are clearing the jungle to build an airfield. Watched in fascination by the native creatures (who, rather strangely for the South Pacific, include kangaroos, elephants, tigers, leopards, and rhinos), they complete it just in time for the arrival of a fleet of transport planes, bringing the animals from the former sequence, as well as a human boy, Commander **MOMOTARO**. While the military creatures get acclimated, the puppy teaches the local child-animals a nursery rhyme about the Rising Sun. Training takes a more meaningful turn when recon planes bring pictures of the British base on the other side of the island. The monkey, bear, and puppy begin parachute training, while the pheasant becomes a pilot. Presenting a history lesson using silhouette animation, Momotaro explains that Europeans have stolen Asia from its rightful rulers, and that the time has come to fight back. The animals attack the British base in a jarringly violent change of tone from the previous sequences, and the cowardly British ogres each try to get the other to take the responsibility for signing the surrender. Back home in Japan, the animals rejoice at the defeat of the British, while children play at parachuting . . . onto a map of the United States.

A sequel of sorts to the **WARTIME ANIME** *Momotaro's Sea Eagles* (1943), *MDSW* was Japan's first full-length animated feature, released on 12 April 1945, scant months before the end of the war. In a coincidental similarity to many later anime "movies," it has a disjointed quality, seemingly resulting from the output of separate teams; one on the opening pastoral, one on the island sequences, and another on the "why-we-fight" exposition. Inspired by Japanese screenings of *Princess Iron Fan* (a Chinese adaptation of **JOURNEY TO THE WEST**), Seo keeps to a slow pacing, with time out for comparisons such as paratroopers to falling dandelions. He also appears to have found native English-speakers to play the British in the surrender scene—perhaps prisoners of war?

In 1983, (ironically, a year dominated by the pacifist **BAREFOOT GEN**), the lost film was rediscovered in Shochiku's Ofuna warehouse and rereleased in 1984. It eventually made it to video, bundled on the same tape as *The Spider and the Tulip* (1943), an unrelated 16-minute short in which a black-faced spider, seemingly modeled on Al Jolson in *The Jazz Singer*, tries to tempt a ladybug into his web. The inclusion of Kichiro Kumaki's film seemed calculated, as in its original year of release, to distract audiences from wartime realities, albeit for different reasons. After the war, director Seo made the featurette *The King's Tail* (1947), before retiring from anime and becoming a children's author and illustrator. Producer Tadahito Mochinaga emigrated to Manchuria shortly before the close of the war. After the Communist revolution, he was instrumental in the foundation of the Shanghai Animation Studio, which would not only rejuvenate the Chinese animation industry, but would also subsequently work as a Japanese subcontractor on many later anime.

MON CHERIE COCO

1972. AKA: *Coco My Darling*. TV series. DIR: Kozo Masanobu, Nobuo Onuki. SCR: Jiro Saito. DES: Sachie Yoshiwara. ANI: Takekazu Kuchida. MUS: N/C. PRD: Nihon TV Doga, NTV. 25 mins. x 13 eps.

French-Japanese Coco Marchand is a scatterbrained girl with design talent, whose playful, dressed down designs all but ruin a stuffy show by the famous Madame Elle. However, her innovative attitude impresses Madame Cheryl, the kindly editor of *Mode* magazine, who takes her under her wing and offers to help her become a fashion designer. Based on a 1972 manga by **SMART-SAN**-creator Waki Yamato, this rags-to-better-rags tale might at first seem like a strange follow-up to the TV Doga studio's **ROAD TO MUNICH**. But the tropes and trials of the fashion world have many similarities to those of sports anime, and *Mon Cherie Coco* sits in the tradition of other girls' stories

like **MASK OF GLASS**, just with more sewing. NB—strictly speaking, the bilingual title probably should have been *Ma Cherie Koko*, but we have kept with both the creator's deliberate evocation of Coco Chanel and her hazy grasp of French grammar. In modern times, compare to **PARADISE KISS**. Fashion designer Miyako Kawamura helped out with some of the artwork.

MONARCH: THE BIG BEAR OF TALLAC

1977. JPN: *Seton Dobutsu Monogatari: Kuma no Ko Jacky*. AKA: *Seton's Animal Tale: Jacky the Bear Cub*. TV series. DIR: Yoshio Kuroda. SCR: Ryuzo Nakanishi, Michio Sato. DES: Yasuji Mori. ANI: Takao Kogawa, Shinichi Tsuji, Koichi Murata, Seiji Okuda, Isao Takahata. MUS: Akehiro Omori. PRD: Nippon Animation, TV Asahi. 25 mins. x 22 eps.

Ran the Native American boy lives high in the Sierra Nevada mountains of California, where he cares for a brother-bear and sister-bear he found as cubs in a cave. Calling them Jacky and Jill, he plays with them and their mother, until the mother bear is killed by Ran's father. Adopting Jacky and Jill as his own, Ran takes them back to his house. An adaptation of one of Ernest **SETON's ANIMAL TALES** that was soon to be followed by **BANNERTAIL THE SQUIRREL**.

MONCHICHI TWINS, THE

1980. JPN: *Futago no Monchichi*. TV series. DIR: Tetsuro Amino, Mariko Oizumi, Ryoji Fujiwara, Tatsuya Matano. SCR: Akiyoshi Sakai, Masaaki Sakurai, Tomomi Tsutsui. DES: N/C. ANI: Mamoru Tanaka, Minoru Tajima. MUS: N/C. PRD: Ashi Pro, Tokyo 12 Channel. 6 mins. x 130 eps.

Monchichi-kun and Monchichi-chan are simian twins who live in the forest. He "likes to play and she likes to be cute," and they get up to many fairy-tale-inspired adventures in the countryside. A long-running cartoon series made to cash in on the dolls made by the Sekiguchi corporation, which were also released by Mattel for the U.S., where they were accompanied by the

less successful all-American cartoon series *The Monchichis*.

MONCOLLÉ KNIGHTS *

2000. JPN: *Rokumon no Moncollé Knight*. AKA: *Mon[ster] Colle[ction] Knight of Rokumon*. TV series. DIR: Yasunaga Aoki, Akitaro Daichi, Akira Kiyomizu, Shunji Yoshida, Akio Sato. SCR: Katsumi Hasegawa, Satoru Akahori, Reiko Yoshida. DES: Atsuko Nakajima. ANI: Hiroko Sugii, Tetsuhito Saito. MUS: N/C. PRD: Studio Deen, TV Tokyo. 25 mins. x 51+ eps. (TV), 25 mins. (m).

Mondo Oya is a hotheaded 12-year-old schoolboy who just loves playing with his Monster Collection Collectable Card Game. One day, Mondo discovers that Rokumon, the world of the CCG, is actually a real place, when he is co-opted to defend the planet from the predations of mad scientist Duke Collection—described in *Newtype*, rather mysteriously, as "a straightforward homosexual."

A pointless addition to the game cash-in phenomenon of **POKÉMON** and **DIGIMON**, artlessly setting itself in the Rokumon "World of Six Gates" to imply a nonexistent connection to its more successful predecessors and tellingly crediting **MAZE**'s Satoru Akahori as a "story generalizer." A theatrical short would pit Mondo against a Fire Dragon and a Lava Chimaera in the magical world of Rokumon, as if anyone cared.

MONEY WARS

1991. JPN: *Money Wars: Nerawareta Waterfront Keikaku*. AKA: *Money Wars: Waterfront Project in Peril*. Video. DIR: Yusaku Saotome. SCR: Shuichi Miyashita. DES: Chuji Nakajima. ANI: Chuji Nakajima. MUS: N/C. PRD: Gainax. 45 mins.

Everyday life at a finance company is upset when a client turns up murdered, and his death is connected to land ownership after the upcoming handover of Hong Kong to the Chinese in 1997. A financial thriller in an exotic Chinese setting that soon relocates to Japan for further conspiratorial investigations, this anime was based on the manga serialized in *Business Jump* by Soichiro Miyagawa, though the animated story was completely original and did not appear in the print version. **NV**

MONKEY AND THE CRAB, THE

1988. JPN: *Saru Kani Kassen*. AKA: *Fight Between the Monkey and the Crab*. TV special. DIR: Yoshikazu Fujita, Minoru Okazaki. SCR: N/C. DES: Minoru Maeda. ANI: Minoru Maeda. MUS: Bimoth. PRD: Studio Juno, Fuji TV. 25 mins.

The monkey agrees to swap his persimmon seed for the crab's rice ball. The monkey eats the rice ball and is soon hungry again, but the crab plants the seed and grows an entire tree. The monkey steals some of the fruit but refuses to bring any down for the crab, and so the two fight until the crab holds the monkey's tail in his pincers. The monkey promises that, if the crab lets him go, he will give him three hairs from his tail, which is why crabs have three hairs on their claws.

The version listed here, screened as part of the *Ponkiki Kids* children's show, is only one of the more recent appearances of the better-known of the JAPANESE FOLK TALES. An early *Saru Kani Kassen* (1917) by Seitaro Kitayama was the second EARLY ANIME ever to be made, and the tale is often referenced—e.g., in MY NEIGHBOR TOTORO, when Satsuki draws Mei as a crab because she is waiting so intently for her seeds to grow.

MONKEY PUNCH'S WORLD: ALICE

1991. JPN: *Monkey Punch no Sekai: Alice*. Video. DIR: Yuzo Aoki. SCR: Tonori Yoshida. DES: Monkey Punch. ANI: Tatsuo Yanagimachi, Etsuji Yamada. MUS: N/C. PRD: Takahashi Studio. 45 mins.

Doctor Stein, a mad scientist, falls in love with his own creation, the female android Alice, though Alice has feelings for the scientist's handsome young son Jiro. In this one-shot adaptation of a minor manga by LUPIN III–creator Monkey Punch, Alice flees the doctor's castle but is pursued by Jiro, either to avenge his father's descent into madness or to have her for himself, or perhaps both.

MONKEY TURN

2004. TV series. DIR: Katsuhito Akiyama. SCR: Atsuhiro Tomioka. DES: Jun Okuda. ANI: PLM. MUS: Daisuke Ikeda. PRD: VAP, Shogakukan, BS Japan. 23 mins. x 25 eps. (TV1), 23 mins. x 25 eps. (TV2).

The Monkey Turn is a cornering technique that shaves seconds off your time in a powerboat race—but it's tricky to pull off and requires skill and daring. Kenji Hatano gets into powerboat racing in high school and promises his would-be girlfriend Sumi Ubukata that he'll be a champion in three years. He gets himself a top coach, Kanichi Koike; the tough and unyielding man puts him through a harsh regimen of training but he's determined to get to the top. His main rival is Takehiro Doguchi, son of a famous father, but there are many others with more experience, and Kenji has to work hard to make good on his promise to Sumi. Based on the manga by Katsutoshi Kawai; the second season was called *Monkey Turn V*.

MONSTER

2004. TV series. DIR: Masayuki Kojima. DES: Kitaro Takasaka, Shigeru Fujita. ANI: Madhouse. MUS: Kuniaki Haishima. PRD: VAP, NTV, Madhouse, Shogakukan. 24 mins. x 74 eps.

Kenzo Tenma, a Japanese brain surgeon working at a top hospital in Germany, is handsome, brilliant, and engaged to a beautiful girl. One night, he faces a terrible decision. A young boy arrives at the hospital after a mysterious shooting, needing surgery; shortly after, the city's mayor is also brought in. Sickened by hospital politics, Kenzo insists on saving the boy because he came in first, despite pressure from his boss. He loses the support of his director, his rank at the hospital, and his fiancée. It seems his career is over; then a series of grisly murders removes the director and the doctors who were promoted over him. Kenzo discovers that the boy he saved was more than he seemed to be, and his life becomes even darker and more dangerous as he follows a trail of murders and political machinations, trying to clear his name and understand why doing the right thing has had such terrible consequences. Based on the manga by creator Naoki Urasawa, with each TV episode corresponding to two chapters, this compelling story takes a man who has it all and throws it away, and asks what it takes to make a monster. A superior anime series that doesn't demand viewers suspend their intelligence in order to be entertained, *Monster* reunites a number of staff from the earlier Urasawa adaptation MASTER KEATON, including composer Haishima, whose ending theme for the first 33 episodes is sung by David Sylvian, late of British New Romantic band "Japan." In spring 2005 New Line Cinema licensed the *Monster* movie rights for a proposed live-action coproduction with Shogakukan. **V**

MONSTER MAN BEM

1968. JPN: *Yokai Ningen Bem*. AKA: *Humanoid Monster Bem*. TV series. DIR: Kujiro Yanagida, Seiji Sasaki, Tadao Wakabayashi. SCR: Akira Naritachi. DES: N/C. ANI: Nobuhide Morikawa. MUS: Masahiro Uno. PRD: Daiichi, Fuji TV. 25 mins. x 26 eps. (TV1), 25 mins. x 2 eps. (V), 25 mins. x 4+ eps. (TV2; 26 projected).

Bem, a gangster with pupil-less eyes, Bero, a young boy, and Bera, a dark, almond-eyed witch, are not humans but creatures from the world of monsters. They wander the Dark Realm as agents of justice, hoping that, by bringing Good into the monster realm, they will eventually be granted the opportunity to become human themselves.

A follow-up to Daiichi's earlier GOLDEN BAT, *MMB* was one of the first Korean coproductions in anime, and an early example of the horror genre that would come to be so popular in the medium. Bero's constant catchphrase of "I just can't wait to be human" resulted in chuckles from audience members of a certain age at Simba's "I just can't wait to be King" in Disney's *The Lion King*. Two pilots produced in 1986 for an abortive "second season" which was never broadcast were released on video with the first television show in 2001. In 2006, the story was resurrected as a projected 26-part TV series, animated by Studio Comet.

MONSTER RANCHER *

1999. JPN: *Monster Farm*. TV series. DIR: Hiroyuki Yano, Yuichiro Yano, Fujio Yamauchi. SCR: Satoshi Nakamura, Masashi Komemura, Takeshi Mochizuki. DES: Minoru Maeda. ANI: Masahiro Sekiguchi. MUS: BMF. PRD: TMS, TBS. 25 mins. x 73 eps.

Eleven-year-old Genki is an expert at the video-game *Monster Battle*. When he wins a video game tournament, he's rewarded with a 200x CD-ROM. But the game transports him from the real world to Monster Rancher Land. There, he meets Holly and her own personal monster, Suezo, and together they team up to fight Moo, accompanied by monsters Mocchi (a large, live personification of the Japanese dessert of the same name), Golem (a giant golem), Tiger of the Wind (a talking horned wolf), and Hamm (called Hare in the American dub, presumably because he is one). The personification of evil, Moo is misbehaving by corrupting all the otherwise good monsters. So Genki and his new friends set off on a quest to find the Phoenix, a mysterious creature with the power to change bad monsters into good ones. A hackneyed rip-off of POKÉMON and its ilk but swiftly snapped up for U.S. broadcast as a partner to DIGIMON on Fox Kids, in spite of poor ratings in Japan. A "special episode" *MR: Circus Caravan* was bundled with a release of the game in Japan.

MONSTER TAMAGON

1972. JPN: *Kaiketsu Tamagon; Eggzilla*. AKA: *Tamagon the Monster*. TV series.

Monster Rancher

DIR: Hiroshi Sasagawa. SCR: Takao Oyama. DES: N/C. ANI: Yuji Nonokawa. MUS: Koba Hayashi. PRD: Tatsunoko, Fuji TV. 5 mins. x 193 eps.

Tamagon helps anyone with a problem to solve it by producing a huge egg that contains exactly the right creature to provide whatever assistance is needed, from cleaning out the bathtub to finding missing objects. For the people who need a babysitter, he creates babysitting monster Peekaboo, for the kid who is falling behind at school, he comes up with Nininger the homework monster, and so on. However, as with the magical remedies of DORAEMON, comedic complications invariably ensue. Made to fill the same daily slot vacated by HIPPO & THOMAS, this show generated immense success for its producers, largely because of the theoretically infinite potential for spin-off toys. A *tama*, of course, is an egg—for more egg-based monsters see TAMAGOTCHI VIDEO ADVENTURES. Compare to the same team's earlier GAZULA THE AMICABLE MONSTER. Note that some Japanese sources claim a much higher episode count of 308, although the Tatsunoko studio's own records only show 193—it is presumed that many of

the "phantom" episodes are misfiled repeat broadcasts.

MONTANA JONES

1994. TV series. DIR: Tetsuo Imazawa. SCR: Marco Pagot, Satoshi Nakamura, Megumi Sugiwara. DES: Marco Pagot. ANI: Yoshiaki Okumura, Masamitsu Kudo, Norio Kaneko. MUS: Mario Pagano, Gianni Bobino, The Alfee. PRD: Studio Juno, NHK. 25 mins. x 52 eps.

It's the 1930s, and Montana Jones, bored with life as a pilot for Onboro Sea-Air Freight, sets off in search of fortune and adventure. His cousin Alfred would prefer a family life, complete with quiet contemplation, decent music, and copious amounts of spaghetti. They couldn't be more dissimilar, which is exactly why they have been thrown together by the sacred fates of buddy-movie plotting. Accompanying the Jones boys is their talkative interpreter, Melissa Sohn, an annoying girl who is obsessed with shopping but is endured by the Joneses because she speaks a zillion languages.

The team travels the world in search of treasure on behalf of Baron Gilt, hounded all the way by the evil Lord Zero, who, with the help of the mad scientist Baron Nitro and his idiot assistants, Slim and Slam, aims to steal all the Jones boys' hard-won treasure. Starting in the Mayan jungles, the globe-trotting fortune-seekers head to the Caribbean for a pastiche of *20,000 Leagues under the Sea*, tour Prague in search of an antique bell, search for a hidden chamber in the Taj Mahal, hunt yetis in Tibet, and raid tombs in Egypt.

A fast, furious, and funny Italian anthropomorphic coproduction in the spirit of SHERLOCK HOUND but with such a blatant pastiche of the *Indiana Jones* series that we can only assume the series was unreleasable in the U.S. "Homages" go both ways, however, and Marco Pagot was the inspiration for a character created by his former collaborator Hayao Miyazaki: PORCO ROSSO. Compare to Disney's similar pulp-serial homage *TaleSpin*.

MOOMINS *

1969. JPN: *Moomin*. TV series, movie. DIR: Masaaki Osumi, Moriyoshi Murano, Masayuki Hayashi, Wataru Mizusawa, Seiji Okuda, Rintaro, Ryosuke Takahashi, Noboru Ishiguro, Toshio Hirata. SCR: Tadaaki Yamazaki, Hisashi Inoue, Yoshiaki Yoshida, Shunichi Yukimuro, Chikara Matsumoto, Keisuke Fujikawa, Kuni Miyajima, Hiroyuki Hoshiyama. DES: Tove Jansson. ANI: Yasuo Otsuka, Tsutomu Shibayama, Toyoo Ashida. MUS: Seiichiro Uno. PRD: Tokyo Movie Shinsha, Mushi Pro, Telescreen, Fuji TV, TV Tokyo. 25 mins. x 65 eps. (TV1), 25 mins. x 52 eps. (*New*), 25 mins. x 104 eps. (*Happy*), 62 mins. (m).
The adventures of a cute little hippo-like troll and his friends and family, based on the series of children's books written between 1945 and 1971 by the Finnish author Tove Jansson (1914–2001) and Jansson's comic versions of the same characters, written for the *London Evening News*. The relationship of the anime series to Jansson's original, however, has been the subject of some controversy, since the original anime adaptation from Tokyo Movie Shinsha introduced anachronisms such as motorcars, much to the author's

annoyance. Consequently, production was moved to Zuiyo (later known as Nippon Animation) for the second season, *New Moomins* (*Shin Moomin*, 1972). While the author was reportedly more satisfied with the designs and stories of the new series, it is the TMS version that remains preferred by most of the Japanese audience. Episode seven of the first series and episode two of the second were also screened in cinemas as part of Toei anthology events in 1971 and 1972 respectively. Hence, they also show up as 25-minute "movies" in some sources.

Tove Jansson's brother Lars, who was responsible for drawing and writing much of the *Moomins* comic strip in the 1960s and 1970s, became one of the producers of a third anime version, *Happy Moomin Family* (*Tanoshii Moomin Ikka*, 1990), in a remake by Hiroshi Saito screened on TV Tokyo. It is this version, made during the heyday of the video era and with far closer ties to merchandising, that established the "Moomin Boom" in Japan—an obsession with plush hippo-troll toys that endures to this day and ensures surprising numbers of Japanese tourists in Finland. The directors changed to Takeyuki Kanda and Tsuneo Tominaga, and the series was renamed *Happy Moomin Family Adventure Diary* (*Tanoshii Moomin Ikka Boken Nikki*, 1991) for episodes 79–104. Jansson's *Comet in Moominland* was brought to the screen as Hiroshi Saito and Masayuki Kojima's *Moomin Tani Suisei* (1992), a movie edition that was later released on video with ten minutes of extra footage. Twenty-eight episodes of the most recent series were dubbed in the U.K. market by the BBC, and subsequently broadcast on Hawaii's K5 channel as *Tales of Moomin Valley*.

Although Jansson had Finnish nationality, she was one of a large ethnic minority of Swedish-speaking Finns, and wrote all her original books in a dialect still sometimes called "Moomin-Swedish," as it invariably reminds native Swedish listeners of Jansson's characters. *The Moomins* is

often erroneously listed as one of the WORLD MASTERPIECE THEATER anime, since it is based on a foreign work and made by the studio that would become known as Nippon Animation.

MOON PHASE *

2005. JPN: *Tsukuyomi Moon Phase*. AKA: *Lunar Chant Moon Phase*. TV series. DIR: Akiyuki Shinbo. SCR: Mayori Sekijima. DES: Masahiro Aizawa. ANI: Masahiro Aizawa; Nobuyuki Takeuchi. MUS: Daisaku Kume. PRD: SHAFT, Victor Entertainment, TV Tokyo. 25 mins. x 25 eps.
Luna Hazuki is a young German girl of Japanese descent, raised as an old-fashioned European lady. She is obsessed with wearing fake cat ears, and although she can be headstrong and selfish she's basically a nice person who just happens to be a vampire—compare to VAMPIRE PRINCESS MIYU and the previous year's PETITE COSSETTE. Photographer Kohei Morioka runs into her when out taking pictures on assignment in an old castle in Germany; it's not a total surprise, as he is descended from a line of psychics and has always had a strange talent for including ghosts and supernatural beings in his shots. Desperate to escape the castle, Luna tries to make Kohei her servant by sucking his blood and fails, but he has managed to set her free of the barriers keeping her within the castle; so, naturally, she follows him to Japan and moves in with him. Unfortunately his cousin Seiji is a demon hunter, and another vampire is hot in her trail. Of all the things the world needs, another magical girlfriend story isn't top of the list, but this one at least looks cute in a slightly different way. Hazuki's late mother soon arrives in the reincarnated form of a cat, which then transforms into a flying cat-like creature. Based on a manga by Keitaro Arima, who simply adds Gothic Lolita fashions to the usual clichés of a magical girlfriend story—URUSEI YATSURA with extra teeth. Part of the relatively recent "Gothic Lolita" subgenre of anime, based on

the fashion fad of the same name and also found in **PETITE COSSETTE** and **MOON PHASE**.

MOONLIGHT LADY *

2001. JPN: *Kao no Nai Tsuki*. AKA: *Faceless Moon, No Surface Moon: The Animation*. Video. DIR: Toshiharu Saito. SCR: Masanobu Arakawa. DES: Megumi Ishihara, Carnelian. ANI: Megumi Ishihara, Noritomo Hattori. MUS: N/C. PRD: Pink Pineapple. 30 mins. x 5 eps.

Suzuna—proud, prissy, mercurial, and needy—is the latest in a long line of hereditary temple priestesses, whose assumption of her duties is a matter of considerable importance for her family, coming as it does at the time of the long-awaited Expectant Moon Ceremony. When she finds that the (orgasmic) preparations have raised her previously suppressed lust, her maids Tomomi and Sayaka (who bears an uncanny resemblance to the recently missing young television actress Ruri) engage her in various sex acts, much to her embarrassment (and pleasure).

Suzuna is additionally haunted by a shadowy dream lover, who makes free with her body—and who is realized in the flesh by the arrival of Koichi, a young man, also endowed with great magical power, who must become her husband as part of the Expectant Moon Ceremony. She is greatly disappointed to find out that he is not her longed-for knight in shining armor, but coarse-mannered and very human. Despite this (and her rape at his hands on the night of his arrival), she begins to fall for him, and he for her.

However, this is all orchestrated by Suzuna's "mother," Yuriko (who has her own liaisons with Tomomi, Koichi, and the gardener Gohei), actually the ghost of a former priestess, in a plot to resurrect herself from her watery grave. She has supplanted Suzuna's family and is using Tomomi's power of forgetfulness as well as the mystical aphrodisiac qualities of a camellia tree to control the other characters and to raise the necessary magical energy from them to bring the ceremony to

her desired conclusion. The result is an increasing atmosphere of eroticism, where the boundaries of dream and reality become almost indistinguishable to those caught in Yuriko's web.

Unfortunately, the last episode discards various subplots—Koichi's university instructor Chikako, who has been using Koichi as her mystical tool, penetrates the barrier which now surrounds the mansion in order to investigate; Suzuna's mute identical twin Mizuna, hidden in a cave behind a waterfall; Suzuna's childhood cousin and childhood friend Io—in order to concentrate on the erotic final ceremony, losing in the process a great deal of the coherence which makes up much of the serial's appeal. The result, though it could have been more, is still an above average erotic anime, which features particularly good art thanks to the designs from Carnelian, who created the original game for the company Root. **OV**

MOONLIGHT MASK

1972. JPN: *Gekko Kamen*. TV series. DIR: Nobuhiro Okaseko. SCR: Tsunehisa Ito, Haruya Yamazaki. DES: Sadayoshi Tominaga, Nobuhiro Okaseko. ANI: Tadashi Yamashita. MUS: Goro Misawa. PRD: Ai Planning Center, Knack, Nippon TV. 25 mins. x 39 eps.

Shavanan, the good king of Paradai, is murdered by the man-monster Great Claw of Satan, an evil figure intent on stealing the fabled treasure hidden somewhere in the small country. He only has one of the three golden keys required to reach the treasure, so he hunts down Shavanan's daughter, Fujiko Kuwata, believing her to have another. However, Fujiko is protected by a group of noble detectives and by the "warrior of love and justice," the mysterious motorcycle-riding superhero Moonlight Mask.

Originating in a 1957 live-action TV series that spun off into four live-action movies, the first two seasons of the anime kept close to the continuity of the TV original, adapting the *Claw of Satan* and *Mammoth Kong* story lines,

while the final part was the *Dragon's Tooth* plot. Curiously, the fourth live *MM* movie, *Last of the Devil* (1957, *Akuma no Saigo*), was to feature a plot very similar to that of **PATLABOR** 2, in which an abandoned soldier decides to avenge himself on the country that betrayed him. Fiercely lampooned in Go Nagai's saucy pastiche **KEKKO KAMEN** (which featured a Great *Toenail* of Satan as a school principal), in 1981, *MM* returned to the live-action theater screens with a new high-kicking female sidekick—martial arts star Etsuko Shiomi. In 2000, it was also remade as a comedy anime designed to hook the original fans and their own very young children. Directed by Toshio Takeuchi and written by Yoshio Urasawa, *Look! It's Little Moonlight Mask!* featured Naoto, who was a humble schoolboy by day and the nemesis of Satan's Claw in the evenings (before bedtime).

MOONLIGHT PIERCE YUMEMI AND THE KNIGHTS OF THE SILVER ROSE

1991. JPN: *Gekko no P.Y. to Gin no Bara no Kishitai*. Movie. DIR: Takeshi Mori. SCR: Shikichi Ohashi. DES: Katsumi Aoshima. ANI: N/C. MUS: Kyosuke Himuro. PRD: Studio Pierrot. 70 mins.

Seventeen-year-old Yumemi Sato is dragged into an interdimensional conspiracy when her handsome upperclassman Masaki Suzukaga reveals that he is a German were-creature who can use magical powers to change shape at will. Hate it when that happens. A pretty-boy anime based on the best-selling novel of the same name by Hitomi Fujimoto.

MOONLIGHT SONATA

2001. Video. DIR: Hayato Nakamura. SCR: Renmu. DES: Shinsuke Terasawa. ANI: Shinsuke Terasawa. MUS: N/C. PRD: Éclair, Museum Pictures, Milky. 30 mins.

The sacred city of Aerial is torn apart by a civil war, in which sword master Lian is overcome with lust for his sister, the queen. He kills her husband King Eril and runs for the hills, where

Mospeada

the couple live briefly in unwedded, incestuous bliss, before being attacked by the agents of justice. Based on an erotic computer game by Éclair. **LNV**

MORAL HAZARD *
2004?. JPN: *Changing Moral Hazard*. Video. DIR: N/C. SCR: N/C. DES: N/C. ANI: N/C. MUS: N/C. PRD: Obtain, Onmitsudo. 30 mins.
A nameless young girl is walking home through a park at night, where she is set upon by a would-be rapist. However, she is saved by a nameless man wielding a baseball bat, who confesses to her that he is a businessman facing bankruptcy and is so depressed that he might as well rape her himself. However, the former thug then fights him off, and the pair of them chase her around the park. Compare to *Dying for a Girl* in the LOLITA ANIME series. **LNV**

MORI, YASUJI
1925–1992. Born in Taipei, Taiwan (at the time part of the Japanese empire), Mori graduated from the design department of the Tokyo University of the Arts in 1949. By 1951, he had joined the animation division of Toei, where he worked on PANDA AND THE

MAGIC SERPENT as a sketch artist and JOURNEY TO THE WEST as a key animator. He left for Zuiyo (now Nippon Animation) in 1973.

MORIMOTO, KOJI
1959– . Born in Wakayama Prefecture, he graduated from the Osaka School of Design and worked briefly as a lowly animator for Annapuru on TOMORROW'S JOE. Inspired by the sight of Takashi Nakamura's work on GOLD LIGHTAN, he went freelance, first achieving fame as one of the animators on NEO TOKYO. Subsequent works have included segments in ROBOT CARNIVAL and MEMORIES (1995), by which time he had founded the Studio 4°C with Eiko Tanaka and Yoshiharu Sato. His involvement in anime has since been largely uncredited, apart from two distinctive Morimoto moments—the concert sequence in MACROSS *Plus* (1994) and the pop promo NOISEMAN (1997). His best-known work today is probably his contribution to THE ANIMATRIX (2002).

MORIYAMA, YUJI
?– . Graduating high school in 1978, Moriyama found work as an animator

on the STAR BLAZERS movie of the same year. He subsequently worked as a key animator on MACROSS and art director on URUSEI YATSURA. His work was also a major feature of the video anime of the early 1980s with high enough quality work to get away with a cinema screening, such as PROJECT A-KO. He sometimes uses the pseudonym Yuji Motoyama.

MOSAICA
1991. JPN: *Eiyu Yoroiden Mosaica*. AKA: *Heroic Armor Tale Mosaica*. Video. DIR: Ryosuke Takahashi. SCR: Ryoei Tsukimura. DES: Norio Shioyama. ANI: Hidetoshi Omori, Hideyuki Motohashi. MUS: Kaoru Wada. PRD: Studio Deen. 30 mins. x 4 eps.
The kingdom of Mosaica is on the verge of being overrun by King Sazara when the great warrior Lee Wu Dante is executed for questioning the King of Mosaica's judgment. His son, Lee Wu Talma, decides to save Mosaica in his father's memory, using ancient giant robots that lie dormant in a forgotten valley. Taking the advice of the hermit Ritish, Talma gathers an army but must first rescue Princess Menoza, who has been taken prisoner by his enemies. An SF fantasy deliberately designed to evoke memories of the crew-members' earlier VOTOMS and RONIN WARRIORS.

MOSPEADA *
1983. JPN: *Kiko Soseiki Mospeada*. AKA: *Armored Genesis Mospeada; Genesis Climber Mospeada*. TV series. DIR: Katsuhisa Yamada, Tatsuya Kasahara, Masayuki Kojima, Kazuhito Akiyama, Norio Yazawa. SCR: Sukehiro Tomita, Akira Koson, Kenji Terada. DES: Yoshitaka Amano, Shinji Aramaki, Hideki Kakinuma. ANI: Kazuhiko Udagawa. MUS: Joe Hisaishi, Hiroshi Ogasawara. PRD: Tatsunoko, Fuji TV. 25 mins. x 25 eps.
In the year 2083, the last remnants of the human race on Mars send a military mission to recapture Earth from the Invid, who overran it a generation before. However, all but young fighter pilot Stick Bernard are wiped out. Crash-landing in the Amazon jungle,

he resolves to head north and attack the Invid base single-handed, even though this is sure to be a suicide mission. En route, he meets Rei, an inexperienced kid with a natural talent for piloting robots, and the pair hone their skills with the Legioss and Mospeada Ride Armor transforming motorcycles. Slowly, the duo gather other revolutionaries around them in order to fight a guerrilla war against the Invid, though their struggle was curtailed by poor ratings in Japan. A famous SF anime featuring several famous designers, whose plot was supposedly based on writer Tomita's interpretation of the medieval standoff between Christianity and Islam! However, it also bears an uncanny resemblance to his unproduced story outline for *Terrahawks* (see **THUNDERBIRDS 2086**). The series was cut together with **MACROSS** and **SOUTHERN CROSS** to form the basis for the English-language **ROBOTECH**, long before it was released subtitled in its unadulterated form as part of the *Robotech Perfect Collection.*

Yellow Dancer (Yellow Belmont), a cross-dressing singer from the series, lived on after its cancellation to record an album, *Live from the Pit Inn*, and the *Love, Live, Alive* music video (chiefly comprising recycled footage, as with *Macross Flashback 2012*).

MOST SPIRITED MAN IN JAPAN

1999. JPN: *Nippon-ichi no Otoko no Tamashii*. TV series. DIR: Toshio Yoshida. SCR: Masashi Sogo. DES: Masaaki Kawanami. ANI: Bob Shirahata. MUS: N/C. PRD: Studio Deen, TBS. 5 mins. x 48 eps.
Tales of sex and sadomasochism, based on the manga in *Young Sunday* by Masahiko Kikuni, creator of **HEARTBROKEN ANGELS**. Japan's highest-ever-rated late-night anime, with a TV share of 9.1% in the graveyard slot, it was broadcast as part of the *Wonderful* anthology program. **⓵Ⓝ✖**

MOTHER ♣

1993. JPN: *Mother: Saigo no Shojo Eve*. AKA: *Mother: Eve, the Last Girl*. Movie.

DIR: Akira Suzuki. SCR: Soji Yoshikawa. DES: Shuichi Seki. ANI: N/C. MUS: Naoki Nishimura. PRD: Nippon Skyway. 75 mins.
Amnesiac boy Dew and pretty girl Eve set out on a quest to find out how the human race came to die out. An "international version" was reputedly released, dubbed into English with Japanese subtitles.

MOUNT HEAD

2002. JPN: *Atamayama*. Movie. DIR: Koji Yamamura. SCR: Shoji Yonemura. DES: Koji Yamamura. ANI: Chie Arai. MUS: Takeharu Kunimoto. PRD: Yamamura Animation. 10 mins.
A miserly old man eats a cherry pit, only to discover a cherry tree growing out of his head. When the tree begins to blossom, people begin throwing parties beneath it, much to the old man's annoyance, in a stop-motion adaptation of one of the **JAPANESE FOLK TALES**, which achieved great fame when it was nominated for a Best Short Animation Oscar in 2002. Despite being an impressive achievement liable to set newsgroups alight for weeks (the authors still remember the excitement in fandom when **POMPOKO** was *almost nominated* for an Academy Award), its thunder was rather stolen by the success of **SPIRITED AWAY**, which won Best Animated Feature the same year.

MOURETSU ATARO

1969. AKA: *Exaggerator Ataro; Extraordinary Ataro; Furious Ataro*. TV series. DIR: Isao Takahata (TV1), Kunihiko Ikuhara (asst TV1, dir TV2). SCR: Shunichi Yukimuro (TV1). DES: Fujiko-Fujio. MUS: Taku Izumi. PRD: Toei, TV Asahi (TV1). 8 mins. x 90 eps. (TV1); 25 mins. x 34 eps. TV2).
Batsugoro is an idle father whose hobby is telling fortunes. After his death, his young son Ataro runs the local grocery store, only to discover that the ghost of his father has missed out on his chance to get into heaven and is now obliged to hang around offering unwelcome advice. Based on a manga by **DORAEMON**-cocreator Fujio Akatsuka,

the first half of this series adhered to the setups of the original story. Later episodes veered away in favor of the supporting cast, such as Nyarome the cat, resulting in a series of stories far removed from Akatsuka's original manga. The show was remade in 1990 under the helmsmanship of Kunihiko Ikuhara, who, it was claimed, directed two episodes of the original, although that would have made him only five years old at the time.

MOUSE *

2003. JPN: *Møuse*. TV series. DIR: Yorifusa Yamaguchi. SCR: Hiroyuki Kawasaki. DES: Shunji Murata, Toshiharu Murata. ANI: Studio Deen. MUS: Naoki Sato, Shigeru Chiba. PRD: Media Factory, Studio DEEN, Broccoli. 14 mins. x 12 eps.
Young teacher Sorata Muon has a secret identity. Following centuries of family tradition, he moonlights as master thief Mouse. Since the original manga was written by **SORCERER HUNTERS**-creator Satoru Akahori and drawn by Hiroshi Itaba, he is assisted by three nubile and scantily dressed young ladies who abuse him and teach by day and wear revealing costumes by night, willingly submitting to (and encouraging) his lecherous advances. Similarly interested in his hide, though for different reasons, is a secret society of art lovers who have recruited a former ally of the Mouse to trap him once and for all. A short, lightweight piece in every sense, but you don't go to the man who gave the world **SABER MARIONETTES** for deep social significance. **Ⓝ**

MUCHABEI

1971. JPN: *Chingo Muchabei*. AKA: *Glorious Muchabei; Extravagant Muchabei*. TV series. DIR: Tadao Nagahama. SCR: Hideko Yoshida, Masaki Tsuji. DES: Kenji Morita. ANI: Daikichiro Kusakabe, Shingo Araki. MUS: N/C. PRD: Tokyo Movie Shinsha, TBS. 25 mins. x 46 eps.
In the early days of the Edo period, masterless samurai Muchabei is forced to eke out a living making umbrellas. He is the sworn guardian of Bokemaru,

a disinherited prince, who is the rightful heir to the riches of the Toyotomi family. They dream of reviving the family's fortunes, but Bokemaru is not the smartest of men and is often outwitted by Kaburezukin, a government spy, in a comedy period piece.

Originally conceived as a standard anime series, the show was broken up into smaller chunks for daily screening when it was discovered that the production was ahead of schedule! The story seems inspired by kabuki dramas about Matajuro Yagyu, the outcast brother of Jubei Yagyu (see **NINJA SCROLL**), who famously bested an opponent by fighting with twin umbrellas instead of swords. There, however, any classical allusions end, since the rest of the show is clogged with anachronisms—there are road signs on the streets of Edo, and Muchabei fights with modern umbrellas seemingly inspired by John Steed in *The Avengers* (itself broadcast in Japan in 1967 under the title *Oshare Mitsu Tantei—Dandy Secret Detectives*). Created by Kenji Morita.

MUKA-MUKA PARADISE

1993. JPN: *Nauseous/Angry Paradise*. TV series. DIR: Katsuyoshi Yatabe, Kunihisa Sugishima. SCR: Yasushi Hirano, Shikichi Ohashi, Miho Maruo, Mayumi Koyama. DES: Hiromitsu Morita, Masayuki Hiraoka. ANI: Masayuki Hiraoka, Akio Watanabe. MUS: N/C. PRD: Nippon Animation, Mainichi Broadcasting. 25 mins. x 51 eps.

Thanks to a messy accident with the professor's time machine, little Eiba arrives in a world where humans never evolved and cutesy talking dinosaurs still walk Earth. He befriends the baby dinosaur Nikanika, tries to avoid provoking the wrath of Nikanika's father Gojigoji, and is (sort of) adopted by long-lashed brontosaurus mother Dosudosu. Based on a manga by **BONOBONO**-creator Mikio Igarashi.

MUNTO *

2003. Video. DIR: Yoshiji Kigami, Tomoe Aratani. SCR: Yoshiji Kigami. DES: Tomoe Aratani. ANI: Yoshiji Kigami.

Tomoe Aratani. MUS: N/C. PRD: Kyoto Animation. 52 mins. (v1), 57 mins. (v2).

Two kingdoms beyond our world are fighting over an energy source known as *akuto*. To save the Kingdom of the Heavens and the Magical Kingdom, Magical King Munto must find a human girl, Yumemi, whom a prophetic vision has suggested will save the universe. Yumemi is just an ordinary schoolgirl, but she's the only human who can see the islands of the Heavens floating above us. As a result, she's not even certain she's sane, and persuading her to find the courage to believe Munto and save his people will be a tough task. A sub-**ESCAFLOWNE** or **BRIGADOON** fantasy, which feels curiously old-fashioned, this also harks back to the remarkable **LEDA: FANTASTIC ADVENTURES OF YOKO**, though without its powerful sexual and emotional tension. A sequel, *M2: Toki no Kabe wo Koete*, followed in 2004.

MURAKAMI, TERU

1933– . Also credited as Jimmy T. Murakami. Born in San Jose to first- and second-generation Japanese immigrant parents, Murakami and his family were sent to an internment camp in Oregon when the U.S. entered World War II. He subsequently studied Fine Arts at the Chouinard Institute in Los Angeles (now part of CalArts) and worked as a commercial artist before becoming an animator on the America series *Gerald McBoing Boing*. He worked briefly for Toei Animation in Japan, returning to America and cofounding the animation studio Murakami-Wolf, with Fred Wolf. Later moving to Ireland, he worked with Roger Corman as an executive producer on the live-action *Battle Beyond the Stars* (1980) before founding another animation studio, Quateru, working chiefly in the European market. His most recognizable works are arguably the two cartoons he made based on the works of cartoonist Raymond Briggs—Dianne Jackson's Christmas classic *The Snowman* (1982), for which he was supervi-

sor, and the nuclear satire *When the Wind Blows* (1986), which he directed himself. He subsequently directed the feature-length cartoon *Christmas Carol: The Movie* (2001). With a career path rivaled only by Tadahito Mochinaga's for sheer variation, Murakami does not technically qualify for inclusion in an encyclopedia of *Japanese* animation. We include him here in anticipation of questions arising from his name.

MURATA, YASUJI

1896–1966. Sometimes Yasushi Murata. Born in Yokohama as the son of a sake seller, Murata left school in his mid-teens and began his career drawing film posters. Joining Yokohama Cinema in 1923, he moved onto drawing the intertitles for silent movies and cartoons. Inspired by the sight of foreign cartoons imported by Yokohama Cinema, he set up his own animation company, debuting with *Why Is the Giraffe's Neck So Long?* (1927, *Giraffe no Kubi wa Naze Nagai?*). Murata used paper-cut animation, but used his paper like anime cels, in anticipation of later developments in animation, his most famous work arguably being *Animal Olympics* (1928, *Dobutsu Olympic Taikai*). He joined the Nippon Manga Eiga company after World War II, but retired soon after due to illness.

MUSASHI ROAD

1990. JPN: *Karakuri Kengoden Musashi Road*. AKA: *Tales of the Trickster Swordsmaster Musashi Road*. TV series. DIR: Akira Torino, Satoshi Nishimura, Noriyuki Abe, Akiyuki Shinbo, Yoshitaka Fujimoto. SCR: Akira Torino, Tsunehisa Ito, Isao Shizuoka, Yoshihisa Araki, Shikichi Ohashi. DES: Tsuneo Tominaga, Kunio Okawara. ANI: N/C. MUS: Kenji Kawai. PRD: Studio Pierrot, Nippon TV. 25 mins. x 50 eps.

Musashi and Kojiro are two squashed-down robots in the spoof sci-fi samurai world of Edotopia. This anime car-crashes plots from **JAPANESE FOLK TALES**, historical events and legends, including Empress Himiko (see **ZEGUY**), the Japanese civil war, and the tale of

YAMATO TAKERU. See also YOUNG MIYA-MOTO MUSASHI.

MUSHI PRODUCTION

Studio founded by Osamu Tezuka in direct competition with Toei Animation, its most notable successes being the 1963–65 boom in television animation started by ASTRO BOY. The company stumbled in the climate of the late 1960s and collapsed in the early 1970s, declaring bankruptcy in 1973. The dispersal of its staff led to the foundation of many of the independent studios of today, such as Madhouse. In 1975, the company's works were the subject of a "masterpiece" retrospective in Yoyogi. Tezuka's work is represented today by Tezuka Productions, a different company.

MUSHISHI

2005. TV series. DIR: Hiroshi Nagahama, Shinpei Miyashita, Tatsuyuki Nagai. SCR: Kinuko Kuwabata, Aki Itami, Yuka Yamada. DES: Yoshihiko Umakoshi. ANI: Yoshihiko Umakoshi, Noboru Sugimitsu, Masayoshi Tanaka. MUS: Toshio Masuda. PRD: ARP Japan, Fuji TV. 25 mins. x 24 eps.
Ginko is a wandering expert in *mushi*, the most basic life-forms in the universe, representing primal energy. Their manifestations often appear to the uninitiated to be supernatural, in the form of hauntings or unexplained phenomena. In other words, a pseudo-scientific gloss on everyday GHOST STORIES, based on the manga by Yuki Urushibara, which began running in *Comic Afternoon* in 2000. A movie adaptation of the series is supposedly in production with Katsuhiro Otomo—a fitting job for the man whose own term for "primal energy" was AKIRA.

MUSHKA AND MISHKA

1979. JPN: *Hokkyoku no Mushka Mishka*. AKA: *Mushka and Mishka of the Arctic*. Movie. DIR: Chikao Katsui. SCR: Akira Kato. DES: Shinichi Tsuji. ANI: N/C. MUS: Reijiro Komutsu. PRD: Mushi Pro, Nikkatsu. 80 mins.
Two polar bears and their friendly seal acquaintance share adventures in this film supervised by Osamu Tezuka and based on the children's book by Tomiko Inui, also known as the writer of *The Tedious Penguin* and *We Are Kangaroos*.

MUSIC IN ANIME

From the early days of silent film, when theater owners paid a pianist to provide appropriate accompaniment, sound has heightened the impact of the image onscreen.

Anime is supported by a phalanx of talented composers, many of whom also work on live-action or game soundtracks and a few with distinguished careers outside the motion picture industry in classical, jazz, or other musical forms. The leader of the pack is Yoko Kanno, whose scores cover every musical angle from the jazz of COWBOY BEBOP to the church-influenced chorals of ESCAFLOWNE. Joe Hisaishi, who has been Studio Ghibli's house composer since he scored 1984's NAUSICAÄ OF THE VALLEY OF WIND, started out as a minimalist. LUPIN III–composer Yuji Ono is a leading purveyor of lounge jazz, and one of the main reasons why the series' reputation as one of the coolest shows ever is still intact after more than three decades. Kohei Tanaka excels at martial themes and variations on Mozart, most notably in his score to GUNBUSTER. Kenji Kawai's pulsing compositions have added extra menace to the scores of GHOST IN THE SHELL and PATLABOR; and Shiro Sagisu's multiple variations on both Beethoven and Burt Bacharach add a distinctive tone to EVANGELION.

Composers from other musical areas also dip into anime. Some of Osamu Tezuka's works were scored by famous mainstream composers Isao Tomita and Kaoru Wada. Ryuichi Sakamoto, formerly of pop trio Yellow Magic Orchestra, and best known to moviegoers for *Merry Christmas, Mr. Lawrence* and *The Last Emperor*, was one of the three composers for WINGS OF HONNEAMISE while his Yellow Magic Orchestra colleague Haruomi Hosono scored THE TALE OF GENJI. Some of these "guests" in the anime world are notable for their distinctively different voices—particularly Shoji Yamashiro, whose thumping, south-Asian influenced score for AKIRA was later reclaimed by the composer as the middle sequence of a symphonic trilogy beginning with *Reincarnated Orchestra* and ending with *Ecophony Rinne*.

Foreign pop luminaries who have scored anime include Jean-Jacques Burnel of the Stranglers, composer for the elegant and original GANKUTSUOU, while Western singers who have sung themes include David Sylvian, of New Romantic band Japan, on MONSTER. *Babylon 5* composer Christopher Franke provided the music for the first TENCHI MUYO! movie. In imitation of Japanese live-action drama, some modern opening and closing themes are deliberately designed as advertisements for music tie-ins. Whereas American serials often reduce their opening themes to mere musical stings—e.g., *Will & Grace* or *Frasier*—in order to lessen the temptation to switch channels, anime capitalizes both on the ritual quality of viewing for younger audiences and on the fact that a recyclable opening sequence saves on animation budgets, and is hence preferably extended for as long as possible. This has led to unexpected appearances by pop stars on the credit listings for anime—such as the use of a Franz Ferdinand track on PARADISE KISS, the surprise showing by the Backstreet Boys on YOUNG HANADA, or the appearance of Radiohead's "Paranoid Android" on ERGO PROXY. Real-life performers also crop up in anime, including a cameo by the boy-band Tokio in CHILD'S TOY and a similar appearance by SMAP in HIME-CHAN'S RIBBON.

Anime scores are complemented by so-called image albums: CDs with music "inspired by" popular titles, abound in Japan. Sometimes the music is composed after the event to cash in on a strong market; sometimes it includes material that didn't make it into the show's final cut, or additional songs by whichever popular singer or composer is working on the rest of the project. Occasionally a composer and director will build up a special relationship: Joe Hisaishi works closely with Hayao Miyazaki from the early stages of a new project, providing sketches of possible themes which the director also uses for inspiration and which are amended and expanded as the movie grows. With a number of shows getting their own spin-off CD and radio dramas, each needing some kind of soundtrack, there's a whole other strand of releases, both with and without the accompanying dialogue.

The music attached to anime in its native land doesn't necessarily travel overseas. Foreign releases quite often get their own theme songs or even soundtracks, whether the borrowed 1980s pop on *Macron One*, the U.S. release of **GOSHOGUN**, or songstress Chantal Goya, who provided the French theme for **MONARCH: THE BIG BEAR OF TALLAC**. Claude Lombard sang themes for over 40 animated shows in France, from **QUEEN OF A THOUSAND YEARS** and **STAR OF THE SEINE** to American cartoons like *The Adventures of Teddy Ruxpin*. Italy has its own anime theme stars, like the Micronauts of **DAITARN 3**, Christina D'Avena of **THREE MUSKETEERS**, or Massimo Dorati, whose energetic performance of the Italian **DIRTY PAIR** opening theme *Kate & Julie* deserves immortality. Popular local themes are treasured by their fans, but using current chart hits or locally popular styles is not always the best strategy. Excessive use of popular music dates and places a show with great precision, which can work to create an instant identification point for audiences at the time, but usually shortens the shelf life of the product—for which see, or rather, hear **BUBBLEGUM CRISIS** and **SAMURAI CHAMPLOO**. Of course, as the French, Italians, Spanish, and other importers of anime have demonstrated, a soundtrack isn't all that hard to replace, either wholly or in part; but hiring composers like Kanno and Sakamoto is likely to produce a more

interesting result than using hand-me-down songs based on transient fads. Sometimes, however, the inspiration can travel both ways—it was the French group Daft Punk who hired Leiji Matsumoto to create pop promos for them, which eventually led to the movie **INTERSTELLA 5555**. Similarly, the musicians of the British group Boa were to use their performance of the opening theme to **SERIAL EXPERIMENTS LAIN** as a means to break into the American market that had previously eluded them.

Music in anime can also be a story element in itself. Stories inspired by or themed around music include lives of famous musicians or **GREAT COMPOSERS**, wish-fulfillment tales of wannabe musicians, and stories where the role of music or sound in our lives is the central idea. The concept of stealing sound is the focus of shows from the highly traditional **CAROL** to the experimental **NOISEMAN**. The struggle to become a performer is depicted in so many shows it could form a book in itself, covering all musical genres from pop musicians like those in **BLACK HEAVEN**, **WANDERING SUN**, or **BECK**, CLASSICAL ARTISTS LIKE **KANON**, or wannabe idols like **CREAMY MAMI**. Real-life performers also crop up in anime like **NITABOH**, the story of a Japanese folk musician. But perhaps anime music's finest moment of inspiration was when **MACROSS** floated the idea that a pretty girl could save humanity from alien annihilation with the power of a heartfelt love song—such a simple and beautiful idea that it still brings a tear to the eye, even for cynical old anime historians.

MUSICAL WANDERINGS OF JIRONAGA KIYOMIZU

2000. JPN: *Anime Rokyoku Kiko Kiyomizu Jironaga*. TV series. DIR: Mitsuo Kobayashi, Tatsuo Suzuki. SCR: Kazuo Kosuga. DES: Mitsuo Kobayashi. ANI: Michishiro Yamada, Nanpei Mitsunori. MUS: N/C. PRD: Piman House, Mainichi Broadcasting. 25 mins. x 27+ eps. Tales of samurai derring-do, set to old-time tunes for the entertainment of the elderly. The target audience for

this anime was the over-sixties, though since it was shown at 5:45 a.m., it's difficult to imagine that *anyone* saw it at all.

MUTEKING

1980. JPN: *Tondemo Senshi Mutaking*. AKA: *Invincible Warrior Mutaking*. TV series. DIR: Seitaro Hara, Koichi Mashimo, Hiroshi Sasagawa, Shinya Sadamitsu, Kenjiro Yoshida, Kazuo Yamazaki, Yutaka Kagawa. SCR: Kazuo Sato, Akiyoshi Sakai, Haruya Yamazaki, Takeshi Shudo, Masaru Yamamoto. DES: Ippei Kuri, Kunio Okawara. ANI: Shizuo Kawai. MUS: Koba Hayashi. PRD: Tatsunoko, Fuji TV. 25 mins. x 56 eps. Law enforcement officer Takuro leaves planet Tako in pursuit of the fugitive Kurodako (Black Octopus) crime family: Takokichi, Takomaro, Takosaku, and Takomi. Arriving on Earth, the octopoid gang disguise themselves as humans and prepare to conquer the planet with their transforming minions. Takoro enlists Earth boy Rin Yuki as his deputy. Rin can now transform into the dashing warrior MuteKing, a superhero (on roller skates) who both fights off the bad guys and wins the heart of Takomi, the female octopus invader who finds his charms irresistible. He also has Takoro's seemingly endless supply of **TIME BOKAN**–inspired robots at his disposal. Transforming robot vehicles, Las Vegas-inspired musical interludes, and roller-skating superhero action from the usual suspects at the Tatsunoko studio, whose most popular chapter was the "MuteQueen" incident in which Takoro's transformation ray accidentally misses Rin and makes his girlfriend the hero of the hour—compare to **MOLDIVER**.

MY AIR RAID SHELTER

2005. JPN: *Boku no Bokugo*. TV special. DIR: Toshio Takeuchi. SCR: Toshio Takeuchi. DES: Seitaro Kuroda. ANI: Ryutaro Hirai. MUS: N/C. PRD: Shinei Doga, TV Asahi. ca. 80 mins. An old man remembers the time 60 years earlier when he huddled with his mother Yuko in the family's air raid shelter, while American B-29 bombers flew overhead. Based on a story by Aki-yuki Nosaka, better known for **GRAVE OF THE FIREFLIES**, it deals with similar issues of death and trauma, beginning with young Yusuke's pride that his father is going away to war to fight the Americans. His father Tetsuo, however, is concerned for his family's well-being, and devotes his last days before marching off to building a suitably secure air raid shelter for his family. Some time after all the neighborhood families assembled to wave off their menfolk (in the style of **CHOCCHAN'S STORY**), Yusuke hears chilling news on the radio of the fall of Saipan. When the war eventually, inevitably comes to Japan in the form of bombing raids, Yusuke is left alone in the shelter when his mother inexplicably walks out into danger. Alone in the dark, he begins to believe that his father's soul inhabits the shelter and is talking to him. Compare to **GLASS RABBIT**, which was similarly released in the 60th-anniversary year of the end of the war.

My My Mai

© 1993 YAMAGUCHI MASAKAZU/AKITA SHOTEN/APPLE

MY ALL-DAY ALL-COLOR
1987. JPN: *Boku no All-Day All-Color*. Video. DIR: Yoji Takatsuki. SCR: Seizo Watase. DES: Seizo Watase. ANI: Seizo Watase, Mikie Maeda. MUS: Tyrone Hashimoto. PRD: Tatsunoko. 30 mins.
Five short manga stories from **HEART COCKTAIL**–creator Seizo Watase, set to musical standards such as "Fly Me to the Moon" and "Love Me Tender." The tales adapted include *Riding the Wave for Ten Miles, 20 Minutes till Princess Kaguya, 250 Km, A Couple Requesting Gentle Rain*, and *Long-Distance Call from the West Side*. The experiment was repeated the following year with **CHALK-COLORED PEOPLE**.

MY FAIR MASSEUSE *
1996. JPN: *Soap no Moko-chan*. AKA: *Moko the Soap Girl*. Video. DIR: Shunji Yoshida. SCR: Naruo Kyujukawa. DES: Naruo Kyujukawa. ANI: Kawase Toshine. MUS: N/C. PRD: Sente Studio. 40 mins.
The perky, sex-starved Moko takes a job in a "soapland" massage parlor, where she cheerfully helps the clien-

tele fulfill their fantasies. This involves sex with old men, a threesome with a couple who want to spice up their love life, and the need to tactfully brush off a priapic grandfather who wants to "save her" from a life she fully enjoys. A porno anime remarkable only for the consensual nature of its sex scenes—a welcome change from the rape and domination that seems to occupy so much space on anime shelves. Based on the manga by Naruo Kyujukawa in *Young Champion* magazine. The story was also adapted into live-action, as the 64-minute TV "movie" in 1992, and an 86-minute video release, *Leave It to Moko* (1994, *Moko ni Omakase*). **N**

MY FATHER'S DRAGON
1993. JPN: *Elmer no Boken*. AKA: *Elmer's Adventure*. Movie. DIR: Masami Hata. SCR: N/C. DES: Shuichi Seki. ANI: N/C. MUS: Naoto Kine. PRD: Shochiku. 98 mins.
Elmer Elevator runs away with an old alley cat to rescue Boris, a young drag-on imprisoned on the faraway Wild Island. The everyday items he needs to help himself include some pink lolli-pops, rubber bands, chewing gum, and

a comb. Based on the children's book by Ruth Stiles Gannett, whose title reflected the original premise that the heroic youngster Elmer is actually the narrator's father as a boy.

MY LIFE AS... *
1999. AKA: *My Life As... Stage 1: A Chicken*. Video. DIR: Akebi Haruno. SCR: Ippei Taira. DES: Akira Ina. ANI: Akira Ina. MUS: N/C. PRD: Five Ways. 35 mins.
Teenager Yasunari runs away from a broken home and is saved from sinking into a life of prostitution by two women, Fumi and Rino. They take him in, along with his friend Chie, and make him their pet. When he publishes the story of his new life of bondage, domination, and group sex in a magazine, it is read by his brother Tomoyasu, who has been searching for him ever since he left home. Tomoyasu is devastated to find his brother loves his new life, so much so that he forces himself on his new tutor, Serina, without knowing that she is a good friend of his brother's new own-ers. A much more toned down version of the same themes could be found on live-action Japanese television in *You Are My Pet* (*DE). **LNV**

MY MY MAI *

1993. JPN: *Sono Ki ni Sasete yo.* AKA: *Get Me In the Mood.* Video. DIR: Osamu Sekita. SCR: Yumi Nakamura, Osamu Sekita. DES: Masakazu Yamaguchi. ANI: N/C. MUS: Koichi Ota, Koji Tajima. PRD: Apple, Beam Entertainment. 22 mins. x 4 eps.

Mai is a psychic investigator who specializes in consultancy jobs—putting members of the public together with the right healer, surgeon, or cure for strange phobias. As with the heroine of the similar **PRIVATE PSYCHO LESSON**, she prefers hands-on treatment, which she administers with a mix of psychobabble, flashes of her lingerie, and as a common last resort, her bounteous nude charms. Based on the *Shonen Champion* manga by *Heart Boiled Papa*–creator Masakazu Yamaguchi and presented as four "episodes," though this anime's release only spreads across two tapes. Similar psychosexual investigations turn up in **REI REI**. ◐

MY NEIGHBOR TAMAGETA

1974. JPN: *Tonari no Tamageta-kun.* AKA: *Little Traveller Tamageta.* TV series. DIR: Shotaro Ishinomori, Noboru Ishiguro. SCR: Shotaro Ishinomori, Shinichi Suzuki. DES: Shotaro Ishinomori. ANI: Nobuyoshi Sohara. MUS: N/C. PRD: Studio Zero, Studio Uni, Tohoku Shinsha. 5 mins. x 60 eps.

Yasushi is an average Japanese boy who gains a series of weird new playmates when his new neighbors turn out to be Mr. Gyoten, a time-traveler from the future, Gyoten's son Tamageta, and the family pet Pochi (i.e., Pooch) the dinosaur. Whenever Tamageta switches on the time machine, trouble inevitably ensues in the style of the "help" offered by **DORAEMON**. Quite often, the playmates are forced to undo other problems created by Yasushi's would-be girlfriend, local girl Yotchan, and her occasional associates Gorilla, Racoon (i.e., Tanuki), and Fox. Based on a manga by Shotaro Ishinomori, this kids' show was put into production by Tohoku Shinsha, but ultimately animated wholly in-house by Studio Zeo.

It sat around on the shelf for almost five years before its broadcast, in small chunks on the *Ohayo Kodomo Show* (*Good Morning Kids Show*). *Tamageta* literally means "Astonished."

MY NEIGHBOR TOKORO

1990. JPN: *Tonari no Tokoro.* TV series. DIR: Haruya Mizutani. SCR: Joji Tokoro. DES: Joji Tokoro. ANI: Tokuhiro Matsubara. MUS: Hiroaki Nakamura. PRD: Pasteoinc. 40 mins.

Parodies of several **JAPANESE FOLK TALES** and others, starring an animated version of star-of-the-moment Joji Tokoro, whose bright idea this was. Originally broadcast as part of the *Not the Real Mr. Tokoro* (*Tokoro-san no Tadamono dewa Nai*) show, these feeble pastiches of *Urashima Taro*, *Little Red Riding Hood*, and several "comedy" skits were bulked out on video by a "making-of" documentary, starring the camera-hungry Mr. Tokoro. The name manages, not quite accidentally enough, to get the show filed next to **MY NEIGHBOR TOTORO** in both English and Japanese, as if somehow the greatness of the latter would improve its chances. The comedian returned in computerized form as *Mr. Digital Tokoro* (2001).

MY NEIGHBOR TOTORO *

1988. JPN: *Tonari no Totoro.* Movie. DIR: Hayao Miyazaki. SCR: Hayao Miyazaki. DES: Hayao Miyazaki. ANI: Yoshiharu Sato. MUS: Joe Hisaishi. PRD: Studio Ghibli. 86 mins.

While their mother is in the hospital convalescing from a long illness, Satsuki and her little sister, Mei, are taken by their father, Professor Kusakabe, to an old house in the country. They clean the house of lurking "dustbunnies" and turn it into a home. Father takes the bus to the university where he lectures, Satsuki attends the local school, and Mei gets lost in the undergrowth, where she discovers a family of round, fluffy woodland creatures. Mispronouncing "troll," from the *Three Billy-Goats Gruff*, she calls them Totoros. Adults cannot see these Totoros, who befriend the children when Satsuki lends one an

umbrella. He returns the favor by growing them a tree with magic acorns and taking them on a magical ride through the countryside on the Catbus—a many-legged feline transport with a Cheshire Cat's grin straight out of **ALICE IN WONDERLAND**. Mei resolves to take her mother a gift but becomes lost on the way. Fearing the worst, the adults send out search parties, and a distraught Satsuki calls on the Totoros' aid.

Hayao Miyazaki's greatest work, and hence probably the best anime ever made, *MNT* is also a very personal film, set in the disappearing countryside of the creator's childhood and featuring a child's love for a bedridden parent—Miyazaki's own mother suffered from spinal tuberculosis. *MNT* has the widest appeal of any of Miyazaki's films, aimed as it is at an audience so young that it can genuinely be described as family entertainment, unlike his more adult-themed works such as **PORCO ROSSO** or teen adventures like **NAUSICAÄ**. *MNT* sees everything through the unquestioning, uncritical, undaunted eyes of a child, and it is an uplifting film of unadulterated hope, originally shown on a double bill with its heartrending opposite, **GRAVE OF THE FIREFLIES**. There are many echoes of other productions from Studio Ghibli, particularly in *MNT*'s depiction of a disappearing pastoral existence, with a ghostly rural world superimposed on modern times, much like the studio's more serious **POMPOKO**. Miyazaki's Japan is a nation very much rooted in its own past, with ancient local shrines overlooking the contemporary action, and the Totoros leading the girls in a stirringly primal fertility ritual. It also mixes the magical with the mundane in the charming style of **KIKI'S DELIVERY SERVICE** and, like the creator's much more downbeat **PRINCESS MONONOKE**, refuses to point a formulaic finger at a bad-guy scapegoat. This latter point was of particular importance to Miyazaki, exasperated at modern parents' willingness to use the TV as a babysitter and disgusted with the conflict-based story lines of most modern children's cartoons.

MNT's appeal has not diminished since its appearance. Now the center of a huge industry of tie-in products, it is that rare case of a film whose spin-offs were created *by audience demand* after the fact, instead of generated by the company as part of a publicity offensive. The most recent spin-off is a ten-minute short anime, *Mei and the Kittenbus*, which premiered at Tokyo's new Studio Ghibli Museum in 2001.

At one critical point in the plot, the "next stop" sign on the Catbus revolves to reveal a destination of particular importance. Whereas modern anime distributors would have digitally replaced it with English letters in translation, the dub released in the U.S. in 1994 was actually made in 1989 at a time when such technology was unavailable. Consequently, the Catbus has a warm, fluffy voice to announce the next stop in the English version—provided by Streamline Pictures' producer Carl Macek.

MY NEIGHBORS THE YAMADAS *

1980. JPN: *Ojamanga Yamada-kun; Hohokekyo Tonari no Yamada-kun.* AKA: *Troublesome Manga Yamadas.* TV series, movie. DIR: Hiroe Mitsunobu (TV), Isao Takahata (m). SCR: Masaki Tsuji, Tomoko Konparu, Noboru Shiroyama (TV), Isao Takahata (m). DES: Hisaichi Ishii. ANI: Hikuji Kanezawa (TV), Kenichi Konishi (m). MUS: Makoto Kawanabe (TV), Akiko Yano (m). PRD: Herald, Fuji TV, Studio Ghibli. 25 mins. x 102 eps. (TV1; 3 stories per ep.), 104 mins. (m), 25 mins. x 61 eps. (*Nono-chan*).

The Yamada family comprises retired couple Yoshio and Ine, their daughter Yoneko and her husband Komugi, eternal retake student Shigeru (who has failed to pass his university entrance exams three times), hapless high school baseball player Noboru, early teen Minoru, and toddler Sanae. In addition, the house is often visited by the occupants of the family's dormitory, several university students, and the local doctor—and soon the stork brings Yoneko and Komugi a new baby

of their own. Designer Hisaichi Ishii, who also created Go FOR IT, TABUCHI and FABLED UNDERGROUND PEOPLE, deliberately used flat, two-dimensional artwork for *Meet the Yamadas* (1980, *Ojamanga Yamada-kun*). Scheduled straight after SAZAE-SAN, the show continued the slot of gentle humor, although leavened in this case with chunks of satire, parody, and even science-fiction adventures. Later remade for theaters as *My Neighbors the Yamadas* (1999, *Hohokekyo Tonari no Yamada-kun*) in a deliberately washed-out sketch style. This version was released in Japan with English subtitles on the DVD.

In 1997, Ishii began serializing *Nono-chan*, a follow-up to the original manga. Featuring very similar comic situations but concentrating this time on the misadventures of a cheeky third-grader, *Nono-chan* was picked up for TV broadcast late in 2001. It was directed for Toei Animation by Nobutaka Nishizawa, using fully digital animation in imitation of the *Yamadas* movie, and shown on TV Asahi in 61 episodes.

MY PLACE

2002. JPN: *Atashi n Chi.* AKA: *My Family.* TV series, movie. DIR: Akitaro Daichi, Tetsuo Yasumi. SCR: Kazuyuki Morosawa, Natsuko Takahashi. DES: Eiko Kera. ANI: N/C. MUS: Motoi Sakuraba. PRD: TV Asahi, Yumeta, ADK, Media Factory, Shinei Animation, Toei Animation. 19 mins. x 123 eps. (TV), 95 mins. (m). The Japanese title is short for "at my home," and this anime based on the comic strip by Eiko Kera is an everyday slice-of-life with the Tachibana family—mother, father, perky daughter Mikan, who tells the story, and son Yuzuhiko. Originally published in the Sunday edition of *Yomiuri Shimbun* newspaper and running since 1995, it has been described as the present-day SAZAE-SAN.

MY SEXUAL HARASSMENT *

1994. JPN: *Boku no Sexual Harassment.* Video. DIR: Yosei Morino. SCR: Yosei Morino. DES: Aki Tsunaki. ANI: Aki Tsunaki. MUS: Burnheads. PRD: Seiyo, KSS. 35 mins. x 3 eps.

Jun Mochizuki is one of the best salesmen for his computer company, a position he has achieved by seducing the bosses of the companies to which he sells. He travels Japan and, in a later episode, even heads off to Boston, bedding his colleagues, his superiors, and his clients in a gay pornographic anime. Based on the series of erotic novels by Sakura Momo. **◐**

MY SKY

1991. JPN: *Ore no Sora: Deka Hen.* AKA: *My Sky: Cop Chapter.* Video. DIR: Takeshi Shirato. SCR: Hiroshi Motomiya. DES: Masami Suda. ANI: Masami Suda. MUS: Takeshi Yasuda, Chage & Asuka. PRD: APPP. 45 mins. x 2 eps.

A thriller revolving around political connections with a multinational corporation as a lone cop, son of the company boss, tracks down the murderer of a female university student, finding that there is a conspiracy to prevent him from discovering the truth. Based on the manga in *Young Jump* magazine by GOODFELLA and CLIMBING ON A CLOUD–creator Hiroshi Motomiya. **◐**

MY WIFE IS A HIGH SCHOOL STUDENT

2005. JPN: *Okusama wa Joshi Kosei.* TV series. DIR: N/C. SCR: Hideo Takayashiki. DES: Kazuo Watanabe. ANI: N/C. MUS: Kei Wakakusa. PRD: Madhouse, TV Saitama, TVK. 25 mins. x 13 eps. Teenage bride Asami Onohara is forced to keep her marriage secret when she is transferred to the high school where her husband Kyosuke is a teacher. High jinks ensue as the couple conceal their cohabitation from fellow students and staff, as colleagues try to set their "single" friend Kyosuke up with a date, and Asami dodges scandal in the classroom. An extra twist: Asami is not the only student with a relative on the staff—one of her classmates is the little brother of the haplessly single English teacher Miss Iwasaki. A late-night anime based on the manga by Hiyoko Kobayashi in *Young Jump* weekly, but part of a long tradition in Japanese TV that stretches back to the

1970 show *My Wife is 18* (*DE), whose plot was virtually identical. Note that Japanese TV has a large number of "My Wife is a…" shows, most of which are translations of American sitcoms, including *My Wife is a Big Star* (*Mona McCluskey*) and *My Wife Is a Witch* (*Bewitched*). BEWITCHED AGNÈS, aka *My Wife Is a Magical Girl*, ended shortly after this knock-off began.

MY-HIME *

2004. JPN: *Mai-HiME*. AKA: *Mai Princess; Princess Mai; Mai-Otome*. TV series. DIR: Masakazu Obara, Tatsuyuki Nagai. SCR: Hiroyuki Yoshino, Noboru Kimura. DES: Hirokazu Hisayuki, Tomoyuki Aoki, Saori Naito, Mutsumi Inomata, Hisashi Hirai, Hiroyuki Okawa, Junichi Akutsu, Kazutaka Miyatake. MUS: Yuki Kajiura. PRD: Sunrise, TV Tokyo. 25 mins. x 26 eps. (TV1) 25 mins. x ?? eps(TV2).
Mai Tokiha and her younger brother Takumi have won scholarships to attend prestigious Fuka Academy. On the long journey, two girls start a supernatural battle on the ferry and Mai begins to learn that she has some of the same powers. Thirteen girls known as HiME—for the Highly Advanced Materializing Equipment power they wield—fight monsters and risk the lives of those they love most. Adapted from the manga written by Noboru Kimura with art by Kenetsu Sato, in which high school boy Yuichi Tate discovers that he is the "key," or essential fighting partner, of two HiME, the anime shifts the emphasis away from the boy-girl partnership of the manga into a less demanding fantasy for guys too lazy to read—VIRGIN FLEET meets ALICE ACADEMY. A second series, entitled *Mai-Otome* (2005), stars Arika, a minor character in series one, and is set in a European-style castle, with the uniforms inspired by French maids rather than Japanese schoolgirls.
A video follow-up, *My Otome Zwei* (2006) was not a sequel so much as a wholesale sci-fi revision in the style of later TENCHI MUYO! serials, relocating the original cast to almost completely different settings and situations; in this case, the faraway land of Windbloom, where heroine Arika Yumemiya is searching for her mother, enrolling en route into the hothouse competitive environment of Garderobe Academy.

MYSTERIES OF THE WORLD

1978. JPN: *Sekai no Fushigi Tanken Series*. AKA: *Investigating World Mysteries*. TV series. DIR: Masahiko Soga, Sadao Nozaki. SCR: Keiji Kubota, Takeshi Shudo, Kyoko Tsuruyama, Junji Takegami. DES: N/C. ANI: N/C. MUS: N/C. PRD: Heart Media, TBS. 25 mins. x 10 eps.
Documentaries combining anime with live action, exploring a mixed bag of mysteries and historical topics, including the statues of Easter Island, the search for a lost continent, the Bermuda Triangle, the NAZCA Lines, the Sphinx and the Pyramids, the Greenwich Meridian, the Leaning Tower of Pisa, and the Great Buddha of Nara. Confusing in its inability to decide whether it wants to be history, geography, travelogue, or the titular "mysteries."

MYSTERIOUS CITIES OF GOLD *

1982. JPN: *Taiyo no Ko Esteban*. AKA: *Esteban the Child of the Sun; Esteban and the Cities of Gold; Esteban the Sun-Kissed Boy*. TV series. DIR: Eiko Toriumi, Bernard Deyries, Kyosuke Mikuriya, Mizuho Nishikubo. SCR: Michiru Umadori, Michiru Kaneko, Soji Yoshikawa, Jean Chalopin. DES: N/C. ANI: Toshiyasu Okada, Hiroshi Kawanami, Yutaka Oka, Norio Yazawa, Hajime Hasegawa, Mitsuki Nakamura, Shingo Araki, Kazutoshi Kobayashi, Yukihiro Takahashi, Toyoo Ashida, Takashi Nakamura. MUS: Nobuyoshi Koshibe (Haim Saban, Shuki Levy, Western version). PRD: MK, Studio Pierrot, NHK. 25 mins. x 39 eps.
In 1532, the orphan Esteban sets out from Barcelona in search of the fabled South American Cities of Gold. He's accompanied by the young Inca girl Zia, the adventurous Spaniard Mendoza, who found the baby Esteban adrift on the open sea, and (later) Tao, the last survivor of the sunken kingdom of Mu (Heva in the English dub).
Set in the time when Japan was "discovered" by the West but made at a time when old-fashioned adventure yarns were rediscovered by the *Indiana Jones* mob, *MCoG* was a Franco-Japanese coproduction undertaken after the completion of ULYSSES 31. There are a few concessions to kiddie programming, such as an infuriating parrot and some comic-relief bunglers, but there is also much in this series to recommend it. It was loosely based on the books *The King's Fifth* (1966) and *City of Seven Serpents* (so claim the producers, though no work of that name exists in the Library of Congress) by Scott O'Dell, better known in the U.S. as the award-winning author of *Island of the Blue Dolphins* (1961). According to O'Dell's widow, Elizabeth Hall, *City of the Seven Serpents* was briefly a working title of *The Captive* (1979), a book by O'Dell relating to Mayan civilization. Full of unexpected changes in gear, *MCoG* starts as a straightforward sea voyage, before giving the first indications of its sci-fi leanings in episode nine when the crew of the Spanish galleon Esperanza jump ship onto the flying ship Solaris. Needless to say, as the quest begins in earnest in South America, Esteban discovers he is the offspring of an Inca princess (with an absent father who turns out to be not so absent)—hence, in true anime tradition, the perfect pilot for the show's supermachine, the solar-powered Golden Condor. Ancient technologies, lost cities, and warring tribes create an exciting mix, and though there are occasional anachronistic bloopers (a tribe of Amazons, *in* the Amazon, for example), the Japanese version closed each episode with a mini historical documentary explaining the actual events and personages that inspired the fictional characters—explaining the differences between Aztecs, Olmecs, Mayas, and Incas, or filling in the background about Pizarro or Magellan. However, these documentaries were dropped from many foreign-language

territories, including the U.K. Though made primarily for the French market, *MCoG* was also popular with the Japanese audience, particularly with those who could spot the irony of staff members from GOLD LIGHTAN animating the flight of the Golden Condor using similar glare effects and shot compositions. Perhaps the most compelling element of *MCoG* is the way in which it genuinely conveys a feel for the age. There was, literally, a whole New World to conquer, and the sense of anticipation and adventure is gripping. Predating the similar SECRET OF BLUE WATER by several years, *MCoG* remains an original, not the least because it presented a positive, sympathetic view of Native American peoples unique to children's television. When the series was rereleased on French DVD, there were rumors that producer Chalopin was in negotiations with Japan about a remake (or perhaps a sequel, since the children only manage to find one of the seven fabled cities), though there has yet to be any confirmation. See also PEPELO, BOY OF THE ANDES.

MYSTERY OF THE NECRONOMICON *

1999. JPN: *Kuro no Dansho*. AKA: *Black Fragment*. Video. DIR: Hideki Takayama, Yoshitaka Makino. SCR: Ryo Saga. DES: Yutaka Sunadori. ANI: Koichi Fuyukawa, Masaki Kaneko. MUS: Kazuhiko Izu, Hiroaki Sano. PRD: Discovery/78. 35 mins. x 2 eps.
After a savage mass murder at a remote Nagano ski resort, most of the guests leave the mountain complex. As a storm brings down the phone lines and cuts off the hotel, vacationing private investigator Satoshi Suzusaki hunts down the killer as further murders occur. Accompanied by his foster-daughter Asuka, he interviews a succession of suspects, discovering a web of intrigue that includes blackmail, sexual

assault, black magic, and experimental gene therapies.
Despite the usual cavalcade of sick sex and gratuitous violence one would expect from UROTSUKIDOJI-director Takayama, the first half of *MotN* is also a simplistic but engaging whodunit. Satoshi collects a number of carefully balanced clues and artifacts, interviewing suspects and collating information that regularly contradicts the viewers' expectations and even prompts suspicion that perhaps *he* is really the murderer. However, with the arrival of his lover, Mina, the dramatic tension snaps. Bearing a satellite phone that allows Satoshi to reconnect to the outside world and the Internet, Mina throws in several extra variables, and the plot spins wildly out of control. Instead of a sedate unmasking in the drawing room, the finale breaks the rules of detective fiction by keeping several last-minute surprises up its sleeve, stretching the viewer's suspension of disbelief with a series of disguises and linking events to a previously unmentioned gang rape at a distant pharmaceuticals company.
In its continual return to computer-screen research, *MotN* betrays its origin as a game for the Sega Saturn. The characters and their quirks are meticulously distributed—onscreen titles give extra details about people's names and the times of critical events, while sudden revelations come accompanied by fast-forward flashbacks, which are cheap and easy with digital animation. Asides reveal that this is only the middle chapter in a loosely linked trilogy—Satoshi is the amnesiac survivor of a former crime, and the killer escapes to set up a sequel. If there's any real "mystery," it's what was *cut* for the anime version, as early scenes belabor the point that Asuka's adopted status has been somehow revoked, setting up but forgetting an incestuous subplot,

while Abdul Al-Hazred's titular Book of the Dead appears but only as the most tantalizing of MacGuffins. A rare case of a game plot that seems to have genuinely required the traditional 30 hours' immersion to make proper sense, reduced here to 60 minutes of sleuthing, dotted with moments of brutal sex and slasher-movie gore. Part of the DISCOVERY SERIES.

MYTHICAL DETECTIVE LOKI RAGNAROK *

2003. JPN: *Matantei Loki Ragnarok*. AKA: *Detective Loki; Demon Detective Loki*. TV series. DIR: Hiroshi Watanabe. SCR: Kenichi Kanemaki. DES: Mariko Oka. ANI: Studio Deen. MUS: Kei Haneoka. PRD: TV Tokyo. 25 mins. x 26 eps.
The Norse trickster Loki annoys the father of the gods Odin once too often and is banished from Heaven. Sent to Earth in the body of a child (shades of CONAN THE BOY DETECTIVE), he lives a comfortable enough life in a huge mansion but schemes to get back to his own world. Loki is the target of constant attacks by other gods whom he's teased and tricked in the past. To regain his powers and be readmitted to Heaven, he has to outwit them, collect the mischievous spirits that infest the human world, and use them to enhance his natural abilities. Consequently, he sets himself up as a detective with the help of his loyal assistant Ryusuke Yamino and cute, bespectacled schoolgirl mystery fan Mayuri Daidoji. Among the many Norse legends that show up to cause problems is Verdandi, better known to anime fans as Belldandy from OH MY GODDESS!, who crashes the wedding of one of Mayuri's friends to kill Loki. Also appearing are her Norn sisters Urd and Skuld, love goddess Freya and her older brother Frey, and Heimdall. Based on a manga by Sakura Kinoshita, and no relation to RAGNAROK: THE ANIMATION.

N

NADESICO *
1996. JPN: *Kido Senkan Nadesico.* AKA: *Robot Warship Pink (Sweet William); Martian Successor Nadesico.* TV series, movie. DIR: Tatsuo Sato, Nobuyuki Habara, Kenichi Hamasaki. SCR: Noboru Aikawa, Takeshi Shudo, Hiroyuki Kawasaki. DES: Kia Asamiya, Keiji Goto, Takeshi Takakura, Takumi Sakura, Rei Nakahara, Yasuhiro Moriki. ANI: Keiji Goto, Natsuki Egami, Masayuki Hiraoka. MUS: Takayuki Hattori. PRD: Xebec, Studio Tron, TV Tokyo. 25 mins. x 26 eps. (TV), 30 mins. (*Gekiganger*), 90 mins. (m).

In the year 2195, while Earth prevaricates about sending troops to fight invaders from Jupiter, a brave civilian takes matters into her own hands and steals a privately owned warship. With a rogue captain straight out of SILENT SERVICE, an unwinnable war out of GUNBUSTER, and a plaster of irony over any cracks, Earth's last hope against the Jovian "lizards" is the ragtag crew of the Nadesico—a ship named after the *nadeshiko* flower that is said to represent Japanese womanly perfection. Captain Yurika and her mostly female crew are determined to meet the challenge, while their cook (and Yurika's childhood sweetheart) Akito is a former pilot ace on the run from his fears, pilot Jiro Yamada is an anime addict bent on living his favorite show, and the military is out to take control by fair means or foul.

Based on a manga in *Monthly Ace* magazine by Kia Asamiya and supposedly set in the same universe as his SILENT MÖBIUS, *Nadesico* is one of the better 1990s shows, particularly for a hard-core fan audience that can spot the in-jokes and identify the fine line between a *satire* of cheesy shows and the cheesy shows themselves. Parodies and homages are handled lightly, and the anime's characters and situations are cleverly scripted to avoid the repetitive tedium of TENCHI MUYO!, whose adoring-female-of-the-week policy it often imitates. The most striking example of this is cute moppet Ruri— a mixture of Wednesday Addams and *Tenchi*'s Sasami, marrying intelligence and competence with sullen cynicism.

Often playing like a superfast trailer for a much longer series, the viewer is left dazed by the compression of information, events, and background. Director Sato cuts conversations as if they were fight scenes; tone and mood change without a by-your-leave, and there's an incredible amount of shouting. The camp giant-robot show-within-the-show *Gekiganger Three* is more than mere comic-relief pastiche of GETTER ROBO and its ilk—a viewing experience that turns the crew into anime fans, it eventually becomes a cultural bridge between the warring worlds. With a wink to the fan audience, anime saves the universe in much the same way as the power of song in the earlier MACROSS. The *Gekiganger* segments were compiled and released with extra footage straight to video in 1997.

The movie release *Nadesico: Prince of Darkness* (1998) closes the series with a flash-forward redolent of the second PATLABOR movie. Years after the original series, the two main leads are missing, presumed dead, and an older Ruri is now the commander of the Nadesico B, fighting an enemy that's not all it seems.

NAGAHAMA, TADAO
1932–1980. Born in Kagoshima, Nagahama graduated in drama from Nippon University, and found early work in puppetry, such as on the TV series of MADCAP ISLAND (see also *DE). He joined the animation studio A Pro (later Shin'ei Doga) as an animator on QTARO THE GHOST, BEFORE SPENDING A PRODUCTIVE THREE YEARS ON SUCH SHOWS AS STAR OF THE GIANTS and ROSE OF VERSAILLES. He went freelance, and subsequently joined Tokyo Movie Shinsha, playing a key role as the director of the French coproduction ULYSSES 31, but he died partway through the project.

NAGAI, GO
1945– . Born in Ishikawa Prefecture, Nagai became an assistant to the manga artist Shotaro Ishinomori after completing high school. He enjoyed early and controversial success as a manga artist, with titles such as SHAMELESS SCHOOL introducing nudity and crudity in abundance to young readers' great

enjoyment and the eternal annoyance their parents. He subsequently copied the model of Osamu Tezuka's Mushi Production to set up his own company, Dynamic Planning, which has overseen Nagai's works in their anime forms, including DEVILMAN, CUTEY HONEY, and KEKKO KAMEN. His greatest influence, however, has been in the world of giant robots, including such important works as GETTER ROBO, GRANDIZER, and MAZINGER Z, anime's first pilotable robot. Although he does have an English-language following, his work still seems much better known in Europe and the Arab world. He was also notably a designer on the puppet series *X-Bomber* (*DE, as *Star Fleet*), including the impressive combining robot Dai-X.

NAGANO, MAMORU

1960– . Born in Kyoto, Nagano's anime debut was HEAVY METAL L-GAIM in 1984. Later design credits include BRAIN POWERED, although he is chiefly known as the creator of FIVE STAR STORIES.

NAGAOKA, AKINORI

1954– . Born in Nagasaki Prefecture, Nagaoka began studying literature at Chuo University, but dropped out and became an animator on THE GARDLES. He subsequently contributed as a key animator on shows such as TOUCH and DOCTOR SLUMP, before his directorial debut on the latter.

NAJICA

2001. JPN: *Najica Dengeki Sakusen.* AKA: *Najica Explosion Battle, Najika Blitz Tactics.* TV series. DIR: Katsuhiko Nishijima, Takeshi Mori. SCR: Takeshi Mori, Kenichi Kanemaki, Kazunori Chiba, Mayori Sekijima. DES: Noriyasu Yamauchi. ANI: Noriyasu Yamauchi. MUS: N/C. PRD: Studio Fantasia, Amber Films. 25 mins. x 12 eps.
Thirty years after ecological disaster has sunk 17% of Earth's surface below rising seas, perfumier Najica Hiragi, age 27, moonlights as a secret agent, using her knowledge of 500 different scents to save the world from terror-

Nadesico

© XEBEC/PROJECT NADESICO • TV TOKYO

ism. Pretty girls and unlikely plotting from the people who brought you AGENT AIKA.

NAKAMURA, TAKASHI

1955– . Born in Yamanashi Prefecture, Nakamura is one of the unsung heroes of modern anime, with a strong resumé of work that often seems to be better known and more highly respected by other animators than by the public at large. He performed key animation duties on both NAUSICAÄ OF THE VALLEY OF WIND and AKIRA, but his directorial work has remained limited to relatively obscure titles such as CATNAPPED and TREE OF PALME. He deserves to be considered alongside Mamoru Oshii (q.v.) as one of the distinctive creators in modern Japanese animation.

NAKAZAWA, KAZUTO

?– . Animator and illustrator whose debut work was on the second of the FATAL FURY TV movies. Has subsequently been a character designer on shows including EL HAZARD and a popular choice as key animator. He is credited with a "unit director" role on KILL BILL: THE ORIGIN OF O-REN.

NAMCO–BANDAI

A vast conglomerate formed in 2005 by the merging of Namco and Bandai. Namco was founded as a mechanical toy company in 1955, trading as Namura Manufacturing until 1972. It acquired the Japanese division of Atari in 1974, bringing it into the coin-operated arcade market and leading to the creation of many games, including *Pac-Man* and *Final Lap*.

Bandai began as a toy company in 1950, subsequently becoming a powerful player in anime through its sponsorship of children's television shows—it was highly instrumental in the introduction and constant recycling of robot toy designs that led to shows such as BRAVE SAGA, GUNDAM, and TRANSFORMERS and the ubiquitous live-action franchise *Mighty Morphin' Power Rangers* (*DE). Bandai subsequently set up its own animation division, Bandai Visual or "Emotion"—the name is a pun on "E," Japanese for picture, and "Motion"—whose distinctive Easter Island heads logo can be found on many anime aimed at older teens. Subsidiaries include the Sunrise studio, Ashi Pro, and Happinet.

NANA

2006. TV series. DIR: Morio Asaka. SCR: Tomoko Konparu, Ryosuke Nakamura. DES: Kunihiko Hamada. ANI: Kunihiko Hamada, Toshihiko Fujisawa. MUS: N/C. PRD: Madhouse, NTV. 25 mins. x 50 eps.

Two girls called Nana, one a naïve middle-class lady, the other a streetwise punk, meet on the train to Tokyo and end up sharing an apartment. Based on the manga by Ai Yazawa serialized in both *Cookie* and *Shojo Beat* magazines, and also adapted into a 2005 live-action movie.

NANAKA 6/17 *

2003. TV series. DIR: Hiroaki Sakurai. SCR: Tomoko Konparu. DES: Masayuki Onji, Yoshiki Yamagawa. ANI: Masayuki Onji. MUS: Toshio Masuda. PRD: JC Staff, GENCO. 23 mins. x 12 eps.

After suffering a brain injury, 17-year-old Nanaka Kirisato becomes convinced that she is a 6-year-old trapped in an older body. From being an intelligent, serious young woman she becomes a cute little girl who just wants to watch anime all day, especially her favorite show, *Magical Domiko*. She believes that, just like her cartoon heroine, she's been placed under a magic spell. Her best friend Renji Nagihara, who feels partly responsible for the action that caused this trouble, teams up with her father to help her grow up again and to keep her injury secret to keep her life as normal as possible. Japanese teenagers acting like 6-year-olds.... Who's going to notice? Based on the *Shonen Champion* weekly manga by Ken Yagami, which artfully reverses many of the clichés of magical-girl shows, *N6/17* essentially plays PETITE PRINCESS YUCIE or MARVELOUS MELMO in reverse. It also contains within it the seed of an arch commentary on fandom itself in the style of GENSHIKEN—so many anime tropes began as aspirational entertainment for children, only to become the chosen obsession of teenagers.

NANAKO SOS

1983. AKA: *Nana the Supergirl*. TV series. DIR: Akira Shigino, Yoshihiko Yamatani, Yoshinobu Shigino, Tetsuro Amino, Tsukasa Sunaga. SCR: Masaru Yamamoto, Shikichi Ohashi, Asami Watanabe, Tomoko Ishizuka. DES: Tsuneo Ninomiya. ANI: Geki Katsumata, Shiro Murata, Tsuneo Ninomiya, Yoshiyuki Kikuchi, Masami Abe. MUS: Ichiro Nitta. PRD: Kokusai Eiga, Movie International, Fuji TV. 25 mins. x 39 eps.

An alien girl crash-lands on Earth, losing her memory in the process but keeping her superpowers. "Rescued" by a boy, who has a knack for making money, and his dopey friend, she agrees to work for them for room and board. They set up the Supergirl Company investigation agency, and Nana gets to work bringing villains to justice, solving love problems, and dodging the unwanted attentions of a mad scientist out to use her for his own ends. Based on an original *Just Comic* manga by POLLON-creator Hideo Azuma, this is one of the most neglected of the magical-girl series, eclipsed in its year of release by the more famous CREAMY MAMI. Mercifully, it has nothing whatsoever to do with AMAZING NURSE NANAKO.

NANIWA SPIRIT

1992. JPN: *Naniwa Yukyoden*. AKA: *Tales of Naniwa Heroism*. Video. DIR: Teruo Kigure. SCR: Haruyuki Maeda. DES: Dokuman Pro. ANI: Teruo Kigure. MUS: Jiro Takemura. PRD: Knack. 58 mins. x 2 eps.

Taido Kaimon is the leader of the Kinshu Group gangster syndicate in Japan's Kansai region. His gang is a cluster of wisecracking madmen, eternally running into trouble with the law, each other, and the local girls who give as good as they get. It's a fast and furious Osaka comedy (see COMPILER) in an adaptation of the gag manga in *Asahi Geino* magazine by Dokuman Pro. The same year saw the release of a three-part video series based on another Dokuman manga: the Osaka motorcycle gang comedy *Nanbono Monjai*, directed by Masamune Ochiai and written by Yoshihisa Araki. ⬤▶

NARUTARU *

2003. JPN: *Narutaru: Mukuro Naru Hoshi—Tama Tana Ko*. AKA: *Shadow Star Narutaru*. TV series. DIR: Toshiaki Iino. SCR: Chiaki Konaka. DES: Masahiko Ota, Keiji Hashimoto. ANI: N/C. MUS: Susumu Ueda. PRD: Kid's Station. 23 mins. x 13 eps.

Cheerful schoolgirl Shiina Tamai lives alone with her jet pilot father. Swimming during a summer vacation with her grandparents, she almost dies when she is swept out to sea. Her life is saved by a strange star-shaped creature. She names him Hoshimaru—the Round Star—and they become friends. He can fly, transform into different shapes, and absorb objects into his body, and even though he doesn't talk, he and Shiina can understand each other. When she returns to school for the new year, Hoshimaru disguises himself as her backpack; but they learn that other children have also met strange creatures, some with their masters—and they're not all friendly. The creatures are called "dragons" and some of their young friends are easily manipulated through their own weaknesses—like arrogant Satomi who thinks she should be one of the elite running the world, or knife-crazy Akinori. A tale of alien invasion that starts out cute and perky and gets darker, based on the 1998 manga in *Comic Afternoon* by Mohiro Kito.

NARUTO *

2002. TV series, video, movie. DIR: Hayato Date, Tensai Okamura, Hirotsugu Kawasaki (m2). SCR: Katsuyuki Sumizawa, Akatsuki Yamatoya, Hirotsugu Kawasaki, Yuka Miyata. DES: Hirofumi Suzuki, Tetsuya Nishio, Shinji Aramaki. ANI: Atsuho Matsumoto, Hiroto Tanaka, Tatsuya Tomaru, Tetsuya Nishio. MUS: Toshiro Masuda, Musashi Project. PRD: Studio Pierrot, TV Tokyo, Aniplex, Dentsu, Bandai, Shueisha, Toho. 23 mins. x 167+ eps. (TV), 17 mins. (v1), 40 mins. (v2), 82 mins. (m1), c. 80 mins. (m2), ? mins. (v3).

Before Naruto Uzumaki was born, a great fighter called Yondaime battled evil nine-tailed fox Kyuubi, and sealed him into a human body—Naruto's. The people of his home village of Konoha fear and distrust what is inside the boy, and as a result of this distrust—and of being orphaned—he's hot-headed and a bit of a troublemaker; but Naruto is determined to show them he is a human being who can be loved and trusted, not a demon. He plans to do this by succeeding to Yondaime's title of Hokage, given to the strongest ninja of the Fire Country. To reach this goal he has to travel, train, study, and fight many opponents, making enemies and allies along the way. This sets up an ongoing tournament/fight scenario with multiple opportunities to introduce new characters, and as with DRAGONBALL and HATTORI THE NINJA, this proved hugely popular.

Several "movies" toured as part of the *Jump Festa* cinema roadshow—a vacation diversion to keep kids off the streets. Their increasing length is a fair indicator of *Naruto*'s growing stature—strictly speaking these are video releases premiered in theaters rather than actual movies, a distinction which was once a big issue in 1980s anime, but now only really applies to the *Jump Festa*. *Find the Crimson Four-Leaf Clover* (2003) was only 17 minutes long and featured a story about the grandson of the third Hokage and his crush on a local girl. *Battle At Hidden Falls—I am the Hero!* (2004), occupied a more significant slot on the bill, at 40 minutes. *Naruto* became the top billed movie for that winter's *Naruto: It's the Snow Princess's Ninja Art Book!* (2004, *Naruto Dai Katsugeki!! Yuki Hime Shinobu Hojo Datte Bayo!*) in which our hero and friends are ordered to escort his favorite film actress to the Snow Country to film a new movie. Its status was assured with the stand-alone *Naruto the Movie: The Great Clash! The Phantom Ruins in the Depths of the Earth* (2005, *Gekijoban Naruto Daigekitotsu! Maboroshi no Chiteiiseki Datte Bayo!*) in which our heroes get caught up in a huge battle with a moving castle while on the highly dangerous and significant errand of

delivering a lost pet. If this sounds like the plots are increasingly an excuse for the battles, it could be because all ninja shows eventually face this problem—when you have to slot in the rumble-of-the-week, give the favorite characters screentime, and keep your audience happy, a good plot and tight writing are usually the first casualties. Based on the manga in *Shonen Jump* by Masashi Kishimoto.

NASTY OLD LADY

1970. JPN: *Ijiwaru Baasan*. AKA: *Bullying Old Woman*. TV series. DIR: Satoshi Murayama, Hiroshi Yamazaki, Yoshio Okamoto, Shoichi Sugiyama. SCR: Susumu Yoshida. DES: Shoichi Hayashi. ANI: Sadayoshi Tominaga, Hiromitsu Morita. MUS: Yasuhiro Koyama. PRD: Knack, Nippon TV. 25 mins. x 40 eps., 25 mins. x 46 eps. (remake).

Based on a 1966 manga by SAZAE-SAN–creator Machiko Hasegawa, this is another slice-of-everyday-life tale, centered around a spiteful old woman who causes trouble for neighbors with her constant bumbling and grumbling. The first show from anime production house Knack, with a leading "lady" voiced in pantomime-dame fashion by gravely male voice actor Shigeo Takamatsu to add to the horror. The story was brought back for a new generation as *New NOL* (1996), a TV remake directed by Yoshimitsu Morita.

NASU: SUMMER IN ANDALUSIA

2003. JPN: *Nasu: Andalusia no Natsu*. Movie. DIR: Kitaro Kosaka. SCR: Kitaro Kosaka. DES: Naoya Tanaka. ANI: Hisao Shirai. MUS: Toshiyuki Honda. PRD: Madhouse. 45 mins.

Pepe is a minor competitor in a Spanish cycling race not unlike the Tour de France, charged with working as a support rider to ensure that the team's star rider gains maximum points on each leg. However, with his team threatening to drop him, Pepe must also face up to his past, as the race blows through his hometown, where his former girlfriend Carmen is preparing to marry his elder brother Angel.

Based on the manga in *Comic Afternoon* by Io Kuroda.

NATSUKI CRISIS

1993. Video. DIR: Koichi Chiaki, Junichi Sakata. SCR: Mayori Sekijima. DES: Futoshi Fujikawa. ANI: Futoshi Fujikawa. MUS: Yasuhiko Shigemura. PRD: Madhouse. 30 mins. x 2 eps.

Natsuki is a karate ace in a private high school where martial arts are a major part of the curriculum. There's fierce rivalry between Natsuki's team and another local school's with an even better reputation for fighting skills. A transfer student from the rival school is attacked by her former classmates, the student president authorizes spying missions, and there are romantic complications, too. The designs are attractive, even though contemporary school stories can date fast because the background detail—what to wear, what bags and accessories are cool, how hair is styled—changes very quickly. This one, based on a 1990 manga from *Business Jump* by Hirohisa Tsuruta, has enough heart and punch to retain its charm.

NAUGHTY DETECTIVES

1968. JPN: *Wanpaku Tankentai*. TV series. DIR: Rintaro, Toshio Hirata, Masami Hata, Masami Murano. SCR: Keiji Abe, Aritsune Kato, Masaki Tsuji. DES: Osamu Tezuka. ANI: Kiyomi Numamoto, Akehiro Kaneyama. MUS: Takeo Yamashita. PRD: Mushi Pro, Fuji TV. 25 mins. x 35 eps.

A group of young boys (plus a token girl and her little brother, the obligatory brat) form a detective club, pooling their talents for brain, brawn, invention, and driving skills to solve crimes in Tokyo. Much to the consternation of police chief Nakamura, they often succeed where the professionals fail. The first show made by Tezuka's studio from a non-Tezuka work, this series adapts the juvenile *Boy Detectives Club* stories of Ranpo Edogawa, a 19th-century novelist better known today for his Poe-inspired tales of horror and suspense, some of which were adapted for the ANIMATED CLASSICS OF JAPANESE

LITERATURE. A watershed show that transferred the literary penchant for amateur sleuthing into the anime market, setting up a formula that survives to this day in CONAN THE BOY DETECTIVE and the YOUNG KINDAICHI FILES.

NAUGHTY DOTAKON

1981. JPN: *Mechakko Dotakon*. AKA: *Robot Kid Dotakon*. TV series. DIR: Takeshi Shirato, Kazumi Fukushima. SCR: Masaru Yamamoto, Takao Yotsuji, Kenichi Matsuzaki, Tetsuya Michio. DES: Takeshi Shirato, Iwamitsu Ito, Mitsue Ito. ANI: Takeshi Shirato. MUS: Shunsuke Kikuchi. PRD: Kokusai Eiga, Toei, Fuji TV. 25 mins. x 28 eps. Geeky genius Michiru has already got her PhD in atomic physics (from a California university) by the age of 11. But she still longs for a little brother, so she builds her own. Robot boy Dotakon is soon joined by their little robot sister, Chopiko, and the trio embarks on a series of fantastic adventures fueled by Michiru's inventions. Luckily for their little town, and the sanity of Michiru's bulky guardian Gorilla Capone, nothing ever gets too out of hand. Eclipsed in its year of release by a far more successful android child, Arale from DOCTOR SLUMP.

NAUGHTY NURSES *

2003. JPN: *Heisa Byoin*. AKA: *Closed Hospital*. Video. DIR: Ichiro Meiji. SCR: Naruhito Sunaga. DES: Ryosuke Morimura. ANI: Ryosuke Morimura. MUS: Yoshi. PRD: Digital Works, YOUC, Vanilla. 30 mins. x 2 eps. Yusuke Nimura is a chronically shy boy, unable to bring himself to have sexual intercourse with his perky girlfriend Mayu Mizuno. The couple separate, only to discover that coincidence brings them back together when they both find work at Aoshima General Hospital. Before long, Yusuke is dodging the attentions of amorous patients, sex-crazed nurse Satsuki, and the lustful senior nurse Ryoko. Meanwhile, he continues to struggle with his feelings for Mayu, who herself is not immune from the attentions of the patients. Relatively everyday hospital high jinks in this erotic anime—though it suffers from excessive use of digital animation loops in the sex scenes—for which the moaning talents of the voice actresses cannot fully compensate; and somewhat oversimplified. Compare with less mainstream stuff in NIGHT SHIFT NURSES and NURSE ME. **⊘Ⓝ**

NAUSICAÄ OF THE VALLEY OF WIND *

1984. JPN: *Kaze no Tani no Nausicaä*. AKA: *Warriors of the Wind*. Movie. DIR: Hayao Miyazaki. SCR: Hayao Miyazaki. DES: Hayao Miyazaki. ANI: Kazuo Komatsubara, Takashi Nakamura, Kazuyoshi Katayama, Hideaki Anno, Takashi Watanabe. MUS: Joe Hisaishi. PRD: Nibariki, Tokuma, Hakuhodo, Toei. 116 mins. (95 mins. as *Warriors of the Wind*). A thousand years after a great war, in a world dominated by the pollution-induced Sea of Corruption, Princess Nausicaä grows up in a peaceful valley shielded from the devastation by its prevailing winds from the sea. These keep the deadly spores that spread the Sea of Corruption away from its fertile lands—survival by a combination of geographical and meteorological chance. Terrible insect-like creatures roam the Sea of Corruption and the desert lands around. Mightiest of all are the huge crustaceans, the Ohmu. One of these can wipe out most human threats, but in a herd, they are unstoppable. Outside the valley, while smaller communities struggle to survive, factions within the Tolmekian Empire are fighting for supremacy. Princess Kushana of Tolmekia finds one of the superweapons that made the ancient war so terrible, the last God Warrior embryo, and plans to use it to ensure that her people stay on top, even if it means upsetting the fragile balance Nature has struggled to regain after the long-ago war.

When the ship carrying her superweapon crashes in the valley, it brings Kushana's army down on the agrarian enclave to retrieve the terrible cargo. Nausicaä's father dies in the struggle, but she can't give herself up to the lust for vengeance—she is the only one with the vision to see that understanding, tolerance, and patience might give a better outcome than aggression, not only with the Tolmekians, but also with the Sea of Corruption and its giant denizens. Faced with the God Warrior's awakening, an Ohmu stampede, and even the failure of the wind that has protected her Valley for generations, she must also face up to her own fears and make the ultimate sacrifice to preserve everything she loves.

It would have been easy to make this a hero-villain tale in the Hollywood mold (something the woefully inferior 1986 U.S. edit *Warriors of the Wind* attempts), but what emerges is a far richer, more complex world. Shunning more conventional firepower, Nausicaä uses her brains, her heart, and her courage to find a solution with compassion for everyone involved. The result is a film that is superbly put together on all levels, with messianic and ecological subtexts that don't weigh down a story packed with action and adventure.

After his initial success as a director-for-hire on CASTLE OF CAGLIOSTRO, Hayao Miyazaki directed this short segment of his own epic 1982 manga, originally serialized in *Animage* magazine. Despite an ending that seems to owe a debt to David Lynch's movie of *Dune* (1984), *Nausicaä* draws on a variety of other sources, including *The Princess Who Loved Insects* (one of the JAPANESE FOLK TALES) and, for its scenes beneath the poisonous-yet-cleansing Sea of Corruption, the 1959 adaptation of Jules Verne's *Journey to the Center of the Earth*. It even pastiches *Bedknobs and Broomsticks* (1971) with an opening montage that ends with Nausicaä in flight where Disney has a witch. As with many of Miyazaki's later characters, there are powerful echoes of the work of British historical fantasy novelist Rosemary Sutcliffe, whose hero-kings are defined by the extent to which they willingly live and die for others. Nausicaä has much in common with

Ashitaka, her spiritual heir in **PRINCESS MONONOKE**, and the art direction of both films spares no effort in the quest for perfection. *Nausicaä*'s access to cutting-edge technology, however, was more limited; the Ohmu were animated by a range of techniques which included cut-paper segments. Despite the notoriously short-lived attention spans of the anime-watching public (see **BRAVE SAGA**), *Nausicaä* polled high in Japanese top-ten lists for two decades after its original release. It influenced many imitators, particularly the incoherent eco-babbling of **GREEN LEGEND RAN**, and even films with little direct relation—**WIND OF AMNESIA** and **WINGS OF HONNEAMISE** both had their original titles altered to reflect the cadences of *Nausicaä* in an attempt to inspire Pavlovian ticket-buying in the Japanese audience.

NAYUTA

1986. Video. DIR: Masami Hata. SCR: Akiyoshi Sakai. DES: Akio Sugino. ANI: Akio Sugino. MUS: Masamichi Amano. PRD: Circus Production, Toshiba EMI. 75 mins.
Nayuta is on her way home from high school when she saves a mother and son from an accident and takes them to the hospital. The son, Kiro, wears a strange metal headband and seems to have some extrasensory powers. Then his mother is abducted, and Nayuta finds her good deed has drawn her into conflict with a strange group of activists known as Jarna and aliens called Hazard. Based on Junko Sasaki's 1981 manga published by Flower Comics.

NAZCA *

1998. JPN: *Jiku Tensa Nazca*. AKA: *Time Reincarnation Nazca*. TV series. DIR: Hiroko Tokita. SCR: Tsunehiro Ito. DES: Hirotoshi Sano. ANI: N/C. MUS: Suneyoshi Saito. PRD: Pioneer, TV Tokyo. 25 mins. x 12 eps.
Kyoji is a high school student who loves kendo and adores his charismatic instructor, art teacher Masanare Tate. Kyoji and Tate's fiancée, Yuka, see him transform into an Incan warrior at

a kendo match. Long ago they were all Incan nobles, and Kyoji's past self betrayed Tate's just before the conquistadors rolled in and destroyed their empire for good. As history seems set to repeat itself, the two meet again as deadly enemies, dressed in implausibly large feather headdresses and enough spandex to cover a chorus line. Not only this trio but everyone they know in modern Tokyo, right down to Kyoji's dog, has counterparts in 16th-century South America. Flashbacks retell the original fight between Bilka (lieutenant of the last Incan general, Huascar) and Yawaru (lieutenant of his usurper brother, Atahualpa) over both priestess Akulia and the Incan doomsday device Ilya Tesse. In a parallel story line, their reincarnations repeat their previous lives, loves, and conflicts in modern Tokyo, as Tate attempts to revive Ilya Tesse and destroy the modern world.

Amid this hokey plot, screenwriter Ito mixes Aztecan and Incan myths and history with impunity, throwing in a spaceship straight out of von Däniken (or **MYSTERIOUS CITIES OF GOLD**) and vague musings about the "close genetic ties" between the Incas and the Japanese. Sano's design work has all the edge he brought to **BOUNTY DOG**, but, as with that show, design alone won't make things work. Also adapted into manga form by the pseudonymous female duo "Akira Hinakawa." As a historical footnote, the real Atahualpa's brother was actually called Manko, presumably omitted from the anime version because *manko* is Japanese for pussy. Alien Incas also appeared in the 1960 kids' TV show *National Kid* (*DE).

NEGIMA *

2005. JPN: *Maho Sensei Negima*. AKA: *Magical Teacher Negima; Master Negi Magi*. TV series. DIR: Nobuyoshi Habara, Nagisa Miyazaki. SCR: Ichiro Okochi. DES: Hatsue Kato. ANI: Hatsue Kato. MUS: Shinkichi Mitsumune. PRD: Xebec, TV Tokyo. 25 mins. x 26 eps.
Preteen wizard-in-training Negi Springfield discovers, as did the heroine of **KIKI'S DELIVERY SERVICE**, that he must

pass a final test before he can become a full-fledged sorcerer. He must relocate from his Welsh magic school to Japan, where he must become a homeroom teacher for a class full of girls. His arrival immediately engenders the hatred of schoolgirl Asuna Kagurazaka, who threatens to tell his wizardly secret to the school. However, the two soon become reluctant partners in the face of a series of magical assaults on the school, while Negi conducts a search for his missing father, the legendary "Thousands Master."

LOVE HINA–manga creator Ken Akamatsu shamelessly crashes his most famous work (several characters from which seem to have doppelgangers here) into *Harry Potter* for this tale of school wizardry—often jokingly termed "Love Hogwarts" in fandom. Three seven-minute trailers featuring elements of the series were used to sell it before its release or as bonuses on *Negima* audio CDs, and are filed in some sources as the Negima "specials."

NEIGHBORHOOD STORY

1995. JPN: *Gokinjo Monogatari*. TV series. DIR: Atsutoshi Umezawa. SCR: Aya Matsui, Yumi Kageyama, Motoki Yoshimura. DES: Yoshihiko Umakoshi. ANI: Chuji Nakajima. MUS: Masahiro Kawasaki. PRD: Toei, TV Asahi. 25 mins. x 50 eps. (TV), 30 min (m).
One of the freshest and most stylish TV shows of its season, *NS* goes back to the 1960s for its look and atmosphere. Childhood friends and neighbors Mikako and Tsutomu head off to art college (he for photography, she for fashion), where they slowly fall for each other. A bubbly adaptation of the 1995 manga in *Ribbon* magazine by **I'M GONNA BE AN ANGEL**–creator Ai Yazawa, there was also a short theatrical release, *NS: The Movie* (1996). Compare to **HIS AND HER CIRCUMSTANCES**, which tells a similar story, but with a more negative slant. The manga sequel, **PARADISE KISS**, was also adapted into an anime in 2005.

NEO TOKYO *

1987. JPN: *Manie Manie Meikyu Mono-*

gatari. AKA: *Labyrinth Tales.* Movie. DIR: Yoshiaki Kawajiri, Katsuhiro Otomo, Rintaro. SCR: Yoshiaki Kawajiri, Katsuhiro Otomo, Rintaro. DES: Rintaro, Katsuhiro Otomo, Yoshiaki Kawajiri, Takashi Watanabe, Atsuko Fukushima. ANI: Takashi Nakamura, Atsuko Fukushima, Koji Morimoto, Kunihiko Sakurai. MUS: Micky Yoshino. PRD: Project Team Argus, Kadokawa. 50 mins.

A slender anthology brackets two dark shorts by Kawajiri and Otomo inside the titular *Labyrinth,* a chiller by veteran Rintaro. Little Sachiko is warned by her mother about playing with strangers and staring into mirrors, but she ignores the warnings with results as predicted by the Brothers Grimm. She and her cat stray into a carnival straight out of a Ray Bradbury story—the kind where you don't want to stay after dark but can't find the exit. Otomo's story, *Order to Stop Construction,* is a classic SF essay on the possibilities of chaos inherent in the most efficient automated system. Kawajiri contributes *Running Man,* the tale of a top racing driver who finds he just can't quit. Despite its futuristic trappings, it's anime for the couch-potato audience, a warning against machine addiction that they'll forget while slavering over the gleaming, roaring engines, and the least interesting of the three plot premises. All three selections ooze dark, edgy style. See **ROBOT CARNIVAL** and **MEMORIES** for anthologies on a different theme.

NEORANGA *

1998. TV series. DIR: Jun Kamiya. SCR: Sho Aikawa. DES: Hiroto Tanaka. ANI: Hirofumi Suzuki. MUS: Kuniaki Haishima. PRD: Pierrot, Pony Canyon, Marubeni. 15 min. x 48 eps. (#1–#24 1st series / #25–#48 2nd series)

A giant robot, a relic of an ancient South Sea civilization, threatens to destroy Tokyo, but it can be controlled by the three teenage Shimabara sisters, who are descended from its makers. Despite their reservations about inheriting this relic of their previously unknown ancestry, the 18-foot-tall robot becomes "one of the family"—with sometimes comic consequences. Originated by Aikawa, with striking designs, backgrounds, and music, this show begins as a *Godzilla* pastiche but soon transforms into a slice-of-life drama with occasional city-stomping. The short and variable episode lengths stem from its original existence as just one of several anime shown on TV's *Anime Complex* anthology slot, though it is a measure of its quality that it was at least optioned for a follow-up season—few of its fellow short shows shared such success.

NERIMA DAIKON BROTHERS

2006. JPN: *Oroshitate Musical Nerima Daikon Brothers.* AKA: *Dress-up Musical Nerima Daikon Brothers.* TV series. DIR: Shinichi Watanabe. SCR: Yoshio Urasawa. DES: Takamitsu Kondo. ANI: N/C. MUS: N/C. PRD: Studio Hibari, Aniplex. 25 mins. x 12 eps.

Hideki cherishes the dream of putting on a concert in a performance dome he hopes to build in his native town of Nerima. Along with his brother Ichiro (a nightclub host), the pretty cousin he adores, and their surreal panda associate, he hustles for dimes in a series of adventures, occasionally leaning on the assistance of "Nabeshin," a strange man who rents him devices to fight evil, and evading the clutches of local law enforcer Inspector Karakuri. As the appearance by "Nabeshin" suggests, this is another comedy from **EXCEL SAGA**'s Shinichi Watanabe, set in the Tokyo district where so many small anime studios sprang up in the shadow of Toei Animation.

NESTING CRANES

1971. JPN: *Tsuru no Sugomori.* AKA: *Cranes in their Nests.* Movie. DIR: Kazuo Saito (pseudonym for Tsutomu Shibayama). SCR: Kazuo Saito. DES: Kazuo Saito. ANI: Kazuo Saito. MUS: Yasuji Kiyose. PRD: Japanese Film Collective. 17 mins.

An earnest tale of animal cooperation, as two out-of-place chickens try to make their home on an island inhabited by cranes. When they are attacked by an eagle, their adoptive parent cranes are killed, but the chickens organize a counterstrike. Eventually, peace is restored to the island. Based on a story by Teru Takakura, this anime was made over a three-year period by around 80 members of the Japan Film Broadcasting Industry Association under the pseudonymous lead of Shibayama.

NETTI'S MARVELOUS STORY

1977. JPN: *Alps no Ongaku Shojo Netti no Fushigi na Monogatari.* AKA: *Musical Alpine Girl Netti's Marvelous Story; The Wonderful Story of Netti, Musical Girl of the Alps.* TV special. DIR: Hiroshi Shirai, Isao Takahata. SCR: N/C. DES: N/C. ANI: Isao Takahata, Ryosuke Takahashi, Shinichi Tsuji. MUS: N/C. PRD: TV Man Union, Mushi Pro, Nippon Animation, TV Asahi. ca. 80 mins.

Netti is the six-year-old daughter of a musical family in an Austrian mountain village. Nervous at the thought of the town mayor coming to see her first performance, Netti makes many errors in rehearsals, before fleeing into the forest in anguish. Lost in the woods, she is rescued by a mysterious old man who calls himself a "snow wizard" and gives her a magic flute to practice on.

This frightfully obscure TV special, mixing live-action footage with animation, was screened in Japan to mark the imminent arrival of the Engel family, a group of Tirolean performers, further details of which we have been unable to trace. The animation sequences comprised three folktales told by the snow wizard, directed in part by future Studio Ghibli giant Isao Takahata. One features a character study of the lonely old man Karzermandel and another features a boy who scares away devils with a magic flute. The final tale is one of chickens escaping from a henhouse and dancing, for some reason, in the farmyard to the pop song "SOS" by the Japanese pop duo Pink Lady (see **GLORIOUS ANGELS**). Although framed as an Alpine adventure in the style of **TREASURES OF THE SNOW** or **HEIDI**—or indeed,

THE SOUND OF MUSIC—such similarities are only superficial. Compare to YOUNG PRINCESS DIANA, which was another bizarre attempt to educate the Japanese public about a real-life visitor to their country with the aid of fictional cartoon stories.

NEW KARATE HELL

1990. JPN: *Shin Karate Jigoku Hen*. Video. DIR: Kozo Kusuba, Toshiyuki Sakurai. SCR: Hideo Nanbu. DES: Kenzo Koizumi, Shunji Saida. ANI: Kenzo Koizumi, Shunji Saida. MUS: Nobuyuki Nakamura. PRD: Nippon Animation. 50 mins. x 2 eps.

A single karate master is all that stands between beautiful women and a group of neo-Nazi rapists. Hellbent on revenge ever since the Gestapo murdered his father and sister, our hero pursues his quarry from the United States to the Amazon rainforests. Based on a manga by Ikki Kajiwara, creator of KARATE-CRAZY LIFE (with Jiro Tsunoda and Joya Kagemaru), this anime devotes equal screen time not only to the hero's flying fists of vengeance, but to questionable audience titillation in the form of the baddies' many crimes.

NHK

Nippon Hoso Kyokai, or Japan Broadcasting Corporation. Japan's public broadcaster, formed in 1925 by the integration of three radio stations, and subsequently offering television broadcasting from 1953. Japan's first TV channel, the conservative NHK has a large number of anime shows, most clustered around the lower age group—for NHK, cartoons generally remain "kid's stuff," and are used to entertain preschoolers. There are, however, notable exceptions, such as THE SECRET OF BLUE WATER. NHK's sister channel NHK Educational often reaches older age groups, with shows such as KASUMIN.

NIEA_7 *

2000. AKA: *Nia Under Seven; NieA_7– Domestic Poor @nimation*. TV series. DIR: Takuya Sato, Tomokazu Tokoro. SCR: Takuya Sato. DES: Yoshitoshi Abe, Yoshiaki Yanagida. ANI: Tsuneo Kobayashi. MUS: Yoshio Owa. PRD: Triangle Staff, WOWOW. 25 mins. x 13 eps.

On an Earth still struggling to come to terms with making contact with aliens, failed college student Mayuko, forced to live in Tokyo while she retakes her exams, shares a flat with a zany alien girl (cat-ears and all) called Niea. Niea is an Under-7, one of the strange underclass of aliens that hasn't integrated into this neat near future. Made by the same studio as the surreal SERIAL EXPERIMENTS LAIN and intended as a "fantasy sitcom" by original creator Yoshitoshi Abe, *NieA_7* is a gentle examination of the immigrants' plight not unlike DEARS—RATHER THAN DEALING WITH GALAXY-SPANNING INVASIONS OR WORLD-SAVING PLOTS, THE CAST ARE MORE CONCERNED WITH EVERYDAY LIFE IN TOKYO AND HOW TO KEEP THEIR BATHHOUSE FROM GOING BANKRUPT. A MANGA VERSION IN *Ace Next* magazine preceded the show, but was created as a promotional tool—it is not fair to say that *NieA_7* was "based on" the *Ace Next* manga.

NIGHT FOR LOVING

1983. JPN: *Ai Shite Night*. AKA: *Kiss Me Licia*. TV series. DIR: Osamu Kasai, Kazumi Fukushima, Yugo Serikawa, Shigeo Koshi. SCR: Mitsuru Majima, Sukehiro Tomita, Tajio Tamura. DES: Yasuhiro Yamaguchi. ANI: Yasuhiro Yamaguchi, Akira Kasahara, Tsuneo Komuro. MUS: Nozomu Aoki. PRD: Toei, TV Asahi. 25 mins. x 42 eps.

Cute schoolgirl Yaeko helps out in the family restaurant in the evenings. Dad disapproves of her friend Satomi, a big fan of the rock band Beehive, and when the pair meet Hashizo, little brother of Beehive's lead singer Takeshi, things get even worse. Yaeko falls for Takeshi and Satomi resents his friend's new infatuation, much to the annoyance of his *own* fiancée. Based on Kaoru Tada's 1981 manga in *Margaret*, and popular in Europe in its day, it has probably passed its sell-by date in the English language.

NIGHT SHIFT NURSES *

2000. JPN: *Yakin Byoto*. AKA: *Night Shift Ward*. Video. DIR: Hisashi Okezawa. SCR: Ryo Saga. DES: Kuniyoshi Hino. ANI: Hiroya Iijima. MUS: Hiroaki Sano. PRD: Tatsuya Tanaka, Hiromi Chiba, Discovery, Mink, Studio 9MAIami. 30 mins. x 12 eps. (v); 30 mins. (5.5); 30 mins. (10.5); 30 mins. x 4 eps. (*YB2*); 30 mins. x 1+ eps. (*YB3*).

Although he hasn't practiced medicine for a decade following an experiment that went wrong, Doctor Ryuji Hirasaka is put on call for a month at Saint Juliana's Hospital. He spends much of his time daydreaming about making the attractive, perky nurses his slaves, but eventually meets the chief medical officer, who turns out to be the self-same woman that caused his career to stall all those years before. Blackmail, rape, and bondage duly ensue, in what would become the largest and most successful franchise in the DISCOVERY SERIES—representing roughly 20 percent of the label's entire output since 2000. Compare to NURSE ME and LESBIAN WARD, both of which attempt to emulate its success. Not that erotic movie makers require a reason to write a show about nurses, but *NSN* was commissioned in the year when the long-running live-action serial *Leave it to the Nurses* (*DE) approached the height of its popularity. The show's actual origin can be traced to a 1999 computer game and its sequels, all by Mink.

Although not distinguished by a title of its own in the Japanese market, the fourth and fifth episodes were rebranded *NSN: RN's Revenge* (2001) in America, with Hirasaka using a nurse's hospitalized sister as leverage to blackmail her into doing his bidding. The American release also included several sequences of scatology and bodily insertions that had been cut from episodes 1–3. Note that this installment appears to draw on the plot from the sequel to the original *NSN* game, but with the male protagonist from the original, a change in cast that would later be revoked in the remake *Yakin Byoto 2* (see below).

An "episode 5.5," otherwise billed as a "director's cut" of the earlier story, reintroduced the series to the Japanese audience for further episodes. Released in America as *NSN: Clinical Confessions* (2003), it continued with Hirasaka's abuse of his compliant nurses, particularly Ren Nanase, a poor waif who only wants a normal romantic life with her would-be love object Naoya, only to be denied it by Hirasaka's "experiments," which continue to involve enemas, insertions, and scatology. However, the emphasis also adds a new voyeuristic element, told through the eyes of a detective investigating reports of "crimes" at the hospital. The detection angle continued with *NSN: Carnal Corruption* (2003), comprising episodes 8 and 9 of the Japanese series, in which the nurses are confronted with evidence of their crimes—a handy excuse for recycling footage from earlier shows. The story is retold of Ryuji's first-ever guinea pig, Narumi Shinguji, and how she discovered her love for him after he took her virginity by force, before introducing feelings of murderous intent. As the Japanese press release so earnestly put it: "The shudder that ran through the industry will come back again."

The series reached another turning point in 2004 with episode "10.5" in Japan, which revisited the "Golden Moments" (their words, not ours!) of episodes 6–10. Since our own episode count seems one short, we can only assume that one episode is missing outside Japan, or a stand-alone "episode 10" is yet to come in the U.S. Episodes 11 and 12, rebranded in Japan as *NSN: Kranke* (2005), feature nurse Hikaru inexplicably falling in love with Dr. Hirasaka and agreeing to marry him, before becoming his willing assistant in breaking in his latest victim, Nurse Ai, her stepsister.

A variant version of *NSN* exists in Japan, based on the sequel to the original game and distributed as part of the **D3 SERIES**. In a futile effort at avoiding confusion, we shall retain the Japanese title for this series, *Yakin Byoto 2*

(2004), and note that it revisits the plot surrounding Ren Nanase from *Clinical Confessions*, but with a new protagonist, Dr. Kuwabara, whereas *Clinical Confessions* simply retained Dr. Hirasaka from the previous installment.

Yet another spin-off, this time as part of the *Discovery Series* once more, presumably based on the third game in the series, came in the form of *Yakin Byoto 3* (2005), in which a critically injured man is found dumped at the hospital entrance. He is saved by earnest young nurse Yu Yagami, but is then asked to participate in a "new experiment" run by beautiful hospital chief Reika Mikage. 🅛🅝🅥

NIGHT TRAIN TO THE STARS *

1985. JPN: *Ginga Tetsudo no Yoru.* AKA: *Night on the Galactic Railroad.* Movie. DIR: Gisaburo Sugii. SCR: Minoru Betsuyaku. DES: Takao Kodama. ANI: Marisuke Eguchi, Koichi Mashimo, Yasunari Maeda. MUS: Haruomi Hosono. PRD: Hiroshi Masumura, Asahi, Herald, Tac. 115 mins.

Based on Kenji Miyazawa's 1927 novel, this dark but gentle fantasy of life and death is a demanding, rewarding film with some dazzling animation and a script by avant-garde playwright Betsuyaku. Giovanni is a lonely child in unhappy circumstances. Late one night, he boards a strange steam train in a meadow on the outskirts of town. He has no plans or expectations; he's simply along for the ride, and finding his classmate and only friend, Campanella, on board is an unexpected bonus. The fantastic voyage takes them along the Milky Way, through landscapes symbolic of death and rebirth, based on Miyazawa's beliefs as a Nichiren Buddhist and student of Christianity and his background as a naturalist. Only when the train comes full circle and deposits him back at home does Giovanni understand that Campanella's journey had a different destination—in the real world he is dead by his own hand.

Director Sugii isn't afraid to take things slowly or to take liberties with a text when necessary (see **TALE OF GENJI**).

Here he turns all Miyazawa's characters into cats, creating a distancing effect that blurs the edges of the film's tragedy and helps us to accept its overriding sense of wonder and optimism. The imagery of the novel, using a railroad as a metaphor for life's journey, is interpreted with superb attention to detail. The steam train and the stations are as rich and credible as any real-world setting, and the poetic beauty of the imagery combines with this richness to give the long journey a powerful emotional weight. Yellow Magic Orchestra–cofounder Hosono's music perfectly fits this visually stunning film, with its imagery of almost hallucinogenic beauty and power, though even he takes a back seat for Handel's *Hallelujah* chorus. Compare to **GALAXY EXPRESS 999**, with a similar interstellar train, also pastiched in Tsui Hark's Hong Kong cartoon, *A Chinese Ghost Story* (1999). The story was also directed by Kazuki Omori as the live-action film *Night Train to the Stars* (1996).

NIGHT WALKER: MIDNIGHT DETECTIVE *

1998. JPN: *Mayonaka no Tantei.* TV series. DIR: Kiyotoshi Sasano, Yutaka Kagawa. SCR: Ryota Yamaguchi. DES: Miho Shimokasa, Ryoichi Makino, Satoshi Isono. ANI: Satoshi Isono, Ikuo Sato. MUS: Akifumi Tada. PRD: AIC, Studio Gazelle, TV Tokyo. 25 mins. x 12 eps.

Half-vampire detective Shido takes a job with Yayoi Matsunaga, a beautiful investigator from the secret NOS government organization, devoted to hunting down the evil "Nightbreed." His orphaned (and lovestruck) assistant, Riho, believes Yayoi and Shido are having an affair, but Yayoi only pays Shido by letting him drink her blood.

Though Buck-Tick's moody industrial rock opening theme disappointingly fades away to reveal yet another man surrounded by adoring girls, *NW* soon steers clear of the comedy path taken by **MASTER OF MOSQUITON**—with the possible exception of a pointless devil-Tinkerbell sidekick. A melting pot of contemporary horror influences, particularly *Nightbreed* (1990) and *Buffy the Vampire Slayer* (1992), it throws a demons-stalk-Tokyo plot out of **WICKED CITY** into a conspiracy inspired by the *X-Files*. Soon, Shido is on the run from the *good* guys, protecting a human woman bearing a Nightbreed child, facing off against the vampire who created him, and saving Riho's life in a predictable fashion that will link them for eternity.

Despite a short run on late-night TV like **PET SHOP OF HORRORS**, *NW* still manages some original twists, particularly in the second episode that focuses on the suicide of an actress. Selling her soul for fame, she eats human hearts to feed the demon within her and cannot bear to live without her possessor when it dumps her in favor of her understudy. *NW* has a pragmatic attitude toward the supernatural, running with Ayana Itsuki's original story for *Dengeki Comic Gao*, and suggesting that anyone who knew what was waiting in the afterlife would stoop to *any* level to avoid death. In this tale of addiction where life itself is the drug, Shido duels with a sword literally made of his own blood, all the while fighting the distrust of the NOS.

Such moments clash with less polished incidents, particularly Riho's naïve solo "investigation," in which she hitches a ride with two strangers, hoping to be attacked by a Nightbreed before they can molest her. Shido condescendingly tells Riho that her crucifix is "fake," even though it clearly satisfies the important criterion of being cross-shaped. On several occasions, most notably in a scene lifted from *Interview with the Vampire* (1994), Shido claims to be unable to endure the sun, even though we have already seen him wandering around in broad daylight. As in **PHANTOM QUEST CORP**, it would seem that a simple pair of shades will protect modern-day vampires from burning alive. An above-average dub from USMC completes the package, along with a closing theme by rockers Lacrima Christi, who inexplicably sing in Japanese with a Canadian accent. **NV**

NIGHT WARRIORS: DARKSTALKERS' REVENGE *

1997. JPN: *Vampire Hunter*. Video. DIR: Shigeru Ikeda. SCR: Tatsuhiko Urahata, Shigeru Ikeda. DES: Shuko Murase. ANI: Shuko Murase, Hiroyuki Tanaka, Hideki Takayama. MUS: Ko Otani. PRD: Madhouse. 40 mins. x 4 eps.

Demitri Maximoff, the most powerful and most feared of vampires, plots to use the psychic energy raised by his human followers to take over the power of the other Darkstalkers, who have always regarded him as an undesirable element. Given that his hair resembles a squeeze of toothpaste, it's hard to blame them completely, but the alternatives aren't so attractive. Meanwhile, the elderly band of advisers to luscious Darkstalker clan chief Morrigan, the girl who put the suck in succubus, is concerned about her general flightiness and the constant infighting between clans, which weakens their chances of retaining dominion. But their lady just wants to fight, seeking out Demitri for that purpose and turning the end of episode one into a duel with erotic overtones. Some of the other game characters put in cameo appearances—dour half-Darkstalker Donovan, tiny psychotic Anita, kitten-girl Felicia, and zombie serial killer/rock-star Raptor. Volume two sees Donovan fighting some cursed armor and meeting sisters Hsien-Ko and Ling-Ling, who have become Darkstalkers to help them free their late mother's soul from the dark powers she died fighting.

Amid all the rumbles (which recreate the original game's battles onscreen with real punch and conviction), there is the glimmer of a plot surrounding the Darkstalkers' removal of light from Earth. This has divided humankind into their servants and the rest, preventing the rest from growing much food or progressing against the faux religiosity that rules their lives. The mysterious Pyron seems to offer humankind the promise of renewed light from his artificial suns, but he's really out to destroy Earth.

Ninja Nonsense: The Legend of Shinobu

Things turn nasty as the Darkstalkers struggle to fight Pyron off before Donovan saves the day.

Films based on games have to overcome major structural problems before they can work as anything but cynical merchandising exercises. *Night Warriors* comes close to sustaining a narrative, but as with **STREET FIGHTER II**, the characters are too firmly embedded in the endless repetitions of gameplay to develop much. There are some interesting subplot possibilities—Donovan's self-hatred and his quest for enlightenment, Morrigan's *Gormenghast* ennui, Anita's shattered childhood, the spiritual and material impoverishment of humankind—but they're flagged rather than explored, relegated to the status of motivation for yet another rumble. **LNV**

NIGHTMARE CAMPUS *

1995. JPN: *Blackboard Jungle: Gaido Gaikuen*. AKA: *Blackboard Jungle: Outerway College*. Video. DIR: Koji Yoshikawa. SCR: Koji Yoshikawa. DES: Keiichi Sato, Kenji Hayama. ANI: Kenji Hayama. MUS: Masamichi Amano. PRD: Phoenix Entertainment. 50 mins. x 5 eps.

Teenager Masao is visiting his father at an archaeological dig in the Himalayas with his mother. When demonic creatures overrun the site, he shoots the one who kills his mother, only to see the corpse turn into his father. A huge earthquake shakes the area, and his school friends back in Japan believe Masao has been killed, but his eventual reappearance is far from the strangest event in school. Masao and his best friend are the embodiment of powerful demonic beings. Other beings, seemingly angelic but in fact completely evil, are trying to take control of the school and the world by unleashing the "demon" in everyone and controlling the powers so released. It's up to the teenage demons to save the world.

Blood, pain, and sadism abound, and there is much nasty sexual content, with the depiction of genitals ranging from the absurdly absent, to suggestive shadows, to explicit realism. The design, art, and animation also vary wildly, with every kind of character style from an Adam Warren-type bimbette to gag-manga goons and retro-styled escapees from early Go Nagai series such as the similarly themed **DEV-ILMAN**. The unevenness may be partly blamed on budget problems (even Amano's music budget cuts corners with public-domain Beethoven), but it also indicates Yoshikawa's willingness to experiment with aspects of a genre that can simply be run by the numbers, so uncritical is its audience. This typical (but minor) Toshio Maeda offering has interesting possibilities but sadly never really gets off the ground. The same creator's **UROTSUKIDOJI** was saved from an early finish by export sales (that means us), but this never took off to the same extent in the West, and so the series climaxed prematurely—a fate with which its target audience is probably in sympathy. ●N●

NIKONIKOPUN

1988. JPN: *Nikonikopun*. TV series. DIR: Yasuo Kageyama. SCR: N/C. DES: Yoshishige Kosako. ANI: Takaaki Ishiyama, Kazuo Iimura, Mitsuo Hikabe. MUS: Takao Ide. PRD: Visual 80, NHK. 23 mins. x 40 eps.
Anime spin-off from a children's show that featured out-of-work actors dressed up as a giant mouse, penguin, and lion, itself part of the Japanese *Watch with Mother* TV strip for the preschool audience. With episode titles like *I Am a Pirate*, *Let's Play*, and *The Picnic March*, the show primed a generation for the later import *Teletubbies*.

NILS' MYSTERIOUS JOURNEY *

1980. JPN: *Nils no Fushigina Tabi*. AKA: *Nils Holgersson*. TV series. DIR: Hisayuki Toriumi, Mamoru Oshii, Yukimatsu Ito. SCR: Narumitsu Taguchi, Ryo Nakahara. DES: Toshiyasu Okada, Mitsuki Nakamura. ANI: Toshiyasu Okada, Noboru Furuse, Jun Tanaka. MUS: Kawauchi Chito. PRD: Studio Pierrot, Gakken, NHK. 25 mins. x 52 eps.
A horrible little boy who torments animals is reduced to the size of a mouse. Rather than seeking revenge, a flock of wild geese take pity on him and ask him along on their migration. In an anime version of Nobel laureate Selma Lagerlof's classic Swedish novel, Nils is finally restored to his normal size a nicer person. Future **GHOST IN THE SHELL**–director Mamoru Oshii helmed several episodes. Toshiyasu Okada went on to greater things with **MYSTERIOUS CITIES OF GOLD**. The first production for Studio Pierrot.

NINE

1983. Movie, TV special. DIR: Gisaburo Sugii, Hideaki Tsuruta. SCR: Hirokazu Nunose. DES: Mitsuru Adachi. ANI: Minoru Maeda, Hiroshi Wagatsuma. MUS: Hiroaki Serizawa, Yasuo Tsuchida. PRD: Group Tac, Toho, Fuji TV. 83 mins., 80 mins., 71 mins., 75 mins.
Misfit middle-schoolers Karasawa and Katsuya, one a transfer student, sign up for the Seishu school baseball team chiefly because they think it will impress Yuri, the girl they both desire. Before long, their shallow initial reasons have transformed into a burning desire to win the All-Japan championships, in a predictable plotline based on a *Shonen Sunday* manga by Mitsuru Adachi, who also dramatized baseball stories in **H2**, **TOUCH**, **SLOW STEP**, and this show's immediate predecessor **MIYUKI**. The popular movie adaptation was followed by two TV movies the same year, *Nine* and *Nine 2: Declaration of Love*. In 1984, it all ended with *Nine: The Conclusion*, in which Katsuya and his teammates, now high school juniors, win the regional qualifying tests in an effort to meet Coach

Nakao's expectations. However, Karasawa is suffering from a "hitter's block" and is lampooned by school reporter Yoko, who secretly loves him. Inspired by her attention, Karasawa hits a home run just for her, and Katsuya becomes suspicious that his friend has scored with Yuri when he smells that both are using the same shampoo. However, as with all Adachi manga, such minor misunderstandings cannot stop the path of true love, and they all live happily ever after, ending with a double-date at the Koshien baseball stadium.

NINE LOVE STORIES

1992. JPN: *Ai Monogatari*. AKA: *Love Stories*. Video. DIR: Tomomi Mochizuki, Koji Morimoto, Mamoru Hamazu, Hiroshi Hamazaki, Hidetoshi Omori, Takashi Anno. SCR: Kaiji Kawaguchi. DES: Kaiji Kawaguchi. ANI: N/C. MUS: The Beatles. PRD: Toho. 92 mins.
A feature-length anthology of short romantic tales from the pen of **SILENT SERVICE**–creator Kaiji Kawaguchi, joined by an underlying theme of Beatles songs. The roster of famous directors is matched by a similarly high-ranking group of voice talents.

NINE O'CLOCK WOMAN *

2001. JPN: *21-ji no Newscaster Miki Katsuragi*. AKA: *Nine O'Clock Newscaster Miki Katsuragi*. Video. DIR: Yoshio Shirokuro. SCR: Reiji Izumo. DES: Sadaharu Nakamura, Midori Okuda. ANI: N/C. MUS: N/C. PRD: Milky, Museum Pictures. 30 mins. x 3 eps.
Miki Katsuragi has achieved her dream—she's landed the job as anchorwoman for the evening news. But despite the success, respect, and popularity this brings her, the young journalist can't beat her addiction to nonstop masturbation. When lowly cue card holder Satake catches her in the act in her dressing room, she agrees to do anything he wants if he'll keep her secret. With the massive success of reality TV, one would hardly imagine it would harm her career; but this is a porn anime, so "publish and be damned" was never a likely response. Only the first

two episodes were released in the U.S. Based on the manga in *Core* magazine by Akira Goto. Miki's program, *News 9*, seems to have been conceived as a direct pastiche of NHK's *News 21*. **ⓛⓝ**

NINETEEN

1990. Video. DIR: Takaichi Chiba. SCR: Koji Kawahara. DES: Sho Kitagawa. ANI: N/C. MUS: Toshiku Kadomatsu. PRD: Madhouse, Victor Music. 42 mins. Kazushi, university student and football player, sees the girl of his dreams in an advertisement. She's really a medical student, who models as a sideline, and one day they meet. As love blossoms against a background of well-to-do student life, can their romance survive the pressures of the 1990s? A tale of yuppie love isn't what most Westerners expect from the Madhouse team, renowned abroad for horror like **WICKED CITY**, but this exudes quiet charm and elegance. Made for an audience of young, rich Tokyoites, this anime was based on the manga in *Young Jump* by **BLUE BUTTERFLY FISH**–creator Sho Kitagawa.

NINJA *

2003. JPN: *Kunoichi Gakuen Ninpocho*. AKA: *Female Ninja Academy Ninpocho*. Video. DIR: N/C. SCR: N/C. DES: N/C. ANI: N/C. MUS: N/C. PRD: D3, Onmitsudo. 30 mins. x 7 eps.
Three girls from the Koga ninja clan run into trouble when they spot boys from the rival Iga clan at a restaurant. Aya and then her friend Shinobu are captured, sexually assaulted, and infected with a parasite that causes them to lose control of their sexual lusts. Their friend Lena resolves to break in to the enemy stronghold to retrieve the antidote, whereupon she must fight her way through a series of sexually-oriented traps and pitfalls. Legendary conflict between rival ninja clans has been a staple of anime for many years, from the innocuous fun of **HATTORI THE NINJA** and **NARUTO** through to the guiltier pleasures of **LA BLUE GIRL**. This porn release, however, is distinguished only by the surprisingly large amounts of recycled footage.

The term *kunoichi* ("female ninja"), is assembled from the three disassembled strokes that form the character for woman (*onna*) in Japanese: making the sounds *ku* in the hiragana syllabary, *no* in the katakana syllabary, and the kanji for *ichi*. The first and most successful release in the **D3 SERIES**. **ⓛⓝⓥ**

NINJA CADETS *

1996. JPN: *Ninja Mono*. Video. DIR: Eiji Suganuma. SCR: Mitsuhiro Yamada. DES: Nobuhito Sue, Keiji Goto. ANI: Fumitomo Kizaki. MUS: N/C. PRD: AIC. 30 mins. x 2 eps.
The Kabuso clan's seizure of Byakuro Castle is marred by the disappearance of the infant princess, who is carried off into hiding by an honorable ninja. Years later, an energetic young group of ninja wannabes are about to be put through their final exam—a mission into the occupied Byakuro Castle to steal the MacGuffin Scrolls of Power. The evil Kabuso clan has hired highly skilled mercenaries to follow them, knowing that one of the young cadets is actually the missing princess.

Often looking like a spin-off of designer Sue's work on **EL HAZARD**, *Ninja Cadets* is a lazy afternoon's *D&D* with a sushi flavor—wandering monsters, a bit of comedy business, and a satisfyingly big fight finale. There is a promising monochrome beginning as Byakuro Castle is stormed by evil hordes, but the story soon collapses into a pastoral idyll in which the life of an outcast assassin is presented as a summer camping trip, where you get to play with knives while a mommy ninjette cooks supper. Faced with innumerable foes and a map seemingly drawn by a bored teenage Dungeon Master (you can go any direction you want, as long as it's over the single bridge), the daftest ninja in the world decide it would be a good idea to split up. Then they wander listlessly around the countryside like bored kids on a school trip, which is probably the distant genesis of this whole story.

Luckily, when they reach the impregnable fortress, it's guarded by

the daftest samurai in the world, and the scene is set for a walk through all the set pieces of chop-socky ninja films—tiger claws, throwing stars, singing floors, and reconnaissance kites. Our elite assassins try some really smart moves like throwing fire around in a room full of paper scrolls, and voice actress Maria Kawamura steals the show as a suicide-blonde evil minion with an electric-chair hairdo, seemingly inserted at the last minute to inject some much-needed evil into the proceedings. Armed with the Scrolls of Power, the ninja set off to depose the bad guys, just as the ending credits roll—further episodes were not forthcoming. Forgettable fun, but while this does indeed boast both scrolls and ninja, **NINJA SCROLL** it ain't. **ⓛ**

NINJA NONSENSE: THE LEGEND OF SHINOBU *

2004. JPN: *Ninin ga Shinobuden*. AKA: *2 x 2 = Shinobuden; 2 x 2 = Tale of Stealth; The Nonsense Kunoichi Fiction*. TV series DIR: Hitoyuki Matsui, Haruo Sotozaki. DES: Jun Shibata. ANI: Ufotable Zippers. MUS: Harukichi Yamamoto. PRD: Ufotable Zippers, Media Works. 24 mins. x 12 eps.
Girl ninja Shinobu attends a secret ninja school—no outsiders are allowed on campus. Like all good Japanese school story heroines, she has boundless enthusiasm but very little ability. She has a partner, a magical creature called Onsokumaru, a bright yellow ball with arms, wings, and perverted tastes. The school principal Ninja Master is the same type of creature, but with a white beard. Her other companions include talking alligator Devil and her genius younger sister Miyabe. Onsokumaru gives her a test of ninja skill as part of her exam—she has to steal an ordinary schoolgirl's underwear. The target is Kaede Shiranui, who coincidentally is also studying for an exam. But Shinobu is such an incompetent ninja that she's immediately spotted by her intended victim. When Kaede challenges her, she bursts into tears and the story of

Ninja Scroll

© 1993/1995 YOSHIAKI KAWAJIRI/MAD HOUSE/
JVC/TOHO CO., LTD./MOVIE INC.

her total failure comes tumbling out. Kind-hearted Kaede gives her a pair of panties so she can pass, and a friendship is forged in vague imitation of that to be found in E-CHAN THE NINJA GIRL. But when Shinobu invites Kaede to look around the ninja academy campus as a thank-you for helping her to pass her test, the principal tells them that any non-ninja who sees the campus cannot be allowed to leave. Fortunately this doesn't apply to the audience. Based on a manga by Ryoichi Koga.

NINJA RESURRECTION: THE REVENGE OF JUBEI *

1997. JPN: *Makai Tensho*. AKA: *Reborn from Hell*. Video. DIR: Yasunori Urata. SCR: Kensei Date. DES: Kenji Haneyama. ANI: Kenji Haneyama. MUS: Masamichi Amano. PRD: Amuse Video, Phoenix. 40 mins. x 2 eps.
Out of favor, Jubei the ninja roams Japan alone. He believes that a new, dark menace is lurking, waiting to enter the world of men. The great swordsman Musashi, now retired to a monastery, senses the same evil. The Tokugawa shogunate has banned the Western fad of Christianity and is slaughtering its followers. The survivors believe that a new Messiah will be born among them, but the prophecy has a dark side—the Savior could turn bad and become Satan himself. Charismatic Christian leader Shiro Amakusa isn't all he seems, and the believers inside his stronghold are in as much danger from the evil forces within as from the Shogun's armies. Jubei and his associates are sent to infiltrate the

Christian citadel of Shimabara, where they find that the peaceful messiah Amakusa has turned to devilry.

Inspired by the same popular novels that informed NINJA SCROLL but misleadingly advertised abroad as a sequel, *NR* is a ninja film for the post-EVANGELION generation, with cruciform explosions in the streets, aliens invading the minds of Japanese citizens, and the use of alien weaponry to fight an alien threat. The eerie, unworldly sight of samurai raising Christian banners and working their foreign magic is truly chilling in this context. Shiro Amakusa's ambiguous position as gentle messiah *and* tormented devil brings echoes of the UROTSUKIDOJI saga—a parallel aided by beautiful music from Masamichi Amano.

NR boasts some classy moments, but the running time is simply too small to contain such multitudes. The mix of fact and fiction is something that really warrants liner notes, and the intense compression of Futaro Yamada's story results in a messy rush of incidental characters. After a promising, portentous beginning with samurai huddling in a Kurosawa rainstorm and turning foreign guns on their convert countrymen, the film rushes headlong into a final battle with no time for a middle act. A completely unnecessary sex scene adds to the collapse of the latter half into substandard anime hackery—described by one of its own producers as "horrendous." The U.S. edition follows the Japanese pattern, with two separate releases, *TROJ* being followed by a second tape, *Hell's Spawn*. In the U.K., both were condensed onto one 80-minute tape. ⬤🅝🆅

NINJA SCROLL *

1993. JPN: *Jubei Ninpocho*. AKA: *Jubei the Wind Ninja, Wind Ninja Chronicles*. Movie. DIR: Yoshiaki Kawajiri. SCR: Yoshiaki Kawajiri. DES: Yutaka Minowa. ANI: Yutaka Minowa. MUS: Kaoru Wada. PRD: Madhouse, Toho, Movic. 94 mins. (m), 25 mins. x 13 eps. (TV).
After 1603, the people of Japan might as well have lived on another planet

for two and a half centuries. Foreign barbarians (that's us) were expelled, along with their corrupting religious influences (Christianity) and their superpowerful, alien weaponry (guns). Under the rule of the Tokugawa family any uprising was ruthlessly suppressed, and stories began to spread about the ninja, a mythical class of superhuman peasants who could beat the samurai through trickery and cunning. Ninja master Jubei occupies a similar position in Japanese popular culture to Robin Hood in ours. A semihistorical figure who mysteriously disappeared, this sword master to the shogun has inspired many plays, novels, and films. It was Jubei's father, Mataemon, who founded the Yagyu school, and his brother Matajuro who became the hero of a kabuki play, *True Tale of Twin Umbrellas* (1887). It wasn't until the 20th century that his own fan base really grew, stirred up by Futaro Yamada's potboiler novels and turned into anime that eventually made him better known abroad than the rest of his family. *Ninja Scroll*, ironically, has contributed significantly to this reputation, even though its own "Jubei" officially bears no relation to the Jubei Yagyu of popular legend. Matters were kept nicely vague in the first movie, but later incarnations were obliged to explain that he is actually "Jubei Kibagami," a generic wandering swordsman who just happens to have had a series of adventures and encounters remarkably similar to that of Futaro Yamada's *Jubei* novels. In *NS*, he has a set number of superpowered opponents (on this occasion, eight of them) to defeat on a quest for justice against an evil sorcerer. Jubei's ultimate aim is to stop Spanish muskets from reaching the shogun's enemy and toppling the fragile order.

The same basic plotting can be found in Yamada's *Jubei* novels, the "real" Jubei anime NINJA RESURRECTION, Kinji Fukasaku's live-action Sonny Chiba vehicle *Darkside Reborn* (1981), and its remake, Masakazu Shirai's *Samurai Armageddon* (1996). *NS*, however, beats the cheap special effects of its live-action rivals hands-down and comes complete with a menagerie of flawed heroes, each with distinct magical abilities. The main love interest is one of anime's most interesting female characters, a woman whose very touch is poison. The set pieces are wonderful, from a duel in a bamboo grove to the explosive finale on a sinking ship. Made for a cinema release, *NS* boasts a coherent plot instead of, say, several TV episodes cut together, and a larger budget than many similar anime. The consequently higher production values have made it an enduring anime favorite in the English language. The character has a brief cameo in JUBEI-CHAN THE NINJA GIRL, which purports to be a comedy about his modern-day reincarnation. The TV series *Ninja Scroll Dragon Stone Chapter* (*NS: Ryuhogoku-hen*, 2003) features an older Jubei who acquires the titular artifact and becomes embroiled in a conflict between a rival ninja clan and demons. A second *Ninja Scroll* movie, supposedly a direct sequel to the movie, has been announced as forthcoming in 2006. ●ⓃⓋ

NINJA THE WONDERBOY

1964. JPN: *Shonen Ninja Kaze no Fujimaru*. AKA: *Young Fujimaru the Wind Ninja*. TV series. DIR: Daisaku Shirakawa, Kimio Yabuki, Takeshi Shirato, Hiromi Uchida, Michiru Takeda. SCR: Satoshi Iijima, Jiro Yoshino, Daisaku Shirakawa, Minoru Tanaka. DES: N/C. ANI: Daikichi Kusube, Akira Okuwara. MUS: Koichi Fukube. PRD: Toei, NET. 25 mins. x 65 eps.
The first animated version of one of Sanpei Shirato's popular ninja manga about a young boy who is carried away by an eagle and brought up by ninja, who instruct him in secret combat techniques and almost magical fighting arts. The warlords of Japan are fighting over the mystical Book of Dragon Smoke, a scroll detailing how to make special weapons (presumably gunpowder). Fujimaru becomes involved in the conflict with his pacifist love-interest, Midori, and fights against his rival, Jupposai of the Fuma clan, as well as

the Iga ninja and the evil southern barbarians.
Shirato was determined to show Japanese life in the Tokugawa shogunate as faithfully as possible, with attention to historical detail, but, although the style of the TV series is quite realistic, it was aimed at a relatively young audience. Shirato's SASUKE follows the same pattern, though he would get to appeal to a more adult audience with LEGEND OF KAMUI. The original manga in *Bokura* magazine was originally known as *Ninja Clan* but had a name change for the anime designed to associate it closer with the show's sponsor—Fujisawa Pharmaceuticals.

NINJAMAN IPPEI

1982. JPN: *Ninjaman Ippei*. TV series. DIR: Hideo Takayashiki, Saburo Hashimoto, Masakazu Yasumura, Yoshihiro Kowata. SCR: Hideo Takayashiki, Masaaki Sakurai, Tomoko Konparu. DES: Saburo Hashimoto, Naoto Hashimoto. ANI: Shunsaburo Takahata. MUS: Kiyoshi Suzuki. PRD: Tokyo Movie Shinsha, Nippon TV. 25 mins. x 13 eps.
Way out in the sticks, the fourth-graders of the local school in Tokio village all come with their own superpowers of doubtful merit, including flying eyeballs and missile-hair. Ippei and his friends study hard at being ninja, but they are constantly under threat from the arrogant cheats over in the neighboring village of Techno. A strange mix of assassins and school comedy, based on a children's manga by Kazuyoshi Kawai in *100-ten Comics* magazine.

NINKU *

1995. JPN: *Ninku*. TV series, movie. DIR: Noriyuki Abe. SCR: Hiroshi Hashimoto, Ryu Tamura. DES: Tetsuya Nishio, Mari Kitayama, Shigenori Takada. ANI: Kazunori Mizuno. MUS: Yusuke Homma. PRD: Studio Pierrot, Fuji TV. 25 mins. x 55 eps. (TV), 26 mins. (m).
Adapted from Koji Kiriyama's 1993 *Shonen Jump* manga, the anime follows the adventures of the Ninku ninja clan. Since the third year of the Edo period, the clan has brought about a fragile

peace through its command of esoteric martial arts, but others are constantly trying to steal their techniques and take over the country. The primary target is Fusuke Ninku, a geeky-looking kid but one of the clan's most vital members; the kidnappers hope he will give them access to its secrets. In the summer "movie" *Ninku: Headstone of a Knife* (1995), screened while the series was still on the air and so separate from its continuity, a gang of impostors is traveling round the country pretending to be the Ninku clan, and the real clan members have to find out what they're up to. The *Ninku* characters also appeared in *Ninku Extra*, a 35-minute video released to popularize the series.

NIPPON ANIMATION

Formed in 1975 as Zuiyo Enterprises to create animation for HEIDI, the studio was split into two legal entities: plain Zuiyo, which retained the rights to the *Heidi* anime, and also its mounting debts; and "Nippon Animation," which continued to employ Zuiyo's staff on other projects. The studio is best known for the WORLD MASTERPIECE THEATER series, which adapted many foreign children's stories, including ANNE OF GREEN GABLES and FUTURE BOY CONAN. Local works include CHIBI MARUKO-CHAN. References to a "Nippon Animation" predating the 1970s are likely to be to the unrelated "Nippon Doga" (*doga*—animation), a company that was eventually absorbed by Toei.

NISHIJIMA, KATSUHIKO

?– . Co-founder of Studio Fantasia and one of the creators credited with PROJECT A-KO. Other work includes direction and key animation on URUSEI YATSURA and direction on AGENT AIKA, NAJICA, and LINGERIES.

NISHIKUBO, MIZUHO

1958– . Often credited as Toshihiko Nishikubo—Japanese sources cannot agree which is the pseudonym and which the real name; he uses Mizuho on GHOST IN THE SHELL. After graduating in sociology from Waseda University in 1976, he became an animator at Tatsunoko. He went freelance in 1979 and worked as an animator on ROSE OF VERSAILLES and MYSTERIOUS CITIES OF GOLD. His directorial debut was STREET CORNER FAIRYTALES; he has also written scripts for anime.

NISHIMURA, JUNJI

1955– . Born in Saga Prefecture, Nishimura graduated in sociology from Meiji Gakuin University in 1980. At the studio Nishiko Pro, he learned animation from director Kazuyuki Hirokawa, working as a key animator on shows such as URUSEI YATSURA. He became the supervising director on PROGOLFER SARU and oversaw the video adaptation of SHUTENDOJI.

NISHIZAKI, YOSHINOBU

1934– . Pseudonym for Hirofumi Nishizaki. Sometimes credited as Yoshinori Nishizaki. Born in Tokyo to a family that specialized in ancient Japanese dancing traditions, Nishizaki rebelled by founding a jazz club in 1957, the year of his graduation from Nippon University. He moved into music production in 1962, setting up his own company, Office Academy, in 1963 and becoming a general manager for Osamu Tezuka's Mushi Production. With the collapse of Mushi, Nishizaki was somehow able to wrest copyrights for WANSA-KUN and TRITON OF THE SEA from their creator, producing them under the auspices of his newly founded Anime Staff Room. His biggest hit, however, came with STAR BLAZERS—a franchise he has continually revised in the decades since. Prolonged legal action has ensued between him and Leiji Matsumoto over who has the right to claim to be the creator of the series. Nishizaki now has the moral right to claim himself as the author of the series and the movies, but Matsumoto is free to make his own new versions. Office Academy was subsequently renamed Westcape Corporation, under which auspices Nishizaki was the executive producer of ODIN and UROTSUKIDOJI, before the

company was declared bankrupt in 1997. Nishizaki was arrested in 1999 over drugs and weapons charges and served five and a half years in prison. The authors submit that while Nishizaki's production career often makes him appear something of a one-hit wonder, perpetually refashioning his one cash cow, even to the extent of the substandard marine knock-off THUNDERSUB, he is now ideally placed to sell his greatest untold story—his own autobiography.

NISHIZONO, SATORU

1962– . Born in Kagoshima Prefecture, Nishizono studied law at Waseda University. He worked briefly at an educational company before becoming a scriptwriter for anime including CRAYON SHIN-CHAN and BONOBONO.

NITABOH

2004. JPN: *Nitaboh: Tsugaru-jamisen Shisho Nitaboh Gaiden*. AKA: *Another Tale of Nitaboh, Father of Tsugaru Guitar*. TV special. DIR: Akio Nishizawa. SCR: Akio Nishizawa, Koji Tanaka. DES: N/C. ANI: N/C. MUS: N/C. PRD: WOW-World. 90 mins.
Born in 1857 to a poor family, Nitaro was orphaned early and lost his sight at the age of eight. He learns to play the *shamisen*, and his love of the instrument gives him the will to go on living. He becomes known as Nitaboh of Kambara, and he and his pupils forge the modern Tsugaru shamisen style before his death in 1928.

Tsugaru shamisen is a folk music style from Tsugaru in Aomori prefecture in snowy Northern Japan. It's based on the traditional meter-long, three-string picked instrument, which came from China by way of Okinawa over 500 years ago. By the late Meiji era, the instrument was widely used by street entertainers and beggars. Many performers were blind, as music was one of the few ways open to blind people to make a living. Nitaro Akimoto was such a player, and this movie tells his story.

The classical shamisen style is heav-

ily formalized, but *tsugaru* encourages free-form jamming and is often compared to Western jazz. Nitaboh's influence was so central that two monuments to him were dedicated near his hometown in 1988 and 1993; this TV movie is another mark of respect. The animation style is traditional, and the backgrounds are particularly pretty, showing his hometown and its environs as a pastoral idyll unspoilt by the encroaching tide of modernity.

NO GOOD DADDY

1974. JPN: *Dame Oyaji*. TV series. DIR: Hisashi Sakaguchi, Fumio Ikeno. SCR: Tomohiro Ando, Susumu Yoshida. DES: Mitsutoshi Furuya. ANI: Fumio Ikeno. MUS: Amp. PRD: Family Planning, Knack, TV Tokyo. 26 mins. x 26 eps.
Poor salaryman Damesuke is married to Onibaba, the Demon-Wife from Hell, who rules him with an iron fist. Every time he tries to assert himself, his family turns on him and beats him up, for they think of him as the world's worst waste of space.

Though in the latter part of the original comic Dad eventually made good and became the boss of a small company, the anime version was canceled before reaching that point in the story. Created by Mitsutoshi Furuya in 1970 for *Shonen Sunday* magazine, this spiteful, violent series was toned down for an early evening TV audience, and each two-chapter episode involved a greater concentration on son Takobo and his school life. Ⓥ

NOBODY'S BOY

1970. JPN: *Chibikko Remi to Meiken Capi; Rittai Anime Ie Naki Ko; Le Naki Ko*. AKA: *Little Remi and His Famous Dog Capi; 3D Animation: Child without a Family; Sans Famille; Homeless Child*. Movie, TV series. DIR: Yugo Serikawa. SCR: Masaharu Segawa. DES: Akira Okuwara. ANI: Akira Okuwara, Yasuji Mori, Katsuya Oda, Akihiro Ogawa. MUS: Tadashi Kishimo. PRD: Toei, TMS, Nippon TV. 81 mins., 25 mins. x 51 eps., 25 mins. x 26 eps.
Hector Malot's 1878 novel *Sans Famille*

inspired Tezuka veteran Serikawa to animate the story of little Remi and his search for his lost parents in the early 20th century. Accompanied by his faithful dog, Remi is forced to join a band of traveling players, but after many adventures he finally finds his mother, who thought he was dead, and is no longer a child without a family.

In 1977, a TV series, *3D Animation: Child Without a Home (Ie Naki Ko)*, followed from Tokyo Movie Shinsha. Directed by Osamu Dezaki with character designs by Akio Sugino and a soundtrack by Takeo Watanabe, it covered the same story at much greater length. "3D" was a grandiose claim, but the characters are well designed, and the skill of the animation is considerable, making use of moving backgrounds to give a sense of depth. Another Malot adaptation, **NOBODY'S GIRL**, followed the next year. In 1980, TMS edited the TV series into another movie, *Child Without a Home*. But the concept still had possibilities—perhaps an influence on the success of the live-action **OSHIN** in 1983, the concept was revived once more, this time with a female lead, as another live-action series, again called *Child Without a Home* (1994). The story was brought back *again* as *Remi: A Child Without a Home* (1996), a 26-episode series directed by Kozo Kusuba for Nippon Animation's **WORLD MASTERPIECE THEATER** franchise. However, the newest version introduced major changes to the story line, switching Remi's gender and transforming *her* into a child singer in order to showcase the talents of voice actress Mitsuko Horie, for whom the series was a glorified star vehicle. With a shorter running time and such major alterations contravening the worthy spirit of previous shows, the series received the lowest ratings ever for the *WMT* and was the death knell for the franchise. See also a further great boy-and-his-dog epic **BELLE AND SEBASTIAN** and another oft-adapted tale of an orphan's quest, **FROM THE APENNINES TO THE ANDES**.

NOBODY'S GIRL

1978. JPN: *Perrine Monogatari*. AKA: *En Famille; Her Own Folk; Story of Perrine*. TV series. DIR: Hiroshi Saito, Shigeo Koshi. SCR: Akira Miyazaki, Kasuke Sato. DES: Shuichi Seki. ANI: Takao Kogawa. MUS: Takeo Watanabe. PRD: Nippon Animation, Fuji TV. 25 mins. x 53 eps. Young Perrine travels with her father around Bosnia, where he is a photographer. After his death, Perrine and her mother are forced to move to France, making ends meet with their own photo business, until Perrine's mother also dies. Perrine continues on the journey with only her dog, Baron, for company, heading for the mansion of her rich grandfather Bilfranc. He turns out to be a cruel man, and instead of announcing herself, Perrine takes a job as a humble worker in his string factory. After many trials of cruelty, he comes to trust Perrine, appointing her as his interpreter and awaiting a fairy-tale ending where she reveals that she has been his granddaughter all along.

Another entry in the **WORLD MASTERPIECE THEATER** series, this family anime was based on an 1893 novel by Hector Malot and is not to be confused with the 1996 sex-change remake of his earlier **NOBODY'S BOY**. Since Malot's original begins with the death of Perrine's mother, all that precedes it in the above synopsis is the creation of scriptwriter Akira Miyazaki. This was a first-time collaboration between writer Miyazaki and Hiroshi Saito, who would become stalwarts of the *WMT* franchise in the absence of an "old guard," such as Hayao Miyazaki and Isao Takahata, who had gone on to better things. Their next entry in the series would be **TOM SAWYER**.

NOBUMOTO, KEIKO

1964– . Born on Hokkaido, Nobumoto graduated from the Asahikawa School of Nursing before attending the Third Anime Scenario House workshop in 1987; she won a Fuji TV new writer's prize two years later. She has written many live-action TV scripts, largely for the channel that first nurtured her talent, including *Give Me Good Love*

(*DE) and *LxIxVxE* (*DE), and movies, including **TOKYO GODFATHERS** and the live-action *World Apartment Horror* (1991) and *Nurse Call* (1993). She has written many of the better anime scripts of recent years, justifying comparisons with Kazunori Ito. Her greatest achievements include the superb recycling of old themes in **MACROSS** *Plus*, and many crucial episodes of **COWBOY BEBOP**. Her recent work includes **WOLF'S RAIN**, and she has also written novels, including the prose adaptation of her own *Macross Plus* scripts.

NOEIN *

2005. JPN: *Noein—Mo Hitori no Kimi e*. AKA: *Noein—To My One and Only*. TV series. DIR: Kazuki Akane, Hiroyuki Tsuchiya, Kenji Yasuda, Kiyoshi Matsuda, Naoki Horiuchi, Mamoru Enomoto. SCR: Kazuki Akane, Hiroshi Onogi, Hiroaki Kitajima, Miya Asakawa, Kazuharu Sato. DES: Takahiro Kishida. ANI: Kensuke Ishikawa, Akira Takada, Haruo Sotozaki, Yukari Kobayashi. MUS: N/C. PRD: Satelight, Viewworks, Chiba TV. 25 mins. x 24 eps. Preteen Haruka Kaminogi lives with her divorced mother in the Hokkaido port of Hakodate and frets over her lifelong friend Yu, a thoughtful boy who is studying hard to get into a private school in distant Tokyo. Their everyday existence is thrown into turmoil by Karasu, a shadowy man who claims to have traveled in time from the year 2020, when the rival dimensions of Lacrima and Shangri La are locked in conflict.

NOEL'S MYSTERIOUS ADVENTURE

1983. JPN: *Noel no Fushigina Boken*. Movie. DIR: Tadao Takakuwa, Yasuo Maeda. SCR: Ryohei Suzuki. DES: Iruka. ANI: Nobukazu Otake, Chikao Katsui. MUS: Iruka. PRD: Iruka Office. 72 mins. On a hot summer's day, Noel and his faithful dog, Kinnosuke, get into a plane to buy some ice cream for the sun. En route, they stop off at the planet Kikazari, where dressing up is compulsory. After meeting with the sun, Noel encounters the master of smog, and must wrestle a sludge monster on the bottom of the ocean.

A vehicle for the singer-songwriter Iruka, who wrote the original story and also provides the voice of Noel, while her three-year-old son plays the dog. The film was shown on a double bill with another of the musician's creations, the short film *Iruka's Christmas: Jeremy's Tree*, in which a lonely orphan finds a bird in the snow who tells him that she lost her home when her tree was cut down. Jeremy agrees to steal the tree from a family's living room but is shot in the process. As he loses consciousness, he has a vision of Santa Claus. This story of sub-Wildean pathos was made by *Noel*-assistant director Maeda—a seasonal outing somewhat ruined by being released in April.

NOIR

2001. TV series. DIR: Koichi Mashimo. SCR: Ryoei Tsukimura. DES: Yoko Kikuchi, Minako Shiba. ANI: N/C. MUS: Yuki Kajiura. PRD: B-Train, TV Tokyo. 25 mins. x 26 eps.
Near-future replay of GUNSMITH CATS, as sexy hitwoman Mireille Bouquet, searching the Tokyo underworld for the assassin who killed her parents, teams up with traumatized Japanese girl Kirika Yumura. Neither can remember the full details of their pasts, but both are dragged into a conspiracy that shows that they are linked by more than mere amnesia.

NOISEMAN

1997. JPN: Onkyo Seimetai Noiseman. AKA: Noiseman Sound Insect. Movie. DIR: Koji Morimoto. SCR: Hideo Morinaka. DES: Koji Morimoto, Masaaki Yuasa. ANI: Masaaki Yuasa. MUS: Yoko Kanno. PRD: Bandai Visual, Studio 4°C. 16 mins.
The future, in the city of Camphon: a scientist has creatured a synthetic life-form called Noiseman, which can turn music into crystals, thus making it inaudible over the airwaves. A teenage biker gang decides to defeat the scientist and his "sound insect." Mixing 2D and 3D animation, the film was originally conceived as a 45-minute

movie with an opening linear narrative sequence that could then open out into various interactive possibilities, along the lines of a game. The film has an arresting design that manages to be both wacky and edgy, a color palette of dusty pastels in the style of the studio's later MIND GAME, intense lighting, and steam punk visuals forshadowing STEAM BOY. Initially given away free to anyone who bought certain models of Pioneer DVD players in 1997, and only later released in 2003 as part of a Studio 4°C retrospective DVD.

NONOMURA HOSPITAL *

1996. JPN: Nonomura Byoin no Hitobito. AKA: People of Nonomura Hospital. Video. DIR: Nobuyoshi Ando. SCR: Oji Miyako. DES: Jun Sato. ANI: Jun Sato. MUS: The Pinks. PRD: Pink Pineapple, KSS. 30 mins. x 2 eps.
After breaking his leg, detective inspector Umihara is sent to Nonomura Hospital to recuperate. When the hospital owner dies, the convalescing Umihara goes to work. Unsure of whether the death was suicide or murder, Umihara questions the victim's beautiful wife, the three attractive nurses, and his charming fellow patient. An anime based on an erotic computer game, it consequently boasts more sex than suspense. Released in the U.S. as *The Mystery of Nonomura Hospital*. **N**

NONTAN

2003. JPN: Genki! Genki! Nontan. AKA: Happy Happy Nontan. TV series. DIR: Yutaka Kagawa. SCR: Kei Muto. DES: N/C. ANI: N/C. MUS: N/C. PRD: Itochu, Polygon Pictures, Columbia Music Entertainment. ca. 6 mins. x 24 eps.
This 3D animated series for young children is based on the adventures of perky white kitten Nontan. With his friends, fun-loving Tanuki, strong Bear, and the pink Rabbit triplets and his rival, Pig, he teaches children positive lessons about the beauty and wonder of life. Originally created as a picture-book series by Sachiko Kiyono, Nontan's adventures have sold a million copies in Japan and there are six volumes on

DVD, each containing four episodes and a short educational segment.

NOOZLES, THE *

1984. JPN: Fushigina Koala Blinky. AKA: Blinky the Mysterious Koala; Blinky and Printy. TV series. DIR: Taku Sugiyama, Noboru Ishiguro. SCR: Taku Sugiyama, Michiru Tanabe. DES: Isamu Noda. ANI: Eimi Maeda. MUS: Reijiro Komutsu. PRD: Nippon Animation, Nippon TV. 25 mins. x 26 eps.
Ten-year-old girl Sandy Brown stays with her grandmother while her archaeologist father is away on a research trip. She is given a toy koala, only to discover that when she "noozles" her nose against it, it transforms into a real koala, Blinky, a refugee from Koalawalla Land. On the run from (literally) a kangaroo court with kangaroo cops, Blinky has come to Earth to hide, his only possession a magical watch that can stop time. His sister, Printy (Pinky in the U.S. dub), also arrives in search of her brother—Printy has a magical makeup compact that can open dimensional gateways. Blinky and Printy take Sandy on many adventures as they study Earth and pop back on occasion to Koalawalla Land, also hiding out from the two evil poachers Frankie and Spike.

Back in the real world, 1984 saw the arrival of six koalas in Japan, sent as goodwill ambassadors by Australia. Japan went into a koala frenzy, lapping up this otherwise unremarkable anime and its rival on TV Tokyo, LITTLE KOALA. The same production team specialized in animal cartoons, most notably DOGTANIAN AND THE THREE MUSKEHOUNDS. The series was broadcast on the U.S. children's channel Nickelodeon.

NORA

1985. Video. DIR: Satomi Mikuriya. SCR: Satomi Mikuriya, Reiko Nakada. DES: Satomi Mikuriya, Yuki Motonori. ANI: Masami Suda. MUS: Yuji Ono. PRD: Mik Mak Pro, Toyo Links, Pony Canyon. 56 mins., 45 mins.
In the year 2097, a beautiful girl and two scientists must prevent their fron-

tier space-town's governing computer from going haywire and starting Armageddon. This adaptation differs considerably from the original 1980 manga from GARAGA-creator Mikuriya, but, since the creator performed so many tasks on the staff, we can assume the changes were made with her approval. A second episode, *Twinkle Nora Rock Me*, completed the story.

NORAKURO

1970. JPN: *Norakuro-kun*. AKA: *Black Stray*. TV series, movie. DIR: Yonehiko Watanabe, Satoshi Murayama. SCR: Masaki Tsuji, Ichiro Wakabayashi, Shunichi Yukimuro. DES: N/C. ANI: Tsuneo Komuro, Toshitaka Kadota. MUS: Hidehiko Arashino. PRD: TCJ, Fuji TV. 11 mins., 25 mins. x 28 eps., 25 mins. x 48 eps.

Shiho Tagawa's *Norakuro* began as a 1931 manga in *Shonen Club* with the story of a brave stray dog's fight against oppressive monkeys. The popular character was soon put to use promoting Japan's militaristic expansion in the 11-minute short *Corporal Norakuro* (1934, *Norakuro Gocho*), a WARTIME ANIME directed by Yasuji Murata, in which the loyal doggy joins the army, beats his monkey allies at rifle practice, has some fun with fireworks, and then wakes up to discover it was all a dream.

The *Norakuro* manga enjoyed a new lease on life during the nostalgia boom that followed the 1968 centenary of the Meiji Restoration. Transferring to *Comic Bon-Bon*, where it ran for another decade, it was brought back for a young audience as the TV series *Norakuro* (1970), in which the low-ranking soldier returned once more, ever jostling for power within an army dominated by General Bull and kept strictly under control by Captain Mole. Playing up the military comedy angle in skits that were crammed two to each episode, Norakuro also had time to fall for Miko, a pretty nurse and troops' pinup.

Never one to admit defeat, the franchise jumped to *Comic Morning* in the 1980s to promote Norakuro's latest incarnation, making this one of the earliest retro anime. The original character's grandson was the lead character in *Norakuro-kun* (1987), a lighthearted Studio Pierrot series directed by future KISHIN CORPS–crew member Takaaki Ishiyama. The child of a poor family is visited by the titular canine, now resembling less a military cartoon than a man in a life-sized Mickey Mouse costume, courtesy of character designs by Yuji Moriyama. The children are soon enlisted in war games, as General Bull arrives and warns of the approaching pig forces of Jimmy Butagawa.

NOTARI MATSUTARO

1990. Video. DIR: Toshio Takeuchi. SCR: Tadaaki Yamazaki, Seiji Matsuoka, Shunichi Yukimuro. DES: Akehiro Kaneyama. ANI: Masayoshi Kitazaki. MUS: Masayoshi Kitazaki. PRD: Mushi Pro. 60 mins. x 6 eps.

A teenage school dropout finds new meaning in his life when he discovers sumo wrestling, heading off to Tokyo for the bright lights and training with an aging master of the sport. Based on a 1973 *Big Comic* manga by TOMORROW'S JOE–creator Tetsuya Chiba, *NM* packs two "episodes" into each 60-minute tape to give the impression that it is actually a 12-part TV series, even though it was never broadcast.

NOW AND THEN, HERE AND THERE *

1999. JPN: *Ima, Soko ni Iru Boku*. AKA: *Now I'm There*. TV series. DIR: Akitaro Daichi. SCR: Hideyuki Kurata. DES: Atsushi Oizumi. ANI: Michinori Nishino. MUS: Migaku Iwazaki, Toshio Masuda. PRD: AIC, WOWOW. 25 mins. x N/D eps.

Schoolboy Shu Matsutani climbs a chimney to rescue a girl he sees sitting at its summit, but he falls into an alternate world. There, the damsel he tried to rescue is revealed as Lala Lu, the bearer of a magic pendant that can control the water element in this new world. The evil Hamdo needs Lala's pendant so that he can construct his fortress in a place called Hellywood— and now Shu isn't just visiting, he's the point man in a war against the forces of darkness. Despite a plot redolent of the comedy EL HAZARD, childish designs, and a sub-Miyazaki look, *N&TH&T* is a remarkably adult show that refuses to stint on images of violence and abuse. Shown on more forgiving satellite TV, this anime was compared to Alex Haley's epic *Roots* by screenwriter Kurata—a trifle optimistic from the man who wrote BATTLE ATHLETES. **V**

NTV, NIPPON TV, I.E. JAPAN TV

TV channel, formed in 1953 as Japan's first commercial broadcaster, and a direct competitor with the license-funded NHK. The TV channel has strong ties with the Yomiuri Group, including not only the Yomiuri TV channel affiliate in some outlying regions, but the *Yomiuri Shimbun* newspaper and the baseball team Yomiuri Giants. It is thus perhaps no surprise that one of the channel's biggest anime successes in early years was the baseball anime STAR OF THE GIANTS. Anime on NTV remains in children's slots and clustered in the late-night graveyard shift.

NUBO: THE DISAPPEARING MEDAL

1990. JPN: *Nubo Kieta Medal*. Video. DIR: Hiromitsu Ota. SCR: N/C. DES: N/C. ANI: Hiromitsu Ota. MUS: Hiroaki Ran. PRD: Aubec. 25 mins.

In the green and pleasant village of Nubo, the summer festival is ruined when a gold medal (first prize in the Pie Eating Contest) disappears. All the local inhabitants, who happen to be the mascot characters from the various types of Morinaga chocolate, go hunting for the missing medal. A cynical exercise in product placement, designed to sell chocolate to kids, and, presumably, get them to eat more pies.

NURSE ANGEL LILIKA SOS

1995. TV series. DIR: Akitaro Daichi. SCR: Akitaro Daichi. DES: Koi Ikeno. ANI: Hajime Watanabe. MUS: Shinkichi Mitsumune. PRD: Studio Gallop, TV Tokyo. 25 mins. x 35 eps.

Ten-year-old Ririka is a typical Japanese elementary-school heroine—cute, sweet, kindhearted, and always willing to help others. When a very handsome older boy returning from his travels gives her a present from the exotic, mysterious realm of England, it turns out to be the device that transforms her into the latest of a long line of anime heroines dating back to LITTLE WITCH SALLY. Earth is under threat from the playing-card-themed forces of Dark Joker (see also WILD CARDZ), and whenever his minions, complete with ace-of-spades tattoos, threaten Earth, Ririka puts on her magic nurse's cap and becomes Lilika, the Nurse Angel. She uses the power bestowed on her to fight evil, extend her powers of healing to the world, and also to sell the many items of product-placement accessories that she wields in the commercially savvy post–SAILOR MOON world. At the halfway point, the series suddenly becomes much darker and more unpredictable—heading for a tear-jerker ending with a real twist. A manga was published the same year by Yasushi Akimoto and Koi Ikeno, who also created TOKIMEKI TONIGHT.

NURSE ME! *

2002. JPN: Seijun Kango Gakuen. AKA: Sexy Nurse Academy. Video. DIR: Juhachi Minamisawa. SCR: Joichi Michigami. DES: Tetsuya. ANI: Tetsuya. MUS: Hiroaki Sano, Takeshi Nishizawa. PRD: Discovery. 30 mins. x 3 eps.
Hospital manager Doctor Miura and head nurse Etsuko hit upon an innovative new way of avoiding malpractice suits; well, innovative if you haven't seen LESBIAN WARD or DOCTOR SHAMELESS. They decide to train their nubile young nurses to perform sexual services for the patients and each other, hoping to ensure a happy hospital. Not all the nurses are easily won over, particularly when they discover that part of their duties include whoring themselves to difficult patients in order to avoid legal action. Virginal new recruit Yumi's lifelong dream of being a nurse is soon shattered after she is broken in by the powers that be. A better than average nurse porn anime, if you like

that sort of thing, with higher than usual production values that extend to generally decent animation, and a rare widescreen presentation. Another entry in the DISCOVERY SERIES, conceived in an apparent attempt to replicate the success of the franchise's similar NIGHT SHIFT NURSES, and based on an erotic novel by Domu Kitahara. **ⒸⓃⓋ**

NURSE WITCH KOMUGI *

2002. JPN: Nurse Witch Komugi-chan; NWK Magical Te; NWK Magicarte Z. AKA: Nurse Witch Komugi-chan It's Magic. Video. DIR: Yasuhiro Takemoto, Yoshitomo Yonetani, Toshihiro Ishikawa, Masato Tamagawa, Masatsugu Arakawa, Ko Matsuzono. SCR: Armstrong Takizawa, Tsuyoshi Tamai. DES: Akio Watanabe. ANI: Yoshinobu Ito. MUS: Ryuji Takagi. PRD: Kyoto Animation, Pioneer, Rondo Robe, Tatsunoko, Toshiba. 25 mins. x 5 eps. (v1), 30 mins. (v2), 30 mins. x 2eps (v3).
Komugi Nakahara is a hyperactive airhead whose main ambition in life is to wear costumes based on famous characters—compare to COSPLAY COMPLEX. When she gets a job at a café where she can dress up all day, she's in heaven. She doesn't even dream that there's such a place as Vaccine World, or that Ungrar the King of Viruses has escaped from prison there, but when the Goddess of Vaccine World sends cute critter Mugimaru to Earth to find a suitable candidate to accept the powers of the Nurse Witch and defend mankind (or at least Akihabara) from the Virus King, she's ready and willing, if not particularly able.
    This parody offshoot of the SOUL TAKER anime series has its amusing moments. In one episode Komugi dresses up as the whole BATTLE OF THE PLANETS team without even taking off her trademark rabbit ears, and Tokyo's Big Sight convention center turns into giant robot Big Sightron during Comic Market. Most of the Soul Taker cast turns up at some point, and throughout Komugi is tormented by her cosplay rival, Magical Maid Koyori. A half hour "special" NWK Magical Te

(2002) appeared two weeks before the series was released, and just to confuse matters it's set between episodes 2 and 3 of the series. It is included on the English language DVD as episode 2.5, in which tortured hero Kyosuke, object of Komugi's obsessive desire, becomes a rock star. The two-part NWK Magicarte Z followed in 2004.
    Parody can be a rewarding genre, but if the parody is the only thing the show has going for it the jokes need to be plentiful and broad enough for anyone to catch. As anyone who's ever been stuck in the middle of the row at a Worldcon Masquerade watching a group of Danes performing a skit on the complete works of Michael Moorcock can tell you, jokes which go down a storm to an audience of hardcore fans don't always play outside that narrow circle. A handful of nods and winks in the direction of industry giants is small reward for three hours of your life.

NYMPHS OF THE STRATOSPHERE *

2004?. JPN: Stratosphere no Yosei. AKA: Fairies of the Stratosphere. Video. DIR: N/C. SCR: N/C. DES: N/C. ANI: N/C. MUS: N/C. PRD: N/C. 30 mins. x 3 eps.
Five young abuse victims turn out to be imperfect angels sent down to earth in order to bring pleasure to the human race—somehow, this is supposed to save the environment, although we are not sure how. One falls in love with a computer programmer and half-heartedly tries to avoid his advances before giving herself to him, in an anime whose plot only really makes sense when read off the box, since much of the early action comprises disparate sex scenes featuring the five girls before their angelic secret identity is known. Although these creatures have breasts and look feminine, like the original Biblical angels they have no sexual organs. Luckily for the animators, they do have fully operational digestive systems, leading to a predictable concentration on either end of same and a focus on non-consensual sex. Compare to ANGELIUM. **ⒸⓃⓋ**

O

OBARI, MASAMI

1966– . Born in Hiroshima Prefecture, Obari went to Tokyo and joined Ashi Production after leaving high school. His early work included low-level animation on TRANSFORMERS and mechanical designs on DANCOUGAR, before he broke into directing when offered the opening sequence of DRAGONAR. He has subsequently become known for the large-breasted, vulpine look of his female characters, as seen in shows such as VIRUS and TOSHINDEN, as well as such pornographic anime as VIPER GTS and MARINE A GO GO, usually as the head of Studio G-1 Neo.

OCEAN WAVES *

1993. JPN: *Umi ga Kikoeru.* AKA: *I Can Hear the Ocean.* TV special. DIR: Tomomi Mochizuki. SCR: N/C. DES: Yoshifumi Kondo. ANI: Katsuya Kondo. MUS: N/C. PRD: Studio Ghibli, Tokuma, Nippon TV. 72 mins.

En route to a high school reunion, Taku Morisaki reflects on his past. Ten years earlier, transfer student Rikako fell for Taku's friend Matsuno, perhaps to hide the alienation she felt at an unwelcoming school. On a trip to Hawaii, her money was stolen, and she surprisingly turned to Taku for help—a simple and possibly innocent act that changed the trio's relationships forever.

Based on a Saeko Himura novel originally serialized in *Animage* magazine, this is Studio Ghibli's only television drama and was made by the studio's younger members for a themed broadcast during the Golden Week holiday. The stress of making *OW* and HERE IS GREENWOOD simultaneously would leave director Mochizuki briefly hospitalized. The studio also made two animated shorts to celebrate the 40th anniversary of broadcaster Nippon TV.

ODA, KATSUYA

1932– . Born in Fukuoka Prefecture, he graduated in Western-style art from Musashino College of Fine Arts (now Musashino Art University) in 1961, but had already been working as an animator for two years at Toei on such titles as PANDA AND THE MAGIC SERPENT and TALES OF HANS CHRISTIAN ANDERSEN. Although he continued to work as an animator on TV shows such as CALIMERO, he drifted away from anime in the 1970s, organizing film festivals and writing film criticism. He subsequently wrote the book *How to Become an Animator* (*Animator ni Nareru Hon*).

ODIN *

1985. JPN: *Odin—Koshi Hansen Starlight.* AKA: *Odin—Photon Ship Starlight; Odin: Photon Space Sailer Starlight, Odin: Starlight Mutiny.* Movie. DIR: Takeshi Shirato, Toshio Masuda, Eiichi Yamamoto. SCR: Kazuo Kasahara, Toshio Masuda, Eiichi Yamamoto. DES: Geki Katsumata, Shinya Takahashi. ANI: Eiichi Yamamoto, Kazuhito Udagawa. MUS: Hiroshi Miyagawa, Kentaro Haneda, Noboru Takahashi, Masamichi Amano, Fumitaka Anzai, Loudness. PRD: Westcape Corp. 139 mins. (93 mins., English-language version).

The photon ship Starlight sets sail from the orbital space colony City of Einstein, en route for Jupiter. Along the way, crew member Akira picks up Sarah, the last survivor of the spacewreck Alford. Sarah is receiving telepathic messages from what she believes to be an alien spacecraft near one of the moons of Uranus. Disobeying orders, the younger members of the crew change course for the alien craft's distant destination, planet Odin.

A beautifully designed film, its already shaky story line was dealt irreparable damage through the removal of 45 minutes of footage and a dire English-language script and dub. The story of a youthful crew and experienced skipper setting out in a spacegoing sailing ship on a dangerous mission inspired by a mysterious and beautiful girl had already been done with enormous success in STAR BLAZERS, and less so with THUNDERSUB. Either producer Yoshinobu Nishizaki wanted to prove that he could repeat that success without help from his former collaborators Leiji Matsumoto and Noboru Ishiguro, or else he is a one-trick pony when it comes to story-lining SF shows. Yet despite the gorgeous design and a skilled crew including Tezuka veteran Yamamoto and "advice" from NORA-creator Satomi Mikuriya, Nishizaki's new version never takes off.

OFFICE AFFAIRS *

1996. JPN: *Me Chi Ku*. AKA: *Female Animal, Bitch*. Video. DIR: Mitsuhiro Yoneda. SCR: Rokurota Marabe. DES: Mitsuhiro Yoneda. ANI: Toshiyuki Nishida, Mitsuhiro Yoneda. MUS: Yoshi. PRD: FAI International, YOUC. 30 mins.

Ono is a new publishing recruit, assigned to one of the fastest-rising new titles under editor-in-chief Megumi Sugiyama. His girlfriend since college days, Rie works at the same company, though she's "only in the administration department." Still the two have a good relationship until he gets the hots for his boss. As he gradually "learns the ropes" he is admitted to the department's elite corps of workers who put in overtime satisfying their editor-in-chief's need for sex and humiliation in the name of stress relief. Eventually Rie finds out and dumps him, and he leaves the company, rationalizing that his boss's kinky sexual needs are the inevitable result of giving women too much responsibility in the workplace.

The tawdry, predictable story line is the benchmark for the standard of work in every department. The most memorable images from this sad video are shots of the door of Ono's apartment, the rejection box into which his manager tosses most of his writing efforts, and the cigarettes and ashtray by his bed—memorable because these are the frames you see most often, with dialogue, orgasmic moans, or panting heard over them to indicate action that's too expensive to draw. Much of the "animation" consists of intercut stills. The characters appear catatonic because they hardly move, even in the grip of passion. For the English dub, Kitty Video gave this lackluster effort as much attention as it deserves, with an undistinguished cast yawning through the tedious script under a director who can't be bothered. *Office Affairs* was later combined with the unrelated **SLEAZY ANGELS** to make a one-hour video under the title *Co-Ed Affairs*. **Ⓝ**

OFFSIDE

1992. JPN: *Offside*. Video. DIR: Takao Yotsuji, Hisashi Abe. SCR: Takao Yotsuji. DES: Hisashi Abe. ANI: Hisashi Abe. MUS: Saburo Takada. PRD: Holly Production, Leona, Visual House Egg. 50 mins.

The world's worst soccer team has never won a single match despite being made up of eager young boys who desperately crave success. Their prayers are answered in the form of new manager Nagisa, who puts them through a sporting regimen punched out of the standard **AIM FOR THE ACE** template. Based on Natsuko Heiuchi's "original" 1987 manga serialized in *Shonen Magazine*, this anime is from the same artist who created the tennis manga *Fifteen-Love*. Compare to **CAPTAIN TSUBASA** and the actionably similar **KICKERS**. As the 2002 World Cup approached, the series was revived on Japanese satellite TV in an anime series directed by Seiji Okuda.

OFUJI, NOBURO

1900–1961. Pseudonym of Shinshichiro Ofuji. Born in Tokyo's Asakusa district as the seventh of eight children, Ofuji was raised by his eldest sister after their mother died in 1907. At age 18, he became an apprentice at Junichi Kouichi's Sumikazu Eiga. Ofuji's paper-cut fairy tales led to a series of innovative experiments at the periphery of the medium—he pioneered silhouette animation and sound in *Whale* (1927, *Kujira*) and made the brief but ground-breaking *Black Cat* (1929, *Kuroneko Nyago*), in which two cats dance in sync to a jazz tune. He also experimented with color in the unreleased *Golden Flower* (1929, *Ogon no Hana*) and stop-motion techniques in *Pinocchio* (1932). He enjoyed considerable success within the foreign arts community, with a 1952 remake of *Whale* placing second in competition at the Cannes Film Festival and his *Ghost Ship* (1956, *Yureisen*) exhibited in Venice. The Noburo Ofuji Prize, an annual award for achievement in animation, was inaugurated in his memory in 1962.

OGENKI CLINIC *

1991. AKA: *Welcome to the O-Genki Clinic; Come to Ogenki Clinic; Return to Ogenki Clinic*. Video. DIR: Takashi Watanabe. SCR: Haruka Inui. DES: Takashi Watanabe. ANI: N/C. MUS: N/C. PRD: AC Create. 45 mins. x 3 eps. (four stories per ep.).

Dr. Ogeguri and his pretty assistant, Nurse Tatase, run a clinic specializing in sexual problems. Ever ready to apply hands-on therapy, the doctor and his assistants help those who can't help themselves, with problems varying from the sexually dysfunctional to the just plain weird.

Based on Haruka Inui's manga from *Play Comic*, this somewhat dated tale of everyday working life in a sex clinic has one redeeming feature—everybody in it is obviously a consenting adult, even if their adulthood is signified by the disproportional body shapes in keeping with the art-style of the original manga. Humor plays a central part, leavening the sex scenes with moments of "comedy," such as Ogeguri's talking penis, and Nurse Tatase's ongoing attempts to convince her mother that Ogeguri would make a good husband. The stage is set for a series of smutty *Carry On*–style tales where the pair give their all to their professional duties while yearning for each other. Refused a release in the early 1990s by the British Board of Film Classification, it is hence only available in the U.S. The Japanese-language version allegedly features famous voice actors using pseudonyms, but the English dub is poor quality. The live-action porn movie *The Ladies' Phone Sex Club*, also created by Haruka Inui, repeats many of the same jokes. **Ⓝ**

OGRE SLAYER *

1994. JPN: *Onikirimaru*. Video. DIR: Yoshio Kato. SCR: Norifumi Terada. DES: Masayuki Goto. ANI: Masayuki Goto. MUS: Kazuhiko Sotoyama. PRD: KSS, TBS. 30 mins. x 4 eps.

A young man who is really the child of an ogre is destined to wander Earth slaying his own kind. When he has killed every ogre, he believes he will become fully human; until then, he is known only by the name of the sword he bears, Ogre Slayer. In each separate story, all set in modern Japan, he meets humans in trouble and deals death and destruction to ogres, but he isn't in the business of "happy endings." An episodic, melancholy quest with a resemblance to Tezuka's **Dororo** but actually inspired by scenes of sword-swinging schoolboys in Paul Schrader's *Mishima* (1985), *OS* has limited animation but attractive artwork and design. The ogres, superbly gross and amoral, are the best things in this short series based on Kei Kusunoki's 1988 manga in *Shonen Sunday* magazine. The same artist also created **Yagami's Family Troubles** and **Yoma: Curse of the Undead**.

Oh My Goddess!

OH! FAMILY

1986. TV series. DIR: Masamune Ochiai, Takashi Hisaoka, Hideki Tonokatsu. SCR: Shunichi Yukimuro, Yoshiaki Yoshida, Tsunehisa Ito, et al. DES: Fumio Sasaki. ANI: Mikio Tsuchiya, Isao Kaneko, Minoru Kibata. MUS: Tadanori Matsui. PRD: Knack, TV Tokyo. 25 mins. x 26 eps.

A comedy soap based on the everyday lives of the Andersons, a "typical" California household, as seen through the eyes of Taeko Watanabe, on whose 1981 Flower Comic manga *Family* it was based. Mom, Dad, and kids Kay, Tracey, and Fay, along with Fay's boyfriend, Rafe, get on with their lives, though much of the comedy arises from the fact that Kay displays every sign of being gay, and his efforts at concealment cause embarrassment to the family. Meanwhile, Dad starts receiving calls from Jonathan, a stranger who claims to be his long-lost son, much to the consternation of Mrs. Anderson. Shown in Italy, where it was much admired, though one episode was banned. ●

OH! HARIMANADA

1992. JPN: *Aa Harimanada*. TV series. DIR: Yukio Okazaki. SCR: Shizuo Noha, Shunichi Nakamura, Hitoshi Yasuhira.

DES: Yutaka Arai. ANI: Ichiro Fukube, Katsumasa Kanezawa, Yutaka Arai, Shunichi Nakamura. MUS: Masamichi Amano. PRD: Horman Office, EG Film, TV Tokyo. 25 mins. x 23 eps.

The unconventional adventures of Harimanada, a sumo wrestler who attains the top rank of *yokozuna* but fights in a ring that seems to owe a lot more to the masked wrestlers and strange tricks of **Kinnikuman**. As with other sports anime such as **Aim for the Ace** and **Tomorrow's Joe**, the series progresses through hardships (an opponent undefeated through 26 bouts), conflicts outside the ring (the Masked Wrestler's fiancée), forbidden techniques (the Murder Mackerel Snap!), and mysterious challengers (the "Mysterious Wrestler," naturally). Based on the 1988 manga in *Comic Morning* by Kei Sadayasu.

OH MY GODDESS! *

1993. JPN: *Aa Megamisama*. AKA: *Ah! My Goddess*. Video, movie, TV series. DIR: Hiroaki Goda. SCR: Naoko Hasegawa, Kunihiko Kondo. DES: Hidenori Matsubara, Hiroshi Kato, Atsushi Takeuchi, Osamu Tsuruyama. ANI: Hidenori Matsubara, Nobuyuki

Kitajima, Yoshimitsu Ohashi, Masanori Nishii. MUS: Takeshi Yasuda. PRD: AIC, WOWOW. 30 mins. x 40 eps., 40 mins. x 1 ep. (v1), 8 mins. x 48 eps. (TV1), 106 mins. (m), 25 mins. x 24 eps. (TV2), 25 mins. x 2 eps. (v2), 25 mins. x 3+ eps. (TV3; 26 eps. planned).

Hapless student Keiichi phones for takeout and accidentally gets through to the Goddess Helpline. When Belldandy (Verthandi—the Norse embodiment of the concept of Being) turns up in his bedroom and offers to grant him a wish, he wishes for her to be his girlfriend, and they're stuck with each other. In the video series, she's a divine doormat who waits on him hand and foot, exerts her powers very discreetly and then only to make life easier for him, and includes both their siblings in the household without a murmur—a parody of ideal Japanese femininity. The 1988 *Comic Afternoon* manga by Kosuke Fujishima does more justice to all the characters, but the anime compresses the whole tale into a romance between the wettest pair of lovers since Noah, a wimp and a doormat whose excuse is that they were fated to be that way. A soft-soap rendition of alien-spouse drama tradition that traces a line back through URUSEI YATSURA and BELOVED BETTY all the way to the American sitcom *Bewitched*, Kosuke Fujishima's story posits a boy who is pure of heart and gives him the perfect girlfriend, whose role seems to be to look pretty, cook, and clean. The story is sugary enough to rot teeth, but the animation and design are remarkably faithful to Fujishima's stunning original art.

Surprisingly, given the fad for mawkish romance à la TENCHI MUYO!, *OMG* did not graduate to a TV series. While other shows jumped onto its formulaic bandwagon, it was Fujishima's other big manga, YOU'RE UNDER ARREST!, that got a TV broadcast. Instead, fans had to contend with a series of short, squashed-down comedy skits, *The Adventures of Mini-Goddess* (1998, *OMG: Chichaitte Koto wa Benri da ne!*, aka *The Adventures of Mini-Goddesses in the Handy "Petite" Size*), directed by Yasuhiro Matsumura. Running as part of the *Anime Complex* anthology TV show, the series was a predictable rush of sight gags as cartoon versions of Belldandy's sisters Urd and Skuld, accompanied by Gan-chan the rat, rushed through comedy business seemingly inspired by old Warner Bros. cartoons. Belldandy's original voice actress, Kikuko Inoue, is conspicuously absent from the first 14 episodes. There were also, however, brief cameos by *OMG* manga characters not seen in the previous anime version, as well as parodies of contemporary anime, such as BERSERK.

After much hype and delays (reputedly occasioned at one point by a go-slow from animators convinced that the world would end according to the prophecies of Nostradamus, so there was little point in doing overtime!), the feature-length *OMG: The Movie* (2000) was finally released, reuniting director Goda and many of the video staff. Originally planned as an adaptation of the "Welsper" story arc from the manga, the film's plot changed through many rewrites into a simpler setup in which Belldandy is approached by her mentor, Celestin, a one-time member

of the Gods' Council. Discredited and imprisoned on the moon, Celestin seeks Belldandy's help, though Keiichi is initially suspicious of her association with the newcomer.

The show was pastiched on many occasions, particularly in erotic variants such as EVOCATION and CAN CAN BUNNY. The *OMG* story itself did not receive a bona fide TV adaptation until 2005, with Hiroaki Goda's 24-episode TBS series which we have listed here as 26 episodes, on account of the two bonus chapters included on the DVD release. This was followed by another TV series, *OMG: Everyone Has Wings* (*Sorezore no Tsubasa*, 2006). A different "Verdandi" would also appear in MYTHICAL DETECTIVE LOKI RAGNAROK.

OH! MY KONBU
1991. TV series. DIR: Tetsuo Imazawa, Mineo Fuji, Shingo Kaneko, Katsunori Kosuga. SCR: Riko Hinokuma, Tatsuhiko Muraame, Aki Tanioka, Shunsuke Suzuki, Yutaka Hayashi, Megumi Sugiwara. DES: Takahiro Kamiya. ANI: Yukio Otaku. MUS: N/C. PRD: Narumi, TBS. 12 mins. x 44 eps.
Fifth-grader Konbu Nabeyama is the son of a cook in a slice-of-life gourmet comedy that tries to add an element of adventure to slaving in the kitchen. Konbu helps his father solve problems in the world through the judicious use of seasonings, the right choice of menu, and the pleasing of fickle customers.

OI RYOMA!
1992. AKA: *Hey Ryoma!; Rainbow Samurai*. TV series. DIR: Hiroshi Sasakawa, Yutaka Kagawa. SCR: Masao Ito, Michio Yoshida, Makoto Noriza, Nobuaki Kishima. DES: Katsumi Hashimoto. ANI: Katsumi Hashimoto, Hideo Kawauchi, Takeshi Shirato. MUS: N/C. PRD: Animation 21, NHK. 25 mins. x 13 eps.
In the 19th century, Japan is in the grip of the shogunate, with the shogun wielding power in the name of a puppet emperor. Young Ryoma Sakamoto is growing up with dreams of being a samurai and doing heroic deeds for his country. He witnesses the arrival of

Commodore Perry's black ships, and realizes that, although he is a samurai, the time has come to challenge the authority of the shogun, who wishes to keep Japan trapped in a feudal time warp. In this adaptation of a manga by Tetsuya Takeda and GO FOR IT, GENKI–creator Yu Koyama, after successfully completing his training, Ryoma leaves Chiba town for a life of adventure.

A famous figure in Japanese history, Ryoma brokered the fateful alliance between the rebel domains of Satsuma and Choshu, and he wrote an eight-point plan for modernizing Japan. His greatest moment was the bloodless coup of 1867, when he and his companions managed to negotiate the "return" of power to the emperor, which ended centuries of rule by the shogunate. Barely a month later, he was assassinated at age 33 without living to see the Japan he helped create. Three weeks after Ryoma's death, the emperor came to power in the Meiji Restoration, beginning Japan's modern era. Ryoma would appear in many other anime, including DRIFTING CLOUDS and ARMORED CHRONICLE HIO.

OISHINBO
1988. AKA: *Feast; Taste Quest*. TV series. DIR: Toshio Takeuchi, Kunihisa Sugishima, Masayuki Kojima. SCR: Ryuzo Nakanishi, Yasuo Tahada. DES: Masaaki Kawanami. ANI: Masaaki Kawanami, Shigetaka Kiyoyama. MUS: Kazuo Otani. PRD: Shinei, Nippon TV. 25 mins. x 136 eps.
Banzai! Oishinbo started in 1975 and ran for 25 years. A short slot where celebrities sampled various regional delicacies, it started a craze for gourmet food shows and the 1983 *Big Comic Spirits* manga *Oishinbo* by Tetsu Kariya and Akira Hamasaki. The anime version sticks close to the original, in which two young reporters go in search of the ultimate celebration menu for their newspaper's hundredth anniversary. A live-action movie version followed in 1996. After the resolution of the original quest, the anime story focuses on comedy and romance, as

chef Jiro aims for the top in an elegant Tokyo restaurant. Despite Jiro's youth, his boss has put him in sole charge of the menu, and he works hard to ensure that he deserves such trust. As in the manga, as much care is given to the depiction of food as to Jiro, his lovely costar Yuko, and the other characters. Several interrelated episodes were also edited into TV specials *Oishinbo: Jiro vs. Katsuyama* (#2, 10, 12, and 36) and *Oishinbo: The Ultimate Full Course* (#1, 6, 23, and 62). The characters also appeared in spin-offs, including *Oishinbo: Ultimate Shopping* (1992), which was an animated segment of the *Magical Brain Power* TV quiz game, and the topical TV special *Oishinbo: The U.S.-Japan Rice War* (1993). See also MISTER AJIKKO and the live-action series *Iron Chef* (1993). Original creator Kariya would also inadvertently cook up a giant robot show: UFO ROBOT DAI APOLLON. COOK DADDY's unorthodox ingredients put it in a different category despite the similarity of the Japanese title.

OJARUMARU

1999. JPN: *Ojarumaru*. AKA: *Prince Mackaroo*. TV series, movie. DIR: Akitaro Daichi. SCR: Rin Futomaru. DES: Hajime Watanabe. ANI: N/C. MUS: Harukichi Yamamoto. PRD: Adobe Pictures, Nippon Crown, NHK Educational, NHK. 8 mins. x 270 eps. (TV), 30 mins. (m). A short series for young children tells the story of a chirpy nobleman's child from Heian-era Japan who time-slips into the modern world. He has wacky adventures living with an ordinary Japanese family, whose son Kazuma becomes his special friend. References to 11th-century culture and modern aspirations mix with artwork that looks naïve but is calculated for comic effect. Like *Teletubbies*, it's paced slowly and simply for easy assimilation by the young. A short film, *Summer of Promises* (2000), introduces Semira, a strange boy who comes to play with Ojaru and his chums and bears a marked resemblance to a boy of the same name who spent a summer with the village elders when they were boys, long ago. A very

different blast from the past would characterize director Daichi's JUBEI-CHAN THE NINJA GIRL.

OKADA, TOSHIO

1958– . Born in Osaka, Okada opened the General Products sci-fi store in 1982. The store would become a focal point for Gainax, the studio of which Okada would eventually become president. He subsequently became an adjunct professor of fan and audience studies at Tokyo University—his *Introduction to Otakuology* (1996, *Otakugaku Nyumon*) remains one of the best studies of the anime world. He is often self-styled as the "Otaking," the King of Otaku.

OKAMA REPORT

1991. JPN: *Okama Hakusho*. AKA: *Homosexual Report; Homosexual White Paper*. Video. DIR: Teruo Kigure. SCR: Ippei Yamagami, Sheila Shimazaki. DES: Teruo Kigure. ANI: Jiro Sayama. MUS: Jiro Takemura. PRD: Knack. 45 mins. x 3 eps.
Shinya Okama (a surname that's a Japanese pun on "homosexual") is a university student who gets a part-time job in a gay bar. He puts on a dress and calls himself Catherine, then finds himself falling in love with a pretty customer, Miki. Miki is a real girl—and thinks "Catherine" is, too. The first video was followed by *Okama Report: Midsummer Happening* and a year later by *OR: Man's Decision*, in which Shinya's high school pal Dan (who doesn't wear dresses) also falls for Miki, presenting Shinya with the dilemma of whether or not he should risk revealing his true nature and losing Miki altogether. Based on the *Young Sunday* manga by Hideo Yamamoto, another of whose sexually themed manga is available in English as *Voyeur*.

OKAMOTO, TADANARI

1932–1990. Born in Osaka, Okamoto graduated in law from Osaka University in 1955 and in film from Nihon University in 1961. He worked as one of the puppeteers at Tadahito Mochi-

naga's MOM Films until 1963, before founding Echo Productions in 1964 and working as a director on such titles as *The Mysterious Medicine* (*Fushigina Kusuri*) and THE MOCHI MOCHI TREE. He also produced many TV commercials and won the Noburo Ofuji Prize in 1965, 1970, and 1975.

OKAWA, KOGI

1966– . Sketch artist on works including VENUS WARS, GHOST IN THE SHELL, and EVANGELION.

OKAWARA, KUNIO

1947– . Sometimes miscredited as Kunio Daikawara. A designer on parts of the TIME BOKAN SERIES and VOTOMS, but best known as the founding father of "real robot design," which strives to make robots credible as real machines made by humans, instead of the quasi-magical creations of the 1970s. Okawara is hence credited with the trend for more scientifically plausible robots-as-vehicles—beginning with his own work on GUNDAM, and continuing with other "real robot" shows such as DOUGRAM: FANG OF THE SUN, VOTOMS, SPT LAYZNER, VIFAM, and DRAGONAR. Okawara also designed more traditional fantasy super-robots for the BRAVE SAGA.

OKAZAKI, MINORU

1942– . Born in Osaka, Okazaki's first credit was on Mushi Production's ASTRO BOY series in 1964. His subsequent work demonstrates his fame as a chief director on TV productions, including LITTLE WITCH SALLY, STAR OF THE GIANTS, SPOOKY KITARO, and AIM FOR THE ACE. His movie debut came with the theatrical spin-offs of DOCTOR SLUMP (1984), on which he had also worked as a TV director.

OKIURA, HIROYUKI

1966– . After work as a character designer and key animator on both MEMORIES and GHOST IN THE SHELL, Okiura achieved directorial fame with JIN-ROH, based on a script by Mamoru Oshii (q.v.).

OKUDA, SEIJI

1943– . Born in Tokyo, he was one of the animators on the original GIGANTOR series, subsequently finding work at TCJ, Tatsunoko, and Art Fresh, before going freelance. His directorial debut came with PSYCHO ARMOR GOBARIAN.

OLD CURIOSITY SHOP, THE

1979. JPN: *Sasurai no Shojo Nell*. AKA: *Wanderings of the Girl Nell*. TV series. DIR: Hideo Makino, Katsumi Kosuga, Hajime Sawa, Mineo Fuji, Keinosuke Tsuchiya. SCR: Keisuke Fujikawa, Kazumi Asakura. DES: Norio Kashima. ANI: Norio Kashima, Hiroshi Kuzuoka. MUS: Harumi Ibe. PRD: Dax, TV Tokyo. 25 mins. x 26 eps.

Nell is a perky girl in 19th-century London, who lives with her grandfather, Trent, above his antique shop, while her mother and brother live in a place evocatively named Paradise. When Grandfather loses all his money gambling and the principal creditor wants to marry Nell to his slimy nephew, she has to flee and try to reach her family. A less permanent abode than the Paradise of Charles Dickens's original novel, Nell's destination still takes some hardship to reach, pursued all the while by the feckless Quilp, who wants her for himself. Dickens's *A Christmas Carol* was also turned into anime as THE STINGIEST MAN IN TOWN.

OLD MAN'S SURVIVAL GUIDE, THE

1990. JPN: *Ojisan Kaizo Koza*. Movie. DIR: Tsutomu Shibayama. SCR: Chinami Shimizu. DES: Tsutomu Shibayama. ANI: Kuniyuki Ishii. MUS: Kazz Toyama. PRD: TMS. 92 mins.

In this anime adaptation of the popular *Weekly Bunshun* manga by Chinami Shimizu and Yoshi Furuya, an old man confesses his secrets of business success to an attentive Office Lady, imparting such gems of wisdom as How to Say the Right Thing, Better Commuting, and Etiquette for Meetings. Compare to the same idea from another angle—SURVIVAL IN THE OFFICE.

OME-1

1985. JPN: *Ome-1*. Video. DIR: Nobuyoshi Sugita. SCR: N/C. DES: N/C. ANI: Hajime Iwasaki. MUS: N/C. PRD: Towa Creation. 30 mins. x 2 eps.

Two science-fiction adventures attempting (and failing) to cash in on the earlier success of the CREAM LEMON and LOLITA ANIME releases. In the first, *Torture Chamber at Penius Base*, pretty schoolgirl Momoko is found to be an interstellar spy and punished for her deception. In the second part, *The Model Is a Soap-Girl*, Momoko goes to work at a "soapland" bathhouse/brothel in order to track down her missing friend, Yuko. A low-quality entry in an already low-rent genre. ⓝⓥ

ON A PAPER CRANE *

1993. JPN: *Tsuru ni Notte*. AKA: *Riding a Crane*. Movie. DIR: Seiji Arihara. SCR: Seiji Arihara. DES: Yoshio Kabashima. ANI: Takaya Ono. MUS: Reijiro Komutsu. PRD: Mushi Pro. 30 mins.

Modern Japanese schoolgirl Tomoko visits the Hiroshima Peace Memorial Museum, where she has to write a report as part of a school assignment. The twelve-year-old finds the museum's story so shocking that she has to leave, going into the nearby Peace Memorial Park, where children are playing happily. She meets a girl her own age, but when Sadako tells her story, Tomoko realizes she is a ghost. When she was two years old, Sadako Sasaki was exposed to radiation in the bombing of Hiroshima, and she contracted leukemia at the age of six. She folded a paper crane every day in the hope that it would help her recover, but the girl died before reaching her teens. Tomoko comes to understand that the bombings affected far more people than those who were killed and injured at the time, then she wakes up and sees the statue of Sadako. A short film shown on a double bill with KAYOKO'S DIARY and sharing much of its crew along with director Arihara, this Hiroshima anime in the spirit of BAREFOOT GEN dwells on the long-term effects of radiation poisoning in the fashion of BENEATH THE BLACK RAIN. The first part gives what is almost an animated tour of the museum and the last half is devoted to Sadako's flashback autobiography. The animation was inspired by the efforts of Miho Cibot-Shimma, a Japanese woman living in France, who decided to spread the word about the evils of nuclear war after seeing children in her adopted homeland playing "atomic war games." Her Japanese friends started raising funds to make OAPC in 1989. Given very limited exposure in the U.S. through subtitled screenings at film festivals.

ON A STORMY NIGHT

2005. JPN: *Arashi no Yoru ni*. AKA: *Stormy Night*. Movie. DIR: Gisaburo Sugii. SCR: Yuichi Kimura, Gisaburo Sugii. DES: Marisuke Eguchi. ANI: Yasuo Maeda. MUS: Keisuke Shinohara. PRD: Arayoru Committee, TBS. ca. 90 mins.

May the goat takes shelter in a mountain hut during a fierce storm, only to find himself sharing it with Gub, a wolf. Despite their differences, the two animals become friends and promise to meet again, using the phrase "on a stormy night" as a password. Gub wrestles with his in-built desires to eat May, but restrains himself at their successive meetings. However, both animals must deal with others of their kind; both wolves and goats are initially disapproving, and then slyly suggest that each spy on the other on future occasions. Realizing that their friendship is no longer a secret and that they risk ostracism by both species, the pair jump into a fast-moving river, hoping that they can meet each other safely "on the other side." A tale of a love that dare not speak its name in the style of the earlier RINGING BELL, based on the best-selling 1994 children's book by Yuichi Kimura.

ON YOUR MARK

1995. Video. DIR: Hayao Miyazaki. SCR: Hayao Miyazaki. DES: Hayao Miyazaki, Masashi Ando. ANI: Masashi Ando. MUS: Chage and Asuka. PRD: Ghibli. 7 mins.

In a futuristic supercity, armed police

raid the headquarters of a religious cult. One of them finds an angel chained in a corner, and the winged girl is rushed into quarantine. The officer who found her and his partner break into the science facility to rescue her, but the story then divides into one of two endings. In the first, the officers fall to their deaths as their stolen truck spins off a collapsing bridge. In the second version, the truck develops wings of its own and flies away from the city, revealed to be an oasis amid a desolate, postindustrial polluted landscape. The angel flies free, and the cops return to face the music.

A short promo-video made by Miyazaki for the pop duo Chage and Asuka (whose likenesses can be discerned in the police characters), it was eventually shown in theaters alongside **Whisper of the Heart** and reputedly tested some of the digital techniques he would reuse in **Princess Mononoke**. It's prettily made, but the reduction of Miyazaki's standard ecological concerns to the time limit and formulae of a pop video makes the story line seem a trifle pretentious. The Japanese video release bulked out the running time with the storyboards and animatics used in production and the live-action video version of the same song.

ONCE UPON A TIME: SPACE *

1981. JPN: *Ginga Patrol PJ*. AKA: *Galactic Patrol PJ*. TV series. DIR: Eiken Murata. SCR: Hideo Takayashiki, Masamichi Nomura. DES: Lune Valgue, Manchu. ANI: Tetsuo Shibuya, Jiro Tsuno. MUS: Koji Makaino, Michel Legrand. PRD: Eiken, Fuji TV. 27 mins. x 26 eps.
A Franco-Japanese coproduction that, like **Ulysses 31**, was not shown in Japan until several years after it was made, *GPPJ* is virtually unknown in Japan, where it was buried in an early-morning TV slot. The story supplied by the French for the Japanese to animate involves Captain Jumbo and his loyal servants Jim, Putty, and Metro the robot, who work to keep law and order in the Omega Alliance of Peaceful Planets. Sworn to abstain from using

deadly weapons, as befits the representatives of a multiracial coalition of spacefaring life-forms, they must solve every hazard they meet by negotiation and quick thinking. Perhaps the absence of much fighting might have also contributed to the series' swift disappearance.

Better known throughout Europe under local language translations of its French title, *Il Était Une Fois: Éspace*, the show was broadcast in English on *Irish* television, and we have unconfirmed reports that it was also shown on Nickelodeon in the U.S. Taking a leaf from Osamu Tezuka, the leads in the show were stock characters (or reincarnations) recycled from French director Albert Barille's first work for the French Studio Procidis, *Il Était Une Fois l'Homme* (*Once Upon a Time: Man*), an explicitly educational series.

ONE HIT KANTA

1977. JPN: *Ippatsu Kanta-kun*. AKA: *One Hit Kanta; Kanta the Batsman*. TV series. DIR: Hiroshi Sasagawa. SCR: Jinzo Toriumi. DES: Akiko Shimomoto. ANI: Mamoru Oshii. MUS: Akisuke Ichikawa, Koba Hayashi. PRD: Akira Inoue, Tatsunoko. 25 mins. x 53 eps.
Based on a manga by Tatsuo Yoshida, this is the story of how little monkey Kanta honors his dead father's memory. Because father was a baseball champion, Kanta forms a baseball squad in his memory with his numerous siblings. With his mother's help, he sets up games with other animal teams and eventually wins the interschool championship in his father's name. This series featured debut work from Mamoru Oshii, who went on to become one of the most famous directors in anime, most notably for **Ghost in the Shell**.

ONE HUNDRED PER CENT

1990. JPN: *Hyakku Per Cent*. Video. DIR: Yoshihisa Matsumoto. SCR: Oki Ike. DES: Kazuo Iimura. ANI: Akio Takami. MUS: Yuki Nagasaka. PRD: JC Staff. 50 mins.
A pretty 22-year-old girl leaves university and gets her dream job as a TV news-

caster, only to discover that life is tough at the top. In this adaptation of the *Young Action* manga by Michio Yanagisawa, she must juggle the demands of her career with her troubled love life. Compare with **Weather Report Girl**, which approaches the same idea, but for laughs.

100% STRAWBERRIES

2005. JPN: *Ichigo 100%*. TV series. DIR: Osamu Sekita. SCR: Tatsuhiko Urahata. DES: Kiyotaka Nakahara. ANI: N/C. MUS: Takayuki Negishi. PRD: Madhouse. 25 mins. x 4 eps. (v), 25 mins. x 24 eps. (TV).
Junpei Manaka heads up to the school roof for a view of his hometown, but instead gets a view of the distinctive strawberry pattern panties being worn by a girl who falls on him. Deciding that the scene would be interesting if recreated for an amateur film (it certainly wasn't in this supposedly professional one!), he seeks out the owner of the panties, only to discover that many of the girls in his school have similar underwear. *100%S* is based on the 2002–2005 *Shonen Jump* manga by Mizuki Kawashita and manages the remarkable feat of recreating the sensation of watching a dull dating sim, despite no relation to any actual game. In an equally impressive anti-achievement, the manga's three-year run in *Shonen Jump* actually ended shortly after the broadcast of the show; one would expect TV to create renewed interest in a franchise, but apparently not in this case.

The TV version was preceded by the video "special" with the self-explanatory title *100% Strawberries: Love Begins!? Photography Training Camp, Indecisive Heart Going East to West* (2004), in which Junpei manages to get a girl alone in a deserted mountain hut during a storm.

ONE PIECE

1998. TV series, movie. DIR: Goro Taniguchi, Kannosuke Uta. SCR: Michiru Shimada, Atsushi Takegami. DES: Noboru Koizumi. ANI: Hisashi Kagawa.

MUS: Kohei Tanaka. PRD: Toei, Fuji TV. ? mins. x ? eps. (v), 25 mins. x 263+ eps. (TV), 50 mins. (m1), 55 mins. (m2/*Clockwork*), 6 mins. (*Django's*), 56 mins. (m3/*Chopper's*), 6 mins. (*Dream*), 95 mins. (m4/*Dead End*), ca.45 mins. (sp3/*Open Upon*), ca.45 mins. (sp4/*Protect!*), 90 mins. (m5/ *Curse*), 5 mins. (*Take Aim*), 90 mins. (m6/*Baron Omatsuri*), 95 mins. (m7/ *Soldier*).

Impetuous, headstrong 16-year-old Monkey D. Luffy eats a piece of magic fruit that renders his whole body elastic and almost invulnerable. Now he wants to be a pirate and find the fabled "One Piece" treasure of Gold Rogers. He saves the life of the red-haired Junx, who gives him his trademark lucky hat. He meets a motley crew of fortune hunters and misfits, and wacky adventures ensue as they hunt the treasure. A movie, also entitled *One Piece*, appeared in summer 2000, in which Luffy and Zorro are captured by the pirate El Dragon and have to escape. Based on Eiichiro Oda's *Shonen Jump* manga, with some debt to **JOURNEY TO THE WEST** in the lead character. Subsequent *One Piece* movies have included *OP: Clockwork Island Adventure* (*Nejima-ki-shima no Boken*, 2001), which played in cinemas with a featurette, *OP: Django's Dance Carnival*; *OP: Chopper's Kingdom of Strange Animals* (*Chinju-jima no Chopper Okoku*, 2002), which ran along with the featurette *Dream Soccer King*; *OP: Dead End Adventure* (*Dead End no Boken*, 2003); *OP: Curse of the Sacred Sword* (*Norawareta Seiken*, 2004) which ran with the featurette *Take Aim! The Pirate Baseball King*; *OP: Baron Omatsuri and the Sacred Island* (*Omatsuri Danshaku to Himitsu no Shima*, 2005), and *OP: The Giant Mechanical Soldier of Karakuri Castle* (*Karakuri-jo no Mecha Kyohei*, 2006). There is also a relatively rare video series of *OP*, which preceded the original TV series as part of the *Super Jump* road show, and which was available to readers who sent in a number of redeemable coupons to the magazine.

One Piece, along with **NARUTO**, is one of the defining children's anime of the early 21st century, with a remarkable following in Japan and abroad—it's difficult to go too wrong with pirates, particularly when Hollywood rediscovered this with the initiation of a movie franchise for *Pirates of the Caribbean* (2003). *One Piece* has been subject to the usual issues in **CENSORSHIP AND LOCALIZATION** in the U.S. market, including some scenes trimmed for length; the replacement of its original score with a synthesizer soundtrack; the removal of alcohol references, tobacco paraphernalia, blood, and many weapons; and the digital alteration of characters deemed to be unwelcome racial stereotypes. There is also an alternate English dub recorded and broadcast in Singapore, which is far more faithful to the intent of the Japanese original, although it lacks much of the American version's finesse and budget. See also **RAVE MASTER**, a pale imitation.

1+2 = PARADISE

1989. Video. DIR: Junichi Watanabe. SCR: Nobuaki Kishima. DES: Akiyuki Serizawa. ANI: Keiichi Sato. MUS: Jun Watanabe. PRD: Uemura/Toei. 30 mins. x 2 eps.

A strange relationship develops between college-boy Yusuke and the beautiful twins, Yuika and Rika, he saves from a wild dog. The girls fall for their dauntless hero, but Yusuke is pathologically scared of women. The girls eventually help him overcome his fear, only to find that he's stopped fantasizing about them and has fallen for the new girl in the school—rich corporate heiress Barako.

A two-part erotic adaptation of Junko Uemura's *Shonen Magazine* series and an early directorial job for **SUPER ATRAGON**'s Watanabe. **N**

ONE POUND GOSPEL *

1988. JPN: *Ichi Pondo no Fukuin*. Video. DIR: Makura Saki (Osamu Dezaki), Masaya Mizutani. SCR: Hideo Takayashiki, Tomoko Konparu. DES: Katsumi Aoshima. ANI: Shojuro Yamauchi. MUS: N/C. PRD: Studio Gallop. 55 mins.

Sister Angela is a novice nun. Kosuke Hatakana is a young boxer who has a problem keeping to his fighting weight, which means that he has never fulfilled his real potential. Angela's concern for Kosuke and his future goes beyond the detached compassion expected of a nun, and his determination to justify her faith in his ability makes him try to prove himself one more time. His despairing trainer can't believe he really means it this time, but Kosuke has another chance at success and seems ready to take it.

Manga creator Rumiko Takahashi is better known to American fans for her lighthearted romantic fantasies **URUSEI YATSURA** and **RANMA ½**, but her heart lies in exploring offbeat events and relationships in the real world, and this is a good example. The director of **GOLGO 13** turns in a crisp, professional job on this very different story.

1001 NIGHTS *

1999. Video. DIR: Mike Smith. SCR: Yoshitaka Amano. DES: Yoshitaka Amano. ANI: N/C. MUS: David Newman. PRD: 1001 Nights Prd Cttee, Bell System 24, Hyperion. 25 mins.

The Demon King Darnish plots to ruin the lives of mortals, engineering a meeting between Princess Budhu and Prince Kamahl solely to make the pair fall in love and to heighten the suffering when they are inevitably parted. The princess cannot bear the separation and throws herself from a tower, but is saved by the fairy Mamune. The angry Darnish chases the lovers, who escape forever when they are transformed into a shining star.

A film commissioned by the Los Angeles Philharmonic Orchestra, featuring music by *The Brave Little Toaster*–composer Newman and showcasing **ANGEL'S EGG**–creator Amano's artistic talents in the U.S.

ONE: TRUE STORIES *

2001. JPN: *One: Kagayaku Kisetsu e*. AKA: *One: To the Glorious Season*. Video. DIR: Yosei Morino (v1), Kan Fukumoto (v2). SCR: Tetsuro Oishi. DES:

Jun Sato. ANI: N/C. MUS: Yoshiro Hara, Tomomi Nakamura. PRD: KSS, ARMS, Nexton, Cherry Lips. 27 mins. x 4 eps. (v1), 30 mins. x 3 eps. (v2).

Orphan Kohei Orihara lives with his aunt and suffers from memory loss, in particular with regard to a childhood friend who was a great help to him in a time of crisis (the death of his sister). Now, in the style of LOVE HINA, he is trying to work out which of several neighborhood girls is The One, although the prime candidate actually turns out to be Mizuka, the surrogate sister who has known him for so long that he has not realized she has become a beautiful teenager. So, that would make her a "childhood friend," then? Based on a 1998 game from Tactics, the anime version constantly returns to Kohei's childhood—an interesting way of approaching the multiple routes of computer games, but also of recycling footage.

The action, such as it is, spreads out across the four seasons of a Japanese school year in the style of SLOW STEP, beginning with the rains that herald the end of summer vacation, and taking us through fall winds, winter snow, and the inevitable cherry blossoms that signify spring and GRADUATION. This sounds like a rerun of a number of other anime because it is. Director Morino has handled the premise of childhood friends separated for years in Masakazu Katsura's I"s. Note that there are two versions of this series—a mainstream one released by KSS in 2001 and the later Cherry Lips erotic variant released in 2003. Technically, the subtitle "True Stories" only applies to the second series, which is the one released in America. **Ⓝ**

ONE-CHOP MANTARO

1990. JPN: Ippon Hocho Mantaro. AKA: One Knife-slice Mantaro. Video. DIR: Toshio Takeuchi. SCR: Megumi Hikichi. DES: Hidetoshi Omori. ANI: Keiichi Sato. MUS: Kosuke Kanadome. PRD: JC Staff, Animate Film. 45 mins. x 2 eps.

Downtown cook Ginpei's prodigal son Mantaro returns after several years

traveling. When he offers to help out in the restaurant, Ginpei notices that the guests eagerly consume Mantaro's pork cutlets but leave his untouched. Mantaro teaches his old-town friends and family the many tricks he has learned on his travels, before setting off to Osaka for a repeat performance. An anime spin-off of the 1973 Business Jump manga One-Chop Ajimei, by an artist known as "Big Jo," this kitchen tale was based on an original book by MISTER HAPPY–creator "Gyujiro." The original manga was way ahead of OISHINBO but only made it to anime in the wake of its successor—perhaps this subtle irony is what led the production staff to concentrate on a "new generation."

ONI

1995. JPN: Toma Kishin Oni. AKA: Fighting Devil Divinity Oni. TV series. DIR: Akira Suzuki. SCR: Natsuko Hayakawa. DES: Masayuki Goto. ANI: N/C. MUS: N/C. PRD: JC Staff, TV Tokyo. 8 mins. x 25 eps.

Human beings can transform into powerful creatures, at which point they fight each other. A series designed to cash in on the Gameboy game of the same name, it was broadcast during the early morning Anime Asaichi children's program. No relation to the more recent Oni PC game from Bungie, which featured anime-style cut-scenes outsourced to real-life anime studio AIC.

ONI TENSEI *

2001. Video. DIR: Nobuhiro Kondo. SCR: Ryota Yamaguchi. DES: Jingi Miyafuji. ANI: Yuji Mukoyama. MUS: N/C. PRD: AIC, Studio Gazelle, Green Bunny. 30 mins. x 4 eps.

Sexy lady investigator Reiko is looking for the murderer responsible for the gruesome deaths of 13 gangsters—her only clue, the timid girl Ema Nozomi, who always seems to be somewhere near the scene of a crime. That would be suspicious even for people who had not seen KEKKAI, and Ema, whose name is shared with that of a king of hell, is soon revealed to have a demonic tattoo on her back that can come to

life to wreak havoc on our world. The result is an intriguing horror anime in which the story takes second place to the obligatory sex, exploring the urban myth that a perfect tattoo will come to life, and placing Reiko in the midst of a crime conspiracy that mixes elements of CRYING FREEMAN and JOJO'S BIZARRE ADVENTURES. **ⒸⓃⓋ**

ONIMARU

1990. Video. DIR: Osamu Dezaki. SCR: Osamu Dezaki. DES: Setsuko Shibunnoichi. ANI: Yukari Kobayashi. MUS: Eimi Sakamoto. PRD: Magic Bus. 45 mins.

During the Onin wars in Japan's medieval Muromachi era, five superpowered warriors hire out their services to the highest bidder. Leader Onimaru can beat two hundred mercenaries singlehandedly, Bo handles demolitions, Saru is as agile as a monkey, Osamu is a cool tactician, and Kiri is the obligatory token swordswoman. This prefabricated group (who might as well be a group of superheroes like those in BATTLE OF THE PLANETS for all the difference the period setting makes) gain an extra unwelcome member when Onimaru rescues Princess Aya, who naturally falls in love with him and refuses to go away. Not to be confused with Onikirimaru, which was released in English as OGRE SLAYER.

ONLY YESTERDAY *

1991. JPN: Omohide Poroporo. AKA: Tearful Thoughts. Movie. DIR: Isao Takahata. SCR: Isao Takahata. DES: Yoshifumi Kondo, Yoshiharu Sato. ANI: Yoshifumi Kondo. MUS: Joe Hisaishi. PRD: Hayao Miyazaki, Studio Ghibli. 119 mins.

The action skips back and forth between 1966 and 1982 as Office Lady Taeko Okajima, visiting the country for a working sabbatical on a farm, recalls events from her childhood—achievements, embarrassments, hopes, dreams, and people. She's trying to decide whether to return to the city and go on with her career or to marry and settle in the countryside, and her reminiscences, at first seemingly aim-

Orguss 02

© 1993/1995 BIGWEST/ORGUSS 02 PROJECT

less, help to shape her decision just as those events and people helped to shape the person she has become.

Hotaru Okamoto's and Yuko Tone's original 1987 story, serialized in *Myojo* weekly, concentrated on the misadventures of the 10-year-old Taeko—the 1982 framing device was conceived by Takahata solely for the film. Beautiful animation and design are almost taken for granted in a Studio Ghibli production, and the script is excellent. The overall emphasis on the importance of marriage, and the assumption (still widespread in Japan at the time) that a real career and family life are mutually exclusive for women, may offend some viewers. Sexual politics aside, Takahata's tale of one woman's choice recreates everyday life in town and the Yamagata countryside with loving care and a marvelous eye for detail, imparting the weight of a historical document without overwhelming the delicate human story.

ORCHID EMBLEM *

1996. JPN: *Rei-Lan Orchid Emblem*. Video. DIR: Hideaki Kushi. SCR: Toshihiko Kudo, Jutaro Nanase. DES: Taro Taki, Shoichiro Sugiura. ANI: Makoto Fuji-

sake. MUS: Hajime Takakuwa. PRD: Dandelion, Beam Entertainment. 40 mins. Rei-Lan is a virginal cop on a stakeout of a drug baron when her team is captured and her boyfriend, Doug, is forced to watch while she has wildly enthusiastic sex with crime lord Tojo. Then she stays on Tojo's ship and has more sex with him, naively accepting his word that Doug has "gone ashore." The pair get matching tattoos of great mystical force that make it impossible for either of them to attain ecstasy without the other. Then Rei-Lan finds Doug's body in a barrel on the ship, escapes, goes to live with a cute little lesbian, becomes a top martial artist, and plots revenge on Tojo. But the dragon tattoo is too powerful, and she ends up back with him, carrying on her martial arts career as a sideline.

Based on an erotic novel from the same Napoleon imprint that gave us EROTIC TORTURE CHAMBER, you could drive a fleet of very large trucks through the holes in the plot, and the defects are in no way concealed by the average animation. As for the English dub, the pseudonymous actors turn in shamefully wooden work, though Rei-Lan's impressions of a Dalek having

an orgasm have some comic value. In their defense, however, given the awful script, any cast picked at random from the greatest classical actors would have struggled to do better.

ORDIAN

2000. JPN: *Ginso Kido Ordian*. AKA: *Attack Armor Ordian; Silver Knight Ordian*. TV series. DIR: Masami Obari. SCR: Kengo Asai, Hiroyuki Kawasaki. DES: Fumihide Sai, Masami Obari, Tsukasa Kotobuki. ANI: Fumihide Sai. MUS: N/C. PRD: Prime, WOWOW. 25 mins. x 24 eps. High school student Yu Kananase is crazy about combat, and even though he's never actually fought anything, he's recruited by the International Military Organization as a potential test pilot for new mobile armor. There are other young recruits in the running, and he has to prove he's the best to achieve his dream. Realizing that game-based anime such as his FATAL FURY and TOSHINDEN were hardly rocket science, director Obari decided to create his own world, inspired by the mismatched design follies and action-heavy plotting of the genre. Sadly the story isn't hugely original; the low quality of Obari's inspiration causes him to throw his creative efforts behind a show that looks like a hundred other robot serials (see BRAVE SAGA), whether inspired by computer games or not. However, the character designs have the pointy-nosed charm of VIRUS, albeit without sulky homoerotic pouts.

ORGUSS *

1983. JPN: *Chojiku Seiki Orguss*. AKA: *Superdimensional Century Orguss*. TV series. DIR: Noboru Ishiguro, Yasuyoshi Mikamoto, Kazuhito Akiyama, Osamu Nabeshima, Hiroshi Yoshida, Masakazu Iijima. SCR: Kenichi Matsuzaki, Sukehiro Tomita, Hiroshi Nishimura. DES: Haruhiko Mikimoto, Yoshiyuki Yamamoto. ANI: Haruhiko Mikimoto, Akiyoshi Nishimori. MUS: Kentaro Haneda. PRD: Magic Bus, Big West, TBS. 25 mins. x 35 eps. (TV), 30 mins. x 6 eps. (v). In 2062, Kei is an officer in one of the two forces fighting over the latest scientific-military advance, the Orbital Elevator, and he is sent to blow it up to avoid its capture by the enemy. Caught in the blast of his own time-oscillation bomb, he is flung into an alternate world, one of many created by the explosion. There he meets his daughter, conceived on a one-night stand just before his mission. She's now 18, fighting on the other side in a terrible war, and in love with his best friend. He also has problems with cute but not-at-all-disposable alien girlfriend Mimsy. Her species has to mate before they're 17 or not at all, and her ex-boyfriend is still very much on the scene. The fate of the patchwork of worlds fragmented by the bomb, with all their diverse citizens and cultures, and the future of all his relationships hangs in the balance. By now Kei must have realized that casual sex brings its own complications.

One of the big SF series of its day, *Orguss* wasn't cut into **ROBOTECH** (with **MACROSS**, **MOSPEADA**, and **SOUTHERN CROSS**) because, coming from a different studio, it couldn't be bought in the same package. Its Mikimoto-designed characters would have fitted perfectly, and its ethos, a giant-robot show in which robots weren't the only item on the agenda, looks forward to **PATLABOR**, as well as fitting the prevailing fashion for heavy mecha and heavy emotion.

The series returned straight to video as *Orguss 02* (1993), directed by Fumihiko Takayama, featuring character designs "inspired" by Mikimoto's originals from Toshihiro Kawamoto and an industrial rock soundtrack from Torsten Rasch. Set 200 years after the close of the original series, in a steampunk world not dissimilar to that of **WINGS OF HONNEAMISE**, the opposing nations of Zafrin and Revillia send archaeologists to find "Decimators" (giant robots left over from the original series). Though the technology is half-forgotten, the reconditioned robots are important weapons in a fast-approaching war. Lean, a young officer on the Revillan side, is excavating a Decimator from the seabed when an

Orphen: Scion of Sorcery

ambush forces him into the machine to survive the attack and discover piloting skills he never suspected. He is sent behind enemy lines to destroy their Decimators, and he meets a girl (a distant descendant of Mimsy) who holds the key to a secret and is a target for all sides. As the conflict escalates, he learns that his own prince plans to use the most powerful Decimator ever discovered to subjugate the world, while an ancient stranger (the "General," the only surviving character from the original series) seeks to bring peace once more. There are byzantine court machinations—the queen poisons the ruler to allow her general to rule in the name of a retarded prince. There are even echoes of more recent Japanese history, as soldiers are forced to choose between their allegiance to the throne itself and the throne's current occupant. The script, from **SOL BIANCA**'s Mayori Sekijima and **BLUE SIX**'s Hiroshi Yamaguchi, manages to pull strong political overtones out of a story that would have been good enough if it were just a straightforward actioner. A superior giant-robot series.

ORPHEN: SCION OF SORCERY *
1998. JPN: *Majutsushi Orphen*. AKA: *Orphen the Magician; Sorcerous Stabber Orphen*. TV series. DIR: Hiroshi Watanabe, Akira Suzuki. SCR: Mayori Sekijima, Masashi Kubota, Yasushi Yamada, Kenichi Araki, Kenichi Kanemaki. DES: Masahiro Aizawa. ANI: Masahiro Aizawa. MUS: Hatake, Sharan Q. PRD: JC Staff, TBS. 25 mins. x 47 eps. Growing up in an orphanage after losing his parents at a very young age, "Orphen" and his two adopted elder sisters, Azalea and Letitia, are selected to study sorcery under the famous Childman at the Tower of Fang. At age 15, Orphen becomes a sorcerer to the Royal Family, but his life is plunged into new difficulties when one of Azalea's spells backfires, transforming her into a monster. Even though he has fallen in love with Azalea, Childman is honor-bound to hunt down the beast that she has become, and Orphen decides to stop him.

Based on a series of over a dozen fantasy novels by Yoshinobu Akita, the *Orphen* TV series begins *in media res* with our hero already a powerful wizard, training a young boy called Majiku. As with **BERSERK**, the majority of the story is told in flashback, as Orphen is threatened by the return of the demon-dragon "Bloody August" only to reveal that it was once the girl he called his sister. Sharing much of the crew of the earlier **SLAYERS**, *Orphen* fortunately lacks much of its predecessor's comedy, opting instead for hard-core fantasy adventure. However, despite a rocking opening theme from pop group Sharan Q, much of the background music sounds like computer-game filler muzak. *Orphen: The Revenge* (1999) is simply the umbrella title for the "second season" of the last 23 episodes. A game based on the series was the first incarnation to reach the U.S., preceding the anime version by several months.

ORUORANE THE CAT PLAYER

1992. JPN: *Nekohiki no Oruorane*. Video. DIR: Mizuho Nishikubo. SCR: Mayori Sekijima. DES: Shunji Murata. ANI: Shunji Murata. MUS: Moto Shiraishi, Kawaji Ishikawa. PRD: JC Staff. 30 mins.
An out-of-work musician mooching round the streets just before Christmas befriends a cat who is fond of good wine. The cat, Iruneido, is one of a feline trio owned by Oruorane, a mysterious old man who can "play" cats as if they were musical instruments. Our hero, always on the lookout for another string to his bow, decides he wants to learn cat-playing for himself. This surreal curio was based on the first novel written by successful writer Baku Yumemakura, who also created **AMON SAGA** and **BATTLE ROYALE HIGH SCHOOL**.

OSHII, MAMORU

1951– . Born in Tokyo's Ota district, Oshii graduated from the education department of Tokyo Gakugei University, where he experimented with his own moviemaking while still a student. With a passionate interest in film (he once claimed to have watched a thousand movies in one year), he joined the Tatsunoko studio and

debuted as an animator on **ONE-HIT KANTA**. Moving to Studio Pierrot (later just Pierrot) in 1980, he met Yoshitaka Amano and Kazunori Ito, who would become frequent collaborators with him on his landmark works of the 1980s and 1990s. Work as a storyboarder and episode director on **URUSEI YATSURA** secured him the chance to direct the *UY* movie *Only You* (1983). His next *UY* movie, *Beautiful Dreamer* (1984), was the first of many Oshii projects to divide critics with surreal imagery and unfocused plotting. He directed **DALLOS** (1983), the first anime made for home video, before going freelance. After **ANGEL'S EGG** (1985) and an abortive association with Hayao Miyazaki and Isao Takahata (whose views on plot and filmmaking seem ever to clash with Oshii's), he began his association with the Headgear collective, which would eventually collaborate on **PATLABOR** (1988). Oshii also began a series of live-action experiments, including *The Red Spectacles* (1987) and *Stray Dog* (1991), which would form the background to **JIN-ROH** (1991), for which he wrote the script. He achieved wider recognition with the superb *Patlabor* movies in the early 1990s, leading directly to his commission to direct **GHOST IN THE SHELL** (1995), for which he pioneered techniques in integrating cel and digital animation.

Oshii's work is characterized by more realistic characters, an aversion to the bright, flat colors of most anime, and an obsession with recreating reality, even down to its mistakes and imperfections, through lens flares, focus-pulls, and other trickery. Owing to the number of his theatrical features released during anime's diaspora abroad, Oshii has become one of the most recognizable directors in the medium, despite a relatively low output in recent years comparable to that of Katsuhiro Otomo. His recent work has included the Polish-language live-action *Avalon* (2001) and the *Ghost in the Shell* sequel, *Innocence* (2004). His basset hound, Gabriel, appears in cameo roles in many of his films.

OSHIN

1984. JPN: *Oshin*. Movie. DIR: Eiichi Yamamoto. SCR: Sugako Hashida. DES: Akio Sugino. ANI: Nobuko Yuasa, Keizo Shimizu. MUS: Koichi Sakata. PRD: Sanrio. 122 mins.
Oshin is a young girl who lives in Japan's northern Yamagata Prefecture at the turn of the 20th century. She endures terrible hardships and poverty, eventually being sold into domestic service at the age of eight. Separated from her mother, she escapes from the timber merchant who treats her like a slave and briefly finds happiness working at a rice shop.

An anime spin-off from one of the landmark Japanese live-action melodramas, *Oshin* focuses on the early episodes of the 300-part 1983 TV drama, reusing both Sugako Hashida's scripts and the voice of child-star Ayako Kobayashi, who played the young Oshin in the TV version. Supposedly based on true stories, cut-and-pasted from hundreds of letters sent to a women's magazine, the live-action *Oshin* was an immense hit all around the world, screened in over 40 countries. After the events of the anime version, the character would continue to struggle for many more onscreen decades, through two changes of actress. Accused of stealing from the rice shop, she would be cast out, rescued by a deserting soldier, married to a southern weakling, left penniless by the 1923 Tokyo earthquake, abused by her mother-in-law, and widowed by her husband's suicide caused by his shame at supplying Japan's military machine during the Pacific War. Eventually, she would become the rich boss of a grocery business, but that would not be until her 83rd year—the year in which the original series was screened. A different female experience of Yamagata can be seen in **ONLY YESTERDAY**, while a very different dramatization of the years around the 1923 earthquake can be found in **DOOMED MEGALOPOLIS**.

OSOMATSU-KUN

1966. AKA: *Young Sextuplets*. TV

series. DIR: Makoto Nagasawa, Hiroe Mitsunobu. SCR: Fujio Akatsuka, Kon Kitagawa. DES: Makoto Nagasawa. ANI: Jiro Murata, Kazuo Komatsubara. MUS: Urahito Watanabe. PRD: Fujio Pro, Studio Zero, Children's Corner, NET. 25 mins. x 57 eps. (1966), 25 mins. x 86 eps. (1988).

Osomatsu, Kazumatsu, Karamatsu, Choromatsu, Todomatsu, and Jushimatsu are six identical brothers who are continually making trouble in their town, chasing after the fishmonger's daughter Totoko, and harassing the local snob, Francophile Iyami. Based on a manga in *Shonen Sunday* by Fujio Akatsuka, who also created GENIUS IDIOT, *Osomatsu-kun* was derided by the PTA as "one of the worst programs ever made," and was consequently very popular with children; compare to the modern-day excesses of the similarly criticized CRAYON SHIN-CHAN. It was remade in 1988 by Studio Pierrot into 86 episodes, which retained its former popularity, soon gaining a 20% audience rating.

OTAKU NO VIDEO *

1991. JPN: *1982 Otaku no Video; 1985 Zoku Otaku no Video*. AKA: *Fan's Video; Thy Video*. Video. DIR: Takeshi Mori. SCR: Toshio Okada. DES: Kenichi Sonoda. ANI: Hidenori Matsubara. MUS: Kohei Tanaka. PRD: Studio Fantasia, Gainax. 50 and 45 mins.

This fan-favorite fantasy by the Gainax studio, which would also produce WINGS OF HONNEAMISE and EVANGELION, is wry and affectionate, self-parody and wish-fulfillment. Inspired by events from the team's own real-life history, it recounts the story of one ordinary young man's efforts to follow the way of the true fan, or "otaku." He loses his girl, his social standing, and his business. His story is counterpointed by a series of spoof live-action "interviews" with fandom personalities such as a cel thief, a costume freak, and a pornography junky. In the second video, merged with the first for Western release, our hero, his devotion undimmed by age, indignity, and failure, triumphs

over the sordid cynicism of the world through the purity of the fanboy spirit, aspiring to become the Ota-King. An English translation by Shin Kurokawa and the Ledoux/Yoshida team plus AnimEigo's excellent liner notes provide a wonderful snapshot of an era of fandom and allow us to laugh with and cry for the true otaku.

OTOGI ZOSHI

2004. AKA: *Story Scroll; Otogi Zoshi—Legend of Magatama*. TV series. DIR: Mizuho Nishikubo, Toshiyasu Kogawa, Hideyo Yamamoto, Jun Takahashi, Junichi Sakata, Yu Ko, Yumi Kamakura, Hisashi Ezura. SCR: Yoshiki Sakurai, Yutaka Omatsu, Junichi Fujisaku, Midori Goto, Hidetoshi Kezuka. DES: Sho-u Tajima, Kazuchika Kise. ANI: Kazuchika Kise. MUS: Hideki Taniuchi, Kenji Kawai. PRD: NTV, VAP, Production I.G., Animax Asia. 23 mins. x 26 eps.

It is A.D. 972. With the capital Kyoto falling into a mire of corruption and sleaze, and both samurai and priests only looking after their own interests, the imperial court sends champion archer samurai Minamoto no Raiko on a mission to find the Magatama, a legendary gem (see BLUE SEED) reputed to contain the power to bring peace. When he succumbs to disease, his 17-year-old sister Hikaru has to step in to save the family honor and the capital, much as other girls took on men's roles in KAI DOH MARU and YOTODEN.

The story and characters of the first half of the series are loosely based on actual events—Minamoto really was a famous hero of old Kyoto, who slew the demon SHUTENDOJI. His four real-life retainers, known as the Shitenno or Four Kings after the heavenly guardians of Buddhist mythology, all turn up in the anime to help Hikaru on her quest, and Abe no Seimei, one of Hikaru's advisers, really was a renowned priest and scholar and appears in numerous other anime and manga, as well as the *Onmyoji* movie series (see *DE, as *The Yin-Yang Master*).

The link to reality gets stronger from episode 14 when the action

moves to present-day Tokyo for a series of stand-alone episodes, linked to local history and mythology in the style of DOOMED MEGALOPOLIS. In a bizarre mythic retelling of the boardinghouse stories of MAISON IKKOKU, Hikaru is recast as a teenage landlady, while many other cast members are reincarnated as some of her strange tenants, most notably Tsuna, a writer on occult subjects. Many anime feature modern incarnations of ancient warriors, but none spend several hours beforehand explaining who was who. Consequently *OZ* has the ancient resonances of SUIKODEN, KARAS, or IKKI TOUSEN, but much less of the confusion of those shows. We have already grown to love these characters in the opening half, making our emotional investment in them considerably stronger. If it is remembered for nothing else, *OZ* will go down in history as a story with a truly unexpected change in direction (compare to FULLMETAL ALCHEMIST), which puts the rehashes and more-of-the-sames of lesser shows to shame. In uniting ancient and modern so firmly and inextricably, it also plays into the urban mythologies made more famous by SPIRITED AWAY and POMPOKO.

OZ is based on a real story scroll, a 17th-century collection of myths and folktales, some of which predate their written versions by several hundred years. The *Comic Blade* manga spin-off series is not the first modern version; novelist Osamu Dazai rewrote some of the stories for his 1945 compilation released in English as *Crackling Mountain and Other Stories*.

OTOHIME CONNECTION

1991. Video. DIR: Takayuki Goto. SCR: Satoru Akahori. DES: Takayuki Goto. ANI: N/C. MUS: Jun Watanabe. PRD: Animate Film, ING, Aniplex. 45 mins.

Schoolgirl Yuki finds a part-time job at a TV station, but while this might be glamor enough, she also latches on to handsome, pretty-boy private investigators Nagisa and Michio. Based on the manga in *Bessatsu Shojo Comic* by Kazumi Oya.

Outlanders

OTOMO, KATSUHIRO

1954– . Born in Miyagi Prefecture, Otomo failed to get into the art college of his choice, and went to Tokyo after finishing high school in 1973, where he began selling comics professionally to *Manga Action*. Like many young manga artists, he found occasional work as a commercial designer, and on anime— notably as a designer on Rintaro's **HARMAGEDON**, which he did not enjoy. However, Otomo's realistic art style was enough to get him promoted off the shop floor and into direction, and he subsequently became one of the prodigies selected for the anthology movies **ROBOT CARNIVAL** and **NEO-TOKYO**. His true claim to fame, however, is his own adaptation of his landmark **AKIRA**. A notorious perfectionist, Otomo's creative control caused the production to run far over budget, although its subsequent foreign success has made him one of the poster boys of Japanese animation, particularly with foreign fans. However, in Japan, he retreated from the anime world, making a live-action low-budget movie of his own, *World Apartment Horror* (1990), and restricting himself to minor roles on a select few films—scripting duties on

ROUJIN Z and **METROPOLIS**, a codirecting credit on **MEMORIES**, and the nebulous "supervising" role on **SPRIGGAN**. It was only with **STEAMBOY** that Otomo returned to full-length anime feature directing, over 15 years after his most famous success. He was subsequently hired to direct a live-action version of **MUSHISHI**, in pre-production at the time of our deadline.

OTSUKA, YASUO

1931– . Born in Shimane Prefecture, he went to Tokyo in 1951 to seek a career as a political cartoonist. Joining Toei Animation in 1957, he worked on a **JOURNEY TO THE WEST** anime and **LITTLE PRINCE AND THE EIGHT-HEADED DRAGON** as a sketch artist, before becoming a key animator on **LITTLE NORSE PRINCE**, where he was a mentor to Isao Takahata and Hayao Miyazaki. He left the company in 1969 and worked for A Production (now Shin'ei Doga), Nippon Animation, and Telecom. He remained a prominent key animator on works including **THE MOOMINS** and **LUPIN III**, but refused to direct, citing Takahata's unpleasant experiences on *Little Norse Prince*. However, in a training capacity, he became one of

the guiding lights of Studio Ghibli. The studio honored him in 2004 with a documentary: *Yasuo Otsuka's Joy of Animating*.

OURAN HIGH SCHOOL HOST CLUB

2006. JPN: *Oran Koko Host Club*. TV series. DIR: Takuya Igarashi, Masayuki Imura. SCR: Yoji Enokido. DES: Kumiko Takahashi. ANI: Kumiko Takahashi. MUS: N/C. PRD: Bones. 25 mins. x 26 eps. Haruhi Fujioka is the only student at Ouran High School not from an incredibly rich family. This lands her in deep trouble when she breaks a valuable vase and is forced to pay it off by working as an indentured servant to the Host Club—a group of impossibly handsome boys who have made a hobby of running a bar for lonely women seeking chaste male companionship. Since Haruhi is rather androgynous herself, she is soon mistaken for a man, and finds a new vocation in pouring drinks and making small talk with the customers, in a male impersonator variation on the rich-boy harem of **BOYS OVER FLOWERS** and **PARADISE KISS**.

OUTLANDERS *

1986. JPN: *Outlanders*. Video. DIR: Katsuhisa Yamada. SCR: Kenji Terada. DES: Hiroshi Hamazaki. ANI: Hiroshi Hamazaki. MUS: Kei Wakakusa. PRD: Tatsunoko. 48 mins.
Earth is invaded by the galaxy-spanning Santovasku Empire in its organic spaceships. Princess Kahm first appears slicing up unsuspecting Earthmen as part of her imperial father's great invasion plan; then she falls into the arms of photographer Tetsuya and decides to save him from the destruction that the empire has planned for the rest of humankind. This puts both lovers and their friends in serious danger from Kahm's conquest-mad daddy and his nasty minions. Based on Johji Manabe's 1985 manga for Hakusensha, with affectionate nods to *Star Wars* and **URUSEI YATSURA**, the story has considerable charm despite a fairly high violence quotient. Manabe has

done little except repeat it since (see **RAI** and **CAPRICORN**), but this doesn't detract from the original. **NV**

OUTLAW STAR *

1998. JPN: *Seiho Bukyo Outlaw Star*. AKA: *Stellar Chivalry Outlaw Star*. TV series. DIR: Mitsuru Hongo. SCR: Katsuhiko Chiba. DES: Takuya Saito, Junya Ishigaki. ANI: Takuya Saito, Hiroyuki Hataike. MUS: Ko Otani. PRD: Sunrise, Sotsu, TV Tokyo. 25 mins. x 24 eps.
Hajime Yadate (Sunrise's name for its in-house idea machine) and Takehiko Ito (**ANGEL LINKS**) adapted an alternate future from Ito's 1988 *Space Hero Tales* manga for the late-night slot on TV Tokyo. A loose and unstable galactic alliance is trying to bring order to the chaos of the expanding space frontier. Hot Ice Hilda is on the wrong side of the law, on the run, in disguise, and in search of a fabulous treasure when she runs across Gene Starwind, a Han Solo wannabe running a rather sleazy, jack-of-all-trades business with his 11-year-old "brother," Jim Hawking, who is definitely the brains of the outfit. Gene's career is severely hampered by space phobia; as a child he watched his father die in space, and by a weird coincidence he thinks one of the gangs chasing Hilda is responsible. Hilda hires the duo to help her with a nebulous "repair job," but before long they've gotten aboard a hidden prototype spaceship and its cybernetically engineered living navigation computer, a cute girl named Melfina. Then Hilda gets killed and Gene & Co. suddenly have more enemies than they ever expected. The Outlaw Star and Melfina are targets for every powerful group in the galaxy; it's widely believed that, aside from the value of the ship itself, it contains clues that will lead to the fabled treasure known as Galactic Leyline (refer to **SOL BIANCA**). As they struggle to survive, they run into comic tropes like Suzuka, a deadly Japanese assassin who's so friendly she joins the crew, and Aisha, a cat-girl who does likewise. The writers rely on such tropes to liven up a plot whose guid-

ance is mostly inertial. Arms mounted on the "grappler" ships turn space combat into something more like a mechanized wrestling match, and, while there are some good flashes of humor (like the OTT opening narrations), this is no competition for **COWBOY BEBOP** in terms of style, content, or execution. When screened on the Cartoon Network, the anime was edited for nudity, violence, gambling, drinking, and lechery because those things don't happen in America.

OUTSIDE THE LAW

1969. JPN: *Roppo Yabure-kun*. AKA: *Yabure Roppo*. TV series. DIR: Eiji Okabe. SCR: Masaki Tsuji, Ichiro Wakabayashi, Haruya Yamazaki, Yoshiaki Yoshida, Hideko Yoshida, Tsunehisa Ito, Takashi Hayakawa, Shigeru Omachi, Seiji Matsuoka, Kinzo Okamoto. DES: N/C. ANI: Takeo Kitahara. MUS: Yasuhiro Koyama. PRD: Tokyo Movie Shinsha, NTV. 5 mins. x 110 eps.
Yabure Roppo is a perfectly average salaryman, remarkable only for his incredible run of bad luck—comparable only to that of Ataru Moroboshi in **URUSEI YATSURA**. He becomes the victim of a series of outrageous scams and accidents, many based on modern urban myths. A girl he sees socially suddenly demands that he marry her. A conman rips him off, and then attempts to blackmail him. He agrees to help out a friend by cosigning a contract, only to discover that his friend has absconded and he is now responsible for the debt. He endures all this torment in order to instruct the viewers on thorny problems within modern Japanese civil law, based on an idea by Sen Saga, who became a mystery novelist after thirty years as a lawyer. Compare to **LAW OF DIVORCE AND INHERITANCE**.
Mr. Roppo gets his name from two Japanese concepts: *Happo Yabure*, meaning "without preventions," and *Roppo Zensho*, a "compendium of laws." His name thus translates as something like Outside the Law, with the emphasis on its inability to protect him, rather than criminal intent.

OVERMAN KING GAINER *

2002. TV series. DIR: Yoshiyuki Tomino. SCR: Ichiro Okochi. DES: Kenichi Yoshida, Kinu Nishimura, Yoshihiro Nakamura, Akira Yasuda, Kimitoshi Yamane. ANI: Kenichi Yoshida. MUS: Kohei Tanaka. PRD: Bandai, Sunrise, WOWOW. 25 mins. x 26 eps.
In a distant future, mankind has wrecked the Earth's environment and retreated to domed cities, leaving the ecosystem to take its chances. The cities are run and supplied by private corporations, overseen by a worldwide authority based in London, but not everyone believes that these corporations are working for the public good. In any event, they have captive markets—any movement outside the cities must be authorized, and any unauthorized excursions are severely punished—compare to similar setups in **THE BIG O** and **HEAT GUY J**. Teenage gamer Gainer Saga is arrested on suspicion of being involved with the Exodus movement, a nebulous group wanting to leave the confines of the domes in search of a better life. In prison he meets mercenary Gain Bijo, and together they commandeer an Overman robot, take the daughter of the city's duke hostage, and lead an exodus out of the city under cover of a festival headlined by idol singer Meeya Laujin. Their destination is the fabled land of Yapan.
Gainer was such a hotshot at virtual combat that he was known in gaming circles as "King Gainer"—now he has to transfer his skills to the real world as he defends the group of travelers from the elite Saint Regan squad sent from London to stop them and the troops of the Siberian Railway.
Director Tomino takes his basic **GUNDAM** mix—gifted but disengaged young pilot, political conflict, and struggle for a promised land—and throws in elements from **MACROSS**: rakish big brother figure, idol singer, journey in constant jeopardy. Unfortunately, he also includes some of today's fashionable high school romance elements. Several members of Gainer's

high school escaping the city with him is plausible enough, but stretches credibility to its limits when they continue classes while on the run and under fire. Tomino has had characters switch sides in earlier work, but having the enemy commander not only switch sides but also become the hero's teacher and roommate is a definite postmodern touch. The statutory cute child, Princess Ana, has statutory cute pets, in this case three ferrets. Although these unnecessary refinements don't slow things down too much, it seems a pity that the man who has led the field in robot anime with a serious human dimension for so long should borrow from less creative minds than his own to satisfy an industry which is increasingly less discerning and less interested in originality.

OVERSEAS DISTRIBUTION AND PIRACY

Although there was some international contact among filmmakers in the days of EARLY ANIME, Japanese animation made its first major steps abroad after the Second World War. Toei Animation became involved at an early stage when its first feature film, PANDA AND THE MAGIC SERPENT was a prizewinner at the 1959 Venice Film festival. It was followed by Osamu Tezuka's first feature *Alakazam the Great* (see JOURNEY TO THE WEST), in a dubbed version that had great longevity.

Television anime began its export drive early, with ASTRO BOY, screened in America mere months after its Japanese premiere. Few American viewers realized they were watching a Japanese show, and were indeed encouraged not to, through CENSORSHIP AND LOCALIZATION. Seven more anime series were sold to U.S. TV in the 1960s—8TH MAN, GIGANTOR, PRINCE PLANET, MARINE BOY, KIMBA THE WHITE LION, SPEED RACER, and THE AMAZING THREE. Many were also screened in other English-speaking territories such as Australia and South Africa, although of all these early TV translations, only *Marine Boy* made it to Britain. The same period

saw Japanese animators from the Topcraft studio working on "American" cartoons for Rankin/Bass. The 1970s saw only two major U.S. TV screenings, but STAR BLAZERS and BATTLE OF THE PLANETS achieved something new—winning fans in high schools and colleges all over the country.

Anime enjoyed similar paths to success in Europe. French TV screened children's series from the early 1970s, some of which later reappeared in North America on French-speaking channels in Canada. *Kimba the White Lion* aired in 1972 as *Le Roi Leo*, with PRINCESS KNIGHT (*Prince Saphir*) shown two years later alongside Italian-Japanese coproduction CALIMERO. Movies were also screened on television and theatrically, starting with the 1969 Toei PUSS IN BOOTS (*Le Chat Botté*) in 1978; but the major event in French anime history was the screening of GRANDIZER (*Goldorak*) in 1978. Summer vacation was considered a wasteland for children's programming in France, but by the time the schools reopened in September Go Nagai's robot show was a word-of-mouth hit. The series is still selling strongly today; Toei found it necessary to issue writs against pirate *Goldorak* DVD releases across French-speaking Europe in 2004.

Goldorak was part of an anime viewing schedule which consisted for the most part of retold fairy tales and innocuous series: CANDY CANDY (as *Candy*) made her French debut just two months after Nagai's epic, but was followed in 1979 by CAPTAIN HARLOCK (*Albator, le Corsaire de l'Espace*) on Antenne 2, and *Battle of the Planets* (*La Bataille des Planetes*) on TF1. Meanwhile, *Goldorak* was dubbed into Spanish as *Goldrake* and into Arabic as *Grandizer*. Go Nagai's giant robot shows became a staple of Spanish TV and created a strong demand for preteen and teenage animated shows, while in Italy they were so successful that Nagai set up an Italian company, Dynamic Italia, to manage his work there.

In 1979, *Spectreman* (*DE) became the first Japanese live-action show to hit

French television, with Haim Saban and Shuki Levy on the crew list—15 years later, they would launch the *Mighty Morphin' Power Rangers* (*DE). Following on from CALIMERO, French studio DIC collaborated on ULYSSES 31 and MYSTERIOUS CITIES OF GOLD (*Les Mysterieuses Cités d'Or*). Nippon Animation's coproduction with Spain's BRB International, AROUND THE WORLD IN 80 DAYS (*Le Tour de Monde en 80 Jours*) was shown in both France and Spain. The same studio's co-production with Apollo Films, ALICE IN WONDERLAND, was screened in Europe in 1985, as was the French release of the Topcraft/Rankin/Bass fantasy *The Last Unicorn* (*La Derniere Licorne*). 1985 also saw the Western debut of *Rainbow Brite*, DIC's collaboration with U.S. and Japanese studios.

Classics of world literature have always attracted Japanese audiences, and created an interesting market in which children watch their culture's stories, interpreted by foreign artists, then redubbed into their native tongues. LITTLE EL CID was shown in Spain and France in 1981, with LES MISÉRABLES in France the same year. Monkey Punch's LUPIN III has enjoyed huge success in France and Italy since 1985, and ROSE OF VERSAILLES (*Lady Oscar*) sold the French Revolution back to France. Scandinavian stories have charmed European children in Japanese versions, including NILS' MYSTERIOUS JOURNEY (European debut 1983) and AUNTY SPOON (European debut 1984). Less success awaited in Finland, where MOOMINS met with criticism from its original author, and KATRI THE MILKMAID, based on a Finnish children's book, was never screened at all. Meanwhile, Hayao Miyazaki's fascination with all things exotically European, including Italian airplanes, Scandinavian cities, Welsh miners, and Welsh writers, has helped to make his work popular across the continent.

Anime also enjoyed success across East Asia, even in countries such as South Korea where Japanese associations and imports were discouraged. DORAEMON in particular became a local icon in Korea and Taiwan. Indonesian broadcasters feigned a complete lack of interest in Japanese television programming, only to find themselves screening it by proxy when they bought the supposedly "American" serials of *Robotech* and *G-Force*. Anime's popularity in East Asia also led to a rise in the piracy of animated titles; this was particularly prevalent in Taiwan, which was not a member of the United Nations, and hence not a signatory to several important copyright conventions. Pirate editions of both anime and manga built entire publishing industries in many East Asian countries, in a boom that ironically worked to the advantage of the Japanese. In Korea, where Japanese imports were banned until the 1990s, since anime and manga did not officially exist, they were not subjected to strict government censorship. For transgressive Korean youths, the best way to annoy their parents was to become an anime or manga fan. In other parts of Asia, most notably Taiwan and Hong Kong, the tsunami of cheap, unlicensed Japanese material, springing into the market as fully-formed serials and tie-in comic stories, often with merchandise and gaming spin-offs already present, undercut and outperformed many local artists, stifling native talent and leaving local comics and animation industries far behind the Japanese. Although there are numerous local talents and creators today, many East Asian creators find themselves pressured or steered into drawing "pseudomanga" in imitation of the now-legal Japanese titles which so dominate the medium.

In the 1980s, as the exponential expansion of TV channels created still more demand for cheap programming, American television saw Go Nagai's 1972 hit **Mazinger Z** (screened in 1985 as *TranZor Z*) and **Queen of a Thousand Years.** Two hybrid series were created by splicing several entirely unrelated Japanese originals into a new American entity. **Force Five** (1980) and **Robotech** (1985) not only filled syndication schedules but also

sold robot toys to American boys with great success.

Television before the general availability of the home video recorder had a captive audience. Viewers were unable to time-shift in order to follow their favorite programs, a limitation networks could exploit with repeat showings. Just as the video recorder put an end to cinema theater re-screenings of "favorite" anime episodes in Japan, it also made it possible for Japanese television to travel to America without the need to pass through a broadcaster. Legend has it that anime first entered America through science fiction fandom on the east and west coasts, where a large Japanese immigrant community, anime broadcasts on Japanese-language local television, and a strong science fiction audience combined to make convention screenings, with and without translations, a possibility. Behind the scenes, certain anime companies were active collaborators in this supposed "grassroots" movement. Some of the first convention screenings used VCR or even 16mm prints donated by Japanese agents.

The rise of the household VCR brought a new market into being, although some might argue that the combination of videocassette and personal computer was a deadly genie that the anime industry has been unable to stuff back into its bottle. Thanks to the Amiga (and much later to PCs and Macintoshes), it was now possible to add amateur subtitles, or "fansubs," to anime videos, rendered easier in America than in Europe through the fact that Japan and the U.S. shared the NTSC video format. Fansubs were soon circulating unofficially and helping to build demand for Japanese animation in cult TV circles.

The 1990s saw the return in syndication of serials first screened in the previous three decades, most notably the early morning screening of *Speed Racer* on MTV, which would in turn lead to a prominent *Speed Racer* poster seen on the wall of the apartment in the sitcom *Friends*. Also screened in

1995 were *Battle of the Planets* (in new variants) and **Ronin Warriors,** a test for later screenings of **Dragon Ball** and **Sailor Moon** with the newer **Teknoman.** This did not result in spectacular ratings, but American licensing company Funimation persevered with a further series, **Dragon Ball Z.** A new Cartoon Network slot, Toonami, aired in March 1997 bringing back old U.S. and Japanese shows like *Thundercats* and **Voltron,** and the following year the Warner Brothers network hit back with Nintendo's latest Japanese merchandising gambit, **Pokémon. Pokémon** was followed by **Digimon** and **Monster Rancher,** setting the scene for a new millennium of exploitation, not merely through television, but through merchandising and tie-ins, in imitation of the model already in place in Japan.

At first traded via the convention circuit and the existing network of anime fan clubs, copies of anime found even wider circulation as Americans accessed the Internet and created an unregulated, fast-moving market in information and goods. At a time in the 1990s when there might have been only 100 anime fans per *state*, Internet access helped establish virtual communities in order to encourage interest in the medium. As a predominantly young, technologically knowledgeable interest group, many with access to computers at home or college, anime fans were also able to use the Internet for the preparation and distribution of fansubs in unprecedented quantities. The prevalence of unlicensed translations has been a subject of unending debate within the American anime industry—many industry employees admit to an early interest fostered by fansubs and argue that fansubs often function as free samples that encourage a later purchase or rental. However, fansubbing is also undeniably open to extreme abuse, and regardless of the motives of many fansubbers to popularize a medium they love, the phenomenon creates ready-made materials for video pirates prepared to sell fansubs for personal profit. Consequently, what was once deemed a harmless activity not unlike borrowing a book from a friend, has escalated into a multi-million dollar copyright infringement industry, and one which has periodically led companies to litigate against persistent offenders. The arrival of Bit Torrent and other peer-to-peer file-sharing systems has made it even easier to obtain anime without paying for it.

Fandom itself, legal, illegal, or in the gray area of fansubbing (which is illegal but often overlooked), remains an influential distribution channel for anime. With weekend attendances often climbing into five figures, the convention circuit has formed its own micro-ulture, effectively unionizing consumers. Some anime companies, particularly those whose sales rely on titles popular only in fandom rather than with the general public, often present a friendly brand identity at conventions by sending representatives to announce new releases and deflect criticism. Such trips can make or break smaller releases—they would have a negligible effect on a major distributor, like Buena Vista, but a thousand fans reaching for their wallets in a single weekend can make the difference between profit and a loss. The precise power of fandom is a paradox—some argue that fandom is small and insignificant, and that, for example, fansubbing consequently represents a negligible loss in business when set against its promotional value. Others claim that fandom's power is so great that companies should obey its every (contradictory) whim, which would suggest that fansubbing and Internet downloading represent a significant danger to anime's increased profitability abroad, and hence the future of the foreign language anime business itself. Since piracy is by its very nature shadowy, it is difficult to determine what difference it makes to the anime business.

As anime moves into its sixth decade in the U.S., science fiction and fantasy remain the dominant genres, with animated pornography gaining a higher profile than in its home market. A Japanese origin is no longer hidden from viewers, but boldly (sometimes falsely) proclaimed, particularly in cases where American networks are involved directly with a Japanese studio. There is also a relatively small but significant theatrical market, which was bolstered when SPIRITED AWAY won the Oscar for Best Feature Animation in 2003.

As we write early in 2006, anime is screened regularly on TV and sold for home viewing not just in America but also in every part of Europe, including its Eastern borders: Poland and Russia have embraced Japanese cartoons with as much enthusiasm as their Western neighbors. With foreign companies now eagerly buying the rights to new anime, often before they are even made, the new frontier for the Japanese industry is now China, a vast territory of one billion potential fans, many already acquainted with the medium through viewings of Sino-friendly anime like RANMA ½ and CHINA NUMBER ONE. Many anime are now at least partially made in China, sometimes for financial reasons, but increasingly also because a significant contribution by Chinese staff helps qualify a title as an international coproduction, and hence not subject to local broadcasting restrictions. In years to come, however, it is likely that national and geographical concerns will cease to be an issue for the animation business. Broadcasting's increasing reliance on direct downloads and the Internet has presented many anime companies with the opportunity to cut out all middlemen. The future of anime may well rest on hard drives and mobile phones, with foreign language versions released simultaneously in order to minimize the potential losses through fansubbing and piracy.

OYO MY HUGGABLE CAT
1984. JPN: *Oyoneko Bunichan.* TV series. DIR: Hiroshi Sasakawa, Hiroshi Fujioka, Kenjiro Yoshida, Teruo Kigure, Katsumi Kosuga. SCR: Hiroshi Kaneko, Hideki Sonoda, Tsunehisa Ito, Hideo Takayashiki, Yoshio Urasawa, Miho Maruo, Hiroko Naka. DES: Misako Ichikawa. ANI: Shinichi Suzuki. MUS: Takeo Watanabe. PRD: Shinei, TV Asahi. 25 mins. x 31 eps.

The comical adventures of bad-tempered fat cat Oyoyo who charms his idiot human family but fights an ongoing battle with other neighborhood pets. Based on the manga *Mr. Happy* (*Shiawase-san*) by Misako Ichikawa (no relation to MISTER HAPPY), serialized in several magazines, including *Shojo* and *Ciao.* Unmatched in anime for feline humor until WHAT'S MICHAEL? appeared a year later.

OZ
1992. Video. DIR: Katsuhisa Yamada. SCR: Asami Watanabe. DES: Toyomi Sugiyama. ANI: Toyomi Sugiyama. MUS: Yoichiro Yoshikawa. PRD: Madhouse. 35 mins. x 2 eps.

A nuclear war kills 60% of humanity and splits the U.S. into six warring states. By 2021, a legend has grown amid the hunger, chaos, and devastation—the fabled city of Oz, where high technology has survived to serve humankind, and hunger and war are unknown. Scientist Felicia sets out to find Oz with mercenary Muto and Droid #1019. At the end of the road they find a madman dreaming of world dominion in a military base with enough firepower to create a new nightmare for the world. Natsumi Itsuki's original 1988 manga in *Comic Lala* was based very loosely on THE WIZARD OF OZ but owed a greater debt to the same studio's WIND OF AMNESIA in this anime adaptation. For reasons known only to the distributor, the *Oz* soundtrack was released in the U.K., though the anime has never been translated.

OZEKI, MASAYUKI
1950– . Joined Studio Mates in 1970 to work on COWBOY ISAMU, before going freelance. His directorial debut was the LUPIN III "movie" *The Fuma Conspiracy* (1987).

P

PACHISLO KIZOKU GIN
2001. JPN: *Pachisuro Kizoku Gin*. AKA: *Pachinko Slot Aristocrat Gin*. TV series. DIR: Hidehito Ueda. SCR: Hiroyuki Hoshiyama, Tsunehisa Ito. DES: Junichi Haneyama. ANI: N/C. MUS: N/C. PRD: A Line, Atlas, Fuji TV. 25 mins. x 23 eps. University student Ginya Otonashi writes articles for a pachinko magazine, but would really prefer to be a famous novelist. He discovers a new and unexpected skill when he finds himself taking part in a secret pachinko contest run by the "Slotium" pachinko consortium. The authors suspect that a "Pachislo Aristocrat" is something similar to a "Pinball Wizard," but there is no direct connection to Ken Russell's rock musical *Tommy* (1975), which was released in Japan under its original title. The name *Gin*, however, literally means "silver," as in the silver balls of both pursuits.

PALE COCOON
2005. Video. DIR: Yasuhiro Yoshiura. SCR: Yasuhiro Yoshiura. DES: Yasuhiro Yoshiura. ANI: Yasuhiro Yoshiura. MUS: Toru Okada. PRD: Studio Rikka. 23 mins.
In a claustrophobic future world Ura reconstructs old images and archives from the past. His latest project turns out to be a music video, whose singer offers up a message from the Moon, where she has just arrived, to dwellers on "the rust-covered Earth." Realizing that the location of the recording seems familiar, the archivist resolves to climb through the abandoned upper levels of his underground home to see for himself, in an interesting, albeit derivative, sci-fi short. Made over a two-year period, and largely the work of a single creator, *Pale Cocoon*'s clearest debt is to **VOICES FROM A DISTANT STAR**, whose attitude, length, and tone it often mirrors. As with so many modern "home brew" anime, it lifts plot elements from earlier fan favorites—in this case the **COWBOY BEBOP** episode "Speak Like a Child" and the underlying conceit of **MEGAZONE 23**. A singer's trip to the Moon is also the starting point of **A.LI.CE**, although this is probably a coincidence. The final moment refers, perhaps inadvertently, to the closing shot of the first-ever straight-to-video anime, Mamoru Oshii's **DALLOS**. *Pale Cocoon* is also a creation of its time—its action reflects the sedentary computer-bound life of modern teenagers (and of modern animators!), its setting a world in environmental crisis, and its ending, a note of mournful hope, with a noninterventionist tone familiar from many other ecological anime. The creator's website gives a 2005 copyright date, although the DVD only appeared in Japanese stores in the early weeks of 2006. **L N V**

PA-MAN
1967. JPN: *Pa-man*. TV series. DIR: Tadao Nagahama, Eiji Okabe, Shinichi Suzuki. SCR: Fujiko-Fujio, Tadao Nagahama, Masaki Tsuji, Koji Miharu, Tatsuo Tamura. DES: Fujiko-Fujio. ANI: Shinichi Suzuki, Tsutomu Shibayama. MUS: Hiroshi Tsutsui. PRD: Studio Zero, Tokyo Movie Shinsha, TBS. 25 mins. x 54 eps. (b/w; two stories per episode), 25 mins. (m1), 15 mins. x 526 eps. (TV2), 32 mins. (m2), 33 mins. (m3).
Four children and Boobie the chimpanzee are recruited to protect their hometown by a mysterious masked man. He gives them helmets that endow the wearers with superstrength and cloaks that let them fly at 91 kph. Lead male Pa-man #1, chimp superhero Pa-man #2, token female Pa-ko, Osaka-born miser Pa-yan, and baby Pa-bo must try to solve the town's problems, great and small, and help its people. After a brief cameo in the final episode of the same creators' **QTARO THE GHOST**, Pa-man got his own series in order to keep money rolling in from the TBS sponsors. The franchise was revived many years later for a short film, *Pa-Man: The Coming of Birdman* (1983), directed by Shinichi Suzuki, a former animator on the original series. Inevitably, the film was revealed as a preview of a coming series, the extremely long-running *New Pa-man* that began soon after on TV Asahi. The update revealed Pa-ko's real identity (she is really the pop star Sumi Hoshino) and introduced a new character, Yuki. *Paman the Movie* (2003) followed.

PANDA AND THE MAGIC SERPENT*

1958. JPN: *Hakujaden*. AKA: *Legend of the White Serpent; Tale of the White Serpent; The White Snake Enchantress*. Movie. DIR: Taiji Yabushita. SCR: Taiji Yabushita, Soichi Yashiro. DES: Akira Okuwara, Yasuji Mori. ANI: Yasuo Otsuka, Kazuko Nakamura, Reiko Okuyama, Taku Sugiyama, Gisaburo Sugii. MUS: Masayoshi Ikeda. PRD: Toei. 78 mins.

The beautiful snake princess Bai-Niang falls in love with the young boy Xu-Xian. His parents make him put the snake back in the fields where he found her, but he never stops missing his pet. Years later, magically transformed into a beautiful girl during a storm, the snake goddess changes a rainbow fish into her handmaid Xiao Chin, sets up house in the town, and seeks Xu-Xian out again. Both grown up, the two fall in love. Local wizard Fa Hai, convinced Bai-Niang is a vampire out to harm Xu-Xian, tries to break up their romance, and banishes Xu to hard labor in a distant city, reasoning that it's the only way to save him. Xu's two clever pets, Panda and Mimi, set out to follow him and become the leaders of the local animal Mafia, using the gang's skills to find him. Determined to save Xu from what he sees as a terrible supernatural evil, Fa whisks him off to his castle by the ocean, and the devoted Panda and Mimi follow him again through a terrible storm. Xiao has to intervene with the gods to save them, while Bai-Niang fights Fa for Xu's freedom. Even after saving Xu from death, she must give up her magical powers and become human before Fa accepts that her love is genuine. The two young lovers can finally marry, Xiao returns to her true form as a pretty fish, and Panda, Mimi and their animal friends all live happily ever after.

Often regarded as the "first" modern anime, this variant on LITTLE MERMAID was originally adapted from Chinese mythology as a story by Shin Uehara. Featuring uncharacteristically "oriental" character designs and serious trials and hardships for the young lovers and their animal friends, it inspired many others to become animators, including the young Hayao Miyazaki, on whom it made a deep impression. It won honors at the Venice Children's Film Festival in 1959 but reaction to its U.S. release in 1961 was disappointing. Mimi, a small "red" panda, is mistakenly referred to as a cat in some sources.

PANDA GO PANDA *

1972. JPN: *Panda Kopanda*. AKA: *Panda; Panda Cub; Panda and Child*. Movie. DIR: Isao Takahata. SCR: Hayao Miyazaki. DES: Hayao Miyazaki. ANI: Yasuo Otsuka, Yoichi Otabe, Yoshifumi Kondo, Seiji Kitara, Takao Kasai, Minoru Maeda. MUS: Teruhiko Sato. PRD: A-Pro, Tokyo Movie Shinsha. 33 mins., 38 mins.

Miyazaki's first original work as a screenwriter is a charming tale of a little girl who befriends a panda and his cub. Left home alone when her grandmother has to go away for a few days, little Mimiko is surprised to find a panda and his cub moving in. They very soon form a little family of their own, with Father Panda offering the fatherless Mimiko the paternal affection she's always wanted, and Mimiko mothering the motherless cub. Everything is going well until the local policeman discovers exactly who Mimiko's houseguests are. The father-bear, a model of good parenthood foreshadowing Miyazaki's ongoing concern with the parent/child relationship, can also be seen as one of the stages in the creation of MY NEIGHBOR TOTORO, and the young protagonist has much in common with the heroine Miyazaki had sketched for TMS's abortive *Pippi Longstocking* project. The sequel, *Panda Go Panda: Rainy Day Circus*, also directed by Takahata, followed a year later. Pandas were big box office in the 1970s after the arrival of a Chinese panda at Tokyo Zoo, and other unrelated appearances during the period included Yugo Serikawa's *Panda's Great Adventure* (1973) and the Sino-Japanese coproduction TAOTAO

THE PANDA. The following decade would see a similar obsession with koalas—see THE NOOZLES.

PANDA-Z THE ROBONIMATION *

2004. AKA: *Robonimal Panda-Z*. TV series. DIR: Mamoru Kanbe. SCR: N/C. DES: Shuichi Oshida. ANI: N/C. MUS: Panda-Z Band. PRD: Bandai Visual, Dynamic Planning, Megahouse Corp., Kid's Station. 5 mins. x 30 eps.

In Robonimal World, where robots are shaped like animals, seven-year-old Pan Taron finds a Super P-Z engine under the research facility headed by his grandfather Doctor Pan Ji, a mad scientist complete with lightbulb on his head to show when he has a really bright idea. The Doctor and Pan's father use it to build superrobot Panda Z, complete with flying fist to deliver a rocket punch, abdominal missiles for a really powerful six-pack, and a bright red jet-pack to fly with. Aimed at younger children, but also exploiting the retro interests of fans-turned-parents who yearn for the pre-GUNDAM days of mighty robot action, the characters are named in simple, picture-book fashion—Denwan the telephone dog gets his name by crashing the Japanese words for "phone" and "bark" together, Rabinna is a pink rabbit nurse, Etekki the monkey is named for the sound monkeys make in Japanese, lumbering Zoutank's name starts with the word for "elephant," and Moo-Gyuu's ends with the Japanese word for cow.

Taron, however, is the only one who can bond with Panda-Z to battle the evil machinations of SkullPanda. Like the Emperor in Go Nagai's puppet show *Star Fleet* (*DE), SkullPanda's body is entirely hidden under a long cloak; he commands his forces from a mobile floating fortress. His chief henchman is evil mustachioed Doctor Jangar, who leads the Warunimal forces in his deadly Black Ham Gear, a giant robot hamster. Warunimal is a hybrid of the Japanese word *warui* (bad) and animal.

Created by MAZINGER Z fan Shuichi Oshida when he was learning

Adobe Illustrator on his Mac, this Go Nagai–inspired heroic robot and his cohorts were picked up by Megahouse when he went freelance, and appeared as a highly successful merchandise line before they were animated. Go Nagai's name appears on the show credited with "original concept," in reflection of the number of distinct Nagai ideas that Oshida lampoons.

PANI PONI DASH

2005. TV series. DIR: Akiyuki Shinbo. SCR: Kenichi Kanemaki, Katsuhiko Takayama. DES: Kazuhiro Oda. ANI: Kazuhiro Oda. MUS: Kei Haneoka. PRD: Gansis, Shaft, TV Tokyo. 25 mins. x 15+ eps.

Rebecca "Becky" Miyamoto is a diminutive 12-year-old genius shorter than the children she is supposed to teach at Momotsuki High School. Pretty girls and a rabbit, with occasional swimsuits. Suspiciously similar to DOKI DOKI SCHOOL HOURS, but why not just keep wringing that idea until it's totally dry?

PANZER DRAGOON *

1996. JPN: Panzer Dragoon. Video. DIR: Shinji Takagi. SCR: Yosuke Kuroda. DES: Atsushi Takeuchi, Kazuhiro Kishita. ANI: Atsushi Takeuchi. MUS: Azuma. PRD: Production IG. 30 mins.

Kyle's girl is stolen from him by the Black Dragon, which also kills his obviously expendable fat friend. When he meets blue dragon Blau, Kyle is suspicious, but only Blau can help him save Alita, who will otherwise be enslaved by the Dark Tower and become the catalyst for the destruction of the entire world.

If a bored director and crew copied a few pages from the *Beginner's Book of Fantasy Gaming*, then lost the important bits like plot and characterization, this is what might emerge. The Sega game's distinctive look is matched by what, at the time of release, must have been a truly innovative combination of cel and digital animation. There are set pieces that recall the game itself and quirkily mismatched compositions of technology and magic, setting up a damsel in

distress, cross-species buddy business, a rescue, and a big fight in just 30 minutes.

With a fallen empire, a blind sorceress, human/dragon symbiosis, and a quest to defeat the ultimate evil, *Panzer Dragoon* had truly epic potential. People have spun trilogies out of less, but the paltry running time isn't up to it. What little space there is for dialogue that doesn't advance the plot, writer Kuroda fills with poetic meditations on sight and seeing. The blind Alita cannot *see* the color red, instead she must *experience* it. "So this is what the sky feels like!" proclaims Kyle during his first dragon flight—a throwaway line that belongs in a much better story.

AD Vision's dub is far better than the spartan original deserves, but this remains a heroic rescue attempt by both Japanese and U.S. crews, fighting impossible odds of budget and (lack of) inspiration. **V**

PANZER WORLD GALIENT

1984. JPN: Kikokai Galient. AKA: Mechanical Armor World Galient. TV series, video. DIR: Ryosuke Takahashi. SCR: Ryosuke Takahashi, Hajime Yadate. DES: Norio Shioyama. ANI: Norio Shioyama. MUS: Toru Fuyuki. PRD: Sunrise, Nippon TV. 25 mins. x 26 eps., 55 mins.

Young Jordy is fighting his father, Madar, who is bent on world domination using giant robots. His brother, Hai Shartart, is also fighting Madar, but not to save the people from dominion; instead he plans to take his father's place, and so he sees Jordy and their sister, Chururu, as rivals. Legend tells of a mysterious avenger, known only as the Iron Giant, who will come to overthrow the tyrant. The video, subtitled *Iron Emblem*, covered the same dramatic ground two years later: ruthless ambition, family conflict, and massively overspecified armor.

The golden age of the robot was in full swing in 1984; *God Mazinger* (see MAZINGER Z) and SOUTHERN CROSS among the multitude onscreen, MACROSS in the theaters, and toys every-

where. Takahashi is renowned as one of the prime movers of the "real robot" style spun off from Tomino's GUNDAM, but the introduction of more realistic elements into future fantasy didn't preclude designs of baroque splendor. The *Galient* robots are among the best—a magnificent fusion of futuristic technology, steampunk weightiness, and off-the-wall neoclassical design. Robot centaurs—you gotta love 'em. **V**

PAPA MAMA BYE-BYE

1980. JPN: Papa Mama Bye-Bye. Movie. DIR: Hiroshi Shidara. SCR: Atsushi Yamagata. DES: Katsumi Aoshima. ANI: Katsumi Aoshima. MUS: Tadahito Mori. PRD: Toei. 75 mins.

Dungaree-wearing teenage tomboy Kaori lives next door to the brothers Ko and Yasu. One day they find an injured pigeon and nurse it back to health. As Kaori is walking to school soon afterward, a U.S. Phantom jet screams overhead and crashes near the boys' house. A heavy-handed juxtaposition of animal hospital and international friendship, inspired by a real-life incident in 1977 when a U.S. jet did indeed make a forced landing in Yokohama. For another U.S. plane ending up where it shouldn't, see SEA OF THE TICONDEROGA.

PAPUA-KUN

1992. JPN: Nangoku no Shonen Papuwa-kun. AKA: Southern-Kingdom Boy Papua. TV series, video. DIR: Jun Takagi, Masahiro Hosoda. SCR: Nobuyuki Fujimoto. DES: Hiroshi Takeuchi, Ken Kawai. ANI: Satoshi Takeuchi, Takao Osone. MUS: Nobuyuki Nakamura. PRD: Nippon Animation, TV Asahi. 25 mins. x 42 eps. (TV), 30 mins. x 2 eps., 25 mins. (v).

Papua is a little boy living a quiet life with his dog Chappy on a small island in the South Pacific. Then Shintaro turns up. Not only is he carrying valuable jewelry, but he's being chased by gangsters. When Chappy steals the jewel, the stage is set for insane high jinks of a kind not normally associated with the creators of WORLD MASTERPIECE

THEATER. This anime was based on a 1991 manga by Ami Shibata, who also created JIBAKU-KUN, though a similar dogs-and-jewels caper can be found much earlier in HONEY HONEY. The series returned on video with the two-part *Papua-kun Encyclopedia* (1993, *Papua-kun Daihyakka*), which included an "extra" episode, the pilot film for a nonexistent sequel, and some interviews with the cast and crew. A final video release in 1994 comprised an unbroadcast "dream" episode, in which Papua-kun gets a fever and hallucinates a bizarre journey among the stars.

PARADE PARADE *

1996. Video. DIR: Motoaki Isshu. SCR: N/C. DES: Toshimitsu Kobayashi. ANI: N/C. MUS: N/C. PRD: Pink Pineapple, AIC. 30 mins. x 2 eps.
Two short stories, supposedly of an erotic nature, based on Satoshi Akifuji's manga exposé of the entertainment world. In the first, a pop star and her manager pleasure each other after her first concert. In the second, rival stars play a dangerous game that involves avoiding the toilet for as long as possible, with a payoff that may indeed be erotic for someone, somewhere. A similar stretching of the boundaries of good taste can be found in PROFESSOR PAIN. ◐

PARADISE KISS

2005. TV series. DIR: Osamu Kobayashi. SCR: Osamu Kobayashi. DES: Nobuteru Yuki. ANI: Nobuteru Yuki, Yuichi Tanaka, Akiko Asaki, Hiroyuki Hashimoto. MUS: Hiroaki Sano. PRD: Madhouse, Twinkle, Fuji TV. 25 mins. x 12 eps.
Teenager Yukari thinks that she spends her whole life trying to live up to the expectations of her pushy mother. Her life of books and constant studying is interrupted by the not entirely unwelcome attentions of a group of fashion students, who think that she would make an ideal model for their clothes label, the titular Paradise Kiss. She initially refuses their offer, although they are able to blackmail her into her first show by threatening to reveal the

identity of her secret crush, which they have discovered by reading her mislaid notebook. With friends like these, who needs enemies?

Yukari begins to hang out at a bar with the bad boy, the pretty boy, the mysterious girl, and the one who is supposed to be cute. Before long, however, she begins to appreciate that these people are more than just another rack of off-the-peg schoolday archetypes, there is more to life than school, and that even if these misfits are not behaving conventionally, they are nevertheless choosing their own path. In becoming their muse, Yukari is inspired to become her own person. Combining the fashion obsessions of COSPLAY COMPLEX or MON CHERIE COCO with the questionable associates of BOYS OVER FLOWERS, this series is actually a sequel of sorts to TV Asahi's NEIGHBORHOOD STORY, and is similarly based on a manga by Ai Yazawa. The closing theme of the Japanese broadcast is "Do You Want To?" by Franz Ferdinand, liable to secure more interest from outside anime fandom than one might normally expect—compare to INTERSTELLA 5555.

PARADISE WITHOUT STARS

1991. JPN: *Hoshikuzu Paradise*. Video. DIR: Masato Namiki. SCR: Takuya Kubo. DES: Fumio Sasaki. ANI: Fumio Sasaki. MUS: Takeshi Kusao. PRD: OB Planning, Pastel. 55 mins.
A love comedy about Hiroshi, a normal teenage boy who discovers after his mother's death that his real father is a famous singer. Moving in with his new-found parent, Hiroshi must cope with having a stepmother who is closer in age to himself than her husband, and who until the previous week, he used to fantasize about whenever he saw her on TV. Based on a *Shonen Sunday* manga by Katsu-Aki, who would also draw the manga adaptation of ESCAFLOWNE several years later. ◐

PARANOIA AGENT *

2004. JPN: *Moso Dairinin*. AKA: *Paranoia*. TV series. DIR: Satoshi Kon. SCR:

Seishi Minakami, Tomomi Yoshino. DES: Masashi Ando. ANI: Akiko Asaki, Hideki Hamazu, Mamoru Sasaki, Toshiyuki Inoue, Satoru Utsunomiya, Hisashi Eguchi, Tadashi Hiramatsu. MUS: Susumu Hirasawa. PRD: Madhouse, WOWOW. 25 mins. x 13 eps.
Detectives Keiichi Ikari and Mitsuhiro Maniwa are assigned to the case of Tsukiko Saki, the designer of a popular cute animal character in the style of HELLO KITTY, who has been the victim of a vicious attack. They are not the only people on Tsukiko's trail; so, too, is tabloid journalist Akio, although he soon falls prey to the same criminal. The attacker is "Li'l Slugger," a shadowy vigilante wielding a battered metal bat (some might say, a GOLDEN BAT), who stalks a series of victims in a dark and forbidding Tokyo. What the investigators fail to realize is that they may not be hunting a single human at all, but a complex social malaise, starting with one small exaggeration that gets progressively larger until the victims' stories of a baseball bat and golden in-line skates feed an urban myth that rampages out of control. Is the kid real, or is he called into being by the stress, unease, and sheer paranoia of living in the big city?

The first TV project from Satoshi Kon is a masterpiece of urban legend, combining the psychological knots of Kon's earlier PERFECT BLUE and the perverted gamesmanship of David Fincher's *Se7en* (1995). Kon exploits the longer running time of TV for all it's worth, setting up supposedly disconnected events that soon reveal a mortifying ripple effect. What at first seems to be a simple police procedural soon gains new complexity. The viewer's attention is drawn first to clues in the background and script, such as the relationship of character names to phases of the moon or the names of animals hidden in their names. This, too, is a red herring, as later episodes reveal *PA* to be an involved meditation on the futility of false hopes and sanitized dreams. As with *Perfect Blue* and MILLENNIUM ACTRESS, *PA* often makes the entertainment industry itself the subject of its ire, with suspicious deaths at an anime studio and later satirical references to superheroics. But Kon also homes in on more general modern issues, opening with crowds of commuters in the style of GANTZ, each studiously ignoring the other while yammering inanities on a mobile phone to a distant listener. Asides and moments in each episode point to a series of unseen connections between the characters in the style of HUMAN CROSSING, particularly with relation to an Internet chatroom in which three buddies make a suicide pact, only for one of them to turn out not to be a dying man, but a young girl—shades here of Hiroshi Shimizu's movie *Ikinai* (1998). Kon also loves postmodern angles on familiar clichés, focusing in one episode on a day in the life of a cop whose main contribution will be to apprehend a character later on. **LV**

PARAPPA THE RAPPER

2001. JPN: *Para Parappa*. TV series. DIR: Hiroaki Sakurai. SCR: N/C. DES: Rodney Alan Greenblat, Takayuki Goto. ANI: N/C. MUS: Masaya Matsuura. PRD: JC Staff, Production IG, Fuji TV. 25 mins. x N/D eps.

The adventures of a happy dancing dog in his ongoing attempts to impress a flower called Sunny. Based on the surreal 1996 PlayStation game, the series features new characters and music from the original designers.

PARASITE HEAVEN

1996. JPN: *Isoro Tengoku*. AKA: *Homestay Heaven; Heaven of a Hanger-on*. Video. DIR: Teruo Kigure. SCR: Satoshi Aoyama. DES: Teru Aranaga. ANI: Kazuyoshi Ota. MUS: N/C. PRD: Beam Entertainment. 30 mins., 40 mins.

Eighteen-year-old Masahiko Kisugi is sent to stay with his Aunt Mizuhara so he can study at a nearby college. In an erotic anime based on the manga by Teru Aranaga in *Comic Lies* magazine, he soon begins an affair with his aunt, and with her three daughters. **N**

PARASOL HENBE

1989. JPN: *Parasol Henbe*. TV series. DIR: Masakazu Higuchi, Takami Fujikawa, Shigeru Fujikawa, Masaya Mizutani, Yugo Serikawa. SCR: Megumi Sugiwara, Aya Matsui, Satoru Akahori. DES: Motoo Abiko. ANI: Takao Yamazaki. MUS: Reijiro Komutsu. PRD: Fujiko Studio, NHK. 8 mins. x 109 eps.

Japanese boy Megeru meets Henbe, a strange hippo-like creature from another world. Henbe and his trademark magical parasol have many adventures with Megeru in this series for the very young, with episode titles such as *I Can't Stand the Rain, A Broadcast from Parasol World, A Butterfly from Another World*, and *The Flying Bicycle*. Based on a manga by BILLY DOG–creator Fujiko-Fujio "A," and featuring the screenwriting debut of Satoru Akahori, whose "zany" output would dominate comedy anime for the coming decade.

PASTEL YUMI

1986. JPN: *Maho no Idol Pastel Yumi*. AKA: *Magical Idol Pastel Yumi*. TV series. DIR: Akira Torino, Yutaka Kagawa, Hiroshi Yoshida, Mitsuru Hongo, Toshio Okabe, Miho Maruo, Kazuyoshi Katayama. SCR: Shoji Imai, Azuma Tachibana, Yoshiyuki Suga, Yoshihisa Araki. DES: Yumiko Hirosawa. ANI: Yumiko Hirosawa. MUS: Koji Makaino. PRD: Studio Pierrot, Nippon TV. 25 mins. x 25 eps.

Schoolgirl Yumi Hanazono lives happily with her parents. She loves nature and all living things. On carnival day, two little imps called Keshimaru and Kakimaru give her a magic baton and a magic ring; anything she draws in the air now becomes real. Using their power, she can transform into the magical idol Pastel Yumi. Another magical-girl story from the people who brought you CREAMY MAMI.

PATALIRO

1982. JPN: *Pataliro! Boku Pataliro!* AKA: *Pataliro! I'm Pataliro!*. TV series, movie. DIR: Nobutaka Nishizawa, Satoshi Hisaoka, Yugo Serikawa, Hiroshi Shidara, Yasuo Yamakichi. SCR: Masaki

Tsuji, Akiyoshi Sakai, Tomomi Tsutsui, Tomoko Konparu. DES: Mineo Maya. ANI: Yasunori Kanemori. MUS: Nozomu Aoki. PRD: Toei, Fuji TV. 25 mins. x 49 eps. (TV1), 48 mins. (m), ca. 9 mins. x 24 eps. (TV2), ca. 9 mins. x 2 eps. (v). Based on Mineo Maya's 1978 manga in *Hana to Yume* magazine, the series was the first to introduce homosexuality to TV anime audiences, and the nudity is reasonably tasteful (allowing for some floral backgrounds) and mostly male. A fantastical plot revolves around Jack Bankolan, a former British agent licensed to kill, who has somehow ended up working on the fabulously wealthy diamond-trading South Sea island of Marinera as a nursemaid to Pataliro VIII, the superpowered brat who is head of state. The joke is that this 007 is gay and the foes he faces are gorgeous men, transposing the machismo of the Bond mythos into lighthearted camp. Originally called just *Pataliro!*, the longer version of the title was used from episode 27 on. Nishizawa's movie, *Pataliro: Stardust Project* (1983), featured the titular plan by the international Tarantella crime syndicate to raid Marinera's diamond vaults. Typically, they send in an advance assassin to remove Bankolan, but the tall, handsome Andersen instead falls in love with his quarry. Kenichi Maejima's *Pataliro Saiyuki* (2005) remodeled the characters as the cast of JOURNEY TO THE WEST. **N**

PATLABOR *

1989. JPN: *Kido Keisatsu Patlabor*. AKA: *Mobile Police Patlabor*. Video, TV series, movies. DIR: Mamoru Oshii, Naoyuki Yoshinaga, Fumihiko Takayama, Yasunori Urata. SCR: Kazunori Ito, Mamoru Oshii, Michiko Yokote. DES: Akemi Takada, Yukata Izubuchi, Hiroki Takagi, Yoshinori Sayama. ANI: Hiroki Takagi, Hiroyuki Kitakubo, Kisaraka Yamada. MUS: Kenji Kawai. PRD: Headgear, Sunrise, Nippon TV. 30 mins. x 7 eps., 30 mins. x 16 eps. (video), 25 mins. x 47 eps. (TV), 118 mins. (m1), 113 mins. (m2).

At the close of the 20th century, a rise

Patlabor

in global sea levels forces a massive building program in Japan, causing the creation of new "labor" construction robots. In a series that effortlessly incorporates human drama and comedy with hard science fiction, the police set up a Pat[rol] Labor division to deal with the new crime that the new technology brings.

The team behind *Patlabor* is arguably the finest assembly of talents in modern anime, rivaled only by Hayao Miyazaki's cohorts at Studio Ghibli and the erratic Gainax collective. Written in direct opposition to the gung ho conflicts of GUNDAM and the postapocalyptic violence of *The Road Warrior*, *Patlabor*'s creators posit a future world where humanity muddles through regardless, and being a giant-robot pilot is just another job—taken, as with the space-force in WINGS OF HONNEAMISE, by misfits unable to secure work in more glamorous sectors. The tribulations of Special Vehicle Division 2 are consequently dogged by idle bureaucrats, budget cuts, interfering R&D officers, and feuds within the group. Girlish rookie Noa Izumi, disaffected techno-millionaire's son Azuma Shinohara, and ultracool Captain Goto occupy central stage, though the other cast members are some of the most well-realized characters in anime. From bad-tempered gun-nut

Ota to henpecked husband Shinshi, down to the gentle giant Hiromi and competent-but-snooty half-American visitor Kanuka Clancy (whose role was greatly expanded from the original manga), all contribute to a truly marvelous ensemble. The series is loaded with subplots that put many live-action shows to shame, including the unrequited love of Goto for his better-qualified opposite number Shinobu (hilariously telegraphed in a spoof episode that featured the pair forced to share a room in a love hotel), Ota's desperately lonely existence (in a *Blade Runner* pastiche scripted by Oshii), and Noa's deeply respectful love for her "pet" labor Alphonse. Made on video because sponsorship was initially unavailable to make it for TV, the show was soon heading for broadcast and movie success. Some of the TV and video stories are downright goofy, like the white-alligator-in-the-sewers urban myth and a ghost story with spirits that need to be appeased; but there's also a long and carefully evolved story line about industrial espionage between rival labor manufacturers, the exploitation of children, and the lengths people go to for money.

Theatrical outings extend this dark agenda further. *Patlabor: The Movie* (1990), directed by Oshii, uses a threat of destruction by a suicidal vision-

ary terrorist to examine the extent to which man depends on technology and the dangers involved in that dependency. Noa and the returning American labor captain Kanuka have to overcome their antagonism to save Tokyo from flood and disaster. *Patlabor 2* (1993) rounded off the series in a brilliantly contrived manner. Set in 2002, after the original team members have gone their separate ways, it features the attempt of a disaffected ex-soldier to orchestrate a military coup. The former members of the Patlabor team reunite one last time to stop him, and the film includes some real treats for long-term fans, including an explanation for Shinobu's eternal spinsterhood and the rare sight of Goto losing his temper. The second movie secured Oshii's chances of directing GHOST IN THE SHELL and shares with its successor a similar mood, pace, and political cynicism. It also features chilling images of a Japan returning all too swiftly to martial law, a topic that Oshii would approach again in JIN-ROH, as well as "guest" designs from Shoji Kawamori and Hajime Katoki.

Christophe Gans, who directed the live-action movie of CRYING FREEMAN, has reportedly optioned *Patlabor 2* for a remake, impressed with its ability to involve its cast in action to which they always seem to arrive a minute too late. This marginalization of the "little people" is a motif that runs through the entire series and adds to the realism. It is also a fundamental feature of the third *Patlabor* movie *WXIII* (2002), in which Tokyo is threatened by a mutant monster. With Oshii conspicuously absent as director (as he was from the inferior *Jin-Roh*), *WXIII* retells an early story from Masami Yuki's *Patlabor* manga but concentrates on the "guest stars," relegating the central cast almost completely to cameo roles.

Sadly for *Patlabor*, accidents in rights acquisitions have had a similar effect on the series itself. The two movies were well dubbed and promoted by Manga Entertainment but reached a far larger audience than the video and TV incarnations, which were sold to the smaller distributor USMC. The series was also lampooned in the erotic pastiche TOKIO PRIVATE POLICE.

PAUL'S MIRACLE WAR

1976. JPN: *Paul no Miracle Dai-sakusen*. AKA: *Paul's Miraculous Adventures*. TV series. DIR: Hiroshi Sasakawa, Mizuho Nishikubo. SCR: Junzo Toriumi, Masaru Yamamoto. DES: Akiko Shimomoto. ANI: Hayao Nobe. MUS: Shunsuke Kikuchi. PRD: Tatsunoko Pro, Fuji TV. 25 mins. x 50 eps.
Little Paul has a very special cuddly toy—Pakkun is really a spirit from an alternate world under threat from the evil invader Belt Satan. Pakkun has come in search of help from Earth, and Paul is obliged to get involved when Belt Satan kidnaps his friend Nina. This charming series is hardly in the traditional science-fiction mold of the studio known as the "home of heroes," but for younger viewers, it's magic.

PEACEMAKER KUROGANE *

2003. AKA: *Peacemaker; Peacemaker: Gunning For Trouble*. TV series. DIR: Tomohiro Hirata. SCR: Naoko Hasegawa, Hiroshi Yamaguchi. DES: Akemi Hayashi. ANI: Tadashi Hiramatsu. MUS: Keiichi Oku. PRD: Gonzo Digimation, Imagica, TV Asahi. 25 mins. x 24 eps.
In the 1860s, as disorder and unrest signify the imminent fall of the Tokugawa Shogunate and the end of the Edo period, an elite military corps of skilled and ruthless swordsmen becomes a major force in Kyoto. When 15-year-old Tetsunosuke Ichimura's parents are killed by Choshu revolutionaries, he and his elder brother Tatsunosuke join the Shinsengumi, the elite band of warriors in Kyoto. Employed as a page to Toshizo Hijikata, he vows to acquire the skills to avenge his parents' murder. Vice Commander Hijikata is a stern, seemingly cold leader. His underling, Captain Souji Okita is a complete contrast, a cheerful, laid-back type—until he unsheathes his sword, when he shows

himself to be the deadliest fighter of them all. The diminutive Tetsunosuke is reckless, unsophisticated, and often mistaken for someone younger than his years. He befriends another orphan, Suzu Ichimura, not realizing that their lives mirror each other, since Suzu's parents were killed by the Shinsengumi. Ichimura senior was devoted to peace; the man who brought about his death was devoted to political reform, and in that cause he is willing to do anything, even burn Kyoto to the ground.

Drawing, like SHINSENGUMI FARCE, on real historical events, director Hirata focuses on a very minor character from history, using Tetsunosuke as a sort of everyman, in much the same way as TREE IN THE SUN, exemplifying the need to find one's own center in the confusion and danger of life in interesting times. A number of famous people play roles in the story—including Ryoma Sakamoto of OI RYOMA!, who appears under an alias and wearing dreadlocks in a manner more befitting SAMURAI CHAMPLOO, and Sanosuke Harada and Hajime Saito, who also show up in RURO NI KENSHIN—but, just as in life, great events and political change occupy Tetsunosuke's mind far less than his personal concerns. A mix of broad comedy, violent action, and vivid characterization helps maintain interest in the journey of the sympathetic but not very original young hero, with his height hang-up, attitude problem, and thirst for revenge, allied to the perky klutziness of a magical-girl show heroine.

Based on the manga by Nanae Chrono, the anime's soft, earthy color palette gives a period feel without looking too much like a history lesson. After this show, the Gonzo studio stayed with the martial theme for SAMURAI 7. It represents a return to swordplay for designer and animation director Hayashi, whose resumé of gentler shows like FRUITS BASKET also includes a stint on UTENA. The DVD box in some territories left the *Kurogane* part of the title in Japanese, lead-

ing many to assume that the title was simply *Peacemaker*, with an inscrutable squiggle next to it. **Ⓥ**

PEACH-COLORED SISTERS

1998. JPN: *Momoiro Sisters*. TV series. DIR: Bob Shirahata. SCR: Satoru Akahori, Satoru Akahori Office. DES: Masaaki Kawanami, Tomoko Kosaka. ANI: N/C. MUS: N/C. PRD: Studio Deen, TBS. 7 mins. x 24 eps.
A love comedy about Momoko ("peach girl"), a hapless 17-year-old who can't seem to snare herself a man, and whose Office Lady sister is very little help at all. Broadcast as part of the *Wonderful* program on TBS, this series of shorts was originally based on a 1993 manga by Tamami Momose. **Ⓝ**

PEACOCK KING *

1988. JPN: *Kujaku-o; Shin Kujaku-o*. Video. DIR: Katsuhito Akiyama, Ichiro Itano, Rintaro. SCR: Noboru Aikawa, Hajime Inaba, Tatsuhiko Urahata. DES: Takuya Wada, Takahiro Kishida, Ken Koike. ANI: Masahiro Tanaka, Takahiro Kishida. MUS: Satoru Kogura, Kit Kat Club, Yas-Kaz, Toshiyuki Honda. PRD: AIC, Studio 88, Madhouse. 55 mins., 60 mins., 50 mins., 45 mins. x 2 eps. (*True PK*).
Kujaku is a young monk and an avatar, the incarnation of a god. His friend and cute blonde fellow-avatar Ashura, his teacher Ajari, and the leather-clad biker/magic master Onimaru band together to fight the demons released by Tatsuma from the ancient temple statues at Nara. Tatsuma is a powerful psychic, but he's never learned proper control of his abilities, and in seeking to test his powers, he puts humankind in terrible danger in the first episode, *Feast for Returning Demons*. In the second story, *Castle of Illusion*, Onimaru and graduate student Hatsuko are the sole survivors of a team digging up relics of medieval warlord and supposed black magician Nobunaga Oda (see YOTODEN). If the two scrolls found by the team are joined, Azuchi Castle will rise again and the warlord will unleash hell on Earth. For the third story,

Harvest of Cherry Blossoms, the threat is undead shogun Ieyasu Tokugawa, who has joined forces with the restless ghost of an actress murdered during WWII and intends to sink Japan beneath the waves.

The story of Kujaku-myo'o (to some esoteric Buddhist sects, a manifestation of Gautama Buddha often depicted riding on a giant peacock) was updated by Makoto Ogino for his 1985 manga in *Young Jump*, using the idea of avatars of the gods as inspiration for a modern-day adventure. The franchise returned as *True PK* (1994, *Shin Kujaku-o*), more faithful to Ogino's original, and it replaced the Madhouse-lookalike animation of AIC with *actual* animation from the Madhouse studio itself, under veteran director Rintaro. His versions throw much of their budget into the movie-quality opening scenes, creating impressive images that soon devolve into less expensive animation. Trawling outside Japan for villains, it features twin avatars, a boy and a girl, born to reincarnate god of light Kujaku-o and god of darkness Tenja-o. The boy, Akira, is a member of a Buddhist sect charged with guarding the Dragon Grail, a mystic vessel that has the power to release Tenja-o into the world. Power-crazed neo-Nazi Siegfried von Mittgard plans to steal the grail and reincarnate himself as Tenja-oh; this will prevent Akira's twin, Tomoko, from fulfilling her destiny, but Siegfried has another role in mind for her.

Like the director's earlier **DOOMED MEGALOPOLIS**, *PK* suffers in English simply through the weight of the original source material—American actors, working with the Japanese names for the Chinese versions of Buddhist takes on Hindu gods, create a predictably confusing roster, though translators Bill Flanagan and Yuko Sato make a heroic effort to incorporate the original Sanskrit. A live-action Japanese–Hong Kong coproduction, *PK: Legend of the Phoenix* (1988), was directed by **STORY OF RIKI**'s Nam Nai Choi and starred martial-arts legend Yuen Biao.

Another Kujaku appears in CLAMP's **RG VEDA**. ⬤Ⓛ🅝Ⓥ

PEKKLE *

1993. JPN: *Ahiru no Pekkle*. AKA: *Pekkle the Duck*. Video. DIR: Akira Shimizu. SCR: Mitsukuni Kumagai. DES: Toshikazu Ishiwatari. ANI: Takashi Asakura, Kennosuke Tokuda. MUS: Yasunori Honda. PRD: Sanrio. 30 mins. x 4 eps.

Another of Sanrio's cute kiddie characters, this time a sweet little duck, accompanied by his girlfriend, Ruby, reenacts tales from the **ARABIAN NIGHTS** for his U.S. video release—*PtD: Aladdin and the Magic Lamp* and *PtD: Sindbad the Sailor*. The final two adventures, unreleased in the U.S., were the shark-infested *PtD: Trouble at the Swimming Gala* and the *Indiana Jones* pastiche *PtD: In Search of the Secret Treasure*. The character, however, was a lame duck when compared to the successes of his Sanrio stablemate **HELLO KITTY**.

PELICAN ROAD CLUB CULTURE

1986. JPN: *Pelican Road Club Culture*. Video. DIR: Eiichi Yamamoto. SCR: Eiichi Yamamoto. DES: Koichi Igarashi. ANI: Kazuhiko Udagawa. MUS: Kazuo Kogure. PRD: Studio World, Nippon Columbia. 55 mins.

High school boy Kenichi Watanabe is crazy about his MBX50 motorcycle. He and his buddies organize a motorcycle club, which they call Culture. In among the engine oil and spark plugs, however, they begin to learn that there's more to life than bikes, chiefly when they are approached by reporter Kanako, who is interested in their stories . . . particularly Kenichi's. Based on Koichi Igarashi's 1982 manga *Pelican Road*, which was a contemporary of **BOMBER BIKERS OF SHONAN** in the same *Shonen King* magazine.

PENDANT

1997. JPN: *Pendant*. Video. DIR: Yoshihiro Oka. SCR: Kaori Nakase, Takao Nitta. DES: Masaki Takei. ANI: Akio Watanabe. MUS: N/C. PRD: Beam Entertainment. 30 mins. x 3 eps.

Tales of young love, based on a computer game by Masaki Takei, creator of **END OF SUMMER**, starting with a lonely summer holiday enlivened by a chance meeting of an old flame and building up to a romantic "climax" on Christmas Eve. Unlike many adaptations of games that simply dump a male protagonist into a sea of women in the style of **TENCHI MUYO!**, this one separates the various female characters into separate stories with different male love interests, which is slightly more realistic, if no less boring. Ⓝ

PENGUINS MEMORY

1985. JPN: *Penguins Memory Shiawase Monogatari*. AKA: *Penguins Memory Happy Tale*. Movie. DIR: Satoshi Kimura. SCR: Hiroshi Kawano, Ryo Yamazaki, Rei Kuno, Dodekagon. DES: Ginjiro Suzuki. ANI: Norio Hikone, Akinori Nagaoka. MUS: Seiko Matsuda. PRD: Animation Staff Room, CM Land. 101 mins.

Mike, a traumatized penguin who once fought in the Delta War, returns to his hometown of Lake City and takes a job as a librarian. He falls in love with Jill, a would-be singing penguin who is the daughter of the owner of the local penguin hospital. Jill meets a record producer and embarks on a successful career, but Mike waddles away alone—he has discovered that she is engaged to marry Jack the penguin doctor, and he doesn't wish to get in the way.

A film made to cash in on the unexpected popularity of a 1984 series of Suntory Beer commercials that replayed famous American films such as *Casablanca* and *The Deer Hunter* but with a cast of cartoon penguins.

PEPELO, BOY OF THE ANDES

1975. JPN: *Andes Shonen Pepelo no Boken*. AKA: *Adventures of Pepelo the Andes Boy*. TV series. DIR: Kazuhiko Udagawa, Yasuo Hasegawa, Seiji Okada, Takashi Anno, Fumio Ikeno. SCR: Shunichi Yukimuro, Soji Yoshikawa, Masaji Tsuji. DES: Yasuhiro Okaoi. ANI: Moriyasu Taniguchi, Yasuhiro Okaoi. MUS: Takeo Yamashita. PRD: Wako, Telescreen, NET (TV Asahi). 25 mins. x 26 eps.

In the 19th century, Pepelo's father sets off to find the mythical city of Eldorado and the Golden Condor, said to lie in Central America. When he hasn't returned a year later, Pepelo sets out to find him. On the way, Pepelo joins forces with Titicaca, an old man, Quena, a girl who has lost her memory, and an Aztecan boy called Azteco. They walk into the Andes using only a condor talisman as a guide. With a certain resemblance to FROM THE APENNINES TO THE ANDES, this series was a reasonable success in Europe, but largely eclipsed seven years later by MYSTERIOUS CITIES OF GOLD, which revisited many of its themes. Perhaps the strangest name on the credits, though, is lyricist Kazuo Umezu, who went on to fame as a writer of gory manga like THE BOY WITH CAT'S EYES.

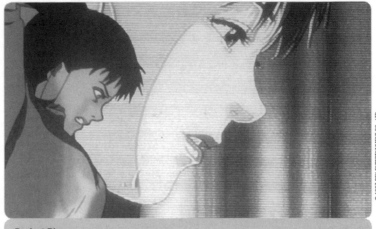

Perfect Blue

© 1997 REX ENTERTAINMENT CO., LTD.

PERFECT BLUE *

1997. Movie. DIR: Satoshi Kon. SCR: Sadayuki Murai. DES: Hisashi Eguchi, Hideki Hamazu, Satoshi Kon. ANI: Hideki Hamazu, Hisao Shirai. MUS: Masahiro Ikumi. PRD: Madhouse, Oniro. 82 mins.

Singer Mima Kirigoe leaves the pop trio Cham to become a serious actress. Her change in careers causes a slow decline into insanity, as forces conspire to keep her from changing her public persona, to the extent of interfering directly in her private life. Matters aren't helped by a murderous stalker, egged on by e-mails from someone claiming to be the real Mima. Eventually, Mima's hold on reality is thoroughly undermined as she sinks into the mother of all neuroses. And she's not on her own—this film is told from the viewpoints of three characters, and each one of them is going slowly insane.

Based on a novel by Yoshikazu Takeuchi and originally planned as a live-action film, *PB* features obvious influences from Hitchcock's *Vertigo* (1958), *Stage Fright* (1950), and Dario Argento's *Suspiria* (1977), but it has ultimately a less bleak and more humane agenda. Murai's script, which adds the film-within-a-film *Double Bind*

to really confuse matters, remains one of anime's best since Kazunori Ito's for PATLABOR. The obsessive fan stalker, who was merely a red herring in the novel, is given a succession of *actual* murders to perform in the anime version, though the blurred line between fantasy and reality is one of *PB*'s greatest achievements—the director deliberately cut all transition shots that signified dream sequences or flashbacks, leaving the audience floundering in a confused world cleverly matching the protagonists' own. Kon, the former animator on the surreal JOJO'S BIZARRE ADVENTURES who created environments full of faux-live-action clutter in ROUJIN Z, makes a virtue of a limited animation budget, depicting crowd scenes with empty faces and playing up the ghostly pallor of fluorescent lighting. The cinematography is gorgeous, as loving a rendition of real-life contemporary Tokyo as the dark, glittering forward-projection of the city in AKIRA (whose creator Katsuhiro Otomo has a production credit for introducing the producers to his protégé Kon, although some press releases implied his involvement in *PB* was far greater). The increasing influence of the Internet and cyber-reality on mass perceptions is seriously examined here (and further explored on TV in SERIAL EXPERIMENTS LAIN), but *PB* is also strong

on traditional story values—beautifully paced plot development and a craftsman's ability to subvert the conventions of the medium. Most notable and controversial remains a scene in which Mima's character is raped, played out as a pastiche of *The Accused* (1988) but continually taunting the viewer with the question of whether *this* time it is really for real. The prosaic movements of lights and camera, and the whispered apologies of the actor playing one of the rapists who has to stay in position during a shooting break, heighten the surreality precisely because they remind us that Mima is being assaulted in a "respectable" professional context—later in the movie, she is attacked for real.

The English version is excellent despite some inevitable losses in translation. Japan may look like every other modern, industrialized, media-led country, but both language and social interaction are hugely important in this tale of fishes out of water. Some of the bowing, scraping, and statement of the obvious (culturally, an attempt to ingratiate oneself by appearing more clueless than the next person) just seems insincere with American voices. Mima's oft-repeated "Who are you?" loses some of its clout when lip-synching considerations force the actress to add a mitigating "Excuse me." The English dub also loses an extra level of emphasis—two scenes when Mima slips into her native dialect, demonstrating to the Japanese audience that not even the girl we see in private is the real Mima. The city girl-next-door whom the fans worship is actually another mask—a pretty country maid who forgets her elocution lessons when Mom phones from back home. This shift is also heard in the film's final line, when Mima announces that she is "herself" at last (and uses her native accent, not the well-spoken Tokyo dialect she's been taught to use on TV). Despite these minor cavils, *PB* remains one of the best anime of the late 1990s. The remake rights were optioned by director Darren Aronofsky, who lifted a shot from the film (of Mima crouching in her bathtub) for his live-action movie *Requiem for a Dream* (2000). Director Kon and writer Murai would return with another peek behind dramatic masks: MILLENNIUM ACTRESS. Sequences from *PB* were shown onstage by Madonna as part of her Drowned World concerts in 2001. The live-action movie *Perfect Blue: If This Is a Dream Wake Me Up* (2002) is based on a later book in the series, and not the one that informed the anime production. **L N V**

PET SHOP OF HORRORS *

1998. TV. DIR: Toshio Hirata, Norihiko Nagahama, Yoshiaki Kawajiri, Satoshi Nishimura. SCR: Yasuhiro Imagawa, Matsuri Akino. DES: Hisashi Abe, Hiroshi Kato. ANI: Hisashi Abe. MUS: N/C. PRD: Madhouse, TBS. 25 mins. x 4 eps.
In Chinatown, in a generic U.S. city (on the Japanese release, *Newtype* magazine claimed it was New York, but *Animage* and *AX* both noted the visual references to Los Angeles), "Count D," a fey Faustian pet shop owner, sells personified desires as "pets" to society's misfits, including a mother who refuses to accept that her own weak will turned her daughter into a drug addict, a faithless husband who cannot admit he drove his bride to suicide, and a proud gangster who wants people to fear his power. Signing deceptively simple contracts, they discover that deals made

with the supernatural should never be taken lightly. Leon, a loud-mouth cop who encapsulates several anime stereotypes of Americans, is convinced that the count is up to something, but the count is strangely welcoming and hospitable toward him. The "horrors" happen when purchasers ignore the strict instructions provided for the care of the unusual creatures they buy—*Gremlins* parallels are obvious. Old meets new and East meets West, not just in the mixture of mythologies, but in the mismatched central characters. Everyday laws cannot touch these criminals, but the count cuts through the red tape and delivers punishment where Leon cannot, without fear or favor toward a would-be president, or even a child star prepared to sell his soul for adult fame. Though our wise-acre policeman is too boneheaded to realize it, the count is on his side, transforming the story from a humdrum chiller into a moral *X-Files*, in which hell's own angel teams up with an earthy cop to mete out peculiar justice.

Matsuri Akino's original 1990 manga ran for over a dozen volumes in *Mitzi Comics DX*, and yet this 1999 TBS series was never planned as more than four episodes. Limited animation is bolstered by flashy effects (from some big names, including DOOMED MEGALOPOLIS–director Rintaro on the opening animation), but the biggest mystery is why there was no more. Perhaps wisely, the show canceled itself before the "sin of the week" angle could become too predictable. Compare to similar rough justice in JUDGE. **V**

PETER PAN AND WENDY *

1989. JPN: *Peter Pan no Boken*. AKA: *Peter Pan's Adventure*. TV series. DIR: Yoshio Kuroda, Fumio Kurokawa, Kozo Kusuba. SCR: Shunichi Yukimuro, Michiru Shimada. DES: Takashi Nakamura, Shohei Kawamoto. ANI: Hirotsuge Kawasaki, Tomihiko Okubo, Moriyasu Taniguchi. MUS: Toshiyuki Watanabe. PRD: Nippon Animation, Fuji TV. 25 mins. x 41 eps.
J.M. Barrie's 1911 novel is given a new

twist as Wendy, *not* wanting to grow up, travels with her two little brothers and Peter Pan to Never Land where he must fight the terrible pirate leader Captain Hook and face many other perils, including Darkness, an evil sorcerer who joins forces with Hook. Nakamura's presence may surprise those who know him only from AKIRA and ROBOT CARNIVAL, as would that of future SPRIGGAN-director Kawasaki. A compilation video of the first three episodes was released in the U.K. on an obscure children's label, featuring new music from Haim Saban and Shuki Levy.

PETITE COSSETTE *

2004. JPN: *Cossette no Shozo; Le Portrait de Petit* [sic] *Cossette*. AKA: *Portrait of Little Cossette*. Video. DIR: Akiyuki Shinbo. SCR: Mayori Sekijima. DES: Hirofumi Suzuki. ANI: Hirofumi Suzuki. MUS: Yuki Kajiura. PRD: Aniplex, Studio Hibari. 38 mins. x 3 eps.
Art student Eiri Kurahashi works part-time in his uncle's Tokyo antique shop, where he finds an antique Venetian glass goblet in which he can see visions of a beautiful young girl with long blonde hair. Her name is Cossette d'Auvergne and she's been dead for 250 years. She's looking for someone to help her—a man with the courage to risk everything, even his own life, to release her from her prison. Eiri's friends start to notice he's acting strangely; previously his life has been bound up with his art, and though he has lots of female friends there hasn't been a special girl. He becomes completely absorbed by his visions and fantasies, losing track of where his life ends and Cossette's begins. His best friend Shoko Mataki is so concerned that her aunt, the local doctor, gets involved, along with tarot reader Michiru and priestess Shakodo. Meanwhile Yu, a young girl with latent talents and a secret crush on Eiri, is drawn into Cossette's dangerous web. Her sweet face hides a calculating heart and an insatiable lust for vengeance. Eiri can only free her by atoning for the

betrayal of her former lover through a blood pact, swearing to love her and her alone and taking on another's soul—compare to similar entrapment in MEMORIES.

Putting a Gothic spin on both the harem show and the magical girlfriend theme reprised in MOON PHASE the following year, *PC* plays elegantly at darkness and foreboding. The three video episodes were edited together into a TV movie, *Le Portrait de Petit Cossette*, in 2005. Based on the manga by Asuka Katsura in *Magazine Z*. Part of the relatively recent "Gothic Lolita" subgenre of anime, based on the fashion fad of the same name, also found in ROZEN MAIDEN and MOON PHASE.

PETITE PRINCESS YUCIE *
2002. JPN: *Petit Puri[ncess] Yushi*. TV series. DIR: Masahiko Otsuka. SCR: Hiroyuki Yamaga. DES: Kazuko Tadano. ANI: Hideaki Anno, Mitsuro Obunai, Tadashi Hiramatsu. MUS: Seiko Nagaoka. PRD: Gainax, AIC, NHK. 25 mins. x 26 eps.
Yucie lives long ago and far away, in a Ruritanian magical land with her foster father and the family's young but fiercely loyal butler, Cube. She's 17 years old, but because of a magical curse, she looks like a 10-year-old girl—compare to NANAKA 6/17. Her positive attitude makes her seem even cuter and perkier—she never lets anything get her down, although she desperately wants to look her real age and become a beautiful, elegant lady with a handsome husband of her own. She has the chance to make her dreams come true when she's chosen as a Petite Princess, one of the elite girls from many different realms who will be trained in the ways of femininity and elegance. If she can defeat the competition, she may even become the Platinum Princess, and win the prize of a magic tiara that will grant her any wish—no prizes for guessing what Yucie's wish will be.

Takami Akai, who created the *Princess Maker* game series in which Cube first appeared, isn't about to let

a winning concept drop. Crashing the countless fairy tales of enchanted princesses into every little girl's impatience to acquire those arcane skills that define a grown-up woman, she's produced the finishing school version of DRAGON BALL. Our heroine is trying to find her true self. Along the way, just like Toriyama's perky hero Son Goku, she makes loyal friends and converts former enemies to friendship.

PETOPETO-SAN
2005. TV series. DIR: Akira Nishimori, Tetsuya Endo, Tamaki Nakatsu, Yasuyuki Shinozaki, Toru Kitahata, Satomi Nakamura, Kenichi Ishikura. SCR: Megumi Ikeno. DES: Mari Tominaga. ANI: Mari Tominaga, Masakazu Iguchi, Hiroyuki Shimizu, Miwa Oshima. MUS: Masami Kurihara. PRD: Xebec M2, TV Saitama. 25 mins. x 13 eps.
After centuries of antagonism and misunderstanding, the Japanese finally welcome "monsters" into their community. In an attempt at species integration, normal children begin attending school with paranormal creatures—see similarly unlikely acceptance of foreigners, sorry, otherworldly creatures, in DEARS. Japanese boy Shingo Ohashi finds himself developing feelings for Hatoko "Petoko" Fujimura, a girl from the sorcerous realm whose main power appears to be the ability to make anything she regards as "cute" cling inescapably to her bare flesh until she falls asleep—compare to URUSEI YATSURA.

PHANTOM BUSTER MIKO
2000. JPN: *Reino Tantei Miko*. AKA: *Spirit Investigator Miko*. Video. DIR: Hiroshi Furuhashi. SCR: Tetsuo Tanaka. DES: Masashi Kojima. ANI: Waki Noguchi. MUS: N/C. PRD: Maxam. 30 mins.
This is a sexually charged variant of the ghostbusting anime typified by PHANTOM QUEST CORP or GHOST SWEEPER MIKAMI, as a sexy exorcist takes on the legions of hell. ◐

PHANTOM HEROES
1991. JPN: *Phantom Yusha Densetsu*.

AKA: *Legend of the Phantom Heroes*. Video. DIR: Satoshi Dezaki. SCR: Kazumi Koide. DES: Keizo Shimizu. ANI: Toshifumi Takizawa. MUS: Kyan Marie with Medusa. PRD: Magic Bus. 45 mins.
Yazawa, a former aircraft carrier F4 Phantom pilot, becomes embroiled in a South American coup when his lover is killed during a CIA operation in El Salvador. A violent thriller based on a best-selling novel by DARK WARRIOR–creator Sho Takejima, this video was rushed out in the year of his untimely death. ◑◆

PHANTOM MASTER
2004. JPN: *Shin Angyo Onshi*. AKA: *Phantom Master—Dark Hero from a Ruined Empire; New History of the Dark Ways*. Movie. DIR: Joji Shimura. SCR: Joji Shimura, Mitsuru Hongo. DES: Hideki Takahashi. ANI: Hideki Takaha-shi. MUS: Ko Otani. PRD: Klockworkz, Oriental Light & Magic, Character Plan. 87 mins.
A Korean-Japanese coproduction based on a Korean comic by author Youn In-Wan and artist Yang Kyung-Il, this is a reversioning of an ancient Asian folktale. In the fictional land of Jushin, the Angyo Onshi are secret agents who roam the land in disguise, rooting out and punishing corrupt officials. Agent Monsu wanders out of the desert into a town where the locals are losing their life forces to a cruel overlord. Justice ensues. The comic was printed in Japan in *Shonen Sunday GX*. ◆

PHANTOM QUEST CORP *
1994. JPN: *Yugen Kaisha*. AKA: *Phantom Company/Limited Company, Private Company*. Video. DIR: Koichi Chigira, Morio Asaka, Takuji Endo. SCR: Asami Watanabe, Tatsuhiko Urahata, Satoshi Kimura. DES: Hitoshi Ueda. ANI: Yasuhito Kikuchi. MUS: Junichi Kanezaki. PRD: Madhouse. 30 mins. x 4 eps.
Ayaka is a modern girl running her own successful business—a freelance psychic agency, supplying the power to deal with any problem. Ayaka is also a hopeless lush who can't stay ahead of her finances, blows all her money on designer clothes and karaoke bars, and

relies on her child butler, Mamoru, to run her home and her life and to make sure she gets up in the morning. The police's own ghostbusting squad, Section U, headed up by a crumpled-but-cute detective with a soft spot for our heroine, causes even more complications. And as for her staff—she's stuck with a dropout priest, a twisted firestarter, a psychic who only works to enhance her meager pension, and her own rich family's hereditary butler.

Like its longer-running contemporary GHOST SWEEPER MIKAMI, *PQC* is packed with gentle digs at what has become of Japan. The money-culture of the late 1980s produced many unreal phenomena of its own (the bubble economy, Generation X) while simultaneously trying to forget the spiritual past. The title, with a double meaning in the real and ghostly worlds, sets the tone for a witty, wacky post-*X-Files* series, but it didn't get the success it deserved at home or abroad. Takuji Endo and Morio Asaka cram their episodes with innovative jerky camera effects to play up the feel of a horror B-movie, just one of the little touches that made *PQC*, but somehow failed to ignite the audience. Other noticeable presences include Yoshiaki Kawajiri as a "guest" director for the striking opening credits and future TENCHI MUYO!–director Kimura as a humble scriptwriter. Creator Juzo Mutsuki has several other underrated series—the similar ancient-meets-modern clashes of DEVIL HUNTER YOHKO and CYBER CITY OEDO 808. The dub from Pioneer is of high quality, and even boasts a hilarious English-language version of one of Ayaka's excruciatingly melancholy karaoke sessions—the single thirtysomething modern girl singing a widow's song that likens herself to "a riderless horse."

PHANTOM: THE ANIMATION *
2004. AKA: *Phantom of Inferno*. Video. DIR: Keitaro Motonaga. SCR: Shoji Harimura. DES: Koji Watanabe. ANI: N/C. MUS: N/C. PRD: KSS, Earth Create. 30 mins. x 3 eps.

Teenage tourist Reiji Agatsuma accidentally runs across pretty girl assassin Ai (codenamed Ein, aka Phantom) while out late at night on the streets of Los Angeles. He witnesses her at work, but when she attacks him he evades her. This makes the Inferno organization think he has the aptitude to join her. He is captured, has his memories erased, and is trained as an assassin in the style of CRYING FREEMAN. Given the name Zwei, he struggles to regain his freedom and his memories. As he and Ein grow closer, she begins to look at her own life and question the emotions she has always suppressed—compare to GUNSLINGER GIRL. Initially released as the interactive title *Phantom of Inferno* (2001), the original involved the use of the DVD remote to steer the course of the game. This adaptation makes all the viewer's choices for them—if that's all that was necessary, what was the point of having "interactivity" in the first place? The original game was later bundled with the anime in a single release.

PHAROAH'S SEAL
1988. JPN: *Oka no Monsho*. Movie. DIR: Daisuke Yasaku. SCR: Chieko Hosokawa. DES: Chieko Hosokawa. ANI: N/C. MUS: Joe Hisaishi. PRD: Toei. 40 mins.
Two lovers are caught up in civil unrest in 1000 B.C. Egypt. Based on Chieko Hosokawa's 1977 manga, which has been reprinted over 130 times by its publishers Princess Comics, this is best described as a "costume drama" since, while the setting is ancient Egypt, the characters' concerns speak to any modern schoolgirl, perhaps explaining the series' runaway success in manga form.

PHOTON *
1997. JPN: *Photon*. AKA: *The Idiot Adventures*. Video. DIR: Koji Masunari. SCR: Yosuke Kuroda. DES: Masaki Kajishima, Shinya Takahashi, Koji Watanabe. ANI: Shinya Takahashi. MUS: Haruhiko Nishioka. PRD: AIC. 45 mins. x 6 eps.
On Sandy Planet, where the locals are so stupid they worship Magic Markers, chieftain's daughter Aun goes AWOL

because she's got a crush on a troubadour, and laconic local boy Photon is sent to find her before she causes trouble. But Photon discovers a crashed spaceship and wakes its beautiful pilot, Keyne, from her cryogenic slumber. Accidentally marrying her by writing the word "Idiot" on her forehead, Photon is forced to protect Keyne from the evil spacefaring prince Papacha.

Planned, like its stablemate TENCHI MUYO!, as a multimedia promotion involving animation, radio drama, novels, and a manga, *Photon* is distinguished by BATTLE ATHLETES–director Masunari allowing the designers free rein with their insane visual conceits, from a girl who can stop time in selected places, to levitation garters, wind-powered landspeeders, and a girl trying to proclaim her love through a mouthful of sand. Sadly, the script doesn't live up to the visual promise, relying on puerile nudie gags and a charmless lead, though moments remain when it looks as if a mad scientist has combined DRAGON HALF and NAUSICAÄ in a secret laboratory. **N**

P.I. PERVERSE INVESTIGATIONS *
2003. JPN: *Sei Sai*. AKA: *Sex Judge*. Video. DIR: Kanzaburo Oda. SCR: Shinji Rannai. DES: Ryosuke Morimura. ANI: Ryosuke Morimura. MUS: Yoshi. PRD: YOUC, Digital Works (Vanilla Series). 30 mins. x 2 eps.
When much loved schoolteacher Yuko falls from the roof under suspicious circumstances, four of her favorite pupils form a team to investigate. Their most important clue is her diary, which shows meetings scheduled with seven female students on the night of her death. The boys duly start hunting for further clues among the girls and are prepared to use any methods at their disposal, soon transforming this anime into the usual cavalcade of rape and abuse, particularly over at the photography club and the swimming club. The U.S. release cunningly found a title and font that would recall the TV series *C.S.I.: Crime Scene Investigation*. Part of the VANILLA SERIES. **LNV**

PIA CARROT *

1997. JPN: *Pia Carrot e Yokoso*. AKA: *Welcome to Pia Carrot*. Video. DIR: Kan Fukumoto, Nobuyoshi Ando. SCR: Katsumasa Kanezawa. DES: Cocktail Soft. ANI: Katsumasa Kanezawa. MUS: N/C. PRD: Pink Pineapple, KSS. 30 mins. x 3 eps. (v1), 30 mins. x 3 eps. (v2), 30 mins. x 6 eps. (v3 *DX*), 50 mins. (m).

In an anime based on a computer-dating simulation game, a lusty teenage boy gets a part-time job at a restaurant, where he is soon seducing the waitresses. By episode three, even the crew tired of the setting, and the cast relocates to Okinawa. For the grand finale, manager Kyoko invites the girls back to her place, everyone gets drunk, and formulaic high jinks ensue. After a manga adaptation appeared in *Comic Gao*, the franchise was renewed for *Pia Carrot 2 DX* (1999), in which, predictably, a new branch of the restaurant opens up, a new boy gets a summer job, and a new rack of girls finds him irresistibly attractive. Released in the U.S. as *Welcome to Pia Carrot* (2001). A short *Pia Carrot* "movie" *PC: Sayaka's Love Story* (*Sayaka no Koi Monogatari*, 2002) was directed by Yuji Muto. **N**

PIANO *

2002. TV series. DIR: Norihiko Sudo. SCR: Mami Watanabe. DES: Kosuke Fujishima. ANI: N/C. MUS: Hiroyuki Kozu. PRD: Marine Entertainment, Animate, Pioneer LDCE, Kid's Station. 24 mins. x 10 eps.

Eighth-grader Miu Nomura has been taking piano classes since she was small. Her parents, big sister Akiko, teachers, and friends know her as a shy, quiet girl, and she lacks self-confidence. Her music teacher feels that her playing, though almost note-perfect, lacks emotion. As Miu gets older, she finds that approaching adulthood affects her whole life, even her playing. Maybe she'll be able to let her feelings out on the keyboard if handsome Kazuya Takahashi ever notices her.

Guaranteed almost supernatural prettiness through the presence of **OH MY GODDESS!**–creator Kosuke

Fujishima, this series also exploited the persona of its lead—voice actress Ayako Kawasumi supposedly started piano classes in childhood, and both composed and performed the series' opening theme. Not to be confused with *Pianist*, which is an episode of the erotic **SECRET ANIMA SERIES**.

PICCOLINO

1976. JPN: *Pinocchio Yori: Piccolino no Daiboken*. AKA: *The Adventures of Piccolino, after Pinocchio*. TV series. DIR: Hiroshi Saito, Masaharu Endo, Shigeo Koshi. SCR: Masao Maruyama. DES: Takao Kogawa, Michiyo Sakurai, Marty Murphy. ANI: Takao Kogawa, Michiyo Sakurai, Koichi Murata. MUS: Karel Svoboda. PRD: Nippon Animation, TV Asahi. 25 mins. x 52 eps.

Lonely toymaker Gepetto constructs a puppet son to keep him company and names him Piccolino. The boy lives as a normal child but yearns to be *real*. This German-Japanese coproduction of Carlo Collodi's 1881 tale involves one of Disney's stalwarts, Marty Murphy. Despite the renaming, the series remains close to the original, with sculpting by old Gepetto, the learning of worldly wisdom, and achieving real humanity—the story is the same. See also **ADVENTURES OF PINOCCHIO**.

PICTURES AT AN EXHIBITION

1966. JPN: *Tenrankai no E*. Movie. DIR: Osamu Tezuka, Shingo Matsuo, Taku Sugiyama. SCR: Osamu Tezuka. DES: Osamu Tezuka. ANI: Akihiro Mori, Shigeru Yamazaki. MUS: Modest Mussorgsky. PRD: Mushi Pro. 34 mins.

This short film by **ASTRO BOY**'s Tezuka sets ten short vignettes of his own devising to music by Mussorgsky originally based on scenes created by a friend of the composer. The Tezuka stories, like the originals, are contemporary social satires: *The Critic, The Artificial Gardener, The Plastic Surgeon, The Factory Owner, The Tough Guy, The Champion, The TV Star, The Zen Funeral, The Soldier,* and *The Finale*. The music is an original arrangement of Mussorgsky's score by Isao Tomita; he was later to make

an arrangement of the same work for synthesizer, but this one is fully orchestrated, making for interesting comparisons. Definitely one to file in the "art house" section of Tezuka's output, here in an unmistakable homage to Disney's *Fantasia* (1940).

PIGGYBACK GHOST

1955. JPN: *Onbu Obake*. AKA: *Knapsack Ghost; Ghost in a Knapsack*. TV series. DIR: Ryuichi Yokoyama. SCR: Ryuichi Yokoyama. DES: Ryuichi Yokoyama. ANI: Mitsuhiro Machiyama. MUS: N/C. PRD: Fuji, Eastman Color, Yomiuri TV (Nippon TV). 55 mins. (m), 25 mins. x 54 eps. (TV).

Green-eyed spirit Onbu is created when lightning strikes jade in a river. He loves swimming through the air but is adopted by Ojie the village blacksmith, who carries him in a knapsack. Onbu plays with the cheeky Kanchan brothers, Ojo the gentle girl, Chinnen the young priest, and the other kindly villagers. Lifting many ideas from **JAPANESE FOLK TALES**, this series was based on a manga by Ryuichi Yokoyama, who also created **FUKU-CHAN**, shared many staff members with the more successful **SAZAE-SAN**, and was remade for TV by Hajime Watanabe at the Eiken Studio in 1966.

PIKKOMAN'S DEVIL TRAINING *

1999. JPN: *Pikkoman no Oni Chikudo: Midnight Milk Party*. AKA: *Pikkoman's Way of Devil Taming*. Video. DIR: Rion Kushiro. SCR: Tedokoro Imaike. DES: Piko Fujikatsu (Pikkoman). ANI: Ken Raibi. MUS: N/C. PRD: Tsuyusha, Akatonbo. 30 mins.

Teenager Chiho Chino wants to have an adventure before she leaves her school days behind, so she auditions for a role in a schoolgirl porn video, believing that her performance will be of a wholly solo nature. However, when she reaches the set, she is raped on camera. Another of anime's more distasteful offerings, this one based on a manga by Piko Fujikatsu. Released in the U.S. in 2002 under the title *Midnight Milk Party*. **N**❤

PILOT CANDIDATE *

1999. JPN: *Megami Kohosei*. AKA: *Candidate for Goddess*. TV series. DIR: Mitsuru Hongo. SCR: Akira Oketani, Miho Sakai. DES: Shinichi Yamaoka. ANI: N/C. MUS: N/C. PRD: Production IG, Xebec. 25 mins. x 12 eps. (TV), 23 mins. (v).

Rei "Zero" Enna and a group of other teenagers from various space colonies must train together at an interstellar academy in order to protect Zion, the last human colony, from the devastating alien invaders known only as "Victim." In a setup that will be familiar to anyone who has followed sports anime or military training movies, the teenage pilots bond, with the exception of a ruthless candidate determined to out-score everyone else. Typically, they idolize their tough, no-nonsense Coach (compare to GUNBUSTER) and the upperclassmen who are so good at the tasks which Zero and company are only just learning. Meanwhile, there are hints that something untoward is going on—as in *The Matrix* (1999), which featured a hero who was "The One," not a Zero, and a bastion of freedom called Zion—what first appear to be design problems or story inconsistencies take on more sinister meanings. Zero's offhand comment that he can't remember his family turns out to be a statement of the literal truth. Meanwhile, the pilots get on with their pilot training, flying five (and only five—why not make more?) robots modeled on Greco-Roman goddesses, color-coded like the creations of a live-action team-show like *Goranger* (*DE).

This anime was based on a manga in *Comic Ga* by DNANGEL creator Yukiru Sugisaki and influenced by the existential musings of EVANGELION, but it features slapstick and a cat-girl thrown in for good measure. As with other anime made at the turn of the century (see DUAL), the transition to digital animation makes for clever camerawork but a sanitized, "clean" feel to all the art. Note that the episodes are numbered "00" through

"11," apparently in order to cause confusion to anime encyclopedists. A one-shot 2002 video spin-off retold the TV series story from the point of view of one of the other pilots.

PINCH AND PUNCH

1969. JPN: *Pinch to Punch*. TV series. DIR: Fumio Ikeno. SCR: Noboru Ishiguro, Toyohiro Ando. DES: N/C. ANI: Tadao Wakabayashi. MUS: N/C. PRD: Fuji TV Enterprise. 5 mins. x 162 eps.

Pinch and Punch are genius twins with a mean streak, easily annoyed with their associates, particularly with the hypocrisy of adults. Their main nemesis is Mamagon, their education-obsessed mother, against whom they soon form a rebel alliance, in the company of their friend Dotako, pet Ijibuta the pig, and little sister Chibigon—note that the *gon* suffix in Japan is usually only applied to dangerous creatures, such as MONSTER TAMAGON.

Pinch and Punch is, quite literally, an anime that just happened—as FRECKLES POOCH came to an end, the staff slowly transferred to this new production, which briefly shared *FP*'s slot before taking it over. The story, so Japanese sources claimed, was not actually pitched to the network; it was simply assumed that a cartoon of equivalent value to *FP* would replace it, and that's what occurred.

PING PONG CLUB *

1995. JPN: *Ike! Inachu Ping-Pong Club*. AKA: *Let's Go! Inachu Ping Pong Club; Make Way for the Ping Pong Club*. TV series. DIR: Masami Hata. SCR: Sukehiro Tomita, Tsunehisa Ito, Kenji Terada, Yoshihiro Sasa. DES: Minoru Furuya. ANI: Mamoru Tanaka. MUS: Katsuyoshi Kobayashi. PRD: Grouper Production, KSS, TBS. 25 mins. x 26 eps.

The boys' table-tennis club consists of earnest captain Takeda, school dreamboat Kinoshita, and four deadbeats who constantly goof off instead of practicing. Their coach, Mr. Shibazaki, is a pushover for all the other teachers. The girls' club is a large group of dedicated, gifted young athletes,

whose coach, Mr. Tachikawa, despises the boys' club and covets its premises. But the clubroom is about more than just ping-pong; it's a refuge for a group of misfits, no-hopers, and adolescents trying to cope with the petty pains and embarrassments of growing up. To keep it, the boys will have to find that old fighting spirit they all seem to lack—a plan helped by the pretty Kyoko, who offers a personal "sex pass" to the highest scorer.

It's hard to describe this short series, based on Minoru Furuya's 1993 *Young Magazine* manga, as anything other than insane. The raging of teenage male hormones and the nonoperational status of the related brain cells is conveyed in a fractured visual and directorial style, complete with a LUPIN III pastiche, mom-and-pop gags, enka and taiko, male impersonators, crossdressers, St. Francis Xavier, the legend of MOMOTARO, volcanic eruptions, smelly foreigners, feats of *Endurance*, and every conceivable offensive reference to sexual habits and bodily functions. There are more naked penises in this low-rent "buddy movie" series than in many erotic anime—falling out of shorts, stuffed into bird's heads for a SWAN LAKE ballet skit, accidentally revealed during exercise—and all the tropes normally used to peek at female nudity, but there's hardly a hint of any real possibility of sexual action. The overall effect is as directionless and futile as the average teenager's life, but it's hard not to feel a creeping sympathy for its hopeless, dogged solidarity with those facing hormonal challenge and social failure.

The throwaway nature is so determinedly pursued as to obscure the solid track record of its crew. This isn't a team of young punks talking dirty to their peers (see BITE ME!: CHAMELEON), but a rack of seasoned professionals with an instinct for video sales. Their work is full of knowing nudges and winks, entirely unashamed of itself. Despite the multitude of monocultural references, the overall *Beavis and Butthead* atmosphere would have spoken loud and clear to legions of hormonally challenged males too young to get most of the cultural digs, but that's hardly the audience for the subtitled version that was released in the U.S. No relation to the 2002 live-action movie, written by Kankuro Kudo and directed by Fumihiko Sone, which was adapted from a different 1996 manga by Taiyo Matsumoto. **Ⓑ Ⓝ Ⓥ**

PINK CURTAIN

1985. JPN: *Pink no Curtain*. Video. DIR: Yoshiharu Kurahashi. SCR: Masahito Nishio. DES: N/C. ANI: Minoru Kichoda. MUS: Hikaru Onda. PRD: Bip. 30 mins. Virgin boy Okuyama is a stocker at the supermarket who has no luck with women. His life is thrown upside down when his sister Noriko unexpectedly moves into his house. Okuyama is overcome with lustful thoughts for her, but she regards him simply as a brother. With more incest from the era that gave us **CREAM LEMON**, this story was based on the strip in *Manga Action* magazine by Joji Akiyama, who also created **KOIKO'S DAILY LIFE**. **Ⓝ**

PINMEN

2000. AKA: *PiNMEN: Workers From Space Video*. DIR: Bak Ikeda. SCR: Bak Ikeda. DES: Bak Ikeda. ANI: Bak Ikeda. MUS: Homo Sapiens Sapiens. PRD: Trilogy Future Studio, Pierrot, Animax, Dentsu. 7 mins.
A group of superadvanced, superpeaceful aliens have locked away all knowledge of warfare deep in their distant past—the flipside of the Zentraedi from **MACROSS**. Learning of a distant blue-green planet where all kinds of "fun" are available, a group of them resolve to come to Earth. Since they are industrious, frugal aliens, they intend to work hard so that they can earn enough money to pay for the entertainment they bring back to their homeworld. An innocuous short animation by an artist calling himself Bakuhatsuro "Bak" Ikeda—a pseudonym meaning *Explodey Ikeda*.

PIPI THE ALIEN

1965. JPN: *Uchujin Pipi*. TV series. DIR: Yuichiro Konnai. SCR: Sakyo Komatsu, Kazumasa Hirai. DES: Toshikazu Fukuhara. ANI: N/C. MUS: Isao Tomita. PRD: NHK, TV Doga, NHK. 25 mins. x 52 eps.
Toshihiko and Ryoko meet the gnomelike alien Pipi and his friends, who have one year (the length of a lunch break on Pipi's world) to learn all they can about planet Earth. Since these two Japanese children are the first people they have met who are close to them in size, they tag along with them as they explore their neighborhood, repaying them by taking them on fantastic space journeys during their own school lunch breaks. A series that mixes live action and animation.

PIPI THE FLIGHTLESS FIREFLY

1995. JPN: *Pipi Tobenai Hotaru*. Movie. DIR: Shinichi Nakada. SCR: Yoshimi Kato. DES: Akimi Kozawa. ANI: Takaya Ono. MUS: N/C. PRD: Office CHK, Success Road, Mushi. 90 mins.
In a heavy-handed "educational" film that also finds the time to tackle environmental issues, a young firefly is bullied by his fellow insects because he cannot actually fly. Government approved, it says here.

PIPOPAPO PATROL

2000. JPN: *Pipopapo Patrol-kun*. AKA: Pip Pop Pattle. TV series. DIR: Mitsuo Hashimoto. SCR: Aya Matsui. DES: Birthday, Izumi Todo. ANI: N/C. MUS: Toshiyuki Takizawa. PRD: Toei Animation, BS Fuji. 25 mins. x 65 eps.
In Sunflower City, technology is so advanced that vehicles are able to think and speak. Perky little police patrol car Pattle (Patrol) and his driver Hajime are partners: both rookies, but eager to learn from more experienced officers and vehicles and determined to do their bit to keep the peace on their patch. A show that takes *Starsky and Hutch*, extracts the cardigans and comedy pimp, and whisks in a dash of *Bob the Builder*, or if you prefer, **BUBU CHACHA** meets **YOU'RE UNDER ARREST**.

Created by Izumi Todo, who was also responsible for **STUMBLING WITCH DOREMI** and **PRECURE**.

PIROPPO

2001. JPN: *Aibo*. TV series. DIR: Katsuhito Ishii. SCR: Katsuhito Ishii, Yumiko Fujimura. DES: Katsuhito Ishii. ANI: Yumi Chiba, Shigeko Sakuma, Rie Nishino. MUS: Eiko Sakurai. PRD: Studio 4°C, Sony, Fuji TV. 20 secs x 54 eps.
A series based on Sony's hugely popular range of robot pets, *Piroppo* stars two new robots, Latte and Macaron, designed by Katsura Moshino, which went on sale in Japan two weeks before the October 11th series premiere. The series was planned as 54 episodes of 20 seconds each, but shown in 5-minute and 10-minute compilations. There's also a web comic on Sony's *AIBO-Life* site. It's hard to see 20-second animations as anything other than commercials, despite the PR claims of a "lavish anime staff." The design is deliberately wacky, with references to pop culture icons like masked wrestlers and cowboys, and a collar-and-tie wearing hammerhead shark.

PITA TEN

2002. TV series. DIR: Yoshiaki Okamura, Yuzo Ten. SCR: Akemi Menda, Yasuko Kobayashi. DES: Kyuta Sakai. ANI: Toshifumi Kawase, Shinichiro Minami. MUS: Hikaru Nanase. PRD: Madhouse, Broccoli, TV Osaka. 24 mins. x 26 eps.
Kotaro Higuchi has recently lost his mother, and his businessman father works long hours and is only around at breakfast. Kotaro is a quiet boy who looks after the house and hangs out with his best friends from childhood, Takashi Ayanokoji, aka Ten-chan, and Koboshi Uematsu, who has been sweet on Kotaro ever since they were small and he comforted her after she hurt herself playing. Ten-chan is the boy with everything—looks, intelligence, great sporting ability, and a wealthy family—but Kotaro has his own special gift: he can see the supernatural. This leads him into a meeting with apprentice angel Misha, a clumsy, tactless but

kind-hearted spirit who succumbs to a huge crush on him and invades his life. She moves in next door to him, starts at his school, and becomes his very own cute and perky stalker. When apprentice devil Shia, who is in big trouble because she's far too nice to succeed as a demon, gets a crush on Ten-chan and moves in with Misha, the stage is set for a comedy romance based on the manga by DIGI CHARAT author Koge Donbo. All this was done far better in URUSEI YATSURA two decades ago, but the twist of adding quasi-infantile cuteness to overt teen sexuality has hooked many fans.

PLACE PROMISED IN OUR EARLY DAYS, THE *

2004. JPN: *Kumo no Muko, Yakusoku no Basho.* AKA: *The Place of Promise in the Clouds; Beyond the Clouds, the Promised Place.* Movie. DIR: Makoto Shinkai. SCR: Makoto Shinkai. DES: Ushio Tazawa. ANI: Ushio Tazawa. MUS: Tenmon. PRD: CoMix Wave. 91 mins.
In an alternate universe, Japan is partitioned after WWII. Hokkaido is annexed by the Soviet Union, while Honshu and the southern islands go to the USA. A huge tower is built on Hokkaido, now known as Ezo, which can be seen across the waters of the Tsugaru Strait from Aomori, the northernmost town on Honshu. Four decades later, in 1996, two teenagers vow to take the girl they both love to see the tower's mysteries in their homemade aircraft, the Bella Ciela. Then Sayuri Sawatari falls ill with a strange narcolepsy and is transferred to Tokyo for treatment by a specialist. Her friends Hiroshi Fujisawa and Takuya Shirakawa abandon their dream and get on with their lives, but when Hiroshi learns that Sayuri is still in a coma three years later, they decide to try and help her. The world is on the brink of war again, and Sayuri's dreams are the key to a mystery which will bring her two childhood friends in touch with parallel worlds and political tensions as she tries to dream herself back to a place where unfulfilled childhood promises can finally be kept.

Makoto Shinkai has developed greatly since he drafted VOICES OF A DISTANT STAR virtually single-handed on his home computer. Mixing the Hokkaido quest of DIAMOND DAYDREAMS with the girlfriend-in-a-coma of THE ETERNITY YOU DESIRE and the alternate history of FULLMETAL ALCHEMIST, this project shows almost the same level of hands-on control—he created, wrote, directed, and storyboarded, and also handled art direction, color design, editing, postproduction, and sound direction. This, plus the use of elements such as flight and hand-built aircraft with Italian names, has led some critics to make comparisons with Hayao Miyazaki. Beautiful as this second work is, such comparisons are extremely premature. Shinkai the writer is still fixated on the theme of his early work—the agony of loss imposed by time, distance, and age. He creates beautiful characters, real and engaging, but they are entirely caught up in yearning and reminiscence, reluctant to move in any direction except back. His promising plot is simply left to unravel, its threads unresolved. His assured handling of lighting, color, and music creates and sustains atmosphere so well that it seems almost unkind to highlight the deficiency, but this is not yet the output of a mature and rounded creator. Like its story, it's a youthful promise, a shining dream that still awaits fulfillment.

PLANET BUSTERS *

1984. JPN: *Birth.* AKA: *World of the Talisman.* Video. DIR: Shinya Sadamitsu. SCR: "Kaname Pro." DES: Koretaku Kaneda, Makoto Kobayashi. ANI: Shinya Sadamitsu, Mutsumi Inomata, Shigenori Kageyama. MUS: Joe Hisaishi (Randy Miller in U.S. version). PRD: Idol, Kaname. 80 mins.
Namu Shurugi (Prince Talon) and his sister Rasa Jupiter (Princess Rasa) are descended from a race wiped out by the people of planet Aquaroid (Pandora), who are engaged in a devastating global war with the android Inorganics race. They fall into the company of Bao (Mo) and Kim (Keen),

two treasure hunters in search of the mystic talisman. This planet, it seems, is a "testing ground" to reveal the one destined to become the leader of the Galactic Empire. In an arrangement similar to KING ARTHUR AND THE KNIGHTS OF THE ROUND TABLE, whoever gets the talisman will become the new ruler. The fight for the talisman is a conflict that begins *every* cycle of cosmic existence, as factions compete to determine whether the dominant life-form throughout the universe will be flesh or metallic.

Though the American dub unsurprisingly reduces this to the usual simplistic Good Humans vs. Evil Robots, this sci-fi story, which features lots of action, cool machines, and frequent shots of Rasa's cute rear end, is a paradoxical and densely layered parable of reincarnation. This makes it very unsuitable for the audience of under-fives at whom the U.K. video release was aimed. Even with the script revamped to minimize the spiritual dimension and make the goal of their quest the "Planet Buster," a secret weapon made by the creator of the universe (who would really need one, right?), it still makes no sense, but it's fun to watch. Ending with the destruction of this cycle of existence, and only the four main characters preserved in spirit form, it is liable to have befuddled many a preteen viewer, especially with the finale, when two alien superbeings sit down and start debating the transient nature of existence. Made for video but shown in Japanese theaters, a "Special Edition" on video includes the 22-minute *Making of Birth* documentary.

PLANET MASK

1966. JPN: *Yusei Kamen.* TV series. DIR: Yonehiko Watanabe, Tsutomu Yamamoto. SCR: Akira Adachi. DES: Takaji Kusunoki. ANI: Masakazu Tanokura. MUS: Hidehiko Arano. PRD: TCJ, Eiken, Fuji TV. 25 mins. x 39 eps.
In the 21st century, the discovery of the inhabited tenth planet, Pineron, out past Pluto, is happy news for the

solar system. Earthman Johansen and Pineron girl Maria fall in love and become the proud parents of the first mixed-race child, Peter. Fifteen years later, Earth and Pineron are thrown into a state of war when Pineron warships mistake an Earth vessel in trouble for an attack ship. A lone masked figure riding on a rocket tries to keep the spacefaring powers apart. This Cold War superhero thriller was inspired in equal chunks by the troubles in Vietnam, Japan's conflicts with the USSR over its northern islands, and the children of mixed-race parents after WWII—children who would shortly be entering their teens. With typical TV double standards, the theme song cried "stop the war," even as the show encouraged kids to go out and *fight* for peace.

Plastic Little

PLANETES *

2003. TV series. DIR: Goro Taniguchi, Tatsuya Igarashi, Megumi Yamamoto, Hiroshi Ishiodori. SCR: Ichiro Okochi. DES: Yuriko Senba, Seiichi Nakatani, Takeshi Takakura. ANI: Eiji Nakata, Hisashi Saito, Masashi Kudo, Yuriko Senba. MUS: Kotaro Nakagawa. PRD: Sunrise, AD Cosmo, NARA Animation, Bandai, NHK. 25 mins. x 26 eps.
By the year 2075, decades of missions and projects have left Earth's orbit cluttered with space junk—bits of rocket, defunct satellites, and other debris. Such space garbage needs to be collected, a task farmed out to private corporations such as Technora. Hachirota "Hachimaki" Hoshino is a young employee who has always wanted to own his own spaceship, but now seems stuck in a workaday rut as little more than a glorified dumpster driver. To his annoyance, he is saddled with rookie recruit Ai Tanabe, who has yet to appreciate that life in space is fraught with dangers—the slightest mistake in a jet firing or the smallest tear in a space suit can spell instant death. Their fellow employees include American Fée Carmichael, a compulsive smoker whose habit is doubly dangerous in oxygen-rich environments,

and Russian Yuri Mihalkov, a widower whose wife was killed when a tiny screw hit a low-orbit craft's window at high velocity. Their troubles in orbit include confrontations with illegal dumpers, terrorists who want mankind to stay Earthbound, and lunar eccentrics who use the low gravity to imitate the flying leaps of ninja.

The idea behind *Planetes* is not new—it lifts elements of both STAR DUST and MIGHTY SPACE MINERS—but its execution is sublime. Its future is not the wish-fulfillment fantasy of GUNDAM, but a mundane, troubled place like something out of Larry Niven's *Known Space* series. Space travel is possible, but only within extremely limited confines—a trip to the Moon still takes several days, and later episodes include the immensely detailed preparations for the first manned flight to Jupiter; compare this to less realistic sci-fi shows like GUNBUSTER, which can happily encase Jupiter in a steel shell in a simple throwaway gag. Yes, it's true that anime's potential is infinite, and creators can show us whatever they can draw. But, like PATLABOR before it, *Planetes* gives equal weight to the science and the fiction, and is all the better

for it. Based on a manga by Makoto Yukimura in weekly *Comic Morning*.

PLASTIC LITTLE *

1994. Video. DIR: Kinji Yoshimoto. SCR: Mayori Sekijima. DES: Satoshi Urushibara, Studio Nue. ANI: Satoshi Urushibara. MUS: Tamiya Terashima. PRD: Animate Film, SME. 45 mins.
Orphaned teenager Tita takes over her father's pet shop hunter business, collecting and selling exotic animals from all over the galaxy. In port on planet Yietta (where, to feebly justify the title, there's very *little plastic*) she rescues a young girl who is being pursued by the local authorities. Elysse Nalerov is in big trouble; her father designed a new weapon, she has the arming codes, and the government will stop at nothing to get them. Tita and her crew decide to help her out, and mayhem ensues.

A lightweight but enjoyable sci-fi adventure made, like its predecessor LEGEND OF LEMNEAR, solely to show off the artistic talents of Urushibara and Yoshimoto. While lacking a particularly strong story line, it succeeds most perfectly in the rendition of an individual artist's style into moving pictures. Unfortunately for the genre,

Urushibara's style isn't SF illustration but cheesecake. The artist on numerous books of cutie-girl illustrations, he renders lush young flesh with glowing perfection. Yoshimoto transfers this perfection exactly to celluloid and puts a remarkable range of motions onto it, so before they take on the evil overlord, the girls can stop for a bath scene where they can compare their breasts. Not only every jiggle of every curve, but the characters' expressions and movements all give the impression of seeing the creator's original art come to life on the page. When one considers the violence often done to original design art in the cause of simplifying it enough to animate cheaply (see **VAMPIRE HUNTER D**), the achievement is all the more remarkable.

At the time of its release, the creators claimed that it was only a prequel to a set of other stories—though as time passed, the only evidence was a brief *PL* audio drama that described Elysse as a "guest star," thereby implying there was more to come. In 1999, Urushibara and Yoshimoto unveiled artwork from a new project, *Femme Femme Buccaneers,* charting the progress of Ann and Ricorne, a two-piece idol-singer act known collectively as Virginity. Though they promised that these two girls, along with the unshaven male pirates of the Yiettan isle of Espaniola, would soon grace anime screens alongside Tita and her crew, the wait continues, making *PL2* the most delayed project in anime, beating even Otomo's *Steam Boy.* Owing to accidents of international pricing and rights negotiation, *PL* is available in separate U.K. and U.S. translations. **NV**

PLATONIC CHAIN

2003. TV series. DIR: Takeshi Okazaki. SCR: N/C. DES: N/C. ANI: Takahiro Goto. MUS: N/C. PRD: AciD Films, TV Tokyo. 5 mins. x 25 eps.
The day after tomorrow, when videophones and constant Internet access are available to everyone. And where there's a network, there's a hacker. Someone has broken into the government's information archive and created the Platonic Chain website, through which anyone can discover anything about anyone else via his or her cellphone. You can find your double and try a life swap, or find the double of your secret crush and practice on him until you're confident enough to hit on your love. You can even find out where the cute guy you just passed on the escalator in the mall goes to school. Teenage friends Hitomi Tanaka, Rika Kagura, and Kanae Mizuhara use the site to help them deal with the problems of everyday life—a nicer attitude than that exhibited in the later **HELL GIRL**. Manga artist Okazaki makes his directorial debut on this version of Koji Watanabe's SF novel, and makes extensive use of CG and motion-capture to help give his characters and settings the Shibuya look. Okazaki and Watanabe have also collaborated on color manga *@Run-city,* which appeared in *Ikki* magazine.

PLAWRES SANSHIRO

1983. TV series. DIR: Kunihiko Yuyama, Masahisa Ishida, Masamune Ochiai, Osamu Sekita, Katsumi Endo, Susumu Ishizaki. SCR: Keisuke Fujikawa, Kenji Terada, Junji Tagami. DES: Mutsumi Inomata, Shigenori Kageyama, Shigeru Katsumata. ANI: Mutsumi Inomata, Hitoshi Yoshinaga, Kazuhiro Ochi, Hirotoshi Sano, Takashi Sogabe, Satoshi Yamazaki. MUS: Yasunori Tsuchida. PRD: Kaname Productions, TBS. 25 mins. x 37 eps.
Pla[stic] wres[tlers] are miniature robot toys that can be operated to fight each other. Orphan Sanshiro Sugata (see **SANSHIRO SUGATA**) has inherited a superb plawres from his vanished father and wants to make it a champion, while his grandfather wants him to put away childish things and focus on becoming a judo champion.

The conflict between a child's and an adult's view of "achievement," the symbolism of inheritance, and the way in which toys provide an interface with a world that seems too big and scary to handle directly are interesting concepts for a series. Sadly, the need to keep things on a child's level restricts what Yuyama can do with his material. He can't have minded, though—14 years on, he made **POKÉMON**. Jiro Uma and Minoru Kamiya produced the spin-off manga in the same year, but strangely enough, the expected toy line didn't materialize.

PLAY BALL

2005. TV series. DIR: Satoshi Dezaki. SCR: Koji Ueda, Makoto Ohama, Mitsuya Suenaga. DES: Keizo Shimizu, Ryosuke Senbo. ANI: Ippei Masui. MUS: Kaoru Wada. PRD: Eiken. 25 mins. x 13 eps.
Junior-high baseball captain Takao Taniguchi ruins his sporting future when he heroically continues to play a game with broken fingers—compare to **H2**. Later, as a student at Sumitani High, he is approached by the captain of the soccer club, who sees him watching a baseball game with a sad look in his eye. Takao begins playing on the soccer team, but baseball remains his first love. Eventually, he decides to return to baseball, only to discover a lackluster club full of apathetic, uncaring players. A predictable tale of overcoming sporting odds then ensues. Based on a manga by Akio Chiba, and broadcast in Japan on a series of syndicated channels, including Kansai TV, Kumamoto TV, TV Miyazaki, and Sendai Broadcasting. **LNV**

PLEASE OPEN THE DOOR

1986. JPN: *Tobira o Akete.* Movie. DIR: Keizo Shimizu, Tsuneo Tominaga. SCR: Kazumi Koide, Satoshi Dezaki. DES: Setsuko Shibunnoichi. ANI: Toshihiro Kawamoto, Mayumi Hirota. MUS: Mark Goldenberg. PRD: Kitty Film, Magic Bus. 81 mins.
Miyako Negishi is a seemingly ordinary high school girl but has amazing powers of ESP, while her friend Keiichiro can transform into a were-lion, and her friend Kaori has the power of teleportation. On a night when the moon is full, they are transported to the alternate "Middle Kingdom," where Miyako

is the fair princess Neryura, fighting a losing battle against the Western king Duran III. Forming an alliance with the Eastern king Dimida, Miyako and her friends use their powers to save the world, hoping eventually to return home. Based on an SF novel by Motoko Arai, better known in the English-speaking world for her story *Green Requiem*. Compare to **Fushigi Yugi**.

PLEASE SAVE MY EARTH *

1993. JPN: *Boku no Chikyu o Mamotte*. Video. DIR: Kazuo Yamazaki. SCR: Kazuo Yamazaki. DES: Takayuki Goto, Yuji Ikeda. ANI: Takayuki Goto. MUS: Hajime Mizoguchi. PRD: Victor Entertainment. 30 mins. x 6 eps., 30 mins. (music video).

Seven schoolchildren have a recurring collective dream in which a team of alien scientists on the moon gather data about Earth. Seeking each other's company, they begin to suspect that the dreams are really suppressed memories of their distant past lives. Past relationships replay themselves, as teenage Alice Sakaguchi is desired by eight-year-old Rin, while he in turn is pursued by the mature woman Mokuren. But love is not the only thing that survives reincarnation, as the members of the group discover that their former incarnations ended in tragedy—a tragedy fated to repeat itself.

One of a glut of mid-1990s lunar reincarnation stories, but it is far more mature than the populist **Sailor Moon** and better executed than the shoddy **Bounty Dog**. This emotive tale of love, loss, and anger echoing through reincarnation was based on a manga serialized in *Hana to Yume* by Saki Hiwatari, whose other manga works include *A Favor of the Devil* and *Tower of the Future*. Only a fraction of the 21-volume original would fit into the anime, and the story was compressed further into a 100 minute "movie" edit concentrating on the Alice/Rin relationship. There was also an animated music video, comprising eight tracks of the wonderful Mizoguchi music that featured

guest contributions from Yoko Kanno. Though released before the series to publicize it, the video actually contained some footage of later chapters and the manga's conclusion, unseen in the anime series proper.

PLEASE TEACHER *

2002. JPN: *Onegai Teacher*. AKA: *Teacher, Please*. TV series. DIR: Yasunori Ide. SCR: Yosuke Kuroda. DES: Hiroaki Goda, Yasuhiro Moriki, Yoshihiro Watanabe, Taraku Uon. ANI: Dome. MUS: Kazuya Takase, Shinji Orita, Tomoyuki Nakazawa. PRD: Bandai, Studio Orphee. 22 mins. x 12 eps. (TV1), 21 mins. (v), 22 mins. x 12 eps. (TV2), 26 mins. (v).

High school boy Kei Kusanagi lives a quiet life with his feisty aunt and lecherous but kind-hearted uncle. He's eighteen, but looks a lot younger as a result of a rare disease that put him in a coma for three years and arrested his physical growth. He is prone to passing out anytime his spirits are low. His cute new schoolteacher is a redhead with glasses who is really an alien—Kei knows because they've already met by accident. Mizuho Kazami has a spaceship with a living control unit, a tiny yellow-clad gnome named Marie. Mizuho is an observer for the Galactic Federation but she's come to Earth on a private mission—to try and find out about her human father. Her mother Hatsuho met him when the 2009 expedition to Mars got lost and was rescued by a Galaxy Federation ship. Kei marries Mizuho, purely as a matter of form, to help conceal her secret; but as their families and friends cause endless complications the pair fall in love. Hatsuho, who turns out to be something of a minx, along with her interfering younger sister Maho (Mizuho's aunt), also make appearances, notably in the 2003 video sequel in which they attempt to engineer a situation so that Kei and Mizuho can finally consummate their marriage. Both the series and its manga adaption with art by Shizuru Hayashiya are out in English, from Bandai and ComicsOne, respectively. There is also an untranslated

CD drama spin-off, *Onegai Friends*.

A second TV series, *Please Twins* (2003, *Onegai Twins*), dumped its predecessor's dogged adherence to a **Tenchi Muyo!** paradigm in favor of one that owed more to **Love Hina**—a truly rarefied distinction in harem shows, if you care about that sort of thing. Its protagonist is Maiku Kamishiro, a student at the school where Mizuho teaches and classmate of characters from the previous series, who has no family and is supporting himself through high school by working as a freelance computer programmer. His only memento of his childhood is an old photograph showing two children, a boy and a girl, playing outside a blue house. He hopes that finding the house might help him find his family, so he tracks it down and moves in—the tracking down of a similar domicile forms an important plot point in **Popotan**. Then two cute girls turn up to visit, both with a copy of the same photograph, each with the same blue eyes as Maiku, and each claiming to be his twin sister. He decides they can both stay until they know for sure which one is his sister. Miina Miyafuji is a feisty redhead, given to saying exactly what she thinks and constantly bickering with Maiku; Karen Onodera is gentle, easily frightened, and ultra-dependent. She's also fond of a biscuit snack called Prech Salad (a pastiche of Japanese Pretz snacks, whereas Mizuho was obsessed with Pochy, a thinly-disguised homage to the real-world Pocky snack), and this has led to a tiny little gnome-like creature dressed all in yellow (the first serial's Marie) following her everywhere hoping for titbits. Meanwhile, Maiku must also dodge the amorous intentions of Tsubaki Oribe, a girl, and Kosei Shimazaki, a boy. Fans of this type of anime will recognize the fantasy setup where, without actually having to make any effort to woo a girl, a guy suddenly finds that there's always one around and she's always cute—like being a rock star, but without the need for drugs or talent. However, *Please Twins* is notably more "mature" than others of its ilk, and mercifully lacks much of the endemic male character lechery or indignant female-induced slapstick of similar shows. Instead, Maiku conceals his interest in the female characters so well that some of them wonder if he might be gay, and then, of course, do everything they can to test the hypothesis. **N**

PLUSTERWORLD

2003. JPN: *Bouken Yuuki Pluster World*. AKA: *Adventure Bravery Pluster World; Journey of Adventure Pluster World*. TV series. DIR: Yuji Himaki. SCR: Sukehiro Tomita. DES: Hiroshi Kugimiya. ANI: N/C. MUS: Motoi Sakuraba. PRD: Nippon Animation, TV Tokyo, Takara. 25 mins. x 52 eps.

Pluster World is a magical realm in which tribes of strange creatures are at war. The tribes resemble various different Earth creatures and are further divided into those who want peace and justice, and those who don't. The Plusters, heroic creatures to whom legend attributes the power to "plus on," or merge with humans to create mighty warriors, battle the evil Minusters. Beetma, a Pluster of the Kabuto tribe, sets out to become the strongest Pluster in the world. On his journey he meets Wyburst, of the Grip tribe, who wants to find the legendary Gonggorahgong, a being who can bring peace to Pluster World. Then he is badly beaten in a fight with a Minus beast, and thrown down the fabled passage into the world of humans. There he meets 11-year-old Tohma and "plusses on" with him to become Plust Beetma. Returning to Pluster World, the pair meet Wyburst and join him in trying to find a power that can defeat the Minusters.

The legendary toy company name in the credits is a clue to the show's intent: to sell as many items of merchandise to children as possible. Like TRANSFORMERS and POKÉMON it's a 25-minute commercial. While Yoshiyuki Tomino used GUNDAM to show that a TV series can be something more, rookie director Himaki is not terribly ambitious.

POCHACCO *

1992. TV series. DIR: Masami Hata, Akira Kiyomizu, Katsumasa Kanezawa, Seiichi Mitsuoka. SCR: Kyoko Kuribayashi. DES: Rie Oshima. ANI: N/C. MUS: N/C. PRD: Sanrio. 10 mins. x 4 eps.

Adventures of a cute little puppy and his animal friends from the team that gave you HELLO KITTY and PEKKLE. Pochacco rescues tiny chicks, hunts down a carrot thief, looks for a pink mushroom, and has other adventures to thrill the under-threes. Despite the mushrooms, *Magic Roundabout* fans must look elsewhere for drug references; this is pure, clean, and sweet.

POKÉMON *

1997. JPN: *Pocket Monster*. TV series, movie. DIR: Kunihiko Yuyama, Masamitsu Hidaka, Yoshitaka Fujimoto. SCR: Atsuhiro Tomioka, Takeshi Shudo, Hideki Sonoda, Junji Takegami. DES: Satoshi Tajiri. ANI: Shunya Yamada. MUS: Junji Miyazaki. PRD: SOFTX, TV Tokyo. 25 mins. x c.279 eps. (TV1), 75 mins. (m1/*Mew2*), 23 mins. (m1s/*Vacation*), 81 mins. (m2/*Lugia*), 24 mins. (m2s/*Rescue*), 74 mins. (m3/*Emperor*), 23 mins. (m3s/*Pichu*), 99 mins. (m4/*Encounter*), 23 mins. (m4s/*Hide & Seek*), 70 mins. (m5/*Heroes*), 23 mins. (m5s/*Pika Pika*), 81 mins. (m6/), 23 mins. (m6s/*Dancing*), 100 mins. (m7/*Destiny*), 103 mins. (m8/*Mew*), ? mins. (m9/*Rangers*).

Ash (Satoshi) oversleeps and is late for the distribution of the trainers' manual giving details of how to capture and train wild Pocket Monsters (Pokémon), fighting-pets much coveted by children. Since the manual sets out which Pokémon are most desirable and how to find them, the other kids have all the "best" catches, and he is stuck with the only one he can find without help from the manual, an "electric mouse" called Pikachu. After a shaky start, the two soon become firm friends, as Pikachu helps Ash capture many more Pokémon and head toward his goal of becoming the world's greatest Pokémon trainer. However, at every turn, Ash and his friends are dogged by

the evil Team Rocket, intent on stealing the best Pokémon for themselves. Officially let off school to hunt their Pokémon, they trek around a safe and supportive world, always finding a bed for the night, and a sisterly type to help out with meals and other necessities. It's a child's dream, with the joys of independence but without the tedium.

Pokémon is a perfectly average TV anime tied into the huge marketing machine of a successful game and, consequently, immeasurably more successful than its contemporaries. Giving children an ongoing adventure, the chance to pit their monsters against each other, and a vast menagerie of creatures guaranteed to befuddle their parents, the game was an immense success, its cross-promotional anime and manga spin-offs reaching the West in record time, arguably creating the most important influence on the medium since AKIRA. Though the stars of TAMAGOTCHI VIDEO ADVENTURES can claim to be the first "virtual pets," it was the interactive quality of Nintendo's *Pokémon* game that seized the high ground. First broadcast in Japan in April 1997, the *Pokémon* phenomenon came to the notice of the West that December in a news item about strobe-like effects in one episode that caused seizures among the Japanese audience (see YAT BUDGET! SPACE TOURS). Popular myth accords the effects of this as a form of mass hysterics, although subsequent examination of medical records has suggested that perhaps less than a tenth of the alleged "800 cases" required medical attention. Others appear to be viewers who may have felt slightly queasy, jumping on the bandwagon to be part of a national event, and whose experience made for entertaining tabloid journalism abroad, but may not have been quite the broadcasting disaster first reported. Despite this initial stumble, the *Pokémon* juggernaut descended on the Western world, with millions of dollars in advertising eventually generating billions of dollars in sales. Compare this investment with the desultory way

SAILOR MOON was dumped on the U.S. Though *Pokémon* was undoubtedly a hit, it was also something of a self-fulfilling prophecy. The transition was not completely smooth—several episodes were "lost," chiefly for content comprising the womanizing antics of Ash's friend Brock, or cross-dressing by the zany Team Rocket.

Thanks to the runaway success of *Pokémon* in English, anime became relatively commonplace on American TV. After years of equating the medium with sex and violence, producers suddenly saw it as a cash cow in the children's market. Clone shows DIGIMON and MONSTER RANCHER swiftly followed, along with unrelated serials such as CARDCAPTORS, GUNDAM W, and FLINT THE TIME DETECTIVE. Early attempts at selling anime for an older audience foundered, with ESCAFLOWNE flopping on American TV, but the early years of the 21st century could well be characterized by a rush to keep the Western *Pokémon*-boom generation watching anime as they grow up.

The TV series went through several name changes to reflect the exact brand of game being promoted. After the initial 82 episodes, it became the more U.S.-friendly *Pokémon: Orange Island* until episode 118, when it returned to previous form in *Pokémon G[old &] S[ilver]*. The franchise also reached theaters in several film outings. *Pokémon the Movie: Mew vs. Mew-two* (1998) gained Japan's second-largest domestic box office for an animated film, at least for a while, until it was beaten by PRINCESS MONONOKE and then SPIRITED AWAY. It featured a fight against an embittered mutant monster, crazily flipping from promising, cautionary SF in the style of Tezuka's BAGHI, through cartoon comedy, to a patronizing moral ending that weakly argued against fighting all the time, even though such activities characterize the rest of the series! The 70-minute film was shown accompanied by the saccharine "let's cooperate" children's short, *Pikachu's Summer Vacation* (*Pikachu no Natsuyasumi*).

Pokémon

Despite a slow decline of interest, the film series continued with *Revelation Lugia* (1999, aka *Power of One*), anime history's *third*-largest Japanese box-office draw, in which yet another very, *very* rare form of Pokémon is the object of the quest. This time, Lugia can only be called forth by bringing three sacred birds together in one spot. The show was accompanied by the short film *Pikachu's Rescue Adventure* (*Pikachu Tankentai*). A year later, the *Pokémon* movie was *Emperor of the Crystal Tower* (2000, translated in 2001 as *Spell of the Unown* [*sic*]), a fairy-tale variant of *Sleeping Beauty* about an imprisoned princess accidentally kidnapping Ash's mother when she wishes for one of her own. The film was accompanied by another short for toddlers, this time *Pichu and Pikachu*, displaying "baby" versions of some of the lead Pokémon. A fourth film, *Encounter Beyond Time* (aka *Pokémon 4Ever*, 2001) features the very, very, *very* rare Pokémon Celebi from the GS game, accompanied by

the short *Pikachu's Hide and Seek* (*Pikachu no Doki-doki Kakurenbo*). *Pokémon Heroes Latias and Latios* (*Mizu no Miyako no Mamorigami*, i.e. *Guardian Spirits of the Water Capital*) accompanied by the short *Glittering Starlit Sky Camp* (*Pika Pika Hoshizora Camp*, both 2002); *Pokémon Jirachi Wish Maker* (*Nana-Yo no Negai Boshi Jiraachi*) and the short *The Dancing Pokémon Secret Base* (*Odoru Pokémon Himitsu Kichi*, both 2003); *Pokémon: Destiny Deoxys* (2004, *Rekku no Homonsha Deokishisu*, aka *Visitor from Above, Deoxys*), *Pokémon: Mew and the Wave Hero* (2005, *Myu to Hado no Yusha*), and *Pokémon Rangers and the Sea King* (2006, *Pokémon Ranger to Umi no Oji*) continue the franchise, while on television, the *Pokémon GS* season transformed into *Pokémon Ranger* and *Pokémon Advanced Generation*.

Often held in snooty disregard by a hard-core anime fandom that would prefer its hobby to be forever outside the mainstream, *Pokémon* is nevertheless the most commercially important anime of the 1990s in terms of brand recognition and the investment it attracted to the medium—many more obscure anime and manga translations were funded with Pikachu's profits. As befits a cultural icon, the series has been mercilessly lampooned in other media, most notably as the "Battling Seizure Robots" in an episode of the *The Simpsons*, and the brainwashing Chinpokomon in *South Park*.

POKONYAN

1993. AKA: *Raccoon Miaow; Rocky Rackat*. TV series. DIR: Hiroshi Sasakawa, Seitaro Hara. SCR: N/C. DES: N/C. ANI: N/C. MUS: Man Brothers Band. PRD: Nippon Herald, NHK. 8 mins. x 170 eps.

A Japanese girl discovers a *tanuki* (a Japanese raccoon dog; see POMPOKO) in her backpack during a camping trip. He proclaims that she is his sister and follows her everywhere. He can use his powers to turn Amy's dreams into real-life adventures, though his good intentions, like those of the creators' earlier DORAEMON, do not always work according to plan. Based on a manga by Fujiko F. Fujio, this anime was also spun off into the *Pokonyan Christmas* and *Pokonyan Summer Holiday* specials.

POLLON

1982. JPN: *Ochamegami Monogatari Korokoro Polon*. AKA: *The Story of Little Goddess Roly-Poly Pollon; Roly-Poly Pollon: The Tallest Tales of the Gods; Little Pollon*. TV series. DIR: Takao Yotsuji. SCR: Masaru Yamamoto, Kenji Terada, Tomohiro Ando. DES: Toshio Takagi, Tsutomu Fujita. ANI: Hirokazu Ishiyuki, Toshio Takagi. MUS: Masayuki Yamamoto. PRD: Kokusai Eiga, Movie International, Fuji TV. 25 mins. x 46 eps.

Pollon, the little daughter of the God Apollo, wants to be a powerful and beautiful goddess when she grows up. Somewhat neglected by her single godly parent, she often assists him in his womanizing ways in the vain hope that she will get a new mommy. With her little friend Eros, she plagues the

Olympians in various comical ways as she attempts to earn the trappings of godhood. Sadly (if predictably), her good deeds often backfire, leaving her in hot water with some deity or other and causing chaos for gods and humans alike. But, because she's a kindhearted girl, she will eventually achieve her aim and become a proper, respectable grown-up goddess. This sweet little series for children was the first to be produced in its entirety by Kokusai, based on the manga *Pollon of Olympus* by NANAKO SOS–creator Hideo Azuma, originally serialized in *100-ten Comic*. Combining stories about the Greek and Japanese sun gods (with Apollo taking the role of Japan's female Amaterasu for a few tales), the story also contained comic-relief characters absent from Greek mythology, such as the Hollywood-stereotype mad scientist Dr. Nya-ha-ah. Compare to BIT THE CUPID.

POLLYANNA

1986. JPN: *Ai Shojo Pollyanna Monogatari*. AKA: *The Story of Loving Child Pollyanna*. TV series. DIR: Kozo Kusuba, Norio Yazawa, Shigeo Koshi, Fumio Kurokawa, Harumi Sugimura. SCR: Saiko Kumasen, Tamao Kunihiro. DES: Yoshiharu Sato, Ken Kawai. ANI: Yoshiharu Sato. MUS: Reijiro Komutsu. PRD: Nippon Animation, Fuji TV. 25 mins. x 51 eps.

Eleven-year-old pastor's daughter Pollyanna is sent to live with her aunt, Polly Harrington, after her father's death in 1920s America. Auntie doesn't like children at all and is brusque and distant, but Pollyanna is an irrepressibly buoyant child and softens her aunt's hard heart with her affectionate, gentle personality. Then she has a tragic accident and loses the use of her legs. After a dangerous operation, and with the help and encouragement of the friends she's made in her new life, Pollyanna recovers and is able to join the party for her aunt's wedding.

Based on the 1913 novel and its sequel by Eleanor Hodgman Porter, this is part of the WORLD MASTERPIECE

THEATER series, and in the true *WMT* tradition, ends in happiness all around after a touching, not to say tear-jerking, series of trials. Sato went on to work with Studio Ghibli and has built on his U.S. links, most recently with work for Disney on *The Tigger Movie* (2000).

POLTERGEIST REPORT *

1992. JPN: *Yu Yu Hakusho*. TV series, movie. DIR: Noriyuki Abe, Masakatsu Iijima, Shigeru Ueda, Katsunori Mizuno, Akiyuki Shinbo. SCR: Yoshiyuki Ohashi, Sukehiro Tomita, Katsuyuki Sumizawa, Yoshihiro Togashi. DES: Minoru Yamazawa, Yuji Ikeda. ANI: Saburo Soya, Yoshinori Kanno. MUS: Yusuke Honma. PRD: Studio Pierrot, Fuji TV. 25 mins. x 112 eps. (TV), 25 mins. (m1), 93 mins. (m2).

Middle school tough-guy Yusuke Urameshi is killed trying to save a child in a car accident. In a fustily bureaucratic hell, his name is found to be missing from the Big Book of Dead People, and his "application" is rejected. The son of the ruler of hell (see DORORON ENMA) comes to his rescue and offers him a chance to return whence he came. Repatriated to Earth, he teams up with Death, two demons, and his former rival and becomes a psychic investigator, fighting battle after battle against evil spirits.

Based on the 1990 *Young Jump* manga by HUNTER X HUNTER–creator Yoshihiro Togashi, *PR* sets up a milieu not dissimilar to the background of UROTSUKIDOJI. The human, spirit, and demon worlds coexist, along with a more nebulous, barely glimpsed hell said to be worse than all the others combined. Like the "Wandering Child" Amano, Yusuke does good deeds in the human world, but there the resemblance ends, since *PR* is far more interested in fight-of-the-week stand-offs in the manner of DRAGON BALL. A very successful series, particularly by the short runs of many 1990s anime, *PR* returned in the 30-minute short *PR: The Movie* (1993). Shown as part of a triple bill of TV tie-ins, it took the traditional summer-special route, as

Yusuke's vacation is interrupted by the kidnapping of his boss, Koenma. The kidnappers demand the King of Hell's seal as ransom, and Yusuke is torn between his loyalty to his friend and savior and his fears of what will happen if the seal falls into the wrong hands.

A full-length feature, *PR: Fight for the Netherworld* (1994), featured the Lord of the Netherworld returning after several millennia to conquer Earth by seizing five power sites around Tokyo. The lush, rich, expensive animation was almost totally wasted on a tired plot, making the *PR* feature look remarkably like a bad remake of several other shows, some of which it actually predated—geomancy from SILENT MÖBIUS, a demon invasion à la SAILOR MOON, and modern-day ghostbusting straight out of USHIO AND TORA. Sadly, this suffered the usual flaws of movies released out of context: the overlarge, idle cast of TENCHI MUYO! and the missing backstory of PATLABOR. *PR* isn't an outstanding show of its type, but the TV series might well have fared better than the movie on English release.

There were also several half-hour spin-off videos, whose self-indulgence only goes to show just how popular *PR* was in Japan. The best fight scenes were excerpted on the two-part video compilation *PR: Image Report* (1994; *YYH: Eizo Hakusho*), followed swiftly by five themed clip-shows, compiled as *PR: Image Report II* (1995; *YYH: Eizo Hakusho II*), one for each of the leads. For the ultimate in futile nostalgia, the "next episode" bumpers that closed each episode were released in their own three-part set, *PR: In Next Week's Episode* (1992-94), allowing viewers to spend 90 minutes watching nothing but ads. ●

POMPOKO *

1994. JPN: *Heisei Tanuki Gassen Pompoko*. AKA: *Heisei [Modern-day] Raccoon Wars Pompoko; Defenders of the Forest*. Movie. DIR: Isao Takahata. SCR: Isao Takahata. DES: Megumi Kagawa, Shinji Otsuka. ANI: Shinji Otsuka. MUS: Joe Hisaishi. PRD: Studio Ghibli. 119 mins.

A group of *tanuki* (Japanese raccoon dogs) finds its country life threatened by the construction of a human New Town. At the instigation of the town elder, these tanuki use their powers of transformation to oppose the human encroachment. Unwilling to declare all-out war on humans (they would miss human food), they fake ghostly hauntings, though the supply of human construction workers appears inexhaustible. An 800-year-old super-tanuki orchestrates a ghostly parade down the main street, but the humans are more intrigued than scared—possibly because some of the "ghosts" include cameo appearances from the stars of Hayao Miyazaki's PORCO ROSSO, MY NEIGHBOR TOTORO, and KIKI'S DELIVERY SERVICE. Any spooky effects are ruined when a local theme park takes credit for the parade, falsely claiming that it was a stunt to showcase its special effects technology. The horrified tanuki discover that the theme park is run by foxes, who have given up fighting humanity and instead live among them in disguise. After outwitting the foxes, the tanuki meet for one last trick, transforming the built-up landscape all too briefly into the virgin countryside it once was. Admitting defeat, they scatter among the human race, though sometimes they meet in secret to briefly walk once more in tanuki form.

Familiar characters from JAPANESE FOLK TALES, the mischievous tanuki are used here to tell a touching variant of Studio Ghibli's oft-repeated ecological message—supposedly inspired by the 1960s real-life construction of a suburb in Tama Hills, west of Tokyo. Lamenting the destruction of a way of life in much the same way as NAUSICAÄ and PRINCESS MONONOKE, it also recalls the happy pastorals of *Totoro*. Tanuki were certainly "in" at this point in the 1990s—the unrelated POKONYAN was a big hit at the same time. An English-subtitled print was shown in very limited release in American theaters in advance preparation for a failed attempt to gain the film an Oscar nom-

ination. However, unlike the universal *Totoro*, *Pompoko*'s appeal is, to some extent, ethnocentric. Gags come at the expense of Japanese history and folklore, and some of the humor is a little too earthy for the sanitized Disney market. The end result is often a foreign-language variant on *Watership Down* (1978), with time out for wacky satire, tear-jerking whimsy, and an unforgettable scene in which a tanuki distracts a driver by flattening his testicles against the windshield. Ghibli's usual standard-setting art direction and design are much in evidence. "Pompoko," by the way, is the sound you get when you tap gently on a tummy stretched full of food. The Tama Hills development also featured in UNTIL THE UNDERSEA CITY and WHISPER OF THE HEART.

PONY CANYON

Formed in 1966 as Nippon Broadcasting System Inc., a record label subsidiary of the radio station NBS, the company's name was changed to Pony in 1970 and, following a merger with the record company Canyon, to Pony Canyon in 1987. The company was an early innovator in the field of computer games, but its chief involvement in the anime world is as the music producer on many titles, contributing to such unlikely bedfellows as AIM FOR THE ACE, EMMA, and MAD BULL 34. As Pony Canyon Enterprises, it has also become more directly involved in anime production on titles including GREEN GREEN.

POPOTAN *

2003. TV series. DIR: Shinichiro Kimura. SCR: Jukki Hanada. DES: Rondo Mizukami, Poyoyon Rock, Haruka Sakurai. ANI: Haruka Sakurai. MUS: Osamu Tezuka (b). PRD: SHAFT, Bandai, BS-I. 24 mins. x 12 eps.

Sisters Ai, Mai, and Mii and their android housekeeper Mea live in an old house which travels through time, jumping ahead on each occasion. The sisters are searching for someone, but the search means constantly having to leave the friends they make behind.

Based on the erotic PC computer game of the same name, which is a play on *tanpopo*, the Japanese word for dandelion, *Popotan* features nudity in keeping with its original incarnation, but also an intriguing variant on a perennial anime theme. Whereas childhood memories of a beloved location or friend form background elements in many harem anime such as LOVE HINA, *Popotan*'s periodic temporal relocations allow shifts in relative ages and perspectives like those found in GUNBUSTER and VOICES OF A DISTANT STAR. At its heart, it reflects a yearning for a carefree childhood and a terror of creeping age that feature in many anime for an audience on the cusp of adulthood. **N**

PORCO ROSSO *

1992. JPN: *Kurenai no Buta*. AKA: *The Crimson Pig*. Movie. DIR: Hayao Miyazaki. SCR: Hayao Miyazaki. DES: Hayao Miyazaki, Megumi Kagawa, Toshio Kawaguchi, Katsu Hisamura. ANI: Megumi Kagawa, Toshio Kawaguchi, Katsu Hisamura. MUS: Joe Hisaishi. PRD: Studio Ghibli. 93 mins.
The Adriatic, 1929—the Balkans may go up in flames at any moment, and the Fascists are on the rise in Italy. Mercenary pilots, survivors of the last Great War, work for hire defending transports from marauding pirates, and Marco is the best of them. But as his idealistic youth fades behind him, the former handsome flyer has undergone a strange transformation. He has literally turned into a pig, but nobody seems to mind, least of all him. His life is tranquil and simple; he owns a tiny island and when he isn't flying, he's dozing on the beach with his radio, a newspaper, and a cigarette, or he's meeting his childhood friend, Gina, now a beautiful widow. But Marco's own world is tipped out of balance by the arrival of an American cad, Curtis, who sets out to make his name by shooting down the Crimson Pig. Taking his beloved plane to Milan for repairs after their duel, Marco meets the irrepressible Fio, just 17 but already an aircraft designer of formidable talent. He also finds the secret police are on his tail, along with a gang of angry aerial pirates who want Marco out of the sky for good. Fio mollifies the pirates by appealing to their sense of pride, reminding them that it took an American to shoot down Marco. The pirates, mortified at this threat to their Italian spirit, wager on a rematch, with a victorious Marco winning the costs of his repairs, whereas a victorious Curtis (already rebuffed by Gina) would win the hand of Fio. As the Italian air force arrive to break up the illegal match, Marco and Curtis prepare to hold them off while the others escape. An epilogue implies that Marco has returned to human form, and that he and Gina live happily ever after.

Miyazaki's most "adult" film, initially conceived for an audience of middle-aged men who had forgotten their youthful aspirations, *PR* was the fourth-biggest animated box-office draw ever in Japan, beaten only by two POKÉMON films and PRINCESS MONONOKE. By turns touching, comic, romantic, and edge-of-the-seat gripping, it is a grown-up's fantasy with a child's directness and innocence. It reflects many of its creator's passions and obsessions and also restates many of his central themes, yet the film has its own freshness and originality. Based loosely on a three-part series Miyazaki wrote in 1990 for *Model Graphix* magazine, *PR* was originally planned as a 45-minute in-flight feature for Japan Air Lines. Eventually produced as a full-length movie, a dub was prepared for the English-language audio channel on JAL flights, and subsequently broadcast on British TV. The idea of porcine transformation would return in Miyazaki's SPIRITED AWAY in which a girl must restore her parents to human form.

PORTRISS

2003. JPN: *Mugen Senki Potriss*. AKA: *Tank Knights Portriss; Infinite Military History Portriss*. TV series. DIR: Akira Shigino, Nam Jong-sik. SCR: Shinzo Fujita, Junichi Iioka. DES: Yoshikazu Takaya. ANI: N/C. MUS: N/C. PRD: Bandai, NAS, Sunrise, TV Tokyo. 25 mins. x 52 eps.
Long ago, Portriss Planet was hit by a meteor, and its humanoid population was almost wiped out. To cope with the changed environment, the few survivors evolved into a race of beings with body chemistry based on heavy metallic elements. An elite fighting sect, the Portriss Knights, rose to fight a dictator, and several hundred years later they continue to protect freedom. They have evolved the Portriss Rise function, which enables them to convert their bodies into humanoid tanks during battle and incorporate more weapons. When another evil dictator, Dark Portriss, appears and sets out to construct the ultimate weapon, three Knights stand ready to thwart his plans. Dragon Blue, the leader, Tiger Barrel, the muscle, and birdlike female Rozze Kyaree, who can split into two separate beings with different weapon functions, infiltrate the enemy headquarters at Babel Tower. Dragon Blue loses his Portriss Rise function after a direct hit from Dark Portriss' superweapon, but in Babel the team encounter a boy with no memories who can merge with Dragon Blue and restore his full functions. They name the boy Yuema. Dark Portriss is out to find four mythical ultimate weapons evolved by their ancient humanoid ancestors, and, analyzing Yue-ma's DNA, he uses the boy's strange powers to produce a new life-form with the same abilities as the Portriss Knights. He names it Black Dragon and sends it to destroy the Knights and their Resistance supporters.

A coproduction with South Korea, based on an online computer game, this has tank-tread robots and quasi-comical design aimed at a child audience. Codirector Nam has direction credits for the Korean animated SF TV series *BASToF Syndrome* and movie *Armageddon*. The GUNDAM and TRANSFORMERS influences are obvious in design and plot, with a love child of the Guntank leading a group of young people to change the world, but the nods to *Star Wars* are also unmissable.

POTOMAS THE HIPPO

1988. JPN: *Kaba no Potomas*. Movie. DIR: Taku Sugiyama. SCR: Hitoshi Yokota. DES: N/C. ANI: Shunji Saita. MUS: Takeo Watanabe. PRD: OH Pro. 25 mins.

Potomas the Hippo has a secret—he can speak like a human being, but only the young kids Maki and Toshi realize it. He also wears a bright green T-shirt with a giant letter "P" on it, but this is supposed to be nicely inconspicuous. Momentarily forgetting to keep quiet, Potomas speaks to a child he has just saved from drowning. Rumors soon spread about a talking hippo, and Potomas is forced to go on the run.

POWER DOLLS *

1995. Video. DIR: Tsuneo Tominaga, Masamitsu Hidaka. SCR: Midori Uki, Atsuhiro Tomioka. DES: Masayuki Goto, Yasuhiro Nishinaka. ANI: Masayuki Goto. MUS: Hiroto Saito, Innerbrain. PRD: Kogado Studio, Artmic, VAP. 25 mins. x 2 eps.

It's A.D. 2540, and rebels on the colony world of Omni have been holding out against the Terran government for five years. Without a standing army, the breakaway colonists have fought back by adapting robotic Power Loaders. Originally used to unload spaceships, the machines have been turned into humanoid battle-tanks. A handful of young female pilots (who serve in the Detachment of Limited Line Service to justify the title acronym) is assigned to blow up the dam at Chatteau Village.

Based on a Japanese computer game of the same name, *PD* taps into many well-established conventions designed to appeal to male fans: girls in battledress, girls in robots, girls with guns, girls sniping at other girls. The characters and situations are all stolen stereotypes, and not especially well handled, with competent but limited animation. There's a heroic effort to establish char-

acter depth by delving into the parental relationships of one of the lead characters, and there's a passable fight toward the end, but since its appeal in Japan was predicated on a love of the game, it's difficult for a foreign audience to feel anything except cheated. None of them would stand a chance in a fight with Ripley from *Aliens*, however big their power loaders.

A sequel, *PD2*, reunited the girls in another adaptation of a game scenario, this time a mission to recapture a stolen prototype. This episode in particular was further damaged in the English-language version by an overdose of reverb effects in the dubbing studio, though the pointlessly flashy audio matched the halfhearted attempt by the original crew to polish the *visuals* with some unnecessary digital effects. In 1997, the series continued in Japan on CD-ROM with a story set after the war, as the newly free state starts to pick up the pieces. The Power Dolls unit is disbanded but antigovernment rebels start causing trouble, and former leader Hardy Newland starts gathering the old crew for one more mission as poachers-turned-gamekeepers.

POWER STONE *

1999. TV series. DIR: Masahiro Omori. SCR: Shikichi Ohashi, Masashi Yokoyama, Kenichi Araki. DES: Tadashi Shida. ANI: Yuji Moriyama, Kazuya Miura, Hideyuki Motohashi. MUS: N/C. PRD: Kokusai Eiga, Studio Pierrot, TBS. 25 mins. x 26 eps.

Fokker is on a quest to retrieve the mystical power stones hidden by his father. In a 19th-century world modeled on the foggy London of SHERLOCK HOUND and an olde-worlde Tokyo populated by ninja, Fokker's quest brings him into contact with the British princess Julia, the ninja-girl Ayame, Ryoma the samurai (see OI! RYOMA), Wang Tang the Chinese brawler (actually Won-ton in Japanese, but the jokey name was altered), Garuda the Red Indian [sic], and Rouge the belly-dancing dusky maiden. Then they fight.

Based on a popular game from CAP-

COM, creators of STREET FIGHTER II, *PS* began as a launch title for the Sega Dreamcast, featuring a true 3D environment packed with useful items and a "power stone" collection theme that allowed the players to transform into more powerful versions of themselves. A few years earlier, such a concept might have barely made it straight to video, but in the late 1990s climate heavy with gaming money and short on options, *PS* became a TV series shown in the prime five-o'clock slot, with the characters regressed from the game to create a slightly younger look designed to appeal to children.

PRECURE

2004. JPN: *Futari wa Precure*. AKA: *Together We're Precure; Together We're Pretty Cure; Pretty Cure TV series*. Movie. DIR: Daisuke Nishio, Akinori Yabe, Takao Iwai, Takenori Kawada, Toru Yamada, Yasuo Yamakichi. SCR: Ryo Kawasaki. DES: Akira Inagami. ANI: Hiroyuki Kawano, Masumi Hattori, Mitsuru Aoyama, Toshie Kawamura, Yasuhiro Namatame. MUS: Naoki Sato. PRD: ABC, Asatsu DK, Toei Animation, TV Asahi. 25 mins. x 49 eps. (TV1), 25 mins. x 37 eps. (TV2), ?? mins. (m1), ?? mins. (m2).

Athletic, energetic Nagisa Misumi and her schoolmate, bookish Honoka Yukishiro have nothing in common until they see a shower of shooting stars, and find that two otherworldly visitors have invaded their lives. Pretty pink Mipple and heroic yellow Mepple are refugees from the Garden of Light, which has been overrun by the forces of darkness led by the wicked king Dusk Zone. But instead of a standard trawl through the tropes and clichés of magical-girl anime, this series owes a substantial debt to martial arts serials, such as director Nishio's earlier AIR MASTER. Dusk Zone wants to steal seven magical life-stones that will make him immortal, and the Queen of Light has sent the girls to find help from humankind, with special powers to transform into Cure Black and Cure White, defenders of light. Together, they are Pretty Cure, or Precure—compare to the Beauty Pair, the wrestlers who ultimately inspired the **DIRTY PAIR**. The forces of evil infiltrate their school disguised as student teachers and transfer students, but are no match for Precure, especially when one of them falls for Honoka. The second half of the first series was particularly influenced by **DRAGONBALL Z** (another Nishio production), with the appearance of muscle-bound warriors that could power-up with a glowing aura, just like Super Saiyajins.

At the end of the first season, the wicked King was defeated and the amnesiac Queen came to Earth in the shape of a 12-year-old girl named Hikari Kujo, or Shiny Luminous in her magical incarnation. The second season, *Pretty Cure Max Heart* (2005), featured the return of Nagisa and Honoka, complete with new powers and new costumes, to help her find 12 new magic artifacts. Two months after the second series premiered, *Pretty Cure Max Heart The Movie* (*Eiga Futari Wa Precure Max Heart*) hit Japanese cinemas, and a second movie, *Pretty Cure Max Heart The Movie 2: Friends of the Snow-Laden Sky* (*Eiga Futari Wa Precure Max Heart 2: Yukizora no Tomodachi*), followed in October 2005. The show was created by **STUMBLING WITCH DOREMI**'s Izumi Todo.

PREFECTURAL EARTH DEFENSE FORCE *

1986. JPN: *Kenritsu Chikyu Bogyo Gun.* AKA: *Earth Defense Force.* Video. DIR: Keiji Hayakawa. SCR: Kazunori Ito. DES: Katsumi Aoshima. ANI: Katsumi Aoshima. MUS: Kentaro Haneda. PRD: Shogakukan. 49 mins.
A parody anime in the spirit of writer Ito's **URUSEI YATSURA** about schoolyard feuds being blown out of all proportion—compare to **PROJECT A-KO**. Realizing that the ominous-sounding Telegraph Pole Society (who wish to conquer the world) are probably students at his school, Mr. Roberi forms a Defense Force. Students Shogi Morita (the handsome blond), Kuho Tasuke (his beefy dark-haired pal), and token

girl Akiko Ifukube are ranged against an army of inept ninja. Meanwhile, the high school's mad scientist, Dr. Inogami, has turned local boy Kami Sanchin into a cyborg, and both sides try to recruit him. While the TPS boasts an army of ninja, the pretty pink-haired Captain Baradaga, and "Scope" Tsuzaki, a hulking brute with many high-tech devices, the EDF is somewhat underfunded—after initial promises of supervehicles and amazing gadgets, the best Roberi can rustle up for the fighters is a ramen cart. The two organizations attempt to steal each other's secrets and poach each other's members, while, amid much comic angst about his condition (see **CASSHAN** or **CYBORG 009**), Sanchin tentatively falls in love with the professor's daughter, Yuko, who has been similarly cyberized. Their romance is truncated by their unerring habit of setting off their built-in military hardware anytime they get angry. Once the TPG have been defeated, the professor reluctantly concedes that he can return the couple to human form, but the reversion process accidentally switches their genders. The couple get used to it, while Morita starts going out with his former enemy Baradaga. Based on the 1983 *Shonen Sunday* manga by Koichiro Yasunaga, this send-up was presented as three fake episodes and a fake preview for a nonexistent episode four.

PRETEAR *

2001. JPN: *Shin Shirayuki Densetsu Preytia.* AKA: *New Snow White Legend Pretear.* TV series. DIR: Kenichi Tajiri, Kiyoko Sayama, Yoshitaka Fujimoto, Yoshimasa Hiraike, Takaaki Ishiyama, Yukio Nishimoto. SCR: Hiroyuki Kawasaki, Kenichi Kanemaki, Yoshimi Narita. DES: Akemi Kobayashi. ANI: Itsuko Takeda, Nobuhito Akada, Michinori Chiba, Megumi Kadonosono, Akemi Kobayashi. MUS: Toshiyuki Omori. PRD: Digimation, Group TAC, Anime R, Hal Filmmaker. 25 mins. x 13 eps.
The happy life of 16-year-old Himeno Awayuki is thrown into turmoil when her hard-drinking author father mar-

ries a wealthy fan who is so obsessed with his work that she has named her own daughters after characters in his books. Shunned by her snobbish new stepsisters, Himeno drifts into depression until she meets a group of seven young men on the grounds of the family mansion. They are the Leafe Knights, denizens of the land of Leafeania, here to save the world from the evil Princess of Disaster and her Demon Larva. The Princess has come to Earth to suck all the Leafe—the life-force of all living things—out of the world and use it for her own ends. The Knights are looking for a special girl, the Pretear, who has the ability to merge with any one of them and become a single, all-powerful defender of life. Although the leader of the Knights, hunky 18-year-old Hayate, doubts it, it seems Himeno is the Pretear. His six companions, cute guys aged from 17 down to 5, all take to Himeno; instead of two snooty sisters she suddenly has a band of brothers.

Based on a manga by Junichi Sato and Kaori Naruse, *Pretear* deliberately invokes fairy-tale antecedents, chiefly **CINDERELLA** and **SNOW WHITE**. The style is generic girl's fantasy, with absurdly nasty siblings and cookie-cutter guys, from the moody but fiercely loyal loner playing hard to get to the adorable surrogate kid brothers for mothering practice. The show has a certain amount of charm, but not many outside its target audience of 10-year-old girls will find much to impress.

PRIDE THE MASTER THIEF

1965. JPN: *Kaiketsu Pride.* TV series. DIR: Yuichi Fujiwara. SCR: Takehiko Maeda. DES: Yuichi Fujiwara. ANI: Taku Sugiyama, Motoyoshi Matsumoto, Noboru Ishiguro. MUS: Seiichiro Uno. PRD: TV Doga, Fuji TV. 5 mins. x 115 eps.
Professor Pride and his faithful dog Dry are masters of crime who boast that they can steal anything from the Eiffel Tower to Mount Fuji itself. Pursued across the world by the hapless Detective Scope, Pride stars in the first-ever crime-caper anime, a distant

ancestor of the later **Lupin III** and **Cat's Eye**. The first anime made by TV Doga, a company formed in 1963 by a coalition between the Tokyo advertising company Koei and Fuji TV. The black-and-white series was completely remade in color in 1967 but never broadcast.

PRIME ROSE

1983. JPN: *Time Slip 10,000-nen Prime Rose*. AKA: *10,000 Year Time Slip Prime Rose*. TV special. DIR: Osamu Dezaki, Naoto Hashimoto. SCR: Keisuke Fujikawa. DES: Osamu Tezuka. ANI: Keizo Shimizu, Yukari Kobayashi, Kenichi Onuki. MUS: Yuji Ono. PRD: Magic Bus, Tezuka Pro, Nippon TV. 98 mins.

An accident on the orbiting military satellite Death Mask wipes out cities in Japan and America, but the occupants have not been killed. Danbala Gai, a member of the time patrol, travels 10,000 years into the future, when Earth is ruled by strange creatures, and the occupants of the two cities have formed their own nations. Though he is not supposed to interfere, Gai becomes involved with Prime Rose, a girl who vows to avenge the murder of her fiancé by learning to fight and killing his murderer, Prince Pirar. But the time patrolman shares her ultimate goal—the restoration of true peace to the world. Based loosely on his manga serial in *Shonen Champion*, creator Tezuka intended the title to refer to the "primrose" flower, though his pronunciation recalls the old English origins of the word, not its modern spelling.

PRINCE OF SNOW COUNTRY

1985. JPN: *Yukiguni no Ojisama*. Movie. DIR: Tomoharu Katsumata. SCR: Yugo Serikawa, Tadahiro Shimafuji. DES: Takao Kasai. ANI: Takao Kasai. MUS: Seiji Yokoyama. PRD: Shinano, Toei. 88 mins.

Koichi and his sister Yuki befriend Hanaguro, a swan who has flown to Japan from Siberia. Hanaguro is attacked by a dog, and the cowardly Koichi flees, but that night he has a dream in which he is whisked away to

the Kingdom of the Snow Prince, where he finds the bravery to help the other swans. A moral fable from the Buddhist Soka Gakkai leader Daisaku Ikeda, who also created **Rainbow Across the Pacific** and **Fairground in the Stars**.

PRINCE OF TENNIS

2001. JPN: *Tennis no Ojisama*. AKA: *TeniPuri (short for Tennis Prince)*. TV series, movie. DIR: Takayuki Hamana. SCR: Jun Maekawa. DES: Akiharu Ishii. ANI: Trans Arts. MUS: Cheru Watanabe. PRD: NAS, Production I.G., JC Staff. 22 mins. x 178 eps. (TV) 40 mins. (v) 65 mins. (m).

Ryoma Echizen is a tennis prodigy, haunted by the fame of his father, a former top player who retired unexpectedly at the height of his career—compare to **Yawara**. With four championships under his belt after several years in America, Ryoma returns to Japan to join Seishun Gakuen (Youth Academy) because of its reputation as one of the best junior high schools for tennis, but also because it was Dad's old school. Not everyone else in the school is as focused on the game or as driven by family rivalry, but there's plenty of competition, and he is the first freshman to make it onto the squad. Ryoma is ambidextrous and often switches hands during a game; he's also a loner, and can come across as arrogant, but his veneer of coolness is ignored by friendly Takeshi Momoshiro, who takes him under his wing, and wise-cracking Eiji Kikumaru. Most high school and sports-show tropes make an appearance, but the talented crew gives the show genuine freshness and charm.

Based on a manga by Takeshi Konomi in *Shonen Jump*, with a huge number of characters and the constant challenge of new teams to face, sports soap opera *PoT* replicated the success of basketball series **Slam Dunk** for the female market. A video followed: *PoT: A Day on Survival Mountain (TnO: Sonzokuyama no Hi)*. In the movie *PoT: The Two Samurai: The First Game* (2005, *TnO: Futari no Samurai: The First Game*),

Ryoma and his classmates play an exhibition game on a luxury cruise ship, only to learn that they're being used as pawns in a corrupt millionaire's web of gambling and deceit, while Ryoma meets his supposed brother. **①Ⓥ**

PRINCE PIRATE

1966. JPN: *Kaizoku Oji*. TV series. DIR: Yoshio Kuroda, Kimio Yabuki, Kenji Araki. SCR: Jiro Yoshino, Minoru Hamada, Hiroyasu Yamaura, Yasuo Yamaguchi, Okichi Harada, Ichiro Wakabayashi. DES: Shotaro Ishinomori. ANI: Tameo Ogawa, Eisuke Kondo, Shinichi Suzuki, Hiroshi Wagatsuma. MUS: Hisayuki Miyazaki. PRD: Toei, NET. 25 mins. x 31 eps.

Kidd's dying father tells him of Morgan, a pirate who yearns to rule the seven seas. Kidd tracks down Morgan's ship, the Hurricane, wins over its skipper, an old sailor called Crapp, and becomes the new captain. However, his dreams of a life on the open sea are soon scrapped by the arrival of the Barracuda and its nasty captain, Fugg Hook.

Mixing equal parts of **Peter Pan and Wendy** with **Sindbad the Sailor**, and adapted from **Cyborg 009**–creator Ishinomori's manga in *Shonen King*, *PP* also featured a genuine kid playing Kidd—the lead voice actor was the 13-year-old Satoshi Furuya, better known today as King Philip in **Alexander**. Captain Kidd's treasure would also feature in **Dagger of Kamui**.

PRINCE PLANET *

1965. JPN: *Yusei Shonen Papi*. AKA: *Planet Boy Papi*. TV series. DIR: Tsutomu Yamamoto, Yonehiko Watanabe, Tadao Wakabayashi, Takeshi Kawauchi. SCR: Ichiro Kanai, Jusaburo Futaba, Satoshi Ogura. DES: Hideoki Inoue. ANI: Tadao Wakabayashi. MUS: Keiro Miki. PRD: TCJ, Eiken, Fuji TV. 25 mins. x 52 eps.

Unwilling to admit Earth into the Galactic Council of Planets until its warlike ways are curbed, the council appoints a prince from the pacifist planet Radion as an Earth-based ambassador. Crash-landing in the American

Southwest, he befriends local oil heiress Diana Worthy, who helps him blend in with Earth society. Before long, "Bobby," as he is now known, moves to the urban sprawl of New Metropolis, where his superpowered pendant from Radion bestows superhuman strength and the ability to fly. With his sometime associates Ajababa the magician and wrestler Dan Dynamo, he fights crime in a predictable but earnest cross of AMAZING THREE and ASTRO BOY. Based on a manga by Hideoki Inoue, a former assistant of Mitsuteru Yokoyama. As was customary in the American market at the time, the original Japanese theme was replaced with a new track, on this occasion by the Carol Lombard Singers.

PRINCESS ANMITSU

1986. JPN: *Anmitsu Hime*. TV series. DIR: Masami Annai, Rei Hidaka, Takaaki Ishiyama. SCR: Yoshio Urasawa, Tomoko Konparu, Hideo Takayashiki, Yoshiyuki Suga, Masaru Yamamoto. DES: Shosuke Kurogane. ANI: Yoshiyuki Kishi. MUS: Hiroshi Ogasawara. PRD:Studio Pierrot, Fuji TV. 25 mins. x 51 eps. A cheeky, vivacious little medieval Japanese princess is bored with life in her father's castle of Amakara. With her best friend Takemaru in sometimes reluctant pursuit, she sets about livening things up. Luckily, as her father's sole heir, she's unlikely to get into real trouble, and since she really loves Takemaru, she'll try and make sure he doesn't either.

Shosuke Kurogane's original manga began in 1949 in *Shojo Comic* magazine, finished in 1955, and was first approached as an anime project in 1961. Abandoned by the inexperienced team because of soaring costs, it took Studio Pierrot to give it all the charm and energy the author hoped for 25 years later, presenting a sweetly fantasized picture of the ideal Japanese childhood, in which preschool- and kindergarten-age children are secure, loved, and much indulged, and their little naughtinesses always innocent and always forgiven.

PRINCESS ARITE

2001. JPN: *Arite-hime*. Movie. DIR: Sunao Katabuchi. SCR: Sunao Katabuchi. DES: Keiko Morikawa. ANI: Kazusane Ozaki. MUS: N/C. PRD: Studio 4°C, Omega Project. ca. 90 mins. Princess Arite, a little girl who lives in a small room on top of a tower, yearns to learn magic and escape to the town below. This fairy tale from Katabuchi, former assistant to Miyazaki on KIKI'S DELIVERY SERVICE, was made inside a computer, though it retains the appearance of traditional cel animation. Based on the novel *The Clever Princess* by Diana Coles.

PRINCESS ARMY

1992. Video. DIR: Osamu Sekita. SCR: Miyuki Kitagawa. DES: Yumi Yamada. ANI: Yumi Yamada. MUS: Yuichi Takahashi. PRD: Group Tack, Animate Film. 30 mins. x 2 eps. Rescued from a drunken attacker by a judoist, Aida Nonoka resolves to become as good as her savior, hoping one day to recognize him by the scar on his back. Transferred to a new high school, she meets two older boys who could possibly be the person to whom she owes her life and wants to give her heart—see UTENA. Multiple unrequited yearnings as three judo girls and three judo boys fall in and out of love while they're supposed to be throwing each other around a room—with matters greatly exacerbated by the sudden arrival of a forgotten fiancé from Holland. Based on the manga in *Shojo* magazine by Miyuki Kitagawa, this is an even gentler judo soap opera than YAWARA, whose earlier success it was doubtless trying to emulate.

PRINCESS KNIGHT *

1967. JPN: *Ribon no Kishi*. AKA: *Knight of the Ribbon; Choppy and the Princess; The Adventures of Choppy and the Princess; Princesse Saphir*. TV series. DIR: Chikao Katsui, Nobuo Onuki, Yoshiyuki Tomino, Masami Hata, Ryosuke Takahashi, Hideo Makino, Seiji Okuda, Norio Hikone. SCR: Osamu Tezuka, Masaki Tsuji. DES: Kazuko

Nakamura, Sadao Miyamoto, Minoru Nishida. ANI: Sadao Miyamoto. MUS: Isao Tomita. PRD: Tezuka Pro, Fuji TV. 25 mins. x 52 eps., 25 mins. (pilot). Thanks to an accident in heaven, where the mischievous cherub Tink is responsible for giving out hearts to babies, Princess Sapphire of Silverland is born with two—a man's *and* a woman's. This is fortunate for her father the king, who proclaims to the populace that the new child is a boy, and, consequently, that any succession problems are over. The secret is kept, since if it becomes known that the heir is a girl, the succession will pass to the corrupt Duke Jeralmin. She grows up as a boy, learning all the masculine skills and doing her utmost to excel and make her father and her people proud. But when she falls in love with the charming prince Franz Charming, she faces a terrible dilemma. Revealing her womanhood would throw away her own achievements, her father's dreams, and the stability of her country—but staying a man means she must sacrifice her dream of love forever.

Beginning as a 1953 manga in *Nakayoshi*, Osamu Tezuka's *PK* was the ASTRO BOY–creator's tribute to the many Takarazuka musical revues he saw as a child, where the all-female cast made cross-dressing a narrative necessity. This gem of a series, much loved in Europe, is less well known in the English-speaking world despite several English-language releases, but its enduring influence can be seen in the massive success of its immediate heirs ROSE OF VERSAILLES and UTENA, as well as in the prevalence of cross-dressing battle-babes throughout anime. It also has powerful links with the magical-girl shows in the princess's masquerade under another identity, her fight against supernatural evil, and her friend and protector-sprite Tink. Its style and pace seem dated now, but the themes, ideas, and plots Tezuka generated are still being reexamined by modern directors and writers who were not even born when it was first broadcast. Versions of *PK* will probably go on being retold forever, but however modern the trappings, they will stand or fall on how they measure up to the power and simplicity of Tezuka's original.

It had a limited American TV release in 1972 under the title *Princess Knight*. Licensees Joe Oriolo and Burt Hecht did better with three episodes edited into a movie entitled *Choppy and the Princess*. With Tink renamed Choppy, this was shown frequently on syndicated TV throughout the U.S. in the 1970s and 1980s. The series also made it onto Australian screens under the *PK* title, and a number of 25-minutes episodes were released on British video by two different distributors. Movie Makers released seven episodes under the general title *The Adventures of Choppy and the Princess* and at least three more under individual episode titles without the *AoCatP* surtitle. Tasley Leisure of Leeds released six episodes as *Choppy and the Princess, Adventures 1–6*. The English dubs lose one of Tezuka's beloved jokes—he named the good characters and countries in his fable after precious stones and metals, with the bad guys named after cheap synthetics like nylon and plastic, but the names have been mangled in translation. Following Tezuka's death in 1989, the series was released on Japanese laser disc in 1991, with the original unbroadcast pilot included as a bonus extra.

PRINCESS MEMORY *

2001. Video. DIR: Ko Tomi. SCR: Mirin Muto. DES: Akira Kano. ANI: Yuji Ushijima. MUS: N/C. PRD: Lemon Heart. 30 mins. x 2 eps.
Collin is a serving boy in a tavern, haunted by dreams of a naked pink-haired damsel in distress, begging for him to rescue her. His fellow workers, pretty girls Pony and Sallion, refuse to take him seriously and force him to get on with his chores until flame-haired adventurer Lily arrives. She has come into town to explore a forbidden cave on its outskirts. Deciding to accompany her on her quest, Collin discovers that there was an element of truth in his

Princess Knight

dreams—one Felina is being held captive, but her soul has been split into separate personality shards, each of which must be collected like **POKÉMON**. If he is able to win them all over, then she shall be restored and accept him as her knight in shining armor, but not before he has had sex with the other cast members—compare to **DVINE** [**LUV**]. **N**

PRINCESS MINERVA *

1995. Video. DIR: Mihiro Yamaguchi. SCR: Hideki Sonoda. DES: Tokuhiro Matsubara. ANI: Tokuhiro Matsubara, Hanchi Rei, Hokukan Sen. MUS: Kenji Kawai. PRD: Pastel. 45 mins.
Without a male heir, the kingdom of Wisler has a girl for its next leader. Minerva is a vain, headstrong, selfish princess who's bored with her role and wants to excel at combat and spellcasting. Despite the best efforts of her chief guard, Blue Morris, to keep her safe (and keep her in check), she disguises herself to fight in a big tournament for girl fighters. Unfortunately, evil sorceress Dynastar hates Minerva and sets out to kidnap her, but grabs Blue Morris instead. The Princess realizes the error of her ways, gets the warrior girls to help her, and sets out to rescue her long-suffering bodyguard.

PM is sweetly predictable, signaling its next move so far ahead that suspense is not one of its outstanding qualities. Based on a computer game/manga/novel multimedia offensive by Ko Maisaka and Run Ishida, its origins are betrayed in an outsized cast to showcase everyone's favorite from the original. Gently poking fun at **PRINCESS KNIGHT** and other tomboy heroines (at one point, the narrator tries to explain how kindhearted Minerva is, only to choke on his own words), the result is a lackluster cousin to **DRAGON HALF** but without its predecessor's insane charm. The character designs are cute but not very original; ditto the story. Uncritical fans of babes in battle bikinis may be amused.

PRINCESS MONONOKE *

1997. JPN: *Mononoke Hime*. AKA: *Princess Ghost; Phantom Princess*. Movie. DIR: Hayao Miyazaki. SCR: Hayao Miyazaki. DES: Hayao Miyazaki. ANI: Masashi Ando, Kitaro Kosaka, Yoshifumi Kondo. MUS: Joe Hisaishi. PRD: Studio Ghibli. 133 mins.
Young Prince Ashitaka defeats a supernatural beast plaguing the remote Eastern lands in which his tribe dwells but is left with a wound that refuses to heal. Because its origin is supernatural, it

© 1997 NIBARIKI/TNDG

Princess Mononoke

has a strange effect that gives Ashitaka superhuman strength and accuracy, enabling his arrows to take the heads or arms off his enemies, but it will also kill him, slowly but surely. Finding that the beast was maddened by an iron ball in its flesh, he goes in search of the culprits, hoping they can provide some way of curing him. As he wanders through the Western forests, he finds a village of ironworkers, the source of the bullet. Tataraba, the ironworkers' fort, is in conflict with both the local overlord and the creatures of the forest, which are led by a wild girl who rides on a wolf. San, an abandoned child adopted by the wolf god Moro and raised as one of her own cubs, now hates the humans who abandoned her. All her loyalty and devotion is given to her new family, the ancient beast gods whose lands are threatened by the incursions of the growing human population. Eboshi, the tough, pragmatic leader of the ironworkers, is consumed with hatred for San, and Ashitaka, a natural peacemaker whose wish is to see everyone live in harmony, tries in vain to settle their differences. He has another agenda; apart from his hope that he may find healing in the forest, he is falling in love with San. The distant, unseen emperor, who claims to be the Son of Heaven, authorizes the death of Shishigami, the woodland god who is responsible for the natural (and

supernatural) resistance to Tataraba. Stealthy humans massacre many of the forest creatures, but the wrath of Shishigami is unstoppable . . . almost.

Purportedly set in medieval Japan but depicting a symbolic *neverwhen* clash of three proto-Japanese races (the Jomon, Yamato, and Emishi), *PM* is the ultimate prequel to Studio Ghibli's ecological concerns in films such as NAUSICAÄ and POMPOKO. It is set at the very point in time when humankind pushed Nature into submission, toppling the old "natural" order and starting the long chain to the present day, when Nature itself seems under threat of extinction. Twenty years in conception and three in production, the highest-grossing Japanese *movie* in any genre at least until SPIRITED AWAY beat Miyazaki's own record, and the first of Miyazaki's films to be released theatrically in America through the Disney/Tokuma marketing deal, *PM* has built a cinematic legend of its own. Born from the creator's own dissatisfaction with the end of *Nausicaä*, which required a miraculous *deus ex machina* to resolve the human/nature conflict, *PM* is consequently far more downbeat and melancholy. Though a minority of critics still regard it as a tedious harangue, even the many who call it Miyazaki's masterpiece agree it's a difficult film for U.S. movie audiences, who are simply unaccustomed

either to animation as polemic, or to the level of violence depicted. Preview audiences, not expecting a Tarantino image in a Disney movie, reacted with nervous laughter to a sequence where a man gets his arm shot off. Producer Toshio Suzuki's strict and noble "no cuts" policy may have preserved Miyazaki's creative vision but made the film difficult to sell into markets that still believed cartoons were kids' stuff. Technically, *PM* is a remarkable achievement, especially on the level of art direction and design; the primeval forests of Japan and the first stirrings of industrial society are depicted with ravishing realism. The characters are well drawn in every sense, each with his or her own motivations and needs, not cardboard heroes and villains but humans struggling to get by in a hostile world. This is a grown-up fantasy, and unlike the vast run of anime that gives us stock figures in pretty clothes and wish-fulfillment situations, *PM* presents real people in a real world that is beautiful and fascinating but must be taken on its own terms.

The U.S. dub, which featured a script rewrite by *Sandman* author Neil Gaiman, was the first theatrical anime production since the ARMITAGE III movie to use "name" actors, with a cast including Billy Crudup, Claire Danes, Minnie Driver, and Gillian Anderson. *PM* was widely reported as being Miyazaki's last film, but he has since completed SPIRITED AWAY and HOWL'S MOVING CASTLE. **Ⓥ**

PRINCESS NINE *
1998. TV series. DIR: Tomomi Mochizuki. SCR: Hiro Maruyama. DES: Akihiko Yamashita, Yoshimi Hashimoto. ANI: Yoshimi Hashimoto. MUS: Masamichi Amano. PRD: Phoenix/NEP21, NHK2. 25 mins. x 26 eps.
Girls don't play baseball, they play softball. But 15-year-old Ryo Hayakawa is a natural ace pitcher, just about to finish junior high and leave so she can help her widowed mother with the family noodle bar. Instead, Mrs. Himuro, Chairperson of the prestigious Kisaragi

High School, persuades Ryo to continue her education by handing her a scholarship. Keiko Himuro plans to take on the male-dominated "hard" sports with an all-girl team, deliberately designed to irritate the snooty and chauvinistic male teachers and staff who think that a girl's education should only aspire to motherhood and housewifery. But sporty girls are competitive by nature, and Ryo is soon butting heads with Izumi Himuro, the prideful, overly competitive daughter of the chairwoman and the school's tennis champion. Despite her initial opposition, Izumi eventually joins the team, adding much-needed batting power. Rivalries soon break out on and off the field, as the girls fight over token boy Hiroki and corporate sponsorship comes attached to corporate scandal. This typical baseball anime in the fashion of **H2** was dumped onto satellite TV in the impecunious late 1990s as the post-**EVANGELION** anime TV boom turned into a slump.

PRINCESS ROUGE *

1997. AKA: *Legend of the Last Labyrinth*. Video. DIR: Isato Date. SCR: Mamoru Takeuchi. DES: Minoru Yamazawa. ANI: Minoru Yamazawa. MUS: N/C. PRD: Beam Entertainment. 30 mins. x 2 eps.
Recently orphaned teenager Yusuke Mizuki struggles to live alone, until a dimensional portal opens while he is cycling to school, literally dumping a pretty girl in his lap. Reluctantly he takes care of the amnesiac green-haired girl who can only remember her name, Rouge. As a mawkish romance develops between them, **OH MY GODDESS!** comparisons become actionably obvious, as the couple is besieged by Rouge's supernatural sisters, Kaige and Meige. Discovering that Rouge is a princess of the underworld, the pair is forced to flee from other family members, chiefly a man called Raiga and his sword-wielding minions. Raiga wants Rouge to help him unseal Gaia's Sword, an artifact of great power. As with so many video anime, the cliff-

hanger ending and lack of follow-up aren't the fault of Western distributors. Six episodes were projected, but after poor sales, only the two on the American video release were ever made.

PRINCESS 69 *

2002. JPN: *Shintaiso Kari*. AKA: *New Gymnastics Kari* (i.e., *Rhythmic Gymnastics Kari*). Video. DIR: N/C. SCR: N/C. DES: N/C. ANI: N/C. MUS: N/C. PRD: Pink Pineapple. 30 mins. x 2 eps. (v1), 30 mins. x 2 eps. (v2)
In an erotic pastiche of the school sports genre of **AIM FOR THE ACE**, rich, privileged Tomomi is the star of her school gymnastics club, determined to break the will of shy, innocent new arrival Miku by indoctrinating her in the sadistic rituals of the Gymnastics of Darkness. This involves torture and bondage after school, both at the hands of Tomomi and her sometime lover, the coach Nikasuke. Other girls are soon recruited, some willingly, some less so, such as Madoka, who confesses to her friend Wakana that she has seen the secret rituals, only to discover that Wakana is already an initiate. Later episodes collapse from the silly into the disturbing as the tortures get increasingly sadistic. For some reason, the sequel *Rhythmic Gymnastics Makoto* (2005) appears to have been released by a different company, as part of the **DISCOVERY SERIES**. ⬤🅝🆅

PRINCESS TUTU *

2002. JPN: *Princess Tutu/Chuchu*. TV series. DIR: Junichi Sato, Shogo Kawamoto, Ikuko Ito, Kiyoko Sayama, Osamu Sekita, Yu Ko. SCR: Chiaki Konaka, Mamiko Ikeda, Michiko Yokote, Rika Nanase, Takuya Sato. DES: Ikuko Ito. ANI: Akemi Kobayashi, Takashi Shiokawa, Yuji Ushijima, Nobuto Akada, Shinichi Yoshikawa. MUS: Kaoru Wada. PRD: Hal Film Maker, Kid's Station, Imagica. 30 mins. x 13 eps. (TV1) 15 mins. x 26 eps. (TV2).
Gangly, clumsy but determined, Ahiru (whose name is Japanese for duck) studies ballet at Kinkan Academy—a duckling training to become a swan,

just in case that wasn't obvious. She adores Mythos, the school's star male dancer, from afar, but he's so remote and passive that he hardly seems to notice anything. His sinister friend Fakir protects and bullies him in equal measure, and elegant and self-centerd Rue, the school's star ballerina, wants him for herself.

This fairy tale redolent of **TALES OF HANS CHRISTIAN ANDERSEN** is also a magical-girl story, a high school romance in which the clumsiest but most determined and kind-hearted girl in the class struggles to win the school hunk; a drama fable along the lines of **MASK OF GLASS** (featuring much music from famous ballets), and the tale of a hero's fight against the forces of darkness seen through the eyes of the princess. The characters inhabit a reality not dissimilar to that of **RANMA ½,** in which an ordinary town can be populated with animal-human hybrids subject to strange enchantments.

The reason is supposedly rooted in an ancient fairy tale, in which a handsome, noble prince fought an evil raven. The story teller died before the story could be finished, and, determined to fulfill their destinies despite the death of their creator, the prince and the bird escaped from the story. In our own world, the prince sacrificed his heart to seal the raven's powers away and protect the world from her malice. But since a story demands an ending a duck is magically transformed into a human girl—with help and advice from mechanical doll musician Edel, Ahiru can use a magic pendant to transform herself into Princess Tutu. When she has retrieved every piece of the prince's lost heart, he will be free. But the raven princess is also free, and determined to fight the swan princess, and Ahiru has a hitherto unsuspected handicap. She transforms back into her duck self whenever she quacks, and she quacks when she's startled. It takes a splash of water to get her back to normal.

The charm of *PT* is its attempt to subvert the formulae of its genres, such as allowing the princess to save the hero. The sensual yearning at the heart of all school romances mixes with the fear of the adult world, in which everything is unfamiliar and safety nets are few; but stronger than the powerful mix of fear and sex is a passion for stories and storytelling, for the magic of making a new world. Borrowing from European folklore already familiar to many Japanese through earlier anime, it deftly creates an internal reality where perception is just a medium for filtering dreams to find the one your heart holds dearest. Writer Konaka brings in a mechanical being wiser and more reliable than most organic ones, just as he did in ARMITAGE III and MALICE DOLL, and keeps the story closer to the terrifying undercurrents of SWAN LAKE than the sugarplum fairy tale of *The Nutcracker*. There's a wonderful echo of LITTLE MERMAID each time Tutu gives the Prince back a piece of his heart; with each piece he gains the power to express new emotions and ideas, but not always pleasant ones. The things she unleashes in him often tear at her own heart like knives. The series is divided into two parts, the first 13 half-hour episodes known as the Egg Chapter, and the following 26 15-minute episodes, shown two at a time, known as the Chick Chapter. **V**

PRISM SEASON

1989. JPN: *Nagata Megumi Prism Season*. AKA: *Megumi Nagata's Prism Season*. Video. DIR: Yuichi Ito. SCR: Yuichi Ito. DES: Megumi Nagata. ANI: Yuichi Ito. MUS: Ami Osaki. PRD: Grouper Pro. 30 mins.
In a gentle adaptation of Megumi Nagata's book *Flowers Wait for the Moon*, a girl grows up, falls in love, and becomes a mother, realizing that her childhood is now forever behind her. The same illustrator's distinctive pastels, Victorian-style fairies, and falling flowers could also be seen in later follow-ups, 1994 Japanese-style adaptations of THUMBELINA, Mimei Ogawa's children's book *The Coloring Magician*, and *Mermaid and the Red Candle*,

though, as a combination of still pictures and narration, none of them is technically anime.

PRIVATE PSYCHO LESSON *

1996. JPN: *Kojin Jugyo*. AKA: *U-Jin's Personal Tuition*. Video. DIR: Tetsuro Amino. SCR: Ryusei. DES: Makoto Takahata. ANI: N/C. MUS: N/C. PRD: JC Staff, Blue Mantis. 35 mins. x 2 eps.
Sara Iijima of Stunford [*sic*] University is a psychotherapist working in the field of higher education—which means most of her patients are high school or college students, coincidentally the target audience for this video. The traditional watch-on-a-chain method is not for her; to hypnotize patients she whips her top off, gets into a state of sexual excitement, and rotates her breasts in opposite directions. Once the patients are under her hypnotic influence, she regresses them to the point of trauma and sorts it out with a bit of fan service. This sex-solves-everything school of analysis has made her very successful—she travels to assignments in her own helicopter gunship and disciplines inadequate teachers with a few hundred well-aimed bullets. A variant on the elder erotic initiatress also seen in REI REI, but the script's treatment of rape—a punishment for bad Japanese girls dealt out by foreign men—is particularly offensive. U-Jin, who wrote the original manga, knows what his audience wants, but he's capable of delivering it more cleverly; see the TALES OF . . . series. **LNV**

PRIVATE SESSIONS *

2001. AKA: *Tokubetsu Jugyo Video*. DIR: Hiroyuki Yanase. SCR: Rokurota Makabe. DES: Hiroyuki Yanase. ANI: Hiroyuki Yanase. MUS: Yoshi. PRD: YOUC Digital Works (Vanilla Series). 30 mins. x 2 eps. (v1) 30 mins. x 2 eps. (v2).
Takumi Mikami is unable to find full-time work as a teacher because he has a record for sexually abusing his pupils. However, such foibles are no bar to employment in the world of anime pornography, and so he is soon taking a temporary teaching job at a

high-class girls' school famed for its discipline. By a remarkable coincidence, discipline is what Takumi is best at, and his sex slave Sahi Azuma is already working at the school in another teaching post. His first victim is Natsuki, the heroine of the basketball club, whom he rapes in his office after practice, while Sahi captures the incident on video. Meanwhile, the brother of one of Takumi's other victims decides that it is more important for his sister's honor for him to regain the tape of her rape than it is for him to report it to the police.

The seemingly unrelated *Private Sessions* 2 (2003) features Juichiro Aoki, a famous painter who lives in a mansion in the leafy suburbs of Kyoto. His wife Reika is 30 years younger than he, and only married him in order to pay off the debts of her father, the *ikebana* master. Although the marriage is technically loveless, Juichiro's wife has come to enjoy their bondage games, as does Juichiro's new apprentice Kaoru, who witnesses their activities in secret.

For the second part of *PS2*, the scene changes once more to a school, where Tomoya Ishiguro realizes that he is the spitting image of one of the real teachers, and so is able to smuggle himself into the daily life of the school. His schoolgirl victims include computer geek Yumi, librarian Seira and art student Asuka. Based on a computer game by Bishop. Another entry in the VANILLA SERIES. **LNV**

PRODUCTION IG

Founded in 1987 by Mitsuhisa Ishikawa and Takayuki Goto as an offshoot of Tatsunoko Productions, the company was first known by a name that combined its founders' initials—IG Tatsunoko. Its first major role was as a production house on the first PATLABOR movie—the authors speculate that, had the movie been a failure, the existence of a separate company would have shielded the parent from liability. Renamed Production IG, it was subsequently merged with ING, another of Ishikawa's companies, to form the entity as it is known today, with credits ranging from **Ghost in the Shell** to **Blood: The Last Vampire** and a prominent position as a subcontractor on Studio Ghibli's **Princess Mononoke**. Notable staffers include Ishikawa himself, Hiroyuki Kitakubo, Toshihiro Kawamoto, and computer animator Norifumi Kiyozumi. Production IG has benefited greatly from its association with director Mamoru Oshii and also from its high profile in the Western fan community, bolstered by a U.S. office. The company is a major player in digital animation, and pioneered "screen architecture"—that is, the pre-visualizing of effects that will be applied to a scene, allowing animators to get a better idea of how their work will look when it is finally composited with multiple effects and filters. Production IG also created the "anime" sequence of **Kill Bill: The Origin of O-Ren** and "Last Orders" (1997), a superb one-minute pastiche of Madhouse Studios' future dystopias as an animated commercial for Murphy's Stout in the U.K. Production IG's advertising work for other companies includes commercials for Kirin Lemon, T-Mobile, and Samsung. The animation studio Xebec is a subsidiary of the company.

PROFESSOR PAIN *

1998. JPN: *Gakuen Sodom*. AKA: *Sodom Academy*. Video. DIR: Genkuro Shizuka. SCR: Genkuro Shizuka. DES: Saki Kuradama. ANI: Saki Kuradama. MUS: N/C. PRD: Beam Entertainment. 25 mins. x 2 eps.
Frustrated teacher Mr. Ohse plants high explosives all over the school (a *university* in the U.S. dub), locks his students in the chemistry lab, and subjects them to sexual torments. A female teacher tries to negotiate and becomes Ohse's next victim. Eventually, however, the secret behind Ohse's madness is revealed. Distraught at his sister's suicide after a gang rape and livid that the press assumed she led her assailants on, Ohse has been encouraged, in a pastiche of the previous year's **Perfect Blue**, to wire up the school and kill his

pupils by anonymous e-mails sent by someone posing as his sister. His aim is to create an over-the-top circus of depravity for the media he so despises. In other words, *PP* wants the best of both worlds—a snide pop at media perversity as an excuse for an hour of orgiastic bondage.

Whereas the original computer game had one of the hapless boys ("forced" by Ohse to copulate with the girl he secretly adores) as a point-of-view character, Genkuro Shizuka's script concentrates on Ohse himself, though the result is still one of anime's most filthily degenerate videos. Merely summarizing the plot is pushing the boundaries of decency—lowlights include grateful rape victims, sexual assault with a mop, a girl forced to evacuate her bowels at the front of the class, needles stuck into breasts, and a lactating teacher providing nourishment for her pupils. **ⒸⓃⓋ**

PROFESSOR POPPEN AND THE SWAMP OF NO RETURN

1982. JPN: *Poppen Sensei to Kaerazu no Numa*. TV special. DIR: Shiro Ii, Yoshimitsu Morita. SCR: Akiteru Yokomitsu. DES: Shinya Takahashi. ANI: Kazuyoshi Yoshida. MUS: Kuni Kawauchi. PRD: Heruhen, Mainichi, TBS. 90 mins.
The assistant professor of biology at Udo University is dispatched to the local marshes to write a paper on the food chain. However, he is unable to formulate a thesis and angrily decides to stop time. Transforming himself into an insect, he then changes shape into a fish, a kingfisher, and a weasel in order to experience the struggle for life firsthand. Based on the *Professor Poppen* series of stories by Katsuhiko Funahashi.

PROGOLFER SARU

1982. AKA: *Progolfer Monkey*. TV special, TV series, movie. DIR: Hiroshi Fukutomi, Junji Nishimura, Minoru Arai, Yasuhiro Imagawa, Tameo Ogawa, Tsukasa Sunaga. SCR: Noboru Shiroyama, Seiji Matsuoka. DES: Shinichi Suzuki. ANI: Toshiyuki Honda, Hideyuki Moto-

hashi. MUS: Hiroshi Tsutsui. PRD: Shinei Doga, TV Asahi. 111 mins. (TVm1), 25 mins. x 147 (TV), 96 mins. (TVm2), 44 mins. (m1), 75 mins. (m2).
Sarumaru Sarutani is a professional golfer, determined to defeat the shadowy Mr. X and his syndicate of evil golfers, including Dragon the kung-fu golf master. This TV special was based on the 1974 manga by Motoo Abiko, one half of the Fujiko-Fujio duo who created **Doraemon**. Splitting from his working partner Hiroshi Fujimoto in the 1980s, he produced several titles under the name Fujiko-Fujio "A," including **Parasol Henbe**, **Laughing Salesman**, and **Billy Dog**—*PGS* is his longest and most successful creation. Serialized in publications for the very young, such as *Mommy, Baby Book*, and *Corocoro Comic*, the story was never intended for the adult audience, except perhaps as a way of making Dad's weekend hobby look more interesting to his children. The hero's much more akin to the Man with No Name than to the irrepressible Stone Monkey of **Journey to the West**, but these games are played strictly for laughs.

Bringing new meaning to the term "crazy golf," *PGS* returned as a TV series in 1985, with a series of fantastical tournaments in which players used absurd special powers, and the simian Saru remained determined to triumph. Amid kung-fu masters, dragon warriors, and fairway fairies, his opponents include Death himself. In the midst of these adventures, he went to America in another TV movie *PGS: Saru in USA* (1985) for a duel against the Native American golf-shaman Hawkwild. The movies beckoned with *PGS: Challenge of Super Golf World* (1986), set in the eponymous theme park where our hero faced the world greats at a tournament run by the ever-present Mr. X. A second movie, *PGS: Koga's Secret Zone—the Shadow Ninja Golfer* (1987), took Saru to a hidden valley in the Japanese Alps, where Saru and his family must battle a trio of golf-assassins. More adult golfing activities would be the focus of **Beat Shot**.

PROJECT A-KO *

1986. JPN: *Project A-Ko*. Movie, video. DIR: Katsuhiko Nishijima; Yuji Moriyama. SCR: Yuji Moriyama, Katsuhiko Nishijima, Tomoko Kawasaki; Takao Koyama. DES: Yuji Moriyama. ANI: Yuji Moriyama, Tomohiro Hirata. MUS: Richie Zito, Joey Carbone. PRD: APPP, Studio Fantasia. 80 mins. (m), 70 mins., 50 mins., 60 mins., 55 mins. x 2 eps. (all video). An alien spaceship crashes on Graviton City. Nobody clears it away, people get used to it being there, and gradually the district is rebuilt on an island around the hulk. Years later, two new girls arrive in class—late, as they always will be—at the Graviton Institute for Girls. Eiko ("A-Ko") Magami is a normal Japanese schoolgirl hero, apart from superstrength and superspeed inherited from superparents who are only revealed at the end of the film—one of its many in-jokes. She's cheerful, loyal, and always tries her best. Her best friend, C-Ko Kotobuki, is very, very stupid but so unbelievably cute that she reawakens an intense crush in rich, clever, and beautiful B-Ko Daitokuji. B-Ko decides that she'll break up the friendship between A-Ko and C-Ko, and then C-Ko will be *her* best friend.

Starting out looking like just another girls' school story in the tradition of TWINS AT ST. CLARE'S, *PA* was actually named after Jackie Chan's *Project A* (1984), and the inspiration of the master of slapstick martial-arts mayhem is obvious. The film pokes fun at such anime staples as the heroic CAPTAIN HARLOCK, here transformed into a cross-dressing dipsomaniac, and the alien-princess-school-love-triangle so successful in URUSEI YATSURA, as well as throwing in foreign jokes like the rotund American fast-food icon Colonel Sanders, in a parody of a scene from HARMAGEDON depicting a terrifying warrior emerging from a dark alley toward the hero. (Kentucky Fried Chicken had just opened its franchise in Japan and the lifesize statue of the colonel outside every restaurant became a target for comedians for

years—see JUNK BOY.) C-Ko isn't what she seems—she is really the princess of a lost alien civilization, and the captain was coming to find her when he accidentally crashed his ship.

In the video sequel *PA2: The Plot of the Daitokuji Corporation* (1987), directed by Moriyama from Koyama's script, B-Ko's millionaire industrialist father, from whom she inherited all her least charming characteristics, is plotting to acquire the alien technology for his own ends, but he reckons without his daughter's determination to win C-Ko's affection or A-Ko's loyalty to her annoying little friend. The pair unite to stop the aliens taking C-Ko home. Moriyama also directed the Kawasaki-scripted video *PA3: Cinderella Rhapsody* (1988), about an unusual love quadrangle forming when A-Ko and B-Ko fall for Kei, who loves C-Ko, who can't stand him because he's taking A-Ko's attention away from her. The whole thing culminates in a huge party on the crashed battlecruiser, which the captain and his crew have converted into the best disco in town. Opening and closing sequences have stunning artwork by Yasuomi Umezu, and the ending reassures us that men come and go, but friends are always friends. Moriyama and Kawasaki teamed up again for *Project A-Ko: Final* (1989, aka *PA4*), in which Kei's matrimonial negotiations with the girls' teacher, C-Ko's origins as an alien princess, and the captain's continuing failure to complete his mission culminate in the arrival of C-Ko's mother in a spaceship modeled on a George Lucas Star Destroyer. But the world's cutest bubble-brain doesn't go home after all, and the video ends, as the first movie began, with our heroines late for school again.

Final wasn't so final after all. A video two-parter, *A-Ko the Versus* (1990, aka *PA5*), took our heroines into an alternate universe to reprise their story with a new twist and new opponents but still the same theme—rivalries, friendships, love, and massive rumbles with bigger collateral damage

than most medium-sized wars.

Nishijima and Moriyama (also known as CREAM LEMON's Yuji Motoyama) wrote the story for *PA* with Kasumi Shirasaka reputedly as a pitch for the soft-core franchise, mercifully dropped. Allowed to flourish as comedy instead of erotica, *PA* throws in parodies of and references to just about every area of popular Japanese and American youth culture. Just like its pornographic precursor, *PA* is cunningly telling the same story with the same ingredients, spinning it just enough to hold the audience's attention. The team added two saving graces: good comic timing and a complete failure to comprehend the meaning of the word "excess." The whole canon—especially the first film and *Cinderella Rhapsody*—is still watchable, whether you have seen enough anime to get the in-jokes or just enjoy comedy that goes completely over the top. Nishijima would reprise the character relationships for the 1990s in the less successful AGENT AIKA.

PROJECT ARMS

2001. TV series. DIR: Hirotoshi Takaya. SCR: Aya Yoshinaga, Shuichi Miyashita. DES: Masaki Sato. ANI: Masako Shimizu and Hideyuki Motohashi. MUS: N/C. PRD: TMS, TV Tokyo. 25 mins. x 26 eps. Teenager Ryo Takatsuki almost loses his left arm in an accident, only to discover his wounds taking on a life of their own—he hasn't lost an arm, so much as gained a symbiotic bioweapon. Sub-GUYVER action based on the *Shonen Sunday* manga by SPRIGGAN-cocreator Ryoji Minagawa. ▼

PROTECTING FROM THE SHADOWS

2006. JPN: *Kage Kara Mamoru*. AKA: *Mamoru from the Shadows*. TV series. DIR: Yoshitaka: Fujimoto. SCR: Ryunosuke Kingetsu, Toshimitsu Takeuchi. DES: Sai Madara, Natsuki Watanabe. ANI: Ichiro Hattori. MUS: Tsuyoshi Watanabe. PRD: Group Tac, Studio Tulip, TV Tokyo, TV Osaka. 25 mins. x 12 eps. Shy, unkempt, bespectacled teenager

Mamoru is really the latest in a long line of ninja, who, for the last 400 years, have been sworn to protect the nearby Konyaku family from harm. The pretty Yuna Konyaku is thus safe from danger for as long as her benevolently geeky stalker is nearby. Based on an idea by Taro Achi, the creator of **Dokkoida**. Note that the last two episodes were broadcast in a single time block, and so may be filed in some sources as a single double-length "eleventh" episode.

PSAMMEAD, THE

1985. JPN: *Onegai, Samiadon!* AKA: *Samiadon, I Wish . . . ; Psammead the Sand Imp.* TV series. DIR: Osamu Kobayashi, Hideharu Iuchi, Fumiko Ishii, Tomomi Mochizuki, Mitsuru Hongo, Kazuhiko Kobayashi. SCR: Toshiyuki Yamazaki, Eiichi Tachi, Haruya Yamazaki. DES: Tsutomu Shibayama. ANI: Hideo Kawauchi. MUS: Kentaro Haneda. PRD: Tokyo Movie Shinsha, NHK. 25 mins. x 39 eps. (2 stories per ep.).

In a deserted English chalk quarry, the older siblings of the five Turner children—Jill, Robert, and Jean—find a strange creature buried in the sand and decide to "take care" of it. It looks like Pikachu in a pointy hat and is allergic to water, but the children have found the powerful and capricious Psammead in this adaptation of E. Nesbit's novel *Five Children and It* (1902). The sand-imp can grant one wish every day, but the wish only lasts until sundown, and like many such magical "advantages" (see **Doraemon**), it doesn't always work as the wishers intend. The children ask for all sorts of toys and adventures, including becoming a mermaid, going into space, and having a robot of their own. Despite the mishaps some of their wishes bring, they learn valuable lessons from their strange friend.

TMS relocated the story to the present-day "English countryside," a half-timbered neverland of green fields and friendly policemen. The sand-imp character was renamed Samiadon (a Japanese wind spirit) in order to bring

an oriental association not present in the original. Several TV episodes were also cut into a feature-length edition for video.

PSYCHIC ACADEMY *

2002. JPN: *Psychic Academy Ora Bansho.* AKA: *Aura Bansho.* TV series. DIR: Shigeru Yamazaki. SCR: Mitsuhiro Yamada. DES: Miho Shimogasa. ANI: N/C. MUS: Michihiko Ota. PRD: E. G. Films, Gansis, Starchild Records. 9 mins. x 24 eps.

Ai Shiomi is an insecure teenager following his gifted older brother to a school for students with psychic abilities. All the female pupils seem to manifest their biggest talents at chest level, providing a clue that this is just another formulaic wish-fulfillment show. The love triangle between Ai, his sweet-and-pneumatic childhood friend Orina, and his tomboyish-but-pneumatic classmate Myu is interrupted by random psychic battles and rough-and-ready wisdom from his crusty psychic coach. Much eye candy, plus boys' uniforms shamelessly stolen from *Harry Potter,* may please the undiscerning. Based on a manga by Katsu Aki, who produced the boys' manga version of **Escaflowne**, this show's sole attempt at innovation was being released straight to the Internet, although in its American incarnation it was released on DVD. **N**

PSYCHIC FORCE

1998. Video. DIR: Fujio Yamauchi. SCR: Hiroyuki Kawasaki, Kenichi Onuki, Katsuhiko Takayama. DES: Kenichi Onuki. ANI: Hideki Araki. MUS: N/C. PRD: Triangle Staff, Broccoli. 40 mins. x 2 eps.

In 2007, the world is under martial law. As telepathic powers manifest in the young, the army begins conducting its own experiments, hoping to create its own elite Psycorps, known as the Psychickers. One day, Keith Evans escapes from the American compound. Evans is taken in by the kindly Griffiths family, but he goes on the run with the Griffiths boy Verne

when the family is attacked by soldiers. Griffiths and Evans then fall in with the international Noah cartel, led by the eccentric Richard Wong, and the fight for freedom begins. This anime was based on an arcade fighting game but bizarrely uses Welsh names for the lead characters.

PSYCHIC WARS *

1991. JPN: *Soju Senshi Psychic Wars.* AKA: *Bestial Warrior Psychic Wars.* Video. DIR: Tetsuo Imazawa. SCR: Yasushi Ishiguro. DES: Masami Suda. ANI: Masami Suda. MUS: Tetsuro Kashibuchi. PRD: Toei. 50 mins.

In this disappointingly trite adaptation of Yasuaki Kadota's SF novel, a recently qualified Kyoto doctor discovers that prehistoric Japan was the site of an ancient war between demons and ninja. Injecting Julian May's *Saga of the Exiles* with a Japanese attitude toward honor, obligation, and love, the *PW* novel was clearly optioned for its time-traveling messiah and prehistoric demon wars, as with **Dark Myth**, hinging on a threat that Japan's ancient enemies are returning to continue a vendetta older than time. But its fascinating take on Japanese history is dumped in a mix of breakneck exposition and supposedly arty pauses. Director Imazawa tries to jolly things along by playing up the rich historicity of the Kansai region and the (literally) many-colored land of the past, but he doesn't have the time or budget to do it properly. He is not helped in this by a particularly poor U.K. dub that has academics discussing the mysteries of Japan's lost Jomon culture (see **Princess Mononoke**) without being able to pronounce its name. **V**

PSYCHO ARMOR GOBARIAN

1983. TV series. DIR: Seiji Okuda, Satoru Kumazaki, Kazuya Miyazaki, Hiroshi Yoshida, Tatsuya Sasahara, Yasuo Ishigawa, Hiroshi Negishi, Kazuhiro Okaseko. SCR: Yoshihisa Araki, Hideki Sonoda, Katsuhiko Taguchi, Jiyu Watanabe, Tsukasa Takahashi. DES: Kiyoshi Fukuda, Yuki Kinoshita. ANI:

Kiyoshi Fukuda, Yuki Kinoshita. mus: Tatsumi Yano. prd: Knack, Dynamic, TV Tokyo. 25 mins. x 26 eps.

Sometime in the 21st century, Earth is threatened by the Galadine, evil psychics from another dimension. The world's last line of defense is the giant robot Gobarian and its teenage pilot, Isamu Napoto, who moves the huge weapon using his immense powers of ESP. He's aided in his fight by his companions Kult Buster and Hans in their robots Reido and Garom. If you think that the robot Gobarian and, indeed, the whole setup are strongly reminiscent of **Mazinger Z**, it won't surprise you to learn that this is another of Go Nagai's many robot tales—though not one of his best.

PSYCHO DIVER: SOUL SIREN *

1997. jpn: *Psycho Diver Masei Rakuryu*. Video. dir: Mamoru Kobe. scr: Toshiaki Kawamura, Tatsuhiko Urahata. des: Makoto Koga, Masafumi Yamamoto. ani: Makoto Koga. mus: Akihiko Hirama, SORMA, TA-1. prd: Toei, AIC, APPP, Madhouse. 60 mins.

Yuki Kano has it all—fame, wealth, the world at her feet—but she's occasionally unable to sing (and for a pop star, this is probably bad). Enter Bosujima, a "psycho diver" with the capability to enter people's heads and straighten out what's wrong with them. Well, most of the time, anyway. Based on a novel by **Amon Saga**–creator Baku Yumemakura, this production has a list of distinguished animation houses in its credits as long as your arm. The look is urban-hard, cool, and savvy with just enough retro and pop-culture references; check out the psychodiving machine for echoes of the brain-swap apparatus from cult 1960s series *The Prisoner*. The voice cast is full of fan favorites headed by Junko Iwao as Yuki. **NV**

PUGYURU

2004. TV series. dir: Hajime Kurihara. scr: Hiroyuki Nakaki. des: Tohiro Konno. ani: N/C. mus: Yasunori Koda. prd: 2000 Creators.com, Dex, Kids' Sta-

tion, Kodansha, Media Factory, MOVIX. 3 mins. x 13 eps.

Not so much a series as a televised gag strip, Tohiro Konno's surreal manga was animated as part of the *Anime Paradise!* TV segment. High school girl Maa... (the rest of her name is inaudible) meets Cheko when her mother hires a maid so that Maa… won't be alone when she has to go away on a long trip. Cheko has allegedly come from the Maid Village, where real maids live and train, but she's not an ordinary maid; she can dissolve, grow roots, fly, and separate her head from her body. She's been sent to change Maa…'s life, and Maa… and her friends have wacky moments with their new little friend, water-gun toting gangsters, an overbearing American, and other strange creatures. Director Kurihara plays a character called Kurihara in episode 5, and the kind of food gag commonly found in juvenile shows like **Anpanman** is a staple of the story, with Cheko's head replaced with dumplings in one episode while in another she eats another appropriately named character's head with syrup. Self-consciously strange, and made using limited animation techniques liable to make it easier to port into mobile phone delivery systems in future.

PUMPKIN WINE

1982. jpn: *The Kabocha Wine*. TV series, movie. dir: Kimio Yabuki. scr: Shunichi Yukimuro, Mitsuru Majima, Shinji Shimizu. des: Megumu Ishiguro, Fumihiro Uchikawa. ani: Megumu Ishiguro, Akira Shimizu. mus: Osamu Shoji. prd: Toei, TV Asahi. 25 mins. x 95 eps. (TV), 60 mins. (TVm), 24 mins.

Shy teenager Shunsuke is terrified of girls. He's grown up surrounded by his sisters, and his mother owns a lingerie shop. When he moves to a new high school thinking it's for boys only but finds it's actually a coed establishment, he's in danger of letting his phobia ruin his schooldays. His fellow pupil, the lovely Natsumi "Call Me L" Asaoka, is a lot bigger than he is in every way.

But despite being kindhearted, taller, and stronger, she falls in love with short, neurotic Shunsuke. And even though he feels he's being run over by a well-meaning bulldozer, he comes to appreciate her finer qualities.

Based on Mitsuru Miura's *Shonen Magazine* manga, the series jars modern audiences because of the dated design and Rubensesque physique of the heroine, but the story has charm, and the French dub was very successful. The TV movie *PW: Is She Really on a Honeymoon with Him!?* (1982) features predictable misunderstandings in a remote ski lodge, following a winter wonderland formula also found in **Kimagure Orange Road** and **Urusei Yatsura**. A short movie, *PW: Nita's Love Story* (1984), ran on the Toei Manga Matsuri summer double bill alongside **Kinnikuman: Ultimate Muscle**. In it, the titular dog, who lives in the school dormitory at the Sunshine academy, has a puppy sired by the pet of the wealthy Takizawa family. Nita steals milk for her offspring but disappears. While searching for the dog, Natsumi is lured onto the Takizawas' yacht by their wayward son, who claims to have the dog on board but really has designs on Natsumi herself.

PUNI PUNI POEMI

2001. Video. dir: Shinichi Watanabe. scr: Yosuke Kuroda. des: Satoshi Ishino. ani: Satoshi Ishino. mus: Toshiro Soda. prd: JC Staff. 30 mins. x 2 eps.

Poemi Watanabe is a cheerful student at Inunabe elementary school who lives happily with her parents until they are attacked and killed by mysterious aliens. Adopted by the parents of her classmate Futaba Memesu, she finds that the seven Memesu sisters have secret lives as the Earth Protect Unit, defending humankind against the aliens who killed her family and are now popping up in war machines all over the place. The snag is that, like *Thunderbirds'* International Rescue, they are sworn to save life, not threaten it—they can defend but not attack. But Poemi has no such scruples, and, with

a bit of magical help, she transforms
into Puni Puni Poemi, magical girl and
enemy of Earth's attackers. A spin-off
of EXCEL SAGA, with Poemi resembling
Excel, and Futaba her associate Hyatt.

PUPPET MASTER SAKON
1999. JPN: *Karakuri Soji Sakon*. AKA:
Sakon the Ventriloquist. TV series. DIR:
Hitoyuki Matsui, Hideki Tonokatsu,
Kazuo Nogami. SCR: Chiho Katsura,
Daisuke Hanebara. DES: Toshimitsu
Kobayashi, Tetsu Koga. ANI: Toshimitsu
Kobayashi. MUS: Norihiro Tsuru, Yuriko
Nakamura. PRD: Kyoiku, Tokyo Movie
Shinsha, WOWOW. 25 mins. x 26 eps.
Scooby-Doo meets *Child's Play*? Sakon is
following in the footsteps of a master
puppeteer who took the art of ventrilo-
quism to undreamed-of levels centuries
ago, but not even his studies in these
ancient arts and his great talent can
explain why his doll Ukon seems to
have a life of its own. Realizing that his
skills and Ukon's unexpected independence could be very useful in solving
mysteries and crimes, Sakon starts to
develop a new sideline as an investigator of unusual problems. Based on the
1995 *Shonen Jump* manga by Ken Obata
and Maro Sharaku, with attractive
designs and an evocative score, *PMS*
nonetheless boasts one of the most
unlikely premises in detective history.
About as believable as Sherlock Holmes talking to a sock puppet, though
sleuthing tales such as CONAN THE BOY
DETECTIVE and YOUNG KINDAICHI FILES
are hardly less strange. ●

PUPPET PRINCESS *
2000. JPN: *Karakuri no Kimi*. Video. DIR:
N/C. SCR: N/C. DES: N/C. ANI: N/C. MUS:
N/C. PRD: N/C. N/D mins.
Lord Ayawatari is not interested in
governing his territory or in conflicts
between the other warlords but instead
only lives to create puppets. Knowing
Ayawatari's nature, the evil warlord
Sadayoshi Karimata invades Ayawatari's
castle and kills almost all his family.
Princess Rangiku, the daughter of
Ayawatari, is forced to seek out the
legendary ninja Danzo Kato to oppose

Puppetry and Stop-motion

the evil Karimata, but Danzo's assistance comes at a cost. Together these
unlikely heroes must find a way to
infiltrate Karimata's castle and restore
the mysterious stolen puppet. Based on
a *Shonen Sunday* manga by USHIO AND
TORA–creator Kazuhiro Fujita.

PUPPETRY AND STOP-MOTION
The first stop-motion animation in
Japan was *Princess Tsumeko and the Devil*
(*Tsumeko-hime to Amanojaku*, 1955)
produced by Tadahito Mochinaga,
who had left cel-based anime behind
after MOMOTARO'S DIVINE SEA WARRIORS.
Mochinaga learned the techniques
of stop-motion animation in China
during his sojourn at the Shanghai
Animation Studio and took them back
to Japan in 1953. He oversaw several
other stop-motion shorts in the 1950s,
his collaborators including Yoshikazu
Inamura and Kiichi Tanaka. Their
highest profile work was the German
sequence in *Beer Through the Ages* (*Beer
Mukashimukashi*, 1956), a 12-minute
commercial commissioned by the
Asahi brewing company to celebrate
its 50th anniversary—compare to PEN-
GUINS MEMORY. The authors presume
that it was commissioned as several

separate TV commercials, and only
later edited together into its full running time as listed in Japanese sources.
Beginning with dancing, drunken
Babylonians, it traces the story of
intoxicants through to ancient Egypt
and medieval Germany, before a brief
Italian interlude that comprises cut-cel-
lophane animation from Noburo Ofuji. The trail, of course, finally reaches
Japan, a nation so taken with the
commercial's achievement that *Kinema
Junpo* magazine voted it the ninth best
cultural work of the year.

Other works included *Little Black
Sambo* (*Chibikuro Sambo no Torataiji*,
1956), exhibited at the Vancouver
International Film Festival, and *Five
Little Monkeys* (*Gohiki no Kozarutachi*,
1956), which won an education award
in the year of its release. Often funded
by Dentsu Eigasha, early stop-motion
appeared to reach the limit of its development with *Penguin Boys Lulu and Kiki*
(*Penguin Boya Lulu to Kiki*, 1958) and
Removing the Lump (*Kobutori*, 1958),
the latter of which reached the heady
heights of a 21-minute running time.
Stop-motion, however, has all the labor
intensive difficulties of cel animation,
but few of its advantages. Sets must

still be constructed, gravity still limits special effects, and the chances of mistakes that ruin an entire scene are greatly increased. Furthermore, the success of the feature-length cel animation of PANDA AND THE MAGIC SERPENT in 1958 was a damaging blow to future investment in stop-motion.

The potential for production-line techniques allowed the output of cel animators to swiftly outstrip stop-motion animators, and cels soon took over. Stop-motion enjoyed limited success on Japanese television, with Tadahito Mochinaga's series *Prince Ciscon* (*Ciscon Oji*, 1963), based on a manga by DORAEMON-creators Fujiko-Fujio. However, *Rudolph the Red-Nosed Reindeer* (*Akabana no Tonakai Rudolph Monogatari*, 1964), based on a script by Romeo Muller, was undertaken by Mochinaga's team as work-for-hire for Videocraft (later known as Rankin/Bass). Not broadcast in Japan until three years after its American premiere, this TV special remains a Yuletide regular in the English-speaking world, but was the last significant use of stop-motion on Japanese TV for some years. However, the efforts of Japan's stop-motion animators were utilized to a great extent on international coproductions, often unseen by the Japanese. Mochinaga's MOM Films company turned out a number of stop-motion works for Rankin/Bass, including *The New Adventures of Pinocchio* (1961), *Willy McBean and His Magic Machine* (1963), *Andersen's Fairy Tales* (1966), *Ballad of Smokey the Bear* (1967, broadcast in Japan as *Smokey Bear no Uta*, 1970), and *Mad Monster Party* (1967), all animated to match prerecorded soundtracks and scripts supplied from America.

It is notable that MOM Films limited itself to short TV specials, as serial stop-motion animation at 24 minutes a week was simply unworkable. A long-running stop-motion series was Ichiro Komuro's *Little Battles of the Salaryman* (*Salaryman Minimini Sakusen*, 1970), but even that only managed a 27-episode run by keeping the episodes at a manageable four minutes each. As Jap-

anese children's television succumbed to the onslaught of live-action rubber monster shows, there was some experimentation with the use of animation for effects work (for the cel variant of this, see BORN FREE). *Devil Hunter Mitsurugi* (*Majin Hunter Mitsurugi*, 1971), featured three live-action children, wielding ceremonial swords themed on Wisdom, Humanity, and Love, which allow them to combine into the stop-motion giant Mitsurugi, who can fight giant monster invaders from Scorpio. Made by animator Takeo Nakamura and his wife Ayako Magiri, the show was innovative, but suffered from production processes that made it inevitably more time-consuming than cels. The TBS network tried something similar with *Transform! Pompoko Jewels* (*Henshin! Pompoko Tama*, 1973) a live-action series about two feuding Japanese families whose children were able to switch identities and genders—shades here of the gender-swapping comedy of RANMA ½. As with MARVELOUS MELMO, the engines of transformation were red and blue magic items (jewels here); as with POMPOKO, *tanuki* were involved, although here they were regarded as interfering creatures from another world who happened to *resemble* Japanese raccoon dogs. As with *Mitsurugi*, the stop-motion elements were only employed very briefly, since the transformative powers of the magical jewels would only last for a maximum of ten minutes. Such an artificial time limit was common in special effects shows, whatever the medium, since it allowed the filmmakers to limit their effects budgets—similar excuses were tried in the live-action ULTRAMAN and later pastiched in the perilously short battery life of EVANGELION.

Stop-motion seemed fated to slip into the world of film festival awards for worthy effort, the prerogative of hobbyists and artists but unlikely to attract much interest from the money-minded producers of the rest of commercial animation. Kazuhiko Watanabe's *The Crane Returns a Favor* (*Tsuru no Ongaeshi*, 1966) won an edu-

cational prize at that year's Mainichi Film Concours, and Katsuo Takahashi's *Issun Boshi* (1967) was voted one of the top ten movies of the year by *Kinema Junpo*. However, many of the early pioneers in stop-motion found alternative employment in puppetry, a creative medium that never escaped from children's television but remained a lucrative field, largely on the license-funded channel NHK—NHK derives its funding from a monthly fee charged to each household which possesses a television. The animator Tadanari Okamoto made TV's first marionette series, *Tamamonomae* (1953), a short-lived tale about a fox who is able to transform herself into a beautiful human girl.

The original puppet version of CHIRORIN VILLAGE (1956, see also *DE) lasted for over a thousand episodes on television, its stars becoming familiar voices to an entire generation, including Tetsuko Kuroyanagi (see CHOCCHAN'S STORY). Other TV experiments in puppetry included the space-voyaging vessel *Silica* (*DE), created by science fiction author Shinichi Hoshi, and Osamu Tezuka's *Space Patrol* (*DE), which was chiefly a puppet show, but also used cel animation for certain special effects and its opening sequence. MADCAP ISLAND (see also *DE) ran for more than a thousand episodes and received that ultimate of TV accolades—complaints about violence and bad language! As a mark of its fame to Japanese viewers of a certain age, it even appeared in a cameo role playing on a TV screen in ONLY YESTERDAY.

Further discussion of the development of puppetry is beyond the scope of this book, except to note *Aerial City 008* (1969, see also *DE), *11 People of Nekojara City* (*Nekojara-shi no Juichinin*, 1970), and the samurai epic *Hakkenden* (*DE), widely acknowledged by the makers of the anime HAKKENDEN to have been a greater influence on them than the 19th-century original. Other puppet shows of the 1970s include the original of SANADA'S TEN BRAVE WARRIORS, (see also *DE, as *Ten Brave*

Warriors of Sanada), an adaptation of the radio drama *The Flutist* (*DE), and 1978's *Kujaku-o* (a Japanese retelling of the same myth that later became **PEACOCK KING**). The early 1980s saw the flourishing of both *Prin Prin* (*DE) and a puppet version of **GREAT CONQUEST** (see also *DE as *Romance of the Three Kingdoms*), for which the accomplished Kihachiro Kawamoto made over 400 puppets.

Regarded as a highly disposable medium, with many thousands of episodes lost or wiped soon after their original broadcast, TV puppetry foundered in the 1980s, particularly after the ill-fated attempt of the commercial channel Fuji TV to make its own puppet show, the sci-fi spectacular *X-Bomber* (1980). Despite creative input from **DEVILMAN**-creator Go Nagai and a truly gripping plot, *X-Bomber* was canceled partway through its run amid whispers of low ratings and enjoyed better success abroad under the title *Star Fleet* (*DE). Fuji TV's attitude also seemed to influence NHK, the home of TV puppetry, whose *Farewell Higeyo* (*Higeyo Saraba*, 1984) was the last puppet series to be shown on the channel for some years. The channel revived puppetry with *Tale of the Heike* (*Heike Monogatari*, 1993), which also featured puppets designed by Kihachiro Kawamoto, and *Drum Canna* (*DE), a significantly shorter puppet series broadcast in seven-minute segments as part of another program.

The traditions of puppetry found new relevance in the late 1990s in digital animation, as an example to the manipulators of *virtual* 3D models in 3D environments. Early digital anime often borrowed from puppetry, particularly in attempts to depict realistic human movement. As with puppets in the physical world, virtual models often have difficulty interacting with the environment around them—figures are best filmed from the waist up to avoid notably unrealistic leg movements and foot placements, and characters in early digital animation such as **A.LI.CE** and **BLUE REMAINS**

Pure Love

spend prolonged periods sitting in vehicles or floating in space, water, or cyberspace. **MALICE DOLL** took the links between puppetry and stop-motion to extremes, with a cast of *of* puppets that comes to life.

Stop-motion continues to flourish outside the commercial world of cel or digital animation, particularly at film festivals. In particular, Kihachiro Kawamoto (see **KIHACHIRO KAWAMOTO FILM WORKS**) has continued to keep Japanese stop-motion in the eyes of festival crowds. While the majority of the Japanese animation in this book reflects Western preconceptions of what "anime" should be, it is worth noting that it is Kawamoto who is the president of the Japan Animation Association, and that Koji Yamamura's **MOUNT HEAD** was nominated for a Best Short Animation Academy Award in the same year as Hayao Miyazaki's **SPIRITED AWAY**. For the average Western viewer, however, the most likely encounter with stop-motion animation is probably the special effects in Shinya Tsukamoto's surreal live-action movie *Tetsuo: The Iron Man* (1991) or the claymation credit sequences of **NINJA**

NONSENSE and many **CRAYON SHIN-CHAN** movies.

PURE LOVE *
1998. JPN: *Rhythm*. Video. DIR: Miyo Morita. SCR: N/C. DES: N/C. ANI: Chuji Nakajima. MUS: N/C. PRD: Daiei. 30 mins. x 2 eps.
In a fantasy world modeled loosely on medieval Europe, knight Hiro sneaks into the king's secret chambers one evening to meet with the queen. Then, the two of them go at it like rabbits, because this is a porn anime, and she is a nymphomaniac. **N**

PURE MAIL *
2001. Video. DIR: Shinichi Masaki, Yuji Yoshimoto. SCR: Yoshio Takaoka. DES: Eta Nishi. ANI: Yuji Yoshimoto. MUS: N/C. PRD: Green Bunny. 30 mins. x 2 eps.
Highschooler Kei Ogata is a loner who has constructed a different persona and life on the Internet, where he chats with girls as "A.W." He begins to suspect that his online friend Eve is also his classmate Midori Nagawa, someone he would love to get to know in real life. However, he fears he'll never be as attractive as A.W.; the other

problem is that he once had a disastrous relationship with her friend Miki, behaved like a monster, and fears he can't control himself outside the safety of the Net. Meanwhile, Kei is caught using the school's servers to log into the chatroom, and is blackmailed into becoming the slave of the cruel tech support lady. **CN**

PURPLE EYES IN THE DARK

1988. JPN: *Yami no Purple Eye*. AKA: *Purple Eye of Darkness*. Video. DIR: Mizuho Nishikubo. SCR: Asami Watanabe. DES: Chie Shinohara. ANI: N/C. MUS: Derek Jackson, Purple Gar, Mayumi Seki. PRD: Youmex, Toei. 30 mins.

Rinko has always had a strange birthmark on her arm but discovers that it indicates she is *not like other girls*. The teenager's young body hides a murderous beast that threatens to transform her at any moment, manifesting itself as glowing, savage purple eyes. An "image video" consisting of images from Chie Shinohara's 1984 *Comic Margaret* manga set to seven musical interludes in the style of CIPHER THE VIDEO. A full-blown anime, however, was not forthcoming, as instead the franchise was adapted for live-action television in 1996 (*DE). The same author also created SEA'S DARKNESS: MOON SHADOW and *Red River* (aka *Anatolia Story*).

PUSS IN BOOTS *

1969. JPN: *Nagagutsu o Haita Neko*. AKA: *Wonderful World of Puss 'n Boots*. Movie. DIR: Kimio Yabuki. SCR: Hisashi Inoue, Morihisa Yamamoto. DES: Yasuo Otsuka. ANI: Yasuji Mori, Reiko Okuyama, Takao Sakano, Hayao Miyazaki, Akio Fukube. MUS: Seiichiro Uno. PRD: Toei. 80 mins. (m1), 53 mins. (m2), 58 mins. (m3), 25 mins. x 26 eps. (TV).

Pierre, youngest of three brothers, befriends Perrault, a cat-musketeer in boots on the run from the henchmen of the evil, rat-loving Nekoboss. Perrault helps Pierre pose as the Marquis of Carabas in order to woo the beautiful Princess Rosa. She, however, is betrothed to the Demon King Lucifer,

who kidnaps her on the night of the full moon. Perrault and Pierre set off to rescue Rosa from Lucifer's castle.

This delightful if free version of Charles Perrault's 18th-century fairy tale was given a limited U.S. release to the Saturday morning kids' market, along with several other Toei anime including JACK AND THE WITCH and TREASURE ISLAND. Featuring nods to SWAN LAKE and *Beauty and the Beast*, it was such a success in Japan that the feline hero became Toei Animation's mascot. The comic elements of the movie owe much to the characterization of the extremely stupid transforming ogre who gets all the best bits of slapstick business. Note the presence of a young Hayao Miyazaki in the lower ranks of the animators.

Tomoharu Katsumata's movie sequel *Three Musketeers in Boots* (1972) dispatched Perrault to the Wild West, where he accompanies the young Annie and Jimmy to Gogo Town, a frontier staging post. Annie's father is killed, and the characters' lives are all endangered when the town boss discovers they know about his counterfeiting operation that he runs out of the basement of the town saloon. Annie is kidnapped, and it is time for a replay of the rescue scenario from the first film, as Perrault and Sheriff Jimmy save her from the bad guys.

A third movie, *PiB: Around the World in 80 Days* (1976), was directed by Hiroshi Shidara for the same film studio—its feline version of Jules Verne a distant precursor of AROUND THE WORLD WITH WILLY FOGG. Perrault bets Grumon the pig industrialist that he can travel around the world in 80 days but is pursued by cat assassins, Carter the obstructive hippo, and Grumon's sneaky lupine agent Professor Garigari.

The unrelated TV series *The Adventures of Puss in Boots* (1992) was directed by Susumu Ishizaki and broadcast on TV Tokyo, featuring young boy Hans and his cat Kusuto. Their adventures include cameos by characters from many other fairy tales and sto-

ries, including SNOW WHITE, DON QUIXOTE, *Hansel and Gretel*, DRACULA, *The Little Match Girl*, and THE THREE MUSKETEERS. This series is currently being repromoted in the U.S. as *Puss 'n' Boots* along with a 75-minute feature, *The Journey of Puss 'n' Boots*, which is probably three episodes edited together. The original 1969 film was restored in 1998 and shown with GALAXY EXPRESS 999 as part of the regular Toei Anime Fair theater run. An adaptation of *Puss in Boots* was also included in the anime series GRIMMS' FAIRY TALES.

PUT IT ALL IN THE RING

2004. JPN: *Ring ni Kakero 1*. TV series. DIR: Toshiaki Komura, Shigeyasu Yamauchi et al. SCR: Yosuke Kuroda. DES: Michi Himeno, Shingo Araki. ANI: Eisaku Inoue, Keiichi Ichikawa, Shingo Araki, Hideji Ishimoto. MUS: Susumu Ueda. PRD: Toei Animation, Marvelous Entertainment, TV Asahi. 25 mins. x 12 eps.

The Takane siblings are determined to fulfill their late father's wish that a Takane should become a champion boxer. Ryuji sets out to develop special techniques that will make him unstoppable in the ring, trained by his sister Kiku and aiming for the national squad. But first he has to take the junior high school championship against his archrival Jun Kenzaki. Based on the manga by Masami Kurumada, this old-fashioned saga of a boy's growth into manhood by way of extreme physical pain (see TOMORROW'S JOE) has a mix of old and new names on the crew. **V**

PUTSUN MAKE LOVE

1987. Video. DIR: Minoru Okazaki. SCR: Wataru Amano. DES: Masaki Kajishima. ANI: Masaki Kajishima. MUS: N/C. PRD: Agent 21, Toei. 25 mins. x 6 eps.

The fall and rise of a loving couple's fortunes, in which cute high school girl Saori begins barely speaking to Yuji, putting him through a series of trials as she slowly realizes that he's the boy for her. As her parents try to fix her up with a husband in an *omiai* ("arranged") marriage meeting, Saori convinces Yuji to impersonate her at the meal, with predictably comedic results. Realizing there is fun to be had in impersonating a girl, Yuji disguises himself again and sneaks into the girls' locker room with a camera, only to be waylaid by his teacher, Miss Akimoto, who confiscates his film. A traditional anime love triangle enters the plot, as Yuji schemes and matchmakes to ensure that Saori's new suitor and the girl who is chasing *him* are maneuvered safely into each other's arms. Yuji and Saori head off to the seaside in the final episode but are kept from consummating their budding relationship by the attentions of their teacher and Yuji's unexpected heroism when he stops a suicidal girl from jumping in front of a train. Based on the manga by Jun Amemiya in *Scholar* magazine, this is an early work for TENCHI MUYO!'s Masaki Kajishima in the playful spirit of SLOW STEP and KIMAGURE ORANGE ROAD.

PYUNPYUNMARU

1967. TV series. DIR: Yugo Serikawa, Yasuo Yamaguchi, Kazuya Miyazaki. SCR: Jiro Yoshino, Tsuneaki Nakane, Kenji Urakawa, Enrico Dolizoni, Tomohiro Ando, Masashi Hayashi, Shunichi Yukimuro. DES: Jiro Tsunoda. ANI: Keijiro Kimura, Hiroshi Wagatsuma, Tetsuhiro Wakabayashi. MUS: Yoshioki Ogawa. PRD: Toei, Shin Production, NET. 25 mins. x 26 eps.

Pyunpyun Maru is a ninja of the Iga clan, in charge of their Nandemo OK (Anything Goes) Office. Lumbered with the crybaby ninja Chibi Maru, downtrodden by his boss, and secretly enamored of the lady ninja Sayuri, Pyunpyun must also fend off the unwelcome advances of Kemeko, the office man-eater. This funny mix of office life and ninja japery was based on the manga *Ninja Awatemaru* by KARATE FOR IDIOTS–creator Jiro Tsunoda serialized in *Shonen King* magazine.

Q

QTARO THE GHOST *
1965. JPN: Obake no Qtaro. TV series, movie. DIR: Eiji Okabe, Tadao Nagahama. SCR: Jiro Yoshida, Kuniaki Kashima, Susumu Yoshida, Chikara Matsumoto, Hisashi Oi, Masaki Tsuji, Nanaba Sakai, Seiji Matsuoka, Asako Shiozawa. DES: Fujiko-Fujio. ANI: Dai-kichiro Kusube, Tsutomu Shibayama, Yasuhiro Yamaguchi, Sadayoshi Tomi-naga, Moriyasu Taniguchi, Susumu Shiraume. MUS: Hiroshi Tsutsui. PRD: Tokyo Movie Shinsha, Shinei, Nippon TV. 25 mins. x 97 eps. (original), 25 mins. x 70 eps. (new), 25 mins. x 96 eps. (new new), 13 mins. (m).
Shota Ohara is a klutzy kid who finds an egg that hatches Qtaro, a large big-eyed blob. The Ohara family takes him in, and predictable misunderstandings ensue, with a normal Japanese house-hold gaining an extra member who can fly, make things disappear, and has a whole host of supernatural friends who insist on dropping in. Qtaro's chums include General Godzilla (no relation to the giant monster), the rich Kizao, the Professor, and Doronpa, the comic-relief American ghost. Qtaro is a Fujiko-Fujio project that, like the same creators' more successful **DORAEMON**, features an otherworldly playmate foisted on a hapless boy.

The original monochrome series was remade in color as New Qtaro (1971) and moved to new produc-tion house Shinei after a long hiatus. The second remake, confusingly also called New Qtaro (1985), was directed by Shinichi Suzuki and represented a concerted effort to update the postwar character for a new generation. A few episodes of this version were translated by the Hawaiian Japanese-language sta-tion KIKU and shown subtitled in some U.S. TV areas with Japanese communi-ties. In 1986, Qtaro starred in his first "movie," Jump, Qtaro! BakeBake's Grand Strategem, which uses 3D technology. Another short film followed in 1987, Go Qtaro! War at 100th Size, in which Shota and the Professor try to enlarge a cake but only end up shrinking them-selves, setting up a fantastic voyage across the new terrors of an oversized living room.

QUEEN AND SLAVE *
2002. JPN: Jo-o Sama wa M Dorei. AKA: The Queen Is a Masochist. Video. DIR: Hiei Tadokoro. SCR: Rokutaro Makabe. DES: Gekka. ANI: Raizo Kitagawa. MUS: N/C. PRD: Five Ways. 28 mins.
Yumi is a sweet and gentle nurse, who moonlights as a whip-wielding domina-trix. Traumatized in childhood by her parents' separation, she sees all men as copies of her womanizing father. Hiroyuki, one of her patients, falls in love with her, only to get annoyed when her darker side is revealed. Dis-appointed that she has more than one side to her character (how dare she!), he "teaches her a lesson" which, pre-dictably, unleashes her inner masoch-ist—compare to **RAPEMAN**. Based on a manga by Beauty Hair, also known for **ORGY TRAINING**. **LNV**

QUEEN EMERALDAS *
1998. JPN: Queen Emeraldas. Video. DIR: Yuji Asada. SCR: Baku Kamio. DES: Masahito Sawada, Katsumi Itabashi. ANI: Masahito Sawada. MUS: Michiru Oshima. PRD: OLM. 30 mins. x 2 eps.
In the distant future, the Afressians are out to dominate the galaxy, and humankind's only hope for freedom is the pirate known as Queen Emeraldas. Driven by the memory of a long-lost love, she sails the seas of space in her namesake ship, fighting evil on her own terms—more like Robin Hood than a traditional pirate. She is fiercely determined to protect the "good name" of her vocation, and when an Afressian crew flies the Skull and Crossbones she insists they cease, employing her usual forceful argu-ments when reason fails. In a remote corner of space she meets a young man who has no faith in humanity and a group of ordinary folk who do their best to revive that faith. When the Afressians under Captain Eldomain come looking for revenge, they take these ordinary folk hostage as bait for a trap for Emeraldas.

Leiji Matsumoto has spent most of his career constructing a huge personal universe in which to develop his notions of honor, justice, courage, and what it means to be a real human being. At the center are his two most glorious creations, the heroic pirate-knight **Captain Harlock** and his friend and ally Emeraldas. Around them revolve a huge cast of friends and foes, people who define their own place in the universe by their responses to its trials and hardships. The video series shows us a young boy with a hard, sad past setting out to make a hard, sad future for himself, until pirate queen Emeraldas and an unlikely crew of galactic deadbeats show him that an open heart is as vital as courage.

Emeraldas is the active facet of Matsumoto's ideal woman, most fully embodied in Maetel of **Galaxy Express 999**. In a sense, every Matsumoto story is the same story, and so the viewer always knows what to expect and is drawn into Matsumoto's world without any protest or difficulty. An enticing introduction to Matsumoto's old values and never-changing style, combined here with up-to-the-minute animation techniques. Though limited in places, the animation itself is stylish, and while the computer graphics vary in quality, they don't impede the flow of the story.

QUEEN OF A THOUSAND YEARS *
1981. JPN: *Shin Taketori Monogatari Sennen Jo-o.* AKA: *Queen Millennia; Captain Harlock and the Queen of a Thousand Years.* TV series, movie. DIR: Masayuki Akehi. SCR: Keisuke Fujikawa, Leiji Matsumoto. DES: Yasuhiro Yamaguchi, Yoshinori Kanemori, Geki Katsumata. ANI: Yasuhiro Yamaguchi. MUS: Kitaro. PRD: Toei, Fuji TV. 25 mins. x 42 eps. (TV), 121 mins. (m). Yayoi Yukino seems like any other young woman; she's secretary to the chief of Tsukuba Observatory, and her father owns a noodle bar. Then she commissions Hajime Amemori's father to construct a strange building for her, and Hajime's own house is blown up. The orphaned Hajime learns that she is actually an alien whose home planet is fated to crush Earth at nine minutes and nine seconds past midnight on the ninth day of the ninth month of 1999. She is the Queen of a Thousand Years,

Queen Emeraldas

and she wants to ensure that Earth will survive into a new millennium. Just as Hajime is beginning to believe her, another alien arrives. Selen, the Thief of a Thousand Years, tells Hajime that Yayoi is really Earth's enemy, and he no longer knows who to believe. This being a Leiji Matsumoto film, the obvious answer is the one who most resembles Maetel of **Galaxy Express 999**, Matsumoto's archetype of perfect womanhood. Based on Matsumoto's manga serialized in the newspaper *Sankei Shinbun*, the TV series was also followed by an original movie production that was released in theaters as *Queen of a Thousand Years* (1982) and featured a theme song sung by Neil Sedaka's daughter Dara.

It was later acquired by U.S. company Harmony Gold and combined by **Robotech**'s Carl Macek with **Captain Harlock** to create the 65-episode U.S. series *Captain Harlock and the Queen of a Thousand Years.* Even though they were two different stories from two completely different studios, Macek welded them together by switching the action constantly between two war fronts separated by light-years, thus sidestepping the fact that the major characters could never appear together.

QUIET DON, THE
1990. JPN: *Shizukanaru Don: Yakuza Side Story.* AKA: *The Quietened Don: Yakuza Side Story.* Video. DIR: Hajime Kamegaki. SCR: Kuniaki Oshikawa.

DES: Osamu Nabeshima. ANI: Osamu Nabeshima. MUS: Shinji Miyazaki. PRD: TMS. 40 mins.

Soft-spoken, mild-mannered Shizuya works by day at a respected underwear factory but at night leads a double life as the third most powerful gangster boss in the Tokyo region. Based on the 1988 manga serialized in *Shonen Sunday* magazine by Tatsuo Nitta, this story was also adapted into a live-action TV drama.

QUINTUPLETS *

2001. JPN: *Go Go Itsutsugo Land*. AKA: *Go!Go! Quintuplets Land*. TV series. DIR: N/C. SCR: N/C. DES: N/C. ANI: Yukari Kobayashi. MUS: Taku Iwasaki. PRD: Eiken, TBS. 22 mins. x 50 eps.

A formulaic comedy for small children featuring five elementary school siblings (two girls, three boys) and their dog. The Kabuto quints are designed like a typical live-action team—there's the bespectacled smart one, the cute girl, the loner, the dashing hero, and the fat but good-hearted one—in this instance, also a girl. The show uses these stereotypes to emphasize that they have "totally different personalities" despite being born just a few minutes apart and focuses on everyday adventures with a fantasy twist at home and school. Broadcast in English in Europe, but more successful in Spanish as *Los Quintillizos*, it has also, sadly, been the subject of pervy fanzines. Nothing's sacred, not even infant stories.

R

RACING BROTHERS LETS AND GO
1996. JPN: *Hasshire Kyodai Lets to Go*. TV series, movie. DIR: Tetsuro Amino, Yoshio Kado. SCR: Hiroyuki Hoshiyama. DES: Akio Takami, Michiru Ishihara. ANI: Akio Takami. MUS: Koji Tsuno. PRD: Xebec, TV Tokyo. 25 mins. x 117 eps. (TV), 81 mins. (m).
Lets and Go are a pair of preteen brothers obsessed with mini racing cars—half lawn mower, half Formula One. In this long-running series based on a manga by Tetsuhiro Koshita, the boys work for genius inventor Professor Tsuchiya to defeat the agents of his rival, Professor Inugami, both on and off the tracks. After the first 51 episodes, the series was rebranded as *L&G: WGP* (1997) and trailed with a feature-length theatrical release. The series proper finished after 98 episodes, but it was brought back as *L&G: MAX* (1998), renumbered back to 1, and featured a new look courtesy of new designer Ishihara. A junior version of **CYBERFORMULA GPX**, whose sci-fi racing drama was still running when *L&G* began.

RAGNAROK THE ANIMATION
2004. TV series. DIR: Seiji Kishi, Lee Myung-jin. SCR: Hideki Mitsui. DES: Kenji Shinohara, Lee Myung-jin. ANI: N/C. MUS: Noriyuki Asakura. PRD: TV Tokyo, G&G Entertainment, Gonzo. 24 mins. x 26 eps.
Swordsman Roan is really a complete wimp, but he and his childhood friend the trainee priest Yufa are on a dangerous mission—a journey to the kingdom of Rune-Midgard to investigate a mysterious event. Yufa is very cute and Roan wants to impress her with his sophisticated talents, but she treats him like a moron. She's pretty naïve herself, but as the journey goes on her talents in healing and magic develop alongside her understanding of people. Along with stern female mage Takius, rough and rowdy female Hunter Judia, and little Maya, who is good at negotiating the best deals thanks to her upbringing with merchants and sailors, the pair travel through a world based on the online game *Ragnarok Online*, developed by the South Korean company Gravity Corp. and the enchantingly named Gungho Online Entertainment Inc. It is stuffed with a whole shopping basket of cultural and anime references from Egyptian gods and Crusaders to vanished older brothers, Dark Lords, and cute but cynical moppets. Seasoned fans and cynics will recognize elements of the classic gaming quest party crashed into the harem show, but director Kishi says it's all about "the drama of human interaction." The game also spun off into a Korean comic.

RAHXEPHON *
2002. TV series, movie. DIR: Yutaka Izubuchi. SCR: Chiaki Konaka, Hiroshi Onogi, Ichiro Okochi. DES: AkihiroYamada, Hiroki Kanno, Michiaki Sato, Yoshinori Sayama. ANI: Hiroki Kanno, Kenji Mizuhata, Takashi Tomioka, Tsunenori Saito, Shiho Takeuchi. MUS: Ichiko Hashimoto. PRD: Asatsu DK, BONES, Media Factory, Fuji TV, Victor Entertainment. 23 mins. x 26 eps. (TV), ca. 80 mins. (m), 15 mins. (v).
In the year 2027, teenager Ayato Kamina is living with his scientist mother in Tokyo Jupiter, the new name for the Japanese capital, which now exists under a huge protective dome after alien invaders destroyed the rest of civilization 15 years earlier. The danger from the alien Mu race and its Dolem monsters is still present, and would-be artist Ayato is caught up in an attack with a remote and mysterious girl, Reika Mishima. They witness the defense of Tokyo by huge, beautiful sonic weapons in female form, redolent of the gorgeous machines of **MAPS**. Haruka Shitow, an older woman and feisty fighter, tells him she has the answers to his many questions, but instead of fleeing the city with her, he follows Reika and witnesses the "hatching" of the godlike giant weapon RahXephon from an egg in a great shrine. Entering the creature, he becomes its perfect partner and pilot; but as he explores his new skills, he also learns that he and the citizens of Tokyo are living in a different time line to the rest of the world, which has not been completely destroyed, and that they are being ruled by the aliens—a revelation with elements of **MEGAZONE**

RahXephon

23, but more likely to have been inspired by *The Matrix* (1999). His own mother is caught up in the conspiracy, and Haruka is part of the Earth forces fighting the aliens. Another girl enters the equation when Quon Kisaragi appears to Ayato in a vision. Part of the anti-alien forces through her adopted family, she is also a vital part of the mystery.

Despite the efforts of **EVANGELION** to become the last word on the giant robot genre, it continued unabated with *RahXephon* as one of the better emulators. Where *Evangelion* had angels, *R* has "dolems," a name derived from the *do-re-mi* of a musical scale and the mythical clay *golem*, each named after elements of musical notation—*Arpeggio*, for example, or *Mezzo Forte*. While much of its influence may seem derived from modern shows, at heart it is a clever, atmospheric, and beautifully designed retread of the science fiction robot shows of the 1970s and 1980s, complete with an alien culture inspired by Mayan ruins (see **SUPER ATRAGON**), whose first attack occurs on December 21st, 2012, the end of the current 400-year Maya age, or *baktun*. Some may also like to see in it an allegorization of

the relationship of the Meiji Restoration–era Japanese toward the West: vastly advanced invaders that force the local population to make incredible leaps in science and technology, ready for a rematch.

Go Nagai's "psychic linkage" between pilot and craft is crashed into Yoshiyuki Tomino's classic format of a boy's rite of passage through an unjust world in which war sets friend against friend and his own blood betrays the hero. Many TV shows simply leech from the past for a ragbag plot with poorly crafted design and script, relying on the fact that the current TV audience is too young to have seen its source material or developed much in the way of critical faculty; but this show doesn't disgrace its antecedents.

In 2003 the series was edited into a 116-minute movie version *R: Pluralitas Concentio* (*R: Tagen Hensokyo*), with Izubuchi as chief director and Tomoki Kyoda as director. The same year saw the video *R Interlude: Thatness and Thereness*, a 15-minute existential dialogue between Quon and a fragment of herself, also directed by Tomoki Kyoda, and given away free as a bonus extra with the RahXephon PS2 game. The

2002 manga tells a slightly different version of the story, starting in 2001 instead of 2012.

RAI: GALACTIC CIVIL WAR CHRONICLE

1994. JPN: *Ginga Sengoku Gunyu Den Rai*. AKA: *Galactic Civil War Rivalry Between Chiefs: Rai; Thunder Jet*. TV series. DIR: Seiji Okuda. SCR: Junzo Toriumi, Satoshi Fujimoto. DES: Makoto Takehoko, Takashi Watabe, Kenji Teraoka, Mitsuki Nakamura. ANI: Makoto Takehoko. MUS: Kaoru Wada. PRD: IG Film, TV Tokyo. 25 mins. x 52 eps. The Galactic Empire is in shreds after the emperor's death, and the universe is consumed by conflict. Young warrior Rai Ryuga, descendant of an old samurai line, wants to bring peace to the warring clans and enlists the help of Shimon, daughter of the late emperor. A replay of Japan's civil war, but in space with fighting robots, *Rai* was a huge success in its original manga form. Serialized in *Dengeki Comic Gao* magazine by Johji Manabe, it shares character archetypes and graphic style with his earlier **OUTLANDERS** and sold over two million copies, making the anime adaptation a foregone conclusion. It has a martial feel courtesy of **DANCOUGAR**-director Okuda and oriental music from **KISHIN CORPS'** Wada.

RAIJIN-OH

1991. JPN: *Zettai Muteki Raijin-o*. AKA: *Completely Invincible Raijin-o*. TV series, video. DIR: Toshifumi Kawase, Nobuhiro Kondo, Takuya Sato. SCR: Hideki Sonoda, Noriko Hayasaka. DES: Satoshi Takeuchi, Takahiro Yamada, Shige Ikeda. ANI: Shinichi Sakuma, Satoshi Takeuchi. MUS: Kohei Tanaka. PRD: Sunrise, TV Tokyo. 25 mins. x 51 eps., 30 mins. x 3 eps. Earth is under threat of invasion from another dimension. Balzeb, Taldar, and their shapeshifting underlings, the Akudama (Evil Orbs), create part-cyborg monsters based on problems humankind has created for itself, like pollution, litter, and noise. There is a solution—three robots stored in a secret hangar that can combine to form the mighty fighting machine Raijin-Oh. When a pilot crashes Raijin-oh into an elementary school and is too badly hurt to carry on, he asks the pupils to take his place and become the Earth Defense Group. Once again, the government has no alternative but to put the safety of Earth in the hands of its children. Although 3 of them will be pilots, all 18 classmates have to learn to work together unselfishly for the good of all humanity. With such a large regular cast, one would expect most to be sidelined, but each of the regulars is featured strongly and has his or her own importance to the team and the story.

Another series created by Sunrise house pseudonym Hajime Yadate, *Raijin-Oh* follows in the tradition of giant-robot shows begun by Mitsuteru Yokoyama's GIGANTOR and Go Nagai's MAZINGER Z, which Sunrise raised to the level of an art form in the late 1970s with shows for a slightly older audience, like GUNDAM. Sunrise was also responsible in no small part for the use of very young children—the target audience for merchandising—as heroes in these shows, and the success of *Raijin-Oh* came shortly after the beginning of their long-running BRAVE SAGA.

RAIL OF THE STAR *

1993. JPN: *O-hoshisama no Rail.* Movie. DIR: Toshio Hirata. SCR: Tatsuhiko Urahata. DES: Yoshinori Kanemori. ANI: Katsutaka Iizuka. MUS: Koichi Saito. PRD: Madhouse. 79 mins.

As a Japanese national growing up in occupied Korea during World War II, young Chiko learns that soldiers on the battlefield are not the only casualties of armed conflict. As the Japanese Empire reaps the increasingly bitter harvest of a failing war effort, her well-to-do middle-class family is rocked by tragedy, losing friends and loved ones to the everyday domestic hazards of life in the 1940s, before peace brings the greatest danger of all. Korea is divided between the victors, and Chiko's family is in Pyongyang, in the northern

half. The Soviet Army begins a search for Japanese veterans like her father, a factory manager called up for military service. Chiko and her surviving relatives embark upon an epic journey to the U.S. Occupied Zone below the 38th parallel. They must rely on the help of the Korean people to get them to safety. Many Koreans suffered during the Japanese colonization, but in this sanitized true-life story (based on a book by Chitose "Chiko" Kobayashi), everything works out tidily. The threadbare but clean and perky-looking Japanese survivors manage to reach safety with the help of forgiving Korean villagers who put human life above race, nationality, or revenge, and Chiko grows up in modern, prosperous Japan, remembering the war through the eyes of a child.

It's not an exclusively Japanese tendency to present war stories in the best possible light—every nation talks about the suffering of its own civilians and the terrible impact of war on children, though sadly only after the event. For this approach, children make the ideal protagonists, since they can't be held responsible for any of the events they observe. A very similar story premise, also based on semiautobiographical memoirs, was transformed into something sublime by the artistry of Studio Ghibli in GRAVE OF THE FIREFLIES, whose success encouraged a number of imitators, of which *Rail of the Star* is perhaps the most blinkered. Compared to the deeply romanticized view of war presented in THE COCKPIT or the realistic yet humane outlook of BAREFOOT GEN, it's pap, used by the Japanese to assure themselves that World War II was some sort of unexpected natural disaster, and that Koreans don't hold much of a grudge for 50 years of colonial rule. Ironically, *RotS*'s artificial worthiness made it more marketable abroad, where American distributors warmed to its deluded cultural relativism, the "bring me your poor" concept of the U.S. zone as refuge, and the opportunity to demonstrate that not all of their anime output was guns and hooters.

RAINBOW ACROSS THE PACIFIC

1992. JPN: *Taiheiyo ni Kakeru Niji.* Video. DIR: Masayuki Akehi. SCR: Yugo Serikawa, Tadahiro Shimafuji. DES: N/C. ANI: Takao Kasai. MUS: Seiji Yokoyama. PRD: Toei. 30 mins.

Schoolgirl Mitsuko tries to protect half-Chinese transfer student Yu-Lian from bullies. That night, she discovers Emily, an old American doll. Given to a Japanese child during an exchange in 1921, it was hidden from the "doll burnings" of the anti-Western war period and saved by a brave young girl (Mitsuko's grandmother) from bayonet practice. At the next day's show-and-tell, Mitsuko tells the story of Emily and encourages Yu-Lian, who has brought her own doll, the beautiful Feng-Qun. When Feng-Qun's ribbon blows away and is caught in a tree, even the bullies cooperate in retrieving it.

Combining treacly internationalism with inadvertent comedy, especially when a girl donates her underwear to help make a rope, this story also suffers from flabby editing (why have a talking doll *and* a doll fairy?) characteristic of a creator with whom nobody dares argue, in this case Daisaku Ikeda, the leader of the Soka Gakkai Buddhist organization. But it is superior to his FAIRGROUND IN THE STARS, cleverly appealing to children by using toys as allegories for human suffering and heroism.

RAINBOW BATTLETEAM ROBIN

1966. JPN: *Rainbow Sentai Robin.* TV series. DIR: Yugo Serikawa, Takeshi Tamiya, Tomoharu Katsumata, Michiru Takeda, Yasuo Yamaguchi. SCR: Kazuhiko Kojima, Hiroshi Ozawa, Minoru Hamada, Hiroaki Hayashi, Michio Suzuki. DES: Studio Zero. ANI: Yoichi Otabe, Keishiro Kimura, Tetsuhiro Wakabayashi, Shinya Takahashi. MUS: Koichi Fukube. PRD: Toei, Studio Zero, NET. 25 mins. x 48 eps.

The people of the dying planet Palta choose Earth as their new home, much to the annoyance of the human race. In an animated pastiche of live-action shows such as ULTRAMAN, teenage

Robin and his six color-coded friends (nurse-robot Lily, Wolf the werewolf, Benkei the warrior-mage, Bell the cat, the know-it-all Professor, and Pegasus the transforming rocket) form a heroic team to save the planet. Inspired in part by Edmond Hamilton's CAPTAIN FUTURE novels, the original concept was thought up by CYBORG 009–creator Shotaro Ishinomori, then calling himself Ishimori.

RAINBOW MAN

1982. JPN: *Ai no Senshi Rainbow Man*. AKA: *Love Warrior Rainbow Man*. TV series. DIR: Kazuhiro Okaseko. SCR: Tsunehisa Ito. DES: Yasunori Kawauchi, Kazuhiro Okaseko. ANI: Kazuhiro Okaseko. MUS: Jun Kitahara. PRD: Ai Planning, Hayama Art, Oscar Studio, Studio Pop, MBS. 25 mins. x 22 eps.

Takeshi Yamato has spent years as a student of yogic master Devadatta. He now has superpowers that allow him to transform himself in seven ways and operate seven kinds of machinery. By combining his powers with an organic V Armor, which he can call up at will, he becomes Rainbow Man. In this form, he fights to defend Japan against the evil machinations of the Death-Death Group. This animated adaptation of the live-action SFX series *Rainbow Man* (1972) recreates the feel of the original, even down to the theme song taken from the earlier series. Compare to ULTRAMAN, which also has both live-action and anime incarnations.

RAINING FIRE

1988. JPN: *Hi no Ame ga Furu*. Movie. DIR: Seiji Arihara. SCR: Toshiaki Imaizumi, Seiji Arihara. DES: Yoshitsuge Hasegawa. ANI: Takaya Ono. MUS: N/C. PRD: Space, Nikkatsu, Mushi Pro. 80 mins.

On the 19th of June 1945, 230 American B-29s bomb Fukuoka while two horror-struck Japanese children watch the incendiary devices make the night sky look as if it is "raining fire." Funded in part by the Kyushu Film Center, jealous at the attention lavished on other towns in anime such as GRAVE OF THE FIREFLIES (Kobe) and BAREFOOT GEN (Hiroshima), *RF* fatuously claims to be an antiwar film, though it conveniently neglects to mention that the sleepy harbor town of Fukuoka was actually a major military port. Conventional weaponry killed more Japanese during the war than the much-hyped A-Bombs at Hiroshima and Nagasaki—in addition to Arihara's look-alike follow-up KAYOKO'S DIARY, a similar study of the firebombing of civilian and industrial targets was directed by Tsuneharu Otani as *After the Unhealable Wounds: Osaka the Sea of Fire* (1991, *Kiesaranu Kizu Ato: Hi no Umi Osaka*).

RAMAYANA *

1998. AKA: *Ramayana: The Legend of Prince Rama, Prince of Light*. Movie. DIR: Ram Mohan, Yugo Sako. SCR: Krishna Shah. DES: N/C. ANI: Kazuyuki Kobayashi. MUS: N/C. PRD: Nippon Ramayana Film Co. 96 mins.

The God-King Rama and his devoted young wife, Sita, are exiled by political intrigue but determined to prove Rama's right to his ancestral throne. In the course of their long wanderings through the forests and kingdoms of ancient India, they meet many friends and allies, including an old friend of Japanese animation, the Monkey God Hanuman, who was the original template for Monkey King Sun Wu-Kong, hero of JOURNEY TO THE WEST. But the beautiful Sita also attracts unwelcome attention from the Demon King Ravana, who kidnaps her and holds her captive in his island fortress. Rama and their friends set out to rescue her and destroy Ravana; before he can recover his throne he must recover his bride. Shapeshifting vampires, flying fortresses, and epic battles provide plenty of action and interest in a film as stuffed with over-the-top weaponry, weird martial arts, and romance as any fantasy anime.

The story, one of the great religious texts of Hinduism, is credited to a half-mythical robber-poet who is said to have given it its present form around 300 B.C. Like the Greek poet Homer, unwitting originator of ULYSSES 31, Valmiki could scarcely have suspected where his tale would end up. This first Indian-Japanese coproduction took years of heroic effort on the part of Mohan and Japanese producer Yugo Sako. Licenses from the Hindu religious authorities were required before work on the animation could go ahead in India, and local artists and animators were trained to work to Japanese standards and methods. Every aspect of the story was carefully constructed to avoid any offense to Hindu religious sensibilities. The end result did not score the hoped-for success either in India or Japan or among film-fan Hindi communities overseas. Less faithful adherence to Hindu myth can be found in RG VEDA.

RANCE: GUARDIAN OF THE DESERT

1994. JPN: *Rance: Nessa no Guardian*. Video. DIR: Hisashi Fujii. SCR: Satoru Akahori. DES: Kazuto Nakazawa. ANI: Kazuto Nakazawa, Koji Matsuyama. MUS: N/C. PRD: Alice Soft, Tokuma. 50 mins.

Lecherous knight Rance decides that all the women in the world belong to him, and that he should start claiming his rights by getting naked with as many of them as possible. This smutty spin-off from a fantasy role-playing computer game featured big names from the mainstream, including BEAST WARRIORS' Akahori and EL HAZARD's Nakazawa. ○

RANCOU CHOKYO: ORGY TRAINING *

2001. JPN: *Ranko Chokyo Maid ni Natta Shojo*. AKA: *Orgy Training: The Girl Became a Maid Video*. DIR: N/C. SCR: N/C. DES: N/C. ANI: N/C. MUS: N/C. PRD: Five Ways, Wide Road. 30 mins.

A poor little rich boy is completely in thrall to his brutal, arrogant father, whose womanizing with the servants drove his mother away. When he finally plucks up the courage to date a girl from school, he tries to copy Dad and have his way with her, and she rejects him. Next day he's walking to school feeling sorry for himself when he meets a beautiful girl who's lost. When he gets home that night, he finds she's the new live-in maid. His father has paid off her father's loan shark debts in exchange for the girl; she has to do whatever her master tells her to work off the debt. He means to challenge his father and "save" her, so as to make her his own sex slave. Based on a manga by Beauty Hair, author of QUEEN AND SLAVE, the show adds another layer to the depersonalization of characters in porn by not giving anyone a name. Curiously, it is also rather lacking in both the orgy and training departments, although it is extremely explicit in its depiction of rape. ⦿ⓛⓝⓥ

RANMA ½ *

1989. JPN: *Ranma Nibunnoichi*. TV series, movie, video. DIR: Tsutomu Shibayama, Hideharu Iuchi, Akira Suzuki, Junji Nishimura, Kazuhiro Furuhashi. SCR: Shigeru Yanagawa, Ryota Yamaguchi. DES: Atsuko Nakajima, Torao Arai. ANI: Tomomi Mochizuki, Takeshi Mori, Masako Sato, Masamitsu Kudo. MUS: Eiji Mori, Kenji Kawai. PRD: Kitty Film, Studio Deen, Fuji TV. 25 mins. x 161 eps., 74 mins. and 60 mins. (m), 30 mins. x 9 eps. (v). Ranma (*luan ma*, Chinese for "wild horse") Saotome and his father, martial artist Genma, fall into magical pools while training in a region of China. Henceforth, Ranma will change into a girl whenever doused in cold water and back to a boy when doused in hot. Genma fares even worse—he becomes a giant panda. The pair leave exotic, dangerous China and return home to safe, familiar Japan, where years ago Saotome senior agreed with his old friend Tendo that Ranma would marry one of the Tendo daughters and take over the family dojo. The Tendo girls are underwhelmed by their prospective bridegroom. Youngest sister Akane, who draws the short straw, is a feisty young lady with formidable fighting skills and considerable contempt for

the teenage boys who attempt to defeat and date her. She and boy-Ranma (Ranma-kun) strike antagonistic sparks off each other right away. Ranma tries to keep his inadvertent sex changes secret at school by posing as his/her own sibling, resulting in Akane and girl-Ranma (Ranma-chan) becoming rivals for supremacy among their classmates. Ranma-chan attracts unwelcome attention from the guys in class, while Ranma-kun is a babe magnet. The stories revolve around the familiar world of teenage home and school life, with the magical element providing injections of fantasy and romance. Just about every stranger who wanders into town has fallen into some kind of magical pool, and the resulting transformations turn school and dojo into a veritable zoo. Meanwhile Ranma and Akane grow to love each other but can't admit it, their various friends and rivals start to pair off, often unwittingly, and the quest to find a cure for the curse goes on.

Based on a 1988 manga in *Shonen Sunday* from URUSEI YATSURA–creator Rumiko Takahashi, *Ranma ½* duplicated her earlier success, but this time with a lead character that is both boy and girl and a strangeness that comes not from extraterrestrial origins but from magic. The story was soon picked up for TV, where it lasted for several years despite *Shonen Sunday*'s sales sinking to their lowest-ever ebb while the manga was running in it. Chunks of the TV series are available in the U.S. under the titles *Ranma ½, R: Anything Goes Martial Arts, R: Hard Battle*, and *R: Outta Control*. However, real success has come abroad, particularly in Asia, where the kung fu and comedy, dubbed into local languages, make it the most China-friendly anime series. It is even shown in the censorious People's Republic, where its repetitive, lighthearted obsessions with romance, food, fighting, and sibling rivalries are not regarded as much of a threat to Communism.

The first movie, directed by Iuchi, was not based on incidents from the

© 1989 RUMIKO TAKAHASHI/SHOGAKUKAN/KITTY FILM/FUJI TV

Ranma ½

manga but had a specially created story based on Chinese legend. In *Ranma ½ The Movie: Big Trouble In Nekonron, China* (1991), Akane is kidnapped by prince Kirin, who wants to marry her, Ranma and the gang rescue her (in a battle scene that pays open homage to SAINT SEIYA, reflecting the involvement of Arai in both movies), and everything ends as usual with the leads refusing to admit their love for each other. The second, *Nihao My Concubine* (1992), directed by Suzuki, has the girls shipwrecked in the South Seas with a crazed young illusionist who forces them to compete in various skill tests to select his bride. To save Akane and the others from this fate worse than death, Ranma-chan has to compete in wacky activities such as survival flower arranging and obstacle-course cooking.

Several video releases also kept the series in the public eye throughout the 1990s, many of which have also been released in English. *Dead Heat Music Match* (1990) started a new career for the three Tendo girls, Ranma-chan, and Chinese interloper Shampoo: they formed the band DoCo and their voice actresses went on to release numerous *Ranma ½* music CDs and videos. It was followed in rapid succession by more videos, many of which have been released in English with desperately labored titles punning on famous Western films. Thus it was that the *R Special* video series (1993) was released in America as *Desperately Seeking Shampoo, Like Water for Ranma ½,* and *Akane and Her Sisters.* A second video series, *R Super* (1995), was similarly altered into *An Akane to Remember, One Flew Over the Kuno's Nest* (paired with a 30-minute "movie" *Ranma ½ Team vs. The Legendary Phoenix*), and *Faster, Kasumi! Kill! Kill!.* Nishimura directed most of the videos.

With animation that has not aged as badly as *UY*'s and a seamless dub in the U.S., *Ranma ½* has attracted fanatical Western devotees, but Takahashi had already covered the territory thoroughly, and a huge amount of plot and character recycling goes on. She cleverly exploits the factors that made *UY* such a success but with less inventiveness and humor, eventually dumbing down to sheer predictability. Takahashi's talent is far greater than *Ranma ½* reveals; but her commercial success comes from giving her audiences exactly what they want, as often as they want it, and the *Ranma ½* franchise delivers honestly on that basis. This makes it popular with a young teenage audience, which doubtless appreciates a series so interchangeable that the episodes do not need to be numbered, making little difference whether one is watching a TV episode or a video special. Likely to gain a new lease on life as the **POKÉMON** generation reaches its teens and discovers new obsessions, but for a better measure of Takahashi's work, see **MAISON IKKOKU** and **ONE-POUND GOSPEL**.

RANPO

1984. JPN: *Ranpo*. TV series. DIR: Ken Basho, Shin Misawa, Junichi Fukuwara. SCR: Yasushi Hirano, Keiko Maruo, Kenji Terada, Hideki Sonoda, Yoshio Urasawa. DES: Hikuji Kanezawa, Masatoshi Uchizaki. ANI: Hikuji Kanezawa, Toshiyuki Honda, Kaoru Kogawa, Masayuki, Moriyasu Taniguchi. MUS: Chito Kawauchi. PRD: NAS, Fuji TV. 25 mins. x 20 eps.

Mild-mannered Japanese kid Ranpo is kidnapped by aliens whose UFO-based experiments turn him into a "warp boy" who truly believes that he can do anything. Back at school on Earth, he enlists his classmates in a number of wacky schemes, and comedic misunderstandings ensue. Based on a 1979 manga in *Shonen Champion* magazine by Masatoshi Uchizaki, *Ranpo* was swiftly yanked off the air—though the official excuse was that its slot was required for baseball games, the series never returned. Years after its original release, the only traces it left behind were praise for Hiroshi Watanabe's Beatles-pastiche opening credits and an unbroadcast 21st episode.

RANTARO

1993. JPN: *Nintama Rantaro*. AKA: *Rantaro the Little Ninja, Ninja Boys*. TV series. DIR: Tsutomu Shibayama. SCR: Yoshio Urasawa. DES: Sobei Amako. ANI: N/C. MUS: Koji Makaino. PRD: Asia-do. 12 mins. x 91 eps. (TV1), 12 mins. x 72 eps., 20 mins. x 18 eps. (TV2), 45 mins. (m).

Well, the ninja have to learn their trade *somewhere*. Rantaro is a little boy who wants to grow up to be a highly trained assassin. So he goes to a ninja school, where he gets to clown around and meet famous people from Japan's civil-war period. Featuring high-profile theme music from bands-of-the-moment Hikaru Genji and Super Monkeys, this lighthearted kids' comedy, based on a manga by Sobei Amako, returned after 91 episodes as *New Rantaro* (1994), which similarly featured ninja whose favorite food was mushrooms, a warrior forced to work part-time at a launderette, and time out from learning about poisons so the gang can go shopping. Several episodes of the second series were "specials" that ran for almost double the time, and the central cast's best moments were later rereleased in the four-part *Rantaro Masterworks* series (1996). The same year saw a short *Rantaro* movie, in which the little ninja, trained for cunning and deceit, must

somehow convince his elders that he is not responsible for thefts at the school. Compare to **HATTORI THE NINJA**.

RAPEMAN, THE

1994. JPN: *Za (The) Rapeman*. Video. DIR: Kinta Kunte, Kazuo Sawada, Hiroshi Ono. SCR: Shintaro Miyawaki. DES: Keiko Aizaki. ANI: Hidemi Kuma. MUS: N/C. PRD: Pink Pineapple, KSS. 45 mins.

Shotoku and his nephew Keisuke are vigilante rapists. With a company motto of "Righting Wrongs through Penetration," they will don black hockey masks and rape females who have somehow offended their clients by dumping them, refusing their advances, or otherwise treating them inappropriately. After teaching their victims a "good lesson," they donate the money they earn to Keisuke's former home at the Sunflower Orphanage. This deeply offensive series was based on the controversial manga by Shintaro Miyawaki and Keiko Aizaki. The anime version was released roughly halfway through the live-action video series, directed by Takao Nagaishi between 1990 and 1998. **L N V**

RASCAL RACCOON *

1977. JPN: *Araiguma Rascal*. TV series. DIR: Seiji Endo, Shigeo Koshi, Hiroshi Saito. SCR: Akira Miyazaki. DES: Seiji Endo. ANI: Seiji Okuda, Noboru Kameyama, Nobuo Fujisawa, Sadahiko Sakamaki, Yoichi Otabe, Toshiko Nakagawa, Hayao Miyazaki, Hirokazu Ishino. MUS: Takeo Watanabe. PRD: Nippon Animation, Fuji TV. 25 mins. x 52 eps.

Young Sterling lives on a farm in Wisconsin with his parents in the early years of the 20th century. One day, he finds an abandoned baby raccoon in the forest and decides to take it home. The pair soon become inseparable. The raccoon's antics keep the neighborhood in quite a stir, but Sterling also finds his little companion a great comfort in the difficult times of his life, including his mother's illness and the terrible storm that devastates the farm and threatens the family's livelihood.

Based on the writings of Sterling North about his own boyhood, this is part of Nippon Animation's WORLD MASTER-PIECE THEATER series and includes Hayao Miyazaki among its animators.

RATINGS AND BOX OFFICE

In general, anime's ratings on Japanese television are not particularly high. Those anime regarded in the Western market as fan favorites are often broadcast in the late-night slots when literally nobody is watching—even the fans are expected to set their video recorders and get some sleep, as "How-to-Timeshift" articles in late 20th-century magazines showed. Japanese TV ratings are not precisely the same as America's Nielsen ratings, and are designed to show the percentage of televisions switched on in Japan, and tuned in to a particular channel at any given time. This has tended to grossly distort comparative ratings over time—since, for example, it was not all that difficult for the George Reeves *Adventures of Superman* to gain a rating of 73% in the 1950s, when there was only a handful of channels to choose from. Consequently, although we may boast that ASTRO BOY's ratings peaked at 40%, they did so at a time when viewers had little option for channel surfing.

Arguably the biggest television program in Japanese history was the opening of the Tokyo Olympics in 1964, for which many consumers bought their first color television set, thereby helping to contribute to its massive 89.9% audience share. Live-action television continues to enjoy ratings vastly superior to animation on Japanese television, with notable peaks including the live-action OSHIN in 1983, with 62.9%. Popular primetime drama shows and NHK historical dramas regularly gain ratings around the 30% mark. Contrary to misleading publicity in America, the live-action GTO was never "the most watched TV program in Japan," since its peak ratings were a respectable 36.8%, an impressive figure, but one which is regularly trounced, and

was in fact beaten by *Hero* (*DE) that same season.

Average anime tend to have ratings below the 10% mark, and it is not unusual for ratings to fall below 2%. The highest rating achieved by an anime in recent memory was for an episode of CHIBI MARUKO-CHAN in 1990, at 39.9%, beating the previous record of 39.4% that had been held by SAZAE-SAN since 1979. STAR OF THE GIANTS (in 1970) and DOCTOR SLUMP (in 1981) tie for third place with 36.9%. The television broadcast of PRINCESS MONONOKE secured a rating of 35.1%, while other shows with peaks in the thirties include THE GUTSY FROG, JAPANESE FOLK TALES, TIGER MASK, TOUCH, and TOMORROW'S JOE.

Unsurprisingly, anime's ratings are higher when adult viewers are discounted and analysis is restricted solely to the juvenile audience. Statistics compiled by NHK's Cultural Research Bureau suggest not only that very young viewers are encouraged by their parents to see shows such as *Watch with Mother* (*Okaasan to Issho*) and *Playing in English* (*Eigo de Asobo*), but also that they comprise a large viewing component of the audiences for primetime programming such as SAZAE-SAN at ages as young as two. In recent years, the only statistically noteworthy anime challenge to juvenile classics has been presented by POKÉMON, which still regularly snatches a large proportion of the young audience.

The picture of anime at cinemas is very different. Arguably, we are living in the Golden Age of anime cinema, since recent years have seen anime movies becoming the highest-grossing movies of any kind at the Japanese box office. However, until the coming of Studio Ghibli, anime's box office performance was significantly less impressive. Anime movies were aimed at children during seasonal vacations, and often took the form of "roadshow" anthologies in which popular TV anime characters of the moment would briefly shine in a theatrical release. The emphasis, as in children's movies

around the world, is often a choice between pablum for a child-only market, in the hope that parents can earn a two hour rest by leaving their offspring at a cinema, or a genuine "family" movie with cross-generational appeal, designed to ensure that the parents have to buy tickets for themselves along with those for their kids.

The Japanese cinema industry was in a notorious slump for many years, never quite recovering from the arrival of TV, with many "movie" releases simply taking the form of very limited theatrical runs for promotional purposes. The difference, in such cases, between a video release and a cinema release is that screening in a cinema anywhere, however brief, obligates dedicated cinema magazines to at least review a movie, and thereby helps gain additional press attention ahead of the inevitable video release. Sometimes, the difference can be quite astonishing—Mamoru Oshii's GHOST IN THE SHELL, hailed around the globe as a masterpiece of modern anime, played in Tokyo theaters for barely two weeks.

Japanese box office records were dominated for almost two decades by two live-action movies—Spielberg's *E.T.* (1982) and Koreyoshi Kurehara's *Antarctica* (*Nankyoku Monogatari*, 1983). It was not until the late 1990s that a sudden rush of blockbusters leapt ahead—*A.I., Mission Impossible 2, Independence Day, Star Wars Episode I: The Phantom Menace, Jurassic Park*, and *Armageddon*. The number one spot at the Japanese box office then fell in quick succession to PRINCESS MONONOKE, *Titanic*, and then SPIRITED AWAY. Hype for HOWL'S MOVING CASTLE tends to emphasize its record-breaking opening weekend, avoiding mention of the fact it failed to outperform its predecessors overall. Such high numbers for Ghibli movies are a relatively recent phenomenon, and only really date from 1997, when *Princess Mononoke*'s takings were four times that of its Miyazaki predecessor, PORCO ROSSO, which had until that point been the best performing Ghibli film in cinemas. Previously, Studio

Ghibli's real strength had been in the home video market—its films performed reasonably at cinemas, breaking records for *anime* if not for movies in general, and were the only films that seriously competed for the cartoon market share of Buena Vista Japan's Disney videos and DVDs. Even in the 1990s, the best-selling non-Ghibli cartoons in Japan were works such as *Beauty and the Beast* and the *Lion King*, with only a handful of works such as EVANGELION and OH MY GODDESS! even scraping into top tens.

Ghibli encourages a certain brand loyalty in the Japanese public—a survey conducted for Toho discovered that the Studio Ghibli name enjoyed an impressive 43% trust rating from filmgoing respondents. The score rose to an even more impressive 64.2% if the name Miyazaki appeared on a movie, perhaps helping to explain Ghibli's controversial decision to hire Hayao Miyazaki's son Goro to direct TALES OF EARTHSEA.

The Japanese successes of Ghibli, or indeed of any other anime, are not necessarily repeated abroad. At the American box office, three of the top four best-performing anime are POKÉMON films, with the number one spot going to the $85 million gross of *Pokémon: The First Movie* (1999). The YUGI-OH movie is at number 3 with $19.8 million, and by the time we reach the highest-grossing Ghibli movie, SPIRITED AWAY at number five, takings have fallen to a more modest $10 million. The COWBOY BEBOP movie, at number 11, is the last American anime release to earn over a million dollars in theaters; takings in the lower half of the top 20 for movies such as PERFECT BLUE and TOKYO GODFATHERS barely break into six figures. To put such figures in their business context, DreamWorks spent over $30 million on prints and advertising alone for *Shrek* (2001), which went on to take more than a quarter of a *billion* dollars at the U.S. box office. Anime may be growing in popularity, but it still has a long way to go before it presents a serious challenge to big

movie business. In fact, it is arguable that without Hayao Miyazaki and Pikachu, anime's standing in cinemas would be almost unnoticeable.

RAVE MASTER *

2001. JPN: *Rave*. AKA: *Groove Adventure Rave*. TV series. DIR: Takashi Watanabe. SCR: Nobuaki Kishima. DES: Akira Matsushima. ANI: Studio DEEN. MUS: Kenji Kawai. PRD: Kazunori Noguchi, RAVE Production Committee, Studio DEEN, TBS. 24 mins. x 51 eps. Teenager Haru Glory inherits the Rave Sword, a weapon wielded 50 years earlier by the legendary Rave Master Shiba. Shiba managed to forestall disaster by scattering the evil Shadow Stones throughout the world in a mighty explosion, but in the process also lost the "good" Rave Stones. When Haru fishes a weird looking dog, Plue, out of the sea, he also inherits Shiba's faithful canine companion. Heading to the city of Hip Hop with Plue, Haru joins forces with the feisty Elie and soon finds himself on a quest to collect the scattered stones, while evading the Shadow Guards and their General Shuda. Can the pair and their allies succeed in their quest? Well, this is a strictly-by-the-numbers quest story so of course they can, but take our word for it rather than spending 24 hours of your life to find out. Despite quite attractive character design, this show is limited in both concept and animation; POKÉMON, CARDCAPTORS, and ONE PIECE were here long before. Using pseudo-cool references to music and pop culture instead of a decent script is *so* last century; nothing dates a weak show faster. In outbreaks of sub-Tezuka whimsy, there's a Punk Street and a Ska Village as well as Hip Hop City, and Haru's battle cry is "Rave-olution!" Need we go on? Viewers chained to a chair and forced to watch it, however, may pass the time by drawing Cold War analogies—fifty years elapsing since the world was transformed by a large explosion, itself caused by the splitting of a magic stone. Based on the manga by Hiro Mashima.

RAYCA

2002. AKA: *Reika*. Video. DIR: N/C. SCR: N/C. DES: Haruhiko Mikimoto. ANI: N/C. MUS: N/C. PRD: Digital Frontier, Bandai Visual. 30 mins. In the 31st century, individuals exist only as data in computer networks. Rayca, a beautiful young idol character, comes back ten thousand years to our time to explore memories of ancient Tokyo and its subcultures. Created by Mikimoto and delicately lit and animated by Digital Frontier, who were also involved in ZOIDS, the 2004 remake of APPLESEED, and a whole clutch of games, this is a slight but pretty work divided into ten short chapters. The DVD package includes an artbook.

RAYEARTH *

1994. JPN: *Maho Kishi Rayearth*. AKA: *Magic Knight Rayearth*. TV series, video. DIR: Toshihiro Hirano, Keitaro Motonaga, Hajime Kamegaki, Koichi Chiaki, Hitoyuki Matsui. SCR: Keiko Maruo, Osamu Nakamura, Nanase Okawa. DES: Atsuko Ishida, Masahiro Yamane. ANI: Atsuko Ishida, Keiji Goto, Hideyuki Motohashi, Masahiro Yamane, Madoka Hiroyama. MUS: Hayato Matsuo. PRD: TMS, Yomiuri TV. 25 mins. x 49 eps., 45 mins. x 3 eps. Hikaru Shido, Umi Ryuzaki, and Fu Ho-oji are three ordinary Japanese schoolgirls who suddenly find themselves transported to Cephiro, a world of magic and monsters in another dimension. Clef, a very youthful looking ancient wizard, tells them that they have been summoned by the guardian of Cephiro, Princess Emeraude. The princess is a "pillar" of Cephiro, the link that holds the magic kingdom together, but she has been kidnapped by the evil High Priest Zagato. In order to save this fragile world, the three girls must literally win their spurs and become Magic Knights, for only the combined powers of the Knights can hope to challenge Zagato and save the world. Clef helps them from time to time, and they have another friend, the rabbit-like Mokona, whose cuddly exterior hides many secrets. Nothing else is quite as it seems either; the sorcerer is in love with the princess, and each of the girls has her own secret strengths and weaknesses. If they are ever to see Tokyo again, they must work together to save Cephiro.

In the second season, the three girls are once again summoned to Cephiro, once again on the brink of oblivion. With Emeraude absent, the three kingdoms of Autozam, Farhen, and Cizeta begin an invasion of Cephiro to overthrow the pillar system. They must also contend with a girl called Nova, who seems to be Hikaru's nemesis and attacks everything she loves.

The three-part 1997 video series keeps the same basic premise but changes the story. To reflect the change, the title became simply *Rayearth*. Cephiro is slowly materializing in Tokyo and the meeting of two dimensions is causing huge earthquakes on Earth. To avert the impending disaster, Guru Clef and Lantis must find the Magic Knights whose powers can put things right. High school girl Hikaru is waiting for her friends Umi and Fu under a cherry tree with supposed magic connections when there's another strong quake, and a strangely cute rabbit-like creature, Mokona, falls out. As Hikaru chases the white rabbit and her friends follow, they are all whisked to the Tokyo Tower where they learn that they must summon the Mashin Gods, powerful sentient fighting machines, and use their powers to defeat the sorcerer Eagle Vision and his Mashin if both worlds are to be saved.

Based on a manga in *Nakayoshi* that combined elements of girls' manga with boys' action-adventure, this magical romance was a huge hit for its creators, manga collective CLAMP, whose work has not always been served well on video (see RG VEDA) and had considerable success in the U.S. The three heroines, linked specifically with the elements of fire, water, and air, are more "magical" in origin than anything on Cephiro, where many people and places are named for popular Japanese

Real Bout High School

cars. There are references not only to anime tropes, such as destined heroes who alone can control powerful armor, and popular locations, like the Tokyo Tower that features in numerous shows, but also to Western classics—as in ALICE IN WONDERLAND and CLAMP's earlier MIYUKI-CHAN IN WONDERLAND, the girls are guided by a white rabbit.

READY FOR ADVENTURE
1989. JPN: *Boken Shitemo Ii Goro*. Video. DIR: Masamune Ochiai. SCR: Masaru Yamamoto. DES: Nami Saki. ANI: Akihiro Izumi. MUS: Toshiya Uchida. PRD: Knack. 45 mins. x 3 eps.
Forced to wait a year to retake his university exams, would-be film director Junpei jumps at the chance to leave Hokkaido and head for the big city for a job in the film business. But when he arrives, he discovers he's volunteered to work as a porn actor for the beautiful Apollo Productions director Mika. Rising through the ranks, he becomes a talent scout, "road-testing" would-be actresses in a Harajuku love hotel. Eventually, there is trouble on the set as new star Masako turns out to be understandably afraid of men. Luckily, Junpei is on hand to show her just how

nice men can be. This smutty respray of JUNK BOY was based on the 1986 manga in *Big Comic Spirits* by Nonki Miyasu. **N**

REAL BOUT HIGH SCHOOL *
2001. AKA: *Samurai Girl*. TV series. DIR: Shinichi Tokaibayashi. SCR: Aya Matsui. DES: Keiji Goto. ANI: Yoshiyuki Kobe. MUS: Takeshi Yasuda. PRD: Gonzo, Kid's Station. 25 mins. x 13 eps.
Ryoko Mitsurugi is a bubbly teenager who enjoys martial arts, both in practice and on TV in old samurai shows. The star of the school kendo team, she takes up the all-new K-Fight martial art, and soon beats all comers. Her training, however, is not as it seems and has a more practical use. One day, time stops, and the surprised Ryoko is forced to defend the frozen world from an attacking monster. Based on a manga in *Dragon* magazine by Reiji Shiga and Sora Inoue.

REAL SCHOOL GHOST STORIES
1996. JPN: *Honto ni Atta Gakko Kaidan*. AKA: *School Ghost Stories That Really Happened*. Video. DIR: Moriyasu Taniguchi, Noriyuki Abe. SCR: Toshimitsu Himeno, Hiroshi Hashimoto. DES:

Moriyasu Taniguchi, Masaya Onishi. ANI: Moriyasu Taniguchi. MUS: Satoshi Hirata. PRD: Matsutake Home Video, Studio Pierrot, SPE Special Works, Fuji TV. 30 mins. (v), 25 mins. x N/D eps. A "true-life" variant of the school ghost stories that characterized the **HERE COMES HANAKO** phenomenon, the idea remained popular into the 21st century, where it was repackaged as simply **GHOST STORIES**, a TV series with a larger framing device. Heroic schoolgirl Satsuki must protect her cry-baby brother, Keiichiro, from ghosts at their new school while fending off the amorous advances of class lothario Hajime. The trio are accompanied by Momoko, a pallid, withdrawn girl who always attracts the attention of spirits, good and otherwise.

REC

2006. TV series. DIR: Ryutaro Naka-mura. SCR: Reiko Yoshida. DES: Hideyuki Morioka. ANI: Hideyuki Morioka. MUS: Kei Haneoka. PRD: Shaft, TBS. 12 mins. x 9 eps.
Luckless twentysomething Fumihiko Matsumaru has been stood up again by another date, and is just about to hurl his tickets into the trash when he meets Aka Onda, a pretty red-haired wannabe actress. Later that night, her apartment burns down and so she moves in "temporarily" with him, leading to yet another twist in the anime subgenre of not-quite-lovers becoming roommates. They must also work together without revealing their living arrangements, since Fumihiko works for a snack-food company, which hires Aka to voice the role of its mascot "cat-tree" in commercials. However, REC's charm stems in part from its blatant appeal to an anime fan crowd, since while Aka may be obsessed with Audrey Hepburn, her personal vocation seems to lie in anime voice acting. If more proof were ever needed that anime has become its own self-referential fantasy world, this is it, with the "magical girlfriend" of anime cliché now transformed into a girl from the anime business itself, in an anime about people making anime.

Based on the 2003 manga series by Q-taro Hanamizawa in the monthly *Sunday GX* magazine.

RECORD OF LODOSS WAR *

1990. JPN: *Lodoss to Senki*. Video, TV series. DIR: Akinori Nagaoka. SCR: Asami Watanabe, Akinori Endo. DES: Yutaka Izubuchi, Nobuteru Yuki, Hidetoshi Kaneko. ANI: Eiko Yamauchi. MUS: Mitsuo Hagita. PRD: Madhouse. 30 mins. x 13 eps., 80 mins. (*Crystania Movie*), 40 mins. x 3 eps. (*Crystania*), 30 mins. (*Welcome to Lodoss*), 25 mins. x 27 eps. (*Heroic Knight*).
This video series based on the novels and gaming scenarios created by Ryo Mizuno and Hiroshi Yasuda presents role-playing games as they never were but should have been. In a world still reeling in the aftermath of a war between gods, a classic D&D party of warrior Parn, elf Deedlit, dwarf Ghim, magic-user Slayn, cleric Etoh, and thief Woodchuck set out to seek the aid of Wort the sage, a former adventurer whose early years were chronicled in the spin-off manga *Lady of Pharis*. The land of Lodoss is under threat from a revival of the power of darkness. A heroic king and his noble warlord have been turned to the dark side by an evil counselor, and the heroes of a former struggle are lending what support they can to the new young team as they travel to Wort's stronghold only to learn that he regards himself simply as an observer and is unwilling to use his great power to intervene. The dungeon party must travel on, trying to recruit allies for the fight against darkness among exotic kingdoms and dank forests, meeting evil Dark Elves, desert princes, and dragons guarding ancient treasures deep below the earth. At the end of the story, it seems that evil has been stopped in its tracks for the moment, and the young hero Parn has completed his journey from boyhood to manhood, his quest for himself.
The villains are dark and deadly enough to satisfy the keenest good-ver-sus-evil aficionado, but they're neither motiveless nor entirely unsympathetic.

One of the most tear-jerking scenes in the whole of anime occurs in episode ten, when tough-guy Ashram the Black Knight, noble servant of dark powers, affirms his eternal love for his elven mistress, Pirotessa, simply in the way he says her name as she dies in his arms. The "little people"—soldiers commanding outpost forts, thieves, and farmers—are shown in a sympathetic light, often more honorable and honest than the great kings and mages, and we learn that some of those who fought for the triumph of Light in days of yore are now on the side of Darkness. In his way the "good" sage Wort is more amoral than his dark counterpart, Karla the Gray Witch, who possesses men and topples empires to keep faith with her unshakable belief that good and evil must be kept in balance, and that when one has ruled for too long the balance must be made to shift.
Seductive music, especially the opening and ending themes, powerful faux-medieval and Art Nouveau design, and strong characters make for an attractive package. There's an effective opening sequence by veteran Rintaro, but the animation is generally undistinguished. The plotting circles and strays in places, and many elements of the dense backstory are hinted at though not explored, but the whole is involving enough to carry the viewer over such minor hiccups.
The first two videos also enjoyed a limited release in a "movie" edition in order to drum up support for the series. Ryutaro Nakamura's later movie and video sequel *Legend of Crystania* (1995 and 1996) proves less than satisfying. A promising concept is let down by low-rent designs, appalling animation, and editing that verges on the deranged in places—add to this a poor English dub and a different U.S. distributor with a nonexistent numbering policy. Set 300 years after the original and featuring characters who were supposed to be dead last time we looked, Ashram is possessed by the evil god Barbas, while Pirotessa

assembles a new band of heroes to fight back. The already confusing plot of warring were-beasts is made even harder to unravel when the tape called "A New Beginning" turns out to be the last episode, coming after "Cave of the Sealed" and "Resurrection of the Gods' King."

The franchise returned briefly for Chiaki Koichi's theatrical short *Welcome to Lodoss Island* (1997), a squashed-down cartoon version rereleased on video with extra footage. In the post-**EVANGELION** boom, when producers desperately searched for anything to expand, the franchise was brought back once more, this time as Yoshihiro Takamoto's TV series *Record of Lodoss War: Chronicles of the Heroic Knight* (1998). Set five years after the original video series, *CotHK* features a number of former supporting characters in major roles, along with members of the original cast, who have hardly changed a bit. Young Spark fills the would-be paladin role occupied by Parn, now a bona fide hero, in the original video series. Barely competent mercenaries Shiris and Orson attack a free village and meet apprentice mage Cecil, a prissy, just-masculine version of elfin babe Deedlit from series one. Deedlit and Parn show up in time to stop a bloodbath when gentle giant Orson goes into berserker mode, and grown-up mage Slayn, also from series one, shows up with his wife and daughter in time to fill some of those expository gaps and get everyone organized into a dungeon party without too much bickering. Nothing much has changed in five years. There's another threat to the peace of the island and the supremacy of Light. Parn still idolizes the ultracool "mercenary king" Kashue and has no idea how to handle women. Deedlit still isn't sure of their relationship after five *years* of adventuring together. The world is still a reactionary place where Kashue can urge Parn, with complete sincerity, to become a king so that he can have the pleasure of treating him as an equal, and the lip service paid

to serious issues with a brief refugee crisis doesn't hold up the real, important action of suborning priests and killing dragons. Despite a wonderful opening sequence, *CotHK* contains all of its predecessor's low-budget faults without any of its earnest, adventuring virtues. Yet the original, loaded with atmosphere and style, still has magic.

RED BARON

1994. TV series. DIR: Akio Saga. SCR: Junji Takegami, Kazuhiko Kobe, et al. DES: Ryu Noguchi. ANI: Satoshi Hirayama. MUS: N/C. PRD: Tokyo Movie Shinsha, NTV. 25 mins. x 49 eps.
In the year 2020, the gladiatorial sport of Mecha Fighting (Metal Fighting in some sources) is the most popular spectator event. One hotheaded boy decides to become the champion pilot, operating his Red Baron robot against all comers. A remake of a 1973 live-action series that featured men dressed up as giant robots—and they say there's no such thing as progress.

RED SHADOW

1987. JPN: *Kamen no Ninja Akakage.* AKA: *Masked Ninja Red Shadow.* TV series. DIR: Susumu Ishizaki, Kunihisa Sugishima, Tomoharu Katsumata, Kazuhisa Takenouchi. SCR: Yoshiyuki Suga, Toshiki Inoue, Asami Watanabe. DES: Akehiro Kaneyama. ANI: Akehiro Kaneyama, Michio Kondo. MUS: Shunsuke Kikuchi. PRD: Toei, Nippon TV. 25 mins. x 23 eps.
In medieval Japan, young temple boy Gennosuke disguises himself as the Red Shadow in order to fight the Cult of the Golden Eye, teaming up with color-coded allies that include the White and Blue Shadows. Another boy-ninja tale, this was one of the first "retro anime," since this nostalgic production was designed to remind parents of their own youth in 1967, when they could have read Mitsuteru Yokoyama's original manga and watched the live-action spin-off adventure TV series. The story was revived for Hiroyuki Nakano's live-action movie *Red Shadow* (2001).

RED-BLOODED ELEVEN

1970. JPN: *Akakichi no Eleven.* AKA: *Here Come The Superboys; Soccer Boy; Goal!.* TV series. DIR: Takeshi Yamada, Yoshiyuki Tomino, Kazuyuki Okaseko. SCR: Tsunehisa Ito, Yoshi Suzuki. DES: Masahiro Ioka. ANI: Yoshiyuki Tomino, Masayuki Hayashi, Seiji Okada. MUS: N/C. PRD: NTV, DOGA Productions. 25 mins. x 52 eps.
At Shinsei high school, soccer is almost a combat sport and new team coach Teppei Matsuki is a fully paid up sadist who will push his team as hard as necessary to win. Headstrong school bad boy Shingo Tamai and his friend Ohira are determined not to be bullied into joining Matsuki's team; instead they set up a squad of their own, and at first play just for fun and struggle to keep up with Matsuki's team. As their skills progress, they play other teams and get stronger and craftier, until they face the crack Asakase high school squad and its star player Misugi Yan in the schools' final. In a tangle of subplots involving old rivalries and injuries, and a mixed-race player seeking his identity and his lost mother (who turns out to be in jail), Shingo develops his skills as a center forward and looks forward to playing a visiting Brazilian squad. He is seriously injured in a game, but his talent, which even the legendary Brazilian Pele recognizes, is equaled by his determination. With the help of a friend of his old rival Matsuki, he recovers to help the team to victory. Definitely melodrama rather than a sports series proper, this is the first in the line of Japanese soccer soaps that stretches to **CAPTAIN TSUBASA** and beyond. Based on a manga by Ikki Kajiwara and Kosei Sonoda.

REDBREAST SUZUNOSUKE

1972. JPN: *Shakudo Suzunosuke.* AKA: *Red-Hips Suzunosuke.* TV series. DIR: Isao Takahata, Shigetsugu Yoshida, Tetsuo Imazawa, Minoru Okazaki. SCR: Haruya Yamazaki, Yoshitake Suzuki. DES:. ANI: Yoichi Kotabe, Shingo Araki, Hideo Kawauchi, Yoshinori Kanada, Tetsuo Imazawa, Yasuo Yamaguchi,

Yoshifumi Kondo, Eiji Tamura, Hayao Miyazaki, Osamu Dezaki. mus: Takeo Watanabe. prd: Tokyo Movie Shinsha, Fuji TV. 25 mins. x 52 eps.

Suzunosuke Shakudo wishes to become a sword master, and begins to study with Shusaku Chiba, the leader of the Kitatatsu Single Sword School. Suzunosuke trains hard and also attracts the attention of his teacher's pretty daughter Sayuri. Meanwhile, the threat of civil war looms in Japan, with the mysterious Kimengumi group selecting opponents of their beliefs for attack. Suzunosuke stands up to them with his famous "swordless vacuum attack."

Based on a manga by animator Eiichi Fukui, and formerly the subject of a popular radio show, the reins in this anime production were handed to Tsunayoshi Takeuchi when Fukui died shortly after production commenced. Director Shigetsugu was nominally in charge, but temporarily obliged to hand things over to a young Isao Takahata when he was taken ill. Hayao Miyazaki and Osamu Dezaki also worked on this production as humble storyboarders, and the staff roster includes a number of Miyazaki's later collaborators, including Kanada and Kondo. The Suzunosuke story also became the subject of a live-action movie series directed by Bin Kado, Kimiyoshi Yasuda and Kazuo Mori.

REFRAIN BLUE

2000. Video. dir: Norio Kashima. scr: Takao Yoshioka. des: Mayumi Watanabe. ani: Mayumi Watanabe. mus: N/C. prd: Pink Pineapple. 30 mins. x 3 eps.

Nao is a girl in a state of some mental distress who walks into the sea and is rescued in the nick of time by Yoshihiro, a boy to whom she now latches on. He is returning to his home town to fulfill a promise made seven years ago. It soon transpires that both are struggling to overcome the loss of a loved one, although their personal journey to healing is (a) being supervised by a mysterious spirit girl playing cupid, and (b) likely to result in nudity

before the end of the show, this being from Pink Pineapple, and based on a game by elf. **N**

REI REI *

1993. jpn: *Utsukushiki Sei no Dendoshi Rei Rei*. aka: *Rei Rei the Sensual Evangelist*. Video. dir: Yoshiki Yamamoto, Mihiro Yamaguchi. scr: Michiru Mochizuki. des: Kenichi Ishimaru. ani: Oji Suzuki. mus: Hiroyuki Ishizuka. prd: KSS, AIC. 30 mins. x 2 eps.

Kaguya is a sexy spirit who wafts down from her home near the moon to solve sexual problems. Aided by cheeky goblin-cum-butler Pipi, she saves humanity from disaster by spreading the gospel of sexual freedom—as long as it's the freedom of *men* to have sex with whomever they choose, as long as they "really love" her. In the first story, schoolboy Mamoru lusts after arrogant Ikuko, who has no time for him since she has been corrupted by her lesbian teacher. Miss Manami, for her part, lusts after hunky local doctor Okabe, deciding to kill Ikuko so she can run off with him. Kaguya doesn't save the girl, but she does show Manami and Okabe the error of their ways and ensures that Ikuko, now properly appreciative of Mamoru, is restored to life before her cremation. A final scene cut from the Japanese version during production showed Manami and Okabe getting their just desserts—each other.

Kaguya returns to help the nerdy Satoshi, a boy whose heart of gold is concealed under an obsession with astronomy that's boring his girlfriend Mika. No, Kaguya doesn't teach him social skills, just helps him "work through" his breast fixation, before turning him into bathwater so he can experience a girl up close. Everything works out in the end, but not before Satoshi is trapped inside a computer game, and Kaguya must endure the obligatory tentacle-rape to save him. Newly rejuvenated, Satoshi becomes a "real man" at last, ready to treat Mika in a fittingly dominant manner.

With an amusing pseudo-psychotherapy subplot and some semblance

of a story, *Rei Rei* compares very favorably to the lackluster erotica of the decade that followed it—thus making it even more of a surprise that this picaresque porno did not return for more than just these two episodes. Based on a manga by **Airbats**-creator Toshimitsu Shimizu, *Rei Rei* draws distantly on the *Taketori Monogatari*, one of the more famous **Japanese Folk Tales**—the story of celestial Princess Kaguya whose search for an Earthbound husband proved fruitless. The same legend was pastiched very differently in **Queen of a Thousand Years** and **Gu-Gu Gunmo**. **N**

REIKO SHIRATORI I PRESUME

1990. jpn: *Shiratori Reiko de Gozaimasu*. aka: *I'm Reiko Shiratori*. Video. dir: Mitsuru Hongo. scr: Ayako Okina. des: Yumiko Suzuki. ani: Keiko Hayashi, Takuya Saito. mus: N/C. prd: Asia-do. 40 mins.

Nineteen-year-old Reiko Shiratori is a true material girl, devoted to style, snobbery, and snide put-downs. Thanks to her rich family, she feels superior to everyone she meets, but her high-class schooling has not prepared her for affairs of the heart. Refusing to admit her feelings for classmate Tetsuya Akimoto before it is too late, Reiko pursues him to Tokyo, where she enrolls at his university to try and win him back. Based on a manga by Yumiko Suzuki, *RSIP* encapsulates the spirit of the money-mad 1980s, and was later adapted into a live-action TV series of the same name (*DE). Compare to the later **His and Her Circumstances**, which also features a homecoming queen whose mask and halo slip.

RELIC ARMOR LEGACIUM

1987. Video. dir: Hiroyuki Kitazume, Hideki Takayama. scr: Akinori Endo. des: Hiroyuki Kitazume, Hidetoshi Omori. ani: Hiroyuki Kitazume. mus: Tatsumi Yano. prd: Atelier Giga. 50 mins.

The inhabitants of planet Libatia are under the mind control of the evil Daats. Professor Grace, escaping from this control, steals the giant robot Legacium and modifies it into a powerful weapon against them. When he is captured, his daughter Arushya manages to flee with the Legacium. Her friends Dorothy and Bric join her to fight Daats and liberate their homeworld.

RELIGION AND BELIEF

It is often said that the Japanese are "born Shinto, marry Christian, and die Buddhist," in recognition of their pragmatic attitude toward multiple beliefs. The same might be said of anime, in which the young are inculcated into rural traditions based on agrarian animism, dazzled in their teens with romance and marriage paraphernalia that is often drawn directly from Christian wedding iconography, and finally encouraged in old age to sacrifice their all for the greater good, be it as pestered parents or tormented mentors. One might interpose an additional stage, that anime children "grow up heathens," steeped as so many adventure anime are in the iconography of foreign myths.

Anime is a magpie medium, stealing flashy objects and solid building materials without discrimination; the exotic religions of the West offer rich pickings, especially as a source for icons and fetishes. As an ordinary teenage girl hearing voices, deemed to have magical powers, and defeating far stronger opponents to save her people, Joan of Arc is a prototype "magical girl": anime has used her story as inspiration for frothy shows like KAMIKAZE THIEF JEANNE and more serious works like TRAGEDY OF BELLADONNA. A shattered, bleeding statue of the Virgin lends resonance to the climactic final battle between good and evil in WICKED CITY—set in a Christian church, where the heroine wields the combined powers of Death and the Madonna. Christ-like figures offer redemption in everything from FIST OF THE NORTH STAR to NAUSICAÄ OF THE VALLEY OF WIND. Of course, Europe and America also mine their own religious iconography for media purposes, which can lead to some confusion about which idols are being paid their

due homage. The crucifix around the hero's neck in TOKYO BABYLON was inspired by pop icon Madonna, and not any Biblical character, while much of the Biblical analogies in SPRIGGAN and GHOST IN THE SHELL seem like so much set dressing.

It is sometimes difficult to make a distinction between religion, faith, and tradition. Faith, as in the individual response to the idea of the divine, is naturally less conspicuous than public practice, being also less open to examination and challenge. Tradition is where belief, religion, and history fade into the timeworn ritual backdrop of everyday life, particularly in the countryside, and hence often appears in anime for or about the very young. In their different ways both BOTTLE FAIRY and MY NEIGHBOR TOTORO allude to Japan's native Shinto religion, while JAPANESE FOLK TALES supply legendary inspirations for most anime, even if they are modernized or reimagined, as in the cases of USHIO AND TORA or SPIRITED AWAY. The anime KAMICHU goes even further and elevates a character to Shinto godhood. In PEACOCK KING the devotions of a young Buddhist monk are both set dressing and part of the storyline in a supernatural action-adventure. TENCHI MUYO!, USHIO AND TORA, ZENKI: THE DEMON PRINCE, and SHRINE OF THE MORNING MIST are all set in and around places of worship.

Like American comic creator Stan Lee before them, anime writers love mythology, with the gods of Greece, Rome, and Scandinavia cropping up in numerous guises, from the supervillains of SAINT SEIYA and ULYSSES 31 to the dysfunctional families of ARION or OH MY GODDESS!. There's even an occasional nod to more exotic traditions, like the Polynesian tribal god NEORANGA, although once in Japan he quickly transmutes into a clunky yet devoted family retainer—a cross between Lurch the butler from *The Addams Family* and an oversized, unstable rockery. While anime has yet to suffer a scandal like that which engulfed Lego's *Bionicles* in 2001, in which

Maori representatives protested that their religion was demonstrably not a forgotten belief system, nor as open for abuse as the creators had thought, it has often stumbled into conflicts over what constitutes fair game in the inspirational stakes. Although many of Osamu Tezuka's works show a great respect for foreign religions and often used the crucifix as an icon of justice and transcendence, he was also the man who sanctioned the infamous "Christ's Eyeball" episode of ASTRO BOY—see CENSORSHIP AND LOCALIZATION. Cruciform imagery, much of it seemingly drawn from its appearance in misunderstood foreign movies rather than direct religious experience, often appears in anime. Examples include the Christ metaphors of EVANGELION and an infamous episode of SAILOR MOON, heavily cut in the U.S. release, in which the supporting cast were all held captive on crystal crucifixes. Anime seems particularly enamored of Judaeo-Christian angels, either as figures of demure, cherubic innocence or gentle parental authority, in everything from the dramatic EARTHIAN to pornography like ANGEL CORE.

As in the West, many creators confuse witchcraft with Satanism, mixing their elements with impunity liable to shock some viewers. A similar confusion often substitutes the five-pointed pentagram of witchcraft (and/or demonology) with the six-pointed Jewish Star of David, witnessed as a symbol of sorcery in anime ranging from UROTSUKIDOJI to SILENT MÖBIUS. Notably, the artist Leiji Matsumoto refused to allow the use of a Star of David in this manner in an abortive remake of CAPTAIN HARLOCK, citing his unwillingness to cause religious offense.

When anime uses religion as a story element, it is usually because of its ability to generate conflict. In HELLSING, the great schism of Christianity, which set Catholics against Protestants and devastated Europe for centuries, lives on despite a common enemy so powerful that both sides must fight it. In ANGEL SANCTUARY the conflict is the war of the fallen angels against the forces of Heaven, another concept born of Christian culture. Nuns and priests are authority figures or protectors of the weak, but more often their supposed disengagement from the world is subverted for dramatic effect, as with sexy priest Nicholas Wolfwood, heavily armed even by the standards of TRIGUN, or Sister Angela of ONE POUND GOSPEL. The sexual potential of nuns has been exploited in porn anime like HOLY VIRGINS and LEATHERMAN, but the concept of a woman vowed to gentleness and virtue, yet powerful and detached enough to deal in death, enhances the shock of violent retribution in such shows as SUIKODEN and CHRONO CRUSADE—a heavy weapon having more impact when wielded by a woman in a wimple.

In the late 1990s, *Animage* critic Maki Watanabe complained that too many anime followed Hollywood's lead in presenting Muslims as blood-crazed terrorists or ignorant peasants like those in LITTLE EL CID or GOSHO-GUN, although it should also be noted that a significant number of postwar anime movies and TV specials drew on stories from the ARABIAN NIGHTS. The scourge of history, religious fundamentalism, features in a few thoughtful modern anime like YUGO THE NEGOTIATOR and MASTER KEATON. Anime has also often embraced an educational role in the dissemination of religions. IN THE BEGINNING and SUPERBOOK both dramatized Bible stories, while Osamu Tezuka regularly used Buddhist and Shinto elements in his *Phoenix* stories (see SPACE FIREBIRD), and both Buddhism and humanism are strong influences on NIGHT TRAIN TO THE STARS. Anime's influence on the young and impressionable has also seen its use for preaching and recruitment, most conspicuously with the lavish movie productions of LAWS OF THE SUN and HERMES for the Institute for Research in Human Happiness, but also in lesser known works such as RAINBOW ACROSS THE PACIFIC or FAIRGROUND IN THE STARS, made as promotional

vehicles for the Soka Gakkai Buddhist association. There was also a promotional anime made for the AUM Shinrikyo organization before the Tokyo sarin gas attack, appearing to feature character designs by Shinji Aramaki, although the authors have not been able to obtain a credit list, and AUM representatives did not answer our requests for information.

Real religious figures and events appear in their historical context, as well as forming story elements in other shows, including the anime life of CONFUCIUS (although his belief system is still arguably not a religion) and the use of the martyrdom of Japanese Christians as a backdrop to NINJA RESURRECTION.

RENTAMAN
1991. JPN: *Anime V Comic Rentaman*. Video. DIR: Takashi Watanabe, Osamu Tsuruyama, Masakazu Iijima, Eiko Toriumi. SCR: N/A. DES: N/A. ANI: N/A. MUS: N/A. PRD: Studio Pierrot. 74 mins. x 4 eps.
A short-lived, unrepeated experimental concept, *Rentaman* was a video magazine show serializing several short, episodic anime such as ABASHIRI FAMILIES, AKAI HAYATE, the comedy *Hisashi Eguchi's Hisagoro Show*, and the thriller *Baku Yumemakura's Twilight Theater*. The serials were later compiled into stand-alone tapes, though the episodic nature of their origins goes some way toward explaining the cut-up storytelling of the two available in English.

RENZU *
2004. JPN: *Renzu—Futari no Kyori*. AKA: *The Distance Between The Two; Lens*. Video. DIR: Sanpo Edogawa. SCR: Isamu Hori. DES: Naomi Hayakawa. ANI: N/C. MUS: N/C. PRD: Five Ways, Wide Road. 30 mins.
Toru Shioda pushes his childhood friend Asuka Misaki out of the way of a speeding car—which saves her life, but causes him to have a leg injury that ruins his promising soccer career. He takes up photography instead, but his resentment and frustration lead him

to try and rape Asuka, and the couple subsequently break up. His cram school teacher, a sexy and dominant woman, provides an outlet for these feelings, as does an attractive redhead he picks up while out girl-hunting with a friend, but his thoughts keep returning to Asuka, who still loves him despite his being so mixed up. A handful of explicit scenes gives the viewer what he bought this tape for, but there isn't time for much in the way of story or character development. Instead, this tale takes many of the childhood associations of romance anime like LOVE HINA and injects a note of bitterness and contempt—its message seemingly that sacrifice is all right, as long as it doesn't cost you anything. The title is a pun on both "lens" and *ren-zu*, "depictions of love." ⓃⓁⓋ

REPORTER BLUES
1990. TV series. DIR: Kenji Kodama. SCR: Ryuzo Nakanishi, Shuichi Miyashita. DES: Akio Sugino, Yukihiro Yokoyama. ANI: N/C. MUS: Pino Massara. PRD: TMS, Rever, RAI. 25 mins. x 52 eps.
Paris in the 1920s: Toni, a pretty young reporter for a daily newspaper, is crazy about the new jazz music that's sweeping Europe. In her spare time, she plays saxophone in a little jazz cellar. As she goes about her daily work, she keeps running across the trail of one woman, Madame Lapin, who seems to be a very respectable lady, wealthy and influential and yet also involved in other, more dubious events. Toni's nose for a story could get her into serious trouble as she uncovers clues to a dangerous game.

One of the many Japanese-Italian coproductions masterminded by SHERLOCK HOUND's Marco Pagot, who co-wrote the story with his brother Gi, this ran for two 26-episode series. The jazzy score and apealing designs from the designer of COBRA and CAT'S EYE make it attractive despite the somewhat run-of-the-mill detective stories. Broadcast on Japan's second satellite TV channel in 1991, the series ran on French TV early in the 1990s, but its biggest success has been in Italy.

REQUIEM FROM THE DARKNESS *
2004. JPN: *Kyogoku Natsuhiko Kosetsu Hyaku Monogatari*. AKA: *Kyogoku Natsuhiko KH Monogatari; Natsuhiko Kyogoku's Worldly Horror Stories*. TV series. DIR: Hideki Tonokatsu. SCR: Hiroshi Takahashi, Sadayuki Murai, Yoshinaka Fujioka, Yuu Kanbara. DES: Shigeyuki Miya. ANI: N/C. MUS: Kuniaki Haishima. PRD: Digiturbo, Nitroplus, Tokyo Movie Shinsha. 22 mins. x 13 eps.

The last years of the Tokugawa Shogunate were a time of upheaval in Japan as the fast-changing 19th-century world invaded its ancient culture; yet the old tales of demons and goblins remained popular through the new era into the present. Author Momosuke Yamaoka, weary of writing for children, is on the road gathering material for a planned horror anthology book, which he intends to call *A Hundred Stories*. He meets three strange companions, shapeshifting bird caller Nagamimi, puppeteer Ogin, and trickster monk Mataichi, who call themselves the Ongyo—see YIN YANG MASTER. They are "legend detectives," investigating the old tales to find the truth behind them and bring those responsible for wrongdoing to justice—compare to MUSHISHI. Each time he meets them, supernatural events and strange incidents follow, such as the capture of a tanuki rumored to be a shapeshifter (see POMPOKO), or a criminal who keeps coming back from the dead.

Author Natsuhiko Kyogoku's original novel has echoes of JUDGE and *Zatoichi* (*DE), since Momosuke and his associates often act as agents of justice where no other justice can touch their victims, or classic tales of wanderers taking on jobs too dirty for the locals, such as YOJIMBO. His earlier horror works have won literary honors and found their way to the movie screen—*Kwaidan: Eternal Love (Warau Iemon)* and live-action TV, but this is the first anime based on his work. The color palette is limited and the worst of the gore implied rather than shown, which gives the show the spooky feel of

Rg Veda

late-night movies watched in a quiet, dark house. Many of the other staffers have backgrounds in both anime and live-action horror: Haishima composed the score for *Night Head* (*DE), for example, while PERFECT BLUE scenarist Murai also wrote episodes of *Wizard of Darkness* (*DE). **NV**

RESCUE KIDS
1991. JPN: *Kinkyu Hasshin Saver Kids*. AKA: *Saver Kids; Emergency Departure Rescue Kids*. TV series. DIR: Hajime Kamegaki, Keitaro Motonaga, Yasushi Nagaoka, Masanori Iijima. SCR: Shuichi Miyashita, Tadaaki Yamazaki. DES: Yasuo Otsuka, Osamu Nabeshima. ANI: Osamu Nabeshima. MUS: N/C. PRD: Studio OX, Tokyo Movie Shinsha, Sotsu Agency, TV Tokyo. 25 mins. x 50 eps.
Brothers Ken and Go and their sister Ran band together to defeat an evil genius in a Darth Vader-style helmet, plotting to take over the world with his "destroid" robot. They use all the resources of the family robot rental business to stop him in this domestic comedy. Any family-based science fiction series runs the risk of comparison with *Lost in Space*, especially if it throws in a villainous nemesis with delusions

of grandeur. *RK* uses science fiction in the same way, as an exotic backdrop for the sibling bickering and minor domestic incidents that reflect its own society, rather than an exploration of alternative possibilities—although Japan has embraced the principle of the domestic robot more thoroughly than America. TMS marketed the show in Europe in the 1990s under the title *Rescue Kids*, and it was dubbed into Spanish and screened in South America. Based on an idea by LUPIN III–creator Monkey Punch.

RG VEDA *
1991. JPN: *Seiden Rg Veda*. AKA: *Holy Scripture R(i)g Veda*. Video. DIR: Hiroyuki Ebata, Takamasa Ikegami. SCR: Nanase Okawa. DES: Mokona Apapa, Tetsuro Aoki, Kiichi Takaoka, Futoshi Fujikawa. ANI: Tetsuro Aoki. MUS: Nick Wood. PRD: Animate Film. 45 mins. x 2 eps.
Ashura the Lord of Heaven is betrayed by his wife and murdered by her lover, his chief general. The usurper rules for 300 years, until the day when the prophesied band of six warriors arrives to defeat him. But there are only five of them, so they wander around a bit

looking for the missing slowpoke, while various people go on about "things that shall be" and "that which is written." By the time they find the latecomer, it's time for the credits to roll.

Based on a manga by the CLAMP artistic collective who gave us **CARDCAPTORS**, *RV* is one of many of their works that has been poorly served in anime form. Like many anime designed as ads for much longer manga (e.g., **COMPILER**), *RV* finishes before it's even begun, with the band of heroes heading off to do great deeds, frustrating English-speaking fans who want to know how the story ends but cannot read the original.

The English dub uses genuinely British accents with mixed success; plummy goddesses ordering around minions sound rather good, but the iconoclastic gang of farting, bickering heroes seem like the Famous Five on safari. Although George Roubicek's script is fine, *Rg Veda* suffers (like many anime) from being transliterated instead of translated. The fact that we're watching a Japanese fantasy retelling of Hindu myth is interesting, but the script keeps names in their Japanese form, so we never find out that Taishakuten is really Indra, Karura is Garuda (see **KARULA DANCES**), Kujaku is Mahamayuri Vidyarajni (see **PEACOCK KING**), Kendappa is Gandharva, and Yasha is Yaksha. There are a few nice moments of fantasy, like the butterflies who are "messengers of darkness," and the mad Princess Aizen Myoo (Ragaraja, a red-skinned, three-eyed, six-armed *male* demon in the original), who imprisons Yasha in a castle of ice, but it's all been done better elsewhere—chiefly in the pious Indian coproduction **RAMAYANA**.

The production company pretentiously used Sanskrit orthography to write the title, not expecting the English distributors to mistake the opening two letters for initials—it's thus pronounced "Rig Veda" not "Argie Veda."

RIDING BEAN *
1989. Video. DIR: Yasuo Hasegawa.

SCR: Kenichi Sonoda. DES: Kenichi Sonoda, Kinji Yoshimoto, Satoshi Urushibara, L. Lime, Yoshihisa Fujita. ANI: Masahiro Tanaka, Osamu Kamijo, Hiroya Ohira, Jun Okuda. MUS: David Garfield, Phil Perry. PRD: Artmic, AIC. 45 mins.
Bean Bandit is known as the Roadbuster; he's one of the best driver/couriers in the business. He makes a living on the outside edge of the law, but he's one of the good guys down deep, a true antihero with a heart of gold. He and his business partner, Rally Vincent, unwittingly get involved with psychotic kidnapper Semmerling, who sets them up to take the rap when her victim is killed, but they fight their way out in a hail of bullets and a screech of brakes. The story ends with nobody the winner and few survivors, but the kidnapper is "retired," permanently, and Bean and Rally live to keep on hustling.

This is one of the most interesting and watchable of anime actioners—made with a real love of Hollywood chase movies including *The Blues Brothers*, *Bullitt*, and *The French Connection*. Watch, too, for Japanese references to such anime as **LUPIN III**, especially in the cat-and-mouse relationship of cop and criminal. Some of the best car chases in anime are routed along the streets of Sonoda's beloved city of Chicago. Director Hasegawa also lets the darker side of Sonoda's manga show through the lighthearted take on an American genre; the violence and amorality of Semmerling's lifestyle are real and chilling, and her abusive, sadomasochistic relationship with an adoring child-slave is clearly spelled out without any need for sexual explicitness. Following the same studio disputes that truncated **BUBBLEGUM CRISIS**, ownership of the *Riding Bean* property became difficult to determine, and the franchise seemed finished. However, Sonoda recycled some of the characters and situations in his later **GUNSMITH CATS**—a radically different Rally becomes a bounty hunter, the child-sex subplot returns in the form of her partner Minnie May, and Bean himself has many

cameo roles in the manga, though he does not appear in the anime. **LV**

RINGING BELL *
1978. JPN: *Chirin no Suzu*. AKA: *Chirin's Bell*. Movie. DIR: Masami Hata. SCR: Takashi Yanase. DES: Takashi Yanase. ANI: Shigeru Yamamoto, Sadao Miyamoto, Toshio Hirata. MUS: Taku Izumi. PRD: Sanrio. 46 mins.
Chirin the lamb is orphaned when the bad wolf Wor (the "Wolf King" in the U.S. dub) kills his mother. Chirin sets out for revenge but has a change of heart. Despairing of his weak nature, he begs the wolf to teach him how to be tough and learns how to be a predator from his parent's killer. Battered, bruised, and half drowned, the lamb is put through a heartless regime of torment until he is toughened into a vicious ram with a "reputation for ruthless killing." Two years later, Chirin is led by Wor in an attack on the farm where he was born. Seeing a ewe vainly fighting to protect her offspring, Chirin is reminded of his mother and turns on the wolf—killing his surrogate father. However, the rest of the flock is afraid of Chirin, and he remains an outcast, forced now to wander without any companionship at all. Chirin is "never seen again," though it is said that sometimes the sheep hear the distant tinkle of the bell around his neck.

A mind-bogglingly disturbing "children's film" that makes *Bambi* look like a comedy, **ANPANMAN**-creator Takashi Yanase's children's book is an unexpectedly nasty outing for the **HELLO KITTY** studio Sanrio, featuring sing-along lyrics such as "We will travel, wolf and ram, and we'll ravage all the land." **V**

RINTARO
1941– . Pseudonym for Masayuki Hayashi, often miscredited outside Japan as Taro Rin. Born in Tokyo, Rintaro graduated from Takada Middle School and began working in 1958 for Toei Animation. Subsequently, he has managed to turn up on the credits listings for most of the landmark

anime of the latter half of the twentieth century, beginning with **Panda and the Magic Serpent** (1958). He moved to Mushi Production in 1963 in time to work on both **Astro Boy** and **Kimba the White Lion**. After going freelance in the late 1960s, he worked on **Captain Harlock**, before gaining his feature direction debut with one of the **Galaxy Express 999** spin-offs in 1979. He was one of three directors of note deemed worthy of inclusion in the **Neo Tokyo** anthology (1987), and subsequent work has included further feature films and video work, such as **Dagger of Kamui**, **Final Fantasy**, **Doomed Megalopolis**, and **Metropolis**.

RISE AND FALL OF THE DINOSAUR KINGDOM, THE

1976. JPN: *Kyoryu Okoku no Kobo*. TV series. DIR: Eiichi Yamamoto. SCR: Eiichi Yamamoto. DES: Shigeo Itahashi. ANI: N/C. MUS: Hiroki Takaragi. PRD: Eizo Kiroku, Yomiuri TV, Nippon TV. 25 mins. x 6 eps.

After the first life-forms evolve on Earth, the world explodes into giant, terrifying action as the dinosaurs arrive. They are the strongest, largest creatures ever to walk on land; their achievements are chronicled in this brief documentary series that mixes diagrams, live-action photography (*not* of dinosaurs), and disappointingly cartoony dinosaur animation closer to *Barney* than *Jurassic Park*.

RISKY SAFETY *

1999. JPN: *Omishi Maho Gekijo: Risky/Sefty*. AKA: *Omishi Magical Theater Risky Safety*. TV series. DIR: Koji Masunari. SCR: Yosuke Kuroda. DES: Takuya Saito. ANI: Kazushi Nomura, Kenichi Hirano. MUS: Tamiya Terashima. PRD: APPP, Victor Entertainment, WOWOW. 8 mins. x 24 eps.

Tomboy apprentice Risky is trying to graduate as a fully-fledged agent of Death. She fixes on schoolgirl Moe Katsuragi as the victim who will prove she can handle the job. Unfortunately for her, she has been accidentally conjoined with apprentice angel Safety,

a perky type who's always doing good and cheering things up. Whenever somebody says something nice, the good side of the duo takes over and Risky turns into Safety. Death-gods can only take someone's life when the person is feeling sad, and while Safety keeps Moe cheerful, Risky has no chance of succeeding. Ray Omishi's manga combines the shifting changes of **Ranma ½** and the "angel/demon on my shoulder" concept and wraps them in spun sugar, with the dark side as cute and lovable as the agent of light and Moe treating both like pets or toys, using them as confidantes and friends through mini-adventures based on Japanese folklore, festivals, and everyday life—compare to **Bottle Fairy**. Shown as part of the *Anime Complex* slot on WOWOW with other short form shows including **Neoranga** and **Rizelmine**.

RIZELMINE

2002. TV series. DIR: Yasuhiro Muramatsu, Hiroyuki Okuno. SCR: Naruhisa Arakawa. DES: Miwa Oshima. ANI: N/C. MUS: Toshihiko Sahashi. PRD: IMAGIN, m.o.e, Madhouse, WOWOW, Kid's Station. 15 mins. x 24 eps.

Fifteen-year-old Tomonori Iwaki comes home from school one day to find that the Japanese Government has married him to an insufferably perky twelve-year-old girl. Rizel is the result of a government experiment in artificial humans, a prototype with the unfortunate design flaw of unleashing incredible destructive power by crying explosive tears when she feels sadness at being unloved. Merely adopting such replicants into a loving family with suitable role models doesn't seem to be an option, so they decide to make her happy by marrying her to a boy who doesn't want her—compare to **Final Approach**. The result is the search for love common to all *Pinocchio* clones from **Astro Boy** onward, combined with the pathological neediness of **Key the Metal Idol** and the many, many "romantic" anime aimed at teenage couch potato boys who think if they sit in their room long enough,

FedEx will *deliver* them a girlfriend, and one who actively seems to enjoy being treated like a doormat. Based on a manga by **DNAngel** creator Yukiru Sugisaki and part of the *Anime Complex Night* slot on WOWOW and Kid's Station, with 12 episodes shown between April and June and 12 between October and December, alongside **Hanaukyo Maid Team** and the live-action *Steel Angel Kurumi Pure* (*DE). In the latter part of the run, Rizel gained the ability to transform into a well-endowed, older version of herself, in the style of **Marvelous Melmo**, thereby completing the box-ticking references to old magical-girl shows. **N**

ROAD TO MUNICH

1972. JPN: *München e no Michi*. TV series, TV special. DIR: Masaaki Osumi. SCR: Soji Yoshikawa, Seiji Matsuoka. DES: Takeshi Osaka. ANI: Norio Yazawa. MUS: Takeo Watanabe. PRD: Nihon TV Doga, TBS. 25 mins. x 15 eps. (TV), 25 mins. (sp).

After winning a bronze medal in the 1964 Tokyo Olympics and silver in Mexico in 1968, it seems like the Japanese men's volleyball team is in with a chance for gold. A harsh training regime begins in 1972 as the world prepares for the Munich Olympics, with the Japanese team under the firm management of Yasutaka Matsudaira.

Each episode introduces one of the players from the real-life team, often using real-world backgrounds, but using anime to depict the players themselves, since filming them for real would have been in contravention of Olympic rules on amateurs and sponsorship. Although the series ended before the final result, as with **Yawara** life imitated art, and the men's team won. A bonus "16th" episode, *Gold Medal of Tears* (*Namida no Kin Medal*), was made after the victory and broadcast in September 1972, in the timeslot that had been taken by *RtM*'s successor, **Mon Cherie Coco**. Considering the tragic implications of the title, it seems possible that the subject included not only the Japanese team's victory, but also some treatment of the effect on the competition of the infamous Munich Massacre, in which Palestinian terrorists kidnapped Israeli athletes and eventually gunned down their surviving hostages during an airport shootout with German police.

ROBIN HOOD

1990. JPN: *Robin Hood no Daiboken.* AKA: *Great Adventures of Robin Hood; Robin Hood Junior.* TV series. DIR: Koichi Mashimo. SCR: Tsunehisa Ito, Katsuhiko Chiba, Hiroyuki Kawasaki. DES: Masamitsu Kudo, Tomohiro Hirata, Torao Arai. ANI: Masamitsu Kudo, Chuichi Iguchi. MUS: Fuminori Iwasaki. PRD: NEP, NHK, Tatsunoko. 25 mins. x 52 eps. (TV), 75 mins. (m).

In 12th-century England, the evil Baron Alwine and Abbot Hereford are in league with the devil in their quest for power. Alwine burns the entire Huntingdon family in their castle; only 14-year-old Robin and his three cousins Will, Winifred, and Barbara escape into the forest where they meet Friar Tuck, an old friend of Robin's father. He guides and protects the young orphans as best he can, and when they meet Little John and his band of teenage outlaws, they determine to fight for justice. The beautiful Marian Lancaster, daughter of a noble family, is kidnapped by the abbot, supposedly for marriage but really because he needs the crucifix she wears around her neck to unlock the magical secrets of Sherwood. Robin, Will, and Little John rescue Marian; then the refugees stay in the forest and fight the baron's agents, chiefly Gilbert, the Knight of the Black Rose, who is Robin's rival for Marian's love. A character of contradictions, Gilbert is a good man bound to serve Alwine because the baron saved his sister's life.

Originally broadcast in a 39-episode run, extra episodes were made for the overseas market, particularly Italy and Germany, where the series was a great success. Though written by Tatsunoko producer Ippei Kuri, *RH* claimed to rely on the legend as retold by *Ivanhoe*

creator Walter Scott. It was the first of Tatsunoko's 1990s "fairy tale" series and was soon followed by the same studio's SNOW WHITE. Part of the story was also released as a feature-length movie edit.

ROBIN JUNIOR

1989. JPN: *Seisenshi Robin Jr.* AKA: *Holy Warrior Robin Jr.* TV series. DIR: Masaharu Okuwaki. SCR: Hideki Sonoda, Satoru Nishizono. DES: Minoru Maeda, Satoshi Hirayama. ANI: Kazuyoshi Takeuchi. MUS: Hiroyuki Nanba. PRD: Tokyo Movie Shinsha, TV Tokyo. 25 mins. x 24 eps.

A set of superheroes modeled, as in the case of BIKKURIMAN, on the characters found on packets of candy. Their mission is to fight the attractively labeled Dark Power, a race of aliens intent on conquering the solar system.

ROBOT CARNIVAL *

1987. Video. DIR: Katsuhiro Otomo, Atsuko Fukushima, Hiroyuki Kitazume, Mao Lamdo, Hideyuki Omori, Koji Morimoto, Yasuomi Umezu, Hiroyuki Kitakubo, Takashi Nakamura. SCR: Katsuhiro Otomo, Atsuko Fukushima, Hiroyuki Kitazume, Mao Lamdo, Hideyuki Omori, Koji Morimoto, Yasuomi Umezu, Hiroyuki Kitakubo, Takashi Nakamura. DES: Katsuhiro Otomo, Atsuko Fukushima, Hiroyuki Kitazume, Mao Lamdo, Hideyuki Omori, Koji Morimoto, Yasuomi Umezu, Hiroyuki Kitakubo, Takashi Nakamura. ANI: Katsuhiro Otomo, Atsuko Fukushima, Hiroyuki Kitazume, Mao Lamdo, Hideyuki Omori, Koji Morimoto, Yasuomi Umezu, Hiroyuki Kitakubo, Takashi Nakamura. MUS: Joe Hisaishi, Isaku Fujita, Masahisa Takeshi. PRD: APPP. 90 mins.

This anthology of robot stories is a sampler for some of the big names of anime and an excellent example of how one theme can be approached in a variety of different ways both in terms of script and design. It's also one of the easiest anime to show to foreign audiences because it has very little dialogue and lots of visual variety. The opening

and closing sequences by Otomo and Fukushima take a wry look at what can happen when a seductive new diversion hits a tiny, poor community. A gigantic mechanical carnival rolls into town, a tinsel juggernaut crushing everything in its tracks, all bells and whistles and '30s-style dancing puppets, providing an opportunity for pure whiz-bang pyrotechnics on the part of the animators. The machine itself forms the title lettering, a neat conceit. At the end of the movie, this shimmering shrine to trash self-destructs taking the open-mouthed peasants with it. Kitazume's *Starlight Angel* is a boy-meets-girl-meets-giant-robot love story set in an amusement park and steeped in the style and atmosphere of the early 1980s; all the characters could have stepped straight out of the GUNDAM universe. Mao's *Cloud* is a more abstract piece whose narrative is buried in a series of beautiful, slow-moving images and hypnotic music, as a childlike robot walks slowly through a gathering storm into sunlight. Its purposely retro design and simple monotone pencil-sketch style look surprisingly contemporary in the 21st century. *Deprive* by Omori is another boy-girl-robot romance though with more of a heavy-metal edge. A young girl is torn from the arms of a handsome young man and kidnapped by an evil entity in KISS-type makeup. To rescue her, he must become his true self—a robot. Morimoto's *Franken's Gears* is a funny, quirky look at the limitations of science, in which an inventor overlooks the importance of tidiness and attention to detail and wrecks his own experiment. Kitakubo's *Tale of Two Robots* is a slapstick take on nationalism; a Japanese robot made of wood and operated by a band of kids must fight off the evil intentions of a mad white scientist and his brick-built alien war machine. *Nightmare* by Nakamura will make you very, very worried about being stranded in town after a drinking binge, as the detritus of urban life takes on ominous new shapes, and a drunk who misses his last train home is forced to watch their rampage and flee their strange leader. Umezu's *Presence* is the crown of a superb collection, a gem of a love story wrapped in a fable about the obsolescence of both people and technology and the responsibilities of the creator to his creation, enhanced by a seductive score whose main theme is unforgettable. The dialogue for this segment was dubbed into laughable "British" by Americans, which is unfortunate, but that's the only flaw in a superbly watchable film that is aging very gracefully, especially in comparison with some of the overhyped new material. Compare to the same year's NEO TOKYO and the later "showcase" anime MEMORIES.

ROBOT KING DAIOJA

1981. JPN: *Saikyu Robo Daioja*. AKA: *Strongest Robot Daioja*. TV series. DIR: Katsuyoshi Sasaki. SCR: Hiroyuki Hoshiyama, Yoshihisa Araki, Tsunehisa Ito, Akifumi Yoshida, Kosuke Yoshida, Sukehiro Tomita. DES: Nobuyoshi Sasaemon, Kunio Okawara, Yutaka Izubuchi. ANI: Akehiro Kaneyama. MUS: Michiaki Watanabe. PRD: Sunrise, TV Asahi. 25 mins. x 50 eps.

In the Edon protectorate of some 50 planets, the heir to the throne must make a grand tour of his realm at age 16, the better to serve his subjects. Traveling with Prince Edward Mito are Baron Kaikusu, Duke Skead, and female ninja Flora Shinobu. In their travels they run across many foul plots (the deadliest of which comes in the latter episodes, aimed at the heart of the monarchy itself!) that they unravel in the name of Mito's father, King Tokugar. At these times, Mito's, Kaikusu's, and Skead's small robots combine into one larger unit with the symbol of Edon on its chest—Robot King Daioja.

With a federation name that's a pun on Edo and a ruler's that's a pun on Tokugawa, *RKD* was inspired in part by the long-running samurai show *Mito Komon* (see MANGA MITO KOMON). *RKD* used many of the staff from UNCHAL-LENGEABLE TRIDER G7, but this show represents the end of the early Sunrise "combining robot" era that began with

Robotech

ZAMBOT 3. Sunrise wouldn't produce anything comparable until *Exkaiser* launched the BRAVE SAGA in 1990.

ROBOTAN *

1966. TV series. DIR: Hiroshi Ono. SCR: Tsuyoshi Danjo, Takuya Yamaguchi, Kasei Matsubara, Renso Agishita, Takashi Taka. DES: Moriyasu Taniguchi, et al. ANI: Moriyasu Taniguchi. MUS: Robotan Group. PRD: Ohiro, Fuji TV. 25 mins. x 104 eps., 25 mins. x 33 eps. Based on a manga by Kenji Morita, the series revolves around alien household robot Robotan, who comes from planet Roborobo and lives with an everyday Japanese family as a domestic servant and friend to the children. Like DORAE-MON, his good intentions don't always work out, with comic consequences. The original series was made in Osaka by the short-lived Ohiro Planning. Production moved to Tokyo Movie Shinsha for the 20th-anniversary color remake *New Robotan* (1986) under director Masaharu Okuwaki.

ROBOTECH *

1985. TV series, video. DIR: Robert Barron, Jim Wager. SCR: Gregory Sne-goff, Robert Barron, Greg Finlay, Steve

Kramer, Mike Reynolds, Steve Flood, Ardwight Chamberlain. DES: (see original shows). ANI: (see original shows). MUS: Ulpio Minucci. PRD: Tatsunoko Productions, Harmony Gold. 25 mins. x 85 eps. (TV), 80 mins., 90 mins., 90 mins. (m3), 90 mins. (m3).

In 1999, a giant alien battlecruiser crashes on Earth. The human race decides to stop fighting each other and unite in case the aliens ever come looking for their missing ship. Ten years on, the ship has been renamed the SDF-1 and reconstructed, but the global celebrations are interrupted by an alien attack. Earth's forces under Captain Gloval fight off the threat. As the SDF-1 attempts to save Earth, it uses its untested Spacefold drive and is transported deep into space, where it must fight a prolonged war with the invading Zentraedi fleet. Young pilot Rick Hunter finds himself in a complex triangular relationship with two very different women, ship's officer Lisa Hayes and singing star Lynn Minmay. After 36 episodes, known as the MACROSS SAGA, encounters with giant aliens, and big emotional tangles, the soap-in-space ended with the devastation of Earth and the deaths of several important characters. Fifteen years on, the story takes a new turn with the *Robotech Masters* saga. Rick Hunter has set off in SDF-3 to find the world of the Robotech Masters, but the Masters themselves are already heading the other way. Young cadet Dana Sterling, offspring of the first interspecies marriage, is thrown into the thick of the fighting when the Robotech Masters attack Earth in search of their lost "protoculture factory." She and her young comrades encounter a strange man who has spent years with the invaders and whose motives are unclear, but who finally destroys his own culture to save them. In the interval between this Second Robotech War and the third season, New Generation, the Invid aliens arrive and conquer Earth. Terran defenders are too exhausted to resist, but a generation later, Scott Bernard and his reinforcements arrive to try and liberate their homeworld. Their task seems hopeless, but if they can somehow contact Admiral Rick Hunter and link up with his space fleet, Earth may have a chance.

The *Robotech* phenomenon is a curious hybrid of Japanese material and American ambition. Originally conceived as a U.S. video release, it was handed to Carl Macek to dub, and the first *Macross* tape, starring Japanese-American hero "Rick Yamada," was premiered at the 1984 World SF Convention. However, Harmony Gold made further deals to bring the show to TV and asked Macek to find a way of expanding it beyond 36 episodes, which is too small for TV syndication. He acquired SOUTHERN CROSS and MOSPEADA from the same studio, providing another 49 half-hour episodes of *similar* design and background. Macek renamed many of the characters, creating cross-generational links that were absent in the completely unlinked original series, and devised the concept of an ancient alien technology that could generate robots and weapons for space combat, rooted in a mysterious concept called "protoculture." The

model-kit company Revell, owners of the *Macross* merchandise rights, already had a trademark line called *Robotech*, and a tie-in was born. The *Robotech* line, having been established before the series was conceived, included robots from shows not involved in Macek's rewrite, like DOUGRAM and ORGUSS, and did not include anything from *Southern Cross* or *Mospeada*.

The success of the concept led to the construction of *Robotech the Movie*, a dub for the U.S. market of the first part of MEGAZONE 23. Since this had absolutely nothing to do with the characters or story lines of any of the three original series, it was presented as a "side story" happening within the chronology of the Robotech Wars. Extra footage was animated for the film in Japan and included as a bonus on the Japanese *Megazone 23* release.

The story was to have continued in a fourth segment focusing on the forgotten SDF-3. Though all 65 episodes were written for a Japanese-American coproduction, the project was never completed. The footage already shot (four partly completed episodes plus other material) was used to make up a single feature-length video, *Robotech II—The Sentinels*, the last animated installment of the saga.

Robotech gained such a hold on its American fans that it spun off into print with greater success. A series of novels by Jack McKinney (a pseudonym for James Luceno and Brian Daley) fills in many narrative gaps and explores many of the minor characters in greater depth, while *Robotech* comics have been produced by four different publishers over 14 years. Many of the comics and novels are based on the completed scripts for *Sentinels*, even though most were never filmed. The "close" of the *Robotech* saga is the final novel, *End of the Circle*. Similar recycling went on in Japan, where Tatsunoko placed some of the unused designs in the unrelated ZILLION.

Robotech attracts passionate response; fans either love or loathe it. Like NAUSICAÄ's U.S. reedit, it is variously viewed

as a welcome adaptation of unfamiliar material for a new, less adventurous audience, or a watered-down travesty of its origins. Its supporters cite a complex story line with material rarely seen in U.S. animation—the unexpected deaths of much-loved characters, the fact that the good guys (humans) usually ended up losing, or even the introduction of a cross-dressing hero. Its detractors point out that all this was present in the original Japanese series and that the destruction of the internal logic and character relationships was unnecessary and excessive. The best way to describe it is probably not as anime but as an American reworking of the Japanese original, but, unlike most palimpsests, enough of the original text remains to entice viewers back to the source material.

Robotech: Shadow Chronicles (2005) is a 90-minute video sequel to the series, but is not technically anime as it was made by a predominantly American and Korean staff. It features the search for the missing Admiral Hunter and the introduction of a new adversary.

R.O.D. *

2000. JPN: *R.O.D.* AKA: *Read or Die*. Video. DIR: Koji Masunari. SCR: Hideyuki Kurata. DES: Takaru Hane, Shinji Ishihama, Kuniyuki Jinguji. ANI: Shinji Ishihama. MUS: N/C. PRD: Studio Deen, Studio Orfee, SPE Visual Works. 30 mins. x 3 eps. (v), 25 mins. x 26 eps. (TV). Bespectacled Yomiko Readman is a teacher whose passion is collecting books. She's also a secret agent for the Royal British Library's Division of Special Operations, a crack squad of bookhunters whose mission is to save literature for posterity. The two sides cross over when she has a run-in with a giant cricket and a strange old man out to steal a book she's just acquired. It's very rare, and the division assigns her a partner to work on finding volume two before the alien bugs get her. We never expected to see the British Library in anime; there's no topic or setting too arcane for the Japanese fantasy romance. Based on a manga in *Ultra*

Jump magazine by Hideyuki Kurata and Shutaro Yamada.

The later TV series drops the original cast in favor of sisters Michelle, Maggie, and Anita, who become rescuers and then bodyguards to author Nenene Sumiregawa—one of Yomiko's favorite authors, and a character in the first episode of the video series. Two years later, the author is trying to find Yomiko, but her path and that of the sisters keep crossing with other British Library agents from the Special Engineering Force and with their sinister assassins. A rogue agent is plotting to conquer first Japan, and then the world.

Recalling CAT'S EYE with its trio of sisters going undercover to steal artworks linked to their father's disappearance, the series uses the trio format to provide a range of types and ages, maximizing the chance of viewers finding a character to identify with. As in GRRL POWER and KOKORO LIBRARY, the producers try to cover all bases with the sisters—one quiet and standoffish, one extrovert and gossipy, one headstrong; one loving Hemingway, one into Harry Potter, and one not keen on books at all; teens, twenties, and prepubescent; brown, blonde, and pink hair.

ROKUDENASHI BLUES

1992. JPN: *Rokudenashi Blues*. Movie. DIR: Takao Yoshisawa. SCR: Yoshiyuki Suga. DES: Masanori Morita. ANI: Yoshitaka Yashima. MUS: Fuminori Iwasaki. PRD: Toei. 25 mins.
A short "movie" based on Masanori Morita's 1988 manga in *Shonen Jump* magazine, in which Taison Maeda determines to be the toughest kid in his school, ruling over his fellow students with the power of his fists. Another distant homage to the U.S. boxer Mike Tyson was carefully buried in STREET FIGHTER II.

ROLLING RYOTA

1990. Video. DIR: Masamune Ochiai. SCR: Yuki Kuroiwa. DES: Shinichi Nagasawa. ANI: Natsuki Aikawa, Shinichi

Romance and Drama

© 2006 STEVE KYTE

Nagasawa. MUS: N/C. PRD: Knack. 45 mins. x 3 eps.
Former biker Takao Ryota becomes a bus driver, causing havoc in the streets by racing his bus against other vehicles. This anime was based on a manga by Hiroyuki Murata, who also created VOLLEY BOYS. Ryota, who sports a distinctive gangster punch-perm hairstyle, was originally voiced by Jutaro Kosugi, but he was replaced by Hiroya Ishimaru, the voice of Koji Kabuto in MAZINGER Z. ⓝⓥ

ROMANCE AND DRAMA

The nature of anime production favors spectacle—anime's mode of production often makes it better suited to special effects, science fiction, and fantasy. Human interest drama or romance can usually be made cheaply with live-action materials, and consequently appears in anime only rarely—HUMAN CROSSING is one of its best examples, although drama can also feature in crime shows such as DOMAIN OF MURDER and in psychological horror like PERFECT BLUE.

Regarded primarily as a children's medium, anime concentrated on comedic stories for its first decade. Its

first demonstrably dramatic work was Noburo Ofuji's *Whale* (*Kujira*, 1927), in which a beautiful woman survives a shipwreck along with three male passengers who immediately begin fighting over her. They are distracted by the arrival of a whale, their hunting of which encourages its vengeful return, in a story that ends with the woman the sole survivor, riding on the whale's back. Early anime romances dealt with comedy and tragedy in equal parts, from the faithless husband's antics in THE WORLD OF POWER AND WOMEN (1932) to the heartbreak of MADAME BUTTERFLY (1940).

Some WARTIME ANIME remained humorous, although others put joking aside in order to warn audiences of the dangers lurking unseen, as in Sanae Yamamoto's *Defeat of the Spies* (*Spy Gekimetsu*, 1942). The postwar period brought increased access to Disney films such as *Bambi* (1942), encouraging Japanese animators to consider tragic scenes alongside the comedy of traditional children's entertainment. This maturing attitude to storytelling helped lift anime out of the single funny vignettes of cartoon shorts and into feature-length storytelling as found in THE LITTLEST WARRIOR (1961). However, the desire to appeal to a children's market continued to limit romantic plots or the seriousness of certain topics—WOOF WOOF 47 RONIN (1963) adapted a famous tragedy from the kabuki stage, tempered by the use of a cast of talking cartoon dogs which detracted from its dramatic weight.

As the cinema market slumped in the 1960s with the onslaught of television, Osamu Tezuka attempted to find a new niche with his erotic romances ARABIAN NIGHTS (1969) and CLEOPATRA: QUEEN OF SEX (1970). Anime, however, has never shied away from drama and tragedy, even in works intended for children, such as the harrowing RINGING BELL (1978) and KIMBA THE WHITE LION (1965).

The growth in the 1970s of the female manga market led to the adaptation of many more romance stories for animation. CANDY CANDY (1976) established many durable conventions of the girl's anime, including the orphan heroine victimized and persecuted like CINDERELLA, enjoying the attentions of a secret benefactor or admirer such as that found in DADDY LONG-LEGS, and enduring a series of torments while waiting for her Prince Charming, often in the company of a small furry animal. Such dramatic traditions even influenced the plots of anime supposedly based on historical fact, such as the breathless excitement of YOUNG PRINCESS DIANA (1986).

Homosexual longing and romance did not solely rely on the arrival of video, first appearing in the TV series PATALIRO (1982). However, video made it far easier for anime with more mature themes to go into production, such as the gay subtexts of SONG OF WIND AND TREES (1987). As the niche market expanded for amateur and professional comics featuring love between handsome young men, gay characters in anime gained wider acceptance. Science fiction and fantasy settings were also popular, as TIES OF LOVE and TOKYO BABYLON showed in 1992, but anime also made use of "real life" backdrops

to tales of gay sexuality and its social consequences, like the family in OH FAMILY, football and music in ZETSUAI, and organized crime in KIZUNA. Girl-on-girl crushes are usually portrayed as innocent adoration, but sometimes with a lesbian subtext, as in UTENA.

The same period, however, also saw maturation of themes on TV, with extended romantic dramas such as TOUCH (1985) and MAISON IKKOKU (1986). Following the success of the alien spouse of URUSEI YATSURA (1981), romance in the 1990s often took on the characteristics of a dating simulation computer game, in which a male protagonist was obliged to work out which of several contenders would be the most appropriate choice for a happy ending. This has led to the "harem" tradition typified by TENCHI MUYO!, in which a single boy is surrounded by a cast of adoring females. The extremes to which this has been carried are exemplified by NEGIMA and HANAUKYO MAID TEAM, where the (underage) male protagonist is surrounded by literally dozens of women from whom to choose. Slacker mentality comes to the fore, with pretty girls that materialize by accident in lonely geeks' closets, or memory loss subplots that offer hope from forgotten childhood contacts. The archetypal lead for the harem show is often a solitary shut-in with borderline Asperger's Syndrome, alienated from friends and family and so inept and passive that his only hope of romance is either a past association occluded by amnesia (he was once loved, but has forgotten, as in LOVE HINA), or a future event about which he is told by time travelers, such as that in DNA² or KIRARA. There is no *now* for the harem show's point of identification; *now* is a miserable, dull, pointless time, although there may have been a dreamtime *then* when he was popular with girls, and might one day be a dreamtime *soon*, when he will be again. The tropes of the harem show have also been inverted for girls, as with the male love-interests of BOYS OVER FLOWERS or PARADISE KISS. Many love objects

also appear to be childhood friends, which is both a way of introducing ready-made love objects and a form of nostalgia—modern urban Japanese yearning for the simpler associations of their rural pasts, when people genuinely could go to the same school as their parents, and everyone in a town would know each other from childhood, a concept known as *osana-najimi*.

The proliferation of quasi-incestuous titles (e.g., SISTER PRINCESS or ONEGAI TEACHER's sequel *Onegai Twins*) may be another symptom of modern life—perhaps related to the shortage of real-world siblings noted in BUBU CHACHA. Living in close proximity to a sibling, humans in the real world are subject to the Westermarck Effect, a deadening of any mating impulses—in effect, the onset of a lack of sexual interest. Traditional China and Japan, however, both have many cases of "adopted" daughters, brought into a family as potential marriage candidates for the family's son, making the idea of romantic attraction to a stepsister less odd than it may at first appear in shows such as MARMALADE BOY (1995). However, it is worth noting that, to the modern, sedentary, couch potato teenager, the appeal of a love interest in one's own household may simply be that it does not involve having to walk so far.

ROMANCE IS IN THE FLASH OF THE SWORD II *

2001. JPN: *Romance wa Tsurugi no Kagayaki II*. Video. DIR: Yosei Morino. SCR: Yosei Morino. DES: Jun Sato, Takeshi Nakamura. ANI: Tomohiro Shibayama. MUS: N/C. PRD: Lemon Heart, Triple X. 30 mins. x 6 eps. Keith (exotic name) is an adventurer and "honorable thief"—but don't expect LUPIN III. In a generic fantasy world, a series of repetitive scenarios with disposable characters have Keith rescuing and/or satisfying various women who either have plans for his body or have been molested by assorted unpleasant beings human and otherwise, usually with spectators—or both. Keith's "bodily fluids" are smeared on a stone to release a powerful demon, whom he then defeats; a demonic monster molests priestesses for their sexual elixirs, but Keith sorts that out too; an evil duke hunts down and molests girls and men and plots against the crown until Keith arrives. He has sex in temples, in dungeons, on a swing, at a unicorn race, with a masseuse possessed by a ghost who's really a she-demon, and in a variety of other circumstances, while saving the world from various agents of darkness. Based on the 1999 erotic game, which was itself a sequel, hence the numerals "II" in the title—as with **STREET FIGHTER II**. ⓛⓝⓥ

ROMEO'S BLUE SKY

1995. JPN: *Romeo no Aoi Sora*. AKA: *Romeo and the Black Brothers*. TV series. DIR: Kozo Kusuba, Shinpei Miyashita, Yasuo Iwamoto, Tomomitsu Matsukawa. SCR: Michiru Shimada. DES: Yoshiharu Sato. ANI: Yoshiharu Sato, Ei Inoue, Katsu Oshiro, Masaki Abe. MUS: Kei Wakakusa. PRD: Nippon Animation, Fuji TV. 25 mins. x 33 eps.

Romeo lives happily with his family in the Swiss Alps until a series of crop failures and his father's illness bring about tragic changes. To save his loved ones from ruin, he sells himself into slavery for 25 francs to Luini, called "God of Death," who travels poor country districts searching for child laborers to fuel the growing cities of Europe. He is taken to Milan and sold to a chimney sweep, and so becomes one of the "Black Brothers," the boys who keep the city's chimneys clear in great hardship. On the way he meets Alfredo, a boy with a mysterious past whose main aim in life is to find his beloved little sister, Bianca, and the two boys become close friends. In Milan he meets the fragile Angeletta, but her brother Anselmo is part of a local gang, the Wolf Pack, and despite Romeo's overtures of friendship, Anselmo begins a gang war. The Wolf Pack are not the only ones out for blood, as Alfredo is threatened by those who know his secret and will stop at nothing to prevent him claiming his rightful inheritance.

The story was based on the 1941 novel *The Black Brothers* (*Die Schwarzen Brüder*) by Lisa Tetzner, a German forced to flee the Nazi regime to Switzerland because of her husband's Marxist leanings. She wrote her book to highlight the real-life scandal of child slavery in Europe—compare to **24 EYES**, a similar protest. The anime adapted the story freely, though it retained the basic elements of the typical **WORLD MASTERPIECE THEATER** production—a classic tale of emotion and melodrama, set at a safe distance in time and space, with vulnerable but heroic young people enduring testing times in the struggle for survival. The lead character's name was changed from Giorgio, new characters were added, and the plot and conclusion altered, partly to fit a schedule originally planned for 39 episodes but finally forced to squeeze the story into 33.

RONIN WARRIORS *

1989. JPN: *Yoiroden Samurai Troopers*. AKA: *Armor Legend Samurai Troopers; Samurai Troopers*. TV series, video. DIR: Makoto Ikeda, Mamoru Hamazu. SCR: Junzo Toriumi, Yuki Onishi. DES: Norio Shioyama, Hideo Okamoto, Yusho Okada. ANI: Norio Shioyama, Kisaraka Yamada. MUS: Osamu Tezuka. PRD: Sunrise, Nagoya TV. 25 mins. x 39 eps. (TV), 30 mins. x 3 eps. (v1), 30 mins. x 4 eps. (v2), 30 mins. x 5 eps. (v3).

SAINT SEIYA—style action, as the evil Lord Arago (Talpa in the U.S.) sends denizens of the Phantom World to invade Earth, and five teenage prettyboys are given mystic suits of samurai armor that will enhance their own natural gifts, enabling them to fight back. Wildfire Ryo, Torrent Shin (Cye), Halo Seiji (Sage), Strata Toma (Rowen), and Hardrock Shu (Kento) can unite their suits to form Hariel's White Armor of Fervor. But Arago has already infiltrated the whole world. The boys' suits, plus all those worn by Arago's champions, are parts of a single incredibly powerful battle armor, broken up when Arago was defeated eons

© 1995 NIPPON ANIMATION CO., LTD.

Romeo's Blue Sky

ago; now he wants to reunite them and make sure his conquest can't be overturned. The team members must overcome their own fears and weaknesses and face terrible dangers—their friends, too, are liable to be used by Arago as bait or bribes.

Looking suspiciously like an entire unbroadcast season cut into sections, the adventures continued on video with Mamoru Hamazu's *ST: Extra Story* (1989), in which our heroes go to the U.S. to investigate a mysterious news report that may point to new activity from Arago. One of them is captured and tortured by a demon who has teamed up with a human scientist to find the secrets of the Troopers' armor and use them to take over all five suits. A second series, *ST: Empire Legend* (1989), contains another tale of courage against supernatural evil, this time in Africa. In a kabuki-themed story arc redolent of **GASARAKI**, the final adventure of Makoto Ikeda's *ST: Message* (1991) has the boys returning to Japan to investigate mysterious forces at work in Shinjuku. While other members of the team face off against their female adversary Suzunagi, Seiji discovers evidence of an Edo-period play about "five boy warriors."

The series was screened as *Ronin Warriors* (1995) on American TV, with a title change occasioned by two other similarly named shows on the air at the time. Its Japanese origins remain clear, with onscreen Japanese text left in place and the lead character's name unchanged. It's very violent by U.S. standards even though there are few flesh-and-blood casualties, and the overall atmosphere of cruelty and menace is very powerful. **V**

ROOMMATE, THE

2005. JPN: *Ki ni Naru Roommate*. AKA: *Horny Roommate*. Video. DIR: P Nakamura. SCR: P Nakamura. DES: Takafumi Hino. ANI: Takafumi Hino. MUS: N/C. PRD: Milky, Studio Ten, Image Works, GP Museum Pictures. 30 mins.
Failing his university entrance exam and dumped by his girlfriend, Yu rents a room and prepares for another try. But when he arrives at his new residence, he discovers that it is situated above a strip club, and performer Rei Asagiri is already living there. Before long, Yu is unable to cope with the distractions and decides to stop studying books and start studying girls. Based on the manga by Kaoru Yunagi, serialized in *Young Comic* monthly. **N**

ROOTS SEARCH *

1986. JPN: *Roots Search: Shokushin Buttai X*. AKA: *Roots Search: Life Devourer X*. Video. DIR: Hisashi Sugai. SCR: Michiru Shimada. DES: Sanae Kobayashi, Yasushi Moriki. ANI: Hiroshi Negishi. MUS: N/C. PRD: Production Wave. 44 mins.
The Tolmeckius Research Institute is impressed with its latest find, a psychic girl called Moira, who astounds them all when she starts experiencing terrible visions. When the orbital station is approached by a runaway ship, Moira's insight reveals that all is not as it seems. The ship has been occupied by a fearsome alien intelligence that mentally tortures its victims until they beg for the release of death. When the creature proves to be invincible, Moira resolves to make the ultimate sacrifice, although even death, it seems, cannot end the suffering.

There are shades of the more recent hit EVANGELION in this SF tale that mixes Biblical elements with an *Alien* pastiche and a far more sinister interpretation of "God's" purpose. But that is where the resemblance ends for this creaky anime, unreleased in English until 1992, a time on the shelf that did not find it aging gracefully. **L**

ROSE OF VERSAILLES

1979. JPN: *Versailles no Bara*. AKA: *Lady Oscar*. TV series. DIR: Tadao Nagahama, Osamu Dezaki, Yasuo Yamakichi, Minoru Okazaki, Tetsuo Imazawa, Akinori Nagaoka. SCR: Yoshimi Shinozaki, Masahiro Yamada, Yukio Sugie, Hajime Hazama. DES: Shingo Araki, Michi Himeno, Akio Sugino, Ken Kawai, Tadao Kubota. ANI: Shingo Araki, Michi Himeno. MUS: Koji Makaino. PRD: Tokyo Movie Shinsha, Nippon TV. 25 mins. x 40 eps.
In 18th-century France, revolution is in the air, but for Oscar François de Jarjayes, the ties of tradition are all-powerful. Sole heir of an ancient family, she is given a man's name at birth and becomes the son her father wants. She succeeds so completely that she is soon one of the best fencers in France, promoted to Captain of the Guard of Marie Antoinette, Austrian child-wife of the Crown Prince. Both Oscar and Antoinette are women alone, forced into roles they did not choose and barred from love by duty. The Crown Princess of France loves a foreign nobleman, while the Captain of the Guard loves a childhood friend who is also a servant of her family. Both loves seem doomed, but both women must continue to live artificial public lives concealing real private agonies. A tangle of fascinating subplots and well-developed supporting characters, some historical and some invented, make this one of the most powerful and credible of anime TV series. As in Riyoko Ikeda's original 1972 manga, the sublime tale of love and loss ends with Antoinette going to the scaffold and Oscar leaving her life behind to share the struggle for freedom

with her beloved André, dying in the assault on the Bastille.
Yet the two deaths are very different. Oscar's is a triumph of the human spirit, Antoinette's a failure. By stealing private happiness while supporting the feudal system that imprisons her as surely as the peasants, the proud, brave Antoinette has colluded in the lies and injustices that have made revolution inevitable. She dies because of her public role as a glittering cog in an increasingly useless machine, but in finally rejecting a system that separates people with artificial barriers of rank and property, Oscar asserts her own right to be fully human, regardless of gender or status. She dies, not because of, but rather *for* who and what she is. This cleverly subverts the familiar format of forbidden love between beautiful men (which would give birth to the *shonen ai* manga genre) by making one of the pair a woman, but one so gifted in traditionally "masculine" skills that the idea of a truly equal relationship, with no element of dependency or weakness, can still be maintained.
The renowned Araki/Himeno team transformed Ikeda's black-and-white manga art into a colorful fantasy, and while the action is played strong, the romance is played with delicacy and pathos, keeping melodrama in check. Its roots are clearly in Tezuka's magical PRINCESS KNIGHT, and its influence is still strong in the 1990s TV hit UTENA. It is so popular in France that it is still screened occasionally on French TV and was also adapted as a live-action film, *Lady Oscar* (1979), directed by Jacques Demy. A live-action musical version is the jewel in the crown of Japan's Takarazuka theater troupe. *Rose of Versailles* deserves its classic rank. Despite its age and technical deficiencies, it still delivers powerful entertainment.

ROUGE

1997. JPN: *Ladies' Comic Video Rouge*. Movie. DIR: N/C. SCR: Haruko Kanzaki, Mizuki Iwase, Kei Misugi, Chika Taniguchi. DES: Haruko Kanzaki, Mizuki Iwase,

Kei Misugi, Chika Taniguchi. ANI: N/C. MUS: N/C. PRD: Komine Communications. 40 mins. x 2 eps.
Bereaved strangers lose themselves in a sordid double life of prostitution but find love with each other. A loveless marriage blossoms through bondage. A trainee gets more than she bargained for when the head nurse takes the biology lesson to the limit. And a male beautician uses unorthodox methods to put color in a makeup artist's cheeks. Four erotically charged tales animated for a female audience, based on stories originally printed in the manga magazine *Rouge*. **Ⓝ**

ROUJIN Z *
1991. AKA: *Old Man Z*. Movie. DIR: Hiroyuki Kitakubo. SCR: Katsuhiro Otomo. DES: Hisashi Eguchi. ANI: Satoshi Kon. MUS: Bun Itakura. PRD: APPP. 80 mins.
Old Mr. Takizawa, unable to care for himself, is selected as the guinea pig for an experimental robot bed designed to administer to his every need. Despite the protests of his nurse Haruko, the project gets underway, but the patient proves to be more trouble than he's worth when he decides to take a trip to the seaside. The bed's true purpose becomes apparent; it's not for the care of the elderly at all, it's the prototype for a military model designed to revolutionize modern warfare. But with Mr. Takizawa at the controls, even the defanged civilian version manages to wreak considerable havoc, with the help of an ornery gang of geriatric hackers and despite the army's efforts to stop it. The ending, an AKIRA pastiche in which an ambulance is riddled with cybernetic tentacles, is followed by a surprise, which, on repeat viewing, you will see was planned all along.

There aren't many anime that begin with an old man wetting himself, but that's part of *Roujin Z*'s originality. AKIRA-creator Otomo took a back seat for this satire on the developed world's aging population, limiting himself to script and design duties. Ridiculing the health service as HUMMINGBIRDS lampooned the privatization of the military, *Roujin Z* is entertaining and thought-provoking, with a witty script in the English-language version from George Roubicek. Arguably a superior story, it's fated to remain in *Akira*'s shadow owing to a drastically smaller animation budget. Watch for some clever touches, such as an underground battle lit in old-fashioned sepia tones and artificial scan lines on a TV screen, showing real attention to detail. Satoshi Kon worked on the backgrounds and later put this experience of designing lived-in environments to good use as the director of PERFECT BLUE.

ROURAN
2002. JPN: *Kiko Sen'nyo Rouran*. AKA: *Mysterious Steel Fairy Rouran*. TV series. DIR: Toshihiro Hirano. SCR: Noboru Aikawa, Sho Egawa. DES: Naomi Miyata, Yutaka Izubuchi, Rei Nakahara, Masunori Osawa, Masakazu Okada, Katsuyuki Tamura. ANI: Kazuhiro Sasaki, Naomi Miyata. MUS: Yoshiro Kakimi. PRD: ZEXCS, Starchild Records, Kid's Station. 15 mins. x 28 eps.
A secret society is using monsters to invade Tokyo, and the peacekeeping force ASY opposes it with huge robots called Steel Hermits (Kosen), recruiting pilots wherever it can. Teenager Yamato Mikogami is sent out as a pilot of the Hermit Ginko when a huge monster attacks the city. After he lures the monster far out to sea and destroys it, a girl appears floating in the air, enveloped in a strange light. Named Rouran, she doesn't know who she is or where she comes from, but it seems she is fated to become the destroyer of worlds. Toshihiro Hirano is a hugely talented designer and director whose preferred scenarios involve cute girls in love with other cute teenagers (of either gender) being menaced by slime-dripping monsters or piloting heavy metal; he tends to favor gothic horror over straight tentacle porn. This show combines his great loves—cute girls, occult horror, and big robots—with the strongest emphasis on robots.

Rouran bears an uncanny resemblance to director Hirano's earlier ICZER ONE, even to the extent of battling a rival counterpart in the manner of Iczers One and Two. See also SAIKANO.

ROZEN MAIDEN
2002. TV series. DIR: Mamoru Matsuo. SCR: Jukki Hanada, Mari Okada, Tsuyoshi Tamai. DES: Kumi Ishii. ANI: Kumi Ishii. MUS: Shinkichi Mitsumune. PRD: Memory Tech, Novic, Pony Canyon, TBS. 24 mins. x 12 eps. (TV1), 24 mins. x 12 eps. (TV2).
Spoiled teenager Jun Sakurada uses an incident at school as an excuse to shut himself in his room. Ordering everything he needs through his computer (and returning most of the packages just before payment is due), with a loving and supportive big sister to take care of everything else, he is stagnating in a comfortable cocoon. Then he receives a package he doesn't expect, containing an elaborate and beautiful antique doll—compare to STEEL ANGEL KURUMI and RIZELMINE. When he winds her mechanism, she springs into life and speaks to him. Her name is Shinku, and she's one of an elite "sisterhood" of dolls who take sibling rivalry to combative extremes. She has a rose-red gown, sweet face, and long blonde hair, but she also has a very powerful personality and Jun is forced to metamorphose out of his chrysalis of comfort and meet other doll owners as Shinku's "medium"—or her slave. A second series, *RM: Traumend*, followed in 2005 from the same crew. Based on a manga by "Peach Pit," the fanzine-turned-pro collective that also created DEARS, picking up neatly on the craze for expensive customized dolls (like Volks' *Super Dollfie* line) which become as much part of their owners' lives as real people. Part of the relatively recent "Gothic Lolita" subgenre of anime, based on the fashion fad of the same name, and also found in PETITE COSSETTE and MOON PHASE.

RUBENKAISER
1977. JPN: *Gekiso! Rubenkaiser*. AKA:

Go Fast! Rubenkaiser; Rough Racer Rubenkaiser, Formula One. TV series. DIR: Yasuo Hasegawa, Takashi Anno, Masahisa Ishida. SCR: Tajio Tamura, Atsuo Murayama. DES: Kazuyoshi Hoshino. ANI: Yuji Tanabe. MUS: Shunsuke Kikuchi. PRD: Wako, Green Box, Toei Animation, TV Asahi. 25 mins. x 17 eps.

Maverick racing driver Shunsuke Hayami is fired from the Arrow team when he disobeys a direct order from the pit. Before long, he is signed up by racing boss Ginjiro Arashi to drive the Rubenkaiser, a prototype Formula One vehicle designed by the late West German master racer George Kaiser, who also turns out to be Shunsuke's long-lost father, in a twist that will come as little surprise. Following their 1976 series MACHINE HAYABUSA, Toei made this further foray onto the tracks of Formula one racing. With an almost identical setup—keen young drivers, a supportive pit and admin team, cute girl, cute kid, and fierce on-track rivalry—it did exactly the same job. However, forced to run opposite the new series of LUPIN III, *Rubenkaiser* suffered understandably low ratings and early cancellation. Manga versions were published in *Terebi Land* and *Terebi-kun* magazines.

RUIN EXPLORERS *

1995. JPN: *Hikyo Tantei Fam and Ihrlie.* AKA: *Ruin Explorers Fam and Ihrlie.* Video. DIR: Takeshi Mori. SCR: Takeshi Mori. DES: Toshihisa Umitani. ANI: Toshihisa Umitani, Yoshiaki Yanagida, Takuya Saito. MUS: Masamichi Amano. PRD: Animate Film, Asia-do. 30 mins. x 4 eps.

In a world filled with the relics of fallen civilizations, elf-catgirl Fam and her human companion Ihrlie search for a treasure known as the Ultimate Power. They meet Galuf, a traveler who claims to have a map revealing its location. Since Fam finds it hard to stay focused for more than a few seconds and Ihrie has a "horrible curse," it seems less than likely they will succeed, even if they weren't facing some

stiff competition from the greatest evil wizard who ever lived. But they have a serious motive that says more about their friendship than their constant bickering. The Ultimate Power is the only thing that can free Ihrlie from her curse and enable her to fulfill her great magical potential. When she was a young apprentice, her carelessness so annoyed her teacher that he cast a spell to prevent her from using her powers. Every time she does so, she transforms out of human shape. She's been avoiding the problem by taking magical pills that enable her to transform back again, but they're almost all used up, so she can only use her magic in dire emergencies. They usually have to rely on Fam's less powerful magic instead.

Galuf, a sleazy merchant out for the treasure himself, is terrified of the various traps and defenses around the Ultimate Power, and he wants our heroines to go in there first. He also hires a crack pair of ruin explorers, sorceress Rasha and swordsman Migel, to make sure the Ultimate Power winds up in his hands. But the Ultimate Power alone won't actually do anything; it must be combined with a magic sword and mirror. Handsome Prince Lyle also wants the Ultimate Power, but for unselfish ends—to fight Rugodorull, a wise cleric corrupted by Dark Powers. Rugodorull has killed everyone else in Lyle's homeland and now wants to destroy all life on Earth. The six finally agree to work together to defeat Rugodorull. Their quest takes them across the seas to a magic island as they try to collect the items that will enable them to summon the Ultimate Power and save the world.

This D&D-style adventure was based on characters created by Kunihiko Tanaka for *Hobby Japan* magazine; compare its more successful contemporary, the lighthearted fantasy SLAYERS. The four episodes were released on two tapes by U.S. label ADV, which subtitled the first *Tales IN the Crypt* while the second is *Ruin Explorers 2: Profits and Prophecies.*

RUN MELOS

1981. JPN: *Hashire Melos.* AKA: *Run for Life.* TV special, movie, video. DIR: Tomoharu Katsumata. SCR: Keinosuke Uekusa. DES: Toshio Mori. ANI: Toshio Mori. MUS: Katsuhiro Tsuboiri. PRD: Toei, Visual 80, Fuji TV. 87 mins. (TV), 107 mins. (m).

Melos is a simple Sicilian farmer traveling to see his sister's wedding when he is sentenced to death by Dionysius, the tyrant of Syracuse. He asks for a few days' grace to go to the wedding and promises to return immediately. The king agrees, but only if Melos can provide a hostage to guarantee his return—to be executed in his place if he fails. His old friend Selinuntius volunteers, and Melos sets off for the wedding. Despite many misadventures and temptations along the way, Melos keeps his word and returns in the nick of time. Dionysius is so impressed by Melos' honesty and Selinuntius' trust in him that he frees them both.

Osamu Dazai's 1940 short story was based on Greek legend filtered through a poem by Schiller, but it has become a classic of *Japanese* literature. The simple story, hinging on the nature of friendship and the ability to keep faith, has a happy resolution that is bitterly ironic when one remembers that Dazai committed suicide.

Toei's TV special was followed in 1992 by a longer theatrical release directed and written by Masaaki Osumi. Despite the overall simplicity of the story, he manages to infuse the film with real tension and urgency, and he has excellent art direction and design to support his work, from the future directors of PERFECT BLUE and JIN-ROH, Satoshi Kon and Hiroyuki Okiura. Melos runs through ravishing backgrounds by Hiroshi Ono, whose talents also enhance such stellar titles as KIKI'S DELIVERY SERVICE and have recently been put to use by Hollywood on *The Tigger Movie.* This movie version was former pop idol Kazumasa Oda's first anime score and also a voice-acting debut for the singer Akina Nakamori, who played Melos' sister. The story was animated twice more for video—for the *Classic Children's Tales* series (1992), as a 30-minute stop-motion short, and again for the *Famous Japanese Fables* series (1997), as a 10-minute short directed by Keisuke Morishita.

RUN=DIM

2001. TV series. DIR: Yasunori Kato. SCR: Shingo Kuwana, Yasunori Kato. DES: Yoshiaki Sato. ANI: N/C. MUS: N/C. PRD: Idea Factory, TV Tokyo. 25 mins. x 12+ eps.

In the 21st century, much of Japan lies underwater after a rise in sea levels. The nation becomes more expansionist in its outlook as it loses more *lebensraum*, and JESAS, an arm of the military, is implicated in a corruption scandal. Green Frontier, an international ecology organization, discovers that JESAS has been earning foreign currency by taking nuclear disposal contracts but then illegally dumping the waste in space. After such promising sub-**PATLABOR** beginnings, the two sides then start fighting each other with giant robots piloted by 14-year-old children. It's 3-D CG, so the look changes for a new century, if not the plot.

RUNE SOLDIER

2001. JPN: *Maho Senshi Riui.* AKA: *Magical Soldier Riui, Louie the Rune Soldier.* TV series. DIR: Yoshitaka Koyama. SCR: Katsuhiko Chiba, Nobuaki Kishima, Jiro Takayama. DES: Kazunori Iwakura. ANI: Takeshi Wada. MUS: Kenji Kawai. PRD: JC Staff, WOWOW. 25 mins. x 24 eps.

Louie is the adopted son of the headmaster of the prestigious Magician's Guild, and a beginning wizard. Unfortunately, he is also a hot-headed, muscle-bound lunk who prefers to use his fists to bash his way out of (and usually before that, into) trouble than to use magic. When a party of female adventurers—warrior Genie, thief Merrill, and priestess Melissa—discover that they need a magician to complete their planned raid on a dungeon, the only one they can find who is willing is

Rune Soldier

© RYO MIZUNO · MAMORU YOKOTA / LOUIE THE RUNE SOLDIER PRODUCTION GROUP

Louie. Merrill and Genie, having already encountered him in less-than-ideal circumstances, reject his application. However, when he interrupts Melissa in the midst of a holy ritual to find the "hero" whom she is to serve (a man she imagines to be a stainless paladin), she discovers to her horror that her god has instead chosen Louie as her hero-designate. Mayhem ensues, in a combination of the role-playing-inspired adventure of **SLAYERS** with the boy-meets-babes setup of **TENCHI MUYO!**. Created by **RECORD OF LODOSS WAR**'s Ryo Mizuno, who wrote the manga (with art by Mamoru Yokota), which was serialized in *Dragon* magazine and *Dragon Jr.*

RUNNING BOY

1986. JPN: *Running Boy Star Soldier no Himitsu.* AKA: *Running Boy: Secrets of Star Soldier.* Movie. DIR: Tameo Ogawa. SCR: Junichi Ishihara, Kasumi Oka. DES: Oji Suzuki. ANI: Oji Suzuki, Hidemi Kamata. MUS: Yoichi Takahashi. PRD: Toho, Film Link International. 49 mins. Genta Shinoyama is a kindhearted boy and video-game freak who helps drunken Nomoto in the street. Nomoto, a programmer for a major games company, befriends Genta but falls under

suspicion when Genta's notes for a computer game are stolen. However, it is not Nomoto but Genta's friend Hideki who is the thief, a fact proven when Hideki sends the stolen idea to a magazine. Genta challenges Hideki to a duel, his chosen weapon—Nomoto's unfinished computer game *Bee's Hive*. The boys are trapped inside the game and must be guided out by Nomoto, who enlists the help of the famous Master Takahashi.

One of the first in the self-indulgent gaming tie-in subgenre (released the same day as **SUPER MARIO BROTHERS**), this anime was made by Hudson Soft, creators of the *Star Soldier* game, and it features a cameo by their popular designer Takahashi, who also sang the theme songs. It bombed at Japanese theaters, but game-based anime would dominate the 1990s, reaching their apotheosis with **POKÉMON**.

RURAL LEADER

1970. JPN: *Inakappe Taisho.* AKA: *Little Country Chief.* TV series. DIR: Hiroshi Sasakawa. SCR: Noboru Shiroyama, Naoko Miyake, Ryosuke Sakurai, Shigeru Yanagigawa, Toshito Hiraya, Tsunehisa Ito, Yoshiaki Yoshida. DES:

Noboru Kawasaki. ANI: Tsuneo Ninomi-ya, Katsumi Endo. MUS: Katsuhiko Nakamura. PRD: Tatsunoko, Fuji TV. 25 mins. x 104 eps.

Creator Noboru Kawasaki allegedly based his story on the early career of a real Japanese judo champion, but turned it on its head for this comedy sports series. Northern boy Daizaemon Kaze is determined to become a great judo champion, with the help of his special trainer—Nyanko the cat. Comical high jinks ensue, in the first Tatsunoko series to be based on a preexisting manga, in this case from *Shonen Sunday*.

RURONI KENSHIN *

1996. JPN: *Ruroni Kenshin*. AKA: *Sword of Ruro; Vagabond Sword; Kenshin the Wanderer; Kenshin the Ronin; Samurai X*. TV series, movie, video. DIR: Kazuhiro Furuhashi, Hatsuki Tsuji. SCR: Michiru Shimada, Yoshiyuki Suga. DES: Hideyoshi Hamazu, Kuniyuki Ishii, Fumie Muroi, Hatsuki Tsuji. ANI: Masami Suda. MUS: Noriyuki Asakura. PRD: Studio Gallop, Studio Deen, Fuji TV. 25 mins. x 94 eps. (TV), 25 mins. x 1 eps. (v1), 90 mins. (m), 30 mins. x 4 eps. (v2), 125 mins. (m2), 40 mins. x 1 eps. (*Themes*), ca. 60 mins. x 2 eps. (v3/*Seiso Hen*).

It's 1878 in Japan, 11 years after the Meiji Restoration (see OI! RYOMA), and most of the revolutionaries have become just as corrupt as the government they once opposed. "Weakening" foreign influences have become ever stronger, and samurai have lost many of their past rights. Kenshin Himura is a former member of the revolutionary Isshin Shishi group—a reformed assassin who now uses a reverse-bladed sword to avoid ever killing again. He falls for the beautiful Kaoru Kamiya, the impoverished daughter of a swordsmaster whose school has fallen on hard times in the modern age. Kenshin stays at Kaoru's dojo, cooking and cleaning, while also finding the time to deal with some old enemies and scare off local ruffians and disaffected former students of Kaoru's school.

RnK began as a 1994 manga in *Shonen Jump* by Nobuhiro Watsuki, inspired in part by the true-life story of Gensai Kawakami, a 19th-century killer whose good looks often distracted his foes from his cold-blooded nature. Kawakami was useful to Japan's revolutionaries during the pre-Restoration period of civil unrest, but, a danger to the new order, he was imprisoned and executed on trumped-up charges in 1871. To add to the drama, Watsuki threw in a love interest and two more characters, the bratty kid Yahiko (supposedly based on the author's younger self, who was picked last for his school kendo team), and the supertough Sanosuke (based on the semihistorical Sanosuke Harada, hero of Ryotaro Shiba's novel *Burning Sword*). The TV series adapts two major story arcs, beginning with the "Tokyo" sequence mentioned above, followed by the "Kyoto" plotline in which another former revolutionary, Makoto, takes up Kenshin's old job, and with it a certain bitterness that the revolution hasn't gone the way he wanted it. Consequently, he plots to return Japan to chaos, but is thwarted by the actions of Kenshin and his associates.

The final sequence from the manga, "Revenge" was unfinished at the time that the anime reached that point in the story. Consequently, the "Revenge" arc was not adapted for the screen; instead, episodes 63 through 95 (the final episode being video-only) of the series went their own way, largely with "filler" episodes that had nothing to do with the manga. It is the loss in quality of these filler episodes that is credited with the serial's removal from the air, although such a criticism seems churlish when the filler episodes alone run for longer than many of *RnK*'s contemporaries.

Surprisingly popular in the U.S. in spite of featuring a hero who would have happily kicked Americans out of Japan, the *Ruro* TV series occasionally lapses into pointless comedy at the expense of its overall serious tone. The depiction of martial arts, however,

while often not realistic, is respectful and detailed. Luckily this doesn't slow down the action; the battle sequences are well staged and directed. Attractive design and characterization, and the emotional and spiritual intensity of the main characters, make this an interesting and involving show. The *RnK* movie (1997, *Ishin Kokorozashi Samurai eno Chinkonka, Requiem for Ishin's Knight*, aka *Samurai X: The Motion Picture*) takes the characters to Yokohama, where Kenshin once more faces a figure from his past. He saves the life of a man being attacked by bandits and finds that he and Shigure have a link—in his old, violent life, he killed Shigure's friend. Now, Shigure is planning a coup against the Meiji Government, which he believes to be as corrupt as its precursor, but his revolt has been infiltrated by elements in the government seeking to advance their own position. It fails, and Shigure is killed after he has surrendered by one of his treacherous supporters. Kenshin faces the betrayer of his former enemy and tests his vow never to kill again.

The 1999 video series, released in English as *Samurai X: Reflection* (*RnK: Tsuioku Hen*), is a flashback to Kenshin's youth, detailing the story of how he got the distinctive cross-shaped scar on his cheek. Free of the restrictions of TV broadcast, it is much darker than the TV version. The video series also exists in a 125-minute "movie" edit, with a fake widescreen appearance and cast/crew interviews. During the serial's long run, crucial moments of the plot were rerun in three clip-shows (billed as TV "specials"), while two more compilations of previous footage were rerun as "summer holiday specials." There was also an eight-part video release, *RnK: Popular Characters*, that purported to portray fan-favorite moments, though one is tempted to point out that a "fan" would buy the episodes anyway. A two-part sequel, released in English as *Samurai X: Trust & Betrayal* (2001, *RnK: Seiso Hen, RnK: Time Chapter*), features an appearance by Kenshin's son. ▼

RXXX: PRESCRIPTION FOR PAIN *

2004. JPN: *Shuchu Chiryoshitsu*. AKA: *Examination in Progress / Sick Bay of Domination*. Video. DIR: Aim. SCR: American Pie. DES: Mario Yaguchi. ANI: Mario Yaguchi. MUS: Yoshi. PRD: YOUC, Digital Works (Vanilla Series). 30 mins. x 2 eps.

Junichi Sugiura is a young doctor, looking forward to the imminent retirement of his boss Tadahiko Mizuno, and the subsequent handover of the Mizuno hospital to him. Imagine, then, his irritation when Tadahiko's pert, sexy, competent daughter Serika arrives. Junichi now realizes that his sure-fire promotion is likely to go to the boss's daughter, unless he can stealthily take over the hospital through a dedicated campaign of bondage, degradation, and humiliation—yes, it's one of those anime. Accordingly, he begins molesting the nurses, some of whom enjoy it, and some of whom don't. Most are relatives of Serika and she, of course, is the grand prize, in an anime from the VANILLA SERIES, based, as usual, on an erotic computer game. For reasons we do not comprehend, the publicity for the American release calls the protagonist Junichi, whereas his name in the original Japanese version was Makoto. We don't think anyone's losing any sleep over it, though. **ⒸⓃⓋ**

RYU THE STONE AGE BOY

1971. JPN: *Genshi Shonen Ryu*. AKA: *Ryu the Early Man; Ryu the Cave Boy*. TV series. DIR: Masayuki Akehi. SCR: Tadashi Kondo, Kuniaki Oshikawa, Toyohiro Ando. DES: Kazuo Komatsubara. ANI: Mataharu Urata, Eiji Tanaka, Kazuo Hayashi, Hiroshi Wakabayashi. MUS: Takeo Watanabe. PRD: Toei Doga, TBS. 25 mins. x 22 eps.

Ryu is born with white skin in a primitive land where everyone else is dark-skinned. Left as a sacrifice to dinosaurs, he is found and reared by an ape, Kitty. When she is killed by a one-eyed Tyrannosaurus Rex, he sets out to avenge her and find his real mother. He makes friends with the beautiful Ran and her kid brother Don, but meets savagery and danger from men who fear his skin color and dinosaurs who just want to eat him, including a confrontation with the tyrannosaur which is scary despite the limitations of animation of the time.

The animation style mixed both adult, dramatic images from Kazuo Komatsubara and more angular, primitive artwork for which Mataharu Urata used knives instead of brushes to apply the paint.

Based on Shotaro Ishinomori's manga *Ryu's Road* (*Ryu no Michi*), what first appears to be an anachronistic combination of *Tarzan* and *One Million Years B.C.* (1966) is later revealed as part of the plot. Ryu's mother is not a cavewoman at all, but an agent from the distant future, which helps explain not only Ryu's strange features, but eventually, the reasons that supposedly extinct dinosaurs are seen coexisting with cavemen. Ryu, Ran, and Don are also time travelers, and, in a lovely paradox, the enmity between Ryu and the tyrannosaur actually predates Ryu's own birth, since it was an adult Ryu that caused/will cause the dinosaur to lose an eye in the first place. Compare to FLINT THE TIME DETECTIVE, although the most obvious echoes are of Hanna-Barbera's *Dino Boy* (1965), in which a child of our own time falls out of a plane into a lost valley populated by dinosaurs.

S

SABER MARIONETTES *
1995. Video, TV series. DIR: Masami
Shimoda, Koji Masunari. SCR: Mayori
Sekijima, Kenichi Kanemaki. DES: Tsukasa Kotobuki, Hidekazu Shimamura,
Kazuo Nagai. ANI: Eiji Suganuma. MUS:
Parome. PRD: Studio Juno, TV Tokyo.
30 mins. x 3 eps. (v/R), 25 mins. x
25 eps. (TV/J), 25 mins. x 6 eps. (v/J
Again), 25 mins. x 25 eps. (TV/J-X), 25
mins. x 1 ep. (v/J-X).
In the late 22nd century, humanity
spreads out from an overpopulated
Earth. The colony ship Mesopotamia
crashes on a distant world, and the six
male survivors christen the planet Terra 2. Maintaining the species through
cloning, the men establish six countries, each ruled by the pure clone of
its founder: Japones, Sheien (probably
China), New Texas, Peterburg (Russia), Geltland (Germany), and Romana
(Italy).

Based on Satoru Akahori's comic
novel in *Dragon* magazine, *SM* is a
laughable simplification of the same
body/soul concepts that informed
the same year's GHOST IN THE SHELL.
It takes the ADVENTURES OF PINOCCHIO
theme buried in so many robot anime
and marries it to the ultimate variant
on the magical-girlfriend and TENCHI
MUYO! genres—a lone boy on a whole
world of tailor-made women. It also
features the most haphazard release
schedule of any anime, jumping
from video to TV, back to video, then
back to TV, and finally finishing on

video again! Two hundred years after
mankind's arrival on Terra 2, clones of
the originals live on, served by female-
form "marionette" androids. Most are
simply machines incapable of emotion
or thought, but over time some have
become more advanced. However
the greatest leap—to androids with a
"heart"—has yet to be made. An evil
scientist and a psychotic villain are
out to take over the state and double-
cross each other, when the scientist
is mowed down by a newly created
android, Lime, made for Villey Junior,
teenage son of a Romana dignitary.
She and her fellow-marionettes Cherry
and Bloodberry help Junior to save
the day after fighting the bad guys and
their powerful, vicious "sexadolls,"
depraved marionettes who get off on
violence rather than sweet submission.

Resetting the plot to zero and recycling the same or similar characters in
much the same way as *Tenchi Muyo!*, the
series proper began the following year
on TV with the prequel *Saber Marionette
J*, set 200 years earlier. Japonese teenager Otaru discovers the marionette
Lime in a hidden basement beneath
a deserted museum (refer to the similar discovery of Ifrita in EL HAZARD).
Otaru is considered odd because he
prefers his relationship with his cute
little puppet to the normal male-male
relationships on his world. Lime is
the first marionette to have a special
"girly circuit," like a human heart,
which gives her feelings. A little later,

Otaru accidentally finds more such
marionettes, Cherry and Bloodberry,
with the same special circuit. The few
marionettes with this circuit are "saber
marionettes," and they have a secret
purpose. They must achieve spiritual
growth, seemingly by playing out the
same corny fantasies as countless other
anime babes, like getting into bed
naked with their embarrassed man,
fighting to be top bitch in his pack,
participating in "talent" contests, cooking for him, and so on. Should this
unlikely program of spiritual discipline
enable them to transcend themselves,
human females will "revive." The
franchise itself revived on video with
SM J Again (1997), which appeared
to be six unbroadcast TV episodes
of a tiresomely domestic nature, was
released straight to video, and continued straight on from the series. The
series bounced back onto TV as *SM J to
X* (1998), with the predictable return
of the previous series' bad-guy Faust,
along with his team of pretty "Saber
Dolls." The final episode was not
broadcast on TV but is only available
on video. **NV**

**SABER RIDER AND THE STAR
SHERIFFS** *
1984. JPN: *Seijushi Bismarck*. AKA:
Star Gunner Bismarck. TV series. DIR:
Masami Annai, Tadamasa Takahashi,
Hiroyuki Yokoyama, Norio Kabeshima,
Akira Torino, Hiroshi Yoshida, Rei Hida-
ka. SCR: Michiru Umadori, Tsunehisa

Ito, Kazusane Hisajima. DES: Shigeru Kato, Yasushi Moriki. ANI: Tadamasa Takahashi, Moriyasu Taniguchi. MUS: Satoshi Etsuka. PRD: Studio Pierrot, Nippon TV. 25 mins. x 52 eps.
The New Frontier is an untamed region of space where the only law is the Star Sheriffs. From its space station, a team of brave young people—Saber Rider, Colt, Fireball, and April—ride out in their sheriff-shaped giant robot to defend the galaxy from bad guys like the Outriders. Before "versioning" for the U.S. market where, with its Wild West theme, it was inevitably headed, *SR&tSS* was set in the solar system, where the alien Deskula invaders had conquered Ganymede, and Earth was defended by the all-Japanese hero Shinji and his buddies, whose names were regarded (by the Japanese) as suitably Western—Bill, Richard, Marian, and Walter. When the series was altered for U.S. consumption, story editor Marc Handler (who went on to produce **VOLTRON**) had to make teen Texan Colt into the hero and sideline the original lead, Japanese kid Fireball, resulting in some hilarious scenes where other characters are looking at Fireball but supposedly listening to Colt. He also had problems with the amount of teenage drinking in the original, editing out all drunken behavior and moving many scenes from saloons to the "coffee shops" and "soda fountains" that were so much a part of the Old West.

SABU AND ICHI INVESTIGATE

1968. JPN: *Sabu to Ichi Torimonohikae.* TV series. DIR: Rintaro, Mori Masaki, Shinichi Suzuki, Fumio Kurokawa, Eiji Kojima, Mami Murano, Kunihiko Okazaki, Masayuki Hayashi, Takeshi Tamiya, Tomoharu Katsumata, Noboru Ishiguro. SCR: Takao Suzuki, Keiichi Abe, Takashi Umebayashi, Yoji Nishikawa. DES: Shotaro Ishinomori. ANI: Akio Sugino, Mami Murano. MUS: Takeo Yamashita. PRD: Mushi, Studio Zero, Toei, NET. 25 mins. x 52 eps.
A detective story from Shotaro Ishinomori in which two Sherlock Holmes

types solve a range of crimes in old Edo. Sabu, a young man in search of adventure, comes to the big city and becomes assistant to Saheiji, police chief of the Ryusenji quarter, who is almost crippled by rheumatism and spends much of his time bedridden. A local character, the masseur Ichi, turns out to be a very useful contact and helps Sabu in his efforts to keep Edo crime-free on behalf of his boss.

SACRILEGE *

2002. JPN: *Kaishun.* AKA: *Rejuvenation.* Video. DIR: Katsumasa Kanezawa. SCR: Kazuhiro Oyama. DES: Hiroya Iijima. ANI: Shigenori Awai. MUS: N/C. PRD: Studio Kuma, Miami Soft. 30 mins. x 2 eps.
Lesbian cops Atsuko and Kei investigate a drug deal that has gone wrong, only to blunder into the activities of an evil cult. A sinister cabal of old men in search of immortality has found a drug that *almost* works. However, when tested on unsuspecting members of the public, it transforms them into crazed demonic rapists. Meanwhile, the shaven-headed female servants of the cabal realize that the cops are on their trail and do what they can to scare them off, which, with sad predictability, involves capture, bondage, torture, and sexualized violence. *Sacrilege* appears strangely old-fashioned, with rather ugly characters, a retro look and a rapacious plot that recalls 1990s tits-and-tentacles titles like **NIGHTMARE CAMPUS**. ○NV

SADAMOTO, YOSHIYUKI

1962– . Born in Yamaguchi Prefecture, Sadamoto sold his first manga work while still at university. He began working for the animation studio Telecom, before joining Gainax as a character designer on **WINGS OF HONNEAMISE**. He has subsequently been an animator on **THE SECRET OF BLUE WATER** and **GUNBUSTER** and was the character designer on **EVANGELION** and **.HACK**. He was also the author of the *Evangelion* manga, which achieved best-seller status before the series even aired, and is regarded as an alternate but valid continuity.

SAIKANO *

2002. JPN: *Saishu Heiki Kanojo.* AKA: *She, The Ultimate Weapon.* TV series, video. DIR: Mitsuko Kase. SCR: Itaru Era. DES: Hisashi Kagawa, Hiroyuki Kanbe, Tomohiro Kawahara. ANI: Jeong Ho-Jang, Keuk Sun-Jeon, Seong Yong-An, Sun Hak-Jeon, Won Cheol-Seo, Yong Il-Park, Kazuhiro Tanaka, Ryo Sato. MUS: Takeo Miratsu. PRD: Shogakukan, Tohokushinsha, Toshiba EMI, Gonzo, CBC. 23 mins. x 13 eps. (TV), 30 mins. x 2 eps. (v).
Hokkaido teenager Shuji had a love affair with an older woman that has made him distant and mistrustful. Passive, shy fellow high school senior Chise has a crush on him, but she's the kind of girl who is constantly apologizing for needing to breathe. She finally steels herself to ask him out, and the pair are actually starting a real relationship, when a mass of bombers whose origin is unknown suddenly attacks Sapporo and flattens the city. It looks as if everyone will be killed, when a small point of red light streaks from the Sapporo television tower into the sky and destroys the bombers. Shuji is stunned to learn that the girl he's seeing is actually a cyborg weapon in the Japan Self Defense Force.

Saikano employs real-world Hokkaido settings, which were in vogue at the time thanks to the end of the long-running live-action TV show *From The North* (*DE, see also **DIAMOND DAYDREAMS**). It also shares that combination of teenage yearning and sci-fi combat that formed such a vital component of the same year's **VOICES OF A DISTANT STAR**. However, its clearest influences lie in the apparently doomed romance and fetishized girlfriend weapons of **MAHOROMATIC** and **LIMIT THE MIRACLE GIRL**. Where 20th-century anime might have allegorized pubescent or emotional turmoil with animal analogies or quasi-religious mysticism, the **CHOBITS** generation is more apt to understand human interactions in terms of hardware interfaces and software conflicts. So it is that Chise's ongoing "development" as a robot weapon causes her to overreact to an impending earthquake as if it is another attack. Meanwhile, Shuji develops a strange revulsion to his would-be girlfriend's declining humanity, and neither is able to cope with collateral damage caused by Chise's attempts to defend the Earth.

Some of anime's best drama springs from the marriage of teenage angst with physical events. The Japan of *Saikano* stands alone in a war against an unnamed foe (although in one scene a downed enemy pilot speaks English), beset by disasters both natural and military, with peripheral characters affording glimpses of the harsh life on the front line—shades here of GUNPARADE MARCH and GUNBUSTER. This could be read as an effective evocation of the modern world—as in HOWL'S MOVING CASTLE, civilization marches on regardless while contested in a savage war elsewhere—but is all the more striking for its relation to the traumas of the teen target audience. Later episodes allude to the closing scenes of Ridley Scott's *Blade Runner* (1982), as Chise and Shuji seek a life, of sorts, together. *Saikano* is also an anime with a brutally blunt and uncompromising antiwar message, rivaling GRAVE OF THE FIREFLIES in the accusatory way it approaches not the battles themselves, but their aftermath. Technology is regarded, even by the avuncular scientist who is Chise's "creator," as a curse that will drag the entire human race on a course for destruction, toward a truly pessimistic denouement.

In the autumn of 2005, a two-part DVD from the same director gave another slant on the story. *Saikano: Another Love Song* tells the story of Chise's prototype, career officer Mizuki, who watches Chise's terrible potential unfolding while she must face the fact that she has reached the end of her own powers. Although billed as a "side story" to the original series, these two chapters are so integrated into the main story that they could have easily been inserted into its midpoint as two more episodes. The art style in both versions also manages to capture the delicate watercolor look of Shin Takahashi's original manga from *Big Comic Spirits* magazine. A live-action movie adaptation, *Saikano: The Last Love Song on this Little Planet*, was premiered at the Tokyo International Film Festival in 2005 and went on general release in Japan in 2006. ◉

SAILOR MOON *

1992. JPN: *Bishojo Senshi Sailor Moon*. AKA: *Pretty Soldier Sailor Moon*. TV series, movie. DIR: Junichi Sato, Kazuhisa Takenouchi, Kunihiko Ikuhara, Yuji Endo, Hiroki Shibata, Masahiro Hosoda, Takuya Igarashi. SCR: Sukehiro Tomita, Yoji Enokido, Ryota Yamaguchi, Jun Maekawa, Kazuhiko Kobe, Chitose Mizuno. DES: Kazuko Tadano, Ikuko Ito, Katsumi Igai. ANI: Kazuko Tadano, Ikuko Itoh, Masahiro Ando, Hisashi Kagawa, Hideyuki Motohashi. MUS: Takanori Arisawa, Tetsuo Komuro, Kazuo Sano. PRD: Toei, Aoi, TV Asahi. 25 mins. x 200 eps., 60 mins. x 3 movies, 16 mins. (m/*Ami-chan*), 42 mins. (m/*Make Up*).

Usagi Tsukino (Serena in the U.S. version) is a cheerful but clumsy teenage crybaby. Nevertheless, she is fated to become Sailor Moon, leader of a team of brave girls: Ami (Amy/Mercury), Minako (Mina/Venus), Rei (Raye/Mars), and Makoto (Lita/Jupiter). Collectively, they are known as the Sailor Warriors (Sailor Senshi), or Sailor Scouts in the U.S. She meets a magical cat, Luna, and receives classic magical-girl items (including a wand and tiara) and superpowers to help her transform. In a past life, she was Moon Princess Serenity, beloved of Prince Endymion. That love will be reborn because Endymion has also been reincarnated as a human with the ability to magically transform into dashing hero (and occasional boy-damsel in distress) Tuxedo Kamen (Tuxedo Mask).

SM began as *Codename Sailor V* (1991, often confused with the unrelated GRADUATION spin-off *Sailor Victory*), a short-lived manga by Naoko Takeuchi in *Run-Run* magazine in which a teenage girl moonlights as a superhero wearing a distinctive sailor-style Japanese schoolgirl uniform. Reworked as a sequel which was published in *Nakayoshi* magazine as part of a cross-media promotion with the anime, the refashioned story now featured several color-coded heroines in the fashion of live-action team shows, as well as a supernatural spin—lunar reincarnations would also crop up in its contemporaries PLEASE SAVE MY EARTH and BOUNTY DOG. There are echoes of *Power Rangers* in the "monster-of-the-week" fight sequences in which our heroines take on ever more outrageously costumed baddies, but the show is saved from banality by the strength of its plotting, its earnest, honest romance, and its refusal to talk down to its audience. With reincarnation a given, the show is unafraid of death; the first season closes with a harrowing assault on the icy lair of the evil Queen Beryl, in which the entire cast is killed off (albeit temporarily). Needless to say, the sanitized U.S. release unconvincingly pretends they have merely been detained elsewhere.

It is unlikely that many of the girls who watched the first season were still glued to their TVs by the last episode in 1996, a ratings disaster the producers attempted to avoid by rebranding and refashioning the series to entice younger audiences. As *SM R[eturns]* in 1993, it introduced new foes from the Black Moon, who intend to destroy present-day Tokyo in order to prevent the founding of Crystal Tokyo in the future. It also introduced Chibi-Usa (Rini), Serena and Endymion's future daughter, who time-travels to stay with the girl who is/was/will be her mother. Rebranded again as Kunihiko Ikuhara's *SM S[uper]* in 1994, it introduced the controversially homoerotic Sailors Uranus and Neptune, who are in search of three mystic talismans. The talismans must be united to summon the Holy Grail, which is needed to locate the Messiah but must be kept out of the hands of Professor Tomoe and the Death Busters lest it summon the *Dark* Messiah. The new Sailors suspect (rightly) that Sailor Saturn is the Dark Messiah, splitting the group with in-fighting. By 1994's season *SM S[uper] S* (note the easy-to-confuse typography!), the focus of the show was gradually shifting away from Usagi and onto Chibi-Usa, thought to be more appealing to younger girls as the original target audience put childish things (i.e., merchandise) behind them. However, ratings hit an all-time low, partly because Chibi-Usa was unpopular, but also because Ikuhara's growing obsessions with fairy tales and subtexts (see his later **UTENA**) were lost on the target audience. Chibi-Usa befriends Pegasus, a flying horse, who enlists her help in keeping an important Golden Crystal from the evil Queen Nephrenia, leader of the Dead Moon Circus, who needs it to escape from her prison (inside a mirror) and conquer Earth. There was also a 48-minute *Super S* TV special, containing a trilogy of stories— a summary of the preceding seasons; a cruise ship cutaway with Neptune and Uranus explaining why they are not appearing in this season; and a final part in which Chibi-Usa fights a monster inside a vampire castle.

For the final season, *SM Sailor Stars*, Chibi-Usa returns to the future, Mamoru leaves to study abroad, and the remaining Sailor Scouts must hold off Shadow Galactica, a group of evil Scouts led by Sailor Galaxia. They are aided in this by the Three Lights (aka *Starlights*), a boy band who can transform into leather-clad girls in times of need.

There were also several theatrical outings—Ikuhara's *Sailor Moon R* (1993) takes place during the Nega Moon story in the TV series. An alien boy befriends the child who will grow up to be Tuxedo Mask, but, when they meet again as young adults, a misunderstanding leads to tragedy. The same year saw his *Make Up Sailor Senshi!* (aka *Dreaming Moon*), a short film of animated character biographies and gossip. *Sailor Moon S The Movie* (1994) focuses on Luna, Sailor Moon's feline friend, who is rescued by and falls in love with

a young astronomer caught up in the battle to save Earth when evil Princess Kaguya (see **REI REI**) plots to freeze it. Hiroki Shibata's *Sailor Moon SS* (1995) features Chibi-Usa's new friend, a modern-day Pied Piper, who leads all the local children toward a spaceship, and the Sailors must save them from being abducted. On the same bill was the short feature *Ami-chan's First Love* starring Sailor Mercury (always popular with the series' unexpectedly large audience of boys, because she did stuff with computers). The series was eventually brought to the U.S. with an indifferent dub, where it flopped, chiefly because it was shown at an insanely early time of the morning, edged into dead airtime by more powerful local interests. *SM*'s failure was an object lesson in how a multimedia sensation, heavily reliant on merchandising tie-ins, can crash without adequate support—Bandai would not make the same mistake with the later **POKÉMON**. Much imitated in modern anime such as **WEDDING PEACH**, *SM* has also been the subject of erotic parodies in **VENUS FIVE** and *Sailor and the Seven Balls*.

As the original *SM* viewers matured into a whole new demographic, a live-action TV series, with the official English title of *Pretty Guardian Sailor Moon* (2003) ran for 49 episodes and two DVD specials—somewhat longer than average in the world of Japanese TV, although its ratings were never quite as high as those of the anime. The release of the series coincided with a republication of the *SM* manga, with some sections rewritten or altered to make it conform closer to its latest "adaptation." The live version also introduced some new Sailors—Luna the cat occasionally transforming into the human-form Sailor Luna; a "Dark" version of Sailor Mercury after she is possessed by an antagonist; and a "Princess" form of Sailor Moon herself, when she is temporarily possessed by the spirit of her older self.

SAINT BEAST

2005. TV series. DIR: Harume Kosaka.

SCR: Mayu Sugiura, Ryu Tamura. DES: Sakura Asagi. ANI: Toshiko Sasaki. MUS: N/C. PRD: Wonderfarm. 25 mins. x 6 eps.

Two mighty angels angered the gods and were cast out of Heaven and sealed in prison. When they finally break free, Yuda the Kirin and Ruka the Phoenix decide to take revenge by conquering their former heavenly home. Soon the guardian spirits of Earth are disappearing. The Goddess calls upon the four Saint Beasts, angelic beings with the powers of their totem animals, to investigate. The four take human form and descend to Earth to live among humans and try to solve the mystery. The story is loosely based on Chinese legend, with shades here of Sun Wukong's uproar in heaven from **JOURNEY TO THE WEST**, but also of the angelic angst of **SAINT SEIYA** and **EARTHIAN**, since it soon focuses on the relationships and pasts of the characters, whose chosen human forms are young, beautiful, and male. Yuda is a hunky, muscular redhead in his mid-twenties, Ruka is a cute, spiky blond a year or so younger, and the Four Saint Beasts sent after them are 22-year-old Seiryu no Go, a dark-haired heroic hunk; 21-year-old Genbu no Shin, whose long green ponytail, spectacles, and interest in nature denote the brains of the party; purple-haired 20-year-old princeling Suzaku no Rei; and cute blond 19-year-old Byakko no Gai, the baby of the party, obsessed, like most teen gods, with TV, food, and shopping. Almost immediately, the Saint Beasts are diverted from their primary mission to find two missing brother Saints, half-human and half-angel, and settle into a country estate with them for some sub–**TENCHI MUYO!** domestic bickering. Ryusei no Kira is a bad boy in black leather who used to torment Go in childhood, and his kid brother Fuuga no Maaya immediately becomes Gai's soulmate and partner in goofing off. The primary plotline does reemerge as Yuda and Ruka wreak havoc among the lower ranks of the angels, and our heroes wrestle with the idea that their old friends could turn to the Dark Side. The character development and promising plot setup isn't resolved in the short running time, leaving a sense of missed opportunity that detracts from the pretty art and design. Of course, what Western anime viewers lack is the vast backstory available in Japan in the manga and CD dramas. All the anime is intended to do is provide pretty moving pictures for the story's existing fans. Despite the boy-on-boy overtones, there's nothing sexually explicit here—go to the CD dramas for that. The music is undistinguished and the animation no more than acceptable, but boy-band fans will love it. Kei Arisugawa created *SB*, and **PHANTOM QUEST CORP**'s Juzo Mutsuki is credited on planning for the anime. The show is also packaged for promotion on mobile phone screens, at time of writing merely in terms of extras and character-based screen themes, although it would not surprise us at all if that is merely the beginning of a mobile broadcast effort like that of **LEGEND OF DUO**.

SAINT ELMO: APOSTLE OF LIGHT

1987. JPN: *Saint Elmo Hikari no Raihosha*. TV special. DIR: Tomoharu Katsumata. SCR: Hiroyasu Yamaura. DES: Katsumi Itahashi. ANI: Yasuhiro Yamaguchi. MUS: Michiru Oshima. PRD: Toei, Yomiuri TV. 84 mins.
A Jovian cloud-cruiser disappears in a strange accident, its pilot feared lost. The master "electrician" Issei Yuki is recalled to Osaka from his current project in Africa and dispatched to investigate. He discovers that there are problems on the giant orbital power station Saint Elmo that are creating electrical storms and threatening to plunge Earth into eternal darkness. In order to save his father's great project, and Mayu, the girl he loves, he tries to stop the Saint Elmo from falling into the sun. A very obscure TV anime, not broadcast in the Tokyo area, and therefore unknown to a large proportion of the *Japanese* audience. Despite a development credit from **CAPTAIN HARLOCK**-

creator Leiji Matsumoto, *Saint Elmo* had its true genesis as a vanity project for the Kansai Electric Company, which wanted to do something to commemorate its 30th anniversary. Apparently, this hokey sci-fi show was it.

SAINT LUMINOUS COLLEGE

1998. JPN: *Sei Luminous Gakuen*. AKA: *St. Luminous Mission High School*. TV series. DIR: Tetsuro Amino. SCR: Akira Oketani. DES: Hisashi Kagawa. ANI: Hisashi Kagawa, Tadashi Yoshida. MUS: Michiya Katakura. PRD: Pioneer, TV Tokyo. 25 mins. x 13 eps.
Two lucky guys become the first male pupils to attend the all-girl St. Luminous College, gaining a seemingly limitless supply of adoring classmates who can't wait to find out about the world of psychic investigation. A predictable rehash of Pioneer's **TENCHI MUYO!** franchise with a cursory *X-Files* twist, this anime was based on an "original" idea by Kenji Terada.

SAINT SEIYA *

1986. JPN: *Seitoshi Seiya*. AKA: *Holy Fighters Seiya; Star Arrow; Zodiac Knights*. TV series, movie. DIR: Shigenori Yamauchi, Kozo Morishita, Kazuhito Kikuchi, Masayuki Akehi, et al. SCR: Takao Koyama, Yoshiyuki Suga, Tadaaki Yamazaki, et al. DES: Shingo Araki, Michi Himeno, Masahiro Naoi, Tadao Kubota, Fumihiro Uchikawa. ANI: Shingo Araki, Tetsuro Aoki. MUS: Seiji Yokoyama. PRD: Toei, TV Asahi. 25 mins. x 114 eps. (TV), 45 mins. (m1), 45 mins. (m2), 75 mins. (m3), 45 mins. (m4), 25 mins. x 13 eps. (*Hades*), 115 mins. (m5), 30 mins. x 6 eps. (v2).
Young martial artist Seiya and the Bronze Saints are sworn to protect Saori, the reincarnation of the Goddess Athena. Their magical armor is at the lower end of a divinely initiated pecking order that moves up through Silver and Gold Saints and even encompasses the sinister Black Saints, servants of a dark power who see Athena as the only barrier to their dominion. In the first series, Ikki and his Black Saints

steal the legendary Gold armor. The battle to retrieve it seems hopeless, but the boys have their Cosmo, a kind of power in every living being that can be developed for good or evil. Combining their Cosmo with their individual skills and courage, they can beat seemingly invincible powers. Since evil can be reborn, their adversaries can reincarnate to fight them again. A complex plot builds through multiple story arcs in the TV series and the self-contained but linked movies, featuring mythologies from Greece, Scandinavia, China, and Christendom. The series ends with a multiepisode tale in which Poseidon captures Athena as part of a plot to create a new Great Flood; the Saints of Athena must defeat him and save the goddess, to save the world as we know it.

Based on the *Shonen Jump* manga by **BT'X**-creator Masami Kurumada, four movie outings followed: the first, Morishita and Kikuchi's *Saint Seiya* (1987, aka *Legend of the Golden Apple*) pitted the boys against Eris, the goddess of Discord. The same year's *SS: Vicious Fight of the Gods* (*Kamigami no Nekki Tatakai*) was designed as the lead-in for the Norse-themed second season of the TV series, moving the action to the frozen wastes of Siberia (not quite Scandinavia, but easier for Japanese kids to find on a map) for a battle with the gods of Midgard over Odin's shield. The only full-length feature was *Legend of the Crimson Youth* (1988, *Makka no Shonen Densetsu*), in which Athena must fight Abel (the reincarnation of her elder brother, the sun god Apollo), and his cohorts Berenice and Jow, who wish to create a "new world of peace" by distinctly unpeaceful methods. Masayuki Akehi's *Armageddon Warriors* (45 mins., 1990) involves the awakening of Lucifer by the powers of the various evil deities Seiya and his companions have sent to Hades. It coincided with the ending of the TV series and proved to be the final outing for the Saints of Athena. The last incarnation of the series to date is the 13-part *Hades* chapter (*SS: Tenkai-hen,*

2002) which some sources file as a video series, as the makers intended, and others file as a television show, since it was made to resemble a TV series in 25-minute episodes and first appeared on pay-per-view television in Japan. A movie sequel to the Hades chapter was released in 2004 (*SS: Tenkai Hen Joso: Overture, SS: Heaven Chapter Defrost: Overture*), followed by a six-episode video spin-off *SS: Hades Chapter Inferno* (2005, *SS: Meio Hades Meikai-hen*).

Designers Araki and Himeno (ROSE OF VERSAILLES) work magic in both the series and movies, except for the last film, where Naoi's design is less successful. Yokoyama's music is suitably grand. Director Yamauchi stretches the series' tension like a bowstring for cliffhanger endings and mid-battle episode breaks that kept audiences coming back for more. But despite its apparent teen appeal, a show that achieves much of its emotional impact through older boys and men fighting brave but naïve teenagers is disturbing, especially when strength and courage are rewarded with ever shinier weapons. *SS* and its close cousin RONIN WARRIORS should come with parental warning attached—though their influence, even into the girls' market, can be discerned throughout the SAILOR MOON–dominated 1990s. For those old enough to separate the complex strands of the story and keep its brutally seductive heroism in perspective, *SS* has many rewards.

The series was also adapted into a live stage musical in 1991, starring members of the boy-band SMAP. The anime itself was acquired for U.S. broadcast as *Knights of the Zodiac* by DIC Entertainment.

SAINT TAIL *

1995. JPN: *Kaito Saint Tail*. AKA: *Master Thief Saint Tail*. TV series. DIR: Osamu Nabeshima. SCR: Masaaki Sakurai, Masahiro Yokoyama. DES: Junko Abe, Shiro Kobayashi. ANI: Junko Abe. MUS: Seiji Suzuki. PRD: Tokyo Movie Shinsha, TV Asahi. 25 mins. x 43 eps.

Meimi is an ordinary Catholic school-girl who transforms at night into the daring thief Saint Tail. It's in the genes, as her mother was a notable burglar before marrying her stage-magician father, but she only steals from those who deserve it, or to help others. Her best friend, Seira, is a novice nun who somewhat heretically hears confessions from troubled parishioners and then blurts out the details to Meimi. Meimi then yells out, "It's showtime!" whereupon God Almighty transforms her into an angelic superthief in a costume based on a magician's female assistant: top hat, revealing bodysuit, and fishnet stockings. While Saint Tail restores valuable items to their true owners, the hapless police are unable to compete with her divinely assisted crime spree, though Meimi's classmate Asuka is the son of the beleaguered chief of police, determined to track down Saint Tail and hoping to capture Meimi's heart as well. A resurrection of two of the most successful themes of the 1980s—magical girls and TMS's own burglars-for-justice series CAT'S EYE—with a dash of Las Vegas showmanship and Catholic guilt. Meimi regrets the embarrassment she causes Asuka's father as she carries out God's work. Based on Megumi Tachikawa's manga.

SAKURA

1946. AKA: *Cherry Blossom*. Movie. DIR: Sanae Yamamoto, Kenzo Masaoka. SCR: N/C. DES: Tatsumi Masae, Yosuke Kurosaki, Yasui Koyata. ANI: N/C. MUS: Carl Maria von Weber. PRD: Nippon Manga Eiga. ca. 5 mins.

Made in the aftermath of WWII by the surviving animators in Tokyo, *Sakura* depicts Kyoto in the springtime, concentrating on the traditional image of a trainee geisha, before moving on to shots of two puppies playing amid a shower of cherry blossoms, and butterflies who turn out to have human faces. Considering the style of a vignette set to classical music, the most obvious influence is likely to have been Disney's *Fantasia* (1940), although there is no record of the movie being screened in Japan during the war years—possibly the directors were inspired by the idea of *Fantasia*, rather than the actual sight of it, just as Osamu Tezuka's METROPOLIS was written without its creator having seen the film of the same name. *Sakura* was a bold effort at restarting Japan's collapsed animation industry, but was understandably substandard, considering the poor conditions in which it was made.

SAKURA DIARIES *

1997. JPN: *Sakura Tsushin*. AKA: *Sakura Communications*. Video. DIR: Kunitoshi Okajima. SCR: Kenji Terada. DES: Nobuyuki Takeuchi. ANI: Nobuyuki Takeuchi. MUS: Mitsuo Hagita. PRD: Kitty Films, Victor, Shaft. 25 mins. x 12 eps. (released on 6 tapes).

Toma Inaba is a dreamer, eager to get into university and begin adult life, but cursed to drift permanently around the outskirts. Arriving in Tokyo from the country to take his university entrance examinations, he fails after catching a bad cold. Said virus was contracted from his cousin and childhood friend, the pretty Urara Kasuga, who had visited him in his hotel room disguised as a prostitute as joke in an effort to boost his spirits, but whom he threw out after not recognizing her. Meanwhile, he has fallen in love with the beautiful but unattainable Mieko Yotsuba, who will only go out with a fellow student of the elite Keio University. He thus begins a life of boarding with Urara (who continues to chase him, and whose widower father is conveniently out of town) while attending a cram school to pass the next year's entrance exam and chasing Mieko (with whom he pretends to be a Keio student).

"When it comes to sex, she wrote the book on it," leers the hopeful box blurb, but the very fact that *SD* is released by ADV, rather than their erotic subsidiary brand Soft Cel, speaks volumes about its confused identity. While *SD* looks superficially like a faithful adaptation of the *Young Sunday* manga by U-Jin, the anime loses much of the original's appeal. Despite being U-Jin's most mature and entertaining

Sakura Diaries

© SHOGAKUKAN/KITTY FILM/VICTOR ENTERTAINMENT

work, *SD* was clearly optioned with the audience of ANGEL and TALES OF . . . in mind, vacillating between the sex farces of U-Jin's better-known works and the far more involving story of the original.

There are some clever moments that duplicate the spirit of the original. Each episode begins with a striking scene, as little-girl-lost Urara sits at her dresser and contemplates her reflection in the mirror, applying her warpaint and contemplating her next covert operation in this battle of the sexes. For the opening credits, Urara is filmed as if she is the only girl in the world, much the same as in the beginning of VIDEO GIRL AI. As with OH MY GODDESS!, the leads' association begins when they are children, but this is not a simple case of love at first sight—in the manga, it is the seven-year-old Touma who risks his life to protect Urara from her abusive father.

But like so many anime romances aimed at the onanistic male, *SD* paints a picture of a strange viewer, old enough to vote but somehow cursed with the emotional maturity of a child. Consequently, its female characters are dragged down to the level of the

wanton Lolitas of CREAM LEMON, while its male lead becomes little more than a priapic TENCHI MUYO!. Despite the more sophisticated story line of the original manga, the anime incarnation often slips into tawdriness, seemingly because the production team refused to believe that they could make an U-Jin anime without some eye candy. Released initially as a video series, and then broadcast the following year in a bowdlerized edition on television. ◍

SAKURA WARS *

1997. JPN: *Sakura Taisen*. Video, TV series. DIR: Takaaki Ishiyama, Ryutaro Nakamura. SCR: Hiroyuki Kawasaki, Satoru Akahori. DES: Hidenori Matsubara, Kosuke Fujishima. ANI: N/C. MUS: Kohei Tanaka. PRD: Bandai, TBS/MBS. 30 mins. x 4 eps. (v1), 30 mins. x 6 eps. (v2), 25 mins. x 25 eps. (TV), 85 mins. (m), 24 mins. x 1 ep. (v3/*Sumire*), 30 mins. x 3 eps. (v4/*École*), 30 mins. x 3 eps. (v5/*Nouveau*).
At the beginning of the 20th century, Earth fends off invading demons from another dimension. Suspecting that another attack is coming, a group of Japanese scientists perfect clunky war machines in the early 1920s, discover-

ing that they can only be effectively piloted by women with the right sort of virtuous energy. Assembling a team of anime archetypes (big-sisterly platoon leader Maria, tomboy Kanna, child Iris, maidenly Sumire, and alien Chinese girl Koh-ran/Hong-Lan), the scientists eventually find their perfect Girl Next Door, Sakura the swordswoman from Sendai. The Imperial Flower Combat Troop (since the platoons are chiefly named, Takarazuka theater style, after flowers) then prepares to resist the alien menace.

SW races through four years and a couple of flashbacks in order to set up the beginning of the Sega console game—hence occasional cutaways to the otherwise irrelevant life of Ichiro Ogami, the hapless naval officer who is the player's point of view in the game proper, as well as the introduction of Kanna, only to remove her, since she is absent at the beginning of the game. Designed to complement the game, it is nevertheless entertaining in its own right, with an appeal that crosses several anime subgenres—including robot combat, gaggles of girls à la TENCHI MUYO!, retro adventure in the style of SUPER ATRAGON, and hefty multimedia promotion. Fans were asked to buy into a complete "universe," including not just the novelization, but also a CD-ROM encyclopedia, two games, and the Taisho Romantic Society, a fan club of alternate historians with its own magazine. To top it all, the actresses appeared in several live-action musicals, drawing further parallels between the look of the show and the cross-dressing Takarazuka musical tradition (particularly ROSE OF VERSAILLES) that inspired it.

Though *SW* does a masterful job of overcoming its computer-game origins, like KISHIN CORPS and creator Hiroi Oji's later VIRGIN FLEET, its innocuous revisionism leaves a nasty taste in the historian's mouth—in the *real* 1920s, the only aliens the Japanese military were preparing to fight were the hapless inhabitants of Manchuria. Somewhat ironically, the period detail is quite exacting, with obsolete terms used for foreign countries, right-to-left writing in the prewar style, and even a character named Koh-ran, after a Japanese actress who specialized in Chinese roles in prewar propaganda films. Each of the first four episodes focused on two of the members (including the two added for the second game, Orihime and Leni, both from the disbanded European Star Division), while the last two featured a two-part story about the entire troop. The franchise was upgraded to a TV series in 2000, which retold the story from the beginning, with the team forming a musical comedy troupe and setting off on a nationwide tour. For the game *SW3*, the action shifts to Paris in 1926, where Ichiro Ogami is put in charge of a new team of girls—big-sisterly part-time thief Roberia, tomboy duchess Grecine, Vietnamese child Kokuriko, and girl-next-door Hanabi, a French-born Japanese girl. *Sakura Wars: The Movie* (*ST: Katsudo Shashin*, lit. *SW: The Motion Picture*), set in Tokyo after the events of *SW3* in Paris, appeared late in 2001. A new member, Lachette, formerly of the Star Division, joins the Imperial Flower Combat Troop to gain field experience in preparation for the founding of the New York team. Meanwhile, an American industrial magnate, Brent Furlong, plots to replace the Troop with automated anti-demon robots, and then to conquer first Tokyo, next Japan, and eventually the world. The hackneyed plot is well presented, with lovingly detailed high-grade animation and art.

Three further video series duly followed, *SW: Sumire* (2002), *SW: École de Paris* (2003), and *SW: Le Nouveau Paris* (2004), the first a one-shot, and the latter two comprising three parts, each part 30 minutes long. *SW: Sumire* commemorates the retirement of both the character Sumire Kanzaki and her voice actress Michie Tomizawa. The multipart series both comprise three parts, each part 30 minutes long. Both related to the Paris-set third game, although by this time a fourth game was already out, set in 1927 and incorporating 14 characters from the preceding installments of the franchise. A fifth game moves the action to New York with mainly new characters—if there is ever a new *SW* anime, this incarnation is a likely source.

SAKYO KOMATSU'S ANIME THEATER

1989. JPN: *Komatsu Sakyo Anime Gekijo*. TV series. DIR: Akira Nishimori. SCR: Sakyo Komatsu. DES: Jun Ishikawa. ANI: Jun Ishikawa. MUS: N/C. PRD: Gainax, MBS. 3 mins. x 27 eps.

A series of adaptations of short stories, this anime's chief source of material is the *Punk Dragon* short-story collection by Sakyo Komatsu, best known for his novels *Japan Sinks* and *Resurrection Day* (the latter adapted into the live-action film *Virus*, 1980). In the anime world, Komatsu also worked with Tezuka on **Space Firebird** and as a voice actor in **Arabian Nights**.

SALAMANDER *

1988. Video. DIR: Hisayuki Toriumi. SCR: Kazuhito Hisajima. DES: Haruhiko Mikimoto, Yasuhiro Moriki. ANI: Toshiyasu Okada. MUS: Tatsushi Umegaki. PRD: Studio Pierrot. 60 mins., 50 mins., 60 mins.

In the year 2381, the aggressive galaxy-devouring parasites known as the Bacterians are heading for planet Gradius. In the first video, *Salamander Basic Saga: Meditating Paola*, ace pilot Stephanie and her teammates, Eddie and Dan, find a beautiful girl in an abandoned spaceship. As she warns of the imminent Bacterian invasion, they wonder if she's an innocent victim or an agent of destruction. The lovely Paola reveals herself to be a Bacterian agent, and Stephanie's father makes the ultimate sacrifice to save Gradius from the invaders. For the second video, *Intermediate Saga*, Dan and Stephanie are called to planet Lotus, whose ruler, Lord British, needs their help. Despite courtly intrigues from rivals embittered at needing foreign aid, the Gradian pilots hold off another invasion. In *Advanced Saga: The Ambition of Gofar*, British comes to Gradius to sign a peace treaty and woo the reluctant Stephanie. She, however, is kidnapped by the Bacterians and taken to their HQ on the artificial sun of Salamander, where they plan to rip out her brain and sew it into the skull of their agent Gofar. Stephanie's father, who has turned to the dark side, figures that her knowledge of the Gradian defenses will turn the battle in the invaders' favor. Needless to say, British and Dan save the day.

A brave stab at adapting the Konami arcade game *Gradius*, *Salamander* is ultimately defeated by the poverty of its source material. The love triangle between Stephanie and the men is well-handled; she is tempted by riches, royalty, and marriage in the form of British as well as by career and camaraderie in the form of Dan. The ex-refugee Eddie is another intriguing character, drawn to the enemy agent Paola because she too does not really belong. A surprisingly cogent hard-science script and well-realized sequences that duplicate moments of gameplay for the fans are ruined by the worst subtitling in anime history, courtesy of Western Connection.

SALARYMAN KINTARO *

2001. TV series. DIR: Tomoharu Katsumata. SCR: Chikako Kobayashi, Sukehiro Tomita. DES: Masami Suda. ANI: N/C. MUS: N/C. PRD: 81 Produce, TBS. 25 mins. x 20 eps.

Kintaro Yajima was a biker gang leader with a ton of charisma and an attitude, until he fell in love and decided to settle down and have a family. Then tragedy struck when his young wife died in childbirth, leaving him alone to bring up their baby son. But Kintaro's biker past has given him a certain fearlessness that leads him to save the life of the CEO of Yamato Construction Company, immediately fast-tracking him into a management position for which his rough past often seems strangely suited.

Any similarities to **GTO** are purely intentional. Like its predecessor, *Salary-*

© MANGLOBE/SHIMOIGUSA CHAMPLOOS

Samurai Champloo

man Kintaro is based on a manga, on this occasion by Hiroshi Motomiya in *Young Jump* magazine. Both titles enjoyed live-action incarnations (*DE) on primetime television, only converting to the anime format when interest (and budgets) had begun to die down. And, of course, both feature mavericks made good—handsome boys with hearts of gold, fighting to raise themselves out of an underclass youth into a respectable middle-class lifestyle.

The methods are often identical. Kintaro breaks up a fight on the day before he is due to start at Yamato Construction, leading to a chain of events that has him arriving for his first day at work in a police car—as with *GTO*, an old friend of his is now a cop. He must dodge the attentions of Yuki, a schoolgirl who makes it very clear that he can have anything he wants, and to whom he finds himself playing a surrogate father role—if, indeed, a surrogate father role includes breaking the jaw of her would-be boyfriend. Meanwhile, romance of sorts begins to unfurl in the style of SLOW STEP, as Kintaro gains the adoring attentions of Misuzu, a bar proprietess with a daughter of her own—this is a slight devia-

tion from the plot of the live-action version, where Misuzu was the younger sister of Kintaro's late wife. Under the title *Kintaro*, the live-action series has also been broadcast with English subtitles on Hawaii's KIKU TV channel. There is also a 1999 live-action movie directed by Takashi Miike.

Salaryman Kintaro is a perfectly harmless anime, although its benign exterior hides tensions behind the scenes. This is an anime that really, really wants to be a live-action TV drama. Its setups and action all seem tailor-made for the real world, and there is little attempt to play to the strengths of the animated medium. As with HUMAN CROSSING, its action remains resolutely mundane, leaving the viewer with the nagging sensation that this ought to have stayed live, and its animated status is a reflection of the fact that its star was already on the wane—nobody, not even an anime viewer, likes to feel they are backing a losing horse. However, the possibility remains that the producers knew what they were doing all along, since *Salaryman Kintaro* enjoyed a new lease of life as one of the first TV shows to be made available for paid Internet download in

Japan—the animated format makes for a better transfer and saving on memory for slower computers, while the live-action connection makes it more likely to appeal to viewers outside the limited anime "fan" bracket. In that regard, far from being a lame duck, this anime production may turn out to have been the kind of business decision that a corporate warrior like Kintaro would be proud of.

SAMURAI, THE

1987. Video. DIR: Kazuo Yamazaki. SCR: Takahiro Miki. DES: Takayuki Goto. ANI: Takayuki Goto. MUS: N/C. PRD: Studio Deen. 45 mins.
Takeshi Chimatsuri is a young martial artist whose rare sword is a gift from his father. He won it in a fair fight from the brilliant swordsman Kagemaru Akari, who was killed in the struggle. Now Akari's twin daughters, Toki and Kagedi, have come looking for Takeshi to avenge their father's death and retake the sword. Based on the manga serialized in *Young Jump* by Mitsuhiro Harunichi, this samurai soap opera fast devolves into a love comedy.

SAMURAI CHAMPLOO *

2004. TV series. DIR: Shinichiro Watanabe, Akira Yoshimura, Hiroyuki Imaishi, Kazuki Akane, Kazuyoshi Katayama, Tsukasa Sunaga. SCR: Dai Sato, Seiko Takagi, Shinji Obara. DES: Kazuto Nakazawa, Mahiro Maeda. ANI: Kazuto Nakazawa, Yumiko Ishii, Shinji Takeuchi. MUS: Fat Jon, Force of Nature, Nujabies, Tsutchie. PRD: Fuji TV, Manglobe. 25 mins. x 26 eps.
Two fighters in Edo-period Japan develop an instant dislike for one another, but keep crossing paths nonetheless. Mugen is a hick from the far south, while Jin is a self-styled noble—a literal odd couple with different class backgrounds, or at least, aspirations. All that unites them is their lack of interest in each other, and their indubitable fighting skills, leading to Fuu, a waitress, to hire them to find a missing man— her father. The plot might sound like a thousand other samurai dramas, but

SC's play for originality comes in its unique style, in which the entire drama is framed with modern-day assumptions and music, as if a focus group of 14-year-old mallrats were obliged to recount a Kurosawa movie, and did so in their own distinctive argot.

As with his earlier COWBOY BEBOP, itself a deliberate mix of disparate musical and story genres, director Watanabe combines self-conscious cool with a tale of nobility fallen on hard times. His heroes are rake-thin free lances with hearts of gold, railing against institutions run by fat, pampered old men—the story not only of *SC*, but of conditions in the modern anime industry itself, and of its attitude towards its fellow samurai TV serials.

SC makes a fine virtue out of what could have been a terrible vice. It is, at heart, a crushingly old-fashioned show, with a studied punkishness dating back to the Vietnam-era *Monjiro* (*DE). Nor is its irreverent anime attitude anything new: SAMURAI GOLD was mixing up Edo period stories before *SC*'s target audience was even born. It dresses itself up with scratch editing and self-consciously anachronistic hip hop, perhaps less in the hope of attracting modern youth than in ensuring the censure of their elders—the ultimate test of *cool*, of course, is that your parents hate it. Sadly, its showy use of oh-so-20th-century music will cause it to age faster than it deserves; compare to similar faddery in BUBBLEGUM CRISIS.

However, *SC* also successfully reclaims the samurai drama for modern teens—a bold affirmation that stories about Japan's past do not have to be boring, staid Sunday night NHK epics for Dad. It boasts of its Internet generation's disrespect towards history, with onscreen cards that proclaim no interest in period accuracy, but while it may feign ignorance, it is made by people with a genuine and deep-seated appreciation of samurai lore. It steals ideas and setups from kabuki, TV, film, novels, and comics, uniting them all in an extended glorification of everything that ever made samurai worth pastich-

ing in the first place. It mixes the thuggery of "Beat" Takeshi Kitano's 2003 postmodern *Zatoichi* with the sedate travelogue of MANGA MITO KOMON and all points in between, named after an Okinawan dish that is a mash-up of everything: *champloo*. Like Pink Floyd's *The Wall* (1976), it is a very smart, well-schooled product, which brags to an impressionable audience that it doesn't need an education. It is only in one episode, when a Japanese village takes on brutish American invaders in a symbolic baseball match, that the extent of the anachronisms and stereotypes are more likely to become obvious to a non-Japanese audience.

Its use of comedy is also sneakily subtle. Mugen and Jin might bicker like Tarantino hit men, but their odd-couple pairing is a timeless play-off between high and low culture, not dissimilar to other mismatched buddies like those in SAMURAI DEEPER KYO. Their humor is also often subtly directed at their underclass audience—Fuu is looking for a man who "smells of sunflowers," but Mugen, like most urban viewers, doesn't actually have a clue what a sunflower smells like.

The design work is heavily stylized, a cunning recognition of the fact that mismatched elements of period dramas and B-movies have established a wholly un-Japanese "samurai norm" in foreign countries, distracting us from the fact that the various episodes of this road movie don't really hang together. The show is so stylish, so maniacally energetic, and so involved in its own mythology that it's easy to forgive its lack of substance, but it is an interesting experiment rather than a complete success. In years to come, it may be seen as a bridge that unites old traditions of Japanese TV and film with postmodern pastiches like AFRO SAMURAI. 🅛🅥

SAMURAI DEEPER KYO *

2002. TV series. DIR: Junji Nishimura, Toshiya Shinohara, Masakazu Hashimoto. SCR: Hiroyuki Kawasaki, Masashi Sogo, Rika Nakase, Tetsuo Tanaka.

DES: Manabu Fukuzawa, Michinori Chiba, Tamotsu Shinohara, ANI: Saburo Tanaka, Shinpei Tomo'oka, Noriko Kondo. MUS: N/C. PRD: Starchild Records, Studio Deen, TV Tokyo. 24 mins. x 26 eps.

At the great battle of Sekigahara in 1600, two great warriors fight a battle that ends in mystery. Kyoshiro Mibu and "Demon Eyes" Kyo both disappear when a meteor strikes the battleground. Four years later, in a land plagued by monsters, Kyoshiro is a traveling medicine salesman who has lost his memories of the past. He runs into female bounty hunter Yuya Shiina, on the road seeking her brother's killer, shortly before an attack by a powerful snake monster. Kyoshiro destroys it and Yuya uncovers his secret—Kyoshiro and Kyo now share one body in the style of ULTRAMAN or BASTARD, and Kyoshiro's mild-mannered persona is the host for Kyo's murderous one. Yuya decides to stick with him and turn him in for Kyo's bounty if she can; Kyo wants to find his own body and needs Kyoshiro until then—compare to the similar quest of a disembodied samurai in DORORO. As the "trio" travel through Japan, meeting more people from their pasts, they learn that the evil Nobunaga Oda was resurrected by the Mibu clan for their own ends and is responsible for the monsters plaguing Japan. The only hope for the country lies in the swordsmith Muramasa, Kyoshiro's former mentor, who has fashioned five magical weapons whose wielders stand the only chance of taking down Nobunaga. Kyoshiro finally manages to kill Nobunaga, only to see him resurrected again by his own clan, this time in Kyo's old body. The pair must work together to defeat him by forging the Muramasa swords into one, incredible dimension-warping weapon.

An additional Jekyll-and-Hyde twist is introduced when we discover that the two-in-one are also one-in-two—Kyo really *is* Kyoshiro, or rather his fighting self. When he fell in love with pacifist beauty Sakuya, Kyoshiro tried to divorce his warrior instincts from the rest of his personality and succeeded in creating another self to embody all the samurai battle instincts and fighting code. He has thus been at war with himself for the whole series. Adapted from Akimine Kamijyo's manga in *Shonen Jump*, the story includes references to many other historical and semi-historical characters like Sasuke Sarutobi (see **MAGIC BOY**) and, of course, Japan's arch-bogeyman Nobunaga himself. ⬤Ⓥ

SAMURAI GIANTS

1973. AKA: *The Star Pitcher*. TV series. DIR: Tadao Nagahama, Tetsu Dezaki, Osamu Dezaki, Yoshiyuki Tomino. SCR: Seiji Matsuoka, Tetsu Dezaki, Haruya Yamazaki, Tomohiro Ando, Asako Tani. DES: Hideo Kawauchi. ANI: Yasuo Otsuka. MUS: Shunsuke Kikuchi. PRD: Eiken, TMS, Yomiuri TV (Nippon TV). 25 mins. x 46 eps.

The Giants baseball team is scouting for new talent and finds a high school player who can hit one massive home run after another. But the school star's great physical strength has a balancing weakness—he lacks control and can't pitch to save his life. Worried about this basic problem, he's not sure whether he should join the team or forget baseball and look for another, more conventional career. His girlfriend convinces him that he should join the Giants and work with the team on his weak point. With her encouragement, he's determined to become a star pitcher. Based on yet another baseball manga by **STAR OF THE GIANTS**–creator Ikki Kajiwara, working here with Ko Inoue.

SAMURAI GOLD *

1988. JPN: *Toyamazakura Uchucho Yatsu no Na wa Gold*. AKA: *Cosmic Commander of the Toyama Cherry Trees; The Guy's Name Is Gold*. Video. DIR: Atsutoshi Umezawa. SCR: Akiyoshi Sakai. DES: Hiroyuki Kitazume. ANI: Hiroyuki Kitazume. MUS: Kentaro Haneda. PRD: Toei. 60 mins.

Late in the 21st century, Earth and its colonies are controlled by five Overseers working through EDO, a vast computer system. When Overseer Redklaad Mount is wounded by a would-be assassin, his estranged son, Gold, is dragged from a seedy downtown bar to investigate. On the space colony of Fedovar, Gold discovers that Redklaad is implicated in the death of the local ruler Duke Plenmatz, who died when the liner Ovconia crashed on its maiden voyage. After fighting with Plenmatz's vengeful son, Ion (his girlfriend Midi's brother), Gold goes missing, presumed dead. Posing as Gold, Ion returns to Earth, where he almost succeeds in sentencing Redklaad to death. Gold saves the day by baring his unique cherry-blossom tattoo, thus unmasking Ion's deception. Gold reveals that all the Overseers, not just his father, are guilty of orchestrating the crash of the Ovconia and murdering the shipbuilders who arranged it. Having challenged his rulers, Gold prepares to commit suicide but is stopped by EDO herself, who admits that she ordered the removal of Plenmatz without thinking of the consequences. EDO exonerates the Overseers, who were only following her orders, and sentences herself to deactivation. Gold becomes an Overseer, but still has time to return to his favorite bar, where Midi plays the piano, Ion serves the drinks, and Ion's former henchman, the Gay Blade, waits on tables.

A lighthearted sci-fi romp, distantly inspired by the life of Kinshiro Toyama, a figure who lived from 1793 to 1855. The character was popularized first in the kabuki play *Toyama no Kinsan* (1893), in which he is portrayed as a tattooed playboy who makes good when he becomes a magistrate, fighting corruption in Edo (old-time Tokyo) in the style of **MANGA MITO KOMON**. Dramatized by several novelists, including *SG*'s credited Tatsuro Jinde (who died in 1986) and Kyosuke Yuki, the character is best known in Japan through several live-action TV series (*DE). *SG*, however, is just an excuse for some laser swordplay and mild detective work, rounded off by an overlong courtroom finale. Very 1980s in both good and bad senses—Gold boasts a hideous mullet haircut, and the Gay Blade takes camp beyond the funny into the insulting, but Kitazume's stark pop-art colors and designs still retain a certain freshness. Similar samurai retellings occur in **JUBEI-CHAN THE NINJA GIRL** and **CYBER CITY OEDO 808**, while Toyama was parodied again in **U-JIN BRAND**. Another descendant of the original Toyama would turn up in **DETECTIVE ACADEMY Q**.

SAMURAI GUN *

2004. TV series. DIR: Kazuhiko Kikuchi. SCR: Hideki Sonoda. DES: Kenichi Onuki. ANI: N/C. MUS: Akifumi Tada. PRD: ADV Films, Avex, Inc., Studio Egg. 25 mins. x 12 eps., 25 mins. (v).

A group of renegade samurai use forbidden firearms to fight an oppressive political system in the 1860s, masking up like ninja to take on the Shogun and his corrupt supporters. But you don't stay Shogun for long without a fair degree of low cunning, and the ruler creates his own force to take down the Samurai Guns by recruiting people with nothing to lose from the lowlife of the streets and taverns. Meanwhile, suspicions begin to arise about the true purpose of the Samurai Guns. The series focuses on one small Samurai Gun unit; half-blind half-breed Ichimatsu, Daimon, their liaison to their boss, and female performer Kurenai ("Scarlet"). Hard-drinking, low-living Ichimatsu's tragic past makes him hate violence, but his need to avenge his parents and sister explains why he's joined a group of assassins. He's also in love with a prostitute. All this goes to make up a suitably modern antihero—although readers might be forgiven for thinking this was a higher-tech variant on **RURO NI KENSHIN**. A final episode was released as a "video exclusive."

As with so many other modern anime, from **SAKURA WARS** to **PEACEMAKER KUROGANE**, *SG* wants the best of both worlds—the freedom to do whatever it wants and the solid grounding that comes with historical references. The result, as ever, is a show that hopes its audience will know enough of its background to preempt its omissions, but still be ignorant enough to forgive its mistakes. Playing games with history is a difficult temptation, and simply piling in any interesting artifact makes a historical setting counterproductive. The gun was certainly known in Japan long before the 19th century, but other elements of *SG*'s *mise en scene*, such as the submachine pistols on display, the zippers, and (although this is a churlish complaint considering other anime) even the Hollywood-implant breast sizes of female characters, come far later than the alleged time period in which this is set. The juxtaposition of Western and Eastern fight systems isn't as easy as *Kung Fu* and Terence Young's *Red Sun* made it look, and the fit here is sometimes awkward—as is the show's use of technology. The producers offer the spurious explanation that these are just "advances" on already existing technology that could theoretically have been carried this far by a secret organization with means and motivation. Based on a manga by Kazuhiko Kumagai in *Young Jump* magazine, and one of several productions in the early 21st century funded with a large injection of American money; ADV Films presumably hoping to find something that pleased audiences in both East and West. **L N V**

SAMURAI PIZZA CATS *

1990. JPN: *Kyatto Ninden Teyande.* AKA: *Stealth Tales of the Kool Kat Gang.* TV series. DIR: Kunitoshi Okajima, Takeshi Serizawa, Shinji Sakai, Katsumi Kosuga. SCR: Satoru Akahori, Mayori Sekijima, Yumi Kageyama, Hiroyuki Kawasaki. DES: Noritaka Suzuki, Mayori Sekijima. ANI: Noritaka Suzuki, Yoshio Kabashima. MUS: Kenji Kawai (Shuki Levy, Haim Saban in Western version). PRD: Tatsunoko, TV Tokyo. 25 mins. x 54 eps. (TV).

In the high-tech streets of Edolopolis (Little Tokyo), a fox (a rat in the English-language version) who has found his perfect role in life, cross-

Samurai Gun

©KAZUHIRO KUMAGAI ? SHUEISHA / AVEX / ADV FILMS

dressing politician Ko'on-no-Kami (Big Cheese), and his avian sidekicks, Kara-maru and Gennari-sai (Bad Bird and Jerry Atrick), plot against Shogun Iei-Iei Tokugawa (Emperor Fred) and his ditzy, romance-obsessed rabbit daughter, Usa-hime (Princess Vi). To save the city from their evil plans, loyal dog retainer Wanko-no-kami (Big Al Dentei) calls for help from the Ninja Team Nyanki (Samurai Pizza Cats), who moonlight as superheroes while making and delivering the best pizza in town. Yattaro (Speedy Cerviche) is the leader of the team and fights with the unbeatable Magical Ginzu Sword. Sukoshii (Guido Anchovy), his smooth-talking comrade in arms and rival for the love of the beautiful Miss Omitsu (Lucille), fights with the Samurai Sunspot Umbrella. Pururun (Polly Esther), the hotheaded sex-kitten of the trio, uses the Cat's Paw Attraction technique, raising her paw like the "beckoning cat" statues in Japanese shops, while electromagnetic waves (represented by streams of fluttering hearts) pull her victims to her. She also throws heart-shaped *shuriken*. In a sly reference to the live-action show *Cyber Ninja*, for most of their missions, the

Pizza Cats are launched from a giant revolver on the roof of the Pizza Parlor by their loyal (and frequently sarcastic) assistant, Otama (Francine). When they need extra clout they can use their own magnificent armored vehicle, Nyago-sphinx (Golden Sphinx); it can even transform into a giant robot, Nyago-king (The Great Catatonic).

With pizza-loving martial artists inspired by the *Teenage Mutant Ninja Turtles*, early writing credits for Satoru "Mr. Zany" Akahori, and even music from **GHOST IN THE SHELL**'s Kenji Kawai in the original version, *SPC* is an anime classic. Many shows are ruined in translation, but *SPC* simply shrugged off the change of language and stayed insanely itself—in one memorable scene in the English version, the characters panic *because* they have been sent a note in Japanese. Brought to the West by Saban soon after its release, *SPC* was perhaps one of the last "translations" in the old 1970s *let's-just-make-it-up* style (see **ROBOTECH**). The improvised nature of the English-language version is, by definition, a very bad translation, but, luckily, one that succeeds in retaining the madcap spirit of the original. Saban International, execrated in many quarters for its editing jobs on Asian material, brought together a team that not only understood what the show needed but actually seems to have enjoyed itself—an object lesson for the bored crews of many English anime dubs with grander pretensions. Edited episodes of the TV series were released on video in the U.S. as *SPC The Movie* (1991). The series made it into U.S. syndication in 1996; it had already been screened in Canada and Britain with some success and remains a fan favorite. Subsequent French, Spanish, and German editions were based on the English version, which means that a true translation of *SPC* has yet to be attempted in any Western language.

SAMURAI 7 *

2004. JPN: *Shichinin no Samurai*. AKA: *Seven Samurai; Akira Kurosawa's Samurai 7*. TV series. DIR: Toshifumi Takizawa, Hiroyuki Okuno. SCR: Atsuhiro Tomioka. DES: Hideki Hashimoto, Takuhito Kusanagi, Makoto Kobayashi. ANI: Hiroyuki Okuno, Katsuhisa Oono. MUS: Eitetsu Hayashi, Kaoru Wada. PRD: Gonzo, Sony Pictures Entertainment, Animax. 25 mins. x 26 eps.

Akira Kurosawa's classic 1954 movie gets the modern treatment with the question "What if *Seven Samurai* had been made in color as a science fantasy show with cooler, younger heroes?" This is, of course, a pointless query, and it's a tribute to the skills of the team rather than the money thrown at this version, allegedly made in "high definition" at double cost of a normal anime series, that the answer is not as awful as one might expect. We start with the basic Kurosawa story—seven penniless fighters are recruited by a group of yokels desperate to stop bandits from stealing their rice crop again. The pay is just their food, but they are all so far down on their luck (for a variety of reasons) that they accept. The story has been moved from the Edo period into a steampunk-pastiche future, in the aftermath of a great war

in which the samurai lost their status and influence all over again.

Our heroes have been updated along with their world. The Toshiro Mifune character, Kikuchiyo, is now a tin man with an exhaust pipe on his head so he can let off steam, played for light relief rather than pathos. Seiji Miyaguchi's stoic samurai Kyuzo, who valued honor and sword skill above everything, has become an assassin for a crime boss. The leader of the gang, shaven-headed, dignified Kanbei, now has a mane of flowing hair. The villains too have been updated—the Nobushi bandit gang are augmented humans with metal body modifications, living weapons capable of flight. In order to keep the link to the rice crop and the land as the essential story element, the remake postulates that these cyborg warriors can only be powered by eating rice, which is a fairly silly proposition in a starfaring society. The design is gorgeous, although it is sometimes betrayed by a poor interface between 2D and 3D animation—which, given the amount reputed to have been spent, and the number of shows that have handled this well, is inexcusable. So, too, is the noticeable drop in animation quality partway through; flashy openers that tail off into substandard animation are commonplace in modern anime, but most of the other offenders do not tempt fate by bragging about their high budgets.

As with **SAMURAI CHAMPLOO**, the show contains many references to other tales of Japan's past—there is even a nod to Goemon Ishikawa from **LUPIN III**, in a sequence where Kanbei leaps from a space cruiser and slices a destroyer in half in mid-air. But where Kurosawa's original depicted real people struggling with life-and-death problems at a time when the nation was in turmoil, *S7* is trying to be cool enough to catch the stunted attention spans of a generation for which poverty, danger, and personal responsibility are concepts more alien than tinplate warriors with exhaust pipes on their heads. **LNV**

SAMURAI SHODOWN: THE MOTION PICTURE *

1993. JPN: *Samurai Spirits*. TV special, video. DIR: Hiroshi Ishiodori, Kazuhiro Sasaki. SCR: Nobuaki Kishima, Masamuro Takimoto. DES: Kazunori Iwakura, Aoi Nanase. ANI: Kazunori Iwakura. MUS: Osamu Tezuka (the other one). PRD: SNK, Asia-do. 80 mins. (TVm), 30 mins. x 2 eps. (v).

One hundred years after their deaths at the hands of a former colleague, six legendary holy warriors are reborn to seek justice against the teammate who betrayed them into the hands of an evil god. Charlotte, Wan Fu, Nakoruru, Galford, and Tam Tam search the feudal province of Edo questing for their lost comrade, Haohmaru, and their sworn nemesis, Shiro Amakusa (see **NINJA RESURRECTION**). Will the followers of the divine light triumph over the forces of the dark, or is the course of history destined to repeat itself? Yes to both, as our heroes fight and fight again. Based on a video game by SNK for the Neo Geo, this video series edited into a "movie" was widely considered a disappointment by game fans. Instead of blood, characters leak a milky white liquid, and the violence levels have been watered down to match. American fans suffered even worse—the androgynous lead villain was rewritten as a woman for the U.S. release.

In the video sequel *SS: Defeat of Ashura* (1999), spiky-haired Haohmaru is back with Rimururu, Nakoruru, and Galford and they're faced with a problem. Shiki, an old enemy of theirs, shows up badly hurt. Nakoruru wants to take her in, but Galford and Rimururu have other plans. They believe she should be destroyed because she's working for an agent of corruption that could destroy them all. Haomaru takes up his sword once again, to save Shiki's life and destroy the dark influence.

After the character of Nakoruru starred in a PC text adventure game, plans were announced to adapt it into a 13-part TV series. However, this project eventually transformed into a video "series," only the first chapter of which was ever released, as the 28-minute *Nakoruru* (2002).

SAMURAI: SPIRIT OF THE SWORD *
1999. JPN: *Kaito Ranma*. AKA: *Swift-Blade Ranma ½*. Video. DIR: Masahiro Sekino. SCR: Mitsuhiro Yamada. DES: Hidekazu Shimamura. ANI: Hidekazu Shimamura. MUS: N/C. PRD: AIC, Animate Film. 30 mins. x 2 eps.
Edo-era swashbuckling with a touch of romance, based on a PC and PlayStation game. **V**

SAMURAI XXX *
2004. JPN: *Yoka no Ken*. AKA: *Blade of Fragrant Phantoms*. Video DIR: Naomi Hayakawa, Haruo Furuki. SCR: Rokurota Makabe. DES: Naomi Hayakawa. ANI: Fun Lee, Ganchan, Haru, Kero, MANE, Nagapon, Yasha. MUS: Yui Takase. PRD: Green Bunny, Kunoichi Partners, Hyper Space. 30 mins. x 2 eps.
Matagoro is a samurai who has no skills with any weapon except the one between his legs. So he's sent on a mission to find a treasure map hidden on the backs of several female ninja. It will only show when they climax, which rather restricts the range of positions possible, though not as much as this kind of lame setup restricts the story. A premise that was pretty weak in THOSE WHO HUNT ELVES has to support the usual grind of sex scenes strung around a disposable plot. Matagoro is also searching for his long-lost sister, who was (a) kidnapped by ninja as a child, and (b) isn't really his sister, thereby ensuring that not-quite-incest is in the cards before the show is over. Based on an "original story" by Naomi Hayakawa, who also brought us BEAST CITY. Not to be confused with *Samurai X,* for which see RURO NI KENSHIN. **LNV**

SAMURAIDER
1991. Video. DIR: Hideaki Oba. SCR: Masaru Yamamoto. DES: Moriyasu Taniguchi. ANI: Moriyasu Taniguchi MUS: Mitsuo Takahama. PRD: Studio TV. 50 mins.

In a weak combination of samurai movie and BOMBER BIKERS OF SHONAN, Tokyo street-punk Masao buys a treasured FZR "katana" motorcycle and becomes a knight of the road, attacking criminals with a genuine *katana* sword. Based on the manga by Shinichi Sugimura in *Young Magazine.*

SANADA'S 10 BRAVE WARRIORS
2005. JPN: *Shinshaku Sengoku Eiyu Densetsu Sanada Ju Yushi The Animation*. AKA: *New Civil War Hero Legend of Sanada's Ten Samurai The Animation; Sanada's Samurai; Sanada 10*. TV series, TV special. DIR: Keizo Shimizu. SCR: Shimao Kawanaka. DES: Keizo Shimizu. ANI: Satoshi Anakura. MUS: N/C. PRD: T.P.O., Group TAC, G&G Direction, Magic Bus, WOWOW. 25 mins. x 12 eps. (TV) 60 mins. (special).
Warlord Yukimura Sanada hires a band of brave fighters to help him in the struggle against Ieyasu Tokugawa (see YOUNG TOKUGAWA IEYASU). Their number includes the legendary Sasuke Sarutobi (see MAGIC BOY), the white-skinned foreigner Saizo Kirigakure, and deadly beauty Kiyomi Miyoshi. Although Sanada himself existed as a great warlord, his ten legendary warriors are just that—legendary, and best known to the Japanese TV audience through the 1975 puppet series *Ten Brave Warriors of Sanada* (*DE). As with the earlier HAKKENDEN, this anime remake capitalizes on the crew's fond childhood memories of the puppet show, and hopes to recreate the historical fiction that brings them into conflict with Ieyasu Tokugawa and then allies them with the followers of defeated warlord Toyotomi for a display of heroism in defeat. The TV special was an hour-long prequel.

SANCTUARY *
1996. Video. DIR: Takashi Watanabe. SCR: Kenishi Terada. DES: Hidemi Kuma, Hiroshi Kato. ANI: Hidemi Kuma. MUS: N/C. PRD: OB Planning, Toho. 70 mins.
Two Japanese survivors of the Khmer Rouge massacres in Cambodia vow to find a sanctuary even if they have

to build it themselves. Returning to Japan, they take seemingly opposite paths—one becomes a politician, the other a gangster. As Asami and Hojo work their way through the linked worlds of politics and crime in modern Japan, they don't hesitate to do anything necessary to secure their own positions and stay true to their vow. Loyal to no one else, they find their friendship increasingly tested as they rise in their chosen fields. A prequel to the 1990 *Big Comic* manga by Sho Fumimura and CRYING FREEMAN–creator Ryoichi Ikegami, the style is glossy and international, the protagonists two sharp-suited young sharks navigating the murky seas of the 1990s without a scruple. It was also made as a live-action film. **NV**

SANPEI THE FISHERMAN
1980. JPN: *Tsurikichi Sanpei*. TV series. DIR: Eiji Okabe, Yoshimichi Nitta, Tameo Ogawa, Kiyoshi Harada, Yasuhiro Yamaguchi, Kazuyoshi Yokota, Fumio Kurokawa, Katsuhiko Yamazaki, Shigeo Koshi, Yasuhiro Imagawa. SCR: Michiru Umadori, Tajio Tamura, Sukehiro Tomita. DES: Takao Yaguchi. ANI: Kazuyuki Okaseko, Takashi Saijo, Hidehito Kojima. MUS: Tatsuaki Sone, Hideyuki Yamamoto. PRD: Nippon Animation, Fuji TV. 25 mins. x 109 eps.
Having grown up in a distant mountain village in northeastern Japan, Sanpei Nihira is a gifted teenage fisherman, and this long-running series is the story of his struggle to catch as many fish as possible, all over Japan and even overseas. The bigger and meaner, the better he likes it, as he invents new techniques and exploits old ones learned from seasoned anglers to their limits in pursuit of more and more powerful fishy opponents. Based on Takao Yaguchi's 1973 manga that ran in both the weekly and monthly editions of *Shonen Magazine*—among the few attempts to present fishing as a combat sport (also see GRANDAR).

SANPEI THE KAPPA
1992. JPN: *Kappa no Sanpei*. Movie.

DIR: Toshio Hirata. SCR: Shunichi Yukimuro. DES: Shigeru Mizuki. ANI: Tatsuo Kitahara. MUS: Kazuki Kuriyama. PRD: Nikkatsu. 90 mins.

Japanese boy Sanpei befriends a *kappa* water-sprite and is soon accepted into a world of spiritual fun that lurks beneath the surface of modern Japan (see POMPOKO). This movie was based on the 1962 manga by SPOOKY KITARO–creator Shigeru Mizuki and selected by the Japanese Ministry of Education as a worthy title.

SANSHIRO SUGATA

1981. JPN: *Sugata Sanshiro*. AKA: *Judo Story*. TV special. DIR: Kyomi Mikamoto. SCR: Fumio Shinbo, Kiyohide Ohara. DES: Monkey Punch. ANI: Kazuhide Yoshinaga. MUS: Talisman, Susumu Akitagawa. PRD: Tokyo Movie Shinsha, Fuji TV. 84 mins.

In the Tokyo of 1882, Sanshiro is a promising young martial artist who seeks a worthy teacher. He proves his ability by defeating 39 masters of jujitsu (who ridicule his choosing judo) and is taken in by their teacher, who continually tests him. He falls for local girl Sayo Murai and must fight her father at judo before defeating his greatest rival on the plain of Ukyogahara. Based on a novel by Tsuneo Tomita, best known in the West through its 1943 movie adaptation by a young Akira Kurosawa—though Kurosawa's version lacks the anime's comic-relief cat. The story, also included in ANIMATED CLASSICS OF JAPANESE LITERATURE, was an inspiration for the toy combat serial PLAWRES SANSHIRO, which supposedly starred the grandson of the original. Kurosawa's 1945 sequel was pastiched in later episodes of IRONFIST CHINMI, when Chinmi fights a foreign sailor. For more judo fun, see YAWARA.

SASAGAWA, HIROSHI

1936– . Sometimes miscredited as Hiroshi Sasakawa. Born in Fukushima Prefecture he graduated from middle school and went to Tokyo, where he found work as an art assistant to Osamu Tezuka in 1956. His manga

works included the original basis for GAZULA THE AMICABLE MONSTER, but in 1964 he left manga behind when he joined Tatsunoko Production, for which he animated SPACE ACE and parts of the TIME BOKAN series. He also wrote several science fiction novels.

SASUGA NO SARUTOBI

1982. AKA: *Idiot Ninja*. TV series. DIR: Koichi Sasaki, Masahisa Ishida. SCR: Takeshi Shudo, Masaki Tsuji, Tomoko Komparu, Shigeru Yanagawa. DES: Hiroshi Kanezawa, Jiro Kono. ANI: Hiroshi Kanezawa, Mutsumi Inomata, Masayuki, Shinichi Suzuki, Moriyasu Taniguchi. MUS: Joe Hisaishi. PRD: NAS, Tsuchida Pro, Fuji TV. 25 mins. x 69 eps.

Sarutobi is the best pupil in his ninja school, but to look at him you'd never know it—he's as round as a butterball, and his superb fighting abilities are masked under a dozy demeanor. Both Mako, the prettiest girl in the school, and local bad-girl Mika see through his appearance to the hero underneath. Rivalry with the neighboring Spiner martial arts school is intense, but Sarutobi and his chums always come out on top. This cheerful comedy was based on Fujihiko Hosono's manga for Shogakukan, itself inspired by the earlier SASUKE and MAGIC BOY.

SASUKE

1968. JPN: *Sasuke*. TV series. DIR: Kiyoshi Onishi, Takeshi Kawanai. SCR: Junzo Tashiro. DES: Sanpei Shirato. ANI: Toyoo Ashida. MUS: Masashi Tanaka. PRD: TCJ, TBS. 25 mins. x 29 eps. (TV1), 25 mins. x 24 eps. (*MSS*).

Sasuke's father sends him away to learn ninja techniques to defend the oppressed of feudal Japan from their overlords, the Tokugawa shogunate. Although just a little boy, he must fight the best warriors, armed to the teeth with swords, *shuriken*, nunchaku, and other deadly weapons. Based on the 1961 manga by Sanpei Shirato, which in its turn was inspired by a novel by Kazuo Den, the story of Sasuke was remade by Eiji Okabe for a much

younger audience as *Manga Sarutobi Sasuke* (1979), a 24-episode series on Tokyo Channel 12, concentrating on Sasuke's feud with the rival ninja of the Iga clan. *Manga Sasuke Sarutobi* appears to have been released in an English compilation "movie" dub by Jim Terry Productions under the title NINJA THE WONDERBOY, despite bearing no relation to the other show released in America under that title.

SATISFACTION, THE

1984. Video. DIR: N/C. SCR: N/C. DES: N/C. ANI: N/C. MUS: N/C. PRD: Zeros, Midnight 25, Sai Enterprise. 21 mins.

A campus beauty is admired by her fellow students, but her practiced air of coolness is actually a façade to hide her strong sex drive. She fantasizes about a series of sexual incidents, including a scene featuring a blue-furred demon seemingly inspired by DEVILMAN, who not only has a revolving phallus, but possibly the first appearance of tentacles in Japanese animated erotica. Subsequently, she is raped and degraded for real. **NV**

SATO, GEN

?– . Born in Tokyo, he found part-time work at Toei Animation while still a student, but immediately after graduation he found work as a computer programmer outside the animation industry. He did not stay away from animation for long, and was lured back in by freelance work and then as a staffer at Ashi Production. After moving to Sunrise, he was assigned to work for Yoshikazu Yasuhiko. His design work and key animation have appeared in installments of the GUNDAM series, TOMORROW'S JOE, and CRUSHER JOE, among others.

SATO, JUNICHI

1960– . Born in Aichi Prefecture, he studied film at the Fine Arts department of Nippon University, but dropped out to join Toei Animation in 1981. His animation debut was on the series TENMARU THE LITTLE TENGU (1983), but he is perhaps best known for his directorial work on **Sailor Moon**. Sometimes works under the pseudonyms Hajime Tendo or Kiichi Hadame. He is also the creator of more recent shows, such as **Kaleido Star** and **Pretear**.

SATO, YOSHIHARU

1958– . Born in Kanagawa Prefecture, he worked as a sketch artist on **Anne of Green Gables** and other children's anime, rising to key animator on **Treasures of the Snow** and **Katri the Milkmaid**. He was also a character designer on **Pollyanna**.

SATO, YUZO

1960– . Born in Hiroshima Prefecture, he dropped out of Tokyo Design College to work for Sanrio on **Sea Prince and the Fire Child**. Subsequently going freelance, his directorial debut was **Bio Hunter**, and he has also worked as a sketch artist on **Confucius**, among others.

SAVE ME, GUARDIAN SHAOLIN

1998. JPN: Mamotte Shugogetten. AKA: Protect Me Shugogetten, Guardian Angel ShugoGetten. TV series, video. DIR: Tatsuo Misawa, Satoshi Yamada, Keiji Hayakawa, Tetsuya Watanabe. SCR: Kenichi Yamada, Yasutoshi Yamada. DES: Ken Ueno. ANI: Masayuki Takagi, Hideyuki Motohashi. MUS: N/C. PRD: Toei, TV Asahi. 25 mins. x 22 eps. (TV), 30 mins. x 5 eps. (v).
Teenager Tasuke Shichiri is home alone while his parents travel China. His father sends occasional presents; the first is a ring with a note—if someone of pure heart peers into it, a guardian from heaven will appear to protect them. No surprise that the heavenly body is a gorgeous teenage girl called Shaolin, whose sole destiny is to protect the "master" who releases her from 4,000 years of imprisonment. However, her naïveté about the modern world causes Tasuke more trouble (in the style of **Doraemon**). Still, she has access to powerful spirits called Star Gods, who can use their special skills to help her. Father's second

package contains a rod found in the same place as the ring, containing another spirit, also a gorgeous teenage girl whose sole destiny is to please her "master." Lu-An, confined for 1,652 years, can bring inanimate objects to life. By another strange coincidence, she and Shaolin are sworn rivals, often getting into fights over Tasuke. To complicate matters even further, several of Tasuke's friends fall for the girls and do all in their power to entice the goddesses away, while a younger girl at Tasuke's school has a huge crush on him and is constantly trying to get rid of his supernaturally stacked slaves.

Based on the manga written by Sakurano Minene for *Shonen GanGan*, the similarity to **Oh My Goddess!** reaches actionable proportions when a third goddess, Huang-Long, shows up to give Tasuke challenges (presumably to strengthen his character, which is normally the scriptwriter's job). Amazing—an average Japanese boy waits all through junior high school for a goddess to worship him, and then three show up at once! A video series, *New Legend: SMGS* (2000), further augmented by five CD dramas and a weekly radio show hosted by the characters, make up the grandly titled *Shugogetten Millennium Project*.

SAZAE-SAN

1969. TV series. DIR: Kazuo Kobayashi, Satoshi Murayama, Takeshi Yamamoto, Yonehiko Watanabe. SCR: Masaki Tsuji, Noboru Shiroyama, Shunichi Yukimuro. DES: Toshiyuki Osumi. ANI: N/C. MUS: Nobuyoshi Koshibe. PRD: Fuji TV. 25 mins. x 1600+ eps.
Sazae Isono, her husband, Masato, their two children, and her mother live together in a small house in a quiet suburb of Tokyo. Each episode is simply a snippet of their daily life, running the gamut of putting up with noisy neighbors, sharing a public phone, or being polite to unwanted visitors.

Based on a 1946 manga serialized in the *Asahi Shinbun* newspaper until 1974, *Sazae-san* was the most successful work by **Nasty Old Lady**–creator

Machiko Hasegawa. Still running 37 years later, the program has outlived both its manga incarnation and its creator, who died in 1992. Appealing to a vast mainstream audience who do not otherwise watch animation, it remains the highest-rated anime on Japanese television, consistently maintaining an audience share around 25% (**Pokémon** can barely manage 14%, while major hits like **Chibi Maruko-chan** and **Conan the Boy Detective** hover around the 13% mark). *Sazae-san* is thus the most popular anime in Japan and makes a mockery of *The Simpsons'* claim to be the longest-running TV cartoon series in the world as it enters its fifth decade of continuous, quiet, small-screen triumph. Compare to the similar tone of **My Neighbors the Yamadas**.

The story also exists in a live-action version starring Chiemi Eri, which ran on TBS from 1965 to 1967 (*DE), while the creation of the story and the life of Hasegawa became the subject of an NHK series in 1979. Modern-day episodes of *Sazae-san* end with the character appearing on screen and playing a *janken* (scissors-paper-stone) match with the viewer. This extra replaces the previous closing sequence, which ran from 1969 to 1991, in which *Sazae-san* would throw a peanut up in the air and catch it in her mouth. The peanut trick was swiftly taken off air in 1991 after a child choked to death while trying to imitate this feat.

SCARLET DEMON

1989. JPN: *Shuri Iro no Yoma*. Video. DIR: Wayu Suzumiya. SCR: Wayu Suzumiya. DES: Wayu Suzumiya, Atsushi Matoba. ANI: Atsushi Matoba. MUS: Kaoru Wada. PRD: Mushi. 20 mins. x 4 eps.
A "video comic" based on Wayu Suzumiya's manga about twin boys born to mixed human and dragon-god parentage. Passing their happy teens at a normal Japanese school, they are forced to defend their classmates from demonic attackers—a task made easier by their magical blood. Compare to **Legend of the Four Kings**.

SCARLET SANSHIRO

1969. JPN: *Kurenai Sanshiro.* AKA: *Judo Boy.* TV series. DIR: Jinzo Toriumi, Ippei Kuri, Hiroshi Sasagawa. SCR: Jinzo Toriumi. DES: Eiji Tanaka, Mitsuki Nakamura. ANI: Eiji Tanaka. MUS: Nobuyoshi Koshibe. PRD: Tatsunoko, Fuji TV. 25 mins. x 26 eps.

Saburo's father is a martial artist who dies in a fight with a mysterious one-eyed man outside the city gates. The boy sets out in search of his father's killer with only one clue: the killer left his glass eye at the scene of the crime. He meets, and fights, a lot of one-eyed people before he finally reaches the end of his quest, accompanied by his blood-red motorcycle, his mischievous junior pal Ken, and his faithful canine companion, Stupid. A run-of-the-mill adventure series of combat against mutants and mummies, characterized by some innovative filming techniques from Tatsunoko, including limited rotoscoping, strobe effects, and clever lighting.

SCHOOL FOR THIEVES

1998. JPN: *Dorobo Gakko.* Video. DIR: Katsumi Hashimoto. SCR: Naoyuki Sakai. DES: Satoshi Hako. ANI: Katsumi Hashimoto, Kenzo Koizumi. MUS: Kenichi Kamio. PRD: Toei. 20 mins.
Based on a best-selling children's book by Satoshi Hako, this short features the self-explanatory goings-on at an educational institute with a difference. Also released as a double cassette with the same crew's 20-minute *Mr. Crow the Baker* (*Karasu no Panya-san*), another Hako story.

SCHOOL GIRL: SPECIAL LESSON *

2000?. JPN: *Heisei Jogakuen.* AKA: *Modern Girls School.* Video. DIR: N/C. SCR: N/C. DES: N/C. ANI: N/C. MUS: N/C. PRD: Obtain. 20 mins.
When Nakamura falls behind in class, she is summoned to school on a Sunday for some extra tutoring. It should come as no surprise to anyone who has seen DESPERATE CARNAL HOUSEWIVES that her teachers have only come in on the weekend because they have a secret plan to abuse and molest her in the name of education. A day of cruel "punishments" and lessons duly follows—or does it? A final twist questions whether Nakamura really didn't enjoy herself, and perhaps whether it happened at all. Possibly related to the *Heisei Jogakuin* series of live-action cheesecake DVDs—if it isn't, then the title is deliberately intended to imply that it is. **LNV**

SCHOOL OF BONDAGE *

2004. JPN: *Inbaku Gakuen.* AKA: *School of Masochists.* Video DIR: Takefumi Goda. SCR: Miki Kano. DES: Yoshiten. ANI: Haraki. MUS: N/C. PRD: Studio Jam, Concept Films, Milky. 30 mins. x 3 eps. (v), 80 mins. (Best Of).
Keisuke Shimizu has many problems at home, and as a result becomes a delinquent who treats women as sexual objects. But this is Japanese porn, so instead of youth custody or a sharp slap on the face from the nearest girl, he gets a visit from his class representative, the lovely Orie, who promises to be his sex slave for three months in an attempt to change his views about the power of true love. Stupidity of that order is fortunately rare in real life; the only possible category for this is fantasy. A "fourth" episode in the series is actually a "Best Of" compilation, the 80-minute movie edit released in America by a different company under the title *School of Masochists.* Based on a story in *Core* magazine by Nariaki Funabori. **LN**

SCHOOL OF DARKNESS *

1995. JPN: *Inju Onna Kyoshi.* AKA: *Lust Beast Woman Teacher.* Video. DIR: N/C. SCR: N/C. DES: N/C. ANI: N/C. MUS: N/C. PRD: Pink Pineapple. 40 mins. x 3 eps.
When her boyfriend Taki becomes increasingly abusive toward her, school teacher Yoko is driven from him to seek lesbian comfort in the arms of her friend Ayano, who kindly offers to help her out by reading spells from a forbidden scroll shaped like a penis and supposedly made of demon skin. The mind boggles as to how anyone expects this to work out well—the scroll soon burrows inside her in the style of DEMON BEAST INVASION, turning her into a succubus intent on draining men of their life force. As in CAMBRIAN, BIBLE BLACK, and any number of other erotic anime you care to mention, an ancient evil has awoken, and now wishes to travel into our dimension to rape and abuse young girls. Considering how much of it goes on in other anime, the ancient evil will have to join the queue.

Episodes two and three take a slightly different tack and are only tenuously related, packing a number of schoolfriends off to the countryside with their teacher Miss Mizuno and her suspicious-looking fiancé. Countryside high jinks duly ensue, with the girls running into the woods for some furtive fumblings, before a storm disrupts the campsite and forces them to seek refuge in dark, forbidding woods.

With achingly predictable B-movie logic, the girls decide that the wisest move would be to split up. Instead of looking for help as agreed, two of them strip off at the first opportunity to go skinny-dipping. Meanwhile, their classmate Kyoko uses the separation of the group as a chance to seduce Miss Mizuno's fiancé, while men who have been overcome by the forces of lustful evil pursue other classmates around the woods. This is, as it turns out, because of the presence of a laughably Freudian giant vagina creature, lurking underground and hoping to lure the cast into damnation. The authors only wish that there were a transcript of the pitch meeting for that one. Not to be confused with ANGEL OF DARKNESS, or any of the myriads of other tits-and-tentacles titles out there. **LNV**

SCHOOL RUMBLE

2004. TV series, video. DIR: Shinji Takamatsu. SCR: Tomoko Konparu, Miho Maruo, Natsuko Takahashi, Yuki Enatsu, Reiko Yoshida. DES: Hajime Watanabe. ANI: Katsuaki Kamata. MUS: Toshiyuki Omori. PRD: Marvelous Entertainment, Media Factory, Sotsu Agency, Starchild, Studio Comet, TV

Tokyo. 23 mins. x 26 eps. (TV) 23 mins. x 2eps (v).

Tenma Tsukamoto gets into the same class as the boy she's crazy about, only to hear that Oji Karasuma will transfer to another school next year. Desperate to get her man before the year is up, she tries everything to win his love, from shooting an arrow with a love letter attached straight at him to disguising herself as a nurse; she even ropes in her sister and her friends to help out. Meanwhile class troublemaker Kenji Harima has his eye on her, but she's no more interested in him that Oji is in her. Based on the manga in *Shonen Magazine* by Jin Kobayashi, and followed in 2005 by a two-part video sequel comprising a series of "outtakes" and bonus scenes that fill in gaps and add extra spin to situations already seen in the TV series.

SCHOOL SPIRITS

1995. JPN: *Gakko no Yurei.* AKA: *Spirits/ Ghosts of the School.* Movie. DIR: Norio Kabeshima. SCR: Masatoshi Kimura, Shigenori Kurii. DES: Shigenori Kurii. ANI: Shigenori Kurii. MUS: N/C. PRD: Toei. 45 mins. x 6 eps.

Another entry in the spooky-school genre typified by HERE COMES HANAKO, this anime is presented as short vignettes split roughly 50/50 between animation and live action. Based originally on chilling tales written for *My Birthday* magazine, it was disgracefully repackaged after the rental release as ten 15-minute tapes for retail. See also REAL SCHOOL GHOST STORIES.

SCIENCE FICTION AND ROBOTS

SF is anime's youngest genre, commencing only with ASTRO BOY (1963), a future fable deliberately planned by Osamu Tezuka in opposition to the fantasies and fairy tales that otherwise dominated the medium. Tezuka's clean, spartan world also allowed for an extreme economy of animation, helping him to save money in the studio. Anime has favored science fiction ever since, not the least because more mundane genres can be less expensively reproduced with live-action, whereas the ability to integrate special effects so readily makes anime a better choice for greater, cheaper spectacle.

The success of *Astro Boy* ushered in dozens of imitators, seemingly caught up in Japan's defeat "by aliens" and its subsequent reconstruction. Like *Superman*, the heroes of PRINCE PLANET (1965) and SPACE ACE (1965) are new arrivals on Earth, with quasi-magical powers or devices that can help their newfound allies. Like GIGANTOR (1963) and BIG X (1964), the Japanese emerge from World War II as the inheritors of a shameful history that may return to haunt them, but with great hope in industry and technology.

Whereas Astro Boy began as little more than a high-tech *Pinocchio* with superpowers, he was also the ultimate playmate for the average Japanese boy. Love of robots reflected a faith in the future that was not always justified, most famously in DORAEMON (1970), in which a time-traveling rescue mission goes periodically awry, courtesy of inadequate materials.

Go Nagai's MAZINGER Z (1972) presented robots not as radio-controlled toys or android companions, but as pilotable machines. Nagai's GETTER ROBO also featured a regular transformation sequence, in which separate modules would combine to form a super-robot—not only permitting the recycling of footage of the transformation sequence, but also encouraging the sales of not one, but three tie-in toys. The show was soon followed by a number of sequels, as well as anime based on Go Nagai's other manga in the same vein.

The broadcast of Gerry Anderson's *Thunderbirds* and *Captain Scarlet* in Japan ensured that by the 1970s, team shows fighting alien menaces were commonplace in live-action TV, combining the ensemble cast with the talents of miniature- and model-makers. In anime such as SKYERS 5 (1967), this led to color-coded teams of youths, often a cookie-cutter composition of leader, maverick, token girl, token child/comic relief, and "the other one." As with the live-action shows postdating *Goranger* (*DE; 1975) such shows were also likely to be unified around an arbitrary theme—cards, dinosaurs, or, in the case of BATTLE OF THE PLANETS, birds who were also ninja. The underlying themes of disparate entities combining into a transcendent whole was seen not only as a wonderful metaphor for teamwork, but also as an excellent excuse to sell multipart vehicle sets requiring all other elements to create one super-toy.

Star Trek (broadcast in Japan as *Great Battle in Space: Star Trek*) helped encourage a similar galactic quest in Japan, in the form of Leiji Matsumoto's (or, depending on which judge you obey, "Yoshinobu Nishizaki's") *Space Cruiser Yamato* (1974), which made it to America as STAR BLAZERS. However, it would not do so until much later, in 1979, after the worldwide success of *Star Wars* (1977). Science fiction was the new fad, resulting in adaptations of classic American SF such as LENSMAN (1984) and CAPTAIN FUTURE (1978). Local competition came in the form of CAPTAIN HARLOCK (1984), but also most notably in GUNDAM (1979), a franchise still running to this day. Featuring angst-ridden combatants in giant robots, *Gundam* codified the concept of the "newtype." The baby boom generation, known as the "new breed" in Japan, was thus allegorized as a literal evolutionary leap, humans with psychic powers, radically different in abilities and expectations from the generation that preceded them. "Newtype" achieved a currency equivalent to that of *slan* in early American SF fandom, or *otaku* in modern anime—it remains the name of the world's best-selling anime magazine.

Gundam's only real rival was MACROSS (1982), which kept with the pilotable robots (although these could transform into space fighter-planes), and introduced the concept of defeating an enemy by singing at them. The concept offered considerable potential for new merchandise formats—spin-off albums. **Votoms** (1983) also offered an angle on "real robots," introducing the notion of a robot as merely a tool in a military arsenal, alongside more traditional technology. Hereafter, the "real robots" largely replaced the "super robots" of earlier genre shows like *Mazinger*.

Although *Gundam* and *Macross* presented some fresh angles on perennial themes, and **Nausicaä of the Valley of Wind** (1984) was a landmark in cinemas, anime SF only truly came into its own through video. It was the arrival of the video recorder that brought the potential for true science fiction, as opposed to the limited "sci-fi" of television. After the early experiment of **Dallos** (1983), science fiction was established as a strong part of the anime world, with works including **Megazone 23** (1985), **Bubblegum Crisis** (1987), and the first **Appleseed** (1988). Video SF came into its own with **Gunbuster** (1988), conceived in loving homage to the sci-fi of the 1960s, and **Patlabor** (1989), produced in an indignant reaction to the brutal apocalyptic world envisioned by *Mad Max 2: The Road Warrior* (1981) and **Fist of the North Star** (1984). SF also flourished in cinemas, in the form of two productions for which critical success came far in advance of actual profits—**Wings of Honneamise** (1987) and **Akira** (1988). Notably, this period also saw the beginning of the long-running **Legend of Galactic Heroes** (1988), a video series that survived primarily through subscriber orders, largely bypassing even video stores.

In the 1980s, Japan (and particularly Tokyo) became a motif in SF all its own, the future metropolis of William Gibson's novel *Neuromancer* (1984) and the Asian influences on the Los Angeles of Ridley Scott's *Blade Runner* (1982) helping to create further interest abroad in science fiction *from* Japan. In seeming inverse correlation to Japan's rising power on the world stage, the robots got smaller. The hulking, city-stomping behemoths of old reduced in size, evolving into the

smaller personal vehicles of **Mospeada**, and the feminized "hard-suit" armor of **Bubblegum Crisis** (1987)—perhaps creators had less to prove, or, in the age of the Sony Walkman, saw that miniaturization was the new cool. Realizing that a primarily male audience would rather watch scantily clad girls, science fiction gained increasing numbers of female characters, until, after a decade of the likes of **Dirty Pair** (1985) and **Sol Bianca** (1990), it was male characters that became the token cast members. *Blade Runner* motifs returned in the android women of **AD Police** (1990), **Armitage III** (1994), and **Ghost in the Shell** (1995). Hideaki Anno's watershed **Evangelion** (1995) was intended as the final word on the tropes and clichés of the giant robot genre, but instead ushered in another cycle of imitators such as **Brain Powered** (1998) and **RahXephon** (2002). As the millennium approached, Japanese SF also began to look backward, both to the retro camp of shows like **Giant Robo** (1993) and **Super Atragon** (1995) and the martial fervor of **Kishin Corps** (1993) and **Sakura Wars** (1997). **Cowboy Bebop** (1998) stood out in the crowd simply for its sense of style—it began life as a Sunrise show deliberately written *without* giant robots, a refreshing change in a medium that seemsto be overrun with them.

Modern science fiction anime occupy a gloriously wide selection of niches, from the intimate sensuality of **Chobits** (2002) to the dingy, dirty low-orbit world of **Planetes** (2003) and the existential rebellion of **Blame** (2003). The Wachowski brothers' *The Matrix* (1999) may have set many of the standards of modern-day media SF, but it did so in a manner that built on anime—its inspirations and homages can be clearly seen, both in the continuing hard-SF explorations of the *Ghost in the Shell* franchise, and in the large number of Japanese contributors to **The Animatrix** (2002).

SCI-FI HARRY

2000. TV series. DIR: Yasuhito Kiku-

chi, Katsuyuki Odera. SCR: Kenichi Takashima, Mitsuhiro Yamada, Takeo Tsutsui. DES: Shinya Takahashi. ANI: Yuji Shigekuni, Keiji Tani. MUS: Jeanne D'Arc, Luca. PRD: APPP, TV Asahi. 25 mins. x 11+ eps.

Harry McQueen is a shy 17-year-old who gets picked on by school bully Chris and his gang because they know he won't fight back. Harry's imagination is his escape route; fantasizing that he's the hero of one of his favorite TV shows, he retreats behind the screen into an imaginary world where he can kick Chris's butt. Then we begin to see another side to Harry. When his friend Kate, who has always stood up for him, is kidnapped by the bullies, Harry suddenly appears to save her, though he has no idea how or why. And then a bizarre series of murders occur. Based on the manga by *Night-Head*–creator Joji "George" Iida and Asami Tojo, set in the fantasyland of the U.S. (and loaded with American names, clearly aimed squarely at a foreign release from the get-go), this might at first sight seem an unlikely project for the studio that brought you **Jojo's Bizarre Adventures**, but events soon take a turn for the surreal.

SCOOPERS

1987. Video. DIR: Jun Hirabayashi, Hideo Watanabe. SCR: Monkey Punch. DES: Monkey Punch, Masakazu Abe. ANI: Hirohide Yashikijima. MUS: N/C. PRD: ACC, Video Tech. 58 mins.

It's 2016, and Shambhala city reporter Yoko and her android boyfriend/bodyguard/cameraman Vito are hunting the enigmatic criminal Mr. X. Their search leads them to the Rainbow Tower, where Yoko is taken hostage and Vito must battle to save her by destroying the program of the Tower's central computer to prevent X's escape. Based on a manga by **Lupin III**–creator Monkey Punch.

SCRAPPED PRINCESS *

2003. AKA: *Sutepri*. TV series DIR: Soichi Masui. SCR: Reiko Yoshida, Atsushi Yamatoya. DES: Takahiro Komori (aka

Mogudan). ANI: Takahiro Komori. MUS: Hikaru Nanase. PRD: Kadokawa Shoten. 25 mins. x 24 eps.

Princess Pacifica Casull suffers from a bad case of fairy-tale curse, since her family was informed at the time of her birth that she was "the poison that will destroy the world"—a prophecy fated to come to pass on her 16th birthday, unless she dies first. Consequently, her parents the king and queen order their baby daughter's execution, although in a moment reminiscent of SNOW WHITE, the knight ordered to carry out the task cannot bring himself to do it. She is found and raised by a farmer's family, until she and her adopted siblings are forced to go on the run from followers of the evil god Mauser, and, despite brother Shannon's ability with the sword and sister Racquel's magical expertise, the attempts on her life get increasingly inventive. Meanwhile, the good knight Sir Leo has decided that Pacifica is his true love and insists on trying to protect her, although his efforts often cause more harm than good. As if that weren't enough, Pacifica's *real* twin brother back at the palace discovers that his sister is still alive and is forced to choose sides.

Often playing like SLAYERS with comedy teen angst, as Pacifica eternally frets that the world would be a happier place if she simply died, *Scrapped Princess* maintains a steady series of opponents and missions-of-the-week, while building up to Pacifica's final redemption and absolution. This fantasy series has attractive design and good character development and interaction to enliven the well-worn premise of a fantasy world growing out of a sci-fi global war. Based on an illustrated novel by Ichiro Sakaki and Yukinobu Asami, which was itself later adapted into a manga by Go Yabuki and serialized in the monthly *Comic Dragon*.

SCRYED
2001. TV series. DIR: Goro Taniguchi. SCR: Yosuke Kuroda. DES: Hisashi Hirai. ANI: N/C. MUS: N/C. PRD: Sunrise. 25 mins. x 26 eps.

Science Fiction and Robots

© 2006 STEVE KYTE

In the near future, Kanagawa Prefecture becomes the "Lost Ground," an alternate reality where light and darkness duel for control of the locals' hearts. Sixteen-year-old Kazuma is an "Inner," a child who has never left the world of the Lost Ground, forced into conflict with powerful beings known as the Altered.

SEA CAT
1988. Movie DIR: Shunji Saida. SCR: N/C. DES: N/C. ANI: N/C. MUS: N/C. PRD: Oh Production, Anido. 20 mins.

Cats have nine lives. The central character of this experimental film needs them all. Lost at sea and adopted by a sea otter, he's abducted by a UFO as nuclear war breaks out and the oceans evaporate in the ensuing holocaust. Director Saida, a talented animator who worked on NAUSICAÄ OF THE VALLEY OF WIND and GRAVE OF THE FIREFLIES, pulled in a team of animators to contribute one shot each. The movie was never distributed but loaned out for small screenings, a method called "hall projection" in Japan.

SEA OF THE TICONDEROGA
1991. JPN: *Ticonderonga no iru Umi*.

Movie. DIR: Yuji Nichimaki. SCR: Koji Kawakita. DES: Takao Kasai. ANI: Takao Kasai. MUS: N/C. PRD: Urban Project, Asmik, Kobushi Pro. 28 mins.

On December 5, 1965, a U.S. aircraft carrier is en route from Vietnam to Yokosuka, Japan. While conducting training exercises 80 miles off Okinawa, an A4 strike aircraft is loaded with a B43 hydrogen bomb, but it falls overboard and sinks in 16,000 feet of water. Based on the true story of the USS Ticonderoga, which reached Japan two days later (on the anniversary of Pearl Harbor; nice touch). Neither side revealed the incident, nor that she was carrying atomic weapons in contravention of U.S. treaties with Japan. The plane, its pilot, and the bomb were never recovered, and the incident was only declassified in 1989, causing an outcry in Japan and resulting in this environmentally themed anime. The extra "n" in *Ticonderonga* may be a genuine error in transcription or an attempt to distance the story from real events, since the anime continues with Ashika, a boy from a Japanese fishing town, contacted by telepathic whales who bring him visions of fearful sea-monsters. Then again, if you were a whale given a choice between nuclear contamination and talking to Japanese fishermen, which would you choose? For more fun with the U.S. Navy, see **Space Family Carlvinson**.

SEA PRINCE AND THE FIRE CHILD *

1981. JPN: *Sirius no Densetsu*. AKA: *Legend of Sirius*. Movie. DIR: Masami Hata, Takuo Suzuki. SCR: Chiho Katsura. DES: Shigeru Yamamoto. ANI: Shigeru Yamamoto, Mikiharu Akabori. MUS: Koichi Sugiyama. PRD: Sanrio. 108 mins. Prince Sirius comes from a family of water spirits and Princess Malta, daughter of Hyperia, from a family of fire spirits. The long and bitter war between the two makes the love of the two young protagonists impossible. When Sirius and Malta try to escape their parents' wrath, they are enveloped in a powerful storm conjured by the evil Algorac, Lord of the Winds. The Disneyesque animation style looks charming.

SEA'S DARKNESS: MOON'S SHADOW

1988. JPN: *Umi no Yami, Tsuki no Kage*. AKA: *Darkness of the Sea, Shadow of the Moon*. Video. DIR: Tetsu Dezaki. SCR: Hirokazu Mizude. DES: Setsuko Shibunnoichi. ANI: Akio Sugino, Yukari Kobayashi. MUS: N/C. PRD: Visual 80. 40 mins. x 3 eps.
These SF-horror adventures that were based on the 1987 manga in *Shojo Comic* by **Purple Eyes in the Dark**–creator Chie Shinohara feature twin girls Ryusui and Ryufu, who discover they have unearthly powers that increase as the moon waxes. As a bonus, tape two contains a ten-minute anime based on Miyuki Kitagawa's *That Girl Is 1,000%* (*Ano Ko wa 1,000%*), a similar tale of haunting romance.

SECRET AKKO-CHAN *

1969. JPN: *Himitsu no Akko-Chan*. AKA: *Akko-chan's Secret*. TV series. DIR: Hiroshi Ikeda, Keiji Hisaoka, Masayuki Akehi, Takeshi Tamiya, Yoshio Takami. SCR: Shunichi Yukimuro, Tomohiro Ando, Masaki Tsuji, Tadaaki Yamazaki.

DES: Fujio Akatsuka. ANI: Shinya Takahashi. MUS: Yasei Kobayashi. PRD: Toei, NET. 30 mins. x 94 eps.
Helpful 10-year-old Akko usually takes good care of her belongings, especially her old mirror, brought back as a present from India by her father. She polishes it carefully every night before she goes to bed, but one night she accidentally breaks it. Very sad, she buries the pieces in the garden. That night, the spirit of the mirror wakes her and gives her another mirror to thank her for cherishing the old one. Her new present is a compact with the power to transform the owner into any person or animal she chooses if she says a magical word; but the fairy warns Akko that she must keep the spell, and the powers of the mirror, a secret. Akko uses her new powers to solve the problems of friends and neighbors in her quiet hometown, and, as her confidence grows, she transforms into animal shapes and even goes to other countries. Based on the 1962 manga series by Fujio Akatsuka, who also created **Osomatsu-kun** and **Genius Idiot Bakabon**, *SA* was the next "magical girl" series after **Little Witch Sally** and confirmed the appeal of the formula. The series was remade for Fuji TV in 1988, with Hiroki Shibata as director and new character designs from Yoshinori Kanemori. Shibata returned for a *third* 28-episode TV season on TV Asahi in 1998, with character designs from Toshio Deguchi.

SECRET ANIMA SERIES *

1997. AKA: (see below). Video. DIR: Kunimitsu Ikeda, Kaoru Tomioka, Hachi Saiga. SCR: Susumu Nanase, Doctor Emu. DES: Ran Hiryu, Protonsaurus, Mon-Mon, Yokihi, Yoshimasa Watanabe. ANI: Ruthie Tanaka, Jiro Makigata. MUS: N/C. PRD: Beam Entertainment. 30 mins. x 8 eps.
An umbrella series of adaptations of pornographic manga, which, unlike the similar **Cool Devices**, was broken up and released abroad as *separate* titles. *Mama* (#1–2, released in the U.S. as *Mama Mia*) was based on a manga

by Ran Hiryu and features Yuichi, an orphaned boy who discovers that his frisky stepsister Mika has been seducing her own mother to prevent her getting her kicks from making any more porn videos. For the second part, a completely different boy (confusingly also called Yuichi) loses his adoptive father in the same traffic accident that leaves his adoptive mother in a wheelchair. Now the man of the house, Yuichi discovers that Dad used to play pervy games with Mom and Rika the maid, and Yuichi carries on the noble family tradition. *Chu²* (#3) consists of three far shorter tableaux from Protonsaurus, with a similar S/M theme to his work in *Cool Devices*. For U.S. release, it was combined with *Momone* (#4, aka *The Naughty Professor*), another tale of bondage from Kazu Yoshinaga, under the title *Twisted Tales of Tokyo*. In *Dream Hazard* (#5), based on a manga from **Cream Lemon**'s Mon-Mon, timid schoolgirl Kaori buys a virtual-reality date in order to sublimate her desires for an upperclassman. Needless to say, things go horribly wrong, and she finds herself "virtually" subjected to the usual porn anime cavalcade of abuse, assault, rape, and torture. In *Four Play* (#6–7), based on the manga *2x1* by **Etchiis**-creator Yokihi, two boys are sent to an absent classmate's home to deliver notes. However, the malingering Noriko instead seduces the sporty Junichi and eventually succumbs to the geekier charms of his quiet friend Satoshi. All three of them begin a series of sexual experiments, scandalizing their contemporaries in a Tokyo suburb. After several different scenes of naughtiness the foursome (Junichi's sister Miyuki turning up as an afterthought) agree that it's okay to do whatever they want, as long as nobody gets hurt. Junichi delivers an impassioned speech to that effect (at least, it might have been impassioned before the dubbers got hold of it) and the credits roll. In *Pianist* (#8), based on a manga by Yoshimasa Watanabe, concert pianist Seiji injures his wrist (sure he does) in a car accident, develops a crush on his robot nurse, and buys a slave-robot to remind him of her. When robot Yuna turns out to be a piano prodigy, he tries to secure her a record deal, only to discover that prejudice exists against nonhuman musicians. Finally, in Serina Kamuro's *Love2Police* (#9), three girls carry out secret missions in order to rescue boys from their virginity and any other frustrations.

Unsurprisingly, these titles register a very low level of interest from all parties concerned—starting with the original creators, since only *Pianist* has a remotely interesting plot, and even that is riddled with holes. The sex is even less entertaining, let down by substandard animation. Most noticeable is the overuse of flashbacks, a relatively easy trick using digital animation, allowing, for example, multiple scenes of video playback as *Mama Mia*'s protagonist watches his stepmother's porno appearances on tape. The low budget also shows in traditional ways, such as very limited backgrounds in several episodes and heavy reliance on pans across single images. With such bad workmanship at the Japanese end, it comes as little surprise that the U.S. dubbing crews seem similarly disinterested in their material—both *Dream Hazard* and *Mama Mia* feature particularly bad performances from actors who clearly wish they were somewhere else. Producing porn will always be a thankless task, but *Secret Anima* is a particularly low-rent example of the genre, unlikely to satisfy fans of anime or erotica.

Mama Mia was later rereleased in the U.S. by Nu-Tech under the title *Ma Ma*. ●NV

SECRET DESIRES *
2002. JPN: *Midara*. AKA: *Lewdness; Secret Desires: Passions of the Midara*. Video. DIR: N/C. SCR: N/C. DES: N/C. ANI: N/C. MUS: N/C. PRD: Museum Video, Milky. 30 mins. x 3 eps.
College student Yuto Sawada picks up a video cassette that turns out to be magic—but all resemblance to **VIDEO GIRL AI** ends there. The tape shows the

The Secret of Blue Water

© 1989 NHK/SOGO VISION/TOHO

viewer his or her secret desires. Yuto sees himself winning an auction for the right to have sex with his stepsister. Anachronistic settings, bondage, and domination are a common theme of the fantasies on the tape; the idea of jerking off while watching *yourself* have sex is an uncomfortable one, especially when the sex you're having is nonconsensual. Based on a computer game by Mink. Compare to *Dream Hazard* in the **SECRET ANIMA SERIES**. ●NV

SECRET GARDEN, THE
1991. JPN: *Anime Himitsu no Hanazono*. AKA: *Anime Secret Garden*. TV series. DIR: Tameo Ogawa. SCR: Kaoru Umeno. DES: Hidemi Kuma, Aiko Katsumata. ANI: Hideki Kubo, Hiroshi Suzuki. MUS: Masaaki Matsumoto, Shiro Sagisu. PRD: Aubec, NHK. 25 mins. x 39 eps.
Plain, awkward Mary is neglected by her pretty mother and military father. Orphaned in India, she is sent to live with her uncle in the north of England. She discovers that her cousin Colin is as lonely as she is—after his mother's death while giving birth to him, he is both indulged and neglected by his heartbroken father and often kept locked away. But Mary's company and

the fascinating project she has uncovered—finding and reviving his mother's secret garden—soon gets Colin back on his feet. When her uncle finally comes home, he finds a welcome he never imagined. Frances Hodgson Burnett's 1909 novel has been filmed many times in the West, and even made into a Broadway musical. The same author wrote **LITTLE LORD FAUNTLEROY** and **A LITTLE PRINCESS**.

SECRET OF BLUE WATER, THE *
1990. JPN: *Fushigi na Umi no Nadia*. AKA: *Nadia of the Mysterious Seas; Nadia*. TV series, movie. DIR: Hideaki Anno, Shigeru Morikawa, Masayuki, Koji Masunari, Takeshi Mori. SCR: Toshio Okada, Hisao Okawa, Kaoru Umeno. DES: Yoshiyuki Sadamoto. ANI: Kazuto Nakazawa, Shunji Suzuki, Kazunori Matsubara, Yoshiaki Yanagida, Hideaki Anno. MUS: Shiro Sagisu. PRD: Gainax, Group Tac, NHK. 25 mins. x 39 eps. (TV), 90 mins. (m).
Paris is the scene of the 1889 International Exposition. Young inventor Jean meets circus acrobat Nadia. He rescues her from a strange gang of comical villains out to steal her necklace, and the pair set off on an amazing adventure that takes them far beneath the seas,

and all around the world. They face racism in France and cold-blooded killing on a remote Pacific island, see a flying contest with Chitty-Chitty Bang-Bang as one of the entrants, and share a dream sequence in which they ride in something suspiciously like Thunderbird 2 (see **THUNDERBIRDS 2086**). They face the last remnants of Atlantis and join the fight to save the world from domination by a mad genius. Along the way they learn that their origins are less important than what they make of themselves, and that while love can conquer all, it doesn't guarantee a happy ending. The 1993 movie *Nadia of the Mysterious Seas the Movie: Fuzzy's Secret* takes up the story some years later, with Jean rescuing a mysterious girl and the impact this has on his stormy relationship with Nadia.

While working at Toho Studios in the 1970s, the young Hayao Miyazaki pitched a scenario to his bosses inspired by Jules Verne, creator of **ADRIFT IN THE PACIFIC**. Set in the late 19th century, *Around the World in 80 Days by Sea* would use two Vernean concepts—a trip around the world by two plucky characters on the run from bad guys, and the mighty submarine Nautilus, commanded by Captain Nemo, who has a secret past of his own. Toho didn't make the series but held onto the option. Miyazaki later used various elements of the idea in **FUTURE BOY CONAN** and **CASTLE IN THE SKY**, but it wasn't until the critical triumph of **WINGS OF HONNEAMISE** that Toho dusted off the outline and approached Gainax to turn it into a TV series.

SBW was conceived as a blatant pitch to the mass audience. Very rarely has this approach produced a show of such enduring charm and emotional validity. The combination of Vernean adventure, Dickensian richness of characterization (particularly in the comical semivillains Grandis, Sanson, and Hanson), nods and winks to more contemporary classics, and steampunk technology was irresistible, propelling the series to success and Nadia to an enduring place in the list of fans' favor-

ite characters. In Nadia, the Gainax team created a heroine who was beautiful and independent yet alone and unsure of her place in the world, capable of anger and courage yet completely opposed to killing, a heroine of color and an animal rights advocate ahead of her time. Young hero Jean, a brilliant but naïve kid with total faith in technology and innocent of the world's deceits and cruelties, is an orphan as she is. The two are bonded by loss and alienation; despite the sunny color palette of the show and its upbeat pacing and music, the audience quickly realizes that a dark and terrible fate is always waiting just out of shot, threatening to engulf the young couple—the same team's later hit **EVANGELION** brought the lurking darkness into the foreground. The impact of several violent scenes—which are never gratuitous but likely to be shocking to a modern Western audience in a children's series—foiled an attempt in the mid-1990s to get the show onto U.K. television screens. *SoBW* was rereleased on DVD as *Nadia: SoBW* in the U.S. in 2001, just in time to invite insidious comparisons between it and the new Disney cartoon *Atlantis: The Lost Empire*. Though the filmmakers admitted to an interest in the works of Hayao Miyazaki, they denied any knowledge of *SoBW*—compare to the controversy surrounding **KIMBA THE WHITE LION**. **Ⓥ**

SECRET OF CERULEAN SAND
2002. JPN: *Patapata Hikosen no Boken*. AKA: *Patapata Airship Adventure*. TV series. DIR: Yuichiro Yano, Kim Echoul, Go Yoonjae. SCR: Yuka Yamada, Koichi Masajima, Noriko Tanimura. DES: Kenji Yazaki, Kazuhide Tomonaga. ANI: Yuichi Takiguchi, Kazuhide Tomonaga. MUS: Daisuke Ikeda, Toshio Nakagawa. PRD: TAF, Tokyo Movie Shinsha, WOWOW, Koko Animation, Sega, ZET. 25 mins. x 26 eps.
Fifteen-year-old Jane Buxton hears that her eldest brother George has been executed for treason while off exploring distant lands. Meanwhile, her stepbrother William storms out

of the family home as a result of an ongoing feud with Jane's father, who is soon on trial for embezzlement. Some time later, Jane receives a parcel in the mail containing a strange shard of blue stone (the "cerulean sand" of the English title). Realizing that this might be the mystical energy source for which George had been searching at the time of his reported death, Jane sets off to discover the truth and clear the family name.

The adventures of a plucky British teenager, in a world of deserts and airships in which the idea of honor is still important, may seem to echo the works of Hayao Miyazaki and Isao Takahata. However, any resemblance to **CASTLE IN THE SKY** stems from both stories drawing on the same source—the works of one of the most popular science fiction authors in Japan, the French writer Jules Verne (1828-1905). *SoCS* takes its inspiration from two of Verne's works, the first being *For the Flag* (1896, *Face au Drapeau*), in which an inventor discovers an incredibly powerful explosive and initially resolves to sell it to the highest bidder, regardless of his duty to his country. The second is *City in the Sahara* (1919, *L'Etonnante Aventure de la Mission Barsac*), Verne's last work, which was finished posthumously by his son. This anime version, a Japanese-Korean coproduction, changes the heroine's name from Joan to Jane, but otherwise clings to the broad strokes of the original, including its melodramatic face-off between the true-hearted Buxtons and the cruel intentions of their stepsiblings—shades here of an even more traditional family drama, stretching back to **CINDERELLA**. Both Verne's original stories dealt with scientists who must come to terms with their complicity in the use of their inventions for evil purposes—shades here for the Japanese audience of **KIKAIDER** and other antiheroes, but also of a genuine old-time fascination with technology and progress that was pastiched in **STEAMBOY**. The plot also revolves around Jane's discovery of a stone with a mysterious power—echoing the

SECRET OF BLUE WATER, which was itself inspired by the works of Verne. Such "coincidences" aside, the authors do not doubt for a moment that commercial concerns steered the producers' choice of material—Verne may have been conveniently out of copyright, but the chance to claim to be using his story while actually pastiching Miyazaki's must have been irresistible.

SECRET OF THE SEAL, THE *
1991. JPN: *Tottoi*. Movie. DIR: Noboru Ishiguro. SCR: Ryuzo Nakanishi. DES: Haruhiko Mikomoto, Masamichi Takano. ANI: Haruhiko Mikimoto. MUS: Koichi Sakata. PRD: Nippon Animation, Nikken Academy. 90 mins.
After the death of his mother, little Alexander moves with his father and sister to the Mediterranean island of Sardinia, where he is nicknamed Tottoi. In a grotto by the sea, he finds a baby seal and its mother. They've been thought extinct in the area for ten years, and he fears that if discovered they'll be shut up in an aquarium for scientific study or experimentation. But he is not sure he can even trust his friends among the islanders to help him keep the rare animals safe. Based on the novel by Gianni Padoan, the story has very strong similarities to **FLY PEEK**, although the character style is more naturalistic.

SECRET SEX STORIES *
2003. JPN: *Soken Rensa*. AKA: *Chain of Debauchery*. Video. DIR: Tomoyori Sasaki. SCR: Shigeaki Serida. DES: Aki Midori. ANI: Aki Midori. MUS: N/C. PRD: Animac. 30 mins.
Two short erotic vignettes appear in this anthology. The first features two hoodlums who break into a widow's house, hoping to steal her late husband's valuables. Instead, all they find are the widow and her daughter and proceed to hold them prisoner and subject them to sexual torment until the burglars get what they want.

The second story takes place in an art class, where the students' complaints about the unrealistic nature of mannequins has finally led the teacher to persuade a pretty young coed to pose for life drawing. The students gradually convince her to doff her clothes, in a striptease that ends with predictable results. In both cases, however, the female victims manage to some extent to turn the tables on their tormentors. Compare to the episode *Five Hour Venus* in the **CREAM LEMON SERIES**. **LNV**

SECRETS OF THE TELEPHONE CLUB
1991. JPN: *Terekura no Himitsu*. AKA: *Secret of the Teleclub*. Movie. DIR: Kan Fukumoto. SCR: Satoshi Yagi. DES: Akira Narita. ANI: Kan Fukumoto. MUS: N/C. PRD: Japan Home Video. 45 mins. x 2 eps.
A lonely man discovers the seedy world of the telephone club, where he can wait to receive calls from women desperate for sex. Soon he becomes a happy escort, taking the virginity of an appreciative client and helping an unhappy housewife find fulfillment. Sometimes they just want to talk, but this adaptation of Akira Narita's manga doesn't dwell for too long on those ones. Compare to **CALL ME TONIGHT**.**N**

SEE IN AO *
2004. AKA: *See in Blue Video*. DIR: Yoshikazu Yabe. SCR: Goro Mimyo. DES: Akira Kano. ANI: Sora Akino. MUS: N/C. PRD: Green Bunny. 30 mins. x 2 eps.
In a futuristic city on the sea, Kyoya teaches at an oceanography institute, where he has lived ever since he was rescued at sea by local girl Miyu. Miyu's twin sister Yui realizes that Miyu is attracted to Kyoya and plays matchmaker until the two are a happily copulating couple. It's only then that we are told Yui is not a human at all, but an android programmed to ensure that Miyu is always safe and happy. Yui has feelings for Kyoya herself, which conflict with her own programming and threaten to cause her entire system to crash—compare to other girlfriends with time limits, like **VIDEO GIRL AI** and **MAHOROMATIC**. After Miyu's unexpected death, Yui is on hand to help Kyoya mourn, which she does by taking her sister's place in Kyoya's bed.

With an erotic perspective on Isaac Asimov's "Laws of Robotics" (themselves adapted for Tezuka's **ASTRO BOY**), *See in Ao* has interesting potential, although it sorely lacks in execution with substandard digital animation and a ponderous pace. We also wonder how Kyoya can lose so much of his memory that he forgets who he is and how he got there, but not so much that he isn't able to function as a teacher. Based on a computer game from Alice Soft. In the U.S. release, the lead characters' names were pointlessly changed to Jim, Amy, and Mizi, even though the show was subtitled and not dubbed—compare to **HERITAGE FROM FATHER**, which suffered similarly in its American release. **N**

SEIZE THE WIND
1988. JPN: *Kaze o Nuke*. Video. DIR: Kazunori Ikegami, Noboru Furuse. SCR: Noboru Aikawa. DES: Noboru Furuse. ANI: Noboru Furuse. MUS: Masahiro Takami. PRD: Madhouse. 60 mins.
In a sports anime that takes place in the world of motocross, 16-year-old Satoshi Ichimonji fights his way from the novice grade up to the Junior Cross championship. Motorcycle trickery abounds, alongside sporting hardships, and, of course, feckless foreign rival Jeff Anemoth. Based on the manga by **SWORD OF MUSASHI**–creator Motoka Murakami in *Shonen Sunday*.

SEKI, SHUICHI
1946– . Born in Tokyo, he studied at a design college before finding work with TCJ (now Eiken). He worked as a sketch artist on **LEGEND OF KAMUI** and eventually made his way up the ranks to character designer. Representative works include **THE WIZARD OF OZ** and **TOM SAWYER**.

SENBON MATSUBARA
1992. Movie. DIR: Tetsu Dezaki. SCR: Tetsuaki Imaizumi. DES: Setsuko Shibunnoichi. ANI: Keizo Shimizu. MUS:

Masato Nichiyoshi. PRD: Magic Bus. 100 mins.

After suffering severe floods in 1753, the people of Senbon Matsubara in Shizuoka cooperate on flood prevention around the Kiso, Nagara, and Yuhi rivers. The people of Satsuma (Kumamoto Prefecture) endure great hardships after being forced to undertake the work by the central government, a subtle indication of the bad feeling that would foment into open rebellion the following century—see OI RYOMA!

SENSITIVE PORNOGRAPH *
2004. Video. DIR: Iroko Omma, Hiroshi Kuruo. SCR: N/C. DES: Takebon. ANI: Takebon. MUS: N/C. PRD: Digital Works (Slash), Phoenix Entertainment. 30 mins.

Young manga artist Seiji is thrilled when he meets Sono, an older manga artist who has been an inspiration in his own career. He is surprised that Sono is equally thrilled to meet him, and the mutual admiration soon turns to mutual attraction. Meanwhile, in an apparently unrelated second chapter, a young male pet sitter is given a "rabbit" to look after which turns out to be a man on a leash. Predictable couplings ensue; compare to **DARLING** and **MY SEXUAL HARRASSMENT**. Based on a manga by Ashika Sakura in *Magazine Magazine* [*sic*]. **Ⓝ**

SENSUALIST, THE *
1990. JPN: *Ihara Saikaku: Koshoku Ichidai Otoko*. AKA: *Ihara Saikaku's Life of an Amorous Man*. Video. DIR: Yukio Abe. SCR: Eiichi Yamamoto. DES: Yukio Abe. ANI: Tomoko Ogawa, Masaharu Endo, Hiroyuki Kondo. MUS: Keiji Ishikawa. PRD: Groupier Productions. 53 mins.

The merchant Yonosuke decides to help his underling Juzo, a comical peasant who has made an unwise bet with a malicious acquaintance. The fool has bet his manhood that he will sleep with the famous courtesan Komurasaki on their first meeting, when any cultured person would know she would not dream of doing so for the richest and most intelligent man in the land, let alone this hayseed. Yonosuke has known her for a long time, and at his request, she agrees to help the poor fool out, not only giving him a night beyond his wildest dreams, but even writing a certificate of the event on his underwear in her most elegant calligraphy. Novelist Saikaku Ihara chronicled the follies and dramas of old-time Japan in his works. This film was based on just part of his *Life of an Amorous Man* (1682), retelling a few of the adventures of Yonosuke. The exquisite, jewellike animation makes use of techniques that recall the traditional crafts of old Japan. Cels were not simply painted but embossed with the textures of leaves or fine fabrics. Genitals are not just pixilated or blacked out, they are transformed into symbolic representations from old woodcuts—a penis becomes the head of a tortoise, a vagina a splitting fruit or unfolding flower. Director Abe's pace is as slow and precisely calculated as a courtesan's every move, producing a hothouse atmosphere of elegant eroticism as far removed from the teenage crudities of most porn anime as Edo is from modern Tokyo. A beautiful anime. **Ⓝ**

SENTIMENTAL JOURNEY *
1998. TV series. DIR: Kazuyoshi Katayama, Keiichi Sato. SCR: Tsunehisa Arakawa. DES: Keiichi Sato, Madoka Hirayama. ANI: Madoka Hirayama. MUS: Toshiyuki Okada. PRD: Sunrise, TV Tokyo. 25 mins. x 12 eps.

Twelve friends are the heroines of this high school romance series, based on the game *Sentimental Graffiti*. Each episode focuses on one of them and her boyfriend problems—getting one, keeping one, making sure he's the right one. Aki is a violinist, Chie wants to be a folk guitarist, Chiho is the tough, sporty daughter of an *okonomiyaki* chef, Wakaba is an archer, Asako wants to be an artist, and Miyuki is fascinated with old-fashioned clothes. Players/viewers who insist on something out of the ordinary can plump for Emiru, who can see ghosts, or Honoka, who is afraid of *all* men. If that's not good enough for you, there are plenty of wounded souls to nurture—Yu pines for the man she last saw eight years ago, while Manami is consumptive, weak, and in need of a good cuddle. Asuka is a perky events manager whose bright exterior conceals a broken heart, while Rurika is bullied at school. A show about the everyday lives and little romantic problems of 12 teenage girls isn't exactly what we expect from the Sunrise studio, but since over a dozen **GUNDAM** kits have been sold for every inhabitant of Japan, doubtless there was an ulterior motive: selling new models and figurines to the chiefly male target audience. The same motivation inspires game-anime tie-ins like **TO HEART** and **SERAPHIM CALL**.

SEO, MITSUYO
1911– . Pseudonym for Norikazu Seo; sometimes also billed as Taro Seo. Born in Hyogo Prefecture, Seo went to Tokyo in the hopes of becoming an artist. After working briefly as one of Kenzo Masaoka's animators in Kyoto, he returned to Tokyo to make the talkie *Sankichi the Monkey* (1933, *Osaru Sankichi*; see **WARTIME ANIME**) and the *Norakuro* series. Inevitably drawn into the propaganda machine, Seo's *Momotaro's Sea Eagles* (1943, *Momotaro no Umiwashi*) was a success with both audiences and the Japanese Navy. Commissioned to make Japan's first full-length animated feature, **MOMOTARO'S DIVINE SEA WARRIORS** (1945), he completed the movie in time for an April 1945 release, although most children had been evacuated from Tokyo by that time. After the war, he made *The King's Tail* (1949, *Osama no Shippo*) before retiring from animation to illustrate children's books.

SEQUENCE
1992. Video. DIR: Naoto Takahashi. SCR: Tsunehisa Arakawa. DES: Ryunosuke Otonashi. ANI: N/C. MUS: Toshiyuki Watanabe. PRD: Studio Giants, Aoi Pro. 40 mins.

Suffering from a crippling memory loss ever since an accident at the age of six, Kara finds new hope, and a new mystery, when he is visited by a girl from his own future. Based on a manga in *Wings* magazine by Ken Mizuki.

SERAPHIM CALL
1999. TV series. DIR: Tomomi Mochizuki. SCR: Go Sakamoto, Sadayuki Murai. DES: Aoi Nanase, Maki Fujii. ANI: Maki Fujii. MUS: Akifumi Oda. PRD: Media works, Sunrise, TV Tokyo. 25 mins. x 12 eps.
A sci-fi respray of SENTIMENTAL JOURNEY, in which 11 beautiful girls between the ages of 12 and 25—the Seraphim—live in the future city of Yokohama Neo Acropolis. Each of them has a different talent or hangup (in place of characterization), and each has a story devoted to her. Yukina is a high school science genius, but she's so afraid of men that she can't so much as pick up a pencil when one of them is looking at her. Tanpopo is 12, collects stuffed animals, and worries about growing up. Chinami is 16 and wants to open her own bakery and bring her divorced parents back together. Hatsumi is a sporty tomboy who's never been seen in a skirt in all her 18 years, but she's suddenly asked to model for an artist. Sakura and Shion are 16-year-old twins worried that romance may drive them apart. Their classmate Kurumi is a wannabe cartoonist in a slump, while Urara, also 16, is the daughter of the man who designed Neo Acropolis, and she loves him so much that she can't love a boy just yet. Ayaka is a spoiled rich kid whose father decides she needs to learn the value of money by getting a job at the age of 14. Saeno is the oldest at 25, an English teacher whose true passion is mathematics, but who runs into an equation she can't solve unless she uses her heart. The eleventh girl is a legend: 18-year-old Kasumi, the goddess of Acropolis whom no one has ever seen. But on Christmas Eve all the Seraphim gather at the Acropolis Tower, hoping for their personal miracles to happen. . . . This collection

of adolescent fantasies, some with an SF twist like Yukina's *Turn-A* GUNDAM parody robot, is designed to promote a game and sell related merchandise. Players can pick their favorite Seraph and get the idol card, *gachapon* toy (see VILLGUST), action figure, and so on.

SERENDIPITY THE PINK DRAGON *
1983. JPN: *Serendipity Monogatari yori, Pure Shima no Nakamatachi.* AKA: *The Story of Serendipity: Friends of Pure Island.* TV series, movie. DIR: Nobuo Onuki, Masayoshi Osaki, Mitsuo Hikabe, Susumu Ishizaki, Keiji Hayakawa, Shigeru Omachi, Hiroyuki Yokoyama, Satoshi Inoue. SCR: Takeshi Matsuki, Tsunehisa Ito, Himiko Nakao. DES: Kazuo Tomizawa, Yoichi Otabe, Yoshiniki Nishi. ANI: Kazuo Tomizawa, Yutaka Oka. MUS: Takeo Watanabe. PRD: Hokuto, Zuiyo Enterprise, Nippon TV. 25 mins. x 26 eps. (TV), 90 mins.
Based on an illustrated book by Steven Cosgrove and Robin James, this children's series tells the story of Corna, a little boy separated from his parents after an accident at sea washed him ashore on a remote South Pacific island with a large pink egg. The egg hatches and a cute little pink creature is born that soon grows into a large dragon. It's Serendipity, who is really a sea spirit, and who becomes the lost boy's friend. Corna's new home is governed by a queen who allows him to stay. A pretty little mermaid called Laura and many strange creatures live there. When the island is threatened by a pirate band come to steal its fabled treasure, the Mermaid's Tears, Corna and his comical friends fight to protect their home. Several episodes were also compiled into a 90-minute "movie" in 1989.
    The theatrical release and TV series production were started by a subsidiary of Mizutaka Enterprises, but work was abandoned with 10 episodes in the can. Only after the completion of a further 16 episodes were the series and movie released. Both have been screened in Europe, and the movie is available on video in the U.S.

SERGEANT FROG
2004. JPN: *Keroro Gunso.* TV series. DIR: Yusuke Yamamoto, Junichi Sato. SCR: Satoru Nishizono, Mamiko Ikeda. DES: Fumitoshi Oizaki, Kunio Okawara. ANI: Asako Nishida, Fumitoshi Oizaki. MUS: N/C. PRD: Sunrise, NAS, Bandai Visual, TV Tokyo. 24 mins. x ?? eps.
Keroro is leading the advance guard of a frog-like alien army to planet Pokopen, which the locals call Earth. But he is captured by the natives and abandoned by his invasion fleet. Siblings Natsumi and Fuyuki Hinata take him home, where he has to do housework in return for a room in a haunted basement. He gradually settles in, comes to like his new home, and loses all interest in military glory when he discovers the delights of making plastic model kits. The other members of his platoon also find homes on Earth and comic mayhem ensues.
    The theme of the alien observer of human foibles has been used in TV comedy from *My Favorite Martian* to *Third Rock from the Sun.* But Keroro follows a Japanese tradition dating back to EMPEROR OF THE PLUM PLANET, and also brings the army-issue kero ball, a device akin to Batman's utility belt, functioning as weapon, communicator, and general situation-saving MacGuffin—compare to DORAEMON. Supposedly based on Mine Yoshizaki's manga, but with an "original creator" credit for Yoshiyuki Tomino and Sunrise house pseudonym Hajime Yadate, the show is packed with references to Japanese science fiction like *Space Giants* (*DE, the live-action version of AMBASSADOR MAGMA) but the PlayStation 2 game packs in even more homages to all kinds of anime weapons, from GUNDAM's beam rifles to EVANGELION's Lance of Longinus. A movie followed in 2006. **LNV**

SERIAL EXPERIMENTS LAIN *
1998. TV series. DIR: Ryutaro Nakamura, Shigeru Ueda, Akihiko Nishiyama, Masahiko Murata, Johei Matsuura. SCR: Chiaki Konaka. DES: Takahiro Kishida, Yoshitoshi Abe, Hiroshi Kato. ANI: Yuichi Tanaka, Masahiro Sekiguchi, Yoshihiro

Sugai. MUS: Reichi Nakaido, Bôa. PRD: Pioneer, Triangle Staff, TV Tokyo. 25 mins. x 13 eps.

Shy 14-year-old Rein Iwakura meets a school friend on the Wired, a super-Internet that allows almost total immersion in cyberspace—but Chisa died by her own hand days ago. Now she says God is in the Wired. Understandably shaken, Rein is further baffled by a strange encounter in a club, where a junkie is so scared by her sudden, chilling response to his pestering that he kills himself. Rein learns more about the Wired, drawing her further into another existence, one where Lain, her second self, lives an independent life in the electronic impulses. In an identity crisis redolent of PERFECT BLUE, Lain starts putting in appearances in the real world, causing her double to wonder which of them is real. Uncertain of her true origins or existence, or of reality itself, Rein/Lain crosses paths with the godlike entity Deus (creator of the Wired, now dwelling inside it) in a surreal struggle. The listless analogue world of the late 20th century and the digital dream of the Wired combine to present a vision of the dominance of technology so nihilistic that at times it makes EVANGELION look almost sunny.

Real originality is rare in any field, but *SEL* skillfully perverts the two-as-one magical-girl tradition in an interesting Internet-inspired direction, fused with a paranoid Luddite technophobia. Much of the credit goes to ARMITAGE III–veteran Konaka and newcomer Abe, who has since created NIEA_7. Director Nakamura deliberately plays up the low-budget animation, making a virtue of 1990s cost-cutting by contrasting Rein's flat, unnatural daily life with the luxuriant, swirling CG images of the Wired itself. Much of the "action" takes place in cyberspace or inside Rein/Lain's skull, and the blurring of links and walls between objective and subjective reality is chillingly effective. Unlike in KEY THE METAL IDOL, Rein finds ordinary life messy and banal; weighing the so-called advantages of humanity, she is prepared to trade up, a sentiment guaranteed to appeal to troubled teens.

The concept would be refined in more magical terms in HAIBANE RENMEI, a later anime based on an earlier manga by Abe.

SERIKAWA, YUGO

1931– . Born in Tokyo, he studied German literature at Waseda University, before joining Toho as an assistant director after graduation. Inspired by the Japanese release of earlier Disney movies, he transferred to Toei Animation in 1959, soon rising to the rank of director. His works as director include NOBODY'S BOY and CYBORG 009.

SETON'S ANIMAL TALES

1989. JPN: *Seton Dobutsuki*. TV series. DIR: Takeshi Shirato, Eiji Okabe, Keiji Kawanami, Hiromitsu Morita, Masao Ito. Yoshikata Nitta. SCR: Yu Mizugi, Haruya Yamazaki, Sukehiro Tomita, Haruya Yamazaki, Tsunehisa Ito. DES: N/C. ANI: Kazutoshi Kobayashi, Hirohide Yashikijima. MUS: N/C. PRD: Nippon Animation, Eiken, TV Asahi. 25 mins. x 45 eps.

A series of stories taken from the work of Ernest "Black Wolf" Thompson Seton, the creator of BANNERTAIL THE SQUIRREL and MONARCH, THE BIG BEAR OF TALLACH. Born in England but a Canadian emigrant, Seton was the leader of the North American Boy Scout movement from 1910 to 1915, until he left over disagreements about the "military" aspects promoted by Lord Baden-Powell and James West. Setting up the "Woodcraft League," he promoted the healthy outdoor life with his 60 books and over 400 short stories and articles. A fraction of these were adapted for this anime series, including *Monarch* (again), *Wari the Fox, Bingo the Famous Dog, Link the Puppy, The Beaver of the Poplar Tree, Fox of Springfield, Snap the Heroic Puppy, Wolf of the Badlands,* and *Silver Fox of Yellowstone,* among others.

SEVEN CITIES

1994. JPN: *Nanatoshi Monogatari*. AKA: *Story of Seven Cities*. Video. DIR: Akinori Nagaoka. SCR: Tomomi Nobe. DES: Katsumi Matsuda. ANI: Kasumi Matsuda. MUS: Hiroshi Sato. PRD: Sony Music Entertainment. 30 mins. x 2 eps.

In 2099, Earth has shifted off its axis and begins to rotate at an angle of 90% to the 20th-century equator. Three years of natural disasters follow, and when things settle down, Earth's ten billion population has died and only two million moon colonists remain. Some return to begin the repopulation of the world in seven new cities. The remaining colonists on the moon fear that their former neighbors might pose a threat and construct a ring of defense satellites to trap them on the newly repopulated homeworld—the Olympus system destroys anything that travels more than 500 meters above the surface. Then the lunar colonists are wiped out by plague. Trapped beneath a defensive ring that will operate automatically for the next 200 years, the seven newly founded cities begin to fight one another. Moorbridge Jr., the son of the exiled ruler of Aquionia, becomes the ruler of New Camelot and leads a force to recapture his homeland. His superior tactician, Kenneth Guildford, leads an attack on an Aquionian supply base, but his victorious troops are subject to a counterattack by the Aquionian hero Almaric Ashvail—compare to the similar well-matched foes of LEGEND OF GALACTIC HEROES, based on another novel by *SoSC* creator Yoshiki Tanaka.

SEVEN OF NANA *

2002. JPN: *Shichinin no Nana*. AKA: *Seven of Seven; NaNa 7 of 7*. TV series. DIR: Yasuhiro Imagawa. SCR: Mamiko Ikeda, Michiko Yokote, Yasuhiro Imagawa, Yasuko Kobayashi. DES: Asako Nishida, Mine Yoshizaki. ANI: N/C. MUS: Yoshihisa Hirano. PRD: AT-X, GENCO. 22 mins. x 25 eps.

Schoolgirl Nana Suzuki's dotty grandfather is using a crystal to separate light from the rainbow into its component seven colors. Unfortunately, he is using the family microwave as part of the experiment, and when Nana opens the door, the crystal explodes and splits her into six clones, each demonstrating just one aspect of the original. On one hand, there's the downbeat depressed Nana, the cheerful chirpy Nana, the clever Nana, the not-so-bright Nana, the nasty Nana, and the hypersensitive Nana. On the other hand, they've all acquired mystic powers, like the ability to fly. The original must now attempt to live with six wacky incarnations of herself—although the authors would like to point out that grandfather's "accident" presents an ideal solution to the problem Japan faces in RIZELMINE.

One of the constant gripes about team shows is that the team members are usually cardboard cutouts displaying one simplistic stereotype who have to work together to succeed. *7oN* could have made this a virtue by actually showing the process of an undeveloped young girl, looking at each aspect of her behavior and working out how to balance them into a rounded personality. Instead it crashes SAILOR MOON into TENCHI MUYO!, as the seven Nanas converge on the original's school crush. Based on a story by director Imagawa.

SEX DEMON QUEEN *

2000. JPN: *Yarima Queen*. Video. DIR: Takeshi Aoki. SCR: Michiru Yari. DES: Mamoru Yasuhiko. ANI: Naoyuki Owada. MUS: N/C. PRD: AIC, Green Bunny. 30 mins.
Blue-haired sorceress Kuri/Cooley and her red-haired assistant Rima travel to a fantasyland with every intention of righting wrongs. When they rescue the green-haired girl Sour from a gang rape, she insists on paying back her saviors by taking them to an inn and having sex with them. Conveniently, Sour is a virgin reared in a secluded convent where the only form of education was a prolonged course in bestowing sexual pleasure. However, the Sex Demon Queen has other plans and dispatches her doglike demons to attack the girls—this is something to do with

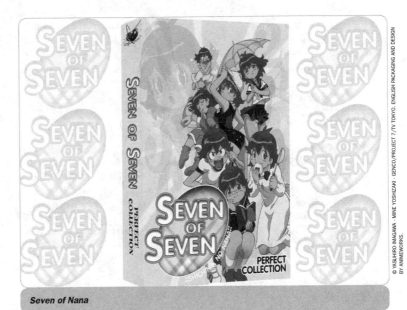

Seven of Nana

some missing magic rings, although they would be strange rings indeed if they were kept where the dogs end up looking.

After the many, many incidences in anime of not-quite-incest, *SDQ* tries something new with not-quite-bestiality—the demons only *look* like dogs, you see. The result is an anime with all the insane campery of VENUS FIVE, coupled with the forbidden acts hinted at in the backstory of the more mainstream HAKKENDEN. 🄻🅽🅥

SEX TAXI *

2002. JPN: *Kojin Taxi*. AKA: *Private (Owned) Taxi*. Video. DIR: Ahiru Koike. SCR: Doji Sozoro. DES: Makoto Amamiya. ANI: Makoto Amamiya. MUS: N/C. PRD: Studio Jam, Milky. 30 mins. x 5 eps.
A nameless protagonist arrives in a new town and gets a job as a taxi driver, using his peripatetic profession as a way to dig up dirt on local beauties. As in Martin Scorsese's *Taxi Driver* (1976), to which this erotic anime otherwise bears no resemblance, passengers tend to forget their manners and their reticence in his presence and often inadvertently spill useful details about their private lives. He has a particular

fetish for upper-class girls, especially in uniforms, and strikes it lucky with a pair of pretty twins who have suppressed lesbian feelings for each other. This being one of *those* anime, they aren't suppressed for long, and our hero is soon dragging the girls back to his abandoned school lair for the usual rounds of domination and abuse. They are followed shortly afterward by more victims, as he compiles further blackmail evidence of the sort that would frighten only sheltered anime schoolgirls. A "Best Of" compilation is filed in some sources as a phantom sixth episode. 🄻🅽🅥

SEX WARD *

2001. JPN: *Heisa Byoto*. Video. DIR: 1862 Kuboyama. SCR: Rokurota Makabe. DES: Joki Satsumaya. ANI: Mamoru Sakisaka. MUS: Yoshi. PRD: Digital Works (Vanilla Series). 30 mins. x 2 eps.
Satsuki Aoyanagi is the new recruit among the nurses, unaware that her long-time rival Naho has also signed up for the same ward. Before long, Satsuki is trying and failing to dodge the petty humiliations of Naho, as well as the lecherous attentions of the hospital chief Yutaka Ishikawa. Not to be

confused with the similarly titled *Heisa Byoin*, filed in this book as NAUGHTY NURSES. Both titles, however, are entries in the erotic VANILLA SERIES. *Sex Ward* is filed as a "completed" title on its manufacturer's web page, despite an ending that was clearly intended to leave things open for a sequel. ●NV

SEX WARRIOR PUDDING *
2004. JPN: *Famiresu Senshi Purin*. AKA: *Fami[ly] Res[taurant] Warrior Purin*. Video. DIR: Katsumasa Kanezawa. SCR: Katsumasa Kanezawa. DES: Isshi Hinoki. ANI: N/C. MUS: N/C. PRD: Milky. 30 mins. x 3 eps.
Shuta is an idle slacker devoted to pornographic computer games in the manner of the protagonist of AKIBA GIRLS. Imagine, then, his surprise (and our lack of it) when he inherits a restaurant from his father. The À La Mode diner is also the workplace for Shuta's would-be girlfriend Purin "Pudding" Nishimura and sex with the staff soon ensues. One would hope that was enough for any erotic anime, but no, the restaurant is not merely packed with sexy waitresses in the style of VARIABLE GEO, but also with *operatives* in a Global Defense Agency, fighting against incursions from the heretofore unknown underground kingdom of Lividoll. Before long, the hordes of Lividoll have decided that the best way to conquer the world is to open a rival restaurant across the street, and then seduce all the customers away from the À La Mode. As plans go, it's hardly Operation Desert Storm, but it's a start. In one of the strange moves of the adult anime industry, the rights to the third and final episode were snapped up by a different company in America. ●

SEXFRIEND *
2002. Video DIR: Kurige Katsura. SCR: Kurige Katsura. DES: Tadashi Shida. ANI: Tadashi Shida, Jiro Yamada. MUS: Toru Yukawa. PRD: Anime House, Green Bunny, Shinkukan. 30 mins. x 2 eps.
The sex-mad schoolgirl is a popular trope in porn; the male can abrogate

all responsibility because she "made" him do it. The girl in this story is Mina Hayase and her target is classmate Tomohiro Takabe. Mina tells Tomohiro she doesn't want a boyfriend; she wants a "sexfriend," just for physical diversion with no strings attached. Aided and abetted by the school nurse, the pair spend most of their days in the nurse's office studying anatomy. At least it's consensual and, as is often the case with Green Bunny productions, well executed. "Sex Friend," or its contraction "SF," was a documented term in Japanese slang as early as 1992, making the only mystery with this title the length of time it took to appear. Based on a video game by Codepink/Stone Heads. ●N

SEXORCIST *
1996. JPN: *Ningyo Tsukai*. AKA: *Puppet Masters*. Video. DIR: Shigeru Yazaki. SCR: Kazuhiko Godo. DES: Kenji Teraoka, Kenichi Harada. ANI: Masao Tsutsumi. MUS: Kazuhiko Izu. PRD: Sente Studio. 45 mins.
The Silhouette robots of 2114 are virtual-reality "puppets" whose sensations of pleasure and pain can be passed on to their human operators. Enter Rika, a beautiful Silhouette manipulator thrown into a corporate underworld where Silhouette-gladiators fight in death matches, and women are forced to endure assaults through the machines to which they are wired.

Despite being another smut session of screaming girls and leering perverts, *Sexorcist* has a lot to teach other game adaptations. The SF/erotica combination gives two extra angles to the dreary combat of TEKKEN or TOSHINDEN. Avoiding the halfhearted hackery of most porn, it really makes use of the SF setting—particularly in the separation of body and mind. In one chilling moment, Rika sees herself through the eyes of the Silhouette she is operating and notices that an assailant is sneaking up behind her.

In legal terms, the Silhouettes are not human, so they can perform more explicit acts than normally allowed by

the Japanese censor. They also speak without moving their lips, allowing the animators to concentrate their budget on the fights and naked flesh. But while it may be an outstanding example of the genre, the genre is porn, and this offering also features bondage, tentacles, hypnotism, drugs, electric whips, and ceremonial rape. The PC game sequel to the original, featuring Rika's granddaughter, was released in the U.K. as *Bishojo Fighter*. ●V

SEXTRA CREDIT *
2003. JPN: *Mejoku*. AKA: *Female Torture*. Video. DIR: Taifu Suginami. SCR: American Pie. DES: Taifu Suginami. ANI: Taifu Suginami. MUS: Yoshi. PRD: YOUC, Digital Works (Vanilla Series). 30 mins. x 2 eps.
Jotaro is a lonely teacher, frustrated by the utter lack of interest shown in him by the five sexy lady teachers at his school. He gains a new mission in life when he keeps a rebellious pupil behind after school and learns that the pair of them make a great team at hunting down female victims. Rape and abuse duly follow in another entry in the VANILLA SERIES, based on a computer game by LiLiM. ●NV

SEXY MAGICAL GIRL *
2003. JPN: *Maho Shojo Ai*. AKA: *Magical Girl Ai*. Video. DIR: Hirohide Shikishima. SCR: Tsunekazu Murakami. DES: Seitsuki. ANI: Seitsuki. MUS: N/C. PRD: Milky (Red), GP Museum Pictures. 30 mins. x 5 eps.
Akitoshi is an average boy in an average Tokyo suburb who suddenly starts noticing the very pretty Ai—although acquaintances inform him that she has always been in the neighborhood, merely escaping his notice in the past. While walking down a back alley, he disturbs a creature in the process of raping local girl Mikage and *almost* intervenes. Before he can truly behave in an active or heroic way, Ai herself steps in to fight the monster, which is an old-fashioned tentacled alien menace. After two episodes of saving Earth through tentacle sex, Ai suddenly dis-

appears, leaving Akitoshi in a strange position akin to the one he had earlier—whereas previously he seemed to be the only person who hadn't noticed Ai, now he is the only one who seems to remember her. As with DEMON BEAST INVASION, this strange reset to zero is in fact a means of restarting a franchise that had already reached its natural end, with a substandard "second half" that plays more like an afterthought sequel. Ai duly returns and saves the day, again, after more tentacle rapist monsters, again. Based on a computer game by Colors. **LNV**

SHADOW SKILL *

1995. JPN: *Kagewaza/Shadow Skill*. Video, TV series. DIR: Hiroshi Negishi, Hiroyuki Kuroda, Tsukasa Sunaga. SCR: Mayori Sekijima, Masashi Sogo. DES: Toshinari Yamashita, Fumitoshi Kizaki. ANI: Yoshio Murata, Fumitoshi Kizaki. MUS: Osamu Tezuka (the other one), Tsutomu Ohira. PRD: Zero-G Room, Shadow Skill Project; Studio Deen, TV Tokyo. 45 mins. (v1), 30 mins. x 3 eps. (v2), 25 mins. x 26 eps. (TV).

In the kingdom of Kuldar (Karuta in the dub), there is only one way out of servitude—by becoming a gladiator in the arena (a thinly disguised Colosseum). Gladiators can become shavals (sevilles), the chosen knights of the kingdom. Ele Rag is the youngest of the 59 shavals, a mistress of the secret fighting art known as the Shadow Skill. She cares for Gau Ban of the Black Howling, a traumatized young orphan she found four years earlier. But Gau lives in a secret internal turmoil of honor and duty, watching Ele Rag's every move so that he may learn the Shadow Skill and become the brother she deserves.

SS was based on the 1992 *Comic Gamma* manga by Megumu Okada, praised in Japan for its meticulous internal logic. Okada has some great ideas, such as the Shadow Skill itself (a psychic martial art for slaves whose hands are bound) and magic in which each spell must be engaged in con-

versation before being unleashed. Okada's clan terminology creates "families" of people who aren't really related, defending the memories of "fathers" who weren't necessarily their biological parents. Like sumo wrestlers, clan adoption brings a new name, and like the samurai codes of old, the ignoble death of one's master forces a period of exile while the outcast seeks revenge. It also forbids the exile to use his or her former name, so *SS* contains a lot of people with very long and cumbersome handles. The man known as Screep Lohengrin of the White Running in the original manga is just plain "Louie" here, for example. Similar compressions devalue the rest of the production: mere moments after we're told that Gau is mute, he breaks his vow of silence to chat with the first stranger he meets. The anime *SS* is reduced to a simple kung-fu revenge tragedy, as a party that consists of two warriors (Ele and Gau), a magic-user (Fowari), and a ranger/cleric (Kiao Yu) square off against people who killed their fathers, and now must prepare to die (etc.). We're occasionally reminded of the original's evil Sorphan Empire, with tales of the King of the Moon or shots of a young Gau hunting a centaur, but the invaders are greatly underused.

The one-shot video *SS* soon made it to the U.K. through Manga Entertainment. It performed way beyond expectations in Japan and was followed in 1996 by an additional three-part series, also released in English, though cut into the feature-length *SS the Movie*. The dub was done in Wales, a land known for its own arcane language, though that's no excuse for the clunky dialogue or the outrageous moment when Kiao yells away soundlessly, presumably because nobody was paying attention to the visuals. The 1998 TV series, produced after the manga had switched publication to *Comic Dragon Junior*, was screened in a late-night slot and restored much of the manga's backstory. However, it still awaits English-language release. **LNV**

SHAKOTAN BOOGIE

1991. Video. DIR: Hiromitsu Sato, Junichi Tokaibayashi. SCR: Shikichi Ohashi. DES: Hiroyuki Horiuchi. ANI: Hiroyuki Horiuchi, Hirotaka Kinoshita. MUS: Noriyuki Asakura. PRD: Studio Pierrot. 55 mins. x 4 eps.

It's girls, gangs, and cars in this adaptation of the 1985 manga in *Young Magazine*, by LULLABY FOR WEDNESDAY'S CINDERELLA–creator Michiharu Kusunoki. Local tough guys steal cars, switch the plates, and sell them, but not without racing them for a while against rival gangs. The anime continues the story where the 1987 live-action movie starring Kazuya Kimura left off. Compare to INITIAL D.

SHAKUGAN NO SHANA

2005. AKA: *Shana of the Burning Eyes*. TV series. DIR: Takashi Watanabe. SCR: Yasuko Kobayashi. DES: Mai Otsuka. ANI: Shingo Fukuyo. MUS: Ko Otani. PRD: JC Staff, Animax, Chiba TV. 25 mins. x 26 eps.

Everyday Japanese student Yuji Sakai is attacked by a strange creature and saved by a girl with red hair and red eyes. Shana, for it is she, is a Flame Haze agent, whose job it is to hunt down Crimson Denizens, creatures from the Crimson Realm who are attempting to break into our world. Shana's mission is to protect Yuji, since there is supposedly something special about him that only gorgeous, nubile alien amazons can detect. Although initially presented as a tough, uncaring fighter, Shana inevitably warms to Yuji, particularly after they are forced to set up home in an URUSEI YATSURA–inspired cohabitation. Learning about the world through the highly inadvisable route of watching TV, Shana is soon asking Yuji to explain more about this "love" of which the soap operas continually speak. The authors are tempted to point out that a more realistic approach would have had her flicking through channel after channel and finding nothing but TENCHI MUYO! clones, questioning her existence, and debating the point of it all. Nevertheless, Shana and her associates are soon battling to save Yuji and his planet from Alastor, the ruler of the Crimson Realm, using a variety of fire-themed magic. Based on a series of books by Yashichiro Takahashi, illustrated by Noizi Ito. As with SLAYERS, calling them "novels" is a little presumptuous, as they are low on word count and high on illustrations, more like novelettes.

SHAMAN KING *
2001. TV series, specials. DIR: Seiji Mizushima. SCR: Katsuhiko Koide. DES: Akio Takami, Shinichi Yamaoka. ANI: Akio Takami. MUS: Toshiyuki Omori. PRD: NAS, TV Tokyo, Animax, Xebec. 23 mins. x 64 eps., 30 mins. x 3 eps. (specials).
Shamans are people who can communicate with the supernatural and join with the spirits of the dead to use their skill and power. Teenager Yoh Asakura is a shaman, engaged to the ambitious Anna. She wants to marry the greatest shaman of all, the Shaman King. Once every 500 years a great contest, the Shaman Fight, gives the winner the chance to become Shaman King and wield great power by controlling the strongest spirits. The winner also gets to meet God. Yoh goes to Tokyo for the contest, along with his three faithful friends—Manta Oyamada, an undersized junior-high student who is scared of spirits but is able to see them, and whom Yoh has taken on as a de-facto apprentice; his spirit partner, a samurai named Amidamaru; and Anna, who is also a medium and is acting as his trainer. Along the way they meet strong opposition, misfit ghosts and would-be magicians, in a series whose high concept could be summed up as PHANTOM QUEST CORP meets DRAGON BALL. Based on a manga by Hiroyuki Takei, serialized in Shonen Jump. **CNV**

SHAMANIC PRINCESS *
1996. Video. DIR: Mitsuru Hongo, Hiroyuki Nishimura. SCR: Asami Watanabe. DES: Atsuko Ishida. ANI: Atsuko Ishida, Masahiko Ogura, Hiroyuki Nishimura. MUS: Yoshikazu Suo. PRD:

Bandai, Movic, Animate Film. 30 mins. x 6 eps.
Accompanied by Japolo, her ermine-like familiar (or "Partner"), Princess Tiara is sent from the Guardian World into our own dimension to prevent an imbalance in the cosmos. As a Magic User, this is her royal duty, since the Guardians must police the actions of indestructible, unpredictable Shadows. Disguised as a schoolgirl, Tiara must find Kagetsu, a being loyal to Yord, the godlike entity that is the Guardian World's source of power. Not only has Kagetsu stolen the Throne of Yord (a direct link to unfathomable powers), but he is also her ex-beloved, and the brother of her missing best friend, Sarah.

SP refers on occasion to the story of Daphne, who in Greek mythology was turned into a laurel tree to avoid the advances of Apollo—Sarah is actually trapped inside the Throne, which looks like a painting of laurel trees. But such literary pretensions are a red herring in themselves, since the six-strong committee that provided SP's "story concept" are more interested in providing good-looking images. With painstakingly animated CG rose petals in the opening credits and ribbon-like adornments worthy of OH MY GODDESS!, they are not unsuccessful; girls duel with swords made of shadows and Tiara's luscious red hair transforms into unearthly wings beneath the light of the moon (a "moon-tree" in Japanese is a laurel). There are faint echoes of KIKI'S DELIVERY SERVICE in the European setting and mundane witchery, but SP is very much a designer's film, with sharp characters from RAYEARTH's Ishida and lush green backgrounds from SPRIGGAN's Hajime Matsuoka. It also has magical powers entrapped in sigils on the sorcerers' own skins, a peculiar fad from the mid-1990s also found in TATTOON MASTER. The switch in directors for the final two episodes also brings a switch in plotting—parts five and six are a prequel to the first four, creating an intriguing circular structure that plays with ideas of memory, dream, and reality.

SHAME ON MISS MACHIKO
1981. JPN: Maitchingu Machiko Sensei. TV series. DIR: Masami Annai, Keiichiro Mochizuki. SCR: Seiko Taguchi, Chiho Shioda, Kenji Terada, Yasuko Hoshikawa. DES: Kazuya Kaminashi, Keiko Aono. ANI: Kazuya Kaminashi, Norio Hirayama. MUS: N/C. PRD: Studio Pierrot, Studio Gallop, TV Tokyo. 25 mins. x 95 eps.
Machiko is a young elementary-school teacher who does her utmost to solve the everyday problems faced by her little pupils. Unfortunately the situations and traps created by the little moppets always seem to involve Teacher losing some or all of her clothes, much to the delight of her class, and the utter disapproval of the Japanese PTA, which fulminated against lechery in a "children's" show (albeit one broadcast at 7:30 p.m.). The later CRAYON SHIN-CHAN would bring similar criticisms.

The story was remade as the live-action movie Machiko Begins (2005) starring Sayaka Isoyama. **N**

SHAMELESS SCHOOL
1995. JPN: Heisei Harenchi Gakuen. AKA: Modern-Era Shameless School. Video. DIR: Koichi Kobayashi. SCR: N/C. DES: Go Nagai. ANI: Kimiyo Ono, Taseiko Hamazu. MUS: N/C. PRD: Pink Pineapple, KSS. 47 mins.
Yamanegi is determined to enjoy his school days—a desire made easier by attending a place of learning where the teachers are more interested in looking at girls' underwear and the classes are a nonstop party. This one-shot anime revived Go Nagai's controversial 1968 manga, originally run in Shonen Jump, much to the annoyance of PTA organizations all over Japan. Compare to Nagai's equally silly KEKKO KAMEN. **N**

SHERLOCK HOUND *
1984. JPN: Meitantei Holmes. AKA: Famous Detective Holmes. TV series, movie. DIR: Hayao Miyazaki, Keiji Hayakawa, Seiji Okuda. SCR: Toshiyuki Yamazaki, Yoshihisa Araki, Hayao Miyazaki, Tsunehisa Ito. DES: Yoshifumi Kondo. ANI: Tsukasa Tannai, Seiji

Kitahara. MUS: Kentaro Haneda. PRD: Tokyo Movie Shinsha, RAI, TV Asahi. 25 mins. x 26 eps. (TV), 45 mins. x 2 (m).

The great detective Sherlock Holmes and his faithful friend Dr. John Watson are in constant demand in Edwardian London to foil the evil schemes of Professor Moriarty, who is constantly out to steal some exotic treasure or cause havoc with his minions, Todd and Smiley. In this charming adventure series for children, they are transformed into anthropomorphic dogs (see also DOG-TANIAN AND THE THREE MUSKEHOUNDS). Their adventures are full of charm, wit, and energy as they search for a missing train, track three mysterious lobsters, and defeat a "monster" in the Thames that is more than it seems. Adapted by MONTANA JONES–creator Marco Pagot from the original novels by Arthur Conan Doyle, this was Pagot's first work with Ghibli's giants. The series was very popular on TV in the U.K. and is still available on video in the U.S. The episodes *Blue Carbuncle* (#5) and *Sunken Treasure* (#9) were combined to make a 1984 theatrical release shown on a double bill with Miyazaki's NAU-SICAÄ. A further two, *The Kidnapping of Mrs. Hudson* (#4) and *Air War Over the Cliffs of Dover* (#10), were combined to create a 1986 "movie" shown on a double bill with CASTLE IN THE SKY. A more realistic Sherlock Holmes would get on the trail of a French master thief: see LUPIN THE MASTERTHIEF AND THE ENIGMA OF 813. The first episode also exists in an alternate dub made by TMS for promotional purposes, which showcases more realistic British accents and renames Todd and Smiley as Nigel and Bruce.

SHE'S NO ANGEL

1994. JPN: *Tenshi Nanka Janai*. AKA: *Somewhat Unangelic*. Video. DIR: Hiroko Tokita. SCR: Tomoko Konparu. DES: Yasuomi Umezu. ANI: Chuji Nakajima. MUS: Fujio Takano. PRD: Group Tac. 30 mins.

Based on the manga in *Ribbon* magazine by NEIGHBORHOOD STORY–creator Ai Yazawa, this anime features the drama and romance centering on one girl's attempt to transfer schools.

SHIBAI TAROKA

1993. JPN: *Shibai Taroka*. AKA: *Puttin' it On*. Video. DIR: Teruo Kigure. SCR: Shunsuke Amemura. DES: Shigeru Koshiba. ANI: Teruo Kigure. MUS: Toshio Okazawa. PRD: Toei, Knack. 30 mins. x 2 eps.

Hard-faced tough-guy Kusuta transfers to the Osaka area, where everyone is a hard-faced tough guy (see COMPILER). But appearances can be deceptive: he likes flowers and fairy stories. The girls love him, the guys hate him. There's trouble. Based on the 1993 manga in *Young Champion* by Shigeru Koshiba.

SHIBAYAMA, TSUTOMU

1941– . Born in Tokyo, he studied drama at Meiji University, joining Toei Animation after graduation and working on shows including KEN THE WOLF BOY and HUSTLE PUNCH. He moved to A Production (now Shin'ei Doga), and continued to work as a key animator and director, although his feature debut did not come until GO FOR IT, TABUCHI (1978).

SHIBUYA HONKY TONK

1988. Video. DIR: Masamune Ochiai. SCR: Masaru Yamamoto. DES: N/C. ANI: Tadashi Abiko. MUS: BORO. PRD: Tokuma Japan, Knack. 35 mins. x 4 eps.

Set in 1945, this is the story of teenager Naoya Abe, who comes from a good family but is fixated by the seeming glamour of organized crime. He manages to talk his way into working for the Todogumi, the clan that controls Tokyo's fashionable Shibuya area, but it's a lot tougher and less glamorous than he hoped. When his girlfriend is threatened and he kills a rival clan member, he decides to escape to London. Volume two sees him working in London as an assistant to photographer Aoki, but he manages to get himself involved in the theft of military secrets. When his criminal past comes to light, he's sent back to Japan to face the music, but he survives and rises through the ranks of the Todogumi. Based on the semiautobiographical novel by Joji Abe, who also appears in a live-action section.

SHIDARA, HIROSHI

1936– . Born in Yamagata, he studied drama at Nippon University, and joined Toei's Kyoto office after graduation. He moved to Toei Animation in 1962, and his credits begin appearing on SPACE PATROL HOPPA by 1965. He was a supervising director on CANDY CANDY.

SHIHO-CHAN

1996. JPN: *Maho no Shiho-chan*. AKA: *Magical Shiho-chan*. Video. DIR: Takashi Abe. SCR: N/C. DES: Minato Koimoro. ANI: Yasuhito Kikuchi. MUS: N/C. PRD: Pink Pineapple, KSS. 30 mins. 2 eps.

Released from an icy tomb in the Antarctic, Vaj the talking penguin goes in search of a girl to protect Earth from danger by transforming into a more "adult" version of herself. This porno based on a *Young Magazine* manga by Minato Koimoro contains oblique references to EVANGELION that serve no purpose whatsoever. Ⓝ

SHIMOKAWA, OTEN

1892–1973. Pseudonym of Sadanori Shimokawa, sometimes Hekoten Shimokawa. Born in Okinawa, Shimokawa moved to Tokyo at the age of seven after the death of his father, a school principal. He worked for the cartoonist Raiten Kitazawa both before and after a stint in the Army General Staff as a trainee engineer. By 1912, he was a cartoonist for the satirical magazine *Tokyo Puck* and was commissioned in 1916 to make short animated cartoons for the Tenkatsu Studio. None of his animation work survives, but his *Mukuzo Imokawa the Doorman*, made in 1916 and released in January 1917, is widely regarded as the "first anime"—see EARLY ANIME. His work appears to have been made using the "chalk board" method, in which a single image on a blackboard is photographed and rephotographed with minor alterations.

Shimokawa's fifth film, *An Animation about Fishing* (1917, *Chamebozu, Uotsuri no Maki*), was also his last. Although he never worked in animation again, he enjoyed success in the 1930s writing manga for the *Sunday Yomiuri*, and postWorld War II as an artist for *Nippon Manga Shinbun*.

SHIN HAKKENDEN

1999. JPN: *God Hakkenden*. TV series. DIR: Katsuyoshi Yatabe, Toshiaki Suzuki, Kenji Yoshida. SCR: Yasushi Hirano. DES: Atsuko Ishida, Masahiko Okura. ANI: Moriyasu Taniguchi, Shinichiro Minami. MUS: N/C. PRD: Beam Entertainment, TV Tokyo. 25 mins. x 26 eps.
The year is 2588 in the system of God-world and its eight satellites. Humanity came here in the distant past, after a long journey across the stars from Earth. Now the system is ruled by a loose coalition of powerful families: House Owari, House Meed, and House Iigy. The story begins when Kai, the heir to House Owari, attacks an icy planet. Living in a humble village on the surface is Ko, a young boy who is perpetually arguing with his father. When Kai's navy arrives, Ko takes his father's mighty Murasame sword to fight back, and his adventures begin. A sci-fi remake of HAKKENDEN. (Not to be confused with Pioneer's continuation of the original *H* series, *Shin [New] Hakkenden*).

SHIN'EI DOGA

Literally "New Image Animation," or "New A Animation." Originally formed as A Productions (A Pro) in late 1965, its releases include the early Hayao Miyazaki work PANDA GO PANDA. The company was reorganized into its new form in 1976 by Daikichiro Kusube, a former employee of Tokyo Movie Shinsha. Its first notable work in its new incarnation was on DORAEMON. Prominent staffers have included Toshihide Yamada, Eiichi Nakamura, Susumu Watanabe, Keiichi Hara, and Toshihiko Ando. The company is still active today on productions such as CRAYON SHIN-CHAN.

SHINESMAN *

1995. JPN: *Tokumu Sentai Shinesman*. AKA: *Special Duty Battle Team Shinesman*. Video. DIR: Shinya Sadamitsu. SCR: Hideki Sonoda. DES: Kiyoharu Ishii, Atsuo Kobu. ANI: Kiyoharu Ishii. MUS: N/C. PRD: Sony, Animate Film. 30 mins. x 2 eps.
Hiroya Matsumoto is a bright young salesman working for Right Trading Company, devoted to his job and to his younger brother, Yota. But after work he swaps his business suit for red combat armor and puts in overtime as leader of the company's Special Duty Combat Unit division. He and his four colleagues Ryoichi Hayami (green), Shojo Yamadera (gray), Shotaro Ono (sepia), and Riko Hidaka (pink) are the Shinesman team. They're under the command of Kyoko Sakakibara of Human Resources and helped by support staff Hitomi Kasahara and Tsukasa Nakamura, and their sworn mission is to defend the Right Trading Company and the world from the invaders from Planet Voice, who are bent on conquering Earth. Sasaki, the prince of Voice, and his strategist sidekick, Seki, are already on Earth implementing the devious plan—through their company Science Electronics, they plan to take over the world through building a great business empire. They've started out with theme parks and a TV show that's wowing kids everywhere; Yota is one of its biggest fans. This is a bizarre combination of *Power Rangers* and *Wall Street*, based on Minamu Tachibana's manga in *Comic Bokke*. Bad acting, recycled footage, silly dialogue, and insane plotting are presented as a satire—though since one gets plenty of that in anime anyway, it's tempting to suggest this is the same old same-old, just presented "ironically." Another allegory of corporate competition, this time about video formats, can be discerned beneath the surface of ARMITAGE III.

SHINGU: SECRETS OF THE STELLAR WARS

2001. JPN: *Gakuen Senki Muryo*. TV series. DIR: Tatsuo Sato. SCR: Tatsuo Sato. DES: Takahiro Yoshimatsu. ANI: Takahiro Yoshimatsu. MUS: Yuji Ono. PRD: Madhouse. 25 mins. x 8+ eps.
In the year 2070, the Japanese government finally admits the existence of aliens after an "unidentified" flying object in Tokyo identifies itself as "the Seeker." A few days later, new student Subaru Muryo transfers to a school in Tenmo, a new town in Kanagawa Prefecture. He dresses and behaves oddly, inspiring fellow student Hajime Murata to investigate further—no prizes for guessing that Subaru is not of this Earth.

SHINIGAMI'S BALLAD

2006. JPN: *Shinigami no Ballad*. AKA: *Ballad of the God of Death; Momo the God of Death*. TV series. DIR: Tomomi Mochizuki, Ryuichi Kimura. SCR: Reiko Yoshida. DES: Hiroyuki Horiuchi. ANI: Hiroyuki Horiuchi. MUS: Moka. PRD: Gingaya, Group Tac, WOWOW. 25mins. x 6 eps.
Momo, an attractive girl clad in gothic clothes, is a classier, prettier version of the Grim Reaper. Assisted by her talking cat Daniel, she interferes in the lives of humans—her mission is supposedly only to do so at the times of their deaths, when she collects their souls, but Momo is often tempted to other duties, including helping people. *Highway to Heaven*, but with a scythe, based on a novel by Keisuke Hasegawa.

SHINSENGUMI FARCE

1989. JPN: *Shogeki Shinsengumi*. Video. DIR: Hiromi Noda, Takenori Kawata. SCR: Hiromi Noda. DES: Hiromi Noda. ANI: Michi Sato. MUS: N/C. PRD: ACC, Tanihara Studio, Random. 30 mins.
A comical depiction of the unrest caused by the arrival of Commodore Perry's black ships in 1853, as nationalists and *ultra*-nationalists fight over who should rule Japan in the name of the emperor (see OI RYOMA!). As the rival domains of Satsuma and Choshu jostle for power, the Shinsengumi organization becomes the emperor's "protectors" in Kyoto. Hyped on

release as "the Shinsengumi as you've never seen them before," somewhat ironically since anime *never* seems to have portrayed the Shinsengumi as the vigilante extremists they actually were. Similarly sanitized versions would appear in ZEGUY and in Nagisa Oshima's live-action *Gohatto* (2000), which romanticized them as sexually confused pretty-boys.

SHIOYAMA, NORIO

1940– . After his debut with HARRIS'S WIND, he joined forces with Ryosuke Takahashi to become one of the prime movers of the great era of robot anime. His first work as a character designer was on DAITARN 3, although he is probably best remembered today for RONIN WARRIORS.

SHIRAKAWA, DAISUKE

1935– . Pseudonym for Kenichi Takahashi. After early training in economics, he joined Toei Animation and worked on MAGIC BOY before working directly with Osamu Tezuka on JOURNEY TO THE WEST (1960). He subsequently worked as an animator on LITTLE NORSE PRINCE, MADCAP ISLAND, and many others, before leaving hands-on animation in 1968 to work as a producer for radio and television. He became a section leader at Media Center, a production planning house, in 1974.

SHIRATO, TAKESHI

1944– . After a debut as a key animator on TIGER MASK in 1969, he played a similar role in the productions of works including STAR BLAZERS and IKKYU. He has also been a sketch artist and character designer and was the director of BENEATH THE BLACK RAIN.

SHIROW, MASAMUNE

1961– . Pseudonym for Masanori Ota. Born in Kobe, Shirow graduated from Osaka University of Arts. He achieved early fame as a manga creator, leading to an ill-starred role as director on his own BLACK MAGIC M-66, from which he eventually stepped down in favor

of Hiroyuki Kitakubo mid-production. Subsequent adaptations of Shirow's manga work, such as GHOST IN THE SHELL, have traded on his name, but have been made without his direct involvement. Others, such as LANDLOCK and GUNDRESS, have utilized the bare minimum of Shirow's contribution (a single character design, for example) and trumpeted it as if he has made every frame.

SHOCKING PINK GIRL MOMOKO

1990. Video. DIR: Masakatsu Tonokawa. SCR: Tetsuya Aikawa. DES: Tetsuya Aikawa. ANI: Hiroyoshi Sugawara. MUS: N/C. PRD: Apollon, Mook, Central AV. ca. 40 mins. x 2 eps.
The misadventures of a large-chested bimbo, based on Tetsuya Aikawa's manga in *Manga Sunday* magazine. She wants to be a star like Marilyn Monroe, but it's a tough route to the top, and it unsurprisingly involves taking off her clothes. **N**

SHOGUN WARRIORS

1977.
This is not an anime show, but it was the first major impact of anime robots on U.S. consciousness since ASTRO BOY. It's a brand name created by Mattel for a range of unrelated anime robot toys imported from Japan. Monogram also produced plastic kits of the toys, and in 1979 Marvel acquired permission to produce a comic book featuring the first three robots licensed, although the story lines and characters bear no relationship to the original Japanese series. The comic ran for 20 issues. By 1980, the line was at an end, but it was massively influential at the time; when FORCE FIVE was advertised in 1981, Jim Terry Productions' flier for the show labeled it "for the kids who have already bought $75 million worth of these Super Robot toys marketed by Mattel under the name of *The Shogun Warriors*." See also GODAIKIN. The names used in the U.S. included (in order of U.S. release) Raydeen (*Brave Reideen*, see BRAVE RAIDEEN), Combatra (COMBATTLER V), Dangard Ace (DAN-

GARD ACE), Mazinga and Great Mazinga (see MAZINGER Z), Daimos (see STARBIRDS), Dragun, Raider, and Poseidon (see GETTER ROBO G), GRANDIZER, and Voltus V (VOLTUS).

SHOJYO KOAKUMA KEI *

2002. JPN: *Shojo Koakuma Kei*. AKA: *Girl Prostitution Kei; The Writhing Women*. Video. DIR: Noboru Yumejima. SCR: Sarasa. DES: Maruta. ANI: Makoto Motoguchi. MUS: N/C. PRD: IKIK Room, Five Ways (Wide Road). 30 mins.
Kyoichi is an ambitious young businessman who hopes to be the best in his field—it's just that his field happens to be prostitution. We first meet him setting up a client who likes young girls with Ayaka, who looks, sounds, and acts young but is no helpless schoolgirl. The real female lead, though, is Yuri, who has a crush on Kyoichi and believes he helped her out of a bad situation. To repay him, she comes to work as a maid in his business and ends up servicing clients, unaware that Kyoichi actually set up her misfortune to put her in his debt. But there's more to Yuri than meets the eye, and Kyoichi's joke that his girls are "little devils" may not be a mere casual remark. The sex is adult and consensual, though tasteless, so this isn't one of the worst porn anime you'll ever see—but please be aware that this is no recommendation. **LN**

SHOOT!

1994. JPN: *Aoi Densetsu Shoot*. AKA: *Blues Legend Shoot*. TV series, movie. DIR: Daisuke Nishio, Akinori Yabe, Takenori Kawata, Masahiro Hosoda, Tatsuo Misawa, Hiroyuki Kadono. SCR: Junji Takegami, Kazuhiko Kobe. DES: Shingo Araki. ANI: Shingo Araki, Masami Abe, Toshio Takahashi. MUS: Yusuke Honma. PRD: Toei, Fuji TV. 25 mins. x 58 eps. (TV), 25 mins. (m).
Toshi joins his high school soccer team and is enjoying the training and social life to the full. Then, in the middle of the series, Kubo, the popular captain of the team, has a cardiac arrest on the pitch and dies. The rest of the series

is the story of how Toshi and his teammates cope with this shattering loss (see Touch for a baseball drama along the same lines). The short film of the same title, also released in 1994, brings back many memories for the team members of their match against a squad from Germany, including an old friend of Kubo's. Based on the 1990 *Shonen Sunday* manga by Tsukasa Oshima.

SHOOTFIGHTER TEKKEN *

2003. JPN: *Koko Tekken-den Tough*. AKA: *High School Exciting Story: Tough*. Video. DIR: Yukio Nishimoto. SCR: Jin Munesue. DES: Fumitomo Kizaki. ANI: Yasuo Hasegawa. MUS: N/C. PRD: AIC, Spike. 45 mins. x 3 eps.
Iron Kiba, champion of the World Pro Wrestling circuit, is tough. Miyazawa is just as tough, if not tougher, and the pair have a long history in the dark and criminal underbelly of the pro wrestling scene. Miyazawa's boy Kiichi looks harmless, but with Dad's training and support from other fighters he becomes a master of the Nanshin Shadow style. Eventually Kiichi and Kiba will face each other in the ring, but not before you've watched three episodes of piledriver punches, bodyslams to the concrete, crushed bones, and buckets of gore. Yet another tournament series, but with no dragonballs, cute critters, or underwear jokes—instead it's a return to Japanese professional wrestling, which has been an obsession with TV audiences ever since the earliest days of TV, when programmers fell in love with the sport because it only required one camera above the ring. The series also attempts to inject comedy, with stumbling results. Based on a manga by Tetsuya Saruwatari, who gave us even more ludicrous fighting in RIKI-OH. Inadvertently or otherwise, the English-language release title implies a non-existent link with TEKKEN. ●V

SHOTARO ISHINOMORI'S HISTORICAL ADVENTURES

1991. JPN: *Ishinomori Shotaro no Rekishi Adventure*. Video. DIR: Fuyu Kanno, Ura Sato. SCR: Masayuki Oseki. DES:

Shotaro Ishinomori. ANI: N/C. MUS: N/C. PRD: Media Design. 50 mins. x 2 eps.
A two-part video series in which Dr. Teng (a researcher at the Time Institute) and his faithul kappa (river creature) assistant Pasuke travel through time, first to the Battle of Sekigahara (1600) and then to the fourth Battle of Kawanakajima (1561). In the second installment, they then look in on the last stand of the Japanese underdog hero Yoshitsune in Hiraizumi (1189) and then, after spending so much time on the Genpei War, suddenly leap several centuries into the future, to cover the first time Nobunaga Oda used firearms in battle, at Nagashino (1575, see also YOTODEN). A mixture of live-action and anime, described by Japanese sources as a "documentary with a touch of story," and presumably related in some way to Shotaro Ishinomori's multivolume manga history of Japan.

SHOYONOID MAKOTO-CHAN

1998. Video. DIR: Sassai Ima. SCR: Sassai Ima. DES: Sassai Ima. ANI: Sassai Ima. MUS: N/C. PRD: JVD. 30 mins. x 2 eps.
A deceased superheroine is brought back from the dead when her inventor father combines her with the body of a slightly underage-seeming android. Then she takes her clothes off. An early entry in the notorious VANILLA SERIES. ◐

SHRINE OF THE MORNING MIST *

2002. JPN: *Asagiri no Miko*. AKA: *Priestess of the Morning Mist; Maidens of the Morning Mist*. TV series. DIR: Yuji Moriyama. SCR: Ryoe Tsukimura. DES: Shoko Nakamoto. ANI: N/C. MUS: Tsuneyoshi Saito. PRD: Chaos Project. 12 mins. x 26 eps.
Teenager Tadahiro Amatsu has different colored eyes—one brown, one light hazel. One conceals a dark secret, which sets masked sorcerer Michimune Ayatachi and his band of demonic aides chasing after Tadahiro. The eye is linked to the spirit world, and what it sees there is able to cross into the human world. Michimune wants to use

Tadahiro to bring the Monster God into the world of men; meanwhile he'll settle for unleashing lesser monsters on mankind. But just when you need a spiritual defender, a whole harem of them turn up. Tadahiro's cousin, klutzy-but-kind trainee priestess Yuzu Hieda recruits four school friends to a shrine maiden defense force, and makes her older sister Kurako their trainer. Now the town has a fighting team to make them safe from demonic attack, and Tadahiro has a cousin who has had a crush on him since they were children, plus four of her friends, clogging up his life and our screen. The short run-time and monster-of-the-week format leaves little room for character development or plot innovation, but it's cute and repetitive enough to sell to both lovers of TENCHI MUYO! clones and those who go misty-eyed at the sight of traditionally dressed shrine maidens. Based on Hiroki Ukawa's manga, serialized in *Young King Ours*, the show was "conceived" by Ryoe Tsukimura, whose previous ideas have included the far superior EL HAZARD.

SHUFFLE!

2005. TV series. DIR: Naoto Hosoda. SCR: Katsuhiko Takayama, Katsumi Hasegawa, Masashi Suzuki. DES: Eiji Hirayama, Aoi Nishimata, Hiro Suzuhira. ANI: Eiji Hirayama. MUS: Kazuhiko Sawaguchi, Minoru Maruo. PRD: Shuffle! Media Partners. 24 mins. x 24 eps.
The gateways to the kingdoms of gods and demons are opened and can't be closed. In an ordinary suburb, the King of the Gods and his family move in on one side of the Tsuchimi family home, the King of the Demons and his family on the other. The teenage daughters of these two households set their sights on the human boy next door. Apparently they both fell in love with him years ago and have always wanted the chance to be near him, so the sudden availability of real estate in the human world is heaven-sent. But Rin already has a girl living with him—a childhood friend who is also in love with him.

The three love rivals and their object all go to the same high school and … well, you can fill in the rest for yourself. We have to admit we never expected a high concept that melds **UROTSUKIDOJI** with **URUSEI YATSURA,** but sadly that's *Shuffle*'s only claim to originality. Based on a computer game by Navel.

SHURA NO TOKI *

2004. JPN: *Mutsu Enmei-ryu Gaiden Shura no Toki*. AKA: *Untold Tales of the Mutsu Enmei School: Agent of Chaos*. TV series. DIR: Shin Misawa. SCR: Junji Takegami. DES: Takehiro Hamatsu. ANI: Takehiro Hamatsu. MUS: Yutaka Minobe (Wave Master). PRD: Studio Comet, Marvelous Music Publishing, Media Factory, Sotsueizo, TV Tokyo. 25 mins. x 26 eps.

The Mutsu clan practices an ancient unarmed martial art in Edo in the early 1600s. Big brother Yakumo crosses the path of swordmasters Musashi Miyamoto and Jubei Yagyu, and of young nobleman Kisshoumaru. Kisshoumaru is really a girl, Shiori, imitating a boy to protect the family inheritance, in the style of **YOTODEN** and **KAI DOH MARU.** An evil uncle wants "him"out of the way, and when Yakumo becomes "his" bodyguard the situation threatens to become even more complicated. Later episodes continue with later generations of the Mutsu clan, in the same family saga style as **JOJO'S BIZARRE ADVENTURES.** Consequently, after episode eight it focuses more on Iori, Musashi's young pupil, and his sometime rival Takato (a Mutsu clan member), thereby allowing the action to move 20 years further on, and engineer a number of new conflicts with a number of new swordsmen from history and legend.

The action leaps ahead again, this time to the Meiji Restoration of the 19th century for the final tale, which features yet another descendant of the Mutsu clan, Izumi, who is caught up with the conflicts of the Shinsengumi in Kyoto—compare to **PEACEMAKER KUROGANE.** We are thus able to see a number of other famous figures,

including Ryoma Sakamoto, in the final struggle over the supremacy of the samurai, which would eventually lead to the fall of the shogunate and the establishment of modern Japan.

Based on a manga by Masatoshi Kawahara in *Shonen Magazine*, it's easy to see *SnT*'s appeal—its dynasty of stubbly-faced, good-hearted heroes sits astride samurai history like the Yagyu clan (see **NINJA SCROLL**), benefiting from action-packed careers with a vague nod toward educational storylines.

SHURATO

1989. JPN: *Tenku no Senki Shurato*. AKA: *Heavenly Chronicle Shurato*. TV series, video. DIR: Mizuho Nishikubo, Takao Koyama, Ippei Kuri, Kazuhiro Mori, Shinji Takahashi, Satoshi Okada, Kiyoshi Murayama, Koji Masunari. SCR: Mayori Sekijima, Takao Koyama, Akinori Endo, Go Mihara. DES: Matsuri Okada, Masaki Nakao, Ammonite, Torao Arai. ANI: Masaki Nakao, Nobuyoshi Habara, Kenichi Okazaki. MUS: Hiroya Watanabe. PRD: Tatsunoko, TV Tokyo. 25 mins. x 36 eps. (TV), 30 mins. x 6 eps. (v).

Close friends Shurato and Gai are fighting in a martial arts tournament in modern-day Tokyo when they are hauled into another dimension and find that they have new powers bestowed by Asian gods and by *shakti*, animal totems with strange powers of their own. Shurato is one of the Eight Warriors of Vishnu, whose celestial kingdom is under threat of invasion from Asura. Gai is also one of these mystic warriors, but when Vishnu's treacherous general, Indra, turns the goddess into a statue and blames Shurato, Gai sides with Indra. The two close friends are now mortal enemies. Branded a traitor, can Shurato save Vishnu, her kingdom, and his friend? Can the two get back to their own lives? The series ended tragically, but six further episodes were released on video in 1991 and 1992, extending the story.

Though possessing a Hindu-mythos setting redolent of **RG VEDA,** this is a

series aimed squarely at the teenage boy market; a decade on, transforming the shakti into flying skateboards looks like a mistake. With the guiding hand of Tatsunoko's legendary producer Ippei Kuri on the tiller, *Shurato* delivers the goods. It was the number-one series in Japan in its year of release.

SHUSAKU *

1999. JPN: *Shusaku*. AKA: *Shameful*. Video. DIR: Jun Fukuda. SCR: Sakura Momoi. DES: Toshihide Masudate. ANI: Toshihide Masudate. MUS: N/C. PRD: Pink Pineapple, KSS. 30 mins. x 3 eps.

Secret lusts abound in a music school, where the teacher instructs his students in more than just carrying a tune. Based on a computer game by "Elf," and shamefully similar to **WAKE UP ARIA.** Ⓝ

SHUTENDOJI *

1989. AKA: *Star Hand Kid; Star Demon*. Video. DIR: Junji Nishimura, Masaaki Sudo, Jun Kawagoe. SCR: Masashi Sogo. DES: Satoshi Hirayama. ANI: Hideyuki Motohashi. MUS: Fumitaka Anzai. PRD: Dynamic Planning, Studio Signal. 50 mins. x 4 eps.

The childless Mr. and Mrs. Shutendo are praying for divine intervention at a shrine when two giant ogres crash through the space-time continuum. One of them is carrying a baby in his mouth, leaving it with them and promising to return in 15 years. Jiro, as they call the child, grows up to be a fine young man (albeit one who casts a giant, horned shadow) and is reluctant to return to his real parents when the allotted time expires.

Based on Go Nagai's 1977 manga for *Shonen Magazine*, *Shutendoji* replays the creator's earlier **DEVILMAN** but with solely Japanese mythical references. Drawing on one of the **JAPANESE FOLK TALES** in which Minamoto no Yorimitsu and several other warriors defeated an ogre who abducted a local maid, *Shutendoji* begins with two monsters fighting across time, crashing from medieval Kyoto, past the mystified crew

Shutendoji

© 1989 GO NAGAI/DYNAMIC PLANNING, INC. • NIPPON COLUMBIA CO., LTD.

of a spaceship, before ending up in modern Japan. The first two episodes are concerned with Jiro's attempts to come to terms with his heritage and fight off his supernatural relatives. His teacher, possessed by evil, kidnaps Jiro's girlfriend, Miyuki, intending to use her as a sacrifice to open the interdimensional barrier that holds back the demons. He must also kill off the evil monk Jawanbo, whose son swears vengeance. By this point, however, Jiro has been thrown forward to the year 2100. He arrives in time to save the Iron Kaiser, a war cyborg sent on a suicide mission to protect its ship, the Alfard. Captain Persis Mahmoud (a CUTEY HONEY look-alike) promises to help return Jiro to his own time, a plan delayed by the revelation that Iron Kaiser is Jawanbo's son, whose life has been prolonged for decades with cybernetic implants, as he waits for the chance to avenge his father's death. For the finale, Jiro and his band must fight their way out of hell, while his adoptive human mother goes slowly insane, decorating the walls of her cell with pictures of hell, until Jiro's adoptive father destroys the pictures and saves Jiro's life. One of the better adaptations of Nagai's work, with a clever script, chilling visuals, and inspired plot twists that bridge time and space.

The original Shutendoji is a figure from medieval Japanese mythology: an ogre bested in combat by a famous

samurai, who died at the foot of Mount Oe, and is still celebrated in a local festival each October. The name can be translated as "An Unearthly Child." See also KAI DOH MARU and OTOGI ZOSHI, which approach the same tale from a very different direction. **LNV**

SIAMESE CAT

2001. JPN: *Siam Cat*. AKA: *Siam Neko, Siam Neko: First Mission*. Movie. DIR: Masahiro Hosoda. SCR: Kihiro Ono. DES: Shingo Araki, Michi Himeno. ANI: Masuo Nakayama. MUS: Nao Kisugi. PRD: Buyu. 90 mins.

Jun and Naomi are two pretty disc-jockeys who comprise "Siamese Cat," a secret government antiterrorist rapid-response team. Jun handles guns and martial arts, Naomi does communications and demolitions, while Mr. Kuritagachi, vice president of the Cabinet Research Room, is their government contact. When the terrorist Shunsuke Kaido (aka Asian Tiger) kidnaps the Japanese prime minister, Siamese Cat goes into action, competing against a rival government's special force, Major Isurugi's Mighty Dog. *Charlie's Angels*, Japanese style, courtesy of LUPIN III–creator Monkey Punch.

SIBLING SECRET *

2002. JPN: *Unbalance*. Video. DIR: Juha-chi Minamisawa. SCR: Miki Naruse. DES: Haruo Okawara. ANI: Haruo Okawara. MUS: Hiroaki Sano, Takeshi Nishizawa.

PRD: Discovery. 30 mins. x 3 eps. Mika has always had a crush on Jun, ever since he became her elder sister's boyfriend. Imagine, then, her guilty delight when her sister dies, leaving her free to chase Jun herself, and all in the name of mutual condolences. In this entry in the DISCOVERY SERIES, Jun initially tries to resist her charms, but eventually succumbs, although it is only then that he reveals that he and Mika's sister used to indulge in prolonged games of bondage and domination, to which he now subjects the shocked Mika. The third episode introduces a new character, Ritsuko, whose father is hoping to use her as leverage in order to take over the restaurant where Mika works. Coincidentally, another *Unbalance* (*DE) was the name of a coffee shop where psychic investigators would meet in early drafts of the script for the famous live-action TV series *Ultra Q*. The mind boggles at what they would have made of this. **LNV**

SIGN OF THE OTAKU

1994. JPN: *Otaku no Seiza*. AKA: *Fanboy Constellation*. Video. DIR: Junji Nishimura, Akira Nishimori. SCR: Masashi Sogo. DES: Hisashi Eguchi, Noboru Furuse, Hiroshi Motomiya. ANI: Tatsuo Okano. MUS: Aurora 5. PRD: KSS. 30 mins. x 2 eps.

A new idol group, the Aurora Girls, are the greatest threat to humankind ever known. They plan to wipe out civilization by spreading the otaku disease, a deadly virus that transforms ordinary people into hard-core anime fans. Packed with anime parodies, including affectionate homages to OTAKU NO VIDEO, this was based on an NES game that featured designs from Hisaishi Eguchi and Hiroshi Motomiya, better known for ROUJIN Z and MY SKY.

SILENT MÖBIUS *

1991. Movie, TV series. DIR: Kazuo Tomizawa, Michitaka Kikuchi, Hideki Tonokatsu, Kunitoshi Okajima. SCR: Michitaka Kikuchi, Kei Shigema, Hiroyuki Kawasaki, Kenichi Kanemaki, Nami Narita, Katsuhiko Takayama. DES:

Kia Asamiya (pseudonym for Michitaka Kikuchi), Michitaka Kikuchi, Yasuhiro Moriki, Yutaka Izubuchi, Masaki Tanaka. ANI: Michitaka Kikuchi, Masahide Yanasawa, Kunihiro Abe, Tetsuro Aoki, Nobuyuki Kitajima, Moriyasu Taniguchi. MUS: Kaoru Wada. PRD: AIC, Radix, TV Tokyo. 54 mins., 60 mins. (m), 25 mins. x 26 eps. (TV).

In the year 2028, Tokyo is overcrowded, polluted, and (unlike present-day Tokyo) occasionally attacked by demonic entities known as the Lucifer Hawks, who are using Japan's luckless capital as an interdimensional portal. Hence the formation of the Attacked Mystification Police Department, a unit designed to prevent the Lucifer Hawks from causing havoc. In a setup not dissimilar to **BUBBLEGUM CRISIS**, the tough half-human leader Rally Cheyenne heads a group of uniformed beauties—cybernetic medium Lebia Maverick, Australian cyborg Kiddy Phenil, old-school Japanese mystic Nami Yamigumo, psychic dispatcher Yuki Saiko, and newest recruit Katsumi Liqueur, daughter of the arch-mage Gigelf and wielder of his sword Grospoliner. In mixing a cyberpunk look with occult imagery, *SM: The Motion Picture* is a visual feast. This is a dark, brooding anime aimed at an audience familiar with Kia Asamiya's original 1988 manga in *Comic Comp*, an assumption that may leave the uninitiated viewer feeling confused. Matters are not helped by the extensive use of flashbacks—as with the manga, the narrative pattern is one of introducing "present-day" action in order to bracket a story from a character's past. Thus, for part of the action, Katsumi Liqueur is a hardened Lucifer-Hawk hunter and a member of the team, though several scenes also depict her as a fresh-faced arrival in 2024, unaware of the secrets that will be imparted to her by her dying mother. Though the first film ends in 2028, *SM 2* (1992), released on a triple bill with **WEATHERING CONTINENT** and the second part of **HEROIC LEGEND OF ARSLAN**, continues in 2025, with Katsumi's permission to leave Tokyo

revoked, and her reluctant recruitment into the AMPD. Both movies share the same dark, brooding elegance; the ambience is definitely that of *Blade Runner*, with "spinner" vehicles flying through an almost permanently rain-swept Tokyo hiding terrors under its shiny carapace. They are triumphs of mood and atmosphere, with little in the way of narrative variety but lashings of cyber-noir style. There was also a 54-minute *Making of SM* video in the same year—*SM* was *very* popular in the Japanese fan community, which lapped up not only the manga and movies, but several novels, including a series of spin-offs set in the 19th century (during the last invasion of the Lucifer Hawks), a computer game from Gainax, and a series of CD dramas.

As studios scrambled for TV product in the wake of the success of **EVANGELION**, many old favorites were snapped up. *SM* was one of them, but the opportunity to reset to zero and remake the series was somewhat defeated by the low budgets of 1990s TV. Though 13 hours of running time allow for better fleshing-out of character backgrounds, the TV version disappointingly dumps much of the movies' style without adding much substance. Its animation and scripting are trite and undistinguished, limited time and budget watering down the impressive look of manga and movies; even the terrifying Lucifer Hawks now look more **ULTRAMAN** than Asamiya.

SILENT SERVICE, THE *

1995. JPN: *Chinmoku no Kantai*. TV special, video. DIR: Ryosuke Takahashi, Masamitsu Hidaka, Koji Koshigoe. SCR: Soji Yoshikawa, Akira Nishimori, Takeshi Ashizawa. DES: Shigeru Kato, Hisashi Hirai, Kimitoshi Yamane. ANI: Shigeru Kato, Keizo Shimizu, Hisashi Hirai. MUS: Akira Senju. PRD: Sunrise, Video Champ, TBS. 100 mins. (TVm), 57 mins. 60 mins. (v).

As part of the surrender terms set at the end of WWII, Japan does not have an army so much as a "Defense Force." However, various interests have

been developing the Seabat—a secret nuclear submarine created by both U.S. and Japanese ingenuity. It's on the cutting edge of military technology, armed with 50 of the most powerful nuclear weapons ever developed, manned by a crew believed to be dead, and led by Shiro Kaieda, an officer so devoted to the principle of peace that he will go to any lengths to uphold it. His ideas, however, differ somewhat from his superiors', as he steals the Seabat, renames it Yamato (see **STAR BLAZERS**), and declares it to be an independent nation. Now former Japanese comrades and U.S. allies alike are equally determined to capture or destroy them. Kaieda is playing for the ultimate prize, by the rules he learned from America, with the most powerful weapon in the world to back him up.

Based on Kaiji Kawaguchi's controversial 1988 manga in *Comic Morning*, *SS* asked pertinent questions about Japan's role in the modern world, when, during the bubble economy of the 1980s, it was a major player on the world stage but hamstrung and embarrassed by its reliance on the unpredictable U.S. for defense (see **SEA OF THE TICONDEROGA** and **PAPA MAMA BYE-BYE**). The anime version, however, was made after a succession of events that diluted the stirring message of the original, commencing with the collapse of the Soviet Union. After the Gulf War, from which the resource-hungry Japan benefited at the expense of other nations' soldiers, Japan was "invited" to join policing actions in Cambodia, negating much of the impact of the postwar restrictions on sending troops abroad. The war in the Balkans (a heavy influence on **GASARAKI**), with its succession of broken truces and pyrrhic victories, made foreign military involvement look distinctly unappealing. Accordingly, the pacifist movement in Japan now had two factions, those who opposed war itself on moral grounds (see **BAREFOOT GEN**) and a growing number who simply couldn't see the point in wasting any money on it when the U.S. was doing such a fine job on its own. In other words, by the time *SS* got its premier as a TV movie on TBS, it had already been overtaken by history—though still a chilling controversy redolent of **WARTIME ANIME**, it was less of an anti-American manifesto than a modern-day **DEEP BLUE FLEET**—the opportunity to set up war-gaming scenarios between nominally friendly nations. Two further installments went straight to video but were not released abroad. Two other Kawaguchi manga, **NINE LOVE STORIES** and **HARD AND LOOSE**, were also adapted for anime. The flagship of the U.S. 7th Fleet, the Carl Vinson, would appear again in **SPACE FAMILY CARLVINSON**.

SILVER FANG *

1986. JPN: *Ginya: Nagareboshi Gin.* AKA: *Silver Tooth: Shooting Star Silver.* TV series. DIR: Tomoharu Katsumata, Yugo Serikawa, Kazumasa Horikawa, Nobutaka Nishizawa, Masayuki Akehi, Tatsuo Higashino. SCR: Michiru Umadori, Kenji Terada. DES: Joji Yanagise. ANI: Koji Yanagise, Masaharu Endo, Tetsuro Aoki. MUS: Goro Omi. PRD: Toei, TV Asahi. 25 mins. x 21 eps., 25 mins. x 26? eps. (*Weed*).

Gin, a beautiful dog with a silver-white coat, is third in a line of attack dogs trained by their master Gobei to fight with Aka Kabuto, the fearsome bear of the mountain. While hunting with Gobei, Gin meets his father, Riki, now the amnesiac leader of a pack of wild dogs determined to kill Aka Kabuto. The wild Riki and the domesticated Gin join forces and go in search of other brave dogs. Yoshihiro Takahashi's manga from *Shonen Jump* ran for several years, but the anime didn't do as well as other shaggy-dog tales like **CALL OF THE WILD**.

Legend of the Silver Fang: Weed (2005) draws inspiration from **KIMBA THE WHITE LION**. Fourteen years after Gin's heroic battle with the great bear, another beast invades the peaceful valley where the dogs have been living. Gin's pregnant mate escapes, guarded by the fierce GB, a former hench-dog of Gin's who reveals a cruel streak in

exile. Gin's son Weed endures torment at the paws of GB, until one fateful day when he stands up for himself and exhibits some of the heroic spirit that made his father famous.

SIN SORORITY *

2002. JPN: *Utsukushii Emonotachi no Gakuen.* AKA: *School of Beautiful Games; Bigaku.* DIR: Yuji Uchida. SCR: Hideo Ura. DES: Shigenori Kurii. ANI: Haruto Fuyurai. MUS: Kenichi Kunshima. PRD: Mink, Milky, Museum Pictures. 30 mins. x 2 eps.

Shy girl Asuna has transferred to a select private school and is desperate to be accepted into its exclusive sorority. Student president Yurika, who prefers to be addressed as "Mistress," will only let her join if she agrees to a perverted sexual initiation ritual. Asuna doesn't like being raped at first but then finds she does, in an erotic anime based on the game by Mink. The title is sometimes contracted as Bigaku—which uses the characters for "Beautiful" and "School," but uses their alternate pronunciations. **ⓛⓃⓋ**

SIN: THE MOVIE *

2001. Video. DIR: Yasunori Urata. SCR: Carl Macek. DES: Dan Kongoji, Makoto Kobayashi. ANI: Dan Kongoji. MUS: Masamichi Amano. PRD: ADV Films, Phoenix Entertainment. 60 mins.

Late in the 21st century, Freeport is plagued by crime and corruption. Crack paramilitary unit HARDCORPS is there to sort it out. Hardman Colonel John Blade comes up against an enemy worthy of his steel in his latest case. Ruthless mogul Elixis Sinclaire, founder of multimillion-dollar biotechnology corporation SinTEK, has recently been developing something really big; at the same time, a wave of kidnappings in the city is baffling the regular law enforcement service. A U.S.-Japanese coproduction with two different subtitle scripts giving two story lines, this is an interesting experiment that's at least an effort to do something new with DVD's many possibilities. The original *Sin* computer game was bundled onto the same DVD.

SINDBAD THE SAILOR *

1962. JPN: *Arabian Night Sindbad no Boken.* AKA: *Arabian Night Sindbad Adventure.* Movie. DIR: Taiji Yabushita, Yoshio Kuroda. SCR: Osamu Tezuka, Morio Kita. DES: Yasuo Otsuka. ANI: Sanae Yamamoto. MUS: Isao Tomita, Masao Yoneyama. PRD: Toei. 81 mins.

Sindbad and his friend Ali meet an old man on the seashore who gives them the map to an island of treasure. They sail off in search of it but are imprisoned in one of the countries they visit. Released through the efforts of the beautiful Princess Samir, they head off once more but are pursued by the evil Grand Vizier, who wants the treasure for himself.

After this popular, big-name movie inspired by the **ARABIAN NIGHTS**, Sindbad would return for the unrelated *Arabian Nights: Sindbad's Adventure* (1975, *Sindbad no Boken*), a 52-episode Nippon Animation series on Fuji TV, directed by Fumio Kurokawa. Though aimed at a younger audience, the series crammed in more of the original, including the stories of Ali Baba (see **ALIBABA'S REVENGE**) and **ALADDIN AND THE WONDERFUL LAMP**.

SINS OF THE SISTERS *

1990. JPN: *Sei Michaela no Gakuen Hyoryuki.* AKA: *Tales of Saint Michaela's Academy.* Video. DIR: Hiroshi Fukutomi, Yorifusa Yamaguchi. SCR: Ryo Motohira, Masaru Yamamoto. DES: Michitaka Kikuchi. ANI: Tetsuro Aoki, Mitsuru Takanashi. MUS: N/C. PRD: Visual SD, Production Eureka, OL Production. 40 mins. x 2 eps., 45 mins. x 2 eps.

During the ill-fated Children's Crusade of A.D. 1212, Pope Innocent III double-crosses the loyal Christian soldiers and sells them to African slavers. Distraught at his betrayal by the very church he is sworn to serve, the children's leader, Hans, throws himself into the sea. Centuries later, he is reincarnated as a hermaphrodite in a convent school, where he seduces the girls and leads them in a bloody revolt against the oppressive nuns. Seizing control of the nuns' time tunnel,

Hans (now called Aiko) and his/her chums travel back to Japan's Amakusa Rebellion (see NINJA RESURRECTION), where they fight the evil Christians. Eventually, all religions are wiped out in a worldwide atheist jihad, and the battle-hardened schoolgirls decide to go back in time again to save the original Hans from the slavers. Meanwhile, Hans/Aiko's lesbian lover, Rika, is brought back to life by Aron/Yuki, an evil nun out to retrieve her kamikaze pilot boyfriend from hell.

An everyday story of multiverse revenge, bare-breasted zombies, mass murder, and kung-fu schoolgirls—prime candidate for the most mind-boggling plot in anime, further mangled on U.S. release when only the final two episodes were released. Thus, the opening half of Hide Takatori's original novel is only discernable through flashbacks and occasional asides, while the complex (and paradoxical) rewrite of both European and Japanese history is buried amid a flurry of leaden dialogue and lesbian titillation. One of the funniest anime since DRAGON HALF, albeit unintentionally, with immortal lines like, "I must avert Yuki's evil plot, or else I will evaporate!" **N**

SISTER PRINCESS

2001. TV series. DIR: Kiyoshi Ohata, Kazuo Nogami. SCR: Masaharu Amiya, Koichi Taki. DES: Yasunari Nitta. ANI: Osamu Kobayashi, Yasuo Okawara. MUS: N/C. PRD: Sunrise, TV Tokyo. 25 mins. x 26 eps., 25 mins. x 13 eps. (TV2).

Disgraced when he fails his high school entrance exam, Wataru Minakami is sent by his father to a remote island school, where he is the sole boy in a population of 12 pretty girls. A bizarre mixture of TENCHI MUYO! and *The Prisoner* ensues.

Ultimately, Wataru's island idyll is disrupted by Akio, a confident, brash individual much like Wataru once was, who arrives with official notification that Wataru has finally gained a place in the educational institution of his choice—in fact, it transpires that Wataru never failed the examination in the first place. He is consequently faced with a difficult decision: to remain in the solipsistic, anodyne world of his sisterly companions, or to take a chance on improving his lot in life by accepting his place at college. A second TV series, *SP Re Pure* (2002), offered even more of the same.

SIX ANGELS

2002. Movie. DIR: Makoto Kobayashi. SCR: Yasushi Hirano. DES: Hiromi Kato, Makoto Kobayashi. ANI: Shoichi Masuo. MUS: Masamichi Amano. PRD: Eighty One Entertainment, Jpec System Co. Ltd. 100 mins.

In a postapocalyptic world, the death penalty has been revoked. A nuclear test site in America has been converted into "Neo Purgatory," a prison for the worst criminals. The inmates are revolting, even before the Canyon family takes control of the prison to gain access to radioactive material and use it to wipe the world's slate clean. As the USA and Soviet Union face off, and mankind stands on the brink of extinction, a team of nubile young women in ludicrous outfits get an unexpected chance to save them. Doris, Marilyn, Naomi, and Maki are the "Rose Guard," a special police unit out to protect women from male brutality. Katherine is a stowaway on their patrol helicopter when it is shot down by Don Canyon and crashes into the test site. The Angels must now take down Don and his three psycho sons to save the world, with only their cute little rabbit-shaped pet high-grade war machine to help out. You may be surprised to learn that one of the rewards of success is to take over the Oval Office.

Created by Yasushi Akimoto, this movie lines up an experienced staff that knows its stuff. Given all that experience and talent, an end result like *Six Angels* is both baffling and disappointing—apart from some good CGI, there is very little onscreen to hold one's attention. Of course, the days when shows using scantily clad girl teams as weapons of mass entertainment were the hottest ticket in town are long past, but given the right slant the concept can still fly. Here, it doesn't. A preview/pilot, featuring a larger cast and somewhat different character designs, was prepared roughly a year before the release of the film, leading to differing release dates in some sources. **LNV**

SKYERS 5

1967. TV series. DIR: Seiji Sasaki, Takeshi Yamamoto, Takeshi Kawauchi, Satoshi Murayama. SCR: Norimasa Mayumi, Kenji Nakano. DES: Noboru Kawasaki. ANI: Shuichi Seki. MUS: Ichiro Tsukasa, Sanpei Akasaka. PRD: TCJ, Eiken, TBS. 25 mins. x 12 eps., 25 mins. x 26 eps. (TV2).

When he receives a microfilm from a dying man, Shotaro becomes the target of the international arms syndicate Ghost, which kills his mother and sister. He is enlisted in Japanese International Secret Police, along with the agents Captain, Polka, Yuri, and Sampson. With Shotaro as their fifth team member, they form the "Skyers," a group of secret agents with high-tech gadgets, ready for the (almost) impossible mission of defeating Ghost's plans for world domination. Perhaps the earliest anime to introduce a five-strong team of Hero, Rogue, Big Guy, Comic Relief, and Token Girl (see BATTLE OF THE PLANETS). In 1971, the series was remade in color.

SLAM DUNK

1994. TV series, movie, TV specials. DIR: Hiromichi Matano, Nobuaki Nishizawa, Hiroyuki Kadono, Masayuki Akehi, Kazuhisa Takenouchi, Satoshi Nakamura. SCR: Yoshiyuki Suga, Nobuaki Kishima. DES: Masaki Sato, Hidemi Kuma. ANI: Masaki Sato, Yoichi Onishi, Takahiro Kagami. MUS: Takanobu Soda, BMF. PRD: Toei, TV Asahi. 25 mins. x 130 eps. (TV), 30 mins., 48 mins., 45 mins., 40 mins. (m), 50 mins. x 3 (TVm).

Hanamichi Sakuragi joins Shohoku High School as a senior and falls in love with gorgeous Haruko Akagi. But his romantic record in junior high was terrible—he's been dumped by 50 girls. This could have something to do with the fact that he's tall and skinny, with red hair, an attitude with very little respect for others, and tremendous fighting abilities; but whatever it is, he's determined to overcome his problem and win Haruko. She has a crush on someone else, Kaede Rukawa, who's only crazy about hoops, and when Hanamichi learns that her beloved older brother, Takenori, is captain of the Shohoku basketball team, he decides to take up the sport. He gradually learns that there's a lot more to basketball than he ever imagined, and as he gets more and more involved with his teammates, he starts to use his strength for something other than fistfights.

Like Takehiko Inoue's original 1990 manga in *Shonen Jump*, SD depicts basketball games with loving realism, but with character development and plotting good enough to interest nonaddicts. More of the same would follow in the movie editions, *Slam Dunk* (1994), *SD: National Championships, Hanamichi Sakuragi* (1994, *SD: Zenkoku Seiha Da! Sakuragi Hanamichi*), *Shohoku's Biggest Crisis: Enter the Hanamichi* (1995, *Shohoku Saida no Kiki: Moero Sakuragi Hanamich*), and *Roaring Basketman Soul! Hanamichi and Ryukawa's Hot Summer* (1995, *Hoero Basketman Damashi: Hanamichi to Ryukawa no Nekki Natsumi*). There were also three "TV specials"—*SD: Decisions at Shohoku Basketball Club* (1994, *Ketsui no Shohoku Basuke-bu*); reedited versions of episodes 40 and 41, *SD: King of the Rebound* (1995, *Rebound-O*); and episodes 62 and 63, *SD Special* (1995).

SLAVE MARKET *
2002. JPN: *Dorei Ichiba*. Video. DIR: Michiru Takizawa. SCR: Naoki Tsuruoka. DES: Michiru Takizawa. ANI: Shoji Yanagisawa. MUS: Hiroaki Sano. PRD: Discovery. 30 mins. x 3 eps.
As the clouds of war beckon in the 17th century, Cassius arrives in Constantinople as an assistant to the European ambassador—yes, we know that Constantinople (Istanbul) is *in* Europe, but this is an erotic anime, not a geography lesson. His old friend Falco immediately takes him to the city's slave market where Bianca, a silver-haired slave girl who addresses him as "brother," soon catches his eye. However, even as Cassius takes his new acquisition home so he can begin manfully resisting the urge to molest her, Bianca's own stalker begins to stalk her new owner.

Later episodes continue the pattern, as Cassius and his associates drift halfheartedly toward a plot involved with the beginning of the Thirty Years War, which is somehow reflected in whichever slave Cassius happens to pick up at the market. In episode two, the slave-of-the-month is Cecilia, a girl who once believed she was betrothed to a prince, but somehow ends up sold at auction, already pregnant with her betrayer's child. Cassius's third purchase is Miya, an "African" slave whose vocal chords have been cut—"African" meaning that she has a slight tan. Cassius busily molests and degrades her, as is his wont, but becomes so obsessed with her that he refuses to hand her over to the mercenaries who come looking for her. Another entry in the DISCOVERY SERIES, complete with whips, chains, scatology, and water sports, like John Norman's *Gor* series without the feminist charm—yes, we are kidding. ⓛⓝⓥ

SLAVE NURSES *
2003. JPN: *Dorei Kaigo*. Video. DIR: Katsumasa Kanezawa. SCR: Yoshio Takaoka. DES: Jiro Iwata. ANI: Jiro Iwata. MUS: Satoshi Shura. PRD: CherryLips, ARMS, Super Seven. 25 mins. x 3 eps.
All the "nurses" in the "hospital" have been seized by raging lusts. Every night sees them satisfying their urges with doctors, patients, and anyone else who passes by. Newly hired male caregiver Yosuke has his own theories about what's behind this sudden surge of libido—but he doesn't want to uncover the truth too quickly because he's having too much fun joining in. It soon transpires that the music piped into the wards has additional, hypnotic side effects—it would be a rare anime medical institution that *wasn't* also a front for an unsanctioned experiment that had strange effects on the inhabitants! As the division of the female characters into standard wish-fulfillment archetypes (older woman, tomboy, the one with glasses…) suggests, this is based on a 2001 erotic computer game, on this occasion from Silkies. We would like to point out, for those that care about this sort of thing, that there are no actual nurses in this anime—the leading ladies are all unskilled teenage caregivers in a nursing home. Despite what is, considering the title, a rather important omission, this remains notable for its high production values—a welcome relief from run-of-the-mill CG animated dreck. ⓛⓝⓥ

SLAVE SISTERS *
1999. JPN: *Shimai Ijiri*. AKA: *Sisters Enslaved/Tormented*. Video. DIR: Mitsuhiro Yoneda. SCR: Nikukyu. DES: Meka Morishige. ANI: Y.O.U.C. MUS: Yoshi. PRD: YOUC, Digital Works (Vanilla Series). 30 mins. x 2 eps.
Yukari Isshiki and her younger sister Miku lose their parents and inherit their massive debts to a crime syndicate. They are given a choice—become sex slaves or die. Shunji Iwashiro is given the task of training them to please their new masters. Part of the VANILLA SERIES—compare to LOVE LESSONS. ⓛⓝⓥ

SLAVES TO PASSION *
2001. JPN: *Hana Dorei*. AKA: *Glorious Slaves*. Video. DIR: Naomi Hayakawa. SCR: Rokurota Makabe, DES: N/C. ANI: Hayoto Teshima. MUS: Yoshi. PRD: YOUC, Digital Works (Vanilla Series). 30 mins. x 2 eps.
Painter's apprentice Kaoru fantasizes about his master's beautiful wife, until the fateful day when his mentor dies, leaving his pretty spouse as a frustrated widow. Kaoru duly steps in to console her by tying her up and subjecting her to bondage games. Another entry in the VANILLA SERIES and based on a

manga by Naomi Hayakawa, creator of
Beast City.

SLAYERS *
1995. TV series, movie, video. DIR:
Takashi Watanabe, Susumu Ishizaki,
Kazuo Yamazaki, Masahito Sato,
Yoshiaki Iwasaki, Moto Kawaguchi,
Seiji Mizushima, Eiji Sato. SCR: Takao
Koyama, Katsuhiko Chiba, Jiro
Takayama, Tetsuko Watanabe, Yasushi
Yamada, Katsumi Hasegawa. DES: Nao
mi Miyata, Kenji Teraoka, Toshihasa
Higashi. ANI: Naomi Miyata, Kazuhiro
Sasaki, Seiji Kikuchi, Mitsuru Abunai.
MUS: Osamu Tezuka (the other one),
Vink. PRD: IG Film, SoftX, TV Tokyo. 25
mins. x 78 eps., (TV), 65 mins. (m1),
85 mins. (m2), 80 mins. (m3), 64
mins. (m4), 40 mins. (m5), 30 mins. x
3 eps. (v1), 30 mins. x 3 eps. (v2).
Hoping to obtain the Sword of Light,
a powerful artifact wielded by the slow-
witted Gourry Gabriev, flat-chested
teen sorceress Lina Inverse decides to
accompany him on his travels. The pair
wander a sub–D&D world in search
of fortune, helped and hindered by a
changing stock company of sidekicks
and adversaries, which include Amelia,
a self-proclaimed Champion of Justice,
the cursed swordsman Zelgadis, and
the priestly prankster Xelloss. One of
the most popular anime franchises of
the 1990s, along with **Tenchi Muyo!**,
Slayers remained a popular choice
throughout the teens of its original 12-
year-old target audience, leaping from
Hajime Kanzaka's original 1989 short
stories in *Dragon* magazine, illustrated
by Rui Araizumi, to a long-running set
of novels and the inevitable manga and
anime spin-offs, eventually sliding from
TV to video. Set in a complicated fantasyland supposedly in a neighboring
plane of existence to the same creator's
Lost Universe, it is the antidote to the
deadly serious **Record of Lodoss War**,
with a cynical cast modeled on argumentative role-players. *Slayers* makes
light of its own lumpen predictability,
with the characters constantly bickering about food, being double-crossed
by feckless clients, and lamenting the

formulaic setups they face. Ridiculing its own shortcomings, *Slayers* has
successfully kept a strong following
that watches for what some might call
biting satire, and others bad workmen
blaming their tools.

The three 26-episode TV seasons
(branded *Slayers*, *S Next*, and *S Try*)
also came accompanied by a set of
theatrical releases, beginning with
Slayers: The Movie (1995). In order not
to disturb the continuity of the ongoing TV series, writer/director Kazuo
Yamazaki opted for a story from a spin-
off continuity, the *S Special* tales set two
years before Lina's first meeting with
Gourry. While the TV show contained
many running "gags" about breasts and
the effect of menstruation on magic
powers, it remained essentially asexual.
However, with the absence of TV
restrictions, the first and subsequent
movies retain Naga from the stories, a
large-breasted, cackling sorceress and
self-appointed traveling companion for
the young Lina, her one-time enemy
and sometime sidekick. Four further
films followed: *S Return* (1996), *S Great*
(1997), *S Gorgeous* (1998), and *S Pre-
mium* (2001). Meanwhile, the prequels
also made it straight to video with *S
Special* (1996, released in the U.S. as *S

Dragon Slave* and *S Explosion Array*, aka
S Book of Spells on DVD) and *S Excellent*
(1998). Naga and her breasts have
become three very popular characters
in the series, and long-term fans of
the series wait eagerly to see how the
writers can explain not only her disappearance between the end of *S Special*
and the beginning of the original
series, but also why she is never even
mentioned after the events of the videos. Other spin-offs include the *Slayers*
game for the SNES and *S Royal* for the
Sega Saturn, the CD *S Etcetera*, and
the CD-ROM *S Hyper*. In a final irony,
the *Slayers* universe was sold as an add-
on to the *Magius* role-playing game,
bringing it full circle to the format that
originally inspired it.

SLEAZY ANGELS *
1998. JPN: *Koin Tenshi*. Video. DIR: Sassai Ima. SCR: Sassai Ima. DES: Sassai
Ima. ANI: Sassai Ima. MUS: N/C. PRD: Uill
Animation, JVD. 30 mins.
Three pretty girls decide to make their
own erotic video, are unsurprisingly
surprised to find that they enjoy it,
and want to do it again. *Sleazy Angels*
was later combined with the unrelated
Office Affairs to make a one-hour
video under the title *Co-Ed Affairs*.

Slayers

SLIGHT FEVER SYNDROME *

1996. JPN: *Binetsubyo Kogun*. Video.
DIR: Taiichi Kitagawa, Kozo Shirakawa.
SCR: Rumi Miyamoto. DES: Kazunami
Ota. ANI: Kazunami Ota. MUS: Hideyuki
Tanaka. PRD: Yang Corporation, Karasu
Communications, Knack. 45 mins. x
2 eps.

Nubile, easily stimulated Mizuki combines the roles of nurse and health education teacher at a private high school (or "college" in the U.S. version). In other words, a feeble framing device for a succession of pornographic scenes in which students and teachers alike confess their experiences or seek her "help" with sexual problems. Mizuki tends to use a very hands-on approach with her students, especially when demonstrating all the various functions of the female anatomy. Then she starts to fall for Kirishima, one of her very attractive male students. In the second video, Mizuki catches him peeping at her sex session with a female colleague. She invites him to her apartment, finally starting to bring her work home with her. Based on the erotic manga by Rumi Miyamoto in *Penguin Club*. 🄽

SLIPPY DANDY

1987. TV series. DIR: Tameo Ogawa.
SCR: N/C. DES: N/C. ANI: Hisatoshi
Motoki. MUS: N/C. PRD: Meruhen, Fuji
TV. 5 mins. x 4 eps.

Farcical thievery in the style of CAT'S EYE, as the pretty blonde photographer Audrey pursues the burglar Slippy Dandy, unaware that he is really Steve, the young college boy who worships her from afar. This series of shorts was shown as part of the variety show *Midnight Treasure Chamber* and made in a deliberately "American" style (meaning brashly bright colors and redundant sound effects plastered over the action in the style of the 1960s TV *Batman*).

SLOW STEP *

1991. Video. DIR: Kunihiko Yuyama.
SCR: Toshimichi Saeki, Kenji Terada.
DES: Tokuhiro Matsubara. ANI: Tokuhiro
Matsubara. MUS: Hiroya Watanabe. PRD:

Pastel, Youmex, OB. 45 mins. x 5 eps.

Minatsu is a lively, popular teenager and star of the girls' softball team. Her chief admirers are her childhood sweetheart, Akiba, and her perverse softball coach, Yamazakura. But while Minatsu falls for Kadomatsu, the boxing champ from a rival school, he is not interested in her. In fact, he is only interested in "Maria," a pretty girl with glasses, though he is unaware that "Maria" is really a disguise Minatsu uses to avoid a gang of thugs that's intent on getting back at her for reporting them in a hit-and-run incident. Kadomatsu and Akiba soon come to blows over their love for the same girl, and Coach Yamazakura, a former high school boxer himself, agrees to teach Akiba how to defend himself. Meanwhile, Coach's orphaned niece, Chika, is desperate to find a wife for him so she can have a new mommy *and* daddy. Throw into this mix Somei, the newest teacher at the school, who's a gorgeous hunk but is scared of *all* women . . . except Sawamura, the school bad-girl who wants Yamazakura for herself.

An addictive blend of softball, boxing, and nostalgic school-day intrigues that adapts the entirety of the short 1987 manga by Mitsuru Adachi in *Ciao* magazine. Not as well known as the same creator's TOUCH, H2, NINE, or MIYUKI, *SS* remains unavailable in the U.S. and has achieved the questionable distinction of being the U.K.'s worst-selling anime from 1995 to 2000, a record broken only by the release of the KIMAGURE ORANGE ROAD videos. This is a great shame because it retains Adachi's masterful qualities of character interaction and observational comedy. The early episodes of quick-change farce are soon discarded for a complex mating dance, as Minatsu deftly deals with her suitors and tries to decide which (if any) to choose. Needless to say, after much comedy business divided, like the original manga, into seasonal chapters, the show ends happily with a spring wedding attended by several couples formed from the supporting cast.

SS is fascinating both for its portrayal of everyday Japan and for the "everyday" aspects that seem so alien to the Western viewer. These include the Japanese attitude toward smoking and sexual harassment, teen rebellion expressed through littering or (the horror!) buying alcohol from a vending machine, as well as the Japanese concept of what makes a man marriage material, and what aspirations a 17-year-old schoolgirl should have. A charmingly conservative story, with beautiful backgrounds and some wonderful humor, including the boys' vehement complaints about the service at a holiday resort, chiefly because they are unable to peek at the girls bathing. Parts three and four were run together as a single feature-length episode in the British version in a feeble attempt to avoid having to pay the classification board for two separate titles.

SLUTTY PRINCESS DIARIES *

2004. JPN: *Kijoku*. AKA: *Princesses Tortured*. Video. DIR: N/C. SCR: N/C. DES:
N/C. ANI: N/C. MUS: N/C. PRD: Animac.
30 mins. x 3 eps.

Distol is a disinherited prince of Astaria, a small kingdom that has been bullied and invaded by its ruthless neighbor Bastarauge. Forced to live at the Bastarauge court with his stepmother as royal hostages, Distol is obliged to endure his incarceration alone when the former queen dies only a few days after arriving. He devotes the next eight years to learning the way of the sword, in the hope that one day he will be able to avenge his kingdom and stepmother, and perhaps also protect his stepsister Princess Qoona, who might be forced to take the late queen's place at the mercies of Bastarauge. Distol also discovers that his stepmother was raped by the king of Bastarauge (so now he *really* wants to avenge her), and that Qoona is fated to be sacrificed in order to enact a sacred ceremony to keep a demon king imprisoned in an alternate dimension.

One way of helping Qoona is to ensure that Elena, a princess of Bastarauge, is corrupted, abused, and raped—this is something to do with magical spells and destinies, apparently. Consequently, Distol breaks into Elena's chambers and carries her off at the very beginning of this complex erotic fantasy anime, before pausing to recount the incidents described above in a long flashback that uses up much of the first episode.

The final episode finds Distol successfully breaking the "seal" that lies inside the body of Elena. It is only then that he realizes that he has been double-crossed, and that by doing so he has allowed the demon back *into* the world—his adviser in this was a witch who now turns out to be a servant of the demon lord Distol was hoping to keep away. Compare to **EROTIC TORTURE CHAMBER**, which similarly devoted massive amounts of time to setting up a story leaving comparatively little time for the sex which is, we suggest, the reason that most people would be buying an anime with a title like that. **LNV**

SMART-SAN

1978. JPN: *Haikara-san ga Toru*. AKA: *Miss "High Collar"; Fashionable Girl Passing By*. TV series. DIR: Yoshihiko Umakoshi, Kazuyoshi Yokota. SCR: Fumi Takahashi. DES: Tsutomu Shibayama. ANI: Tatsuhiro Nagaki, Eiji Tanaka, Takashi Saijo. MUS: Masuhiro Yamaguchi. PRD: Nippon Animation, TV Asahi. 25 mins. x 44 eps.

Early in the 20th century, pretty teenage tomboy Benio Hanamura is the spoiled only child of a major in the army. She studies martial arts and is much more direct than is considered proper for a young lady, even if it is the modern fashion. Benio is caught up in Japan's conflict between progress and tradition when her father decides to arrange her marriage to rich boy Shinobu, much against her will. According to custom, she is sent to her future husband's family home, but he is called up for war service and sent to the Russian front. Soon his family hears that he is missing, believed dead.

Benio eventually becomes a journalist and is astounded to meet Shinobu again some years later; he has lost his memory and believes he is Mikhailov, the husband of a Russian noblewoman. Benio becomes engaged to another man, but on their wedding day, Shinobu arrives at the ceremony, memory restored, to reclaim his bride just as a terrible earthquake hits the capital (see **DOOMED MEGALOPOLIS**).

Waki Yamato's original 1975 manga in *Shojo Friend* was hugely successful, but the anime didn't do as well; Nippon Animation cut it short earlier than planned. *Haikara* ("high collar") is a mild term of ridicule in 1920s Japanese slang—a fashion victim who slavishly adopts Western trends and fads.

SNOW QUEEN, THE

2005. JPN: *Yuki no Jo-O*. TV series. DIR: Osamu Dezaki, Kenji Hachizaki. SCR: Masashi Togawa, Makoto Nakamura, Michiru Shimada, Sukehiro Tomita, Tomoko Konparu. DES: Akio Sugino. ANI: Izumi Shimura, Miyuki Goto. MUS: Akira Chisumi. PRD: Tokyo Movie Shinsha, NHK. 25 mins. x 39 eps.

Kay and Gerda are childhood friends, separated when the evil actions of the legendary Snow Queen cause a shard of a mirror to become embedded in Kay's heart. He tearfully forces Gerda to leave him alone and heads off to the realm of the Snow Queen. Despite the admonitions of adults that Kay is lost to the world, Gerda insists on looking for him. An adaptation of one of the **TALES OF HANS CHRISTIAN ANDERSEN**, in apparent imitation of the earlier **WORLD MASTERPIECE THEATER** series, featuring the long-standing team of Dezaki and Sugino. As with **CINDERELLA**, there are a few alterations in the anime version, most notably the queen's quest to retrieve the many scattered shards of the "troll-mirror"—as in **POKÉMON**, she's gotta catch 'em all.

SNOW WHITE

1994. JPN: *Shiroyuki-hime no Densetsu*. AKA: *Story of Princess Snow White*. TV series. DIR: Kunitoshi Oka-

jima. SCR: Tsunehisa Arakawa. DES: Yoshio Kabeshima. ANI: N/C. MUS: N/C. PRD: Tatsunoko, NHK2. 25 mins. x 52 eps.

The evil Lady Crystal is affronted to hear that she is not "the fairest of them all" and orders the hunter Sampson to take her stepdaughter Snow White out into the forest and kill her. But Snow White escapes into the forest and hides with seven dwarves, hoping that some day her Prince Richard will come to save her and restore justice in the kingdom. This retelling of one of the most famous of **GRIMMS' FAIRY TALES**, like the same studio's later **CINDERELLA**, expands the original to fill out an extended running time. In this case, Tatsunoko ensures that Snow White meets her Prince Charming early on in the events so that her intrigues, letters, and clandestine meetings with him allow for plenty of extra action. The finale returns to the original, poisoned apple and all. See also **VIDEO PICTURE BOOK** and **HELLO KITTY**.

SAILOR MOON–director Junichi Sato would also create the "new *SW* story" **PRETEAR**, first as a manga drawn by Kaori Naruse for *Asuka* magazine, then as a TV anime. Refracting the legend through the prism of **UTENA**, it features Himeno Awayuki, a Japanese teenager who discovers she is the "Snow Princess," fated to save the world from evil, assisted by seven bold "knights," who are, of course, fearsomely pretty boys.

SOCCER FEVER

1994. TV series. DIR: Hitoshi Oda. SCR: Marco Pagot. DES: N/C. ANI: Kazuyoshi Takeuchi. MUS: N/C. PRD: RAI, Tokyo Movie Shinsha, NHK2. 26 mins. x 52 eps.

In the year of the World Cup tournament in the U.S., this series features British journalist Brian Thompson recounting anecdotes from various earlier World Cup games in other countries. Created by Marco Pagot (**SHERLOCK HOUND**, **REPORTER BLUES**), the animation of this Japanese-Italian coproduction has much in common with European styles and shows characters considerably older than the usual school or college-age heroes like **Captain Tsubasa.** Korean animators followed the same lead with a special called *Spin Kicker* (1997) to cash in on the run-up to the 2002 World Cup.

SOL BIANCA *

1990. Video. DIR: Katsuhito Akiyama, Hiroki Hayashi, Hiroyuki Ochi. SCR: Mayori Sekijima, Hideki Mitsui. DES: Naoyuki Onda, Atsushi Takeuchi, Koji Watanabe, Kenji Teraoka, Satoshi Shimura. ANI: Kazuhiro Konishi, Naoyuki Onda, Koichi Arai, Takashi Takeuchi. MUS: Toru Hirano, Kosei Kenjo, Seiko Nagaoka. PRD: AIC, Pioneer. 60 mins. x 2 eps., 30 mins. x 6 eps.

Rim Delapaz wants to rescue his mother from the evil dictator Battros. He disobeys his father, stows away on a cruiser, and hopes that the rest of a plan will come to him before he arrives. But the cruiser is hijacked by pirates, the crew of the Sol Bianca, who are ready to throw Rim out of the airlock before he tempts them with the treasure that lies in Battros's vaults. The pirates decide to help Rim in his mission, but their landing team is ambushed by Battros's minions. As their fellow buccaneers mount a rescue mission, Rim's father decides it's time to mount a revolution, in which the crew of the Sol Bianca are caught.

Take a bunch of girls and a spaceship and you have a very wide range of possibilities. Luckily not all of them are pornographic (though see **Spaceship Agga Ruter**). Strangely redolent of *Blake's 7*'s Liberator, Sol Bianca is an alien ship faster than any other vehicle in space, while its pirate crew, in the eye-candy tradition of **Bubblegum Crisis**, are all female: laid-back, wine-drinking captain Feb; butch Janny, good with weapons and inclined to fly off the handle; complex, tough-but-fair April; intelligent but reserved June, whose empathic link with the ship and its guidance computer, G, has mysterious origins; and the very young May, with a penchant for frilly clothes but an ace engineer in the

bargain. After the promising beginning, the second *SB* video slid into anime hackery, with the girls chased around by a rival pirate whose gun can disintegrate their clothes, and the ship overrun by clunky "viruses" that look like cybernetic worms. Though it ends on a cliffhanger with the suggestion that the Sol Bianca's original builders want her back, a third chapter of *Sol Bianca* never arrived—this is despite a popular reception in the English-speaking world, where it's available in two translations, of which Kiseki's, in the U.K., is the better. In the U.S., AD Vision published a short-lived spin-off comic called *SB: Treasure of the Lost Sun*, which featured the girls on an *Indiana Jones*–style treasure hunt, with no mention of their video antics.

Pioneer remade the series from scratch with *SB: The Legacy* (1999), featuring all-new character designs from Onda, a new script from Hideki Mitsui, and contributions from two stalwarts of the company's 1990s success: **Armitage III**–director Ochi and **El Hazard**–composer Nagaoka. The revamped version takes the concept from the earlier series that Earth is semilegendary to the people of the far future, and then postulates a group of religious fanatics, the "Earthians," determined to preserve artifacts from the homeworld. This turns the crew of the Sol Bianca, somewhat pointlessly, from devil-may-care pirates into iconoclastic art thieves. *SB: The Legacy* also "updates" the characters, mostly ignoring the precedents of the first series. April is now captain, having found the Sol Bianca and put together a crew. Janny is still the muscle. June is still the brains, with a powerful symbiotic relationship with the ship and its computer. The biggest changes are in Feb, who still drinks but doesn't really seem to have a role in the crew, and May (now Meiyo), who supplants Rim as a stowaway and ship's mascot, though she too can link with the computer as June does. The computer can also take the form of a huge, shadowy woman, sometimes resembling the Christian

Madonna and sometimes the goddess Diana. As with most TV anime of the late 1990s, digital animation gives the show an overly "clean" look, though it adds considerable charm to the spaceships. Released almost simultaneously in Japan and the U.S., *SB: The Legacy* was derided in Japan for "smelling of butter;" in other words, it was a little too Americanized for Japanese tastes—though art connoisseurs will find a treasure trove of cultural references, from Dante's *Inferno* to Alphonse Mucha paintings.

SOLTY REI *

2005. TV series. DIR: Yoshimasa Hiraike, Masashi Abe, Ryuichi Kimura, Yoshihiko Iwata. SCR: Noboru Kimura. DES: Shujiro Hamakawa. ANI: Shujiro Hamakawa, Sawako Yamamoto, Shuichi Hara, Toshiharu Murata. MUS: Toshiyuki Omori. PRD: AIC, Gonzo, TV Asahi. 25 mins. x 13 eps.

An amnesiac android girl is adopted by a bounty hunter as his own daughter, despite being on the run from an interstellar security bureau. In an act of stunning originality, the pursuing agents are named after cars. Oh no, wait a moment, see **Rayearth** and **Viper GTS**. A manga spin-off later appeared in monthly *Comic Rex*, written by scenarist Kimura and drawn by Kazutaka Takimiya.

SOMEDAY'S DREAMERS *

2003. JPN: *Maho Tsukai ni Taisetsu na Koto; What is Important For Magic Users.* AKA: *Important Things for Magic Users.* TV series DIR: Masami Shimoda. SCR: Norie Yamada. DES: Michinori Chiba, Nobue Yoshinaga. ANI: Keiko Kawashima. MUS: Takefumi Haketa. PRD: Daiei, JC Staff, Pioneer LDC, Rondo Robe, Viewworks, TV Asahi. 25 mins. x 12 eps.

Country girl Yume Kikuchi has magical powers. That's not so unusual—in a nod to the *Harry Potter* fad, she lives in a land exactly like modern Japan, except for the presence of wizards as capable members of society, using their magic to do all kinds of jobs—in hospitals, schools, the police force, just about anywhere. When Yume's skills develop, she too will use them to help others under the guidance of the Ministry that controls magical activity. First, though, she has to pass her apprenticeship to the handsome mage Masami Oyamada, get used to life in the big city, and work out what's most important to her. If you thought KIKI'S DELIVERY SERVICE was a low-key movie, wait until you see this. Despite ravishing art direction, the story is so slow and the characters so quiet, you could be back in YOKOHAMA SHOPPING LOG. Based on the manga in *Comic Dragon* by Kumichi Yoshizuki and Norie Yamada, this show is so laid back it's as if it never came off the page—pretty, sweet, and soporific; and often inverting the conventions of guy-gets-girls harem shows. In this story, we have a single hapless girl who ends up living amidst a group of guys—the gullible Yume having inadvertently applied to live with Masami on the assumption that she would be living with a girl.

SONG OF RAIYANTSUURI

1993. JPN: *Raiyantsuuri no Uta*. AKA: *Song of Liang Chu Li* [?]. Movie. DIR: Seiji Arihara. SCR: Seiji Arihara, Toshiaki Imaizumi. DES: N/C. ANI: Takaya Ono. MUS: N/C. PRD: Mushi, Ringoro. 90 mins.
An indentured Chinese laborer, brought to Japan to work in a coal mine during WWII, manages to escape his captors. He hides out in the Japanese countryside, so far from human habitation that he does not realize when the war ends, with ultimately tragic results. Based on a story by Yoichi Takashi.

SONG OF THE BASEBALL ENTHUSIAST

1977. JPN: *Yakyukyu no Uta*. TV special, TV series, movie. DIR: Tameo Ogawa, Eiji Okabe, Hiroshi Fukutomi. SCR: Eiji Okabe, Haruya Yamazaki, Ryuzo Nakanishi, Shunichi Yukimuro. DES: Shinji Mizushima. ANI: Hidenori Kondo. MUS: Michiaki Watanabe. PRD: Nippon

Animation, Fuji TV. 50 mins. (TVm), 25 mins. x 24 eps. (TV), 90 mins. (m).
Yuki Mizuhara is a teenage southpaw pitcher with outstanding ability, spotted by a talent scout for the Tokyo Mets. Brought into the team, "Yuki" is forced to reveal that he is really a she, but *Yuko* Mizuhara soon wins the affections of the scandalized players when she helps them in their ongoing feud against their rivals, the Hanshin Tigers. Based on the 1977 manga by MAN'S AN IDIOT–creator Shinji Mizushima, *SotBE* began as a double-length pilot episode released as a TV special just before Christmas, with the series proper starting in May of the following year. Episodes 3–6 were also screened as full-length "specials" before being retailored as standard 25-minute chapters. Later episodes tried to move away from the Mizuhara story line (which was only one part of the original), but tales about other players on the team did not attract the same ratings—25 years on, it's the Mizuhara episodes that are still available on video. A movie, shown on a double bill with FUTURE BOY CONAN in 1979, focused on two players, the Northern Wolf and the Southern Tiger, whose rivalry gathers extra drama when it is revealed that they are twins separated at birth.

SONG OF THE CHIMNEY GHOSTS

1993. JPN: *Obake Entotsu no Uta*. Movie. DIR: Yutaka Ozawa. SCR: Yoko Yamamoto. DES: Takao Kasai. ANI: Takao Kasai. MUS: N/C. PRD: Asmik. 42 mins.
One day in 1945, children in Tokyo mistake the distant factory smoke of Shitamachi for ghosts in the sky, though their happy playtime is soon destroyed by the arrival of American bombers. Yet another childhood-innocence-obliterated-by-heartless-Allied-cruelty movie, this one based on a story by Katsumoto Saotome. Compare to the worthy BAREFOOT GEN or GRAVEYARD OF THE FIREFLIES, and their many inferior successors.

SONG OF THE LADYBUGS

1974. JPN: *Tento Mushi no Uta*. TV

series. DIR: Masami Annai, Yukihiro Takahashi. SCR: Akiyoshi Sakai. DES: Noboru Kawasaki. ANI: N/C. MUS: Shunsuke Kikuchi. PRD: Tatsunoko, Fuji TV. 25 mins. x 104 eps.
Seven orphaned children decide to stay together and earn their own living. Even though their grandfather is very wealthy, he does nothing to help them, so they struggle to survive in difficult conditions. Based on the 1974 manga by STAR OF THE GIANTS–creator Noboru Kawasaki, another of whose works, *Inakappe Taisho*, was animated by Tatsunoko in 1970. No relation to the Candies pop trio's 1970s nuptial ditty "Ladybug Samba," sung in karaoke form at a wedding scene in EVANGELION.

SONG OF THE SHEEP

2003. JPN: *Hitsuji no Uta*. AKA: *Lament of the Lamb*. Video. DIR: Gisaburo Sugii. SCR: Gisaburo Sugii. DES: Yasuhiro Seo. ANI: Madhouse. MUS: N/C. PRD: Madhouse. 30 mins. x 4 eps.
Kazuna's family has a gene that dare not speak its name—every now and then they have a child with a strange thirst for blood, but never call it vampirism and keep it quiet. Kazuna is afflicted as a child, and sent to live with the Eda family after his mother dies when he is only three years old. He has a normal, quiet family life and his foster mother wants to adopt him. Kazuna is unaware of his condition until he is a teenager and suffers several devastating attacks triggered by the sight of blood. His sister Chisana, a fellow sufferer, comes back into his life, and Kazuna learns the family secret and has to cope with the knowledge that his life is not going to be anything he expected. How does a young vampire live a normal life in the human world—presumably in a different way than the VAMPAIYAN KIDS? The original manga is by Kei Toume, author of WOLF'S RAIN. There is also a live-action theatrical version. **V**

SONG OF WIND AND TREES

1987. JPN: *Kaze to Ki no Uta: Sei ni Naru ka na*. AKA: *Song of Wind and Trees: Sanctus—Can This Be Holy?*.

Video. DIR: Yoshikazu Yasuhiko, Tatsuya Hiramatsu. SCR: Keiko Takemiya. DES: Keiko Takemiya, Yoshikazu Yasuhiko. ANI: Yoko Kamimura. MUS: Nobuyuki Nakamura. PRD: Studio Gallop, Konami Kogyo, Herald. 60 mins.

At the end of the 19th century, a new academic year starts in a European boarding school for boys. Serious, devoutly religious Serge finds himself sharing a room with beautiful blond Gilbert Cocteau, an incorrigible flirt whom Serge correctly suspects of being homosexual. Gilbert's sweet nature and considerable physical charms gradually win over his suspicious and hostile roommate, and the pair become friends and lovers. But their relationship is under pressure from Serge's religious convictions and Gilbert's naturally flirtatious personality, which attracts plenty of offers from other boys, staff, and visitors. This tender, starry-eyed romantic melodrama was based on the 1976 manga by **Toward the Terra**–creator Keiko Takemiya.

SONIC SOLDIER BORGMAN *

1988. JPN: *Cho-on Senshi Borgman*. AKA: *Borgman; Supersonic Soldier Borgman*. TV series, movie, video. DIR: Hiroshi Negishi, Hiroshi Yoshida, Kiyoshi Murayama. SCR: Hideki Sonoda, Nobuaki Kishima, Noboru Aikawa, Kiyoshi Murayama. DES: Michitaka Kikuchi, Koichi Ohata, Torao Arai, Takehiro Yamada. ANI: Masamitsu Kudo, Hideyuki Motohashi. MUS: Hiromoto Tobisawa. PRD: Ashi Pro, Nippon TV. 25 mins. x 35 eps. (TV), 25 mins. (m), 60 mins., 30 mins. x 3 eps. (v).

In the late 1990s, Tokyo is destroyed by four meteorites. In 2030, Megalo City in Tokyo Bay is infiltrated by a secret organization. Check: natural disaster, rebuilding, sinister organization—now all we need is a group of armored vigilantes. Our heroes Anice, Chuck, and Ryo are actually cyborgs (hence Borgman) created for a peaceful international deep-space probe, but the project head, Memory Geen, is the first to have been infiltrated by the alien Yoma, who plan to inherit the Earth

since their own world is dying. The five battle-suited female cops of the World Criminal Police at first distrust and oppose the Borgman team, since fighting the Yoma is what they've been specially created and trained to do. Sound familiar? Post–**Bubblegum Crisis** but curiously more old-fashioned, *Borgman* is a stylistic bridge between earlier team shows and the dystopian heroes ushered in by *Alien, Blade Runner,* and *Terminator,* though none of them used a teaching career as cover for their hard-suited heroes. If you can ignore the presence of the annoying infants that this tactic welds into the story line and the somewhat simplistic characterization, this is a pleasant enough adventure for teens. Originator Kikuchi's design skills, helped by Ohata's monsters, propelled the show to success in Japan and a video revival four years later. The first video, *Midnight Gigs,* is a music compilation from the series, with some cast and crew information. The video release *The Borgman: The Last Battle* (1989), Murayama's movie *Lover's Rain* (1990), and the three-part video series *Borgman 2: New Century 2058* (1993, *B2: Shinseiki 2058*) carry the story forward to 2058 and a new Yoma attack. The survivors of the previous conflict unite with new allies to fight the old battles. Compare to the similarly themed **Virus**.

SONIC THE HEDGEHOG *

1996. Video. DIR: Kazunori Ikegami. SCR: Mayori Sekijima. DES: Tsuneo Ninomiya, Haruo Miyakawa. ANI: Tsuneo Ninomiya. MUS: Mitsuhiro Oda. PRD: Sega, Taki Corporation. 25 mins. x 2 eps., 25 mins. x 78 eps. (*Sonic X*).

Sonic the Hedgehog's archnemesis, Dr. Robotnik, has been banished from the Land of Darkness by an evil Metal Robotnik. He tells Sonic that the Robot Generator has been sabotaged and will blow Planet Freedom to kingdom come. Sonic is reluctant to get involved until the president's daughter Sara turns on the charm, but as he sets off on his mission, he must defeat the Hyper Metal Sonic, a robot hedgehog

(and *Terminator 2* homage) who's after his girl and his life.

Based on the video game series of the same name, the anime was released in English as *Sonic the Movie* to imply a budget and quality that simply weren't there. *StH* retains many favorites from the original, though Sonic's original hedgehog girlfriend, Amy, is replaced with the more human Sara. Hajime Kamegaki's later TV series *Sonic X* (2003) has Sonic and pals getting blown through the dimensions to Earth, where they team up with a 12-year-old boy to stop evil Dr. Eggman from collecting all seven Chaos Emeralds, which will give him absolute power. The first season ran a full year and was followed by a 26-episode second season.

SONODA, KENICHI

1962– . Born in Kumamoto, he worked for the Artmic studio as a designer of machinery and characters on shows such as **Gall Force** and **Riding Bean**. He retrieved elements of the latter story from the collapse of Artmic by writing them into a new manga story, **Gunsmith Cats**, which was subsequently adapted into anime. His design work also appears in shows including Gainax's **Wings of Honneamise** and **Otaku no Video**.

SORAN THE SPACE BOY

1965. JPN: *Uchu Shonen Soran*. TV series. DIR: Tatsuo Ono. SCR: Kazuya Fujimoto, Ryu Mitsuse, Morimasa Matsumoto, Shota Fujimura, Masaki Tsuji. DES: N/C. ANI: Shizuko Sumeoka, Norio Yazawa. MUS: Kazuo Iba, Taku Izumi. PRD: TCJ, Eiken, TBS. 25 mins. x 96 eps.

Professor Tachibana invents the Antisolar Bomb. Fearing it might be "put to the wrong uses" (it's a bomb!), he flees from Earth with his wife and child, but an accident befalls their capsule, and their son is the sole survivor. Raised by aliens on the planet Soran, the boy returns to Earth 15 times stronger than humans. Accompanied by his sidekick, Chappy the space squirrel, Soran rights wrongs on Earth, searching all the while for his long-lost sister. A muddled mixture of *Superman* and the James Bond movies.

SORCERER HUNTERS *

1995. JPN: *Bakuretsu Hunter*. AKA: *Explosion Hunter*. TV series, video. DIR: Koichi Mashimo, Nobuyoshi Habara. SCR: Satoru Akahori, Hiroyuki Kawasaki, Masaharu Amiya. DES: Keiji Goto, Toshihisa Kogawa. ANI: N/C. MUS: Kenji Kawai. PRD: Xebec. 25 mins. x 26 eps. (TV), 30 mins. x 3 eps. (v).

The place is the Spooner Continent. The benevolent Big Mama's last lot of defenders of peace and justice, the Haz Knights, failed to rid the land of evil sorcerers. Instead, she finds some unlikely replacements and names them the Sorcerer Hunters. Two are brothers, goofy lecher Carrot Glace, who's always hungry, and Marron Glace, who's quiet and refined. Despite their constant backbiting, they're devoted to each other. Then there's a big blond hunk named Gateau Mocha, who may be gay and secretly lusting after pretty-boy Marron. The other two are sisters, Tira Misu and Chocolate Misu, who dress in S/M style clothing when they go to work, complete with spike-heeled shoes and whips. They're both fixated on Carrot but don't fight over him because they're devoted to each other. They're all theoretically named after desserts, though to Western palates it's stretching things to call glazed carrots and chestnuts—literally carrot and marron *glacé*—a dessert.

The plot is riddled with internal contradictions. Many of the people our heroes are called on to help are stupid, superstition-ridden chumps not much better than the sorcerers who plague them. The supreme being, despite having a reassuringly maternal name and a sidekick whose name sounds like Daughter, has not been entirely honest with them. She's actually using each mission she gives them to train them for a bigger mission, one that will save the whole world from destruction, and she hasn't told them that Carrot is the

ultimate weapon. Carrot (like innocent Rushe Lenlen in **BASTARD**) has the ultimate evil locked inside him. He can transform into a monster of enormous power, but he is completely unaware of this power and unable to control it. It only emerges when he is struck by magic, which happens rather a lot. The bad guy, Sacher Torte, is actually an ex-good guy, one of the Haz Knights who was driven to the dark side by despair over their failure to save the world from evil last time around. He knows about Carrot's power and wants to use it to destroy everything and start again with a clean slate. The survival of a planet depends on a hormonally challenged kid and his love for his brother and friends. No wonder Big Mama is keeping it to herself. The three-episode video series is somewhat saucier than the TV anime, with more flesh on show and more gags. The first episode is a hot-springs story in which an unnaturally advanced child chases Tira and Chocolate while Carrot goes after his unnaturally youthful mother; amid all the fan service the producers allow the child to break the fourth wall repeatedly, getting into heated debate with the narrator. Episode two brings in the leader of the Haz Knights, androgynous swordsman Millefeuille, and once again shows the difference between TV and video; the restrained androgyne of the series is a gleeful, girl-fondling pervert. Carrot's multiple manga transformations, ignored in the TV series, are also showcased in the climactic final fight. The final episode flashes back to the characters' early lives but also provides comic relief, including Big Mama's karaoke turn.

Based on a manga in *Dengeki Comic Gao* by Satoru Akahori and Rei Omishi, *SH* is actually a rather enjoyable series, with more on offer than its slapstick wrappings indicate, including fun characters and wild designs. Though individual episodes may often stray into the banal territory that Akahori has done his utmost to claim, there are some interesting premises and plot twists like Sacher's origins, the Gateau-Marron

relationship, and the genuine devotion between the two sisters competing for Carrot's affections. The second season of the TV series, which features Sacher's attempts to waken the destructive god slumbering inside Carrot, was renamed *Spell Wars; Sorcerer Hunters' Revenge* in the U.S.

SORCERER ON THE ROCKS *

1999. JPN: *Chivas 123*. Video. DIR: Kazuhiro Ozawa. SCR: Hiroyuki Kawasaki. DES: Yuki Mirai. ANI: Hisashi Abe. MUS: Nobuo Ito. PRD: Toho Video. 30 mins. x 2 eps.

Chivas Scotch is a loud, self-centered Chasemancer (magical bounty hunter) determined to tame the god Loki for a big reward, accompanied by his shape-shifting servant Kiss and nurse-out-of-water (and occasional bunny girl) Gin Phase. Beginning life in *Comic Gao* as yet another off-the-peg creation from **BEAST WARRIORS'** Satoru Akahori and pseudonymous collaborator Yuki Mirai, it nevertheless stayed on video. In the cutthroat conditions of the early 21st century, it would take something more than 60 minutes of hackneyed magic to win a lucrative TV contract...we hope. Bought for translation by ADV Films, though the name had to be changed in the U.S., where Chivas is a trademark.

SOUL HUNTER *

1999. JPN: *Sendai den Hoshin Engi*. AKA: *Immortal Tales of Hoshin Engi; Fengshen Yanyi*. TV series. DIR: Junji Nishimura. SCR: Koji Ueda, Atsuhiro Tomioka, Masashi Sogo. DES: Masashi Kojima. ANI: N/C. MUS: Ryo Sakai. PRD: Studio Deen. 25 mins. x 26 eps.

In the 11th century B.C., the world is divided into two realms that coexist without any problem: Earth for humans and Heaven (actually Mount Kunlun, the Chinese Olympus), for immortals. Heaven has conferred on the young Immortal, Taikoubou, the mission of delivering Earth from the threat of the demon Immortal, Dakki, by capturing the 365 demons who are rampaging all over China. She and her aides have taken Emperor Zhou and

Southern Cross

in his name are bringing misfortune, famine, and slavery to the land. Taikoubou sets out to find warriors to support him in his mission and is joined by "Raishinshi" and Nataku, while at the Imperial Palace Lord Chancellor Bunchu and Duke Kou Hiko seek to protect the imperial princes.

Based on Ryu Fujisaki's 1996 manga for *Shonen Jump*, which adapted a Chinese ghost story for a modern Japanese audience, it was noteworthy for the originality of his characters and his remarkable graphic treatment of drapery and costume. Although set in a specific time, everything seems deliberately incoherent, notably the presence of a hi-fi setup during festivals (also seen in the *Monkey* live-action series). Occasional laziness in the animation is obscured behind flashy computer graphics.

SOUL TAKER, THE
2001. TV series. DIR: Akinori Arafusa. SCR: Mayori Sekijima. DES: Akio Watanabe, Noriaki Tetsura. ANI: Haruo Sotozaki, Toshiaki Aida. MUS: N/C. PRD: Tatsunoko, WOWOW. 25 mins. x 13 eps.
Kyosuke Date comes home on a visit

from his college dormitory to a devastating scene. His mother, Mio, has been assaulted and is dying in a sea of blood, a knife gripped in her shaking hand. Beautiful Maya Misaki is somehow or other on hand to help. The bewildered Kyosuke learns things he never knew about his family. He has a twin sister, Runa, who has a group of "other selves," beings called Flickers. She's on the run from both the mysterious organization known as the Hospital, men in white with seemingly magical powers, and from robots sent by Kirihara Kontzern, a giant corporation. Kyosuke has to find his sister so that he can find out why their mother died, and why so much mystery surrounds his family. See also the *SoulTaker* spin-off, **NURSE WITCH KOMUGI**.

SOUND OF MUSIC, THE
1991. JPN: *Trapp Ikka Monogatari*. AKA: *Story of the Trapp Family, Trapp Family Story, The.* TV series. DIR: Kozo Kusuba, Jiro Saito, Fujino Sadohara, Nobuaki Nakanishi. SCR: Ayo Shiroya. ANI: Katsu Oshiro, Hiromi Kato, Nobuhiro Hosoi, Koji Ito, et al. MUS: Shinsuke Kazato. PRD: Nippon Animation, Fuji TV. 25 mins. x 40 eps.

In pre-WWII Austria lives the von Trapp family—widowed Baron Georg and his seven children—who find their lives transformed by their new nanny, who reinforces their love of music, and eventually helps them escape the Nazis. This anime was based on Maria Augusta Kutschera von Trapp's account of her family's struggles that was published as *The Story of the Trapp Family Singers* (1949) and made world famous by the 1959 Rodgers and Hammerstein musical and the subsequent 1965 film starring Julie Andrews, which fictionalized the events considerably. Part of the **WORLD MASTERPIECE THEATER** series, this anime also takes many liberties with the story, chiefly to make it palatable to a younger audience. The series was also cut down into an 85-minute feature-length TV movie that covered roughly the same pacing and ground as the live-action movie. Compare to **NETTI'S MARVELOUS STORY**.

SOUTHERN CROSS *
1984. JPN: *Chojiku Kitai Southern Cross*. AKA: *Superdimensional Cavalry Southern Cross.* TV series. DIR: Yasuo Hasegawa, Tsukasa Sunaga, Masakazu Yasumura, Katsuhisa Yamada, Hiroshi Yoshida. SCR: Jinzo Toriumi, Hisato Kaganai, Tomoko Kawasaki, Kenji Terada. DES: Miya Sonoda, Hiroshi Ogawa, Hiroyuki Kitazume. ANI: Yutaka Arai. MUS: Tsutomu Sato. PRD: Tatsunoko, TBS. 25 mins. x 23 eps.
The human colony world of Grolier is attacked by the savage alien Zor. Jeanne Francaix, hotheaded commander of the 15th Squadron of the Southern Cross army, is on the front line. Her close friend Bowie Emerson, a passionate music lover, is one of her troop, and when he is taken prisoner by the Zor, he falls in love with alien singer Musika. Believing that most of the Zor don't want war but are being forced into it by their commanders, he escapes, promising Musika that he will come back for her. Meanwhile Jeanne has fallen in love with Seifrietti Weisse, an enemy pilot who has been captured in battle and lost his memory.

She convinces him that he should join the human side and enlists him in her squadron despite the protests of her commander, who is not convinced by his courage and success in battle. The lovers find new hope in a hidden outcrop of beautiful, thriving flowers uncontaminated by the devastation that both races have wrought. They also learn that the leaders of Zor are planning the total extinction of humanity. Seifrietti's memory returns, and he decides to return to the Zor base alone and eliminate the leaders in the hope that his people can live in peace with humans and that their world can survive.

SC was only one of a rich crop of robot series from this period, and not the most successful, but it achieved fame in the West when it became part of **ROBOTECH**, with changes to character names and relationships made to support the new continuity. Jeanne became Dana, half-breed daughter of Max and Miriya Sterling from the *Macross Saga* segment. It would be more than a decade before Max and Miriya's "real" daughter, Mylene Jenius, took to the screen in **MACROSS 7**. The rewrite also brought a different kind of ecological emphasis. Carl Macek's *SC* removed one of Grolier's moons in order to claim the story was set on a polluted Earth: as in **GUN-BUSTER**, it is humans, not aliens who now present the greatest threat to the environment. Humanity is presented as a race of shortsighted idiots whose fight for survival obscures the fact that they have wrecked their own planet, forcing other species into extinction just as the Zor leaders seek to wipe them out.

SOUTHERN RAINBOW
1982. JPN: *Minami no Niji no Lucy*. AKA: *Lucy of the Southern Rainbow*. TV series. DIR: Hiroshi Saito, Shigeo Koshi, Kozo Kusuba, Takayoshi Suzuki. SCR: Akira Miyazaki. DES: Shuichi Seki. ANI: Eimi Maeda, Koichi Murata, Fumiko Morimoto, Noboru Takano. MUS: Koichi Sakata. PRD: Nippon Ani-

mation, Fuji TV. 25 mins. x 50 eps. Lucy May is the youngest daughter of the Popple family. In 1836, she sets out with her mother, father, brothers Ben and Tob, and sisters Clara and Kate on the long voyage from England to Australia, which was then a mysterious and hazardous continent where colonists faced hardship but had the opportunity to become rich in their new homeland. The series covers four years during which, after many struggles, the family sets up a successful business in the new city of Adelaide. Part of the **WORLD MASTERPIECE THEATER** series, this anime was based on a novel by Phyllis Piddington serialized in the Japanese magazine *Living Book*.

SPA OF LOVE *
2005. JPN: *Ryojoku Hitozuma Onsen*. AKA: *Rape Wife Onsen*. Video. DIR: P Nakamura. SCR: Shima Iizaki. DES: Kenji Fukube. ANI: Takahiro Toyomasu. MUS: N/C. PRD: Waki Pro, GP Museum Soft, Image House, Milky. 30 mins. x 2 eps. Yuji arrives at a traditional Japanese inn with impeccable references, but soon things start to go wrong. He rapes the young hostess and the maids, and also targets three innocent housewives who are staying at the inn. More domination and abuse, in a traditional setting similar to that of **SWALLOWTAIL INN**—the Japanese publicity specifies sex in the bath and lactating breasts as two of the "delights" awaiting within. Based on a computer game by Strikes.
🅛🅝🅥

SPACE ACE *
1965. JPN: *Uchu no Ace*. AKA: *Ring-O*. TV series. DIR: Hiroshi Sasagawa, Toshio Kinoshita, Ippei Kuri, Tatsuo Yoshida, Seiji Okuda. SCR: Jinzo Toriumi. DES: Tatsuo Yoshida. ANI: Akiyuki Kuma, Tatsuo Yoshida, Seiji Okuda. MUS: Taku Izumi. PRD: Tatsunoko, Fuji TV. 25 mins. x 52 eps. (b/w).
The survivors of an alien race set out in search of an uninhabited planet where their civilization can be rebuilt. During the voyage, a single ship piloted by one little alien leaves the convoy and

lands on Earth. Professor Tatsunoko of the Tatsunoko Institute discovers what he thinks is a giant shell on the sea bed and opens it to find the childlike pilot. A creature from planet Parum, "Ace" can use "space fuse" energy to perform amazing feats of strength and can fly through the air on a silver ring. With the professor's daughter Asari (Ginger), cub reporter Yadokari (Flash Scoop), and Ebo (Ibo) the robot dog, Space Ace fights off alien monsters and invaders by using a high-energy food supply maintained by Asari and stored in Ebo's flip-top nose. The Tatsunoko Studio's first production, planned as an answer to Osamu Tezuka's **ASTRO BOY**. *SA* featured Rei Osumi as a "science fiction adviser"—the author took the studio's money in return for such suggestions as shooting one's way out of trouble with a "platina ray." Broadcast on Australian TV; the first episode was remade in color in an unsuccessful attempt to gain a U.S. sale. Not to be confused with the American animation by Don Bluth for the wholly unconnected *Space Ace* game.

SPACE ADVENTURE COBRA *
1982. JPN: *Space Cobra* (TV); *Space Adventure Cobra* (m). TV series, movie. DIR: Osamu Dezaki, Toshio Takeuchi, Shunji Oga, Masaharu Okuwaki. SCR: Kenji Terada, Haruya Yamazaki, Kazuo Terada, Kosuke Miki. DES: Akio Sugino, Shinji Otsuka. ANI: Akio Sugino, Koji Morimoto, Ryutaro Nakamura, Atsuko Fukushima, Chuji Nakajima, Jun Kawagoe, Hideo Nanba, Takuya Wada. MUS: Kentaro Haneda (TV), Osamu Tokaibayashi (m). PRD: Tokyo Movie Shinsha, Fuji TV. 103 mins. (m), 25 mins. x 31 eps. (TV).
Bored 24th-century salaryman Mr. Johnson buys a virtual vacation at the Trip Movie Corporation only to discover that his chosen holiday (the life of a space pirate) triggers real memories that he has suppressed. He discovers that he really *is* Cobra, a rogue with a price on his head who has a false arm hiding the mentally powered "psycho-gun." Fleeing the Galactic Guild, he

encounters beautiful bounty hunter Jane Royale (Jane Flower), who has part of a treasure map tattooed on her shapely back. Her sisters Dominique and Catherine have the other pieces that reveal the location of the Supreme Weapon. Cobra springs Catherine from prison before tracking down Dominique, a police officer who has infiltrated the all-female Snow Guerrillas gang. Though Cobra claims to want the Supreme Weapon (and, like any Buichi Terasawa hero worth his salt, to see the girls naked), he is also intent on protecting the ladies from Crystal Boy, his golden cyborg rival, who lacks Cobra's qualms about skinning them alive to make the map more portable.

Keeping relatively close to Buichi Terasawa's 1978 manga in *Shonen Jump* magazine, the first season's quest for the MacGuffin Supreme Weapon ends with Cobra recruited by Dominique for undercover work. Investigating Guild drug-smuggling on planet Laloux, he joins the Red Saxons, a sports team that plays the rugby/baseball hybrid *rugball*. Amid violent matches reminiscent of *Rollerball* (1975), he rises through the ranks to crack the case and win the championship. The series ends with a third arc, as Cobra locates Salamander, the entity behind the guild that's revealed to be an energy field controlled by the spirit of Adolf Hitler.

Predating *Total Recall* with its original premise, *SAC* is typical Terasawa, crammed full of leggy, disposable beauties who turn up, wiggle their assets, snog the hero, and then get shot. It's got plenty of ray-gun action, as well as the artist's other trademark—madly futurist designs based on contemporary technologies like motorcycles, cars, and planes.

The TV series was preceded by a feature, with a script written by Terasawa himself and Haruya Yamazaki—Miyazaki's amanuensis on CASTLE OF CAGLIOSTRO. The movie script shuffles the characters into a slightly different setting—in this version Jane Flower and her sisters Catherine and Dominique form the three aspects of the Empress of the Universe, ruler of the planet Myras, who will manifest when all fall in love with the same man (guess who?). Crystal Boy (aka Necron) is now the personification of Death itself, tracking Cobra as he springs Catherine from jail and encounters Dominique on the Planet of the Snow Guerrillas. Clearly a dry run for the later series, changes made between the two include a new composer and the replacement of the original Cobra voice actor Shigeru Matsuzaki with Nachi Nozawa. *SAC* also steals from many SF movies, including *Barbarella* (1967), *Flash Gordon* (1980), the Genesis project from *Star Trek: Wrath of Khan* (1982), and the carbonite-freezing episode from *The Empire Strikes Back* (1980). The movie is often claimed as a sequel set two years *after* the TV events, though it requires remarkable suspension of disbelief to accept that Cobra would meet two trios of virtually identical girls with the same names, occupations, and troubles. Similarly, the movie version does not allude to Mr. Johnson's induction at the Trip Movie Corporation; Japanese audiences familiar with the manga could disregard any of the film's more far-fetched or hallucinatory episodes as yet more evidence that this is all "really a dream"—not an option available to most English-speaking viewers. When dubbed for the U.K. market, Manga Entertainment replaced the Japanese soundtrack with all-new material from the group Yello. The decision gained *SAC* extra press coverage and papered over the cracks to make this antique film seem up-to-date, while the 1995 copyright date for the new score helped imply it was newer than it really was.

The series is popular to this day and has an ardent fan following in Japan and Europe. Scenes from the feature were also recycled for Matthew Sweet's pop promo "Girlfriend." However, its influence was strongest in Korea, where Cobra's relationship with Jane was shoddily rehashed with Hyesong and Marie Kim in Lee Hyun-se's *Armageddon* (1996). Other Terasawa works adapted as anime include GOKU: MIDNIGHT EYE and KABUTO.

SPACE DEFENSE OFFICER TAA-BO

1991. JPN: *Uchu Jieitai Taa-bo*. AKA: *Space Self Defense Force Taa-Bo*. Movie, video. DIR: Masami Hata. SCR: Joji Iida, Anzu Nemuru. DES: Koichi Kadowaki. ANI: Toshiharu Akahori. MUS: Toyomi Kojima. PRD: Sanrio. 34 mins., 30 mins.

Interstellar crime-fighter Taa-bo fights the evil Scorpion Brothers in a short-lived attempt to introduce a more traditional hero to the Sanrio lineup. After his movie debut *Taa-Bo on the Planet of the Dragon Pavilion* (1991, *Taa-bo no Ryumiyasei Daitanken*), the character devolved to video, where he disappeared from view after *Taa-Bo on the Planet Where Time Stopped* (1993, *Taa-bo no Toki no Tomatta Sei*). The "movie" was also bundled onto a Sanrio anthology tape with mini-features of more popular stars HELLO KITTY and KEROPPI.

SPACE DEMON DAIKENGO

1978. JPN: *Uchu Majin Daikengo*. AKA: *Space Machine Daikengo; Space Devil/God Daikengo*. TV series. DIR: Asahi Yahiro, Noriyasu Furukawa, Hiroshi Yamanouchi, Hideyoshi Ojika. SCR: Akiyoshi Sakai, Jinzo Toriumi, Satoshi Toyama, Ichiro Yamamura, Michio Fukushima, Hajime Mori. DES: Kunio Okawara, Mitsuki Nakamura, Motohiro Takahashi, Tadakazu Iguchi. ANI: Tadanori Tanabe, Kenzo Koizumi, Tadakazu Iguchi, Tsuneo Ninomiya. MUS: Hiroshi Tsutsui. PRD: Tori Pro, Studio Nue, Toei Animation, TV Asahi. 25 mins. x 26 eps.

There's intrigue afoot on planet Emperius. Prince Zamuson is murdered, but urges his younger brother Rygar to escape before dying at the hands of alien invaders. Believing the attackers were aided by local traitors, Rygar flees to avoid imprisonment. He has his sympathizers—beautiful Cleo, daughter of the corrupt Prime Minister, and two helpful robots, Anike and Otoke. Rygar revives the legendary giant space robot Daikengo, and he and his supporters fight the invading soldiers of the Magellan Empire, commanded by the evil Lady Baracross and her protege Roboleon, until peace is restored to Emperius and the galaxy. This is supposedly the first giant robot anime not to be focused on Earth (BATTLE OF THE PLANETS only acquired its deep-space focus in non-Japanese versions), and Daikengo is certainly the first robot to be able to open his mouth, show pointed fangs, and spit fire. The show was made by "Tori Pro," a group of defectors from the Tatsunoko studio, with whose productions this has many similarities.

SPACE FAMILY CARLVINSON

1988. JPN: Uchu Kazoku Carlbinson. Video. DIR: Kimio Yabuki, Tatsuo Suzuki. SCR: Michiru Shimada. DES: Yoshito Asari. ANI: Masahiro Kanno. MUS: Hiroya Watanabe. PRD: Toei. 45 mins.
A traveling-show troupe of aliens are playing cards when a vessel comes out of warp space and nearly crashes into their ship before crashing on planet Anika. The only survivor is a baby human girl, Corona. They decide to look after her, at least until somebody shows up to claim her. In order to equip themselves to play the part of the "normal" human family and friends the baby will need, they research information from the crashed ship's data banks and embark on one of the longest-running shows of their entire career. But they identify more and more with their roles, and when a ship comes for Corona five years later, they have *become* her family and friends.

Yoshito Asari's 1985 manga in *Shonen Captain* was a revamp of the popular SWISS FAMILY ROBINSON castaway theme that also inspired the U.S. comic *Space Family Robinson*, later known as *Lost in Space*. Mysteriously, the Nimitz-class U.S. aircraft carrier Carl Vinson visited Japan in the 1980s, though it seems likely that the use of its name is either coincidence or one of those meaningless puns that the Japanese find so entertaining (see SORCERER

HUNTERS). As Chairman of the House Naval Affairs Committee from 1931 to 1947, the original Carl Vinson could be said to be personally responsible for the support and maintenance of the U.S. Navy during WWII, which hardly seems likely to have endeared him to the Japanese.

SPACE FIREBIRD *

1980. JPN: Hi no Tori 2772: Ai no Cosmozone. AKA: Firebird 2772: Love's Cosmozone; Phoenix 2772. Movie. DIR: Taku Sugiyama. SCR: Osamu Tezuka, Taku Sugiyama. DES: Shinji Ito, Tsuyoshi Matsumoto, Noboru Ishiguro. ANI: Kazuko Nakamura, Noboru Ishiguro. MUS: Yasuo Higuchi. PRD: Kadokawa, Tohoku Shinsha. 122 mins. (m), 60 mins. (v1/Karma), 48 mins. (v2/Yamato), 48 mins. (v3/Space), 25 mins. x 13 eps. (TV).
In the 22nd century, humans are bred to order, raised in laboratories, and selected for their roles from birth by a tyrannical government exploiting the planet to the verge of ecological collapse. Godot is lucky enough to be raised by the robot Olga, a warm, gentle mother-figure who looks like a fetishist's dream girl in her shiny red outfit and can transform into a whole range of fabulous toys and vehicles. He grows up to be a sensitive and intelligent young man who rebels against the harshness and cruelty of his society. While training to be a space pilot, he learns that he has a brother, Rock, who is one of the ruling class, selected for his intelligence and ruthlessness. He also falls in love with Lena, an upper-class girl, and, because this is a crime against the State (and against Rock, her fiancé!), he is sent to a harsh prison planet. He is offered his freedom if he will capture the Space Firebird, a mystical creature whose blood can bestow immortality and everlasting power. The faithful Olga, who has followed him through all his troubles, joins him on his mission; she has always loved him and is determined to help him use the powers of the Firebird to revive the dying Earth.

Based on Osamu Tezuka's long-running series of 12 interlinked tales first begun in 1967 in the manga magazine *Com*, this magical love story contains many elements common in his work—the recycling of characters (BLACK JACK is the prison planet commandant), the use of comic characters and musical numbers straight out of Disney, the contrast between inner beauty and outer sham, supportive and exploitative relationships, and the visual inventiveness that makes every frame a pleasure. There are unexpected roles for Frederik L. Schodt and his fellow translator Jared Cook, credited along with SF writer Sakyo Komatsu as "planning brains."

The phoenix in *Space Firebird* is an eternal being who visits all parts of space and time in the course of the long-running *Phoenix* manga, which only finished in 1988, shortly before Tezuka's death in February 1989. The earliest chapters, created at the height of Tezuka's powers when he was also writing ASTRO BOY, are said to be the best. The third, fourth, and fifth chapters of the original were also animated for video by the Madhouse studio. The one-shots were supervised by Rintaro and seem to be a short-lived attempt to follow *SF* with the ten remaining chapters, though only these three were made. Rintaro's *Phoenix: Karma* (1986, Hi no Tori: Hoo Hen), also shown in cinemas on a double bill with TIME STRANGER, features the firebird's manifestation in ancient India, where it witnesses a conflict between a pirate king and a sculptor, who is, of course, making a statue of a phoenix. Toshio Hirata's *Phoenix: Yamato* (1987, Hi no Tori: Yamato Hen) moves to Japan for a retelling of the story of YAMATO TAKERU. The last episode, Yoshiaki Kawajiri's *Phoenix: Space* (1987, Hi No Tori: Uchu Hen), features the Earthbound starship ZFX-302 finding an icy planet whose occupants prefer death to life.

A 13-episode *Phoenix* TV series (Hi no Tori, 2004) was directed by Ryosuke Takahashi, and spanned the various incarnations of the story from Dawn to Future. It was coproduced by New York's WNET/13 PBS station.

SPACE PATROL HOPPER

1965. JPN: *Uchu Patrol Hopper*. AKA: (see below). TV series. DIR: Taiji Yabushita, Yoshio Ishihara, Yoshio Kuroda, Hiroshi Shidara, Masayuki Akehi. SCR: Taiji Yabushita, Susumu Ginga, Fumi Takahashi. DES: N/C. ANI: Masao Kumogawa. MUS: Shunsuke Kikuchi. PRD: Toei, NET. 25 mins. x 44 eps.

After being severely injured in a space accident, Earth boy Jun is saved by the Hopper Aliens, who give him a new cyborg body. With superhuman powers, Jun signs up for the space patrol along with fellow operatives Donkey, Pooh, Dar, Hook, and Professor Doc. After episode 27, the title was changed to *Patrol Team: Space Boy Jun (Patrol Tai: Uchukko Jun)*. One of many 1960s also-rans in the wake of **ASTRO BOY**, including **PRINCE PLANET**, **SORAN THE SPACE BOY**, and **SPACE ACE**.

SPACE PIRATE MITO

1999. JPN: *Uchu Kaizoku Mito no Daiboken*. AKA: *Stellarbusters, Great Adventures of Space Pirate Mito*. TV series. DIR: Takashi Watanabe, Koji Yasuda, Yoshio Nitta, Masahiko Murata, Shigeru Ueda, Kunitoshi Okajima. SCR: Hidefumi Kimura, Junko Okazaki. DES: Reibanji Ishigami. ANI: Masahiro Sekiguchi, Hitoshi Kanezawa. MUS: Hikaru Nanase. PRD: Sunrise, TV Tokyo. 25 mins. x 26 eps.

Fifteen-year-old Aoi discovers that his mother is not a model working abroad at all. He discovers this when she is attacked in the cemetery by members of the space patrol, where she reveals that her adult body harbors Mito, a childlike female space pirate. Mito is his real mother, but, because she is an alien, she does not appear old enough to be. She reveals that Aoi is actually the heir to the throne of the Great Kingdom of the Milky Way, and they are chased by Lanban, the corrupt leader of the space patrol, who wants an artifact that can make *him* king of

the galaxy instead. A sci-fi take on the stories of Mitsukuni Tokugawa (see **MANGA MITO KOMON**), with a space pirate straight out of **TENCHI MUYO!**, this series only got more bizarre for its second season. After episode 13, Aoi suddenly transforms into a girl. The newly female Aoi becomes Queen of the Milky Way but also continues to attend Japanese high school in disguise. The former Queen, Hikari, returns as a ghost and demands her throne back, setting the stage for more space piracy (in the name of the established order) and motherly interference from Mito (who seems to have been passed over in the succession). When released on DVD, the series also included a bonus short, *Mito Wars*, an early experiment in full digital animation.

SPACE RUNAWAY IDEON

1980. JPN: *Densetsu Kyoshin Ideon*. AKA: *Legendary God-Giant Ideon*. TV series, movie. DIR: Yoshiyuki Tomino, Masanori Miura, Toshifumi Takizawa. SCR: Sukehiro Tomita, Jiyu Watanabe, Arata Koga. DES: Yukien Kogawa, Submarine. ANI: Yukien Kogawa. MUS: Koichi Sugiyama. PRD: Sunrise, TV Tokyo. 25 mins. x 39 eps. (TV), 90 mins. (m).

In 2400, the human race and the Buff Clan are at war, but one young pilot believes that peace can be made between the two enemies. Meanwhile humankind has one last line of defense: advanced war machines retrieved from the destroyed colony world Solo, which can be combined into the super-robot Ideon—piloted by Cosmo Yuki, Casha Imhof, Sherril Formosa, and Bes Jordan. Devised by Yoshiyuki Tomino in large part as a reworking of his popular **GUNDAM**, *SRI* had an even more outrageous main robot. It was formed from three giant trucks (Sol-Amber, Sol-Vainer, and Sol-Conver), each of which could become an independent war machine (Ideo-Delta, Ideo-Nova, or Ideo-Buster) and was armed with massive quantities of weaponry, including a small black-hole cannon. Any fan would call that seri-

ous play value, but the merchandising of *SRI* never took off as *Gundam's* did. Two films followed in 1982, shown on the same double bill. The first was a digest of episodes 1–32, the second of the finale, with bonus footage from the canceled episodes 40-43. Within five years, the coming of video would make such "movies" much rarer, and less popular with audiences—witness the outrage at the discovery that much of the **EVANGELION DEATH AND REBIRTH** double bill was recycled TV footage.

SPACE SAGITTARIUS

1986. JPN: *Uchusen Sagittarius*. AKA: *Spaceship Sagittarius*. TV series. DIR: Kazuyoshi Yokota, Jiro Saito, Keiji Hayakawa. SCR: Nobuyuki Isshiki, Nobuyuki Fujimoto. DES: Sadahiko Sakamaki, Shuichi Seki, Noboru Takano. ANI: Hiroyoshi Sugawara. MUS: Haruki Mino. PRD: Nippon Animation, TV Asahi. 25 mins. x 77 eps.

Mr. Giraffe, a scientist, commissions Toppie and Lana, a mouse and frog with their own space haulage company, to take him in search of his teacher Anne, who disappeared while trying to prove her scientific theories on the dangerous planet Vega III. The pilots are dragged away from their loved ones (in Toppie's case, his pregnant wife, while Lana simply kisses his lasagna goodbye), and they are soon in trouble when facing a death sentence on the first planet they reach. Saved by the minstrel Sibip, they continue their journey. Based on the Italian comic *Altri Mondi* by Andrea Romoli, this charming little fantasy series brings together three animal astronauts who cruise the galaxy in the good ship Sagittarius, with anthropomorphic adventures in the style of **SHERLOCK HOUND** and **MONTANA JONES**.

SPACE TRAVELERS: THE ANIMATION *

2000. Video. DIR: Takashi Ui. SCR: Katsuhiko Koide. DES: Chikara Okazaki. ANI: Noboru Takahashi. MUS: Toshiyuki Watanabe. PRD: Amuse Video, Fuji TV, Robot. 60 mins.

Plucky hero Hayabusa Jetter, his ingenue sidekick Irene Bear, muscle-moun-
tain Crush Bomber, slimy Chinese
trader Hoi, slinky femme fatale Gold
Papillon, boomerang-throwing kid
Black Cat, unstoppable space samurai
Dragon Attack, mechanic Electric
Sunny, and funky cyberhipster Karl
Hendrix fight to restore the honor
of planet Earth after an apocalyptic
interstellar incident. A parody of the
giant-robot space operas of the 1980s,
with homages to *Star Wars* and *Star Trek*
thrown in, *ST* is cheap and derivative,
though the producers would argue
that this was at least *part* of the plan.

It began as a throwaway gag in Katsuyuki Motohiro's popular live-action
movie *Space Travelers* (2000) in which a
Tokyo bank robbery goes disastrously
wrong. As the police surround the
building, the staff and hostages volunteer to help the robbers bluff their way
out; each is given a code name based
on a character from the robbers' favorite cartoon, a nonexistent show called
Space Travelers—hence the ridiculously
large cast of anime archetypes. Scraps
of animation were made as inserts
for the original movie and are reused
here—hence the strange pacing of the
overlong opening credits that were
not originally intended to be shown
in this manner. The plot is a tired
succession of fight scenes, a ludicrous
transformation sequence, and an in-
joke as the crew flies past the ruins of
the Fuji TV building. An afterthought
following the movie's success, *ST* was
reputedly inspired by Motohiro's love
of STAR BLAZERS, GUNDAM, and EVANGE-
LION, though in execution it is a pale
imitation of the 1970s hacksploitation
of COWBOY BEBOP and all too obviously a product of the terminally low
budgets of many 1990s anime. Ironically, it was Motohiro's previous film
Bayside Shakedown (1999) that was said
to have sounded the death knell for
anime—not understanding its appeal
to the teen audience, certain producers backed away from making shows for
that age group, only to discover that
Motohiro's follow-up was just that.

SPACE WARRIORS *

1980. JPN: *Uchu Senshi Baldios*. AKA:
Space Warrior Baldios; Baldios. TV
series, movie. DIR: Kazuyuki Hirokawa,
Takao Yotsuji, Kunihiko Yuyama,
Kazuya Yamazaki, Seiji Yamamuro,
Junji Nishimura, Osamu Sekita. SCR:
Akiyoshi Sakai, Jinzo Toriumi, Tomomi
Tsutsui, Takeshi Shudo. DES: Osamu
Kamijo, Hajime Kamegaki. ANI: Takeshi
Tanaka, Tooyo Ashida. MUS: Kentaro
Haneda. PRD: Ashi Productions, Tokyo
12 Channel. 25 mins. x 31 eps. (TV),
117 mins. (m).
Marin Reagan, a native of planet S1,
flees a radioactive atmosphere and
the persecutions of dictator Gattler,
making his way to Earth. Gattler and
the S-1 armies are on their way to take
over the planet as a replacement for
their hopelessly polluted homeworld,
and Marin joins the team working to
defend Earth from alien attack as the
pilot of super-robot Baldios. Earth
and S-1 are fated to come into final
conflict, and the love-hate relationship
between Marin and Aphrodia, commander of the S-1 forces, will finally
be resolved. The show went off the air
with another eight episodes to go, leading to protests from Japanese fans. The
partly completed finale was assembled
with some new footage from Tooyo
Ashida to make a movie release, *Space
Warrior Baldios* (1981, aka *Revenge of the
Space Warriors*, aka *SW: Battle for Earth
Station S-1*), showing the last battle
between Gattler's spaceship Aldebaran
and the Earth satellite base Blue Fixer
under Commander Tsukikage. Gattler
offers Aphrodia the chance to avenge
her dead brother by killing Marin, but
she can't do it and commits suicide.
The ensuing battle destroys both
armies and their weapons, and Marin,
the sole survivor, is left to return to a
devastated Earth with the body of the
woman he truly loved. A 98-minute
version of the movie was screened in
Japan and is also available on video in
the U.S.

SPACEKETEERS *

1978. JPN: *SF Saiyuki Starzinger*. AKA:
SF Journey to the West Starzinger. TV
series. DIR: Yugo Serikawa, Kozo Morishita, Kazumi Fukushima. SCR: Tatsuo
Tamura, Michiru Umadori, Sukehiro
Tomita. DES: Masami Suda. ANI: Masami
Suda, Satoshi Kamimiya. MUS: Shunsuke Kikuchi. PRD: Toei, Fuji TV. 25
mins. x 73 eps.
As the Queen of the Great Planet at
the center of the universe grows old,
the harmony of the universe becomes
unbalanced. Minerals and planets
transform into evil starmen and attack
other planets. In order to restore
peace, the old queen must be replaced
with a young, strong ruler who can
keep her subjects in order. Princess
Aurora is saved by scientist Dr. Kitty
when the starmen attack the moon.
He knows that she has the power to
restore the harmony of the universe as
the new ruler of the Great Planet, so
she sets out in the spaceship Cosmos
Queen with three companions charged
to keep her safe: Sir Jogo (Arimos)
from the planet of water, Don Hakka
(Porkos) from the planet of fire, and
rebel cyborg Jan Kugo (Jesse Dart),
who wears a control circlet around his
head. The starmen and other monsters
try to stop them, but Aurora won't
allow any creatures who were originally
peaceful to be killed. She knows that
if she fulfills her destiny, they will be
restored to their former shapes and
will once again live in harmony with
their fellow beings.

Based on the *Terebi* magazine manga
by CAPTAIN HARLOCK–creator Leiji Matsumoto, this SF retelling of JOURNEY TO
THE WEST was rebranded as *SFSS "II"*
for its final nine episodes, in which
the four have replenished the galactic
energy provided by the old queen and
go to the solar system of Girara, which
is still unbalanced and needs Princess
Aurora to restore it to normalcy. This
time, the farewell to their princess is a
final one, and her three companions
must take their leave of her, but all
of them (especially Kogo) leave their
hearts in her keeping. Edited down to
26 episodes for U.S. release as part of
the FORCE FIVE series, Jim Terry's new

title and character names now misleadingly implied a space-going THREE MUSKETEERS. For the U.S. version, the characters are on a mission to the Dekos Star System, whose evil power source has caused the once-peaceful creatures of the universe to change into evil mutants.

SPACESHIP AGGA RUTER *

1998. JPN: *Space Opera Agga Ruter*. Video. DIR: Shigeru Yazaki. SCR: Masaki Kajishima, Hideyuki Kurata. DES: Masaki Kajishima, Kenji Teraoka. ANI: Katsuhisa Ito. MUS: T.K. Crow. PRD: AIC, Beam Entertainment. 30 mins. x 4 eps.
The evil Shiunk kills Taiyo's parents and leaves him to die in space. Rescued by the kindly android Kei, Taiyo is raised without human companionship for 15 years aboard her ship the Agga Ruter. Kei tells Taiyo to call her "Mother" and instructs him in the arts of love in a succession of Oedipally suspect scenes. When captured by the shrill space pirate Janis (who has been hired by Shiunk to steal the Agga Ruter), the pair prove to be perkily cooperative hostages, volunteering to cook and clean, rummaging in her underwear drawer, and reading out the funny bits from her diary. Janis is a descendant of Re-Formed Humans, ancient members of the Fighter civilization who recombined their DNA to survive on hostile worlds. Though she appears human, she turns into a were-tiger when reminded of abuse at the hands of her circus-ringmaster stepfather. Endowed with superhuman strength *and* bedroom prowess, Taiyo is the only man who can satisfy her, and the sexually sated Janis agrees to switch sides. The Agga Ruter, itself a Fighter relic (see the similar SOL BIANCA), lacks a vital component, which has been mistaken for a precious gem and put on display on the Millennium Mule cruise liner. The gang sneak in to steal it, but Shiunk (now disguised as the Joker with a bad blond wig) has followed them and arranged for their capture by a vicious green-eyed blonde, who is luckily not immune to Taiyo's charms.

A sci-fi porno made by the thinly disguised cast and crew of the TENCHI MUYO! series, whose audience was probably old enough by this point to appreciate the "joke." Even the humor is familiar, with Kei setting up a mock Japanese living room on the bridge of Janis's warship in order to teach her how to be a good wife (sexually available and a great cook). Taiyo is a dead ringer for the older but still passive hero of *Tenchi in Tokyo*, the Agga Ruter is a ship with all the weird properties of Jurai vessels, and the females are cookie-cutter *Tenchi* girlies. Compare to MASQUERADE, which also appears to be reheated leftovers from the franchise. **Ⓝ **

SPARKLING PHANTOM

1990. JPN: *Sparkling Phantom: Runohara Meikyu*. AKA: *SP: Runohara Labyrinth*. Video. DIR: Narumi Kakinouchi. SCR: Narumi Kakinouchi. DES: Kana Hoshino. ANI: N/C. MUS: N/C. PRD: Victor Entertainment. 45 mins.
This SF fantasy about a Japanese girl who is transported to an alternate world populated by fairies was based on the manga in *Hana to Yume* magazine by Kana Hoshino.

SPECTRAL FORCE

1998. JPN: Spectral Force. Video. DIR: Yoshiaki Sato. SCR: Yoshiaki Sato. DES: Shinnosuke Hino, Tatsunori Nakamura, Yoshiaki Tsubata. ANI: Katsuaki Tsubata. MUS: Toru Kobayashi. PRD: Idea Factory, Toon Works. 30 mins. x 2 eps.
This heroic fantasy has fighters duelling for supremacy in the world of Neverland (no relation to PETER PAN AND WENDY). Featuring copious computer graphics, it was based on the *Spectral Force* video game.

SPECTRE

1991. JPN: *Hosai Sengoku Shi Spectre/Requiem*. AKA: *Racing Civil War Chronicle Spectre/Requiem*. Video. DIR: Yoichiro Shimatani. SCR: Yoichirio Shimatani, Ranko Ono. DES: Fumihide Sai, Hiroshi Kiyomizudera. ANI: Fumihide Sai. MUS: Takahiko Kanemaru. PRD:

Apples, Miyuki Pro. 45 mins. x 2 eps.
Modern-day bikers make and break alliances with neighboring gangs, fight over the right to use a local petrol station, and are eventually united under a powerful leader. It's a replay of the events of Japan's 16th-century civil war, but with bikes instead of horses and knives instead of swords. Based on the manga by Jiro Ueno in *Weekly Playboy*. **Ⓥ**

SPEED GRAPHER *

2005. TV series. DIR: Kunihisa Sugishima, Masashi Ishihama. SCR: Shin Yoshida, Yasuyuki Suzuki. DES: Yusuke Kozaki, Masashi Ishihama. ANI: Masashi Ishihama, Toyoaki Fukushima. MUS: Shinkichi Mitsumune. PRD: Gonzo, TAP, TV Asahi. 25 mins. x 24 eps.
Cameraman Tatsumi Saiga used to have a real job as a war photographer, but a strange chain of circumstances led him into the unprincipled end of the market among the paparazzi. Hanging around Tokyo scrabbling for saleable shots, his perfectionism works against him. When he's hired to snap the exclusive Roppongi Club, he can't afford to say no, despite the difficulties. The club's location is secret, it's open only to the A-list, and rumor says that members get access to extraordinary powers through secret ceremonies and forbidden fantasies. When Saiga sneaks in and photographs one of these strange ceremonies, he's caught out by a goddess who, far from being angry, enables him to change into Speed Grapher, a superhuman entity with the power to make anything or anyone he photographs explode—an update of the old superstition that taking someone's photograph will steal his soul. Gorgeous 15-year-old Kagura wants to get away from the club before she becomes a bit player in someone else's twisted fantasy. They get out, but now face retribution from the cult.

SPEED RACER *

1967. JPN: *Mach Go Go Go*. AKA: *Mach 5, Go Go!*. TV series. DIR: Tatsuo Yoshida, Ippei Kuri, Hiroshi Sasagawa,

Seitaro Hara, Hiroyuki Fukushima. scr: Jinzo Toriumi, Tadashi Hirose, Takashi Hayakawa, Masaaki Sakurai, Masashi Kubota. des: Ippei Kuri, Hiroshi Sasagawa. ani: Masami Suda, Takashi Saijo. mus: Nobuyoshi Koshibe, Michiru Oshima. prd: Tatsunoko, Fuji TV, Tatsunoko, TV Tokyo. 25 mins. x 52 eps. (TV1), 25 mins. x 34 eps.

Go Mifune (Speed) is a young racing driver for his father Daisuke's (Pops Racer) Mifune Motors team (nameless in the U.S. version). His mother Aya (Mom Racer), irritating kid brother Kuo (Sprite), and pet monkey Senpei (Chim Chim) all work on the team along with Go's girlfriend, Michi (Trixie), and mechanic Sabu (Sparks). Go's success and the superb engineering of his racing car the Mach Five lead other jealous racers to try and put a spanner in the works, but they are foiled by the mysterious Masked Racer (Racer X), who also fends off master criminals and foreign spies. He's really Go's older brother Kenichi (Rex), a government agent who, for a variety of top-secret reasons, is compelled to work anonymously and cut himself off from his family. The series contained a surprising amount of violence and tension, and it had all the technical limitations of 1960s TV animation, but since distributors K. Fujita had successfully sold **MARINE BOY** to U.S. company Trans-Lux, it had a ready market for this new product.

Accepted by many of its fans as an American product from the first American TV screening in 1967, *Speed Racer* amended the Japanese original considerably. Actor/writer Peter Fernandez was entrusted with the task of toning down the Japanese version for U.S. consumption, and he ensured that no *Speed Racer* villain was ever killed by amending the scripts and inserting shots of stunned bad guys with cartoon planets and stars circling their heads.

A revival on MTV led to the making of a new 13-episode series, *The New Adventures of Speed Racer* (1993) by Fred Wolf Films in 1993; this really *was* an American cartoon. A proposed live-action feature film didn't get beyond concept stage, but 1994 brought us *Speed Racer the Movie*—a compilation of two series episodes with an episode of *Colonel Bleep* interspersed with classic animated TV commercials of the 1960s to bulk out the running time to 80 minutes. Speed would also appear in a commercial for Volkswagen and a music video for Ghost-Face Killah. He returned to Japan, this time to TV Tokyo, in a 34-episode "30th anniversary" remake in 1997, with Pops renamed Daisuke Hibiki and new character Mai Kazami (photographer/love interest) along with her brother, Wataru (brat). The final season neglected the racing plot in favor of time travel. After hitting 555 kph while trying to outrun a tornado, Speed is catapulted through time to the year 2555, when the world is ruled by the evil dictator Handler. With his car newly converted to a fully operational time machine, Speed and the gang set off in search of the Ezekiel Wheel, an energy source that can change the future.

SPIRAL *

2002. jpn: *Spiral: Suiri no Kizuna*. aka: *Spiral: Bonds of Reasoning, Lines of Reasoning*. TV series. dir: Shingo Kaneko. scr: Chinatsu Hojo, Katsuhiko Koide, Mitsuyasu Sakai, Tetsuo Tanaka. des: Yumi Nakayama. ani: Yumi Nakayama. mus: Akira Mitake. prd: SME VisualWorks, Sotsu Agency, TV Tokyo. 25 mins. x 25 eps.

Teenager Ayumu Narumi's older brother Kiyotaka, a renowned detective and pianist, disappeared two years ago. Now, Ayumu is accused of murder. School journalist Hiyono Yuizaki is determined to prove his innocence, and the pair team up to investigate both mysteries. A strange group calling themselves the Blade Children, who seem to know Kiyotaka, is at the center of a series of deaths and mysteries. Kiyotaka's wife Madoka, a police inspector, is investigating them with her partner, but is ordered by her boss to back off. It seems there is more to the Blade Children than meets the eye, for they're also being killed off one by one by the ominous "Hunters." From the manga by Kyou Shirodaira with art by Eita Mizuno, serialized in *Shonen Gangan* and wholly unconnected to Junji Ito's manga *Spiral* (*Uzumaki*). A conspiracy story with real suspense is rare in any medium, and this is a good one, well served by a good script and nicely paced direction. **V**

SPIRIT OF WONDER *

1992. jpn: *Spirit of Wonder China-san no Yutsu*. aka: *SoW: Miss China's Melancholy; SoW: Miss China's Ring*. Video. dir: Mitsuru Hongo, Takashi Anno. scr: Michiru Shimada. des: Yoshiaki Yanagida. ani: Yoshiaki Yanagida. mus: Kohei Tanaka. prd: EMI, Asia-do. 45 mins. (v1), 45 mins. x 2 eps. (v2).

Miss China runs a bar and boarding house in a small town. Her long-term residents are mad scientist Professor Breckenridge and his assistant, Jim Floyd (named for Heywood Floyd in *2001: A Space Odyssey*), whom she secretly loves. But she thinks Jim is smitten with local florist Lily and that her love is hopeless, until, for her birthday, he flies her to the moon and gives her a real moonstone ring.

Based on Kenji Tsuruta's delicately beautiful manga short stories serialized in *Afternoon* from 1986 onward, *SoW* harks back to a bygone age of Jules Verne, H.G. Wells, and similar Victorian-era science fiction. Tsuruta's output is fearfully slow, so it was little surprise that the anime incarnation was similarly tardy. A second *SoW* release, the *Scientific Boys' Club* (2001, *SoW: Shonen Kagaku Kurabu*), chiefly features Wendy Lindberg, a leading interplanetary ether theorist, who believes that light oscillates in "ether" just as sound oscillates in air and that one can therefore travel in space by airship using "ether convection." Her father, Gordon, and his eccentric old buddies from the Scientific Boys' Club plan to celebrate the club's 50th anniversary by flying to Mars using this method, a crackpot idea, which, like other insanely romantic schemes in Tsuruta's universe, pays off eventually. The two 35-minute *SBC* episodes each came with a 10-minute short to tie them in with the original 1992 video titled *China-san's Reduction* (*C-san no Shukusho*). Yanagida, who turned Tsuruta's fragile art into animation with such skill, returns on character design and art direction, and Anno directs.

SPIRITED AWAY *

2001. JPN: *Sen to Chihiro no Kami-kakushi*. AKA: *Sen and Chihiro's Spirited Away*. Movie. DIR: Hayao Miyazaki. SCR: Hayao Miyazaki. DES: Hayao Miyazaki. ANI: Masashi Ando. MUS: Joe Hisaishi. PRD: Studio Ghibli. ca. 125 mins.

Young girl Chihiro must journey from modern-day Japan to the Spirit World in order to rescue her parents, who have been turned into pigs. This is a surreal mixture of the childhood adventure of MY NEIGHBOR TOTORO with the threatening other-world of PRINCESS MONONOKE and the transformations of PORCO ROSSO.

After taking a wrong turn on the way to their new house, Chihiro's family end up in what appears to be the ruins of a theme park. As night falls, it transforms into a literal "ghost town." Chihiro's parents are changed into pigs, and she is forced to work in an unearthly bathhouse. Like many Miyazaki heroines before her, she is kind to those in need, and the new friends she meets come to her aid when her fellow indentured servant Haku is placed in grave danger.

Like a maverick diamond cutter, Miyazaki has made some innovative choices in the facets he carves. Like Mamoru Oshii's PATLABOR films, the leads in *SA* often seem like clueless bystanders in someone else's story. Its chills are sometimes lost on an audience that cannot read Japanese, such as the creepy moment when Chihiro walks through a harmless-seeming village, although the signs over the cafés in the background offer "Flesh," "Fresh Eyeballs," and "Dog." The most obvious "hidden" plotline is a romance

between a human child and a river god, one of many forbidden loves in Japanese mythology, seen before in USHIO AND TORA. Another is a tale of warring sisters who live close by and continue to feud incessantly. The witch Yubaba's bathhouse is a meeting place for innumerable folk tales old and new, some of which only have a single scene to charm us. We see the end, but not the beginning, of the tale of a river god polluted by litter dumping (Miyazaki's obligatory environmental moment), the last part of the tale of a dragon-thief, and curious scenes from the life of No Face, a lonely, violent god desperate to be loved.

Miyazaki's eye for the fantastic does not disappoint, with desolate vistas of a world knee-deep in water, a train to nowhere (perhaps it shares a terminus with MY NEIGHBOR TOTORO's Catbus?), and a truly Grimm sense of the horrors that lie beneath the surface of the most innocent story. One critic controversially suggested that *SA* was a subtle allegory of life in a brothel, and like all the best fairy tales, the film is innocent, child-friendly, and psychologically disturbing all at once.

It shares the impenetrable ethnocentric references of Isao Takahata's POMPOKO and a Japanese obsession with bathing and the smell of outsiders, but it seems to lack the humanity of KIKI'S DELIVERY SERVICE. Considering this is a story about a girl in a very inhuman world, that's probably part of the point, but the result could so easily have been the same as with PRINCESS MONONOKE—Nebraska mallrats prefer to watch the latest Jerry Bruckheimer, another Miyazaki film tanks in the U.S., and the fans blame Disney, who would really very much prefer it if Miyazaki remade MY NEIGHBOR TOTORO anyway and stopped doing animated pastiches of Tarkovsky and comedy allegories of union demarcation disputes involving a collective of soot-creatures. However, *Spirited Away* defied many expectations by winning an Academy Award for Best Animated Feature in 2003, gaining the film a new lease on life, and pushing

Miyazaki to the forefront of anime's expansion abroad, despite the fact that much of his work is made in reaction to mainstream Japanese animation and is not really representative of it. His next directorial outing was HOWL'S MOVING CASTLE.

SPOOKY KITARO

1968. JPN: *Gegege no Kitaro*. AKA: *Spooky Ooky Kitaro*. TV series, movie. DIR: Yoshio Kuroda, Masao Murayama, Yasuo Yamaguchi, Yoshio Takami, Masayuki Akehi, Hiroshi Shidara, Keiji Hisaoka, Fusahito Nagaki, Hideo Furusawa, Masamune Ochiai, Hiroshi Wagatsuma, Tomoharu Katsumata, Isao Takahata, Takeshi Tamiya. SCR: Susumu Takahisa, Masaki Tsuji, Shunichi Yukimuro, Tomohiro Ando. DES: Shigeru Mizuki, Yoshinori Kanemori. ANI: Mitsuo Hosoda, Masamune Ochiai, Hiroshi Wagatsuma, Shinya Takahashi. MUS: Taku Izumi. PRD: Toei, Fuji TV. 25 mins. x 65 eps. (TV1, b/w), 25 mins. x 45 eps. (TV2, color), 25 mins. x 108 eps. (TV3), 25 mins. x 7 eps. (TV4), 24 mins. (m1), 40 mins. (m2), 49 mins. (m3), 48 mins. (m4), 25 mins. x 92 eps. (TV5), 50 mins. (m5), 30 mins. (m6), 24 mins. (m7).

Kitaro is a little boy who lives with a gang of phantoms and figures from JAPANESE FOLK TALES, including his friends Rat Man, Cat Girl, and Piece-of-Paper. The spirit of his father possesses one of his eyeballs, which has grown tiny arms and legs and can climb about from its perch in his hair. His life may be strange in some of its details, but Kitaro is actually just a nice, ordinary Japanese boy who uses various magical artifacts, like his traditional coat and wooden shoes, to assist him in helping his human and nonhuman friends to resolve the problems that arise in their lives. Despite (or perhaps because of) reprising basic magical-girl and school-story concepts (the great thing about ghosts, of course, is that they *don't* have to go to school, as the theme song gleefully informs us), the series is charming and funny, with Kitaro's supernatural surrogate family presented as regular folks whose ditherings, weaknesses, and prosaic good-heartedness wouldn't be *too* out of place in SAZAE-SAN. LITTLE DEVIL–creator Shigeru Mizuki's 1965 manga in *Shonen Magazine* led to the first TV series, which then returned in color in 1971. The fashion for ghoulies and ghosties at the time was influenced by American TV and inspired other anime like VAMPIRE, LITTLE GOBLIN, and MONSTER MAN BEM. After a long hiatus, *SK* returned for a third series in 1985, now overseen by Osamu Kasai and Hiroki Shibata—in many ways a complete remake of the preceding two versions but with a few nods to the modern audience, such as the introduction of super-deformed "SD" scenes of a squashed-down Kitaro at humorous moments. Some later stories were all-new ideas based on viewer suggestions. During the same period, Toei also took the franchise into movie theaters, commencing with *SOK* (1985), which drew less on the original manga than on Mizuki's picaresque *Ghoulish Travels in Kitaro's World* (*Kitaro no Sekai o Bake Ryoko*), then running in *Shonen King* magazine. Three more short movies followed in 1986: *Great Ghost War* (*Yokai Daisakusen*), featuring cameos from DRACULA, FRANKENSTEIN, and the Wolfman, *Great Ghost Army—Destructive Monsters Arrive in Japan* (*Saikyo Yokai Guntai! Nippon Joriku*), and *The Big Revolt of Monsters from Another Dimension* (*Kyojigen Yokai no Dai Hanran*). The short-lived TV series *SOK: Hell Chapter* (1988, *Jigoku Hen*) retold the story of Kitaro's origins, prompted by the opportunity to meet his parents' ghosts in the underworld. After that, the franchise lay dormant again until revived in 1996 by director Daisuke Nishio. This most recent incarnation, confusingly termed the "fourth" TV series, though technically being the fifth, also spun off into three more movies, Tomoharu Katsumata's *Giant Sea Monster* (1996, *Dai Kaiju*), Junichi Sato's *Ghost Knighter* (1997, *Obake Knighter*), and Takao Yoshizawa's *Monster Express! Ghost Train* (1997, *Yokai Tokkyu! Maboroshi no Kisha*). There was also a brief live-action series featuring Mizuki in a cameo role.

In interviews, Mizuki has been heard to suggest that traditional Japanese spirits are driven out of the modern world by the prevalence of electric light—that they need the shadows cast by candles and starlight to survive. This elegiac quality, alluding both to the advance of modernity and the transient nature of youth, can also be seen in modern fairy tales such as POMPOKO and SPIRITED AWAY.

SPORTS ANIME

Sports anime have formed a vital part of the medium since its earliest days—the sublimated conflict of a sporting event, allowing both dramatic tension and a finishing line for which the opponents can strive, is readily appreciable by a younger audience. One of AESOP'S FABLES was adapted by Sanae Yamamoto in his single-reel *Tortoise and the Hare* (1924), but the first identifiable "sports anime" was Yasuji Murata's *Animal Olympics* (1928), in which a duck successfully wins the 800-meter gold, besting a bulldog, hippo, and camel. Inspired by the Amsterdam Olympics of the same year but played largely for laughs, the short film also includes a polar bear attempting to pole vault, and a cheating pig, whose attempt to win the hurdles with the aid of a balloon is brought crashing back down to earth through the intercession of an elephant's well-thrown javelin.

As war loomed in the 1930s, sports anime ironically clung to an American import, with animals competing again in Yasuji Murata's *Our Baseball* (1930) and Seiichi Harada's *Baseball in the Forest* (*Mori no Yakyu-dan*, 1934).

Firmly supported as a wholesome pursuit by the postwar Occupation forces, the game returned in Sanae Yamamoto's *Animal Great Baseball Battle* (*Dobutsu Daiyakyu Sen*, 1949). The same year saw Hideo Furusawa's *Sports Tanuki* (*Sports Kotanuki*, 1949), in which a Japanese raccoon dog competes as a jockey in a horse race.

Real-world sporting events, particularly ones such as baseball, pro wrestling, or sumo, which could be covered by a single, unmoving camera, were early ratings draws for live-action TV, which had the effect of discouraging animators. Early TV producers followed the lead of Osamu Tezuka in ASTRO BOY, who saw that anime's true potential lay in showing audiences sci-fi and fantasy—things they would not get so easily from live-action. However, experiments in anime sports inevitably followed the national hysteria surrounding the 1964 Tokyo Olympics, in which the Japanese women's volleyball team took an unexpected gold medal. This success would generate a vast wave of sporting *manga*, which, once proving their popularity in print, would tempt producers to buy the rights for anime adaptation.

Although the protagonist of HARRIS'S WIND (1966) dabbled in many different disciplines, the first true TV sports anime did not arise until STAR OF THE GIANTS (1968)—tellingly, a show about the real-life Yomiuri Giants baseball team, part-owned by the same conglomerate that also owned the broadcaster, NTV. *SotG* pioneered techniques that have become mandatory in modern anime—framing a sporting contest with the zooms and freeze-frames of martial arts combat. Before long, many sports were represented in anime, including volleyball in ATTACK NUMBER ONE (1969), wrestling in ANIMAL 1 and TIGER MASK (both 1969), boxing in TOMORROW'S JOE (1970), soccer in RED-BLOODED ELEVEN (1970), kick-boxing in KICK FIEND (1970), tennis in AIM FOR THE ACE (1973), and the self-evident A KARATE-CRAZY LIFE (1973) and IN PRAISE OF JUDO (1974). Almost all gravitated toward the common sports story— plucky outsiders winning against overwhelming odds, often in the face of personal bereavement, with family members and coaches seeming to have the life expectancy of the average rock drummer. Later seasons would replay the same story, but at a regional,

Spriggan

national, or international level. In an interesting curio, **ROAD TO MUNICH** (1972) used animation in order to bypass Olympic competition restrictions concerning the use of players' images for "professional" purposes.

As merchandising began to play a bigger part in anime production, sports anime began to favor activities that offered better toy potential, most notably vehicular stories such as **SPEED RACER** (1967), **MACHINE HAYABUSA** (1976), and **ARROW EMBLEM** (1977). Baseball shows made a brief return in the late 1970s, only to be drowned in the merchandise-oriented sci-fi and fantasy of the 1980s. With most sports now relegated to one-shots or videos like **PROGOLFER SARU** (1982), baseball hung on by introducing romance, particularly in series based on the works of manga creator Mitsuru Adachi, such as **MIYUKI** (1983), **NINE** (1983), and **TOUCH** (1985). Other producers embraced commercial pressures with original cunning, making shows with improved foreign sales potential, such as the soccer favorite **CAPTAIN TSUBASA** (1983), which had guaranteed export audiences around the world, despite comparably little domestic interest. The more merchandise-oriented used sport as their excuse rather than their reason, with Olympic mascot shows like **EAGLE SAM** (1983) and **MISHA THE**

BEAR CUB (1979), or completely unrelated releases that sought to exploit newfound awareness of event locations—it is no coincidence that **TWELVE MONTHS** went into production in the year of the Moscow Olympics, nor that **YAWARA** enjoyed a revival in time for Atlanta. Arguably the most successful use of sports anime clichés in the late 1980s was not a sports anime at all, but the sci-fi pastiche **GUNBUSTER** (1987).

Since the early 1990s, sports anime have featured periodic revivals of baseball, soccer, and volleyball, among a scattering of ever stranger attempts to push the envelope with more obscure pursuits, such as the fishing of **GRANDAR** (1998) or the speedboat racing of **MONKEY TURN** (2004). Producers have also shied away from real-world games, preferring fantastical concoctions such as **BATTLE ATHLETES** (1997) and **EYESHIELD 21** (2005). Modern children nowadays are less likely to play catch than they are to engage in more sedentary activities, such as the board gaming of **HIKARU'S GO** (2001) or the pachinko of the same year's **PACHISLO KIZOKU GIN**, though **PRINCE OF TENNIS** (also 2001) bucked the trend. The act of playing with a computer has itself become the subject of anime inquiry, from **RUNNING BOY** (1986) to **BPS** (2003). The greatest change, however, has been in a marked increase in mar-

tial arts tales, thanks to their relation to computer gaming—the ubiquitous **STREETFIGHTER II** (1994) and its clones. It could also be argued that "collecting" is the new sport, be it of digitized monsters in **POKÉMON** (1997), or of cards in **DUEL MASTERS** (2002). Sports even made its way into erotica, in the form of the volleyball-themed **ANGELS IN THE COURT** (2001) and the rhythmic gymnastics of **PRINCESS 69** (2002).

SPOTLIGHT *

2002. Video. DIR: 1862 Kuboyama. SCR: Rokurota Makabe. DES: Hayato Nankodo. ANI: Hayoto Nankodo. MUS: Yoshi. PRD: Digital Works (Vanilla Series), Blue Gale. 30 mins. x 2 eps.
Pretty, pert Saori would love to be a pop idol, which is fortunate, because her mother Emiko has just inherited a music management company from her newly deceased second husband. However, she has also inherited a stepson, Masaki, who has an unhealthy obsession with his stepsister. In an updated and erotic inversion of the **CINDERELLA** motif, Saori gets the chance to front the Teinkle pop trio, much to the annoyance of the other two girls, Yuna and Erica, who begin bullying her for being such a privileged upstart. Masaki soon teaches them the error of their ways by tying them up and molesting them, in typical **VANILLA SERIES** style—for this is one of *those*, based on a story by Blue Gale. Meanwhile, Masaki plots to make a move on Saori, while also enjoying the attentions of his stepmother, who sees in him something of his father, and offers to bed him for mutual companionship and general stress release. In the tradition of certain erotic computer games, some scenes neglect to put much effort into the male characters, drawing them instead as virtual silhouettes so that the "spotlight" is literally on the female victim. Compare to **PARADE PARADE** and **PERFECT BLUE.** **ⒷⓃⓋ**

SPRIGGAN *

1998. AKA: *Striker*. Movie. DIR: Hirotsuge Kawasaki. SCR: Katsuhiro Otomo,

Hirotsuge Kawasaki, Yasutaka Ito. DES: Hisashi Eguchi. ANI: Hisashi Eguchi. MUS: Kuniaki Haishima. PRD: TBS, Toho, Bandai, Studio 4°C. ca. 90 mins.

Explorers in Turkey find "Noah's Ark," a spaceship frozen in layers of ice. The clandestine ARCAM research organization, dedicated to recovering the artifacts of a lost prehistoric civilization, sends in its researchers but comes under attack from American agents who want the Ark's secrets for themselves. Yu Ominae, a Japanese schoolboy who is really one of ARCAM's elite "Spriggan" agents, heads for Turkey for a battle of wits against the Pentagon's high-powered Machiners Platoon led by the supersoldiers Fatman and Little Boy. They, however, report to the evil McDougal, a child prodigy whose powers are dangerously out of control. McDougal has realized that the Ark is a weather control device, and he intends to start a new Ice Age.

Inspired by the final shot of *Raiders of the Lost Ark* (itself an homage to *Citizen Kane*), Hiroshi Takashige and **PROJECT ARMS**–creator Ryoji Minagawa's 1989 manga in *Shonen Sunday* posited a secret society fighting to claim all the world's paranormal artifacts for good, with agents named after Celtic fairies that "protect important treasures in ancient ruins."

From the English lettering to the Chinese theme song, this is an anime made with the foreign audience in mind—the script was translated before the film was made in an attempt to secure foreign backing. The manga was originally translated into English as *Striker*, in a version that hid its strong anti-Americanism, though the film was made and released in the U.S. amid a post–*X-Files* willingness to cast the Pentagon as the bad guy. The anime project began life as a video of *Spriggan*'s "Berserker" chapters but was changed to the Ark plotline and upgraded to a theatrical release—close up it still looks like a video production inflated with extra capital. In a succession of bloody battles punctuated with Biblical apocalypse and government con-

spiracy, director Kawasaki recalls the whip-like cuts of **GHOST IN THE SHELL**, tearing from shot to shot to distract us from the sparse animation—*Spriggan* has less than a third of **AKIRA**'s cel count, which it hides with a breakneck pace worthy of Tsui Hark. "Supervisor" Katsuhiro Otomo's influence is clearest in the design of the Ark and the portrayal of the evil McDougal. Like the mutant children of *Akira*, he has a bluish pallor, a vocabulary that belies his age, and a voice provided by a genuine child actor.

A sequence from Kuniaki Haishima's score was lifted and reused in the Korean movie *Joint Security Area* (2001) and also in a British TV commercial for the Carphone Warehouse.

SPRING AND CHAOS *

1996. JPN: *Ihatov no Kenso: Kenji no Haru*. AKA: *Iwate Fantasy: Kenji's Spring*. TV special. DIR: Shoji Kawamori. SCR: Shoji Kawamori. DES: Takahiro Kishida. ANI: Takahiro Kishida. MUS: Shang-Shang Typhoon. PRD: Group Tac, Magic Bus, Animal, Triangle Staff, NTV. 53 mins.

A brief survey of the life and works of Kenji Miyazawa, animated for theatrical screenings in his hometown of Iwate during the centenary of his birth but only combined in this form for a December TV special. As in the adaptation of the same author's earlier **NIGHT ON THE GALACTIC RAILROAD**, the main roles are taken by cats, and all visible signs are written in Esperanto in honor of the author's devotion to the artificial language—hence Ihatov and not Iwate. Young Kenji, a pacifist, is at odds with Japan's increasingly militaristic society in the days before WWII. He is also determined to pursue a career as an author and poet, much to the chagrin of his levelheaded father. The story of Miyazawa's brief life (he died in his thirties) is punctuated by brief interludes from his stories, in a style similar to the **DIARY OF ANNE FRANK**. Director Kawamori is better known today for **ESCAFLOWNE** and **MACROSS**.

SPRITE: BETWEEN TWO WORLDS *

1996. JPN: *Manami to Nami Sprite*. AKA: *Manami and Nami Sprite*. Video. DIR: Takeshi Yamaguchi. SCR: Tsutomu Senogai. DES: Shinobu Arimura. ANI: Takashi Wada. MUS: Plectrum. PRD: Toei. 40 mins. x 2 eps.

When his mother is taken ill, the irritating Toru is packed off to stay with "relatives" in Tokyo, where he meets the shapely Manami. Immediately smitten, he discovers that this demure girl next door has a hidden side, a second bad-girl personality called Nami who's ready to put out at the drop of a hat.

Ever since the early days of **CREAM LEMON**, the tawdry genre of anime Lolita porn has suggested that inside every underage girl there's a sexually mature adult bursting to get out, if only the right boy comes along with the magic password. You couldn't get much better than Toru—so pathologically shy he can only search for sexual partners among his own family. And he's not the only one—this adaptation of Shinobu Arimura's manga alludes to a victim of childhood abuse, returning to the scene of the crime to face her demons. Blink and you'll miss it: a moment when Manami compares the size of Toru's member to her father's.

Where animation is limited, as it is here, voices have to carry a lot of the emotional weight, but the dubbing crew simply can't be bothered. The end result contains many silent hiatuses as the cast seemingly waits for canned laughter that never comes, and though **DEEP BLUE FLEET**–director Takeshi Yamaguchi tries to inject some arty moments (schoolgirls fighting with martial-arts moves based on common sports, waving grasses as lovers talk by a river), this is, like so many others of its ilk, a morally dubious attempt to package human pain as entertainment. **GN**

SPT LAYZNER

1985. JPN: *Aoki Ryusei SPT Layzner*. AKA: *Blue Meteor SPT Layzner*. TV series, video. DIR: Ryosuke Takahashi, Tetsuro Amino, Takashi Imanishi, Toshifumi Takizawa, Yoshitaka Fujimoto. scr: Hiroyuki Hoshiyama, Fuyunori Gobu, Yasushi Hirano, Tsunehisa Ito, Ryosuke Takahashi. des: Moriyasu Taniguchi, Kunio Okawara. ani: Moriyasu Taniguchi. mus: Hiroki Inui. prd: Sunrise, Nippon TV. 25 mins. x 38 eps. (TV), 55 mins. x 3 eps. (v).

In 1996, Mars has been colonized by humans, with Russia and the U.S. both having established settlements on the planet. A group of Russian students, including Anna, David, Simone, and Arthur, is welcomed to an American base as part of a student exchange program. Eiji Asuka, child of a human father and a mother from planet Glados, is caught up in the beginnings of hostilities between the Americans and Russians and manages to save most of the students, but when Glados attacks Earth, he comes under suspicion purely because of his mixed blood. He and his giant robot, the "Blue Meteor" SPT (Super Powered Tracer) Layzner, are fated to play a key role in the conflict between planets. He is imprisoned by the Americans, considered a traitor by Glados, and has to fight his own sister Julia in a war that results in the occupation of Earth under Glados leader Le Kain. The second part of the TV series begins on Earth in 1999, when three years of oppression have all but crushed human culture; the books, art, and learning of humankind are destroyed wherever they are found. Eiji and his young friends are living a hand-to-mouth existence as part of the resistance, while Julia has become the leader of a cult and a target for the aliens. As Eiji and Kain face each other for the last battle, Julia prepares to use her mystic powers to save Earth. The series is laden with emotional tension, with a dark emphasis on the cruelty of war and the corrupting effects of power. The early deaths of innocent civilians—including one of the original school party—set the tone; these are battles where nobody really wins and the good don't always survive. The series was taken off the air after episode 38, resulting in a confusing ending with Eiji simply left floating in space and a complex transfer to video. Initially, the series was released as three tapes: *Eiji 1996* and *Lu Kain 1999* (digests of episodes 1–24 and 26–37 respectively), incorporating extra, previously unseen footage, and *Act III: Seal 2000*, which contained the unbroadcast episodes 39 and 40. Set after the end of the war, Kain is still spoiling for a fight and prepares to reopen hostilities, but he is killed by his son Lu who takes control of Glados. Lu faces off against Eiji, but Julia manages to stop the fighting by warping Earth to a different part of the universe. *SPTL* was also released as another video series, the first two tapes comprising episodes 1–4, while the third contained episodes 15 and 28, supposedly because they were fan favorites. The entire 38-episode broadcast run was not released on video until 1997.

SPY OF DARKNESS *

1996. jpn: *Inju vs. Onna Spy.* aka: *Lust-Beast vs. Female Spy.* Video. dir: Hisashi Tomii, Tai Fujimoto. scr: N/C. des: N/C. ani: Hideki Araki. mus: N/C. prd: Pink Pineapple, KSS. 45 mins. When the government develops a high-tech cyborg as a secret military weapon, a failure in gene manipulation causes the experimental creature to become a sex beast, fueled only by its insatiable lust for women and utter destruction. The creature escapes and starts to abduct women, so the government assigns Anne, a sexy spy, to solve the crimes. When Anne finds the hideout where the creature is keeping the abducted women, she is caught in "an erotic battle of the sexes!" Another one for the pile. **❶❷❸**

SQUARE OF THE MOON *

2002. jpn: *Yoru ga Kuru.* aka: *Night Is Coming.* Video. dir: Yoshiyuki Okano. scr: N/C. des: Sachiko Yamamoto. ani: Sachiko Yamamoto. mus: N/C. prd: Green Bunny, Alice Soft. 30 mins. x 4 eps.

College student Izumi and her fellow members of the Astronomy Club are in fact warriors from the Blue Moon, who have come to Earth to protect humanity from the evil Light Hunters. These evil creatures suck the life force out of their victims, by enveloping them with their tentacles and using psionic powers to make them believe that their sexual fantasies are being fulfilled. So, yes, it's **SAILOR MOON** and/or **VENUS FIVE** meets **DEMON BEAST INVASION**, based on the game from Alice Soft. **❶❷❸**

SRUNGLE *

1983. jpn: *Aku Dai Sakusen Srungle.* aka: *Great Subspace War Srungle; Gorilla Force.* TV series. dir: Kazuya Miyazaki, Kenzo Koizumi, Tatsuya Kasahara. scr: Masaru Yamamoto, Juzo Tsubota. des: Yoshitaka Amano, MIC Group. ani: Asao Takahashi, Satoshi Yamaguchi, Tsukasa Dokite. mus: Masayuki Yamamoto. prd: Kokusai Eiga, TV Asahi. 25 mins. x 53 eps. Garrick Space Town, built in the habitable zone between the twin planets Baxas, is under threat from a criminal organization, calling itself, rather pathetically, Crime. Led by an android known as Fork-Razor, the police are powerless against its daring exploits. To help the forces of law to contain this android crime wave, Doctor Mandi (Captain Chance) forms the Gorilla team of brave space cops Jet, Sexy, Superstar, Magician, and Baby's-Face, equipped with powerful robotic weapons like the mighty Srungle. In this golden age of robot shows, there was plenty of dross around; with a TV run starting the week before Tomino's magical **DUNBINE**, this pedestrian cop show was never likely to fly. It isn't one of the more frequently highlighted entries on Amano's resume. However, it was picked up by Saban, crashed into another show, dressed up with a Top 40 soundtrack, and syndicated on American TV in 1985 as *Macron One* (see **GOSHOGUN**).

STAFF-ROOM AFTER SCHOOL

1994. jpn: *Hokago Shokuinshitsu.* aka: *Staff-room after Class.* Video. dir: Kazuko Hirose. scr: Mieko Koide. des: Masayoshi Sudo. ani: Masayoshi

Sudo. MUS: N/C. PRD: Daiei, Tokuma. 30 mins. x 2 eps.

Despite his normal appearance, schoolteacher Mitsuo is a whirlwind of homosexual lusts, and he can contain his desires no longer when, on his birthday, he blurts out his feelings to fellow art teacher Toshiaki. A secret romance develops, but, a year later, Mitsuo's parents try to fix him up with a nice girl. Based on the pretty-boy manga by Mieko Koide, who also wrote the script. **N**

STAINLESS NIGHT *

1995. Video. DIR: Ryunosuke Otonashi. SCR: Akira Takano. DES: Ryunosuke Otonashi, Yuriko Chihane. ANI: Ryunosuke Otonashi. MUS: N/C. PRD: Pink Pineapple, KSS. 30 mins. x 2 eps.

In the year 2020, hiking teenagers Mirei and Sayaka find a broken android in the mountains. It is the beautiful Linnear, who, once repaired, repays their kindness by having lesbian sex with them. Based on the manga by Kei Amaki, whose erotic works also appear in the **CREAM LEMON** collection. **N**

STAIRS *

2001. Video. DIR: Masashi Minamite. SCR: N/C. DES: N/C. ANI: Haraki. MUS: N/C. PRD: Milky, Museum Pictures. 30 mins.

Childhood friends Makoto and Une are attending cram school together. Makoto secretly lusts after Une and is crushed to discover that she now has a boyfriend. However, he soon discovers solace in the arms of new arrival Nonoka. Based on the erotic manga by Mikan R. **LNV**

STAR BLAZERS *

1974. JPN: *Uchu Senkan Yamato*. AKA: *Space Cruiser Yamato; Space Battleship Yamato*. TV series, movie, video. DIR: Noboru Ishiguro, Leiji Matsumoto, Eiichi Yamamoto, Yoshinobu Nishizaki, Takeshi Shiraji, Toshio Sodota. SCR: Keisuke Fujikawa, Maru Tamura, Eiichi Yamamoto, Yasushi Hirano. DES: Leiji Matsumoto, Studio Nue, Kazuyuki Okaseko, Toshiyuki Kubooka, Hiroyuki

Star Blazers

Kitazume, Aki Tsunaki, Nobuaki Nagano, Makoto Kobayashi, Atsushi Takeuchi, Keiji Hashimoto, Syd Mead. ANI: Toyoo Ashida, Yoshikazu Yasuhiko, Takeshi Shirato. MUS: Hiroshi Miyagawa, Kentaro Haneda. PRD: Westcape, Studio Take Off, Yomiuri TV (Nippon TV). 25 mins. x 26 eps. (TV1), 25 mins. x 26 eps. (TV2), 25 mins. x 25 eps. (TV3), 130 min. (m1), 151 mins. (m2), 93 mins. (TVm/m3), 93 mins., 145 mins. (m4), 163 mins. (m5), 30 mins. x 3 eps. (v).

In 2199, the evil emperor Desslar (Desslock) orders the destruction of Earth. Radiation bombs from his planet Gamilas (Gamilon) have devastated the planet's surface and will make it uninhabitable within a year. Enemy cruisers have Earth under heavy surveillance so there's no chance to build a starship to fight back or escape. But the radiation that has dried up the oceans has exposed many old hulks, including the 250-year-old wreck of the WWII battleship Yamato (Argo). Tunneling under the surface, the authorities have secretly built a starship within the old hull. When Queen Starsha from the distant world of Iscandar offers Earth a device that can rid them

of the deadly radiation if they'll just send a ship to fetch it, Captain Okita (Avatar) and a handpicked crew set out on the hazardous journey in the reborn Yamato. Young pilot Susumu Kodai (Derek Wildstar) has a grudge against the captain, who survived the battle that claimed Kodai's beloved older brother, Mamoru (Alex), but as time goes on, Kodai and the whole crew come to see the captain as a heroic father-figure whose responsibility to do everything in his power to save Earth is a heavy burden.

Despite looking faintly ridiculous to modern eyes, *Space Battleship Yamato* is one of the watersheds in anime history. A Japanese respray of *Star Trek*, it replaces pioneer exploration (or gunboat diplomacy) with oblique references to WWII—a desperate suicide mission, hounded by enemy vessels in red, white, and blue. The titular ship itself is the most obvious—at the time the greatest battleship ever built, it was sunk during a one-way mission to hold off the U.S. attack on Okinawa in 1945. Naval and aerial battle sequences are clumsily transposed to a space setting: ships "list" when holed in the hull and fighters are shot "down," although in space there isn't supposed to be a "down." Beyond the risible pseudophysics, however, *SBY* contained a supremely strong story line. *SBY* changed the way TV programmers thought about SF; previously it had been supposed that only very young audiences watched TV anime, and so there was no point in screening anything but giant-robot and *sentai* shows. The influence of the original series on a whole generation of Japanese animators is incredible, and it resulted in homages and cameos for the ship in many anime works. The green-skinned aliens seem to have inspired the design of the Zentraedi in MACROSS, while the teacher-pupil relationship of Okita and Kodai, born out of the captain's guilt over the loss of the pilot's close relation, never had a better reprise than in GUNBUSTER, where Coach Ota played the captain role to the full, even to the extent of dying before the end.

The show was the brainchild of writer Eiichi Yamamoto and THUNDERSUB-producer Yoshinobu Nishizaki, who poached many staff from his former employers Mushi Pro. It also features heavy involvement from CAPTAIN HARLOCK–creator Matsumoto, who drew many of the initial designs and also the spin-off manga. The show lived out a lukewarm and unremarkable initial run of 26 episodes, but in 1977 the advent of *Star Wars* rejuvenated network interest in sci-fi. The first movie, *SBY* (1977), is a compilation of the first TV series that gained a new lease on life abroad as *Space Cruiser*, with the Gamilas hordes renamed the Gorgons. Back in Japan, Tomoharu Katsumata's movie *Farewell to SBY: In the Name of Love* (*Saraba Uchusenkan Yamato: Ai no Senshitachi*, aka *SBY: Warriors of Love*, 1978) seemed intended as the last word on the series, which ended with the Yamato destroyed, along with most of the main characters. Plainly, this would not be very useful for prolonging the franchise, leading to the same year's *SBY 2* TV series, which retold the events of the movie, but with a

more open-ended finish that didn't kill everyone off. Earth's new age of peace is disrupted in 2201 by Emperor Zorder's Comet Empire. This was soon followed by Takeshi Shirato's *SBY: The New Voyage* (1979, *USY: Aratanaru Tabitachi*), a 95-minute TV special broadcast on Fuji TV, in which the Yamato has the chance to come to the aid of Earth's savior Queen Starsha when she suffers attacks by the Black Star Cluster Empire. *The New Voyage* was shown in 1981 in theaters on a double bill with the next genuine movie edition, Katsumata's *Be Forever Yamato* (1980, *Yamato yo Towa ni*), featuring Kodai and a crew that includes Starsha and Mamoru's daughter, Sasha, defeating the invading forces of commander Kazan of the Dark Empire.

However, *SBY*'s reissue as *Space Cruiser* was by no means the last of its English-language incarnations. The series made it to American TV screens as *Star Blazers* (1979). Claster Studios had acquired the first two series with its sights on marketing tie-ins for its toy division, Hasbro. Some changes were made for the U.S. market, notably to character names. Comic relief robot Analyzer and cyborg mechanic Sandor had been created well in advance of George Lucas's knockabout robot duo in *Star Wars*, but Analyzer was named IQ-9 in imitation of C-3PO. Some changes were made to cushion U.S. sensibilities; violence was toned down, and Dr. Sado's copious drinking became nonalcoholic. Despite an early lukewarm reception, American anime fans, as passionately loyal as their Japanese counterparts to the show they loved, began to screen episodes in convention video rooms. Its classic status on both sides of the Pacific was secured by fan interest and activity, to the extent where the full series and all five movies are still selling on video in the U.S. and Japan.

In 1980, a third Japanese TV series (also brought to the U.S.) moved the action further forward again to the year 2205, when new danger appeared in the Bolar Wars. During a battle

between Galman Gamilas and the Bolar Commonwealth, a stray missile flies into the sun and renders it unstable. With only a year before the sun explodes, Kodai must restaff the Yamato with a crew fresh out of the academy and find a new Earth for the human race. In fact, by the end, the sun's stability is restored, leaving the grande finale of the Yamato's adventures to Takeshi Shirato's movie release *Final Yamato* (1983, *USY: Kanketsu*). For this conclusion, Okita (returned from the dead as an admiral) takes command of the ship in 2203 to defend Earth from Lugarl, priest-king of Dengil, a planet destroyed by a near-miss with the rogue planet Aquarius. The Aquarians are descendants of an advanced race that fled Earth during Noah's flood, and now they want to come home. The Yamato saves the galaxy once again, then sinks into the watery grave from which it was raised at the very beginning of the saga, there to remain until *Blade Runner*–futurist Syd Mead resurrected it in his much-trumpeted designs for the video series *Yamato 2520* (1995). Top-heavy with directors (Shirato, Nishizaki, and Shigenori Kageyama) and adding a stellar design team to rework Matsumoto and Kitazume's originals, this relaunch of the old ship failed to fly. It looks pretty, but the repetition of the teens-save-Earth concept lacks the passion and conviction of the old series. Sometimes the latest fashion just can't compete with the classics.

In recent years, the story has remained in the headlines largely through the acrimonious court battle that has raged between the two men claiming to be its creators. This seems to stem from their conflicting ideas of who was responsible for what in the original, with producer Yoshinobu Nishizaki claiming that the series was his idea, and artist Leiji Matsumoto counter-claiming that while the extant TV versions may belong to Nishizaki, it is he who has the right to make his own new versions.

STAR CHILD PORON

1974. JPN: *Hoshi no Ko Poron*. AKA: *Polon, Girl from the Stars; Poron the Star Child*. TV series. SCR: Tetsuyoshi Onuma, Setsuko Murayama. DES: N/C. ANI: Fumio Sakai. MUS: N/C. PRD: Nippon Animation, Jiho Eigasha. 5 mins. x 260 eps.

Poron is an alien child who comes in a flying saucer from the distant reaches of space to Earth. There, he soon encounters the native life-forms, although as a new arrival, he is unaware that he has ignored humans, and instead befriends a rabbit, a bear, and a fox. This little-known science fantasy is not to be confused with CHOBIN THE STARCHILD, which started its TV run a month earlier.

STAR DUST

1992. Video. DIR: Ichiro Itano. SCR: N/C. DES: Kazutoshi Kobayashi. ANI: Kazutoshi Kobayashi. MUS: Junichi Kanezaki. PRD: Yoyogi Animation Gakuin. 30 mins.

A misguided sci-fi tale of ecological police keeping *space* free from pollution in 2061. The quality of this anime is at least partly forgivable, though, for being an apprentice film made by students at the Yoyogi Animation academy. Only a few years later, budgets would become so tight in the anime business that members of the same college would become cheap labor on the far longer-running but equally amateurish GANDHARA.

STAR OCEAN EX *

2001. TV series. DIR: Hiroshi Watanabe. SCR: Mayori Sekijima, Kenichi Kanemaki. DES: Ayako Kuroda. ANI: Ryoko Hata, Akira Matsushima. MUS: Motoi Sakuraba. PRD: Studio Deen, TV Tokyo. 25 mins. x 26 eps.

Claude is transported to Exvel, a world beyond time, where the fantasy adventures are what one might expect of an anime adaptation of a novel adaptation of a PlayStation game. This anime was based on *Star Ocean Second Story* serialized in *Shonen Gan Gan* magazine, itself based on a computer game.

STAR OF DAVIDE

1989. JPN: *Davide no Hoshi*. Video. DIR: Yoichiro Shimatani. SCR: Akio Sato, Yoichiro Shimatani, Ranko Ono. DES: Masaaki Sato. ANI: Tatsuya Sotomaru. MUS: Takahiko Kanemaru. PRD: Apples, Miyuki Pro. 45 mins. x 5 eps.

Lustful creatures from another dimension are invading Earth, starting with the women, for a change. Based on the manga by Masaaki Sato, the fifth episode of this video series was rebranded *New SoD* (1991) and moved the sex and violence to the English countryside. A less fantastic (but equally distasteful) version of the story was also turned into *Star of David: Beauty Hunter* (1979), a live-action film directed by Norifumi Suzuki. **NV**

STAR OF THE GIANTS

1968. JPN: *Kyojin no Hoshi*. TV series, movie. DIR: Tadao Nagahama, Yoshio Kabashima (TV1); Tetsuro Imazawa, Tetsu Dezaki, Minoru Okazaki, Akinori Nagaoka (TV2). SCR: Tadaaki Yamazaki, Mamoru Sasaki, Masaki Tsuji, Ryohei Suzuki, Sumiko Hayashi, Tsunehisa Ito, Toru Sawaki, Yoshiaki Yoshida, Seiji Matsuoka (TV1); Toshiaki Imaizumi, Noboru Shiroyama, Yoshihisa Araki (TV2). DES: Noboru Kawasaki. ANI: Daikichiro Kusube, Hideo Kawauchi, Yasuo Otsuka, Yoshifumi Kondo, Tetsuo Imazawa, Toshiyuki Honda, Tetsuro Wakabayashi, Noboru Ishiguro, Soji Yoshikawa, Masaru Inoue, Shingo Araki, Takao Kasai. MUS: Takeo Watanabe. PRD: Tokyo Movie (Shinsha), Magic Bus, Yomiuri TV (Nippon TV). 25 mins. x 182 eps. (TV1), 90 mins. (m1), 70 mins. (m2), 70 mins. (m3), 60 mins. (m4), 30 mins. (TV sp.), 25 mins. x 52 eps. (TV2/*New*), 25 mins. x 23 eps. (TV3/*New 2*), 25 mins. x 13 eps. (TV4/*Hanagata*).

Hyuma Hoshi is a promising young baseball player who dreams of becoming a top star like his father before him. When he joins the famous Giants team, his father and friends all do their utmost to make sure he achieves his full potential of becoming the star of the Giants. Based on the 1966 *Shonen Maga-zine* manga by Noboru Kawasaki and Ikki Kajiwara, *SotG* was the first sports anime, the direct ancestor of the rest of the genre, including Kawasaki's later ANIMAL 1, as well as the girls' variants AIM FOR THE ACE, ATTACK NUMBER ONE, and their many imitators. In bringing a sports plot to a medium previously dominated by juvenile adventure and sci-fi, it paved the way for other aspects of manga's diversity to cross over into animation. During the course of the original TV run, several reedits were screened in theaters as part of vacation anime festivals. The first, *SotG* (1969), was billed as the only chance for many viewers to see their favorite show in *color*—black-and-white TV sets being more common at the time. Other movie edits included *SotG: Big League* (1970, *Dai League Ball*), and the final game against the Yakult Swallows, *SotG: Confrontation at Shinjuku* (1970, *Shinjuku no Taiketsu*). Though *SotG* was popular in Japan, the mundane nature of its struggles, albeit leavened with some far-fetched training techniques lifted from martial arts, left it unlikely to be exported to the West. Hyuma's only appearance in the English-language was in the 30-minute TV special *Star of the Giants vs. the Mighty Atom* (1969), a friendly match between the Giants and the characters from ASTRO BOY, which reached the U.S. as part of the latter series—renamed *Astro Boy vs. the Giants*. The series was followed by SAMURAI GIANTS, adapted from another Kawasaki manga, and by a later, much less successful sequel. *New [Shin] SotG* (1977) is set five years after the original and was broadcast at a time when the Yomiuri Giants were facing anime competition from the Tokyo Mets (see SONG OF THE BASEBALL ENTHUSIAST) and the Seibu Lions (see GO FOR IT, TABUCHI). The final 23 episodes, rebranded as *New SotG II* (1979), deviated most from the original manga, introducing new regular characters, dumping Hyuma's girlfriend, and even killing off his father in the final episode, much to the original creators' annoyance.

The story was rereleased as a 13-

episode series in October 2002, which used both footage from the original and newly animated scenes in order to retell the story from the point of view of supporting character Mitsuru Hanagata.

STAR OF THE SEINE

1975. JPN: *La Seine no Hoshi.* AKA: *Star of La Seine; The Black Tulip.* TV series. DIR: Masaaki Osumi, Yoshiyuki Tomino, Tetsu Dezaki. SCR: Soji Yoshikawa, Michiru Umadori. DES: Akio Sugino. ANI: Kazuo Yamazaki, Toshio Takagi. MUS: Shunsuke Kikuchi. PRD: Unimax, Fuji TV. 25 mins. x 39 eps.

Simone, illegitimate daughter of the King of Austria and an opera singer, is taken from court as a baby into the care of a Parisian florist and grows up as just another working-class girl in the French capital at the end of the 1700s. When the king's old friend the Comte de Voudrel recognizes her, he adopts her, and she discovers the secret of her birth. She learns to fence and teams up with the comte's son Robert, who secretly helps out the poor and needy using his secret identity as the Black Tulip. Thus is born the Star of La Seine, heroine of the Revolution. But despite her support of the people in their struggle to overthrow the nobility, Simone also has sympathy for her half-sister, Queen Marie Antoinette, and when the Revolution finally overthrows the monarchy, she and Robert rescue the queen's children and adopt them as their own. A popular adventure series that leaves the nods to historical accuracy to ROSE OF VERSAILLES (the heroine of the Revolution dresses in hotpants and boots more suited to 1970s disco than 1780s swordfights), *SotS* did well in Europe, though Italy made Robert rather than Simone the titular hero. The *Black Tulip* title seems to have been engineered to imply an association with an unrelated 1850 novel of the same name by THREE MUSKETEERS-creator Alexandre Dumas.

STARBIRDS *

1978. JPN: *Tosho Daimos.* AKA: *Fighter/ Champion Daimos; Fighting General Daimos.* TV series. DIR: Tadao Nagahama, Yoshikazu Yasuhiko, Kazuo Terada, Yoshihiro Takahashi. SCR: Masaki Tsuji, Fuyunori Gobu, Masaaki Sakurai. DES: Akehiro Kaneyama, Studio Nue, Yutaka Izubuchi. ANI: Akehiro Kaneyama. MUS: Shunsuke Kikuchi. PRD: Sunrise, Toei, TV Asahi. 25 mins. x 44 eps. (TV).

Winged aliens from the dying planet Baam decide to conquer Earth and make it their new home. Heading up the resistance is Kazuya Ryusaku in the giant robot Daimos. During an enemy attack, Kazuya saves a girl called Erika. She's lost her memory, so both are completely unaware that she's the princess of the invading aliens, and they fall in love. When the truth emerges, she returns to her people to try and stop the war, while Kazuya is considered a traitor by his own people because he supports her wish for peace. The evil Emperor Olbam compels Erika to shoot her human lover; he survives and, not knowing that she is being forced to act against her will, decides to destroy the alien base in revenge. *Romeo and Juliet* with giant robots, the series didn't achieve the stellar popularity of Go Nagai's robot epics like GRANDIZER, its one claim to fame being the debut of PATLABOR's Yutaka Izubuchi as a guest robot designer on one episode. A 1980 "movie" was simply a theatrical showing of episode 24. In the U.S., the show was also edited into a 90-minute feature by New Hope Productions (see VOLTUS), broadcast on the Showtime cable network under the title *Starbirds*, with the robot renamed Dynamo and a new soundtrack deliberately redolent of *Star Wars.* See also SHOGUN WARRIORS.

STARCAT FULL HOUSE

1989. JPN: *Hoshineko Full House.* Video. DIR: Noboru Ishiguro. SCR: Noboru Ishiguro. DES: Noboru Sugimitsu, Haruhiko Mikimoto. ANI: Masahito Kitagawa. MUS: Kaoru Wada. PRD: Artland. 30 mins. x 4 eps.

This slapstick comedy is about three pretty girls struggling to earn a living as pilots of the Iron Goblin delivery vessel. The computer answers back, the space pirates are on their tail, and romantic entanglements with their clients cause friction in the trio. The final episode throws the alien Eterna race into the mix, but it's hardly GUNBUSTER.

STARCHILD RECORDS

Subsidiary of King Records, itself a subsidiary of the publishing house Kodansha, the Starchild label appears on many anime thanks to the dabbling of its chairman Toshimichi Otsuki in anime production, such as FLCL and MAGICAL SHOPPING ARCADE ABENOBASHI.

STARLIGHT NOCTURNE

1989. JPN: *Gasei Yakyoku.* Video. DIR: Osamu Dezaki. SCR: Toshiaki Imaizumi. DES: Akio Sugino. ANI: Akio Sugino. MUS: Akira Mioka. PRD: Magic Bus. 30 mins. x 4 eps.

Complicated romance in early 20th-century Japan, as a baron's only daughter switches places with the maid who shares her birthday, causing confusion when each is more attracted to a man from the other's social background. The 1923 Tokyo earthquake (see DOOMED MEGALOPOLIS) brings matters to a close. Based on the manga by Masako Hirata.

STARSHIP OPERATORS *

2005. TV series. DIR: Takashi Watanabe. SCR: Yoshihiko Tomizawa. DES: Fumio Matsumoto, Kimitoshi Yamane. ANI: N/C. MUS: Kenji Kawai. PRD: JC staff, Geneon, TV Tokyo. 25 mins. x 13 eps.

In a mix-up of NADESICO and GUNDAM, a group of cadets on a starship decide to take matters into their own hands when their homeworld Kibi is attacked by invaders. The crew of the Amaterasu declare war on the invaders, hoping to fund their unilateral defense effort by selling the TV rights to a galactic network—a sort of reality show, where instead of getting voted off, weekly losers are killed in the line of fire. The military plotline is leavened with plenty of girls in uniform and budding romance. Compare to STELLVIA.

STARSHIP TROOPERS

1988. JPN: *Uchu no Senshi*. AKA: *Space Warriors*. Video. DIR: Tetsuro Amino. SCR: Tsunehisa Ito, Noboru Aikawa. DES: Hiroyuki Kitakubo, Yutaka Izubuchi, Kazumasa Miyabe, Studio Nue. ANI: Yoshinobu Inano. MUS: Hiro Tsunoda. PRD: Sunrise, Bandai. 50 mins. x 3 eps.

Johnnie Rico loves the beautiful, willful Carmen, his high school sweetheart. When she signs up for the war against Earth's alien assailants, he follows suit in the hope of impressing her, but they get different assignments—she as a trainee pilot, he as an infantry grunt. From the studio that brought you GUNDAM, cited by its creator Tomino as one of his inspirations, this is an animated version of the Hugo-award winning 1959 novel by Robert Heinlein. Amino's version retains the scenes of training and combat but also focuses on time off the battlefield. His soldiers get into barroom brawls with disgruntled civvies, bury one of their comrades, and are then forced to attend his girlfriend's wedding to a new lover. The romance between Johnnie and Carmen becomes more central, ending with their tearful reunion in the hospital, to which they have both been evacuated with injuries. Carmen, absent for the bulk of the novel, has regular appearances in the anime to remind viewers what Johnnie is fighting for. In addition, each episode closes with Carmen bouncing along a beach in a bikini.

Johnnie's mother, Maria, also has a larger part to play. In the anime, she opposes Johnnie's enlistment, slapping his face as he prepares to leave. Her death is also made far more immediate; Amino's version keeps the trainees closer to Earth so that we see Johnnie and his platoon fighting fires at the Fall of Buenos Aires, unaware that his mother is breathing her last nearby. The only Japanese character in the original book, Private Shujumi, is not

Steam Detectives

present in the anime, perhaps because a Japanese audience would not warm to a stereotypical martial artist. He is replaced by the jug-eared, happy-go-lucky Private Azuma, who has "dead meat" written all over him from day one.

Directing the adaptation amid the post–*Top Gun* glut of gung ho Hollywood movies, Amino tried to defang Heinlein's militarist text with some home truths about the evils of war, but he still ran into criticism at home for "over-Americanizing" the anime. Maybe he shouldn't have turned his Filipino hero into an all-American blond, but Paul Verhoeven's live-action *Starship Troopers* (1997) later followed the same route with Caspar van Dien looking about as Filipino as Bugs Bunny. One of Heinlein's references to his own military past managed to survive untouched in the anime; Johnnie's ship, the Rodger Young, is named after a real-life Ohio private who was posthumously decorated for singlehandedly destroying a Japanese gun emplacement in 1943.

STARZAN S

1984. JPN: *Okawari Boy Starzan S*.

AKA: *Transforming Boy Starzan S*. TV series. DIR: Hidehito Ueda, Hiroyuki Tanaka, Mazakazu Higuchi, Shinya Sadamitsu, Masayuki Kojima, Takaaki Ishiyama. SCR: Takao Koyama, Mayori Sekijima, Yoshiyuki Suga, Miho Maruo. DES: Yoshitaka Amano, Ammonite. ANI: Masayuki Hayashi. MUS: Kazunori Ishida. PRD: Tatsunoko, Fuji TV. 25 mins. x 32 eps.

The beautiful Jun Yagami sets out in search of her father, Mamoru, who was last seen searching for the world of Paratopia, where nobody ever grows old. Caught in a space storm with a group of feckless bounty hunters, she lands on the unexplored world of Kirakira. The world is riven by a war between the Zenobi tribe and a group of evil robots led by the metallic Darth Bellow. The bounty hunters join forces with Darth Bellow, while Jun supports the Zenobi and their "forest god," the human boy Starzan, who possesses a transforming vehicle known as the Tobida Star. Conceived as a rather obvious mixture of *Star Wars* and *Tarzan*, this anime had robot toy tie-in potential ahead of the TRANSFORMERS sensation the following year.

STEALTH! KARATE CLUB

1990. JPN: *Onin! Karate-bu*. Video. DIR: Osamu Sekita. SCR: Hideo Nanbu. DES: Koichi Endo. ANI: Koichi Endo. MUS: Akira Yamazaki. PRD: JC Staff, Nippon Eizo. 50 mins. x 4 eps.

Supertough high school kids duke it out in the Osaka area (see COMPILER), which, naturally, means that they're all in league with gangsters. Based on the 1985 manga by Koji Takahashi in *Young Jump* magazine. ♥

STEAM DETECTIVES *

1998. JPN: *Kaiketsu Shoki Tanteidan*. AKA: *Handsome Steam Detectives*. TV series. DIR: Kiyoshi Murayama. SCR: Tsunehisa Arakawa, Kenichi Araki. DES: Akio Takami, Satoshi Hashimoto. ANI: Akio Takami. MUS: N/C. PRD: Xebec, TV Tokyo. 25 mins. x 26 eps.

Ten-year-old smartass Narutaki fights crime in the steampunk environs of Steam City. He is assisted by his loyal butler (shades of *Batman*) who has looked after him since his parents were killed by the malevolent Phantom Menace, and also by curvy 16-year-old nurse Ling Ling, daughter of a dead scientist, who not only shops, cooks, and wears a cute uniform, but also has her own magnificently clunky giant robot, Goriki. This intriguing mix of the diminutive CONAN THE BOY DETECTIVE with the nostalgic technology of GIANT ROBO is frittered away with low-quality animation and poorly conceived plots. Based on the 1995 manga by SILENT MÖBIUS–creator Kia Asamiya serialized in *Ultra Jump*.

STEAMBOY *

2004. Movie. DIR: Katsuhiro Otomo. SCR: Katsuhiro Otomo, Sadayuki Murai. DES: Katsuhiro Otomo. ANI: Shinji Takagi, Tatsuya Tomaru, Atsushi Irie, Katsumi Matsuda, Tsutomu Awada, Yasuyuki Shimizu, Hisashi Eguchi, Hirotsugu Kawasaki. MUS: Steve Jablonsky. PRD: Studio 4°C, Sunrise, Mash Room. 126 mins. (original version), 104 mins. (international version).

In Manchester, England, in 1866, young James "Ray" Steam hopes to be an inventor like his father and grandfather. Receiving a parcel in the mail from his grandfather Lloyd, Ray becomes the new owner of the "steam ball," a prototype energy source that utilizes a supercompressed liquid—a similar catalyst to that in THE SECRET OF CERULEAN SAND. Ray's father Eddie is working with Scarlett O'Hara, the owner of the American O'Hara Foundation, whose impressive Steam Tower will be a feature of the Great Exhibition in London—compare to THE SECRET OF BLUE WATER which uses the earlier Paris Exhibition as a conduit to adventure. However, Lloyd and Eddie have fallen out over the tower's uses. Ray joins forces with inventor Robert Stephenson in order to thwart the O'Hara organization's plan to sell advanced steam-powered weapons at London's Great Exhibition, a trade fair that will attract the great and the good from all over the world.

As with many other anime hyped for their technical achievement (MACROSS PLUS comes to mind, as does METROPOLIS, for which Otomo wrote the screenplay), *Steamboy* seems obsessed with the matter of its own creation. Eddie boasts to his son that the Steam Tower merely needs to exist and be seen to achieve its end. Some might argue the same for *Steamboy* itself, trumpeted as a flagship for anime abroad, ten years and $20.2 million in the making, constantly tweaked and remodeled to keep up with its notoriously perfectionist director's desire to remain at the cutting edge. However, this long-awaited follow-up, Otomo's first full-length anime feature as director since AKIRA, replays its predecessor's military-industrial conspiracy, dressed up in period costume and the exotic, inscrutable setting of England. As in Otomo's most famous work, the characters are plunged into a race over the mastery of an earth-shattering energy source, culminating in a long battle that levels buildings citywide with the cavalier attitude of a Godzilla. Like ASTRO BOY, *Steamboy*'s protagonist is torn between positive and negative father figures,

but much of it comprises an overlong chase sequence, even in the "international version" that discards 20 minutes of footage from the original Japanese release—much of the jettisoned material coming from the early Manchester scenes.

Steamboy was commissioned in the mid-1990s, amid the same retro mood that saw other steampunk stylings such as SAKURA WARS or SUPER ATRAGON, with arch references to *Gone With the Wind* (1939) in its choice of leading lady. Its imagery recalls that of Otomo's "Cannon Fodder" segment in MEMORIES, while its love of steam power suggests the clunky contraptions of Hayao Miyazaki's CASTLE IN THE SKY and SHERLOCK HOUND. In its final moments, however, it also resembles the reconciliation and truce of HOWL'S MOVING CASTLE, with weapons of mass destruction temporarily thwarted and family values asserting themselves, however briefly, in the race to save London from the Steam family's FRANKENSTEIN technology. There is a certain irony that Otomo should employ so many devices from the 21st century in order to recreate a fantasy ideal of the 19th, particularly when if anything lets *Steamboy* down, it is the humble, low-tech want of an editor to take a red pencil to an overblown and strangely paced script. The movie enjoyed a new lease on life on DVD and was one of the first releases in the new Blu-Ray format, in 2006. ♥

STEEL ANGEL KURUMI *

1999. JPN: *Kotetsu Tenshi Kurumi*. TV series. DIR: Naohito Takahashi, Kazuya Murata, Norihiko Sudo. SCR: Tsunehisa Arakawa. DES: Yuriko Senba, Takeshi Ito, Toshihiko Sato. ANI: Yuriko Senba. MUS: N/C. PRD: Kadokawa, Pony Canyon, WOWOW. 15 mins. x 24 eps. (TV1), 15 mins. x 4 eps. (v), 15 mins. x 12 eps. (TV2).

In a 1920s Japan not unlike that of SAKURA WARS, a mad scientist (we know he's mad because he's called Professor Demon) has devoted the full power of his weird science to producing a robot whose deadly weapons are pink hair, a cute voice, and a French maid outfit. When a teenage boy sneaks into the basement for a peek, Kurumi decides *he's* her master. The 15-minute running time restricts what can be done to move the story along, but the audience's short attention span might work in favor of a concept that was hackneyed about three TENCHI MUYO! clones back. Realizing that a respray was all the audience's low expectations required, the producers returned in 2001 with a new series, which was just like the old one but set in the present day, with everyone's name now bearing the suffix "Mark Two." That was worth it. A live-action version of the series was also made, under the title *Steel Angel Kurumi Pure* (2002, *DE).

STEEL DEVIL

1987. JPN: *Daimaju Gekito Hagane no Oni*. AKA: *Violent Encounter Demon of Steel*. Video. DIR: Toshihiro Hirano. SCR: Noboru Aikawa. DES: Naoyuki Onda, Koichi Ohata. ANI: Koichi Ohata. MUS: Masahiro Kawasaki. PRD: AIC, Tokuma Japan Communications. 60 mins.
An experimental laser brings down a UFO on a remote island, and scientists Haruka and Takuya risk their lives to investigate. Accidentally opening a door to another dimension, Haruka is transformed into a giant mechanical warrior. In this derivative apocalyptic anime from ICZER-ONE-creator Hirano, ancient entities rise from their slumber of ages and fight in the sky above Shinjuku to herald the end of the rule of humanity. See also CYGUARD and GENOCYBER.

STEEL JEEG

1975. JPN: *Kotetsu Jeeg*. TV series. DIR: Masayuki Akehi, Yoshio Nitta, Kazuya Miyazaki, Masayuki Akehi, Yugo Serikawa, Masamune Ochiai, Nobutaka Nishizawa, Yasuo Yamakichi. SCR: Hiroyasu Yamaura, Keisuke Fujikawa, Tomohiro Ando. DES: Kazuo Nakamura, Geki Katsumata. ANI: Kazuo Nakamura, Seiji Kikuchi, Koji Uemura, Sadao Tominaga. MUS: Michiaki Watanabe. PRD: Toei, NET. 25 mins. x 46 eps.

Hiroshi Shima is mortally injured in a racing accident but restored to life as a cyborg by his scientist father. Professor Shima is also investigating the relics of the ancient Jamatai kingdom, and he is murdered by the henchmen of their Queen Himika when he discovers a tiny bronze bell with supposed sorcerous powers. The modern inhabitants of Japan are attacked by the bell's ancient makers, but Hiroshi holds them off by interfacing with the head of a giant robot, Steel Robot Jeeg, also created by his father (a multitalented physiologist-cum-archaeologist-cum-robot designer, it would seem). To complete its body and launch into space, he needs parts released by the space jet Big Shooter, piloted by his father's lovely assistant, Miwa Satsuki. The enemy has huge *haniwa* robots, called "clay phantoms," buried under the soil of Japan, and only Jeeg can destroy them and save the world; but can cyborg Hiroshi suppress his human feelings for Miwa? After episode 29, the Jamatai invaders were replaced by a new enemy, the Ryoma Empire. Based on an idea by Tatsuya Yasuda and Go Nagai, creator of GRANDIZER, GETTER ROBO, and MAZINGER Z, *SJ* also ran as a manga in several children's publications. *Haniwa* in Japanese archaeology are literally "circles of clay"—barrel-shaped terracotta cylinders topped by sculptures, used to mark the borders of burial grounds in ancient Japan. They date from the period when Queen *Himiko* ruled the state of *Yamatai* in the 3rd century A.D. (see DARK MYTH). Compare to similar ghosts of the past in PSYCHIC WARS and BLUE SEED.

STEIN OF TRASH STREET

2003. JPN: *Garakuta-dori no Stein*. AKA: *Stain in Trash Street*. TV series. DIR: Ryuji Masuda. SCR: Ryuji Masuda. DES: Wakako Masuda. ANI: Daisuke Suzuki. MUS: Meina Co. PRD: Kid's Station. 7 mins. x 13 eps. (TV1), 7 mins. (sequel).
The adventures of society dropout Stein and his cat Balban, who find themselves living on a forgotten,

trash-strewn street in the middle of an unforgiving city. The trash, however, has a life of its own; like him, it ends up cast away for a reason, leading Stein to discover the tales associated with it—compare to TOKYO GODFATHERS. As with VOICES OF A DISTANT STAR, this CGI animation, created by Masuda and designed by his wife, demonstrates how technology has enabled anime to go back to cottage industry roots, with individual creators in far greater control. The design is quirky and charming, with more than a touch of antique British children's series like *The Flowerpot Men* (1952) about the hero and his fat cat friend, and displays a deep, unsettling color and lighting palette. A one-shot sequel, *GnS: Epilogue* followed later in 2003.

STELLVIA *

2003. JPN: *Uchu no Stellvia*. AKA: *Stellvia of Space*. TV series. DIR: Tatsuo Sato. SCR: Ichiro Okochi, Katsuhiko Chiba, Katsuhiko Koide, Miho Sakai, Tatsuo Sato. DES: Makoto Uno, Naohiro Washio. ANI: Shigeru Ueda. MUS: Seiko Nagaoka. PRD: Foundation II, Xebec. 25 mins. x 26 eps.
A distant supernova triggered a huge electromagnetic pulse that brought mankind to the verge of extinction 189 years ago. With 99% of Earth's population destroyed, humanity has built huge space stations called "foundations" to try and prevent another such catastrophe. In 2356, 15-year-old Shima Katase passes the entrance exams for the Space Academy and sets out for the foundation Stellvia, hoping that she'll be ready to help out with the Great Mission, a plan to stop the aftershock from the first disaster causing more damage. First, though, she has to make friends, enemies, and rivals, and overcome her own fears and grow up. Yes, it's a high school story set in space. We've been on similar territory before, with the sublime GUNBUSTER exploring the insecurities of growing up enhanced by the time dilation effect, and a whole host of lesser stories starring an overly large cast of cute,

slightly klutzy girls who are not the star student but try so hard that they eventually save the day. Parallels grow even stronger when the crew of the Stellvia find themselves having to deal with an alien attack. Writer-director Sato doesn't bring anything new to the table for *Stellvia*, despite its pretty design and animation—compare to **BATTLE ATHLETES**.

STEPMOTHER'S SIN *

2001. JPN: *Gibo*. AKA: *Stepmother*. Video. DIR: Takayoshi Mizuno. SCR: Rokurota Makabe. DES: Matsuri Ohana. ANI: Matsuri Ohana. MUS: Yoshi. PRD: Digital Works (Vanilla Series). 30 mins. x 2 eps.

Ever since witnessing a primal scene of his mother being unfaithful, Yusuke has developed a hatred of women that he directs in particular at members of his own family. Now divorced, his father is posted to a distant office, leaving Yusuke to live with his new stepmother-to-be Misako and Shiina, her daughter from a previous marriage. Meanwhile, Yusuke is conducting a secret affair with his cousin Mio, but also resolves to humiliate his new stepfamily. Shiina fantasizes about her stepbrother, but is then raped by him in front of her mother, who is so aroused by the incident that she then begs to be taken herself. Traumatized by the experience, Shiina allows herself to fall in with a street gang who end up raping her, too. Somewhat belatedly, Yusuke realizes the errors of his ways and that he actually loves Misako. He seeks her forgiveness, but she tells him that she has learned to love the sadistic sex he has taught her. This revelation causes Yusuke to lose control of his senses (as if he hadn't already!), and he is arrested after attacking a loving couple in the park. The police drag him back to Misako's house, where she is found in the middle of an orgy. She begs Yusuke to give her what she needs, but, in a surprise twist, the anime ends with the death of one of the leading characters. Precisely who is left to the viewer's imagination. **LNV**

STEPSISTER *

2002. JPN: *Gibomai*. Video. DIR: Toshihito Yura. SCR: Kentaro Mizuno. DES: Selen. ANI: Hitoshi Haga. MUS: Hiroaki Sano, Takeshi Nishizawa. PRD: Discovery. 30 mins. x 2 eps.

Kyosuke has never really liked his stepmother Megumi, holding her personally responsible for the separation of his parents and his mother's untimely death soon after. But he rallies around when his famous painter father dies, and soon discovers that Megumi wants to hang onto a number of valuable paintings. As the negotiations over Kyosuke's father's estate continue, Megumi offers her daughter Yuna for Kyosuke's sexual diversion. Kyosuke begins a sadistic relationship with his stepsister, in an entry in the **DISCOVERY SERIES**, based on an erotic computer game by Selen. **LNV**

STEREOTYPES AND ARCHETYPES

Although we do not wish to draw too many links between Japan's traditional past and its modern-day entertainment, it is worth noting that much of the shorthand employed in story meetings and brainstorming sessions can break down into the *yakugara* character clichés established in the Japanese theater. In kabuki, for example, roles are broadly divided into protagonists and antagonists, with heroes divided into the gruff, "hot-headed" *aragoto*, and the more refined, elegant, even effeminate *wagoto* role—see **SAMURAI CHAMPLOO**, which copies these divisions to the letter. Other kabuki character clichés include the *jitsugoto*, who oppose evil with divine strength, although they are often broken and destroyed by their efforts. Female characters in kabuki were more simply divided into *wakaonnagata* (youthful princesses, courtesans, and other damsels in likely distress), *kashagata* (samurai wives, often good with a sword or a frying pan), and *akuba* (archetypal bad-girls, with street smarts, tattoos, and sass). These basic classes of character are further multiplied by three age groups—young, middle-aged, and old—to create most main characters of the Japanese stage, although we have left out several subclasses, such as clowns, due to space limitations. Similarly, kabuki has six basic types of villain—evil princes (aka "nation demolishers"), evil samurai, evil retainers, dishonest clerks, henchmen (often used for comic relief), and apprentices. Multiplied by the three age groups, they form 18 basic templates for villainy, from beautiful boy-villains who threaten the hero's would-be girlfriend, to scheming old uncles who are secretly in league with an enemy clan.

Anime in the early days of TV, particularly but not exclusively those with a sporting basis, would often use similar character archetypes. The viewer's point of identification is usually the character closest in age to the target audience, and often a supposed "natural" at the anime's central sport/activity, with a rough, unhoned talent that requires hard work and perseverance (**GUNBUSTER**'s oft-repeated "*doryoku to konjo*") to turn into true ability. The catalyst that drives them into action in many instances is the loss of an elder family member—a father or sibling—although the lost relation may eventually reappear working for the enemy. The mentor figure is an associate of the one who is lost, attempting to assuage his/her own guilt or bereavement by pushing the lead character into ever better achievements. The mentor figure will also be likely to have a tragic fate, possibly due to some disease or affliction that s/he has kept from the protagonist, or otherwise a moment of supreme sacrifice. Note also that these archetypes are far from unique, as they delineate a mythic "hero's journey" that can also be found in Western media, most obviously *Star Wars* (1977), itself famously using Joseph Campbell's *Hero with a Thousand Faces* to define its archetypes. There will also be a childish sidekick, often for comic relief, and probably a dark mysterious stranger, who may turn out to be the long-lost relative. These dynamics, plus a few sports matches or battles, can normally carry a story healthily for 26 episodes. By the time the audience might notice they have seen it all before, they are probably already in a different year at school or following a different show—that, at least, is how the more cynical producers might excuse the use of such stereotypes.

The rise of merchandising led many manga and anime creators to follow larger cast templates, chiefly inspired by foreign imports. It was Gerry Anderson's *Thunderbirds* that introduced the Japanese to the toy-selling, audience-pleasing potential of an entire family of protagonists, most noticeable in SKYERS 5 (1967) and *Goranger* (*DE; 1975), which introduced the character roster of Hero, Rogue, Big Guy, Comic Relief, and Token Girl, often working for an avuncular scientist, and perhaps most recognizable in BATTLE OF THE PLANETS (1972).

Five lead characters allows for a healthy group dynamic and helps justify the sale of five toys instead of one. This format was further refined in girls' anime to remove men from the equation, creating groups of five heroines—or more precisely, a single point of identification, with four supporting cast members. HUMMINGBIRDS and early seasons of SAILOR MOON offer the best examples, with our klutzy, ugly-duckling Girl Next Door heroine, a hapless, self-doubting center, surrounded by a brusque Tomboy, a demure Maiden, a sophisticated Older Girl, and a Child (occasionally a feral one). Other female characters might include Foreign Girls, often depicted as blonde, loud, large-breasted, and stupid. It should be noted, however, that blonde hair, or indeed any other hair color, including green and purple, is not a racial signifier in anime, which often gives its characters ludicrous hair colors in order to aid identification. Similar concerns often lead to heavy accessorizing in female characters' hair.

Foreignness also plays an important part in the subject of gay erotica—many relationships in such anime being describable as a meek, submissive, dark-haired character, who is acted upon, dominated, or seduced by a more experienced, often elder, blonder character—even if the seducer is not demonstrably foreign, their actions will often be the least stereotypically Japanese.

The arrival of the dating simulation genre has also utilized the basic female archetypes of the team show, often turning game play into a form of personality test in which the computer tries to work out what kind of mate the player would most prefer—a bratty pop idol Child, perhaps, or a librarian Maiden, both likely candidates for *moe*, the modern fan obsession with unthreatening, childlike girls like something out of the LOLITA ANIME. Many dating sims introduce more than the basic character set (which, incidentally, the authors first divined by comparing the programming flowcharts of erotic dating sims), but additional girls are often variations on the basic themes. Such themes are readily translated into erotic anime, many of which are based directly on the games where the archetypes are most clearly used. Where romance is part of the story, even in mundane anime not related to dating sims, it is often assumed that the Girl Next Door character among a hero's love objects will be the eventual lucky lady—time-slip chapters of both the URUSEI YATSURA and DORAEMON stories imply that their heroes settle for their hometown girl, and not any exotic alien princesses or demon queens.

Japanese critics are often reluctant to admit that so many characters can be so easily delineated. Takashi Kondo's *Guide of Fantastic Beauties* (*Kusou Bishojo Tokuhon*, 1997), for example, prefers to plot female anime characteristics on six axes—Town vs. Country, Warlike vs. Peaceful, Adult vs. Child, Real vs. Ethereal, Fresh vs. Bitter, and the rather vague Sun vs. Moon. Furthermore, attempts by press liaisons to make something sound palatable to journalists can reduce any anime plot to predictable and unappealing stereotypes. Consequently, the phrase "Hot-headed and/or shy boy gets robot and/or several would-be girlfriends, and/or a childhood sweetheart who is a mysterious girl" is applicable to a depressingly large number of anime. Where a title first appeared in comic form, it has also become a hoary cliché to say "based on the popular manga," regardless of whether the manga was popular or not.

STINGIEST MAN IN TOWN, THE *

1978. JPN: *Machi Ichiban Kechinbo*. TV special. DIR: Katsuhisa Yamada. SCR: Romeo Muller. DES: Paul Coker Jr. ANI: Kazuyuki Komori. MUS: Fred Spielman. PRD: Top Craft, Rankin/Bass, TV Asahi. 55 mins.

On a cold Christmas Eve in 1880s London, notorious miser Ebenezer Scrooge is visited in his sleep by three ghostly apparitions who teach him the errors of his ways and the meaning of Christmas. This U.S.-Japan coproduction based on Charles Dickens's 1843 novel *A Christmas Carol* was designed as a musical for the American market and made to order by the Japanese from a prerecorded voice and music track. Character designer Coker seems to have worked almost solely on festive cartoons back in the U.S., including *Frosty's Winter Wonderland* and *The Year without a Santa Claus*—he is better known as one of the artists on *Mad* magazine and an old hand at designing greetings cards for Hallmark. For the subsequent Japanese version, a new script was synchronized to the existing pictures: a rare case of an anime that genuinely has been *dubbed* in Japanese. The Japanese edition was broadcast on Christmas Eve 1978, a mere 24 hours after the U.S. premiere. Director Yamada would go on to make a variety of more obviously Japanese cartoons, including the high-spirited JUNK BOY and the spirit-slaying DEVIL HUNTER YOHKO. Dickens's OLD CURIOSITY SHOP was animated the following year by an unconnected crew.

STOP HIBARI-KUN

1983. JPN: *Stop Hibari-kun*. TV series. DIR: Satoshi Hisaoka, Tetsuo Imazawa, Yoshiaki Kawajiri, Hiroshi Sasagawa. SCR: Shigeru Yanagawa, Hiromi Asano, Tokio Tsuchiya, Hiroshi Koda, Tomomi Tsutsui, Takeshi Shudo. DES: Yoshinori Kanemori. ANI: Makoto Ito, Kazuo Tomizawa, Kiyoshi Matsumoto, Takao Kasai, Yasuomi Umezu. MUS: Koji Nishimura. PRD: Toei, Fuji TV. 25 mins. x 35 eps.

Yusaku Sakamoto is sent to live with a friend of the family after his mother's death—or should that be, a friend of the Family. Now he's living with Ibari Ozora, head of the Ozora crime syndicate, and Ozora's pretty daughters Tsugumi, Tsubame, Suzume, and Ko-chan. The prettiest "girl" of all, however, is Hibari, Ozora's eldest son, who has decided he likes life better if he dresses as a girl. This bizarre forerunner of TENCHI MUYO! combined with a cross-dressing *Godfather* was based on the 1982 manga in *Shonen Jump* by EIJI-creator Hisashi Eguchi.

STORIES FROM A STREET CORNER *

1962. JPN: *Aru Machikado no Monogatari*. Movie. DIR: Eiichi Yamamoto. SCR: Osamu Tezuka. DES: Osamu Tezuka. ANI: Shigeyuki Hayashi (Rintaro), Masaharu Mitsuyama, Tetsuro Amino, Gisaburo Sugii. MUS: Tatsuo Takai. PRD: Mushi Pro. 38 mins.

Posters on a street corner each tell their own story—a circus poster and several advertisements briefly come to life, and a pianist and a violinist from separate pictures fall in love. Meanwhile, a little girl in a nearby garret apartment loses her doll, which finds a new friend in the mouse, playing in the gutter, who saves it from being swept away in a rainstorm. Military posters are slapped over the peacetime images, and the buildings are destroyed by enemy bombs. However, in the aftermath, the girl, the mouse, and her doll are all safe, and the military posters have blown away, revealing the originals underneath. There is no dialogue;

the film tells its stories visually. The first work to be produced by Tezuka's Mushi Productions; the second would be ASTRO BOY. See also STREET CORNER FAIRYTALES.

STORY OF DONBE

1981. JPN: *Donbe Monogatari*. TV special. DIR: Fusahito Nagaki. SCR: Shota Tatsumachi, Keisuke Fujikawa. DES: Takashi Keuchi, Akira Fukuda. ANI: Akira Fukuda. MUS: Hiroshi Takada, Kiyoshi Suzuki. PRD: Eiken, NTV. 84 mins.

Researcher Mutsugoro takes his family to a remote and uninhabited island near Hokkaido, to study the local population of wild bears. Nearby poachers make his life difficult, and he "inherits" an orphaned bear cub, whom the family call Donbe and raise as one of their own. A dramatization of one Tadashi Hata's essays from his book *The Hokkaido Animal Kingdom*, the author himself provided authentic bear impersonations for the voice track, and is hence credited as Donbe's "voice actor."

STORY OF LITTLE LOVE

1984. JPN: *Chiisana Koi no Monogatari*. TV special. DIR: Toshio Hirata, Tetsu Dezaki. SCR: Shunichi Yukimuro. DES: Yoshiyuki Momose. ANI: Yoshishige Kosako. MUS: Shinsuke Kazato. PRD: Visual 80, MK, TBS. 84 mins.

Tiny schoolgirl Chiiko develops a crush on older boy Saly and believes herself to be his girlfriend, although Saly is already involved in a love triangle with Tonko, the girl he met on his summer vacation in the mountains. Based on a 1962 manga by Chikako Mitsuhashi.

STORY OF LITTLE MONICA *

2002. JPN: *Little Monica Monogatari*. Movie. DIR: Joki Satsumaya. SCR: Roku-rota Makabe. DES: Joki Satsumaya. ANI: Mamoru Yasaki. MUS: Yoshi. PRD: YOUC, Digital Works (Vanilla Series). 30 mins. x 2 eps.

Little Monica is a place, not a person, the idyllic seaside town to which protagonist (and accomplished ladies' man) Will returns after a long absence. However, the town is a shadow of its

former self, having fallen under the sway of the evil ruler Kajo. Will finds out how much things have changed when he travels to the local theater, which has been turned into a strip joint where Meow, a girl he has just met on the boat over, takes off her clothes before selecting a lucky audience member to have intercourse with her onstage—on this occasion, it is Will who is selected. Will has actually come back to Little Monica in order to be reunited with his childhood friend Celia, whose younger sisters Tina and Mei are intensely curious about boys and encourage Will to teach them the facts of life. He eventually does so, while helping out around the trio's restaurant (their mother having gone missing years before) and planning to make an honest woman out of Celia, while still fantasizing about Meow. He might also do something about the previously unmentioned prophecy as well, which predicts that someone will overthrow Kajo and restore the city's goodness—though presumably that would mean no more stripper freebies for our hero. The series is notable for its high-gloss character designs and skilled use of CG animation—unlike many of its brethren in the VANILLA SERIES, the staff seems to know how bodies actually move. **LNV**

STORY OF RIKI

1989. JPN: *Riki-O*. AKA: *Power King; King Riki*. Video. DIR: Tetsu Dezaki. SCR: Kazumi Koide. DES: Akio Sugino. ANI: Yasuhiro Seo. MUS: Yoshimasa Nakajima. PRD: Magic Bus. 45 mins. x 2 eps.

In the near future, supertough guy Riki is sent to a private prison for a crime he didn't commit. He thrives, however, in the ultraviolent prison environment, fighting his way to the top of the pack and then out to freedom. Based on a manga by Masahiko Takakumi in *Business Jump*, this story was also made into Nam Nai Choi's live-action Hong Kong film *Story of Riki* (1992). **V**

STORY OF SUPERCONDUCTORS

1988. JPN: *Chodendo Monogatari*. TV

special. DIR: Masayuki Oseki, Kenji Naito. SCR: Takashi Yamada, Hiroshi Aoki. DES: Isao Oji. ANI: Isao Oji. MUS: N/C. PRD: Studio Twinkle, Tokai TV. 60 mins.

The science department of the *Tosai Shinbun* newspaper investigates a story on superconductors, learning all about the mysterious world of subzero electrical conductivity, the Meissner Effect, Brian Josephson's work on "tunneling" (flow across an insulating layer without application of voltage), and implications for super-*computer* technology in the 21st century. Meanwhile, attractive reporter Miss Ohashi begins to find bespectacled scientist Dr. Arai rather attractive.

STORY OF THE SOYA

1984. JPN: *Soya Monogatari*. TV series. DIR: N/C. SCR: Masaru Yamamoto. DES: Shiro Murata, Hiroki Hayashi. ANI: Shiro Murata. MUS: Toshi Fukui. PRD: Kokusai Eiga, TV Tokyo. 25 mins. x 21 eps.

In 1978, the Antarctic survey vessel Soya calls in at Yamaguchi Prefecture's Moji port on her final voyage. Watching are Susumu Kozaki, a shipbuilder's son who was born on the day the Soya was launched, and his own son, Hiroshi. Susumu tells Hiroshi the story of the Soya, how it was commissioned by the Russians, and how the contract was canceled soon after launch. Renamed the Jishin Maru, the Soya bears witness to the events of the 1930s, as the dark clouds of war gather.

STRAIGHT AHEAD

2003. JPN: *Massugu ni Iko*. AKA: *Let's Go Straight*. TV series. DIR: Kiyotaka Isako. SCR: Aki Itami, Atsushi Yamatoya, Yoichi Kato. DES: Aki Tsunaki, Nanae Morita. ANI: Aki Tsunaki. MUS: Michiru Oshima. PRD: Yumeta, Yomiuri TV. 20 mins. x 4 eps., 25 mins. x 5 eps. (TV2).

In the tradition of **I AM A CAT** and **THE CALL OF THE WILD**, a story is told from the point of view of an animal, in this case Mametaro the mongrel dog, who offers comment and insight into the personal life of his owner, Iku, a Japa-

nese high school girl. Based on the 1993 manga from *Bessatsu Margaret* and *Chorus* magazines by "Kira." A second TV series followed in 2005, premiering on the Internet but later broadcast on Yomiuri TV.

STRANGE DAWN

2000. TV series. DIR: Shogo Kawamoto, Junichi Sato. SCR: Michiko Yokote. DES: Akihiko Yamashita. ANI: Miho Shimokasa. MUS: Kaoru Wada. PRD: HAL Filmmakers, WOWOW. 25 mins. x 13 eps.

Eri and Yuko are high school girls summoned into another world by Queen Aria. Her kingdom, Guriania, is at war with neighboring Barujitan, and she believes the two girls are witches who can use their mighty powers to end the conflict. But they don't have any powers, don't like each other, and don't want to work together—except that it seems like it's the only way they can get back to their own world. Predictably cute character designs, including a couple of childlike fantasy creatures that at least make a change from the usual magical animal sidekicks. But what sets *Strange Dawn* apart is the uses to which it puts its designs—the childish-seeming characters belie a plotline that is unafraid to jump feet-first into war, bloodshed, and death. This is, unfortunately, exactly the sort of thing that TV companies don't want in their cutesy cartoons, leading to a patchy history of broadcast, suspension, and burial that has left *Strange Dawn* one of anime's forgotten shows, at least abroad. As with **EL HAZARD**, Junichi Sato's story concentrates on the mundane annoyances that might beset human beings in a fantasy world—regardless of the world that needs saving, the girls are more worried about finding a working toilet and how far they can stretch their limited laundry resources. Cunningly, the series also refuses point-blank to deal with the sort of questions that another series, such as **ESCAFLOWNE**, would have answered in the very first episode. We don't find out why the girls are so

antagonistic toward each other, nor anything about their life in our own world—the lack of an introduction scene misleading the viewers and keeping them guessing throughout, and all for the better.

STRANGE LOVE *

1996. JPN: *Hen*. AKA: *Strange*. Video. DIR: Oji Suzuki. SCR: Mayori Sekijima. DES: Yasuomi Umezu. ANI: Chuji Nakajima. MUS: Koji Tsuno. PRD: Group Tac. 40 mins. x 2 eps.

Nerdy teacher (sorry, college professor) Sushiaki develops an obsession with one of his pupils, the impossibly proportioned Chizuru Yoshida. Torn with conflicting feelings in the hypocritical manner of **HOMEROOM AFFAIRS**, he discovers that she has been secretly appearing in commercials, in contravention of a school (sorry, college) rule that specifies no part-time jobs. Hoping to use this to his advantage, he realizes too late that he has become the plaything of a masterful tease. The "virginal" Chizuru is already sleeping with a rock star, but both men are left in the lurch when Chizuru falls for a *female* transfer student, Azumi Yamida. Despite several notable names in the crew, this is a creatively barren and often incoherent jailbait fantasy in the spirit of **CREAM LEMON**, complete with a few halfhearted homages to other anime such as **PROJECT A-KO**. Based on just part of the 1991 manga in *Young Jump* by Hiroya Oku, which sold more than five million copies, the story (and viewers) deserved better than this. Though the USMC release labels this as only *possibly* unsuitable for minors, it's probably unsuitable for anyone. **Ⓝ**

STRATOS FOUR *

2003. TV series, video. DIR: Takeshi Mori. SCR: Katsuhiko Takayama. DES: Noriyasu Yamauchi, Tomohiro Kawahara. ANI: Noriyasu Yamauchi. MUS: Masamichi Amano. PRD: Bandai Visual, Columbia Music Entertainment, Studio Fantasia, TV Saitama. 23 mins. x 13 eps. (TV), 30 mins. x 2 eps. (v1), 30 mins. x 6 eps. (v2).

In an Earth suffering a cometary bombardment (shades here of **STAR BLAZERS**), two new defensive programs keep the world safe. The front line is held by the Comet Blasters, top gun pilots based in space stations beyond Earth, armed with nuclear warheads to destroy meteors before they can penetrate the atmosphere. The second line is the Meteor Sweepers, ground-based pilots in hypersonic planes who deal with any debris resulting from the space blasts. Heroine Mikaze is a teenager Meteor Sweeper trainee (in Okinawa, of course—see **GUNBUSTER**) who longs to become one of the elite Comet Blaster pilots. Like all teenage anime heroines, but most notably like her predecessor pilot in **HUMMINGBIRDS**, she has to struggle with her own shortcomings first, as she and her teammates learn the ropes.

Although the most obvious inspirations for *Stratos Four* are *Deep Impact* (1998) and *Armageddon* (1998), it often plays more like Gerry Anderson's *UFO* (1970), seen from the viewpoint of the Interceptor pilots and then filtered through teenage insecurity and powerlessness. Mikaze is a classic anime archetype: the daughter of renowned pilots, she flutters between an innate belief in her destiny to follow in the "family business" and teenage fretting that she should be choosing her own path, and not merely aping her parents. Later episodes inject a note of seriousness—there may be on-base high jinks like any school anime, and sops to the anime audience like a comic-relief cat, not to mention the outrageous suspension of disbelief required to watch a bunch of inept schoolgirls flying jet fighters, and yet *Stratos Four* does not shy away from moments of danger and tension. Later episodes include subplots about how the loneliness of a space station posting can turn a girl's mind to same-sex relationships and the obligatory alien menace, although the former eventually turns out to have been created as a viral infection by the latter. For this, we largely have Studio Fantasia

to thank—while the people who gave us **AGENT AIKA** have toned down their legendary obsessions a little, there is still much ogling of technical hardware and ample provision of female pulchritude for the male viewer. This may also explain the wholly unnecessary subplot that finds part-time work for some of the pilots in a Chinese restaurant, thereby permitting the animators to put them into slinky *cheongsam* dresses on occasion.

The TV series was followed by two video sequels: *Stratos Four: Return to Base,* in which the girls have to deal with a space station threatening to fall out of the sky, and *Stratos Four: Advance,* the first episode of which was broadcast on TV before its Japanese release. Director Mori gets a coscripting credit on the two-part video and is the sole writer on the six-parter, but otherwise the principal crew is unchanged. After the DVD release of *Stratos Four: Advance,* later episodes were also broadcast on TV, leading some sources to file it as a TV anime. The titular *Battle-Fairy Mave-chan* (2005), in a spin-off of the plane-oriented **YUKIKAZE** series, was an avowed *Stratos Four* fan.

STRAWBERRY EGGS *

2001. JPN: *Ai! Mai! Mi! Strawberry Egg.* TV series. DIR: Yuji Yamaguchi. SCR: Yasuko Kobayashi. DES: Maki Fujii. ANI: Tetsuya Yanasawa. MUS: Keiichi Nozaki. PRD: TNK, WOWOW. 25 mins. x 13 eps. Twenty-three-year-old hothead Hibiki Amawa is a boy from the far north of the Japanese mainland who wants to be a schoolteacher. With funds running low, he accepts the first job he can find, teaching (in drag!) at a school whose man-hating principal only hires female staff. Hibiki must then earn his students' respect, while keeping his true identity secret and battling the principal to keep the school from becoming girls-only—and to keep from falling in love, in a comedy from the studio that brought you **HAND MAID DAY**.

STRAWBERRY MARSHMALLOW
2005. JPN: *Ichigo Mashimaro.* TV

series. DIR: Takuya Sato, Kazuhiro Ozawa, Mamoru Kanbe. SCR: Takuya Sato, Michiko Yokote, Jukki Hanada. DES: Kyuta Sakai. ANI: Kyuta Sakai, Tatsuya Abe. MUS: Tsuyoshi Watanabe. PRD: Domu, TBS, Geneon USA. 25 mins. x 13 eps.

Nobue Ito is a chain-smoking twentysomething who is forced to endure the company of her little sister Chika and Chika's friends, who are supposedly cute, thereby marrying the comedy setups of **AZUMANGA DAIOH** with the world-weary surrogate mother of **EVANGELION**'s Misato. Based on a manga by "Barasui" ("Rose Water") in *Dengeki Daioh.*

STREET CORNER FAIRYTALES
1984. JPN: *Machikado no Meruhen.* Video. DIR: Mizuho Nishikubo. SCR: Takeshi Shudo. DES: Yoshitaka Amano. ANI: Heihachi Tanaka. MUS: Virgin VS. PRD: Kitty Film. 52 mins.

Hiroshi, a student in a Shinjuku high school, dreams of one day writing a children's book and is working hard to save enough money so that he can do it. He falls in love with a girl he meets by chance on the subway, and Hiroko becomes very important to the eventual realization of his dreams. Set to 17 pop tunes in the style of **CIPHER**, this is not to be confused with Tezuka's **STORIES FROM A STREET CORNER**, though the producers rather hoped it would be.

STREET FIGHTER II *
1994. JPN: *Street Fighter II; Street Fighter II Victory; SF Zero.* AKA: *Street Fighter II: The Movie; SF II TV; SF Alpha.* Movie, TV series, video. DIR: Gisaburo Sugii (m/TV); Eiichi Sato, Takuya Sato, Yukio Takahashi, Kuniaki Komura, Hideaki Shimada, Shigeru Yamazaki, Yutaka Arai (TV); Shigeyasu Yamauchi (v). SCR: Kenichi Imai, Gisaburo Sugii (m); Reiko Yoshida, Naoyuki Sakai (TV). DES: Shuko Murase, Minoru Maeda (m); Akira Kano, Junichiro Nishikawa, Yasuhiro Oshima, Satoshi Matsuoka (TV); Yoshihiko Umakoshi (v). ANI: Minoru Maeda (m); Yoshihiko Umakoshi. MUS: Tetsuya Komuro (m/

TV); Chage & Asuka, Hayato Matsuo, Masahiro Shimada (TV). prd: Group Tac. 104 mins. (m), 25 mins. x 29 eps. (TV), 45 mins. x 2 eps. (v). Evil Vega (M. Bison) is one of the leaders of the Shadowlaw organization intent on world domination. He is brainwashing martial artists in order to use them as secret agents and has kidnapped Ken Masters, a prominent street fighter. Ken's former sparring partner, Ryu, teams up with Interpol to track him down.

A film based on the sequel to CAP-COM's original computer *game*, *SFII*'s thin premise is a weak hook on which to hang a succession of fight scenes. However, Sugii's theatrical release sets the standard for the entire game-adaptation subgenre and has been much imitated by titles including Toshinden, Art of Fighting, Fatal Fury, and Sexorcist. Though not the first game-based anime (see Super Mario Brothers), *SFII* was arguably the most successful until Pokémon. Many anime "movies" such as Tekken aren't "motion pictures" at all but straight-to-video nonsense given a pretentious title for foreign release. *SFII*, however, is a genuine theatrical feature, with computer graphics, lifelike fight animation, and a big budget. Unlike the live-action version released the same year starring Kylie Minogue and Jean-Claude Van Damme, the anime didn't have to try for a younger audience by cutting out the fights, nor was it limited by some cast members without any martial arts experience—the fights in *SFII* were coordinated by real-life fight choreographer Shinichi Shoji and, since this is animated, every one's superb.

The derivative plot is a cunning conceit to gain as much of the feel of the game as possible without wasting too much time. Stealing from *Enter the Dragon* (1973), *SFII* maneuvers its characters into a set of standoffs engineered through a fighting contest and the idea that several of them are working as secret agents or in law enforcement. It also adds two elements that would become staples of fighting-game

Street Fighter II V

adaptations—a mind-control subplot to orchestrate fights between supposed allies, and a shower scene to showcase a female character in the nude.

Characters' billing comes partly determined by their popularity among fans and partly from their seniority. The American Ken and Japanese Ryu are two characters from the first game (1987), and the two gave the filmmakers the chance to have a male American in distress getting rescued by a hunky Japanese guy. Chun-Li and Guile (Interpol agents in the anime) were popular characters from the *SFII* game (1991), while Cammy's cameo role (as a brainwashed assassin) was largely determined by her standing with fans. Though a relative latecomer in *Super SFII* (1993), she gets to climb further up the billing by virtue of being a girl. The other characters get a chance to show their special moves in various bouts, but most of the film belongs to this central cast. Each featured character gets an obligatory rumble, but Sugii creates moments of genuine drama, most notably in a marvelously choreographed fight between Chun Li and Balrog (Vega), enhancing the tension with most of the

violence offscreen or in partial shot. As in the game, the bad guys' names have been confusingly shuffled for legal reasons—M(ike) Bison, originally the name of the big African-American boxer character, was assigned to the supreme baddie in the Western release, while M. Bison's name is changed to Balrog, and Balrog's to Vega. The anime feature was resurrected for a *game* called *Street Fighter II Movie* (1996), which combined a normal *SFII*-style game with a semi-interactive version of the film, utilizing footage from the anime. This variant also included a few scenes of bridging animation not found in the bona fide anime release.

The TV series *Streetfighter II V* (1995) serves as a prequel to the game, in which teen versions of Ryu and Ken are trounced by a young Guile and set off on an around-the-world trip to learn from "the best of the best." Though there is a heroic effort to introduce deeper backstories for the kung-fu clotheshorses of the game (Chun Li is a young Hong Kong tour guide, Fei Long is an action film star, etc.), the TV series is undistinguished, and even Sugii's direction rarely rises above the barely necessary. Matters

Street Fighter Alpha

© 1999 CAPCOM/POLYDOR, MANGA ENTERTAINMENT, INC.

are not helped by an English dub that persistently mispronounces "Ryu" throughout—an achievement roughly equivalent to dubbing *Star Wars* with Han *Sulu*. However, amid the relatively undemanding audience of fighting-game fans, the TV series could be considered a success—it certainly outlasted many of its more "popular" contemporaries.

A final incarnation of the franchise was the two-part video series *SF Zero* (1999, renamed *SF Alpha* in the West, like its game incarnation). With a new director and scenarist better known for **Boys Over Flowers**, *Zero* keeps the "early years" aspect of the TV series, focusing on an even younger audience by introducing the game's popular schoolgirl fighter Sakura, as well as Ryu's previously unmentioned brother, Shun, who arrives from Brazil. Somewhat cynically dumping the previous continuity (Chun Li and Ryu meet for the first time, *again*, as if the producers do not expect any of the original audience to still be watching), *Zero* runs through a predictable set of clichés, as Ryu discovers his father's evil

secret, is tempted by the dark side, and avenges the death of his teacher. *Zero* was partly funded by U.S. distributor Manga Entertainment, which edited it into a single feature-length edition in the expectation it would do as well as its predecessor. But while it often matches the kinetic action of its illustrious ancestor, complete with some good backgrounds, after half a decade of inferior copies of the original *SFII* movie, *Zero* simply looks like just another one. *Street Fighter II Ryu vs. Yomigaeru Fujiwara Kyo* (2004) was a manga boxed set featuring a complete run of Masaomi Kanzaki's manga and a 23-minute anime exclusive in which Ryu, Ken, Chun Li, and E. Honda are transported back in time. *Street Fighter Alpha Generations* (*Street Fighter Zero 2*, 2005) is a 50-minute video in which Ryu returns to the site of his education to pay homage to the spirit of his dead mentor, only to be tormented by the memory of his master's death and his desire to wreak revenge on his arch-rival, Goki. **Ⓥ**

STUDENT COUNCIL ALMIGHTY
2005. JPN: *Gokujo Seitokai*. AKA:

Best Student Council. TV series. DIR: Yoshiaki Iwasaki. SCR: Yosuke Kuroda. DES: Tsuyoshi Kawada. ANI: Tsuyoshi Kawada. MUS: Yoko Shimomura. PRD: JC Staff, Konami. 24 mins. x 26 eps. Orphan schoolgirl Rino is clearly losing it—her best friend is a hand puppet, albeit a self-aware one for as long as he is installed. She transfers to a new school, the all-girl Miyagami Academy, only to discover on her first day that her lodgings have burned down. She manages to apprehend the arsonist, and is hence invited onto the influential student council.

A touch of politics arrives in the everyday school anime genre, in a show that concentrates, not on classes, but on their class representatives. Often portrayed in other anime as the dull class grinds always sucking up to the teachers, these hall monitors and council reps are presented here as the heroes—with something of a debt to the satirical Reese Witherspoon vehicle *Election* (1999).

STUDIO DEEN
Formed in 1975 by a group of colorists from Sunrise, the studio took its name from **Brave Raideen**, the first of the Sunrise shows on which it worked. It gained an Osaka regional subsidiary in 1991 and a Chinese subsidiary in 1994, thereby allowing it to cut costs on animation during the impecunious mid-1990s. The studio continues to enjoy a close relationship with the company that supposedly spawned it and can often be found on the credit listings of Sunrise anime. Notable works as a leading animation partner include **Diamond Daydreams**, **Fruits Basket**, and the **Patlabor** videos.

STUDIO FANTASIA
Formed in 1983 by former staffers from Tsuchida Production, Studio Fantasia appears to have been intended as a liability shield for what turned out to be the lucrative new world of straight-to-video animation. Its early works included stints on **Cream Lemon** and later installments of **Project A-**

KO, establishing a reputation for "fan service"—wholly gratuitous nudity or quasi-nudity—that has made it a popular studio to this day, and led to the ludicrously unsubtle **AGENT AIKA** and **NAJICA**.

STUDIO 4°C
Sometimes Studio Yondo Shii. Formed by a group that includes former Studio Ghibli and Nippon Animation employee Kyoko Tanaka and animator Koji Morimoto. Particularly prominent in anime that integrate digital animation, notably **SPRIGGAN** and **STEAMBOY**, but also found in such fluff as **TWEENY WITCHES**. The studio primarily focuses on producing experimental and postmodern animation shorts including its *Sweat Punch* shorts, segments of **THE ANIMATRIX** segments, **NOISEMAN**, and music videos for Glay, Ayumi Hamasaki, and Hikaru Utada.

STUDIO GALLOP
A smaller animation studio founded in 1979 by a former employee of Tokyo Animation Film. Its first conspicuous role was on **AUNTIE SPOON**, and it continues today on productions such as **TRANSFORMERS** and **YUGI-OH**.

STUDIO GHIBLI
Formed in 1985 by Tokuma Shoten for Hayao Miyazaki and Isao Takahata, and initially mostly staffed by former employees of Topcraft (q.v.), Ghibli's first notable work was on Miyazaki's **CASTLE IN THE SKY**. It has subsequently produced many of the most popular and acclaimed anime of the last 20 years, including **MY NEIGHBOR TOTORO**, **GRAVE OF THE FIREFLIES**, and **KIKI'S DELIVERY SERVICE**. Notable members include Hayao Miyazaki and Isao Takahata, and producer Toshio Suzuki, a former editor of Tokuma's *Animage* magazine, whose contacts ensure that the publication continues to get Ghibli-related exclusives. Ghibli became nominally independent of its parent company in 1992, but merged with Tokuma in 1997, after a deal struck the previous year with Disney to distribute Ghibli

titles outside Japan—technically, it is now known as the Studio Ghibli Company. The most conspicuous effect was the higher profile distribution of **PRINCESS MONONOKE** in the United States. Miyazaki's next film, **SPIRITED AWAY**, was the first anime to win a Best Feature Animation Oscar. The studio became fully independent from Tokuma once more in 2005. As the founder generation nears retirement, the studio shows signs of diversifying, Disney-style, into other market sectors peripheral to filmmaking. There is now a Ghibli clothes label and a Ghibli Museum, and in a controversial decision, the studio's **TALES OF EARTHSEA** was directed by Hayao Miyazaki's son Goro, in what appears to have been an attempt to establish the word "Miyazaki" itself as a brand independent of the man who made it famous.

STUDIO LIVE
Founded by Toyoo Ashida in 1976, it became a public limited company in 1994. Notable staffers besides the founder include Kenichi Takeshita, Noriyasu Yamauchi, and Satoshi Nishimura. Production credits range from **BAREFOOT GEN** to **GUYVER**.

STUDIO PIERROT
Founded in 1979 by former employees of Tatsunoko, Pierrot soon acquired a reputation as the creator of the softer side of anime, particularly "magical girl" **PASTEL YUMI**, **CREAMY MAMI**, or **FANCY LALA**, many of which featured character designs by Akemi Takada and Koji Motoyama. Its roster of productions, however, is just as wide as any other company's—reputation aside, it also worked on **HYPER POLICE** and **GTO**. Usually billed today as just plain Pierrot, its modern successes include **EMMA** and **SUGAR SUGAR RUNE**.

STUDIO Z-5
The fifth incarnation of a company that initially went by the name of Studio Z, Z-5 was founded in 1980. Its high profile staffers have included Hajime Kamegaki and Hideyuki Moto-

hashi, and works include **LOVE HINA** and **FIRE FIGHTER DAIGO**.

STUMBLING WITCH DOREMI
1999. JPN: *Ojamajo Doremi*. TV series. DIR: Junichi Sato, Takuya Igarashi, Akinori Yabe. SCR: Reiko Yoshida, Yumi Kageyama, Atsushi Yamatoya, Midori Kuriyama. DES: N/C. ANI: Yoshihiko Umakoshi, Chuji Nakajima. MUS: N/C. PRD: Toei, TV Asahi. 25 mins. x 46+ eps.

Doremi is an average third-grade girl who wishes she could be a witch. She meets Lika, the owner of a magic shop, and correctly guesses that she is a genuine witch. Unfortunately, the lucky guess transforms Lika into a frog, and Doremi can only transform her back by becoming a qualified witch herself. Doremi minds the store with her schoolmates Hazuki and Aiko, beginning her adventures in witchery. This child-oriented variant on **SAILOR MOON** features innovative crayon and watercolor backgrounds in the style of children's books. The third season, which began in 2001, transforms the girls' magic shop into a bakery and introduces a "funny" American, Momoko, who only speaks halting Japanese. The show was created by house pseudonym Izumi Todo, who is also credited with the similar **PRECURE**.

SUBMARINE 707
1996. JPN: *Shinkai no Guntai Submarine 707F*. AKA: *Undersea Fleet Submarine 707F*. Video. DIR: Teruo Kigure, Jiro. SCR: Satoru Ozawa. DES: Masaaki Sudo. ANI: Masaaki Sudo, Teruo Kigure. MUS: N/C. PRD: Knack. 45 mins. x 2 eps.

Investigating a "Bermuda triangle" effect in the Pacific, the damaged submarine 707 is led to a vast undersea cavern by a white whale. 707 rests on the seabed for repairs but sinks beneath it to find the lost undersea empire of Mu (see **SUPER ATRAGON**). Queen Chiaka, ruler of Mu, has been thrown into a conflict with the surface world by bad-guy Red Silver's illegal drilling operations near her kingdom, and the crew of 707 must end the crisis before it destroys the world. An old-fashioned yarn based on Satoru Ozawa's 1963 submarine manga in *Shonen Sunday*, it was revived for the 1990s thanks to the dual influence of the nostalgic "retro" fashion ushered in by **GIANT ROBO** and the new-found popularity of submarine dramas post–**SILENT SERVICE**. A year later, Ozawa's **BLUE SUBMARINE NO. SIX** was also adapted into an anime, with far greater success.

SUBMARINE 707R *
2003. AKA: *Submarine 707 Revolution*. Video. DIR: Shoichi Masuo; Yuichi Wada, Kobun Shizuno. SCR: Hiroshi Onogi. DES: Jun Takagi, Minoru Murao, Kazutaka Miyatake. ANI: Minoru Murao, Nobuaki Nagano. MUS: Hideaki Kobayashi, Tatsuya Kozaki, Wave Master, Yutaka Minobe. PRD: Aniplex, Group TAC, Sony Music Entertainment. 48 mins. x 2 eps.
Under threat from an international terrorist organization, eleven nations form the Peace-Keeping Navy (PKN), only for the evil Admiral Red to crash his submarine into the PKN fleet and almost destroy it at the opening ceremony. Only commander Hayami of the Japanese sub 707R stands between him and victory, leading to a cat-and-mouse game on the high seas.

The submarine genre is understandably limited in its potential, leading elements of *Submarine 707R* to play like innumerable other underwater thrillers, most notably **SILENT SERVICE** and *The Hunt for Red October* (1990). Its clearest parallels, however, are with the criminal mastermind and plucky Japanese supersub of **BLUE SUBMARINE NO. SIX**, whose creator, Satoru Ozawa, also wrote the original 1963 manga of *707R*. *707R* really plays up its retro origins, often looking more like **ASTRO BOY** or **GIGANTOR**, both in its cartoonish design and the deliberate juxtaposition of it with more serious themes—it is worth remarking that where *707R* has an Admiral Red, there is a *Duke* Red in Tezuka's **METROPOLIS**.

Ozawa's work has been cited

by many animators of the modern generation as a prime influence on their obsession with technology and sci-fi. Notable among them is **EVANGELION**-director Hideaki Anno, who is acknowledged here as the director of the opening credit sequence, leading some sources (and unscrupulous foreign distributors) to credit him with direction of the entire series.

SUBMARINE SUPER 99
2003. TV series. DIR: Hiromichi Matano. SCR: Keisuke Fujikawa. DES: Leiji Matsumoto, Katsumi Itabashi, Kichiro Harada. ANI: N/C. MUS: Shinichiro Mizobuchi. PRD: Vega Entertainment, AT-X, Tsuburaya. 25 mins. x 13 eps.
When the genius submarine designer Doctor Oki and his grandson Goro go missing, his other grandson Susumu immediately suspects the worst—that he has been kidnapped by the evil Helmet Party organization before he can spill their secrets to the world. Told that both his grandfather and elder brother are dead in an accident, Susumu sets off in Oki's prototype submarine, number 99. Susumu knows the 99 like the back of his hand, and is soon proving to be a useful addition to the crew. Before long, the crew of the 99 are at odds with the ruling clique of the undersea Ocean Empire, but even their supposed enemies have honorable men among them—faking the destruction of the 99 in order to allow it to escape.

It will come as no surprise to the reader that Dr. Oki and Goro are still alive and are being held prisoner by the ruler of the Ocean Empire, whose name is Hell Deathbird.

Deathbird wants Oki's latest superinvention, a powerful engine, in order to outfit a fleet of supersubs to seize control of the surface world. As in **SUPER ATRAGON**, the menacing "aliens" are actually from within the Earth, in this case a deep trench that leads to an "Underground Sea"—an "Undersea Sea," if you want to split hairs. Their world is under threat from the ever-growing spread of radiation poisoning,

leading Susumu, once reunited with his family, to realize that the inhabitants of the Ocean Empire are not evil but simply misguided and misled by their leaders.

It is with a weary sigh that we note Leiji Matsumoto dusting off his old character designs yet again and reprising the basic plot of **STAR BLAZERS** underwater. The rationale, as ever, is that if something is not broken it should not be fixed, and that children's television is repetitive because it regularly finds itself addressing a completely new audience. That is all very well, but the hype for Matsumoto's work often clings defensively to his past glories, as if expecting more of the audience to be adults revisiting golden childhood memories than children who have never experienced them before. Consequently, this straight swap of new money for old rope is somewhat halfheartedly hyped as being in the "retro style," although even the most forgiving of modern day viewers surely must concede that the end result often seems less like a celebration of a popular creator's work than yet another tired, cynical rehash of it. Compare to **THUNDERSUB**, an earlier title for which Matsumoto plundered his own work, years before many of the target audience for *Submarine Super 99* were even born.

SUBMISSION CENTRAL *
2002. JPN: *Dokusen*. AKA: *Monopoly*. Video. DIR: Mitsuhiro Yoneda. SCR: Rokurota Makabe. DES: Meka Morishige. ANI: Meka Morishige. MUS: Yoshi. PRD: YOUC, Digital Works (Vanilla Series). 20 mins. x 2 eps.
Two boys make an Internet pact to take turns abusing and "training" a pair of kidnapped girls on camera, to be screened for an Internet audience that will later vote on who deserves to keep them. One of their victims, the hapless Tsumugi, does not initially realize that one of her captors is her own boyfriend Kyoshiro. Based on a computer game from "ruf"; another entry in the **VANILLA SERIES**. ⓁⓃⓋ

SUE CAT

1980. TV series. DIR: Takao Yotsuji. SCR: Tsunehisa Ito. DES: Front Publicity. ANI: Shinnosuke Mina. MUS: Akira Ito. PRD: Knack, Tokyo 12 Channel. 15 mins. x 40 eps.

Sue is a suburban Tokyo cat who enjoys climbing up on the roof to scat sing, beating out the rhythm with her tail, hoping that one day she'll become a star singer just like the human vocalists on TV. She talks her way onto the set of the NTV talent show *Who's the Star?* and becomes an overnight celebrity, soon forgetting all about her past life. As her life becomes a whirl of music hits, recording contracts, and product endorsements, she begins to wonder if she has sacrificed her personal life for stardom. As she reminisces about her happy kittenhood, she is found by her sisters, Lan and Miki, who convince her to return home to obscurity.

NTV and Crown Records, both real-life companies, have manufactured starlets before, so it's no surprise that they should do the same with a cat. This silly anthropomorphic "star is born" series was broadcast in double chunks in the Kansai region, and hence is listed as "30 mins. x 20 eps." in some sources. Later, very different satires of the idol-singer's life include PERFECT BLUE and HUMMINGBIRDS, while *Mis Print* (1997) was a much shorter-lived anime series about feline pop stars.

SUEZEN

Pseudonym for Shiro Iida, animator, born in Tokyo and often associated with Tatsunoko Production as a key animator and designer. His name appears on WINGS OF HONNEAMISE and YADAMON, and, so claim Japanese sources, the artist has also worked in secret for foreign studios including Disney and 20th Century Fox, although in what capacity nobody seems willing to say.

SUGAR *

2001. JPN: *Chicchana Yukitsukai Sugar.* AKA: *Cute Snowmancer Sugar; Little Snow Fairy Sugar, A.* TV series. DIR:

Shinichiro Kimura. SCR: Akiko Horii, Seishi Minakami, Tomoyasu Okubo, Yasunori Yamada. DES: Keiko Kawashima. ANI: N/C. MUS: Shinkichi Mitsumune. PRD: TBS, Broccoli, JC STAFF, Kadokawa, Pioneer, BS-i. 25 mins. x 24 eps. (TV1), 24 mins. x 2 eps. (special).

Sugar is a trainee snow fairy who, with her friends Salt and Pepper, aspires to become a season fairy and help to create and control the weather on Earth using special musical instruments. In the town of Muhlenberg (based, after an extensive production crew "research trip," on one of three real-world Rothenburgs in Germany), they enlist the help of human schoolgirl Saga. As a mid-European girl who helps out in her grandmother's coffee shop, Saga has elements of the lead in KIKI'S DELIVERY SERVICE about her, but also happens to be one of the very few humans who can see fairies and who can help them in their quest to find the mythic "Twinkles" that makes flowers grow—compare to BOTTLE FAIRY. The search for Twinkles soon takes second place to other adventures, as the fairies report in to their elderly fairy boss and even, on one occasion, turn to the (cute) dark side when they fall in with a crowd of bad fairies. Later episodes suggest, as subtly and cutely as possible, that Saga is less helping the fairies than they are helping her, as the orphan girl tries to regain ownership of her late mother's piano—an allegory of grief and growing up like the many other imaginary friends found in other anime. Their adventures spun off a two-part TV summer special in 2003, in which Saga reminisces about the good old days. Based on a manga by Haruka Aoi and PITA TEN's Koge Donbo. Relentlessly, criminally cute, but after day upon day of sex and samurai-related anime, a welcome change to anime encyclopedists.

SUGAR SUGAR RUNE

2005. JPN: *Sugar² Rune.* TV series. DIR: Yukihiro Matsushita, Hiroyuki Tomita, Kunitoshi Okajima, Masayuki Matsumoto. SCR: Reiko Yoshida, Mamiko Ike-

da, Tomoko Konparu, Masahiro Okubo. DES: Noriko Otake. ANI: Noriko Otake, Park Sang-jin, Sawako Yamamoto. MUS: Shinkichi Mitsumune. PRD: Studio Pierrot, TV Tokyo. 25 mins. x 29 eps.

Chocola Meilleur and Vanilla "Ice" Mieux (no, really) are two sorceresses from the Magical Realm, each charged with the mission of collecting as much love as possible from the humans they meet, in the form of crystallized hearts that symbolize warm feelings. At stake is the throne of the Magical Realm itself, with the sweet-natured, mild-mannered Vanilla seemingly gaining much more human attention than the plucky redhead Chocola. In other words, another magical girl show revisiting the well-trodden ground of LITTLE WITCH SALLY, although this one appears to have fast-tracked into production thanks to its familial connections—the "original" manga serialized in *Nakayoshi* magazine was created by Moyoko Anno, the wife of EVANGELION-director Hideaki Anno, who guests as an animation director on the opening sequence here. Chocola seems to have gained her name from the Japanese spelling of the French movie *Chocolat* (2000), which has a silent "t," and is hence no relation to Chocula in DON DRACULA. Compare to BEWITCHED AGNÈS, one of many magical-girl shows with which *Sugar Sugar Rune* shared the airwaves in its year of broadcast.

SUGII, GISABURO

1940– . Born in Shizuoka Prefecture, he left school at sixteen and had many jobs, eventually joining Toei Animation in 1958. By 1961, he was working at Mushi Production, where he became a key animator and then director on ASTRO BOY. He left Mushi in 1967 to found Art Fresh with the Dezaki brothers, in which capacity he contributed as a key animator to shows including JOURNEY TO THE WEST and DORORO, on which he was a supervising director. In 1969, he was one of the founding members of Group Tac, although he subsequently went fully freelance in 1985. Although his directorial work incorporates everything from **The Tale of Genji** to **Touch**, arguably his most long-standing influence on the medium is his work on the first **Street-fighter II** movie, which established a series of tropes and traditions for game adaptations that remain much imitated to this day.

SUGIYAMA, TAKU

1937– . Sometimes miscredited as Suguru Sugiyama. Born in Tokyo, he worked as an animator on **Panda and the Magic Serpent**, **Journey to the West**, and **The Littlest Warrior**, while still pursuing his education at night school. He left anime to complete his education, graduating in Western-style art from Musashino College of Fine Arts (now Musashino Art University) in 1962. He returned to anime after graduation, working as an art director and assistant director for Iwanami Films, including a stint on the *Dolphin Prince* (see **Marine Boy**), which was intended to become Japan's first color TV anime. He became a writer and director at Nippon Animation on shows including **Dogtanian and the Three Muskehounds**, **Dororo**, and **Alice in Wonderland**. He is also the author of several books on animation, including *The Anime Handbook, Young Anime Graffiti*, and *A Compendium of TV Anime*.

SUIKODEN *

1993. JPN: *Yokai Seki Suikoden*. AKA: *Demon Century Water Margin, Suikoden: Demon Century*. Video. DIR: Hiroshi Negishi. SCR: Mayori Sekijima. DES: Nobuyuki Tsuru. ANI: Nobuyuki Tsuru. MUS: N/C. PRD: JC Staff. 46 mins. Hotheaded country boy Nobuteru Sugo goes to town when his sister is abducted by an evil gang boss who is trying to buy up land in Shinjuku by blackmail and intimidation. Sugo meets other heroes who help him in his quest: one is a crossdressing martial artist who can disable a man without breaking a fingernail; another a Christian priest who believes in muscular, not to say aggressive, evangelism; and

yet another a psychotic nun who is gentle as a lamb with orphan children but freaks out if anyone catches a glimpse of her tattoo.

Based on a story by **Irresponsible Captain Tylor**–creator Hitoshi Yoshioka that retold Shi Nai-an and Luo Guanzhong's 14th-century Chinese novel *Water Margin* in a sci-fi setting, the final scene reveals that the characters are the reincarnations of the novel's Lin Chung, Hu San-Niang, and company, but this allusion is left unclear in an English dub that appears ignorant of the distant literary origins. Mitsuteru Yokoyama's unrelated 1969 *Water Margin* manga in *Kibo Life* was much more faithful to the original. It was never animated, but several of the characters were lifted wholesale for the later **Giant Robo**. For another rehash of the *Water Margin*, see **Hakkenden**. 🅝🅥

SUKEBAN DEKA *

1991. JPN: *Sukeban Deka*. AKA: *Bad Girl Cop*. Video. DIR: Takeshi Hirota. SCR: Takeshi Hirota. DES: Nobuteru Yuki. ANI: Masahiro Kase. MUS: Takashi Takao. PRD: JH Project, SIDO. 50 mins. x 2 eps.
Former high school tearaway Saki Asamiya soon ends up on the wrong side of the law and is stuck in the slammer just like her wayward mother. She is offered the chance to redeem herself by returning to school as an undercover agent to spy on the Mizuchi sisters' crime ring. It's an offer she can't refuse since it's the only way to gain her mother a reprieve from Death Row. Armed only with a police-issue yo-yo and a very bad attitude, Saki goes back to school and finds herself facing the Mizuchis and their father, a criminal hiding behind a cloak of respectability. As allies she has only a boy so fixated on her that he shaves his head to get her attention and Junko, an innocent young artist whose talents make her a target for one of the sisters.

Played in a deadly serious, deadpan manner that only accentuates its essential silliness, *SD* is an entertaining

one-joke knockabout. Based on a 1976 manga by Shinji Wada in *Hana to Yume* magazine, it was soon co-opted for the male gaze in Hideo Tanaka's live-action TV series the same year. The anime version was released partway through a later series of live-action movie adaptations that also showcased cute young actresses in school uniforms. Ultimately, however, like its female lead, it's too bad to be good, and too good to be bad. After a DVD rerelease of the live-action *Sukeban Deka* series sold a surprising 130,000 copies in 2005, Toei announced that a new live-action movie was in the offing for 2006.

SUKISHO *

2003. JPN: *Suki na Mono wa Suki Dakara Shoganai!!*. AKA: *If I Like Something Then There's Nothing You Can Do, Sukisyo*. TV series. DIR: Haruka Ninomiya. SCR: Mamiko Ikeda. DES: Mami Yamaguchi, Yuzu Tsutae. ANI: Zexcs. MUS: N/C. PRD: Zexcs, Chiba TV. 24 mins. x 12 eps.
Blue-haired, impulsive Sora Hashiba is good looking but goofy. He falls out of a third storey window, goes into the hospital, and emerges with gaps in his memory. He has a new dorm-mate: pink-haired, enigmatic Sunao Fujimori claims to be a childhood friend but Sora can't remember him. As he begins to suspect his accident was no such thing and goes in search of the truth, he also starts to feel dangerously attracted to Sunao. Meanwhile, Sora and Sunao both begin to exhibit darker, hidden personalities, respectively called Yoru and Ran.

This originated as a computer game from Platinum Label, aimed at fans of "boys' love" stories, which spun off into a dozen novels. The anime version supposedly boasts an all-female staff, at least at the top echelons, presumably to assure the fangirls that all the right buttons will be pushed—though since the game seems to have managed this despite the presence of nasty unwelcome men, it seems like unnecessary hype.

SUNNY BOARDINGHOUSE

1987. JPN: *Yo Atari Ryoko*. AKA: *Ray of Sunshine; Staring into the Sun*. TV series, movie. DIR: Hiroko Tokita, Gisaburo Sugii, Satoshi Inoue, Hayato Ikeda, Mitsuru Hongo. SCR: Satoshi Yagi, Michiru Shimada, Tomoko Konparu, Higashi Shimizu, Hiroko Naka. DES: Minoru Maeda. ANI: Yoshihiro Kawamura, Kazuya Takeda, Kazuyuki Okaseko. MUS: Hiroaki Serizawa (TV), Kohei Tanaka (m). PRD: Group Tac, Fuji TV. 25 mins. x 48 eps. (TV), 70 mins. (m).

Kasumi lives in a student hostel run by her aunt while studying and enjoying her other passion, running. Her fiancé, Kazuhiko, is at college in America. As she makes friends in the hostel, one boy, Yusaku, becomes especially close to her. Their friendship develops through comic moments, misunderstandings, and day-to-day events, with Kasumi's betrothal hanging over them like the Sword of Damocles. Based on a 1979 manga by Fumi Yamazaki and Mitsuru Adachi (creator of TOUCH), this is another of Adachi's specialty soap operas with sympathetic female characters, often with a sporting connection and a relationship dilemma. The movie finale *You Were in My Dreams Kasumi* (1988, *Kasumi Yume no Naka Kimi ga Ita*), shown on what must have been a weepy double bill with the KIMAGURE ORANGE ROAD feature, has the tanned Kazuhiko returning from the U.S. to become a motorcycle racer and demanding to marry Kasumi right away. Yusaku tries to keep a low profile, but at the last moment—literally, on the steps of the altar in church—he finally tells her he loves her, and she realizes that she really loves him. Luckily Kazuhiko is a good sport and encourages them to be together. Though credited to Sugii, the bulk of the movie was actually a directorial debut for Kimiharu Ono, Sugii's assistant on TALE OF GENJI.

SUNRISE

Formed as Sotsueisha in 1972 by refugees from the collapse of Mushi Production, rebranded as Nippon Sunrise in 1977 and as Sunrise in 1987. A part of the Bandai group since 1994. Its most famous work remains GUNDAM, but it has also worked on numerous other giant-robot shows, as well as DIRTY PAIR, CITY HUNTER, OUTLAW STAR, and MAI-HIME. It continues to refashion and update the "real robot" tradition, with more recent shows such as GASARAKI. See also Namco-Bandai. The company's most famous "employee" is the nonexistent Hajime Yatate/Yadate, a house pseudonym credited as a creator on various works to ensure that the company owns the intellectual property it generates.

SUNSET GUARDSMAN

1968. JPN: *Yuyake Bancho*. TV series. DIR: Renzo Kinoshita, Yoshiyuki Tomino. SCR: Yoshiaki Yoshida, Shunichi Yukimuro. DES: Renzo Kinoshita. ANI: Renzo Kinoshita, Kazuhiro Okaseko. MUS: Kenjiro Hirose. PRD: Tokyo TV Doga, Nippon TV. 10 mins. x 156 eps.

Tadaharu Akagi is a small but tough boy, transferred to Kiso Junior High, which is infamous for its badly behaved children. He is literally from the wrong side of the tracks—orphaned, he lives with his grandfather in a ramshackle house near the railway. One day at school, two of his classmates ask for his help in dealing with bullies. Though he is a strong fighter, he refuses, until the bullying becomes intolerable and he loses his temper. Samurai ethics at a modern school, as a bold hero resists violence and gets dewy-eyed whenever he sees a sunset.

SUPER ADDICTIVE

1994. JPN: *Cho Kusei ni Nariso*. AKA: *Heart Mark*. TV series. DIR: Tetsuya Endo, Mitsuo Hikabe, Yasuhiro Matsuyama, Yoshiaki Iwasaki. SCR: Yorimichi Nakano, Takeshi Shudo, Tsutomu Nagai. DES: Toshiko Sasaki. ANI: Kazuyoshi Sasaki, Seiji Kikuchi. MUS: Yo Sakamoto. PRD: Studio Sensen, Video Champ, NHK2. 25 mins. x 39 eps.

Idol singer Nagisa Shiratori disguises herself as a boy to attend school, hoping to prove her prowess at fighting and gain applicants for her father's undersubscribed martial arts school. Based on a manga in *Nakayoshi* magazine by Anzu Yoshimura and Yayoi Takano.

SUPER GALS *

2001. JPN: *Super Gals Kotobuki Ran*. TV series. DIR: Tsuneo Kobayashi. SCR: Masashi Kubota. DES: Yoshiko Kuzumoto, Hirohito Tanaka. ANI: Keiichi Ishiguro, Takahiro Kitano. MUS: N/C. PRD: Studio Pierrot, TV Tokyo. 25 mins. X 12+ eps.

Ran Kotobuki is the girliest girl in the fashion-conscious, shopping-crazy Tokyo district of Shibuya, but her parents and elder brother desperately want her to be a police officer like themselves. Based on the manga in *Ribbon* magazine by Miho Fujii.

SUPER ATRAGON *

1995. JPN: *Shin Kaitei Gunkan*. AKA: *New Undersea Battleship*. Video. DIR: Kazuyoshi Katayama, Michio Fukuda. SCR: Nobuaki Kishima. DES: Yoshikazu Yasuhiko, Makoto Kobayashi, Masami Kosone. ANI: N/C. MUS: Masamichi Amano. PRD: Toho. 50 mins. x 2 eps.

In the troubled 1930s, the alien inhabitants of the sunken Pacific kingdom of Mu test the people of Earth by giving them a huge power source and waiting to see if they use it for good or evil. This classic case of bad timing leads to the U.S. and Japan each building a supersubmarine. Consumed with grief over his brother's death at Hiroshima (see BAREFOOT GEN), a gunner on the prototype battlesub Ra disobeys his captain's orders and opens fire on the American sub Liberty. The Ra and the Liberty ram each other and sink, and the Mu experiment is called off for fifty years.

Fast forward to the present, where Mu attack craft are spotted at the north and south poles. The United Nations prepare for battle, unaware that they have no chance of defeating the Mu battleships. Only the Ra itself, lovingly restored in secret by the surviving first mate and his patriotic colleagues, can save the day, captained by the son of the original captain. Go, whose father went missing when he was a small child, is on a UN vessel sent to investigate the Mu weapons and is rescued by the Ra. Needless to say, he is troubled by the thought that the remote, forbidding "captain" may be his missing father, as the Ra takes on its enemy in naval action that recalls both SILENT SERVICE and STAR BLAZERS.

Shunro Oshikawa's original novel *Kaitei Gunkan* (1900) was a militaristic scientific romance, as if Jules Verne's Captain Nemo had decided to wage war on the Western powers in the Pacific. Combined with *Undersea Kingdom* (*Kaitei Okoku*), an unrelated "lost civilization" story by Shigeru Komatsuzaki, it was adapted into Ishiro Honda's live-action *Atragon* (1963, *Kaitei Gunkan*, aka *Atoragan the Flying Supersub*), which featured special effects by Eiji Tsuburaya (see ULTRAMAN) and designs by Komatsuzaki, who was also one of Toho's senior illustrators.

Made in the middle of the retro boom ushered in by GIANT ROBO, the 1995 anime version keeps WWII, but now has to include three generations of the hero's family in the story in order to establish a link with Japan's martial past. As well as supremely Vernean technology like gravity lenses, *SA* injects an ambiguous note of 1990s conspiracy, suggesting that the battle between Terrans and Mu-ites is an accident in communication. Annette, exiled from Mu since the 1940s and prepared to help the Terrans, suggests that the entire conflict is a misunderstanding engendered by Avatar, the unbalanced Earth envoy of the Mu Empire. Sadly, however, none of these questions are answered, since *SA* is left open-ended, with the crew of the Ra preparing to dive beneath the sea and go in search of the Mu Empire itself. This was not in either of the previous versions of the story, and, although a journey to the center of the Earth seems quite fitting, *SA* never made it beyond episode two. Mu (or Lemuria)

is a "lost continent" in the Pacific that was originally suggested as an explanation for the distribution of Polynesians before Thor Heyerdahl's 1947 Kon-Tiki expedition demonstrated that they had probably scattered across the ocean on boats. As Asia's Atlantis, the place appears in many anime, including WHITE WHALE OF MU, SUBMARINE 707, BRAVE RAIDEEN, MARINE EXPRESS, and FIGHT! OSPA.

SUPER BABY

1994. JPN: *Osawaga Super Baby*. Movie. DIR: Junichi Sato. SCR: Junichi Sato. DES: Akira Inagami. ANI: Akira Inagami. MUS: N/C. PRD: Toei. 30 mins.
Kazuyoshi the bratty baby causes trouble for his long-suffering mother and elder sister, though he is often placated by his grandfather's creations—toy animals that can come to life. Then, when that plot idea seems to run out of steam, he transforms into Super Baby to fight crime. One of the few theatrical outings so forgettable as to never get a release on video.

SUPER JETTER

1965. JPN: *Super Jetter Mirai kara Kita Shonen*. AKA: *Super Jetter, the Boy from the Future*. TV series. DIR: N/C. SCR: Ichiro Kanai, Takao Tsutsui, Masao Yamamura, Masaki Tsuji. DES: N/C. ANI: Kiyoshi Onishi. MUS: Takeo Yamashita. PRD: TCJ, Eiken, TBS. 25 mins. x 52 eps.
Time patrolman Jetter comes back from the 30th century in pursuit of the evil criminal Jagger, enlisting the help of pretty contemporary photographer Kaori Mizushima and her friend Professor Nishigoro. He fights crime in our time with three of the professor's inventions—a paralyzer ray, an anti-gravity belt, and a device that can stop time for 30 seconds.

SUPER KUMA-SAN

2003. AKA: *Super Bear*. TV special. DIR: Yukio Kaizawa. SCR: Hiromasa Tani. DES: Daisuke Yoshida. ANI: Daisuke Yoshida, Ayako Kurata, Haruki Miura, Nobuyoshi Hoshikawa. MUS: N/C. PRD:

Toei Animation, Animax. 25 mins.
A large blue bear turns into a superhero to thwart bank robbers, in a one-shot anime based on the script that won the first Animax screenplay contest in 2002. Compare to AZUSA WILL HELP, which won the following year.

SUPER MARIO BROTHERS

1986. JPN: *SMB Peach Hime Kyushutsu Dai Sakusen*. AKA: *SMB: Struggle to Rescue Princess Peach*. Movie. DIR: Masami Hata. SCR: Hideo Takayashiki. DES: Nintendo, Shigeru Miyamoto, Takashi Tezuka. ANI: Maya Matsuyama. MUS: Toshiyuki Kimori. PRD: Nintendo. 60 mins.
Italian plumber Mario is playing a computer game when Princess Peach calls out to him from the screen, begging for help. He dives in to help save her from the evil Turtle tribe, aided by his loyal brother, Luigi. He must head for the game's Mushroom land, there to seek advice from the Mushroom sage. Released on the same day as RUNNING BOY, hence tied in the race to become the first anime based on a video game, *SMB* features the lovable character who first appeared in Nintendo's hit game *Donkey Kong*. A slightly different plot, involving the characters' efforts to save Princess *Daisy* from *dinosaurs*, would form the basis for Rocky Morton's live-action *SMB* (1993), starring Bob Hoskins. The franchise also returned as a short-lived three-part video anime in 1989, pointlessly retelling the fairy tales of MOMOTARO, SNOW WHITE, and *Rumplestiltskin*, but with the cast of the game *Super Mario Brothers 3*. The online Japanese Movie Database also contains a cryptic reference to a 21-minute film called *Super Mario Brothers 2* (1986), written by and starring one Jimmy Kobayashi. However, we have been unable to determine what it is.

SUPER MILK-CHAN *

1998. JPN: *Oh! Super Milk-chan*. TV series. DIR: Hideyuki Tanaka, Yoshio Nitta. SCR: Kiki Shiina. DES: Hideyuki Tanaka. ANI: Atsuko Nakajima. MUS:

N/C. PRD: Pioneer, Fuji TV. 5 mins. x 14 eps. (TV1), 25 mins. x 25 eps. (TV2). This spoof on 1970s spy thrillers and Bond movies has the cute and childlike Milk, a greedy, immoral brat with a passion for sushi, battling invading aliens, toxic monsters, and enemy snipers. After starting life as a short segment in the late-night *Flyer TV* show, Milk's adventures moved up to full half-hour status on satellite, with the same gang of regulars augmented by new characters like ghastly genius Professor Eyepatch. As the new series opens, Milk is holed up in her apartment with her two sidekicks, bottle-shaped and somewhat paranoid robot Tetsuko and little green blob Hanage ("nose hair"), who resembles a particularly cute booger, complete with round eyes, bright pink nose, and stringy black mustache. Milk is beset by creditors and can't pay the rent. After her inept attempt at extortion from the local ant family fails, she is saved by a job offer from the president himself. He wants her to catch a counterfeiter with a Belgian waffle fixation. Visiting Eyepatch, who may have been Tetsuko's creator but now has a new toy, Robodog, a sniffer hound that can detect fakes, our little band sets up a roadside waffle stand to lure the villain into their net.

SUPER PIG *

1994. JPN: *Ai to Yuki no Pig-Girl Tonde Burin*. AKA: *Pig Girl of Love and Justice—Fly Burin*. TV series. DIR: Takayoshi Suzuki, Tatsuya Hirakawa, Masahiro Hosoda, Masahito Kitagawa, Kunihisa Sugishima, Teppei Matsuura. SCR: Minori Ikeno, Tomoko Ishizuka. DES: Hiromi Kato, Masamichi Takano. ANI: Kazuyoshi Sekiyuki, Takao Yamazaki, Kenichi Imaizumi. MUS: Goro Omi. PRD: Nippon Animation, Mainichi Broadcasting (MBS). 25 mins. x 51 eps. Young Karin receives magical powers from a pig. Of all the magical girls, she gets the roughest deal, since instead of transforming her into a curvy, long-legged singing idol or magician, she gets to be the Pig of Justice. Not too happy at first, she buckles down and

makes the best of her new powers. Everyone in town loves their cute little pink hero, and every time she does a good deed, she gets a magic pearl. When she's collected enough, she'll be allowed to choose her own transformation. But her father, a reporter, has sworn to find Pig's true identity. Based on a manga in *Ciao* magazine from Taeko Ikeda and Mari Mori, it's a somewhat original take on the magical-girl genre of LITTLE WITCH SALLY.

SUPER ROBOT GALATT

1984. JPN: *Choriku Robo Galatt*. AKA: *Change Robo Galatt*. TV series. DIR: Takeyuki Kanda, Osamu Sekita, Tetsuro Amino, Mamoru Hamazu, Hiroshi Negishi, Hideki Tonokatsu, Susumu Ishizaki, Shinya Sadamitsu. SCR: Hiroyuki Hoshiyama, Tsunehisa Ito, Yasushi Hirano, Takao Koyama. DES: Toyoo Ashida, Kunio Okawara, Koichi Ohata. ANI: Toyoo Ashida, Hiroshi Watanabe, Megumu Ishiguro. MUS: Masanori Sasaroku. PRD: Sunrise, Fuji TV. 25 mins. x 25 eps. Ceaselessly inventing for 30 years in spite of recriminations and complaints from his neighbors, mad scientist Dr. Kiwi finally cooks up an "expanding super alloy" (see GODAIKIN) by combining scrap iron, sugar, Japanese radish, and boogers. He builds Jamboo, a superchange roboid, to ferry young Michael Marsh to and from school. Michael's associates Patty Pumpkin and Camille Cashmere have their own robots, too. But Jamboo changes into the powerful robot Galatt to fight the minions of the Space Real Estate Company, which plans to parcel Earth up and sell it on the open market. Not one of Sunrise's longer-running robot shows, *SRG* treats giant-robot combat primarily as a topic for gag and parody—compare to PREFECTURAL EARTH DEFENSE FORCE.

SUPER ROBOT WARS

2005. JPN: *Super Robot Wars Origin Generation: The Animation*. Video. DIR: Jun Kawagoe. SCR: Satoru Nishizono. DES: Ryo Tanaka, Yasuhiro Saiki. ANI:

N/C. MUS: JAM Project. PRD: Brains Base. 30 mins. x 3 eps. A series of robots built as an alien defense project cause more trouble than they are worth when they go rogue. Lesser, human-interfaced models go into combat against them—whichever way you want to dress it up, this means robots fighting, again, but this time the reason for the cliché is that this is a spin-off of a series of games, specifically *Super Robot Wars Original Generation*, that were made in a pastiche of the robot shows of the past and featured cameo appearances by many famous anime machines and pilots. So it is not derivative and disposable nonsense, then. However, this story takes place after the second release in the game series and restricts itself to robots and characters specifically created for the game, doubtless for copyright and licensing reasons.

SUPER ZUCAN

1992. JPN: *Midnight Gamble Anime Super Zucan*. TV series. DIR: Junji Nishimura. SCR: N/C. DES: N/C. ANI: N/C. MUS: Haruo Mitsunami. PRD: Kitty Film, Fuji TV. 12 mins. x 42 eps. This late-night mahjong anime using many of the staff from RANMA ½ dredges through the clichés of sporting anime but adds more girls in states of undress. Based on a manga by Sayuki Katayama.

SUPERBOOK: VIDEO BIBLE *

1981. JPN: *Anime Oyako Gekijo*. AKA: *Anime Mother and Child Theater*. TV series. DIR: Masakazu Higuchi, Kenjiro Yoshida, Osamu Sekita, Susumu Ishizaki, Norio Yazawa. SCR: Akiyoshi Sakai, Kiichi Takayama, Tomomi Tsutsui, Kazuo Sato. DES: Akiko Shimomoto, Hajime Fukuoka. ANI: Kenjiro Yoshida, Osamu Sekita. MUS: Masashi Maruyama, Hiro Takada. PRD: Tatsunoko, Production Roots, TV Tokyo. 25 mins. x 26 eps. (TV1), 25 mins. x 52 eps. (TV2), 25 mins. x 26 eps. (TV3). Professor's son Sho (Christopher) and his girlfriend, Azusa (Joy), are cleaning the attic when they discover an

SCRAMBLE WARS © 1992 ARTMIC, TEN LITTLE GALL FORCE © 1988 MOVIC/SONEY M.E.

Super-Deformed Double Feature *

old Bible among the scattered books. A magical "Time Bible," it transports them to the Old Testament era, where they watch the greatest story ever told as it happens around them.

A different take on biblical studies from Tezuka's IN THE BEGINNING, this series was seemingly made to cash in on the Bible's status as a worthy international best-seller rather than through any overt religious impetus. The writers introduced Zenmaijikake (Gizmo), a wind-up crusader toy that is brought to life by the Time Bible, and attempted to involve the children in the stories, though events are predestined, so all they can do is *try* to change them—for example, Eve bites into the apple because Zenmaijikake's clockwork winds down before he can stop her, and, though he shoots up a flare to warn Sho, the children cannot get there in time to stop Adam from taking a bite himself.

Bought for the U.S. market and reedited for the Christian Broadcast Network under the title *Superbook,* by the time the series reached video, its Japanese origins were almost completely occluded, though the voice actors in the English version included many from the cast of SPEED RACER. It was discredited in Christian circles for the introduction of modern charac-

ters—instead of making the original more accessible, it was more likely to confuse its young audience who were disappointed not to find robots and time-travelers in the *real* Bible.

A sequel the following year, *Adventures at Tondera [Flying] House*, kept the same TIME BOKAN–inspired kids-and-robot lineup for another 52 episodes; this time young Gen and female foil Kanna are caught in the rain and find shelter in a Western-style house in the forest. The guardian robot Kandenchin is building a time machine that, when struck by lightning, catapults the group into the past, where they witness further biblical events up to and including the story of Christ (though the Nativity and Resurrection had already been included in the former series). The sequel, *PC Travel Detectives* (1983, aka *Trouble Shooters*), was set five years after their original adventures with the Time Bible, with an older Chris and Joy, accompanied by Chris's younger brother, Hisashi, thrown into the past by a magic computer.

SUPERCAR GATTIGER *

1977. JPN: *Cho Supercar Gattaiger.* TV series. DIR: Yukihiro Takahashi, Tadashi Hosono, Tsutomu Murai. SCR: Michiru Umadori, Sukehiro Tomita, Haruya Yamazaki, Hideharu Iuchi, Hisashi Chiaki. DES: Shiro Yamaguchi (pseudonym for Shiro Murata), Mechaman. ANI: Shiro Yamaguchi (pseudonym for Shiro Murata). MUS: Hiroya Ishikawa. PRD: Eiwa, Tokyo 12 Channel. 25 mins. x 26 eps.

Racing driver Jo Kabuki is abandoned by his mother soon after his birth, and his scientist father dies in strange circumstances when a bomb explodes under his car. Now Jo is a member of the five-man Tiger Team—Hiroki, Ken, Katsumi, and, as in SPEED RACER, a token girl who is the professor's daughter, in this case Sachiyo Tabuchi, daughter of the inventor of the 300-mph Solar Energy engines. When not racing all around the world, the team's supervehicles combine to form

Gattiger, a mighty weapon that fights those of evil intent. Many of their races bring them up against the Demon Empire, whose leader, Emperor Black Demon, is not only Jo's grandfather, but also his father's murderer. Jo's mother, Queen Demon, was compelled to leave her loved ones out of loyalty to her own father. She works to support the Empire's semi-evil schemes (Black Demon only wants to conquer the world to put an end to war, though his assistant, Erich Bergen, has his own sadistic motives), but at moments of extreme danger, she shows up masked and disguised to save her son. Even though she always obeys her father (as a good daughter should), she still protects her child (as a good mother should)—for instance, when ordered to shoot Jo through the heart while Black Demon watches, she uses a tranquilizer instead of a bullet. Much loved by early American fandom for its hilariously over-the-top melodrama, it was based on an original idea by Hitoshi Chiaki and given a limited U.S. broadcast on some local TV stations for the Japanese community. Compare to CYBERFORMULA GPX.

SUPER-DEFORMED DOUBLE FEATURE *

1988. JPN: *Scramble Wars To'Hasshire! Genom Trophy Rally.* AKA: *Scramble Wars Get Going! Race for the Genom Trophy Rally; Scramble Wars; Ten Little Gall Force.* Video. DIR: Kenichi Yatagai, Hiroyuki Fukushima. SCR: N/C. DES: Kenichi Sonoda, Kimitoshi Yamane, Hiroyuki Kitazume. ANI: Toshiko Sasaki. MUS: Takehito Nakazawa. PRD: Artmic, Movic. 67 mins.

GENOM, the malevolent corporation of BUBBLEGUM CRISIS, is sponsoring a road race through the desert to the town of Bangor. "Super-deformed" (i.e., cute and squashed-down) versions of characters from *BGC,* GALL FORCE, GENESIS SURVIVOR GAIARTH, and AD POLICE are all taking part, and they all mean to win. The ensuing mayhem is straight out of *Wacky Races,* parodying the original shows with insane humor. The *GF* gals return in *Ten Little Gall Force*, a 1992 parody in which more super-deformed characters return to the studio to make a documentary about the making of their movie and interact with animated versions of the crew.

The Western release combines the two completely separate Japanese videos of just over half an hour each, linked by their super-deformed art style of characters with heads out of all proportion to their squat, comical bodies. It's pure coincidence that the British release company also had its headquarters in a town called Bangor, though Wales has no deserts at present.

SUPERDIMENSION ROMANESQUE SAMY

1986. JPN: *Chojiku Romanesque Samy Missing 99*. Video. DIR: Seiji Okuda, Hidemi Kama. SCR: Seiji Okuda. DES: Moriyasu Taniguchi, Toru Yoshida. ANI: Yutaka Arai, Moriyasu Taniguchi. MUS: Hideo Goto. PRD: Aubec, Anime R. 59 mins.

The universe created by God is not eternal but can collapse if Satan has his way. Luckily, the forces of good are lined up to save the cosmos. This is all news to average Japanese teenager Samy, who is chased by supernatural pursuers and escapes from them into a place "beyond time." Samy and her friends Tokyo, Silver, and Dews must oppose the might of the evil Noa, with the aid of swords, sorcery, and cybernetic battle-suits. A mixture of **ALICE IN WONDERLAND** and **PLANET BUSTERS**.

SURFSIDE HIGH SCHOOL

1999. TV series. DIR: Nobuyoshi Yoshida, Kenichi Maejima. SCR: N/C. DES: Tsutomu Ishigaki. ANI: N/C. MUS: N/C. PRD: Shogakukan, PolyGram, TBS. 7 mins. x 16 eps.

Late-night lineup of high school surfer dudes who dress like gangsters for TBS's after-midnight series of shorts. Drawn in a hard-edged caricature style, this series of shorts was based on a 1996 *Young Sunday* manga by Ken Sawai and screened as part of the *Wonderful* program.

SURVIVAL IN THE OFFICE

1990. JPN: *OL Kaizo Koza*. AKA: *O(ffice) L(adies) Remodeling Lecture*. Video. DIR: Hajime Ishigaki. SCR: Megumi Hikichi, Hiroshi Hashimoto. DES: Shinobu Arima. ANI: Yasushi Nagaoka. MUS: Michiru Oshima. PRD: TMS. 91 mins.

An Office Lady forgets to make a single photocopy, threatening the very fabric of existence in a Japanese company—or not. She muses on the ways to get through the week, including helpful advice on Goofing Off on Different Weekdays and The Right Thing to Say to Your Boss. Inspired by the column *Drop Dead! Stupid Office Ladies* in *Monthly Gendai* magazine. Released straight to video shortly after the same studio's **OLD MAN'S SURVIVAL GUIDE**, this is not to be confused with Risu Akizuki's manga *Survival in the Office* (*OL Shinka Ron*), which was released in English.

SURVIVAL: NO MAN'S PLANET

2003. JPN: *Mujin Wakusei Survive*. AKA: *Deserted Planet Survive; Uninhabited Planet Survive*. TV series. DIR: Yuichiro Yano. SCR: Shoji Yonemura. DES: Sadaichi Takiguchi, Hisashi Eguchi. ANI: Noriko Hara, Shuji Takahara. MUS: Takefumi Haketa. PRD: Madhouse, Telecom, NHK. 25 mins. x 52 eps.

In the 22nd century, a series of natural disasters on Earth has caused humanity to move away into space and onto colony worlds. Fourteen-year-old Luna has been reared on colony Rocca A2 by her pet/nanny Chako, a pink catlike robot, until she transfers to a new school, Soria Academy. However, her cosseted life is thrown into upheaval during a school trip to Jupiter's moon Io, where their craft is pulled into a giant gravitational storm. Only seven of the pupils make it into the escape pod with Chako and land on a blue planet, complete with monsters, ominously giant footprints, ancient ruins, mysterious voices, and a dwindling water supply. Meanwhile, their rescue ship is hijacked by three escaped prisoners who have no intention of using it to get them home.

Playing like a re-versioning of *Lost*

In Space (1965) or, if you prefer, a foreshadowing of *Lost* (2004) in space, this series even has its own man you love to hate in the form of the clever but selfish school dreamboat Howard, who tries to buy a passage off-planet with the convicts in exchange for spare parts. When he fails, the best hope for the party comes from a mysterious amnesiac boy named Adam, whose people may have left a space vessel somewhere on the planet. Compare also to **ADRIFT IN THE PACIFIC** and its sci-fi reprise **VIFAM**, both of which also marooned school children, although leaving plucky youngsters to find self-reliance is a staple of most anime aimed at a teenage audience—see **GUNDAM**. Some may also detect a few parallels with *They Were Eleven* (*DE).

This adventure series should not be confused with *Survival 2.7D*, a five-minute music video for Japanese pop group Glay, directed and designed by Koji Morimoto and animated and produced by Studio 4°C in 2004.

SUSIE AND MARVIE

1999. JPN: *Susie to Marvie*. TV series. DIR: Shinya Sadamitsu, Scott Frazier. SCR: Noma Sabear. DES: Sonomi Makino. ANI: Nobuyoshi Habara. MUS: N/C. PRD: ShoPro, Xebec, NHK. 4 mins. x 104 eps.

Ten-year-old Susie is a daydreamer, while her one-year-old brother, Marvie, is a mischievous scatterbrain. They like to play with their neighbor Aunt Nana, and her lovable golden retriever, Hana. They also like to play with Professor Peabney, a dachshund inventor with a remarkable resemblance to *Rocky and Bullwinkle*'s Professor Peabody. In the style of **DORAEMON**, the professor's inventions never quite go according to plan. These happy-go-lucky playtime adventures in a 1950s style were based on the 1994 manga by Noma Sabear serialized in *Sunshine* magazine.

SUZUKI, TOSHIMICHI

?– . Anime producer and founder of the Artmic studio, whose credits only show up on a limited number of video anime produced in a brief period between the mid-1980s and early 1990s. Since this straddled the post-AKIRA period where many in Western fandom discovered anime, Suzuki's works gained great attention—particularly BUBBLEGUM CRISIS, RIDING BEAN, and GALL FORCE. However, Artmic soon faced financial difficulties, leading to an exodus of creators and licenses that still has repercussions today. Some titles were abandoned mid-story, others picked up later under slightly different names and continuities. This confusion has even affected rights deals—the authors recall several occasions when rival companies have both believed themselves to be the sole sales agent for former Artmic products. Artmic licenses now largely reside with former coproduction partners Youmex and AIC—hence the remake *Bubblegum Crisis 2040*, on which Suzuki has a credit for being the "original creator," not for direct involvement with the actual production.

SUZUKI, TOSHIO

1948– . Born in Nagoya, Suzuki found employment at the publisher Tokuma Shoten shortly after graduating in literature from university—where, at age 18, he read the novel of GRAVE OF THE FIREFLIES and resolved one day to make a movie of it. After initial work on the magazine *Asahi Geino* ("Asahi Arts"), he became the editor of *Animage* magazine in 1978, in which capacity he commissioned Hayao Miyazaki's manga version of what was then a failed movie pitch—NAUSICAÄ OF THE VALLEY OF WIND. After assuring Miyazaki that he would not turn it into an anime, Suzuki subsequently talked his friend around. Suzuki is also credited with gaining a decent distribution deal for MY NEIGHBOR TOTORO. Formally joining Studio Ghibli in 1991, Suzuki produced many movies for the company, as well as GHOST IN THE SHELL: *Innocence* for Mamoru Oshii, joining it in mid-production, at the same time as he was producing HOWL'S MOVING CASTLE. Suzuki is also believed to be the author of the stern noninter-

ference policy that prevented Buena Vista from bowdlerizing Ghibli movies for an American audience, famously sending a sword to his fellow producer Harvey Weinstein with the message attached: "No Cuts."

SWALLOWTAIL INN *

2003. JPN: *Ryokan Shirasagi*. AKA: *White Heron Inn*. Video. DIR: Juhachi Minamizawa. SCR: Joichi Michigami. DES: Dodoitsu, Tatsuya. ANI: Hanya. MUS: Hiroaki Sano, Takeshi Nishizawa, Sentaro. PRD: Discovery, AT-2 Project. 30 mins. x 2 eps.
When the owner of a traditional Japanese inn dies, the only way his widow Yuriko Shiratori can keep the inn going is by offering sexual services to selected guests, though even this scheme seems to fail due to her lack of skill. When a vagrant with memory loss is found wandering in the woods, kindhearted Yuriko takes him in, names him Kenji, and employs him to help out with odd jobs. Evidently his memory hasn't completely disappeared, as he is a good chef and has other hidden talents. He soon picks up on the specialty of the house, and offers Yuriko some tuition in unusual techniques to increase their income by improving the services they offer to their customers. Yuriko's husband's energetic younger sister Fuyuka soon arrives, and after mistaking Kenji for one of the special customers, pitches in to help with the guest parties. Her performance is disappointing and she also receives Kenji's special tutoring as they work toward the inn's profitability. Pretty visuals are unfortunately often marred by off-model characters, as well as a varying level of detail, but a resemblance to the female lead in AI YORI AOSHI may interest connoisseurs of the genre. For us, it's sadly refreshing to find a porn anime where most of the sex is between consenting adults. Another entry in the DISCOVERY SERIES, based on a game by Speed.🅒🅝

SWAN LAKE *

1981. JPN: *Hakudori no Mizuumi*.

Movie. DIR: Kimio Yabuki. SCR: Hirokazu Fuse. DES: N/C. ANI: Takuo Noda, Hiroshi Wagatsuma, Shunji Saita, Takashi Abe. MUS: Peter Tchaikovsky. PRD: Toei. 75 mins.
Princess Odette is bewitched by the wicked magician Rothbart; by day she is a swan, by night a girl. Prince Siegfried sees her transformation and falls in love with her. He vows to break the spell and save the princess, but the spell may only be broken by the man who proclaims his undying love for her. At a ball, Siegfried dances with several girls, eventually finding the one whom he assumes to be Odette. Proclaiming his love, he discovers too late that it is Odile, Rothbart's daughter, breaking Odette's heart. Toei's animated version of Tchaikovsky's 1877 ballet won an award at the 1981 Moscow Film Festival. In a backhanded compliment to its artistic merits, 2,500 cels were stolen during production.

SWEET MINT

1990. JPN: *Maho no Angel Sweet Mint*. AKA: *Magical Angel Sweet Mint*. TV series. DIR: Toshitaro Oba, Norio Takase, Kazuhiro Ozawa. SCR: Takao Koyama, Aya Matsui, Yoshimasa Takahashi, Masaharu Amiya. DES: Toshiyuki Tsuru. ANI: Himiko Ito, Hiroaki Sakurai, Yoshitaka Fujimoto. MUS: Osamu Morizuka. PRD: Ashi Pro, TV Tokyo. 25 mins. x 47 eps.
Another magical-girl series whose sweet heroine has a cute little bluebird as her magical friend and uses a magic compact (harking back to SECRET AKKO-CHAN) that transforms into anything she needs. The compact is a gift from Grandmother Herbe; when 12-year-old Mint opens the lid, the design of a crossbow engraved there actually turns into a bow whose arrow is tipped with a crystal heart. When she fires the arrow, the streaks of light from its facets transform her into a Magical Angel. From the studio that brought you GIGI, Mint has a similar origin—she is really a princess from the land of magic, sent to Earth to bring happiness to humans, taking up residence in the "Happy

Shop" in the little town of Toal so she can carry out her mission.

SWEET SPOT

1991. Video. DIR: Gisaburo Sugii. SCR: N/C. DES: Kiyosuke Eguchi. ANI: Kiyosuke Eguchi. MUS: N/C. PRD: Tomason, Group Tac. 45 mins.

These "amusing" adventures of a golf-crazy Office Lady were based on a manga from *Weekly Spa!* magazine by Yutsuko Chudoji.

SWEET VALERIAN

2004. AKA: *Sweet Valerians.* TV series. DIR: Hiroaki Sakurai. SCR: Sayuri Oba. DES: Yoshiki Yamakawa. ANI: N/C. MUS: Double Oats. PRD: Madhouse, MBS, TBS. 4 mins. x 26 eps.

Stress is a killer in Japan, the country which has a specific word for working oneself to death—*karoshi.* In CLAMP's fictional Ajaran City, a group known as the Stress Team floats over the city spotting those whose stress levels are heading for meltdown and transforming them into monsters. To fight this menace, the "living enigma" Ear Hermit (a huge-eared purple head on legs) is on the lookout for a special team, and he finds it when Kanoko, Kate, and Pop go to take the test for a moped licence. The Hermit ensures that instead they receive a "Valerian Licence" which enables them to transform into Sweet Valerian, defenders of justice in the form of prettily costumed fluffy bunnies—thereby obviating the need for them to have cute mascot sidekicks, since they are *their own* mascot animals. CLAMP's ability to run endless riffs on cute is truly staggering, especially as it is mixed with visual inventiveness, strong character and story skills, and a sense of fun. The style of this short series is flat, bright, and colorful, with a happy 1960s vibe, and the addition of elements like a whole UFO full of cute aliens and a talking mobile phone with a bad attitude only confirms our long held view that whatever CLAMP are on, we'd like some. In the real world, the herb valerian is supposedly a stress retriever. Note that

Sword for Truth

© 1990 TAKESHI NARUMI/PROMISE CO., TOEI VIDEO CO., LTD.

some of the episodes were not initially broadcast on television, although it is unlikely that this minor snub would have been something that CLAMP got stressed about.

SWIMMY

1991. JPN: *Ganbare Swimmy.* AKA: *Go for It, Swimmy!.* Movie. DIR: Hidetoshi Omori. SCR: Hideharu Iguchi. DES: Hidetoshi Omori. ANI: Hidetoshi Omori. MUS: Hideo Sato. PRD: OH Productions. 26 mins.

Swimmy, a black fish born into a shoal of red fish, tries to fit in amid adventures as he is chased by tuna and must evade the Great Octopus. Originally based on a children's picture book.

SWISS FAMILY ROBINSON *

1981. JPN: *Kazoku Robinson Hyoryuki: Fushigi na Shima no Flowne.* AKA: *Swiss Family Robinson: Mysterious Island of Flowne.* TV series. DIR: Yoshio Kuroda, Seiji Okuda, Michiyo Sakurai, Shigeo Koshi, Fumio Kurokawa, Hideo Fukuzawa, Fumio Ikeno, Takayoshi Suzuki, Taku Sugiyama. SCR: Shozo Matsuda. DES: Shuichi Seki. ANI: Michiyo Sakurai, Koichi Murata. MUS: Koichi Sakata. PRD: Nippon Animation, Fuji TV. 25 mins. x 50 eps.

The Robinsons leave Switzerland for Australia, but shipwreck strands them alone on a Pacific island. Gradually they build a home and a life there, but then find they are not alone—an old sailor and a young aborigine are also on the island. Helped by their new friends, they build a raft to try and reach Australia. One of Nippon Animation's WORLD MASTERPIECE THEATER series, this retelling of Johann David Wyss's 19th-century shipwreck tale has been adapted for TV and film many times before, but rarely with such charm. A series with moments of real beauty, owing much to Masahiro Ioka's backgrounds. See also SPACE FAMILY CARLVINSON. Dubbed by Saban and broadcast on the Family Channel (later known as Fox Family Channel).

SWORD FOR TRUTH *

1990. JPN: *Shuranosuke Zanmaken.* AKA: *Demon-slaying Sword of Shuranosuke.* Video. DIR: Osamu Dezaki. SCR: Jo Toriumi. DES: Akio Sugino. ANI: Akio Sugino. MUS: Toshiyuki Watanabe. PRD: Toei. 50 mins.

Lone samurai Shuranosuke strolls into 1636 Edo (the capital of Ieyasu, first Tokugawa shogun) and with one swipe of his legendary blade Onimaru, nonchalantly dispatches the giant white tiger that has been terrorizing the citizenry. The tiger is only the first wave of an assault by evil forces using demonic powers to kidnap Princess Mio then swap her for a magical dagger. Shuranosuke agrees to make the exchange but must then get the princess safely past a series of magical traps to return her to her no less treacherous household. But while the enemy has magic on its side, he has his own superb skills and the love of beautiful ninja-thief Orin.

Based on a novel by **YOTODEN**-creator Jo Toriumi, *SfT* oozes style and mystery, with gorgeous art direction by Yukio Abe. However, the limited animation that characterizes Dezaki's direction (e.g., **BLACK JACK**) lets it down—though optioned by Manga Entertainment in the hope it would be another **NINJA SCROLL**, it is nowhere near as good. To add insult to injury, the anime was infamously advertised with the fiendishly inaccurate line, "Ancient feudal Japan was ruled by clans of shoguns." A live-action version, *Legend of the Devil* (1998), directed by Masaru Tsushima and starring the incandescently gorgeous Masaki Kyomoto as Shuranosuke, contains more of our hero's story than *SfT*, and retains plenty of the sex scenes, but has less convincing supernatural perils. **NV**

SWORD OF MUSASHI

1985. JPN: *Musashi no Ken*. AKA: *Sword of Musashi*. TV series. DIR: Toshio Kadota, Katsumi Minoguchi, Masamune Ochiai, Yuji Asada, Akinori Yabe, Hideki Tonokatsu, Kazutoshi Kobayashi, Kenjiro Yoshida. SCR: Masaru Yamamoto, Haruya Yamazaki. DES:

Motoka Murakami. ANI: Makoto Kuniyoshi. MUS: Hidemi Sakashita. PRD: Eiken, TV Tokyo. 25 mins. x 72 eps. (TV1), 25 mins. x 72 eps. (TV2).

Born on the same day as Japan's legendary "Sword Saint" and named after him, too, the young Natsuki Musashi hopes one day to become as good with a sword as his famous namesake. Training hard at kendo at his home in Iwate, he is devastated by his father's death and transfers to a new dojo. There, however, he encounters not only new challenges, but also the bitter enmity of a new rival. Based on a manga by **SEIZE THE WIND**–creator Motoka Murakami in *Shonen Sunday*, *SoM* was rebranded after episode 49 as *SoM: The Teen Years* (1986, *Seishun-hen*), featuring Musashi's ongoing feuds with rival "samurai" from neighboring high schools. All set in the present day, this mixture of the clichés of sports anime and samurai period drama drew its inspiration from the life of Musashi Miyamoto (see **YOUNG MIYAMOTO MUSASHI**).

SWORD OF THE DESTROYER

1992. JPN: *Hayo no Ken*. AKA: *Sword of the Destructive Phantom*. Video. DIR: Setsuko Shibunnoichi, Shinichiro Kimura. SCR: Kazumi Koide. DES: Yukari Kobayashi. ANI: Yukari Kobayashi. MUS: Makihiko Araki. PRD: Magic Bus. 30 mins. x 2 eps.

Heroic fantasy in the ancient kingdom of Gandia, as the Fairy and Human realms choose their Princess of the Red Lotus, the only one who may wield the Sword of the Destroyer. Lots of Talking With Capital Letters, as battle-maid Raethril takes on the minions of the Prince of Darkness, rather unfortunately named Redial.

Based on a best-selling novel by Shuko Maeda. **V**

SYMPHONY DREAM STORY

1985. JPN: *Symphony Yume Monogatari*. Video. DIR: Dojiro, Satoshi Harada, Yutaka Kuramoto. SCR: Gokiburi, Yuka Kurokawa. DES: N/C. ANI: N/C. MUS: N/C. PRD: Nippon Soft System. 75 mins.

Three short pornographic tales in the tradition of **CREAM LEMON**: *Shining May*, in which an idol singer takes to the spotlight in more ways than one; *Telepathist Love Q315*, in which Earth can only be saved from alien invaders by the nubile bodies of young telepaths; and, finally, *Barefoot after Class*, in which two school girls find something else to do with each other beyond helping with their homework. Supposedly "humorous." **N**

SYNAPI *

2001. Movie. DIR: Bak Ikeda. SCR: Bak Ikeda. DES: Bak Ikeda. ANI: N/C. MUS: N/C. PRD: Genome Entertainment Inc., Imagica Entertainment Inc. 5 mins.

This CG short about "the essence of communication" features a faceless female character who is desperately trying to communicate with the unseen hordes rushing around her and tries various ways to make contact. Shown at the Yubari International Fantastic Film Festival and New York's FantAsia film festival in 2001, it went on the festival circuit to worldwide acclaim. See also Ikeda's similar **PINMEN**. Not to be confused with *Schnappi the Little Crocodile*, a German cartoon character whose name romanizes in the same way when moved into Japanese letters.

T

TABOO CHARMING MOTHER *
2003. JPN: *Enbo.* AKA: *Captivating/ Charming Mother; Erotic Heart Mother.* Video. DIR: Kan Fukumoto. SCR: Chiho Hananoki. DES: Tsuzuru Miyabi. ANI: Yuji Uchida, Kan Fukumoto, Shigenori Imoto. MUS: N/C. PRD: Big Wing, Milky, Museum Pictures. 30 mins. x 6 eps.
Only a year after marrying a significantly older man, Misako already feels that she is in a rut. Her stepson Kazuhiko treats her with distant disdain, and she hasn't had sex with husband Yosuke for two whole months. Initially, she is insulted and appalled by nuisance phone calls, although as time goes by, her frustrations in her private life cause her almost to welcome them. Over the course of several calls, her stalker talks her into using a sex toy he has left by her front gate in exchange for stopping the calls. Despite his telephonic absence, she begins using it obsessively—and even acquires another—unable to control her lust. When he telephones again, he persuades her to confess her fantasies. As time passes, it almost seems as if her life is improved by her illicit interludes of semi-forced onanism and phone sex—even her stepson seems to warm to her and addresses her at one point as "Mom." The identity of her caller is initially unclear, although considering the *Scooby Doo* size of the list of potential suspects, it shouldn't take anyone long to work out who it is. Later episodes introduce Misako's sister, Emiko, who

is drawn into the maelstrom. Within the limited demands of anime porn, *TCM* is an intriguing title, much longer than the norm, and consequently able to stretch its suspense and sex scenes over several episodes. This is probably due at least in part to the size of the adult manga by Tsuzuru Miyabi that inspired it; compare to U-jin's **SAKURA DIARIES**. **LN**

TA-CHAN KING OF THE JUNGLE
1994. JPN: *Jungle no Osama Ta-chan.* TV series. DIR: Hitoshi Nanba, Akitaro Daichi, Shigeru Ueda, Teppei Matsuura, Takaaki Ishiyama. SCR: Jinzo Toriumi, Akihiro Arashima, Satoshi Fujimoto, Toshiyuki Otaki, Takeshi Ito. DES: Hiroka Kudo. ANI: Shigeru Kato, Chuji Nakajima, Kiyoshi Matsumoto, Masahiko Murata. MUS: Masatake Yamada. PRD: Amuse, TV Tokyo. 25 mins. x 50 eps.
A muscle-bound man in a loincloth fights evil kung-fu masters and vampires in darkest Africa. Though distantly inspired by Edgar Rice Burroughs's *Tarzan of the Apes* (1912), this series was filtered through a popular *Shonen Jump* manga by Masaya Tokuhiro.

TACTICAL ROAR
2006. TV series. DIR: Yoshitaka Fujimoto. SCR: Kazuho Hyodo. DES: Takeshi Ito. ANI: Takeshi Ito. MUS: Hikaru Nanase. PRD: Actas, TV Kanagawa. 25 mins. x 13 eps.
In the aftermath of a catastrophic rise

in global sea levels, a token boy heads out pirate hunting in the company of a group of girls, on a Pacific Ocean dominated by a massive, mystery storm.

TACTICS
2004. TV series DIR: Hiroshi Watanabe, Kazuhiko Inoue, Chiaki Ima, Shigeru Ueda. SCR: Kenichi Kanemaki, Hiroyuki Kawasaki, Katsuhiko Takayama, Masashi Kubota. DES: Mariko Oka. ANI: Mariko Oka. MUS: Kei Haneoka. PRD: Medianet, MAG Garden, Studio Deen, TV Tokyo. 24 mins. x 25 eps.
Scholar Kantaro Ichinomiya researches folklore by day and goes ghostbusting by night in the manner of **MUSHISHI**. Hunting for an ogre-eating goblin, he releases a different kind of man-eater—hunky goblin Haruka, sealed inside a shrine and now out to form a very unusual monster-busting partnership with Kantaro. Kantaro's cute fox-spirit housekeeper Yoko doesn't approve of Haruka and Kantaro's partnership at first; nor does green blob Mu-chan, married to white goblin Sugino but carrying a torch for Kantaro. Based on the manga in *Comic Blade* by Sakura Kinoshita and Kazuko Higashiyama, this anime adaption adds a new character created specifically for TV—schoolgirl Suzu Edogawa falls for Haruka on sight. An old-time harem of spirits is a twist on the familiar theme geek-gets-girls, and this has more charm than the usual.

TAIL OF TWO SISTERS *
1999. JPN: *Sister's Rondo: Charm Point 1.* Video. DIR: Yoshimaro Otsubo. SCR: Tedokoro Imaike. DES: Maron Kurase. ANI: N/C. MUS: N/C. PRD: Beam Entertainment, Akatonbo. 30 mins.
In this typical tale of anime abuse replaying the vengeful student/teacher setup from ADVENTURE KID, new teacher Serina Kawano strikes up a very strange relationship with her pupil Masaya, submitting to his sadistic demands. Meanwhile, Serina's little sister, Yumi, is having boyfriend "troubles" of her own and doesn't understand how to keep her man. Needless to say, Serina has some advice for her. Not to be confused with the Korean horror movie, *Tale* [sic] *of Two Sisters* (2003). **N**

TAIMAN BLUES
1987. Video. DIR: Tetsu Dezaki. SCR: Machiko Kondo. DES: Yukari Kobayashi. ANI: Yukari Kobayashi. MUS: N/C. PRD: Magic Bus. 30 mins. x 5 eps.
A series grouping together two different stories linked by the biker theme. The three-part *Naoto Shimizu Chapter* is a tale of rivalry between two gangs, MND and Laku, and the personal vendetta between MND's Naoto and Laku's Yota, which lands Naoto in prison in the second (1988) episode. The third part of his story, his life after prison, was released in 1989. *Lady's Chapter* (1990) is devoted to a different set of characters, this time focusing on biker girls. Fifteen-year-old Mayumi has to move to the rough end of Osaka when her parents split and remarry. She meets Noriko, who helps her settle into her new life, and eventually moves in with her. Through Noriko's job at a petrol station, they get to know regular customer Big Bear and his biker gang, and eventually get into their own gang of girl racers. Based on a manga by Yu Furusawa.

TAITO ROAD
1996. JPN: *Shinken Densetsu Taito Road.* AKA: *True Fighting Legend Taito Road.* TV series. DIR: Tatsuo Misawa. SCR: Kenichi Kanemaki, Kazuhiko

Kobe, Yoshihiko Tomizawa. DES: Michio Fukuda. ANI: Masahiro Masai. MUS: Koji Tsunoda. PRD: Toei, TV Tokyo. 25 mins. x 13 eps.
In a lackluster picaresque that tries to cash in on the successful STREET FIGHTER II franchise, a young man sets out to fight lots of people. **V**

TAKADA, AKEMI
?– . Born in Tokyo, Takada graduated from Tama Art University, and in the same year gained employment at Tatsunoko, where she worked for four years as a character designer on shows such as URUSEI YATSURA, before going freelance. An accomplished illustrator, her anime work includes a soft touch on KIMAGURE ORANGE ROAD and CREAMY MAMI, although she is perhaps best known for her membership in the Headgear collective and the key role she played with husband Kazunori Ito in the creation of PATLABOR.

TAKAHASHI, KATSUO
1932– . Born in Nagasaki, Takahashi grew up in Korea, which was a Japanese colony at the time. He was repatriated in 1945, and studied drama, film, and puppetry for four years before founding Chuo Productions (now Tokyo Chuo Productions) in 1958, specializing in children's entertainment and puppetry. He also wrote *Children's Education in the Age of Television,* an influential book in early Japanese broadcast media.

TAKAHASHI, RUMIKO
1957– . Born in Niigata Prefecture, Takahashi graduated from the history department of Japan Women's University. She had already been attending a manga workshop and found work as an assistant to Kazuo Umezu. She won a Shogakukan new writers prize in 1977 and went on to create the original manga for URUSEI YATSURA, MAISON IKKOKU, and RANMA ½, three of the defining manga works of the 1980s. She also appears as a "guest" designer on the credits for a few anime, as a design assistant on ADRIFT IN THE PACIF-

IC, and as the designer of a single character in CRUSHER JOE. Subsequently, her role in anime has been limited to that of the author of the manga on which many shows are based, notably the long-running INU YASHA, but also ONE-POUND GOSPEL and MERMAID'S FOREST. Her design credit on MOEYO KEN is for work on the original game on which the anime is based.

TAKAHASHI, RYOSUKE
1943– . Born in Tokyo, Takahashi dropped out of the literature department at Meiji University in order to begin full-time employment at Mushi Production, where he had already been working part-time. He went freelance in 1969, and became supervising director on ZERO TESTER. As a writer and director on VOTOMS, he was a key figure in the move toward the depiction of "realistic robots" (see Okawara, Kunio). He was also a supervising director on the 1979 remake of CYBORG 009, MAMA IS A FOURTH GRADER, and the *Knight of the Iron Dragon* segment in THE COCKPIT.

TAKAHATA, ISAO
1935– . Sometimes credited with the pseudonym Tetsu Takemoto. Born in Mie Prefecture, Takahata graduated from the French literature department of Tokyo University in 1959. Inspired by viewing Paul Grimault's cartoons in his student days, he joined Toei Animation in 1961 and worked on THE LITTLEST WARRIOR and THE LITTLE PRINCE AND THE EIGHT-HEADED DRAGON. His directorial debut came with LITTLE NORSE PRINCE, a financial flop despite critical acclaim, which led to his temporary retreat into television animation. Directorial posts followed at A Production (now Shin'ei Doga) and Zuiyo (now Nippon Animation), where he worked with his protégé and long-time collaborator Hayao Miyazaki on the landmark HEIDI and ANNE OF GREEN GABLES. Moving on to Tokyo Movie Shinsha and then freelance, he entered independent production with Miyazaki on NAUSICAÄ OF THE VALLEY OF

WIND and had a pivotal role in Studio Ghibli, not only directing his own movies, such as the groundbreaking **GRAVE OF THE FIREFLIES** and **POMPOKO**, but serving as producer on many of "Miyazaki's" masterpieces. In any other country, Takahata would be regarded as a national treasure—in an anime industry fixated on the successes of Miyazaki, the quiet achievements of this master filmmaker are often overlooked, despite a career rivaled only in length and achievement by that of Rintaro (q.v.).

TAKAMARU

1991. JPN: *Cho-Bakumatsu Shonen Seiki Takamaru*. AKA: *Super 19th-Century Boy Takamaru*. Video. DIR: Toyoo Ashida, Satoshi Nishimura. SCR: Toyoo Ashida, "Mindanao," Yuichiro Takeda. DES: Toyoo Ashida. ANI: Takahiro Yoshimatsu. MUS: Kohei Tanaka. PRD: JC Staff, Studio Live. 25 mins. x 6 eps.
Set in the world of the Champion Kingdom, an imaginary island whose inhabitants follow a traditional samurai lifestyle, this is a tale of friendship and courage aimed at preteens. Based on director Ashida's manga in *Animedia* magazine. Compare to **SHINSENGUMI FARCE**.

TAKAYASHIKI, HIDEO

1947– . Born in Iwate Prefecture, Takayashiki dropped out of Toyo University to pursue a career in scriptwriting, including work on **LUPIN III**, **TOMORROW'S JOE**, and the screenplay for the **URUSEI YATSURA** movie *Always My Darling*. He has also written many novelizations, including ones for the anime of **DRAGON QUEST** and **SUKEBAN DEKA**.

TAKE THE X TRAIN

1987. JPN: *X Densha de Iko*. AKA: *Let's Take the X Train*. Video. DIR: Rintaro, Tatsuhiko Urahata. SCR: Rintaro, Yoshio Urasawa. DES: Yoshinori Kanemori. ANI: Yoshinori Kanemori. MUS: Yosuke Yamashita. PRD: Madhouse. 50 mins.
Public-relations man Toru Nishihara is waiting on an underground station platform when he sees a phantom train. Ghosts are about to invade the human world, and Toru is co-opted by a secret military unit that has gathered the world's psychics to hold them off. Toru is threatened and cajoled into taking part, though the phantom train lays waste to the armed forces in a cataclysmic battle. The jazz number "Take the A-Train," whose title inspired Koichi Yamano's original short story, appears at several points in this elegant little chiller and is sung over the closing credits by Akiko Yano.

TAKEGAMI *

1990. JPN: *Ankoku Shinden Takegami*. AKA: *Guardian of Darkness Takegami*. Video. DIR: Osamu Yamazaki. SCR: Osamu Yamazaki. DES: Masami Obari. ANI: Masanori Nishii. MUS: Seiko Nagaoka. PRD: JC Staff. 45 mins. x 3 eps.
The lonely, homely Terumi has a crush on Koichi and sells her soul for beauty, agreeing to be possessed by an ancient dragon lord, who in return will make her more popular at school. Now everywhere she goes she is greeted by hissing cats and wilting flowers. And next time the school bullies come calling, she tears their souls apart. But Koichi has also been possessed, by a "kindly" spirit called Susano, although he (and anyone else who knows their **JAPANESE FOLK TALES**) has his doubts about who the good guys are, as the powerful beings fight an age-old war in modern Tokyo.
Despite a U.S. dub that adds to the suspense by not scrimping on the demonic voice effects, *Takegami* is a derivative tale of violent transformations that sits somewhere between **GUYVER** and **SHUTENDOJI**, with a dose of misogyny and lackluster fight scenes. Compare to **LEGEND OF THE FOUR KINGS** and **DARK MYTH**, which similarly retell ancient myth in a modern setting, but not as an excuse for getting into fights with girls. **OWV**

TAKIZAWA, TOSHIFUMI

1953– . Born in Nagano Prefecture, Takizawa joined Tokyo Animation Film as an animator, soon moving on to Shin'ei Doga. He worked on **CYBORG 009** and had his directorial debut working for Yoshiyuki Tomino on **SPACE RUNAWAY IDEON**. He subsequently went freelance.

TALE OF GENJI *

1987. JPN: *Murasaki Shikibu Genji Monogatari*. AKA: *Murasaki Shikibu's Tale of Genji*. Movie. DIR: Gisaburo Sugii, Kimiharu Ono, Naoto Hashimoto. SCR: Tomomi Tsutsui. DES: Yasuhiro Nakura. ANI: Yasuo Maeda, Masahiko Murata, Masayuki, Yoshiyuki Sadamoto, Minoru Maeda, Mahiro Maeda. MUS: Haruomi Hosono. PRD: Tac, Herald. 110 mins.
Hikaru Genji, son of Japan's Kiritsubo Emperor, is a brilliant and gifted young man stifled by the conventions of Heian court life, which offers no real outlet for his talent and energy except the arts and illicit love affairs. He is also haunted by memories of his mother, Lady Kiritsubo, who died when he was very young. He falls in love with his father's consort, Fujitsubo, but his own wife, Lady Aoi, and another lover, Lady Rokujo, will not give him up. The battle for sole possession of his heart is at the core of this film; despite being fought with courtly grace, it's a vicious and ultimately fatal contest, observed by the child Murasaki Shikibu, an orphan in Genji's care who will later become one of his loves.
Facetiously advertised as a "faithful adaptation" of Murasaki Shikibu's 11th-century novel, *ToG* was commissioned to mark the centenary of the *Asahi Shinbun* newspaper and the minor anniversaries for some of its affiliates. It unsurprisingly ditches most of the 1,000-page original, concentrating on a love triangle that formed just chapters 4–10 out of a total of 54. Though highly compromised by a recognizably modern script featuring several anachronisms of manner and etiquette, it is nevertheless a brave representation of the *spirit* of the original, and it is as stylistically rich as **THE SENSUALIST**. Sometimes, however, its attempt to be

faithful can backfire—most notably in the confusingly "real" predominance of black hair, demonstrating all too well why so many anime prefer to differentiate characters with brighter colors and styles. Director Sugii takes enormous risks with pacing, composition, and narrative flow; he utilizes early computer graphics and live-action footage of flames and cherry blossoms. Many scenes are composed of static shots, and the exquisite delicacy of the imagery is given plenty of time to sink in—this film is *slow*. Heavy with the beauty and mood of a vanished age, the hothouse emotions of the court reflect Genji's own emotional turmoil, somewhat ill-served by a translation and U.S. release that plays up the original's classical credentials but shies from offering any notes on the surviving poetic allusions. However, the true value of *ToG* does not lie in its relation to the original book at all but in its position as one of the small number of available anime that demonstrate the true diversity of the medium. Composer Hosono was one-third of the Yellow Magic Orchestra with Ryuichi Sakamoto and Yukihiro Takahashi. An erotic pastiche, "Bareskin Gen-chan," appeared as one of the stories in the historical porn series *Classical Sex-Zone* (1988).

TALE OF HIKARI
1986. JPN: *Hikari no Densetsu*. TV series. DIR: Tomomi Mochizuki, Shinya Sadamitsu, Toriyasu Furusawa, Tetsuya Komori, Hirotsugu Hamazaki. SCR: Hideki Sonoda, Mayori Sekijima, Asami Watanabe, Yasushi Hirano. DES: Toyoko Hashimoto, Ammonite. ANI: Chuichi Iguchi. MUS: Koji Kawamura. PRD: Tatsunoko, TV Asahi. 30 mins. x 19 eps.
Teenage gymnast Hikari struggles to succeed in bitter rivalry with school supergymnast Diana Groichiva. A typical sports anime in the tradition of AIM FOR THE ACE, the series was taken off the air before finishing the standard 26-episode run despite injecting a contrived romance with a young rock star. Based on the 1985 manga in *Comic Margaret* by Izumi Aso.

TALE OF THE NINJA RYUKEN
1991. JPN: *Ninja Ryuken Den*. Video. DIR: Mamoru Kobe, Minoru Okazaki. SCR: Katsuhiko Nobe. DES: Satoshi Horiuchi. ANI: Satoshi Horiuchi. MUS: Toshiya Okuda. PRD: Studio Juno. 50 mins.
The scene is New York, where bioresearcher Ned Freidman announces a cure for cancer, although there are rumors of strange goings-on—screams are heard from his house, and large crates are transported from there to his laboratory. Modern-day ninja Ryu, along with CIA operative Robert and his team, go to investigate. But Ryu is really the avatar of ancient dragon gods, and this is only another stage in the eternal battle between good and evil.

Based on the video game known in the U.S. as *Ninja Gaiden*, *TNR*'s action is its biggest selling point. The beginning of the story, a running midnight brawl, is fluid and well depicted, with no dialogue, just the sound of footsteps and blade on blade. The characterization can be strange—if presenting feisty game character Irene as quiet and shy seems a contradiction in terms, making her a CIA operative scared to fire a gun is downright silly. There's an underdeveloped romantic subplot, and Robert gets more emphasis than game stars Ryu and Irene, as well as the video's best line, "Men love three things. We love fighting, we love alcohol, and we love women." **Ⓥ**

TALES FOR SLEEPLESS NIGHTS
1992. JPN: *Nemurenu no Chiisana Ohanashi*. AKA: *Small Stories for Sleepless Nights*. Video. DIR: Kimiharu Ono. SCR: Eto Mori. DES: Shinji Nomura. ANI: Shinji Nomura. MUS: Yuko Hara. PRD: Group Tac, Victor Music Production. 33 mins. x 3 eps.
Three videos about cats—*Cat's Best Friend*, *Cat's Adventure*, and *Cat's Christmas*—each containing three smaller stories of feline fun. Based on a 1989 column in *Monthly Kadokawa* magazine by Yuko Hara, better known as the keyboard player/vocalist with the Southern All-Stars.

TALES OF . . . *
1990. JPN: *Konai Shasei*. AKA: *Pictures from High School*. Video. DIR: Toshiyuki Sakurai, Takamasa Ikegami. SCR: Toshiyuki Sakurai. DES: Yuji Moriyama, Kinji Yoshimoto, Satoshi Urushihara. ANI: Yuji Moriyama, Kinji Yoshimoto, Satoshi Urushihara, Satoshi Hirayama. Masamune Ochiai. MUS: Takeshi Yasuda. PRD: Studio Fantasia. 40 mins. x 3 eps.
Barefaced and bawdy anime porn based on short manga from SAKURA DIARIES–creator U-Jin. Broken into several short tableaux, it includes the infamous spoof ULTRAMAN episode where a giant businessman humps skyscrapers until a giant schoolgirl helps him out. It's the one with the naughty nurse looking for a soft spot in a bodybuilder, the college girls who will do absolutely *anything* for a free pizza, and the little match-girl who turns out to be the Ghost of Christmas Porn. Humor is the order of the day, with pastiches of AIM FOR THE ACE and ASTRO BOY—U-Jin isn't afraid to laugh at himself, and at other dirty old men. His male characters are pathetic, hormonal losers in thrall to capricious little minxes. Everybody is desperate for sex, although, in a refreshing change from the rape fantasies that characterize so much anime porn, everybody has a good time. Strangely, the U.S. distributors have switched the running order, so that the second Japanese release is actually the first in the translated version. This means that the salaryman we see growing into a giant monster and being destroyed in "Sailor Warrior Akko" is inexplicably brought back from the dead for his cameo role on the train in "Lusty Long-Distance Commute." But since this anime is still on sale in Japan 11 years after its original release, whereas lesser erotica are swiftly deleted, such minor continuity bloopers are unlikely to put off the U.S. audience. Released in America as *Tales of Misbehavior, Tales of Titillation*, and *Tales of Sintillation*. The unrelated *Tales of Seduction* was a 2004 retitling of the anime filed in this book as U-JIN BRAND. **Ⓝ**

TALES OF EARTHSEA *

2006. JPN: *Gedo Senki*. AKA: *Ged's Chronicle; Wizard of Earthsea*. Movie. DIR: Goro Miyazaki. SCR: Goro Miyazaki, Keiko Tanba. DES: N/C. ANI: N/C. MUS: Tamiya Terashima. PRD: Studio Ghibli. ca. 80 mins.

An adaptation of Ursula K. LeGuin's *Earthsea* books, in particular the third volume, *The Farthest Shore*, controversially directed by a man whose former qualifications in the anime world had extended only as far as being the director of the Studio Ghibli museum, and, perhaps more handily, being the son of Hayao Miyazaki. Forthcoming at the time we went to press.

TALES OF ETERNIA *

2001. TV series. DIR: Shigeru Ueda, Takeshi Nagasawa, Satoshi Sato. SCR: Hiroyuki Kawasaki, Satoru Nishizono, Katshuiko Takayama. DES: Akihisa Maeda, Mutsumi Inomata. ANI: Akihisa Maeda, Miko Nakajima. MUS: N/C. PRD: Xebec, Production IG, WOWOW. 25 mins. x 13 eps.

Inferia and Celestia are in the midst of a religious war, which the locals (with the arrogance of religious fanatics everywhere) call the Extreme Light War. As diplomacy breaks down and things get nasty, a young girl meets three teenagers near the borders of Inferia. She is Meldy, a Celestian, and according to her, both countries face a disaster called Grand Fall if they don't stop fighting. 18-year-old Lid Harshel and his 17-year-old friends, Keal Zaibel and Fara Elstead, agree to help her, and together they set off for Belcarnu, legendary isle of everlasting summer, in search of a solution. Based on the PlayStation RPG of the same name, a follow-up to *Tales of Fantasia* and *Tales of Destiny*, the series credits Toshinori Otsuki as "Exclusive Production Director." No, we don't know what that means either.

TALES OF HANS CHRISTIAN ANDERSEN *

1968. JPN: *Andersen Monogatari*. AKA: *Andersen Tales; The World of Hans*

Tales of...

Christian Andersen. Movie, TV series. DIR: Kimio Yabuki (m), Masami Hata, Ichiro Fujita, Taku Sugiyama, Noboru Ishiguro, Makura Saki (pseudonym for Osamu Dezaki), Tetsu Dezaki (TV). SCR: Hisashi Inoue, Morihisa Yamamoto (m), Yoshiaki Yoshida, Shunichi Yukimuro, Eiichi Tachi, Koji Ito, Haruya Yamazaki, Seiji Matsuoka, Takeyuki Kanda, Keisuke Fujikawa. DES: Reiji Koyama (m), Toshihide Takeuchi, Shuichi Seki, Keiichi Makino (TV). ANI: Akira Okuwara (m), Masami Hata. Shuichi Seki (TV). MUS: Seiichiro Uno (both). PRD: Toei (m), Zuiyo (Nippon Animation), Fuji TV. 80 mins. (m), 25 mins. x 52 eps. (TV).

Toei's 1968 movie interweaves the most famous of Andersen's stories into a Disneyesque musical around the tale of young Hans trying to get a ticket for the opera and gradually discovering his talent for telling stories. It focuses particularly on *The Red Shoes* and *The Little Match Girl*. A 73-minute version was dubbed for U.S. release as *The World of Hans Christian Andersen* (1971). Toei would mine Andersen's works for two further movies, LITTLE MERMAID and a version of THUMBELINA in 1978.

The 1971 TV series, also entitled *Andersen Monogatari*, retold many of the best-loved fairy tales collected by the Danish author, some in a single episode and some as an extended tale over several episodes. It employs the framing device of Candy, a girl who wishes to enter the Magic University and must collect 100 cards to do so by performing 100 good deeds—one shudders to think at the uses to which such a concept would be put post-POKÉMON. The large number of different staff members were encouraged to vary their styles (see JAPANESE HISTORY). This led to a wide range of looks and moods (some episodes are lighthearted, some darker) and some interesting stylistic experimentation. Compare to GRIMMS' FAIRY TALES.

TALES OF PHANTASIA

2005. JPN: *Tales of Phantasia: The Animation*. Video. DIR: Takuo Tominaga, Shinjiro Shigeki. SCR: Ryunosuke Kingetsu. DES: Kosuke Fujishima. ANI: Noriyuki Matsutake. MUS: N/C. PRD: Namco, Geneon, Actus, Frontier Works. 30 mins. x 4 eps.

Warrior Cless Alvein is sent back in time to confront Dhaos, an evil sorcerer imprisoned by his parents. He is accompanied by Mint Adnade, a girl who has mastered the arts of healing, and a number of other companions forming an archetypal (dare we suggest, stereotypical) party of adventurers. As the character roster suggests, this is based on a role-playing game, in this case the long-running *Tales...* series that began in 1995 with the Super Famicom (SNES) game of the same name. TALES OF ETERNIA is based on a later game in the same series.

TALES OF YAJIKITA COLLEGE

1991. JPN: *Yajikita Gakuen Dochuki.* Video. DIR: Osamu Yamazaki, Yoshihisa Matsumoto. SCR: Ayumu Watanabe. DES: Minoru Yamazawa. ANI: Minoru Yamazawa. MUS: Nobuhiko Kajiwara. PRD: JC Staff. 40 mins. x 2 eps.
Forbidden love triangles at Mura'ame College, as Junko and Reiko become involved with boys they shouldn't, then discover that they are the last inheritors of the secrets of the ninja. Your average, everyday mix of romance and assassins, based on the 1982 girls' manga in *Bonita* magazine by Ryoko Shito.

TAMA AND FRIENDS *

1994. JPN: *Uchi no Tama Shirimasen ka.* AKA: *Have You Seen/Do You Know My Tama?.* TV series. DIR: Hiroshi Takefuji, Seiko Sayama (TV), Hitoshi Nanba (m). SCR: Masumi Hirayanagi, Shige Sotoyama. DES: N/C. ANI: N/C. MUS: Michiko Yamakawa. PRD: Sony, TBS. 12 mins. x 36 eps. (TV), 40 mins. (m).
Puppies and kittens hang out together in an infants' playground, where they get involved in numerous saccharine adventures. Tama, Doozle, Tiggle, and Momo then "share in fun-filled adventures that impart important social values." The anime was aimed at the very young and marketed in Japan as a kind of "Where's Waldo?"—its posters demanding "Have You Seen My Tama?" That it was optioned and "re-imagined" for broadcast in the U.S. by 4Kids almost makes one wish for the days of tentacle porn once more.

TAMA PRO

An animation house set up by Eiji Tanaka, a former employee of Mushi Production, Tama Pro became a limited company in 1970. It subsequently relocated much of its animation work to studios in China, particularly Shanghai in 1996. The studio also did minor work on foreign productions, such as the straight-to-video *American Tail: Mystery of the Night Monster* (1999).

TAMAGOTCHI VIDEO ADVENTURES *

1997. JPN: *Eiga Tamagotchi Honto no Hanashi.* AKA: *True Tamagotchi Tales.* TV series. DIR: Masami Hata, Mitsuo Hashimoto. SCR: Hideki Mitsui, Narimi Narita. DES: Kenji Watanabe, Hideki Inoue. ANI: Kenji Watanabe. MUS: N/C. PRD: Bandai, Fuji TV. 9 mins. x 2 mins.
The Tamagotchi Museum doesn't have a display from Earth, so a group of Tamagotchi friends decide to go and collect appliances and artifacts from our world to make a display before the Great Gotchi realizes there isn't one. A blatant cash-in broadcast on Japanese TV in the wake of the Tamagotchi "virtual pet" boom, which combined the get-a-life-factor of pet rocks with the sonic irritation of other people's mobile phones. They were a brief fad in the mid-1990s, soon superseded by their "third generation" fighting versions, the DIGIMON. Both, however, were trounced in the marketplace by the multimedia phenomenon of Nintendo's POKÉMON.

TAMALA 2010 *

2003. AKA: *A Punk Cat in Space.* Movie. DIR: Tol ("Tree of Life"). SCR: Tol. DES: Kentaro Nemoto, Tol. ANI: Kentaro Nomoto (2D), Michiro Tsutsumoto (3D CG). MUS: Homei Tanabe, PRD: Tol. 92 mins.
Orphan kitty Tamala heads off to Orion, much to the annoyance of her snake-charming human foster parent. En route, she finds herself in the city of Hate on Planet Q, where she befriends a cat called Michelangelo. Michelangelo later believes that Tamala has been murdered by Kentauros, an evil stalker who we also see sexually tormenting his pet mouse Penelope. Tamala, however, has a secret of her own, which is eventually revealed to Michelangelo by a maggot-infested zombie.

Loaded with ambient music, aimless vignettes, super-retro animation in a 1960s style, and highbrow bricolage, *Tamala 2010* has very little to do with punks, and much more to do with the art-house notion that audiences will be too afraid to say that something makes no sense. A well-known Japanese shipping company, whose logo is a cute little cat, once reputedly complained about the exploitation of their brand identity in KIKI'S DELIVERY SERVICE. Back then, their grievances were supposedly curtailed by making them coproducers. But the same company is liable to be less than happy with *Tamala 2010,* which dares to suggest that a feline-themed postal service is really the modern-day front for an ancient cult of human sacrifice, which now lays waste in a different way, by encouraging the pointless consumption of worthless trash goods.

But *Tamala 2010* isn't quite as smart as it thinks it is. Like HELLO KITTY scripted by Samuel Beckett, with all the futile pretension that implies, it bolts together a series of random scenes, united only by grasping attempts to gain gravity by association. Visual and textual allusions abound, to everything from *Querelle* to METROPOLIS, THE HAPPY PRINCE to *2001: A Space Odyssey,* but beneath its knowing surfaces, *Tamala 2010* has little to say. Ultimately, it's a brilliant five-minute feline conspiracy thriller, ludicrously and counterproductively stretched to feature-length.

Shot primarily in a faux-monochrome that recalls *Felix the Cat,* its black and white frames are cunningly augmented with subtle spots of earth tones—browns, blues, and greens that give the film a surreal edge. There are also moments of computer graphics, color animation, and even a prolonged sequence of a real-life highway. *Tamala 2010* plays like the combined graduation shorts of a fine arts college, stuck in a blender and randomly reassembled. But if you want to put on a beret, stroke your goatee, sip espresso and tell the freshman semiotics class that it's all incredibly meaningful, then you'll help perpetuate the latest outing for the Emperor's new clothes.

One gets the impression that *Tamala 2010*'s makers realized this themselves, as much of what passes for "plot" is delivered in a rambling voice-over at the end of the movie, as if their tutor had told them they weren't going to get a grade at all unless they talked some sense. Until then, it comprises little more than self-conscious wackiness and an irritating feline ingenue, wandering through cheap animation that polite reviewers would call a triumph of irony. Since *Tamala 2010* soon gained its own merchandising line in the style of *Hello Kitty*, it is tempting to add that whatever worthy point its creators thought they were making has been well and truly blunted.

TANSA 5

1979. JPN: *Kagaku Boken Tai Tansa 5*. AKA: *Science Adventure Command Tansa 5*. TV series. DIR: Shigeru Suzuki, Tameo Ogawa, Akira Suzuki, Kunihiko Okazaki, Osamu Sekita, Toshifumi Takizawa. SCR: Yoshihisa Araki, Sukehiro Tomita, Hiroyuki Hoshiyama, Tsunehisa Ito, Kenichi Matsuzaki, Takao Yotsuji, Jiyu Watanabe. DES: Michiru Suzuki, DM Design. ANI: Michiru Suzuki. MUS: Goro Omi. PRD: Sunrise, TV Tokyo. 25 mins. x 33 eps.

Tansa 5 is a five-member patrol team comprising Ryu, Daichi, Rui, Yumeto, and Hajime, whose Land, Aqua, and Sky Tansa vehicles can combine to form the predictably giant robot, Big Tansa. They also have the Time Tansa, a vehicle that allows them to travel an hour into the past, though they must return within their time limit or risk creating a paradox and leaving them lost forever. Their opponents are relics of the past—the forgotten civilization of Lemuria (see **SUPER ATRAGON**), found to be responsible for the statues

on Easter Island—a handy ad for sister-company Bandai, which use the statues as the logo for its Emotion video range. In the tradition of team shows dating back to **BATTLE OF THE PLANETS**, one of the team members was doomed, in this case Yumeto, who was replaced halfway through the run by new team member Johnny.

TAOTAO THE PANDA

1981. JPN: *Shunmao (Xiong Mao) Monogatari Taotao*. AKA: *Panda Story Taotao*. Movie, TV series. DIR: Tatsuo Shimamura (m), Shuichi Nakahara, Kazuhiko Ikegami, Taku Sugiyama. SCR: Takeshi Takahashi (m), Keiji Kubota, Takeshi Shudo, Nobuko Morita, Osamu Kagami. DES: Shuichi Nakahara. ANI: Yusaku Sakamoto (m), Masao Kumagawa (TV). MUS: Masaru Sato (m), Yasuo Tsuchida (TV). PRD: Shunmao; Shunmao, TV Osaka. 90 mins. (m), 25 mins. x 50 eps. (TV).

Chinese panda Taotao and his mate, Ang, are forced to flee when humans encroach on their natural habitat in Sichuan. Trapped and taken to a zoo in Europe, he becomes popular with the visitors, though animal psychologist Marie realizes that he is pining for his homeland. The first ever Sino-Japanese coproduction, this harks back to the panda boom of the 1970s (see **PANDA GO PANDA**) and was shown on a double bill with the live-action film *Tora-san's Promise* (see **TORA-SAN: THE ANIME**). Many of the same team went on to make the German coproduction *Taotao's Library—World Animal Stories* (1983, *Taotao Ehonkan Sekai Dobutsu Banashi*), in which a baby panda, coincidentally called Taotao, hears a number of stories at his mother's knee.

TARE PANDA

2000. AKA: *Lazy Panda; Papa Panda*. Video, TV series DIR: Yui Takashi (aka Takashi Ui). SCR: N/C. DES: Hikaru Suemasa. ANI: Keitaro Mochizuki. MUS: N/C. PRD: Bandai Visual, San-X, Green Camel. 30 mins. (v), ca. 3 mins. x ca. 5 eps. (TV).

Tare Panda is a flat, lifeless panda,

who excels at doing almost nothing. The slothful bear appears here in his own one-shot video, in which he is seen rescuing a Rapunzel bear, playing panda sumo, and racing in a very slow grand prix. The joke wears thin, however, when you realize you've just paid to watch a panda roll with tortuous slowness for several minutes, and that the "animation" ends all too soon to be replaced with an interview with the creature's creator and a live-action "Making Of" that shamelessly recycles much of the animation you've just seen. An obvious attempt by Bandai to seize some of the merchandising-led **HELLO KITTY** market—compare to the same company's **AFRO KEN**.

Designed in 1995 by Hikaru Suemasa for a range of character goods, Tare Panda was voted most popular toy in Japan in a 1999 magazine poll, and competitions to see how tall a stack could be built from his soft fabric body resulted in a record of 9.5 metres. In other words, to the delight of copyright owners San-X, a huge number of floppy little stuffed pandas were sold, and this animated video was made, with a later TV series shown on Sony's Animax channel—although we believe that TV series to have comprised much of the footage already contained here, in short bursts.

TARO MAEGAMI

1979. JPN: *Maegami Taro*. TV special. DIR: Hiroshi Saito. SCR: Akira Miyazaki. DES: Yoshiyuki Momose. ANI: Yoshiyuki Momose. MUS: Shinichi Tanabe. PRD: Nippon Animation, Fuji TV. 70 mins. An elderly couple, childless through many years of love and sacrifice, is finally rewarded with the birth of a son whom they name Taro. Determined to help his impoverished home village, young Taro travels the world in search of the Water of Life, which legend says brings both peace and wealth. However, the water is guarded by an evil serpent which uses its powers as a weapon.

Based on the book by Miyoko Matsutani considered a children's

Taro Maegami

© 1979 NIPPON ANIMATION CO., LTD.

masterpiece, this story was also adapted into another anime—**TARO THE DRAGON BOY**.

TARO THE DRAGON BOY *

1979. JPN: *Ryu no Ko Taro.* AKA: *Taro the Dragon's Son.* Movie. DIR: Kirio Urayama. SCR: Kirio Urayama, Takashi Mitsui. DES: Yoichi Otabe, Reiko Okuyama. ANI: Yoichi Otabe, Yuji Endo, Osamu Kasai. MUS: Riichiro Manabe. PRD: Toei. 75 mins.

A young mountain boy named Taro searches for his mother who has been changed into a dragon. During his dangerous quest, he risks his own life to save others and fulfill his mission. Finally, Taro engages in a ferocious battle with the enchanted dragon. A beautifully animated film featuring animation from Otabe, who also worked on the Miyazaki/Takahata **HEIDI**. Released on video in the U.S. in 1985, it was based on the same Miyoko Matsutani book adapted into **TARO MAEGAMI**, a TV special screened the following month. For another suspicious case of "simultaneous creation," see **THE WIZARD OF OZ**.

TATSUNOKO PRODUCTION, ALSO TATSUNOKO PRO

Founded in 1964 by manga artist Tatsuo Yoshida with his brothers Kenji and Toyoharu (who used the pseudonym Ippei Kuri), Tatsunoko soon established a reputation in influential television shows, including **SPEED RACER** and **BATTLE OF THE PLANETS**. The studio has also established many sister companies and spin-off subsidiaries, including IG Tatsunoko, now better known as Production IG. Notable staffers include Hiroshi Sasagawa, Hidehito Ueda, and Tetsuya Kobayashi. Many famous creators had their first break working for Tatsunoko, including illustrators such as Yoshitaka Amano and Akemi Takada. The studio celebrated its 40th anniversary with the Madhouse-influenced **KARAS**. The company's products are easily identified by its seahorse logo, a *tatsunoko* in Japanese being a "dragon's child," the word for a seahorse/seadragon, but also a reflection that the founding father of the company was "Tatsuo" Yoshida. Tatsunoko was bought in 2005 by the toy company Takara. See also Bee Train and Xebec.

TATTOON MASTER *

1996. Video. DIR: Kazuyuki Hirokawa. SCR: Yosuke Kuroda. DES: Hiroyoshi Iida. ANI: Hideki Araki. MUS: Harukichi Yamamoto. PRD: AIC, KSS. 30 mins. x 2 eps.

While his anthropologist mother is off studying the remote Tattoon tribe, Hibio (Eric) sulkily does the housework for his inept father, a pornographic filmmaker. He believes his mother to be dead, and she very nearly was, since she angered the Tattoons, who were ready to kill her. Unbeknownst to Hibio, his mother has bought her life by offering his hand in marriage to the Tattoon chieftainess Nima (Bala), who arrives in Tokyo weapons in hand, magical powers at the ready, and all set to marry him. This is not a welcome thought to the misogynist Hibio, whose sole experience of women has been his father's models, his feckless mother, and his militant feminist class president Fujimatsu (Lisa), a keen archer who carries her bow everywhere, and, for reasons utterly incomprehensible, wants Hibio for herself. Yet another alien-girl-adores-geek scenario, it traces a long line back to **URUSEI YATSURA** but is sadly lacking any of its predecessor's

virtues—a failed attempt to take the well-worn clichés in a new direction resulting in a uniformly unlikable cast. Based on a manga in *Ultra Jump* by Masahisa Tadanari.

TBS, OR TOKYO BROADCASTING SYSTEM

TV channel originally established as "KRT" in 1955, and the original home of the *Adventures of Superman*, a foreign import that may have inspired rival channel Fuji TV to commission **ASTRO BOY** in competition. In more recent times it continues to fight Fuji TV for market share, often scheduling its own anime in direct opposition to its competitor. TBS screens anime in all three major blocks, early morning for the kids, prime time for an older audience, and in the graveyard shift for fans. The Mainichi Broadcasting System (MBS) is an affiliate of TBS, as is the *Mainichi Shinbun* newspaper.

TEACHER TANK ENGINE

1996. JPN: *Kikan Kuruma Sensei.* Movie. DIR: Kozo Kusuba. SCR: Takuro Fukuda. DES: Shuichi Seki. ANI: Shunji Saita. MUS: N/C. PRD: Nippon Animation. 100 mins.

A modern spin on **BOTCHAN**, as a clueless city boy becomes a supply teacher on a remote Japanese island, slowly gaining the trust of the canny locals. Based on a novel by Shizuka Ijuin, the anime features live-action stars as many of the voices, including Yumi Adachi, Kin Sugai, and Shigeru Muroi.

TEACHER'S PET *

2000. JPN: *Natural.* Video. DIR: Kan Fukumoto. SCR: Fairy Tale. DES: Mizuki Sakisaka. ANI: Tadaji Tamori. MUS: N/C. PRD: Beam Entertainment, Green Bunny. 30 mins. x 2 eps.

New teacher Haruhiko Shimotsuki comes home to find pretty student Chitose Misawa in his apartment, offering herself and her undying love to him. Naturally he takes her up on her proposal, though matters are complicated by the fact that she is the younger sister of his ex-girlfriend Mariko, by the covert nature of their relationship, and his insistence on training her as his sex slave in time-honored S/M fashion.

In *Natural Another*, the direct sequel (issued in America with *Natural* under the title *Teacher's Pet*), Haruhiko further complicates matters by sleeping with another student and by accepting his colleague "Professor" Takagi's (this taking place per the English translation at a "college") advances, only to abuse her in the same fashion as Chitose, all in the name of breaking their wills to comply with his. Still, this is one of the better instances of the "training" genre of erotic anime, if only because the participants are (mostly) willing, the training mostly refrains from physical violence (emotional violence is another matter) and bodily fluids, and the production values are relatively high (as is to be expected from Green Bunny). These episodes were followed by *Natural2 Duo* and were based on the games by F&C. Not to be confused with Izumi Aso's 1989 romantic manga of the same name. **Ø**

TECHNOLOGY AND FORMATS

We cover several anime "firsts" in our section on **EARLY ANIME**, and reiterate here that the development of anime remains directly tied to new developments and applications of media technology—film from 1917, television from 1961, and video from 1983. When the only resource available was a film camera, anime remained beholden to the film medium, with Oten Shimokawa drawing his *Mukuzo Imokawa the Doorman* (*Imokawa Mukuzo Genkanban no Maki*, 1917) in chalk.

Animators all over the world soon realized that while foreground figures would need to move on a frame-by-frame basis, background images could often remain unchanged from shot to shot. Paper-cut animators began to experiment with translucent paper in order to create multiple layers of action on a screen. The animation "cel," a clear piece of celluloid (nitro-cellulose), presented the ideal

solution, allowing animators to draw partial images on uniformly shaped, identically sized squares of transparent film. These could be layered one on top of the other on a rostrum and then photographed by an overhead camera in order to create a multilayered image. This "rostrum camera" setup was already in use outside Japan, and first reached Japan in 1941, when Tadahito Mochinaga built one for Mitsuyo Seo's *Ant Boy* (*Ari-chan*, 1941).

Cels and rostrum cameras became the basic tools of the anime world for the next fifty years. Images could be kept in exact "registration" from shot to shot by the use of sprocket holes at their edges. These are not seen in the finished film, since they occur beyond "TV Safety"—that is, beyond the area of the image that will actually be photographed. Jimmy T. Murakami reported his frustration at Toei in the late 1950s, where animators still insisted on holding cels together by the less exacting means of paperclips.

The ability to reuse elements also led to certain choices in filmmaking, such Osamu Tezuka's decision to have a spartan, barely furnished future in **ASTRO BOY**, and a robot protagonist whose limb positions, once drawn on cels, could be reused from episode to episode. Although cels are transparent, too many of them stacked one on top of another can cause lower levels to appear murky, generally limiting the number of cels in use to three—a foreground, a background, and some kind of change onscreen, be it a hand gesture or a moving mouth. Five levels of cel are usually considered to be the maximum, although the need to pour in extra light can cause a leeched, bleached quality reducing the vivacity of any colors. This, however, was exploited by Mamoru Oshii, who adopted a "bled" color scheme for his **PATLABOR** movies. The need for light in order to ensure good photography also makes it time-consuming to realistically depict night sequences in cel animation, as it requires animators to use murkier, grayer grades of standard

colors. Katsuhiro Otomo's **AKIRA**, which contains many night sequences, is a particularly good example of the painstaking efforts required.

The opportunity to reuse backgrounds also led to an understandable craftsmanship—anime can have wonderful skies, sunsets, and lush backgrounds, since the painters can afford to concentrate their efforts on an image that will be used for more than a single 24th of a second. Animators can also treat the image through the use of camera filters or effects placed on the rostrum camera itself, often using improvised methods, such as those employed in some episodes of **FIST OF THE NORTH STAR**. Not all cels are the regulation screen shape. Long panning shots, for example, might be drawn onto elongated cels, in order to keep a single unbroken image onscreen. Horizontal movement is thereby achieved by moving the *cel*. Vertical movement, such as zooms, can be achieved by moving the *camera*, which is attached to a fixed rail.

Anime were shot on 16mm and then transferred to video for broadcast using a standard telecine process. However, some anime were shot on other forms of film—**MAGIC BOY** (1959) was the first anime to be shot using the Cinescope process, a deliberate attempt to match the same methods used on Disney's *Lady and the Tramp* (1955). Disney's *Sleeping Beauty* (1959) was the first feature cartoon to be shot on 70mm film, although this achievement largely passed the Japanese by, since prints of the film in Japan were in 35mm. Consequently, Japanese sources in search of the opportunity to discuss Japan's "first" 70mm film tend to fall back on **METAMORPHOSES/WINDS OF CHANGE** (1978), which was an American-Japanese coproduction, but did contain a 70mm sequence directed by Sadao Miyamoto. Other technological breakthroughs in anime include 3D, first used for the final episode of **NOBODY'S BOY** (1977) and occasionally wheeled out for children's movies, and stereo sound, first used in the BATTLE OF THE PLANETS movie (1978).

Anime, particularly in television, tends not to keep to the "full animation" tactics of Disney, in which an image can go through 24 adjustments in a second, once for each frame. Instead, it tends to be "shot on threes," meaning that a single image may occupy three frames of film. This can give Japanese animation a jerky quality when compared to more expensive animation techniques. There is nothing physically preventing the Japanese from doing "full" animation—nothing, that is, except the financial restrictions born of the relatively low returns that the Japanese animation industry usually expects—see RATINGS AND BOX OFFICE.

The arrival of video anime with DALLOS (1983) changed anime's method of distribution, not the technology that actually made it. The lower overheads required to put video cassettes and laser discs, then DVDs, into stores allowed producers to try more experimental works. Video also allowed for private viewing, and hence the return of EROTICA AND PORNOGRAPHY.

In addition, video permitted the ready export of anime abroad, where original formats were sometimes confused. AI CITY, made as a movie for screening in cinemas, went straight to video outside Japan, whereas the original APPLESEED, released straight-to-video in Japan, was released in cinemas in Britain, blowing up artwork originally intended for the small screen to the work's arguable detriment. The mixture of original formats often led to false expectations among rights-buyers and audiences abroad. Anime's initial boom in the English-speaking world was spearheaded by *movies*—AKIRA, UROTSUKIDOJI, and CASTLE OF CAGLIOSTRO—but largely comprised *videos*, with a predictable drop in quality. Nor were many of the videos stand-alone titles, leading to increased confusion, particularly in cases such as RG VEDA, where a Japanese release was left open-ended, with the expectation that audiences would follow the rest of the story in a manga version simply unavailable to the American mainstream at the time.

In the mid-1990s, the expansion of television networks and the reduction in video budgets led to a new form of distribution. Instead of releasing niche programming onto video, some producers sold it at a cheap rate to television networks, who would then broadcast it during the late-night "graveyard shift." What once might have been released in the 1980s as a video series of six one-hour episodes would now be broken into 12 or 13 half-hour episodes, with the concomitant budgetary savings of more recyclable opening and ending credit sequences. Essentially, the idea was to have a video release in which the fan was expected to bring his own tape— Japanese magazines even published guides on how to get the best from home taping. The rise of the late-night anime led to a different type of content, with the late-night anime largely unsuitable for primetime. Although not a problem in Japan, this has led to more confused expectations abroad, as anime distributors buy "TV serials" that they find to be almost impossible to sell for broadcast without cuts.

The ability to store and manipulate images digitally is the most crucial innovation in the anime business since the adoption of the cel, and its repercussions are still playing out. The cel animation industry has now been replaced by new methods of production since the 1990s, which we cover in greater detail in our entry on GAMING AND DIGITAL ANIMATION. But the new technology has also exerted a strong influence on the type of anime that gets made. Just as anime once favored TV serials or videos, it now favors increasingly smaller episodes, easier to stream online, download, and view on personal devices such as a PSP or iPod. This also allows many anime producers to invent a new excuse for what they have always done—cutting their budgets.

TECHNOPOLICE 21C *
1982. JPN: *Technopolis 21C*. AKA: *Techno Police*. Movie. DIR: Masashi Matsumoto, Shoji Kawamori. SCR: Mamoru Sasaki, Kenichi Matsuzaki, Masaru Yamamoto, Hiroyuki Hoshiyama. DES: Yoshitaka Amano, Kazumasa Miyabe. ANI: Norio Hirayama, Kogi Okawa. MUS: Joe Hisaishi. PRD: Studio Nue, Artmic, Toho, Dragon Production. 79 mins.
In the year 2001 (which still seemed quite a long way off in 1982), the police force uses robots to minimize risk to human personnel in fighting crime. The Technopolice is the special squad of cops and robots set up to use the new technology to its best effect. But a crime wave is sweeping Centinel City, and the police have almost lost control. When a powerful experimental tank is hijacked, hotheaded rookie cop Kyosuke (Ken) is thrown in at the deep end. In a high-tech Road Ranger car (a step up from his own beloved Lotus Seven, which he proudly describes as a "collector's item"), he sets out on a death-defying chase through the streets. Luckily he's got the best Techroid (Technoid) backup on the force, three superb robots: his own Blader (Blade), who throws a pair of cuffs to catch villains as they flee; pretty Scanny, the computer hacker partner of token girl Eleanor; and Vigoras (Vigorish), a big, strong robot to partner his big, strong sidekick Kosuga. With their help, he may just manage to stay alive long enough to capture the crooks, disarm the tank, and save Eleanor; but not even his instinct for outguessing the criminals can help him outwit the political machinations behind the hijack and bring the culprits to justice. Based on an idea by Toshimitsu Suzuki, who would return in BUBBLEGUM CRISIS with hardsuits bearing a certain resemblance to the Techroids. Also note the cameo appearance of two cute girl traffic cops in a small car, distantly foreshadowing YOU'RE UNDER ARREST!

TEKKAMAN *
1975. JPN: *Uchu Kishi Tekkaman*. AKA:

Tekkaman the Space Knight; Space Knight Tekkaman. TV series, video. DIR: Hiroshi Sasagawa, Hideo Nishimaki, Eiko Toriumi, Seitaro Hara (TV1), Hiroshi Negishi, Akihiko Nishiyama, Kazuya Yamazaki, Hideki Tonokatsu (TV2), Hideki Tonokatsu (v). SCR: Jinzo Toriumi, Akiyoshi Sakai, Hiroshi Sakamoto (TV1), Mayori Sekijima, Hiroyuki Kawasaki, Satoru Akahori, Tetsuko Watanabe, Katsuhiko Chiba (TV2), Hiroyuki Kawasaki (v). DES: Yoshitaka Amano, Kunio Okawara (TV1), Yoshinori Sayama Hirotoshi Sano, TO III O [*sic*] (TV2), Hirotoshi Sano, Yoshinori Sayama, Rei Nakahara (v). ANI: Masami Suda, Tsuneo Ninomiya (TV1), Shigeru Kato (TV2), Akira Kano (v). MUS: Bob Sakuma (TV1), Kaoru Wada (TV2), Shigeki Kuwara (v). PRD: Tatsunoko, NET (now TV Asahi) (TV1), Tatsunoko, TV Tokyo (TV2). 25 mins. x 26 eps. (TV1), 25 mins. x 49 eps. (TV2), 30 mins. x 6 eps. (v).

A space-borne version of **BATTLE OF THE PLANETS**, as the invading Waldstar aliens (Waldarians in the U.S. dub) are opposed by Joji Minami (Barry Gallagher), a young man who can wear the powerful Tekkaman battle armor designed by Professor Amachi (Dr. Edward Richardson). The professor's daughter, Hiromi (Patricia), the teleporting alien Andro Umeda, and space furball Mutan support him in his fight on the starship Terra Azzura. Not unlike Vega in **HARMAGEDON**, Andro is a survivor from another world ravaged by the enemy, helping humans avert a similar disaster on their own world. In the Japanese version, the situation was considerably more desperate, since Earth is on the verge of ecological collapse, and the human race will perish without a new home. Conversely, in the U.S. version, the human ships that first encounter the Waldarians are simply looking for new worlds to colonize. Created by Jinzo Toriumi and Akira Toyama from an idea by Ippei Kuri, the original TV series ends with Earth saved, but at the price of the hero's life—though it is highly likely that his "death" was only a cliffhanger that

would have been revealed as a red herring in episode 27, had the unpopular series not been pulled off the air only halfway through its original planned run of 52 episodes.

The concept was revived for a new series, *SK Tekkaman Blade* (1992), screened in the U.S. as *Teknoman*. This time, the alien Radamu kidnap humans to use them as living weapons, almost invincible once they conjure up the alien Tekkaman armor. One such human, known only as D-Boy, escapes from their control and makes his way to Earth, whose defenders, undecided as to how far to trust him, still need his armor and its power to have a chance of saving the planet. The classic team-show jealousies, misunderstandings, and romantic love tangles back up a plot with plenty of fighting action, and D-Boy's past tragedy is gradually revealed. In the video series *SK Tekkaman Blade* 2 (1994), ten years have elapsed since the events of the second TV series, and D-Boy returns to save Earth again. The marketing-led emphasis on starlets in the 1990s means that this time the Tekkaman Support Team consists of several beautiful young girls, each of whose voice actresses made a tie-in single. **V**

TEKKEN *

1998. AKA: *Iron Fist*. Video. DIR: Kunihisa Sugishima. SCR: Ryota Yamaguchi. DES: Masaaki Kawabata. ANI: Masaaki Kawabata. MUS: Kazuhiko Sotoyama. PRD: Foursome. 30 mins. x 2 eps., 58 mins.

Sometime in the near future, cloning has been outlawed by the Darwin Treaty, but an international crime-fighting organization suspects that super-rich weapons magnate Heihachi Mishima is planning something nasty. Meanwhile Kazuya, Mishima's son, is out to kill him. Mishima thought the best way to train his gentle, good-hearted son was by throwing him into a ravine. The boy survived only thanks to his raging thirst for revenge and has now become a superb martial artist in his own right. A prestigious martial arts tournament

on Mishima's private island off Hong Kong, attended by the best fighters from all over the world, offers Kazuya the chance to achieve his aims. His childhood friend Jun wants to bring him back from his chosen path of hatred, but his father aims to Turn Him To The Dark Side.

This game-based anime incorporates characters from all three *Tekken* versions then available. *Tekken* pays lip service to the police thriller angle exploited in the past by **STREET FIGHTER II**, casting Jun Kazama as a lady investigator with an international crime-busting syndicate. Both in anticipation of the large Chinese market and in recognition of the ideal way to engineer as many fight scenes as possible, it also pastiches Bruce Lee movies—hence the martial arts tournament on a millionaire's private island, the promised fight through the floors of a central tower, and the Hong Kong setting. Though the plot meanders toward a massive fight at Mishima's lair, which would, of course, be the tournament featured in the game itself, the events of the game only take place off-screen for a few fleeting seconds. The script takes the macho posturing of games to mind-boggling extremes, and as a rundown of all the available clichés, *Tekken* has the lot, including a childhood flashback, bad dreams, sibling rivalry, a shower scene, an evil corporation, a female assassin, a psychic girl agent, graphic breaking bones, a gentle giant, a girl in a sailor suit, a broken punching bag, incompetent minions, Russian androids, a self-destruct sequence, and a baddie who lives to fight another day. As a small bonus, it also includes stealth dinosaurs and a boxing kangaroo. As well as adding the pretentious subtitle "the motion picture," the English-language release replaced the original soundtrack with music from popular beat combos, including Offspring and Corrosion of Conformity. **V**

TEMPLE THE BALLOONIST

1977. JPN: *Fusen Shojo Temple-chan*. AKA: *Hot Air Balloon Girl Temple;*

Tiffany's Traveling Band; Sabrina's Journey. TV series DIR: Seitaro Hara. SCR: Jinzo Toriumi, Shigeru Yanagawa. DES: Akiko Shimamoto. ANI: Kazuhiko Udagawa. MUS: Nobuyoshi Koshibe. PRD: Tatsunoko, Fuji TV. 25 mins. x 26 eps.

Deep in the Alps lies the tiny village of Green Grass, the home of Temple, a pretty, curly-haired girl who wears a drum majorette's outfit and dreams of becoming a musician. On a stormy night, she meets Puffy the cloud, who whisks her away to a magical hot-air balloon. Riding in the balloon, Temple and Puffy see several musicians fleeing from robbers. Rescuing them in the nick of time, they discover that their new traveling companions are animal musicians—Tommy the cat, who plays his whiskers like a mouth harp, Quincy the horn-playing duck, Nicky the flutist mouse, along with Scrapper the orphan drummer boy. Picaresque adventures ensue, with a halfhearted aim of eventually returning Temple to her home—compare to THE WIZARD OF OZ—in a Tatsuo Yoshida creation whose little leading lady's bright attitude and golden curls seem designed to recall the Shirley Temple whose name she appears to share. There were several attempts to sell the story to the American TV market in the 1980s, hence the multiple alternate titles employed in advertising flyers by Harmony Gold. However, we have no record of the show's translation or broadcast in English.

TEN LITTLE FROGS

1998. JPN: *10-piki no Kaeru.* Video. DIR: Masahiro Hosoda. SCR: Miyako Ando. DES: Hirokazu Ishiyuki. ANI: Hirokazu Ishiyuki. MUS: Kenichi Kamio. PRD: Toei, Trans Arts. 20 mins. x 2 eps.

Ten frogs set out in search of adventure in their swamp, sailing in a boat made from a running shoe. Based on the children's book by Hisako Madokoro and Michiko Nakagawa, the story of the frogs returned in a second episode, in which they went to a summer festival.

TEN TOKYO WARRIORS *

1999. JPN: *Tokyo Jushoden.* AKA: *Ten Captains of Tokyo.* Video. DIR: Hikaru Takanashi, Noboru Ishiguro. SCR: Tetsuya Oishi. DES: Sawako Yamamoto. ANI: Sawako Yamamoto. MUS: N/C. PRD: Five Ace, Beam Entertainment. 27 mins. x 6 eps.

Long ago, ten brave warriors defeated the Demon King and his legion of "Kyoma" warriors. But in present day Tokyo, Shindigan, a servant of the Kyoma, is determined to resurrect her master and restore his rule on Earth. You will not be surprised to hear that the warriors are reborn in the manner of IKKI TOUSEN, since schoolboy Jutto Segu discovers that he is the reincarnation of one of the original heroes, and that the time has come for him to fight again. A rehash of DOOMED MEGALOPOLIS, doomed by a repetitive monster-of-the-moment format with formulaic plots and characters, based on a novel by Taku Atsushi that was also adapted into a manga by Satoru Kiga, whose illustrations were used as the basis for the characters in this anime version. A CD drama was also produced in Japan. **🅛🅥**

TEN TOP TIPS FOR PRO BASEBALL

1983. JPN: *Proyakyu o 10 Tanoshiku Miru Hoho.* AKA: *How to Make Pro Baseball Ten Times More Exciting.* Movie. DIR: Kiyoshi Suzuki. SCR: Junichi Ishihara, Toshiharu Iwaida. DES: Hisaichi Ishii. ANI: Tsutomu Shibayama, Osamu Kobayashi, Tetsu Dezaki, Tsukasa Sunaga. MUS: Kazuo Otani. PRD: Tokyo Movie Shinsha for Film Link (1), Magic Bus for Film Link (2). 95 mins., 106 mins.

Based on the two books of career reminiscences by real-life Hanshin Tigers baseball star Takenori Emoto. Mixing live action and animation to tell humorous anecdotes from professional baseball (nine short tales in nine "innings"), the film was followed by a sequel in 1984.

TENAMONYA VOYAGERS *

1999. Video. DIR: Katsuhito Akiyama,

Akiyuki Shinbo. SCR: Ryoei Tsukimura. DES: Masashi Ishihama, Noriaki Tetsura, Naoyuki Konno. ANI: Takashi Azuhara. MUS: Masamichi Amano. PRD: Studio Pierrot. 30 mins. x 4 eps.

Rookie schoolteacher Ayako Hanabishi volunteers for a posting in the middle of nowhere only to find that the school has closed down before she arrives. Far from home with no money, she meets Wakana Nanamiya, a Japanese girl on a sports scholarship, who is also stranded. The brash, tough girl Paraila has never seen the girls' homeland, and she inspires the others to pool their resources and head for home. However, their train is attacked en route, and the girls realize too late that Paraila is wanted by the police and using them as cover. So begins a road-movie setup that would make a perfect live-action film of the week, somewhat redundantly transformed into an anime space opera. Compare to AWOL, which similarly augmented a real-world drama with pointless sci-fi trappings. An inferior Japanese fish-out-of-water comedy to Tsukimura's earlier EL HAZARD, *TV* mixes obvious quick fixes (a space-going *bullet*-train after GALAXY EXPRESS 999) with halfhearted visual gags (spaceships like battering rams that deposit a 20th-century police car inside a criminal's ship). There are regular breaks for cheesy shots of Tatsue Yokoyama, the dogged police officer who never quite catches them—the filmmakers would have you believe that this is an "homage" to pulp detective shows of the 1970s, though it looks suspiciously like a poverty of ideas masquerading as irony. There are some genuinely funny moments born of the onscreen ensemble, and occasionally some tongue-in-cheek observations in the style of a poor man's GUNBUSTER, but like so many 1990s anime comedies, *TV* thinks it's a lot funnier than it really is (see also JUBEI-CHAN THE NINJA GIRL), and it stops abruptly with a cynical narration that unhelpfully adds, "And for some reason, this is the end." It will, however, remain forever in the anime history books as the first to be released in the U.S. straight to DVD without ever gracing the old-fashioned VHS format.

TENCHI MUYO! *

1992. JPN: *Tenchi Muyo! Ryo Oh Ki.* AKA: *This Way Up!; No-Good Tenchi; No Need for Tenchi; Heaven and Earth Prince.* Video, TV series, movie. DIR: Hiroki Hayashi, Kenichi Yatagai, Kazuhiro Ozawa, Yoshiaki Iwasaki, Shinichi Kimura, Koji Masunari, Satoshi Kimura. SCR: Naoko Hasegawa, Masaki Kajishima, Hiroki Hayashi, Ryoei Tsukimura, Yosuke Kuroda, Satoru Nishizono. DES: Masaki Kajishima, Atsushi Takeuchi, Takeshi Waki. ANI: Takchiro Nakayama, Wataru Abe. MUS: Seiko Nagaoka, Christopher Franke, Ko Otani, Tsuneyoshi Saito. PRD: AIC, Pioneer, TV Tokyo. 30 mins. x 6 eps. (v/*Ryo-ohki* 1), 45 mins. (v sp./*Carnival*), 30 mins. x 6 eps. (v/*Ryo-ohki* 2), 40 mins. (v sp./*Mihoshi*), 25 mins. x 26 eps. (TV1/*Universe*), 40 mins. x 3 eps. (v/*Sammy*), 95 mins. (m1/*In Love*), 25 mins. x 26 eps. (TV2/*Sammy*), 25 mins. x 26 eps. (TV3/*Tokyo*), 60 mins. (m2/*Daughter*), 95 mins. (m3/*Forever*), 25 mins. x 26 eps. (TV4/*GXP*), 30 mins. x 6 eps. (v/*Ryo-ohki* 3), 30 mins. (v/*Ryo-ohki* finale), 25 mins. x ?? eps. (TV5/*Sasami*). Tenchi Masaki is a quiet, average teenager who lives in the family shrine with his father and grandfather, goes to school, and does nothing much—until the day he accidentally releases a malevolent creature from the family shrine (compare to USHIO AND TORA). It transforms into a hot babe, space pirate Ryoko, and her hots are aimed at Tenchi. Then another alien babe, Jurai Princess Ayeka, arrives with her sweet little sister, Sasami. She too fancies Tenchi, but she's got another reason for hating Ryoko—a past tragedy that robbed her of her intended husband. When ditzy Space Officer Mihoshi falls out of the skies onto the Masaki houschold and pink-haired alien professor Wasshu shows up, the scene is set for a romantic farce in which the girls fight for Tenchi's affec-

Tenchi Muyo!

© AIC • PIONEER LDC

tions while he fights off various galactic threats and gradually uncovers the truth about his family. There's also a mascot "cabbit" (cat/rabbit), the titular Ryo-Oh-Ki, which likes carrots and will one day grow into a spaceship.

The "unwelcome guest" genre, in which a hapless boy is saddled with a magical babe, is a popular high concept in anime. It's a genre rich in mind-boggling situation comedies: girlfriend-as-alien (URUSEI YATSURA), girlfriend-as-elfin-nymphomaniac (ADVENTURE KID), girlfriend-as-the-Norse-embodiment-of-the-concept-of-Being (OH MY GODDESS!), girlfriend-as-time-traveling-ghost-of-future-dead-wife (KIRARA). *Tenchi* is its 1990s apotheosis; a show about a boy stuck with more girls than he can shake a stick at, every one of them feverishly competing for a chaste peck on the cheek. Originally conceived as a spoof vacation episode of BUBBLEGUM CRISIS, *Tenchi* reached screens in this heavily rewritten form—however, along with the girl-heavy cast, the idea that it was okay to just goof off for an episode or two became ingrained. Sasami's regular plea that things can always stay the

same "forever and ever" is perhaps the most bowel-emptyingly fearsome line in televisual history, striking greater dread into the audience than any horror movie. Though the first video series of *Tenchi* was witty, funny, and charming, the premise was repeated *ad nauseam* by a creative team happy to simply coast along. Later incarnations of the series reorder a few plot elements into what some might call alternate universes, and others lazy continuity.

The Pioneer corporation, searching for an easily repeatable franchise to rival Sunrise's BRAVE SAGA or Tatsunoko's TIME BOKAN, hyped *Tenchi* to insane extremes, and someone eventually believed it—the series clambered onto TV screens with the new-look *Tenchi Universe* (Ryoko *crashes* on Earth while being *pursued* by Mihoshi; see the subtle difference?), which moves the action into space for its second season. A further TV series, *Tenchi in Tokyo*, packed our boy off to college—but a dimensional portal let his harem pop up for "unexpected" visits. At the time of its U.S. release, Pioneer's blurb proclaimed it was the "same old Tenchi," which was at least honest.

The series proper "ended" with three expensive movies, beginning with *Tenchi Muyo in Love* (1996), which paid out for music from *Babylon 5*–composer Christopher Franke. Shamelessly ripping off *Back to the Future*, Tenchi must travel back in time to unite his courting parents. Despite high production values and an involving plot, the movie is let down by the serial's vastly overpopulated cast—the number of characters demanding a scene to steal often makes it resemble crowded game-based anime like **Street Fighter II**. In typical *Tenchi* style, the movie *Daughter of Darkness* (1997, aka *Midsummer's Eve*) halfheartedly inverts the previous plot, featuring the cast visited by a character from the *future*, claiming to be Tenchi's daughter. The final movie, *Tenchi Forever* (1999), features Tenchi kidnapped by yet another obsessive female and spirited into a parallel world where his adoring harem have to find him. *Tenchi Muyo GXP* (2002) is yet another retelling, a 26-episode TV series supposedly rooted more in the continuity of the video serials, moving the focus away from Tenchi, who joins the galactic police, and onto his young classmate Seina Yamada, a shy, retiring child who believes that he, like Ataru in **Urusei Yatsura**, has the worst luck in the world. Amid a main plot about a pirate guild's plan to seize control of the galaxy, the usual geek-gets-girls "comedy" ensues.

A third video series ran for six episodes, and a bonus finale (the "20th" episode in the cumulative video continuity), ran from 2003 to 2005.

With both the appeal and dogged staying power of a mutant cockroach, the franchise might not necessarily have pleased the crowds (ratings were unremarkable), but it certainly pleased studio executives. *Tenchi* was a fertile breeding ground for other shows during the 1990s—most notably the superior **El Hazard**, which was made by bored staffers Hayashi and Tsukimura, and the pornographic pastiches **Spaceship Agga Ruter** and

Masquerade. Two video "specials" also introduced a superheroine, who returned in her own video series *Magical Princess Pretty Sammy*, which followed the classic magical-girl-show pattern (see **Little Witch Sally**), and, predictably, ran a string of subplots about the grown-up girls competing for first place in Tenchi's affections. Little Sasami, however, was safely remodeled as his sister, allowing an 8-year-old girl to adore a 17-year-old guy without a hint of impropriety and simultaneously securing her claim to be big bro's Number One. The series has some enjoyable moments—one episode is a wholly unsubtle dig at Bill Gates's Microsoft empire—but ultimately it's a show about cute little girls for much older boys who really should know better. The video series was itself rehashed for Japanese TV as the jaw-droppingly camp 26-episode *Magical Girl Pretty Sammy* (*Magical Project S*). The relationships and premises are completely reworked, but this time, apart from the odd cameo appearance, Tenchi and friends are sidelined. Sammy has a mother and father and a whole bunch of elementary school friends and is more interested in talking to her best friend Misa (who is also her unwitting adversary Pixie Misa) than mooning over boys. Marketed in Japan for the little-girl audience, the series received inexplicably high ratings in Nagoya but has proved unpopular with Western *Tenchi* fans, perhaps because it abandons most of the series' established tropes in favor of those of standard magical-girl shows.

Pretty Sammy returned in the TV series *Sasami's Magical Girl Club* (2006). **Ⓝ**

TENJHO TENGE *
2004. JPN: *Tenjo Tenge*. AKA: *Everything Above Heaven; Everything Under Heaven*. TV series, video, TV special. DIR: Toshifumi Kawase. SCR: Toshiki Inoue. DES: Takahiro Umehara. ANI: Takahiro Umehara, Studio Madhouse. MUS: Yasunori Iwasaki. PRD: DR Movie, Madhouse, Nagoya Broadcasting Network,

TV Asahi. 23 mins. x 24 eps. (TV), 24 mins. x 2 eps. (v), 92 mins. (special). Young punks Soichiro Nagi and his best friend, Afro-Japanese Bob Makihara, join Todo Academy, a high school with a high delinquent population and a number of martial arts clubs that fight for supremacy under the iron regulation of the student council. They meet up with the stunningly beautiful Natsume twins, Maya and Aya, and are drawn into a closed world of highly advanced skills and unruly emotions. Both sisters see something special in Soichiro; Aya falls for him, and Maya, whose ex-boyfriend allegedly killed his best friend, their brother, sees him as a fighter with huge but as yet untapped potential. The pair find themselves in the twins' exclusive Juken club, opposed to the student council and its powerful, mysterious leader Mitsuomi, who also happens to be Maya's ex. The combination of teenagers simultaneously flouting authority and regulating their own anarchy through hierarchies as arcane and restrictive as anything in the adult world is familiar—just compare to **Boys Over Flowers** or **Utena**. But don't come here for philosophy because you'll get eye candy instead; *TT* is all about defying the laws of physics and gravity with slam-bang fighting action and enormous breasts. Based on the manga by "Oh! Great," the TV series led to a two-part video spin-off from the same director, entitled *TT: Ultimate Fight*, and a prequel "special," *TT: Past Chapter* (2005). **ⒸⓃⓋ**

TENMARU THE LITTLE TENGU
1983. JPN: *Kotengu Tenmaru*. TV series. DIR: Hiroshi Shidara, Yuji Endo, Atsutoshi Umezawa, Takeshi Shirato, Junichi Sato. SCR: Tadaaki Yamazaki, Akiyoshi Sakai, Katsuhiko Taguchi. DES: Kiichiro Suzuki. ANI: Masami Abe, Takeshi Shirato. MUS: Hiroshi Tsutsui. PRD: Toei, Fuji TV. 25 mins. x 19 eps. Prince Tenmaru leaves the land of the tengu (crow-spirits) in pursuit of 108 evil creatures who have invaded the human realm. He hides out at the apartment of pretty Earth girl Yoko. A

mixture of the gentle humor of **Dorae-mon** with the ghost-busting of **Dororon Enma**, *Tenmaru* was the anime debut of future **Sailor Moon**–director Junichi Sato.

TEPPEN
1995. AKA: *Summit*. Video. DIR: Yota Minagawa, Fumi Shirakawa. SCR: Tomohiro Ando, Masashi Reishi. DES: Masashi Yusono. ANI: Hidemizu Kita. MUS: N/C. PRD: Toei. 50 mins. x 2 eps.
In an adaptation of Takanori Onari's manga from *Young Jump* magazine, teenage tough-guy Satoshi gets into fights at school and has run-ins with the police. **V**

TEXHNOLYZE *
2003. TV series DIR: Hirotsugu Hamazaki, Koujirou Tsuruoka, Sayo Yamamoto, Takayuki Hirao. SCR: Chiaki Konaka, Noboru Takagi, Shin Yoshida, Takeshi Konuta. DES: Shigeo Akahori, Morifumi Naka, Toshihiro Nakajima. ANI: Shigeo Akahori. MUS: Hajime Mizoguchi, Keishi Urata. PRD: Fuji TV, Madhouse, Pioneer, Rondo Robe. 24 mins. x 22 eps.
Centuries after mankind first burrowed underground to live in "experimental" cities, the descendants of the original colonists are fighting for control of the near-derelict city of Lux. Orphan Ichise is a prizefighter who gets involved with a corrupt promoter and literally loses an arm and a leg. He becomes the guinea pig of a female scientist working on the Texhnolyze project, and receives new limbs and enhanced fighting powers. This in turn makes him the favored protégé of Onishi, leader of an organization with a mysterious power over Lux. Girl prophet Ran offers him the chance to find out who he really is and what his destiny holds. Created by Yoshitoshi Abe, whose fascination for labyrinths and processes of evolution led to the modern anime classics **Serial Experiments Lain** and **Haibane Renmei**, this is a beautifully designed dystopia, although built on foundations set by many others—see *Robocop*, **Megazone**

23, **AD Police**, and even the previous year's **Tokyo Underground**. **LV**

TEZUKA, OSAMU
1928–1989. Born in Osaka Prefecture, Tezuka graduated in medicine from Osaka University, although he was already writing manga in his teens, and never practiced as a doctor—his pursuit of a medical education may have been a form of conscientious objection in wartime Japan. He is often termed the "God of Manga" or "Father of Manga." He is one of the giants of postwar Japanese comics, and the author of over 500 volumes of comics, although his manga output need not concern us here, save in his youthful associations with other artists, dramatized in **We're Manga Artists: Tokiwa Villa**. He was able to be so prolific, at least in part, through his adoption of a "production line" system that institutionalized the practices already present in the comics industry of farming out different work to multiple assistants. Tezuka's ability to delegate not only set paradigms for other comics artists, but also encouraged him to diversify into animation. Seeing TV as an opportunity to advertise his comics, and vice versa, Tezuka helped create anime as we know it with his groundbreaking **Astro Boy**, **Kimba the White Lion,** and **Princess Knight**. His early successes stumbled in the late 1960s, as Mushi Production began to lose money, causing Tezuka to embark on more "adult" fare such as **Arabian Nights** and questionable deals which found creations such as his **Triton of the Sea** ending up in the hands of others. Tezuka left Mushi Pro in 1971 as the company spiraled into chaos, and returned with Tezuka Production, a new company that continued to make meaningful contributions to the anime world, particularly in the often overlooked world of TV specials such as **Prime Rose**. For details of the lifelong work by which Tezuka would probably have preferred to be remembered, see **Space Firebird**. Tezuka is one of the founding fathers of Japanese animation, since it was he,

along with Shotaro Ishinomori and Mitsuteru Yokoyama, who first created many of the tropes and traditions that are replayed every season in modern anime. He was also active in selling anime to America, visiting the U.S. and encouraging its fledgling fanbase. He was the president of the Japan Animation Association until his death, and was succeeded by Kihachiro Kawamoto. See also Mushi Production, Tezuka Production. Some older sources repeat Tezuka's claim that he was born in 1926: a deception that he maintained in order to convince his editors that he was an adult manga creator and not a teenage prodigy.

TEZUKA PRODUCTION
Also Tezuka Pro. Founded by Osamu Tezuka in 1968 as a company to produce *comics*, Tezuka Pro was a separate entity, and therefore shielded from any liability when the anime company Mushi Production collapsed in the early 1970s. It was able to continue operating and diversified into animation production; its first anime, **Marvelous Melmo**, was released before Mushi even officially closed. Tezuka Pro is hence the company responsible for most of Tezuka's anime output in the last two decades of his life, such as TV specials like **Bandar Book**. Since his death, the company has maintained a strong presence in the industry, with an unofficial mission statement to ensure that everything Tezuka ever wrote will eventually be animated. Recent applications of this policy have seen anime of **Metropolis**, **Black Jack,** and an **Astro Boy** remake, all designed to keep Osamu Tezuka's legacy alive.

THAT'LL DO NICELY
1991. JPN: *Nyuin Bokki Monogatari: O Daiji ni*. AKA: *Hospitalization Surprise Story: That'll Do Nicely*. Video. DIR: Sadamune Koyama, Naoko Kuzumi. SCR: Sadamune Koyama. DES: Koichi Arai. ANI: Yoshio Mizumura. MUS: Michiya Katakura. PRD: Tokyo Kids. 45 mins. x 2 eps.

Ayumu Nerima is hospitalized after a motorcycle accident, but he soon perks up when he discovers that everyone on the ward is desperate for sex, from the nurses to the unwed-teenager mother next door. A predictable farce based on a manga by Maki Otsubo in *Manga Action* magazine—compare to **O-GENKI CLINIC**. **N**

THERE GOES SHURA

1994. JPN: *Shura ga Yuku*. Video. DIR: Masamune Ochiai. SCR: Yu Kawanabe. DES: Aiko Kamada. ANI: Teruo Kigure. MUS: Hideyuki Tanaka. PRD: Knack. 50 mins. x 2 eps.

The assassination of a Shinjuku gang boss starts a trail of blood-soaked revenge, ending with a nasty shoot-out between yakuza in Kyushu. Based on the original manga in *Comic Goraku* by Yu Kawanabe (who also wrote **EMPEROR OF THE SOUTH SIDE**) and Masato Yamaguchi. **V**

THERE GOES TOMOE

1991. JPN: *Tomoe ga Yuku*. Video. DIR: Takaaki Ishiyama. SCR: Asami Watanabe. DES: Matsuri Okuda. ANI: Masayuki Goto. MUS: Katsuhiro Kunimoto. PRD: Beam Entertainment. 45 mins. x 2 eps.

In this adaptation of Yumi Tamura's manga from *Bessatsu Shojo Comic*, Tomoe Oshima is a bad-girl biker who cherishes a hidden love for stuntman Tokoro. Since the heroine takes her name from Tomoe Gozen, the famous 12th-century woman-warrior, it might be prudent to file this story with **SPECTRE**, another adaptation of Japanese history into a modern setting.

THEY WERE ELEVEN *

1986. JPN: *Juichi-nin Iru*. Movie. DIR: Tetsu Dezaki, Tsuneo Tominaga. SCR: Toshikai Imaizumi, Katsumi Koide. DES: Akio Sugino, Keizo Shimizu. ANI: Keizo Shimizu, Yukari Kobayashi, Kenichi Maejima. MUS: Hirohiko Fukuda. PRD: Kitty Film. 91 mins.

An interplanetary group of 10 military academy cadets set out on their end-of-course test. They have to take an elder-ly spaceship out into space and survive 53 days without outside help. Any one of them can give up, but if so, they all fail. Then they find there are 11 people on board. One of them is an imposter, and they can't contact the academy to find out who it is or whether it's all part of the test. A series of incidents and accidents, trivial at first, grow increasingly threatening, and their personal strengths and weaknesses, as well as the social and political agendas of their different races, have a wider impact than on the outcome of this test alone. The anime version of Moto Hagio's suspenseful 1975 manga is delicate but powerful, a miniature gem.

30,000 MILES UNDER THE SEA

1970. JPN: *Kaitei Sanman Mile*. Movie. DIR: Takeshi Tamiya. SCR: Katsumi Okamoto. DES: Makoto Yamazaki. ANI: Reiko Okayama, Sadao Kikuchi, Torihiro Kaneyama. MUS: Takeo Watanabe. PRD: Toei. 60 mins.

Returning home from an ocean trip, young Isamu meets the beautiful sea-dweller Angel on a volcanic island. Attacked by a fiery dragon, Isamu and Angel escape on the observation boat See Through (a punning reference to the Sea View in Irwin Allen's 1961 *Voyage to the Bottom of the Sea*), and Angel invites Isamu to see her undersea kingdom of Atlas. As Isamu is preparing to return to dry land, Atlas is attacked by the evil king, Magma VII, who reveals that he is planning to use the dragon to seize control of the surface world. The fate of Earth and Ocean is placed in the hands of Isamu and Angel for the final battle against the invading king.

This was the fourth Toei adaptation of a Shotaro Ishinomori story (the previous one was **FLYING GHOST SHIP**), but this popular manga artist's work continue to appear in a variety of different anime for many decades to come, from the SF of **CYBORG 009** to the economics education of **JAPAN INC**. Director Tamiya would go on to direct another kids-save-the-world extravaganza in 1973 with **BABEL II**.

THIS UGLY AND BEAUTIFUL WORLD

2004. JPN: *Kono Minikuku mo Utsukushii Sekai*. AKA: *Konomini; The Ugly & Beautiful World*. TV series. DIR: Shoji Saeki. SCR: Tomoyasu Okubo, Sumio Uetake, Shin Itagaki, Shoji Saeki. DES: Kazuhiro Takamura, Yo Yoshinari. ANI: Kazuhiro Takamura. MUS: Tsuyoshi Watanabe. PRD: Gainax, SHAFT, Geneon, Rondo Robe, MOVIC, TBS. 24 mins. x 12 eps.

Bored part-time motorcycle courier Takeru Takemoto has a close encounter of the third kind when he finds two alien girls in the glow of a strange light in the woods. Later, one of his friends encounters a second, similar girl. Based on an original concept by Hiroyuki Yamaga and Shoji Saeki, this science-fiction tale introduces alien entities that are not "living" organisms by our definition, but can mimic human beings. Their function is to help humans experience the beauty of emotion, such as joy or surprise—they often seem to achieve this by jiggling, the true hallmark of a Gainax anime. This is the 20th-anniversary work from the renowned studio, which previously collaborated with the SHAFT production house on **MAHOROMATIC**.

THOMAS THE RAPE ENGINE

2004. JPN: *Chikansha Thomas*. AKA: *Thomas the Pervert Train*. Video. DIR: Kenji Matsuda. SCR: Hiroshi Sasaki. DES: Hirotaka. ANI: Takashi Tsukamoto. MUS: N/C. PRD: Dream Entertainment, Studio March, Milky, Museum Soft. 30 mins.

A man with nothing better to do tries to "teach the women of the world about the pleasures of sex" by feeling them up on a crowded train. He has a special technique, it says here. Based on a computer game by Xuse. Compare to **MIDNIGHT SLEAZY TRAIN** and **XPRESS TRAIN**. **OOOO**

THOSE WHO HUNT ELVES *

1996. JPN: *Elf o Karu Monotachi*. AKA: *Elf Hunters*. TV series. DIR: Kazuyoshi Katayama, Tatsuo Okazaki, Hiroshi

Fukutomi. SCR: Masaharu Amiya, Masashi Kubota. DES: Keiji Goto, Akira Furuya. ANI: Keiji Goto. MUS: Susumu Akitagawa. PRD: Group Tac, TV Tokyo. 25 mins. x 24 eps.

A trio of adventurers is transported (with their T-74 tank) to a world inhabited by elves. Elven leader Celcia accidentally destroys the spell to send them back. Luckily fragments were copied onto the skin of five elves (and you can bet they aren't fat, old male elves, either) so fighter Junpei, actress Airi, and schoolgirl tank pilot Ritsuko must find them to get home. Crashing quest into skin-flick, with the emphasis on stripping the elves rather than skinning them, there are a few plot twists designed to amuse *Beavis and Butthead* viewers (firebrand Celcia transforms herself into an ugly dog and gets stuck, ho ho) and some with wider appeal (all the spell fragments our heroes find are easily visible without removing a stitch of clothing from their hosts.) There are nods to **DOMINION** in Ritsuko's devotion to her tank, and **EL HAZARD** in Junpei's obsession with finding decent curry in this alien world. Based on an "original" manga by Yutaka Yagami in *Dengeki Comic Gao*. **◐◍**

THREE MUSKETEERS, THE

1987. JPN: *Anime Sanjushi*. TV series, TV special, movie. DIR: Kunihiko Yuyama, Tetsuro Amino, Takashi Watanabe, Keiji Hayakawa, et al. SCR: Yasuo Tanami, Jack Production. DES: Mitsuki Nakamura, Shingo Ozaki, Hatsuki Tsuji. ANI: Hatsuki Tsuji, Shojuro Yamauchi. MUS: Kohei Tanaka. PRD: Studio Gallop, Gakken, Toei, NHK. 25 mins. (TVm), 25 mins. x 52 eps. (TV), 45 mins. (m).

In 17th-century France, young D'Artagnan leaves his home village to travel to Paris and find fame and fortune, serving his King as a Musketeer like his father before him. So far, so close to the 1844 novel by Alexandre Dumas *père*. In Paris, he defeats the plots of evil Cardinal Richelieu and Milady against Louis XIII, aided by his fellow Musketeers and mentors Athos, Porthos, and Aramis, and by the

Those Who Hunt Elves

queen's beautiful maid, Constance. The familiar Dumas tale was popularized in Japan by *D'Artagnan's Story*, an 11-volume series of novels by Yoshihiro Suzuki, with accompanying artwork by **LUPIN III**–creator Monkey Punch. The *3M* anime adapts the first volume of this version, with two major additions to the Dumas original—D'Artagnan's orphan boy assistant Jean, and the fact that Aramis is actually a *woman*, in a cross-dressing homage to **ROSE OF VERSAILLES**. The series, which began in October, was piloted the previous May with a 25-minute TV special *Chase the Iron Mask* (*Tekkamen o Oe*). For the latter half of the series, the animators would draw on the same events, from Dumas' *Man in the Iron Mask* through the tenth book in Suzuki's series. The series was recut again into the movie *Aramis' Adventure* (1989, *Aramis no Boken*), which rearranged flashbacks with new footage set a year after the final episode. Lune is a 16-year-old girl from the Swiss Alps, who falls in love with François, a young man she meets in the forest. Believing him to have been murdered, she adopts a man's disguise and changes her name to Aramis, hoping to track down the

man who ordered his death. Naturally, this turns out to have been his twin brother, Louis XIII, in a surprise that dovetails beautifully with the original source material. For very different animated versions, see **DOGTANIAN AND THE THREE MUSKEHOUNDS**, **KEROPPI**, and **PUSS IN BOOTS**.

3X3 EYES *

1991. JPN: *Sazan Eyes*. Video. DIR: Daisuke Nishio, Kazuhisa Takenouchi. SCR: Akinori Endo, Yuzo Takada. DES: Koichi Arai, Tetsuya Kumagai, Hiroshi Kato. ANI: Koichi Arai, Tetsuya Kumagai. MUS: Kaoru Wada. PRD: Tabac, Toei. 30 mins. x 4 eps., 45 mins. x 3 eps.

Yakumo Fuji loses his father in an accident in Tibet but gains a new responsibility. He must help a 300-year-old immortal, the last of the race that once ruled Earth, who lives in a symbiotic relationship with a 16-year-old girl called Pai. Yakumo is killed rescuing Pai but is brought back to life as her zombie protector. Now both of them begin a quest to become human.

Creator Yuzo Takada began as an assistant to **JUDGE**'s Fujihiko Hosono, and here combines the "walking dead" hero of ULTRAMAN with the ancient immortals of Tezuka's THREE-EYED PRINCE. Takada's *3x3 Eyes* manga suggests that all myths are the vestigial race-memory of a great conflict between extradimensional entities. Mixing the treasure-hunting elements of *Indiana Jones* with a mythopoeic buddy-movie, Pai and Yakumo search the world for artifacts that might help them. The mawkish romance between the two (made frankly irritating in an English dub that gives Pai a grating screech in place of a voice) is nicely contrasted with their magical personae—shy-boy Yakumo is an indestructible zombie, and puppy-fat ingenue Pai disappears completely when her third eye opens, revealing a powerful being with a demonic disregard for human life. In this way, *3x3 Eyes* is perhaps the most dramatically interesting spin-off from CREAM LEMON's schizophrenic "Lolita" concept and is mercifully asexual.

A second series followed in 1995 after Takada's successful BLUE SEED, with Pai losing her memory in Hong Kong and living as a schoolgirl in Japan. The new story, featuring input from Takada himself, takes the pair to Mount Kunlun, China's version of Olympus, where they join forces with some priests and a man with a really bad Australian accent to find the "key" to Pai's dimension. Covering only the first five volumes of the ongoing original, *3x3 Eyes* remains one of those truncated anime series consistently beset with rumors of its imminent return to the screen.

THREE-EYED PRINCE

1985. JPN: *Mitsume ga Toru; Akumajima no Prince Mitsume ga Toru.* AKA: *The Three-eyed Prince on Devil's Island.* TV special, TV series. DIR: Yugo Serikawa (TVm), Hidehito Ueda, Yusaku Saotome, Keiichiro Mochizuki, Shichi Matsumi (TV). SCR: Haruya Yamazaki (TVm), Mayori Sekijima, Reiko Naka, Tsunehisa Arakawa. DES: Osamu Tezuka (TVm), Kazuhiko Udagawa (TV). ANI: Shigetaka Kiyoyama, Hiroshi Wagatsuma, Masami Abe (TVm),

Kazuhiko Udagawa, Yoshiaki Matsuhira (TV). MUS: Kazuo Otani (TVm), Toshiyuki Watanabe (TV). PRD: Toei, Tezuka Pro, Nippon TV, Tezuka Pro, TV Tokyo. 85 mins. (TVm), 25 mins. x 47 eps. (TV). Sharaku is a high school student but his naïve manner, youthful face, and bald head make him look like a kindergarten kid, and he usually has some kind of bandage or dressing on his forehead. If he didn't, the world would be in trouble, for he is the last descendant of a three-eyed race who once ruled the world with advanced technology and vast intelligence. His mother left him to be raised at Dr. Inumochi's home shortly before she was killed by a mysterious lightning blast. Sharaku's friend is the local priest's daughter, Wato, a tomboy and aikido expert who knows his secret. She loves his "true" self, an arrogant but lonely superbeing, and looks after and protects his childlike human persona. She's also the one who usually has to take off his third-eye covering so he can save the situation when they get into some kind of trouble with magical phenomena, and she puts it back on again to prevent him taking over the world once the danger is past. Based on a manga by Osamu Tezuka, in which he hoped to combine the look of Elmer Fudd with the adventures of Sherlock Holmes—note an investigative character "Sha-rak," whose faithful assistant is addressed as "Wat-san." A heavy influence on the later **3x3 EYES**.

THUMBELINA

1978. JPN: *Andersen Dowa: Oyayubi-hime.* AKA: *Andersen's Tale: Thumbelina; Princess Thumb.* Movie, TV series. DIR: Yugo Serikawa (m), Hiromitsu Morita, et al. (TV2). SCR: Yuko Oyabu (m), Akiyoshi Sakai, Shigeru Yanagawa, Yu Mizugi (TV1). DES: Osamu Tezuka, Satoshi Fukumoto (m), Usagi Morino (TV). ANI: Tatsuji Kino (m), Usagi Morino (TV). MUS: Shunsuke Kikuchi (m), N/C (TV). PRD: Toei, Tezuka Pro (m), Enoki Film, TV Tokyo (TV). 64 mins. (m), 25 mins. x 26 eps. (TV).

The movie made by Tezuka's studio for

Toei is a straightforward adaptation of the classic fairy tale. A tiny girl, only as long as a man's thumb, is born to a childless woman, abducted by frogs who want her to marry their son, but escaping instead (with the help of a kindly bumblebee, a Tezuka addition) to find a real prince without having to kiss the frog first. It's utterly charming. One of the ever-popular TALES OF HANS CHRISTIAN ANDERSEN, the story was adapted again by Megumi Nagata (see PRISM SEASON), and again as a TV series, *The Story of Princess Thumbelina* (1994, *Oyayubi-hime Monogatari*). A feature-length edit of this series was apparently released on home video in the U.S. as *Thumbelina*. The series was also shown in Spanish on Puerto Rican TV.

THUNDERBIRDS 2086 *

1982. JPN: *Kagaku Kyujotai Technovoyager.* AKA: *Scientific Rescue Team Technovoyager.* TV series. DIR: Noboru Ishiguro, Yasuo Hasegawa, Katsuhito Akiyama, Hiromichi Matano, Shigeo Koshi. SCR: Hideki Sonoda, Noboru Ishiguro, Kazuo Yoshioka, Takayuki Kase, Shiro Ishimori, Keiji Kubota. DES: Kenzo Koizumi, Kunio Aoii, Kazuto Ishikawa. ANI: Katsu Amamizu, Mitsuru Ishii, Yasushi Nakamura. MUS: Kentaro Haneda, Koji Makaino. PRD: Jin, Green Box, AIC, Tohoku Shinsha, Fuji TV. 25 mins. x 24 eps.

In 2066, the World Federation Supreme Council appoints former astronaut Dr. Gerard Simpson (pointlessly renamed Warren Simpson in the U.S. dub) to run the International Rescue Organization. Based on a remote Pacific island, he leads a group of kids who pilot the "Techno Voyager" vehicles to save people in danger—Captains Raiji Hidaka (Dylan Beyda) in One, Sammy Edkins Jr. (Johnathan Jordan Jr.) and Eric Jones (Jesse Rigel) in Two, Gran Hanson (Gran Hansen) in Three, Catherine Heywood (Kallan James) in Four, and token brat Paul Simpson ("Skipper" Simpson) getting under everyone's feet.

The concept of the five-strong team had already been popularized in anime by **BATTLE OF THE PLANETS**, but the other similarities between *Technovoyager* and the British cult puppet show *Thunderbirds* (1966) might be considered actionably obvious. Luckily for him, producer Banjiro Uemura was head of Tohoku Shinsha and also of ITC Japan, part of the international corporation that owned the Thunderbirds copyright—*if* he found the resemblance too close for comfort, he would have had to sue *himself*. Uemura had already made **ZERO TESTER**, which by his own cautious admission "learned from" *Thunderbirds*. In 1977, he had held extensive talks with *Thunderbirds*-creator Gerry Anderson about a new animated series to be called first *Thunderhawks*, then *Terrahawks: Order to Recapture Earth*. During the outlining process, much of Anderson's original idea was discarded in favor of new plot elements from Sukehiro Tomita and designs from Yoshikazu Yasuhiko. Set in the year 2085, it was to be the story of second-generation immigrants from the rest of the solar system, returning to reconquer their homeworld, which has been overrun by aliens led by the evil "Queen Mother." The show stalled in the early stages, because the Japanese network MBS claimed there was no call for sci-fi. *Star Wars* opened in Japan just a few months later, by which time the project was already canceled.

However, several parties reused elements of the proposal in later shows—writer Tomita with **MOSPEADA**, Anderson with his puppet show *Terrahawks* (1983), and Uemura with *Technovoyager*.

Technovoyager flopped in Japan (only 18 episodes were screened on its initial run), but in his capacity as head of ITC Japan, Uemura was able to sell it to ITC's American arm, and, in 1983, the full run was broadcast in America as "*Thunderbirds 2086*, an ITC Entertainment Production"—transformed into a *bona fide* ITC production after the fact. The new title recognized the show's debt to *Thunderbirds*, but where the British only allowed for a handful of rescue craft, the Japanese team could call on no less than 17, enabling them to investigate crime and save lives on land, under the sea, in the air, and in space. The coincidental and remarkably convenient confusion of the letters B and V in Japanese allowed for the "Techno Voyager" vehicles to have the letters "TB" on their sides. The extensive vehicle lineup and stock hero team characters were close to the Japanese *Terrahawks* outline, while the *Terrahawks* puppet series released in Britain reputedly had many elements of the British outline—with the Queen Mother renamed Zelda. In another moment of chance cross-cultural pollination, both *Terrahawks*' Zeroids and **GUNDAM**'s Haro were spherical robots.

The confusion continued when the six unbroadcast episodes of *Technovoyager* were exported back to Japan as part of *Thunderbirds 2086*, two 90-minute videos with the U.S. dub (by **SPEED RACER**'s Peter Fernandez) left intact for added exoticism. Meanwhile, in a final irony, an "anime" version of *Terrahawks* did eventually reach Japanese screens; when the puppet show was broadcast in Japan, its opening sequence was replaced with new Japanese-made animated footage, directed by Tetsu Dezaki. Hideaki Anno, a big enough fan of the original *TB* to produce the Japanese-made documentary *The Complete Thunderbirds*, would acknowledge his own debt to Gerry Anderson with numerous homages in **EVANGELION**.

THUNDERBOYS
1995. JPN: *Itsuka no Main*. AKA: *Forever Main*. Video. DIR: Hiromichi Matano. SCR: Isao Shizudani. DES: Shushi Mizuho. ANI: Mitsuharu Otani. MUS: Teppei Sato. PRD: Toei. 45 mins.
Tokyo bikers race and fight, and race, and fight. Based on the manga in *Young Jump* by Shushi Mizuho. **LV**

THUNDERSUB *
1979. JPN: *Uchu Kubo Blue Noah*. AKA: *Space Carrier Blue Noah*. TV series. DIR: Kazunori Takahashi, Tomoharo Katsumata, Masahiro Sasaki, Kunihiko Okazaki, Shiro Murata, Teppei Matsu-ura. SCR: Hideaki Yamamoto, Kiyoshi Matsuoka, Takashi Yamada. DES: Akinobu Hane. ANI: Kenzo Koizumi. MUS: Masaaki Hirao. PRD: Westcape Corporation, Yomiuri TV (Nippon TV). 25 mins. x 27 eps.
In the year 2050, Earth is invaded by the alien Godom race, known rather more grandly in the Western version as the Force of Death. Ninety percent of humanity is wiped out, but their last hope lies in the secret Point N1 Base on Minamidori Island. There, the great aircraft carrier Blue Noah is nearing completion. With a young crew led by the inventor's son Makoto Kusaka (Earth commander's son Colin Collins in the U.S. version), it launches fighters to save the world, but the project isn't yet complete, and the ship must get to other secret Points to complete its construction, powered by a pendant passed on to the hero by his dying father.

As if taking a WWII battleship and sending it on a star trek wasn't ludicrous enough, this Earthbound follow-up to **STAR BLAZERS** somehow failed to recapture the magic of its predecessor. It wasn't until episode 21 that the ship justified its "Space Carrier" title, picking up a star drive at Point N9 that finally allowed it to get out of the water. Though 27 episodes were made, the first 4 were not shown in their original form but cut together into a feature-length "TV special" to open the series. Unlike the Yamato, however, the Blue Noah did not return for a sequel. See also **ODIN**, another attempt by producer Yoshinobu Nishizaki to make money out of ships sailing in space.

TICO OF THE SEVEN SEAS
1994. JPN: *Nanatsu no Umi no Tico*. AKA: *Tico and Nanami*. TV series. DIR: Jun Takagi, Jiro Fujimoto, Shinpei Miyashita, Kozo Kuzuba, et al. SCR: Hideki Mitsui, Aya Matsui, Noriyuki Aoyama, Asako Ikeda, Toru Nobuto. DES: Satoko Morikawa, Shigeru Morimoto, Kazue Ito. ANI: Yoshiharu Sato, Masaru Oshiro, Koichiro Saotome, Ei Inoue, Azumayami Sugiyama. MUS:

Tico of the Seven Seas

© 1994 NIPPON ANIMATION CO., LTD.

Hibiki Mikazu. PRD: Nippon Animation, Fuji TV. 25 mins. x 39 eps.
Little Nanami travels the world's oceans with her father, Scott Simpson, an oceanographer, in search of adventure and on the track of a legendary luminous whale said to have played a vital role in the evolution of life on Earth. Their captain is Alphonso, a brave fishermen and the owner of the good ship Peperonchino. Rich, beautiful Cheryl Melville talks her way on board in search of adventure, with her butler, and refuses to leave. Nanami's special friend, the orca Tico, swims alongside their boat as they search for the whale through the seven seas. When an unscrupulous team of scientists gets to the whale first, Nanami and Tico rescue it in the hope of learning its secrets and sharing them with the rest of the world. This is one of Nippon Animation's rare series *not* based on a classic novel; the story was created for the company by Akira Hiroo. Beautiful designs and a plot combining adventure with ecological correctness make a charming children's series. Episode 31 was not broadcast but included on the laserdisc release.

TIDE-LINE BLUE
2005. TV series. DIR: Umanosuke Iida, Dan Odawara, Keiko Oyamada. SCR: Yuka Yamada, Megumi Sasano. DES: Sadakazu Takiguchi, Kimitoshi

Yamane, Akihiko Yamashita. ANI: Kazuhide Tomonaga, Mineko Ueda. MUS: Tsuneyoshi Saito. PRD: Telecom, TV Asahi. 25 mins. x 13 eps.
It has been 14 years since the terrifying Hammer of Eden disaster, in which a meteorite strike on the Earth wiped out six billion lives and caused a massive rise in the sea levels. Aoi, the secretary-general of what's left of the United Nations, hopes to persuade the remnants of the globe to pull together, while Gould, a maverick submarine captain, stands up to the New United Nations by declaring war on them in the Ulysses, a rogue nuclear submarine. So, EVANGELION meets SILENT SERVICE, with the unsurprising presence of Satoru Ozawa, creator of BLUE SUBMARINE NO. SIX, among the committee members who came up with the plot. Compare also to SUBMARINE SUPER 99, which similarly featured two brothers separated by conflict—in this case, a boy called Keel is our teenage point-of-view character in the town of Yabitsu, attacked by Gould, while Keel's brother Tean is one of the men onboard Gould's sub.

TIES OF LOVE
1992. JPN: *Ai no Kusabi*. AKA: *Ties of Affection, Bonds of Love*. Video. DIR: Akira Nishimori, Kazuhito Akiyama. SCR: Naoko Hasegawa, Reiko Yoshiwara. DES: Katsumi Michihara, Naoyuki Onda. ANI: Koichi Arai, Takeyoshi Nakayama. MUS: Toshio Yabuki. PRD: AIC. 60 mins. x 2 eps.
The future city of Tanagra is governed by a computer entity known as Jupiter but administered by the Parthia syndicate, whose members are drawn from the aristocratic group known as Blondys. Social tensions bubble under its serene, ordered surface; disaffected political groups are plotting to kill the most important syndicate member, Jason Mink. But there's an even more pressing destabilizing factor in Jason's life: he has fallen deeply and embarrassingly in love with his "pet" Riki, a boy from the wrong side of the tracks who, like many young men and women

with no other options, has voluntarily become a sex slave. Neither Jason nor Riki can admit the ties that hold them, even to themselves; leaving aside their pride, both would be outcasts. Jason gives Riki a vacation, a chance to go back to the slums and find his old friends again, but a meeting with his former lover leads to tragedy.
Based on the novel by Reiko Yoshiwara, which was illustrated by JOKER's Katsumi Michihara, *ToL's* society is reminiscent of ancient Greece; not only are the institutions of power restricted to a certain class, but women are completely excluded from significant roles. All the key power relationships we see, including sexual ones, are between men. Ironically, the Jupiter computer manifests as feminine: like Kusanagi in GHOST IN THE SHELL, she's a man-made idea of the female in a world run by masculine elites. There is sexually explicit material but the violence is mostly emotional. Like most anime about homosexual love, this was originally made for a *female* audience. **NV**

TIGER MASK
1969. TV series, movie. DIR: Takeshi Tamiya, Kimio Yabuki, Tomoharu Katsumata, Fusahito Nagaki, Hiroshi Shidara, Yoshio Kuroda, Yasuo Yamaguchi (TV1), Kozo Morishita, Shigenori Yamauchi, Hideki Takayama, Tomoharu Katsumata, Masayuki Akehi, Kazuo Yamazaki, Osamu Sekita (TV2). SCR: Masaki Tsuji, Tadashi Kondo, Tomohiro Ando (TV1), Haruya Yamazaki (TV2). DES: Naoki Tsuji. ANI: Keijiro Kimura, Koichi Murata (TV1), Tsukasa Abe (TV2). MUS: Shunsuke Kikuchi (both). PRD: Toei, Yomiuri TV (Nippon TV) (TV1), Toei, TV Asahi (TV2). 25 mins. x 105 eps. (TV1), 47 mins., 53 mins., 25 mins. (m), 25 mins. x 33 eps. (TV2).
Naoto Date has a secret identity as masked wrestler Tiger Mask, part of a crude school of fighting that is more violence than art. Overcome by guilt when an opponent's death puts his little son in an orphanage, the hard man devotes himself to the well-being of the orphans and works to improve

their lives in the only way he knows how—by fighting. He also aims to raise the standards of the ring and ensure that fighting is recognized as an honorable art, not mere violence.

Based on a 1968 manga in *Bokura* magazine by KARATE-CRAZY LIFE's Ikki Kajiwara and ZERO SEN HAYATO–creator Naoki Tsuji, *TM* soon made it to theaters, as episodes were edited into seasonal "movies"—*TM* (1970, #9), *TM: War Against the League of Masked Wrestlers* (1970, #23, 25 and 26), and *TM: The Black Demon* (1971, #56).

A 1981 follow-up series is set after Naoto's death—he was killed saving the life of a child. A new opponent, Outer Space Mask, not endorsed by any of the national wrestling federations, bullies his way into the ring and injures a young wrestler. Tatsuo, a great fan of Tiger Mask who once lived in the orphanage he supported, intervenes wearing his hero's old mask and is accepted into the fraternity of masked wrestlers, where he becomes a major star. Champion of the oppressed and weak, he hides his secret wrestling identity under the everyday clothes of a sports journalist, echoing that other champion of the weak, *Superman*. ❷

TIME BOKAN

1975. AKA: *Time Fighters, Time Machine.* TV series. DIR: Hiroshi Sasagawa, Takao Koyama, Katsuhisa Yamada, Hideo Nishimaki (TV1), Seitaro Hara (TV2), Takao Yotsuji (TV4). SCR: Jinzo Toriumi, Haruya Yamazaki, Keiji Kubota, Tsunehisa Ito, Shigeru Yanagawa (TV1), Akiyoshi Sakai (TV2), Masaru Yamamoto (TV4), Satoru Akahori. DES: Tatsuo Yoshida, Yoshitaka Amano, Kunio Okawara. ANI: Eiji Tanaka, Hidemi Kama, Hitoshi Sakaguchi. MUS: Masayuki Yamamoto, Masaaki Jinbo. PRD: Tatsunoko, Fuji TV. 25 mins. x 61 eps. (TV1), 25 mins. x 108 eps. (TV2), 25 mins. x 53 eps. (TV3), 25 mins. x 52 eps. (TV4), 25 mins. x 52 eps. (TV5), 25 mins. x 58 eps. (TV6), 25 mins. x 20 eps. (TV7), 30 mins. x 2 eps. (v), 25 mins. x 26 eps. (TV8).

Junko and Tanpei are the grandchildren of a mad inventor who produced a time machine, went off into history, and simply vanished. They're determined to find him, but they're not the only ones. The scandalously dressed villain Madame Margot, with her hapless sidekicks, Birba and Sgrinfia, are also on his trail, and on the trail of a massive diamond lost somewhere in time. The ending could be viewed as an anticlimax—the professor returns to the present under his own steam—but in this case the journey, with its slapstick perils, crazy creatures, and interventions by wicked but inept villains, is more than the destination.

Time Bokan was only the first chapter in an epic saga of insanity on every level: design, characterization, and plot. With often-cited similarities to *Wacky Races*, and machines and performances that went further and further over the top, Ippei Kuri produced the first series based for Tatsunoko Production and remained in charge throughout its increasingly silly but lovable progress to classic status.

Like Sunrise's BRAVE SAGA, both the crew and central concept of the series remained through successive sequels, with only superficial changes. Only the characters' looks and the wonderful machines, designed to spin off into toy merchandising, displayed any variation—the robots and vehicles became so lucrative that a new one was introduced every episode.

Its successor, *TB Series Yattaman* (1977), came only a week later. Ganchan, descendant of a line of inventors, has made his own robot car, Yatta One, and takes his girlfriend and mechanic for a celebratory meal. Unfortunately they go to a restaurant run by sexy Miss Doronjo and her comic sidekicks, Tonzura and Boyakei. They are members of a gang under orders to find a powerful artifact, the Dokurostone (Skullstone), which can locate hidden treasure and is really the head of a mighty extraterrestrial called Dokurobei, who is just using the crooks to retrieve it. Ganchan and his friends must stop the crooks, but the quest takes them all over the world and through time. Though the plot is an obvious respray, art directors Toyo'o Ashida, Kazuhiko Itada, and Takashi Nakamura brought *visual* freshness and invention.

Once again, as one series ended another began, the following year's *TBS Zendaman* (1978). This time young Tetsu and his girlfriend Sakura race through time in their robots, Zendalion and Zendagorilla, to fight the trio of villains headed by sexy Miss Mujo. A short *Zendaman* movie premiered in spring 1980, but the new series *TBS Time Patrol Tai [Team] Otasukeman* was already on the air. In an achingly familiar setup, Miss Atasha, Dovalski, and Sekovitch are seeking an artifact that will enable the shadowy Tonmanomanto to dominate the world. Hikaru and Nana spring to the rescue in their increasingly incredible machines, chasing or chased by the villains through time and space. An *Otasukeman* movie was screened in spring 1981 as once again the new series *TBS Yattodetaman* had just begun on TV. Princess Domenica's rule is challenged by the theft of the Cosmopavone, a magical bird whose powers (like Tezuka's SPACE FIREBIRD) can bring peace and healing. She calls on two of her ancestors, a boy and a girl from the 1980s, for help against hot-tempered Princess Mirenjo and her henchmen.

The sixth series, *TBS Gyakuten Ippatsuman* (1982, aka *Ippatsuman Returns*), revolved around Homuran and Harubo, owners of the time delivery company Timelease, who set off to make a delivery to another era and find themselves pursued by Munmun, Kosuinen, and Kyokanchin, representatives of rival firm Sharecowbellies, who are now calling themselves the Clean Aku Trio. Then Ippatsukiman shows up to help Timelease, and they realize that there's more to this job than they thought. The final series, *TBS Itadakiman* (1983), moves the starting point for the journey to Oshaka Academy, where the headmaster orders three students, Hoshi, Sagosen, and Hatsuo, to find the pieces of an artifact called the Oshakapuzzle, now scattered throughout the world. Meanwhile three "ronin" (students waiting to retake entrance exams) called Yanyan, Dasainen, and Tonmentan are also looking for the puzzle, which will give the finder strange powers. As before, the titular hero comes to the aid of the good guys.

Falling ratings brought the show to an end after reasonably long innings, though it returned to video once its young audience was old enough to rent. Members of the original crew reunited one last time for the *Wacky Races* homage *Time Bokan Royal Revival* (1993), which pits all seven trios of villains from the original series in a race against each other. The prize is supposedly the leading role in the next episode.

However, there was no next episode until *Thieving Kiramekiman* (2000, *Kaito Kiramekiman*), an eighth series that reordered the archetypes to make good-natured criminals the protagonists. The handsome Puff is sent back 500 years to our time to rescue his ancestor, Professor Rikkid. Everybody needs the treasure known as the Gold Eye, and Puff teams up with the pretty teenager Lips to form the Kiramekiman cat-burglar team. They are pursued by a trio of bumbling French cops, while Lips' own father is the chief of police—a combination of elements of CAT'S EYE and LUPIN III. This most recent incarnation in the franchise was shown on TV Tokyo. There was also an unrelated Fuji TV series *Time Travel Tondekeman* (1989), directed by Kunihiko Yuyama.

TIME STRANGER

1986. JPN: *Toki no Tabibito Time Stranger*. AKA: *Time Traveler Time Stranger*. Video. DIR: Mori Masaki. SCR: Atsushi Yamatoya, Mori Masaki, Toshio Takeuchi. DES: Moto Hagio, Koji Morimoto. ANI: Takuo Noda, Hiroshi Fukutomi, Toshio Hirata, Yoshiaki Kawajiri, Kunihiko Sakurai, Yasuomi Umezu.

MUS: Ryoichi Kuniyoshi. PRD: Project Team Argos, Madhouse. 91 mins. A minibusload of modern-day teenagers is hijacked by Jiro Agino, a time-traveler from the future, who drags them back to WWII Tokyo, and then to feudal Japan. They arrive at Azuchi Castle in 1582, just before the surprise attack that will/did/could result in the death of Nobunaga Oda. Jiro has determined that this is a critical moment in history, and that, had Nobunaga survived, Japan would have been spared the seclusion and stagnation of the Tokugawa period—forecasting that when Western powers arrived in the 19th century they would not have been able to treat Japan as a second-class nation. This in turn would have created a better political climate in the Pacific, and averted Japan's involvement in WWII! The gang is faced with a dilemma—to change history by warning Nobunaga (portrayed with a sympathy rare in his other anime appearances such as YOTODEN), or to keep quiet and risk dying in the coming "surprise" attack. Meanwhile, far-future assassin Toshito Kutajima arrives to terminate Jiro's meddling, while schoolgirl Tetsuko "Teko" Hayasaka unhelpfully falls in love with Nobunaga's page-boy Ranmaru. Sometimes confused with GOSHOGUN spin-off *Etranger*, this has more in common with FIRE TRIPPER minus the cute infant. Considering the famous names all over the crew (note THEY WERE ELEVEN's Hagio designing alongside future MEMORIES-director Morimoto), it's a real mystery why this was never picked up for U.S. release. Based on a young adult SF novel by Taku Mayumura. In 2003, the unrelated anime *Goshogun* was released in the U.S. under the confusing title of *Time Stranger*, in what we can only assume was a deliberate attempt to annoy the authors of the *Anime Encyclopedia*.

TIME STRANGER KYOKO

2001. JPN: *Jiku Iho Kyoko Chokora ni Makase*. AKA: *Time Stranger Kyoko: Leave it to Chocola*. Video. DIR:

Masatsugu Arakawa. SCR: Fumihiko Shimo. DES: Hiroyoshi Iida. ANI: Hiroyoshi Iida. MUS: Koshu Inaba. PRD: Production IG, Transarts. 11 mins. A number of girls stand watch as guardians for the future of the world, their sub-SAILOR MOON ranks including Sakataki the Crystal Stranger, Hizuki the Ice Stranger, and of course, Kyoko Suomi, the Time Stranger. None of that's important right now, however, because the king's robot assistant is trying to organize a birthday party for him, in a spin-off tale that only tenuously relates to the 2000 manga in *Ribon* magazine by FULL MOON–creator Arina Tanemura. Although made for video, this short was shown in a few venues as part of a *Ribon* promotional tour, hence its being filed as a "movie" in some sources. **CNV**

TIME TRIO

1988. JPN: *Zukkoke Sanningumi Zukkoke Jiku Boken*. AKA: *Bumbling Trio's Time Travel Adventure*. Video. DIR: Hidehito Umeda. SCR: Takao Koyama. DES: Kazuo Maekawa. ANI: Takashi Saijo. MUS: Masayuki Yamamoto. PRD: Tama. 57 mins.
Hachibe, Mochan, and Hakase are three young newshounds for their elementary-school newspaper. While trying to spy on their pretty teacher, Yukiko, they are flung back into the Edo period where they meet another beautiful authority figure, this time a princess struggling to control her domains. Based on a best-selling children's book by Masayoshi Nasu. Compare to ZEGUY.

TIMID VENUS

1986. JPN: *Okubyo Venus*. Video. DIR: Hiroyuki Kadono. SCR: Koichi Arai. DES: Hiroyuki Kitakubo, Shingo Araki, Michi Himeno. ANI: Michi Himeno. MUS: Ami Osaki. PRD: Victor. 20 mins.
Young singer Hiromi is packed off to New York shortly after the release of her debut single and told to train hard for her first concert. A short anime made with a semidocumentary feel.

TO HEART

2000. TV series. DIR: Naohito Takahashi. SCR: Hiroshi Yamaguchi. DES: Yuriko Senba. ANI: Shichiro Kobayashi. MUS: N/C. PRD: KSS, Sun TV. 25 mins. x 13 eps.

Akari and her boyfriend, Hiroyuki, walk to high school together every day. In the evenings, Akari chats to her old friend Shiho on the phone, or the two girls hang out at restaurants and karaoke bars. Their classmates include a rich girl who belongs to the school's Black Magic Club and a robot maid sent to school to collect data on Japanese student behavior. So it's just another typical Japanese high school, and Hiroyuki is just another typical Japanese high school boy who, despite being a nice quiet guy with no outstanding talents, finds himself surrounded by pretty girls who would do anything for him. But the trouble is, they don't seem to have much idea of anything *to* do. Episode one revolves around selecting seating assignments for the class, which involves much making and ripping up of lists. Episode two shows extended footage of Akari getting ready for a date with Hiroyuki, but those anticipating fan service should note she spends most of the time brushing her teeth and their date consists of drinking coffee and talking. Created by a group of artists calling itself AQUAPLUS, this is another anime based on a 1997 "love simulation game" (see also SERAPHIM CALL) for the PlayStation and designed to sell merchandise depicting the cute characters. The anime shifts the original's focus from Hiroyuki to Akari, presumably to lure in a female audience who wouldn't take kindly to being regarded as the "prize" in a game. It's not overtly sexual; rather it creates the fantasy life most lonely Japanese teenagers would apparently like to have, which, on the evidence of this show, is a quiet one.

TOBIDAZE BATCHIRI

1966. AKA: *Jump to It, Batchiri.* TV series. DIR: Kumi Yamamoto. SCR: Hitoshi Narihashi. DES: Mitsuteru Okamoto. ANI: Batchiri Group. MUS: Kunio Miyauchi. PRD: Nippon TV. 10 mins. x 132 eps.

The adventures of jug-eared schoolboy detective Batchiri, who can solve cases that baffle the police, thanks to his brilliantly ingenious mind. An early precursor of CONAN THE BOY DETECTIVE.

TOBIWAO IS TAKEN ILL

1982. JPN: *Tobiwao no Boya wa Byoki Desu.* AKA: *The Boy Tobiwa Is Taken Ill.* Movie. DIR: Kazuya Miyazaki. SCR: Tomiko Inui. DES: Renzo Kinoshita. ANI: Tatsuhiro Nagaki. MUS: Tadashi Kinoshita. PRD: Mushi. 19 mins.

Flying fish Tobiwao is happily frolicking in the waters of the Pacific when there is a bright flash in the sky and white ash starts to rain down on him. He dives for cover beneath the sea, but that night, he goes to his mother complaining of feeling very ill indeed. An anthropomorphic parable, set on March 1, 1954—the day of the infamous Bikini Bomb Test. The same event prompted producer Ishiro Honda to wonder if the test could do so much damage to fish, what would it do to other animals? The result of his speculation was released as *Godzilla* (1954).

TODO, IZUMI

A house pseudonym used by workers at Toei Animation in the creation of some anime serials, including PRECURE and TOMORROW'S NADJA. Compare to Hajime Yatate, the nonexistent man who invents stories for Sunrise, or Saburo Yade, who has supposedly dreamed up many of the teamshows made by Tsuburaya.

TOEI ANIMATION

Founded in 1956 as the animation arm of the film studio Toei, the company's first and most important acquisition was Nippon Doga, the small studio formed in 1947 by Sanae Yamamoto and Kenzo Masaoka. The company was known as *Toei Doga* until 1998, when the *doga* part of its name was translated into English as Toei Animation. For simplicity's sake, we have referred to the company as Toei Animation throughout this book. As the inheritor of Japan's prewar EARLY ANIME tradition, and as the instigator of Japan's postwar feature anime, Toei can be seen as the cradle of the modern Japanese animation business. Its movie releases included early classics of Japanese feature animation, including LITTLE NORSE PRINCE and PUSS IN BOOTS, whose leading feline Perrault remains the studio's mascot character. Despite its successes, it was unable to compete at a local level with the higher-budget releases of Disney, and enjoyed longer term success in television—some of its early work including KEN THE WOLF BOY, LITTLE WITCH SALLY, and TIGER MASK. As a feature of the move into TV and the same general slump in finances that killed off Mushi Production, Toei put many staff on temporary or freelance contracts in the early 1970s. A number of them responded by forming their own limited companies as suppliers to Toei, leading to the foundation of many of the small studios of today. As one of the largest production studios, Toei's home in north Tokyo's Nerima Ward attracted other anime specialty companies, both spin-offs and originals (the situation is analogous to Hewlett-Packard and California's Silicon Valley). Today, Nerima is the site of dozens of other production houses, as well as several of the best-known manga creators. More recent successes for the studio have included INTERSTELLA 5555, PRETTY CURE, and ONE PIECE, which took the studio's work to a wide international audience.

TOHO

Founded in 1932 as the Tokyo-Takarazuka Theater company (the characters for which contract to "To-Ho" in Japanese, and conveniently also mean "Eastern Treasure"), Toho's international reputation is largely founded on its production of the movies of Akira Kurosawa and the famous *Godzilla* series. However, it has also produced or distributed many anime productions, including **LUPIN III**, **TOUCH**, and the movies of Studio Ghibli.

TOKAIDO GHOST STORIES

1981. JPN: *Tokaido Yotsuya Kaidan*. AKA: *Ghost Stories of Tokaido/Yotsuya*. TV special. DIR: Hajime Suzuki. SCR: Sadatoshi Yasunaga. DES: N/C. ANI: N/C. MUS: N/C. PRD: TMS, Telecom, Fuji TV. 54 mins.
Set in 1636, this is the story of Iemon, who plans to kill his wife, Oiwa, hoping to inherit her wealth and marry his new, rich ladylove. Though his slow poisoning scheme pays off, he escapes justice in this world but not in the next, as Oiwa's shade returns to haunt him at every turn. A TV special based on Japanese ghost stories, for which one segment consisted of an animated tale.

TOKIMEKI MEMORIAL

1999. AKA: *Heartbeat Memorial*. Video. DIR: Hajime Kamegaki, Akira Nishizawa. SCR: Yosuke Kuroda. DES: Hideyuki Motohashi. ANI: Hideyuki Motohashi, Yasunori Tokiya. MUS: N/C. PRD: Studio Pierrot. 40 mins. x 2 eps.
Kirameki High School has a beautiful romantic legend. If on graduation day a girl confesses her love to a boy under the old tree in the school grounds, the two will have a long and happy life together. Twelve girls are in their last five months before graduation: Shiori Fujisaki, the principal character; her best friend Megumi Mikuhara; the beautiful but vain Mira Kagami; and the others consisting of Saki Nijino, Ayako Katagiri, Nozomi Kiyokawa, Yuko Asahina, Yuina Himoo, Yukari Koshikii, Yumi Saotome, and Miharu Tatebayashi. The first episode is essentially an introduction to all the characters, but in the second, as Rei Ijuin's Christmas party approaches, Shiori must decide whether to let her beloved know her true feelings.
Based on a 1994 dating game by Konami, which required the player to win one of the girls' hearts over a game span that was supposed to occupy three years of high school and

end at graduation, this video spin-off matches the game story closely and uses the same voice actresses, though the character designs are slightly different. Launched for the PC Engine, the original game spun off ten further titles in PlayStation, Sega Saturn, Game Boy, PC, Mac, and arcade incarnations, plus a radio chat show, radio dramas, and a long list of merchandise.

TOKIMEKI TONIGHT

1982. AKA: *Heartbeat Tonight*. TV series. DIR: Hiroshi Sasagawa, Akinori Nagaoka, Tsutomu Shibayama, Teruo Kigure, Hideo Yoshisawa, Noboru Ishiguro, Tomomi Mochizuki. SCR: Toshio Okabe, Takao Koyama, Tomomi Tsutsui, Fuyunori Gobu, Akiyoshi Sakai. DES: Koi Ikeno. ANI: Keiichi Takahashi, Keiko Yoshimoto, Gisaburo Sugii. MUS: Kazuo Otani. PRD: Group Tac, Nippon TV. 25 mins. x 34 eps.
Ranze looks like any other teenage girl, but she's the daughter of a vampire and a female werewolf. You can imagine how that would cramp your style bringing friends home after school, so she leaves her family to try and live a normal life. But then, just as she's enjoying falling in love with school hunk Shinpeki, she begins to manifest powers of her own. Strict laws forbid creatures of the night from marrying humans, and it seems that everything's going to go wrong for her—but in the end, luckily, Shinpeki turns out to be the long-lost son of Satan. Based on the 1982 manga by **NURSE ANGEL LILIKA SOS**–creator Koi Ikeno.

TOKIO PRIVATE POLICE *

1997. JPN: *Tokio Kido Police*. AKA: *Tokio Mobile Police*. Video. DIR: Moriichi Higashi. SCR: Yu Yamato. DES: Harunaga Kazuki, Satoshi Teraoka. ANI: Harunaga Kazuki. MUS: An Fu. PRD: Beam Entertainment. 30 mins. x 2 eps.
In 2034 Tokyo is beset by a giant-robot crime wave. With personnel numbers slashed on the police force, the government is forced to subcontract to private companies—compare to similar privatizations in **HUMMINGBIRDS**. Hence the

Tokio [*sic*] Private Police, although the subject of this anime is less concerned with fighting future crime and more with erotic diversions. A cast roster that is a thinly disguised reference to **PATLABOR** duly assembles, with section chief Shibata trying to keep his affair with a captain under wraps, and new recruit Noriko arriving at the run-down Ginza branch, and getting laid on her first day.
Episode two features some robot action as well, although that's not the kind of action that viewers of this short-lived series are likely to be looking for. The authors are not entirely sure why the world needs an erotic parody of *Patlabor*, but here it is. **N**

TOKYO BABYLON *

1992. Video. DIR: Koichi Chiaki, Kumiko Takahashi. SCR: Tatsuhiko Urahata, Hiroaki Jinno. DES: Kumiko Takahashi. ANI: Kumiko Takahashi. MUS: Toshiyuki Honda. PRD: Animate Film. 50 mins., 55 mins.
Subaru Sumeragi lives in Tokyo with his twin sister, Hokuto. A fey, gentle young man, he's a psychic by heritage and by trade, often called on by the police to assist on investigations that stump all normal crime-fighting methods. Each of the two videos (the second appeared in 1994) focuses on one case: the first a murder for power and money that is complicated when a bereaved young woman, out for revenge, unleashes psychic forces she can't control; and the other a genuinely chilling look into the world of a psychopathic serial killer. The stories contrast Subaru's unworldly gentleness with the cynical and self-seeking city dwellers around him. The religious symbols are leftover 1980s fashion statements rather than deep philosophical references—a superficial quality only emphasized by a truly awful English-language musical interlude. The real importance of *TB* is its part in the movement of elements from girls' manga into the commercial mainstream—though the U.K. distributors did hype it by falsely claiming that the

tape contained scenes of phone sex! Both videos are enjoyable in their own right but are only fragmentary glimpses of CLAMP's much larger manga universe, missing many of its facets. Subaru has a part in the earth-shaking events of **X: The Movie**, in which the genial vet who has been his friend, suitor, and mentor, reveals his darker side, and the ancestral links between their two families are finally resolved.

TOKYO GODFATHERS *

2004. Movie. DIR: Satoshi Kon, Shogo Furuya. SCR: Keiko Nobumoto, Satoshi Kon. DES: Kenichi Konishi, Satoshi Kon. ANI: Kenichi Konishi. MUS: Keiichi Suzuki. PRD: Madhouse. 92 mins. Three tramps—alcoholic Gin, transvestite Hana, and teen runaway Miyuki—find an abandoned baby while searching through the trash on Christmas Eve. They decide to return it to its mother, only to plunge into a whirl of scandal, kidnapping, and attempted murder, all on the one day when Tokyo is supposed to be quiet.

Like Satoshi Kon's earlier **Perfect Blue**, *TG* initially seems like a strange choice for animation. With so many real world locations, why not film it with real people? But nobody in the metropolitan government was going to approve a live-action film depicting a shanty town in the shadow of Tokyo's distinctive twin tower metropolitan government offices, nor were many of today's TV idols likely to sign up for a tale of grunge and poverty, however happy the ending. The clincher would have been the snow. It is popularly believed that it only falls in Tokyo once every ten years—the presence of snow being the first of this movie's many Christmas miracles, and far cheaper to achieve with animation.

Satoshi Kon's choice of subject matter is an act of faith in itself—framing the relentless hope and happiness of a Christmas comedy in the stark, realist tones of his other work. The baby's arrival sends the tramps scurrying to buy water instead of booze at their local convenience store, much to the

Tokyo Babylon

© 1992 CLAMP/SHINSHOKAN/MOVIC/SONY MUSIC ENTERTAINMENT (JAPAN) INC.

shop assistant's surprise. Hana jokes in the soup line that he is "eating for two," only to shock the charity worker the following day when he does indeed turn up with a babe in arms. In its comedy and sentimentality, *TG* is the closest thing we'll see to an anime pantomime, an end-of-year revel that turns everything on its head—even down to the Japanese voice actors, who are often cast against type, and with some amusing cameos. The opening sequence cunningly inserts production credits into the storefronts and graffiti surrounding the action; the ending is a souped up version of Beethoven's *Ode to Joy*—to the Japanese, the ultimate Christmas song.

TG also finds divine inspiration and beauty in everyday events, such as a wounded tramp seeing an angel, who turns out to be a bar girl in fancy dress. It may have three wise men (one and a half of whom are actually female), but its nativity story is not limited to Christian lore. A cemetery becomes a treasure trove as the tramps search for votive offerings of *sake*, and the film's stand-in for Santa Claus, white beard and all, can only perform his task properly if he dies doing it. The movie

alludes to Akira Kurosawa's *Rashomon*, which similarly features old men bickering over a foundling child in a storm, but at its heart is a search for kindness and warmth in materialist Japan.

TG shows a side of Tokyo that tourists rarely see, a side that many anime fans will find less believable than the heroic ninja, giant monsters, and transforming robots produced by audience chasers whose talent only extends to riffs on the latest fashion. It is also, like **Akira**, a love letter to the city. Kon renders its back alleys, shabby corners, and blue-collar areas with the same devotion that Otomo gave to the neon overload of its glittering uptown districts. Kon's leading characters are mostly confused and hapless but with an inner core of humanity that redeems their weakness. Ultimately, all are attempting to reunite themselves with "families" they have abandoned, believing their crimes to be unpardonable, whereas all their loved ones want for Christmas is for them to walk back in through the door. The story is compassionate but unsentimental—a work of honest emotion on the level of **My Neighbor Totoro** or Frank Capra's Christmas masterpiece *It's A Wonderful*

Life—and we can't, sadly, say that about very many anime. **LV**

TOKYO KIDS

Studio formed in 1990 by former employees of Studio Gallop and Tokyo Movie Shinsha, and particularly strong in digital compositing. Representative works include HIKARIAN and SUSIE AND MARVIE.

TOKYO MOVIE SHINSHA

Also known as TMS. Founded in 1964 by former puppeteer Yutaka Fujioka as a company to work on BIG X, the company originally operated as plain "Tokyo Movie" until 1976, when a refinancing deal led to the appendation of the phrase "New Company," or *Shinsha*, to its name. It has also traded variously as Kyoiku Tokyo Shisha (Education Tokyo Office) and Thomas Entertainment. The company has worked on many anime serials and movies, including AKIRA, GOLGO 13, ROSE OF VERSAILLES, MONSTER RANCHER, and LUPIN III. In 2005, the games corporation Sega announced that it had acquired a 50.2% stake in TMS, linking the animation studio to Sega's products in much the same way as the relationship of the component companies within Namco-Bandai. Just as Toei's Nerima location has attracted related industries to settle nearby, Tokyo Movie Shinsha shares its neighborhood in Tokyo's northwestern Suginami district with many other animation companies, including Sunrise and Madhouse.

TOKYO PIG

1988. AKA: *Fairweather Pig; Clear Day with Occasional Pig*. Movie, TV series. DIR: Toshio Hirata. SCR: Toshio Takeuchi, Hideo Takayashiki. DES: Kazuo Komatsubara. ANI: Kazuo Komatsubara. MUS: N/C. PRD: OH! Productions, TV Tokyo. 45 mins. (m), 25 mins. x 61 eps. (TV). Eight-year-old Noriyasu writes and draws in his diary, discovering later that *everything* he writes in it comes true, even if it involves talking pigs and strange adventures. This adaptation of the children's picture book by Shiro

Yadakara was revived for a TV series in 1997, directed by Shinichi Watanabe and written by Yoshio Urasawa, with Harebuta's ("Sunny Pig"'s) ability to "smell" people's true intentions getting him into many scrapes.

TOKYO REQUIEM *

2005. JPN: *Tokyo Chinkonka*. Video. DIR: Kazuyuki Honda. SCR: Kazuyuki Honda. DES: Akira Kano. ANI: Kazuyuki Honda. MUS: N/C. PRD: Milky, Studio Jam. 30 mins. x 2 eps.
A secret society in Tokyo is intent on kidnapping four "priestesses," each the mistress of a particular element of Fire, Water, Earth, or Wind. Their use in a clandestine, and no doubt unpleasant, ceremony is prophesied to herald the return of an evil god—as one might expect, if one has seen DOOMED MEGALOPOLIS. Having already captured and ritually ravished the Priestess of Earth, their second target is Homura Kamishiro, an attractive red-haired schoolgirl and part-time prostitute, who is soon infected with a magical feather that causes her to be constantly aroused and in need of satisfaction. Hiroto "The Avenger" Nambu steps in—he is an agent of another society, dedicated to opposing the previous one, and now functioning as the girl's protector and occasional sexual partner. Based on a manga by Nishiki Nakamura published in 2002, this is supposedly a multipart complete adaptation, although so far only two episodes have appeared. **LNV**

TOKYO REVELATION *

1995. JPN: *Shin Megami Tensei: Tokyo Mokushiroku*. AKA: *True Goddess Reborn: Tokyo Revelation*. Video. DIR: Osamu Yamazaki. SCR: Mamiya Fujimura. DES: Kenichi Onuki. ANI: Minoru Yamazawa. MUS: Hiroshi Ikeyori. PRD: JC Staff. 29 mins. x 2 eps., (v) 25 mins. x 52 eps. (TV).
Pale loner Akito Kobayashi sells his soul to Satan, and swears to assemble large quantities of the element Magnetite in order to open a gateway to hell. He transfers to a new school, where

he swiftly turns all the local girls into vessels of demonic possession and sets his sights on class beauty Saki, whose pliant young body contains massive amounts of Magnetite. Ranged against him are a motley crew of schoolkids, including two ninja in disguise, a teen witch, and handsome occult hobbyist Kojiro. This junior version of UROTSUKIDOJI has sorcerous computer geeks summoning devils through the Internet, necromantic heavy petting, a harpy who's an obvious rip-off of DEVILMAN's Silene, a clueless cast who don't know their Hecate from their athame, and some of the cheesiest dialogue known to man, including, "It's not every day I meet ninjas who are demon slayers. . . . I wouldn't be surprised if you were the reincarnation of some great goddess." Kojiro is the reincarnation of Tokyo's guardian deity Masakado (see DOOMED MEGALOPOLIS), his golden retriever has been possessed by the Hound of Hell (see CARD CAPTORS), and, if the plot wasn't trashy enough for you, it's actually a remake—this is a slightly more faithful adaptation of the novel and computer game already available in anime form as DIGITAL DEVIL STORY. Before you can say "Buffy," Satan is stalking Tokyo, teen witch Kyoko's been excommunicated for performing sex magic, and there's a faint whiff of homoeroticism redolent of the later X: THE MOVIE, as Akito confesses his love for Kojiro, albeit in a doomed, unrequited sort of way. The whole thing is tied up in a fiendishly rushed ending, with the characters yelling plot details at each other while the credits roll over them.

In 2000, the franchise was revived to promote a new version of the game on the Nintendo Gameboy. In *Goddess Reborn Devichil* (*Shin Megami Tensei Devichil*), 11-year-old soccer-loving schoolboy Setsuna flees indoors when rocks begin to rain from the sky. He meets token female Mirai Kaname and her scientist father, Kokai, who explains that the raining rocks are a sign that Magical King Lucifer has returned to terrorize the planet and is trying to break out of the parallel "magic" Earth to subdue the everyday world. Mirai, however, is one of the "Devil Children," a carrier of the "Devil Genome" that will allow her to fight Lucifer in the style of Go Nagai's *Devilman*. As demonstrated by the younger age group, the early morning broadcast, and the availability of the game in "Black" and "Red" editions, the new generation of the franchise has more in common with **POKÉMON** than with the story that originally inspired it. *Tokyo Revelation 2* (2002), a new version of the game, featured CG animation as part of its gameplay. **LV**

TOKYO UNDERGROUND *

2002. TV DIR: Hayato Date. SCR: Satoru Nishizono. DES: Yuji Moriyama. ANI: Shim Hyunok. MUS: Akifumi Tada. PRD: Studio Pierrot, TV Tokyo, Dentsu. 24 mins. x 26 eps.

Based on the manga in *Shonen Gangan* magazine by Akinobu Uraku, this is the story of a world under the streets and subway tunnels of Tokyo, where a group of powerful children with the ability to control the elements live a secret life. Rumina Asagi meets them after his first day at high school, when he comes home to a big hole in his back yard and two strange girls, fragile Ruri and feisty Chelsea, in his house. When Ruri is dragged back to the netherworld below Tokyo, Rumina joins forces with Chelsea and his schoolfriend Ginnosuke to get her back from the adults who hold her prisoner—he feels obliged to do this, because he has already died once rescuing her, and has now been brought back from the dead with new elemental powers into the bargain—compare to **POLTERGEIST REPORT**.

Director Hayato Date was a key member of the team that made **NARUTO**, a fan favorite of the early 21st century that similarly made light of more serious questing issues. He also made **BUBU CHACHA**, a kid's show for the very young that subtly revealed the strains of modern life, featuring a protagonist in need of rescue and companionship.

TU's Ruri is not merely a damsel in distress, she is a girl reared in a hermetically sealed world, cut off, as characters observe, from the sun and sky. Japanese comics and animation have seen many such exiles, both in times gone past, and in a recent resurgence since 9/11 and the invasion of Iraq. Like Japan itself, the fantasy realms of anime are often cut off from the rest of the globe. In the hidden worlds of *TU*, we see a similar distant conflict to that in **HOWL'S MOVING CASTLE**, and a nation under siege like that of **HEAT GUY J**. *Tokyo Underground* also reflects the iPod generation's general lack of affect. In a reversal of the twists of *The Matrix*, our intrepid heroes face a completely new environment, unlike anything they have ever encountered. Their first thought, however, is how much it reminds them of a film set—similar designer apathy for slightly older kids appears in *TU*'s contemporary, **GANTZ**.

TOKYO UNIVERSITY STORY

2005. JPN: *Tokyo Daigaku Monogatari: Kamen Ronin Ban*. AKA: *Tokyo University Story: Episode of the Masked Ronin*. Video. DIR: Jiro Fujimoto. SCR: Tatsuya Egawa. DES: Tadashi Shida. ANI: N/C. MUS: N/C. PRD: Sega, HMP, Shogakukan. 30 mins. x 2 eps.

Handsome, promising student Naoki finds his academic prospects crumbling around him when he is distracted by the pretty Haruka. Despite apparent similarities to **SAKURA DIARIES**, this video series is based on a much older manga in *Big Comic Spirits* from **GOLDEN BOY**–creator Tatsuya Egawa, which celebrated the tenth anniversary of its first publication in 2003. The story was also adapted into a 1994 live-action TV series (*DE), and a live-action movie, directed by Egawa himself and due for release in 2006. The anime features bonus commentary tracks from the Japanese voice actors—which are relatively rare in Japanese anime releases, although such extras have long been a staple of the English-language anime community.

TOKYO VICE *

1988. Video. DIR: Osamu Yamazaki. SCR: Minami Machi Bugyosho. DES: Kenichi Onuki. ANI: Osamu Tsuruyama. MUS: Karioka. PRD: Minami Machi Bugyosho. 60 mins.

Teenagers Junpei, Akira, and Keiko get involved in corruption on a grand scale when one of them is slipped a computer disk in a Shinjuku club by someone whose life is just about to be terminated. The bad guys are prepared to do anything to recover the disk, including tracking Junpei with a military satellite, kidnapping his sister Kumiko, chasing him in a helicopter gunship, and suppressing all media coverage of the cataclysmic aftermath. As usual, the police (in the form of Inspector Sakamoto and his team) are some way behind the young heroes in getting to the root of the problem, which leads to an explosive showdown with the corrupt corporation's secret weapon, a heavily armed robot. Like its U.S. inspiration *Miami Vice*, *TV* flirts with low life but is basically clean-cut, cute, and earnest. The action (the main point of an action show) is rather patchy; apart from the admittedly good final fight, there's a motorcycle/helicopter chase and a shootout with some suits, and that's your lot. We know that real investigators spend most of their time playing with computers and questioning suspects, but we don't necessarily want to watch the whole process.

Later rereleased in the U.S. by Media Blasters as *Tokyo Project*.

TOM OF T.H.U.M.B. *

1967. JPN: *001/7 Oyayubi Tom*. AKA: *Tom Thumb, 001/7*. TV series. DIR: Yasuji Mori. SCR: Toshio Shino (translator). DES: N/C. ANI: Yasuji Mori, Takao Kasai. MUS: Yasei Kobayashi. PRD: Toei, Videocraft, NET. 6 mins. x 26 eps.

Secret agent Tom and his faithful assistant, Swinging Jack, are accidentally zapped by a Miniaturization Ray, and are now small enough to fit into pockets. This actually makes them more, not less, effective as secret agents, and they become employees of the

Tiny Humans Underground Military Bureau. From their new secret hide-away inside a desk, they pop out in a tiny sportscar, ready to battle against MAD, an organization hellbent on world conquest.

A diminutive variant on James Bond, with the U.S. title a reference to *The Man From U.N.C.L.E.*, ToT was a coproduction between Toei Animation and the U.S. company Videocraft, made as a companion piece to **THE KING KONG SHOW**. The same companies also produced several other cartoons, including *The Mouse on the Mayflower* and *The Smokey Bear Show*. Among the many other "American" shows that technically qualify as anime are **MIGHTY ORBOTS**, the **ROBOTECH** sequel *Sentinels*, and **THE STINGIEST MAN IN TOWN**.

TOM SAWYER *

1980. JPN: *Tom Sawyer no Boken*. AKA: *Adventures of Tom Sawyer; Tom and Huck*. Movie, video, TV series. DIR: Hiroshi Saito, Shigeo Koshi, Takayoshi Suzuki. SCR: Akira Miyazaki, Mei Kato, Yoshiaki Tomita, Tadahiko Isogai, Takeshi Shise, Seijiro Kamiyama. DES: Shuichi Seki. ANI: Yoshishige Kosako, Yoshitaka Gokami, Noboru Takano, Michiyo Sakurai, Akio Sugino. MUS: Katsuhisa Hattori. PRD: Nippon Animation, Fuji TV. 25 mins. x 49 eps., 105 mins. (m).

Tom is a boy who lives in a small town on the banks of the Mississippi River in 19th-century America. He and his best friend, orphan Huck, hang out together and make mischief in and out of school. Their shenanigans include a balloon ride, a river trip, and a rescue of an innocent person from the false accusations of Indian Joe. Based on Mark Twain's 1876 novel, this **WORLD MASTERPIECE THEATER** series was edited into a feature-length movie entitled *Tom and Huck* for U.S. video release. An English dub of the series by Saban was shown as part of HBO's Family Showcase, alternating in the 7:30 a.m. timeslot with **LITTLE WOMEN**. Twain's follow-up, **HUCKLEBERRY FINN**, was also turned into an anime.

TOMATO-MAN

1992. JPN: *Sarada Ju Yushi Tomato Man*. AKA: *Tomato-man and the Knights of the Salad Table*. TV series. DIR: Hiroshi Sasagawa, Teppei Matsuura, Shinichi Watanabe, Hiromichi Matano. SCR: Masaaki Sakurai, Shikichi Ohashi. DES: Futako Kamikita, Yoshiko Hashimoto. ANI: Michio Shindo, Hiroshi Kagawa. MUS: N/C. PRD: Animation 21, TV Tokyo. 25 mins. x 50 eps.

The Kingdom of Salad is a beautiful dreamland where vegetables, fruits, and insects try, often unsuccessfully, to live together in peace and harmony. When the wicked Bug-Bug gang casts an evil sleep spell on beautiful Princess Peach, King Boo-Melon sends for "the Withered Plum," an old hermit believed to have magical powers, to awaken the princess from her eternal sleep. To help protect the king, Plum uses his magical powers to create a group of mighty warriors from ordinary food, the Knights of the Salad Table. Tomato-man, the last of the knights created by Plum, is the hero of the show. One of the few TV shows to attribute disruptive political intent to fruit and vegetables.

TOMINO, YOSHIYUKI

1941– . Born in Kanagawa Prefecture, he graduated in film from the Fine Arts department of Nippon University. He joined Mushi Production in 1964, where he soon became a writer and director on **ASTRO BOY**. He went freelance after three years, and studied advertising production at Tokyo Designer Gakuin College, before being tempted back into the anime business as a director on **TRITON OF THE SEAS**, **BRAVE RAIDEEN**, and **STAR OF THE SEINE**. His greatest contribution to the anime world came with his involvement in giant-robot shows, adding notes of pathos and tragedy to **DAITARN 3**, **ZAMBOT 3**, and his most famous creation, **GUNDAM**. For this and the realization that in his anime no major character was safe, he later gained the nickname "Kill 'em All Tomino." He also wrote the lyrics to many of the songs

associated with his shows, using the pseudonym Iogi Rin, and is credited with several novels, including the trilogy released in English as *Mobile Suit Gundam: Awakening, Escalation, Confrontation*. Tomino has occasionally struck out at the success of *Gundam*, protesting that it is all he is known for in fandom, despite a varied resumé that stretches all the way back to the earliest days of Japanese television animation.

TOMITA, KUNI

?– . A former storyboard artist for Madhouse on productions such as **CYBER CITY OEDO 808** and **WICKED CITY**, Tomita relocated to America in 1990. She subsequently brought a Japanese touch to local shows such as *Invasion America* (1998) and *X-Men: Evolution* (2000).

TOMITA, SUKEHIRO

1948– . Sometimes miscredited as Yukihiro Tomita; a pseudonym for Hiroshi Tomita. Born in Saitama Prefecture, Tomita worked briefly in the business world before becoming a screenwriter on **SPACEKETEERS**. Subsequent work has included **SPACE RUNAWAY IDEON**, **MACROSS**, and **GALL FORCE**, for which he wrote a novel spin-off. He also works as a manga scriptwriter, and hence is often associated with the manga adaptations or precursors of his anime work.

TOMORROW'S ELEVEN

1979. JPN: *Ashita no Yusha Tachi*. AKA: *Heroes of Tomorrow*. TV special. DIR: Kozo Morishita. SCR: Seiji Matsuoka. DES: Hiroshi Motomiya. ANI: Susumu Shiraume. MUS: N/C. PRD: Toho, Nippon TV. 85 mins.

In 1978, as the World Under-21 Soccer Championships draw near, amateur Jiro Ipponji is still living on a Hokkaido ranch with his sister Yuki, caring for his beloved horse, Golden Leg, and romancing his girlfriend, Yoko. The withdrawn loner is approached by Shin Mizuki and coach Matsumoto to play for Japan's national team. He agrees, becoming a formidable attacker. I think they make him leave his horse at home, though. Made as part of the hype for the 1979 championships, which were held in Japan. Compare to CAPTAIN TSUBASA.

TOMORROW'S JOE

1970. JPN: *Ashita no Joe.* AKA: *Rocky Joe.* TV series, movie. DIR: Osamu Dezaki, Hideo Makino, Seiji Okuda, Yuki Kobayashi, Toshio Hirata. SCR: Shunichi Yukimuro, Tadaaki Yamazaki, Seiji Matsuoka, Haruya Yamazaki, Hiroshi Saito, Tsunehisa Ito. DES: Akio Sugino, Hiroaki Kaneyama, Shingo Araki. ANI: Akio Sugino, Hiroaki Kaneyama, Shingo Araki. MUS: Tadao Yagi (TV1); Ichiro Araki (TV2). PRD: Mushi, Fuji TV; TMS, Nippon TV. 25 mins. x 79 eps. (TV1), 153 mins. (m1), 25 mins. x 47 eps., 120 mins. (m2).

One of anime's great sporting legends, this is the story of Joe Yabuki, a 15-year-old from the wrong side of the tracks living by his wits in Tokyo, who meets Danbei, a once-great boxing coach now seeking refuge from his past in drink. Both see something they need in the other—Joe a source of free meals, Danbei a potentially great fighter and a reason to live. Under the cloak of training with Danbei, Joe carries on a life of petty crime, eventually getting caught and sent to prison. Over a year inside, he finally realizes that Danbei was offering him both friendship and a future, and he carries on with the training regime the two had set up. On his release, he begins a successful boxing career. As he rises through the ranks, his main rival is Toru Rikiishi, a prison acquaintance, who dies tragically in a bout with Joe at the end of the series, leaving the champion devastated.

TJ is the most famous creation of Tetsuya Chiba, also known for WEATHER PERMITTING, I'M TEPPEI, and NOTARI MATSUTARO. His 1968 *Shonen Magazine* manga was drawn from a script by KARATE CRAZY LIFE's Ikki Kajiwara, who used the pseudonym Asao Takamori since he was also writing STAR OF THE GIANTS for a rival magazine at the time. The story was also adapted as a 1970 live-action film. It continued to attract

readers after the series it inspired had ended, and in 1980, with a second series in production for Nippon TV, the first series was edited to feature length for theatrical release, providing background for new fans and a reminder of the story for older ones. Though many of the old crew returned to work on the sequel, *TJ2* also featured new directors, including Mizuho Nishikubo and Toshio Takeuchi. It opens as Joe, having given up boxing after Riki's death, is brought back to the ring through the encouragement of his friends. This time, as in the manga, the tragic death at the end of the series is Joe's own, and fans were inconsolable. The second anime movie, premiered in 1981 was an edit of this series. The title *Rocky Joe* was adopted for Western sale in an attempt to cash in on the popularity of Sylvester Stallone's live-action film series, obscuring the fact that Joe was there first. ❺

TOMORROW'S NADJA

2003. JPN: *Asu no Nadja.* AKA: *Nadja of Tomorrow.* TV series. DIR: Takuya Igarashi. SCR: K. Y. Green, Tomoko Konparu, Yoshimi Narita, Yumi Kageyama. DES: Kazuto Nakazawa. ANI: Akira Inagami, Mitsuru Aoyama. MUS: Keiichi Oku. PRD: Toei Animation, TV Asahi. 25 mins. x 50 eps.

Over a century ago, pretty blonde thirteen-year-old Nadja lives in an orphanage in an unspecified part of Europe, until the arrival of a mysterious package makes her think her mother may still be alive. She joins a traveling circus in an effort to find her origins. Two mysterious men attempt to steal her heart-shaped brooch, but she is rescued by handsome, aristocratic Francis Harcourt. When you learn that the strangers keep chasing after her to try and get her heirloom jewel, you may detect a certain similarity to SECRET OF BLUE WATER; this will quite probably be enhanced by the arrival of a perky boy Nadja's age, a cute red-headed preschool moppet and not one, but two, friendly young lions. Based on the manga in *Nakayoshi* magazine, writ-

ten by Izumi Todo and drawn by Yui Ayumi, this mines the long tradition of children in search of their loved ones, like NOBODY'S BOY and NOBODY'S GIRL. A game spin-off duly followed.

TONDE MON PE

1982. JPN: *TondeMon Pe.* AKA: *Mon-Pe.* TV series. DIR: Shigetsugu Yoshida, Junzo Aoki, Hideharu Iuchi, Saburo Kawashima, Masaharu Okuwaki. SCR: Chifude Asakura, Yoshiaki Yoshida, Masaaki Sakurai, Kenji Terada. DES: Kazu Mitsui. ANI: Takao Kasai. MUS: Yuikihide Takekawa. PRD: Tokyo Movie Shinsha, TV Asahi. 25 mins. x 42 eps.

Fifteen-year-old country girl Mon-Mon dreams of being a fashion designer and gets a job as an au pair to a rising star designer, Mrs. Kano, her baby girl PePe, and her silly writer husband. But PePe can make toys and animals do very odd things. Mon's employers don't seem to notice anything odd is going on, and she finds her dream job turning into a chaotically cute trial of wits she has no chance of winning. She's a sweet girl, hardworking and kind, but very unsophisticated and simply not used to walking teddy bears and talking stuffed animals. She eventually decides to leave her job and go home, but psychic baby PePe, who has come to love her, finds a way to make sure she stays.

TOPCRAFT

Animation company formed in 1972 by several former employees of Toei, including Toru Hara, a former producer on LITTLE NORSE PRINCE. Although the studio's first work was on MAZINGER Z for its "parent" company Toei, it was soon lured away by the American Rankin/Bass company to work on foreign animation. Its first job was on episodes of the series *Kid Power* (1972). Amid the local chaos caused by the collapse of Mushi Production, Topcraft employees worked on TV specials for Rankin/Bass, including *20,000 Leagues Under the Sea* and TOM SAWYER. Later years saw the company working on anime only when times were lean; while Topcraft may have done occasional work on bona fide anime such as TIME BOKAN, LUPIN III, and LITTLE KOALA, the company's efforts were aimed at chasing dollars from Rankin/ Bass specials such as *The First Easter Rabbit* (1976). Topcraft thereby managed to appear on the credits of many supposedly foreign cartoons, including *Barbapapa* (1973), *Doctor Snuggles* (1979), and *The Hobbit* (1977). Topcraft had no connection with Ralph Bakshi's animated *Lord of the Rings*, but when Bakshi's work finished partway, Topcraft and Rankin/Bass cunningly fashioned their own *Return of the King* (1980) as a sequel of sorts to *The Hobbit*! However, most of Topcraft's work in this period was unknown in Japan, with only THE STINGIEST MAN IN TOWN being broadcast in Topcraft's home country. The high points of Topcraft's work for the U.S. include *The Last Unicorn* (1982) and *The Flight of Dragons* (1982). Subsequently, Topcraft was commissioned to work on Hayao Miyazaki's NAUSICAÄ OF THE VALLEY OF WIND. Those remaining members of Topcraft's staff who had not left during the high-pressure creation of *Nausicaä* stayed on and formed the core of the new Studio Ghibli. Their first work as Ghibli was CASTLE IN THE SKY. Some members of Topcraft split to form Pacific Animation Corporation (PAC), under which auspices they continued to work for Rankin/Bass on such productions as *Thundercats* (1985).

TOPO GIGIO

1988. TV series. DIR: Shigeo Koshi, Noboru Ishiguro, Masahito Kitagawa, Shigeru Omachi. SCR: Noboru Ishiguro, Chiyu Tadaoki. DES: Susumu Shiraume. ANI: Tadaichi Iguchi, Hirokazu Ishino. MUS: Nobuyoshi Koshibe. PRD: Nippon Animation, TV Asahi. 25 mins. x 34 eps.

By the 25th century, mice have evolved into a sentient species, gaining bigger heads, shorter tails, and the power of speech. Topo Gigio is a mouse space pilot sent on an exploration mission who accidentally returns to the 20th century, before the establishment of peaceful diplomatic relations between humans and mice. Landing in Santa Catalina City, he finds that humans still think of mice as either pets or pests, cats are still the enemy, and mouse society is still underground, but a nine-year-old girl, Jean, learns his secret and helps him.

Created by the Italian author Maria Perego, the famous mouse was introduced to Japanese children in a series of adventures getting his friends into and out of trouble (compare to future cat DORAEMON). These included rescuing mouse rebel Kurt and his fat friend Per from numerous scrapes, foiling the plots of head cat Megalo, helping mouse inventor Doc with his devices, and even meeting with Dracula. After episode 21, the series was rebranded as *Dreaming Topo Gigio (Yume Miru Topo Gigio)*.

TOPPUKU VIOLENT RACERS

1996. JPN: *Toppuku Kyoso Kyoku*. AKA: *Symphony of Violent Racers in Battledress*. Video. DIR: Yoshimasa Yamazaki. SCR: Narihiko Tatsumiya. DES: Kenzo Koizumi. ANI: Kenzo Koizumi. MUS: N/C. PRD: Taki. 42 mins. x 2 eps.

The Sea Monkey biker gang fights over its turf. Yet another bikers-beat-each-other-up anime, this one based on a manga by Yu Furuzawa. Compare to BOMBER BIKERS OF SHONAN. ⬤🄥

TOPSTRIKER

1991. JPN: *Moero Topstriker!*. AKA: *Burn Topstriker; Enter the Topstriker*. TV series. DIR: Ryo Yasumura, Akira Kiyomizu, Shigeru Yamazaki, Masahito Kitagawa. SCR: Yoshiyuki Suga, Yoshimasa Takahashi. DES: Kazuyuki Okaseko. ANI: Kazuyuki Okaseko. MUS: N/C. PRD: Nippon Animation, TV Tokyo. 25 mins. x 49 eps.

Hikari Yoshikawa arrives in Italy to develop his soccer skills with the Columbus team under top trainer Bertini and Dr. Robson, who used to be a top-level English player—he is, as anyone acquainted with the current state of the English game would realize, rather old. Hikari has some problems with rival player Cesare but eventually leads the team to the final, losing with honor, and is selected by Robson for a new international team, the Jupiter Wings. This consists of talented players from all over the world who haven't been selected for their national teams. The aim is to compete with the best at the international level, but with so many strong personalities involved, it will take time and effort to get them to work together. The story has a similar premise to 1992's FREE KICK FOR TOMORROW, but without the focus on the family relationships of the hero; the presentation of the game itself was more realistic than in many earlier series. It was screened in France as *School for Champions*, with Hikari renamed Benjamin, Cesare called Mark, and almost every Japanese name removed from the credits—a yellow card for local boy Thibault Chatel for crediting himself as director.

TORA-SAN: THE ANIME

1998. JPN: *Otoko wa Tsurai yo: Torajiro no Wasurenakusa*. AKA: *It's Tough to Be a Man: Torajiro's Forget-Me-Not*. TV special. DIR: Setsuko Shibunnoichi, Tetsu Dezaki. SCR: Tadao Hayashi. DES: Kenichiro Takai. ANI: Kenichiro Takai. MUS: Naoki Yamamoto. PRD: Eiken, TBS. 95 mins.

Torajiro Kuruma is an itinerant peddler, eternally unlucky in relationships but forever prepared to help others in need. In this case it is the singer Madonna Lily, who asks for his aid in Hokkaido but rejects his offer of love. A tragicomedy spun off from Yoji Yamada's long-running "Tora-san" series, which produced 48 movies, starting with *It's Tough to Be a Man* (1969, *Otoko wa Tsurai yo*). The franchise, arguably the most successful movie series on the planet, was thrown into chaos by the death of its leading man Kiyoshi Atsumi late in 1996. The character had a brief cameo, played by a double, in Yamada's live-action *The Man Who Caught the Rainbow* (1997), but this anime version can be seen as an attempt to move into a medium where the absence of the star would be less noticeable. The original was pastiched in the anthropomorphic anime **Dorataro**, and its 28th installment was shown on a double bill with **Tao-tao the Panda**.

TORIUMI, HISAYUKI
1941– . Sometimes miscredited as Eiko Toriyumi. Born in Kanagawa Prefecture, he graduated in law and politics from Chuo University in 1966. He found work as a writer and director at Tatsunoko on **Battle of the Planets** and subsequently wrote many other anime, including **Salamander**, **Tekkaman**, and **The Mysterious Cities of Gold**. He was a founding member of Studio Pierrot, but is now a freelance novelist.

TOSHINDEN *
1996. JPN: *Toshinden*. Video. DIR: Masami Obari. SCR: Masaharu Amiya, Jiro Takayama. DES: Tsukasa Kotobuki, Kazuto Nakazawa, Masahiro Yamane. ANI: Hiroshi Kato. MUS: Kensuke Shina. PRD: Animate Film. 30 mins. x 2 eps.
Uranus, leader of a powerful secret organization cleverly called "The Organization," wants to build an army of indestructible, invincible warriors. To foil the plan, the world's indestructible, invincible warriors reunite. Eiji, Sophia, and tooth-rottingly cute little Ellis are among the chosen ones, but Uranus' minions are gradually picking off the opposition and time is running out. Yet another game-based clone in the **Street Fighter II** mode—a large cast of two-dimensional video game "characters" brought to the screen in a cynical promotion, each given barely enough screentime to have a fight and use their little combat catchphrases or moves. Meanwhile, the big-haired Eiji embarks on a halfhearted quest for his missing brother, with risible attempts at depth resulting in immortal dialogue like, "We both know your brother killed my dad."
Obari's direction starts off well, with a line of soldiers aiming guns upstaged by a journalist aiming a camera. He pas-

tiches the **Akira** manga as the robotic Sho takes on a U.S. aircraft carrier, then shifts the scene to a Chinatown setup redolent of his later **Virus**. But this remains an anime-by-numbers that ticks every perfunctory box of a game adaptation—including a female character in a shower scene (Sofia actually manages to put her clothes back on while jumping through a window), fights between allies engineered through "mind-control," and a big fight at a secret hideout (in this case, two nicely inconspicuous skyscrapers). **V**

TOUCH
1985. TV series, movie, TV special. DIR: Gisaburo Sugii, Hiroko Tokita, Naoto Hashimoto, Akinori Nagaoka. SCR: Yumiko Takahoshi, Shigeru Yanagawa, Tomoko Konparu. DES: Minoru Maeda, Shichiro Kobayashi. ANI: Yasuo Maeda, Masako Goto, Hajime Watanabe. MUS: Hiroaki Serizawa. PRD: Toho, Group TAC, Fuji TV. 25 mins. x 101 eps. (TV), 93 mins., 80 mins., 85 mins. (m), 60 mins. x 2 (TVm).
When his popular twin brother is killed in an accident, Tatsuya tries to fill his shoes, both on their high school baseball team and romantically with Minami, the team's manager. A moving and involving story based on the 1981 manga in *Shonen Sunday* by **Slow Step**–creator Mitsuru Adachi. *Touch* the anime was a huge hit, both in Japan, where its rating topped 30%, and in Europe. The series transferred into theaters for three movie editions—*T: Ace without a Backstop* (1986, *Sebango no Nai Ace*), *T2: Goodbye Gift* (1986, *Sayonara Okurimono*), and *T3: You Are Too Right* (1987, *Kimi wa Torisugi Daa to ni*)—ending with the team about to play the national championship finals and Tatsuya asking himself if he has succeeded either on the field or in love. The closing credits of the series rolled without showing fans the outcome of the big game, or giving answers to either of Tatsuya's questions. Over a decade later, released in a period that also saw the long-delayed ending of **Kimagure Orange Road**, the

TV special *Miss Lonely Yesterday—Are kara, Kimi wa . . .* (1998, *MLY: Since Then, You've . . .*) takes place three years after that fateful match and shows us how Tatsuya and Minami have dealt with life and their own relationships outside the protective routines of school days. Series director Sugii and original designer Maeda returned for this follow-up. After it gained outstanding 23.3% ratings, it was only a matter of time before a further follow-up was announced: *Crossroads: Whereabouts of the Wind* (2001, *Crossroads: Kaze no Yukue*). In this latest installment, Tatsuya joins the minor U.S. team the Emeralds, and he soon finds himself courted by the team owner's young daughter, Alice Vormont. Meanwhile, Minami becomes a sports photographer's assistant, and the two nonlovers' paths are fated to cross once again. Adachi's baseball manga also reached anime in **H2**, **Miyuki**, and **Nine**.

TOUR CONDUCTOR
2005. JPN: *Shinjin Tour Conductor Rina*. AKA: *Tour Guide Tour Conductor Rina*. Video. DIR: Toshiaki Kanbara, Shigeru Yazaki. SCR: Guts Maro. DES: Masaki Hosoyama. ANI: Masaki Hosoyama. MUS: N/C. PRD: Ypsilon, Studio Matrix, Film Works, Movie King, GP Museum Soft. 30 mins.
Rina is a new recruit working for a travel firm placed in charge of the ominous sounding Demon Princess Tour. Her job is to take a tour group to the spooky village of Murasawa, famous for a local ghost legend. However, she discovers that at least part of the legend is true and that a terrible fate awaits the women on the tour bus when they are delivered into the clutches of rapacious local men in the remote country village. Based on an erotic novel. **LNV**

TOURNAMENT OF THE GODS *
1997. JPN: *Toshin Toshi II*. AKA: *Battle City II*. Video. DIR: Takehiro Nakayama. SCR: Takehiro Nakayama. DES: Takehiro Nakayama. ANI: Takehiro Nakayama. MUS: N/C. PRD: Pink Pineapple, KSS. 30 mins. x 3 eps.

At the Battle Tournament, fighters struggle to become proclaimed the supreme "Battle God." The victor of each gladiatorial bout gets the possessions of the vanquished, including their female partner. Sid, a mere fourth-level fighter, enters the tournament not because he wants to find his way through the maze and become an "angel eater" (use your imagination), but rather because he wants to win the hand of his beloved Azuki. Even though Sid wins the day with his pure heart, he is infected with a bizarre drug by the evil Aquross and becomes subject to incredible sexual urges that must be satisfied by copulation with angels. Though the superior **Sexorcist** got there first, this erotic anime is based on a computer game that came even closer to the original inspiration—even the Japanese title is designed to look almost, but not quite, exactly like **Toshinden**. **LNV**

TOWARD THE TERRA *

1980. JPN: *Terra e*. Movie. DIR: Hideo Onchi. SCR: Hideo Onchi, Chiho Shioda. DES: Masami Suda. ANI: Masami Suda. MUS: Masaru Sato. PRD: Toei. 119 mins. Earth is a distant memory. Five hundred years after a revolution replaced human government with computer-aided totalitarianism, machines control every aspect of human life. Artificially created children are examined on reaching adulthood—telepaths are weeded out and destroyed. These "Mu" rejects marshal their strength in a desperate attempt to escape this hostile environment. They need a dynamic leader who can take them to a world of their own, where they can live without fear of persecution. Meanwhile the computers declare that a fugitive Mu is at large, and Keith, one of the elite caste who work for the computers, realizes that his servant Jonah is more than he seems to be.

Keiko Takemiya, author of **Song of Wind and Trees**, wrote this science-fiction epic for *Manga Shonen* in 1977, and the anime remains close to the original style—boys' manga from a girls' artist. Despite the old-fashioned character designs, the film has held up well. The story handles familiar science-fiction concepts with assurance: Orwellian social and political oppression, computers that dictate humankind's every move, mutant monsters shunned and hunted by humans, and pilgrims braving danger for a freer world. The film does not shy away from death, and, though violence and gore are kept low-key, some scenes are disturbing. **N**

TOWER OF ETRURIA

2003. Video. DIR: Motoaki Ishu. SCR: Yuji Suzuki. DES: Ryosuke Morimura. ANI: Ryosuke Morimura. MUS: N/C. PRD: Milky, Museum Pictures. 30 mins. x 2 eps.
In an erotic variant on the fairy tales of Rapunzel and Sleeping Beauty, an evil witch kidnaps the beautiful princess Cecilia, imprisoning her in a supposedly impregnable tower. While the princess is abused and tortured, her royal parents decree that they will offer her hand in marriage to the brave knight who rescues her. The warrior Albion duly volunteers, although this is an anime that concentrates more on the princess's misery than the quest to end it—compare to **Blood Royale**. Based on a manga by Hiyo Hiyo in *Core* magazine. **LNV**

TO-Y

1987. Video. DIR: Mamoru Hamazu. SCR: Izo Hashimoto. DES: Naoyuki Onda. ANI: Naoyuki Onda. MUS: Masayuki Matsuura. PRD: Studio Gallop. 60 mins. To-Y, leader of the up-and-coming band Gasp, has an intense rivalry with another young musician, Yoji. An ambitious manager, Miss Kato, tries to use this to persuade him to dump his band and let her manage his solo career. She plays him and Yoji off against each other and threatens to stop Gasp playing a big open-air concert that is vital to their career. In the end To-Y decides that playing his own kind of music with his own kind of people is more important than manufactured pop success, and this commitment pays off when he and Gasp set up their own gig near the open-air concert and draw a good crowd. An enjoyable pop soap opera based on Atsushi Kamijo's 1985 manga from *Shonen Sunday Comics Wide*, it had added cred thanks to music director Matsuura, a member of hit band PSY-S, who also have a single on the soundtrack, along with Zelda, Barbee Boys, Street Sliders, Kujira, and more.

TP TIME PATROL BON

1989. TV series. DIR: Kunihiko Yuyama. SCR: Shunichi Yukimuro. DES: Tsukasa Fusanai. ANI: Tsukasa Fusanai. MUS: Hiroshi Tsutsui. PRD: Studio Gallop. 25 mins. x 26 eps.
A lackluster **Time Bokan** rip-off from **Doraemon**-creators Fujiko-Fujio, in which Japanese schoolboy Heibon is enlisted in the efforts of the time patrol to keep the past out of trouble. Compare to **Flint the Time Detective**.

TRAGEDY OF BELLADONNA

1973. JPN: *Kanashimi no Belladonna*. Movie. DIR: Eiichi Yamamoto. SCR: Eiichi Yamamoto, Yoshiyuki Fukuda. DES: Kuni Fukai. ANI: Gisaburo Sugii, Shinichi Tsuji, Yasuo Maeda. MUS: Nobuhiko Sato. PRD: Mushi Pro. 89 mins.
In medieval France, country-boy Jean falls in love with country-girl Jeanne. As part of a strange ritual, the local landlord forces himself on Jeanne, and then allows his soldiers to gang rape her. Jean's hand is cut off when he fails to raise enough funds for the war coffers. Losing faith in God, Jeanne starts to have conversations with the Devil. Both Jean and the villagers throw her out, believing her to be possessed, and the disillusioned girl devotes herself to the Devil. Based on the 1862 novel *La Sorcière* by Jules Michelet, it adapts the story of Joan of Arc for an adult art-house audience, using a combination of still frames and full animation deliberately aimed at breaking free of the full-animation mold and extending anime's "artistic" potential. Compare this with **The Sensualist**, aimed at

the same kind of artsy audience, and **Heroic Legend of Arslan**, which uses the still-frame device with considerable artistic invention purely to reduce costs. It is the last of three films made for an adult audience by Mushi, though before production began, Osamu Tezuka had already lost control of the company. New president Eiichi Kawabata appointed Yamamoto to direct *Belladonna*, and the result is different in mood and tone from **Arabian Nights** and **Cleopatra: Queen of Sex**, made by Mushi under Tezuka.

Transformers

TRAGIC SILENCE *

2005. JPN: *Shojo Yugi*. AKA: *Girl Game*. Video. DIR: Tsuyoshi Kano. SCR: Miki Kano. DES: Wataru Yamaguchi. ANI: N/C. MUS: N/C. PRD: Onion Studio, Five Ways. 30 mins. x 2 eps.

Luticia is a girl from a clan of vampires, who finds herself falling into forbidden love with Sho, her human childhood friend. Luticia's vampire relatives are very strict about avoiding human relationships—normal people are to be regarded as a food source, not potential bedmates, although this does not seem to have prevented Luticia's clan-mate Rick sleeping with Elana, a woman in a nearby town. This sets up an obvious tension between the humans of the village and the vampires that they now realize are dwelling in their midst. Although many vampires and humans appear to be in forbidden relationships, it's the one between Luticia and Sho that forms the focus of this short erotic anime—dumping the angst of *Romeo and Juliet* into a setting more akin to **Dracula: Sovereign of the Damned**. Based on an original story by Hashiba Hayase. **CNV**

TRANSFORMERS *

1985. JPN: *Tatakae Cho Robot Seimetai Transformers*. AKA: *Fight Super Living Robots Transformers*. TV series, movie. DIR: (Japan) Takayuki Nakano, Shoji Tajima (TV1–2), Katsutoshi Sasaki, Takao Yoshizawa (TV3–5), Mika Iwanami (BW), Osamu Sekita (Car-Robot). SCR: (Japan) Katsushige

Hirata (translator, TV1–2), Keisuke Fujikawa (TV3–5) Tomohiro Ando (v), Mika Iwanami (BW). DES: (Japan) (TV1–2), Ban Magami (TV3–5, v). ANI: N/C. MUS: Shiro Sagisu (TV1–2), Kazunori Ishida (TV3–5, v). PRD: Toei, Nippon Animation, Toei; TV Asahi; TV Tokyo. 25 mins. x 64 eps. (TV1), 25 mins. x 30 eps. (TV2), 25 mins. x 35 eps. (TV3), 25 mins. x 35 eps. (TV4), 25 mins. x 35 eps. (TV5), 25 mins. x 36 eps. (*Beast Wars*, TV1), 25 mins. x 36 eps. (*BW*, TV2), 25 mins. x 36 eps. (*BW*, TV3), 25 mins. x 39 eps. (*Car-Robot*), 25 mins. x 39 eps. (*Car Robot*), 25 mins. x 52 eps. (*Armada*), 25 mins. x 52 eps. (*Energon*), 25 mins. x 52 eps. (*Galaxy Force*).

Far out in the galaxy is a planet where life has evolved in mechanical, rather than organic, form: Cybertron, a world of intelligent transforming robots. Two forces struggle for control of the planet—the evil Destrons (Decepticons in the U.S. version) led by Megatron (later upgraded to Galvatron), and the heroic Cybertrons (Autobots), led by Convoy (Optimus Prime). The energy that sustains the planet is running out and the good guys build a huge starship, the Ark, to look for new energy

sources. The Destron too have their own starship, and after their plotting leads to both ships being flung far back in time to Earth, good and bad robots are buried under the crust of our planet until, in the 20th century, they are awakened by the eruption of a volcano. Remodeling themselves to allow transformation into automobiles, jets, and other indigenous technology in order to conceal their presence from the local population, they plan to carry on their war on Earth. The Cybertrons team up with a few humans who stumble across their base, but the Destrons see humankind as inferiors to be enslaved or removed.

A U.S.-Japanese coproduction and the **Pokémon** of its day, *Transformers* was originally made to order by Toei from scripts and designs prepared in the U.S. It was based on a toy line by Takara that was not originally known as *Transformers* until it was licensed to Hasbro for Western markets. Though nothing particularly new (**Macross** was way ahead of the game with transforming robots) or believable (a consistent sense of scale disappearing for good), the concept of two-toys-in-one wormed its way into boys' hearts, and there it stayed.

Transformers: The Movie (1986) was notable for a voice cast including Orson Welles, Eric Idle, and Leonard Nimoy. It moved the action back to the robots' homeworld in 2005. Supposedly designed to bridge the gap between the first and second series, it was not shown in Japan, creating the first wobbles of confusion that would eventually split the franchise into four distinct and contradictory continuities. Optimus Prime dies, handing on leadership of the Cybertrons to Ultra Magnus, who in turn passes on the leadership to Rodimus Prime. On the dark side, Megatron is remodeled by the mighty Unicron, an even nastier Force of Evil that goes around the galaxy eating planets, into a new leader named Galvatron—possibly after his Japanese self, who appeared in a new TV series the same year.

Transformers 2010 (1986) continued the story without reference to the movie continuity, ending with another heroic self-sacrifice for Convoy and featuring a whole range of new transforming toys. The format of "new transformations to fight new battles" was set, and from here on the complications multiplied, with U.S. and British comics from Marvel taking the story in separate directions, while the animated version continued in Japan. Originated completely in Japan, the third series, *Transformers Headmasters* (1987), has the goodies led by Fortress Maximus and Galvatron still leading the Destrons, as the search for new energy sources goes on across the galaxy.

The fourth series, *Transformers Chojin Master Force* (1988), introduces a new breed of robots, known as Pretenders, that can mix with human beings. The Destron have been driven off Earth, but under their leader Metalhawk, the few remaining Cybertron Pretenders are fighting to defend humans from a demonic force. The transformations that sold toys were still paramount, with the robot characters changing into other forms such as starfighters. The fifth season, *Transformers: Victory* (1989), focuses around Star Saber, the Galaxy's greatest swordsman, who leads the

Cybertron to protect Earth from the menace of Deathsaurus.

Transformers Z[one] (1990), in which a supernatural evil has resurrected the Destron, was canceled, and instead it was released straight to video as a 25-minute special. The series returned with a vengeance as *Beast Wars* (1998) on TV Tokyo, which reduplicated its checkered origins for a whole new generation. Though now using computer animation (from *ReBoot* creators Mainframe) the franchise began once more as a U.S.-Japan coproduction, which was then continued in Japan as *Beast Wars Second* (1998), *Beast Wars Neo* (1999), and *Beast Wars Metals* (1999). Just to confuse things, there was an additional non-anime Beast Wars sequel, *Beast Machines* (2000), animated in Canada by Mainframe, and only later exported back to Japan as *Beast Wars Returns*. A twist was borrowed from *Jurassic Park* as the two opposing robot ships crashed on planet Gaea and the good guys merged with local animals, while the bad guys linked up with fossil dinosaur DNA, enabling the protagonists to transform into cyberversions of the local fauna both alive and extinct. The Destron (Predacon in the English version) under souped-up T-Rex Galvatron (Megatron) want the planet's mysterious energy source, and the Cybertron (Maximals) under Live-Convoy (giant gorilla Optimus Primal) mean to stop them.

Transformers: Car-Robot (2000, released in America as *Transformers: Robots in Disguise*) returned to cel animation and the basic vehicle-to-robot transformation on which the series originally made its name. At the beginning of 2001, it was rebranded as *Transformers: Powerful Cars*. The next series was a true international coproduction between America and Japan, the 52-episode *Transformers: Armada* (2002, subsequently released in Japan as *Transformers: Micron Legend*), focusing on a group of special, smaller Transformers known as Mini-cons in America (Microns in Japan), who flee to Earth being pursued by the larger, bullying

versions. The difference between the American and Japanese versions is not limited to the language track—the American version was rushed into production and onto the airwaves, resulting in numerous bloopers and substandard animation that were cleaned up for the localized version in Japan, which had more time to work on the materials.

Despite such embarrassments, the coproduction method clearly made things a little easier for both sides, and the cross-Pacific collaboration continued in *Transformers: Energon* (2004, released in Japan as *Transformers: Super Link*), set ten years after the events of the previous series and featuring two new twists. The Transformers themselves are locked in a struggle to seize the powerful element known as Energon, but the series also introduces the other great robot gimmick—the *Energon* continuity robots can not only transform, but they can also *combine*.

The emphasis on quests and collection was continued in the next international coproduction, *Transformers: Cybertron* (2005, released in Japan as *Transformers: Galaxy Force*), in which a black hole threatens to destroy the galaxy, and both Autobots and Decepticons rush to acquire the MacGuffins of the season—the Planet Forces (Cyber Planet Keys in Japan) that will allow them to control the energies involved and save the universe, or conquer it, or something.

With the concept still selling toys to a new generation of six-year-old fans, and "vintage" 1980s items acquiring collectible status, it seems the *Transformers* concept will run and run. Edits of various series were also rebroadcast as seven "TV specials" throughout the period and were also shown as *Beast Wars* "movies" in 1998 and 1999. There have also been two computer-animated *Robotmaster* DVDs released as special deals with toy packets, which feature characters from several of the continuities. *Transformers Takara* is a special DVD release of episodes from the original series previously unseen outside

Japan. An American *Transformers* "live-action" movie (the term seems strange considering how much CG animation will doubtless be used) is forthcoming in 2007.

TRANSLATION

Translation is the rendering of any text into another language, replicating the original author's intent and tone. A difficult enough task in simple conversation, it is even more difficult when languages are as different in structure as Japanese and English. Since an anime is not the work of a single creative, translating Japanese animation requires a series of decisions concerning the intent, not only of the original author, but also of some actors. Translation in the anime world is often a labor of love—it is no coincidence that many translators are surprisingly young, idealistic, and ready to take intern-level salaries for complex work that in other sectors would usually require at least one, if not two university degrees and a decade of linguistic experience.

The basic form of translating anime is the subtitle—a text-based translation superimposed on the film. When movies are screened at film festivals, distributors sometimes supply a print with white subtitles. When viewed at a high resolution on a cinema screen, such subtitles are clear and easily read; however, the same subtitles can often fade into the image when viewed on a television screen. This is a handy means of discouraging piracy, although some distributors have not realized the qualitative loss inherent in using "white on white" subtitles for home video releases, where they tend to bleed and disappear into white backgrounds.

"Hard subtitles" are part of the finished image; "soft subtitles" are digital in origin, and can be turned on or off depending on the language needs of the viewer. Preferred subtitles in anime are usually yellow or white outlined in black (a type style called drop shadow), although some companies use multiple colors to denote different speakers or

even onscreen titles to translate signs or background details not part of the main dialogue.

True translation requires a rare set of skills—a mastery of the Source Language (in this case, Japanese) and the ability to write fluently and professionally in the Target Language (English). In order to facilitate sales abroad, some Japanese companies provide a "spotting list"—a very basic translation, often prepared by someone in the Japanese office who is not an English native-speaker. Some Western distributors, particularly before the 1990s, liked to believe that spotting lists were close enough to the original dialogue to completely remove the need for a translator. However, many spotting lists, summarizing rather than translating dialogue, missing jokes, puns, and exact meanings, often neglecting songs or onscreen credits altogether, are next to useless in preparing a professional quality translation.

Translators usually require a copy of the source program with a burned-in timecode (BITC)—an onscreen counter that allows each line's location to be identified to the precise fraction of a second. It is also usual to request a copy of the Japanese script. Anime scripts were often hand-written until the mid-1990s, but today are largely word-processed, and divide neatly into descriptions of onscreen action (at the top of the page), and dialogue (on the lower half of the page). In this regard, they bear a closer resemblance to scripts used in English-language commercials, rather than the playbook format used for English-language screenplays and theater scripts. Subtitle scripts must be fitted within a limited space on screen, forcing subtitlers to limit their language, often condensing or summarizing meaning. As with all translation, one must walk a delicate line between the communicative (what people say) and the referential (what they mean). This is particularly difficult translating Japanese into English, since word order, honorifics, and cultural differences can often ruin punch

lines or moments of drama and need to be carefully considered. A perennial problem is translating simple forms of address, since Japanese are often apt to call one another by titles rather than names, creating a dissonant sense in a viewer who hears the word: "Senpai!" but reads the translation "Motoko!"

The fees offered for translation vary widely. The lowest payment we have seen for an anime script was barely 0.03% of the highest, reflecting the variation in both skills and expectations in the industry. The ideal translators are fluent speakers of both source and target languages, with an appropriate level of skill in the target language to have sold books or scripts of their own, but the prices for such individuals often proves prohibitive. Company accountants argue that it makes far better economic sense to hire a translator to do a "basic" translation into English and a rewriter who will then polish the script. This can lead to generational loss, also known as semantic drift, where the meanings of certain phrases will mutate from the original author's intent, since the rewriter rarely understands enough of the original to check. It also leads to a form of job-title inflation—merely having a "translation" is no longer enough; instead we must now talk of "English-language adaptations," or "trans-creations."

Subtitled releases appeal to roughly 10% of the anime-buying market. Outside the fan community, in some mainstream sectors and particularly on television, it is more normal to see "dubbed" anime—that is, anime whose Japanese language track has been replaced by an English-language track. As a rule of thumb, a dubbed release costs ten times as much to produce, but can sell ten times as many copies and is more easily sold to television. The expense is incurred through the need to hire voice actors and a recording studio. Early dub releases, made for the children's market and often subject to drastic CENSORSHIP AND LOCALIZATION, often had dub scripts with names, plots, and even locations differing entirely from the original—the location of Battle of the Planets was moved into space, that of Mospeada back to Earth. Since the 1990s, when the Japanese origin of anime became a selling point in itself, even dub translations have aspired to a more faithful reproduction of the original. There are, however, still some exceptions, such as the brief vogue for "fifteening," in which anime were refitted for an older audience by the addition of superfluous bad language, and the occasional improvisational throwback such as Ghost Stories. Some English-language rewriters even go so far as to credit themselves as the "authors" of a script, regardless of the person who actually wrote it or the often uncredited figure who translated the script into English.

The voice track in an anime is usually separate from the Music and Effects track (or M&E). This allows for a far easier process, although there have been cases in the anime world where the M&E track has been lost or damaged—such as the original Gunbuster, which has never been dubbed into English owing to the prohibitive costs of reconstructing the audio from the ground up. Recording is usually done using an Automated Dialogue Replacement process (ADR, known as post-synching in Britain), in which single lines or scenes can be dropped in and manipulated digitally, one at a time. Digital editing processes allow for lines to be moved fractionally ahead or behind, speeded up or slowed down in order to achieve synchronized lip movements (lip sync), although the limited nature of Japanese animation sometimes means that lips do not necessarily sync completely, even in the Japanese original. The movement of characters' mouths is sometimes known as "lip flaps" in America, and the process of synching known as "fitting the flaps"—a term which did not survive in Britain, where it sounds laughably obscene.

Dialogue recording for actors is commonly done one voice at a time,

in order to allow for audio manipulation, and to avoid paying a performer by the hour to largely sit and watch other actors work. Some anime dubs are recorded with ensemble casts, although the immediacy and interactivity of such performances is often outweighed by the extra studio time spent doing retakes. Actors are sometimes brought in to the studio in twos and threes to record all the sequences in which they share screen time. There is thus no single method employed in recording dialogue, but often a mix of all three, even over the course of dubbing a single title. "Making Of" documentaries often imply a prevalence of ensemble casts, purely because they are usually shot for technical reasons on the "crowd-scene" day when most of the cast will be available for interviews.

A subtitle script is subject to further rewrites for performance, both for ease of delivery and fitting the flaps. The worst cases of semantic drift can often occur on the spot, as actors misread, mispronounce or misinterpret lines. For this reason, the best choice for ADR directors is usually whoever wrote the ADR script—there are several in the modern anime industry who started as voice actors or translators and progressed through ADR rewriting to directing.

Translators are also obliged to make a judgment call on "ad libs" in the original script, where the Japanese screenwriter calls for the cast to improvise. Whether to faithfully reproduce whatever the Japanese actors said on the day of their recording, or to interpret the "author's intent" as being one of letting the English-language actors similarly improvise, is one of the no-win situations of anime translation. Incidences of semantic drift are more common in dubbing, and the subject of increased indignation among fans at the liberties they believe to have been taken with the original script. Matters are often confused further by the use of "Japlish," English words adorning box art or press materials in Japan, frequently misspelled, which then

establish themselves within fandom as the "approved" terms.

Translators on dubs are often obliged to make another judgment call, particularly with humor, as to whether they should reproduce the exact meaning of a line, or instead substitute it with a different line that will induce the same effect in the viewer—be it a belly laugh, shocked surprise, or a groan. It appears traditional in anime fandom for the translator to take the blame for anything a fan doesn't like, particularly if the fan has learned a little Japanese and can use the occasion to boast of his own supposed skill. The best example of this is the controversy over Kosuke Fujishima's *Aa Megamisama*, which was initially (and excellently) translated as Oh My Goddess!, only to incur the wrath of fans who knew enough Japanese to read the letters "*aa*" but not enough to know that it could be a contraction of "*anna ni*." A later incarnation of the series was subsequently released as *Ah My Goddess*, an inferior translation that nevertheless matched the Japlish title already seen on Japanese materials, and hence greeted as somehow more "correct." Similarly, Streamline pictures felt obliged to release the Lupin III movie *Secret of Mameux* under the title *Secret of Mamo*, since the latter title was already popular in fandom, and the producers had given up fighting.

Some humor can be unintentional, leaving translators with a further problem—to faithfully translate an author's text if doing so would make it seem laughable to foreign audiences. Even the great Osamu Tezuka was unable to resist making a few English puns with his character's names, which often makes them difficult to translate, while spelling and names in Gundam and Captain Harlock have been a source of constant argument between self-appointed interpreters of the original creators' will.

Fans, however, are not the worst enemy of translators, and can often lend diligent and impressive support. Fandom has potentially limitless time to debate and correct its understanding of any anime it chooses, whereas translators are unable to predict what project will be the next to land in their laps. Time itself can be the most crushing limitation on a translator's performance. In one case, the translator was driven to an airport freight terminal at two in the morning to meet the tape directly from the plane, with eight hours to translate the script, for a producer who wanted a master ready for one o'clock in the afternoon, ready for review copies to be made and biked over to magazines by two. He made the deadline, although SAMURAI GOLD hasn't won any awards.

Another controversy in the anime world concerns "dubtitling," in which a distributor uses a dubbing script as the source for subtitling. This often creates subtitles that do not appear to translate the onscreen Japanese dialogue at all, and is greatly frowned upon in fandom. However, fandom's censure sometimes extends too far, occasionally deriding perfectly reasonable translation decisions as dubtitling, simply because they do not match the critic's preferred translation to the precise letter.

Semantic drifts can sometimes range further than the original target language, in cases where a "second generation" translation is prepared from the English text. Although most European distributors claim to translate direct from Japanese, there are cases of companies using some or all of an English-language translation in the preparation of the version in their own language. In the eyes of anime companies, this is usually a victimless crime, although it can be galling for English-language translators to see others taking the credit for their work and hard-won skills. This practice was common in the early 1990s, but now seems to have faded away, largely because many European anime translators are now better paid and better trained than their English-language counterparts.

TRAVELER IN DARKNESS WITH HAT AND BOOKS

2004. JPN: *Yami to Boshi to Hon no Tabibito*. AKA: *Yamibo*. TV series. DIR: Yuji Yamaguchi. SCR: Hideki Shirane, Rika Nakase, Tomomi Mochizuki, Toshifumi Kawase. DES: Asako Nishida. ANI: Kyuta Sakai. MUS: Akifumi Tada. PRD: Studio Deen, MBS. 25 mins. x 13 eps.

Eve is one of the overseers at the Great Library, an interdimensional institution where multiple realities from the entire universe are contained within books—at least, that is how it appears in our dimension. Eve, however, has lived many lives in these other worlds and has had many names, all while searching for a particular girl, in a multiverse drama recalling the works of Neil Gaiman and Roger Zelazny. Compare to READ OR DIE. Based on an erotic game by Root, with designs by Carnelian.

TREASURE ISLAND *

1965. JPN: *Shin Tarakajima; Dobutsu Takarajima*. AKA: *New Treasure Island; Animal Treasure Island*. TV special. DIR: Osamu Tezuka (TVm), Hiroshi Ikeda (m1), Osamu Dezaki, Toshio Takeuchi, Hideo Takayashiki (TV1). SCR: Osamu Tezuka (TVm), Satoshi Iijima, Hiroshi Ikeda (m1), Haruya Yamazaki, Hajime Shinozaki (TV1). DES: Osamu Tezuka (TVm), Yasuji Mori (m1), Akio Sugino (TV1). ANI: Gisaburo Sugii (TVm), Yasuji Mori (m1), Akio Sugino (TV1). MUS: Isao Tomita (TVm), Naoki Yamamoto (m1), Kentaro Haneda (TV1). PRD: Mushi, Fuji TV (TVm), Toei (m1); Tokyo Movie Shinsha, Nippon TV (TV1). 52 mins. (TVm), 78 mins. (m1), 25 mins. x 26 eps. (TV1), 90 mins. (m2).

Jack the wolf sea-pirate is killed in a harbor inn. The innkeeper's rabbit son, Jim, finds a treasure map on the old sea-wolf and sets out to find the booty, berthing on a ship crewed by other animals, chartered by the deer Dr. Livesay and financed by the pig Squire Trelawney. He befriends Silver, another wolf, who is revealed as the leader of the local pirates when they seize control of the ship. Eventually, the pirates find the island on the map and go in search of buried treasure. The anime then deviates from Robert Louis Stevenson's original 1881 story, in a style that not only contains elements of creator Osamu Tezuka's occasional heavy-handed moralizing, but also his genius. As the animals near the treasure, they lose their anthropomorphic characteristics, devolving back to a feral state and running off into the jungle. Eventually, only Silver and Jack are left, and Silver struggles between the two states. Reasoning that no treasure is worth losing one's "humanity" to animal greed, Silver and Jack leave the treasure behind. This anthropomorphic adaptation should not be confused with Shichima Sakai and Osamu Tezuka's 1947 manga *Shin Takarajima*, which shares the title but not the concept. Some sources list this as the first-ever anime "TV special," a somewhat pointless distinction since it was not the first one-shot anime to be broadcast—see INSTANT HISTORY. The U.S. release was colorized for Fred Ladd by animators in Seoul, who ensured that it was the South Korean flag, not the Japanese one, that the animals accidentally raise in a throwaway visual gag.

Hiroshi Ikeda's *Animal Treasure Island* (1971, *Dobutsu Takarajima*) deviated further from the original. The human Jim Hawkins and his mouse companion Lex set sail in a toy boat, pursued by a porcine Long John Silver (perhaps thanks to animator Hayao Miyazaki, who worked on the production). Jim also joins forces with a third party in search of the map, Captain Flint's granddaughter Cathy. At the climax, the treasure is found to be at the bottom of a drained lake, a conceit later reused in Miyazaki's CASTLE OF CAGLIOSTRO and ripped off in other anime, including LADIUS and BEAST WARRIORS. It was released in the U.S. as just plain *Treasure Island*, coincidentally featuring many of the same voice actors from the U.S. dub of the earlier version.

A more faithful version came in the form of the TV series *Treasure Island* (1978), director Dezaki's follow-up to his **NOBODY'S BOY** for TMS. This version restored the human characters from the original but did insist on giving Jim Hawkins a leopard cub for a pet. As well as directing, Dezaki provided storyboards under his pseudonym of Makura Saki, and this version was also reedited into a "movie" release, with Takeuchi credited as director and Dezaki as assistant. The series has been screened in Europe and run in Spanish on Puerto Rican TV.

TREASURES OF THE SNOW
1983. JPN: *Alps Monogatari: Watashi no Annette*. AKA: *My Annette: Story of the Alps*. TV series. DIR: Kozo Kusuba. SCR: Kenji Yoshida. DES: Issei Takematsu. ANI: Issei Takematsu, Eimi Maeda, Yoshiharu Saito. MUS: Ryohei Hirose. PRD: Nippon Animation, Fuji TV. 25 mins. x 48 eps.
In the remote Swiss village of Rossiniere, local bully Lucien causes Annette's younger brother Dani to fall into a valley and break his leg. The 13-year-old Annette vows revenge on Lucien, determined to damage his life in any way she can, although she eventually realizes that a truly good person should forgive others, even if they do wrong to them. Based on the 1950 children's book with a heavy Christian subtext by Patricia M. St. John, the anime version added many sequences not found in the original story, taking several episodes, for example, to cover the years leading up to the fateful leg-breaking incident. Compare to another **WORLD MASTERPIECE THEATER** Alpine story, Johanna Spyri's **HEIDI**.

TREE IN THE SUN, A *
2000. JPN: *Hidamari no Ki*. TV series. DIR: Gisaburo Sugii, Rei Mizuno. SCR: Tatsuhiko Urahata. DES: Marisuke Eguchi. ANI: Noriyuki Fukuda, Masahiro Kitazaki. MUS: Reiko Matsui. PRD: Madhouse, Nippon TV. 25 mins. x 25 eps.
At the end of the Tokugawa period, as Americans enter feudal Japan, two young men come of age. Manjiro Ibutani is a samurai through and through, beholden to his lord and obliged to lay down his life before his honor. But Manjiro's code is put to the test by a succession of humiliations, such as guarding the U.S. consul and commanding a unit composed of lowly farmers. Eventually, Manjiro becomes one of the fundamentalists who refuse to modernize (see **OI RYOMA!**); he is unable to survive in the brave new world of the late 19th century. But Ryoan, the doctor who tends his wounds, is very different. Ryoan has studied Western-style medicine and appreciates all the good that can be learned from the foreign powers. Both love their country and want to help their people, but in very different ways—compare to **SANCTUARY**, which similarly observes life from two very different perspectives. Based on the 1981 manga by Osamu Tezuka and partly inspired by the life of his own great-grandfather, Ryoan Tezuka, a 19th-century doctor. Broadcast with English subtitles in the U.S. on Asahi Homecast.

TREE OF PALME *
2001. JPN: *Parumu no Ki*. AKA: *Palm Tree; Wooden Palm*. Movie. DIR: Takashi Nakamura. SCR: Takashi Nakamura. DES: Toshiyuki Inoue. ANI: Mamoru Sasaki. MUS: Takashi Harada. PRD: Palm Studio, GENCO, Kadokawa, Toho. 136 mins.
On planet Arcana, a mystic tree is said to absorb the memories of the civilization where it takes root. A sentient android boy, Palme, is made from this wood to care for his maker's sick wife. When she dies, he is paralyzed with grief and loses all sense of purpose. Then blue-skinned Koram, a woman warrior of the Sol tribe, arrives at their home fleeing a group of armed pursuers, and he mistakes her for his dead mistress. She asks Palme and his maker to take a mysterious egg to the sacred region of Tama. When his maker is killed by Koram's attackers, Palme takes over and journeys through Arcana, encountering danger and friendship and learning what it is to be human. This Japanese take on *Pinocchio* is beautifully rendered, with backgrounds by Mutsuo Koseki, whose work is better known from **NAUSICAÄ OF THE VALLEY OF WIND** and **CASTLE IN THE SKY**. Attractive and interesting designs show stylistic echoes of **CATNAPPED**; but it's poorly paced and the character of Palme himself is not sympathetic. **Ⓥ**

TRIANGLE *
1998. JPN: *Terra Story*. Video. DIR: Yukihiro Makino. SCR: Yutaka Hidaka. DES: Hiro Asano. ANI: Hiro Asano. MUS: N/C. PRD: Daiei. 30 mins. x 2 eps.
Nineteen-year-old Keisuke gets a whirlwind education in the art of love from several enthusiastic ladies. Will they help him win the woman of his dreams? And will she mind some extra company? Based on a computer game, so the answers are probably yes and no. **Ⓝ**

TRIANGLE HEART—SWEET SONGS FOREVER
2000. Video DIR: Akiyuki Shinbo. SCR: Maki Tsuzuki. DES: Satoshi Ishino. ANI: Satoshi Ishino. MUS: Hiroaki Sano. PRD: Starchild. 30 mins. x 4 eps.
Fiasse Christella, headmistress of a renowned music school, is a former singer who still does a charity World Tour every year. Her mother left her very wealthy, and mysterious evildoers covet both her and her inheritance. Her old friends Ellis McGaren and brother/sister sword masters Kyoya and Miyu Takamachi are drafted to protect her. The World Tour is coming up and Fiasse is determined that the show must go on. The story is based on a computer game by Ivory. It took two and a half years to release the four episodes on video, but Tsuzuki spun a creator credit for two **LYRICAL NANOHA** TV series off them in 2004 and 2005.

TRIANGLE STAFF
Company formed in 1987 by defectors from numerous anime companies, the first work for which was animation on the video remake of **DEVILMAN**.

Notable staffers have included Ryotaro Nakamura, Noriyuki Suga, and Takashi Hirokawa.

TRIGUN *

1998. JPN: *Trigun*. TV series. DIR: Satoshi Nishimura. SCR: Yosuke Kuroda. DES: Takahiro Yoshimatsu. ANI: Yoshimitsu Ohashi. MUS: Tsuneo Imahori. PRD: Madhouse, TV Tokyo. 25 mins. x 26 eps.

A space Western in the style of EAT-MAN, set in one of those star systems that look exactly like the fantasy American West, if you ignore the two suns and the presence of a pair of female insurance investigators. Derringer Meryl and Stungun Millie, both as cute as pie, are there to keep an eye on a one-man destruction machine named Vash the Stampede, to try and minimize the collateral damage and expense of his shootouts. But Vash, a fabled gunman chased by every bounty hunter in the area, is not just another bad guy. He avoids killing at any cost and only fires off one of his mighty weapons to prevent injury to others. When you get right down to it, he's just a skinny geek with spiky hair and a good nature, whose main passions in life are food and girls. With hot lead flying from just about every other direction, Vash doesn't fire a single shot until episode five. He also raises issues such as exploitation of natural resources and the ethics of murder. And in Nicholas Wolfwood, a sexy young Christian priest whose weapons (wielded only in a good cause) include a portable confessional and a huge cross packed with weaponry, he's created an unusual antagonist. Ranged against him are his real enemies, the Gung-Ho Guns, whose secret agenda is to blacken his reputation by provoking him into murder. Based on Yasuhiro Nightow's original manga in *Young King Ours*. ◐

TRINITY BLOOD *

2005. TV series. DIR: Tomohiro Hirata, Daisuke Chiba. SCR: Atsuhiro Tomioka, Yuji Hosono, Masahiro Sekino, Masayuki Kojima. DES: Atsuko Nakajima,

Trinity Blood

Thores Shibamoto. ANI: Atsuko Nakajima, Yasuomi Umezu. MUS: Takahito Eguchi. PRD: AIC, Madhouse, Hanjin, FAI, Angle, Anime Aru, Gonzo. 24 mins. x 24 eps.

In a postapocalyptic scenario not dissimilar from that in VAMPIRE HUNTER D, a race of vampires faces up to a new threat, long-lived humans who have modified their bodies with cybernetic implants and nanotechnology. Peter Abel Nightroad is an agent for the Vatican but is also a secret operative in Ax, a special tactical unit run by the maverick Cardinal Catherina—compare to HELLSING and CHRONO CRUSADE. Based on a novel by the late Sunao Yoshida, although it is likely that the anime made it into production more through the artwork that accompanied the text, since artist Kiyo Kujo later adapted it into a manga for *Asuka* magazine. ◐ⓃⓋ

TRISTIA OF THE DEEP BLUE SEA *

2004. JPN: *Aoi Umi no Tristia*. AKA: *Tristia; Blue Ocean of Tristia*. Video. DIR: Hitoyuki Matsui. SCR: Kazuharu Sato. DES: Eiji Komatsu. ANI: ufotable zippers. MUS: Norihiko Tsuru, Yuriko Nakamura. PRD: Kogado Studio, Inc., Kumasan

Team, Inc., The Klockworx. 30 mins. x 2 eps.

It's been ten years since the ocean city of Tristia was ravaged by dragon attacks, and Nanoca, granddaughter of the great inventor Prospero Flanka, still dreams of carrying on his work and restoring the city to its former glory. That's enough plot for a Miyazaki movie, but not for an anime based on a computer game like this one. Accordingly, Nanoca's rival Panavia Tornado challenges her to enter the upcoming Golem Building Contest, in which inventors compete to create a useful household magical robot. Many of the characters are named after aircraft, which, we're sure you'll agree, more than makes up for any other elements that may seem derivative or futile. Cute girls and Roman centurion-inspired robot designs hint that this may not be rocket science, although a leading lady who aspires to be a great engineer is at least a welcome change from the usual anime roster of wannabe pop idols and doormats. ◐ⓃⓋ

TRITON OF THE SEA

1972. JPN: *Umi no Triton*. TV series, movie. DIR: Yoshiyuki Tomino. SCR: Seiji

Matsuoka, Masaki Tsuji, Yuki Miyata, Chikara Matsumoto, Minoru Onotani. DES: Osamu Tezuka. ANI: Akiyoshi Hane. MUS: Yoshimasa Suzuki. PRD: Animation Staff Room, Westcape; Office Academy. 25 mins. x 27 eps. (TV), 74 mins. (m).

Poseidon rules the depths of the sea cruelly, imposing his will through armies of vicious creatures. Little Triton's parents died resisting him, and now the boy carries on their struggle, helped by the intelligent and gentle female dolphin Lukar and by little mermaid Pipi. *Triton* began life as a 1969 manga in the *Sankei Shinbun* and was first animated as the unreleased eight-minute pilot *Blue Triton* (1971, *Aoi Triton*). Taken from Osamu Tezuka by skullduggery behind-the-scenes, both *Triton* and WANSA-KUN may have been birthed by the ASTRO BOY creator, but they were reared by other hands.

TRI-ZENON
2000. JPN: *Muteki Trizenon*. TV series. DIR: Takashi Watabe, Matsuo Asami, Hiroshi Kimura. SCR: Katsumi Hasegawa, Takao Yoshioka. DES: Naomi Miyata, Rei Nakahara. ANI: Naomi Miyata, Naoko Yamamoto. MUS: Kenji Kawai. PRD: Ganges, Kadokawa, TBS. 25 mins. x 22 eps.

"Hot-blooded and straightforward" Akira Kamui lives with his father and kid brother, Ai. His mother is mysteriously missing, and Japan is under threat from alien invaders. To fight the enemy, Akira has help from his childhood friend Kana, with whom he constantly squabbles, his dog Gon, the enigmatic but cute Shizuku, and sisters Uma and Riku (complete opposites), as well as Rama, a girl from an old Japanese family, and Umu, the standoffish singer of a local amateur band. Akira's rival Jin, who is strong, handsome, cool, and really nice, and Jin's sister Ena make up the rest of the team. Conceived as a multimedia project by Rui Araizumi, its publicity claims that *Tri-Zenon* will simultaneously encompass manga, anime, and novels, with each freestanding enough to be enjoyed

independently, but together forming a complex interweaving story. A man's reach should exceed his grasp, but this may be rather too ambitious for the creator and team that gave us SLAYERS.

TROPES AND TRANSFORMATIONS
Anime's most common stylistic device is the appearance of the characters themselves. Many, but not all, creators take their lead from Osamu Tezuka (himself working in imitation of the Fleischers' Betty Boop and Disney's Mickey Mouse) in using visual "pedomorphism"—many anime characters have skulls more like those of babies than adults, with large, widely spaced eyes and a drastically reduced lower jaw line, often creating a pointed chin and small mouth. Much imitated by foreign artists who claim to draw in a "manga style," this tradition is more related to the concerns of anime, with large eyes to help convey expression and emotion, and a reduced mouth size to lessen the time spent animating lip movements. Perfected with Tezuka's ASTRO BOY, this drawing style is now commonplace in anime, in manga based on anime designs, and consequently in much graphic art from Japan. It is merely one of many art styles used in Japanese comics, but the one most likely to appear in the kinds of works that are usually adapted for animation.

Unreal proportions do not merely apply to the faces of anime characters. In anime for the young, the baby motif is often continued for the whole body, with an outsized head and, occasionally, feet and short legs. In anime for older viewers, torso and leg dimensions are elongated to create tall, elfin body shapes, although, as in Western comics, the boys are sometimes given carved, muscular physiques, and many girls get large breasts. Regardless of the proportions of characters in a show, they may sometimes devolve into squashed down, "super-deformed" (SD) cartoon versions of themselves in moments of intense agitation, or sometimes in entire SD spin-offs in

which the cast remains permanently in a cartoon parody state.

Anime hairstyles have their own traditions. Period pieces like THE TALE OF GENJI will sometimes use natural shades for all characters, but the combination of black Asian hair and limited animation can make it difficult to tell them apart. In general, anime characters are differentiated by blatantly unreal coloring—it is not unusual in a cast of all-Japanese characters to find black hair alongside foreign variants like red, blond, and brown, and artificial shades like pink, blue, and green. Similarly, many characters have instantly recognizable hairstyles. Anime boys have quiffs and spikes in their hair that remain in constant position for ease of animation (but may occasionally droop into their line of sight), while girls have complex accessorizing. Drawing plaits or braids is unnecessarily fiddly for artists on a short deadline, but bows or ponytails with distinctive scrunchies are much quicker to draw and often present another excuse for brightly colored adornment. Such hairstyles can make anime girls seem younger than their age, but help make a hero's five love-objects at least a little different.

Anime clothing is similarly differentiated, with a cast line-up of girls likely to be dressed in mini-skirts, trousers, shorts, and long dresses, usually in direct reflection of their characters. Some anime, such as HUMMINGBIRDS, even feature the rather desperate inclusion of a pair of pants with one long leg and one short—an apparent attempt to do something offbeat. The only place where clothing is not set apart in this way is in female underwear, for reasons based on animation concerns and erotic subtexts. Animators at Studio Fantasia, long-time purveyors of soft-core titillation like AGENT AIKA, reported that overly lacy or frilly underwear was simply too time-consuming to animate. Distinguishing underwear with straightforward colors often backfired, since a pair of red or blue panties could look too much like gym-wear or a swimsuit, and hence lost much of its erotic edge. Instead, the default setting for anime underwear became plain white panties (Studio Fantasia taking this to an extreme, where they had their own identifiable style of panty, worn by both protagonists and antagonists), which are not only easier to draw, but can also carry an erotic charge based on Japanese censorship—a blank space in the image as a substitute for what is hidden beneath it.

The slapstick and externalized emotions common to cartoons around the world also play a major part in anime comedy. Lechery can be signaled by drool or nosebleeds (a sign of high blood pressure caused by sexual arousal), or an elongated philtrum that accentuates pursed lips; anger by enlarged and throbbing veins, red face, or steam coming out of the ears; panic or relief by an exaggerated sweat drop on the brow or hair; romance by the sudden eruption in the frame of hearts and flowers. Sight gags can work even when the visual grammar of the medium is a little unfamiliar. One does not have to know much about Japan to enjoy many of the visual gags in PROJECT A-KO, whose very title is a spoof on a Jackie Chan movie, or to get the joke when LUPIN III, eyes bugging out and body suddenly rigid as an arrow, spots yet another cute girl.

Another visual trope in anime is the exaggerated freeze-frame. The use of a single still image for a prolonged period represents an obvious saving in animation costs (taken to ludicrous extremes in later episodes of EVANGELION), but also accentuates moments of high drama. A samurai holding still, waiting for his opponent's head to fall off, or a freeze-frame of kung-fu action, inadvertently resembles the *mie*—a held-pose used to similar effect in kabuki drama. It has since been much copied in live-action science fiction, most notably the "bullet time" sequences of *The Matrix* (1999), which ironically spent large amounts of money imitating an anime trope originally designed to save on a budget. Some-

times, a heroic pose is accompanied by a gleam of highlighting on a character's sword or armor with a chiming sound effect. This can also be parodied by a self-confident (male) character producing the same effect from his white teeth, or even his glasses. Unconfirmed popular myth asserts that this is the origin of the Jamaican slang term *bling*, for jewelry or other conspicuous accessories.

Anime excels at adapting visual devices from manga and inserting them into action. Sudden crash-zooms into character's eyes, often accompanied by a *bling* sound effect and the narrowing of the screen, can denote steely resolve or intense rivalry between two characters. Watery, starry eyes and a sudden outbreak of hearts, flowers, or soft-focus is used to show a girlish crush or adoration. Silence itself can be illustrated by a sound effect, with an uncomfortable pause, perhaps in the wake of an unfunny joke, marked only by the calling of distant crows. A clonking sound of hollow bamboo is a reference to the *shishi odoshi* ("deer-scarer"), a pivoted bamboo tube used as part of a Japanese water landscape that fills up with water until it tips, hitting against a stone, and denotes the passage of time. Sometimes anime will even steal sound effects directly from manga and write them onscreen. There is even a manga "sound effect" for total silence—the word *shiin*, which can sometimes be seen onscreen as an additional visual gag.

Until the advent of video, anime's audience was primarily juvenile, and anime fictions often deal with the politics of exclusion and inclusion, filial duties, and family obligations—such as ASTRO BOY's *Pinocchio*-inspired yearning to become a real child and, when that fails, his *Superman*-inspired quest to do good for the human race. Juvenile and teenage anime viewers are in an a permanent liminal state, facing the pressures of puberty and adolescence, and wishing both to grow up fast and never to grow up at all. Anime deals with these concepts by injecting story lines

of transformation, allowing its characters to experiment with becoming something different—the superhero duality of Clark Kent and Superman, later remodeled with the symbiotic existence of ULTRAMAN, but also that of the "magical girls" like MARVELOUS MELMO (1971), able to transform into an older, more sophisticated version of herself.

Anime for girls had often drawn directly on the cross-dressing traditions of the Takarazuka musical theater, particularly Osamu Tezuka's PRINCESS KNIGHT (1967) and Riyoko Ikeda's ROSE OF VERSAILLES (1979), creating a subgenre running all the way to UTENA (1997), in which heroines become their *own* knights in shining armor. The notion of girls assuming men's clothing is given the weight of history in YOTODEN (1987) and OTOGI ZOSHI (2004), where the heroines assume the roles of dead or sick brothers. Despite the inclusion in MOSPEADA (1983) of a hunky hero who likes women and also dresses up as one, men's cross-dressing efforts often get less respectful presentation—such as a gentle comic sideswipe at school cross-dressing in HERE IS GREENWOOD (1991). In the same year, OKAMA REPORT and 3x3 EYES presented more sympathetic cross-dressers, but in 1992 Go Nagai lowered the tone of the whole girls' school genre with DELINQUENT IN DRAG. The right and wrong way for a samurai to cross-dress is graphically illustrated in PEACEMAKER KUROGANE (2003). Note that transvestism is distinct from transsexuality, a topic most famously treated in RANMA ½ (1989), whose hero regularly transformed into a heroine and back again, forcing him to deal with both sides of the battle of the sexes.

One of the most important innovators in the anime of transformation is Go Nagai, who gave male viewers the sight of a superheroine whose clothes regularly disintegrated in CUTEY HONEY, and another whose "costume" left her almost completely naked in KEKKO KAMEN. These, however, were mere diversions compared to his true achievements in the boys' market, notably the pilotable robot MAZINGER Z, which could combine with other robots to form a super-robot. This simple device not only generated a powerful pester factor among children who would demand all the toys in order to re-enact their favorite moments from the show, it also allowed for a prolonged transformation sequence, and hence the weekly reuse of preexisting anime footage.

Such transformations have been a common feature of anime ever since, reaching their apotheosis with MACROSS and the TRANSFORMERS, created during a general reduction in the size of toys during the 1980s. Smaller toys were easier to store and transport, not just for children but for toy companies, and the reduction in size was compensated for by increased variation—more intricate moving parts that allowed each model to be "two toys in one."

Anime is currently engaged in one of its biggest transformations, its format and scheduling shifting from a communal experience delivered at set times in theaters and on TV to infinitely mutable packets of data accessed on a handheld device. This reflects a change in society, camouflaging the big idea in a colorful wrapper. New tropes and transformations will doubtless emerge as a result.

TROUBLE CHOCOLATE *

1999. TV series. DIR: Tsuneo Tominaga. SCR: Hideki Sonoda. DES: Sachiko Hikabe. ANI: Robot, Junichi Takaoka. MUS: N/C. PRD: AIC, TV Asahi. 25? mins. x 20 eps.
Timid teenager Cacao, a student at the Microgrand Academy, spends more time lusting after gorgeous green-haired Hinano next door than studying, even though the classes on offer include magic. His magic professor, Professor Garner, reveals that, since he's over 120 years old, it's time for him to stop goofing around and move on to the next stage of his magical education. As Cacao slowly starts to regain his memory, he recalls that not

only has he already achieved his ends with Hinano, but she also isn't quite as human as she seems. Most males forget how old they are at some point, but very few forget who they've slept with, so Cacao isn't the brightest apple in the barrel, and his continuing progress may be problematic.

TROUBLED TIMES

1991. JPN: Michiteru Kuru Toki no Muko ni. AKA: Toward a Time of Trouble. TV special. DIR: Eiko Toriumi. SCR: Eiko Toriumi. DES: Takayuki Goto. ANI: Hisatoshi Motoki. MUS: Teruhiko Sato. PRD: Studio Pierrot, Nippon TV. 80 mins.
It's a fantasy adventure as tribal boy Bokudo, his red-deer guardian spirit, and the chieftain's pretty daughter Faya go hunting in the Gobi Desert. A one-shot adaptation of Koji Suzuki's novel Paradise, which won the 1991 Japan Fantasy Novel Award.

TRUE LOVE STORY

2003. AKA: True Love Story: Summer Days, and yet... Video. DIR: Hidehito Ueda. SCR: Masashi Takimoto, Naotaka Hayashi. DES: Tatsuya Oka. ANI: N/C. MUS: Ryo Sakai. PRD: KSS. 30 mins. x 3 eps.
Another story set in a high school where a bevy of cute girls covering all the teenage wish-fulfillment stereotypes surround one ordinary teenage boy.

TRUSTY GINJIRO

1991. JPN: Koha Ginjiro. Video. DIR: Koichi Ishiguro. SCR: Hirokazu Mizude. DES: Kazuya Takeda. ANI: Kazuya Takeda. MUS: N/C. PRD: Animate Film, Visual 80. 45 mins. x 3 eps.
After the death of his elder brother, Ginjiro Yamazaki appoints himself his parents' protector. Transferred to a new school, he gets into a lot of fights, as one might expect in an anime from MY SKY–creator Hiroshi Motomiya, this one based on a 1975 manga originally serialized in Shonen Jump. ◆

TSUBASA CHRONICLE *

2005. TV series, movie. DIR: Koichi Mashimo. SCR: Hiroyuki Kawasaki.

DES: Minako Shiba. ANI: Minako Shiba, Yukiko Ban, Takao Takegami. MUS: Yuki Kajiura. PRD: Bee Train, Production IG, NHK. 25 mins. x 26 eps. (TV), 60 mins. (m).
Wannabe archaeologist Xiaolang is dragged in an unexpected career direction when his childhood friend, Sakura the Clow Princess, loses her memory. Xiaolang is advised by a witch that he must recover the scattered pieces of Sakura's memory from a number of points in space and time—a quest tinged with tragedy, since if he succeeds, she will still not know who he is. Memory loss might be an apt subject to bring up for the CLAMP collective of creators as well, who, in imitation of the eternal self-referential recycling of Leiji Matsumoto (see SUBMARINE SUPER 99), have simply dumped characters from some of their earlier works into a vaguely defined quest narrative. So it is that we have two characters from CARDCAPTORS joining forces with a number of elements and creatures from RAYEARTH to chase after a new MacGuffin. As in the case of the "original" manga, also created by CLAMP, there are also frequent crossovers with xxxHOLIC—most notably in the case of the Tsubasa Chronicles movie spin-off, TC: Chronicles of the Princess of Birdcage-land (2005, Tsubasa Chronicle: Torikago no Kuni no Himegimi), which was shown in a double bill with the xxxHOLIC movie A Midsummer Night's Dream.

TSUKIKAGE RAN: CARRIED BY THE WIND *

2000. JPN: Kaze ni Omakase Tsukikage. AKA: Moonshadow Drifting on the Wind, Lordless Retainer Tsukikage. TV series. DIR: Akitaro Daichi. SCR: Yosuke Kuroda. DES: Hajime Watanabe. ANI: Takahiro Yoshimatsu. MUS: N/C. PRD: Madhouse, WOWOW. 25 mins. x 13 eps.
In the olde-worlde nostalgia spirit of the turn of the century that also created ARMORED CHRONICLE HIO and TREE IN THE SUN, this anime is a jokey retelling of old samurai dramas, written by JUBEI-CHAN THE NINJA GIRL's Akitaro Daichi, and broadcast on Japanese TV

while the latter show was still on-air. As with *Jubei-chan*, Daichi takes an old favorite (in this case Moonshadow, a wandering samurai originally popularized by heartthrob Jushiro Konoe, star of *Zatoichi Challenged* and *Sworn Brothers*), switches the character's sex, and gives her a gimmicky favorite food in place of any personality. Ran Tsukikage is a wandering samurai *lady*, righting wrongs and doing good deeds all around Japan, accompanied by Miao, a female specialist in Chinese kung fu. Tsukikage likes drinking sake and eating bean-curd dregs (see **AKANE-CHAN**)—a meal that *Newtype*, without a scrap of irony, recommended its readers eat in front of the TV for the ultimate viewing experience.

TSURU-HIME

1990. JPN: *Tsuru Hime Jaaaa!*. AKA: *Princess Tsuru, Crane Princess*. TV series. DIR: Tameo Ogawa, Yoshihiro Yamaguchi, Yoshiko Sasaki, Shigeru Ueda, Koichi Sasaki. SCR: Hirokazu Mizude, Tadashi Hayakawa, Tameo Ogawa. DES: Yoshiko Tsuchida. ANI: Hiromi Muranaka. MUS: N/C. PRD: Aubec, Nippon TV. 17 mins. x 67 eps.

The ugly Princess Tsuru makes life hell for everyone in the samurai-era Hagemasu Castle. This gag anime was based on the manga in *Margaret* magazine by Yoshiko Tsuchida.

TSURUPIKA HAGEMARUKUN

1988. AKA: *Little Baldy Hagemaru*. TV series. DIR: Hiroshi Sasagawa, Tetsuo Yasumi, Tsukasa Sunaga, Hiroyuki Sasaki, Teruo Kigure, Koichi Sasaki, Junji Nishimura. SCR: Masaaki Sakurai. DES: Munekatsu Fujita. ANI: Akira Kawajima, Katsuhiko Yamazaki. MUS: Kuni Kawauchi. PRD: Shinei Doga. 25 mins. x 58 eps.

In this adaptation of the four-panel gag strip by Shinbo Nomura, ten-year-old brat Hagemaru Hageda causes mischief all over his small Japanese suburb.

TV ASAHI

Often abbreviated in Japanese broadcast listings as "EX," this channel began life in 1957 as NET—Nippon Educational Television. Subsequently renamed Asahi National Broadcasting (ANB—Zenkoku Asahi Hoso) in 1962. Asahi has a large number of children's titles and often appears to stick to long-running family franchises instead of short bursts of riskier entertainment like TV Tokyo. It is the home of both **DORAEMON** and **CRAYON SHIN-CHAN**. The newspaper the *Asahi Shinbun* is a related company.

TV TOKYO

Established as Television Tokyo Channel 12 in 1964 by the Foundation for Science and Technology, TV Tokyo, or "TX," is a subsidiary of the *Nihon Keizai Shinbun* newspaper. A smaller channel with a far greater interest in niche programming, TV Tokyo is the home of many of the anime series recognizable to Western teenagers, particularly the short-run shows lasting for 13 episodes. The channel's biggest anime successes are arguably **POKÉMON** and **NARUTO**, although it was also the home of many modern favorites, including **EVANGELION** and **COWBOY BEBOP** (see also WOWOW). TV Tokyo also runs the dedicated anime satellite channel Anime Theater X (AT–X).

TWD EXPRESS: ROLLING TAKEOFF

1987. Video. DIR: Kunihiko Yuyama. SCR: Izo Hashimoto. DES: Kazuyuki Kobayashi. ANI: Kazuyuki Kobayashi. MUS: Minoru Yamazaki. PRD: Gakken, Shochiku. 55 mins.

Space cargo workers Ken Kato, Duke Stern, and Ivan Sernikov run the Tiger Wolf Dragon Express service, but they land themselves in big trouble when they rescue the beautiful android Rina. She is being pursued by the evil Baron Gohdam, who wants her so he can seize control of the superpowerful Hydra. Based on a manga in *Comic Nora* by Yuki Hijiri, it was also shown in some theaters on a double bill with the **MAPS** movie.

TWEENY WITCHES

2004. JPN: *Maho Shojo Tai Arusu*. AKA: *Magical Girl Squad Alice*. TV series. DIR: Yoshihari Ashino, Yasuhiro Aoki, Toru Yoshida. SCR: Shinji Obara. DES: Daisuke Nakayama. ANI: Studio 4°C. MUS: Tamiya Terashima. PRD: Tohoku-shinsha, Dentsu, Beyond C, NHK. 9 mins. x 40 eps.

Fifth-grade schoolgirl Alice dreams of having magical powers. One day she's pretending to study in class, but the book on her desk is a magical one that transports her to a forest. She meets and befriends witches-in-training Eva and Sheila, and it seems her dreams are about to come true. This is not, perhaps, what one would immediately expect from a creation of **IRIA**'s Keita Amemiya, whose remarkable live-action fantasies (*Hakaider, Moon over Tao*) have a grittier edge. However, that darkness soon emerges. Alice, who has always imagined that magic powers are there to be used for good, finds her wonderland can be as harsh and unjust as her own world—senior witches are enslaving other magic beings. She and her new witch sisters free an elf from captivity, but like many Amemiya characters, they find the price of doing good is high. In the magic world releasing a captured elf is a criminal act, and they are punished by a curse that will prevent them from growing up until the elf is recaptured—shades here of **THOSE WHO HUNT ELVES**, without the kinky undertones.

TWELVE KINGDOMS *

2002. JPN: *Juni Koku-ki; Juni Kokki*. AKA: *Chronicle of Twelve Kingdoms; Record of Twelve Countries*. TV series. DIR: Tsuneo Kobayashi. SCR: Noboru Aikawa. DES: Hiroto Tanaka, Yuko Kusumoto. ANI: Hiroto Tanaka. MUS: Kunihiko Ryo. PRD: Studio Pierrot, NHK, Sogovision. 25 mins. x 45 eps.

Unhappy teenager Yoko Nakajima is suddenly confronted by a strange man who says she is his queen and he is her sworn subject. He fights off a group of beast demons before taking her and two of her classmates into another world, where people from Earth are hunted fugitives. The friends and their protectors wander the lands, trying to survive and find out why they are there and how to get home.

Based on a series of novels begun in 1991 by Fuyumi Ono, the first story arc in *Twelve Kingdoms* often plays like a new version of ESCAFLOWNE or FUSHIGI YUGI. We have, of course, a Japanese girl transported to an otherworldy kingdom—the early episodes coincidentally based on the book SEA'S DARKNESS: MOON'S SHADOW, although they have no relation to the Chie Shinohara story of the same name. Yoko's "difference" is telegraphed from the earliest moments by her naturally red hair. Whereas anime hair colors are often wholly random and unrealistic, the script soon calls attention to Yoko's, when her parents urge her to dye it black in order to fit in. A brown-red deviation from the normal black is what happens when you try to bleach Japanese hair and is often used in fiction to suggest a girl is something of a wild-child. This has led, ironically, to Japanese girls who genuinely do not have standard issue black hair being forced to dye their hair black in the manner to which Yoko's parents are alluding. Yoko, it is alleged, is one of the latter, a straight-A student who has been voted class president, but who is being led away from her previous childish things by the allegorical temptations of the twelve kingdoms.

By the sixth episode, however, the story has taken a radical departure, dumping Yoko into the company of a number of beast-like creatures in a more surreal setting. Yoko's adventures start to take on elements of THE WIZARD OF OZ, or, more properly, *The Lion, The Witch and the Wardrobe*, as Yoko discovers that she really is fated to be queen of one of the lands and that only her successful ascension to the thrown can restore the sundered and ruined kingdoms. In another parallel with the Narnia books, or perhaps even John Norman's *Gor* series, the focus of the story leaves its original protagonist for long periods of time, concentrating on some of

her associates. In the next story arc, based on the Ono novel *Sea's Wind: Maze's Shore*, there are also elements of the lost children of HAIBANE RENMEI, in a series of fairytales that unite the stories of mundane, urban tragedy in our own world with the incarnation of fantastic creatures in the twelve kingdoms.

Later chapters, based on the novel *Ten Thousand-League Wind: Dawn's Sky*, see Yoko becoming ruler of one of the kingdoms and forced to deal with the aftermath of her less than illustrious predecessor, alongside politicking by some of her rival queens and long tangents that discuss some of their own backstories. A few final stories prepare the ground for a last battle, as Yoko rides off to save her newfound home.

The original novels presented a sprawling saga, distantly inspired, in the fashion of LIKE A CLOUD, LIKE A BREEZE, by Chinese history and mythology. However, it is worth noting that the stories have been shuffled and rearranged for this anime version. Two of them, "Correspondence" and "Ally of the Moon," were originally short stories, and are dealt with in just two episodes, while others stretch over many chapters. The final story arc, five episodes that draw on the novel *Eastern Sea God, Western Ocean*, almost exhausts the original source material featuring Yoko, although other books about other cast members still remain unadapted. As with IRONFIST CHINMI, the exhaustion of the original material left the producers with the difficult choice of pressing on regardless and diverging from the original even further, or calling a hiatus with the vague hope of restarting if the material became available. Hence, although originally planned as a 68-episode series, *Twelve Kingdoms* currently grinds to a halt at episode 45 with some plot elements left unresolved; an unfortunate fate for an anime that has gained a large and appreciative following for its literally novelistic density and complex relationships. Two PlayStation 2 spin-offs also followed.

TWELVE MONTHS *

1980. JPN: *Mori wa Ikiteiru.* AKA: *The Forest Is Alive.* Movie. DIR: Kimio Yabuki, Tetsuo Imazawa. SCR: Tomoe Takashi, Kimio Yabuki. DES: Yasuhiro Yamaguchi. ANI: Takashi Abe, Takao Kasai, Shinya Takahashi. MUS: Vladimir Grifutsov. PRD: Toei. 65 mins.

Sent out to collect spring flowers in midwinter by the wicked queen, Anya believes her life is lost, but she is saved by the spirit of her mother, who chases the snow from the forest. Anya is helped by the twelve spirits of the months of the year, each one a handsome prince, and within an hour, the once-barren winter wood is awash with the colors of spring. A Cinderella-like fairy tale based on a story by Soviet poet Samuel Marshack and featuring powerful orchestrations from the Leningrad Symphony Orchestra.

24 EYES

1980. JPN: *Nijushi no Hitomi.* TV special. DIR: Akio Jissoji, Shigetsugu Yoshida. SCR: Sumie Tanaka. DES: Kazuyuki Honma. ANI: Shunsaburo Takahata, Hiromi Yokoyama, Kanetsugu Kodama. MUS: Takeo Watanabe. PRD: TMS, Fuji TV. 84 mins.

Young Miss Oishi is the new school teacher on the island of Shodoshima in 1928. When she injures her leg, her 12 students visit her at home and discover that she cycles nine miles every day to teach them. Miss Oishi transfers to a new school in time to see her students five years later (1933). In 1941, the boys go off to war, preferring a glorious military career to a humdrum home life. Four years later, a widowed Miss Oishi comes out of retirement to teach once again—her new students including a sister and a daughter of the original class. The surviving class of 1928 arrange a reunion and buy her a new bicycle.

Based on the book by Sakae Tsuboi, *24 Eyes* draws lightly on Tsuboi's years at the periphery of Japanese anarchist counterculture and her disgust that "pacifist" Japan was rearming during the Korean war. The book was also adapted into a live-action film by former propagandist Keisuke Kinoshita in 1954. Made after the previous year's **DIARY OF ANNE FRANK** made WWII an acceptable subject for TV, this anime remake mixes animation with live action (old Tsuburaya studio hand Jissoji handling the former, **HELLO SPANK**–director Yoshida the latter) to depict different times of Miss Oishi's life. The story was remade again as the fully live-action *Children on the Island* (1987). Many other anime would copy *24 Eyes'* concentration on children, recognizing that a cast too young to have started WWII need not be held accountable for those who really did. Hideaki Anno would pay homage to *24 Eyes* in **GUNBUSTER** with a scene in which a teacher bids farewell to a class including the daughter of her former classmate.

21 EMON WELCOME TO SPACE

1981. JPN: *21 Emon: Uchu e Irasshai.* Movie. DIR: Tsutomu Shibayama. SCR: Masaki Tsuji. DES: Yuko Yamamoto. ANI: Michishiro Yamada. MUS: Shunsuke Kikuchi. PRD: Fujiko F, Shogakukan, Shinei. 93 mins.

In the 21st century, would-be space pilot Emon discovers that he is the sole heir to the dilapidated Tsuzureya Inn in Tokyo. But the inn hasn't changed since the 19th century, and customers no longer find it quaint. Realizing that Emon can be "persuaded," the owners of the Galaxy Hotel chain invite him on a space holiday to get him away from his inheritance. Emon is accompanied on the trip by his wacky potato-digging robot, Gonsuke, and the all-powerful alien, Monga.

The Fujiko-Fujio team behind **ESPER MAMI** and **MOJACKO** were heavily involved in this adaptation of their series from *Corocoro Comic*, even to the extent of singing the theme song themselves. The film was shown on a double bill with another Fujiko-Fujio production, the **DORAEMON** short *What Am I for Momotaro?*, and reuses the footage for one scene in which Doraemon and Emon briefly share each other's movie.

TWILIGHT OF THE COCKROACHES *

1987. JPN: *Gokiburi no Tasogare.* AKA: *Cockroach.* Movie. DIR: Hiroaki Yoshida. SCR: Hiroaki Yoshida. DES: Yoshinori Kanemori. ANI: Toshio Hirata. MUS: Morgan Fisher. PRD: TYO, Kitty Film. 105 mins.

Naomi, an attractive young cockroach, enjoys the easy life with her boyfriend, Ichiro, and other roaches in Mr. Saito's apartment. This is because the lazy Saito lets the roaches eat the scraps from his table and never tries to hurt them. Hans, a hard-bitten fighter-roach from the other side of the yard, is a rival for Naomi's affections, but he eventually returns to his own people. Naomi embarks on the long quest across the yard (50 human feet, an incredible distance) to find him. There, she discovers that Hans did not lie, and that other humans are engaged in an all-out war to exterminate the roaches; Hans and his people are fighting a suicidal battle they cannot win. The unthinkable happens when Momoko, the woman across the yard, moves in with Saito—a newly house-proud Saito kills off the roaches. Soon, only Ichiro and the pregnant Naomi are left, then he too is killed. Naomi escapes to give birth to a new litter, and a new generation of cockroaches, just that little bit more resistant to human poisons, is ready for a rematch.

A very *Japanese* insect movie that mixes a neighborly human romance with the anthropomorphized characters of *Hoppity Goes to Town* and the apocalyptic armageddon of WWII—*A Bug's Death*, if you will. Beginning with Naomi's first encounter with the human female, the film is chiefly told in flashback, lending it the weight of inevitable tragedy that also characterizes **GRAVE OF THE FIREFLIES**. Shot in a mixture of live action (the humans) and animation (the roaches) that is all the more impressive in these days of digital easy-fixes, it mixes the comic spectacle of humans battling their only serious rivals for planetary domination,

with the heroic defensive actions of a tiny community facing impossible odds. The director reportedly thought of his cockroaches as a metaphor for the way the Japanese appear to the rest of the world—he meant as selfish, parasitical trading partners, though many foreign critics saw other parallels, particularly in *TotC*'s glorification of fanatical suicide missions and its insect cast's self-assured belief that they will, eventually, become the masters of Earth. A fascinating and unexpectedly entertaining experiment, comparable in some regards with the U.S. movie *Joe's Apartment* (1996), which also featured a single guy who shared his apartment with roaches. ●

TWILIGHT OF THE DARK MASTER *

1997. JPN: *Shihaisha no Tasogare.* AKA: *Twilight of the Master.* Video. DIR: Akiyuki Shinbo. SCR: Duanne Dell'Amico, Tatsuhiko Urahata. DES: Hisashi Abe. ANI: Hisashi Abe. MUS: Keiji Urata. PRD: Madhouse. 46 mins.

In the beginning, the Great Mother created a Demon Master, an adversary designed to test the mettle of human beings. However, the Demon Master exceeded its design specifications, and the Great Mother had to create a Guardian to protect humankind. Eons later, in the year 2089, a strange force transforms the Japanese Eiji—he turns on his lover Shizuka, mutilates her, and escapes into the city. Determined to give her mutated fiancé the release of death, Shizuka pursues him, accompanied by a police detective and Shijo, an androgynous man who is the current Guardian. As in **DOOMED MEGALOPOLIS**, the monster terrorizing the city is simply a pawn of the true evil, in this case the Demon Master himself, who is asserting his powers through a new illegal muscle-enhancement drug. This predictable sci-fi gorefest was based on the manga by Saki Okuse and originally serialized in *Wings* magazine. ●●●

TWILIGHT Q

1987. JPN: *Twilight Q Toki no Musibume—Reflection; Twilight Q*

Twilight of the Dark Master

2—*Meikyu Bukken File 538.* AKA: *TQ: A Knot in Time; TQ2 Labyrinth Article File 538.* Video. DIR: Tomomi Mochizuki, Mamoru Oshii. SCR: Kazunori Ito. DES: Akemi Takada, Katsuya Kondo. ANI: Shinji Otsuka. MUS: Kenji Kawai. PRD: Studio Deen. 30 mins. x 2 eps.
Mayumi is on holiday when she finds an old camera while swimming. Out of curiosity she has the film developed—only one frame can be saved. The picture shows her with a young man she has never met. Returning to her holiday base to investigate, she learns from the camera manufacturer that this model hasn't even been made yet. She finds herself caught up in weird events that take her back in time to WWII and forward to her own graveside. This unsettling paradoxical tale is seemingly without meaning, a bizarre entry in the girls' anime catalog. The second story takes matters even further into fantasy, opening with the transformation of an airship into a giant carp and focusing on a small girl, seemingly the reincarnation of a powerful deity, and a mysterious detective in shades. He's a Tokyo detective who wants to find out why every aircraft over his town has suddenly vanished without a trace. The magic of the transformation sequence is unforgettable, but there's little that could be described as action.

The surreal goings-on in this short-lived "twilight zone" were made by the crew of **PATLABOR** but owe a heavy debt to the 1960s live-action show *Ultra Q[uestion]* (a forerunner of **ULTRAMAN**). Whereas its predecessor threatened to "apart your soul and going into the mystery zone [*sic*]," this modern update preferred to "take over your reality and disable the stop button."

TWIN
1989. JPN: *Hassai Circuit Roman Twin.* AKA: *Racing Circuit Romance Twin.* Video. DIR: Noboru Ishiguro, Osamu Sekita. SCR: Takashi Yamada. DES: Tsuneo Ninomiya. ANI: Tsuneo Ninomiya, Koichi Endo. MUS: N/C. PRD: Japan Home Video. 80 mins.
Hyo Hibino grows up a confused orphan after his mother dies giving birth to him—alternately blaming himself for her death and believing himself to be invulnerable. He gets the perfect opportunity to prove it when he becomes a motorcycle racer. An anime based on the 1986 *Young Sunday* manga by **F** and **DASH KAPPEI**–creator Noboru Rokuda.

TWIN BEE PARADISE
1999. Video. DIR: Kazuhiro Takamoto. SCR: Yasunori Ide. DES: Akihiro Asanuma. ANI: Akihiro Asanuma. MUS: N/C. PRD: Public & Basic, Beam Entertainment. 30 mins. x 3 eps.
Fresh from the video game that spawned them, the Twin Bee team is carted off for an intergalactic adventure, complete with big hair, babies, and UFOs. The series was preceded by a 1994 "episode zero," which must have made for one of the slowest anime productions in history.

TWIN DOLLS *
1994. JPN: *Seijuden Twin Dolls; Inju Seisen Twin Angels.* AKA: *Holy Beast Story Twin Dolls; Lust Beast Crusade Twin Angels.* Video. DIR: Kan Fukumoto. SCR: Oji Miyako. DES: Rin Shin. ANI: Akira Ojo. MUS: Teruo Takahama. PRD: Dandelion. 45 mins. x 2 eps. (*Dolls*), 30 mins. x 4 eps. (*Angels*).
The one thing you can be pretty sure of in anime is that people who look like ordinary high school girls rarely are. Mai and Ai are professional demon hunters, descended from an immortal being, dedicated to defending mankind (and, in particular, high school grrrl-kind) from the demons of the Pleasure Underworld. They are appointed guardians of the infant Messiah who will save the world. For once tentacles aren't used as penis substitutes—instead the crew animates optimistic renditions of the real thing. This openness doesn't last long as the story introduces one of the most mericious of all plot devices, the "orb of orgasm"; pop it in a woman's mouth and she'll *enjoy* being raped. Historical and mythical figures are used as set dressing in the background of an unpleasant exercise in taking money for old rope.

For reasons we've never been quite able to fathom, the franchise not only changed its Japanese title to *Twin Angels*, but also gained itself a new U.S.

distributor, moving from Softcel to Anime 18 for the distribution of the 1995 sequel.

For *Angels*, the sorcerer-nuns must defend their charge, Lord Onimaro (who is 21, allegedly), from another demon assault, when Kama and Sutra, the King and Queen of Seduction, drag him off to a ritual orgy. Onimaro's guardian Dekinobu worries that if he succumbs to his demonic heritage, he will become the Demon King and his legion of sex-crazed monsters will subdue the world. He makes a predictable choice and has the twins stripped and tortured for his pleasure, planning to have them sacrificed. But Dekinobu is determined to rescue Onimaro from his destiny, even if it costs him his life.

Angels adds staggering naiveté to its other offenses—what hormonally normal male, offered the career choice of ordinary human or Demon King with ultimate power, is going to be persuaded into the paths of righteousness by two "19-year-old" bimbos who can't even find sensible underwear? It is difficult, however, to completely write off any show that has immortal dialogue like, "Commence creation of an evil sex barrier!" and a scene featuring two miniskirted girls on a stormy school roof trying to hang onto a magic staff while lightning transforms it into a giant penis. ●NV

TWIN LOVE

2004. JPN: *FUTAKOI/Futakoi Alternative*. TV series. DIR: Nobuo Tomizawa, Takayuki Hirao, Matsuri Ose. SCR: Tomoko Konparu, Miho Maruo, Masahiro Yokotani, Katsumi Terato, Kazuharu Sato, Matsuri Ose, Ryunosuke Kingetsu. DES: Mineko Ueda, Toshimitsu Kobayashi. ANI: Toshimitsu Kobayashi. MUS: So Kikuchi, Shunsuke Suzuki, Tatsuya Murayama, Toshimichi Isoe. PRD: Feel, Flag, UFO Table, Media Works. 25 mins. x 13 eps. (TV1), 25 mins. x 13eps (TV2).

Ninth-grader Nozomu Futami moves back to his childhood hometown to live alone, boarding and helping out in a temple so he can go to school while his father works overseas. He welcomes the chance to get reacquainted with his childhood friends, twins Sumireko and Kaoruko Ichijo, and hopes to get closer to them both; but his school is overrun with girl twins, plus a few pairs of siblings for variety. There's a local legend about twin girls falling in love with the same boy, and he is set to become the beneficiary. However, as with the **D3 SERIES** tales *Lustful Mother* and *Lustful Sister*, this twin story has a literal twin story—a second tale runs in parallel, in which redheads Sara and Souju Shirogane work as assistants in a private detective agency that has recently been taken over by the son of the original owner. The trio run into trouble with local gangsters, and high jinks ensue. This series was also adapted as a manga in *Comic Dengeki Daioh* with art by Kanao Araki. Yes, it's yet another geek-gets-girls show, this time based originally on a magazine story and illustrations by Hina Futaba and Mutsumi Sasaki.

TWIN SIGNAL

1995. Video. DIR: Takashi Sogabe. SCR: N/C. DES: Toshiko Sasaki. ANI: Toshiko Sasaki. MUS: Takeshi Suzuki. PRD: Tokyo Kids. 28 mins. x 3 eps.

A-S Signal is the newest, most sophisticated Human Formed Robot (HFR) in the Atrandom series, created by Professor Shinnosuke Otoi, a brilliant engineer. Signal looks like a cute 16-year-old boy, programmed to be "big brother" to the professor's grandson, Nobuhiko. Made of the revolutionary material MIRA by a secret process, Signal is the constant target of kidnap attempts and other efforts to steal the Professor's secrets. But there's one small problem with the process—whenever Nobuhiko sneezes, Signal transforms from a normal teenage boy into a sweet three-year-old super-deformed dwarf. Chibi Signal, as he's known in this state, is phenomenally cute and obsessed with eating chocolate, but his powers as a bodyguard are severely compromised.

Luckily, lots of pretty boy robots pop up to help Signal out. They are earlier models in the Atrandom series. Signal's older brother and prototype, Pulse, also lives with the Otoi family as does Code, a robot bird also made by the same secret techniques. Based on the early chapters of the *Shonen GanGan* manga by Sachi Oshimizu, which has also spun off novels and drama CDs.

TWINKLE HEART

1986. Video. DIR: Seiji Okuda. SCR: Kenji Terada. DES: Sachiko Yamamoto. ANI: Moriyasu Taniguchi. MUS: N/C. PRD: Project Team Argos. 45 mins.

On a distant planet, the treasure of Love is being sought by planetary ruler Ogod. Three insufferably cute aliens—Cherry, Lemon, and Berry—join in the search and finally reach Earth. In order to look for information about the treasure, they decide that the best course would be to turn their spaceship into a hamburger bar, so as to blend in with the natives and listen for any intelligence. A comedy, in case you were wondering.

TWINS AT ST. CLARE'S

1991. JPN: *Ochamen Futago Clare Gakuen Monogatari*. AKA: *Story of Mischievous Twins at Clare College*. TV series. DIR: Masaharu Okuwaki, et al. SCR: Haruya Yamazaki, Michiru Shimada. DES: Shuichi Seki. ANI: Keiko Sasaki, Satoshi Hirayama, Toshiharu Mizutani. MUS: Masahiro Kawasaki. PRD: Tokyo Movie Shinsha, Nippon TV. 25 mins. x 26 eps.

Patricia and Isabel are identical twins whose rich parents decide that their girls should learn the true values of life. They don't feel their expensive, luxurious school is making a very good job of this, so instead they send them to St. Clare's, a much simpler school. At first the girls resent this, seeing it as a step down the social ladder. Their privileged background doesn't help them adjust to life as members of a community unimpressed by wealth. They are determined to win respect, but because they're completely unused to communal life, they rebel against the rules, going on strike, stealing, and causing all sorts of trouble. Instead of the school's best students they become its biggest troublemakers, but they eventually settle down, make friends, and learn to value and respect others while having lots of fun. There are midnight feasts, adventures, and all the things people do at boarding school in novels like the 1941 book by Enid Blyton that inspired this series. Unfortunately real English boarding schools were never so exciting, but Japanese audiences didn't care; nor did those across Europe. TMS followed with another twin story, **Me and I: The Two Lottes.**

TWO DOWN, FULL BASE

1982. AKA: *Two Out, Bases Loaded.* TV special. DIR: Tsutomu Shibayama. SCR: Seiichi Yashiro. DES: Michishiro Yamada, Hideo Kawauchi. ANI: Tsutomu Shibayama, Kenichi Onuki. MUS: Takeyoshi Hoguchi, Joe Hisaishi. PRD: Group Tac, Asia-do, Toho, Fuji TV. 85 mins.
Musuke "Shorty" Sato is a shortstop for the local junior baseball team, the Eggs, who is asked by his mother to look after some money for her. He foolishly lends it to Tower and Dump, the school badboys, and must enlist the help of the pitcher's pretty little sister.

TWO ON THE ROAD

1992. JPN: *Itsumo Futari.* AKA: *Always the Two of Us.* Video. DIR: Hirotoshi Hayasaka, Seizo Watase. SCR: Seizo Watase. DES: Seizo Watase. ANI: N/C. MUS: BEGIN. PRD: Cure. 37 mins., 30 mins.
Two anthologies of short stories, 13 in all, based on originals by **Chalk-Colored People**–creator Seizo Watase. As with other adaptations of Watase's

work, they are set to music—stories here include *Ashes of Love, White Fish/ Blue Fish, Dance on the Sands, Glider, Handbag Mirror, Blue Snow,* and *Living in the World.* Though several early ones were broadcast on the WOWOW satellite channel, this qualifies more as a video production.

TWO TAKAS, THE

1984. JPN: *Futari no Taka.* TV series. DIR: Takao Yotsuji, Hiroko Tokita, Junichi Sakata, Hiroshi Negishi. SCR: Sukehiro Tomita, Hideo Takayashiki, Jiyu Watanabe, Yasushi Hirano. DES: Shiro Murata, Akira Nakanishi. ANI: Shiro Murata, Yasuhiro Moriguchi. MUS: Joe Hisaishi. PRD: Movie International, Fuji TV. 25 mins. x 32 eps.
Two boys both named Taka ("Hawk") are both passionate motorcyclists and both determined to be champions. The similarity ends there; one's a rich kid from a good family, one's from the wrong side of the tracks, constantly fighting with his mother. Then they learn that, following a fire in the maternity unit where they were born, two babies were accidentally swapped over.
 Based on Kaoru "**Area 88**" Shintani's 1981 manga in *Shonen Sunday,* this was the last Movie International production. The studio closed down before it could be completed, so only by reading the manga could fans find out how the story ended; but the series gave them Hisaishi's music by way of compensation.

2001 NIGHTS

1987. JPN: *Space Fantasia 2001 Nights.* Video. DIR: Toshio Takeuchi. SCR: Chiho Katsura. DES: Akio Sugino, Takashi Watanabe. ANI: Hisatoshi Motoki, Noboru Tatsuike. MUS: Satoshi

Kadokura. PRD: TMS. 57 mins.
In 2085, a sleeper ship carrying the embryos of the "Robinson Family" launches for planet Ozma. A community begins to thrive onboard the ship, and when it reaches Ozma 375 years later, the terraformed planet is settled peacefully. Then, a second ship arrives, captained by yet another Robinson, who urges the colonists to help spread the human race even further into space. Owing much more to *2001: A Space Odyssey* than **Swiss Family Robinson**, this majestic video was shot in "Super Perspective Technique" (whatever that is) to capture the photo-real quality of Yukinobu Hoshino's original 1984 *Action Comics* manga. Note also the homages to **The Wizard of Oz.**

TWO'S COMPANY

1998. JPN: *Futari Kurashi.* AKA: *Two People Living Together.* TV series. DIR: Futa Morita. SCR: Fumihiko Shimori. DES: Masayuki Hirooka. ANI: Masayuki Hirooka. MUS: Katsuo Ono. PRD: TBS. 5 mins. x 36 eps.
The romantic misadventures of an out-of-work manga artist, based on a manga by working manga artist Kenjiro Kakimoto. These shorts were broadcast as part of the late night *Wonderful* program. **N**

TYPHOON IN ISE BAY

1989. JPN: *Ise-wan Taifun Monogatari.* AKA: *Story of the Typhoon in Ise Bay.* Movie. DIR: Seijiro Kamiyama, Yasuo Iwamoto. SCR: Seijiro Kamiyama. DES: Masahiro Kitazaki. ANI: Masahiro Kitazaki. MUS: Masao Haryu. PRD: Mushi. 90 mins.
This self-explanatory true story of a 1959 storm that decimated Western Japan was directed by Kamiyama, who also wrote the original book.

U

UDAGAWA, TOKI

?– . Born in Kanagawa, Udagawa went to Tokyo to study drama at Waseda University, but soon found part-time work as a puppeteer and performed on the original puppet version of **MADCAP ISLAND**. Dropping out of Waseda, he became a full-time performer in the Hitomi-za puppetry troupe. In 1983, he moved into anime by becoming the producer of **KAKKUN CAFÉ**.

UFO ROBOT DAI APOLLON *

1976. JPN: *UFO Senshi Dai Apollon.* AKA: *UFO Warrior Dai Apollon, Shadow World.* TV series. DIR: Tatsuo Ono. SCR: Takao Koyama, Okihara Matsumoto, Noboru Shiroyama, Soji Yoshikawa, Seiji Matsuoka. DES: Toyoo Ashida. ANI: Keijiro Kimura, Takashi Kakuta, Konio Okoto, Toyoo Ashida, et al. MUS: Masahisa Takeshi. PRD: Eiken, TBS. 25 mins. x 39 eps.
Sixteen-year-old Takeshi forms a football team at the Blue Sky Orphanage. One day after a game, he's alone on the field when a warrior of light on a mighty steed appears and points his sword at Takeshi's chest. Takeshi loses consciousness, waking later to find a mark in the shape of a sun over his heart. He is really the son of the king of planet Apollon, spirited away to Earth by his father's faithful retainer, Rabi, in order to avoid the prince's death at the hands of the usurper General Dazaan. His heart contains the "Key Energy" of his planet, which allows him to control the space ship Rabi cunningly hid on the ocean floor—it contains several flying saucers, a dart-shaped flyer with detachable motorcycle, and the three component vehicles Edda (Head), Trangu (Trunk), and Legga (Leg) that combine to form the giant robot Dai Apollon. Using his Key Energy, Takeshi can painfully synchronize with the robot, allowing him to operate it as an extension of his own body. The separate vehicles are piloted by his teammates Miki, Choko, and Goro, whose clothes magically change into their football jerseys whenever they shout "U! F! O!" Using the robot, Takeshi hopes to set his planet free and release his mother from imprisonment. Based on the 1974 *Shonen King* manga by **OISHINBO**-creator Tetsu Kariya and Shigeru Tsuchiyama, though since the original featured a 15-year-old orphan called Akira defeating demons with the powers of 108 heroes (see **SUIKODEN**), and no giant robot anywhere to be seen, it's a wonder the producers bothered to pay for the rights at all.

UFO SUMMER

2005. JPN: *Iria no Sora, UFO no Natsu.* AKA: *Iria's Sky, UFO Summer.* Video. DIR: Naoyuki Ito. SCR: Michiko Yokote. DES: Eiji Komatsu, Yoshinori Sayama, Takeyasu Kurashima. ANI: N/C. MUS: Hiroshi Takagi. PRD: Toei Animation, Happinet. 30 mins. x 6 eps.
Naoyuki Asaba is a withdrawn boy who likes watching the sky and daydreaming about UFOs. One summer night, he sneaks into his school's swimming pool and encounters a distant-seeming girl who claims her name is Iria Kana. The two shyly become friends as Naoyuki teaches her to swim, but she is soon whisked away by stern-faced minders. Naoyuki begins to suspect, as does anyone who has seen **MAHORO-MATIC** or **SAIKANO**, that Iria is part of a clandestine military project, fighting a "secret" war in parts unknown, but he must also contend with the predictable arrival of Iria at his school at the beginning of the new semester. But while this might appear to have all the hallmarks of innumerable other anime, its closest influence is not the above-mentioned tales, but the elegiac longing and tragedy of **VOICES OF A DISTANT STAR**. Based on a novel by Mitsuhito Akiyama.

UFO ULTRAMAIDEN VALKYRIE *

2002. JPN: *Enban Ojo Walküre.* AKA: *UFO Princess Valkyrie; UFO Battlemaiden Valkyrie, UFO Princess Valkyrie.* TV series, video. DIR: Shigeru Ueda, Nobuhiro Takagi. SCR: Ryoe Tsukimura. DES: Maki Fujii. ANI: Tetsuya Yanagisawa, Hiroshi Kubo. MUS: Kenji Kawai. PRD: Toshiba EMI, Kid's Station, Media Factory, UHF Group, TNK. 24 mins. x 12 eps. (TV1), 24 mins. x 12 eps. (TV2), 30 mins. x 6 eps. (V).
Princess Valkyrie crash-lands on Earth, right on top of bathhouse owner

U-Jin Brand

© 1991 YUJIN/SEIYO/ANIMATE FILM CO., LTD.

Kazuto. She can only save him from death by giving him part of her soul. Naturally, she gives him the teenage half and reverts to her child persona. Kazuto and his friends have to try and get her back to normal and explain away the space ship stuck in the roof, although this becomes less of a talking point as more crashes occur. Alien girls crashing into the human world and developing crushes on an ordinary boy with an old-fashioned occupation may sound familiar, but nonetheless Ryoe Tsukimura, creator and screenwriter of EL HAZARD, is credited with the series concept. The pseudonymous Kaishaku, creator of KANNAZUKI NO MIKO, "originated" the idea in the manga of the same name, although similarities to TENCHI MUYO! and BIRDY THE MIGHTY are obvious. The second series, *December Nocturne* (*Junigatsu no Yasokyoku*), followed in October 2003 with the arrival of the mysterious Valkyrie Ghost, another alien girl whose main agenda is getting Kazuto for herself but who also reveals more of the mysterious past of Valkyrie's home planet of Valhalla. A third series, subtitled *Deluxe*, was announced for 2004 but instead our happy band of Tenchi

clones got a video series, *Bride of the Star Spirit Season* (*Seiretsu no Hanayome*). The show's Japanese title reflects the German pronunciation of the word *valkyrie*, presumably better known to the Japanese than the Anglo-Saxon variant thanks to the Richard Wagner opera *Die Walküre* (1862).

U-JIN BRAND *
1991. Video. DIR: Osamu Sekita. SCR: Satoru Akahori. DES: Yumi Nakayama. ANI: Yumi Nakayama. MUS: Nobuo Ito. PRD: JC Staff, Animate. 45 mins.
Three short stories based on U-Jin's erotic manga, similar in style to ANGEL and TALES OF.... In the first story, a songwriter can produce hits for teenage idol singers—but only after he gets to know the girl *really* well. Despite his constant calendar of seductions, he secretly loves innocent Akiyo, with whom he must one day work and try on his irresistible charm. The other two chapters are linked tales of Toyama no Benbei, a righter of wrongs in the tradition of Toyama no Kinsan (see SAMURAI GOLD). In the first, he is called in to avenge a girl wronged by a serial seducer, who claims he will still respect her if they do the deed then

dumps her because she is no longer a virgin. In the second, he is brought in to solve the problem of a young man who doesn't want to dump his career prospects along with his unwelcome engagement to the boss's daughter. In 2004 the title was rereleased in the U.S. as *Tales of Seduction*. **N**

ULTIMATE GIRLS
2005. JPN: *U.G.: Ultimate Girl* [sic]. TV series. DIR: Yuji Moto. SCR: Satoru Nishizono. DES: Hideyuki Morioka. ANI: Seiji Matsuda. MUS: Moka. PRD: m.o.e., Studio Matrix. 13 mins. x 12 eps.
In a retread of the premise for ULTRAMAN, three young girls decide that they want to get a closer look at one of the giant monsters that has been periodically attacking their city. They get what they wanted, only to be crushed to death by UFO-man, the giant superhero who has been protecting humanity from danger by battling the creatures. However, UFO-man is a kindly and public-spirited individual, who brings the girls back from the dead on the condition that they agree to take over the task of saving the world. A sequel was originally hinted later the same year, although this had transformed into a mere audio-drama bonus extra on the DVD release of the TV series. However, low budget transformations form part of the appeal of this series, which cheekily makes a comedy virtue out of ever decreasing funding for animation. Whereas old-school anime often used transformation sequences to recycle footage, *Ultimate Girls* does not even go that far, instead showing a picture of the city from a distance, an arrow pointing to the street where one of the girls is transforming and a thermometer-style horizontal menu, as if a file is downloading, with the message "Please Wait." Meanwhile, it even finds a new excuse for cheesecake, since the girls' embarrassment at losing their clothes is what powers the release of their destructive energies. At least, that is how things are supposed to work, except team member Tsugumi is such an exhibitionist that she rarely gets

embarrassed enough to generate any monster-destroying energy of her own. A manga version also ran in *Dengeki Gao* magazine.

ULTIMATE SUPERMAN R

1991. JPN: *Kyukyoko Chojin R*. Video. DIR: Ayumi Shibuki. SCR: Toshiko Uehara. DES: Toyomi Sugiyama. ANI: Toyomi Sugiyama. MUS: Masayuki Yamamoto. PRD: Studio Core. 75 mins.
Average Japanese teenager Ichiro Tanaka is really an android, programmed to take over the world by mad scientist Hiroshi Narihara. He enlists the help of the school photography club, which is probably a bad idea. Based on the comedy manga by PATLABOR-creator Masami Yuki, this anime was also spun off into several audio dramas.

ULTIMATE TEACHER *

1988. JPN: *Kyofun no Bio-Ningen: Saishu Kyoshi*. AKA: *Fearsome Bio-Human: The Last Teacher*. Video. DIR: Toyoo Ashida. SCR: Monta Ibu. DES: Atsuji Yamamoto, Mandrill Club. ANI: Noriyasu Yamauchi. MUS: Miyuki Otani. PRD: Studio Live, SME. 60 mins.
Ganpachi Chabane, half-man, half-cockroach, is the result of a genetic experiment. This makes him a natural teacher in the eyes of many teenagers, so when he escapes from the lab where he was created, he heads straight for Emperor High School and installs himself on the staff. His idea of education agrees with that of the pupils—both see it as a battleground where only the strong survive. The school is overrun by student gangs; Chabane has to defeat the leader of the strongest gang, pretty martial artist Hinako Shiratori, if he's to keep his class in line. Luckily Hinako has a weakness; if she isn't wearing her lucky blue bloomers emblazoned with a cute white cat, she has no confidence at all in her fighting skills and changes from powerhouse to pushover. The U.S. translation calls these "lucky gym shorts," but the U.K. version's "velvet pussy panties" is much more in line with the crude tone of the whole package. Mystifyingly released in theaters on a double bill with the LEGEND OF GALACTIC HEROES movie, it features a theme song by famous Japanese pop band the Kome-Kome Club. Atsuji Yamamoto also wrote a manga version for *Animage Comics*. ⓥ

ULTRA B

1987. TV series, movie. DIR: Hiroshi Sasagawa, Tetsuo Yasumi, Teruo Kigure, Kazuhiro Mori, Fusahito Nagaki. SCR: Masaaki Sakurai, Masaru Yamamoto, Nobuaki Kishima, Hirokazu Mizude. DES: Fujiko-Fujio "A." ANI: Keisuke Mori. MUS: Shunsuke Kikuchi. PRD: Shinei Doga, TV Asahi. 25 mins. x 51 eps., 20 mins. (m).
One night, Michio chases a UFO to see where it lands. He is taken inside it and encounters a mysterious baby, Ultra B (aka UB). Though at first the only strange thing about him is his pathological obsession with drinking milk, UB soon reveals that he has superpowers when he moves in with Michio's family—a fact that causes humorous misunderstandings in the style of DORAEMON. Based on a manga by Fujiko-Fujio "A" for *Fujiko-Fujio Land* magazine, its appearance in a glorified vanity publication perhaps explaining the tiredness of the idea. The 1988 "movie" outing *UB: Dictator B.B. from the Black Hole* featured the arrival of the evil, pterodactyl-riding "Black Baby," whom UB defeats with the aid of his cohorts Super Baby Robot and Muscle Bird. Another work from PROGOLFER SARU–creator Motoo Abiko, formerly half of the Fujiko-Fujio duo.

ULTRA GRAN

1982. JPN: *Hitotsuboshi-ke no Ultra Baa-san*. AKA: *Ultra Granny of the Hitotsuboshi Family; Super Grandma*. TV series. DIR: Kenji Hirata, Satoshi Inoue. SCR: Yoshiyuki Suga, Shigeru Mizuno, Hiroko Naka. DES: Toshio Kitahara. ANI: Takumi Manabe, Takao Yamazaki. MUS: Masayuki Yamamoto. PRD: Knack, Yomiuri TV (Nippon TV). 25 mins. x 13 eps.
Seventy-year-old Granny Hitotsuboshi acts like a teenager and cares nothing about the effect her quick tongue and accident-prone nature have on those around her. Her crazy schemes create chaos for her family, which includes hard-pressed salaryman Eitaro, exam-obsessed mother Kinuko, consumptive grandson Kenichi, toddler Todome, and Antonio the local tramp. Based on a gag manga by Meme Akutagawa—compare to SAZAE-SAN and MY NEIGHBORS THE YAMADAS.

ULTRA MANIAC *

2003. TV series, video. DIR: Shinichi Masaki, Nanako Shimazaki. SCR: Hisayoshi Kato, Miho Maruo, Shiki Masuda, Yasuko Oe. DES: Miho Shimogasa. ANI: Maki Fujii . MUS: Toru Yugawa. PRD: Animax, Ashi Pro, Studio Aqua, Studio Jack, Studio Ox. 30 mins. (v), 23 mins. x 26 eps. (TV).
Nina is in line for the title of Princess of the Magic Kingdom. To qualify for consideration, she and her transforming talking cat Rio have to travel to Earth to improve their magic skills, in the sorcerously self-improving manner of LITTLE WITCH SALLY and KIKI'S DELIVERY SERVICE. But she is involved in an accident on her flying scooter, and as a result she meets and befriends Ayu Tateishi, a sporty, kindhearted, and popular girl in her second year at middle school. She tries to use her magic to help her friend's romantic endeavors, with comic results; but she also has to decide if she will follow her destiny or stay on Earth. From the age of its protagonists and the trappings (cute magic creature sidekick, magic equipment, and transformation sequences) this appears to be a magical-girl show, but it deviates from the classic canon by making the magical girl second lead in the style of E-CHAN THE NINJA. There are also a few nods to a more modern magic—Nina doesn't have a wand or bracelet, but a sentient PDA that she plugs into a treasure casket to work her spells. Her aim in the TV series is to retrieve five magical stones, although once she achieves this she realizes, like BEWITCHED AGNÈS, that she rather likes the human world and would prefer

to stay. The original manga in *Ribon* magazine is by MARMALADE BOY–creator Wataru Yoshizumi, but designed to appeal to a younger audience. A one-shot video, which we presume to be related to *Ribon*-reader screenings like that of FULL MOON, featured Nina helping Ayu win a tennis match.

ULTRAMAN *

1979. JPN: *The Ultraman*. Movie, TV series. DIR: Eiko Toriumi, Masahisa Ishida, Takashi Anno, Katsuyuki Tsuji, Takeshi Shirato, et al. (TV1), Masayoshi Ozaki (TV2), Mitsuo Hikabe (*USA, Company*), Hiroshi Sasagawa (v), Tetsuro Amino (*Tsuifun*), Mitsuo Hikabe (*Company*), Hiroko Tokita (*Love and Peace*). SCR: Keiichi Abe, Soji Yoshikawa, Hiroyuki Hoshiyama, Yasushi Hirano (TV1), Hiroko Naka, Keiji Kubota (TV2), John Eric Seward (*USA*), Hiroshi Hashimoto (v). DES: Tsuneo Ninomiya, Kunio Okawara, Shoji Kawamori (TV1), Yoshihiko Shinozaki (TV2), Kazuo Iimura (*USA*), Tsuneo Ninomiya (v), N/C (*Love and Peace*). ANI: Tsuneo Ninomiya (TV1), Osamu Kamijo (TV2), Kazuo Iimura (*USA*), Tsuneo Ninomiya, Hiroko Minamimoto (v), Yutaka Miya (*Tsuifun*), Noriko Nishimiya (*Company*), Haruo Takahashi (*Love and Peace*). MUS: Kunio Miyauchi (TV1, TV2), Shinsuke Kazato (*USA*), N/C. PRD: Sunrise, Tsuburaya, TBS, Tsuburaya, NHK2, Tsuburaya, Hanna-Barbera, Tsuburaya, Triangle Staff. 30 mins. x 50 eps. (TV1) , 25 mins. (*Kids* m), 10 mins. x 26 eps. (TV2/*Kids*), 10 mins. x 26 eps. (TV3/*Mother*), 80 mins. (*USA*), 30 x 6 eps. (v), 30 mins. (*Tsuifun*), 60 mins. (*Company*), 80 mins. (*Love and Peace*).

After an apprenticeship in special effects on films ranging from *The War at Sea from Hawaii to Malaya* (see WARTIME ANIME) through the original *Godzilla* to Kurosawa's *Throne of Blood* (for which he made the forest move), Eiji Tsuburaya started the famed "monster studio" that bears his name. The live-action *Ultraman*, one of the enduring icons of Japanese TV, evolved from *Ultra Q* (1966), an SF drama series in the *X-Files* mode featuring the investigation of mysterious beings and events. As *Ultraman* (also 1966), it was taken over by the monsters and became a battle between the heroic Ultrans, citizens of Nebula M78, and their human allies, against often absurd but compelling monster opponents. It is still one of the most popular toy lines in Japan, with legions of new plastic monsters released every year.

The Ultraman (1979), broadcast during the period that reruns of the live-action series prepared the audience for *Ultraman 80*, commences with glowing symbols appearing over major cities like Tokyo, Paris, and New York. A new tactical team, the Space Garrison, is set up by the Earth Defense Force and discovers they are signs of a higher civilization from another dimension, the Ultrans, who came to Earth in ancient times. To fight evil in our dimension, they need human help. Young pilot Hikari flies out into space to investigate and is transported by a beam of light into another dimension, where he meets an Ultran and agrees to the merging of their life forces. Hikari can now use the star-shaped "Beam Flasher" on his forehead to transform into Ultraman Joneas (aka Joe). He can fight the monsters and aliens that menace Earth, and thanks to the lower cost of animation, he has a much wider range of power-rays than any of his live-action brothers. Episodes from this series were edited into a feature-length video, *The Adventures of Ultraman* (1982), for the U.S. market only. It focuses on Hikari's journey and meeting with the Ultran, and the space warfare elements. A few translated episodes were also released in the U.S. video market on one tape as *Ultraman II*.

Ultraman Kids (1984) was more humorous, a short movie of cute kiddie versions of the Ultraman family and their monster rivals. In April 1986 they got their own series, *Ultraman Kids Proverb Stories* (*U.K.: Kotowaza Monogatari*), in which Ultraman Zoffy and friends reenact wise maxims for little ones. The two final episodes were not broadcast. A second kids' series moved from Ultraman's home on TBS to the NHK2 satellite channel—the FROM THE APENNINES TO THE ANDES pastiche *30 Million Light Years in Search of Mother* (1991, *U.K.: Haha o Tazunete 3,000 Man Konen*).

The serious movie *Ultraman: The Adventure Begins* (1987; retitled *Ultraman USA* in Japan) was a Japanese-American coproduction between Tsubaraya and Hanna-Barbera and based on a story by Noboru Tsubaraya. Three stunt pilots survive a fatal crash thanks to three aliens from M78, who have linked life forces with the pilots and made them part of the Ultra-Force. The aliens' mission is to destroy four evil Sorkin Monsters hatched from asteroids that have crashed onto New Orleans, San Francisco, Denver, and New York. Ultra-Scott, Ultra-Chuck, and token woman Ultra-Beth now have a secret base inside Mount Rushmore and another under a golf course, plus three robots to help them out.

The video series *Ultraman Graffiti* (1990) featured more cartoony adventures for mini-versions of the Ultra brothers—a style that continues to dominate the franchise, at least in its animated incarnation. It was followed by Tetsuro Amino's video release *Ultra-Violent Battle—Comet War-God Tsuifun* (1996, *Chotoshi Gekiden—Suisei Senshin Tsuifun*). In the late 1990s, the live-action *Ultraman* was influenced by the postmodern angst of EVANGELION, resulting in the more serious *Ultraman Gaia* TV series, written in part by SERIAL EXPERIMENTS LAIN's Chiaki Konaka. The Sturm und Drang of the *Gaia* movies was balanced in theaters by new cartoon Ultrakids features, Mitsuo Hikabe's *Ultraman Company* (1996) and Hiroko Tokita's *Ultraman: Love and Peace* (1999), featuring animation by Triangle Staff. This is the most recent animated incarnation of the series to date, though the original is often referenced in shows including BIRDY THE

MIGHTY, PROJECT A-KO, URUSEI YATSU-RA, PATLABOR, DOCTOR SLUMP, and the feline parody *Ultranyan* (1997).

ULYSSES 31 *

1981. JPN: *Uchu Densetsu Ulysses 31*. AKA: *Space Legend Ulysses 31*. TV series. DIR: Bernard Deyries, Tadao Nagahama, Kazuo Terada, Seiji Okuda. SCR: Ryohei Suzuki, Jean Chalopin, Nina Wolmark. DES: Shingo Araki, Michi Himeno, Studio Nue, Manchu, Noboru Tatsuike, Shinji Ito, Yuki Motonori. ANI: Shingo Araki, Tooyo Ashida. MUS: Kei Wakakusa (Denny Crokett, Ike Egan, Haim Saban, Shuki Levy for Western version). PRD: DIC, Tokyo Movie Shin-sha, TV Nagoya (TV Asahi). 25 mins. x 26 eps. (only 12 shown in Japanese broadcast, 1988).

Preparing for a routine journey back to his home on 31st-century Earth, star-ship captain Ulysses runs into trouble on planet Troy when his son, Telema-chus, is captured by the disciples of the Cyclops. Killing the Cyclops to save Telemachus, Ulysses brings down the wrath of the god Zeus, who puts his crew into suspended animation and wipes the navigation systems of his ship, the Odyssey. Accompanied only by Telemachus, Numinor, and Yumi, the alien siblings from planet Zotra, and the intensely annoying robot No-no, Ulysses must wander the stars in search of the Kingdom of Hades to awaken his crew and find the way back home.

A ridiculously contrived sci-fi reworking of Homer's *Odyssey*, accom-plished in such an endearing and exciting fashion as to become one of the best-loved anime in Europe, *Ulysses 31* was the first French-Japanese coproduction. It was also the last for ROSE OF VERSAILLES' Tadao Nagahama, who died during production. Producer Jean Chalopin would return with the equally memorable MYSTERIOUS CITIES OF GOLD, before his output sank into the financially lucrative but creatively impoverished doldrums of the toy tie-ins *Rainbow Brite* (also made with Japanese staff) and *Care Bears*. He next surfaced in the anime world when his Studio DIC provided the English dub of SAILOR MOON.

The basis of the story (the gods, their human servants, and the obstacles they place in Ulysses' way) has hardly changed, except that Telemachus accompanies our hero rather than staying at home to fight off his mother Penelope's suitors as he did in the original. The addition of new characters doesn't jar; there are so many fantastic beings in the story already that a sweet alien telepath and an annoying robot with an appetite for metal fit right in. The design team makes the best of what it has, with classy machines from Manchu (aka French designer Phillippe Bouchet), reworked by Studio Nue and SAINT SEIYA–designer Araki. His version of Ulysses had to be toned down by Deyries at final approval stage; the director wanted a pacifist hero, so most of the Japanese-originated futuristic sidearm designs were discarded. The show remains deservedly popular, despite the annoying little robot—most notable among its many achievements, a Homeric episode in which the SF Ulysses travels back in time to meet the Greek original and the faithful Penelo-pe. For this episode alone, *Ulysses 31* is an anime classic.

UNCHALLENGEABLE TRIDER G7

1980. JPN: *Muteki Robo Trider G7*. AKA: *Invincible Robo (T) Rider G7*. TV series. DIR: Katsutoshi Sasaki, Seiji Kikuchi, Akira Suzuki, Takao Yoshikawa. SCR: Hiroyuki Hoshiyama, Tsunehisa Ito, Kenichi Matsuzaki, Katsutoshi Sasaki, Sukehiro Tomita, Fuyunori Gobu. DES: Nobuyoshi Sasakado, Kunio Okawara, Yutaka Izubuchi. ANI: Nobuyoshi Sasakado, Akehiro Kaneyama, Keijiro Kimura, Norio Shioyama. MUS: Kurodo Kaya. PRD: Sotsu Agency (Sunrise), TV Nagoya (TV Asahi). 25 mins. x 50 eps. When his father dies in 1985, young Watta Takeo inherits the family space transport firm. Despite the fact that the president is just a schoolkid, the company has to fight for survival in a competitive world with rivals and space pirates at every turn. Watta manages to succeed and keep the company going thanks to Professor Navarone's giant robot, Trider G7. Looking forward to the workhorse robots of PATLABOR and back to the boy-and-his-bot sagas of Go Nagai, the series mixes school and home scenarios with space battles—compare to John Stanley's American comic *O.G. Whiz*, which similarly featured a boy "dragged" away from school and forced to play with expen-sive supertoys.

UNDERSEA ENCOUNTER *

1981. JPN: *Kaitei Daisenso Ai no Niman Mile*. AKA: *War Beneath the Sea: 20,000 Miles for Love*. TV special. DIR: Ippei Kuri. SCR: Mamoru Sasaki. DES: Akemi Takada, Kunio Okawara. ANI: Takashi Saijo. MUS: Hiroaki Suzuki. PRD: Tatsunoko, Nippon TV. 72 mins. All the nations of Earth are crumbling before the might of Darius, ruler of the Gabia Empire. Meanwhile, childhood friends Ben and Ricky are sailing on the oceans in search of the lost city of Atlantis. When their ship is sunk, they are rescued by Captain Nemo in his submarine Nautilus. The captain reveals that he knows the location of Atlantis and offers to take them there.

Dubbed in the early 1980s by Har-mony Gold and broadcast as afternoon filler in several U.S. cities, this obscure TV movie was two years in the mak-ing, shot on 35mm film, and the first lead design job for PATLABOR's Akemi Takada. Directorial assistant Koichi Mashimo would later be given charge of another ship's commander, the less heroic IRRESPONSIBLE CAPTAIN TYLOR. The character of Nemo would reap-pear in SECRET OF BLUE WATER, an even freer adaptation of Jules Verne's origi-nal story.

UNICO *

1981. Video, movie. DIR: Toshio Hirata, Mami Murano. SCR: Masaki Tsuji. DES: Osamu Tezuka. ANI: Shigeru Yamamoto, Akio Sugino, Yoshiaki Kawajiri, Kazuo Tomizawa. MUS: Yukihide Takakawa,

Micky Yoshino, Godiego, Ryo Kitayama, Iruka. PRD: Madhouse, Sanrio Eiga, Tezuka Pro. 25 mins. (v), 90 mins. x 2 (m).

Exiled from Paradise by a malevolent goddess, Unico the baby unicorn is blown on the West Wind, finding troubled souls and helping them before he moves on again. Originally appearing as a color Osamu Tezuka manga in *Lyrica* magazine, Unico first showed up on TV in the pilot *U: Black Cloud, White Feather* (1979, *Kuroi Kumo Shiroi Hane*), eventually released straight to video. In this version, he arrives in a heavily polluted city, where he is befriended by a rat. While sharing a meager meal with the rat, Unico finds out that the sick girl upstairs can only be cured by the destruction of the local factories and chemical plants. As soon as Unico has brought sunlight back to the town, the West Wind returns to carry him away, before depositing him in yet another desolate place, alone and with no memory of the past.

The TV series wasn't picked up, but the movie *Fantastic Adventures of Unico* (1981) presents the backstory, showing the gods jealous of baby Unico's happiness. They command the West Wind to take him away from his mother and abandon him on the Hill of Oblivion, but the West Wind hasn't the heart to do it, instead leaving Unico in the Land of Mists. When the gods learn of the deception, they send the evil Night Wind to finish the job, and the West Wind saves Unico's life by racing to the Land of Mists and snatching Unico away from the friends he has made there. A second movie, *U in the Land of Magic* (1983, *Maho no Shima e*), again opens with the amnesiac Unico in a strange place, once more making friends thanks to his open, happy nature and willingness to help those in trouble. This time a puppet, maltreated by humans, has been brought to life and given magical powers by the mysterious energy of sunlight. Kuruku has vowed to revenge himself on all humanity by turning humans and animals into puppets and imprisoning

them on his magical island. Helped by a little girl and boy, Unico tries to save Kuruku but cannot convince him there is more to life than hate. As Unico's new friends are reunited with their families, he is once again torn away by the West Wind, who tells him the gods will soon find him because of the happiness he has created. Given such a bleak scenario, it's perhaps not surprising that the TV series was not picked up, but the movies—whose art style is not the same as the pilot episode—have acquired their own overseas following thanks to U.S. video release. Compare to similar Sanrio-sponsored misery in **RINGING BELL**.

UNINHABITED ISLAND, THE *
1998. JPN: *Mujin Shima Monogatari X*. AKA: *Story of X the Uninhabited Island*. Video. DIR: Hiroshi Ogawa. SCR: Mirin Takefuji. DES: Hirohito Kato. ANI: Shigenori Kurii. MUS: N/C. PRD: Pink Pineapple, KSS. 50 mins. x 2 eps.
Seven beautiful Japanese girls are shipwrecked on a deserted island, where they are overcome with madness and desire, much to the benefit of the men who have arranged for their castaway status. Released in the U.S. as *Desert Island Story*. ◐

UNIVERSITY GIRLS *
2005. JPN: *Joshidai H Sodanshitsu*. AKA: *Female Student Perverse Consultation Room*. Video. DIR: N/C. SCR: N/C. DES: N/C. ANI: N/C. MUS: N/C. PRD: Obtain. 30 mins.
Schoolgirl, sorry, college student Madoka goes to see her counselor for advice on her studies, only to find herself submitting to a series of sexual advances. Compare to **DESPERATE CARNAL HOUSEWIVES**, which has the same basic premise. ◐

UNTIL THE MOONRISE
1991. JPN: *Takeda Tetsuya Tsuki Noboru made ni*. AKA: *Tetsuya Takeda, Until the Moonrise*. Video. DIR: Eiichi Yamamoto. SCR: Eiichi Yamamoto. DES: Kazuo Tomozawa. ANI: Kazuo Tomozawa, Sai Imazaki, Neri Mimana.

MUS: N/C. PRD: Grouper Productions. 40 mins.
A father and daughter in Japan climb to the top of a ridge to watch the moonrise. As they wait, an old man tells them his story. An adaptation of Tetsuya Takeda's story about the relationship between a Japanese child and an American soldier.

UNTIL THE UNDERSEA CITY
1969. JPN: *Kaitei Toshi ga Dekiru made (31 Nen no Nippon)*. AKA: *Until the Undersea City: Japan in 31 Years*. TV special. DIR: Eiichi Yamamoto, Yusaku Sakamoto. SCR: Tadaaki Yamazaki. DES: Shuji Kimura. ANI: Jiro Fujimoto. MUS: N/C. PRD: Mushi, Nippon TV. 45 mins.
Taro Yamamoto has devoted his life to designing an undersea city. In 1972, he joins Tokyo Electronics, where he meets and eventually marries the pretty submariner Kazuko. He moves out to Tama New Town (see **POMPOKO**) and is present at the launch of the submarine Mambo in 1983. In 1986, construction finally begins on the undersea city of Oceanacopia. It is completed in 1997, and three years later, in the futuristic-sounding year of 2000, Taro finally gets to gaze on his creation.

URAHATA, TATSUHIKO
1963– . Born in Wakayama Prefecture, he joined Madhouse in 1983 as a writer. His subsequent scripts have included **RAIL OF THE STAR** and **FLY! DREAMERS**.

URBAN SQUARE
1985. JPN: *Urban Square Kohaku no Tsuigeki*. AKA: *Urban Square: Chasing Amber*. Video. DIR: Akira Nishimori. SCR: Kazunori Ito. DES: Akemi Takada, Chiharu Sato. ANI: Hideyuki Motohashi. MUS: Chicken Chuck. PRD: Network. 55 mins.
Ryu Matsumoto is a screenwriter who sees a murder in Kobe, but his testimony is ignored by police because the body has vanished without a trace. Eager to prove he's not crazy and worried that he may have attracted the attention of the murderers, Ryu hires

private detective Mochizuki to protect him and investigate. Similarities with cult live-action movie *Blow-Up* (1966) are unlikely to be coincidental. **Ⓥ**

URDA THIRD REICH *

2003. AKA: *Urda*. Online series. DIR: Romanov (Kazuhiro) Higa. SCR: Romanov Higa. DES: Romanov Higa, Tetsuya Watanabe. ANI: Romanov Higa. MUS: Junki Shimizu. PRD: Romanov Films. 5 mins. x 5 eps.

In the summer of 1943, Nazis in Europe uncover a crashed spaceship that allows them to manipulate time and change the course of the war—a hackneyed concept in science fiction, but one that achieved new prominence in Asia with the release of the Korean-Japanese alternate history movie *2009: Lost Memories* (2002). Hitler sets up the URDA project to exploit the technology, and the Allies send in spy Erna Kurtz. Ex-commando Erna uncovers the plot and finds that she is already closely linked to it through her relationship to project commander Glimhild Kurtz. She tries to rescue the young girl who is the subject of the URDA tests—and claims to be from the future. This one-man show with an almost entirely unknown cast is a prime example of how the Internet is changing the way we get our entertainment. Made in CGI but intended to look like full cel animation, its only link with the anime establishment is the presence of designer, producer, and director Watanabe, who also has a background in CGI, but is here credited with the design of the vehicles. The short format works well for streaming and new platforms like mobile phones, but it takes a very skillful director to do anything other than make eye candy in such a restricted timeslot. A generation with its attention span attuned to MTV is unlikely to worry about such details as depth of character and plot development, but those who love anime for the freedom it gives the writer have legitimate cause for concern and may be reassured by this confident debut, which packs a lot into its tiny parcels.

Urda Third Reich

The *URDA* series was also cut together and shown as a "movie" at the Tokyo International Film Festival in 2005. Compare to **VOICES OF A DISTANT STAR** and **LEGEND OF DUO**, both of which also showcase potential new directions for the anime world in the early 21st century. **ⓛⓥ**

URIQPEN: ANIMAL RESCUE LEAGUE *

1974. JPN: *Uriqpen Kyudotai*. TV series. DIR: Hiroshi Sasagawa, Seitaro Hara. SCR: Jinzo Toriumi . DES: Akio Sugino. ANI: Jun Tanaka. MUS: Shunsuke Kikuchi. PRD: Tatsunoko, Fuji TV. 5 mins. x 156 eps. (also broadcast as 26 different 30-min. strips).

Four young animals, rabbit Seitaro Usagi, squirrel Risu, bear Kuma, and penguin Penguin (U-Ri-Ku-Pen), are part of a team of brave young animals that rescues others in peril—a sort of animal **THUNDERBIRDS 2086**. Other team members included a dog, a boar, a deer, a koala, a mouse, a seagull, and a lion, but the title would have become too unwieldy even for such a long-running show if they'd all been included in the acronym, although it would have been fun listening to announcers say, "And now, it's time for *Uriqpen-inu-bu-shi-ko-nezu-kamome-shi.*"

The animals would win a prize for completing a mission, as would the viewers, who were encouraged to write in and guess which of the creatures would save the world by each Friday (a single mission stretched over a week of TV). Created by Mitsuru Kaneko, this show was given a limited broadcast on some American local TV stations for the Japanese community.

UROTSUKIDOJI *

1987. JPN: *Chojin Densetsu Urotsukidoji*. AKA: *Legend of the Overfiend: Wandering Child; Wandering Kid*. Video, movie. DIR: Hideki Takayama. SCR: Noboru Aikawa, Goro Sanyo, et al. DES: Rikizo Sekime, Shiro Kasami, Sumito Ioi, Keiichi Sato, Tetsuya Yanasawa. ANI: Tetsuya Yanasawa. MUS: Masamichi Amano. PRD: JAVN, Angel. 45 mins., 55 mins., 55 mins. (v1–*U1*), 55 mins., 50 mins. (v1 part 2), 108 mins. (m1–*U1*), 88 mins. (*U2*), 60 mins., 50 mins., 50 mins. (v3, aka *U3*), ca. 80 mins. (m3 aka *U3*), 40 mins. x 3 eps. (v4, aka *U4*), ca. 40 mins. (v5, aka *U5*), 45 mins. x 3 eps. (v6, aka *The Urotsuki*).

Every three thousand years, a superbeing is born who will unite the three separate dimensions of humans, demons, and Jujin "man-beasts," bringing about a new world. Man-beast Amanojaku is determined to track down this "Chojin," and after 300 years of wandering, locates demonic forces at work in 1993 Japan. Teenager Nagumo impregnates schoolgirl Akemi, rupturing the fabric of the universe and ushering in the apocalypse. Akemi goes into hibernation for a century to await the birth of her child (the Chojin), and Earth is ravaged by a nuclear war. Decades later, in a Japan ruled by former industrialist Caesar, the Chojin is born early because of the arrival in Tokyo of his diametrical opposite, the Kyo-O (translated variously as Mad King, or Lord of Chaos). Buju, a man-beast hybrid, elopes with Caesar's daughter, Alecto, and finds the Kyo-O in a temple shortly before he is killed. Buju is brought back to life by the Kyo-O (a young girl called Himi whose growth is rapidly accelerated) and overthrows Caesar. He vows to take Himi to Osaka to confront the Chojin. Despite the efforts of the Chojin to stop him, he eventually succeeds—Chojin drinks a drop of the blood from Himi's first menstruation, and the world is restored to normality.

Based on the violent and pornographic 1985 manga by Toshio Maeda for *Wani* magazine, **Urotsukidoji** is the best-known of the anime "nasties" released in English in the 1990s. A fiercely complex cycle of rape and redemption, it even seems to have confused its Japanese crew—the first three episodes take place in Osaka, the next two are set *before* the third episode, with the same characters inexplicably moved to Tokyo. This leap backward seems designed to incorporate the Kyo-O subplot, vital to the rest of the series, but unnecessary if the series were to end early; though considering that the series has a fiendishly cyclical plot (like its contemporary **Gall Force**), it is conceivable that one is set several eons after the other! Perplexity continued in the English-language market, where the series was dubbed by three different companies using different actors and contradictory

translations. The first five-part video series was edited into the two "movies," *Legend of the Overfiend* and *Legend of the Demon Womb*. Note that *Demon Womb* was numbered in Roman numerals as "Urotsukidoji II," thereby causing the *second* series, *Return of the Overfiend*, to gain the misleading numeral of *Urotsukidoji III*. In the U.S. all five video episodes appeared, numbered 1 to 5 in order of release, not action, to add to the confusion. The massive and (to the Japanese originators) completely unexpected success of the series in English led to the making of two sequels. The four-part *Return of the Overfiend* (1993) featured the postholocaust chapters, followed by *Inferno Road* (1995), which concludes the saga in three parts. However, though the series is complete in the U.S., *Inferno Road* was delayed by the British censor for three years. Eventually, the final chapter alone was permitted a release in 2001—the British DVD sheepishly includes the scripts of the banned episodes to compensate. *Urotsukidoji V: The Final Chapter* (1996) is a mysterious curio in the history of the saga, intended as the first installment of yet another series. Despite being abandoned partway through production, with some of the animation still jerky and incomplete, it was nonetheless released in Japan and Germany and claims to introduce the real Chojin at last, dropping many of the newer characters and returning to a continuity that seems to owe more to the earlier episodes of the series. This, however, could have made no difference—as with some installments of **Gall Force**, the ending of *Urotuskidoji IV* implied that some characters had been shoved back through a time or dimensional loop, and hence would be reexperiencing certain elements of the saga again, albeit with some changes.

The story was remade again as *Urotsukidoji: New Saga* (aka *The Urotsuki*, 2002), a three-part video series made as part of the erotic **Vanilla Series**. In a return to the subject matter and characters of the original series,

Amanojaku evades prison and hides out at a Japanese high school; along with the usual sex and violence, there is an increased concentration, in the style of *Inferno Road*, on the childhoods of the protagonists, designed to show how they might grow up into the kind of beastly people they ultimately turn out to be. In this version, the Chojin is renamed the Ultra God.

Urotsukidoji amply achieves Maeda's overriding narrative aim—to demonstrate that the only way to win in this world is to die young before your dreams are shattered. The question for his critics, in both the pro- and anticensorship lobbies, is whether the poetry of the end justifies the gross extremity of the means. Since *Urotsukidoji*, many other Maeda works have been adapted, including **Demon Beast Invasion**, **Adventure Kid**, **La Blue Girl**, **Nightmare Campus**, and **Demon Warrior Koji**. Though the *Urotsukidoji* saga is now complete in manga form, recent spin-offs have included stories of the Chojin's earlier manifestations in human history, leaving a rich vein of material for potential further anime installments. Scenes from *Urotsukidoji*, **Md Geist**, and **Perfect Blue** were shown onstage as part of Madonna's *Drowned World* tour in 2001. **CNV**

URUSEI YATSURA *

1981. AKA: *Those Obnoxious Aliens; Weird Folk from Planet Uru; Noisy People.* TV series, movie, video. DIR: Mamoru Oshii, Keiji Hayakawa, Tameo Ogawa, Kazuo Yamazaki, Tetsu Dezaki, Katsuhisa Yamada, Setsuko Shibunnoichi. SCR: Hiroyuki Hoshiyama, Masaru Yamamoto, Shunsuke Kaneko, Ichiro Izumi, Takao Koyama, Kazunori Ito, Michiru Shimada, Tomoko Konparu, Hideo Takayashiki. DES: Akemi Takada, Torao Arai, Setsuko Shibunoichi, Kumiko Takahashi. ANI: Katsumi Aoshima, Yuichi Endo, Tsukasa Dokite, Yukari Kobayashi, Kumiko Takahashi. MUS: Shinsuke Kazato, Izumi Kobayashi, Fumitaka Anzai, Masamichi Amano, Toshiyuki Omori, Mitsuru Kotaki. PRD: Studio Pierrot, Kitty Film,

Fuji TV. 25 mins. x 218 eps. (TV), 101 mins., 98 mins., 90 mins., 95 mins., 85 mins., 77 mins. (m), 45 mins. x 2 eps., 57 mins., 30 mins. x 2 eps., 25 mins. x 6 eps. (v).

The alien Oni race decide to invade Earth but offer to leave if Earth's champion can defeat theirs at a game of tag. But the randomly selected Earth champion is Ataru Moroboshi, a hapless Japanese teenage lecher. Racing the beautiful Princess Lum, Ataru tricks her by stealing her bikini top and wins the game. Earth is saved, but he has gained an alien fiancée living in his closet. She may be sexy, but she has the power to electrocute him if he goes near another girl and is fiercely jealous of his many love interests, including his Earth-girl paramour, Shinobu.

One of Western fandom's favorites, based on the 1978 *Shonen Sunday* manga by Rumiko Takahashi, this romantic comedy mixes sci-fi with **Japanese Folk Tales** and suburban life. Takahashi has a dark side, but she keeps it for her horror stories like **Mermaid's Forest**; in most of her work, creatures of all planets share the same failings and desires, and there is more of a gulf between male and female than there can ever be between human and alien.

The TV series (sadly showing its age in terms of animation quality) introduces us to Lum, her unlikely beloved Ataru, the unluckiest, laziest, and most lecherous boy on Earth, and their associates, including his helplessly uncomprehending parents, her dreamboat ex-boyfriend, Rei, her bratty cousin, Ten-chan, and her many pretty friends. The original series is loaded with topical domestic humor in the manner of a Japanese *Simpsons*, but though little of this survives translation, the fresh, funny slapstick and situations do, along with an educational quantity unforeseen by the original filmmakers. *UY*'s depiction of mundane *Japanese* life is a window onto a culture alien to many Western fans, a fact cleverly exploited in the studiously annotated subtitled releases from AnimEigo. The TV series is a delight from beginning to end and

Urusei Yatsura

© 1981 RUMIKO TAKAHASHI / SHOGAKUKAN • KITTY • FUJI TV

absolutely deserves its fan-favorite status; its stablemate **Ranma ½**, originally made for an audience too young to remember the early *UY*, has attained a similar status simply by copying it.

The movies and videos are all variations on the same theme—love, and the crazy deceptions we play in its name. The first two movies are directed by **Ghost in the Shell**'s Mamoru Oshii and designed by Kazuo Yamazaki. *Only You* (1983) introduces another alien fiancée for Ataru, and shows Lum's desperate attempts to save him from walking to the altar with Elle, a girl who rules a planet with décor straight out of a rose-strewn Harlequin fantasy. In the surreal *Beautiful Dreamer* (1984), the characters are caught up in Ataru's recurring dream, enabling Oshii to play with perceptions of reality within the conventional format of a romantic comedy. Yamazaki moved up to direct *Remember My Love* (1985) with character designs by Takada. This tale of transdimensional travel, obsessive love, and the line between childhood and adulthood remains, for all its lunatic wrappings (such as Ataru transformed into a pink hippo and a Bradburyesque nightmare circus that later showed up

in **Neo-Tokyo** and **Sailor Moon**), the purest SF story ever achieved by the *UY* team. *Lum the Forever* (1986) was again directed by Yamazaki and designed by Takeda, with **Dirty Pair**'s Dokite directing the animation. The gang is making a film, with Lum as the star, but all the surrounding activity, including the cutting down of an ancient cherry tree, has awakened a curse that may change their lives forever and lead to the loss of the things they value most. *UY The Final Chapter* (1988, *Kanketsuhen*) puts the romantic boot on the other foot; instead of Ataru running after some cute girl, Lum is carried off by an alien hunk named Lupa, to whom, it appears, her grandfather promised her in marriage when she was still a baby. Neither Ataru nor Carla (Lupa's girlfriend) is pleased, and the chaos culminates in yet another game of tag to decide the fate of Earth. Dezaki directed Konparu's screenplay with designs by Shibunnoichi. Typically, the "final chapter" wasn't—the last *UY* movie was actually *Always (Itsudatte) My Darling* (1991), made when *UY* had been supplanted on TV by *Ranma*, reversing the previous plot for a kidnap tale in which Ataru is carried off by an alien princess named Lupica, and Lum sets out to get him back with a little help from biker goddess Benten and snow princess Oyuki. It was made by a new team, with Yamada in the director's chair, Takayashiki joining Konparu on screenplay, another Takahashi (Kumiko) designing and directing the animation, and music from Koteki.

The ever-increasing cost of moviemaking coincided with the rise of the video format that started with **DALLOS** in 1983. In 1986, the Japanese *UY* fan club began screening "exclusive" mini-movies at public events, soon revealed to be advance copies of the straight-to-video *UY* releases *Ryoko's September Tea Party* and *Memorial Album*. Both stories used flashback footage from the series with about 15 minutes of new framing animation to recount the past history of the characters and episodes from the story line—a useful way of hooking new video buyers to boost TV series sales on video. A new story, *Inaba The Dream Maker* (1987), featured a transdimensional white rabbit and answered the question of what happens when you unlock doors in time and space without knowing where they lead. Next up was the insanely funny *Raging Sherbet* (1988), in which flying alien ice-cream cones carry out kamikaze revenge attacks on Lum's greedy girlfriend Ran. Ghost love story *Nagisa's Fiancé* appeared the same year. Then 1989 brought four new romantic comedy stories. *I Howl at the Moon* has Ataru gobbling Lum's cooking and turning into a wolf. *Catch the Heart* has hard-nosed Ran involved in chaos when a spirit gives her a candy that makes capturing the heart of the one you love a breeze. *Goat and Cheese* shows the problems of ancient and incomprehensible family curses when Mendo's father breaks one by taking a picture in front of the statue of great-grandfather's goat, and *The Electric Household Guard* gives Mendo a new servant with eyes only for his sister, Kyoko. In 1991 the series was rounded off with *Terror of Girly-eye Measles,* in which Ataru's womanizing ways spread

an alien virus all over town, and *Date with a Spirit,* in which he tries to date a pretty ghost haunting sorceress Sakura's fiancé. An improvisational dub of two episodes by minor British celebrities was screened as *Lum the Invader Girl* (2000) as part of a "Japan Night" on a U.K. cable channel.

URUSHIHARA, SATOSHI

1966– . Sometimes credited as Satoshi Urushibara. Although briefly employed by Toei Animation, Urushihara soon went freelance, peddling his distinctive illustration work as a character designer for games and anime, and was founder of the manga studio Ars Work [*sic*]. **ANOTHER LADY INNOCENT** is representative of his style—a master with flesh tones and the female form, which has often led him to erotica such as **TALES OF...**, where his talents seem best employed. Attempts have also been made to put him to work in more mainstream areas, such as **LEGEND OF LEMNEAR** or **PLASTIC LITTLE**, but his best-known successes are probably as a designer on the *Langrisser* and *Glowlancer* computer games.

USELESS ANIMALS

2005. JPN: *Damekko Dobutsu.* TV series. DIR: Setsuko Shibuichi. SCR: Mitsuyo Suenaga. DES: Yukari Kobayashi. ANI: Yukari Kobayashi. MUS: Tsunta Kobayashi. PRD: Magic Bus, Kid's Station. 5 mins. x 26 eps.
When he is not found to be suitably savage or lupine in demeanor, Uruno is declared to be a useless wolf and cast out. He wanders the world until he finds the Useless Forest, populated solely by animals that have similarly failed to live up to their stereotypical characteristics. This, however, is not all good—a near-sighted owl may be no threat, but Uruno is threatened and harangued by a bad-tempered rabbit whose "useless" quality is to be violent, not cute at all, and rather dangerous. However, he is tempted to stay in the forest when he falls for the cute cheetah Chiiko, in an anime that mixes the out-of-character anthropomorphics

of **ON A STORMY NIGHT** with a cast that often resembles children dressed up as animals for a kindergarten play. Nor are the animals "realistic" in our own sense, since there is space in the Useless Forest for fantasy creatures like an alcoholic unicorn and a timid winged horse. Beneath the cutesy subtext is a staple of many Japanese movies and live-action TV serials—a group of comical no-hopers somehow finding their way in life through their friendship.

USHIO AND TORA *

1992. JPN: *Ushio to Tora.* Video. DIR: Kunihiko Yuyama. SCR: Kenji Terada, Kunihiko Yuyama. DES: Tokuhiro Matsubara. ANI: Tokuhiro Matsubara. MUS: Shiro Sagisu. PRD: Pastel, Toho. 30 mins. x 11 eps.
Ushio Aotsuki is the grandson of a priest and guardian of an ancient temple, where (so he is told) the malevolent spirit Nagatobimaru (Lord Long-Flyer) has been imprisoned for centuries, impaled on the magical Spear of Beast. He discovers the old legends are true when he inadvertently releases the spirit. Invisible to others, Tora (as Ushio calls Nagatobimaru) claims he would dearly love to eat Ushio but cannot get close to him while Ushio hangs onto the spear. The second-sight provided by the spear allows Ushio to see a whole world of spirits living amid our own and, in an unlikely team with Tora, he sets out busting ghosts in the neighborhood. These include a stone centipede in a school storeroom, sickle-carrying weasels, a group of flying heads, and floating clouds of bad vibes.

Combining a reluctant-buddies/unwelcome-guest plot with modern rewrites of **JAPANESE FOLK TALES**, *U&T* began as a 1990 *Shonen Sunday* manga by Kazuhiro Fujita, only parts of which are adapted here. Despite the obvious potential for a long-running TV series (the manga tops 30 volumes), *U&T* stayed on video and fizzled out in the mid-1990s, while its inferior contemporary **TENCHI MUYO!** ripped off its premise before swapping the ghostbusting for interminable flirting. The show comes laden with arch observations on modern Japan in the style of POMPOKO—the samurai-era Tora cannot eat today's people because they daub themselves with sickly perfumes; the sickle-weasels must disguise themselves as humans to survive; and a sea monster made of drowned souls is rendered invulnerable by modern pollution. As in DEVIL HUNTER YOHKO, new construction disturbs the ancient dead, while modern children are their inheritors and saviors—Ushio is the descendant of a warrior-mage, and his friend Mayuko the reincarnation of an exorcist. This anime also features some unexpected changes of tone—despite their antagonism, Ushio and Tora complement each other like signs of the Chinese zodiac (*ushi*/ox and *tora*/tiger), and it is Ushio who leaps to Tora's defense when he is pursued by talisman master Piao, a Cantonese exorcist who mistakenly believes Tora killed his family. Similarly, while Ushio spars constantly with local tomboy Asako, he is prepared to fight for her against Tsubura, the spirit of a water wheel who wishes to carry her away (this episode is the only one not taken directly from the manga). The series ends with a spoof episode, the *C[omical] D[eforme] Theater*, in which cartoon versions of the characters fight, sing songs, and eventually appear in their own zany silent movie. There was also an audio spin-off on the *U&T Original Album*, which featured music "inspired by" the series from Seikima-II guitarist Ace Shimizu (see HUMANE SOCIETY).

A welcome antidote to the teen wish-fulfillment pap that dominated much of the anime market throughout the 1990s, *U&T* is by turns funny, exciting, and reflective, distinguished by two separate translations, of which the U.S. version by ADV is the superior. ⬤Ⓥ

UTA—KATA

2004. AKA: *One Song/Poem Piece*. DIR: Keiji Goto. SCR: Hidefumi Kimura. DES: Megumi Kadonosono. ANI: Akiko Nagashima, Koichiro Ueda. MUS:

Utena

Harumi Ono. PRD: TV Kanagawa, Bandai Visual, gimik, HAL Filmmaker. 24 mins. x 12 eps. (TV), 30 mins. (v).

In a reprise of the premise of E-CHAN THE NINJA, Japanese schoolgirl Ichika stares into a mirror to discover another girl staring back at her. Her new companion is Manatsu (literally: "Midsummer"), who grants her magical powers that will only last for the summer, in an allegory of the end of childhood and one last vacation before the responsibilities of the grown-up world start to impinge—compare to MAHOROMATIC. However, all is not sweetness and light, as there are hints that this has happened before and that Ichika is the target of a mysterious plot conceived by the woman next door. A number of well-known manga illustrators, including Ken Akamatsu and Koshi Rikudo, provide "guest" designs for the costumes into which Ichika changes in each episode.

A one-shot video sequel followed,

Twin Summers of the First Winter (2005, *Shoto no Futanatsu*) in which Satsuki, believing herself to be alone once more, encounters an apparent doppelganger of Manatsu during the winter. The new girl claims to be Mafuyu (or "Midwinter"), in a rather pointless rehash that to some minds betrays the elegiac quality of the original series—if everything can be reset and reprised à la TENCHI MUYO!, where's the drama?

UTENA *

1997. JPN: *Shojo Kakumei Utena*. AKA: *Revolutionary Girl Utena; La Fillette Revolutionnaire Utena; Ursula's Kiss*. TV series, movie. DIR: Kunihiko Ikuhara, Shingo Kaneko, Toru Takahashi, Tatsuo Okazaki, Akihiko Nishiyama, Katsushi Sakurabi, Takafumi Hoshikawa, Shigeo Koshi, Hiroaki Sakurai. SCR: Yoji Enokido, Noboru Higa, Kazuhiro Uemura, Ryoei Tsukimura. DES: Chiho Saito, Shinya Hasegawa. ANI: Shinya Hasegawa, Tomoko Kawasaki, Yuji

Matsukura. mus: Shinkichi Mitsumune, J.A. Seazar. prd: Be-Papas, JC Staff, TV Tokyo. 25 mins. x 39 eps. (TV), 75 mins. (m).

Pink-haired tomboy Utena Tenjo (a surname infuriatingly mispronounced throughout the U.S. dub) is an eighth grader at Otori Academy. She clings to the memory of her childhood encounter with a mysterious "prince" as she wept by the grave of her parents. Though she cannot remember his face (refer to CANDY CANDY), she treasures the rose signet ring he gave her and, for reasons not totally clear, resolves to dress and behave as a boy until she finds him again.

Otori is a teen fantasy, where teachers live in fear of the student council and sputter impotently at pupils' "witty" comebacks, the boys and girls are all beautiful, and dueling is the number-one occupation. Fencers regularly meet for ritual combat within a gargantuan hall (part of the school, yet also a separate dimension), where they fight for the right to the hand of Anthy, the "Rose Bride" whose body is a living sheath for a sword. Victorious in battle, Utena becomes Anthy's betrothed, though the student council do what they can to topple her because they are searching for the ultimate duelist who will summon forth the divine power known as "Dios."

Portentous and pretentious in equal amounts, *Utena* quite literally invests teenage crushes and schoolgirl intrigues with world-shattering significance. Created by director Ikuhara, with several other staffers from his earlier SAILOR MOON S, and Chiho Saito, who drew the *Utena* manga for *Ciao* magazine, it artfully perverts mundane school life into a quest of fantastic proportions. It also features swordplay and cross-dressing in the swashbuckling tradition of PRINCESS KNIGHT and ROSE OF VERSAILLES, to which it owes a heavy aesthetic debt. Director Ikuhara acknowledges a strong influence from TRAGEDY OF BELLADONNA, the film that inspired him to work in anime. Like the tarot-themed episodes of ESCAFLOWNE, *Utena*

presents its heroine with a series of subtext-laden duels to test her mettle, forging her into a suitable messiah. Highly sensual though rarely explicit, its premise is ironically close to that of an UROTSUKIDOJI that replaces sex and violence with pure, infinite yearning. On Japanese TV, *Utena* thrived in the vacuum left by the conclusion of EVANGELION, though it was not without controversy—in a ludicrous outbreak of racism, the TV Tokyo switchboard received complaints that love interest Anthy was "black."

Many better-known fairy tales are mixed and matched with situation comedy: one character proudly displays a "designer pendant" that is nothing more than a cowbell, then slowly transforms into a cow before the others' eyes. In another, tomboy Utena and twee Anthy swap personalities after a particularly hot curry. Amid all the school high jinks, the central story continues, as girls pine for their princes, boys for their princesses, and a plot with the vague aims of "bringing revolution and attaining eternity" advances ever onward. Ikuhara brings sensibilities and themes from his own *Sailor Moon S* episodes to this unlikely confection of swords and roses, mirroring the rollercoaster of teenage emotions in a whirl of seductive imagery. Unlike SLAYERS, which mixes "real" elements into its fantasy world for comic effect, *Utena* coats the real world in fantasy but lets the sharp edges show through. Beautiful clothes and skill with a sword can't ward off the pain of inadequacy and loss—though they certainly *look* good. The series too places increasing emphasis on style over substance as it progresses, becoming ever more surreal, with additional digital effects in the last season.

The movie *Adolescence of Utena* (1999) wraps up the story with a fantasy that summarizes its main themes in a succession of vignettes rather than providing a logical conclusion. It's therefore incomprehensible to anyone who has not seen the preceding series; a hallucinogenic whirl of tortured

relationships, floating roses, flying cars, flashing blades, and gorgeous costumes.

UTSUNOMIKO

1989. aka: *Celestial Prince*. Movie, video. dir: Fumio Kurokawa (m), Tetsuo Imazawa (v). scr: Kenji Terada, Sukehiro Tomita (m), Junji Takegami, Sukehiro Tomita (v). des: Mutsumi Inomata (m), Teruyoshi Yamazaki (v). ani: Chuichi Iguchi, Kazuya Kise. mus: Chiyoshi Kawano (m), Masahiro Kawasaki (v). prd: Nippon Animation, Toei Animation. 83 mins. (m1), 30 mins. x 13 eps., 75 mins. (m2).

Based on Keisuke Fujikawa's novel of mythical 7th-century Japan, the first movie, subtitled *Earth Chapter*, introduces the divine child Utsunomiko, born with a tiny horn on his head but otherwise a normal mystic hero. Trained with a group of friends by the mysterious priest Ojino, he is a fine fighter but will only ever use a bamboo staff. When the group is forced to fight a cruel overlord and his diabolical allies, they must prove their courage and strength to save their friends. In the video series, subtitled *Heaven Chapter*, Imazawa used Inomata's designs but completely changed the staff. Yamazaki redesigned the characters, and new music was provided by Kawasaki. Ojino gives the friends a magic Phoenix ship that takes them to heaven, but Utsunomiko finds the gods can be just as cruel as humans, and he fights them for the rights of the people, eventually changing into his god-form as the only way to win and finally meet his father, the supreme lord of heaven. The clash between the "new" Buddhist practices and native Shinto spirits, as well as the civil disorders of the time, form the backdrop to a series of richly designed adventures, and the video animation is (unusually) better than that of the 1988 film, allowing for better appreciation of the subtlety of Inomata's work. The 1990 film *U: Heaven Chapter* was a short reworking of the video series.

V

VAMPIRE

1968. TV series. DIR: Tsutomu Yamada, Tei Mabune. SCR: Yasuhiro Yamaura, Masaki Tsuji, Toshiro Fujinami, Tomohiro Ando, Shunichi Yukimuro, Yoshiyuki Fukuda. DES: Osamu Tezuka. ANI: Renzo Kinoshita. MUS: Hikaru Hayashi. PRD: Mushi Pro, Fuji TV. 25 mins. x 26 eps.

Toppei Tachibana is an everyday worker at the Mushi Pro company, who is secretly one of the Clan of Night's Weeping, a were-creature. Mr. Morimura, a reporter from the *Daily Times* researching vampires, discovers that Toppei transforms into a wolf whenever he sees a full moon and starts to chronicle both his activities and his secret feud with other clan members. A self-referential series from Tezuka, disastrously mixing animated supernatural creatures with live-action footage, shot in and around his own studios—the **ASTRO BOY**–creator would later do his best to edge *Vampire* out of his biography. Tezuka, Toppei's boss in real life and onscreen, plays himself in the series, while behind the scenes are several staff borrowed from **ULTRAMAN**'s Tsuburaya studios and respected art-house animator Renzo Kinoshita (see **WARTIME ANIME**). Compare to the later **BORN FREE**.

VAMPIRE HUNTER D *

1985. JPN: *Vampire Hunter D*. Movie. DIR: Toyoo Ashida. SCR: Yasuhiro Hirano. DES: Yoshitaka Amano, Noriyasu Yamaura. ANI: Hiromi Matsushita. MUS: Tetsuya Komuro. PRD: Ashi Pro. 80 mins., ca. 120 mins.

Ten thousand years in the future, humanity lives in a quasi-medieval society overrun by the vampires who keep them in a state of feudal subjugation and terror. When Count Lee claims Doris as his next bride, a mysterious cloaked stranger in a big hat, known only as "D," rides into town on a huge horse and saves her. The townspeople want to give her up to pacify the count, but Doris has fallen in love with her vampire-hunter savior. "D" has to clean out the nest of vampires, but he's not without problems of his own. His hand has an independent life and nags him mercilessly, and his own background as a half-vampire is the cause of much inner conflict.

The film is based on a long series of novels by Hideyuki Kikuchi, who also created **WIND OF AMNESIA**, **WICKED CITY**, and **DARKSIDE BLUES**. Despite the Hammer-horror trappings, at heart *VHD* is more like a vampire Western. The character designs, based on Amano's illustrations for the novels, may entice lovers of his smoky, elegant watercolors and baroque game characters, but they were radically simplified to cut animation costs, with only traces of the artist's hand remaining, mostly in still frames.

Based on Kikuchi's third novel, *D: Demon Deathchase*, and shown unfinished and unedited as a "work in progress" at the Fantasia 2000 festival, the new version, *VHD Bloodlust*, is directed and scripted by **NINJA SCROLL**'s Yoshiaki Kawajiri. As with the original, the story is based on part of Kikuchi's epic novel series but adds a greater emphasis on action. D, revealed as a half-vampire or "dhampir," is one of several hunters hired to rescue Charlotte, the daughter of a wealthy family, who has been kidnapped by a vampire; but she has fallen in love with her captor. Does he kill them both, or allow her to escape the misery of human life and flee to another planet with her lover? Characters are designed by Yutaka Minowa, monsters by Yasushi Nirasawa, and animation is by Madhouse. **NV**

VAMPIRE PRINCESS MIYU *

1988. JPN: *Kyuketsuki Miyu*. AKA: *Vampire Miyu*. Video, TV series. DIR: Toshihiro Hirano. SCR: Noboru Aikawa, Yuji Hayami. DES: Narumi Kakinouchi, Yasuhiro Moriki (v), Megumi Kadonosono, Kenji Teraoka (TV). ANI: Narumi Kakinouchi, Masahiro Nishii. MUS: Kenji Kawai. PRD: AIC, Pony Canyon. 30 mins. x 4 eps. (v), 25 mins. x 26 eps. (TV).

Himiko is a cynical, charlatan "medium" faced with a real-life case of demonic possession in Japan's former capital of Kyoto. There, amid sleepy, leafy lanes, she witnesses a battle between the Shinma, evil "demon-god" creatures from another dimension,

ANIMEIGO, INC. © SODEISHINSHA & PONY CANYON, INC.

Vampire Princess Miyu

and Earth's only protector, a vampire princess called Miyu.

Like Claudia in Anne Rice's *Interview with the Vampire*, Miyu is a former human who bears a vampire curse, trapped forever in a world of teenage angst. Motivated sometimes less by a sense of justice than by her own raging hormones, she pushes a succubus away from a man she secretly wants herself, parades Lolita-fashion around her devoted servant (and former enemy) Larva, and slowly worms her way into Himiko's life. Like PET SHOP OF HORRORS, *VPM* features the ghostbusting odd-couple of a mundane person from our world and a flashy spellcaster from the next. The olde-worlde charm of Kyoto makes a nice change from the sprawling city of Tokyo, particularly when the animation has aged so well. But amid the long, long silences and dark, meaningful glances, *VPM* is a mass of contradictions. As Himiko points out in a rare moment of lucidity, Miyu walks around in daylight, licks up holy water, and can crush a crucifix in her bare hands—so for the peculiarly picky audience of vampire folklorists, *VPM* is little more convincing than the execrable BEAST CITY.

Furthermore, since she often seems only to be protecting people so she can chow down on their jugular veins, what exactly makes her any better than the creatures she is supposed to be fighting? Don't expect any answers, because Miyu (and, it would seem, her creator Narumi Kakinouchi) would rather smile condescendingly and tell you that you could never understand rather than admit they don't know either.

Sometimes this approach pays off, especially when the story reverses the roles of the sexes. It makes a change to see a predatory succubus chasing after a young *male* virgin, or indeed to see a vain pretty-*boy* selling his soul to the devil to keep his looks forever. There are some great ideas, such as the girl who loses her mind because she is kept alive by blood transfusions from her dying parents, or alien parasites that feed off people's dreams. But such moments are few, making for an elegantly chilling and curiously watchable anime that constantly promises more than it delivers.

The video series is based on Kakinouchi's 1988 manga and directed by her husband, one of Japan's masters of horror and creator of ICZER-ONE.

In 1997, it was snapped up for TV adaptation amid the post-EVANGELION boom when so many old video shows were reborn as cheap but at least *partly* market-tested TV. The TV series, conceived by Kakinouchi, Hirano, and Yuji Hayanami, introduced new characters such as Miyu's little bat-winged rabbit Shina, and another servant, Reiha, a snow demon who detests Miyu and also has the power to send Shinma back to the shadows. Reiha confides in her doll while chirpy human schoolgirl Chisato balances Miyu's coldness and further enhances the disturbing links between magic and childhood. Megumi Kadonosono reworks the character designs without obvious disharmony, and Kenji Kawai's music is just as evocative and elegant. Hirano (by this point using his real first name of Toshiki) disliked some of the changes required by Japanese TV censorship, including the removal of much of the projected second episode story line, and restored the deletions for the video release in 1998. Another Kakinouchi project, *Vampire Princess Yui*, the story of a girl whose mother was bitten by Miyu while pregnant, was published in manga form but not animated. **Ⓥ**

VAMPIRE WARS *
1990. Video. DIR: Kazuhisa Takenouchi. SCR: Hiroyuki Hoshiyama. DES: Hideki Hamazu, Hiroyuki Kitazume. ANI: Hideki Hamazu. MUS: Kazz Toyama. PRD: Toei. 50 mins.
Japanese agent Kosaburo Kuki (sort of) hides out in Paris in the company of dialogue-challenged whores and meets Lamia Vindaw, a girl who's sort of chummy with "vampires," who are really a galaxy-spanning alien race that have achieved immortality by storing life-giving energy in their bodies. Human blood provides a weak source of this energy, but Lamia's altered body chemistry has a uniquely powerful version. It's just what the aliens need to revive their king, trapped in a deep sleep in Transylvania ever since the visitors arrived five thousand years ago. Meanwhile, Monsieur Lassar of

the French Secret Service thinks there is a connection between a terrorist attack on a NASA base in Arizona and the murder of a CIA man in Paris, and he hires Kuki to find out. Naturally, it's Lamia that is the key, though the more interesting elements of the backstory are only revealed in the final moments of this awful anime, which is little more than an ad for the opening chapters of the best-selling Kiyoshi Kasai novel on which it is based. Most but not all anime novel adaptations suffer in the transition, mainly from being cut down to fit a 50-minute running time—barely enough to contain the average short story. However, such bastard children of the industry are often sold off at a bargain price to foreign companies (for obvious reasons), though any who pay for them discover at their cost that there is negligible pressure to rush out the next part—thus the interminable wait over the next episodes of HEROIC LEGEND OF ARSLAN.

The original Lamia of vampire legend was Queen of Libya and one of Zeus's many lovers. She was transformed into a child-eating monster, giving her name to a race of ghoulish female demons with a craving for blood. This tired story does no credit to its ancient antecedents. **LNV**

VAMPIYAN KIDS

2001. JPN: *Nanchatte Vampiyan*. AKA: *Vampire Vegetarians*. TV series. DIR: Masaaki Yuasa (pilot), Masatsugu Arakawa. SCR: N/C. DES: Suzuka Yoshida (pilot), Kayoko Nabeta (pilot), Miyako Yazu. ANI: Hiroyuki Nishimura, Kanami Sekiguchi, Kayoko Nabeta, Masahiro Sato, Takayuki Hamana, Taketomo Ishikawa, Tsuyoshi Ichiki, Yuichiro Sueyoshi. MUS: Ko Otani (pilot), Toshihiko Sahashi. PRD: Fuji TV, Production IG, IKIF +, Ogura Workshop. 25 mins. x 26 eps.

A vampire family that survives on orange juice instead of blood can't call itself "vampire"—hence the name *vampiyan*. The father can't even scare humans and is sent into exile in the human world to scare 1,000 people

before he is permitted to return home. But his daughter Sue falls in love with human boy Ko and doesn't want to go back. The whole show appears to have undergone a transfusion between the pilot (screened at the 2004 Future Film Festival in Italy) and release—the main crew and cast members, except for Ko and Mama, were all replaced. Notably, the voice of "Papa" in the pilot was provided by Kenji Utsumi, who has voiced vampires on other occasions, such as the similarly comedic DON DRACULA and the more traditional DRACULA: SOVEREIGN OF THE DAMNED.

VANDREAD *

2001. TV series. DIR: Takeshi Mori, Hitoyuki Matsui. SCR: Atsuhiro Tomioka, Natsuko Takahashi. DES: Mahiro Maeda, Kazuya Kuroda, Tomohiro Kawahara. ANI: Takahiro Fujii, Satoshi Kawano. MUS: N/C. PRD: Gonzo, Media Factory, WOWOW. 23 mins. x 12 eps. (TV1), 23 mins. x 12 eps. (TV2), 75 mins. (*Integral*), 75 mins. (*Turbulence*).

War has been raging for generations between the all-male planet Talac and the all-female planet Majel. Suspend disbelief as to how they keep this up, then imagine that they are invaded by a common enemy and forced to settle their differences for a united counter-attack. The first meeting of 16-year-old Talac engineer Hibiki Tokai and Majel babe Dirda is unplanned; he gets tired of his mundane job assembling robots and plots to steal one of his own. He stows away on a Talac immigration ship, but then the ship is attacked by a Majel pirate. But, despite their races' history of separate development, Hibiki and Dirda will eventually work things out.

The script cleverly exploits the mutual attraction/repulsion of teenagers of opposite sexes, though the visuals resort to standard fan-service ogling of female charms. *Vandread Integral* (aka *Vandread: Taidohen*, 2001) was a feature-length edit of the first series broadcast as a TV movie to set the scene for part two. *Vandread: Turbulence*

(aka *Vandread: Gekitohen*, 2003) was a similar recapitulation of the second season.

VANILLA SERIES *

1997. Video. DIR: Rion Kujo, Norihiko Nagahama, Teruaki Murakami, Mitsuhiro Kometa, Rokurota Makabe, Sotsuki Mitsumura, Kanzaburo Oda, Takayoshi Mizuno, Naomi Hayakawa, Hiroyuki Yanase. SCR: Nikukyuu, Rokurota Makabe, Naruhito Sunaga. DES: Raihiken (aka Ken Raika), Matsuri Ohana, Ryosuke Morimura. ANI: Raihiken Tetsuya Ono, Meka Morishige, Takeshi Okamura, Shinichi Omata. MUS: Yoshi. PRD: YOUC, Digital Works. 30 mins. x 4 eps. (*Love Doll*), 2 eps. (*Shoyonoid Makoto-chan*), 1 ep. (*Sleazy Angels*), 3 eps. (*A Heat for All Seasons*), 4 eps. (*Mei King*), 2 eps. (*Slave Sisters*), 1 ep. (*Office Affairs*), 1 ep. (*Sins of the Flesh*), 2 eps. (*Bondage Mansion*), 1 ep. (*Endless Serenade*), 2 eps. (*Girl Next Door*), 2 eps. (*Dark*), 4 eps. (*Nightmare Campus*), 2 eps. (*Campus*), 2 eps. (*Holy Virgins*), 2 eps. (*Private Sessions*), 2 eps. (*Punishment*), 2 eps. (*Sex Ward*), 2 eps. (*Slaves to Passion*), 2 eps. (*Stepmother's Sin*), 2 eps. (*Hooligan*), 2 eps. (*I Love You*), 2 eps. (*Classroom of Atonement*), 2 eps. (*Spotlight*), 2 eps. (*Submission Central*), 2 eps. (*Story of Little Monica*), 3 eps. (*The Urotsuki/New Saga*), 2 eps. (*Debts of Desire*), 2 eps. (*Rxxx: Prescription for Pain*), 2 eps. (*Maid Service*), 1 ep. (*Ingoku Byouto*), 2 eps. (*Hardcore Hospital*), 2 eps. (*Voyeur's Digest*), 2 eps. (*Perverse Investigations*), 2 eps. (*Xpress Train*), 2 eps. (*Wicked Lessons*), 2 eps. (*Private Sessions 2*), 2 eps. (*Hot For Teacher*), 2 eps. (*Chains of Lust*), 2 eps. (*Naughty Nurses*), 2 eps. (*Bondage 101*), 2 eps. (*Milk Money*), 3 eps. (*Angel Blade*), 2 eps. (*Anyone You Can Do*), 2 eps. (*Internal Medicine*), 2 eps. (*My Brother's Wife*), 2 eps. (*Sextra Credit*), 2 eps. (*Duchess of Busty Mounds*), 2 eps. (*Invasion of the Boobie Snatchers*), 2 eps. (*Group Groper Train*), 2 eps. (*Incontinent Helena*), 2 eps. (*Mother Knows Breast*), 2 eps.

(*Virgin Auction*), 2 eps. (*Invisible Man*), 2 eps. (*Stepsister*).

The Vanilla Series is the Digital Work company's umbrella title for numerous unrelated pornographic anime in the style of Cool Devices or the Discovery Series, largely based on lecherous computer games. With many unrelated one-shot or two-part titles, the Vanilla Series has been greatly overrepresented in the American market, since its titles have been separated, renamed, and sold as several dozen anime releases—many have their own entries in this book, but we have assembled this chronological umbrella entry in an attempt to make some sense of it. Most of the original games are erotic variants of the "dating simulation" engine, in which a protagonist's choices in a role-playing environment lead him not to treasure or freedom, but to the perfect girl of his dreams. Consequently, plotlines often revolve around a roster of half a dozen female stereotypes, differentiated through hair color and non-threatening personality traits.

The first release from the production team was Love Doll in 1997, although its role as the inaugural title for the franchise was only really assigned retroactively. Similar membership to a Vanilla "line" would be assigned to the 1998 releases Shoyonoid Makoto-chan and Sleazy Angels.

The Sega Saturn-originated *Heat for All Seasons* (*Kiss Yori*, 1999) features Masato, an aspiring novelist who moves to a seaside town for a working vacation while looking for candidates for a summertime fling. Masato's friend Oka finds his dream girl working at a restaurant, but Masato rekindles his love with his old high school sweetheart, Chisato, before juggling her with a succession of other girls in the style of an erotic Tenchi Muyo!. Released originally in three seasonally-themed chapters, the English-language version initially featured a title change to *Summer Heat, Autumn Heat,* and *Winter Heat,* before being repackaged as *Heat for All Seasons.*

Mei King (1999) is another outbreak of the Cream Lemon virus, as a man called Cane falls in love with the spirit of a woman trapped inside the body of a young girl called Charlotte. In *Sins of the Flesh* (*Ikenie,* aka *Holy Sacrifice,* 1999), talented artist Adolfo wants to enter the Church and live out his days painting angels, though temptations of the flesh present themselves in the form of the country girl Michaela, with predictable results. Slave Sisters and Office Affairs followed the same year, demonstrating Vanilla's ongoing obsessions with both young girls and scenarios of bondage, coercion, and domination.

Bondage Mansion (*Kinbaku no Yakata,* 2000) featured extensive scenes of the same in a secluded forest hideaway, perpetrated by a father upon his daughters. A different variant on the incest theme was presented in the same year's Endless Serenade, while Girl Next Door presented a vaguely consensual variant on the dating sim theme, whereas *Dark* (*Daraku,* aka *Degeneration,* 2000), featuring more coerced sex, didn't.

In 2001, the Vanilla Series almost doubled its output, jumping on the erotic horror bandwagon with an adaptation of Toshio Maeda's Nightmare Campus, classroom bondage in Private Sessions, Classroom of Atonement, *Campus,* and *Punishment* (*Korashime*). The "gentler" side of pornography continued with I Love You, while bondage and wife coveting continued in Slaves to Passion and Stepmother's Sin. The year also saw a further concentration on fantasy in the literal sense, with Angel Blade and *Hooligan: The Quest for the Seven Holy Dildos* (released in Japan as just plain *Hooligan*), in which a botched "science experiment" transports a Japanese boy to another time and place where he must obtain a series of magical artifacts from the usual roster of stereotyped females—a more quest-oriented variant on the erotic dating sim. The same year saw the nursing craze in Japanese erotica reaching its peak—a line the authors suspect can be traced from the mainstream TV show *Leave It to the Nurses* (*DE), through to erotic rip-offs in the computer games world in 1999, and the subsequent success of Night Shift Nurses, the flagship title of the rival Discovery Series. Not to be outdone, the Vanilla Series retaliated with Sex Ward, and by mixing nurses *and* nuns in Holy Virgins.

The nursing themes continued into 2002, with the release of Vanilla's Ingoku Byouto, and Hardcore Hospital. Erotic horror continued with the release of *The Urotsuki,* the newest incarnation of the Urotsukidoji franchise (released in America as *Urotsukidoji: New Saga*), while less violent fantasies appeared in The Story of Little Monica. Coercion and domination returned in Submission Central and Debts of Desire, while Spotlight mixed the not-quite-incest genre with a tale of a female singer seeking the big time. *Maid Service* (*Maid no Yakata: Zetsubo-hen,* aka *Maid Mansion: Chapter of Despair,* 2002) featured an orphan, Momoko, who must perform menial services for the rich youth Takaaki if she is to earn enough to pay for her college tuition.

By 2003, Vanilla appeared to be establishing an annual roster of subgenres in those areas of anime erotica proven to work in the market. In *Wicked Lessons* (*Gakuen no Shuryosha,* aka *Hunter of the Campus,* 2002), an abusive youth forces his raped and orphaned stepsister to help him chase girls at a college, all "to get back at his father." Meanwhile, school (or "college") abuse and sex continued in Hot for Teacher, P.I.: Perverse Investigations, and *Private Sessions 2.* Hospitals continued to perform beyond the call of duty in Naughty Nurses, while *Chains of Lust* (*Ryojoku no Rensa,* 2003) featured two workers at an erotic video store who decide to make a porn movie without acquiring the consent of their female performers—the authors wonder if this is an erotic variant on the contemporary self-referential genre in the mainstream that also gave us Anime Shop-Keeper.

A similar spread of titles covered all of the Vanilla Series' main bases in 2004, with school bondage in SEXTRA CREDIT and BONDAGE 101, and hospital abuses in RXXX: PRESCRIPTION FOR PAIN. However, the year also saw a marked increase in the number of incest and not-quite-incest tales, particularly involving a fetish for lactating women. This is nothing new in erotic anime, and dates at least as far back as PROFESSOR PAIN in 1998, but 2004 alone saw the Vanilla Series releasing MILK MONEY, ANYONE YOU CAN DO... I CAN DO BETTER, and *My Brother's Wife* (*Aniyome*, 2004).

The new direction, with its concentration on older, fuller-figured women (at least compared to the jailbait of earlier incarnations), continued with *Duchess of Busty Mounds* (*Mama Haha*, 2005), INVASION OF THE BOOBIE SNATCHERS, and *Mother Knows Breast* (*Chibo*, 2005, lit. *Perverse Mother*). The franchise also released *Group Groper Train* (*Shudan Chikan Densha*, 2005), INCONTINENT HELENA, and *Virgin Auction* (*Shojo Auction*, 2005).

The year 2006 was presumably some cause for celebration for the Vanilla Series, having reached its 100th title. The vagaries of release schedules make it unclear exactly which DVD represented Vanilla's attainment of three-figure smut, but by our unreliable calculations, it was probably *Invisible Man* (*Tomei Ningen*, 2006). Male characters in some erotic anime games have often been rendered invisible or translucent in the past, and some anime have found ways to remove the image of male participants from the action in order to show more female flesh (be it through tentacles at a distance in erotic horror, or transforming a character into a girl's bathwater as in REI REI). *Invisible Man* takes the concept literally, often allowing for the anime to incorporate the genre of live-action pornography known as "POV" (point-of-view), in which the girls address and interact with the camera as if it is the male viewer himself. *Invisible Man* features an old man who

takes supreme advantage after ingesting a drug that makes him disappear. A similar concept can be seen in the Japanese box art to *Stepsister* (2006, the characters say *Gimai* but the *furigana* alongside demands it be read as "Imoto," or "Younger Sister")—not to be confused with the Discovery Series title of the same name—which features a semi-naked girl about to perform a sexual act on her knees, smiling up at the viewer/buyer. However, the onscreen action itself is more traditional, both in terms of the way it is filmed and in the plotting the title suggests, which is old-school Vanilla Series not-quite-incest. **Ⓝ**

VARIABLE GEO *

1996. Video. DIR: Toru Yoshida. SCR: Yosuke Kuroda. DES: Takahiro Kimura. ANI: Takahiro Kimura. MUS: Harukichi Yamamoto. PRD: KSS. 30 mins. x 3 eps.

This ridiculously puerile anime was based on a video game that must have seemed like a really good idea at the time. Waitresses from rival restaurants meet in public fighting bouts in which they pound each other into submission (see STREET FIGHTER II). The ultimate winner gets $10 million and some prime real estate in the city of her choice. The loser must strip off her clothes and humiliate herself in front of the audience (see SEXORCIST). Meanwhile, a shadowy secret organization (see TOSHINDEN) is planning to use the ultimate winner's DNA to breed the ultimate warrior (see TEKKEN). Plucky heroine Yuka Takeuchi punches and kicks her way through a series of opponents from the game (see all of the above), in a succession of ludicrous set pieces that show off fighting catchphrases and special moves (ditto). Working conditions in the fighting-evil trade have obviously gone downhill—this never happened to the Knight Sabers. It lasts 90 minutes. Life's too short, really. Trust us. **Ⓝ Ⓥ**

VENUS FIVE *

1994. JPN: *Sailor Senshi Venus Five*.

AKA: *Sailor Warriors Venus Five*. Video. DIR: Satoshi Inoue, Kan Fukumoto. SCR: Wataru Amano. DES: Rin Shin. ANI: N/C. MUS: N/C. PRD: Daiei. 45 mins. x 2 eps.

Five beautiful teenage girls are destined to battle the evil Inma Empire led by the perverted Necros. The empire aims to revive the god Apollo from his ten-thousand-year slumber in order to gain his near-infinite power. And the only thing that will revive a god is . . . yes, you've guessed it, the sexual secretions of certain beautiful high school girls. Unfortunately for the bad guys, our heroines have been recruited by the Goddess of Love to ensure that the power of evil doesn't triumph, and Aphrodite has even sent them a talking cat to help them. A shameless SAILOR MOON parody based on a manga by Jin Ara, *V5* is aimed straight at the fans who dream of seeing more than just a flash of thigh in those transformation sequences. The girls mimic the Sailor Scouts every way they can—fighting poses, speeches, costumes, all are so close to the original that they could be twins. There, however, all similarity ends, as the cat talks dirty, the tentacles multiply, and the smut takes over. This is for all those out there who snicker at a bad guy called Count Uranus, as well as connoisseurs of Immortal Dialogue like, "Let me entice you to the very summit of lust." **Ⓛ Ⓝ Ⓥ**

VENUS WARS *

1989. JPN: *Venus Senki*. AKA: *Venus War Chronicle*. Movie. DIR: Yoshikazu Yasuhiko. SCR: Yuichi Sasamoto, Yoshikazu Yasuhiko. DES: Hiroyoshi Yokoyama, Yoshikazu Yasuhiko, Sachiko Kamimura, Hirotoshi Sano, Makoto Kobayashi, Shichiro Kobayashi. ANI: Yoko Kamimura. MUS: Joe Hisaishi. PRD: Triangle Staff, Kugatsu-sha. 104 mins.

Young journalist Susan Sommers arrives on Venus to cover the war between its two nation-states just before the troops of Ishtar take the capital and overcome the armies of Aphrodia. She meets a group of young motorcycle punks, the Killer Commandos, led by Hiro. Previously engaged in racing other gangs around a makeshift circuit in scenes reminiscent of *Rollerball*, Hiro and some of his team fight a guerrilla action against the occupying forces of Ishtar, and Susan soon loses her journalistic objectivity as she is drawn into the struggle. Based on one of Yasuhiko's own manga, and with music by the man who has given both Hayao Miyazaki and Beat Takeshi some unforgettable themes, this glossily produced and well-designed film ought to be a classic, but it just misses the mark. Sasamoto contributes an intelligent script in which our young hotheads learn that not all adults are brain-dead, not all organization is tyranny, and not all action is sensible. There's plenty to interest the genre fan, including some good action sequences and fine mecha designs, yet the film lacks the emotional edge and perverse power of Yasuhiko's earlier **ARION**. A similar Venusian Cold War standoff would appear in **BLACK MAGIC**.

VERY PRIVATE LESSON *

1998. JPN: *Kyokasho ni Nai!*. AKA: *Not in the Textbook!*. Video. DIR: Hideaki Oba. SCR: Hideaki Oba. DES: Masahiko Yamada. ANI: Etsuro Tokuda, Masahiko Yamada. MUS: Ryuichi Katsumata. PRD: AIC. 30 mins. x 2 eps.
High school teacher Oraku and his colleague Satsuki hope to marry one day. Meanwhile, one of his students has fallen in love with him. Aya is a beautiful and spoiled delinquent; her father, a very wealthy man, only wants his princess to be happy, so much so that he insists she moves in with the man she loves. So what's the problem with having a beautiful teenager move in, with Daddy's blessing? Aya is a Mob princess in the style of **THE GOKUSEN**; her father's money comes from organized crime, and while he's happy for her to do whatever she wants, if she doesn't stay a virgin he'll kill whoever is responsible. So Oraku has to become Aya's chaperone. Meanwhile, if anyone finds out he is living with one of his students, his career and his

future marriage to Satsuki will both go down the drain. You may recall **HOMEROOM AFFAIRS**, **MY WIFE IS A HIGH SCHOOL STUDENT**, or **HAPPY LESSON** at this point. **LN**

VICIOUS *

2001. Video DIR: Sakura Harukawa. SCR: N/C. DES: N/C. ANI: N/C. MUS: N/C. PRD: Five Ways. 30 mins. x 2 eps.
In what appears to be Victorian or Edwardian Britain at the turn of the 20th century, a household is still struggling to come to terms with the death of its much-loved mother in a fall down the stairs six months earlier. Daughter Angela feels that her father is cold-hearted and distant and despises him for seeking solace in the arms of the maid, Bridget. Perhaps out of spite, perhaps in an attempt to assuage her own loneliness, Angela decides that she will lose her virginity to John the butler. Although John is initially reluctant (he fears reprisals from his boss), he eventually succumbs to Angela's charms. However, Angela's mood changes when she learns that John and Bridget plan to leave her father's employment, turning the latter half of this erotic anime into a tale of murder and revenge. **LNV**

VICKY THE VIKING *

1974. JPN: *Chiisana Viking Vickie*. AKA: *Vickie the Little Viking*. TV series. DIR: Hiroshi Saito, Noboru Ishiguro, Kiyoshi Harada. SCR: Yuji Fusano, Hiroshi Kaneko, Akira Saiga, Takeshi Hidaka, Chikao Katsui. DES: Shuichi Seki. ANI: Shinichi Tsuji. MUS: Seiichiro Uno. PRD: Zuiyo, Taurus Film, Fuji TV. 25 mins. x 77 eps.
Vicky is the son of Halvar, chief of a little Viking village. He'd rather play than learn to fight, but he is compelled to go on one of the village's raiding expeditions where he manages to foil the plans of the enemy, Sven the Terrible, through his quick wits and courage. Adapted from a series of stories by Runer Jonsson, this German-Japanese coproduction holds the seeds of a great tradition—Zuiyo later became

Nippon Animation, whose **WORLD MASTERPIECE THEATER** series was dedicated to bringing classic stories from the West to Japanese TV.

VICTORY PITCHER

1987. JPN: *Shori Tosha*. Video. DIR: Hiroki Shibata. SCR: Akane Nishiura. DES: Noriko Umeda. ANI: Katsumi Aodori. MUS: Akihiko Matsumoto. PRD: Toei. 72 mins.
Baseball coach Hoshiyama offers a chance to turn professional to Katsumi Kunimasa, a star member of the student squad that won the summer tournament. The young girl becomes a star pitcher for the Chunichi Dragons (conveniently, the team her father owns), and, after a year of triumphs, she leads them to victory in the national championships at legendary Koshien Stadium. Based on the manga by Noriko Umeda, this anime may be compared to the other girl-playing-baseball story **SONG OF THE BASEBALL ENTHUSIAST**. The Dragons team members are all based on the real-life team, though their opponents are fictional. At the time, the real-life Hoshiyama was a commentator, but fact was eventually true to fiction, and he became the manager for the real-life Dragons.

VIDEO GIRL AI *

1992. JPN: *Denno Shojo Ai*. AKA: *Cyber Girl Ai; Electric Girl Ai*. Video. DIR: Mizuho Nishikubo. SCR: Satoru Akahori. DES: Takayuki Goto. ANI: Takayuki Goto. MUS: Nobuyuki Shimizu. PRD: Production IG, Tatsunoko. 30 mins. x 6 eps.
Average-guy Yota loves girl-next-door Moemi. But Moemi has a crush on local hero Takashi, and to make it worse, Takashi is a nice guy and Yota's best friend. Enter Ai, a disposable alien girl who escapes from a dating video and resolves to get Yota together with his true love. But before you can say "Cyrano de Bergerac," Ai secretly longs for Yota, too. Ai is a "video girl," designed to distract and amuse, programmed, like all video, with a definite time limit. When her relationship with Yota moves from being a dispos-

able, casual entertainment into more dangerous territory, the "copyright authorities" step in. Yota, Moemi, Ai, and their friends move through the tortuous dance of teenage emotion and sexual longing, beautifully conveying the agonies of alienation and embarrassment inherent in growing up, and also learning that time will not always be on their side.

An unwelcome guest/magical girlfriend tale in the tradition of URUSEI YATSURA and OH MY GODDESS!, playing straight to the gallery with fan-service asides and a loving appreciation of the loser male psyche. Satoru Akahori's script masterfully recreates a world of teenage desperation, far from the madcap comedies for which he is normally known. From the opening shot in which Ai addresses the audience directly, through the regular stuck-record repetition of Moemi's declaration of love for the wrong man, Akahori demonstrates that there's more to him than the slapstick of SORCERER HUNTERS. But occasional moments of unnecessary physical comedy intrude on what could have been a great emotional farce, and sporadic outbreaks of Katsura's trademark panty shots further undermine a show that, at heart, is all heart. After shoving the couple together, Ai immediately breaks them up—a schizophrenic characterization that is one of Ai's biggest flaws. She fluctuates unevenly between bitchy best friend, infuriating tease, and doormat mother-substitute, while Moemi is part drippy little girl, part sassy schemer. Yota himself is half lovable dork, half *annoying* dork, his own wavering interest in his love objects often reduced to comparisons of breast size or cooking ability.

Director Nishikubo's clever camerawork fades the entire world into the background so that only the self-obsessed leads get any screen time, overexposing shots of school life to turn every dingy corridor into a pathway of dreamy bright nostalgia. He puts similar thought into the opening credits, which feature a fully rendered Ai skipping through a world that's often only half-formed, as if the camera itself has eyes only for her. Nishikubo's pauses emphasize the secret language of women, lingering for long moments as Ai and Moemi alternate between friendship and rivalry. The series considerately ends before outstaying its welcome (see TENCHI MUYO!), and an excellent dub completes the package. A live-action movie, *Video Girl Ai* (1991), was directed by Ryu Kaneda from a script credited to both creator Katsura and scenarist Masahiro Yoshimoto.

VIDEO PICTURE BOOK

1988. JPN: *Video Anime E-Bon*. Video. DIR: Noriaki Kairo. SCR: Noriaki Kairo, Shin Yukuba. DES: N/C. ANI: Shunji Saita. MUS: Masahito Maekawa. PRD: Mushi Pro. 12 mins. x 50 eps.
A vast library of classic tales animated in bite-sized chunks, including a number from AESOP'S FABLES, GRIMMS' FAIRY TALES, TALES OF HANS CHRISTIAN ANDERSEN, and the ARABIAN NIGHTS. Some of the titles include JOURNEY TO THE WEST, *Jack and the Beanstalk*, CINDERELLA, ALICE IN WONDERLAND, SNOW WHITE, A LITTLE PRINCESS, THE WIZARD OF OZ, LITTLE WOMEN, *Little Red Riding Hood, Hansel and Gretel*, LITTLE MERMAID, *The Ugly Duckling*, HEIDI, TREASURE ISLAND, PETER PAN AND WENDY, *The Little Match Girl, Gulliver's Travels*, DADDY LONG-LEGS, ROBIN HOOD, LITTLE LORD FAUNTLEROY, SECRET GARDEN, *Frog Prince*, THREE MUSKETEERS, NOBODY'S BOY, NOBODY'S GIRL, and ADRIFT IN THE PACIFIC. A similar concept was on sale at the same time in Aubec's 26-volume *Video Anime Picture Book Theatre: World Masterpiece Children's Stories*.

VIEWTIFUL JOE *

2004. TV series. DIR: Takaaki Ishiyama. SCR: GGB. DES: Yukiko Ohashi, Nobuaki Nagano. ANI: Masaki Kubomura. MUS: N/C. PRD: Capcom, Group Tac, TV Tokyo. 25 mins. x 51 eps.
Everyday slacker Joe has only two interests in life, and arguably, the screen hero Captain Blue takes precedence over Silvia, Joe's often neglected girlfriend. But when villains from the Movieworld snatch Silvia from a cinema and drag her into an alternate dimension, Joe chases after her into the screen. He gets to be Viewtiful Joe, a superhero in training who tries to rescue his beloved, while learning tips on the superhero lifestyle from the aging, portly Captain Blue. Incorporating heavy doses of the underrated Arnold Schwarzenegger vehicle *The Last Action Hero* (1993), *Viewtiful Joe* dutifully recreates the look of the Capcom game that premiered the year before. It contains loving sideswipes at Japanese-style superheroes like ULTRAMAN, but also a terrifying English dub, with slacker slang and wanna-be streetwise hip hop argot that already sounds self-conscious and dated—compare to SAMURAI CHAMPLOO.

VIFAM

1983. JPN: *Ginga Hyoryo Vifam*. AKA: *Galactic Tales of Vifam; Galactic Wanderer Vifam; Round Vernian Vifam*. TV series. DIR: Takeyuki Kanda, Susumu Ishizaki, Tetsuro Amino, Osamu Sekita, Seiji Okuda, Junji Nishimura, Kazuo Yamazaki. SCR: Hiroyuki Hoshiyama, Yasushi Hirano, Tsunehisa Ito. DES: Toyoo Ashida, Kunio Okawara, Shoji Sato. ANI: Toyoo Ashida, Hiroshi Watanabe, Hideyuki Motohashi, Yasushi Nagaoka, Makoto Ito. MUS: Toshiyuki Watanabe. PRD: Sunrise, TBS. 25 mins. x 46 eps. (TV), 50 mins. x 4 eps. (v), 25 mins. x 12 eps. (TV2).
The Terran colony of Kreado is attacked by alien Kuktonian invaders, and when the adult crew of its orbiting space station are all killed, it is up to their 13 surviving children to fight back. Eventually, they reactivate the old starship Janus from dry dock and prepare to head for their homeworld—a trip fraught with perils both on the planets they pass and within the labyrinthine corridors of the Janus itself. It's a sci-fi remake of ADRIFT IN THE PACIFIC, and *Vifam*'s ludicrously overpopulated cast returned in 1984 for video adventures *V: News from Catcher* (*Catcher kara no Benri*), *V: Gathering of*

the Thirteen (*Atsumatta Jusanbito*), *V: The 12 Fade Away* (*Kieta Junibito*, also shown in theaters), and *V: Kate's Reflections* (*Kate no Kioku*). The fact that the 4 video episodes follow on from the TV series, break down into eight 25-minute acts, and would have taken the series to a full year's 52 episodes makes it likely that they were the final unbroadcast episodes of the series.

The series was remade by Toshifumi Kawase as *Vifam 13* (1998), reuniting many of the old crew for a production that used previously unfilmed scripts as its basis. For the *V13* story arc, the crew rescue baby Kukto twins from a derelict ship and are forced to juggle child-care with their continuing mission.

VILLGUST
1992. JPN: *Kyoryu Densetsu Villgust*. AKA: *Armored Dragon Legend Villgust*. Video. DIR: Katsuhiko Nishijima. SCR: Satoru Akahori. DES: Katsuhiko Nishijima. ANI: Katsuhiko Nishijima. MUS: Kohei Tanaka. PRD: Animate Film. 30 mins. x 2 eps.
Two separate groups of adventurers meet up in a faux-medieval European village in the alternate universe of Villgust. Wannabe paladins Kui, Yuta, and cute girls Kris and Fanna are full of high ambitions to protect the land and rid it from evil, while catgirl Ryugia, Marobo the dog-man, Bostof the elf, and cute little girl Lemi are more interested in finding something to eat. They've actually been sent by the presiding goddess of the land to rid Villgust of a dark, evil force that looks suspiciously like Jabba the Hutt. Gabadi is a wicked oppressor with a large band of thoroughly nasty disposable minions, but he's devoted only to his pet frog, Antoinette. Gabadi succeeds in tricking Kui and company into fighting Ryugia (who has a penchant for bikini-style armor, an infantile food fetish, and a set of claws borrowed from X-Man Wolverine) and her friends—the very people intended by Heaven to be their allies! He wants them to destroy each other so that there is no opposition to his evil plans.

More through luck than judgment, our heroes eventually start fighting his minions instead of each other, and they battle their way through a tornado, flying slabs of rock, snake-headed monsters, and tentacles to rid the land of his evil and bring peace back to Villgust.

Bandai originated the *gachapon* concept—small plastic toys enclosed in egg-shaped cases and sold for small change in street-corner vending machines. The name is said to be the sound of the egg-shaped cases falling from the machine. These sweet little creatures influenced video games, card games, and manga—Nintendo created the *Villgust* role-playing game based on them, and from that came this video series. So if anyone asks you which came first, it was definitely the egg.

VIOLENCE JACK *
1986. JPN: *Violence Jack Harlem Bomber; Violence Jack Jigokugai; Violence Jack Hell's Wind*. AKA: *VJ Slumking; VJ Hell Town [Evil Town]; VJ Hell's Wind*. Video. DIR: Seiji Okuda, Ichiro Itano. SCR: Noboru Aikawa, Takuya Wada, Makio Matsushita. DES: Takuya Wada, Moriyasu Taniguchi. ANI: Takuya Wada, Moriyasu Taniguchi. MUS: Hiroshi Ogasawara. PRD: Ashi Pro, Studio 88, Dynamic Planning. 30 mins. x 2 eps. (*Harlem/Slumking*), 30 mins. x 2 eps. (*Hell Town*), 60 mins. (*Hell's Wind*).
A comet strikes Earth and causes a chain reaction of other cataclysms. In Japan, the fault line gives way in the mother of all earthquakes, while the long-dormant volcano Mount Fuji erupts in a spectacular cloud of ash and lava. Survivors trapped in the Tokyo subway system turn into savage tunnel tribes. Gangs of motorcycle bandits roam the land in search of resources. And through the midst of it all walks Violence Jack, a mountain of a man with superhuman strength, inhuman fangs, and absolutely no scruples. Jack is an elemental force, wandering the desolate land like hell's own lawman, coming to the rescue of the assaulted, raped, and injured survivors,

but not before the camera has permitted us a long, lingering look at their torments. These include stabbings, shootings, eviscerations, chainsaw decapitation, and someone eating his dead lover.

Often thought to be an inferior remake of **FIST OF THE NORTH STAR**, *VJ* actually predates it, starting as a 1973 manga in *Goraku* magazine, as the sequel to Go Nagai's **DEVILMAN**. The video necessarily condensed much of the epic original (Nagai's longest) into a broader, more basic, and much less shocking package, though it remains extremely violent and nasty even when censored—the U.K. running time is considerably shorter than the original. The lead character, with "the strength of a gorilla and teeth of a wolf, blood boiling with the fire of prehistory," is named for the huge jackknife he carries, and the anime focuses on his volcanic nature rather than the tangle of subplots and reincarnations of the manga. The basic postapocalyptic plots of the video version (with knowing winks to *Mad Max*) were originally intended to have some internal coherence but were released in the wrong order outside Japan. The first episode, showing the comet hitting Earth and explaining that Jack is the personification of the Grim Reaper, born from a mound of skulls, is actually *Slumking*, which was inexplicably the *last* episode to be released in the English version. To be fair, the muddled running order hardly makes any difference. The then boss of U.K.'s Manga Entertainment, Mike Preece, coined the term "beer-and-curry movie" for those anime destined to be watched by a group of inebriated teenage boys in search of sex and violence, and *VJ* is exactly what he meant. Those with higher hopes for the anime industry find the show embarrassingly infantile, including the English-language voice cast, who all appear to be using pseudonyms. 🄻🄽🅅

VIOLIN OF THE STARRY SKY
1995. JPN: *Hoshizora no Violin*. Movie. DIR: Setsuo Nakayama. SCR: Toshikai

Imaizumi. DES: Mitsuharu Miyamae. ANI: Kazunori Tanabashi. MUS: Kazuki Kuriyama. PRD: Takahashi Studio. 90 mins. Based on Noboru Wada's true story of the life of the Shinshu violinmaker Kikuji Ozawa (1916–98), who pursued his dream to make and play violins even as the clouds gathered for World War II. Violin music is provided by soloist Mio Umezu.

VIOLINIST OF HAMELIN, THE

1996. JPN: *Hamelun no Violin*. AKA: *Violin of Hamelin*. Movie, TV series. DIR: Takashi Imanishi, Junji Nishimura, Hiroshi Morioka, Akira Kiyomizu. SCR: Takashi Imanishi, Yasuhiro Imagawa. DES: Toshimi Kato. ANI: Toshimi Kato. MUS: Kohei Tanaka. PRD: Nippon Animation, Studio Deen, TV Tokyo. 50 mins. (m), 25 mins. x 25 eps. (TV).
Fifteen years ago, Queen Horn of Sforzando tried to shut evil out of the world of Staccato with a powerful spell, but not even the strongest spell lasts forever, and now Horn's strength is failing. Evil Hell King Bass is trying to break through the barrier and release the "supreme leader" Great Chestra (in Japanese "Oh-kestra"), a dark being of unparalleled power who is trapped somewhere in Staccato. Horn's estranged daughter, Flute, is the only person who can save Sforzando from the inrush of darkness. She's been in hiding for 15 years, but now she is called by her mother to return to Sforzando. She sets out for the capital with her childhood friend and guardian, Hamel, but on the way they have many strange adventures and meet old and new friends. Hamel learns more about the mystery of his past and the strange horn on his head.

Based on a 1991 manga in *Shonen GanGan* by Michiaki Watanabe, *VoH* mixes tragedy and suspense with humor. On the way to becoming a moving picture the story developed a split personality. In 1996, it became a funny movie and was followed soon after by a much darker and more serious TV series—insofar as anything can be dark and serious when the protagonists'

main weapons, as well as their names, are musical instruments. The animation in the TV series is noticeably low-budget, too, which caused controversy when the director himself publicly complained about the limited materials he had to work with.

VIPER GTS *

2002. Video. DIR: Masami Obari. SCR: P. Warrior, Kunitoshi Watanabe. DES: Kenichi Hamazaki. ANI: Kenichi Hamazaki, Kazuhiro Yamada. MUS: Takehiro Kawabe. PRD: Frontline, Moonrock, Studio G 1 Neo. 30 mins. x 3 eps.
Girl-demon Carrera and her partner Rati and self-appointed rival Mercedes form part of a demonic sales force, like Avon ladies but with spells. Their mission is to attract the attention of humans in need of magical aid, which they then grant in exchange for their victims' immortal souls. Teenage wimp Ogawa summons Carrera looking for vengeance on everyone who's ever picked on him. When she turns up to grant his wish, he takes one look at her oiled and wobbling endowments and decides to wish for something else instead. In a surprising plot twist, she discovers that he is massively well endowed and develops a crush on him. However, her contract fulfilled, she returns to whence she came, much to Ogawa's disappointment. She is duly punished for overstaying her time, and Ogawa begins summoning other demons in an attempt to regain her company, resulting in Mercedes' appearance, after which she also conceives a longing for him. But they aren't his only fans—the angels also muscle in. It's their duty to save Ogawa and the demonic duo, so they kidnap Carrera and Rati to Heaven, and despite being cute females, they sprout penises and anoint the sinners liberally with "holy water from God's Tool." Ogawa and Mercedes thereafter mount a rescue mission, to assault Heaven and save the victims from the fate of salvation-by-rape. Nobody can say Masami Obari lacks a sense of the

ridiculous—although divine sperm has been done before in MASQUERADE—nor the ability to produce high quality animated pornography. *Viper GTS*, despite its simple plot, shines above the great majority of anime porn for its excellence in character design, art, and animation. Combining two geeky wet dreams in one (the characters are named after top-marque cars, Rati being *Mase*rati, and the series is named for the $90K Dodge dream machine), he must be laughing himself silly all the way to the bank. Based on a computer game by Sogna, which was little more than an erotic, satanic take on OH MY GODDESS!—if you accept naming elements after automobiles as originality, then Sogna's claim to have created an "original story" won't annoy you. ●

VIRAGO IN DUNGEON

1991. JPN: *Ozanari Dungeon*. AKA: *Perfunctory Dungeon*. Video. DIR: Hiroshi Aoyama. SCR: Hideki Sonoda. DES: Minoru Maeda. ANI: Yoshikazu Takiguchi, Yasuo Otsuka. MUS: Kazz Toyama and Secret Plans. PRD: Tokyo Movie Shinsha. 30 mins. x 3 eps.
Three adventurers are hired by King Gazelle to steal the Dragon Head relic from the Shrine of Fire. Mocha (sexy elf-babe warrior), Blueman (funny animal cat-thief), and Kilieman (dog-wizard) are startled out of their larcenous intentions when the relic introduces itself to them as Morrow and asks to be taken, not to Gazelle's Tower of Fire, but to the Tower of Wind. Morrow is an organic program that can transform the Tower of Wind into an ultimate weapon called the Space Dragon. Gazelle, he says, is just a frontman for the real enemy, a mysterious being out to control the Space Dragon and destroy the world. Based on the 1987 *Comic Nora* manga by Motoo Koyama, who named the characters after the brands of coffee he was drinking while drawing the series–Mocha, Blue Mountain, and Kilimanjaro.

VIRGIN FLEET *

1991. JPN: *Seishojo Kantai Virgin Fleet*.

AKA: *Holy Maiden Fleet Virgin Fleet.* Video. DIR: Masahiro Hosoda. SCR: Yasuhiro Imagawa. DES: Hiroyuki Kitazume. ANI: Hiroyuki Kitazume. MUS: Masanobu Ito. PRD: Beam Entertainment. 30 mins. x 3 eps.

In the 1930s, a group of teenage girls in a Japanese military academy train with a mysterious psychic energy that includes, among other things, weather control and telekinesis and can only be controlled by a few young female virgins. Many years before in WWI, a similar team called the 36 minstrels somehow succeeded in controlling this force and was able to put an end to the fighting. With the political situation growing ever more tense, Russia spying on its neighbors and trying to steal military secrets, and internal squabbling between the leaders of Japan, the nation desperately needs that power once more. A survivor of the Minstrel force is now highly placed in the military command and her daughter heads the academy—but she hasn't inherited her mother's power, which causes some friction between them. And out of the squabbling, shallow band of young ladies in her care, the one who emerges as able to release virgin energy is Shiokaze, who is engaged and whose boyfriend is pressuring her to leave the academy and marry him right away. Sadly, he's not the only man in the story who takes sexism to comic levels—the local military leaders trot out all the clichés about a woman's place in war without any sense of irony, though in the U.S. dub the director and actors substitute a level of overacting that approaches talent in itself.

VF is part of the subgenre that includes creator Hiroi Oji's earlier **SAKURA WARS**, in which 20th-century military history isn't quite the way the West remembers it. In Oji's cute, squeaky-clean universe, Japan only wants to unleash the massive destructive force of virgin energy to *prevent* more killing—compare to similarly farfetched avoidances of history in **KISHIN CORPS** and **SUPER ATRAGON**. However, this anime remains curiously endear-

ing, full, like **GUNBUSTER**, of the martial enthusiasm of an undefeated Japan (see **WARTIME ANIME**), with well-animated backgrounds, sepia-toned flashbacks, and intriguing *neverwhen* aircraft designs. The story has some interesting moments and makes a few pointed observations on the real thoughts and feelings of teenagers about jealousy, love, and sex, but like many video anime, it starts a whole raft of subplots that don't go anywhere.

VIRGIN MARY IS WATCHING, THE

2004. JPN: *Maria-sama ga Miteru.* AKA: *Maria is Watching; Marimite.* TV series, special. DIR: Yukihiro Matsushita. SCR: Chiaki Manabe, Genki Yoshimura, Natsuko Takahashi, Reiko Yoshida. DES: Reine Hibiki, Akira Matsushima. ANI: Hirofumi Morimoto, Akira Matsushima, Yukiko Akiyama, Miyako Tsuji et al.. MUS: Mikiya Katakura. PRD: Rondo Robe. 25 mins. x 13 eps. (TV1), 24 mins. x 13 eps. (TV2), 2 mins. x 13 eps. (sp).

Elite Catholic girls' school Lillian Academy has a system whereby senior students adopt freshmen as their "little sisters," signifying the relationship by giving their chosen freshman a rosary. The two are then known as *soeurs*— French for sisters. Yumi Fukuzawa is asked by junior Sachiko Ogasawara to be her *soeur*, and is drawn into the inner circle of the Roses, the name given to members of the student council, setting the stage for a whole hothouse of blooming passions, rivalries, and non-incidents. Getting elected to the council, giving Valentine's Day chocolate (normally only given to men), and buying jeans all assume massive significance. Based on a series of novels by Oyuki Konno, the 13-episode series spun off a sequel, *VMiW: Spring (MSgM: Haru).* Spring is the season of change, covering New Year parties, graduation ceremonies, and the start of the Japanese school year in April, but despite this, nothing much happens in the second series, either. Humorous "out-takes" from the series were added to the DVD in 2004, as the two-minute "specials" *Don't Tell the Vir-*

gin Mary (Maria-sama ni wa Naisho). A video series followed in 2006.

VIRGIN TOUCH *

2002. JPN: *Flutter of Birds: Toritachi no Habataki.* Video. DIR: Yoshitaka Fujimoto. SCR: Sumishi Aran, Rei Tachibana. DES: Masaki Takei, Tatsuhito Kurashiki. ANI: Tatsuhito Kurashiki. MUS: N/C. PRD: Pink Pineapple. 30 mins. x 2 eps.

After eight years away in the big city, Yusaku is invited to come back to his remote hometown and work for a while in his uncle's clinic. He arrives back home to find that much has changed. Although he left as just another teenager, he returns as a respected authority figure, and his childhood friend Ibuki has grown into a pretty doctor herself. Yusaku is a heartthrob for the impressionable local nurses and some of the patients at the clinic. Not all the afflictions seem to be serious—some appear to be curable through the handy expedient of sexual intercourse, but it's not as if viewers of this mildly erotic anime wouldn't have been expecting that. Based on a computer game released the previous year by Silkies. **🅝**

VIRTUA CALL 2 *

1997. Video. DIR: Kaoru Tomioka. SCR: Tetsuya Oseki. DES: N/C. ANI: Mitsuru Fujii. MUS: N/C. PRD: Fairy Dust. 45 mins. x 2 eps.

Virtuacall is the latest development in phone-sex clubs—a virtual meeting service that lets you see, hear, and even touch the man or woman of your dreams. Emily decides to use the service to help Hasegawa, a friend from her apartment building. She desires him, but he seems reluctant to make a move. She plans to assist in building his confidence and improving his chances of scoring by introducing him to Virtuacall for some online practice sessions. The anime is based on a Sega Saturn game; compare to similar cybersex in **SECRET ANIMA**'s *Dream Hazard.* **🅝**

VIRTUA FIGHTER *

1995. TV series. DIR: Hideki Tonokatsu.

SCR: Tsutomu Kamishiro, Kuniaki Kasai, Natsuko Chizumu. DES: Ryo Tanaka, Hiroshi Ono. ANI: Ryo Tanaka. MUS: Kaori Ohori. PRD: Tokyo Movie Shinsha, TV Tokyo. 25 mins. x 35 eps. Based on Sega's successful video game, the story hinges around young martial artist Akira Yuki and his travels in search of his inner self. This involves lots of fighting. Luckily he meets lots of other people who also want to find themselves through fighting. He teams up with Pai Chan, a Chinese girl who is fighting to find her fiancé, and Jacky, who is fighting to find his sister Sara, and they fight lots of people "for honor, love, and revenge." The almost concurrent appearance of the **STREET FIGHTER II** TV series obviously had nothing to do with it, and an artist like Ono, who did the ravishing backgrounds for **DOG OF FLANDERS**, is wasted here. **V**

Visitor

© 1998 GAGA PICTURES/AVEX/JIC

VIRUS

1997. JPN: *Virus Buster Serge*. TV series. DIR: Masami Obari. SCR: Masami Obari, Jiro Kaneko, et al. DES: Masami Obari, Natsuki Mamiya. ANI: Masami Obari, Kazuto Nakazawa. MUS: Toshiyuki Omori. PRD: JC Staff, Plum, TV Tokyo. 30 mins. x 13 eps.
In 2097 Hong Kong, virtuality is preferable to the real world. The Internet has a mind of its own. Cloning is outlawed. Vast supercomputers run on biological software, but the combination of genetics and cybernetics places human beings at the mercy of digital viruses, some of which are accidents, some of which are the work of the infamous "Incubator." The STAND is an elite task force that terminates viruses with extreme prejudice. Serge is a brainwashed assassin, plotting the death of STAND captain Raven. But when Serge is "cured" of his desire for vengeance, he joins the team. Impossibly proportioned token female Erika is just dying to get to know him better. But Serge is less popular with the two gunslinging officers, Macus and Joichiro, who don't want an ex-assassin for backup. The team must learn to work together and

to exorcise the demons from their own past—the viruses feed on skeletons in the mental closet.
With its possessed human hosts, *Virus* shares themes with **GHOST IN THE SHELL** and glossy horror moods out of **SILENT MÖBIUS**. It combines the angst of **EVANGELION** and the superheroes of **SONIC SOLDIER BORGMAN**, artfully concealing a tiny budget and breakneck schedule with great splashes of special effects, clever uses of shadow, and superfast cuts. Its appeal to audiences is nicely, if perhaps cynically, manufactured; the makers assume that a male SF audience is already guaranteed, so they concentrate on the brooding, pouting, pretty-boys to drag in female fans. Fight scenes are carefully interwoven with character development; the end-of-episode cliffhanger is just as likely to be a terrifying revelation from the past as a physical threat. However, like the equally beautiful **DARKSIDE BLUES**, *Virus* has a frustrating tangle of subplots and relationships running into dead ends with no time to resolve them. For those who really can't wait to get more of the high-tensile battle action and the darkly erotic aura of the male cast, the Sega Saturn game and later PlayStation spin-off *Virus: The Battle Field* use the original cast voices and design. The hip-hop group Dragon Ash had its big break with the anime's opening theme, going on to

record music for **DT EIGHTRON** and Kinji Fukasaku's live-action *Battle Royale* (2001). **V**

VISIONARY *

1995. AKA: *Vixens*. Video. DIR: Teruo Kigure, Taiichi Kitagawa. SCR: Ryo Saga. DES: Tomohiro Ando. ANI: Tomohiro Ando. MUS: Masahiko Kikuchi. PRD: Knack, Beam Entertainment. 30 mins., 45 mins., 30 mins.
Ujita is a geeky high school boy who has no luck whatever with women and gets grief from the local bully, until he hits the wrong key on his computer by mistake. Up pops sexy Doreimon, back from the future to solve all his problems in a cheeky parody of **DORAEMON** with no panties. Just like the hapless robot cat, she can answer all of Ujita's prayers, but things don't always work out as she plans or he hopes. Later episodes continue the short pornographic comedies in the style of creator U-Jin's similar **TALES OF . . .** , with scenes including nymphomaniac vampires on a college campus and skydiving love. The series was later repackaged under the title *Vixens*. **NV**

VISITOR

1998. TV series. DIR: Atsushi Tokuda. SCR: Kazunori Ito. DES: Akemi Takada. ANI: N/C. MUS: Keiichi Matsuzaki. PRD: COM NT, WOWOW. 50 mins. x 3 eps.
In the year 2099, one of NASA's Apollo

rocket capsules is found in the Mongolian desert, where it appears to have been for 65 million years. Meanwhile on Mars, a strange black artifact of unknown origins is eating one of the planet's moons. Earth ship Davide is sent to investigate and is sucked into the vortex. Lila Mochizuki and her companions are suddenly a long, long way from home. Entirely computer-generated animation faintly reminiscent of Supermarionation is one of the earliest in a style of animation likely to dominate the medium in the 21st century—motion-capture against CG backgrounds fast becoming the only viable means of making anime in an age of atrophied artistic skills and cheap computer power. This anime was intended for video but premiered on the satellite channel WOWOW. Later repackaged as a feature-length movie-edit. Compare to **A.Li.Ce** and **Aurora**.

VOICE ACTING

Voice acting in the earliest of the **Early Anime** was not part of the finished work, since anime was in existence for a decade before the introduction of audio. Instead, anime would be screened to a musical accompaniment, although many would also employ a live *benshi* (narrator) to fill in dialogue and story elements in the style of similar performances in the Japanese puppet theater or magic lantern shows. Voice work in early anime was often of secondary concern, with "actors" pulled in from available staff. When casting the two combatants in **Benkei vs. Ushiwaka** (1939) animator Kenzo Masaoka chose Mrs. Masaoka to play the diminutive hero, and himself as the hulking brute Benkei.

Dialogue from several American films was stolen to add exotic foreign language scenes to **Wartime Anime**, including snatches from Popeye's enemy Bluto, who appears as an Allied soldier in *Momotaro's Sea Eagles* (1943). Sometimes the effect can be unintentionally surreal—in the middle of the battle sequence in **Momotaro's Divine Sea Warriors** (1945), an American

voice can be heard hailing a taxi. The first genuine English-language voice actor in anime appears in the closing moments of the same film, as the tremulous and cowardly British soldier who attempts to renegotiate the terms of his surrender. The uncredited actor is clearly a native speaker, but with a strange delivery that seems either to be a calculated attempt to make his dialogue unusable, or perhaps, more chillingly, the sign of a man in genuine fear for his life.

In the 1950s, as Toei and Mushi began to make animated features in imitation of Disney, famous Japanese personalities were often chosen to appear in anime, although not always on account of their acting skills. Osamu Tezuka's **Arabian Nights** (1969) and **Cleopatra: Queen of Sex** (1970) bizarrely include vocal performances from a number of famous Japanese authors, including Shusaku Endo, Yasutaka Tsutsui and Sakyo Komatsu.

The rise of television saw an exponential rise in the number of vocal performers in Japan, creating an entire voice acting industry in order to dub foreign television productions into Japanese. Anime voice acting often exploited this fact with casting decisions whose relevance is all but lost on a non-Japanese audience, hiring the Japanese "voices" of famous American screen stars to portray anime characters with similar profiles. Yasuo Yamada, who was until his death the voice of **Lupin III**, was also renowned for playing Clint Eastwood, while Lupin's sidekick Jigen was played by Kiyoshi Komori, the Japanese voice of Lee Marvin. Similar casting "coincidences" continue to the present day, with numerous big name anime voice actors also playing big names from Hollywood, although it is less common for a Hollywood star to have one single Japanese actor play all their roles.

The popular anime voice actors of today include Akio Otsuka, best known as Batou in **Ghost in the Shell**, who is also the voice of Jonathan Frakes (Commander William Riker) in *Star

Trek: The Next Generation*. Yasunori Matsumoto played both V-daan in **Beast Warriors** and Brad Pitt in *Se7en*; Kappei Yamaguchi is the voice of **Inu Yasha** and Bugs Bunny; and the versatile Koichi Yamadera has voiced not only **Cowboy Bebop**'s Spike Spiegel, but also Jim Carrey, Eddie Murphy, Robin Williams, and Tom Hanks. Many famous voice actors end up typecast—consistently given the same kind of role, be it as a juvenile lead, a maverick rebel, or a slow lunk. This can limit the audience's perception of their abilities, but can also prove to be beneficial on fast schedules—an actor who has played three hot-headed heroes in the past week probably knows what he's doing when given a fourth. Sometimes anime can exploit these associations in reverse—**Evangelion** famously cast several prominent voice actors against type, in a decision that generated superb performances. Anime voice actors are also liable to enjoy spin-off careers in radio and music, and many have their own radio shows or albums. Modern anime exploits this by using voice actors in radio dramas or games as an experiment to test the market for a later anime version.

Voice acting in Japan is usually recorded while the actors watch the animatics (in Japanese, the "Leica reel")—a precisely timed video of storyboards that allows them a sense of how the finished product will look. Many voice recording facilities in Japan run around the clock in order to get the best returns from their investment in expensive machinery. This, along with union rules, has made child actors rare in anime voice work: they tend only to appear in movie productions, which require less studio time than a long-running series, and can also afford the higher prices of daytime booking. In the cheaper, longer-running worlds of video and TV, child parts are often played by adult women, notably Masako Nozawa, who is the Japanese voice of both talking pig *Babe* (1995) and **Dragon Ball Z**'s Goku, and Megumi Ogata, who has voiced male anime protagonists from **Evangelion** to **Yugi-oh**. Most Japanese voice actors are professionally trained as such, and hence know to monitor and preserve the talent that earns their living. In one notable choice, Akira Kamiya, the voice of Ken in **Fist of the North Star**, decided upon his trademark high-pitched attacks because falsetto yells would be easier to repeat and maintain over a long series than gruff growls. Such considerations can often elude less experienced actors abroad, some of whom have temporarily damaged their vocal chords, lost their voices, or been forced to drop out of long-running productions.

The concept of a voice acting fan-dom first arrived in Japan in the early 1980s, with newly founded magazines such as *Newtype* and *Animage* in search of fresh subjects for articles, and the rise in voice acting spin-offs occasioned by Mari Iijima's role as the singer Lin Minmei in **Macross**. For the video-based anime industry, with a primarily male fan-base, a heavy concentration on voice *actresses* was inevitable, with some of the most popular stars including Megumi Hayashibara (the female **Ranma ½**, but also Audrey Tautou in *Amélie*), Kotono Mitsuishi (the lead in **Sailor Moon**, but also sometimes heard as Cameron Diaz and Natalie Portman), Aya Hisakawa (Sailor Mercury *and* Natalie Portman, again), and Chisa Yokoyama (Pretty Sammy in **Tenchi Muyo!**, but also Winona Ryder and Alicia Silverstone). Anime voice actors are also popular choices as columnists in magazines, and not merely those associated directly with the anime world. Fumi Hirano, who was once the voice of Lum in **Urusei Yatsura**, still writes a column on the world of fish for *Big Comic*. This is not quite as bizarre as it may first seem, since she left the acting business to marry a wealthy fish market entrepreneur. Although, on second thought, it is still pretty weird.

Voice acting in the Western world has developed similar personality cults, beginning with the realization that many American voice actors were often locally available, easy on the eye and good with crowds—all excellent reasons to invite them to conventions. Many American voice actors have become fixtures on the convention circuit, including stars from anime of yesteryear such as Corinne Orr (**Speed Racer**) and Amy Howard Wilson (**Star Blazers**). Voice actor attendance at conventions has grown exponentially during the 1990s and beyond, particularly since Japanese guests can be expensive to invite and may not speak English. It is not uncommon for American anime conventions to have many more American voice actors than Japanese guests.

Whereas video anime tend to use relative unknowns, often rendered all the more unknowable by the use of pseudonyms to preserve union status, anime movie releases in America regularly use "stunt-casting"—the use of actors famous elsewhere. Incidences date back to the use of Frankie Avalon in *Alakazam the Great* (1960, see **Journey to the West**), and have included cameo anime performances from Orson Welles and Leonard Nimoy (in the **Transformers** movie). This has even happened in Japan, where the producers of the **Armitage III** movie *Polymatrix* decided to make it extra exotic by hiring foreign actors and releasing the movie in English in Japan, with the voices of Kiefer Sutherland and Elizabeth Berkley.

American stunt-casting roles have become even more noticeable in recent years with the release of Studio Ghibli films in America, utilizing such talents as Lauren Bacall and Jean Simmons (**Howl's Moving Castle**), or Kirsten Dunst and Debbie Reynolds (**Kiki's Delivery Service**). Similar casting decisions have been made with regard to the voices in some modern porn anime, in which erotic stars such as Asia Carrera, Kobe Tai, and Alexa Rae are used to dub anime, in the presumed hope that fans of their live-action work will also pick up their porn voice-overs for the sake of completeness. This was also tried with some erotic anime in Japanese, such as the casting of adult video starlets in the original Japanese language track of **Adventure Kid**. Players of the actor game "Six Degrees of Kevin Bacon" will be disappointed to hear that although he voiced the eponymous *Balto* (1995), he has not appeared in an anime. However, he did costar with Kiefer Sutherland in *Flatliners* (1990), which should help anyone playing a version that links to the anime world.

VOICES OF A DISTANT STAR *

2002. JPN: *Hoshi no Koe*. AKA: *Voice of the Stars*. Video. DIR: Makoto Shinkai. SCR: Makoto Shinkai. DES: Makoto Shinkai. ANI: Makoto Shinkai. MUS: Tenmon. PRD: CoMix Wave International, Mangazoo. 25 mins.

Noboru and Mikako are ordinary Japanese teenagers in love: they walk each other home from high school, hang out at the convenience store, and dream of a future together. When mysterious aliens attack a human colony on Mars, Mikako is accepted for a United Nations military program. She becomes a Tracer, piloting a giant robotic combat suit on a series of training missions, before circumstances force her mothership to take successively greater warp jumps away from home. Her would-be boyfriend waits back in Japan, hoping for his mobile phone to ring with a text message from his 15-year-old girlfriend. Every now and then, it does ... but Mikako's texts can only travel at the speed of light. Her *now* becomes his *then*, separated by days, then weeks, then months....

Such tales of robots and romance initially seem little removed from a hundred other anime since the groundbreaking **Zambot 3**, but *Voices* remains a touchstone of 21st-century anime not for its story, but for the means of its execution. This is a work so saturated with its creator's sensibility and personality that watching it is like reading a private diary—its strongest literary influences are the phantom girlfriends in the works of novelist

Voltage Fighter Gowkaiser

VOLLEY BOYS

1996. Video. DIR: Kunihiko Yuyama.
SCR: Hiroshi Koda. DES: Hiroyuki Murata.
ANI: N/C. MUS: N/C. PRD: Toho. 50 mins.
x 2 eps.

Sex-starved teenage boys at Kudo high school sign up for the *girls'* volleyball team—hoping that if they build it, the girls will come, to a year that has no girls in it at all. This spin-off from Hiroyuki Murata's 1988 manga in *Young Magazine* mixes *Field of Dreams* with **Ping Pong Club**.

VOLTAGE FIGHTER GOWKAISER *

1996. JPN: *Chojin Gakuen Gowkaiser*.
AKA: *Superhuman Academy Gowkaiser*.
Video. DIR: Masami Obari. SCR: Kengo Asai. DES: Masami Obari. ANI: Masahiro Yamane. MUS: Airs. PRD: JC Staff, GaGa.
45 mins. x 3 eps.

Isato Kaiza's (Isato Goka's) athletic skills have won him a place at the Belnar Institute, a school for those with some outstanding gift, and this being an Obari anime, all the female students have at least two. But the institute's mysterious founder has a hidden agenda—he is using the arcane powers of his Caizer Stones to control his students by giving them superhuman fighting skills, while he is controlled by a beautiful, seemingly female but definitely inhuman entity. Isato's friend Kash has given him a Caizer Stone and with it the power to transform into armored hero Gowkaizer; he learns that just about everyone else he knows has similar powers of transformation. Alas, the script doesn't. It starts with some interesting ideas, but many never develop. A subplot about incest between a brother and sister at school is well developed, largely because it provides an excuse for more sex and fighting; another, about a teacher's involvement in the government's attempts to keep an eye on things at the institute, is more or less ignored because it doesn't. The interesting relationship between the founder and his control remains unexplained. Perhaps the plan was to take all these ideas further if the video had spun off into a TV

Haruki Murakami, separated from a narrator by obstacles both physical and metaphysical. Its brevity is a great virtue, forcing Shinkai to enhance the emotional charge. This is useful, too, since unforgiving critics might otherwise focus on its minor flaws, such as the "future" technology that simply slaps spaceships and robots onto the present day (the phones already look dated), or a closing song that often sounds like a cat in pain. However, *Voices* is truly one of the most beautiful and powerful anime of recent years and its creator has become a poster boy for the new generation of have-a-go amateur animators. Shinkai assembled much of it solo, using software packages liberated from his day job at a computer games company, and originally played the lead himself while conscripting his fiancée to play Mikako. In pushing for the fan-friendly audience, in his designs and plotting, in incidents, in scenes, and even in some shots, Shinkai's debt to **Gunbuster** is so great that it verges on the actionable. But Shinkai's constant reference to the 1988 classic is only one of several homages—look out, too, for passing train cars destined for

the "U.N. Spacy" of the **Macross** saga.

As multimedia corporations fight over increasingly smaller TV ratings shares and pump out endless dross based on bad computer games, *Voices* shows what one man can achieve in his living room. Of course, Shinkai had a little help from the Mangazoo corporation, which eventually provided financial and logistic support (including revoicing the cast for the mass-market release), but *Voices* is essentially put together with a high-end personal computer and commercially available software. In that regard, it brings the medium full circle, to the homemade concoctions of **Early Anime**.

The DVD release includes both Japanese voice tracks, as well as Shinkai's earlier short film *She and Her Cat*. Compare also to the same year's **Saikano**, with which it shares several story elements and attitudes. *Voices* also enjoyed an extensive run at a small western Tokyo cinema, so is filed in some sources as a "movie." Shinkai followed *Voices* with the feature-length **The Place Promised in Our Early Days**, which revisits many of the same themes.

series, but it never happened. Based on a computer game (though it only uses some of the characters), with plenty of action and plenty of Obari's trademark fan service, *Gowkaizer* remains just another beat-'em-up with fantasy tropes thrown in. The videos were also edited into a feature-length *Gowkaiser* "movie." **NV**

VOLTRON *

1981. JPN: *Hyakujuo Go-Lion, Kiko Kantai Dairugger XV*. AKA: *Beast Centurion Go-Lion, Machine Platoon Dairugger XV; Lion Force Voltron*. TV series. DIR: Katsuhiko Taguchi, Kazuyuki Okaseko, Kazushi Nomura, Hiroshi Sasagawa. SCR: Susumu Takahisa, Ryo Nakahara, Masaaki Sakurai. DES: Kazuo Nakamura. ANI: Kazuo Nakamura, Moriyasu Taniguchi, Akira Saijo. MUS: Masahisa Takeshi. PRD: Toei, Tokyo 12 Channel. 25 mins. x 125 eps.

Reptile Emperor Dai Bazal of planet Garla (aka Zarkon of planet Doom in the American version) has built a galaxy-conquering army by transforming kidnapped enemies into fighting monsters. On a mission to Earth his forces kidnap some of its people, including our unsuspecting heroes Akira, Takashi, Tsuyoshi, Isamu, and Hiroshi. They are carried off to a conquered world for transformation. Stealing an enemy ship, they escape and manage to reach the palace of Princess Fara, where they learn that five ancient robot lions can combine to form one mighty robot. Impressed by their courage, the dead emperor (in hologram form) gives them the power to operate the machines, form the robot, and free the galaxy from the forces of evil in just 52 episodes.

In the U.S. version, Earth was the headquarters of the peace-loving planetary federation known as the Galaxy Alliance, and Sven, Keith, Lance, Pidge, and Hunk were Space Explorers sent on a mission to planet Arus, recently devastated by Zarkon. Their objective was the Lion Force, Arus's five greatest weapons, which could merge to form the super-robot Voltron.

They find that Princess Allura has survived the devastation of her world and is struggling to overthrow Zarkon's evil rule, and they join her as the pilots of the five robot lions that combine to make up Voltron. In the original story Akira is killed in battle (Sven is merely wounded, since American heroes can't die) and Fara/Allura takes his place on the team.

The *Golion* series was bought for U.S. syndication as *Voltron: Defender of the Universe!*, with scripts "written" by Jameson Brewer and Howard Albrecht. Presaging the later treatment of **ROBOTECH**, it was combined with an unrelated show to bulk out the running time. *Dairugger XV* (1982) was a 56-episode show, also from Toei, renamed *Vehicle Team Voltron* in the U.S. In the original Japanese version, Earth is enjoying a period of unparalleled prosperity thanks to its alliances with the people of the planets Mila and Sara. The president of the Terran League initiates a mission to explore space beyond our galaxy, and the starship Rugger-Guard sets out on its mission. Attacked by a ship of the Galveston Empire, Rugger-Guard sends out its best line of defense—Dairugger XV, a giant robot made up of 15 different mecha, each with its own pilot. As with **GOLD LIGHTAN** and other shows of the period, there is a far-fetched origin—15 players on a team in rugby, a sport whose only other anime appearance is in **WARTIME ANIME**.

In the U.S. version, Voltron technology was brought back to Earth after the struggle with Zarkon in the earlier *Lion Force Voltron* segment of the series. The Galaxy Alliance used it to build their own, even larger Voltron made up of 15 smaller robots and sent it out of our galaxy on the spaceship Explorer to find habitable new planets. The Drule dictatorship, whose homeworld was dying of pollution, sent ships to tag along behind the Explorer and try to steal any habitable worlds for themselves. The 15 pilots of the Explorer had to do battle both with natural forces like volcanoes on the worlds they

discovered and with the Drule. Eventually the Drule population revolted, the planet exploded, and the "good" Drule were rescued by Voltron and relocated to new homes.

The producers intended to refashion **LIGHTSPEED ELECTRON ARBEGAS** as the third part of the series, but the show was canceled. However, merchandising by U.S. toy distributors Matchbox further confused matters by including the "stackable" robot hero from *Arbegas* as "Voltron II." The toy boxes show stills from all three anime, with Dairugger as "Voltron I" and GoLion as "Voltron III," claiming that the Arbegas robot is part of the Voltron story line, though he never appears in the TV show. Riding on the momentum created by *Star Wars* and sales of space battle toys, *Voltron* was successfully rerun on U.S. cable TV in the early 1990s. World Events Productions ran a 90-minute special in 1983 then syndicated the series as a half-hour daily show, tied into the merchandising of toy weaponry. *Lion Force* did better than *Vehicle Team Voltron* with its new audience, to the extent that new episodes were commissioned from Japan specially for the American market—creating a total run for the combined *Voltron* series of 125 episodes. In one of these, the "recovered" Sven rejoined the team just in time to help defeat Zarkon. The sequel *Voltron: The Third Dimension* (1998, aka *Voltron 3D*) was an all-American 3-D CG motion-capture version made by *Babylon 5*'s effects company Netter Digital. In this version, the team is joined by Zarkon himself, who has seen the error of his ways, and fights to defeat Zarkon's evil son Lotor—you can tell he's evil because he has a *scar*.

VOLTUS *

1977. JPN: *Cho Denji Machine Voltes V*. AKA: *Super Electromagnetic Machine Voltes 5*. TV series. DIR: Tadao Nagahama, Yoshiyuki Tomino, Yukihiro Takahashi. SCR: Koichi Taguchi, Masaki Tsuji, Fuyunori Gobu. DES: Akehiro Kaneyama, Nobuyoshi Sasakado. ANI: Akehiro Kaneyama. MUS: Hiroshi Tsutsui. PRD: Sunrise, Toei, TV Asahi. 25 mins. x 40 eps.

The three Go brothers, Kenichi, Daijiro, and Hiyoshi, and their friends Ippei Mine and Megumi Oka pilot the giant robot Voltes V in the battle against the people of planet Bozan, who are trying to add Earth to their galactic empire. But the prince of Bozan, Hainel, claims to be the Go boys' half-brother; he says their father was an alien, sent to Earth many years before. How can they fight their own flesh and blood, can Earth trust them, and might this point to a way forward for both peoples?

After Sunrise made **COMBATTLER V** for Toei, it followed up with this repeat performance—the undisputed star of which is Hainel, the first baddie to be a real hit with the female audience, who wrote in demanding that he survive. Originally dubbed in Japan by William Ross for a U.S. theatrical release, the relatively faithful version was scrapped by new owners "New Hope Productions," which replaced it with a soundtrack more like *Star Wars* and eventually sold it to the Christian Broadcast Network. The company similarly tried to capitalize on George Lucas' success by refashioning **STARBIRDS**.

VOOGIE'S ANGEL *

1997. JPN: *Denno Sentai Voogie's Angel.* AKA: *Cyber Battle Team Voogie's Angel.* Video. DIR: Mamoru Takeuchi. SCR: Mamoru Takeuchi. DES: Masami Obari. ANI: Masami Obari. MUS: Satoshi Yuyama. PRD: JC Staff, Beam Entertainment. 30 mins. x 3 eps.

A hundred years after Earth is invaded by aliens, the last remnants of the human race dwell in underwater "Aqua Bases." A team of five cybernetically enhanced women is trained for the purpose of carrying out guerrilla attacks against the occupying forces. Earth's last best hope for salvation is Voogie's Angel. Playing like a warped version of *Stingray, VA* delivers some interesting moments. The cutesy-conventional girl cyborg team (good sort, tough girl, kid sister, nice Japanese girl) and their scientist father-figure go

from the aliens-invade-earth scenario, via space battles and embarrassing "comic" scenes, to the extremely violent fight in the second episode in which our heroes are smashed almost to a pulp. Then there's the black-and-white **GUNBUSTER** homage in episode three, which shows how each of the cyborgs died tragically and was then rebuilt in enhanced form. The fight for human freedom shows the cyborgs what it means to be truly human but doesn't explain why cyber-enhanced women usually have gravity-defying breasts or why swimwear is the battle dress of preference in Obari-designed shows. A radio and CD drama in 1996 preceded the video release. Spin-offs include a manga in *Comic Gamma* and a "side story" *Onward! Super Angels* that features the characters in super-deformed (see **SUPER-DEFORMED DOUBLE FEATURE**) mode. The series was also released on DVD in the 70-minute feature-length "director's cut" *VA: Forever and Ever* (1998), containing extra footage. **Ⓥ**

VOTOMS *

1983. JPN: *Sokokihei Votoms.* AKA: *Armored Trooper Votoms; ScopeDog.* TV series, video. DIR: Ryosuke Takahashi, Haruka Miyako, Tatsuya Matsuno, Toshifumi Takizawa, Hiroshi Yoshida, Yukihiro Takahashi, Masakazu Yasumura. SCR: Fuyunori Gobu, Soji Yoshikawa, Jinzo Toriumi, Ryosuke Takahashi, Takashi Imanishi. DES: Norio Shioyama, Ryosuke Takahashi, Kunio Okawara (TV, v), Yutaka Izubuchi (v94). ANI: Norio Shioyama. MUS: Hiroki Inui. PRD: Sunrise, TV Tokyo. 25 mins. x 52 eps. (TV), 60 mins. x 3 eps. (v), 30 mins. x 4 (v94).

On a distant world, the Perfect Soldier is finally created after genetic manipulation and a breeding program lasting centuries, but by the time this happens, the war has almost ended. The politicians and scientists who bred him either want him dead or want to use him in other, more sinister ways. But Chirico Cuve isn't a machine—he's a human being, and he's determined

to find out who is responsible for all this. As the war ends he is separated from his unit, thrown into a series of desperate situations, enslaved, used as a gladiator in robot combat, enlisted as a mercenary, and meets the love of his life, only to discover that she too is a Perfect Soldier.

The first video, *The Last Red Shoulder* (1985), is a continuation of the story after the end of the TV series. Chirico leaves Udo City in search of his beloved Fiana. In *Big Battle* (1986), he finds her being held hostage by Bararant in an experimental facility near Koba City, and he and his comrades have to fight their way in to save her. 1987's *Red Shoulder Document: The Roots of Treachery* is a prequel to the TV series and shows Chirico's origins as part of a genetic experiment and recruitment into the Red Shoulder group. In 1994 Takahashi brought the same team together for a four-part video adventure set 32 years after the end of the TV series. Chirico and Fiana have been in cryo-sleep together for all that time, but now a new threat has arisen, and it's time for them to fight again. An extra item on the first tape, *Votoms Briefing*, filled in the backstory for those who missed the series 11 years earlier.

The "real robot" concept was born out of a conviction that the weapons of the future would not be made of shiny metal in clean, bright primary colors. Designer Okawara wanted to create suits that looked as if they could be made in a 20th-century factory, designed so that the toys that would inevitably be spun off the series could be posed and moved exactly like their animated inspirations (unlike many of the suits he'd designed for **GUNDAM**) and smaller in scale than his designs for **DOUGRAM**.

Robots, which started out in anime primarily as cool toys to even up the odds for the little guy (children, the human race, or the Japanese) against a big, hostile world (adults, alien invaders, or foreign competition), had been seen right from the first as having as much potential for destruction as for good. GIGANTOR could be used by evil men just as easily as by perky little Jimmy Sparks—the power lay in the hands of whoever held the remote control. Takahashi and his fellow writers and directors extended this idea into the whole range of future military technology (VOTOMs is an acronym for Vertical One-man Tank for Offensive Maneuvers), showing robots and scientifically enhanced superbeings as just another weapon in the arsenal of the politicians, and war as a vicious, dehumanizing process in which honor and courage came from the individual, rather than any religion or value system, and could be crushed as easily as an insect (see GREY: DIGITAL TARGET). It also didn't hurt that *Votoms'* hero resembled Steve McQueen (lead character in the Western *Junior Bonner*, an early inspiration for the anime), whose laconic combination of little-boy charm and man's-man toughness was hugely popular with Japanese audiences.

The concept and the appealingly gritty realism of Takahashi's future war vision spun off another video series set in the same universe, as the title signals. Written by Takahashi but directed by Takeyuki Kanda, *Armored Trooper Votoms: Armor Hunter Merowlink* (1988, *Kiko Ryohei Merowlink*) is the story of a young rookie who is the sole survivor of a platoon cut down by bungling and treachery higher up the ranks. Framed for desertion and the deaths of his colleagues, he vows to avenge them; each of the twelve 25-minute episodes shows one act of vengeance on an individual betrayer. A

brilliantly paced series richly meriting a Western release, it combines good character development and edge-of-the-seat tension. There are points when *Merowlink* doesn't simply suspend disbelief but knocks it out cold, especially in the final episode with an escape sequence as silly on calm reflection as it is absolutely convincing while you watch. Sequences of extreme violence and deliberate cruelty are carefully calculated to enhance the effect of this stunning rite-of-passage tale. The series was a major inspiration for the *Heavy Gear* role-playing war- and video-game franchise, which now has its own CGI cartoon series. Note that *Votoms* has many recap episodes and fix-ups of preexisting videos, which are sometimes mistaken for original episodes. These recapitulations are *ATV: Highlights, Stories of the ATV 2, Woodo, Kammen, Sansa,* and *Quant.* ⬤Ⓥ

VOYAGE OF THE TSUSHIMA

1982. JPN: *Tsushima-maru: Sayonara Okinawa.* AKA: *The Tsushima: Farewell Okinawa.* Movie. DIR: Osamu Kobayashi. SCR: Shoichiro Okubo, Koji Senno. DES: Osamu Kobayashi. ANI: Tsutomu Shibayama, Hideo Kawauchi. MUS: Haruya Sugita. PRD: Asia-do. 70 mins.
On August 22, 1944, the Japanese freighter Tsushima Maru flees Okinawa for the mainland with a cargo consisting primarily of evacuees, the crew divided over whether to steer a zigzag course or simply to steam at full speed for safety. Her luck runs out off Akuseki Island, Kagoshima, when she is struck three times by torpedoes from an American submarine. The ship

sinks with the loss of 1,484 lives, including 738 children. Based on a true story dramatized by Tatsuhiro Oshiro in book form in 1961, this movie ends with a roll call of those who did not survive. The wreck of the Tsushima Maru itself was not located until 1997.

VOYEUR'S DIGEST *

2002. JPN: *Bad End.* Video. DIR: Kanzaburo Oda. SCR: Rokurota Makabe; Designer/s: Mario Yaguchi. ANI: Mario Yaguchi. MUS: Yoshi. PRD: YOUC, Digital Works (Vanilla Series). 30 mins. x 2 eps.
Student Toshiki Mikimoto is the secret proprietor of an underground newspaper, which exposes trouble and corruption in his school. At least, that's how he rationalizes it to himself; in fact, his newsletter is more of a scandalous gossip column, making slanderous accusations about certain coeds, in the hope that Toshiki's fellow students will take it upon themselves to "punish" the alleged transgressors. When a group of students duly take the bait and rape one of their number, Toshiki is on hand to record everything for prosperity. In the second episode, he similarly stalks another voluptuous coed, in an erotic anime in the VANILLA SERIES, based on a computer game. The original title was presumably changed in the American release in order to prevent people like us making snide and unjustified remarks about the beginning and middle not being all that good either. Compare to CLASSROOM OF ATONEMENT, which shares many plot elements. ⬤ⓃⓋ

W

WAKE UP ARIA *
1998. Video. DIR: Komari Yukino. SCR: N/C. DES: N/C. ANI: Hideo Ura. MUS: N/C. PRD: Cosmos Plan. 30 mins. Pretty young musician Aria goes to Golden Breast Island in search of an education and finds herself in the company of several other pretty, musically minded girls, including the Chinese Yang, Hiren, and the Indian twins Luna and Monica. However, the Royal Elegance Music School is just a front for the lusts of its principal and vice-principal, Mr. Karma and Ms. Shinbi. Every student they see ends up brainwashed into performing sexual acts for and with the perverse pair. Aria must escape the island alive, but not before she gets a good "education" in this predictable porno. **LNV**

WANDABA STYLE *
2003. JPN: *Moso Kagaku Series Wandaba Style*. AKA: *Delusion Science Series Wandaba Style; Fantasy Chemistry Series Wandaba Style*. TV series. DIR: Nobuhiro Takamoto. SCR: Juzo Mutsuki. DES: Shoji Hara, Gaku Miyao, Koji Nakakita. ANI: TNK. MUS: Try Force. PRD: Wonderfarm, TNK, Kid's Station, Chiba TV. 25 mins. x 12 eps.
Top manager Michael Hanagata cobbles together girl band Mix Juice from four has-been singers whose careers are going nowhere. Ayame Akimo is a folk singer whose brain is away with the fairies most of the time. Himawari Natsuwa sings Japanese classics with so little success that she also has to work on a construction site. Former child star Sakura Haruno is getting by selling her panties over the Internet. Yuri Fuyude plays such hard-edged rock that she can't get a gig anywhere. Michael's plan is to make a fortune by getting the girls to play the first ever concert on the moon. That suits boy genius billionaire Susumu Tsukumo (aged 13) who wants to find an eco-friendly means of space travel and thinks the girls will make excellent test subjects to supplement his cute personal android Kiku 8. Homages to anime like **EXCEL SAGA** and **PUNI PUNI POEMI** as well as Gerry Anderson's *Thunderbirds* and the *Super Mario* games make this a lightweight cavalcade of sight gags. Creator Juzo Mutsuki also edited and wrote the lyrics for the theme song.

The slang term *wandaba* originates in the martial music by Toru Fuyuki that once accompanied scenes of military preparation or launch in the old live-action *Ultraman Returns* (*DE, 1971)—parodied in fandom as a tune that went "wandabadabadabadaba." It has come to signify any launch sequence or scene of steely, belligerent resolve, and was also appropriated for the name of the male protagonist, Wan Dabada, in **BEAST WARRIORS**.

WANDERING SUN
1971. JPN: *Sasurai no Taiyo*. TV series. DIR: Chikao Katsui, Yoshiyuki Tomino, Masayuki Hayashi, Ryosuke Taka-hashi. SCR: Hiroyuki Hoshiyama, Shunichi Yukimuro, Michio Suzuki, Tadaaki Yamazaki, Haruya Yamazaki, Tsunehisa Ito, Isao Okishima. DES: Yoshikazu Yasuhiko. ANI: Hayao Nobe. MUS: Taku Izumi. PRD: Mushi, Fuji TV. 25 mins. x 26 eps.
Miki and Nozomi are two would-be singers. Miki's rich parents will go to any lengths to give their little princess her heart's desire, but the more talented Nozomi comes from a deprived background. The daughter of a deceased noodle seller, Nozomi must struggle to support her blind mother and make sacrifices on the way to achieving the success that her natural guitar-strumming ability deserves. Based on a manga in *Shojo Comic* by Keisuke Fujiwara and Mayumi Suzuki.

WANNA-BE'S *
1986. Video. DIR: Yasuo Hasegawa. SCR: Toshimichi Suzuki. DES: Kenichi Sonoda, Yoshiharu Shimizu, Shinji Araki, Kimitoshi Yamane, Hideki Kakinuma. ANI: Yoshiharu Shimizu. MUS: Hiroshi Arakawa, Seikima-II. PRD: Artmic, Animate Film, AIC. 45 mins.
Eri Fuma and Miki Morita are young female pro-wrestlers who fight under the professional name Wanna-Be's. They struggle to rise through the ranks and challenge the champions, not realizing that they are embroiled in a plot to test a secret muscle-enhancing drug. Will it be enough to help them defeat mutated monsters, though? A

hilarious look at the sport that's so popular in Japan, with some thinly disguised "guest appearances" by real girl wrestling stars—compare to the similar wrestling in-jokery of CRUSHER JOE and METAL FIGHTERS MIKU.

WANSA-KUN

1973. AKA: *Little Wansa*. TV series. DIR: Eiichi Yamamoto, Minoru Tanaka, Masami Hata, Noboru Ishiguro, Norio Yazawa, Minami Asa. SCR: Keisuke Fujikawa, Maru Tamura, Fumio Ikeno, Eiichi Yamamoto, Hitoshi Hidaka. DES: Shinji Nagashima. ANI: Hiromitsu Morita, Toyoo Ashida. MUS: Yasushi Miyakawa. PRD: Tomi Pro, Anime Room, Mushi, Fuji TV. 25 mins. x 26 eps. Wansa the little white dog comes to town and befriends neighborhood boy Kota. His "people," however, are the neighborhood dogs, who introduce him to a hidden life of triumph and tragedy as the local canines fight a vicious turf war with their cat enemies. Wansa falls in love with local puppy Midori and pines for his mother, *presumed* dead in typical anime fashion. Based on the 1971 manga written by Tezuka for *Tezuka Magazine Leo* and starring the mascot character of the Sanwa Bank, this musical comedy, faintly redolent of *Lady and the Tramp*, was the last TV series made by the beleaguered Mushi studio. It, along with TRITON OF THE SEA, was effectively lost to its creator through copyright foul-ups and is not a "true" Tezuka work.

WARTIME ANIME

With the Japanese invasion of China in the 1930s, the fairy tales and fables of EARLY ANIME were gradually co-opted into the military machine, the anime creators tempted by offers of funding and, for the first time, wide distribution.

Early emphasis was on austerity and unity in the face of potential threats. Yasuji Murata's *Masamune and the Monkeys* (*Saru Masamune*, 1930) dwells on the virtues of righteous intervention, depicting an incident in which the

Wartime Anime—*Sky Over the Shanghai Battle Line*

swordsmith Masamune comes to the aid of a monkey, and is consequently bestowed with the blade that will one day save his own life. Like many other anime from the period, it tacitly advanced Japan's demands for an East Asian "co-prosperity sphere," and her right to interfere in the affairs of other countries in order to overthrow Western imperialism. Murata's *Aerial Momotaro* (*Sora no Momotaro*, 1931) featured a war between penguins and albatrosses on a remote island near the South Pole, broken up by the timely arrival of the Japanese hero Momotaro. Yoshitaro Kataoka's *Bandanemon the Monster Exterminator* (*Bandanemon: Bakemono Taiji no Maki*, 1935) focused on a tough Japanese hero who comes to the aid of oppressed villagers, volunteering to clear an infestation of tanuki from a nearby castle. The shape-changing creatures have disguised themselves as beautiful women (with shades of Betty Boop) in order to distract him from his mission. Yasuji Murata revisited the plot of DREAMY URASHIMA with his *One Night at a Bar* (*Izakaya Hitoya*, 1936), the Dragon King's Palace of legend presented as a drunken hallucination by a man who, like the Japanese nation itself, has yet to wake up to reality—in this case, the inevitability of conflict.

In the wake of the League of Nations' condemnation of Japan's expansion into Manchuria, attacks on foreign powers became more blatant. In Takao Nakano's *Black Cat Banzai* (*Kuroneko Banzai*, 1933), a peaceful parade of toys is disrupted by a fleet of flying bat-bombers, each ridden by a clone of Mickey Mouse. Snake-marines with machine gun mouths land on the beach, and the invaders kidnap a doll. The islanders beg for help from a book of JAPANESE FOLK TALES, which obligingly disgorges Momotaro, Kintaro, and several other Japanese folk icons. The story ends with a celebration, as all the dead trees sprout cherry blossoms.

Shiho Tagawa's popular manga character NORAKURO joined up in Yasuji Murata's *Corporal Norakuro* (*Norakuro Gocho*, 1934). This comprised another warning about drunkenness, in which the titular stray dozed off and dreamed he was attacked by monkeys. The emphasis on humor continued with the uncredited *Sky Over the Shanghai Battle-Line* (*Sora no Shanhai Sensen*, 1938), in which two comical Japanese pilots observed the Chinese war theater in a biplane. Similarly, Noboru Ofuji's *Aerial Ace* (*Sora no Arawashi*, 1938) featured another pilot fighting giant clouds in the shape of Popeye

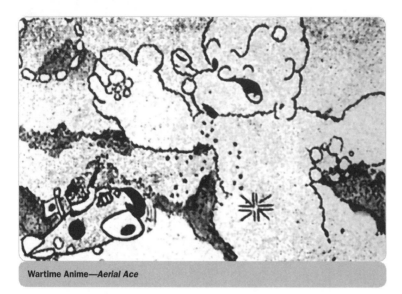

Wartime Anime—*Aerial Ace*

and Stalin—FOREIGN INFLUENCES were no longer welcome.

In 1939, the increasingly oppressive Japanese government passed a Film Law bringing the media under greater central control. The onset of war with America in 1941 brought greater funding, but also greater pressures on filmmakers. Kajiro Yamamoto completed *The War at Sea from Hawaii to Malaya* (*Hawaii-Marei Okikaisen*, 1942) in just six months, recreating Pearl Harbor with special-effects footage from Eiji Tsuburaya, creator of *Ultraman* (*DE). Its success prompted the Japanese Navy to attempt similar triumphs with animation, ordering Mitsuyo Seo to make *Momotaro's Sea Eagles* (*Momotaro no Umiwashi*, 1943). Retelling the Momotaro folktale with enemy caricatures, the film pushed the boundaries of animation in Japan with an unprecedented running time of 37 minutes. With animation cels in short supply (nitro-cellulose was a crucial ingredient in gunpowder), Seo's animators were forced to wash their materials in acid and reuse them for this tale of the bombing of Pearl Harbor in fairy-tale form, destroying the original artwork even as they shot each frame of animation. In order to get the right voice for a caricature of *Popeye*'s Bluto, seen on

the deck of a sinking ship, they also sampled the original straight from a reel of the American print—copyright law hardly being an issue at the time. The film was immensely popular with children on release, and was even screened in the palace for Prince Akihito (the current Heisei Emperor). The Navy authorized Seo to make an even longer sequel, and the result was Japan's first full-length animated feature, MOMOTARO'S DIVINE SEA WARRIORS.

Other anime of the 1940s show signs of increasing desperation, as Japanese defeats become harder to ignore. Sanae Yamamoto's *Defeat of the Spies* (*Spy Gekimetsu*, 1942) depicts Roosevelt and Churchill sending three agents onto Japanese soil, although they are swiftly unmasked. In Ryotaro Kuwata's *Human Rugby Bullets* (*Tokkyu Nikudan Sen*, 1943), a sports match between Japanese dogs and foreign monkeys attempts to make light of Japan's use of the *taiatari* ramming attack—a chilling precursor to the following year's *kamikaze* attacks. Animation was also a major component of the ten-minute short *Nippon Banzai* (1943), best described as Japan's *Why We Fight*. In it, evil British soldiers are shown oppressing the natives of Asia beneath a hot sun, which segues into the rising sun

of Japan's flag. Cartoon fish dance in and out of the wreck of the HMS *Prince of Wales*, while Chiang Kai-Shek is first portrayed as a marionette (with his wife, operated by Allied "advisers"), then as a gleeful child with a toy plane (a snide reference to the Flying Tigers). The anime sequence ends with Roosevelt impeached and Churchill's trademark cigar falling from his mouth in shock, before returning to live-action footage exhorting young men to join up.

In the aftermath of the war, the surviving animators in Tokyo worked on SAKURA. Anime struggled for some time amid conditions of deprivation in which many had understandably more pressing problems, and early postwar anime are largely feel-good FANTASY AND FAIRY TALES such as *The Magic Pen*. Sanae Yamamoto would help recreate anime with the establishment of his studio Nippon Doga in 1947. Bought by Toei in 1956, the company would form the foundations of Toei Animation, and with it, the beginnings of the anime industry as we know it today.

The war, however, remained a taboo subject for a decade, with the anomalous exception of ZERO SEN HAYATO and occasional references as origin stories in shows such as GIGANTOR and BIG X. As the babyboomers reached maturity, several anime began alluding to the war through future allegories such as STAR BLAZERS, and the devastation wrought by the giant aliens of MACROSS.

After the success of the anime DIARY OF ANNE FRANK, producers realized the value of children as protagonists—caught up in a conflict not of their own making, the brutalized innocents of BAREFOOT GEN, GRAVE OF THE FIREFLIES, and their many imitators allowed history without discussion of responsibility. The Hiroshima Peace Festival film prize became dominated by Renzo Kinoshita, whose short anime included *Pica-Don* (1978, the nickname of the bomb that destroyed Hiroshima), TOBIWAO IS TAKEN ILL, *Last Air Raid Kumagaya* (1990), and the unfinished project *Okinawa*. Outside the art-house theaters however, popular representations of the war became increasingly fantastic, as a nostalgic craze for "retro" anime transformed into an obsession with rewriting history—**KISHIN CORPS** and **SAKURA WARS** would have met with joyous approval from the government censor in 1941.

WAT PO AND US

1988. JPN: *Wat Po to Bokura no Ohanashi*. AKA: *The Story of Us and Wat Po*. Video. DIR: Shigenori Kageyama. SCR: Shozo Uehara. DES: Mutsumi Inomata, Shohei Kohara, Takahiro Tomoyasu, Torao Arai. ANI: Mutsumi Inomata. MUS: Satoshi Kadokura. PRD: Diva, Konami. 55 mins.

The life of a tiny fishing village is disrupted when Wat Po, a horned white whale who is the village's guardian spirit, vanishes. The creature used to attract fish for the people to catch. Local boy Jam, hearing strange music wafting down from the mountains, sets out with three friends and his dog in search of the sound. Attacks by monsters scare his friends away, but he finds a mountain lake where a lovely young girl called Selene is playing music to Wat Po. At first she's afraid and tries to flee in winged armor. Her people, the Birdoes, are technologically far in advance of the village folk, but they hid inside the mountain generations ago after a terrible war devastated and polluted the land. They used their power of flight to bring Wat Po from the sea to the landlocked lake. Selene and Jam decide to rescue Wat Po and try to bring their peoples back together, but Jam's disappearance is arousing old hatreds and may even rekindle the long-ago war.

An eco-saga with a strong antiwar message in the vein of **FUTURE BOY CONAN** and **GREEN LEGEND RAN**, it fails to match up to the same team's work on **WINDARIA** and **LEDA: FANTASTIC ADVENTURES OF YOKO**.

WATANABE, KAZUYUKI

1932– . Born in Tokyo and a graduate of Tokyo University of Fine Arts, Wata-

Wartime Anime—*Black Cat Banzai*

nabe's first anime work was a paper-cut animation version of **AESOP'S FABLES**. His subsequent animations have included the prize-winning *Princess Kaguya* and *The Little Match Girl*—much of his work comprises fairy tales and parables drawn from **JAPANESE FOLK TALES** and the **TALES OF HANS CHRISTIAN ANDERSEN**.

WATANABE, SHINICHI

?– . Aka Nabeshin. Often appearing as a cameo character in his own work (look out for someone with an afro hairdo, particularly in **EXCEL SAGA** and its spin-offs), Watanabe is a modern director with a strong track record in comedy and parody, although his stature often seems artificially inflated through the coincidental resemblance of his own name to that of Shinichiro Watanabe (q.v.).

WATANABE, SHINICHIRO

?– . After early work on **MACROSS** *Plus*, Watanabe soon established a reputation as a modern, "groovy" director, overseeing both **COWBOY BEBOP** and **SAMURAI CHAMPLOO**. He also featured as one of the directors on **THE ANIMATRIX**, setting him apart as one of Japan's top anime creatives, despite a very limited cinema output so far. Not to be confused with Shinichi Watanabe (q.v.).

WATARU

1988. JPN: *Majin Eiyuden Wataru*. AKA: *Legend of Devilish Heroism Wataru*. TV series, video. DIR: Hideharu Iuchi, Michio Fukuda, Masamitsu Hidaka, Nobuhiro Kondo, Katsuoshi Yatabe, Yutaka Kagawa. SCR: Yoshiaki Takahashi, Ryosuke Takahashi, Hiroyuki Kawasaki, Takao Koyama, Hiroko Naka. DES: Toyoo Ashida, Kazunori Nakazawa. ANI: Toyoo Ashida. MUS: Junichi Kanezaki, Satoshi Kadokura. PRD: Sunrise, Nippon TV. 25 mins. x 45 eps., 25 mins. x 28 eps., 30 mins. x 4 eps. (v).

After school, ten-year-old Wataru doesn't go straight home—instead he slips into an alternate world where he is the pilot of a huge super-deformed comical robot and fights to deliver the world from the oppression of an evil magician with the help of the cute but overexciteable Tora-chan. Luckily these adventures only last a few seconds in our world, or his mother would wonder why he was late for dinner. A huge success in Japan, the first series spun off a remake series with the prefix *Cho* [*Super*] and the four-part video series *W: Tales of Endless Time* (*W: Owarinaki Toki no Monogatari*).

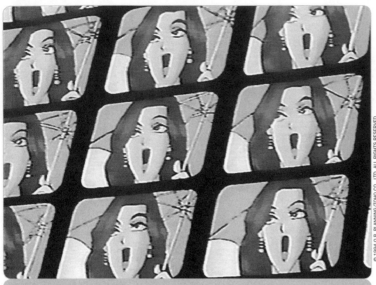

Weather Report Girl

WATCH WITH MOTHER

1988. JPN: *Mama Ohanashi o Shikikasete*. TV series. DIR: Keiji Hayakawa. SCR: Shunichi Yukimuro. DES: Yuzo Sato. ANI: N/C. MUS: N/C. PRD: Staff 21, Nippon TV. 8 mins. x 15 eps.

Short animated films of well-known **JAPANESE FOLK TALES**, including the stories of **TARO MAEGAMI**, *The Riceball Family, The Master of Catching Stars, Thunder Is the Bridegroom,* and *The Elephant's Sneeze.* Shown as part of the children's variety program, *Tondeke Gutchonpa.*

WAVE OF RAGE

1998. JPN: *Soliton no Akuma*. AKA: *Sea of Angels—Waves of Devils; Devil of the Solitons*. Movie. DIR: Toshio Takeuchi, Jun Kawagoe. SCR: Masashi Sogo. DES: Hisatoshi Motoki. ANI: Hisatoshi Motoki. MUS: N/C. PRD: Locomotion, Japan Cinema Associates. 90 mins. Deep below the sea off the coast of Okinawa, the Ocean Technopolis is at the forefront of humankind's efforts to adapt to catastrophically rising sea levels, but it's caught in the middle of escalating tensions between Japan and Taiwan. Taiwan is already blaming Japan for the disappearance of its submarine Shui Long, though the vessel

was actually destroyed by an underwater monster enraged by the testing of a new Japanese holophonic sonar device. Fleeing the creature, the Japanese submarine Hatsushio inadvertently leads its pursuer to Technopolis. The serpentine creature attacks the underwater city, trapping several tourists on the sea floor. Atsushi Kurase, head of the nearby Helios Oil underwater drilling rig, is trying to organize a rescue operation—his estranged wife and daughter, Qiu Hua and Mei Ling, are trapped on a stricken tour submarine. He sees the Hatsushio and calls on it for aid. The sub cannot publicly refuse, but its commander is given orders that if Atsushi or any rescuees should realize the top-secret nature of its mission, they are to have a "fatal accident." Though the tourists are saved, the cast is now trapped on the damaged Sea Turtle 200, Helios Oil's underwater platform. They are contacted by the Solitons, underwater creatures made from pure energy, who reveal that a rogue one of their race is responsible for the attacks and that only a human mutated into Soliton form can stop it. To save his daughter, Kurase volunteers, destroying the menace with the aid of the

Hatsushio. This derivative combination of *The Abyss* and *The Hunt for Red October* was redeemed in Japanese eyes by its well-conceived setting—a 21st-century Asia riven by international tension, with Japan, Taiwan, and China provocatively cast as superpowers in a new Cold War. Based on the 1995 novel by Katsufumi Umehara. For more underwater action, see **BLUE SUBMARINE No. SIX** and **SILENT SERVICE**. **Ⓥ**

WEATHER PERMITTING

1984. JPN: *Ashita Tenki ni Naare*. AKA: *Tomorrow If the Weather Holds*. TV series. DIR: Hisaya Takabayashi, Hiroe Mitsunobu, Kenjiro Yoshida. SCR: Noboru Shiroyama. DES: Tetsuya Chiba. ANI: Hikuji Kanezawa, Kazuo Tomizawa, Akira Kasahara. MUS: Masakazu Togo. PRD: Fuji TV, NAS. 25 mins. x 47 eps. Taro is a short, fat food-addict who is obsessed with golf—the one sport that doesn't object if its players meander around the field slowly. He astounds observers with his golfing skill but eventually becomes so devoted to the game that he excludes everything else from his life. Based on a 1980 manga by **TOMORROW'S JOE**–creator Tetsuya Chiba.

WEATHER REPORT GIRL *

1994. JPN: *Otenki Oneesan*. AKA: *Weather Woman*. Video. DIR: Kunihiko Yuyama, Takashi Watanabe. SCR: Kunihiko Yuyama. DES: Naomi Miyata. ANI: Shinji Sato. MUS: Fumihiko Kurihara. PRD: OB Planning, Toho. 45 mins. x 2 eps.

A determined young woman gets her big break in TV when the regular weather girl goes on vacation. Regardless of the barometer, Keiko sets temperatures and ratings soaring as she uses her clothing, or lack of it, to illustrate the trends and turns the serious stuff of the weather report into a song and dance routine. When the original weather girl gets back from her holiday and finds her replacement so popular, the fur begins to fly! Not everyone at the TV station likes the new style weather report, though, and rivals in the boardroom and on the screen are out to end Keiko's career. Based on the 1992 manga in *Young Magazine* by Tetsu Adachi, *WRG* also spawned the live-action film *Weather Woman*, directed by Tomoaki Hosoyama, starring Kei Mizutani as the exhibitionist heroine. ◐

WEATHERING CONTINENT, THE

1992. JPN: *Kaze no Tairiku*. AKA: *Continent of Wind*. Movie. DIR: Koichi Mashimo. SCR: Koichi Mashimo. DES: Mutsumi Inomata, Nobuteru Yuki. ANI: Kazuya Yokose. MUS: Michiru Oshima. PRD: IG, Kadokawa. 60 mins.

The long history of the continent of Atlantis is coming to an end; its once-great cities are crumbling to dust, and it is almost completely deserted after a series of natural disasters. Its few surviving people are under constant threat from scavengers and bandits. Water is increasingly scarce; the winds that scour the land carry no rainclouds, and most of the rivers and springs have long dried up. Across this desolate landscape walk three travelers: Tieh, an androgynous young mystic devoted to the Moon Goddess, Boyce, a mercenary warrior, and Lakshi, a feisty young person who is really the princess Lakshi Arun Ard. Through a series of strange events, they find themselves in a long-dead city where they face the anger of departed souls disturbed by a group of pirates plundering their comfortable afterlife. Tieh and Lakshi must confront their own demons, and all three of the companions must fight to escape the grip of Death and return to a world that, while dying, still has something to offer them.

Originally released on a triple bill with SILENT MÖBIUS 2 and HEROIC LEGEND OF ARSLAN 2, this hypnotically slow tale was based on a novel by Sei Takekawa with illustrations by Mutsumi Inomata, on which Yuki's character designs are based. A manga by Masaeda Hashimoto followed in *Dragon* magazine.

WEB DIVER

2001. JPN: *Denno Boken-ki Web Diver*. AKA: *Cyber Adventure Web Diver*. TV series. DIR: Hiroshi Negishi, Kunitoshi Okajima. SCR: Mayori Sekijima. DES: Shigetsugu Takahashi. ANI: N/C. MUS: N/C. PRD: NAS, Radix, TV Tokyo. 25 mins. x N/D eps.

In the year 2100, children are able to transform themselves into data, allowing them to interact in a "magical" cyberworld. When the cyberworld is attacked by the evil Wills Program Deletron, Japanese kids Kenta and Aoi hold them off with the aid of the Web Knight Gradion, which looks uncannily like a giant robot.

WEDDING PEACH

1995. JPN: *Ai Tenshi Densetsu Wedding Peach*. AKA: *Legend of Love Angel WP*. TV series, video. DIR: Kunihiko Yuyama, Norihiko Sudo, Yuji Asano, Toshiaki Suzuki, Yoshitaka Fujimoto. SCR: Sukehiro Tomita, Kenji Terada, Hideki Sonoda, Shikichi Ohashi. DES: Kazuko Tadano. ANI: Yuri Isseki, Mariko Fujita, Moriyasu Taniguchi. MUS: Toshiki Hasegawa. PRD: NAS, KSS, TV Tokyo. 25 mins. x 51 eps., 30 mins. x 4 eps. (v).

Three adolescent girls—one good, one bad, one silly—band together to fight evil as the Love Angel and her, er, bridesmaids. Yes, where SAILOR MOON fought evil with the power of love and makeup, *WP* uses bridal finery. Naturally, the ditzy one (Momoko, aka Wedding Peach) is the bride and lead fighter of evil, with the intellectual and the bad girl (Yuri and Hinagiku, aka Angel Lily and Angel Daisy, respectively) as her sidekicks. All this has its roots in an ancient battle between the devils, led by Reine Devilla, who wants to banish all love from Earth, and the angels, led by Queen Aphrodite, who wants to preserve it. So the queen picked three ordinary high school girls and gave them magical items to enable them to transform into their wedding-day alter egos. Unlike most magical girls, they transform in three stages—from school uniform to wedding dress or bridesmaid's outfit to sexy lightly armored battlesuits. (Why wedding dress, you ask? To build up the power of Love, *obviously*!) The series ended with the

world made safe for Love, but in 1997 our heroes returned in the four-part video series *WP DX*; they're enjoying a quiet vacation when a monster attacks Earth, and Aphrodite gives them back their powers to fight once more for love and truth. Tomita, who wrote the manga of *WP* for *Ciao* magazine, was also a writer on SAILOR MOON, and Tadano worked as a designer on the first two *SM* TV series.

WEISS KREUZ

1998. AKA: *White Cross; Night Hunters*. TV series, video. DIR: Kiyoshi Egami, Masami Obari. SCR: Isao Shizuoka, Shigeru Yanagawa, Sukehiro Tomita. DES: Tetsuya Yanasawa. ANI: Tetsuya Yanasawa. MUS: Weiss. PRD: Animate Film, TV Tokyo. 25 mins. x 25 eps. (TV), 25 mins. x 2 eps. (v), 25 mins. x 13 eps. (TV2).

Why *shouldn't* four pretty teenage male florists fight evil when the shop closes for the night? Our heroes hate the crime and murder stalking the big city and harming the innocent, so they roam the night streets offing as many of the bad guys as they can—and I do mean permanently; they may be florists, but they're no shrinking violets when it comes to pest control. Unlike the Knight Sabers (but like *Charlie's Angels*), they have an external authority—a mystery man known only as Persia. As the series progresses they find that more of the drug rings and terrorist factions they take out are connected to one hugely powerful family, pointing to a coldly planned conspiracy.

With a concept straight from BUBBLEGUM CRISIS and a cast out of SAINT SEIYA via GUNDAM W, *WK* was made to promote Weiss, a band manufactured from four young voice actors, purportedly based on an idea by their lead singer, Takehito Koyasu, and first serialized as a novel in *Animage*. A number of interesting *Doomwatch*-style SF concepts lurk in the plotlines (like the attempt to infest the water supply with flesh-eating bacteria), but relentless cuteness always wins out, and every episode has a downbeat ending

What's Michael?

designed to pluck at the heartstrings of the intended junior-high-school-girl audience. Giving one of the boys a Wolverine-style steel claw and making him a biker jock isn't enough to give the show real teeth; it loses out in the crime-fighter stakes to *BGC* and can't compete with ZETSUAI for angst. For sheer prettiness, though, the characters take some beating, and the series is fabulous eye-candy. Released in the U.S. under the title *Knight Hunters.*

Weiss Kreuz Glühen (aka *Knight Hunters Eternity,* 2002) was a second TV series, in which the boys find themselves at a mysterious academy, troubled by student suicides and violence in a similar setup seemingly inspired by *Challenge From the Future* (*DE). The series introduced two new pretty boys, Sena and Kyo, and radically different character designs by Toshimitsu Kobayashi, as an indirect result of an ongoing dispute with the original character designer Kyoko Tsuchiya. Three of the original *WK* voice actors also appeared together in GET BACKERS, leading to a boost among fans for the latter series among *WK* aficionados.

WE'RE MANGA ARTISTS: TOKIWA VILLA
1981. JPN: *Bokura Mangaka: Tokiwa So Monogatari.* AKA: *WMA: Tokiwa Villa Story.* TV special. DIR: Shinichi Suzuki, Kazumi Fukushima, Atsutoshi Umezawa. SCR: Masaki Tsuji, Kazuo Koike. DES: Shotaro Ishinomori. ANI: Takao Kasai. MUS: Nozomu Aoki. PRD: Toei, Aoi, TBS. 84 mins.
Possibly the single most influential address in the postwar history of Japanese comics, Tokiwa was the apartment complex where a group of stellar artists lived in 1953. Hiro Terada, Motoo Abiko and Hiroshi Fujimoto (the pair who worked as Fujio-Fujiko), Shotaro Ishinomori (then plain Ishimori), and Fujio Akatsuka shared the trials and tribulations of being struggling young artists and writers with no money and no luck with editors or girls, with a spirit of insane youthful enthusiasm that enabled them to survive the lean years and emerge as stars of the manga firmament. The Tokiwa building was demolished in 1981, prompting both this anime and NHK's rival live-action documentary *Tokiwa Villa of My Youth.* In allowing the manga characters to come to life for some sequences, the anime version was the greater success. The story was revived for Jun Ichikawa's live-action movie *Tokiwa: The Manga Apartment* (1996).

WET SUMMER DAYS *
2003. JPN: *Suika.* AKA: *Melon.* Video. DIR: Yasuhito Kikuchi. SCR: Mitsuhiro Yamada, Kazuhiro Ota. DES: Kazuhiro Ota. ANI: Shigeru Ikehata. MUS: Kamin. PRD: Studio A.P.P.P., Moon Rock, Circus. 30 mins. x 3 eps.
Tokiwa is a quiet seaside hamlet far from the city and the hometown of Sayaka Shirakawa, an artist's daughter going steady with a local boy. It's based on a dating sim game, hence the swift divergence of the story into tales of five girls who are so "different" that it takes different hats and hairstyles to remind you which is which. The storyline, however, takes on an element of doom and gloom—such as the rumor in the village that Sayaka's father paints corpses—in accordance with the Japanese tradition that holds that summertime is the best occasion for ghost stories, in order to keep the blood cold. Later episodes veer away from Sayaka to incorporate Akira, a student returning to the town for the summer vacation who discovers that his childhood friend Itsuki appears to have become a shrine maiden. A third man, Hiroshi, also encounters a local girl in the third episode, and once more what appears to be a simple tale of young love drifts into unexpected revelations and implications of tragedy. As with ONE: TRUE STORIES and several other anime of recent years, this title appears to exist in two incarnations back in Japan, both with and without the more explicit scenes. Ⓝ

WHAT'S MICHAEL?
1985. Video, TV series. DIR: Yuichi Higuchi, Katsumi Kosuga, Norio Yazawa, Kunitoshi Okajima, Hideki Hirojima, Satoshi Okada, Seiji Okuda. SCR: Masaaki Sakurai, Yoshio Urasawa, Koji Tanaka, Osamu Nakamura, Nobuaki Kishima, Mayumi Shimazaki, Tomoko Konparu, Megumi Sugiwara. DES: Norio Kabeshima, Katsuyoshi Kanemura. ANI: Norio Kabeshima. MUS: Makoto Kobayashi, Koji Makaino. PRD: Kitty Film, TV Tokyo. 56 mins. (v1), 60 mins. (v2), 25 mins. x 45 eps. (TV).
Michael is a fat orange cat who lives with a pair of well-meaning but very stupid humans who fondly imagine he is their pet. But Michael's own daily life is rich in all kinds of little incidents and upheavals—avoiding local bad cat Nyazilla, a monster against whom Michael knows he'll always come out worse, scrounging food from local stores, meeting up with his animal friends, and keeping the humans amused as best he can. And Michael also has a fantasy life even his fellow feline Garfield would envy, with cat corporations, cat nightclubs, and his own imitation of a dancing American megastar also called Michael. His adventures continued in 1988 with another video and a TV series. Based on the 1984 manga in *Comic Morning* by Makoto Kobayashi, itself the happy musings of an indulgent pet-owner rather than the more biting satire of I AM A CAT. *WM* was the first show to

begin on video and then transfer to TV, and it is a must for cat-lovers and fans of observational humor.

WHAT'S UP MECHADOC?

1984. JPN: *Yoroshiku Mechadoc*. TV series. DIR: Hidehito Ueda, Takaaki Ishiyama, Hiroyuki Tanaka, Masayuki Kojima, Shinya Sadamitsu. SCR: Kenji Terada, Hirohisa Soda, Takao Koyama, Mayori Sekijima. DES: Tatsunoko Anime Office, Ammonite. ANI: Hideyuki Motohashi, Chuichi Iguchi. MUS: Hirokazu Takahashi. PRD: Tatsunoko, Fuji TV. 25 mins. x 30 eps.

Jun Kazama is crazy about cars and loves to tune their engines to top performance; he can make even a standard manufacturer's model run above spec. With Kazumichi Nakamura and Kiyoshi Noro, he sets up a tuning shop called Mechadoc in Yokohama, helped by Kanzaki, the owner of the nearby Paddock teashop. Competing with a rival store owned by the scheming Wataru Hochi, they tune up biker gangs and befriend female car-nut Reiko Ono. Eventually Jun is so drawn into the world of custom cars that he races against rival mechanics' masterpieces—compare to the much later INITIAL D. Based on the 1982 *Shonen Jump* manga by Ryuji Tsugihara.

WHISPER OF THE HEART *

1995. JPN: *Mimi o Sumaseba*. AKA: *Prick Up Your Ears; If You Listen Closely/Carefully*. Movie. DIR: Yoshifumi Kondo. SCR: Hayao Miyazaki. DES: Yoshifumi Kondo, Satoshi Kuroda. ANI: Kitaro Kosaka. MUS: Yuji Nomi. PRD: Studio Ghibli. 111 mins.

Imaginative, intelligent 14-year-old Shizuku Tsukishima secretly longs to be a writer, reading anything she lays her hands on. Observing that the same name continually crops up on the borrower's lists of books she takes from both the school library and from the public library where her father works, she wonders who this Seiji Amasawa, who shares her taste in reading, might be. When they do finally meet, Seiji upsets her by criticizing her work, and

she storms off. Idly following a cat she sees getting off her train, she finds herself in a chic residential area. Wandering into an antique store, she befriends the shopkeeper (eventually revealed as Seiji's grandfather) and becomes intrigued by Baron, an elegantly dressed German cat-doll. Shizuku and Seiji learn that they share a love of music, and with his violin playing and her singing, they soon become closer.

Baron himself appears in Shizuku's dream and shows her a magical fantasy world, which Shizuku begins to turn into a story. Grandfather encourages her to continue writing, while reminiscing about his prewar youth in Germany, where he loved and lost the owner of Baron's lady-doll companion. But Seiji's future plans threaten their growing friendship—he is taking two months off school to have special violin tuition. If he shows promise, his father has agreed to let him go to Italy and study to become a professional musician. Meanwhile, their friendship and her writing project are distracting Shizuku from her schoolwork and may even mean she fails her exams.

A gentle, beautifully executed movie based on a manga by Aoi Hiiragi, which, like KIKI'S DELIVERY SERVICE, juxtaposes flights of fantasy (Shizuku's daydreams of journeys with Baron) with commonplace realities (Shizuku's "failure" in the eyes of her teachers). It revolves around the stresses of love and ambition, the need to lay the groundwork of both careers and relationships, and the difficulty of balancing it all when your head and heart are awhirl. It marries the lush production values common to Studio Ghibli productions with a new directorial vision that, sadly, developed no further. Director Kondo died, tragically just into his forties, soon after the film was released. A sequel, *Happy Times* (*Shiawase na Jikan*), exists in manga form, while the real-world location, Tama Hills, also got the Ghibli treatment in POMPOKO. It is implied that one of the stories that Shizuku ends up writing is the basis for another anime, THE CAT RETURNS.

WHISTLE!

2002. TV series. DIR: Hiroshi Fukutomi, Shin Misawa. SCR: Shunichi Yukimuro, Takashi Yamada, Nobuaki Kishima. DES: Tadami Komura. ANI: Tadami Komura, Masateru Kudo. MUS: Toshihiko Sahashi. PRD: Marvelous Entertainment, Animax. 24 mins. x 39 eps.

Sho Kazamatsuri wants to be a pro soccer player. He's not very talented, but that's a perfect qualification for the role of hero in a TV anime series about developing your own skills through effort and determination while learning to work as part of a team. Leaving a prestigious high school because he's unable to rise very far in its renowned soccer team, he enrolls at Sakura Junior High and finds that at last he can get to play, albeit for the underdogs. Based on the *Shonen Jump* manga by Daisuke Higuchi, this is a standard boys' sports series, the bread and butter of anime.

WHITE FANG

1982. JPN: *Shiroi Kiba White Fang Monogatari*. AKA: *White Fang Story*. TV special. DIR: Soji Yoshikawa, Takeyuki Yokoyama. SCR: Shiro Hagiwara. DES: Yoshikazu Yasuhiko. ANI: Yoshikazu Yasuhiko, Tsuneo Ninomiya. MUS: Hitoshi Komuro. PRD: Sunrise, TBS. 85 mins.

A hunter living in the forests of North America rears and trains a superb white wolf to become his faithful companion. Based on the classic novel by Jack London, author of CALL OF THE WILD, this was the first non-SF show from GUNDAM studio Sunrise.

WHITE WHALE OF MU, THE

1980. JPN: *Mu no Hakugei*. AKA: *Moby Dick 5*. TV series. DIR: Tetsuo Imazawa, Yasuo Yamakichi, Akinori Nagaoka, Minoru Okazaki, Satoshi Dezaki. SCR: Hiroyuki Hoshiyama, Kenichi Matsuzaki, Masaaki Sakurai, Hideo Takayashiki. DES: Shunzo Aoki. ANI: Takao Kasai. MUS: Kentaro Haneda. PRD: Toyko Movie Shinsha, Yomiuri TV (Nippon TV). 25 mins. x 26 eps.

The people of Atlantis are defeated by the people of Mu (see SUPER ATRAGON) and send their planet through a time slip to escape. Thirty thousand years later, at the end of the 20th century, the White Whale, last remnant of the forgotten civilization of Mu, awakes from her slumber, causing massive natural disasters all over Earth. The escaped Atlanteans have emerged from their time tunnel, and the flying cybernetic White Whale assembles a group of young children on Easter Island to protect the Earth. Ken (the leader), Mamoru (the cocky one), Rei (the token girl), Shin (the fat one), and Manabu (the bratty brain) serve Princess Madora, daughter of King La-Mu. This far-fetched mixture of **BATTLE OF THE PLANETS** and **BLUE SUBMARINE NO. SIX** was based on an original story by Motoo Fukuo and is infamous in early U.S. fandom for its naked winged cherub, who was quite obviously male. A transforming whale would also appear in **LADIUS**.

WICKED CITY *
1987. JPN: *Yoju Toshi*. AKA: *Demon Beast City; Supernatural Beast City; Monster City*. Video. DIR: Yoshiaki Kawajiri. SCR: Kisei Cho. DES: Yoshiaki Kawajiri, Masao Maruyama, Kazuo Oga. ANI: Kenichi Ishikawa. MUS: Takeshi Nakazawa, Hironobu Kagoshima. PRD: Madhouse. 80 mins.
A state of stalemate exists between our world and the next dimension, and while "Black Guard" agents from both sides play a game of espionage, representatives from the two worlds prepare to sign a treaty. Renzaburo Taki is an undercover human, forced to partner up with the sexy, deadly Makie. Charged with guarding the uncooperative and lecherous old ambassador Giuseppe Maiyart, the pair become attracted to each other, though relationships between a human and a denizen of the Dark Realm are most inadvisable. In the climactic final battle between good and evil they learn that they are vital to the future of both worlds, and the love they have developed is more than just coincidence.
Made for the theaters with a

relatively large budget, *WC* is vastly superior to the later straight-to-video **DEMON CITY SHINJUKU**, with which it is often confused, and indeed shares a writer, director, and studio. However, it still comes lumbered with risible *"Oh Taki!"/ "Oh, Makie!"* dialogue, perfunctory sex scenes, and a misogynistic obsession with Bad Girls From The Dark World. The final showdown in a church also throws in a contrived twist to wrap up the story, tearing vast holes in the preceding plot as it does so.
DARKSIDE BLUES–creator Hideyuki Kikuchi's original novel cleverly exploited the fantasies of bored businessmen. Taking the viewer from bar to office to airport to hotel, it walks through the scenery of a company rep's humdrum life, enlivening each familiar place with dangerous sex and vicarious violence. *WC* was the first film to show the distinctive style of **NINJA SCROLL**'s Kawajiri, whose trademark blue-red lighting is leavened here with artful fog effects and moody shadows. The first set piece says it all: a fight to the death beneath the wheels of a taxiing jumbo jet, with superfast fists making a virtue of the low animation cel count, an imitation shaky-cam effect right out of a Sam Raimi film, and superfast cutting to hide the joins, borrowed from Hong Kong action master Tsui Hark. Tsui would repay the compliment in 1993 when he produced a live-action version of *WC* in Hong Kong, featuring Leon Lai as Taki and Michele Reis as Makie.
Amid the dark palette and piano-wire tension, Kawajiri demonstrates a marvelously gothic sense of the unbreakable link between sex and death. The predatory nature of most sexual relationships, set out in Taki's opening encounter with a spider-woman whose vagina is lined with teeth, is contrasted in true Hammer-horror fashion with the purity of his relationship with Makie, whose inner self is affected but not changed by the sexual horrors she endures. For Makie, transformation and transcendence come when the deadly power of her fight-

ing skill is lifted to another level by motherhood; Death and the Madonna become one. **LNV**

WIDOW *
2004. JPN: *Mibojin: Numeriau Niku-yoku yo Midara ni Nureru Mitsuko*. AKA: *Widow: Slimy Lust and a Dirty Wet Honey Pot*. Video. DIR: Ahiru Koike. SCR: Sosuke Kokubunji. DES: KAZU. ANI: Ahiru Koike. MUS: N/C. PRD: Milky, Studio Jam. 30 mins. x 2 eps.
Some time after the death of his brother, Kaoru returns to Japan to help settle the estate. This requires him meeting his brother's widow Taeko for the first time. Kaoru soon discovers that his old flame Miyuki is now the tutor to Taeko's younger sister Chiyoko and that all the residents of the house have a history of sex games in a secret underground basement. As might be expected in an erotic anime such as this, it is not all that long before Kaoru is offering sexual condolences to his widowed sister-in-law, thereby exercising erotic anime's perennial obsessions with not-quite-incest and the use of bereavement as a means of sexual entrapment. **LNV**

WIFE COSPLAY CAFÉ
2004. JPN: *Hitozuma Cosplay Kissa*. Video. DIR: Hiroshi Shirasui. SCR: N/C. DES: Haruo Fuyuki. ANI: Haruo Fuyuki, PILGRIM. MUS: N/C. PRD: Atelier Kaguya, Milky, Aiko, J. Fox. 30 mins. x 2 eps.
Tomoya Asahina is the deputy manager of Noel, a café staffed by lonely housewives. He decides to lure in more customers by creating a new uniform, with a very high miniskirt and a low-cut top. His plan is greeted enthusiastically by the waitresses, who are soon "educating" Tomoya on the feelings and desires of older women, both in and out of their costumes. Based on a 2003 computer game by Atelier Kaguya—the *hitozuma* of the title literally refers to "someone else's wife," since in erotic movies these are invariably more fun than one's own. **LNV**

WIFE EATER *

2003. JPN: *Tsumamigui*. Video. DIR: Hiromi Yokoyama. SCR: Himajin Planning, Taifu Sekimachi. DES: Toshide Matsudate. ANI: N/C. MUS: N/C. PRD: Pink Pineapple, SOFTGARE. 30 mins. x 2 eps.

The work of Rumiko Takahashi has inspired many imitations, some of which do their inspiration little credit. MAISON IKKOKU's young widow in a rooming house has become something of a porno paradigm, here crashed into the "unexpected alien visitor" genre, with a dash of SLOW STEP in its little girl latching on to every passing adult to try and find a new family. To vary things a bit and avoid any unjustified claims of copyright infringement, it's an apartment complex, not a boarding house, and the landlord runs a sex shop from his room. The widow is shy Chiho, and the guy with a crush on her is Satoru. He has no idea how to win her heart, but sex with new tenant Kanae, an experienced married woman who knows what women want, will surely help him to his goal, in an erotic anime that spends much longer than usual setting up its prescribed sex scenes. An "episode 0" was released, with a preview of the first episode and some additional bonus footage. The title plays with puns and slang terms for transitory affairs and eating with one's fingers. Based on a computer game from Alice Soft. **ⓁⓃ**

WIFE WITH WIFE *

2005. JPN: *Tsuma Tsuma*. AKA: *Tsuma X Tsuma*. Video. DIR: Ao Tengen. SCR: Kazunari Kume. DES: Naoki. ANI: Naoki, Ao Tengen. MUS: N/C. PRD: Animac. 30 mins. x 2 eps.

In a setup seemingly ripped from the derivative world of Japanese TV, Kotaro inherits Sakura Market from his late father, only to discover that his small, independent grocery business is under assault from the grasping Kaneyu Corporation, which is run by his long-lost brother. Since this is an erotic anime, the plot soon veers off the competitive track into the grow-ing feelings between Kotaro and his stepmother, an "older woman" who was still significantly younger than her first husband. Meanwhile, Kotaro also finds out that service with a smile can lead to a different kind of servicing, when he offers to carry groceries home for lonely housewife Toko, and she repays him with sexual favors.

The second story is unrelated to the first, and features newlyweds Yosuke and Akira (Akira being a girl's name here), whose sex life gets off to a bumpy start thanks to the tiring process of moving house so soon after their wedding. But their union comes under even stronger pressure when Yosuke begins his new job as an assistant director and is almost immediately seduced by red-haired actress Atsuko. The first episode is based on the game *Tsuma X Tsuma* 3, while the second is based on the game *Tsuma X Tsuma* 1.5—note that as with GUN X SWORD and HUNTER X HUNTER, the "X" in the Japanese title is silent. The the art and animation of the series are above the usual par for CGI anime porn, and although these episodes are currently all there are, with two other *TXT* games still unadapted, other installments may follow. Not even the two episodes here have fully conclusive endings—in the first, the takeover attempt is unresolved and two characters remain untouched (with one's backstory untold as well); in the second, Atsuko remains determined to get Yosuke. **ⓁⓃⓋ**

WILD ARMS *

1999. TV series. DIR: Toshiaki Kawasaki. SCR: Aya Matsui, Hideki Mitsui. DES: Kanami Sekiguchi, Yasuo Miyazawa. ANI: Minoru Yamazawa, Kanami Sekiguchi. MUS: Miyuki Otani. PRD: B-Train, WOWOW. 25 mins. x 22 eps.

On the planet Far Gaia, Loretta, a dark and deadly Crest Sorceress who wields a powerful magic based on tarot cards (flavor of the month since ESCAFLOWNE and CARDCAPTORS) leads a team of strange talents. Shaian looks like a little boy, but he's really a 25-year-old sci-entist and a sharpshooter of no mean skill. His main aim is to get his grown-up body back. But he's not the only one around who conceals his age—team genius Jerusha is a cute pink bunnykin who won't see 5,000 again. Even cute little turquoise-haired Mirabelle is really a Noble Red Vampire under that sweet exterior. A "macaroni" Western that mixes cute fantasy and frontier adventure based on the PlayStation RPG, this doesn't have the same protagonists as the game; producer Sony decided to throw in a few little kids.

WILD CARDZ *

1997. JPN: *The Crown Knights: Jaja Uma Quartet*. AKA: *Crown Knights: Wild Horse Quartet*. Video. DIR: Yasushi Nagaoka. SCR: Hideki Sonoda, Hiromitsu Amano. DES: Noritaka Suzuki. ANI: Keisuke Watanabe. MUS: N/C. PRD: Animate Film. 25 mins. x 2 eps.

The story follows the four defenders of the Card Kingdom as they try to defend it from a series of game-themed aggressors such as battle mecha shaped like giant chessmen and oversize mahjong tiles. As usual, the four defenders are girls of high school age and uniform cuteness who possess supernatural powers. The two episodes released form one long battle sequence, giving the impression that they come from the middle of a much longer story that might as a whole possess some substance. Or it might not.

WILD 7 *

1994. Video. DIR: Kiyoshi Egami. SCR: Ginzo Choshiya. DES: Hisashi Hirai, Akira Takeuchi. ANI: Hisashi Hirai. MUS: Kazushi Umezu. PRD: Animate Film. 50 mins. x 2 eps.

A team of seven killers from Death Row, led by a reform school escapee, is equipped with motorcycles and a license to terminate with extreme prejudice, Police Captain Kusanami showing touching but wholly unjustified faith in their ability to discriminate between bad guys and innocent bystanders. Their first assignment, bringing in a gang of bank robbers,

Willow Town

turns into a running firefight through downtown Tokyo that piles taxpayers' bodies on the sidewalks. *W7: Biker Knights* followed in 1995. A shady politician and his crime-lord buddy decide to discredit our heroes even more by forming their own look-alike gang which will race through Tokyo and—here's the twist—kill innocent bystanders *deliberately*. Based on a 1969 manga by Mikiya Mochizuki, inspired by the *Dirty Dozen* (1967), and predating **Cyber City Oedo 808**, the anime version does its utmost to outgross **Mad Bull 34**, with which it also shares the same standard of writing and English dubbing—so bad it's almost good. *Wild 7 Another* (2002) was a TV version of the franchise, directed by Sumio Watanabe. The series also existed in a live-action variant, broadcast in 1972 (*DE). **ⓥ**

WILD STRIKER
2002. JPN: *Hungry Heart Wild Striker*. TV series. DIR: Satoshi Saga. SCR: Yoshiyuki Suga. DES: Kenichi Imaizumi. ANI: Tetsuro Aoki. MUS: Nobuyuki Nakamura. PRD: Animax, Fuji TV, Nippon Animation. 24 mins. x 52 eps.
Sixteen-year-old Kyosuke Kano is in the first year of high school. He quit soccer in junior high, but when he is inveigled into managing the female soccer team at his new high school, his love for the game rekindles and he starts to play again, eventually becoming one of the world's best strikers. Yoichi Takahashi, who wrote and drew the original man-

ga *Hungry Heart*, also wrote and drew the manga that became Japan's most famous soccer anime, **Captain Tsubasa**, and was formerly married to Akari Hibino, voice of the young Tsubasa. Broadcast in Latin America, Portugal, and the Philippines but as yet unshown in English, despite sponsorship from sports shoe maker Puma.

WILD SWANS, THE
1977. JPN: *Hakucho no Oji*. AKA: *Swan Princes*. Movie. DIR: Nobutaka Nishizawa, Yuji Endo. SCR: Tomoe Ryu. DES: Takashi Abe, Hideo Chiba. ANI: Takashi Abe. MUS: Akihiro Komori. PRD: Toei Animation. 62 mins.
A widowed king remarries, but his frequent visits to his six sons and daughter annoy his new bride. Since she's the daughter of a witch, she is in a position to solve the problem in an interesting way; her spell transforms the six brothers into swans. Only their sister, Elisa, escapes, and she must follow her brothers and find a way to break the spell and bring them home. Based on a dark story found in both the **Tales of Hans Christian Andersen** and **Grimms' Fairy Tales**.

WILLFUL IDOL
1990. JPN: *Kimama ni Idol*. Video. DIR: Junichi Sato. SCR: Koichi Yomogi. DES: Kenichi Koya. ANI: Seiji Kikuchi. MUS: Toshitaro. PRD: Tabac. 50 mins.
Three pretty girls want to make it big as pop stars, but it's tough on their way to the top. Based on a manga in *Comic Burger* by Kenichi Koya, *WI* was distinguished by a marketing gimmick that had the three lead voice actresses taking the stage for real in an early attempt at multimedia promotion. Compare to the earlier **Glorious Angels**, which didn't try to manufacture its own hype, or the later **Perfect Blue**, which documented what can happen when you do.

WILLOW TOWN
1993. JPN: *Tanoshii Willow Town*. AKA: *Happy Willow Town; Wind in the Willows*. TV series. DIR: Tameo Ogawa,

Masahito Sato, Yasuo Yamakichi, Shigeru Omachi, Yutaka Kagawa. SCR: Takao Koyama, Hideki Mitsui, Yoshimasa Takahashi, Yumi Kageyama, Toshiyuki Machida, Kenichi Yamada. DES: Toshiyasu Okada. ANI: N/C. MUS: N/C. PRD: Enoki Films, TV Tokyo. 25 mins. x 25 eps.
Kenneth Grahame's enchanting novel *The Wind in the Willows* (1908) is the basis for a series about the happy little world of the animals who live along the riverbank. Toad's boastful nature and the evil ferrets and weasels who live in the Wild Wood threaten everyone's quiet lives until the brave Ratty, Mole, Badger, and Toad band together to ensure that they can all live happily ever after. The series ends with them all saying their farewells before hibernating for the winter.

WIND: A BREATH OF HEART
2004. Video, TV series. DIR: Tsuneo Tominaga (v), Mitsuhiro Togo (TV). SCR: Asami Watanabe (v), Akiko Horii, Takamitsu Kono (TV). DES: Koji Watanabe (v), Shinichi Yoshino (TV). ANI: Koji Watanabe (v), N/C (TV). MUS: N/C (v), Tatsuya Murayama (TV). PRD: venet, KSS (v), Radix, AT-X (TV). 30 mins. x 3 eps. (v), 12 mins. x 13 eps. (TV).
Makoto Okano and his sister Hinata return to their hometown, a mysterious, remote place where everyone except him seems to have a magical power. They settle in for lessons with their smooth-tongued classmate Tsutomu and Makoto's childhood friend Kasumi, until the day that the sound of a harmonica draws Makoto to the roof of the school. There, he finds Minamo, his childhood sweetheart, in a romantic anime seemingly designed to marry the teen troubles of **Love Hina** to the muggle-headed adventures of **Alice Academy** and **Cromartie High**, which similarly featured "mundane" attendees in a place where everyone else was gifted. In such a glorification of the merely average, we can see elements of Japanese media's perennial obsession with klutzy ugly ducklings such as **Sailor Moon**. This anime exists in two

versions, which inexplicably appear to have entered production simultaneously. Since both are based on a gaming franchise created by "minori," the authors assume that different incarnations of the game were licensed separately—compare to similar simultaneous creation problems that have led to confusion with **NIGHT SHIFT NURSES.** The differing versions take their origins from different branches of the game's potential endings. One rendition, given away free with one of the games, presents the story from the point of view of one character. The video version condenses the entire plot, while the longest incarnation, the TV version, concentrates on just two endings available from the story. The original game featured a sequence of animation by Makoto Shinkai, creator of **VOICES OF A DISTANT STAR.**

WIND NAMED AMNESIA, A *

1990. JPN: *Kaze no Na wa Amnesia*. AKA: *The Wind's Name Was Amnesia; Wind of Amnesia*. Movie. DIR: Kazuo Yamazaki. SCR: Kazuo Yamazaki, Yoshiaki Kawajiri. DES: Satoru Nakamura, Morifumi Naka. ANI: Satoru Nakamura. MUS: Kazz Toyama, Hidenobu Takemoto. PRD: Madhouse. 80 mins.
In 1997, a mysterious wind wipes the minds of most of the human race. In a Montana research facility, crippled cyborg Johnny retains human memories; when he is saved from an attack by a bestial human, he names his rescuer Wataru ("drifter") and starts teaching him to talk. When Johnny dies, Wataru sets off to search for other survivors. In San Francisco he meets Sophia, who listens to his story and pointedly refuses to tell him hers. They wander across America until Sophia feels like telling Wataru the story behind the wind, 20 minutes before the end. Then there's a showdown with a law-enforcement robot that's been stalking Wataru since San Francisco, a perfunctory sex scene, and a finale that implies there's hope, even when the rest of the film has demonstrated that there isn't.

Wind of Amnesia has a fascinating "high concept," based on a novel by **DARKSIDE BLUES**–creator Hideyuki Kikuchi, but after the bold, broad strokes of the original idea (coincidentally similar to Thomas Calvert McClary's 1934 story *Rebirth*), it swiftly devolves into mundane cliché little better than **FIST OF THE NORTH STAR.** Transforming into an aimless road movie, it shifts gear into a quest to rescue a damsel in distress whose people still have the intelligence of chimps but have nonetheless managed to set up a society based around ritual human sacrifice. Wataru then teaches a former policeman how to be human again (by showing him how to use a shotgun), before making a brief stop at the obligatory "false paradise." In other words, despite being made for the movies as a stand-alone production, it still has the picaresque feel of a cut-up TV series, amateurishly crashing George R. Stewart's *Earth Abides* (1949) into Harlan Ellison's *A Boy and His Dog* (1969). The script suggests early on that the "wind" could be a psionic experiment gone wrong, or perhaps even rather stupid aliens who prefer to wipe humanity's mind as part of a preemptive strike, but there's no mystery here. Despite having the answers to everything, Sophia refuses to tell Wataru (or us) for a full 60 minutes, preferring instead to play devil's advocate with mind-boggling inconsistency, railing against the civilized charade of a computer-controlled city in the Nevada desert but vigorously defending the rights of savages who want to sacrifice virgins. Quite possibly, she is simply too embarrassed to tell the truth about an alien intervention plot device whose incoherence would not be matched until **GREEN LEGEND RAN.** The rest of the script is similarly shoddy—no thought is given as to why people wear clothes, considering that they have forgotten what they were for, and an "Eternal City" is supposedly built "at the beginning of the 21st century" when we've already been told that the film is set in 1999. There is a brief treatment of the idea that humanity might be better off this way, but it was done far more convincingly in **GREY: DIGITAL TARGET.** Artistically, this is a departure for the Madhouse studio, full of airy, wide-open spaces that are a far cry from the dark urban sprawls of **WICKED CITY.** 🔞🅥

WIND OF EBENBOURG *

2003. JPN: *Ebenbourg no Kaze*. Video. DIR: Yosei Morino. SCR: Yosei Morino. DES: N/C. ANI: N/C. MUS: Satoshi Shura. PRD: Amumo, Studio Ego. 30 mins. x 2 eps.
Ronsard is a small town in the Grand Duchy of Ebenbourg in exotic 19th-century Europe. Its new lord is Claude MacDonald, who was a poor student in even more exotic England until the former lord, Eric, was exiled. Claude finds out about his inheritance when the counselor for Ronsard, beautiful bespectacled Sophie, seeks him out. They are both virgins, and to seal the pact of his new inheritance they have to have sex. That done and an assassination attempt foiled, Claude learns that as well as inheriting Eric's title and mansion, he also inherits his maid. Mylene is quite willing to serve the new master exactly as she served the old one, but carries on seeing Eric off duty. The pair plot to kill the Grand Duke and implicate Claude so Eric can take power over all Ebenbourg. Meanwhile Claude starts to remember his past, when he made a childhood promise to another maid, Charlotte. *The Prisoner of Zenda* crashes into Japan's French maid fetish with predictably pretty and vacuous results. 🔞🅛🅝🅥

WINDARIA *

1986. JPN: *Windaria Senki Densetsu*. AKA: *Legend of Windaria Chronicle; Once Upon a Time*. Movie. DIR: Kunihiko Yuyama. SCR: Keisuke Fujikawa. DES: Mutsumi Inomata, Shigenori Kageyama, Shohei Kohara, Shigeru Katsumata, Toshihiko Sato. ANI: Mutsumi Inomata. MUS: Satoshi Kadokura. PRD: Kaname Pro. 101 mins.
After centuries of peace, the Kingdom of Paro (the Shadowlands) is under the reign of an arrogant king, Draco,

who sees himself as a mighty conqueror. The neighboring Kingdom of Isa (Lunaria), realizing that it would be the first target for any expansionist plans, tries to keep Paro peacefully under control by rationing the fresh water flowing through Isa's system of locks and canals. As war looms, their heirs Prince Jil (Roland) and Princess Aanasu (Veronica) love one another, but family loyalty makes their union impossible; she chooses death for both in a twist on *Romeo and Juliet*. A happily married farming couple, Izu (Alan) and Malin (Marie), are drawn into the conflict when the agents of both countries try to buy Izu's services. Seeing a chance for adventure and wealth working for Paro, he tries to sneak out of his home in the middle of the night, but Malin wakes and makes him promise to return to her even as she promises to wait for him, no matter what happens. His betrayal of his country and his marriage buys him the sophisticated toys he covets—elegant clothes, a fast bike, an upper-class girl who would never look at a mere farmer—but costs him dearly. His new masters try to have him killed; when he runs for home he finds it destroyed, his village devastated, most of his old friends dead. Only the ghost of his beautiful wife lingers to say a final farewell. Painfully, he learns that he can't buy his way back into the past he has betrayed. Presiding over the conflict between tradition and modernity, a huge "tree of life" symbolizes the enduring power of nature.

Based on Keisuke Fujikawa's novel, written at a time when Japan was beginning to realize how much it had already thrown away in its rush to modernize, this Asian romance has wider meaning for a world whose small economies and ecosystems are increasingly under threat. Katsumata's backgrounds are pure delight, and although the robots of Windaria are rarely mentioned among its many pleasures, this is partly because Kohara does such a good job of integrating them carefully into their faux-feudal societies. This genuinely thoughtful fantasy has

a good mix of action and reflection and a score whose sweeping grandeur reflects the beauty of the visuals.

WINDY TALES

2004. JPN: *Fujin Monogatari*. TV series. DIR: Junji Nishimura. SCR: Hiroaki Jinno. DES: Masatsugu Arakawa. ANI: Nobutoshi Ogura. MUS: Kenji Kawai. PRD: Production IG, Sky PerfecTV. 25 mins. x 13 eps.

After her new schoolteacher Taiki uses a miraculous control over the wind to save her life, schoolgirl Nao Ueshima resolves to travel to his home village to find out more. She discovers that Taiki's powers are nothing strange in his birthplace, since everyone in the remote mountain village is also a "wind handler" or *kazetsukai*. The anime is distinguished by a strangely angular art style reminiscent of **RYU THE STONE AGE BOY**. The anime was adapted from a screenplay that won the Best Anime Plan Grand Prix in 2002.

WINGMAN

1984. JPN: *Yume Senshi Wingman*. AKA: *Dream Warrior Wingman*. TV series. DIR: Tomoharu Katsumata, Yugo Serikawa, Masayuki Akehi, Hideo Watanabe, Hiroyuki Kadono, Shigeo Koshi. SCR: Akiyoshi Sakai, Sukehiro Tomita, Shigeru Yanagawa. DES: Yoshinori Kanemori. ANI: Masamune Ochiai. MUS: Keiichi Oku. PRD: Toei, TV Asahi. 25 mins. x 47 eps.

Some of the greatest battles take place not in the waking world, but in dreams. Warriors capable of transforming into powerful armored beings can intervene in our world to save those in danger. When superhero-obsessed teenager Kenta sees a girl literally fall out of the sky, he has no idea what's about to happen. Aoi has a "dream note," a kind of promissory paper: whatever you write on it will come true. Kenta writes that he wants to be the superhero Wingman, protecting everyone from the evil Rimel, ruler of the fourth-dimensional land of Powdream. And it happens—he's a superhero! But Rimel sends his minions into the real world in disguise

to steal the dream note and so prevent Wingman from foiling his plans. He also wants to break up the growing friendship between Kenta and Aoi. Based on the 1983 *Shonen Jump* manga by Masakazu Katsura, creator of **VIDEO GIRL AI** and **DNA²**.

WINGS OF HONNEAMISE *

1987. JPN: *Oneamisu no Tsubasa*. AKA: *Royal Space Force, Royal Space Force: A Wing of Honnêamise*. Movie. DIR: Hiroyuki Yamaga. SCR: Hiroyuki Yamaga, Hiroshi Onogi. DES: Yoshiyuki Sadamoto. ANI: Hideaki Anno, Yuji Moriyama, Fumio Iida, Yoshiyuki Sadamoto. MUS: Ryuichi Sakamoto, Yuji Nomi, Koji Ueno. PRD: Bandai, Gainax. 120 mins. Shiro Lhadatt is a dropout, a wannabe pilot who wasn't good enough to get into the navy air corps. Instead, he joins the only organization that will have him, a ragtag group of misfits called the Royal Space Force. Underfunded, undermotivated, and under extreme pressure, they race to get a man in space, but nobody believes it's possible. Nobody, that is, except for Shiro and his would-be girlfriend, a religious zealot called Lequinni. Space is waiting for humanity as a whole, but the project to reach it is the result of two nations' political and military agendas. Our hero joins up for all the wrong reasons but eventually realizes that he can turn the "fake dream" of his government's PR campaign into a real dream, and he becomes the first man in space. Despite the political skullduggery that follows, he refuses to let go of the hope that the reality just might redeem all the failure and sacrifice of history and give us another chance to soar.

One of anime's greatest successes and greatest failures, *WoH* is a peculiarly Japanese take on the U.S.-Soviet space race—an outsider's view of the gung ho ideals of *The Right Stuff*, moved to an alien world to emphasize the viewer's own alienation. Made by the young, fiendishly talented Gainax collective, it was so expensive and so badly received in Japan that it didn't break even until 1994. One of the shining examples of how cerebral and intelligent anime can be, it's far removed from the sex and violence that stuffs Western anime catalogues. It's a film that rewards repeat viewings if only for the meticulous design of every aspect of its world. The language, the names, the maps, and even the telegraph poles all scream to be recognized as triumphs of world-building almost unequalled elsewhere in science-fiction film. Even the minutiae of everyday life are knocked ever-so-slightly out of kilter, with little touches like triangular spoons, unidentifiable foods, and sunrise in the north.

Gainax, which later made **GUN-BUSTER** and **EVANGELION**, is made up of *true* science-fiction fans. Space is their religion; they fervently believe that it's humankind's destiny to leave the cradle of Earth and spread out among the stars. The film's closing moments are their manifesto: a march of progress from the earliest times until the climactic moment, a final leap into space as war rages around the launch-pad. *WoH* is a marvelous film, improved all the more by music from *Merry Christmas, Mr. Lawrence*'s Ryuichi Sakamoto and a fluent adaptation (though allegedly far removed from the original) from LA Hero, which was bought out during production and rebranded as the American arm of Manga Entertainment. A sequel, *Blue Uru,* has been promised for a decade but thus far has only materialized in the form of a Gainax video game. *WoH* also exists in an ill-fated 1987 dub version from Go East, under the title *Star Quest*—which rearranged some scenes, changed some names, and was reputedly so bad that it was hidden from sight after its poorly received LA premiere. Compare to the similarly unfortunate treatment suffered by **NAUSICAÄ** as *Warriors of the Wind.* ◐

WITCH HUNTER ROBIN *
2002. TV series. DIR: Shuko Murase, Yohei Miyahara, Kumiko Takahashi. SCR: Aya Yoshinaga, Shuko Murase, Toru Nozaki. DES: Kumiko Takahashi,

Wings of Honneamise

Hajime Sato, Michiaki Sato, Yoshinori Sayama, Shinji Aramaki, Toshihiro Nakashima. ANI: Hiromitsu Morishita, Iwao Teraoka, Toshihiro Nakashima. MUS: Taku Iwasaki. PRD: Bandai Visual, Sunrise. 24 mins. x 26 eps.
In present-day Japan, use of magic—called CRAFT—is an everyday occurrence. It's more about extrasensory perception and enhanced mental powers than the spells-and-potions variety of magic. Anyone using CRAFT for evil is branded a witch, likely to be hunted down by an official body, the STN (*Solomon Tokatsu Nindantai*—or Solomon Secret Action Group). But it goes even further; STN mastermind Solomon, based in Europe, tracks down individuals with witch genes in their ancestry and takes action against anyone with emerging latent abilities, visiting the sins of their forebears on later generations. Six skilled witch hunters form the operational arm of STN-Japan, out to protect the population from misuse of magic. The team's father figure, Takuma Zaizen, combines the roles of M and Q from the James Bond mythos, as the man who gets the hottest weapons for the team and the controller of their field activities. When one of the team is lost in action and a new member joins them, the team's equilibrium is upset. Gentle, reserved Robin Sena, Japanese but raised in an Italian convent, is

just fifteen and has an uncanny ability to control fire, but her relationships with her new teammates prove more difficult to manage, and the political undercurrents of their work create more conflict. A moody, grey-black color palette and restrained design create an atmosphere of repressed emotion—later episodes play up the literal witch hunts in a new form of cold war, marrying the paranoia of Arthur Miller's *The Crucible* (1953) to the paranoid conspiracies and switches in allegiance of *Alias* (2001). Compare to **HELLSING** and **CHRONO CRUSADE**, which similarly allegorized modern conflicts with myth and magic. The original concept is credited to Sunrise's house pseudonym Hajime Yadate and director Murase. A live-action version was supposedly planned by the American Sci-Fi channel, but dropped in 2005.

WITCHBLADE *
2006. TV series. DIR: Yoshimitsu Ohashi. SCR: Yasuko Kobayashi. DES: Kazuyuki Matsubara, Makoto Uno. ANI: N/C. MUS: Kazunori Miyake. PRD: Gonzo, CBC, TBS. 25 mins. x 26 eps.
Police officer Masane Amo suffers from amnesia in 22nd-century Japan, initially unaware that she is the latest in a long line of blade wielders—fierce warrior women who deploy the legendary "witchblade" in the service of justice. Based on the American comic

created by Marc Silvestri, which was set in the 1990s, this science-fiction spin-off uses the hereditary nature of the witchblade to establish a continuity sufficiently far from the original to allow a different story.

WITCHES

1992. JPN: *Nozomi Witches*. Video. DIR: Gisaburo Sugii. SCR: Gisaburo Sugii. DES: Kosuke Eguchi. ANI: Kosuke Eguchi. MUS: Hiroaki Serizawa. PRD: Tac. 45 mins. x 2 eps.

Ryutaro is an average high school student until the beautiful Nozomi takes an interest in him. Clever, a superb athlete, and fancied by every boy in class, she decides that Ryutaro has real potential, and her belief in him soon pushes him all the way to the Olympic boxing trials. But does she see him as anything but a sporting project? Based on the *Young Jump* manga by Toshio Nobe. **V**

WIZARD OF OZ, THE *

1984. JPN: *Oz no Maho Tsukai*. Movie, TV series. DIR: Masaru Tenkauchi, Masaharu Endo, Hiromitsu Morita. SCR: Akira Miyazaki, Takafumi Nagamine, Hiroshi Saito. DES: Shuichi Seki (TV), N/C (m). ANI: Shinya Takahashi, Minoru Kobata, Akio Sakai, Joji Yanase, Toshio Kaneko. MUS: K. S. Yoshimura (TV), Joe Hisaishi (m). PRD: Itoman, Panmedia, TV Tokyo. 25 mins. x 52 eps. (TV), 60 mins. (m, 78 mins. in the U.S.).

Brunette Kansas girl Dorothy Gale and her dog, Toto, are whisked away to the magical land of Oz, where she joins forces with a Tin Woodman, a Scarecrow, and a Cowardly Lion, following the Yellow Brick Road to the Emerald City, from whence she hopes to return home. Based on *The Wonderful Wizard of Oz* (1900), *The Marvelous Land of Oz* (1904), *Ozma of Oz* (1907), and *The Emerald City of Oz* (1910) from L. Frank Baum's 14-volume series, *WoO* was first broadcast abroad in 1984 but not shown in Japan until 1986. It was dropped by NHK and eventually screened on TV Tokyo, though the final two episodes were crammed into an hour-long special. On video, the

separate story arcs were condensed into 90 minutes each and released across four two-tape sets—thereby existing in feature-length chunks, often leading to their confusion with the Fumihiko Takayama anime movie version. The Takayama *Wizard of Oz* (1982, though not released in Japan until 1986) is a 60-minute movie (78 in the U.S.) with a blonde Dorothy. It keeps closer to the plot of the first book only, just like the famous live-action 1939 Judy Garland adaptation. Curiously, Akira Miyazaki is credited as a screenwriter in both blonde and brunette versions, which, despite the contradictory international release dates, must have begun production almost simultaneously! Both were seen in the U.S. before being shown in Japan.

A video of a Japanese Oz puppet show, *WoO: Dorothy's Adventure* (1991, *Dorothy no Daiboken*), is also filed in some anime sources. See also the sci-fi remake GALAXY ADVENTURES OF SPACE OZ, the distantly related OZ, and VIDEO PICTURE BOOK.

WIZARDRY

1990. Video. DIR: Shunsuke Shinohara. SCR: Masaru Terajima. DES: Satoshi Hirayama, Yasushi Hirayama. ANI: Yasushi Nagaoka. MUS: Soji Kawamura. PRD: TMS. 50 mins.

Evil wizard Werdna has stolen a powerful amulet from crazy King Trebor and constructed a ten-level dungeon right under the king's own castle, where he and the amulet are hiding. The king offers a reward for the recovery of his property, so hero Shin Garland takes up the challenge and joins a band of adventurers to descend into the wizard's lair. Based on the computer game of the same name designed by AnimEigo founder Robert Woodhead and Roe R. Adams III.

WOLF GUY

1992. Video. DIR: Naoyuki Yoshinaga. SCR: Toshikazu Fujii. DES: Osamu Tsuruyama. ANI: Atsushi Aono. MUS: Kenji Kawai. PRD: JC Staff. 30 mins. x 6 eps. Akira Inugami is infected with a ter-

rible poison. The only known antidote has an unfortunate side effect—it turns him into a werewolf. He opts for survival but then has to cope with his new desires and with the attention of the military, which is interested in using his affliction for its own purposes. Based on the series of novels by Kazumasa Hirai, who also wrote HARMAGEDON and episodes of 8TH MAN.

WOLF'S RAIN *

2003. TV series, video. DIR: Tensai Okamura. SCR: Keiko Nobumoto, Aya Yoshinaga, Dai Sato, Doko Machida, Miya Asakawa, Tensai Okamura. DES: Toshihiro Kawamoto, Shinji Aramaki, Shingo Takeba, Tomoaki Okada. ANI: Ayumi Karashima, Hiroki Kanno, Keiichi Sato, Kenji Mizuhata, Koichi Horikawa, Koji Osaka, Masahiro Koyama, Naoyuki Onda, Ryuji Tomioka, Satoshi Osawa, Shigeki Kuhara, Takahiro Omori, Tomoaki Kato, Toshihiro Kawamoto, Toshihiro Nakajima. MUS: Yoko Kanno. PRD: Bandai Visual, BONES, Fuji TV. 25 mins. x 26 eps. (TV), 30 mins. x 4 eps. (v).

In a postapocalyptic future, humans think wolves have been hunted to extinction; but some survive, and have learned to pass for human in a new twist on the werewolf legend (or indeed on POMPOKO). Lone wolf Kiba is on a quest to find the legendary Lunar Flowers, whose scent can lead the wolves to a paradise where they can live freely and without fear. Tsume is a renegade wolf who betrayed his pack and now lives as a human-form scavenger. Full of self-loathing, he first opposes Kiba but then joins him. Hige and Toboe are hardly more than cubs, but once they learn about Kiba's quest they join him. The pack meets Cheza, a girl engineered from plants, who can open the way to the paradise of the Lunar Flowers; but others are seeking the key for their own ends. Only after tragedy and suffering will the four young wolves attain paradise—which, in a typical anime twist, soon turns out to be more than originally expected, with the science-fictional future of the original setting also alluding to a secret past that links humans, wolves, and another, even more sinister foe. This, however, can stretch the viewer's patience a little—despite a relatively low running time, the series suffered from production delays and scheduling conflicts that led to its broadcast in several different slots, with hiatuses that led to four recap episodes. If the makers had spent less time recounting the story so far, they might have had more than enough space to finish the entire run within the requisite 26 episodes. Instead, the story wasn't finished on TV, but on video, numbered as if to comprise TV episodes 27-30. Yoko Kanno's musical team and the Warsaw Philharmonic do a beautiful job of supporting the atmosphere and character development. The art and design are moody, dark, and understated, making for a technically unadventurous but attractive series. Original creator Keiko Nobumoto, who similarly documented a loner's quest in the future world of **COWBOY BEBOP**, delegated story and art duties on the manga adaptation to Toshitsugu Iida. On a historical note, wolves were worshipped by northern Japan's indigenous Ainu racc, but were wiped out by 1905—the extinction of wolves regarded as a sign of the march of progress and the dismissal of the old gods, in the style of **PRINCESS MONONOKE**.

Wolf's Rain

© 2003-2004 BONES • KEIKO NOBUMOTO / BV

WONDERBEAT SCRAMBLE

1986. JPN: *Wonderbeat S.* TV series. DIR: Satoshi Dezaki, Seiji Arihara. SCR: Toshiaki Imaizumi, Kazumi Koide, Noboru Shiroyama, Hideo Takayashiki, Toshiyuki Tanabe, Yoshihisa Araki. DES: Setsuko Shibunnoichi, Keizo Shimizu, Yuichi Higuchi. ANI: Toshio Nitta. MUS: Ko Komemitsu. PRD: Mushi, Magic Bus, TBS. 25 mins. x 24 eps.

In the year 2121, Professor Sugida disappears during an experiment in medical miniaturization, for which he has been inserted within a patient's body. His son, Susumu, is allowed to join the White Pegasus team sent to rescue him and is miniaturized to board the mini-vessel Wonderbeat. The seven-man crew discovers that the professor, far from being dead, has been kidnapped by the alien creature Hieu as the first step in its quest for world domination. It's anime's homage to *Fantastic Voyage* (1966), or, if you'd rather, *Invasion of the Body Snatchers* (1956), seen from the inside out. Each episode finishes with a live-action mini medical lecture, from **ASTRO BOY**'s Osamu Tezuka, who was also the executive producer. Compare to the similar **MICROID S**.

WONDERFARM

Production company established in 1996, whose works include **COSPLAY COMPLEX**, **HAND MAID MAY**, and **SAINT BEAST**.

WONDERFUL GENIE FAMILY *

1969. JPN: *Hakushon Daimao.* AKA: *Bad King Haxion/Atchoo.* TV series. DIR: Hiroshi Sasakawa, Tsuneo Ninomiya. SCR: Junzo Toriumi. DES: Tatsuo Yoshida. ANI: Shigeru Yamamoto, Yukihiro Takahashi, Takashi Saijo. MUS: Shosuke Ishikawa. PRD: Tatsunoko, Fuji TV. 25 mins. x 52 eps.

In this modern-day parody of **ALADDIN AND THE WONDERFUL LAMP**, a jinni and his family can be summoned from their imprisoning bottle by a Sneeze (Dad), a Sniff (Mom), and a Yawn (the eternally tired daughter). Created by producer Tatsuo Yoshida, the series bears a strong resemblance to the original **COMET-SAN**, sharing with it an original inspiration in *I Dream of Jeannie* and *Bewitched* (see **BEWITCHED AGNÈS**) and a remake in the early years of the 21st century. Original director Hiroshi Sasakawa returned for *Akubi-chan* (*Yobarete Tobidete Akubi-Chan/ Call Her Up and Out She Flies: Akubi-chan*), a 26-part TV series on Kid's Station that was successful enough to generate a 13-part TV sequel in 2002. However, at the time of writing, only the original 1969 series has been broadcast in the U.S.

WOOF WOOF 47 RONIN

1963. JPN: *Wan Wan Chushingura.* AKA: *Woof Woof Chushingura; Doggie March.* Movie. DIR: Daisaku Shirakawa, Hiroshi Ikeda. SCR: Satoshi Iijima, Daisaku Shirakawa. DES: Seiichi Toriizuka. ANI: Akira Okuwara, Hayao Miyazaki. MUS: Urahito Watanabe. PRD: Toei. 81 mins.

Lock the puppy lives happily in the peaceful forest until outlaws Kira the tiger and Akamimi the fox murder his mother. Lock enlists Goro, an aging stray dog, to help him in his quest for revenge, and they assemble a band of dogs to bring justice against the killers where the law has failed. Based an idea by executive producer Osamu Tezuka, itself inspired by the kabuki play *Chushingura* (which exists in many forms, the earliest known dating from 1706), also known as *Treasury of Loyal Retainers* or *The 47 Ronin*. The original story dates from 1701, when Lord Asano of Ako Castle was provoked into drawing his sword and wounding his guest, the high-ranking samurai Kira. Asano was forced to commit suicide, but the castle steward Oishi assembled 46 loyal retainers, who murdered Kira, and then committed ritual suicide in 1703. The anime version is far simpler, dumping matters of etiquette and loyalty in favor of an archetypal quest for revenge, with only Oishi (Lock) and Kira surviving in any recognizable form. The final showdown in the snow, also present in the original, made the film ideal for its release just before Christmas. Compare to the similarly canine DOGTANIAN AND THE THREE MUS-KEHOUNDS. A young Hayao Miyazaki was one of the animators.

WORDS WORTH *

1999. Video. DIR: Kan Fukumoto. SCR: N/C. DES: Rin Shin. ANI: Rin Shin. MUS: N/C. PRD: Beam Entertainment, Green Bunny. 30 mins. x 5 eps.
The forces of light and darkness fight to obtain the scattered pieces of the Words Worth, a stone monolith with magical powers. This sensual fantasy epic was based on the pornographic computer game from Elf. As per usual, there is a prophecy about a legendary swordsman, ladies in diaphanous veils, and lots of shagging. **Ⓝ**

WORLD MASTERPIECE THEATER

After the success of Isao Takahata and Hayao Miyazaki's HEIDI, Nippon Animation began a long-term project to adapt numerous Western children's favorites into anime. Originally sponsored by the soft drink company Calpis, the *WMT* (*Sekai Meisaku Gekijou*) series began in 1975 with DOG OF FLANDERS. The Calpis sponsorship continued in the following years with FROM THE APENNINES TO THE ANDES, RASCAL RAC-COON, and NOBODY'S GIRL. Without Cal-pis, but firmly established as Nippon Animation's yearly cash cow by 1979 (compare to Tatsunoko's TIME BOKAN, Sunrise's BRAVE SAGA and GUNDAM, or Tokyo Movie Shinsha's LUPIN III), the *WMT* series continued with ANNE OF GREEN GABLES, TOM SAWYER, SWISS FAMILY ROBINSON, SOUTHERN RAINBOW, TREA-SURES OF THE SNOW, KATRI THE MILKMAID, A LITTLE PRINCESS, POLLYANNA, LITTLE WOMEN, LITTLE LORD FAUNTLEROY, PETER PAN AND WENDY, DADDY LONG-LEGS, THE SOUND OF MUSIC, THE BUSHBABY, LITTLE MEN, TICO OF THE SEVEN SEA, and ROMEO'S BLUE SKY. By 1996, however, the franchise was showing signs of increasing strain—LASSIE was taken off the air and replaced with *Remi: A Child without a Home*, a remake of NOBODY'S BOY that deviated so far from the original as to betray the entire raison d'etre of the franchise. The *WMT* never recovered and was laid to rest after 21 years, though the earlier shows were soon given a new lease on life through video. Though the English-language market has been dominated in succes-sive waves by the likes of ROBOTECH, AKIRA, UROTSUKIDOJI, and POKÉMON, anime in Europe is far more likely to be known through the high-quality children's entertainment for which the *WMT* became justly famous. By the early 21st century, most if not all of the *WMT* anime had also been released in 90-minute movie edits on DVD.

WORLD OF AIKA-CHAN, THE

1993. JPN: *Aika-chan no Chikyu*. Video. DIR: Kusa Sugiyama. SCR: Kusa Sugiya-ma. DES: Shunji Saita. ANI: Shunji Saita. MUS: N/C. PRD: Tech. 33 mins.
The author of the manga *Secrets of the World* was only 12 years old, and she died only days after completing it. Aika Tsubota's parents published her environmentally themed story in her memory, and this one-shot anime was the eventual result, sponsored in part by a charity opposing the pollution of the oceans. In 1995, *Secrets of the World* itself was animated as a two-part video series under the auspices of the Japa-nese Department of the Environment.

WORLD OF AKIRA TORIYAMA, THE

1990. JPN: *Pink Mizudorobo Amedoro-bo; Kennosuke-sama*. AKA: *Pink Thieves Water and Rain; Kennosuke-sama*. Movie. DIR: Toyoo Ashida, Minoru Oka-zaki. SCR: Aya Matsui. DES: Akira Tori-yama. ANI: Toyoo Ashida, Katsuyoshi Nakatsuru. MUS: Takeshi Kazuchi. PRD: Toei. 31 mins. x 2 eps.
Two minor works from DRAGON BALL–creator Toriyama, shown on their own dedicated double bill under this umbrella title. *Pink*, the first story, is set in a town where no rain has fallen for three years. The corrupt Silver Compa-ny has monopolized the water supply and charges high prices even for drink-ing water. Bath-loving girl Pink starts stealing water from Silver Company's tankers, soon teaming up with spiky-haired guy Cobalt Blue to rob from the water-rich and give to the poor. The second story, *Kennosuke-sama*, is a squashed-down cartoon comedy about a family of old-fashioned samurai living in modern-day Tokyo whose young son has to head out for an important date.

WORLD OF NARUE *

2003. JPN: *Narue no Sekai*. TV series. DIR: Toyoo Ashida, Hiromitsu Morita. SCR: Yu Sugitani. DES: Takaaki Hirayama. ANI: Mika Takahashi, Takaaki Hirayama. MUS: Takayuki Negishi. PRD: BeSTACK, Imagica, Media Factory, Pony Canyon, Toshiba Digital Frontier. 25 mins. x 12 eps.
Kazuto Iizuka is an ordinary Japanese 14-year-old until his new classmate Narue Nanase bludgeons a puppy with a bat, claiming that it is an alien invad-er about to eat him. In fact, Narue is not lying. Although she has been raised on Earth, she is the daughter of a man who works for the Galactic Fed-eration. Kazuto thereby gains the alien girlfriend common to so many anime since URUSEI YATSURA, who is not mere-ly a love interest, but also a defender of the Earth—see SAIKANO, MAHOROMATIC, and … well, most of the anime on the

shelves of your local anime store. Later episodes tick further boxes of the modern harem show, since cute cyborg girls are soon also hanging around with Kazuto, while time-dilation effects à la **GUNBUSTER** ensure that Narue's older sister is actually younger than her, and also comes to stay. There are several superficial references in the story to classic science-fiction novels, particularly Robert Heinlein's *Door into Summer* (1957) and A.E. van Vogt's *World of Null-A* (1948) to which the title is a punning reference.

WORLD OF POWER AND WOMEN, THE

1932. JPN: *Chikara to Onna no Yo no Naka*. AKA: *In a World of Power and Women*. Movie. DIR: Kenzo Masaoka. SCR: Tadao Ikeda. DES: Tadao Ikeda. ANI: Mitsuyo Seo, Seiichi Harada, Saburo Yamamoto. MUS: Choki Imazawa. PRD: Shochiku, Masaoka Eiga. ca. 10 mins. A nameless husband and father of four lives in fear of his wife, a statuesque beauty who towers above him. One night, she hears him talking in his sleep, either dreaming or reminiscing about an affair with a typist at his place of work. The angry wife turns up at the company on the pretext of delivering lunch for her husband and loses her temper when she sees him flirting with the typist. The husband helpfully suggests that the women settle their differences with a boxing match. The typist overcomes her opponent with tickling, but the victory goes to the wife, in anime's first "talkie." Despite a 1932 production date, the movie did not receive its premiere until April the following year.

WOUNDED MAN

1986. JPN: *Kizuoibito*. Video. DIR: Satoshi Dezaki, Takao Takeuchi. SCR: Tetsuaki Imaizumi, Kazuo Koike. DES: Keizo Shimizu. ANI: Keizo Shimizu. MUS: Noriaki Yamanaka. PRD: Toei, Magic Bus. 30 mins. x 5 eps. TV reporter Yuko Soka visits gold-rush Brazil in order to interview Keisuke Ibaragi, aka Rio Baraki, the quarterback of the football team. After predictably becoming lovers, the pair go in search of an Amazon treasure in the company of Peggy, a shipbuilder. The girls eventually meet with death for the crime of being eye candy in a macho anime—this one based on a manga by the same team of Kazuo Koike and Ryoichi Ikegami that produced **CRYING FREEMAN** and **SANCTUARY**. Keisuke discovers that his mother, Natsuko, Yuko, and Peggy were killed by the mysterious secret group GPX. Boiling with revenge, he finally confronts the two men responsible in a showdown on a sinking aircraft carrier. **LNV**

WOW! MR. MASARU!

1998. JPN: *Sexy Commando Gaiden! Wow!, Masaru-san*. AKA: *Sexy Commando Side Story!, Wow! Mr. Masaru*. TV series. DIR: Akitaro Daichi. SCR: Kyosuke Usuta. DES: Toshihide Masudate. ANI: Toshihide Masudate. MUS: Harukichi Yamamoto. PRD: M-BAS, TBS. 10 mins. x 48 eps. Teenager Masaru is the top fighter at his school in a number of martial arts—karate, judo, boxing, and more. But he wants to get even better. He goes off into the mountains for three months and returns as the "Sexy Commando." His new special technique is to stun opponents with weird fighting poses, then attack before they can gather their wits. Based on the 1995 *Shonen Jump* manga by Kyosuke Usuta, these shorts were serialized as part of the *Wonderful* variety program. **V**

WOWOW

Sometimes rendered as "World Wide Watching." A subscription satellite broadcaster formed in competition with NHK's satellite services in 1991, WOWOW soon became the home of many foreign movies and import television, including *The Simpsons* and *South Park*. The channel was also host to some of the more controversial anime of the 1990s—**COWBOY BEBOP** may have been shown on TV Tokyo, but its missing episodes were only restored on WOWOW. Other representative works for the channel include **PARANOIA AGENT** and **ERGO PROXY**.

X: THE MOVIE *

1996. JPN: *X: 1999*. Movie. DIR: Rintaro.
SCR: Nanase Okawa, Asami Watanabe.
DES: Nobuteru Yuki. ANI: Nobuteru Yuki.
MUS: Yasuaki Shimizu, X-Japan. PRD:
Madhouse. 98 mins. (m), 25 mins. (v),
25 mins. x 24 eps. (TV).
Two groups of psychic warriors,
known as the Seven Seals of the Earth
Dragon and the Seven Harbingers
of the Heaven Dragon, fight to save
the world or destroy it. The battle is
fought in modern Tokyo but draws on
landmarks of the city's historic and
spiritual past as both shields for Earth
and levers to trigger its destruction.
Subaru and Seishiro (characters from
CLAMP's earlier TOKYO BABYLON)
fight on opposing sides and end up by
destroying each other without resolving the struggle. Kamui, a psychic of
enormous power, witnesses the fight
and is so devastated that he flees
Tokyo. But running can't save him; it
is his destiny to join one side or the
other and decide the fate of Earth. He
finally returns to Tokyo to avenge the
death of his mother, but to protect his
friends Fuma and Kotori (whom he
has loved since childhood), he refuses
to take sides in the decisive battle. But
Fate has decided otherwise. Fuma is
Kamui's opposite number, the balance
to his powers in the scales of destiny.
When Fuma is seduced by the Earth
Dragon's powers and kills his own
sister, Kotori, Kamui finally joins the
other side. The two friends must fight

each other to decide if the world survives or ends.

Based on the manga in *Asuka*
magazine from the CLAMP collective,
X was preceded by lots of hype and a
25-minute music video made with the
rock group X-Japan, suitably titled
X2. But the amount that has to be cut
from a huge, unfinished saga to make
it into a coherent feature-length script
can destroy the subtlety of a story and
alienate fans of the original. Faced
with compressing the massive melodrama without upsetting its fans, director
Rintaro opted for style and emotion
over clarity and substance. The look
and mood of the original are there,
just don't expect it to make much
sense in terms of plot. The "1999" was
dropped from the title for its English-
language release since it didn't reach
video until 2000. Yoshiaki Kawajiri's *X*
TV series followed in 2001, preceded
by an "episode zero" released on video, which included teasers of the show
to come, but also footage that was not
re-used in the TV series proper. Put
into production when the direction of
the manga storyline was clearer, and
taking advantage of the longer running time afforded by TV, the series
revisits the story of the movie, but with
greater opportunities for character
development.

XABUNGLE

1982. JPN: *Sento Mecha Xabungle*. AKA:
Battle Mecha Xabungle; The Bungler.
TV series, movie. DIR: Yoshiyuki Tomi-
no, Toshifumi Takizawa, Osamu Sekita,
Akira Suzuki, Yasuhiro Imagawa. SCR:
Tsunehisa Ito, Soji Yoshikawa. DES:
Kunio Okawara, Yutaka Izubuchi. ANI:
Tomonori Kogawa, Akehiro Kaneyama.
MUS: Koji Makaino. PRD: Sunrise, TV
Asahi. 25 mins. x 50 eps. (TV), 86
mins. (m).
On planet Zola, the purebred Innocents live inside a sealed dome, unable
to survive in the inhospitable environment. The Civilian underclass, who live
out in the wilderness, regard the Innocents' rocket launches as "ascensions
of light" and do not question their
assigned roles as rockmen (bluestone
miners), freighters (traders), and sand-
rats (desert-dwellers). Civilian Jiron
Amos believes his rockman father was
murdered and steals the new Walker
Machine Xabungle, quarrelling all the
way with the pretty land-ship captain
Elche. He sets out on the land-ship
Iron Gear to learn the truth about his
father's death, but the whole planet
has another truth to learn. For generations all Zolans have believed that they
were descended from colonists from
the planet Earth, but they never left
the homeworld—Zola *is* the Earth, devastated by centuries of exploitation.

A more jocular robot show than its
contemporaries, *Xabungle* (i.e., "The
Bungler") featured an inept hero and
giant robot battles often played for
laughs, set against a background that
mixes parts of GREY and NAUSICAÄ with

Westerns—homages extend as far as having a Clint Eastwood clone among the characters, along with a look-alike of Sunrise's all-time great antihero Char Aznable. A deliberate attempt to break the serious mold of Sunrise robot shows (by Tomino, the man whose name remains synonymous with GUNDAM), it also predates PATLABOR in its depiction of robots as everyday working tools. The story reappeared in 1983 in a feature-length edit, *Xabungle Graffiti*, screened alongside the two DOUGRAM short movies. The Wild West imagery would return years later in TRIGUN and EAT-MAN.

X: The Movie

XANADU: LEGEND OF DRAGONSLAYER

1988. JPN: *Xanadu Dragonslayer Densetsu*. Video. DIR: Atsutoshi Umezawa. SCR: Haruya Yamazaki. DES: Koichi Arai. ANI: Koichi Arai. MUS: Seiji Yokoyama. PRD: Nippon Falcom, Toei. 50 mins.

The evil magician Reichswar has killed the King to gain possession of a magic crystal; now he means to use its power to rule the whole of Xanadu. Then the widowed Queen Rieru is kidnapped. One brave young warrior, wielding the magic blade Dragonslayer, goes to her rescue. It's all based on the role-playing game *Xanadu*, as if you couldn't guess.

XEBEC

Formed in 1995 by former employees of Tatsunoko, Xebec functions as a subsidiary of its parent company, contributing animation to shows including ZOIDS, PILOT CANDIDATE, AND LOVE HINA. Prominent staffers include Takashi Sudo, Nobuyoshi Habara, Akio Takami, and Makoto Uno. The company takes its name from a three-masted Mediterranean pirate ship.

XENOSAGA: THE ANIMATION

2005. TV series. DIR: Shigeyasu Yamauchi. SCR: Yuichiro Takeda. DES: Nobuteru Yuki, Hiroyuki Okawa. ANI: Masayuki Sato. MUS: Kosuke Yamashita. PRD: Happinet, Toei, TV Asahi. 25 mins. x 12 eps.

Four thousand years after humanity abandoned the Earth, a human vessel carrying a KOS-MOS battle android is attacked by alien enemies. In an inversion of the perils of BLACK MAGIC M-66, KOS-MOS turns out to be a model that resembles a pretty girl, which self-activates in order to save the life of its creator Shion. The ship destroyed, Shion and her creation are thrust into the middle of the ongoing war between humanity and the Gnosis aliens in an anime based on the PlayStation game of the same name—in fact, it is *so* based on the game that the cast often seem to assume that the viewer only requires summaries of plot details from the PlayStation version, often making it impenetrable to viewers who do not already know what is going to happen.

XPRESS TRAIN *

2003. JPN: *Chikan Densha*. AKA: *Groper Train; Lovely Train*. Video. DIR: Taifu Suginami. SCR: Yuta Takahashi. DES: Takashi Itani. ANI: Yuji Kamizaki. MUS: Yoshi. PRD: YOUC, Digital Works (Vanilla Series). 28 mins. x 2 eps.

Salaryman Kazuo loses his job after he is wrongfully accused of groping a woman on the subway. The actual culprit is an old lecher who calls himself the "God of Groping," who takes the down-at-heels Kazuo on as his 500th apprentice. Soon Kazuo is learning the way of successful groping—and picking up handy tips like avoiding women in groups, women on mobile phones, or women who look like they might put up a fight—all targets which the talented Kazuo goes after with relish. However, both gropers are in for a surprise when they run into Reiko, a woman who actually enjoys being felt up by strangers. Making a comedy out of one of Japan's most prevalent commuting annoyances, this entry in the VANILLA SERIES even manages to turn tragedy into porn, as the dying old groper persuades one of his victims to administer hand relief to the only part of his body that still has any blood in it. **LN**

XTRA CREDIT *

2002. JPN: *Reiju Gakuen*. AKA: *Domination Academy*. Video. DIR: Shigeru Kohama. SCR: Rokurota Makabe. DES: Yoshihito Kato. ANI: Motokazu Murakami. MUS: Hiroaki Sano, Takeshi Nishizawa. PRD: Discovery. 30 mins. x 2 eps.

Keiko is a young, attractive school teacher, sorry, professor at an elite academy, who secretly enjoys being the pin-up of all the boys. Feeling under threat by the arrival of the equally attractive new teacher Miyuki, Keiko arranges for her rival to be "taught" her true place in the order of things, which involves molestation, rape, and assault, as per usual. An entry in the **Discovery Series**, not to be confused with the similarly titled **Sextra Credit**. ●●●

X-TREME TEAM

1998. JPN: *Totsugeki! Pappara Tai*. AKA: *Attack! Sprinkle Squad*. TV series. DIR: Kenichi Maejima. SCR: Natsuki Matsuzawa. DES: Yukari Kobayashi. ANI: N/C. MUS: N/C. PRD: Media Works, TV Tokyo. 25 mins. x 26 eps.

This spoof of anime's teens-save-Earth genre starts with rumors of an imminent alien invasion. The world mobilizes to establish the United Earth Defense Forces, the most powerful of whom are, of course, in Japan. When the promised alien invasion doesn't arrive, however, the SWAT teams resort to mercenary activities, fighting crime, chasing terrorists, and even delivering valuables as security guards. They also organize "friendly" competitions with rival defense teams. A tongue-in-cheek comedy about what might have happened if, say, the cast of **Evangelion** was all ready for the Angels, but the Angels forgot to come.

XXXHOLIC

2005. Movie, TV series. DIR: Tsutomu Mizushima. SCR: Ageha Okawa, Michiko Yokote. DES: Kazuchika Kise. ANI: N/C. MUS: N/C. PRD: Production IG, TBS. 60 mins. (m), 60 mins. x ?? eps. (TV).

In anime's answer to *The Sixth Sense* (1999), Kimihiro Watanuki has the ability to see and interact with ghosts. He is approached by a woman called Yuko, who offers to cure him of his affliction, but only if he agrees to work for her. Based on the manga by CLAMP, which began running in *Young* magazine in 2003. After the movie *XXXholic: A Midsummer Night's Dream* (*Manatsu no Yoru no Yume*), which shared a double bill and several plot elements with CLAMP's **Tsubasa Chronicle**, a TV series followed in 2006.

Y

YABUKI, KIMIO

1934– . Born in Fukushima Prefecture, Yabuki graduated from Tokyo National University of Fine Arts and Music in 1958 and found work with Toei's Kyoto studios as an assistant director in live-action. Transferring to Toei Animation in 1962, his anime directorial debut was on KEN THE WOLF BOY, and his breakthrough work was on PUSS IN BOOTS. He moved to Toei's advertising division in 1970, officially leaving anime behind, although he subsequently went freelance in 1973, returning to the anime world to work on such titles as CALIMERO.

YABUSHITA, TAIJI

1903–1986. Born in Osaka, Yabushita graduated from the photography department of Tokyo School of Arts (now Tokyo National University of Fine Arts and Music) in 1925. He worked briefly for Shochiku before leaving to make films for Monbusho, the Ministry of Education. Joining Nippon Doga, he made *A Baby Rabbit's Tale* (1952, *Ko-usagi Monogatari*) and *Kappa Kawataro* (1955). With Nippon Doga's sale to Toei, Yabushita became the director of production for Toei Animation. After the 13-minute *Lost Kitten* (1957, *Koneko no Rakugaki*), he oversaw the flowering of Toei's animated features, including PANDA AND THE MAGIC SERPENT (1958), MAGIC BOY (1959), and JOURNEY TO THE WEST (1960).

YADAMON

1992. TV series. DIR: Kiyoshi Harada, Masaya Mizutani, Yoshiko Sasaki, Koichi Takada. SCR: Minami Okii. DES: SUEZEN. ANI: Masahiko Murata, Hideaki Sakamoto, Kenichi Shimizu. MUS: Koji Makaino. PRD: Group Tac, NHK. 8 mins. x 170 eps.

Yadamon is a little witch who lives with Jan and his parents in the near future. Maria, Jan's mother, is a biologist and spends her time performing experiments. Yadamon is an inquisitive girl, and, like most magical friends (see DORAEMON), she frequently gets Jan into trouble. Like all good magical girls, she has a cute little magical pet, Taimon, who can not only talk but also stop time for a short while.

The series aired every weekday; the 21-week first run accounted for 110 episodes. Starting out on NHK, the second series aired on NHK's Educational Channel in 1993. For the linguistically curious, *iya-damon* is a cute way for little girls to say "no," which might be useful for the heroine of YOIKO.

YADATE, HAJIME

Also sometimes Hajime Yatate. A house pseudonym employed by Sunrise in order to assign some or all of the intellectual property in a new concept to the studio itself. Yadate's name appears on most of the company's giant robot shows.

YAGAMI'S FAMILY TROUBLES

1990. JPN: *Yagami-kun no Katei no Jijo*. AKA: *Yagami's Family Circumstances; Affairs at the House of Yagami*. Video. DIR: Shinya Sadamitsu. SCR: N/C. DES: Kei Kusunoki, Kazuya Yokose. ANI: Kazuya Yokose. MUS: Ichiro Nitta. PRD: IG Tatsunoko, Kitty Film. 30 mins. x 3 eps., 55 mins.

Yagami's mother looks as if she's just 16 and is as cute as anything; despite finding this embarrassing, he can't help lusting after her in a combination of Oedipus *and* Lolita complexes! All his classmates, and his teacher, and the local delinquent, are in love with his mother; as well as fighting each other over who loves her most, they get together to plot ways of getting rid of their common enemy, Yagami's father. Dad has problems of his own as the love object of a secretary in his office, but once his coworker discovers he has such a pretty "young" wife, she turns her affections instead to Yagami. No wonder the poor boy's confused. Things could hardly get worse when a new student who looks almost exactly like Yagami's mother joins his class—and it's a boy. The 1986 *Shonen Sunday* manga by OGRE SLAYER–creator Kei Kusunoki pushed the envelope of family values, but the spin-off video is a low-budget effort aimed at exploiting the manga fan base. The series was repackaged into an edited one-shot *Decisions* (*Yorinuki*) the same year.

YAIBA

1993. JPN: *Kenyu Densetsu Yaiba*. AKA: *Legend of Brave Swordsman Yaiba*. TV series. DIR: Kunihiko Yuyama, Norihiko Sudo, Sadao Suzuki, Hiroshi Yoshida, Osamu Sekita, Akitaro Daichi, Kazuya Murata, Yasuhiro Matsumura, Eiichi Sato. SCR: Kenji Terada, Shikichi Ohashi, Isao Shizuoka. DES: Tokuhiro Matsubara, Katsuyoshi Kanemura. ANI: Tokuhiro Matsubara, Tadashi Hirota, Kazuto Nakazawa. MUS: Kohei Tanaka. PRD: Pastel, TV Tokyo. 25 mins. x 52 eps.

Leaving the distant isle where he and his father studied samurai skills, Yaiba Kurogane comes home with his animal friends—a tiger and a vulture. He stays with his father's old adversary, Raizo, and Raizo's cute daughter, Sayaka, enrolling in her high school. Here he has to face school kendo champion Takeshi Onimaru, possessor of a demonic sword. Yaiba goes into the mountains to learn from ancient sword master Musashi (see YOUNG MIYAMOTO MUSASHI) and gets not just new skills but also a magic sword of his own, the legendary Sword of the Thunder God. All he has to do is stay true to the samurai spirit within him and collect seven magic spheres to enhance his sword's power, and then he can vanquish all evil. But he and Takeshi aren't the only people with conquest in mind. Princess Moon, the Thunder God's old adversary, is out to conquer Earth, and Yaiba and Takeshi must forget their quarrel and unite to save the world. Adapted from the first successful manga by CONAN THE BOY DETECTIVE–creator Gosho Aoyama, *Yaiba* has many similarities with its smarter younger brother, mixing action, drama, and humor.

YAMAGA, HIROYUKI

1962– . Born in Niigata Prefecture, Yamaga was an obsessive fan whose love of film found new directions at Osaka University of Arts. After making a live-action wine commercial, he made the inaugural movie for the 1981 Daicon III SF convention with fellow students Hideaki Anno and Takami Akai. Yamaga was only 24 years old when work began on WINGS OF HONNEAMISE (1987), which he was to direct, before becoming the president of the Gainax animation company formed in expectation of profits. Despite acclaimed directorial work on GUNBUSTER (1988), Yamaga soon disappeared behind the scenes as Gainax involved itself in computer games. He was technically "president-at-large" for 14 years, only returning actively to direction with MAHOROMATIC (2001).

YAMAMOTO, EIICHI

1939– . Born in Kyoto Prefecture, he attended several schools in different parts of Japan before leaving high school to work at a pharmaceutical company. He quit in 1958 to pursue an animation career, joining Mushi Production in 1961, and soon gaining directorial credits on ASTRO BOY and KIMBA THE WHITE LION. He also directed TRAGEDY OF BELLADONNA (1973) before leaving the troubled Mushi to work on STAR BLAZERS. Yamamoto left anime entirely in the late 1970s to work on the NTV series *Wonderful World Travel*, in the course of which he spent much time filming abroad. He returned to anime with OSHIN (1984) and a number of video works, including THE SENSUALIST, which he scripted. He also worked in an advisory capacity on UROTSUKIDOJI, and published an account of his days at Mushi.

YAMAMOTO, SANAE

1898–1981. Pseudonym of Zenjiro Yamamoto. Born in Chiba Prefecture, he began working part-time for Seitaro Kitayama's animation company Kitayama Eiga, while still a student of Japanese art. After the Great Kanto Earthquake and Kitayama's subsequent relocation to Osaka, Yamamoto stayed in Tokyo to found Yamamoto Manga Productions. His *Mountain Where Old Women Are Abandoned* (1923, *Obasuteyama*) was the earliest anime extant until the discovery of Seitaro Kitayama's *Taro the Guardsman* (1918)—the Naoki Matsumoto discovery of 2005 has yet to be satisfactorily dated. He labored for some time on *Jar* (not dated, *Tsubo*), an instructional film for Monbusho, the Ministry of Education, and moved into political advertisements and propaganda in the 1930s. His most notable propaganda work was *Defeat of the Spies* (1942, *Spy Gekimetsu*). Post–World War II, he assembled surviving animators in the Tokyo area to form Nippon Doga, a company eventually merged into Toei to form Toei Animation. Yamamoto consequently played an executive role in Japan's early features PANDA AND THE MAGIC SERPENT, MAGIC BOY, and *Alakazam the Great* (see JOURNEY TO THE WEST).

YAMAMOTO YOHKO *

1995. JPN: *Sore Yuke! Uchu Senkan Yamamoto Yoko*. AKA: *Go! Space Cruiser Yoko Yamamoto, Starship Girl Yamamoto Yohko*. Video. DIR: Akiyuki Shinbo. SCR: Yuji Kawahara, Mayori Sekijima, Masashi Kubota. DES: Kashiro Akaishi, Kazuto Nakazawa (v) Akio Watanabe (TV). ANI: Hiroyuki Morinobu. MUS: N/C. PRD: JC Staff, Tee-Up, TV Osaka. 30 mins. x 7 eps. (v), 25 mins. x 26 eps. (TV).

In A.D. 2990, the human race has been split into two spacefaring empires, Terra and Ness. With Terra on a losing streak in the ritualized "war games," scientist Rosen creates a time machine, sending emissaries back to 20th-century Earth to recruit new warriors by testing them with familiar-looking arcade games. He finds schoolgirl Yoko and convinces her to time-travel after school to the battlefront, where she and several other girls from her school must adapt their arcade game skills to real combat. This is yet another spin on *The Last Starfighter* (see also BATTLE ATHLETES), with video-game style duels in advanced machines that look like a cross between a Formula One racing car and a goldfish. The alleged "girl power" is presented, in the tradition of GUNBUSTER, for the titillation of a male audience, but there are a few fun visual tricks, like cockpits that disappear in battle, leaving the pilot apparently floating in space. Based on a novel by Taku Atsushi, also adapted as an audio drama. Episode four is renumbered "episode zero," and reintroduces the characters for the second "season." This episode "zero" was never released in the U.S. *YY* returned as a TV series in 1999.

YAMAMURA, KOJI

1964– . Born in Aichi Prefecture, he began a career making corporate videos after graduating from university in 1987. He had already made several short cartoons in his student days and moonlighted on several anime productions, including a stint as a character designer on the NHK educational program *Playing in English* (*Eigo de Asobo*). He also worked as an illustrator on a very simple show designed to teach Japan's *kana* syllabary to very young viewers. He made his name, however, with several 8mm short films, one of which, **MOUNT HEAD**, was nominated for a Best Short Animation Oscar. Yamamura's accolade would have made him one of the most famous figures in the anime world, were it not for **SPIRITED AWAY**'s Oscar win for Best Feature Animation the same year, news of which largely swamped his own quiet achievement.

YAMATO TAKERU

1994. JPN: *Yamato Takeru*. TV series. DIR: Hideharu Iuchi, Shinichi Masaki, Nobuhiro Kondo, Jiro Saito, Takeshi Yoshimoto. SCR: Masaharu Amiya, Kenichi Araki. DES: Koichi Ohata. ANI: Takahiro Kishida, Moriyasu Taniguchi, Akira Kasahara. MUS: Takahiro Kishida. PRD: Nippon Animation, TBS. 25 mins. x 39 eps.
On planet Yamato, a twin birth is a bad omen for the throne, so when two brothers are born to the queen, one of them must be killed. But Takeru is saved through the intervention of the gods and survives to return and claim the throne (and the beautiful princess) as fate has decreed. For this sci-fi clash of robotic armor indistinguishable from "magic," creator Masami

Yuki took his inspiration from one of Japan's oldest stories. The original Yamato Takeru's epic expedition was recorded in two of Japan's oldest historical texts, the *Kojiki* (A.D. 712) and *Nihon Shoki* (A.D. 720), and he and Princess Ototachibana are jointly credited as founders of many real shrines. Ancient sources sometimes embroider the bare cloth of supposed history— Takeru is alleged to have defeated Kumaso warriors by disguising himself as a woman and getting them drunk, and he was to have saved the plains from Ainu arsonists by cutting away the burning brush with his sword. The weapon, known thenceforth as *Kusanagi* ("Grass-Cutter"), became one of the Imperial Treasures of Japan, lending its name to several anime protagonists, most notably Motoko Kusanagi in **GHOST IN THE SHELL**.

The final two episodes were not broadcast but released on video in 1997. The beginning of a fourth season that never materialized, they are set three years after the original, with Takeru now 16 years old, having to defend his homeworld from samurai-style robot invaders from planet Izumo in a "flying magic fortress." See also **LITTLE PRINCE AND THE EIGHT-HEADED DRAGON** and the live-action version of the legend released in the West as *Orochi the Eight-Headed Dragon*.

YAMAZAKI, KAZUO

1949– . Born in Tokyo, Yamazaki dropped out of high school to work in anime, gaining credits on shows for Madhouse, Sunrise, and Studio Deen, among others. His directorial debut came with an episode of the live/animation hybrid show **BORN FREE** in 1976. Later works have included the remake of **TIGER MASK**, **URUSEI YATSURA**, and **MAISON IKKOKU**. More recent years have seen him move away from directing into storyboarding on shows such as **ARGENTO SOMA**.

YAMAZAKI KING OF SCHOOL

1997. JPN: *Gakko O Yamazaki*. AKA: *School King Yamazaki*. TV series. DIR:

Tsuneo Tominaga. SCR: Kazumi Koide, Taku Ichikawa. DES: Hiroshi Ikeda. ANI: Shinichi Suzuki. MUS: N/C. PRD: Bandai, TV Tokyo. 25 mins. x 33 eps.
A bratty six-year-old declares himself the "King of School." In a rip-off of the earlier **CRAYON SHIN-CHAN**, this adaptation of Manabu Kashimoto's manga from *Corocoro Comic* features kleptomania, disobedience, and fighting.

YAMAZAKI, OSAMU

1962– . Born in Kumamoto Prefecture, Yamazaki began his animation career at Kaname Productions in 1981, before going freelance in 1985, just in time to cash in on the boom in production caused by the arrival of video. After a directorial debut on **YOTODEN** (1987), he also worked as director on **TAKEGAMI** (1990) and **TOKYO REVELATION** (1995).

YANBO, NINBO AND TONBO

1995. JPN: *Yanbo Ninbo Tonbo*. TV series. DIR: Seitaro Hara, Tatsuo Okazaki, Shigeo Koshi, Mamoru Kobe. SCR: Satoshi Nakamura. DES: Takumi Izawa. ANI: Katsumi Hashimoto, Hiroshi Kagawa, Kazuhiko Udagawa. MUS: N/C. PRD: Image K, NHK2. 25 mins. x 39 eps.
An old 1950s NHK radio drama featuring the three titular monkey brothers, this anime updates the story for the '90s audience of the original broadcasters' new satellite channel. The brothers try some crow soup, start a fire on the mountain, and race the king of the Pig People—like kids do.

YANKI: RIDE LIKE THE WIND

1989. JPN: *Yanki Reppu Tai*. AKA: *Yanki Wind Gang*. Video. DIR: Tetsuro Imazawa. SCR: Ryunosuke Ono, Yasushi Ishikura. DES: Masahide Hashimoto. ANI: Hideki Kakinuma. MUS: Tetsuro Kashibuchi. PRD: Toei. 50 mins. x 6 eps.
Impossibly tough and hairsprayed biker boys and girls fight turf wars in the streets, with much revving of motors and "you killed my buddy, prepare to die" dialogue. This lackluster latecomer to the genre typified by **BOMBER BIKERS OF SHONAN** was based on the *Shonen Magazine* manga by Masahide

Hashimoto, whose hero was *so* tough that he transferred schools 20 times. Only a Japanese tough guy would continue to go at all! **LV**

YASUHIKO, YOSHIKAZU

1947– . Born in Hokkaido, he dropped out of Hirosaki University midway through a degree in Western history in order to go to Tokyo and become an animator at Mushi Production. His early anime work included stints on WANDERING SUN and the second series of MOOMINS. With the demise of Mushi Pro, he was one of the early defectors to what would become Sunrise, ideally placing him to work as a director and character designer on that studio's output, most notably as a defining character designer in the GUNDAM and DIRTY PAIR series. His other works in anime include CRUSHER JOE and GIANT GORG, and he has also contributed to anime adaptations of his manga work, including ARION and VENUS WARS. Also known as "YAS," the name with which he signs his artwork.

YASUJI'S PORNORAMA

1971. JPN: *Yasuji no Pornorama Yachimae!* AKA: *Yasuji's Pornorama: How About That!* Movie. DIR: Takamitsu Mitsunori. SCR: Yoshiaki Yoshida. DES: Yasuji Tanioka. ANI: Michiru Suzuki. MUS: Kiyoshi Hashijo. PRD: TV Tokyo. 101 mins.
Three incidents in the life of Busuo ("Fatso"), the lecherous hero of Yasuji Tanioka's anarchic 1970 manga *Yasuji's Course on Being an Utter Brat* (*Yasuji no Metameta Gaki Michi Koza*). Though produced by TV Tokyo, these cartoon erotica were "too hot for television" and screened instead in theaters. With the failure of CLEOPATRA: QUEEN OF SEX the previous year, anime pornography would disappear for a generation after this, until straight-to-video releases made LOLITA ANIME possible.

YAT BUDGET! SPACE TOURS

1996. JPN: *YAT Anshin! Uchu Ryoko.* TV series. DIR: Hitoshi Nanba, Takuya Sato, Tsuneo Kobayashi, Kazuhiro

Sasaki. SCR: Keiko Hagiwara, Ryo Motohira, Mineo Hayashi, Yutaka Hirata. DES: Hiroka Kudo. ANI: Hiroka Kudo. MUS: Kenji Kawai. PRD: Tac, NHKEP. 25 mins. x 75 eps.
The Yamamoto Anshin Travel Company's latest luxury space tour hits an unexpected setback when the ship warps into an unknown part of space, ruled by a race of fishlike humanoids called the Gannon, who don't like their visitors. "Luxury" is a misnomer; the ship is a pile of junk, the captain is fat and grumpy, and, with the exception of the stewardess—his daughter Katsura—and the boy who's crazy about her, most of the crew are robots or aliens, and all of them are weird. Beset by pretty shark-boys out for their blood, with restless passengers, and the normally quiet Katsura ready to bash someone with her monkey wrench, how will our gang of misfits get their passengers home? To make matters worse, they've got a stowaway—squirrel-girl Marron, who can turn herself into a little pink ball but doesn't seem to have many other useful survival skills. This cute, colorful slapstick SF show, created by Shinji Nishikawa, was a departure for NHK's educational division. Something the anime industry *itself* should have learned from was a stroboscopic sequence in the final episode, which produced fainting and convulsions in some viewers in March 1997. Nine months later, a similar sequence in POKÉMON would make international headlines.

YAWARA! *

1989. JPN: *Yawara! The Gentle Judo Girl.* AKA: *A Fashionable Judo Girl.* TV series, movie, TV special. DIR: Hiroko Tokita, Katsuhisa Yamada, Akio Sakai, Junichi Sakata. SCR: Toshiki Inoue, Yoshiyuki Suga. DES: Yoshinori Kanemori. ANI: Kunihiko Sakurai, Hirotsugu Yamazaki. MUS: Eiji Mori. PRD: Kitty Film, Yomiuri TV. 25 mins. x 124 eps. (TV), 60 mins. (m), 90 mins. (TVm).
Teenage judo genius Yawara Inokuma (who shares the surname of the gold medalist from the 1960 Tokyo Olym-

pics) wants to get to the Barcelona Olympics and fulfill her grandfather Jigoro's dream of making her a judo champion under his coaching. But she also wants a life of her own outside of training schedules and competitions—her best friend, the plain Fujiko, also strives hard to be a top-class sportswoman. Yawara attracts two suitors, playboy Kasamatsuri and young sports reporter Matsuda. With them come rivals to create anime love polygons—Matsuda is also desired by the buxom photographer Kuniko, while rich-bitch judoist Sayaka sees herself as the perfect companion to Kazamatsuri. To make matters even more complicated, Sayaka's trainer is Yawara's own estranged father, Kojiro—determined that his daughter is toughened by a truly worthy opponent.

Based on the 1986 manga in *Big Comics Spirits* by MASTER KEATON–creator Naoki Urasawa, *Yawara* is one of the better successors to AIM FOR THE ACE, always ready to lay sports aside for more human-interest drama. Her love for her crusty old grandfather is equal to her determination to go to school, have fun with her friends, and maybe even fall in love; this is the main cause of conflict in both manga and anime. The first season ends, in true sports-anime style, with Yawara's defeat of her Soviet rival, Tereshkova, as *glasnost* takes hold. The series was a hit with more than just the female audience. Life imitated art as it drew to a close with Tokita's movie *Wiggle Your Hips* (1992, *Soreyuke Koshinuke Kids*), shown on a double bill with the RANMA ½ feature *Nihao My Concubine*. As the anime *Yawara* went off to the Barcelona Olympics in 1992, 16-year-old real-life judoist Ryoko Tamura won a silver medal at the actual Barcelona games and was immediately christened "Yawara-chan" by the Japanese media. Four years later, the series was revived for a feature-length TV special, Morio Asaka's *Yawara: Only You* (*Y: Zutto Kimi no Koto ga . . .*), in which Yawara defeats Sayaka in Atlanta and faces another of her father's protégés in the finals, the

French Marceau. The real-life Tamura dutifully obliged by winning another silver at the real-life Atlanta Olympics. Four more years later, Tamura finally won gold in Sydney, wearing the fictional Yawara's trademark yellow ribbon in her hair. For other judo-related struggles, see SANSHIRO SUGATA.

YEARLING, THE

1983. JPN: *Koshika Monogatari*. AKA: *Little Deer Story*. TV series. DIR: Masaaki Osumi. SCR: Shunichi Yukimuro, Eiichi Tachi, Michiru Umadori, Soji Yoshikawa. DES: Shuichi Seki. ANI: Shuichi Seki. MUS: Koichi Sugiyama. PRD: MK Production, NHK. 25 mins. x 52 eps.
Based on the book by Marjorie Kinnan Rawlings about an orphaned fawn and the 12-year-old boy who finds it and rears it. Jody lives in grinding poverty on an isolated homestead in the Florida swamps in 1807. As he grows toward manhood and the fawn grows into an adult deer, Jody struggles with the difficulties of keeping a relationship going with a wild thing while still respecting its own nature. *The Yearling* was Osumi's last anime directing job—he left to work in the theater.

YESTERDAY ONCE MORE

1997. JPN: *Dosokai Y.O.M.* AKA: *Same Window Club: Y.O.M.* Video. DIR: Kan Fukumoto. SCR: Miyuki Takahashi. DES: Shinichi Takagi. ANI: Shinichi Takagi. MUS: N/C. PRD: Pink Pineapple, KSS. 30 mins. x 4 eps.
Meeting for a reunion after a long time apart, the former members of a school tennis club discover new, forbidden pleasures in each other's company and agree to meet again, to catch up on old times, of course. Based on the erotic computer game from Fairy Tale, in the style of END OF SUMMER.

YIN-YANG MASTER

2003. JPN: *Onmyoji: Yoen Emaki*. AKA: *Yin-Yang Master: Scroll of Passionate Phantoms; Yin-Yang Mistress*. Video. DIR: Kazuhiko Yagami. SCR: Rokurota Makabe. DES: N/C. ANI: N/C. MUS: Salad. PRD: Milky, T-Rex,

Museum Pictures. 30 mins. x 2 eps.
In the Taisho period of the early 20th century (see ARISA), Japan is drifting inexorably toward war, and dark evils stalk the streets of Tokyo. Baffled detective Hiromasa Miyamoto decides to seek supernatural help by visiting the Master of Yin and Yang (or should that be Mistress?), Abe no Seimei, a voluptuous sorceress who has the power to command and control the nymphlike goddesses who rule the four directions of the compass. Then everybody's clothes come off and they have sex. Not to be confused with the medieval supernatural TV series *The Yin-Yang Master* (*DE), the movie adaptations of which would have been in Japanese video stores at the same time as this erotic anime was released. Based on a computer game. ●Ⓝ❤

YIN-YANG WAR

2004. JPN: *Onmyo Taisenki*. TV series. DIR: Masakazu Hishida. SCR: Junko Okazaki. DES: Michio Fukuda. ANI: Ayako Kurata. MUS: Yoko Fukushima. PRD: NAS, Sunrise, TV Tokyo. 25 mins. x 52 eps.
Riku Tachibana is raised by his grandfather, a strange old man who teaches him innumerable hand positions and signals in an impenetrable code. It gets so that this form of sign language comes as second nature to Riku, much to his classmates' amusement, until the day that he discovers they have a purpose. Grandfather is a sorcerer, who has secretly taught Riku the movements necessary to summon magical powers. Now all Riku needs to do is work out which sign creates which sorcery—and of course, save the world, while combating a number of other kids who use devices and signals to summon their own monsters, in the manner of DIGIMON.

YOIKO

1998. AKA: *Pretty Girl, Pretty Child*. TV series. DIR: Takahiro Omori, Jun Matsumoto, Kiyotaka Matsumoto, Kenichi Takeshita. SCR: Sukehiro Tomita, Shikichi Ohashi, Shigeru Yanagawa. DES:

Yugo Ishikawa. ANI: N/C. MUS: Shigeru Chiba. PRD: Studio Pierrot, TBS. 25 mins. x 20 eps.
The agenda of this late-night series is hinted at by the title's wordplay. Kazahana Ezumi is just a little girl at elementary school, but her body is almost that of a grown woman. This gets her into all kinds of problematic situations that a little girl her age isn't equipped to handle. Same old same-old (see CREAM LEMON) gets new names, faces, and clothes. Based on Yugo Ishikawa's *Big Spirits* manga, this anime incongruously mixes childish schoolroom gags with prurient nudity. Ⓝ

YOKOHAMA SHOPPING LOG

1998. JPN: *Yokohama Kaidashi Kiko*. AKA: *Going Shopping in Yokohama*. Video. DIR: Takashi Anno. SCR: Takashi Anno. DES: Atsushi Yamagata. ANI: Atsushi Yamagata. MUS: Gontiti. PRD: Asiado. 29 mins. x 2 eps.
This is either a sweet tale of a young girl's everyday life in a quiet suburb or a mold-breaking SF adventure in which an android searches for meaning in a world plagued by global warming. Alpha Hasseno is a humanoid robot girl who lives in the countryside of a future Japan, near what used to be Yokohama. Though Yokohama today is a big coastal city partly built on reclaimed marshland, in this future much of Japan's urban infrastructure has been destroyed as global warming has put much of the world underwater. Her area is safe for the moment, but storms and floods are a constant threat. She runs a coffee shop, Café Alpha, in the absence of her owner, but she doesn't know where he is or when he will return. She's happy to wait, meanwhile serving coffee to the local characters. But in the course of her daily life and her shopping trip into Yokohama city—a trip that shows us how her world differs from ours—she meets other people, even another robot, and starts to wonder about her own life and purpose. The arrival of a parcel containing her creator's diary adds to the mystery. Based on the

Yoma: Curse of the Undead

manga by Hitoshi Ashinano in *Comic Afternoon* magazine from 1994 onward.

YOKOHAMA THUGS

1993. JPN: *Yokohama Bakurettai*. Video. DIR: Mineo Goto, Masamune Ochiai. SCR: Shunsuke Amemura. DES: Satoshi Kuzumoto. ANI: N/C. MUS: N/C. PRD: Toei. 50 mins. x 4 eps.
It's all gags and fighting as gangster Tsunematsu Narita (the "biggest idiot in Yokohama") causes havoc in the neighborhood with his two henchmen. Based on the *Shonen Champion* manga by Satoshi Kuzumoto. ⓥ

YOKOHAMA'S FAMOUS KATAYAMA

1992. JPN: *Yokohama Meibutsu Otoko Katayamagumi*. AKA: *Yokohama's Famous Male Katayama Gang*. Video. DIR: Yoshinori Nakamura, Osamu Sekita. SCR: Hideo Nanba. DES: Masafumi Yamamoto. ANI: Masafumi Yamamoto. MUS: Quarter Moon. PRD: JC Staff, Nippon Eizo. 50 mins. x 2 eps.
Motorcycle gangsters with "a comical touch," as Hiromi Katayama, leader of the Yokohama biker gang Crazy Babies, tries to proclaim a one-month moratorium on violence while he trains new recruits, though his Tokyo rival, the

Mad Emperor, has other ideas. Based on the manga in *Shonen Magazine* by Akira Yazawa. Compare to **BOMBER BIKERS OF SHONAN**.

YOKOYAMA, MITSUTERU

1934–2004. Born in Kobe, he left high school and worked for four months in a bank before quitting to become a manga artist. He is one of the most influential manga artists of the postwar era, fully deserving of consideration alongside Osamu Tezuka and Shotaro Ishinomori, although his role specifically in anime is largely limited to that of the creator of a couple of important titles. With **GIGANTOR**, he defined many of the tropes and traditions that would lead to Japan's giant robot anime; with **LITTLE WITCH SALLY**, he established much of what is now taken for granted in the "magical girl" tradition. His other works include **BABEL II**, and a manga adaptation of *The Water Margin*, which was used as the basis for the TV series of the same name (*DE).

YOMA: CURSE OF THE UNDEAD *

1988. JPN: *Yoma*. AKA: *Blood Reign; Curse of the Undead*. Video. DIR:

Takashi Anno. SCR: Noboru Aikawa. DES: Matsuri Okuda. ANI: Matsuri Okuda. MUS: Hiroya Watanabe. PRD: Animate Film, JC Staff. 40 mins. x 2 eps.
In medieval Japan, the constant battles between rival warlords have left the land ravaged and prey to evil; the spirit world is ever-present. When the great warlord Shingen Takeda dies, one of his ninja, Maro, tries to escape from the clan, and his best friend, Hikage, is sent to hunt him down. He comes to a village where people seem to have no memory of their earlier lives, and he falls in love with Aya, a woman he meets there; but he learns that it's really just a fattening ground for people who don't want to live because of past sadness. They are kept in a state of happy forgetfulness while being held as sacrificial food for a demonic giant spider that has drawn Maro into its coils. When he destroys the god and breaks the spell, his beloved Aya remembers her past sorrows and kills herself. The second part of the story, *Maro's Evil Fang*, released in 1989, reveals that the spider god was only part of a huge conspiracy to allow the Demon Kings of the Land and Sea to unite as one and unleash all the devils in the world on mankind. Through a ninja girl named Aya, who looks exactly like his dead love, and the ghost of Maro's beloved Kotone, Hikage learns that only by killing his friend can he prevent this evil, but Maro offers him the chance to become a Lord of Hell. After a final bloody battle, it seems that evil has been defeated; but on the road, Aya and Hikage take a baby from the arms of a dead woman and see that it looks exactly like Maro. Is evil simply reborn again and again? Based on an original story by Kei Kusunoki, creator of **OGRE SLAYER** and **YAGAMI'S FAMILY TROUBLES**, this is an elegant and chilling story, much subtler than the blockbuster **UROTSUKIDOJI**, with which it shares the rebirth-of-evil theory. ⓥ

YOSHI

A pseudonym credited with almost all of the musical accompaniments to the erotic Vanilla Series, thereby inadvertently becoming one of the most prolific composers in anime.

YOSHIDA, TATSUO

1932–1977. Born in Kyoto, Yoshida grew up in the war years, and found work in 1945 as an illustrator for newspapers including the *Kyoto Shinbun.* He subsequently moved into manga creation, and was one of the early innovators who realized the cross-promotional possibilities of television, founding the Tatsunoko studio in 1962 with his brothers Kenji and Toyohiro (aka Ippei Kuri). His output included Space Ace, Hutch the Honeybee, and the Time Bokan series, although Tatsunoko is probably best known in the west for Battle of the Planets and Speed Racer.

YOSHIMOTO, KINJI

?– . Animator and illustrator whose work has included character design on La Blue Girl, mechanical design on Riding Bean, and several collaborations with Satoshi Urushihara, most notably Legend of Lemnear and Plastic Little.

YOTODEN *

1987. JPN: Sengoku Kitan Yotoden. AKA: Civil War Chronicle of the Magic Blades; Wrath of the Ninja. Video. DIR: Osamu Yamazaki. SCR: Noboru Aikawa. DES: Kenichi Onuki, Junichi Watanabe. ANI: Kenichi Onuki. MUS: Seiji Hano. PRD: MTV, JC Staff. 40 mins. x 3 eps.
In 1582, demons possess the warlord Nobunaga Oda, acting through his adviser Ranmaru Mori. The only weapons that can fight the demons are three magical weapons—a sword, a pike, and a dagger—each in the possession of a different ninja clan. The Kasami clan holds the dagger, and when the demons wipe out the rest of her family, teenage Ayame assumes the masculine name Ayanosuke and sets out to avenge her clan. Sakon of the Hyuga clan has the sword, and Ryoma of the Hakagure clan the pike. As the demons try to prevent them

from using the magic weapons, their loved ones are killed and their homes destroyed. They think they have foiled the plot by killing Nobunaga and Ranmaru, but the dead were only impersonators. Ranmaru has a master plan, centuries in the making, to build a bridge between hell and Earth and give the world over to the rule of the Demon God. The three blades reunite in a titanic battle at Azuchi Castle, where victory is won at a terrible cost (compare to Time Stranger, which approaches the same events from a science-fictional viewpoint).

As with most ninja stories, Sword for Truth–creator Jo Toriumi's original *Yotoden* novel owes more to 20th-century fiction than 16th-century fact. Treading the same ground as Ninja Scroll, it assumes that the real-life events of Japan's civil war went hand-in-hand with black magic, and that Nobunaga united Japan, not with the foreign guns of the history books, but with demon armies. Ninja with '80s haircuts duck and dive their way in and out of real historical events like superpowered Forrest Gumps with throwing-stars, led by an ice-cool heroine whose gorgeous voice is from the refreshingly unsqueaky Keiko Toda. The story ends with a demonic battle that carries visceral, ultraviolent overtones of the contemporary Urotsukidoji series, also written by scenarist Aikawa. ⓝⓥ

YOUMEX

Anime company established in 1985 by Junji Fujita, a former employee of the music company King Records. Youmex was a coproducer in several of the video anime of the 1980s and early 1990s, including Slow Step, AD Police, and Hummingbirds, although Youmex's achievements were marred by the financial difficulties it inherited from its collapsed Bubblegum Crisis–partner Artmic. The company was subsequently bought out by Toshiba EMI (aka TOEMI), for whom Fujita went to work in 1998.

YOUNG ASHIBE

1991. JPN: *Shonen Ashibe.* TV series, video. DIR: Noboru Ishiguro. SCR: Oki Ike, Toshiaki Sasae, Katsuhide Motoki. DES: Hiromi Morishita. ANI: Kiyotoshi Aoii. MUS: Toshiyuki Arakawa. PRD: Nippon Eizo, TBS. 8 mins. x 75 eps.
The story of a cute little boy and his pet white sea lion was a successful *Young Jump* 4-panel strip by Hiromi Morishita, selling five million copies of its six collected volumes by the end of 1992. The first TV series starring Chika Sakamoto in the leading role spun off 25 more episodes of *YA2* in 1992, with Minami Takayama taking over the role. The fourth season (#64–75) was not broadcast on TV but released straight to video.

YOUNG HANADA

2002. JPN: *Hanada Shonen Shi.* AKA: *History of Young Hanada.* TV series. DIR: Masayuki Ojima. DES: Yoshinori Kanemori. ANI: Satoshi Yoshimoto. MUS: Yoshihisa Hirano. PRD: Madhouse, NTV. 25 mins. x 25 eps.
Elementary schoolboy Ichiro Hanada is the kind of kid who gets into constant trouble. He receives nine stitches on his head after he is hit by a truck, only to discover that his accident has given him the new ability to see ghosts. What's worse, they all want him to help them out with their unfinished business around his home village, in this lighthearted comedy from the manga in *Uppers* magazine by Makoto Isshiki. Although rather obscure in its home country, *Young Hanada* enjoyed a new lease on life in Asia, particularly in Taiwan, where it rode a trend born in equal parts of *The Sixth Sense* (1999) and a local Chinese cartoon, Wang Shaudi's *Grandma and Her Ghosts* (1998). Its sunny, simple rural backgrounds are deceptive—it won the Best Animation prize at the 2003 Asian Television Technical and Creative Awards. The theme songs were provided by the Backstreet Boys.

YOUNG KINDAICHI FILES

1996. JPN: *Kindaichi Shonen no Jiken*

Bo. AKA: *Young Kindaichi's Casebook.*
Movie, TV series. DIR: Daisuke Nishio.
SCR: Takeya Nishioka, Michiru Shimada, Hiroshi Motohashi, Akinori
Endo, Toshiki Inoue. DES: Shingo Araki;
Hidemi Kuma. ANI: Shingo Araki. MUS:
Kaoru Wada. PRD: Toei Animation, Nippon TV. 90 mins. (m), 25 mins. x 148
eps., 90 mins. (m).
Hajime Kindaichi, grandson of a
famous detective, swears on the name
of his grandfather to solve every
murder case he finds. He's 17, a bit
of a delinquent with a bad record of
attendance at his high school, but he's
got a mind like a steel trap, a gift for
sleight-of-hand, and a lot of help from
childhood friend Miyuki Nanase.

Based on the 1992 manga in *Shonen
Magazine* by Yozaburo Kanari and Fumiya Sato, *YKF* features the descendant
of a famous sleuth—the Kosuke Kindaichi created by crime novelist Seishi
Yokomizo in 1946, whose most famous
cases include *The Man with Three Fingers*
and the live-action movie *The House of
Inugami* (1976). As with LUPIN III, there
were legal wrangles with the indignant
executors of the original, though these
were resolved with an out-of-court settlement as the series' popularity steadily
increased. The manga spun off into
a 1995 live-action TV series, and the
first volume was adapted into Nishio's
anime movie *YKF: Murder at the Hotel
Opera* (1996). *YKF* rode a post–
X-Files wave of interest in detective stories, making it and rival CONAN THE BOY
DETECTIVE two of the greatest anime
hits of the 1990s. Rather than limiting
the mysteries to the 25-minute sessions
of single episodes, writers favored
two- and three-part dramas, increasing
the suspense and readily lending themselves to feature-length video releases.
Just some of Kindaichi's TV cases
include *The Waxworks Murders, Death by
the Devil's Symphony,* and *The Killer on
the Haunted Train.* Araki's designs for
the 1997 TV series were revamped by
Hidemi Kama for the 1999 movie *Deep
Blue Slaughter,* in which Kindaichi hunts
a murderer stalking a newly built Okinawa beach-resort.

YOUNG MIYAMOTO MUSASHI

1982. JPN: *Shonen Miyamoto Musashi:
Wanpaku Nitoryu.* AKA: *Young Miyamoto
Musashi: Naughty Way of Two Swords.*
TV special. DIR: Yugo Serikawa, Hideo
Watanabe. SCR: Shizuo Nonami. DES:
Kazumi Fukube, Hiroshi Wagatsuma.
ANI: Hiroshi Wagatsuma, Moriyasu
Yamaguchi, Satoshi Hirayama. MUS:
N/C. PRD: Toei, Fuji TV. 84 mins.
Four-year-old Bennosuke sees his
father, a great swordmaster, killed by
an even better man, Hirata. Since he
knows he isn't old enough or skilled
enough to take revenge, he becomes
Hirata's disciple. When he's mastered
the secrets of the sword and invented
the technique of fighting with two at
once, he kills Hirata and assumes the
name Musashi. Based on the life of
Musashi Miyamoto (Miyamoto Musashi, 1584–1645), often said to be the
greatest swordsman in Japanese history, author of *The Book of Five Rings,*
and subject of Eiji Yoshikawa's famous
series of novels. In this incarnation,
however, his life bears an uncanny similarity to the plot of RINGING BELL. This
anime version of Musashi's life was
based on Renzaburo Shibata's novel
The Duellist, with character designs lifted from Kazumi Fukube's later manga
adaptation. See SWORD OF MUSASHI.

YOUNG PRINCESS DIANA

1986. JPN: *Niji no Kanata e: Shojo
Diana-hi Monogatari.* AKA: *End of the
Rainbow: Young Princess Diana Story.*
TV special. DIR: Hidemi Kama. SCR: Seiji
Matsuoka. DES: Yutaka Arai. ANI: Oji
Suzuki, Animation 501. MUS: N/C. PRD:
Tachyon, Aubec, NTV, TV Asahi. 114
mins.
Born in 1961, Diana Spencer is a child
of the British aristocracy. Her parents
divorce when she is six years old, and
she goes to live with her father and
grandmother. Sent away to boarding
school, Diana is shy and withdrawn,
but a sweet-natured girl who helps the
maid with the washing-up and excels
at pet care—winning the best-guinea-pig contest. Isolated when her father
remarries, Diana throws herself into

swimming and ballet, hoping that one
day her prince will come. Then she
meets Charles, the heir to the throne,
never imagining that one day she will
become his wife.

Screened a few days before the arrival of the real-life Charles and Diana
on a royal visit to Japan, this could
well be described as the highlight of
scenarist Matsuoka's career—his later
KAMA SUTRA hardly compares! The
early life of the late Princess Diana is
plundered with, in anime terms, only
minor alterations; voiced by NAUSICAÄ-actress Sumi Shimamoto. The mind
boggles at how this might have been
"improved" with a few giant robots and
invading aliens, but sadly it was not to
be. The appeal is obvious to a Japanese
audience reared on CINDERELLA and
denied intrusive media access to their
own royals—though the upbeat ending
is particularly ironic considering the
protagonist's later fate.

YOUNG TOKUGAWA IEYASU

1975. JPN: *Shonen Tokugawa Ieyasu.*
DIR: Takeshi Tamiya, Kimio Yabuki.
SCR: Hisao Okawa. DES: Shingo Araki,
Takeshi Shirato. ANI: Shingo Araki, Shoji
Iga. MUS: Takeo Watanabe. PRD: Toei
Animation, NET (TV Asahi). 25 mins. x
20 eps.
At the age of six, young Takechiyo Matsudaira (the future Ieyasu Tokugawa) is
involved in a hostage exchange
between his beleaguered samurai family and the powerful Oda clan. At 14,
he officially reaches manhood, and is
given the name Motoyasu Matsudaira.
He begins his military career by opposing the Oda clan before deciding to
ally himself with its new leader, Nobunaga.

Historical series on TV are a safe
bet—parents think they're educational
and advertisers like to be associated
with worthy cultural products. Tokugawa was the third of the three great
warlords who ended Japan's Civil War
period, Nobunaga Oda being the first.
The series glamorizes his boyhood with
demons and ninja, poking a finger at
parents who thought it was all going to

be high school curriculum stuff. Manga spin-offs ran in *Terebiland* magazine, among others.

YOU'RE UNDER ARREST! *
1994. JPN: *Taiho Shichauzo*. Video, TV series, movie. DIR: Hiroshi Watanabe, Kazuhiro Furuhashi, Junji Nishimura, Takeshi Mori. SCR: Michiru Shimada, Michiko Yokote, Kazuhisa Sakaguchi (TV), Masashi Sogo (m). DES: Atsuko Nakajima, Toshihiro Murata, Hiroshi Kato. ANI: Yasuhiro Aoki. MUS: Ko Otani (TV), Kenji Kawai (m). PRD: Studio Deen, Toci, TBS. 30 mins. x 4 eps. (v), 25 mins. x 47 eps. (TV), 24 mins. x 1 ep. and 6 mins. x 20 eps. (special), 25 mins. x 26 eps. (TV2), 88 mins. (m), 26 mins. (v2).
Miyuki is a gentle, reserved young woman, but for all that she's an ace driver in her working life as one of Tokyo's police officers. Natsumi is hot-headed, impulsive, and disorganized. She too is a Tokyo police officer, in the motorcycle division, and, when the two are teamed up, she doesn't think she and Miyuki will ever hit it off. But from their first important case, a pursuit of a reckless driver with a deadly agenda, they come to rely on each other and value each other's good qualities.

This pretty, innocuous, and astoundingly sanitized cop show takes the mismatched-partners cliché, removes almost all jeopardy, and hopes to muddle through on infantile foolery, female flesh, and an anal attention to audio effects—particularly engine noises. Based on the manga by **OH MY GODDESS!**–creator Kosuke Fujishima, *YuA* flips incessantly between car chases and mawkish flirting at the station house, creating a peculiar combination of *CHiPs* and a school disco. The 1996 TV series that followed the four videos—quite literally, with the first episode numbered as episode five—is pure soap opera, following day-to-day life at the station and expanding the roles of their colleagues, in particular Officer Ken Nakajima, whose romance with Miyuki forms an ongoing subplot. The

You're under Arrest!

episodes pack in much fan service and even a little violence, like Miyuki trying to electrocute a pervert, but there's nothing to merit real concern on these counts. A new series, *YuA: Special* (1999), comprised much shorter episodes, screened as part of the *Wonderful* program. The 1999 movie, directed by Nishimura, did much the same thing with a bigger budget for its story of an abandoned car full of weaponry and the danger that arises from its discovery. The series also spun off into audio dramas, wittily written by former **PATLABOR**-scenarist Michiko Yokote, including *Police Stories* and *Only One*. The latter CD features the girls getting jobs as the pop group "Tokyo Policewoman Duo," in which guise they record the worst song ever made, the "We Are Policewomen" rap. In taking the genre that gave us "Cop Killer" and using it to extol the virtues of driving safely, the song is the perfect summary of the series as a whole. It returned for a 26-episode TV season in spring 2001. In 2002, the show was also adapted into a live-action TV series (*DE), and returned to anime form with *YUA: No Mercy* (aka *YUA in America*), in which the girls are

transferred to the LAPD, and end up chasing a former Japanese detective who has stolen Miyuki's car—not quite *The Shield*.

YS *
1989. Video. DIR: Jun Kamiya, Takashi Watanabe. SCR: Tadashi Hayakawa, Katsuhiko Chiba. DES: Tetsuya Ishikawa, Hideaki Matsuoka, Hiroyuki Nishimura. ANI: Tetsuya Ishikawa, Hiroyuki Nishimura. MUS: Michio Fujisawa. PRD: Urban Project; Tokyo Kids. 30 mins. x 7 eps. (v), 30 mins. x 4 eps. (v2).
Adol, a young swordsman in the magical kingdom of Esteria, must save the world from demonic destruction by gathering six sacred books and bringing them to the Goddesses on Precious Mountain. Based on the NES game by Nippon Falcom that has also spun off a manga by Sho Hagoromo, a series of novels, and other merchandise. *Ys: Palace of the Celestial Gods* (1992, *Tenku no Shinden*) was a second video series based on the events of the second game. Set on the flying island of Ys, it featured Adol in another quest. There was also a 60-minute animated music video, *Ys Special Collection: All About Falcom*.

YUGI-OH *

1998. AKA: *King of Games*. TV series, movie. DIR: Hiroyuki Kadono, Yoko Ikeda, Satoshi Nakamura, Keiji Hayakawa, Kunihisa Sugishima. SCR: Junji Takegami, Toshiki Inoue, Yasuko Kobayashi, Kenichi Kanemaki, Katsuhiko Chiba. DES: Shingo Araki, Michi Himeno. ANI: Masayuki Takagi. MUS: BMF. PRD: Studio Gallop, Nippon Animation, TV Asahi. 25 mins. x 27 eps. (TV1), 25 mins. x 40+ eps. (TV2), 25 mins. (m).

Game-mad Japanese boy Yugi is victimized by the school bullies and obsessed with an ancient Egyptian Millennium Puzzle. The successful player acquires a second thoroughly evil and nasty persona. Yugi can now transform into a vengeful, powerful figure; he can bring game monsters to life and deal out retribution to local evildoers, as well as to those who used to bully him, by forcing them to play a "dark game" on his terms. When he accidentally awakens the Guardian of Darkness, he and his friends are dragged into an adventure that features his own father reincarnated as a Pegasus and a showdown at a real-world gaming convention against his archenemy, who in our dimension is the president of the Industrial Illusion Company. Armed with another Egyptian artifact, the Millennium Eye, Yugi becomes the strongest duelist, in an anime/manga/collectible card game tie-in commissioned in the wake of POKÉMON. Based on the manga by Kazuki Takahashi serialized in *Shonen Jump*, it was followed by a second season, *YO: Duel Fighters*. This is a kids-get-even fantasy so some sequences are quite violent—like the one where our hero pours petrol down the trousers of an armed robber and keeps him at bay with a cigarette lighter. A 30-minute movie formed part of 1999's Toei Anime Fair bill. ⓥ

YUGO THE NEGOTIATOR *

2004. DIR: Seiji Kishi, Shinya Hanai. SCR: Kazuharu Sato, Kenichi Kanemaki. DES: Takahiko Matsumoto, Kenichi Imaizumi. ANI: N/C. MUS: N/C. PRD: G&G Direction, Artland, Kid's Station. 25 mins. x 13 eps.

Based on the manga by Shinji Makari and Shu Akana, this is the story of Yugo Beppu, a negotiator who works to free hostages, resolve standoffs, and save lives in tense situations all around the world. Yugo is a young man of high intelligence who speaks many languages fluently; he is physically and mentally strong enough to withstand any form of torture; but the qualities that make him stand out above others in his field are his humanity, compassion, and his superb instinct for when and how far to trust others. His missions in this series take him first to Pakistan, where he agrees to negotiate for the lost-cause handover of a girl's father, and then Siberia, where he is tasked with locating a rich man's lost granddaughter, whose wing of the family was separated from her relatives by the upheavals of the Russian revolution.

Yugo has little of the menace-of-the-week setups so common to anime. Instead, it divides into two broad story arcs, more like two three-hour movies than a 13-episode TV series, and each animated by a different production team. It also flies in the face of many anime conventions, without recourse to the robots or science-fictional distractions of many other shows. Yugo may have a quiet assistant, but her origin story is nasty in the extreme—she isn't mute because she is shy, she is mute because one of her parents cut out her tongue. In its reliance on tension and psychological profiling, its portrayal of a man of peace in a brutal world, Yugo is one of the more interesting anime of modern times, mixing up the intelligent protagonist of MASTER KEATON with real-world issues far removed from much of modern anime's content.

YUKI

1981. Movie. DIR: Tadashi Imai. SCR: Akira Miyazaki. DES: Tetsuya Chiba. ANI: Shinichi Tsuji. MUS: Chito Kawauchi. PRD: Mushi, Nikkatsu. 89 mins.

Demons threaten the peaceful existence of a group of peasants who live in Japan's far north during the Muromachi period (1338–1573). However, the villagers have the aid of Yuki, a snow fairy who dwells among them in human form, and her beloved horse, Fubuki (Snowstorm). Though based on the story by Takasuke Saito, itself drawing on JAPANESE FOLK TALES, elements of this anime seem to coincidentally foreshadow the far more famous PRINCESS MONONOKE.

YUKI TERAI—SECRETS *

2000. JPN: *Yuki Terai Secret Films*. TV series. DIR: Kenichi Kutsugi. SCR: N/C. DES: N/C. ANI: N/C. MUS: N/C. PRD: Fuji TV, Frog Entertainment. 79 mins.

The virtual idol Yuki Terai is a lively 17-year-old who supposedly lives just outside Tokyo. She stars in this entirely computer-generated animation made up of six short segments, mostly SF and fantasy, but including a sequence where she is a singer in a French café-bar and another where she must shut down a critical machine at the other end of a space ship—yes, this involves running down a very long corridor while klaxons blare and lights flash. There is also a trailer for an unmade World War II epic seemingly inspired by *Pearl Harbor* (2001). These disparate shorts are little more than showreels for computer animators, made at that point in the early 21st century when developments in computer animation could still surprise on a monthly basis. The production credits imply that they were first seen as part of a larger show on Fuji TV, hence our classification of them as "television," and neither the "video" nor "movie" that some foreign distributors have attempted to imply. In the wake of *Final Fantasy: The Spirits Within* (2001), of course, computer animation has gone underground again, and prides itself on *not* being noticed, making Yuki Terai one of the creations of the brief flurry of CG-hype that also gave us VISITOR, AURORA, MALICE DOLL, and BLUE REMAINS. The rights for *Yuki Terai* were picked up by Escapi and released in the U.K. and northern Europe, alongside DVDs of similar showreels, *Virtual Stars* (1999) and *Cybervenus Feifei* (2001). The discs are sometimes sold under the umbrella label for the whole series: *Virtually Real.*

YUKIKAZE *

2002. JPN: *Sento Yosei Yukikaze.* Video. DIR: Masahiko Okura. SCR: Hiroshi Yamaguchi, Yumi Tada, Masahiko Okura, Masashi Sogo, Ikuto Yamashita, Seiji Kio. DES: Yumi Tada, Masahiro Aizawa, Koichi Hashimoto, Ikuto Yamashita, Seiji Kio, Atsushi Takeuchi, Kanetake Ebikawa, Masahiko Sekino, Masaru Kato. ANI: Koichi Hashimoto, Masahiro Sekino. MUS: Satoshi Mishiba, Dogen Shiono (The KANI), Clara. PRD: Bandai Visual, Victor Entertainment, Gonzo. 25 mins. x 4 eps. (v1) 30 mins. (v2).

Thirty years after secretly opening an interdimensional gate beneath Antarctica, the alien Jam commence their invasion plan. Beaten back by human defenders, the Jam retreat to their homeworld, which has been given the human codename "Fairy," and to which the portal now serves as a possible conduit for counterattack. Mankind's Special Air Force is its main line of defense, using fighters with AI so sophisticated that one, Yukikaze, is actually sentient. Rei Fukai is its designated pilot, and supported by a multinational force under General Lydia Cooley, he and his fellow pilots fight an enemy they can never see clearly and about which they know very little. In an ideological twist reminiscent of GUN-BUSTER, the Jam are a machine-based race who regard humans as parasites, stealing the Earth from its rightful owners, the machines. This places Yukikaze in an interesting dilemma, as it actually has more in common with the enemy it has been created to defeat.

Just as Shoji Kawamori did for MACROSS *Plus*, the team based its fighter technology on study visits to the Komatsu air force base, so the mecha designs are state-of-the-art and the whole show is imbued with a passion for *Top Gun* antics. The Gonzo

Yukikaze

© 2002 OK. H / B.V.G.

team pulls out all the visual stops, with the work of color coordinator Eriko Murata looking particularly strong and providing a wonderful sense of atmosphere—compare to BLUE SUBMARINE NO. SIX and AREA 88.

The series began as a collection of linked short stories published in 1984 by Chohei Kanbayashi, in which the Jam have their portal at the *north* pole, and which revealed that Yukikaze ("Blizzard") took its name from the most famous destroyer in the Japanese navy in World War II. Publicity at the time of *Yukikaze*'s American release mystifyingly boasted that it had recently won the "Japanese Nebula" Seiun award, but it first achieved that honor some 20 years earlier—its true publication date being a much surer indicator of its cutting-edge originality, since many foreign audiences may have otherwise assumed it to be a rip-off of the movie *Stealth* (2005). Anniversaries seem to have played an important part in the commissioning process, since *Yukikaze*'s anime incarnation went into production to mark the 20th anniversary of Bandai's Emotion video label. Much was made at the time of its amazingly realistic animation of planes; the

show does seem to spend an inordinate amount of time presenting fetishized views of aerial battles, which may have been entertaining then but may seem to the more jaded to look like so many modern-day combat flight simulators.

Yukikaze also generated an odd spin-off in the form of *Yukikaze Mave-chan* (2005), a one-shot video based on some doodles drawn by designer Ikuto Yamashita when his hard drive was temporarily down. Elfin Mave is one of a group of girls fighting the alien Jam in another world. When she runs into a strange boy, she naturally leaps into the attack with her knives. Her companion Super Sylph rescues the boy, who turns out to be a human called Rei; he has no idea how he was sucked into the girls' world, because he was just minding his own business at an anime convention. It turns out that the world was created by the desires of anime fans, and the girls represent the archetypes fans like best—at least it's honest!

Mave is a happy person, fun to be around, but her two big knives warn anyone not to mess with her. Super Sylph is a gentle, quiet girl, tall and curvy. Sly and slinky chatterbox Sylph bickers constantly, and childlike Fand is strange and silent. But the worst danger is not from aliens but from the fans' minds shifting on to home and dinner—as the convention draws to an end, the world created from its collective dream starts to collapse. An intriguing adaptation of the guilt trip attitude of KEY OF THE METAL IDOL, itself an emotional approach to the brutal realities of the entertainment industry.

YUKIMURO, SHUNICHI

1941– . Born in Kanagawa Prefecture, he enrolled in the Eighth Scenario Writing Workshop for television drama, "graduating" in 1961. His early work was for Nikkatsu, although subsequently his name has somehow found its way onto over 3000 scripts for television, including many anime such as SAZAE-SAN, KIMBA THE WHITE LION, MOOMINS, and SPOOKY KITARO.

YUMERIA *

2004. TV series. DIR: Keitaro Motonaga. SCR: Makoto Uezu, Yosuke Kuroda. DES: Shinobu Nishioka, Yasuhiro Moriki. ANI: N/C. MUS: N/C. PRD: Studio Deen, BS-i. 24 mins. x 12 eps.
Tomokazu Mikuri discovers that in his dreams he can visit the alternate world of Yumeria, populated by pretty girls, where he is welcomed as a hero who can save the oppressed kingdom from destruction at the hands of the Faydoom invaders. Sub–TENCHI MUYO! "comedy" soon ensues, as Tomokazu and a number of real-world associates get to travel to the alternate world and, well, hang out. Not an erotic anime, although it is loaded with puerile excuses to ogle girls, many of who either appear underage, act like they might as well be, or are Tomokazu's relatives. Based on a video game—*yume* is Japanese for dream.

YU-NO *

1998. Video. DIR: Katsumasa Kanezawa. SCR: Osamu Kudo. DES: Tetsuro Aoki. ANI: Takeo Takahashi, Yasushi Nagaoka. MUS: N/C. PRD: Pink Pineapple, KSS. 30 mins. x 4 eps.
Takuya falls for the woman his father marries after his mother's death. Yes, it's yet another almost-but-not-quite incest story; compare to CREAM LEMON and COOL DEVICES. Announced as forthcoming in the U.S. from Nu-Tech at the time of our deadline. **Ⓝ**

YUN-YUN PARADISE

1995. JPN: YunYun Paradise. Video. DIR: Hiroshi Yamakawa. SCR: N/C. DES: N/C. ANI: Inatsugi Kiyomizu. MUS: N/C. PRD: Pink Pineapple, AIC. 30 mins.
This "love comedy" features Yun-Yun, a suspiciously young-looking Chinese girl, falling in love with a Japanese boy. Based on a novel from the same Napoleon imprint that gave us EROTIC TORTURE CHAMBER. **Ⓝ**

YUYAMA, KUNIHIKO

1952– . Born in Tokyo and developing an interest in animation while still at high school, Yuyama worked as an inbetweener on episodes of STAR BLAZERS and BRAVE RAIDEEN. He was a sketch artist and storyboarder on the foreign coproduction *Barbapapa* (1973) and joined Aoi Productions in 1978. The same year, he had his directorial debut while working for Aoi on GALAXY EXPRESS 999, and soon struck up a successful working partnership with the screenwriter Takeshi Sudo on GOSHO-GUN. By 1982, he had been promoted to "chief director," an overseeing role on GIGI AND THE FOUNTAIN OF YOUTH. While remaining in TV during the 1980s, he also played a leading role in anime's exodus into video. His work also showed a mastery of elements for a female audience, most obvious in his THREE MUSKETEERS spin-off, *Aramis' Adventure*. After his underrated USHIO AND TORA, he gained true fame through his involvement with two later works –SLAYERS and POKÉMON.

Z

ZAION: I WISH YOU WERE HERE *
2001. AKA: *I Wish You Were Here*. TV series. DIR: Seiji Mizushima. SCR: Natsuko Takahashi. DES: Yasuhiro Oshima. ANI: Yasuhiro Oshima, Yasufumi Soejima. MUS: N/C. PRD: Gonzo. 25 mins. x 4 eps.
In May 2002, a terrorist group sets off a gas explosion in Atlanta, Georgia. It is the first of many incidents across the U.S., though the perpetrators' motives are a mystery. Only unclear photographs of (surprise, surprise) a "mysterious girl" provide any clue. They seem to be linked in some way to Project I, a top secret operation by an international collective of scientists, who are rumored to be working on a "Multipurpose Operative Being" experiment in sentient cybernetics. A mixture of conspiracies and espionage from Gonzo, combining CG elements of the studio's earlier BLUE SUBMARINE No. SIX with the identity crisis of SERIAL EXPERIMENTS LAIN.

ZAMBOT 3
1977. JPN: *Muteki Chojin Robot Zambot 3*. AKA: *Invincible Superman Zambot 3*. TV series. DIR: Yoshiyuki Tomino, Minoru Onodani, Susumu Yukita, Takao Yotsuji, Shinya Sadamitsu, Kazuyuki Hirokawa, Kazuya Yamazaki. SCR: Fuyunori Gobu, Yoshihisa Araki, Soji Yoshikawa. DES: Yoshikazu Yasuhiko, Ryoji Hirayama, Studio Nue. ANI: Tadaichi Iuchi, Green Box, Kazuo Tomozawa. MUS: Takeo Watanabe, Hiroshi Matsuyama. PRD: Sunrise, Nagoya TV

(TV Asahi). 25 mins. x 23 eps.
The last descendants of an extraterrestrial race take refuge on 19th-century Earth when their homeworld of Bial is destroyed by the treacherous Gaizoku. Several generations later, a Gaizoku advance force led by "Killer the Butcher" attacks Earth, and the local population accuses the descendants of the original refugees of bringing down trouble on the planet. They decide to use the ships their fathers arrived in to fight the mechanical monsters. These ships include the giant robot Zambot 3, made up by combining three different machines. Young Kappei, the robot's pilot, is assisted by Uchita and Keiko. The enemy has a very nasty way of killing; they implant explosive devices in their prisoners' bodies and can set them off at any time, even after the prisoners have returned to their homes and families. The tragic climax has Uchita and Keiko killed in a valiant effort to fight off the enemy, presaging the angst to come in Tomino's GUNDAM, for which this can reasonably be regarded as a test run. Notable for beginning as a lighthearted parody of earlier robot shows, before descending into tragedy—compare with GUNBUSTER and EVANGELION. **V**

ZANKAN
1996. AKA: *Killer Mischief*. Video. DIR: Motoaki Isshu. SCR: N/C. DES: N/C. ANI: Sugiko Enkai. MUS: N/C. PRD: Pink Pineapple, KSS. 30 mins. x 2 eps.

At the turn of the 21st century, Earth is conquered by demons, and only the two sexy "Riot" girls can save the universe, by having lots of sex. That's a surprise. Based on a manga by EVOCATION-creator Ryoga Ryuen. **N**

ZATCH BELL *
2003. JPN: *Kinshoku no Zatch; Konjiki no Zatch Bell*. AKA: *Gash Bell; Golden Zatch Bell*. TV Series, movie. DIR: Tetsuji Nakamura, Atsuji Shimizu. SCR: Atsushi Yamatoya, Hiro Masaki, KOHEI-MUSHI, Takashi Yamada, Yoshimi Narita, Yuji Hashimoto. DES: Ken Otsuka. ANI: Ken Otsuka, Hideki Hashimoto. MUS: Ko Otani. PRD: Fuji TV, Toei Animation, Yomiko Advertising Inc. 25 mins. x 140 eps. (TV), 85 mins. (m1), 83 mins. (m2).
There can be only one, and that doesn't just apply in *Highlander*. The mamono, a race of tiny demons, is trying to find a new ruler. Candidates are sent into the human world to pick a human master and then fight other demon contenders, using spells from their different colored magic books, until only one is left alive. Perky little blond demon Zatch started out wanting to win so he could be a benevolent demon king and stop them fighting each other, but then lost all memory of his past life: clues to the past are hidden in his magical red book. He pairs up with lonely, apathetic schoolboy Kiyomaro Takamine, who is isolated at school because his classmates are

Zeorymer Hades Project

jealous of his intelligence. The scene is thereby set for another tale of a child with a strange playmate, combining the otherworldly mentor of HIKARU'S GO with the seemingly endless quest for material acquisition of POKÉMON. It's perhaps no coincidence that Zatch's voice actress is Ikue Otani, the voice of Pikachu. The series also spawned two movies, *Konjiki no ZB: Unlisted Demon 101* (*KnoZB: 101 Banme no Mamono*, 2004), in which Zatch and Kiyomaro stumble into another world and risk being stuck there forever unless they can solve a crime, and *KnoZB: Attack of the Mechavulcan* (*KnoZB: Mechavulcan no Raishu*, 2005), in which Zatch's friend Vulcan 300 is transformed into a giant menacing robot. Based on the manga by Makoto Raiku in *Shonen Jump*.

ZEGUY *
1992. JPN: *Unkai no Meikyu Zeguy*. AKA: *Labyrinth of the Sea Clouds: Zeguy*. Video. DIR: Shigenori Kageyama. SCR: Shigenori Kageyama. DES: Aki Tsunaki. ANI: Akinobu Takahashi. MUS: Soichiro Harada. PRD: KSS. 40 mins. x 2 eps.
Time-traveling troubleshooters Toshizo and Gennai (from the ultranationalist

Shinsengumi organization of 19th-century Japan) must prevent the evil Himiko (Japan's ancient ruler, see DARK MYTH) from opening a gateway to our world. They have two sailor-suited schoolgirls to help them but are lined up against a squad of smart enemies, including Leonardo da Vinci. Sadly, however, da Vinci is one of the only historical references that have survived in the dub version of this comedy romp—many of the clever references of the original script are sanded away by a distributor uneasy with "ethnocentric" allusions. Fun despite the dumbing-down, it's notable for a rare moment in a Manga Entertainment release when a character is chastised for using a rude word. Rereleased in 2004 in the U.S. as *Mask of Zeguy*.

ZENKI: THE DEMON PRINCE *
1995. JPN: *Kishin Doji Zenki*. AKA: *Demon-God Boy Zenki*. TV series. DIR: Junji Nishimura. SCR: Ryota Yamaguchi, Masashi Sogo, Hitoshi Tokimura. DES: Hideyuki Motohashi, Torao Arai. ANI: Hideyuki Motohashi. MUS: Koji Tsuno. PRD: Studio Deen, Kitty Film, TV Tokyo. 25 mins. x 51 eps.
A thousand years ago, a sorcerer sealed

the demon Zenki in stone to protect the world. Chiaki, a direct descendant, lives in modern Tokyo, where her grandmother has taught her the forbidden spell that breaks Zenki's bonds. To save her own world, she must use the spell, set Zenki free, and try to harness his power to fight off the spirits that are attacking modern Japan. The problem is, this involves his living with her in the family temple, and when he isn't casting spells as a superb hunk of menacing magical manhood, he takes the form of an annoying little brat who's every girl's worst nightmare of a kid brother. The director of RANMA ½ must know something about milking a franchise for its last drop of humor, but he doesn't have much to work with here—just an average kids' TV series and not a patch on USHIO AND TORA. Based on the manga in *Shonen Jump* by Hide Taniguchi and Yoshihiro Kuroiwa.

ZENO: LOVE WITHOUT LIMITS
1999. JPN: *Zeno: Kagirinaki Ai ni*. Movie. DIR: Takashi Ui. SCR: Takashi Ui, Shigeki Chiba. DES: N/C. ANI: Satoshi Mutsukura. MUS: N/C. PRD: Robot, Media Vision. 90 mins.
Father Zeno is a Polish priest who lived in Japan during the 1930s and fell in love with the land and its people. In the aftermath of World War II, he comes back with a mission to help the children of Japan who have been orphaned by war, fire, flood, or earthquake.

ZEORYMER HADES PROJECT *
1988. JPN: *Meio Kikaku Zeorymer*. AKA: *Hades Project Zeorymer*. Video. DIR: Toshihiro Hirano. SCR: Noboru Aikawa. DES: Michitaka Kikuchi, Yasuhiro Moriki. ANI: Michitaka Kikuchi. MUS: Eiji Kawamura. PRD: AIC, Artmic. 30 mins. x 4 eps.
Scientist Masaki Kihara rebels against his employers, the Haudragon crime syndicate. He destroys seven of the huge Hakkeshu robots he created for their top-secret Hades Project and hides the eighth and most powerful, the Zeorymer. Fifteen years later, the Haudragon have almost rebuilt the

Hakkeshu, but the government has the Zeorymer and means to use it to thwart the criminals' plans. It needs the right pilot—a clone of its creator. Luckily, the government has one it had made earlier. Fifteen-year-old Masato is about to find out that his whole life so far has been a lie, and that he was created in a test tube for the sole purpose of going into battle as the pilot of the greatest war machine the world has ever seen. Unless he can destroy the Hakkeshu and thwart Haudragon's plans, the world will plunge into an abyss of nuclear destruction.

Hirano gives this dark, tense scenario all the menace and nastiness that he brought to **ICZER-ONE** a year earlier, while the atmosphere and design work foreshadow Kikuchi's later **SILENT MÖBIUS**. But there are no nasty alien invaders here—all the evil and suffering, as well as all the near-magical technology that created the magnificently spiky robots, is the work of humans; like **GUNDAM**, this reminds us that science fiction doesn't need aliens. Masato's emotional struggle and the near-disintegration of his personality are portrayed with melodramatic emphasis. This is a minor work by the standards of its stellar team but still has much of interest to offer. **LV**

ZERO G ROOM
Studio founded in 1991 by director Hiroshi Negishi, along with fellow animators Takuya Saito and Toshinari Yamashita, eventually merged into the planning company Radix. Works include **SAKURA WARS** and the **TENCHI MUYO!** movies.

ZERO NO MONO *
2001. AKA: *Nothing; Worthless.* Video. DIR: Ryuichi Kimura. SCR: Saki Hosen. DES: Akira Kano. ANI: Haruo Okuwara. MUS: N/C. PRD: Studio March, Milky, Museum Pictures. 30 mins.
A nameless slacker protagonist fantasizes about abusing and humiliating the girls in his dull college class. After he is snubbed by snooty coed Riko, he stalks her and attempts to torment

her with a thrown jar of semen. She instead reacts with interest, much to his surprise, and he follows her to her destination—a house where her "Master" is busily abusing another girl. Riko actually enjoys the pain, and soon it is she who is in charge, in yet another bondage anime. Our language warning is stronger than usual on this title, since the dub by Nutech inserts outrageous quantities of swear words. Not that anyone buying this sort of thing is likely to be shocked by anything so mild as bad language. Based on an anonymous story by the artist "Zero no Mono," from the series *Women at the Crossroads* (*Onna no Ko no Tsuji*), in the publication *Waning Moon* (*Tsuki ga Kakeru*). **LNV**

ZERO SEN HAYATO
1964. TV series. DIR: Kazuo Hoshino, Tomio Sagisu. SCR: Satoru Kuramoto, Tomio Sagisu. DES: Tomio Sagisu. ANI: Saburo Sakamoto, Fujio Watanabe. MUS: Takeo Watanabe. PRD: P Productions, Oricomi, Fuji TV. 25 mins. x 41 eps.
Hayato Azuma, grandson of one of the Iga ninja clan, becomes a Zero-sen fighter pilot in the South Seas. Launching from Atsugi Island, he and his 34 ace pilot associates (including other descendants of ninja) fight as the Bakufu Team, under their commander Miyamoto, against a large number of opponents from nations whose insignia and nationality remain coyly unidentified. The only postwar anime for a generation after **WARTIME ANIME** to refer to WWII itself, this was based on the manga by **TIGER MASK**–creator Naoki Tsuji. In one memorable scene, the animators used footage from the live-action *War at Sea from Hawaii to Malaya* (see **ULTRAMAN**) as a background.

ZERO SUM GAME *
2001. JPN: *Sex Crime: Zero Sum Game.* Video. DIR: Kaoru Toyooka, Hotaru Arisugawa. SCR: Guts Maro. DES: N/C. ANI: Shigeru Sasaki. MUS: Yasuaki Fujita. PRD: Blue Eyes, Picol Aibu. 30 mins.
A romantic future seems to beckon for

Yuka and her boyfriend Yazaki, until a fateful night when he takes her to see the band Zero Sum in concert. Lead singer Keith knows Yazaki from their student days and also carries a torch for Yuka. At the backstage party, he ensures that Yazaki gets drunk and volunteers to escort him home, leaving Yuka at the mercy of a gang rape by the other band members. In the aftermath, Yuka decides to tell Yazaki what has happened, but Keith, who wants her for himself, convinces her instead to work through her trauma—unsurprisingly, this involves repeatedly having sexual intercourse with him. The result is yet another erotic anime that requires its female victims to be "broken in" through rape and domination. Based on a manga by Naizo Kudara. **LNV**

ZERO TESTER
1973. TV series. DIR: Ryosuke Takahashi, Yoshiyuki Tomino, Seiji Okuda. SCR: Fuyunori Gobu, Haruya Yamazaki, Kazushi Inoue, Soji Yoshikawa. DES: John Dettault, Crystal Art Studio. ANI: Kazuo Nakamura, Kazuhiko Udagawa, Yoshikazu Yasuhiko. MUS: Naoki Yamamoto. PRD: Tohoku Shinsha, Soei, Kansai TV (Fuji TV). 25 mins. x 66 eps.
A series of space accidents turn out to be the work of the Armanoid aliens, who plan to conquer Earth. Professor Tachibana gathers a team around him at the Future Science Invention Center and prepares five state-of-the-art vehicles for Shin, Go, Lisa, and Captain Kenmotsu. Three of the Tester vehicles combine to make the giant Zero Tester robot, which successfully sees off the Armanoid invasion in 39 episodes. The rest of the series, retitled *ZT: Save the Earth!* (*Chikyu o Mamotte!*), was aimed at a younger age group and featured an attack by the new Gallos aliens.

An early gathering of many of anime's future greats, particularly for the **GUNDAM** series, this Gerry Anderson "homage" escaped complaint from the Japanese division of ITC because *Thunderbirds* (1965) was distributed in Japan by Tohoku Shinsha, who also produced *ZT!* Tohoku producer Banjiro Uemura would eventually work with Gerry Anderson himself on the abortive *Terrahawks* anime, and he would go it alone with the blatant THUNDERBIRDS 2086. Crystal Art was eventually renamed Studio Nue.

ZETSUAI *

1992. JPN: *Zetsuai 1989.* AKA: *Desperate Love 1989; Everlasting Love 1989.* Video. DIR: Takuji Endo, Kazuo Yamazaki. SCR: Tatsuhiko Urahata. DES: Tetsuro Aoki, Kazuya Kise. ANI: Tetsuro Aoki. MUS: Kenji Kawai, Yasunori Honda. PRD: Madhouse. 45 mins., 33 mins., 45 mins.
Takuto Izumi, a high school soccer star, has a dark family secret—his mother's obsessive love for his father led to murder. Superstar idol singer Koji Nanjo has a terrible family background, with long-standing animosity between him and his eldest brother, and his middle sibling clinging to the elder. With their problems, the two should never even contemplate a relationship, but Koji has fancied Izumi since he first saw him; even when he finds out Izumi isn't, as he thought, a girl, he can't get him out of his mind. His obsessive love is the last thing Izumi needs, but as Koji pursues the relationship and Koji's friend Katsumi Shibuya becomes a friend to Izumi, too, love grows between the desperately needy pair despite Izumi's reluctance to accept it. It's tested by the hostility of Koji's family, which doesn't hesitate to threaten Izumi's chance of an international soccer career.
Bronze Cathexis (1994), a 33-minute "image" video concentrating on Koji, features five pop promos set to animation (as with CIPHER) directed by some of the star directors of the Madhouse studio: Katsuyuki Kodera, Yoshiaki Kawajiri (who storyboarded *Zetsuai*), Koichi Chiaki, Toshio Hirata, and Rintaro.
A further video, *Bronze: Zetsuai since 1989* (1996), directed by Yamazaki and designed by Kise, shows Izumi leaving for a soccer tour. When Koji doesn't

show up to see him off, he gets worried and starts to wonder why. In fact, Koji has had a minor car accident, but as a result Izumi starts pondering over their whole relationship.
Based on the ongoing 1990 manga in *Margaret* by Minami Ozaki, *Zetsuai* is one of the greatest icons of *shonen ai*—gay erotica for a female audience. The video versions show only a tiny segment of the angst-ridden multi-character story, and though there's not much explicit sex, there is a lot of blood—accidents and self-inflicted wounds abound. Koji and Izumi have become *shonen ai*'s Romeo and Juliet, and a similarly tragic ending probably awaits. "Everlasting Love" is Ozaki's preferred English title, either through deliberate irony or simply poor translation. **NV**

ZETTAI SHONEN

2005. AKA: *Absolute Boy.* TV series. DIR: Tomomi Mochizuki, Hiroshi Negishi, Kenichi Imaizumi. SCR: Kazunori Ito, Miwa Kawasaki, Tatsuya Hamazaki. DES: Masayuki Sekine. ANI: Hiroshi Kawaguchi, Hiroyuki Horiuchi, Kenichi Imaizumi, Koji Watanabe, Yuko Yamamoto, Nobuyuki Hata. MUS: Hikaru Nanase. PRD: Studio One Pack, Asia-do, Studio Fuga, Trilogy Future, Anime Aru, NHK. 25 mins. x 26 eps.
Ayumu Aizawa is sent by his mother to stay with his father—a posting he initially regards with some reluctance, although his consent is bought with the bribe of a mountain bike. But on his rides around the remote village of Tana, he encounters a series of strange phenomena that lead him to believe that something weird is going on in the woods—glowing lights through the trees, a local girl who knows more than she lets on, and a small child eerily attired in the clothes that Ayumu himself wore when he was younger. It's all due to fairies, apparently, in a surreal take on *The X Files.*

ZILLION *

1987. JPN: *Akai Kodan Zillion.* AKA: *Red Tracer Zillion; Red Photon Zillion.* TV

series, video. DIR: Hiroshi Hamazaki, Tetsuya Kobayashi. SCR: Tsunehisa Ito, Mayori Sekijima. DES: Mizuho Nishikubo, Kunio Aoii, Ammonite. ANI: Takayuki Sato. MUS: Jun Irie. PRD: Tatsunoko, Nippon TV. 25 mins. x 31 eps., 45 mins. (v).
In the year 2387, a group of human colonists live on the planet Maris, hailed as a "second Earth." However, the colonists are attacked by the Noza aliens—Maris' only hope is a captured alien weapon system known as the "Zillion Gun." Three of these fall into the hands of the defenders, and a team of brave young freedom fighters calling themselves the White Nauts/Nuts (White Knights in the U.S. release) fight for their people's survival. The 1988 video release *Burning Night* was a one-shot written and directed by Nishikubo, set in the peacetime after the aliens have been seen off. Former comrades Champ, Dave, JJ, and cute girl Apple form a rock band (see DANCOUGAR) but have to call on their old combat skills again when Apple is kidnapped by a criminal gang. Made just after ROBOTECH *Sentinels* was canceled, *Zillion* incorporated some of the design work undertaken for the aborted project by Tatsunoko. The whole series was based on a toy—a photoelectric gun used for Lazer Tag—and only 5 of the 31 episodes, plus *Burning Night* (released as *Zillon Special: BN*) appeared on video in the U.S.

ZIPANG

2004. TV series. DIR: Kazuhiro Furuhashi, Daisuke Tsukushi, Hideki Okamoto, Hiromichi Matano, Takashi Yamana, Yukihiro Matsushita. SCR: Kazuhiro Furuhashi, Yuichiro Takeda. DES: Yoshihiko Umakoshi, Sanpei Ohara, Yasuhiro Nishinaka. ANI: Akira Kasahara, Hirofumi Morimoto, Masashi Matsumoto. MUS: Toshihiko Sahashi. PRD: Studio Deen, TBS. 25 mins. x 26 eps.
The modern-day Japanese Kongo-class AEGIS destroyer Mirai ("Future") is transported back in time to the eve of

the Battle of Midway and faced with the difficult decision to intervene in World War II or to sit back and watch its countrymen die in the battle. The commander initially adopts a strictly defensive position (itself an ironic pastiche of Japan's own postwar constitutional stance), only to find trouble coming his way when the crew inadvertently rescue Major Kusaka, an officer who was, historically, supposed to have died at Midway. After much bickering, the ship heads for Singapore, where executive officer Kadomatsu discovers that the presence of the Mirai has already altered the timeline too far for history to play out as they remember it. Consequently, after seven episodes of hand-wringing indecision, they decide to weigh in on the Japanese side, and set course for Guadalcanal. Ultimately, the Mirai is destined for a showdown involving the quintessential WWII vessel, the Yamato—see STAR BLAZERS for its better-known appearance in an earlier anime. Based on the 2001 manga by SILENT SERVICE–creator Kaiji Kawaguchi, serialized in *Comic Morning* magazine, this series also owes obvious debts of inspiration to Don Taylor's *Final Countdown* (1980), in which an American aircraft carrier falls through time to witness Pearl Harbor, and the Sonny Chiba vehicle *Time Slip* (1981), in which modern Japanese soldiers stumble across time into Japan's civil war. Compare to DEEP BLUE FLEET.

Z-MIND *

1999. JPN: *Omoharuki Shojo Gattai Robo Zee-Mine*. AKA: *Spring Term Pretty-Girl Synchro Robot Z-Mine*. Video. DIR: Yasuhiro Matsumura. SCR: Fuyunori Gobu. DES: Kamo Manimaru, Kenta Aoki. ANI: N/C. MUS: Toshiki Inoue. PRD: Sunrise. 25 mins. x 6 eps.

Ayame, on her way home from viewing the cherry blossoms, is attacked by strange men and dragged, along with three other girls, into a new role as a transforming-robot pilot. It was made in a deliberate 1970s style (compare to the '60s retro of GATE KEEPERS), even

down to a mysterious male who pops up to give advice (shades of *Charlie's Angels*). Displaying all the hallmarks of an EVANGELION clone that arrived too late, only to discover that the TV boom had slumped, it sidled out sheepishly onto video.

ZOIDS

1999. TV series. DIR: Yoshio Kado, Nobuyoshi Habara, Shingo Kobayashi. SCR: Kazuhiko Sumizawa, Kazuhiko Koide. DES: Tadashi Sakazaki. ANI: Taro Ikegami. MUS: Akira Takahashi. PRD: Xebec, Sho-Pro, MRS, JRK, TBS. 25 mins. x 67 eps. (TV1), 25 mins. x 26 (TV2).

Van is just an ordinary kid, but his life changes forever when a capsule crashes outside his village and he defends it from bandits. The occupants are a sleek metallic dinosaur and a beautiful girl. The girl, Phina, says that her companion, Jeek, is a zoid. Van sets off with them on an adventure he could never have imagined, a battle against Deathsaura.

Promoting toys is what kids' robot shows are all about; Bandai's GUNDAM franchise is just one example. Here, though, is a show that starts out with a range of toys that have been on sale since 1982, a motor-driven range of construction kit toys by Tomy, with a name made from a Japlish combination of *ju* ("beast") and "android," making *ju-oids*. The artwork has a split personality, using CG on the Zoids (under the supervision of Nobuyoshi Habara) but aiming for a cel-animated look overall. At the beginning of 2001, the series was rebranded as *New Century Zoid Slash Zero* (*Zoid Shinseki/0*) with episode 68, moving away from the martial theme of the earlier episodes and concentrating instead on gladiatorial zoid combat. A manga spin-off was serialized in *Corocoro Comic*.

ZONE OF ENDERS

2001. Video, TV series. DIR: Tetsuya Watanabe. SCR: Shin Yoshida. DES: Madoka Hirayama, Tsutomu Suzuki, Tsutomu Miyazawa. ANI: Kumi Horii.

MUS: Hikaru Nanase. PRD: Sunrise, TV Tokyo. 55 mins. x N/D eps. (v), 25 mins. x 26 eps.

In A.D. 2167, humankind has established colonies in space. Jupiter colony Antilla is the farthest human settlement from Earth, so its residents are called Enders. Leo Stenbuck, an introverted Ender, goes along with his friends (who bully him most of the time) to a UN Space Force facility to steal from their junkyard, but he gets caught. At the same time, fanatical Martian military ruling party Z.O.E. hijacks the Antilla colony. His home turned into a battlefield, Leo witnesses the deaths of his friends. Scared and weighed down with guilt, he runs from the scene determined to find the reasons behind the attack. In April 2001, the video *ZoE 2167* and the *ZoE Dolores* TV series were both released alongside the PlayStation game, which itself has a solid crew including GUNDAM and *Metal Gear Solid* veteran Nobuyoshi Nishimura. The anime version is set five years before the events of the game.

ZOO WITHOUT AN ELEPHANT

1982. JPN: *Zo no Inai Dobutsuen*. Movie. DIR: Yasuo Maeda. SCR: Hikaru Saito. DES: Junji Nagashima. ANI: Minoru Aoki. MUS: Kuni Kawauchi. PRD: Tac, Herald. 80 mins.

After the war, concerned brother Hide promises his critically ill sister Miyoko that he will arrange for her to see a real elephant. But when he goes to the zoo to find one, an old man tells him of the tragic day when the zoo animals were slaughtered. Compare to GOODBYE LITTLE HIPPO, a similar tale of wartime deprivation.

ZORRO THE MAGNIFICENT

1996. JPN: *Kaiketsu Zorro*. AKA: *Magnificent Zorro; Z for Zorro*. TV series. DIR: Katsumi Minoguchi, Kenichi Hirano, Yasuhiro Matsumura, Masakazu Amiya, Takeshi Yamaguchi, Akiyuki Shinbo. SCR: Sukehiro Tomita, Yasushi Hirano, Takashi Yamada, Hideki Sonoda, Isao Shizuoka. DES: Hisashi Kagawa. ANI: Hirotoshi Takaya, Masaaki Endo. MUS:

N/C. PRD: Tohoku, Ashi productions, NHK2. 25 mins. x 52 eps.

Based on the stories by Johnston McCulley, which first appeared in *All-Story Weekly* in 1919, the series chronicles the adventures of a heroic freedom fighter (*El Zorro:* "The Fox") struggling to defend the independence of the people of 19th-century California from their Spanish rulers. Like the Hollywood feature film *Mask of Zorro* (1999), *ZtM* is set a generation later, with Zorro's son taking up the mantle and rapier. The idea has previous history in animation—Hayao Miyazaki planned a *Kaiketsu Zorro* series in 1982 but it never appeared. Other animated adventures of Zorro include the 1981 Filmation series and a 2000 Warner Bros. remake. *Zorori the Magnificent* (1993, *Kaiketsu no Zorori*) is an unrelated 30-minute feature directed by Toshio Takeuchi, which featured two popular episodes from a Zorro-pastiche children's book by Miho Mizushima and Yutaka Hara, with animals in all the main roles. Zorro, of course, is played by a fox.

This Zorori returned as the hero of a 52-episode series on Nagoya TV in 2004, directed by Hiroshi Nishikiori. Zorori, accompanied by his twin boar assistants, and with a self-proclaimed desire to become the Prince of Mischief, came back once more in his own 53-minute anime movie *Kaiketsu Zorori: The Race for the Mysterious Treasure* (*Nazo no O-Takara no Daisakusen*, 2006).

Selected Bibliography

Index

SELECTED BIBLIOGRAPHY

BOOKS

Acuff, D. with Robert Reiher. *What Kids Buy and Why: The Psychology of Marketing to Kids.* New York: Free Press.

Akiyama, F. *Current Japanese Robots and Heroes.* Volume. 1. Tokyo: privately published, 1993.

Animage. *The Art of Japanese Animation I: 25 Years of Television Cartoons.* Tokyo: Tokuma Shoten, 1989.

_____. *The Art of Japanese Animation II: 70 Years of Theatrical Films.* Tokyo: Tokuma Shoten, 1989.

Buckley, S. *Encyclopedia of Contemporary Japanese Culture.* London: Routledge, 2002.

[Black and Blue] *Japanese Animation: Nippon no Anime – Owarinaki Ogon Jidai [The Unending Golden Age].* Tokyo: Neko Cinema Books, 2000.

Clements, J. and Motoko Tamamuro. *The Dorama Encyclopedia: A Guide to Japanese Television Drama since 1953.*

Berkeley: Stone Bridge Press, 2003.

Constantine, P. *Japanese Street Slang.* New York: Tengu Books, 1992.

Cremin, S. *The Asian Film Library Reference to Japanese Film.* 2 vols. London: Asian Film Library, 1998.

Galbraith, S. *Japanese Science Fiction, Fantasy, and Horror Films.* Jefferson, North Carolina: McFarland, 1994.

Haraguchi, M., ed. *Animage Pocket Data Notes.* Annual. Tokyo: Tokuma Shoten, 1989–2000.

Hiramatsu, K., ed. *Terebi 50 nen in TV Guide: The TV History of 50 Years.* Tokyo: Tokyo News Tsushinsha, 2000.

Ikeda, H. *A Type and Motif Index of Japanese Folk Literature.* Helsinki: Academia Scientiarum Fennica, 1969.

Ikeda, K. and Hideaki Ito. *NHK Renzoku Ningyogeki no Subete 1953–2003. [All About NHK Puppet Serials].* Tokyo: Enterbrain, 2003.

Inoue, S., ed. *Anime DVD Kanzen* [Complete] *Catalogue 2000.* Tokyo: Kadokawa Shoten, 2000.

Inoue, T., ed. *Niju Seiki Anime Daizen* [Encyclopedia of 20th-Century Anime]. Tokyo: Futabasha, 2000.

Iwasaki, A. et al. *Pia Cinema Club Gaikoku Eigaban [Guide to Foreign Films Released in Japan].* Tokyo: Pia, 2005.

Kawai, H. *The Japanese Psyche: Major Motifs in the Fairy Tales of Japan.* Dallas: Spring Publications, 1982.

Kondo, T. *Kusou Bishojo Tokuhon [The Guide of Fantastic Beauties].* Tokyo: Takarajimasha (Bessatsu Takarajima #349).

_____, ed. *Nihon-ichi no Manga o Sagase!* [Find the Best Manga in Japan!]. Tokyo: Bessatsu Takarajima (#316), 1996.

Ledoux, T., and D. Ranney, eds. *The Complete Anime Guide: Japanese Animation Video Direc-*

tory and Resource Guide. Issaquah, Washington: Tiger Mountain Press, 1996.

_____ et al., eds. *Anime Interviews: The First Five Years of Animerica Anime and Manga Monthly.* San Francisco: Cadence Books, 1997.

Lent, J., ed. *Animation in Asia and the Pacific.* Eastleigh, U.K.: John Libbey, 2001.

Levi, A. *Samurai from Outer Space: Understanding Japanese Animation.* Chicago: Open Court Press, 1996.

Mayer, F., ed. *The Yanagita Kunio Guide to the Japanese Folk Tale.* Bloomington: Indiana University Press, ND.

McCarthy, H. *Hayao Miyazaki: Master of Japanese Animation.* Berkeley: Stone Bridge Press, 1999.

[NHK Hoso Bunka Kenkyusho] *Terebi Shicho no 50-nen [50 Years of Television Ratings].* Tokyo: NHK Shuppan.

[Nichigai Associates

inc.] *Writers of Comics in Japan: A Biographical Dictionary [Mangaka Anime Sakka Jinmei Jiten]*. Tokyo: Nichigai Associates, 1997.

Okada, T. *Otakugaku Nyumon* [Introduction to Otakuology]. Tokyo: Ota, 1996.

Otani, R., ed. *Anime Video Sogo* [General] *Catalogue '99*. Tokyo: Hinode, 1999.

Patten, F. *Watching Anime, Reading Manga: 25 Years of Essays and Reviews*. Berkeley: Stone Bridge Press, 2004.

Schilling, M. *Encyclopedia of Japanese Pop Culture*. New York: Weatherhill, 1997.

_____. *Contemporary Japanese Film*. New York: Weatherhill, 1999.

Schodt, F. *Manga! Manga! The World of Japanese Comics*. Tokyo: Kodansha International, 1984.

_____. *Dreamland Japan: Writings on Modern Manga*. Berkeley: Stone Bridge Press, 1996.

Seto, T. et al. *Nippon no Anime: All About Japan Anime*. Tokyo: Takarajima-sha (Bessatsu Takarajima #638), 2002.

Smith, T., and M. Graham, eds. *Japanese Animation Information: Baycon Guide*. Bay Area Animation Society (California), 1986.

Sunrise. *Sunrise Anime Super Data File*. Tokyo: Tatsumi Shuppan, 1997.

Takefuji, T. *Newtype Animesoft Kanzen* [Complete] *Catalog*. Tokyo: Kadokawa Shoten, 1993.

Tatsunoko. *Tatsunoko Pro Anime Super Data File*. Tokyo: Tatsumi Shuppan, 1999.

Tezuka Productions. *Tezuka Osamu Gekijo* [The Animation Filmography of Osamu Tezuka]. Tokyo: Tezuka Productions, 1991.

Tokyo Movie Shinsha. *TMS Anime Super Data File*. Tokyo: Tatsumi Shuppan, 1998.

Tsukada, H., ed. *Nihon Onsei Seisakusha Meikan [Directory of Japanese Audio Production Workers]*.Vol. 1. Tokyo: Shogakukan and the Union of Japanese Audio Production Workers, 2004.

Weisser, T., and Y. M. Weisser. *Japanese Cinema Encyclopedia: Horror, Fantasy, Science Fiction*. Miami: Vital Books, 1997.

Yamaguchi, Y. *Nippon no Anime Zenshi [History of Japanese Animation]*. Tokyo: Ten Books, 2004.

MAGAZINES

Animage (Japan). 1978–.

Anime UK/Anime FX (U.K.). 1991–96.

Animeland (France) 1991–.

Animerica (U.S.). 1993–.

AX (Japan). 1998–2001.

Manga Mania/Manga Max (U.K.). 1993–2000.

Newtype (Japan). 1984–.

Newtype USA. 2002—

Protoculture Addicts (Canada). 1988–.

ONLINE SOURCES (JAPANESE)

http://www.jmdb.ne.jp

http://www3.justnet.ne.jp/~a_matsu/Ashi.HTM

http://tvgroove.com

http://www.fujitv.co.jp

http://www.tv-asahi.co.jp

http://www.geocities.co.jp/Playtown/3064/

http://www.ntv.co.jp

http://www.tbs.co.jp

http://www.ktv.co.jp

http://www.ytv.co.jp

ONLINE SOURCES (ENGLISH)

www.akadot.com

www.allanime.org

www.animeacademy.com

www.animenewsnetwork.com

www.animeondvd.com

www.animeresearch.com

www.anipike.com

www.google.co.jp

www.hentaineko.com

www.imdb.com

www.wikipedia.org

INDEX

Anime whose titles begin with numerals are listed *twice* in this index, at the very beginning in numerical order and within the alphabetical entries according to spelling based on pronunciation; e.g., the anime *1001 Nights* appears at the beginning of the listings as well as under the (reasonably assumed) pronunciation/spelling *One Thousand and One Nights*. Alphabeticization is by the "word first" method, so that the anime *Ai Oboeteimasu ka* is listed before *Aika*. **Boldface type** indicates a main text entry for an anime that has been released in English. **Boldface** numerals are used with Japanese and alternative English titles to lead you to their corresponding main entries; cross-references follow in normal type. This index also includes the names of key figures, studios, and some rare but known alternative titles that are not listed in the main text, as well as books, magazines, and other creative works.

ABOUT THE AUTHORS

Clements, Jonathan. (1971–). Born in southern England, Clements' first anime translations were released in 1994, the year he graduated in Japanese from Leeds University. He wrote his Master's thesis at the University of Stirling on anime and manga exports, having translated over 70 himself, including SAMURAI GOLD, GREY: DIGITAL TARGET and SOL BIANCA. He was the editor of *Manga Max* magazine from 1998–2000, and a contributing editor of *Newtype USA* from 2002–2004. He has scripted many audio plays for Big Finish Productions, including episodes of *Doctor Who, Judge Dredd,* and *Strontium Dog.*

McCarthy, Helen. (1951–). Born in northern England, McCarthy was the founding editor of Anime *UK magazine,* editor of *Manga Mania* magazine, and the author of *Anime! A Beginner's Guide,* the first book in the English language on the medium. She appeared in several anime as a voice actress and produced the UK release of BEAST WARRIORS. Her subsequent publications have included *Hayao Miyazaki: Master of Japanese Animation* and *500 Manga Heroes and Villains.*

OTHER TITLES OF INTEREST FROM STONE BRIDGE PRESS

Obtain any of these books online or from your local bookseller.
sbp@stonebridge.com • www.stonebridge.com • 1-880-947-7271

The Dorama Encyclopedia

A Guide to Japanese TV Drama Since 1953

JONATHAN CLEMENTS AND MOTOKO TAMAMURO

Over 1,000 entries cover Japanese TV and examine the close connections among broadcast, anime, and print media.

480 pp, 7 x 9", paper, 100+ b/w photos and illustrations, 978-1-880656-81-5, $24.95

Cosplay

Catgirls and Other Critters

GERRY POULOS

Cosplay—short for "costume play"—is sweeping the anime con scene from coast to coast, and once again we're leading the way with a new book for both beginning and veteran cosplayers.

80 pp, 7 x 9", paper, 100 color photos and illustrations, 978-1-933330-02-0, $16.95

The Anime Companion

What's Japanese in Japanese Animation?

GILLES POITRAS

With more than 500 glossary-style entries, this book is a complete guide to anime's distinctive visual style. Includes illustrations, film citations, and numerous references to the related art of manga.

176 pp, 7 x 9", paper, 50 b/w illustrations, 978-1-880656-32-7, $16.95

The Anime Companion 2

More What's Japanese in Japanese Animation?

GILLES POITRAS

This long-awaited "companion" volume boasts over 500 all-new glossary-style entries to help you decipher anime's distinctive content.

168 pp, 7 x 9", paper, 35 b/w photos and illustrations, 978-1-880656-96-9, $18.95

Anime Essentials

Every Thing a Fan Needs to Know

GILLES POITRAS

Answering just about every question a fan (or curious parent) has, *Anime Essentials* is an easy-to-read and fun-to-look-at overview of the pop culture phenomenon sweeping America.

128 pp, 7 x 9", paper, 50 b/w anime images, 978-1-880656-53-2, $16.95

Anime Explosion!

The What? Why? & Wow! of Japanese Animation

PATRICK DRAZEN

Anime is . . . exploding. But where did Japanese animation come from, and what does it all mean? Written for fans and culture watchers this is an engaging tour of the anime megaverse.

320 pp, 6 x 9", paper, 100+ b/w images, 978-1-880656-72-3, $18.95

Hayao Miyazaki

Master of Japanese Animation

HELEN MCCARTHY

Mixing first-hand interviews and personal insights with critical evaluations of art, plot, production qualities, and literary themes, this book provides a film-by-film appraisal of the man often called "the Walt Disney of Japan."

240 pp, 7 x 9", paper, 60+ b/w illustrations, 8 pp in color, 978-1-880656-41-9, $18.95

Watching Anime, Reading Manga

25 Years of Essays and Reviews

FRED PATTEN; FOREWORD BY CARL MACEK

Fred Patten helped establish anime as a serious art form in America back in the early days. This collection of his writings is an incisive history of how anime came to America.

360 pp, 5⅜ x 8⅜", paper, 40 b/w illustrations+photos, 978-1-880656-92-1, $18.95